SOLD
4/05

CAPT.
WE

D0498415

HOME
4/05

CAPT. FELIX WRIGHT
RR#1, S6, C30
4389 FRANCIS PENNINSULA RD.,
MADEIRA PARK, B.C.
CANADA V0N 2H0

RENT

FELIX WRIGHT
SUITE 1004
151 EAST KEITH RD.
NORTH VANCOUVER B.C.
CANADA V7L 4M3

Forward

FELIX V. WRIGHT
POST OFFICE BOX 786
8668 N.E. HILLCREST DRIVE
MOSES LAKE, WA 98837

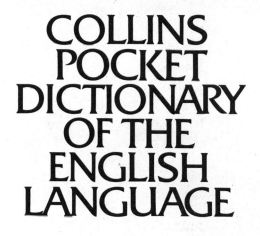

COLLINS POCKET DICTIONARY OF THE ENGLISH LANGUAGE

COLLINS POCKET DICTIONARY OF THE ENGLISH LANGUAGE

Collins
London and Glasgow

First Published 1981
Reprinted 1981 (twice); 1982; 1983; 1984; 1985; 1986
© Wm. Collins Sons & Co. Ltd. 1981
ISBN 0 00 433050 1

Computer typeset by C. R. Barber & Partners,
Wrotham, England.

Printed and bound in Great Britain
by William Collins Sons & Co. Ltd.
P.O. Box, Glasgow G4 0NB.

CONTENTS

FOREWORD

COLLINS POCKET ENGLISH DICTIONARY is an up-to-date survey of the contemporary language. Like its larger brother, *Collins English Dictionary,* COLLINS POCKET DICTIONARY caters for today's needs by placing the current core meaning of words at the head of the definition, where it belongs for most purposes, and treating specialized and obsolete meanings only after current senses have been established.

Like the larger volume, too, the present book puts emphasis on ease of use and ready availability of information by placing all vocabulary items including compounds, prefixes and suffixes, abbreviations, and foreign terms in a single alphabetical listing; and by ensuring that all words that require defining are entered as independent headwords. Only idioms and items that consist of the headword plus standard ending are placed within another entry.

In addition, simplicity and clarity have been sought by framing definitions in direct, straightforward language and by marking off different meanings clearly with bold numbers. The result is a body of dictionary information instantly accessible to all who consult it, irrespective of their degree of verbal sophistication, a dictionary truly suitable for Everyman.

Another feature that will commend itself to most users is the emphasis on spelling aids. Not only the 'standard' irregular forms are shown: our rule has been to show *any* form of the headword that might pose a spelling difficulty: for example, the plurals of *all* nouns ending in *-o* or *-y* are given, not just those considered irregular.

The present convenient, compact volume has been achieved by concentrating on a judicious selection of general and special vocabulary that excludes rarer and highly technical words and meanings (for which the reader is referred to *Collins English Dictionary*); and by omitting proper names.

Etymologies, though brief, preserve the essential elements; and no economies have been made in respect of pronunciations, like spelling difficulties, a very frequent reason for referring to one's dictionary. The pronunciation scheme uses a minimum of special symbols, again in the interests of clarity and simplicity.

The result is a compact all-purpose dictionary that we hope will serve the needs of large numbers of people all over the world who speak and write English and may need occasional help with it.

W.T.M.

GUIDE TO THE USE OF THE DICTIONARY

1. HEADWORDS

1.1 Single alphabetical listing
All main entries in the dictionary, whether single words, compounds, combining forms (see 1.3, below), abbreviations, or foreign words, are entered in alphabetical order in the main text.

1.2 Alternative spellings
Alternative spellings that are alphabetically close and both common are placed together at the head of the article. Where one form is less common it is placed *after* the relevant definition.

Alternative spellings that are alphabetically distant are given separate main entries, with the less common form cross-referred to the more common form.

Common North American spellings are given in this way.

Although only *-ize* and *-ization* spellings are shown, the reader should understand that spellings in *-ise* and *-isation* are equally acceptable.

1.3 Combining forms
Prefixes, suffixes, and other combining forms are generously represented among the headwords since they enable the reader significantly to expand the vocabulary shown in the dictionary.

Combining forms that are added to the beginning of words are distinguished thus: *dis-; in-; self-.* Those that are added to the end of words are shown thus: *-able; -or; -ship.*

1.4 Homographs
Headwords that have the same spelling but are different words are entered separately and distinguished by small superior numbers, thus:

mine¹
mine²

1.5 Cross-references
Cross-references from one main entry to another are shown by placing the headword to which the reader is referred in small capitals, thus:

microchip same as CHIP (*n.* 6)
plywood [PLY¹ + WOOD]

2. PRONUNCIATION

2.1 General note
The pronunciations shown are those commonly used by educated speakers of English. The few special symbols used will be readily understood from the sample words shown in the key (2.2, below) and are devised to allow a wide range of speakers of English to interpret them in the light of their own pronunciation.

2.2 Pronunciation Key
Only special symbols are shown in the key. Letters not shown have their normal values.

English Sounds

ā   as in acre, rate, gait
ä   as in calm, far, father
ē   as in fee, meat, funny
ī   as in pipe, why, buy
ō   as in tone, groan, though
ô   as in call, corn, awl
oo   as in book, full, soot
ōō   as in food, soup, through, brew
yoo as in sinuous, globular
yōō as in few, tune, due
oi   as in boil, boy, loiter
ou   as in shout, aloud, allowed
ʉr   as in demur, fern, bird
ə   as in alone (ə lōn′), potter (pot′ər),
       timorous (tim′ər əs), nation
       (nā′shən)
ər   as in perhaps, partner, undergo
ēə   as in fear, mere, beer
āə   as in fair, vary, bear, bare
ōōə as in moor, cure, furious
īə   as in fire, lyre
ouə as in our, flour
ch   as in church, chair, lurch
sh   as in shin, cushion, bashed
zh   as in leisure, fusion, azure
th   as in think, both, nothing
th as in this, bother, loathing
ŋ   as in sing, anger, anxious
′   as in apple (ap′′l), happen (hap′′n)
kh   as in Scottish loch (see also below)

Foreign Sounds

å   as in Fr. *bal,* halfway between (a) and (ä)
ë   as in Fr. *coeur:* the sound (e) pronounced with lips rounded as if for (o)
ö   as in Fr. *feu* or Ger. *Goethe:* the sound (ā) pronounced with lips rounded as if for (ō)
ð   as in a range of sounds as heard in Fr. *coq,* Ger. *doch,* Ital. *poco,* Sp. *torero*
ü   as in Fr. *duc* or Ger. *grün:* the sound (ē) pronounced with lips rounded as if for (ōō)
kh   as in Ger. *doch:* a prolonged (h) sound with the lips and tongue positioned as if for (k)
H   as in Ger. *ich:* as the previous sound but formed in the front of the mouth with the tongue raised towards the front of the palate
n   as in Fr. *bon, vin, blanc,* etc.: indicates that the preceding vowel sound is nasalized
r   as in the uvular or tongue-point trill of the 'r' in Fr. *rare,* Ger. *recht,* Ital. *trarre,* Sp. *reserva,* etc.
′   as in Fr. *lettre* (let′r′)

Guide to the Dictionary

2.3 Notes

(i) Though words like castle, path, fast are shown as pronounced with an (ä) sound, many speakers use an (a). Such variations are acceptable and are to be assumed by the reader.

(ii) The letter 'r' in some positions is not sounded in the speech of Southern England and elsewhere. However, many speakers in other areas do sound the 'r' in such positions with varying degrees of distinctness. Again, such variations are to be assumed, and though the dictionary shows an 'r' in such pronunciations as **fern** (fu̇rn), **fear** (fēər), **arm** (ärm), the reader will sound or not sound the 'r' according to his speech habits.

(iii) The symbol (ə), the schwa, represents the neutral vowel heard in a wide range of unstressed syllables. In some such words, however, among some speakers an (i) sound is heard, as in **listless** (list′ləs or list′lis). Again, such variations should be assumed.

(iv) Though the widely received pronunciation of words like *which, why* is with a simple (w) sound and is so shown in the dictionary, many speakers, in Scotland and elsewhere, preserve an aspirated sound: (hw). Once again this variation is to be assumed.

(v) A primary or main stress is shown by an accent (′) after the stressed syllable. A secondary or weaker stress is shown by a lighter tick (′) after the syllable carrying secondary stress.

(vi) When a pronunciation is not shown, it is the same as that of the preceding headword or can easily be deduced from it, or, in the case of compounds, from the pronunciations given for the separate parts. Partial pronunciations are given when this can be done without loss of clarity.

3. PART-OF-SPEECH LABELS

Part-of-speech function is shown for headwords and derived forms within articles, but not for prefixes, suffixes, abbreviations, and multiple word entries. When a word functions as more than one part-of-speech, each change of function is shown by a bold dash and a new part-of-speech label.

When two or more part-of-speech labels are attached to an entry without an intervening definition (**joggle ... vt., vi** ...) each applies equally to what follows.

4. INFLECTED FORMS

Inflected forms regarded as irregular or offering difficulty in spelling are shown in small bold type after the part-of-speech label. The following notes amplify this general statement.

4.1 Plurals of nouns

The following are regarded as regular: plurals formed simply by adding -s to the singular or by adding -es when the singular ends in s, x, z, ch, or sh.

Plurals formed in *any* other way are shown.

4.2 Verbal forms

The following are regarded as regular:

(i) present tenses formed simply by adding -s to the infinitive or by adding -es after s, x, z, ch, and sh.

(ii) past tenses and past participles formed simply by adding -ed to the infinitive with no other change.

(iii) present participles formed simply by adding -ing to the infinitive with no other change.

Verbal parts formed in *any* other way are shown, including verbs which drop a final e in forming the present participle.

Where *two* inflected verbal parts are given, the first is the past tense *and* the past participle, and the second is the present participle.

Where *three* inflected verbal parts are given, the first is the past tense, the second is the past participle, and the third is the present participle.

make ... vt. made, mak′ing ...
swim ... vi. swam, swum, swim′ming ...

4.3 Comparatives and Superlatives

The following are regarded as regular: comparatives and superlatives formed simply by adding -er or -est to the base.

Comparatives and superlatives that involve any further change in the base word are shown.

4.4 Irregular forms that are alphabetically distant from the base form are entered in their alphabetical place as headwords and cross-referred to the base form.

5. ETYMOLOGIES

A brief account of the origin of most words is placed within square brackets before the definitions. Occasionally the reader is referred to the etymologies given at the component parts of a word (see example at 1.5, above). The presence of [< ?] indicates that the etymology is uncertain.

6. DEFINITIONS

6.1 Numbering of Senses

Where the definition embraces two or more distinct meanings, the different senses are marked off with consecutive bold numbers. The senses of each part of speech and idiomatic phrase are numbered separately. Sometimes a numbered sense is subdivided

Guide to the Dictionary

into *a)*, *b)*, etc., especially to denote specific applications of a general meaning.

In general, the meaning given first in the dictionary is not the oldest (and often obsolete) meaning, but the core meaning common in current usage.

6.2 *Capitalization*

Where a headword has a capital initial, that word is always so written or printed in generally accepted usage. Where a word is usually (but not always) capitalized or usually (but not always) used with a small initial, these facts are indicated. The reader is also told when a word is capitalized for a specific meaning (or meanings) or, conversely, not capitalized for a specific meaning or meanings.

6.3 *Plural usages*

Where a word is only used in the plural (or often or usually) this is clearly indicated. Where a word is used in the plural (or often or usually) for a specific meaning or meanings, this, again, is indicated.

If a noun that is plural in form is used as a singular in all or some meanings, this information is provided.

6.4 *Prepositional usage*

When a verb is followed by a certain preposition or prepositions in some or all of its meanings, this information is provided. Such prepositional usage is not to be confused with idioms that consist of verb + preposition/adverb with a special meaning ("phrasal verbs," eg. *get on, get over, get up*). Such phrasal verbs are entered as idiomatic phrases.

6.5 *Additional information*

Background information or comment has been added to the definition proper when this seemed helpful. Such additional material is usually introduced by a colon.

6.6 *Examples*

Examples of how a word is used have been provided where this helps to clarify the definition. Such examples are placed within italic square brackets.

7. USAGE LABELS

Certain words and certain meanings are restricted in usage in any of a number of ways. A word or meaning may be technical or slang or vulgar or poetic, and so on. Words or meanings that occur in technical or specialized contexts have a *field label* attached to them to indicate the area in which they are likely to be encountered (*Music, Physics, Aeronautics,* and so on).

In addition, as a help to appropriate usage the following restrictive labels are employed with meanings as indicated.

[Colloq.] Colloquial: characteristic of relaxed conversation or informal writing, but not substandard or illiterate.

[Slang] Slang: characteristic of speech in highly informal contexts, not generally regarded as accepted or standard.

[Derog.] Derogatory: describing a use that could be offensive, whether intended to be so or not.

[Vulg.] Vulgar: a word or meaning usually considered taboo in most contexts.

[Archaic] Archaic: a word or sense no longer in common use but still found in certain restricted contexts (eg. church ritual) and earlier literature.

[Obs.] Obsolete: no longer in use but found in earlier literature.

[Poet.] Poetic: characteristic of poetry (especially poetry of the 18th and 19th centuries) or of poetic prose.

[Dial.] Dialect: a word or meaning regularly used only in some geographical areas.

In addition, where a word or meaning is typical of the USA, Canada, Australia, New Zealand, S Africa, etc., this fact is noted.

8. IDIOMATIC PHRASES

Idiomatic phrases are listed in alphabetical order after the completed definition of the headword. Idioms are entered under the key word, that is, the word that contains the main idea, and this will often not be the first word in the phrase. For example:

eat one's heart out; set one's heart on will be found under **heart; give someone his head; keep (or lose) one's head** under **head.**

Where part of a phrase is placed within brackets, that part is either optional or shows an acceptable variation.

9. DERIVED ENTRIES

Derived entries are formed by adding a standard ending to the headword and are run-in in alphabetical order at the end of the entry block. However, any derived word that has developed a distinct meaning of its own that cannot be deduced from the base word has been entered as a separate headword and fully defined. Only when no definition is required are they run in. (See 1.3, above).

The number of such possible derived words in English is indefinitely great. They are listed here when they are a standard part of the current language; but less common forms and many adverbs ending in -ly are omitted. The reader should understand that almost any English adjective can be turned into an adverb by adding -ly.

ABBREVIATIONS AND SYMBOLS USED IN THE DICTIONARY

abbrev. abbreviated; abbreviation
abl. ablative
Abor. Aboriginal (in etym.)
acc. accusative
adj. adjective
adv. adverb
Aeron. Aeronautics
Afr. African
Afrik. Afrikaans
alt. alternative
Am. American
AmInd. American Indian
AmSp. American Spanish
Anat. Anatomy
Anglo-Ind. Anglo-Indian
Anglo-Norm. Anglo-Norman
Ar. Arabic
Aram. Aramaic
Archaeol. Archaeology
Archit. Architecture
Arith. Arithmetic
art. article
assoc. associated
Astrol. Astrology
Astron. Astronomy
Aust. Australian

Beng. Bengali
Biochem. Biochemistry
Biol. Biology
Bot. Botany
Braz. Brazilian
Brit. British

C Celsius; Central
c. century (in etym.); circa
Canad. Canada; Canadian
Celt. Celtic
cent. century; centuries
cf. compare
Ch. Church
Chem. Chemistry
Chin. Chinese
cm centimetre(s)
Colloq. colloquial
comp. compound
compar. comparative
conj. conjunction
contr. contracted; contraction

Dan. Danish
dat. dative
deriv. derivative
Derog. derogatory
Dial., dial. dialect
dim. diminutive
Du. Dutch

E East; eastern
E. East; English (in etym. & pronun.)
Early ModDu. Early Modern Dutch
Early ModG. Early Modern German
Eccles. Ecclesiastical
Ecol. Ecology
Econ. Economics

Educ. Education
e.g. for example
Elec. Electricity
Eng. English
equiv. equivalent
esp. especially
etym. etymology
Ex. example
exc. except

fem. feminine
ff. following (entry, sense, etc.)
fig. figurative(ly)
Finn. Finnish
Fl. Flemish
Fr. French
Frank. Frankish
freq. frequentative
fut. future

g gram(s)
G. German (in etym. & pronun.)
Gael. Gaelic
gen. genitive
Geog. Geography
Geol. Geology
Geom. Geometry
Ger. German
ger. gerund
Gmc. Germanic
Goth. Gothic
Gr. Greek
Gram. Grammar

Haw. Hawaiian
Heb. Hebrew
Hist. Historical; History
Hort. Horticulture
Hung. Hungarian
hyp. hypothetical

Ice. Icelandic
i.e. that is
imper. imperative
imperf. imperfect
incl. including
Ind. Indian
indic. indictative
inf. infinitive
intens. intensive
interj. interjection
Ir. Irish
irreg. irregular
It. Italian

Jap. Japanese
Jav. Javanese

kg kilogram(s)
km kilometre(s)

l litre(s)
L Late
L. Latin
LGr. Late Greek

Abbreviations and Symbols (*cont.*)

Linguis. Linguistics
lit. literally
LL. Late Latin
LME. Late Middle English

m metre(s)
M Middle; Medieval
Math. Mathematics
MDu. Middle Dutch
ME. Middle English
Mech. Mechanics
Med. Medicine; Medieval
M. Meteorology
Mex. Mexican
MexInd. Mexican Indian
MFr. Middle French
MGr. Middle Greek
MHG. Middle High German
Mil. Military
ML. Medieval Latin
MLowG. Middle Low German
Mod., Mod Modern
ModE. Modern English
ModGr. Modern Greek
ModL. Modern Latin
Myth. Mythology

N North; northern
N. North
n. noun
Naut., naut. nautical usage
NE northeastern
neut. neuter
n.fem. noun feminine
n.masc. noun masculine
nom. nominative
Norm. Norman
Norw. Norwegian
n.pl. plural form of noun
n.sing. singular form of noun
N.T. New Testament
NW northwestern
N.Z. New Zealand

O Old
Obs., obs. obsolete
occas. occasionally
OE. Old English
OFr. Old French
OHG. Old High German
OIr. Old Irish
ON. Old Norse
ONormFr. Old Norman French
orig. originally
OS. Old Saxon
O.T. Old Testament

p. page
part. participle
pass. passive
Per. Persian
perf. perfect
pers. person
Philos. Philosophy
Phonet. Phonetics
Photog. Photography
phr. phrase
Phys. Ed. Physical Education
Physiol. Physiology
PidE. Pidgin English
pl. plural
Poet. Poetic
Pol. Polish

pop. popular
Port. Portuguese
poss. possessive
pp. pages; past participle
Pr. Provençal
prec. preceding
prep. preposition
pres. present
prin. pts. principle parts
prob. probably
pron. pronoun
pronun. pronunciation
prp. present participle
Psychol. Psychology
pt. past tense

R.C.Ch. Roman Catholic Church
redupl. reduplication
refl. reflexive
Rom. Roman
Russ. Russian

S South; southern
S. South
S Afr. South African
Sans. Sanskrit
Scand. Scandinavian
Scot. Scottish
SE southeastern
Sem. Semitic
sing. singular
Slav. Slavic
Sp. Spanish
sp. spelled; spelling
specif. specifically
subj. subjective
superl. superlative
SW southwestern
Swed. Swedish

Theol. Theology
trans. translation
Turk. Turkish
TV, T.V. television

ult. ultimately
U.S. United States

v. verb
var. variant; variety
v.aux. auxiliary verb
Vet. Veterinary Medicine
vi. intransitive verb
VL. Vulgar Latin
voc. vocative
vt. transitive verb
Vulg. vulgar; Vulgate

W West; western
W. Welsh; West
WAfr. West African
WInd. West Indian

Yid. Yiddish

Zool. Zoology

‡ foreign word or phrase
+ plus
< derived from
? uncertain; possibly; perhaps
& and

A

A, a (ā) *n., pl.* **A's, a's** 1. the first letter of the English alphabet 2. *a symbol for* the first in a sequence or group —**from A to Z** from start to finish

A (ā) *n. Music* the sixth tone in the ascending scale of C major —*adj.* shaped like *A*

A *Physics the symbol for* ampere

a (ə; *stressed* ā) *adj., indefinite article* [< AN] 1. one; one sort of 2. each; any one 3. [< OE. *an*] per *[once a day] A* is used before words beginning with a consonant sound or a sounded *h [a* child, *a* home, *a* uniform*]*

a are(s) (metric measure of land)

a- *a prefix meaning:* 1. [OE. a-] up, out *[awake]* 2. [OE. *of-, af-*] off, of *[akin]* 3. [Gr. a-, an-] not *[atypical]*

Å angstrom unit

A. 1. absolute 2. ampere 3. angstrom

A., a. *Music* alto

a. 1. acre(s) 2. adjective 3. answer

AA, A.A. 1. Alcoholics Anonymous 2. antiaircraft 3. Automobile Association

AAA, A.A.A. Amateur Athletics Association

A1 (ā′wun′) 1. [Colloq.] first-class; excellent 2. a designation of first-class ships as in Lloyd's Register

aardvark (ärd′värk′) *n.* [obs. Afrik., earth pig] a nocturnal burrowing mammal of Africa feeding off termites: also called *ant bear*

Aaron's beard (âar′ənz) the popular name of various plants, esp. St. John's Wort

ab- [L.] *a prefix meaning* away, from, off, down *[abdicate]*

A.B. able-bodied seaman

aba (a′bə) *n.* [Ar.] a sleeveless robe worn by Arabs

aback (əbak′) *adv.* 1. pressed backwards against the mast, as sails in a wind from ahead 2. [Archaic] backwards —**taken aback** startled and confused

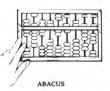

ABACUS

abacus (ab′ə kəs) *n., pl.* **-cuses, -ci** (-sī′) [< Gr. *abax*] 1. a frame with beads sliding on wires, for doing arithmetic 2. *Archit.* a slab forming the uppermost part of the capital of a column

abaft (ə bäft′) *adv.* [< OE. *be,* by + *æftan,* behind] at or towards the stern of a ship; aft —*prep. Naut.* behind

abalone (ab′ə lō′nē) *n.* [AmSp.] a sea mollusc with a spiral shell lined with mother-of-pearl

abandon (ə ban′dən) *vt.* [< OFr. *mettre à bandon,* put under (someone else's) ban] 1. to forsake; desert 2. to give up (something) completely 3. to yield (oneself) completely, as to a feeling —*n.* unrestrained freedom of action or emotion —**aban′donment** *n.*

abandoned *adj.* 1. forsaken; deserted 2. unrestrained 3. shamefully wicked; immoral

abase (ə bās′) *vt.* **abased′, abas′ing** [< L. *ad-,* to + LL. *bassus,* low] to humble or humiliate —**abase′ment** *n.*

abash (ə bash′) *vt.* [< L. *ex* + *ba,* interj.] to make ashamed and ill at ease —**abashed′** *adj.*

abate (ə bāt′) *vt.* **abat′ed, abat′ing** [< OFr. *abattre,* beat down] 1. to make less 2. *Law* to put a stop to; end —*vi.* to become less; subside —**abate′ment** *n.*

abattoir (ab′ə twär′) *n.* [see ABATE] a slaughterhouse

abbacy (ab′ə sē) *n., pl.* **-cies** an abbot's or abbess's position, jurisdiction, or term of office

abbé (a′bā) *n.* [Fr.: see ABBOT] a French title of respect for a priest

abbess (ab′es) *n.* [see ABBOT] a woman who is head of an abbey of nuns

abbey (ab′ē) *n.* 1. a monastery or convent 2. a church belonging to an abbey

abbot (ab′ət) *n.* [< Aram. *abbā,* father] a man who heads an abbey of monks

abbr., abbrev. 1. abbreviated 2. abbreviation

abbreviate (ə brē′vē āt′) *vt.* **-at′ed, -at′ing** [< L. *ad-,* to + *brevis,* short] 1. to shorten (a word) by leaving out letters 2. to make shorter —**abbre′via′tion** *n.*

A B C (ā′bē′sē′) *n., pl.* **A B C's** 1. the alphabet 2. the basic elements (*of* a subject) 3. an alphabetically arranged reference or guide book

ABC Australian Broadcasting Commission

abdicate (ab′də kāt′) *vt., vi.* **-cat′ed, -cat′ing** [< L. *ab-,* off + *dicare,* proclaim] 1. to give up formally (a high office, etc.) 2. to surrender (a right, etc.) —**ab′dica′tion** *n.*

abdomen (ab′də mən) *n.* [L.] 1. the lower part of the body containing the intestines, etc.; belly 2. in arthropods, the hind part of the body —**abdominal** (ab dom′ə n'l) *adj.*

abduct (ab dukt´) *vt.* [< L. *ab-*, away + *ducere*, to lead] to kidnap (a person) —**abduc´tion** *n.* —**abduc´tor** *n.*

abeam (ə bēm´) *adv.* at right angles to a ship's side

Aberdeen Angus (ab´ər dēn´aŋ´gəs) any of a breed of black, hornless cattle, originally from Scotland

Aberdeen terrier a long-bodied, wire-haired terrier

aberration (ab´ər ā´shən) *n.* [< L. *ab-*, from + *errare*, wander] **1.** a departure from what is right, true, normal, etc. **2.** mental derangement **3.** *Astron.* the apparent displacement of a heavenly body **4.** *Optics* the failure of light rays from one point to converge to a single focus

abet (ə bet´) *vt.* **abet´ted, abet´ting** [< OFr. *a-*, to + *beter*, to bait] to incite or help, esp. in wrongdoing —**abet´ment** *n.* —**abet´tor, abet´ter** *n.*

abeyance (ə bā´əns) *n.* [< OFr. *a-*, at + *bayer*, gape] temporary suspension, as of an activity or function

abhor (ab hôr´) *vt.* **-horred´, -hor´ring** [< L. *ab-*, from + *horrere*, to shudder] to shrink from in disgust or hatred —**abhor´rence** (ab hor´əns) *n.*

abhorrent (ab hor´ənt) *adj.* **1.** causing disgust, hatred, etc.; detestable **2.** opposed (*to*) [*abhorrent* to his principles] —**abhor´rently** *adv.*

abide (ə bīd´) *vi.* **abode´** or **abid´ed, abid´ing** [< OE. *a-* (intens.) + *bidan*, remain] **1.** to remain **2.** [Archaic] to reside —*vt.* **1.** to tolerate **2.** to submit to **3.** to await —**abide by 1.** to live up to (a promise, etc.) **2.** to submit to and carry out —**abid´ance** *n.*

abiding *adj.* enduring; lasting —**abid´ingly** *adv.*

ability (ə bil´ə tē) *n., pl.* **-ties 1.** skill or talent; competence **2.** a being able; power to do

-ability (ə bil´ə tē) *pl.* **-ties** [L.] *a suffix used to form nouns from adjectives ending in* -ABLE [*durability*]

abject (ab´jekt) *adj.* [< L. *ab-*, from + *jacere*, throw] **1.** of the lowest degree; miserable **2.** lacking self-respect; servile —**ab´jectness, abjec´tion** *n.*

abjure (ab jooər´) *vt.* **-jured´, -jur´ing** [< L. *ab-*, from + *jurare*, swear] to give up (rights, allegiance, etc.) on oath; renounce —**abjuration** (ab´jooə rā´shən) *n.*

ablate (ab lāt´) *vt.* **-lat´ed, -lat´ing** [see ff.] **1.** to remove, as by surgery **2.** *Astrophysics* to melt, vaporize, etc. (surface material) **3.** *Geol.* to wear away, as by the action of water —**abla´tion** *n.*

ablative (ab´lə tiv) *n.* [< L. *ab-*, away + *ferre*, carry] the grammatical case in Latin expressing removal, direction from, cause, etc. —*adj.* of or in the ablative

ablaut (ab´lout) *n.* [G. < *ab-*, off + *Laut*, sound] the change of vowels in related words to show changes in tense, meaning, etc. (Ex.: drink, drank, drunk)

ablaze (ə blāz´) *adj.* **1.** flaming **2.** greatly excited

able (ā´b'l) *adj.* **a´bler, a´blest** [< L.

habere, have] **1.** having enough power, skill, etc. (*to* do something) **2.** skilled; talented —**a´bly** *adv.*

-able (ə b'l) [< L. *-abilis*] *a suffix meaning:* **1.** able to [*durable*] **2.** capable of being [*drinkable*] **3.** worthy of being [*lovable*] **4.** having qualities of [*comfortable*] **5.** tending or inclined to [*peaceable*]

able-bodied (ā´b'l bod´ēd) *adj.* healthy and strong

able-bodied seaman *same as* ABLE RATING

able rating *see* MILITARY RANKS, table

ablution (ab loo´shən) *n.* [< L. *ab-*, off + *luere*, lave] **1.** a washing of the body, esp. as a religious ceremony **2.** [*pl.*] [Colloq.] washing facilities

-ably (ə blē) *a suffix used to form adverbs from adjectives ending in* -ABLE [*peaceably*]

ABM anti-ballistic missile

abnegate (ab´nə gāt´) *vt.* **-gat´ed, -gat´ing** [< L. *ab-*, from + *negare*, deny] to give up (rights, claims, etc.); renounce —**ab´nega´tion** *n.* —**ab´nega´tor** *n.*

abnormal (ab nôr´m'l) *adj.* not normal, average, or typical; irregular —**ab´normal´ity** (-mal´ə tē) *n.*

Abo (a´bō) *n., pl.* **-bos** [< ABORIGINE] [Aust. Slang] an Australian aborigine —*adj.* aboriginal

aboard (ə bôrd´) *adv.* **1.** on, in, or into a ship, aircraft, etc. **2.** alongside —*prep.* on board

abode¹ (ə bōd´) *n.* [see ABIDE] a home; residence

abode² *alt. pt. and pp. of* ABIDE

abolish (ə bol´ish) *vt.* [< L. *abolere*, destroy] to do away with; put an end to —**abol´ishment** *n.*

abolition (ab´ə lish´ən) *n.* **1.** an abolishing or being abolished **2.** [*occas.* A-] the abolishing of slavery —**ab´oli´tionary** *adj.* —**ab´oli´tionist** *n.*

A-bomb (ā´bom´) *n.* *same as* ATOMIC BOMB

abominable (ə bom´ə nə b'l) *adj.* **1.** disgusting; vile **2.** very bad —**abom´inably** *adv.*

Abominable Snowman a large, hairy, manlike animal reputed to live in the Himalayas

abominate (ə bom´ə nāt´) *vt.* **-nat´ed, -nat´ing** [< L. *abominari*, regard as an ill omen] **1.** to feel hatred and disgust for; loathe **2.** to dislike very much —**abom´ina´tion** *n.* —**abom´ina´tor** *n.*

aboriginal (ab´ə rij´ə n'l) *adj.* **1.** existing from earliest days; first; indigenous **2.** of aborigines, esp. [A-] those of Australia —*n.* *same as* ABORIGINE

aborigine (ab´ə rij´ə nē´) *n., pl.* **-nes´** [L. < *ab-*, from + *origine*, beginning] any of the earliest known inhabitants of a region, esp. [A-] those of Australia

abort (ə bôrt´) *vi.* [< L. *aboriri*, to miscarry] **1.** to have a miscarriage **2.** to fail to be completed —*vt.* **1.** to cause to have an abortion **2.** to cut short (an operation of an aircraft, missile, etc.)

abortion (ə bôr´shən) *n.* **1.** deliberate

termination of pregnancy **2.** expulsion of a foetus from the womb before it is viable **3.** anything immature and incomplete **4.** anything grotesquely misshapen

abortive *adj.* **1.** coming to nothing; unsuccessful **2.** *Biol.* rudimentary **3.** *Med.* causing abortion

abound (əbaund') *vi.* [< L. *ab-*, away + *undare*, rise in waves] **1.** to be plentiful **2.** to teem (*with*)

about (əbaut') *adv.* [< OE. *onbutan*, around] **1.** all round **2.** here and there **3.** near **4.** in the opposite direction **5.** in succession or rotation [play fair—turn and turn *about*] **6.** approximately —*adj.* **1.** active [up and *about* again] **2.** in the vicinity —*prep.* **1.** on all sides of **2.** here and there in **3.** near to **4.** with; on (one's person) [have your wits *about* you] **5.** attending to [go *about* your business] **6.** intending; on the point of **7.** concerning —**how** (or **what**) **about** [Colloq.] what is your opinion concerning? —**how about that!** [Colloq.] isn't that interesting!

about-turn (əbaut'turn'; *for v.*, əbaut'-turn') *n.* **1.** a sharp turn to the opposite direction **2.** a sharp change, as in opinion —*vi.* -**turned', -turn'ing** to turn or face in the opposite direction Also **about'face'**

above (əbuv') *adv.* [OE. *abufan*] **1.** in a higher place; up **2.** in heaven **3.** at a previous place (in a piece of writing) **4.** higher in status, etc. —*prep.* **1.** higher than **2.** beyond; past **3.** upstream from **4.** better or more than **5.** too honourable or good for [not *above* cheating] —*adj.* mentioned earlier —*n.* something that is above —**above all** most of all; mainly

aboveboard (əbuv'bôrd') *adv., adj.* without dishonesty

abracadabra (ab'rəkədab'rə) *n.* [LL.] **1.** a word supposed to have magic powers, used in incantations, etc. **2.** foolish or meaningless talk

abrade (əbrād') *vt.* -**rad'ed, -rad'ing** [< L. *ab-*, away + *radere*, scrape] to rub off; wear away by scraping

abrasion (əbrā'zhən) *n.* **1.** a scraping or rubbing off, as of skin **2.** an abraded spot or area

abrasive *adj.* causing abrasion —*n.* a substance used for grinding, polishing, etc.

abreast (əbrest') *adv., adj.* **1.** side by side **2.** informed (*of*) or conversant (*with*) recent developments

abridge (əbrij') *vt.* **abridged', abridg'ing** [< LL. *abbreviare*: see ABBREVIATE] **1.** to shorten by using fewer words **2.** to reduce in scope, extent, etc. —**abridg'er** *n.* —**abridg'ment, abridge'ment** *n.*

abroad (əbrôd') *adv.* **1.** to or in foreign countries **2.** circulating [a report is *abroad* that he is ill] **3.** far and wide **4.** outdoors —**from abroad** from a foreign land

abrogate (ab'rəgāt') *vt.* -**gat'ed, -gat'ing** [< L. *ab-*, away + *rogare*, propose] to cancel or repeal; annul —**ab'roga'tion** *n.* —**ab'rogative** *adj.* —**ab'roga'tor** *n.*

abrupt (əbrupt') *adj.* [< L. *ab-*, off + *rumpere*, break] **1.** sudden; unexpected **2.** brusque **3.** very steep **4.** jumping from topic to topic; disconnected —**abrupt'ly** *adv.* —**abrupt'ness** *n.*

abscess (ab'ses) *n.* [< L. < *ab(s)-*, from + *cedere*, go] a swollen, inflamed area in body tissues, in which pus gathers —*vi.* to form an abscess —**ab'scessed** *adj.*

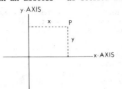

ABSCISSA
(x, the abscissa of P; y, the ordinate of P)

abscissa (ab sis'ə) *n., pl.* -**sas, -sae** (-ē) [< L. *ab-*, from + *scindere*, to cut] *Math.* in a system of coordinates, the distance of a point from the vertical axis as measured along a line parallel to the horizontal axis: cf. ORDINATE

abscond (əb skond') *vi.* [< L. *ab(s)-*, from + *condere*, hide] to run away and hide, esp. in order to escape the law —**abscond'-er** *n.*

abseil (ab'sāl) *vi.* [< G. *ab-*, down + *Seil*, rope] *Mountaineering* to descend by means of a double rope secured from above —*n.* a descent so made

absence (ab'səns) *n.* **1.** the state of being absent **2.** the time of being away **3.** a lack [in the *absence* of proof]

absent (ab'sənt; *for v.* ab sent') *adj.* [< L. *ab-*, away + *esse*, be] **1.** not present; away **2.** not existing; lacking **3.** not attentive —*vt.* to keep (oneself) away

absentee (ab'sən tē') *n.* a person who is absent, as from work —*adj.* designating or of a person who lives away from his property, office, etc. [an *absentee* landlord]

absenteeism *n.* absence from work, school, etc., esp. when deliberate or habitual

absent-minded *adj.* **1.** not attentive; preoccupied **2.** habitually forgetful

absinthe, absinth (ab'sinth) *n.* [< Gr. *apsinthion*] **1.** wormwood **2.** a green liqueur with the flavour of wormwood and anise

absolute (ab'sə loot') *adj.* [see ABSOLVE] **1.** perfect; complete **2.** not mixed; pure **3.** unrestricted [an *absolute* ruler] **4.** positive; definite **5.** actual; real [an *absolute* truth] **6.** *Gram.* a) forming part of a sentence, but syntactically independent [in the sentence "The weather being good, they went," *the weather being good* is an *absolute* construction] b) with no expressed object: said of a verb usually transitive —*n.* something that is absolute —**the Absolute** *Philos.* that which is thought of as existing in and by itself, without relation to anything else —**ab'solute'ness** *n.*

absolutely (ab'sə loot'lē; *for interj.*, ab'-

sə lōōt′lē) *adv.* in an absolute manner
—*interj.* yes indeed; definitely
absolute majority 1. a majority of over half 2. a majority that beats the combined opposition
absolute pitch the ability to identify or sing any note, or to sing a given tone, without having a known pitch sounded beforehand
absolute temperature temperature measured from absolute zero
absolute zero a point of temperature theoretically equal to -273.15°C: the hypothetical point at which a substance would have no molecular motion and no heat
absolution (ab′sə lōō′shən) [see ABSOLVE] 1. a formal freeing (*from* guilt); forgiveness 2. remission (*of* sin or its penalty)
absolutism (ab′sə lōō′tiz′m) *n.* government in which the ruler has unlimited powers —**ab′solut′ist** *n., adj.*
absolve (əb zolv′) *vt.* -solved′, -solv′ing [< L. *ab-*, from + *solvere*, to loose] 1. to pronounce free from guilt 2. to give religious absolution to 3. to free (someone *from* an obligation) —**absolv′ent** *adj., n.*
absorb (əb sôrb′) *vt.* [< L. *ab-*, from + *sorbere*, drink in] 1. to suck up 2. to engross 3. to take in and incorporate 4. to take in (a shock, jolt, etc.) with little or no recoil or reaction 5. to take in and not reflect (light, sound, etc.) —**absorbed′** *adj.* —**absorb′ent** *adj., n.* —**absorb′ing** *adj.*
absorption (əb sôrp′shən) *n.* 1. an absorbing 2. great interest 3. *Biol.* the passing of nutrient material into the blood or lymph —**absorp′tive** *adj.*
abstain (əb stān′) *vi.* [< L. *ab(s)-*, from + *tenere*, hold] 1. to do without voluntarily; refrain (*from*), esp. alcohol 2. to choose not to vote —**abstain′er** *n.*
abstemious (əb stē′mē əs) *adj.* [< L. *ab(s)-*, from + *temetum*, strong drink] moderate, esp. in eating and drinking —**abste′miously** *adv.* —**abste′miousness** *n.*
abstention (əb sten′shən) *n.* an abstaining; specif., a refraining from voting on some issue
abstinence (ab′stə nəns) *n.* an abstaining from some or all food, drink, or other pleasures —**ab′stinent** *adj.*
abstract (ab′strakt; *also, and for n.* 1 & v. 3 always, ab strakt′) *adj.* [< L. *ab(s)-*, from + *trahere*, draw] 1. thought of apart from material objects 2. expressing a quality so thought of [“beauty” is an *abstract* word] 3. theoretical 4. not easy to understand 5. *Art* seeking to make an effect through form and colour alone —*n.* 1. a summary 2. an abstract thing, condition, etc. —*vt.* 1. to take away 2. to think of (a quality) apart from any object that has it 3. to summarize —**in the abstract** in theory as distinct from practice —**abstract′ly** *adv.*
abstracted *adj.* withdrawn in mind; preoccupied
abstraction *n.* 1. mental withdrawal 2.

an abstracting 3. an abstract idea 4. an unrealistic notion 5. an abstract picture, sculpture, etc. —**abstrac′tionism** *n.* —**abstrac′tionist** *n.*
abstruse (ab strōōs′) *adj.* [< L. *ab(s)-*, away + *trudere*, thrust] hard to understand; deep —**abstruse′ly** *adv.*
absurd (əb surd′) *adj.* [< L. *ab-*, intens. + *surdus*, deaf] so clearly inconsistent or unreasonable as to be laughable or ridiculous —**absurd′ity**, **absurd′ness** *n.*
abundance (ə bun′dəns) *n.* [see ABOUND] 1. a great supply; more than sufficient quantity 2. wealth —**abun′dant** *adj.* —**abun′dantly** *adv.*
abuse (ə byōōz′; *for n.*, ə byōōs′) *vt.* abused′, abus′ing [< L. *ab-*, away + *uti*, to use] 1. to use wrongly 2. to mistreat 3. to insult; revile —*n.* 1. wrong use 2. mistreatment 3. a corrupt practice 4. insulting language —**abus′er** *n.* —**abu′sive** *adj.*
abut (ə but′) *vi.* abut′ted, abut′ting [< OFr. *a-*, to + *bout*, end] 1. to touch or lean against end-on 2. to adjoin —*vt.* to border upon

ABUTMENT

abutment *n.* the supporting structure of a bridge, arch, etc.
abysmal (ə biz′m′l) *adj.* 1. of or like an abyss; bottomless 2. [Colloq.] immeasurably bad —**abys′mally** *adv.*
abyss (ə bis′) *n.* [< Gr. *a-*, without + *byssos*, bottom] 1. a bottomless gulf; chasm 2. anything too deep for measurement [*an abyss of shame*] 3. *Theol.* the primeval chaos before the Creation —**abyssal** (ə bis′′l) *adj.*
-ac (ak, ək) [< Fr. < Gr.] a suffix meaning: 1. relating to [*cardiac*] 2. affected by or having [*maniac*]
Ac *Chem.* actinium
AC, A.C., a.c. alternating current
A.C. aircraft(s)man
A/C, a/c *Bookkeeping* account
acacia (ə kā′shə) *n.* [< Gr. *akakia*, thorny tree] a tree or shrub with clusters of yellow or white flowers: some yield gum arabic or dyes
academic (ak′ə dem′ik) *adj.* [see ACADEMY] 1. of colleges, universities, etc. 2. merely theoretical [*an academic question*] 3. having to do with liberal rather than technical education Also **ac′ademical** —*n.* a person at university, esp. a teacher —**ac′adem′ically** *adv.*
academic freedom freedom of a teacher or student to express views without arbitrary interference
academy (ə kad′ə mē) *n., pl.* -mies [< Gr. *akadēmeia*, place where Plato taught]

1. a school offering training in a special field 2. an association of scholars, writers, artists, etc., for advancing literature, art, or science 3. a secondary school, esp. in Scotland

acanthus (ə kan′thəs) *n., pl.* **-thuses, -thi** (-thī) [< Gr. *akē̆*, a point] 1. a plant with lobed, often spiny leaves 2. *Archit.* a conventional representation of its leaf

A.C.A.S., ACAS Advisory, Conciliation, and Arbitration Service

acc. 1. accompanied 2. account 3. accusative

A.C.C.A. Association of Certified and Corporate Accountants

accede (ak sēd′) *vi.* **-ced′ed, -ced′ing** [< L. *ad-*, to + *cedere*, to yield] 1. to assent; agree (*to*) 2. to enter upon the duties (of an office) —**acced′ence** *n.* —**acced′-er** *n.*

accelerando (ak sel′ə ran′dō) *adv., adj.* [It.] *Music* with gradually quickening tempo

accelerate (ək sel′ə rāt′) *vt.* **-at′ed, -at′-ing** [< L. *ad-*, to + *celerare*, hasten] 1. to increase the speed of 2. to cause to happen sooner —*vi.* to go faster —**accel′era′tion** *n.* —**accel′erative** *adj.*

accelerator *n.* 1. a device, as the foot throttle of a motor vehicle, for speeding up something 2. *Chem.* a substance that speeds up a reaction 3. *Nuclear Physics* a device that accelerates charged particles to high energies

accent (ak′sent; *for v. also* ak sent′) *n.* [< L. *ad-*, to + *canere*, to sing] 1. the emphasis given to a syllable or word in speaking it 2. a mark used to show this emphasis or to distinguish various sounds for the same letter 3. a distinguishing regional or national way of pronouncing 4. [*pl.*] speech 5. special emphasis [to put the *accent* on safety] 6. *Music* emphasis or stress on a note or chord 7. *Prosody* rhythmic stress or beat —*vt.* 1. to stress 2. to mark with an accent

accentor (ak sen′tər) *n.* [< L. *ad*, to + *cantor*, singer] any of a genus of small songbirds, as the hedge sparrow

accentuate (ak sen′tyōo wāt′) *vt.* **-at′ed, -at′ing** 1. to pronounce or mark with an accent or stress 2. to emphasize —**accen′tua′tion** *n.*

accept (ək sept′) *vt.* [< L. *ad-*, to + *capere*, take] 1. to receive willingly 2. to say "yes" to [to *accept* an invitation] 3. to agree to 4. to believe in 5. to approve 6. to understand as having a certain meaning 7. to agree to pay —*vi.* to accept something offered —**accept′er** *n.*

acceptable *adj.* worth accepting; satisfactory or, sometimes, merely adequate —**accept′abil′ity** *n.* —**accept′ably** *adv.*

acceptance *n.* 1. an accepting or being accepted 2. approval 3. assent 4. a promise to pay

accepted *adj.* generally regarded as true, proper, etc.; conventional; approved

acceptor *n.* 1. one who accepts, esp. a bill of exchange 2. *Electronics* an impurity added to a semiconductor that increases its conductivity

access (ak′ses) *n.* [see ACCEDE] 1. approach 2. a means of approaching 3. the right to enter, use, etc. 4. an outburst [an *access* of anger] 5. the onset (of a disease)

accessary (ək ses′ər ē) *adj., n., pl.* **-ries** *same as* ACCESSORY

accessible (ək ses′ə b′l) *adj.* 1. that can be approached or entered 2. easy to approach or enter 3. obtainable 4. open to the influence of (with *to*) [not *accessible* to pity] —**acces′sibil′ity** *n.* —**acces′sibly** *adv.*

accession (ak sesh′ən) *n.* 1. the act of attaining (a throne, power, etc.) 2. assent 3. *a*) increase by addition *b*) an item added, as to a library —**acces′sional** *adj.*

accessory (ək ses′ər ē) *adj.* [see ACCEDE] 1. extra; additional 2. *Law* helping in an unlawful act —*n., pl.* **-ries** 1. something extra, as an article to complete one's costume or a piece of optional equipment 2. *Law* an accomplice —**accessory before** (or **after**) **the fact** one who aids another before (or after) the commission of a crime —**accessorial** (ak′sə sôr′ē əl) *adj.*

access time in computers, the time between a request for information from storage and its delivery

accident (ak′sə dənt) *n.* [< L. *ad-*, to + *cadere*, to fall] 1. a happening that is not foreseen or intended 2. an unintended happening that results in injury, loss, etc. 3. chance [to meet by *accident*] 4. an attribute that is not essential

accidental (ak′sə den′t'l) *adj.* 1. happening by chance 2. belonging but not essential —*n.* 1. a nonessential quality 2. *Music* a sign, as a sharp or flat, placed before a note to show a change of pitch —**ac′ciden′tally** *adv.*

acclaim (ə klām′) *vt.* [< L. *ad-*, to + *clamare*, to cry out] 1. to greet with strong approval 2. to announce with much applause or praise [they *acclaimed* him victor] —*n.* loud applause or strong approval

acclamation (ak′lə mā′shən) *n.* 1. loud applause or strong approval 2. an approving vote by voice without an actual count 3. [Canad.] an unopposed election —**acclamatory** (ə klam′ə tôr′ē) *adj.*

acclimatize (ə klī′mə tīz′) *vt., vi.* **-tized′, -tiz′ing** [see AD- & CLIMATE] to accustom or become accustomed to a different climate or environment —**accli′matiza′tion** *n.*

accolade (ak′ə lād′) *n.* [ult. < L. *ad*, to + *collum*, neck] 1. anything done or given as a sign of great respect, appreciation, etc. 2. a touch with a sword used in conferring knighthood

accommodate (ə kom′ə dāt′) *vt.* **-dat′ed, -dat′ing** [< L. *ad-*, to + *com-*, with + *modus*, a measure] 1. to help by supplying (with something) 2. to do a favour for 3. to adjust; adapt 4. to reconcile 5. to have room for —*vi.* to become adjusted, as the lens of the eye in focusing —**accom′-modative** *adj.* —**accom′moda′tor** *n.*

accommodating *adj.* ready to help; obliging

accommodation (ə kom′ə dā′shən) *n.* 1. adjustment 2. lodgings or space, as in a hotel, on a ship, etc. 3. reconciliation of differences 4. willingness to do favours 5. a help or convenience

accommodation address an address to which letters, etc. may be sent, although the addressee does not live or work there

accompaniment (ə kum′pə nē mənt) *n.* 1. anything that accompanies something else 2. *Music* a part played as a subsidiary to a song, or to another part

accompanist (ə kum′pə nist) *n.* a person who plays an accompaniment

accompany (ə kum′pə nē) *vt.* -nied, -nying [see AD- & COMPANION[1]] 1. to go or be together with 2. to supplement 3. to play an accompaniment for or to

accomplice (ə kum′plis) *n.* [see COMPLEX] a person who knowingly helps another in an unlawful act

accomplish (ə kum′plish) *vt.* [< L. ad-, intens. + *complere*, complete] to do; succeed in doing; complete

accomplished *adj.* 1. done; completed 2. skilled; proficient 3. trained in the social arts or skills

accomplishment *n.* 1. completion 2. something done successfully; achievement 3. a social art or skill

accord (ə kôrd′) *vt.* [< L. ad-, to + cor, heart] to grant or concede —*vi.* to agree or harmonize (*with*) —*n.* mutual agreement; harmony —**of one's own accord** willingly, without being asked —**with one accord** all agreeing —**accord′ance** *n.*

according *adj.* in harmony —**according as** to the degree that —**according to** 1. in agreement with 2. in the order of 3. as stated by

accordingly *adv.* 1. in a way that is fitting and proper 2. therefore

ACCORDION

accordion (ə kôr′dē ən) *n.* [< G., prob. < It. *accordare*, be in tune] a musical instrument with a bellows which is pressed to force air through reeds operated by fingering keys or studs —*adj.* having folds like an accordion's bellows [*accordion* pleats] —**accor′dionist** *n.*

accost (ə kost′) *vt.* [< L. ad-, to + *costa*, rib, side] to approach and speak to, esp. in a bold or forward manner

account (ə kount′) *n.* [< L. *computare*:

see COMPUTE] 1. a report 2. an explanation 3. worth; importance 4. a record of financial transactions 5. *same as* BANK ACCOUNT —*vt.* to consider to be —*vi.* 1. to furnish a reckoning of money received and paid out 2. to make amends (*for*) 3. to give reasons (*for*) 4. to be the cause of (with *for*) 5. to put out of action by killing, defeating, etc. (with *for*) —**by all accounts** according to all opinions —**call to account** 1. to demand an explanation of 2. to reprimand —**give a good account of oneself** to acquit oneself well —**on account** as partial payment —**on account of** because of —**on no account** under no circumstances —**take account of** 1. to allow for 2. to take notice of —**take into account** to take into consideration —**turn to (good) account** to get use or profit from

accountable *adj.* 1. obliged to account for one's acts; responsible 2. that can be accounted for; explainable —**account′a-bil′ity** *n.* —**account′ably** *adv.*

accountant *n.* a person whose work is to inspect or keep financial accounts —**account′ancy** *n.*

accounting *n.* the principles or practice of setting up and auditing financial accounts

accoutrements (ə kōōt′trə mənts) *n.pl.* [< L. con-, together + *suere*, to sew] 1. clothes; dress 2. equipment; furnishings

accredit (ə kred′it) *vt.* [see CREDIT] 1. to attribute 2. to certify as meeting certain standards 3. to give credentials to (an ambassador, representative, etc.) 4. to take as true —**accred′ita′tion** *n.*

accretion (ə krē′shən) *n.* [< L. ad-, to + *crescere*, grow] 1. growth in size, esp. by addition 2. a growing together of parts 3. accumulated matter 4. a whole resulting from such growth —**accre′tive** *adj.*

accrue (ə krōō′) *vi.* -crued, -cru′ing [see ACCRETION] 1. to come as a natural growth 2. to be added periodically as an increase —**accru′al** *n.*

acct. account

acculturation (ə kul′chə rā′shən) *n.* a conditioning or becoming adapted to a different culture

accumulate (ə kyōōm′yə lāt′) *vt., vi.* -lat′-ed, -lat′ing [< L. ad-, to + *cumulare*, to heap] to pile up or collect, esp. over a period of time —**accu′mulative** *adj.*

accumulation (ə kyōōm′yə lā′shən) *n.* 1. an accumulating; collection 2. accumulated or collected material

accumulator (ə kyōōm′yə lāt′ər) *n.* 1. a storage battery 2. a device, as in a computer, that stores a quantity and that will add to it, storing the sum 3. a bet on several successive races, both the stake and the winnings being carried forward from one race to the next

accuracy (ak′yoo rə sē) *n.* the quality or state of being accurate; precision

accurate (ak′yoo rət) *adj.* [< L. ad-, to + *cura*, care] 1. careful and exact 2. free from errors —**ac′curately** *adv.*

accursed (ə kur′sid) *adj.* 1. under a curse 2. deserving to be cursed Also **accurst′**

accusation (ak′yŏŏ zā′shən) *n.* 1. an accusing or being accused 2. the wrong that one is accused of

accusative (ə kyŏŏ′zə tiv) *adj.* [see ACCUSE] *Gram.* designating or in the case of an object of a verb or prepositions —*n.* 1. the accusative case 2. a word in this case —**accu′sati′val** (-tī′v′l) *adj.*

accusatory (ə kyŏŏ′zə tər ē) *adj.* making or containing an accusation; accusing

accuse (ə kyŏŏz′) *vt.* **-cused′, -cus′ing** [< L. *ad-*, to + *causa*, lawsuit] 1. to blame 2. to bring charges against (of breaking the law, etc.) —**the accused** *Law* the person charged with committing a crime —**accus′er** *n.* —**accus′ingly** *adv.*

accustom (ə kus′təm) *vt.* to make used (*to* something) as by custom or regular use; habituate

accustomed *adj.* 1. customary; usual; characteristic 2. used (*to*); in the habit of

ace (ās) *n.* [< L. *as*, unit] 1. a playing card, domino, etc. with one spot 2. a serve, as in tennis, that one's opponent is unable to return 3. *Golf* a hole in one 4. a combat pilot who has destroyed many enemy aircraft 5. [Colloq.] an expert —*adj.* [Colloq.] first-rate; expert —**ace up one's sleeve** a hidden and powerful advantage —**within an ace of** on the verge of; very close to

-aceous (ā′shəs) [L.] *a suffix meaning* of the nature of, like, belonging to, producing, etc.

acerbate (as′ər bāt′) *vt.* **-bat′ed, -bat′ing** 1. to make sour or bitter 2. to irritate; vex

acerbity (ə sur′bə tē) *n., pl.* **-ties** [< L. *acerbus*, bitter] 1. sharpness or harshness of temper, words, etc. 2. a sour, astringent quality —**acer′bic** *adj.*

acetaldehyde (as′ə tal′də hīd′) *n.* [ACET(O)- + ALDEHYDE] a colourless, soluble, volatile liquid used as a solvent

acetate (as′ə tāt′) *n.* a salt or ester of acetic acid

acetic (ə sēt′ik) *adj.* [< L. *acetum*: see ACETO-] of, like, containing, or producing acetic acid or vinegar

acetic acid a sour, colourless liquid having a sharp odour: it is found in vinegar

aceto- [< L. *acetum*, vinegar] *a combining form meaning* of or from acetic acid

acetone (as′ə tōn′) *n.* a colourless, flammable, volatile liquid used as a solvent for certain oils, etc.

acetylene (ə set′ə lēn′) *n.* a colourless gas used for lighting and, with oxygen, in blowlamps, etc.

acetylsalicylic acid (ə sēt′ əl sal′ə sil′ik) aspirin

ache (āk) *vi.* **ached, ach′ing** [OE. *acan*] 1. to have or give dull, steady pain 2. to yearn —*n.* a dull, continuous pain

achieve (ə chēv′) *vt.* **achieved′, achiev′-ing** [< OFr. *a-*, to + *chief:* see CHIEF] 1. to succeed in doing; accomplish 2. to get by exertion; attain; gain —**achiev′-er** *n.*

achievement *n.* 1. an achieving 2. a thing achieved, esp. by skill, work, etc.; feat

Achilles' heel (ə kil′ēz) [< *Achilles,* Gr. hero killed by an arrow in his vulnerable heel] (one's) vulnerable spot

Achilles' tendon the tendon connecting the back of the heel to the muscles of the calf of the leg

achromatic (ak′rə mat′ik) *adj.* [< Gr. *a-*, without + *chrōma,* colour] 1. colourless 2. refracting white light without breaking it up into its component colours

acid (as′id) *adj.* [L. *acidus,* sour] 1. sharp to the taste; sour 2. sharp or sarcastic in speech, etc. 3. of an acid 4. having too much acid —*n.* 1. a sour substance 2. [Slang] same as LSD 3. *Chem.* any compound that reacts with a base to form a salt —**ac′idly** *adv.*

acidic (ə sid′ik) *adj.* 1. forming acid 2. acid

acidify (ə sid′ə fī′) *vt., vi.* **-fied′, -fy′ing** 1. to make or become sour or acid 2. to change into an acid

acidity (ə sid′ə tē) *n., pl.* **-ties** 1. acid quality or condition; sourness 2. the degree of this

acid test [orig., a *test* of gold by *acid*] a crucial, final test of value or quality

acidulous (ə sid′ yŏŏ ləs) *adj.* 1. somewhat acid or sour 2. somewhat sarcastic Also **acid′ulent**

-acious (ā′shəs) [< L.] *a suffix meaning* inclined to, full of [*tenacious*]

-acity (as′ə tē) *a n.-forming suffix corresponding to* -ACIOUS [*tenacity*]

ack-ack (ak′ak′) *n.* [echoic] [Colloq.] an antiaircraft gun or its fire

acknowledge (ək nol′ij) *vt.* **-edged, -edging** [ult. < OE. *oncnawan,* to understand] 1. to admit to be true 2. to recognize the authority or claims of 3. to recognize and answer (a greeting or introduction) 4. to express thanks for 5. to state that one has received (a letter, gift, etc.)

acknowledgment, acknowledge-ment *n.* 1. an admission 2. something done or given in acknowledging, as thanks 3. recognition of the authority or claims of

acme (ak′mē) *n.* [Gr. *akmē,* a point, top] the highest point; peak

acne (ak′nē) *n.* [? < Gr. *akmē:* see prec.] a skin disease characterized by inflammation of the sebaceous glands, causing pimples on the face, etc.

acolyte (ak′ə līt′) *n.* [< Gr. *akolouthos,* follower] 1. *R.C.Ch.* a member of the highest of the four minor orders, who serves at Mass 2. an attendant 3. a novice

aconite (ak′ə nīt′) *n.* [< L. < Gr. *akoniton*] 1. a poisonous plant with blue, purple, or yellow hoodlike flowers 2. a drug made from the dried roots

acorn (ā′kôrn′) *n.* [< OE. *æcern,* nut] the fruit of the oak tree

acoustic (ə kŏŏs′tik) *adj.* [< Gr. *akouein,* hear] 1. having to do with hearing or with acoustics 2. detonated by sound vibrations [an *acoustic* mine] 3. designating a musical instrument whose tones are not electronically altered Also **acous′tical** —**acous′tically** *adv.*

acoustics *n.pl.* 1. the qualities of a room, etc. that relate to how clearly sounds can be heard in it **2.** [*with sing. v.*] the branch of physics dealing with sound

acquaint (əkwānt′) *vt.* [< L. *ad*, to + *cognoscere*, to know] **1.** to make familiar (*with*) **2.** to make aware

acquaintance *n.* **1.** a person whom one knows only slightly **2.** knowledge gained from personal experience —**make the acquaintance of** to come into social contact with —**acquaint′anceship′** *n.*

acquiesce (ak′wē es′) *vi.* **-esced′, -esc′-ing** [< L. *ad-*, to + *quiescere*, to keep quiet] to consent quietly without protest, but without enthusiasm —**ac′quies′cence** *n.* —**ac′quies′cent** *adj.*

acquire (əkwīr′) *vt.* **-quired′, -quir′ing** [< L. *ad-*, to + *quaerere*, seek] **1.** to gain by one's own efforts **2.** to get as one's own —**acquisition** (ak′wə zish′ən) *n.*

acquired taste 1. a liking for something at first considered unpleasant **2.** the thing so liked

acquisitive (əkwiz′ə tiv) *adj.* eager to acquire wealth, ideas, etc. —**acquis′itively** *adv.* —**acquis′itiveness** *n.*

acquit (əkwit′) *vt.* **-quit′ted, -quit′ting** [< L. *ad*, to + *quietare*, to quiet] **1.** to declare not guilty of a charge **2.** to release from a duty, etc. **3.** to conduct (oneself); behave —**acquit′tal** *n.* —**acquit′-ter** *n.*

acre (ā′kər) *n.* [OE. *æcer*, field] **1.** a measure of land, 43 560 square feet or 4046 m² **2.** [*pl.*] specific holdings in land; lands

acreage (ā′kər ij) *n.* acres collectively

acrid (ak′rid) *adj.* [< L. *acris*, sharp] **1.** bitter, or irritating to the taste or smell **2.** bitter or sarcastic in speech, etc. —**acrid-ity** (a krid′ə tē) *n.* —**ac′ridly** *adv.*

acrimony (ak′rə mə nē) *n.* [< L. *acer*, sharp] bitterness or harshness of manner or speech; asperity —**ac′rimo′nious** (-mō′nē əs) *adj.*

acro- [< Gr. *akros*, at the end or top] *a combining form meaning* highest, at the extremities

acrobat (ak′rə bat′) *n.* [< Gr. *akros* (see prec.) + *bainein*, to go] an expert performer of tricks in tumbling or on the trapeze, tightrope, etc. —**ac′robat′ic** *adj.* —**ac′robat′ically** *adv.*

acrobatics (ak′rə bat′iks) *n.pl.* [*also with sing. v.*] **1.** the skill or tricks of an acrobat **2.** any activity requiring agility and skill [*mental acrobatics*]

acromegaly (ak′rō meg′ə lē) *n.* [see ACRO- & MEGALO-] abnormal enlargement of the head, hands, and feet, resulting from overproduction of growth hormone by the pituitary gland —**ac′romegal′ic** (-məgal′ik) *adj.*

acronym (ak′rə nim) *n.* [< ACRO- + Gr. *onyma*, name] a word formed from the first (or first few) letters of a series of words, as *radar*, from *ra*dio *d*etecting *a*nd *r*anging

acrophobia (ak′rə fō′bē ə) *n.* [ACRO- + PHOBIA] an abnormal fear of being in high places

acropolis (əkrop′ə lis) *n.* [< Gr. *akros*

(see ACRO-) + *polis*, city] the fortified upper part of an ancient Greek city, esp. [A-] that of Athens, on which the Parthenon was built

across (əkros′) *adv.* **1.** crossed **2.** from one side to the other —*prep.* **1.** from one side to the other of **2.** on the other side of **3.** into contact with by chance [he came *across* a friend]

acrostic (əkros′tik) *n.* [< Gr. *akros* (see ACRO-) + *stichos*, line of verse] a verse or arrangement of words in which certain letters in each line, as the first or last, spell out a word, motto, etc. —**acros′ti-cally** *adv.*

acrylic fibre (əkril′ik) [< ACR(ID)] a synthetic fibre derived from hydrogen cyanide and acetylene

acrylic resin any of a group of transparent thermoplastic resins, as Per-spex

act (akt) *n.* [< L. *actum*, pp. of *agere*, to do] **1.** a thing done **2.** an action **3.** a decision (of a legislative body, etc.) **4.** one of the main divisions of a drama or opera **5.** any of the separate performances on a variety programme **6.** insincere behaviour —*vt.* **1.** to play the part of **2.** to perform in (a play) —*vi.* **1.** to perform on the stage **2.** to behave as though playing a role **3.** to behave; comport oneself **4.** to function **5.** to serve as spokesman (*for*) **6.** to have an effect (*on*) **7.** to appear to be —**act on** (or *upon*) to behave in accordance with —**act up** [Colloq.] **1.** to misbehave **2.** to become inflamed, painful, etc.

A.C.T. Australian Capital Territory

acting *adj.* **1.** temporarily taking over the duties of a position **2.** functioning —*n.* the art of an actor

actinic rays (ak tin′ik) violet or ultraviolet rays that produce chemical changes, as in photography

actinide series (ak′tə nid′) a group of radioactive chemical elements from element 89 (actinium) to element 103 (lawren-cium)

actinium (ak tin′ē əm) *n.* [< Gr. *aktis*, ray] a radioactive chemical element found in pitchblende: symbol, Ac

action (ak′shən) *n.* [see ACT] **1.** the doing of something **2.** a thing done **3.** [*pl.*] behaviour **4.** bold and energetic activity **5.** an effect [the *action* of a drug] **6.** the way of moving, as of a machine **7.** the moving parts, as of a gun **8.** the happenings in a story or play **9.** a lawsuit **10.** military combat **11.** [Colloq.] activity or excitement —**out of action** not functioning

actionable *adj.* *Law* that gives cause for a lawsuit

action painting an art form using the spattering of paint to create random compositions

action stations points manned instantly by troops when enemy attack is imminent

activate (ak′tə vāt′) *vt.* **-vat′ed, -vat′ing** **1.** to make active **2.** to make radioactive

3. to treat (sewage) with air so as to purify it —**ac′tiva′tion** *n.* —**ac′tiva′tor** *n.*

activated carbon a highly porous carbon that can adsorb gases, vapours, and colloidal particles

activated sludge aerated sewage added to untreated sewage to hasten bacterial decomposition

active (ak′tiv) *adj.* [see ACT] **1.** acting, working, etc. **2.** capable of acting, functioning, etc. **3.** causing motion or change **4.** lively, quick, etc. **5.** necessitating action [*active* sports] **6.** liable to erupt [an *active* volcano] **7.** *Gram.* denoting the voice of a verb whose subject is shown as performing the action —*n.* *Gram.* the active voice —**ac′tively** *adv.*

active list the list of those who can be called on for military duty (**active service**) in the armed forces

activism (ak′tə viz′m) *n.* the policy of taking direct action, esp. for political or social ends —**ac′tivist** *adj., n.*

activity (ak tiv′ə tē) *n., pl.* -**ties** **1.** the state of being active **2.** liveliness **3.** any specific action or pursuit [recreational *activities*]

act of God *Law* an unforeseeable occurrence, esp. a disaster, caused by the forces of nature

actor (ak′tər) *n.* a person who acts in plays, films, etc. —**ac′tress** *n.fem.*

A.C.T.U. Australian Council of Trade Unions

actual (ak′chōō wəl) *adj.* [see ACT] **1.** existing in reality **2.** existing at present or at the time

actuality (ak′chōō wal′ə tē) *n.* **1.** reality **2.** *pl.* -**ties** an actual thing or condition; fact

actually (ak′chōō wəl ē) *adv.* really

actuarius (ak′chōō wāər′ē əs) *n.* *S Afr. Hist.* the actuary of the synod of a Dutch Reformed church

actuary (ak′chōō wər ē) *n., pl.* -**aries** [< L. *actuarius*, clerk] a person who calculates risks, premiums, etc. for insurance —**actuarial** (ak′chōō wāər′ē əl) *adj.*

actuate (ak′chōō wāt′) *vt.* -**at′ed, -at′ing** **1.** to put into action **2.** to cause to take action —**ac′tua′tion** *n.*

acuity (ə kyōō′ə tē) *n.* [< L. *acus*, needle] keenness, as of thought or vision; acuteness

acumen (ə kyōō′mən) *n.* [< L. *acuere*, sharpen] keenness and quickness of mind

acupuncture (ak′yōō puŋk′chər) *n.* [< L. *acus*, needle + PUNCTURE] *Med.* the practice of piercing parts of the body with needles to treat disease or relieve pain

ACUTE ANGLE

acute (ə kyōōt′) *adj.* [see ACUMEN] **1.** keen of mind; shrewd **2.** sensitive [acute

hearing] **3.** very serious **4.** having a sharp point **5.** severe and sharp, as pain **6.** severe but short, as some diseases; not chronic **7.** of less than 90° [an acute angle] —**acute′ly** *adv.* —**acute′ness** *n.*

acute accent a mark (′) used to show : *a)* the quality or length of a vowel, as in French *idée* *b)* primary stress

-acy (ə sē) [< Gr.] *a suffix meaning* quality, condition, position, etc. [*celibacy, curacy*]

ad (ad) *n.* [Colloq.] an advertisement

ad- [L.] *a prefix meaning* motion towards, addition to, nearness to: assimilated to **ac-, af-, ag-, al-, an-, ap-, ar-, as-, at-,** and **a-** before certain consonants

A.D. [L. *Anno Domini*, in the year of the Lord] of the Christian era: used with dates

adage (ad′ij) *n.* [Fr. < L. *ad-*, to + *aio*, I say] an old saying that has been popularly accepted as a truth

adagio (ə dä′jē ō) *adv.* [It.] *Music* slowly —*n., pl.* -**gios** a slow movement in music

Adam¹ (ad′əm) *Bible* the first man : Gen. 1–5 —**not know (a person) from Adam** not to know (a person) at all

Adam² *adj.* [< the 18th c. Brit. architects] of a style of architecture and furniture based on classical designs

adamant (ad′ə mənt) *n.* [< Gr. *a-*, not + *daman*, subdue] a substance of unbreakable hardness —*adj.* **1.** too hard to be broken **2.** unyielding —**ad′aman′-tine** (-man′tīn) *adj.* —**ad′amantly** *adv.*

Adam′s apple the projection formed in the front of the throat by the thyroid cartilage, seen chiefly in men

adapt (ə dapt′) *vt.* [< L. *ad-*, to + *aptare*, to fit] **1.** to make suitable by changing **2.** to adjust (oneself) to new circumstances —*vi.* to adjust oneself —**adapt′abil′ity** *n.* —**adapt′able** *adj.*

adaptation (ad′əp tā′shən) *n.* **1.** an adapting **2.** a thing resulting from adapting **3.** *Biol.* a change in structure, function, etc. that produces better adjustment to the environment Also **adaption** (ə dap′shən)

adapter, adaptor *n.* **1.** a device for adapting apparatus to new uses **2.** a device for connecting several electrical appliances to a single mains socket

A.D.C., ADC aide-de-camp

add (ad) *vt.* [< L. *ad-*, to + *dare*, give] **1.** to combine (numbers) into a total **2.** to join (*to*) so as to increase **3.** to state further —*vi.* **1.** to calculate a total **2.** to cause an increase (*to*) —**add up 1.** to find the total of **2.** to seem reasonable —**add up to** [Colloq.] to mean; signify

addend (ad′end) *n.* [< ff.] a number or quantity to be added to another

addendum (ə den′dəm) *n., pl.* -**da** [L. : see ADD] a thing added; esp., an appendix or supplement

adder (ad′ər) *n.* [< OE. *nædre*] a small poisonous snake; common viper

addict (ə dikt′; *for n.* ad′ikt) *vt.* [< L. *ad-*, to + *dicere*, say] to give (oneself) up (*to* some strong habit): usually in the passive —*n.* 1. one addicted, esp. to a drug 2. [Colloq.] a person devoted to something —**addic'tion** *n.* —**addic'tive** *adj.*

addition (ə dish'ən) *n.* 1. an adding of numbers to get a total 2. a joining of a thing to another thing 3. a part added —**in addition (to)** besides; as well (as) —**addi'tional** *adj.*

additive (ad'ə tiv) *adj.* 1. relating to addition 2. to be added —*n.* a substance added, as a preservative

addle (ad''l) *adj.* [< OE. *adela*, mud] 1. rotten: said of an egg 2. muddled; confused —*vt., vi.* -**dled,** -**dling** to make or become rotten or confused

address (ə dres') *n.* [< L. *dirigere*, to direct] 1. the place to which letters, etc. can be sent to one; place where one lives or works 2. the writing on letters or parcels showing their destination 3. a speech, esp. a formal one 4. the location in a computer's storage compartment of an item of information 5. social skill and tact 6. [*pl.*] attentions paid in courting a woman —*vt.* 1. to write the destination on (a letter or parcel) 2. to speak or write to 3. to direct words (*to*) 4. to apply (oneself)

addressee (ad'res ē') *n.* the person to whom a letter, etc., is addressed

adduce (ə dyōōs') *vt.* -**duced',** -**duc'ing** [< L. *ad-*, to + *ducere*, to lead] to give as a reason or proof; cite —**adduc'er** *n.* —**adduc'ible** *adj.*

-ade (ād) [ult. < L.] *a suffix meaning:* 1. the act of [*blockade*] 2. the product of [*pomade*] 3. participant(s) [*brigade*]

adeno- [< Gr. *adēn,* gland] *a combining form meaning* of a gland or glands

adenoidal (ad'ən oid''l) *adj.* 1. having difficult breathing due to enlarged adenoids 2. *a*) glandular *b*) of lymphoid tissue: also **ad'enoid'** 3. having adenoids

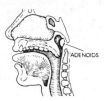

ADENOIDS

adenoids (ad'ən oidz') *n.pl.* [< ADEN(O)-] lymphoid growths in the throat behind the nose

adept (ə dept'; *for n.* ad'ept) *adj.* [< L. *ad-*, to + *apisci,* to attain] highly skilled; expert —*n.* an expert —**adept'ness** *n.*

adequate (ad'ə kwət) *adj.* [< L. *ad-*, to + *aequare,* to make equal] 1. sufficient; suitable 2. barely satisfactory —**ad'e-quacy, ad'equateness** *n.*

‡à deux (à dö') [Fr.] 1. of or for two 2. intimate

adhere (əd hēar') *vi.* -**hered',** -**her'ing** [< L. *ad-*, to + *haerere,* to stick] 1. to stick fast 2. to stay firm in supporting or approving —**adher'ence** *n.* —**adher'er** *n.*

adherent *n.* a supporter (*of* a person, cause, etc.) —*adj.* 1. sticking fast; attached 2. *Bot.* grown together

adhesion (əd hē'zhən) *n.* 1. a sticking or being stuck together 2. devoted attachment 3. *Med. a*) the joining together, by fibrous tissue, of bodily parts normally separate *b*) such fibrous tissue

adhesive (əd hē'siv) *adj.* 1. sticking 2. gummed; sticky —*n.* an adhesive substance, as glue —**adhe'sively** *adv.*

ad hoc (ad'hok') [L., to this] for a special case only

adieu (ə dyōō') *interj., n., pl.* **adieus', adieux'** [Fr.] goodbye

ad infinitum (ad in'fə nīt'əm) [L., to infinity] endlessly; forever; without limit

adipose (ad'ə pōs') *adj.* [< L. *adeps,* fat] of, or containing animal fat —*n.* animal fat —**ad'ipos'ity** (-pos'ə tē) *n.*

adj. 1. adjective 2. adjourned 3. adjutant

adjacent (ə jā's'nt) *adj.* [< L. *ad-*, to + *jacere,* to lie] near or close (*to*) —**adja'-cency** *n.* —**adja'cently** *adv.*

adjective (aj'ik tiv) *n.* [< L. *ad-*, to + *jacere,* to throw] a word used to qualify a noun [*good, every,* and *Aegean* are adjectives] —**ad'jecti'val** (-ti'v'l) *adj.*

adjoin (ə join') *vt., vi.* [< L. *ad-*, to + *jungere,* to join] to be next to —**adjoin'-ing** *adj.*

adjourn (ə jurn') *vt.* [< L. *ad,* to + *diurnus,* daily] to put off until a future day —*vi.* 1. to close a session for a time 2. [Colloq.] to go (*to* another place) —**adjourn'ment** *n.*

adjudge (ə juj') *vt.* -**judged',** -**judg'ing** [< L. *ad-*, to + *judicare,* to judge] 1. to decide by law 2. to order by law 3. to award (costs, etc.) by law 4. [Rare] to deem

adjudicate (ə jōō'də kāt') *vt.* -**cat'ed,** -**cat'ing** [see prec.] *Law* to hear and decide (a case) —*vi.* to serve as a judge (*in* or *on*) —**adju'dica'tion** *n.* —**adju'dica'-tor** *n.*

adjunct (aj'uŋkt) *n.* [see ADJOIN] 1. a thing added, but secondary 2. a subordinate associate 3. *Gram.* a modifier —*adj.* connected in a subordinate way —**adjunc'tive** *adj.* —**adjunc'tively** *adv.* —**ad'junctly** *adv.*

adjure (ə jōōr') *vt.* -**jured',** -**jur'ing** [< L. *ad-*, to + *jurare,* to swear] 1. to charge solemnly, often under oath 2. to entreat —**adjura'tion** *n.*

adjust (ə just') *vt.* [< OFr. < L. *justus,* lawful] 1. to regulate [*to adjust a watch*] 2. to change so as to make suitable, etc. 3. to settle rightly 4. to decide how much is to be paid on (an insurance claim) —*vi.* to adapt oneself —**adjust'able** *adj.* —**adjust'er** *n.*

adjustment *n.* 1. an adjusting 2. a means by which parts are adjusted 3. the settlement of a claim

adjutant (aj'ə tənt) *n.* [< L. *ad-*, to + *juvare,* to help] 1. an assistant 2. *Mil.* a staff officer who is an administrative assistant to the commanding officer **3.** a large stork of India and Africa

adjutant general *pl.* **adjutants general 1.** an army officer who is the chief administrative assistant of a commanding general **2.** the head of a department of a general staff

ad-lib (ad´lib´) *vt., vi.* **-libbed´, -lib´bing** [< ff.] [Colloq.] to improvise; extemporize —*adj.* spoken or done extemporaneously —*adv.* **1.** [Colloq.] extemporizing freely **2.** without restriction Also **ad lib**

ad libitum (ad´lib´i təm) [ML.] as one pleases

Adm. 1. Admiral **2.** Admiralty

adman (ad´man´) *n.* a man whose work or business is advertising: also **ad man**

admin (ad´min) *n.* [Colloq.] administration

administer (əd min´ə stər) *vt.* [< L. *ad-*, to + *ministrare*, to serve] **1.** to manage or direct **2.** to dispense, give, or apply (medicine, justice, etc.) **3.** to direct the taking of (an oath, etc.) **4.** *Law* to act as executor of Also **admin´istrate** —*vi.* **1.** to act as administrator **2.** to furnish help —**admin´istrant** *n.*

administration (əd min´ə strā´shən) *n.* **1.** management, specif. of the affairs of a government **2.** *a)* the executive officials of a government *b)* the government **3.** the administering (*of* medicine, an oath, etc.) —**admin´istrative** *adj.*

administrator (əd min´ə strāt´ər) *n.* **1.** one who administers **2.** *Law* one appointed by a court to settle an estate

admirable (ad´mər ə b'l) *adj.* deserving admiration —**ad´mirabil´ity** *n.* —**ad´mirably** *adv.*

admiral (ad´mər əl) *n.* **1.** [< Ar. *amir a'ālî*, high leader] *see* MILITARY RANKS, table **2.** [orig. *admirable*] any of certain colourful butterflies

admiral of the fleet *see* MILITARY RANKS, table

admiralty *n., pl.* **-ties 1.** the rank, position, or authority of an admiral **2.** [often A-] the governmental department for naval affairs, as formerly in Britain

admire (ad´mīr´) *vt.* **-mired´, -mir´ing** [< L. *ad-*, at + *mirari*, to wonder] **1.** to regard with wonder and approval **2.** to have high regard for —**admiration** (ad´mə rā´shən) *n.* —**admir´er** *n.* —**admir´ingly** *adv.*

admissible (əd mis´ə b'l) *adj.* **1.** that can be accepted [*admissible* evidence] **2.** that ought to be admitted

admission (əd mish´ən) *n.* **1.** an admitting or being admitted **2.** the right to enter **3.** an entrance fee **4.** a conceding **5.** a thing conceded or confessed —**admis´sive** *adj.*

admit (əd mit´) *vt.* **-mit´ted, -mit´ting** [< L. *ad-*, to + *mittere*, to send] **1.** to concede **2.** to acknowledge **3.** to permit or entitle to enter or use **4.** to permit to practise [*admitted* to the bar] **5.** to leave room for **6.** to have room for —*vi.* to allow or warrant (with *of*)

admittance *n.* **1.** an admitting or being admitted **2.** permission or right to enter

admittedly (əd mit´id lē) *adv.* by admission or agreement; confessedly [*admittedly* afraid]

admixture (ad miks´chər) *n.* [< L. *ad-*, to + *miscere*, to mix] **1.** a mixture **2.** a thing added in mixing

admonish (əd mon´ish) *vt.* [< L. *ad-*, to + *monere*, to warn] **1.** to reprove mildly **2.** to caution; warn **3.** to urge or exhort —**admon´ishment** *n.*

admonition (ad´mə nish´ən) *n.* **1.** an admonishing, or warning to correct some fault **2.** a mild rebuke; reprimand

ad nauseam (ad´nô´zē əm) [L., to nausea] to the point of disgust or tedium

ado (ə dōō´) *n.* [ME. < dial. *at do*, to do] fuss; trouble

adobe (ə dō´bē) *n.* [Sp.] **1.** unburnt, sun-dried brick **2.** the clay of which it is made **3.** a building of adobe

adolescence (ad´ə les´'ns) *n.* the time of life between puberty and maturity

adolescent *adj.* [< L. *adolescere*, to mature] **1.** developing from childhood to maturity **2.** of or characteristic of adolescence —*n.* a boy or girl from puberty to adulthood; person in his teens

Adonis (ə dō´nis) *n.* [< a young man loved by Aphrodite] any very handsome young man

adopt (ə dopt´) *vt.* [< L. *ad-*, to + *optare*, to choose] **1.** to take into one's family by legal process and raise as one's own child **2.** to take and use (an idea, etc.) as one's own **3.** to choose or accept —**adopt´able** *adj.* —**adopt´er** *n.* —**adop´tion** *n.*

adoptive *adj.* **1.** of adoption **2.** having become so by adopting [*adoptive* parents]

adorable (ə dôr´ə b'l) *adj.* **1.** [Colloq.] delightful; charming **2.** worthy of adoration —**ador´ably** *adv.*

adore (ə dôr´) *vt.* **adored´, ador´ing** [< L. *ad-*, to + *orare*, to speak] **1.** to love or honour greatly; idolize **2.** to worship as divine **3.** [Colloq.] to like very much —**ad´ora´tion** (ad´ə rā´shən) *n.* —**ador´er** *n.*

adorn (ə dôrn´) *vt.* [< L. *ad-*, to + *ornare*, to deck out] **1.** to add beauty or distinction to **2.** to put decorations on; ornament —**adorn´ment** *n.*

ADP Automatic Data Processing

adrenal (ə drē´n'l) *adj.* [AD- + RENAL] **1.** near the kidneys **2.** of or from the adrenal glands —*n.* same as ADRENAL GLAND

adrenal gland either of a pair of endocrine organs lying immediately above the kidney

adrenalin (ə dren´'l in) **1.** a hormone secreted by the adrenal gland, that stimulates the heart, etc. **2.** this substance extracted from animal adrenals or prepared synthetically Also **adren´aline**

adrift (ə drift´) *adv., adj.* **1.** drifting **2.** without any particular purpose **3.** [Colloq.] wrong; amiss

adroit (ə droit´) *adj.* [Fr. < L. *ad*, to

+ *dirigere*, to direct] skilful in a physical or mental way; clever —**adroit′ly** *adv.* —**adroit′ness** *n.*

adsorb (ad sôrb′) *vt.* [< AD- + L. *sorbere*, to drink in] to collect (a gas, etc) in condensed form on a surface —**adsor′bent** *adj., n.* —**adsorp′tion** (-sôrp′-) *n.*

A.D.T. [U.S. & Canad.] Atlantic Daylight Time

adulate (ad′yo͞o lāt′) *vt.* -lat′ed, -lat′ing [< L. *adulari*, fawn upon] to praise or flatter too greatly —**ad′ula′tion** *n.* —**ad′ula′tor** *n.* —**ad′ulatory** *adj.*

adult (ad′ult) *adj.* [see ADOLESCENT] 1. grown up; fully developed 2. of or for adult persons —*n.* a mature person, animal, or plant —**adult′hood** *n.*

adulterant (ə dul′tər ənt) *n.* a substance used to adulterate something —*adj.* adulterating

adulterate (ə dul′tə rāt′) *vt.* -at′ed, -at′ing [< L. *adulter*, adulterer < *ad-*, to + *alter*, other] to make inferior, impure, etc. by adding a harmful, inferior, or unnecessary substance —**adul′tera′tion** *n.*

adulterer (ə dul′tər ər) *n.* a person (esp. a man) who commits adultery —**adul′teress** *n.fem.*

adultery *n., pl.* -teries [see ADULTERATE] voluntary sexual intercourse between a married person and another not the spouse —**adul′terous** *adj.*

adumbrate (ad′əm brāt′) *vt.* -brat′ed, -brat′ing [< L. *ad-*, to + *umbra*, shade] 1. to outline vaguely 2. to foreshadow vaguely 3. to overshadow —**ad′umbra′tion** *n.* —**adum′brative** *adj.*

adv. 1. adverb 2. adverbial 3. advertisement

ad valorem (ad′və lôr′əm) [L.] in proportion to the value : said of duties levied on imports according to their invoiced value : abbrev. **ad val.**

advance (əd vans′) *vt.* -vanced′, -vanc′-ing [< L. *ab-*, from + *ante*, before] 1. to bring forward 2. to raise in rank, etc. 3. to help; further 4. to propose 5. to raise the rate of 6. to pay (money) before due 7. to lend —*vi.* 1. to go forward 2. to improve; develop 3. to rise in rank, etc. —*n.* 1. a moving forward 2. an improvement 3. a rise in value or cost 4. [*pl.*] approaches to gain favour, become acquainted, etc. 5. a payment made before due 6. a loan —*adj.* 1. in front 2. beforehand [*advance* information *]* —**in advance** 1. in front 2. ahead of time —**advance′ment** *n.*

advanced *adj.* 1. beyond in complexity, etc. [*advanced* studies *]* 2. old 3. progressive in opinion [*advanced* views *]* 4. in front

Advanced Level 1. the higher standard of the General Certificate of Education 2. a pass in a particular subject at this standard

advantage (əd vän′tij) *n.* [< L. *ab ante*, from before] 1. a more favourable position 2. a favourable circumstance 3. gain or benefit 4. *Tennis* the first point scored after deuce —*vt.* -taged, -taging to give

an advantage to —**take advantage of** 1. to use for one's own benefit 2. to impose upon the weakness, good nature, etc. of 3. to seduce

advantageous (ad′vən tā′jəs) *adj.* favourable

Advent (ad′vent) *n.* [< L. *ad-*, to + *venire*, to come] 1. the period including the four Sundays just before Christmas 2. *Theol.* a) Christ's birth b) *same as* SECOND COMING 3. [**a-**] a coming or arrival

Adventist (ad′vən tist) *n.* a member of a Christian sect based on the belief that Christ's second coming will soon occur —**Ad′ventism** *n.*

adventitious (ad′ven tish′əs) *adj.* [see ADVENT] 1. added from outside; accidental 2. *Biol.* occurring in unusual places —**ad′-venti′tiously** *adv.*

adventure (əd ven′chər) *n.* [see ADVENT] 1. an exciting and dangerous undertaking 2. an unusual, stirring experience 3. a business venture 4. the encountering of, or a liking for, danger —*vt.* -tured, -tur-ing to risk or venture —*vi.* 1. to engage in adventure 2. to take a risk —**adven′tur-ous** *adj.*

adventure playground a playground where children make imaginative use of everyday materials

adventurer *n.* 1. a person who has or likes to have adventures 2. *same as* SOLDIER OF FORTUNE 3. a financial speculator 4. a person who seeks to become rich, powerful, etc. by dubious schemes —**adven′turess** *n.fem.*

adventurism *n.* actions regarded as reckless and risky

adverb (ad′vurb) *n.* [< L. *ad-*, to + *verbum*, a word] a word used to modify a verb, adjective, or another adverb, by expressing time, place, manner, degree, cause, etc. —**adver′bial** *adj., n.* —**adver′bi-ally** *adv.*

adversary (ad′vər sər ē) *n., pl.* -saries an opponent; enemy

adverse (ad′vərs) *adj.* [< L. *adversus*, turned opposite to : see ADVERT[1]] 1. unfavourable 2. opposite in position —**ad′-versely** *adv.*

adversity (əd vur′sə tē) *n.* wretchedness; trouble

advert[1] (əd vurt′) *vi.* [< L. < *ad-*, to + *vertere*, to turn] to call attention (*to*); refer or allude

advert[2] (ad′vurt) *n.* [Colloq.] an adver-tisement

advertise (ad′vər tīz′) *vt.* -tised, -tis′ing [see ADVERT[1]] 1. to tell about or praise (a product, etc.), as through newspapers or television so as to promote sales 2. to make known —*vi.* 1. to call the public's attention to things for sale, etc. 2. to ask (*for*) publicly by printed notice, etc. [*advertise* for a maid *]* —**ad′vertis′er** *n.*

advertisement (əd vur′tiz mənt) *n.* 1. a public announcement, usually paid for, as of things for sale, needs, etc. 2. the act of advertising

advice (əd vīs′) *n.* [< L. *ad-*, at + *videre*, to look] 1. opinion given as to what to do **2.** notification of transaction **3.** [*usually pl.*] information —**take advice 1.** to act in accordance with advice received **2.** to seek advice from a specialist

advisable (əd vī'zə b'l) *adj.* to be recommended —**advis'abil'ity** *n.* —**advis'ably** *adv.*

advise (əd vīz') *vt.* -**vised',** -**vis'ing 1.** to give advice to **2.** to recommend **3.** to notify —*vi.* **1.** to give advice **2.** [Chiefly U.S.] to consult (*with*) —**advis'er, advi'sor** *n.*

advised *adj.* showing or resulting from thought or advice : now chiefly in *well-advised, ill-advised*

advisedly (əd vī'zid lē) *adv.* deliberately

advisory *adj.* **1.** advising or empowered to advise **2.** relating to, or containing, advice

advocaat (ad'vō kä') *n.* [Du.] a liqueur with a raw egg base

advocacy (ad'və kə sē) *n.* an advocating; a speaking or writing in support (*of* something)

advocate (ad'və kət; *for v.* -kāt') *vt.* -**cat'- ed, -cat'ing** [< L. *ad-*, to + *vocare*, to call] to support; be in favour of —*n.* **1.** a person who pleads another's cause, esp. in a law court **2.** a person who supports something

advowson (ad vou'z'n) *n.* [< L. *advocatio,* a summoning] the right to name the holder of a benefice

advt. *pl.* **advts.** advertisement

adze (adz) *n.* [OE. *adesa*] an axelike tool with a curved blade at right angles to the handle

AEA, A.E.A. Atomic Energy Authority

A.E.C., AEC [U.S.] Atomic Energy Commission

aegis (ē'jis) *n.* [< Gr. *aigis,* goatskin] **1.** *Gr. Myth.* a shield borne by Zeus and, later, Athena **2.** a protection **3.** sponsorship

aegrotat (ī'grō tat, ē-) *n.* [L., he is ill] a certificate allowing a candidate to pass an examination although he has missed all or part of it through illness

-aemia (ē'mē ə) [< Gr. *haima,* blood] a suffix meaning a (specified) condition of the blood [*leukaemia*]

aeolian (ē ō'lē ən) *adj.* [< *Aeolus,* in Gr. myth. the god of the winds] of the wind

aeolian harp a boxlike stringed instrument that makes musical sounds when air blows on it

aeon (ē'ən) *n.* [< Gr. *aiōn,* an age] an extremely long, indefinite time

aerate (āər'āt') *vt.* -**at'ed,** -**at'ing** [see AERO-] **1.** to charge (liquid) with gas, as in making soda water **2.** to expose to air, or cause air to circulate through —**aer- a'tion** *n.* —**aer'ator** *n.*

aeri- same as AERO-

aerial (āər'ē əl) *adj.* [< L. *aer,* air] **1.** of, in, or like air **2.** unreal; imaginary **3.** high up **4.** of, for, or by aircraft or flying —*n. Radio & T.V.* an arrangement of wires, metal rods, etc. used in sending and receiving electromagnetic waves —**aer'ially** *adv.*

aerialist *n.* an acrobat who performs on a trapeze

aerie (āər'ē) *n.* same as EYRIE

aero (āər'ō) *adj.* of or for aeronautics or aircraft

aero- [< Gr. *aēr,* air] a combining form meaning : **1.** air **2.** aircraft or flying **3.** gas

aerobatics (āər'ə bat'iks) *n.pl.* [AERO- + (ACRO)BATICS] precisely controlled manoeuvres performed by aircraft in other than straight and level flight —**aer'obat'- ic** *adj.*

aerodrome (āər'ə drōm') *n.* [AERO- + Gr. *dromos,* a running] a landing area for aircraft, with its buildings, etc.

aerodynamics (āər'ō dī nam'iks) *n.pl.* [*with sing. v.*] the branch of mechanics dealing with the forces exerted by air or other gases in motion —**aer'odynam'- ic** *adj.*

aero-engine (āər'ō en'jin) *n.* an engine for powering an aircraft, esp. a jet engine

aerofoil (āər'ō foil') *n.* a part with a curved surface, as a wing, etc., designed to give an aircraft lift

aerolite (āər'ə līt') *n.* [AERO- + -LITE] a stony meteorite —**aer'olit'ic** (-lit'ik) *adj.*

aeronautics (āər'ə nôt'iks) *n.pl.* [*with sing. v.*] [AERO- + Gr. *nautēs,* sailor] the science of aerial navigation —**aer'o- nau'tical, aer'onau'tic** *adj.*

aeroplane (āər'ə plān') *n.* [< Fr. *aéro-,* AERO- + *planer,* soar] a power-driven aircraft, heavier than air, that is kept aloft by the aerodynamic forces of air upon its wings

aerosol (āər'ō sol') *n.* [AERO-+ SOL^2] **1.** a suspension of colloidal particles in a gas **2.** a spray can dispensing deodorant, paint, etc. under pressure

aerospace (āər'ō spās') *n.* the earth's atmosphere and the space outside it —*adj.* of spacecraft or missiles designed for flight in aerospace

aerostatics (āər'ō stat'iks) *n.pl.* [*with sing. v.*] the branch of mechanics dealing with the equilibrium of air or other gases, and with the equilibrium of solid bodies floating in air or other gases —**aer'ostat'- ic** *adj.*

aery (āər'ē) *n.* same as EYRIE

aesthesia (ēs thē'zē ə) *n.* [< Gr. *aisthēsis,* perception] the ability to feel sensations

aesthete (ēs'thēt') *n.* [Gr. *aisthētēs,* one who perceives] **1.** a person highly sensitive to art and beauty **2.** a person who artificially cultivates artistic sensitivity or makes a cult of art and beauty —**aestheti- cism** (ēs thet'ə siz'm) *n.*

aesthetic (ēs thet'ik) *adj.* **1.** of aesthetics **2.** sensitive to art and beauty; artistic —**aes- thet'ically** *adv.*

aesthetics *n.pl.* [*with sing. v.*] the study or theory of beauty; specif., the branch of philosophy dealing with art and its forms, effects, etc.

aestival (ēs'tə v'l) *adj.* [< L. *aestas,* summer] of or for summer

aestivate (ēs'tə vāt') *vi.* -**vat'ed,** -**vat'-**

ing [see prec.] to spend the summer in a dormant condition

aether (ē′thər) *n.* *earlier var. of* ETHER —**aethereal** (i thēər′ē əl) *adj.*

aetiology (ēt′ē ol′ə jē) *n.* [< Gr. *aitia*, cause + *logos*, discourse] **1.** the study of causation **2.** *Med.* the study of the causes of diseases

a.f., A.F. audio-frequency

afar (ə fär′) *adv.* [Poet. or Archaic] at or to a distance

A.F.C., AFC 1. Air Force Cross **2.** Association Football Club **3.** automatic frequency control

affable (af′ə b'l) *adj.* [< L. *ad-*, to + *fari*, to speak] **1.** easy to approach and talk to; friendly **2.** gentle and kindly —**af′-fabil′ity** *n.* —**af′fably** *adv.*

affair (ə fãər′) *n.* [< OFr. < L. *ad-*, to + *facere*, to do] **1.** a thing to be done **2.** [*pl.*] matters of business or concern **3.** any matter, or event **4.** a sexual relationship outside marriage

affect[1] (ə fekt′) *vt.* [< L. *ad-*, to + *facere*, to do] **1.** to have an effect on; influence **2.** to move or stir the emotions of

affect[2] *vt.* [see prec.] **1.** to pretend to have, feel, like, etc.; feign [*to affect indifference*] **2.** to like to have, use, wear, etc. [*she affects plaid coats*]

affectation (af′ek tā′shən) *n.* **1.** artificial behaviour meant to impress others **2.** show or pretence

affected[1] (ə fek′tid) *adj.* **1.** emotionally moved **2.** influenced; acted upon **3.** attacked by disease

affected[2] *adj.* **1.** assumed for effect; artificial **2.** behaving in an artificial way to impress people

affecting *adj.* emotionally touching

affection *n.* **1.** fond or tender feeling; warm liking **2.** a disease **3.** an affecting or being affected

affectionate *adj.* full of affection; tender and loving —**affec′tionately** *adv.*

afferent (af′ər ənt) *adj.* [< L. *ad-*, to + *ferre*, to bear] *Physiol.* bringing inward; specif., designating nerves that transmit impulses towards a nerve centre

affiance (ə fī′əns) *vt.* **-anced, -ancing** [< ML. *ad-*, to + *fidare*, to trust] to pledge, esp. in marriage

affidavit (af′ə dā′vit) *n.* [ML., he has made oath] a written statement made on oath

affiliate (ə fil′ē āt′; *for n.* -it) *vt.* **-at′ed, -at′-ing** [< L. *ad-*, to + *filius*, son] **1.** to take in as a member **2.** to connect (oneself *with*) —*vi.* to associate oneself; join —*n.* an affiliated person or organization —**affil′-ia′tion** *n.*

affiliation order a court order that a man judged to be the father of an illegitimate child should contribute to its maintenance

affinity (ə fin′ə tē) *n.*, *pl.* **-ties** [< L. *ad-*, to + *finis*, end] **1.** mutual attraction **2.** close relationship **3.** relationship by marriage **4.** a similarity of structure implying common origin **5.** the force that causes atoms to combine —**affin′itive** *adj.*

affirm (ə furm′) *vt.* [< L. *ad-*, to + *firmare*, to make firm] **1.** to assert to be true **2.** to confirm; ratify —*vi.* *Law* to declare solemnly, but not under oath —**affirm′-able** *adj.* —**af′firma′tion** (af′ər mā′-shən) *n.*

affirmative (ə fur′mə tiv) *adj.* **1.** answering "yes" **2.** positive, as in asserting —*n.* **1.** a word indicating assent **2.** an affirmative statement —**affirm′atively** *adv.*

affix (ə fiks′; *for n.* af′iks) *vt.* [< L. *ad-*, to + *figere*, to fix] **1.** to fasten; attach **2.** to add at the end —*n.* **1.** a thing affixed **2.** a prefix or suffix —**affix′ture** *n.*

afflatus (ə flāt′əs) *n.* [< L. *ad-*, to + *flare*, to blow] inspiration, as of an artist

afflict (ə flikt′) *vt.* [< L. *ad-*, to + *fligere*, to strike] to cause suffering to; distress very much

affliction *n.* **1.** an afflicted condition; pain; suffering **2.** anything causing pain or distress

affluence (af′loo wəns) *n.* [< L. *ad-*, to + *fluere*, to flow] **1.** wealth **2.** abundance

affluent *adj.* **1.** wealthy **2.** abundant —*n.* a stream flowing into a river; tributary —**af′fluently** *adv.*

affluent society a community in which the majority of people are able to enjoy a high standard of living

afford (ə fôrd′) *vt.* [OE. *geforthian*, to advance] **1.** to have enough or the means for: usually with *can* or *be able* **2.** to be able (*to* do something) with little risk **3.** to give; yield [*it affords* much pleasure] —*adj.*

afforest (ə for′əst) *vt.* [ML. *afforestare*] to turn (land) into forest; plant many trees on

affray (ə frā′) *n.* [< OFr. < L. *ex*, out of + Gmc. base *frith-*, peace] a noisy brawl or quarrel

affront (ə frunt′) *vt.* [< L. *ad-*, to + *frons*, forehead] **1.** to insult openly **2.** to confront —*n.* an open insult

Afghan (af′gan) *n.* **1.** a native of Afghanistan **2.** a dog with silky hair and a long, narrow head: also **Afghan hound** —*adj.* of Afghanistan, its people, etc.

aficionado (ə fish′yə nä′dō) *n.*, *pl.* **-dos** (-dōz) [Sp.] a devoted follower of some sport, art, etc.; fan

afield (ə fēld′) *adv.* **1.** away (from home) **2.** astray

aflame (ə flām′) *adv.*, *adj.* **1.** in flames **2.** glowing **3.** greatly excited

afloat (ə flōt′) *adv.* **1.** floating freely **2.** on board ship; at sea **3.** flooded **4.** drifting about **5.** in circulation [*rumours are afloat*] **6.** free of trouble, debt, etc.

A.F.M. Air Force Medal

afoot (ə foot′) *adv.* **1.** in motion or operation; in progress; astir **2.** on foot; walking

afore (ə fôr′) *adv.*, *prep.*, *conj.* [Archaic or Dial. except in compounds and nautical use] before

aforementioned *adj.* mentioned before

aforesaid *adj.* spoken of before

aforethought *adj.* premeditated

a fortiori (ā fôr′tē ôr′ī′) [L., for a stronger (reason)] all the more : said of a conclusion following with even greater logical necessity another already accepted

Afr. 1. Africa 2. African

afraid (ə frād′) *adj.* [< ME. *affraien*, to frighten] feeling fear; frightened (with *of*, *that*, or an infinitive) : often used colloquially to indicate regret [I'm *afraid* I can't go]

afresh (ə fresh′) *adv.* again; anew

African (af′ri kən) *adj.* of Africa, its peoples, etc. —*n.* a native or inhabitant of Africa

Africana (ä fri kä′nə) *n.pl.* objects of cultural or historical interest of S African origin

Africander (af′ri kan′dər) *n.* a breed of large hump-backed beef cattle originating in S Africa

African lily a S African plant with rounded clusters of funnel-shaped flowers

African time [S Afr. Slang] unpunctuality

African violet a tropical African plant with violet, pink, or white flowers and hairy, dark-green leaves

Afrikaans (af′ri käns′) *n.* [Afrik.] one of the two official languages of South Africa, closely related to Dutch and Flemish

Afrikaner (af′ri kän′ər) *n.* [Du.] a white native of South Africa with Afrikaans as mother tongue

Afro (af′rō) *adj.* [< ff.] designating or of a full, bouffant hair style, orig. modelled on a Negro style

Afro- *a combining form meaning* Africa(n)

Afro-American (af′rō ə mer′ə kən) *adj.* of Negro Americans, their culture, etc. —*n.* a Negro American

afrormosia (af′rôr mō′sē ə) *n.* a hard teaklike wood used in furniture

aft (äft) *adv.* [< OE. *afta*, behind] at, near, or towards the stern of a ship or rear of an aircraft

after (äf′tər) *adv.* [OE. *æfter*] behind in place or time; later or next —*prep.* 1. behind in place or time 2. in search of 3. as a result of 4. in spite of 5. next to in rank 6. in the manner of 7. in honour of 8. concerning —*conj.* following the time when —*adj.* 1. next; later 2. nearer the rear (esp. of a ship or aircraft)

afterbirth *n.* the placenta and foetal membranes expelled from the womb after childbirth

afterburner *n.* 1. a device for obtaining additional thrust in a jet engine by using the hot exhaust gases to burn extra fuel 2. a device, as on an incinerator, for burning undesirable exhaust gases

aftercare *n.* the supervision given to a patient recovering from an illness or operation

afterdamp *n.* an asphyxiating gas left in a mine after an explosion of firedamp

aftereffect *n.* a later or secondary result

afterglow *n.* 1. the glow remaining after sunset 2. a pleasant feeling after an enjoyable experience

afterlife *n.* 1. life after death 2. one's later years

aftermath (äf′tər math′) *n.* [AFTER + OE. *mæth*, cutting of grass] 1. a result, esp.

an unpleasant one 2. a second crop of grass after the earlier mowing

aftermost *adj.* 1. last 2. nearest to the stern

afternoon (äf′tər nōōn′) *n.* the time of day from noon to evening —*adj.* of, in, or for the afternoon

afterpains *n.pl.* pains from contraction of the uterus following childbirth

afters *n.pl.* [Colloq.] the sweet course of a meal

aftershave *n.* a lotion, often perfumed, applied to the face by men after shaving

aftertaste *n.* a taste lingering, as after eating

afterthought *n.* 1. an idea, etc. added later 2. a thought coming too late to be useful

afterwards *adv.* later

Ag [L. *argentum*] *Chem.* silver

ag (akh) *interj.* [S Afr.] a general exclamation of irritation, disgust, etc.

again (ə gen′) *adv.* [< OE. *on-*, towards + *gegn*, direct] 1. once more 2. back into a former condition 3. besides 4. on the other hand —**as much again** twice as much

against (ə genst′) *prep.* [see AGAIN] 1. in opposition to 2. towards so as to strike 3. opposite to the direction of 4. in contrast with [green *against* the gold] 5. in contact with [leaning *against* the wall] 6. in preparation for 7. as a charge on [a bill entered *against* his account] 8. to the detriment of —**over against** 1. opposite to 2. as compared with

agape[1] (ə gāp′) *adv.*, *adj.* 1. with the mouth wide open, as in wonder 2. wide open

agape[2] (ag′ə pē) *n.* [< Gr. *agapē*, love] *Christian Theol.* 1. God's love for man 2. spontaneous, altruistic love 3. a religious meal taken by early Christians

agar-agar (ä′gər ä′gər) *n.* [Malay] a gelatinous extract of seaweed, used for bacterial cultures, etc.

agaric (ag′ər ik) *n.* [< Gr. *agarikon*] any gill fungus, as the common edible mushroom, etc.

agate (ag′ət) *n.* [< Gr. *achatēs*] a hard, semiprecious stone with striped or clouded colouring

agave (ə gä′vē) *n.* [< Gr. *Agauē*, proper name, lit., illustrious] any of several American desert plants, having tall flower stalks and fleshy leaves

age (āj) *n.* [< L. *aetas*] 1. the time that a person or thing has existed 2. the lifetime 3. a stage of life 4. the condition of being old 5. a generation 6. a period in history or in prehistoric or geologic time 7. [often pl.] [Colloq.] a long time —*vi.*, *vt.* **aged**, **ag′ing** or **age′-ing** to grow or cause to become old or mature —**(come) of age** (to reach) the age of full legal rights —**under age** not having reached the required or legal age

-age (ij, əj) [< LL.] *a suffix meaning*: 1. act, condition, or result [usage] 2. amount or number [acreage] 3. cost

[postage] 4. place *[steerage]* 5. collection *[peerage]* 6. home *[hermitage]*
aged (ā'jid *for* 1 & 2; ājd *for* 3 & 4) *adj.*
1. grown old 2. of old age 3. brought to a desired state of aging 4. of the age of —**the aged** (ā'jid) old people

ageless *adj.* 1. not growing older 2. eternal

agelong *adj.* lasting a very long time

agency (ā'jən sē) *n., pl.* **-cies** [see AGENT]
1. an organization offering a particular kind of service 2. the business or place of business of any person, firm, etc. authorized to act for another 3. action; power 4. means

agenda (ə jen'də) *n., pl.* **-das** [< L. *agere,* do] a list of things to be dealt with

agent (ā'jənt) *n.* [< L. *agere,* do] 1. a person, firm, etc. authorized to act for another 2. [Colloq.] a travelling representative, as for an insurance company 3. a person or thing that performs an action or produces an effect —**agential** (ā jen'shəl) *adj.*

‡**agent provocateur** (à zhän′prŏ vô kà-tēr′) *pl.* **agents provocateurs** [Fr.] a secret agent hired to join a group and incite its members to commit unlawful acts to weaken or discredit it

age-old (āj'ōld') *adj.* ages old; ancient

agglomerate (ə glom'ə rāt'; *for adj. & n.* -ər ət) *vt., vi.* -at'ed, -at'ing [< L. *ad-,* to + *glomerare,* to form into a ball] to gather into a mass or ball —*adj.* so gathered —*n.* a jumbled mass, esp. of fragments of volcanic rock fused by heat —**agglom′era′tion** *n.*

agglutinate (ə glōōt''n ət; *for v.* -āt') *adj.* [< L. *ad-,* to + *gluten,* glue] stuck together, as with glue —*vt., vi.* -nat'ed, -nat'ing to stick or clump together —**agglu′tina′tion** *n.* —**agglu′tinative** *adj.*

aggrandize (ə gran'dīz') *vt.* -dized', -diz'-ing [< Fr. < L. *grandis,* great] 1. to make greater, more powerful, etc. 2. to make seem greater —**aggran′dizement** (-dīz mənt) *n.*

aggravate (ag'rə vāt') *vt.* -vat'ed, -vat'-ing [< L. *ad-,* to + *gravis,* heavy] 1. to make worse 2. [Colloq.] to annoy —**ag′grava′tion** *n.*

aggregate (ag'rə gət; *for v.* -gāt') *adj.* [< L. *ad-,* to + *grex,* a herd] total —*n.* a group of distinct things gathered into a whole —*vt.* -gat'ed, -gat'ing 1. to gather into a whole 2. to amount to; total —**in the aggregate** taken all together; on the whole —**ag′grega′tion** *n.* —**ag′gregative** *adj.*

aggression (ə gresh'ən) *n.* [< L. *ad,* to + *gradi,* to step] 1. an unprovoked attack or warlike act 2. the habit of being aggressive

aggressive (ə gres'iv) *adj.* 1. ready to fight; quarrelsome 2. ready to engage in direct action 3. bold and active —**aggres′sively** *adv.* —**aggres′sor** *n.*

aggrieve (ə grēv') *vt.* -grieved', -griev'-ing [see AGGRAVATE] 1. to cause grief or injury to; offend 2. to injure in one's legal rights

aggro (ag'rō) *n.* [< *aggravation* or *aggression*] [Slang] aggressive behaviour; trouble-making

aghast (ə gäst') *adj.* [< OE. *gæstan,* terrify < *gast,* ghost] feeling great dismay; horrified

agile (aj'īl) *adj.* [< L. *agere,* do] quick of movement; nimble; lively —**ag′ilely** *adv.* —**agility** (ə jil'ə tē) *n.*

agin (ə gin') *prep.* [< obs. *again,* against] [Dial. or Colloq.] against

agitate (aj'ə tāt') *vt.* -tat'ed, -tat'ing [< L. *agere,* do] 1. to stir up or shake up 2. to excite the feelings of 3. to keep discussing so as to stir up support for —*vi.* to stir up support *[to agitate for reform]* —**ag′itat′edly** *adv.* —**ag′ita′-tion** *n.* —**ag′ita′tor** *n.*

agitprop (aj'it prop') *adj.* [< Russ. *agit(atsiya) prop(aganda),* agitation propaganda] of or for agitating and propagandizing

agley (ə glē', -glā') *adv.* [Scot.] awry

aglitter (ə glit'ər) *adv., adj.* glittering

aglow (ə glō') *adv., adj.* in a glow

A.G.M. annual general meeting

agnail (ag'nāl') *n.* [< OE. *ange,* pain + *nægl,* nail (metal)] 1. a sore round a fingernail 2. a hangnail

agnostic (ag näs'tik) *n.* [< Gr. *a-,* not + *gignōskein,* know] a person who believes that one cannot know whether there is a God, or anything beyond material phenomena —*adj.* of or characteristic of an agnostic —**agnos′tically** *adv.* —**agnos′ticism** *n.*

Agnus Dei (ag'nəs dē'ī; äg'nōōs dā'ē) [L., Lamb of God] 1. a representation of Christ as a lamb 2. *R.C.Ch.* a prayer in the Mass, beginning *Agnus Dei*

ago (ə gō') *adj.* [< OE. *a-,* away + *gan,* go] gone by; past *[years ago]* —*adv.* in the past *[long ago]*

agog (ə gog') *adv., adj.* [OFr. < *a-,* to + *gogue,* joyfulness] with eager interest or excitement

agonize (ag'ə nīz') *vi.* -nized', -niz'ing 1. to make convulsive efforts; struggle 2. to be in agony —*vt.* to torture —**ag′o-niz′ingly** *adv.*

agony (ag'ə nē) *n., pl.* -nies [< Gr. *agōn,* a contest] 1. great mental or physical pain 2. death pangs 3. a convulsive struggle 4. a sudden outburst *(of* emotion)

agony column 1. a newspaper feature offering sympathetic advice to readers on their personal problems 2. a section of a newspaper containing advertisements for lost relatives, personal messages, etc.

agoraphobia (ag'ər ə fō'bē ə) *n.* [< Gr. *agora,* market place + -PHOBIA] an abnormal fear of open spaces or public places

agrarian (ə grāər'ē ən) *adj.* [< L. *ager,* field, land] 1. relating to land or to the ownership of land 2. of agriculture —*n.* one who favours a more even division of land

agree (ə grē') *vi.* -greed', -gree'ing [< L. *ad,* to + *gratus,* pleasing] 1. to be of the same opinion 2. to consent or accede *(to)* 3. to arrive at an understanding **4.** to be suitable, healthful, etc. (followed by *with*) **5.** to be in harmony **6.** *Gram.* to correspond in number, person, case, or gender —*vt.* to acknowledge —**agree to differ** to accept divergence of opinion

agreeable *adj.* **1.** pleasing **2.** willing **3.** conformable ;—**agree'abil'ity** *n.* —**agree'ably** *adv.*

agreement *n.* **1.** an agreeing **2.** an understanding between people, countries, etc. **3.** a contract

agriculture (ag'ri kul'chər) *n.* [< L. *ager*, field + *cultura*, cultivation] the work of raising crops and livestock —**ag'ricul'tural** *adj.* —**ag'ricul'turist** *n.*

agrimony (ag'rə mə nē) *n.*, *pl.* **-nies** [< Gr. *argemōnē*] a plant having little yellow flowers on spiky stalks

agronomy (ə gron'ə mē) *n.* [< Gr. *agros*, field + *nemein*, manage] the science and economics of crop production —**agron'o-mist** *n.*

aground (ə ground') *adv.*, *adj.* on or onto the shore, a reef, etc. *[*the ship ran *aground]*

agt. agent

agterskot (akh'tər skot') *n.* [< Afrik. *agter*, afterwards & *skot*, payment] in South Africa, final payment to a farmers' cooperative, etc. for a crop or wool clip

ague (ā'gyo͞o) *n.* [< ML. (*febris*) *acuta*, violent (fever)] **1.** a fever, usually that of malaria, marked by regularly recurring chills **2.** a fit of shivering

ah (ä) *interj.* an exclamation of pain, delight, etc.

A.H. [L. *Anno Hegirae*] in the year of the Hegira

aha (ä hä', ə hä') *interj.* an exclamation of satisfaction, pleasure, triumph, etc.

ahead (ə hed') *adv.*, *adj.* **1.** in or at the front **2.** forwards; onwards **3.** in advance **4.** winning or leading **5.** having something as a profit or advantage —**get ahead** to advance socially, financially, etc.

ahem (ə hem'; *conventionalized pronun.*) *interj.* a cough or similar sound made to get attention, fill a pause, etc.

ahoy (ə hoi') *interj.* *Naut.* a call used in hailing *[*ship *ahoy!]*

A.I. artificial insemination

aid (ād) *vt.*, *vi.* [< L. *ad-*, to + *juvare*, to help] to give help (to); assist —*n.* **1.** assistance **2.** a helper **3.** a helpful device —**in aid of** [Colloq.] for the purpose of

A.I.D. artificial insemination by donor

aide (ād) *n.* [Fr.] **1.** an assistant **2.** *same as* AIDE-DE-CAMP

aide-de-camp (ād'ə kän') *n.*, *pl.* **aides-de-camp** [Fr., lit., camp assistant] an officer in the army, navy, etc. serving as assistant and confidential secretary to a superior

aigrette, aigret (ā'gret) *n.* [see EGRET] the white plumes of the egret, once worn for ornament

ail (āl) *vt.* [< OE. *egle*, harmful] to be the cause of pain to; trouble —*vi.* to be in poor health; be ill

aileron (ā'lə ron') *n.* [Fr. < L. *ala*, wing]

a movable hinged section of an aeroplane wing for controlling rolling movements

ailing (āl'iŋ) *adj.* in poor health; sickly

ailment *n.* an illness, esp. a mild one

aim (ām) *vi.*, *vt.* [< L. *ad-*, to + *aestimare*, to estimate] **1.** to point (a weapon) or direct (a blow, remark, etc.) **2.** to direct (one's efforts) **3.** to try or intend (*to* do or be) —*n.* **1.** the act of aiming **2.** the direction of a blow, etc. **3.** purpose —**take aim** to point a weapon

aimless *adj.* having no aim or purpose —**aim'lessly** *adv.*

ain't (ānt) [< *amn't*, contr. of *am not*] a dialectal or substandard contraction for *am not*, *is not*, *are not*, *has not*, and *have not*

air (āər) *n.* [< Gr. *aēr*] **1.** the invisible mixture of gases (chiefly nitrogen and oxygen) that surrounds the earth; atmosphere **2.** space above the earth; sky **3.** a movement of air **4.** an outward appearance **5.** a person's manner or bearing **6.** [*pl.*] affected, superior manners **7.** public expression *[*give *air* to your opinions *]* **8.** transportation by aircraft **9.** a song or melody —*adj.* of aircraft, air forces, etc. —*vt.* **1.** to let air into or through **2.** put where air can dry, etc. **3.** to publicize —*vi.* to become aired, etc. —**in the air 1.** prevalent **2.** not decided —**on** (or **off**) **the air** Radio & TV that is (or is not) broadcasting or being broadcast —**take the air** to go outdoors

air bag a bag of nylon, plastic, etc. that inflates automatically within a motor vehicle on impact

air base a base of operations for military aircraft

air bladder a sac with air or gas in it, found in most fishes and in some other animals and some plants

airborne *adj.* **1.** carried by the air **2.** aloft; flying

air brake 1. a brake operated by compressed air **2.** any flap on an aircraft for reducing speed in flight

air brick a brick with holes in it, for ventilation

airbus *n.* a short-range or medium-range passenger aircraft

air chief marshal *see* MILITARY RANKS, table

air commodore *see* MILITARY RANKS, table

air conditioning a method of regulating humidity and temperature in buildings, etc. —**air'condi'tion** *vt.*

air-cooled *adj.* cooled by having air passed over, into, or through it —**air'-cool'** *vt.*

aircraft *n.*, *pl.* **-craft'** any machine designed for flying, whether heavier or lighter than air

aircraft carrier a warship that carries aircraft, with a large, flat deck for taking off and landing

aircraftman *n.* a junior rank in the RAF —**air'craftwom'an** *n.fem.*

air curtain (or **door**) a downward

draught of air at an open entrance for maintaining even temperatures within

air cushion   **1.** an inflatable cushion **2.** the pocket of air that supports a hovercraft **3.** a form of pneumatic suspension consisting of an enclosed volume of air

AIREDALE
(58 cm high
at shoulder)

Airedale (āər′dāl′) *n.* [< *Airedale* in W. Yorkshire] a large terrier having a hard, wiry coat

airfield *n.*   a field where aircraft can take off and land

air force   the aviation branch of the armed forces

air gun   a gun operated by compressed air

air hole   **1.** a hole that permits passage of air **2.** an unfrozen place in ice covering a body of water

air hostess   a stewardess on an airliner or aeroplane

airily *adv.*   in an airy or gay, light manner; jauntily; breezily

airiness *n.*   **1.** a being airy, or full of fresh air **2.** lightness; jauntiness

airing *n.*   **1.** exposure to the air, as for drying **2.** exposure to public knowledge **3.** a walk or ride outdoors

airing cupboard   a cupboard in which laundry, etc. is exposed to warm air

airless *adj.*   **1.** without air or without fresh air **2.** without wind or breeze

air letter   a single sheet of lightweight paper which forms an envelope, and is sent by airmail

airlift *n.*   a system of transporting troops, supplies, etc. by aircraft —*vt.* to transport by airlift

airline *n.*   a system or company for moving cargo and passengers by aircraft —*adj.* of an airline

airliner *n.*   a large aircraft for carrying passengers

air lock   **1.** an airtight compartment, with adjustable air pressure, between places that do not have the same air pressure **2.** a blockage caused by trapped air

airmail *n.*   **1.** the system of transporting mail by aircraft **2.** letters, etc. so transported

airman *n.*   an aviator

air marshal   see MILITARY RANKS, table

air pocket   an atmospheric condition that causes an aircraft to make sudden, short drops

airport *n.*   a place where aircraft can land and take off, usually with facilities for passengers, etc.

air pressure   the pressure of atmospheric or compressed air

air pump   a machine for removing or compressing air

air raid   an attack by aircraft, esp. bombers

air rifle   a rifle operated by the force of compressed air

air sac   any of the air-filled cavities in a bird's body, having connections to the lungs

air-sea rescue   **1.** an air rescue at sea **2.** an organization which rescues people from ship or aircraft disasters

airship *n.*   any self-propelled aircraft that is lighter than air and can be steered

airsick *adj.*   unwell or nauseated from travelling in an aircraft —**air′sick′ness** *n.*

airspace *n.*   the space above a particular land area

airspeed *n.*   the speed of an aircraft relative to the air rather than to the ground

airstrip *n.*   a hard-surfaced area used as a temporary aircraft runway

air terminal   a building in a city where transport is available to and from an airport outside the city

airtight *adj.*   too tight for air or gas to enter or escape

air-to-air *adj.*   operating between aircraft in flight

air vice-marshal   see MILITARY RANKS, table

airwaves *n.pl.*   the medium through which radio signals are transmitted

airy *adj.* **-ier, -iest**   **1.** in or of air **2.** open to the air; breezy **3.** unsubstantial **4.** light as air **5.** gay **6.** flippant **7.** [Colloq.] putting on airs

aisle (īl) *n.* [< L. *ala*, wing] **1.** a part of a church set off by a row of columns or piers **2.** a passageway, as between rows of seats —**aisled** (īld) *adj.*

aitch (āch) *n.* the letter H, h —**drop one's aitches**   to miss off the initial aspiration from words

aitchbone (āch′bōn′) *n.* [< ME. *a nache bone* < OFr. *nache*, buttock] **1.** the rump bone **2.** a cut of beef around the rump bone

ajar[1] (ə jär′) *adv., adj.* [< OE. *cier*, a turn]   slightly open, as a door

ajar[2] *adv., adj.* [A-, on + JAR[1]]   not in harmony

akimbo (ə kim′bō) *adv., adj.* [ME. < ON. *keng*, bent + *bogi*, a bow]   with hands on hips and elbows bent outwards

akin (ə kin′) *adj.*   **1.** of one kin; related **2.** similar

-al (əl, ′l) [< L.]   a suffix meaning: **1.** of, like, or suitable for [*comical, hysterical*] **2.** the act or process of [*avowal*] **3.** [AL(DEHYDE)] *Chem.* a) an aldehyde [*chloral*] b) a barbiturate [*phenobarbital*]

Al   *Chem.* aluminium

à la, a la (ä′lä) [Fr.]   **1.** to, in, or at the **2.** in the manner or style of **3.** according to

alabaster (al′ə bäs′tər) *n.* [< Gr. *alabastros*]   **1.** a translucent, whitish variety of gypsum **2.** a streaked or mottled variety of calcite

à la carte (ä′lä kärt′) [Fr.]   with a separate price for each item on the menu

alack (ə lak´) *interj.* [A(H) + LACK] [Archaic] an exclamation of regret, surprise, dismay, etc.

alacrity (ə lak´rə tē) *n.* [< L. *alacer*, lively] eager willingness shown by quick, lively action —**alac´ritous** *adj.*

Aladdin's cave (ə lad´inz) [< *Aladdin* in *The Arabian Nights*] an apparently inexhaustible store of riches

à la mode (ä´lä mōd´) [Fr.] in fashion; stylish

alarm (ə lärm´) *vt.* [< It. *all'arme*, to arms] 1. to frighten 2. to warn of danger —*n.* 1. fear caused by danger 2. a signal, sound, etc. to warn of danger 3. a mechanism designed to warn of danger 4. the bell, etc. of an alarm clock 5. [Archaic] a sudden call to arms

alarm clock a clock that can be set to ring or buzz at any particular time, as to awaken a person from sleep

alarming *adj.* frightening —**alarm´ingly** *adv.*

alarmist *n.* one who habitually spreads alarming rumours, etc. —*adj.* of or like an alarmist

alarum (ə lar´əm) *n.* [Archaic] alarm —**alarums and excursions** noisy disturbance; confusion

alas (ə las´) *interj.* [< OFr. < L. *lassus*, weary] an exclamation of sorrow, pity, regret, etc.

alate (ā´lāt) *adj.* [< L. *ala*, wing] having wings

alb (alb) *n.* [ult. < L. *albus*, white] a long, white linen robe worn by a priest at Mass

albacore (al´bə kôr´) *n.* [< Ar. *al*, the + *bakūrah*, albacore] a fish of the tuna family

albatross (al´bə tros´) *n.* [< Sp. < Ar. *al qādūs*, water container] any of several large, web-footed sea birds related to the petrel

albeit (ôl bē´it) *conj.* [ME. *al be it*, al(though) it be] although; even though

albert (al´bərt) *n.* [< Prince *Albert*, husband of Queen Victoria] a kind of watch chain usually attached to a waistcoat

Albertan (al bur´tən) *n.* a native or inhabitant of Alberta —*a.* of or having to do with Alberta

albino (al bē´nō) *n., pl.* **-nos** [< L. *albus*, white] 1. one who lacks normal colouring: albinos have a white skin, whitish hair, and pink eyes 2. any animal or plant lacking in colour —**albinism** (al´bə niz'm) *n.*

Albion (al´bē ən) [Chiefly Poet.] Britain or England

album (al´bəm) *n.* [< L. *albus*, white] 1. a book with blank pages for mounting pictures, stamps, etc. 2. a) a booklike holder for gramophone records *b)* a single long-playing record, not part of a set

albumen (al´byoo mən) *n.* [L. < *albus*, white] 1. the white of an egg 2. same *as* ALBUMIN

albumin (al´byoo mən) *n.* [see prec.] any of a class of water-soluble proteins found in milk, egg, muscle, blood, and in many plants

albuminous (al byoo´mə nəs) *adj.* of, like, or containing albumin or albumen

alchemy (al´kə mē) *n.* [< Ar. *al-kīmiyā*] a form of chemistry studied in the Middle Ages: its chief aim was to change the baser metals into gold —**alchemic** (al kem´-ik), **alchem´ical** *adj.* —**al´chemist** *n.*

alcohol (al´kə hol´) *n.* [< Ar. *al kuhl*, powder of antimony] 1. a colourless volatile liquid: it can be burned as fuel, is used in industry and medicine, and is the intoxicating element in whisky, wine, beer, etc. 2. any intoxicating liquor with this liquid in it 3. any of a series of similarly constructed organic compounds

alcoholic (al´kə hol´ik) *adj.* 1. of, containing, or caused by alcohol 2. suffering from alcoholism —*n.* one who has chronic alcoholism

alcoholism *n.* the habitual drinking of alcoholic liquor to excess, or a diseased condition caused by this

alcove (al´kōv) *n.* [< Ar. *al*, the + *qubba*, arch] 1. a recessed section of a room 2. a secluded bower in a garden

aldehyde (al´də hīd´) *n.* [< AL(COHOL) + L. *de*, without + HYD(ROGEN)] a colourless, volatile fluid obtained from alcohol by oxidation

alder (ôl´dər) *n.* [< OE. *alor*] any of a group of trees and shrubs growing in moist regions

alderman (ôl´dər mən) *n.* [< OE. *eald*, old + *man*] in England and Wales, formerly, a senior member of a county or borough council, elected by the other councillors —**al´derman´ic** (-man´ik) *adj.*

Alderney (ôl´dər nē) *n., pl.* **-neys** any of a breed of small dairy cattle originally from Alderney, one of the Channel Islands

ale (āl) *n.* [< OE. *ealu*] 1. an alcoholic drink made by fermenting a cereal, originally differing from beer by being unflavoured by hops 2. [Colloq.] beer

aleatory (ā´lē ə tər ē) *adj.* [< L. *alea*, chance] depending on chance or luck

alehouse (āl´hous´) *n.* 1. [Obs.] a place where ale is sold and served; tavern 2. [Colloq.] a public house

alembic (ə lem´bik) *n.* [< Ar. *al*, the + *anbīq*, still < Gr. *ambix*, cup] 1. an apparatus of glass or metal, formerly used for distilling 2. anything that refines or purifies

aleph (ä´lif) *n.* the first letter of the Hebrew alphabet

alert (ə lurt´) *adj.* [< It. *all' erta*, on the watch] 1. watchful; vigilantly ready 2. active; nimble —*n.* a warning signal, as of an expected air raid —*vt.* to warn to be ready or watchful —**on the alert** watchful; vigilant

A level same *as* ADVANCED LEVEL

alexandrine (al´ig zan´drīn) *n.* [*occas.* A-] *Prosody* an iambic line having six feet —*adj.* of an alexandrine

alexandrite (al´ig zan´drīt) *n.* [< Russian tsar *Alexander II*] a chrysoberyl that appears dark green in daylight and deep red in artificial light

alexia (ə lek′sē ə) *n.* [< Gr. *a-*, without + *lexis*, speech] a loss of the ability to read

alfalfa (al fal′fə) *n.* [< Ar. *al-faṣfaṣah*, the best fodder] a deep-rooted plant used for fodder and as a cover crop

al fine (al fē′nē) [It.] *Music* to the end

alfresco (al fres′kō) *adv.* [It.] outdoors —*adj.* outdoor

alg. algebra

algae (al′jē) *n.pl., sing.* **al′ga** (-gə) [< L.] a group of plants, one-celled or multicellular, containing chlorophyll and other pigments, found in water and including seaweeds —**al′gal** (-gəl) *adj.*

algebra (al′jə brə) *n.* [< Ar. *al,* the + *jabr,* reunion of broken parts] a mathematical system used to generalize certain arithmetical operations by using letters to stand for numbers —**al′gebra′ic** (-brā′ik) *adj.* —**al′gebra′ical** *adj.* —**al′gebra′ically** *adv.* —**al′gebra′ist** *n.*

-algia (al′jə, -jē ə) [< Gr.] *a suffix meaning pain* [*neuralgia*]

algid (al′jid) *adj.* [< L. *algidus*] cold; chilly —**algid′ity** *n.*

ALGOL (al′gol) *n.* [*Alg(orithmic) O(riented) L(anguage)*] a computer programing language designed for mathematical and scientific purposes

algorism (al′gər iz′m) *n.* [< 9th-c. Ar. mathematician] the Arabic, or decimal, system of counting

algorithm (-iᵺ′m) *n.* [< prec.] *Math.* any special method of solving a certain kind of problem

alias (ā′lē əs) *n., pl.* **a′liases** [< L. *alius,* other] an assumed name —*adv.* otherwise named

alibi (al′ə bī′) *n., pl.* **-bis′** [< L. *alius ibi,* elsewhere] 1. *Law* the plea that an accused person was elsewhere than at the scene of the crime 2. [Colloq.] an excuse —*vi.* **-bied′, -bi′ing** [Colloq.] to offer an excuse

alien (āl′yən) *adj.* [< L. *alius,* other] 1. foreign 2. repugnant (*to*) 3. of aliens —*n.* 1. a foreigner 2. a foreign-born resident who is not a naturalized citizen 3. a being from another world

alienable *adj.* capable of being transferred to a new owner —**al′ienabil′ity** *n.*

alienate *vt.* **-at′ed, -at′ing** 1. to cause a transference of (affection) 2. to make unfriendly; estrange 3. to transfer the ownership of (property) to another —**al′iena′tion** *n.* —**al′iena′tor** *n.*

alienist (āl′yən ist) *n.* [U.S.] a psychiatrist

alight¹ (ə līt′) *vi.* **alight′ed** or **alit′, alight′ing** [< ME. *a-,* off + *lihtan,* dismount] 1. to get down or off; dismount 2. to come down after flight

alight² *adj.* lighted up; glowing

align (ə līn′) *vt.* [< Fr. *a,* to + *ligne,* line] 1. to bring into a straight line 2. to bring (parts, as the wheels of a car) into proper coordination 3. to bring into agreement, etc. —*vi.* to line up —**align′ment** *n.*

alike (ə līk′) *adj.* [< OE. *gelic*] like one another; similar —*adv.* 1. similarly 2. equally

aliment (al′ə mənt) *n.* [< L. *alere,* nourish] 1. food 2. means of support —**al′imen′tal** (-men′t'l) *adj.*

alimentary (al′ə men′tər ē) *adj.* 1. connected with food or nutrition 2. nourishing

alimentary canal (or **tract**) the passage in the body through which food passes to be digested: it extends from the mouth to the anus

alimony (al′ə mə nē) *n.* [< L. *alere,* nourish] an allowance paid, esp. to a woman, by the spouse or former spouse after a legal separation or divorce

aline (ə līn′) *vt., vi.* **alined′, alin′ing** same as ALIGN

A-line (ā′līn′) *adj.* slightly flared from the waist or shoulders : said of garments

aliphatic (al′ə fat′ik) *adj.* [< Gr. *aleiphar,* fat] *Chem.* of or obtained from fat; specif., of compounds with carbon atoms in open chains

aliquant (al′ə kwənt) *adj.* [< L. *alius,* other + *quantus,* how much] *Math.* that does not divide a number evenly [8 is an *aliquant* part of 25]

aliquot (al′ə kwət) *adj.* [< L. *alius,* other + *quot,* how many] *Math.* that divides a number evenly

alive (ə līv′) *adj.* [< OE. *on,* in + *life,* life] 1. having life; living 2. in existence, etc. 3. lively; alert —**alive to** fully aware of —**alive with** teeming with; full of

alkali (al′kə lī′) *n., pl.* **-lis′, -lies′** [< Ar. *al,* the + *qili,* ashes (of saltwort)] any base, as soda, etc., or any mineral salt capable of neutralizing acids

alkaline (al′kə lin′) *adj.* of, like, or containing an alkali; basic —**al′kalin′ity** (-lin′ə tē) *n.*

alkaloid *n.* any of a number of basic organic substances, as caffeine, etc., found in certain plants

Alkoran (al′kor än′) *n.* the Koran

all (ôl) *adj.* [OE. *eall*] 1. the whole quantity, extent, or number of 2. every one of 3. the greatest possible [in all sincerity] 4. any [beyond all question] 5. alone; only —*pron.* 1. [with pl. v.] everyone [all are present] 2. everything 3. every part —*n.* 1. everything one has [give your all] 2. a totality; whole —*adv.* 1. wholly [all worn out] 2. apiece [a score of thirty all] —**after all** nevertheless —**all but** 1. all except 2. almost —**all for** [Colloq.] wholeheartedly in support of —**all in** [Colloq.] very tired —**all in all** as a whole —**all out** to one's maximum effort or capacity —**all the** (better, worse, etc.) so much the (better, worse, etc.) —**all there** [Colloq.] in possession of all one's mental faculties —**all the same** 1. nevertheless 2. of no importance —**at all** 1. in the least 2. in any way 3. under any conditions —**for all** in spite of —**in all** altogether

all- *a combining form denoting* entirety;

comprehensiveness [*all*-electric, *all*-powerful]

alla breve (äi′ə brā′ve) [It.] *Music* the time signature ¢, representing 2/2 time

Allah (al′ə) *the Moslem name for* GOD

allay (ə lā′) *vt.* -layed′, -lay′ing [< OE. *a-*, down + *lecgan*, lay] 1. to lessen or relieve (pain, etc.) 2. to put (fears, etc.) to rest; calm

all-clear (ôl′klēər′) *n.* a signal that an air raid is over

allegation (al′ə gā′shən) *n.* 1. an alleging 2. an assertion, esp. one made without proof

allege (ə lej′) *vt.* -leged′, -leg′ing [ult. < L. *ex-*, out of + *litigare*, to dispute] 1. to declare or assert 2. to assert without proof 3. to give as a plea, excuse, etc. —allege′able *adj.*

alleged *adj.* 1. so-called 2. so declared, but without proof —alleg′edly (-id lē) *adv.*

allegiance (ə lē′jəns) *n.* [< OFr. < L. *ligare*, to bind] 1. the obligation of support and loyalty to one's ruler, government, or country 2. loyalty or devotion, as to a cause, etc.

allegorize (al′ə gə rīz′) *vt.* -rized′, -riz′-ing to treat as an allegory —*vi.* to use allegories —al′legoriza′tion *n.*

allegory (al′ə gər ē) *n., pl.* -ries [< Gr. *allos*, other + *agoreuein*, speak] a story, picture, etc. in which things and events have a symbolic meaning: allegories are used for explaining ideas, moral principles, etc. —al′legor′ical (-gor′-) *adj.*

allegretto (al′ə gret′ō) *adj., adv.* [It.] *Music* moderately fast

allegro (ə läg′rō) *adj., adv.* [It.] *Music* fast

alleluia (al′ə lōō′yə) *interj., n.* same as HALLELUJAH

allergen (al′ər jən) *n.* [ALLERGY + -GEN] a substance inducing an allergic reaction —al′lergen′ic (-jen′ik) *adj.*

allergic (ə lur′jik) *adj.* 1. of or caused by allergy 2. having an allergy

allergy (al′ər jē) *n., pl.* -gies [< Gr. *allos*, other + *ergon*, work] 1. abnormal sensitivity to a specific substance (such as a food, pollen, etc.) or condition (as heat or cold) which is harmless to most people 2. [Colloq.] a strong dislike

alleviate (ə lē′vē āt′) *vt.* -at′ed, -at′ing [< L. *ad-*, to + *levis*, light] 1. to relieve (pain, etc.) 2. to reduce or decrease [to *alleviate* poverty] —alle′via′tion *n.* —alle′viative *adj.* —alle′via′tor *n.*

alley[1] (al′ē) *n., pl.* -leys [< OFr. *aler*, go] 1. a narrow street or walk; specif., one behind a row of buildings 2. *Bowling* the long, narrow lane along which balls are rolled 3. a lane in a garden or park —up (one) one's alley [Slang] suited to one's tastes or abilities

alley[2] *n., pl.* -leys [< ALABASTER] a fine marble used as the shooter in playing marbles: also al′ly

alleyway *n.* 1. an alley between buildings 2. any narrow passageway

all found including meals, heating, etc. without extra charge

Allhallows (ôl′hal′ōz) *n.* [< OE. *eall*,

all + *halig*, holy] [Archaic] *same as* ALL SAINTS' DAY

alliaceous (al′ē ā′shəs) *adj.* [< L. *allium*, garlic] 1. of a group of strong-smelling bulb plants including onion, garlic, etc. 2. tasting or smelling of onions or garlic

alliance (ə li′əns) *n.* [see ALLY] 1. an allying or being allied 2. *a)* a close association for a common goal, as of nations, parties, etc. *b)* the countries, groups, etc. in such association 3. similarity in characteristics

allied (al′īd) *adj.* 1. united by kinship, treaty, etc. 2. closely related [*allied* sciences]

Allies (al′īz′) *n.pl.* 1. in World War I, the nations allied by treaty against Germany and the other Central Powers 2. in World War II, the nations associated against the Axis; esp., Great Britain, the Soviet Union, and the U.S.

ALLIGATOR (2.4-3.6 m long)

alligator (al′ə gāt′ər) *n.* [< Sp. *el lagarto* < L. *lacerta*, lizard] a large reptile like the crocodile found in tropical rivers and marshes of the U.S. and in China

alligator pear same as AVOCADO

all-in (ôl′in′) *adj.* 1. with all expenses included 2. *Wrestling* denoting a style in which various types of holds or attacks are allowed

alliterate (ə lit′ə rāt′) *vi., vt.* -at′ed, -at′-ing to show or cause to show alliteration

alliteration (ə lit′ə rā′shən) *n.* [< L. *ad-*, to + *littera*, letter] repetition of a beginning sound in two or more words of a phrase, etc. —allit′erative *adj.*

allocate (al′ə kāt′) *vt.* -cat′ed, -cat′ing [< L. *ad-*, to + *locus*, a place] 1. to set apart for a specific purpose 2. to distribute in shares; allot 3. to fix the place of —al′locable *adj.* —al′loca′tion *n.*

allopathy (ə lop′ə thē) *n.* [< Gr. *allos*, other & -PATHY] treatment of disease by remedies that produce effects different from those produced by the disease —allopathic (al′ə path′ik) *adj.*

allot (ə lot′) *vt.* -lot′ted, -lot′ting [< OFr. *a-*, to + *lot*, lot] 1. to distribute in shares; apportion 2. to give or assign as one's share —allot′table *adj.* —allot′ter *n.*

allotment *n.* 1. a portion 2. a plot of public land for cultivation rented by an individual

allotrope (al′ə trōp′) *n.* an allotropic form

allotropy (ə lot′rə pē) *n.* [< Gr. *allos*, other + *tropos*, manner] the property that certain chemical elements have of existing in two or more different forms:

also **allot′ropism** —**al′lotrop′ic** (al′ə-trop′ik) *adj.*

all-out (ôl′out′) *adj.* complete or whole-hearted

allow (əlou′) *vt.* [< OFr. < L. *ad-*, to + *locus*, a place + *laudare*, to praise] **1.** to let happen, etc.; permit **2.** to let have [*allowed* no holiday] **3.** to acknowledge as true **4.** to provide (an amount, etc.) for a purpose —**allow for** to keep in mind —**allow′able** *adj.*

allowance *n.* **1.** something allowed, as money, food, etc. given regularly for a specific purpose **2.** a reduction in price, as for a trade-in, etc. —*vt.* **-anced, -anc-ing 1.** to put on an allowance **2.** to apportion economically —**make allowance (or allowances) for 1.** to excuse because of mitigating factors **2.** to leave room, time, etc. for

allowedly (ə lou′id lē) *adv.* admittedly

alloy (al′oi; *also, and for v. usually,* ə loi′) *n.* [see ALLY] **1.** a substance that is a mixture of two or more metals **2.** *a)* formerly, a less valuable metal mixed with a more valuable one *b)* something that lowers the value of another thing —*vt.* **1.** to mix (metals) to form an alloy **2.** to debase by mixing with something inferior

all-purpose (ôl′pur′pəs) *adj.* useful in many ways

all right 1. satisfactory **2.** unhurt; safe **3.** correct **4.** yes; very well **5.** [Colloq.] certainly

all-round (ôl′round′) *adj.* **1.** versatile [an *all-round* player] **2.** comprehensive —**all-round′er** *n.*

All Saints′ Day an annual church festival (November 1) in honour of all the saints

All Souls′ Day in some Christian churches, a day (usually November 2) of prayer for the dead

all-spice (ôl′spīs′) *n.* **1.** the berry of a West Indian tree **2.** the spice made from this berry

all-time (ôl′tīm′) *adj.* unsurpassed up to the present time

allude (ə lood′) *vi.* **-lud′ed, -lud′ing** [< L. *ad-*, to + *ludere*, to play] to refer in an indirect way (*to*)

allure (əlyooər′) *vt., vi.* **-lured′, -lur′ing** [< OFr. *a-*, to + *lurer*, to lure] to tempt with something desirable; attract —*n.* fas-cination —**allure′ment** *n.* —**allur′er** *n.*

alluring *adj.* tempting strongly; highly attractive; charming —**allur′ingly** *adv.*

allusion (ə loo′zhən) *n.* **1.** an alluding **2.** an indirect reference; casual mention —**allu′sive** *adj.*

alluvial (ə loo′vē əl) *adj.* of or found in alluvium

alluvium (ə loo′vē əm) *n.* **-viums, -via** [< L. *ad-*, to + *luere*, to wash] sand, clay, etc. gradually deposited by moving water, as along a river bed

ally (ə lī′; *also, and for n. usually,* al′ī) *vt.* **-lied′, -ly′ing** [< L. *ad-*, to + *ligare*, to bind] **1.** to unite for a specific purpose **2.** to relate by similarity of structure, etc. —*vi.* to become allied —*n., pl.* **-lies 1.** a country or person joined with another

for a common purpose **2.** [A-] [*pl.*] *see* ALLIES **3.** an associate; helper

alma mater (al′mə mät′ər, mät′ər) [L., fostering mother] the university or school that one attended

almanac (ôl′mə nak′) *n.* [< LGr. *almenichiaka,* calendar] **1.** a calendar with astronomical data, weather forecasts, etc. **2.** a book published annually, containing information, usually statistical, on many subjects

almighty (ôl mīt′ē) *adj.* **1.** all-powerful **2.** [Slang] great —*adv.* [Slang] extremely —**the Almighty** God

almond (ä′mənd) *n.* [< Gr. *amygdalē*] **1.** the edible, nutlike kernel of a small, dry, peachlike fruit **2.** the tree bearing this fruit —**al′mondlike′** *adj.*

almoner (ä′mən ər) *n.* **1.** one who distributes alms **2.** formerly, a hospital social worker responsible for the welfare and aftercare of patients

almost (ôl′mōst) *adv.* very nearly; all but

alms (ämz) *n., pl.* **alms** [< Gr. *eleos,* pity] money, food, etc. given to poor people —**alms′giv′er** *n.*

almshouse *n.* a building, endowed by charity for housing the poor

aloe (al′ō) *n., pl.* **-oes** [< Gr.] **1.** a South African plant with fleshy, spiny leaves **2.** [*pl., with sing. v.*] a laxative drug made from the juice of certain aloe leaves

aloft (ə loft′) *adv.* [see LOFT] **1.** high up; up above **2.** in the air; flying **3.** high above a ship's decks

alone (ə lōn′) *adj., adv.* [< ALL + ONE] **1.** apart from anything or anyone else **2.** without any other person **3.** only —**let alone 1.** to refrain from bothering **2.** not to mention [we hadn't a penny, *let alone* a pound]

along (ə loŋ) *prep.* [< OE. *and-*, over against + *-lang,* long] **1.** on or beside the length of **2.** in conformity with —*adv.* **1.** in a line **2.** progressively onward **3.** as a companion **4.** with one [she took her book *along*] —**all along** from the very beginning —**be along** [Colloq.] to come or arrive [I'll *be along* soon]

alongshore (ə loŋ′shôr′) *adv.* near or beside the shore

alongside (ə loŋ′sīd′) *adv.* at or by the side; side by side —*prep.* at the side of; side by side with

aloof (ə loof′) *adv.* [a-, on + Du. *loef,* to windward] at a distance but in view —*adj.* **1.** at a distance **2.** distant in sympathy, etc. [an *aloof* manner] —**aloof′-ly** *adv.*

alopecia (al′ə pēsh′ə) *n.* [< Gr. *alōpekia,* fox mange] baldness

aloud (ə loud′) *adv.* **1.** with the normal voice [read the letter *aloud*] **2.** loudly

alp (alp) *n.* [< L. *Alpes*] a high mountain; esp. [*pl.*] [A-] those in Switzerland and adjoining countries

alpaca (al pak′ə) *n., pl.* **-pac′as, -pac′a** [Sp. < SAmInd. *allpaca*] **1.** a S American mammal related to the llama, with long, fleecy wool **2.** this wool **3.** a cloth woven from this wool **4.** a glossy cloth of cotton and wool

alpenstock (al'pən stok') **n.** [G., Alpine staff] an iron-pointed staff used by mountain climbers

alpha (al'fə) **n.** **1.** the first letter of the Greek alphabet (A, α) **2.** the beginning of anything

alpha and omega **1.** the first and last letters of the Greek alphabet **2.** the beginning and the end

alphabet (al'fə bet') **n.** [< Gr. *alpha* + *beta*] **1.** the letters of a language, arranged in a traditional order **2.** a system of signs to indicate letters

alphabetical (al'fə bet'i k'l) **adj.** of or using an alphabet —**al'phabet'ically adv.**

alphabetize (al'fə bə tīz') **vt.** -**ized', -iz'-ing** to arrange in alphabetical order —**al'phabetiza'tion n.**

alphanumeric (al'fə nyōō mer'ik) **adj.** having or using both alphabetical and numerical symbols

alpha particle a positively charged particle given off by certain radioactive substances : it consists of two protons and two neutrons

alpha ray **1.** *same as* ALPHA PARTICLE **2.** a stream of alpha particles, less penetrating than a beta ray

Alpine (al'pīn) **adj.** **1.** of the Alps **2.** [a-] of or like high mountains

already (ôl red'ē) **adv.** **1.** by or before the given or implied time **2.** even now or even then

alright (ôl rīt') **adv.** *var. of* ALL RIGHT : a disputed sp., but in common use

Alsatian (al sā'shən) **n.** a large, powerful, somewhat wolflike dog, used in police work, etc.

also (ôl'sō) **adv.** [< OE. *eal*, all + *swa*, so] in addition; too : sometimes used in place of *and*

also-ran **n.** [Colloq.] any loser in a race, competition, election, etc.

alt. **1.** alternate **2.** altitude **3.** alto

Alta. Alberta

altar (ôl'tər) **n.** [ult. < L. *altus*, high] **1.** a raised platform where sacrifices are made to a god, etc. **2.** a table, stand, etc. used for sacred purposes in a place of worship —**lead to the altar** to marry

altarpiece **n.** an ornamental carving, painting, etc. above and behind an altar

alter (ôl'tər) **vt.** [< L. *alter*, other] **1.** to make different **2.** to resew parts of (a garment) for a better fit —**vi.** to become different; change —**al'terable adj.**

alteration (ôl'tə rā'shən) **n.** **1.** an altering or being altered **2.** the result of this; change

altercate (ôl'tər kāt') **vi.** -**cat'ed, -cat'-ing** [< L. *altercari*, to dispute] to argue angrily —**al'terca'tion n.**

alter ego (al'tər eg'ō) [L., lit., other I] **1.** another aspect of oneself **2.** a very close friend

alternate (ôl'tər nət, *for v.* ôl'tər nāt') **adj.** [< L. *alternus*, one after the other < *alter*, other] **1.** succeeding each other **2.** every other **3.** alternative —**n.** a substitute —**vt.** -**nat'ed, -nat'ing** to do,

use, or make happen by turns —**vi.** **1.** to act, happen, etc. by turns **2.** to take turns —**alter'nately adv.** —**al'terna'tion n.**

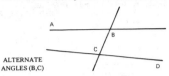

ALTERNATE
ANGLES (B,C)

alternate angles two angles at opposite ends and on opposite sides of a line crossing two others

alternating current an electric current that reverses its direction periodically

alternative (ôl tur'nə tiv) **adj.** providing a choice between two (or loosely, more than two) things —**n.** **1.** a choice between two or more things **2.** any of the things to be chosen —**alter'natively adv.**

alternator (ôl'tər nāt'ər) **n.** an electric generator or dynamo producing alternating current

althaea (al thē'ə) **n.** [< Gr.] *same as* ROSE OF SHARON

althorn (alt'hôrn') **n.** a brass instrument, the alto saxhorn : also **alto horn**

although (ôl thō') **conj.** [ME. < *all* + *though*] in spite of the fact that; though

altimeter (al'tə mēt'ər) **n.** [< L. *altus*, high + -METER] an instrument for measuring altitude

altitude (al'tə tyōōd') **n.** [< L. *altus*, high] **1.** height; esp., above the earth's surface or sea level **2.** a high place **3.** a high level, eminence, etc. **4.** *Astron.* the angular height of a planet, etc. above the horizon —**al'titu'dinal adj.**

alto (al'tō) **n.**, *pl.* -**tos** [It. < L. *altus*, high] **1.** the range of the lowest female voice or, esp., formerly, the highest male voice **2.** a voice or singer with such range **3.** an instrument with a similar range —**adj.** of, in, for, or having this range

alto clef *see* C CLEF

altogether (ôl'tə geth'ər) **adv.** **1.** wholly; completely **2.** in all **3.** on the whole —**in the altogether** [Colloq.] nude

altruism (al'trōō iz'm) **n.** [< L. *alter*, another] unselfish concern for the welfare of others —**al'truist n.** —**al'truis'tic adj.**

alum (al'əm) **n.** [< L. *alumen*] a double sulphate, esp. of potassium and aluminium, used in medicine and in making dyes, etc.

alumina (ə lōō'mi nə) **n.** an oxide of aluminium found as forms of corundum, including emery, sapphires, etc.

aluminium (al'yōō min'yəm) **n.** [< L. *alumen*, alum] a silvery, lightweight, metallic chemical element that resists corrosion, and is found only in combination : symbol, Al

aluminize (ə lōō'mə nīz') **vt.** -**nized', -niz'-ing** to cover, or treat, with aluminium

aluminum (ə lōō'mə nəm) **n.** *U.S. var. of* ALUMINIUM

alumnus (ə lum'nəs) **n.,** *pl.* -**ni** (-nī) [L.,

foster son] [U.S.] one who is a graduate of a school, college, etc.

alway (ôl′wā) *adv.* [Archaic] always

always (ôl wāz) *adv.* [see ALL & WAY] 1. in every instance 2. all the time 3. if need be

alyssum (a′lis əm) *n.* [< Gr. *alyssos*, curing madness] a plant with white or yellow flowers

am (am; *unstressed* əm) [OE. *eom*: see BE] *1st pers. sing., pres. indic., of* BE

Am *Chem.* americium

AM amplitude modulation

Am. 1. America 2. American

A.M., a.m., AM [L. *ante meridiem*] before noon

Amadhlozi (am′a hloz′ē) *n.pl.* [< Zulu pl. *amadlozi*] [S Afr.] ancestral spirits: also **Amadlozi**

amadoda (am′a dod′a) *n.pl.* [< Bantu] [S Afr.] men, esp. black

amah (ä′ma) *n.* [Anglo-Ind. < Port] in the Orient, a woman servant, esp. one who serves as a baby's nurse

amain (a main′) *adv.* [A-, on + MAIN[1]] [Archaic or Poet.] 1. forcefully 2. at great speed

amalgam (a mal′gam) *n.* [< Gr. *malagma*, emollient < *malassein*, soften] 1. any alloy of mercury with another metal [silver *amalgam* is used as a dental filling] 2. any mixture or blend

amalgamate (-ga māt′) *vt., vi.* **-mat′ed, -mat′ing** to combine; unite —**amal′gama′-tion** *n.*

amanuensis (a man′yoo wen′sis) *n., pl.* **-ses** [L. < a-, from < *manus*, hand + -*ensis*, relating to] an assistant who takes dictation; secretary

amaranth (am′a ranth′) *n.* [< Gr. *a-*, not + *marainein*, die away] 1. any of a genus of plants, usually with colourful leaves 2. [Poet.] an imaginary flower that never dies 3. a dark purplish red —**am′aran′thine** (-ran′thīn) *adj.*

amaryllis (am′a ril′as) *n.* [< Gr.; name for a shepherdess] a bulb plant bearing several white, pink, or red lilylike flowers on a single stem

amass (a mas′) *vt.* [< L. *massa*, mass] 1. to accumulate (esp. wealth) 2. to pile up —**amass′er** *n.*

amateur (am′a tar) *n.* [Fr. < L. *amare*, to love] 1. one who engages in some art, sport, etc. for pleasure rather than as a profession 2. one who does something without skill —*adj.* of or done by or as by an amateur or amateurs —**am′ateur-ish** *adj.* —**am′ateurism** *n.*

amatory (am′a tər ē) *adj.* [< L. *amare*, to love] of or showing love, esp. sexual love

amaze (a māz′) *vt.* **amazed′, amaz′ing** [see MAZE] to fill with great surprise or wonder; astonish —**amaz′edly** (-id lē) *adv.* —**amaze′ment** *n.* —**amaz′ingly** *adv.*

amazon (am′a zən) *n.* [< Gr. < ?, but derived by folk etym. < a-, without + *mazos*, breast] a large, strong, or aggressive woman; after a race of female warriors in Greek mythology —**amazonian** (am′a zō′nē ən) *adj.*

ambassador (am bas′a dər) *n.* [< Pr. < hyp. *ambaissa*, mission] 1. the highest-ranking diplomatic representative appointed by a government to represent it in another country 2. an official messenger —**ambas′sado′rial** (-dôr′ē əl) *adj.* —**ambas′sadress** *n. fem.*

amber (am′bər) *n.* [< Ar. ʻanbar, ambergris] 1. a brownish-yellow translucent fossil resin used in jewellery, etc. 2. the colour of amber 3. the light between the green and red of traffic lights —*adj.* made of or like amber

ambergris (-grēs′) *n.* [< OFr. *ambre gris*, grey amber] a greyish, waxy substance from the intestines of sperm whales, used in some perfumes

ambi- [L. < *ambo*, both] a combining form meaning both

ambiance (am′bē əns) *n.* [Fr.: see AMBIENT] an environment or milieu: also **am′bience**

ambidextrous (am′ba dek′strəs) *adj.* [< L. AMBI- + *dexter*, right hand] 1. able to use both hands with equal ease 2. deceitful —**am′bidexter′ity** (-dek ster′-ə tē) *n.*

ambient (am′bē ənt) *adj.* [< L. *ambi-*, around + *ire*, go] surrounding; on all sides

ambiguity (am′ba gyoo′a tē) *n.* the quality or state of being ambiguous

ambiguous (am big′yoo wəs) *adj.* [< L. *ambi-*, around + *agere*, act] 1. having two or more possible meanings 2. not clear; indefinite; vague —**ambig′uously** *adv.*

ambit (am′bit) *n.* [see AMBIENT] 1. scope; extent 2. boundary; circumference

ambition (am bish′ən) *n.* [< L. *ambitio*, a going around (to solicit votes)] 1. a strong desire for success, power, etc. 2. the thing so desired

ambitious *adj.* 1. full of or showing ambition 2. needing great effort, skill, etc. —**ambi′tiously** *adv.*

ambivalence (am biv′a ləns) *n.* [AMBI- + VALENCE] simultaneous conflicting feelings towards a person or thing, as love and hate —**ambiv′alent** *adj.*

amble (am′b'l) *vi.* **-bled, -bling** [< L. *ambulare*, to walk] 1. to walk in a leisurely manner 2. to move at a smooth, easy gait: said of a horse, etc. —*n.* 1. a leisurely walking pace 2. a horse's ambling gait —**am′bler** *n.*

ambrosia (am brōz′ēə) *n.* [< Gr. a-, not + *brotos*, mortal] 1. *Gr. & Rom. Myth.* the food of the gods and immortals 2. anything that tastes or smells delicious —**ambro′sial, ambro′sian** *adj.*

ambry (am′brē) *n., pl.* **-bries** [< L. *armarium*, chest for arms] a recessed cupboard in the wall of a church

ambulance (am′byoo ləns) *n.* [< L. *ambulare*, to walk] 1. a specially equipped vehicle for carrying the sick or wounded 2. orig., a mobile field hospital

ambulate (am′byoo lāt′) *vi.* **-lat′ed, -lat′-ing** [< L. *ambulare*, to walk] to move about; walk —**am′bulant** *adj.* —**am′bula′-tion** *n.*

ambulatory (-lə tər ē) *adj.* **1.** of or for walking **2.** able to walk **3.** movable —*n.*, *pl.* **-ries** any sheltered place for walking, as in a cloister

ambuscade (am′bəs kād′) *n.*, *vt.*, *vi.* **-cad′ed, -cad′ing** [see ff.] *same as* AMBUSH —**am′buscad′er** *n.*

ambush (am′boosh) *n.* [< ML. *in-*, in + *boscus*, woods] **1.** the act of waiting in a concealed place to launch a surprise attack **2.** the surprise attack **3.** the place of hiding —*vt.*, *vi.* **1.** to lie in wait (for) **2.** to attack from ambush —**am′bushment** *n.*

ameer (ə mēar′) *n.* *same as* AMIR

ameliorate (ə mēl′yə rāt′) *vt.*, *vi.* **-rat′ed, -rat′ing** [< L. *melior*, better] to make or become better; improve —**amel′iora′-tion** *n.* —**amel′iorative** *adj.*

amen (ā′men′, ä′-) *interj.* [< Heb. *āmēn*, truly] may it be so!: used after a prayer or to express approval

amenable (ə mē′nə b′l) *adj.* [< OFr. < LL. *minare*, to drive (animals) < L. *minare*, to threaten] **1.** responsible or answerable **2.** responsive; submissive —**ame′nabil′ity** *n.* —**ame′nably** *adv.*

amend (ə mend′) *vt.* [< L. *emendare*, to correct] **1.** to make better; improve **2.** to correct **3.** to change or revise (a law, etc.) —*vi.* to improve one's conduct —**amend′able** *adj.* —**amend′atory** *adj.* —**amend′er** *n.*

amendment *n.* **1.** a change for the better; improvement **2.** a correction of errors, etc. **3.** a revision or addition proposed or made in a law, etc.

amends *n.pl.* something given or done to make up for injury, loss, etc. that one has caused

amenity (ə mē′nə tē) *n.*, *pl.* **-ties** [< L. *amoenus*, pleasant] **1.** a useful or desirable facility or service **2.** pleasant quality; attractiveness

amenorrhoea (ā men′ə rē′ə) *n.* [< Gr. *a-*, not + *mēn*, month + *rhein*, to flow] abnormal absence or suppression of menstruation

amerce (ə murs′) *vt.* **amerced′, amerc′-ing** [< OFr. *a merci*, at the mercy of] to punish by imposing a fine —**amerce′-ment** *n.*

American (ə mer′ə kən) *adj.* **1.** of or in America **2.** of, in, or characteristic of the U.S., its people, etc. —*n.* **1.** a native or inhabitant of America **2.** a citizen of the U.S. —**Amer′icanize′** *vt.*, *vi.*

American Indian *same as* INDIAN (*n.* 2)

Americanism *n.* **1.** a word, phrase or usage originating in or peculiar to American English **2.** a custom, characteristic, or belief of or originating in the U.S. **3.** devotion or loyalty to the U.S., or to its traditions, etc.

americium (am′ə rish′ē əm) [< *America*] a chemical element, one of the transuranic elements produced from plutonium: symbol, Am

Amerind (am′ə rind′) *n.* an American

Indian or Eskimo —**Am′erin′dian** *adj.*, *n.* —**Am′erin′dic** *adj.*

amethyst (am′ə thist) *n.* [< Gr. *a-*, not + *methystos*, drunken] **1.** a purple or violet variety of quartz, used in jewellery **2.** popularly, a purple corundum, used in jewellery **3.** purple or violet —**am′ethys′-tine** (-this′tin) *adj.*

Amharic (am har′ik) *n.* the Semitic language used officially in Ethiopia

amiable (ā′mē ə b′l) *adj.* [< L. *amicus*, friend] having a pleasant, friendly disposition; good-natured —**a′miabil′ity** *n.* —**a′miably** *adv.*

amicable (am′i kə b′l) *adj.* [see AMIABLE] friendly in feeling; showing good will [an *amicable* discussion] —**am′icabil′ity** *n.* —**am′icably** *adv.*

amice (am′is) *n.* [< L. *amictus*, cloak] an oblong cloth of white linen worn about the neck and shoulders by a priest at Mass

amicus curiae (ə mī′kəs kyooar′i ē′) [L., friend of the court] *Law* a person who offers, or is called in, to advise a court on some legal matter

amid (ə mid′) *prep.* [ME. < *on*, at + *middan*, middle] in the middle of; among

amide (am′īd, -id) *n.* [< AMMONIA] any of a group of organic compounds containing the CO·NH₂ radical in place of one hydrogen atom of an ammonia molecule —**amidic** (ə mid′ik) *adj.*

amidships (ə mid′ships) *adv.*, *adj.* in or towards the middle of a ship

amidst (ə midst′) *prep.* *same as* AMID

amine (ā′mēn, am′ēn) *n.* [< AMMONIA] *Chem.* a derivative of ammonia in which hydrogen atoms have been replaced by radicals containing hydrogen and carbon atoms

amino acids (ə mē′nō) a group of organic compounds that contain the amino radical and are units of structure of proteins

amir (ə mēar′) *n.* [Ar.] in some Moslem countries, a ruler, prince, or commander: see also EMIR

amiss (ə mis′) *adv.* [see A- & MISS¹] astray, wrongly, etc. —*adj.* wrong, faulty, improper, etc.

amity (am′ə tē) *n.*, *pl.* **-ties** [< L. *amicus*, friend] peaceful relations, as between nations; friendship

ammeter (am′ēt′ər) *n.* [AM(PERE) + -METER] an instrument for measuring an electric current in amperes

ammo (am′ō) *n.* [Slang] ammunition

ammonia (ə mōn′ē ə) *n.* [ult. < a substance found near Libyan shrine of Jupiter *Ammon*, Roman-Egyptian god] **1.** a colourless, pungent gas, used in fertilizers, cleaning fluids, etc. **2.** a water solution of this gas: in full, **ammonia water** —**ammonia-cal** (am′ə nī′ə k′l) *adj.*

ammonite (am′ə nīt′) *n.* [< L. (*cornu*) *Ammonis*, (horn) of Ammon] a coiled fossil shell

ammonium (ə mō′nē əm) *n.* the radical NH₄, present in salts produced by the reaction of ammonia with an acid

ammunition (am′yoo nish′ən) *n.* [see MUNITIONS] **1.** anything hurled by a weapon or exploded as a weapon, as bullets, shells, grenades, etc. **2.** any means of attack or defence

amnesia (am nē′zē ə) *n.* [< Gr. *a-*, not + *mnasthai*, remember] partial or total loss of memory —**amne′siac′** (-zē ak′), **amne′sic** *adj., n.*

amnesty (am′nəs tē) *n., pl.* **-ties** [< Gr. *amnēstia*, a forgetting] a general pardon, esp. for political offences

amnion (am′nē ən) *n., pl.* **-nions, -nia** [< Gr. *amnos*, lamb] the innermost membrane of the sac enclosing the embryo of a mammal, reptile, or bird —**am′niot′-ic** (-ot′ik) *adj.*

AMOEBA

NUCLEUS

VACUOLE

PSEUDOPODIUM

amoeba (ə mē′bə) *n., pl.* **-bas, -bae** (-bē) [< Gr. *ameibein*, to change] a microscopic, one-celled animal found usually in stagnant water —**amoe′bic** *adj.*

amok (ə mok′) *adj., adv.* [Malay *amoq*] in a frenzy to kill; in a violent rage, esp. in **run amok**

among (ə muŋ′) *prep.* [< OE. *on*, in + *gemang*, a crowd] **1.** surrounded by [*among* friends] **2.** in the group or class of **3.** by or with many of **4.** with a share for each of **5.** with one another [*talking among* ourselves] **6.** by the joint action of

amongst (ə muŋst′) *prep.* same as AMONG

amoral (ā mor′əl) *adj.* **1.** neither moral nor immoral **2.** without moral principles —**amorality** (ā′mə ral′ə tē) *n.*

amorous (am′ər əs) *adj.* [< L. *amare*, to love] **1.** fond of making love **2.** full of love **3.** of sexual love or lovemaking —**am′orously** *adv.* —**am′orousness** *n.*

amorphous (ə môr′fəs) *adj.* [< Gr. *a-*, without + *morphē*, form] **1.** shapeless **2.** indefinite, vague, etc. **3.** *Biol.* without specialized structure **4.** *Chem., Mineralogy* not crystalline —**amor′phism** *n.*

amortize (ə môr′tīz) *vt.* **-tized, -tizing** [< L. *ad*, to + *mors*, death] to put money aside at intervals, as in a sinking fund, for gradual payment of (a debt, etc.) —**am′-ortiz′able** *adj.* —**am′ortiza′tion** *n.*

amount (ə mount′) *n.* [< L. *ad*, to + *mons*, mountain] **1.** the sum of two or more quantities; total **2.** a principal sum plus its interest **3.** a quantity —*vi.* **1.** to add up; total **2.** to be equal in meaning, value, or effect

amour (ə mooər′) *n.* [Fr. < L. *amor*, love] a love affair, esp. one that is illicit or secret

‡**amour-propre** (à mooər prô′pr′) *n.* [Fr.] self-respect

amp. **1.** amperage **2.** ampere(s)

ampelopsis (am′pə lop′sis) *n.* [< Gr. *ampelos*, vine + *opsis*, appearance] a climbing shrub like the vine

amperage (am′pər ij) *n.* the strength of an electric current, measured in amperes

ampere (am′pāər) *n.* [< A. M. *Ampère*] the SI unit of electric current

ampersand (am′pər sand′) *n.* [< *and per se and*, lit., (the sign) & by itself (is) *and*] a sign (&) meaning *and*

amphetamine (am fet′ə mēn′) *n.* a compound used as a drug to overcome depression, fatigue, etc.

amphi- [< Gr.] *a prefix meaning:* **1.** on both sides or ends **2.** of both kinds **3.** around; about

amphibian (am fib′ē ən) *n.* [see ff.] **1.** any of a class of vertebrates, including frogs, toads, salamanders, etc., that usually begin life in the water as tadpoles with gills, and later develop lungs **2.** any amphibious animal or plant **3.** an aircraft that can take off from and come down on either land or water **4.** a vehicle that can travel on either land or water

amphibious *adj.* [< Gr. *amphi-*, AMPHI- + *bios*, life] **1.** that can live or operate both on land and in water **2.** of or for a military operation involving the landing of troops from seaborne transports —**amphib′iously** *adv.*

amphitheatre (am′fə thē′ə tər) *n.* [see AMPHI- & THEATRE] **1.** a round or oval building with an open space (arena) surrounded by rising rows of seats **2.** a level place surrounded by rising ground

amphora (am′fər ə) *n., pl.* **-rae** (-ē) [< Gr. *amphi-*, AMPHI- + *pherein*, to bear] a Greek or Roman jar with a narrow neck and base and two handles

ample (am′p′l) *adj.* **-pler, -plest** [< L. *amplus*] **1.** more than enough; abundant **2.** enough; adequate **3.** large in size, extent, etc. —**am′pleness** *n.*

amplifier (am′plə fī′ər) *n. Electronics* a device used to increase electrical signal strength

amplify (am′plə fī′) *vt.* **-fied′, -fy′ing** [< L. *amplus*, ample + *facere*, make] **1.** to make stronger **2.** to develop more fully **3.** *Electronics* to strengthen (an electrical signal) by means of an amplifier —*vi.* to speak or write at length —**am′plifi-ca′tion** *n.*

amplitude (am′plə tood′) *n.* [< L. *amplus*, ample] **1.** extent; largeness **2.** abundance; fullness **3.** scope or breadth, as of mind **4.** the extreme range of a fluctuating quantity, from the average or mean to the extreme

amplitude modulation the changing of the amplitude of the transmitting radio wave in accordance with the signal being broadcast : distinguished from FREQUENCY MODULATION

amply (am′plē) *adv.* to an ample degree

ampoule (am′pool) *n.* [see ff.] a small, sealed glass container for one dose of a medicine

ampulla (am pool′ə) *n., pl.* **-pul′lae** (-ē)

[< L. *ampulla*, bottle] **1.** a nearly round Greek and Roman bottle with two handles **2.** a container used in churches

amputate (am'pyŏŏtāt') *vt.* **-tat'ed, -tat'-ing** [< L. *am-*, for AMBI- + *putare*, prune] to cut off (an arm, leg, etc.), esp. by surgery —**am'puta'tion** *n.*

amuck (ə muk') *adj., adv.* same as AMOK

amulet (am'yŏŏlit) *n.* [< L.] something worn on the body as a charm against evil

amuse (ə myŏŏz') *vt.* **amused', amus'ing** [< Fr. à, at + OFr. *muser*, stare fixedly] **1.** to occupy or entertain **2.** to make laugh, smile, etc. —**amus'able** *adj.*

amusement *n.* **1.** the condition of being amused **2.** something that amuses or entertains

amusement park an outdoor place with devices for entertainment, as side shows, roundabouts, etc.

amylase (am'əlās') *n.* an enzyme that helps change starch into sugar, found in saliva, pancreatic juice, etc.

amylum (am'ələm) *n.* [< Gr.] *Chem.* starch

an¹ (ən; *stressed* an) *adj., indefinite article* [< OE. *an*, one] **1.** one; one sort of **2.** each; any one **3.** to each; for each

an², an' (an) *conj.* [< *and*] [Archaic] if

an- same as A- (not, without): used before vowels

-an (ən, 'n) [< L.] *a suffix meaning:* **1.** (one) belonging to or having some relation to [*diocesan*] **2.** (one) born in or living in [*American*] **3.** (one) believing in or following [*Mohammedan*]

an. · **1.** [L. *anno*] in the year **2.** anonymous

Anabaptist (an'ə bap'tist) *n.* [< Gr. *ana-*, again + *baptizein*, baptize] a member of a 16th-cent. Swiss sect of the Reformation, that practised baptism of adults —*adj.* of this sect —**An'abap'tism** *n.*

anabolism (ə nab'əliz'm) *n.* [< Gr. *anabolē*, a rising up] the process in a plant or animal by which food is changed into living tissue —**anabolic** (an'ə bol'ik) *adj.*

anachronism (ə nak'rəniz'm) *n.* [< Gr. *ana-*, against + *chronos*, time] **1.** the representation of something as existing or occurring at other than its proper time **2.** anything out of its proper time in history —**anach'ronis'tic, anach'ronous** *adj.* —**anach'ronis'tically** *adv.*

anaconda (an'ə kon'də) *n.* [< ?] a long, heavy S American snake similar to the boa

anadromous (ə nad'rə məs) *adj.* [< Gr. *ana-*, upward + *dramein*, run] going up rivers to spawn: said of salmon, shad, etc.

anaemia (ə nē'mē ə) *n.* [< Gr. *a-, an*, without + *haima*, blood] a condition in which there is a reduction of the number of red blood corpuscles in the bloodstream

anaemic *adj.* **1.** suffering from anaemia **2.** pale; lacking vitality —**anae'mically** *adv.*

anaerobe (an âar'ōb) *n.* [< Gr. *an-*, AN- + *aero-*, AERO- + *bios*, life] a microorganism that can live where there is no free oxygen —**anaerobic** (an'âar ō'-bik) *adj.*

anaesthesia (an'əs thē'zē ə) *n.* [< Gr. *an*, without + *aisthesis*, feeling] **1.** partial or total loss of the sense of pain, touch, etc., produced by disease **2.** a loss of sensation induced by an anaesthetic

anaesthetic (an'əs thet'ik) *n.* a drug, gas, etc. used to produce anaesthesia, as before surgery —*adj.* producing anaesthesia —**an'aesthet'ically** *adv.*

anaesthetist (ə nēs'thə tist) *n.* a person who administers anaesthetics

anaesthetize *vt.* **-tized', -tiz'ing** to cause anaesthesia in, as by giving an anaesthetic —**anaes'thetiza'tion** *n.*

anaglypta (an'ə glip'tə) *n.* [< L., work in bas relief] a textured wallpaper designed to be painted over

anagram (an'ə gram') *n.* [< Gr. *ana-*, back + *gramma*, letter] a word or phrase made from another by rearranging its letters (Ex.: *now — won*) —**an'agrammat'-ic** (-grə mat'ik), **an'agrammat'ical** *adj.*

anal (ā'n'l) *adj.* of or near the anus

analects (an'əlekts') *n.pl.* [< Gr. *ana-*, up + *legein*, gather] collected literary excerpts: also **an'alec'ta**

analgesia (an'l jē'zē ə) *n.* [< Gr. *an-*, without + *algēsia*, pain] a state of not feeling pain although fully conscious —**an'-alge'sic** *adj., n.*

analogize (ə nal'ə jīz') *vi.* **-gized', -giz'-ing** to use, or reason by, analogy —*vt.* to explain or liken by analogy —**anal'o-gist** *n.*

analogous *adj.* [see ANALOGY] similar or comparable in certain respects —**anal'o-gously** *adv.*

analogue (an'ə log') *n.* a thing or part that is analogous

analogue, analog (an'ə log') *adj.* of or by means of an analogue computer

analogue computer an electronic computer that uses voltages to represent the numerical data of physical quantities Also **analog**

analogy (ə nal'ə jē) *n.,* pl. **-gies** [< Gr. *ana-*, according to + *logos*, ratio] **1.** similarity in some respects **2.** a comparing of something point by point with something similar **3.** *Linguis.* the formation of new words based on the pattern of older ones [*energize* is formed from *energy* by analogy with *apologize* from *apology*] —**an'alog'ical** *adj.*

analyse (an'ə līz') *vt.* **-lysed', -lys'ing** **1.** to separate into parts so as to find out their nature, function, etc. **2.** to examine in detail so as to determine the nature of

analysis (ə nal'ə sis) *n.,* pl. **-ses'** [< Gr. *ana-*, up, throughout + *lysis*, loosing] **1.** *a)* a breaking up of any whole into parts so as to find out their nature, function, etc. *b)* a statement of these findings **2.** same as PSYCHOANALYSIS **3.** *Chem.* the separation of compounds and mixtures into their constituents to determine their nature or proportion

analyst (an'ə list) *n.* **1.** a person who analyses **2.** same as PSYCHOANALYST

analytic (an'ə lit'ik) *adj.* of, or skilled in analysis: also **an'alyt'ical**

analytics *n.pl.* [*with sing. v.*] the part of logic having to do with analysing

analyze (an'ə līz') *vt.* **-lyzed', -lyz'ing** *U.S. sp. of* ANALYSE

anapaest (an'ə pest') *n.* [< Gr. *ana-*, back + *paiein*, strike] a metrical foot consisting of two unaccented syllables followed by an accented one **—an'apaes'tic** *adj.*

anaphora (ənaf'ər ə) *n.* [< Gr. *ana-*, back + *pherein*, to bear] the repetition of a word or phrase at the beginning of successive clauses or sentences as a rhetorical device

anarchism (an'ər kiz'm) *n.* **1.** the theory that all forms of government interfere with individual liberty **2.** resistance, sometimes by terrorism, to government

anarchist (an'ər kist) *n.* one who believes in or advocates anarchism **—an'archis'tic** *adj.*

anarchy (an'ər kē) *n.* [< Gr. *an-*, without + *archos*, leader] **1.** political disorder and violence **2.** the complete absence of government **3.** disorder in any sphere of activity

anastigmatic (an as'tig mat'ik) *adj.* free from, or corrected for, astigmatism

anat. **1.** anatomical **2.** anatomist **3.** anatomy

anathema (ənath'ə mə) *n.,* *pl.* **-mas** [< Gr., thing devoted to evil < *anatithenai*, dedicate] **1.** a thing or person greatly detested **2.** a formal curse, as in excommunicating a person from a church **3.** a thing or person accursed

anathematize *vt., vi.* **-tized', -tiz'ing** to curse

anatomize (ənat'ə mīz') *vt., vi.* **-mized', -miz'ing** **1.** to dissect (an animal or plant) in order to examine the structure **2.** to analyse in great detail **—anat'omiza'tion** *n.* **—anat'omist** *n.*

anatomy (ənat'ə mē) *n., pl.* **-mies** [< Gr. *ana-*, up + *temnein*, to cut] **1.** the science of the structure of animals or plants **2.** the structure of an organism **3.** the dissecting of an animal or plant in order to study its structure **4.** a detailed analysis **—an'atom'ical** (an'ə tom'i k'l) *adj.* **—an'atom'ically** *adv.*

-ance (əns, 'ns) [< L.] *a suffix meaning:* **1.** the act of [*utterance*] **2.** the state of being [*vigilance*] **3.** a thing that [*conveyance*] **4.** a thing that is [*dissonance*]

ancestor (an'ses'tər) *n.* [< L. *ante-*, before + *cedere*, go] **1.** any person from whom one is descended **2.** an early type of animal from which later kinds have evolved **3.** a predecessor **—an'ces'tress** *n.fem.*

ancestral (an ses'trəl) *adj.* of or inherited from ancestors **—ances'trally** *adv.*

ancestry (an'səs trē) *n., pl.* **-tries** **1.** family descent or lineage **2.** ancestors collectively

anchor (aŋ'kər) *n.* [< Gr. *ankyra*, hook] **1.** a heavy object, usually a shaped iron weight, lowered to the bottom of water

to keep a ship from drifting **2.** anything regarded as giving stability or security **—vt.** to hold secure by or as by an anchor **—vi.** **1.** to lower the anchor overboard **2.** to become fixed **—drop (cast) anchor 1.** to lower the anchor overboard **2.** to settle (*in a place*) **—weigh anchor 1.** to raise the anchor **2.** to leave

anchorage *n.* **1.** money charged for the right to anchor **2.** a place to anchor **3.** something that can be relied on

anchorite (aŋ'kə rīt') *n.* [< Gr. *ana-*, back + *chōrein*, retire] a person who lives alone for religious meditation; hermit : also **an'choret** (-rit) **—an'choress** *n.fem.*

anchor man 1. the final contestant, as on a relay team **2.** *Radio & TV* that member of a team of broadcasters who coordinates various items

anchovy (an'chə vē) *n., pl.* **-vies** [< Port. *anchova*] a very small, herringlike fish

anchusa (aŋ kyōō'sə) *n.* [< Gr. *anchousa*] any of several plants related to borage

‡ancien régime (än syan' rā zhēm') [Fr., old order] the former social and political system, esp. that in France before the Revolution of 1789

ancient (ān'shənt) *adj.* [ult. < L. *ante*, before] **1.** of times long past; esp., before the end of the Western Roman Empire in 476 A.D. **2.** very old **3.** antiquated **—n.** **1.** one who lived in ancient times **2.** an aged person **—the ancients** people who lived in ancient times; esp., the writers and artists of Graeco-Roman times

anciently *adv.* in ancient times

ancillary (an sil'ər ē) *adj.* [< L. *ancilla*, maidservant] **1.** subordinate (*to*) **2.** auxiliary

-ancy (ən sē, 'n sē) *same as* -ANCE

and (ənd, ən, 'n; *stressed* and) *conj.* [OE.] **1.** also; in addition; as well as **2.** plus **3.** as a result [*he told her and she wept*] **4.** [Colloq.] to [*try and get it*]

andante (an dan'tē) *adj., adv.* [It.] *Music* moderate in tempo

andantino (an'dan tē'nō) *adj., adv.* [It.] *Music* slightly faster than andante

ANDIRONS

andiron (an'dī'ərn) *n.* [< OFr. *andier* (altered after iron)] either of a pair of metal supports with front uprights, used to hold the wood in a fireplace

and/or either and or or, according to what is meant [*personal and/or real property*]

andro- [< Gr. *anēr, andros*, man] a com-

bining form meaning : 1. man, masculine 2. anther, stamen

androgen (an′drə jən) *n.* [ANDRO- + -GEN] a male sex hormone that can give rise to masculine characteristics —**an′drogen′ic** (-jen′ik) *adj.*

androgynous (an droj′ə nəs) *adj.* [< Gr. *anēr, andros,* man + *gynē,* woman] 1. hermaphroditic 2. *Bot.* bearing both staminate and pistillate flowers in the same cluster —**androg′yny** *n.*

android (an′droid) *n.* in science fiction, an automaton that looks human

Andromeda (an drom′ə də) 1. *Gr. Myth.* a princess whom Perseus rescued from a sea monster 2. *Astron.* a N constellation just south of Cassiopeia

anecdote (an′ik dōt′) *n.* [< Gr. *anekdotos,* unpublished]   a short, entertaining account of some happening —**an′ecdot′al** *adj.* —**an′ecdot′ist** *n.*

anechoic (an′e kō′ik) *adj.* [AN- + ECHOIC] free from echoes [an *anechoic* recording chamber]

anemia (ə nē′mē ə) *n.* U.S. var. sp. of ANAEMIA

anemometer (an′ə mom′ə tər) *n.* [< Gr. *anemos,* the wind + -METER] a gauge for determining the force or speed of the wind —**an′emom′etry** *n.*

anemone (ə nem′ə nē′) *n.* [< Gr. *anemos,* wind] 1. a plant with cup-shaped flowers, usually white, purple, or red 2. *same as* SEA ANEMONE

anent (ə nent′) *prep.* [< OE. *on efen, on even* (with)]   [Archaic or Scot.] concerning; as regards

aneroid (an′ər oid) *adj.* [< Gr. *a-,* without + *nēros,* liquid]   not using liquid —*n. same as* ANEROID BAROMETER

aneroid barometer   a barometer in which changes in atmospheric pressure cause the elastic top of a box to bend in or out, thus moving a pointer

anesthesia (an′es thē′zē ə) *n.* U.S. var. sp. of ANAESTHESIA

aneurysm, aneurism (an′yoor iz′m) *n.* [< Gr. *ana-,* up + *eurys,* broad] a sac formed when the wall of an artery becomes enlarged

anew (ə nyoo′) *adv.* 1. again 2. in a new manner

angel (ān′j′l) *n.* [< Gr. *angelos,* messenger] 1. *Theol.* a) a messenger of God b) a supernatural being 2. a guiding spirit 3. a conventionalized image of a human figure with wings and a halo 4. a person regarded as beautiful, good, etc. 5. a former English gold coin 6. [Colloq.] a supporter who provides money, as for producing a play

angel cake   a light, spongy, white cake made with egg whites and no fat : also **angel food cake**

angelfish *n.*   a brightly coloured tropical fish with spiny fins

angelic (an jel′ik) *adj.* of or like an angel or the angels : also **angel′ical** —**angel′ically** *adv.*

angelica (an jel′i kə) *n.* [ML., angelic (herb)] 1. any of a number of related plants used in flavouring, etc. 2. its candied stems, used in cookery

Angelus (an′jə ləs) *n.* [L.: see ANGEL] [*also* a-] *R.C.Ch.* 1. a prayer said at morning, noon, and evening in commemoration of the Incarnation 2. a bell rung to announce the time for this

anger (aŋ′gər) *n.* [ON. *angr,* distress] a feeling of displeasure and hostility resulting from injury, opposition, etc. —*vt.* to make angry; enrage

Angevin, Angevine (an′jə vin) *adj.* [Fr.] of Anjou or the Plantagenets

angina (an jī′nə) *n.* [< Gr. *anchein,* to squeeze] 1. any inflammatory disease of the throat 2. *same as* ANGINA PECTORIS —**angi′nal, angi′nous** *adj.*

angina pectoris (pek′tər is) [L., angina of the breast] recurrent pain in the chest and left arm, caused by a sudden decrease of blood to the heart

angiosperm (an′jē ə spʉrm′) *n.* [< Gr. *angeion,* capsule + *sperma,* seed] any flowering plant having the seeds enclosed in an ovary

Angl. 1. Anglican 2. Anglicized

angle[1] (aŋ′g′l) *n.* [< L. *angulus,* corner] 1. *a)* the shape or space formed by two straight lines or plane surfaces that meet *b)* the degrees of difference in direction between them 2. a sharp corner 3. point of view —*vt., vi.* **-gled, -gling** 1. to move or bend at an angle 2. [Colloq.] to give a specific point of view to (a story, etc.)

angle[2] *vi.* **-gled, -gling** [OE. *angul,* fishhook] 1. to fish with a hook and line 2. to use tricks to get something

ANGLE IRON

angle iron   an angled piece of iron or steel used for joining or reinforcing two beams, girders, etc.

angle of incidence   the angle that a light ray or electromagnetic wave striking a surface makes with a line perpendicular to the surface

angler *n.* 1. a fisherman 2. a saltwater fish that feeds on other fish

Angles (aŋ′g′lz) *n.pl.* a Germanic people that settled in NE and E England in the 5th cent. A.D. —**An′glian** *adj., n.*

Anglican (aŋ′gli kən) *adj.* [< ML. *Anglicus,* of the Angles] of the Church of England —*n.* a member of an Anglican church —**An′glicanism** *n.*

Anglicism (aŋ′glə siz′m) *n.* a word, idiom or trait peculiar to the English

Anglicize (aŋ′glə sīz′) *vt., vi.* **-cized′, -ciz′-ing** [*also* a-] to change to English idiom, pronunciation, customs, etc.

angling (aŋ′gliŋ) *n.* the act or skill of fishing with hook and line

Anglo (aŋ'glō) *n., pl.* -glos [Canad.] an English-speaking Canadian, esp. one of Anglo-Celtic origin; Anglo-Canadian

Anglo- (aŋ'glō) *a combining form meaning* English

Anglo-French (aŋ'glō french') *adj.* English and French —*n.* the French spoken in England from the Norman Conquest

Anglo-Indian (aŋ'glō in'dē ən) *adj.* 1. of England and India 2. of Anglo-Indians —*n.* 1. a person of British and Indian ancestry 2. a British citizen who lives or has lived in India, esp. when it was part of the British empire

Anglo-Norman (aŋ'glō nôr'mən) *adj.* English and Norman —*n.* 1. a Norman settler in England after the Norman Conquest 2. the Anglo-French dialect spoken by such settlers

Anglophilia (aŋ'glə fil'ē ə) *n.* [*often* a-] extreme admiration for England, its people, customs, etc. —**An'glophile'** (-fīl') *n.*

Anglophobia (aŋ'glə fō'bē ə) *n.* [*often* a-] hatred or fear of England, its people, customs, etc. —**An'glophobe'** (-fōb') *n.* —**An'glopho'bic** *adj.*

Anglo-Saxon (aŋ'glō sak's'n) *n.* 1. a member of the Germanic peoples (Angles, Saxons, and Jutes) living in England at the time of the Norman Conquest 2. *same as* OLD ENGLISH —*adj.* 1. of the Anglo-Saxons or their language 2. of their descendants; English

Angora (aŋ gôr'ə) *n.* [former name of *Ankara*] 1. a kind of cat with long, silky fur *b)* a kind of goat with long, silky hair *b)* a cloth made from this hair 3. *a)* a long-eared rabbit with long, silky hair *b)* a soft yarn made from this hair

angostura (bark) (aŋ'gəs tyoͦər'ə) [< *Angostura*, now Ciudad Bolivar, in Venezuela] a bitter bark used as a tonic and as a flavouring in bitters

angry (aŋ'grē) *adj.* -grier, -griest 1. feeling or showing anger 2. stormy 3. inflamed —**an'grily** *adv.*

angstrom (aŋ'strəm) *n.* [< 19th-c. Swed. physicist] one hundred-millionth of a centimetre

anguish (aŋ'gwish) *n.* [< L. *angustia*, tightness] great suffering, as from grief or pain; agony —*vi., vt.* to feel or make feel anguish —**an'guished** *adj.*

angular (aŋ'gyoͦo lər) *adj.* 1. lean; bony 2. awkward 3. having or forming an angle or angles 4. measured by an angle —**an'gularly** *adv.*

angularity (aŋ'gyoͦo lar'ə tē) *n., pl.* -ties 1. the quality of being angular 2. [*pl.*] angular forms; angles

anhydrous (an hī'drəs) *adj.* [< *Gr.* an-, without + *hydōr*, water] 1. without water 2. *Chem.* having no water of crystallization

anil (an'il) *n.* [< Ar. *al*, the + *nīl*, indigo] a West Indian shrub from which indigo is made

aniline (an'i lēn') *n.* [see prec.] a colourless, oily liquid, a derivative of benzene, used in making dyes, etc.

aniline dye 1. any dye made from aniline

2. commonly, any synthetic dye made from coal tar

anima (an'ə mə) *n.* [L.] life principle; soul

animadversion (an'ə mad vʉr'shən) *n.* 1. a critical, esp. unfavourable, comment (*on* or *upon* something) 2. the act of criticizing adversely

animadvert (-vʉrt') *vi.* [< L. *animus*, mind + *advertere*, turn] to comment (*on* or *upon*), esp. with disapproval; criticize adversely

animal (an'ə m'l) *n.* [< L. *anima*, breath, soul] 1. any living organism except a plant or bacterium : most animals can move about 2. any such organism other than a human being 3. a brutish or inhuman person —*adj.* 1. of, like, or from an animal 2. gross, bestial, etc. —**an'imally** *adv.*

animalcule (an'ə mal'kyoͦol) *n.* [< prec.] a very small or microscopic animal —**an'imal'cular** *adj.*

animal husbandry the raising of cattle, sheep, etc.

animalism (an'ə m'liz'm) *n.* 1. the activity, appetites, nature, etc. of animals 2. the doctrine that man is a mere animal with no soul —**an'imalist** *n.* —**an'imalis'tic** *adj.*

animality (an'ə mal'ə tē) *n.* 1. the animal kingdom; animal life 2. the animal instincts in man

animalize (an'ə mə līz') *vt.* -ized, -iz'ing to make (a person) resemble a beast; brutalize

animal magnetism the power to attract others

animal spirits healthy, lively vigour

animate (an'ə māt'; *for adj.* -mit) *vt.* -mated, -mat'ing [see ANIMAL] 1. to bring to life 2. to make gay or spirited 3. to inspire 4. to give motion to —*adj.* 1. living; having life, esp. animal life 2. lively; spirited

animated cartoon a film made by photographing a series of drawings, each slightly changed from the one before, so that the figures in them seem to move

animation (an'ə mā'shən) *n.* 1. life 2. vivacity; liveliness 3. *same as* ANIMATED CARTOON

animato (an'i mä'tō) *adj., adv.* [It.] *Music* with animation

animism (an'ə miz'm) *n.* [see ANIMAL] 1. the belief that all natural objects and phenomena have souls 2. a belief in the existence of spirits, demons, etc. —**an'imist** *n.* —**an'imis'tic** *adj.*

animosity (an'ə mos'ə tē) *n., pl.* -ties [see ff.] ill will; hostility

animus (an'ə məs) *n.* [L., passion] 1. an animating force 2. a feeling of ill will; animosity

anion (an'ī'ən) *n.* [< Gr. *ana-*, up + *ienai*, go] a negatively charged ion —**anionic** (an'ī on'ik) *adj.*

anise (an'is) *n.* [< Gr. *anēson*] a plant with fragrant seeds used for flavouring

aniseed (an'ə sēd') *n.* the seed of anise

ankh (aŋk) *n.* [Egypt., life, soul] a cross

with a loop at the top, an ancient Egyptian symbol of life

ankle (aŋ'k'l) *n.* [OE. *ancleow*] 1. the joint that connects the foot and the leg 2. the part of the leg between the foot and calf

anklet (aŋ'klit) *n.* anything worn around the ankle as an ornament or fetter

ankylosis (aŋ'kə lō'sis) *n.* [< Gr. *ankylos*, bent] *Med.* an abnormal growing together and stiffening of a joint

anna (an'ə) *n.* [Hindi *ānā*] a former coin of India, Pakistan, and Burma

annals (an''lz) *n.pl.* [< L. *annus*, year] 1. a written account of events year by year in chronological order 2. historical records; history 3. any journal containing reports of a society, etc. —**an'nalist** *n.*

annates (an'āts) *n.pl.* [< L. *annus*, year] *Eccles.* the first year's revenue of a see, etc., paid to the Pope

anneal (ə nēl') *vt.* [OE. *anælan*, burn] 1. to heat (glass, metals, etc.) and then cool slowly to prevent brittleness 2. to temper (the mind, will, etc.) —**anneal'er** *n.*

annelid (an'ə lid) *n.* [< L. *anulus*, ring] a worm with a body made of joined segments, as the earthworm

annex (ə neks'; *for n.*, an'eks) *vt.* [< L. *ad-*, to + *nectere*, tie] 1. to attach, esp. to something larger 2. to add as a condition, consequence, etc. 3. to incorporate into a state, etc. the territory of (another state, etc.) 4. to take, esp. without asking —*n.* Chiefly U.S. *sp. of* ANNEXE —**an'nexa'tion** *n.*

annexe (an'eks) *n.* 1. a wing added to a building 2. a nearby building used as an addition to the main building 3. something added, as to a document

annihilate (ə nī'ə lāt') *vt.* -lat'ed, -lat'ing [< L. *ad-*, to + *nihil*, nothing] 1. to destroy completely 2. to kill —**anni'hila'tion** *n.* *adj.* —**anni'hila'tor** *n.*

anniversary (an'ə vur'sər ē) *n.*, *pl.* -ries [< L. *annus*, year + *vertere*, turn] 1. the date on which some event occurred in an earlier year 2. the celebration of such a date —*adj.* of, being, or connected with an anniversary

‡**anno Domini** (an'ō dom'ə nī) [L., in the year of the Lord] in the (given) year since the beginning of the Christian Era —*n.* [Colloq.] old age

annotate (an'ə tāt') *vt.*, *vi.* -tat'ed, -tat'ing [L. *ad-*, to + *notare*, to mark] to provide critical or explanatory notes for (a literary work, etc.) —**an'nota'tion** *n.*

announce (ə nouns') *vt.* -nounced', -nounc'ing [< L. *ad-*, to + *nuntiare*, to report] 1. to give notice of publicly; proclaim 2. to say 3. to make known the arrival, etc. of 4. *Radio & TV* to be an announcer for —*vi.* to serve as an announcer —**announce'ment** *n.*

announcer *n.* a person who announces; specif., one who introduces radio or television programmes

annoy (ə noi') *vt.* [< L. *in odio*, in hate] 1. to irritate, bother, or make somewhat angry 2. to harm by repeated attacks —*vi.* to be annoying —**annoy'ance** *n.* —**annoy'ing** *adj.*

annual (an'yoo wəl) *adj.* [< L. *annus*, year] 1. of or measured by a year 2. happening once a year 3. for a year's time, work, etc. 4. living for only one year or season —*n.* 1. a yearly publication 2. a plant that lives only one year or season —**an'nually** *adv.*

annuity (ə nyoo'ə tē) *n.*, *pl.* -ties [< L. *annus*, year] 1. a payment of a fixed sum of money at regular intervals, esp. yearly 2. an investment yielding such payments

annul (ə nul') *vt.* -nulled', -nul'ling [< L. *ad-*, to + *nullum*, nothing] 1. to do away with 2. to invalidate; cancel —**annul'lable** *adj.*

annular (an'yoo lər) *adj.* [< L. *anulus*, ring] of, like, or forming a ring —**an'nular'ity** (-lar'ə tē) *n.*

annular eclipse an eclipse in which a ring of sunlight can be seen around the disc of the moon

annulate (an'yoo lāt') *adj.* [see ANNULAR] marked with, or made up of, rings : also **an'nulat'ed**

annulment (ə nul'mənt) *n.* 1. an annulling or being annulled 2. an invalidation, esp. of a marriage

annunciate (ə nun'sē āt') *vt.* -at'ed, -at'ing [< L. *annuntiare*] to announce

annunciation (ə nun'sē ā'shən) *n.* 1. an announcing 2. [A-] *a)* the angel Gabriel's announcement to Mary that she was to give birth to Jesus *b)* the church festival (March 25) commemorating this

annunciator (ə nun'sē āt'ər) *n.* an electric indicator, as in hotels, to show the source of calls

anode (an'ōd) *n.* [< Gr. *ana-*, up + *hodos*, way] 1. a positively charged electrode, as in an electron tube, etc. 2. the negative electrode in a battery supplying current

anodize (an'ə dīz') *vt.* -dized', -diz'ing to put a protective film on (a metal) by an electrolytic process

anodyne (an'ə dīn') *adj.* [< Gr. *an-*, without + *odynē*, pain] relieving or lessening pain —*n.* anything that relieves pain or soothes —**an'odyn'ic** (-din'ik) *adj.*

anoint (ə noint') *vt.* [< L. *in-*, on + *ungere*, smear] 1. to rub oil or ointment on 2. to put oil on in a ceremony of consecration —**anoint'ment** *n.*

Anointing of the Sick *R.C.Ch.* the sacrament in which a priest anoints a person dying or critically ill

anomalous (ə nom'ə ləs) *adj.* [< Gr. *an-*, not + *homos*, same] 1. deviating from the general rule 2. being or seeming inconsistent —**anom'alously** *adv.*

anomaly *n.*, *pl.* -lies 1. departure from the usual; abnormality 2. anything anomalous

anomie, anomy (an'ə mē) *n.* [< Gr. *a-*, without + *nomos*, law] lack of purpose or ethical values in a person or in a society —**anomic** (ə nom'ik) *adj.*

anon (ə non') *adv.* [OE. *on an*, in one]

[Archaic. or Lit.] soon; shortly —**ever and anon** now and then

anon. anonymous

anonym (an'ə nim) *n.* [see ANONYMOUS] 1. a person whose name is not known 2. a pseudonym

anonymity (an'ə nim'ə tē) *n.* the condition or fact of being anonymous

anonymous (ə non'ə məs) *adj.* [< Gr. *an-*, without + *onyma*, name] 1. with no name known 2. given, written, etc. by one whose name is withheld or unknown 3. lacking in distinctive features —**anon'y·mously** *adv.*

anorak (an'ə rak') *n.* [< Eskimo] a waterproof jacket, usually with a hood

anorexia (an'ə rek'sē ə) *n.* [< Gr. *an-*, without + *orexis*, desire] chronic lack of appetite for food

another (ə nuth'ər) *adj.* [ME. *an other*] 1. one more 2. a different 3. one of the same kind as —**pron.** 1. one additional 2. a different one 3. one of the same kind

ans. answer

anserine (an'sər in') *adj.* [< L. *anser*, goose] 1. of or like a goose 2. stupid; foolish

answer (än'sər) *n.* [< OE. *and-*, against + *swerian*, swear] 1. a reply to a question, letter, etc. 2. any retaliation 3. a solution to a problem —*vi.* 1. to reply in words, by an action, etc. 2. to respond (*to*) 3. to be sufficient 4. to be responsible (*to* a person *for* an action, etc.) 5. to correspond (*to*) —*vt.* 1. to reply to in some way 2. to respond to the signal of (a telephone, etc.) 3. to comply with; serve 4. to refute (an accusation, etc.) 5. to suit —**answer back** [Colloq.] to reply rudely or impertinently

answerable *adj.* 1. responsible; accountable 2. that can be answered

WORKER ANT

ant (ant) *n.* [OE. *æmete*] any of a family of insects, generally wingless, that live in colonies with a complex division of labour

-ant (ənt, 'nt) [Fr. < L.] *a suffix meaning:* 1. that has, shows, or does [*defiant*] 2. a person or thing that [*occupant*]

antacid (ant'as'id) *adj.* counteracting acidity

antagonism (an tag'ə niz'm) *n.* 1. opposition or hostility 2. an opposing force, principle, etc.

antagonist *n.* an adversary; opponent

antagonistic (an tag'ə nis'tik) *adj.* showing antagonism; acting in opposition —**antag'onis'tically** *adv.*

antagonize (an tag'ə nīz') *vt.* -nized', -niz'ing [< Gr. *anti-*, against + *agōn*, contest] 1. to incur the dislike of; make an enemy of 2. to oppose or counteract

antalkali (ant al'kə lī') *n.* a substance that counteracts alkalinity

antarctic (ant ärk'tik) *adj.* [< Gr. *anti*,

opposite + *arktikos*, arctic] of the South Pole or the region around it

Antarctic Circle [*also* a- c-] an imaginary circle parallel to the equator, 66°33' south of it

ant bear 1. a large anteater of tropical S America 2. the aardvark

ante (an'tē) *n.* [L., before] 1. *Poker* the stake that one must put into the pot before receiving cards 2. [Colloq.] the amount one must pay as one's share —*vt.*, *vi.* -**ted** or -**teed**, -**teing** [Colloq.] to pay (one's share)

ante- [< L. *ante*, before] *a prefix meaning:* 1. before, prior (to) [*antecedent*] 2. in front (of) [*anteroom*]

anteater (ant'ēt'ər) *n.* a mammal that feeds mainly on ants: anteaters have a long, sticky tongue

antecede (an'tə sēd') *vt.*, *vi.* -ced'ed, -ced'ing [< L. *ante*, before + *cedere*, go] to go before; precede —**an'teced'ence** *n.*

antecedent *n.* 1. any thing prior to another 2. [*pl.*] one's ancestry, past life, etc. 3. *Gram.* the word, phrase, or clause to which a pronoun refers —*adj.* previous —**an'teced'ently** *adv.*

antechamber (an'ti chām'bər) *n.* a smaller room leading into a larger or main room

antedate (an'ti dāt') *vt.* -dat'ed, -dat'ing 1. to come before 2. to put a date on that is earlier than the actual date

antediluvian (an'ti də loo'vē ən) *adj.* [< ANTE- + L. *diluvium*, a flood] 1. of the time before the Biblical Flood 2. very old or old-fashioned

antelope (an'tə lōp') *n.* [< MGr. *antholops*, deer] 1. a swift, cud-chewing, deerlike animal related to oxen and goats 2. leather made from an antelope's hide

ante meridiem (an'tē mə rid'ē əm) [L.] before noon: abbrev. A.M., a.m., AM

antenatal (an'tē nā't'l) *adj.* before birth

antenna (an ten'ə) *n.* [< L. *antemna*, sail yard] 1. *pl.* -**nae** (-ē), -**nas** either of a pair of movable sense organs on the head of an insect, crab, etc.; feeler 2. *pl.* -**nas** *Radio & TV same as* AERIAL

antenuptial contract in South Africa, a marriage contract effected prior to the wedding

antepenult (an'ti pi nult') *n.* [see ANTE- & PENULT] the third last syllable in a word, as -*lu-* in *antediluvian*

antepenultimate (-pi nul'tə mət) *adj.* third from the end —*n.* anything third from the end

anterior (an tēr'ē er) *adj.* [L., compar. of *ante*, before] 1. at or towards the front 2. coming before in time, etc.

anteroom (an'ti room') *n.* a room leading to a larger one; waiting room

anthem (an'thəm) *n.* [< Gr. *anti-*, over against + *phōnē*, voice] 1. a religious choral song usually based on words from the Bible 2. a song of praise or devotion

anther (an'thər) *n.* [< Gr. *anthos*, flower] the part of a stamen that contains the pollen

anthill (ant'hil') *n.* the soil carried by

ants from their underground nest and heaped around its entrance

anthology (an thol′ə jē) *n.*, *pl.* **-gies** [< Gr. *anthos*, flower + *legein*, gather] a collection of poems, etc. —**anthological** (an thə loj′i k'l) *adj.* —**anthol′ogist** *n.*

anthracene (an′thrə sēn′) *n.* [< Gr. *anthrax*, coal] a product of coal-tar distillation used in making dyes

anthracite (an′thrə sīt′) *n.* [< Gr. *anthrax*, coal] hard coal, which gives much heat but little flame and smoke

anthrax (an′thraks) *n.* [< Gr., (burning) coal, hence carbuncle] an infectious disease of animals that can be transmitted to man

anthropo- [< Gr.] *a combining form meaning* human

anthropocentric (an′thrə pə sen′trik) *adj.* [prec. + -CENTRIC] viewing everything in terms of human values

anthropoid (an′thrə poid′) *adj.* [SEE ANTHROPO-] manlike; esp., designating or of any of the most highly developed apes —*n.* any anthropoid ape

anthropology (an′thrə pol′ə jē) *n.* [ANTHROPO- + -LOGY] the study of the variety, distribution, characteristics, cultures, etc. of mankind —**an′thropolog′ical** (-pə loj′i k'l) *adj.* —**an′thropol′ogist** *n.*

anthropomorphism (an′thrə pə môr′fiz′m) *n.* [see ff.] the attributing of human shape to a god, animal, or inanimate thing —**an′thropomor′phic** *adj.* —**an′thropomor′phist** *n.*

anthropomorphous (-pə môr′fəs) *adj.* [< Gr. *anthrōpos*, man + *morphē*, form] having a human shape

anti (an′ti, -tē) *n.*, *pl.* **-tis** [< ff.] [Colloq.] a person opposed to some policy, proposal, etc.

anti- [< Gr. *anti*, against] *a prefix meaning:* **1.** against; hostile to **2.** that operates against **3.** that prevents, cures, or neutralizes **4.** opposite **5.** rivalling

antiaircraft (an′tē âer′kraft) *adj.* used for defence against hostile aircraft [*antiaircraft gun*]

antiballistic missile (an′ti bə lis′tik) a ballistic missile intended to destroy another ballistic missile in flight

antibiosis (an′ti bī o′sis) *n.* [< ANTI- + Gr. *bios*, life] *Biol.* an association between organisms which is harmful to one of them

antibiotic (an′ti bī ot′ik) *n.* a substance capable of destroying, or stopping the growth of, bacteria and other microorganisms —*adj.* of antibiotics

antibody (an′ti bod′ē) *n.*, *pl.* **-bod′ies** a protein produced in the body in response to contact with an antigen, serving to neutralize the antigen

antic (an′tik) *n.* [< L. *antiquus*: see ANTIQUE] a playful or silly act, trick, etc. —*adj.* [Archaic] fantastic; queer —*vi.* **-ticked**, **-ticking** to perform antics

antichrist (an′ti krist′) *n.* an opponent of Christ —[A-] *Bible* the great antagonist of Christ: I John 2:18

anticipate (an tis′ə pāt′) *vt.* **-pat′ed**, **-pat′ing** [< L. *ante-*, before + *capere*, take] **1.** to look forward to **2.** to forestall **3.** to foresee and take care of in advance **4.** to use or enjoy in advance **5.** to be ahead of in doing something —**an′tic′ipatory** *adj.*

anticipation (an tis′ə pā′shən) *n.* **1.** an anticipating **2.** something expected **3.** foreknowledge

anticlerical (an′ti kler′ə k'l) *adj.* opposed to the influence of the clergy or church, esp. in public affairs

anticlimax (an′ti klī′maks) *n.* **1.** a sudden drop from the dignified or important to the commonplace or trivial **2.** a final event which is in disappointing contrast to those coming before —**an′ticlimac′tic** *adj.*

anticline (an′ti klīn′) *n.* [< ANTI- + Gr. *klinein*, incline] *Geol.* a fold of stratified rock in which the strata slope downwards in opposite directions from the central axis

anticlockwise (an′ti klok′wīz) *adj.*, *adv.* in a direction opposite to that in which the hands of a clock move

anticoagulant (an′ti kō ag′yoo lənt) *n.* a drug or substance that delays or prevents the clotting of blood

anticyclone (an′ti sī′klōn) *n.* an area of high barometric pressure, with the winds blowing outwards

antidepressant (an′ti di pres′ənt) *adj.* designating or of any drug used to treat emotional depression

antidote (an′tə dōt′) *n.* [< Gr. *anti-*, against + *didonai*, give] **1.** a remedy to counteract a poison **2.** anything that works against an evil or unwanted condition

antifreeze (an′ti frēz′) *n.* a substance of low freezing point added esp. to the water in car radiators to prevent freezing

antigen (an′tə jən) *n.* [ANTI- + -GEN] an enzyme, toxin, etc. to which the body reacts by producing antibodies

antihero (an′ti hēer′ō) *n.* the main character of a novel, play, etc. who lacks the virtues of a traditional hero

antihistamine (an′ti his′tə mēn′) *n.* any drug used to minimize the action of histamine in allergic conditions such as hay fever

antiknock (an′ti nok′) *n.* a substance added to the fuel of internal-combustion engines to reduce noise caused by too rapid combustion

antilogarithm (an′ti log′ə riⁱh′m) *n.* the number corresponding to a given logarithm: also **antilog**

antimacassar (an′ti mə kas′ər) *n.* [ANTI- + *macassar* (oil), a former hair oil] a small cover to protect the back or arms of a chair, etc. from soiling

antimagnetic (an′ti mag net′ik) *adj.* made of metals that resist magnetism [an *antimagnetic* watch]

antimatter (an′ti mat′ər) *n.* a form of matter in which the electrical charge of each constituent particle is the reverse of that in the usual matter of our universe

antimony (an′ti mə nē) *n.* [< ML.] a silvery-white, metallic chemical element,

found only in combination: symbol, Sb
—an′timo′nic *adj.* —an′timo′nous *adj.*

antinomian (an′ti nō′mē ən) *n.* [<
ANTINOMY] [*also* A-] *Christian Theol.*
a believer in the doctrine that faith alone
is necessary for salvation

antinomy (an tin′ə mē) *n., pl.* -mies [<
Gr. *anti*, against + *nomos*, law] a
contradiction or inconsistency between two
apparently reasonable principles or laws

antinovel (an′ti nov′l) *n.* a work of prose
fiction in which the author's intention is
to violate such traditional aspects of the
novel as plot, etc.

antiparticle (an′ti pär′tə k'l) *n.* any of
the constituent particles of antimatter

antipasto (an′ti pas′tō) *n.* [It. *anti*-, before
+ *pasto*, food] a dish of salted fish,
meat, olives, etc. served as an appetizer

antipathy (an tip′ə thē) *n., pl.* -thies [<
Gr. *anti*-, against + *pathein*, feel] 1. a
strong dislike 2. the object of such dislike
—an′tipathet′ic (-thet′ik) *adj.*

antipersonnel (an′ti pur′sə nel′) *adj.*
directed against, or intended to destroy,
people rather than material objects

antiperspirant (an′ti pur′spər ənt) *n.* a
substance applied to the skin to reduce
perspiration

antiphon (an′tə fon′) *n.* [see ANTHEM]
a hymn, psalm, etc. chanted or sung in
responsive, alternating parts —antiph′onal
(-tif′ə n'l), an′tiphon′ic *adj.*

antipodes (an tip′ə dēz′) *n.pl.* [< Gr.
anti-, opposite + *pous*, foot] 1. any two
places directly opposite each other on the
earth 2. [*with pl. or sing. v.*] in British
usage, New Zealand and Australia 3. two
opposite things —antip′odal *adj.* —antip′-
ode′an (-dē′ən) *adj., n.*

antipope (an′ti pōp′) *n.* a pope set up
against the one chosen by church laws,
as in a schism

antipyretic (an′ti pī ret′ik) *adj.* [ANTI- +
PYRETIC] reducing fever —n. anything
that reduces fever

antiq. 1. antiquarian 2. antiquity; antiquities

antiquarian (an′tə kwäer′ē ən) *adj.* 1.
of antiques or antiquities 2. of antiquaries
3. of, or dealing in, rare old books —n.
an antiquary

antiquary (an′tə kwər ē) *n., pl.* -quaries
one who collects or studies antiquities
and ancient art

antiquate (an′tə kwāt′) *vt.* -quat′ed,
-quat′ing [see ANTIQUE] to make old
or obsolete; cause to become old-fashioned
—an′tiquat′ed *adj.* —an′tiqua′tion *n.*

antique (an tēk′) *n.* [< L. *antiquus*,
ancient] 1. a piece of furniture, silverware, etc. of a former period 2. an ancient
relic —adj. 1. of, or in the style of,
a former period 2. dealing in antiques
3. of ancient times 4. [Colloq.] old-
fashioned —vt.-tiqued′,-tiqu′ing to make
look antique —antique′ly *adv.* —antique′-
ness *n.*

antiquity (an tik′wə tē) *n., pl.* -ties 1.
the early period of history, esp. before

the Middle Ages 2. great age 3. [*pl.*]
relics, customs, etc. of the distant past

antirrhinum (an′ti rī′nəm) *n.* [< Gr.
anti-, like + *rhis, rhinos*, nose] a plant
with two-lipped flowers, esp. the
snapdragon

antiscorbutic (an′ti skôr byoo′tik) *adj.*
that cures or prevents scurvy

anti-Semitic (an′ti sə mit′ik) *adj.*
showing prejudice, discriminating against,
or persecuting Jews —an′ti-Sem′ite
(-sem′īt) *n.* —an′ti-Sem′itism (-sem′-
ə tiz′m) *n.*

antisepsis (an′ti sep′sis) *n.* [ANTI +
SEPSIS] 1. the technique of preventing
infection, etc. 2. the use of antiseptics

antiseptic (an′ti sep′tik) *adj.* 1.
preventing infection, decay, etc. by
inhibiting the action of microorganisms
2. using antiseptics 3. free from infection
—n. any antiseptic substance —an′tisep′-
tically *adv.*

antiserum (an′ti sēer′əm) *n.* a serum
with antibodies in it

antisocial (an′ti sō′shəl) *adj.* 1.
unsociable 2. harmful to the welfare of
the people generally

antistatic (an′ti stat′ik) *adj.* reducing
static electric charges, as on textiles,
polishes, etc.

antitank (an′ti taŋk′) *adj.* for use against
tanks in war

antithesis (an tith′ə sis) *n., pl.* -ses′[<
Gr. *anti*-, against + *tithenai*, place] 1.
a contrast of thoughts 2. a contrast or
opposition 3. the exact opposite —an′ti-
thet′ic (an′ti thet′ik), an′tithet′ical *adj.*

antitoxin (an′ti tok′sin) *n.* 1. an antibody
formed by the body to act against a specific
toxin 2. a serum containing an antitoxin
injected into a person to prevent a disease
—an′titox′ic *adj.*

antitrades (an′ti trādz′) *n.pl.* winds that
blow above and opposite to the trade winds

antitrust (an′ti trust′) *adj.* [Chiefly U.S.]
opposed to, or regulating trusts, or business
monopolies

antitype (an′ti tīp′) *n.* [< Gr. *anti*,
corresponding to + *typos*, form] 1. that
which is represented by a type 2. an
opposite type

antivivisection (an′ti viv′ə sek′shən) *n.*
opposition to medical research on living
animals —an′tiviv′isec′tionist *n., adj.*

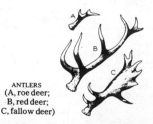

ANTLERS
(A, roe deer;
B, red deer;
C, fallow deer)

antler (ant′lər) *n.* [< OFr. *antoillier*] the

branched, deciduous horn of any animal of the deer family —**ant'lered** *adj.*

antonym (an'tə nim') *n.* [< Gr. *anti-*, opposite + *onyma*, name] a word that is opposite in meaning to another

antrum (an'trəm) *n., pl.* **-tra, -trums** [< Gr. *antron*, cave] *Anat.* a cavity; esp., either of a pair of sinuses in the upper jaw

anuresis (an'yoo rē'sis) *n.* [< AN-+ Gr. *ourēsis*, urination] the condition of being unable to pass one's urine

anus (ā'nəs) *n., pl.* **a'nuses** [L., ring] the opening at the lower end of the alimentary canal

anvil (an'vəl) *n.* [< OE. *anfilt*] an iron block on which metal objects are hammered into shape

anxiety (aŋ zī'ə tē) *n., pl.* **-ties** 1. a state of being worried about what may happen 2. an eager desire

anxious (aŋk'shəs) *adj.* [< L. *angere*, choke] 1. uneasy in mind; worried 2. causing anxiety 3. eagerly wishing —**anx'iously** *adv.* —**anx'iousness** *n.*

any (en'ē) *adj.* [< OE. *ænig*] 1. one, no matter which, of more than two 2. some, no matter what amount or kind 3. without limit 4. every —*pron. sing. & pl.* any one or ones; any amount or number —*adv.* to any degree or extent

anybody *pron.* 1. any person; anyone 2. a person of fame, importance, etc.

anyhow *adv.* 1. no matter in what way 2. in any case 3. carelessly

any more now; nowadays

anyone *pron.* any person; anybody

any one any single (person or thing)

anything *pron.* any object, fact, etc. —*n.* a thing, no matter of what kind —*adv.* in any way —**anything but** not at all

anyway *adv.* 1. at least; anyhow 2. haphazardly; carelessly 3. in any manner or way

anywhere *adv.* in, at, or to any place —**get anywhere** [Colloq.] to have any success

anywise *adv.* in any manner; at all

Anzac (an'zak') *n.* [acronym] a soldier in the Australian and New Zealand Army Corps

A.O.B., a.o.b. any other business

aorist (ā'ə rist) *n.* [Gr. *aoristos*, indefinite] a past tense of Greek verbs, denoting an action without indicating whether completed

aorta (ā ôr'tə) *n., pl.* **-tas, -tae** (-tē) [< Gr. *aeirein*, raise] the main artery of the body carrying blood from the left ventricle of the heart to arteries in all parts

apace (ə pās') *adv.* at a fast pace; swiftly

Apache (ə pach'ē) *n.* [prob. < Zuñi *ápachu*, enemy] *pl.* **Apach'es, Apach'e** a member of a tribe of Indians of the SW U.S.

apart (ə pärt') *adv.* [< L. *ad*, to + *pars*, part] 1. to one side; aside 2. away in place or time 3. separately in use, etc. [viewed *apart*] 4. in or to pieces 5. notwithstanding [all joking *apart*] —*adj.* separated —**apart from** 1. besides 2. with the exception of —**take apart** to

reduce (a whole) to its parts —**tell apart** to distinguish one from another

apartheid (ə pärthīt') *n.* [Afrik., apartness] the official S African government policy of racial segregation: this term was superseded in the 1970's by e.g. separate development

apartment (ə pärt'mənt) *n.* [< Fr. < It. *parte*, part] 1. a room in a building 2. [U.S.] *same as* FLAT² 3. [*pl.*] a set of rented rooms; lodgings

apathy (ap'ə thē) *n., pl.* **-thies** [< Gr. *a-*, without + *pathos*, emotion] 1. indifference 2. lack of emotion —**ap'athet'ic** (-thet'ik) *adj.*

apatite (ap'ə tīt') *n.* [< Gr. *apatē*, deceit: so named from being mistaken for other minerals] a mineral consisting essentially of calcium phosphate

ape (āp) *n.* [OE. *apa*] 1. a chimpanzee, gorilla, orangutan, or gibbon 2. any monkey 3. a mimic —*vt.* **aped, ap'ing** to imitate —**ape'like'** *adj.*

A.P.E.C. [Canad.] Atlantic Provinces Economic Council

ape-man *n.* an extinct primate with characteristics between those of man and the higher apes

aperient (ə pēər'ē ənt) *adj., n.* [< L. *aperire*: see APERTURE] *same as* LAXATIVE

aperiodic (ā'pēər ē od'ik) *adj.* 1. occurring irregularly 2. *Physics* without periodic vibrations

aperitif (ə per'i tēf) *n.* [see ff.] an alcoholic drink, esp. a wine, taken before meals

aperture (ap'ər tyooər) *n.* [< L. *aperire*, open] 1. an opening 2. the diameter of the opening in a camera, etc., through which light passes into the lens

apex (ā'peks) *n., pl.* **a'pexes, ap'ices** (ā'pə sēz') [L., a point] 1. the highest point 2. the pointed end 3. a climax

aphasia (ə fā'zhə) *n.* [< Gr. *a-*, not + *phanai*, to speak] a total or partial loss of the power to use or understand words —**apha'sic** (-zik) *adj., n.*

APHELION
(planet at aphelion A and at perihelion P)

aphelion (ə fē'lē ən) *n., pl.* **-lions, -lia** [< Gr. *apo*, from + *hēlios*, sun] the point farthest from the sun in the orbit around it of a planet, comet, or man-made satellite: cf. PERIHELION

aphid (ā'fid) *n.* [ModL. *aphis*] a small insect that sucks the juice from plants —**aphidian** (ə fid'ē ən) *adj., n.*

aphis (ā′fis) *n., pl.* **aphides** (af′ə dēz′) an aphid

aphorism (af′ə riz'm) *n.* [< Gr. *apo-*, from + *horizein*, to limit] 1. a concise statement of a principle 2. a maxim or adage —**aph′orist** *n.* —**aph′oris′tic** *adj.* —**aph′oris′tically** *adv.*

aphrodisiac (af′rə diz′ē ak′) *adj.* [< *Aphroditē*, Gr. goddess of love] arousing or increasing sexual desire —*n.* an aphrodisiac substance

apiary (ā′pyər ē) *n., pl.* **-aries** [< L. *apis*, bee] a place where bees are kept —**a′piarist** *n.*

apical (ap′i k'l) *adj.* of, at, or constituting the apex

apices (ā′pə sēz′) *n. alt. pl. of* APEX

apiculture (ā′pə kul′chər) *n.* [< L. *apis*, bee] the raising and care of bees; beekeeping —**a′picul′turist** *n.*

apiece (ə pēs′) *adv.* for each one

apish (āp′ish) *adj.* 1. like an ape 2. foolishly imitative 3. silly, affected —**ap′-ishness** *n.*

aplomb (ə plom′) *n.* [Fr., perpendicularity < *à*, to + *plomb*, PLUMB¹] self-possession; poise

apo- [< Gr.] *a prefix meaning* from, or away from

Apoc. 1. Apocalypse 2. Apocrypha

apocalypse (ə pok′ə lips′) *n.* [< Gr. *apokalyptein*, disclose] a religious writing depicting symbolically the end of evil; specif., [A-] the last book of the New Testament; book of Revelation —**apoc′a-lyp′tic, apoc′alyp′tical** *adj.*

apocrypha (ə pok′rə fə) *n.pl.* [< Gr. *apo-*, away + *kryptein*, hide] 1. any writings of doubtful authenticity 2. [A-] fourteen books of the Septuagint that are rejected in Judaism and regarded by Protestants as not canonical : eleven are fully accepted in the Roman Catholic canon

apocryphal *adj.* 1. of doubtful authenticity 2. not genuine; counterfeit 3. [A-] of or like the Apocrypha

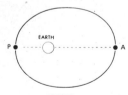

APOGEE
(moon at apogee A and at perigee P)

apogee (ap′ə jē′) *n.* [< Gr. *apo-*, from + *gē*, earth] 1. the point farthest from the earth, the moon, or another planet, in the orbit of a satellite or spacecraft around it : opp. to PERIGEE 2. the highest or farthest point —**ap′oge′an, ap′oge′al** *adj.*

apolitical (ā′pə lit′ə k'l) *adj.* not concerned with political matters

apologetic (ə pol′ə jet′ik) *adj.* showing realization of and regret for a fault, wrong, etc. : also **apol′oget′ical** —**apol′oget′ically** *adv.*

apologetics *n.pl.* [*with sing. v.*] the branch of theology dealing with the defence of Christianity

apologia (ap′ə lō′jē ə) *n.* an apology, esp. a formal defence of an idea, religion, etc.

apologist (ə pol′ə jist) *n.* a person who writes or speaks in defence of a doctrine, faith, action, etc.

apologize (ə pol′ə jīz′) *vi.* **-gized′, -giz′-ing** to make an apology; esp., to express regret for a fault

apologue (ap′ə lôg′) *n.* [< Gr.] a short allegorical story with a moral; fable

apology (ə pol′ə jē) *n., pl.* **-gies** [< Gr. *apo-*, from + *logos*, word] 1. an expression of regret for a fault, wrong, etc. 2. an inferior substitute 3. a formal defence of some idea, doctrine, etc.

apophthegm (ap′ə them′) *n.* [< Gr. *apo-*, from + *phthengesthai*, utter] a short, pithy saying —**ap′ophthegmat′ic** (-theg-mat′ik), **ap′ophthegmat′ical** *adj.*

apoplectic (ap′ə plek′tik) *adj.* 1. of, like, causing, or having apoplexy 2. [Colloq.] seemingly about to have apoplexy Also **ap′oplec′tical**

apoplexy (ap′ə plek′sē) *n.* [< Gr. *apo-*, down + *plēssein*, to strike] sudden paralysis with some loss of consciousness and feeling, caused when a blood vessel in the brain breaks or becomes clogged; stroke

apostasy (ə pos′tə sē) *n., pl.* **-sies** [< Gr. *apo-*, away + *stasis*, a standing] an abandoning of something that one once believed in, as a faith, cause, etc.

apostate (ə pos′tāt′) *n.* a person guilty of apostasy; renegade —*adj.* guilty of apostasy

a posteriori (ā′ pos ter′ē ôr′ī) [L.] from effect to cause, or from particular instances to a generalization Opposed to A PRIORI

apostle (ə pos′'l) *n.* [< Gr. *apo-*, from + *stellein*, send] 1. a person sent out on a special mission; specif., [*usually* A-] any of the twelve disciples sent out by Jesus to teach the gospel 2. an early advocate or leader, as of a reform movement —**apos′tleship′** *n.*

Apostles′ Creed an early statement of belief in the basic Christian doctrines

apostolate (ə pos′tə lət) *n.* the office, duties, or period of activity of an apostle

apostolic (ap′əs tol′ik) *adj.* 1. of the Apostles, their teachings, work, or times 2. [*often* A-] of the Pope; papal Also **ap′os-tol′ical**

Apostolic See *R.C.Ch.* the Pope′s see at Rome

apostrophe¹ (ə pos′trə fē) *n.* [< Gr. *apo-*, from + *strephein*, turn] words addressed to a person or thing, whether absent or present —**apostrophic** (ap′ə strof′ik) *adj.*

apostrophe² *n.* [Fr. : see prec.] the mark (′) used: 1. to show the omission of a letter or letters from a word (Ex.: *it′s* for *it is*) 2. to indicate the possessive case (Ex.: *Mary's* dress) **3.** in forming some plurals (Ex.: five *6's*, dot the *i's*)

apostrophize *vt., vi.* **-phized', -phiz'ing** to speak or write an apostrophe (to)

apothecaries' measure a system of units used in measuring liquids in pharmacy

apothecaries' weight formerly, a system of weights used in pharmacy

apothecary (ə poth'ə kər ē) *n.,* *pl.* **-caries** [< Gr. *apothēkē*, storehouse] a chemist licensed to prescribe, prepare, and sell drugs

apothegm (ap'ə them') *n.* same as APOPHTHEGM

apothem (ap'ə them') *n.* [< APO- + Gr. *thema*: see THEME] *Math.* the perpendicular from the centre of a regular polygon to any one of its sides

apotheosis (ə poth'ē ō'sis) *n.,* *pl.* **-ses'** (-sēz') [< Gr. *apo-*, from + *theos*, god] **1.** the act of raising a person to the status of a god **2.** the glorification of a person or thing **3.** an ideal or exact type

apotheosize (ə poth'ē ə sīz') *vt.* **-sized', -siz'ing 1.** to deify **2.** to glorify; idealize

appal (ə pôl') *vt.* **-palled', -pal'ling** [< L. *pallidus*, pale] to fill with horror or dismay; shock

appalling *adj.* **1.** causing horror, shock, or dismay **2.** [Colloq.] very bad —**appal'lingly** *adv.*

appanage (ap'ə nij) *n.* [< L. *ad*, to + *panis*, bread] **1.** money, land, etc. set aside by a monarch for the support of his younger children **2.** a benefit that is a perquisite or adjunct Also **a'panage**

apparatus (ap'ə rāt'əs) *n.,* *pl.* **-ra'tus, -ra'tuses** [< L. *ad-*, to + *parare*, prepare] **1.** the instruments, equipment, etc. for a specific use **2.** any complex device or system

apparel (ə par'əl) *n.* [< L. *apparare*: see prec.] clothing; attire —*vt.* **-elled, -elling 1.** to clothe; dress **2.** to adorn; bedeck

apparent (ə par'ənt) *adj.* [see APPEAR] **1.** readily seen **2.** readily understood **3.** seeming See also HEIR APPARENT —**appar'ently** *adv.* —**appar'entness** *n.*

apparition (ap'ə rish'ən) *n.* [see APPEAR] **1.** anything that appears unexpectedly or remarkably **2.** a ghost; phantom —**ap'pari'tional** *adj.*

appeal (ə pēl') *n.* [< L. < *ad-*, to + *pellere:* see COMPEL] **1.** an urgent request for help, etc. **2.** interest; attraction **3.** a call upon some authority for a decision, etc. **4.** *Law* the review by a higher court of the decision of a lower tribunal **5.** *Cricket* a request to the umpire to declare a batsman out —*vi.* **1.** to make an urgent request (for help, etc.) **2.** to be attractive, interesting, etc. **3.** to apply (to a higher court) for the alteration of a decision made by a lower one **4.** to resort (to) for decision, etc. **5.** *Cricket* to ask the umpire to declare a batsman out —*vt.* to make a request to a higher court for the rehearing of (a case) —**appeal'ing adj.**

appear (ə pēər') *vi.* [< L. *ad-*, to + *parere*, come forth] **1.** to come into sight or being **2.** to become understood [it appears he left] **3.** to seem; look **4.** to present

oneself formally or publicly **5.** to act as counsel in a court of law **6.** to be published

appearance *n.* **1.** an appearing **2.** the outward aspect of anything **3.** an outward show **4.** [*pl.*] the way things seem to be —**keep up appearances** to try to give the impression of being proper, well-off, etc. —**put in an appearance** to be present for a short time

appease (ə pēz') *vt.* **-peased', -peas'ing** [ult. < L. *pax*, peace] **1.** to make peaceful or quiet, esp. by giving in to the demands of **2.** to satisfy or relieve —**appeas'er** *n.*

appeasement *n.* the policy of giving in to demands of a hostile power in an attempt to keep peace

appellant (ə pel'ənt) *adj. Law* relating to appeals —*n.* a person who appeals, esp. to a higher court

appellate *adj. Law* relating to, or having jurisdiction to review, appeals [an *appellate* court]

appellation (ap'ə lā'shən) *n.* [< L. *appellare*, appeal] **1.** the act of calling by a name **2.** a name or title

appellative (ə pel'ə tiv) *adj.* of appellation; naming —*n.* a name or title —**appel'latively** *adv.*

append (ə pend') *vt.* [< L. *ad-*, to + *pendere*, to suspend] to attach or affix; add as an appendix —**append'age** *n.*

appendicectomy (ə pen'di sek'tə mē) *n., pl.* **-mies** the surgical removal of the vermiform appendix: also **appendectomy** (ap'ən dek'tə mē)

appendicitis (ə pen'də sīt'əs) *n.* inflammation of the vermiform appendix

appendix (ə pen'diks) *n., pl.* **-dixes, -dices'** (-də sēz') [see APPEND] **1.** additional material at the end of a book **2.** *Anat.* an outgrowth of an organ; esp., a small sac (**vermiform appendix**) extending from the large intestine

apperception (ap'ər sep'shən) *n.* [< L. *ad*, to + *percipere*, perceive] the state of the mind in being conscious of its own consciousness —**ap'percep'tive** *adj.*

appertain (ap'ər tān') *vi.* [see PERTAIN] to belong properly as a function, part, etc.; pertain

appetency (ap'ə tən sē) *n., pl.* **-cies** [see ff.] a strong desire or longing Also **ap'petence**

appetite (ap'ə tīt') *n.* [< L. *ad*, + *petere*, to seek] a desire or craving, esp. for food —**ap'petitive** (-tə tiv) *adj.*

appetizer *n.* a small portion of food or a drink to stimulate the appetite at the beginning of a meal

appetizing *adj.* **1.** stimulating the appetite **2.** savoury; tasty —**ap'petiz'ingly** *adv.*

applaud (ə plôd') *vt., vi.* [< L. *ad*, to + *plaudere*, clap hands] **1.** to show approval (of) by clapping the hands, etc. **2.** to praise; approve —**applaud'er** *n.*

applause (ə plôz') *n.* approval or praise, esp. as shown by clapping hands, cheering, etc.

apple (ap''l) *n.* [OE. *æppel*] a round,

firm, fleshy fruit growing on any of a genus of trees in temperate regions

apple of one's eye 1. the pupil of one's eye 2. any person or thing that one cherishes

apple-pie bed a bed in which the sheets are so folded that one cannot stretch one's legs

apple-pie order [Colloq.] neat order

appliance (ə plī′əns) *n.* a device or machine for a specific task

applicable (ap′li kə b'l) *adj.* that can be applied; appropriate —**ap′plicabil′ity** *n.* —**ap′plicably** *adv.*

applicant (ap′li kənt) *n.* a person who applies, as for employment, help, etc.

application (ap′li kā′shən) *n.* 1. the act or a way of applying or being applied 2. anything applied, esp. a remedy 3. a request, or the form completed in making a request 4. continued effort 5. relevance

applicator (ap′lə kāt′ər) *n.* any device for applying medicine or paint, polish, etc.

applied (ə plīd′) *adj.* used in actual practice or to work out practical problems [*applied* science]

APPLIQUÉ

appliqué (a plē′kā) *n.* [Fr. < L.: see ff.] a decoration made of one material attached by sewing, etc. to another —*vt.* **-quéd, -quéing** to decorate with appliqué

apply (ə plī′) *vt.* **-plied′, -ply′ing** [< L. *ad-*, to + *plicare*, to fold] 1. to put on [*apply* salve] 2. to use practically [*apply* one's knowledge] 3. to concentrate (one's faculties) —*vi.* 1. to make a formal request 2. to be suitable or relevant [this rule *applies* to everyone] —**appli′er** *n.*

appoint (ə point′) *vt.* [ult. < L. *ad*, to + *punctum*, a point] 1. to name for an office, etc. [to *appoint* a chairman] 2. to set (a date, place, etc.); decree 3. to furnish [well-*appointed*] —**appointee′** *n.*

appointment *n.* 1. an appointing or being appointed; specif., a naming for an office, etc. 2. a person so named 3. an office held in this way 4. an arrangement to meet a person; engagement 5. [*pl.*] furnishings

apportion (ə pôr′shən) *vt.* to divide and distribute in shares according to a plan —**appor′tionment** *n.*

appose (ə pōz′) *vt.* **-posed′, -pos′ing** [< L. *ad-*, near + *ponere*, put] to put side by side, next, or near

apposite (ap′ə zit) *adj.* [see prec.] appropriate; apt

apposition (ap′ə zish′ən) *n.* 1. an apposing or the position resulting from this 2. *Gram.* the placing of a word or expression beside another so that the second explains and has the same grammatical construction as the first (Ex.: Mary, my cousin, is here) —**ap′posi′tional** *adj.*

appraisal (ə prā′z'l) *n.* 1. an appraising 2. an appraised value Also **appraise′ment**

appraise (ə prāz′) *vt.* **-praised′, -prais′-ing** [< L. *ad*, to + *pretium*, price] 1. to set a price for, esp. officially 2. to estimate the quantity or quality of —**apprais′able** *adj.*

appreciable (ə prē′shə b'l) *adj.* enough to be perceived; noticeable —**appre′ciably** *adv.*

appreciate (ə prē′shē āt′) *vt.* **-at′ed, -at′-ing** [see APPRAISE] 1. to recognize gratefully 2. to be fully or sensitively aware of 3. to think well of; enjoy 4. to estimate the quality or worth of 5. to raise the price of —*vi.* to rise in value —**appre′cia′tor** *n.*

appreciation (ə prē′shē ā′shən) *n.* 1. grateful recognition, as of a favour 2. sensitive awareness or enjoyment, as of art 3. a rise in value or price

appreciative (ə prē′shə tiv) *adj.* feeling or showing appreciation —**appre′ciative-ness** *n.*

apprehend (ap′rə hend′) *vt.* [< L. *ad-*, to + *prehendere*, to seize] 1. to take into custody; arrest 2. to perceive or understand 3. to dread

apprehension *n.* 1. anxiety; dread 2. capture or arrest 3. perception or understanding

apprehensive *adj.* uneasy or fearful about the future

apprentice (ə pren′tis) *n.* [see APPRE-HEND] 1. a person under legal agreement to work for a master craftsman in return for instruction 2. any beginner —*vt.* **-ticed, -ticing** to place or accept as an apprentice —**appren′ticeship′** *n.*

apprise¹, apprize¹ (ə prīz′) *vt.* **-prised′** or **-prized′, -pris′ing** or **-priz′-ing** [see APPREHEND] to inform or notify

apprize², apprise² (ə prīz′) *vt.* **-prized′** or **-prised′, -priz′ing** or **-pris′-ing** *same as* APPRAISE

appro (ap′rō) *n.* [Colloq.] approval: chiefly in the phrase **on appro**

approach (ə prōch′) *vi.* [< L. *ad*, to + *prope*, near] to draw nearer —*vt.* 1. to come near or nearer to 2. to be similar to; approximate 3. to bring near (to something) 4. to make a proposal or a request to 5. to begin dealing with —*n.* 1. a coming closer 2. an approximation 3. an advance or overture (*to* someone) 4. a way of getting to a person, place, or thing; access 5. the act of bringing an aircraft into position for landing 6. *Golf* a stroke from the fairway onto the green —**approach′able** *adj.*

approbation (ap′rə bā′shən) *n.* [< L. *approbare*, APPROVE] official approval, permission, or praise

appropriate (ə prō′prē ət; *for v.* āt′) *adj.* [< L. *ad,* to + *proprius,* one's own] suitable —*vt.* -at′ed, -at′ing 1. to take for one's own use 2. to take improperly, as without permission 3. to set aside for a specific use —**appro′priately** *adv.* —**appro′priative** *adj.*

appropriation (ə prō′prē ā′shən) *n.* 1. an appropriating or being appropriated 2. a thing appropriated; esp., money set aside for a specific use

approval (ə prōo′v'l) *n.* 1. an approving 2. favourable opinion 3. consent —**on approval** for the customer to examine and decide whether to buy or return

approve (ə prōov′) *vt.* -proved′, -prov′-ing [< L. *ad-,* to + *probare,* to test] 1. to give one's consent to 2. to judge to be satisfactory —*vi.* to have a favourable opinion (*of*)

approx. 1. approximate 2. approximately

approximate (ə prok′sə mət; *for v.* -māt′) *adj.* [< L. *ad,* to + *proximus,* nearest] 1. not exact, but almost so 2. resembling 3. near in position —*vt.* -mat′ed, -mat′-ing to come near to; be almost the same as —*vi.* to be almost the same —**approx′i-mately** *adv.* —**approx′ima′tion** *n.*

appurtenance (ə pur′tin əns) *n.* [< L. *appertinere,* APPERTAIN] 1. something added to a more important thing 2. [*pl.*] accessories —**appur′tenant** *adj., n.*

Apr. April

après (a′prā′) *prep.* [Fr.] after

apricot (āp′rə kot′) *n.* [ult. < L. *praecoquus,* early matured] 1. a small, yellowish-orange fruit related to the peach 2. yellowish orange

April (ā′prəl) *n.* [< L.] the fourth month of the year, having 30 days: abbrev. **Apr.**

April fool a victim of jokes on April Fools' Day

April Fools' Day April 1, All Fools' Day

a priori (ā′prī ôr′ī) [L.] 1. from cause to effect or from a generalization to particular instances 2. based on theory instead of on experiment Opposed to A POSTERIORI

apron (ā′prən) *n.* [< ME. *a napron* < OFr. *naperon* < L. *mappa,* napkin] 1. a garment worn over the front part of the body to protect one's clothes 2. anything like an apron, as the part of a stage in front of the curtain

apron string a string for tying an apron on —**tied to one's mother's** (or **wife's,** etc.) **apron strings** dominated by one's mother (or wife, etc.)

apropos (ap′rə pō′) *adv.* [Fr. *à propos*] 1. at the right time; opportunely 2. by the way —*adj.* relevant; apt —**apropos of** with regard to

apse (aps) *n.* [< Gr. *haptein,* to fasten] a semicircular or polygonal projection of a building, esp. one at the east end of a church, with a domed roof

apsis (ap′sis) *n., pl.* -sides (-sə dēz′) [L., arch] that point in the orbit of the moon, a planet, etc. nearest to (**lower apsis**), or that farthest from (**higher apsis**), the centre of attraction

apt (apt) *adj.* [< L. *aptus,* pp. of *apere,* to fasten] 1. appropriate; fitting 2. tending or inclined; likely 3. quick to learn —**apt′ly** *adv.* —**apt′ness** *n.*

apteryx (ap′tər iks) *n.* [< Gr. *a-,* without + *pteryx,* wing] *same as* KIWI

aptitude (ap′tə tyōod′) *n.* [see APT] 1. a natural tendency, inclination, or ability 2. quickness to learn 3. the quality of being appropriate; fitness

aqua (ak′wə) *n., pl.* **aq′uas, aq′uae** (-wē) [L.] water —*adj.* [< AQUAMARINE] bluish-green

aqua fortis (fôr′təs) [L., strong water] *same as* NITRIC ACID

aqualung (ak′wə luŋ′) *n.* [AQUA + LUNG] a kind of self-contained underwater breathing apparatus

aquamarine (ak′wə mə rēn′) *n.* [L. *aqua marina,* sea water] a bluish-green beryl —*adj.* bluish-green

aquanaut (ak′wə nôt′) *n.* [AQUA + (ASTRO)NAUT] a person using a watertight underwater chamber as a base for oceanographic experiments

aquaplane (ak′wə plān′) *n.* [AQUA + PLANE⁴] a board on which one rides as it is pulled over water by a motorboat —*vi.* -planed′, -plan′ing 1. to ride on such a board 2. to skim uncontrollably over a road surface on a thin film of water: said of a motor vehicle

aqua regia (rē′jē ə) [L., kingly water: it dissolves gold] a mixture of nitric and hydrochloric acids

aquarium (ə kwär′ē əm) *n., pl.* -iums, -ia [< L. *aquarius,* of water] 1. a tank, etc., for keeping live water animals and plants 2. a building where such collections are exhibited

Aquarius (ə kwär′ē əs) [L., the water carrier] 1. a large S constellation 2. the eleventh sign of the zodiac

aquatic (ə kwat′ik) *adj.* [< L. *aqua,* water] 1. growing or living in water 2. done in or upon the water [*aquatic sports*] —*n.* 1. an aquatic plant or animal 2. [*pl.*] aquatic sports —**aquat′ically** *adv.*

aquatint (ak′wə tint′) *n.* [< It. *acqua tinta,* dyed water] 1. a process using acid to produce an etching that looks like a water colour 2. such an etching

aqua vitae (vīt′ē) [L., water of life] 1. *Alchemy* alcohol 2. brandy or other strong drink

aqueduct (ak′wə dukt′) *n.* [< L. *aqua,* water + *ducere,* to lead] 1. a large pipe or conduit for bringing water from a distant source 2. a bridgelike structure for carrying a water conduit or canal across a valley

aqueous (ā′kwē əs) *adj.* 1. of, like, or containing water 2. formed by the action of water

aqueous humour a watery fluid in the space between the cornea and the lens of the eye

aquiline (ak′wə līn′) *adj.* [< L. *aquila,* eagle] 1. curved like an eagle's beak 2. of or like an eagle

-ar (ər) [< L.] 1. *a suffix meaning*

of, relating to, like *[polar]* **2.** *a suffix denoting agency [vicar]*

Ar *Chem.* argon

Ar. **1.** Arabic **2.** Aramaic

ar. **1.** arrival **2.** arrives

Arab (ar'əb) *n.* **1.** a native of Arabia **2.** any of a Semitic people originating in Arabia **3.** a swift, graceful horse native to Arabia —*adj.* *same as* ARABIAN

ARABESQUE

arabesque (ar'əbesk') *n.* [< It. < Ar. '*arab*] **1.** an elaborate design of intertwined flowers, foliage, etc. **2.** *Ballet* a position in which one leg is extended backwards and the arms are extended

Arabian (ə rā'bē ən) *adj.* of Arabia or the Arabs —*n.* *same as* ARAB

Arabic (ar'əbik) *adj.* **1.** of Arabia **2.** of the Arabs —*n.* the Semitic language of the Arabs

Arabic numerals the figures 1, 2, 3, 4, 5, 6, 7, 8, 9, and the 0 (zero)

arable (ar'əb'l) *adj.* [< L. *arare*, to plough] suitable for ploughing and producing crops —*n.* arable land —*ar'abil'ity n.*

Araby (ar'əbē) [Archaic or Poet.] Arabia

arachnid (ə rak'nid) *n.* [< Gr. *arachnē*, spider] any of a group of arthropods, including spiders, scorpions, and mites, with eight legs —**arach'nidan** *adj., n.*

arak (ar'ək) *n.* *same as* ARRACK

Aram. Aramaic

Aramaic (ar'əmā'ik) *n.* a group of Semitic languages of Biblical times

arbiter (är'bə tər) *n.* [L.] **1.** a person selected to judge a dispute; umpire; arbitrator **2.** a person having control (of something) *[an arbiter of fashion]* —*ar'bitral adj.*

arbitrary (är'bə trər ē) *adj.* [see ARBITER] **1.** left to one's own choice **2.** based on one's whim **3.** absolute; despotic —*ar'bitrarily adv.* —*ar'bitrariness n.*

arbitrate (är'bə trāt') *vt., vi.* -trat'ed, -trat'ing [see ARBITER] **1.** to decide (a dispute) as an arbitrator **2.** to submit (a dispute) to arbitration

arbitration (är'bə trā'shən) *n.* settlement of a dispute by someone chosen to hear both sides and come to a decision —*ar'bitra'tional adj.*

arbitrator (är'bə trāt'ər) *n.* one chosen to arbitrate

arbor[1] (är'bər) *n., pl.* **ar'bores'**(-bə rēz') [L.] *Bot.* a tree

arbor[2] *n.* [< L. *arbor*, tree] *Mech.* **1.** a shaft; beam; axle **2.** a bar that holds cutting tools

arboraceous (är'bə rā'shəs) *adj.* **1.** of or like a tree **2.** wooded

arboreal (är bôr'ē əl) *adj.* **1.** of or like a tree **2.** living in trees

arborescent (är'bə res'ənt) *adj.* treelike

arboretum (är'bə rēt'əm) *n., pl.* **-tums, -ta** [L.] a place where many kinds of trees and shrubs are grown for exhibition or study

arboriculture (är'bər ə kul'chər) *n.* [< L. *arbor*, tree + *cultura*, culture] the scientific cultivation of trees and shrubs —*ar'boricul'turist n.*

arborvitae (är'bər vīt'ē) *n.* [L., tree of life] an evergreen tree related to the cypress

arbour (är'bər) *n.* [< L. *herba*, herb] a place shaded by trees or climbing plants —*ar'boured adj.*

arbutus (är byōōt'əs) *n.* [L., wild strawberry tree] a tree or shrub with dark-green leaves and berries like strawberries

arc (ärk) *n.* [< L. *arcus*, arch] **1.** a bowlike curved line or object **2.** the band of incandescent light formed when an electric discharge is conducted from one electrode to another **3.** any part of a curve, esp. of a circle —*vi.* **arced** or **arcked**, **arc'ing** or **arck'ing** **1.** to move in a curved course **2.** to form an arc

arcade (är kād') *n.* [< L. *arcus*, arch] **1.** a covered passageway, esp. one lined with shops **2.** a line of arches and their supporting columns

Arcadian (är kā'dē ən) *adj.* [< *Arcadia*, in ancient Greece] ideally rustic —*n.* a person who leads a simple rural life

arcane (är kān') *adj.* [< L. *arcere*, to shut up] **1.** hidden or secret **2.** understood by only a few; esoteric

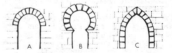

ARCHES
(A, semicircular; B, horse-shoe; C, pointed)

arch[1] (ärch) *n.* [< L. *arcus*, arch] **1.** a curved structure that supports the weight of material over an open space, as in a doorway, etc. **2.** the form of an arch **3.** anything shaped like an arch —*vt., vi.* **1.** to form (into) an arch **2.** to span with or as an arch

arch[2] (ärch) *adj.* [< ff.] **1.** main; chief **2.** gaily mischievous; pert —**arch'ly** *adv.* —**arch'ness** *n.*

arch- [< Gr. *archos*, ruler] *a prefix meaning* main, chief *[archbishop, archduke]*

-arch (ärk; *occas.* ərk) [< Gr. *archos*, ruler] *a suffix meaning* ruler *[matriarch]*

arch. **1.** archaic **2.** architecture

Archaean (är kē'ən) *adj.* [< Gr. *archē*, beginning] *Geol.* of the oldest period of geological time: also [Chiefly U.S.] **Arche'an**

archaeology (är'kē ol'ə jē) *n.* [< Gr.

archē, beginning + -LOGY] the scientific study of the life of ancient peoples, as by excavation of ancient cities —ar'chaeo·log'ical (-ə loj'i k'l) *adj.* —ar'chaeol'o·gist *n.*

archaeopteryx (ar'kē op'tər iks) *n.* [< Gr. *archaias*, ancient + *pteryx*, wing] an extinct, reptilelike bird

archaic (är kā'ik) *adj.* [< Gr. *archaios*, ancient] 1. ancient 2. old-fashioned 3. seldom used except in poetry, church ritual, etc. —archa'ically *adv.*

archaism (är'kā iz'm) *n.* 1. the use of archaic words, technique, etc. 2. an archaic word, usage, etc. —ar'chaist *n.* —ar'cha·is'tic *adj.*

archangel (ärk'ān'j'l) *n.* a chief angel

archbishop (ärch'bish'əp) *n.* a chief bishop

archbishopric *n.* the office, rank, term, or church district of an archbishop

archdeacon (-dē'k'n) *n.* a church official ranking just below a bishop —arch'dea'con·ry *n.*

archdiocese (ärch'dī'ə sis) *n.* the diocese of an archbishop —arch'dioc'esan (-dī os'ə sən) *adj.*

archduchess (ärch'duch'is) *n.* the wife of an archduke

archduchy (ärch'duch'ē) *n.*, *pl.* -ies the territory of an archduke or of an archduchess

archduke (ärch'dyook') *n.* a chief duke, esp. a prince of the former Austrian royal family

archenemy (ärch'en'ə mē) *n.*, *pl.* -mies a chief enemy —the archenemy Satan

archer (ärch'ər) *n.* [< L. *arcus*, bow] one who shoots with bow and arrow —[A-] the constellation Sagittarius

archery *n.* the practice, art, or sport of shooting with bow and arrow

archetype (är'kə tīp') *n.* [< Gr. *archos*, first + *typos*, model] 1. the original pattern or model; prototype 2. a perfect example —ar'chetyp'al, ar'chetyp'ical (-tip'i k'l) *adj.*

archfiend (ärch'fēnd') *n.* a chief fiend —the archfiend Satan

archidiaconal (är'kə dī ak'ə n'l) *adj.* of an archdeacon or archdeaconry —ar'chidi·ac'onate *n.*

archiepiscopal (är'kē ə pis'kə p'l) *adj.* of an archbishop or archbishopric —ar'chi·epis'copate *n.*

archipelago (är'kə pel'ə gō') *n.*, *pl.* -goes', -gos' [< Gr. *archi-*, chief + *pelagos*, sea] 1. a sea with many islands 2. such a group of islands

architect (är'kə tekt') *n.* [< Gr. *archi-*, chief + *tektōn*, carpenter] 1. a person whose profession is designing plans for buildings, bridges, etc. and administering construction 2. any builder or creator

architectonic (är'kə tek ton'ik) *adj.* 1. of architecture 2. having structure or design like that of architecture 3. *Philos.* having to do with the systematizing of knowledge

architecture (är'kə tek'chər) *n.* 1. the science or profession of designing and

constructing buildings, etc. 2. a style of construction 3. design and construction —ar'chitec'tural *adj.* —ar'chitec'turally *adv.*

architrave (är'kə trāv') *n.* [< L. *archi-*, first + *trabs*, a beam] *Archit.* 1. the lowest part of an entablature, a beam resting directly on the tops of the columns 2. the moulding around a doorway, window, etc.

archives (är'kīvz) *n.pl.* [< Gr. *archē*, the beginning] 1. a place where public records, documents, etc. are kept 2. the documents kept there —archival (är kī'-v'l) *adj.*

archivist (är'ki vist) *n.* one having charge of archives

archpriest (ärch'prēst') *n.* a chief priest

archway (ärch'wā') *n.* a passage under an arch

-archy (är kē, ər kē) [< Gr. *archien*, to rule] *a suffix meaning* a ruling, or that which is ruled [*monarchy*]

arc lamp a lamp in which the light is produced by an arc between electrodes: also **arc light**

arctic (ärk'tik) *adj.* [< Gr. *arktikos*, of the Bear (Gr. *arktos*), northern] 1. of or near the North Pole 2. very cold —the Arctic the region around the North Pole

Arctic Circle [*also* a- c-] an imaginary circle parallel to the equator, 66°33' north of it

Arcturus (ärk tyooər'əs) [< Gr. *arktos*, bear + *ouros*, a guard] the brightest star in the constellation Boötes

-ard (ərd) [< MHG. *hart*, bold] *a suffix* denoting one who carries an action too far [*drunkard*]

ardent (är'dənt) *adj.* [< L. *ardere*, burn] 1. passionate 2. intensely enthusiastic; zealous 3. glowing; radiant 4. burning; aflame —ar'dency *n.* —ar'dently *adv.*

ardour (är'dər) *n.* [< L. *ardere*, burn] 1. emotional warmth; passion 2. zeal 3. intense heat

arduous (är'dyoo wəs) *adj.* [L. *arduus*, steep] 1. difficult to do; laborious 2. using much energy; strenuous

are[1] (är; *unstressed* ər) [OE. *aron*] *pl.* & *2nd pers. sing., pres. indic.*, of BE

are[2] (är) *n.* [< L. *area*: see ff.] a unit of area equal to 100 square metres

area (âar'ē ə) *n.* [L., vacant place] 1. a part of the earth's surface; region 2. the size of a surface, in square units 3. a sunken space outside the basement of a building 4. a particular part of a house, district, etc. [*dining area*] 5. scope or extent —ar'eal *adj.*

arena (ə rē'nə) *n.* [L., sand] 1. the central part of an ancient Roman amphitheatre, for gladiatorial contests 2. any place like this 3. any sphere of struggle

arenaceous (ar'ə nā'shəs) *adj.* [L. *arenaceus*] sandy

aren't (ärnt) are not

areola (ə rē'ə lə) *n.*, *pl.* -lae (-lē'), -las [L., dim. of AREA] a small, surrounding area, as the dark ring around a nipple

Also **areole** (ar′ē̇ōl′) —**are′olar** adj. —**are′olate** adj.

arête (ə rāt′) n. [Fr., fish skeleton] a sharp, narrow ridge or crest of a mountain

argent (är′jənt) n. [< L. argentum] [Archaic or Poet.] silver —adj. [Poet.] of silver: also **argen′tal** (-jen′t'l)

argon (är′gon) n. [Gr., inert] a chemical element, that is an inert, odourless gas forming nearly one percent of the atmosphere: symbol, Ar

argosy (är′gə sē) n., pl. -sies [< It. (nave) Ragusea, (vessel of) Ragusa, ancient Dalmatian port] [Poet.] 1. a large ship 2. a fleet of such ships

argot (är′gō) n. [Fr. < ?] the specialized vocabulary of a particular group, as the secret jargon of criminals

argue (är′gyoo) vi. -gued, -guing [< L. arguere, prove] 1. to have a disagreement; quarrel 2. to give reasons (for or against) —vt. 1. to debate 2. to contend 3. to give evidence of; indicate 4. to persuade by giving reasons —**ar′guable** adj. —**ar′guably** adv. —**ar′guer** n.

argument (är′gyoo mənt) n. 1. a disagreement; dispute 2. a reason or reasons offered for or against something 3. a summary

argumentation (är′gyoo men tā′shən) n. 1. the process of arguing 2. debate; discussion

argumentative (-men′tə tiv) adj. 1. apt to argue 2. controversial —**ar′gumen′tativeness** n.

Argus (är′gəs) n. [< giant in Gr. myth. with a hundred eyes] an alert watchman

argy-bargy (är′jē bär′jē) n. [< Scot. < ? ARGUE] [Colloq.] a wrangling argument

aria (är′ē ə) n. [It. < L. aer, air] an air or melody in an opera or oratorio, esp. for solo voice

Arian[1] (âer′ē ən) n., adj. same as ARYAN

Arian[2] adj. of Arius or Arianism —n. a believer in Arianism

-arian (âer′ē ən) [< L.] a suffix denoting: age, sect, social belief or occupation [antiquarian]

Arianism n. the doctrines of Arius, who taught that Jesus was not of the same substance as God

arid (ar′id) adj. [< L. arere, to be dry] 1. dry and barren 2. not interesting; dull —**aridity** (ə rid′ə tē), **ar′idness** n.

Aries (âer′ēz) [L., the Ram] 1. a N constellation 2. the first sign of the zodiac

aright (ə rīt′) adv. in a right way; correctly

arise (ə rīz′) vi. **arose′**, **aris′en** (-riz′'n), **aris′ing** [OE. < a-, out + risan, rise] 1. to originate 2. to result (from something) 3. to get up 4. to ascend

aristocracy (ar′ə stok′rə sē) n., pl. -cies [< Gr. aristos, best + kratein, to rule] 1. government by a privileged minority, usually of inherited wealth 2. a country with such government 3. a privileged ruling class; nobility 4. those considered the best in some way

aristocrat (ar′is tə krat′) n. 1. a member of the aristocracy 2. a person with the manners, beliefs, etc. of the upper class

—**a′ristocrat′ic** adj. —**a′ristocrat′ically** adv.

Aristotelian (ar′is tə tēl′yən) adj. of Aristotle or his philosophy —n. 1. a follower of Aristotle 2. a person who is empirical in his thinking —**Ar′istote′lianism** n.

arithmetic (ə rith′mə tik; for adj. ar′ith met′ik) n. [< Gr. arithmos, number] the science of computing by positive, real numbers —adj. of or using arithmetic: also **ar′ithmet′ical** —**ar′ithmet′ically** adv.

arithmetician (ar′ith mə tish′ən) n. a person skilled in arithmetic

arithmetic mean the average obtained by dividing a sum by the number of its addends

arithmetic progression a sequence of terms derived by adding to or subtracting from the preceding one a constant quantity (Ex.: 5, 9, 13)

ark (ärk) n. [< L. arcere, enclose] 1. Bible the boat in which Noah, his family, and two of every kind of creature survived the Flood 2. same as ARK OF THE COVENANT

ark of the covenant Bible the chest containing the stone tablets inscribed with the Ten Commandments

arm[1] (ärm) n. [OE. earm] 1. an upper limb of the human body 2. anything like this in structure, function or position 3. anything commonly in contact with the human arm; esp., a) a sleeve b) a support for the arm, as on a chair 4. power to seize, control, etc. [the arm of the law] —**arm in arm** with arms interlocked —**at arm's length** at a distance —**with open arms** in a warm and friendly way —**arm′less** adj. —**arm′like′** adj.

arm[2] n. [< L. arma, weapons] 1. any weapon: usually used in pl. 2. [pl.] warfare; fighting 3. [pl.] heraldic insignia 4. any branch of the military forces —vt. 1. to provide with weapons, etc. 2. to prepare for or against attack —vi. to equip oneself with weapons, etc., esp. for war —**take up arms** 1. to go to war 2. to enter a dispute —**to arms!** get ready to fight! —**up in arms** 1. prepared to fight 2. indignant (with about) —**armed** adj.

armada (är mä′də) n. [Sp. < L. arma, weapons] 1. a fleet of warships 2. [A-] such a fleet sent against England by Spain in 1588

armadillo (är′mə dil′ō) n., pl. -los [Sp. < L. armare, to arm] a burrowing mammal of the S U.S. and South America, having a covering of bony plates

Armageddon (är′mə ged′'n) Bible the scene of the last, deciding battle between good and evil: Rev. 16:16

armament (är′mə mənt) n. [< L. armare, to arm] 1. [often pl.] all the military forces and equipment of a nation 2. all the military equipment of a warship, fortification, etc. 3. an arming or being armed for war

armature (är′mə tyooər) n. [see prec.] 1. any protective covering 2. a soft iron bar placed across the poles of a magnet 3. the iron core wound with wire, usually a revolving part, in a generator or motor 4. *Sculpture* a framework for supporting the clay, etc. in modelling

armchair (ärm′chāer′) *n.* a chair with supports at the sides for one's arms or elbows

armed forces all the military, naval, and air forces of a country or group of countries

armhole *n.* an opening for the arm in a garment

armistice (är′mə stis) *n.* [< L. *arma*, arms + *sistere*, cause to stand] a temporary stopping of warfare by mutual agreement; truce

Armistice Day November 11, the anniversary of the armistice of World War I in 1918

armlet (ärm′lit) *n.* 1. a band worn for ornament around the upper arm 2. a small inlet of the sea

armoire (är mwär′) *n.* [< L. *armarium*, chest for arms] a large cupboard or clothespress

armorial (är môr′ē əl) *adj.* of coats of arms; heraldic

armour (är′mər) *n.* [< L. *armare*, to arm] 1. covering worn to protect the body against weapons 2. any defensive or protective covering 3. a quality, etc. serving as a defence difficult to penetrate —*vt., vi.* to put armour on

armoured *adj.* 1. covered with armour 2. equipped with tanks and other armoured vehicles

armourer *n.* 1. a maker of firearms 2. *Mil.* a man in charge of small arms

armour plate a protective covering of steel plates, as on a tank —ar′mour plat′-ed *adj.*

armoury *n., pl.* -mouries [see ARM[2]] a storehouse for weapons; arsenal

armpit (ärm′pit′) *n.* the hollow under the arm where it joins the shoulder

armrest *n.* a support for one's arm

army (är′mē) *n., pl.* -mies [< L.: see ARMADA] 1. a large, organized body of soldiers for waging war 2. [often A-] a large organization of persons for a specific cause [the Salvation *Army*] 3. any large number of persons, animals, etc.

arnica (är′ni kə) *n.* [ModL.] 1. a plant bearing bright yellow flowers 2. a preparation made from this, formerly used for treating sprains, bruises, etc.

aroma (ə rō′mə) *n.* [< Gr. *arōma*, spice] 1. a pleasant odour; fragrance 2. a characteristic quality

aromatic (ar′ə mat′ik) *adj.* 1. of or having an aroma 2. *Chem.* containing one or more benzene rings in the molecule —*n.* an aromatic plant, substance, or chemical —ar′omat′ically *adv.*

arose (ə rōz′) *pt. of* ARISE

around (ə round′) *adv.* [ME. < *a-*, on + *round*] 1. round; esp. *a)* in every direction *b)* in various places [to shop *around*] 2. [Colloq.] nearby —*prep.* 1. round; esp., *a)* so as to encircle or envelop *b)* on the border of 2. [Chiefly U.S.] about [*around* 1890] —*adj.* 1. on the move

[up and *around*] 2. [Colloq.] existing —have been around [Colloq.] to have had wide experience

arouse (ə rouz′) *vt.* aroused′, arous′ing 1. to awaken 2. to stir, as to action 3. to excite —arous′al *n.*

arpeggio (är pej′ē ō) *n., pl.* -gios [It. < *arpa*, a harp] the playing of the notes of a chord in quick succession

arquebus (är′kwə bəs) *n.* [< Du. *haak*, hook + *bus*, gun] an early type of portable gun

arr. 1. arranged 2. arrival

arrack (ar′ək) *n.* [< Ar. *'araq*, liquor] in the Orient, strong alcoholic drink

arraign (ə rān′) *vt.* [< L. *ad*, to + *ratio*, reason] 1. to bring before a law court to answer charges 2. to call to account —arraign′er *n.* —arraign′ment *n.*

arrange (ə rānj′) *vt.* -ranged′, -rang′ing [< OFr. *a-*, to + *renc*, rank] 1. to put in the correct or suitable order 2. to classify 3. to prepare or plan 4. to settle or adjust (matters) 5. *Music* to adapt (a composition) to particular instruments or voices —*vi.* 1. to come to an agreement (*with* a person) 2. to make plans —arrange′able *adj.* —arrang′er *n.*

arrangement *n.* 1. an arranging 2. something made by arranging parts in a particular way 3. [*usually pl.*] a plan or preparation 4. a settlement 5. *Music* an adaptation of a composition for other instruments, voices, etc.

arrant (ar′ənt) *adj.* [< ERRANT] that is plainly such; out-and-out [an *arrant* fool] —ar′rantly *adv.*

arras (ar′əs) *n.* [< Arras, in France] 1. an elaborate kind of tapestry 2. a wall hanging, esp. of tapestry

array (ə rā′) *vt.* [ult. < L. *ad-*, to + Gmc. base *raid-*, order] 1. to put in the proper order; marshal (troops, etc.) 2. to dress in finery —*n.* 1. an orderly grouping, esp. of troops 2. an impressive display 3. fine clothes

arrears (ə rēarz′) *n.pl.* [< L. *ad*, to + *retro*, behind] 1. overdue debts 2. unfinished work, etc. —in arrears (or arrear) behind in paying a debt, in one's work, etc.

arrest (ə rest′) *vt.* [< L. *ad-*, to + *restare*, to stop] 1. to seize by authority of the law 2. to stop or check 3. to catch and keep (one's attention, etc.) —*n.* an arresting or being arrested —under arrest in legal custody —arrest′er, arres′tor *n.*

arresting *adj.* attracting attention; interesting; striking —arrest′ingly *adv.*

‡**arrière-pensée** (a ryer′pän sā′) *n.* [Fr.] a mental reservation; ulterior motive

arrival (ə rī′v′l) *n.* 1. the act of arriving 2. a person or thing that arrives or has arrived

arrive (ə rīv′) *vi.* -rived′, -riv′ing [< L. *ad-*, to + *ripa*, shore] 1. to reach one's destination 2. to come [the time has *arrived*] 3. to attain fame, etc. —arrive at to reach by thinking, etc.

‡**arrivederci** (ä rē′ve der′chē) *interj.* [It.] goodbye

‡**arriviste** (à rē vēst′) *n.* [Fr.] same as PARVENU

arrogance (ar′ə gəns) *n.* overbearing pride or self-importance: also **ar′rogancy**

arrogant *adj.* [see ff.] full of or due to arrogance; overbearing; haughty —**ar′rogantly** *adv.*

arrogate (ar′ə gāt′) *vt.* -gat′ed, -gat′ing [< L. ad-, for + *rogare*, ask] 1. to claim or seize without right 2. to ascribe or attribute without reason —**ar′roga′tion** *n.*

arrow (ar′ō) *n.* [OE. *earh, arwe*] 1. a slender shaft, usually pointed at one end and feathered at the other, for shooting from a bow 2. a sign used to indicate direction

arrowhead *n.* 1. the pointed tip of an arrow 2. a marsh plant with arrow-shaped leaves

arrowroot *n.* [from its use as an antidote for poisoned arrows] 1. a tropical American plant with starchy roots 2. the edible starch made from its roots

arse (ärs) *n.* [< OE. *ærs*] [Vulg.] the buttocks

arsenal (är′s'n əl) *n.* [< Ar. *dār (ēs) ṣinā′a,* workshop] a place for making or storing weapons and other munitions

arsenic (är′snik; *for adj.* är sen′ik) *n.* [ult. < Per. *zar*, gold] 1. a silvery-white, brittle, very poisonous chemical element, compounds of which are used in making insecticides, medicines, etc.: symbol, As 2. loosely, arsenic trioxide, a poisonous, tasteless, white powder —*adj.* of or containing arsenic

arsenical (är sen′ə k'l) *adj.* of or containing arsenic

arson (är′s'n) *n.* [< L. *ardere*, to burn] the crime of purposely setting fire to property —**ar′sonist** *n.*

art¹ (ärt) *n.* [< L. *ars, artis*, art] 1. human creativity 2. skill 3. any specific skill or its application 4. any craft or profession, or its principles 5. a making of things that have form and beauty 6. any branch of creative work, esp. painting, sculpture, etc. 7. products of creative work 8. a branch of learning; specif., [*pl.*] the liberal arts as distinguished from the sciences 9. cunning 10. trick; wile: *usually used in pl.*

art² *archaic 2nd pers. sing., pres. indic., of* BE: *used with* thou

-art (ərt) *same as* -ARD

art. 1. article 2. artificial

artefact (är′tə fakt′) *n.* var. sp. of ARTIFACT

arterial (är tēər′ē əl) *adj.* 1. of or like an artery 2. of or being a main road with many branches —**arte′rially** *adv.*

arteriosclerosis (är tēər′ē ō sklə rō′sis) *n.* [see ff. & SCLEROSIS] a thickening, and loss of elasticity, of the walls of the arteries, as in old age —**arte′riosclerot′ic** (-rot′ik) *adj.*

artery (är′tər ē) *n., pl.* -teries [prob. < Gr. *aeirein*, raise] 1. any of the tubes carrying blood from the heart 2. a main road or channel

ARTESIAN WELL

artesian well (är tē′zhən) [< *Artois,* former Fr. province] a well in which ground water is forced up by hydrostatic pressure

art form an accepted mode of artistic composition, as the novel

artful (ärt′fəl) *adj.* 1. sly or cunning 2. skilful or clever —**art′fully** *adv.* —**art′fulness** *n.*

arthritis (är thrīt′əs) *n.* [Gr. < *arthron,* joint] inflammation of a joint or joints —**arthrit′ic** (-thrit′ik) *adj.* —**arthrit′ically** *adv.*

arthropod (är′thrə pod′) *n.* [< Gr. *arthron,* joint + -POD] any of a large group of invertebrate animals with jointed legs and a segmented body, as insects, crustaceans, arachnids, etc.

artic (är tik′) *n.* [Colloq.] an articulated lorry

artichoke (är′tə chōk′) *n.* [< Ar. *al-haršūf*] 1. a thistlelike plant 2. its flower head, cooked as a vegetable 3. *short for* JERUSALEM ARTICHOKE

article (är′ti k'l) *n.* [< L. *articulus,* dim. of *artus,* joint] 1. a separate item [an *article* of luggage] 2. a commodity 3. a complete piece of writing, as in a newspaper 4. *Gram.* the words *a, an,* or *the,* used as adjectives 5. a section of a written document —*vt.* -cled, -cling to bind by the articles of an agreement

articular (är tik′yoo lər) *adj.* [see prec.] of a joint or joints [an *articular* inflammation]

articulate (är tik′yoo lət; *for v.* -lāt′) *adj.* [see ARTICLE] 1. expressing oneself clearly 2. able to speak 3. made up of distinct syllables or words 4. jointed: usually *articulated* —*vt.* -lat′ed, -lat′ing 1. to pronounce carefully 2. to express clearly 3. to put together by joints —*vi.* 1. to speak distinctly 2. to be jointed

articulated lorry a large lorry made in two sections connected by a pivoted bar

articulation (är tik′yoo lā′shən) *n.* 1. enunciation 2. a spoken sound 3. a jointing or being jointed 4. a joint between bones or similar parts

artifact (är′ti fakt′) *n.* [see ff.] any object made by human work; esp., a primitive tool, etc.

artifice (är′ti fis) *n.* [< L. *ars,* art + *facere,* make] 1. skill or ingenuity 2. trickery 3. a sly trick

artificer (är tif′ə sər) *n.* 1. a skilled craftsman 2. an inventor 3. a military mechanic

artificial (är'ti fish'əl) *adj.* [see ARTIFICE] **1.** made by human work or art; not natural **2.** simulated [*artificial* teeth] **3.** affected [an *artificial* smile] —ar'tifi'cial'ity (-fish'ē al'ə tē) *n.* —ar'tifi'cially *adv.*

artificial insemination the impregnation of a female by the introduction of semen without sexual intercourse

artificial respiration the artificial maintenance of breathing, as by forcing breath into the mouth

artillery (är til'ər ē) *n.* [< OFr. *artillier*, to arm] **1.** heavy mounted guns **2.** the science of guns —**the artillery** the military branch specializing in the use of artillery —artil'lerist, artil'leryman *n.*

artisan (är'ti zan') *n.* [ult. < L. *ars*, art] a skilled workman; craftsman

artist (är'tist) *n.* [< L. *ars*, art] **1.** a person skilled in any of the fine arts **2.** a person who does anything very well **3.** same as ARTISTE

artiste (är tēst') *n.* [Fr.] a professional in any of the performing arts

artistic (är tis'tik) *adj.* **1.** done skilfully and tastefully **2.** of art or artists —artis'tically *adv.*

artistry (är'tis trē) *n.* artistic work or skill

artless (ärt'lis) *adj.* **1.** without guile or deceit; ingenuous **2.** simple; natural **3.** lacking skill or art **4.** uncultured; ignorant —art'lessly *adv.* —art'lessness *n.*

†**art nouveau** (ärnoo̅vō') [Fr.] an art movement of the late 19th and early 20th cent., emphasizing stylized curvilinear designs

arty (ärt'ē) *adj.* art'ier, art'iest [Colloq.] showing artistic pretensions —art'iness *n.*

arty-crafty *adj.* [Colloq.] of arts and crafts: usually a disparaging term

arum (âer'əm) *n.* [< Gr. *aron*] a plant bearing small flowers on a fleshy spike enclosed by a hoodlike leaf

-ary (ə rē) [< L.] a suffix meaning: **1.** related to; connected with [*auxiliary*] **2.** a place for [*granary*]

Aryan (âer'ē ən) *n.* [< Sans. *ārya*, noble] **1.** formerly, the hypothetical language from which all Indo-European languages are supposed to be descended **2.** a person supposed to be a descendant of the prehistoric peoples who spoke this language **3.** loosely, esp. in Nazi usage, a non-Jewish Caucasoid

as[1] (az; *unstressed* əz) *adv.* [< ALSO] **1.** to the same amount or degree [he's just as happy at home] **2.** for instance [a card game, as bridge] **3.** when related in a specified way [romanticism as contrasted with classicism] —*conj.* **1.** to the same amount or degree that [straight as an arrow] **2.** in the same manner that [do as he does] **3.** at the same time that [she wept as she spoke] **4.** because **5.** that the consequence is [so obvious as to need no reply] **6.** though [full as he was, he kept eating] —*pron.* **1.** a fact that [he is tired, as anyone can see] **2.** that [the same colour as yours (is)] —*prep.* **1.** in the role or function of [he poses as a friend] —**as for**

concerning —**as if** (or **though**) **1.** as it (or one) would if **2.** that [it seems as if she's never home] —**as it were** as if it were so —**as of** on or from (a specified time) [as of Friday, he'll be retired]

as[2] (as) *n., pl.* **as'ses** (-əz) [L.] an ancient Roman coin

As *Chem.* arsenic

AS., A.S., A.-S. Anglo-Saxon

A.S.A. Amateur Swimming Association

asafoetida (as'ə fet'i də) *n.* [< Per. *āzā*, gum + L. *foetida*, fetid] a bad-smelling gum resin formerly used in medicine to repel disease

asbestos (az bes'təs) *n.* [< Gr. *a-*, not + *sbennynai*, extinguish] a fire-resistant, fibrous mineral used in insulation, roofing, etc.

ascend (ə send') *vi.* [< L. *ad-*, to + *scandere*, climb] to move upwards; rise —*vt.* **1.** to climb **2.** to succeed to (a throne) —**ascend'able, ascend'ible** *adj.*

ascendancy, ascendency *n.* a position of control or power: also **ascend'ance, ascend'ence**

ascendant, ascendent *adj.* **1.** ascending **2.** in control; dominant —*n.* **1.** a dominating position; ascendancy **2.** *Astrol.* the sign of the zodiac just above the eastern horizon —**in the ascendant** at or approaching the height of power, fame, etc.

ascension (ə sen'shən) *n.* an ascending —**the Ascension** *Bible* the bodily ascent of Jesus into heaven

Ascension Day the fortieth day after Easter, celebrating the Ascension

ascent (ə sent') *n.* **1.** an ascending or rising **2.** an upward slope

ascertain (as'ər tān') *vt.* [< OFr. *a-*, to + *certain*, CERTAIN] to find out with certainty —**as'certain'able** *adj.* —**as'certain'ment** *n.*

ascetic (ə set'ik) *adj.* [< Gr. *askein*, to train the body] self-denying; austere: also **ascet'ical** —*n.* one who leads a life of contemplation and self-denial, esp. for religious purposes —**ascet'ically** *adv.* —**ascet'icism** *n.*

ascorbic acid (ə skôr'bik) [A- + SCORB(UTIC)] a water-soluble vitamin occurring in citrus fruits, tomatoes, etc.: it prevents and cures scurvy; vitamin C

ascribe (ə skrīb') *vt.* **-cribed', -crib'ing** [< L. *ad-*, to + *scribere*, write] **1.** to put down (to a supposed cause); attribute **2.** to regard as belonging (to) or coming from someone [poems *ascribed* to Homer] —**ascrib'able** *adj.* —**ascription** (ə skrip'shən) *n.*

asepsis (ā sep'sis) *n.* **1.** the condition of being aseptic **2.** aseptic treatment or technique

aseptic *adj.* **1.** not septic **2.** free from microorganisms that cause disease —**asep'tically** *adv.*

asexual (ā sek'shoo wəl) *adj.* **1.** having no sex **2.** of reproduction without the union of male and female germ cells —**asex'ually** *adv.*

ash[1] (ash) *n.* [OE. *æsce*] **1.** the white or greyish powder left after something has been thoroughly burned **2.** fine, volcanic lava See also ASHES

ash² *n.* [OE. æsc] a timber and shade tree having tough, elastic, straight-grained wood

ashamed (əshāmd') *adj.* **1.** feeling shame **2.** feeling reluctant because fearing shame —**ashamedly** (əshā'midlē) *adv.*

ashcan (ash'kan') *n.* [U.S.] a dustbin

ashen *adj.* **1.** like ashes, esp. in colour; pale; pallid **2.** of ashes

ashes *n.pl.* **1.** the unburned particles and greyish powder left after a thing has been burned **2.** human remains, esp. after cremation **3.** [A-] [< mock In memoriam notice of England's defeat (1882)] Cricket the mythical trophy for which England and Australia compete in test matches

ashlar, ashler (ash'lər) *n.* [< L. assis, board] **1.** a square, hewn stone used in building **2.** a thin, dressed, square stone used for facing masonry walls

ashore (əshôr') *adv., adj.* **1.** to or on the shore **2.** to or on land

ash pan a removable receptacle for ashes under a grate

ashram (ash'rəm) *n.* [< Sans ā, towards + śrama, penance] a secluded place for religious meditation

ashtray (ash'trā') *n.* a container for smokers' tobacco ashes: also **ash tray**

Ash Wednesday the first day of Lent: from the putting of ashes on the forehead in penitence

ashy *adj.* **-ier, -iest** **1.** of, like, or covered with ashes **2.** of ash colour; pale

Asian (ā'shən) *adj.* of Asia —*n.* an inhabitant of Asia Also **Asiatic** (ā'shēat'-ik)

Asian influenza influenza caused by a virus first isolated in Singapore: also **Asian flu**

aside (əsīd') *adv.* **1.** on or to one side **2.** away **3.** apart —*n.* an actor's words spoken as to the audience and supposedly not heard by the other actors

asinine (as'ənīn') *adj.* [< L. asinus, ass] **1.** like an ass **2.** stupid, obstinate, etc. —**as'inin'ity** (-nin'ətē) *n.*

ask (ăsk) *vt.* [OE. ascian] **1.** to use words in seeking the answer to (a question) **2.** to put a question to (a person) **3.** to request or demand **4.** to be in need of **5.** to invite —*vi.* **1.** to make a request (for) **2.** to inquire (about, after, or for) —**ask'er** *n.* —**ask'ing** *n.*

askance (əskans') *adv.* [< ?] **1.** with a sideways glance **2.** with suspicion, disapproval, etc.

askew (əskyōō') *adv., adj.* to or on one side; awry

asking price the price asked by a seller

aslant (əslänt') *adv.* on a slant; slantingly —*prep.* on a slant across —*adj.* slanting

asleep (əslēp') *adj.* **1.** sleeping **2.** inactive; dull **3.** numb [my arm is asleep] **4.** dead —*adv.* into a sleeping or inactive condition

A.S.L.E.F. (az'lef) Associated Society of Locomotive Engineers and Firemen

asocial (ā sō'shəl) *adj.* **1.** not social;

characterized by withdrawal from others **2.** selfish

asp (asp) *n.* [< Gr. aspis] a small, poisonous snake of Africa and Europe

asparagus (əspar'əgəs) *n.* [L. < Gr. asparagos, a sprout] a plant with small, scalelike leaves and tender, edible shoots

aspect (as'pekt) *n.* [< L. ad-, to, at + specere, to look] **1.** the way one appears or looks **2.** the appearance of an idea, problem, etc. from a specific viewpoint **3.** a side facing in a given direction [the eastern aspect of the house] **4.** Astrol. the position of stars in relation to each other or to the observer

aspen (as'pən) *n.* [OE. æspe] a poplar tree with leaves that flutter in the least breeze —*adj.* trembling

asperity (as per'ətē) *n., pl.* **-ties** [< L. asper, rough] **1.** sharpness of temper **2.** roughness or harshness, as of surface, sound, etc.

asperse (əspʉrs') *vt.* **-persed', -pers'ing** [< L. ad-, to + spargere, to sprinkle] to slander —**aspers'er** *n.*

aspersion *n.* **1.** a defaming **2.** a damaging or disparaging remark; slander

asphalt (as'falt) *n.* [< Gr.] **1.** a brown or black tarlike variety of bitumen **2.** a mixture of this with sand or gravel, for paving, roofing, etc. —*vt.* to pave, roof, etc. with asphalt —**asphal'tic** *adj.*

asphodel (as'fədel') *n.* [< Gr. asphodelos] **1.** a kind of lily with white or yellow flowers **2.** Gr. Myth. the immortal flower growing in the Elysian fields

asphyxia (asfik'sēə) *n.* [< Gr. a-, not + sphyzein, throb] loss of consciousness as a result of too little oxygen and too much carbon dioxide in the blood; suffocation —**asphyx'iant** *adj., n.*

asphyxiate *vt.* **-at'ed, -at'ing** **1.** to cause asphyxia in **2.** to suffocate —**asphyx'ia'tion** *n.*

aspic (as'pik) *n.* [< OFr. aspe] a jelly of meat juice moulded with meat, seafood, etc., and eaten as a relish

aspidistra (as'pədis'trə) *n.* [< Gr. aspis, a shield] a plant with stiff, glossy evergreen leaves

aspirant (as'pər ənt, əspīr'ənt) *adj.* aspiring —*n.* a person who aspires, as after honours, etc.

aspirate (as'pə rāt'; for n. & adj. -pər ət) *vt.* **-rat'ed, -rat'ing** [see ASPIRE] **1.** to begin (a word or syllable) with the sound of English h **2.** to follow (a consonant) with a puff of suddenly released breath **3.** to remove (fluid or gas), as from a body cavity, by suction —*n.* **1.** the speech sound represented by English h **2.** an expiratory breath puff —*adj.* preceded or followed by an aspirate: also **as'pirat'ed**

aspiration (as'pə rā'shən) *n.* **1.** strong desire or ambition **2.** aspirating **3.** an aspirate

aspirator (as'pə rāt'ər) *n.* a suction apparatus for removing air, fluids, etc. as from a body cavity

aspiratory (əspīr'ətər ē) *adj.* of breathing or suction

aspire (ə spīr′) *vi* -pired′, -pir′ing [< L. *ad*-, to + *spirare*, to breathe] to be ambitious (*to* get or do something lofty); seek (*after*) —aspir′er *n.*

Aspirin (as′pər in) *Trademark* [Canad.] aspirin

aspirin (as′pər in) *n.* a white, crystalline powder, acetylsalicylic acid, used for reducing fever, relieving headaches, etc.

ass (as) *n.* [< L. *asinus*] 1. an animal related to the horse but having longer ears 2. a silly person

assafoetida (as′ə fet′i də) *n. same as* ASA-FOETIDA

assail (ə sāl′) *vt.* [< L. *ad*, to + *salire*, to leap] 1. to attack violently 2. to attack with arguments, etc. —assail′able *adj.* —assail′ant *n.*

assassin (ə sas′in) *n.* [Fr. < Ar. *hash-shāshīn*, hashish users] a murderer who strikes suddenly; esp., the killer of a politically important person

assassinate *vt.* -nat′ed, -nat′ing 1. to murder (esp. a politically important person) 2. to ruin (a reputation, etc.), as by slander —assas′sina′tion *n.*

assault (ə sôlt′) *n.* [< L. *ad*, to + *saltare*, to leap] 1. a violent attack, physical or verbal; sometimes, specif., rape 2. *Law* a threat or attempt to physically harm another —*vt.*, *vi.* to make an assault (upon) —assault′ive *adj.*

assault and battery *Law* the carrying out of threatened physical harm or violence

assay (ə sā′) *n.* [OFr. *essai*, test < L. *ex*-, out + *agere*, to act] 1. the analysis of an ore, etc. to find out the nature and proportion of the ingredients 2. the report of such analysis —*vt.* 1. to make an assay of; analyse 2. to try; attempt —assay′er *n.*

assegai, assagai (as′ə gī′) *n.* [Port *azagaia* < Ar.] in South Africa, a sharp, light spear made esp. from the wood of the **assegai tree**

assemblage (ə sem′blij) *n.* 1. an assembling 2. a group of persons or things gathered together; assembly

assemble (ə sem′b'l) *vt.*, *vi.* -bled, -bling [< L. *ad*-, to + *simul*, together] 1. to gather into a group; collect 2. to fit together the parts of —assem′bler *n.*

assembly (ə sem′blē) *n.*, *pl.* -blies 1. an assembling 2. a group of persons gathered together 3. a legislative body 4. *a*) a fitting together of parts to form a complete unit *b*) such parts

assembly line an arrangement by which each worker does a single operation in assembling work as it is passed along, often on a moving belt or track

assent (ə sent′) *vi.* [< L. *ad*-, to + *sentire*, to feel] to express acceptance; agree (*to*); concur —*n.* consent —assent′er *n.*

assert (ə surt′) *vt.* [< L. *ad*-, to + *serere*, to join] 1. to state positively; declare 2. to insist on or defend (one's rights, etc.) —assert oneself to insist on one's rights, or on being recognized —assert′er, asser′tor *n.*

assertion *n.* 1. a positive statement; declaration 2. an asserting

assertive *adj.* positive or confident in a dogmatic way —asser′tively *adv.* —asser′tiveness *n.*

assess (ə ses′) *vt.* [< L. *ad*-, to + *sedere*, to sit] 1. to set an estimated value on (property, etc.) for taxation 2. to set the amount of (damages, a fine, etc.) 3. to impose a fine, tax, etc. on 4. to impose (an amount) as a fine, tax, etc. 5. to estimate the value of —assess′ment *n.*

assessor *n.* 1. one who assesses, esp., *a*) property, etc., for taxation *b*) damage to property for insurance purposes *c*) school work submitted for certain examinations 2. a person called in to advise a court on a matter requiring specialist knowledge —assessorial (as′ə sôr′ē əl) *adj.*

asset (as′et) *n.* [< L. *ad*, to + *satis*, enough] 1. anything owned that has exchange value 2. a valuable or desirable thing 3. [*pl.*] *a*) all the resources of a person or business, as accounts and notes receivable, cash, property, etc. *b*) *Law* property, as of a bankrupt

asseverate (ə sev′ə rāt′) *vt.* -at′ed, -at′ing [< L. *ad*-, to + *severus*, earnest] to state seriously or positively; assert —assev′era′tion *n.*

assiduity (as′ə dyoo′ə tē) *n.*, *pl.* -ties 1. the quality of being assiduous; diligence 2. [*pl.*] constant personal attention

assiduous (ə sid′yoo wəs) *adj.* [see ASSESS] working with constant and careful attention; persevering —assid′u-ously *adv.* —assid′uousness *n.*

assign (ə sīn′) *vt.* [< L. *ad*-, to + *signare*, to sign] 1. to set apart for a specific purpose; designate 2. to place at some task or duty 3. to give out as a task 4. to ascribe (a motive, etc.) 5. *Law* to transfer (a claim, etc.) to another —*vi.* *Law* to transfer property, etc. to another —*n.* [*usually pl.*] an assignee —assign′a-ble *adj.* —assign′er, *Law* assign′or *n.*

assignation (as′ig nā′shən) *n.* 1. an appointment to meet, esp. one made secretly by lovers; rendezvous 2. an assigning 3. anything assigned

assignee (ə sī′nē′) *n.* *Law* a person to whom a claim, property, etc. is transferred

assignment (ə sīn′mənt) *n.* 1. anything assigned, as a task, etc. 2. *Law a*) a transfer of a claim, etc. *b*) a deed, etc. authorizing this

assimilate (ə sim′ə lāt′) *vt.* -lat′ed, -lat′-ing [< L. *ad*-, to + *similis*, like] 1. to absorb (food) into the body 2. to incorporate into one's thinking 3. to absorb (groups of different cultures) into the main culture 4. to make like or alike (with *to*) —*vi.* to become assimilated —assim′i-lable *adj.* —assim′ila′tor *n.*

assimilation (ə sim′ə lā′shən) *n.* 1. an assimilating; specif., *a*) the absorption of a minority group into the main culture *b*) *Phonet.* the process by which a sound becomes like a neighbouring sound [the p in *cupboard* has been lost by assimilation to *b]* c) *Physiol.* the change of digested or absorbed food into living tissue

assist (ə sist′) *vt.* [< L. *ad-*, to + *sistere*, to make stand] to help; aid —*vi.* to give help; aid —**assist at** to be present at; attend

assistance *n.* help; aid

assistant *adj.* helping —*n.* **1.** a person who assists or serves; helper **2.** *same as* SHOP ASSISTANT

assize (ə sīz′) *n.* [see ASSESS] **1.** [*pl.*] formerly, a) court sessions held periodically in each county of England and Wales b) the time or place of these **2.** [Archaic] a) a law regulating standards of weight, price, etc. for goods to be sold b) these standards

assn. association

assoc. **1.** associate **2.** associated **3.** association

associate (ə sō′shē āt′; *for n. & adj. usually* -it) *vt.* -**at′ed**, -**at′ing** [< L. *ad-*, to + *sociare*, to join] **1.** to connect in the mind **2.** to bring into relationship as companion, etc. **3.** to join; combine —*vi.* **1.** to join (*with*) as a companion, etc. **2.** to unite —*n.* **1.** a friend, partner, etc. **2.** a member of less than full status, as of a society **3.** anything joined with another thing or things —*adj.* **1.** joined with others, as in some work **2.** of less than full status

association (ə sō′sē ā′shən) *n.* **1.** an organization of persons having the same interests, purposes, etc.; society **2.** the act of associating; companionship; partnership **3.** a connection in the mind between ideas, feelings, etc. —**asso′cia′tional** *adj.*

association football a game in which players try to propel a ball into their opponents′ goal, only the goalkeepers being allowed to touch the ball with their hands

associative (ə sō′shə tiv) *adj.* **1.** of, characterized by, or causing association **2.** *Math.* of an operation in which the result is the same however the elements are grouped

assonance (as′ə nəns) *n.* [< L. *ad-*, to + *sonare*, to sound] **1.** likeness of sound **2.** a partial rhyme in which the stressed vowel sounds are alike as in *late* and *make* —**as′sonant** *adj.*, *n.*

assort (ə sôrt′) *vt.* [< OFr. *a-*, to + *sorte*, sort] to separate into classes; classify —*vi.* to match or harmonize (*with*) —**assort′ative** *adj.* —**assort′er** *n.*

assorted *adj.* **1.** miscellaneous **2.** sorted into groups **3.** matched [a poorly *assorted* group]

assortment *n.* **1.** an assorted group; variety **2.** an assorting; classification

ASSR, A.S.S.R. Autonomous Soviet Socialist Republic

asst. assistant

assuage (ə swāj′) *vt.* -**suaged′**, -**suag′ing** [< L. *ad*, to + *suavis*, sweet] **1.** to lessen (pain, etc.) **2.** to calm (passion, etc.) **3.** to satisfy (thirst, etc.) —**assuag′er** *n.*

assume (ə syoom′) *vt.* -**sumed′**, -**sum′ing**

[< L. *ad-*, to + *sumere*, to take] **1.** to take for granted; suppose **2.** to take upon oneself; undertake **3.** to pretend to have; feign **4.** to take on (the role, etc. *of*) **5.** to seize; usurp

assuming *adj.* presumptuous

assumption (ə sump′shən) *n.* **1.** the act of assuming **2.** a supposition **3.** presumption **4.** [A-] *R.C.Ch.* a) the taking up of the body and soul of the Virgin Mary into heaven b) a festival on August 15 celebrating this

assurance (ə shooar′əns) *n.* **1.** the act of assuring **2.** sureness; confidence **3.** something that inspires confidence, as a promise, etc.; guarantee **4.** self-confidence **5.** impudent forwardness **6.** insurance, esp. providing for events that are certain to occur, as death

assure (ə shooar′) *vt.* -**sured′**, -**sur′ing** [< L. *ad* to + *securus*, secure] **1.** to make (a person) sure of something; convince **2.** to give confidence to **3.** to declare to or promise confidently **4.** to guarantee **5.** to insure against loss, esp. of life —**assur′er** *n.*

assured *adj.* **1.** certain **2.** confident **3.** insured —**assuredly** (ə shooar′id lē) *adv.*

Assyrian (ə sir′ē ən) *adj.* of Assyria —*n.* **1.** a native of Assyria **2.** the language of the Assyrians

A.S.T. [U.S. & Canad.] Atlantic Standard Time

astatine (as′tə tēn′) *n.* [< Gr. *astatos*, unstable] a radioactive chemical element formed from bismuth bombarded by alpha particles: symbol, At

aster (as′tər) *n.* [< Gr. *astēr*, star] a plant with purplish, pink, or white daisylike flowers

asterisk (as′tər isk) *n.* [< Gr. *astēr*, star] a starlike sign (*) used in printing to indicate footnote references, omissions, etc. —*vt.* to mark with this sign

astern (ə sturn′) *adv.* **1.** behind a ship or aircraft **2.** at or towards the back of a ship or aircraft **3.** backwards

asteroid (as′tə roid′) *adj.* [< Gr. *astēr*, star] like a star or starfish —*n.* **1.** any of the small planetary bodies between Mars and Jupiter **2.** a starfish

asthma (as′mə) *n.* [Gr.] a chronic disorder characterized by wheezing, coughing, difficulty in breathing, and a suffocating feeling —**asthmat′ic** *adj.* —**asthmat′ically** *adv.*

astigmatic (as′tig mat′ik) *adj.* **1.** of or having astigmatism **2.** correcting astigmatism —**as′tigmat′ically** *adv.*

astigmatism (ə stig′mə tiz′m) *n.* [< Gr. *a-*, without + *stigma*, a mark] an irregularity in a lens, esp. of the eye, so that light rays do not meet in a single focal point and images are distorted

astir (ə stur′) *adv.*, *adj.* **1.** in motion **2.** out of bed

astonish (ə ston′ish) *vt.* [< L. *ex-*, emphatic + *tonare*, to thunder] to fill with wonder or surprise; amaze —**aston′ishing** *adj.* —**aston′ishment** *n.*

astound (ə stound′) *vt.* [see ASTONISH]

to astonish greatly —**astound'ing** *adj.* —**astound'ingly** *adv.*

astraddle (ə strad'ʼl) *adv.*   in a straddling position

astrakhan (as'trə kan') *n.*   1. a loosely curled fur from the pelt of very young lambs orig. bred near Astrakhan   2. a fabric made to look like this   Also sp. **as'trachan'**

astral (as'trəl) *adj.* [< Gr. *astēr*, star] of, from, or like the stars

astray (ə strā') *adv.*   off the right path; in error

astride (ə strīd') *adv.*   1. with a leg on either side   2. with legs far apart —*prep.*   1. with a leg on either side of (a horse, etc.)   2. extending across

astringent (ə strin'jənt) *adj.* [< L. *ad-*, to + *stringere*, to draw]   1. that contracts body tissues and checks capillary bleeding, etc.   2. harsh; austere —*n.*   an astringent substance —**astrin'gency** *n.* —**astrin'gently** *adv.*

astro- [< Gr. *astron*, star]   *a combining form*   meaning   of   a   star   or   stars [*astrophysics*]

astrol.   1. astrologer   2. astrology

astrolabe (as'trə lāb') *n.* [< Gr. *astron*, star + *lambanein*, take]   an instrument once used to find the altitude of stars, etc.

astrology (ə strol'ə jē) *n.* [< Gr. *astron*, star + -LOGY]   a study based on the belief that the positions of the moon, sun, and planets affect human affairs —**astrol'oger** *n.* —**astrological** (as'trə loj'i k'l) *adj.*

astron.   1. astronomer   2. astronomy

astronaut (as'trə nôt') *n.* [see ff.]   a person trained to make rocket flights in outer space

astronautics (as'trə nôt'iks) *n.pl.* [with *sing. v.*] [< ASTRO- + Gr. *nautēs*, sailor]   the science that deals with spacecraft and with travel in outer space —**as'tronau'tical** *adj.*

astronomical (as'trə nom'i k'l) *adj.*   1. extremely large, as the numbers used in astronomy   2. of astronomy   Also **as'tronom'ic** —**as'tronom'ically** *adv.*

astronomy (ə stron'ə mē) *n.* [< Gr. *astron*, star + *nemein*, arrange]   the science of the stars, planets, and all other heavenly bodies —**astron'omer** *n.*

astrophysics (as'trō fiz'iks) *n.pl.* [with *sing. v.*]   the science of the physical properties of the stars, planets, etc. —**as'trophys'ical** *adj.* —**as'trophys'icist** *n.*

astute (ə styoot') *adj.* [< L. *astus*, cunning]   shrewd; keen

asunder (ə sun'dər) *adv.* [see SUNDER]   1. into parts or pieces   2. apart or separate

asylum (ə sī'ləm) *n.* [< Gr. *a-*, without + *sylē*, right of seizure]   1. formerly, a sanctuary, where criminals, etc. were safe from arrest   2. any refuge   3. the protection given by one country to refugees from another: also **political asylum**   4. [Obs.] a place for the care of the mentally ill, or of the aged, poor, etc.

asymmetry (a sim'ə trē) *n.*   lack of symmetry —**asymmetrical** (a'sə met'ri k'l), **a'symmet'ric** *adj.*

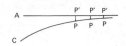

ASYMPTOTE (A, asymptote of curve C)

asymptote (as'im tōt') *n.* [< Gr. *a-*, not + *syn-*, together + *piptein*, fall]   a straight line always approaching but never meeting a curve —**as'ymptot'ic** (-tot'ik) *adj.*

at (at; *unstressed* ət) *prep.* [OE. æt]   1. on; in; near; by   2. to or towards   3. from [get the facts *at* their source]   4. attending [*at* the party]   5. busy with [*at* work]   6. in the state or manner of [*at* a trot, *at* war]   7. because of [terrified *at* the sight]   8. according to [*at* his discretion]   9. with reference to [good *at* tennis]   10. in the amount, degree, price, etc. of [*at* five pounds each]   11. from an interval of [visible *at* fifty metres]   12. on or close to the time or age of [*at* five o'clock]

At   *Chem.* astatine

at.   1. atmosphere   2. atomic

atavism (at'ə viz'm) *n.* [< L. *at-*, beyond + *avus*, grandfather]   the appearance in an individual of a characteristic found in an early ancestor but not in recent ones; reversion to a former type —**at'avis'tic** *adj.*

ataxia (ə tak'sē ə) *n.* [< Gr. *a-*, not + *tassein*, arrange]   inability to coordinate voluntary muscular movements

A.T.C.   1. Air Traffic Control   2. Air Training Corps

ate (et, āt)   *pt.* of EAT

-ate[1] (āt *for 1*; ət, āt *for 2*) [< L.]   *a suffix meaning:*   1. to become, cause to become, produce, form, or provide with [*maturate, vaccinate*]   2. of or characteristic of, having or filled with [*passionate*]

-ate[2] (āt, ət) [< L.]   *a suffix denoting* a function, agent, or official [*directorate, potentate*]

atelier (at'əl yā') *n.* [Fr.]   a studio or workshop

atheism (ā'thē iz'm) *n.* [< Gr. *a-*, without + *theos*, god]   the belief that there is no God —**a'theist** *n.* —**a'theis'tic**, **a'theis'tical** *adj.*

athenaeum (ath'ə nē'əm) *n.* [after the temple of Athena at Athens]   1. an institution for the promotion of learning, as a literary or scientific society   2. a building containing a reading room or library, esp. one used by such an institution

atherosclerosis (ath'ə rō sklə rō'sis) *n.* [< Gr. *athērōma*, tumour + SCLEROSIS]   a thickening of the walls of arteries, with the formation of fatty nodules —**ath'erosclerot'ic** (-rot'ik) *adj.*

athirst (ə thurst') *adj.*   1. eager (for)   2. thirsty

athlete (ath'lēt') *n.* [< Gr. *athlon*, a prize]   a person trained in exercises, games, or contests requiring physical strength, skill, speed, etc.

athlete's foot   a common fungous

infection of the skin of the feet; ringworm of the feet

athletic (ath let′ik) *adj.* 1. physically strong, skilful, etc. 2. of athletes or athletics —**athlet′ically** *adv.*

athletics *n.pl.* [*sometimes with sing. v.*] the practice of, or contests in, track and field events

at-home (ət hōm′) *n.* an informal reception at one's home, usually in the afternoon

athwart (ə thwôrt′) *prep.* 1. from one side to the other of; across 2. in opposition to 3. *Naut.* across the course of —*adv.* 1. crosswise 2. so as to block or thwart

-atic (at′ik) [< Gr.] *a suffix meaning* of, of the kind of [*lymphatic, chromatic*]

atingle (ə tiŋ′g′l) *adj.* tingling; excited

-ation (ā′shən) [< Fr. or L.] *a suffix meaning:* 1. the act of [*alteration*] 2. the condition of being [*gratification*] 3. the result of [*compilation*]

-ative (ə tiv, āt′iv) [< Fr. or L.] *a suffix meaning* of or relating to, serving to, tending to

Atlantic (ət lan′tik) *adj.* [< L.] of, in, on, or near the ocean touching Europe and Africa to the east and the American continents to the west

Atlantic Provinces in Canada, the provinces of New Brunswick, Newfoundland and Labrador, Nova Scotia, and Prince Edward Island

Atlantis (ət lan′tis) legendary island or continent west of Gibraltar, supposed to have sunk in the Atlantic

atlas (at′ləs) *n.* [< Gr. *Atlas*, Titan forced to hold the heavens on his shoulders] 1. a book of maps 2. a book of tables, charts, etc. on a specific subject

atm. 1. atmosphere 2. atmospheric

atmosphere (at′məs fēar′) *n.* [< Gr. *atmos*, vapour + *sphaira*, sphere] 1. all the air surrounding the earth 2. the gaseous mass surrounding any star, etc. 3. the air in any given place 4. general feeling; mood 5. *Physics* a unit of pressure equal to 101 325 pascals —**at′mospher′ic** (-fer′ik) *adj.*

atmospherics (at′məs fer′iks) *n.pl.* *same as* STATIC

at. no. atomic number

atoll (a′tol) *n.* [< Maldive Is. term] a ring-shaped coral island nearly or completely surrounding a lagoon

atom (at′əm) *n.* [< Gr. *a-*, not + *temnein*, cut] 1. a tiny particle; jot 2. *Chem. & Physics* any of the smallest particles of an element that combine with similar particles of other elements to produce compounds: atoms consist of electrons revolving about a positively charged nucleus —**the atom** *same as* ATOMIC ENERGY

atom bomb *same as* ATOMIC BOMB —**at′om-bomb′** *vt.*

atomic (ə tom′ik) *adj.* 1. of an atom or atoms 2. of or using atomic energy or atomic bombs —**atom′ically** *adv.*

atomic bomb an extremely destructive bomb, the power of which comes from

the energy that is suddenly released when a chain reaction of nuclear fission is set off

atomic energy the energy released from an atom in nuclear fission or nuclear fusion, or by radioactive decay

atomic mass unit a unit of mass, one twelfth of the mass of an atom of the most common isotope of carbon

atomic number *Chem.* a number representing the relative position of an element in the periodic table; number representing the number of protons in an atomic nucleus

atomic theory the theory that all material objects and substances are composed of atoms

atomic weight *Chem.* a number representing the weight of one atom of an element as compared with the weight of one atom of another element taken as the standard (now usually carbon at 12)

atomize (at′ə mīz′) *vt.* **-ized′, -iz′ing** 1. to separate into atoms 2. to reduce (a liquid) to a fine spray

atomizer *n.* a device used to shoot out a fine spray, as of medicine or perfume

atom smasher *same as* ACCELERATOR

atonality (ā′tō nal′ə tē) *n.* *Music* lack of tonality through intentional disregard of key —**aton′al** *adj.*

atone (ə tōn′) *vi.* atoned′, aton′ing to make amends (*for* wrongdoing, etc.) —**aton′er** *n.*

atonement *n.* [ME. *at-onement*, in harmony] 1. an atoning 2. satisfaction given for wrongdoing, etc.; expiation 3. [A-] *Theol.* the reconciliation of God to man by means of Jesus' sufferings and death

atop (ə top′) *adv.* on the top —*prep.* on the top of

-atory (ə tər ē) [< L.] *a suffix meaning* of, characterized by, produced by [*accusatory*]

atrium (ā′trē əm) *n., pl.* **a′tria, a′triums** [L.] 1. the main room of an ancient Roman house 2. *Anat.* either of the upper chambers of the heart —**a′trial** *adj.*

atrocious (ə trō′shəs) *adj.* [< L. *atrox*, fierce] 1. very cruel, evil, etc. 2. appalling or dismaying 3. [Colloq.] very bad —**atro′ciously** *adv.* —**atro′ciousness** *n.*

atrocity (ə tros′ə tē) *n., pl.* **-ties** 1. atrocious behaviour 2. an atrocious act 3. [Colloq.] a very offensive thing

atrophy (at′rə fē) *n.* [< Gr. *a-*, not + *trephein*, nourish] a wasting away, or failure to grow, of an organ, etc. —*vi.* **-phied, -phying** to waste away or fail to develop —*vt.* to cause atrophy in

atropine (at′rə pin) *n.* [< Gr. *Atropos*, the Fate who cuts the thread of life] a poisonous, crystalline alkaloid obtained from belladonna: also **at′ropin**

att. 1. attention 2. attorney

attach (ə tach′) *vt.* [< OFr. *estachier*, fasten] 1. to fasten by tying, etc. 2. to join [*he attached* himself to us] 3. to connect by ties of affection 4. to affix (a signature, etc.) 5. to ascribe 6. *Law* to take (property or a person) into custody by writ —*vi.* to be attributable; belong

attaché (ə tash′ā) *n.* [Fr., see ATTACH] a person with special duties on the staff of an ambassador

attaché case a flat, rectangular case for carrying documents, papers, etc.

attachment (ə tach′mənt) *n.* 1. anything that attaches; fastening 2. devotion 3. anything attached 4. an accessory for an electrical appliance, etc. 5. the act of attaching something 6. *Law* a taking of a person, property, etc. into custody, or a writ for this

attack (ə tak′) *vt.* [< OFr. *atachier*] 1. to use force against in order to harm 2. to speak or write against 3. to begin working on energetically 4. to begin acting upon harmfully —*vi.* to make an assault —*n.* 1. an attacking; onslaught 2. an onset of a disease 3. a beginning of a task —**attack′er** *n.*

attain (ə tān′) *vt.* [< L. *ad-*, to + *tangere*, to touch] 1. to gain through effort; achieve 2. to arrive at —*vi.* to succeed in reaching or coming (*to* a goal)

attainder (ə tān′dər) *n.* [OFr. *ataindre*, attain] the loss of a person's civil rights and property because he has been sentenced to death or outlawed

attainment (ə tān′mənt) *n.* 1. an attaining or being attained 2. anything attained, as a skill

attaint (ə tānt′) *vt.* to punish by attainder

attar (at′ər) *n.* [< Ar. *'itr*, perfume] a perfume made from the petals of flowers, esp. of damask roses

attempt (ə tempt′) *vt.* [< L. *ad-*, to + *temptare*, to try] to try to do, get, etc. —*n.* 1. a try; endeavour 2. an attack, as on a person's life —**attempt′able** *adj.*

attend (ə tend′) *vt.* [< L. *ad-*, to + *tendere*, to stretch] 1. to be present at 2. to accompany as a result [success *attended* his efforts *]* 3. to go with 4. [Now Rare] to take care of —*vi.* 1. to pay attention 2. to wait (*on* or *upon*) 3. to give care or attention (*to*)

attendance *n.* 1. an attending 2. the number of persons attending 3. regularity in attending

attendant *adj.* 1. attending or serving 2. accompanying [*attendant* difficulties *]* —*n.* one who attends or serves

attention *n.* 1. *a)* concentration *b)* readiness for concentration 2. notice 3. care or consideration 4. an act of courtesy: *usually used in pl.* 5. *Mil.* the erect, motionless posture of soldiers in readiness for a command

attentive *adj.* 1. paying attention 2. courteous, devoted, etc. —**atten′tively** *adv.* —**atten′tiveness** *n.*

attenuate (ə ten′yoo wāt′) *vt.* -at′ed, -at′ing [< L. *ad-*, to + *tenuis*, thin] 1. to make slender or thin 2. to dilute or weaken —*vi.* to become thin, weak, etc. —**atten′uable** *adj.* —**atten′ua′tion** *n.*

attest (ə test′) *vt.* [< L. *ad-*, to + *testis*, a witness] 1. to declare to be true 2. to certify, as by oath 3. to serve as proof of —*vi.* to testify (*to*) —**attesta-**

tion (at′es tā′shən) *n.* —**attest′er, attes′tor** *n.*

attested *adj.* certified to be free of a disease, esp. tuberculosis; said of cattle, etc.

Attic (at′ik) *adj.* 1. of Attica 2. Athenian 3. elegant; restrained [an *Attic* style *]* —*n.* the Greek dialect of Attica, the literary language of ancient Greece

attic (at′ik) *n.* [< prec.] 1. the room below the roof of a house 2. a storey above the cornice of a façade

attire (ə tīər′) *vt.* -tired′, -tir′ing [< OFr. *a*, to + *tire*, order] to dress, esp. in fine garments —*n.* clothes; finery

attitude (at′ə tyood′) *n.* [< L. *aptus*, APT] 1. one's disposition, outlook, etc. 2. the posture of the body 3. the position of an aircraft or spacecraft in relation to a given line or plane —**at′titu′dinal** *adj.*

attitudinize (at′ə tyood′ən īz′) *vi.* -nized′, -niz′ing to pose for effect

attorney (ə tur′nē) *n., pl.* -neys [< OFr. < *a-*, to + *torner*: see TURN] 1. any person having the legal power to act for another 2. [U.S.] a lawyer

attorney general *pl.* attorneys general, attorney generals the chief law officer of a government

attract (ə trakt′) *vt.* [< L. *ad-*, to + *trahere*, to draw] 1. to draw to itself or oneself 2. to get the admiration, etc. of —*vi.* to be attractive

attraction *n.* 1. an attracting or the power of attracting; esp., charm or fascination 2. anything that attracts 3. *Physics* the mutual action by which bodies tend to draw together

attractive *adj.* that attracts or has the power to attract

attribute (ə trib′yoot; *for n.* a′trə byoot′) *vt.* -uted, -uting [< L. *ad-*, to + *tribuere*, to assign] to think of as belonging to; assign or ascribe (*to*) —*n.* 1. a characteristic or quality of a person or thing 2. an object used as a symbol for a person, office, etc. —**at′tribu′tion** *n.*

attributive (ə trib′yoo tiv) *adj.* 1. attributing 2. *Gram.* coming just before the noun it modifies: said of an adjective —*n.* an attributive adjective, as *black* in *black cat* —**attrib′utively** *adv.*

attrition (ə trish′ən) *n.* [< L. *ad-*, to + *terere*, to rub] 1. a wearing away by friction 2. any gradual wearing, or weakening [war of *attrition*]

attune (ə tyoon′) *vt.* -tuned′, -tun′ing 1. to bring into harmony or agreement 2. to tune

A.T.V. Associated Television

at. wt. atomic weight

atypical (ā tip′i k'l) *adj.* not typical —*atyp′ically adv.*

Au [L. *aurum*] *Chem.* gold

aubergine (ō′bər zhēn′) *n.* [Fr. < Ar. < Per.] 1. the fruit of the eggplant, used as a vegetable 2. the colour of this vegetable, a dark purple

aubrietia (ô brē′shə) *n.* [< Claude *Aubriet*, 18th-c. Fr. painter] a rock plant with flowers in a range of pink and purple shades

auburn (ô′bərn) *adj., n.* [< L. *albus*,

white; meaning infl. by ME. *brun,* brown] reddish brown, esp. of hair

auction (ôk′shən) *n.* [< L. *augere,* increase] a public sale at which each item is sold to the highest bidder —*vt.* to sell at auction

auctioneer (ôk′shə nēar′) *n.* one whose work is selling things at auction —*vt.* to auction

aud. 1. audit 2. auditor

audacious (ô dā′shəs) *adj.* [< L. *audere,* dare] 1. bold or daring; fearless 2. rudely bold; brazen; insolent —**audac′ity** (-das′-) *n.*

audible (ô′də b'l) *adj.* [< L. *audire,* hear] loud enough to be heard —**au′dibil′ity** *n.* —**au′dibly** *adv.*

audience (ô′dē əns) *n.* [< L. *audire,* hear] 1. a group assembled to see and hear a play, concert, etc. 2. those reached by a certain radio or TV programme, book, etc. 3. a formal interview

audio (ô′dē ō) *adj.* [< L. *audire,* hear] 1. of frequencies corresponding to sound waves that are normally audible 2. of or relating to sound reproduction

audio-frequency (ô′dē ō frē′kwən sē) *adj.* of the band of audible sound frequencies or corresponding electric current frequencies, from about 20 to 20 000 hertz

audiometer (ô′dē om′ə tər) *n.* an instrument for measuring hearing

audiotypist (ô′dē ō tī′pist) *n.* a typist trained to type from a dictating machine

audiovisual (ô′dē ō vizh′ oo wəl) *adj.* involving both hearing and sight: used esp. of teaching aids

audit (ô′dit) *n.* [< L. *audire,* hear] a formal examination of accounts —*vt., vi.* to examine (accounts, etc.)

audition (ô dish′ən) *n.* 1. a hearing to test the ability of an actor, etc. 2. the act or sense of hearing —*vt., vi.* to give an audition (to)

auditor (ô′də tər) *n.* 1. a person who is authorized to audit accounts 2. a hearer or listener

Auditor General in Canada, an officer appointed by the Governor General to audit the accounts of the Federal Government and report to Parliament

auditorium (ô′də tôr′ē əm) *n.* the area of a concert hall, theatre, etc. in which the audience sits

auditory (ô′də tər ē) *adj.* of hearing

A.U.E.W. Amalgamated Union of Engineering Workers

au fait (ō fā′) [Fr.] 1. acquainted with the facts; well-informed 2. proficient; expert

‡auf Wiedersehen (ouf vē′dər zā′ən) [G.] goodbye

Aug. August

Augean (ô jē′ən) *adj.* 1. *Gr. Myth.* of Augeas or his filthy stable, which Hercules cleaned in a day 2. filthy

auger (ô′gər) *n.* [< OE. *nafu,* nave (of wheel) + *gar,* spear] a tool for boring holes in wood

aught (ôt) *n.* [< OE. *a,* one + *wiht,*

creature] 1. anything 2. [< *a naught*] a zero

augment (ôg ment′) *vt., vi.* [< L. *augere,* increase] to increase —**aug′menta′tion** *n.* —**augment′er** *n.*

augmentative *adj.* augmenting —*n.* an intensifying word or affix

au gratin (ō grat′an) [Fr., with scrapings] with a lightly browned crust of bread crumbs and grated cheese

augur (ô′gər) *n.* [L.] 1. in ancient Rome, one who interpreted omens as favourable or unfavourable 2. a fortuneteller; soothsayer —*vt., vi.* 1. to foretell 2. to be an omen (of) —**augur ill** (or **well**) to be a bad (or good) omen —**au′gural** (ô′-gyər əl) *adj.*

August (ô′gəst) *n.* [L. < *Augustus* (Caesar)] the eighth month of the year, having 31 days: abbrev. **Aug.**

august (ô gust′) *adj.* [L. *augustus*] 1. inspiring awe; imposing 2. worthy of respect; venerable

Augustan (ô gus′tən) *adj.* 1. of or like Augustus Caesar or the literary achievements of his times 2. of any similar literary period; classical; elegant

GREAT AUK
(to 75 cm high)

auk (ôk) *n.* [< ON. *alka*] a diving bird of the northern seas, with webbed feet and short wings used as paddles

‡au lait (ō lā′) [Fr.] with milk

auld (ôld) *adj.* [Dial. & Scot.] old

auld lang syne (ôld′ laŋ′ sīn′) [Scot., old long since] old times; the good old days

aumbry (ôrm′ brē) *n.* same as AMBRY

‡au naturel (ō nà tü rel′) [Fr.] 1. naked 2. prepared simply

aunt (änt) *n.* [< L. *amita,* paternal aunt] 1. a sister of one's mother or father 2. the wife of one's uncle

auntie, aunty (än′tē) *n.* aunt

Aunt Sally (sal′ē) 1. a figure used as a target in a fairground game 2. any target for insults or criticism

au pair (ō pāər′) [Fr., as an equal] designating the system whereby a girl receives board and lodging with a family, usually in a foreign country, in return for household help —*n.* such a girl

aura (ôr′ə) *n., pL* -ras, -rae (-ē) [< Gr., breeze] 1. a particular atmosphere or quality that seems to surround a person or thing 2. an invisible emanation

aural (ôr′əl) *adj.* [< L. *auris,* ear] of or received through the ear or the sense of hearing —**au′rally** *adv.*

aureate (ôr′ē it) *adj.* [< L. *aurum,* gold]

1. golden; gilded 2. splendid or brilliant, often affectedly so

aureole (ôr'ē ōl') *n.* [< L. *aureola* (*corona*),' golden (crown)] 1. a halo 2. the sun's corona

au revoir (ō'rə vwär') [Fr.] till we meet again; goodbye

auric (ôr'ik) *adj.* [< L. *aurum*, gold] 1. of gold 2. *Chem.* of compounds in which gold has a valence of three

auricle (ôr'ə k'l) *n.* [< L. *auris*, ear] 1. the external part of the ear 2. an atrium of the heart

auricula (ô rik'yoo lə) *n., pl.* -**las, -lae'** (-lē') [see prec.] a species of primula with leaves shaped like a bear's ear

auricular (ô rik'yoo lər) *adj.* 1. of the ear or sense of hearing 2. spoken directly into the ear 3. ear-shaped 4. *Anat.* of an auricle —**auric'ularly** *adv.*

auriferous (ô rif'ər əs) *adj.* [< L. *aurum*, gold + *ferre*, bear] bearing or yielding gold

aurochs (ô'roks) *n., pl.* **au'rochs** [< G.] 1. the extinct wild ox of Europe 2. the nearly extinct European bison

aurora (ô rôr'ə) *n., pl.* -**ras, rae** (-ē) [L., dawn] the dawn —**auro'ral, auro'rean** *adj.*

aurora australis (ô strā'lis) [L.: see prec. & AUSTRAL] luminous bands of light like the aurora borealis, but in the Southern Hemisphere

aurora borealis (bôr'ē ăl'is) [L. < AURORA & Gr. *Boreas*, north wind] luminous bands appearing in the night sky of the Northern Hemisphere; northern lights

auscultation (ôs'kəl tā'shən) *n.* [< L. *auscultare*, listen] a listening to sounds in the chest, abdomen, etc., as in diagnosis

auspice (ôs'pis) *n., pl.* -**pices'** (-pə sēz) [< L. *auspicium*] 1. [*pl.*] guiding sponsorship; patronage 2. an omen, esp. a favourable one

auspicious (ôs pish'əs) *adj.* 1. favourable 2. successful

Aussie (oz'ē) *adj., n.* [Slang] Australian

austere (o stēar') *adj.* [< Gr. *austēros*, dry] 1. stern; forbidding 2. showing strict self-discipline; ascetic 3. very plain —**austere'ly** *adv.* —**austere'ness** *n.*

austerity (o ster'ətē) *n., pl.* -**ties** 1. an austere quality 2. tightened economy, as from shortages of goods

austral (ôs'trəl) *adj.* [< L. *auster*, the south] 1. southern; southerly 2. [A-] Australian

Australasian (ôs'trə lā'zhən) *adj.* of the islands of the SW Pacific; esp. Australia and New Zealand

Australian (o strāl'ē ən) *adj.* of Australia —*n.* an inhabitant of Australia

Austro-¹ *a combining form meaning* Austria

Austro-² [< L. *auster*, south] *a combining form meaning* South, Southern

autarchy (ô'tär kē) *n., pl.* -**chies** [< Gr. *autos*, self + *archos*, ruler] 1. absolute rule; autocracy 2. a country under such rule —**autar'chic, autar'chical** *adj.*

autarky (ô'tär kē) *n.* [< Gr. *autos*, self + *arkein*, suffice] economic self-sufficiency as a national policy

auth. 1. author 2. authority 3. authorized

authentic (ô then'tik) *adj.* [< Gr. *authentikos*] 1. that can be believed; reliable 2. genuine; real —**authen'tically** *adv.* —**authenticity** (ô'thən tis'ə tē) *n.*

authenticate *vt.* -**cat'ed, -cat'ing** 1. establish as authentic, or true, valid, genuine, etc. —**authen'tica'tion** *n.* —**authen'tica'tor** *n.*

author (ô'thər) *n.* [< L. *augere*, to increase] 1. the writer (*of* a book, article, etc.) 2. one who makes or originates something; creator

authoritarian (ô thor'ə täər'ē ən) *adj.* believing in or characterized by unquestioning obedience to authority —*n.* a person who believes in or enforces such obedience —**author'itar'ianism** *n.*

authoritative (ô thor'ə tət iv) *adj.* 1. having authority; official 2. reliable because coming from an authority 3. dictatorial —**author'itatively** *adv.*

authority (ô thor'ə tē) *n., pl.* -**ties** [see AUTHOR] 1. *a)* the power or right to give commands, take action, etc. *b)* the position of one having such power *c)* such powers as delegated; authorization 2. influence resulting from knowledge, prestige, etc. 3. a writing, etc. cited in support of an opinion 4. *a)* [*pl.*] persons, esp. in government, having the power to enforce laws, etc. *b)* a body with powers to enforce bylaws, levy rates, etc. in a given area 5. evidence or testimony [we have it on his *authority*] 6. an expert 7. self-assurance based on expertness

authorize (ô'thə rīz') *vt.* -**ized', -iz'ing** 1. to give official approval to 2. to empower; commission 3. to justify —**au'-thoriza'tion** *n.* —**au'thoriz'er** *n.*

Authorized Version the revised English translation of the Bible published in 1611, authorized by James I

authorship (ô'thər ship') *n.* 1. the profession of a writer 2. the origin (of a book, idea, etc.)

autism (ô'tiz'm) *n.* [see AUTO-] *Psychol.* a state of mind characterized by self-absorption, fantasy, and a disregard of external reality —**autis'tic** *adj.*

auto (ôt'ō) *n., pl.* -**tos** [U.S.] a motor car

auto- [Gr. *autos*, self] *a combining form meaning:* 1. self [*autobiography*] 2. by oneself or itself [*automobile*]

autobahn (ôt'ə bän') *n.* [G.] in Germany, a motorway

autobiography (ôt'ō bī og'rə fē) *n., pl.* -**phies** the story of one's own life written by oneself —**au'tobiog'rapher** *n.* —**au'to-bi'ograph'ical** (-bī'ə graf'i k'l), **au'tobi'o-graph'ic** *adj.*

autoclave (ôt'ə klāv') *n.* [Fr. < *auto-*, AUTO- + L. *clavis*, a key] a container for sterilizing, cooking, etc. by superheated steam under pressure

autocracy (ô tok'rə sē) *n., pl.* -**cies** [see ff.] a government in which one person has supreme power; dictatorship

autocrat (ôt'ə krat') *n.* [< Gr. *autos*,

self + *kratos*, power] **1.** a ruler with absolute power; despot **2.** any domineering, self-willed person —**au′tocrat′ic** *adj.* —**au′tocrat′ically** *adv.*

auto-da-fé (ôt′ō də fā′) *n., pl.* **au′tos-da-fé′** [Port., act of the faith] **1.** the public ceremony in which the Inquisition judged those tried as heretics **2.** the execution of the sentence; esp., the public burning of a heretic

autogiro, autogyro (ôt′ə jī′rō) *n., pl.* **-ros** [< AUTO- + Gr. *gyros*, circle] an early kind of aircraft having both a propeller and a large horizontal rotor

autograph (ôt′ə gräf′) *n.* [< Gr. *autos*, self + *graphein*, write] **1.** a person's own signature or handwriting **2.** a thing written in one's own handwriting —*vt.* to write one's signature on or in —**au′tograph′ic** *adj.* (-graf′ik)

automat (ôt′ə mat′) *n.* [see AUTOMATIC] [Chiefly U.S.] a restaurant in which patrons get food from small compartments opened by putting coins into slots

automate (ôt′ə māt′) *vt.* **-mat′ed, -mat′ing** [< automation] **1.** to convert to automation **2.** to use the techniques of automation in

automatic (ôt′ə mat′ik) *adj.* [Gr. *automatos*, self-moving] **1.** done without conscious thought or volition **2.** involuntary or reflex **3.** operating by itself **4.** occurring as a necessary consequence [such action incurs *automatic* dismissal] **5.** *Firearms* using the force of the explosion of a shell to eject, reload, and fire again, so that shots continue in rapid succession —*n.* **1.** an automatic pistol, etc. **2.** a motor vehicle having automatic transmission —**au′tomat′ically** *adv.*

automatic pilot an instrument that keeps an aircraft, etc. to a predetermined course and altitude

automatic transmission a transmission system in a motor vehicle in which the gears can be set to change automatically

automation (ôt′ə mā′shən) *n.* **1.** in manufacturing, a system in which many or all of the processes are automatically performed or controlled by machinery, electronic devices, etc. **2.** any system using equipment to replace people

automatism (ô tom′ə tiz′m) *n.* **1.** the quality or condition of being automatic **2.** automatic action

automaton (ô tom′ə tən) *n., pl.* **-tons′, -ta** [see AUTOMATIC] **1.** anything that can move or act of itself **2.** an apparatus that works or moves by responding to preset controls or computerized instructions **3.** a person acting in a mechanical way

automobile (ôt′ə mə bēl′) *n.* [Fr.: see AUTO- & MOBILE] [Chiefly U.S.] a motor car

automotive (ôt′ə mōt′iv) *adj.* [AUTO- + -MOTIVE] **1.** self-moving **2.** having to do with motor vehicles

autonomous (ô ton′ə məs) *adj.* [< Gr. *autos*, self + *nomos*, law] **1.** having self-government **2.** functioning independently

autonomy *n.* self-government

autopilot (ôt′ō pī′lət) *n.* *same as* AUTOMATIC PILOT

autopsy (ô′top′sē) *n., pl.* **-sies** [< Gr. *autos*, self + *opsis*, sight] an examination of a dead body to discover the cause of death, damage done by a disease, etc.

autoroute (ôt′ō rŏŏt′) *n.* [Fr.] in France, a motorway

autostrada (ôt′ə strä′də) *n.* [It.] in Italy, a motorway

autosuggestion (ôt′ō sə jes′chən) *n.* suggestion to oneself arising within oneself

autumn (ôt′əm) *n.* [< L. *autumnus*] **1.** the season between summer and winter **2.** any period of incipient decline —**autumnal** (ô tum′nəl) *adj.*

aux. auxiliary

auxiliary (ôg zil′yər ē) *adj.* [< L. *auxilium*, aid] **1.** giving help; assisting **2.** acting in a subsidiary capacity **3.** additional; reserve —*n., pl.* **-ries** *adj.* **1.** an auxiliary person or thing **2.** [*pl.*] foreign troops aiding a country at war

auxiliary verb a verb that helps to form tenses, moods, or voices of other verbs, as *have* or *be*

AV 1. audiovisual **2.** Authorized Version (of the Bible)

Av., av. avenue

av. average

avail (ə vāl′) *vi., vt.* [< L. *ad*, to + *valere*, to be strong] to be of use, help, or advantage (to) —*n.* effective use or help [of no *avail*] —**avail oneself of** to take advantage of (an opportunity, etc.)

available (ə vā′lə b'l) *adj.* **1.** that can be used **2.** that can be got or reached —**avail′abil′ity** *n.* —**avail′ably** *adv.*

avalanche (av′ə länsh′) *n.* [Fr. < L. *labi*, to slip] **1.** a large mass of loosened snow, earth, etc. suddenly and swiftly sliding down a mountain **2.** anything that comes suddenly in overwhelming numbers

avant-garde (a voṇ′gärd′) *n.* [Fr.] the leaders in new movements, esp. in the arts —*adj.* of such movements, ideas, etc. —**avant′-gard′ism** *n.*

avarice (av′ər is) *n.* [< L. *avere*, to desire] greed for riches —**avaricious** (av′ə rish′əs) *adj.*

avast (ə väst′) *interj.* [< Du. *houd vast*, hold fast] *Naut.* stop! cease! halt!

avatar (av′ə tär′) *n.* [Sans. *avatāra*, descent] *Hinduism* a god's coming down in bodily form to earth

avaunt (ə vônt′) *interj.* [< L. *ab*, from + *ante*, before] [Archaic] begone! go away!

avdp. avoirdupois

ave (ä′vā, -vē) *interj.* [L., be well] **1.** hail! **2.** farewell! —*n.* [A-] the prayer AVE MARIA

Ave., ave.

Ave Maria (ä′vä mə rē′ə, -vē) [L. (Luke 1:28)] **1.** "Hail, Mary," the first words of a prayer to the Virgin Mary used in the Roman Catholic Church **2.** this prayer

avenge (ə venj′) *vt., vi.* **avenged′, aveng′-ing** [< L. *ad*, to + *vindicare*, claim] **1.** to get revenge for (an injury, etc.) **2.**

to take vengeance on behalf of —**aveng'-er** *n.*

avenue (av'ə nyōō') *n.* [see ADVENT] 1. a road, path, or drive, often bordered with trees 2. a way of approach 3. a street, esp. a wide, principal one

aver (ə vur') *vt.* **averred', aver'ring** [< L. *ad*, to + *verus*, true] 1. to declare to be true; affirm 2. *Law* to state formally; assert —**aver'ment** *n.*

average (av'ər ij) *n.* [< Fr. < It. < Ar. *'awar*, damaged goods; sense development from *n.* 3] 1. the usual or normal kind, amount, etc. 2. the result obtained by dividing the sum of two or more quantities by the number of quantities 3. *Marine Law a*) loss incurred by damage to a ship *b*) division of such a loss among the interested parties —*adj.* 1. usual; ordinary 2. being a numerical average —*vi.* **-aged, -aging** to be or amount to on the average —*vt.* 1. to calculate the average of 2. to do, take, etc. on the average —**average out** to arrive at an average eventually —**on the** (or an) **average** as an average quantity, rate, etc. —**av'er-ageness** *n.*

averse (ə vurs') *adj.* [see AVERT] not willing; reluctant; opposed (*to*) —**averse'-ly** *adv.* —**averse'ness** *n.*

aversion *n.* 1. a strong dislike; antipathy 2. the object arousing such dislike

avert (ə vurt') *vt.* [< L. *a-*, from + *vertere*, turn] 1. to turn away [*avert* one's eyes] 2. to keep from happening; prevent [to *avert* a catastrophe]

Avesta (ə ves'tə) *n.* [< Per.] the sacred writings of Zoroastrianism —**Aves'tan** *adj., n.*

aviary (āv'yər ē) *n.,* pl. **-aries** [< L. *avis*, bird] a large cage or building for keeping many birds

aviation (ā'vē ā'shən) *n.* [< L. *avis*, bird] the science of flying aircraft

aviator (ā'vē āt'ər) *n.* an aeroplane pilot; flier

avid (av'id) *adj.* [< L. *avere*, to desire] 1. greedy [*avid* for power] 2. eager [an *avid* reader] —**avidity** (ə vid'ə tē) *n.* —**av'-idly** *adv.*

avocado (av'ə kä'dō) *n.,* pl. **-dos** [< MexSp.] a pear-shaped tropical fruit with yellow, buttery flesh

avocation (av'ə kä'shən) *n.* [< L. *ab-,* away + *vocare,* call] something one does in addition to one's regular work; hobby —**av'oca'tional** *adj.*

avocet (av'ə set') *n.* [< Fr. < It.] a long-legged wading bird with a slender bill that curves upwards

avoid (ə void') *vt.* [< OFr. *esvuidier,* to empty] 1. to keep away from; shun 2. to keep from happening 3. to make void; annul (a plea, etc. in law) —**avoid'able** *adj.* —**avoid'ably** *adv.* —**avoid'ance** *n.*

avoirdupois (av'ər də poiz') *n.* [< OFr. *aveir de peis,* goods having weight] *same as* AVOIRDUPOIS WEIGHT

avoirdupois weight a system of weights based on a pound of 16 ounces

avouch (ə vouch') *vt.* [see ADVOCATE] 1.

to vouch for; guarantee 2. to declare the truth of; affirm 3. to acknowledge openly; avow —**avouch'ment** *n.*

avow (ə vou') *vt.* [see ADVOCATE] to declare openly; acknowledge —**avow'al** *n.* —**avowed'** *adj.* —**avowedly** (ə vou'id lē) *adv.* —**avow'er** *n.*

avuncular (ə vuŋ'kyoo lər) *adj.* [< L. *avunculus,* maternal uncle] of or like an uncle

await (ə wāt') *vt.* [< ONormFr. *a-,* to + *waitier,* wait] 1. to wait for 2. to be in store for —*vi.* to wait

awake (ə wāk') *vt.,* *vi.* **awoke', awok'-en,** or **awaked', awak'ing** [< OE. *awacan*] 1. to rouse from sleep; wake 2. to rouse from inactivity —*adj.* 1. not asleep 2. active or alert

awaken (ə wāk'ən) *vt., vi.* to wake up; rouse —**awak'ener** *n.*

awakening *n., adj.* 1. (*a*) waking up 2. (an) arousing, as of impulses, interest, etc.

award (ə wôrd') *vt.* [< ONormFr.] 1. to give as the result of judging, as in a contest 2. to give by the decision of a law court or arbitrator —*n.* 1. something awarded; prize 2. a decision, as by a judge or arbitrator

aware (ə wāər') *adj.* [< OE. *wær,* cautious] knowing or realizing; conscious; informed —**aware'ness** *n.*

awash (ə wosh') *adv., adj.* 1. just above the surface of the water and washed over by it 2. flooded with water

away (ə wā') *adv.* [< OE. *on,* on + *weg,* way] 1. from any given place; off [to run *away*] 2. in another place or direction [look *away*] 3. far [*away* behind] 4. off; aside 5. from one's possession [give it *away*] 6. out of existence [to fade *away*] 7. at once [fire *away*] 8. without stopping [to work *away* all night] —*adj.* 1. absent; gone 2. at a distance [a mile *away*] 3. *Sport* played on an opponent's ground [an *away* match] —*n. Sport* a game played on an opponent's ground —*interj.* 1. begone! 2. let's go! —**away with** 1. take away 2. go or come away —**do away with** 1. to get rid of 2. to kill

awe (ô) *n.* [< ON. *agi*] a mixed feeling of reverence, fear, and wonder, caused by something sublime, etc. —*vt.* **awed, aw'-ing** to inspire awe in; fill with awe —**stand** (or **be) in awe of** to respect and fear

aweigh (ə wā') *adj.* *Naut.* clearing the bottom; being weighed : said of an anchor

awesome (ô'səm) *adj.* inspiring or showing awe

awe-struck (ô'struk') *adj.* filled with awe or wonder

awful (ô'fəl) *adj.* [see AWE] 1. [Colloq.] *a*) very bad, unpleasant, etc. *b*) great [an *awful* bore] 2. causing fear; terrifying 3. inspiring awe —**aw'fulness** *n.*

awfully *adv.* 1. [Colloq.] badly 2. [Colloq.] extremely 3. in a way to inspire awe

awhile (ə wīl') *adv.* for a while; for a short time

awkward (ôk'wərd) *adj.* [< ON. *ǫfugr,*

turned backwards + OE. -*weard*, -WARD]
1. clumsy; bungling **2.** unwieldy **3.**
inconvenient; uncomfortable **4.** embarrassed or embarrassing **5.** not easy to
deal with; requiring tact *[* an *awkward* situation *]* —**awk′wardly** *adv.*

awl (ôl) *n.* [< OE. æl, *awel*] a small,
pointed tool for making holes in wood,
leather, etc.

AWN

awn (ôn) *n.* [ON. ǫgn, chaff] the bristly
fibres on a head of barley, oats, etc. —**awned**
adj.

awning (ô′niŋ) *n.* [< ?] a structure
of canvas, metal, etc. extended before a
window, etc. as a protection from sun
or rain

awoke (əwōk′) *alt. pt. & occas. pp. of*
AWAKE

awoken (əwōk′′n) *occas. pp. of* AWAKE

AWOL, awol (ā′wol′) *adj.* [*a(bsent)*
w(ith)o(ut) *l(eave)*] *Mil.* absent without
leave, but without intention of deserting

awry (ərī′) *adv., adj.* [< a- (OE. *on*)
on, + WRY] **1.** with a twist to a side;
askew **2.** wrong; amiss *[* our plans went
awry]

axe (aks) *n., pl.* **ax′es** [OE. *eax*, *æx*]
a tool with a long handle and a bladed
head, for chopping wood, etc. —*vt.* axed,
ax′ing **1.** to trim, split, etc. with an
axe **2.** a) to dismiss (employees) b) to
reduce; restrict (expenditure, etc.) —**get**
the axe [Colloq.] to be discharged from
one's job —**have an axe to grind** [Colloq.]
to have an object of one's own to promote

axes¹ (ak′siz) *n. pl. of* AXE

axes² (ak′sēz) *n. pl. of* AXIS¹

axial (ak′sē əl) *adj.* **1.** of, like, or forming
an axis **2.** round or along an axis —**ax′i-**
ally *adv.*

axil (ak′sil) *n.* [< L. *axilla*, armpit] the
upper angle between a leaf, etc. and the
stem from which it grows

axiom (ak′sē əm) *n.* [< Gr. *axios*, worthy]
1. a statement widely accepted as true

2. an established principle of a science,
art, etc. **3.** a statement that needs no
proof because its truth is obvious

axiomatic (ak′sē ə mat′ik) *adj.* **1.** like
an axiom; self-evident **2.** full of axioms
—**ax′iomat′ically** *adv.*

axis (ak′sis) *n., pl.* **ax′es** [L.] **1.** a
real or imaginary straight line on which
an object rotates or is regarded as rotating
2. a central line or lengthwise structure
around which the parts of a thing, system,
etc. are evenly arranged **3.** a straight
line for reference, as in a graph —**the**
Axis Germany and Italy, and later Japan
as allies in World War II

axle (ak′s′l) *n.* [< ff.] **1.** a rod on which
a wheel turns, or one connected to a
wheel so that they turn together **2.** a
bar connecting opposite wheels, as of a
vehicle

axletree (ak′s′l trē′) *n.* [< ON. ǫxull,
axle + *tre*, beam] a bar connecting
two opposite wheels of a wagon, etc.

Axminster (aks′min stər) *n.* [<
Axminster, in Devon] a type of carpet
with a cut pile

axolotl (ak′sə lot′′l) *n.* [< Nahuatl, water
toy] a salamander of Mexico and the
W U.S.

ayah (ī′yə) *n.* [< Hindi < Port. *aia*,
governess] a native nursemaid or lady's
maid in India, esp. formerly

ayatollah (ī′ə tol′ə) *n.* [< Per. < Ar.]
one of a class of Islamic religious leaders

aye¹ (ā) *adv.* [ON. *ei*] [Poet.] always;
ever: also sp. **ay**

aye² (ī) *adv.* [< ? prec.] yes; yea —*n.*
an affirmative vote or voter Also sp. **ay**

Ayrshire (āar′shər) *n.* [the former Scot.
county] any of a breed of brown and
white dairy cattle

azalea (əzāl′ē ə) *n.* [< Gr. *azaleos*, dry]
a shrub allied to the rhododendron, having
variously coloured flowers and leaves that
are usually shed in the autumn

azimuth (az′ə məth) *n.* [< Ar. *al*, the
+ *samt*, path] *Astron., Surveying*, etc.
distance in angular degrees in a clockwise
direction from the north point or, in the
Southern Hemisphere, south point —**az′i-**
muth′al (-muth′əl) *adj.*

Aztec (az′tek) *n.* [< *Aztatlán*, their
legendary place of origin] **1.** *pl.* **-tecs,**
-tec a member of a people who lived
in Mexico before the conquest by Cortés
in 1519 **2.** their language, usually called
Nahuatl —*adj.* of the Aztecs

azure (azh′ər) *adj.* [OFr. < Ar. < Per.
lāzhuward, lapis lazuli] of the colour
of a clear sky; sky-blue —*n.* **1.** sky-blue
or any similar blue **2.** [Poet.] the blue sky

B

B, b (bē) *n.*, *pl.* **B's, b's** 1. the second letter of the English alphabet 2. *a symbol for* the second in a sequence or group

B (bē) *n.* 1. *Cinema* designating a supporting film 2. *Music* the seventh tone in the ascending scale of C major

B 1. *Chess* bishop 2. *Chem.* boron

B. 1. Baron 2. Bible 3. British

B., b. 1. bachelor 2. bacillus 3. *Music* bass 4. bay 5. book 6. born 7. brother

b. *Cricket* 1. bowled 2. bye

Ba *Chem.* barium

B.A. [L. *Baccalaureus Artium*] Bachelor of Arts

baa (bä) *n.* [echoic] the cry of a sheep or goat; bleat

B.A.A. British Airports Authority

Baal (bā′əl) *n.*, *pl.* **Ba′alim** (-im) 1. an ancient Semitic fertility god 2. a false god; idol —**Ba′alism** *n.*

baas (bäs) *n.* in South Africa, a word for boss, used esp. by nonwhites and coloureds when addressing a European overseer, etc.

baaskap (bäs′kap′) *n.* [< BAAS + Afrik. *skap*, ship] in South Africa, control of nonwhites by whites

baba (bä′bä) *n.* [Fr.] a sponge cake saturated in spirits and served as a dessert [a rum *baba*]

babalas (bab′ə las′) *n.* [< Zulu *ibhabhalasi*] [S Afr.] a hangover

Babbitt metal (bab′it) [< I. *Babbitt*] a soft alloy of tin, copper, and antimony, used to reduce friction in bearings, etc.

babble (bab′'l) *vi.* **-bled, -bling** [echoic] 1. to make incoherent sounds, as a baby does 2. to talk foolishly or too much 3. to make a low, bubbling sound —*vt.* to say indistinctly or incoherently —*n.* 1. confused, incoherent vocal sounds 2. foolish or meaningless talk 3. a low, bubbling sound —**bab′bler** *n.*

babe (bāb) *n.* 1. a baby 2. a naive or helpless person 3. [Chiefly U.S. Slang] a young woman

babel (bā′b'l) *n.* [< the city in the Bible: Gen. 11:1-9] [also **B-**] 1. a confusion of voices, languages, or sounds 2. a place of such confusion

BABOON
(90-150 cm long, including tail)

baboon (bə bōōn′) *n.* [< OFr. *babuin*, ape, fool] any of various large and fierce, short-tailed monkeys of Africa and Arabia, having a doglike snout and cheek pouches —**baboon′ery** *n.*

baby (bā′bē) *n.*, *pl.* **-bies** [ME. *babi*] 1. a very young child; infant 2. one who behaves like an infant 3. a very young animal 4. the youngest or smallest in a group 5. [Colloq.] favourite scheme; responsibility —*adj.* 1. of or for an infant 2. extremely young 3. small of its kind —*vt.* **-bied, -bying** to treat like a baby —**be left holding the baby** to be left to take the responsibility —**ba′byish** *adj.* —**ba′bylike′** *adj.*

baby bonus in Canada, a regular government payment to parents of children up to a certain age

baby grand a small grand piano

Babylonian (bab′ə lō′nē ən) *n.* an inhabitant of ancient Babylon or Babylonia —*adj.* of ancient Babylonia

baby-sit (bā′bē sit′) *vi.*, *vt.* **-sat′, -sit′-ting** to act as a baby sitter (to)

baby sitter one who takes care of a child while the parents are out

B.A.C. British Aircraft Corporation

baccalaureate (bak′ə lôr′ē ət) *n.* [< ML. *baccalaris*, young nobleman seeking to become a knight] the degree of Bachelor of Arts (or Science, etc.)

baccarat, baccara (bak′ə rä′) *n.* [Fr. < ?] a gambling game played with cards

bacchanal (bak′ə nəl) *n.* 1. a worshipper of Bacchus 2. a drunken carouser 3. a drunken orgy —*adj.* of Bacchus or his worship

Bacchanalia (bak′ə nā′lē ə) *n.pl.* 1. an ancient Roman festival honouring Bacchus 2. [**b-**] a drunken party; orgy —**bac′chana′-lian** *adj.*, *n.*

bacchant (bak′ənt) *n.*, *pl.* **-chants, -chan′-tes** (-kan′tēz) 1. a priest or worshipper of Bacchus 2. a drunken carouser —**bac-chante** (-kan′tē) *n.fem.* —**bacchan′tic** *adj.*

Bacchic (bak′ik) *adj.* [< *Bacchus*, ancient Gr. & Rom. god of wine and revelry] *same as* BACCHANAL

baccy (bak′ē) *n.* Colloq. clipped form of TOBACCO

bachelor (bach′əl ər) *n.* [see BACCALAUREATE] 1. a man who has not married 2. a person who is a BACHELOR OF ARTS (or SCIENCE, etc.) —*adj.* of or for a bachelor —**bach′elorhood′** *n.*

bachelor flat a small flat suitable for a person living alone

bachelor girl an unmarried young woman who leads an independent life

Bachelor of Arts (or **Science**, etc.)

1. a degree given by a college or university **2.** one who has this degree
bachelor's button a plant like the buttercup, having flowers shaped like buttons
bacillary (bə sil′ər ē) *adj.* [see ff.] **1.** rod-shaped: also **bacilliform** (bə sil′ə fôrm′) **2.** consisting of rodlike structures **3.** of, like, or caused by bacilli
bacillus (bə sil′əs) *n., pl.* **-cil′li** [< L. *baculus*, stick] **1.** any of the rod-shaped bacteria **2.** [*usually pl.*] loosely, any of the bacteria, esp. those causing disease
back (bak) *n.* [OE. *bæc*] **1.** the rear part of the body from the nape of the neck to the end of the spine **2.** the backbone **3.** the part that supports or fits the back **4.** the rear part of anything **5.** the part that is less often used, seen, etc. **6.** *Sports* a defensive player or position in many different games —*adj.* **1.** at the rear **2.** of or for a time in the past [*back* pay] **3.** backward; reversed —*adv.* **1.** at, to, or towards the rear **2.** to or towards a former condition, time, etc. **3.** in concealment **4.** in return [to pay one *back*] —*vt.* **1.** to cause to move backwards (often with *up*) **2.** to stand behind **3.** to support or help **4.** to bet on **5.** to provide with a back or backing —*vi.* **1.** to go backwards **2.** to shift anticlockwise: said of the wind —**at the back of one's mind** dimly recalled but not receiving one's conscious attention —**back and forth** to and fro —**back down** to withdraw from a position, etc. —**back out (of)** **1.** to withdraw from an enterprise **2.** to break a promise or engagement —**back up** to support —**be (flat) on one's back** to be ill, bedridden, etc. —**behind one's back** without one's knowledge or consent —**get (or put) one's back up** to make or be obstinate —**go back on** [Colloq.] **1.** to betray **2.** to fail to keep (a promise, etc.) —**put one's back into it** apply oneself energetically to a task
backbencher (bak′ben′chər) *n.* a member of parliament who is not a leader in his party
backbite *vt., vi.* **-bit′**, **-bit′ten**, **-bit′ing** to slander (an absent person) —**back′bit′-er** *n.*
back-blocks *n.pl.* the far interior of Australia and New Zealand
backboard *n.* **1.** a board that forms or supports the back of something **2.** *Basketball* a flat surface just behind the basket
back boiler a tank behind a fireplace for heating water
backbone *n.* **1.** the spine **2.** main support **3.** willpower, courage, etc.
backbreaking *adj.* very tiring
back chat [Colloq.] saucy or insolent retorts
back-comb *vt.* to fluff (the hair) by brushing or combing the hair ends towards the scalp
back country [Aust.] remote and sparsely inhabited areas
backdate (bak′dāt′) *vt.* **-dat′ed**, **-dat′-**

ing to date or put into effect from before the actual date [a *backdated* pay rise]
backdoor *adj.* secret; underhand
backdrop *n.* a curtain hung at the back of a stage, often a painted scene: also **backcloth**
backer *n.* **1.** a patron; supporter **2.** one who bets on a contestant
backfire (bak′fīr′) *n.* a premature explosion in a cylinder of an internal-combustion engine —*vi.* **-fired′**, **-fir′ing** **1.** to explode as a backfire **2.** to go awry; boomerang
back-formation *n.* a word formed from, but looking as if it were the base of, another word (Ex.: *burgle* from *burglar*)
backgammon *n.* [BACK + ME. *gammen*, game] a game for two people, with pieces moved as dice are thrown
background *n.* **1.** the part of a scene towards the back **2.** an unimportant position **3.** *a)* one's social environment *b)* the whole of one's study, training, and experience **4.** events or conditions leading up to something
background music sound effects or music accompanying action, as in films
backhand *n.* **1.** handwriting that slants backwards, up to the left **2.** a stroke, as in tennis, with the back of the hand turned forward —*adj.* performed with a backhand —*adv.* with a backhand
backhanded *adj.* **1.** *same as* BACKHAND **2.** indirect or sarcastic; equivocal —*adv.* with a backhand
backhander *n.* **1.** a blow with the back of the hand **2.** [Slang] a bribe
backing *n.* **1.** something forming a back for support or strength **2.** support given to a person or cause **3.** those giving such support **4.** musical accompaniment, esp. for a pop singer
backlash *n.* **1.** a quick, sharp recoil **2.** a sudden, strong reaction, as to a political or social movement or development
backlog *n.* **1.** a reserve **2.** an accumulation of unfilled orders, etc. —*vi., vt.* **-logged′**, **-log′ging** to accumulate as a backlog
backmarker *n.* **1.** a competitor in a race who concedes an initial advantage to his opponents **2.** a competitor who is behind the others at any stage
back number **1.** an old issue of a periodical **2.** [Colloq.] an old-fashioned person or thing
backpack *n.* *same as* RUCKSACK —*vi.* to go hiking with a backpack —**back′pack′-ing** *n.*
backpedal (bak′ped′′l) *vi.* **-ped′alled**, **-ped′alling** **1.** to press backwards on bicycle pedals in braking **2.** to move backwards **3.** to retreat from an opinion
backroom *adj.* doing important research without any publicity and often in secret
back seat a secondary or inconspicuous position
back-seat driver a passenger in a motor car who offers unwanted advice about driving

backside (bak′sīd′) *n.* 1. the back part 2. the rump

backslide (bak′slīd′) *vi.* -slid′, -slid′ing to slide backwards in morals or religious enthusiasm —back′slid′er *n.*

backspace *vi.* -spaced′, -spac′ing to move a typewriter carriage back a space at a time

backspin *n.* backward spin given to a propelled ball, etc. that causes it, upon hitting a surface, to change its normal direction

backstage *adv., adj.* in the wings or dressing rooms of a theatre

backstairs *adj.* involving intrigue or scandal

backstroke *n.* a stroke made by a swimmer lying face upwards —*vi.* -stroked′, -strok′ing to perform a backstroke

back-to-back (bak′tə bak′) *adj.* 1. of houses built with backs adjoining 2. [Colloq.] one after another

backtrack *vi.* 1. to return by the same path 2. to withdraw from a position, etc.

backup, back-up *adj.* 1. alternate or auxiliary 2. supporting —*n.* 1. an accumulation because of a stoppage 2. a support or help

backward *adv.* 1. towards the back 2. with the back foremost 3. in reverse 4. into the past 5. from a better to a worse state Also **back′wards** —*adj.* 1. turned towards the rear or in the opposite way 2. hesitant or shy 3. retarded —**bend (or lean) over backwards** 1. to try earnestly (to please, pacify, etc.) 2. to offset a tendency, bias, etc. by an effort in the opposite direction —**back′wardness** *n.*

backwash *n.* water or air moved backwards,′as by a ship, propeller, etc.

backwater *n.* 1. stagnant water in a stream 2. a place where there is no progress —*adj.* stagnant; backward

backwoods *n.pl.* [*occas.* with *sing. v.*] heavily wooded, remote areas —*adj.* in, from, or like the backwoods: also **back′-wood**—**back′woods′man** *n.*

backyard (bak′yärd′) *n.* 1. a yard or area of enclosed ground behind a house 2. somewhere within easy reach

bacon (bāk′'n) *n.* [< OS.] cured meat from the back or sides of a pig —**bring home the bacon** [Colloq.] 1. to earn a living 2. to succeed; win

Baconian (bā kō′nē ən) *adj.* of Francis Bacon, 16th cent. Eng. philosopher, or his system of philosophy —*n.* an adherent of this philosophy

bacteria (bak tēar′ē ə) *n.pl., sing.* -**rium** [< Gr. *baktron,* staff] one-celled microorganisms which have no chlorophyll and multiply by simple division: some cause diseases, but others are necessary for fermentation, etc. —**bacte′rial** *adj.* —**bacte′rially** *adv.*

bacteriology (bak tēar′ē ol′ə jē) *n.* the study of bacteria, as in medicine, or for agriculture, etc. —**bacte′riol′ogist** *n.*

Bactrian camel (bak′trē ən) [< *Bactria,*

ancient country in W Asia] a camel with two humps, native to C Asia

bad[1] (bad) *adj.* **worse, worst** [ME.] 1. not good; not as it should be 2. defective in quality 3. unfit 4. unfavourable 5. rotten; spoiled 6. incorrect; faulty 7. a) wicked; immoral b) mischievous 8. harmful 9. severe 10. ill —*n.* anything bad —**not bad** [Colloq.] good; fairly good: also **not half bad, not so bad** —**bad′ness** *n.*

bad[2] *archaic pt. of* BID

bad blood a feeling of (mutual) enmity

bad debt a debt which is unpaid and not collectable

bade (bad; *occas.* bād) *alt. pt. of* BID

bad egg [Slang] a mean or dishonest person: also **bad actor, bad apple, bad hat, bad lot,** etc.

badge (baj) *n.* [ME. *bage*] 1. an emblem worn to show rank, etc. 2. any distinguishing mark

badger (baj′ər) *n.* [< ?] a carnivorous, burrowing mammal with thick, short legs, and long claws on the forefeet —*vt.* to nag at

badinage (bad′ə näzh′) *n.* [Fr. < ML. *badare,* to gape] playful, teasing talk; banter —*vt.* -naged′, -nag′ing to tease with playful talk

badly (bad′lē) *adv.* 1. in a bad manner 2. [Colloq.] very much; greatly

badminton (bad′min tən) *n.* [< *Badminton,* estate of the Duke of Beaufort] a game in which a shuttlecock is batted back and forth with rackets across a net

baffle (baf′'l) *vt.* -fled, -fling [16th-c. Scot.] 1. to confuse; puzzle; confound 2. to hinder; impede —*n.* a wall or screen to deflect the flow of liquids, gases, etc., or to check sound waves —**baf′flement** *n.* —**baf′fler** *n.* —**baf′fling** *adj.*

bag (bag) *n.* [ON. *baggi*] 1. a nonrigid container made of fabric, paper, etc., with an opening at the top that can be closed 2. a piece of hand luggage 3. a woman's handbag 4. *a)* a container for game *b)* the amount of game caught or killed 5. an udder or sac 6. [*pl.*] [Colloq.] plenty 7. [Slang] an unattractive woman —*vt.* **bagged, bag′ging** 1. to make bulge 2. to capture 3. to kill in hunting 4. [Slang] to get —*vi.* 1. to swell 2. to hang loosely —**bag and baggage** [Colloq.] with all one's possessions —**in the bag** [Slang] having its success assured —**bags** (I)! [Slang] I claim it! it's mine!: used esp. by children

bagatelle (bag′ə tel′) *n.* [< It. *bagatella* < ML. *baga,* bag] 1. something of little value 2. a game somewhat like billiards 3. a short musical composition

baggage (bag′ij) *n.* [< ML. *baga,* bag] 1. the bags, etc. of a traveller 2. the supplies and gear of an army 3. *a)* [ult. < Ar. *bagija,* adulteress] formerly, a prostitute *b)* a saucy girl

baggy *adj.* **bag′gier, bag′giest** 1. puffed in a baglike way 2. hanging loosely —**bag′-gily** *adv.* —**bag′giness** *n.*

bagnio (bän′yō) *n., pl.* -**ios** [< Gr. *balaneion,* bath] a house of prostitution; brothel

BAGPIPE

bagpipe (bag′pīp′) *n.* [*often pl.*] a shrill-toned musical instrument with a double-reed, fingered pipe and drone pipes, all sounded by air forced from a leather bag —**bag′pip′er** *n.*

bah (bä) *interj.* an exclamation expressing scorn or disgust

Bahaism (bə hä′iz'm) *n.* [Ar. *ba-hā*, splendour] a modern religion, developed orig. in Iran, that advocates universal brotherhood, etc. —**Baha′ist** *n., adj.*

baie dankie (bī′ə daŋ′kē) *interj.* [S Afr.] thank you very much

bail¹ (bāl) *n.* [< L. *bajulus,* porter] 1. money deposited with the court to obtain the release of an arrested person until his trial 2. the release thus brought about 3. the person giving bail —*vt.* 1. to have (an arrested person) set free by giving bail 2. to help out of financial or other difficulty (often with *out*)

bail² *n.* [see prec.] a bucket for removing water from a boat —*vi., vt.* 1. to remove water from (a boat) 2. to ladle out (water, etc.) Also **bale** —**bail out** 1. to make a parachute jump from an aircraft 2. [Colloq.] to help out or rescue —**bail′er** *n.*

bail³ *n.* [< ON. *beygla*] a hooped-shaped handle for a bucket, etc.

bail⁴ *n.* [ult. < L. *bajulus,* porter] 1. *Cricket* either of two pieces of wood laid across the three stumps to form a wicket 2. [*pl.*] formerly, an outer fortification made of stakes

bailey (bā′lē) *n.* [ME. *baili,* BAIL⁴] the outer wall or court of a medieval castle

Bailey bridge (bā′lē) [< Sir D. C. *Bailey*] *Mil. Engineering* a portable bridge consisting of a series of prefabricated steel sections

bailie (bā′lē) *n.* [Scot.: see ff.] in Scotland, a municipal councillor who serves as a magistrate

bailiff (bā′lif) *n.* [OFr.: see BAIL¹] 1. a sheriff's officer who serves writs, etc. 2. an overseer or steward of an estate 3. [Chiefly U.S.] a court officer who guards jurors, etc.

bailiwick (bā′lə wik) *n.* [ME. < *bailif,* bailiff + OE. *wic,* village] 1. a bailiff's district 2. [Chiefly U.S.] one's particular area of activity, authority, etc.

bain-marie (ban mà rē′) *n., pl.* **bains-marie′** (ban-) [Fr. < ML., bath of Maria] an open pan of hot water in which other containers are placed to warm

bairn (bāərn) *n.* [< OE. *beran,* to bear] [Scot.] a child

bait (bāt) *vt.* [< ON. *bīta,* bite] 1. to put food, etc. on (a hook or trap) so as to lure animals or fish 2. to torment or harass with unprovoked attacks 3. to set attacking dogs against for sport —*n.* 1. food, etc. put on a hook or trap as a lure 2. any lure; enticement —**bait′er** *n.*

baize (bāz) *n.* [< L. *badius,* chestnut-brown] a feltlike, thick woollen cloth used as a covering

bake (bāk) *vt.* **baked, bak′ing** [OE. *bacan*] 1. to cook (food) by dry heat, esp. in an oven 2. to dry and harden (esp. glazed stoneware) by heat —*vi.* 1. to bake bread, etc. 2. to become baked

baked beans cooked haricot beans in tomato sauce

Bakelite (bā′kə līt′) [< L. H. *Baekeland*] *Trademark* a synthetic resin and plastic

baker (bāk′ər) *n.* one whose work or business is baking bread, etc.

baker's dozen thirteen

bakery *n., pl.* **-eries** a place where bread, cakes, etc. are baked or sold

baking powder a leavening agent containing sodium bicarbonate and an acid substance, such as cream of tartar

baksheesh, bakshish (bak′shēsh) *n.* [< Per. *bakhshidan,* give] in Turkey, India, etc., a tip or gratuity

bal. balance

Balaklava helmet (bal′ə klä′və) [< *Balaklava,* in the Crimea] a woollen covering for the whole head, leaving only the face exposed

balalaika (bal′ə lī′kə) *n.* [Russ.] a Russian stringed instrument somewhat like a guitar

balance (bal′əns) *n.* [OFr. < L. *bis,* twice + *lanx,* scale] 1. an instrument for weighing, esp. one with two matched pans hanging from either end of a poised lever 2. a state of equilibrium in weight, value, etc. 3. bodily or mental stability 4. the pleasing harmony of various elements in a work of art 5. a weight, force, etc. that counteracts another or causes equilibrium 6. *a)* equality of debits and credits in an account *b)* the difference between credits and debits 7. the amount still owed after a partial settlement 8. a remainder 9. *same as* BALANCE WHEEL —*vt.* **-anced, -ancing** 1. to weigh in or as in a balance 2. to compare as to relative value, etc. 3. to counterpoise or counteract; offset 4. to put or keep in a state of equilibrium 5. to make or be equal to in weight, force, etc. 6. *a)* to find any difference between the debit and credit sides of (an account) or to equalize them *b)* to settle (an account) —*vi.* 1. to be in equilibrium 2. to be equal in value, weight, etc. 3. to have the credit and debit sides equal —**in the balance** in a critical, undecided state —**on balance** considering everything —**bal′anceable** *adj.* —**bal′ancer** *n.*

balance of (international) payments

a balance for a given period showing an excess or deficit in total payments of all kinds between one country and another

balance of power an even distribution of military and economic power among nations

balance of trade the difference in value between the imports and exports of a country

balance sheet a summarized statement showing the financial status of a business

balance wheel a wheel that swings back and forth to regulate the movement of a timepiece, etc.

balata (bal′ə tə) *n.* [Sp. < Tupi] the dried milky sap of a tropical American tree, used commercially

balcony (bal′kə nē) *n.*, *pl.* **-nies** [< It., akin to OHG. *balcho*, beam] 1. a platform projecting from a building and enclosed by a balustrade 2. an upper floor of seats in a theatre, etc., often jutting out over the main floor

bald (bôld) *adj.* [ME. *balled* < ?] 1. lacking hair on the scalp 2. not covered by natural growth 3. plain; blunt 4. worn, of a tyre 5. having white fur or feathers on the head, as some animals and birds —**bald′ly** *adv.*

balderdash (bôl′dər dash′) *n.* [< ?] nonsensical talk or writing

balding (bôl′fəl) *adj.* becoming bald

baldric (bôl′drik) *n.* [< OFr.] a belt worn over one shoulder and across the chest to support a sword, etc.

bale (bāl) *n.* [< OHG. *balla*, ball] a large bundle, as of cotton, hay, or straw, compressed and bound —*vt.* **baled, bal′-ing** to make into bales —**bal′er** *n.*

baleen (bə lēn′) *n.* [< L. *balaena*, whale] *same as* WHALEBONE

baleful (bāl′fəl) *adj.* harmful or evil; sinister —**bale′fully** *adv.* —**bale′fulness** *n.*

balk (bôk) *vi.* [OE. *balca*, bank] 1. to stop and refuse to move or act 2. to hesitate (*at*) —*vt.* 1. to miss or let slip by 2. to obstruct or thwart —*n.* 1. a roughly hewn piece of timber 2. a check, hindrance, etc. 3. a ridge of unploughed land between furrows

Balkan (bôl′kən) *adj.* of the countries of the Balkan Peninsula in SE Europe, their people, etc.

ball¹ (bôl) *n.* [ME. *bal*] 1. any round object; sphere; globe 2. a round or egg-shaped object used in various games 3. a throw of a ball 4. a solid missile for a cannon or firearm 5. a rounded part of the body 6. [*pl.*] [Vulg. Slang] the testicles —*vi., vt.* to form into a ball —*interj.* [*pl.*] a vulgar expression of contempt —**be on the ball** [Slang] to be alert —**get** (or **keep**) **the ball rolling** [Colloq.] to start (or maintain) some action —**have the ball at one's feet** [Colloq.] to have everything in one's favour —**play ball** [Colloq.] to cooperate

ball² *n.* [< LL. *ballare*, to dance] 1. a formal social dance 2. [Slang] an enjoyable time or experience

ballad (bal′əd) *n.* [< OFr. *ballade*, dancing song, ult. < LL. : see prec.] 1. a sentimental song with the same melody for each stanza 2. a song or poem that tells a story in short stanzas and simple words 3. a slow, sentimental popular song —**bal′ladeer′** *n.* —**bal′ladry** *n.*

ballade (ba läd′) *n.* [Fr. : see prec.] 1. a verse form with three stanzas of eight or ten lines each and an envoy of four or five lines 2. a romantic musical composition

BALL-AND-SOCKET JOINT

ball-and-socket joint a joint allowing limited movement in any direction

ballast (bal′əst) *n.* [< ODan. *bar, bare + last*, load] 1. anything heavy carried in a ship, vehicle, etc. to give stability 2. anything giving stability to character, human relations, etc. 3. crushed rock used to make a firm bed for railway sleepers —*vt.* to furnish with ballast

ball bearing 1. a bearing in which the moving parts revolve on freely rolling metal balls 2. any of these balls

ball boy *Sport* a person who retrieves balls, esp. in tennis

ball cock a device in a cistern which controls the flow of water by means of a floating ball and valve

ballerina (bal′ə rē′nə) *n.* [It. < LL. : see BALL²] a woman ballet dancer

ballet (bal′ā) *n.* [see BALL²] 1. an intricate group dance using pantomime and conventionalized movements to tell a story 2. a company of such dancers

balletomane (ba′let ō mān′) *n.* [BALLET + Fr. *manie*, mania] a ballet enthusiast —**bal′letoma′nia** *n.*

ballgame (bôl′gām) *n.* 1. [Colloq.] scene of action 2. [Colloq.] set of circumstances [*a different ballgame*]

ballista (bə lis′tə) *n.*, *pl.* **-tae** (-tē) [L. < Gr. *ballein*, to throw] a device used in ancient warfare to hurl heavy stones, etc.

ballistic missile a long-range missile guided automatically in flight, but free-falling at its target

ballistics (bə lis′tiks) *n.pl.* [*with sing. v.*] 1. the science dealing with the motion and impact of projectiles 2. the study of the effects of firing on a firearm or bullet, etc. —**ballis′tic** *adj.*

ballocks (bol′əks) *n.pl.* [< OE. *beallucas*, testicles] [Vulg. Slang] the testicles —*interj.* [Vulg. Slang] nonsense!

balloon (bə loon′) *n.* [< It. *palla*, ball] 1. a large, airtight bag that rises when filled with a gas lighter than air 2. such a bag with a car for passengers or instruments 3. an inflatable rubber bag, used as a toy —*vt.* to cause to swell like a balloon —*vi.* 1. to ride in a balloon 2. to swell —*adj.* like a balloon —**balloon'-ist** *n.*

ballot (bal'ət) *n.* [< It. *palla*, ball] 1. the democratic process of choosing or deciding according to the number of votes cast 2. the total number of votes cast 3. the actual vote or paper on which it is marked —*vi.* to decide by means of the ballot —**bal'loter** *n.*

ballot box a sealed container into which completed ballot papers are inserted

ballot paper a form on which a vote is marked

ball point pen a pen having instead of a point a small ball bearing

ballroom (bôl'rōōm') *n.* a large hall for dancing

ballroom dancing dancing in which two people dance as partners to a waltz, fox trot, etc.

balls-up (bôlz'up) *n.* [Vulg. Slang] a muddle or confusion

bally (bal'ē) *adj., adv.* a euphemism for BLOODY

ballyhoo (bal'ē hōō') *n.* [< ?] 1. loud talk 2. sensational advertising —*vt., vi.* -**hooed'**, -**hoo'ing** [Colloq.] to promote by sensational methods

balm (bäm) *n.* [< Gr. *balsamon*] 1. an aromatic resin obtained from certain trees and used as medicine; balsam 2. any fragrant ointment or oil 3. anything healing or soothing

balmy *adj.* -**ier**, -**iest** 1. soothing, pleasant, etc. 2. [var. of BARMY] [Slang] crazy or foolish —**balm'ily** *adv.* —**balm'iness** *n.*

baloney (bə lō'nē) *n.* [< ? *bologna*, sausage] [Slang] nonsense —*interj.* [Slang] nonsense!

B.A.L.P.A. (bal'pə) British Airline Pilots' Association

balsa (bol'sə) *n.* [Sp.] 1. a tropical American tree that yields an extremely light and buoyant wood used for rafts, etc. 2. a raft

balsam (bôl'səm) *n.* [see BALM] 1. an aromatic resin obtained from certain trees 2. any of various aromatic oils or fluids 3. anything healing or soothing 4. any of various trees that yield balsam —**balsamic** (bôl sam'ik) *adj.*

Baltic (bôl'tik) *adj.* 1. of the Baltic Sea 2. of the Baltic States —*n.* the Baltic Sea

baluster (bal'əs tər) *n.* [< Gr. *balaustion*, flower of the wild pomegranate: from resemblance in shape] any of the small posts supporting a stair rail

balustrade (bal'ə strād') *n.* a railing held up by balusters

bamboo (bam bōō') *n.* [Malay *bambu*] a treelike, tropical grass with springy, jointed, often hollow stems, used for furniture, canes, etc.

bamboozle (bam bōō'z'l) *vt.* -**zled**, -**zling** [< ?] 1. to deceive; cheat 2. to confuse —**bamboo'zlement** *n.*

ban (ban) *vt.* **banned**, **ban'ning** [OE. *bannan*, summon] to prohibit or forbid, as by official order —*n.* 1. a condemnation

by church authorities 2. an official prohibition 3. strong public disapproval

banal (bə näl') *adj.* [Fr.] dull because of overuse; trite —**banality** (bə nal'ə tē) *n.* —**banal'ly** *adv.*

BANANA

banana (bə nän'ə) *n.* [Sp. & Port. < native name in W Africa] 1. a treelike, tropical plant with large clusters of edible fruit 2. the narrow and somewhat curved fruit, having a sweet, creamy flesh and a yellow skin

banana oil a liquid acetate with a bananalike aroma, used in flavourings, etc.

banana republic any small country whose economy is controlled by foreign capital

band¹ (band) *n.* [ON.] 1. something that binds, ties together, etc., as a strip or ring of wood or metal 2. a stripe 3. a narrow strip of cloth used to line, decorate, etc. [*hatband*] 4. [*usually pl.*] two strips hanging in front from the neck, as part of certain academic or clerical dress 5. a division of a long-playing gramophone record 6. a specific range of frequencies, as in radio broadcasting 7. a belt to drive wheels or pulleys in machinery —*vt.* 1. to put a band on or round 2. to put schoolchildren into groups according to ability

band² *n.* [Fr. *bande*, troupe < Goth. *bandwa*, sign] 1. a group of people united for a common purpose 2. a group of musicians playing together —*vi., vt.* to unite for a common purpose (usually with *together*)

bandage (ban'dij) *n.* [Fr. < *bande*, a strip] a strip of cloth or other dressing used to bind or cover an injury —*vt.* -**aged**, -**aging** to put a bandage on

bandanna, bandana (ban dan'ə) *n.* [Hindi *bāndhnū*, method of dyeing] a large, coloured handkerchief, usually with a printed pattern

B & B, b. and b. bed and breakfast

bandbox (band'boks') *n.* a light box of wood or pasteboard to hold hats, collars, etc.

bandeau (ban'dō) *n., pl.* -**deaux** (-dōz) [Fr.] a narrow ribbon worn around the head

banderole, banderol (ban'də rōl') *n.* [Fr. < It.] 1. a narrow flag or pennant, as one attached to a lance 2. a ribbonlike scroll carrying an inscription

bandicoot (ban'di kōōt') *n.* [< Telugu, pig rat] 1. a large rat found in India and Ceylon 2. a ratlike animal of Australia that carries its young in a pouch

bandit (ban'dit) *n., pl.* **-dits, banditti** (ban dit'ē) [It. *bandito*] 1. a robber, esp. one who robs travellers 2. anyone who cheats, steals, etc. —**ban'ditry** *n.*

bandmaster (band'mäs'tər) *n.* the leader or conductor of a band, esp. a military or brass band

bandoleer, bandolier (ban'də lēar') *n.* [< Fr. < Sp. *banda*, scarf] a broad shoulder belt with pockets for carrying ammunition, etc.

band saw a power saw consisting of an endless, toothed steel belt running over pulleys

bandsman *n.* a member of a band of musicians

bandstand *n.* a platform for a band or orchestra, esp. outdoors

bandwagon *n.* a wagon for the band to ride in, as in a parade —**on the bandwagon** [Colloq.] on the popular or apparently winning side, as in an election

bandy[1] (ban'dē) *vt.* **-died, -dying** [< ?] 1. to exchange (words), as in arguing 2. to pass (gossip, etc.) about carelessly 3. to toss or hit (a ball, etc.) back and forth

bandy[2] *adj.* [< ?] bent or curved outwards

bandylegged *adj.* bowlegged

bane (bān) *n.* [OE. *bana*, slayer] 1. the cause of distress, death, or ruin 2. [Poet.] ruin 3. deadly poison: now obs. except in *ratsbane*, etc. —**bane'ful** *adj.*

bang[1] (baŋ) *vt.* [ON. *banga*, pound] to hit or shut noisily —*vi.* 1. to make a sharp, loud noise 2. to strike sharply (*against, into*, etc.) —*n.* 1. a hard blow or loud knock 2. a sudden, loud noise —*adv.* 1. hard and noisily 2. suddenly or exactly —**bang on** [Slang] absolutely right

bang[2] *vt.* [< ?] [Chiefly U.S.] to cut (hair) short and straight across

banger *n.* [< BANG[1]] [Colloq.] 1. a sausage 2. a noisy old car 3. a firework that explodes loudly

bangle (baŋ'g'l) *n.* [Hindi *bangrī*] a decorative bracelet, armlet, or anklet

banian (ban'yan) *n.* same as BANYAN

banish (ban'ish) *vt.* [< OFr. *banir*] 1. to send into exile 2. to dismiss —**ban'ishment** *n.*

banister (ban'əs tər) *n.* [< BALUSTER] 1. [often *pl.*] a railing and the balusters supporting it 2. this railing

banjo (ban'jō) *n., pl.* **-jos, -joes** [< U.S. pronun. of *bandore* < Gr. *pandoura*, musical instrument] a stringed musical instrument having a long neck and a circular body —**ban'joist** *n.*

bank[1] (baŋk) *n.* [< OHG. *bank*, bench] 1. a) an establishment for receiving, lending, or, sometimes, issuing money b) its building 2. the fund held, as by the dealer, in some gambling games 3. *Med.* any place for gathering and distributing blood or body parts —*vi.* to put money in or do business with a bank —*vt.* to deposit (money) in a bank —**bank on** [Colloq.] to depend on —**bank'able** *adj.*

bank[2] *n.* [< ON.] 1. a long mound or heap 2. a steep slope, as of a hill 3. a stretch of rising land at the edge of a stream, etc. 4. a shallow place, as in a sea 5. the sloping of an aircraft laterally on a turn —*vt.* 1. to cover (a fire) with ashes and fuel so that it will burn longer (sometimes with *up*) 2. to pile up so as to form a bank 3. to slope (a curve in a road, etc.) 4. to slope (an aircraft) laterally on a turn —*vi.* 1. to form a bank or banks 2. to bank an aircraft

bank[3] *n.* [< OHG. *bank*, bench] 1. a row or tier of objects eg. oars 2. a row of keys in a keyboard —*vt.* to arrange in a bank

bank account money deposited in a bank and subject to withdrawal by the depositor

bankbook *n.* the book in which the account of a depositor in a bank is recorded

bank card same as CHEQUE CARD

banker *n.* 1. one who owns or manages a bank 2. the keeper of the bank in some gambling games

bank holiday a day on which banks are closed by law and which is usually a general holiday

banking *n.* the business of a bank

bank manager the head of a local branch of a bank

bank note a promissory note issued by a bank, payable on demand : it is a form of paper money

Bank of Canada a central bank owned by the Canadian government, which issues bank notes, controls the amount of credit given by commercial banks, etc.

Bank of England the government bank responsible for keeping the country's gold reserves

bank rate the official rate at which the Bank of England will discount approved bills of exchange

bankrupt (baŋk'rupt) *n.* [< It. *banca*, bench + *rotta*, broken] a person legally declared unable to pay his debts: his property is divided among his creditors —*adj.* 1. that is a bankrupt 2. lacking in some quality [morally *bankrupt*] —*vt.* to make bankrupt —**bank'ruptcy** *n.*

banner (ban'ər) *n.* [< OFr. *baniere*] 1. a piece of cloth bearing a design, motto, etc. 2. a flag

banner headline a headline extending across a newspaper page

bannister (ban'əs tər) *n.* same as BANISTER

bannock (ban'ək) *n.* [< OE. *bannue*, cake] [Scot.] a flat cake of oatmeal or barley meal

banns (banz) *n.pl.* [see BAN[1]] the proclamation of an intended marriage

banquet (baŋ'kwit) *n.* [Fr. < It. *banca*, table] 1. a feast 2. a formal dinner —*vt.* to honour with a banquet —*vi.* to dine at a banquet —**ban'queter** *n.*

banshee (ban shē') *n.* [< Ir. *bean*, woman + *sith*, fairy] *Ir. & Scot. Folklore* a female spirit believed to wail outside a house to warn of an impending death in the family

bantam (ban'təm) *n.* [< *Bantam,* in Java] 1. [*often* B-] any of various dwarf varieties of breeds of domestic fowl 2. a small but aggressive person

bantamweight *n.* see BOXING AND WRESTLING WEIGHTS, table

banter (ban'tər) *vt.* [< ?] to tease in a playful way —*vi.* to exchange banter (*with* someone) —*n.* good-natured teasing —**ban'terer** *n.*

Bantu (ban'tōō') *n., pl.* **-tus, -tu** [Bantu *ba-ntu,* mankind] 1. a group of African languages including the majority of principal languages spoken from the equator to the Cape of Good Hope 2. [Derog.] a black speaker of a Bantu language

Bantustan (ban'tōō stän') *n.* [BANTU + Per. *stān,* place] [Derog.] in South Africa, black homeland, partially self-governing

bantubeer (ban'tōō bēər) *n.* in South Africa, a malted drink of partially fermented and germinated Kaffir corn

banyan (ban'yən) *n.* [from a tree of this kind under which the *banians* (Hindu merchants) had built a pagoda] an East Indian fig tree whose branches take root

baobab (bā'ō bab') *n.* [< EAfr. name] a tall tree of Africa and India, characterized by a thick trunk and angular branches

bap (bap) *n.* [< ?] [Chiefly Scot.] a soft bread roll

baptism (bap'tiz'm) *n.* [< Gr. *baptizein,* immerse] 1. the rite of admitting a person into a Christian church by dipping him in water or sprinkling water on him 2. any experience that initiates, tests, etc. —**baptis'mal** *adj.*

baptism of fire [see Matt. 3:11] any experience that tests one's courage, strength, etc. for the first time

Baptist (bap'tist) *n.* 1. John the Baptist 2. a member of a Protestant denomination holding that baptism should be only by immersion

baptize (bap tīz') *vt.* **-tized', -tiz'ing** 1. to administer baptism to 2. to purify; initiate 3. to christen

bar¹ (bär) *n.* [< ML. *barra,* barrier] 1. any piece of wood, metal, etc. longer than it is wide or thick, often used as a barrier, lever, etc. 2. an oblong piece [*bar* of soap] 3. anything that obstructs, hinders, or prevents 4. a strip, band, or broad line 5. the part of a law court where prisoners are brought to trial 6. a law court 7. lawyers collectively 8. *a)* a counter at which alcoholic drinks are served *b)* a place with such a counter 9. a part of a shop that offers a particular service [*heel bar*] 10. *Heraldry* a horizontal stripe on a shield or bearing 11. *Music a)* any of the vertical lines across a staff *b)* the notes or rests, or both, contained between two such lines —*vt.* **barred, bar'-ring** 1. to fasten as with a bar 2. to

obstruct; close 3. to oppose; prevent 4. to exclude 5. to mark with stripes —*prep.* excluding; excepting [the best, *bar* none] —**be called to the bar** to be admitted as a barrister —**behind bars** in prison

bar² *n.* [< Gr. *baros,* weight] a unit of pressure

barb (bärb) *n.* [< L. *barba,* beard] 1. a sharp point projecting away from the main point of a fishhook, arrow, etc. 2. a cutting remark 3. a beardlike growth near the mouth of certain animals —*vt.* to provide with a barb or barbs —**barbed** *adj.*

barbarian (bär bāər'ē ən) *n.* [see BARBAROUS] 1. a member of a ‚people with a civilization regarded as primitive, etc. 2. a coarse or unmannerly person 3. a savage, cruel person —*adj.* uncivilized, cruel, rude, etc. —**barbar'ian-ism** *n.*

barbaric (bär bar'ik) *adj.* 1. uncivilized; primitive 2. wild, crude, etc. —**barbar'i-cally** *adv.*

barbarism (bär'bər iz'm) *n.* 1. the state of being primitive or uncivilized 2. a barbarous act, custom, etc. 3. *a)* the use of words and expressions not standard in a language *b)* a word or expression of this sort (Ex.: "youse" for "you")

barbarity (bär bar'ə tē) *n., pl.* **-ties** 1. cruel or brutal behaviour 2. a cruel or brutal act 3. a crude or coarse taste, manner, etc.

barbarous (bär'bər əs) *adj.* [< Gr. *barbaros,* foreign] 1. uncivilized 2. crude, coarse, etc. 3. cruel; brutal 4. characterized by substandard usages in speaking or writing —**bar'barously** *adv.* —**bar'barousness** *n.*

Barbary ape (bär'bər ē) [< area in N. Afr.] a tailless, apelike monkey of North Africa and Gibraltar

barbecue (bär'bə kyōō') *n.* [< Sp. < Haitian *barbacoa,* framework] 1. a pig, ox, etc. roasted whole over an open fire 2. any meat grilled over an open fire 3. a party or picnic at which such meat is served 4. a portable outdoor grill —*vt.* **-cued', -cu'ing** to prepare (meat) outdoors by roasting on a spit or over a grill, often with a highly seasoned sauce

barbed wire twisted wire with sharp points all along it, used for barriers: also **barb wire**

barbel (bär'b'l) *n.* [ult. < L. *barba,* beard] 1. a threadlike growth from the jaws of certain fishes 2. a large European freshwater fish with such growths

barbell (bär'bel') *n.* [BAR¹ + (DUMB)BELL] a metal bar to which discs of varying weights are attached at each end, used for weight-lifting exercises: also **bar bell, bar-bell**

barber (bär'bər) *n.* [< L. *barba,* beard] a person whose work is cutting hair, shaving and trimming beards, etc. —*vt.* to cut the hair of, shave, etc.

barberry (bär'bər ē) *n., pl.* **-ries** [< Ar.

barbāris] a spiny shrub with sour, red berries

barber's pole a pole with spiral stripes of red and white, a symbol of the barber's trade

barbican (bär'bi kən) *n.* [< OFr., prob. < Per.] a fortification at the gate or bridge leading into a town or castle

barbiturate (bär bit'yoo rət) *n.* any salt or ester of barbituric acid, used as a sedative or to induce sleep

barbituric acid (bär'bə tyooər'ik) [< G. *Barbitursäure*] a crystalline acid, derivatives of which induce sleep

barcarole, barcarolle (bär'kə rōl') *n.* [Fr. < It. *barca*, boat] 1. a song sung by Venetian gondoliers 2. a piece of music imitating this

bard (bärd) *n.* [Gael. & Ir.] 1. an ancient Celtic poet 2. any poet —**bard'ic** *adj.*

bare (bäər) *adj.* [OE. *bær*] 1. *a)* without the customary covering [*bare* floors] *b)* without clothing; naked 2. without equipment or furnishings; empty 3. simple; plain 4. mere —*vt.* **bared, bar'ing** to make bare; uncover —**lay bare** to uncover —**bare'ness** *n.*

bareback *adv., adj.* on a horse with no saddle

barefaced *adj.* 1. shameless; brazen 2. unconcealed; open 3. with the face uncovered —**bare'fac'edly** (-fās'id lē) *adv.* —**bare'fac'edness** *n.*

barefoot *adj., adv.* without shoes and stockings —**bare'foot'ed** *adj.*

bareheaded *adj., adv.* wearing no hat or other head covering

barelegged *adj., adv.* with the legs bare

barely *adv.* 1. only just; scarcely 2. scantily [*barely* furnished]

bargain (bär'gin) *n.* [< OFr. *bargaignier*, to haggle] 1. something sold at a price favourable to the buyer 2. a mutual agreement between parties on what should be given or done 3. such an agreement in terms of its worth to one of the parties [a bad *bargain*] —*vi.* 1. to haggle 2. to make a bargain —*vt.* to barter —**bargain for** 1. to try to get cheaply 2. to expect —**bargain on** to count on —**into the bargain** in addition —**bar'gainer** *n.*

barge (bärj) *n.* [< ML. *barga*] 1. a large, flat-bottomed boat for carrying freight on rivers, etc. 2. a large pleasure boat, used for pageants, etc. —*vi.* 1. to move slowly and clumsily 2. to come or go (*in* or *into*) in a rude, abrupt way 3. to collide (*into*)

bargee (bär jē') *n.* [< *barge*] a man who operates, or works aboard, a barge

barge pole a long pole used to propel a barge —**not touch with a barge pole** to refuse to have anything to do with (something or someone)

bar graph a graph with parallel bars representing in proportional lengths the figures given in the data

baritone (bar'ə tōn') *n.* [< Gr. *barys*,

deep + *tonos*, tone] 1. the range of a male voice between bass and tenor 2. a singer or instrument with such a range 3. a part for such a voice or instrument

barium (bäar'ē əm) *n.* [< Gr. *barys*, heavy] a silver-white, metallic chemical element: symbol, Ba

barium meal a thick mixture containing barium sulphate used for examination of the stomach and intestines

bark[1] (bärk) *n.* [ON. *bǫrkr*] the outside covering of trees and woody plants —*vt.* 1. to take the bark off (a tree) 2. [Colloq.] to scrape some skin off

bark[2] *vi.* [OE. *beorcan*] 1. to make the sharp, abrupt cry of a dog 2. to make a sound like this 3. to speak sharply; snap 4. [Colloq.] to cough —*vt.* to say with a bark or a shout —*n.* a sound made in barking —**bark up the wrong tree** to misdirect one's attack, energies, etc.

barley (bär'lē) *n.* [< OE. *bere*, barley] 1. a cereal grass 2. its grain, used in making malts, in soups, etc.

barleycorn *n.* barley or a grain of barley

barley sugar a clear, hard sweet made by melting sugar, formerly with a barley extract added

barley water a drink made by boiling barley in water

barm (bärm) *n.* [OE. *beorma*] the foamy yeast that appears on the surface of fermenting malt liquors

barmaid (bär'mād') *n.* a waitress who serves alcoholic drinks in a bar

barman (bär'mən) *n.* a bartender

bar mitzvah, bar mizvah (bär mits'-və) [Heb., son of the commandment] [*also* B- M-] 1. a Jewish boy who has arrived at the age of thirteen years 2. the ceremony celebrating this

barmy (bär'mē) *adj.* **-ier, -iest** 1. [Slang] silly; idiotic 2. full of barm; foamy

barn (bärn) *n.* [< OE. *bere*, barley + *ærn*, building] a farm building for sheltering harvested crops, livestock, etc.

barnacle (bär'nə k'l) *n.* [< Fr. *bernicle*] 1. a saltwater shellfish that attaches itself to rocks, ship bottoms, etc. 2. a person or thing hard to get rid of —**bar'nacled** *adj.*

barnacle goose a species of wild goose

barn dance 1. a lively country dance 2. [U.S.] a party, orig. held in a barn, at which people dance square dances

barney (bär'nē) *n.* [< ? Dial.] [Colloq.] 1. a fight 2. a noisy quarrel

barn owl a species of brown and grey owl with a spotted white breast, commonly found in barns

barnstorm *vi., vt.* to tour in small towns and rural districts, performing plays —**barn'storm'er** *n.* —**barn'storm'ing** *adj.*,

barnyard *n.* the yard or ground near a barn —*adj.* of, like or fit for a barnyard

barograph (bar'ō gräf') *n.* a barometer that records variations in atmospheric pressure automatically

barometer (bə rom'ə tər) *n.* [< Gr. *baros*, weight + -METER] **1.** an instrument for measuring atmospheric pressure, used in forecasting the weather or finding height above sea level **2.** anything that indicates change —**barometric** (bar'ō met'rik), **bar'omet'rical** *adj.*

baron (bar'ən) *n.* [OFr., man] **1.** a member of the lowest rank of the British hereditary peerage **2.** a European nobleman of like rank **3.** a powerful businessman or industrialist —**bar'oness** *n.fem.* —**baronial** (bə rō'nē əl) *adj.*

baronet *n.* a man holding the lowest hereditary British title —**bar'onetcy** *n.*

baron of beef a joint of meat consisting of both sides of the back; a double sirloin

barony *n., pl.* **-onies** **1.** a baron's domain **2.** the rank or title of a baron

baroque (bə rok') *adj.* [Fr. < Port. *barroco*, imperfect pearl] **1.** *a)* of a style of art and architecture with much ornamentation and curved lines *b)* of a style of music with highly embellished melodies **2.** of the period in which these styles flourished (c. 1550–1750) —*n.* baroque style, baroque art, etc.

baroscope (bar'ə skōp') *n.* [< Gr. *baros*, weight + -SCOPE] an instrument indicating changes in atmospheric pressure —**bar'o-scop'ic** (-skop'ik) *adj.*

barouche (bə rōōsh') *n.* [< G. < L. *bi-*, two + *rota*, wheel] a four-wheeled carriage with a collapsible hood and two double seats

barque, bark (bärk) *n.* [< Fr. < L. *barca*] **1.** a sailing vessel with two forward masts, and its rear mast rigged fore-and-aft **2.** [Poet.] any boat

barrack[1] (bar'ək) *n.* [< Fr. < Sp. *barro*, clay] [*pl., often with sing. v.*] **1.** a building or group of buildings for housing soldiers, etc. **2.** a large, plain building

barrack[2] *vi., vt.* [< Abor. *borak*, banter] to shout to encourage or discourage a player, as in cricket —**bar'racking** *n., adj.*

barracuda (bar'ə kyōō'də) *n., pl.* **-da, -das** [Sp.] a fierce, pikelike fish of tropical seas

barrage (ba'räzh) *n.* [Fr. < *barrer*, to stop] **1.** a curtain of artillery fire laid down to keep enemy forces from moving, etc. **2.** a prolonged attack of words **3.** a man-made barrier in a river —*vi., vt.* **-raged, -raging** to lay down a barrage (against)

barrage balloon an anchored balloon with cables attached for entangling low-flying attacking aircraft

barratry (bar'ə trē) *n.* [< OFr. *barater*, to cheat] fraud or negligence on the part of a ship's officers or crew that results in a loss to the owners

‡**barre** (bär) *n.* [Fr.] the practice bar in a ballet studio

barrel (bar'əl) *n.* [< ML. *barillus*] **1.** a large, wooden, cylindrical container with slightly bulging sides and flat ends **2.** any somewhat similar cylinder, drum, etc. as the tube of a gun **3.** a unit of capacity, as in the oil industry, normally equal to

35 Imperial gallons —*vt.* **-relled, -relling** to put in a barrel —**have (someone) over a barrel** [Slang] to have (someone) completely at one's mercy

barrel organ a mechanical musical instrument having a revolving cylinder studded with pins which open pipe valves, producing a tune

barrel roll a complete revolution made by an aircraft around its longitudinal axis while in flight

barrel vault *Archit.* a vault shaped like half a cylinder

barren (bar'ən) *adj.* [< OFr. *baraigne*] **1.** that cannot produce offspring **2.** not producing crops or fruit **3.** unproductive; unprofitable **4.** dull; boring —**bar'renly** *adv.* —**bar'renness** *n.*

Barren Grounds a sparsely-inhabited region of tundras in N Canada : also **Barren Lands**

barricade (bar'ə kād') *n.* [< Fr. *barique*, cask] a barrier, esp. one thrown up hastily for defence —*vt.* **-cad'ed, -cad'ing** **1.** to shut in or keep out with a barricade **2.** to obstruct

barrier (bar'ē ər) *n.* [< OFr. *barre*, BAR[1]] **1.** an obstruction, as a fence or wall **2.** anything that holds apart or separates [*racial barriers*]

barrier cream a cream used to protect the skin from dirt, harmful substances, etc.

barrier reef a long ridge of coral parallel to the coastline, separated from it by a lagoon

barrister (bar'is tər) *n.* [< BAR[1]] a member of the legal profession qualified to plead cases in the higher courts

barrow[1] (bar'ō) *n.* [< OE. *beran*, to bear] **1.** *same as* WHEELBARROW **2.** a two-wheeled handcart, used by street vendors

barrow[2] *n.* [OE. *beorg*, hill] a heap of earth or rocks marking an ancient grave

bar sinister *same as* BEND SINISTER

Bart. Baronet

barter (bär'tər) *vi.* [< OFr. *barater*, cheat] to trade by exchanging goods or services without using money —*vt.* to exchange (goods, etc.) —*n.* **1.** the practice of bartering **2.** anything bartered —**bar'-terer** *n.*

baryon (bar'ē on') *n.* [< Gr. *barys*, heavy + (ELECTR)ON] a heavy atomic particle, as the proton

baryta (bə rīt'ə) *n.* [< ff.] **1.** barium oxide **2.** barium hydroxide —**baryt'ic** (-rit'ik) *adj.*

barytes (bə rīt'ēz) *n.* [< Gr. *barys*, weighty] a white, crystalline mineral composed mainly of barium sulphate

basal (bā's'l) *adj.* **1.** of, at, or forming the base **2.** basic; fundamental —**bas'-ally** *adv.*

basalt (bas'ôlt) *n.* [< L. *basaltes*, dark marble] a dark, tough, volcanic rock

bascule bridge (bas'kyōōl) [Fr.] a drawbridge counterweighted so that it can be raised and lowered easily

base[1] (bās) *n., pl.* **bas'es** [< L. *basis*,

basis] 1. the thing or part on which something rests; foundation 2. the main part, as of a system, on which the rest depends 3. the principal or essential ingredient 4. a basis 5. a place of safety in certain games, as rounders 6. the point of attachment of a part of the body 7. a centre of operations; headquarters 8. *Chem.* any compound that reacts with an acid to form a salt 9. *Geom.* the line or plane upon which a figure is thought of as resting 10. *Math.* the number which is the foundation of a system of logarithms or numeration —*adj.* forming a base —*vt.* based, bas'ing 1. to make a base for 2. to put or rest (*on*) as a base 3. to place (*in* or *at* a base)

base² *adj.* [< VL. *bassus*, low] 1. with little or no honour, courage, etc.; contemptible 2. menial or degrading 3. inferior in quality 4. of comparatively low worth [iron is a *base* metal] —**base'-ly** *adv.* —**base'ness** *n.*

baseball *n.* a game played, chiefly in the U.S., with a ball and a bat by teams of nine players on a field with four bases

baseborn *adj.* 1. of humble birth or origin 2. of illegitimate birth 3. mean or ignoble

baseless *adj.* having no basis in fact; unfounded

base line 1. a line serving as a base 2. *Tennis* the line at the back at either end of a court

basement (bās'mənt) *n.* the lowest storey of a building, wholly or partly below ground surface

basenji (bə sen'jē) *n.* [Bantu] an African breed of small dog with a reddish-brown coat

bases¹ (bās'əz) *n.* *pl.* of BASE¹

bases² (bā'sēz) *n.* *pl.* of BASIS

bash (bash) *vt.* [echoic] [Colloq.] to strike with a violent blow; smash (*in* or *into*) —*n.* [Colloq.] a violent blow —**have a bash at** [Slang] to make an attempt at

bashful *adj.* [< ABASH] timid, shy, and easily embarrassed —**bash'fully** *adv.* —**bash'fulness** *n.*

BASIC (bā'sik) *n.* [B(*eginner's*) A(*ll-purpose*) S(*ymbolic*) I(*nstruction*) C(*ode*)] a computer language that uses common English terms

basic (bā'sik) *adj.* 1. of or forming a base; fundamental 2. of a minimum rate [*basic* pay] 3. *Chem.* of or containing a base —*n.* a basic principle, factor, etc.: usually used in *pl.* —**bas'ically** *adv.*

Basic English a copyrighted simplified form of English devised by C. K. Ogden

basic industry an industry that is fundamental to a country's economy

basic slag a by-product in the manufacture of steel, now widely used as a fertilizer

basil (baz''l) *n.* [< Gr. *basilikon*, royal] a fragrant herb used for flavouring

basilica (bə sil'i kə) *n.* [< Gr. *basilikē* (*stoa*), royal (portico)] 1. in ancient Rome, a rectangular building with colonnaded aisles, used as a courtroom, etc. 2. a Christian church in this style —**basil'ican** *adj.*

basilisk (baz'ə lisk') *n.* [< Gr. *basileus*, king] 1. a mythical, lizardlike monster with fatal breath and glance 2. a tropical American lizard with a crest

basin (bās''n) *n.* [< VL. *bacca*, water vessel] 1. a wide, shallow container, as for liquid 2. a washbowl or sink 3. any shallow, esp. water-filled, hollow, as a pond 4. a harbour 5. all the land drained by a river and its branches 6. a depression in the earth's surface

basis (bā'sis) *n.*, *pl.* **ba'ses** [< Gr., base] 1. the base or foundation of anything 2. a principal constituent 3. a basic principle or theory

bask (bäsk) *vi.* [ME. *basken*, wallow] 1. to warm oneself pleasantly, as in sunlight 2. to enjoy any pleasant feeling

basket (bäs'kit) *n.* [ME.] 1. a container made of interwoven cane, strips of wood, etc. 2. anything like a basket 3. the structure hung from a balloon to carry persons, etc. 4. *Basketball a)* the goal, a round, open net hanging from a ring *b)* a score made by tossing the ball through this

basketball *n.* 1. a game played by two teams of five players each, in a zoned floor area: points are scored by tossing a ball through a basket at the opponent's end of the court 2. the large, round, inflated ball used in this game

basket chair a chair that is made of basketwork

basket weave a weave of fabrics resembling the weave used in basketwork

basketwork *n.* work that is interlaced or woven like a basket

basking shark a large shark that feeds on plankton

Basque (bask) *n.* 1. any member of a people living in the W Pyrenees 2. their unique language —*adj.* of the Basques, their language, etc.

basque (bask) *n.* [Fr. < ?] a woman's tightfitting bodice or tunic

bas-relief (bas'rə lēf') *n.* [Fr. < It.: see BASSO & RELIEF] sculpture in which figures are carved in a flat surface so that they project only a little

bass¹ (bās) *n.* [ME. *bas*, low] 1. the range of the lowest male voice 2. a singer or instrument with such a range; specif., *same as* DOUBLE BASS —*adj.* of, in, for, or having this range

bass² (bas) *n.* [OE. *bærs*] a spiny-finned food and game fish of fresh or salt water

bass³ (bas) *n.* *same as* BAST

bass clef (bās) *Music* a sign on a staff, indicating the position of F below middle C on the fourth line

basset (bas'it) *n.* [< OFr. *bas*, low] a kind of hunting hound with a long body, short legs, and long ears

basset horn a rich-toned wind instrument, similar to a clarinet in tone and fingering

bassinet (bas'ə net') *n.* [< Fr. *berceau*,

cradle] an infant's basketlike bed, often hooded and on casters

basso (bas´ō) *n., pl.* **bas´sos** [It. < VL. *bassus,* low] a bass voice or singer

BASSOON

bassoon (bə soon´) *n.* [< Fr.] a double-reed woodwind instrument —**bassoon´ist** *n.*

bass viol (bās) *same as* VIOLA DA GAMBA

bast (bast) *n.* [OE. *bæst*] fibre obtained from phloem, for making ropes, etc.

bastard (bas´tərd) *n.* [< OFr.] **1.** a person born of parents not married to each other **2.** anything spurious, inferior, etc. **3.** [Vulg.] one regarded with contempt, pity, etc. or, sometimes, with playful affection **4.** [S.Afr.] a person with mixed white and coloured parents: also **bastaard** —*adj.* **1.** of illegitimate birth or uncertain origin **2.** not genuine or authentic —**bas´tardly** *adj.* —**bas´tardy** *n.*

bastardize (bas´tər dīz´) *vt.* -**ized´,** -**iz´-ing 1.** to make, declare, or show to be a bastard **2.** to make corrupt or inferior —**bas´tardiza´tion** *n.*

baste[1] (bāst) *vt.* **bast´ed, bast´ing** [< OHG. *bastjan,* sew with bast] to sew temporarily with long, loose stitches

baste[2] *vt.* **bast´ed, bast´ing** [< ?] to moisten (meat) with melted butter, etc. during roasting

baste[3] *vt.* **bast´ed, bast´ing** [ON. *beysta*] **1.** to beat soundly **2.** to attack with words; abuse

bastille, bastile (bas tēl´) *n.* [Fr.: see BASTION] a prison —**the Bastille** a prison in Paris destroyed (July 14, 1789) in the French Revolution

bastinado (bas´tə nā´dō) *n., pl.* -**does** [< Sp. *bastón,* stick] a beating with a stick, usually on the soles of the feet —*vt.* -**doed,** -**doing** to inflict a bastinado on

basting (bās´tiŋ) *n.* **1.** the act of sewing with loose, temporary stitches **2.** such stitches

bastion (bas´tē ən) *n.* [Fr. < It. *bastire,* build] **1.** a projection from a fortification **2.** any strong defence or bulwark —**bas´-tioned** *adj.*

bat[1] (bat) *n.* [< OE. *batt*] **1.** any stout club or stick, esp. one used to strike the ball in cricket and baseball **2.** a disc with a short handle used to strike the ball in table tennis, etc. **3.** a turn at batting **4.** a batsman at cricket **5.** [Colloq.] a blow or hit —*vt.* **bat´ted, bat´-ting** to strike with or as with a bat —*vi.* to take a turn at batting —**bat around**
[Slang] to travel or roam about —**off one's own bat** without any assistance

bat[2] *n.* [< Scand.] a mouselike mammal with a furry body and membranous wings, usually seen flying at night —**blind as a bat** quite blind —**have bats in the (or one's) belfry** [Slang] to be insane; have crazy ideas

bat[3] *vt.* **bat´ted, bat´ting** [< OFr. *battre,* beat] [Colloq.] to blink; flutter —**not bat an eye (or eyelid)** [Colloq.] **1.** not show surprise **2.** not sleep

batch (bach) *n.* [OE. *bacan,* bake] **1.** the quantity of anything needed for or made in one operation or lot **2.** a group of things or persons **3.** the amount (of bread, etc.) produced at one baking

bate (bāt) *vt., vi.* **bat´ed, bat´ing** [< ABATE] to abate or lessen —**with bated breath** with the breath held in because of fear, excitement, etc.

bath (bäth) *n., pl.* **baths** (bä*th*z) [OE. *bæth*] **1.** a large moulded container in which one washes oneself **2.** [*usually pl.*] a building for bathing or swimming **3.** a washing, esp. of the body, in water **4.** water or other liquid for bathing, or for regulating temperature, etc. **5.** a container for such liquid —*vt.* to wash —*vi.* to take a bath

Bath chair (bäth) a wheelchair of a kind used at Bath

bath cube a soluble cube that scents or softens water

bathe (bā*th*) *vt.* **bathed, bath´ing** [OE. *bathian*] **1.** to put into a liquid; immerse **2.** to wet or moisten **3.** to cover as if with a liquid —*vi.* **1.** to go into or be in water so as to swim, cool oneself, etc. **2.** to soak oneself in something —*n.* a swim or dip

bathing cap a tightfitting cap of rubber, etc., worn to keep the hair dry, as while swimming

bathing suit a garment worn for swimming

bathmat (bäth´mat´) *n.* a mat used next to a bathtub

bathometer (bə thom´ə tər) *n.* [< Gr. *bathos,* depth + -METER] an instrument for measuring water depths

bathos (bā´thos) *n.* [Gr., depth] **1.** an abrupt change from the lofty to the trivial; anticlimax **2.** false pathos —**bathetic** (bə thet´ik) *adj.* —**bathet´ically** *adv.*

bathrobe (bäth´rōb´) *n.* a long, loose coat for wear before or after a bath, swimming, etc.

bathroom *n.* a room with a bathtub and usually a toilet, washbasin, etc.

bath salts a substance which is added to bath water to scent or soften it

bathyscaph (bath´ə skaf´) *n.* [< Gr. *bathys,* deep + *skaphē,* boat] a deep-sea diving compartment

bathysphere (bath´ə sfēər´) *n.* [< Gr. *bathys,* deep + SPHERE] a round, watertight observation chamber lowered by cables into sea depths

batik (bat´ik) *n.* [Malay] **1.** a method of dyeing designs on cloth by coating with removable wax the parts not to be dyed **2.** cloth so decorated —**adj.** of or like batik

batiste (ba tēst′) **n.** [Fr. < supposed original maker, *Baptiste*] a fine, thin cloth of cotton, linen, etc.

batman (bat′mən) **n.** [< Fr. *bat*, packsaddle] an officer's personal servant

baton (bat′ən) **n.** [Fr. < VL. hyp. *basto*, stick] **1.** a slender stick used by a conductor in directing an orchestra, choir, etc. **2.** the short rod passed in a relay race **3.** a staff serving as a symbol of office

batrachian (bə trā′kē ən) **adj.** [< Gr. *batrachos*, frog] of or like amphibians without tails, as frogs and toads —**n.** an amphibian without a tail

batsman (bats′mən) **n.** the batter in cricket

battalion (bə tal′yən) **n.** [< Fr. < VL. *battalia*, BATTLE] **1.** a large group of soldiers arrayed for battle **2.** any large group joined together in some activity

batten[1] (bat′'n) **n.** [var. of BATON] **1.** a sawed strip of wood, etc. **2.** a strip of wood put over a seam between boards as a fastening **3.** a strip used to fasten canvas over a ship's hatchways —**vt.** to fasten with battens

batten[2] **vi.** [ON. *batna*, improve] to grow fat; thrive

batter[1] (bat′ər) **vt.** [< L. *battuere*, beat] **1.** to beat or strike with blow after blow **2.** to injure by pounding, hard wear, or use —**vi.** to pound noisily

batter[2] **n.** [< OFr. : see BATTER[1]] a flowing mixture of flour, milk, eggs, etc. esp. for making pancakes

battered baby a young child with serious physical injuries caused by a parent or other adult

battering ram **1.** an ancient military machine having a heavy beam for battering down walls, etc. **2.** anything used like this

battery (bat′ər ē) **n.**, **pl.** **-teries** [see BATTER[1]] **1.** a connected group of cells storing an electrical charge and capable of furnishing a current, as in a car, radio, etc. **2.** a group of similar things used together **3.** *Law* any illegal beating of another person : see ASSAULT AND BATTERY **4.** *Mil.* an emplacement or fortification equipped with heavy guns —**adj.** of poultry or cattle intensively reared in cages

battle (bat′'l) **n.** [< L. *battuere*, to beat] **1.** a large-scale fight between armed forces **2.** armed fighting; combat **3.** any conflict —**vt.**, **vi.** **-tled**, **-tling** to oppose, fight, or struggle —**give** (or **do**) **battle** to fight —**bat′tler** **n.**

battle-axe **n.** **1.** a heavy axe formerly used as a weapon **2.** [Colloq.] a woman who is harsh, etc.

battle cruiser a large warship with longer range and greater speed than a battleship, but less heavily armoured

battle cry a cry or slogan used to encourage those in a battle, struggle, contest, etc.

battledore (bat′'l dôr′) **n.** [< ? Pr. *batedor*, beater] a bat or racket used to hit a shuttlecock back and forth in a game (called **battledore and shuttlecock**) like badminton

battle dress the standard everyday uniform of a soldier

battlefield **n.** **1.** the place where a battle is fought or was fought **2.** any area of conflict

BATTLEMENTS

battlement (bat′'l mənt) **n.** [< OFr. *batailler*, fortify] a low wall, as on top of a tower, with open spaces for shooting —**bat′tlement′ed** (-men′tid) **adj.**

battle royal *pl.* **battles royal** a fight involving many contestants; free-for-all

battleship **n.** a large warship with the biggest guns and very heavy armour

batty (bat′ē) **adj.** **bat′tier**, **bat′tiest** [< BAT[2]] [Slang] **1.** insane; crazy **2.** odd; eccentric

bauble (bô′b'l) **n.** [< OFr. *baubel*, plaything] a showy trinket; trifle

baulk (bôk) **n.**, **vt.**, **vi.** *same as* BALK

bauxite (bôk′sīt) **n.** [Fr. < (Les) *Baux*, town in France] the claylike ore from which aluminium is obtained

bawd (bôd) **n.** [< ? OFr. *baud*, licentious] [Now Literary] a person, esp. a woman, who keeps a brothel

bawdy (bô′dē) **adj.** **-ier**, **-iest** characterized by references to sex —**bawd′ily** **adv.** —**bawd′iness** **n.**

bawdyhouse **n.** a house of prostitution

bawl (bôl) **vi.**, **vt.** [< ML. *baulare*, to bark] **1.** to shout or call out noisily; bellow **2.** to weep loudly —**bawl out** [Slang] to scold angrily

bay[1] (bā) **n.** [< ML. *baia*] a part of a sea or lake, indenting the shoreline; wide inlet

bay[2] **n.** [< OFr. *baer*, gape] **1.** *a)* an opening or alcove marked off by columns, etc. *b)* a recess in a wall, as for a window *c)* *same as* BAY WINDOW **2.** a compartment or space : cf. BOMB BAY

bay[3] **vi.**, **vt.** [< OFr.] to bark (at) in long, deep tones —**n.** **1.** the sound of baying **2.** the situation of a hunted animal forced to turn and fight —**at bay** **1.** with escape cut off **2.** held off —**bring to bay** to force into a situation that makes escape impossible

bay[4] **n.** [< L. *baca*, berry] **1.** *same as* LAUREL **2.** [*pl.*] *a)* a wreath of bay leaves given to poets and conquerors *b*) honour; fame

bay⁵ *adj.* [< L. *badius*] reddish-brown: said esp. of horses —*n.* 1. a horse of this colour 2. reddish brown

bayberry (bā′bər ē) *n., pl.* -ries a tropical American tree yielding an aromatic oil used in bay rum

bay leaf the dried leaf of the laurel, used as a herb

bayonet (bā′ə nit) *n.* [< Fr. *Bayonne*, in France] a detachable blade put on a rifle muzzle for hand-to-hand fighting —*vt., vi.* -neted, -neting to stab or kill with a bayonet

bay rum an aromatic liquid formerly obtained from leaves of a bayberry tree: it is used in medicines, etc.

bay window a window or set of windows jutting out from the wall of a building

bazaar (bə zär′) *n.* [Per. *bāzār*] 1. in Oriental countries, a market or street of shops 2. a sale of various articles, usually to raise money for a club, church, etc.

bazooka (bə zōōk′ə) *n.* [term orig. coined for a comic musical horn] a weapon of metal tubing, for aiming and launching electrically fired, armour-piercing rockets

BB 1. Boys' Brigade 2. double black (of pencil lead)

BBC British Broadcasting Corporation

B.C. 1. before Christ 2. British Columbia

BCG [*Bacillus Calmette-Guérin*] anti-tuberculosis vaccine

B.D. Bachelor of Divinity

BDA British Dental Association

bdellium (del′ē əm) *n.* [< Gr. *bdellion*, of Oriental origin] a myrrhlike gum resin

B.D.S. Bachelor of Dental Surgery

be (bē, bi) *vi.* was or were, been, be′-ing [OE. *beon*] 1. to exist; live [Caesar *is* no more] 2. to happen or occur [the party *is* tonight] 3. to remain or continue [will he *be* here long?] 4. to have a place, position, or outlook [the door *is* on your left] Note: *be* is used to link its subject to a predicate complement (Ex.: he *is* brave, that hat *is* ten pounds, let x *be* y) or as an auxiliary: (1) with a past participle to form the passive voice [he will be paid] (2) with a past participle to form an archaic perfect tense [Christ *is* risen] (3) with a present participle to express continuation [the motor *is* running] (4) with a present participle or infinitive to express futurity, possibility, obligation, intention, etc. [he *is* going next week, she *is* to wash the dishes] *Be* is conjugated in the present indicative: (I) am, (he, she, it) *is*, (we, you, they) *are*; in the past indicative: (I, he, she, it) *was*, (we, you, they) *were* —**be off** go away

be- [OE. < *be*, about] *a prefix* meaning: 1. around [beset] 2. completely; thoroughly [bedeck] 3. away [bereave] 4. about [bethink] 5. make [besot] 6. furnish with; affect by [becloud]

Be *Chem.* beryllium

B.E. Bachelor of Engineering

beach (bēch) *n.* [< ?] a sandy shore, esp. one used by swimmers, sunbathers, etc. —*vt., vi.* to ground (a boat) on a beach

beachcomber *n.* a man who loafs on beaches or wharves, living on what he can beg or find

beachhead *n.* a position established by invading troops on an enemy shore

beacon (bēk′′n) *n.* [OE. *beacen*] 1. a signal fire, esp. one on a hill, pole, etc. 2. any light for warning or guiding 3. a lighthouse 4. a radio transmitter that sends out signals for guiding aircraft 5. anything that warns 6. *same as* BELISHA BEACON —*vt.* to provide or mark with beacons

bead (bēd) *n.* [< OE. *biddan*, pray] 1. a small, usually round piece of glass, wood, metal, etc., pierced for stringing 2. [*pl.*] *a*) a string of beads *b*) a rosary 3. any small, round object, as the front sight of a rifle 4. a drop or bubble 5. foam, as on beer 6. a narrow, half-round moulding —*vt.* to decorate or string with beads —*vi.* to form a bead or beads —**draw a bead on** to take careful aim at —**bead′ed** *adj.*

beadle (bē′d'l) *n.* [< OFr.] 1. in Scotland, a church official attending on the minister 2. formerly, a minor parish officer in the Church of England

beadsman (bēdz′mən) *n.* a person who prays for another's soul, esp. one hired to do so

beady *adj.* -ier, -iest 1. small, round, and glittering like a bead 2. decorated with beads

beagle (bē′g'l) *n.* [< ? Fr. *bégueule*, wide-throat] a small hound with a smooth coat, short legs, and drooping ears

beak (bēk) *n.* [< L. *beccus*] 1. a bird's bill 2. the beaklike mouthpart of various insects, etc. 3. the spout of a jug 4. the ram projecting from the prow of an ancient warship 5. [Colloq.] the nose 6. [Slang] a magistrate or schoolteacher —**beaked** (bēkt) *adj.* —**beak′like** *adj.*

beaker (bē′kər) *n.* [< ON. *bikarr*, cup] 1. *a*) a goblet *b*) a cup having a wide mouth [a plastic *beaker*] 2. a jarlike container of glass or metal used by scientists

Beaker folk a Bronze Age people named after the bell-shaped beakers found in graves

beam (bēm) *n.* [OE.] 1. a long, thick piece of wood, or of metal or stone used in building 2. the part of a plough to which the handles, etc. are attached 3. the crossbar of a balance, or the balance itself 4. any of the heavy, horizontal crosspieces of a ship 5. a ship's breadth at its widest point 6. a slender shaft of light or other radiation, as of X-rays 7. a radiant look, smile, etc. 8. a stream of radio or radar signals for guiding aircraft or ships —*vt.* 1. to give out (shafts of light) 2. to direct or aim (a radio signal, etc.) —*vi.* 1. to shine brightly 2. to smile warmly —**off the beam** 1. not following a guiding beam, as an aeroplane 2. [Colloq.] wrong; incorrect —**on the beam** 1. following a guiding beam, as an aircraft 2. [Colloq.] working or functioning well —**beam′ing** adj.

beam-ends (bēm′endz′) n.pl. the ends of a ship's beams —**on her beam-ends** tipping so far to the side as to be in danger of overturning —**on one's beam-ends** at the end of one's resources, money, etc.

bean (bēn) n. [OE. bean] 1. a plant of the legume family, with edible, smooth, kidney-shaped seeds 2. any such seed 3. a pod with such seeds, eaten as a vegetable when still unripe 4. any of various beanlike seeds [coffee beans] —**full of beans** [Colloq.] lively; ebullient —**not a bean** [Colloq.] no money at all —**spill the beans** [Colloq.] to divulge secret information

beanbag n. a small cloth bag filled with beans, and thrown in some games

bean-feast n. 1. an annual dinner or outing for workers 2. any celebration

beano (bēn′ō) n. [Slang] any celebration or party

bear[1] (bâər) vt. bore, borne or born, bear′ing [OE. beran] 1. to carry; transport 2. to have or show [it bore his signature] 3. to give birth to 4. to produce or yield 5. to support or sustain 6. to put up with; tolerate [to bear pain] 7. to require [his actions bear watching] 8. to carry or conduct (oneself) 9. to carry over or·hold [to bear a grudge] 10. to bring and tell (a message, etc.) 11. to move as if carrying [the crowd bore us along] 12. to give or supply [to bear witness] —vi. 1. to be productive 2. to lie, point, or move in a given direction 3. to have bearing (on) [his story bears on the crime] 4. to tolerate 5. to weigh [grief bears heavily on her] —**bear arms** to serve as a soldier —**bear down** 1. to press down 2. to make a strong effort —**bear down on** 1. to make a strong effort towards accomplishing 2. to approach —**bear out** to confirm —**bear up** to endure —**bring to bear on** (or upon) to cause to have an effect on

bear[2] n. [OE. bera] 1. a large, heavy mammal with shaggy fur and a very short tail 2. [B-] either of two N constellations, the **Great Bear** and the **Little Bear** 3. one who is clumsy, rude, etc. 4. one who sells shares, in the expectation of buying them later at a lower price —adj. falling in price [a bear market] —**like a bear with a sore head** [Colloq.] bad-tempered

bearable adj. that can be endured —**bear′ably** adv.

beard (bēərd) n. [OE.] 1. the hair growing on the lower part of a man's face 2. any beardlike part, as the awn of certain grains —vt. to face or oppose courageously; defy —**beard′ed** adj.

bearer (bâər′ər) n. 1. a person or thing that bears, carries, or supports 2. a person presenting a cheque, etc. for payment

bear garden any rough, noisy, rowdy place

bear hug a tight embrace

bearing n. 1. way of carrying and conducting oneself; carriage 2. a support or supporting part 3. the act of producing young, fruit, etc. 4. endurance 5. a) direction or position with reference to some known point, etc. b) [pl.] awareness of one's position or situation [to lose one's bearings] 6. relevant meaning; application 7. Heraldry any figure in a coat of arms 8. Mech. any part of a machine on which another part revolves, etc. —adj. that bears, or supports weight

bearskin n. 1. the pelt of a bear 2. a rug, etc. made of this 3. a tall fur hat worn as part of a uniform

beast (bēst) n. [< L. bestia] 1. any large, four-footed animal 2. a person who is brutal, vile, etc. 3. qualities like those of an animal

beastly adj. -lier, -liest 1. [Colloq.] disagreeable; unpleasant 2. of or like a beast; bestial, brutal, etc. —adv. [Colloq.] very —**beast′liness** n.

beat (bēt) vt. beat, beat′en, beat′ing [OE. beatan] 1. to strike repeatedly 2. to punish by so striking 3. to dash repeatedly against 4. to form (a path, etc.) by repeated treading 5. to shape by hammering 6. to mix by stirring; whip 7. to move (esp. wings) up and down 8. to drive game out of cover 9. a) to defeat in a contest or struggle b) to outdo or surpass 10. to mark (time) by tapping, etc. 11. [Colloq.] to baffle or puzzle —vi. 1. to strike repeatedly 2. to throb, pulsate, etc. 3. to hunt through woods, etc. for game —n. 1. a beating, as of the heart 2. any of a series of blows or strokes 3. a pulsating movement or sound 4. a habitual route [a policeman's beat] 5. a) the unit of musical rhythm [four beats to a bar] b) the accent in the rhythm of verse or music —adj. 1. [Slang] tired out; exhausted 2. of a group of young persons, esp. of the 1950's, rebelling against conventional attitudes [the beat generation] —**beat down** 1. to shine with dazzling light and intense heat 2. to put down; suppress 3. [Colloq.] to force to a lower price —**beat it!** [Slang] go away! —**beat off** to drive back —**beat up** [Slang] to give a beating to; thrash

beaten (bēt′'n) adj. 1. struck with repeated blows 2. shaped by hammering 3. flattened by treading 4. defeated —**off the beaten track** (or **path**) unusual, unfamiliar, etc.

beater n. 1. an implement or utensil for beating 2. one who drives game from cover in a hunt

beatific (bē′ə tif′ik) adj. 1. making blissful or blessed 2. full of bliss or joy [a beatific smile]

beatify (bē at′ə fi′) vt. -fied′, -fy′ing [< Fr. < L. beatus, happy + facere, make] 1. to make blissfully happy 2. R.C.Ch. to declare one who has died to be among the blessed in heaven —**beat′ifica′tion** n.

beatitude (bē at′ə tyo͞od′) n. [< L. beatus, happy] perfect blessedness or happiness —**the Beatitudes** the blessings on the meek, the peacemakers, etc. in the Sermon on the Mount: Matt. 5: 3-12

beatnik (bēt′nik) *n.* [BEAT + Russ. (via. Yid.) *-nik*] a member of the beat generation

beau (bō) *n.*, *pl.* **beaus, beaux** (bōz) [Fr. < L. *bellus*, pretty] 1. a dandy 2. [Chiefly U.S.] suitor

Beaufort scale (bō′fərt) [< Sir F. *Beaufort*] *Meteorol.* a scale of wind velocities ranging from 0 (calm) to 17 (hurricane)

Beaujolais (bō′zhə lā′) *n.* a rich red wine from the region of Beaujolais near Burgundy, France

beauteous (byōōt′ē əs) *adj.* same as BEAUTIFUL —**beau′teously** *adv.*

beautician (byōō tish′ən) *n.* a person who does facials, manicuring, etc. in a beauty salon

beautiful (byōōt′ə fəl) *adj.* having beauty; very pleasing to the eye, ear, mind, etc. —**beau′tifully** *adv.*

beautify (byōōt′ə fī′) *vt.*, *vi.* **-fied′, -fy′-ing** to make or become beautiful —**beau′tifica′tion** *n.* —**beau′tifi′er** *n.*

beauty (byōōt′ē) *n.*, *pl.* **-ties** [< L. *bellus*, pretty] 1. the quality of being very pleasing, as by colour, form, tone, behaviour, etc. 2. a thing having this quality 3. good looks 4. a very good-looking woman 5. any attractive feature [that's the *beauty* of it]

beauty queen a woman who has won a beauty contest

beauty salon (or **shop** or **parlour**) a place where women go for hair styling, manicuring, etc.

beauty sleep [Colloq.] 1. sleep before midnight, popularly thought to be most restful 2. any extra sleep

beauty spot 1. a tiny black patch formerly applied by women to the face 2. a natural mark or mole on the skin 3. any place noted for its beauty

BEAVER
(81-120 cm long, including tail)

beaver¹ (bē′vər) *n.* [OE. *beofor*] 1. a large, amphibious rodent with soft, brown fur, webbed hind feet, and a flat, broad tail 2. its fur 3. a hat made of this fur —**beaver away** to work hard and steadily

beaver² *n.* [< OFr. *bave*, saliva] the chinpiece of a helmet

be-bop (bē′bop′) *n.* *orig.* name for BOP

becalm (bi käm′) *vt.* 1. to make calm 2. to make (a sailing ship) motionless from lack of wind

became (bi käm′) *pt.* of BECOME

because (bi koz′) *conj.* [< ME. *bi*, by + *cause*] for the reason that; since —**because of** on account of

béchamel (bāsh′ə mel′) *n.* [Fr. < Louis de *Béchamel*] a rich white sauce

beck¹ (bek) *n.* [< BECKON] a beckoning

gesture of the hand, etc. —**at the beck and call of** at the service of

beck² *n.* [< ON. *bekkr*, brook] a little stream, esp. one with a rocky bottom

beckon (bek′'n) *vi.*, *vt.* [< OE. *beacen*, beacon] 1. to summon by a gesture 2. to attract; lure

become (bi kum′) *vi.* **-came′, -come′, -com′ing** [OE. *becuman*] to come or grow to be —*vt.* to be right for or suitable to [that hat *becomes* you] —**become of** to happen to

becoming *adj.* 1. that is suitable or appropriate 2. suitable to the wearer

becquerel (bek′ə rel′) [< A. H. *Becquerel*] the SI unit of activity of a radioactive source

bed (bed) *n.* [OE.] 1. a piece of furniture for sleeping or resting on 2. any place or thing used for sleeping or reclining 3. a plot of soil where plants are raised 4. the bottom of a river, lake, etc. 5. rock, etc. in which something is embedded 6. a geological layer —*vt.* **bed′ded, bed′-ding** 1. to provide with a sleeping place 2. to put to bed 3. to have sexual intercourse with 4. to embed 5. to plant in a bed of earth: also **bed out** 6. to arrange in layers —*vi.* 1. to go to bed; rest 2. to form in layers —**bed and board** sleeping accommodation and meals —**bed down** to prepare and use a sleeping place —**get out of the wrong side of the bed** to be cross or grouchy

B.Ed. Bachelor of Education

bed and breakfast overnight accommodation and breakfast, as offered by a hotel or boarding house, etc.

bedaub (bi dôb′) *vt.* to make daubs on; smear over

bedbug (bed′bug′) *n.* a small, wingless, reddish-brown, bloodsucking insect that infests beds, etc.

bedclothes *n.pl.* sheets, blankets, quilts, etc. used on a bed

bedding *n.* 1. mattresses and bedclothes 2. straw, etc., used to bed animals 3. *Geol.* stratification

bedding plant an immature plant bedded out in the garden

bedeck (bi dek′) *vt.* to decorate; adorn

bedevil (bi dev′'l) *vt.* **-illed, -illing** 1. to plague; torment 2. to confuse; muddle —**bedev′ilment** *n.*

bedew (bi dyōō′) *vt.* to make wet as with dew

bedizen (bi dī′z'n) *vt.* [BE- + Low G. *diesse*, of flax] to dress in a cheap, showy way —**bedi′zenment** *n.*

bed jacket a woman's short, loose upper garment sometimes worn in bed over a nightgown

bedlam (bed′ləm) *n.* [< (St. Mary of) *Bethlehem*, old insane asylum in London] any place or condition of noise and confusion —**bed′lamite** (-īt′) *n.*

bed linen bed sheets, pillowcases, etc.

Bedlington terrier (bed′lin t'n) [< town in Northumberland] a woolly-coated terrier resembling a small lamb

bed of roses [Colloq.] a situation of ease and luxury

Bedouin, Beduin (bed′ōō win) *n.*, *pl.* **-ins, -in** [< Fr. < Ar., desert dwellers] [*also* **b-**] 1. an Arab of the nomadic desert tribes of Arabia, Syria, or N Africa 2. any wanderer

bedpan *n.* a shallow pan for use as a toilet by a person confined to bed

bedraggle (bi drag′'l) *vt.* **-gled, -gling** to make wet, limp, and dirty, as by dragging through mud

bedridden (bed′rid′'n) *adj.* having to stay in bed, usually for a long period, because of illness, infirmity, etc.

bedrock *n.* 1. solid rock beneath the soil and superficial rock 2. a secure foundation 3. the very bottom 4. basic principles

bedroom *n.* a room to sleep in

Beds. Bedfordshire

bedside *n.* the space beside a bed —*adj.* 1. beside a bed 2. as regards patients [a *bedside* manner]

bed-sitting room furnished accommodation consisting of a combined bedroom and sitting room: also **bed′sit′ter, bed′-sit′n.**

bedsore *n.* a sore on the body of a bedridden person, caused by chafing or pressure

bedspread *n.* a cover spread over the blankets on a bed, mainly for ornament

bedstead (bed′sted′) *n.* a framework for supporting the springs and mattress of a bed

bedstraw *n.* [from its former use as straw for beds] a small plant with white or coloured flowers

bed-wetting *n.* urinating in bed

bee¹ (bē) *n.* [OE. *beo*] 1. a four-winged, hairy insect that gathers pollen and nectar 2. a busy person —**have a bee in one's bonnet** to be obsessed by an idea

bee² *n.* [< OE. *ben*, service] [U.S.] a meeting of people to work together or to compete [a sewing *bee*]

beeb (bēb) *n.* [Colloq.] British Broadcasting Corporation

beebread (bē′bred′) *n.* a yellowish-brown mixture of pollen and honey, made and eaten by some bees

beech (bēch) *adj.* [OE. *bece*] designating a family of trees including the beeches, oaks, and chestnuts —*n.* a tree of the beech family, with smooth bark, hard wood, dark-green leaves, and edible nuts —**beech′en** *adj.*

beechmast (-mäst′) *n.* beechnuts, esp. as they lie on the ground: also **beech mast**

beechnut *n.* the small, three-cornered, edible nut of the beech tree

beef (bēf) *n.*, *pl.* **beeves**; also, and for 4 always, **beefs** [< L. *bos, bovis*, ox] 1. meat from a full-grown ox, cow, or bull 2. such an animal, esp. one bred for meat 3. [Colloq.] muscle or strength 4. [Slang] a complaint —*vi.* [Slang] to complain —**beef up** [Colloq.] to strengthen by addition, etc.

beefeater (bēf′ēt′ər) *n.* 1. *same as* YEOMAN OF THE GUARD 2. a guard at the Tower of London

beef tea a drink made from beef extract or by boiling lean strips of beef

beefy *adj.* **-ier, -iest** fleshy and solid; brawny —**beef′iness** *n.*

beehive (bē′hīv′) *n.* 1. a shelter for a colony of bees 2. a place of great activity

beekeeper *n.* a person who keeps bees for producing honey —**bee′keep′ing** *n.*

beeline *n.* a straight, direct route —**make a beeline for** [Colloq.] to go straight towards

Beelzebub (bē el′zə bub′) [< Heb. *Ba'al zebūb*, god of flies] *Bible* the chief devil; Satan

bee moth a moth whose larvae, hatched in beehives, eat the wax of the honeycomb

been (bēn) *pp. of* BE

beer (bēar) *n.* [OE. *beor*] 1. an alcoholic, fermented beverage made from malted barley and hops 2. a drink of this 3. a soft drink made from roots, etc.

beer and skittles a time of pleasure and amusement

beergarden *n.* an open-air enclosure where beer and other drinks are served

beer parlour [Canad.] a licensed place in which beer is sold to the public

beery *adj.* **-ier, -iest** 1. of or like beer 2. showing the effects of drinking beer —**beer′iness** *n.*

beestings (bēs′tiņz) *n.pl.* [*often with sing. v.*] [OE. *bysting*] the first milk of a cow after having a calf

beeswax (bēz′waks′) *n.* wax secreted and used by bees to build their honeycomb

beeswing (bēz′wiŋ′) *n.* a gauzy film that forms in some old wines, esp. port

beet (bēt) *n.* [< L. *beta*] a plant with edible leaves and a thick, fleshy, white or red root

beetle¹ (bēt′'l) *n.* [< OE. *bitan*, to bite] an insect with hard front wings that cover the membranous hind wings when these are folded —**beetle off** [Colloq.] to scurry away like a beetle

beetle² *n.* [OE. *betel*] 1. a heavy, wooden mallet 2. a household mallet or pestle for mashing or beating

beetle³ *vi.* **-tled, -tling** [prob. < ff.] to project or jut; overhang —*adj.* jutting; overhanging: also **bee′tling**

beetle-browed *adj.* [ME.] 1. having bushy or overhanging eyebrows 2. frowning; scowling

beetroot (bēt′rōot) *n.* a variety of beet: its dark red root is eaten as a vegetable

beet sugar sugar extracted from sugar beets

befall (bi fôl′) *vi.*, *vt.* **-fell′, -fall′en, -fall′-ing** [< OE. *be-* + *feallan*, fall] to happen (to)

befit (bi fit′) *vt.* **-fit′ted, -fit′ting** to be suitable or proper for —**befit′tingly** *adv.*

before (bi fôr′) *adv.* [< OE. *be-*, by + *foran*, before] 1. ahead; in front 2. in the past; previously 3. earlier; sooner —*prep.* 1. ahead of in time, space, rank, or importance 2. just in front of 3. in the sight, presence, etc. of 4. being considered by *[* the bill *before* the assembly *]* **5.** earlier than **6.** in preference to —*conj.* **1.** earlier than the time that **2.** rather than

before Christ in the year before the beginning of the Christian Era: it is fixed by counting backwards from 1 A.D.

beforehand *adv., adj.* **1.** ahead of time; in advance **2.** in anticipation

befoul (bi foul') *vt.* to dirty or sully; foul

befriend (bi frend') *vt.* to act as a friend to; help

befuddle (bi fud' 'l) *vt.* **-dled, -dling** to confuse or stupefy as with alcoholic drink —**befud'dlement** *n.*

beg (beg) *vt.* **begged, beg'ging** *[* < OFr. *begand,* beggar*]* **1.** to ask for as charity **2.** to ask for as a kindness or favour —*vi.* **1.** to be a beggar **2.** to entreat —**beg off** to ask to be released from —**go (a-)begging** to be unwanted

began (bi gan') *pt.* of BEGIN

beget (bi get') *vt.* **-got', -got'ten** or **-got', -get'ting** *[* < OE. *begitan,* acquire *]* **1.** to be the father of **2.** to produce *[* tyranny *begets* rebellion *]* —**beget'ter** *n.*

beggar (beg' ər) *n.* **1.** a person who begs **2.** a very poor person **3.** [Colloq.] a person; fellow —*vt.* **1.** to make poor **2.** to make seem useless *[* beauty *beggars* description *]* —**beg'gardom** *n.* —**beg'garly** *adj.*

begin (bi gin') *vi.* **began', begun', begin'-ning** *[* < OE. *beginnan]* **1.** to start doing something **2.** to come into being **3.** to commence **4.** to be or do in the slightest degree *[* they don't *begin* to compare *]* —*vt.* **1.** to cause to start **2.** to originate **3.** to be the first part of —**begin'ner** *n.*

beginner's luck the exceptional luck that is believed to accompany beginners

beginning *n.* **1.** a commencing **2.** the time or place of starting **3.** the first part **4.** [*usually pl.*] an early stage —**beginning of the end** the last stage

begone (bi gon') *interj., vi.* (to) be gone; go away; get out

begonia (bi gōn' yə) *n.* *[* < M. *Bégon]* a plant with showy flowers and ornamental leaves

begot (bi got') *pt. & alt. pp.* of BEGET

begotten *alt. pp.* of BEGET

begrudge (bi gruj') *vt.* **-grudged', -grudg'-ing** **1.** to feel resentment at the possession of (something) by another **2.** to give with ill will —**begrudg'ingly** *adv.*

beguile (bi gīl') *vt.* **-guiled', -guil'ing** **1.** to charm or delight **2.** to pass (time) pleasantly **3.** to mislead by guile **4.** to deprive (*of* or *out of*) by deceit —**beguile'-ment** *n.* —**beguil'er** *n.* —**beguil'ingly** *adv.*

beguine (bi gēn') *n.* *[* < Fr. *béguin,* infatuation *]* a native dance of Martinique or its music

begum (bā' gəm) *n.* *[* < Hindi *begam,* lady *]* in India, a Moslem princess or lady of high rank

begun (bi gun') *pp.* of BEGIN

behalf (bi häf') *n.* *[* < OE. *be,* by + *healf,* side *]* support or interest *[* speak on his *behalf]* —**on behalf of** in the interest of; for

behave (bi hāv') *vt., vi.* **-haved', -hav'-ing** *[* see BE- & HAVE *]* **1.** to conduct (oneself or itself) or act in a specified way **2.** to conduct (oneself) properly; do what is right

behaviour (bi hāv' yər) *n.* the way a person behaves or acts; conduct —**behav'-ioural** *adj.*

behavioural science any of the sciences, as sociology, psychology, or anthropology, that study human behaviour

behaviourism *n.* the doctrine that observed behaviour provides the only valid data of psychology —**behav'iourist** *n., adj.*

behead (bi hed') *vt.* to cut off the head of

beheld (bi held') *pt. & pp.* of BEHOLD

behemoth (bi hē' moth) *n.* [Heb. *behēmāh,* beast] **1.** *Bible* a huge animal, assumed to be the hippopotamus : Job 40 : 15-24 **2.** any huge animal or thing

behest (bi hest') *n.* [OE. *behæs,* vow] an order, command, or earnest request

behind (bi hīnd') *adv.* [OE. *behindan*] **1.** in or to the rear **2.** in a former time, place, etc. **3.** into a retarded state **4.** into arrears **5.** slow; late —*prep.* **1.** remaining after **2.** at the back of **3.** lower in rank, etc. **4.** later than **5.** on the farther side of **6.** supporting or advocating **7.** hidden by —*adj.* that follows *[* the person *behind]* —*n.* [Colloq.] the buttocks

behindhand *adv., adj.* late or slow in payment, time, or progress

behold (bi hōld') *vt.* **-held', -held', -hold'-ing** [OE. *bihealdan,* to hold] to look at; regard —*interj.* look! see! —**behold'er** *n.*

beholden *adj.* obliged to feel grateful; indebted

behove (bi hōv') *vt.* **-hoved', -hov'ing** [OE. *behofian,* need] to be necessary or fitting for; incumbent upon *[* it *behoves* you to do this *]*

beige (bāzh) *n.* [Fr.] **1.** a pale brown sandy colour **2.** a soft, unbleached wool fabric —*adj.* greyish-tan

being (bē' iŋ) *n.* [see BE] **1.** existence; life **2.** basic or essential nature **3.** one that lives or exists *[* a human *being]* —**being as** (or **that**) [Dial. or Colloq.] since; because —**for the time being** for now

bejewel (bi jōō' əl) *vt.* **-elled, -elling** to decorate with or as with jewels

bel (bel) *n.* *[* < A.G. *Bell] Physics* a unit for comparing two power levels, equal to 10 decibels

belabour (bi lā' bər) *vt.* **1.** to beat severely **2.** to attack verbally **3.** *popularly, same as* LABOUR, *vt.*

belated (bi lāt' id) *adj.* late or too late; tardy —**belat'edly** *adv.* —**belat'edness** *n.*

belay (bi lā') *vt., vi.* **-layed', -lay'ing** *[* < OE. *be- + lecgan,* lay *]* **1.** to make (a rope) secure by winding round a pin (**belaying pin**), cleat, etc. **2.** [Naut. Colloq.] to hold; stop **3.** to secure (a person or thing) by a rope

belch (belch) *vi., vt.* [OE. *bealcian*] **1.** to expel (gas) through the mouth from the stomach **2.** to throw forth (its contents) violently *[* the volcano *belched* flame *]* —*n.* **1.** a belching **2.** a thing belched

beldam, beldame (bel'dəm) *n.* [see BELLE + DAME] [Obs.] an old woman; esp., a hideous old woman

beleaguer (bi lē'gər) *vt.* [< Du. *leger,* a camp] 1. to besiege by encircling 2. to beset; harass

belfry (bel'frē) *n., pl.* -fries [< OHG. *bergen,* to protect + *frid,* peace] 1. a bell tower 2. the part of a steeple that holds the bell or bells —**bel'fried** *adj.*

Belial (bēl'yəl) *n.* [< Heb. *belīya'al,* worthlessness] *Bible* wickedness, personified as Satan

belie (bi lī') *vt.* -lied', -ly'ing 1. to give a false idea of; misrepresent 2. to leave unfulfilled 3. to show to be untrue —**beli'-er** *n.*

belief (bə lēf') *n.* [< OE. *geleafa*] 1. the state of believing 2. faith, esp. religious faith 3. trust or confidence 4. a creed, tenet, etc. 5. an opinion; expectation

believe (bə lēv') *vt.* -lieved', -liev'ing [< OE. *geliefan*] 1. to take as true, real, etc. 2. to have confidence in a statement or promise of 3. to suppose or think —*vi.* 1. to have confidence (*in*) 2. to have religious faith 3. to suppose or think —**believ'abil'ity** *n.* —**believ'able** *adj.* —**believ'ably** *adv.* —**believ'er** *n.*

Belisha beacon (bə lē'shə) [< *Hore-Belisha*] a flashing orange light mounted on a post and marking a pedestrian crossing

belittle (bi lit'') *vt.* -tled, -tling to make seem little, less important, etc. —**belit'tle-ment** *n.* —**belit'tler** *n.*

bell[1] (bel) *n.* [OE. *belle*] 1. a hollow object, usually cuplike and of metal, which rings when struck 2. the sound made by a bell 3. anything shaped like a bell 4. *Naut.* a bell rung every half hour to mark the periods of the watch —*vt.* to attach a bell to —**bell, book, and candle** instruments used formerly in excommunications in the R.C. Church —**bell the cat** to hazard one's safety for the sake of others —**sound as a bell** in perfect condition

bell[2] *n., vi., vt.* [< OE. *bellan*] bellow; roar; bay

belladonna (bel'ə don'ə) *n.* [< It., beautiful lady] 1. a poisonous plant with bell-shaped flowers; deadly nightshade: it yields atropine 2. atropine

bell-bottom *adj.* designating trousers flaring at the ankles: also **bell'-bot'tomed**

belle (bel) *n.* [Fr., fem. of BEAU] a pretty woman or girl; often, one who is the prettiest

belles-lettres (bel let'rə) *n.pl.* [Fr.] fiction, poetry, drama, etc. as distinguished from technical writings

bellicose (bel'ə kōs') *adj.* [< L. *bellicus,* of war] quarrelsome; warlike —**bel'licose'-ly** *adv.* —**bellicosity** (bel'ə kos'ə tē) *n.*

belligerence (bə lij'ər əns) *n.* belligerent or aggressively hostile attitude or quality

belligerent *adj.* [< L. *bellum,* war + *gerere,* carry on] 1. showing readiness to fight or quarrel 2. warlike 3. of war; of fighting 4. at war —*n.* a belligerent person or nation —**bellig'erently** *adv.*

bell jar a bell-shaped cover made of glass, used to keep gases, moisture, etc. in or out: also **bell glass**

bell metal an alloy of copper and tin used in bells

bellow (bel'ō) *vi.* [OE. *bylgan*] 1. to roar as a bull 2. to cry out loudly, as in anger —*vt.* to utter loudly or powerfully —*n.* a bellowing sound

bellows (bel'ōz) *n.sing. & pl.* [see BELLY] 1. a device that produces a stream of air when its sides are pumped together: used for blowing fires, in pipe organs, etc. 2. the folding part of some cameras

bellpull *n.* a handle or cord pulled to operate a bell

bellpush *n.* a button that operates an electric bell

bellringer *n.* 1. a person who rings church bells 2. a performer on musical handbells

bellwether (bel'weth'ər) *n.* a male sheep, usually wearing a bell, that leads the flock

belly (bel'ē) *n., pl.* -lies [< OE. *belg,* leather bag] 1. the part of the human body between the chest and thighs; abdomen 2. the underside of an animal's body 3. the stomach 4. the deep interior *[the belly of a ship]* 5. any part, etc. that curves outwards —*vt., vi.* -lied, -lying to swell out; bulge

bellyache *n.* pain in the abdomen —*vi.* -ached', -ach'ing [Slang] to complain —**bel'lyach'er** *n.*

bellybutton *n.* [Colloq.] the navel: also **belly button**

belly dance a dance characterized by a twisting of the abdomen, sinuous hip movements, etc. —**bel'ly-dance'** *vi.* -danced', -danc'ing —**belly dancer**

belly-flop *vi.* -flopped', -flop'ping [Colloq.] to dive awkwardly, with the belly striking flat against the water —*n.* such a dive

bellyful *n.* 1. enough or more than enough to eat 2. [Colloq.] all that one can bear

belly-landing *n.* the landing of an aircraft with the undercarriage up, esp. in an emergency

belly laugh [Colloq.] a hearty laugh

belong (bi loŋ') *vi.* [< ME.] 1. to be owned (with *to*) 2. to be a member (with *to*) 3. to be related (*to*) 4. to have a proper place *[it belongs here]*

belonging *n.* 1. [*pl.*] possessions; property 2. close relationship; affinity *[a sense of belonging]*

beloved (bi luvd') *adj.* dearly loved —*n.* a dearly loved person

below (bi lō') *adv., adj.* [see BE- & LOW[1]] 1. in or to a lower place; beneath 2. in a later place (of a book, etc.) 3. in hell 4. on earth 5. in or to a lesser rank, function, etc. —*prep.* 1. lower than, as in position, rank, worth, etc. 2. unworthy of

belt (belt) *n.* [< L. *balteus,* belt] 1. a band of leather, etc., worn about the waist 2. any encircling thing like this 3. an endless band for transferring motion from one wheel to another 4. an area with some distinctive feature 5. [Slang] a hard blow —*vt.* l. to encircle or fasten as with a belt 2. to hit hard, as with a belt —*vi.* [Colloq.] to move at high speed —**below the belt** unfair(ly) —**belt up** l. [Colloq.] to become silent 2. to fasten a safety belt —**tighten one's belt** to live more thriftily —**under one's belt** [Colloq.] as part of one's experience

beluga (bə lōo′gə) *n., pl.* **-ga, -gas** [< Russ. *byeli*, white] l. a large, white sturgeon of the Black and Caspian seas 2. a white whale

belvedere (bel′və dēər′) *n.* [It., beautiful view] a summerhouse, or an open, roofed gallery in an upper storey, built to give a view of the scenery

B.E.M. British Empire Medal

bemoan (bi mōn′) *vt., vi.* to moan about or lament (a loss, grief, etc.) [to bemoan one's fate]

bemuse (bi myōoz′) *vt.* **-mused′, -mus′-ing** [BE- + MUSE] to muddle, confuse, or stupefy —**bemuse′ment** *n.*

ben¹ (ben) *n.* [< Gael. *beann*, peak] [Scot. & Ir.] a mountain peak [Ben Nevis]

ben² *adv., prep* [OE. *be-* + *innan*, in] [Scot.] within; inside —*n.* [Scot.] the inner room of a cottage

bench (bench) *n.* [OE. *benc*] l. a long, hard seat for several persons 2. a worktable, esp. for a mechanic, etc. 3. the place where judges sit in a court 4. [sometimes B-] *a*) the office of a judge *b*) judges collectively *c*) a law court —**on the bench** serving as a judge or magistrate

bencher *n. Law* a senior member of the Inns of Court

bench mark l. a surveyor's mark made on a landmark for use as a reference point 2. a standard in judging quality, value, etc. Also **bench′mark′** *n.*

bend¹ (bend) *vt.* **bent, bend′ing** [OE. *bendan*, to bind] l. to force (an object) into a curved or crooked form 2. to turn from a straight line 3. to make (someone) submit 4. to turn or direct (one's attention, etc. *to*) 5. to incline or tend (*to* or *towards*) —*vi.* l. to turn from a straight line 2. to yield by curving, as from pressure 3. to curve the body; stoop (*over* or *down*) 4. to give in; yield —*n.* l. a bending or being bent 2. a curving part, as of a river —**round the bend** [Colloq.] crazy, mad, insane, etc.

bend² *n.* [ME. < prec.] any of various knots used in tying ropes —**the bends** [Colloq.] decompression sickness

bender *n.* [Slang] a drinking bout; spree

bend sinister *Heraldry* a diagonal band on a coat of arms: a sign of bastardy in the family line

beneath (bi nēth′) *adv.* [< OE. *be-* + *neothan*, down] in a lower place; below; underneath —*prep.* l. lower than; below 2. underneath 3. unworthy of [it is beneath him to cheat]

Benedictine (ben′ə dik′tin; *for n. 2* -tēn) *adj.* l. of Saint Benedict 2. of the monastic order based on his teachings —*n.* l. a Benedictine monk or nun 2. [b-] a liqueur, orig. made by Benedictine monks

benediction (ben′ə dik′shən) *n.* [< L. *bene*, well + *dicere*, speak] a blessing, esp. one ending a religious service —**ben′e-dic′tory** *adj.*

benefaction (ben′ə fak′shən) *n.* [< L. *bene*, well + *facere*, do] l. the act of doing good or helping those in need 2. money or help freely given

benefactor (ben′ə fak′tər) *n.* a person who has given help, esp. financial help —**ben′efac′tress** *n.fem.*

benefice (ben′ə fis) *n.* [< L. *beneficium*, kindness] l. an endowed church office providing a living for a vicar, etc. 2. its income —*vt.* **-ficed, -ficing** to provide with a benefice

beneficence (bə nef′ə səns) *n.* [see BENEFACTION] l. the fact or quality of being kind or doing good 2. a charitable act or generous gift —**benef′icent** *adj.*

beneficial (ben′ə fish′əl) *adj.* producing benefits; advantageous; favourable —**ben′-efi′cially** *adv.*

beneficiary (ben′ə fish′ər ē) *n., pl.* **-aries** l. a person named to receive the income or inheritance from a will, insurance policy, etc. 2. a holder of a benefice —*adj.* holding a benefice

benefit (ben′ə fit) *n.* [see BENEFACTION] l. anything helping to improve conditions; advantage 2. [*often pl.*] payments made by an insurance company, public agency, etc., as during sickness or retirement 3. a public performance, dance, etc. whose proceeds go to help a certain person, cause, etc. —*vt.* **-fited, -fiting** to aid —*vi.* to receive advantage; profit —**give someone the benefit of the doubt** to assume a person is innocent

benefit of clergy the exemption which the medieval clergy had from trial except in a church court

benefit society same as FRIENDLY SOCIETY

benevolence (bə nev′ə ləns) *n.* [< L. *bene*, well + *velle*, to wish] l. an inclination to do good; kindliness 2. a kindly, charitable act —**benev′olent** *adj.*

Bengali (beŋ gôl′ē) *n.* l. a native of Bengal 2. the Indo-European, Indic language of Bengal

Bengal light (beŋ gôl′) a firework or flare with a steady blue light, used, esp. formerly, as a signal, etc.

benighted (bi nīt′id) *adj.* l. surrounded by darkness 2. intellectually or morally backward

benign (bi nīn′) *adj.* [< L. *bene*, well + *genus*, birth] l. good-natured; kindly 2. favourable; beneficial 3. *Med.* doing little or no harm —**benign′ly** *adv.*

benignant (bi nig′nənt) *adj.* [< prec.] l. kindly or gracious, sometimes in a patronizing way 2. favourable; beneficial —**benig′nancy** *n.*

benignity *n., pl.* **-ties** l. kindliness 2. a kind act

benison (ben′ə z'n) *n.* [see BENEDICTION] a blessing; benediction

bent¹ (bent) *pt.* and *pp. of* BEND¹ —*adj.* l. curved or crooked 2. strongly determined **3.** [Slang] dishonest; corrupt —**n.** **1.** a tendency **2.** a mental leaning; propensity [a bent for art] —**to** (or **at**) **the top of one's bent** to (or at) the limit of one's ability

bent² **n.** [OE. beonot] any of various wiry, low-growing grasses: also called **bent'grass'**

Benthamism (ben'thəm iz'm) **n.** the philosophy of Jeremy Bentham (1748-1832), Brit. economist, which holds that the greatest happiness of the greatest number should be the goal of society

BENTWOOD CHAIR

bentwood (bent'wood') **adj.** designating furniture made of wood permanently bent into various forms by heat, moisture, and pressure

benumb (bi num') **vt.** **1.** to make numb **2.** to deaden the mind, will, or feelings of

benzene (ben'zēn) **n.** [< BENZOIN] a flammable, poisonous liquid, obtained from coal tar and used as a solvent

benzine (ben'zēn) **n.** [< BENZOIN] a colourless, flammable liquid obtained in the distillation of petroleum and used as a motor fuel

benzoin (ben'zō in) **n.** [< Ar. lubān jāwi, incense of Java] the resin from certain tropical Asiatic trees, used in medicine, perfumery, etc. —**benzoic** (ben zō'ik) **adj.**

benzol (ben'zol) **n.** same as BENZENE

bequeath (bi kwēth') **vt.** [< OE. be- + cwethan, say] **1.** to leave (property) to another by last will and testament **2.** to hand down —**bequeath'able** **adj.** —**bequeath'al** **n.**

bequest (bi kwest') **n.** [see prec.] **1.** a bequeathing **2.** anything bequeathed

berate (bi rāt') **vt.** **-rat'ed, -rat'ing** [BE- + RATE²] to scold or rebuke severely

Berber (bʉr'bər) **n.** **1.** any of a Moslem people living in N Africa **2.** their language

berceuse (bāar söz') **n.,** pl. **-ceuses** (Fr. -söz') [Fr.]. **1.** a lullaby **2.** a piece of instrumental music that has a rocking or lulling effect

bereave (bi rēv') **vt.** **-reaved'** or **-reft'** (-reft'), **-reav'ing** [< OE. be- + reafian, rob] **1.** to deprive: now usually in the pp. (bereft) [bereft of hope] **2.** to leave in a sad or lonely state, as by death —**the bereaved** the survivors of a recently deceased person —**bereave'ment** **n.**

beret (ber'ā) **n.** [see BIRETTA] a flat, round cap of felt, wool, etc.

berg (bʉrg) **n.** same as ICEBERG

bergamot (bʉr'gə mot') **n.** [< Fr. < ? Turk. beg-armûdī, prince's pear] **1.** a pear-shaped citrus fruit grown in S Europe for its oil, used in perfumery **2.** an aromatic herb

Bergie (bʉr'gē) **n.** [< Afrik. berg, mountain] [S Afr. Colloq.] a vagabond, esp. one living on the slopes of Table Mountain in the Western Cape of South Africa

bergwind (berkh'vənt) **n.** in South Africa, a hot, dry wind blowing from the high interior region to the coastal regions

beriberi (ber'ē ber'ē) **n.** [Singh. beri, weakness] a deficiency disease caused by lack of thiamine (vitamin B_1) in the diet

berk (bʉrk) **n.** [< Berkshire Hunt] [Slang] a stupid person; fool

berkelium (bʉr'klē əm) **n.** [< University of California at Berkeley] a radioactive chemical element: symbol, Bk

Berks. Berkshire

Bermuda shorts (bər myōō'də) [< island in W Atlantic] short trousers extending to just above the knee

berry (ber'ē) **n.,** pl. **ber'ries** [OE. berie] **1.** any small, juicy, fleshy fruit, as a raspberry, etc. **2.** the dry seed of various plants, as a coffee bean **3.** Bot. a fleshy fruit with a soft wall and thin skin, as the tomato, etc. —**ber'rylike' adj.**

berserk (bər sʉrk') **adj., adv.** [< ON. ber, a bear + serkr, coat] in or into a state of violent rage or frenzy —**n.** Norse Legend a frenzied warrior: also **berserk'er**

berth (bʉrth) **n.** [< base of BEAR¹] **1.** a built-in bed or bunk on a ship, train, etc. **2.** Naut. a) space to keep clear of another ship, etc. b) space for anchoring c) a place of anchorage **3.** a position, job, etc. —**vt.** to put into or furnish with a berth —**vi.** to occupy a berth —**give a wide berth to** to stay well away from

beryl (ber'əl) **n.** [< Gr. bēryllos] beryllium aluminium silicate, a very hard, crystalline mineral: emerald and aquamarine are two gem varieties of beryl

beryllium (bə ril'ē əm) **n.** [< prec.] a hard, rare, metallic chemical element: symbol, Be

beseech (bi sēch') **vt.** **-sought'** or **-seeched', -seech'ing** [see BE- & SEEK] **1.** to ask (someone) earnestly; implore **2.** to ask for earnestly —**beseech'ingly adv.**

beset (bi set') **vt.** **-set', -set'ting** [see BE- & SET] **1.** to attack from all sides; harass **2.** to surround **3.** to set thickly with —**beset'ment n.**

besetting adj. constantly harassing or attacking

beside (bi sīd') **prep.** [OE. bi sidan] **1.** at the side of; near **2.** in comparison with **3.** in addition to; besides **4.** other than; aside from **5.** not pertinent to [beside the point] —**beside oneself** wild with fear, rage, etc.

besides adv. **1.** in addition **2.** except for that mentioned **3.** moreover —**prep.** **1.** in addition to **2.** other than

besiege (bi sēj') **vt.** **-sieged', -sieg'ing**

[ME. < be- + segen, to lay siege to]
1. to hem in with armed forces 2. to
close in on 3. to overwhelm [besieged
with queries] —**besieg'er** n.

besmirch (bi smurch') vt. [BE- + SMIRCH]
1. to make dirty; soil 2. to bring dishonour
to; sully

besom (bē'zəm) n. [< OE. besma, broom]
a broom, esp. one made of twigs tied
to a handle

besot (bi sot') vt. -sot'ted, -sot'ting 1.
to stupefy, as with alcoholic drink 2.
to make silly —**besot'ted** adj.

besought (bi sôt') alt. pt. and pp. of
BESEECH

bespangle (bi spaŋ'g'l) vt. -gled, -gling
to cover with or as with spangles

bespatter (bi spat'ər) vt. to spatter, as
with mud or slander; soil or sully by
spattering

bespeak (bi spēk') vt. -spoke' (-spōk'),
-spo'ken or -spoke', -speak'ing 1. to
speak for or engage in advance 2. to
be indicative of; show 3. to foreshadow

bespectacled (bi spek'tə k'ld) adj.
wearing eyeglasses

bespoke (bi spōk') pl. and alt. pp. of
BESPEAK —adj. custom-made; making or
made to order

Bessemer process (bes'ə mər) [< Sir
H. Bessemer] a method of making steel
by blasting air through molten pig iron
in a large container (**Bessemer converter**)
to burn away impurities

best (best) adj. superl. of GOOD [OE.
betst] 1. of the most excellent sort 2.
most suitable, etc. 3. largest [the best
part of an hour] —adv. superl. of WELL²
1. in the most excellent or suitable manner
2. in the highest degree —n. 1. the person
or people, thing, action, etc. of the greatest
excellence, worth, etc. 2. the utmost 3.
one's finest clothes —vt. to defeat or
outdo —**all for the best** turning out to
be fortunate after all —**as best one can**
as well as one can —**at best** under the
most favourable conditions —**at one's best**
in one's best mood, form, health, etc. —**had
best** ought to —**make the best of** to
do as well as one can with

bestial (bes'tē al) adj. [< LL. bestialis]
like a beast; savage, vile, etc. —**bestial-
ity** (bes'tē al'ə tē) n. —**bes'tially** adv.

bestiary (bes'tē ər ē) n., pl. -aries [<
L. bestia, beast] a type of medieval natural
history book with moralistic or religious
fables about animals

bestir (bi stur') vt. -stirred', -stir'ring to
stir to action; exert or busy (oneself)

best man the principal attendant of the
bridegroom at a wedding

bestow (bi stō') vt. [see BE- & STOW]
1. to give as a gift (often with on or
upon) 2. to apply; devote —**bestow'al** n.

bestrew (bi strōō') vt. -strewed',
-strewed' or -strewn', -strew'ing 1. to
cover over (a surface); strew 2. to scatter
or lie scattered over or about

bestride (bi strīd') vt. -strode' (-strōd'),
-strid'den (-strid''n), -strid'ing 1. to sit

on, mount, or stand over with a leg on
each side 2. [Archaic] to stride over

best seller a book, gramophone record,
etc. currently outselling most others

bet (bet) n. [prob. < ABET] 1. an agreement
between two persons that the one proved
wrong about the outcome of something
will do or pay what is stipulated; wager
2. the thing or sum thus staked —vt.
bet or **bet'ted, bet'ting** 1. to declare
in or as in a bet 2. to stake (money,
etc.) in a bet 3. to wager with (someone)
—vi. to make a bet —**you bet** (you)!
[Colloq.] certainly!

beta (bēt'ə) n. 1. the second letter of
the Greek alphabet (B, β) 2. the second
of a group or series

betake (bi tāk') vt. -took', -tak'en, -tak'-
ing to go (used reflexively) [he betook
himself to his castle]

beta particle an electron or positron
ejected from the nucleus of an atom during
radioactive disintegration

betatron (bēt'ə tron') n. [BETA &
ELECTRON] an electron accelerator that
uses a rapidly changing magnetic field
to accelerate the particles to high velocities

betel (bēt''l) n. [Port. < Malay] a tropical
Asian climbing plant whose leaf is chewed
by some Asians

betel nut the fruit of the betel palm,
chewed together with lime and leaves of
the betel (plant) by some Asians

betel palm a palm grown in SE Asia

bête noire (bāt'nwär') pl. **bêtes noires**
(bāt'nwär')[Fr.] a person or thing feared,
disliked, and avoided

bethel (beth'əl) n. [< Heb. bēth 'ēl, house
of God] a place of worship esp. for seamen

bethink (bi thiŋk') vt. -thought', -think'-
ing to bring (oneself) to think of, consider,
or recollect; remind (oneself)

betide (bi tīd') vi., vt. -tid'ed, -tid'ing
[< BE- + OE. tid, time] to happen (to);
befall

betimes (bi tīmz') adv. [ME. < bi-,
& TIME] early or early enough

betoken (bi tō'k'n) vt. [< ME. be- &
TOKEN] 1. to be a token or sign of;
show 2. to show beforehand

betony (bet'ə nē) n. [< L. betonica] a
plant formerly used for dyeing and in
medicine

betray (bi trā') vt. [ult. < tradere, to
hand over] 1. to help the enemy of (one's
country, etc.) 2. to fail to uphold [to
betray a trust] 3. to lead astray; specif.,
to seduce and then desert 4. to reveal
unknowingly 5. to reveal or show signs
of —**betray'al** n. —**betray'er** n.

betroth (bi trōth') vt. [< ME. < be- +
OE. treowth, truth] to promise in marriage
—**betroth'al** n.

betrothed adj. engaged to be married
—n. the person to whom one is betrothed

betted (bet'id) alt. pt. and pp. of BET

better (bet'ər) adj. compar. of GOOD [<
OE. betera] 1. superior 2. more suitable,
etc. 3. larger [the better part of an hour]
4. improved in health —adv. compar.
of WELL² 1. in a more excellent or more

suitable manner **2.** in a higher degree —*n.* **1.** a person superior in authority, position, etc. **2.** the thing, condition, etc. that is more excellent, etc. —*vt.* **1.** to surpass **2.** to improve —**better off** in more favourable circumstances, esp. financially —**get** (or **have**) **the better of 1.** to outdo **2.** to outwit —**had better** would be wise; ought to

better half [Colloq.] one's wife or one's husband

betterment *n.* a being made better; improvement

betting shop a licensed off-course bookmaker's premises

bettor, better *n.* a person who bets

between (bi twēn') *prep.* [< OE. *be*, by + *tweon(um)*, by twos] **1.** in the space, time, etc. that separates (two things) **2.** that connects [a bond *between* friends] **3.** by the joint action of **4.** in or into the combined possession of [they had fifty pounds *between* them] **5.** from one or the other of [choose *between* love and duty] —*adv.* in an intermediate space, position, or function —**between ourselves** in confidence; as a secret: also **between you and me** —**in between** in an intermediate position

betweentimes *adv.* in the intervals: also **between'whiles'**

betwixt (bi twikst') *prep., adv.* [OE. *betwix*] between: now archaic except in **betwixt and between,** neither altogether one nor altogether the other

bevel (bev''l) *n.* [< ?] **1.** a tool that is a rule with a movable arm, for measuring or marking angles, etc.: also **bevel square 2.** a sloping edge between parallel surfaces —*adj.* sloped; bevelled —*vt.* **-elled, -elling** to cut to an angle other than a right angle —*vi.* to slope at an angle

BEVEL GEAR

bevel gear a gearwheel meshed with another so that their shafts are at an angle

beverage (bev'ər ij) *n.* [< L. *bibere,* imbibe] any liquid for drinking, esp. other than plain water

beverage room [Canad.] same as BEER PARLOUR

bevy (bev'ē) *n., pl.* **bev'ies** [< ?] **1.** a group, esp. of girls or women **2.** a flock: now chiefly of quail

bewail (bi wāl') *vt.* to wail over or complain about; lament; mourn

beware (bi wāar') *vi., vt.* [prob. < OE. *be-* + *warian,* be wary] to be wary (of); be on one's guard (against)

bewilder (bi wil'dər) *vt.* [BE- + archaic *wilder,* lose one's way] to confuse hopelessly, as by something complicated;

befuddle; puzzle —**bewil'dered** *adj.* —**bewil'dering** *adj.* —**bewil'derment** *n.*

bewitch (bi wich') *vt.* [< OE. *wicca,* witch] **1.** to fascinate **2.** to cast a spell over —**bewitch'ing** *adj.*

bey (bā) *n.* [Turk.] **1.** in the Ottoman Empire, the governor of a Turkish province **2.** a Turkish title of respect and former title of rank

beyond (bi yond') *prep.* [< OE. *be-* + *geond,* yonder] **1.** farther on than **2.** later than **3.** outside the reach of [beyond help] **4.** more or better than —*adv.* **1.** farther away **2.** in addition —**the (great) beyond** whatever follows death

bezel (bez''l) *n.* [< OFr.] **1.** a sloping, cutting edge as of a chisel **2.** a slanting face of a cut jewel **3.** the groove and flange holding a watch crystal in place

bezique (bi zēk') *n.* [Fr. *bésigue*] a card game for two players

B/F, b.f. brought forward

b.f. bloody fool

BFPO British Forces Post Office

B'ham Birmingham

bhang (baŋ) *n.* [Hindi < Sans. *bhangā*] **1.** the hemp plant **2.** its dried leaves and flowers which have intoxicating properties

bhindi (bin'dē) *n.* [Hindi] *Indian name for* okra

b.h.p. brake horsepower

bi- (bī) [L.] *a prefix meaning:* **1.** having two **2.** doubly **3.** happening every two **4.** happening twice during every **5.** using two or both **6.** joining or involving two **7.** *Chem.* having twice as many atoms or chemical equivalents as the other constituent of the compound [sodium bicarbonate]

Bi *Chem.* bismuth

biannual (bī an'yoo wəl) *adj.* coming twice a year; semiannual: see also BIENNIAL —**bian'nually** *adv.*

bias (bī'əs) *n., pl.* **bi'ases** [Fr. *biais,* slant] **1.** a mental leaning; prejudice; bent **2.** a slanting or diagonal line, cut or sewn across the weave of cloth **3.** *Bowls* the weight in the side of the ball that causes it to roll in a curve —*adj.* slanting; diagonal —*adv.* diagonally —*vt.* **-ased** or **-assed, -asing** or **-assing** to cause to have a bias; prejudice —**on the bias** diagonally

bias binding a strip of material cut on the bias and used for binding hems or for decoration

biaxial (bī ak'sē əl) *adj.* having two axes, as some crystals —**biax'ially** *adv.*

bib¹ (bib) *n.* [< L. *bibere,* drink] **1.** an apronlike cloth tied under a child's chin at meals **2.** the front upper part of an apron or overalls

bib² (bib) *n.* [< ?] a food fish related to the cod, found in the North Sea and the Arctic

bibcock (bib'kok') *n.* a tap whose nozzle is bent downwards

‡bibelot (bib'lō) *n.* [< OFr. *belbel,* bauble] a small object whose value lies in its beauty or rarity

Bibl., bibl. **1.** Biblical **2.** bibliographical

Bible (bī′b′l) *n.* [< Gr. *biblos*, papyrus] **1.** the sacred book of Christianity; Old Testament and New Testament **2.** [b-] any book regarded as authoritative —**Biblical** (bib′li k′l) *adj.*

Bible-thumper *n.* a clergyman or other person who is a vigorous exponent of his beliefs

biblio- [< Gr. *biblion*] *a combining form meaning :* **1.** book; of books [*bibliophile*] **2.** of the Bible

bibliography (bib′lē og′rə fē) *n.,* pl. **-phies** [see BIBLE & -GRAPHY] **1.** a list of writings on a given subject, by a given author, etc. **2.** a list of the books, articles, etc. referred to by an author **3.** the study of the editions, dates, authorship, etc. of books and other writings —**bib′liog′rapher** *n.* —**bib′liograph′ic** (-ə graf′ik), **bib′liograph′ical** *adj.* —**bib′liograph′ically** *adv.*

bibliomania (bib′lē ə mā′nē ə) *n.* [BIBLIO- + -MANIA] a craze for collecting books, esp. rare ones —**bib′liomane′** *n.* —**bib′liomа′niac** *n., adj.*

bibliophile (bib′lē ə fīl′) *n.* [BIBLIO- + -PHILE] **1.** one who loves or admires books **2.** a book collector Also **bib′liophil′**(-fil), **bibliophilist** (bib′lē of′ə list) —**bib′liophil′ic** (-ə fil′ik) *adj.*

bibulous (bib′yoo ləs) *adj.* [< L. *bibere*, drink] **1.** highly absorbent **2.** addicted to or fond of alcoholic drink

bicameral (bī kam′ər əl) *adj.* [< BI- + L. *camera*, chamber] having two legislative chambers

bicarb (bī cärb′) *n.* [Colloq.] short for SODIUM BICARBONATE

bicarbonate (bī kär′bə nit) *n.* an acid salt of carbonic acid containing the radical HCO_3

bicarbonate of soda *same as* SODIUM BICARBONATE

bicentenary (bī′ sen tēn′ər ē) *adj., n., pl.* **-naries** *same as* BICENTENNIAL

bicentennial (bī′ sen ten′ē əl) *adj.* **1.** happening once in a period of 200 years **2.** lasting for 200 years —*n.* a 200th anniversary or its celebration

biceps (bī′seps) *n., pl.* **-ceps** [L. < *bis*, two + *caput*, head] a muscle having two points of origin; esp., the large muscle in the front of the upper arm

bicker (bik′ər) *vi.* [ME. *bikeren*] to have a petty quarrel; squabble —*n.* a petty quarrel —**bick′erer** *n.*

bicolour (bī′kul′ər) *adj.* of two colours : also **bi′col′oured**

BICUSPID

bicuspid (bī kus′pid) *adj.* [< BI- + L. *cuspis*, pointed end] having two points :

—*n.* any of eight adult teeth with two-pointed crowns

bicycle (bī′ si k′l) *n.* [Fr. : see BI- & CYCLE] a vehicle consisting of a metal frame mounted on two wheels, one behind the other, and equipped with handlebars, a saddlelike seat and foot pedals —*vi.,* **-cled, -cling** to ride on a bicycle —**bi′cyclist, bi′cycler** *n.*

bid (bid) *vt.* **bade** or **bid, bid′den** or **bid, bid′ding** [< OE. *biddan,* urge & OE. *beodan,* command] **1.** to offer a (certain amount) as the price that one will pay or accept **2.** to express in greeting or taking leave [to bid farewell] **3.** to command, ask, or tell **4.** to declare openly **5.** *Card Games* to state (the number of tricks one expects to take) and declare (trumps) —*vi.* to make a bid —*n.* **1.** a bidding of an amount **2.** the amount bid **3.** a chance to bid **4.** an attempt or try **5.** *Card Games* the act of bidding —**bid fair** to seem likely —**bid′der** *n.*

biddable *adj.* **1.** obedient; docile **2.** worth bidding on [a *biddable* bridge hand]

bidding *n.* **1.** a command or request **2.** an invitation or summons **3.** the bids in a card game or auction

biddy (bid′ē) *n., pl.* **-dies 1.** a hen **2.** [Slang] a woman, esp. an elderly, gossipy one

bide (bīd) *vi.* **bode** or **bid′ed, bid′ed, bid′ing** [OE. *bidan*] [Archaic or Dial.] **1.** to continue **2.** to dwell **3.** to wait —*vt.* [Archaic or Dial.] to endure —**bide one's time** *pt.* **bid′ed** to wait patiently for an opportunity

bidet (bē′dā) *n.* [Fr.] a low, bowl-shaped bathroom fixture with running water, used for washing the genitals

biennial (bī en′ē əl) *adj.* [< L. *bis,* twice + *annus,* year] **1.** happening every two years **2.** lasting for two years —*n.* *Bot.* a plant that lasts two years, usually producing flowers and seed the second year

bier (bēər) *n.* [OE. *bær,* bed] a portable framework on which a coffin or corpse is placed

biff (bif) *n.* [prob. echoic] [Colloq.] a blow; strike; hit —*vt.* [Colloq.] to strike; hit

bifid (bī′fid) *adj.* [< L. *bis,* twice + *findere,* cleave] divided into two equal parts by a cleft —**bifid′ity** *n.*

bifocal (bī fō′k′l) *adj.* adjusted to two different focal lengths —*n.* a lens with one part ground to adjust the eyes for close focus, and the rest ground for distant focus

bifocals *n.pl.* a pair of glasses with bifocal lenses

bifurcate (bī′fər kāt′; for *adj.* also -kit) *adj.* [< L. *bi-* + *furca,* fork] having two branches —*vt., vi.* **-cat′ed, -cat′ing** to divide into two branches —**bi′furca′tion** *n.*

big (big) *adj.* **big′ger, big′gest** [ME. < ?] **1.** of great size, extent, force, etc. **2.** a) full-grown b) elder [his *big* sister] **3.** loud **4.** important or outstanding **5.** boastful; ambitious [*big* talk] **6.** noble [a big heart] —*adv.* [Colloq.] **1.**

boastfully [to talk *big*] **2.** impressively **3.** showing imagination [think *big!*] —**too big for one's boots** pompous; conceited —**big′ness** *n.*

bigamy (big′ə mē) *n., pl.* **-mies** [< L. *bis,* twice + Gr. *gamos,* marriage] the act of marrying a second time while a previous marriage is still legally in effect —**big′amist** *n.* —**big′amous** *adj.* —**big′a-mously** *adv.*

Big Brother [< G. Orwell's *1984*] a person or organization with total control over others, esp. of a dictatorial nature

big end the crankpin end of a connecting rod at its point of attachment in an internal-combustion engine

big game large wild animals hunted for sport, as lions, etc.

bighearted (big′här′tid) *adj.* generous or magnanimous —**big′heart′edly** *adv.*

bight (bīt) *n.* [ME. *byht*] **1.** a loop or slack part in a rope **2.** *a)* a curve in a river, coastline, etc. *b)* a bay formed by such a curve

big money [Colloq.] very high pay or large profit

bignonia (big nō′nē ə) *n.* [< Abbé *Bignon*] a tropical American plant

bigot (big′ət) *n.* [< OFr.] a narrow-minded person who is intolerant of other creeds, opinions, races, etc. —**big′oted** *adj.* —**big′otedly** *adv.* —**big′otry** *n.*

big shot [Chiefly U.S. Slang] an important, influential person: also **big noise, big wheel,** etc.

big stick [< use of term by T. Roosevelt] [also **B- S-**] a policy of acting or negotiating from a position backed by a show of strength

big time [Colloq.] the highest level in any profession, etc. —**big′-time′** *adj.*

big top [Colloq.] the main tent of a circus

bigwig (big′wig′) *n.* [Colloq.] a person of great importance or influence

bijou (bē′zhōō) *n., pl.* **-joux** (-zhōōz) [Fr.] **1.** a jewel **2.** an exquisite trinket

bike (bīk) *n., vt., vi.* **biked, bik′ing** [< BICYCLE] [Colloq.] **1.** bicycle **2.** motorcycle

bikini (bi kē′nē) *n.* [< *Bikini,* atoll in the Marshall Islands] a brief two-piece bathing suit for women

bilateral (bī lat′ər əl) *adj.* [BI- + LATERAL] **1.** of, on, or having two sides, factions, etc. **2.** affecting both sides equally **3.** symmetrical on both sides of an axis —**bilat′eralism** *n.*

bilberry (bil′bər ē) *n., pl.* **-ries** [ult. < ON. *bollr,* BALL[1] + *ber,* berry] **1.** a European plant having edible blue or blackish berries **2.** the berry: also called **blaeberry, whortleberry**

bile (bīl) *n.* [< L. *bilis*] **1.** the bitter, greenish fluid secreted by the liver and found in the gall bladder: it helps in digestion **2.** [< ancient belief in bile as the humour causing anger] bitterness of spirit; anger

bilge (bilj) *n.* [var. of BULGE] **1.** the rounded, lower part of a ship's hold **2.** stagnant, dirty water that gathers there: also **bilge water 3.** [Slang] worthless

talk or writing —*vt.* **bilged, bilg′ing** to break open in the bilge: said of a ship —*vi.* to spring a leak in the bilge

biliary (bil′yər ē) *adj.* **1.** of or involving the bile **2.** bile-carrying **3.** bilious

bilingual (bī liŋ′gwəl) *adj.* [< L. *bis,* two + *lingua,* tongue] **1.** of or in two languages **2.** capable of using two languages, esp. with equal facility —*n.* a bilingual person —**bilin′gually** *adv.*

bilingualism *n.* **1.** the ability to use two languages **2.** [Canad.] the government's official policy of using both French and English in its communications with the public

bilious (bil′yəs) *adj.* **1.** of the bile **2.** having or resulting from some ailment of the bile or the liver **3.** bad-tempered —**bil′iously** *adv.* —**bil′iousness** *n.*

bilk (bilk) *vt.* [? < BALK] **1.** to cheat or swindle **2.** to elude —*n.* a bilking or being bilked —**bilk′er** *n.*

bill[1] (bil) *n.* [< L. *bulla,* knob] **1.** a statement of charges for goods or services **2.** a list, as a menu, theatre programme, etc. **3.** a poster or handbill, esp. one announcing a circus, etc. **4.** a draft of a law proposed to a lawmaking body **5.** a bill of exchange **6.** any promissory note **7.** [U.S.] a bank note **8.** *Law* a declaration of certain facts in legal proceedings —*vt.* **1.** to make out a bill of (items) **2.** to present a statement of charges to **3.** *a)* to advertise by bills *b)* to book (a performer) —**fill the bill** [Colloq.] to meet the requirements

bill[2] *n.* [OE. *bile*] **1.** a bird's beak **2.** a narrow promontory —*vi.* **1.** to touch bills together **2.** to caress lovingly: now only in **bill and coo,** to kiss, talk softly, etc. in a loving way

bill[3] *n.* [OE. *bill*] an ancient weapon having a hook-shaped blade with a spike at the back

billabong (bil′ə boŋ′) *n.* [Abor. < *billa,* water] in Australia, a backwater channel that forms a lagoon or pool

billboard (bil′bôrd′) *n.* [U.S.] a hoarding

billet[1] (bil′it) *n.* [see BILL[1]] **1.** *a)* a written order to provide lodging for military personnel, as in private buildings *b)* the quarters thus occupied **2.** a position or job —*vt.* to assign to lodging by billet

billet[2] *n.* [< OFr. *bille,* tree trunk] **1.** a short, thick piece of firewood **2.** an unfinished metal bar

billet-doux (bil′ē dōō′) *n., pl.* **billets-doux** (bil′ē dōōz′) [Fr.] a love letter

billhead (bil′hed′) *n.* a letterhead used for statements of charges

billhook (bil′hook′) *n.* a tool with a curved or hooked blade at one end, for pruning and cutting

billiards (bil′yərdz) *n.* [Fr. *billard;* orig., a cue] a game played with hard balls on an oblong table covered with cloth and having raised, cushioned edges: a cue is used to hit the balls —**bil′liard** *adj.*

billion (bil′yən) *n.* [Fr. < *bi-,* BI- + *million*] **1.** in Great Britain and Germany, a million millions (1,000 000 000 000) **2.** in the U.S. and France, a thousand millions

(1,000 000 000) **3.** an indefinite but very large number —**bil′lionth** *adj., n.*

billionaire (bil′yən âar′) *n.* one whose wealth comes to at least a billion pounds, dollars, etc.

bill of attainder formerly, a legislative enactment pronouncing a person guilty, without a trial, of an alleged crime (esp. treason)

bill of exchange a written order to pay a certain sum of money to the person named; draft

bill of fare a list of the foods served; menu

bill of health a certificate stating whether there is infectious disease aboard a ship or in a port —**clean bill of health 1.** a bill of health certifying the absence of infectious disease **2.** [Colloq.] a good record

bill of lading a contract issued by the master of a ship listing the goods received and promising their delivery

billow (bil′ō) *n.* [ON. *bylgja*] **1.** a large wave **2.** any large, swelling mass or surge, as of smoke, sound, etc. —*vi., vt.* to surge, swell, or cause to swell like or in a billow —**bil′lowy** *adj.*

billsticker (bil′stik′ər) *n.* a person hired to paste advertisements on walls, etc.: also **bill′post′er**

billy (bil′ē) *n., pl.* **-lies** [< Abor. *billa*, water] [Aust.] a can or kettle used in outdoor cooking: also **billycan**

billy goat a male goat

biltong (bil′toŋ) *n.* [Afrik. < *bil*, rump + *tong*, tongue] strips of meat dried and cured in the sun

B.I.M. British Institute of Management

bimetallic (bī′mə tal′ik) *adj.* **1.** containing or using two metals **2.** of or based on bimetallism

bimetallism (bī met′əl iz′m) *n.* the use of two metals, usually gold and silver, as the monetary standard, with fixed values in relation to each other —**bimet′allist** *n.*

bin (bin) *n.* [OE., manger] **1.** a box or enclosed space for storing foods, etc. **2.** a container for rubbish —*vt.* **binned, bin′-ning** to store in a bin

binary (bī′nər ē) *adj.* [< L. *bini*, two by two < *bis*, double] **1.** made up of two parts or things; double **2.** designating a number system that has 2 as its base —*n., pl.* **-ries** something made up of two parts or things

binary star two stars revolving around a common centre of gravity; double star

bind (bīnd) *vt.* **bound, bind′ing** [< OE. *bindan*] **1.** to tie together, as with a rope **2.** to hold or restrain **3.** to encircle with a belt, etc. **4.** to bandage (often with *up*) **5.** to make stick together **6.** to constipate **7.** to strengthen by a band, as of tape **8.** to fasten together sheets of (a book) and enclose within a cover **9.** to obligate, as by duty **10.** to compel, as by legal restraint —*vi.* **1.** to be constricting or restricting **2.** to be obligatory —*n.* [Colloq.] an annoyance; a bore —**bind over** to put under legal bond

binder *n.* **1.** a person who binds; specif.,

a bookbinder **2.** a thing that binds; specif., *a)* a substance, as tar, that binds things together *b)* a detachable cover for holding sheets of paper together **3.** a device attached to a reaper, for tying grain in bundles

bindery *n., pl.* **-eries** a place where books are bound

binding *n.* a thing that binds, as *a)* the fastenings on a ski for the boot *b)* a band or bandage *c)* tape used in sewing for strengthening seams, etc. *d)* the covers and backing of a book —*adj.* that binds; esp., that holds one to an agreement, etc.

bindweed *n.* convolvulus

bine (bīn) *n.* [dial. form of BIND] any climbing, twining stem, as of the hop

binge (binj) *n.* [< dial. *binge*, soak] [Colloq.] a drunken or unrestrained spree

bingo (biŋ′gō) *n.* [< ?] a gambling game using cards marked with numbers : counters are placed on those numbers corresponding to numbered discs drawn by lot

binnacle (bin′ək′l) *n.* [ult. < L. *habitaculum*, dwelling] the case enclosing a ship's compass

BINOCULARS

binocular (bi nok′yə lər; *also, esp. for n.,* bi-) *adj.* [< L. *bini*, double + *oculus*, eye] using, or for the use of, both eyes —*n.* [*usually pl.*] a binocular instrument, as field glasses —**binoc′ular′ity** (-lar′ə tē) *n.*

binomial (bī nō′mē əl) *n.* [< *bi-* + Gr. *nomos*, part] *Math.* an expression consisting of two terms connected by a plus or minus sign —*adj.* **1.** composed of two terms **2.** of binomials

binomial theorem a general formula expressing any power of a binomial as a sum (Ex.: $(a + b)^2 = a^2 + 2ab + b^2$)

bio- [Gr. < *bios*, life] *a combining form meaning* life, of living things, biological [*biography*]

bioastronautics (bī′ō as′trə nô′tiks) *n.pl.* [*with sing. v.*] the science dealing with the effects of space travel upon living organisms

biochemistry (bī′ō kem′is trē) *n.* the branch of chemistry that deals with plants and animals and their life processes —**bi′o-chem′ical** *adj.* —**bi′ochem′ist** *n.*

biocoenosis (bī′ō si nō′sis) *n.* [< BIO- + Gr. *koinōsis*, mingling] a community of biologically integrated and interdependent plants and animals

biodegradable (bī′ō di grä′də b'l) *adj.* [BIO- + DEGRAD(E) + -ABLE] that can be readily decomposed by biological, esp. bacterial, action, as some detergents

bioengineering (bī′ō en′jə nēar′in) *n.* a science dealing with the application of engineering science to problems of biology and medicine

biogenesis (bī′ō jen′ə sis) *n.* [BIO- + GENESIS] the principle that living organisms derive only from other similar organisms —**bi′ogenet′ic** (-jə net′ik) *adj.*

biography (bī og′rə fē) *n.* [see BIO- & -GRAPHY] 1. *pl.* **-phies** an account of a person's life written by another 2. such writings, collectively —**biog′rapher** *n.* —**biographical** (bī′ə graf′i k'l), *adj.*

biol. 1. biological 2. biologist 3. biology

biological (bī′ə loj′i k'l) *adj.* 1. of biology; of plants and animals 2. used in or produced by practical biology Also **bi′olog′ic** —**bi′olog′ically** *adv.*

biological control the control of destructive organisms, esp. insects, by various, usually nonchemical means

biological warfare the use of disease-spreading microorganisms, toxins, etc. as a weapon of war

biology (bī ol′ə jē) *n.* [BIO- + -LOGY] the science that deals with the origin, history, life processes, structure, etc. of plants and animals —**biol′ogist** *n.*

biomedicine (bī′ō med′ə s'n) *n.* a branch of medicine combined with research in biology that studies the effects of environmental stress —**bi′omed′ical** *adj.*

bionic (bī on′ik) *adj.* designating a living organism, parts of which are artifical

biophysics (bī′ō fiz′iks) *n.pl.* [*with sing. v.*] the study of biological phenomena in relation to physics —**bi′ophys′ical** *adj.* —**bi′ophys′icist** *n.*

biopsy (bī′op′sē) *n.*, *pl.* **-sies** [< BIO- & Gr. *opsis*, sight] the removal of bits of living tissue, fluids, etc. from the body for diagnostic examination

biorhythm (bī′ō rith′′m) *n.* any of three separate biological cycles which are held to affect a person's physical, emotional, and intellectual energy levels

bioscope (bī′ə skōp′) *n.* [S Afr.] cinema

bioscopy (bī os′kə pē) *n.* [< BIO- & Gr. *skopein*, to see] a medical examination to find out if life is present

biosphere (bī′ə sfēar′) *n.* [BIO- + SPHERE] that portion of the earth and its atmosphere which contains living organisms

biosynthesis (bī′ō sin′thə sis) *n.* the formation of chemical compounds by living organisms

biotin (bī′ə tin) *n.* [< Gr. *bios*, life] a factor of the vitamin B group, found in liver, egg yolk, and yeast

bipartisan (bī′pär tə zan′) *adj.* of or representing two parties —**bi′partisan′-ship.** *n.*

bipartite (bī pär′tīt) *adj.* [< L. *bi-*, two + *partire*, divide] 1. having two parts 2. with two involved —**bipar′titely** *adv.*

biped (bī′ped) *n.* [< L. *bi-* + *pes, pedis,* foot] any two-footed animal —*adj.* two-footed: also **biped′al**

biplane (bī′plān′) *n.* an aircraft with two sets of wings, one above the other

bipolar (bī pō′lər) *adj.* having two poles —**bipolarity** (bī′pō lar′ə tē) *n.*

birch (burch) *n.* [OE. *beorc*] 1. a tree having smooth bark and hard, closegrained wood 2. this wood 3. a birch rod used for whipping —*vt.* to beat with a birch —*adj.* of birch

bird (burd) *n.* [OE. *bridd,* young bird] 1. any of a class of warmblooded, two-legged, egg-laying vertebrates with feathers and wings 2. [Slang] a person, esp. a mildly eccentric one 3. [Slang] a young woman —**bird in the hand** something sure because already in one's possession: opposed to **bird in the bush,** something unsure, etc. —**birds of a feather** people with the same characteristics —**for the birds** [Slang] ridiculous, worthless, etc. —**get the bird** to be rudely dismissed —**bird′er** *n.*

birdbath *n.* a basinlike garden ornament for birds to bathe in

birdcall *n.* 1. the sound or song of a bird 2. an imitation of this 3. a device for imitating bird sounds

birdie *n.* 1. a small bird: child's word 2. *Golf* a score of one stroke under par for a hole

birdlime *n.* a sticky substance spread on twigs to catch birds

bird of paradise a brightly coloured bird found in and near New Guinea

bird of passage 1. any migratory bird 2. anyone who travels or roams about constantly

bird of prey any bird, as the hawk, owl, etc., that kills and eats mammals and other birds

birdseed *n.* seed for feeding caged birds

bird's-eye *adj.* 1. a) seen from above b) general 2. having markings like birds' eyes

bird watching the hobby of observing wild birds in their habitat —**bird watcher**

BIRETTA

biretta (bə ret′ə) *n.* [< L. *birrus,* hood] a square cap with three projections, worn by Roman Catholic clergy

Biro (bī′rō) *Trademark* a kind of ballpoint pen

birth (burth) *n.* [< OE. *beran,* to bear] 1. the act of bringing forth offspring 2. the act of being born 3. origin or descent 4. the beginning of anything 5. natural inclination or talent [an actor by *birth*]

—**give birth to** 1. to bring forth (offspring) 2. to be the cause of

birth certificate an official document stating the date and place of a person's birth

birth control control of how many children a woman will have, as by contraception

birthday *n.* 1. the anniversary of a person's birth . 2. the day of a person's birth or a thing's beginning

birthmark *n.* a skin blemish present at birth

birthplace *n.* the place of one's birth

birthrate *n.* the number of births per year per thousand of population in a given group

birthright *n.* the rights that a person has by birth

birthstone *n.* a precious or semiprecious gem symbolizing the month of one's birth

biscuit (bis′kit) *n., pl.* **-cuits, -cuit** [< L. *bis*, twice + *coquere*, cook] 1. a small, crisp, flat cake, often sweetened 2. light brown 3. pottery before glazing

bisect (bī sekt′) *vt.* [< L. *bi-* + *secare*, cut] to cut in two 2. *Geom.* to divide into two equal parts —*vi.* to divide; fork —**bisec′tion** *n.* —**bisec′tor** *n.*

bisexual (bī sek′syoo wəl) *adj.* 1. sexually attracted to both sexes 2. hermaphroditic —*n.* one that is bisexual —**bisex′ual′ity** (-wal′ə tē), **bisex′ualism** *n.*

bishop (bish′əp) *n.* [< Gr. *episkopos*, overseer] 1. a high-ranking Christian clergyman supervising a diocese 2. a chessman that can move only diagonally

bishopric (bish′ə prik) *n.* the diocese, office, authority, or rank of a bishop

bismuth (biz′məth) *n.* [< G. *Wismut*] a hard, brittle, metallic chemical element: symbol, Bi

bison (bī′s′n) *n., pl.* **bi′sons** [< L. < Gmc.] a four-legged bovine mammal with a shaggy mane, short, curved horns, and a humped back, as the European wisent or the American buffalo

bisque¹ (bisk) *n.* biscuit ceramic ware left unglazed

bisque² *n.* [Fr.] a handicap of one point per set in tennis, one turn per game in croquet, or one or more strokes per game at match play in golf

bistre (bis′tər) *n.* [Fr. *bistre*] a yellowish-brown to dark-brown pigment made from the soot of burned wood

bistro (bēs′trō) *n., pl.* **-tros** [Fr.] a small restaurant or bar

bit¹ (bit) *n.* [< OE. *bite*, a bite] 1. the metal mouthpiece on a bridle, used for controlling the horse 2. anything that curbs or controls 3. a drilling or boring tool for use in a brace, etc. —*vt.* **bit′ted, bit′ting** to put a bit into the mouth of (a horse) —**take the bit between one's teeth** to be beyond control

bit² *n.* [< OE. *bita*, a piece] 1. *a)* a small piece or quantity *b)* a limited degree [*a bit* bored] *c)* a short time 2. [U.S. Colloq.] 12¹/₂ cents 3. a small part, as in a play —*adj.* very small [a *bit* role]

—**bit by bit** little by little —**do one's bit** to do one's share

bit³ *n.* [*b(inary)* (*dig*)*it*] *Computers* a unit of information representing the physical state of a system having one of two values, such as *on* or *off*

bitch (bich) *n.* [< OE. *bicce*] 1. the female of the dog, wolf, etc. 2. [Derog.] a bad-tempered, malicious, woman 3. [Slang] anything unpleasant —*vi.* [Slang] to complain —**bitch′iness** *n.* —**bitch′y** *adj.*

bite (bīt) *vt.* **bit** (bit), **bitten** (bit′′n) or **bit, bit′ing** [< OE. *bitan*] 1. to seize or cut with or as with the teeth 2. to cut into, as with a sharp weapon 3. to sting, as an insect 4. to hurt in a sharp, stinging way 5. to eat into; corrode 6. to seize or possess —*vi.* 1. to press or snap the teeth (*into, at,* etc.) 2. to cause a biting sensation 3. to press hard; grip 4. to seize a bait 5. to be caught, as by a trick —*n.* 1. the act of biting 2. biting quality; sting 3. a wound or sting from biting 4. *a)* a mouthful *b)* a light meal or snack 5. a tight hold or grip 6. [Colloq.] an amount removed —**bit′er** *n.*

biting *adj.* 1. cutting 2. sarcastic —**bit′ingly** *adv.*

bitter (bit′ər) *adj.* [< OE. *bitan*, to bite] 1. having a sharp, often unpleasant taste; acrid 2. causing or showing sorrow, pain, etc. 3. sharp; harsh; piercing 4. characterized by hatred, etc. —*n.* 1. something bitter [take the *bitter* with the sweet] 2. bitter, strongly hopped beer —**to the bitter end** until the end, however difficult —**bit′terly** *adv.* —**bit′terness** *n.*

bittern (bit′ərn) *n.* [prob. < L. *butio*] a wading bird of the heron family

bitters (bit′ərz) *n.pl.* a drink containing bitter herbs, etc. and usually alcohol, used in some cocktails

bittersweet (bit′ər swēt′) *n.* same as WOODY NIGHTSHADE —*adj.* 1. both bitter and sweet 2. pleasant with sad overtones

bitty (bit′ē) *adj.* lacking unity; disjointed

bitumen (bi′tyōo mən) *n.* [L.] 1. any of several substances obtained as asphaltic residue in the distillation of coal tar, petroleum, etc., or occurring as natural asphalt 2. [Aust. Colloq.] a tarred road —**bitu′minous** *adj.*

bituminous coal coal that yields pitch or tar when it burns; soft coal

bivalent (bī vā′lənt) *adj.* 1. having two valences 2. having a valence of two —**biva′lence, biva′lency** *n.*

bivalve (bī′valv′) *n.* any mollusc having a shell of two parts, or valves, hinged together, as a mussel, clam, etc. —*adj.* having such a shell: also **bi′valved′**

bivouac (biv′ōo wak′) *n.* [< OHG. *bi-*, by + *wacht*, guard] a temporary encampment (esp. of soldiers) in the open —*vi.* **-acked′, -ack′ing** to encamp in the open

biz (biz) *n.* [Slang] business [show *biz*]

bizarre (bi zär′) *adj.* [Fr. < Sp. *bizarro*,

bold] odd; grotesque; eccentric —**bizarre′-ly** adv. —**bizarre′ness** n.

Bk Chem. berkelium

bk. pl. **bks.** 1. bank 2. book

B.L. Bachelor of Law

blab (blab) vt., vi. **blabbed, blab′bing** [ME. blabben] 1. to give away (a secret) in idle chatter 2. to chatter; prattle —n. 1. gossip 2. a person who blabs

blabber vt., vi. [ME. blabberen, of echoic origin] [Dial. or Colloq.] to blab or babble —n. one who blabs: also [Colloq.] **blab′-bermouth′**

black (blak) adj. [OE. blæc] 1. opposite to white; of the colour of coal : see COLOUR 2. having dark-coloured skin and hair; esp., Negro 3. in complete darkness 4. without cream, milk, etc. : said of coffee 5. soiled; dirty 6. wearing black clothing 7. evil; wicked 8. sad; dismal 9. sullen or angry 10. humorous in a morbid or cynical way [black comedy] —n. 1. black colour, pigment, etc. 2. black clothes, esp. worn for mourning 3. a Negro —vt. 1. to blacken 2. to polish with blacking 3. to boycott cargo, work, etc. as a form of industrial action —**black out** 1. to cause a blackout in 2. to lose consciousness —**in the black** operating at a profit —**black′ish** adj. —**black′ly** adv. —**black′-ness** n.

blackamoor (blak′ə mooər′) n. [Archaic] a dark-skinned person; specif., an African Negro

black-and-blue (blak′ən blōō′) adj. discoloured from congestion of blood under the skin, due to a bruise

Black and Tans the unofficial name for the semimilitary force sent to Ireland in 1920 to combat Sinn Fein activities

black and white writing or print

black art same as BLACK MAGIC

blackball n. a secret vote against a person or thing —vt. 1. to vote against 2. to ostracize

black bear 1. the common N American bear 2. any of several dark-coloured bears of Asia

black belt a black-coloured belt awarded to an expert in judo or karate

blackberry n., pl. **-ries** the black, edible fruit of various brambles

blackbird n. a songbird of the thrush family, the male of which is almost entirely black

blackboard n. a smooth, usually dark surface, originally of slate, on which to write or draw with chalk

black book a book with the names of those to be punished, blacklisted, etc.

black box a popular term for FLIGHT RECORDER

blackcap n. a small songbird, the male of which has a black head

blackcock n. the male of the black grouse

Black Country the heavily industrialized region of the Midlands of England

blackcurrant (blak′kur′ənt) n. 1. the small black fruit of a garden shrub 2. the shrub itself

blackdamp n. a suffocating gas, a mixture of carbon dioxide and nitrogen, found in mines

Black Death a deadly disease, probably bubonic plague, which devastated Europe and Asia in the 14th cent.

blacken vi. to become black or dark —vt. 1. to make black 2. to slander; defame —**black′ener** n.

black eye a discolouration of the skin surrounding an eye, resulting from a sharp blow or contusion

black flag the flag of piracy, usually with a white skull and crossbones on a black background

Black Friar a Dominican Friar

blackguard (blag′ärd) n. a scoundrel —adj. vulgar, abusive, etc. —vt. to revile —**black′guardly** adj., adv.

blackhead (blak′hed′) n. 1. a black-tipped pimple in a skin pore 2. a bird with a black head

black hole a collapsed star so condensed that neither light nor matter can escape its gravitational field

blacking n. a black polish, as for shoes

black lead graphite, as used in lead pencils, etc.

blackleg n. a worker who refuses to join a strike —vi. to work during a strike —vt. to take the place of a striking worker

blacklist n. a list of persons being discriminated against —vt. to put on a blacklist

black magic magic with an evil purpose; sorcery

blackmail n. [lit., black rent < ON. mal, discussion] payment extorted to prevent disclosure of information that could bring disgrace —vt. 1. to try to get blackmail from 2. to coerce (into doing something) —**black′mail′er** n.

Black Maria (məri′ə) a police van used to transport prisoners

black mark an unfavourable item in one's record

black market a place or system for selling goods illegally, esp. in violation of rationing —**black marketeer**

Black Mass [also b- m-] 1. a Requiem Mass 2. a parody of the Mass by worshippers of Satan

Black Monk a Benedictine Monk

Black Muslim [Chiefly U.S.] a member of a militant Islamic sect of American Negroes

blackout n. 1. a concealing of all lights that might be visible to enemy air raiders at night 2. a temporary electrical power failure or cut 3. a temporary loss of consciousness, vision, memory, etc. 4. the extinguishing of all stage lights to end a scene, etc. 5. suppression, as of news by censorship

black pepper a hot seasoning made by grinding the whole dried, black berries of the pepper plant

black power [also B- P-] political and economic power sought by Negroes in the struggle for civil rights

black pudding a sausage made of blood, suet, etc.

Black Rod the chief usher to the Order of the Garter and the House of Lords

black sheep a person regarded as not so respectable as the rest of his family or group

Black Shirt a member of any fascist organization having a black-shirted uniform

blacksmith *n.* a smith who works in iron, making and fitting horseshoes, etc.

black spot a dangerous place, esp. a part of a road where there are many accidents

black tea tea withered and fermented before being dried by heating

blackthorn *n.* 1. a thorny shrub with plumlike fruit; sloe 2. a walking stick made of its stem

black tie 1. a black bow tie, properly worn with a dinner jacket 2. a dinner jacket and the proper accessories

black velvet a drink made of stout and champagne

Black Watch a Highland regiment, so called from the dark colour of the tartan

black widow an American spider the female of which sometimes eats its mate

bladder (blad′ər) *n.* [OE. *blæddre*] 1. a sac in the bodies of many animals, that inflates to receive and contain liquids or gases; esp., the **urinary bladder** in the pelvic cavity, which holds urine 2. a bag, etc. resembling this 3. an air sac, as in some water plants

bladderwort (blad′ər wurt′) *n.* a plant growing in water and having leaves with bladders that trap prey

bladderwrack (blad′ər rak) *n.* a seaweed having branched brown fronds and air sacs

blade (blād) *n.* [OE. *blæd*] 1. the cutting part of a knife, tool, etc. 2. *a)* the leaf of a plant, esp. of grass *b)* the flat part of a leaf 3. a broad, flat surface, as of an oar 4. a flat bone 5. formerly, a dashing young man —**blad′ed** *adj.*

blain (blān) *n.* [< OE. *blegen*] a pustule or blister

blamable, blameable (blām′ə b'l) *adj.* that deserves blame; culpable —**blam′ably** *adv.*

blame (blām) *vt.* **blamed, blam′ing** [see BLASPHEME] 1. to accuse of being at fault; condemn (*for*) 2. to put the responsibility of (an error, fault, etc. *on*) —*n.* 1. condemnation 2. responsibility for a fault or wrong —**be to blame** to be blamable —**blame′less** *adj.* —**blame′lessly** *adv.* —**blame′lessness** *n.*

blameworthy *adj.* deserving to be blamed —**blame′wor′thiness** *n.*

blanch (blänch) *vt.* [see BLANK] 1. to make white; bleach 2. to make pale 3. to scald (vegetables, almonds, etc.) 4. to bleach (leeks, celery, etc.) by covering to keep away light —*vi.* to turn pale

blancmange (bla monzh′) *n.* [Fr., white food] a sweet, moulded dessert made with starch, milk, etc.

bland (bland) *adj.* [< L. *blandus*, mild] 1. *a)* mild and soothing *b)* tasteless, insipid, dull, etc. 2. agreeable; suave —**bland′ly** *adv.* —**bland′ness** *n.*

blandish (blan′dish) *vt., vi* [< L. *blandiri*, flatter] to flatter or coax; cajole —**blan′dishment** *n.*

blank (blaŋk) *adj.* [OFr. *blanc*, white] 1. *a)* not written on [*a blank* paper] *b)* having empty spaces to be filled in 2. empty of thought or expression 3. utter; complete [*a blank* denial] 4. lacking certain elements, as a wall without an opening —*n.* 1. an empty space, esp. one in a printed form 2. such a printed form 3. an empty place or time 4. a piece of metal, etc. to be finished by stamping, etc. 5. a powder-filled cartridge without a bullet: in full, **blank cartridge** 6. a mark, often a dash, written in place of a word —**draw a blank** [Colloq.] 1. to be unsuccessful in an attempt 2. to be unable to remember —**blank′ly** *adv.* —**blank′ness** *n.*

blank cheque a cheque carrying a signature only and allowing the bearer to fill in any amount

blanket (blaŋ′kit) *n.* [< OFr. *blanc*, white] 1. a large, soft piece of cloth used for warmth, esp. as a bed cover 2. anything like a blanket —*adj.* covering a group of conditions or items —*vt.* 1. to cover 2. to suppress; obscure

blanket stitch a wide buttonhole stitch used to reinforce the edges of blankets and other thick material

blank verse unrhymed verse; esp., unrhymed verse having five iambic feet per line

blare (blāər) *vt., vi.* **blared, blar′ing** [ME. *bleren*, bellow] 1. to sound out with loud, trumpetlike tones 2. to exclaim loudly —*n.* a loud, brassy sound

blarney (blär′nē) *n.* [< stone in Blarney Castle, Ireland, supposed to give the gift of flattery] smooth talk; flattery —*vt., vi.* **-neyed, -neying** to use blarney (on)

blasé (blä′zä) *adj.* [Fr.] indifferent to something because of familiarity or surfeit

blaspheme (blas fēm′) *vt.* **-phemed′, -phem′ing** [< Gr. *blasphēmein*, speak evil of] 1. to speak irreverently or profanely of or to (God or sacred things) 2. to curse or revile —**blasphem′er** *n.*

blasphemy (blas′fə mē) *n., pl.* **-mies** 1. words or action showing disrespect for God or anything held sacred 2. any irreverent remark or action —**blas′phemous** *adj.*

blast (bläst) *n.* [< OE. *blæst*] 1. *a)* an explosion *b)* a charge of explosive causing this 2. the sound of a sudden rush of air or gas, as through a trumpet 3. a strong rush of air 4. a sudden outburst, as of criticism —*vi.* 1. to set off explosives, etc. 2. to make a loud, harsh sound —*vt.* 1. to blow up; explode 2. to blight; wither 3. [Colloq.] to criticize sharply —*interj.* an expression of annoyance, impatience, etc. —**blast off** to take off with explosive force, as a rocket —**(at) full blast** at full speed or capacity

blasted *adj.* 1. blighted 2. damned

blast furnace a smelting furnace into

which a blast of air is forced from below for intense heat

blastoff, blast-off *n.* the launching of a rocket, space vehicle, etc.

blatant (blāt′ənt) *adj.* [prob. < L. *blaterare*, babble] 1. glaringly conspicuous or obtrusive 2. disagreeably loud —**bla′-tancy** *n.* —**bla′tantly** *adv.*

blather (blath′ər) *n., vi., vt.* same as BLETHER

blaze[1] (blāz) *n.* [< OE. *blæse*] 1. a brilliant burst of flame; fire 2. any very bright light 3. a spectacular outburst [a blaze of oratory] 4. a vivid display 5. [pl.] hell: a euphemism, esp. in **go to blazes!** —*vi.* **blazed, blaz′ing** 1. to burn rapidly or shine brightly 2. to be stirred, as with anger —**blaze away** 1. to fire a gun repeatedly 2. [Colloq.] to work energetically

blaze[2] *n.* [< ON. *blesi*] 1. a white spot on an animal's face 2. a mark made on a tree by cutting off a piece of bark —*vt.* **blazed, blaz′ing** to mark (a tree or trail) with blazes —**blaze a trail in** to pioneer in

blaze[3] *vt.* **blazed, blaz′ing** [< OE. or ON.] to make known publicly

blazer (blā′zər) *n.* [< BLAZE[1]] a lightweight jacket, sometimes in the colours of a sports club or school

blazon (blā′z′n) *n.* [OFr. *blason*, shield] a coat of arms —*vt.* 1. to make widely known; proclaim 2. to describe or portray (coats of arms) 3. to adorn colourfully —**bla′zonment** *n.* —**bla′zonry** *n.*

bleach (blēch) *vt., vi.* [< OE. *blac*, pale] to make or become white or colourless —*n.* a substance used for bleaching —**bleach′er** *n.*

bleaching powder chloride of lime or any other powder used in bleaching

bleak (blēk) *adj.* [< ON. *bleikr*, pale] 1. exposed to wind and cold; unsheltered 2. cold and cutting; harsh 3. not cheerful or hopeful; gloomy —**bleak′ly** *adv.* —**bleak′ness** *n.*

blear (blēar) *adj.* [< ME. *bleren*, have watery eyes] 1. made dim by tears, etc. 2. blurred —*vt.* 1. to dim with tears, etc. 2. to blur —**blear′y** *adj.*

bleary-eyed *adj.* having bleary eyes

bleat (blēt) *vi.* [< OE. *blætan*] to make the cry of a sheep, goat, or calf, or a sound like this —*vt.* to say in a bleating voice —*n.* a bleating cry —**bleat′er** *n.*

bleed (blēd) *vi.* **bled** (bled), **bleed′ing** [< OE. *blod*, blood] 1. to lose blood 2. to suffer wounds or die in a cause 3. to feel sympathy; suffer [my heart bleeds] 4. to ooze sap, juice, etc. 5. to run together, as dyes in wet cloth —*vt.* 1. to draw blood from 2. to ooze (sap, juice, etc.) 3. to empty of liquid, air, or gas 4. to take sap or juice from 5. [Colloq.] to extort money from —**bleed like a pig** to bleed profusely

bleeding *adj., adv.* [Vulg.] a euphemism for BLOODY

blemish (blem′ish) *vt.* [< OFr. *blesmir*, injure] to mar, as by some flaw or fault —*n.* 1. a mark that mars the appearance 2. any defect

blench (blench) *vi.* [< OE. *blencan*, deceive] to shrink back, as in fear; flinch

blend (blend) *vt.* [< OE. *blendan*] 1. to mix or mingle (varieties) 2. to mix so the parts are no longer distinct —*vi.* 1. to mix or merge 2. to shade gradually into each other, as colours 3. to harmonize —*n.* a mixture of varieties [a blend of coffee] —**blend′er** *n.*

blende (blend) *n.* [G. < *blenden*, deceive] sphalerite or any of certain other sulphides

blenny (blen′ē) *n., pl.* **blen′nies, blen′-ny** [< Gr. *blenna*, slime] small sea fish covered with a slimy substance

blesbok (bles′buk′) *n.* [< Afrik.] an antelope of South Africa, characterized by lyre-shaped horns and a white blaze

bless (bles) *vt.* **blessed** or **blest, bless′-ing** [< OE. *bletsian*, consecrate with blood] 1. to make holy 2. to ask divine favour for 3. to endow (with) [blessed with health] 4. to make happy or prosperous 5. to glorify 6. to make the sign of the cross over —**bless me** (or **you,** etc.)! an exclamation of surprise, dismay, etc.

blessed (bles′id) *adj.* 1. holy; sacred 2. fortunate 3. beatified 4. bringing joy 5. cursed: an ironical oath —**bless′edly** *adv.* —**bless′edness** *n.*

blessing *n.* 1. a benediction 2. a grace said before or after eating 3. the gift of divine favour 4. good wishes or approval 5. a benefit

blest (blest) *alt. pt. & pp.* of BLESS —*adj.* blessed

blether (bleth′ər) *n.* [ON. *blathr*] 1. foolish talk 2. a person who chatters foolishly —**bleth′erer** *n.*

blew (bloo) *pt.* of BLOW[1]

blight (blīt) *n.* [? < ON. *blikja*, turn pale] 1. any insect or disease that destroys or stunts plants 2. anything that destroys, frustrates, etc. 3. an area of decay and neglect, esp. in a city —*vt.* 1. to wither 2. to destroy 3. to frustrate

blighter *n.* a contemptible or annoying person

blighty (blīt′ē) *n.* [< Hindi, foreign land] [Mil. Slang] 1. [often B-] Britain; home 2. a wound involving a return to Britain: also **a blighty one**

blimey (blī′mē) *interj.* [< (God) blind me] [Colloq.] an exclamation of surprise, wonder, etc.

blimp (blimp) *n.* [echoic] 1. a soundproof cover for a cine camera 2. [Colloq.] a small, nonrigid or semirigid airship 3. [< Col. *Blimp*, creation of Brit. cartoonist David Low] a person, esp. a military officer, who is complacent and highly conservative

blind (blīnd) *adj.* [OE.] 1. without the power of sight 2. of or for sightless persons 3. not able or willing to understand 4. without adequate directions or knowledge [a blind search] 5. reckless 6. hard to see; hidden 7. closed at one end 8. not controlled by intelligence [blind destiny] 9. [Slang] drunk 10. Aeron.

by the use of instruments only [*blind flying*] —*vt.* **1.** to make sightless **2.** to dazzle **3.** to deprive of insight **4.** to obscure **5.** to hide —*n.* **1.** anything that obscures or prevents sight **2.** a screen for a window **3.** a person or thing used to mislead —*adv.* **1.** blindly **2.** recklessly **3.** sight unseen [to buy a thing *blind*] —**the blind** blind people —**blind′ly** *adv.* —**blind′ness** *n.*

blind alley **1.** a lane shut off at one end **2.** any undertaking, idea, etc. that leads to nothing

blind date [Colloq.] a social engagement arranged for a man and a woman previously unacquainted

blindfold *vt.* [< ME. *blindfeld*, struck blind] to cover the eyes of, as with a cloth —*n.* something used to cover the eyes —*adj.* **1.** with the eyes covered **2.** reckless

blind gut *same as* CAECUM

blindman's buff (blīnd′manz buf′) a game in which a blindfolded player has to catch and identify another

blind spot **1.** the small area, insensitive to light, in the retina of the eye where the optic nerve enters **2.** an area where vision is obscured **3.** a prejudice, or area of ignorance, that one has but is often unaware of

blindworm *n.* *same as* SLOWWORM

blink (bliŋk) *vi.* [see BLENCH] **1.** to wink quickly **2.** to flash on and off **3.** to look with eyes half shut —*vt.* to cause (eyes, light, etc.) to blink —*n.* **1.** a blinking **2.** a glimmer —**blink at** to ignore or condone (a mistake) —**on the blink** [Colloq.] not working properly

blinker *n.* either of two flaps on a horse's bridle that shut out the side view

blinking *adj., adv.* *a euphemism for* BLOODY

blip (blip) *n.* [echoic] **1.** a luminous image, as on a radar screen **2.** a quick, sharp sound

bliss (blis) *n.* [< OE. *blithe*, blithe] **1.** great joy or happiness **2.** spiritual joy —**bliss′ful** *adj. adv.* —**bliss′fulness** *n.*

blister (blis′tər) *n.* [< ? ON. *blastr*] **1.** a raised patch of skin filled with watery matter and caused by burning or rubbing **2.** anything resembling a blister —*vt.* **1.** to raise blisters on **2.** to lash with words —*vi.* to form blisters —**blis′tery** *adj.*

blithe (blīth) *adj.* [OE.] gay; cheerful; carefree —**blithe′ly** *adv.* —**blithe′ness** *n.*

blithering (blith′ər iŋ) *adj.* [< BLETHER] talking without sense; jabbering

blithesome (blīth′səm) *adj.* blithe; gay

B.Litt., B.Lit. [L. *Baccalaureus Lit(t)erarum*] Bachelor of Letters (or Literature)

blitz (blits) *n.* [< ff.] **1.** a sudden, overwhelming attack **2.** [B-] the German air raids on Britain during 1940 (preceded by *the*) —*vt.* to subject to a blitz; overwhelm

blitzkrieg (-krēg) *n.* [G. < *Blitz*, lightning + *Krieg*, war] **1.** sudden, swift, large-scale offensive warfare intended to win

a quick victory **2.** any sudden, overwhelming attack

blizzard (bliz′ərd) *n.* [U.S. dial. *bliz*, violent blow] a violent storm with driving snow and cold winds

bloat¹ (blōt) *vt., vi* [< ON. *blautr*, soaked] **1.** to swell, as with water or air **2.** to puff up, as with pride

bloat² *vt.* [< ME. *blote* < ON. *blautr:* see prec.] to cure by soaking in salt water and smoking

bloated *adj.* **1.** cured by salting and smoking: said of fish **2.** swollen, as with pride, wealth, etc.

bloater *n.* a herring that has been bloated

blob (blob) *n.* [echoic] a small drop or mass

bloc (blok) *n.* [Fr. < LowG. *block*, log] a group of legislators or nations, acting together in some common cause

block (blok) *n.* [see prec.] **1.** any large, solid piece of wood, stone, or metal **2.** a blocklike stand for chopping, beheading, mounting a horse from, etc. **3.** a large building divided into offices, flats, etc. **4.** an obstruction or hindrance **5.** a pulley in a frame **6.** a large, hollow building brick **7.** a child's toy brick **8.** any number of things regarded as a unit **9.** a group of buildings bounded by intersecting streets **10.** [Colloq.] a person's head **11.** *Printing* a piece of engraved wood, etc. with a design —*vt.* **1.** to impede; hinder **2.** to sketch with little detail (often with *out*) **3.** *Cricket* to play (a ball) defensively —**block up** to shut in; enclose —**block′age** *n.* —**block′er** *n.*

blockade (blo kād′) *n.* **1.** a shutting off of a port or region by hostile troops or ships to prevent passage **2.** any strategic barrier —*vt.* -**ad′ed,** -**ad′ing** to subject to a blockade —**blockad′er** *n.*

blockade runner a ship or person that tries to go through or past a blockade

block and tackle pulley blocks and ropes or cables, used for hoisting large, heavy objects

blockbuster (blok′bus′tər) *n.* [Colloq.] **1.** a large, highly destructive aerial bomb **2.** a successful, heavily promoted film, novel, etc.

blockhead *n.* a stupid person

BLOCKHOUSE

blockhouse *n.* **1.** [U.S.] formerly, a wooden fort with openings in the walls to shoot from **2.** *Mil.* a small structure of concrete for defence or observation

blockish *adj.* stupid; dull —**block′ishness** *n.*

block letter a plain capital letter used in writing for its legibility

block release the release of employees

from work, usually for several weeks, to enable them to attend a training course

block system a system of dividing a railway line into sections, ensuring by signals that only one train can be in the section at a time

block vote a vote in which a delegate's influence is in accordance with the number of people he represents

blocky *adj.* 1. like a block 2. stocky

bloke (blōk) *n.* [< ?] [Colloq.] a fellow; chap

blond (blond) *adj.* [Fr. < ?] 1. having yellow or yellowish-brown hair, often with fair skin 2. yellow or yellowish-brown: said of hair —*n.* a blond person —**blond'-ness** *n.* —**blonde** *adj., n.fem.*

blood (blud) *n.* [< OE. *blod*] 1. the fluid, usually red, circulating in the arteries and veins of vertebrates 2. murder 3. the essence of life 4. sap or juice, esp. if red 5. passion or disposition 6. parental heritage; ancestry 7. kinship; family relationship 8. people, esp. youthful people [new *blood* in the firm] 9. a dandy —*vt.* 1. to let (a hunting dog) taste or see the blood of its prey 2. to initiate (a person) in any new experience —**bad blood** anger; hatred —**in cold blood** 1. with cruelty 2. dispassionately; deliberately —**in one's blood** to be a natural or inherited characteristic —**make one's blood boil** to make one angry —**make one's blood run cold** to terrify one

blood bath a massacre; slaughter

blood brother 1. a brother by birth 2. a person bound to one by mingling his blood with one's own

blood count the number of red corpuscles and white corpuscles in a given volume of blood

bloodcurdling *adj.* very frightening

blood group any of several groups into which human blood is classified

blood heat the normal temperature of human blood, approximately 36.8°C (98.4°F)

bloodhound *n.* a large, keen-scented dog used in tracking fugitives, etc.

bloodless *adj.* 1. without blood 2. without bloodshed 3. anaemic or pale 4. having little energy —**blood'lessly** *adv.* —**blood'lessness** *n.*

bloodletting *n.* the opening of a vein to remove blood; bleeding

blood money 1. money paid to a hired killer 2. money paid as compensation for a murder

blood orange a variety of orange with a red pulp

blood poisoning any disease in which the blood contains microorganisms or other poisonous matter

blood pressure the pressure exerted by the blood against the inner walls of the blood vessels

blood relation a person related by birth

bloodshed *n.* the shedding of blood; killing

bloodshot *adj.* red because the small blood vessels are swollen or broken: said of an eye

blood sport any pastime, as fox-hunting, in which killing is involved

bloodstained *adj.* 1. soiled or discoloured with blood 2. guilty of murder

bloodstone *n.* a dark-green variety of quartz spotted with red jasper, used as a gem

bloodstream *n.* the blood flowing through the circulatory system of a body

bloodsucker *n.* 1. an animal that sucks blood, esp. a leech 2. a person who extorts from others

bloodthirsty *adj.* murderous; cruel

blood vessel a tube through which the blood circulates in the body; artery, vein, or capillary

bloody *adj.* -ier, -iest 1. of, like, or covered with blood 2. involving bloodshed 3. bloodthirsty 4. [Vulg. Slang] cursed; damned —*adv.* [Vulg. Slang] very —*vt.* **blood'ied, blood'ying** to stain with blood —**blood'ily** *adv.*

bloody-minded *adj.* [Colloq.] intentionally awkward or uncooperative —**blood'y-mind'edness** *n.*

bloom[1] (bloom) *n.* [< ON. *blomi*, flowers] 1. a flower 2. the state or time of flowering 3. the time of most vigour, etc. 4. a youthful, healthy glow 5. the powdery coating on some fruits or leaves —*vi.* 1. to bear flowers; blossom 2. to be in one's prime; flourish 3. to glow as with health —**bloom'ing** *adj.*

bloom[2] *n.* [OE. *bloma*, lump of metal] an oblong mass of metal in an intermediate stage of manufacture

bloomer *n.* 1. a plant with reference to its blooming [an early *bloomer*] 2. [Slang] a stupid mistake

bloomers *n.pl.* [< Amelia J. *Bloomer*] 1. baggy trousers gathered at the knee, formerly worn by women 2. an undergarment somewhat like this

blossom (blos'əm) *n.* [< OE. *blostma*] 1. a flower, esp. of a fruit-bearing plant 2. a state or time of flowering —*vi.* 1. to open into blossoms 2. to begin to thrive

blot (blot) *n.* [< ?] 1. a spot or stain, esp. of ink 2. anything that spoils or mars 3. a disgrace —*vt.* **blot'ted, blot'-ting** 1. to spot; stain 2. to erase or get rid of 3. to dry, as with blotting paper —*vi.* 1. to make blots 2. to become blotted 3. to be absorbent —**blot one's copybook** to spoil one's reputation by a mistake

blotch (bloch) *n.* [? < BLOT] 1. a discoloured patch or blemish on the skin 2. any large stain —*vt.* to mark with blotches —**blotch'y** *adj.* -ier, -iest

blotter (blot'ər) *n.* a pad of blotting paper

blotting paper a thick, soft, absorbent paper used to dry a surface freshly written on in ink

blotto (blot'ō) *adj.* [< ?] [Slang] very drunk

blouse (blouz) *n.* [Fr., peasant's smock] 1. a shirtlike garment worn by women 2. the jacket of a military uniform —*vi.*, *vt.* **bloused, blous'ing** to gather in and drape at the waistline

blouson (blōō′zon) *adj.* [Fr. < *blouse*] styled with a full, bloused top —*n.* a blouson dress, top, etc.

blow¹ (blō) *vi.* blew, blown, blow′ing [< OE. *blawan*] 1. to move with some force: said of the wind 2. to send forth air, as with the mouth 3. to pant 4. to sound by blowing 5. to spout water and air, as whales do 6. to be carried by the wind 7. to burst suddenly, as a tyre, or melt, as a fuse (often with *out*) 8. to lay eggs: said of flies —*vt.* 1. to force air from, onto, into, or through 2. to drive by blowing 3. to sound by blowing 4. to form by blown air or gas 5. to burst by an explosion 6. to melt (a fuse) 7. [Colloq.] to spend (money) freely 8. [Slang] to bungle and fail in —*n.* 1. a blowing 2. a blast of air —*interj.* [Colloq.] damn! —**blow hot and cold** to be favourable towards and then opposed to; vacillate —**blow one's top** (or **lid**) [Slang] to lose one's temper —**blow one's own trumpet** to boast of one's achievements —**blow over** 1. to move away, as rain clouds 2. to be forgotten —**blow up** 1. to fill with air or gas 2. to explode 3. to become intense, as a storm 4. to enlarge (a photograph) 5. to exaggerate (an incident, etc.) 6. [Colloq.] to lose one's temper —**blow′er** *n.*

blow² *n.* [ME. *blowe*] 1. a hard stroke, as with the fist 2. a sudden misfortune; shock —**come to blows** to begin fighting

blow-by-blow *adj.* told in great detail

blow-dry (blō′drī′) *vt.* -dried′, -dry′ing to dry and style (hair) with an electric device (**blow′-dry′er**) that sends out heated air —*n.* the act of blow-drying the hair

blowfly *n. pl.* -flies′ [BLOW¹ + FLY²] any of various flies that deposit eggs in meat, open wounds, etc.

blowhole *n.* 1. a nostril in the head of whales, etc. 2. a hole through which gas or air can escape 3. a hole in the ice to which seals, etc. come for air

blowlamp *n.* a small burner that shoots out a hot flame intensified by a blast of air

blown *pp.* of BLOW¹ —*adj.* 1. swollen or bloated 2. out of breath 3. made by blowing

blowout *n.* 1. the bursting of a tyre 2. the melting of an electric fuse 3. the uncontrolled escape of oil or gas from a well 4. [Slang] a large meal

blowpipe *n.* 1. a tube for forcing air or gas into a flame to increase its heat 2. a metal tube used in blowing glass 3. a tubelike weapon through which darts are blown

blowy *adj.* -ier, -iest windy

blowzy (blou′zē) *adj.* -ier, -iest [< obs. *blouze*, wench] 1. fat and coarse-looking 2. slovenly

blubber¹ (blub′ər) *n.* [ME. *blober*, bubble] the fat of the whale and other sea mammals

blubber² *vi.* [see prec.] to weep loudly —*vt.* to say while blubbering —*n.* loud

weeping —*adj.* thick or swollen —**blub′-berer** *n.*

bludgeon (bluj′'n) *n.* [< ?] a short club with a thick, heavy, or loaded end —*vt., vi.* 1. to strike with a bludgeon 2. to bully or coerce

blue (blōō) *adj.* [< OFr. *bleu*] 1. having the colour of the clear sky 2. having a blue tinge through cold or anger: said of the skin 3. sad and depressing 4. [Colloq.] indecent —*n.* 1. the colour of the clear sky 2. any blue pigment or dye 3. anything coloured blue 4. a supporter of the British Conservative party 5. a) a sportsman who has represented his university, esp. at Oxford or Cambridge b) the badge awarded to him 6. [*pl.*] [Colloq.] a depressed, unhappy feeling 7. [*pl., also with sing. v.*] Negro folk music, or the jazz evolved from it, with slow tempo and melancholy words —*vt., vi.* blued, blu′ing or blue′ing to make or become blue —**once in a blue moon** very seldom —**out of the blue** as if from the sky; unexpected —**blue′ness** *n.*

blue baby a baby born with cyanosis

bluebell *n.* a plant with blue, bell-shaped flowers

blue blood descent from nobility: also **blue′blood′** *n.* —**blue′-blood′ed** *adj.*

blue book [*also* B- B-] an official government publication, often having a blue cover

bluebottle *n.* 1. a large blowfly with a steel-blue abdomen 2. [Old Slang] a policeman

blue cheese a cheese in which a blue mould has been intentionally produced, as Roquefort, Danish Blue, etc.

blue-collar *adj.* designating or of industrial workers, esp. the semiskilled and unskilled

blue-eyed boy [Colloq.] a favourite; pet

blue-pencil (blōō′pen′s'l) *vt.* -cilled, -cilling to edit, cross out, etc. with or as with a blue pencil

blue peter [*also* B- P-] a blue signal flag with a white square in the centre, displayed on a vessel about to leave port

blueprint *n.* 1. a photographic reproduction in white on a blue background, as of architectural plans 2. any detailed plan —*vt.* to make a blueprint of

blue-ribbon (blōō′rib′ən) *adj.* outstanding of its kind

bluestocking *n.* [< blue stockings worn at literary meetings in 18th-c. London] a learned, bookish, or pedantic woman

blue tit a common European tit having a blue crown, wings and tail and yellow underparts

blue whale a whalebone whale with a dark blue-grey body: probably the largest animal that has ever lived

bluff¹ (bluf) *vt., vi.* [prob. < Du. *bluffen*, baffle] 1. to mislead or frighten by a false, bold front 2. to get (one's way) by bluffing —*n.* a person who bluffs —**call someone's bluff** to challenge someone to give proof of his claims —**bluff′er** *n.*

bluff² *adj.* [< Du. *blaf*, flat] 1. having

a broad, flat front that slopes steeply **2.** having a rough, frank, but affable manner —*n.* **1.** a high, steep bank **2.** [Canad.] a clump of trees on a prairie; copse —**bluff'**-**ly** *adv.*

bluish (bloo'ish) *adj.* somewhat blue : also sp. **blue'ish**

blunder (blun'dər) *vi.* [< ON. *blunda,* shut the eyes] **1.** to move clumsily; stumble **2.** to make a foolish mistake —*vt.* to do poorly; bungle —*n.* a foolish mistake —**blun'derer** *n.* —**blun'deringly** *adv.*

blunderbuss (blun'dərbus') *n.* [Du. *donderbus,* thunder box] an obsolete short gun with a broad muzzle

blunt (blunt) *adj.* [< ?] **1.** having a dull edge or point **2.** plain-spoken and abrupt **3.** slow to perceive; dull —*vt.* **1.** to make dull or insensitive **2.** to make less effective —**blunt'ly** *adv.* —**blunt'**-**ness** *n.*

blur (blur) *vt., vi.* **blurred, blur'ring** [< BLEAR] **1.** to smear or smudge **2.** to make or become less distinct —*n.* **1.** the state of being blurred **2.** an obscuring stain **3.** anything indistinct to the sight or mind —**blur'ry** *adj.*

blurb (blurb) *n.* [arbitrary coinage] [Colloq.] an exaggerated advertisement, as on a book jacket

blurt (blurt) *vt.* [echoic] to say suddenly, without stopping to think (with *out*)

blush (blush) *vi.* [< OE. *blyscan,* shine] **1.** to become red in the face from embarrassment, etc. **2.** to be ashamed (*at* or *for*) **3.** to become rosy —*n.* **1.** a reddening of the face, as from shame **2.** a rosy colour —*adj.* rosy [*blush*-pink] **blusher** *n.* a cosmetic colouring for the cheeks, etc.

bluster (blus'tər) *vt.* [< LowG. *blüstern*] **1.** to say noisily and aggressively **2.** to force by blustering —*vi.* **1.** to speak or behave in a noisy, bullying way **2.** to blow stormily : said of wind —*n.* **1.** noisy, bullying talk **2.** noisy commotion —**blus'**-**teringly** *adv.* —**blus'tery, blus'terous** *adj.*

B.M. **1.** Bachelor of Medicine **2.** British Museum

B.M.A. British Medical Association

B.Mus. Bachelor of Music

BO, B.O. **1.** [Colloq.] body odour **2.** box office

boa (bō'ə) *n.* [L.] **1.** any of a number of tropical snakes that crush their prey in their coils, as the anaconda **2.** a woman's long, fluffy scarf, as of feathers

boa constrictor a species of boa which reaches a length of 3 to 4.5 metres

boar (bôr) *n.* [OE. *bar*] **1.** an uncastrated male pig **2.** a wild pig

board (bôrd) *n.* [< OE. *bord,* plank] **1.** a long, flat piece of sawn wood **2.** a flat piece of wood or other material for some special use [a notice *board*] **3.** *a*) a construction material made in thin, flat sheets [*fibreboard*] *b*) pasteboard or stiff paper, used in book covers **4.** *a*) a table for meals *b*) food, esp. meals provided regularly for pay **5.** a council table **6.** *a*) the directors of a company

b) a group of examiners or interviewers **7.** the side or border [*seaboard*] **8.** (pl.) a wooden wall about 1m high forming the enclosure in which ice hockey or box lacrosse is played —*vt.* **1.** to get on (an aircraft, etc.) **2.** to come onto the deck of (a ship) **3.** to provide with meals, or room and meals, regularly for pay **4.** to cover (*up*) with boards **5.** in ice hockey and box lacrosse, to bodycheck an opponent against the boards —*vi.* to receive meals, or room and meals, regularly for pay —**across the board** including all classes or groups —**board out** to arrange for someone to receive food and lodging away from home —**go by the board** to be discarded, ignored, or abandoned —**on board** on or in a ship, aircraft, bus, etc. —**the boards** the stage (of a theatre)

boarder *n.* **1.** one who boards at a boarding house, boarding school, etc. **2.** one who boards a ship, etc.

boarding *n.* *Ice Hockey* etc. an act of bodychecking an opponent against the boards

boardinghouse *n.* a house where room and meals can be had for pay : also **boarding house**

boarding school a school providing lodging and meals for the pupils

Board of Trade a British government department supervising commerce and industry

boardroom *n.* a room in which a board of administrators, directors, etc. regularly holds meetings

boast (bōst) *vi.* [< Anglo-Fr.] to talk about deeds, abilities, etc. with too much pride and satisfaction —*vt.* **1.** to brag about **2.** to glory in (something) —*n.* **1.** the act of one who boasts **2.** anything boasted of —**boast'er** *n.* —**boast'ingly** *adv.*

boastful *adj.* inclined to brag; boasting

boat (bōt) *n.* [OE. *bat*] **1.** a small, open watercraft propelled by oars, sails, or engine **2.** a ship: landsman's term **3.** a boat-shaped dish —*vi.* to row, sail, or cruise in a boat —**in the same boat** in the same unfavourable situation —**miss the boat** [Colloq.] to fail to make the most of an opportunity —**rock the boat** [Colloq.] to disturb the status quo

boater *n.* a stiff, flat straw hat with a brim

boathook *n.* a long pole with a metal hook on one end for manoeuvring boats

boathouse *n.* a building for storing a boat

boatman *n.* a man who operates, works on, rents, or sells boats

boatswain (bō's'n) *n.* a ship's warrant officer or petty officer in charge of the deck crew, the rigging, anchors, etc.

boat train a train scheduled to take passengers to or from a particular ship

bob¹ (bob) *vt.* **bobbed, bob'ing** [ME. *bobbe,* hanging cluster & *bobben,* knock against] **1.** to move, esp. up and down, with short, jerky motions **2.** to cut (hair) short —*vi.* to move with short, jerky motions —*n.* **1.** a quick, jerky motion **2.** a woman's short haircut **3.** a weight at the end of a plumb line, etc. **4.** a docked tail, as of a horse —**bob up** to appear unexpectedly

bob² *n., pl.* **bob** [< ?] [Old Slang] a shilling

bobbejaan (bob'ə yän') *n.* [S Afr.] a baboon

bobbejaan spanner *n.* [S Afr.] a monkey wrench

bobbin (bob'in) *n.* [Fr. *bobine*] a reel or spool for thread used in spinning, weaving, machine sewing, etc.

bobble (bob''l) *n.* [< BOB¹] a small tufted ball for decoration, as on a woollen hat

bobby (bob'ē) *n., pl.* **-bies** [< Sir Robert (*Bobby*) Peel] a policeman

bobcat (bob'kat') *n.* a wild cat of temperate N America: also **bay lynx**

bobotie (booboo'tē) *n.* [S Afr.] a dish made of curried mincemeat with a beaten egg crust

bobsleigh *n.* a long sledge with two sets of runners one behind the other

bobtail *n.* **1.** a tail cut short; docked tail **2.** a horse or dog with a bobtail

Boche (bosh) *n.* [Fr. < *tête de caboche*, hard head] [*also* b-] [Derog.] a German, esp. a German soldier

bod (bod) *n.* [< BODY] [Colloq.] a person

bode¹ (bōd) *vt.* **bod′ed, bod′ing** [< OE. *boda*, messenger] to be an omen of; presage —**bode ill** (or **well**) to be a bad (or good) omen —**bode′ful** *adj.*

bode² *alt. pt. of* BIDE

bodega (bə dē′gə) *n.* [Sp.] a wine shop, esp. in Spanish-speaking countries

bodge (boj) *vt.* [Colloq.] *same as* BOTCH

bodice (bod′is) *n.* [< *bodies*] **1.** the upper part of a dress **2.** a kind of vest for women worn as an undergarment or over a blouse or dress

bodily (bod′ə lē) *adj.* of, in, by, or to the body —*adv.* **1.** in person; in the flesh **2.** as a single body

bodkin (bod′kin) *n.* [ME. *boidekyn* < ?] **1.** a pointed instrument for making holes in cloth **2.** a long hairpin **3.** a thick, blunt needle

body (bod′ē) *n., pl.* **bod′ies** [< OE. *bodig, cask*] **1.** the whole physical substance of a person, animal, or plant **2.** the trunk of a man or animal **3.** a corpse **4.** the flesh, as opposed to the spirit **5.** [Colloq.] a person **6.** a group regarded as a unit *[an advisory body]* **7.** the main part of anything **8.** a mass of matter *[a body of water]* **9.** density or consistency **10.** richness of tone or flavour —*vt.* **bod′ied, bod′ying** to give substance to —**in a body** as a single unit, esp. to show shared opinion or purpose —**keep body and soul together** to stay alive

bodycheck *vt.* *Ice Hockey* to obstruct another player

bodyguard *n.* a person or persons, usually armed, assigned to guard someone

body politic the people who collectively constitute a political unit under a government

body stocking a tightfitting garment,

usually of one piece, that covers the torso and, sometimes, the legs

Boer (boo͞ər) *n.* [Du. *boer*, peasant: see BOOR] a descendant of the Dutch or Huguenot colonists of South Africa

boerbul (boo͞ər′bəl) *n.* [S Afr.] a crossbred mastiff used esp. as a watchdog

boeremusiek (boo͞ə′rə mü′sik) *n.* [S Afr.] light music associated with the culture of the Afrikaners

boerewors (boo͞ə′rə vôrs) a traditional mincemeat sausage of South Africa

boerperd (boo͞ər′purt) *n.* a S African breed of rugged horse, often palomino

boet (boot) *n.* [< Afrik., brother] [S Afr. Colloq.] a friend: also **boetie**

boffin (bof′in) *n.* [< ?] [Colloq.] a scientist, esp. one engaged in military or government research

bog (bog) *n.* [< Gael. & Ir. *bog*, soft] **1.** wet, spongy ground; a small marsh **2.** [Slang] a lavatory —*vt., vi.* **bogged, bog′-ging** to sink or become stuck in or as in a bog (often with *down*) —**bog′giness** *n.* —**bog′gy** *adj.* **-ier, -iest**

bogan (bō′gən) *n.* [Canad.] a sluggish side stream

bogey (bō′gē) *n., pl.* **-geys** **1.** *same as* BOGY **2.** [after Colonel *Bogey*, imaginary first-rate golfer] *Golf* par or, now usually, one stroke more than par on a hole

boggle (bog′′l) *vi.* **-gled, -gling** [< Scot. *bogle*, spectre] **1.** to be startled or frightened (*at*) **2.** to hesitate (*at*)

bogie (bō′gē) *n., pl.* **-gies** [< Dial.] **1.** an undercarriage on a railway carriage **2.** a small, low, swivelling truck

bog oak oak or other wood preserved in peat bogs

bogtrotter *n.* [Derog.] an Irishman

bogus (bō′gəs) *adj.* [< ?] not genuine

bogy (bō′gē) *n., pl.* **-gies** [see BOGGLE] **1.** an evil spirit; goblin **2.** anything causing great fear

bogyman, bogeyman *n.* an imaginary frightful being

Bohemian (bō hē′mē ən) *n.* **1.** a native of Bohemia **2.** *same as* CZECH **3.** [*often* b-] one who lives in an unconventional way —*adj.* **1.** of Bohemia; Czech **2.** [*often* b-] characteristic of a Bohemian (*n.* 3) —**Bohe′mianism** *n.*

boil¹ (boil) *vi.* [< L. *bulla*, bubble] **1.** to bubble up and vaporize by being heated **2.** to seethe like boiling liquids **3.** to be agitated, as with rage **4.** to cook in boiling liquid —*vt.* **1.** to heat to the boiling point **2.** to cook in boiling water —*n.* the act or state of boiling —**boil away** to evaporate by boiling —**boil down** to lessen in quantity, as by boiling —**boil down to** to amount to —**boil over** **1.** to come to a boil and spill over **2.** to lose one's temper

boil² *n.* [< OE. *byl*] an inflamed, painful, pus-filled swelling on the skin, caused by infection

boiler *n.* **1.** a container in which things are boiled **2.** a tank in which water is turned to steam for heating or power **3.**

a device burning oil, gas, etc., which provides hot water, esp. for central heating

boiler suit a one-piece suit worn for dirty work

boiling point 1. the temperature at which a liquid boils. 2. a state of high excitement

boisterous (bois′tər əs) *adj.* [ME. *boistreous*, crude] 1. *a)* noisy and unruly *b)* loud and exuberant 2. rough and stormy —**bois′terously** *adv.*

bokmakierie (bok′mə kēər′ē) *n.* a large yellow shrike of South Africa

bold (bōld) *adj.* [< OE. *beald*] 1. daring; fearless 2. impudent 3. prominent and clear —**make bold** to dare (*to*) —**bold′ly** *adv.* —**bold′ness** *n.*

bole (bōl) *n.* [ON. *bolr*] a tree trunk

bolero (bə lāər′ō; *for 3 also* bol′ər ō) *n.*, *pl.* **-ros** [Sp.] 1. a Spanish dance 2. music for this 3. a short, sleeveless or sleeved jacket that is open in front

boll (bōl) *n.* [< OE. *bolla*, bowl] the roundish seed pod of a plant, esp. of cotton or flax

bollard (bol′ərd) *n.* [< BOLE] 1. a post on a ship or wharf for securing ropes 2. a post used: *a)* to mark a traffic island *b)* to close a road to vehicles

bollocks (bol′əks) *n.pl. same as* BALLOCKS

Bolshevik (bol′shə vik′) *n.* [Russ. < *bolshe*, majority] [*also* b-] 1. a member of a majority faction in Russia, which formed the Communist Party after seizing power in 1917 2. a Communist, esp. of the Soviet Union 3. loosely, any radical: hostile usage —*adj.* [*also* b-] of the Bolsheviks or Bolshevism —**Bol′shevism** *n.* —**Bol′shevist** *n.*, *adj.*

Bolshie, Bolshy (bol′shē) *adj.* [< prec.] [*also* b-] [Colloq.] 1. difficult to manage; rebellious 2. bad-tempered 3. left wing: hostile usage —*n.* a Bolshevik

bolster (bōl′stər) *n.* [OE.] 1. a long, narrow pillow 2. any bolsterlike object or support —*vt.* to prop up as with a bolster; support (often with *up*) —**bol′sterer** *n.*

bolt[1] (bōlt) *n.* [OE.] 1. a sliding bar for locking a door, etc. 2. a metal rod with a head, threaded and used with a nut to hold parts together 3. a sudden dash 4. a flash of lightning 5. an arrow shot from a crossbow 6. a roll (*of* cloth, etc.) —*vt.* 1. to swallow (food) hurriedly 2. to fasten as with a bolt —*vi.* 1. to dash away suddenly 2. *Hort.* to produce seed prematurely —*adv.* straight; erectly [*bolt* upright] —**bolt from the blue** a sudden, unforeseen occurrence, often unfortunate —**shoot one's bolt** to exhaust one's capabilities —**bolt′er** *n.*

bolt[2] *vt.* [< OFr. *buleter*] 1. to sift (grain, etc.) so as to grade 2. to examine closely —**bolt′er** *n.*

bomb (bom) *n.* [< Gr. *bombos*, hollow sound] 1. a container filled with an explosive, incendiary, etc. for dropping or hurling, or for detonating by a timing mechanism 2. [*often* B-] the atom bomb or similar nuclear device —*vt.* to attack

or destroy with bombs —**like a bomb** [Colloq.] with great success

bombard (bom bärd′) *vt.* [< Fr. *bombarde*, mortar] 1. to attack with artillery or bombs 2. to keep attacking with questions, etc. 3. to direct a stream of particles, as neutrons, against —**bombard′ment** *n.*

bombardier (bom′bə dēər′) *n.* 1. a noncommissioned rank in the Royal Artillery 2. [U.S.] the person who releases the bombs in a bomber 3. [B-] *Trademark* [Canad.] a snow tractor, usually with caterpillar tracks at the rear and skis at the front

bombast (bom′bast) *n.* [< ML. *bambax*, cotton] pompous, high-sounding talk or writing —**bombas′tic** *adj.* —**bombas′tically** *adv.*

Bombay duck (bom′bā′) [< *Bombay*, in India] any of various dried fishes eaten as a relish with curry dishes

bombazine (bom′bə zēn′) *n.* [< ML. *bambax*, cotton] a twilled cloth of silk or rayon with worsted

bomb bay a compartment in the fuselage of a bomber that can be opened to drop bombs

bomber *n.* 1. an aircraft designed for dropping bombs 2. a person who uses bombs as for illegal purposes

bombshell *n.* a devastating surprise

bona fide (bō′nə fī′dē) [L.] in good faith

bonanza (bō nan′zə) *n.* [Sp., prosperity] 1. any source of wealth or profits 2. a rich vein of ore

bonbon (bon′bon′) *n.* [Fr. *bon*, good] a name for various sweets

bond (bond) *n.* [see BAND[1]] 1. anything that binds, fastens, or unites 2. [*pl.*] fetters 3. a binding agreement 4. the status of goods kept in a warehouse until taxes are paid 5. *Chem.* the means by which atoms or groups of atoms are combined in molecules 6. *Finance* an interest-bearing certificate issued by a government or business, promising to pay the holder a specified sum 7. *Law* a written obligation to pay specified sums, do specified things, etc. —*vt.* 1. to fasten or unite as with a bond 2. to place (goods) under bond —*vi.* to hold together by or as by a bond —**bottled in bond** bottled and stored in bonded warehouses for the length of time stated on the label, as some whisky —**bond′able** *adj.* —**bond′er** *n.*

bondage *n.* [< ON. *bua*, inhabit] 1. slavery 2. subjection to some force or influence

bonded *adj.* 1. subject to or secured by a bond or bonds 2. placed in a government-certified, or bonded, warehouse pending payment of taxes

bondman *n.* 1. a feudal serf 2. a man or boy bondservant Also **bondsman** —**bond′maid** *n.fem.*

bond paper a strong, superior stock of paper, esp. of rag pulp, used for documents, letterheads, etc.

bondservant *n.* a slave

bone (bōn) *n.* [OE. *ban*] **1.** any of the pieces of hard tissue forming the skeleton of most vertebrate animals **2.** this hard tissue **3.** [*pl.*] the skeleton **4.** a bonelike substance or part **5.** a thing made of bone —*vt.* **boned, bon'ing** **1.** to remove the bones from **2.** to put whalebone into **3.** [Slang] to steal —**feel in one's bones** to be certain without any real reason —**have a bone to pick** to have something to quarrel about —**make no bones about** [Colloq.] to admit freely —**to the bone** to the bare essentials —**bone'like'** *adj.*

bone china translucent china made with white clay to which bone ash or calcium phosphate has been added

bone-dry (bōn'drī') *adj.* dry as bone; very dry

bone meal crushed or finely ground bones, used as feed for stock or as fertilizer

boneshaker *n.* **1.** an early kind of bicycle with solid tyres **2.** [Slang] any old or rickety vehicle

bonfire (bon'fīər) *n.* [ME. *banefyre*, bone fire] a large fire built outdoors

Bonfire Night the fifth of November, the anniversary of the attempt made by Guy Fawkes to blow up Parliament

bongo (boŋ'gō) *n., pl.* **-gos, -goes** [AmSp. < ?] either of a pair of small joined drums, of different pitch, struck with the fingers: in full, **bongo drum**

bonhomie, bonhommie (bon'ə mē') *n.* [Fr. < *bon*, good + *homme*, man] good nature; amiability

‡**bon jour** (bon zhōor') [Fr.] good day; hello

bonkers (boŋk'ərz) *adj.* [< ?] [Slang] mad; crazy

bon mot (bon'mō') *pl.* **bons mots** (bon'-mōz') [Fr., good word] an apt, clever, or witty remark

bonnet (bon'it) *n.* [OFr. *bonet*] **1.** a flat, brimless cap, worn by men in Scotland **2.** a hat with a chin ribbon, worn by babies or girls **3.** a metal covering, as over the engine of a motor vehicle

bonny, bonnie (bon'ē) *adj.* **bon'nier, bon'niest** [< Fr. *bon*, good] [Chiefly Scot.] **1.** handsome or pretty, with a healthy, cheerful glow **2.** fine; pleasant —**bon'nily** *adv.*

bonsai (bon sī') *n.* [Jap.] *n.* **1.** the art of dwarfing trees, etc. **2.** *pl.* **bonsai'** such a tree or shrub

‡**bon soir** (bon swär') [Fr.] good evening

bonus (bō'nəs) *n., pl.* **bo'nuses** [L., good] **1.** anything given in addition to the customary amount as an incentive, reward, etc. **2.** an extra dividend allotted to shareholders out of profits **3.** a dividend paid to insurance policyholders

bon voyage (bon'voi äzh') [Fr.] pleasant journey: a farewell to a traveller

bony (bō'nē) *adj.* **-ier, -iest** **1.** of, like, or having bones **2.** thin; emaciated —**bon'i-ness** *n.*

bonze (bonz) *n.* [< Jap. *bonsō*] a Buddhist monk

boo (bōō) *interj., n., pl.* **boos** [echoic] a sound made to show disapproval, scorn,

etc., or to startle —*vi., vt.* **booed, boo'-ing** to make this sound (at)

boob (bōōb) *n.* [Slang] **1.** a foolish person **2.** an embarrassing mistake **3.** [Vulg.] a female breast —*vi.* [Slang] to blunder

booby (bōō'bē) *n., pl.* **-bies** [prob. < Sp. *bobo*] **1.** a foolish person **2.** a tropical, diving sea bird related to the gannet

booby prize a prize, usually ridiculous, given in fun to whoever has done worst in a game, race, etc.

booby trap **1.** any device for tricking a person unawares **2.** a mine set to be exploded by some action of the unsuspecting victim —**boo'by-trap'** *vt.* **-trapped', -trap'ping**

boodle (bōō'd'l) *n.* [< Du. *boedel*, property] **1.** something given as a bribe **2.** the loot taken in a robbery

boogie-woogie (bōōg'ē wōōg'ē) *n.* [? echoic] a style of jazz piano playing in which repeated bass figures accompany the melodic variations

book (book) *n.* [OE. *boc*] **1.** a) a number of sheets of paper with writing or printing on them, fastened together between protective covers b) a relatively long literary work **2.** a main division of a literary work **3.** a) a number of blank sheets bound together [an account *book*] b) a record or account **4.** a libretto **5.** a booklike package, as of matches **6.** a record of bets —*vt.* **1.** to record in a book; list **2.** to engage (rooms, etc.) ahead of time **3.** to record charges against on a police record —*adj.* in, from, or according to books or accounts —**book in** **1.** to make a reservation **2.** to register at a hotel —**bring to book** **1.** to force to explain **2.** to reprimand —**by the book** according to the rules —**in someone's good** (or **bad**) **books** in (or out of) someone's favour, or good graces —**keep books** to keep a record of business transactions —**know like a book** to know well —**the Book** the Bible —**throw the book at** [Slang] **1.** to place all possible charges against **2.** to give the maximum punishment to —**book'er** *n.*

bookbinding *n.* the art, trade, or business of binding books —**book'bind'er** *n.*

bookcase *n.* a set of shelves or a cabinet for holding books

book club an organization that sells books, usually at reduced prices, to members who undertake to buy a minimum number of them annually

bookend *n.* an ornamental weight or bracket at the end of a row of books to keep them upright

bookie *n.* [Colloq.] *same as* BOOKMAKER

booking *n.* **1.** a reservation of a room, seat, etc. **2.** an engagement, as for a lecture, performance, etc.

bookish *adj.* **1.** inclined to read and study; scholarly **2.** having mere book learning; pedantic —**book'ishness** *n.*

bookkeeping *n.* the work of keeping a record of business transactions —**book'-keep'er** *n.*

bookmaker *n.* a person in the business

of taking bets, as on horse races —**book′-mak′ing** *n.*

bookmark *n.* anything slipped between the pages of a book to mark a place

bookplate *n.* a label pasted in a book to identify its owner

book review an article or talk in which a book is discussed and critically analysed

bookseller *n.* the owner of a bookshop

bookshop *n.* a shop where books are sold

bookstall *n.* a stand where books are sold

book value the value as shown in account books; specif., the value of the capital stock of a business

bookworm *n.* 1. an insect that harms books by feeding on the binding, etc. 2. an avid reader

boom[1] (boom) *vi., vt.* [echoic] to make, or utter with, a deep, hollow, resonant sound —*n.* a booming sound

boom[2] *n.* [Du., beam] 1. a spar extending from a mast to hold the bottom of a sail outstretched 2. a long beam extending as from an upright to lift and guide something [a microphone *boom*] 3. a barrier of chains or timbers across a harbour, etc.

boom[3] *vi.* [< ? BOOM[1]] to grow swiftly; flourish [business *boomed*] —*n.* a period of business prosperity, etc. —*adj.* of or resulting from a boom in business [a *boom* town]

boomslang (boom′slaŋ) *n.* a green, venomous tree snake of South Africa

boomerang (boom′ərang′) *n.* [Abor.] 1. a flat, curved stick that can be thrown so that it will return to the thrower: used by Australian aborigines 2. something that recoils on its originator and results in his disadvantage —*vi.* to act as a boomerang

boon (boon) *n.* [ON. *bon*, petition] 1. a welcome benefit; blessing 2. [Archaic] a request or favour

boor (boor) *n.* [Du. *boer*, peasant] a rude, awkward, or ill-mannered person —**boor′-ish** *adj.* —**boor′ishly** *adv.* —**boor′ishness** *n.*

boost (boost) *n.* [< ?] 1. an act that helps or promotes 2. a push upwards or forwards 3. an increase —*vt.* 1. to urge others to support 2. to raise as by a push from below 3. to increase

booster *n.* 1. any device providing added power, thrust, etc. 2. any of the early stages of a multistage rocket

booster shot (or **injection**) a later injection of a vaccine for maintaining immunity

boot[1] (boot) *n.* [OFr. *bote*] 1. a protective covering of leather, etc. for the foot and part of the leg 2. the luggage compartment of a motor car 3. [Colloq.] a kick —*vt.* 1. to kick 2. [Slang] to dismiss (often with *out*) —**lick the boots of** to be servile towards —**put the boot in** 1. to kick a person when he is already down 2. to torment a person who is already overcome —**the boot** [Slang] dismissal

boot[2] *n., vt., vi.* [< OE. *bot*, advantage] [Archaic] profit —**to boot** besides; in addition

bootee (boot′ē) *n.* a baby's knitted or cloth shoe

Boötes (bō ō′tēz) [< Gr., ploughman] a N constellation including the star Arcturus

booth (booth) *n. pl.* **booths** (boothz) [< ON. *buth*, temporary dwelling] 1. a stall for the sale of goods, as at a market 2. a small enclosure for telephoning, voting, etc.

bootleg *vt., vi.* **-legged′, -leg′ging** [< concealing objects in the leg of a boot] to make or sell (esp. alcoholic liquor) illegally —*adj.* bootlegged; illegal —**boot′-leg′ger** *n.*

bootless *adj.* useless —**boot′lessly** *adv.*

booty (boot′ē) *n., pl.* **-ties** [< MLowG. *bute*] 1. spoils of war 2. loot 3. any valuable gain

booze (booz) *vi.* **boozed, booz′ing** [< Du. *buizen*] [Colloq.] to drink too much alcoholic liquor —*n.* [Colloq.] alcoholic liquor —**booz′y** *adj.*

boozer *n.* [Colloq.] 1. a person who is fond of drinking alcohol 2. a public house or bar

bop (bop) *n.* [< ?] a style of jazz with complex rhythms and harmonies, etc.

bor. borough

boracic (bəras′ik) *adj.* same as BORIC

borage (bor′ij) *n.* [< ML. *burra*, coarse hair] an annual plant with blue flowers and hairy leaves

borax (bôr′aks) *n.* [< Per. *būrah*] a white, crystalline salt used in glass, soaps, etc.

Bordeaux (bôr dō′) *n.* red or white wine from the region around Bordeaux

Bordeaux mixture a mixture of lime, water and copper sulphate, used to kill insects and fungi

border (bôr′dər) *n.* [< OHG. *bord*, margin] 1. an edge or a part near an edge; margin 2. a dividing line between countries, etc. 3. a narrow strip along an edge —*vt.* 1. to provide with a border 2. to bound —*adj.* of or near a border —**border on** (or **upon**) 1. to be next to 2. to be like —**the Borders** the district on or near the boundary between Scotland and England

borderland *n.* 1. land forming or near a border 2. a vague, uncertain condition

borderline *n.* a boundary —*adj.* on the boundary of what is acceptable, normal, etc.

bore[1] (bôr) *vt.* **bored, bor′ing** [< OE. *bor*, auger] 1. to make a hole in or through with a drill, etc. 2. to make (a hole, tunnel, etc.) as by drilling —*vi.* to bore a hole or passage —*n.* 1. a hole made by boring 2. *a)* the hollow part of a gun barrel, etc. *b)* its inside diameter

bore[2] *n.* [< ON. *bara*, billow] a high, abrupt tidal wave in a narrow channel

bore[3] *vt.* **bored, bor′ing** [< ?] to weary by being dull or monotonous —*n.* a tiresome, dull person or thing

bore[4] *pt.* of BEAR[1]

boredom *n.* the condition of being bored or uninterested; ennui

boric (bôr′ik) *adj.* of or containing boron

boric acid a white, crystalline, weakly acid compound, used as a mild antiseptic

born (bôrn) *alt. pp. of* BEAR[1] —*adj.* 1. brought into life 2. by birth 3. natural

borne (bôrn) *alt. pp. of* BEAR[1]

boron (bôr'on) *n.* [< BORAX] a non-metallic chemical element occurring in borax, etc.: symbol, B

borough (bur'ə) *n.* [< OE. *burg*, town] 1. a town with a municipal corporation granted by royal charter 2. a town that sends representatives to Parliament

borrow (bor'ō) *vt., vi.* [< OE. *borgian*, borrow] 1. to take or receive (something) with the understanding that one will return it 2. to adopt (something) as one's own —**borrow trouble** to worry prematurely —**bor'rower** *n.*

borsch (bôrsh) *n.* [Russ.] a Russian beetroot soup: also **bortsch**

Borstal (bôr'st'l) *n.* [< *Borstal*, town in England] [*also* b-] a treatment centre for young offenders

BORZOI
(70–80 cm high
at shoulder)

borzoi (bôr'zoi) *n.* [Russ., swift] a breed of large dog with a narrow head and silky coat

bosh (bosh) *n., interj.* [Turk. worthless] [Colloq.] nonsense

bo's'n (bōs''n) *n.* *contracted form of* BOATSWAIN

bosom (booz'əm) *n.* [OE. *bosm*] 1. the human breast 2. the breast regarded as the source of feelings 3. the enclosing space formed by the breast and arms in embracing 4. the midst 5. the part of a garment that covers the breast —*adj.* close; intimate

boss[1] (bos) *n.* [Du. *baas*, master] an employer or supervisor —*vt.* 1. to act as boss of 2. [Colloq.] to order (a person) about

boss[2] *n.* [< OFr. *boce*, swelling] a raised part on a flat surface; esp., a decorative knob, stud, etc.

bossa nova (bos'ə nō'və) [Port., new bump] 1. jazz samba music originating in Brazil 2. a dance for couples performed to this music

bossy *adj.* **-ier, -iest** [Colloq.] domineering or dictatorial —**boss'ily** *adv.* —**boss'iness** *n.*

bosun (bōs''n) *n.* *same as* BOATSWAIN

bot. 1. botanical 2. botanist 3. botany 4. bottle

botany (bot'ə nē) *n.* [< Gr. *botanē*, plant] the science that deals with plants, their life, structure, growth, etc. —**botanical** (bə tan'i k'l) *adj.* —**bot'anist** *n.*

botch (boch) *vt.* [ME. *bocchen*, repair] 1. to patch clumsily 2. to bungle —*n.*

a bungled piece of work —**botch'er** *n.* —**botch'y** *adj.*

botfly (bot'flī') *n., pl.* **-flies'** [< ? Gael. *boiteag*, maggot + FLY[2]] a fly whose larvae are parasitic in horses, sheep, etc.

both (bōth) *adj., pron.* [< OE. *ba tha*, both these] the two [*both* (birds) sang] —*conj., adv.* together; equally; as well: with *and* [*both* tired *and* sick]

bother (both'ər) *vt., vi.* [prob. Anglo-Ir. for POTHER] 1. to worry, annoy, etc. 2. to concern (oneself) —*n.* 1. worry; trouble 2. a person who gives trouble —*interj.* an expression of annoyance, etc.

botheration (both'ə rā'shən) *n., interj.* [Colloq.] *same as* BOTHER

bothersome *adj.* troublesome

bothy, bothie (both'ē) *n.* [< BOOTH] [Scot.] 1. a small roughly-built shelter or outhouse 2. a poorly-finished dwelling for farm workers

bo tree (bō) [Sinhalese *bo*] a fig tree sacred to Buddhists and Hindus

bottle (bot''l) *n.* [< LL. *buttis*, cask] 1. a container, esp. for liquids, usually of glass, with a narrow neck 2. the amount that a bottle holds —*vt.* **-tled, -tling** 1. to put into bottles 2. to store under pressure in a cylinder, etc. [*bottled* gas] —**bottle up** 1. to suppress (emotions) 2. to shut in (enemy troops, etc.) —**hit the bottle** [Slang] to drink much alcoholic liquor —**bot'tleful** *n.* —**bot'tler** *n.*

bottle green a dark green colour

bottleneck *n.* 1. a place, as a narrow road, where traffic is slowed down or halted 2. any point at which progress is slowed down

bottlenose *n.* a kind of dolphin, grey or greenish, with a bottle-shaped snout

bottle party a party to which guests bring drink with them

bottle store [S Afr.] an off-licence

bottom (bot'əm) *n.* [< OE. *botm*, ground] 1. the lowest part or position 2. the farthest part 3. the part on which something rests 4. the side underneath 5. the seat of a chair 6. the ground beneath a body of water 7. *a)* a ship's keel *b)* a ship 8. basic meaning 9. [Colloq.] the buttocks —*adj.* of, at, or on the bottom; lowest, last, etc. —*vt.* 1. to provide with a bottom 2. to understand; fathom 3. to base (*on* or *upon*) —*vi.* 1. to reach the bottom 2. to be based —**at bottom** fundamentally —**be at the bottom of** to be the real reason for —**bottoms up!** [Colloq.] drink deep!: a toast

bottom drawer a woman's collection of linen, clothing, etc., made in preparation for marriage

botulism (bot'yoo liz'm) *n.* [< L. *botulus*, sausage] poisoning resulting from the toxin produced by a certain bacillus sometimes found in foods improperly preserved

bouclé (boo'klā) *n.* [Fr.] 1. a curly yarn that gives the fabric made from it a tufted or knotted texture 2. fabric made from this yarn

boudoir (bōōd'wär) *n.* [Fr., pouting room] a woman's private room

bouffant (bōō'fän) *adj.* [< Fr. *bouffer*, puff out] puffed out, as some skirts or hairstyles

bougainvillaea, bougainvillea (bōō'-gən vil'ē ə)' *n.* [< L. A. de *Bougainville*] a woody tropical plant having flowers with large, showy, purple or red bracts

bough (bou) *n.* [OE. *bog*, shoulder] a branch of a tree, esp. a main branch

bought (bôt) *pt. & pp.* of BUY

bouillon (bool'yon) *n.* [Fr.] a clear broth

boulder (bōl'dər) *n.* [< ME. *bulderstan* < Scand.] a large rock worn smooth by weather and water

boulder clay unstratified material left by a glacier, consisting of fine clay, boulders and pebbles

boule[1] (bōō'lē) *n.* [Gr.] 1. the ancient Greek senate 2. the modern Greek parliament

boule[2] (bōōl) *n.* [Fr., ball] [*usually pl.*] a French game similar to bowls

boulevard (bōōl'ə värd', bōōl'vär') *n.* [< MDu. *bolwerc*, bulwark] a broad street, often lined with trees

boult (bōlt) *vt.* same as BOLT[2]

bounce (bouns) *vt.* bounced, bounc'ing [akin to Du. *bonzen*, thump] to cause to hit against a surface so as to spring back —*vi.* 1. to spring back after striking a surface; rebound 2. to leap 3. to boast 4. [Slang] to be returned to the payee by a bank: said of a worthless cheque —*n.* 1. *a)* a bouncing *b)* a leap 2. capacity for bouncing 3. impudence; bluster 4. [Colloq.] energy; zest —**bounce back** [Colloq.] to recover strength, spirits, etc. quickly —**bounc'y** *adj.*

bouncer *n.* [Slang] a man hired to remove disorderly people from a nightclub, etc.

bouncing *adj.* big, healthy, strong, etc.

bound[1] (bound) *vi.* [Fr. *bondir*, to leap] 1. to move with a leap or series of leaps 2. to bounce or rebound, as a ball —*n.* 1. a jump; leap 2. a bounce

bound[2] *pt. & pp.* of BIND —*adj.* 1. tied 2. closely connected 3. certain [*bound* to win] 4. obliged [legally *bound* to pay] 5. provided with a binding, as a book —**bound up in** (or **with**) 1. devoted to 2. involved in

bound[3] *adj.* [< ON. *bua*, prepare] going; headed [*bound* for home]

bound[4] *n.* [< ML. *bodina*, boundary] 1. a boundary 2. [*pl.*] a place enclosed by a boundary —*vt.* 1. to limit; confine 2. to be a limit or boundary to —*vi.* to have a boundary (*on*) —**beat the bounds** to walk ceremoniously around the boundaries of a parish —**out of bounds** 1. beyond the boundaries 2. forbidden —**bound'less** *adj.*

boundary (boun'dər ē) *n., pl.* -ries 1. anything marking a limit 2. *Cricket a)* the marked limit of the playing area *b)* a stroke that reaches this limit, scoring four or six runs

bounden (boun'dən) *adj.* [old pp. of BIND]

1. under obligation 2. obligatory [*bounden* duty]

bounder *n.* [< BOUND[1]] [Colloq.] a cad

bountiful (boun'tə f'l) *adj.* 1. giving freely and graciously 2. abundant Also **boun'te-ous** —**boun'tifully** *adv.*

bounty *n., pl.* -ties [< L. *bonus*, good] 1. generosity 2. a generous gift 3. a reward or premium, as one given by a government for the performance of certain services

bouquet (bōō kā') *n.* [Fr.] 1. a bunch of cut flowers 2. a fragrant smell, esp. of a wine or brandy

‡**bouquet garni** (bōō'kā gär nē') a bunch of herbs tied together and used for flavouring soups, stews, etc.

bourbon (bur'bən, booər'-) *n.* [< *Bourbon* County, Kentucky, U.S.] [U.S.] [*sometimes* **B-**] a whisky made from maize and aged for not less than two years

bourgeois (booər'zhwä) *n., pl.* -**geois** [Fr.] 1. a member of the bourgeoisie 2. a person whose beliefs, attitudes, etc. are middle-class —*adj.* of the bourgeoisie; conventional, materialistic, etc.

bourgeoisie (booər'zhwä'zē') *n.* [with *sing. or pl. v.*] the social class between the very wealthy and the working class; middle class

bourn[1], **bourne**[1] (booərn) *n.* [OE. *burna*, stream] a brook

bourn[2], **bourne**[2] (booərn) *n.* [see BOUND[4]] [Archaic] 1. a boundary 2. a goal 3. a domain

bourrée (boo'rā) *n.* [Fr.] 1. a lively, 17th-cent. French dance in duple time 2. music for this

bourse (booərs) *n.* [Fr., purse] a stock exchange; specif., [**B-**] the stock exchange of Paris

bout (bout) *n.* [< ME. *bught*] 1. a period of some activity, illness, etc. 2. a struggle; contest

boutique (bōō tēk') *n.* [Fr.] a small shop, or a part of a department store, selling fashionable items

bouzouki (bōō zōō'kē) *n.* [< ModGr.] a stringed musical instrument of Greece, somewhat like a mandolin

bovine (bō'vīn) *adj.* [< L. *bos, bovis,* ox] 1. of an ox or cow 2. slow, dull, stupid, stolid, etc.

bow[1] (bou) *vi.* [< OE. *bugan,* bend] 1. to bend the head or body in respect, agreement, etc. 2. to yield, as to authority —*vt.* 1. to bend (the head) in respect, shame, agreement, etc. 2. to weigh (*down*); overwhelm —*n.* a bending of the head or body, as in respect, greeting, etc. —**bow and scrape** to be too polite and ingratiating —**take a bow** to acknowledge applause

bow[2] (bō) *n.* [see prec.] 1. anything curved or bent 2. a flexible, curved strip of wood with a taut cord connecting the ends, designed for shooting arrows 3. a slender stick strung along its length with horsehairs, drawn across the strings of a violin, etc. to play it 4. a decorative knot, usually with two loops, untied by pulling the ends —*vt., vi.* 1. to bend in the shape of a bow 2. to play (a violin, etc.) with a bow

bow³ (baʊ) *n.*·[< LowG. or Scand.] 1. the front part of a ship 2. the oarsman nearest the bow

bowdlerize (baʊd'lə rīz') *vt.* **-ized'**, **-iz'-ing** [< Thomas *Bowdler*, who in 1818 published an expurgated Shakespeare] to expurgate —**bowd'leriza'tion** *n.*

bowel (baʊ'əl) *n.* [< L. *botulus*, sausage] 1. an intestine 2. [*pl.*] the inner part [the *bowels* of the earth] 3. [*pl.*] [Archaic] tender emotions —**move one's bowels** to defecate

bower (baʊ'ər) *n.* [< OE. *bur*, dwelling] 1. a place enclosed by leafy boughs; arbour 2. [Archaic] a boudoir —*vt.* to enclose in a bower —**bow'ery** *adj.*

bowerbird *n.* any of certain brightly-coloured birds of Australia and New Guinea

bowhead (bō'hed') *n.* a whale with an arched upper jaw

bowie knife (bō'ē) [< Col. J. *Bowie*] a long sheath knife with a single edge

bowl¹ (bōl) *n.* [< OE. *bolla*] 1. a deep, rounded dish 2. a thing shaped like a bowl, as the hollowed-out part of a smoking pipe 3. the contents of a bowl

bowl² *n.* [< L. *bulla*, bubble] a heavy ball used in the game of bowls —*vi.*, *vt.* 1. to roll (a ball) or participate in bowling or bowls 2. to move swiftly and smoothly 3. *Cricket a)* to throw (a ball) to the batsman *b)* to dismiss a batsman by delivering a ball that knocks down the wicket (often with *out*) —**bowl over** 1. [Colloq.] to astonish 2. to knock over —**bowl'er** *n.*

bowleg (bō'leg') *n.* a leg that is bowed or curved outwards —**bow'leg'ged** (-leg'-id, -legd') *adj.*

bowler (bōl'ər) *n.* [< name of hat manufacturer] a felt hat with a rounded crown and narrow curved brim

bowline (bō'lin) *n.* [ME. *bouveline*] 1. a rope used to keep the sail taut when sailing into the wind 2. a knot used to tie off a loop : also **bowline knot**

bowling (bōl'iŋ) *n.* 1. a game in which a heavy ball is bowled along a lane (**bowling alley**) to knock over wooden pins set upright at the far end 2. *same as* BOWLS

bowls (bōlz) *n.* a game played on a lawn (**bowling green**) with wooden balls which are rolled in an attempt to make them stop near a target ball (the *jack*)

BOWSPRIT

bowsprit (bō'sprit) *n.* [prob. < Du.] a large, tapered spar extending forwards from the bow of a sailing vessel

bow tie (bō) a small necktie tied in a bow

BOXING AND WRESTLING WEIGHTS

WEIGHTS	PROFESSIONAL BOXING	OLYMPIC BOXING	FREESTYLE WRESTLING
LIGHT FLYWEIGHT		under 48 kg	under 48 kg
FLYWEIGHT	under 50.8 kg	under 51 kg	under 52 kg
BANTAMWEIGHT	under 53.3 kg	under 54 kg	under 57 kg
FEATHERWEIGHT	under 57.2 kg	under 57 kg	under 62 kg
JUNIOR LIGHTWEIGHT	under 59.0 kg		
LIGHTWEIGHT	under 61.2 kg	under 60 kg	under 68 kg
JUNIOR WELTERWEIGHT	under 63.5 kg		
LIGHT WELTERWEIGHT		under 63.5 kg	
WELTERWEIGHT	under 66.7 kg	under 67 kg	under 74 kg
JUNIOR MIDDLEWEIGHT	under 70.0 kg		
LIGHT MIDDLEWEIGHT		under 71 kg	
MIDDLEWEIGHT	under 72.3 kg	under 75 kg	under 82 kg
LIGHT HEAVYWEIGHT	under 79.4 kg	under 81 kg	under 90 kg
MID HEAVYWEIGHT			under 100 kg
HEAVYWEIGHT	over 79.4 kg	over 81 kg	over 100 kg

bow window (bō) a curved, bay window

box¹ (boks) *n.* [< Gr. *pyxos*, boxwood]
1. a container, usually lidded, made of cardboard, wood, or other stiff material
2. the contents of a box 3. the driver's seat on a coach 4. any boxlike thing, as *a*) a small, enclosed group of seats in a theatre *b*) a large, enclosed stall for a horse 5. *same as* HORSE-BOX 6. a small country house used by sportsmen 7. [*often* B-] [Colloq.] television —*vt.* to provide with or put into a box —*adj.*
1. shaped like a box 2. packed in a box —**box in** (or **up**) to shut in —**box'**-like *adj.*

box² *n.* [< ?] a blow struck with the hand, esp. on the ear —*vt.* 1. to strike such a blow 2. to fight in a boxing match with —*vi.* 1. to fight with the fists

box³ *n.* [< Gr. *pyxos*] an evergreen shrub or small tree with small, leathery leaves

boxer *n.* 1. a man who boxes; pugilist; prizefighter 2. a medium-sized dog with a sturdy body and a smooth, fawn or brindle coat

box girder a hollow girder that is square or rectangular in shape

boxing *n.* [< BOX²] the sport of fighting with the fists, esp. in padded leather mittens (**boxing gloves**)

Boxing Day [from the custom of giving Christmas boxes to milkmen, postmen, etc. on this day] the first day after Christmas (26th December), observed as a holiday

box junction a junction marked by yellow cross-hatching on the road: drivers may enter only if their exit is clear

box lacrosse in Canada, lacrosse played indoors: also called **boxla**

box number a number given to newspaper advertisements to which replies may be sent

box office 1. a place where admission tickets are sold, as in a theatre 2. [Colloq.] the power of a show or performer to attract an audience

box pleat a double pleat with the under edges folded towards each other

boxroom *n.* a small room or cubbyhole used for storing articles that are not immediately required

box spring a coiled spring contained in a boxlike frame, used as a base for mattresses, chairs, etc.

boy (boi) *n.* [ME. *boie*] 1. a male child 2. an immature man 3. a man servant, porter, etc. 4. [Colloq.] a son 5. [S Afr. Derog.] a black male servant —**boy'**-ish *adj.* —**boy'ishness** *n.*

boycott (boi'kot) *vt.* [< Captain *Boycott*, Irish land agent so treated in 1880] 1. to join together in refusing to deal with, so as to punish, coerce, etc. 2. to refuse to buy, sell, or use (something) —*n.* the act of boycotting

boyfriend *n.* 1. a sweetheart, or escort of a girl or woman 2. a boy who is one's friend

boy scout a member of the **Scouts**,

a worldwide boys' organization that stresses outdoor life and service

boysenberry (boi'z'nbər ē) *n.*, *pl.* **-ries** [< R. *Boysen*] a large, purple berry, a cross of the raspberry, loganberry, and blackberry

Bp. bishop

B.P. 1. British Petroleum 2. British Pharmacopoeia

Bq *Physics the symbol for* becquerel

Br *Chem.* bromine

Br. 1. Breton 2. Britain 3. British

B.R., BR British Rail

bra (brä) *n.* [< BRA(SSIÈRE)] an undergarment worn by women to support and shape the breasts

braai (brī) *n. short for* BRAAIVLEIS

braaivleis (brī'flās) *n.* [S Afr.] a barbecue

brace (brās) *vt.* braced, brac'ing [< L. *brachium*, arm] 1. to tie or bind 2. to tighten 3. to strengthen or make firm by supporting the weight of 4. to make ready for an impact, etc. 5. to stimulate —*n.* 1. a pair 2. a device that clasps or connects; fastener 3. [*pl.*] straps passed over the shoulders to hold up trousers 4. a device for maintaining tension, as a guy wire 5. either of the signs { }, used to connect words, lines, etc. 6. a device used as a support; prop 7. a device for correcting the position of irregular teeth —**brace up** [Colloq.] to call forth one's courage, etc.

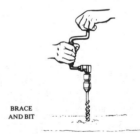

BRACE
AND BIT

brace and bit a tool for boring, consisting of a removable drill (*bit*) in a rotating handle (*brace*)

bracelet (brās'lit) *n.* [< L. *brachium*, arm] 1. an ornamental band or chain worn about the wrist or arm 2. [Colloq.] a handcuff

brachiopod (brā'kē əpod') *n.* [< Gr. *brachiōn*, arm + -POD] a marine animal with two armlike parts with tentacles

brachium (brā'kē əm) *n.*, *pl.* **-chia** [L.] the part of the arm from the shoulder to the elbow —**bra'chial** *adj.*

bracing (brās'iŋ) *adj.* invigorating

bracken (brak''n) *n.* [< ON.] 1. a large, coarse fern 2. a growth of such ferns

bracket (brak'it) *n.* [< L. *bracae*, breeches] 1. any angle-shaped support 2. a wall shelf held up by brackets 3. a wall fixture, as for a small lamp 4.

an architectural support projecting from a wall **5.** either of the signs [ ], or ( ) used to enclose words, figures, etc. **6.** the part of a classified grouping that falls within specified limits —*vt.* **1.** to support with brackets **2.** to enclose in brackets **3.** to classify together

brackish (brak′ish) *adj.* [< MDu. *brak*, salty] somewhat salty, as water in some marshes near the sea —**brack′ishness** *n.*

bract (brakt) *n.* [L. *bractea*, thin metal plate] a leaf, usually small and scalelike, growing at the base of a flower —**bracteal** (brak′tē əl) *adj.* —**brac′teate** *adj.*

brad (brad) *n.* [ON. *broddr*, spike] a thin wire nail with a small or off-centre head

bradawl (brad′ôl) *n.* a hand-boring tool with a chisel edge

brae (brā) *n.* [ON. *bra*, brow] [Scot.] a sloping bank; hillside

brag (brag) *vt., vi.* **bragged, brag′ging** [prob. < OFr. *braguer*] to boast —*n.* **1.** boastful talk or manner **2.** [Colloq.] anything boasted of **3.** an old card game, like poker —**brag′ger** *n.*

braggadocio (brag′ə dō′chē ō) *n., pl.* **-os** [coined by Spenser] **1.** a braggart **2.** noisy boasting

braggart (brag′ərt) *n.* an offensively boastful person —*adj.* boastful

Brahma (brä′mə) [< Sans., worship] *Hinduism* the supreme essence or spirit of the universe

Brahman (brä′mən) *n., pl.* **-mans** a member of the priestly Hindu caste, the highest: also **Brah′min** —**Brahmanic** (brä man′ik), **Brahman′ical** *adj.*

braid (brād) *vt.* [< OE. *bregdan*, move quickly] **1.** to plait (hair, etc.) **2.** to trim with braid —*n.* **1.** a length of braided hair **2.** a woven band of tape, ribbon, etc. used to bind or decorate clothing —**braid′ing** *n.*

Braille (brāl) *n.* [< L. *Braille*] [also **b-**] **1.** a system of printing and writing for the blind, using raised dots felt by the fingers **2.** the characters used in this system —*vt.* **Brailled, Brail′ling** [also **b-**] to print or write in such characters

brain (brān) *n.* [OE. *brægen*] **1.** the mass of nerve tissue in the cranium of vertebrate animals **2.** *a*) [*often pl.*] intelligence *b*) [Colloq.] a person of great intelligence *c*) [Colloq.] the main organizer *d*) [Colloq.] an electronic device able to perform some of the functions of a human brain —*vt.* **1.** to dash out the brains of **2.** [Slang] to hit hard on the head —**beat** (or **rack, cudgel,** etc.) **one's brains** to try hard to remember, etc. —**have on the brain** to be obsessed by

brainchild *n.* [Colloq.] an idea, plan, etc. regarded as produced by one's mental labour

brain drain [Colloq.] depletion of the intellectual or professional resources of a country, etc., esp. through emigration

brainless *adj.* foolish or stupid

brainpower *n.* mental ability

brainstorm *n.* **1.** a sudden attack of insanity **2.** [Colloq.] a mental aberration

brains trust a group of people who answer questions of current or topical interest in public

brain teaser a difficult problem or puzzle, esp. one intended to be solved for entertainment

brainwash *vt.* [Colloq.] to indoctrinate so intensively and thoroughly as to effect a radical transformation of beliefs —**brain′-wash′ing** *n.*

brainwave *n.* **1.** rhythmic electric impulses given off by nerve centres in the brain **2.** [Colloq.] a sudden inspiration or idea

brainy *adj.* **-ier, -iest** [Colloq.] intelligent

braise (brāz) *vt.* **braised, brais′ing** [< Fr. *braise*, live coals] to cook (meat) by browning in fat and then simmering in a covered pan with a little liquid

brak (brak) *n.* [S Afr.] a crossbred dog; mongrel

brake¹ (brāk) *n.* [< BRACKEN] a large, coarse fern

brake² *n.* [< MLowG. or ODu.] **1.** any device for slowing or stopping the motion of a vehicle or machine **2.** a device for beating flax or hemp so that the fibre can be separated **3.** a heavy harrow —*vt.* **braked, brak′ing 1.** to slow down or stop as with a brake **2.** to break up (flax, etc.) —*vi.* **1.** to operate a brake **2.** to be slowed down or stopped by a brake

brake³ *n.* [< MLowG., stumps] a clump of brushwood, brambles, etc.

brake⁴ *archaic pt. of* BREAK

brake band a band with a lining (**brake lining**) of asbestos, fine wire, etc., that creates friction when tightened about the drum of a brake

brake horsepower the rate at which an engine works measured according to the force needed to brake it

brake shoe a block curved to fit the shape of a wheel and forced against it to act as a brake

brake van the railway carriage from which the guard applies the brakes

bramble (bram′b'l) *n.* [< OE. *brom*, broom] **1.** any prickly shrub, esp. the blackberry **2.** a blackberry

brambling *n.* [see prec.] a brightly-coloured finch of Europe and Asia, similar to the chaffinch

bran (bran) *n.* [OFr. *bren*] the husk of grains of wheat, rye, oats, etc. separated from the flour, as by sifting

branch (bränch) *n.* [< LL. *branca*, paw] **1.** any woody extension from the trunk or from a main limb of a tree **2.** anything like a branch, as, *a*) a division of a body of learning *b*) a separately located unit of an organization [a *branch* of a library] —*vi.* **1.** to put forth branches **2.** to come out (*from*) as a branch —*vt.* to separate into branches —**branch off 1.** to separate into branches **2.** to diverge —**branch out 1.** to put forth branches **2.** to extend the scope of interests, activities, etc. —**branched** *adj.*

brand (brand) *n.* [OE.] **1.** *a*) an identifying mark or label on products *b*) the make

of a commodity *[a brand of cigars]*
c) a special kind *[a brand of nonsense]*
2. *a)* a mark burned on the skin with
a hot iron, used on cattle to show ownership
b) the iron thus used **3.** a mark of disgrace;
stigma **4.** a stick that is burning or partially
burned **5.** [Archaic] a sword —*vt.* **1.**
to mark with or as with a brand *[a scene
branded in his memory]* **2.** to mark as
disgraceful —**brand′er** *n.*

brandish (bran′dish) *vt.* [< Gmc. *brand,*
sword] to wave or shake menacingly
or exultantly; flourish —*n.* a brandishing
of something

brand-new (brand′nyōō′) *adj.* [orig.,
fresh from the fire] **1.** entirely new **2.**
recently acquired

brandy (bran′dē) *n., pl.* **-dies** [< Du.
brandewijn, distilled wine] an alcoholic
spirit distilled from wine or fruit juice

brandy snap a crisp, ginger-flavoured
biscuit, rolled and usually filled with cream

bran tub a lucky dip in which parcels
are concealed in bran

brash (brash) *adj.* [< ?] **1.** reckless **2.**
bold, impudent, etc. —**brash′ly** *adv.*
—**brash′ness** *n.*

brass (bräs) *n., pl.* **brass′es** [OE. *bræs*]
1. a yellowish metal that is an alloy of
copper and zinc **2.** things made of brass
3. the brass instruments of an orchestra
4. a brass memorial tablet, in a church
5. [Colloq.] impudence **6.** [Colloq.] money
—*adj.* made of brass

brass band a band of brass and
percussion instruments

brass hat [Slang] **1.** a military officer
of high rank **2.** any high official

brassica (bras′i kə) *n.* [L., cabbage] a
plant of the cabbage and turnip family

brassie (bräs′ē) *n.* [orig. made with a
brass sole] a golf club with a wooden
head, used for long fairway shots

brassière (braz′ē ər) *n.* [< Fr. *bras,* arm]
same as BRA

brass tacks [Colloq.] basic facts;
practical details

brassy *adj.* **-ier, -iest** **1.** impudent **2.**
cheap and showy **3.** blaring **4.** like brass
5. of or decorated with brass —**brass′-
ily** *adv.* —**brass′iness** *n.*

brat (brat) *n.* [OE. *bratt,* cloak] a child,
esp. an impudent, unruly child —**brat′tish-
ness** *n.* —**brat′tish** *adj.*

bravado (brə vä′dō) *n.* [< Sp. *bravo,*
brave] pretended courage or defiant
confidence

brave (brāv) *adj.* [< It. < L. *barbarus,*
barbarous] **1.** not afraid; valiant **2.** fine;
splendid *[brave new world]* —*n.* a N
American Indian warrior —*vt.* **braved,**
brav′ing **1.** to face with courage **2.** to
defy —**brave′ly** *adv.* —**brave′ness, brav′-
ery** *n.*

bravo¹ (brä′vō′) *interj.* [It.] well done!
very good! excellent! —*n., pl.* **-vos′** a
shout of "bravo!"

bravo² (brä′vō) *n., pl.* **-voes, -vos;** [It.]
a hired killer; assassin

bravura (brə vyōōər′ə, -vōōər′-) *n.* [It.,
spirit] **1.** a display of daring; dash **2.**

Music a) a brilliant passage that displays
the performer's skill *b)* brilliant technique
—*adj.* characterized by bravura

brawl (brôl) *vi.* [< ? Du. *brallen,* boast]
1. to quarrel noisily **2.** to flow noisily:
said of water —*n.* a noisy quarrel
—**brawl′er** *n.*

brawn (brôn) *n.* [< OFr. *braon,* flesh]
1. strong, well-developed muscles **2.**
muscular strength **3.** a loaf of jellied,
seasoned meat made from the head and
feet of a pig or calf —**brawn′iness** *n.*
—**brawn′y** *adj.*

bray (brā) *vi.* [< VL. *bragire,* cry out]
to make the loud, harsh cry of a donkey,
or a sound like this —*vt.* to utter thus
—*n.* such a sound

braze¹ (brāz) *vt.* **brazed, braz′ing** [Fr.
braser, solder, var. of *braiser,* braise] to
solder with a metal having a high melting
point

braze² *vt.* **brazed, braz′ing** [< OE. *bræs,*
brass] **1.** to coat with brass **2.** to make
hard like brass

brazen *adj.* [see prec.] **1.** impudent **2.**
of or like brass **3.** harsh and piercing
—**brazen it out** to act boldly as if one
need not be ashamed —**bra′zenly** *adv.*
—**bra′zenness** *n.*

brazier¹ (brā′zhyər) *n.* [see BRAISE] a
metal pan, bowl, etc. to hold burning coals
or charcoal

brazier² *n.* [see BRASS] a person who
works in brass

Brazil nut (brə zil′) a hard-shelled, three-
sided, oily edible seed of a tall S. American
tree

brazilwood *n.* [< *Brazil,* S. America]
a reddish wood obtained from several
tropical American trees

B.R.C.S. British Red Cross Society

breach (brēch) *n.* [< OE. *brecan,* to break]
1. a failure to observe a law, a contract,
public peace, etc. **2.** an opening made
through a wall, defence, etc. **3.** a break
in friendly relations —*vt.* to make a breach
in —**step into the breach** to take on a
responsibility, give help, etc., in an
emergency

breach of promise a breaking of a
promise to marry

bread (bred) *n.* [OE. *bread,* crumb] **1.**
a food baked from a leavened, kneaded
dough made with flour, water, yeast, etc.
2. one's livelihood —*vt.* to cover with
bread crumbs before cooking —**bread and
butter** one's livelihood —**cast one's bread
upon the waters** to do good deeds without
expecting something in return —**know
which side one's bread is buttered on** to
know what is to one's (economic) interest
—**take the bread out of someone's mouth**
to deprive someone of his means of
livelihood

bread-and-butter *adj.* **1.** of the work,
etc. relied on for earnings **2.** basic,
everyday, etc. **3.** expressing thanks, as
a letter to one's host

breadboard *n.* **1.** a board on which
bread is sliced **2.** a board, usually portable,

on which experimental electronic circuits or diagrams can be laid out

breadfruit *n.* a large, tropical fruit with a starchy pulp, that is like bread when baked

bread line [U.S.] a line of poor people waiting to be given food —**on the bread line** at subsistence level

breadth (bredth) *n.* [< OE. *brad,* broad] 1. the distance from side to side of a thing; width 2. openness and lack of restriction [*breadth* of knowledge]

breadwinner *n.* a person who supports dependants by his earnings

break (brāk) *vt.* broke, bro′ken, break′-ing [OE. *brecan*] 1. to cause to come apart by force; smash 2. to cut open the surface of (soil, the skin, etc.) 3. to cause the failure of by force [to *break* a strike] 4. to make inoperative by cracking, disrupting, etc. 5. to tame 6. *a)* to cause to get rid (*of* a habit) *b)* to get rid of (a habit) 7. to demote 8. to reduce to poverty, bankruptcy, etc. 9. to surpass (a record) 10. to violate (a law, etc.) 11. to escape from by force [to *break* prison] 12. to disrupt the order of [to *break* ranks] 13. to interrupt (a journey, electric circuit, etc.) 14. to reduce the force of by interrupting (a fall, etc.) 15. to bring to a sudden end 16. to penetrate (silence, etc.) 17. to disclose 18. to decipher (a code, etc.) 19. to fracture (a bone) —*vi.* 1. to split into pieces; burst 2. to disperse [*break* and run] 3. to force one's way (*through*) 4. to stop associating (*with*) 5. to become inoperative 6. to turn, change, etc. suddenly 7. to move away suddenly 8. to begin suddenly to perform, etc. [*break* into song] 9. to come into being or knowledge [the story *broke*] 10. *a)* to fall apart slowly *b)* to dash away, as a wave on the shore 11. to change in tone [his voice *broke*] 12. to cease temporarily; discontinue —*n.* 1. a breaking 2. a sudden move; dash 3. a broken place 4. a beginning [*break* of day] 5. an interruption of something regular 6. a gap; interval 7. a breach in friendly relations 8. a short rest between periods of work 9. [Slang] a piece of luck 10. *Cricket* a change in direction of a ball on bouncing —**break away** 1. to escape 2. to become detached 3. to secede —**break down** 1. to go out of working order 2. to give way to tears 3. to have a physical or nervous collapse 4. to analyse 5. to crush (opposition, etc.) —**break even** to make neither a profit nor a loss —**break in** 1. to enter forcibly 2. to interrupt 3. to train (a beginner) 4. to work the stiffness out of (new equipment) —**break out** 1. to begin suddenly 2. to escape 3. to become covered with a rash —**break the back of** to get through the greater or worst part of —**break up** 1. to disperse 2. to take apart 3. to put a stop to 4. to begin holidays, as at the end of a school term 5. [Colloq.] to end a relationship —**break′able** *adj.*

breakage *n.* 1. a breaking 2. things

broken 3. damage due to breaking, or the sum allowed for this

breakaway *adj.* of that which has seceded

breakdown *n.* a breaking down; specif., *a)* a failure to function properly *b)* a failure of health *c)* decomposition *d)* a separating into parts; analysis

breaker *n.* a wave that breaks into foam

breakfast (brek′fast) *n.* the first meal of the day —*vi.* to eat breakfast —**break′-faster** *n.*

breaking and entering unauthorized entry into a building with intent to commit a crime

breaking point the point at which material, or one's endurance, etc., collapses under strain

breakneck *adj.* dangerously fast

breakout *n.* a sudden escape, as from prison

breakthrough *n.* 1. a strikingly important advance or discovery 2. the act or place of breaking through against resistance

breakup *n.* 1. a breaking up; specif., *a)* dispersion *b)* disintegration *c)* a collapse *d)* ending 2. *a)* in the Canadian north, the breaking up of the ice on a body of water that marks the beginning of spring *b)* this season

breakwater *n.* a barrier to break the impact of waves, as before a harbour

bream (brēm) *n.* [< OFr. *bresme*] 1. a European freshwater fish related to the minnows 2. any of various saltwater fishes

breast (brest) *n.* [OE. *breost*] 1. either of two milk-secreting glands at the upper, front part of a woman's body 2. a corresponding gland in other animals 3. the upper, front part of the body 4. the part of a garment over the breast 5. the breast regarded as the centre of emotions or as a source of nourishment —*vt.* 1. to face, esp. firmly 2. to reach the top of (a hill) —**make a clean breast of** to confess

breastbone *n.* same as STERNUM

breast-feed *vt.* -fed′ (-fed′), -feed′ing to feed (a baby) milk from the breast; suckle

breastplate *n.* a piece of armour for the breast

breast stroke a swimming stroke in which both arms are simultaneously brought out sideways from the chest

breastwork *n.* a low wall put up quickly as a defence, esp. to protect gunners

breath (breth) *n.* [OE. *bræth,* odour] 1. air taken into the lungs and then let out 2. respiration 3. the power to breathe easily 4. life or spirit 5. air carrying fragrance or odour 6. a whiff of air 7. moisture produced by a condensing of the breath, as in cold air 8. a slight pause 9. a faint hint —**below** (or **under**) **one's breath** in a whisper —**catch one's breath** 1. to gasp 2. to pause or rest —**out of breath** breathless, as from exertion —**save one's breath** not to waste one's time by trying to convince —**take one's breath away** to overwhelm with awe, horror, etc.

Breathalyzer, Breathalyser (breth'-
əliz'er) [*breath (an)alyser*] *Trademark*
a device that tests exhaled breath to
measure the amount of alcohol in the body
breathe (brēth) *vi., vt.* breathed, breath'-
ing [see BREATH] 1. to take (air) into
the lungs and let it out again 2. to live
3. to take in or give out (air, an odour)
4. to instil [*to breathe confidence*] 5.
to blow softly 6. to speak or sing softly
7. to give or take time to breathe; rest
—**breathe again** (or freely) to have a
feeling of relief —**breathe one's last** to
die —**breathable** *adj.*
breather *n.* [Colloq.] a pause as for rest
breathing *adj.* that breathes; living; alive
—*n.* 1. respiration 2. a single breath
or the time taken by this 3. the sound
of *h* in *hit, hope,* etc.; aspirate
breathless (breth'lis) *adj.* 1. out of breath;
gasping 2. unable to breathe easily because
of excitement, fear, etc. 3. still and heavy,
as the air 4. dead —**breath'lessly** *adv.*
—**breath'lessness** *n.*
breathtaking (breth'tāk'iŋ) *adj.* very
exciting; thrilling —**breath'tak'ingly** *adv.*
breath test a chemical test of a driver's
breath to determine the amount of alcohol
in his blood
bred (bred) *pt. & pp.* of BREED
breech (brēch) *n.* [< OE. *broc*] 1. [Obs.]
the buttocks 2. the part of a gun behind
the barrel
breech birth the birth of a baby with
the feet or buttocks appearing first : also
breech delivery

BREECHES

breeches (brich'iz) *n.pl.* trousers reaching
to the knees —**too big for one's breeches**
too forward, presumptuous, etc. for one's
position or status
breeches buoy (brēch'iz) a device for
rescuing people at sea, consisting of a
pair of short canvas breeches suspended
from a life buoy that is run along a rope
breed (brēd) *vt.* bred, breed'ing [< OE.
bredan, keep warm] 1. to bring forth
(offspring) 2. to produce [*ignorance
breeds* prejudice] 3. to raise [to breed
dogs] 4. to train 5. to produce (fissionable
material) in a breeder reactor —*vi.* 1.
to originate 2. to reproduce —*n.* 1. a
stock of animals or plants descended from
common ancestors 2. a kind; type
—**breed'er** *n.*
breeder reactor a nuclear reactor that
produces more fissionable material than
it consumes

breeding *n.* 1. the producing of young
2. good upbringing or training 3. the
producing of plants and animals, esp. so
as to develop new or better types
breeze[1] (brēz) *n.* [< Fr. *brise*] 1. a
gentle wind 2. [Colloq.] commotion 3.
[Colloq.] a thing easy to do —*vi.* breezed,
breez'ing [Colloq.] to move quickly,
jauntily, etc. (often with *along, in*)
breeze[2] *n.* [Fr. *braise,* live coals] a
substance left when coke, coal, or charcoal
is burned
breeze block a building block, usually
hollow, made of concrete and fine cinders
breezy *adj.* -ier, -iest 1. slightly windy
2. lively and carefree [*breezy* manner]
—**breez'ily** *adv.*
Bren (gun) (bren) [< *Bmo,* Czechoslovakia + *Enfield,* England] a light,
fast, gas-operated machine gun used by
the British army in World War II
brent (brent) *n.* [?] any of a number
of related small, dark wild geese of Europe
and N America
brethren (breth'rən) *n.pl.* brothers
Breton (bret''n) *adj.* [see BRITON] of
Brittany, its people, or their language —*n.*
1. a native or inhabitant of Brittany 2.
the Celtic language of the Bretons
breve (brēv) *n.* [< L. *brevis,* brief] 1.
a mark (˘) put over a short vowel or
short or unstressed syllable 2. *Music* a
note ( ) equal to two semibreves
breviary (brēv'yər ē) *n., pl.* -aries [<
L. *brevis,* brief] R.C.Ch. a book of the
daily prayers, hymns, etc.
brevity (brev'ə tē) *n.* [< L. *brevis,* brief]
1. briefness of time 2. conciseness;
terseness
brew (brōō) *vt.* [< OE. *breowan*] 1.
to make (beer, etc.) from malt and hops
by steeping, boiling, and fermenting 2.
to make (tea, etc.) by steeping or boiling
3. to plan (mischief, trouble, etc.); plot
—*vi.* 1. to brew beer, etc. 2. to infuse
3. to begin to form : said of a storm,
trouble, etc. —*n.* 1. a brewed beverage
2. an amount brewed —**brew up** to make
tea —**brew'er** *n.*
brewery (brōō'ər ē) *n., pl.* -eries an
establishment where beer, ale, etc. are
brewed
briar[1] (brī'ər) *n.* same as BRIER[1] —**bri'-
ary** *adj.*
briar[2] *n.* 1. same as BRIER[2] 2. a tobacco
pipe made of brierroot
bribe (brīb) *n.* [< OFr. *briber,* beg]
anything given or promised to induce a
person to do something illegal or wrong
—*vt.* bribed, brib'ing 1. to give a bribe
to 2. to get or influence by bribing —*vi.*
to give bribes —**brib'able** *adj.* —**brib'er**
n. —**brib'ery** *n.*
bric-a-brac (brik'ə brak') *n.* [< Fr.]
small, rare, or artistic objects or
knickknacks
brick (brik) *n.* [< OFr. *brique,* fragment]
1. clay moulded into oblong blocks and
baked, used in building, etc. 2. any of
these blocks 3. bricks collectively 4.
anything shaped like a brick 5. [Colloq.]

a loyal and dependable person —*adj.* of
or like brick —*vt.* to build or pave with
brick —**drop a brick** [Colloq.] to make
a tactless or indiscreet remark —**like a
ton** (or **load**) **of bricks** [Colloq.] with great
force

brickbat *n.* 1. a piece of brick used
as a missile 2. an unfavourable or critical
remark

bricklaying *n.* the act or work of building
with bricks —**brick′lay′er** *n.*

brick red yellowish or brownish red
—**brick′-red′** *adj.*

bridal (brīd′'l) *n.* [< OE. *bryd*, bride +
ealo, ale] a wedding —*adj.* 1. of a bride
2. of a wedding

bride (brīd) *n.* [OE. *bryd*] a woman who
has just been married or is about to be
married

bridegroom *n.* [< OE. *bryd*, bride +
guma, man] a man who has just been
married or is about to be married

bridesmaid *n.* any of the young women
who attend the bride at a wedding

bridge[1] (brij) *n.* [< OE. *brycge*] 1. a
structure built over a river, railway, etc.
to provide a way across 2. a thing that
provides connection or contact 3. the
upper, bony part of the nose 4. the thin,
arched piece over which the strings are
stretched on a violin, etc. 5. a raised
platform on a ship for the commanding
officer 6. *Dentistry* a mounting for false
teeth, attached to real teeth —*vt.* **bridged,
bridg′ing** to build a bridge over or between
—**burn one's bridges** (**behind one**) to
commit oneself to a course from which
there is no retreat —**bridge′able** *adj.*

bridge[2] *n.* [< ? Russ.] any of various
card games that developed from whist

bridgehead *n.* a fortified position
established by an attacking force on the
enemy's side of a river, etc.

bridging loan a short-term loan made
to a person awaiting funds from another
source

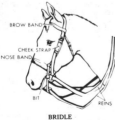

BROW BAND

CHEEK STRAP

NOSE BAND

BIT   REINS

BRIDLE

bridle (brīd′'l) *n.* [< OE. *bregdan*, pull]
1. a head harness for guiding a horse
2. anything that restrains —*vt.* **-dled, -dling**
1. to put a bridle on 2. to curb as with
a bridle —*vi.* to pull one's head back
quickly with the chin drawn in, showing
anger, scorn, etc.

bridle path a path for horseback riding

Brie (**cheese**) (brē) [< *Brie*, in N France]
a ripened soft, white cheese

brief (brēf) *adj.* [< L. *brevis*] 1. of short
duration or extent 2. concise 3. curt
—*n.* 1. a summary 2. a concise statement
of the main points of a law case, as
prepared by a solicitor for a counsel 3.
[*pl.*] closefitting, legless underpants or
panties 4. *R.C.Ch.* a papal letter less
formal than a bull —*vt.* 1. to supply
with all the pertinent information 2. *a*)
to furnish with a legal brief *b*) to hire
as counsel —**hold a brief for** 1. to be
retained as counsel for 2. to argue for
or be in favour of —**brief′ing** *n.* —**brief′-
ly** *adv.* —**brief′ness** *n.*

briefcase *n.* a flat, flexible case, usually
of leather, for carrying papers, etc.

brier[1] (brī′ər) *n.* [< OE. *brer*] 1. any
thorny bush, as a bramble, wild rose, etc.
2. a growth of such bushes

brier[2] *n.* [Fr. *bruyère*] 1. a heath native
to S Europe 2. its root, or a tobacco
pipe made from the root : usually sp. **bri′ar**

Brig. 1. Brigade 2. Brigadier

brig[1] (brig) *n.* [< BRIGANTINE] a two-
masted ship with square sails

brig[2] *n.* *Scot. & N Eng.* var. of BRIDGE[1]

brigade (bri gād′) *n.* [Fr. < It. *briga*,
strife] 1. a large unit of soldiers 2.
a group of people organized as a unit
in some work [a fire *brigade*] —*vt.* **-gad′-
ed, -gad′ing** to organize into a brigade

brigadier (brig′ə dēər′) *n.* see MILITARY
RANKS, table

brigand (brig′ənd) *n.* [see BRIGADE] a
bandit, usually one of a roving band —**brig′-
andage** *n.*

brigantine (brig′ən tēn′) *n.* [< It.
brigantino, pirate vessel] a two-masted
ship with the foremast square-rigged and
a fore-and-aft mainsail

bright (brīt) *adj.* [OE. *bryht*] 1. shining
with light that is radiated or reflected;
full of light 2. clear or brilliant in colour
or sound 3. lively; cheerful 4. mentally
quick 5. *a*) full of happiness or hope
b) favourable 6. splendid; illustrious —*adv.*
in a bright manner —**bright′ly** *adv.*
—**bright′ness** *n.*

brighten *vt., vi.* to make or become
brighter (often with *up*)

Bright's disease [< R. *Bright*] see
NEPHRITIS

brilliance (bril′yəns) *n.* great brightness,
radiance, splendour, intelligence, etc.: also
bril′liancy

brilliant *adj.* [< It. *brillare*, sparkle] 1.
shining brightly; sparkling 2. vivid; intense
3. splendid or distinguished 4. highly
intelligent or skilful —*n.* a gem, esp.
a diamond, cut with many facets to increase
its sparkle

brilliantine (bril′yən tēn′) *n.* [Fr.] an oily
dressing for grooming the hair

brim (brim) *n.* [MHG. *brem*, edge] 1.
the topmost edge of a cup, bowl, etc.
2. a projecting rim or edge, as of a hat
—*vt., vi.* **brimmed, brim′ming** to fill or
be full to the brim —**brim over** overflow
—**brim′less** *adj.*

brimstone (brim′stōn′) *n.* [< OE. *brynstan*, burning stone] *same as* SULPHUR

brindled (brin′d'ld) *adj.* [prob. < ME. *brennen*, burn] grey or tawny, streaked or spotted with a darker colour

brine (brīn) *n.* [OE.] 1. water full of salt 2. *a)* sea water *b)* the sea —*vt.* **brined, brin′ing** to soak in brine

bring (briŋ) *vt.* **brought, bring′ing** [OE. *bringan*] 1. to carry or lead "here" or to a place where the speaker will be 2. to cause to be, happen, appear, etc. 3. to lead, along a course of action or belief 4. to sell for 5. *Law a)* to present in court [*bring* charges] *b)* to advance (evidence) —**bring about** 1. to make happen; effect 2. to turn (a ship) around —**bring forth** 1. to produce (offspring, etc.) 2. to make known —**bring forward** 1. to introduce; show 2. *Bookkeeping* to transfer (a figure) to the top of the next page or column —**bring home to** to prove; make realise —**bring in** 1. to import 2. to produce (income) 3. to introduce 4. to give (a verdict) —**bring off** to accomplish —**bring on** to cause to happen or appear —**bring over** to convince or persuade —**bring round** 1. to persuade 2. to bring back to consciousness —**bring up** 1. to raise; rear 2. to introduce into discussion 3. to cough up 4. to vomit 5. to stop abruptly 6. to cause someone to face a charge in court —**bring′er** *n.*

bring-and-buy sale a bazaar to which people bring items for sale and buy those brought by others

brinjal (brin′jəl) *n.* in India or Africa, the aubergine

brink (briŋk) *n.* [< Dan., shore] the edge, esp. at the top of a steep place; verge

brinkmanship *n.* the policy of pursuing a hazardous course of action to the brink of catastrophe before withdrawing: also **brinks′manship′**

briny (brīn′ē) *adj.* **-ier, -iest** of or like brine; very salty —**the briny** [Slang] the ocean —**brin′iness** *n.*

briquette, briquet (bri ket′) *n.* [< Fr. *brique*, brick] a brick made of compressed coal dust, etc., used for fuel

brisk (brisk) *adj.* [< ? Fr. *brusque*, brusque] 1. quick in manner; energetic 2. cool, dry, and bracing [*brisk* air] 3. active; busy [*brisk* trading] —*vt., vi.* to make brisk; enliven (often with *up*) —**brisk′ly** *adv.* —**brisk′ness** *n.*

brisket (bris′kit) *n.* [ME. *brusket*] 1. the breast of an animal 2. meat cut from this part

brisling (bris′liŋ) *n.* [Norw.] *same as* SPRAT

bristle (bris′'l) *n.* [< OE. *byrst*] 1. any short, stiff, prickly hair of an animal or plant 2. such a hair, or an artificial hair like it, in a brush —*vi.* **-tled, -tling** 1. to become stiff and erect, like bristles 2. to have the bristles become erect, as in fear 3. to become tense with fear, anger, etc. 4. to be thickly covered (with)

[*bristling* with difficulties] —*vt.* 1. to make stand up like bristles 2. to make bristly

bristly *adj.* **-tlier, -tliest** 1. having bristles; rough with bristles 2. bristlelike; prickly —**bris′tliness** *n.*

Brit (brit) *n.* [Colloq.] a British person

Brit. 1. Britain 2. Britannia 3. British

Britannia (bri tan′yə) 1. Great Britain 2. the personification of Britain as a helmeted female warrior

britannia metal [*also* B-] an alloy of tin, copper, and antimony, used in tableware, like pewter

Britannic *adj.* of Britain; British

britches (brich′iz) *n.pl.* [Colloq.] trousers

British (brit′ish) *adj.* [< Celt.] 1. of Great Britain or the British Commonwealth 2. of the English language as spoken and written in Britain —**the British** the people of Great Britain

British thermal unit the heat required to raise the temperature of one pound of water one degree Fahrenheit

Briton *n.* [< L. *Brit(t)o*; of Celt. orgin] 1. a member of an early Celtic people living in S Britain at the time of the Roman invasion 2. a native or inhabitant of Great Britain

brittle (brit′'l) *adj.* [< OE. *breotan*, to break] 1. easily broken; fragile 2. having a sharp, hard quality —**brit′tlely, brit′-tly** *adv.* —**brit′tleness** *n.*

bro. *pl.* **bros.** brother

broach (brōch) *vt.* [< ML. *brocca*, spike] 1. to start a discussion of; bring up 2. to make a hole in so as to let out liquid 3. to open in order to begin to use —*n.* 1. a tapered bit for shaping holes 2. a spit for roasting meat —**broach′er** *n.*

broach (brōch) *vi., vt* [< ?] *Naut.* to turn so that the beam faces the waves and wind

B road a second-class road

broad (brôd) *adj.* [< OE. *brad*] 1. of large extent from side to side; wide 2. spacious 3. clear; full [*broad* daylight] 4. obvious [a *broad* hint] 5. strongly marked [a *broad* accent] 6. coarse or ribald 7. tolerant; liberal [a *broad* view] 8. wide in range [a *broad* survey] 9. main or general —*n.* 1. the broad part of anything 2. [U.S. Vulg. Slang] a woman —**the Broads** in East Anglia, a group of shallow navigable lakes, connected by a network of rivers —**broad′ly** *adv.* —**broad′ness** *n.*

broad arrow a mark in the form of a broad arrow formerly used on British government property

broad bean a plant of the legume family, bearing large, broad pods with flat, edible seeds

broadcast *vt.* **-cast′, -cast′ing** 1. to transmit by radio or TV 2. to spread (information, etc.) 3. to scatter (seed) —*vi.* to broadcast radio or TV programmes —*adj.* of or by radio or TV broadcasting —*n.* a radio or TV programme —*adv.* far and wide —**broad′cast′er** *n.*

broadcloth *n.* a fine, smooth, woollen, cotton, or silk cloth

broaden *vt., vi.* to widen; expand

broad gauge a railway track with a greater distance between the lines than the standard gauge of 56.5 inches (c. 1.44 metres)

broad-leaved *adj.* denoting trees other than conifers; having broad rather than needle-shaped leaves

broad-minded *adj.* tolerant; liberal —**broad**'-**mind**'**edly** *adv.* —**broad**'-**mind**'-**edness** *n.*

broadsheet *n.* a large sheet of paper printed only on one side, as with a political message

broadside *n.* 1. the side of a ship 2. *a)* all the guns that can be fired from one side of a ship *b)* their simultaneous firing 3. an abusive attack in words 4. *same as* BROADSHEET —*adv.* with the side facing

broadsword *n.* a sword with a broad blade, for slashing rather than thrusting

brocade (brō kād') *n.* [< It. *broccare*, embroider] a rich cloth with a raised design woven into it —*vt.* -**cad**'**ed**, -**cad**'-**ing** to weave a raised design into

broccoli (brok'ə lē) *n.* [It. *broccolo*, a sprout] a plant related to the cauliflower but bearing tender shoots with greenish buds, cooked as a vegetable

brochette (brō shet') *n.* [see BROACH[1]] a small spit, as for grilling kebabs

brochure (brō'shər) *n.* [Fr. < *brocher*, to stitch] a pamphlet

broderie anglaise (brō drē än glez') [Fr., English embroidery] fine eyelet embroidery, usually white

broeder (brood'ər) *n.* [S Afr.] a brother

Broederbond (brood'ər bont) *n.* in S Africa, a secret society of Afrikaner Nationalists

brogue[1] (brōg) *n.* [prob. < Ir. *barrōg*, a hold] dialectal pronunciation, esp. that of the Irish

brogue[2] *n.* [Gael. & Ir. *brōg*, shoe] 1. a sturdy walking shoe, usually with decorative perforations 2. a coarse shoe of untanned leather, formerly worn in Ireland

broil[1] (broil) *vt.* [OFr. *bruillir*] [Chiefly U.S.] to grill —*vi.* 1. to be grilled 2. to become heated or angry

broil[2] *n.* [< OFr. *brouillier*, to dirty] a noisy or violent quarrel; brawl

broiler *n.* a young chicken suitable for roasting

broke (brōk) *pt. & archaic pp. of* BREAK —*adj.* [Colloq.] having no money; bankrupt —**go broke** [Colloq.] to become bankrupt

broken *pp. of* BREAK —*adj.* 1. splintered, fractured, etc. 2. not in working condition 3. violated [a *broken* promise] 4. disrupted as by divorce [a *broken* home] 5. weakened or beaten 6. bankrupt 7. not even; interrupted 8. imperfectly spoken [*broken* English] 9. subdued and trained —**bro**'**kenly** *adv.*

broken chord *same as* ARPEGGIO

broken-down *adj.* 1. sick or worn out, as by old age or disease 2. out of order; useless

brokenhearted *adj.* crushed by sorrow

broker *n.* [< OFr. *brochier*, broach] 1. a person hired to act as an agent in making contracts or sales 2. *same as* STOCKBROKER 3. a dealer in second-hand goods

brokerage *n.* 1. the business of a broker 2. a broker's fee

brolly (brol'ē) *n.* [altered < (UM)BRELLA] 1. [Colloq.] an umbrella 2. [Slang] a parachute

bromide (brō'mīd) *n.* [< BROMINE] 1. a compound of bromine with another element or with a radical 2. potassium bromide used as a sedative 3. a trite saying

bromide paper a type of photographic paper coated with an emulsion of silver bromide

bromine (brō'mēn) *n.* [< Gr. *brōmos*, stench] a chemical element, usually a reddish-brown, corrosive liquid volatilizing to form an irritating vapour: symbol, Br

bronchi (broŋ'kī) *n. pl. of* BRONCHUS

bronchial (broŋ'kē əl) *adj.* of the bronchi

bronchitis (broŋ kīt'əs) *n.* [< Gr. *bronchos*, windpipe + -ITIS] an inflammation of the mucous lining of the bronchial tubes —**bronchit**'**ic** (-kit'ik) *adj.*

bronchus (broŋ'kəs) *n., pl.* -**chi** (-kī) [< Gr. *bronchos*, windpipe] either of the two main branches of the trachea, or windpipe

bronco (broŋ'kō) *n., pl.* -**cos** [< Sp., rough] a wild or partially tamed horse of the western U.S.: also sp. **bron**'**cho**, *pl.* -**chos**

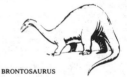

BRONTOSAURUS

brontosaurus (bron'tə sôr'əs) *n., pl.* -**sau**'**ruses**, -**sau**'**ri** (-ī) [< Gr. *brontē*, thunder + -SAURUS] a huge, plant-eating dinosaur

bronze (bronz) *n.* [< It. *bronzo*] 1. an alloy of copper and tin 2. an article made of bronze 3. a reddish-brown colour like bronze —*adj.* of or like bronze —*vt.* **bronzed**, **bronz**'**ing** to give a bronze colour to

Bronze Age a phase of human culture (c. 3500–1000 B.C.) characterized by bronze tools and weapons

bronze medal a medal awarded to an entrant who is placed third in a competition

brooch (brōch) *n.* [see BROACH[1]] a large ornamental pin

brood (brood) *n.* [< OE. *brod*] 1. a group of birds hatched at one time 2. [Colloq.] the children in a family 3. a group of a particular kind —*vi.* 1. to sit on and hatch eggs 2. to keep thinking about something; worry (*on, over,* or *about*) —*vt.* to brood (eggs) —*adj.* kept for breeding [a brood mare] —**brood'ingly** *adv.*

brooder *n.* a heated shelter for raising young fowl

broody *adj.* **-ier, -iest** 1. ready to brood, as poultry 2. inclined to dwell moodily on one's own thoughts

brook[1] (brook) *n.* [OE. *broc*] a small stream

brook[2] *vt.* [OE. *brucan,* to use] to endure

broom (broom) *n.* [OE. *brom,* brushwood] 1. *a*) a bundle of stiff fibres (orig. twigs of broom) fastened to a handle and used for sweeping *b*) any long-handled sweeping brush 2. a shrub of the legume family, with yellow flowers —*vt.* to sweep as with a broom

broomstick *n.* the handle of a broom

bros. brothers

brose (broz) *n.* [< ME. *broues,* broth] [Scot.] a thin porridge eaten with butter, cream, or milk

broth (broth) *n.* [OE.] a clear, thin, meat soup

brothel (broth'əl) *n.* [< OE. *breothan,* go to ruin] a house of prostitution

brother (bruth'ər) *n., pl.* **broth'ers;** chiefly religious, **breth'ren** [OE. *brothor*] 1. a male as he is related to the other children of his parents 2. a close friend like a brother 3. a fellow man 4. a fellow member of the same race, creed, etc. 5. a member of a men's religious order

brotherhood *n.* 1. the state of being a brother 2. an association of men united in a common work, etc.

brother-in-law *n., pl.* **broth'ers-in-law'** 1. the brother of one's husband or wife 2. the husband of one's sister 3. the husband of the sister of one's wife or husband

brotherly *adj.* 1. of or like a brother 2. friendly, kind, loyal, etc. —**broth'erliness** *n.*

BROUGHAM

brougham (broom) *n.* [after Lord *Brougham*] 1. a closed carriage with the driver's seat outside 2. any of various early styles of motor car

brought (brôt) *pt. & pp.* of BRING

brouhaha (broo'hä hä) *n.* [Fr.] a noisy stir or wrangle; uproar

brow (brou) *n.* [< OE. *bru*] 1. the eyebrow 2. the forehead 3. the facial expression [an angry *brow*] 4. a projecting edge, as of a cliff 5. the rounded top of a hill

browbeat *vt.* **-beat', -beat'en, -beat'ing** to intimidate with harsh, stern looks and talk

brown (broun) *adj.* [< OE. *brun*] 1. having the colour of chocolate or coffee, a mixture of red, black, and yellow 2. tanned or dark-skinned —*n.* a brown colour, pigment, or dye —*vt., vi.* to make or become brown, as by exposure to sunlight or heat —**browned off** [Colloq.] disheartened or resentful —**brown'ish** *adj.* —**brown'ness** *n.*

brown coal *same as* LIGNITE

brownie *n.* 1. a small, helpful, brown elf in folk tales 2. [B-] a Girl Guide of the youngest group

browning *n.* a preparation for colouring and thickening gravy

brown paper coarse wrapping paper made from unbleached material

brown rice rice that has not been polished

brown shirt [*often* B- S-] 1. a storm trooper in Nazi Germany 2. any Nazi

brown study deep absorption in thought; reverie

brown sugar sugar crystals with a coating of dark syrup

browse (brouz) *vt.* **browsed, brows'ing** [< OS. *brustian,* to sprout] 1. to glance through a book, etc. casually 2. to nibble at leaves, etc. —*vt.* to nibble at —*n.* 1. casual examination 2. leaves, young shoots, etc. on which animals feed —**brows'er** *n.*

B.R.S. British Road Services

brucellosis (broo'sə lo'sis) *n.* [< Sir David *Bruce*] a disease, esp. in man and cattle, caused by bacteria

Bruin (broo'ən) [Du., brown] [*also* b-] a name for the bear in fable and folklore

bruise (brooz) *vt.* **bruised, bruis'ing** [< OE. *brysan,* crush] 1. to injure (body tissue) without breaking the skin but causing discolouration 2. to injure the surface of (fruit, etc.) 3. to hurt (the spirit, etc.) —*vi.* to be or become bruised —*n.* a bruised area of tissue, etc.

bruiser *n.* a strong, pugnacious man; specif., a professional boxer

bruit (broot) *vt.* [< OFr. *bruire,* rumble] [Archaic or U.S.] to spread (*about*) a rumour of

brumby (brum'bē) *n.* [< ?] [Aust.] a wild horse, esp. one that is descended from runaway stock

brunch (brunch) *n.* [Colloq.] a meal combining breakfast and lunch

brunette (broo net') [< OFr. *brun*] a girl or woman with dark brown hair —*adj.* of a dark brown colour

brunt (brunt) *n.* [< ?] 1. the shock (of an attack) or impact (of a blow) 2. the heaviest or hardest part

brush[1] (brush) *n.* [< OFr. *broce,* bush] 1. a device for cleaning, painting, etc., having bristles, hairs, or wires fastened into a back 2. the act of brushing 3. a light, grazing stroke 4. a bushy tail, esp. of a fox 5. a brief encounter, esp. an unfriendly one 6. *Elec.* a piece of copper, etc. used as a conductor between an external circuit and a revolving part —*vt.* 1. to clean, polish, etc. with a brush 2. to apply, remove, etc. with a brush 3. to touch in passing —*vi.* to graze past something —**brush aside** (or **away**) to dismiss from consideration —**brush off** [Slang] to dismiss abruptly —**brush up** 1. to clean up 2. to refresh one's memory or skill (often with *on*)

brush² *vi.* [ME. *bruschen*] to move with a rush; hurry —*n.* a short, quick fight or quarrel

brushed *adj.* processed by brushing so as to raise the nap, as some fabrics or leather

brushoff *n.* [Slang] an abrupt dismissal: esp. in the phrase **give** (or **get**) **the brushoff**

brush-up *n.* the act or instance of tidying one's appearance, esp. in the phrase **wash and brush-up**

brushwood *n.* 1. chopped-off tree branches 2. a thick growth of small trees and shrubs

brushwork *n.* a characteristic way of putting on paint with a brush [Renoir's *brushwork*]

brusque (broosk) *adj.* [Fr. < It. *brusco*, sour] abrupt in manner or speech; curt —**brusque'ly** *adv.* —**brusque'ness** *n.*

Brussels carpet (brus''lz) a kind of carpet with a thick-looped pile

Brussels lace a lace made by sewing completed patterns on a machine-made net

Brussels sprouts a plant of the cabbage family that bears miniature cabbagelike heads on an erect stem

brutal (broot''l) *adj.* 1. savage, violent, etc. 2. very harsh 3. plain and direct, but disturbing [*brutal* facts]

brutality (broo tal'ə tē) *n.* 1. the quality of being brutal 2. *pl.* **-ties** a brutal act

brutalize (broot'əl īz') *vt.* **-ized'**, **-iz'ing** 1. to make brutal 2. to treat brutally —**bru'-taliza'tion** *n.*

brute (broot) *adj.* [< L. *brutus*, irrational] 1. lacking the ability to reason [a *brute* beast] 2. lacking consciousness [the *brute* force of nature] 3. of or like an animal; brutal, cruel, sensual, stupid, etc. —*n.* 1. an animal 2. a person who is brutal or stupid, sensual, etc.

brutish *adj.* of or like a brute; savage, stupid, sensual, etc. —**brut'ishly** *adv.* —**brut'ishness** *n.*

bryony (brī'ə nē) *n.*, *pl.* **-nies** [< Gr. *bryein*, swell] a climbing plant with greenish flowers

bryophyte (brī'ə fīt') *n.* [< Gr. *bryon*, moss + *phyton*, plant] any moss or liverwort —**bry'ophyt'ic** (-fit'ik) *adj.*

Brythonic (bri thon'ik) *adj.*, *n.* [ult. < same word as BRITON] *see* CELTIC

B.Sc. [L. *Baccalaureus Scientiae*] Bachelor of Science

B.S.I. British Standards Institution

B.S.T. British Summer Time

Bt. Baronet

B.t.u. British thermal unit(s)

bubble (bub''l) *n.* [echoic] 1. a very thin film of liquid forming a ball around air or gas [soap *bubbles*] 2. a tiny ball of air or gas in a liquid or solid 3. any scheme that seems plausible but proves worthless —*vi.* **-bled**, **-bling** 1. to rise in bubbles; boil; foam 2. to make a bubbling sound —**bubble over** 1. to overflow 2. to be unrestrained in one's enthusiasm, etc.

bubble and squeak a dish of cabbage and potatoes, and sometimes meat, fried together

bubble bath 1. a bath perfumed and softened by a solution, crystals, or powder that forms surface bubbles 2. such a solution, powder, etc.

bubble car a car with a transparent, bubble-shaped top

bubble gum chewing gum that can be blown into bubbles

bubbly *adj.* full of bubbles —*n.* [Colloq.] champagne

bubo (byoo'bō) *n.*, *pl.* **-boes** [< Gr. *boubōn*, groin] an inflamed swelling of a lymph gland, esp. in the groin —**bubon'ic** (-bon'-ik) *adj.*

bubonic plague a contagious disease characterized by buboes, fever, and delirium: fleas from rats are the carriers

buccaneer (buk'ə nēr') *n.* [< Fr. *boucanier*] a pirate, or sea robber —**buc'ca-neer'ing** *n.*, *adj.*

buck¹ (buk) *n.* [< OE. *bucca*, male goat] 1. a male deer, goat, etc. 2. the act of bucking 3. [Obs.] a young man —*vi.* to rear upwards quickly in an attempt to throw off a rider: said of a horse, etc. —*vt.* to throw by bucking —*adj.* male —**buck up** [Colloq.] 1. to cheer up 2. to hurry up —**buck'er** *n.*

buck² *n.* [< ?] 1. *Poker* a counter placed before a player as a reminder to deal next, etc. 2. [U.S. & Aust. Slang] a dollar —**pass the buck** [Colloq.] to seek to make someone else take the blame or responsibility

buckboard *n.* [< ?] [U.S.] an open carriage with floorboards whose ends rest directly on the axles

bucket (buk'it) *n.* [< OE. *buc*, pitcher] 1. a container with a handle, for carrying water, etc.; pail 2. the amount held by a bucket: also **buck'etful**, *pl.* **-fuls'** 3. a thing like a bucket, as a scoop on a mechanical shovel 4. [*pl.*] [Colloq.] large amounts —*vt.*, *vi.* 1. to move rapidly or bumpily 2. to rain heavily (with *down*) —**kick the bucket** [Slang] to die

bucket seat a single contoured seat whose back can often be tipped forwards, as in some sports cars

bucket shop an unregistered firm of stockbrokers

buckle¹ (buk''l) *n.* [< L. *buccula*, cheek strap] 1. a clasp for fastening a strap, etc. 2. a clasplike ornament, as for shoes —*vt.*, *vi.* **-led**, **-ling** to fasten with a buckle —**buckle down** to apply oneself energetically

buckle² *vt.*, *vi.* **-led**, **-ling** [prob. < Du. *bukken*, bend] to bend, warp, or crumple —*n.* a bend, bulge, kink, etc. —**buckle under** to give in; yield; submit

buckler (buk'lər) *n.* [OFr. *bocler*] a small, round shield worn on the arm

buckram (buk'rəm) *n.* [prob. < *Bokhara*, in Asia Minor] a coarse cloth stiffened with glue or other size, for use in bookbinding, etc. —*adj.* of or like buckram

Bucks. Buckinghamshire

buckshee (buk shē′) *n.* [< BAKSHEESH] something free; gratuity —*adj.* free of charge

buckshot *n.* a large lead shot for shooting deer and other large game

buckskin *n.* 1. a soft yellowish-grey leather made from the skins of deer or sheep 2. [*pl.*] clothes made of buckskin —*adj.* made of buckskin

buckthorn *n.* a shrub with purple berries formerly used as a purgative

bucktooth *n., pl.* -teeth′ a projecting front tooth —**buck′toothed′** *adj.*

buckwheat *n.* [< OE. *boc*, beech + WHEAT] 1. a plant grown for its black grains 2. the grain of this plant, from which a dark flour is made

bucolic (byōō kol′ik) *adj.* [< Gr. *boukolos*, herdsman] 1. of shepherds; pastoral 2. of country life; rustic —*n.* a pastoral poem —**bucol′ically** *adv.*

bud (bud) *n.* [ME. *budde*, seedpod] 1. *a*) a small swelling on a plant, from which a shoot, or flower develops *b*) a partly opened flower 2. any immature person or thing 3. an outgrowth or swelling in simple organisms, that develops into a new individual —*vi.* **bud′ded, bud′ding** 1. to put forth buds 2. to begin to develop —*vt.* 1. to cause to bud 2. to graft by inserting a bud of (a plant) into the bark of another sort of plant —**nip in the bud** to check at the earliest stage

Buddhism (bōōd′iz'm) *n.* a religion of central and eastern Asia, founded in India by Buddha —**Bud′dhist** *n., adj.* —**Bud′dhis′tic** *adj.*

buddleia (bud′lē ə) *n.* [< Adam *Buddle*] any of a genus of shrubs and trees with purple or orange blossoms

budge (buj) *vti., vi.* **budged, budg′ing** [Fr. *bouger*, move] 1. to move even a little 2. to yield or cause to yield

budgerigar (buj′ə ri gär′) *n.* [Abor.] an Australian parakeet

budget (buj′it) *n.* [< L. *bulga*, leather bag] 1. a plan adjusting expenses to the expected income during a certain period 2. the amount of money needed for a specific use 3. an estimate of revenue and expenditure for a country or organization —*vt.* 1. to put on or in a budget 2. to plan in detail; schedule —*vi.* to make provision (*for*) —**budg′etary** *adj.* —**budg′eter** *n.*

budgie (buj′ē) *n.* [Colloq.] same as BUDGERIGAR

buff (buf) *n.* [< It. *bufalo*, BUFFALO] 1. a brownish-yellow leather 2. a dull brownish yellow 3. [Colloq.] a devotee; fan —*adj.* of the colour buff —*vt.* to shine; polish —**in the buff** naked

buffalo (buf′ə lō′) *n., pl.* -loes′, -los′[< Gr. *bous*, ox] 1. any of various wild oxen, sometimes domesticated, as the water buffalo of India 2. popularly, the American bison

buffer¹ (buf′ər) *n.* [OFr. *buffe*, blow] 1. a device to lessen the shock of collision, esp. of railway vehicles 2. any person

or thing that serves to lessen shock, as between antagonistic forces 3. a substance that tends to stabilize the hydrogen ion concentration in a solution by neutralizing an added acid or alkali

buffer² *n.* [< ?] [Colloq.] a bumbling man, esp. one who is elderly or pompous: also **old buffer**

buffer state a small country located between two antagonistic powers and regarded as lessening the possibility of conflict between them

buffet¹ (buf′it) *n.* [< OFr. *buffe*, blow] 1. a blow with the hand 2. any blow or shock —*vt.* 1. to slap 2. to struggle against —*vi.* to struggle

buffet² (bōō′fā; *for 3 usually* buf′it) *n.* [< OFr. *buffet*, bench] 1. a counter where refreshments are served 2. a meal at which guests serve themselves as from a buffet 3. a piece of furniture with drawers and cupboards for dishes, linen, etc.

buffet car (bōō′fā) a railway coach where light meals or snacks are served

buffoon (bə fōōn′) *n.* [< It. *buffare*, to jest] a person who is always clowning —**buffoon′ery** *n.*

bug (bug) *n.* [prob. < W. *bwg*, hobgoblin] 1. any of various insects with sucking mouthparts and forewings thickened towards the base 2. [Colloq.] any insect, specif. one regarded as a pest 3. [Colloq.] a germ or virus 4. [Slang] a tiny hidden microphone 5. [Slang] a defect, as in a machine 6. [Slang] an enthusiast; devotee —*vt.* **bugged, bug′ging** [Slang] 1. to hide a microphone in (a room, etc.) for secretly recording conversation 2. to annoy, anger, etc.

bugbear *n.* [BUG + BEAR²] 1. an imaginary terror 2. anything causing needless or excessive fear

bugger (bug′ər) *n.* [< ML. *Bulgarus*, a Bulgarian] 1. a sodomite 2. [Vulg. Slang] a contemptible person or thing —*vt.* 1. to commit sodomy with 2. [Vulg. Slang] *a*) to ruin; complicate (often with *up*) *b*) to make weary —*interj.* [Vulg. Slang] a strong exclamation of annoyance —**bugger about** [Vulg. Slang] 1. to fool about 2. to create difficulties —**bug′gery** *n.*

buggy (bug′ē) *n., pl.* **bug′gies** [< ?] a light, one-horse carriage with one seat

bugle (byōō′g'l) *n.* [< L. *buculus*, young ox] a brass instrument like a trumpet but smaller: used chiefly for military calls —*vi., vt.* **-gled, -gling** to call or signal by blowing a bugle —**bu′gler** *n.*

buhl (bōōl) *n.* [< C. A. *Boulle*] 1. decoration of furniture with tortoise shell, brass, silver, etc. inlaid in wood 2. furniture so decorated

build (bild) *vt.* **built, build′ing** [< OE. *bold*, house] 1. to make by putting together materials, parts, etc.; construct 2. to establish [to *build* a theory on facts] 3. to create, develop, etc. —*vi.* 1. *a*) to put up buildings *b*) to have a house, etc.

built **2.** to grow or intensify —*n.* form or figure [a stocky *build*]

builder *n.* a person in the business of constructing buildings

building *n.* **1.** anything that is built **2.** the process or business of constructing houses, etc.

building society a cooperative banking enterprise financed by deposits on which interest is paid and from which mortgage loans are advanced on homes

buildup, build-up *n.* [Colloq.] **1.** favourable publicity or praise **2.** growth or expansion [a military *buildup*] **3.** a gradual approach to a climax

built-in *adj.* **1.** made as part of the building [a *built-in* wardrobe] **2.** intrinsic; inherent

built-up *adj.* **1.** made higher, stronger, etc. by the addition of parts **2.** having many buildings on it

bulb (bulb) *n.* [< Gr. *bolbos*] **1.** an underground bud that sends down roots and has a very short stem covered with leafy scales, as in a lily, onion, etc. **2.** a corm, tuber, or tuberous root resembling a bulb, as in a crocus **3.** a plant that grows from a bulb **4.** anything shaped like a bulb [an electric light *bulb*] —**bulbar** (bul'bər) *adj.*

bulbous *adj.* **1.** of, having, or growing from bulbs **2.** shaped like a bulb

bulge (bulj) *n.* [< L. *bulga*, bag] **1.** an outward swelling **2.** a projecting part **3.** [Colloq.] a sudden increase —*vi., vt.* **bulged, bulg'ing** to swell outwards

bulk (bulk) *n.* [ON. *bulki*, heap] **1.** size or volume, esp. if great **2.** the main part [the *bulk* of one's fortune] **3.** bulky matter that passes through the intestines unabsorbed —*vi.* **1.** to form into a mass **2.** to have size or importance —*vt.* to give more bulk to —*adj.* **1.** total; aggregate **2.** not in individual packets —**in bulk 1.** not in individual packets **2.** in large amounts

bulk buying the purchase of large quantities of a commodity, often on preferential terms

bulkhead (bulk'hed') *n.* [< ON. *balkr*, partition + HEAD] any of the upright partitions separating parts of a ship, aircraft, etc. as for protection against fire or leakage

bulky *adj.* **-ier, -iest 1.** large; massive **2.** awkwardly large; big and clumsy —**bulk'ily** *adv.* —**bulk'iness** *n.*

bull¹ (bool) *n.* [< OE. *bula*, bull] **1.** the adult male of any bovine animal, as the ox, or of certain other large animals, as the elephant, whale, etc. **2.** a person who buys stocks, etc. expecting, or seeking to bring about, a rise in their prices **3.** *a)* the central mark of a target *b)* a direct hit **4.** [Slang] insincere talk; nonsense —[B-] same as TAURUS —*adj.* **1.** male **2.** like a bull in size, strength, etc. **3.** rising in price [a *bull* market] —**bull in a china shop** in a clumsy or tactless manner —**take the bull by the horns** to

deal boldly with a danger or difficulty —**bull'ish** *adj.* —**bull'ishly** *adv.*

bull² *n.* [< LL. *bulla*, seal] an official document or decree from the Pope

bull³ *n.* [<?] a mistake in a statement that is illogical in a ludicrous way

bull- [< BULL¹] a combining form meaning: **1.** of or like a bull **2.** large or male [*bullfrog*]

bulldog *n.* a short-haired, square-jawed, heavily built dog noted for its strong grip

bulldoze *vt.* **-dozed', -doz'ing** [<?] **1.** [Colloq.] to intimidate **2.** to move, make level, etc. with a bulldozer

bulldozer *n.* **1.** a person who bulldozes **2.** a tractor with a large, shovellike blade on the front, for moving earth, etc.

bullet (bool'it) *n.* [< L. *bulla*, knob] a small, shaped piece of metal to be shot from a firearm

bulletin (bool'ə tin) *n.* [< L. *bulla*, knob] **1.** a brief statement of the latest news **2.** a regular publication, as for members of a society

bullfight *n.* a public show in which a bull is first provoked in various ways and then usually killed with a sword by a matador —**bull'fight'er** *n.* —**bull'fight'ing** *n.*

bullfinch *n.* a songbird with a black head and, in the male, a bright red throat and breast

bullfrog *n.* a large N American frog with a deep, loud croak

bullheaded *adj.* blindly stubborn

bullion (bool'yən) *n.* [< OFr. *billon*, small coin] gold and silver regarded as raw material, as before coinage

bullock (bool'ək) *n.* [< OE. *bula*, bull] a castrated bull

bullring *n.* an arena for bullfighting

bull-roarer *n.* a flat piece of wood at the end of a string, which makes a roaring noise when whirled

bull's-eye *n.* **1.** a thick, circular glass in a ship's deck, etc., for admitting light **2.** same as BULL¹ (3) **3.** *a)* a convex lens for concentrating light *b)* a lantern with such a lens **4.** the glass boss at the centre of a plate of glass **5.** a hard, round sweet

bull terrier a strong, lean, white dog, developed by crossing the bulldog and the terrier

bully¹ (bool'ē) *n.,* pl. **-lies** [orig., sweetheart < Du.] a person who hurts, frightens, or browbeats those who are smaller or weaker —*vt., vi.* **-lied, -lying** to behave like a bully (towards) —*adj.* [Colloq.] fine; very good

bully² *n.* [< Fr. *bouillir*, boil] corned beef: also **bully beef**

bully³ *n.* *Hockey* the method of starting play in which two players strike their sticks together and against the ground three times before trying to hit the ball —*vi.* to start play by a bully Also **bully off**

bulrush (bool'rush) *n.* [< OE. *bol*, tree

trunk + *risc*, rush] 1. a tall marsh plant with reedlike leaves 2. *Bible* papyrus

bulwark (bool′wərk) *n.* [< MDu. *bolwerc*] 1. an earthwork or defensive wall; rampart 2. a defence or protection 3. [*usually pl.*] a ship's side above the deck —*vt.* 1. to provide bulwarks for 2. to be a bulwark to

bum¹ (bum) *n.* [prob. < G. *Bummler*, loafer] [U.S. Colloq.] 1. a tramp or derelict 2. any irresponsible person —*vi.*, *vt.* **bummed, bum′ming** [U.S. Colloq.] to live as a bum; cadge —*adj.* **bum′mer**, **bum′mest** [U.S. Slang] poor in quality

bum² *n.* [ME. *bom* < ?] [Colloq.] the buttocks

bumbailiff (bum′bā′lif) *n.* [< ?] a sheriff's officer employed to collect debts and arrest debtors

bumblebee (bum′b'l bē′) *n.* [< ME. *bomblen*, buzz] a large, hairy, yellow-and-black social bee

bumbling (bum′bliŋ) *adj.* [see prec.] self-important in a blundering way

bumf, bumph (bumf) *n.* [< *bumfodder*, lit., toilet paper] [Derog. Colloq.] official documents, etc.

bump (bump) *vt.*, *vi.* [echoic] 1. to hit against; collide with 2. to move with jolts —*n.* 1. a light blow 2. a swelling, esp. one caused by a blow 3. a collision 4. one of the protuberances on the skull, said to give an indication of mental qualities —**bump into** [Colloq.] to meet unexpectedly —**bump off** [Slang] to murder —**bump up** to increase (prices, etc.) —**bumpy′y** *adj.*

bumper¹ *n.* a device for absorbing some of the shock of a collision; specif., a bar across the front or back of a car

bumper² *n.* [< obs. *bombard*, leather jug] 1. a cup or glass filled to the brim 2. [Colloq.] anything unusually large of its kind —*adj.* unusually abundant

bumpkin (bump′kən) *n.* [< MDu. *bommekijn*, small cask] an awkward or simple person from the country

bumptious (bump′shəs) *adj.* [prob. < BUMP] disagreeably conceited, arrogant, or forward —**bump′tiously** *adv.* —**bump′- tiousness** *n.*

bun (bun) *n.* [< OFr. *buigne*, swelling] 1. a small roll or cake usually sweetened 2. hair worn in a roll or knot

bunch (bunch) *n.* [< ?] 1. a cluster of things growing, grouped, or thought of together 2. [Colloq.] a group of people —*vt.*, *vi.* to gather together in a mass or in loose folds (often with *up*) —**bunch′y** *adj.*

buncombe, bunkum (bun′kəm) *n.* [< *Buncombe* county, N Carolina, U.S.] [Colloq.] talk that is empty, insincere, or merely for effect; humbug

bundle (bun′d'l) *n.* [< MDu. *bondel*] 1. a number of things tied together 2. a package 3. a bunch or group 4. *Biol.* an anatomic unit consisting of separate nerve fibres, muscles, etc. banded together —*vt.* **-dled, -dling** 1. to make into a bundle 2. to send hastily (*away, off, out,* or *into*) —*vi.* to go hastily; bustle —**bundle up** to put on plenty of warm clothing

bundu (boon′doo) *n.* [S Afr. Slang] wild, uninhabited country

bung (buŋ) *n.* [< MDu. *bonge*] 1. a stopper for the hole in a barrel 2. a bunghole —*vt.* 1. to close with a stopper 2. to stop up 3. [Slang] to fling; throw

bungalow (buŋ′gə lō′) *n.* [< Hindi *bāṅglā*, thatched house] a small house usually of one storey

bunghole (buŋ′hōl′) *n.* a hole in a barrel or keg through which liquid can be drawn out

bungle (buŋ′g'l) *vt.* **-gled, -gling** [< ?] to spoil by clumsy work; botch —*vi.* to do things badly or clumsily —*n.* 1. a bungling, or clumsy, act 2. a bungled piece of work —**bun′gler** *n.* —**bun′glingly** *adv.*

bunion (bun′yən) *n.* [prob. < OFr. *buigne*, swelling] an inflammation and swelling on the foot, esp. on the big toe

bunk¹ (buŋk) *n.* [prob. < Scand.] 1. a shelf-like bed built into or against a wall, as in a ship 2. [Colloq.] any sleeping place —*vi.* 1. to sleep in a bunk 2. [Colloq.] to use a makeshift sleeping place

bunk² *n.* [Slang] *same as* BUNCOMBE

bunk³ *n.* [< ?] a hurried departure, esp. under suspicious circumstances: only in **do a bunk**

bunk bed a pair of twin beds linked one above the other

bunker *n.* [Scot. < ?] 1. a large bin or tank, as for fuel 2. a weapon emplacement of steel and concrete in an underground fortification system 3. a sand trap serving as an obstacle on a golf course —*vt.* *Golf* to hit (a ball) into a bunker

bunny (bun′ē) *n.*, *pl.* **bun′nies** [dim. of dial. *bun*, rabbit] a rabbit: pet name used by children

Bunsen burner (bun′s'n) [< R. W. *Bunsen*] a small, tubular gas burner that produces a hot, blue flame

bunting¹ (bun′tiŋ) *n.* [< ?] 1. a thin cloth used in making flags 2. flags, or strips of cloth used as decorations

bunting² *n.* [< ?] any of various small birds having a stout bill

buoy (boi) *n.* [< L. *boia*, fetter] 1. a floating object anchored in water to warn of rocks, etc., or to mark a channel 2. *short for* LIFE BUOY —*vt.* 1. to mark with a buoy 2. to keep afloat 3. to lift in spirits; encourage

buoyancy (boi′ən sē) *n.* [< Sp. *boyar*, to float] 1. the ability to float in liquid or air 2. the power to keep something afloat 3. cheerfulness 4. the ability to recover quickly after a setback —**buoy′- ant** *adj.*

BUPA British United Provident Association

bur (bur) *n.* [< Scand.] 1. the rough,

prickly seedcase or fruit of certain plants **2.** a plant with burs **3.** anything that clings like a bur **4.** *same as* BURR

burble (bur'b'l) *vi.* **-bled, -bling** [echoic] **1.** to make a gurgling sound **2.** to babble **3.** [Colloq.] to be verbose

burbot (bur'bət) *n.* [ult. < L. *barba*, a beard] a freshwater fish of the cod family, with barbels on the chin

burden[1] (burd''n) *n.* [< OE. *beran*, to bear] **1.** anything that is carried; load **2.** a heavy load, as of responsibility **3.** the carrying of loads [a beast of *burden*] **4.** the carrying capacity of a ship, or the weight of its cargo —*vt.* to put a burden on; oppress —**bur'densome** *adj.*

burden[2] *n.* [< OFr. *bourdon*, humming] **1.** a chorus or refrain of a song **2.** a repeated, central idea; theme

burdock (bur'dok') *n.* [BUR + DOCK[3]] a plant with purple-flowered heads covered with hooked prickles

bureau (byooər'ō) *n.*, *pl.* **-reaus, -reaux** (-ōz) [Fr., desk] **1.** a desk with drawers for papers **2.** [U.S.] a chest of drawers **3.** an agency providing specified services [a travel *bureau*] **4.** [U.S.] a government department

bureaucracy (byoo͡ə ro'krə sē) *n.*, *pl.* **-cies** [< Fr. *bureau* + -CRACY] **1.** the administration of government through departments managed by officials following an inflexible routine **2.** the officials collectively **3.** governmental officialism **4.** concentration of authority in a complex structure of administrative bureaus

bureaucrat (byoo͡ər'ə krat') *n.* an official in a bureaucracy, esp. one who follows a routine strictly —**bu'reaucrat'ic** *adj.* —**bu'reaucrat'ically** *adv.*

burette (byoo͡ ret') *n.* [Fr.] a graduated glass tube with a stopcock at the bottom, for measuring small quantities of liquid or gas

burgeon (bur'jən) *vi.* [< OFr. *burjon*, a bud] **1.** to put forth buds, shoots, etc. **2.** to grow rapidly; flourish

burgess (bur'jis) *n.* [< LL. *burgus*, castle] **1.** an inhabitant of a borough **2.** formerly, a member of parliament representing a borough, corporate town or university

burgh (bur'ə) *n.* [Scot. var. of BOROUGH] in Scotland, a chartered town —**burghal** (bur'g'l) *adj.*

burgher (bur'gər) *n.* **1.** a citizen of a corporate town, esp. on the continent **2.** *S Afr. Hist.* a citizen of the Cape not employed by the Dutch East India Company

burglar (bur'glər) *n.* [< OFr. *burgeor*, burglar] a person who commits burglary

burglarious (bər glāər'ē əs) *adj.* of, given to, or being burglary —**burglar'iously** *adv.*

burglary (bur'glər ē) *n.*, *pl.* **-ries** the act of breaking into a building to commit theft or other felony

burgle (bur'g'l) *vt.*, *vi.* **-gled, -gling** [< BURGLAR] to commit burglary (in)

burgomaster (bur'gə mäs'tər) *n.* [< MDu. *burg*, town + *meester*, master] the

mayor of a town in the Netherlands, Flanders, Austria, or Germany

burial (ber'ē əl) *n.* the burying of a dead body; interment —*adj.* of or connected with burial

BURIN

burin (byoo͡ər'in) *n.* [Fr.] a pointed cutting tool used by engravers or marble workers

burk, burke (burk) *n.* *same as* BERK

burlesque (bər lesk') *n.* [< It. *burla*, jest] **1.** any broadly comic or satirical imitation; parody **2.** [U.S.] a variety show characterized by striptease acts, etc. —*adj.* comically imitating; parodying —*vi.* **-lesqued', -lesqu'ing** to imitate comically or derisively; parody

burly (bur'lē) *adj.* **-lier, -liest** [ME. *borlich*, excellent] big and strong; muscular —**bur'liness** *n.*

burn[1] (burn) *vt.* **burned** or **burnt, burn'ing** [OE. *biernan*] **1.** to set on fire **2.** to destroy by fire **3.** to injure or damage by fire, heat, friction, or acid **4.** to consume as fuel **5.** to sunburn **6.** to cauterize **7.** to harden (bricks, etc.) by fire **8.** to cause by fire, heat, etc. [to *burn* a hole] **9.** to cause a sensation of heat in —*vi.* **1.** to be on fire; blaze **2.** to undergo combustion **3.** to give out light or heat **4.** to be destroyed, injured or damaged by fire or heat **5.** to feel hot **6.** to be inflamed, as with anger —*n.* **1.** an injury caused by fire, heat, wind, etc. **2.** the process or result of burning —**burn down** to burn to the ground —**burn one's boats** (or **bridges**) to embark on a course of action from which there can be no retreat —**burn oneself out** to exhaust oneself by too much work or dissipation —**burn one's fingers** [Colloq.] to suffer from having meddled —**burn the midnight oil** to stay up late reading or working —**burn up** to burn completely

burn[2] *n.* [see BOURN[1]] [Scot. & North Eng.] a brook

burner *n.* the part of a stove, furnace, etc. from which the flame comes

burning *adj.* **1.** that burns **2.** intense; critical

burning glass a convex lens for focusing the sun's rays so as to set fire to something

burnish (bur'nish) *vt.*, *vi.* [< OFr. *brun*, brown] to make or become shiny by rubbing; polish —*n.* a gloss or polish —**bur'nisher** *n.*

burnoose, burnous (bər noos') *n.* [< Ar. *burnus*] a long cloak with a hood, worn by Arabs and Moors

burnt (burnt) *alt. pt. and pp. of* BURN[1]

burnt sienna *see* SIENNA

burnt umber *see* UMBER

burp (bʉrp) *n., vi.* [echoic] [Colloq.] belch —*vt.* to cause (a baby) to belch by patting its back

burr (bʉr) *n.* [prob. echoic] 1. the trilling of *r*, with uvula or tongue [a Scottish *burr*] 2. a whirring sound —*vi.* 1. to speak with a burr 2. to make a whir

burrow (bʉr'ō) *n.* [see BOROUGH] 1. a hole dug in the ground by an animal 2. any similar hole for shelter, etc. —*vi.* 1. to make a burrow 2. to live or hide in or as in a burrow 3. to search, as if by digging —*vt.* 1. to make burrows in 2. to make by burrowing —**bur'rower** *n.*

bursar (bʉr'sər) *n.* [ML. *bursa*, bag] 1. a treasurer, as of a college 2. the holder of a scholarship at school or university

bursary *n.* 1. a treasury, esp. of a college 2. a scholarship or grant, esp. one awarded in a Scottish school or university —**bursarial** (bər sāar'ē əl) *adj.*

burst (bʉrst) *vi.* burst, burst'ing [< OE. *berstan*] 1. to come apart suddenly and violently; break open 2. to give sudden expression to some feeling; break (*into* tears, etc.) 3. to go, come, start, etc. suddenly and with force 4. *a)* to be as full as possible *b)* to be filled (*with* anger, etc.) —*vt.* to cause to burst —*n.* 1. a bursting; explosion 2. the result of a bursting; break 3. a sudden, violent display of feeling 4. a sudden action; spurt 5. a single series of shots —**burst'er** *n.*

bury (ber'ē) *vt.* bur'ied, bur'ying [OE. *byrgan*] 1. to put (a dead body) into the earth, a tomb, etc. 2. *a)* to hide in the ground *b)* to cover up 3. to put away [to *bury* a feud] 4. to involve oneself deeply in —**bury the hatchet** to stop fighting and become reconciled

bus (bus) *n., pl.* bus'es [< (OMNI)BUS] 1. a large motor coach for carrying many passengers, usually along a regular route 2. [Colloq.] a motor car or aeroplane —*vt.* bussed, bus'sing to transport by bus, esp. to achieve racial integration in schools —*vi.* to go by bus —**miss the bus** to miss an opportunity

busby (buz'bē) *n., pl.* -bies [< ?] a tall fur hat worn by hussars, guardsmen in the British army, etc.

bush[1] (boosh) *n.* [ME.] 1. a woody plant having many stems branching out near ground level; shrub 2. anything resembling a bush; esp., a thickly furred tail 3. shrubby woodland or uncleared country —*vi.* to grow thickly or spread out —**beat about the bush** to talk around a subject without getting to the point

bush[2] *n.* [MDu. *busse*, box] a removable metal sleeve for reducing the effect of friction on a bearing or for decreasing the diameter of a hole —*vt.* to fit with a bush

bush baby any of various nocturnal lemurlike mammals of African forests, with a long, bushy tail and large eyes

bushel (boosh'l) *n.* [< OFr. *boisse*, grain measure] a unit of dry measure for grain, fruit, liquids, etc., equal to 4 pecks or 8 gallons (c. 36.4 litres)

bush jacket in South Africa, a shirtlike jacket with patch pockets designed esp. to be worn in bush country

bush line an airline operating in the bush country of Canada's northern regions

bush lot [Canad.] a tract of woodland

bushman *n.* 1. a person who lives in the Australian bush 2. a backwoodsman 3. [B-] a member of a nomadic people of SW Africa

bush pilot [Canad.] a pilot who operates in the bush country

bushranger *n.* [< BUSH[1] + RANGER] in Australia, an outlaw who makes the bush his hide-out

bush tea in South Africa, a beverage like tea made from the dried leaves of various leguminous shrubs

bush telegraph [Colloq.] the informal but rapid means by which news is spread throughout a community

bushveld (boosh'felt') *n.* [S Afr.] bushy countryside

bushy *adj.* -ier, -iest 1. overgrown with bushes 2. thick and spreading out like a bush

busily (biz'ə lē) *adv.* in a busy manner

business (biz'nis) *n.* [OE. *bisignes*: see BUSY] 1. one's work, occupation, or profession 2. rightful concern 3. a matter, activity, etc. 4. the buying and selling of goods; trade 5. a commercial or industrial establishment; shop, factory, etc. 6. action in a drama to take up a pause in dialogue, etc. —*adj.* of or for business —**business is business** sentiment cannot be allowed to interfere with profit making —**mean business** [Colloq.] to be in earnest —**mind one's own business** to refrain from interfering in the affairs of others

businesslike *adj.* efficient, methodical, etc.

businessman *n.* a man in business, esp. as an owner or executive

busker (bus'kər) *n.* [< Slang *busk*, to be a strolling entertainer] a street singer or strolling entertainer

BUSKINS

buskin (bus'kin) *n.* [< ? MDu. *brosekin*, small leather boot] 1. a boot reaching to the calf or knee, worn long ago 2. *a)* the high, thick-soled, laced boot worn by actors in ancient Greek and Roman tragedy *b)* tragic drama; tragedy

busman's holiday a holiday in which

one's recreation is very similar to one's daily work

buss (bus) *n., vt., vi.* [< ?] [Archaic or Dial.] kiss

bust[1] (bust) *n.* [< It. *busto*] 1. a piece of sculpture representing a person's head, shoulders, and upper chest 2. a woman's bosom

bust[2] *vt., vi.* [< BURST] [Slang] 1. to break 2. to make or become bankrupt or demoted —*n.* [Slang] 1. a financial collapse 2. a spree —*adj.* bankrupt —**bust up** [Colloq.] 1. to put an end to a friendship 2. to disrupt, esp. violently —**go bust** to become bankrupt

bustard (bus′tərd) *n.* [ult. < L. *avis tarda,* slow bird] a large, long-legged game bird

bustle[1] (bus′'l) *vi., vt.* -tled, -tling [< ME. *busken,* prepare] to hurry busily or with much fuss and bother —*n.* busy and noisy activity —**bus′tlingly** *adv.*

bustle[2] *n.* [< ? G. *Buschel,* bunch] *Hist.* padding worn at the back by women to puff out the skirt

bust-up (bust′up) *n.* [Colloq.] a quarrel or brawl

busy (biz′ē) *adj.* -ier, -iest [< OE. *bisig*] 1. occupied; at work; not idle 2. full of activity 3. in use at the moment, as a telephone line 4. meddlesome 5. displeasingly crowded with detail, colours, etc. —*vt.* **bus′ied, bus′ying** to make or keep busy —**bus′yness** *n.*

busybody *n., pl.* -bod′ies one who pries into other people's affairs; meddler

but[1] (but; *unstressed* bət) *prep.* [OE. *butan,* without] 1. except [nobody came *but* me] : sometimes regarded as a conjunction [nobody came *but* I (came)] 2. other than [we cannot choose *but* (to) stay] —*conj.* 1. yet [he is bad, *but* he has some virtues] 2. on the contrary [I am old, *but* you are young] 3. unless [it never rains *but* it pours] 4. that [I don't question *but* you're right] 5. that . . . not [I never think of London *but* I think of fog] —*adv.* 1. only [if I had *but* known] 2. merely [he is *but* a child] 3. just [I heard it *but* now] —*pron.* who . . . not; which . . . not [not a man *but* felt it] —*n.* an objection [ifs and *buts*] —*vt.* to raise an objection —**but for** if it were not for

but[2] (but) *adj.* [akin to prec.] [Scot.] outside —*n.* [Scot.] the outer room —**but and ben** [Scot.] a two-room cottage consisting of an outer and an inner room

butane (byōō′tān) *n.* [< BUTYL] either of two hydrocarbons in the methane series used as a fuel, etc.

butch (booch) *adj.* [< *Butch,* nickname] [Slang] masculine in appearance, manner, etc.; mannish

butcher (booch′ər) *n.* [< OFr. *bouc,* he-goat] 1. one whose work is killing animals or dressing their carcasses for meat 2. one who sells meat 3. anyone who kills as if slaughtering animals —*vt.* 1. to kill or dress (animals) for meat 2. to kill brutally 3. to mangle

butcherbird *n.* a shrike which, after killing prey, impales it on thorns

butchery *n., pl.* -eries 1. the work of a butcher 2. brutal bloodshed 3. a slaughterhouse

butler (but′lər) *n.* [< OFr. *bouteille,* bottle] a manservant, usually the head servant of a household, in charge of wines, pantry, etc.

butt[1] (but) *n.* [< ?] 1. the thick end of anything 2. a stub as of a cigarette 3. an object of ridicule or criticism 4. a mound of earth behind a target 5. [*pl.*] a target range —*vt., vi.* to join end to end

butt[2] *vt.* [< OFr. *buter* thrust against] to ram with the head —*vi.* to make a butting motion —*n.* a thrust with the head or horns —**butt in** (or **into**) [Slang] to interfere in (another's business, a conversation, etc.)

butt[3] *n.* [< LL. *bottis,* cask] a large barrel or cask

butter (but′ər) *n.* [< L. *butyrum* < Gr. *bous,* cow + *tyros,* cheese] 1. the solid, yellowish, edible fat obtained by churning cream 2. a substance like butter [peanut *butter*] 3. any of certain vegetable oils that are solid at ordinary temperatures [cocoa *butter*] —*vt.* 1. to spread with butter 2. [Colloq.] to flatter (with *up*) —**look as if butter would not melt in one's mouth** to look innocent or demure —**but′tery** *adj.*

butter bean a large, dried haricot bean

buttercup *n.* a yellow-flowered plant common in meadows and wet places

butterfingers *n.* one who often fumbles and drops things —**but′terfin′gered** *adj.*

butterfly *n., pl.* -flies [< OE. *buttorfleoge*] 1. any of a large group of insects active by day, having a slender body and four broad, usually brightly coloured wings 2. [*pl.*] [Colloq.] a nervous sensation, esp. in the stomach

butterfly nut *same as* WING NUT

butterfly stroke *Swimming* a stroke in which the arms are plunged forward together in large circular movements

buttermilk *n.* the sour liquid left after churning butter from milk

butter muslin a thin, loosely-woven cotton fabric formerly used for wrapping butter, backing maps, etc.

butterscotch *n.* a hard, sticky sweet made with brown sugar, butter, etc.

buttery (but′ər ē) *n., pl.* -teries [< LL. *bottis,* cask] 1. a storeroom for food and wine 2. in some universities, a bar run for students

buttock (but′ək) *n.* [< OE. *buttuc,* end] 1. either of the two fleshy, rounded parts at the back of the hips 2. [*pl.*] the rump

button (but′'n) *n.* [OFr. *boton*] 1. any small disc or knob used as a fastening, ornament, etc. on a garment 2. anything small and shaped like a button; specif., *a*) a small knob for operating a doorbell, etc. *b*) a small mushroom —*vt., vi.* to fasten with buttons —**not worth a button** of little or no value —**but′toner** *n.*

buttonhole *n.* **1.** a slit or loop through which a button can be fastened **2.** a flower or spray worn pinned to the lapel or in the buttonhole —*vt.* **-holed´, -hol´- ing 1.** to make (a person) listen to one, as if by grasping his coat by a buttonhole **2.** to make buttonholes in

buttress (but´ris) *n.* [< OFr. *buter*: see BUTT²] **1.** a projecting structure built against a wall to support or reinforce it **2.** a support; prop —*vt.* **1.** to support or reinforce with a buttress **2.** to prop up; bolster

butyl (byo͞ot´il) *n.* [< L. *butyrum*: see BUTTER] any of the four isomeric organic radicals C₄H₉

buxom (buk´səm) *adj.* [ME., humble] healthy, plump, jolly, etc.; having a shapely, full-bosomed figure: said of a woman —**bux´omly** *adv.* —**bux´omness** *n.*

buy (bī) *vt.* **bought, buy´ing** [< OE. *bycgan*] **1.** to get by paying money; purchase **2.** to get by exchange or sacrifice **3.** to be the means of purchasing [all that money can *buy*] **4.** to bribe **5.** [Slang] to accept as valid, agreeable, etc. —*vi.* to be a buyer —*n.* **1.** a buying **2.** anything bought —**buy into** (or **in**) to pay money so as to get membership in, etc. —**buy off** to appease by bribery —**buy out** to buy all the stock, rights, etc. of —**buy up** to buy all that is available of —**buy´a- ble** *adj.*

buyer *n.* **1.** one who buys; consumer **2.** one whose work is to buy merchandise for a retail store

buzz (buz) *vi.* [echoic] **1.** to hum like a bee **2.** to talk excitedly **3.** to move with a buzzing sound **4.** to be filled with noisy activity or talk —*vt.* **1.** to make (wings, etc.) buzz **2.** to fly an aircraft low over **3.** to signal with a buzzer —*n.* **1.** a sound like a bee's hum **2.** a confused sound, as of many voices **3.** a signal on a buzzer **4.** [Colloq.] a telephone call —**buzz about** (or **around**) to scurry about —**buzz off** [Colloq.] to hurry away

buzzard (buz´ərd) *n.* [< L. *buteo*, kind of hawk] any of various hawks that are slow and heavy in flight

buzzer *n.* an electrical device that makes a buzzing sound as a signal

B.V.M. [L. *Beata Virgo Maria*] Blessed Virgin Mary

bwana (bwä´na) *n.* [Swahili] [often **B-**] master; sir: native term of address used in parts of Africa

by (bī) *prep.* [< OE. *be, bi*] **1.** near; at [stand *by* the wall] **2.** a) in or during [to travel *by* night] b) for a fixed time [to work *by* the hour] c) not later than [be back´ *by* noon] **3.** a) via b) past [to march *by* the reviewing stand] c) towards [north *by* west] **4.** on behalf of [he did well *by* me] **5.** through the means of [made *by* hand] **6.** a) according to [*by* the book] b) in [to grow dark

by degrees] c) following in series [march two *by* two] **7.** with the sanction of [*by* your leave] **8.** a) in or to the amount of [apples *by* the kilo] b) and in another dimension [two *by* four] c) using (the given number) as multiplier or divisor —*adv.* **1.** close at hand; near [stand *by*] **2.** away; aside [put money *by*] **3.** past [cars sped *by*] —*adj., n. same as* BY —**by and by** after a while —**by and large** considering everything

by- *a prefix meaning:* **1.** close by; near [bystander] **2.** secondary [byproduct]

by-and-by (bī´´n bī´) *n.* a future time

bye (bī) *n.* [see BY] **1.** in sports in which competitors are paired, the status of the extra man, who advances to the next round without playing **2.** *Cricket* a run scored off a ball not struck by the batsman —*adj.* incidental —**by the by(e)** incidentally

byelaw (bī´lô´) *n. same as* BYLAW

by-election (bī´i lek´shən) *n.* a special election held between general elections to fill a vacant parliamentary seat

bygone (bī´gon´) *adj.* gone by; past —*n.* **1.** anything that is past **2.** an object from the past, esp. a small antique —**let bygones be bygones** to let past offences be forgotten

bylaw *n.* [< ME. *bi*, town + *laue*, law] any of a set of rules made by a local authority

byline *n.* a line at the head of a newspaper or magazine article, telling who wrote it

bypass *n.* **1.** a main road built to avoid a city or other congested area **2.** a path, pipe, channel, etc. between two points that avoids or is auxiliary to the main way —*vt.* **1.** to go around instead of through **2.** to furnish with a bypass **3.** to ignore, fail to consult, etc.

byplay *n.* action, gestures, etc. going on aside from the main action, as in a play

byproduct, by-product *n.* anything produced, as from residues, in the course of making another thing; secondary product or result

byre (bīər) *n.* [OE., hut] a cowshed

byroad *n.* a side road; byway

Byronic (bī ron´ik) *adj.* of, like, or characteristic of Byron or his writings; romantic, cynical, ironic, etc.

bystander *n.* a person who stands near but does not participate; onlooker

byway *n.* **1.** a road that is not used very much **2.** a secondary activity, line of study, etc.

byword *n.* **1.** a proverb **2.** a person or thing proverbial for some specific characteristic [his name was a *byword* for cruelty] **3.** a favourite phrase

Byzantine (bi zan´tīn) *adj.* **1.** of Byzantium or the Byzantine Empire **2.** of or pertaining to the Orthodox Eastern Church **3.** *Archit.* designating a style developed in Byzantium, characterized by domes, round arches, mosaics, etc. —*n.* a native or inhabitant of Byzantium

C

C, c (sē) *n., pl.* **C's, c's** 1. the third letter of the English alphabet 2. *a symbol for* the third in a sequence or group

C *n.* 1. a Roman numeral for 100 2. *Music* the first tone in the scale of C major

C 1. *Chem.* carbon 2. *Physics* capacitance 3. *Physics the symbol for* coulomb

C, C. 1. Celsius 2. Centigrade 3. Conservative

C, c copyright

C. 1. Catholic 2. Church

C., c. 1. cathode 2. century 3. *pl.* **CC.** chapter 4. contralto

c. 1. carat 2. cent 3. circa 4. *Cricket* caught

Ca *Chem.* calcium

ca. 1. cathode 2. circa

C.A. 1. Central America 2. Chartered Accountant

C/A current account

CAA, C.A.A. Civil Aviation Authority

cab (kab) *n.* [< CABRIOLET] 1. a taxicab 2. the place in a lorry, crane, etc. where the operator sits 3. *Hist.* a carriage for public hire

cabal (kə bal′) *n.* [Fr., intrigue] 1. a small group of persons joined in a secret intrigue; junta 2. the intrigues of such a group; plot

cabala (kə bäl′ə) *n.* [< Heb. *qabbālāh*, received lore] 1. an occult rabbinical philosophy, based on a mystical interpretation of the Scriptures 2. any secret doctrine Also sp. **cab′bala** —**cab′a-list** *n.*

cabaret (kab′ə rā′) *n.* [Fr., tavern] 1. a restaurant or café with dancing, singing, etc. as entertainment 2. such entertainment

cabbage (kab′ij) *n.* [< ? L. *caput*, head] a common vegetable with thick leaves formed into a round, compact head on a short stalk

cabbage white a common white butterfly whose green larvae feed on cabbage and related plants

cabdriver *n.* a person who drives a cab: also [Colloq.] **cab′by, cab′bie**

caber (kā′bər) *n.* [Gael. *cabar*] a long, heavy pole tossed as a test of muscular strength in the Highland Games

cabin (kab′in) *n.* [< LL. *capanna*, hut] 1. a small house, built simply or crudely 2. a private room on a ship 3. a roofed section of a boat 4. an enclosed section for passengers in an aircraft

cabin boy a boy whose work is to serve and run errands for officers and passengers aboard a ship

cabin cruiser a motorboat with a cabin

cabinet (kab′ə nit) *n.* [Fr., < *cabine*, cabin] 1. a case or piece of furniture with drawers or shelves for holding things 2. a boxlike enclosure for a radio, television, etc. 3. formerly, a private council room 4. [*often* C-] the body of senior ministers in a government

cabinetmaker *n.* a workman who makes fine furniture, etc. —**cab′inetmak′ing** *n.*

cable (kā′b'l) *n.* [< L. *capere*, take hold] 1. a thick, heavy rope, now often of wire 2. a ship's anchor chain 3. *same as* CABLE LENGTH 4. a bundle of insulated wires through which an electric current can be passed 5. *same as* CABLEGRAM —*vt.* **-bled, -bling** 1. to transmit by undersea cable 2. to send a cablegram to —*vi.* to send a cablegram

cable car a car drawn by a moving cable

cablegram *n.* a message sent by undersea cable

cable length a unit of nautical measure: in Britain, one tenth of a nautical mile (185.2m): also **cable's length**

caboodle (kə bōō′d'l) *n.* [< ?] [Colloq.] lot; group [*the whole* caboodle]

caboose (kə bōōs′) *n.* [< MDu.] 1. a ship's galley 2. [U.S.] the guard's van on a goods train, usually at the rear 3. [Can.] a mobile cabin used by lumbermen

cabriolet (kab′rē ə lā′) *n.* [Fr., < *cabriole*, a leap] a light, two-wheeled carriage, usually with a hood that folds, drawn by one horse

cacao (kə kā′ō) *n., pl.* **-ca′os** [Sp. < Mex.Ind.] a tropical American tree, bearing large, elliptical seedpods (**cacao beans**), from which cocoa and chocolate are made

cachalot (kash′ə lot′) *n.* [Fr. < Sp. < ? Port.] *same as* SPERM WHALE

cache (kash) *n.* [Fr. < *cacher*, conceal] 1. a place in which stores of food, supplies, etc. are hidden 2. anything so hidden —*vt.,* cached, cach′ing to hide in a cache

cachet (kash′ā) *n.* [Fr.] 1. a seal on an official letter 2. *a*) a mark indicating superior quality *b*) prestige 3. a commemorative design stamped on letters, etc.

cachinnate (kak′ə nāt′) *vi.* **-nat′ed, -nat′-ing** [< L. *cachinnare*] to laugh loudly —**cach′inna′tion** *n.*

cachou (kə shōō′) *n.* [< Malay *kachu*] 1. *same as* CATECHU 2. a lozenge for sweetening the breath

cacique (kə sēk′) *n.* [Sp. < native word] in Latin America, an Indian chief

cack-handed (kak′han′did) *adj.* [< ?] 1. [Dial.] left-handed 2. [Colloq.] clumsy; awkward

cackle (kak''l) *vi.* **-led, -ling** [echoic] **1.** to make the shrill, broken, vocal sounds of a hen **2.** to laugh or chatter with similar sounds —*vt.* to utter in a cackling manner —*n.* **1.** a cackling **2.** cackling laughter or chatter —**cut the cackle** [Slang] come to the point

caco- [< Gr. *kakos*, bad] *a combining form meaning* bad, poor, harsh [*cacography*]

cacoethes (kak'ō ē'thēz) *n.* [< Gr. *kakos*, bad + *ēthos*, habit] an itch (to do something); mania

cacography (kə kog'rə fē) *n.* [CACO- + -GRAPHY] **1.** bad handwriting **2.** incorrect spelling

cacophony (kə kof'ə nē) *n., pl.* **-nies** [< Gr. *kakos*, bad + *phōnē*, voice] harsh, jarring sound; dissonance —**cacoph'onous** *adj.* —**cacoph'onously** *adv.*

cactus (kak'təs) *n., pl.* **-tuses, -ti** (-tī) [< Gr. *kaktos*, kind of thistle] any of various desert plants with fleshy stems and reduced or spinelike leaves

cad (kad) *n.* [< CADET] a man or boy whose behaviour is considered to be ungentlemanly

cadaver (kə dāv'ər) *n.* [L.] a dead body, esp. of a person; corpse, as for dissection

cadaverous (kə dav'ər əs) *adj.* of or like a cadaver; esp., pale, ghastly, or gaunt and haggard

caddie (kad'ē) *n.* [see CADET] a person who attends a golfer, carrying his clubs, etc. —*vi.* **-died, -dying** to act as a caddie

caddish (kad'ish) *adj.* like or characteristic of a cad

caddis worm (kad'is) the wormlike aquatic larva of the **caddis fly** that lives in a case made of twigs, grains of sand, etc. cemented together with its secreted silk

caddy¹ (kad'ē) *n., pl.* **-dies** [< Malay *kati*, weight of c. 500g] a small container used for storing tea

caddy² *n., vi.* *same as* CADDIE

cadence (kād''ns) *n.* [< L. *cadere*, fall] **1.** fall of the voice in speaking **2.** inflection in tone **3.** a rhythmic flow of sound **4.** measured movement, as in marching **5.** *Music* the harmonic ending, final trill, etc. of a phrase

cadenza (kə den'zə) *n.* [It.: see prec.] **1.** an elaborate passage played by the solo instrument in a concerto **2.** any brilliant flourish in an aria or solo passage

cadet (kə det') *n.* [Fr. < L. *caput*, head] **1.** a student at an armed forces or police academy **2.** a younger son —**cadet'ship'** *n.*

cadge (kaj) *vt., vi.* cadged, cadg'ing [< ?] to beg or get by begging; sponge —**cadg'er** *n.*

cadi (kä'dē) *n.* [Ar. *qādi*] a Moslem magistrate

cadmium (kad'mē əm) *n.* [< L. *cadmia*, zinc ore] a blue-white, metallic chemical element occurring in zinc ores: it is used in electroplating, etc.: symbol, Cd —**cad'-mic** *adj.*

cadre (kä'də) *n.* [< L. *quadrum*, a square] **1.** a framework **2.** a nucleus of trained

men around which a military or political unit can be built

CADUCEUS

caduceus (kə dyōō'sē əs) *n., pl.* **-cei'** (-sē ī') [L.] the winged staff with two serpents twined about it, carried by Mercury: used as an emblem of the medical profession —**cadu'cean** *adj.*

caecum (sē'kəm) *n., pl.* **-ca** (-kə) [< L. (*intestinum*) *caecum*, blind (intestine)] the pouch that is the beginning of the large intestine

Caenozoic (sē'nō zō'ik) *adj.* same as CAINOZOIC

Caerphilly (kāər fil'ē) *n.* [< town in SE Wales] a creamy-white, mild cheese

Caesar (sē'zər) *n.* [< Gaius Julius *Caesar*] **1.** the title of the Roman emperors from Augustus to Hadrian **2.** any emperor or dictator

Caesarean, Caesarian (si zãər'ē ən) *adj.* of Julius Caesar or the Caesars —*n.* same as CAESAREAN SECTION

Caesarean section [< Julius *Caesar*, supposedly born in this way] [also c-s-] a surgical operation for delivering a baby by cutting through the mother's abdominal and uterine walls

caesium (sē'zē əm) *n.* [< L. *caesius*, bluish-grey] a soft, silver-white, ductile, metallic element, used in photoelectric cells: symbol, Cs

caesura (si zyooər'ə) *n., pl.* **-ras, -rae** (-ē) [< L. *caedere*, to cut] a pause in a line of verse: in English verse, usually about the middle of the line —**caesu'ral** *adj.*

café, cafe (ka'fē) *n.* [Fr. *café*, coffee] a small or inexpensive restaurant, serving light meals and refreshments

cafeteria (kaf'ə tēər'ē ə) *n.* [AmSp., coffee shop] a restaurant in which food is displayed on counters and patrons serve themselves

caff (kaf) *n.* [Colloq.] *clipped form of* CAFÉ

caffeine (kaf'ēn) *n.* [< G., ult. < It. *caffè*, coffee] an alkaloid present in coffee, tea, and coca cola: it is a stimulant to the heart and central nervous system

caftan (kaf'tən) *n.* [Turk. *qaftān*] **1.** a long-sleeved robe worn in eastern Mediterranean countries **2.** a similar garment worn in western countries

cage (kāj) *n.* [< L. *cavea*, hollow place] **1.** a box or structure of wires, bars, etc. for confining birds or animals **2.** an openwork structure, as some lift compartments **3.** *Basketball* the basket —*vt.* **caged, cag'ing** to put or confine, as in a cage

cagey, cagy *adj.* **-gier, -giest** [< ?] [Colloq.] wary; careful not to get caught or fooled —**ca'gily** *adv.*

cagoule (kə gōōl′) *n.* [Fr., monk's hood] a form of very light anorak that packs away into a small space

cahoots (kə hōōts′) *n.pl.* [< ?] [Colloq.] partnership; league : implying scheming in the phrase **in cahoots**

caiman (kā′mən) *n., pl.* **-mans** same as CAYMAN

Cain (kān) *n.* [see Gen. 4] any murderer —**raise Cain** [Colloq.] to cause a great commotion or much trouble

Cainozoic (kī′nō zō′ik) *adj.* [< Gr. *kainos,* recent + *zōē,* life] designating or of the geologic era following the Mesozoic and including the present

cairn (kāərn) *n.* [< Gael. *carn*] a conical heap of stones built as a monument or landmark —**cairned** *adj.*

cairngorm (kāərn′gôrm) *n.* [< *Cairngorms,* mountain range in NE Scotland] a yellow or brown variety of quartz, used as a gem

cairn terrier [said to be so named from its burrowing in cairns] a small, shaggy Scottish terrier

caisson (kə sōōn′, kā′son) *n.* [Fr. < L. *capsa,* box] **1.** a chest or wagon for transporting ammunition **2.** a watertight enclosure inside which men can do construction work under water **3.** a watertight box for raising sunken ships

cajole (kə jōl′) *vt., vi.* **-joled', -jol'ing** [< Fr.] to coax with flattery and insincere talk; wheedle —**cajol'ery** *n.*

cake (kāk) *n.* [< ON. *kaka*] **1.** a mixture of flour, eggs, milk, sugar, etc. baked and often covered with icing **2.** a shaped portion of a food mixture *[an oatcake]* **3.** a shaped, solid mass, as of soap **4.** a hard crust or deposit —*vt., vi.* **caked, cak′ing** to form into a hard crust —**have one's cake and eat it** to benefit from opposing courses of action —**piece of cake** (something) very easy to accomplish —**take the cake** [Colloq.] to win the prize : ironic usage —**cak′y** *adj.*

cakewalk *n.* **1.** formerly, a competition among Negroes, judged on the elegance of a promenade to music **2.** anything very easily accomplished

Cal. large calorie(s)

cal. **1.** calendar **2.** calibre **3.** small calorie(s)

calabash (kal′ə bash′) *n.* [< Fr. < Sp. < ?] **1.** a tropical American tree or its gourdlike fruit **2.** *a)* a tropical plant, or its bottle-shaped gourd *b)* a large smoking pipe made from this gourd **3.** the dried, hollow shell of a calabash, used as a bowl, cup, etc.

calamary (kal′ə mər ē) *n., pl.* **-maries** [< L. *calamus,* reed, pen] a squid : so called from its pen-shaped skeleton

calamine (kal′ə mīn′) *n.* [< L. *cadmia :* see CADMIUM] a pink powder consisting of zinc oxide mixed with ferric oxide, used in skin lotions and ointments

calamitous (kə lam′ə təs) *adj.* bringing or causing calamity —**calam′itously** *adv.* —**calam′itousness** *n.*

calamity *n., pl.* **-ties** [< L. *calamitas*] **1.** deep trouble or misery **2.** any extreme misfortune

calandria (kə lan′drē ə) *n.* [< Sp. *calandria,* lark] a sealed vessel used as a heat-exchanger in the core of certain nuclear reactors

calcareous (kal kāər′ē əs) *adj.* [< L. *calx,* lime] of, like, or containing calcium carbonate, calcium, or lime

calceolaria (kal′sē ə lāər′ē ə) *n.* [< L. *calceus,* shoe] a plant with a slipper-shaped flower

calces (kal′sēz) *n.* *alt. pl.* of CALX

calciferol (kal sif′ə rol′) *n.* [CALCIF-(EROUS) + *ergosterol*] vitamin D₂ : it is a crystalline alcohol

calciferous *adj.* [< L. *calx,* lime + -FEROUS] producing or containing calcite

calcify (kal′sə fī′) *vt., vi.* **-fied′, -fy′ing** [< L. *calx,* lime] to change into a hard, stony substance by the deposit of lime or calcium salts —**cal′cifica′tion** *n.*

calcine (kal′sīn) *vt., vi.* **-cined, -cining** [< ML. *calcinare*] **1.** to change to calx or powder by heat **2.** to burn to ashes or powder —**calcination** (kal′sə nā′shən) *n.*

calcite (kal′sīt) *n.* crystalline calcium carbonate

calcium (kal′sē əm) *n.* [< L. *calx,* lime] a soft, silver-white, metallic chemical element found in limestone, marble, chalk, etc. : symbol, Ca

calcium carbonate a white powder or crystalline compound, found in limestone, marble, etc.

calcium hydroxide slaked lime, a white, crystalline compound, used in making alkalis, bleaching powder, etc.

calcspar (kalk′spär′) *n.* same as CALCITE

calculable (kal′kyōō lə b′l) *adj.* that can be calculated

calculate (kal′kyōō lāt′) *vt.* **-lat′ed, -lat′-ing** [< L. *calculare,* reckon] **1.** to determine by using mathematics; compute **2.** to determine by reasoning **3.** to plan **4.** [U.S. Colloq.] to suppose —*vi.* **1.** to make a computation **2.** to rely or count (*on*)

calculated *adj.* **1.** undertaken after the probable results have been estimated **2.** deliberately planned **3.** apt or likely —**cal′-culat′edly** *adv.*

calculating *adj.* shrewd or scheming

calculation (kal′kyōō lā′shən) *n.* **1.** a calculating **2.** something deduced by calculating estimate; plan **3.** careful planning or forethought, esp. with selfish motives

calculator (kal′kyōō lāt′ər) *n.* a device, now usually electronic, for doing rapid mathematical calculations

calculus (kal′kyōō ləs) *n., pl.* **-li′** (-lī′) **-luses** [see CALCULATE] **1.** a method of mathematical analysis using the combined methods of DIFFERENTIAL CALCULUS and INTEGRAL CALCULUS **2.** any abnormal stony deposit formed in the body

caldron (kôl′drən) *n. same as* CAULDRON

calèche (ka lesh′) *n.* [Fr.] [Canad.] a horse-drawn carriage used for taking tourists around in cities such as Montreal and Quebec

Caledonian (kal′ə dō′nē ən) *adj.* Scottish; of or designating the Scottish Highlands —*n.* a Scot

calendar (kal′ən dər) *n.* [< L. *kalendae*, CALENDS] 1. a system of determining the beginning, length, and divisions of a year 2. a chart that shows such an arrangement, usually for a single year 3. a list or schedule, as of pending court cases —*vt.* to enter in a calendar; schedule

calender (kal′ən dər) *n.* [< L. *cylindrus*, cylinder] a machine with rollers between which paper, cloth, etc. is run, to give it a smooth or glossy finish —*vt.* to process (paper, etc.) in a calender —**cal′enderer** *n.*

calends (kal′indz) *n.pl.* [often with sing. *v.*] [< L. *kalendae*] the first day of each month in the ancient Roman calendar : also **kalends**

calendula (kə len′dyoo lə) *n.* [ModL.] a plant of the composite family, with yellow or orange flowers

calf[1] (käf) *n., pl.* **calves** [< OE. *cealf* & ON. *kalfr*] 1. a young cow or bull 2. the young of some other large animals, as the elephant, whale, etc. 3. leather from the hide of a calf; calfskin —**kill the fatted calf** to make a feast of welcome : Luke 15 :23

calf[2] *n., pl.* **calves** [ON. *kalfi*] the fleshy back part of the leg below the knee

calf love the love of an adolescent for a member of the opposite sex

calf's-foot jelly an edible gelatin made by boiling calves' feet

calfskin *n.* 1. the skin of a calf 2. a soft, flexible leather made from this

calibrate (kal′ə brāt′) *vt.* -brat′ed, -brat′-ing [see ff.] 1. to determine the calibre of 2. to fix or correct the scale of (a measuring instrument) —**cal′ibra′tion** *n.* —**cal′ibra′tor** *n.*

calibre (kal′ə bər) *n.* [< Fr. & Sp. < Ar. *qālib*, mould] 1. the size of a bullet or shell as measured by its diameter 2. the diameter of the bore of a gun 3. the diameter of a cylindrical body 4. quality or ability

calices (kāl′ə sēz) *n. pl.* of CALIX

calico (kal′ə kō′) *n., pl.* -coes′, -cos′[< Calicut (now Kozhikode) in India] 1. a plain, white or unbleached cotton fabric 2. [U.S.] a coarse, printed cotton fabric —*adj.* 1. of calico 2. [U.S.] spotted like calico

californium (kal′ə fôr′nē əm) *n.* [< University of *California*] a radioactive chemical element: symbol, Cf

caliper (kal′ə pər) *n. same as* CALLIPER

caliph (kal′if) *n.* [< Ar. *khalifa*] supreme ruler: the title taken by Mohammed's successors as heads of Islam: also **calif, khalif**

caliphate (kal′ə fāt) *n.* the rank or reign of a caliph

calisthenics (kal′əs then′iks) *n.pl. same as* CALLISTHENICS —**cal′isthen′ic, cal′isthen′ical** *adj.*

calix (kā′liks) *n., pl.* **calices** (kāl′ə sēz′) [L.] a cup

calk[1] (kôk) *vt. same as* CAULK —**calk′er** *n.*

calk[2] *n.* [< L. *calx*, heel] the part of a horseshoe that projects downwards to prevent slipping —*vt.* to fasten calks on

call (kôl) *vt.* [< OE. *ceallian* & (or <) ON. *kalla*] 1. to say in a loud tone; shout 2. to summon 3. to convoke [to *call* a meeting] 4. to give or apply a name to 5. to declare to be as specified [I *call* it silly] 6. to awaken 7. to communicate with by telephone 8. to give orders for [to *call* a strike] 9. to utter directions for (a square dance) 10. *Bridge* to name (a suit) —*vi.* 1. to speak in a loud tone; shout 2. to utter its characteristic cry, as a bird 3. to visit for a short while 4. to telephone —*n.* 1. a loud utterance; shout 2. the distinctive cry of an animal or bird 3. a summons 4. an economic demand, as for a product 5. an inner urging towards a certain action or profession 6. power to attract [the *call* of the wild] 7. need; occasion [no *call* for tears] 8. a brief visit 9. *Bridge* a bid or right to bid —**call back** 1. to ask to come back 2. to telephone again or in return —**call for** 1. to demand 2. to come and get 3. to need [this *calls for* action] —**call in** 1. to summon for help or consultation 2. to take out of circulation, as coin 3. to demand payment of (a loan, etc.) 4. [Colloq.] to pay a short visit : also **call in on** —**call in question** to raise doubts about —**call off** 1. to order away 2. to cancel (a scheduled event) —**call on** 1. to visit briefly 2. to ask (a person) to speak —**call out** 1. to shout 2. to summon into action 3. to challenge, as to a duel —**call round** to visit informally —**call up** 1. to make one remember 2. to summon, esp. for military duty 3. to telephone —**call (up)on** 1. to summon 2. to invite (a person) to speak, perform a service, etc. —**on call** 1. available when summoned 2. payable on demand —**within call** in hearing distance

call-box *n.* a soundproof kiosk containing a public telephone

caller *n.* 1. a person or thing that calls, esp. for a square dance 2. a person who makes a short visit

call girl a prostitute with whom appointments are made by telephone

calligraphy (kə lig′rə fē) *n.* [< Gr. *kallos*, beauty + *graphein*, write] 1. beautiful handwriting 2. handwriting —**callig′rapher, callig′raphist** *n.*

calling (kôl′iŋ) *n.* 1. one's profession or trade 2. an inner urging towards some profession; vocation

calliper (kal′ə pər) *n.* [< CALIBRE] 1. [usually pl.] an instrument consisting of a pair of hinged legs, used to measure the diameter of something 2. a splint of metal used to support the leg

calliper rule a graduated rule with one sliding jaw and one that is stationary

callisthenics (kal′əs then′iks) *n.pl.* [< Gr. *kallos*, beauty + *sthenos*, strength] exercises to develop a strong, trim body —**cal′listhen′ic, cal′listhen′ical** *adj.*

callosity (ka los′ə tē) *n.* pl. **-ties** a hardened, thickened place on skin or bark; callus

callous (kal′əs) *adj.* [< L. *callum*, hard skin] 1. unfeeling; insensitive 2. *a)* having calluses *b)* hardened (of skin) —*vt., vi.* to make or become callous —**cal′lousness** *n.*

callow (kal′ō) *adj.* [< OE. *calu*, bald] 1. young and inexperienced; immature 2. [Rare] still lacking the feathers needed for flying —**cal′lowness** *n.*

callus (kal′əs) *n.,* pl. **-luses** [L., var. of *callum*, hard skin] 1. a hardened, thickened place on the skin 2. the hard substance that forms initially at the break in a fractured bone so as to reunite the parts

calm (käm) *n.* [< Gr. *kauma*, heat] 1. lack of wind or motion; stillness 2. lack of excitement; serenity —*adj.* 1. still; quiet 2. not excited; tranquil —*vt., vi.* to make or become calm (often with *down*) —**calm′ative** *adj.* —**calm′ly** *adv.* —**calm′ness** *n.*

calomel (kal′ə mel′) *n.* [< Gr. *kalos*, beautiful + *melas*, black] a white, tasteless powder, formerly used as a cathartic, etc.

calor gas (kal′ər) *Trademark* butane gas liquefied under pressure in containers for cooking, heating, etc.

caloric (kə lor′ik) *adj.* [< L. *calor*, heat] 1. of heat 2. of calories —**calor′ically** *adv.*

calorie (kal′ə rē) *n.* [< L. *calor*, heat] 1. the amount of heat needed to raise the temperature of one gram of water by one degree Celsius: also **small calorie** 2. [C-] the amount of heat needed to raise the temperature of one kilogram of water by one degree Celsius: also **large calorie** 3. a unit equal to the large calorie, used for measuring energy produced by food Also sp. **cal′ory**

calorific (kal′ə rif′ik) *adj.* producing or relating to heat

calorimeter (kal′ə rim′ə tər) *n.* [< L. *calor*, heat + -METER] an apparatus for measuring amounts of heat

calque (kalk) *n.* [< L. *calcare*, tread] *Linguis.* a borrowing by which a specialized meaning of a word or phrase in one language is transferred to another language by a literal translation (Ex: *masterpiece* from German *Meisterstück*)

calumet (kal′yoo met′) *n.* [Fr., < L. *calamus*, reed] a long-stemmed ceremonial pipe, smoked by N. American Indians as a token of peace

calumniate (kə lum′nē āt′) *vt., vi.* **-at′ed, -at′ing** [*see* CALUMNY] to spread false and harmful statements about; slander —**calum′nia′tion** *n.* —**calum′nia′tor** *n.*

calumnious *adj.* full of calumnies; slanderous

calumny (kal′əm nē) *n.,* pl. **-nies** [< L. *calumnia*, slander] a false and malicious statement; slander

Calvary (kal′vər ē) [< L. *calvaria*, skull] the place near Jerusalem where the crucifixion of Jesus took place

calve (käv) *vi., vt.* **calved, calv′ing** [< OE. *cealfian*] to give birth to (a calf)

calves (kävz) *n.* pl. of CALF

Calvinism (kal′vin iz′m) *n.* the theological system of Calvin and his followers, which emphasizes the doctrines of predestination and salvation solely by God's grace —**Cal′vinist** *n., adj.* —**Cal′vinis′tic, Cal′vinis′tical** *adj.*

calx (kalks) *n.,* pl. **calx′es, calces** (kal′-sēz) [L., lime] the ashy powder left after a metal or mineral has been calcined

calypso (kə lip′sō) *n.* [< ?] 1. a W Indian style of singing, with improvised, often satirical words, and syncopated rhythm 2. a song or dance in calypso style

calyx (kā′liks) *n.,* pl. **ca′lyxes, calyces** (kā′lə sēz′) [L., pod] the outer whorl of protective leaves, or sepals, of a flower, usually green

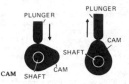

cam (kam) *n.* [Du. *cam*, orig., comb] a wheel, projection on a wheel, etc. which gives an eccentric or reciprocating motion to another wheel, a shaft, etc., or receives such motion from it

camaraderie (kam′ə räd′ər ē) *n.* [Fr.] loyalty and friendly feeling; comradeship

camber (kam′bər) *n.* [< L. *camur*, arched] a slight convex curve of a surface, as of a road, a beam, aerofoil, etc. —*vt., vi.* to arch slightly

Cambrian (kam′brē ən) *adj.* designating or of the first geological period in the Paleozoic Era

cambric (kām′brik) *n.* [< *Cambrai*, N France] 1. a fine, thin linen 2. a cotton cloth like this

Cambs. Cambridgeshire

came (kām) *pt.* of COME

camel (kam′′l) *n.* [< Heb. *gāmāl*] either of two species of large, domesticated mammals with a humped back and long neck: capable of storing water in its body, the camel is the common beast of burden in Asian and African deserts: see BACTRIAN CAMEL and DROMEDARY

cameleer (kam′ə lēər′) *n.* a camel driver

camellia (kə mēl′yə) *n.* [< G. J. *Kamel*] any of a genus of Asian evergreen shrubs with glossy leaves and waxy, roselike flowers

camelopard (kam′ə lə pärd′) *n.* [< Gr. *kamēlos*, camel + *pardalis*, leopard: from its neck and spots] early name for the GIRAFFE

camel's hair 1. the hair of the camel

2. cloth made of this hair, sometimes mixed with wool, etc. —**cam'el's-hair'**, **cam'-el-hair'** *adj.*

camel's-hair brush an artist's small brush, made of hair from a squirrel's tail

Camembert (cheese) (kam'əm bãər') [from *Camembert*, in Normandy] a soft, creamy, rich French cheese

cameo (kam'ē ō') *n., pl.* **-os'** [< ML. *camaeus*] **1.** a carving in relief on certain gems or shells so that the raised design is in a different colour from its background **2.** a gem, shell, etc. so carved **3.** *a)* a small but creative part in a film or play *b)* a fine piece of descriptive writing

camera (kam'ər ə) *n.* [L., vault] **1.** a device for taking photographs, consisting of a closed box containing a sensitized plate or film on which an image is formed when light enters through a lens **2.** *TV* that part of the transmitter containing a plate on which the image to be televised is projected for transformation into electrical signals —**in camera** in privacy or secrecy

camiknickers (kam'ē nik'ərz) *n.pl.* [CAMI(SOLE) + KNICKERS] a one-piece undergarment for women, consisting of knickers attached to a camisole top

camisole (kam'ə sōl') *n.* [see CHEMISE] *Hist.* a woman's underbodice, orig. a corset cover

camomile (kam'ō mīl') *n.* [< Gr. *chamai*, on the ground + *mēlon*, apple] any of several plants with strong-smelling foliage; esp., a plant whose dried, daisylike flower heads have been used in a medicinal tea

camouflage (kam'ə fläzh') *n.* [Fr. < *camoufler*, to disguise] **1.** the disguising of ships, guns, etc. to conceal them from the enemy, as by the use of paint, leaves, etc. in patterns merging with the background **2.** a disguise of this kind **3.** any device or action used to conceal or mislead —*vt., vi.* **-flaged'**, **-flag'ing** to disguise or conceal by camouflage —**cam'-ouflag'er** *n.*

camp¹ (kamp) *n.* [< L. *campus*, field] **1.** a place where tents, huts, etc. are put up, as for soldiers **2.** any temporary lodging composed of tents, huts, etc. [a holiday *camp*, mining *camp*] **3.** a group of people who support a common cause **4.** [S Afr.] a field or pasture —*vi.* **1.** to set up a camp **2.** to live in a camp (often with *out*) —**break camp** to pack up camping equipment and go away —**camp'er** *n.*

camp² *adj.* [< ?] **1.** affectedly theatrical **2.** effeminate; homosexual —*n.* camp behaviour —*vi.* **1.** to act in a bizarre manner **2.** to parade one's homosexuality

campaign (kam pān') *n.* [< Fr. < L. *campus*, field] **1.** a series of organized, planned actions for a particular purpose **2.** a series of military operations with a particular objective in a war —*vi.* to participate in, or go on, a campaign —**cam-paign'er** *n.*

campanile (kam'pə nē'lē) *n., pl.* **-les, -li** (-lē) [It. < L. *campana*, bell] a bell tower, esp. one that stands apart from another building

campanology (kam'pə nol'ə jē) *n.* [< L. *campana*, bell + -LOGY] **1.** the study of bells **2.** the art of bellringing —**cam'pa-nol'ogist** *n.*

campanula (kam pan'yōō lə) *n.* [< L. *campana*, bell] a plant with bell-shaped flowers

camp bed a portable, folding bed used in camping, etc.

camp chair a lightweight folding chair

camp follower **1.** a civilian who goes along with an army **2.** a non-member associated with a certain group

camphor (kam'fər) *n.* [< Sans *karpurah*, camphor tree] a crystalline substance, with a strong odour, derived from the wood of an Asian laurel (**camphor tree**): used as a moth repellent, in medicine, etc. —**camphor'ic** (-fôr'ik) *adj.*

camphorate (kam'fə rāt') *vt.* **-at'ed, -at'-ing** to put camphor in or on [*camphorated* oil]

campion (kam'pē ən) *n.* [< ?] any of various flowering plants of the pink family, with white or pink flowers

campsite (kamp'sīt') *n.* **1.** an area set aside for camping, often equipped with water, toilets, picnic stoves, etc. **2.** any site for a temporary camp

campstool *n.* a light folding stool

campus (kam'pəs) *n., pl.* **-puses** [L., field] the grounds, sometimes including the buildings, of a college or university —*adj.* **1.** on or of the campus **2.** of a college or university [*campus* politics]

camshaft (kam'shäft') *n.* a shaft to which a cam is fastened

can¹ (kan; *as an auxiliary, usually* kən, k'n) *vi. pt.* **could** [< OE. *cunnan*, know] **1.** to know how to **2.** to be able to **3.** to be likely to [*can* it be true?] **4.** to have the right to **5.** [Colloq.] to be permitted to —**can but** can only

can² *n.* [< OE. *canne*, cup] **1.** a container of various kinds, usually made of metal with a separate cover **2.** *same as* TIN **3.** [Chiefly U.S. Slang] *a)* a prison *b)* a toilet —*vt.* **canned, can'ning 1.** to put in airtight cans for preservation **2.** [Slang] to make a recording of —**carry the can** to take the responsibility (*for*) —**can'ner** *n.*

Can. **1.** Canada **2.** Canadian **3.** Canon

Canaan (kā'nən) Promised Land of the Israelites, between the Jordan & the Mediterranean —**Ca'naanite'** *n.*

Canad. Canadian

Canada balsam (kan'ə də) a thick, yellow, resinous fluid from the balsam fir

Canada Council an agency set up by the Canadian government in 1957 to promote the arts and social sciences

Canada Day July 1st, the anniversary of the day in 1867 when Canada became the first British colony to receive dominion status: in Canada, a public holiday

Canada goose a large wild goose of Canada and the northern U.S., grey, with black head and neck

Canada jay a grey, crestless jay, notorious in northern parts of N America for its stealing: also called **camp robber, whiskey jack**

Canadian (kə nā′dē ən) *adj.* of Canada or its people —*n.* a native or inhabitant of Canada

Canadiana (kə nā′dē ä′nə; *in Canad.,* -an′ə) *n.pl.* objects, such as books, furniture, and antiques, relating to Canadian history and culture

Canadianism (kə nād′ē ə niz′m) *n.* 1. the Canadian national character 2. loyalty to Canada, its culture, etc. 3. a Canadian idiom, pronunciation, custom, etc.

Canadianize *vt., vi.* to make or become Canadian by changing customs, ownership, character, content, etc. *[the American textbook was Canadianized before being adopted for use in Canadian schools]*

Canadian Shield a wide area of Precambrian rock, covering most of E and C Canada, and rich in minerals

Canadien (kan′ə dyö′, -dē en′) *n.* a French Canadian —**Canadienne**′ (-dyen′, -dē en′) *fem.*

canaille (kə nī′) *n.* [Fr. < L. *canis*, dog] the mob; rabble

canal (kə nal′) *n.* [< L. *canalis*, channel] 1. an artificial waterway for transportation or irrigation 2. *Anat.* a tubular passage or duct —*vt.* **-nalled**′, **-nal**′**ling** to build a canal through or across

canalize (kan′ə līz′) *vt.* **-ized**′, **-iz**′**ing** 1. to make a canal through 2. to provide an outlet for, esp. by directing into a specific channel —**ca**′**naliza**′**tion** *n.*

canapé (kan′ə pā′) *n.* [Fr.] a small piece of toast, etc. spread with fish, cheese, etc., and served as an appetizer

canard (kə närd′) *n.* [Fr., a duck, hoax] a false, malicious report, as fabricated by a newspaper

canary (kə näər′ē) *n., pl.* **-nar**′**ies** [< *Canary Islands*] 1. a small, yellow songbird of the finch family 2. a light yellow: also **canary yellow** 3. a sweet wine like madeira

canasta (kə nas′tə) *n.* [Sp., basket] a card game for two to six players played with two packs

canc. 1. cancel 2. cancelled 3. cancellation

cancan (kan′kan′) *n.* [Fr.] a lively dance with much high kicking performed by female entertainers

cancel (kan′s′l) *vt.* **-celled**, **-celling** [< L. *cancellare*, draw lines across < *cancer*, lattice] 1. to call off (a meeting, etc.) 2. to cross out with lines or mark over, as in deleting written matter or marking a cheque, etc. as used 3. to annul 4. to abolish; withdraw 5. to neutralize; offset (often with *out*) 6. *Math.* to remove (a common factor from both terms of a fraction, equivalents on opposite sides of an equation, etc.) —*vi.* to offset each other (with *out*) —**can**′**celler** *n.*

cancellation (kan′sə lā′shən) *n.* 1. the act of cancelling 2. something cancelled 3. the mark showing that something is cancelled

cancer (kan′sər) [< L., crab] 1. [C-]

a N constellation 2. [C-] the fourth sign of the zodiac —*n.* 1. a malignant tumour in the body 2. anything harmful that spreads and destroys —**can**′**cerous, can**′**croid** *adj.*

candela (kan dē′lə) *n.* [L., candle] the S1 unit of luminous intensity

candelabrum (kan′də lä′brəm) *n., pl.* **-bra, -brums** [L.: see CHANDELIER] a large branched candlestick: also **can**′**dela**′**bra,** *pl.* **-bras**

candid (kan′did) *adj.* [L. *candidus*, white, sincere] 1. very honest or frank in speech or writing 2. free from bias; fair; impartial —**can**′**didly** *adv.* —**can**′**didness** *n.*

candidacy (kan′di də sē) *n., pl.* **-cies** the fact or state of being a candidate: also **can**′**didature**

candidate (kan′di dət) *n.* [L. *candidatus*, white-robed] 1. a person who seeks, or has been proposed for, an office, an award, etc. 2. a person entered for an examination 3. a person or thing apparently designed for a certain end *[a candidate for fame]*

candid camera a camera, usually small, with a fast lens, used to take informal, unposed pictures

candied (kan′did) *adj.* 1. cooked in sugar or syrup to preserve, glaze, or encrust 2. crystallized into sugar

candle (kan′d′l) *n.* [< L. *candela*] 1. a cylinder of tallow or wax with a wick through its centre, which gives light when burned 2. anything like this in form or use —**burn the candle at both ends** to work or play too much so that one's energy is dissipated —**not hold a candle to** to be not nearly so good as —**not worth the candle** not worth doing —**can**′**dler** *n.*

candlelight *n.* subdued light given as by candles

Candlemas (kan′d′l məs) *n.* [< OE.: see CANDLE & MASS] 1. a church feast, Feb. 2, commemorating the purification of the Virgin Mary: candles for sacred uses are blessed then: also **Candlemas Day** 2. a Scottish Quarter Day

candlepower *n.* the luminous intensity of a light source, now expressed in candelas

candlestick *n.* a holder for a candle or candles

candlewick *n.* a thick, soft cotton yarn —*adj.* designating or of a muslin fabric, bedspread, etc. patterned with tufts of soft cotton yarn

candour (kan′dər) *n.* [< L. *candor*, whiteness] 1. the quality of being fair and unprejudiced 2. honesty in expressing oneself

candy (kan′dē) *n., pl.* **-dies** [< Per. *qand*, cane sugar] 1. crystallized sugar made by evaporating boiled cane sugar, syrup, etc. 2. [Chiefly U.S.] a sweet —*vt.* **-died, -dying** 1. to cook in or with sugar or syrup, esp. to preserve —*vi.* to become candied

candy-floss *n.* a light, fluffy confection consisting of fibres of melted sugar spun around a stick

cane (kān) *n.* [< Gr. *kanna*] 1. the slender, jointed stem of certain plants, as bamboo 2. any plant with such a stem, as sugar

cane 3. the woody stem of a fruiting plant 4. a stick used for flogging 5. a walking stick 6. split rattan, used in weaving chair seats, etc. —*vt.* **caned, can'-ing** 1. to flog with a cane 2. to make or furnish (chairs, etc.) with cane —**can'-er** *n.*

cane sugar sugar (*sucrose*) from sugar cane

canine (kā'nīn) *adj.* [< L. *canis,* dog] 1. of or like a dog 2. of the family of animals that includes dogs, wolves, jackals, and foxes —*n.* 1. a dog or other canine animal 2. a sharp-pointed tooth on either side of the upper jaw and lower jaw: in full, **canine tooth**

canister (kan'is tər) *n.* [< L. *canistrum,* wicker basket] a small box for coffee, tea, etc.

canker (kaŋ'kər) *n.* [< L. *cancer*: see CANCER] 1. an ulcerlike sore that spreads 2. anything that corrupts —*vt.* 1. to infect with canker 2. to debase —*vi.* to become cankered —**can'kerous** *adj.*

cankerworm *n.* any of several moth larvae harmful to fruit trees

cannabis (kan'ə bis) *n.* [L., hemp] 1. hemp 2. the female flowering tops of the hemp

canned (kand) *adj.* 1. preserved in cans 2. [Slang] recorded for reproduction, as on radio [*canned* commercials] 3. [Slang] intoxicated

cannel (coal) (kan''l) [< ? *candle coal*] a variety of bituminous coal that burns with a bright flame

cannelloni (kan'ə lō'nē) *n.* [It.] tubular casings of pasta filled with minced meat, served in a tomato sauce

cannery (kan'ər ē) *n., pl.* **-neries** a factory where foods are canned

cannibal (kan'ə b'l) *n.* [Sp. *canibal,* prob. < Carib] a person or animal that eats its own kind —*adj.* of or like a cannibal —**can'nibalism** *n.* —**can'nibalis'tic** *adj.*

cannibalize *vt., vi.* **-ized', -iz'ing** to strip (old or worn equipment) of parts for use in other units —**can'nibaliza'tion** *n.*

canning (kan'iŋ) *n.* the act, process, or work of putting food in cans for preservation

cannon (kan'ən) *n.* [< L. *canna,* cane] 1. a large, mounted piece of artillery 2. an automatic gun mounted on an aircraft 3. Billiards a shot in which the cue ball strikes both object balls —*vt.* to cannonade —*vi.* 1. to cannonade 2. to collide (with *into*)

cannonade (kan'ə nād') *n.* a continuous firing of artillery —*vi., vt.* **-ad'ed, -ad'-ing** to fire artillery (at)

cannonball (kan'ən bôl') *n.* a heavy ball, esp. of iron, formerly used as a projectile in cannon: also **cannon ball**

cannon bone the bone between hock or knee and fetlock in a four-legged, hoofed animal

cannon fodder soldiers, sailors, etc. thought of as being expended (i.e., killed or maimed) or expendable in war

cannot (kan'ot) can not

canny (kan'ē) *adj.* **can'nier, can'niest** [< CAN¹] 1. careful and shrewd 2. wise and well-informed 3. thrifty —**can'nily** *adv.* —**can'niness** *n.*

canoe (kə nōō') *n.* [< Sp. < Carib] a narrow, light boat moved by paddles —*vi.* **-noed', -noe'ing** to go in a canoe —*vt.* to transport by canoe —**canoe'ist** *n.*

canon¹ (kan'ən) *n.* [< L., a rule] 1. a law or body of laws of a church 2. an established rule or criterion [*the canons* of good taste] 3. *a*) a list of sacred books officially accepted as genuine *b*) a list of the genuine works of an author 4. *a*) [*often* C-] *Eccles.* the fundamental part of the Mass, between the Preface and the Communion *b*) a list of recognized saints 5. *Music* a polyphonic composition in which a melody is repeated at intervals

canon² *n.* [< LL. *canonicus,* one living by the canon: see prec.] a clergyman serving in a cathedral

canonical (kə non'i k'l) *adj.* 1. of, according to, or ordered by church canon 2. authoritative; accepted 3. belonging to a scriptural canon 4. of a canon (clergyman)

canonical hour any of the seven periods of the day assigned to prayer and worship

canonicals *n.pl.* the clothes prescribed by canon for a clergyman when conducting services

canonist (kan'ən ist) *n.* an expert in canon law

canonize *vt.* **-ized', -iz'ing** 1. to declare (a dead person) a saint in formal church procedure 2. to glorify 3. to put into a scriptural canon 4. to give church sanction to —**can'oniza'tion** *n.*

canon law the laws governing the ecclesiastical affairs of a Christian church

canoodle (kə nōō'd'l) *vi.* **-dled, -dling** [< ?] to caress or cuddle (*with*)

canopy (kan'ə pē) *n., pl.* **-pies** [< Gr. *kōnōpeion,* bed with mosquito nets < *kōnōps,* gnat] 1. a covering fastened above a bed, throne, etc. or held over a person 2. anything that covers like a canopy, as the sky 3. the transparent hood over an aeroplane cockpit 4. the part of a parachute that opens up 5. a rooflike projection over a door, pulpit, etc. —*vt.* **-pied, -pying** to place or form a canopy over; cover; shelter

canst (kanst; *unstressed* kənst) *archaic* 2nd pers. *sing., pres. indic.,* of CAN¹: *used with* thou

cant¹ (kant) *n.* [< L. *cantus,* song] 1. insincere, trite talk, esp. when pious or moral 2. the special words used by those in a certain sect, occupation, etc.; jargon 3. the secret slang of beggars, thieves, etc.; argot —*vi.* to use cant —*adj.* of, or having the nature of, cant

cant² *n.* [< L. *cant(h)us,* tyre of a wheel] 1. a slanting surface 2. a sudden movement that causes tilting or overturning 3. the tilt thus caused 4. a corner or outside angle —*vt., vi.* to tilt or slant

can't (känt) cannot

Cantab. Cantabrigian

cantabile (kan tä′bi lē′) *adj., adv.* [< It.] *Music* in an easy, flowing manner

Cantabrigian (kan′tə brij′ē ən) *adj.* [< ML. *Cantabrigia*] of Cambridge or Cambridge University

cantaloupe, cantaloup (kan′tə lōop′) *n.* [< It. < *Cantalupo*, near Rome] a melon with a hard, ribbed rind and sweet, juicy, orange flesh

cantankerous (kan taŋ′kər əs) *adj.* [prob. < ME. *contakour*, troublemaker] bad-tempered; quarrelsome —**cantan′kerously** *adv.* —**cantan′kerousness** *n.*

cantata (kən tät′ə) *n.* [< It. *cantare*, sing] a musical composition with vocal solos, choruses, etc., telling a story that is sung but not acted

canteen (kan tēn′) *n.* [< It. *cantina*, wine cellar] 1. a place where refreshments can be obtained, as by employees 2. a shop providing luxuries, spirits, etc. to the personnel of a military camp 3. a box containing cutlery 4. a small flask for carrying drinking water

canter (kan′tər) *n.* [< *Canterbury gallop*, riding pace of the medieval Canterbury pilgrims] a smooth, easy pace like a moderate gallop —*vi., vt.* to ride or move at a canter

Canterbury bells (kan′tər bər ē) a cultivated bellflower with white, pink, or blue, cuplike flowers

cantharides (kan thar′ə dēz′) *n.pl.* [< Gr. *kantharis*, blistering beetle] a preparation of powdered, dried Spanish flies, formerly used in medicine

canticle (kan′ti k'l) *n.* [< L. *canticum*, song] 1. a song or chant 2. a non-metrical liturgical hymn

CANTILEVER

cantilever (kan′tə lē′vər) *n.* [? < CANT² + LEVER] 1. a bracket or block projecting from a wall to support a balcony, etc. 2. a projecting structure supported only at one end, which is anchored to a pier or wall —*vt.* to support by means of cantilevers —**can′tile′vered** *adj.*

cantilever bridge a bridge whose span is formed by two cantilevers projecting towards each other

canto (kan′tō) *n., pl.* -**tos** [It. < L. *cantus*, song] any of the chapterlike divisions of certain long poems

canton (kan′ton) *n.* [< LL. *cantus*, corner] any of the political divisions of a country or territory; specif., any of the states in the Swiss Republic —*vt.* to divide into cantons —**can′tonal** *adj.*

Cantonese (kan′tə nēz′) *adj.* of Canton, China, or its people —*n.* the Chinese dialect spoken in and around Canton

cantonment (kan tōōn′mənt) *n.* [see

CANTON] 1. the assigning of quarters to troops 2. a permanent military camp in British India

cantor (kan′tôr) *n.* [L., singer] 1. a church choir leader 2. a singer of liturgical solos in a synagogue, who leads the congregation in prayer —**canto′rial** *adj.*

Canuck (kə nuk′) *n., adj.* [< ?] [U.S. & Canad. Colloq.] Canadian

canvas (kan′vəs) *n.* [< L. *cannabis*, hemp] 1. a coarse cloth of hemp, cotton, etc., used for tents, sails, etc. 2. a sail or set of sails 3. *a*) a specially prepared piece of canvas for an oil painting *b*) such a painting 4. a tent or tents —**under canvas** 1. in tents 2. with sails unfurled

canvass (kan′vəs) *vt.* [< *canvas*: ? because used for sifting] to try to get votes, orders, etc. —*vt.* 1. to go through (places) or among (people) asking for (votes, orders, etc.) 2. to examine or discuss in detail —*n.* the act of canvassing, esp. to estimate the outcome of an election, sales campaign, etc. —**can′-vasser** *n.*

canyon (kan′yən) *n.* [Sp. *cañón*, canyon, tube] a long, narrow valley between high cliffs

caoutchouc (kou chōōk′) *n.* [Fr. < SAmInd] crude, natural rubber

cap (kap) *n.* [< LL. *cappa*, cloak] 1. any closefitting head covering, brimless or peaked 2. *a*) a head covering worn as a mark of occupation, rank, etc. [a nurse's *cap*] *b*) a mortarboard 3. a cover or top 4. *same as* PERCUSSION CAP 5. *Sport* a hat awarded to a player selected for his country or national team —*vt.* **capped, cap′ping** 1. to put a cap on 2. to present with a cap, as in sport 3. to cover the top or end of 4. to match, surpass, or top 5. to bring to a high point; climax —**cap in hand** in a humble manner —**cap it all** to give the finishing touch —**if the cap fits** [Colloq.] take it how you please: an expression used to a person who takes a general remark personally

cap. 1. capacity 2. *pl.* **caps.** capital 3. capitalize

capability (kā′pə bil′ə tē) *n., pl.* -**ties** 1. practical ability 2. [*pl.*] abilities, features, etc. not yet developed

capable (kā′pə b'l) *adj.* [< L. *capere*, take] having ability; able; skilled; competent —**capable of** 1. admitting of; open to 2. having the ability or qualities necessary for 3. able or ready to [*capable of* telling a lie] —**ca′pableness** *n.* —**ca′pably** *adv.*

capacious (kə pā′shəs) *adj.* [< L. *capere*, take] roomy; spacious —**capa′ciously** *adv.* —**capa′ciousness** *n.*

capacitance (kə pas′ə təns) *n.* *Elec.* the quantity of electric charge that can be stored in a capacitor, expressed in farads —**capac′itive** *adj.*

capacitor *n.* *Elec.* a device for storing an electric charge; condenser

capacity (kə pas′ə tē) *n., pl.* -**ties** [see CAPACIOUS] 1. the ability to contain, absorb, or receive 2. content or volume

3. mental ability **4.** maximum output [operating at *capacity*] **5.** position, function, etc. [acting in the *capacity* of adviser] **6.** *Law* legal authority

cap-a-pie, cap-à-pie (kap′ə pē′) *adv.* [< L. *caput*, head + *pes*, foot] from head to foot

caparison (kə par′ə s'n) *n.* [< Fr. < ff.] an ornamented covering for a horse; trappings —*vt.* to adorn, as with trappings or rich clothing

cape[1] (kāp) *n.* [< LL. *cappa*, cloak] a sleeveless garment fastened at the neck and hanging over the back and shoulders

cape[2] *n.* [< L. *caput*, head] **1.** a piece of land projecting into a body of water **2.** [C-] the SW region of the Cape Province of South Africa —**the Cape** the Cape of Good Hope

Cape Coloured [S Afr.] a coloured person

Cape doctor [S Afr. Colloq.] a strong SE wind in the area of Cape Town, esp. in summer, believed to blow ills out to sea

Cape Dutch 1. in South Africa, a distinctive style in furniture or buildings **2.** *obs. name for* AFRIKAANS

Cape gooseberry [S Afr.] the strawberry tomato, eaten raw or as jam

caper[1] (kā′pər) *vi.* [< CAPRIOLE] to skip about in a playful manner —*n.* **1.** a gay, playful jump or leap **2.** a wild, foolish action or prank —**cut a caper** (or **capers**) **1.** to caper **2.** to play tricks

caper[2] *n.* [< Gr. *kapparis*] a prickly, trailing Mediterranean bush whose green flower buds are pickled and used to flavour sauces, etc.

capercaillie (kap′ər kāl′yē) *n.* [< Gael. *capull*, horse + *coille*, forest] the largest species of European wood grouse: also **capercail′zie** (-yē, -zē)

Cape salmon [S Afr.] *same as* GEELBEK

Cape sparrow *n.* a very common S African bird: also called **mossie**

Capie (kā′pē) *n.* [S Afr. Slang] a Cape Coloured

capillarity (kap′ə lar′ə tē) *n.* **1.** capillary state **2.** the property of exerting or having capillary attraction **3.** *same as* CAPILLARY ATTRACTION

capillary (kə pil′ə rē) *adj.* [< L. *capillus*, hair] **1.** of or like a hair; very slender **2.** having a very small bore **3.** in or of capillaries —*n.*, *pl.* **-laries 1.** a tube with a very small bore: also **capillary tube 2.** any of the tiny blood vessels connecting the arteries with the veins

capillary attraction a phenomenon occurring in liquids which are in contact with solids, as in a capillary tube, causing the liquid surface to rise or be depressed: also **capillary action**

capital[1] (kap′ət'l) *n.* [< L. *caput*, head] **1.** a city that is the official seat of government of a state, nation, etc. **2.** money or property owned or used in business **3.** an accumulation of such wealth

4. wealth used to produce more wealth **5.** [*often* C-] capitalists collectively **6.** *same as* CAPITAL LETTER —*adj.* **1.** involving or punishable by death **2.** principal; chief **3.** being the seat of government **4.** of capital or wealth **5.** excellent —**make capital of** to make the most of; exploit

CAPITAL

capital[2] *n.* [< L. *caput*, head] the top part of a column or pilaster

capital gain profit from the sale of capital investments, as stock, property, etc.

capitalism *n.* **1.** the economic system in which the means of production and distribution are privately owned and operated for profit **2.** the principles, power, etc. of capitalists

capitalist *n.* **1.** an owner of wealth used in business **2.** an upholder of capitalism —*adj.* capitalistic

capitalistic (kap′ə tə lis′tik) *adj.* **1.** of capitalists or capitalism **2.** upholding or practising capitalism

capitalization (kap′ə tə lī zā′shən) *n.* **1.** the act of converting something into capital **2.** the total capital funds of a company, represented by stock, undivided profit, etc. **3.** the using of capital letters in writing and printing

capitalize (kap′ə tə līz′) *vt.* **-ized′**, **-iz′ing 1.** to use as or convert into capital **2.** to supply capital to or for (an enterprise) **3.** to write in capital letters **4.** to begin (a word) with a capital letter —**capitalize on (something)** to use (something) to one's own advantage

capital letter a large letter of a kind used to begin a sentence or proper name, as A, B, C

capital levy a tax on individual or corporate capital levied in addition to income tax

capitally *adv.* in an excellent manner; very well

capital punishment penalty of death for a crime

capital stock 1. the capital of a company, divided into shares **2.** the value of the issued shares

capital transfer tax a tax levied in many instances when capital is passed as a gift from one person to another

capitation (kap′ə tā′shən) *n.* [< L. *caput*, head] a tax or fee of so much per head

capitulate (kə pi′tyoo lāt′) *vi.* **-lat′ed**, **-lat′ing** [< LL. *capitulare*, draw up in heads or chapters] to give up (*to an* enemy) on prearranged conditions; surrender

capitulation (kə pi'tyŏŏ lā' shən) *n.* 1. a conditional surrender 2. a document containing terms of surrender, etc.; treaty

capo (kä'pō) *n., pl.* **-pos** [< It. *capotasto* < *capo*, chief + *tasto*, key] a device fastened over the fingerboard of an instrument to facilitate a change of key

capon (kā'pən) *n.* [< L. *capo*] a castrated cock fattened for eating —**ca'ponize' vt.**

caprice (kə prēs') *n.* [Fr. < It.] 1. a sudden, impulsive change in thought or action; whim 2. a capricious quality or nature

capricious (kə prish'əs) *adj.* subject to caprices; erratic

Capricorn (kap'rə kôrn') [< L. *caper*, goat + *cornu*, horn] 1. a S constellation 2. the tenth sign of the zodiac

caprine (ka'prēn) *adj.* [< L. *caper*, goat] of, like, or designating a goat

capriole (kap'rē ōl') *n.* [< L. *caper*, goat] 1. a caper; leap 2. an upward leap made by a horse without going forward —*vi.* **-oled', -ol'ing** to make a capriole

caps. capitals (capital letters)

capsicum (kap'sə kəm) *n.* [< L. *capsa*, box] any of various red peppers whose pungent, fleshy pods yield chili peppers, cayenne peppers, etc.

capsize (kap sīz') *vt., vi.* **-sized', -siz'ing** [? < Sp. *cabezar*, sink by the head] to overturn or upset: said esp. of a boat

capstan (kap'stən) *n.* [Fr. & Pr. *cabestan*] 1. an apparatus, mainly on ships, consisting of an upright cylinder around which cables or hawsers are wound for hoisting anchors, etc. 2. a rotating spindle on a tape-recorder that drives the tape past the head

capstone (kap'stōn') *n.* same as COPESTONE

capsule (kap'syŏŏl) *n.* [< L. *capsa*, chest] 1. a small gelatin container enclosing a dose of medicine 2. a detachable compartment to hold men, instruments, etc. in a space vehicle: in full, **space capsule** 3. *Anat.* a sac or membrane enclosing a part 4. *Bot.* a case, pod, or fruit containing seeds, spores, or carpels —*adj.* in a concise form —*vt.* **-suled, -suling** to condense —**cap'sular** *adj.*

capsulize *vt.* **-ized', -iz'ing** 1. to enclose in a capsule 2. to condense

Capt. Captain

captain (kap'tən) *n.* [< L. *caput*, head] 1. a chief or leader 2. *see* MILITARY RANKS, table 3. *a)* the commander or master of a ship *b)* the pilot of a commercial aircraft *c)* the leader of a team, as in sports —*vt.* to be captain or leader of —**cap'taincy** *n.*

caption (kap'shən) *n.* [< L. *capere*, take] a heading, as of a newspaper article, or a legend accompanying an illustration, a film, etc. —*vt.* to supply a caption for

captious *adj.* [see prec.] 1. made for the sake of argument or faultfinding;

sophistical 2. quick to find fault —**cap'tiously** *adv.* —**cap'tiousness** *n.*

captivate (kap'tə vāt') *vt.* **-vat'ed, -vat'ing** [< L. *captivus*, captive] to capture the attention or affection of; charm —**cap'tivat'ingly** *adv.* —**cap'tiva'tor** *n.*

captive (kap'tiv) *n.* [< L. *capere*, take] a person or animal caught and held, as a prisoner, or captivated, as by love —*adj.* 1. *a)* held prisoner *b)* forced to listen or act in a certain way [a *captive* audience] 2. restrained or limited [a *captive* balloon] 3. captivated

captivity (kap tiv'ə tē) *n., pl.* **-ties** imprisonment

captor (kap'tər) *n.* [L.] one who captures or holds captive

capture (kap'chər) *n.* [< L. *capere*, take] 1. a taking or being taken by force, surprise, or skill 2. that which is thus taken —*vt.* **-tured, -turing** 1. to take by force, surprise, or skill 2. to represent (something immaterial) in permanent form [to *capture* her charm on canvas]

Capuchin (kap'yŏŏ shin) *n.* [< Fr. < It. *cappuccio*, cowl] 1. a monk of a branch of the Franciscan order 2. [**c-**] a S American monkey with a hoodlike crown of hair

car (kär) *n.* [< L. *carrus*, chariot] 1. same as MOTOR CAR 2. orig., any vehicle on wheels 3. a name given to certain types of railway carriage [dining *car*] 4. [U.S.] *a)* any vehicle that moves on rails *b)* the cage of a lift 5. the part of a balloon or airship for carrying people

carabineer, carabinier (kar'ə bə nēar') *n.* [Fr. *carabinier*] a soldier armed with a carbine

caracal (kar'ə kal') *n.* [< Turk. *kara*, black + *kulak*, ear] a reddish-brown lynx of SW Asia and E Africa, with black-tipped ears

caracole (kar'ə kōl') *n.* [< Sp. *caracol*, shell of snail] a half turn to the right or left made by a horse with a rider —*vi.* **-coled', -col'ing** to make a caracole

carafe (kə raf') *n.* [prob. < Ar. *gharafa*, draw water] a bottle of glass or metal for water, coffee, etc.

caramel (kar'ə mel) *n.* [Fr.] 1. burnt sugar used to colour or flavour food 2. a toffee made from sugar, milk, etc.

caramelize (kar'ə mə līz') *vt., vi.* **-ized', -iz'ing** to turn into caramel

carapace (kar'ə pās') *n.* [Fr. < Sp. *carapacho*] an upper case or shell, as of the turtle

carat (kar'ət) *n.* [< Gr. *keration*] 1. a unit of weight for precious stones, equal to 200 milligrams 2. one 24th part (of pure gold) [14-*carat* gold is 14 parts pure gold and 10 parts alloy]

caravan (kar'ə van') *n.* [< Per. *kārwān*] 1. a closed vehicle designed to be pulled by a horse or motor vehicle and equipped as a place to live or work in 2. a company of merchants, pilgrims, etc. travelling together for safety, as through a desert —vi. -vanned', -van'ning to go on holiday in or with a caravan

caravanserai (kar'ə van'sə rē) *n.* [< Per. *kārwān*, caravan + *sarāī*, palace] in the Orient, a kind of inn with a central court, where caravans stop for the night

caravan site an area, usually with piped water, electricity, etc. designed to accommodate caravans

caravel (kar'ə vel') *n.* [< Gr. *karabos*] a fast, small sailing ship used in the 16th cent.

caraway (kar'ə wā') *n.* [< Ar. *karawiyā'*] a herb with spicy, strong-smelling seeds used to flavour bread, cakes, etc.

carbide (kär'bīd) *n.* [see CARBO-] a compound of an element, usually a metal, with carbon; esp., calcium carbide

carbine (kär'bīn) *n.* [< Fr.] a rifle with a short barrel

carbineer (kär'bə nēər') *n.* same as CARABINEER

carbo- a combining form meaning carbon

carbohydrate (kär'bō hī'drāt) *n.* [CARBO- + HYDRATE] any of a group of organic compounds, including the sugars and starches, composed of carbon, hydrogen, and oxygen

carbolated (kär'bō lāt'id) *adj.* containing or treated with carbolic acid

carbolic acid (kär bol'ik) same as PHENOL

carbon (kär'bən) *n.* [< L. *carbo*, charcoal] 1. a nonmetallic chemical element found in all organic compounds: diamond and graphite are pure carbon: symbol, C; radioactive isotope (**carbon 14**) is used in dating archaeological specimens 2. a sheet of carbon paper 3. a copy, as of a letter, made with carbon paper: in full, **carbon copy** 4. *Elec.* a stick of carbon used in an arc lamp —*adj.* of carbon

carbonaceous (kär'bə nā'shəs) *adj.* 1. of, consisting of, or containing carbon 2. resembling coal or carbon

carbonate (kär'bə nit; *also, and for v. always*, -nāt') *n.* a salt of carbonic acid —*vt.* -at'ed, -at'ing to charge with carbon dioxide —**car'bona'tion** *n.*

carbon black finely divided carbon produced by the incomplete burning of oil or gas, used esp. in rubber and ink

carbon dating the determination of the approximate age of (fossils, etc.) by measuring the carbon 14 content —**car'-bon-date'** *vt.*

carbon dioxide a colourless, odourless gas : it passes out of the lungs in respiration

carbonic (kär bon'ik) *adj.* of, containing, or obtained from carbon or carbon dioxide

carbonic acid a weak, colourless acid formed by the solution of carbon dioxide in water

carboniferous (kär'bə nif'ər əs) *adj.* [< CARBON + -FEROUS] 1. producing or containing carbon or coal 2. [C-] designating or of a great coal-making period

of the Paleozoic Era : the warm, damp climate produced great forests, which later formed rich coal seams —**the Carboniferous** 1. the Carboniferous Period 2. the rock and coal strata formed then

carbonize (kär'bə nīz') *vt.* -ized', -iz'ing 1. to change into carbon, as by partial burning 2. to treat or combine with carbon —**car'boniza'tion** *n.*

carbon monoxide a colourless, odourless, highly poisonous gas, CO, produced by the incomplete combustion of carbon

carbon paper thin paper coated on one side with a carbon preparation, and used to make copies of letters, etc.

carbon tetrachloride (tet'rə klôr'īd) a nonflammable, colourless liquid used in fire extinguishers, etc.

Carborundum (kär'bə run'dəm) [< CARB(ON) + (C)ORUNDUM] *Trademark* a very hard, abrasive substance, esp. silicon carbide, used in grindstones, abrasives, etc.

carboy (kär'boi) *n.* [< Per. *qarābah*] a large glass bottle enclosed in basketwork or in a wooden crate

carbuncle (kär'buŋ k'l) *n.* [< L. dim. of *carbo*, coal] 1. a smooth, convex-cut garnet 2. a painful, pus-bearing inflammation of the tissue beneath the skin, more severe than a boil —**carbun'cular** *adj.*

carburate (kär'byoo rāt') *vt.* [< *carburet*, carbide] 1. to combine with carbon 2. to mix (gas or air) with volatile carbon compounds —**car'bura'tion** *n.*

carburettor, carburetter (kär'-bə ret'ər, -byoo-) *n.* a device in which air is mixed with vaporized petrol to make an explosive mixture in an internal-combustion engine: U.S. sp. **carburetor**

carcase, carcass (kär'kəs) *n.* [< Fr. < ?] 1. the dead body of an animal 2. [Derog.] the human body, living or dead 3. the worthless remains of something 4. a framework or shell

carcinogen (kär sin'ə jən) *n.* [< ff. + -GEN] any substance that produces cancer —**car'cinogen'ic** *adj.*

carcinoma (kär'sə nō'mə) *n., pl.* -mas, -mata [< Gr. *karkinos*, crab] a cancerous growth —**car'cinom'atous** *adj.*

car coat a short overcoat, esp. for use on car journeys

card[1] (kärd) *n.* [< Gr. *chartēs*, leaf of paper] 1. a flat, stiff piece of thick paper or thin pasteboard; specif., *a*) one of a pack of playing cards *b*) a postcard *c*) a card bearing a message or greeting *d*) a card identifying a person as an agent, member, etc. *e*) any of a series of cards on which information is recorded [an index card] *f*) [*pl.*] [Colloq.] formerly, an employee's insurance card, tax form, etc., kept by his employer 2. a series of events making up a programme, as in horse-racing 3. [Colloq.] an eccentric or entertaining person —**card up one's sleeve** a plan or resource kept secret —**get one's cards** [Colloq.] to be dismissed from one's job

—in (or **on**) **the cards** likely **—play one's cards** (**well**) to act carefully or cleverly **—put** (or **lay**) **one's cards on the table** to reveal one's intentions

card² *n.* [< L. *carere*, to card] a metal comb or a machine for raising nap or combing fibres of wool, cotton, etc. **—vt.** to use a card on (fibres) in preparation for spinning **—card′er** *n.* **—card′ing** *n., adj.*

cardamom (kär′də məm) *n.* [< Gr. *kardamon*, cress + *amōmon*, spice plant] an Asiatic plant with aromatic seeds, used in medicine and as a spice Also **car′damon**

cardboard (kärd′bôrd′) *n.* stiff, thick paper, or pasteboard, used for cards, boxes, etc.

cardiac (kär′dē ak′) *adj.* [< Gr. *kardia*, heart] of, near, or affecting the heart

cardigan (kär′di gən) *n.* [< 7th Earl of *Cardigan*] a sweater or jacket, usually knitted, that opens down the front

cardinal (kärd′n əl) *adj.* [< L. *cardo*, hinge] **1.** principal; chief **2.** deep red **—n. 1.** one of the Roman Catholic officials appointed by the Pope to his council **2.** a deep red, crested American songbird

cardinalate *n.* the rank of a cardinal

cardinal number *Math.* any number used in counting or showing how many (e.g., two, forty, 627, etc.): distinguished from ORDINAL NUMBER

cardinal points the four principal points of the compass; north, south, east, and west

cardinal virtues the basic virtues of Greek philosophy: justice, prudence, fortitude, and temperance

card index cards containing data or records, arranged systematically: also **card catalogue, card file**

cardio- [< Gr. *kardia*, heart] *a combining form meaning of* the heart

cardiogram (kär′dē ō gram′) *n.* *same as* ELECTROCARDIOGRAM

cardiology (kär′dē ol′ə jē) *n.* the branch of medicine dealing with the heart **—car′diol′ogist** *n.*

cards (kärdz) *n.pl.* **1.** a game played with a pack of cards, as bridge, rummy, etc. **2.** card playing

cardsharp (kärd′shärp′) *n.* [Colloq.] a professional cheater at cards: also **card′-sharp′er**

card table a table at which card games are played, esp. a small, square table with folding legs

card vote *same as* BLOCK VOTE

care (kāər) *n.* [< OE. *caru*, sorrow] **1.** *a*) worry or concern *b*) a cause of this **2.** close attention **3.** a liking or regard (*for*) **4.** charge; protection **5.** something to watch over or attend to **—vi. cared, car′ing 1.** to feel concern or interest **2.** to feel love or a liking (*for*) **3.** to provide (*for*) **4.** to wish (*for*) **—care of** at the address of **—have a care** to be careful: also **take care —take care of 1.** to be responsible for **2.** to provide for

careen (kə rēn′) *vt.* [< L. *carina*, keel] **1.** to cause (a ship) to lean on one side, as for repairs **2.** to tip; tilt **—vi.** to lean sideways

career (kə rēər′) *n.* [Fr. *carrière*, racecourse < It. *carro*, car] **1.** one's progress through life or in a particular vocation **2.** a profession or occupation **3.** a swift course **—adj.** pursuing a normally temporary activity as a lifework [a *career* soldier] **—vi.** to rush wildly

careerist *n.* a person interested chiefly in success in his own career, to the neglect of other things **—career′ism** *n.*

carefree (kāər′frē′) *adj.* free from troubles or worry

careful *adj.* **1.** acting or working in a thoughtful, painstaking way **2.** cautious **3.** accurately or thoroughly done **—care′fully** *adv.* **—care′fulness** *n.*

careless *adj.* **1.** done without enough attention, precision, etc. **2.** not thinking before one acts or speaks; inconsiderate **3.** carefree **—care′lessness** *n.*

caress (kə res′) *vt.* [ult. < L. *carus*, dear] to touch lovingly or gently; kiss **—n.** an affectionate touch or gesture **—caress′er** *n.* **—caress′ingly** *adv.*

caret (kar′it) *n.* [L., there is lacking] a mark (ʌ) used in writing or in correcting proofs, to show where something is to be added

caretaker (kāər′tāk′ər) *n.* a person employed to take care of a building, etc. **—adj.** holding office temporarily [a *caretaker* government]

careworn *adj.* showing the effects of troubles and worry; haggard

cargo (kär′gō) *n., pl.* **-goes** [< Sp. *cargar*, to load] the goods carried by a ship, aircraft, lorry, etc.; freight

Carib (kar′ib) *n.* [< Sp.] **1.** a member of an Indian people of the S West Indies and the N coast of S America **2.** the family of languages of the Caribs **—Car′iban** *adj., n.*

Caribbean (kar′ə bē′ən) *adj.* **1.** of the Caribs **2.** of the Caribbean Sea, its islands, etc.

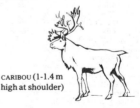

CARIBOU (1-1.4 m high at shoulder)

caribou (kar′ə bōō′) *n.* [CanadFr. < Algonquian name] the N American reindeer

caricature (kar′i kə tyoōər′) *n.* [Fr. < It. *caricare*, exaggerate] **1.** a picture or imitation of a person, literary style, etc. that exaggerates certain features or mannerisms for satirical effect **2.** a ridiculously poor imitation **—vt. -tured′, -tur′ing** to depict as in a caricature **—car′icatur′ist** *n.*

caries (kāər'ē ēz) *n.* [L., decay] decay of bones, or, esp., of teeth

carillon (kar'əl yän) *n.* [Fr., chime of (four) bells, ult. < L. *quattuor*, four] 1. a set of stationary bells, each producing one tone of the chromatic scale 2. a melody played on such bells

carinate (kar'ə nāt') *adj.* [< L. *carina*, keel] with a keeled breastbone: said of a bird

cariole (kar'ē ōl') *n.* [< It. *carro*, car] 1. a small carriage drawn by one horse 2. a light, covered cart

carl, carle (kärl) *n.* [OE. < ON. *karl*] *Hist.* a peasant, bondman, or villein

Carlovingian (kar'lō vin'jē ən) *adj., n. same as* CAROLINGIAN

Carmelite (kär'mə līt') *n.* a friar or nun of the order of Our Lady of Mount Carmel —*adj.* of this order

carminative (kär'mə nə tiv) *adj.* [< L. *carminare*, to card, cleanse] causing gas to be expelled from the stomach and intestines —*n.* a medicine to relieve flatulence

carmine (kär'mīn) *n.* [< Ar. *qirmiz*, crimson] 1. a red pigment obtained from cochineal 2. its colour —*adj.* red or purplish-red; crimson

carnage (kär'nij) *n.* [< L. *caro, carnis*, flesh] bloody and extensive slaughter, esp. in battle; massacre

carnal *adj.* [see prec.] 1. in or of the flesh; material or worldly 2. sensual; sexual —**carnality** (kär nal'ə tē) *n.*

carnation (kär nā'shən) *n.* [< L. *caro:* see CARNAGE] 1. rosy pink 2. a plant of the pink family, with white, pink, or red flowers that smell like cloves

carnelian (kär nēl'yən) *n. same as* CORNELIAN

carnival (kär'nə vəl) *n.* [< Fr. or It.] 1. the period of feasting and revelry just before Lent 2. a festivity; merrymaking 3. [Chiefly U.S.] a funfair

carnivore (kär'nə vôr') *n.* 1. any of an order of fanged, flesh-eating mammals, including the dog, lion, seal, etc. 2. any animal or plant that feeds on animals

carnivorous (kär niv'ə rəs) *adj.* [< L. *caro*, flesh + *vorare*, eat] flesh-eating —**carniv'orously** *adv.* —**carniv'orousness** *n.*

carob (kar'əb) *n.* [< Fr. < Ar.] a leguminous tree of the E Mediterranean, bearing long flat, brown pods used as fodder and sometimes human food

carol (kar'əl) *n.* [< OFr.] a song of joy or praise; esp., a Christmas song —*vi., vt.* -**oled**, -**olling** to sing in joy; warble —**car'oler** *n.*

Carolean (kar'ə lē'ən) *adj.* [L. *Carolus*, Charles] 1. of Charles I or Charles II of England, their reign or period 2. of any other king called Charles Also **Caroline**

Carolingian (kar'ə lin'jē ən) *adj.* [see prec.] of the second Frankish dynasty, founded (751 A.D.) by Pepin the Short, son of Charles Martel

carotid (kə rot'id) *adj.* [< Gr. *karōtides*] of or near either of the arteries, one on each side of the neck, which convey the blood to the head —*n.* a carotid artery

carousal (kə rou'zəl) *n. same as* CAROUSE

carouse (kə rouz') *vi.* -**roused**, -**rous'ing** [< G. *gar aus(trinken)*, (to drink) quite out] to drink heavily, esp. along with others having a noisy, merry time —*n.* a noisy, merry drinking party —**carous'er** *n.*

carousel (kar'ə sel') *n.* [Fr. < It.] *same as* MERRY-GO-ROUND

carp¹ (kärp) *n.* [OFr. *carpe* < Gmc.] any of a group of edible freshwater fishes living in ponds

carp² *vi.* [< ON. *karpa*, brag] to find fault in a petty or nagging way —**carp'er** *n.*

carpal (kär'pəl) *adj.* [ModL. *carpalis*] of the carpus —*n.* a bone of the carpus: also **carpa'le** (-pā'lē)

car park a building or piece of land designed for the parking of cars

carpel (kär'pəl) *n.* [< Gr. *karpos*, fruit] 1. a simple pistil, regarded as a modified leaflike structure 2. any of the segments of a compound pistil —**car'pellary** *adj.*

carpenter (kär'pən tər) *n.* [< L. *carpentum*, cart] a workman who builds and repairs wooden articles, buildings, etc. —*vi.* to do a carpenter's work —*vt.* to make or repair as by carpentry

carpentry *n.* the work or trade of a carpenter

carpet (kär'pit) *n.* [< ML. *carpita*, woollen cloth < L. *carpere*, to card] 1. a heavy fabric for covering a floor, stairs, etc. 2. anything like a carpet [a *carpet* of snow] —*vt.* to cover as with a carpet —**on the carpet** 1. being, or about to be, reprimanded 2. under consideration —**sweep under the carpet** to conceal from sight or knowledge, esp. something unpleasant

carpetbag *n.* an old-fashioned type of travelling bag, made of carpeting

carpetbagger *n.* [U.S.] 1. an adventurer who went South to take advantage of unsettled conditions after the American Civil War 2. any candidate for office without local connections

carpeting *n.* carpets or carpet fabric

carpet slippers slippers made with woollen uppers resembling carpeting

carpet-snake an Australian snake with a patterned skin

carping (kär'piŋ) *adj.* tending to carp, or find fault

car pool 1. a group of vehicles owned by an organization and used by its members 2. an arrangement by a group to rotate the use of their cars

carport *n.* a shelter for a motor car, consisting of a roof supported on posts

carpus (kär'pəs) *n., pl.* -**pi** (-pī) [< Gr. *karpos*, wrist] the wrist, or the wrist bones

carrack (kar'ək) *n.* [< OFr. < Ar.] an armed merchantman of the 15th and 16th cent.

carrageen, carragheen (kar'ə gēn') *n.*

[< *Carragheen*, Eire] a purplish, edible seaweed: also called **Irish moss**

carriage (kar'ij) *n.* [< Anglo-Fr. *carier*, *carry*] 1. a carrying; transportation 2. the cost of carrying 3. the manner of carrying the head and body; posture 4. a passenger coach on a railway train 5. a four-wheeled passenger vehicle, usually horse-drawn 6. a wheeled support [a gun *carriage*] 7. a moving part (as on a typewriter) for supporting and shifting something

carriage clock a portable clock, usually with a case, capable of being carried in any position

carriage forward with the cost of transport to be paid by the consignee

carriage paid with the cost of transport paid by the sender

carriageway *n.* the part of the road for use by vehicles, as distinct from the pavement

carrier (kar'ē ər) *n.* 1. a person or thing that carries something 2. a person or company licensed to carry passengers or goods 3. a receptacle or part for carrying something, as on a bicycle 4. *same as* AIRCRAFT CARRIER 5. a person or animal that carries and transmits disease germs 6. *Electronics* the steady transmitted wave whose amplitude, frequency, or phase is modulated by the signal

carrier bag a large paper or plastic bag, with handles, used for shopping

carrier pigeon a homing pigeon trained to carry a written message fastened to its leg

carrion (kar'ē ən) *n.* [< L. *caro*, flesh] 1. the decaying flesh of a dead body 2. anything very repulsive

carrion crow a black European crow with a thick, black bill, which feeds on carrion and small creatures

carrot (kar'ət) *n.* [< Gr. *karōton*] 1. a plant with a fleshy, orange-red root, eaten as a vegetable 2. the root

carroty *adj.* orange-red, like carrots

carry (kar'ē) *vt.* **-ried, -rying** [< L. *carrus*, car] 1. to hold or support while moving 2. to take from one place to another 3. to lead or impel 4. to transmit [air carries sound] 5. to extend [to *carry* the fight to the enemy] 6. to transfer (a figure, etc.) from one column to the next 7. to bear the weight of 8. to be pregnant with 9. to have as a quality, consequence, etc. [to *carry* a guarantee] 10. to keep with one [to *carry* a watch] 11. to conduct (oneself) in a specified way 12. to include as part of its contents: said of a newspaper, etc. 13. to capture (a fortress, etc.) 14. to win over (a group) 15. to win (an election, argument, etc.) —*vi.* to have or cover a range [his voice *carries* well] —*n., pl.* **-ries** 1. the range or distance covered by a gun, golf ball, etc. 2. a carrying —**be** (or **get**) **carried away** to be moved to unreasoning enthusiasm —**carry forward** to take over to the next page, accounting period, etc. —**carry off** 1. to kill [disease *carries off* many] 2.

to win (a prize, etc.) 3. to handle (a situation), esp. with success —**carry on** 1. to engage in 2. to continue as before 3. [Colloq.] to behave in a wild or childish way 4. [Colloq.] to engage in an illicit love affair —**carry out** 1. to put (plans, etc.) into practice 2. to accomplish —**carry over** 1. to transfer 2. to postpone —**carry through** 1. to accomplish 2. to sustain

carry-cot *n.* a child's portable cot

carryout *adj.* *same as* TAKEAWAY

carsick (kär'sik') *adj.* affected with nausea from riding in a motor car, bus, etc. —**car'sick'ness** *n.*

cart (kärt) *n.* [< ON. *kartr*] a small, strong, two-wheeled vehicle drawn by a horse or pushed by hand —*vt., vi.* to carry as in a cart —**cart off** to carry away —**in the cart** [Slang] in trouble —**put the cart before the horse** to do things backwards —**cart'er** *n.*

carte blanche (kärt'blänsh') [Fr., white (i.e., blank) card] full authority; freedom to do as one thinks best

cartel (kär tel') *n.* [< G. < Fr. < It. *carta*, CARD[1]] an agreement among apparently competing firms to fix prices etc.

Cartesian (kär tē'zhən) *adj.* [< *Cartesius*, L. form of *Descartes*] of Descartes or his philosophical or mathematical ideas —*n.* a follower of Descartes

Cartesian coordinates a set of numbers that locate a point by its distances from axes intersecting at right angles

carthorse *n.* a strong, heavy horse

Carthusian (kär thyoo'zhən) *n.* [< L. name for Chartreuse] a monk or nun of a very strict order founded in 1084 —*adj.* of the Carthusians

cartilage (kärt'il ij) *n.* [< L. *cartilago*] a tough, elastic tissue forming part of the skeleton; gristle —**car'tilag'inous** (-aj'ə nəs) *adj.*

cartogram (kär'tə gram') *n.* [< Fr. *carte*, chart + -GRAM] a map giving statistical data by means of lines, dots, shaded areas, etc.

cartography (kär tog'rə fē) *n.* [see CARD[1] + -GRAPHY] the art or work of making maps or charts —**cartog'rapher** *n.* —**cartographic** (kär'tə graf'ik) *adj.*

carton (kärt'ən) *n.* [Fr. < It. *carta*, card] a cardboard box or container

cartoon (kär toon') *n.* [see prec.] 1. a drawing that caricatures some situation or person 2. *a)* a humorous drawing, often with a caption *b)* *same as* COMIC STRIP 3. *same as* ANIMATED CARTOON 4. a full-size sketch of a design or picture to be copied in a fresco, tapestry, etc. —*vt.* to draw a cartoon of —**cartoon'ist** *n.*

cartouche (kär toosh') *n.* [Fr. < It. *carta*, card] 1. a scroll-like ornament or tablet 2. on Egyptian monuments, an oval or oblong figure containing the name of a ruler or deity

cartridge (kär'trij) *n.* [< Fr. < It. *carta*, card] 1. a cylindrical case of cardboard, metal, etc. containing the charge and primer, and usually the projectile, for a firearm **2.** a small container holding a supply of material for insertion into a larger device, as a protected roll of camera film, or a continuous magnetic tape wound on spools

cartridge belt a belt with pockets or loops for cartridges

cartridge clip a metal container for cartridges, inserted in certain types of firearms

cartridge paper a heavy, unbleached drawing paper

cartwheel (kärt′wēl′) *n.* **1.** the large, spoked wheel of a cart **2.** anything resembling this, as a large coin or hat **3.** a kind of handspring performed sideways

cartwright (kärt′rīt′) *n.* one who makes carts

carve (kärv) *vt.* **carved, carv′ing** [< OE. *ceorfan*] **1.** to shape by or as by cutting **2.** to decorate the surface of with cut designs **3.** to divide by cutting; slice —*vi.* **1.** to carve statues or designs **2.** to carve meat —**carve out 1.** to take a piece from **2.** to appropriate (land, position, etc.) —**carve up** to share out —**carv′er** *n.*

carvel (kär′vəl) *n.* *same as* CARAVEL

carve-up (kärv′up) *n.* [Slang] **1.** a division of illicit gains **2.** a secret agreement to share out jobs, privileges, etc.

carving *n.* **1.** the work or art of a person who carves **2.** a carved figure or design

carving knife a large knife for carving meat

carwash (kär′wosh′) *n.* a facility for washing and polishing motor cars

CARYATID

caryatid (kar′ēat′id) *n., pl.* **-ids, -ides′** (-ə dēz′) [< L. < Gr.] a supporting column that has the form of a draped female figure

Casanova (kas′ə nō′və) *n.* [< Giovanni *Casanova*] a libertine

casbah (kaz′bä) *n.* [Fr. < Ar.] the old, crowded quarter of a N African city, esp. [C-] of Algiers

cascade (kas kād′) *n.* [< L. *cadere*, fall] a small, steep waterfall, esp. one of a series —*vt., vi.* **-cad′ed, -cad′ing** to fall or drop in a cascade

cascara (kas kär′ə) *n.* [Sp. *cáscara*, bark] **1.** a small buckthorn of the U.S. **2.** a laxative made from its bark

case¹ (kās) *n.* [< L. *casus*, accident, pp. of *cadere*, fall] **1.** an example or instance **2.** a person being helped by a doctor or social worker **3.** any matter undergoing study **4.** a statement of the facts, as

in a law court **5.** convincing arguments [he has no *case*] **6.** a lawsuit **7.** [Colloq.] a peculiar person **8.** *Gram. a)* an inflected form taken by a noun, pronoun, or adjective to show syntactic relationship *b)* such relationship —*vt.* **cased, cas′ing** [Slang] to look over carefully, esp. for an intended robbery —**in any case** no matter what —**in case 1.** in the event that **2.** as a precaution against some eventuality

case² *n.* [< L. *capsa*, box] **1.** a container, as a box, sheath, etc. **2.** a protective cover [a *watchcase*] **3.** a full box or its contents **4.** the hard cover of a book **5.** *Printing* a shallow tray in which type is kept —*vt.* **cased, cas′ing 1.** to put in a container **2.** to enclose **3.** to bind (a book) in hard covers

caseharden *vt.* **1.** *Metallurgy* to form a hard, thin surface on (an iron alloy) **2.** to make callous

case history (or **study**) collected information about an individual or group, for use in sociological, medical, or psychiatric studies

casein (kā′sē in) *n.* [< L. *caseus*, cheese] a protein that is one of the chief constituents of milk and cheese

case law law based on previous judicial decisions

caseload *n.* the number of cases being handled by a court, probation officer, etc.

casement (kās′mənt) *n.* [< OFr. *encassement*, frame] a hinged window frame that opens outwards: a **casement window** often has two such frames, opening like French doors —**case′mented** *adj.*

casework *n.* social work in which the worker gives guidance on the basis of a study of individual and family background —**case′work′er** *n.*

cash (kash) *n.* [< Fr. *caisse*, money box] **1.** money that a person actually has; esp., ready money **2.** notes and coins **3.** money or a cheque paid at the time of purchase —*vt.* to obtain cash for —*adj.* of, for, or requiring cash [a *cash* sale] —**cash in** to turn into cash —**cash in on** to get profit or profitable use from

cash-and-carry *adj.* with cash payments and no deliveries

cash crop a crop grown for sale, rather than for subsistence

cash discount a discount allowed a purchaser paying within a specified period

cashew (kə shōō′) *n.* [< Fr. < Port. < Tupi] **1.** a tropical tree bearing edible, kidney-shaped nuts **2.** the nut: also **cashew nut**

cash flow the total amount of money that moves in and out of a business over a given period

cashier¹ (ka shēər′) *n.* [< Fr. *caissier*] a person in charge of cash transactions for a bank, shop, etc.

cashier² *vt.* [< LL. *cassare*, destroy] to dismiss, esp. with dishonour, from a position of command, trust, etc.

cashmere (kash′mēər) *n.* [< *Kashmir* in Asia] **1.** a fine wool from goats of

Kashmir 2. a soft, twilled cloth of this or similar wool

cash on delivery payment in cash when a purchase or shipment is delivered

cash register a business machine, usually with a money drawer, that registers visibly the amount of each sale

casing (kās′iŋ) *n.* a protective covering

casino (kə sē′nō) *n., pl.* **-nos** [It., < L. *casa*, hut] a room or building for dancing, or, esp., gambling

cask (kåsk) *n.* [< Fr. < Sp. *casco*, helmet] 1. a barrel, esp. one for liquids 2. the contents of a full cask

casket (kås′kit) *n.* [prob. < OFr. *casse*, box] 1. a small box or chest, as for valuables 2. [Chiefly U.S.] a coffin

casque (kask) *n.* [Fr.] a helmet —**casqued** *adj.*

Cassandra (kə san′drə) *n.* [< *Cassandra*, daughter of Priam] a person whose warnings of misfortune are disregarded

cassava (kə sä′və) *n.* [< Fr. < WInd.] 1. a tropical plant with edible starchy roots 2. a starch taken from the root, used to make bread and tapioca

casserole (kas′ərōl′) *n.* [Fr., < Gr. *kyathos*, bowl] 1. a baking dish of earthenware or heat resistant glass, often with a cover 2. the food cooked in such a dish —*vt.* to cook in a casserole

cassette (ka set′) *n.* [Fr., dim. < *casse*, case] 1. a case with magnetic tape, for use in a tape recorder 2. a case with roll film in it, for loading a camera quickly

cassia (ka′sē ə) *n.* [< Heb. *qeṣī'āh*] 1. the bark of a tree native to Asia : used as an alternative source of cinnamon 2. any of a genus of herbs, shrubs, etc. of the legume family : the pods of some have a laxative pulp; from others senna is extracted

cassimere (kas′ə mēar′) *n.* [var. of CASHMERE] a woollen cloth, twilled or plain, used for men's suits

cassino (kə sē′nō) *n.* [see CASINO] a simple card game

Cassiopeia (kas′ē ō pē′ə) [< *Cassiopeia*, mother of Andromeda] a N constellation near Andromeda

cassock (kas′ək) *n.* [< Fr. < It.] a long, closefitting vestment, usually black, worn by clergymen, choristers, etc.

cassowary (kas′ə wər ē) *n., pl.* **-waries** [Malay *kasuārī*] any of a genus of large, flightless birds of Australia and New Guinea

cast (kåst) *vt.* **cast, cast′ing** [< ON. *kasta*, throw] 1. to throw with force; hurl 2. to deposit (a ballot or vote) 3. *a*) to direct [to *cast* one's eyes] *b*) to give forth [to *cast* light] 4. to drop (a net, anchor, etc.) at the end of a rope 5. to throw out (a fly, etc.) at the end of a fishing line 6. to draw (lots) or shake (dice) out of a container 7. to shed [the snake *casts* its skin] 8. to throw 9. to calculate (a horoscope) 10. to formulate 11. *a*) to form (molten metal, etc.) by pouring into a mould *b*) to make by such a method 12. *a*) to choose actors for (a play or film) *b*) to select (an actor)

for (a role) —*vi.* 1. to throw dice 2. to throw out a fly, etc. on a fishing line —*n.* 1. a casting; throw; specif., *a*) a throw of dice *b*) a throw of a fishing line 2. something formed in a mould, as a statue; also, the mould 3. a plaster form to immobilize a broken arm, leg, etc. 4. the set of actors in a play or film 5. *a*) an appearance, as of features *b*) kind; quality *c*) a tinge; shade [a reddish *cast*] 6. a slight squint 7. *a*) a pellet ejected from the crop of a bird of prey *b*) same as WORMCAST —**cast about** 1. to search (for) 2. to devise (means for doing something) —**cast down** 1. to turn downwards 2. to sadden; discourage —**cast off** 1. to discard; disown 2. to set free 3. to free a ship from a dock, quay, etc. 4. *Knitting* to make the last row of stitches —**cast on** *Knitting* to make the first row of stitches —**cast out** to expel —**cast up** 1. to throw up 2. to turn upwards 3. to total

castanets (kas′tə nets′) *n.pl.* [< Sp. < L. *castanea*, chestnut] a pair of small, hollowed pieces of hard wood, ivory, etc. held in the hand and clicked together in time to music, esp. in Spanish dances

castaway (kås′tə wā′) *n.* 1. an outcast 2. a shipwrecked person —*adj.* 1. discarded 2. cast adrift, as by shipwreck

caste (kåst) *n.* [< L. *castus*, pure] 1. any of the distinct, hereditary Hindu social classes, each by tradition excluded from social dealings with the others 2. any exclusive social group 3. rigid class distinction based on birth, wealth, etc. —**lose caste** to lose social status

castellated (kas′tə lāt′id) *adj.* [< L. *castellum*, castle] 1. built with turrets and battlements, like a castle 2. crenellated —**cas′tella′tion** *n.*

caster (kås′tər) *n.* 1. a small bottle or container with a perforated top for serving sugar, salt, etc. at the table 2. a wheel or freely rolling ball set in a frame and attached to each leg of a piece of furniture so that it can be moved easily

castigate (kas′tə gāt′) *vt.* **-gat′ed, -gat′ing** [< L. *castigare*, purify < *castus*, pure] to punish or rebuke severely —**cas′tiga′tion** *n.* —**cas′tiga′tor** *n.*

casting (kås′tiŋ) *n.* anything, esp. of metal, that has been cast in a mould

casting vote the deciding vote cast by a chairman in the event of a deadlock in a committee, board meeting, etc.

cast-iron *adj.* 1. made of cast iron 2. very hard, strong, etc. 3. impregnable [a *cast-iron* alibi]

cast iron a hard, unmalleable alloy of iron made by casting : it has a high proportion of carbon

castle (kås′'l) *n.* [< L. *castellum*, dim. of *castrum*, fort] 1. a large building fortified with thick walls, turrets, and often a moat 2. *Chess* same as ROOK² —*vi.* **-tled, -tling** *Chess* to move (a king) two squares to either side and place the castle on the square passed over by the king

castle in the air an imaginary scheme

unlikely to be realized; daydream : also **castle in Spain**

castoff (käst′of) *adj.* thrown away; discarded —*n.* a person or thing cast off

castor¹ (käs′tər) *n.* [< Gr. *kastōr*, beaver] **1.** an oily substance obtained from the beaver, used in perfumery : also **castoreum** (kas′tôr′ē əm) **2.** a hat of beaver fur

castor² *n.* *same as* CASTER

castor-oil plant a tropical plant with large, beanlike seeds (**castor beans**) from which oil is extracted

castrate (kas trāt′) *vt.* -**trat′ed**, -**trat′ing** [< L. *castrare*] **1.** to remove the testicles of; geld **2.** to deprive of real vigour; emasculate —**castra′tion** *n.*

cast steel steel formed by casting, not by rolling or forging —**cast′-steel′** *adj.*

casual (kazh′yoo wəl) *adj.* [< L. *casus*, chance] **1.** happening by chance; not planned **2.** occasional *[a casual worker]* **3.** slight *[a casual acquaintance]* **4.** careless or nonchalant **5.** informal or for informal use —*n.* **1.** a casual worker **2.** *[pl.]* shoes, clothes, etc. for informal occasions —**cas′ually** *adv.* —**cas′ualness** *n.*

casualty (kazh′yoo wəl tē) *n.*, *pl.* -**ties** [see prec.] **1.** a member of the armed forces killed, wounded, captured, etc. **2.** anyone hurt or killed in an accident **3.** the hospital department treating people injured in accidents **4.** anything destroyed, or made useless by some unforeseen happening

casuarina (kaz′yoo wə rē′na) *n.* [Malay *kasuārī*, cassowary : from the similarity of the branches to the bird's feathers] any of several Australian trees with jointed, green branchlets

casuistry (kaz′yoo wis trē) *n.*, *pl.* -**ries** [< L. *casus*, chance] subtle but misleading or false reasoning, esp. about moral issues; sophistry —**cas′uist** *n.*

cat (kat) *n.* [OE.] **1.** any of a family of flesh-eating, predacious mammals, including the lion, tiger, etc.; specif., a small, lithe, soft-furred animal of this family, often kept as a pet **2.** [Derog. Colloq.] a woman who makes spiteful remarks **3.** *same as* CAT-O′-NINE-TAILS **4.** [C-] *same as* CATERPILLAR (tractor) **5.** [Slang] *a)* a jazz enthusiast *b)* any person —**let the cat out of the bag** to let a secret be found out —**like a cat on hot bricks** excessively nervous —**set the cat among the pigeons** to stir up trouble —**the cat's pyjamas** (or **whiskers**) [Colloq.] the very best —**cat′like** *adj.*

cat. catalogue

catabolism (kə tab′ə liz′m) *n.* [< Gr. *kata*-, down + *bolē*, a throw] the process in a plant or animal by which living tissue is changed into waste products of a simpler composition —**catabolic** (kat′ə bol′ik) *adj.*

catabolize *vi.*, *vt.* -**lized′**, -**liz′ing** to change by catabolism

cataclysm (kat′ə kliz′m) *n.* [< Gr. *kata*-, down + *klyzein*, wash] **1.** a sudden, violent change, as an earthquake, war, etc. **2.** a great flood —**cat′aclys′mic** (-kliz′mik) *adj.*

catacomb (kat′ə kōōm′) *n.* [< L. *cata*, by + *tumba*, tomb] a gallery in an underground burial place

catafalque (kat′ə falk′) *n.* [< L. *cata*, by + *fala*, scaffold] a wooden framework, usually draped, on which the body in a coffin awaiting burial lies in state

Catalan (kat′ə lən) *adj.* of Catalonia —*n.* **1.** a native of Catalonia **2.** the Romance language of Catalonia, akin to Provençal

catalepsy (kat′ə lep′sē) *n.* [< Gr. *kata*, down + *lambanein*, seize] a condition in which consciousness and feeling are suddenly and temporarily lost, and the muscles become rigid —**cat′alep′tic** *adj.*, *n.*

catalogue (kat′ə log′) *n.* [< Gr. < *kata*, down + *legein*, collect] a complete list; esp., *a)* an alphabetical card index, as of the books in a library *b)* a list of things exhibited, articles for sale, etc., usually with comments and illustrations —*vt.*, *vi.* **1.** to enter in a catalogue **2.** to make a catalogue of —**cat′alogu′er** *n.*

catalpa (kə tal′pə) *n.* [< AmInd. *kutuhlpa*] a tree with trumpet-shaped flowers, and slender pods

catalyse (kat′ə līz′) *vt.* -**lysed′**, -**lys′ing** to change or bring about as a catalyst —**cat′alys′er** *n.*

catalysis (kə tal′ə sis) *n.*, *pl.* -**ses′** (-sēz′) [Gr. *katalysis*, dissolution] the speeding up of a chemical reaction by the addition of some substance which itself undergoes no change thereby

catalyst (kat′ə list) *n.* **1.** any substance serving as the agent in catalysis **2.** a person or thing that is a stimulus —**cat′a-lyt′ic** *adj.*, *n.* —**cat′alyt′ically** *adv.*

catamaran (kat′ə mə ran′) *n.* [< Tamil] **1.** a boat with two parallel hulls **2.** a narrow log raft or float propelled by sails or paddles

cataplexy (kat′ə pleks′ē) *n.* [< Gr. *kata*-, down + *plessein*, strike] a state of immovability, esp. of animals feigning death

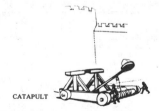

CATAPULT

catapult (kat′ə pult′) *n.* [< Gr. *kata*-, down + *pallein*, hurl] **1.** a weapon for shooting stones, consisting of a piece of elastic fixed to a forked stick **2.** an ancient military device for throwing stones, etc. **3.** a mechanism for launching an aeroplane, rocket, etc., as from a ship's deck —*vt.* to shoot from or as from a catapult; hurl —*vi.* to be catapulted; leap

cataract (kat′ə rakt′) *n.* [< Gr. *katarrhaktēs*, waterfall] **1.** a large waterfall **2.** any rush of water **3.** *a)* an eye disease in which the lens becomes opaque, causing partial or total blindness *b)* the opaque area

catarrh (kə tär′) *n.* [< Gr. < *kata-*, down + *rhein*, flow] inflammation of a mucous membrane, esp. of the nose or throat —**catarrh′al, catarrh′ous** *adj.*

catastrophe (kə tas′trə fē) *n.* [< Gr. *kata-*, down + *strephein*, turn] **1.** any great and sudden disaster **2.** the culminating event of a drama by which the plot is resolved **3.** a disastrous end **4.** a fiasco —**catastrophic** (kat′ə strof′ik) *adj.*—**cat′a-stroph′ically** *adv.*

catatonia (kat′ə tō′nē ə) *n.* [< Gr. *kata-*, down +*tonos*, tension] a syndrome of schizophrenia, marked by stupor alternating with phases of excitement —**cat′aton′ic** *adj.*

cat brier a thorny climbing plant with black berries

cat burglar a burglar who climbs up to upper windows, roofs, etc. to enter

catcall *n.* a shrill shout or whistle expressing derision or disapproval —*vt., vi.* to make catcalls (at)

catch (kach) *vt.* **caught, catch′ing** [< L. *capere*, take] **1.** to seize and hold; capture **2.** to take by or as by a trap **3.** to deceive **4.** to surprise in the act [to be *caught* stealing] **5.** to hit [the blow *caught* him in the eye] **6.** to get to in time [to *catch* a train] **7.** to lay hold of [to *catch* a ball] **8.** to get by chance or quickly [to *catch* a glimpse] **9.** to become infected with **10.** to understand **11.** to captivate; attract **12.** to cause to be entangled [to *catch* one's heel in a rug] **13.** [Colloq.] to hear **14.** *Cricket* to dismiss (a batsman) by catching the ball before it touches the ground —*vi.* **1.** to become held, fastened, or entangled **2.** to start burning **3.** to take and keep hold, as a lock —*n.* **1.** the act of catching **2.** a thing that catches or holds **3.** the person or thing caught **4.** the amount caught **5.** a person worth catching, esp. as a husband or wife **6.** a snatch or bit [*catches* of old tunes] **7.** an emotional break in the voice **8.** [Colloq.] a hidden qualification or difficulty **9.** *Cricket* the dismissal of a batsman by a fielder catching the ball before it touches the ground **10.** *Music* a round for three or more voices —*adj.* **1.** designed to trick [a *catch* question] **2.** attracting attention —**catch as catch can** with any hold, approach, etc.: orig. said of a style of wrestling —**catch it** [Colloq.] to receive a punishment —**catch me!** [Colloq.] you won't find me (doing that) —**catch on 1.** to understand **2.** to become fashionable, popular, etc. —**catch out 1.** to discover (someone) in the act of committing a crime, making an error, etc. **2.** *Cricket* to dismiss (a batsman) by making a catch —**catch up 1.** to take up **2.** to become even, as by hurrying —**catch up on** to engage in more (work, sleep, etc.) so as to compensate for earlier neglect —**catch′-er** *n.*

catching *adj.* **1.** infectious **2.** catchy

catchment *n.* **1.** the catching or collecting of water, esp. rainfall **2.** the water thus caught **3.** all those served by a school, hospital, etc. in a particular catchment area

catchment area 1. the area draining into a river, reservoir, etc. **2.** the area served by a school, hospital, etc.

catchpenny *adj.* cheap and flashy; worthless

catch phrase a phrase that catches or is meant to catch popular attention by repetition

catchword *n.* **1.** a word or phrase repeated so often that it becomes a slogan **2.** a word placed to catch attention

catchy *adj.* **-ier, -iest 1.** catching attention **2.** easily remembered [a *catchy* tune] **3.** meant to trick

catechism (kat′ə kiz′m) *n.* [< Gr. *kata-*, thoroughly + *ēchein*, sound] **1.** a handbook of questions and answers for teaching the principles of a religion **2.** a close questioning —**cat′echis′mal** *adj.* —**cat′e-chis′tic, cat′echis′tical** *adj.*

catechist *n.* a person who catechizes

catechize *vt.* **-chized′, -chiz′ing** [see CATECHISM] **1.** to teach (esp. religion) by the use of questions and answers **2.** to question searchingly Also sp. **cat′echise′**

catechu (kat′ə chōō′) *n.* [Malay *kachu*] a substance obtained from several Asiatic trees: used in dyeing, etc.

categorical (kat′ə gor′i k'l) *adj.* unconditional; absolute; positive Also **cat′e-gor′ic** —**cat′egor′ically** *adv.*

categorize (kat′ə gə rīz′) *vt.* **-rized′, -riz′-ing** to place in a category —**cat′egoriza′-tion** *n.*

category (kat′ə gor ē) *n., pl.* **-ries** [< Gr. *katēgorein*, accuse] a class or division in a scheme of classification

catena (kə tē′nə) *n., pl.* **-nae** (-nē) [L., chain] a linked or connected series, as of excerpted writings, esp. comments on scripture by the Fathers of the Churches

cater (kā′tər) *vi.* [ult. < L. *capere*, take] **1.** to provide food; act as a caterer **2.** to take pains to gratify another's needs or desires (with *to* or *for*)

caterer *n.* one who caters; esp., one whose business is providing food and service for parties, etc.

caterpillar (kat′ər pil′ər) *n.* [< L. *catta pilosa*, hairy cat] the wormlike larva of a butterfly or moth —[C-] *Trademark* a tractor with an endless roller belt over cogged wheels, to move over rough ground

caterwaul (kat′ər wôl′) *vi.* [prob. echoic] to make a shrill, howling sound like a cat —*n.* such a sound

catfish (kat′fish′) *n.* a scaleless fish with long barbels about the mouth

catgut *n.* [CAT + GUT: reason for *cat* uncertain] a tough string or thread made from the dried intestines of sheep, etc. and used for musical instruments, etc.

Cath. 1. Catholic **2.** [*also* c-] cathedral

catharsis (kə thär′sis) *n.* [< Gr. *katharos*, pure] **1.** purgation, esp. of the bowels

2. the relieving of the emotions, esp. by art or psychiatry

cathartic *adj.* of or effecting catharsis; purging: also **cathar′tical** —*n.* a medicine to stimulate evacuation of the bowels

Cathay (ka thā′) *poet. or archaic name of* China

cathedra (kə thē′drə) *n.* [< Gr. *kathedra,* seat] 1. the bishop's throne in a cathedral 2. the episcopal see

cathedral (kə thē′drəl) *n.* the main church of a bishop's see, containing the cathedra —*adj.* of, like, or containing a cathedral

Catherine wheel (kath′ə rin) [< martyrdom of St. *Catherine* of Alexandria] [*also* **c- w-**] a firework in the shape of a wheel, that spins and throws out coloured lights

catheter (kath′ə tər) *n.* [< Gr. *kata-,* down + *hienai,* send] a slender tube inserted into a body passage, esp. for draining urine from the bladder —**cath′eterize** *vt.*

cathode (kath′ōd) *n.* [< Gr. *kata-,* down + *hodos,* way] 1. in an electrolytic cell, the negative electrode, from which current flows: opposed to ANODE 2. in a vacuum tube, the electron emitter 3. the positive terminal of a battery —**cathodic** (ka thod′ik) *adj.*

cathode rays a stream of electrons projected from the surface of a cathode

cathode-ray tube a vacuum tube in which the electrons can be focused on a fluorescent screen, producing a visible pattern on the exterior face

catholic (kath′ə lik) *adj.* [< Gr. *kata-,* completely + *holos,* whole] 1. all inclusive; universal 2. broad in sympathies, tastes, etc.; liberal 3. [*often* C-] of the universal Christian church 4. [C-] Roman Catholic —*n.* 1. [*often* C-] a member of the universal Christian church 2. [C-] a Roman Catholic —**catholically** (kə thol′-ik′lē) *adv.*

Catholicism (kə thol′ə siz′m) *n.* the doctrine, faith, practice, and organization of the Roman Catholic Church

catholicity (kath′ə lis′ə tē) *n.* 1. broadness of taste, sympathy, etc.; liberality, as of ideas 2. universality

cation (kat′ī′ən) *n.* [< Gr. *kata,* down + *ienai,* go] a positive ion: in electrolysis, cations move towards the cathode —**cationic** (kat′ī on′ik) *adj.*

catkin (kat′kin) *n.* [< Du. dim. of *katte,* cat] a drooping, scaly spike of unisexual flowers without petals, as on willows, hazels, etc.

catmint (kat′mint′) *n.* an aromatic plant with blue flowers, attractive to cats; also **cat′nip′**

catnap (kat′nap′) *n.* a short, light sleep; doze —*vi.* **-napped′, -nap′ping** to take a catnap

cat-o′-nine-tails (kat′ə nīn′tālz′) *n.* a whip made of nine knotted cords attached to a handle

CAT'S
CRADLE

cat's cradle a child's game in which a string looped over the fingers is transferred back and forth on the hands of the players to form designs

cat's-eye *n.* 1. a glass marker stud set in a road so as to reflect light from headlights 2. a gem that reflects light in a way suggestive of a cat's eye

cat's-paw *n.* 1. a person used by another to do distasteful or unlawful work; dupe 2. a light breeze rippling the surface of water

cattle (kat′'l) *n.* [< ML. *captale,* property < L. *caput,* head] 1. [Archaic] farm animals 2. cows, bulls, or oxen

cattle-cake *n.* a concentrated, high-protein food for cattle, pressed into cakes

cattle-grid *n.* a device to prevent cattle, etc. from straying, consisting of a shallow pit crossed by parallel bars

catty *adj.* **cat′tier, cat′tiest** 1. spiteful, malicious, etc. 2. of or like a cat —**cat′tily** *adv.* —**cat′tiness** *n.*

catwalk *n.* a high, narrow walk, as along the edge of a bridge or over an engine room

Caucasian (kô kā′zē ən) *adj.* 1. of the Caucasus 2. *same as* CAUCASOID —*n.* 1. a native of the Caucasus 2. *same as* CAUCASOID

Caucasoid (kôk′ə soid′) *adj.* designating or of one of the major groups of mankind that includes the native peoples of Europe, North Africa, India, etc.: loosely called the *white race* —*n.* a member of the Caucasoid group

caucus (kôk′əs) *n.* [< ?] 1. a private meeting of a political party to decide on policy, esp. prior to an open meeting 2. [Often Derog.] a local faction of a political party

caudal (kôd′'l) *adj.* [< L. *cauda,* tail] 1. of or like a tail 2. at or near the tail —**cau′dally** *adv.* —**cau′date** *adj.*

caudle (kôd′'l) *n.* [< L. *cal(i)dus,* warm] a warm drink for invalids; esp., a spiced gruel with wine added

caught (kôt) *pt. & pp. of* CATCH

caul (kôl) *n.* [OE. *cawl,* net] a membrane sometimes enveloping the head of a child at birth

cauldron (kôl′drən) *n.* [< L. *calidus,* warm] a large pot used for boiling, usually with a hooped handle

cauliflower (kol′ə flou′ər) *n.* [< It. < L. *caulis,* cabbage] a variety of cabbage with a compact white head of fleshy flower stalks, eaten as a vegetable

cauliflower ear an ear permanently deformed by injuries from repeated blows, as in boxing

caulk (kôk) *vt.* [< L. *calcare,* tread] 1. to make (a boat, etc.) watertight by filling the seams or cracks with oakum, tar, etc. **2.** to stop up (cracks of window frames, etc.) with a filler —**caulk′er** *n.* —**caulk′ing** *n.*

causal (kôz′′l) *adj.* **1.** of, like, or being a cause **2.** relating to cause and effect —**caus′ally** *adv.*

causality (kô zal′ə tē) *n.,* *pl.* -**ties 1.** causal quality or agency **2.** the interrelation or principle of cause and effect

causation (kô zā′shən) *n.* **1.** the act of causing **2.** causality

causative (kôz′ə tiv) *adj.* **1.** producing an effect; causing **2.** expressing causation, as the verb *fell* (a cause to fall) —*n.* a causative word —**caus′atively** *adv.*

cause (kôz) *n.* { < L. *causa*] **1.** anything producing an effect or result **2.** a reason, motive, or ground; esp., sufficient reason [*cause* for complaint] **3.** any movement that a person or group is interested in and supports **4.** an action or question to be resolved by a court of law —*vt.* **caused, caus′ing** to bring about; effect —**make common cause with** to join forces with —**caus′able** *adj.* —**cause′less** *adj.*

‡**cause célèbre** (kôz′ sə leb′rə) [Fr.] a celebrated trial

causerie (kō′zə rē) *n.* [Fr.] **1.** an informal talk; chat **2.** a short, conversational piece of writing

causeway (kôz′wā′) *n.* { < L. *calx,* limestone + way] **1.** a raised path, as across a marsh **2.** a paved way or road

caustic (kôs′tik) *adj.* [< Gr. *kaiein,* to burn] **1.** that can burn or destroy tissue by chemical action **2.** cutting or sarcastic in utterance —*n.* any caustic substance —**caus′tically** *adv.* —**caustic′ity** (-tis′ə tē) *n.*

cauterize (kôt′ər īz′) *vt.* -**ized′,** -**iz′ing** [< Gr. *kaiein,* burn] to burn with a hot iron or with a caustic substance, so as to destroy dead tissue, etc. —**cau′teriza′-tion** *n.*

caution (kô′shən) *n.* [< L. *cautio* < same base as *cavere,* take heed] **1.** wariness **2.** a warning; admonition, esp. a warning given to a person suspected of an offence, that his words will be taken down and may be used in evidence **3.** [Colloq.] a person or thing provoking notice, surprise, etc. —*vt.* **1.** to warn; admonish **2.** to warn (a person arrested) that he need not speak, but that if he does so, his words may be taken down in writing

cautious *adj.* full of caution; wary —**cau′-tionary** *adj.* —**cau′tiously** *adv.* —**cau′tious-ness** *n.*

cavalcade (kav′′l kād′) *n.* [Fr. < L. *caballus,* horse] **1.** a procession of horsemen, cars, etc. **2.** *a)* any procession *b)* a sequence of events, etc.

cavalier (kav′ə lēər′) *adj.* [Fr. < L. *caballus,* horse] **1.** *a)* casual or indifferent towards matters of some importance *b)* haughty; supercilious *c)* free and easy **2.** [C-] of the Cavaliers —*n.* **1.** [C-] a partisan of Charles I in his struggles with Parliament (1641-49) **2.** a gallant

gentleman **3.** a knight —**cav′alier′ly** *adv.,* *adj.* —**cav′alier′ness** *n.*

cavalry (kav′əl rē) *n.,* *pl.* -**ries** [see CAVALIER] combat troops mounted originally on horses but now often on motorized armoured vehicles —**cav′alryman** *n.*

cave (kāv) *n.* [< L. *cavus,* hollow] a hollow place inside the earth; cavern —*vt.,* *vi.* **caved, cav′ing** to explore caves —**cave in 1.** to collapse **2.** to make collapse **3.** [Colloq.] to give in; yield —**cav′er** *n.*

caveat (kav′ē at′) *n.* [L., let him beware] **1.** *Law* a notice filed with the proper officers directing them to stop an action **2.** a warning

cave-in (kāv′in′) *n.* **1.** a caving in **2.** a place where the ground, a mine, etc. has caved in

cave man 1. a prehistoric human being of the Stone Age who lived in caves: also **cave dweller 2.** a man who is rough and crudely direct, esp. in his approach to women

cavern (kav′ərn) *n.* [< L. *cavus,* hollow] a large cave

cavernous *adj.* **1.** like a cavern; deep-set, hollow, etc. **2.** full of caverns —**cav′-ernously** *adv.*

caviar, caviare (kav′ē är′) *n.* [Fr. < It. < Turk.] the salted eggs of sturgeon, salmon, etc. eaten as an appetizer

cavil (kav′əl) *vi.* -**illed, -illing** [< L. *cavilla,* a jest] to object when there is little reason; carp (*at* or *about*) —*n.* a trivial objection; quibble —**cav′iler** *n.*

cavity (kav′ə tē) *n.,* *pl.* -**ties** [< L. *cavus,* hollow] a hole or hollow place

cavort (kə vôrt′) *vi.* [< ?] to caper; frolic

cay (kā) *n.* [Sp. *cayo*] a low island, coral reef, or sandbank off a mainland

cayenne (kā en′) *n.* [< Tupi] a very hot red pepper made from the dried fruit of a pepper plant, esp. of the capsicum: also **cayenne pepper**

cayman (kā′man) *n.,* *pl.* -**mans** [Sp. < Carib] a reptile of Central and South America similar to the alligator

Cb *Chem.* columbium

CBC Canadian Broadcasting Corporation

CBE Commander of the British Empire

CBI Confederation of British Industry

CC 1. County Council **2.** Cricket Club

cc, c.c. cubic centimetre(s)

cc. chapters

C.C., c.c. carbon copy

C clef *Music* a sign on a staff indicating that C is the note on the third line (*alto clef*) or on the fourth line (*tenor clef*)

Cd *Chem.* cadmium

CD, C.D. 1. Civil Defence **2.** Corps Diplomatique

cd *Physics the symbol for* candela

CDN *international car registration for* Canada

Cdn. Canadian

Cdr. Commander

C.D.T. [U.S. & Canad.] Central Daylight Time

Ce *Chem.* cerium

C.E. 1. Church of England **2.** Civil Engineer **3.** Common Era

cease (sēs) *vt., vi.* **ceased, ceas′ing** [< L. *cessare* < *cedere*, yield] to end; stop; discontinue —*n.* a ceasing: chiefly in **without cease**

ceaseless *adj.* unceasing; continual —**cease′lessly** *adv.*

cedar (sē′dər) *n.* [< Gr. *kedros*] **1.** any of certain coniferous trees of the pine family, having durable, fragrant wood, as the **cedar of Lebanon 2.** the wood of any of these —*adj.* of cedar

cede (sēd) *vt.* **ced′ed, ced′ing** [< L. *cedere*, yield] **1.** to give up one's rights in; surrender **2.** to transfer the title or ownership of **3.** to admit or allow, as an argument

cedilla (si dil′ə) *n.* [< Fr. < Sp. < Gr. *zēta*, zeta] a hooklike mark placed under *c* in some French and Portuguese words (Ex.: *façade, ração*) to show the sound of *s* rather than *k*

Ceefax (sē′faks) *Trademark* the BBC teletext service

ceilidh (kā′lē) *n.* [Gael., visit] [Scot. & Ir.] a gathering, usually in a private house, to sing, tell stories, etc.

ceiling (sēl′iŋ) *n.* [< ?] **1.** the inside top part of a room, opposite the floor **2.** an upper limit set on anything **3.** *Aeron.* the maximum height at which an aircraft can normally fly —**hit the ceiling** [Slang] to lose one's temper

celandine (sel′ən dīn′) *n.* [< Gr. *chelidōn*, a swallow] **1.** a plant related to the poppy, with yellow flowers: also, **greater celandine 2.** a plant of the buttercup family, with yellow flowers: also, **lesser celandine**

celebrant (sel′ə brənt) *n.* [see ff.] one who performs a religious rite, as the priest officiating at the Eucharist

celebrate (sel′ə brāt′) *vt., vi.* **-brat′ed, -brat′ing** [< L. *celebrare*, to honour < *celeber*, populous] **1.** to observe (an anniversary, holiday, etc.) with ceremony or festivity **2.** to perform (a ritual, etc.) **3.** to honour publicly —**cel′ebra′tor** *n.* —**cel′ebra′tory** *adj.*

celebrated *adj.* famous; renowned

celebration (sel′ə brā′shən) *n.* **1.** that which is done to celebrate **2.** the act or an instance of celebrating

celebrity (sə leb′rə tē) *n.* **1.** wide recognition; fame **2.** *pl.* **-ties** a famous person

celerity (sə ler′ə tē) *n.* [< L. *celer*, swift] swiftness

celeriac (sə ler′ē ak′) *n.* [altered < CELERY] an umbelliferous plant eaten as a vegetable

celery (sel′ər ē) *n.* [< Gr. *selinon*, parsley] a plant with long, crisp leafstalks eaten as a vegetable

celestial (sə les′tyəl) *adj.* [< L. *caelum*, heaven] **1.** of the sky **2.** *a)* of heaven; divine *[celestial beings] b)* highest; perfect *[celestial bliss]* —**celes′tially** *adv.*

celestial equator the great circle of the celestial sphere formed by projecting the plane of the earth's equator onto it

celestial sphere an imaginary sphere

of infinite diameter containing the whole universe

celibacy (sel′ə bə sē) *n.* [see ff.] **1.** the state of being unmarried **2.** complete sexual abstinence

celibate (sel′ə bət) *adj.* [< L. *caelebs*, unmarried] of or in a state of celibacy —*n.* a celibate person

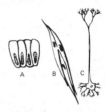

CELLS
(A, epithelial; B, smooth muscle; C, nerve)

cell (sel) *n.* [< L. *cella*] **1.** a small room or cubicle **2.** a very small cavity, as in a honeycomb **3.** any of the smallest organizational units of a movement **4.** *Biol.* a small unit of protoplasm, usually with a nucleus, cytoplasm, and an enclosing membrane **5.** *Elec.* a receptacle for generating electricity by chemical reactions or for decomposing compounds by electrolysis —**celled** *adj.*

cellar (sel′ər) *n.* [< L. *cella*, small room] **1.** a room or rooms below ground level and usually under a building, often used for storing fuel, wines, etc. **2.** a stock of wines kept in a cellar —*vt.* to store in a cellar

cellarage *n.* **1.** space in a cellar **2.** the fee for storage in a cellar

cellaret (sel′ə ret′) *n.* [< CELLAR] a cabinet for wine

cello (chel′ō) *n., pl.* **-los** [< VIOLONCELLO] an instrument of the violin family, between the viola and double bass in size and pitch; violoncello —**cel′list** *n.*

cellophane (sel′ə fān′) *n.* [< CELLULOSE + Gr. *phainein*, appear] a thin, transparent material made from cellulose, used as moistureproof wrapping for foods, etc.

cellular (sel′yoo lər) *adj.* of, like, or containing a cell or cells —**cel′lular′ity** (-lar′ə tē) *n.*

cellule (sel′yool) *n.* a very small cell

cellulite (sel′yoo līt′) *n.* [CELLUL(E) + permanent deposits of subcutaneous fat

Celluloid (sel′yoo loid′) [< CELLULOSE] *Trademark* a flammable substance made from pyroxylin and camphor

cellulose (sel′yoo lōs′) *n.* [Fr. < L. *cella*, cell] the chief substance composing the cell walls or fibres of all plant tissue —**cel′lulos′ic** *adj., n.*

Celsius (sel′sē əs) *adj.* [< A. *Celsius*] designating or of a thermometer on which 0° is the freezing point and 100° is the boiling point of water; centigrade: abbrev. **C**

Celt (kelt, selt) *n.* [< L. *Celta*] 1. a person who speaks a Celtic language : the Bretons, Irish, Welsh, and Highland Scots are Celts 2. an ancient Gaul or Briton

Celtic (kel'tik, sel'-) *adj.* of the Celts, their culture, etc. —*n.* an Indo-European subfamily of languages with a Goidelic branch (Irish Gaelic, Scottish Gaelic, Manx) and a Brythonic branch (Welsh, Breton, and Cornish)

cement (si ment') *n.* [< L. *caementum*, rough stone] 1. a powdered substance made of burned lime and clay, mixed with water, etc. to make mortar or concrete : the mixture hardens when it dries 2. any substance that fastens things together when it hardens, as glue 3. a cementlike substance used in dentistry to fill cavities —*vt.* 1. to unite as with cement 2. to cover with cement —*vi.* to become cemented —**cementation** (sē'men tā'shən) *n.* —**cement'er** *n.* —**cement'like'** *adj.*

cemetery (sem'ə trē) *n.,* *pl.* -teries [< Gr. *koimētērion* < *koiman*, put to sleep] a place for the burial of the dead, esp. one not attached to a church

cenobite (sē'nō bīt') *n.* same as COENOBITE

cenotaph (sen'ə tàf') *n.* [< Gr. *kenos*, empty + *taphos*, tomb] a monument honouring a dead person whose body is somewhere else

Cenozoic (sē'nə zō'ik) *adj.* U.S. sp. of CAINOZOIC

censer (sen'sər) *n.* [see INCENSE[1]] a container in which incense is burned

censor (sen'sər) *n.* [L. < *censere*, to assess] an official with the power to examine publications, films, etc. and to suppress anything considered obscene, objectionable, etc. —*vt.* to subject (a book, letter, etc.) to censorship —**censorial** (sen sôr'ē əl) *adj.*

censorious (sen sôr'ē əs) *adj.* [see prec.] harshly critical —**censo'riously** *adv.* —**censo'riousness** *n.*

censorship (sen'sər ship') *n.* 1. the act or a system of censoring 2. the work or position of a censor

censure (sen'shər) *n.* [see CENSOR] a condemning as wrong; strong disapproval —*vt.* -sured, -suring to condemn as wrong —**cen'surable** *adj.* —**cen'surably** *adv.* —**cen'surer** *n.*

census (sen'səs) *n.* [L.; see CENSOR] an official, usually periodic, count of population and recording of economic status, age, sex, etc.

cent (sent) *n.* [< L. *centum*, hundred] a 100th part of a dollar, rupee, etc., or a coin of this value

cent. 1. centigrade 2. centimetre 3. central 4. century

centaur (sen'tôr) *n.* [< Gr. *Kentauros*] Gr. Myth. any of a race of monsters with a man's head, trunk, and arms, and a horse's body and legs

centenarian (sen'tə nāar'ē ən) *adj.* 1. of 100 years 2. of a centenarian —*n.* a person at least 100 years old

centenary (sen ten'ər ē) *adj.* [< L. *centum*, hundred] 1. of a century 2. of a centennial —*n.,* *pl.* -naries 1. a century 2. same as CENTENNIAL

centennial (sen ten'ē əl) *adj.* [< L. *centum*, hundred + *annus*, year] 1. of 100 years 2. happening once in 100 years 3. 100 years old 4. of a 100th anniversary —*n.* a 100th anniversary or its celebration

centesimal (sen tes'ə məl) *adj.* [< L. *centum*, hundred] 1. hundredth 2. of or divided into hundredths

centi- (sen'tə) [L.] *a combining form meaning :* 1. hundred or hundredfold 2. a 100th part of

centigrade (sen'tə grād') *adj.* [< L. *centum*, hundred + *gradus*, degree] 1. consisting of or divided into 100 degrees 2. same as CELSIUS

centigram, centigramme *n.* [CENTI- & GRAM] a unit of weight, equal to 1/100 gram : abbrev. **cg**

centilitre *n.* [CENTI- & LITRE] a unit of capacity, equal to 1/100 litre : abbrev. **cl**

centime (son'tēm) *n.* [see CENTESIMAL] the 100th part of a franc, an Algerian dinar, etc.

centimetre (sen'tə mēt'ər) *n.* [CENTI- & METRE] a unit of measure, equal to 1/100 metre : abbrev. **cm**

centimetre-gram-second *adj.* of a system of measurement in which the centimetre, gram, and second are used as the units of length, mass, and time

centipede (sen'tə pēd') *n.* [< L. < *centum*, hundred + *pes*, foot] a many-segmented arthropod with a pair of legs to each segment

CENTO (sen'tō) Central Treaty Organization

central (sen'trəl) *adj.* [L. *centralis*] 1. in, at, near, or forming the centre 2. equally accessible from various points 3. main; basic 4. designating that part of the nervous system consisting of the brain and spinal cord (of a vertebrate) —**central'ity** (-tral'ə tē) *n.* —**cen'trally** *adv.*

Central America part of N America between Mexico and S America —**Central American**

central bank a national bank that controls credit, issues banknotes, and acts as the government's banker

central heating a form of heating for buildings in which a central heat source is linked to radiators or air ducts

centralism *n.* the principle or system of centralizing power or authority —**cen'tralist** *adj., n.*

centralize *vt.* -ized, -iz'ing 1. to make central; gather together 2. to organize under one control —*vi.* to become centralized —**cen'traliza'tion** *n.* —**cen'traliz'er** *n.*

central reservation the strip of land that separates the two sides of a motorway or dual carriageway

centre (sen'tər) *n.* [< Gr. *kentron*, sharp point] 1. a point equally distant from all points on the circumference of a circle or surface of a sphere 2. the point around which anything revolves; pivot 3. a place at which an activity is carried on or to which people are attracted 4. the approximate middle point of anything 5. a group of nerve cells regulating a particular function 6. in some sports, a player near the centre of the line 7. [often C-] *Politics* a party between the left and right —*vt.* 1. to place in, at, or near the centre 2. to draw or gather to one place 3. to furnish with a centre —*vi.* to be concentrated or focussed

centreboard *n.* a movable, keellike board lowered through a slot in the floor of a sailing boat to prevent drifting

centrefold *n.* the central facing pages of a magazine, devoted to graphic display

centre-forward *n.* the central position in the forward line of a football team, etc.

centre-half *n.* the central position in the half-back line of a football team, etc.

centre of gravity that point in a body or system around which its weight is evenly distributed or balanced

centrepiece *n.* 1. an ornament for the centre of a table 2. the most important item, as in a display

centric (sen'trik) *adj.* 1. central 2. having a centre 3. of or originating from a nerve centre Also **cen'trical** —**cen'trically** *adv.* —**centric'ity** (-tris'ə tē) *n.*

-centric *a combining form meaning:* 1. having a centre (of a specified kind or number) 2. having (a specified thing) as its centre

centrifugal (sen trif'yoo gəl) *adj.* [< CENTR(O)- + L. *fugere*, flee] 1. moving or tending to move away from a centre 2. using or acted on by centrifugal force —*n.* a centrifuge —**centrif'ugally** *adv.*

centrifuge (sen'trə fyooj') *n.* a machine using centrifugal force to separate particles of varying density

centring (sen'triŋ) *n.* a temporary frame to support an arch or vault during construction

centripetal (sen trip'ət 'l) *adj.* [< CENTR(O)- + L. *petere*, seek] 1. moving or tending to move towards a centre 2. using or acted on by centripetal force —**centrip'etally** *adv.*

centrist (sen'trist) *n.* a member of a political party of the centre

centro- [< L.] *a combining form meaning* centre

centuple (sen'tyoop 'l) *adj.* [< L. *centum*, hundred + *plicare*, fold] hundredfold —*vt.* **-pled, -pling** to multiply by a hundred

centurion (sen tyooər'ē ən) *n.* [see ff.] the commanding officer of a Roman century

century (sen'chər ē) *n.*, *pl.* **-ries** [< L. *centum*, hundred] 1. any period of 100 years, esp. reckoned from the beginning of the Christian Era 2. *Sports* a score of 100, esp. 100 runs in cricket 3. in ancient Rome, a military unit, originally made up of 100 men

cephalic (ke fal'ik) *adj.* [< Gr. *kephalē*, head] of or in the head —**cephal'ically** *adv.*

cephalopod (sef'ə lō pod') *n.* [prec. + -POD] any of a class of molluscs having

a distinct head with a beak, and muscular tentacles about the mouth, as the octopus

ceramic (sə ram'ik) *adj.* [< Gr. *keramos*, clay] 1. of pottery, tile, porcelain, etc. 2. of ceramics —*n.* 1. [*pl.*, *with sing. v.*] the art or work of making objects of baked clay 2. such an object —**ceramist** (ser'ə mist), **ceram'icist** *n.*

cere (sēər) *n.* [< Gr. *kēros*, wax] a waxy, fleshy area at the base of the beak of some birds, as the parrot

cereal (sēər'ē əl) *adj.* [< L. *Cerealis*, of Ceres] of grain —*n.* 1. any grain used for food, as wheat, oats, etc. 2. food made from grain, esp. breakfast food

cerebellum (ser'ə bel'əm) *n.* [L., dim. of *cerebrum*, brain] the section of the brain behind and below the cerebrum: it is the coordinating centre for muscular movement

cerebral (ser'ə brəl) *adj.* of the brain

cerebral palsy a disorder of the central nervous system, characterized by spastic paralysis

cerebrate (ser'ə brāt') *vi.* **-brat'ed, -brat'-ing** [see CEREBELLUM] to use one's brain; think —**cer'ebra'tion** *n.*

cerebrospinal (ser'ə brō spī'n'l) *adj.* of or affecting the brain and the spinal cord

cerebrum (ser'ə brəm) *n.* [L.: see CEREBELLUM] the upper, main part of the brain of vertebrate animals

cerecloth (sēər'kloth') *n.* cloth treated with wax, formerly used to wrap a dead person for burial

ceremonial (ser'ə mō'nē əl) *adj.* of, for, or consisting of ceremony; formal —*n.* 1. an established system of rites connected with an occasion 2. a rite or ceremony —**cer'emo'nialism** *n.* —**cer'emo'nialist** *n.* —**cer'emo'nially** *adv.*

ceremonious *adj.* 1. full of ceremony 2. very polite or formal —**cer'emo'niously** *adv.* —**cer'emo'niousness** *n.*

ceremony (ser'ə mə nē) *n.*, *pl.* **-nies** [L. *caerimonia*]. 1. a set of formal acts established as proper to a special occasion, such as a wedding 2. behaviour that follows rigid etiquette 3. formality 4. meaningless formality —**stand on ceremony** to behave with formality

cerise (sə rēz') *n.*, *adj.* [Fr., cherry] cherry red

cerium (sēər'ē əm) *n.* [< asteroid *Ceres*] a grey, metallic chemical element: symbol, Ce

CERN [C(onseil) E(uropéen pour la) R(echerche) N(ucléaire)] a co-operative European nuclear research organization centred in Geneva, Switzerland

cert (surt) *n.* [Slang] certainty —**a dead cert** something certain to happen, succeed, etc.

cert. 1. certificate 2. certified

certain (surt''n) *adj.* [< L. *certus*, determined] 1. fixed or determined 2. inevitable 3. not to be doubted 4. reliable [*a certain* cure] 5. unerring [his *certain* aim] 6. convinced; positive 7. not named, though definite [*a certain* person] 8. some *[to a certain extent]* —**for certain** without doubt

certainly *adv.* beyond a doubt; surely

certainty *n.* 1. the quality, state, or fact of being certain 2. *pl.* **-ties** anything certain; definite fact

certes (sur'tēz) *adv.* [< L. *certus*, certain] [Archaic] certainly; verily

certificate (sur tif'ə kət; *for v.* -kāt') *n.* [see CERTIFY] a written statement testifying to a fact, qualification, ownership, etc. —*vt.* **-cat'ed, -cat'ing** to attest by a certificate; issue a certificate to —**certif'i-ca'tor** *n.*

Certificate of Secondary Education an examination taken in secondary schools, and of a lower standard than the GENERAL CERTIFICATE OF EDUCATION

certification (sur'tə fi kā'shən) *n.* 1. a certifying or being certified 2. a certified statement

certified (sur'tə fīd') *adj.* 1. guaranteed 2. attested to by a certificate 3. formerly, officially declared insane

certified cheque a cheque certified by a bank as genuine, on which it guarantees payment

certify (sur'tə fī') *vt.* **-fied', -fy'ing** [< L. *certus*, certain + *facere*, make] 1. to declare (a thing) true, certain, etc. by formal statement 2. to guarantee 3. formerly, to declare officially insane —*vi.* to testify (*to*) —**cer'tifi'able** *adj.* —**cer'ti-fi'ably** *adv.*

certitude (sur'tə tyōōd') *n.* [< LL. *certitudo*] 1. a feeling absolutely sure 2. inevitability

cerulean (sə rōō'lē ən) *adj.* [< L. *caeruleus*] sky-blue; azure

cervine (sur'vīn) *adj.* [< L. *cervus*, deer] of or like a deer

cervix (sur'viks) *n.*, *pl.* **-vices'** (-və sēz') **-vixes** [L., neck] 1. the neck 2. a necklike part, esp. of the uterus —**cer'vical** *adj.*

cesium (sē'zē əm) *U.S. spelling of* CAESIUM

cess (ses) *n.* [prob. < ASSESS] [Archaic] a tax

cessation (se sā'shən) *n.* [< L. *cessare*, cease] a ceasing, either final or temporary; stop

cession (sesh'ən) *n.* [< L. *cedere*, to yield] a ceding or giving up of (rights, territory, etc.) to another

cesspit (ses'pit') *n.* *same as* CESSPOOL

cesspool (ses'pōōl') *n.* [< ?] a tank or deep hole in the ground to receive drainage or sewage from the sinks, toilets, etc. of a house

cestus (ses'təs) *n.* [< L. *caedere*, strike] a device of leather straps, sometimes weighted with metal, worn on the hand by boxers in ancient Rome

cesura (si zyōōər'ə) *n.* *same as* CAESURA

cetacean (si tā'shən) *n.* [< Gr. *kētos*, whale] any of an order of water mammals, including whales, porpoises, and dolphins —*adj.* of the cetaceans

cetane (sē'tān') *n.* [< L. *cetus*, whale] a saturated hydrocarbon of the methane family, found as a colourless oil in petroleum

cetane number a number representing the ignition properties of diesel engine fuel oils

CF 1. Canadian Forces 2. cost and freight

Cf *Chem.* californium

cf. [L. *confer*] compare

c/f carried forward

CFB Canadian Forces Base

CFL Canadian Football League

cg centigram(me)(s)

cgs, c.g.s., C.G.S. centimetre-gram-second

Ch. 1. Chaldean 2. China 3. Chinese

Ch., ch. 1. chapter 2. church

cha (chä) *n.* [< Hindi *cā* < Chin. *ch'a*] [Slang] tea

cha-cha (chä'chä) *n.* [echoic] a ballroom dance of Latin American origin Also **cha'-cha'-cha'**

chafe (chāf) *vt.* **chafed, chaf'ing** [< L. *calere*, be warm + *facere*, make] 1. to rub so as to make warm 2. to wear away or make sore by rubbing 3. to annoy; irritate —*vi.* 1. to rub (*on* or *against*) 2. to be irritated or impatient —*n.* an irritation caused by rubbing —**chafe at the bit** to be impatient

chafer (chāf'ər) *n.* [OE. *ceafor*] a large, heavy beetle

chaff (chāf) *n.* [OE. *ceaf*] 1. threshed or winnowed husks of grain 2. anything worthless 3. good-natured teasing —*vt., vi.* to tease in a good-natured way

chaffer (chaf'ər) *vi.* [< OE. *ceapfaru*] [Now Rare] to haggle over price; bargain —**chaf'ferer** *n.*

chaffinch (cha'finch') *n.* [OE. *ceaffinc*] a small European songbird, with black and white wings: the male has a reddish body and blue-grey head

chafing dish (chāf'iŋ) a pan with a heating apparatus beneath it, to cook food at the table or to keep food hot

chagrin (sha'grin) *n.* [Fr., grief] a feeling of embarrassment and distress caused by failure or disappointment —*vt.* **-grined, -grining** to cause to feel chagrin

chain (chān) *n.* [< L. *catena*] 1. a flexible series of joined links 2. [*pl.*] *a)* fetters *b)* captivity 3. a chainlike measuring instrument, or its length: a *surveyor's chain* is 66 feet (20.12m) 4. a connected series of things or events 5. a number of stores, restaurants, etc. owned by one company —*vt.* 1. to fasten with chains 2. to hold down, restrain, confine, etc.

chain gang a gang of prisoners chained together, as when working

chain mail flexible armour made of metal links

chain-react *vi.* to be involved in a chain reaction

chain reaction 1. a series of chemical or nuclear reactions in which the products of the reaction contribute directly to the propagation of the process 2. any sequence of events, each of which results in the following

chain-smoke *vt., vi.* **-smoked', -smok'-ing** to smoke (cigarettes) one straight after the other

chain store any of a number of shops having the same owner

chair (châar) *n.* [OFr. *chaiere* < L. *cathedra*] **1.** a piece of furniture for one person to sit on, having a back and, usually, four legs **2.** a seat of authority or dignity **3.** an official position, as a full professorship **4.** a chairman **5.** *same as:* a) SEDAN CHAIR *b)* ELECTRIC CHAIR —*vt.* **1.** to place in a chair **2.** to preside over as chairman **3.** to carry aloft in, or as in a chair, as a mark of respect —**take the chair** to preside as chairman

chairlift *n.* a line of seats suspended from a power-driven endless cable, used esp. to carry skiers up a slope

chairman *n.* a person who presides at a meeting or heads a committee, board, etc: also, **chair′per′son** —**chair′man-ship′** *n.*

chaise (shāz) *n.* [Fr.] any of certain lightweight carriages, some with a collapsible top, having two or four wheels

chaise longue (shāz′lon′) [Fr., long chair] a couchlike chair with a seat long enough to support the outstretched legs

chalcedony (kal sed′ən ē) *n., pl.* -nies [< Gr. *chalkēdōn*, a precious stone < ?] a kind of quartz with the lustre of wax, variously coloured

chalet (shal′ā) *n.* [Swiss-Fr.] **1.** a herdsman's hut in the Swiss Alps **2.** a type of Swiss house, with balconies and overhanging eaves **3.** a cabin in a holiday camp

chalice (chal′is) *n.* [< L. *calix*, cup] **1.** a goblet **2.** the cup for the wine of Holy Communion —**chal′iced** *adj.*

chalk (chôk) *n.* [< L. *calx*, limestone] **1.** a white limestone that is soft and easily pulverized **2.** a piece of chalk used for writing on a blackboard, etc. —*adj.* made or drawn with chalk —*vt.* **1.** to smear with chalk **2.** to mark with chalk —**as different as chalk from cheese** totally different —**by a long chalk** by a long way —**chalk up 1.** to score or achieve **2.** to charge or credit —**chalk′iness** *n.* —**chalk′y** *adj.*

challenge (chal′ənj) *vt.* -lenged, -lenging [< L. *calumnia*, CALUMNY] **1.** to call to take part in a contest, duel, etc. **2.** to make an objection to; question **3.** to make demands on [to *challenge* the imagination] **4.** to call to a halt for identification **5.** to take formal exception to (a prospective juror) —*n.* **1.** a call to a contest, duel, etc. **2.** a calling into question [a *challenge* to an assertion] **3.** anything that calls for special effort **4.** a demand for identification [a sentry gave the *challenge*] **5.** *Law* a formal objection or exception to a person chosen as a prospective juror —**chal′lenger** *n.*

chalybeate (kə lib′ē ət) *adj.* [< Gr. *chalyps*, steel] containing salts of iron —*n.* a chalybeate liquid

chamber (châm′bər) *n.* [see CAMERA] **1.** an assembly hall **2.** a legislative or judicial body **3.** a council or board [a *chamber* of commerce] **4.** [*pl.*] a) a place where judicial business not requiring to be done in open court is transacted *b)* the rooms where a barrister conducts business **5.** [Archaic] a room, esp. a bedroom **6.** [*pl.*] a suite of rooms used by one person **7.** a cavity **8.** a compartment; specif., the part of a gun that holds the cartridge —**cham′bered** *adj.*

chamberlain (châm′bər lin) *n.* [< OFr. < OHG.] **1.** an officer in charge of the household of a ruler or lord **2.** formerly, a treasurer esp. of a municipality

chambermaid *n.* a woman whose work is taking care of bedrooms, as in hotels

chamber music music for performance by a small group, as a string quartet, orig. in a small hall

chamber of commerce an association established to further the business interests of its community

chamber pot a portable container kept in a bedroom and used as a toilet

CHAMELEON
(to 60 cm long, including tail)

chameleon (kə mēl′yən) *n.* [< Gr. *chamai*, on the ground + *leōn*, lion] **1.** any of various lizards that can change the colour of their skin **2.** a changeable or fickle person —**chame′leon′ic** (-mē′lē on′ik) *adj.*

chamfer (cham′fər) *n.* [< L.: see CANT[2] & FRAGILE] a bevelled edge or corner —*vt.* **1.** to cut a chamfer on; bevel **2.** to make a groove or fluting in

chamois (sham′wä; for 2b & *vt.*, sham′ē) *n., pl.* -ois [Fr.] **1.** a small antelope of Europe and the Caucasus **2.** a) a soft leather made from the skin of chamois, or of sheep, deer, etc. *b)* a piece of this leather, used as a polishing cloth: also **chammy** (sham′ē) —*adj.* made of chamois —*vt.* **-oised** (-ēd), **cham′oising** (-ē in) to polish with a chamois skin

champ[1] (champ) *vt., vi.* [echoic] to chew hard and noisily —*n.* the act of champing —**champ at the bit 1.** to bite upon its bit restlessly: said of a horse **2.** to be restless

champ[2] *n.* [Slang] *same as* CHAMPION

champagne (sham pān′) *n.* **1.** any of various wines produced in Champagne, in NE France **2.** any similar wine **3.** pale, tawny yellow

champers (sham′pərz) *n.* [Slang] champagne

champion (cham′pē ən) *n.* [< LL. *campio*, combatant < L. *campus*, field] **1.** a winner of first place in a competition **2.** a person who fights for another or for a cause; defender —*adj.* **1.** winning first place **2.** [Dial. or Colloq.] excellent —*vt.* to fight for; defend —**cham′pionship′** *n.*

Chan., Chanc. 1. Chancellor 2. Chancery

chan. channel

chance (chäns) *n.* [< L. *cadere,* fall] 1. the happening of events without apparent cause; luck 2. an unpredictable or accidental happening 3. a risk 4. an opportunity 5. a possibility *[a chance that he will live]* —*adj.* accidental —*vi.* **chanced, chanc'ing** to happen —*vt.* to risk *[let's chance it]* —**by chance** accidentally —**chance on** (or **upon**) to find by chance —**chance one's arm** to risk possible failure —**on the off chance** relying on the (remote) possibility

chancel (chän's'l) *n.* [< L. *cancelli,* lattice] that part of a church around the altar, reserved for the clergy and choir

chancellery (chän'sə lə rē) *n., pl.* **-leries** 1. the staff, residence or rank of a chancellor 2. the political section of an embassy 3. a consulate Also sp. **chan'cellory**

chancellor *n.* [< LL. *cancellarius,* keeper of the barrier] 1. [usually C-] any of several high officials in the British government 2. the honorary head of a university 3. the prime minister in W Germany and Austria

Chancellor of the Exchequer the cabinet minister responsible for finance, taxation, etc.

chancery (chän'sər ē) *n., pl.* **-ceries** [< ML. *cancellaria*] 1. a division of the High Court of Justice in England and Wales 2. *same as* CHANCELLERY —**in chancery** 1. in process of litigation in the court of chancery 2. in a helpless situation

chancre (shaŋ'kər) *n.* [Fr.: see CANCER] a venereal sore or ulcer; primary lesion of syphilis —**chan'crous** *adj.*

chancy (chän'sē) *adj.* **-ier, -iest** risky; uncertain

chandelier (shan'də lēər') *n.* [< L. *candela,* candle] a lighting fixture hanging from a ceiling, with branches for candles, electric light bulbs, etc.

chandler (chän'dlər) *n.* [< L. *candela,* candle] 1. a retailer of supplies, etc. of a certain kind *[ship's chandler]* 2. a maker or seller of candles —**chan'dlery** *n.*

change (chānj) *vt.* **changed, chang'ing** [< L. *cambire,* barter] 1. to put or take (a thing) in place of something else; substitute *[to change one's clothes]* 2. to exchange *[let's change seats]* 3. to alter 4. to give or receive the equivalent of (a coin or banknote) in currency of lower denominations or in foreign money 5. to put a fresh covering on —*vi.* 1. to alter; vary 2. to leave one train, bus, etc. and board another 3. to put on other clothes —*n.* 1. the act or process of substitution or variation 2. variety 3. another set of clothes 4. *a)* money returned as the difference between the purchase price and the larger sum given in payment *b)* a number of coins or banknotes whose total value equals a single larger coin or note *c)* small coins 5. a place where merchants meet to do business; exchange: also **'change** 6. [usually *pl.*] Bell Ringing

any order in which the bells may be rung —**change down** to change to a lower gear —**change up** to change to a higher gear —**get no change out of** [Slang] to fail to gain information, help, etc. from —**change'ful** *adj.* —**change'fully** *adv.* —**change'fulness** *n.* —**chang'er** *n.*

changeable *adj.* 1. that can change or be changed; alterable 2. having a changing appearance or colour —**change'abil'ity, change'ableness** *n.* —**change'ably** *adv.*

changeless *adj.* unchanging; immutable

changeling *n.* a child secretly put in the place of another, esp., in folk tales, by fairies

change of life *same as* MENOPAUSE

changeover *n.* 1. a complete change, as in goods produced, equipment, etc. 2. a change of situation, job, etc.

channel (chan''l) *n.* [see CANAL] 1. the bed of a river, etc. 2. the deeper part of a river, harbour, etc. 3. a body of water joining two larger bodies of water 4. a tubelike passage for liquids 5. any means of passage or transmission 6. [*pl.*] the proper or official course of action *[to make a request through army channels]* 7. a long groove 8. a frequency band within which a radio or television transmitting station must keep its signal —*vt.* **-nelled, -nelling** 1. to make a channel in 2. to send through or direct into a channel —**the Channel** the English Channel

chant (chänt) *n.* [< L. *canere,* sing] 1. *a)* a song, esp. one in which a series of words is sung to each tone *b)* words, as of a psalm, to be sung in this way 2. a singsong way of speaking —*vi., vt.* 1. to chant; intone 2. to speak monotonously —**chant'er** *n.*

chanticleer (chan'tə klēər') *n.* [< OFr.: see CHANT & CLEAR] a cock: name used in fable and folklore

chantry (chän'trē) *n., pl.* **-tries** [see CHANT] 1. an endowment to pay for the saying of Masses for the soul of a specified person 2. a chapel or altar endowed, esp. in the Middle Ages, for this purpose

chanty (shan'tē) *n., pl.* **-ties** *same as* SHANTY²

chaos (kā'os) *n.* [L. < Gr. *chaos,* space, chaos (sense 1)] 1. the disorder of formless matter and infinite space, supposed to have existed before the ordered universe 2. extreme confusion or disorder

chaotic (kā ot'ik) *adj.* in a state of chaos; in a completely disordered condition —**chaot'ically** *adv.*

chap¹ (chap) *n.* [< ?] *same as* CHOP²

chap² *n.* [< CHAPMAN] [Colloq.] a man or boy

chap³ *vt., vi.* **chapped, chap'ping** [ME. *chappen*] to crack open or roughen, as the skin from exposure to cold —*n.* a chapped place in the skin

chap. 1. chaplain 2. chapter

chapatti, chapati (chə pa'tē) *n., pl.* **-tis, -ties** [< Hindi] a flat, unleavened bread from India

chapel (chap''l) *n.* [< VL. *capella,* cloak:

orig. sanctuary in which cloak of St. Martin was preserved] **1.** a room used as a place of worship **2.** a part of a church, having its own altar **3.** a religious service in a chapel **4.** any place of worship for those who are not members of an established church **5.** the members of a trade union in a publishing house, etc.

chaperon, chaperone (shap′ə rōn′) *n.* [Fr. < OFr., hood] an older or married woman who accompanies young unmarried people in public to supervise their behaviour —*vt., vi.* -**oned**′, -**on**′**ing** to act as chaperon (to) —**chap′eron′age** *n.*

chaplain (chap′lin) *n.* [see CHAPEL] a clergyman attached to a chapel or serving with the armed forces or in a prison, hospital, etc. —**chap′laincy, chap′lainship′** *n.*

chaplet (chap′lit) *n.* [< OFr.] **1.** a garland for the head **2.** a string of prayer beads one third the length of a full rosary **3.** any string of beads —**chap′leted** *adj.*

chapman (chap′mən) *n.* [< OE. *ceap,* trade] [Archaic] a pedlar; hawker

chappie, chappy *n. same as* CHAP[2]

CHAPS

chaps[1] (chaps, shaps) *n.pl.* [< MexSp. *chaparejos*] leather trousers without a seat, worn over ordinary trousers by cowboys to protect their legs

chaps[2] (chaps) *n.pl. same as* CHOPS

chapter (chap′tər) *n.* [< L. *caput,* head] **1.** a main division, as of a book **2.** a thing like a chapter; part **3.** *a)* a formal meeting of canons of a church or of the members of a religious order *b)* the group of such canons, etc. —**chapter and verse** **1.** the exact reference or authority **2.** detailed information —**chapter of accidents** a chain of unfortunate events

char[1] (chär) *vt., vi.* **charred, char′ring** **1.** to burn to charcoal **2.** to scorch

char[2] *n.* a charwoman —*vi.* **charred, char′-ring** to work as a charwoman

char[3] *n.* [< ?] any of a genus of trout with small scales and a red belly Also sp. **charr**

char[4] *n. same as* CHA

charabanc, char-à-banc (shar′ə baŋ′) *n.* [Fr., car with bench] a sightseeing bus

character (kar′ik tər) *n.* [< Gr. *charassein,* engrave] **1.** the particular personality of an individual or group **2.** a distinctive quality **3.** nature; kind or sort **4.** moral strength **5.** *a)* reputation *b)* good reputation **6.** status; position **7.** a personage [great *characters* in history] **8.** a person in a play, novel, etc. **9.** [Colloq.] an eccentric person **10.** any figure, letter, or symbol used in writing and printing **11.** *Biol.* any attribute, as colour, shape, etc., caused by the action of genes —**char′-acterless** *adj.*

characteristic (kar′ik tə ris′tik) *adj.* typical; distinctive —*n.* **1.** a distinguishing feature or quality **2.** the integer part of a logarithm —**char′acteris′tically** *adv.*

characterize (kar′ik tə rīz′) *vt.* -**ized**′, -**iz**′**ing** **1.** to describe the particular qualities of **2.** to be the distinctive character of; distinguish —**char′acteriza′tion** *n.*

charade (shə räd′) *n.* [Fr.] **1.** [*often pl.*] a game in which a word to be guessed is acted syllable by syllable or as a whole **2.** a mockery; farce

charcoal (chär′kōl′) *n.* [prob. < ME. *charren,* to burn + *cole,* coal] **1.** a form of carbon produced by partially burning wood or other organic matter **2.** a very dark grey or brown —*vt.* to draw with charcoal

chard (chärd) *n.* [< L. *carduus,* thistle] a kind of beet whose leaves are used as food

charge (chärj) *vt.* **charged, charg′ing** [< L. *carrus,* wagon] **1.** to ask as a price **2.** to record as a debt against a person **3.** to make liable for (an error, etc.) **4.** to accuse; censure [he *charged* her with negligence] **5.** to give as a task, duty, etc. to; command **6.** to rush forward and attack **7.** to load or fill with the required material **8.** to add an electrical charge to (a battery, etc.) **9.** to saturate with [air *charged* with steam] —*vi.* **1.** to ask payment (*for*) **2.** to attack vigorously or move forward as if attacking —*n.* **1.** cost or price **2.** accusation; indictment **3.** instruction or command **4.** *a)* an attack or onrush *b)* the signal for this **5.** responsibility or care (*of*) **6.** a person or thing entrusted to someone's care **7.** the amount, as of fuel, gunpowder, etc., used to load something **8.** the amount of chemical energy stored in a battery and dischargeable as electrical energy —**in charge** having the responsibility or control

chargeable *adj.* that can be charged

chargé d′affaires (shär′zhā da fãar′) [Fr.] a diplomat temporarily substituting for an ambassador, or one in charge of a minor diplomatic mission

charger *n.* **1.** a horse ridden in battle **2.** an apparatus for charging storage batteries **3.** [Obs.] a large platter

chariot (char′ē ət) *n.* [see CHARGE] a horse-drawn, two-wheeled cart used in ancient times for war, racing, etc.

charioteer (char′ē ə tēər′) *n.* a chariot driver

charisma (kə riz′mə) *n.* [< Gr., grace] **1.** a special quality of leadership that inspires great popular allegiance Also **char-**

ism (kar′iz′m) **2.** *Christian Theol.* a divinely inspired gift or talent, as for prophesying —**charismatic** (kar′iz mat′-ik) *adj.*

charitable (char′i tə b′l) *adj.* **1.** kind and generous to those in need **2.** of or for charity **3.** kind and forgiving in judging others —**char′itably** *adv.*

charity (char′ə tē) *n., pl.* **-ties** [< L. *caritas*, affection] **1.** a charitable institution, organization, etc. **2.** a voluntary giving of money, etc. to those in need **3.** kindness in judging others **4.** benevolence **5.** an act of good will **6.** *Christian Theol.* the love of man for his fellow men

charlatan (shär′lə t′n) *n.* [Fr. < It.] one who pretends to have expert knowledge or skill that he does not have; fake; mountebank —**char′latanism, char′la-tanry** *n.*

Charles′s Wain (chärl′ziz) *same as* PLOUGH

charleston (chärl′stən) *n.* [< *Charleston*, in S. Carolina, U.S.] [also C-] a lively dance in 4/4 time, characterized by a twisting step

charlie (chär′lē) *n.* [< *Charles*] [Colloq.] a fool

charlock (chär′lok) *n.* [OE. *cerlic*] a weed with yellow flowers

charlotte (shär′lət) *n.* [Fr.] a dessert made of fruit, gelatin, custard, etc. in a mould lined with strips of cake

charm (chärm) *n.* [< L. *carmen*, song] **1.** a quality that attracts or delights **2.** a trinket on a bracelet, etc. **3.** a chanted word or verse, an action, or an object assumed to have magic power —*vt.* **1.** to fascinate; delight **2.** to act on as though by magic —**charm′er** *n.*

charming *adj.* attractive; fascinating; delightful —**charm′ingly** *adv.*

charnel (chär′n′l) *n.* [< L. *caro*, flesh] a building or place where corpses or bones are deposited: in full, **charnel house** —*adj.* of, like, or fit for a charnel

Charon (kāər′ən) *Gr. Myth.* the boatman who ferried dead souls across the river Styx to Hades

chart (chärt) *n.* [see CARD[1]] **1.** a map, esp. one for marine or air navigation **2.** an outline map on which information is plotted **3.** *a)* a group of facts set up in the form of a diagram, graph, etc. *b)* such a diagram **4.** [*chiefly pl.*] a list of the currently most popular gramophone records, etc. —*vt.* **1.** to make a chart of **2.** to plan (a course of action) **3.** to show by, on, or as by, a chart —**chart′-less** *adj.*

charter (chär′tər) *n.* [see CARD[1]] **1.** a written grant of rights given by a monarch or legislature **2.** a document setting forth the aims and principles of a united group **3.** the hire or lease of a ship, bus, etc. —*vt.* **1.** to grant a charter to **2.** to hire for exclusive use —**char′terer** *n.*

chartered accountant an accountant

certified by the Institute of Chartered Accountants

chartered bank in Canada, a privately owned bank incorporated by Parliament to operate in the commercial banking system and usually having a network of branches across the country

Chartism (chär′tiz′m) *n.* a movement for social and political reform in England (1838-48), or its principles set forth in the People's Charter (1838) —**Chart′ist** *n., adj.*

chartreuse (shär trœz′) *n.* [Fr., Carthusian] a pale-green or white liqueur made by Carthusian monks

charwoman (chär′woom′ən) *n.* [see CHORE] a woman who does cleaning or scrubbing, as in office buildings

chary (chāər′ē) *adj.* **-ier, -iest** [< OE. *cearu*, care] **1.** not taking chances; cautious **2.** not giving freely; sparing —**char′ily** *adv.* —**char′iness** *n.*

Charybdis (kə rib′dis) whirlpool off the NE coast of Sicily: see SCYLLA

chase[1] (chās) *vt.* **chased, chas′ing** [see CATCH] **1.** to follow quickly so as to catch **2.** to run after; follow **3.** to drive away **4.** to hunt **5.** [Slang] to court in an unsubtle manner —*vi.* **1.** to go in pursuit **2.** [Colloq.] to rush —*n.* **1.** a pursuit **2.** *a)* the hunting of game for sport *b)* the quarry **3.** *same as* FOREST (sense 2)

chase[2] *n.* [OFr. < L. *capsa*, box] **1.** a groove **2.** a rectangular metal frame in which pages or columns of type are locked

chase[3] *vt.* **chased, chas′ing** [< Fr. *enchâsser*, enshrine] to ornament (metal) by engraving, etc.

chaser *n.* **1.** [Colloq.] a horse for steeplechasing **2.** [Colloq.] a drink taken after another, as beer after spirits

chasm (kaz′′m) *n.* [< Gr. *chainein*, gape] **1.** a deep crack in the earth's surface; abyss **2.** a divergence of feelings, interests, etc.; rift —**chas′mal, chas′mic** *adj.*

chassis (shas′ē) *n., pl.* **-sis** (-ēz) [Fr.: see CHASE[2]] **1.** the frame of a motor vehicle or aircraft **2.** the landing gear of an aircraft **3.** *Radio & TV* the framework to which the parts of a receiver, amplifier, etc. are attached

chaste (chāst) *adj.* [< L. *castus*, pure] **1.** not indulging in extramarital sexual activity **2.** celibate **3.** decent; modest **4.** restrained and simple in style —**chaste′-ly** *adv.* —**chaste′ness** *n.*

chasten (chās′′n) *vt.* [< L. *castigare*, punish] **1.** to punish so as to correct; chastise **2.** to restrain; subdue **3.** to refine in style —**chas′tener** *n.*

chastise (chas tīz′) *vt.* **-tised′, -tis′ing** [see prec.] to punish, esp. by beating —**chastise′ment** *n.* —**chastis′er** *n.*

chastity (chas′tə tē) *n.* **1.** virtuousness **2.** sexual abstinence **3.** decency **4.** simplicity of style

CHASUBLE

chasuble (chaz′y∞ b′l) *n.* [< ML. *casubla*, hooded garment] a sleeveless outer vestment worn over the alb by priests at Mass

chat (chat) *vi.* **chat′ted, chat′ting** [< CHATTER] to talk in a light, informal way —*n.* **1.** an informal conversation **2.** any of various birds with a chattering call —**chat up** [Colloq.] to draw into conversation

château (sha′tō) *n.,* *pl.* **-teaux′** (-tōz) [Fr. < L. *castellum,* castle] a French castle or large country house

chatelaine (shat′ə lān′) *n.* [Fr., ult. < L. *castellum,* castle] **1.** the mistress of a castle **2.** *Hist.* a woman's ornamental chain, esp. for the waist, with keys, a watch, etc. fastened to it

chattel (chat′′l) *n.* [see CATTLE] a movable item of personal property, as a piece of furniture

chatter (chat′ər) *vi.* [echoic] **1.** to make short, indistinct sounds in rapid succession, as birds, apes, etc. **2.** to talk fast, incessantly, and foolishly **3.** to click together rapidly, as the teeth do from cold —*n.* rapid, foolish talk —**chat′-terer** *n.*

chatterbox *n.* an incessant talker

chatty *adj.* **chat′tier, chat′tiest** **1.** fond of chatting **2.** light and informal: said of talk —**chat′tily** *adv.* —**chat′tiness** *n.*

chauffeur (shō′fər) *n.* [Fr., stoker] a person hired to drive a private car for someone else —*vt.* to act as chauffeur to

chauvinism (shō′və niz′m) *n.* [< N. *Chauvin,* fanatical Fr. patriot] **1.** militant, boastful, and fanatical patriotism **2.** unreasoning devotion to one's race, sex, etc. —**chau′vinist** *n., adj.* —**chau′vinis′-tic** *adj.* —**chau′vinis′tically** *adv.*

cheap (chēp) *adj.* [< OE. *ceap,* a bargain] **1.** low in price **2.** charging low prices **3.** spending little **4.** worth more than the price **5.** easily got **6.** of little value **7.** contemptible **8.** available at low interest rates: said of money —*adv.* at low cost —**on the cheap** cheaply —**cheap′ly** *adv.* —**cheap′ness** *n.*

cheapen *vt., vi.* to make or become cheap or cheaper

cheap-jack *n.* [CHEAP + JACK] a seller of cheap, inferior articles —*adj.* cheap, inferior, base, etc.

cheapskate *n.* [Colloq.] a miserly person

cheat (chēt) *vt.* [< ME. *eschete:* see ESCHEAT] **1.** to defraud **2.** to deceive by trickery **3.** to foil by tricks or luck [to *cheat* death] —*vi.* **1.** to practise deception **2.** [Slang] to be sexually unfaithful (often with *on*) —*n.* **1.** one who deceives; swindler **2.** a fraud; deception —**cheat′er** *n.* —**cheat′ingly** *adv.*

check (chek) *n.* [OFr. *eschec,* a check at chess] **1.** a sudden stop **2.** any restraint of action **3.** one that restrains or controls **4.** a supervision or test of accuracy, efficiency, etc. **5.** [U.S.] one's bill at a restaurant or bar **6.** *U.S. sp.* of CHEQUE **7.** a pattern of small squares like that of a chessboard **8.** a fabric with such a pattern **9.** *Chess* a state of play in which the opponent's king could be captured next move **10.** *Hunting* the loss of a quarry's scent by the hounds —*interj. Chess* a call indicating that the opponent's king is in check —*vt.* **1.** to make stop suddenly **2.** to restrain **3.** to repulse or rebuke **4.** to test, measure, verify, or control by investigation or comparison **5.** to mark with a pattern of squares **6.** *Chess* to place (an opponent's king) in check —*vi.* **1.** to agree with one another, item for item [the accounts *check*] **2.** to investigate so as to determine the condition, validity, etc. of something (often with *on*) **3.** *Chess* to place an opponent's king in check **4.** *Hunting* to lose the scent of the quarry: said of hounds —*adj.* **1.** used to check or verify **2.** having a crisscross pattern; checked —**check in 1.** to register at a hotel, airport, etc. **2.** [Colloq.] to report, as by presenting oneself —**check off** to mark as verified, examined, etc. —**check out 1.** to settle one's bill and leave a hotel, etc. **2.** to add up the prices of (purchases) and collect the total: said of a cashier **3.** to examine and verify **4.** to prove to be accurate, sound, etc. upon examination —**check up on** to examine or investigate —**in check** under control

checked *adj.* having a pattern of squares

checkers *n.pl.* [U.S.] *same as* DRAUGHTS

checkmate *n.* [ult. < Per. *shāh māt,* the king is dead] **1.** *Chess a)* the winning move that checks the opponent's king so that it cannot be put into safety *b)* the king's position after this move **2.** complete defeat, frustration, etc. —*interj. Chess* a call indicating checkmate —*vt.* **-mat′-ed, -mat′ing** to subject to checkmate

checkout *n.* the place for checking out purchases, as in a supermarket

checkup *n.* a general medical examination

Cheddar (cheese) (ched′ər) [< *Cheddar,* Avon] [*often* c-] a variety of hard, smooth cheese

cheek (chēk) *n.* [OE. *ceoke,* jaw] **1.** either side of the face, below the eye **2.** either of the buttocks **3.** [Colloq.] sauciness; impudence —*vt.* to speak insolently to —**cheek by jowl** intimately —(with) **tongue in cheek** in a humorously ironic or insincere way

cheekbone *n.* the bone of the upper cheek, just below the eye

cheeky *adj.* -ier, -iest [Colloq.] saucy; insolent —**cheek′ily** *adv.* —**cheek′iness** *n.*

cheep (chēp) *n.* [echoic] the short, faint, shrill sound of a young bird; peep —*vt., vi.* to make such a sound —**cheep′er** *n.*

cheer (chēar) *n.* [< Gr. *kara,* head] 1. a shout of welcome, encouragement, etc. 2. state of mind or of feeling; spirit —*vt.* 1. to fill with joy and hope; gladden; comfort (often with *up*) 2. to urge on, greet, or applaud with cheers —*vi.* 1. to be or become cheerful; feel encouraged (usually with *up*) 2. to shout cheers

cheerful *adj.* 1. joyful 2. bright and attractive 3. willing; ready [a *cheerful* helper] —**cheer′fully** *adv.* —**cheer′fulness** *n.*

cheerio (chēar ē ō′) *interj., n., pl.* -os′ [Colloq.] 1. goodbye 2. good health: a toast

cheerless *adj.* not cheerful; dismal —**cheer′lessly** *adv.* —**cheer′lessness** *n.*

cheers *interj.* [Colloq.] good health: a toast

cheery *adj.* -ier, -iest cheerful —**cheer′ily** *adv.* —**cheer′iness** *n.*

cheese[1] (chēz) *n.* [OE. *cyse*] 1. a food made from curds of soured milk pressed together to form a solid, variously hardened, ripened, etc. 2. a shaped mass of this

cheese[2] *n.* [prob. < Hindi *chīz,* thing] [Slang] an important person or thing: also **big cheese**

cheeseburger (chēz′bur′gər) *n.* [see HAMBURGER] a hamburger topped with melted cheese

cheesecake *n.* 1. a kind of cake made of cottage cheese or cream cheese, eggs, sugar, etc. 2. [Slang] photographs, etc., of women displayed for their sex appeal

cheesecloth *n.* [from use as cheese wrapping] a thin cotton cloth with a loose weave

cheesed off [Slang] bored; fed up

cheeseparing *n.* miserly handling of money —*adj.* stingy; miserly

cheesy *adj.* -ier, -iest 1. like cheese in consistency, smell, etc. 2. [Slang] inferior; poor —**chees′iness** *n.*

cheetah (chēt′ə) *n.* [Hindi *chītā*] a swift, leopardlike animal of Africa and S Asia

chef (shef) *n.* [Fr. < *chef de cuisine,* head of the kitchen] 1. a head cook, as in a restaurant 2. any cook

chela (kē′lə) *n., pl.* -lae (-lē) [< Gr. *chēlē,* claw] a pincerlike claw of a crab, lobster, scorpion, etc.

Chelsea Pensioner (chel′sē) an inmate of the Chelsea Royal Hospital for old soldiers

chem. 1. chemical(s) 2. chemist 3. chemistry

chemical (kem′ik′l) *adj.* 1. of chemistry 2. involving the use of chemicals —*n.* any substance used in or obtained by a chemical process —**chem′ically** *adv.*

chemical engineering the science or profession of applying chemistry to industrial uses

chemical warfare warfare using poisonous gases, flame throwers, defoliants, etc.

chemin de fer (shə man′də fāər′) [Fr., a railway] a kind of baccarat, a gambling game

chemise (shə mēz′) *n.* [< VL. *camisia,* shirt] *Hist.* a woman's undergarment like a loose, short slip

chemist (kem′ist) *n.* [< (AL)CHEMIST] 1. one who sells medicines, toiletries, etc. 2. an expert or specialist in chemistry 3. a pharmacist

chemistry *n., pl.* -tries [see prec.] the science dealing with the composition and properties of substances, and with the reactions by which substances are produced from or converted into other substances

chemotherapy (kem′ō ther′ə pē) *n.* the prevention or treatment of infection or disease by chemical drugs —**chem′other′apist** *n.*

chemurgy (kem′ər jē) *n.* [CHEM(ISTRY) + -URGY] the branch of chemistry dealing with the industrial use of organic products, esp. from farms

chenille (shi nēl′) *n.* [Fr., caterpillar < L. *canicula,* little dog] 1. a tufted, velvety yarn 2. a fabric filled or woven with this

cheque (chek) *n.* [see CHECK] a written order to a bank to pay the stated amount from one's account

cheque card a card issued by a bank to an account-holder to guarantee payment of a cheque up to a stated limit

chequer (chek′ər) *n.* [see CHECK] 1. a small square, as on a chessboard 2. a pattern of such squares —*vt.* 1. to mark off in squares, or in patches of colour 2. to break the uniformity of, with changes in fortune, etc.

chequered *adj.* 1. having a pattern of squares 2. varied in colour and shading 3. marked by diversified features or by varied events [a *chequered* career]

cherish (cher′ish) *vt.* [< L. *carus,* dear] 1. to hold dear; feel or show love for 2. to take good care of; foster [to *cherish* one's rights] 3. to cling to the idea of

cheroot (shə rōōt′) *n.* [< Tamil *churuṭṭu,* a roll] a cigar with both ends cut square

cherry (cher′ē) *n., pl.* -ries [< Gr. *kerasion*] 1. a small, fleshy fruit, yellow to dark red, with a stone 2. any tree which bears this fruit, or its wood 3. the bright-red colour of certain cherries —*adj.* 1. bright-red 2. made with cherries

cherub (cher′əb) *n., pl.* -ubs; for 1-3 usually -ubim (-ə bim) [< Heb. *kerūbh*] 1. *Bible* one of certain winged heavenly beings 2. *Christian Theol.* any of the second order of angels, just below the seraphim 3. a representation of a cherub, usually as a chubby, rosy-faced child with wings 4. a child, with a sweet, innocent face —**cherubic** (chə rōō′bik) *adj.*

chervil (chur′vəl) *n.* [< OE. < L. < Gr.] an aromatic plant, with leaves used to flavour soups, etc.

Cheshire cat (chesh′ər) a proverbial grinning cat from Cheshire, esp. one described in Lewis Carroll's *Alice's Adventures in Wonderland*

chess (ches) *n.* [see CHECK] a game for two, each with 16 pieces moved variously on a chessboard in alternation, the object being to checkmate the opponent's king

chessboard *n.* a board with 64 squares of two alternating colours, for chess and draughts

chessman *n.* any of the pieces used in chess

chest (chest) *n.* [< Gr. *kistē*, box] 1. a) the part of the body enclosed by the ribs b) the outside front of this 2. a box with a lid and, often, a lock 3. *same as* CHEST OF DRAWERS 4. a cabinet for medicines, etc. —**get (something) off one's chest** [Colloq.] to unburden oneself of (some trouble, etc.) by talking about it

chested *adj.* having a (specified kind of) chest, or thorax [hollow-*chested*]

chesterfield (ches′tər fēld′) *n.* [< 19th-c. Earl of *Chesterfield*] 1. a single-breasted overcoat for men, usually with a velvet collar 2. a sofa with upright ends

chestnut (ches′nut′) *n.* [< Gr. *kastaneia*] 1. the smooth-shelled, sweet, edible nut of certain trees 2. one of these trees, or the wood 3. *same as* HORSE CHESTNUT 4. reddish brown 5. a reddish-brown horse 6. [Colloq.] an old, stale joke or story —*adj.* reddish-brown

chest of drawers a set of drawers within a frame

chesty *adj.* -ier, -iest [Colloq.] inclined to or having a disease of the chest

cheval glass (shə val′) [Fr. *cheval*, horse] a full-length mirror on swivels in a frame

chevalier (shev′ə lēər′) *n.* [see CAVALIER] 1. a member of the lowest rank of the French Legion of Honour 2. a cavalier; gallant

Cheviot (chev′ē ət) *n.* [< *Cheviot Hills*] 1. any of a breed of sheep with short, dense wool 2. [*usually* c-] a) a rough wool fabric b) a cotton cloth resembling this

CHEVRON

chevron (shev′rən) *n.* [< OFr., rafter] any V-shaped pattern or device, esp. a bar worn on the sleeve of a military uniform, to show rank or service

chew (chōō) *vt.* [< OE. *ceowan*] 1. to bite and crush with the teeth 2. to think over or discuss (often with *over*) —*n.* 1. a chewing 2. something chewed, as a portion of tobacco —**chew the rag (or fat)** [Slang] to converse idly —**chew′-er** *n.*

chewing gum chicle or other gummy substance, flavoured and sweetened for chewing

chewy *adj.* -ier, -iest needing much chewing —**chew′iness** *n.*

chg. *pl.* **chgs.** charge

chgd. charged

chi (kī) *n.* the 22nd letter of the Greek alphabet (X, χ)

Chianti (kē an′tē) *n.* [It.] a red or white wine, orig. made in Tuscany

chiaroscuro (kē är′ə skyōōar′ō) *n.*, *pl.* -ros [It. < L. *clarus*, clear + *obscurus*, dark] 1. the treatment of light and shade in a painting, drawing, etc., so as to produce an illusion of depth 2. a painting, etc. emphasizing this

chic (shēk) *n.* [Fr.] smart elegance of style and manner —*adj.* smartly stylish

chicane (shi kān′) *n.* [Fr. < *chicaner*, to quibble] 1. *same as* CHICANERY 2. *Motor Racing* an artificial barrier designed to reduce speeds before a bend, etc. —*vi.* -caned′, -can′ing to use chicanery —*vt.* to trick

chicanery *n.*, *pl.* -eries 1. the use of clever but deceptive talk or action to deceive 2. an instance of this

chick (chik) *n.* 1. a young chicken 2. any young bird 3. a child: term of endearment 4. [Slang] a young woman

chicken (chik′ən) *n.* [< OE. *cycen*, little cock] 1. a common farm bird; hen or cock, esp. a young one 2. its flesh 3. a young or inexperienced person 4. [Slang] a cowardly person —*adj.* 1. of chicken 2. [Slang] cowardly —*vi.* [Slang] to lose courage and abandon a plan, action, etc. (usually with *out*)

chicken feed [Slang] a petty sum of money

chicken pox an acute, contagious virus disease, usually of young children, with fever and a series of skin eruptions

chickpea (chik′pē) *n.* [< L. *cicer*, pea] a plant of the legume family with pods containing edible seeds

chickweed *n.* a low-growing weed

chicle (chik′′l) *n.* [AmSp.] a substance made from the juice of the sapodilla tree, used in making chewing gum

chicory (chik′ə rē) *n.*, *pl.* -ries [< Gr. *kichorion*] 1. a plant with blue flowers: the leaves are used for salad 2. its root, roasted and ground for mixing with coffee or for use as a coffee substitute

chide (chīd) *vt.*, *vi.* chid′ed or chid (chid), chid′ed or chid or chidden (chid′′n), chid′-ing [OE. *cidan*] to scold —**chid′er** *n.* —**chid′ingly** *adv.*

chief (chēf) *n.* [< L. *caput*, head] the head or leader of a group, tribe, company, department, etc. —*adj.* 1. highest in rank, office, etc. 2. main; principal —**in chief** in the chief position

chiefly *adv.* 1. above all 2. mainly; mostly

chief petty officer *see* MILITARY RANKS, table

chieftain (chēf′tən) *n.* [< L. *caput*, head] a leader, esp. of a clan or tribe —**chief′-taincy, chief′tainship′** *n.*

chief technician *see* MILITARY RANKS, table

chiffchaff (chif′chaf′) *n.* [echoic] a small, olive-green and brown warbler, feeding mainly on insects and spiders

chiffon (shif′on) *n.* [Fr. < *chiffe*, rag] a sheer, lightweight fabric of silk, nylon, etc. —*adj.* 1. made of chiffon 2. *Cooking* made light as by adding beaten egg whites

chiffonier, chiffonnier (shif′ə nēar′) *n.* [Fr., orig., ragpicker < prec.] a narrow, high cabinet or chest of drawers, often with a mirror

chignon (shēn′yôn) *n.* [Fr. < L. *catena*, chain] a knot or coil of hair worn at the back of the neck by women

chigoe (chig′ō) *n., pl.* -oes (-ōz) [< Wind. name] a flea of tropical S. America and Africa: the female burrows into the skin, causing painful sores: also **chig′ger**

Chihuahua (chi wä′wä) *n.* [< *Chihuahua,* state of Mexico] an ancient Mexican breed of very small dog with large, pointed ears

chilblain (chil′blān′) *n.* [CHILL + BLAIN] a painful sore on the foot or hand, caused by exposure to cold

child (chīld) *n., pl.* **chil′dren** [< OE. *cild*] 1. an infant 2. an unborn offspring 3. a boy or girl before puberty 4. a son or daughter 5. a descendant 6. an immature or childish adult 7. a product *[a child of the Renaissance]* —**with child** pregnant —**child′less** *adj.* —**child′lessness** *n.*

child benefit a regular government payment to the parents of children up to a certain age

childbirth *n.* the act of giving birth to a child

childhood *n.* the time or state of being a child

childish *adj.* 1. of or like a child 2. not fit for an adult; immature; silly —**child′ishly** *adv.* —**child′ishness** *n.*

childlike *adj.* like a child; innocent, trusting, etc.

childminder *n.* someone employed to look after the children of working parents

children (chil′drən) *n. pl.* of CHILD

child's play anything simple to do

chili (chil′ē) *n., pl.* **chil′ies** [MexSp.] 1. the dried pod of red pepper, a very hot seasoning 2. the tropical American plant that bears this pod

chiliad (kil′ē ad′) *n.* [< Gr. *chillioi,* thousand] 1. a group of 1000 2. a thousand years

chill (chil) *n.* [OE. *ciele*] 1. a feeling of coldness that makes one shiver 2. a moderate coldness 3. a discouraging influence 4. a sudden fear 5. unfriendliness 6. a feverish cold —*adj.* same as CHILLY —*vi.* 1. to become cool 2. to shiver from cold, fear, etc. —*vt.* 1. to make cool 2. to cause a chill or 3. to check (enthusiasm, etc.) 4. to depress; dispirit 5. to harden (metal) on the surface by rapid cooling —**chill′er** *n.* —**chill′ingly** *adv.* —**chill′ness** *n.*

chilly *adj.* -ier, -iest 1. moderately cold 2. chilling 3. unfriendly 4. dispiriting —**chill′iness** *n.*

Chiltern Hundreds (chil′tərn) a nominal office under the British crown: appointment to it formally circumvents the rule against resignation from Parliament

Chimaera (kī mēar′ə) *same as* CHIMERA

chime¹ (chīm) *n.* [< L. *cymbalum,* cymbal] 1. [*usually pl.*] a) a tuned set of bells or metal tubes b) the sounds produced by these 2. a single bell in a clock, etc. —*vi.* **chimed, chim′ing** 1. to sound as a chime 2. to sound in harmony, as bells 3. to harmonize; agree —*vt.* 1. to ring (a chime) 2. to indicate (time) by chiming —**chime in** 1. to interrupt, as talk 2. to agree —**chim′er** *n.*

chime² *n.* [ME. *chimb*] the extended rim at each end of a cask or barrel

Chimera (kī mēar′ə) *n.* [< Gr. *chimaira,* she-goat] *Gr. Myth.* a fire-breathing monster with a lion's head, goat's body, and serpent's tail —*n.* [**c-**] an impossible or foolish fancy

chimerical (kī mer′i k′l) *adj.* 1. unreal 2. absurd 3. visionary Also **chimer′ic** —**chimer′ically** *adv.*

chimney (chim′nē) *n., pl.* -neys [< Gr. *kaminos,* oven] 1. the passage through which smoke escapes from a fire; flue 2. a structure containing a flue and extending above the roof 3. a glass tube around the flame of a lamp, etc. 4. a fissure or vent, as in a cliff or volcano

chimney sweep a person whose work is cleaning the soot from chimneys

chimp (chimp) *n.* [Colloq.] a chimpanzee

CHIMPANZEE
(90–150 cm high)

chimpanzee (chim′pan zē′) *n.* [< Fr. < Bantu] an anthropoid ape of Africa, with black hair and large ears

chin (chin) *n.* [OE. *cin*] the part of the face below the lower lip; projecting part of the lower jaw —**keep one's chin up** to bear up bravely —**take it on the chin** [Slang] to suffer defeat, etc., bravely

Chin. 1. China 2. Chinese

china (chī′nə) *n.* 1. *a)* porcelain, orig. from China *b)* vitrified ceramic ware like porcelain 2. dishes, etc. of this 3. any earthenware crockery

china clay *same as* KAOLIN

Chinaman *n.* 1. [Archaic] a native of China 2. *Cricket* an off-break bowled by a left-handed bowler to a right-handed batsman

Chinatown *n.* the Chinese quarter of a city

chincherinchee (chin′chər in chē′) *n.* [< ?] a bulbous S African plant with spikes of white or yellow long-lasting flowers

chinchilla (chin chil′ə) *n.* [Sp. < L. *cimex*, bug] 1. a small rodent of the Andes, bred extensively for its fur 2. its expensive, soft, pale-grey fur

chine[1] (chīn) *n.* [< OFr. *eschine*] 1. the backbone 2. a cut of meat containing part of the backbone 3. a ridge

chine[2] *n.* [< OE. *cine*, fissure] [S Eng. Dial.] a rocky ravine or deep fissure in a cliff

Chinese (chī nēz′; *for adj., often* chī′ nēz′) *n.* 1. *pl.* **-nese′** a native of China or a person of Chinese descent 2. the language of the Chinese —*adj.* of China, its people, etc.

Chinese lantern a lantern of brightly coloured paper, made so that it can be folded up

Chinese puzzle any intricate puzzle

Chink (chiŋk) *n.* [< CHINESE] [Derog.] a Chinese

chink[1] (chiŋk) *n.* [OE. *cine*] a crack; fissure

chink[2] *n.* [echoic] a sharp, clinking sound, as of coins striking together —*vi., vt.* to make or cause to make a sharp, clinking sound

chinless wonder [Colloq.] a weak or cowardly person

chinoiserie (shin′wä′zə rē) *n.* [Fr. < *Chinois*, Chinese] 1. an ornate decorative style based on Chinese motifs 2. articles, designs, etc. in this style

chinook (chi nook′, -nuk′) *n.* [< AmInd.] 1. a warm, dry wind blowing down the E slopes of the Rocky Mountains 2. a warm, moist wind blowing onto the coasts of Washington and Oregon

Chinook salmon a Pacific salmon valued as a food fish

chintz (chints) *n.* [< Hindi *chhīnt*] a cotton cloth printed in colours and usually glazed

chintzy *adj.* **-ier, -iest** 1. like chintz 2. of a style of furnishing typified by chintz curtains, coverings, etc.

chinwag (chin′wag′) *n., vi.* [Colloq.] talk; chat

chip (chip) *vt.* **chipped, chip′ping** [< OE. hyp. *cippian*] 1. *a)* to break or cut a small piece from *b)* to break or cut off (a small piece) 2. to shape by cutting —*vi.* to break off into small pieces —*n.* 1. a small piece of wood, etc. cut or broken off 2. a place where a small piece has been chipped off 3. a slice or strip of potato fried in deep fat 4. [U.S.] a potato crisp 5. a small, round disc used as a token; counter 6. *Electronics* a tiny wafer of semiconductor material processed to form a type of integrated circuit 7. wood, palm leaf, or straw split and woven into baskets, etc. —**chip in** [Colloq.] 1. to share in giving money or help 2. to add one's comments —**chip off the old block** a person much like his father —**chip on one's shoulder** [Colloq.] an inclination to take offence —**have had one's chips** [Colloq.] to be

defeated, dead, etc. —**when the chips are down** [Colloq.] when something is really at stake

chip-board *n.* a wood substitute made from compressed wood chips or shavings bonded in resin

chipmunk (chip′muŋk) *n.* [AmInd.] a small, striped N American squirrel: it lives mainly on the ground

chipolata (chip′ō lä′tə) *n.* [Fr. < It.] a small sausage, esp. of pork sausagemeat

Chippendale (chip′′n dāl′) *adj.* [< T. *Chippendale*] designating or of an 18th-cent. style of furniture with graceful lines and, often, rococo ornamentation

chirography (kī rog′rə fē) *n.* [< Gr. *cheir*, hand + -GRAPHY] handwriting; penmanship —**chirog′rapher** *n.*

chiromancy (kīə′rə man′sē) *n.* [< Gr. *cheir*, hand & *manteia*, prophecy] *same as* PALMISTRY —**chi′roman′cer** *n.*

chiropody (kə rop′ə dē) *n.* [< Gr. *cheir*, hand + -POD] the profession dealing with the care of the feet and with the treatment of foot disorders —**chirop′odist** *n.*

chiropractic (kīə′rə prak′tik) *n.* [< Gr. *cheir*, hand + *praktikos*, practical] a method of treating disease by manipulation of the body joints, esp. of the spine —**chi′roprac′tor** *n.*

chirp (chûrp) *vi., vt.* [echoic] to make, or utter in, short, shrill sounds, as some birds or insects —*n.* a short, shrill sound —**chirp′er** *n.*

chirpy *adj.* [Colloq.] cheerful; merry —**chirp′ily** *adv.* —**chirp′iness** *n.*

chirrup (chir′əp) *vi.* [var. of CHIRP] to chirp repeatedly —*n.* a chirruping sound

chisel (chiz′′l) *n.* [< L. *caedere*, to cut] a sharp-edged tool for cutting or shaping wood, stone, or metal —*vi., vt.* **-elled, -elling** to cut or shape with a chisel —**chis′-eller** *n.*

chit[1] (chit) *n.* [ME. *chitte*, kitten] 1. a child 2. an immature, slender or childish girl

chit[2] *n.* [< Hindi] 1. a memorandum 2. a voucher of a small sum owed 3. [Colloq.] an invoice, etc.

chitchat (chit′chat′) *n.* informal talk; gossip

chitin (kīt′in) *n.* [< Gr. *chiton*, tunic] a tough, horny substance forming the outer covering of insects, etc.

chivalrous (shiv′′l rəs) *adj.* 1. having the attributes of an ideal knight; gallant, honourable, etc. 2. of chivalry Also **chiv′alric** —**chiv′alrously** *adv.*

chivalry (shiv′′l rē) *n.* [< OFr. *chevaler*, knight] 1. the medieval system of knighthood 2. the noble qualities a knight was supposed to have, such as courage, honour, etc. 3. the demonstration of these qualities

chives (chīvz) *n.pl.* [< L. *cepa*, onion] a plant with small, hollow leaves having a mild onion odour

chivy, chivvy (chiv′ē) *vt., vi.* **chiv′ied** or **chiv′vied, chiv′ying** or **chiv′vying** to fret; worry; nag

chloral (klôr′əl) *n.* [CHLOR(O)- +

AL(COHOL)] 1. a colourless liquid with a pungent odour, prepared by the action of chlorine on alcohol 2. *same as* CHLORAL HYDRATE

chloral hydrate a colourless, crystalline compound used chiefly as a sedative

chlorate (klôr'āt) *n.* a salt of chloric acid

chloric (klôr'ik) *adj.* 1. of or containing chlorine with a higher valency than in corresponding chlorous compounds 2. designating or of a colourless acid whose salts are chlorates

chloride (klôr'īd) *n.* a compound in which chlorine is combined with another element or radical

chlorinate (klôr'ə nāt') *vt.* -nat'ed, -nat'ing to treat or combine (a substance) with chlorine; esp., to pass chlorine into (water or sewage) for purification —**chlo'rina'tion** *n.*

chlorine (klôr'ēn) *n.* [see CHLORO-] a greenish-yellow, poisonous, gaseous chemical element with a disagreeable odour, used in water purification, etc.; symbol, Cl

chloro- [< Gr. *chlōros*, pale green] a *combining form meaning:* 1. green 2. having chlorine in the molecule

chloroform (klor'ə fôrm') *n.* [see CHLORO- & FORM(IC)] a sweetish, colourless, volatile liquid used as a general anaesthetic and as a solvent —*vt.* to anaesthetize with chloroform

chlorophyll (klôr'ə fil') *n.* [< Gr. *chlōros*, green + *phyllon*, leaf] the green pigment of plants —**chlo'rophyl'lose, chlo'rophyl'lous** *adj.*

chlorous (klôr'əs) *adj.* of or containing chlorine with a lower valency than in corresponding chloric compounds

chm., chmn. chairman

choc-ice (chok'īs) *n.* an ice cream covered with a thin layer of chocolate

chock (chok) *n.* [ONormFr. *choque*] a block or wedge placed under a wheel, barrel, etc. to prevent motion —*vt.* to provide or wedge fast as with chocks

chockablock (chok'ə blok') *adj.* crowded —*adv.* tightly together

chock-full (chok'fool') *adj.* filled to capacity

chocolate (chok'ə lət) *n.* [< Fr. < Sp. < MexInd. *chocolatl*] 1. a paste, powder, etc. made from cacao seeds that have been roasted and ground 2. a drink made of chocolate, hot milk or water, and sugar 3. a sweet made of or coated with chocolate 4. reddish brown —*adj.* 1. made of or flavoured with chocolate 2. reddish-brown

chocolate-box *adj.* [Colloq.] of a style of painting that is pretty in a sentimental way

choice (chois) *n.* [< OFr.] 1. a choosing; selection 2. the power to choose; option 3. a person or thing chosen 4. the best part 5. a variety from which to choose 6. a supply well chosen 7. an alternative 8. care in choosing —*adj.* 1. of special excellence 2. carefully chosen —**choice'ly** *adv.* —**choice'ness** *n.*

choir (kwīər) *n.* [see CHORUS] 1. a group

of singers trained to sing together, esp. in a church 2. the part of a church they occupy

choke (chōk) *vt.* choked, chok'ing [< OE. *aceocian*] 1. to prevent from breathing by blocking the windpipe; strangle; suffocate 2. to obstruct by clogging 3. to hinder the growth or action of 4. to cut off some air from the carburettor of (a petrol engine) to make a richer petrol mixture —*vi.* 1. to be suffocated 2. to be blocked up —*n.* 1. the act or sound of choking 2. the valve that chokes a carburettor —**choke back** to hold back (feelings, sobs, etc.) —**choke down** to swallow with difficulty —**choke up** 1. to block up; clog 2. [Colloq.] to be unable to speak, because of fear, tension, etc.

choker *n.* a closely fitting necklace

choky[1] *adj.* -ier, -iest 1. inclined to choke 2. suffocating; stifling Also sp. **chok'ey**

choky[2] *n.* [< Hindi *caukī*, shed] [Slang] prison

choler (kol'ər) *n.* [see ff.] 1. [Obs.] bile: from medieval idea about humours 2. [Now Rare] anger or ill humour

cholera (kol'ər ə) *n.* [< Gr. *cholē*, bile] any of several intestinal diseases; esp., Asiatic *cholera*, an acute, infectious disease characterized by severe diarrhoea, cramps, and loss of water from the body

choleric (kol'ər ik) *adj.* [see CHOLER] showing a quick temper or irascible nature

cholesterol (kə les'tə rol') *n.* [< Gr. *cholē*, bile + *stereos*, solid] a crystalline fatty alcohol found esp. in animal fats, blood, nerve tissue, and bile

chomp (chomp) *vt., vi.* same as CHAMP[1]

choose (chōoz) *vt.* chose, cho'sen, choos'ing [OE. *ceosan*] 1. to pick out; select 2. to decide or prefer [to *choose* to remain] —*vi.* 1. to make one's selection 2. to have the desire or wish —**choos'er** *n.*

choosy, choosey *adj.* -ier, -iest [Colloq.] hard to please; fussy

chop[1] (chop) *vt.* chopped, chop'ping [ME. *choppen*] 1. to cut by blows with an axe or other sharp tool 2. to cut into small bits 3. to hit with a short, sharp stroke —*vi.* to make quick, cutting strokes with a sharp tool —*n.* 1. a short, sharp blow 2. a piece chopped off 3. a slice of lamb, pork, veal, etc. cut from the rib, loin, or shoulder —**get the chop** [Slang] 1. to be dismissed from one's job 2. to be killed

chop[2] *n.* [var. of *chap*, jaw] 1. a jaw 2. a cheek See CHOPS

chop[3] *vi.* chopped, chop'ping [OE. *ceapian*, to bargain] to shift or veer suddenly, as the wind; change direction —**chop and change** to change (one's plans, ideas, etc.) constantly —**chop logic** to argue

chop-chop *adv., interj.* [PidE. < Chin.] quickly

chophouse *n.* a restaurant that specializes in chops and steaks

chopper *n.* 1. a small hand-axe, esp. for chopping firewood 2. [*pl.*] [Slang] a set of teeth, esp. false teeth 3. [Colloq.] a helicopter

choppy[1] *adj.* **chop′pier, chop′piest** [< CHOP[3]] shifting constantly and abruptly, as the wind —**chop′piness** *n.*

choppy[2] *adj.* **chop′pier, chop′piest** [< CHOP[1]] 1. rough with short, broken waves, as the sea 2. making abrupt starts and stops; jerky —**chop′pily** *adv.* —**chop′piness** *n.*

chops *n.pl.* [var. of *chap, jaw*] 1. the jaws 2. the mouth and lower cheeks —**lick one's chops** to experience or show pleasure in anticipation of something

chopsticks (chop′stiks′) *n.pl.* [PidE. for Chin. *k'wai-tsze,* the quick ones] two small sticks held in one hand and used in some Asian countries to lift food to the mouth

chop suey (chop′sōō′ē) [< Chin. *tsa-sui,* various pieces] a Chinese-American dish of meat, bean sprouts, celery, mushrooms, etc. cooked together in a sauce

choral (kôr′al) *adj.* [Fr.] of, for, sung by, or recited by a choir or chorus —**cho′rally** *adv.*

chorale, choral (ka räl′) *n.* [< G. *Choral* (*gesang*), choral (song)] 1. a hymn tune 2. a choral composition based on such a tune 3. a group of singers; choir

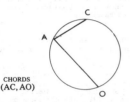

CHORDS
(AC, AO)

chord[1] (kôrd) *n.* [see CORD] 1. a feeling or emotion thought of as being played on like the string of a harp [to strike a sympathetic *chord*] 2. *Geom.* a straight line joining any two points on an arc or circumference

chord[2] *n.* [< ACCORD] *Music* a combination of three or more tones sounded together in harmony —**chord′al** *adj.*

chore (chôr) *n.* [< OE. *cierr*] 1. a small routine task; odd job: *often used in pl.* 2. a hard or unpleasant task

chorea (ko rē′ə) *n.* [< Gr. *choreia,* choral dance] a nervous disorder characterized by jerking movements caused by involuntary muscular contractions; Saint Vitus' dance

choreography (kor′ē og′rə fē) *n.* [Gr. *choreia,* dance + -GRAPHY] 1. the art of devising dances, esp. ballets 2. the arrangement of the movements of a dance 3. dancing, esp. ballet dancing —**chor′eog′rapher** *n.* —**chor′eograph′ic** (-ə graf′ik) *adj.* —**chor′eograph′ically** *adv.*

chorister (kor′is tər) *n.* [see CHORUS] a member of a choir, esp. a boy singer

chortle (chôr′t'l) *vi., vt.* **-tled, -tling** [coined by Lewis Carroll, prob. < *chuckle + snort*] to make, or utter with, a gleeful chuckling

or snorting sound —*n.* such a sound —**chor′tler** *n.*

chorus (kôr′əs) *n.* [< Gr. *choros*] 1. in ancient Greek drama, a group whose singing, dancing, and narration supplement the main action 2. a group of dancers and singers performing together, as in an opera 3. the part of a drama, song, etc. performed by a chorus 4. a group trained to sing or speak something together simultaneously 5. a simultaneous utterance by many [a *chorus* of protest] 6. music written for group singing 7. the refrain of a song following each verse —*vt., vi.* to sing, speak, or say in unison —**in chorus** in unison

chose (chōz) *pt. & obs. pp.* of CHOOSE

chosen *pp.* of CHOOSE —*adj.* selected

chough (chuf) *n.* [ME.] a European bird of the crow family, with red legs and beak and glossy black feathers

choux pastry (shōō) [< Fr. (*pâte*) *choux,* cabbage (dough)] a very light pastry made with eggs

chow (chou) *n.* [< Chin.] 1. a medium-sized dog, originally from China, with a compact, muscular body and thick coat: official name **chow chow** 2. [Slang] food

chow mein (chou mān′) [Chin. *ch'ao,* fry + *mien,* flour] a Chinese-American dish consisting of a thick stew of meat, celery, bean sprouts, etc.

Chr. 1. Christ 2. Christian 3. Chronicles

chrism (kriz′m) *n.* [< Gr. *chriein,* anoint] consecrated oil used in baptism and other sacraments

Christ (krīst) [< Gr. *christos,* the anointed] Jesus of Nazareth, regarded by Christians as the Messiah prophesied in the Old Testament

christen (kris′'n) *vt.* [OE. *cristnian*] 1. to take into a Christian church by baptism 2. to give a name to, esp. at baptism 3. [Colloq.] to use for the first time —**chris′tening** *n.*

Christendom *n.* 1. Christians collectively 2. those parts of the world where most of the inhabitants profess Christianity

Christian (kris′tyən) *n.* a believer in Jesus as the Christ, or in the religion based on the teachings of Jesus —*adj.* 1. of Jesus Christ or his teachings 2. of or professing the religion based on these teachings 3. having the qualities taught by Jesus Christ, as love, kindness, etc. 4. of Christians or Christianity —**Chris′tianly** *adj., adv.*

Christian Era the era beginning with the year formerly thought to be that of the birth of Jesus Christ

Christianity (kris′tē an′ə tē) *n.* 1. Christians collectively 2. the Christian religion 3. a particular Christian religious system 4. the state of being a Christian

Christianize (kris′tyən īz′) *vt.* **-ized′, -iz′ing** 1. to convert to Christianity 2. to cause to conform with Christian character or precepts —**Chris′tianiza′tion** *n.*

Christian name the baptismal name as distinguished from the surname or family name

Christian Science a religion and system of healing founded by Mary Baker Eddy c. 1866: official name, *Church of Christ, Scientist* —**Christian Scientist**

christie, christy (kris′tē) *n.*, *pl.* **-ties** [< *Christiania*, now Oslo] *Skiing* a high-speed turn with skis kept parallel

Christlike (krīst′līk′) *adj.* like Jesus Christ, esp. in character or spirit —**Christ′like′ness** *n.*

Christly *adj.* of Jesus Christ; Christlike

Christmas (kris′məs) *n.* [see CHRIST & MASS] a holiday on Dec. 25 celebrating the birth of Jesus Christ: also **Christmas Day**

Christmas box a sum of money or other present given at Christmas to tradesmen, employees, etc.

Christmas rose *same as* HELLEBORE

Christmas tree an evergreen or artificial tree hung with ornaments and lights at Christmas time

chromate (krō′māt) *n.* a salt of chromic acid

chromatic (krō mat′ik) *adj.* [< Gr. *chrōma*, colour] **1.** of or having colour or colours **2.** *Music* using or progressing by semitones —**chromat′ically** *adv.* —**chro-mat′icism, chro′matic′ity** (-tis′ə tē) *n.*

chromatics *n.pl.* [*with sing.* v.] the scientific study of colours

chromatic scale the musical scale made up of thirteen successive semitones to the octave

chromatin (krō′mə tin) *n.* [< Gr. *chrōma*, colour] a protoplasmic substance in living cells that takes a deep stain: it forms the chromosomes

chromatography (krō′mə tog′rə fē) *n.* [< Gr. *chrōma*, colour & -GRAPHY] the process of separating constituents of a mixture by running a solution of it through an adsorbent on which the substances are separated into bands

chrome (krōm) *n.* [< Gr. *chrōma*, colour] chromium or chromium alloy, esp. as plating —*vt.* **chromed, chrom′ing** to plate with chromium

chromic (krō′mik) *adj.* designating or of compounds containing trivalent chromium

chromite (krō′mīt) *n.* a black mineral that is the chief ore of chromium

chromium (krō′mē əm) *n.* [< CHROME] a metallic chemical element resistant to corrosion: symbol, Cr

chromium plate a thin coating of chromium, esp. on steel, deposited by electrolysis —**chro′mium-plat′ed** *adj.*

chromosome (krō′mə sōm′) *n.* [< Gr. *chrōma*, colour + *sōma*, body] any of the microscopic rod-shaped bodies of a cell nucleus that carry genes, which convey hereditary characteristics —**chro′moso′-mal** *adj.*

chromosphere (krō′mə sfēər′) *n.* [< Gr. *chrōma*, colour + SPHERE] the reddish layer of gases around the sun

chromous (krō′məs) *adj.* designating or of compounds containing bivalent chromium

Chron. Chronicles

chron. **1.** chronological **2.** chronology

chronic (kron′ik) *adj.* [< Gr. *chronos*, time] **1.** lasting a long time or recurring often: said of a disease **2.** having had an ailment for a long time **3.** perpetual; constant **4.** [Colloq.] pitifully bad —**chron′ically** *adv.* —**chronicity** (krə nis′ə tē) *n.*

chronicle (kron′i k′l) *n.* [< Gr. *chronika*, annals] **1.** a historical record of events in the order in which they happened **2.** a narrative; history —*vt.* **-cled, -cling** to tell or write the history of —**chron′icler** *n.*

chronological (kron′ə loj′i k′l) *adj.* **1.** arranged in the order of occurrence **2.** relating to a narrative or history Also **chron′olog′ic** —**chron′olog′ically** *adv.*

chronology (krə nol′ə jē) *n.*, *pl.* **-gies** [< Gr. *chronos*, time + -LOGY] **1.** the science of measuring time and of dating events **2.** an arrangement or list of events in the order of occurrence —**chronol′ogist** *n.*

chronometer (krə nom′ə tər) *n.* [< Gr. *chronos*, time + -METER] an instrument for measuring time precisely —**chronomet′ric** (kron′ō met′rik), **chron′omet′rical** *adj.*

chrysalis (kris′ə lis′) *n.*, *pl.* **chrysalides** (krisal′ə dēz′), **chrys′alises** [< Gr. *chrysos*, gold] **1.** the pupa of a butterfly, when it is in a cocoon **2.** the cocoon Also **chrys′alid**

chrysanthemum (kri san′thə məm) *n.* [< Gr. *chrysos*, gold + *anthemon*, flower] any of a genus of late-blooming plant, cultivated for its showy flowers, in a wide variety of colours

chrysoberyl (kris′ō ber′əl) *n.* [Gr. *chrysos*, gold + BERYL] a yellowish mineral used as a semiprecious stone

chrysolite (kris′ō līt′) *n.* [< Gr. *chrysos*, gold + *lithos*, stone] *same as* OLIVINE

chrysoprase (kri′ō prāz′) *n.* [< Gr. *chrysos*, gold + *prason*, leek] a light-green chalcedony used as a semiprecious stone

chub (chub) *n.* [ME. *chubbe*] a small, freshwater fish

chubby *adj.* **chub′bier, chub′biest** [< prec.] round and plump —**chub′biness** *n.*

chuck[1] (chuk) *vt.* [< ? Fr. *choquer*, strike against] **1.** to tap playfully, esp. under the chin **2.** to toss **3.** [Slang] *a)* to get rid of *b)* to give up (often with *in*) —*n.* a light tap under the chin —**chuck it!** stop!; give it up! —**chuck out** [Colloq.] to throw out

CHUCK
(of a drill)

chuck[2] *n.* [prob. < CHOCK] **1.** a cut of beef including the shoulder blade **2.** a clamplike device, as on a lathe, by which the tool is held

chucker-out (chuk'ər out') *n.* *same as* BOUNCER

chuckle (chuk''l) *vi.* **-led, -ling** [prob. < *chuck*, to cluck] **1.** to laugh softly in a low tone, as in mild amusement **2.** to cluck, as a hen —*n.* a soft, low-toned laugh —**chuck'ler** *n.*

chucklehead *n.* [Colloq.] a stupid person

chuff (chuf) *vi., n.* [echoic] *same as* CHUG

chuffed (chuft) *adj.* [< ?] [Slang] pleased; gratified

chug (chug) *n.* [echoic] a puffing sound, as of a locomotive —*vi.* **chugged, chug'-ging** to make, or move with, such sounds

chukka (boot) (chuk'ər) [< CHUKKER] a man's ankle-high bootlike shoe, orig. worn for polo

chukker, chukkar (chuk'ər) *n.* any of the periods of play, 7 ¹/₂ minutes each, of a polo match

chum (chum) *n.* [prob. < *chamber mate*] [Colloq.] a close friend —*vi.* **chummed, chum'ming** [Colloq.] to be close friends

chummy *adj.* **chum'mier, chum'miest** [Colloq.] intimate; friendly —**chum'mily** *adv.* —**chum'miness** *n.*

chump (chump) *n.* [< ?] **1.** a heavy block of wood **2.** [Colloq.] a stupid person —**off one's chump** [Colloq.] insane

chunk (chuŋk) *n.* [< ? CHUCK²] **1.** a short, thick piece, as of meat, wood, etc. **2.** a considerable portion

chunky *adj.* **-ier, -iest 1.** short and thick **2.** stocky; thickset **3.** containing chunks —**chunk'iness** *n.*

church (chʉrch) *n.* [ult. < Gr. *kyriakē* (*oikia*), Lord's (house)] **1.** a building for public worship, esp. one for Christian worship **2.** public worship **3.** [*usually* C-] *a)* all Christians *b)* a particular denomination of Christians **4.** ecclesiastical, as opposed to secular, government **5.** the profession of the clergy —*adj.* of a church or of organized Christian worship —*vt.* to bring (a woman after childbirth) to church for a service of thanksgiving

Church Commissioners the administrative body responsible for the property of the Church of England

churchgoer *n.* a person who attends church, esp. regularly —**church'go'ing** *n., adj.*

churchly *adj.* of, or belonging to, a church

Church of England the Anglican Church: it is an established church with the Sovereign as its head

churchwarden *n.* **1.** one of two lay officers elected annually by a parish **2.** a long clay pipe

churchyard *n.* the land adjoining a church, often used as a place of burial

churl (chʉrl) *n.* [OE. *ceorl*, freeman] a surly or ill-bred person —**churl'ish** *adj.* —**churl'ishly** *adv.*

churn (chʉrn) *n.* [OE. *cyrne*] **1.** a container in which milk or cream is shaken to form butter **2.** a large vessel for containing milk —*vt.* **1.** to shake (milk or cream) in a churn **2.** to make (butter) in a churn **3.** to stir up vigorously —*vi.* **1.** to use

a churn in making butter **2.** to move as if in a churn; seethe —**churn out** to produce in great numbers

chute¹ (shōōt) *n.* [Fr., a fall] **1.** an inclined or vertical trough down which things may slide **2.** a waterfall

chute² *n.* [Colloq.] a parachute

chutney (chut'nē) *n., pl.* **-neys** [Hindi *chatnī*] a relish made of fruits, spices, and herbs: also sp. **chut'nee**

chyle (kīl) *n.* [< Gr. *chylos* < *cheein*, pour] a milky fluid formed from chyme in the small intestine and passed into the blood —**chy'lous** *adj.*

chyme (kīm) *n.* [< Gr. *chymos*, juice < *cheein*, pour] the mass resulting from digestion of food —**chy'mous** *adj.*

chypre (shē'prə) *n.* [Fr., of Cyprus] a perfume made from sandalwood

C.I. Channel Islands

CIA, C.I.A. Central Intelligence Agency

‡**ciao** (chou) *interj.* [It.] [Colloq.] hello; goodbye

cicada (si kä'də) *n., pl.* **-das, -dae** (-dē) [L.] a large insect with transparent wings : the male makes a loud, shrill sound

cicatrix (sik'ə triks) *n., pl.* **cicatrices** (sik'ə trī'sēz) [L.] **1.** *Med.* the contracted tissue at the place where a wound has healed; scar **2.** *Bot.* the scar left where a branch, etc. was once attached Also **cic'atrice**

cicely (sis'ə lē) *n.* [< L. *seselis*] a perennial plant similar to chervil, used as a herb

cicerone (chich'ə rō'nē) *n., pl.* **-nes** [It. < L. *Cicero*, the orator] a well-informed guide for sightseers

C.I.D. Criminal Investigation Department

-cide (sīd) [< L. *caedere*, kill] a suffix meaning: **1.** killer [*pesticide*] **2.** killing [*genocide*]

cider (sī'dər) *n.* [< Gr. < Heb. *shēkār*, strong drink] an alcoholic beverage made from fermented apple juice

CIF cost, insurance and freight

cigar (si gär') *n.* [Sp. *cigarro*] a compact roll of tobacco leaves for smoking

cigarette (sig'ə ret') *n.* [Fr., dim. of *cigare, cigar*] a small roll of finely cut tobacco wrapped in thin paper for smoking

cigarette card a picture card formerly given away in cigarette packets and collected in sets

CIGS Chief of the Imperial General Staff

cilia (sil'ē ə) *n.pl., sing.* **-ium** [L.] **1.** the eyelashes **2.** *Biol.* small hairlike processes, on some leaves or some cells, as in protozoans —**cil'iate** (-ət) *adj.*

C.-in-C. Commander-in-Chief

cinch (sinch) *n.* [< Sp. < L. *cingulum*, girdle] **1.** [Colloq.] a sure or easy thing **2.** a saddle or pack girth —*vt.* to gird with a cinch

cinchona (siŋ kō'nə) *n.* [< the Countess del *Chinchón*] a tropical S American tree from the bark of which quinine is obtained

cincture (siŋk'chər) *n.* [L. *cinctura*, girdle] **1.** an encircling **2.** anything that encircles as a belt —*vt.* **-tured, -turing** to encircle with a cincture

cinder (sin'dər) *n.* [OE. *sinder*] **1.** any

matter, as coal or wood, burned but not reduced to ashes **2.** a minute piece of such matter **3.** [*pl.*] ashes from coal or wood —**cin′dery** *adj.*

Cinderella (sin′dərel′ə) *n.* [after a character in a fairy tale] any poor or obscure person, organization, etc.

cine camera a camera that takes moving pictures, used esp. by amateur photographers

cinema (sin′ə mə) *n.* [< CINEMA(TO-GRAPH)] a film theatre —**the cinema** the art or business of making films —**cin′e-mat′ic** (-mat′ik) *adj.* —**cin′emat′ically** *adv.*

cinematograph (sin′ə mat′ə gräf′) *n.* [< Gr. *kinēma*, motion + *graphein*, write] a film projector, camera, theatre, etc.

cinematography (sin′ə mə tog′rə fē) *n.* the art of photography in making film —**cin′ematog′rapher** *n.* —**cin′emat′ograph′ic** (-mat′ə graf′ik), **cin′emat′ograph′ical** *adj.*

cineraria (sin′ərāər′ē ə) *n.* [< L. *cinis*, ashes: the leaves have an ash-coloured down] a hothouse plant with heart-shaped leaves and colourful flowers

cinerarium *n.*, *pl.* **-rar′ia** [L. < *cinis*, ashes] a place to keep the ashes of cremated bodies —**cin′erary** *adj.*

cinnabar (sin′ə bär′) *n.* [< Gr. *kinnabari*] **1.** mercuric sulphide, a heavy, bright-red mineral, the principal ore of mercury **2.** artificial mercuric sulphide, used as a red pigment **3.** vermilion

cinnamon (sin′ə mən) *n.* [< Heb. *qinnāmōn*] **1.** the yellowish-brown spice made from the inner bark of a laurel tree native to the East Indies **2.** this bark **3.** yellowish brown —*adj.* **1.** yellowish-brown **2.** flavoured with cinnamon

cinque (siŋk) *n.* [< L. *quinque*, five] a five at dice or on a playing card

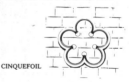

CINQUEFOIL

cinquefoil (siŋk′foil′) *n.* [< L. *quinque*, five + *folium*, leaf] **1.** a plant with compound leaves with five leaflets **2.** *Archit.* a circular design of five converging arcs

Cinque Ports a group of ports in SE England, originally five in number

cipher (sī′fər) *n.* [< Ar. *ṣifr*, nothing] **1.** *a)* secret writing based on a key *b)* a message in such writing *c)* the key to such a system **2.** a person or thing of no importance or value **3.** the symbol 0; nought; zero **4.** an Arabic numeral **5.** a monogram —*vt.*, *vi.* **1.** to write in cipher **2.** [Now Rare] to do arithmetic

cir., circ. 1. circa **2.** circulation **3.** circumference

circa (sur′kə) *prep.* [L.] about: used before an approximate date, figure, etc. [*circa* 1650]

circadian (sər kā′dē ən) *adj.* [< L. *circa*, about + *dies*, day] of certain biological rhythms associated with the 24-hour daily cycles

circle (sur′k'l) *n.* [see CIRCUS] **1.** a plane figure bounded by a single curved line every point of which is equally distant from the point at the centre **2.** the line bounding such a figure **3.** anything shaped like a circle **4.** a section of seats in a theatre, as in a balcony **5.** a complete or recurring series; cycle **6.** group of people bound together by common interests —*vt.* **-cled, -cling 1.** to encompass; surround **2.** to move round, as in a circle —*vi.* to revolve —**come full circle** to return to an original position after going through a cycle —**cir′cler** *n.*

circlet (sur′klit) *n.* **1.** a small circle **2.** a circular band worn as an ornament, esp. on the head

circs (surks) *n.pl.* [Colloq.] circumstances

circuit (sur′kit) *n.* [< L. *circum*, around + *ire*, go] **1.** the length of the line forming the boundaries of an area **2.** the area bounded **3.** a going round something **4.** *a)* the regular journey through a district of a person in his work, as of a judge, minister of religion, etc. *b)* such a district **5.** a chain of theatres, etc. at which plays, films, etc. appear in turn **6.** a motor racing track **7.** *Elec.* a complete or partial path over which current may flow

circuit breaker a device that automatically interrupts the flow of an electric current

circuitous (sər kyoo′ə təs) *adj.* roundabout; devious —**circu′itously** *adv.* —**circu′itousness, circu′ity** *n.*

circuitry (sur′kə trē) *n.* the scheme, system, or components of an electric circuit

circular (sur′kyə lər) *adj.* [L. *circularis*] **1.** in the shape of a circle; round **2.** relating to a circle **3.** moving in a circle **4.** roundabout; circuitous **5.** intended for circulation among a number of people —*n.* a circular advertisement, letter, etc. —**cir′-cular′ity** (-lar′ə tē) *n.* —**cir′cularly** *adv.*

circularize *vt.* **-ized′, -iz′ing 1.** to send circulars to **2.** to canvass **3.** to make circular —**cir′culariza′tion** *n.* —**cir′cular-iz′er** *n.*

circular saw a saw in the form of a disc with a toothed edge, rotated at high speed by a motor

circulate (sur′kyə lāt′) *vi.* **-lat′ed, -lat′-ing** [< L. *circulari*, form a circle] **1.** to move in a circle or circuit, as the blood **2.** to go from person to person or from place to place —*vt.* to cause to circulate —**cir′cula′tor** *n.* —**cir′cula-tory, cir′culative** *adj.*

circulating library a library from which books can be borrowed, sometimes for a subscription

circulation (sur′kyə lā′shən) *n.* **1.** a

circulating or moving round, as of blood through the arteries and veins **2.** the passing of something, as money, news, etc., from person to person **3.** *a)* the distribution of newspapers, magazines, etc. *b)* the average number of a newspaper sold in a given period —**in circulation 1.** in use **2.** participating in activities, etc.

circum- [< L. *circum*] *a prefix meaning* round, about, surrounding, on all sides [CIRCUM- + AMBIENT] surrounding

circumambient (sur′kəm am′bē ənt) *adj.* [CIRCUM- + AMBIENT] surrounding

circumcise (sur′kəm sīz′) *vt.* **-cised′, -cis′ing** [< L. *circum-*, around + *caedere*, to cut] to cut off all or part of the foreskin of —**cir′cumci′sion** (-sizh′ən) *n.*

circumference (sər kum′fər əns) *n.* [< L. *circum-*, around + *ferre*, carry] **1.** the line bounding a circle or other rounded surface **2.** the distance measured by this line —**circum′feren′tial** (-fə ren′shəl) *adj.*

circumflex (sur′kəm fleks′) *n.* [< L. *circum-*, around + *flectere*, bend] a mark (^) used over certain vowels in some languages to indicate a specific sound —*adj.* **1.** of or marked by a circumflex **2.** bending around; curved —**cir′cumflex′ion** *n.*

circumlocution (sur′kəm lə kyoo͞′shən) *n.* [see CIRCUM- & LOCUTION] a roundabout or lengthy way of expressing something —**cir′cumloc′utory** (-lok′yə tər ē) *adj.*

circumnavigate (-nav′ə gāt′) *vt.* **-gat′-ed, -gat′ing** [see CIRCUM- & NAVIGATE] to sail or fly around (the earth, an island, etc.) —**cir′cumnav′iga′tion** *n.*

circumscribe (sur′kəm skrīb′) *vt.* **-scribed′, -scrib′ing** [< L. *circum-*, around + *scribere*, write] **1.** to encircle **2.** *a)* to limit *b)* to restrict **3.** *Geom. a)* to draw a figure around (another figure) so as to touch it at as many points as possible *b)* to be thus drawn around —**cir′cum-scrip′tion** (-skrip′shən) *n.*

circumspect (sur′kəm spekt′) *adj.* [< L. *circum-*, around + *specere*, look] careful to consider all related circumstances before acting —**cir′cumspec′tion** *n.* —**cir′cum-spect′ly** *adv.*

circumstance (sur′kəm stəns) *n.* [< L. *circum-*, around + *stare*, stand] **1.** a fact or event, esp. one accompanying another, either incidentally or as a determining factor **2.** [*pl.*] conditions affecting a person, esp. financial conditions **3.** ceremony; show *[pomp and circumstance]* —*vt.* **-stanced, -stancing** to place in certain circumstances —**under no circumstances** under no conditions; never —**under the circumstances** conditions being what they are or were —**cir′cumstanced** *adj.*

circumstantial (sur′kəm stan′shəl) *adj.* **1.** having to do with, or depending on, circumstances **2.** incidental **3.** complete in detail —**cir′cumstan′tial′ity** (-shē al′ə tē) *n.*

circumstantial evidence *Law* evidence offered to prove certain circumstances from which the existence of the fact at issue may be inferred

circumstantiate *vt.* **-at′ed, -at′ing** to

give detailed proof or support of —**cir′cum-stan′tia′tion** *n.*

circumvent (sur′kəm vent′) *vt.* [< L. *circum-*, around + *venire*, come] **1.** to get the better of; outwit **2.** to surround, as with evils, enmity, etc. —**cir′cumven′-tion** *n.*

circus (sur′kəs) *n.* [L. < Gr. *kirkos*, circle] **1.** a travelling show of acrobats, trained animals, clowns, etc. **2.** [Colloq.] any group of persons who habitually travel together, esp. sportsmen **3.** an open space where streets converge **4.** in ancient Rome, an arena with tiers of seats around it, used for games, races, etc.

cirrhosis (sə rō′sis) *n.* [< Gr. *kirrhos*, tawny + -OSIS] a degenerative disease, esp. of the liver, marked by excess formation of connective tissue —**cirrhot′-ic** (-rot′ik) *adj.*

cirrocumulus (sir′ō kyoo͞′myə ləs) *n.* [< CIRRUS & L. *cumulus*, heap] a high formation of clouds in small, white puffs or streaks

cirrostratus (sir′ō strāt′əs) *n.* [< CIRRUS & STRATUS] a high formation of clouds in a thin, whitish veil

cirrus (sir′əs) *n., pl.,* for 1 **-ri** (-ī); for 2 **-rus** [L., a curl] **1.** *Biol. a)* a plant tendril *b)* a threadlike appendage, as a feeler **2.** a high formation of clouds in wispy filaments —**cir′rose, cir′rous** *adj.*

cisalpine (sis al′pīn) *adj.* [L. *cis*, on this side + ALPINE] on this (the Roman, or southern) side of the Alps

cisco (sis′kō) *n., pl.* **-coes** or **-cos** [ult. < AmInd.] any of various whitefish of deep lakes in N America

cissy (sis′ē) *n. same as* SISSY

cist (sist) *n.* [< Gr. *kistē*, chest] a prehistoric tomb made of stone slabs or hollowed out of rock

Cistercian (sis tur′shən) *adj.* [< ML. *Cistercium* (now *Cîteaux*, France)] of a monastic order following the Benedictine rule strictly —*n.* a Cistercian monk or nun

cistern (sis′tərn) *n.* [< L. *cista*, chest] **1.** a tank for the storage of water, specif., *a)* in the roofspace of a house *b)* above a W.C. for flushing **2.** an underground reservoir for the storage of liquid, esp. rain water

citadel (sit′ə d'l) *n.* [< L. *civitas*, city] **1.** a fortress on a commanding height for defence of a city **2.** a stronghold **3.** a refuge

citation (sī tā′shən) *n.* [see ff.] **1.** a quoting **2.** a passage cited **3.** official honourable mention for meritorious service in the armed forces **4.** a summons to appear before a court of law **5.** a reference to a legal statute, etc. —**cita′tor** *n.* —**cita′-tory** *adj.*

cite (sīt) *vt.* **cit′ed, cit′ing** [< L. *citare*, summon] **1.** to quote (a passage, book, etc.) **2.** to refer to or mention by way of example, etc. **3.** to mention in a citation (sense 3) **4.** to summon to appear before a court of law

cithara (sith′ə rə) *n.* [L. < Gr. *kithara*]

an ancient musical instrument somewhat like a lyre

citified (sit′i fīd′) *adj.* having the manners, dress, etc. attributed to city people

citizen (sit′ə zən) *n.* [see CITY] 1. formerly, an inhabitant of a city 2. a member of a state or nation

citizenry *n.* all citizens as a group

citizenship *n.* 1. the status of a citizen, or his duties and rights 2. one's conduct as a citizen

citrate (si′trāt) *n.* [< CITRUS] a salt or ester of citric acid

citric (si′trik) *adj.* [< CITRUS] 1. of or from lemons, oranges, etc. 2. designating an acid obtained from such fruits, used in making dyes, citrates, etc.

citron (si′trən) *n.* [see CITRUS] 1. a yellow, thick-skinned fruit resembling a lemon 2. the semitropical tree bearing this fruit 3. the candied peel of this fruit

citronella (si′trə nel′ə) *n.* [ModL. < CITRUS] 1. a sharp-smelling oil used in perfume, insect repellents, etc. 2. a grass of S Asia from which it is derived

citrus (si′trəs) *n.* [L., citron tree] 1. any of the trees that bear oranges, lemons, limes, etc. 2. any such fruit —*adj.* of these trees: also **cit′rous**

cittern (sit′urn) *n.* [see CITHERA] an early stringed instrument of the guitar family: also **cith′er**

city (sit′ē) *n., pl.* **cit′ies** [< L. *civis,* citizen] 1. a centre of population larger than a town 2. in Britain, a large town that has been granted a charter from the Crown 3. in the U.S., a self-governing town —*adj.* of or in a city —**the City** 1. the City of London, esp. the financial and commercial institutions located there 2. the financial world in general

city editor the editor of a newspaper, responsible for financial news

city fathers the important officials of a city

city-state *n.* a state made up of an independent city and the territory controlled by it, as in ancient Greece

civ. 1. civil 2. civilian

civet (siv′it) *n.* [< Fr. < Ar.] a yellowish substance with a musklike scent, secreted by the civet cat and used in making perfumes

civet cat a catlike, flesh-eating mammal of Africa and S Asia, with spotted, yellowish fur

civic (siv′ik) *adj.* [see CITY] 1. of a city; municipal 2. of citizens or citizenship —**civ′ically** *adv.*

civic centre a complex of buildings serving the administrative, social, and recreational needs of a town

civics *n.pl.* [*with sing. v.*] the study of civic affairs and the duties and rights of citizenship

civil (siv′′l) *adj.* [see CITY] 1. of a citizen or citizens 2. of a community of citizens 3. civilized 4. polite or courteous 5. not military or religious [civil marriage]

6. *Law* relating to private rights —**civ′-illy** *adv.*

civil defence a system of warning devices, air-raid or fallout shelters, civilian volunteers, etc. for defence of a population against enemy attack

civil disobedience nonviolent opposition to a law by refusing to comply with it

civil engineering the branch of engineering dealing with the design and construction of roads, bridges, etc. —**civil engineer**

civilian (sə vil′yən) *n.* [see CITY] a person not an active member of the armed forces or of an official force having police power —*adj.* of or for civilians

civility (sə vil′ə tē) *n., pl.* **-ties** 1. politeness, esp. of a merely formal kind 2. a civil act or utterance

civilization (siv′ə li′zā′shən) *n.* 1. social organization of a high order 2. the countries and peoples considered to have reached a high social development 3. the total culture of a people, nation, etc. 4. a civilizing or becoming civilized

civilize (siv′ə līz′) *vt.* **-lized′, -liz′ing** [see CITY] 1. to bring out of a primitive or savage condition 2. to improve in habits or manners; refine —**civ′ilized′** *adj.*

civil law 1. the body of law concerning private rights 2. the body of codified law developed from Roman law

civil liberties rights of speaking and acting as one likes without hindrance except in the interests of the public good

civil list in Britain, the annual amount fixed by Parliament for the household expenses of members of the royal family

civil marriage a marriage performed by a public official, not by a clergyman

civil rights 1. the rights of a citizen as a private individual, esp. in relation to the state 2. [Colloq.] the rights of minorities within a society

civil service all those employed in government work except those in the armed forces, legislature, and judicature —**civil servant**

civil war war between factions of the same nation

civvies (siv′ēz) *n.pl.* [Colloq.] civilian clothes

Civvy Street (siv′ē) [Colloq.] civilian life

ck. *pl.* **cks.** cask

Cl *Chem.* chlorine

cl centilitre(s)

cl. 1. claim 2. class 3. clause

clack (klak) *vi.* [echoic] 1. to make a sudden, sharp sound 2. to chatter —*n.* 1. a clacking sound 2. chatter —**clack′-er** *n.*

clad (klad) *alt. pt. & pp. of* CLOTHE —*adj.* 1. clothed 2. having a layer of another metal or stone, wood, etc. bonded to it —**clad′ding** *n.*

claim (klām) *vt.* [< L. *clamare,* cry out] 1. to demand as rightfully belonging to one 2. to call for; require 3. to assert;

maintain —n. 1. a demand for something rightfully due 2. a right to something 3. something claimed, as land 4. an assertion —claim'able adj. —claim'er n.

claimant n. one who makes a claim

clairvoyance (klāer voi′əns) n. the supposed ability to perceive things that are not in sight

clairvoyant adj. [Fr. < clair, clear + voir, see] of or having clairvoyance —n. a clairvoyant person

clam (klam) n. [< OE. clamm, fetter] a hard-shelled, edible, bivalve mollusc —vi. to dig for clams —clam up [Colloq.] to refuse to talk

clamber (klam′bər) vi., vt. [ME. clambren] to climb clumsily or with effort, using both hands and feet —n. a hard or clumsy climb —clam'berer n.

clammy (klam′ē) adj. clam'mier, clam'-miest [prob. < OE. clam, clay] unpleasantly moist, cold, and sticky —clam'mily adv. —clam'miness n.

clamour (klam′ər) n. [< L. clamare, cry out] 1. a loud outcry; uproar 2. a noisy demand or complaint 3. a loud, sustained noise —vi. to cry out, demand, or complain noisily —vt. to express with clamour —clam'orous adj. —clam'orously adv. —clam'orousness n.

clamp[1] (klamp) n. [< MDu. klampe] a device for clasping or fastening things together —vt. 1. to fasten or brace with a clamp 2. to impose forcefully —clamp down (on) to become more strict (with)

clamp[2] n. [< MDu. klamp, heap] a pile, esp. of potatoes, stored under earth or straw —vt. to keep in a clamp

clan (klan) n. [Gael. clann, offspring] 1. a social group, as in the Scottish Highlands, composed of several families descended from a common ancestor 2. a group of people with interests in common

clandestine (klan des′tin) adj. [< L. clam, secretly] secret or hidden; surreptitious —clandes'tinely adv.

clang (klaŋ) vi., vt. [echoic] to make or cause to make a loud, sharp, ringing sound, as by striking metal —n. a clanging sound

clanger n. [< prec.] [Colloq.] a mistake, esp. a social blunder [he dropped a clanger]

clangour (klaŋ′ər) n. [< L. clangere, clang] a clanging sound, esp. a continued clanging —vi. to make a clangour —clan'-gorous adj. —clan'gorously adv.

clank (klaŋk) n. [echoic] a sharp, metallic sound —vi., vt. to make, or cause to move with, a clank

clannish (klan′ish) adj. 1. of a clan 2. tending to associate closely and to avoid others —clan'nishly adv. —clan'nish-ness n.

clap[1] (klap) vi. clapped, clap'ping [OE. clæppan, beat] 1. to make a sudden, explosive sound, as of two flat surfaces being struck together 2. to strike the hands together, as in applauding —vt. 1. to strike together briskly and loudly

2. to strike with an open hand 3. to put, move, etc. swiftly [clapped into jail] —n. 1. the sound of clapping 2. the act of striking the hands together 3. a sharp slap, as in hearty greeting —clap eyes on [Colloq.] to catch sight of; see —clap hold of [Colloq.] to seize; grasp —clapped out [Colloq.] 1. worn out 2. exhausted

clap[2] n. [< OFr.] [Slang] gonorrhoea: with the

clapper n. a thing that makes a clapping noise, as the tongue of a bell —like the clappers [Colloq.] very fast

claptrap n. [CLAP[1] + TRAP[1]] showy, insincere, empty talk, etc. —adj. showy and cheap

claque (klak) n. [Fr. < claquer, to clap] 1. a group of people paid to go to a play, opera, etc. and applaud 2. a group of fawning followers —claqu'eur n.

claret (klar′ət) n. [< L. clarus, clear] 1. a red wine, esp. Bordeaux 2. purplish red —adj. purplish-red

clarify (klar′ə fī) vt., vi. -fied', -fy'ing [< L. clarus, clear + facere, make] 1. to make or become clear and free from impurities 2. to make or become easier to understand —clar'ifica'tion n.

clarinet (klar′ə net′) n. [Fr.: see ff.] a single-reed, woodwind instrument played by means of holes and keys —clar'inet'-tist n.

clarion (klar′ē ən) n. [< L. clarus, clear] a trumpet of the Middle Ages producing clear, sharp, shrill tones —adj. clear, sharp, and ringing [a clarion call]

clarity (klar′ə tē) n. [< L. clarus, clear] clearness

clash (klash) vi. [echoic] 1. to collide with a loud, harsh, metallic noise 2. to conflict; disagree —vt. to strike with a loud, harsh noise —n. 1. the sound of clashing 2. a) conflict b) lack of harmony

clasp (kläsp) n. [ME. claspe] 1. a fastening, as a hook, to hold things together 2. a grasping; embrace 3. a grip of the hand 4. a metal bar attached to the ribbon of a military decoration —vt. 1. to fasten with a clasp 2. to grasp firmly; embrace 3. to grip with the hand 4. to cling to

clasp-knife n. a large pocketknife with one or more folding blades, secured by a catch when open

class (kläs) n. [< L. classis] 1. a number of people or things grouped together because of certain likenesses; kind; sort 2. a group of people of the same social or economic status [the middle class] 3. high social rank 4. a) a group of pupils or students taught together b) a meeting of such a group 5. grade or quality [travel first class] 6. [Colloq.] excellence 7. Biol. a group of animals or plants ranking below a phylum —vt. to put in a class; classify —vi. to be classed —in a class by itself (or oneself) unique

class consciousness an awareness of

belonging to a certain economic class
—**class′-con′scious** *adj.*

classic (klas′ik) *adj.* [< L. *classis*, class]
1. of the highest class; being a model of its kind 2. of the art, literature, and culture of the ancient Greeks or Romans, or their writers, artists, etc. 3. balanced, formal, restrained, regular, etc. 4. famous as traditional or typical 5. [Colloq.] simple in style —*n.* 1. a writer, artist, etc., or a literary or artistic work, recognized as excellent, authoritative, etc. 2. a famous traditional event 3. [Colloq.] a suit, dress, etc. that is classic (sense 5) 4. *Horse Racing* any of the five principal races in the flat racing calendar —**the classics** literature regarded as classic

classical *adj.* 1. *same as* CLASSIC (senses 1, 2, 3) 2. versed in Greek and Roman culture, literature, etc. 3. of the form of language used in standard literary works [*classical* Arabic] 4. of music that conforms to certain established standards of form, complexity, musical literacy, etc. 5. standard and traditional —**clas′sical′ity** (-kal′ə tē) *n.* —**clas′sically** *adv.*

classicism (klas′ə siz′m) *n.* 1. the aesthetic principles or qualities of ancient Greece and Rome 2. adherence to such principles 3. knowledge of the literature and art of ancient Greece and Rome Also **clas′sicalism** —**clas′sicist** *n.*

classification (klas′ə fi kā′shən) *n.* an arrangement according to some systematic division into classes or groups —**clas′sifica′tory** *adj.*

classified advertising newspaper advertising under such listings as situations vacant, for sale, etc.

classify (klas′ə fī′) *vt.* -**fied′**, -**fy′ing** 1. to arrange in classes according to some system or principle 2. to designate (government documents, etc.) as secret or confidential —**clas′sifi′able** *adj.* —**clas′sifi′er** *n.*

classmate (klas′māt′) *n.* a member of the same class in a school

classroom *n.* a room in a school in which classes are taught

classy *adj.* -**ier**, -**iest** [Colloq.] first-class, esp. in style or manner —**class′iness** *n.*

clatter (klat′ər) *vi.*, *vt.* [ME *cláteren*] to make, or cause to make a clatter —*n.* 1. a rapid succession of loud, sharp noises 2. noisy chatter —**clat′terer** *n.* —**clat′teringly** *adv.*

clause (klôz) *n.* [< L. *claudere*, close] 1. a group of words containing a subject and predicate 2. a particular article, stipulation, or provision in a document —**claus′al** *adj.*

claustrophobia (klôs′trə fō′bē ə) *n.* [< L. *claustrum* (see CLOISTER) + -PHOBIA] an abnormal fear of being in an enclosed or confined place —**claus′tropho′bic** *adj.*

clavichord (klav′ə kôrd′) *n.* [< L. *clavis*, key + *chorda*, string] a stringed musical instrument with a keyboard, predecessor of the piano

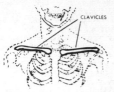
CLAVICLES

clavicle (klav′ə k′l) *n.* [< L. *clavis*, key] a bone connecting the breastbone with the shoulder blade; collarbone

clavier (klə vēər′; *for 1, also* klav′ē ər) *n.* [Fr. < L. *clavis*, key] 1. the keyboard of an organ, piano, etc. 2. any stringed instrument that has a keyboard

claw (klô) *n.* [OE. *clawu*] 1. a sharp, hooked nail on the foot of a bird and of many reptiles and mammals 2. a foot with such nails 3. a pincer of a lobster, etc. 4. anything regarded as a claw, specif., a hammer (**claw hammer**) with one end forked, used to pull out nails —*vt.*, *vi.* to scratch, clutch, pull, dig, or tear with or as with claws —**clawed** *adj.*

clay (klā) *n.* [OE. *clæg*] 1. a firm, plastic earth, used in the manufacture of bricks, pottery, etc. 2. *a)* earth *b)* the human body —**clay′ey** *adj.* —**clay′ish** *adj.*

claymore (klā′môr′) *n.* [Gael. *claidheamhmor*, great sword] a large, two-edged broadsword formerly used by Scottish Highlanders

clay pigeon a disc, as of baked clay, tossed into the air from a trap as a target in trapshooting

CLC Canadian Labour Congress

clean (klēn) *adj.* [OE. *clæne*] 1. free from dirt or impurities; unsoiled 2. recently laundered 3. morally pure 4. sportsmanlike 5. neat and tidy 6. trim 7. skilful; deft 8. without obstructions or flaws; clear 9. complete; thorough 10. producing little immediate fallout: of nuclear weapons —*adv.* 1. in a clean manner 2. [Colloq.] completely —*vt.*, *vi.* to make clean —**clean out** 1. to empty so as to make clean 2. [Slang] to remove or use up, esp. money —**clean sheet** (or **slate**) a new start, esp. when free of earlier mistakes, crimes, etc. —**clean up** 1. to make clean or neat 2. [Slang] to make much profit —**clean up on** [Slang] to make a large profit from —**come clean** [Slang] to confess; tell the truth —**make a clean breast of** [Colloq.] to confess —**clean′able** *adj.* —**clean′ness** *n.*

clean-cut *adj.* 1. clearly and sharply outlined 2. well-formed 3. trim, neat, etc.

cleaner *n.* 1. one who cleans offices, etc. 2. one who dry-cleans 3. a preparation for removing dirt, etc. 4. a machine for cleaning, as a vacuum cleaner

cleanly¹ (klen′lē) *adj.* -**lier**, -**liest** 1. keeping oneself or one's surroundings clean 2. always kept clean —**clean′lily** *adv.* —**clean′liness** *n.*

cleanly² (klēn′lē) *adv.* in a clean manner

cleanse (klenz) *vt.* **cleansed, cleans′ing**
[OE. *clænsian*] to make clean, pure, etc.;
purge —**cleans′er** *n.*

cleanup (klēn′up′) *n.* **1.** a cleaning up
2. elimination of crime, vice, etc. **3.** [Slang]
profit; gain

clear (klēər) *adj.* [< L. *clarus*] **1.** free
from clouds or mist; bright **2.** transparent;
not turbid **3.** having no blemishes **4.**
easily seen or heard; distinct **5.** perceiving
acutely; keen **6.** easily understood **7.**
obvious **8.** certain **9.** free from guilt;
innocent **10.** free from charges or
deductions; net **11.** free from debt or
encumbrance **12.** free from obstruction
—*adv.* **1.** in a clear manner **2.** [Colloq.]
all the way; completely **3.** out of the
way —*vt.* **1.** to make clear or bright
2. to free from impurities, blemishes, etc.
3. to make intelligible or lucid **4.** to rid
of obstructions **5.** to get rid of **6.** to
free (a person or thing) *of* or *from* something
7. to free from guilt or blame **8.** to pass
over, under, by, etc. **9.** to be passed
or approved by **10.** to make (a given
amount) as profit **11.** *Banking* to pass
(a cheque, etc.) through a clearinghouse
—*vi.* **1.** to become clear, unclouded, etc.
2. to vanish **3.** to get clearance, as a
ship leaving port **4.** *Banking* to exchange
cheques, etc., through a clearinghouse
—**clear away 1.** to take away so as to
leave a cleared space **2.** to go away
—**clear off 1.** to remove things from
(a surface) **2.** [Colloq.] to depart —**clear
out 1.** to clear by emptying **2.** [Colloq.]
to depart —**clear the air** (or **atmosphere**)
to get rid of emotional tensions, etc. —**clear
up 1.** to make or become clear **2.** to
make orderly **3.** to explain —**in the clear
1.** in the open **2.** [Colloq.] free from
suspicion, etc. —**clear′ly** *adv.* —**clear′-
ness** *n.*

clearance *n.* **1.** a making clear **2.** the
clear space between a moving object and
that which it passes by **3.** official
authorization to see classified documents,
etc. **4.** *Naut.* a certificate authorizing a
ship to enter or leave port

clear-cut *adj.* **1.** clearly outlined **2.**
distinct

clearheaded *adj.* having a clear mind
—**clear′head′edly** *adv.* —**clear′head′ed-
ness** *n.*

clearing *n.* an area of land cleared of trees

clearing bank any of the principal British
banks, esp. those that are members of
the central clearinghouse in London

clearinghouse *n.* **1.** an office maintained
by a group of banks as a centre for
exchanging cheques, etc. **2.** a central office
for getting and giving information

clearsighted *adj.* **1.** seeing clearly **2.**
understanding or thinking clearly —**clear′-
sight′edly** *adv.* —**clear′sight′edness** *n.*

clearstory (klēər′stər ē) *n., pl.* **-ries**
same as CLERESTORY

clearway *n.* a stretch of road, not a
motorway, where motorists may not stop

cleat (klēt) *n.* [< OE. hyp. *cleat*, lump]
1. a piece of wood or metal, often wedge-

shaped, fastened to something to
strengthen it **2.** *Naut.* a small piece of
wood or metal on which a rope can be
fastened

cleavage (klē′vij) *n.* **1.** the hollow
between a woman's breasts **2.** a cleaving,
splitting, or dividing **3.** the manner in
which a thing splits **4.** a cleft; fissure

cleave[1] (klēv) *vt.* **cleaved** or **cleft** or **clove,
cleaved** or **cleft** or **clo′ven, cleav′ing** [OE.
cleofan] **1.** to divide by a blow; split
2. to pierce —*vi.* to split; separate —**cleav′-
able** *adj.*

cleave[2] *vi.* **cleaved, cleav′ing** [OE.
cleofian] **1.** to adhere; cling (*to*) **2.** to
be faithful (*to*)

cleaver *n.* a heavy cleaving tool with
a broad blade, used by butchers

G CLEF   F CLEF

C CLEFS

TYPES OF CLEF

clef (klef) *n.* [< L. *clavis*, key] a symbol
used in music to indicate the pitch of
the notes on the staff

cleft[1] (kleft) *n.* [< OE. *cleofan*, CLEAVE[1]]
1. an opening made by cleaving; crack;
crevice **2.** a hollow between two parts

cleft[2] *alt. pt. & pp.* of CLEAVE[1] —*adj.*
split; divided

cleft palate a congenital fissure from
front to back along the roof of the mouth

cleg (kleg) *n.* [< ON. *kleggi*] same as
HORSEFLY

clematis (klem′ə tis) *n.* [< Gr. *klēma*,
twig] a woody climbing plant with brightly
coloured flowers

clement (klem′ənt) *adj.* [L. *clemens*] **1.**
lenient; merciful **2.** mild, as weather
—**clem′ency** *n.* —**clem′ently** *adv.*

clench (klench) *vt.* [< OE. *(be)clencan*,
make cling] **1.** to clinch, as a nail **2.**
to close (the teeth or fist) firmly **3.** to
grip tightly —*n.* a firm grip —**clench′-
er** *n.*

clerestory (klēər′stər ē) *n., pl.* **-ries** [<
ME. *cler*, clear + *storie*, storey] the wall
of a church rising above the roofs of
the flanking aisles and containing windows
for lighting the central part of the structure

clergy (klur′jē) *n., pl.* **-gies** [see CLERK]
men ordained for religious service;
ministers, priests, rabbis, etc., collectively

clergyman *n.* a member of the clergy

cleric (kler′ik) *n.* [see CLERK] a clergyman

clerical *adj.* **1.** relating to a clergyman
or the clergy **2.** relating to office clerks
or their work —**cler′ically** *adv.*

clerical collar a stiff, white collar

buttoned at the back, worn by certain clergymen

clerk (klärk) *n.* [< Gr. *klērikos,* priest] 1. an office worker who keeps records, types letters, etc. 2. an official in charge of records, etc. of a court 3. a layman who has minor duties in a church —*vi.* to work as a clerk —**clerk′ly** *adj., adv.* —**clerk′ship** *n.*

clerk of (the) works the agent or overseer responsible for supervising work on a building site, etc.

clever (klev′ər) *adj.* [< ?] 1. skilful in doing something; adroit; dexterous 2. intelligent, quick-witted, witty, etc. —**clev′-erly** *adv.* —**clev′erness** *n.*

clew (klōō) *n.* [< OE. *cliwen*] 1. a ball of thread or yarn 2. same as CLUE 3. *Naut.* a metal loop in the corner of a sail —**clew down** (or **up**)   to lower (or raise) a sail by the clews

cliché (klē′shā) *n.* [Fr. < *clicher,* to stereotype] 1. a trite expression or idea 2. a stereotype printing plate

click (klik) *n.* [echoic] 1. a slight, sharp sound like that of a door latch snapping into place 2. a mechanical device, as a catch, that clicks into position —*vi.* 1. to make a click 2. [Colloq.] *a)* to be suddenly clear *b)* to get along together successfully, esp. with someone of the opposite sex —*vt.* to cause to click —**click′er** *n.*

client (klī′ənt) *n.* [< L. *cliens,* follower] 1. a person or company for whom a lawyer, accountant, etc. is acting 2. a customer —**cliental** (klī en′t'l) *adj.*

clientele (klē′on tel′) *n.* [< Fr. < L. *clientela*] all one's clients or customers, collectively: also **clientage** (klī′ən tij)

cliff (klif) *n.* [OE. *clif*] a high, steep face of rock, esp. one on a coast; precipice —**cliff′y** *adj.*

cliffhanger, *n.,* any story, situation, etc. of high suspense —**cliff′hang′ing** *adj.*

climacteric (klī mak′tər ik) *n.* [< Gr. *klimax,* ladder] a period in a person's life when an important physiological change occurs, esp. the menopause —*adj.* crucial

climate (klī′mit) *n.* [< Gr. *klima,* region] 1. the prevailing weather conditions of a place 2. any prevailing conditions affecting life, activity, etc. 3. a region with certain prevailing weather conditions —**climatic** (klī mat′ik) *adj.* —**climat′ically** *adv.*

climax (klī′maks) *n.* [< Gr. *klimax,* ladder] 1. the final, culminating element or event in a series 2. the decisive turning point of the action, as in drama 3. formerly, an arrangement of ideas, images, etc. with the most forceful last 4. an orgasm —*vi., vt.* to reach, or bring to, a climax —**climac′-tic** *adj.*

climb (klīm) *vi., vt.* [OE. *climban*] 1. to go up by using the feet and often the hands 2. to rise gradually; mount 3. to move (*down, over, along,* etc.) using the hands and feet 4. to rise socially 5. *Bot.* to grow upwards on by winding

round or adhering with tendrils —*n.* 1. a climbing; ascent 2. a place to be climbed —**climb down** to withdraw from a position, etc. —**climb′er** *n.*

clime (klīm) *n.* [see CLIMATE] [Poet.] a region; climate

clinch (klinch) *vt.* [var. of CLENCH] 1. to settle (an argument, deal, etc.) definitely 2. to fasten (a nail, bolt, etc.) by flattening the projecting end —*vi.* 1. *Boxing* to grip the opponent's body with the arms 2. [Slang] to embrace —*n.* 1. clinching, as with a nail 2. *Boxing* an act of clinching 3. [Slang] an embrace

clincher *n.* a decisive point, argument, etc.

cling (kliŋ) *vi.* clung, **cling′ing** [OE. *clingan*] 1. to hold fast by embracing; adhere 2. to be or stay near 3. to be emotionally attached —**cling′er** *n.* —**cling′ingly** *adv.* —**cling′y** *adj.*

Clingfilm *Trademark* a thin polythene material having the power to adhere closely; used for wrapping food, etc.

clinic (klin′ik) *n.* [< Gr. *klinē,* a bed] 1. a place where patients are treated by specialist physicians or surgeons 2. a department of a hospital or medical school where outpatients are treated 3. a private hospital or nursing home

clinical *adj.* 1. of, like, or connected with a clinic 2. having to do with the treatment and observation of patients 3. scientifically impersonal —**clin′ically** *adv.*

clinical thermometer a thermometer with which the body temperature is measured

clink[1] (kliŋk) *vi., vt.* [echoic] to make or cause to make a slight, sharp sound, as of glasses striking together —*n.* such a sound

clink[2] *n.* [< 18th c. London prison] [Colloq.] a jail

clinker *n.* [Du. *klinker*] a hard mass of fused stony matter formed in a furnace, as from impurities in the coal

clinker-built *adj.* [< *clink,* dial. var. of CLINCH] built with overlapping boards or plates, as a boat

clip[1] (klip) *vt.* clipped, **clip′ping** [< ON. *klippa*] 1. to cut as with shears 2. *a)* to cut short *b)* to shorten by omitting syllables, etc. 3. to cut the hair of 4. [Colloq.] to hit with a quick, sharp blow 5. [Slang] to cheat —*vi.* 1. to clip something 2. to move rapidly —*n.* 1. the act of clipping 2. the amount of wool clipped from sheep at one time 3. a sequence clipped from a film 4. a rapid pace 5. [Colloq.] a quick, sharp blow

clip[2] *vi., vt.* clipped, **clip′ping** [OE. *clyppan,* embrace] to grip tightly; fasten —*n.* 1. any device that clips or fastens things together 2. a brooch or other piece of jewellery fitted with a clip

clipboard *n.* a portable writing board with a hinged clip at the top to hold papers

clip joint [Slang] a nightclub, etc. that charges excessive prices

clipped form (or **word**) a shortened form of a word, as *phone* (for *telephone*) or *fan* (for *fanatic*)

CLIPPER
SHIP

clipper *n.* 1. a person who cuts, trims, etc. 2. [*usually pl.*] a tool for cutting or trimming 3. a narrow-beamed sailing ship built for great speed
clippie *n.* [< CLIP¹] [Slang] a bus conductress
clipping *n.* something cut out or trimmed off, as an item clipped from a newspaper, etc.
clique (klēk) *n.* [Fr.] a small, exclusive circle of people; snobbish or narrow coterie —**cliqu′ish, cliqu′ey, cliqu′y** *adj.*
clitoris (klit′ər əs) *n.* [< Gr. *kleitys,* hill] a small, sensitive, erectile organ at the upper end of the vulva —**clit′oral, clitoric** (klī tôr′ik) *adj.*
cloak (klōk) *n.* [< ML. *clocca,* bell: from its shape] 1. a loose, usually sleeveless outer garment 2. something that covers or conceals —*vt.* 1. to cover as with a cloak 2. to conceal; hide
cloak-and-dagger *adj.* dealing with spies, spying, intrigue, etc.
cloakroom *n.* a room where hats, coats, umbrellas, etc. can be left temporarily
clobber¹ (klob′ər) *n.* [< ?] [Colloq.] personal belongings, esp. clothes
clobber² *vt.* [< ?] [Slang] 1. to beat or hit repeatedly; maul 2. to defeat decisively
cloche (klōsh) *n.* [< ML. *clocca,* bell] 1. a raised glass or plastic cover for delicate plants 2. a closefitting, bell-shaped hat for women
clock¹ (klok) *n.* [ME. *clokke* < ML. *clocca,* bell] 1. a device for measuring and indicating time, as by pointers moving over a dial 2. [Colloq.] any device for recording or measuring 3. [Slang] the face —*vt.* 1. to record the time of (a race, runner, etc.) with a stopwatch, etc. 2. [Slang] to punch or strike —**clock in** (or **on**) to report for work, esp. by punching a timeclock —**clock off** to go off duty —**clock up** 1. to reach a given speed, time, etc. in competition 2. to work a given number of hours, days, etc. —**round the clock** day and night
clock² *n.* [< ? prec., because orig. bell-shaped] a woven ornament on the side of a stocking
clockwise *adv., adj.* in the direction in which the hands of a clock rotate
clockwork *n.* 1. the mechanism of a clock 2. any similar mechanism, consisting of springs and gears —**like clockwork** very regularly and precisely
clod (klod) *n.* [OE.] 1. a lump, esp. of

earth or clay 2. a dull, stupid fellow —**clod′dish** *adj.* —**clod′dishness** *n.*
clodhopper *n.* [CLOD + HOPPER] 1. a clumsy, stupid fellow; lout 2. a coarse, heavy shoe
clog (klog) *n.* [ME. *clogge,* lump of wood] 1. a wooden shoe 2. a shoe with a thick, usually wooden sole 3. anything that hinders or obstructs —*vt.* **clogged, clog′ging** 1. to hinder; impede 2. to fill with obstructions —*vi.* to become stopped up —**clog′giness** *n.*
cloisonné (kloi zon′ā) *adj.* [Fr., partitioned] denoting a kind of enamel work in which the decoration is set in hollows formed by thin strips of wire
cloister (klois′tər) *n.* [< L. *claudere,* close] 1. a place of religious seclusion; monastery or convent 2. a covered walk along the inside walls of a monastery, college, etc., with an opening along one side —*vt.* to seclude or confine as in a cloister —**clois′-tered** *adj.* —**clois′tral** *adj.*
clomp (klomp) *vi.* to walk heavily or noisily; clump
clone (klōn) *n.* [< Gr. *klōn,* twig] *Biol.* all the descendants derived asexually from a single individual —*vi., vt.* to propagate as a clone Also **clon**
close¹ (klōs) *adj.* **clos′er, clos′est** [see ff.] 1. with little space between 2. compact; dense [*a close weave*] 3. nearby [*a close neighbour*] 4. very near in interests, affection, etc. [*a close friend*] 5. miserly 6. oppressively warm and stuffy 7. strict; thorough; careful [*close attention*] 8. nearly equal or alike [*close in age*] 9. nearly even [*a close contest*] 10. enclosed or enclosing; shut in 11. confined or confining 12. carefully guarded [*close custody*] 13. hidden; secluded 14. secretive; reserved 15. restricted, as in membership —*adv.* in a close manner —**close′ly** *adv.* —**close′ness** *n.*
close² (klōz) *vt.* **closed, clos′ing** [< L. *claudere,* to close] 1. to shut 2. to block up or stop (an opening, passage, etc.) 3. to bring together; unite 4. to bring to an end; finish 5. to complete (a sale, agreement, etc.) —*vi.* 1. to become shut 2. to come to an end 3. to end or suspend operations 4. to become joined together 5. to come close or together —*n.* a closing; end —**close down** to shut or stop entirely —**close in** to surround, cutting off escape —**close up** 1. to draw nearer together 2. to shut or stop up entirely 3. to heal, as a wound does
close³ (klōs) *n.* [see prec.] 1. an enclosed place 2. enclosed grounds by a building [*a cathedral close*]
closed (klōzd) *adj.* 1. not open; shut 2. covered over or enclosed 3. not open to new ideas, discussion, etc. 4. restricted; exclusive
closed circuit a system of television transmission by cables to receivers on a circuit —**closed′-cir′cuit** *adj.*
closed shop a factory, business, etc. operating under an agreement with a trade union by which only members of the union may be employed

close harmony (klōs) *Music* harmony consisting of chords having all four tones within an octave

closemouthed *adj.* not talking much; taciturn: also **close′lipped′**

close quarters a confined space or position —**at close quarters** in close proximity; very near together

close season the period during which it is not permitted to kill certain game or fish

close shave 1. a shave very close to the skin 2. [Colloq.] a narrow escape: also **close call, close thing**

closet (kloz′it) *n.* [< L. *claudere,* to close] 1. a small room or cupboard for clothes, supplies, etc. 2. a small, private room for reading, etc. 3. a water closet —*vt.* to shut up in a private room for confidential discussion

close-up (klōs′up′) *n.* a photograph, or a film or TV shot, made at very close range

closure (klō′zhər) *n.* [< L. *claudere,* to close] 1. a closing or being closed 2. a finish; end; conclusion 3. anything that closes 4. the parliamentary procedure by which debate is closed —*vt.* **-sured, -suring** to apply the closure to (a bill, debate, etc.)

clot (klot) *n.* [OE. *clott*] 1. a thickened mass or lump [a blood *clot*] 2. [Colloq.] a stupid person —*vt., vi.* **clot′ted, clot′ting** to form into a clot; coagulate

cloth (kloth) *n., pl.* **cloths** (kloths) [OE. *clath*] 1. a woven, knitted, or pressed fabric of fibrous material, as cotton, wool, silk, etc. 2. a piece of such fabric for a special use [*dishcloth*] —*adj.* made of cloth —**the cloth** the clergy collectively

clothe (klōth) *vt.* **clothed** or **clad, cloth′ing** [OE. *clathian* < *prec.*] 1. to put clothes on; dress 2. to provide with clothes 3. to cover over as if with a garment

clothes (klōthz) *n.pl.* [OE. *clathas*] 1. articles, usually of cloth, to cover the body 2. bedclothes

clotheshorse *n.* a frame on which to hang clothes, etc. for airing or drying

clothespeg *n.* a small clip, as of wood or plastic, for fastening clothes on a line

clothier (klō′thē ər) *n.* one who makes or sells clothes

clothing (klō′thiŋ) *n.* 1. wearing apparel; clothes; garments 2. a covering

cloud (kloud) *n.* [OE. *clud,* mass of rock] 1. a visible mass of water vapour in the sky 2. a mass of smoke, dust, steam, etc. 3. a great number of moving things close together [a *cloud* of locusts] 4. a murkiness, as in a liquid 5. anything that darkens, obscures, etc. —*vt.* 1. to cover with clouds 2. to darken; obscure —*vi.* to become cloudy, gloomy, etc. —**in the clouds** 1. fanciful; impractical 2. in a reverie or daydream —**under a cloud** 1. under suspicion of wrongdoing 2. troubled; depressed —**cloud′less** *adj.*

cloudburst *n.* a sudden, very heavy rain

cloud chamber *Physics* a chamber supersaturated with water vapour for tracking the path of charged particles

cloudy *adj.* **-ier, -iest** 1. covered with clouds; overcast 2. of or like clouds 3. opaque or foggy 4. obscure 5. troubled; gloomy —**cloud′iness** *n.*

clough (kluf) *n.* [OE. *clōh*] a steep valley, esp. in N England

clout (klout) *n.* [OE. *clut*] 1. a blow, as with the hand; rap 2. [Colloq.] power or influence; esp., political power —*vt.* [Colloq.] to strike, as with the hand

clove¹ (klōv) *n.* [< L. *clavus,* nail: from its shape] the dried flower bud of a tropical evergreen tree, used as a pungent, fragrant spice

clove² *n.* [OE. *clufu*] a segment of a bulb, as of garlic

clove³ *alt. pt.* of CLEAVE¹

clove hitch a kind of knot for fastening a rope around a spar, pole, or another rope

cloven (klō′v'n) *alt. pp.* of CLEAVE¹ —*adj.* divided; split

cloven foot (or **hoof**) a foot divided by a cleft, as in the ox, deer, and sheep: used as a symbol of the Devil

clover (klō′vər) *n.* [< OE. *clafre*] any of a genus of low-growing herbs with leaves of three leaflets and small flowers in dense heads —**in clover** living in ease and luxury

CLOVERLEAF

cloverleaf *n., pl.* **-leafs′** a motorway interchange in the form of a four-leaf clover, which, by means of an overpass, permits traffic to move in any of four directions

clown (kloun) *n.* [< ?] 1. a performer who entertains, as in a circus, by antics, jokes, tricks, etc. 2. a buffoon 3. a clumsy, boorish person 4. orig., a peasant; rustic —*vi.* to play practical jokes, act in a silly manner, etc. —**clown′ery** *n.* —**clown′-ish** *adj.*

cloy (kloi) *vt., vi.* [ult. < L. *clavus,* nail] to surfeit by too much of something, esp. something sweet, rich, etc. —**cloy′ingly** *adv.*

club (klub) *n.* [< ON. *klumba,* mass] 1. a heavy stick, used as a weapon 2. any stick or bat used to strike a ball in a game [a golf *club*] 3. a group of people associated for a common purpose 4. the room, building, etc. used by such a group 5. a) [*pl.*] a suit of playing cards marked with a black cloverleaf figure (♣) b) a card of this suit —*vt.* **clubbed, club′bing** 1. to strike as with a club

2. to pool (resources, etc.) —*vi.* to unite or combine for a common purpose —**in the club** [Slang] pregnant

clubfoot *n.* a congenital deformity of the foot, often clublike —**club′foot′ed** *adj.*

clubhouse *n.* a building occupied by a club

club root a plant disease in which the root becomes thickened and distorted

cluck (kluk) *vi.* [echoic] to make a low, sharp, clicking sound, as of a hen calling her chickens —*vt.* to utter with such a sound —*n.* the sound of clucking

clue (kloo) *n.* [see CLEW] something that leads out of a maze or helps to solve a problem —*vt.* **clued, clu′ing** 1. to indicate by a clue 2. [Colloq.] to provide with information (often with *in*) —**not have a clue** 1. to be baffled 2. to be incompetent

clueless *adj.* [Colloq.] helpless; stupid

clump (klump) *n.* [< Du. or LowG.] 1. a lump; mass 2. a cluster, as of trees —*vi.* 1. to tramp heavily 2. to form clumps —*vt.* to group together in a cluster —**clump′ish** *adj.* —**clump′y** *adj.*

clumsy (klum′zē) *adj.* **-sier, -siest** [ME. *clumsid*, numb] 1. lacking grace or skill; awkward 2. awkwardly shaped or made —**clum′sily** *adv.* —**clum′siness** *n.*

clung (kluŋ) *pt. & pp.* of CLING

clunk (kluŋk) *n.* [echoic] 1. a dull, metallic sound 2. [Colloq.] a heavy blow —*vi.* to move with a clunk

cluster (klus′tər) *n.* [OE. *clyster*] 1. a number of things of the same sort gathered or growing together 2. a number of persons or animals grouped together —*vi., vt.* to gather or grow in a cluster —**clus′tery** *adj.*

clutch¹ (kluch) *vt.* [OE. *clyccan*, clench] 1. to grasp or snatch with a hand or claw 2. to grasp or hold eagerly or tightly —*vi.* to snatch or seize (*at*) —*n.* 1. *a)* a device for engaging or disengaging an engine *b)* the pedal that operates this 2. a grasp; grip 3. a claw or hand in the act of seizing 4. [*usually pl.*] power; control

clutch² *n.* [< ME. *clekken*, hatch] 1. a nest of eggs 2. a brood of chicks 3. a cluster of things

clutter (klut′ər) *n.* [< CLOT] a number of things scattered in disorder; jumble —*vt.* to put into disorder; jumble (often with *up*) —**clut′tery** *adj.*

Clydesdale (klīdz′dāl′) *n.* [< *Clydesdale,* Scotland] any of a breed of strong draught horse

Cm *Chem.* curium

cm centimetre; centimetres

cmdg. commanding

Cmdr. Commander

C.M.G. Companion (of the Order) of St. Michael and St. George

cml. commercial

CND, C.N.D. Campaign for Nuclear Disarmament

co- a prefix shortened from COM- meaning: *a)* together with [*cooperation*] *b)* joint [*co-owner*] *c)* equally [*coextensive*]

Co *Chem.* cobalt

Co. *pl.* **Cos.** 1. company 2. county

C/O, co. 1. care of 2. carried over

C.O., CO 1. Commanding Officer 2. conscientious objector

coach (kōch), *n.* [< *Kócs,* village in Hungary] 1. a single-decker bus, esp. one used for travel over long distances 2. a railway carriage 3. a large, covered, four-wheeled carriage with an open, raised seat in front for the driver 4. an instructor or trainer, as of athletes, singers, etc. 5. a private tutor —*vt., vi.* to tutor, instruct, or train (athletes, etc.)

coachbuilder *n.* a person or company that builds motor vehicle bodies

coachman *n.* the driver of a coach or carriage

coadjutor (kō aj′ə tər) *n.* [< L. *co-*, together + *adjuvare,* to help] an assistant; helper

coagulate (kō ag′yoo lāt′) *vt.***-lat′ed, -lat′ing** [< L. *coagulare*] to cause (a liquid) to become a soft, semisolid mass; clot —*vi.* to become coagulated —**coag′ulant** *n.* —**coag′ula′tion** *n.* —**coag′ulative** *adj.*

coal (kōl) *n.* [OE. *col*] 1. a black, combustible, mineral solid formed from vegetable matter and used as a fuel 2. a piece or pieces of this substance 3. an ember 4. charcoal —*vt.* to provide with coal —*vi.* to take in a supply of coal —**carry** (or **send**) **coals to Newcastle** 1. to take things to a place where they are plentiful 2. to do an unnecessary thing —**haul** (or **rake, drag, call**) **over the coals** to criticize sharply —**heap coals of fire on** (**someone's**) **head** to cause (someone) to feel remorse by returning good for his evil

coalesce (kō′ə les′) *vi.* **-lesced′, -lesc′ing** [< L. *co-*, together + *alescere,* grow up] 1. to grow together 2. to unite or merge into a single body, group, or mass —**co′a-les′cence** *n.* —**co′ales′cent** *adj.*

coalface (kōl′fās′) *n.* the exposed seam of coal in a mine

coalfield *n.* an area rich in coal deposits

coal gas a gas produced by the distillation of bituminous coal: used for lighting and heating

coalition (kō′ə lish′ən) *n.* [see COALESCE] 1. a combination; union 2. a temporary alliance of political parties, nations, etc. —**co′ali′tionist** *n.*

coal scuttle a metal container for storing and carrying coal for domestic use

coal tar a black, thick liquid obtained by the distillation of coal, used in dyes and medicines

coal-tit *n.* a small songbird with a black head and a white patch on the nape

coaming (kō′miŋ) *n.* [< ?] a raised border around a hatchway, etc. to keep out water

coarse (kôrs) *adj.* [< COURSE in sense of "ordinary or usual order"] 1. of inferior or poor quality 2. consisting of rather large particles 3. not fine in texture, form, etc. 4. for rough work 5. lacking in refinement; vulgar 6. obscene —**coarse′-ly** *adv.* —**coarse′ness** *n.*

coarse fish any freshwater fish not of

the salmon family, and caught other than by fly-fishing

coarsen *vt., vi.* to make or become coarse

coast (kōst) *n.* [< L. *costa*, side] land beside the sea; seashore —*vi.* 1. to sail near or along a coast 2. to continue in motion by momentum alone 3. to let one's past efforts carry one along —*vt.* to sail along or near the coast of —**the coast is clear** there is no apparent danger —**coast′al** *adj.*

coaster *n.* 1. a ship that travels along a coast 2. a small tray, mat, etc. placed under a glass to protect a table

coast guard 1. a governmental force employed to defend a nation's coasts, prevent smuggling, etc. 2. a member of a coast guard —**coast guards′man**

coastline *n.* the outline of a coast

coat (kōt) *n.* [< ML. *cot(t)a*, tunic] 1. a sleeved outer garment opening down the front 2. the natural covering of an animal or plant 3. a layer, as of paint, over a surface —*vt.* to cover with a coat —**coat′ed** *adj.* —**coat′less** *adj.*

coating *n.* a coat or layer over a surface

coat of arms [< Fr. *cotte d'armes,* garment blazoned with one's heraldic arms] a group of emblems arranged on and around a shield and used as an insignia

coat of mail *pl.* **coats of mail** a suit of armour made of linked metal rings or overlapping plates

coattail *n.* the back part of a coat below the waist; esp., either half of this part when divided —**ride** (or **hang,** etc.) **on (someone's) coattails** to have one's success dependent on that of someone else

coax (kōks) *vt.* [< obs. *cokes,* fool] to persuade or urge by soothing words, flattery, etc. —**coax′er** *n.* —**coax′ing** *adj., n.* —**coax′ingly** *adv.*

coaxial (kō ak′sē əl) *adj.* 1. having a common axis : also **coax′al** 2. designating a high-frequency transmission cable with an outer conductor tube surrounding an insulated central conductor

cob (kob) *n.* [prob. < LowG.] 1. a lump 2. a hazelnut : also **cob′nut′** 3. a round loaf of bread 4. a male swan 5. a short, thickset horse

cobalt (kō′bôlt) *n.* [< G. *Kobold,* goblin of the mines] a hard, steel-grey, metallic chemical element : symbol Co : a radioactive isotope (**cobalt 60**) is used in the treatment of cancer —**cobal′tic** *adj.* —**cobal′tous** *adj.*

cobalt blue 1. a dark blue pigment made from cobalt and aluminium oxides 2. dark blue

cobalt bomb a cobalt 60 device used in radiotherapy

cobber (kob′ər) *n.* [< ?] [Aust. & N.Z. Colloq.] a friend

cobble (kob′'l) *vt.* **-bled, -bling** [< ?] 1. to mend (shoes, etc.) 2. to mend or put together clumsily

cobbler[1] *n.* [< ?] an iced drink of wine, whisky, or rum, an orange or lemon slice, sugar, etc.

cobbler[2] *n.* a person whose work is mending shoes

cobblestone *n.* [< ME. *cobel ston*] a rounded stone of a kind formerly much used for paving streets

COBOL (kō′bol) *n.* [*CO(mmon) B(usiness) O(riented) L(anguage)*] a computer programming language for general commercial use

cobra (kō′brə) *n.* [< Port.] a very poisonous snake of Asia and Africa : loose skin around the neck expands into a hood when the snake is excited

cobweb (kob′web′) *n.* [< ME. *coppe,* spider + web] 1. a web spun by a spider 2. a thread of this 3. anything flimsy, gauzy, or ensnaring, like a web —**blow** (or **sweep**) **away the cobwebs** 1. to clear away dirt, etc. 2. to get rid of antiquated ideas, etc. —**cob′web′by** *adj.*

coca (kō′kə) *n.* [SAmInd. *cuca*] any of certain s American shrubs, esp. a species whose dried leaves are the source of cocaine

cocaine, cocain (kō kān′) *n.* [see prec.] a crystalline alkaloid obtained from dried coca leaves : it is a narcotic and local anaesthetic

coccus (kok′əs) *n., pl.* **cocci** (kok′sī) [< Gr. *kokkos,* berry] a bacterium of a spherical shape

coccyx (kok′siks) *n., pl.* **coccyges** (kok sī′jēz) [< Gr. *kokkyx,* cuckoo : from its shape like a cuckoo's beak] a small, triangular bone at the lower end of the vertebral column —**coccyg′eal** (-sij′ē əl) *adj.*

cochineal (koch′ə nēl′) *n.* [< L. *coccinus,* scarlet < *coccum,* berry] a red dye made from the dried bodies of female cochineal insects

cochlea (kok′lē ə) *n., pl.* **-leae** (-ē′), **-leas** [< Gr. *kochlias,* snail] the spiral-shaped part of the internal ear, containing the auditory nerve endings —**coch′lear** *adj.*

cock[1] (kok) *n.* [OE. *coc*] 1. the male of the chicken or of certain other birds 2. a weathercock 3. a leader or chief 4. a valve for regulating the flow of liquid 5. the hammer of a firearm 6. a jaunty, erect position 7. [Colloq.] a friend; fellow : used as a term of address 8. [Vulg. Slang.] the penis —*vt.* 1. to set (a hat, etc.) jauntily on one side 2. to raise; erect [a dog *cocks* his ears] 3. to turn (the eye or ear) towards something 4. to set the hammer of (a gun) in firing position —*vi.* to assume an upright or tilted position —**at half cock** before full preparations have been made —**cock up** [Colloq.] to make a mess of

cock[2] *n.* [ME. *cokke*] a small, cone-shaped pile, as of hay —*vt.* to pile in cocks

cockade (ko kād′) *n.* [Fr. < *coq,* a cock] a rosette worn on the hat as a badge —**cock-ad′ed** *adj.*

cock-a-hoop (kok′ə hōōp′) *adj.* [< Fr., cock with a crest] in very high spirits; elated

cock-a-leekie (kok′ə lē′kē) *n.* [< COCK[1] + *leeky,* leek] [Scot.] a soup made by boiling chicken with leeks

cock-and-bull story an absurd story

cockatoo (kok′ə tōō′) *n., pl.* **-toos′** [Du.

< Malay] a crested parrot of Australia and the East Indies, with white plumage tinged with yellow or pink

cockatrice (kok′ə trīs′) *n.* [< OFr.] a legendary serpent supposedly killing by a look

cockchafer (kok′chāf′ər) *n.* [COCK¹ (? because of size) + CHAFER] a large European beetle

cockcrow *n.* the time when cocks begin to crow; dawn : also **cock′crow′ing**

cocked hat a three-cornered hat with a turned-up brim —**knock into a cocked hat** [Slang] to ruin

cockerel (kok′ər əl) *n.* [dim. of COCK¹] a young cock, less than a year old

cocker (spaniel) (kok′ər) [from use in hunting woodcock] a small spaniel with silky hair, and drooping ears

cockeyed (kok′īd′) *adj.* 1. cross-eyed 2. [Colloq.] a) tilted; crooked; awry b) silly; foolish c) drunk

cockfight *n.* a fight between gamecocks, usually wearing metal spurs —**cock′fight′-ing** *n.*

cockle¹ (kok′'l) *n.* [< Gr. konchē, conch] 1. an edible shellfish with two heart-shaped, radially ridged shells 2. a cockleshell 3. a wrinkle; pucker —*vi., vt.* -**led, -ling** to wrinkle; pucker —**cockles of one's heart** one's deepest feelings

cockle² *n.* [< OE. coccel, tares] any of various weeds that grow in grainfields

cockleshell *n.* 1. the shell of a cockle 2. loosely, a scallop shell, etc. 3. a small boat

cockney (kok′nē) *n., pl.* -**neys** [ME. cokeney, cock's egg] [often C-] 1. a native of London, esp. of the East End 2. the urban dialect of London, esp. the East End —*adj.* [often C-] of or like cockneys or their dialect

cockpit (kok′pit′) *n.* 1. the space in an aeroplane for the pilot 2. in small vessels, a sunken space towards the stern used by the steersman, etc. 3. any place that has been much fought over 4. an enclosed space for cockfighting

cockroach *n.* [Sp. cucaracha] an insect with long feelers, and a flat, soft body

cockscomb (koks′kōm′) *n.* 1. the red, fleshy growth on the head of a cock 2. a plant related to the amaranth

cockshy (kok′shī′) *n.* [COCK¹ + SHY²] 1. a target in throwing games 2. a throw in such a game 3. an object of criticism or ridicule; butt

cocksure *adj.* [COCK¹ + sure] 1. absolutely sure 2. self-confident and overbearing

cocktail *n.* [< ?] 1. an alcoholic drink, usually iced, made of a spirit mixed with a wine, fruit juice, etc. 2. an appetizer, as fruit juice, diced fruits, or seafood

cocky *adj.* -**ier, -iest** [< COCK¹] [Colloq.] jauntily conceited; self-confident in an aggressive or swaggering way —**cock′ily** *adv.* —**cock′iness** *n.*

coco (kō′kō) *n., pl.* -**cos** [Sp. & Port.] 1. a tropical palm 2. its fruit; coconut

cocoa (kō′kō) *n.* [Sp. & Port. < MexInd.] 1. powder made from cacao seeds that

have been roasted and ground 2. a drink made by adding sugar and hot water or milk to this powder 3. a reddish-yellow brown

coconut, cocoanut (kō′kə nut′) *n.* the fruit of the coconut palm, a thick, brown, oval husk enclosing a layer of edible white meat : the hollow centre is filled with a sweet, milky fluid called **coconut milk**

coconut matting matting woven from the fibre of coconut husks

cocoon (kə kōōn′) *n.* [< Fr. < ML. coco, shell] 1. the silky case which certain insect larvae spin about themselves before the pupa stage 2. any protective cover like this —*vt.* to wrap in or protect by a cocoon

cocopan (kō′kō pan) *n.* [S Afr.] a small truck running on rails used esp. on the mines

cocotte (ko kot′) *n.* [Fr.] 1. a prostitute 2. any sexually promiscuous woman 3. a small fireproof dish in which food is cooked and served individually

cod¹ (kod) *n., pl.* **cod, cods** [ME.] an important food fish found in northern seas : also **cod′fish**

cod² *n.* [< OE. codd, bag] 1. [Dial.] a husk or pod, esp. a pea pod 2. [Archaic] the scrotum

C.O.D., c.o.d. cash (or collect) on delivery

coda (kō′də) *n.* [It. < L. cauda, tail] Music a passage formally ending a composition or section

coddle (kod′'l) *vt.* -**dled, -dling** [prob. < CAUDLE] 1. to cook (esp. eggs) gently in water not quite boiling 2. to treat tenderly; pamper

code (kōd) *n.* [< L. codex, wooden tablet] 1. a system of secret writing in which letters, figures, etc. are given certain meanings 2. a set of signals for sending messages, as by telegraph, flags, etc. 3. a body of laws arranged systematically 4. any set of principles —*vt.* **cod′ed, cod′-ing** to put in the form or symbols of a code —**cod′er** *n.*

codeine (kō′dēn) *n.* [< Gr. kōdeia, poppy head] an alkaloid derived from opium, used for pain relief and in cough medicines : also **co′dein**

codex (kō′deks) *n., pl.* **codices** (kō′-də sēz′) [see CODE] a manuscript volume, esp. of an ancient text

codger (koj′ər) *n.* [prob. < cadger : see CADGE] [Colloq.] an eccentric, esp. elderly, fellow

codicil (kod′i sil′) *n.* [< L. codex : see CODE] Law an addition to a will to change, revoke, or add provisions —**cod′i-cil′lary** *adj.*

codify (kō′də fī′) *vt.* -**fied′, -fy′ing** to arrange (laws, etc.) systematically —**cod′i-fica′tion** *n.* —**cod′ifi′er** *n.*

cod-liver oil (kod′liv′ər) oil obtained from the liver of the cod and related fishes : it is rich in vitamins A and D

codpiece *n.* [COD² + piece] [Hist.] a bag or flap fastened over the front opening in men's breeches

coeducation (kō′ed yoo kā′shən) *n.* the educational system in which students of both sexes attend classes together —**co′edu ca′tional** *adj.*

coefficient (kō′ə fish′ənt) *n.* **1.** *Math.* a number, symbol, etc. used as a multiplier **2.** *Physics* a number or constant for a given substance, used as a multiplier in measuring the change in some property of the substance under given conditions

coelenterate (si len′tə rāt′) *n.* [ult. < Gr. *koilos*, hollow + *enteron*, intestine] any of a large group of marine animals, as the jellyfishes, corals, etc. having a large central cavity with a single opening

coeliac disease (sē′lē ak′) [< Gr. *koilia*, belly] an intestinal disorder caused by inadequate absorption of fats

coenobite (sē′nə bīt′) *n.* [< Gr. *koinos*, common + *bios*, life] a member of a religious order in a monastery or convent —**coe′nobit′ic** (-bit′ik), **coe′nobit′ical** *adj.*

coequal (kō ē′kwəl) *adj., n.* equal —**co′equal′ity** (-i kwol′ə tē) *n.* —**coe′qually** *adv.*

coerce (kō urs′) *vt.* -**erced′**, -**erc′ing** [< L. *co-*, together + *arcere*, confine] **1.** to restrain or constrain by force; curb **2.** to force; compel **3.** to enforce —**coer′cible** *adj.* —**coer′cion** *n.* —**coer′cive** *adj.*

coeval (kō ē′v'l) *adj., n.* [< L. *co-*, together + *aevum*, age] contemporary —**coe′vally** *adv.*

coexist (kō′ig zist′) *vi.* **1.** to exist together, at the same time **2.** to live together without conflict despite differences —**co′exist′ence** *n.* —**co′exist′ent** *adj.*

coextend (kō′ik stend′) *vt., vi.* to extend equally in space or time —**co′exten′sion** *n.* —**co′exten′sive** *adj.*

C. of C. Chamber of Commerce

C. of E. Church of England

coffee (kof′ē) *n.* [< Turk. < Ar.] **1.** a dark-brown, aromatic drink made by brewing in water the roasted and ground beanlike seeds of a tall tropical shrub **2.** these seeds : also **coffee beans 3.** the shrub **4.** the colour of coffee with milk or cream in it; brown

coffee bar a snack bar, esp. one serving espresso coffee

coffee break a brief respite from work when coffee or other refreshment may be taken

coffeehouse *n.* a place where coffee and other refreshments are served

coffee mill a small machine for grinding roasted coffee beans: also **coffee grinder**

coffee table a low table usually in a living room

coffer (kof′ər) *n.* [see COFFIN] **1.** a chest or strongbox for keeping valuables **2.** [*pl.*] a treasury; funds **3.** a decorative sunken panel in a dome, etc.

cofferdam *n.* [prec. + DAM¹] a watertight temporary structure in a river, lake, etc. to keep an enclosed area dry so that dams, etc. may be constructed

coffin (kof′in) *n.* [< Gr. *kophinos*, basket] the case or box in which a dead person is buried —*vt.* to put into or as if into

a coffin —**a nail in one′s coffin** anything that brings one's death closer

C. of S. Church of Scotland

cog¹ (kog) *n.* [< Scand.] **1.** one of the teeth on the rim of a wheel, for transmitting or receiving motion; gear tooth **2.** a cogwheel —**cogged** *adj.*

cog² *n.* [< earlier *cock*, to secure] a projection on a beam that fits into a groove in another beam, making a joint

cogent (kō′jənt) *adj.* [< L. *co-*, together + *agere*, drive] forceful and to the point, as a reason or argument; compelling —**co′gency** *n.* —**co′gently** *adv.*

cogitate (koj′ə tāt′) *vi., vt.* -**tat′ed**, -**tat′ing** [< L. *cogitare*, ponder] to think seriously and deeply (about); ponder —**cog′ita′tion** *n.* —**cog′itative** *adj.*

cognac (kon′yak) *n.* [Fr.] **1.** a French brandy distilled from wine near Cognac, France **2.** loosely, any brandy

cognate (kog′nāt) *adj.* [< L. *co-*, together + (*g*) *nasci*, be born] **1.** related by family **2.** derived from a common original form —*n.* **1.** a person related to another **2.** a cognate word, language, or thing —**cog′nateness, cogna′tion** *n.*

cognition (kog nish′ən) *n.* [L. *cognito*, knowledge] **1.** the process of knowing, including perception, memory, judgment, etc. **2.** the result of such a process —**cogni′tional** *adj.* —**cog′nitive** *adj.*

cognizance (kog′nə zəns) *n.* [< L. *cognoscere*, know] **1.** perception or knowledge **2.** official observation **3.** *Heraldry* a distinguishing mark **4.** *Law* the power of dealing with a matter judicially —**take cognizance of** to notice or recognize —**cog′nizant** *adj.*

cognomen (kog nō′mən) *n.*, *pl.* -**no′mens**, -**nom′ina** [L. < *co-*, together + *nomen*, name] **1.** the third name of an ancient Roman **2.** a surname **3.** a nickname —**cognom′inal** *adj.*

cognoscente (kon′yō shen′tē) *n.*, *pl.* -**ti** (-tē) [It. < L. *cognoscere*, know] a connoisseur

COGWHEELS

cogwheel (kog′wēl′) *n.* a wheel rimmed with teeth which mesh with those of another wheel to transmit or receive motion

cohabit (kō hab′it) *vi.* [< L. *co-*, together + *habitare*, dwell] to live together as husband and wife, esp. when not legally married —**cohab′ita′tion** *n.*

coheir (kō′âr′) *n.* a person who inherits jointly with another or others —**co′heir′ess** *n.fem.*

cohere (kō hēar′) *vi.* -**hered′**, -**her′ing** [< L. *co-*, together + *haerere*, stick] **1.** to stick together, as parts of a mass **2.** to be connected naturally or logically

coherent *adj.* **1.** showing logical consistency or intelligibility **2.** sticking together **3.** *Physics* having the same frequency and constant phase difference *[coherent* light *] —***coher′ence** *n.* **—coher′ently** *adv.*

cohesion (kō hē′zhən) *n.* 1. the act of cohering; tendency to stick together 2. *Physics* the force by which the molecules of a substance are held together —**cohe′sive** (-hēs′iv) *adj.* —**cohe′sively** *adv.* —**cohe′siveness** *n.*

cohort (kō′hôrt) *n.* [< L. *cohors,* enclosure] 1. an ancient Roman military unit, one tenth of a legion 2. a band of soldiers 3. any group or band 4. an associate, colleague, or supporter

COHSE (kō′zē) Confederation of Health Service Employees

C.O.I. Central Office of Information

coif (koif; *for n. 2 & vt. 2, usually* kwäf) *n.* [< LL. *cofea,* cap] 1. a cap that fits the head closely 2. a style of arranging the hair —*vt.* **coifed, coif′ing;** *also, and for 2 usually,* **coiffed, coif′fing** 1. to cover as with a coif 2. *a)* to style (the hair) *b)* to give a coiffure to

coiffure (kwä fyooər′) *n.* [Fr.] 1. a headdress 2. a style of arranging the hair

coign of vantage (koin) [archaic var. of *coin*(QUOIN)] an advantageous position

coil¹ (koil) *vt.* [see COLLECT²] to wind (rope) into a circular or spiral form —*vi.* to wind round and round —*n.* 1. anything wound into a series of rings or a spiral 2. a single turn of a coiled figure 3. a contraceptive device consisting of a loop of wire or plastic inserted in the womb 4. *Elec.* a spiral of wire used as an inductor, etc.

coil² *n.* [< ?] [Archaic] commotion; turmoil —**mortal coil** the activities and troubles of life

coin (koin) *n.* [< L. *cuneus,* wedge] 1. a piece of stamped metal issued by a government as money 2. such pieces collectively —*vt.* 1. *a)* to make (coins) by stamping metal *b)* to make (metal) into coins 2. to invent (a new word) —*vi.* to make coins —**coin money** [Colloq.] to earn money rapidly —**false coin** anything spurious —**pay (someone) back in his own coin** to treat (a person) in the same way that he treated others

coinage *n.* 1. the act of coining 2. a system of metal currency 3. an invented word

coincide (kō′in sīd′) *vi.* **-cid′ed, -cid′ing** [< L. *co-,* together + *incidere,* fall upon] 1. to take up the same place in space 2. to occur at the same time 3. to correspond or agree exactly

coincidence (kō in′sə dəns) *n.* 1. a coinciding 2. an accidental and remarkable occurrence of events, ideas, etc. at the same time

coincident *adj.* 1. occurring at the same time or place 2. in agreement; identical —**coin′cident′al** *adj.* —**coin′cident′ally** *adv.*

Cointreau (kwän′trō′) *n. Trademark* an orange-flavoured French liqueur

coir (koiər) *n.* [< Tamil *kayaru,* to be twisted] the fibre of coconuts, used to make rope, etc.

coitus (kō′it əs) *n.* [L. < *co-,* together + *ire,* go] sexual intercourse: also **coition** (kō ish′ən) —**co′ital** *adj.*

coke¹ (kōk) *n.* [< ME. *colke,* core] coal from which most of the gases have been removed by heating —*vt., vi.* **coked, cok′ing** to change into coke

coke² *n.* [Colloq.] cocaine

Col. 1. Colonel 2. Colossians

col (kol) *n.* [< L. *collum,* neck] a gap between peaks in a mountain range, used as a pass

col. 1. colony 2. colour(ed) 3. column

cola (kō′lə) *n.* [< WAfr. name] 1. an African tree whose nuts yield an extract with caffeine, used in soft drinks and medicine 2. a sweet, carbonated soft drink flavoured with this extract

colander (kul′ən dər) *n.* [ult. < L. *colare,* to strain] a vessel with a perforated bottom to drain off liquids

cold (kōld) *adj.* [OE. *cald*] 1. of a temperature much lower than that of the human body 2. without the proper heat or warmth 3. dead 4. feeling chilled 5. without warmth of feeling; not cordial *[a cold personality]* 6. detached *[cold logic]* 7. designating or having colours that suggest cold, as tones of blue, green, or grey 8. faint *[a cold scent]* 9. [Colloq.] with little or no preparation *[to enter a game cold]* 10. [Slang] unconscious *[knocked cold]* —*n.* 1. absence of heat; lack of warmth 2. the sensation produced by a loss or absence of heat 3. cold weather 4. a condition characterized by nasal discharge, malaise, etc., and thought to be viral —**catch (a) cold** 1. to become ill with a cold 2. to encounter unexpected difficulties —**cold comfort** little or no comfort —**have (or get) cold feet** [Colloq.] to be (or become) timid or fearful —**in cold blood** without feeling pity or remorse —**out in the cold** ignored; neglected —**throw cold water on** to discourage —**cold′ish** *adj.* —**cold′ly** *adv.* —**cold′ness** *n.*

coldblooded *adj.* 1. having a body temperature approximating to that of the surrounding air, land, or water, as fishes and reptiles 2. without pity; cruel —**cold′blood′edly** *adv.* —**cold′blood′edness** *n.*

cold chisel a hardened and tempered steel chisel for cutting or chipping cold metal

cold cream a creamy, soothing preparation for softening and cleansing the skin

cold feet [Colloq.] lack or loss of confidence; timidity

cold frame an unheated, boxlike, glass-covered structure for protecting young plants

cold front *Meteorol.* the edge of a cold air mass advancing into a warmer air mass

coldhearted *adj.* lacking sympathy or kindness —**cold′heart′edly** *adv.* —**cold′heart′edness** *n.*

cold shoulder [Colloq.] deliberate

indifference; slight or snub: often with *the* —**cold'-shoul'der** *vt.*

cold sore *same as* HERPES SIMPLEX

cold storage 1. storage of foods, furs, etc. in a refrigerator 2. a state of temporary disuse; abeyance

cold sweat [Colloq.] a physical reaction to fear, anxiety, etc., characterized by chill and moist skin

cold war sharp conflict in diplomacy, economics, etc. between states, without actual warfare

cole (kōl) *n.* [< L. *caulis*, cabbage] any of various plants of the cabbage family, esp., rape

coleopterous (kol'ē op'tər əs) *adj.* [< Gr. *koleos,* sheath + *pteron,* wing] belonging to an order of insects, including beetles, with horny front wings covering membranous hind wings

coleslaw (kōl'slô') *n.* [< Du. *kool,* cabbage + *sla,* salad] a salad made of shredded raw cabbage: also **cole slaw**

coletit *n.* same as COAL-TIT

coleus (kō'lē əs) *n.* [< Gr. *koleos,* sheath] a labiate plant grown for its showy, brightly coloured leaves

coley (kō'lē) *n.* [< ? *coal-fish,* saithe] any of several edible deep-water fish, esp. the saithe

colic (kol'ik) *n.* [< Gr. *kolon,* colon] acute abdominal pain caused by abnormal conditions in the bowels —*adj.* 1. of colic 2. of the colon —**col'icky** *adj.*

coliseum (kol'ə sē'əm) *n.* [< the *Colosseum,* in Rome] a large building or stadium for sports events, shows, etc.: also **colosse'um**

colitis (kō līt'is) *n.* [< Gr. *kolon,* colon + -ITIS] inflammation of the large intestine

coll. 1. collect 2. collection 3. college 4. colloquial

collaborate (kə lab'ə rāt') *vi.* -rat'ed, -rat'ing [< L. *com-,* with + *laborare,* work] 1. to work together, esp. in some literary, artistic, or scientific undertaking 2. to cooperate with an enemy invader —**collab'ora'tion** *n.* —**collab'ora'tionist** *n.* —**collab'orative** *adj.* —**collab'ora'tor** *n.*

collage (kə läzh') *n.* [< Gr. *kolla,* glue] 1. an art form in which bits of objects are pasted together on a surface 2. a composition so made —**collag'ist** *n.*

collagen (kol'ə jen') *n.* [< Gr. *kolla,* glue] a fibrous protein found in bone, cartilage, etc.

collapse (kə laps') *vi.* -lapsed', -laps'ing [< L. *com-,* together + *labi,* fall] 1. to fall down or fall to pieces 2. to break down suddenly 3. to fold or come together compactly —*vt.* to cause to collapse —*n.* the act of collapsing; a falling in or together; failure or breakdown, as in business, health, etc. —**collaps'ibil'ity** *n.* —**collaps'ible** *adj.*

collar (kol'ər) *n.* [< L. *collum,* neck] 1. the part of a garment that encircles the neck 2. a cloth band attached to the neck of a garment 3. a band of leather or metal for the neck of a dog, cat, etc. 4. the part of the harness that fits over the neck of a horse 5. a ring, as on rods or pipes, to connect parts, etc. —*vt.* 1. to put a collar on 2. to seize by or as by the collar 3. [Colloq.] to arrest —**hot under the collar** 1. angry 2. excited 3. ill at ease —**col'lared** *adj.*

collarbone *n.* a slender bone joining the breastbone to the shoulder blade; clavicle

collate (ko lāt') *vt.* -lat'ed, -lat'ing [< L. *collatus* < *com-,* together + *ferre,* bring] 1. to compare (texts, data, etc.) critically 2. to gather (the sections of a book) together in proper order for binding —**colla'tor** *n.*

collateral (ko lat'ər əl) *adj.* [< L. *com-,* together + *latus,* side] 1. side by side; parallel 2. accompanying the main thing in a subordinate way 3. of the same ancestors but in a different line 4. of security given as a pledge for the fulfilment of an obligation —*n.* 1. a collateral relative 2. stocks, bonds, etc. used for collateral security —**collat'erally** *adv.*

collation (ko lā'shən) *n.* 1. the act, process, or result of collating 2. a light meal

colleague (kol'ēg) *n.* [< L. *com-,* with + *legare,* appoint as deputy] a fellow worker; associate

collect[1] (kə lekt') *vt.* [see ff.] 1. to gather together; assemble 2. to gather (stamps, books, etc.) for a hobby 3. to call for and receive (money) for (rent, a fund, bills, etc.) 4. to call for and take away 5. to regain control of (oneself) —*vi.* 1. to gather; assemble [a crowd *collected*] 2. to accumulate —**collect'able, collect'ible** *adj.*

collect[2] (kol'ekt) *n.* [ult. < L. *com-,* together + *legere,* gather] [*also* C-] a short prayer used in certain church services

collected (kə lek'tid) *adj.* 1. gathered together 2. in control of oneself; calm —**collect'edly** *adv.*

collection *n.* 1. the act or process of collecting, specif., post for dispatch 2. things collected [a stamp *collection*] 3. an accumulation 4. money collected, as during a church service

collective *adj.* 1. formed by collecting 2. of or as a group 3. designating any enterprise in which people work together as a group 4. *Gram.* designating a noun which is singular in form but denotes a collection of individuals (e.g., *army, crowd*) —*n.* 1. a collective enterprise or the people involved 2. *Gram.* a collective noun —**collec'tively** *adv.* —**col'lectiv'ity** *n.*

collective bargaining negotiation between organized workers and their employer or employers concerning wages, hours, and working conditions

collectivism *n.* ownership and control of the means of production and distribution by the people collectively —**collec'tivist** *n., adj.* —**collec'tivis'tic** *adj.*

collector *n.* a person or thing that collects; specif., a) a person whose work is collecting taxes, etc. b) a person who collects stamps, etc. as a hobby

collector's item any rare or beautiful object thought worthy of collection

colleen (kol′ēn) *n.* [< Ir. *caile*, girl] [Irish] a girl

college (kol′ij) *n.* [see COLLEAGUE] 1. any institution of higher education not designated as a university 2. an autonomous academic institution within a university 3. a school offering specialized instruction [a secretarial *college*] 4. an institution set up by a profession [the Royal *College* of Surgeons] 5. an association of individuals having certain powers, duties, etc. [Herald's *College*]

college pudding a suet pudding containing dried fruit

collegial (kə lē′jē əl) *adj.* 1. with authority shared equally among colleagues 2. *same as* COLLEGIATE

collegian *n.* a member of a college

collegiate *adj.* 1. of a college or college students 2. made up of colleges, as some universities

collide (kə līd′) *vi.* -lid′ed, -lid′ing [< L. *com-*, together + *laedere*, strike] 1. to strike violently against each other 2. to come into conflict; clash

collie (kol′ē) *n.* [< ?] a silky-haired dog with a long, narrow head: first bred in Scotland to herd sheep

collier (kol′yər) *n.* [see COAL] 1. a coal miner 2. a) a ship for carrying coal b) a member of its crew

colliery *n., pl.* -lieries a coal mine and its buildings, etc.

collimate (kol′ə māt′) *vt.* -mat′ed, -mat′-ing [< L. *com-*, with + *linea*, a line] 1. to make (beams of radiation) parallel 2. to adjust the line of sight of (a telescope, etc.) —**col′lima′tion** *n.* —**col′lima′tor** *n.*

collision (kə lizh′ən) *n.* 1. a colliding 2. a clash or conflict of opinions, interests, etc.

collision course a course bound to end in collision

collocate (kol′ō kāt′) *vt.* -cat′ed, -cat′-ing [see LOCATE] to arrange or place together, esp. side by side

colloid (kol′oid) *n.* [< Gr. *kolla*, glue] a substance made up of insoluble, nondiffusible particles that remain suspended in a medium of different matter —**colloi′dal** *adj.*

collop (kol′əp) *n.* [< Scand.] a small slice of meat, esp. of bacon

colloq. 1. colloquial(ly) 2. colloquialism

colloquial (kə lō′kwē əl) *adj.* [see COLLOQUY] 1. having to do with or like conversation 2. designating words, phrases, and idioms characteristic of informal speech and writing —**collo′qui-ally** *adv.*

colloquialism *n.* 1. colloquial quality, style, or usage 2. a colloquial word or expression

colloquium (kə lō′kwē əm) *n., pl.* -quia, -quiums [see ff.] an organized conference or seminar

colloquy (kol′ə kwē) *n., pl.* -quies [< L. *com-*, together + *loqui*, speak] a conversation, esp. a formal discussion —**col′loquist** *n.* —**col′loquize′** *vi.*

collusion (kə lŏŏ′zhən) *n.* [< L. *com-*, with + *ludere*, to play] a secret agreement

for fraudulent or illegal purpose; conspiracy —**collu′sive** (-siv) *adj.* —**collu′sively** *adv.*

collywobbles (kol′ē wob′′lz) *n.pl.* [often with *sing v.*] [prob. < COLIC + WOBBLE] [Colloq.] 1. pain in the abdomen 2. extreme nervousness

cologne (kə lōn′) *n.* *same as* EAU DE COLOGNE

colon¹ (kō′lən) *n.* [< Gr. *kōlon*, limb] a mark of punctuation (:) used before an extended quotation, example, etc.

colon² *n., pl.* -lons, -la [< Gr. *kolon*] that part of the large intestine extending from the caecum to the rectum —**colonic** (kə lon′ik) *adj.*

colonel (kur′n′l) *n.* [< Fr. < L. *columna*, column] *see* MILITARY RANKS, table —**colo′nelcy** *n.*

colonial (kə lō′nē əl) *adj.* 1. of or living in a colony or colonies 2. [*often* C-] of or relating to the colonies of the British Empire 3. of or characteristic of the thirteen British colonies that became the U.S. —*n.* an inhabitant of a colony —**colo′nially** *adv.*

colonialism *n.* the system of maintaining foreign colonies, esp. for exploitation —**colo′nialist** *n., adj.*

colonist (kol′ə nist) *n.* 1. any of the original settlers of a colony 2. an inhabitant of a colony

colonize *vt., vi.* -nized′, -niz′ing 1. to found or establish a colony or colonies (in) 2. to settle in a colony —**col′oniza′-tion** *n.* —**col′oniz′er** *n.*

COLONNADE

colonnade (kol′ə nād′) *n.* [Fr. < L. *columna*, column] *Archit.* a series of columns set at regular intervals, usually supporting a roof —**col′onnad′ed** *adj.*

colony (kol′ə nē) *n., pl.* -nies [< L. *colere*, cultivate] 1. a) a group of people who settle in a distant land but under the jurisdiction of their native land b) the region thus settled 2. [C-] [*pl.*] the colonies and, loosely, the dominions, of the British Empire 3. a community of people of the same nationality or pursuits concentrated in a particular place 4. *Biol.* a group of similar plants or animals living or growing together

colophon (kol′ə fən) *n.* [< Gr. *kolophōn*, top] 1. a note in a book giving facts about its production, formerly printed at the end 2. the distinctive emblem of the publisher

Colorado beetle (kol′ə räd′ō) [< U.S. State] a widely distributed black-and-yellow beetle that is a destructive pest of potatoes

coloratura (kol′ər ə tooər′ə) n. [It. < L. colorare, colour] 1. brilliant runs, trills, etc., in music used to display a singer's skill 2. a soprano who sings such music: in full, **coloratura soprano**

colossal (kə los′'l) adj. 1. like a colossus in size; huge 2. [Colloq.] extraordinary —**colos′sally** adv.

colossus (kə los′əs) n., pl. -**los′si** (-ī) -**los′suses** [< Gr. kolossos] 1. a gigantic statue; esp., [C-] that of Apollo set at the entrance to the harbour of Rhodes c. 280 B.C. 2. any huge or important person or thing

colostomy (kə los′tə mē) n., pl. -**mies** [COLO(N)² + Gr. stoma, mouth] the surgical operation of forming an artificial opening in the colon

colostrum (kə los′trəm) n. [L., beestings] the first milk produced for several days after the birth of the young

colour (kul′ər) n. [< L. color] 1. the sensation resulting from stimulation of the retina of the eye by light waves of particular wavelengths 2. the property of reflecting light of a particular wavelength: the distinct colours of the spectrum are red, orange, yellow, green, blue, indigo, and violet; the primary colours of the spectrum are red, green, and blue 3. any colouring matter; dye; pigment; paint: the primary colours (red, yellow, and blue) and secondary colours formed from these (green, orange, purple, etc.) are sometimes distinguished from black, white, and grey (achromatic colours) 4. colour of the face; esp. a healthy rosiness 5. the colour of the skin of a nonwhite person 6. [pl.] a) a flag of a country, regiment, etc. b) Sport a badge or cap denoting membership of a team, esp. at school or college 7. [pl.] one's position, opinion, or true nature 8. appearance of truth [the news lent colour to the rumour] 9. authenticity —vt. 1. to give colour to; paint; stain; dye 2. to change the colour of 3. to alter or influence, as by distortion —vi. 1. to become coloured 2. to change in colour 3. to blush; flush —**change colour** 1. to become pale 2. to blush or flush —**colour up** to blush or flush —**lose colour** to become pale —**nail one's colours to the mast** to commit oneself to a particular course of action —**off colour** 1. unwell 2. in bad taste —**under colour of** under the pretext of —**under false colours** deceitfully; as an impostor —**with flying colours** triumphantly —**col′ourer** n.

colourable adj. 1. capable of being coloured 2. apparently plausible, but actually specious; deceptive

colouration, coloration (kul′ə rā′shən) n. 1. the way a thing is coloured 2. the technique of using colours

colour bar a barrier of social, political, and economic restrictions imposed on nonwhites

colourblind adj. unable to perceive colours or to distinguish between certain colours, as red and green —**col′ourblind′ness** n.

coloured adj. 1. having colour 2. of a (specified) colour 3. [sometimes C-] non-Caucasoid; nonwhite; specif., Negro 4. [C-] in South Africa, of racially mixed parentage 5. altered, distorted, or exaggerated —n. 1. [usually C-] a person who is not white 2. [C-] in South Africa, a nonwhite person of racially mixed parentage

colourful adj. 1. full of vivid colours 2. full of interest or variety; distinctive in style, etc.

colouring n. 1. the act or art of applying colours 2. anything applied to impart colour; pigment, dye, etc. 3. same as COLOURATION 4. skin colour 5. false appearance

colourless adj. 1. without colour 2. dull in colour; grey or pallid; drab 3. lacking interest or life; dull —**col′ourlessly** adv. —**col′ourlessness** n.

colour sergeant see MILITARY RANKS, table

colour supplement a magazine printed in colour given away with a newspaper

colt (kōlt) n. [OE.] 1. a young horse, donkey, zebra, etc.; specif., a male racehorse four years of age or under 2. Sport a young or inexperienced player

coltish adj. of or like a colt; esp., frisky, frolicsome, etc. —**colt′ishly** adv.

columbine (kol′əm bīn′) n. [< L. columba, dove] a plant with showy, spurred flowers of various colours

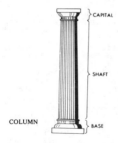

CAPITAL

SHAFT

COLUMN

BASE

column (kol′əm) n. [< L. columna] 1. a slender upright structure, generally a cylindrical shaft with a base and a capital; pillar 2. anything like a column in shape or function 3. a cylindrical body of fluid, as mercury or air 4. a formation of troops, ships, etc. in a file 5. any of the vertical sections of printed matter lying side by side on a page 6. a vertical arrangement of numbers 7. a series of feature articles in a newspaper or magazine, written by a special writer or devoted to a certain subject —**columnar** (kə lum′nər), **col′umned** adj.

columnist (kol′əm nist) n. a person who writes or conducts a column, as in a newspaper

com- [L., with] *a prefix meaning* with or together [*combine*]: also used as an intensive [*command*]

Com. 1. Commander 2. Commission(er) 3. Committee

com. 1. commerce 2. common 3. communication

coma (kō′mə) *n.* [< Gr. *koma*, deep sleep] a state of deep, prolonged unconsciousness, as caused by injury

comatose (kō′mətōs′) *adj.* 1. of, like, or in a coma or stupor 2. as if in a coma; torpid

comb (kōm) *n.* [OE. *camb*] 1. a thin strip of plastic, metal, etc. with teeth, passed through the hair to arrange or clean it, or set in the hair to hold it in place 2. anything like a comb specif., *a*) a tool for cleaning and straightening wool, etc. *b*) a red, fleshy outgrowth on the top of a cock's head 3. a honeycomb —*vt.* 1. to clean or arrange with a comb 2. to remove with or as with a comb; separate (often with *out*) 3. to search thoroughly —*vi.* to roll over; break : said of waves

combat (kom′bat) *vi., vt.* **-bated, -bating** [< L. *com-*, with + *battuere*, beat] to fight; struggle (against) —*n.* battle; conflict; strife —**com′bative** *adj.*

combatant *adj.* 1. fighting 2. ready or prepared to fight —*n.* a person who engages in combat; fighter

combat fatigue a neurotic condition characterized by anxiety, irritability, depression, etc., often occurring after prolonged combat in warfare

combe (kōōm) *n.* *same as* COOMB

comber (kō′mər) *n.* 1. one that combs wool, flax, etc. 2. a large wave that breaks on a beach, reef, etc.

combination (kom bə nā′shən) *n.* 1. a combining or being combined 2. a thing formed by combining 3. an association of persons, firms, etc. for a common purpose 4. the series of numbers or letters used in opening a combination lock 5. [*pl.*] a one-piece undergarment for body and legs 6. a motorcycle with sidecar attached 7. *Math.* any of the various groupings into which a number of units may be arranged without regard to order —**com′bina′tional, com′binative** *adj.*

combination lock a lock with a mechanism operated by a set series of numbers

combine (kəm bīn′; *for. n. & v. 3,* kom′bīn) *vt., vi.* **-bined′, -bin′ing** [< L. *com-*, together + *bini*, two by two] 1. to come or bring into union; unite; join 2. to unite to form a chemical compound 3. to harvest and thresh with a combine —*n.* 1. a machine for harvesting and threshing grain: also **combine harvester** 2. an association of corporations, etc. for commercial or political purposes —**combin′able** *adj.* —**combin′er** *n.*

combings (kō′miηz) *n.pl.* loose hair, wool, etc. removed in combing

combining form a word form that occurs only in compounds or derivatives (Ex.: *-logy* in *cardiology*)

combustible (kəm bus′tə b'l) *adj.* that catches fire and burns easily —*n.* a flammable substance —**combus′tibil′ity** *n.* —**combus′tibly** *adv.*

combustion (kəm bus′chən) *n.* [< L. *com-*, intens. + *urere*, burn] 1. the act or process of burning 2. rapid chemical combination accompanied by heat and, usually, light —**combus′tive** *adj.*

come (kum) *vi.* **came, come, com′ing** [OE. *cuman*] 1. to move from "there" to "here" 2. to approach by moving towards 3. to arrive or appear [help will *come*] 4. to extend; reach 5. to take place [*success came* to him] 6. to take form in the mind [her name *came* to him] 7. to occur in a certain place or order [after 9 *comes* 10] 8. to arrive at a particular state [*come* to grief] 9. to be brought (to an awareness, understanding, etc.) 10. to have a certain descent or origin 11. to result 12. to happen [how did he *come* to hear of it?] 13. to get to be; become [it *came* loose] 14. to be available [this dress *comes* in four sizes] 15. to amount; add up (*to*) 16. [Slang] to have a sexual orgasm —*vt.* [Colloq.] to play the part of [don't *come* the innocent with me] —*interj.* look! see here! —**as good** (or **tough, strong,** etc.) **as they come** extremely good (or tough, strong, etc.) —**come about** to happen; occur —**come across** 1. to find by chance 2. [Colloq] to be effective, etc. 3. [Slang] to give or do what is wanted —**come again?** [Colloq.] what did you say? —**come between** to estrange; divide —**come by** 1. to get; gain 2. to pay a visit —**come clean** to make a confession —**come down** to suffer loss in status, wealth, etc. —**come down on** (or **upon**) to scold; criticize harshly —**come down with** to catch (a disease) —**come in** 1. to enter 2. to come into fashion 3. to finish in a contest 4. [Colloq.] to prove to be [the money came in very useful] 5. *Cricket* to start one's innings as a batsman 6. *Radio* to answer a call or signal —**come in for** [Colloq.] to get; acquire —**come into** 1. to enter into 2. to inherit —**come off** 1. to become detached 2. to occur 3. [Colloq.] to prove successful, etc. —**come off it!** [Colloq.] I don't believe you! —**come on** 1. to make progress 2. to find 3. to appear, make an entrance, etc. —**come one's way** to come to one's notice, into one's possession, etc. —**come out** 1. to be disclosed 2. to go on strike 3. to make a debut 4. to end up; turn out 5. to be published —**come out for** to support; endorse —**come out with** 1. to disclose 2. to say; publish —**come over** 1. to pay a visit from some distance 2. to change sides or one's opinions 3. to make an impression [he *came* over badly] 4. [Colloq.] to feel [he *came* over faint] —**come round** 1. to revive; recover 2. to make a turn 3. to visit casually 4.

to concede or yield —**come through** 1. to complete or endure something successfully 2. [Slang] to do or give what is wanted —**come to** to recover consciousness —**come up** 1. to arise, as in discussion 2. to rise, as in status 3. to be put forward, as for a vote —**come upon** to find —**come up to** 1. to reach to 2. to equal —**come up with** to propose, produce, find, etc. —**how come?** [Colloq.] how is it that? why? —**to come** in the future —**com'er** n.

comeback n. [Colloq.] 1. a return to a previous state or position, as of success 2. a retaliatory action in response to something done or said

Comecon (kom'i kon') Council for Mutual Economic Assistance: a trade organization of Soviet-oriented Communist nations

comedian (kə mē'dē ən) n. 1. an entertainer who tells jokes, sings comic songs, etc. 2. an actor who plays comic parts —**come'dienne'** n.fem.

comedy (kom'ə dē) n., pl. **-dies** [< Gr. kōmōs, festival + aeidein, sing] 1. orig., a drama or narrative with a happy ending or nontragic theme 2. any of various types of play or film with a humorous treatment of characters and situation and a happy ending 3. a novel or any narrative having a comic theme, tone, etc. 4. the comic element in life —**comedic** (kə mē'-dik) adj.

come-hither (kum'hith'ər) adj. [Colloq.] flirtatious or inviting [a come-hither look]

comely (kum'lē) adj. **-lier, -liest** [< OE. cyme, delicate] pleasant to look at —**come'liness** n.

come-on n. [Slang] an inducement

comestible (kə mes'tə b'l) adj. [< L. com-, intens. + edere, eat] [Rare] edible —n. [usually pl.] food

comet (kom'ət) n. [< Gr. komē, hair] a heavenly body having a solid nucleus with a luminous mass (coma) around it, and, usually, a long, luminous tail —**com'etary** adj.

comeuppance (kum'up''ns) n. [Colloq.] deserved punishment; retribution

comfit (kum'fit) n. [see CONFECTION] a sugar-coated sweet, often with a nut, fruit, etc. in the centre

comfort (kum'fərt) vt. [< L. com-, intens. + fortis, strong] to soothe in distress or sorrow; console —n. 1. relief from distress, grief, etc. 2. a person or thing that comforts 3. a state of, or thing that provides, ease and enjoyment —**com'-forting** adj. —**com'fortless** adj.

comfortable adj. 1. providing comfort 2. at ease in body or mind; contented 3. [Colloq.] sufficient to satisfy [a comfortable salary] —**com'fortably** adv.

comforter n. 1. a person or thing that comforts 2. a woollen neckscarf 3. a baby's dummy —**the Comforter** Bible the Holy Spirit: John 14:26

comfrey (kum'frē) n., pl. **-freys** [< L.

confervere, to heal] a plant related to borage, with small blue, purplish, or yellow flowers

comfy adj. **-fier, -fiest** [Colloq.] comfortable; snug

comic (kom'ik) adj. [< Gr. kōmikos] 1. of comedy 2. amusing; funny —n. 1. a comedian 2. the humorous element in art or life 3. a magazine or booklet containing comic strips, esp. for children —**com'ical** adj.

comic strip a series of cartoons, as in a newspaper, telling a humorous or adventurous story

coming (kum'iŋ) adj. 1. approaching; next 2. showing promise of being successful, etc. —n. arrival; advent —**have it (or something) coming to one** to deserve or merit something

comity (kom'ə tē) n., pl. **-ties** [< L. comis, polite] courteous behaviour; politeness

Comm., comm. 1. Commonwealth 2. Communist

comma (kom'ə) n. [< Gr. komma, clause < koptein, cut off] a mark of punctuation (,) used to indicate a slight separation of sentence elements

command (kə mänd') vt. [< L. com-, intens. + mandare, entrust] 1. to give an order to; direct 2. to have authority over; control 3. to have ready for use 4. to deserve and get [to command respect] 5. to control or overlook from a higher position —vi. to exercise authority —n. 1. an order; direction; mandate 2. authority to command 3. power to control by position 4. mastery 5. a military or naval force under a specified authority [Strategic Air Command]

commandant (kom'ən dant') n. a commanding officer of a fort, prisoner of war camp, etc.

commandeer (kom'ən dēər') vt. [< Fr. commander, to command] 1. to seize (property) for military or governmental use 2. [Colloq.] to take forcibly

commander (kə män'dər) n. 1. a person who commands; leader 2. a member of the higher class of some orders of chivalry [Knight Commander of Royal Victorian Order] 3. see MILITARY RANKS, table —**command'ership** n.

commander in chief pl. **commanders in chief** the supreme commander of the armed forces of a nation

commanding adj. 1. being in command 2. having the presence, etc. of one in command; authoritative 3. from which the surrounding countryside may be seen

commandment n. an authoritative command or order; specif., any of the Ten Commandments

commando (kə män'dō) n., pl. **-dos, -does** [< Port.] 1. a small raiding force trained to operate inside enemy territory 2. a member of such a group 3. [S Afr.] a body of armed men esp. raised by Boers in the Boer War

command paper a government

document presented to Parliament by, or as by, royal command, as a white paper

command performance a performance of a play, film, etc. for, or as for, a ruler by command or request

commedia dell' arte (kôm mä'- dyă del lär'te) [It.] a type of Italian comedy of the 16th century, having a stereotyped plot and stock characters

commemorate (kə mem'ə rāt') *vt.* **-rat'- ed, -rat'ing** [< L. *com-*, intens. + *memorare*, remind] **1.** to honour the memory of, as by a ceremony **2.** to serve as a memorial to —**commem'ora'tion** *n.* —**commem'orative, commem'oratory** *adj.* —**commem'oratively** *adv.*

commence (kə mens') *vi., vt.* **-menced', -menc'ing** [< L. *com-*, together + *initiare*, begin] to begin; start; originate —**commence'ment** *n.* —**commenc'er** *n.*

commend (kə mend') *vt.* [see COMMAND] **1.** to put in the care of another; entrust **2.** to recommend **3.** to praise —**commend'- able** *adj.* —**commend'ably** *adv.* —**com'- menda'tion** *n.* —**commend'atory** *adj.*

commensurable (kə men'shər ə b'l) *adj.* [see ff.] measurable by the same standard or measure —**commen'surabil'ity** *n.* —**commen'surably** *adv.*

commensurate *adj.* [< L. *com-*, with + *mensura*, measure] **1.** equal in measure or size **2.** proportionate **3.** commensurate —**commen'surately** *adv.* —**commen'- sura'tion** *n.*

comment (kom'ent) *n.* [< L. *com-*, intens. + *meninisse*, remember] **1.** a note or notes in explanation or criticism of something written or said **2.** a remark or observation —*vi.* to make a comment or comments (*on* or *upon*) —**no comment** I have nothing to say on the matter

commentary (kom'ən tər ē) *n., pl.* **-tar- ies 1.** a series of explanatory notes or annotations **2.** a series of remarks or observations; specif., a description, for radio or TV, of a sporting event, ceremony, etc. —**com'mentar'ial** (-tãər'ē əl) *adj. m*

commentate *vi.* **-tat'ed, -tat'ing** to perform as a commentator

commentator *n.* **1.** a person who describes and comments upon sporting events, etc., as on radio or TV **2.** a person who reports and analyses, etc.

commerce (kom'urs) *n.* [< L. *com-*, together + *merx*, merchandise] **1.** the buying and selling of goods, as between cities, states, or countries **2.** social intercourse

commercial (kə mur'shəl) *adj.* **1.** of or connected with commerce or trade **2.** made or done primarily for profit **3.** offering training in business skills, etc. —*n. Radio & TV* a paid advertisement —**commer'cially** *adv.*

commercial broadcasting radio and TV financed by advertising and generally run to make a profit

commercialism *n.* the practices and

spirit of commerce or business, esp. in seeking profits

commercialize *vt.* **-ized', -iz'ing 1.** to apply business methods to **2.** to make use of for profit, esp. at the expense of quality —**commer'cializa'tion** *n.*

commercial traveller a representative of a firm who visits customers to solicit business, take orders, etc.

Commie (kom'ē) *adj., n.* [*sometimes* c-] [Chiefly U.S. Colloq.] Communist: a derogatory usage

commination (kom'ə nā'shən) *n.* [< L. *comminari*, threaten] a threat or warning, esp. of divine punishment —**comminatory** (kom'i nə tər ē) *adj.*

commingle (kə miŋ'g'l) *vt., vi.* **-gled, -gling** to mingle together; intermix; blend

commis (kom'ē) *n. pl.* **-mis** (-ēz) [Fr.] a junior or apprentice waiter or chef

commiserate (kə miz'ə rāt') *vt.* **-at'ed, -at'ing** [< L. *com-*, intens. + *miserari*, pity] to feel or show pity for —*vi.* to condole or sympathize (*with*) —**commis'er- a'tion** *n.* —**commis'erative** *adj.*

commissariat (kom'ə sãar'ē ət) *n.* **1.** the branch of an army which provides food and supplies for the troops **2.** formerly, a government department in the U.S.S.R.: since 1946, called *ministry* —**commissar** (kom'ə sär') *n.*

commissary (kom'ə sər ē) *n., pl.* **-saries** [< L. *committere*, commit] **1.** a deputy assigned to some duty **2.** formerly, an army officer in charge of providing food and supplies —**com'missar'ial** (-sãər'ē əl) *adj.*

commission (kə mish'ən) *n.* [see COMMIT] **1.** an authorization to perform certain duties or to take on certain powers **2.** a document giving such authorization or instruction **3.** the state of being so authorized **4.** authority to act for another **5.** that which one is authorized to do for another **6.** a committing, as of a crime **7.** *a)* a group of people officially appointed to perform specified duties *b)* a government department set up for a specific purpose [*the Price Commission*] **8.** a percentage or fee paid to an agent for services **9.** *Mil.* an official document conferring a rank of officer —*vt.* **1.** to give a commission to **2.** to authorize **3.** *Naut.* to put (a vessel) into service —**in** (or **out of**) **commission 1.** in (or not in) use **2.** in (or not in) working order

commissionaire (kə mish'ə nãər') *n.* [Fr.] a uniformed doorman at a hotel, cinema, office block, etc., esp. one of a group of ex-servicemen (**Corps of Commissionaires**)

commissioned officer an officer in the armed forces holding rank by a commission

commissioner (kə mish'ə nər) *n.* **1.** a member of a commission (sense 7) **2.** an official in charge of a government agency, territory, etc.

Commissioner for Oaths a solicitor

empowered to administer an oath to one making a sworn statement, affidavit, etc.

commit (kə mit') *vt.* **-mit'ted, -mit'ting** [< L. *com-*, together + *mittere*, send] 1. to give in charge or trust; consign 2. to put officially in custody or confinement [*committed* to prison] 3. to do or perpetrate (an offence or crime) 4. to bind as by a promise; pledge [*committed* to action] —**commit to memory** to learn by heart; memorize —**commit to paper** (or **writing**) to write down —**commit'table** *adj.*

commitment *n.* 1. a committing or being committed 2. official consignment of a person to prison 3. a pledge or promise 4. any obligation or engagement Also **commit'tal**

committee *n.* [see COMMIT] 1. a group of people chosen, as in a legislature or club, to consider or act on some matter 2. [C-] the House of Commons when sitting as a Committee —**in committee** under consideration by a committee, as a resolution or bill

Committee of Supply the House of Commons when sitting as a Committee of the whole house to discuss public expenditure estimates

commode (kə mōd') *n.* [Fr. < L.: see COM- & MODE] 1. a chest of drawers 2. a chair enclosing a chamber pot

commodious (kə mō'dē əs) *adj.* [see prec.] spacious; roomy —**commo'diously** *adv.* —**commo'diousness** *n.*

commodity (kə mod'ə tē) *n., pl.* **-ties** [see COMMODE] 1. any useful thing 2. anything bought and sold

commodore (kom'ə dôr') *n.* [< Fr.: see COMMAND] 1. a courtesy title, as of the president of a yacht club 2. the senior captain of a merchant shipping line 3. *see* MILITARY RANKS, table

common (kom'ən) *adj.* [< L. *communis*, shared by all or many] 1. belonging equally to, or shared by, all 2. belonging to the community at large; public 3. widely existing; general 4. familiar; usual 5. not of the upper classes; of the masses [the *common* people] 6. having no rank [a *common* soldier] 7. below ordinary; inferior 8. vulgar; low; coarse 9. *Gram.* designating a noun that refers to any of a group or class, as *book, apple, street* 10. *Math.* belonging equally to two or more quantities [a *common* denominator] —*n.* 1. [*sometimes pl.*] land owned or used by all the inhabitants of a place 2. [Slang] common sense —**common or garden** of the usual kind; ordinary —**in common** equally with all concerned —**com'monly** *adv.* —**com'monness** *n.*

commonality (kom'ə nal'ə tē) *n.* 1. the common people 2. a sharing of common features, etc.

commonalty (kom'ən əl tē) *n., pl.* **-ties** 1. the common people 2. a general body or group

commoner *n.* 1. one who is not of the nobility 2. at some universities, a student

who is not supported by a university or college scholarship

common fraction a fraction whose numerator and denominator are both whole numbers

common law the law of a country or state based on custom, usage, and the decisions of law courts

common-law marriage *Law* a marriage not solemnized by religious or civil ceremony but effected by agreement to live together as husband and wife

common market an association of countries formed to effect a closer economic union; specif., [C- M-] the European Economic Community

commonplace *n.* 1. a trite remark; platitude 2. anything common or ordinary —*adj.* obvious or ordinary —**com'monplace'ness** *n.*

common room a sitting-room in schools, colleges, etc. for the use of students or staff

commons *n.pl.* 1. the common people 2. [*often with sing. v.*] [C-] same as HOUSE OF COMMONS 3. [*often with sing. v.*] food provided for meals for a whole group —**short commons** a reduced diet

common sense ordinary good sense or sound practical judgment —**com'monsense', com'mon-sen'sical** *adj.*

common time *Music* a metre of four beats to the bar; 4/4 time: also **common measure**

Commonwealth *n.* 1. an association of states, dependencies, and territories formerly ruled by Britain that recognize the reigning British sovereign as titular head 2. the government of England under the Cromwells (1649-60) 3. the official designation of the federated states of Australia

commonwealth *n.* 1. the people of a state viewed politically 2. a state in which the people are taken as sovereign; democracy

commotion (kə mō'shən) *n.* [< L. *com-*, together + *movere*, move] 1. violent motion 2. confusion

communal (kom'yoon 'l) *adj.* 1. designating common ownership of property 2. of the community; public 3. of a commune or communes —**commu'nally** *adv.*

commune[1] (kə myoon') *vi.* **-muned', -mun'ing** [< OFr. *comuner*, to share] 1. to talk together intimately 2. to be in close rapport [to *commune* with nature]

commune[2] (kom'yoon) *n.* [ult. < L. *communis*, common] 1. a small group of people living communally and sharing in work, earnings, etc. 2. the smallest administrative district of local government in France, Belgium, etc. —**the Commune** the revolutionary government of Paris in 1871

communicable (kə myoo'ni kə b'l) *adj.* 1. that can be communicated, as an idea 2. that can be transmitted, as a disease

—commu'nicabil'ity *n.* —commu'nicably *adv.*

communicant *n.* a person who receives Holy Communion

communicate *vt.* -cat'ed, -cat'ing [< L. *communis*, common] 1. to impart; transmit 2. to make known; give (information, etc.) —*vi.* 1. to receive Holy Communion 2. to give or exchange information, etc. 3. to be connected, as by a door [*communicating* rooms] —commu'nica'tor *n.* —commu'nicative *adj.*

communication (kə myōō'nə kā'shən) *n.* 1. a transmitting 2. a) a giving or exchanging of information, etc. by talk, writing, etc. b) the information so given 3. a means of communicating 4. [*often pl.*, *with sing. v.*] the science of transmitting information

communication cord a device in a train enabling a passenger to stop the train in an emergency

communion (kə myōōn'yən) *n.* [< L. *communis*, common] 1. a sharing of one's thoughts and emotions; communing 2. possession in common 3. a Christian denomination 4. [C-] a celebrating of Holy Communion

communiqué (kə myōō'nə kā') *n.* [Fr.] an official communication or bulletin

communism (kom'yōo niz'm) *n.* [see COMMON] 1. a theory or system based on the ownership of all property by the community 2. [*often* C-] a) socialism, formulated by Marx, Lenin, etc., characterized by equal distribution of goods b) the form of government in the U.S.S.R., China, etc.

communist *n.* 1. an advocate or supporter of communism 2. [C-] a member of a Communist Party —*adj.* 1. of, like, advocating, or supporting communism 2. [C-] designating or of a political party advocating Communism —com'munis'tic *adj.*

community (kə myōō'nə tē) *n.*, *pl.* -ties [< L. *communis*, common] 1. a) all the people living in a particular district, city, etc. b) the district, city, etc. where they live 2. a group of people living together and having interests, work, religion, etc. in common 3. society; the public 4. ownership or participation in common 5. friendly association

community centre a meeting place in a community for cultural, recreational, or social activities

community college a Canadian educational institution which trains post-secondary students for skilled trades, offering also courses in continuing education to the people of the community

commutation (kom'yōo tā'shən) *n.* [< L. *commutare*, commute] an exchange; substitution —com'mutate' *vt.*

commutative (kə myōō'tə tiv) *adj.* 1. of or involving interchange or substitution 2. *Math.* designating an operation that is unchanged by altering the order of

symbols [addition of numbers is *commutative*]

commutator (kom'yōo tāt'ər) *n.* a device for changing the direction of an electric current

commute (kə myōōt') *vi.* [< L. *com-*, intens. + *mutare*, to change] 1. to travel as a commuter 2. to be a substitute —*vt.* -mut'ed, -mut'ing 1. to exchange; substitute 2. to change (an obligation, punishment, etc.) to one that is less severe —commut'able *adj.*

commuter *n.* one who travels regularly, esp. by train, bus, etc., between two points at some distance

comp. 1. comparative 2. composition 3. compound

compact (kəm pakt'; *also for adj., and for n. always,* kom'pakt) *adj.* [< L. *com-*, together + *pangere*, fasten] 1. closely and firmly packed; dense 2. taking little space 3. not wordy; terse —*vt.* 1. to pack or join firmly together 2. to condense —*n.* 1. a small cosmetic case, usually containing face powder and a mirror 2. an agreement; covenant —compact'ly *adv.* —compact'ness *n.* —compact'or *n.*

companion[1] (kəm pan'yən) *n.* [< L. *com-*, with + *panis*, bread] 1. one who associates with or accompanies another or others 2. a person employed to live or travel with another 3. a thing that matches another in colour, etc. 4. [C-] a member of the lowest rank in an order of knighthood 5. a guidebook or handbook —compan'ionship' *n.*

companion[2] *n.* [< Du. < It. *compagna*, company] *Naut.* a skylight on the upper deck of a ship, to let light into the cabin below

companionable *adj.* having the qualities of a good companion; sociable —compan'-ionabil'ity, compan'ionableness *n.* —compan'ionably *adv.*

companionway *n.* a stairway leading from the deck of a ship to the cabins or space below

company (kum'pə nē) *n.*, *pl.* -nies [see COMPANION[1]] 1. companionship; society 2. a group of people gathered for some purpose [a business *company*] 3. a guest or guests 4. habitual associates 5. *Mil.* a body of troops, normally composed of two or more platoons 6. *Naut.* the whole crew of a ship: in full, **ship's company** —**keep (a person) company** to stay with (a person) and provide companionship —**part company** 1. to stop associating (with) 2. to separate and go in different directions

company sergeant major *see* WARRANT OFFICER

comparable (kom'pər ə b'l) *adj.* 1. that can be compared 2. worthy of comparison —com'parabil'ity, com'parableness *n.* —com'parably *adv.*

comparative (kəm par'ə tiv) *adj.* 1. involving comparison as a method [*comparative* linguistics] 2. relative *[comparative* joy *]* **3.** *Gram.* designating or of the second degree of comparison of adjectives and adverbs —**n.** *Gram.* the comparative degree —**compar'atively** *adv.* —**compar'ativeness** *n.*

compare (kəm pāər') *vt.* **-pared', -par'ing** [< L. *com-,* with + *par,* equal] **1.** to liken (*to*) **2.** to examine for similarities or differences (often followed by *with*) **3.** *Gram.* to form the degrees of comparison of —*vi.* **1.** to be worthy of comparison (*with*) **2.** to be regarded as similar —**beyond** (or **past** or **without**) **compare** without equal —**compare notes** to exchange views, impressions, etc.

comparison (kəm par'ə s'n) *n.* **1.** a comparing or being compared **2.** likeness; similarity **3.** *Gram.* change in an adjective or adverb to show the positive, comparative, and superlative degrees —**bear** (or **stand**) **comparison** to be capable of being compared with —**in comparison with** compared with

compartment (kəm pärt'mənt) *n.* [< L. *com-,* intens. + *partiri,* divide] **1.** any of the divisions into which a space is partitioned off **2.** a separate section, part, division, or category **3.** a division of a railway carriage —**compart'men'tal** (-men't'l) *adj.* —**compart'mented** *adj.*

compartmentalize (kəm'pärt men'tə līz') *vt.* **-ized', -iz'ing** to put or separate into detached compartments, divisions, or categories

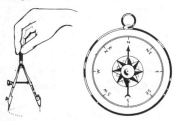

DRAWING COMPASS   DIRECTIONAL COMPASS

compass (kum'pəs) *n.* [< L. *com-,* together + *passus,* a step] **1.** an instrument for showing direction, esp. one consisting of a magnetic needle swinging freely and pointing to the magnetic north **2.** [*often pl.*] an instrument consisting of two pivoted legs, used for drawing circles or for taking measurements **3.** full extent or range; reach; scope **4.** a boundary —*vt.* **1.** to go round **2.** to encircle **3.** to understand **4.** to accomplish or contrive —**com'passable** *adj.*

compassion (kəm pash'ən) *n.* [ult. < L. *com-,* together + *pati,* suffer] sorrow for the sufferings or trouble of another, with the urge to help; deep sympathy

compassionate *adj.* **1.** feeling or showing compassion **2.** given out of compassion *[compassionate* leave *]* —**compas'sionately** *adv.*

compatible (kəm pat'ə b'l) *adj.* [see COMPASSION] **1.** capable of living together harmoniously or getting along well together; in agreement **2.** consistent **3.** that can be used together : said of equipment *[speakers compatible* with the amplifier *]* —**compat'ibil'ity, compat'ibleness** *n.* —**compat'ibly** *adv.*

compatriot (kəm pat'rē ət) *n.* [see COM- & PATRIOT] a fellow countryman —**compa'triotism** *n.*

compeer (kom pēər') *n.* [< L. *com-,* with + *par,* equal] **1.** an equal; peer **2.** a companion

compel (kəm pel') *vt.* **-pelled', -pel'ling** [< L. *com-,* together + *pellere,* drive] **1.** to force to do something **2.** to bring about by force —**compel'lable** *adj.* —**compel'ler** *n.* —**compel'ling** *adj.*

compendious (kəm pen'dē əs) *adj.* [see ff.] containing all the essentials in a brief form; concise but comprehensive —**compen'diously** *adv.*

compendium *n.,* *pl.* **-diums, -dia** [< L. *com-,* together + *pendere,* weigh] a concise but comprehensive treatise

compensate (kom'pen sāt') *vt.* **-sat'ed, -sat'ing** [< L. *com-,* with + *pendere,* weigh] **1.** to make up for; counterbalance **2.** to recompense —*vi.* to make or serve as compensation or amends (*for*) —**compensative** (kəm pen'sə tiv) *adj.* —**com'pensator** *n.* —**compensatory** (kəm pen'sə tər ē) *adj.*

compensation (kom'pen sā'shən) *n.* **1.** a compensating or being compensated **2.** anything given as an equivalent, or to make amends for a loss, etc. —**com'pensa'tional** *adj.*

compère (kom'pâer) *n.* [Fr., godfather] a master of ceremonies, esp. in a variety show —*vt.* to act as a compere —**commère** (kom'mâer') *n.fem.*

compete (kəm pēt') *vi.* **-pet'ed, -pet'ing** [< L. *com-,* together + *petere,* seek] to enter into or be in rivalry; contend; vie (*in* a contest, etc.)

competence (kom'pə təns) *n.* [see prec.] **1.** ability; fitness **2.** sufficient means for one's needs **3.** legal capability, power, or jurisdiction Also **com'petency**

competent *adj.* [see COMPETE] **1.** well qualified; capable; fit **2.** sufficient; adequate **3.** *Law* legally qualified or fit —**com'petently** *adv.*

competition (kom'pə tish'ən) *n.* **1.** competing; rivalry **2.** a contest or match **3.** the person or persons against whom one competes

competitive (kəm pet'ə tiv) *adj.* of, involving, or based on competition : also **compet'itory** —**compet'itively** *adv.* —**compet'itiveness** *n.*

competitor *n.* a person, team, company, etc. that competes

compile (kəm pīl') *vt.* **-piled', -pil'ing** [< L. *com-,* together + *pilare,* compress] **1.** to gather together (statistics, facts, etc.) in an orderly form **2.** to compose (a book, etc.) of materials gathered from various sources —**compilation** (kom′-pə lā′shən) *n.* —**compil′er** *n.*

complacency (kəm plās′′n sē) *n.* [< L. *com-*, intens. + *placere*, please] quiet satisfaction; contentment; often, self-satisfaction, or smugness: also **compla′cence** —**compla′cent** *adj.*

complain (kəm plān′) *vi.* [< L. *com-*, intens. + *plangere*, strike (the breast)] 1. to express pain, displeasure, etc. 2. to find fault 3. to state a grievance, esp. in a court of law —**complain′er** *n.* —**complain′ingly** *adv.*

complainant *n.* *Law* one who states a grievance or makes a complaint in court; plaintiff

complaint (kəm plānt′) *n.* 1. an utterance of pain, displeasure, etc. 2. a cause for complaining 3. an ailment 4. *Law* a formal charge

complaisant (kəm plā′zənt) *adj.* [see COMPLACENCY] willing to please; affably agreeable; obliging —**complai′sance** *n.* —**complai′santly** *adv.*

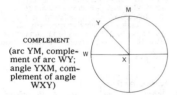

COMPLEMENT

(arc YM, complement of arc WY; angle YXM, complement of angle WXY)

complement (kom′plə mənt; *for v.* -ment′) *n.* [see COMPLETE] 1. that which completes or brings to perfection 2. the amount needed to fill or complete 3. a complete set 4. either of two parts that complete each other 5. the officers and crew needed to man a ship 6. *Gram.* a word or words that complete the meaning of the predicate (Ex.: *foreman* in *make him foreman*) 7. *Math.* the number of degrees added to an angle or arc to make it equal 90 degrees —*vt.* to be a complement to

complementary (kom′plə men′tər ē) *adj.* 1. acting as a complement; completing 2. mutually making up what is lacking —**com′plementar′ily** (-tar′ə tē) *n.*

complete (kəm plēt′) *adj.* [< L. *com-*, intens. + *plere*, fill] 1. lacking no parts; entire 2. ended; finished 3. thorough; absolute [a *complete* scoundrel] —*vt.* -**plet′ed**, -**plet′ing** 1. to end; finish 2. to make whole, full, or perfect —**complete′ly** *adv.* —**complete′ness** *n.*

completion (kəm plē′shən) *n.* 1. a completing, or finishing 2. the state of being completed

complex (kom′pleks) *adj.* [< L. *com-*, with + *plectere*, weave] 1. consisting of two or more related parts 2. complicated —*n.* 1. a complex whole 2. *Psychoanalysis* a) a group of largely unconscious impulses and attitudes towards something, strongly influencing behaviour b)

popularly, an obsession —**complex′ly** *adv.* —**complex′ness** *n.*

complex fraction a fraction with a fraction in its numerator or denominator, or in both

complexion (kəm plek′shən) *n.* [see COMPLEX] 1. the colour, texture, etc. of the skin, esp. of the face 2. general appearance character; aspect

complexity (kəm plek′sə tē) *n.* 1. a complex condition or quality 2. *pl.* -**ties** anything complex or intricate; complication

complex number any number expressed as the formal sum of a real number and a multiple of the imaginary square root of -1

compliance (kəm plī′əns) *n.* 1. a complying with a request, demand, etc. 2. a tendency to give in to others —**in compliance with** complying with —**compli′ant** *adj.*

complicate (kom′plə kāt) *vt., vi.* -**cat′ed**, -**cat′ing** [< L. *com-*, together + *plicare*, fold] to make or become intricate, difficult, or involved

complicated *adj.* intricately involved; hard to solve, analyse, etc. —**com′plicat′edly** *adv.*

complication (kom′plə kā′shən) *n.* 1. a complicated condition or structure 2. a complicating factor, 3. *Med.* a second disease or abnormal condition occurring in the course of a primary disease

complicity (kəm plis′ə tē) *n., pl.* -**ties** [see COMPLEX] the fact or state of being an accomplice in wrongdoing

compliment (kom′plə mənt; *for v.* -ment′) *n.* [ult. < L. *complere*, to complete] 1. a formal act of courtesy 2. something said in praise 3. [*pl.*] respects —*vt.* to pay a compliment to

complimentary (kom′plə men′tər ē) *adj.* 1. paying or containing a compliment 2. given free as a courtesy [a *complimentary* ticket] —**com′plimen′tarily** *adv.*

comply (kəm plī′) *vi.* -**plied′**, -**ply′ing** [see COMPLETE] to act in accordance with a request, order, rule, etc.) —**compli′er** *n.*

component (kəm pō′nənt) *adj.* [see COMPOSITE] serving as one of the parts of a whole —*n.* 1. an element or ingredient 2. an individual part of a mechanism, as of a motor car

comport (kəm pôrt′) *vt.* [< L. *com-*, together + *portare*, bring] to behave (oneself) in a specified manner —*vi.* to agree or accord (*with*) —**comport′ment** *n.*

compose (kəm pōz′) *vt.* -**posed′**, -**pos′ing** [< OFr. *com-*, with + *poser*, place] 1. to make up; constitute 2. to put in proper form 3. to create (a musical or literary work) 4. to settle [to *compose* differences] 5. to calm (oneself) 6. *Printing* to set (type) —*vi.* 1. to create musical or literary works 2. to set type —**compos′er** *n.*

composed *adj.* calm; tranquil; self-possessed —**compos′edly** *adv.* —**compos′edness** *n.*

composite (kom′pə zit) *adj.* [< L. *com-*, together + *ponere*, put] 1. formed of distinct parts; compound **2.** designating a large family of plants, as the daisy, etc., having flower heads composed of dense clusters of small flowers **3.** [C-] *Archit.* combining features of the Ionic and Corinthian orders —**n.** **1.** a thing of distinct parts **2.** a composite plant —**com′positely** *adv.* —**com′positeness** *n.*

composite school [Canad.] a secondary school offering both academic and nonacademic courses

composition (kom′pə zish′ən) *n.* **1.** a composing; specif., *a*) the art of writing *b*) the creation of musical works **2.** the makeup of a thing or person **3.** that which is composed, as *a*) a work of music, literature, or art *b*) an exercise in writing **4.** an aesthetically unified arrangement of parts **5.** a settlement made between a debtor and his creditors —**com′posi′tional** *adj.*

compositor (kəm poz′ə tər) *n.* a person who sets type

‡**compos mentis** (kom′pəs men′tis) [L.] of sound mind

compost (kom′post) *n.* [see COMPOSITE] a mixture of decomposing vegetation, manure, etc. for fertilizing soil

composure (kəm pō′zhər) *n.* [see COMPOSE] calmness; tranquillity; self-possession

compote (kom′pot) *n.* [Fr.: see COMPOST] a dish of fruits stewed in a syrup

compound[1] (kəm pound′; *for n. and, usually, for adj.,* kom′pound) *n.* [see COMPOSITE] **1.** a substance containing two or more elements chemically combined in fixed proportions **2.** a thing formed by the combination of parts **3.** a word composed from existing words and affixes —**vt.** **1.** to mix or combine **2.** to make by combining parts **3.** to settle by mutual agreement **4.** to settle (a debt) by compromise payment **5.** to intensify by adding new elements —**vi.** to agree or compromise —**adj.** made up of two or more separate parts or elements —**compound a felony** (or **crime**) to agree, for payment, not to inform about or prosecute for a crime —**compound′able** *adj.*

compound[2] (kom′pound) *n.* [Malay *kampong*] **1.** in the Orient, an enclosed space with a building or buildings in it, esp. if occupied by foreigners **2.** any similar enclosed area, as in a prison **3.** in South Africa, esp. on the mines, an enclosure containing the living quarters of black workers

compound eye an eye made up of numerous simple eyes functioning collectively, as in insects

compound fracture a bone fracture in which broken ends of bone have pierced the skin

compound interest interest paid on both the principal and the accumulated unpaid interest

compound sentence a sentence consisting of two or more independent, coordinate clauses

compound time *Music* a time in which

each beat in the bar is divisible into three, as 6/4, 9/8, etc.

comprehend (kom′prə hend′) *vt.* [< L. *com-*, with + *prehendere*, seize] **1.** to grasp mentally; understand **2.** to include; comprise —**com′prehen′sible** *adj.*

comprehension *n.* **1.** the act of or capacity for understanding **2.** the fact of including or comprising

comprehensive *adj.* **1.** including much; inclusive **2.** able to comprehend fully **3.** of or relating to an education system including comprehensive schools —**n.** *same as* COMPREHENSIVE SCHOOL —**com′prehen′sively** *adv.* —**com′prehen′siveness** *n.*

comprehensive school a secondary school serving the educational needs of all the children in an area

compress (kəm pres′; *for n.* kom′pres) *vt.* [< L. *com-*, together + *premere*, press] to press together and make more compact —**n.** a pad of folded cloth, often medicated or wet, applied to a part of the body —**compressed′** *adj.* —**compres′sibil′ity** *n.* —**compres′sible** *adj.* —**compres′sive** *adj.*

compression (kəm presh′ən) *n.* **1.** a compressing or being compressed **2.** the compressing of a working fluid in an engine, as of the mixture in an internal-combustion engine just before ignition

compressor *n.* **1.** a machine for compressing air, gas, etc. **2.** a muscle that compresses a part

comprise (kəm prīz′) *vt.* **-prised′, -pris′-ing** [see COMPREHEND] **1.** to include; contain **2.** to consist of —**compris′able** *adj.* —**compris′al** *n.*

compromise (kom′prə mīz′) *n.* [< L. *com-*, together + *promittere*, to promise] **1.** a settlement in which each side makes concessions **2.** the result of such a settlement **3.** something midway between two other things —**vt.** **-mised′, -mis′ing** **1.** to settle by concessions on both sides **2.** to lay open to danger, suspicion, or disrepute **3.** to weaken (one's principles, etc.) —**vi.** to make a compromise —**com′promis′er** *n.*

Comptometer (komp′tom′ə tər) *Trademark* a high-speed mechanical calculating machine

comptroller (kən trō′lər) *n.* [< CONTROLLER] *same as* CONTROLLER (sense 1) —**comptrol′lership** *n.*

compulsion (kəm pul′shən) *n.* [see COMPEL] **1.** a being compelled **2.** a driving force **3.** *Psychol.* an irresistible impulse to perform some act

compulsive *adj.* **1.** of, or resulting from compulsion **2.** acting as if under a compulsion [a *compulsive* liar] —**compul′-sively** *adv.* —**compul′siveness** *n.*

compulsory *adj.* **1.** obligatory; required **2.** compelling; coercive —**compul′sorily** *adv.*

compulsory purchase the enforced purchase of land, etc., as by a local authority

compunction (kəm pungk′shən) *n.* [< L. *com-*, intens. + *pungere*, to prick] a sharp feeling of uneasiness brought on by a sense of guilt; remorse —**compunc'tious** *adj.* —**compunc'tiously** *adv.*

computation (kom'pyoo tā'shən) *n.* 1. a computing; calculation, esp. involving numbers 2. a method of computing 3. a computed amount —**com'puta'tional** *adj.*

compute (kəm pyoot') *vt., vi.* -**put'ed**, -**put'ing** [< L. *com*-, with + *putare*, reckon] 1. to determine (an amount, etc.) by reckoning; calculate 2. to use a computer —**comput'abil'ity** *n.* —**comput'able** *adj.*

computer *n.* a person or thing that computes; specif., an electronic machine that performs rapid calculations or compiles, correlates, and selects data

computerize *vt.* -**ized'**, -**iz'ing** to equip with, or operate by, an electronic computer —**comput'eriza'tion** *n.*

comrade (kom'rād) *n.* [< Sp. *camarada*, roommate < L. *camera*] 1. a friend; close companion 2. an associate 3. a fellow-member of a political party, esp. a fellow communist or socialist —**com'radely** *adj.* —**com'radeship'** *n.*

con[1] (kon) *adv.* [< L. *contra*] against; in opposition [to argue pro and con]

con[2] *vt.* **conned**, **con'ning** [ME. *connen*, to be able : see CAN[1]] to peruse or learn carefully

con[3] *vt.*, **conned**, **con'ning** [< L. *conducere*, conduct] *Naut.* to direct the course of (a vessel)

con[4] *adj.* [Slang] confidence [a con man] —*vt.* **conned**, **con'ning** [Slang] 1. to swindle (a victim) by first gaining his confidence 2. to trick, esp. by glib talk

con[5] *n.* [Slang] a convict

concatenate (kon kat'ə nāt') *adj.* [< L. *com*-, together + *catena*, chain] linked together; connected —*vt.* -**nat'ed**, -**nat'ing** to link or join, as in a chain —**concat'ena'tion** *n.*

concave (kon kāv') *adj.* [< L. *com*-, intens. + *cavus*, hollow] hollow and curved like the inside half of a hollow ball —**concave'ly** *adv.* —**concave'ness** *n.*

conceal (kən sēl') *vt.* [< L. *com*-, together + *celare*, hide] 1. to hide 2. to keep secret —**conceal'ment** *n.*

concede (kən sēd') *vt.* -**ced'ed**, -**ced'ing** [< L. *com*-, with + *cedere*, cede] 1. to admit as true or certain 2. to grant as a right —*vi.* 1. to make a concession 2. to acknowledge defeat in an election, etc.

conceit (kən sēt') *n.* [see CONCEIVE] 1. an exaggerated opinion of oneself, one's merits, etc.; vanity 2. a fanciful or witty expression or notion

conceited *adj.* having an exaggerated opinion of oneself; vain —**conceit'edly** *adv.* —**conceit'edness** *n.*

conceivable (kən sē'və b'l) *adj.* that can be conceived, understood, imagined, or believed —**conceiv'ably** *adv.*

conceive (kən sēv') *vt.* -**ceived'**, -**ceiv'ing** [< L. *com*-, together + *capere*, take] 1. to become pregnant with 2. to form in the mind 3. to imagine 4. to understand —*vi.* 1. to become pregnant 2. to form an idea (*of*)

concentrate (kon'sən trāt') *vt.* -**trat'ed**, -**trat'ing** [< L. *com*-, together + *centrum*, centre] 1. to focus (one's thoughts, efforts, etc.) 2. to increase the strength, purity, or intensity of —*vi.* to fix one's attention (*on* or *upon*) —*n.* a substance that has been concentrated —**con'centra'tive** *adj.* —**con'centra'tor** *n.*

concentration (kon'sən trā'shən) *n.* 1. close or fixed attention 2. a concentrating or being concentrated 3. strength or density, as of a solution

concentration camp a prison camp for people considered undesirable by the state for political or ethnic reasons

concentric (kon sen'trik) *adj.* [< L. *com*-, together + *centrum*, centre] having a centre in common [concentric circles] —**concen'trically** *adv.*

concept (kon'sept) *n.* [see CONCEIVE] an idea, esp. a generalized idea of a class of objects

conception (kən sep'shən) *n.* 1. a conceiving or being conceived in the womb 2. the beginning of some process, etc. 3. the formulation of ideas 4. a concept —**concep'tional** *adj.* —**concep'tive** *adj.*

conceptual (kən sep'tyoo wəl) *adj.* of conception or concepts —**concep'tually** *adv.*

conceptualize *vt.* -**ized'**, -**iz'ing** to form a concept or idea of; conceive —**concep'tualiza'tion** *n.*

concern (kən surn') *vt.* [< L. *com*-, with + *cernere*, sift] 1. to have a relation to 2. to involve; affect 3. to make uneasy or anxious —*n.* 1. a matter of importance to one; affair 2. interest in a person or thing 3. relation; reference 4. worry; anxiety 5. a business firm —**as concerns** in regard to —**concern oneself** 1. to busy oneself 2. to be worried

concerned *adj.* 1. involved or interested (often with *in*) 2. uneasy or anxious

concerning *prep.* relating to; about

concert (kən surt'; *for n. & adj.* kon'sərt) *n.* [< L. *com*-, with + *certare*, strive] 1. a programme of vocal or instrumental music 2. mutual agreement; concord —*vt., vi.* to plan together; devise —*adj.* of or for concerts —**in concert** 1. in unison 2. performing live

concerted (kən sur'tid) *adj.* mutually arranged or agreed upon; done together —**concert'edly** *adv.*

concertina (kon'sər tē'nə) *n.* [< CONCERT] a small musical instrument similar to an accordion —*vi.* to fold like a concertina

concerto (kən chāər'tō) *n., pl.* -**tos**, -**ti** (-tē) [It.] a composition for one or more solo instruments and an orchestra

concert pitch *Music* a pitch, slightly higher than the usual pitch, to which concert instruments are tuned

concession (kən sesh'ən) *n.* 1. a conceding 2. a thing conceded;

acknowledgment, as of an argument **3.** a privilege granted by a government, company, etc., as the right to use land **4.** [Canad.] a land subdivision in a township survey

concessionaire (kən sesh′ə nãer′) *n.* [Fr.] the holder of a concession granted by a government, company, etc.: also **concessionnaire′**

concession road [Canad.] any of a number of roughly parallel roads forming a grid pattern along township survey lines

conch (konch) *n. pl.* **conchs, conches** (kon′chəz) [< Gr. *konchē*] **1.** the spiral, one-piece shell of various sea molluscs **2.** such a mollusc

conciliate (kən sil′ē āt′) *vt.* **-at′ed, -at′-ing** [see COUNCIL] **1.** to win over; make friendly **2.** to gain (regard, good will, etc.) by friendly acts or concessions —**concil′iable** *adj.* —**concil′ia′tion** *n.* —**concil′i-a′tor** *n.*

conciliatory *adj.* tending to conciliate or reconcile: also **concil′iative**

concise (kən sīs′) *adj.* [< L. *com-*, intens. + *caedere*, to cut] brief and to the point; short and clear —**concise′ly** *adv.* —**concise′ness, conci′sion** (-sizh′ən) *n.*

conclave (kon′klāv) *n.* [< L. *com-*, with + *clavis*, key] **1.** R.C.Ch. the private meeting of the cardinals to elect a pope **2.** any private meeting

conclude (kən klo̅o̅d′) *vt.* **-clud′ed, -clud′-ing** [< L. *com-*, together + *claudere*, shut] **1.** to bring to a close; finish **2.** to infer; deduce **3.** to decide (*to* do something) **4.** to come to an agreement about —*vi.* to come to a close; finish

conclusion (kən klo̅o̅′zhən) *n.* **1.** the last part; as, *a*) the last division of a discourse *b*) the last step in a reasoning process; judgment formed after thought *c*) the last of a chain of events **2.** a concluding (*of* a treaty, etc.) —**in conclusion** lastly; in closing

conclusive *adj.* that settles a question; final; decisive —**conclu′sively** *adv.* —**conclu′siveness** *n.*

concoct (kən kokt′) *vt.* [< L. *com-*, together + *coquere*, cook] **1.** to make by combining ingredients **2.** to devise; plan —**concoc′tion** *n.*

concomitant (kon kom′ə tənt) *adj.* [< L. *com-*, together + *comes*, companion] accompanying; attendant —*n.* an accompanying or attendant condition, etc. —**concom′itance** *n.* —**concom′itantly** *adv.*

concord (koŋ′kôrd) ·*n.* [< L. *com-*, together + *cor*, heart] **1.** agreement; harmony **2.** *a*) peaceful relations, as between nations *b*) a treaty establishing this —**concord′ant** *adj.*

concordance (kən kôr′dəns) *n.* **1.** agreement; harmony **2.** an alphabetical list of the words of a book with references to the passages in which they occur

concordat (kon kôr′dat) *n.* [see CONCORD] **1.** a compact; formal agreement **2.** an agreement between a pope and a government concerning church affairs

concourse (koŋ′kôrs) *n.* [see CONCUR] **1.** a coming together **2.** a crowd **3.** a large open space where crowds gather, as in a railway station or airport terminal

concrete (kon′krēt; *also, & for vt. 1 always,* kon krēt′) *n.* [< L. *com-*, together + *crescere*, grow] **1.** a building material made by mixing cement, sand aggregate, and water, which hardens as it dries **2.** a concrete thing, idea, etc. —*adj.* **1.** made of· concrete **2.** specific, not general or abstract **3.** having a material, perceptible existence; real **4.** *Gram.* designating a thing that can be perceived by the senses; not abstract —*vt.* **-cret′ed, -cret′ing 1.** to make of or cover with concrete **2.** to form into a mass; solidify —*vi.* to solidify —**concrete′ly** *adv.* —**concrete′-ness** *n.*

concretion (kon krē′shən) *n.* **1.** a solidifying or being solidified **2.** a solidified mass

concubine (koŋ′kyoo bīn′) *n.* [< L. *com-*, with + *cubare*, lie down] a woman who cohabits with a man although not legally married to him —**concubinage** (kon kyoo′-bə nij) *n.*

concupiscence (kən kyoop′ə səns) *n.* [< L. *com-*, intens. + *cupere*, to desire] strong or abnormal desire or appetite, esp. sexual desire; lust —**concu′piscent** *adj.*

concur (kən kur′) *vi.* **-curred′, -cur′ring** [< L. *com-*, together + *currere*, run] **1.** to agree (*with*) **2.** to act together **3.** to occur at the same time; coincide

concurrence (-kur′əns) *n.* **1.** agreement; accord **2.** a combining to bring about something **3.** a coming or happening together Also **concur′rency**

concurrent *adj.* **1.** occurring or existing at the same time **2.** meeting in the same point **3.** acting together **4.** in agreement —**concur′rently** *adv.*

concuss (kən kus′) *vt.* to give a concussion to

concussion (kən kush′ən) *n.* [< L. *com-*, together + *quatere*, shake] **1.** impaired functioning, esp. of the brain, as a result of a violent blow **2.** a violent shaking; shock, as from impact —**concus′sive** *adj.*

condemn (kən dem′) *vt.* [< L. *com-*, intens. + *damnare*, to harm] **1.** to disapprove of strongly; censure **2.** to declare guilty of wrongdoing; convict **3.** to inflict a penalty upon **4.** to declare unfit for use or service —**condem′nable** (-dem′nə b′l) *adj.* —**condemn′er** *n.*

condemnation (kon′dem nā′shən) *n.* **1.** a condemning or being condemned **2.** a cause for condemning —**condemnatory** (kən dem′nə tər ē) *adj.*

condensation (kon′dən sā′shən) *n.* **1.** a condensing or being condensed **2.** anything condensed

condense (kən dens′) *vt.* **-densed′, -dens′-ing** [< L. *com-*, intens. + *densus*, dense] **1.** to make more dense or compact **2.** to express in fewer words **3.** to change to a denser form, as from a gas to a liquid —*vi.* to become condensed —**condens'able, condens'ible** *adj.*

condensed milk a thick milk made by evaporating part of the water from cow's milk and adding sugar

condenser *n.* a person or thing that condenses; specif., *a*) an apparatus for converting gases or vapours to a liquid state *b*) a lens for concentrating light rays on an area *c*) *Elec. same as* CAPACITOR

condescend (kon'də send') *vi.* [< L. *com-*, together + *descendere*, descend] 1. to descend voluntarily to a level, regarded as lower; deign 2. to deal with others in a patronizing manner —**con'descend'ing** *adj.* —**con'descen'sion** *n.*

condign (kən dīn') *adj.* [< L. *com-*, intens. + *dignus*, worthy] deserved; suitable: said esp. of punishment

condiment (kon'də mənt) *n.* [< L. *condire*, to pickle] a seasoning for food, as pepper, mustard, sauces, etc.

condition (kən dish'ən) *n.* [< L. *com-*, together + *dicere*, speak] 1. anything required before the performance or completion of something else; provision; prerequisite 2. anything that modifies the nature of something else [good business *conditions*] 3. state of being [the human *condition*] 4. *a*) state of health *b*) [Colloq.] an illness [a lung *condition*] 5. a proper or healthy state [athletes out of *condition*] 6. social position; rank —*vt.* 1. to impose a condition or conditions on 2. to be a condition of; determine 3. to affect, modify, or influence 4. to bring into a proper or desired condition —**on condition that** provided that —**condi'tioner** *n.*

conditional *adj.* 1. containing or dependent on a condition; qualified 2. expressing a condition —*n. Gram.* the mood expressing a condition —**condi'tional'ity** *n.* —**condi'tionally** *adv.*

conditioned reflex (or **response**) a reflex in which the response (e.g., secretion of saliva in a dog) is occasioned by a secondary stimulus (e.g., the ringing of a bell) repeatedly associated with the primary stimulus (e.g., the sight of meat)

condole (kən dōl') *vi.* -**doled'**, -**dol'ing** [< L. *com-*, with + *dolere*, grieve] to express sympathy; mourn in sympathy —**condo'latory** *adj.* —**condo'lence** *n.* —**condol'er** *n.*

condom (kon'dəm) *n.* [<?] a thin sheath, esp. of rubber, for the penis, used as a contraceptive

condominium (kon'də min'ē əm) *n.* [< L. *com-*, together + *dominium*, dominion] 1. joint rule by two or more states 2. [U.S.] a block of flats or multiple-unit dwelling in which each tenant owns his own unit

condone (kən dōn') *vt.* -**doned'**, -**don'ing** [< L. *com-*, intens. + *donare*, give] to forgive, pardon, or overlook (an offence) —**condon'able** *adj.* —**condon'er** *n.*

condor (kon'dôr) *n.* [Sp. < SAmInd. *cuntur*] a very large vulture of the S American Andes, with a bare head and a neck ruff of downy white feathers

conduce (kən dyōōs') *vi.* -**duced'**, -**duc'ing** [< L. *com-*, together + *ducere*, lead] to tend or lead (*to* an effect); contribute —**condu'cive** *adj.*

conduct (kon'dukt'; *for v.* kən dukt') *n.* [see CONDUCE] 1. management; handling 2. the way one acts; behaviour —*vt.* 1. to lead 2. to manage, or control 3. to act as conductor of (an orchestra, choir, etc.) 4. to behave (oneself) 5. to be able to transmit [copper *conducts* electricity] —*vi.* 1. to lead 2. to act as a conductor —**conduct'ibil'ity** *n.* —**conduct'ible** *adj.*

conductance (kən duk'təns) *n.* the ability of a component to conduct electricity

conduction (kən duk'shən) *n.* 1. a conveying, as of liquid through a channel 2. *Physics* transmission (*of* electricity, heat, etc.) by the passage of energy from particle to particle

conductivity (kon'duk tiv'ə tē) *n.* the property of conducting heat, electricity, etc.

conductor (kən duk'tər) *n.* 1. a person who conducts; guide 2. one who controls and directs the performance of music by an orchestra or choir 3. one who has charge of the passengers on a bus 4. a thing that conducts electricity, heat, etc. —**conduc'torship'** *n.* —**conduc'tress** *n.fem.*

conduit (kon'dit) *n.* [see CONDUCE] 1. a pipe or channel for conveying fluids 2. a tube or protected trough for electric wires

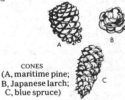

CONES
(A, maritime pine; B, Japanese larch; C, blue spruce)

cone (kōn) *n.* [< Gr. *kōnos*] 1. *a*) a solid with a circle for its base and a curved surface tapering evenly to a point *b*) a surface described by a moving straight line passing through a fixed point and tracing a fixed curve, as a circle or ellipse, at another point. 2. any object shaped like a cone 3. a reproductive structure of certain lower plants, with an elongated central axis bearing overlapping scales, bracts, etc. which produce pollen, spores, or ovules

confab (kon'fab') *n.* [Colloq.] a confabulation; chat —*vi.* -**fabbed'**, -**fab'bing** [Colloq.] to confabulate

confabulate (kən fab'yoo lāt') *vi.* -**lat'ed**, -**lat'ing** [< L. *com-*, together + *fabulari*, to talk] to talk together informally; chat —**confab'ula'tion** *n.*

confection (kən fek'shən) *n.* [< L. *com-*, with + *facere*, make] 1. any sweetmeat or other sweet preparation, as ice cream 2. a frivolous piece of work —**confec'tionary** *adj.*

confectioner *n.* one whose work or business is making or selling sweets, cakes, etc.

confectionery *n.*, *pl.* **-eries** 1. confections or sweets, collectively 2. the business, work, or shop of a confectioner

confederacy (kən fed′ər ə sē) *n.*, *pl.* **-cies** 1. people, nations, etc. united for some common purpose 2. a conspiracy

confederate (kən fed′ər ət; *for v.* -ə rāt′) *adj.* [< L. *com-*, together + *foedus*, a league] united in a confederacy or league —*n.* 1. a person, group, or state united with another or others for a common purpose; ally 2. an accomplice 3. [C-] any supporter of the Confederate States of America during the American Civil War —*vt.*, *vi.* **-at′ed**, **-at′ing** to unite in a confederacy; ally

confederation (kən fed′ə rā′shən) *n.* 1. a uniting or being united in a league or alliance 2. nations or states joined in a league 3. [C-] the federation of Canada, formed (1867) from three British colonies —**confed′eral** *adj.*

confer (kən fur′) *vt.* **-ferred′**, **-fer′ring** [< L. *com-*, together + *ferre*, bring] to give; bestow —*vi.* to have a conference —**confer′ment** *n.* —**confer′rable** *adj.*

conference (kon′fər əns) *n.* 1. a conversing or consulting on a serious matter 2. a formal meeting of a group for discussion —**in conference** occupied in discussion —**conferential** (kon′fə ren′shəl) *adj.*

confess (kən fes′) *vt.*, *vi.* [< L. *com-*, together + *fateri*, acknowledge] 1. to admit or acknowledge (a fault, crime, belief, etc.) 2. *Eccles.* a) to tell (one's sins) to God or a priest b) to hear the confession of (a person): said of a priest —**confess to** to admit or admit having —**confess′edly** (-id lē) *adj.*

confession *n.* 1. a confessing; admission of guilt or sin 2. something confessed 3. a statement of religious beliefs: in full, **confession of faith**

confessional *n.* an enclosed place in a church, where a priest hears confessions —*adj.* of or for confession

confessor *n.* 1. one who confesses, esp. one who avows his religious beliefs 2. a priest authorized to hear confessions

confetti (kən fet′ē) *n.pl.* [*with sing. v.*] [It.] pieces of coloured paper scattered about at weddings

confidant (kon′fə dant′) *n.* a close, trusted friend in whom one confides —**con′-fidante′** *n.fem.*

confide (kən fīd′) *vi.* **-fid′ed**, **-fid′ing** [< L. *com-*, intens. + *fidere*, to trust] to trust (*in* someone), esp. by sharing secrets —*vt.* 1. to tell about as a secret 2. to entrust (a duty, etc.) *to* someone —**con-fid′er** *n.*

confidence (kon′fə dəns) *n.* 1. firm belief; trust; reliance 2. certainty; assurance 3. belief in one's own abilities 4. the belief that another will keep a secret [told in strict *confidence*] 5. something told as a secret

confidence trick a swindle effected by one (**confidence man**) who first gains the confidence of his victim

confident *adj.* full of confidence; specif., a) assured; certain [*confident* of victory] b) sure of oneself; self-confident —**con′fi-dently** *adv.*

confidential (kon′fə den′shəl) *adj.* 1. secret; private; in confidence 2. entrusted with private matters —**con′fiden′tially** *adv.* —**confiden′tial′ity** (-shē al′ə tē) *n.*

confiding (kən fīd′iŋ) *adj.* trustful or inclined to trust —**confid′ingly** *adv.*

configuration (kən fig′yoo rā′shən) *n.* [< L. *com-*, together + *figurare*, to form] 1. arrangement of parts 2. form, outline, or structure —**config′ura′tional** *adj.* —**config′urative** *adj.*

confine (kən fīn′; *for n.* kon′fīn′) *n.* [< L. *com-*, with + *finis*, an end] [*usually pl.*] a bounded region; border; limit —*vt.* **-fined′**, **-fin′ing** 1. to keep within limits; restrict 2. to keep shut up, as in prison, indoors, etc. —**be confined** to be undergoing childbirth —**confin′able** *adj.* —**confine′ment** *n.*

confirm (kən furm′) *vt.* [< L. *com-*, intens. + *firmus*, firm] 1. to strengthen; establish 2. to ratify 3. to prove the validity of; verify 4. to cause to undergo religious confirmation —**confirm′able** *adj.*

confirmation (kon′fər mā′shən) *n.* 1. a ratification; verification 2. something that confirms or proves 3. a ceremony admitting a person to full church membership

confirmed *adj.* 1. firmly established; habitual [a *confirmed* liar] 2. corroborated —**confirm′edly** *adv.*

confiscate (kon′fə skāt′) *vt.* **-cat′ed**, **-cat′ing** [< L. *com-*, together + *fiscus*, treasury] 1. to seize (private property) for the public treasury 2. to seize as by authority; appropriate —**confis′cable** *adj.* —**con′fisca′tion** *n.* —**con′fisca′tor** *n.*

conflagration (kon′flə grā′shən) *n.* [< L. *com-*, intens. + *flagrare*, burn] a big, destructive fire

conflate (kən flāt′) *vt.* [< L. *conflare*, blow together] to combine (texts, etc.) to form a whole

conflict (kən flikt′; *for n.* kon′flikt) *vi.* [< L. *com-*, together + *fligere*, strike] to be antagonistic, incompatible, or contradictory; clash —*n.* 1. a fight or struggle 2. sharp disagreement, as of interests or ideas 3. emotional disturbance —**conflic′tive** *adj.*

confluence (kon′floo əns) *n.* [< L. *com-*, together + *fluere*, to flow] 1. a flowing together, esp. of two or more streams 2. the place where they join, or a stream formed in this way 3. a coming together as of people; crowd; throng —**con′fluent** *adj.*

conform (kən fôrm′) *vi.* [< L. *com-*, together + *formare*, to form] 1. to accept customs, traditions, etc. 2. to be in agreement 3. to be or become similar —*vt.* to bring into harmony or agreement —**conform′er** *n.* —**conform′ism** *n.* —**conform′ist** *n.*, *adj.*

conformable *adj.* 1. that conforms 2.

quick to conform; obedient —**conform'ably** *adv.*

conformation (kon'fôr mā'shən) *n.* 1. a symmetrical arrangement of the parts of a thing 2. the structure of a thing as determined by the arrangement of its parts

conformity *n., pl.* **-ties** 1. agreement; correspondence 2. action in accordance with customs, rules, etc.

confound (kən found'; *for 3, usually* kon'-found') *vt.* [< L. *com-*, together + *fundere*, pour] 1. to mix up indiscriminately; confuse 2. to make feel confused; bewilder 3. to damn: used as a mild oath

confounded *adj.* 1. confused; bewildered 2. damned: a mild oath —**confound'edly** *adv.*

confrere (kon'frāer) *n.* [OFr.] a fellow worker; colleague

confront (kən frunt') *vt.* [< L. *com-*, together + *frons*, forehead] 1. to stand or meet face to face 2. to face or oppose boldly or defiantly 3. to bring face to face (*with*) —**confrontation** (kon'-frun tā'shən) *n.*

Confucianism (kən fyōō'shyən iz'm) *n.* the ethical teachings of Confucius (551?-479? B.C.), Chinese philosopher, emphasizing devotion to parents and the maintenance of justice and peace —**Confu'-cianist** *n., adj.*

confuse (kən fyōōz') *vt.* **-fused', -fus'ing** [see CONFOUND] 1. to mix up; put into disorder 2. to bewilder; perplex 3. to disconcert 4. to fail to distinguish between —**confus'edly** (-id lē) *adv.* —**confus'edness** *n.* —**confus'ing** *adj.*

confusion *n.* a confusing or being confused; disorder, bewilderment, etc. —**covered with confusion** greatly embarrassed

confute (kən fyōōt') *vt.* **-fut'ed, -fut'ing** [< L. *confutare*] to prove (a person, statement, etc.) to be in error or false —**confutation** (kon'fyōo tā'shən) *n.*

conga (koŋ'gə) *n.* [AmSp.] a Latin American dance in which the dancers form a winding line —*vi.* to dance the conga

congé (kôn'zhā) *n.* [Fr. < L. *com-*, intens. + *meare*, go] 1. a dismissal 2. permission to leave

congeal (kən jēl') *vt., vi.* [< L. *com-*, together + *gelare*, freeze] 1. to solidify or thicken by cooling or freezing 2. to thicken; coagulate —**congeal'able** *adj.* —**congelation** (kon'jə lā'shən) *n.*

congener (kon'jə nər) *n.* [< L. *com-*, together + *genus*, kind] a person or thing of the same kind, class, etc.

congenial (kən jēn'ē əl) *adj.* [see COM- & GENIAL¹] 1. kindred; compatible 2. having the same temperament; sympathetic 3. suited to one's needs; agreeable —**conge'nial'ity** (-jēn'ē al'ə tē) *n.* —**congen'ially** *adv.*

congenital (kən jen'ə t'l) *adj.* [see COM- & GENITAL] existing as such at birth —**congen'itally** *adv.*

conger (eel) (koŋ'gər) [< Gr. *gongros*] a large, edible saltwater eel

congest (kən jest') *vt.* [< L. *com-*, together + *gerere*, carry] 1. to crowd or become crowded 2. to block (the nose) with mucus 3. to overload or clog (an organ) with blood —*vi.* to become congested —**conges'tion** *n.* —**conges'tive** *adj.*

CONGLOMERATE ROCK

conglomerate (kən glom'ə rāt; *for adj. & n.* -ər ət) *vt., vi.* **-at'ed, -at'ing** [< L. *com-*, together + *glomus*, a ball] to form into a rounded mass —*adj.* 1. formed into a rounded mass 2. made up of separate substances collected into a single mass 3. *Geol.* made up of rock fragments or pebbles cemented together by clay, silica, etc. —*n.* 1. a conglomerate mass 2. a large corporation formed by merging many diverse companies 3. *Geol.* a conglomerate rock —**conglom'era'tion** *n.*

congratulate (kən grat'yoo lāt') *vt.* **-lat'ed, -lat'ing** [< L. *com-*, together + *gratus*, agreeable] to express to (a person) one's pleasure at his good fortune, success, etc. —**congratulate oneself** to consider oneself fortunate —**congrat'ula'tor** *n.* —**congrat'ulatory** *adj.*

congratulation (kən grat'yoo lā'shən) *n.* 1. a congratulating 2. [*pl.*] expressions of pleasure and good wishes at another's fortune or success

congregate (koŋ'grə gāt') *vt., vi.* **-gat'ed, -gat'ing** [< L. *com-*, together + *grex*, a flock] to gather into a mass or crowd; assemble —*adj.* 1. assembled 2. collective —**con'gregative** *adj.* —**con'grega'tor** *n.*

congregation (koŋ'grə gā'shən) *n.* 1. a gathering; assemblage 2. an assembly of people for religious worship 3. the members of a particular place of worship —**con'grega'tional** *adj.*

Congregationalism *n.* the faith and organization of a Protestant denomination in which each member church is self-governing —**Con'grega'tional** *adj.* —**Con'-grega'tionalist** *n., adj.*

congress (koŋ'gres) *n.* [< L. *com-*, together + *gradi*, to walk] 1. an association or society 2. an assembly or conference 3. any of various legislatures, esp. [C-] the legislature of the U.S. 4. [C-] in India, a major political party : also Congress Party —**congressional** (kən gresh'ən 'l) *adj.*

congruence (koŋ'groo wəns) *n.* the state or quality of being in agreement; harmony Also **con'gruency**

congruent *adj.* [< L. *congruere*, to agree] 1. in agreement; harmonious 2. *Geom.* of the same shape and size —**con'gruently** *adv.*

congruity (koŋ grōō'ə tē) *n., pl.* **-ties** the condition of being congruous or congruent; agreement; appropriateness

congruous (koŋ′grōo wəs) *adj.* 1. *same as* CONGRUENT 2. fitting; suitable; appropriate —**con′gruously** *adv.*

conical (kon′i k'l) *adj.* 1. of a cone 2. resembling or shaped like a cone —**con′ically** *adv.*

conic section (kon′ik) a curve, as an ellipse, circle, parabola, or hyperbola, produced by the intersection of a plane with a right circular cone

conifer (kon′ə fər) *n.* [L. < *conus*, a cone + *ferre*, to bear] a cone-bearing tree or shrub, as the pine, fir, cedar, etc. —**coniferous** (kə nif′ər əs) *adj.*

conjectural (kən jek′chər əl) *adj.* 1. based on or involving conjecture 2. inclined to make conjectures —**conjec′turally** *adv.*

conjecture (kən jek′chər) *n.* [< L. *com-*, together + *jacere*, to throw] 1. an inferring, theorizing, or predicting from incomplete evidence; guesswork 2. a guess —*vt., vi.* -tured, -turing to arrive at by conjecture; guess —**conjec′turable** *adj.* —**conjec′turer** *n.*

conjoin (kən join′) *vt., vi.* [< L. *com-*, together + *jungere*, to join] to join together; unite —**conjoin′er** *n.*

conjoint *adj.* 1. joined together; united 2. of two or more in association; joint —**conjoint′ly** *adv.*

conjugal (kon′jōo gəl) *adj.* [< L. *com-*, together + *jugum*, yoke] of marriage or the relation between husband and wife —**con′jugally** *adv.*

conjugate (kon′jōo gət; *also, and for v. always,* -gāt′) *vt.* -gat′ed, -gat′ing [< L. *com-*, together + *jugum*, a yoke] *Gram.* to inflect (a verb) systematically, according to voice, mood, tense, number, and person —*adj.* 1. joined together, esp. in a pair; coupled 2. *Gram.* derived from the same base and, usually, related in meaning —*n.* a conjugate word —**con′jugative** *adj.* —**con′juga′tor** *n.*

conjugation (kon′jōo gā′shən) *n.* 1. a conjugating or being conjugated 2. *Gram. a)* an arrangement of the inflectional forms of a verb *b)* a class of verbs with similar inflectional forms

conjunction (kən juŋk′shən) *n.* [see CONJOIN] 1. a joining together; union; combination 2. *Astrol., Astron.* the apparent closeness of two or more heavenly bodies 3. *Gram.* a word used to connect words, phrases, clauses, or sentences (Ex.: *and, but, if,* etc.) —**conjunc′tional** *adj.* —**conjunc′tionally** *adv.*

conjunctiva (kon′juŋk tī′və) *n.,* pl. -vas, -vae (-vē) [ModL.] the mucous membrane lining the inner surface of the eyelids and covering the front part of the eyeball —**con′juncti′val** *adj.*

conjunctive (kən juŋk′tiv) *adj.* 1. connective 2. united; combined 3. *Gram.* used as a conjunction —*n.* a conjunctive word; esp., a conjunction —**conjunc′tively** *adv.*

conjunctivitis (kən juŋk′tə vīt′is) *n.* inflammation of the conjunctiva

conjuncture (kən juŋk′chər) *n.* [see CONJOIN] 1. a combination of events or circumstances 2. a crisis

conjuration (kon′joo rā′shən) *n.* 1. [Obs.] a conjuring; invocation 2. a magic spell; incantation

conjure (kun′jər; *for vt. 2* kən jooʹər′) *vi.* -jured, -juring [< L. *com-*, together + *jurare*, swear] 1. to perform tricks that appear to defy natural laws 2. to summon a demon, spirit, etc. by magic 3. to practise magic —*vt.* 1. to entreat solemnly 2. to summon (a devil, etc.) by magic —**conjure up** 1. to cause to appear as by magic 2. to call to mind

conjurer, conjuror (kun′jər ər) *n.* 1. one who performs tricks that appear to defy natural laws, esp. for people's entertainment 2. a magician

conk (koŋk) *n.* [< ?] [Slang] a blow on the head —*vt.* [Slang] to hit on the head —**conk out** [Slang] 1. to fail suddenly in operation 2. to become very tired and, usually, fall asleep

conker (koŋk′ər) *n.* [< dial. *conker*, snail shell] 1. the horse chestnut 2. [*pl.*] a children's game in which a horse chestnut, threaded on a string, is knocked against another to try to break it

connect (kə nekt′) *vt.* [< L. *com-*, together + *nectere*, fasten] 1. to join (two things together, or one thing *with* or *to* another); link; couple 2. to show or think of as related; associate —*vi.* 1. to be joined or be related 2. to meet so that passengers can change to another bus, aeroplane, etc. —**connect′ible, connect′able** *adj.* —**connec′tor, connect′er** *n.*

connection, connexion (kə nek′shən) *n.* 1. a joining or being joined 2. a thing that joins 3. a relation; association 4. *a)* a relative, esp. by marriage *b)* an influential associate: *usually used in pl.* 5. a train, bus etc. timed to allow transfer of passengers between services —**in connection with** 1. together with 2. with reference to —**connec′tional** *adj.*

connective *adj.* connecting —*n.* a connecting word, as a conjunction or relative pronoun —**connec′tively** *adv.*

connective tissue body tissue that connects and supports other tissues and organs in the body

conning tower 1. an armoured wheelhouse on the deck of a warship 2. on submarines, a low observation tower serving also as an entrance to the interior

connivance (kə nī′vəns) *n.* a conniving; esp., passive cooperation, as by consent in wrongdoing

connive (kə nīv′) *vi.* -nived′, -niv′ing [< L. *conivere*] 1. to pretend not to see or look (*at* something wrong), thus giving tacit consent (*with* something wrong), thus giving tacit consent 2. to cooperate secretly (*with* someone), esp. in wrongdoing —**conniv′er** *n.*

connoisseur (kon′ə sur′) *n.* [< Fr. < L. *cognoscere*, know] one who has expert knowledge and keen discrimination in some field, esp. in the fine arts

connote (ko nōt′) *vt.* -not′ed, -not′ing [< L. *com-*, together + *notare*, to mark] to suggest or convey (associations, overtones, etc.) in addition to the explicit, or denoted, meaning —**connotation** (kon'ō tā'shən) *n.*

connubial (kə nyōō'bē əl) *adj.* [< L. com-, together + *nubere*, marry] of marriage; conjugal —**connu'bially** *adv.*

conquer (koŋ'kər) *vt.* [< L. com-, intens. + *quaerere*, seek] 1. to get control of, as by winning a war 2. to overcome; defeat —*vi.* to be victorious; win —**con'querable** *adj.* —**con'queror** *n.*

conquest (koŋ'kwest) *n.* 1. the act of conquering 2. something conquered 3. a) a winning of someone's love *b)* one whose love has been won —**the (Norman) Conquest** the conquering of England by the Normans in 1066

conquistador (kon kwis'tə dôr') *n., pl.* **-dors', -dores'** [Sp., conqueror] any of the Spanish conquerors of Mexico or Peru

Cons. Conservative

consanguineous (kon'saŋ gwin'ē əs) *adj.* [see COM- & SANGUINE] having the same ancestor; closely related —**con'sanguin'ity** *n.*

conscience (kon'shəns) *n.* [< L. com-, with + *scire*, know] a knowledge or sense of right and wrong, with a compulsion to do right —**in (all) conscience** in fairness —**on one's conscience** causing one to feel guilty —**con'scienceless** *adj.*

conscience money money one pays to relieve one's conscience, as for some former dishonesty

conscience-stricken *adj.* feeling guilty or remorseful because of having done some wrong

conscientious (kon'shē en'shəs) *adj.* [see CONSCIENCE] 1. governed by what one knows is right; scrupulous 2. painstaking —**con'scien'tiously** *adv.* —**con'scien'tiousness** *n.*

conscientious objector a person who for reasons of conscience refuses to take part in warfare

conscious (kon'shəs) *adj.* [see CONSCIENCE] 1. having a feeling or knowledge (with *of* or *that*); aware 2. able to feel and think; awake 3. aware of oneself as a thinking being 4. intentional [*conscious* humour] 5. known to or felt by oneself 6. interested in; concerned with [fashion-*conscious*] —**con'sciously** *adv.*

consciousness *n.* 1. the state of being conscious; awareness 2. the totality of one's thoughts, feelings, and impressions; conscious mind

conscript (kən skript'; *for adj. & n.* kon'-skript) *vt.* to enrol for compulsory service in the armed forces —*adj.* conscripted —*n.* a conscripted person

conscription (kən skrip'shən) *n.* [< L. com-, with + *scribere*, write] compulsory military service

consecrate (kon'sə krāt') *vt.* **-crat'ed, -crat'ing** [< L. com-, together + *sacer*, sacred] 1. to set apart as holy; make or declare sacred for religious use 2. to devote entirely; dedicate 3. to cause

to be revered; hallow —**con'secra'tion** *n.* —**con'secra'tor** *n.* —**con'secratory** *adj.*

consecutive (kən sek'yōō tiv) *adj.* [see CONSEQUENCE] 1. following in order, without interruption; successive 2. proceeding in logical order —**consec'utively** *adv.*

consensus (kən sen'səs) *n.* [see ff.] 1. an opinion held by all or most 2. general agreement

consent (kən sent') *vi.* [< L. com-, with + *sentire*, feel] 1. to agree (*to* do something) 2. to give permission (*to* something) —*n.* 1. permission, approval, or assent 2. agreement —**consent'er** *n.*

consequence (kon'sə kwəns) *n.* [< L. com-, with + *sequi*, follow] 1. a result; effect 2. a logical result or conclusion 3. importance —**in consequence (of)** as a result (of) —**take the consequences** to accept the results of one's actions

consequent *adj.* 1. following as a result; resulting 2. proceeding in logical sequence —*n.* anything that follows —**consequent on** (or **upon**) 1. following as a result of 2. inferred from

consequential (kon'sə kwen'shəl) *adj.* 1. following as an effect 2. important —**con'sequen'tial'ity** (-shē al'ə tē) *n.* —**con'sequen'tially** *adv.*

conservancy (kən sur'vən sē) *n.* 1. a commission with jurisdiction over a river or port 2. conservation of natural resources

conservation (kon'sər vā'shən) *n.* 1. a conserving 2. the official care and protection of natural resources, as forests —**con'serva'tional** *adj.* —**con'serva'tionist** *n.*

conservation of energy *Science* the principle that energy is never consumed but only changes form, and that the total energy in the universe remains fixed

conservation of matter (or **mass**) *Science* the principle that matter is neither created nor destroyed during any physical or chemical change

conservative (kən sur'və tiv) *adj.* 1. tending to preserve established institutions and to resist any changes 2. [C-] designating or of the major right-wing political party of Great Britain or of Canada 3. moderate; cautious; safe —*n.* 1. a conservative person 2. [C-] a member of a Conservative party 3. [C-] in Canada, a member of the Progressive Conservative Party —**conser'vatism** *n.* —**conser'vatively** *adv.* —**conser'vativeness** *n.*

conservatoire (kən sur'və twär') *n.* [Fr.] a school or academy of music or art

conservatory (kən sur'və trē) *n., pl.* **-ries** [see ff.] 1. a greenhouse 2. same as CONSERVATOIRE

conserve (kən surv') *vt.* **-served', -serv'ing** [< L. com-, with + *servare*, to guard] 1. to keep from being damaged, lost, or wasted 2. to preserve (a foodstuff, esp. fruit) with sugar —*n.* [often *pl.*] fruit, etc., preserved with sugar —**conserv'able** *adj.* —**conserv'er** *n.*

consider (kən sid'ər) *vt.* [< L. com-, with + *sidus*, a star] 1. to think about in order to understand or decide **2.** to keep in mind **3.** to be thoughtful of (others) **4.** to regard as; think to be —*vi.* to think carefully; reflect

considerable *adj.* **1.** worth considering; important **2.** much or large —**consid′era-bly** *adv.*

considerate *adj.* having or showing regard for others and their feelings; thoughtful

consideration (kən sid′ə rā′shən) *n.* **1.** the act of considering; deliberation **2.** thoughtful regard for others **3.** something considered in making a decision **4.** an opinion produced by considering **5.** a recompense; fee —**take into consideration** to keep in mind —**under consideration** being thought over

considered *adj.* arrived at after careful thought

considering *prep.* in view of; taking into account —*adv.* [Colloq.] all things considered

consign (kən sīn′) *vt.* [L. *consignare*, to seal] **1.** to hand over; deliver **2.** to entrust **3.** to assign; relegate **4.** to send or deliver (goods) —**consign′able** *adj.* —**consignee** (kon′sī nē′) *n.* —**consign′or, consign′er** *n.*

consignment *n.* **1.** a consigning **2.** something consigned, esp. goods sent to an agent for sale

consist (kən sist′) *vi.* [< L. *com*-, together + *sistere*, to stand] **1.** to be formed or composed (*of*) **2.** to be contained or inherent (*in*) **3.** to exist in harmony (*with*)

consistency *n., pl.* **-cies** **1.** conformity with previous practice **2.** agreement; harmony **3.** *a)* firmness or thickness, as of a liquid *b)* degree of this Also **consis′tence**

consistent *adj.* **1.** in agreement or harmony; compatible **2.** holding to the same principles —**consis′tently** *adv.*

consolation (kon′sə lā′shən) *n.* **1.** a consoling or being consoled; solace **2.** a person or thing that consoles

console[1] (kən sōl′) *vt.* **-soled′, -sol′ing** [< L. *com*-, with + *solari*, to solace] to comfort in distress —**consol′able** *adj.* —**consol′ingly** *adv.*

CONSOLE
(of an organ)

console[2] (kon′sōl) *n.* [Fr.] **1.** a bracket for supporting a shelf, cornice, etc. **2.** the desklike frame containing the keys, stops, etc. of an organ **3.** a radio, television, or gramophone cabinet designed to stand on the floor **4.** a control panel for operating aircraft, computers, etc.

consolidate (kən sol′ə dāt′) *vt., vi.* **-dat′-**

ed, **-dat′ing** [< L. *com*-, together + *solidus*, solid] **1.** to combine into one; unite **2.** to make or become strong, stable, etc. [the troops *consolidated* their position] —**consol′ida′tion** *n.* —**consol′ida′tor** *n.*

consols (kon′solz) *n.pl.* [< *consolidated annuities*] British government securities

consommé (kən som′ā) *n.* [Fr.] a clear, strained meat soup

consonance (kon′sə nəns) *n.* [< L. *com*-, with + *sonus*, a sound] harmony, esp. of musical tones

consonant (kon′sə nənt) *n.* [see prec.] **1.** any speech sound produced by obstructing the breath stream as *p, t, l, f,* etc. **2.** a letter representing such a sound —*adj.* **1.** in harmony or agreement **2.** harmonious in tone —**con′sonan′tal** (-nant′-) *adj.*

consort (kon′sôrt; *for v.* kən sôrt′) *n.* [< L. *com*-, with + *sors*, a share] **1.** a wife or husband, esp. of a reigning king or queen **2.** a ship that travels with another —*vi.* **1.** to associate **2.** to agree; be in accord

consortium (kən sôr′tē əm) *n., pl.* **-tia** [see prec.] **1.** an alliance, as of two or more business firms **2.** an international banking agreement or association

conspectus (kən spek′təs) *n.* [see ff.] **1.** a general view; survey **2.** a summary; synopsis; digest

conspicuous (kən spik′yoo wəs) *adj.* [< L. *com*-, intens. + *specere*, to see] **1.** easy to see; obvious **2.** outstanding; striking —**conspic′uously** *adv.* —**conspic′-uousness** *n.*

conspiracy (kən spir′ə sē) *n., pl.* **-cies** **1.** a conspiring, esp. in an unlawful plot **2.** such a plot **3.** the group taking part in such a plot

conspirator *n.* a person who takes part in a conspiracy —**conspiratorial** (kən spir′ə tôr′ē əl) *adj.*

conspire (kən spīr′) *vi.* **-spired′, -spir′-ing** [< L. *com*-, together + *spirare*, breathe] **1.** to plan and act together secretly, esp. in order to commit a crime **2.** to work together for any purpose or effect

constable (kun′stə b′l) *n.* [< LL. *comes stabuli*, lit., count of the stable] **1.** a policeman **2.** the keeper or governor of a royal castle **3.** *Hist.* the highest ranking official of a royal household, court, etc.

constabulary (kən stab′yoo lər ē) *n., pl.* **-ies** the police force of a town or district —*adj.* of constables or a constabulary: also **constab′ular**

constant (kon′stənt) *adj.* [< L. *com*-, together + *stare*, to stand] **1.** not changing; specif., *a)* resolute *b)* faithful *c)* regular; stable **2.** continual; persistent [constant interruptions] —*n.* **1.** anything that does not change or vary **2.** *Math., Physics* a quantity that always has the same value: opposed to VARIABLE —**con′stancy** *n.* —**con′stantly** *adv.*

constellation (kon′stə lā′shən) *n.* [< L. *com*-, with + *stella*, a star] **1.** a group of fixed stars, usually named after a figure that they supposedly suggest in outline

2. any brilliant cluster, gathering, or collection —**constellatory** (kən stel'ə tər ē) *adj.*

consternation (kon'stər nā'shən) *n.* [< L. *consternare*, to throw into confusion] great fear or shock that makes one feel helpless or bewildered

constipate (kon'stə pāt') *vt.* -pat'ed, -pat'ing [< L. *com-*, together + *stipare*, cram] to cause constipation in

constipation (kon'stə pā'shən) *n.* a condition in which the faeces are hard and elimination from the bowels is infrequent and difficult

constituency (kən stit'yoo wən sē) *n.*, *pl.* -cies 1. all the people, esp. voters, served by a particular elected official 2. the district of such voters, etc.

constituent (-yoo wənt) *adj.* [see ff.] 1. necessary in forming a whole; component 2. that can elect 3. authorized to make or revise a constitution [a *constituent* assembly] —*n.* 1. a component 2. a person who appoints another as his representative

constitute (kon'stə tyoot') *vt.* -tut'ed, -tut'ing [< L. *com-*, together + *statuere*, to set] 1. to make up; form 2. to appoint 3. to set up (an assembly, etc.) in a legal form 4. to establish (a law, government, etc.)

constitution (kon'stə tyoo'shən) *n.* 1. a constituting; establishment 2. structure; organization 3. the physical makeup of a person 4. the system of fundamental laws and principles of a government, state, society, etc.

constitutional *adj.* 1. of or in the constitution of a person or thing; basic; essential 2. for improving a person's constitution 3. of or in accordance with the constitution of a nation, society, etc. [*constitutional* right] —*n.* a walk or other exercise taken for one's health —**con'stitu'tional'ity** *n.* —**con'stitu'tionally** *adv.*

constitutive (kon'stə tyoot'iv) *adj.* 1. having power to establish, appoint, or enact 2. basic 3. forming a part (*of*); constituent —**con'stitu'tively** *adv.*

constrain (kən strān') *vt.* [< L. *com-*, together + *stringere*, draw tight] 1. to compel [*constrained* to agree] 2. to hold back by force; restrain 3. to confine —**constrained' ** *adj.*

constraint (-strānt') *n.* 1. compulsion or coercion 2. a forced, unnatural manner 3. confinement or restriction

constrict (kən strikt') *vt.* [see CONSTRAIN] 1. to make smaller or narrower by squeezing, etc. 2. to hold in; limit —**constric'tive** *adj.*

constriction *n.* 1. a constricting 2. a feeling of tightness or pressure

constrictor *n.* 1. that which constricts, as a muscle that contracts an opening 2. a snake that kills by coiling around its prey and squeezing

construct (kən strukt'; *for n.* kon'strukt) *vt.* [< L. *com-*, together + *struere*, pile up] 1. to build, form, or devise by fitting parts together systematically 2. *Geom.*

to draw to specified requirements —*n.* something put together systematically —**construc'tor, construct'er** *n.*

construction (kən struk'shən) *n.* 1. the act of constructing or the way in which something is constructed 2. a structure 3. an interpretation, as of a statement 4. the arrangement of words in a sentence —**construc'tional** *adj.* —**construc'tionally** *adv.*

constructive (kən struk'tiv) *adj.* 1. helping to construct; leading to improvements [*constructive* criticism] 2. inferred or implied by interpretation —**construc'tively** *adv.* —**construc'tiveness** *n.*

construe (kən stroo') *vt.* -strued', -stru'ing [see CONSTRUCT] 1. to interpret [her silence was *construed* as agreement] 2. to analyse (a sentence, etc.) so as to show its syntactical construction 3. to translate 4. *Gram.* to combine in syntax

consul (kon's'l) *n.* [< L. *consulere*, to deliberate] 1. a government official appointed to live in a foreign city and serve his country's citizens and business interests there 2. a chief magistrate of ancient Rome —**con'sular** (kon'syoo lər) *adj.* —**con'sulship'** *n.*

consulate (kon'syoo lət) *n.* 1. the office or residence of a consul 2. the position, powers, and duties of a consul

consult (kən sult') *vi.* [< L. *consulere*, to deliberate] to talk things over; confer —*vt.* 1. to ask advice or information from 2. to consider [*consult* your own wishes] —**consult'er** *n.*

consultant *n.* 1. an expert called on for professional or technical advice 2. a senior hospital physician or surgeon —**consul'tancy** *n.*

consultation (kon's'l tā'shən) *n.* 1. the act of consulting 2. a meeting to discuss or plan something —**consultative** (kən sul'tə tiv), **consul'tatory** *adj.*

consume (kən syoom') *vt.* -sumed', -sum'ing [< L. *com-*, together + *sumere*, to take] 1. to destroy, as by fire 2. to use up; waste (time, money, etc.) 3. to eat or drink; devour 4. to engross or obsess [*consumed* with envy] —**consum'able** *adj.*

consumer *n.* a person or thing that consumes; specif., one who buys goods or services for his own needs and not for resale

consumerism *n.* 1. the movement for consumer protection, esp. in connection with defective and unsafe products 2. the consumption of goods and services

consumer research research conducted to discover the needs and desires of consumers

consummate (kən sum'it; *for v.* kon'sə māt') *adj.* [< L. *com-*, together + *summa*, a sum] 1. complete or perfect 2. highly expert —*vt.* -mat'ed, -mat'ing 1. to bring to completion; finish 2. to make (a marriage) actual by sexual intercourse —**consum'mately** *adv.* —**con'summa'tion** *n.* —**con'summa'tor** *n.*

consumption (kən sump'shən) *n.* 1. a)

a consuming or being consumed *b*) the amount consumed **2.** tuberculosis of the lungs

consumptive *adj.* **1.** destructive; wasteful **2.** of or having tuberculosis of the lungs —*n.* a person who has tuberculosis of the lungs

cont. 1. contents **2.** continued

contact (kon´takt) *n.* [< L. *com-*, together + *tangere*, to touch] **1.** the act of touching or meeting **2.** the state of being in touch or association (*with*) **3.** an acquaintance; connection **4.** a person who has been exposed to a contagious disease and who may transmit it **5.** *Elec.* a connection between two conductors in a circuit —*vt.* **1.** to place in contact **2.** to get in touch with —*vi.* to come into contact

contact lens a tiny, thin correctional lens of glass or plastic placed on the fluid over the cornea of the eye

contagion (kən tā´jən) *n.* [see CONTACT] **1.** the spreading of disease by contact **2.** a contagious disease **3.** the spreading of an emotion, idea, etc.

contagious *adj.* **1.** spread by contact **2.** carrying the causative agent of a disease **3.** spreading from person to person —**conta´giously** *adv.* —**conta´giousness** *n.*

contain (kən tān´) *vt.* [< L. *com-*, together + *tenere*, to hold] **1.** to have in it; hold or include **2.** to have the capacity for holding **3.** to hold back or restrain within fixed limits **4.** to be divisible by, esp. without a remainder [10 *contains* 5 and 2] —**contain´able** *adj.*

container *n.* **1.** a box, tin, jar, etc. **2.** a reusable, standardized receptacle for carrying cargo

containerize *vt.* **-ized´, -iz´ing** to pack (general cargo) in large, standardized containers for more efficient shipment —**contain´eriza´tion** *n.*

containment *n.* the policy of attempting to prevent the influence of an opposing nation or political system from spreading

contaminant (kən tam´ə nənt) *n.* a substance that contaminates another substance, the air, water, etc.

contaminate (kən tam´ə nāt´) *vt.* **-nat´ed, -nat´ing** [< L. *com-*, together + *tangere*, to touch] to make impure, infected, corrupt, radioactive, etc. by contact; pollute; taint —**contam´ina´tion** *n.* —**contam´inative** *adj.* —**contam´ina´tor** *n.*

contemn (kən tem´) *vt.* [< L. *com-*, intens. + *temnere*, to scorn] to treat with contempt; scorn —**contemn´er** *n.*

contemplate (kon´təm plāt´) *vt.* **-plat´ed, -plat´ing** [< L. *contemplari*, to observe (orig., in augury), to mark out a space for observation)] **1.** to look at intently **2.** to think about intently; study carefully **3.** to expect or intend —*vi.* to meditate or muse —**con´templa´tion** *n.* —**con´templa´tor** *n.*

contemplative (kon´təm plāt´iv; *for adj. 2* + *n. usually,* kən tem´plə tiv) *adj.* **1.** of or inclined to contemplation; meditative **2.** designating a religious order dedicated to prayer and meditation —*n.* a member

of a contemplative religious order —**con´templa´tively** *adv.*

contemporaneous (kən tem´pə rā´nē əs) *adj.* [< L. *com-*, with + *tempus*, time] existing or happening at the same time —**contem´porane´ity** *n.*

contemporary (kən tem´pə rer ē) *adj.* [< L. *com-*, with + *tempus*, time] **1.** living or happening in the same period **2.** of about the same age **3.** modern —*n.*, *pl.* **-ries** a person or thing of the same period or about the same age as another or others

contempt (kən tempt´) *n.* [see CONTEMN] **1.** the feeling of a person towards someone or something he considers worthless or beneath notice; scorn **2.** the condition of being despised **3.** *Law* a showing disrespect for the dignity of a court: in full, **contempt of court**

contemptible *adj.* deserving contempt or scorn; despicable —**contempt´ibly** *adv.*

contemptuous *adj.* full of contempt; scornful —**contemp´tuously** *adv.* —**contemp´tuousness** *n.*

contend (kən tend´) *vi.* [< L. *com-*, together + *tendere*, stretch] **1.** to fight **2.** to argue **3.** to compete; vie —*vt.* to hold to be a fact; assert —**contend´er** *n.*

content¹ (kən tent´) *adj.* [see CONTAIN] **1.** happy enough with what one has or is; satisfied **2.** assenting —*vt.* to satisfy —*n.* contentment

content² (kon´tent) *n.* [see CONTAIN] **1.** [*usually pl.*] a) all that is contained in something *b*) all that is dealt with in a writing or speech **2.** meaning or substance **3.** the amount contained

contented (kən ten´tid) *adj.* satisfied —**content´edly** *adv.* —**content´edness** *n.*

contention (kən ten´shən) *n.* [see CONTEND] **1.** strife, struggle, dispute, etc. **2.** a point that one argues for as true or valid

contentious *adj.* **1.** quarrelsome **2.** characterized by contention —**conten´tiousness** *n.*

contentment (kən tent´mənt) *n.* the state, quality, or fact of being contented

conterminous (kon tur´mə nəs) *adj.* [< L. *com-*, together + *terminus*, an end] having a common boundary —**conter´minously** *adv.*

contest (kən test´; *for n.* kon´test) *vt.* [< L. *com-*, together + *testis*, a witness] **1.** to try to disprove; dispute [to *contest* a will] **2.** to fight for —*vi.* to struggle (*with* or *against*) —*n.* **1.** a fight, struggle, or controversy **2.** a competitive race, game, etc. —**contest´able** *adj.* —**contest´er** *n.*

contestant (kən tes´tənt) *n.* [Fr.] **1.** one that competes in a contest **2.** one who contests a claim, decision, etc.

context (kon´tekst) *n.* [< L. *com-*, together + *texere*, to weave] the parts of a sentence, paragraph, etc. surrounding a word or passage and determining its exact meaning [to quote a remark out of *context*] —**contextual** (kon teks´tyoo wəl) *adj.*

contiguous (kən tig´yoo wəs) *adj.* [see

CONTACT] 1. in contact; touching 2. near or adjacent —**contiguity** (kon′tə gyōō′ə tē) *n.* —**contig′uously** *adv.*

continence (kon′tin əns) *n.* [see ff.] 1. self-restraint 2. self-restraint in sexual activity; esp., total abstinence 3. the ability to control urination and defecation

continent (kon′tin ənt) *adj.* [see CONTAIN] 1. characterized by self-restraint, esp. by total abstinence, in sexual activity 2. able to control urination and defecation —*n.* any of the main large land areas of the earth (Africa, Asia, Australia, Europe, N America, S America, and, sometimes, Antarctica) —**the Continent** all Europe except the British Isles —**con′tinen′tal** (-en′t'l) *adj.* —**con′tinently** *adv.*

continental drift the hypothetical drifting of continents caused by currents in the earth's mantle

continental quilt *same as* DUVET

continental shelf the submerged, gradually sloping shelf of land that borders a continent

contingency (kən tin′jən sē) *n., pl.* **-cies** 1. a contingent condition; esp., dependence on chance 2. a possible, unforeseen, or accidental occurrence Also **contin′gence**

contingent *adj.* [see CONTACT] 1. dependent (*on* or *upon* an uncertainty); conditional 2. accidental 3. unpredictable because dependent on chance 4. possible —*n.* 1. a share or quota, as of troops 2. a part of a large group 3. a chance happening —**contin′gently** *adv.*

continual (kən tin′yoo wəl) *adj.* 1. repeated often 2. going on uninterruptedly —**contin′ually** *adv.*

continuance *n.* 1. a continuing 2. duration 3. stay 4. an unbroken succession

continuation (kən tin′yoo wā′shən) *n.* 1. a keeping up or going on without stopping 2. a beginning again; resumption 3. a part added; supplement, sequel, etc.

continue (kən tin′yōō) *vi.* **-ued, -uing** [see CONTAIN] 1. to last; endure 2. to go on in a specified action or condition; persist 3. to extend 4. to stay 5. to resume —*vt.* 1. to go on with 2. to extend 3. to resume 4. to cause to remain; retain —**contin′uable** *adj.* —**contin′uer** *n.*

continuity (kon′tə nyōō′ə tē) *n., pl.* **-ties** 1. a continuous state or quality 2. an unbroken, coherent whole 3. the script for a film, television programme, etc.

continuo (kən tin′yoo wō′) *n.* [It.] *Music* a continuous bass accompaniment played as on a harpsichord or organ

continuous (kən tin′yoo wəs) *adj.* going on without interruption; unbroken —**contin′uously** *adv.*

continuum (-yoo wəm) *n., pl.* **-ua, -uums** [L.] a continuous whole, quantity, or series

contort (kən tôrt′) *vt., vi.* [< L. *com-*, together + *torquere*, to twist] to twist or wrench out of shape; distort —**contor′tion** *n.* —**contor′tive** *adj.*

contortionist (kən tôr′shən ist) *n.* a person who can twist his body into unnatural positions

contour (kon′tooər) *n.* [< L. *com-*, intens. + *tornare*, to turn] the outline of a figure, land, etc. —*vt.* 1. to represent in contour 2. to shape to the contour of —*adj.* conforming to or following the shape or contour of something

contour map a map with lines (**contour lines**) connecting all points of the same elevation

contra- [< L.] a prefix meaning: 1. against, opposite, opposed to 2. lower in musical pitch

contraband (kon′trə band′) *n.* [< L. *contra-*, against + LL. *bandum*, ban] 1. smuggled goods, forbidden by law to be imported and exported 2. war materiel not to be supplied by a neutral to a belligerent : in full **contraband of war** —*adj.* forbidden by law to be imported or exported —**con′traband′ist** *n.*

contraception (kon′trə sep′shən) *n.* [CONTRA- + (CON)CEPTION] intentional prevention of the fertilization of the human ovum —**con′tracep′tive** *adj., n.*

contract (kon′trakt; *for v.* kən trakt′) *n.* [< L. *com-*, together + *trahere*, draw] 1. an agreement, esp. a written one enforceable by law 2. a formal agreement of marriage 3. a document containing the terms of an agreement 4. *Bridge* the number of tricks bid by the highest bidder —*vt.* 1. to reduce in size; shrink 2. to undertake by contract 3. to get or incur 4. to shorten (a word or phrase) by the omission of a letter or sound —*vi.* 1. to become smaller 2. to make a contract —**contract out** to agree not to participate in something, esp. the state pension scheme —**contract′ibil′ity** *n.* —**contract′ible** *adj.*

contractile (kən trak′tīl) *adj.* having the power of contracting —**contractility** (kon′-trak til′ə tē) *n.*

contraction *n.* 1. a contracting or being contracted 2. the drawing up and thickening of a muscle in action 3. the shortened form of a word or phrase (Ex. : aren't for are not) —**contrac′tional** *adj.* —**contrac′tive** *adj.*

contractor (kən trak′tər) *n.* 1. one who contracts to supply certain materials or do certain work for a stipulated sum 2. one of the parties to a contract

contractual (kən trak′chōō wəl) *adj.* of, or having the nature of, a contract —**con-trac′tually** *adv.*

contradict (kon′trə dikt′) *vt.* [< L. *contra-*, against + *dicere*, speak] 1. *a)* to assert the opposite of (a statement) *b)* to deny the statement of (a person) 2. to be contrary to —**con′tradic′tion** *n.* —**con′tradic′tor, con′tradict′er** *n.*

contradictory *adj.* 1. involving a contradiction; inconsistent 2. inclined to contradict or deny —**con′tradic′torily** *adv.* —**con′tradic′toriness** *n.*

contradistinction (kon′trə dis tiŋk′shən) *n.* distinction by contrast —**con′tradis-tinc′tive** *adj.*

contralto (kən tral′tō) *n., pl.* **-tos** [It.] 1. the range of the lowest female voice 2. a singer with this range

contraption (kən trap′shən) n. [< ?] [Colloq.] a contrivance or gadget

contrapuntal (kon′trə pun′t'l) adj. [< It. *contrappunto,* counterpoint] 1. of or characterized by counterpoint 2. according to the principles of counterpoint —con′trapun′tally adv. —con′trapun′tist n.

contrariwise (kon′trər ē wīz′; *for 3, often* kən trâər′-) adv. 1. on the contrary; from the opposite point of view 2. in the opposite way, order, direction, etc. 3. perversely

contrary (kon′trer ē; *for adj. 4, often* kən trâər′ē) adj. [< L. *contra,* against] 1. in opposition 2. opposite in nature, order, etc.; altogether different 3. unfavourable [*contrary* winds] 4. inclined to oppose stubbornly; perverse —n., pl. -ries the opposite —adv. in a contrary way —on the contrary as opposed to what has been said —to the contrary to the opposite effect —con′trarily adv. —con′trariness n.

contrast (kən träst′; *for n.* kon′träst) vt. [< L. *contra,* against + *stare,* to stand] to compare so as to point out the differences —vi. to show differences when compared —n. 1. a contrasting 2. a striking difference, between things being compared 3. a person or thing showing differences when compared with another

contravene (kon′trə vēn′) vt. -vened′, -ven′ing [< L. *contra,* against + *venire,* come] 1. to go against; violate 2. to disagree with; contradict —con′traven′er n.

contravention (-ven′shən) n. violation; infringement —in contravention of violating: said esp. of laws, etc.

contretemps (kôn′trə tän′) n., pl. -temps′ (-tän′) [Fr.] an inopportune happening causing embarrassment

contribute (kən trib′yoot) vt., vi. -uted, -uting [see COM- & TRIBUTE] 1. to give jointly with others to a common fund 2. to write (an article, poem, etc.) for a magazine, newspaper, etc. 3. to furnish (ideas, etc.) —contribute to to have a share in bringing about —contribution (kon′trə byoo′shən) n. —contrib′utor n. —contrib′utory adj.

contrite (kən′trīt) adj. [< L. *com,* together + *terere,* rub] feeling sorrow or remorse for having done wrong —con′tritely adv. —contri′tion (-trish′ən) n.

contrivance (kən trī′vəns) n. 1. something contrived, as an invention, mechanical device, plan, etc. 2. the act, way, or power of contriving

contrive (kən trīv′) vt. -trived′, -triv′ing [< ML. *contropare,* compare] 1. to devise; plan 2. to construct skilfully; fabricate 3. to bring about, as by a scheme —vi. to form plans; scheme —contriv′er n.

control (kən trōl′) vt. -trolled′, -trol′ling [< L. *contra,* against + *rotulus,* a roll] 1. to exercise authority over; direct 2. to restrain 3. to regulate (financial affairs) —n. 1. power to direct or regulate 2. a being directed; restraint 3. a means of controlling; check 4. a standard of

comparison for checking the findings of an experiment 5. [*usually pl.*] an apparatus to regulate a mechanism —control′lable adj.

controller n. 1. a person in charge of expenditures, as in business, government (usually sp. *comptroller*), etc. 2. a person or device that controls —control′lership′ n.

control tower a tower at an airport, from which air traffic is directed

controversial (kon′trə vur′shəl) adj. of, subject to, or stirring up controversy; debatable —con′trover′sialist n.

controversy (kon′trə vur′sē, kən trov′ə-sē) n., pl. -sies [< L. *contra,* against + *vertere,* to turn] 1. a discussion in which opinions clash; debate 2. a quarrel —controvert (kon′trə vurt′) vt.

contumacy (kon′tyoo mə sē) n., pl. -cies [< L. *com-,* intens. + *tumere,* swell up] stubborn refusal to submit to authority —contumacious (kon′tyoo mā′shəs) adj.

contumely (kon′tyoo mə lē) n., pl. -lies [< L. *contumelia,* reproach] 1. humiliating treatment 2. a scornful insult —con′tume′lious (-mē′lē əs) adj.

contuse (kən tyooz′) vt. -tused′, -tus′ing [< L. *com-,* intens. + *tundere,* to beat] to bruise without breaking the skin

contusion (-tyoo′zhən) n. a bruise

conundrum (kə nun′drəm) n. [16th-c. < ?] 1. a riddle whose answer contains a pun 2. any puzzling question

conurbation (kon′ur bā′shən) n. [< COM- + L. *urbs,* city] a densely populated urban area, including suburbs and towns around a large city

convalesce (kon′və les′) vi. -lesced′, -lesc′ing [< L. *com-,* intens. + *valere,* be strong] to recover gradually from illness; regain strength and health

convalescence n. 1. a gradual recovery of health after illness 2. the period of such recovery —con′vales′cent adj., n.

convection (kən vek′shən) n. [< L. *com-,* together + *vehere,* carry] 1. a transmitting 2. a) the movement of parts within a fluid because of differences in density, temperature, etc. b) the transference of heat by such movement —convec′tional adj. —convec′tive adj.

convector (kən vek′tər) n. a heating device which transmits heat to the air by convection

convene (kən vēn′) vi., vt. -vened′, -ven′-ing [< L. *com-,* together + *venire,* come] to assemble for a meeting —conven′er n.

convenience (kən vēn′yəns) n. [see CONVENE] 1. the quality of being convenient 2. personal comfort 3. anything that adds to one's comfort or saves work 4. a lavatory, esp. a public one —at one's convenience at a time, place, etc. that suits one

convenient adj. 1. favourable to one's comfort; easy to do, use, or get to; handy 2. [Colloq.] easily accessible (*for*); near (*for*) —conven′iently adv.

convent (kon′vənt) n. [see CONVENE] 1. a community of nuns or, sometimes, monks, living under strict religious vows 2. the building or buildings occupied by such a group —**conventual** (kən ven'tyoō wəl) *adj.*

conventicle (kən ven'ti k'l) *n.* [< prec.] a religious assembly, esp. an illegal or secret one

convention (kən ven'shən) *n.* 1. an assembly, often periodical, or the delegates to it 2. *a*) an agreement between persons, nations, etc. *b*) general agreement on the usages and practices of social life 3. a customary practice, rule, method, etc.

conventional *adj.* 1. *a*) conforming to accepted rules; not natural, original, or spontaneous *b*) ordinary 2. sanctioned by, or growing out of custom or usage 3. having to do with a convention 4. nonnuclear [*conventional* weapons *]* —**conven'tionalism** *n.* —**conven'tionally** *adv.*

conventionality (kən ven'shə nal'ə tē) *n.*, *pl.* -**ties** 1. a being conventional 2. conventional behaviour or act 3. a conventional form, usage, or rule

conventionalize (kən ven'shən əl īz') *vt.* -**ized**', -**iz'ing** to make conventional —**conven'tionaliza'tion** *n.*

converge (kən vurj') *vi.*, *vt.* -**verged**', -**verg'ing** [< L. *com*-, together + *vergere*, to turn] to come or bring together at a point

convergence *n.* 1. the act, or fact of converging 2. the point at which things converge —**conver'gent** *adj.*

conversable (kən vur'sə b'l) *adj.* 1. easy to talk to; affable 2. liking to converse or talk

conversant (kən vur's'nt) *adj.* [see CONVERSE[1]] familiar or acquainted (*with*); versed (*in*) —**conver'sance, conver'sancy** *n.* —**conver'santly** *adv.*

conversation (kon'vər sā'shən) *n.* [see CONVERSE[1]] a talking together; specif., informal talk

conversational *adj.* 1. of or for conversation 2. given to conversation —**con'versa'tionalist** *n.*

conversation piece an unusual article of furniture, bric-a-brac, etc. that attracts attention or invites comment

converse[1] (kən vurs'; *for n.* kon'vurs) *vi.* -**versed**', -**vers'ing** [< L. *conversari*, to live with] to hold a conversation; talk —*n.* conversation —**convers'er** *n.*

converse[2] (kon'vurs) *adj.* [see CONVERT] reversed in position, order, etc.; contrary —*n.* a thing related in a converse way; the opposite —**converse'ly** *adv.*

conversion (kən vur'shən) *n.* a converting or being converted; specif., *a*) a change from lack of faith to religious belief or from one religion to another *b*) *Rugby* an additional score made after a try by kicking the ball over the crossbar —**conver'sional, conver'sionary** *adj.*

convert (kən vurt'; *for n.* kon'vərt) *vt.* [< L. *com*-, together + *vertere*, to turn] 1. to change; transform [*convert* grain into flour *]* 2. to change from one belief, religion, etc. to another 3. to exchange for something equal in value 4. *Finance* to change (a security, currency, etc.) into

an equivalent of another form —*vi.* 1. to be converted 2. *Rugby* to score extra points after a try —*n.* a person converted, as to a religion

converter (kən vur'tər) *n.* a person or thing that converts; specif., *a*) a furnace for converting pig iron into steel *b*) *Elec.* a device for converting alternating current into direct current Also sp. **conver'tor**

convertible (kən vur'tə b'l) *adj.* that can be converted —*n.* a motor car with a top that can be folded back —**convert'ibil'ity** *n.* —**convert'ibly** *adv.*

convex (kon'veks; *for n.* kon veks') *adj.* [< L. *com*-, together + *vehere*, bring] curving outwards like the surface of a sphere —*n.* a convex surface, object, etc. —**convex'ity** *n.* —**convex'ly** *adv.*

convey (kən vā') *vt.* [< L. *com*-, together + *via*, way] 1. to take from one place to another; transport; carry 2. to transmit 3. to communicate 4. to transfer, as a title to property, to another person —**convey'able** *adj.*

conveyance *n.* 1. a conveying 2. a means of conveying, esp. a vehicle 3. *a*) the transfer of real property from one person to another *b*) a document to effect this —**convey'ancer** *n.* —**convey'ancing** *n.*

conveyor, conveyer *n.* one that conveys; esp., a mechanical contrivance, as a continuous chain or belt (**conveyor belt**)

convict (kən vikt'; *for n.* kon'vikt) *vt.* [see CONVINCE] to prove or find (a person) guilty —*n.* 1. one found guilty and sentenced by a court 2. one serving a sentence in prison

conviction (kən vik'shən) *n.* 1. a convicting or being convicted 2. the state or appearance of being convinced 3. a strong belief —**carry conviction** to be convincing —**convic'tive** *adj.* —**convic'tively** *adv.*

convince (kən vins') *vt.* -**vinced**', -**vinc'ing** [< L. *com*-, intens. + *vincere*, conquer] to persuade by argument or evidence; make feel sure —**convinc'er** *n.* —**convinc'ible** *adj.* —**convinc'ingly** *adv.*

convivial (kən viv'ē əl) *adj.* [< L. *com*-, together + *vivere*, to live] 1. festive 2. fond of eating, drinking, and good company; sociable —**conviv'ial'ity** *n.*

convocation (kon'və kā'shən) *n.* 1. a convoking 2. a group that has been convoked; esp. *a*) *Church of England* a provincial synod *b*) in some universities, a legislative assembly composed of graduates —**con'voca'tional** *adj.*

convoke (kən vōk') *vt.* -**voked**', -**vok'ing** [< L. *com*-, together + *vocare*, to call] to call together; convene —**convok'er** *n.*

convolute (kon'və loōt') *adj.* [see CONVOLVE] rolled up in a spiral; coiled —*vt.*, *vi.* -**lut'ed**, -**lut'ing** to wind around; coil —**con'volut'ed** *adj.* —**con'volute'ly** *adv.*

convolution (kon'və loō'shən) *n.* 1. a twisting, coiling, or winding together 2. a convoluted condition 3. any of the irregular folds or ridges on the surface of the brain

convolve (kən volv′) vt., vi. -volved′, -volv′ing [< L. com-, together + volvere, to roll] to roll, coil, or twist together

convolvulus (kən vol′vyŏŏ ləs) n., pl. -luses, -li′ (-lī′) [see prec.] a trailing or twining plant; bindweed

convoy (kon′voi) vt. [see CONVEY] to escort, esp. in order to protect —n. 1. the act of convoying 2. a protecting escort, as for ships or troops 3. ships, vehicles, etc. travelling together for mutual protection

convulse (kən vuls′) vt. -vulsed′, -vuls′ing [< L. com-, together + vellere, to pluck] 1. to shake violently; agitate 2. to cause to shake with laughter, rage, etc. —convul′sive adj. —convul′sively adv.

convulsion n. 1. a violent, involuntary contraction of the muscles: often used in pl. 2. a fit of laughter 3. any violent disturbance —convul′sionary adj.

cony (kō′nē) n., pl. -nies [< L. cuniculus, rabbit] 1. a rabbit 2. rabbit fur Also sp. co′ney

coo (kōō) vi. [echoic] 1. to make the soft, murmuring sound of pigeons or doves 2. to speak gently and lovingly, as in **bill and coo** —vt. to express lovingly, as with a coo —n. a cooing sound —coo′-ingly adv.

cooee (kōō′ē) interj. a call to attract attention, esp. one used in the Australian bush --vi. coo′eed or coo′eyed, coo′ee-ing or coo′eying to utter the call of cooee

cook (kook) n. [< L. coquere, to cook] a person who prepares food —vt. 1. to prepare (food) by boiling, baking, frying, etc. 2. [Colloq] to alter or falsify [to cook the books] —vi. 1. to act as a cook 2. to undergo cooking —cook someone's goose [Colloq.] 1. to spoil someone's plans 2. to bring about someone's downfall —cook up [Colloq.] to devise —what's cooking? [Slang] what's happening?

cooker n. 1. an apparatus for cooking food, usually consisting of an oven and a hob 2. a fruit more suitable for cooking than for eating raw

cookery n. the art, practice, or work of cooking

cookery book a book with recipes and other information about preparing food: also **cook′book** n.

cookie, cooky (kook′ē) n., pl. -ies [prob. < Du. koek, a cake] [U.S.] a small, sweet biscuit

cool (kōōl) adj. [OE. col] 1. moderately cold 2. tending to reduce discomfort in hot weather [cool clothes] 3. a) calm; composed b) restrained [cool jazz] c) [Slang] dispassionate 4. showing dislike or indifference 5. calmly impudent or bold 6. [Colloq.] without exaggeration [a cool thousand] 7. [U.S. Slang] pleasing —n. 1. a cool place, time, etc. 2. [Chiefly U.S. Slang] dispassionate manner [keep one's cool] —vt., vi. to make or become cool —cool off to calm down —cool one's heels to wait or be kept waiting —play

it cool [Slang] to stay aloof —cool′-ish adj. —cool′ly adv. —cool′ness n.

coolabar (kōō′lə bär′) n. [Abor.] an Australian eucalyptus that grows along rivers: also **coo′labah**

coolant (kōōl′ənt) n. a substance, usually a fluid, used to remove heat, as from an internal-combustion engine

cool drink [S Afr.] a soft drink

cooler n. 1. a container for cooling things or keeping them cool 2. anything that cools 3. [Slang] a jail

coolie (kōō′lē) n. [Hindi qūlī, servant] an unskilled native labourer, esp. formerly, in China, India, etc.

cooling tower a tower used to recycle water used for cooling, as in a nuclear reactor

coomb, coombe (kōōm) n. [< OE. cumb] 1. a deep, narrow valley 2. same as CWM

coon (kōōn) n. 1. short for RACCOON 2. a) [Derog. Slang] a Negro or Aborigine b) in South Africa, esp. a dancer, singer, etc. in the Coon Carnival, a traditional New Year festival presented by Cape Coloureds

coop (kōōp) n. [ult. < L. cupa, cask] 1. a small cage, pen, or building for poultry, etc. 2. any place of confinement 3. a wicker basket for catching fish —vt. to confine in or as in a coop

co-op (kō′op) n. [Colloq.] 1. a cooperative 2. a shop run by a cooperative society

cooper (kōōp′ər) n. [< L. cupa, a cask] a person whose work is making or repairing barrels and casks —vt., vi. to make or repair (barrels and casks)

cooperate, co-operate (kō op′ə rāt′) vi. -at′ed, -at′ing [< L. co-, with + opus, work] to act or work together with another or others —coop′era′tion, co-op′era′tion n. —coop′era′tor, co-op′era′tor n.

cooperative, co-operative (kō op′ər ə tiv) adj. 1. cooperating or inclined to cooperate 2. designating or of an organization, shop, etc. owned collectively by members who share in its benefits —n. a cooperative society, shop, etc. —coop′eratively, co-op′eratively adv. —coop′erativeness, co-op′erativeness n.

cooperative society a commercial enterprise owned and managed by customers or workers, esp. a chain of shops in which profits are distributed to members of the society

co-opt (kō opt′) vt. [< L. co-, with + optare, choose] to add to a group by a vote of those already members —co′-op-ta′tion, co-op′tion n. —co-op′tative adj.

coordinate, co-ordinate (kō ôr′-də nət; also, and for v. always, -də nāt′) vt. -nat′ed, -nat′ing [< L. co-, with + ordo, order] 1. to bring into proper order or relation; adjust; harmonize 2. to make coordinate —n. 1. a coordinate person or thing 2. [pl.] clothes that harmonize or contrast in colour, texture, etc. 3. Math. any of two or more magnitudes used to define the position of a point, line, etc. —adj. 1. of equal order or importance **2.** of coordination or coordinates —**coor′dina′tion, co-or′dina′-tion** *n.* —**coor′dinative, co-or′dinative** *adj.* —**coor′dina′tor, co-or′dina′tor** *n.*

coot (ko͞ot) *n.* [< ? MDu. *koet*] **1.** a ducklike bird **2.** [Colloq.] a foolish or senile person

cop (kop) *vt.* **copped, cop′ping** [< ?] [Slang] **1.** to seize, win, steal, etc. **2.** to suffer, esp. a punishment *[to cop a clout]* —*n.* [Slang] **1.** a policeman **2.** an arrest, esp. in **a fair cop** —**cop it** to get into trouble and be punished —**cop out** [U.S. Slang] **1.** to confess to the police **2.** a) to renege b) to quit —**not much cop** of little worth or value

copal (ko͞o′pəl) *n.* [Sp. < SAmInd. *copalli*] a hard resin from tropical trees

copartner (ko͞o pärt′nər) *n.* a partner, or associate —**copart′nership** *n.*

cope[1] (ko͞op) *vi.* **coped, cop′ing** [< OFr. *coup*, a blow] **1.** to fight or contend (*with*) successfully or on equal terms **2.** to deal with problems, troubles, etc.

cope[2] *n.* [< L. *cappa*, cap] **1.** a large, capelike vestment worn by priests **2.** anything that covers like a cope, as a canopy —*vt.* **coped, cop′ing** to cover with a cope

Copernican system (ko͞o pur′ni kən) [< N. *Copernicus*, (1473-1543) Pol. astronomer] the theory that the planets revolve around the sun and that the earth rotates

copestone (ko͞op′ston) *n.* **1.** the top stone of a wall; stone in a coping **2.** a finishing touch Also **coping stone**

copier (ko͞op′e͞ər) *n.* **1.** one who copies; imitator, transcriber, etc. **2.** a duplicating machine

copilot (ko͞o′pi′lət) *n.* the assistant pilot of an aircraft

coping (ko͞o′piŋ) *n.* [< COPE²] the top layer of a masonry wall, usually sloped

COPING
SAW

coping saw a saw in a U-shaped frame, esp. for cutting curved outlines

copious (ko͞o′pe͞əs) *adj.* [< L. *copia*, abundance] plentiful; abundant —**co′pi-ously** *adv.* —**co′piousness** *n.*

copper[1] (kop′ər) *n.* [< LL. *cuprum* < Gr. *Kyprios*, Cyprus, noted for its copper mines] **1.** a reddish-brown, ductile, metallic element: symbol, Cu **2.** a copper coin, as an old penny **3.** reddish brown **4.** a large metal vessel, used esp. for boiling washing —*adj.* **1.** of copper **2.** reddish-brown —*vt.* to coat with copper —**cop′-pery** *adj.*

copper[2] *n.* [prob. < COP] [Slang] a policeman

copper beech a beech tree with coppery-coloured leaves

copper-bottomed *adj.* **1.** having the bottom sheathed with copper: said esp. of ships **2.** financially reliable

copperhead *n.* a poisonous N American pit viper with a copper-coloured head

copperplate *n.* **1.** a sheet of copper etched or engraved for printing **2.** a print made from this **3.** copperplate printing or engraving **4.** a fine style of handwriting based on that used for copperplate engravings

coppersmith *n.* a person whose work is making utensils, etc. out of copper

coppice (kop′is) *n.* [see COUP.] same as COPSE

copra (kop′rə) *n.* [Port. < Hindi *khoprā*] dried coconut kernel, the source of coconut oil

copse (kops) *n.* [< COPPICE] a thicket of small trees, undergrowth, and shrubs; coppice

Copt (kopt) *n.* **1.** a native of Egypt descended from the ancient Egyptians **2.** an Egyptian Christian

Coptic (kop′tik) *adj.* of the Copts, their language, etc. —*n.* the Afro-Asiatic language of the Copts

copula (kop′yoo lə) *n.,* *pl.* **-las** [< L. *co-*, together + *apere*, to join] something that connects or links together —**cop′u-lar** *adj.*

copulate (kop′yoo lāt′) *vi.* **-lat′ed, -lat′-ing** [see prec.] to have sexual intercourse —**cop′ula′tion** *n.*

copy (kop′e͞) *n.,* *pl.* **cop′ies** [< L. *copia*, plenty] **1.** a thing made just like another **2.** any of a number of books, magazines, etc. having the same printed matter **3.** a manuscript to be printed **4.** subject matter for a writer **5.** the words of an advertisement —*vt.,* *vi.* **cop′ied, cop′ying** **1.** to make a copy of **2.** to imitate

copybook *n.* a book with models of handwriting, for teaching penmanship —*adj.* ordinary; trite

copycat *n.* a person who habitually imitates or mimics: a child's term

copyhold *n.* *Law* tenure of property less than a freehold proved by a written transcript or record in the rolls of a manorial court —**cop′yhold′er** *n.*

copyist *n.* **1.** a person who makes written copies; transcriber **2.** a person who imitates

copyright *n.* the exclusive legal right to the publication, production, or sale of a literary, musical, or artistic work —*vt.* to protect (a book, etc.) by copyright —*adj.* protected by copyright

copy typist a typist who types from copy

copywriter *n.* a writer of copy for advertising or promotional material

coquette (ko ket′) *n.* [Fr. < *coq*, a cock] a girl or woman flirt —*vi.* **-quet′ted, -quet′-ting** to flirt —**co′quetry** *n.* —**coquet′tish** *adj.*

cor (kôr) *interj.* [< GOD] [Slang] an

exclamation of surprise, admiration, irritation, etc.

Cor. 1. Corinthians 2. Coroner

cor. cornet

coracle (kor′ə k'l) *n.* [< W. *corwg*] a small boat of waterproof material stretched over a wooden frame

CORAL
(A, organ-pipe; B, reef; C, mushroom; D, Bermuda)

coral (kor′əl) *n.* [< Gr. *korallion*] 1. the stony skeleton of some marine polyps, often in masses forming reefs and atolls in tropical seas 2. any of such polyps 3. a piece of coral 4. yellowish red : also **coral red** or **coral pink** —*adj.* 1. made of coral 2. coral-red

cor anglais (kôr äŋ′glä) *pl.* **cors anglais** [Fr.] a double-reed instrument of the woodwind family, similar to the oboe

corbel (kôr′bəl) *n.* [< L. *corvus*, raven] a bracket of stone, wood, etc. projecting from a wall to support a cornice, etc. —*vt.* **-belled**, **-belling** to provide with corbels

corbie (kôr′bē) *n.* [see prec.] [Scot.] a crow or raven

cord (kôrd) *n.* [< Gr. *chordē*] 1. thick string 2. *a)* a rib on the surface of a fabric *b)* [*pl.*] corduroy trousers *c)* [*pl.*] corduroy trousers 3. any force acting as a tie or bond 4. *Anat.* any part like a cord [the spinal cord] 5. *Elec. U.S.* var. of FLEX² 6. a measure of wood cut for fuel (128 cubic feet, c. 3.6m³) —*vt.* 1. to fasten with a cord 2. to stack (wood) in cords

cordate (kôr′dāt) *adj.* [< L. *cor, cordis*, heart] heart-shaped —**cor′dately** *adv.*

cordial (kôr′dē əl) *adj.* [see prec.] warm and friendly; hearty —*n.* a drink with a fruit base —**cor′dially** *adv.* —**cor′dialness** *n.*

cordiality (kôr′dē al′ə tē) *n.* 1. a warm, friendly feeling 2. *pl.* **-ties** a cordial act or remark

cordite (kôr′dīt) *n.* [< CORD] a smokeless explosive

cordless (kôrd′lis) *adj.* operated by batteries rather than by current from an outlet

cordon (kôr′d'n) *n.* [see CORD] 1. a line or circle of police, ships, etc. stationed around an area to guard it 2. a cord, ribbon, or braid worn as a decoration —*vt.* to encircle or shut (*off*) with a cordon

‡**cordon bleu** (kôr dôn blö′) [Fr.] any very high distinction, esp. in cookery —*adj.* of food prepared to a very high standard

cordovan (kôr′də vən) *n.* [< Sp. *Cordoba*, in Spain] a fined-grained leather, usually of split horsehide

corduroy (kôr′də roi′) *n.* [< CORD] 1.

a heavy, ribbed cotton fabric 2. [*pl.*] trousers made of this —*adj.* 1. made of, or ribbed like, corduroy 2. made of logs laid crosswise [a corduroy road]

cordwainer (kôrd′wān ər) *n.* [< CORDOVAN] [Archaic] a shoemaker or worker in cordovan leather

core (kôr) *n.* [prob. < L. *cor*, heart] 1. the central part of an apple, pear, etc. 2. the central part of anything 3. the most important part 4. the centre of a nuclear reactor that contains the fissionable fuel 5. *Computers* a ferrite ring used to store one bit of information 6. *Elec.* a mass of iron inside a wire coil : it increases the magnetic field —*vt.* **cored**, **cor′ing** to remove the core of —**cor′er** *n.*

co-respondent (kō′ri spon′dənt) *n.* [CO- + RESPONDENT] *Law* a person charged with having committed adultery with the wife or husband from whom a divorce is being sought —**co′respond′ency** *n.*

corgi (kôr′gē) *n.* [< W. *cor(r)*, dwarf + *ci*, dog] a short-legged dog with a foxlike head, orig. from Wales

coriander (kor′ē an′dər) *n.* [< Gr. *koriandron*] 1. an umbelliferous herb 2. its strong-smelling, seedlike fruit, used in flavouring

CORINTHIAN
CAPITAL

Corinthian (kə rin′thē ən) *adj.* 1. of Corinth, its people, or culture 2. dissolute and loving luxury 3. designating or of an order of Greek architecture, distinguished by a bell-shaped capital with a design of acanthus leaves —*n.* a native or inhabitant of Corinth

cork (kôrk) *n.* [< Sp. *corcho* < ?] 1. the light, thick, elastic outer bark of an oak tree 2. a piece of cork; esp., a stopper for a bottle, etc. 3. any stopper 4. the outer bark of woody plants —*adj.* made of cork —*vt.* 1. to stop with a cork 2. to restrain 3. to blacken with burnt cork

corkage *n.* a charge made for serving wine, etc., esp. if bought off the premises

corked (kôrkt) *adj.* 1. stopped up with a cork 2. tainted by the cork : said esp. of wine

corker (kôr′kər) *n.* [Slang] a remarkable person or thing

corkscrew (kôrk′skrōō′) *n.* a spiral-shaped device for pulling corks out of bottles —*adj.* shaped like a corkscrew —*vi., vt.* to move in a spiral; twist

corm (kôrm) *n.* [< Gr. *kormos*, a lopped tree trunk] the fleshy, scaly, underground stem of certain plants, as the gladiolus

cormorant (kôr′mə rənt) *n.* [< L. *corvus*, raven + *marinus*, marine] 1. a large, voracious, diving bird with webbed toes 2. a greedy person

corn[1] (kôrn) *n.* [OE.] **1.** a small, hard seed, esp. of a cereal grass; kernel **2.** the seeds of all cereal grasses; grain **3.** the leading cereal crop, as wheat in England or oats in Scotland **4.** [U.S.] maize **5.** [Colloq.] ideas, music, etc. considered trite, sentimental, etc. —*vt.* to pickle (meat, etc.) in brine

corn[2] *n.* [< L. *cornu*, a horn] a hard, thick, painful growth of skin, esp. on a toe

corncob *n.* the woody core of an ear of maize

corn-crake *n.* a brown, short-billed rail

cornea (kôr′nē ə) *n.* [< L. *cornu*, a horn] the transparent outer coat of the eyeball —**cor′neal** *adj.*

corned (kôrnd) *adj.* preserved with salt or brine [*corned* beef]

cornel (kôr′n′l) *n.* [< L. *cornus*] a small tree with very hard wood, as the dogwood, cornelian cherry, etc.

cornelian (kôr nēl′yən) *n.* [< L. *cornu*, a horn] a red variety of chalcedony, used in jewellery

corner (kôr′nər) *n.* [< L. *cornu*, a horn] **1.** the point or place where lines or surfaces join and form an angle **2.** the space within the angle formed **3.** the angle formed at a street intersection **4.** something used to form, protect, or decorate a corner **5.** a remote or secluded spot **6.** region; quarter [every *corner* of the world] **7.** an awkward position from which escape is difficult **8.** a monopoly acquired on a stock or commodity **9.** *Sports* a free kick taken from the corner of the field in football and hockey: also **corner kick, corner hit** —*vt.* **1.** to force into an awkward position **2.** to get a monopoly on —*vi.* to turn corners: said of a vehicle : at, on, or for a corner —**cut corners** to economize on time, effort, etc., esp. at the expense of quality —**cor′nered** *adj.*

cornerstone *n.* **1.** a stone laid in the corner of a building, esp. at a ceremony for beginning a building **2.** the basic part; foundation

cornet (kôr′nət) *n.* [< L. *cornu*, a horn] **1.** a brass musical instrument similar to the trumpet **2.** a cone-shaped wafer for holding ice cream **3.** formerly, a cavalry officer —**cornet′ist** *n.*

corn exchange a place where grain is sold

cornflakes *n.pl.* a breakfast cereal of crisp flakes made from hulled maize

cornflour *n.* a finely ground starchy flour made from maize, corn, etc.; used esp. for thickening sauces

cornflower *n.* a plant with white, pink, or blue flowers

cornice (kôr′nis) *n.* [< Gr. *korōnis*, a wreath] **1.** a horizontal moulding projecting along the top of a wall, etc. **2.** the top part of an entablature

Cornish (kôr′nish) *adj.* of Cornwall, its people, or culture —*n.* the Brythonic Celtic language spoken in Cornwall until c. 1800

Cornish pasty same as PASTY[2]

CORNUCOPIA

cornucopia (kôr′nyoo kō′pē ə) *n.* [L. *cornu copiae*, horn of plenty] **1.** a representation of a horn overflowing with fruits, flowers, and grain; horn of plenty **2.** an abundance

corny (kôr′nē) *adj.* **-ier, -iest** [Colloq.] unsophisticated, trite, sentimental, etc. —**corn′iness** *n.*

corolla (kə rol′ə) *n.* [< L. *corona*, crown] the petals, or inner floral leaves, of a flower —**corollate** (kor′ə lāt′), **cor′ollat′ed** *adj.*

corollary (kə rol′ər ē) *n., pl.* **-laries** [see prec.] **1.** a proposition that follows from another that has been proved **2.** an inference or deduction **3.** a normal result

corona (kə rō′nə) *n., pl.* **-nas, -nae** (-nē) [L., crown] **1.** *Astron.* a) a ring of coloured light round the sun or moon b) the outermost part of the sun's atmosphere, seen during a total eclipse **2.** *Bot.* the cuplike part on the inner side of the corolla of certain flowers **3.** *Anat.* the upper part of a tooth, skull, etc. **4.** *Elec.* a sometimes visible electric discharge around a conductor —**coro′nal** *adj.*

coronary (kor′ə nər ē) *adj.* [see CORONA] of the arteries supplying blood to the heart muscle —*n., pl.* **-naries** same as CORONARY THROMBOSIS

coronary thrombosis the formation of an obstructing clot in a coronary artery: also **coronary occlusion**

coronation (kor′ə nā′shən) *n.* [< L. *corona*, crown] the act of crowning a sovereign

coroner (kor′ə nər) *n.* [ME. < L. *corona*, crown] a public officer whose chief duty is to determine by inquest before a jury the causes of any deaths not obviously due to natural causes —**cor′onership′** *n.*

coronet (kor′ə net′) *n.* [< OFr. *corone*, crown] **1.** a small crown worn by nobility **2.** a band, as of jewels or flowers, worn around the head —**cor′onet′ed** *adj.*

corporal[1] (kôr′pər əl) *n.* [< L. *caput*, head] see MILITARY RANKS, table

corporal[2] *adj.* [< L. *corpus*, body] of the body —**cor′poral′ity** (kôr′pə ral′ə tē) *n.* —**cor′porally** *adv.*

corporal punishment punishment inflicted directly on the body, as flogging

corporate (kôr′pər ət) *adj.* [< L. *corpus*, body] **1.** incorporated **2.** of a corporation **3.** shared by all in a group —**cor′porately** *adv.*

corporation (kôr′pə rā′shən) *n.* **1.** a

group of people with a charter granting them certain of the legal powers, rights, and liabilities of an individual **2.** a group of people, as the municipal authorities of a town or city, legally authorized to act as an individual **3.** [Colloq.] a pot belly —**cor′porative** *adj.* —**cor′pora′tor** *n.*

corporeal (kôr pôr′ē əl) *adj.* [< L. *corpus*, body] **1.** of or for the body **2.** material; physical —**corpo′real′ity** (-al′ə tē) *n.* —**corpo′really** *adv.*

corps (kôr) *n.*, *pl.* **corps** (kôrz) [< L. *corpus*, body] **1.** a body of people associated in some work, organization, etc. **2.** *Mil.* a) a specialized branch of the armed forces b) a tactical subdivision of an army

corps de ballet (kôr′də ba lā′) [Fr.] the members of a ballet company

corps diplomatique (dip′lō ma tēk′) the body of diplomatic officials accredited to foreign governments

corpse (kôrps) *n.* [var. of CORPS] **1.** a dead body, esp. of a person **2.** something lifeless and of no use

corpulence (kôr′pyoo ləns) *n.* [< L. *corpus*, body] fatness; obesity: also **cor′pulency** —**cor′pulent** *adj.*

corpus (kôr′pəs) *n.*, *pl.* **-pora** (-pər ə) [L.] **1.** a body; esp., a dead one **2.** a complete collection, as of writings of a specified type **3.** the substance of anything

corpuscle (kôr′pus′'l) *n.* [< L. *corpus*, body] **1.** a very small particle **2.** any of the erythrocytes (**red corpuscles**) or leucocytes (**white corpuscles**) in the blood, lymph, etc. of vertebrates: also **corpuscule** (kôr′pus′kyool) —**corpus′cular** (-kyoo lər) *adj.*

corr. 1. correspondence **2.** corresponding

corral (kə räl′) *n.* [Sp. < L. *currere*, to run] an enclosure for holding or capturing horses, cattle, etc.; pen —*vt.* **-ralled′, -ral′ling 1.** to drive into or confine in a corral **2.** to surround or capture; round up

corrasion (kə rā′zhən) *n.* [< L. *corradere*, scrape together] *Geol.* the erosion of rock by the action of running water or glacial ice

correct (kə rekt′) *vt.* [< L. *com-*, together + *regere*, lead straight] **1.** to make right **2.** to mark the errors of **3.** to make conform to a standard **4.** to scold or punish **5.** to cure or counteract —*adj.* **1.** conforming to an established standard; proper **2.** true; accurate; right —**correc′tive** *adj., n.* —**correct′ly** *adv.* —**correct′ness** *n.* —**correc′tor** *n.*

correction *n.* **1.** a correcting or being corrected **2.** a change that corrects a mistake; rectification **3.** punishment to correct faults —**correc′tional** *adj.*

correlate (kôr′ə lāt′) *n.* [see COM- + RELATE] either of two interrelated things —*adj.* closely and naturally related —*vi., vt.* **-lat′ed, -lat′ing** to be in or bring into mutual relation —**cor′rela′tion** *n.*

correlative (kə rel′ə tiv) *adj.* **1.** having a mutual relationship **2.** *Gram.* expressing mutual relation and used in pairs [*neither . . . nor* are *correlative* conjunctions] —*n.*

1. a correlate **2.** a correlative word —**correl′atively** *adv.* —**correl′ativ′ity** *n.*

correspond (kor′ə spond′) *vi.* [< L. *com-*, together + *respondere*, answer] **1.** to be in agreement (*with* something); match **2.** to be similar or equal (*to*) **3.** to communicate by letters —**cor′respond′ingly** *adv.*

correspondence *n.* **1.** agreement; conformity **2.** similarity; analogy **3.** a) communication by exchange of letters b) the letters written or received

correspondence school a school that gives courses of instruction (**correspondence courses**) by post

correspondent *adj.* corresponding —*n.* **1.** a person who exchanges letters with another **2.** a person hired as by a newspaper to send news regularly from a distant place or write on a special subject

corridor (kor′ə dôr′) *n.* [< L. *currere*, to run] **1.** a long passageway or hall **2.** a strip of land providing passage through foreign-held land **3.** a passageway connecting all the compartments of a railway carriage

corridors of power the Civil Service, etc. considered as a source of influence in administrative decisions

corrie (kor′ē) *n.* [< ScotGael. *coire*, cauldron] [Scot.] a round hollow in a hillside; cirque

corrigendum (kor′ə jen′dəm) *n.*, *pl.* **-da** [L.; see CORRECT] an error to be corrected in a printed work, or [*pl.*] a list of such errors inserted in the work

corrigible (kor′i jə b'l) *adj.* [see CORRECT] capable of being corrected or reformed —**cor′rigibly** *adv.*

corroborate (kə rob′ə rāt′) *vt.* **-rat′ed, -rat′ing** [< L. *com-*, intens. + *robur*, strength] to confirm; bolster; support —**corrob′ora′tion** *n.* —**corrob′ora′tor** *n.*

corroborative (-er ə tiv) *adj.* corroborating; confirmatory: also **corrob′oratory** —**corrob′oratively** *adv.*

corroboree (kə rob′ə rē) *n.* [Abor.] [Aust.] **1.** an Aboriginal festival **2.** any noisy celebration

corrode (kə rōd′) *vt., vi.* **-rod′ed, -rod′ing** [< L. *com-*, intens. + *rodere*, gnaw] to eat into or wear away gradually, as by rusting —**corrod′ible** *adj.*

corrosion (kə rō′zhən) *n.* **1.** a corroding **2.** a substance formed by corroding —**corro′sive** *adj.*

corrugate (kor′oo gāt′) *vt., vi.* **-gat′ed, -gat′ing** [< L. *com-*, intens. + *rugare*, to wrinkle] to shape into parallel grooves and ridges; furrow [*corrugated* iron] —**cor′ruga′tion** *n.*

corrupt (kə rupt′) *adj.* [< L. *com-*, together + *rumpere*, to break] **1.** morally debased; evil; depraved **2.** taking bribes **3.** containing alterations or errors [a *corrupt* text] —*vt., vi.* to make or become corrupt —**corrupt′er, corrup′tor** *n.* —**corrup′tive** *adj.*

corruptible *adj.* that can be corrupted, esp. morally —**corrupt′ibil′ity** *n.* —**corrupt′ibly** *adv.*

corruption *n.* 1. a making or being corrupt 2. depravity 3. bribery 4. decay 5. something corrupted

corsage (kôr säzh′) *n.* [Fr.: see CORPS] a small bouquet for a woman to wear, as at the waist or shoulder

corsair (kôr′sâr) *n.* [< L. *cursus*, course] 1. a privateer 2. a pirate 3. a pirate ship

corselet (kôrs′lət) *n.* [see ff.] 1. a medieval piece of body armour: also sp. **cors′let** 2. a woman's lightweight corset: also sp. cor′**selette**′

corset (kôr′sit) *n.* [see CORPS] [*sometimes pl.*] a closefitting undergarment worn, chiefly by women, to give support to or shape the torso —**cor′-setry** *n.*

cortège (kôr tāzh′) *n.* [Fr. < L.: see COURT] a ceremonial procession, as at a funeral

cortex (kôr′teks) *n., pl.* **-tices** (-tə sēz′) [L., bark of a tree] 1. *a*) the outer part of an internal organ, as of the kidney *b*) the layer of grey matter over most of the brain 2. the bark or rind of a plant —**cor′tical** *adj.*

corticate (kôr′ti kit) *adj.* [< CORTEX] covered with bark: also **cor′ticat′ed, cor′-ticose′**

cortisone (kôrt′ə zōn′) *n.* [< chem. name] an adrenal-gland hormone used in treating various inflammatory and allergic diseases

corundum (kə run′dəm) *n.* [Tamil *kurundam*, ruby] a hard mineral, aluminium oxide, used for grinding and polishing: the ruby, sapphire, etc. are precious varieties

coruscate (kor′əs kāt′) *vt.* **-cat′ed, -cat′-ing** [< L. *coruscus*, vibrating] to glitter; sparkle —**coruscant** (kə rus′kənt) *adj.* —**cor′usca′tion** *n.*

corvette (kôr vet′) *n.* [ult. < L. *corbis*, basket] 1. formerly, a warship smaller than a frigate 2. a small, fast warship used for antisubmarine and convoy duty

corymb (kor′imb) *n.* [< Gr. *korymbos*] a broad, flat cluster of flowers in which the outer stems are long and those towards the centre progressively shorter —**corymbose** (kə rim′bōs), **corym′bous** *adj.*

coryza (kə rī′zə) *n.* [< Gr. *koryza*, catarrh] a cold in the head; acute nasal congestion

cos¹ cosine

cos² (kos) *n.* [< Aegean island] a kind of lettuce with long leaves: also **cos lettuce**

'cos (kos) *conj.* [Colloq.] because: also **cos**

cosec cosecant

cosecant (kō sē′kənt) *n.* *Trigonometry* the ratio between the hypotenuse and the side opposite a given acute angle in a right-angled triangle

cosh (kosh) *n.* [< Romany *koshter*, skewer] [Slang] a blunt weapon, often made from hard rubber; bludgeon —*vt.* [Slang] to strike with a cosh

cosign (kō′sīn′) *vt., vi.* 1. to sign (a promissory note) in addition to the maker, thus becoming responsible if the maker should default 2. to sign jointly —**co′sign′-er** *n.*

cosignatory (kō sig′nə tər ē) *adj.* signing jointly —*n., pl.* **-ries** one of two or more joint signers

cosine (kō′sīn) *n.* *Trigonometry* the ratio between the side adjacent to a given acute angle in a right-angled triangle and the hypotenuse

cosmetic (koz met′ik) *adj.* [< Gr. *kosmos*, order] 1. designed to beautify the complexion, hair, etc. 2. for improving the appearance by correcting deformities —*n.* any cosmetic preparation for the skin, hair, etc. —**cosmet′ically** *adv.*

cosmic (koz′mik) *adj.* [< Gr. *kosmos*, order] 1. of the cosmos 2. vast —**cos′mically** *adv.*

cosmo- [see COSMOS] *a combining form meaning* world, universe [*cosmology*]

cosmogony (koz mog′ə nē) *n.* [< Gr. *kosmos*, universe + *gignesthai*, produce] 1. the origin of the universe 2. *pl.* **-nies** a theory or account of this —**cos′mogon′-ic** (-mə gon′ik), —**cosmog′onist** *n.*

cosmology (koz mol′ə jē) *n.* [COSMO- + -LOGY] the study of the universe as a whole and of its form, nature, etc. as a physical system —**cosmol′ogist** *n.*

cosmonaut (koz′mə nôt′) *n.* [Russ. < COSMO- + Gr. *nautēs*, sailor] an astronaut, esp. a Russian astronaut

cosmopolitan (koz′mə pol′ət'n) *adj.* [< COSMO- + Gr. *polis*, city] 1. representative of all or many parts of the world 2. at home in all countries or places —*n.* a cosmopolitan person —**cos′mopol′itan-ism** *n.*

cosmos (koz′mos) *n.* [Gr. *kosmos*, universe] 1. the universe considered as a harmonious and orderly system 2. any complete and orderly system

Cossack (kos′ak) *n.* a member of a people of S Russia, famous as horsemen —*adj.* of the Cossacks

cosset (kos′it) *vt.* [< ? OE. *cot-sæta*, cot dweller] to make a pet of; pamper —*n.* a pet lamb, or any small pet

cost (kost) *vt.* **cost** or, for 2, **cost′ed, cost′-ing** [< L. *com-*, together + *stare*, to stand] 1. *a*) to be obtained for (a certain price) *b*) to require the expenditure, loss, etc. of 2. *Business* to estimate the cost of producing —*n.* 1. the amount of money, effort, etc. required to obtain or produce something 2. loss; sacrifice 3. [*pl.*] *Law* court expenses of a lawsuit —**at all costs** regardless of the cost or difficulty involved

costal (kos′t'l) *adj.* [< L. *costa*, rib] of or near a rib

costermonger (kos′tər muŋ′gər) *n.* [< *costard*, kind of apple + MONGER] a person who sells fruit or vegetables from a barrow: also **cos′ter**

costive (kos′tiv) *adj.* [see CONSTIPATE] constipated or constipating —**cos′tively** *adv.* —**cos′tiveness** *n.*

costly (kost′lē) *adj.* **-lier, -liest** 1. costing much; dear 2. magnificent; sumptuous —**cost′liness** *n.*

cost of living the average cost of the necessities of life, as food, shelter, and clothes

costume (kos'tyōōm) *n.* [< L. *consuetudo*, custom] **1.** *a)* the style of dress typical of a certain period, people, etc. *b)* a set of such clothes **2.** a set of outer clothes —*vt.* **-tumed, -tuming** to provide with a costume

costumier (kos tyōōm'ē ər) *n.* one who makes, sells, or rents costumes

cosy (kō'zē) *adj.* **-sier, -siest** [< ?] warm and comfortable; snug —*n.*, *pl.* **-sies** a knitted or padded cover to keep a teapot or egg hot —**co'sily** *adv.* —**co'siness** *n.*

cot¹ (kot) *n.* [< Hindi *khāṭ*] **1.** a small bed with high sides for a baby **2.** a narrow, canvas bed.

cot² *n.* [OE.] **1.** [Poet.] a cottage **2.** a cote

cot³ cotangent

cotangent (kō tan'jənt) *n.* Trigonometry the ratio between the side adjacent to a given acute angle in a right-angled triangle and the side opposite

C.O.T.C. Canadian Officers Training Corps

cot death the unexplained, sudden death of a sleeping infant

cote (kōt) *n.* [ME., COT²] a shelter for sheep, doves, etc.

coterie (kōt'ər ē) *n.* [Fr.: see COTTER¹] a close circle of friends with common interests; clique

cottage (kot'ij) *n.* [< OFr. *cote* or ME. *cot*, hut] **1.** a small house in a rural area **2.** [Aust.] a one-storey house —**cot'-tager** *n.*

cottage cheese a soft, white cheese made by straining and seasoning the curds of sour milk

cottage industry an industry in which employees work in their own homes, often using their own equipment

cotter¹, cottar (kot'ər) *n.* [see COT²] [Scot.] a farm-worker who occupies a cottage rent-free

cotter² *n.* [< ?] a bolt or wedge put through a slot to hold together parts of machinery

COTTER PIN

cotter pin a split pin used as a cotter, fastened in place by spreading apart its ends after it is inserted

cotton (kot''n) *n.* [< Ar. *quṭun*] **1.** the soft, white seed hairs of various plants **2.** a plant producing this material **3.** thread or cloth made of cotton —*adj.* of cotton —**cotton on to** [Colloq.] **1.** to take a liking to **2.** to become aware of (a situation) —**cot'tony** *adj.*

cotton gin [see GIN²] a machine for separating cotton fibres from the seeds

cotton wool **1.** fluffy absorbent cotton, used for surgical dressings, etc. **2.** raw cotton

cotyledon (kot'ə lēd'n) *n.* [< Gr. *kotylē*, cavity] the first leaf produced by the embryo of a flowering plant —**cot'yle'don-ous, cot'yle'donal** *adj.*

couch (kouch) *n.* [< OFr. < L. *com-*, together + *locare*, to place] **1.** an article of furniture on which one may sit or lie down; sofa **2.** any resting place —*vt.* **1.** to put in words; express **2.** to lay as on a couch **3.** to bring down; esp., to lower (a spear, etc.) to an attacking position —*vi.* **1.** to recline **2.** to lie in hiding

couch grass (kouch) [var. of QUITCH] a weedy grass that spreads rapidly by its underground stems

cougar (kōō'gər) *n.* [< Tupi] same as PUMA

cough (kof) *vi.*, *vt.* [ME. *coughen*] to expel (air) suddenly and noisily from the lungs —*n.* **1.** a coughing **2.** a condition, as of the lungs, causing frequent coughing —**cough up** **1.** to bring up (phlegm, etc.) by coughing **2.** [Slang] to hand over (money, etc.) —**cough'er** *n.*

cough mixture a medicine for the relief of coughs

could (kood) *v.* **1.** *pt.* of CAN¹ **2.** an auxiliary generally equivalent to *can*, expressing esp. a shade of doubt

coulomb (kōō'lom) *n.* [< *Coulomb*, Fr. physicist] the SI unit of electric charge

coulter (kōl'tər) *n.* [< L. *culter*, ploughshare] a blade on a plough, for making vertical cuts in the soil

council (koun's'l) *n.* [< L. *com-*, with + *calere*, to call] **1.** a group of people called together for consultation, advice, etc. **2.** an administrative or legislative assembly

council house a dwelling built by a local council and often let at a subsidized rent

councillor (koun'sə lər) *n.* a member of a council, esp. of a city or town —**coun'cil-lorship'** *n.*

counsel (koun's'l) *n.* [< L. *consilium*, meeting] **1.** a mutual exchange of ideas, opinions, etc.; discussion **2.** advice **3.** *a)* a lawyer *b)* a barrister —*vt.* **-selled, -sel-ling** **1.** to advise **2.** to urge the acceptance of (a plan, etc.) —**keep one's own counsel** to keep one's thoughts, plans, etc. to oneself

counsellor *n.* **1.** an adviser **2.** [U.S.] a lawyer —**coun'sellorship'** *n.*

count¹ (kount) *vt.* [< L. *computare*, compute] **1.** to name numbers in regular order to (a certain number) [to *count* to five] **2.** to add up, so as to get a total **3.** to check by numbering off **4.** to include **5.** to believe to be [to *count* oneself lucky] —*vi.* **1.** to name numbers or items in order **2.** to have importance, value, etc. **3.** to have a specified value (often with *for*) **4.** to rely or depend (*on* or *upon*) —*n.* **1.** a counting, or adding up **2.** a total reached by counting **3.** a reckoning **4.** Law any of the charges in an indictment —**count out** **1.** to disregard; omit **2.** to end a Parliamentary sitting when there is not a quorum of members present **3.** Boxing to declare (a boxer) defeated when he has remained down for a count of ten —**out for the count** unconscious, esp. because of exhaustion —**count'able** *adj.*

count[2] *n.* [< L. *comes*, companion] a nobleman equal in rank to an English earl

countdown *n.* the counting backwards of units of time, esp. before the firing of a rocket

countenance (koun'tə nəns) *n.* [< L. *continentia*, bearing] 1. facial expression 2. the face 3. approval; support 4. composure, esp. in **keep** (or **lose**) **one's countenance** —*vt.* -**nanced, -nancing** to approve —**put out of countenance** to disconcert

counter[1] (koun'tər) *n.* [see COUNT[1]] 1. a long table, board, etc., as in a shop for the display of goods, serving of food, etc. 2. a small piece of metal, wood, etc., used in some games 3. an imitation coin 4. a person or thing that counts —**under the counter** in a surreptitious manner: said of illegal sales

counter[2] *adv.* [< L. *contra*, against] in a contrary direction, manner, etc. —*adj.* acting in opposition —*n.* 1. the opposite 2. an opposing action 3. a stiff leather piece around the heel of a shoe 4. the part of a ship's stern between the waterline and the curved part 5. *Boxing, Fencing, etc.* a blow given while parrying an opponent's blow —*vt., vi.* 1. to oppose or check (a person or thing) 2. to say or do (something) in reply 3. *Boxing* to strike one's opponent while parrying (his blow)

counter- [< L. *contra-*, against] a combining form meaning: 1. opposite [*counterculture*] 2. in retaliation [*counterplot*] 3. complementary [*counterpart*]

counteract (koun'tər akt') *vt.* to act against; neutralize the effect of with opposing action —**coun'terac'tion** *n.*

counterattack (koun'tər ə tak') *n.* an attack made in opposition to another attack —*vt., vi.* to attack so as to offset the enemy's attack

counterbalance (koun'tər bal'əns) *n.* a weight, force, or influence that balances or offsets another —*vt.* -**anced, -ancing** to be a counterbalance to; offset

counterclockwise (koun'tər klok'wīz) *adj., adv.* [U.S.] anticlockwise

counterespionage (koun'tər es'pē ə näzh') *n.* actions to prevent or thwart enemy espionage

counterfeit (koun'tər fit) *adj.* [< OFr. *contre-*, counter- + *faire*, make] 1. made in imitation of something genuine so as to defraud; forged [*counterfeit* money] 2. pretended; sham —*n.* an imitation made to deceive —*vt., vi.* 1. to make an imitation of (money, etc.) in order to defraud 2. to pretend 3. to resemble closely —**coun'terfeit'er** *n.*

counterfoil *n.* [COUNTER- + FOIL[2]] the stub of a cheque, receipt, etc. kept by the issuer as a record

counterintelligence *n.* actions to counter enemy intelligence or espionage activity, prevent sabotage, etc.

countermand (koun'tər mänd') *vt.* [< L. *contra*, against + *mandare*, command] 1. to cancel (a command) 2. to call back by a contrary order —*n.* a command or order cancelling another

countermarch *n.* a march back or in the opposite direction —*vi., vt.* to march back

countermeasure *n.* action taken to oppose, neutralize, or retaliate against some other action

counterpane (koun'tər pān') *n.* [ult. < L. *culcita puncta*, pricked (i.e., embroidered) quilt] a bedspread

counterpart *n.* 1. a person or thing that closely resembles or complements another 2. a duplicate

counterpoint *n.* [< It.: see COUNTER- & POINT] 1. a melody accompanying another melody 2. the art of adding related but independent melodies to a basic melody, in accordance with the fixed rules of harmony

counterpoise *n.* [see COUNTER[2] & POISE] 1. *same as* COUNTERBALANCE 2. a state of balance —*vt.* -**poised', -pois'ing** *same as* COUNTERBALANCE

counterproductive *adj.* bringing about effects or results that are contrary to those intended

countersign (koun'tər sīn') *n.* 1. a signature added to a previously signed document for confirmation 2. *Mil.* a secret signal which must be given to a sentry by someone wishing to pass —*vt.* to confirm by signing —**coun'tersig'nature** *n.*

countersink (koun'tər siŋk') *vt.* -**sunk', -sink'ing** 1. to enlarge the top part of (a hole in metal, wood, etc.) to make the head of a bolt, screw, etc. fit into it 2. to sink (a bolt, screw, etc.) into such a hole

countertenor (koun'tər ten'ər) *n.* 1. the range of the highest mature male voice, above tenor 2. a voice, singer, or part with such a range

countervail (koun'tər vāl') *vt.* [< COUNTER[2] + L. *valere*, to be strong] 1. to compensate 2. to counteract —*vi.* to avail (*against*)

counterweigh (koun'tər wā') *vt.* *same as* COUNTERBALANCE —**coun'terweight'** *n.*

countess (koun'tis) *n.* 1. the wife or widow of a count or earl 2. a noblewoman whose rank is equal to that of a count or earl

countless (kount'lis) *adj.* too many to count

countrified (kun'tri fid') *adj.* 1. rural; rustic 2. having the appearance, actions, etc. attributed to country people Also sp. **coun'tryfied'**

country (kun'trē) *n., pl.* -**tries** [< L. *contra*, opposite] 1. an area; region 2. the whole territory or people of a nation 3. the land of a person's birth or citizenship 4. land with farms and small towns; rural region 5. the area associated with a poet, novelist, etc. [Burns *country*] —*adj.* rural;

rustic —**go to the country** to dissolve Parliament and hold an election

country club a social club in the country or on the outskirts of a city, with a clubhouse, golf course, etc.

country-dance *n.* an English folk dance, esp. one in which partners form two facing lines

country house a residence in the country, esp. of someone who also owns a residence in town

countryman *n.* 1. a man who lives in the country; rustic 2. a man of one's own country; compatriot —**coun'trywom'-an** *n.fem.*

countryside *n.* a rural region or its inhabitants

county (koun'tē) *n., pl.* -ties [< ML. *comitatus,* jurisdiction of a count] 1. a small administrative district; esp., *a)* a unit of local government in England and Wales *b)* the largest local administrative unit of most states in the U.S. 2. the people in a county, esp. the upper-class families

county council the governing body composed of the elected representatives of the ratepayers of a county

county town a town or city that is the seat of government of a county

coup (kōō) *n., pl.* **coups** (kōōz) [Fr. < Gr. *kolaphos,* a blow] 1. a sudden, successful move or action; brilliant stroke 2. same as COUP D'ÉTAT

‡**coup de grâce** (kōō də gräs') [Fr., lit., stroke of mercy] a finishing stroke

‡**coup d'état** (dā tä') [Fr., lit., stroke of state] the sudden, forcible overthrow of a government

coupé (kōō'pā) *n.* [Fr., *couper,* to cut] a closed, two-door motor car, usually with a sloping back

couple (kup''l) *n.* [< L. *copula,* a link] 1. a man and a woman who are engaged, married, or partners in a dance, etc. 2. two things or persons of the same sort that are somehow associated 3. anything joining two things together; link 4. [Colloq.] a few —*vt.* -**pled,** -**pling** to join together —*vi.* 1. to come together 2. to copulate

couplet (kup'lit) *n.* two successive lines of poetry, esp. two of the same length that rhyme

COUPLING

coupling (kup'liŋ) *n.* 1. a joining together 2. a mechanical device for joining parts or things together

coupon (kōō'pon) *n.* [Fr. < *couper,* to cut] 1. a certificate giving a specified right, as reduced purchase price 2. a part of a printed advertisement for use in ordering goods, etc. 3. a detachable statement on a bond, specifying the interest

due 4. the entry form for various competitions

courage (kur'ij) *n.* [< L. *cor,* heart] a willingness to face and deal with danger, trouble, or pain; fearlessness; bravery; valour

courageous (kə rā'jəs) *adj.* having or showing courage; brave —**coura'geously** *adv.* —**coura'geousness** *n.*

coureur de bois (kōō rēr də bwä') [Fr., runner of the woods] *Canad. Hist.* a French-Canadian woodsman who traded with Indians for furs

courgette (kōōər'zhet') *n.* a variety of marrow that is green-skinned and shaped somewhat like a cucumber

courier (kōōr'ē ər) *n.* [ult. < L. *currere,* to run] 1. a messenger sent with important or urgent messages 2. a person who makes arrangements for, or accompanies, a group of travellers on a journey

course (kôrs) *n.* [< L. *currere,* to run] 1. an onward movement; progress 2. a way, path, or channel 3. the direction taken 4. a regular manner of procedure [the law must take its *course*] 5. *a)* a series of like things in order *b)* a particular succession of events 6. natural development [the *course* of true love] 7. a part of a meal served at one time 8. a horizontal layer, as of bricks, in a building 9. *Educ.* a complete series of lectures, etc., as leading to a degree —*vt.* **coursed, cours'ing** 1. to pursue 2. to cause (esp. hounds) to chase —*vi.* 1. to run or race 2. to hunt with hounds —**in due course** in the usual or proper sequence (of events) —**of course** 1. as is or was to be expected 2. certainly —**on** (or **off**) **course** moving (or not moving) in the intended direction

courser (kôr'sər) *n.* [see prec.] [Poet.] a graceful, spirited, or swift horse

coursing *n.* hunting with dogs trained to follow game, esp. hares, by sight rather than by scent

court (kôrt) *n.* [< L. *cohors,* enclosure] 1. an uncovered space surrounded by buildings or walls 2. a short street 3. an area for playing any of several ball games 4. *a)* the palace of a sovereign *b)* the family, advisers, etc. of a sovereign *c)* a sovereign and his councillors as a governing body *d)* any formal gathering held by a sovereign 5. attention paid to someone in order to get something 6. courtship; wooing 7. *a)* a judge or judges *b)* a place where trials are held, investigations made, etc. *c)* a judicial assembly —*vt.* 1. to pay attention to (a person) in order to get something 2. to try to get the love of; woo 3. to seek [to *court* favour] 4. to make oneself open to [to *court* insults] —*vi.* to woo —*adj.* of or fit for a court —**hold court** to officiate or preside over a group of one's admirers —**laugh out of court** to ridicule completely —**out of court** without a trial —**court'er** *n.*

court card any king, queen, or jack in a pack of cards

courteous (kur'tē əs) *adj.* [see COURT]

polite and gracious —**cour'teously** *adv.*
—**cour'teousness** *n.*

courtesan (kôr'tə zan) *n.* [< Fr. < It.
cortigiana, court lady] a prostitute; esp.,
formerly, a mistress of a king, nobleman,
etc.: also **cour'tezan**

courtesy (kur'tə sē) *n.*, *pl.* **-sies** 1.
courteous behaviour 2. a polite or
considerate act —**by courtesy of** by
consent of (someone)

courthouse (kôrt'hous') *n.* 1. a building
in which law courts are held 2. [U.S.]
a building that houses the offices of a
county government

courtier (kôr'tē ər) *n.* an attendant at
a royal court

courtly *adj.* **-lier, -liest** suitable for a
king's court; dignified, elegant, etc.
—**court'liness** *n.*

court-martial (kôrt'mär'shəl) *n.*, *pl.*
courts'-mar'tial; for 2, now often
court'-mar'tials a court held by personnel
in the armed forces to try offences against
military law —*vt.* **-tialled, -tialling** to try
by a court-martial

Court of St. James [< *St. James Palace*,
former royal residence] the British royal
court

court plaster [< former use by court
ladies for beauty spots] an adhesive
plaster, formerly used to protect cuts, etc.

courtship *n.* the process or period of
courting

court shoe a woman's low-cut shoe
without straps or laces

courtyard *n.* a space enclosed by walls,
adjoining or in a large building

cousin (kuz'’n) *n.* [< L. *com-*, with +
soror, sister] 1. the son or daughter of
one's uncle or aunt: also **cous'in-ger'man**
(-jur'mən), **first** (or **full**) **cousin** 2. loosely,
any relative by blood or marriage 3. a
title of address used by one sovereign
to another or to a nobleman —**cous'inly**
adj., adv. —**cous'inship** *n.*

couture (kōō tyōōr') *n.* [Fr. < L. *com-*,
together + *suere*, to sew] the work or
business of designing new fashions in
women's clothes

couturier (kōō tyōōər'ē ā') *n.* [Fr.] a man
engaged in couture —**couturière**
(-tyōōər'ē er') *n.fem.*

cove[1] (kōv) *n.* [< OE. *cofa*, cave] 1.
a sheltered nook or recess, as in cliffs
2. a small bay or inlet 3. a concave
moulding —*vt., vi.* **coved, cov'ing** to curve
concavely

cove[2] *n.* [<?] [Slang] a boy or man; fellow

coven (kuv'ən) *n.* [see CONVENE] a
gathering or meeting, esp. of witches

covenant (kuv'ə nənt) *n.* [see CONVENE]
1. a binding agreement made by two or
more parties; compact 2. *Law* a formal,
sealed contract 3. *Theol.* the promises
made by God to man, as recorded in
the Bible —*vt., vi.* to promise by or
in a covenant —**cov'enanter, cov'enan-
tor** *n.*

Covenanter *n.* a person who supported
either of the Scottish Presbyterian
Covenants in the 17th cent.

Coventry (kov'ən trē) *n.* [< *Coventry*,
in W Midlands] ostracism [to send a
person to *Coventry*]

cover (kuv'ər) *vt.* [< L. *co-*, intens. +
operire, hide] 1. to place something on
or over 2. to extend over 3. to clothe
4. to coat, sprinkle, etc. thickly 5. to
conceal 6. to protect as by shielding 7.
to take into account 8. a) to protect
against financial loss b) to be sufficient
for payment 9. to travel over 10. to
deal with 11. to point a firearm at 12.
Journalism to get news, pictures, etc. of
13. *Sports* to guard or obstruct (an
opponent, etc.) 14. to mate with (a mare):
said of a stallion —*vi.* 1. to spread over
a surface, as a liquid 2. to provide an
alibi or excuse (*for*) 3. to assume
responsibility for an absent colleague's
work (with *for*) —*n.* 1. anything that
covers, as a lid, top, etc. 2. a) a shelter
or a hiding place b) a pretext, disguise,
or false identity 3. a tablecloth and a
place setting for one person 4. an
envelope, wrapping, etc. for post —**cover
up** to keep blunders, crimes, etc. from
being known —**take cover** to seek
protective shelter —**cov'erer** *n.*

coverage *n.* the amount, extent, etc.
covered by something

cover charge a fixed charge added to
the cost of food and drink, as at a nightclub
or restaurant

cover girl [Colloq.] a girl model whose
picture is often put on magazine covers, etc.

covering letter (or **note**) a letter (or
note) sent with a parcel, another letter,
etc. as an explanation

coverlet (kuv'ər lit) *n.* [< OFr. *covrir*,
cover + *lit*, bed] 1. a bedspread 2.
any covering

cover note a certificate from an insurance
company that provides proof of the
existence of an insurance policy

cover point *Cricket* a fielding position
on the off side and about halfway to the
boundary

covert (kuv'ərt) *adj.* [< OFr. *covrir*, cover]
concealed, hidden, or disguised —*n.* 1.
a protected place; shelter 2. a hiding
place for game —**cov'ertly** *adv.* —**cov'ert-
ness** *n.*

cover-up *n.* something used for hiding
one's real activities, intentions, etc.

covet (kuv'it) *vt., vi.* [< L.: see CUPIDITY]
to want ardently (esp., something that
another has)

covetous *adj.* greedy; avaricious —**cov'-
etousness** *n.*

covey (kuv'ē) *n., pl.* **-eys** [< OFr. *cover*,
to hatch] 1. a small flock of birds, esp.
partridges or quail 2. a small group of
people

cow[1] (kou) *n., pl.* **cows**; archaic **kine** (kīn)
[OE. *cu*] 1. the mature female of domestic
cattle, valued for its milk, or of certain
other animals, as the buffalo, elephant,
etc.: the male is called a *bull* 2. [Vulg.
Colloq.] a woman 3. [Aust. Slang]
something objectionable, esp. in a **fair cow**

cow[2] *vt.* [< ON. *kūga*, to subdue] to

make timid and submissive by filling with fear or awe

coward (kou′ərd) *n.* [< L. *cauda*, tail] one who lacks courage —**cow′ardly** *adj.*

cowardice *n.* lack of courage; esp., shamefully excessive fear of danger, difficulty, etc.

cowbell *n.* a bell hung from a cow's neck

cowboy *n.* [U.S.] a ranch worker who rides on horseback in his job of herding cattle: also **cow′hand′**

cowcatcher *n.* [U.S.] a metal frame on the front of a locomotive to remove obstructions from the line

cower (kou′ər) *vi.* [prob. < ON.] to crouch or huddle up, as from fear; shrink; cringe —**cow′eringly** *adv.*

cowhide *n.* 1. the hide of a cow 2. leather made from it 3. a whip made of this

cowl (koul) *n.* [< L. *cucullus*, hood] 1. *a)* a monk's hood *b)* a monk's cloak with a hood 2. something shaped like a cowl; esp., *a)* a cover for the top of a chimney *b)* the top front part of a motor car body *c)* a cowling —*vt.* to cover as with a cowl —**cowled** *adj.*

cowlick (kou′lik) *n.* [< it looking as if licked by a cow] a tuft of hair on the head that cannot easily be combed flat

cowling (kou′liŋ) *n.* [see COWL] a detachable metal covering for an aircraft engine, etc.

co-worker (kō′wur′kər) *n.* a fellow worker

cow parsley an umbelliferous plant, found in the hedgerows of Europe and Asia

cowpox *n.* a contagious disease of cows: smallpox vaccine is made from the virus

cowrie, cowry (kou′rē) *n.*, *pl.* **-ries** [< Sans. *kaparda*] the shell of a mollusc, formerly used as currency in parts of Africa and S Asia

cowshed *n.* a shelter for cows

cowslip *n.* [< OE. *cu*, cow + *slyppe*, paste] a European primrose with yellow flowers

cox (koks) *n.*, *pl.* **cox′es** [Colloq.] a coxswain —*vt.*, *vi.* to be coxswain for (a boat or crew)

coxcomb (koks′kōm′) *n.* [for *cock's comb*] 1. a jester's cap topped with a notched strip of red cloth 2. a silly, vain, foppish fellow; dandy —**cox′comb′ry** *n.*

coxswain (kok′sən, -swān′) *n.* [< *cock*, small boat + SWAIN] the steersman of a boat or racing shell —*vi.*, *vt.* to act as a coxswain

coy (koi) *adj.* [< L. *quietus*, quiet] 1. bashful; shy 2. affecting innocence or shyness 3. reticent in making a commitment —**coy′ly** *adv.* —**coy′ness** *n.*

coyote (koi′ōt, koi ōt′ē) *n.* [MexInd.] a small wolf of western N American prairies

coypu (koi′pōō) *n.*, [< native name] 1. a S American water-rat similar to the beaver 2. its fur Also **nutria**

cozen (kuz′'n) *vt.*, *vi.* [< ME. *cosin*, fraud] to cheat, defraud, or deceive —**coz′enage** *n.*

cp, c.p. candlepower

cp. compare

C.P. 1. Canadian Pacific Limited 2. Cape Province 3. Communist Party 4. Country Party (in Australia)

CPA critical path analysis

Cpl, Cpl. Corporal

CPO, C.P.O. Chief Petty Officer

cps, c.p.s. cycles per second

Cr *Chem.* chromium

crab¹ (krab) *n.* [< OE. *crabba*] 1. a crustacean with four pairs of legs, one pair of pincers and a flattish shell 2. a machine for hoisting heavy weights —[**C-**] Cancer, the constellation and zodiac sign —*vi.* **crabbed, crab′bing** to fish for crabs —**catch a crab** *Rowing* to unbalance the boat by a faulty stroke —**crab′ber** *n.*

crab² *n.* [< ?] 1. *same as* CRAB APPLE 2. a sour-tempered person —*adj.* of a crab apple —*vi.* **crabbed, crab′bing** [Colloq.] to complain peevishly —**crab′-ber** *n.*

crab apple 1. a small, very sour apple, used for jellies, jams, etc. 2. a tree bearing crab apples: also **crab tree**

crabbed (krab′id) *adj.* [< CRAB²] 1. peevish; cross 2. hard to read; illegible —**crab′bedness** *n.*

crabby *adj.* **crab′bier, crab′biest** [see prec.] peevish; cross —**crab′bily** *adv.* —**crab′biness** *n.*

crab louse a louse, somewhat crablike in shape, infesting the pubic regions, armpits, etc.

crack (krak) *vi.* [< OE. *cracian*, resound] 1. to make a sudden, sharp breaking noise 2. to break or split, usually without complete separation of parts 3. to become rasping or change pitch suddenly, as the voice 4. [Colloq.] to break down [to *crack* under the strain] —*vt.* 1. to cause to make a sharp, sudden noise 2. to cause to break or split 3. to subject (as petroleum) to cracking: see CRACKING² 4. to hit with a sudden, sharp blow 5. to manage to solve [to *crack* a code] 6. [Colloq.] to break open 7. [Slang] to make (a joke) —*n.* 1. a sudden, sharp noise 2. a break, usually partial 3. a chink; fissure 4. an erratic shift of vocal tone 5. a moment; instant [the *crack* of dawn] 6. [Colloq.] a sudden, sharp blow 7. [Colloq.] an attempt 8. [Slang] a joke —*adj.* [Colloq.] first-rate [*crack* troops] —**crack a bottle** [Colloq.] to drink —**crack down (on)** to become strict or stricter (with) —**cracked up to be** [Colloq.] alleged or believed to be —**crack up** [Colloq.] 1. to break down physically or mentally 2. to break into a fit of laughter or tears

crackbrained *adj.* crazy

cracked *adj.* 1. broken without complete separation of parts 2. harsh [a *cracked* voice] 3. [Colloq.] crazy

cracker (krak′ər) *n.* 1. a firework 2. a little paper roll: it contains sweets, mottoes, etc. and pops open when the ends are pulled 3. a thin, crisp, unsweetened biscuit

crackers *adj.* [Slang] crazy

cracking¹ *adj.* [Colloq.] excellent; fine

—get cracking [Colloq.] to start doing something

cracking² *n.* the process of breaking down hydrocarbons by heat and pressure, as in producing petrol

crackle (krak′'l) *vi.* **-led, -ling** [freq. of CRACK] to make slight, sharp popping sounds **—crack′ly** *adj.*

crackling *n.* **1.** the production of slight, sharp popping sounds **2.** the browned, crisp rind of roast pork

crackpot *n.* [Colloq.] a crazy or eccentric person **—adj.** [Colloq.] crazy or eccentric

-cracy (krə sē) [< Gr. *kratos*, rule] a combining form meaning a (specified) type of government; rule by [*autocracy*]

cradle (krā′d'l) *n.* [OE. *cradol*] **1.** a baby's small bed, usually on rockers **2.** infancy **3.** the place of a thing's beginning **4.** a framework for support or protection **5.** *Mining* a boxlike device on rockers for washing out gold **—vt. -dled, -dling** to place, rock, or hold in or as in a cradle

craft (kräft) *n.* [OE. *cræft*, strength] **1.** a special skill or art **2.** an occupation requiring this **3.** the members of a skilled trade **4.** guile **5.** *pl.* **craft** a boat, ship, or aircraft **—vt.** to make with skill

craftsman *n.* **1.** a skilled workman **2.** a skilful artist **—crafts′manship′** *n.*

crafty (kräf′tē) *adj.* **-ier, -iest** sly; cunning **—craft′ily** *adv.* **—craft′iness** *n.*

crag (krag) *n.* [< Celt.] a steep, rugged rock rising above others or projecting from a rock mass **—crag′gy** *adj.*

crake (krāk) *n.* [< ON. *kraka*, crow] any of several birds of the rail family with long legs and a short bill

cram (kram) *vt., vi.* **crammed, cram′ming** [OE. *crammian*, stuff] **1.** to pack full or too full **2.** to stuff; force **3.** to feed to excess **4.** to prepare for an examination in a hurried, intensive way

crammer *n.* a person or institution that prepares students for examinations, esp. by cramming them

cramp¹ (kramp) *n.* [< OFr. *crampe*, bent] **1.** a sudden, painful contraction of a muscle from chill, strain, etc. **2.** partial local paralysis, as from excessive use of muscles [*writer's cramp*] **—vt.** to cause a cramp in

cramp² *n.* [MDu. *krampe*, lit., bent in] **1.** a metal bar bent at each end for holding together timbers, etc.: also **cramp iron 2.** a clamp **—vt. 1.** to fasten as with a cramp **2.** to confine or hamper **—cramp one's style** [Slang] to hamper one's skill, confidence, etc. in doing something

cramped *adj.* **1.** confined; restricted **2.** irregular and crowded, as some handwriting

crampon (kram′pən) *n.* either of a pair of spiked iron plates fastened on shoes to prevent slipping

cranberry (kran′bər ē) *n., pl.* **-ries** [< Du. *kranebere*, crane berry] a firm, sour, edible, red berry of an evergreen shrub

crane (krān) *n.* [OE. *cran*] **1.** a large wading bird with very long legs and neck **2.** a machine for lifting or moving heavy weights by means of a movable projecting arm or a horizontal travelling beam **—vt.,**

vi. **craned, cran′ing** to stretch (the neck) in trying to see over something

crane fly a two-winged, slender fly with very long legs; daddy long-legs

cranial (krā′nē əl) *adj.* of or from the cranium

craniology (krā′nē ol′ə jē) *n.* the scientific study of skulls, esp. human skulls

cranium (krā′nē əm) *n., pl.* **-niums, -nia** [< Gr. *kranion*] **1.** the skull **2.** the bones forming the enclosure of the brain **—cra′nial** *adj.*

crank (kraŋk) *n.* [< OE. *cranc-*, as in *cranstæf*, yarn comb] **1.** a handle or arm at right angles to a shaft of a machine, to transmit or change motion **2.** [Colloq.] an eccentric person **—vt.** to start or operate by a crank **—crank up 1.** to start an engine by using a starting handle **2.** [Colloq.] to begin moving faster

crankcase *n.* the metal casing of the crankshaft of an internal-combustion engine

crankpin *n.* a cylindrical bar or pin, as part of a crankshaft, to which a connecting rod is attached

crankshaft *n.* a shaft having one or more cranks for transmitting motion

cranky *adj.* **-ier, -iest 1.** eccentric **2.** irritable **3.** out of order **—crank′ily** *adv.* **—crank′iness** *n.*

cranny (kran′ē) *n., pl.* **-nies** [< LL. *crena*, a notch] a small, narrow opening; crevice **—cran′nied** *adj.*

crap (krap) *n.* [< OFr., ordure] [Vulg. Slang] **1.** nonsense, insincerity, etc. **2.** trash; junk **3.** faeces **—vi.** to defecate **—crap′py** *adj.*

crape (krāp) *n.* [see CRÊPE] **1.** same as CRÊPE (sense 1) **2.** a piece of black crêpe as a sign of mourning

crapulence (krap′yoo ləns) *n.* sickness from excess in drinking or eating **—crap′u-lent** *adj.*

crapulous *adj.* [< L. *crapula*, drunkenness] sick from intemperance, esp. in drinking

crash¹ (krash) *vi.* [prob. echoic] **1.** to fall, collide, or break with a loud, smashing noise **2.** to move with such a noise **3.** to fall and be destroyed: said of aircraft **4.** to collapse, as a business **—vt. 1.** to smash **2.** to cause to crash **3.** to force or impel with a crashing noise (with *in, out,* etc.) **4.** [Colloq.] to get into (a party, etc.) without an invitation, etc. **—n. 1.** a loud, smashing noise **2.** a crashing **3.** a sudden collapse **—adj.** [Colloq.] using all possible resources, effort, and speed [*a crash course*]

crash² *n.* [prob. < Russ. *krashenina*, coloured linen] a coarse cloth of plain, loose weave

crash dive a sudden submergence of a submarine to escape from attack **—crash′-dive′** *vi.* **-dived′, -div′ing**

crash helmet a thickly padded, protective helmet

crashing *adj.* [Colloq.] thorough [*a crashing bore*]

crash-land *vt., vi.* to bring (an aeroplane)

down in a forced landing, with some damage —**crash landing**

crass (kras) *adj.* [L. *crassus*, gross] grossly stupid, dull, or obtuse —**crass'-ly** *adv.* —**crass'ness**

-crat (krat) [< Gr. *kratos*, rule] *a combining form meaning* participant in or supporter of (a specified kind of) government or ruling body [*democrat*, *aristocrat*]

crate (krāt) *n.* [L. *cratis*, wickerwork] 1. a packing case made of wood slats 2. [Slang] an old, decrepit car or aeroplane —*vt.* **crat'ed, crat'ing** to pack in a crate

crater (krāt'ər) *n.* [< Gr. *kratēr*] 1. a bowl-shaped cavity, as at the mouth of a volcano or on the moon 2. any pit like this, as one made by an exploding bomb

cravat (krə vat') *n.* [< Fr. *Cravate*, Croat] 1. a neckerchief or scarf 2. a necktie

crave (krāv) *vt.* **craved, crav'ing** [OE. *crafian*] 1. to ask for earnestly; beg 2. to long for; desire strongly —*vi.* to have a longing (*for*) —**crav'er** *n.*

craven (krā'vən) *adj.* [? < L. *crepare*, to burst] very cowardly —*n.* a complete coward —**cra'venly** *adv.*

craving *n.* an intense desire or longing

craw (krô) *n.* [ME. *craue*] the crop of a bird or insect —**to stick in the (or one's) craw** to be unacceptable

crawfish (krô'fish') *n.* same as CRAYFISH

crawl (krôl) *vi.* [< ON. *krafla*] 1. to move slowly by drawing the body along the ground, as a worm 2. to go on hands and knees 3. to move slowly 4. to act abjectly 5. to swarm (*with* crawling things) 6. to feel as if insects were crawling on the skin —*n.* 1. a crawling 2. an overarm swimming stroke —**crawl'er** *n.*

crayfish (krā'fish') *n.* [< OFr. *crevice*] a small, lobster-shaped freshwater crustacean

crayon (krā'ən) *n.* [< L. *creta*, chalk] 1. a small stick of chalk, charcoal, or coloured wax, used for drawing, colouring, or writing 2. a crayon drawing —*vt.* to draw or colour with crayons —**cray'on-ist** *n.*

craze (krāz) *vt.* **crazed, craz'ing** [ME. *crasen* < Scand.] to make insane —*n.* 1. a mania 2. a fad

crazy (krā'zē) *adj.* **-zier, -ziest** 1. insane 2. [Colloq.] foolish, fantastic, etc. 3. [Colloq.] enthusiastic 4. cracked or rickety —**cra'zily** *adv.* —**cra'ziness** *n.*

crazy paving a form of paving made from irregular shaped stones fitted together

creak (krēk) *vi., vt.* [see CROAK] to make, cause to make, or move with a harsh, grating, or squeaking sound, as rusted hinges —*n.* such a sound —**creak'y** *adj.*

cream (krēm) *n.* [prob. < L. *chrisma*, oil] 1. the oily, yellowish part of milk 2. any food having a creamy consistency 3. a creamy cosmetic or emulsion 4. the best part 5. yellowish white —*vi.* to form cream or a creamy foam —*vt.* 1. to take cream from 2. to add cream

to 3. to make creamy by beating, etc. —**cream of** creamed purée of —**cream off** to remove the best of (something) —**cream'y** *adj.*

cream cheese a soft, white cheese made of cream or of milk enriched with cream

creamery *n., pl.* **-eries** a place where dairy products are processed or sold

cream of tartar a white, acid, crystalline substance used in baking powder

crease (krēs) *n.* [see CREST] 1. a line made by folding and pressing 2. a fold or wrinkle 3. *Cricket* any of three lines marking positions for the bowler or batsman —*vt.* 1. to make a crease in 2. to graze with a bullet —*vi.* to become creased —**creas'er** *n.*

create (krē āt') *vt.* **-at'ed, -at'ing** [< L. *creare*] 1. to bring into being; originate, design, invent, etc. 2. to bring about; cause 3. to invest with a new rank, function, etc. —*vi.* [Slang] to make a fuss or cause an uproar

creation *n.* 1. a creating or being created 2. the universe 3. anything created; esp., an original design, etc. —**the Creation** *Theol.* God's creating of the world

creative *adj.* 1. creating or able to create 2. imaginative and inventive —**cre'ativ'-ity** *n.*

creator *n.* 1. one who creates 2. [C-] God

creature (krē'chər) *n.* [< L. *creatura*] 1. anything created 2. a living being, animal or human 3. one completely dominated by or dependent on another

crèche (krāsh) *n.* [Fr.] 1. a day nursery for children and very young children 2. a display of a stable with figures, representing a scene at the birth of Jesus

credence (krēd'əns) *n.* [< L. *credere*, believe] 1. belief, esp. in another's testimony 2. *Eccles.* a small side table for the Eucharistic wine, etc.

credential (kri den'shəl) *n.* 1. that which entitles to credit, confidence, etc. 2. [*pl.*] a letter or certificate showing one's right to a certain position or authority

credibility gap an apparent disparity between what is said and the actual facts

credible (kred'ə b'l) *adj.* [< L. *credere*, believe] that can be believed; believable —**cred'ibil'ity, cred'ibleness** *n.* —**cred'i-bly** *adv.*

credit (kred'it) *n.* [< L. *credere*, believe] 1. belief; confidence 2. *a*) good reputation *b*) one's influence based on this 3. praise 4. a source of approval or honour [*a credit* to the team] 5. [*pl.*] a list of acknowledgments in a film, TV programme, etc. 6. *a*) the amount in a bank account, etc. *b*) a sum available for withdrawal by someone specified 7. *a*) acknowledgment of a payment by entry of the amount in an account *b*) the right-hand side of an account, for such entries 8. *a*) trust in one's ability to make payments *b*) time allowed for payment 9. *Educ.* *a*) certification of a successfully completed unit or course of study *b*) a distinction awarded to an examination candidate who performs well —*vt.* 1. to believe; trust

2. to give credit to or commendation for **3.** to give credit in a bank account, etc. —**credit one with** to ascribe to one —**give one credit for 1.** to commend one for **2.** to believe or recognize that one has —**on credit** with agreement on future payment —**to one's credit** bringing approval or honour to one

creditable *adj.* **1.** praiseworthy **2.** ascribable (*to*) —**cred'itabil'ity** *n.* —**cred'-itably** *adv.*

credit card a card issued by banks, etc., enabling the holder to obtain goods and services on credit

Creditiste (kred'i test') *a.* of the Social Credit Rally of Quebec —*n.* a member of this organization

creditor *n.* a person who extends credit or to whom money is owed

credo (krē'dō) *n., pl.* -**dos** [L., I believe] **1.** *same as* CREED **2.** [C-] the Apostles' Creed or the Nicene Creed

credulity (krə dyōō'lə tē) *n.* a tendency to believe too readily

credulous (kred'yoo ləs) *adj.* [< L. *credere*, believe] **1.** tending to believe too readily **2.** indicating credulity —**cred'-ulously** *adv.* —**cred'ulousness** *n.*

creed (krēd) *n.* [< L. *credo*, I believe] **1.** a statement of religious belief, esp. as accepted by a church **2.** any statement of belief, opinions, etc. —**creed'al** *adj.*

creek (krēk) *n.* [< ON. -*kriki*, a winding] **1.** a narrow inlet or bay **2.** [U.S. & Aust.] a small stream —**up the creek** [Slang] **1.** in trouble **2.** crazy

creel (krēl) *n.* [< ?] a wicker basket for fishermen to carry fish caught

creep (krēp) *vi.* **crept, creep'ing** [OE. *creopan*] **1.** to move with the body close to the ground, as on hands and knees **2.** to come on or move slowly, gradually, stealthily, etc. **3.** to grow along the ground, etc., as some plants —*n.* **1.** a creeping **2.** [Slang] an annoying person —**make one's flesh (or skin) creep** to make one fearful, etc., as if insects were creeping on one's skin —**the creeps** [Colloq.] a feeling of fear, repugnance, etc.

creeper *n.* **1.** a person, animal, or thing that creeps **2.** a plant whose stem puts out tendrils for creeping along a surface **3.** [Slang] a thick, crêpe-soled shoe

creepy *adj.* **-ier, -iest 1.** having or causing fear or disgust, as if insects were creeping on one's skin **2.** creeping —**creep'ily** *adv.* —**creep'iness** *n.*

creepy-crawly *n.* [Colloq.] a small, crawling creature; insect

cremate (kri māt') *vt.* **-mat'ed, -mat'ing** [< L. *cremare*, to burn] to burn (a dead body) to ashes —**crema'tion** *n.* —**crema-tory** (krem'ə tər ē) *n., adj.*

crème (krām) *n.* [Fr.] **1.** cream **2.** a thick liqueur

crème de menthe (də mänt') [Fr.] a sweet, mint-flavoured liqueur, green or colourless

crenate (krē'nāt) *adj.* [< VL. *crena*, notch] having a scalloped edge, as certain leaves : also **cre'nated**

crenellate (kren'l āt') *vt.* **-ellat'ed, -ellat'ing** to furnish with battlements —**cren'ella'tion** *n.*

Creole, creole (krē'ōl) *n.* [< Fr. < Sp. < L. *creare*, create] **1.** orig., a person of European parentage born in Latin America or the Gulf States of the U.S. **2.** *a)* a descendant of such persons *b)* a person of mixed Creole and Negro descent **3.** French as spoken by Creoles —*adj.* of Creoles or their languages

creosote (krē'ə sōt') *n.* [< Gr. *kreas*, flesh + *sōzein*, save] a transparent, pungent, oily liquid distilled from wood tar or coal tar : used as an antiseptic and a wood preservative —*vt.* **-sot'ed, -sot'ing** to treat with creosote

crêpe, crepe (krāp) *n.* [Fr. *crêpe* < L. *crispus*, crisp] **1.** a thin, crinkled cloth, as of silk or wool **2.** *same as* CRAPE **3.** a very thin pancake **4.** soft rubber with a wrinkled surface, used for some shoe soles

crepe paper thin paper crinkled like crepe

crepitate (krep'ə tāt') *vi.* **-tat'ed, -tat'-ing** [< L. *crepare*, creak] to crackle —**crep'ita'tion** *n.*

crept (krept) *pt. & pp.* of CREEP

crepuscular (kri pus'kyoo lər) *adj.* [< L. *creper*, dark] of, like, or active at, twilight

Cres. Crescent

crescendo (krə shen'dō) *adj., adv.* [It.: see ff.] *Music* gradually getting louder —*n., pl.* -**dos 1.** a gradual increase in loudness **2.** a passage played crescendo

crescent (kres''nt) *n.* [< L. *crescere*, grow] **1.** the shape of the moon in its first or last quarter **2.** anything of similar shape **3.** a street that curves in a crescent shape **4.** [*also* C-] [< the Turkish crescent emblem] Turkish or Moslem power —*adj.* **1.** [Poet.] increasing; growing **2.** shaped like a crescent

cress (kres) *n.* [OE. *cressa*] a plant, as watercress, with pungent leaves used in salads

crest (krest) *n.* [< L. *crista*] **1.** a comb, tuft, etc. on the heads of some animals or birds **2.** a plume or emblem on a helmet **3.** a heraldic device as used on a coat of arms, note paper, etc. **4.** top; ridge —*vt.* **1.** to provide with a crest **2.** to reach the top of —*vi.* to form or reach a crest —**crest'ed** *adj.*

crestfallen *adj.* dejected or humbled

cretaceous (kri tā'shəs) *adj.* [< L. *creta*, chalk] **1.** of, like, or containing chalk **2.** [C-] designating or of the third geological period of the Mesozoic Era

cretin (kret'in) *n.* [< Fr. *chrétien*, Christian] **1.** a person suffering from cretinism **2.** [Colloq.] an idiot —**cre'ti-nous** *adj.*

cretinism *n.* a congenital thyroid deficiency with resulting deformity and idiocy

cretonne (kre'ton) *n.* [Fr. < *Creton*, in

Normandy] a heavy, printed cotton or linen cloth, for curtains, etc.

crevasse (kri vas′) *n.* [< OFr. *crevace, crevice*] a deep crack or fissure, esp. in a glacier

crevice (krev′is) *n.* [< L. *crepare*, to creak] a narrow opening; fissure; cleft —**crev′iced** *adj.*

crew[1] (krōō) *n.* [< L. *crescere*, grow] a group of people working together or classed together, as the personnel of a ship or an aircraft —*vt., vi.* to serve (on) as a crew member —**crew′man** *n.*

crew[2] *alt. pt. of* CROW[2]

crew cut a man's style of close-cropped haircut

crewel (krōō′əl) *n.* [LME. *crule*] a fine worsted yarn used in fancywork and embroidery —**crew′elwork′n.**

crib (krib) *n.* [OE.] 1. a rack, trough, or box for fodder; manger 2. [U.S.] a baby's cot 3. [Colloq.] *a)* a plagiarism *b)* a translation or other aid used, often dishonestly, in doing schoolwork 4. [Colloq.] the game of cribbage —*vt.* **cribbed, crib′bing** 1. [Colloq.] to plagiarize 2. to confine —*vi.* [Colloq.] to do schoolwork dishonestly, as by using a crib —**crib′ber** *n.*

cribbage (krib′ij) *n.* a card game in which the object is to form combinations that count for points

crick (krik) *n.* [< ?] a painful cramp in the neck, back, etc. —*vt.* to cause a crick in

cricket[1] (krik′it) *n.* [< OFr. *criquer*, creak] a leaping, chirping insect related to the grasshopper

cricket[2] *n.* [< ?] 1. an outdoor game played by two teams of eleven men each, in which a ball, bats, and wickets are used 2. [Colloq.] fair play; sportsmanship —*vi.* to play cricket —**crick′eter** *n.*

cried (krīd) *pt. & pp. of* CRY

crier (krī′ər) *n.* 1. a person who cries 2. a person who shouts out news, proclamations, etc.

crime (krīm) *n.* [< L. *crimen*, offence] 1. an act committed in violation of a law 2. criminal acts, collectively 3. [Colloq.] something deplorable; shame

criminal (krim′ən'l) *adj.* 1. having the nature of crime 2. relating to or guilty of crime 3. [Colloq.] deplorable —*n.* a person guilty of a crime —**crim′inal′ity** (-ə nal′ə tē) *n.* —**crim′inally** *adv.*

criminology (krim′ə nol′ə jē) *n.* [see CRIME & -LOGY] the scientific study and investigation of crime —**crim′inol′ogist** *n.*

crimp (krimp) *vt.* [< OE. *(ge)crympan*, to curl] 1. to press into narrow folds; pleat 2. to make (hair, etc.) wavy 3. to pinch together 4. [Colloq.] to hamper —*n.* anything crimped —**crimp′er** *n.*

crimpy *adj.* **-ier, -iest** curly; wavy

crimson (krim′z'n) *n., adj.* [ult. < Ar. *qirmiz, kermes*] deep red —*vt., vi.* to make or become crimson

cringe (krinj) *vi.* **cringed, cring′ing** [OE. *cringan*, fall (in battle)] 1. to draw back, crouch, as when afraid; cower 2. to act servilely —*n.* a cringing —**cring′er** *n.*

crinkle (kriŋ′k'l) *vi., vt.* **-kled, -kling** [see CRINGE] 1. to wrinkle; ripple 2. to rustle —*n.* 1. a wrinkle, twist, or ripple 2. a rustling sound —**crin′kly** *adj.*

crinoline (krin′ə lēn) *n.* [< L. *crinis*, hair + *linum*, thread] 1. a coarse, stiff, cloth used as lining to stiffen garments 2. *Hist.* a hooped petticoat of this, to puff out a skirt

cripple (krip′'l) *n.* [< OE. *creopan*, creep] a person or animal that is lame or disabled —*vt.* **-pled, -pling** to lame or disable —**crip′pler** *n.*

crisis (krī′sis) *n., pl.* **-ses** (-sēz) [< Gr. *krinein*, decide] 1. a turning point in the course of anything 2. a time of great danger or trouble 3. the turning point in a disease, indicating either imminent recovery or death

crisp (krisp) *adj.* [< L. *crispus*, curly] 1. easily crumbled; brittle 2. fresh and firm, as celery 3. fresh and tidy, as a uniform 4. sharp and clear [a *crisp* analysis] 5. lively 6. invigorating [*crisp* air] 7. closely curled —*n.* a very thin slice of potato fried and eaten cold, esp. as a snack —*vt., vi.* to make or become crisp —**crisp′ly** *adv.* —**crisp′ness** *n.*

crispy *adj.* **-ier, -iest** *same as* CRISPY

crisscross (kris′kros′) *n.* [earlier Christ's cross] a mark or pattern made of crossed lines —*adj.* marked with crossing lines —*vt., vi.* to mark with or move in crossing lines —*adv.* 1. crosswise 2. awry

criterion (krī tēər′ē ən) *n., pl.* **-ia, -ions** [< Gr. *kritēs*, judge] a standard, rule, or test by which something can be judged

critic (krit′ik) *n.* [< Gr. *krinein*, decide] 1. one who writes judgments of books, plays, music, etc. professionally 2. a person given to faultfinding

critical *adj.* 1. tending to find fault 2. characterized by careful analysis 3. of critics or criticism 4. of or forming a crisis; decisive 5. designating the point at which a nuclear chain reaction becomes self-sustaining —**crit′ically** *adv.*

critical path analysis a technique for determining which mode of operation of a particular project involves the lowest cost, least time, etc.

criticism (krit′ə siz′m) *n.* 1. the act, art, or principles of criticizing, esp. literary or artistic work 2. a review, article, etc. expressing this 3. faultfinding; disapproval

criticize *vi., vt.* **-cized′, -ciz′ing** 1. to analyse and judge as a critic 2. to find fault (with) —**crit′iciz′er** *n.*

critique (kri tēk′) *n.* [Fr.] 1. a critical analysis or evaluation 2. the art of criticizing

croak (krōk) *vi.* [echoic] 1. to make a deep, hoarse sound, as that of a frog 2. to talk dismally 3. [Slang] to die —*vt.* 1. to utter in deep, hoarse tones 2. [Slang] to kill —*n.* a croaking sound —**croak′y** *adj.*

Croatian (krō ā′shən) *adj.* of Croatia, its people, language, etc. —*n.* 1. a Croat

2. the South Slavic language of the Croats: see SERBO-CROATIAN

crochet (krō′shā) *n.* [Fr., small hook] needlework in which loops of thread are interwoven with a hooked needle —*vi., vt.* **-cheted** (-shād), **-cheting** to do crochet or make by crochet —**crochet′er** *n.*

crock[1] (krok) *n.* [OE. *crocca*] an earthenware pot or jar

crock[2] *n.* [< ON. *kraki*, bent object] [Slang] anyone or anything worthless or useless, as from age

crockery (krok′ər ē) *n.* [< CROCK[1]] earthenware pots, jars, dishes, etc.

crocodile (krok′ə dīl′) *n.* [< Gr. *krokodilos*, lizard] **1.** a large, lizardlike reptile of tropical streams, with a thick skin, long tail, and long, narrow head with massive jaws **2.** leather made from a crocodile's hide **3.** a party of schoolchildren walking in double file

crocodile tears a hypocritical show of grief

crocus (krō′kəs) *n., pl.* **cro′cuses, cro′ci** (-kē) [< Gr. *krokos*, saffron] **1.** a spring-blooming plant with a fleshy corm and a yellow, purple, or white flower **2.** in the Canadian prairies, the pasqueflower, floral emblem of Manitoba: also **prairie crocus**

Croesus (krē′səs) *n.* [< *Croesus*, fl. 6th c. B.C.; last king of Lydia] a very rich man

croft (kroft) *n.* [OE.] **1.** a small enclosed field **2.** a small farm, esp. one in Scotland or N England —**croft′er** *n.*

Cro-Magnon (krō man′yon) *adj.* [< cave in SW France, where remains were found] belonging to a prehistoric, Caucasoid type of man, tall and erect, who lived in the European continent

cromlech (krom′lek) *n.* [W. < *crom*, bent + *llech*, flat stone] **1.** same as DOLMEN **2.** an ancient monument of monoliths, arranged in a circle around a mound or dolmen

crone (krōn) *n.* [< MDu. *kronje*, old ewe] an ugly, withered old woman; hag

crony (krō′nē) *n., pl.* **-nies** [< ? Gr. *chronios*, long-continued] a close companion

crook (krook) *n.* [< ON. *krōkr*, hook] **1.** a hooked, or curved staff, crosier, etc. **2.** a bend or curve **3.** [Colloq.] a swindler or thief —*vt., vi.* **crooked** (krookt), **crook′-ing** to bend or curve

crooked (krook′id; *for 3* krookt) *adj.* **1.** not straight; bent; curved **2.** dishonest; swindling **3.** having a crook or hook —**crook′edly** *adv.* —**crook′edness** *n.*

croon (kroon) *vi., vt.* [< MDu. *cronen*, to growl] **1.** to sing or hum in a low, gentle tone **2.** to sing (popular songs) in a soft, sentimental manner —*n.* a low, gentle singing or humming —**croon′er** *n.*

crop (krop) *n.* [OE. *croppa*, flower, crop of bird] **1.** any agricultural product, growing or harvested **2.** the yield of any product in one season or place **3.** a group or collection **4.** the handle of a whip **5.** a saclike enlargement of a bird's gullet, in which food is stored before digestion **6.** hair cut close to the head —*vt.* **cropped, crop′ping 1.** to cut off or bite off the tops or ends of **2.** to grow or harvest as a crop **3.** to cut short —*vi.* to grow or bear crops **2.** to feed by grazing —**crop out** to appear at the surface, as a rock formation —**crop up** to happen unexpectedly

crop-eared *adj.* having the ears or hair cut short

cropper *n.* one that crops —**come a cropper** [Colloq.] **1.** to fall heavily or headlong **2.** to fail

croquet (krō′kā′) *n.* [Fr.: see CROTCHET] an outdoor game in which the players use mallets to drive a wooden ball through hoops in the ground

croquette (kro ket′) *n.* [Fr. < *croquer*, to crunch] a small cake or roll of chopped meat, fish, etc., coated with crumbs and fried in deep fat

crosier (krō′zhər) *n.* [< OFr. *croce*] a staff carried by or before a bishop or abbot as a symbol of his office

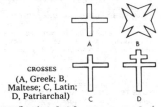

CROSSES
(A, Greek; B, Maltese; C, Latin; D, Patriarchal)

cross (kros) *n.* [< L. *crux*, a cross] **1.** an upright post with a bar across it on which the ancient Romans fastened convicted persons to die **2.** a cross-shaped badge, decoration, etc. **3.** *a)* a monument in the shape of a cross *b)* the place where a cross has been set up **4.** a representation of a cross as a symbol of the crucifixion of Jesus, and hence of the Christian religion **5.** any trouble or affliction **6.** any mark made by intersecting lines **7.** such a mark (X) made as a signature **8.** *a)* a crossing of varieties or breeds *b)* the result of such mixing; hybrid —*vt.* **1.** to make the sign of the cross over or upon **2.** to place across or crosswise [*cross* your fingers] **3.** to intersect **4.** *a)* to draw a line across *b)* to draw two lines across (a cheque) and so make it payable only into a bank account **5.** to go or extend across **6.** to bring into contact, causing electrical interference [the wires were *crossed*] **7.** to thwart; oppose **8.** to interbreed —*vi.* **1.** to intersect **2.** to go or extend from one side to the other **3.** to pass each other —*adj.* **1.** lying or passing across **2.** contrary; opposed **3.** ill-tempered; irritable **4.** involving reciprocation **5.** of mixed variety or breed —**cross off** (or **out**) to cancel as by drawing lines across —**cross one's fingers** to fold one finger over another in the hope of bringing good luck —**cross one's mind** to come suddenly to one's mind —**the Cross 1.** the cross on which Jesus died **2.** Christianity —**cross′ly** *adv.* —**cross′ness** *n.*

crossbar *n.* a bar, line, or stripe placed crossways

crossbench *n.* in the British parliament, a bench reserved for members who belong to neither the government nor the opposition —**crossbench′er** *n.*

crossbill *n.* a finch having a bill with curving points that cross

crossbow *n.* a medieval weapon consisting of a bow set transversely on a wooden stock

crossbreed *vt., vi.* -bred, -breed′ing *same as* HYBRIDIZE —*n. same as* HYBRID

crosscheck *vi., vt.* to verify (a statement, etc.) by consulting other sources —*n.* an act of crosschecking

cross-country *adj., adv.* across open country or fields, not by roads —*n.* a cross-country race

crosscut *adj.* **1.** used for cutting across [a *crosscut* saw] **2.** cut across —*n.* a cut across —*vt., vi.* -cut′, -cut′ting to cut across

cross-examine (kros′ig zam′in) *vt., vi.* -ined, -ining **1.** to question closely **2.** *Law* to question (a witness already questioned by the opposing side) to determine the validity of his testimony —**cross′-exam′ina′tion** *n.*

cross-eye *n.* an abnormal condition in which the eyes are turned towards each other —**cross′-eyed′** *adj.*

cross-fertilize *vt., vi.* -lized′, -liz′ing to fertilize or be fertilized by pollen from another plant or variety of plant —**cross′-fer′tiliza′tion** *n.*

cross fire 1. *Mil.* a firing at an objective from two or more positions so that the lines of fire cross **2.** any complex of opposing forces, opinions, etc.

crossing *n.* **1.** the act of passing across, thwarting, interbreeding, etc. **2.** an intersection, as of lines, streets, etc. **3.** a place where a street, river, etc. may be crossed

cross-legged (-leg′id, -legd′) *adj., adv.* with ankles crossed, or with one leg crossed over the other

crosspatch *n.* [CROSS + dial. *patch*, fool] [Colloq.] a cross, bad-tempered person

cross-ply *adj.* having the fabric cords running diagonally to stiffen the sidewalls: said of a tyre

cross-purpose (kros′pur′pəs) *n.* a conflicting purpose —**be at cross-purposes** to talk, act, etc. along different lines without either party realising it

cross-question (kros′kwes′chən) *vt.* to cross-examine

cross-refer (kros′rifur′) *vt., vi.* -ferred′, -fer′ring to refer from one part to another

cross-reference (kros′ref′ər əns) *n.* a reference from one part of a book, index, etc. to another part

crossroad *n.* **1.** a road that crosses another **2.** a road that connects main roads **3.** [*usually pl.*] the place where roads intersect —**at the crossroads** at the point where one must choose between different courses of action

cross section 1. *a)* a cutting through something, esp. at right angles to its axis *b)* a piece so cut off *c)* a drawing of a plane surface as exposed by such a cutting **2.** a sample with enough of each kind to show what the whole is like —**cross′-sec′tion** *vt.* —**cross′-sec′tional** *adj.*

cross-stitch *n.* a stitch made by crossing two stitches in the form of an X —*vt., vi.* to sew with this stitch

crosstalk *n.* **1.** rapid, witty dialogue **2.** conversation in which two or more people are talking at once **3.** *Radio* etc. undesired sounds heard on a receiving channel

crosswise *adv.* so as to cross; across: also **cross′ways′**

crossword puzzle an arrangement of numbered squares to be filled in with words: numbered synonyms, definitions, etc. are given as clues

crotch (kroch) *n.* [see CRUTCH] a forked place, as where *a)* the legs fork from the human body *b)* the legs of a pair of trousers, etc. meet *c)* a tree trunk divides into two branches —**crotched** *adj.*

crotchet (kroch′it) *n.* [< OFr. *croc*, hook] **1.** *Music* a note having the time value of one quarter of a semibreve **2.** a peculiar whim or stubborn idea

crotchety *adj.* full of whims or stubborn ideas

crouch (krouch) *vi.* [< OFr. *croc*, hook] **1.** to stoop low, as an animal ready to pounce **2.** to cringe in a servile manner —*n.* the act or position of crouching

croup[1] (kroop) *n.* [echoic] an inflammation of the respiratory passages, with laboured breathing and hoarse coughing —**croup′y** *adj.*

croup[2] *n.* [OFr. *croupe*] the rump of a horse, etc.

croupier (kroo′pē ər) *n.* [Fr.] a person in charge of a gambling table, who rakes in and pays out the money

crouton (kroo′ton) *n.* [< Fr.: see CRUST] a small piece of toasted or fried bread, often served in soup

crow[1] (krō) *n.* [OE. *crawa*] a large bird with glossy black plumage and a typical harsh call: the raven, rook, and jackdaw are crows —**as the crow flies** in a direct line —**eat crow** [U.S. Colloq.] to admit an error

crow[2] *vi.* crowed or, for 1, crew (kroo), crowed, crow′ing [OE. *crawan*] **1.** to make the shrill cry of a cock **2.** to boast in triumph **3.** to make a sound of pleasure, as a baby does —*n.* a crowing sound

crowbar (krō′bär′) *n.* a long metal bar, chisellike at one end, used as a lever for prying, etc.

crowd (kroud) *n.* [OE. *crudan*] **1.** a large number of people or things gathered closely together **2.** the common people **3.** [Colloq.] a set or clique —*vi.* **1.** to push one's way (*into*) **2.** to throng —*vt.* **1.** to push or shove **2.** to press closely together; cram **3.** to be or press very near to —**crowd out** to exclude because of insufficient space or time —**crowd′ed** *adj.*

crowfoot (krō′foot′) *n.*, *pl.* **-foots**′ a plant of the buttercup family, with leaves resembling a crow's foot

crown (kraun) *n.* [< Gr. *korōnē*, wreath] **1.** a wreath worn on the head as a sign of honour, victory, etc. **2.** a reward or honour **3.** the emblematic headdress of a monarch **4.** [*often* C-] *a*) the power of a monarch *b*) the monarch as head of the state **5.** a thing like a crown, as the top of the head, of a hat, etc. **6.** a former British coin equal to five shillings (25p) **7.** *a*) the highest point, as of an arch *b*) the centre part of a road **8.** *a*) the part of a tooth projecting beyond the gum line *b*) an artificial substitute for this —*vt.* **1.** *a*) to put a crown on *b*) to enthrone **2.** to honour or reward **3.** to be the highest part of **4.** to put the finishing touch on **5.** [Slang] to hit on the head **6.** *Draughts* to make a king of —**crown′er** *n.*

crown colony a British colony directly under the control of the home government in London

Crown corporation a corporation set up by a Canadian government for the production or sale of specific goods or services independently of government departments

crown court a court of criminal jurisdiction holding sessions throughout England and Wales

Crown Derby a type of fine china

crown jewels the jewellery, including the regalia, used by the sovereign on a state occasion

crown prince the male heir apparent to a throne

crow's-foot *n.*, *pl.* **-feet**′ any of the wrinkles at the outer corners of the eyes: *usually used in pl.*

CROW'S NEST

crow's-nest *n.* a lookout platform close to the top of a ship's mast

crozier (krō′zhər) *n. same as* CROSIER

CRTC Canadian Radio-television and Telecommunications Commission

crucial (krōō′shəl) *adj.* [< L. *crux*, cross] of supreme importance; decisive; critical —**cru′cially** *adv.*

crucible (krōō′sə b'l) *n.* [< ML. *crucibulum*, lamp] **1.** a heat-resistant container for melting ores, metals, etc. **2.** a severe test or trial

crucifix (krōō′sə fiks′) *n.* [see CRUCIFY] **1.** a representation of a cross with the figure of Jesus crucified on it **2.** the cross as a Christian symbol

crucifixion (krōō′sə fik′shən) *n.* **1.** a crucifying **2.** [C-] the crucifying of Jesus, or a representation of this

cruciform (krōō′sə fôrm′) *adj.* cross-shaped

crucify (krōō′sə fī′) *vt.* **-fied**′, **-fy′ing** [< L. *crux*, cross + *figere*, fix] **1.** to execute by nailing or binding to a cross and leaving to die of exposure **2.** to torment **3.** [Colloq.] to defeat; ridicule —**cru′cifi′er** *n.*

crude (krōōd) *adj.* [L. *crudus*, rough] **1.** in a raw or natural condition **2.** lacking grace, style, etc. **3.** not carefully made **4.** stark [*crude* reality] **5.** [Colloq.] vulgar; tasteless —**crude′ly** *adv.* —**crude′ness**, **cru′dity** *n.*

cruel (krōō′əl) *adj.* [< L. *crudus*, rough] **1.** enjoying others' suffering; merciless **2.** causing pain, distress, etc. —**cru′elly** *adv.* —**cru′elty** *n.*

cruet (krōō′it) *n.* [< OFr. *crue*, earthen pot] **1.** a small glass bottle, as for holding vinegar, oil, etc., for the table **2.** a stand for holding such bottles

cruise (krōōz) *vi.* **cruised**, **cruis′ing** [< Du. *kruisen*, to cross] **1.** to sail or drive from place to place, as for pleasure **2.** to move at the most efficient speed for sustained travel —*n.* a cruising voyage

cruiser *n.* **1.** a fast warship somewhat smaller than a battleship **2.** *same as* CABIN CRUISER

cruiserweight *n. Boxing* a light heavyweight: see BOXING AND WRESTLING WEIGHTS, table

crumb (krum) *n.* [OE. *cruma*] **1.** a small piece broken off something, as of bread **2.** any bit or scrap [*crumbs* of knowledge] **3.** the soft, inner part of bread **4.** [Slang] a worthless person —*vt.* **1.** to crumble **2.** *Cooking* to cover with crumbs

crumble (krum′b'l) *vt.* **-bled**, **-bling** [< prec.] to break into crumbs —*vi.* to fall to pieces; decay —*n.* a pudding consisting of a crumbly topping over fruit

crumbly (krum′blē) *adj.* **-blier**, **-bliest** apt to crumble; easily crumbled —**crum′bliness** *n.*

crumby (krum′ē) *adj.* **-bier**, **biest 1.** full of crumbs **2.** [Slang] *same as* CRUMMY —**crum′biness** *n.*

crummy (krum′ē) *adj.* **-mier**, **-miest** [Slang] cheap; inferior; worthless —**crum′miness** *n.*

crumpet (krum′pit) *n.* [< ?] **1.** a light, soft cake baked on a griddle: it is usually toasted before serving **2.** [Slang] sexually attractive womanhood

crumple (krum′p'l) *vt., vi.* **-pled**, **-pling** [< ME. *crimplen*, to wrinkle] **1.** to crush together into wrinkles **2.** to break down; collapse —**crum′ply** *adj.*

crunch (krunch) *vi., vt.* [echoic] to chew,

press, grind, etc. with a noisy, crushing sound —*n.* **1.** the act or sound of crunching **2.** [Colloq.] *a)* a showdown *b)* a tight situation —**crunch′y** *adj.*

Crunchie (krunch′ē) *n.* [S Afr. Derog. Slang] an Afrikaner

crupper (krup′ər) *n.* [< OFr. *crope*, rump] **1.** a leather strap attached to a saddle or harness and passed under the horse's tail **2.** a horse's rump; croup

crusade (krōō sād′) *n.* [ult. < L. *crux*, cross] **1.** [*sometimes* C-] any of the Christian military expeditions (11th - 13th cent.) to recover the Holy Land from the Moslems **2.** vigorous, concerted action for some cause or against some abuse —*vi.* -sad′ed, -sad′ing to engage in a crusade —**crusad′er** *n.*

cruse (krōōz) *n.* [OE. *cruse*] [Obs.] a small container for water, oil, honey, etc.

crush (krush) *vt.* [< OFr. *croisir*, break] **1.** to press between opposing forces so as to break or put out of shape **2.** to grind or pound into small particles **3.** to subdue; overwhelm **4.** to extract by pressing —*n.* **1.** a crushing **2.** a crowded mass of people **3.** a drink prepared by crushing fruit **4.** [Colloq.] an infatuation —**crush′able** *adj.* —**crush′er** *n.*

crust (krust) *n.* [< L. *crusta*] **1.** *a)* the hard, outer part of bread *b)* a piece of this **2.** the pastry covering of a pie **3.** any hard surface layer, as of snow **4.** [Slang] insolence **5.** *Geol.* the solid outer shell of the earth —*vt., vi.* to cover or become covered with a crust —**crus′tal** *adj.* —**crust′ed** *adj.*

crustacean (krus tā′shən) *n.* [< L. *crusta*, crust] any of a class of hard-shelled arthropods, including shrimps, crabs, and lobsters, that usually live in water and breathe through gills —*adj.* of crustaceans

crusty *adj.* -ier, -iest **1.** having a crust **2.** rudely abrupt or surly —**crust′ily** *adv.* —**crust′iness** *n.*

crutch (kruch) *n.* [OE. *crycce*, staff] **1.** a staff with a crosspiece that fits under the armpit, used by lame people as an aid in walking **2.** anything relied on for support; prop —*vt.* to support as with a crutch

crux (kruks) *n., pl.* **crux′es, cruces** (krōō′-sēz) [L., CROSS] **1.** a difficult problem; puzzling thing **2.** the essential or deciding point

cry (krī) *vi.* **cried, cry′ing** [< L. *quiritare*, to wail] **1.** to make a loud vocal sound, as for help **2.** to sob and shed tears; weep **3.** *a)* to plead (*for*) *b)* to show a great need (*for*) —*vt.* **1.** to beg for [to *cry* quarter] **2.** to utter loudly; shout **3.** to call out (wares for sale, etc.) —*n., pl.* **cries 1.** a loud vocal sound expressing pain, anger, etc. **2.** an announcement called out publicly **3.** an urgent appeal; plea **4.** a rallying call **5.** public outcry **6.** a fit of weeping **7.** the characteristic vocal sound of an animal —**a far cry** a great distance or difference —**cry down** to belittle; disparage —**cry off** to withdraw from an agreement or undertaking —**cry out 1.** to shout; yell **2.** to complain

loudly —**cry up** to praise highly —**in full cry** in eager pursuit

crying *adj.* demanding immediate notice

cryogenics (krī′ə jen′iks) *n.pl.* [*with sing. v.*] [< Gr. *kryos*, cold] the science that deals with the effects of very low temperatures on the properties of matter

crypt (kript) *n.* [< Gr. *kryptein*, to hide] an underground chamber; esp., a vault under a church

cryptic (krip′tik) *adj.* [see CRYPT] **1.** hidden or mysterious **2.** obscure and curt —**cryp′tically** *adv.*

cryptogam (krip′tə gam′) *n.* [< Gr. *kryptos*, hidden + *gamos*, marriage] a plant that bears no flowers or seeds but propagates by means of spores, as algae, mosses, ferns, etc. —**cryp′togam′ic** *adj.*

cryptogram (krip′tə gram′) *n.* [< Gr. *kryptos*, hidden + -GRAM] something written in code or cipher: also **cryp′to-graph′** —**cryp′togram′mic** *adj.*

cryptography (krip tog′rə fē) *n.* [< Gr. *kryptos*, hidden + -GRAPHY] the art of writing or deciphering messages in code —**cryptog′rapher** *n.*

CRYSTALS
(A, isometric; B, mono-
clinic; C, triclinic)

crystal (kris′t'l) *n.* [< Gr. *kryos*, frost] **1.** a clear, transparent quartz **2.** *a)* a very clear, brilliant glass *b)* articles made of such glass, as goblets, bowls, etc. **3.** the transparent covering over the face of a watch **4.** anything clear like crystal **5.** a solidified form of a substance made up of plane faces in three dimensions in a symmetrical arrangement **6.** *Electronics* a piezoelectric material, as quartz, used to produce and control a desired frequency, as in transmitters, etc. —*adj.* **1.** of crystal **2.** like crystal; transparent

crystal gazing the practice of gazing into a large glass ball (**crystal ball**) and professing to see images, esp. of future events —**crystal gazer**

crystalline (kris′tə lin) *adj.* **1.** made of crystal or crystals **2.** like crystal in clearness or structure

crystallize *vt.* -lized′, -liz′ing **1.** to cause to form crystals **2.** to give a definite form to **3.** to coat with sugar —*vi.* **1.** to become crystalline in form **2.** to take on a definite form —**crys′talliza′tion** *n.*

crystallography (kris′tə log′rə fē) *n.* [< CRYSTAL & -GRAPHY] the science of the form, structure, properties, and classification of crystals —**crys′tallog′rapher** *n.*

crystalloid (kris'tə loid') *n.* a substance, usually crystallizable, which, when in solution, readily passes through vegetable and animal membranes

Cs *Chem.* caesium

CSC Canadian Services College

C.S.E. Certificate of Secondary Education

C.S. gas [< B. C(arson) & R. S(taughton), its U.S. inventors] a gas causing tears, salivation and painful breathing, used in chemical warfare and civil disturbances

C.S.I.R.O. [Aust.] Commonwealth Scientific and Industrial Research Organization

C.S.T. [U.S. & Canad.] Central Standard Time

ct. 1. carat 2. *pl.* cts. cent 3. court

CTV Canadian Television (Network Ltd.)

Cu [L. *cuprum*] *Chem.* copper

cu. cubic

cub (kub) *n.* [< ?] 1. the young of certain mammals, as the fox, bear, lion, whale, etc. 2. an inexperienced or callow person, esp. a novice reporter —*vt., vi.* to give birth to (cubs) —**cub'bish** *adj.*

cubbyhole (kub'ē hōl') *n.* [< dial. *cub,* little shed + HOLE] a small, enclosed space or room

cube (kyoōb) *n.* [< Gr. *kybos*] 1. a solid with six equal, square sides 2. anything having this shape 3. the product obtained by multiplying a given number by its square; third power [the *cube* of 3 is 27] —*vt.* **cubed, cub'ing** 1. to raise to the third power 2. to cut or shape into cubes

cube root the number or quantity of which a given number or quantity is the cube [the *cube root* of 8 is 2]

cubic (kyoō'bik) *adj.* 1. having the shape of a cube 2. having three dimensions, or having the volume of a cube whose length, width, and depth each measure the given unit [a *cubic* metre] 3. relating to the cubes of numbers

cubicle (kyoō'bi k'l) *n.* [< L. *cubare,* lie down] 1. a small sleeping compartment 2. any small compartment

cubic measure a system of measuring volume in cubic units, esp. that in which 1,728 cubic inches = 1 cubic foot and 1,000 cubic millimetres = 1 cubic centimetre

cubism (kyoō'biz'm) *n.* a movement in art, esp. of the early 20th century, characterized by the use of cubes and other geometric forms —**cub'ist** *n., adj.*

cubit (kyoō'bit) *n.* [< L. *cubitum,* elbow] an ancient measure of length, about 50 cm

Cub Scout a member of a junior division of Boy Scouts

cuckold (kuk'ōld) *n.* [see ff.] a man whose wife has committed adultery —*vt.* to make a cuckold of

cuckoo (kook'oō) *n., pl.* **cuck'oos** [< OFr. *cucu,* echoic] 1. a greyish-brown bird with a long, slender body : the European species lays eggs in the nests of other birds 2. its call —*adj.* [Slang] crazy

cuckoopint *n.* a wild flower with arrow-shaped leaves and a purple spadix

cuckoo spit (or **spittle**) a froth produced on plants by the larvae of certain insects

cucumber (kyoō'kum bər) *n.* [< L. *cucumis*] 1. a creeping plant of the gourd family 2. the long fruit, with a green rind and firm, white flesh, used in salads —**cool as a cucumber** calm and self-possessed

cud (kud) *n.* [OE. *cudu*] food regurgitated from the first stomach of cattle and other ruminants and chewed a second time —**chew the cud** to ruminate; ponder

cuddle (kud'l) *vt.* **-dled, -dling** [< ?] to hold lovingly; embrace and fondle —*vi.* to lie close and snug; nestle —*n.* an embrace; hug —**cud'dlesome, cud'dly** *adj.*

cuddy (kud'ē) *n., pl.* **-dies** [< ?] 1. a small cabin on a ship 2. the cook's galley on a small ship

cudgel (kuj'əl) *n.* [OE. *cycgel*] a short, thick stick or club —*vt.* **-elled, -elling** to beat with a cudgel —**cudgel one's brains** to think hard —**take up the cudgels (for)** to come to the defence (of)

cue[1] (kyoō) *n.* [< *q, Q* (? for L. *quando,* when) found in 16th-c. plays] 1. a short piece of dialogue, action, or music that is a signal for an actor's entrance or speech 2. any signal to do something 3. an indirect suggestion; hint —*vt.* **cued, cue'ing** to give a cue to

cue[2] *n.* [< QUEUE] 1. a long, tapering rod used in billiards, etc. to strike the ball 2. a pigtail —*vt.* **cued, cue'ing** to strike with a cue

cuff[1] (kuf) *n.* [< ME. *cuffe,* glove] 1. a band at the end of a sleeve 2. a trouser turnup 3. a handcuff —**off the cuff** [Colloq.] improvised; impromptu

cuff[2] *vt.* [< ? CUFF[1]] to strike, esp. with the open hand; slap —*n.* a slap or blow

cuirass (kwi ras') *n.* [< L. *corium,* leather] 1. a piece of closefitting armour for protecting the breast and back 2. the breastplate of such armour

Cuisenaire rod (kwē'zə nāar') [< inventor's name] *Trademark* any of a set of rods of various colours and lengths representing different numbers that are used to teach children arithmetic

cuisine (kwē zēn') *n.* [Fr. < L. *coquere,* to cook] style of cooking or preparing food

cul-de-sac (kool'də sak') *pl.* **cul-de-sacs** [Fr., lit., bottom of a sack] a passage with only one outlet

-cule (kyoōl, kyool) [< Fr. or L.] a suffix meaning small

culinary (ku'lə nər ē) *adj.* [< L. *culina,* kitchen] of the kitchen or of cooking

cull (kul) *vt.* [< L. *colligere,* collect] 1. to pick out; select and gather 2. to take out (inferior or surplus animals) from a herd or flock —*n.* something picked out; esp., an animal taken from a herd or flock

culminate (kul'mə nāt') *vi.* **-nat'ed, -nat'ing** [< L. *culmen,* peak] to reach its highest point or climax —**cul'minant** *adj.* —**cul'mina'tion** *n.*

culotte (kyoō lot') *n.* [Fr.] [*often pl.*] trousers made full in the legs to resemble a skirt, worn by women

culpable (kul'pə b'l) *adj.* [< L. *culpa,*

fault] deserving blame —**cul′pabil′ity** n. —**cul′pably** adv.

culprit (kul′prit) n. [< Anglo-Fr. culpable, guilty + prit, ready] a person accused or found guilty of a crime or offence

cult (kult) n. [< L. cultus, care] 1. a system of religious worship 2. devoted attachment to a person, principle, etc. 3. a sect —**cult′ism** n. —**cult′ist** n.

cultivable (kul′tə və b′l) adj. that can be cultivated: also **cul′tivat′able** (-vāt′ə b′l) —**cul′tivabil′ity** n.

cultivate (kul′tə vāt′) vt. -vat′ed, -vat′ing [< L. colere, to till] 1. to prepare (land) for growing crops; till 2. to grow (plants) 3. to develop or improve [cultivate one's mind] 4. to seek to become familiar with —**cul′tivat′ed** adj.

cultivation (kul′tə vā′shən) n. 1. the act of cultivating (in various senses) 2. refinement, or culture

cultivator (kul′tə vāt′ər) n. 1. one who cultivates 2. a tool or machine for loosening the earth around plants

culture (kul′chər) n. [see CULT] 1. the skills, arts, etc. of a given people in a given period; civilization 2. improvement of the mind, manners, etc. 3. development by special training or care [body culture] 4. development or improvement of a particular plant or animal 5. cultivation of the soil 6. a growth of bacteria, etc. in a specially prepared substance (**culture medium**) —vt. -tured, -turing to cultivate —**cul′tural** adj. —**cul′turist** n.

cultured adj. 1. refined in speech, behaviour, etc. 2. produced by cultivation

cultured pearl a pearl induced to grow in the shell of a mollusc by the insertion of a foreign body

CULVERT

culvert (kul′vərt) n. [< ?] a conduit, esp. a drain, under a road or embankment

cum (kum) prep. [L.] with; combined with [a kitchencum-dining room]

cumber (kum′bər) vt. [< OFr. encombrer, obstruct] 1. to hinder; hamper 2. to burden

cumbersome adj. burdensome; unwieldy; clumsy

cumbrance (kum′brəns) n. a troublesome burden

Cumbrian (kum′brē ən) adj. 1. of the ancient British kingdom of Cumbria 2. of the English county of Cumbria —n. a native or inhabitant of Cumbria

cumin (kum′in) n. [< Gr. kyminon] 1. a small plant 2. its aromatic fruits, used for flavouring Also sp. **cum′min**

cummerbund (kum′ər bund′) n. [Hindi & Per. kamarband, loin band] a wide sash worn as a waistband

cumquat (kum′kwot) n. same as KUMQUAT

cumulate (kyōōm′yoo lāt′) vt., vi. -lat′-ed, -lat′ing [< L. < cumulus, a heap] same as ACCUMULATE

cumulative (kyōōm′yoo lə tiv) adj. increasing in effect, size, etc. by successive additions; accumulated —**cu′mulatively** adv.

cumulus (kyōōm′yoo ləs) n., pl. -li′(-lī′) [L., a heap] a thick cloud type with a dark, horizontal base and upper parts resembling domes —**cu′mulous** adj.

cuneiform (kyōō′nē ə fôrm′) adj. [< L. cuneus, a wedge + -FORM] wedge-shaped, as the characters used in ancient Assyrian, Babylonian, and Persian inscriptions —n. cuneiform characters

cunning (kun′iŋ) adj. [< ME. cunnen, know] 1. sly; crafty 2. made with skill or ingenuity 3. [U.S.] pretty —n. slyness; craftiness —**cun′ningly** adv.

cunt (kunt) n. [ME.] 1. [Vulg.] the female genitals 2. [Vulg. Slang] a despicable person

cup (kup) n. [< L. cupa, tub] 1. a small, bowl-shaped container for beverages, often with a handle 2. a cup and its contents 3. a cupful 4. anything shaped like a cup 5. a part of a bra designed to hold a breast 6. an ornamental cup given as a prize 7. the wine chalice at Communion; also, the wine 8. one's portion 9. something served in a cup —vt. **cupped, cup′ping** 1. to shape like a cup 2. to take in or put into a cup 3. Med. to subject to cupping —**in one's cups** drunk

C.U.P. Cambridge University Press

cupboard (kub′ərd) n. a piece of furniture or a recess with a door concealing storage space, often with shelves

cupboard love a pretended affection assumed in the hope of a gain

Cup Final 1. the annual final of the F.A. Cup soccer competition 2. the final of any cup competition

Cupid (kyōō′pid) [< L. cupido, desire] the Roman god of love —n. [c-] a representation of Cupid as a naked, winged cherub with bow and arrow

cupidity (kyōō pid′ə tē) n. [< L. cupere, to desire] strong desire for wealth; greed

cupola (kyōō′pə lə) n. [It. < L. cupa, tub] 1. a rounded roof or ceiling 2. a small dome or similar structure on a roof —**cu′polaed** (-ləd) adj.

cupping (kup′iŋ) n. the use of a glass cup (**cupping glass**) from which the air has been exhausted, to draw blood to the surface of the skin: used, esp. formerly, in medicine

cupreous (kyōō′prē əs) adj. of, like, or containing copper

cupric (kyōō′prik) adj. Chem. of or containing copper with a valence of two

cupriferous (kyōō prif′ər əs) adj. [< L. cuprum, copper + -FEROUS] containing copper

cupronickel (kyōō′prō nik′′l) *n.* an alloy of copper and nickel, used in condenser tubes, some coins, etc.

cuprous (kyōō′prəs) *adj. Chem.* of or containing copper with a valence of one

cup tie *Sport* an eliminating match between two teams competing with others for a cup

cur (kur) *n.* [< ON. *kurra,* to growl] 1. a dog of mixed breed; mongrel 2. a contemptible person

curable (kyōōər′ə b'l) *adj.* that can be cured

curaçao (kyōōər′ə sō′) *n.* [< *Curaçao,* island in the Caribbean] a liqueur flavoured with orange peel

curacy (kyōōər′ə sē) *n., pl.* **-cies** the position, office, or work of a curate

curare, curari (kyōō rä′rē) *n.* [< native (Tupi) name] a black, resinous substance prepared from the juices of certain S. American plants, used as an arrow poison by some Indians and in medicine to relax muscles

curate (kyōōər′ət) *n.* [< L. *curare,* take care] a clergyman who assists a vicar or rector

curative (kyōōər′ə tiv) *adj.* curing or having the power to cure —*n.* a thing that cures; remedy

curator (kyōō rāt′ər) *n.* [< L. *cura,* care] a person in charge of a museum, art gallery, etc. —**curatorial** (kyōōər′ə tôr′ē əl) *adj.* —**cura′torship′** *n.*

curb (kurb) *n.* [< L. *curvus,* bent] 1. anything that checks, restrains, or subdues 2. a raised margin along an edge, to strengthen or confine 3. *same as* KERB 4. a chain or strap attached to a horse's bit, used to check the horse —*vt.* 1. to restrain; control 2. to provide with a curb

curd (kurd) *n.* [< ME. *crud*] [*often pl.*] the coagulated part of sour milk, from which cheese is made

curdle (kur′d'l) *vt., vi.* **-dled, -dling** to form into curd; coagulate —**curdle one's blood** to horrify or terrify one

cure (kyōōər) *n.* [< L. *cura,* care] 1. a healing or being healed 2. a medicine or treatment for restoring health 3. a method of treating a disease, ailment, etc. 4. *same as* CURACY —*vt.* **cured, cur′ing** 1. to restore to health 2. to get rid of (an ailment, evil, etc.) 3. *a)* to preserve (meat, fish, etc.), as by salting or smoking *b)* to process (tobacco, leather, etc.), as by drying

curé (kyōōə′rä) *n.* [Fr.] in France, a parish priest

cure-all *n.* something supposed to cure all ailments or evils; panacea

curet, curette (kyōōə ret′) *n.* [Fr.] a spoon-shaped surgical instrument for the removal of tissue from the walls of body cavities —*vt.* **-ret′ted, -ret′ting** to clean or scrape with a curet —**curet′tage** *n.*

curfew (kur′fyōō) *n.* [< OFr. *covrir,* to cover + *feu,* fire] 1. a time in the evening beyond which people may not appear on the streets 2. *Hist.* the ringing of a bell

every evening as a signal for people to cover fires, put out lights, and retire

Curia (kyōōr′ē ə) *n.* [L.] the administrative body of the Roman Catholic Church, with various courts, officials, etc. under the authority of the Pope: in full, **Curia Romana** (rō mä′nə) —**cu′rial** *adj.*

curio (kyōōr′ē ō′) *n., pl.* **-os′** [contr. of CURIOSITY] any unusual or rare article

curiosity (kyōōr′ē os′ə tē) *n., pl.* **-ties** 1. a desire to learn or know 2. anything curious or rare

curious (kyōōr′ē əs) *adj.* [< L. *curiosus,* careful] 1. eager to learn or know 2. inquisitive; prying 3. arousing attention because unusual or strange —**cu′riously** *adv.*

curium (kyōōr′ē əm) *n.* [< Marie & Pierre *Curie*] a radioactive chemical element: symbol, Cm

curl (kurl) *vt.* [< ME. *crul,* curly] 1. to wind (esp. hair) into ringlets or coils 2. to cause to bend round —*vi.* 1. to become curled 2. to form, or move in, a spiral or curve 3. to play the game of curling —*n.* 1. a ringlet of hair 2. anything with a curled shape —**curl up** 1. to gather into spirals or curls 2. to sit or lie with the legs drawn up 3. [Colloq.] to be embarrassed or disgusted —**in curl** curled —**curl′y** *adj.*

curler *n.* a pin, clasp, etc. for curling hair

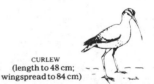

CURLEW
(length to 48 cm;
wingspread to 84 cm)

curlew (kur′lyōō) *n.* [echoic] a large, brownish wading bird with long legs

curlicue (kur′li kyōō′) *n.* [< CURL + CUE²] a fancy curve, flourish, etc.

curling (kur′liŋ) *n.* a game played on ice by sliding a heavy disc (**curling stone**) towards a target circle

curmudgeon (kur muj′ən) *n.* [< ?] a surly, ill-mannered person

currant (kur′ənt) *n.* [< Anglo-Fr. lit., Corinth] 1. a small, seedless raisin from the Mediterranean region 2. *a)* the berry of several species of hardy shrubs, used for jellies and jams *b)* the shrub

currency (kur′ən sē) *n., pl.* **-cies** [see ff.] 1. the money in circulation in any country 2. common acceptance or use

current (kur′ənt) *adj.* [< L. *currere,* run] 1. *a)* in progress *b)* contemporary *c)* of most recent date 2. circulating 3. commonly used or accepted —*n.* 1. a flow of water or air in a definite direction 2. a general tendency or drift 3. the flow or rate of flow of electric charge in a conductor —**cur′rently** *adv.*

current account a bank account against

which the holder may draw cheques at any time

curricle (kur'i k'l) *n.* [see ff.] a two-wheeled carriage drawn by two horses abreast

curriculum (kə rik'yə ləm) *n., pl.* **-ula, -ulums** [L., a course, race] 1. a course of study 2. all the courses offered in a school —**curric′ular** *adj.*

curriculum vitae (vē′tī) [L., course of life] a summary of one's personal, educational, and professional history

curry[1] (kur'ē) *vt.* **-ried, -rying** [< OFr. *correier*, to put in order] 1. to rub down and clean the coat of (a horse, etc.) with a currycomb or brush 2. to prepare (tanned leather) by soaking, cleaning, beating, etc. —**curry favour** to try to win favour by flattery, fawning, etc. —**cur′rier** *n.*

curry[2] *n., pl.* **-ries** [Tamil *kari*, sauce] 1. a powder (**curry powder**) prepared from turmeric and various spices 2. a sauce made with curry powder 3. a kind of stew prepared with curry —*vt.* **-ried, -rying** to prepare with curry powder

CURRYCOMB

currycomb *n.* a comb with teeth or ridges, to curry a horse

curse (kurs) *n.* [OE. *curs*] 1. a calling on God or the gods to send evil to some person or thing 2. a profane oath 3. a thing cursed 4. evil that seems to come in answer to a curse 5. any cause of evil or injury 6. [Colloq.] menstruation (preceded by *the*) —*vt.* **cursed, curs′ing** 1. to call evil down on 2. to swear at 3. to bring evil or injury on; afflict —*vi.* to swear —**be cursed with** to suffer from

cursed (kur′sid) *adj.* 1. under a curse 2. deserving to be cursed; evil —**curs′edly** *adv.* —**curs′edness** *n.*

cursive (kur′siv) *adj.* [< L. *cursus*: see COURSE] designating or of writing in which the letters are joined

cursor (kur′sər) *n.* [L., runner] the sliding part of a measuring instrument, as on a slide rule

cursory (kur′sər ē) *adj.* [< L. *cursor*, runner] hasty and superficial —**cur′sorily** *adv.* —**cur′soriness** *n.*

curt (kurt) *adj.* [L. *curtus*] so brief as to be rude; terse; brusque [a *curt* reply] —**curt′ly** *adv.* —**curt′ness** *n.*

curtail (kur tāl′) *vt.* [< L. *curtus*, short] to cut short; reduce; abridge —**curtail′er** *n.* —**curtail′ment** *n.*

curtain (kur′t'n) *n.* [< L. *cohors*, a court] 1. a piece of cloth, etc. hung, as at a window, to decorate or conceal 2. anything that conceals or shuts off 3. *Theatre* a) the screen at the front of the stage b) the opening or the closing of the curtain

for a play, act, or scene 4. [*pl.*] [Slang] death; the end —*vt.* to provide or shut off as with a curtain

curtain raiser 1. a short play or skit presented before a longer production 2. any brief preliminary event

curtain wall an independently supported outer wall bearing only its own weight

curtsy (kurt′sē) *n., pl.* **-sies** [var. of COURTESY] a woman's gesture of greeting, respect, etc. made by bending the knees and slightly lowering the body —*vi.* **-sied, -sying** to make a curtsy Also sp. **curt′sey**

curvaceous (kur vā′shəs) *adj.* [< CURVE] [Colloq.] having a full, shapely figure: said of a woman

curvature (kur′və tyər) *n.* 1. a curving or being curved 2. a curve; curved part of anything

curve (kurv) *n.* [L. *curvus*, bent] 1. a line having no straight part; bend with no angles 2. a thing or part with the shape of a curve 3. a curving 4. a curved line indicating variations, as in prices 5. a line representing data on a graph —*vt., vi.* **curved, curv′ing** 1. to form a curve by bending 2. to move in a curve

curvet (kur vet′) *n.* [< L. *curvus*, bent] an upward leap by a horse —*vi.* **-vet′ted** or **-vet′ed, -vet′ting** or **-vet′ing** 1. to make a curvet 2. to leap; frolic

curvilinear (kur′və lin′ē ər) *adj.* consisting of or enclosed by a curved line or lines: also **cur′vilin′eal**

curvy *adj.* **-ier, -iest** having curves or a curve

cushion (koosh′ən) *n.* [< L. *culcita*, mattress] 1. a pillow or pad 2. a thing like this in shape or use 3. anything serving to absorb shock, as the inner rim of a billiard table 4. anything that relieves distress, provides comfort, etc. —*vt.* 1. to provide with a cushion 2. to absorb (shock or noise) 3. to act as a cushion in protecting from injury, relieving distress, etc.

cushy (koosh′ē) *adj.* **-ier, -iest** [< Hindi *khush*, pleasant] [Colloq.] easy; comfortable [a *cushy* job]

CUSO Canadian University Services Overseas

cusp (kusp) *n.* [L. *cuspis*, point] 1. a pointed end 2. any of the elevations on the chewing surface of a tooth 3. either horn of a crescent, as of the moon

cuspid (kus′pid) *n.* a canine tooth

cuspidate (kus′pə dāt′) *adj.* 1. having a cusp or cusps 2. having a short, abrupt point Also **cus′pidat′ed**

cuss (kus) *n.* [< CURSE] [Colloq.] 1. a curse 2. a person or animal regarded as queer or annoying —*vt., vi.* [Colloq.] to curse —**cuss′ed** *adj.*

custard (kus′tərd) *n.* [< L. *crusta*, crust] 1. a mixture of eggs, milk, flavouring, and, often, sugar, either boiled or baked 2. a sauce made of milk, sugar, and cornflour

custodian (kus tō′dē ən) *n.* one who has the custody or care of something, esp. a public building; keeper

custody (kus′tə dē) *n., pl.* **-dies** [< L.

custos, guard] a guarding or keeping —**in custody** under arrest —**take into custody** to arrest —**custo'dial** (-tō'dē əl) *adj.*

custom (kus'təm) *n.* [< L. *com*-, intens. + *suere,* be accustomed] **1.** a usual practice; habit **2.** social conventions carried on by tradition **3.** [*pl.*] *a)* duties imposed on imported goods *b)* [*with sing. v.*] the department in charge of collecting these duties **4.** the regular patronage of a business **5.** *Law* such usage as by long-established practice has taken on the force of law —*adj.* [U.S.] made to order

customary *adj.* **1.** in keeping with custom; usual **2.** *Law* holding or held by custom —**cus'tomarily** *adv.* —**cus'tomariness** *n.*

custom-built *adj.* built to order, according to the customer's specifications: also **custom-made**

customer (kus'tə mər) *n.* **1.** a person who buys, esp. one who buys regularly **2.** [Colloq.] any person with whom one has dealings [a rough *customer*]

customhouse *n.* an office where customs or duties are paid: also **cus'tomshouse'**

cut (kut) *vt.* cut, cut'ting [ME. *cutten*] **1.** to make an opening in with a sharp-edged instrument **2.** to pierce sharply so as to hurt **3.** to hurt the feelings of **4.** to grow (a new tooth through the gum) **5.** to divide into parts with a sharp-edged instrument **6.** to carve (meat) **7.** to hew **8.** to mow or reap **9.** to pass across; intersect **10.** to divide (a pack of cards) before dealing **11.** to stop photographing (a film scene) **12.** to reduce [to *cut* salaries] **13.** to trim **14.** to make or do by or as by cutting; specif., *a)* to make (an opening, clearing, etc.) *b)* to type or mark (a stencil) *c)* to cut cloth so as to form (a garment) *d)* to perform [to *cut* a caper] *e)* to hit or throw (a ball) so that it spins *f)* to edit (film) as by deleting scenes *g)* to make a recording of on (a gramophone record) **15.** [Colloq.] to pretend not to see or know (a person) **16.** [Colloq.] to stay away from **17.** [Slang] to stop —*vi.* **1.** to pierce, sever, gash, etc. **2.** to take cutting [pine *cuts* easily] **3.** to swing a bat, etc. (*at* a ball) **4.** to move swiftly **5.** to make a sudden shift to another scene, as in a film —*adj.* **1.** that has been cut **2.** made or formed by cutting —*n.* **1.** a cutting or being cut **2.** a stroke or blow with a sharp-edged instrument **3.** a stroke taken at a ball **4.** an opening made by a sharp-edged instrument **5.** the omission of a part **6.** a piece cut off, as from a meat animal **7.** a reduction **8.** the shortest way across: usually **short cut** **9.** a passage or channel cut out **10.** the style in which a thing is cut; fashion **11.** an act, remark, etc. that hurts one's feelings **12.** [Colloq.] a snub **13.** [Slang] a share, as of profits —**a cut above** [Colloq.] somewhat better than —**cut a figure** to make a (certain) impression —**cut and dried** **1.** arranged beforehand **2.** lifeless; dull —**cut down** to reduce; lessen —**cut in** **1.** to draw in front of another vehicle leaving too

little space **2.** to interrupt **3.** to give a share to —**cut it fine** [Colloq.] to leave only a minimum reserve of time, resources, etc. —**cut it out** [Colloq.] to stop what one is doing —**cut no ice** [Colloq.] to make no impression —**cut off** **1.** to sever **2.** to stop abruptly **3.** to shut off **4.** to interrupt **5.** to intercept **6.** to disinherit —**cut out** **1.** to remove; omit **2.** to eliminate and take the place of (a rival) **3.** to make or form as by cutting **4.** [Colloq.] *a)* to discontinue *b)* to cease to function —**cut out for** suited for —**cut up** **1.** to cut into pieces **2.** [Colloq.] *a)* to criticize harshly *b)* to cause to be dejected —**cut up rough** [Colloq.] to react with anger, resentment, etc.

cutaneous (kyo͞o tā'nē əs) *adj.* [< L. *cutis,* skin] of, on, or affecting the skin

cutaway *n.* a man's formal coat cut so as to curve back to the tails: also **cutaway coat** —*adj.* of a diagram or model having parts cut away to show the inside

cutback *n.* a reduction, as of production, personnel, etc.

cute (kyo͞ot) *adj.* cut'er, cut'est [< ACUTE] [Colloq.] **1.** clever; shrewd **2.** [U.S.] pretty, esp. in a dainty way —**cute'ly** *adv.* —**cute'ness** *n.*

cut glass glass shaped or ornamented by grinding and polishing —**cut'-glass'** *adj.*

cuticle (kyo͞ot'i k'l) *n.* [L. *cuticula,* skin] **1.** *same as* EPIDERMIS **2.** hardened skin at the base and sides of a fingernail or toenail —**cutic'ular** *adj.*

cutis (kyo͞ot'is) *n.* [L.] the vertebrate skin, including both its layers, the dermis and the epidermis

cutlass (kut'ləs) *n.* [< L. *culter,* knife] *Hist.* a short, thick, curved sword used esp. by sailors

cutlery (kut'lər ē) *n.* **1.** any implements used for eating **2.** cutting instruments, such as knives and scissors

cutlet (kut'lit) *n.* [< L. *costa,* a rib] **1.** a small slice of meat from the ribs or leg, often breaded and fried, etc. **2.** a small, flat croquette of chopped meat or fish

cutoff (kut'ôf') *n.* **1.** the limit set for a process, activity, etc. **2.** any device for cutting off the flow of a fluid, a connection, etc.

cut-price *adj.* **1.** available at a lower price than the standard rate **2.** offering cut-price goods or services

cutter (kut'ər) *n.* **1.** a person whose work is cutting, as the sections of a garment **2.** a small, swift vessel; specif., *a)* a boat carried by large ships as a communications tender: also **ship's cutter** *b)* a single-masted sailing boat with a mainsail and two foresails *c)* a small boat, often lightly armed, used in the enforcement of customs regulations **3.** [U.S.] a small, light sleigh

cutthroat *n.* **1.** a murderer **2.** a razor with a long blade that folds into the handle —*adj.* **1.** merciless; ruthless **2.** three-handed: said of card games

cutting *n.* **1.** a piece cut off **2.** a newspaper

clipping: also **press cutting** 3. a shoot cut from a plant for rooting or grafting 4. an excavation for a railway line, road, etc. through high ground —*adj.* 1. that cuts 2. chilling or piercing 3. sarcastic —**cut′tingly** *adv.*

cuttlefish (kut′'l fish′) *n.* [OE. *cudele*] a squidlike sea mollusc with ten sucker-bearing arms: when in danger, some cuttlefish eject an inky fluid: also **cuttle**

Cwlth. Commonwealth

cwm (kōōm) *n.* [W.] 1. [Welsh] a valley 2. *Geol.* a hollow on a mountainside worn by glacial action; cirque

cwt. hundredweight

-cy (sē, si) [< Lat. *-kia*] *a suffix meaning:* 1. condition [*hesitancy*] 2. rank or office of [*curacy*]

cyanic (sī an′ik) *adj.* of or containing cyanogen

cyanic acid a colourless, poisonous acid

cyanide (sī′ə nīd′) *n.* a highly poisonous compound of cyanogen with a metal

cyanogen (sī an′ə jin) *n.* [< Gr. *kyanos*, blue + -GEN] a colourless, poisonous, flammable gas

cyanosis (sī′ə nō′sis) *n.* [< Gr. *kyanos*, blue] a bluish skin colour caused by lack of oxygen in the blood

cybernetics (sī′bər net′iks) *n.pl.* [*with sing. v.*] [< Gr. *kybernētēs*, helmsman] the comparative study of complex electronic computers and the human nervous system —**cy′bernet′ic** *adj.*

cyclamate (sī′klə māt′) *n.* a complex organic compound with an extremely sweet taste

cyclamen (sī′klə mən) *pl.* **-mens** [< Gr. *kyklaminos*] a plant of the primrose family, having heart-shaped leaves and white, pink, or red flowers with reflexed petals

cycle (sī′k'l) *n.* [< Gr. *kyklos*, circle] 1. *a)* a period of time within which a round of regularly recurring events is completed *b)* a complete set of such events 2. a very long period of time 3. a series of poems or songs on the same theme 4. a bicycle, tricycle, etc. 5. *Elec.* one complete period of the reversal of an alternating current —*vi.* **-cled, -cling** 1. to occur in cycles 2. to ride a bicycle, etc.

cyclic (sī′klik) *adj.* 1. of, or having the nature of, a cycle; moving in cycles 2. *Chem.* arranged in a ring or closed-chain structure: said of atoms Also **cy′clical**

cyclist (sī′klist) *n.* a person who rides a bicycle

cyclo- [< Gr. *kyklos*, circle] *a combining form meaning* of a circle or wheel, circular

cyclone (sī′klōn) *n.* [< Gr. *kyklos*, circle] 1. loosely, a tornado or hurricane 2. *Meteorol.* a storm with strong winds rotating about a moving centre of low atmospheric pressure —**cyclonic** (sī klon′ik) *adj.*

Cyclops (sī′klops) *n., pl.* **Cyclopes** (sī klō′pēz) [< Gr. *kyklos*, circle + *ōps*, eye] *Gr. Myth.* any of a race of one-eyed giants —**Cyclopean** (sī klō′pē ən) *adj.*

cyclostyle (sī′klə stīl′) *n.* [CYCLO- +

STYLE] a duplicating apparatus using a pen with a small, toothed wheel which cuts holes in a stencil —*vt.* to duplicate in this way

cyclotron (sī′klə tron′) *n.* [CYCLO- + (ELEC)TRON] an apparatus for giving high energy to particles, usually protons and deuterons: used in atomic research

cyder (sī′dər) *n.* same as CIDER

cygnet (sig′nit) *n.* [< Gr. *kyknos*, swan] a young swan

cylinder (sil′ən dər) *n.* [< Gr. *kylindein*, to roll] 1. a roller-shaped solid or hollow body, of uniform diameter 2. anything with the shape of a cylinder, esp. the chamber in which the piston moves in an engine —**cylindrical** (sə lin′dri k′l) *adj.*

CYMBALS

cymbal (sim′b'l) *n.* [< Gr. *kymbē*, hollow of a vessel] a circular, concave brass plate used as a percussion instrument: it is struck with a drumstick, brush, etc. or used in pairs which are struck together to produce a ringing sound —**cym′balist** *n.*

cyme (sīm) *n.* [< Gr. *kyma*, swelling] a flower cluster in which the central flower blooms first —**cymose** (sī′mōs) *adj.*

Cymric (kim′rik) *adj.* [< W. *Cymru*, Wales] of the Celtic people of Wales or their language

cynic (sin′ik) *n.* [see ff.] 1. a person who believes the worst about people or the outcome of events 2. [C-] a member of a school of ancient Greek philosophers who esteemed virtue and stressed independence from worldly needs and pleasures —*adj.* 1. [C-] of or like the Cynics 2. same as CYNICAL

cynical (sin′i k'l) *adj.* [< Gr. *kyōn*, dog] 1. denying the sincerity of people's motives and actions 2. sarcastic, sneering, etc. 3. [C-] same as CYNIC —**cyn′ically** *adv.* —**cyn′icalness** *n.*

cynicism (sin′ə siz′m) *n.* 1. the attitude or beliefs of a cynical person 2. a cynical remark, idea, or action

cynosure (sin′ə zhooər′) [< Gr. *kynosoura*, dog's tail] [C-] *an old name for* URSA MINOR —*n.* a centre of attention or interest

cypher (sī′fər) *n., vt., vi.* same as CIPHER

cypress (sī′prəs) *n.* [< Gr. *kyparissos*] 1. a dark-foliaged, cone-bearing evergreen 2. cypress branches used as a symbol of mourning

Cypriot (sip′rē ət) *adj.* of Cyprus —*n.* a native or inhabitant of Cyprus Also **Cyp′-riote** (-ōt)

Cyrillic (sə ril′ik) *adj.* of the Slavic alphabet attributed to Saint Cyril, 9th-cent. apostle to the Slavs

cyst (sist) *n.* [< Gr. *kystis,* sac] any of certain saclike structures in plants or animals, esp. one filled with fluid or diseased matter —**cyst′ic** *adj.*

cystic fibrosis a disease of children, characterized by fibrosis and malfunctioning of the pancreas

cystitis (sis tīt′is) *n.* [CYST + -ITIS] an inflammation of the urinary bladder

cystoscope (sis′tə skōp′) *n.* [< CYST + -SCOPE] an instrument for visually examining the interior of the urinary bladder —**cystos′copy** (-tos′kə pē) *n.*

-cyte (sīt) [< Gr. *kytos,* hollow] *a combining form meaning* a cell

cytology (sī tol′ə jē) *n.* [< Gr. *kytos,*

hollow + -LOGY] the branch of biology dealing with cells —**cytol′ogist** *n.*

cytoplasm (sit′ə plaz′m) *n.* [< Gr. *kytos,* hollow + -PLASM] the protoplasm of a cell, exclusive of the nucleus

czar (zär) *var. of* TSAR —**czar′dom** *n.* —**czar′ist** *adj., n.*

czarevitch (zär′ə vich′) *n. var. of* TSAREVITCH

czarina (zä rē′nə) *n. var. of* TSARINA: also **czarit′za** (-rit′sə)

Czech (chek) *n.* 1. a Bohemian, Moravian, or Silesian Slav of Czechoslovakia 2. their West Slavic language —*adj.* of Czechoslovakia: also **Czech′ish**

Czechoslovak (chek′ə slō′vak) *adj.* of Czechoslovakia or its people —*n.* a Czech or Slovak living in Czechoslovakia Also **Czech′oslovak′ian** (-slō va′kē ən)

D

D, d (dē) *n., pl.* **D's, d's** the fourth letter of the English alphabet

D (dē) *n.* **1.** a Roman numeral for 500 **2.** *Music* the second tone in the ascending scale of C major

D *Chem.* deuterium

D. **1.** [Chiefly U.S.] Democrat(ic) **2.** Dutch

d deci-

d. **1.** day(s) **2.** diameter **3.** died **4.** [L. *pl. denarii*] penny; pence (in former Brit. currency)

dab¹ (dab) *vt., vi.* **dabbed, dab'bing** [ME. *dabben*, to strike] **1.** to touch lightly and quickly, esp. with something moist **2.** to put on (paint, etc.) with light strokes —*n.* **1.** a tap; pat **2.** a bit, esp. of a soft or moist thing [a dab of rouge] **3.** [*pl.*] [Slang] fingerprints —**dab'ber** *n.*

dab² *n.* [ME. *dabbe*] a flounder of coastal waters

dab³ *n.* [< ?] [Colloq.] an expert

dabble (dab''l) *vt.* **-bled, -bling** [Du. *dabben*, strike] to spatter or splash —*vi.* **1.** to play in water, as with the hands **2.** to do something superficially (with *in* or *at*) [to dabble in art] —**dab'bler** *n.*

dabchick (dab'chik') *n.* [< OE. *dop*, to dive + CHICK] either of two small grebes of Europe and the Americas

dab hand someone who is skilled at some activity; expert

‡da capo (dä kä'pō) [It.] *Music* from the beginning

dace (dās) *n.* [< OFr. *dars*, dart] a small freshwater fish

DACHSHUND (20-25 cm high at shoulder)

dachshund (daks'hoond) *n.* [G. *Dachs*, badger + *Hund*, dog] a small dog with a long body and short legs

Dacron (dak'ron) *Trademark* a synthetic, crease-resistant fabric

dactyl (dak'til) *n.* [< Gr. *daktylos*, finger] a metrical foot of three syllables, the first accented and the others unaccented —**dac'tylic** (dak til'ik) *adj.*

dad (dad) *n.* [< child's cry *dada*] [Colloq.] father: also **daddy**

dada (dä'dä) *n.* [Fr., hobbyhorse] [*also* D-] a movement (1916-22) in art and literature characterized by fantastic or incongruous creations —**da'daist** *adj., n.*

daddy-longlegs (dad'ē loŋ'legz') *n., pl.* **-long'legs'** *same as* CRANE FLY

dado (dā'dō) *n., pl.* **-does** [< L. *datum*, a die] **1.** the part of a pedestal between the cap and the base **2.** the lower part of a wall if decorated differently from the upper

daemon (dē'mən) *n.* [< Gr. *daimōn*] **1.** *Gr. Myth.* a secondary deity **2.** a guardian spirit **3.** *same as* DEMON —**daemonic** (di mon'ik) *adj.*

daff (daf) *n.* [Colloq.] a daffodil

daffodil (daf'ə dil') *n.* [< Gr. *asphodelos*] **1.** a narcissus, having a yellow flower and a large, trumpetlike crown **2.** the flower, one of the Welsh national emblems

daft (däft) *adj.* [< OE. (ge)*dæfte*, mild] **1.** silly; foolish **2.** insane; crazy —**daft'ly** *adv.* —**daft'ness** *n.*

dagga (dakh'ə) *n.* [< Afrik. < Hottentot *dagah*] in S Africa, a hemp smoked as a narcotic

dagger (dag'ər) *n.* [< ME. *daggere*] **1.** a weapon with a short, pointed blade, used for stabbing **2.** *Printing* a reference mark (†) —**look daggers at** to look at with anger —**at daggers drawn** in a state of hostility

dago (dā'gō) *n.* [< Sp. *Diego*, James] [Derog. Slang] a foreigner, esp. a Spaniard, Portuguese, or Italian

daguerreotype (də ger'ō tīp') *n.* [< L. *Daguerre*] a photograph made by an early method on a plate of chemically treated metal or glass

dahlia (dāl'yə) *n.* [< A. *Dahl*] a perennial plant with tuberous roots and large, showy flowers

Dail Eireann (doil'âar'ən) [Ir., assembly of Ireland] the lower house of the legislature of the Republic of Ireland

daily (dā'lē) *adj.* done, happening, or published every day —*n., pl.* **-lies** **1.** a daily newspaper **2.** a charwoman —*adv.* every day; day after day

dainty (dān'tē) *n., pl.* **-ties** [< L. *dignitas*, worth] a delicacy —*adj.* **1.** delicious and choice **2.** delicately pretty **3.** of refined taste; fastidious —**dain'tily** *adv.* —**dain'tiness** *n.*

daiquiri (dak'ər ē) *n.* [< *Daiquiri*, in Cuba] a cocktail made of rum, sugar, and lime juice

dairy (dâar'ē) *n., pl.* **dair'ies** [< OE. *dæge*, breadmaker] **1.** a commercial establishment that distributes milk and milk products **2.** a place where milk and cream are kept and butter, cheese, etc. are made —*adj.* of milk, cream, butter, cheese, etc.

dairy cattle cows raised mainly for their milk

dairy farm a farm that specializes in producing milk

dairymaid *n.* a girl or woman who milks cows or works in a dairy

dairyman *n.* a man who works in or for a dairy

dairy products milk, cream, cheese, butter, etc.

dais (dā′īs) *n.*, *pl.* **da′ises** [< L. *discus*, discus] a platform raised above the floor at one end of a hall or room, as for seats of honour, a speaker's stand, etc.

daisy (dā′zē) *n.*, *pl.* **-sies** [< OE. *dæges eage*, day's eye] a plant bearing flowers with white rays around a yellow disc —**push up (the) daisies** [Slang] to be dead and buried

Dalai Lama (da′lī lä′ma) [Mongol. *dalai*, ocean + LAMA] the traditional high priest of the Lamaist religion

dale (dāl) *n.* [OE. *dæl*] a valley

dalles (dalz) *n.pl.* [< Canad. Fr., trough] [US & Canad.] the rapids of a river flowing in a narrow channel between high rock walls

dally (dal′ē) *vi.* **-lied, -lying** [< OFr. *dalier*, to converse] **1.** to waste time **2.** to deal lightly or carelessly (*with*) **3.** to make love in a playful way —**dal′liance** *n.*

Dalmatian (dal mā′shən) *n.* a large, short-haired dog with dark spots on a white coat

‡**dal segno** (dal se′nyō) [It.] *Music* from the sign: a direction to return and repeat from the sign (𝄋)

dam[1] (dam) *n.* [ME.] **1.** a barrier built to hold back flowing water **2.** the water thus kept back —*vt.* **dammed, dam′ming** **1.** to build a dam in **2.** to keep back or confine as by a dam (usually with *up*)

dam[2] *n.* [see DAME] the female parent of any four-legged animal

damage (dam′ij) *n.* [< L. *damnum*, loss] **1.** injury or harm resulting in a loss **2.** [*pl.*] *Law* money compensating for injury, loss, etc. **3.** [Colloq.] cost —*vt.* **-aged, -aging** to do damage to —*vi.* to incur damage —**dam′ageable** *adj.*

damask (dam′əsk) *n.* [< *Damascus* (the city)] **1.** a lustrous, reversible fabric as of silk or linen, in figured weave, used for table linen, upholstery, etc. **2.** deep pink or rose —*adj.* **1.** made of or like damask **2.** deep-pink or rose —*vt.* to ornament with flowered designs or wavy lines

damask rose a very fragrant rose important as a source of attar of roses

dame (dām) *n.* [< L. *domina*, lady] **1.** [Obs.] a lady **2.** [D-] the title of a woman who has received an order of knighthood **3.** the role of a comic old woman in a pantomime, usually played by a man **4.** [U.S. Slang] a woman

damn (dam) *vt.* **damned, damn′ing** [< L. *damnare*, condemn] **1.** to condemn to an unhappy fate or *Theol.* to hell **2.** to condemn as bad, inferior, etc. **3.** to swear at by saying "damn" —*vi.* to swear or curse —*n.* the saying of "damn" as a curse —*adj., adv.* [Colloq.] *short for* DAMNED —*interj.* an expression of anger,

annoyance, etc. —**damn all** [Slang] nothing whatever —**damn with faint praise** to condemn by praising mildly —**not give (or care) a damn** [Colloq.] not care at all

damnable *adj.* deserving to be damned; outrageous; execrable —**dam′nably** *adv.*

damnation (dam nā′shən) *n.* a damning or being damned —*interj.* an expression of anger, annoyance, etc. —**dam′natory** *adj.*

damned (damd) *adj.* **1.** condemned or deserving condemnation **2.** [Colloq.] deserving cursing; outrageous [*a damned shame*] —*adv.* [Colloq.] very —**do (or try) one's damnedest** [Colloq.] to do or try one's utmost

damning *adj.* proving or indicative of guilt

damp (damp) *n.* [MDu., vapour] **1.** a slight wetness; moisture **2.** any harmful gas in a mine —*adj.* somewhat moist or wet —*vt.* **1.** to make damp **2.** to reduce or check (energy, action, etc.) —**damp′ish** *adj.* —**damp′ly** *adv.* —**damp′ness** *n.*

damp course a layer of impervious material in a brick wall that prevents damp from rising

dampen *vt.* **1.** to make damp **2.** to deaden, reduce, or lessen —*vi.* to become damp —**damp′ener** *n.*

DAMPER

damper *n.* **1.** anything that deadens or depresses **2.** a movable plate or valve in a flue for controlling the draught **3.** a device to check vibration in the strings of a piano, etc.

damsel (dam′z′l) *n.* [see DAME] [Archaic or Poet.] a girl; maiden

damson (dam′z′n) *n.* [< L. *Damascenus*, (plum) of Damascus] a variety of small, purple plum —*adj.* of the colour of this plum

Dan. **1.** Daniel **2.** Danish

dance (däns) *vi.* **danced, danc′ing** [< OFr. *danser*] **1.** to move the body and feet in rhythm, ordinarily to music **2.** to move lightly, rapidly, or gaily about —*vt.* **1.** to take part in or perform (a dance) **2.** to cause to dance —*n.* **1.** rhythmic movement of the body and feet, ordinarily to music **2.** a particular kind of dance **3.** the art of dancing **4.** a party to which people come to dance **5.** a piece of music for dancing **6.** rapid, lively movement —**dance attendance on** to be always near so as to lavish attentions on —**danc′er** *n.*

D and C dilatation (of the cervix) and curettage (of the uterus)

dandelion (dan′də lī′ən) *n.* [< L. *dens*, tooth + *de*, of + *leo*, lion] a common weed with jagged leaves and yellow flowers

dander (dan′dər) *n.* [< ?] [Colloq.] anger or temper —**get one's dander up** [Chiefly U.S. Colloq.] to become angry

dandify (dan′də fī′) *vt.* **-fied′, -fy′ing** to dress up like a dandy —**dan′difica′tion** *n.*

dandle (dan′d'l) *vt.* **-dled, -dling** [< ?] to dance (a child) up and down on the knee or in the arms

dandruff (dan′druf) *n.* [< ?] little scales or flakes of dead skin formed on the scalp —**dan′druffy** *adj.*

dandy (dan′dē) *n., pl.* **-dies** [< ?] a man excessively attentive to his appearance; fop —*adj.* **-dier, -diest** [U.S. Colloq.] very good —**dan′dyish** *adj.*

Dane (dān) *n.* a native or inhabitant of Denmark

danger (dān′jər) *n.* [< L. *dominus,* master] **1.** liability to injury, damage, loss, or pain **2.** a thing that may cause injury, pain, etc.

danger money extra money paid to compensate for the risks involved in certain dangerous jobs

dangerous *adj.* full of danger; unsafe; perilous —**dan′gerously** *adv.* —**dan′gerousness** *n.*

dangle (dan′g'l) *vi.* **-gled, -gling** [< Scand.] **1.** to hang, swinging loosely **2.** to follow (*after*) —*vt.* to cause to dangle

Danish (dā′nish) *adj.* of Denmark, the Danes, or their language —*n.* the language of the Danes

dank (dank) *adj.* [ME.] disagreeably damp; moist and chilly —**dank′ly** *adv.* —**dank′ness** *n.*

dankie (dan′kē) *interj.* [Afrik.] [S Afr.] thank you

dapper (dap′ər) *adj.* [< ? MDu.] **1.** trim, neat, or smart **2.** small and active —**dap′perly** *adv.*

dapple (dap′'l) *adj.* [< ?] marked with spots: also **dap′pled** —*n.* **1.** a spotted condition **2.** an animal whose skin is spotted —*vt., vi.* **-pled, -pling** to become covered with spots

dapple-grey *adj.* grey spotted with darker grey —*n.* a dapple-grey horse

Darby and Joan (där′bē ən jōn′) [< ? an 18th-cent. song] an old married couple devoted to each other

dare (dãər) *vi., vt.* **dared** or archaic **durst** (dûrst), **dared, dar′ing** [< OE. *durran*] **1.** to have enough courage for (some act) **2.** to oppose and defy **3.** to test the courage of (someone) with a dare —*n.* a challenge —**dare say** to think probable —**dar′er** *n.*

daredevil *adj.* bold and reckless —*n.* a bold, reckless person —**dare′dev′ilry, dare′dev′iltry** *n.*

daring *adj.* having or showing a bold willingness to take risks, etc. —*n.* bold courage —**dar′ingly** *adv.*

dark (därk) *adj.* [< OE. *deorc*] **1.** entirely or partly without light **2.** almost black **3.** not light in colour or complexion **4.** hidden; secret **5.** not easily understood **6.** gloomy **7.** angry or sullen **8.** evil; sinister **9.** ignorant; unenlightened —*n.* **1.** the state of being dark **2.** night —**in the dark** uninformed; ignorant —**keep dark** to keep secret or hidden —**dark′-ish** *adj.* —**dark′ly** *adv.* —**dark′ness** *n.*

Dark Ages the Middle Ages; esp., the early part to the late 10th cent.

Dark Continent Africa

darken *vt., vi.* to make or become dark or darker —**not darken one's door** not come to one's home

dark horse [Colloq.] **1.** an unexpected winner, as in a horse race **2.** one who reveals unexpected talents

darkroom *n.* a room from which all actinic rays are excluded, so that photographs can be developed in it

darling (där′lin) *n.* [OE. *deorling*] a person much loved by another —*adj.* very dear; beloved

darn¹ (därn) *vt., vi.* [< ?] to mend (cloth, etc.) by sewing a network of stitches across the gap —*n.* a darned place in fabric —**darn′er** *n.*

darn² *vt., vi., n., adj., adv., interj.* [Colloq.] a *euphemism for* DAMN (the curse) —**darned** *adj., adv.*

darnel (där′n'l) *n.* [< Fr. dial. *darnelle*] a weedy rye grass which can become poisonous

darning *n.* things to be darned

dart (därt) *n.* [< OFr.] **1.** a small, pointed missile for throwing or shooting **2.** a sudden, quick movement **3.** a tapered, stitched fold in a garment **4.** [*pl.*, *with sing. v.*] a game in which a dart is thrown at a target —*vt., vi.* to throw, move, etc. suddenly and fast

dartboard *n.* a circular piece of wood, cork, etc. used as a target in the game of darts

Dartmoor pony (därt′mooər) a breed of small, strong ponies, originally from Dartmoor

Darwinian theory (där win′ē ən) Darwin's theory of evolution, which holds that all species of plants and animals developed from earlier forms, those forms surviving which are best adapted to the environment: also called **Dar′winism** —**Dar′winist** *adj., n.*

dash (dash) *vt.* [< Scand.] **1.** to throw so as to break **2.** to strike violently (*against*) **3.** to throw, thrust, etc. (with *away, down,* etc.) **4.** to destroy; frustrate [to dash one's hopes] **5.** to depress; discourage **6.** [Colloq.] a *euphemism for* DAMN —*vi.* **1.** to strike violently (*against* or *on*) **2.** to rush —*n.* **1.** a bit of something added **2.** a sudden rush **3.** vigour; verve **4.** showy appearance **5.** the mark (—) used to indicate a break, omission, etc. **6.** *Telegraphy* a long signal, as in Morse code —**dash off 1.** to do, write, etc. hastily **2.** to rush away

dashboard *n.* a panel with instruments and gauges on it, as in a motor car; facia

dasher *n.* [Canad.] the ledge along the top of the boards of an ice hockey rink

dashing *adj.* **1.** full of dash or spirit; lively **2.** showy; stylish —**dash′ingly** *adv.*

dassie (das′ē) *n.* [< Afrik.] in South Africa, a hyrax, esp. a rock rabbit

dastard (das′tərd) *n.* [ME.] a mean, cowardly evildoer —**das′tardly** *adj.*

dat. dative

data (dāt′ə) *n.pl.* [*often with sing. v.*] [L., things given] facts or figures from which conclusions can be inferred; information: the sing. form is **datum**

data bank information stored in a form that can be directly retrieved by a computer

data processing the recording and handling of information by mechanical or electronic means

date¹ (dāt) *n.* [< L. *data*, as in *data Romae*, lit., given at Rome] 1. a statement on a writing, coin, etc. of when it was made 2. the time at which a thing happens or is done 3. the day of the month 4. a) an appointment for a set time b) the person with whom one has such an engagement —*vt.* **dat′ed, dat′ing** 1. to mark (a letter, etc.) with a date 2. to find out or give the date of 3. to show as old-fashioned 4. to have a social engagement with —*vi.* to belong to, or have its origin in, a definite period in the past (usually with *from* or *back to*) —**out of date** old-fashioned —**to date** until now —**up to date** in or into agreement with the latest ideas, styles, etc. —**dat′able, date′able** *adj.*

date² *n.* [< Gr. *daktylos*, a finger] the sweet, fleshy fruit of a cultivated palm (**date palm**)

dateline *n.* 1. the date and place of writing as given in a line in a newspaper, etc. 2. *same as* DATE LINE

date line an imaginary line drawn north and south through the Pacific Ocean, at which each calendar day begins at midnight, so that when it is Sunday just west of the line, it is Saturday just east of it

date stamp 1. a rubber stamp with figures that can be adjusted to show the date 2. the mark made by this

dative (dāt′iv) *adj.* [< L. *dare*, give] designating, of, or in that case which expresses the indirect object of a verb —*n.* 1. the dative case 2. a word in the dative case —**datival** (də tī′v′l) *adj.*

daub (dôb) *vt., vi.* [< L. *de-*, intens. + *albus*, white] 1. to cover or smear with sticky, soft matter, such as plaster, grease, etc. 2. to paint coarsely and unskilfully —*n.* 1. anything daubed on 2. a daubing stroke 3. a poorly painted picture —**daub′er** *n.*

daughter (dôt′ər) *n.* [< OE. *dohtor*] 1. a girl or woman as she is related to either or both parents 2. a female descendant 3. a female thought of as if in the relation of child to parent [*a daughter* of France] —**daugh′terliness** *n.* —**daugh′terly** *adj.*

daughter-in-law *n.*, *pl.* **daugh′ters-in-law′** the wife of one's son

daunt (dônt) *vt.* [< L. *domare*, tame] to make afraid or discouraged; intimidate; dishearten

dauntless *adj.* that cannot be intimidated or discouraged —**daunt′lessly** *adv.* —**daunt′lessness** *n.*

dauphin (dô′fin) *n.* [Fr., lit., dolphin] the eldest son of the king of France: a title used from 1349 to 1830 —**dau′phine, dau′phiness** *n. fem.*

davenport (dav′ən pôrt′) *n.* [< ?] 1. a small writing desk with a hinged writing surface 2. [U.S.] a large sofa

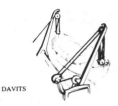

DAVITS

davit (dav′it) *n.* [< OFr. dim. of *David*] either of a pair of uprights projecting over the side of a ship for suspending, lowering, or raising a boat

Davy Jones's locker (dā′vē jōn′ziz) the bottom of the sea; grave of those drowned or buried at sea

Davy lamp [< Sir H. *Davy*] an early safety lamp for miners, with the flame enclosed by wire gauze

dawdle (dôd′'l) *vi., vt.* **=dled, =dling** [< ?] to waste (time) in trifling; loiter —**daw′dler** *n.*

dawn (dôn) *vi.* [< OE. *dæg*, day] 1. to begin to be day; grow light 2. to begin to appear, develop, etc. 3. to begin to be understood [the meaning *dawned* on me] —*n.* 1. daybreak 2. the beginning (*of* something)

dawn chorus the singing of many birds at daybreak

day (dā) *n.* [< OE. *dæg*] 1. a) the period of light between sunrise and sunset b) daylight c) sunshine 2. the time (24 hours) that it takes the earth to revolve once on its axis 3. [often D-] a particular day [Christmas Day] 4. [also pl.] a period of time; era [the best writer of his *day*] 5. a time of power, glory, etc. [he has had his *day*] 6. the time one works each day [an eight-hour *day*] 7. [pl.] one's lifetime —**all in a day's work** part of the usual course of events —**call it a day** [Colloq.] 1. to stop working for the day 2. to decide to stop doing (something) —**day after day** every day —**day by day** each day —**day in, day out** every day —**from day to day** 1. from one day to the next 2. without particular concern about the future

daybed (dā′bed′) *n.* a couch that can also be used as a bed

dayboy *n.* a child who attends a boarding school by day and returns home each night —**day′girl** *n. fem.*

daybreak *n.* the time in the morning when light first appears; dawn

day centre a place where meals, entertainment, etc. are provided for old or disabled people who spend the day there

daydream *n.* 1. a pleasant, dreamlike thinking or wishing; reverie 2. a pleasing but visionary notion —*vi.* to have daydreams —**day′dream′er** *n.*

daylight *n.* 1. the light of day 2. dawn 3. daytime 4. full understanding or knowledge

daylight robbery blatant overcharging

daylight-saving time time that is one hour later than standard time, generally used in the summer

day release a system of vocational training for employees during working hours, usually one day a week

day room a room for recreation, reading, etc., as in a barracks, institution, or the like

day school 1. a school whose pupils live at home 2. a school that has classes in the daytime

day-to-day *adj.* everyday; daily

daze (dāz) *vt.* **dazed, daz′ing** [< ON. *dasi*, tired] to stun or bewilder —*n.* a dazed condition —**daz′edly** (-id lē) *adv.*

dazzle (daz′′l) *vi., vt.* **daz′zled, daz′zling** [< DAZE] 1. to overpower or be overpowered with very bright light 2. to surprise or arouse admiration with brilliant qualities, display, etc. —*n.* 1. a dazzling 2. something that dazzles —**daz′zler** *n.* —**daz′zlingly** *adv.*

db decibel; decibels

D.B.E. Dame Commander of the Order of the British Empire

DC, D.C., d.c. direct current

D.C.B. Dame Commander of the Order of the Bath

D.C.M. Distinguished Conduct Medal

D.D. [L. *Divinitatis Doctor*] Doctor of Divinity

D-day (dē′dā′) *n.* the day for beginning an important operation; specif., June 6, 1944, the day Allied forces invaded W Europe in World War II

D.D.S. Doctor of Dental Surgery

DDT a powerful insecticide effective upon contact

de- [< Fr. or L.] a prefix meaning: 1. away from, off [*derail*] 2. down [*decline*] 3. entirely [*defunct*] 4. reverse the action of [*defrost*]

deacon (dēk′′n) *n.* [< Gr. *diakonos*, servant] 1. a cleric ranking just below a priest 2. a church officer who helps the clergyman, esp. in secular matters —**dea′conate** *n.* —**dea′coness** *n. fem.*

deactivate (dē ak′tə vāt′) *vt.* **-vat′ed, -vat′ing** to make (an explosive, etc.) inactive —**deac′tiva′tion** *n.*

dead (ded) *adj.* [OE.] 1. no longer living 2. without life 3. deathlike 4. lacking vitality, interest, warmth, etc. 5. without feeling, motion, or power 6. extinguished or extinct 7. no longer used or significant 8. unerring; sure [a *dead* shot] 9. exact; precise [*dead* centre] 10. complete [a *dead* stop] 11. *Elec.* without current or uncharged 12. *Sports* no longer in play —*n.* the time of greatest darkness, most intense cold, etc. [the *dead* of night] —*adv.* 1. completely; absolutely [*dead* right] 2. directly [*dead* ahead] —**dead from the neck up** [Colloq.] extremely stupid —**the dead** those who have died

deadbeat *n.* [Slang] a person who is penniless or exhausted

dead duck [Colloq.] a person or thing doomed to death, failure, etc., esp. because of a mistake

deaden *vt.* 1. to lessen the vigour or intensity of 2. to make numb —*vi.* to become as if dead

dead-end (ded′end′) *adj.* 1. having only one exit [a *dead-end* street] 2. giving no opportunity for progress

dead end 1. an end of a street, etc. that has no regular exit 2. an impasse

deadhead *n.* 1. a person who uses a free ticket to go to the theatre, etc. 2. [U.S. & Canad.] a log sticking out of the surface of water as a snag to navigation —*vt.* to remove dead flower heads

dead heat a race in which two or more contestants reach the finishing line at exactly the same time; tie

dead letter 1. a law, practice, etc. no longer enforced or operative but not formally done away with 2. a letter that cannot be delivered or returned

deadline *n.* the latest time by which something must be done or completed

deadlock *n.* 1. a standstill resulting from the action of equal and opposed forces 2. a type of lock that can be locked or unlocked only with a key —*vt., vi.* to bring or come to a deadlock

dead loss 1. a loss for which no compensation is payable 2. [Colloq.] a worthless person or thing

deadly *adj.* **-lier, -liest** 1. causing or likely to cause death 2. to the death [*deadly* combat] 3. typical of death 4. extreme or excessive [*deadly* silence] 5. *Theol.* causing spiritual death —*adv.* 1. as if dead [to lie *deadly* still] 2. extremely or excessively [*deadly* serious] —**dead′liness** *n.*

deadly nightshade same as BELLA-DONNA

dead man's handle a device in trains that requires constant pressure to maintain the power supply

dead march funeral music in slow march tempo

deadpan *adj., adv.* [Colloq.] without expression

dead reckoning [< ? *ded* (for *deduced*) *reckoning*] the finding of a ship's position by an estimate based on data recorded in the log rather than by taking astronomical observations

dead set a resolute attack or effort —*adv.* absolutely and uncompromisingly

dead weight 1. the weight of an inert person or thing 2. the weight of a vehicle without a load

deadwood *n.* 1. dead wood on trees 2. a useless or burdensome person or thing

deaf (def) *adj.* [OE.] 1. unable to hear 2. unwilling to hear or listen —**deaf′ly** *adv.* —**deaf′ness** *n.*

deaf aid a hearing aid

deaf-and-dumb *adj.* 1. deaf-mute 2. of or for deaf-mutes [*deaf-and-dumb* alphabet]

deafen *vt.* 1. to make deaf 2. to overwhelm with noise —**deaf′ening** *adj., n.* —**deaf′eningly** *adv.*

deaf-mute (def′myo͞ot′) *n.* a person who is deaf, esp. from birth, and unable to speak

deal[1] (dēl) *vt.* **dealt, deal′ing** [OE. *dælan*] 1. to portion out or distribute 2. to give or administer (a blow) —*vi.* 1. to have to do (*with*) [books *dealing* with fish] 2. to act or conduct oneself [*deal* fairly with others] 3. to consider or attend to [to *deal* with a problem] 4. to do business; trade (*with* or *in*) 5. to distribute playing cards to the players —*n.* 1. *a*) the act of distributing playing cards *b*) a player's turn to deal 2. a business transaction 3. a bargain or agreement 4. [Colloq.] behaviour or conduct towards another [a square *deal*] —**big deal** [Colloq.] a very impressive thing —**raw** (or **rough**) **deal** very unfair treatment —**deal′er** *n.*

deal[2] *n.* [OE. *dæl*, part] a considerable amount —**a good** (or **great**) **deal** 1. a large amount 2. very much

deal[3] *n.* [MDu. *dele*] 1. a fir or pine board 2. fir or pine wood —*adj.* made of deal

dealing *n.* 1. distribution 2. behaviour 3. [*usually pl.*] transactions or relations

dealt (delt) *pt.* and *pp.* of DEAL[1]

dean[1] (dēn) *n.* [< LL. *decanus*, head of ten soldiers or monks] 1. the presiding official of a cathedral 2. *a*) a university official in charge of a faculty *b*) a fellow of a college with responsibility for undergraduate discipline —**dean′ship** *n.*

dean[2] *n.* [< OE. *denu*, valley] a narrow, wooded valley

deanery *n., pl.* **-eries** 1. the rank, authority, or residence of a dean 2. the parishes presided over by a dean

dear (dēər) *adj.* [OE. *deore*] 1. much loved; esteemed: a polite form of address [*Dear* Sir] 3. high-priced 4. earnest [our *dearest* wish] 5. cherished; precious [for *dear* life] —*adv.* 1. with deep affection 2. at a high cost —*n.* a loved person: also **dear′est** —*interj.* an expression of surprise, pity, etc. —**dear′ly** *adv.*

dearth (durth) *n.* [see DEAR] 1. scarcity of food; famine 2. any scarcity or lack

death (deth) *n.* [OE.] 1. the act or fact of dying; ending of life 2. [D-] the personification of death, usually as a skeleton holding a scythe 3. the state of being dead 4. any end resembling dying 5. the cause of death —**at death's door** nearly dead —**be the death of** likely to cause the death of —**put to death** to execute —**to death** very much [worried *to death*] —**to the death** to the very end of (a struggle, etc.) —**death′like′** *adj.*

deathbed *n.* the bed on which a person dies —*adj.* done in one's last hours of life [a *deathbed* will]

deathblow *n.* 1. a blow that kills 2. a thing destructive or fatal (*to* something)

death certificate a document stating the cause of death and signed by a doctor

death duty a tax levied on property inheritances

deathless *adj.* that cannot die; immortal

deathly *adj.* 1. causing death; deadly 2. like or characteristic of death —*adv.* 1. in a deathlike way 2. extremely [*deathly* ill]

death rate the number of deaths per year per thousand of population

death's-head *n.* a human skull symbolizing death

deathtrap *n.* an unsafe building, vehicle, etc.

death warrant 1. an official order to put a person to death 2. anything that makes inevitable the destruction or end of a person or thing

deathwatch *n.* 1. a vigil kept beside a dead or dying person 2. a beetle that bores into wood and makes a tapping sound: also **deathwatch beetle**

debacle (dā bäk′'l) *n.* [< Fr. *débâcler*, break up] 1. an overwhelming defeat or rout 2. a total, often ludicrous, collapse or failure

debar (di bär′) *vt.* **-barred′, -bar′ring** [< Anglo-Fr.: see DE- & BAR[1]] 1. to exclude (*from* something); bar 2. to prevent or prohibit —**debar′ment** *n.*

debark (di bärk′) *vt., vi.* [< Fr.: see DE- & BARQUE] to disembark —**de′barka′-tion** *n.*

debase (di bās′) *vt.* **-based′, -bas′ing** [DE- + (A)BASE] to make lower in quality, dignity, etc. —**debase′ment** *n.*

debate (di bāt′) *vi.* **-bat′ed, -bat′ing** [< OFr. *debatre*, fight] 1. to discuss opposing reasons; argue 2. to take part in a formal discussion —*vt.* 1. to dispute about, esp. in a meeting or legislature 2. to argue (a question) or argue with (a person) formally 3. to consider reasons for and against —*n.* 1. discussion of opposing reasons; argument 2. *a*) the discussion of a bill, etc. in Parliament *b*) a formal contest in reasoned argument by two opposing teams —**debat′able** *adj.* —**debat′er** *n.*

debauch (di bôch′) *vt.* [< OFr. *desbaucher*, seduce] to lead astray morally; corrupt —*vi.* to dissipate —*n.* 1. debauchery 2. an orgy —**debauch′er** *n.* —**debauch′ment** *n.*

debauchery (di bôch′ər ē) *n., pl.* **-eries** 1. extreme indulgence of one's appetites 2. [*pl.*] orgies

debenture (di ben′chər) *n.* [< L. *debentur*, there are owing] 1. a voucher acknowledging a debt 2. an interest-bearing bond often issued without security

debenture stock shares issued by a company, which guarantee a fixed return at regular intervals

debilitate (di bil′ə tāt′) *vt.* **-tat′ed, -tat′-ing** [< L. *debilis*, weak] to make weak; enervate —**debil′ita′tion** *n.*

debility *n., pl.* **-ties** [< L. *debilis*, weak] bodily weakness; feebleness

debit (deb′it) *n.* [< L. *debere*, owe] 1. an entry in an account of money owed

2. the total of such entries —*vt.* to enter as a debit

debonair (deb′ə nāär′) *adj.* [< OFr. *de bon aire*, of good breed] **1.** genial; affable **2.** carefree in manner; jaunty —**deb′onair′ly** *adv.*

debouch (di bouch′) *vi.* [< Fr. dé-, DE- + *bouche*, mouth] **1.** *Mil.* to come forth from a narrow place into open country **2.** to emerge —**debouch′ment** *n.*

debrief (dē brēf′) *vt.* [DE- + BRIEF] to question (a pilot, etc.) following a flight or mission —**debrief′ing** *n.*

debris, débris (də′brē) *n.* [< OFr. *desbrisier*, break apart] **1.** broken pieces of stone, wood, etc.; rubble **2.** bits of rubbish; litter **3.** a heap of rock fragments

debt (det) *n.* [< L. *debere*, owe] **1.** something owed to another **2.** an obligation to pay or return something **3.** the condition of owing [to be in *debt*]

debt of honour a gambling or betting debt

debtor *n.* one that owes a debt

debug (dē bug′) *vt.* -**bugged′**, -**bug′ging** [DE- + BUG] **1.** [Slang] to correct defects, etc. in **2.** [Slang] to remove hidden listening devices from (a room, etc.)

debunk (dē bunk′) *vt.* [DE- + BUNK²] [Colloq.] to expose the false or exaggerated claims, etc. of —**debunk′er** *n.*

début (dā′bōo, dā′byōo) *n.* [Fr. < *débuter*, lead off] **1.** the first appearance before the public, as of an actor **2.** the formal introduction of a girl into society

débutante (deb′yōo tänt′) *n.* [Fr.] a girl making a début into society

Dec. December

deca- [< Gr. *deka*, ten] *a combining form meaning* ten

decade (dek′ād) *n.* [< Gr. *deka*, ten] **1.** a period of ten years **2.** a group of ten

decadence (dek′ə dəns) *n.* [< L. *de-*, from + *cadere*, fall] a process, condition, or period of decline, as in morals, art, etc. —**dec′adent** *adj., n.*

decagon (dek′ə gən) *n.* [see DECA- & -GON] a plane figure with ten sides and ten angles

decagram, decagramme *n.* [see DECA- & GRAM] a measure of weight, equal to 10 grams

decahedron (dek′ə hē′drən) *n.,* pl. -**drons, -dra** [see DECA- & -HEDRON] a solid figure with ten plane surfaces

decalitre (dek′ə lēt′ər) *n.* [see DECA- & LITRE] a measure of capacity, equal to 10 litres

Decalogue (dek′ə log′) *n.* [< Gr.: see DECA- & -LOGUE] [*sometimes* d- } same as TEN COMMANDMENTS

decametre (dek′ə mēt′ər) *n.* [see DECA- & METRE] a measure of length, equal to 10 metres

decamp (di kamp′) *vi.* [< Fr.: see DE- & CAMP¹] **1.** to break or leave camp **2.** to go away suddenly and secretly

decant (di kant′) *vt.* [< L. *de-*, from + *canthus*, rim] to pour off (a liquid, esp. wine) gently without stirring up the sediment

decanter *n.* a decorative glass bottle, used for serving wine, etc.

decapitate (di kap′ə tāt′) *vi.* -**tat′ed,** -**tat′ing** [< L. *de-*, off + *caput*, head] to cut off the head of; behead —**decap′ita′tion** *n.* —**decap′ita′tor** *n.*

decapod (dek′ə pod′) *adj.* [see DECA- & -POD] ten-legged —*n.* **1.** any crustacean with ten legs, as a lobster, crab, etc. **2.** any cephalopod with ten arms, as a squid

decarbonize (dē kär′bə nīz′) *vt.* -**ized′,** -**iz′ing** to remove carbon from: also **decar′burize′** (-byōo riz′) -**rized′,** -**riz′ing** —**decar′boniza′tion** *n.*

decathlon (dē kath′lon) *n.* [DEC(A)- + Gr. *athlon*, a contest] an athletic contest consisting of ten events

decay (di kā′) *vi.* [see DECADENCE] **1.** to lose strength, prosperity, etc. gradually **2.** to rot **3.** to undergo radioactive disintegration —*vt.* to cause to decay —*n.* **1.** a deterioration **2.** a rotting or rottenness **3.** the spontaneous disintegration of radioactive atoms

decease (di sēs′) *n.* [< L. *de-*, from + *cedere*, go] death —*vi.* -**ceased′,** -**ceas′ing** to die

deceased (di sēst′) *adj.* dead —**the deceased** the dead person or persons

deceit (di sēt′) *n.* [see DECEIVE] **1.** a deceiving or lying **2.** a dishonest action; lie **3.** the quality of being deceitful

deceitful *adj.* **1.** apt to lie or cheat **2.** deceptive; false —**deceit′fully** *adv.* —**deceit′fulness** *n.*

deceive (di sēv′) *vt.* -**ceived′,** -**ceiv′ing** [< L. *de-*, from + *capere*, take] to make (a person) believe what is not true —*vi.* to use deceit —**deceive oneself** to delude oneself —**deceiv′er** *n.* —**deceiv′ingly** *adv.*

decelerate (dē sel′ə rāt′) *vt., vi.* -**at′ed,** -**at′ing** [DE- + (AC)CELERATE] to slow down —**decel′era′tion** *n.*

December (di sem′bər) *n.* [< L. *decem,* ten: the Romans counted from March] the twelfth and last month of the year, having 31 days: abbrev. **Dec.**

decency (dē′sən sē) *n.,* pl. -**cies** a being decent; propriety; proper behaviour, modesty, good taste, etc.

decennial (di sen′ē əl) *adj.* [< L. *decem,* ten + *annus,* year] **1.** of or lasting ten years **2.** occurring every ten years —*n.* a tenth anniversary —**decen′nially** *adv.*

decent (dē′sənt) *adj.* [< L. *decere,* befit] **1.** proper and fitting **2.** not obscene **3.** conforming to approved social standards **4.** adequate [*decent* wages] **5.** [Colloq.] fair and kind —**de′cently** *adv.*

decentralize (dē sen′trə līz′) *vt.* -**ized′,** -**iz′ing** to break up a concentration of (governmental authority, etc.) and distribute more widely —**decen′traliza′tion** *n.*

deception (di sep′shən) *n.* **1.** a being deceived **2.** an illusion or a fraud

deceptive *adj.* deceiving or meant to deceive —**decep′tively** *adv.* —**decep′tiveness** *n.*

deci- [< L. *decem,* ten] *a combining form meaning* one tenth [*decigram*]

decibel (des′ə bel′) *n.* [DECI- + *bel* (after

A. G. *Bell*)] a numerical expression of the relative loudness of a sound

decide (di sīd′) *vt.* **-cid′ed, -cid′ing** [< L. *de-*, off + *caedere*, to cut] 1. to reach a decision about 2. to end (a contest, dispute, etc.) by giving one side the victory —*vi.* to arrive at a judgment —**decid′er** *n.*

decided *adj.* 1. definite; clear-cut 2. unhesitating; determined —**decid′edly** *adv.*

deciduous (di sid′yoo was) *adj.* [< L. *de-*, off + *cadere*, fall] 1. shedding leaves annually 2. falling off at a certain season, as leaves, antlers, etc. —**decid′uously** *adv.*

decigram, decigramme (des′ə gram′) *n.* [see DECI- & GRAM] a metric weight, equal to 1/10 gram

decilitre (des′ə lēt′ər) *n.* [see DECI- & LITRE] a metric measure of volume, equal to 1/10 litre

decimal (des′ə m′l) *adj.* [< L. *decem,* ten] of or based on the number 10; progressing by tens —*n.* a fraction with an unwritten denominator of some power of ten, shown by a point (**decimal point**) before the numerator (Ex.: ·5 = 5/10): in full, **decimal fraction** —**dec′imally** *adv.*

decimal currency a system of currency in which the monetary units are powers of ten: also **decimal coinage**

decimalize *vt.* **-ized′, -iz′ing** to adopt a decimal system for (currency, etc.) —**dec′-imaliza′tion** *n.*

decimal system a system of computation based on the number ten

decimate (des′ə māt′) *vt.* **-mat′ed, -mat′-ing** [< L. *decem,* ten] 1. to destroy a large part of 2. orig., to kill every tenth one of —**dec′ima′tion** *n.*

decimetre (des′ə mēt′ər) *n.* [see DECI- & METRE] a metric measure of length, equal to 1/10 metre

decipher (di sī′fər) *vt.* [DE- + CIPHER] 1. to decode 2. to make out the meaning of (ancient inscriptions, etc.) —**deci′pherable** *adj.*

decision (di sizh′ən) *n.* 1. the act of deciding something 2. a judgment or conclusion 3. determination [a man of *decision*] —**deci′sional** *adj.*

decisive (di sī′siv) *adj.* 1. that settles a dispute, etc. 2. critically important 3. showing decision or determination —**deci′-sively** *adv.* —**deci′siveness** *n.*

deck[1] (dek) *n.* [prob. < MLowG. *verdeck*] 1. a roof over a section of a ship's hold, serving as a floor 2. any platform or floor like a ship's deck —**clear the decks** to get ready for action

deck[2] *vt.* [MDu. *decken,* to cover] to cover with finery or ornaments

deck chair a folding chair, usually with a canvas seat

deckhand *n.* a common sailor

deckle edge (dek′′l) [< G. *Decke,* a cover] a rough, irregular edge sometimes given to a sheet of paper

declaim (di klām′) *vi., vt.* [< L. *de-,* intens. + *clamare,* shout] 1. to recite a speech, poem, etc.) with artificial eloquence 2.

to deliver a tirade (*against*) —**declaim′-er** *n.* —**dec′lama′tion** (dek′lə-) *n.*

declaration (dek′lə rā′shən) *n.* 1. a declaring; announcement 2. a formal statement 3. a statement of taxable goods 4. *Bridge* the winning bid 5. *Cricket* the closing of an innings before all wickets have fallen

declare (di klāər′) *vt.* **-clared′, -clar′ing** [< L. *de-,* intens. + *clarus,* clear] 1. to announce openly, formally, etc. 2. to show or reveal 3. to say emphatically 4. to make a statement of (taxable goods), as at customs 5. *Card Games* to establish (trump or no-trump) by a successful bid —*vi.* 1. to make a declaration 2. to state openly a choice, opinion, etc. 3. *Cricket* to close an innings before all wickets have fallen —**declare oneself** 1. to state strongly one's opinion 2. to reveal one's true character, etc. —**declar′ative** (-klar′-) *adj.* —**declar′er** *n.*

declassify (dē klas′ə fī′) *vt.* **-fied′, -fy′-ing** to make (governmental documents, etc.) available to the public

declension (di klen′shən) *n.* [see DECLINE] 1. a sloping; descent 2. a declining; deterioration 3. *Gram.* a class of nouns, pronouns, or adjectives having the same inflection —**declen′sional** *adj.*

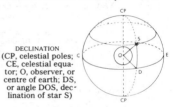

DECLINATION
(CP, celestial poles; CE, celestial equator; O, observer, or centre of earth; DS, or angle DOS, declination of star S)

declination (dek′lə nā′shən) *n.* 1. a bending or sloping downwards 2. the angle formed by a magnetic needle with the line pointing to true north 3. [U.S.] a polite refusal 4. *Astron.* the angular distance of a heavenly body north or south from the celestial equator

decline (di klīn′) *vi.* **-clined′, -clin′ing** [< L. *de-,* from + *clinare,* to bend] 1. to refuse something 2. to approach the end; wane 3. to deteriorate 4. to bend or slope downwards —*vt.* 1. to refuse, esp. politely 2. *Gram.* to give the inflected forms of (a noun, pronoun, or adjective) 3. to cause to bend or slope downwards —*n.* 1. a declining; deterioration; decay 2. a period of decline 3. a wasting disease, esp. tuberculosis 4. a downward slope —**declin′able** *adj.* —**declin′er** *n.*

declivity (di kliv′ə tē) *n.,* pl. **-ties** [< L. *de-,* down + *clivus,* a slope] a downward slope of the ground

declutch (dē kluch′) *vi.* to disengage the clutch which connects the engine and transmission of a motor vehicle

decoct (di kokt′) *vt.* [< L. *de-,* down + *coquere,* cook] to extract the essence of by boiling —**decoc′tion** *n.*

decode (dē kōd') *vt.* -cod'ed, -cod'ing to translate (a coded message) into understandable language

decoke (dē kōk') *vt. same as* DECARBONIZE

décolletage (dā kol'ə täzh') *n.* [Fr.] a low-cut dress, etc.

décolleté (dā kol'tā) *adj.* [Fr., ult. < L. *de*, from + *collum*, neck] 1. cut low so as to bare the neck and shoulders 2. wearing a décolleté dress, etc.

decompose (dē'kəm pōz') *vt., vi.* -posed', -pos'ing [see DE- & COMPOSE] 1. to break up into components or parts. 2. to rot —de'compos'able *adj.* —de'composi'tion (-kom pə zish'ən)

decompress (dē'kəm pres') *vt.* to free from pressure —de'compres'sion *n.* —de'compres'sor *n.*

decompression sickness a condition caused by the formation of nitrogen bubbles in the blood as a result of a sudden lowering of air pressure

decongestant (dē'kən jes'tənt) *n.* a drug, etc. that relieves congestion, as in the nasal passages

decontaminate (dē'kən tam'ə nāt') *vt.* -nat'ed, -nat'ing to rid of a harmful substance, as radioactive products —de'contam'ina'tion *n.*

décor (dā'kôr) *n.* [Fr.] 1. decoration 2. the decorative scheme of a room, stage set, etc.

decorate (dek'ə rāt') *vt.* -rat'ed, -rat'ing [< L. *decus*, an ornament] 1. to adorn; ornament 2. to paint or wallpaper 3. to give a medal or similar token of honour to —decorative (dek'ər ə tiv) *adj.* —dec'orativeness *n.* —dec'ora'tor *n.*

decorated style a richly ornamented style of 14th cent. Gothic architecture

decoration (dek'ə rā'shən) *n.* 1. a decorating 2. an ornament 3. a medal or similar honour

decorous (dek'ər əs) *adj.* [L. *decorus*, becoming] having or showing decorum —dec'orously *adv.*

decorum (di kôr'əm) *n.* [L.: see prec.] 1. whatever is suitable or proper 2. propriety in behaviour, speech, etc.

decoy (di koi'; *for n.* dē'koi) *n.* [< Du. *de kooi*, the cage] 1. a thing, animal, or person used to lure into a trap 2. a place into which wild ducks, etc. are lured for capture —vt. 1. to lure into a trap, danger, etc. 2. [Canad.] *same as* DEKE —vi. to be decoyed

decrease (di krēs'; *for n.*, dē'krēs) *vi., vt.* -creased', -creas'ing [< L. de-, from + *crescere*, grow] to become or cause to become gradually less, smaller, etc. —n. 1. a lessening 2. amount of decreasing —on the decrease decreasing —decreas'ingly *adv.*

decree (di krē') *n.* [< L. de-, from + *cernere*, judge] an official order or decision, as of a government —vt. -creed', -cree'ing to order, decide, or appoint by decree

decree nisi (nī'sī) [L. *nisi*, unless] a provisional divorce order which becomes absolute after a fixed period, unless cause to the contrary is shown

decrepit (di krep'it) *adj.* [< L. de-, intens. + *crepare*, creak] broken down or worn out by old age or long use —decrep'itly *adv.* —decrep'itude' *n.*

decrescendo (dē'krə shen'dō) *adj., adv.* [It.] *Music* with a gradual decrease in loudness —n., *pl.* -dos *Music* a gradual decrease in loudness; symbol <

decretal (di krēt''l) *adj.* [< LL. *decretalis*] of a decree —n. *R.C.Ch.* a decree issued by the Pope

decry (di krī') *vt.* -cried', -cry'ing [see DE- & CRY] to speak out against strongly and openly; denounce

dedicate (ded'ə kāt') *vt.* -cat'ed, -cat'ing [< L. de-, intens. + *dicere*, speak] 1. to devote to a sacred purpose 2. to devote to some work, duty, etc. 3. to address (a book, etc.) to someone as a sign of honour —ded'ica'tor *n.*

dedicated *adj.* devoted; single-minded

dedication (ded'ə kā'shən) *n.* 1. a dedicating or being dedicated 2. an inscription, as in a book, dedicating it to someone 3. wholehearted devotion —ded'icatory *adj.*

deduce (di dyoos') *vt.* -duced', -duc'ing [< L. de-, down + *ducere*, lead] 1. to infer by logical reasoning 2. to trace the course of —deduc'ible *adj.*

deduct (di dukt') *vt.* [see prec.] to take away or subtract (a quantity)

deductible *adj.* that is allowed as a deduction in computing income tax —deduct'ibil'ity *n.*

deduction (di duk'shən) *n.* 1. a deducting or being deducted; subtraction 2. the amount deducted 3. *a)* reasoning from the general to the specific *b)* a conclusion so deduced —deduc'tive *adj.* —deduc'tively *adv.*

deed (dēd) *n.* [OE. *ded*] 1. a thing done; act 2. a feat of courage, skill, etc. 3. action; actual performance 4. *Law* a document which transfers a present interest in property —in deed in fact; really

deed box a strong box used to hold documents

deed of covenant an agreement to pay a certain sum annually, as to a charity, for a stated number of years : the tax on this gift may be reclaimed by the charity

deed poll *Law* a deed made by one party only, esp. one by which a person changes his name

deejay (dē'jā') *n.* [D(ISC) J(OCKEY)] [Colloq.] *same as* DISC JOCKEY

deem (dēm) *vt., vi.* [OE. *deman*, to judge] to think, believe, or judge

deemster (dēm'stər) *n.* the title of either of the two chief judges of the Isle of Man : also demp'ster

deep (dēp) *adj.* [OE. *deop*] 1. extending far downwards, inwards, or backwards 2. extending down, back, or in a specified distance *[two feet deep]* 3. *a)* located far down or back *b)* coming from or going far down or back 4. hard to understand 5. grave or serious 6. strongly felt 7. intellectually profound 8. carefully guarded [a deep secret] **9.** dark and rich [a deep red] **10.** absorbed by [deep in thought] **11.** intense **12.** of low pitch [a deep voice] —n. **1.** a deep place **2.** the part that is darkest, etc. [the deep of the night] **3.** Cricket the area of the field relatively far from the wicket —adv. far down, far back, etc. —**go off the deep end** [Colloq.] to become angry or excited —**in deep water** in trouble or difficulty —**deep'ly** adv. —**deep'ness** n.

deepen vt., vi. to make or become deep or deeper

deepfreeze (dēp'frēz') n. **1.** storage in a deep freezer **2.** same as DEEP FREEZER —vt. -froze', -fro'zen, -freez'ing to subject (foods) to sudden freezing so as to preserve and store

deep freezer any freezer for freezing and storing food

deep-laid adj. carefully worked out and kept secret

deep-rooted adj. **1.** having deep roots **2.** firmly fixed; hard to remove

deep-seated adj. **1.** buried deep **2.** firmly fixed

deer (dēor) n., pl. **deer** [OE. deor, wild animal] any of a family of hoofed, cud-chewing animals, including the reindeer, red deer, etc.

deerskin n. **1.** the hide of a deer **2.** leather or a garment made from this

deerstalker n. a hat with peaks in front and behind

deface (di fās') vt. -faced', -fac'ing [see DE- & FACE] to spoil the appearance of —**deface'ment** n.

de facto (dē fak'tō) [L.] existing in actual fact though not by official recognition, etc.

defalcate (dē'fal kāt) vi. -cated, -cating [< L. de-, from + falx, sickle] to steal or misuse funds entrusted to one's care; embezzle —**defal'ca'tion** n.

defame (di fām') vt. -famed', -fam'ing [< L. dis-, from + fama, fame] to attack the reputation of —**defamation** (def'ə-mā'shən) —**defamatory** (di fam'ə tər ē) adj.

default (di fôlt') n. [< L. de-, away + fallere, fail] failure to do or appear as required; specif., a) failure to pay money due b) failure to take part in or finish a contest —vt., vi. **1.** to fail to do, pay, finish, etc. (something) when required **2.** to lose (a contest, etc.) by default —**go by default** to occur because of absence, lack of action, etc. —**default'er** n.

defeat (di fēt') vt. [< L. dis-, from + facere, do] **1.** to win victory over; beat **2.** to bring to nothing; frustrate —n. a defeating or being defeated

defeatist n. one who too readily accepts defeat —adj. of or like a defeatist —**defeat'ism** n.

defecate (dē'fə kāt) vt., vi. -cat'ed, -cat'-ing [< L. de-, from + faex, faecis, dregs] to excrete waste matter from the bowels Also **def'aecate** —**def'eca'tion** n.

defect (dē'fekt; also, and for v. always, di fekt') n. [< L. de-, from + facere, do] **1.** lack of something necessary for completeness **2.** an imperfection; blemish —vi. to forsake a party, cause, etc. —**defec'tion** n. —**defec'tor** n.

defective (di fek'tiv) adj. **1.** having a defect or defects; faulty **2.** subnormal in intelligence —n. a person with some bodily or mental defect —**defec'tively** adv. —**defec'tiveness** n.

defence (di fens') n. [< L. defendere] **1.** a defending against attack **2.** means of protection **3.** justification or support by speech or writing **4.** self-protection, as by boxing **5.** the side that is defending in any contest **6.** Law a) the arguments of the defendant b) the defendant and his lawyer —**defence'less** adj. —**defence'-lessly** adv. —**defence'lessness** n.

defend (di fend') vt. [< L. de-, away + fendere, strike] **1.** to guard from attack **2.** to support or justify **3.** Law a) to oppose (an action, etc.) b) to act as lawyer for (an accused) —vi. to make a defence —**defend'er** n.

defendant adj. defending —n. Law the person sued or accused

defensible adj. that can be defended or justified —**defen'sibil'ity, defen'sible-ness** n.

defensive adj. **1.** defending **2.** of or for defence —n. a position of defence: chiefly in **on the defensive** in a position that makes defence necessary —**defen'-sively** adv. —**defen'siveness** n.

defer¹ (di fur') vt., vi. -ferred', -fer'ring [see DIFFER] to put off; postpone; delay —**defer'ment, defer'ral** n.

defer² vi. -ferred', -fer'ring [< L. de-, down + ferre, to bear] to give in to the wish or judgment of another

deference (def'ər əns) n. **1.** a yielding in opinion, judgment, etc. **2.** courteous regard or respect

deferential (def'ə ren'shəl) adj. showing deference; very respectful: also **def'erent** —**def'eren'tially** adv.

defiance (di fi'əns) n. open, bold resistance to authority or opposition —**in defiance of** in spite of —**defi'ant** adj. —**defi'antly** adv.

deficiency (di fish'ən sē) n. **1.** a being deficient; absence of an essential **2.** pl. -cies a shortage

deficiency disease a disease, as rickets, caused by lack of vitamins, minerals, etc. in the diet

deficient adj. [see DEFECT] **1.** lacking in some essential; incomplete **2.** inadequate in amount, quality, etc. —**defi'-ciently** adv.

deficit (def'ə sit) n. [< L. deficere, to lack] the amount by which a sum of money is less than the required amount

defile¹ (di fīl') vt. -filed', -fil'ing [< OFr. defouler, tread underfoot] **1.** to make filthy **2.** to corrupt **3.** to profane or sully —**defile'ment** n. —**defil'er** n.

defile² (dē'fīl) vi. -filed', -fil'ing [< Fr. dé-, from + filer, form a line] to march in single file —n. a narrow passage, valley, or mountain pass

define (di fīn') vt. -fined', -fin'ing [<

L. *de-*, from + *finis,* boundary] **1.** to state the meaning of (a word, etc.) **2.** to determine the extent and nature of **3.** to determine the boundaries of —**defin′a-ble** *adj.*

definite (def′ə nit) *adj.* [see prec.] **1.** precise and clear in meaning **2.** certain; positive **3.** having exact limits **4.** *Gram.* limiting or specifying ["the" is the *definite* article] —**def′initely** *adv.*

definition (def′ə nish′ən) *n.* **1.** a defining or being defined **2.** a statement of the meaning of a word, phrase, etc. **3.** a being in clear, sharp outline —**def′ini′-tional** *adj.*

definitive (di fin′ə tiv) *adj.* **1.** decisive; conclusive **2.** most nearly complete and accurate **3.** serving to define —**defin′i-tively** *adv.*

deflate (di flāt′) *vt., vi.* -**flat′ed, -flat′ing** [DE- + (IN)FLATE] **1.** to collapse by letting out air or gas **2.** to make or become smaller or less important **3.** to cause deflation of (currency, prices, etc.)

deflation *n.* **1.** a deflating or being deflated **2.** a lessening of the amount of money in circulation, causing a rise in its value —**defla′tionary** *adj.*

deflect (di flekt′) *vt., vi.* [< L. *de-,* from + *flectere,* bend] to bend or turn to one side; swerve —**deflec′tion, deflex′ion** *n.* —**deflec′tive** *adj.* —**deflec′tor** *n.*

deflower (dē flou′ər) *vt.* [see DE- & FLOWER] **1.** to deprive (a woman) of virginity **2.** to ravage or spoil **3.** to remove flowers from (a plant) —**deflora-tion** (dē′flôr ā′shən) *n.*

defoliate (dē fō′lē āt′) *vt.* -**at′ed, -at′ing** [< L. *de-,* from + *folium,* leaf] to strip (trees, etc.) of leaves —**defo′liant** *n.* —**defo′lia′tion** *n.*

deform (di fôrm′) *vt.* [< L. *de-,* from + *forma,* form] **1.** to impair the form or shape of **2.** to make ugly —**deform′a-ble** *adj.* —**deformation** (dē′fôr mā′shən) *n.* —**de′forma′tional** *adj.*

deformed *adj.* misshapen; ugly

deformity *n., pl.* -**ties 1.** a deformed or disfigured part of the body **2.** ugliness or depravity

defraud (di frôd′) *vt.* [< L. *de-,* from + *fraus,* fraud] to take property, rights, etc. from by fraud

defray (di frā′) *vt.* [< OFr.] to pay (the cost or expenses) —**defray′able** *adj.* —**defray′al, defray′ment** *n.*

defrost (di frôst′) *vt.* **1.** to remove frost or ice from by thawing **2.** to cause (frozen foods) to become unfrozen —*vi.* to become defrosted

deft (deft) *adj.* [see DAFT] skilful in a quick, sure, and easy way —**deft′ly** *adv.* —**deft′ness** *n.*

defunct (di fuŋkt′) *adj.* [< L. *de-,* from + *fungi,* perform] no longer existing; dead or extinct

defuse (dē fyōōz′) *vt.* -**fused′, -fus′ing 1.** to remove the fuse from (a bomb, etc.) **2.** to remove the cause of tension from (a crisis, etc.)

defy (di fī′) *vt.* -**fied′, -fy′ing** [< L. *dis-,*

from + *fidus,* faithful] **1.** to resist boldly or openly **2.** to resist in a baffling way **3.** to dare (someone) to do something

degenerate (di jen′ər ət; *for v.* -ə rāt′) *adj.* [< L. *de-,* from + *genus,* race] having sunk below a former or normal condition, etc.; deteriorated —*n.* a degenerate person, esp. one who is morally depraved —*vi.* -**at′ed, -at′ing** to lose former normal or higher qualities —**degen′eracy** *n.* —**degen′erately** *adv.* —**degen′erative** *adj.*

degeneration (di jen′ə rā′shən) *n.* **1.** the process of degenerating **2.** *Biol.* loss of a function in the course of evolution

degrade (di grād′) *vt.* -**grad′ed, -grad′-ing** [< L. *de-,* down + *gradus,* a step] **1.** to lower in rank or status **2.** to lower in quality, etc. **3.** to dishonour **4.** *Chem.* to convert (an organic compound) into a simpler compound —**degrad′able** *adj.* —**degradation** (deg′rə dā′shən) *n.* —**degrad′ing** *adj.*

degree (di grē′) *n.* [see DEGRADE] **1.** any of the successive steps in a series **2.** a step in the direct line of descent **3.** social or official rank **4.** relative condition; manner or respect **5.** extent, amount, or intensity [hungry to a slight *degree*] **6.** *Algebra* rank as determined by the sum of a term's exponents **7.** *Educ.* a rank given by a college or university to a student who has completed a course of study, or to a distinguished person as an honour **8.** *Gram.* a grade of comparison of adjectives and adverbs [the superlative *degree* of "good" is "best"] **9.** *Law* [Chiefly U.S.] the seriousness of a crime **10.** *Math., Astron., Geog., etc.* a unit of measure for angles or arcs, 1/360 of the circumference of a circle **11.** *Physics* a unit of measure on a scale, as for temperature —**by degrees** gradually

dehisce (di his′) *vi.* -**hisced′, -hisc′ing** [< L. *de-,* off + *hiscere,* gape] to burst or split open, as a seedpod —**dehis′cence** *n.* —**dehis′cent** *adj.*

dehumanize (dē hyōō′mə nīz′) *vt.* -**ized′, -iz′ing** to deprive of human qualities; make inhuman or machinelike

dehydrate (dē hī′drāt) *vt.* -**drated, -drat-ing** to remove water from (a compound, etc.); dry —*vi.* to become dry —**de′hydra′-tion** *n.* —**dehy′drator** *n.*

de-ice (dē īs′) *vt.* -**iced′, -ic′ing** to melt ice from or keep free of ice —**de-ic′er** *n.*

deify (dē′ə fī′) *vt.* -**fied′, -fy′ing** [< L. *deus,* god + *facere,* make] **1.** to make a god of **2.** to look upon or worship as a god —**de′ifica′tion** *n.*

deign (dān) *vi.* [< L. *dignus,* worthy] to condescend; think fit

deism (dē′iz′m) *n.* [< L. *deus,* god] belief in the existence of God based on reason rather than revelation —**de′ist** *n.* —**deis′-tic, deis′tical** *adj.*

deity (dē′ə tē) *n., pl.* -**ties** [< L. *deus,* god] **1.** the state of being a god **2.** a god or goddess —**the Deity** God

‡**déjà vu** (dā zhà vü′) [Fr., already seen] **1.** *Psychol.* the illusion that one has previously experienced something actually

new to one 2. anything which is unoriginal : said esp. of the arts

deject (di jekt') vt. [< L. de-, down + jacere, throw] to dishearten; depress —**dejec'tion** n.

dejected adj. in low spirits; disheartened

de jure (dē jooar'ē) [L.] by right or legal establishment [de jure government]

deke (dēk) vt. [Canad. Slang] in ice hockey or box lacrosse, to draw a defending player out of position by faking a shot or movement —n. [Canad. Slang] such a shot or movement

dekko (dek'ō) n. [Hindi.] [Colloq.] a look

delay (di lā') vt. [< OFr. de-, intens. + laier, leave] 1. to put off; postpone 2. to make late; detain —vi. to stop for a while —n. a delaying or being delayed

delectable (di lek'tə b'l) adj. [see DELIGHT] very pleasing; delightful; delicious —**delec'tabil'ity** n.

delectation (dē'lek tā'shən) n. [see DELIGHT] delight; entertainment

delegate (del'ə gāt'; also for n. -gət) n. [< L. de-, from + legare, send] a person authorized to act for others; representative —vt. -gat'ed, -gat'ing 1. to appoint as a representative 2. to entrust (authority, etc.) to another

delegation (del'ə gā'shən) n. 1. a body of delegates 2. a delegating or being delegated

delete (di lēt') vt. -let'ed, -let'ing [< L. delere, destroy] to take out (a letter, word, etc.) —**dele'tion** n.

deleterious (del'ə tēər'ē əs) adj. [< Gr. dēleisthai, injure] harmful to health, well-being, etc.; injurious —**del'ete'riously** adv. —**del'ete'riousness** n.

delftware (delft'wâer') n. glazed earthenware, usually blue and white, which originated in Delft in the Netherlands Also **delft, delf**

deliberate (di lib'ər ət; for v. -āt') adj. [< L. de-, intens. + librare, weigh] 1. carefully thought out and formed, or done on purpose 2. not rash or hasty 3. unhurried and methodical —vi., vt. -at'ed, -at'ing to consider carefully —**delib'erately** adv. —**delib'erateness** n. —**delib'erative** adj. —**delib'era'tor** n.

deliberation (di lib'ə rā'shən) n. 1. a deliberating 2. [often pl.] consideration and discussion 3. carefulness

delicacy (del'i kə sē) n., pl. -cies 1. the quality or state of being delicate; fineness, weakness, sensitivity, tact, etc. 2. a choice food

delicate (del'i kət) adj. [L. delicatus, delightful] 1. pleasing in its lightness, mildness, etc. 2. beautifully fine in texture, workmanship, etc. 3. slight and subtle 4. easily damaged, spoiled, etc. 5. frail in health 6. a) needing careful handling b) showing tact, consideration, etc. 7. finely sensitive —**del'icately** adv. —**del'i-cateness** n.

delicatessen (del'i kə tes'n) n. [G. pl. < Fr. délicatesse, delicacy] 1. prepared cooked meats, smoked fish, cheeses, salads, relishes, etc., collectively 2. a shop where such foods are sold

delicious (di lish'əs) adj. [< L. deliciae, delight] 1. very enjoyable 2. very pleasing to taste or smell —n. [D-] a sweet, red or green winter apple —**deli'ciously** adv.

delight (di līt') vt. [< L. de-, from + lacere, entice] to give great pleasure to —vi. 1. to give great pleasure 2. to be highly pleased —n. 1. great pleasure 2. something giving great pleasure —**delight'ed** adj. —**delight'edly** adv.

delightful adj. giving delight; very pleasing —**delight'fully** adv. —**delight'fulness** n.

delimit (dē lim'it) vt. to set the limits or boundaries of —**delim'ita'tion** n.

delineate (di lin'ē āt') vt. -at'ed, -at'ing [< L. de-, from + linea, line] 1. to draw; depict 2. to depict in words; describe —**delin'ea'tion** n. —**delin'ea'tor** n.

delinquent (di liŋ'kwənt) adj. [< L. de-, from + linquere, to leave] failing or neglecting to do what duty or law requires —n. a delinquent person; esp., a juvenile delinquent —**delin'quency** n. —**delin'-quently** adv.

deliquesce (del'ə kwes') vi. -quesced', -quesc'ing [< L. de-, from + liquere, to be liquid] 1. to melt away 2. to become liquid by absorbing moisture from the air —**del'iques'cence** n. —**del'iques'-cent** adj.

delirious (di lir'ē əs) adj. 1. in a state of delirium 2. caused by delirium 3. wildly excited —**delir'iously** adv.

delirium n., pl. -iums, -ia [< L. de-, from + lira, a line] 1. a temporary state of mental excitement, marked by confused speech and hallucinations 2. uncontrollably wild excitement

delirium tremens (trē'mənz) [ModL., trembling delirium] a violent delirium resulting chiefly from chronic alcoholism

deliver (di liv'ər) vt. [< L. de-, from + liberare, to free] 1. to distribute [deliver the post] 2. to transfer 3. to set free or save from evil, danger, etc. 4. to assist at the birth of 5. to utter (speech, etc.) 6. to strike (a blow) —vi. 1. to make deliveries, as of merchandise 2. [Colloq.] to produce the expected, or promised, results —**be delivered of** to give birth to —**deliver the goods** [Colloq.] to produce what has been promised —**deliv'erable** adj. —**deliv'erance** n.

delivery n., pl. -eries 1. a transfer 2. a distributing, as of the post 3. a giving birth 4. any giving forth 5. the act or manner of giving a speech, throwing a ball, etc.

dell (del) n. [OE. del] a small, wooded valley

delouse (dē lous') vt. -loused', -lous'ing to rid of lice —**delous'er** n.

Delphic (del'fik) adj. of the oracle of Apollo at Delphi in ancient times Also **Del'-phian**

delphinium (del fin'ē əm) n. [< Gr.

delphin, dolphin] a plant bearing spikes of irregular flowers, usually blue

delta (del′tə) *n.* 1. the fourth letter of the Greek alphabet (Δ, δ) 2. a deposit of soil, usually triangular, formed at the mouth of some rivers

delta wing the triangular shaped wing of certain kinds of jet aircraft

delude (di lōōd′) *vt.* -lud′ed, -lud′ing [< L. *de-*, from + *ludere*, play] to mislead; trick —**delud′er** *n.*

deluge (del′yōōj) *n.* [< L. *dis-*, off + *lavere*, wash] 1. a great flood 2. a heavy rainfall 3. an overwhelming rush of anything —*vt.* -uged, -uging 1. to flood 2. to overwhelm —**the Deluge** *Bible* the flood in Noah's time

delusion (di lōō′zhən) *n.* 1. a false belief or opinion 2. a deluding or being deluded —**delu′sional** *adj.* —**delu′sive, delu′sory** *adj.*

deluxe (də lōōks′) *adj.* [Fr.] of extra fine quality; elegant —*adv.* in a deluxe manner

delve (delv) *vi.* delved, delv′ing [OE. *delfan*] 1. to search (*into* books, etc.) 2. [Archaic] to dig —**delv′er** *n.*

demagnetize (dē mag′nə tīz′) *vt.* -ized′, -iz′ing to deprive of magnetism —**demag′-netiza′tion** *n.*

demagogue (dem′ə gog′) *n.* [< Gr. *dēmos*, the people + *agōgos*, leader] one who tries to stir up people's emotions in order to gain power —**dem′agog′ic** *adj.* —**dem′agog′y** *n.*

demand (di mänd′) *vt.* [< L. *de-*, from + *mandare*, entrust] 1. to ask for boldly or urgently 2. to ask for as a right or with authority 3. to require —*n.* 1. a demanding 2. a thing demanded 3. a strong request 4. an urgent requirement 5. *Econ.* a) the desire for a commodity b) the amount of a commodity, etc. that people are prepared to buy —**in demand** asked for —**on demand** when presented for payment —**demand′able** *adj.* —**demand′er** *n.*

demanding *adj.* making demands on one's patience, energy, etc. —**demand′-ingly** *adv.*

demarcation, demarkation (dē′-mär kā′shən) *n.* [Sp. < *de-*, from + *marcar*, to mark] 1. the act of setting and marking boundaries 2. a limit or boundary

demean (di mēn′) *vt.* [DE- + MEAN²] to degrade

demeanour (di mēn′ər) *n.* [< OFr. < L. *minari*, threaten] outward behaviour; conduct; deportment

demented (di ment′id) *adj.* [< L. *demens*, *dementis*, mad] mentally deranged; insane

dementia (di men′shē ə) *n.* [L. < *de-*, out from + *mens*, the mind] impairment of mental powers from organic causes

demerara (dem′ə räar′ə) *n.* [< *Demerara*, in Guyana] brown crystallized cane sugar from the West Indies

demerit (di mer′it) *n.* a fault; defect

demesne (di mān′) *n.* [see DOMAIN] 1. *Law* possession (of real estate) in one's

own right 2. the land around a mansion 3. a region or domain

demi- [< L. *dimidius*, half] a prefix meaning: 1. half 2. less than usual in size, power, etc.

demigod (dem′ē god′) *n.* 1. *Myth.* a) a minor deity b) the offspring of a human being and a god or goddess 2. a godlike person

DEMIJOHN

demijohn (dem′ē jon) *n.* [Fr. *dame-jeanne*] a large bottle of glass or earthenware, with a narrow neck and a wicker casing and handle

demilitarize (dē mil′ə tə rīz′) *vt.* -rized′, -riz′ing to free from military control —**demil′itariza′tion** *n.*

demimonde (dem′ē mond′) *n.* [Fr. < *demi-*, DEMI- + *monde*, world] formerly, the class of women who had lost social standing because of sexual promiscuity

demise (di mīz′) *n.* [< L. *de-*, down + *mittere*, send] 1. *Law* a transfer of an estate by lease 2. death —*vt.* -mised′, -mis′ing to give or transfer (an estate) by lease

demisemiquaver (dem′ē sem′ē kwā′-vər) *n. Music* a note having 1/32 of the duration of a semibreve

demister (dē mist′ər) *n.* a device for melting ice and frost, as on a windscreen

demo (dem′ō) *n.* [Colloq.] *same as* DEMONSTRATION

demob (dē mob′) *vt.* -mobbed′, -mob′bing [Colloq.] to demobilize

demobilize (dē mō′bə līz′) *vt.* -lized′, -liz′ing 1. to disband (troops) 2. to discharge (a person) from the armed forces —**demo′biliza′tion** *n.*

democracy (di mok′rə sē) *n., pl.* -cies [< Gr. *dēmos*, people + *kratein*, rule] 1. government by the people directly or through elected representatives 2. a country, state, etc. with such government 3. the principle of equality of rights, opportunity, etc.

democrat (dem′ə krat′) *n.* 1. one who upholds and practises democracy 2. [U.S.] [D-] a member of the Democratic Party

democratic (dem′ə krat′ik) *adj.* 1. of or upholding (a) democracy 2. for all or most people 3. treating all people in the same way —**dem′ocrat′ically** *adv.*

demodulation (dē mod′yoo lā′shən) *n. Radio* the recovery, at the receiver, of a signal that has been modulated on a carrier wave

demography (di mog′rə fē) *n.* [< Gr. *dēmos*, the people + -GRAPHY] the statistical study of populations —**demog′-rapher** *n.* —**demographic** (dē′mə graf′ik) *adj.*

demolish (di mol′ish) *vt.* [< L. *de-*, down + *moliri*, build] to tear down; destroy; ruin —**dem′oli′tion** (dem′ə-), **demol′ishment** *n.*

demon (dē′mən) *n.* [L. *daemon*] 1. *same as* DAEMON 2. a devil; evil spirit 3. a person or thing regarded as evil, cruel, etc. 4. one who has great energy or skill —**demonic** (dē mon′ik) *adj.*

demonetize (dē′mun′ə tīz′) *vt.* -**tized′**, -**tiz′ing** to deprive (currency) of its standard value

demoniac (di mō′nē ak′) *adj.* of or like a demon; fiendish Also **demoniacal** (dē′mō nī′ə k'l) —*n.* one possessed by a demon —**de′moni′acally** *adv.*

demonolatry (dē′mə nol′ə trē) *n.* worship of demons

demonology (dē′mə nol′ə jē) *n.* the study of demons or of beliefs about them —**de′monol′ogist** *n.*

demonstrable (dem′ən strə b'l) *adj.* that can be demonstrated, or proved —**demon′-strably** *adv.*

demonstrate (dem′ən strāt′) *vt.* -**strat′-ed, -strat′ing** [< L. *de-*, from + *monstrare*, show] 1. to show by reasoning; prove 2. to explain by using examples, experiments, etc. 3. to show the working of 4. to show (feelings) plainly —*vi.* to show one's feelings or views by taking part in a public meeting, parade, etc.

demonstration (dem′ən strā′shən) *n.* 1. a proving 2. an explanation by example, experiment, etc. 3. a practical showing of how something works 4. a display 5. a public show of opinion, etc., as by a mass meeting

demonstrative (di mon′strə tiv) *adj.* 1. showing feelings openly 2. giving proof (*of*) 3. having to do with demonstration 4. *Gram.* pointing out [*"this"* is a *demonstrative* pronoun] —*n. Gram.* a demonstrative word —**demon′stratively** *adv.* —**demon′strativeness** *n.*

demonstrator (dem′ən strāt′ər) *n.* 1. one who takes part in a public demonstration 2. one who explains the uses of machinery, products, etc.

demoralize (di mor′ə līz′) *vt.* -**ized′**, -**iz′-ing** 1. to lower the morale of 2. to throw into confusion —**demor′aliza′tion** *n.* —**demor′aliz′er** *n.*

demote (dē mōt′) *vt.* -**mot′ed, -mot′ing** [DE- + (PRO)MOTE] to reduce to a lower grade; lower in rank —**demo′tion** *n.*

demotic (dē mot′ik) *adj.* [< Gr. *dēmos*, the people] of the people; popular

demur (di mur′) *vi.* -**murred′, -mur′ring** [< L. *de-*, from + *morari*, to delay] to be unwilling because of doubts or objections; object —*n.* a demurring —**demur′rable** *adv.*

demure (di myoor′) *adj.* [< *de-* (prob. intens.) + OFr. *mëur*, mature] 1. modest; reserved 2. affectedly modest; coy —**demure′ly** *adv.* —**demure′ness** *n.*

demurrer (di mur′ər) *n.* [see DEMUR] a

plea for the dismissal of a lawsuit on the grounds that even if the statements of the opposition are true, they do not sustain the claim

demystify (dē mis′tə fī′) *vt.* -**fied′, -fy′-ing** to remove the mystery from; make clear

den (den) *n.* [OE. *denn*] 1. the cave or other lair of a wild animal 2. a retreat or headquarters, as of thieves 3. a small, cosy room

Den. Denmark

denarius (di nâr′ē əs) *n., pl.* -**nar′ii′**(-ī′) [< L. *decem*, ten] an ancient Roman silver coin

denary (dē′nər ē) *adj.* [see prec.] of the number ten

denationalize (dē nash′ən'l īz′) *vt.* -**ized′**, -**iz′ing** to place (a government-controlled industry) under private ownership —**dena′-tionaliza′tion** *n.*

denature (dē nā′chər) *vt.* -**tured, -turing** 1. to change the nature of 2. to make (alcohol, etc.) unfit for human consumption —**dena′tura′tion** *n.*

dendrology (den drol′ə jē) *n.* the scientific study of trees —**dendrol′ogist** *n.*

Dene (den′ē, -ā) *n.* the official organization of the Indians of the Northwest Territories of Canada

dene (dēn) *n. same as* DEAN[2]

dengue (deŋ′gē) *n.* [WIndSp. < Swahili] an infectious tropical disease transmitted by mosquitoes and characterized by severe pain in the joints

denial (di nī′əl) *n.* 1. a denying; saying "no" (to a request, etc.) 2. a statement in opposition to another 3. a disowning; repudiation

denier (den′yər) *n.* [see DENARIUS] a unit of weight for measuring the fineness of silk, nylon, etc.

denigrate (den′ə grāt′) *vt.* -**grat′ed**, -**grat′ing** [< L. *de-*, intens. + *nigrare*, blacken] to belittle; speak ill of someone —**den′igra′tion** *n.* —**den′igra′tor** *n.*

denim (den′əm) *n.* [< Fr. (*serge*) *de Nîmes*, (serge) of Nîmes, Fr. town] a coarse, twilled cotton cloth used for overalls, jeans, uniforms, etc.

denizen (den′i zən) *n.* [< L. *de intus*, from within] 1. an inhabitant 2. an animal, plant, etc. that has become naturalized

denominate (di nom′ə nāt′) *vt.* -**nat′ed**, -**nat′ing** [< L. *de-*, intens. + *nominare*, to name] to give a specified name to; call

denomination (di nom′ə nā′shən) *n.* 1. a particular religious sect 2. a class or kind with a specific name or value [*coins of different denominations*] 3. a name 4. the act of denominating

denominational *adj.* of, or under the control of, a religious denomination —**denom′ina′tionalism** *n.*

denominator (di nom′ə nāt′ər) *n.* [ML.] the term below the line in a fraction, indicating the number of equal parts into which the whole is divided

denote (di nōt′) *vt.* -**not′ed, -not′ing** [< L. *de-*, down + *notare*, to mark] 1. to be a sign of; indicate **2.** to refer to explicitly; mean —**denot′able** *adj.* —**de′nota′tion** *n.*

dénouement (dā nōō′ män) *n.* [Fr. < *dé-*, out + *nouer*, to tie] the outcome, solution, or unravelling of a plot in a drama, story, etc.

denounce (di nouns′) *vt.* **-nounced′**, **-nounc′ing** [see DENUNCIATION] **1.** to accuse publicly **2.** to condemn strongly **3.** to give formal notice of the ending of (a treaty, etc.) —**denounce′ment** *n.* —**denounc′er** *n.*

dense (dens) *adj.* **dens′er, dens′est** [L. *densus,* compact] **1.** packed tightly together **2.** difficult to get through **3.** stupid —**dense′ly** *adv.* —**dense′ness** *n.*

density *n.,* *pl.* **-ties 1.** the condition of being dense **2.** number per unit, as of area **3.** *Physics* the ratio of the mass of an object to its volume

dent (dent) *n.* [ME., var. of DINT] a slight hollow made in a surface, as by a blow —*vt.* to make a dent in —*vi.* to become dented

dental (den′t'l) *adj.* [< L. *dens, dentis,* tooth] **1.** of or for the teeth or dentistry **2.** *Phonet.* formed by placing the tip of the tongue against or near the upper front teeth —*n.* *Phonet.* a dental consonant (th, *th*)

dental floss thin, strong thread for removing food particles from between the teeth

dental surgeon *same as* DENTIST

dentate (den′tāt) *adj.* [see DENTAL] having teeth or toothlike projections; toothed or notched

dentifrice (den′tə fris) *n.* [< L. *dens,* tooth + *fricare,* rub] any preparation for cleaning teeth

dentine (den′tēn) *n.* [see DENTAL] the hard, calcareous tissue of a tooth, under the enamel

dentist (den′tist) *n.* [< L. *dens,* tooth] one whose profession is the care of teeth, the replacement of missing teeth with artificial ones, etc.

dentistry *n.* the profession or work of a dentist

dentition (den tish′ən) *n.* [see DENTAL] the number and kind of teeth and their arrangement

denture (den′chər) *n.* [see DENTAL] a fitting for the mouth, with artificial teeth

denude (di nyōōd′) *vt.* **-nud′ed, -nud′ing** [< L. *de-*, off + *nudare,* strip] to make bare; strip —**de′nuda′tion** *n.*

denumerable (di nyōō′mər ə b'l) *adj.* *Math.* countable

denunciation (di nun′sē ā′shən) *n.* [< L. *de-*, intens. + *nuntiare,* announce] the act of denouncing —**denun′ciatory, denun′ciative** *adj.*

deny (di nī′) *vt.* **-nied′, -ny′ing** [< L. *de-*, intens. + *negare,* deny] **1.** to declare (a statement) untrue **2.** to refuse to accept as true or right **3.** to refuse to acknowledge as one's own **4.** to refuse to give **5.** to refuse the request of

deodar (dē′ō där′) *n.* [Hindi] a

Himalayan cedar with fragrant, light-red wood

deodorant (dē ō′dər ənt) *adj.* that prevents, destroys, or masks undesired odours —*n.* any deodorant preparation, esp. one used on the body

deodorize *vt.* **-ized′, -iz′ing** to remove or mask the odour of or in —**deo′doriza′-tion** *n.* —**deo′doriz′er** *n.*

deoxyribonucleic acid (dē ok′si rī′-bō nyōō klē′ik) a basic material in the chromosomes of the cell nucleus : it contains the genetic code

dep. 1. department **2.** deposed **3.** deposit **4.** deputy

depart (di pärt′) *vi.* [< L. *dis-*, apart + *partire,* divide] **1.** to go away (*from*); leave **2.** to set out; start **3.** to die **4.** to turn aside (*from* something)

departed *adj.* **1.** gone away; past **2.** dead —**the departed** the dead person or persons

department *n.* [see DEPART] **1.** a separate part or division, as of a government or business **2.** a field of knowledge or activity **3.** an administrative district in France —**depart′men′tal** (-men′t'l) *adj.* —**depart′men′tally** *adv.*

department store a retail store for the sale of many kinds of goods arranged in departments

departure (di pär′chər) *n.* **1.** a departing **2.** a starting out, as on a journey **3.** a deviation (*from* something)

depend (di pend′) *vi.* [< L. *de-*, down + *pendere,* hang] **1.** to rely (*on*) **2.** to be determined by something else **3.** to rely (*on*) for support or aid

dependable *adj.* that can be depended on; reliable —**depend′abil′ity** *n.* —**depend′ably** *adv.*

dependant *n.* a person who depends on someone else for support, etc.

dependence *n.* **1.** a being dependent **2.** reliance (*on* another) for support or aid **3.** reliance; trust

dependency *n.,* *pl.* **-cies 1.** *same as* DEPENDENCE **2.** something dependent **3.** a territory geographically distinct from the country governing it

dependent *adj.* **1.** relying (*on* another) for support **2.** determined by something else **3.** subordinate

depict (di pikt′) *vt.* [< L. *de-*, intens. + *pingere,* paint] **1.** to represent in a drawing, sculpture, etc. **2.** to picture in words; describe —**depic′tion** *n.*

depilatory (di pil′ə tər ē) *adj.* [< L. *de,* from + *pilus,* hair] serving to remove unwanted hair —*n.,* *pl.* **-ries** a depilatory agent, as in cream form

deplete (di plēt′) *vt.* **-plet′ed, -plet′ing** [< L. *de-*, from + *plere,* fill] **1.** to use up (funds, etc.) **2.** to empty wholly or partly —**deple′tion** *n.*

deplorable (di plôr′ə b'l) *adj.* **1.** that can or should be deplored **2.** very bad; wretched —**deplor′ably** *adv.*

deplore (di plôr′) *vt.* **-plored′, -plor′ing**

[< L. *de-*, intens. + *plorare*, weep] **1.** to be regretful or sorry about; lament **2.** to regard as unfortunate or wretched

deploy (di ploi′) *vt., vi.* [< L. *displicare*, to unfold] **1.** to spread out (troops, etc.) so as to form a wider front **2.** to move in accordance with a plan —**deploy′ment** *n.*

depolarize (dē pō′lə rīz′) *vt.* **-ized′, -iz′-ing** to destroy or counteract the polarization of —**depo′lariza′tion** *n.*

deponent (di pō′nənt) *adj.* [< L. *deponere*, set down] *L. & Gr. Gram.* denoting a verb with a passive voice form and an active meaning —*n. Law* a person who gives written testimony under oath

depopulate (dē pop′yoo lāt′) *vt.* **-lat′ed, -lat′ing** to reduce the population of, esp. by violence, pestilence, etc. —**depop′ula′-tion** *n.* —**depop′ula′tor** *n.*

deport (di pôrt′) *vt.* [< L. *de-*, from + *portare*, carry] **1.** to expel (an alien) from a country **2.** to behave (oneself) in a specified way

deportation (dē′pôr tā′shən) *n.* expulsion, as of an undesirable alien, from a country

deportee (dē′pôr tē′) *n.* a deported person

deportment (di pôrt′mənt) *n.* the manner of conducting oneself; behaviour

depose (di pōz′) *vt.* **-posed′, -pos′ing** [< OFr. *de-*, from + *poser*, cease] **1.** to remove from office or a position of power; oust **2.** *Law* to state under oath but out of court

deposit (di poz′it) *vt.* [< L. *de-*, down + *ponere*, put] **1.** to place or entrust, as for safekeeping **2.** to give as a pledge or partial payment **3.** to set down **4.** to leave (sediment, etc.) lying —*n.* **1.** something placed for safekeeping, as money in a bank **2.** a pledge or part payment **3.** a depository **4.** something left lying

deposit account an account in a bank, post office, etc. which pays interest on depositors' savings

depositary *n., pl.* **-taries 1.** a person, firm, etc. entrusted with something for safekeeping **2.** a depository

deposition (dep′ə zish′ən) *n.* **1.** *Law* the written testimony of a witness made under oath **2.** a testifying **3.** a deposing or being deposed **4.** a depositing or being deposited **5.** something deposited

depositor (di poz′ə tər) *n.* a person who deposits something, esp. money in a bank

depository *n., pl.* **-ries 1.** a place where things are put for safekeeping **2.** a depositary

depot (dep′ō) *n.* [< Fr.: see DEPOSIT] **1.** a storehouse **2.** a bus station **3.** *Mil.* a storage place for supplies

deprave (di prāv′) *vt.* **-praved′, -prav′-ing** [< L. *de-*, intens. + *pravus*, crooked] to make morally bad; corrupt —**depraved′** *adj.*

depravity (di prav′ə tē) *n.* **1.** a depraved condition; wickedness **2.** *pl.* **-ties** a depraved act or practice

deprecate (dep′rə kāt′) *vt.* **-cat′ed, -cat′-ing** [< L. *de-*, off + *precari*, pray] **1.** to express disapproval of **2.** to belittle —**dep′recat′ingly** *adv.* —**dep′reca′tion** *n.* —**dep′recatory** *adj.*

depreciate (di prē′shē āt′) *vt.* **-at′ed, -at′-ing** [< L. *de-*, from + *pretiare*, to value] **1.** to reduce in value or price **2.** to belittle —*vi.* to drop in value or price —**depre′cia-tory** *adj.*

depreciation (di prē′shē ā′shən) *n.* **1.** a decrease in value of property through wear, etc. **2.** a decrease in the purchasing power of money **3.** a belittling

depredation (dep′rə dā′shən) *n.* [< L. *de-*, intens. + *praedari*, to plunder] a plundering or laying waste

depress (di pres′) *vt.* [< L. *de-*, down + *premere*, to press] **1.** to sadden **2.** to decrease the activity of **3.** to lower —**depress′ing** *adj.* —**depres′sive** *adj.*

depressant *adj.* lowering the rate of muscular or nervous activity —*n.* a depressant medicine, drug, etc.

depressed *adj.* **1.** gloomy; sad **2.** pressed down **3.** characterized by widespread unemployment, etc. **4.** lowered in intensity, amount, etc.

depression *n.* **1.** a depressing or being depressed **2.** a depressed place **3.** low spirits **4.** a decrease in force, amount, etc. **5.** a period of slackening business activity, much unemployment, etc., esp. [D-] that of the early 1930s

deprive (di prīv′) *vt.* **-prived′, -priv′ing** [< L. *de-*, intens. + *privare*, to separate] **1.** to take something away from forcibly **2.** to keep from having, using, or enjoying —**dep′riva′tion** *n.*

deprived *adj.* lacking adequate food, shelter, education, social facilities, etc.

dept. department

depth (depth) *n.* [ME. *depthe*] **1.** the distance from the top downwards, or from front to back **2.** deepness **3.** intensity, as of colours, etc. **4.** profundity of thought **5.** lowness of pitch **6.** the middle part [the *depth* of winter] **7.** [usually *pl.*] the deep or deepest part, as of the sea —**in depth** in a thorough way —**out of** (or **beyond**) **one's depth 1.** in water too deep for one **2.** past one's understanding

depth charge (or **bomb**) an explosive charge that explodes under water: used esp. against submarines

deputation (dep′yoo tā′shən) *n.* **1.** a deputing or being deputed **2.** a delegation

depute[1] (di pyoot′) *vt.* **-put′ed, -put′ing** [< L. *de-*, from + *putare*, consider] **1.** to give (authority, etc.) to someone else as deputy **2.** to appoint as one's substitute, agent, etc.

depute[2] (dep′yoot) *n.* [< DEPUTY] [Scot.] a deputy

deputize (dep′yoo tīz′) *vt.* **-tized′, -tiz′-ing** to appoint as deputy —*vi.* to act as deputy

deputy (dep′yoo tē) *n., pl.* ′**-ties** [see DEPUTE[1]] **1.** one appointed to substitute for another **2.** a member of a legislature in some countries, such as France and Canada —*adj.* acting as deputy

derail (di rāl′) *vi., vt.* to go or cause to go off the rails: said of a train, etc. —**derail′ment** *n.*

derange (di rānj′) *vt.* **-ranged′, -rang′ing** [< OFr. *des-*, apart + *rengier*, range] **1.** to upset the order or working of **2.** to make insane —**deranged′ adj.**

Derby (där′bē) *n., pl.* **-bies 1.** an annual race for three-year-old horses at Epsom Downs **2.** any similar horse race **3.** any local sporting event

derelict (der′ə likt′) *adj.* [< L. *de-*, intens. + *relinquere*, leave behind] deserted by the owner; abandoned —*n.* **1.** a ship deserted at sea **2.** a destitute person

dereliction (der′ə lik′shən) *n.* **1.** a neglect of, or failure in, duty **2.** an abandoning or being abandoned

derestrict (dē′ri strikt′) *vt.* to remove a speed restriction on motor vehicles in built-up areas —**derestrict′ed** *adj.*

deride (di rīd′) *vt.* **-rid′ed, -rid′ing** [< L. *de-*, down + *ridere*, laugh] to laugh at in contempt or scorn; ridicule —**deri′sion** *n.*

‡de rigueur (də rē gër′) [Fr.] required by etiquette

derisive (di rī′siv) *adj.* showing or provoking derision: also **deri′sory** —**deri′sively** *adv.*

derivation (der′ə vā′shən) *n.* **1.** a deriving or being derived **2.** the source or origin of something **3.** the forming of words from bases

derivative (dəriv′ətiv) *adj.* **1.** derived **2.** not original —*n.* **1.** something derived **2.** a word formed by derivation **3.** *Chem.* a substance derived from another by chemical change **4.** *Math.* the instantaneous rate of change of one variable with respect to another

derive (di rīv′) *vt.* **-rived′, -riv′ing** [< L. *de-*, from + *rivus*, a stream] **1.** to get or receive (*from* a source) **2.** to deduce or infer **3.** to trace from or to a source —*vi.* to come (*from* a source) —**deriv′able** *adj.*

derma (dur′mə) *n.* [< Gr. *derma*, skin] *same as* DERMIS —**der′mal, der′mic** *adj.*

dermatitis (dur′mə tīt′is) *n.* [< Gr. *derma*, skin + -ITIS] inflammation of the skin

dermato- [Gr.] *a combining form meaning* skin

dermatology (dur′mə tol′ə jē) *n.* [DERMATO- + -LOGY] the branch of medicine dealing with the skin and its diseases —**der′matol′ogist** *n.*

dermis (dur′mis) *n.* [< LL. *epidermis*, EPIDERMIS] the layer of skin just below the epidermis

derogate (der′ə gāt′) *vt., vi.* **-gat′ed, -gat′ing** [< L. *de-*, from + *rogare*, ask] to take away (*from*) so as to impair —**der′oga′tion** *n.*

derogatory (di rog′ə tər ē) *adj.* **1.** tending to lessen or impair **2.** belittling Also **derog′ative**

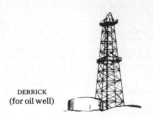

DERRICK
(for oil well)

derrick (der′ik) *n.* [< T. *Derrick*] **1.** a large apparatus for lifting and moving heavy objects **2.** a tall framework, as over an oil well, to support drilling machinery, etc.

derring-do (der′iŋ dōō′) *n.* [ME. *derrynge do*, daring to do] daring action; reckless courage

derv (durv) *n.* [< *d(iesel) e(ngine) r(oad) v(ehicle)*] diesel oil

dervish (dur′vish) *n.* [< Per. *darvēsh*, beggar] a member of any of various Moslem orders: some practise whirling, howling, etc. for religious reasons

desalination (dē sal′ə nā′shən) *n.* [< DE- + SALINE] the removal of salt, esp. from sea water to make it drinkable —**desal′inate′** *vt.* **-nat′ed, -nat′ing**

descant (des′kant; *for vi., also* dis kant′) *n.* [< L. *dis-*, apart + *cantus*, song] *Music* **1.** singing in which there is a fixed melody and a subordinate melody added above **2.** this added melody —*vi.* **1.** to discourse (*on* or *upon*) **2.** to sing —*adj.* of the highest member of a family of instruments

descend (di send′) *vi.* [< L. *de-*, down + *scandere*, climb] **1.** to move from a higher to a lower place **2.** to pass from an earlier to a later time, from general to particular, etc. **3.** to slope downwards **4.** to come down (*from* a source) **5.** to pass by inheritance **6.** to stoop (*to* some act) **7.** to make a sudden visit or attack (*on* or *upon*) —*vt.* to move down

descendant *n.* one who is an offspring, however remote, of a certain ancestor, family, group, etc.

descendent *adj.* descending

descent (di sent′) *n.* **1.** a descending; coming or going down **2.** ancestry **3.** a downward slope **4.** a way down **5.** a sudden attack (*on* or *upon*) **6.** a decline

describe (di skrīb′) *vt.* **-scribed′, -scrib′ing** [< L. *de-*, from + *scribere*, write] **1.** to tell or write about **2.** to picture in words **3.** to trace the outline of

description (di skrip′shən) *n.* **1.** the act or technique of describing **2.** a statement or passage that describes **3.** sort or variety —**answers** (or **fits**) **the description** corresponds to a given description

descriptive *adj.* of or characterized by description

descry (di skrī′) *vt.* **-scried′, -scry′ing** [< OFr. *des-*, from + *crier*, cry] **1.** to

catch sight of (distant or obscure objects)
2. to detect

desecrate (des'ə krāt') *vt.* -crat'ed, -crat'-
ing [DE- + (CON)SECRATE] to violate the
sacredness of —**des'ecra'tion** *n.*

desegregate (dē seg'rə gāt') *vt., vi.* -gat'-
ed, -gat'ing to abolish racial segregation
(in) —**deseg'rega'tion** *n.*

desert[1] (di zurt') *vt., vi.* [< L. *de-*, from
+ *serere*, to join] 1. to forsake (someone
or something); abandon 2. to leave (one's
post, etc.) without permission —**desert'-**
er *n.* —**deser'tion** *n.*

desert[2] (dez'ərt) *n.* [< LL. *desertum*,
a desert: see prec.] 1. an uncultivated
region without inhabitants; wilderness 2.
a dry, barren, sandy region —*adj.* 1.
of a desert 2. wild and uninhabited

desert[3] (di zurt') *n.* [see DESERVE] 1.
the fact of deserving reward or punishment
2. [*often pl.*] deserved reward or
punishment

deserve (di zurv') *vt., vi.* -served', -serv'-
ing [< L. *de-*, intens. + *servire*, serve]
to be worthy (of); merit

deserved *adj.* rightfully earned or
merited; just —**deserv'edly** (-zur'vid lē)
adv.

deserving *adj.* having merit; worthy (of)

déshabillé (dāz'a bē'ā) *n. same as* DIS-
HABILLE

desiccate (des'i kāt') *vt., vi.* -cat'ed, -cat'-
ing [< L. *de-*, intens. + *siccus*, dry] to
dry up completely —**des'icca'tion** *n.*

design (di zīn') *vt.* [< L. *de-*, out + *signum*,
a mark] 1. to make preliminary sketches
of 2. to form (plans, etc.) in the mind
3. to plan and work out (something)
creatively 4. to intend for some purpose
—*vi.* to make original plans, patterns,
etc. —*n.* 1. a plan; scheme 2. purpose;
intention 3. [*pl.*] a secret scheme (with
on or *upon*) 4. a plan or sketch to work
from 5. the arrangement of form, colour,
etc. —**by design** purposely

designate (dez'ig nāt') *adj.* [see prec.]
named for an office, etc. but not yet in
possession of it —*vt.* -nat'ed, -nat'ing
1. to specify 2. to name 3. to appoint

designation (dez'ig nā'shən) *n.* 1. a
pointing out 2. appointment to an office,
etc. 3. a name, title, etc.

designedly (di zīn'id lē) *adv.* purposely

designer *n.* a person who designs, or
makes original sketches, patterns, etc.

designing *adj.* scheming; crafty —*n.*
the art or work of creating designs, patterns,
etc. —**design'ingly** *adv.*

desirable (di zīər'ə b'l) *adj.* 1. worth
having; pleasing 2. designating the best
or the preferable course of action —**desir'a-**
bil'ity, desir'ableness *n.* —**desir'ably** *adv.*

desire (di zīər') *vt.* -sired', -sir'ing [<
L. *de-*, from + *sidus*, star] 1. to long
for; crave 2. to request 3. to want sexually
4. to prefer; consider to be the best [such
a result is much to be *desired*] —*n.* 1.
a strong craving 2. sexual appetite 3.
a request 4. anything desired

desirous *adj.* desiring; wanting

desist (di zist') *vi.* [< L. *de-*, from +

sistere, to cause to stand] to cease (*from*
an action)

desk (desk) *n.* [ult. < L. *discus*, DISCUS]
1. a kind of table with drawers and with
a flat top for writing, etc. 2. a musician's
stand in an orchestra 3. a counter at
which public services are carried out
[*information desk*]

desolate (des'ə lət; *for v.* -lāt') *adj.* [<
L. *de-*, intens. + *solare*, make lonely] 1.
lonely; solitary 2. uninhabited; deserted
3. laid waste 4. forlorn; wretched —*vt.*
-lat'ed, -lat'ing 1. to rid of inhabitants
2. to lay waste 3. to forsake 4. to make
forlorn —**des'olately** *adv.* —**des'olate-**
ness *n.*

desolation (des'ə lā'shən) *n.* 1. a making
desolate 2. a desolate condition or place
3. misery 4. loneliness

despair (di spāer') *vi.* [< L. *de-*, without
+ *spes*, hope] to lose hope (*of*) —*n.*
1. a loss of hope 2. a person or thing
causing despair —**despair'ingly** *adv.*

despatch (di spach') *vt., n. var. sp. of*
DISPATCH

desperado (des'pə rä'dō) *n., pl.* **-does,**
-dos [see DESPAIR] a dangerous, reckless
criminal

desperate (des'pər ət) *adj.* [see DESPAIR]
1. rash or violent because of despair 2.
having a great need 3. extremely serious
4. drastic —**des'perately** *adv.*

desperation (des'pə rā'shən) *n.* 1. the
state of being desperate 2. recklessness
caused by despair

despicable (des'pik ə b'l) *adj.* deserving
to be despised —**des'picably** *adv.*

despise (di spīz') *vt.* -spised', -spis'ing
[< L. *de*, down + *specere*, look at] to
regard with scorn or dislike

despite (di spīt') *prep.* [see prec.] in
spite of —*n.* 1. malice; spite 2. [Archaic]
contempt —**in despite of** in spite of

despoil (di spoil') *vt.* [< L. *de-*, intens.
+ *spoliare*, to plunder] to rob; plunder
—**despoil'er** *n.* —**despoil'ment, despo'li-**
a'tion (-spō'-) *n.*

despond (di spond') *vi.* [< L. *de*, from
+ *spondere*, to promise] to lose courage
or hope —**despond'ent** *adj.* —**despond'-**
ingly *adv.*

despondency *n.* loss of courage or hope;
dejection: also **despond'ence**

despot (des'pot) *n.* [< Gr. *despotēs*,
master] 1. an absolute ruler 2. anyone
who acts like a tyrant —**despot'ic** *adj.*
—**despot'ically** *adv.*

despotism (des'pə tiz'm) *n.* 1. rule by
a despot; autocracy 2. the methods of
a despot; tyranny

dessert (di zurt') *n.* [< OFr. *des-*, from
+ *servir*, serve] 1. a sweet course served
at the end of a meal 2. fruit and nuts
served after the sweet course

dessertspoon *n.* a spoon between a
teaspoon and tablespoon in size

destination (des'tə nā'shən) *n.* 1. the
place towards which someone or something
is going or sent 2. the end for which
something or someone is destined

destine (des'tin) *vt.* -tined, -tining [<

L. *de-*, intens. + *stare*, stand] **1.** to predetermine, as by fate **2.** to set apart for a certain purpose **—destined for 1.** bound for **2.** intended for

destiny (des'tə nē) *n., pl.* **-ies** [see prec.] **1.** the seemingly inevitable succession of events **2.** (one's) fate **3.** that which determines events

destitute (des'tə tyōōt') *adj.* [< L. *de-*, down + *statuere*, set] **1.** lacking (with *of*) **2.** living in complete poverty **—des'ti·tu'tion** *n.*

destroy (di stroi') *vt.* [< L. *de-*, down + *struere*, build] **1.** to demolish **2.** to spoil completely **3.** to put an end to **4.** to kill

destroyer *n.* **1.** a small, fast, heavily armed warship **2.** a person or thing that destroys

destruct (di strukt') *n.* the deliberate destruction of a malfunctioning missile, etc. after its launch **—vi.** to be automatically destroyed

destructible *adj.* that can be destroyed **—destruct'ibil'ity** *n.*

destruction *n.* [see DESTROY] **1.** a destroying or being destroyed **2.** the cause or means of destroying

destructive *adj.* **1.** likely to cause or causing destruction **2.** merely negative **—destruc'tively** *adv.* **—destruc'tiveness** *n.*

destructor *n.* an incinerator for rubbish

desuetude (de syōō'ə tyōōd') *n.* [< L. *de-*, from + *suescere*, to be accustomed] disuse

desultory (des''l tər ē) *adj.* [< L. *de-*, from + *salire*, to leap] **1.** passing from one thing to another in an aimless way **2.** random **—des'ultorily** *adv.*

detach (di tach') *vt.* [< OFr. *de-*, off + *estachier*, attach] **1.** to unfasten and remove **2.** to send (troops) on a special mission **—detach'able** *adj.*

detached *adj.* **1.** not connected; separate **2.** disinterested; impartial

detachment *n.* **1.** the state of being impartial or aloof **2.** a detaching; separation **3.** a unit of troops assigned to some special task

detail (dē'tāl) *n.* [< Fr. *dé-*, from + *tailler*, to cut] **1.** an item or particular **2.** a small part **3.** a dealing with things item by item **4.** a minute account **5.** *a)* one or more soldiers, etc. chosen for a particular task *b)* the task **—vt.** **1.** to tell, item by item **2.** to choose for a particular task **—in detail** item by item **—de'tailed** *adj.*

detain (di tān') *vt.* [< L. *de-*, off + *tenere*, hold] **1.** to keep in custody; confine **2.** to hold back **—detainee'** *n.* **—detain'er** *n.* **—detain'ment** *n.*

detect (di tekt') *vt.* [< L. *de-*, from + *tegere*, to cover] to discover (something hidden or not easily noticed) **—detect'able, detect'ible** *adj.*

detection *n.* **1.** a finding out or being found out **2.** *same as* DEMODULATION **—detec'tor** *n.*

detective *adj.* of detectives and their work **—n.** a person, usually on a police force, whose work is investigating crimes, getting secret information, etc.

détente (dā tänt') *n.* [Fr.] a lessening of tension or hostility, esp. between nations

detention (di ten'shən) *n.* a detaining or being detained; confinement; enforced delay

detention centre a place where young persons may be detained for short periods, by a court order

deter (di tur') *vt.* **-terred'**; **-ter'ring** [< L. *de-*, from + *terrere*, frighten] to discourage (a person) from doing something through fear, etc. **—deter'ment** *n.*

detergent (di tur'jənt) *n.* [< L. *de-*, off + *tergere*, wipe] a cleansing substance that is like soap but not made from fats and lye **—adj.** cleansing

deteriorate (di tēər'ē ə rāt') *vt., vi.* **-rat'ed, -rat'ing** [< L. *deterior*, worse] to make or become worse **—dete'riora'tion** *n.*

determinant (di tur'mi nənt) *adj.* determining **—n.** **1.** a thing or factor that determines **2.** *Math.* the sum of the products formed, following certain rules, from a square array of numbers

determinate (di tur'mi nit) *adj.* [see DETERMINE] **1.** having exact limits **2.** settled; conclusive **—deter'minately** *adv.*

determination (di tur'mə nā'shən) *n.* **1.** a determining or being determined **2.** a firm intention **3.** firmness of purpose

determine (di tur'mən) *vt.* **-mined, -mining** [< L. *de-*, from + *terminus*, an end] **1.** to settle conclusively **2.** to find out exactly **3.** to decide upon **4.** to establish the nature, kind, or quality of [*genes determine* heredity] **5.** to set limits to; define **—vi.** **1.** to decide; resolve **2.** *Law* to come to an end **—deter'minable** *adj.* **—deter'miner** *n.*

determined *adj.* **1.** having one's mind made up; resolved **2.** resolute; unwavering **—deter'minedly** *adv.*

determinism *n.* the doctrine that everything, esp. one's choice of action, is determined by causes independent of one's will **—deter'minist** *n., adj.*

deterrent (di ter'ənt) *adj.* deterring **—n.** a thing or factor that deters **—deter'rence** *n.*

detest (di test') *vt.* [< L. *de-*, down + *testis*, a witness] to dislike intensely **—detest'able** *adj.*

detestation (dē'tes tā'shən) *n.* **1.** intense dislike or hatred; loathing **2.** a detested person or thing

dethrone (dē thrōn') *vt.* **-throned', -thron'ing** to remove from a throne; depose **—dethrone'ment** *n.* **—dethron'er** *n.*

detonate (det'ən āt') *vi., vt.* **-nat'ed, -nat'ing** [< L. *de-*, intens. + *tonare*, thunder] to explode noisily **—det'ona'tion** *n.*

detonator *n.* **1.** a fuse, percussion cap, etc. for setting off explosives **2.** an explosive

detour (dē'tōōər) *n.* [< OFr. *des-*, DE + *tourner*, turn] **1.** a roundabout way **2.** a route used when the usual route is closed to traffic **—vi., vt.** to go or cause to go by way of a detour

detoxify (dē tok'sə fī') *vt.* **-fied', -fy'ing**

[< DE- + TOXIN] to remove a poison from, esp. alcohol —**detox'ifica'tion** n.

detract (di trakt') vt. [< L. de-, from + trahere, draw] to take or draw away —vi. to take something desirable away (from) —**detrac'tion** n. —**detrac'tor** n.

detriment (det'rə mənt) n. [< L. de-, off + terere, rub] 1. damage; injury; harm 2. anything that causes this —**det'rimen'tal** (-men't'l) adj.

detritus (di trīt'əs) n. [L.: see prec.] fragments of rock, etc. produced by erosion

‡**de trop** (də trō') [Fr.] too much; superfluous

detumescence (dē'tyoo mes'əns) n. [< L. detumescere, to stop swelling] a subsidence, or lessening, of a swelling

deuce[1] (dyoos) n. [< L. duo, two] 1. a playing card with two spots 2. the side of a die bearing two spots 3. Tennis a score of 40 each (or five games each) after which one side must get two successive points (or games) to win

deuce[2] n., interj. [< L. deus, God & DEUCE[1]] bad luck, the devil, etc.: a mild oath

‡**deus ex machina** (dā'əs eks'mak'i nə) [L., god from a machine] 1. any unconvincing character or event brought artificially into the plot of a story, play, etc. to settle an involved situation 2. anyone who unexpectedly intervenes in events

Deut. Deuteronomy

deuterium (dyoo tēər'ē əm) n. [< Gr. deuteros, second] the hydrogen isotope having an atomic weight of 2.0141; heavy hydrogen: symbol, D

Deutsche Mark (doi'chə) pl. mark the monetary unit of West Germany

devalue (dē val'yoo) vt. -ued, -uing 1. to lessen the value of 2. to lower the value of (a currency) in relation to other currencies —**deval'ua'tion** n.

devastate (dev'ə stāt') vt. -tat'ed, -tat'ing [< L. de-, intens. + vastare, make empty] 1. to lay waste 2. to overwhelm —**dev'astat'ing** adj. —**dev'asta'tion** n.

develop (di vel'əp) vt. [< Fr. dé-, apart + OFr. voloper, to wrap] 1. to cause to become fuller, larger, stronger, etc. 2. to bring into being; evolve 3. to improve the value or change the use of (land), as by building 4. Music to elaborate (a theme) 5. Photog. to put (an exposed film, etc.) in various chemical solutions in order to make the picture visible 6. to make known gradually; reveal 7. to begin to experience [develop tuberculosis] —vi. 1. to come into being or activity 2. to become larger, fuller, better, etc.; grow or evolve 3. to be disclosed

developer n. a person or thing that develops; esp., Photog. a chemical used to develop film, plates, etc.

developing country a country that is in the process of becoming industrialized

development n. 1. a developing or being developed 2. a stage in growth, advancement, etc. 3. an event or happening —**devel'opmen'tal** (-men't'l) adj.

development area an area in which the government encourages industrial expansion because of unemployment

deviant (dē'vē ənt) adj. deviating, esp. from what is considered normal —n. one whose behaviour is deviant —**de'viancy, de'viance** n.

deviate (dē'vē āt') vi., vt. -at'ed, -at'ing [< L. de-, from + via, road] to turn aside (from a course, standard, etc.) —n. a deviant; esp., one with deviant sexual behaviour —**de'via'tor** n.

deviation (dē'vē ā'shən) n. a deviating or being deviant, as in behaviour, political ideology, etc. —**de'via'tional** adj.

device (di vīs') n. [see DEVISE] 1. an underhanded scheme; trick 2. a mechanical invention 3. something used for artistic effect 4. a design or emblem on a coat of arms 5. a motto —**leave to one's own devices** to allow to do as one wishes

devil (dev''l) n. [ult. < Gr. diabolos, slanderous] 1. [often D-] Theol. a) to turn chief evil spirit; Satan (with the) b) any demon of hell 2. a wicked person 3. one who is mischievous, reckless, etc. 4. an unlucky, unhappy person 5. something difficult, annoying etc. 6. a literary hack 7. a printer's devil —vt. -illed, -illing 1. to prepare (food) with hot seasoning 2. [Chiefly U.S.] to annoy —vi. to work for a lawyer, author, etc. without pay or recognition —**a devil of a** an extreme example of a —**between the devil and the deep (blue) sea** between equally unpleasant alternatives —**give the devil his due** to acknowledge the good qualities of even a wicked person —**play the devil with** to cause havoc

devilish adj. 1. of or like a devil 2. mischievous; reckless 3. [Colloq.] extremely bad —adv. [Colloq.] extremely; very —**dev'ilishly** adv. —**dev'ilishness** n.

devil-may-care (dev''l mā kâar') adj. reckless or careless; happy-go-lucky

devilment n. mischief or mischievous action

devilry n., pl. -ries 1. witchcraft 2. evil behaviour

devil's advocate 1. one who upholds the wrong side for argument's sake 2. R.C.Ch. an official selected to raise objections in the case of one named for canonization

devious (dē'vē əs) adj. [< L. de-, off + via, road] 1. not straightforward or frank 2. roundabout; winding 3. going astray —**de'viously** adv. —**de'viousness** n.

devise (di vīz') vt., vi. -vised', -vis'ing [< OFr. deviser, to distribute] 1. to work out (something) by thinking 2. Law to bequeath (real property) by will —n. Law a gift of real property by will —**devis'al** n. —**devis'er** n.

devoid (di void') adj. [< OFr. des-, from + vuidier, to void] completely without; empty (of)

devolution (dē'və loo'shən) n. a transfer of authority from a central to a regional government

devolve (di volv′) *vt., vi.* **-volved′, -volv′-ing** [< L. *de-*, down + *volvere*, roll] to pass (*on*) to another: said of duties, responsibilities, etc. —**devolve′ment** *n.*

Devonian (de vō′nē ən) *adj.* [< *Devonshire*] *Geol.* of the period after the Silurian in the Paleozoic Era

devote (di vōt′) *vt.* **-vot′ed, -vot′ing** [< L. *de-*, from + *vovere*, vow] to set apart for or give up to some purpose, activity, or person

devoted *adj.* **1.** dedicated **2.** very loving, loyal, or faithful —**devot′edly** *adv.* —**devot′edness** *n.*

devotee (dev′ə tē′) *n.* a person strongly devoted to someone or to something, as a religion

devotion (di vō′shən) *n.* **1.** piety **2.** religious worship **3.** [*pl.*] prayers **4.** loyalty or deep affection —**devo′tional** *adj.*

devour (di vour′) *vt.* [< L. *de-*, intens. + *vorare*, swallow whole] **1.** to eat (up) hungrily or voraciously **2.** to consume; destroy **3.** to take in greedily, as with the eyes **4.** to engross —**devour′er** *n.*

devout (di vout′) *adj.* [see DEVOTE] **1.** very religious **2.** showing reverence **3.** sincere —**devout′ly** *adv.*

dew (dyoo) *n.* [OE. *deaw*] **1.** the moisture that condenses in drops on cool surfaces at night **2.** anything regarded as refreshing, pure, etc., like dew —*vt.* to wet as with dew —**dew′y** *adj.*

dewclaw *n.* a functionless digit on the foot of some animals, as on the inner side of a dog's leg

Dewey Decimal System (dyoo′ē) [< J. *Dewey*] a library system of classifying books by use of numbers with decimals

dewlap *n.* [< ME. < *dew*, prob. dew + OE. *læppa*, fold] a loose fold of skin hanging from the throat of cattle and certain other animals —**dew′lapped′** *adj.*

DEW line (dyoo) [*D(istant) E(arly) W(arning)*] a line of radar stations near the 70th parallel in N America

dew point the temperature at which dew starts to form

dew pond an artificial pond fed by condensation

dew-worm *n.* [Canad. Colloq.] any large earthworm that can be seen at night and is used as fishing bait

dexter (dek′stər) *adj.* [L., right] of or on the right-hand side (on a coat of arms, the left of the viewer)

dexterity (dek ster′ə tē) *n.* [see prec.] skill in using one's hands, body, or mind

dexterous (dek′strəs) *adj.* having or showing skill in the use of the hands, body, or mind: also **dex′trous** —**dex′ter-ously** *adv.*

dextrin (dek′strin) *n.* [Fr.] a soluble, gummy substance obtained from starch: also **dex′trine**

dextrose (dek′strōs) *n.* [ult. < L. *dexter*, right] a glucose found in plants and animals

D.F. Defender of the Faith

D.F.C., DFC Distinguished Flying Cross

D.F.M., DFM Distinguished Flying Medal

dg decigram(me)(s)

‡**dharma** (där′mə) *n.* [Sans., law] *Hinduism, Buddhism* **1.** cosmic order or law **2.** observance of this law

dhow (dou) *n.* [Ar. *dāwa*] a single-masted ship with a lateen sail, used along the Indian Ocean coasts

D.H.S.S. Department of Health and Social Security

di-¹ [Gr. *di-* < *dis*, twice] a prefix meaning: twice, double, twofold: also **dis-**

di-² same as DIS-

di-³ same as DIA-

dia- [< Gr.] a prefix meaning: **1.** through, across [*diaphragm, diagonal*] **2.** apart, between [*diagnose*]

diabetes (dī′ə bēt′ēz) *n.* [< Gr. *dia-*, through + *bainein*, go] any of various diseases characterized by an excessive discharge of urine

diabetes mellitus (mə lit′is) [ModL., honey diabetes] a chronic form of diabetes involving an insulin deficiency and excess of sugar in the blood and urine

diabetic (dī′ə bet′ik) *adj.* **1.** of or having diabetes **2.** prepared for diabetics —*n.* one who has diabetes

diabolic (dī′ə bol′ik) *adj.* [see DEVIL] **1.** of the Devil or devils **2.** very wicked or cruel Also **di′abol′ical**

diaconate (dī ak′ə nit) *n.* **1.** the rank or office of a deacon **2.** a group of deacons —**diak′onal** *adj.*

diacritical (dī′ə krit′i k'l) *adj.* [< Gr. *dia-*, across + *krinein*, separate] **1.** serving to distinguish **2.** able to distinguish —**di′a-crit′ically** *adv.*

diacritical mark a mark, as a macron or a cedilla, added to a letter or symbol to show its pronunciation

diadem (dī′ə dem′) *n.* [< Gr. *dia-*, through + *dein*, bind] **1.** a crown **2.** a jewelled headband or circlet worn as a crown

diaeresis (dī ēər′ə sis) *n., pl.* **-ses′** [< Gr. *dia-*, apart + *hairein*, to take] a mark (··) placed over the second of two consecutive vowels to show that it is pronounced in a separate syllable

diagnose (dī′əg nōz′) *vt., vi.* **-nosed′, -nos′ing** to make a diagnosis of (a disease, etc.)

diagnosis (dī′əg nō′sis) *n., pl.* **-ses** [< Gr. *dia-*, between + *gignōskein*, know] **1.** the act or process of deciding the nature of a disease, problem, etc. by examination and analysis **2.** a decision based on this —**di′agnos′tic** (-nos′tik) *adj.* —**di′agnos-ti′cian** (-nos tish′ən) *n.* —**di′agnos′tics** *n.pl.*

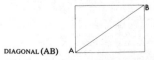

DIAGONAL (AB)

diagonal (dī ag′ən'l) *adj.* [< Gr. *dia-*, through + *gōnia*, angle] **1.** slanting between opposite corners, as of a rectangle **2.** having a slanting direction or slanting

diagram 239 **dice**

markings, lines, etc. —*n.* a diagonal line, plane, course, part, etc. —**diag′onally** *adv.*

diagram (dī′ə gram′) *n.* [< Gr. *dia-*, across + *graphein*, write] a drawing, plan, or chart that explains a thing, as by outlining its parts and their relationships —*vt.* -**grammed′**, -**gram′ming** to make a diagram of —**di′agrammat′ic** (-grə mat′-ik), **di′agrammat′ical** *adj.*

dial (dī′əl) *n.* [< L. *dies*, day] 1. the face of a watch, clock, or sundial 2. the face of a meter, gauge, etc. on which a pointer indicates an amount, degree, etc. 3. a graduated disc or strip on a radio or television set, for tuning in channels 4. a rotating disc on a telephone, used in making connections automatically 5. [Slang] the face —*vt., vi.* -**alled**, -**alling** 1. to measure, regulate, etc. with a dial 2. to call on a telephone by using a dial

dialect (dī′ə lekt′) *n.* [< Gr. *dia-*, between + *legein*, to talk] 1. the form of a spoken language peculiar to a region, community, social group, etc. 2. any language as a member of a group of languages [English is a West Germanic *dialect*] —*adj.* of or in dialect —**di′alec′tal** *adj.* —**di′alec′tally** *adv.*

dialectic (dī′ə lek′tik) *n.* [see prec.] 1. [often pl.] the practice of examining ideas logically, often by question and answer 2. logical argumentation 3. [often pl.] a method of logic used by Hegel and Marx in which opposites are reconciled in a synthesis —**di′alec′tical** *adj.*

dialling tone a low, purring sound indicating to the user of a telephone that a number may be dialled

dialogue (dī′ə log′) *n.* [see DIALECT] 1. a conversation 2. open and frank discussion of ideas, as in seeking mutual understanding 3. the passages of talk in a play, story, etc.

dialysis (dī al′ə sis) *n., pl.* -**ses′** (-sēz′) [< Gr. *dia-*, apart + *lyein*, to loose] the separation of crystalloids from colloids in solution through a semipermeable membrane —**dialyse** (dī′ə līz′) *vt., vi.* -**lysed′**, -**lys′ing** —**dialytic** (dī′ə lit′ik) *adj.* —**di′alyt′ically** *adv.*

diamagnetism (dī′ə mag′nə tiz′m) *n.* the property of being repelled by both poles of a magnet

diamanté (dē′ə mon′tā) *adj.* [Fr.] decorated with rhinestones or other glittering bits of material

diameter (dī am′ət ər) *n.* [< Gr. *dia-*, through + *metron*, measure] 1. a straight line passing through the centre of a circle, sphere, etc. from one side to the other 2. the length of such a line

diametrical (dī′ə met′ri k′l) *adj.* 1. of or along a diameter 2. designating an opposite that is wholly so: also **di′amet′ric** —**di′amet′rically** *adv.*

diamond (dī′ə mənd) *n.* [< Gr. *adamas*, adamant] 1. a mineral consisting of nearly pure carbon in crystalline form: it is the hardest mineral known: used for gems, cutting tools, abrasives, etc. 2. a gem cut from this mineral 3. *a)* a plane figure (◆) *b)* a red mark like this on a suit

of playing cards *c)* [pl.] this suit —*adj.* of, like, or set with a diamond

diamond wedding a sixtieth wedding anniversary

dianthus (dī an′thəs) *n.* [< Gr. *dios*, divine + *anthos*, flower] any of a genus of flowers, including carnations

diapason (dī′ə pās′′n) *n.* [< Gr. *dia*, through + *pas*, all (notes)] 1. the entire range of a musical instrument or voice 2. one of the principal stops of an organ covering the instrument's complete range

diaper (dī′ə pər) *n.* [< MGr. *diaspros*, pure white] 1. *a)* orig., cloth with a pattern of repeated figures *b)* such a pattern 2. [U.S.] a nappy

diaphanous (dī af′ə nəs) *adj.* [< Gr. *dia-*, through + *phainein*, to show] so fine or gauzy in texture as to be transparent

diaphragm (dī′ə fram′) *n.* [< Gr. *dia-*, through + *phragma*, fence] 1. the partition of muscles and tendons between the chest cavity and the abdominal cavity 2. a device to regulate the amount of light entering a camera lens, etc. 3. a thin, vibrating disc that produces sound waves, as in a loudspeaker 4. a contraceptive device placed over the mouth of the cervix —**di′aphragmat′ic** (-frag mat′ik) *adj.*

diapositive (dī′ə poz′ə tiv) *n.* [DIA- + POSITIVE] *Photog.* a positive transparency, as a slide on film or glass

diarist (dī′ ə rist) *n.* a person who keeps a diary

diarrhoea (dī′ə rē′ə) *n.* [< Gr. *dia-*, through + *rhein*, to flow] excessive frequency and looseness of bowel movements

diary (dī′ə rē) *n., pl.* -**ries** [< L. *dies*, day] 1. a daily written record, esp. of the writer's own experiences, thoughts, etc. 2. a book for this, or for keeping notes of future appointments

Diaspora (dī as′pə rə) *n.* [< Gr. *dia-*, across + *speirein*, to sow] 1. the dispersion of the Jews after the Babylonian exile 2. these Jews

diastase (dī′ə stās′) *n.* [< Gr. *dia-*, apart + *histanai*, to stand] an enzyme that changes starches into maltose and later into dextrose

diatom (dī′ət əm) *n.* [< Gr. *dia-*, through + *temnein*, to cut] any of a number of related microscopic algae which are a source of food for marine life

diatomic (dī′ə tom′ik) *adj.* 1. having two atoms in the molecule 2. having two radicals in the molecule

diatonic (dī′ə ton′ik) *adj.* [< Gr. *dia-*, through + *teinein*, stretch] *Music* designating or of any standard major or minor scale of eight tones —**di′aton′ically** *adv.*

diatribe (dī′ə trīb′) *n.* [< Gr. *dia-*, through + *tribein*, to rub] a bitter, abusive criticism or denunciation

dibble (dib′′l) *n.* [ME. *dibbel*] a pointed tool used to make holes in the soil for seeds, bulbs, etc.: also **dib′ber** —*vt.* -**bled**, -**bling** to plant with a dibble

dice (dīs) *n.pl., sing.* **die** or **dice** [see

DIE^2] 1. small cubes marked on each side with from one to six spots and used in games of chance 2. [*with sing. v.*] a gambling game played with dice —*vi.* **diced, dic'ing** to play with dice —*vt.* to cut (vegetables, etc.) into small cubes —**no dice** 1. no 2. no success, etc.

dicey *adj.* [Colloq.] hazardous; risky

dichotomy (dī kot'ə mē) *n., pl.* -**mies** [< Gr. *dicha*, in two + *temnein*, to cut] division into two usually opposed parts or groups —**dichot'omous** *adj.*

dichromatic (dī'krō mat'ik) *adj.* [DI-^{1} + CHROMATIC] having two colours —**dichro'matism** *n.*

dick (dik) *n.* [< *Richard*] [Slang] a detective —**clever dick** [Colloq.] a know-all

Dickensian (di ken'zē ən) *adj.* [< C. *Dickens*] 1. of Dickens or his writings 2. resembling the situations, characters, etc. described by Dickens

dicker (dik'ər) *vi., vt.* [< *dicker*, ten hides (as a unit of barter)] [U.S.] to trade by bargaining; barter; haggle

dicky (dik'ē) *adj.* -**ier**, -**iest** [? < *Dick*] [Colloq.] diseased; unsound; shaky —*n.* a man's detachable, or false, shirt front: also **dick'ey**

dicotyledon (dī'kot ə lēd''n) *n.* a flowering plant with two seed leaves (cotyledons) —**di'cotyle'donous** *adj.*

Dictaphone (dik'tə fōn') [DICTA(TE) + -PHONE] *Trademark* a machine that records and plays back spoken words

dictate (dik'tāt; *for v.* dik tāt') *vt., vi.* -**tat'ed**, -**tat'ing** [< L. *dicere*, speak] 1. to speak or read (something) aloud for someone else to write down 2. to command expressly 3. to give (orders) with authority —*n.* 1. an authoritative command 2. a guiding principle

dictation (dik tā'shən) *n.* 1. the dictating of words for another to write down 2. the words so spoken 3. the giving of orders or commands —**dicta'tional** *adj.*

dictator *n.* 1. a ruler with absolute power 2. a person who is domineering —**dicta'torship'** *n.*

dictatorial (dik'tə tôr'ē əl) *adj.* of or like a dictator; autocratic; tyrannical —**dic'tato'rially** *adv.*

diction (dik'shən) *n.* [< L. *dicere*, say] 1. manner of expression in words 2. enunciation

dictionary (dik'shə nər ē) *n., pl.* -**aries** [see prec.] 1. a book of alphabetically listed words in a language, with definitions, pronunciations, etc. 2. such a book of words in one language with their equivalents in another 3. any alphabetically arranged list of words relating to a special subject

dictum (dik'təm) *n., pl.* -**tums**, -**ta** [< L. *dicere*, to speak] a formal statement of fact; pronouncement

did (did) *pt. of* DO^1

didactic (di dak'tik) *adj.* [< Gr. *didaskein*, teach] 1. intended for instruction 2. morally instructive 3. boringly pedantic

Also **didac'tical** —**didac'tically** *adv.* —**didac'ticism** *n.*

diddle (did''l) *vt., vi.* -**dled**, -**dling** [< ?] [Colloq.] to cheat or swindle —**did'-dler** *n.*

didgeridoo (di'jər ē dōō') *n.* [Abor.] [Aust.] a musical instrument made from a bamboo pipe or hollow sapling

die^1 (dī) *vi.* **died, dy'ing** [< ON. *deyja*] 1. to stop living; become dead 2. to suffer agony like that of death 3. to stop functioning 4. to lose force or activity 5. to fade or wither away 6. [Colloq.] to wish intensely [she's *dying* to tell] —**die away** (or **down**) to become weaker and cease gradually —**die back** (or **down**) to wither to the roots —**die (of) laughing** to be overcome with mirth —**die out** to go out of existence

die^2 *n., pl.,* for 1 **dice** (dīs); for 2 **dies** (dīz) [< L. *dare*, give] 1. *see* DICE 2. any of various tools for stamping, cutting, or shaping —*vt.* **died, die'ing** to mould, stamp, cut, or shape with a die —**the die is cast** the irrevocable decision has been made

die casting 1. the process of forcing molten metal into a metallic mould 2. a casting so made

die-hard, diehard *adj.* extremely stubborn —*n.* a stubborn person, esp. an extreme conservative

dieldrin (dēl'drin) *n.* a highly toxic insecticide

dielectric (dī'ə lek'trik) *n.* [< DI(A)- + ELECTRIC] a material, as rubber, glass, etc., that does not conduct electricity —*adj.* nonconducting

diesel (dē'z'l) *n.* [< R. *Diesel*] [*often* D-] 1. a type of internal-combustion engine that burns fuel oil ignited by heat from air compression: also **diesel engine** (or **motor**) 2. a train, lorry, etc. with such an engine

diesel-electric *n.* a locomotive driven by an electric generator powered by a diesel engine

diesel fuel a heavy oil, distilled from petroleum, used by diesel engines: also **diesel oil**

diesinker (dī'siŋ'kər) *n.* a maker of dies that are used in stamping or shaping —**die'-sink'ing** *n.*

diet^1 (dī'ət) *n.* [< Gr. *diaita*, way of life] 1. a regimen of special or limited food and drink, as for health or to gain or lose weight 2. what a person or animal usually eats and drinks —*vi.* to eat special or limited food, esp. for losing weight —**di'etary** *adj.* —**di'eter** *n.*

diet^2 *n.* [< L. *dies*, day] 1. a formal assembly, esp. formerly 2. in some countries, a national or local legislative assembly

dietetic (dī'ə tet'ik) *adj.* of or for a particular diet of food and drink: also **di'etet'ical**

dietetics *n.pl.* [*with sing. v.*] the study of the kinds and quantities of food needed for health

dietitian, dietician (dī'ə tish'ən) *n.* an

expert in dietetics; specialist in planning meals or diets

differ (dif'ər) *vi.* [< L. *dis-*, apart + *ferre*, to bear] 1. to be unlike; be not the same (often with *from*) 2. to be of opposite or unlike opinions

difference (dif'rəns) *n.* 1. condition or quality of being different 2. the way in which people or things are different 3. the state of holding a differing opinion; disagreement; quarrel 4. *Math.* the amount by which one quantity is greater or less than another —**make a difference** 1. to have an effect 2. to change the situation —**split the difference** to share equally what is left over

different *adj.* 1. not alike; dissimilar (with *from* or *to*) 2. not the same; distinct 3. various 4. unusual —**dif'ferently** *adv.*

differentia (dif'ə ren'shē ə) *n.*, *pl.* **-tiae'** (-shi ē') a distinguishing characteristic

differential (dif'ə ren'shəl) *adj.* 1. of, showing, or depending on a difference 2. making use of differences [a differential gear] 3. *Math.* of or involving differentials —*n.* 1. a differentiating amount, factor, etc. [differentials in salary] 2. *Math.* an infinitesimal difference between values of a variable quantity —**dif'feren'tially** *adv.*

differential calculus the branch of higher mathematics which deals with derivatives and their applications

differential gear (or **gearing**) an arrangement of gears connecting two axles in the same line and allowing one axle to turn faster than the other

differentiate (dif'ə ren'shē āt') *vt.* -**at'ed,** -**at'ing** 1. to constitute a difference in or between 2. to make unlike 3. to distinguish between 4. *Math.* to work out the derivative of —*vi.* 1. to become different or differentiated 2. to note a difference —**dif'feren'tia'tion** *n.*

difficult (dif'i kəlt) *adj.* 1. hard to do, understand, etc. 2. hard to satisfy, please, etc. —**dif'ficultly** *adv.*

difficulty *n.*, *pl.* **-ties** [< L. *dis-*, not + *facilis*, easy] 1. a being difficult 2. an obstacle or objection 3. trouble 4. disagreement —**in difficulties** in distress, esp. financially

diffident (dif'ə dənt) *adj.* [< L. *dis-*, not + *fidere*, to trust] lacking confidence in oneself; timid; shy —**dif'fidence** *n.* —**dif'fidently** *adv.*

diffract (di frakt') *vt.* [< L. *dis-*, apart + *frangere*, break] to break into parts; specif., to subject to diffraction

diffraction *n.* 1. the breaking up of a ray of light into dark and light bands or into the colours of the spectrum, as when it is deflected at the edge of an opaque object 2. a similar breaking up of other waves, as of sound —**diffrac'tive** *adj.*

diffuse (di fyōōs'; *for v.* -fyōōz') *adj.* [< L. *dis-*, apart + *fundere*, pour] 1. spread out; not concentrated 2. using more words than are needed —*vt., vi.* **-fused', -fus'ing** 1. to pour or disperse in every direction

2. *Physics* to mix by diffusion —**diffuse'-ly** *adv.* —**diffuse'ness** *n.* —**diffus'ibil'ity** *n.* —**diffus'ible** *adj.* —**diffu'sive** *adj.*

diffusion (di fyōō'zhən) *n.* 1. a diffusing or being diffused; specif., *a*) a scattering of light rays, as by reflection *b*) an intermingling of the molecules of liquids, gases, etc. 2. wordiness

dig (dig) *vt.* dug, dig'ging [< ? OFr. *digue*, dike] 1. to turn up or remove (ground, etc.) with a spade, the hands, etc. 2. to make (a hole, cellar, etc.) as by doing this 3. to get from the ground in this way 4. to find out, as by careful study 5. to jab or prod 6. [Slang] *a*) to understand *b*) to like —*vi.* 1. to dig the ground 2. to make a way as by digging (*through, into, under*) 3. [Colloq.] to have rooms or lodgings —*n.* 1. [Colloq.] *a*) a poke, nudge, etc. *b*) a sarcastic comment 2. an archaeological excavation 3. [*pl.*, *often with sing. v.*] [Colloq.] living quarters —**dig in** 1. to dig trenches for cover 2. to entrench oneself 3. [Colloq.] to begin eating —**dig one's heels** (or **toes**) **in** to refuse to move or be persuaded

digest (di jest'; *for n.* dī'jest) *vt.* [< L. *di-*, apart + *gerere*, to bear] 1. to change (food, esp. in the stomach and intestines, so that it can be absorbed by the body 2. to think over and absorb 3. to summarize —*vi.* to be digested —*n.* a collection of condensed, systematic information; summary or synopsis, as of legal material —**digest'ible** *adj.*

digestion *n.* 1. the act or process of digesting food 2. the ability to digest food 3. the absorption of ideas

digestive *adj.* of, for, or aiding digestion —*n.* any substance that aids digestion —**diges'tively** *adv.*

digger (dig'ər) *n.* 1. a tool or machine for digging 2. [D-] [Slang] an Australian or New Zealander

diggings *n.pl.* 1. materials dug out 2. [often with sing. v.] a place where digging or mining is carried on 3. [Slang] one's lodgings

digit (dij'it) *n.* [L. *digitus*, a finger, toe] 1. a finger or toe 2. any numeral from 0 to 9

digital *adj.* 1. of, like, or having digits 2. using numbers that are digits to represent all the variables involved in calculation —*n.* a key played with a finger, as on the piano —**dig'itally** *adv.*

digital clock (or **watch**) a timepiece that shows the time in digits rather than by hands on a dial

digital computer a computer that uses numbers to perform calculations, usually in a binary system

digitalis (dij'ə tāl'is) *n.* [see DIGIT: from its flowers] 1. any of a genus of plants with long spikes of thimblelike flowers 2. a medicine made from foxglove leaves, used as a heart stimulant

digitate (dij'ə tāt') *adj.* [see DIGIT] 1. having separate fingers or toes 2. fingerlike —**dig'ita'tion** *n.*

dignified (dig′nə fīd′) *adj.* having or showing dignity

dignify (dig′nə fī′) *vt.* **-fied′, -fy′ing** [< L. *dignus*, worthy + *facere*, make] to give dignity to; honour

dignitary *n.,* *pl.* **-taries** [< L. *dignitas*, dignity] a person holding a high, dignified position or office

dignity *n.,* *pl.* **-ties** [< L. *dignus*, worthy] **1.** the quality of being worthy of esteem or honour **2.** high repute; honour **3.** the degree of worth or honour **4.** a high position or title **5.** stateliness **6.** self-respect

digraph (dī′gräf) *n.* [DI-¹ + -GRAPH] two letters that express a single sound (Ex.: read, show)

digress (dī gres′) *vi.* [< L. *dis-*, apart + *gradi*, go] to depart temporarily from the main subject in talking or writing —**digres′sion** (-gresh′ən) *n.*

DIHEDRAL ANGLE

(angle formed by planes MWON and MWXY)

dihedral (dī hē′drəl) *adj.* [< DI-¹ + Gr. *hedra*, a seat] having or formed by two intersecting plane faces

dike (dīk) *n.* [< OE. *dic*] **1.** a ditch **2.** an embankment or dam made to prevent flooding as by the sea **3.** a low wall, often made of stone —*vt.* diked, dik′ing to protect or enclose with a dike Also **dyke** —**dik′er** *n.*

dikkop (dik′əp) *n.* [< Afrik. *dik*, thick + *kop*, head] [S Afr.] **1.** the stone curlew **2.** [Slang] a fool

dilapidate (di lap′ə dāt′) *vi., vt.* **-dat′ed, -dat′ing** [< L. *dis-*, apart + *lapidare*, throw stones at] to become or make partially ruined —**dilap′idat′ed** *adj.* —**dilap′ida′-tion** *n.*

dilate (dī lāt′) *vt., vi.* **-lat′ed, -lat′ing** [< L. *dis-*, apart + *latus*, wide] **1.** to make or become wider or larger **2.** to expand (*on* or *upon*) —**dilat′able** *adj.* —**dil′ata′-tion** —**dila′tion** *n.* —**dila′tor** *n.*

dilatory (dil′ə tər ē) *adj.* [see DEFER¹] **1.** causing delay **2.** inclined to delay; slow; tardy —**dil′atorily** *adv.* —**dil′atoriness** *n.*

dilemma (di lem′ə) *n.* [< Gr. *di-*, two + *lēmma*, proposition] a situation in which one must choose between unpleasant alternatives

dilettante (dil′ə tan′tē) *n., pl.* **-tantes′, -tan′ti** (-tan′tē) [It. < L. *delectare*, to delight] **1.** a person who dabbles in an art or science in a superficial way **2.** a person who loves the fine arts —*adj.* of or characteristic of a dilettante —**dil′et-tant′ism** *n.*

diligent (dil′ə jənt) *adj.* [< L. *di-*, apart + *legere*, choose] **1.** persevering and careful in work **2.** done with careful, steady effort —**dil′igence** *n.* —**dil′igently** *adv.*

dill (dil) *n.* [OE. *dile*] a plant with bitter seeds and aromatic leaves, used to flavour pickles, etc.

dillydally (dil′ē dal′ē) *vi.* **-lied, -lying** [redupl. form of DALLY] [Colloq.] to waste time in hesitation; loiter

dilute (dī lyo̅o̅t′) *vt.* **-lut′ed, -lut′ing** [< L. *dis-*, off + *lavare*, wash] to thin down or weaken by mixing with water, etc. —*adj.* diluted —**dilute′ness** *n.* —**dilut′-er, dilu′tor** *n.* —**dilu′tion** *n.*

diluvial (di lo̅o̅′vē əl) *adj.* [< L. *diluvium*, a deluge] of a flood, esp. the Deluge Also **dilu′vian**

dim (dim) *adj.* **dim′mer, dim′mest** [OE. *dimm*] **1.** not bright; dull **2.** not clearly seen, heard, or understood **3.** not clearly seeing, hearing, or understanding **4.** [Colloq.] stupid —*vt., vi.* dimmed, dim′-ming to make or grow dim —**take a dim view of** to view with disapproval, gloom, etc. —**dim′ly** *adv.*

dime (dīm) *n.* [< L. *decimus*, a tenth] a coin of the U.S. and of Canada equal to ten cents

dimension (də men′shən) *n.* [< L. *dis-*, off + *metiri*, to measure] **1.** any measurable extent, as length, width, depth, etc. **2.** [pl.] measurements in length and width, and often depth **3.** [often pl.] size or scope —**dimen′sional** *adj.* —**dimen′-sionally** *adv.*

diminish (də min′ish) *vt.* [ult. < L. *deminuere*, make smaller & *minutus*, MINUTE²] **1.** to reduce in size, degree, importance, etc. **2.** *Music* to reduce (a minor interval) by a semitone —*vi.* to become smaller or less —**dimin′ished** *adj.* —**diminution** (dim′ə nyo̅o̅′shən) *n.*

diminished responsibility *Law* a plea in which mental derangement is submitted as demonstrating lack of criminal responsibility

diminuendo (də min′yo̅o̅ wen′dō) *adj., adv., n., pl.* **-dos** [It.] same as DECRE-SCENDO

diminutive (də min′yo̅o̅ tiv) *adj.* **1.** very small; tiny **2.** *Gram.* expressing smallness —*n.* a word or name formed by the addition of a suffix expressing smallness, as *ringlet, sonny* —**dimin′utively** *adv.*

dimity (dim′ə tē) *n., pl.* **-ties** [< Gr. *dis-*, two + *mitos*, a thread] a strong, often corded cotton cloth

dimple (dim′p'l) *n.* [ME. *dimpel*] a small, natural hollow spot, as on the cheek or chin —*vt., vi.* **-pled, -pling** to form dimples (in)

dimwit (dim′wit′) *n.* [Colloq.] a stupid person; simpleton —**dim′wit′ted** *adj.* —**dim′wit′tedly** *adv.*

din (din) *n.* [OE. *dyne*] a loud, continuous noise; confused clamour —*vt.* dinned, din′-ning **1.** to beset with a din **2.** to repeat insistently or noisily —*vi.* to make a din

dinar (dē′när) *n.* [< Ar.: see DENARIUS] the monetary unit of Algeria, Iraq, Jordan, Libya, Tunisia, etc.

dine (dīn) *vi.* **dined, din'ing** [ult. < L. *dis-*, away + *jejunus*, fasting] to eat dinner —*vt.* to provide a dinner for —**dine out** to dine away from home

diner *n.* 1. a person eating dinner 2. *same as* DINING CAR 3. [U.S.] a small restaurant

dinette (dīnet') *n.* an alcove or small, partitioned space used as a dining room

ding (diŋ) *vi.* [< Scand.] to make a sound like that of a bell; ring —*n.* the sound of a bell

ding-dong *n.* [echoic] 1. the sound of a bell struck repeatedly 2. a heated argument —*adj.* [Colloq.] vigorously contested

dinges (dəŋgs) *n.* [< Afrik. *ding*, thing] [S Afr. Colloq.] a jocular word for something whose name is unknown, forgotten, etc.; thingumabob

dinghy (diŋ'gē) *n.*, *pl.* **-ghies** [Hindi *diṅgī*] 1. any small boat used as a tender to a yacht 2. a small single-masted racing boat 3. an inflatable life raft

dingle (diŋ'g'l) *n.* [ME. *dingel*, abyss] a small, deep, wooded valley; dell

dingo (diŋ'gō) *n.*, *pl.* **-goes** [Abor.] the Australian wild dog

dingy (din'jē) *adj.* **-gier, -giest** [< ?] 1. dirty-coloured 2. dismal; shabby —**din'gi-ness** *n.*

dining car a railway carriage equipped to serve meals to passengers

dining room a room where meals are eaten

dinkum (diŋ'kəm) *adj.* [< ?] [Aust. Slang] genuine; true —**dinkum oil** [Aust. Colloq.] the truth

dinky (diŋ'kē) *adj.* **-kier, -kiest** [< Scot. *dink*, trim] [Colloq.] small and neat; dainty

dinner (din'ər) *n.* [see DINE] 1. the chief meal of the day, whether eaten in the evening or about noon 2. a banquet in honour of some person or event

dinner dance an evening event consisting of a dinner followed by a dance, usually formal

dinner jacket a man's tailless jacket for semiformal evening wear, orig. black

dinosaur (dī'nə sôr') *n.* [< Gr. *deinos*, terrible + *sauros*, lizard] any of a large group of extinct, four-limbed reptiles of the Mesozoic Era

dint (dint) *n.* [OE. *dynt*, blow] 1. exertion: now chiefly in by dint of 2. a dent —*vt.* to dent

diocesan (dī os'ə s'n) *adj.* of a diocese —*n.* the bishop of a diocese

diocese (dī'ə sis) *n.* [< Gr. *dia*, through + *oikos*, house] the district under a bishop's jurisdiction

diode (dī'ōd) *n.* [< DI-[1] + Gr. *hodos*, way] an electron tube, etc. conducting electricity in only one direction

dioecious (dī ē'shəs) *adj.* [< DI-[1] + Gr. *oikos*, house] *Biol.* having the male reproductive organs in one individual and the female organs in another

Dionysian (dī'ə niz'ē ən) *adj.* [< *Dionysus*, the Greek god of wine] wild, frenzied, and sensuous

dioptre (dī op'tər) *n.* [< Gr. *dia-*, through + *opsis*, sight] a unit of measure of the power of a lens

diorama (dī'ə räm'ə) *n.* [DI(A)- + (PAN)ORAMA] 1. a picture painted on a set of transparent curtains and looked at through a small opening 2. a miniature scene depicting three-dimensional figures in a naturalistic setting

dioxide (dī ok'sīd) *n.* an oxide containing two atoms of oxygen per molecule

dip (dip) *vt.* **dipped, dip'ping** [OE. *dyppan*] 1. to put into liquid for a moment 2. to dye in this way 3. to wash (sheep or pigs) in disinfectant 4. to make (a candle) by putting a wick repeatedly in melted tallow or wax 5. to take out as by scooping up 6. to lower and immediately raise again 7. to switch car headlights from main to lower beam —*vi.* 1. to plunge into a liquid and quickly come out 2. to sink or seem to sink suddenly 3. to undergo a slight decline 4. to slope down 5. to lower something into liquid, etc., esp. in order to take something out: often figurative [to dip into one's savings] 6. to read or study superficially (with *into*) —*n.* 1. a dipping or being dipped 2. a brief plunge into a liquid 3. a liquid into which something is dipped, as for dyeing 4. a candle made by dipping 5. a downward slope 6. a thick, creamy sauce into which one dips crisps or other appetizers 7. [Slang] a pickpocket

Dip. A.D. Diploma in Art and Design

Dip. Ed. Diploma in Education

diphtheria (dif thēar'ē ə) *n.* [< Gr. *diphthera*, leather] an acute infectious disease characterized by high fever and the formation in the air passages of a membrane-like obstruction —**diphthe'rial** *adj.*

diphthong (dif'thoŋ) *n.* [< Gr. *di-*, two + *phthongos*, sound] *Phonet.* a vowel sound made by gliding from one vowel to another within the same syllable, as (ɑi) in *boy* —**diphthon'gal** *adj.*

diploma (di plō'mə) *n.* [< Gr. *diplōma*, folded letter] 1. a certificate conferring honours, privileges, etc. 2. a certificate conferring a degree from a college or university

diplomacy (di plō'mə sē) *n.*, *pl.* **-cies** 1. (skill in) conducting relations between nations 2. tact in dealing with people

diplomat (dip'lə mat') *n.* [< Fr., ult. < L. *diploma*, DIPLOMA] 1. a representative of a government who conducts relations with another government 2. a tactful person Also **diplomatist** (di plō'mə tist)

diplomatic *n.* 1. of diplomacy 2. tactful and adroit in dealing with people —**dip'lo-mat'ically** *adv.*

diplomatic immunity exemption from court action, etc. abroad, granted to members of the diplomatic service

dipole (dī'pōl') *n.* *Physics* two equal but opposite electric charges or magnetic poles separated by a small distance —**dipo'-lar** *adj.*

dipper (dip'ər) *n.* 1. a container for dipping; esp., a long-handled cup 2. any of a genus of songbirds, as the water ouzel —**dip'perful** *n.*

dipso (dip'sō) *n.* [Colloq.] a dipsomaniac

dipsomania (dip'sō mā'nē ə) *n.* [< Gr. *dipsa*, thirst + -MANIA] an abnormal and insatiable craving for alcoholic drink —**dip'soma'niac** *n.*

dipstick (dip'stik') *n.* a graduated rod for measuring the depth of a substance in its container, as oil in a car engine

dip switch a switch which dips a vehicle's headlights

dipterous (dip'tər əs) *adj.* [< Gr. *di-*, two + *pteron*, wing] having two wings or two winglike appendages

diptych (dip'tik) *n.* [< Gr. *di-*, twice + *ptychē*, fold] 1. an ancient hinged writing tablet 2. a picture painted on two hinged tablets

dire (dīər) *adj.* **dir'er, dir'est** [L. *dirus*] 1. arousing terror; dreadful: also **dire'ful** 2. urgent —**dire'ly** *adv.*

direct (di rekt') *adj.* [< L. *dis-*, apart + *regere*, to rule] 1. by the shortest way; straight *[a direct route]* 2. straightforward; frank 3. with nothing or no one between; immediate 4. in an unbroken line of descent; lineal 5. exact; complete *[the direct opposite]* 6. in the exact words of the speaker —*vt.* 1. to manage; guide; conduct 2. to order or command with authority 3. to turn or point; aim; head 4. to tell (a person) the way to a place 5. to address (words, etc.) to a specific person 6. to write the name and address on (a letter, etc.) 7. to supervise the action of (a play, film, etc.) —*vi.* 1. to give directions 2. to be a director —**direct'ness** *n.*

direct current an electric current flowing in one direction

direct-grant school a day public school that receives a government grant for its non-fee-paying pupils

direction (di rek'shən) *n.* 1. the act of directing; management; supervision 2. [*usually pl.*] instructions for doing, using, etc. 3. an order or command 4. the point towards which one faces or line along which one moves or lies 5. an aspect, way, trend, etc.

directional *adj.* 1. of, aimed at, or indicating (a specific) direction 2. designed for radiating or receiving radio signals most effectively in one or more particular directions —**direc'tionally** *adv.*

direction finder a device for finding out the direction from which radio waves or signals are coming

directive (di rek'tiv) *adj.* directing —*n.* a general instruction or order issued authoritatively

directly *adv.* 1. in a direct way or line; straight 2. with nothing coming between 3. exactly *[directly opposite]* 4. right away —*conj.* [Colloq.] as soon as

direct object the word or words denoting the receiver of the action of a transitive verb

director *n.* a person or thing that directs; specif., *a)* a member of a board chosen to direct the affairs of a company or institution *b)* one who directs the staging of a film, etc. —**directorial** (di rek'tôr'ē əl) *adj.* —**direc'torship'** *n.* —**direc'tress** *n.fem.*

directorate *n.* 1. a board of directors 2. the position of director

directory *adj.* directing or advising —*n.*, *pl.* -ries a book listing the names, addresses, etc. of a specific group of persons

direct speech the reporting of what was said using the exact words and quotation marks

direct tax a tax levied directly on the person who is to pay it, as an income tax or property tax

dirge (durj) *n.* [< L. *dirige*, direct, first word of an antiphon in the Office of the Dead] 1. a funeral hymn 2. a song, poem, etc. expressing grief

dirigible (dir'i jə b'l) *adj.* [see DIRECT] that can be steered —*n.* same as AIRSHIP

dirk (durk) *n.* [< ?] a short, straight dagger

dirndl (durn'd'l) *n.* [< G. *Dirne*, girl] 1. a kind of dress with a full skirt, gathered waist, and closefitting bodice 2. the skirt of such a dress: also **dirndl skirt**

dirt (durt) *n.* [< ON. *dritr*, excrement] 1. any unclean matter, as mud, etc. 2. earth or garden soil 3. dirtiness, corruption, etc. 4. obscene writing, etc. 5. malicious gossip —**do one dirt** [Slang] to harm one

dirt-cheap *adj.* [Colloq.] very inexpensive

dirt track a track of levelled cinders, loose earth, etc. used for motor-cycle racing

dirty *adj.* -ier, -iest 1. soiled or soiling with dirt; unclean 2. muddy or clouded *[a dirty green]* 3. obscene; pornographic 4. mean; nasty 5. unfair; dishonest 6. [Colloq.] showing dislike, irritation, etc. *[a dirty look]* 7. Naut. squally; rough *[dirty weather]* —*vt.*, *vi.* **dirt'ied, dirt'ying** to make or become dirty; soil —*adv.* [Slang] very (with *big* or *great*) —**do the dirty on** to behave unkindly towards —**dirt'ily** *adv.* —**dirt'iness** *n.*

dis- [< L.] *a prefix denoting* separation, negation, or reversal *[dismiss, dishonest, disown]*

disability (dis'ə bil'ə tē) *n.*, *pl.* -ties 1. a disabled condition 2. that which disables, as an illness or injury

disable (dis ā'b'l) *vt.* -bled, -bling 1. to make unable or unfit; cripple 2. to disqualify legally —**disa'blement** *n.*

disabuse (dis'ə byōoz') *vt.* -bused', -bus'ing to rid of false ideas; undeceive

disadvantage (dis'əd văn'tij) *n.* 1. an unfavourable situation; drawback; handicap 2. harm or detriment —*vt.* -taged, -taging to act to the disadvantage of —**at a disadvantage** in an unfavourable situation —**disad'vanta'geous** (-ad'văn tā'jəs) *adj.*

disadvantaged *adj.* deprived of a decent standard of living, education, etc.; underprivileged

disaffect (dis'ə fekt') *vt.* to make discontented or disloyal —**dis'affect'ed** *adj.* —**dis'affec'tion** *n.*

disagree (dis′ə grē′) *vi.* **-greed′, -gree′-ing** **1.** to fail to agree; be different **2.** to differ in opinion **3.** to give distress [*cheese disagrees* with me]

disagreeable *adj.* **1.** not to one's taste; unpleasant **2.** quarrelsome —**dis′agree′a-bly** *adv.*

disagreement *n.* **1.** refusal to agree **2.** failure to agree; difference **3.** difference of opinion **4.** a quarrel

disallow (dis′ə lou′) *vt.* to refuse to allow; reject as invalid or illegal —**dis′allow′-ance** *n.*

disappear (dis′ə pēar′) *vi.* **1.** to go out of sight **2.** to become lost or extinct —**dis′-appear′ance** *n.*

disappoint (dis′ə point′) *vt.* **1.** to fail to satisfy the hopes or expectations of **2.** to frustrate (hopes, etc.)

disappointment *n.* **1.** a disappointing or being disappointed **2.** a person or thing that disappoints

disapprobation (dis′ap′rō bā′shən) *n.* disapproval

disapprove (dis′ə prōōv′) *vt., vi.* **-proved′, -prov′ing** **1.** to have or express an unfavourable opinion (of) **2.** to refuse to approve —**dis′approv′al** *adj.*

disarm (dis ärm′) *vt.* **1.** to take away weapons from **2.** to make harmless **3.** to overcome the hostility of —*vi.* to reduce armed forces and armaments

disarmament (dis′är′mə mənt) *n.* the reduction of armed forces and armaments, as to a limitation set by treaty

disarming *adj.* removing suspicions, fears, or hostility —**disarm′ingly** *adv.*

disarrange (dis′ə rānj′) *vt.* **-ranged′, -rang′ing** to make less neat; disorder —**dis′arrange′ment** *n.*

disarray (dis′ə rā′) *vt.* to throw into disorder; upset —*n.* **1.** disorder; confusion **2.** a state of disorderly or insufficient dress

disassociate (dis′ə sō′shē āt′) *vt.* **-at′ed, -at′ing** to sever association with; separate —**dis′asso′cia′tion** *n.*

disaster (di zäs′tər) *n.* [< L. *dis-* + *astrum*, star] any happening that causes great harm or damage; calamity

disastrous *adj.* being or causing great harm, damage, etc.; calamitous —**disas′-trously** *adv.*

disavow (dis′ə vou′) *vt.* to deny any knowledge or approval of, or responsibility for —**dis′avow′al** *n.*

disband (dis band′) *vt.* to break up (an association or organization) —*vi.* to scatter; disperse —**disband′ment** *n.*

disbar (dis′bär′) *vt.* **-barred′, -bar′ring** to deprive (a lawyer) of the right to practise law —**disbar′ment** *n.*

disbelieve (dis′bə lēv′) *vt., vi.* **-lieved′, -liev′ing** to refuse to believe (*in*) —**dis′be-lief′** *n.* —**dis′believ′er** *n.*

disburse (dis burs′) *vt.* **-bursed′, -burs′-ing** [< OFr. *desbourser*] to pay out; expend —**disburs′al, disburse′ment** *n.*

disc (disk) *n.* [see DISCUS] **1.** any flat, circular thing **2.** anything with the appearance of a disc [the moon's *disc*] **3.** a gramophone record **4.** *Biol.* any disc-

shaped part or structure; specif., *a*) the disc-shaped centre of certain composite flowers *b*) a layer of fibrous connective tissue occurring between vertebrae

discard (dis kärd′; *for n.* dis′kärd) *vt.* [< OFr.: see DIS- & CARD¹] **1.** *Card Games* to throw away (undesired cards) **2.** to get rid of as no longer useful —*vi.* *Card Games* to make a discard —*n.* **1.** something discarded **2.** *Card Games* the card or cards discarded

disc brake a brake, as on a motor vehicle, that causes two friction pads to press on a rotating disc

discern (di surn′) *vt.* [< L. *dis-*, apart + *cernere*, to separate] **1.** to recognize as separate **2.** to make out clearly —**dis-cern′ible** *adj.* —**discern′ibly** *adv.*

discerning *adj.* having or showing good judgment or understanding —**discern′ingly** *adv.*

discernment *n.* keen perception or judgment; insight

discharge (dis chärj′) *vt.* **-charged′, -charg′ing** [< L. *dis-*, from + *carrus*, wagon] **1.** to release or dismiss (a jury, prisoner, etc. **2.** to unload (a cargo) **3.** to shoot (a projectile) **4.** to throw off; emit [to *discharge* pus] **5.** to pay (a debt) or perform (a duty) **6.** *Elec.* to remove stored energy from (a battery or capacitor) —*vi.* **1.** to get rid of a burden, load, etc. **2.** to be released or thrown off **3.** to go off: said of a gun, etc. **4.** to emit waste matter: said of a wound, etc. —*n.* **1.** a discharging or being discharged **2.** that which discharges, as a certificate of dismissal from military service, etc. **3.** that which is discharged **4.** a flow of electric current across a gap, as in a spark —**discharge′able** *adj.* —**discharg′er** *n.*

disciple (di sī′p'l) *n.* [< L. *discere*, learn] **1.** a follower of any teacher or school **2.** an early follower of Jesus, esp. one of the Apostles —**disci′pleship′** *n.*

disciplinarian (dis′ə pli nāar′ē ən) *n.* one who believes in or enforces strict discipline

disciplinary (dis′ə pli nər ē) *adj.* **1.** of or having to do with discipline **2.** that enforces discipline by punishing

discipline (dis′ə plin) *n.* [see DISCIPLE] **1.** *a*) training that develops self-control *b*) strict control to enforce obedience **2.** orderly conduct, obedience, etc. **3.** treatment that corrects or punishes **4.** a system of rules, as for a monastic order **5.** a branch of knowledge —*vt.* **-plined, -plin-ing** **1.** to train; control **2.** to punish —**dis′-ciplinable** *adj.* —**dis′cipliner** *n.*

disc jockey a person who conducts a radio programme of recorded music, interspersed with chatter, etc.

disclaim (dis klām′) *vt.* **1.** to give up any claim to **2.** to repudiate —**disclama-tion** (dis′klə mā′shən) *n.*

disclaimer *n.* **1.** a disclaiming or renunciation, as of a claim, title, etc. **2.** a disavowing

disclose (dis′klōz′) *vt.* **-closed′, -clos′-**

ing 1. to make known 2. to bring into view —**disclo'sure** (-klō'zhər) n.

disco (dis'kō) n. [Colloq.] a discotheque

discobolus (dis kob'ə ləs) n. [< Gr. diskos, discus + ballein, to throw] a discus thrower

discolour (dis kul'ər) vt., vi. to change in colour by fading or staining —**discol'our-a'tion, discol'ora'tion** n.

discomfit (dis kum'fit) vt. [< L. dis- + conficere, prepare] 1. to make uneasy 2. to frustrate the plans of 3. orig., to defeat —**discom'fiture** n.

discomfort (dis kum'fərt) n. lack of comfort; uneasiness —vt. to cause discomfort to

discommode (dis'kə mōd') vt. -mod'ed, -mod'ing [< DIS- + L. commodare, make suitable] to cause bother to; inconvenience —**dis'commo'dious** adj.

discompose (dis'kəm pōz') vt. -posed', -pos'ing to disturb the calm of; disconcert —**dis'compo'sure** n.

disconcert (dis'kən surt') vt. 1. to upset the composure of 2. to upset (plans, etc.) —**dis'concert'ing** adj.

disconnect (dis'kə nekt') vt. to break or undo the connection of; detach —**dis'connec'tion** n.

disconnected adj. 1. incoherent 2. separated, detached, etc. —**dis'connect'edly** adv.

disconsolate (dis kon'sə lət) adj. [see DIS- & CONSOLE¹] so unhappy that nothing will console —**discon'solately** adv.

discontent (dis'kən tent') adj. same as DISCONTENTED —n. lack of contentment; dissatisfaction: also **dis'content'ment** —vt. to make discontented

discontented adj. not contented; wanting something different —**dis'content'edness** n.

discontinue (dis'kən tin'yōō) vt., vi. -ued, -uing to stop; cease; give up —**dis'contin'uance, dis'contin'ua'tion** n.

discontinuous adj. not continuous; broken —**discontinuity** (dis kon'-tə nyōō'ə tē) n.

discord (dis'kôrd) n. [< L. dis-, apart + cor, heart] 1. disagreement 2. a harsh or confused noise 3. Music a lack of harmony in tones sounded together

discordant adj. 1. not in accord; conflicting 2. not in harmony; clashing —**discord'ance, discord'ancy** n. —**discord'antly** adv.

discothèque (dis'kō tek) n. [Fr. < disque, record + bibliothèque, library] a nightclub or other public place for dancing to recorded popular music

discount (dis'kount; for v., also dis kount') n. [see DIS- & COMPUTE] 1. a reduction from a usual or list price 2. the interest deducted in advance by one who lends money on a promissory note, etc. 3. the rate of interest (**discount rate**) charged for this —vt. 1. to allow for exaggeration, bias, etc. 2. to disbelieve or disregard 3. to deduct an amount from (a bill, price, etc.) 4. to sell at less than the regular price 5. to pay or receive the value of (a promissory note, etc.), minus the discount

—**at a discount** below the regular price —**dis'countable** adj.

discountenance (dis koun'tə nəns) vt. -nanced, -nancing 1. to make ashamed or embarrassed; disconcert 2. to refuse approval or support to

discourage (dis kur'ij) vt. -aged, -aging [OFr. descoragier] 1. to deprive of courage; dishearten 2. to persuade (a person) to refrain 3. to try to prevent by disapproving —**discour'agement** n. —**discour'aging** adj. —**discour'agingly** adv.

discourse (dis'kôrs; also, and for v. usually, dis kôrs') n. [< L. dis-, from + currere, to run] 1. talk; conversation 2. a formal treatment of a subject, in speech or writing —vi. -coursed', -cours'-ing 1. to converse; talk 2. to speak or write (on or upon a subject) formally

discourteous (dis kur'tē əs) adj. impolite; ill-mannered —**discour'teously** adv. —**discour'teousness, discour'tesy** n.

discover (dis kuv'ər) vt. [see DIS- & COVER] 1. to be the first to find, see, or know about 2. to find out —**discov'erable** adj. —**discov'erer** n.

discovery n., pl. -eries 1. a discovering 2. anything discovered

discredit (dis kred'it) vt. 1. to disgrace 2. to cast doubt on 3. to reject as untrue —n. 1. something that causes disgrace 2. disgrace 3. loss of belief; doubt —**discred'itable** adj. —**discred'itably** adv.

discreet (dis krēt') adj. [see DISCERN] 1. careful about what one says or does; prudent 2. unobtrusively tasteful —**discreet'ly** adv. —**discreet'ness** n.

discrepancy (dis krep'ən sē) n., pl. -cies [< L. dis-, from + crepare, to rattle] lack of agreement, or an instance of this; inconsistency —**discrep'ant** adj.

discrete (dis krēt') adj. [see DISCERN] 1. separate and distinct 2. made up of distinct parts —**discrete'ly** adv. —**discrete'ness** n.

discretion (dis kresh'ən) n. 1. the freedom or authority to make decisions and choices 2. the quality of being discreet; prudence —**years** (or **age**) **of discretion** maturity —**discre'tionary** adj.

discriminate (dis krim'ə nāt'; for adj. -nət) vi. [see DISCERN] 1. to show partiality or prejudice 2. to see the difference (between things) 3. to be discerning —vt. -nat'ed, -nat'ing 1. to differentiate 2. to distinguish —adj. distinguishing carefully —**discrim'inat'ing** adj. —**discrim'inative** adj.

discrimination (dis krim'ə nā'shən) n. 1. a showing of partiality or prejudice in treatment 2. the act of discriminating, or distinguishing differences 3. the ability to do this

discriminatory (-krim'ə nə tər ē) adj. 1. practising discrimination, or showing prejudice 2. distinguishing

discursive (dis kur'siv) adj. [see DISCOURSE] wandering from one topic to another; rambling; digressive —**discur'sively** adv. —**discur'siveness** n.

DISCUS
THROWER

discus (dis′kəs) *n., pl.* **dis′cuses, disci**
(dis′kī) [< Gr. *diskos*] a heavy disc
of metal and wood thrown in athletic
contests

discuss (dis kus′) *vt.* [< L. *dis-*, apart
+ *quatere*, to shake] to talk or write
about; consider and argue the pros and
cons of

discussion *n.* talk or writing in which
the pros and cons of a subject are considered
—**under discussion** being discussed

disdain (dis dān′) *vt.* [< L. *dis-*, not +
dignari, DEIGN] to regard as beneath one's
dignity; scorn —*n.* aloof contempt or
scorn —**disdain′ful** *adj.*

disease (di zēz′) *n.* [< OFr. *des-*, DIS-
+ *aise*, EASE] **1.** illness in general **2.**
a particular destructive process in an
organism; specific illness **3.** a harmful
condition —**diseased′** *adj.*

disembark (dis′im bärk′) *vt., vi.* to leave,
or unload from, a ship, aircraft, etc. —**dis′-
embarka′tion** (dis′em-) *n.*

disembody (dis′im bod′ē) *vt.* **-bod′ied,
-bod′ying** to free from bodily existence
—**dis′embod′ied** *adj.*

disembowel (dis′im bou′əl) *vt.* **-elled,
-elling** to take out the bowels, or entrails,
of —**dis′embow′elment** *n.*

disenchant (dis′in chänt′) *vt.* to set free
from an enchantment or illusion —**dis′en-
chant′ment** *n.*

disencumber (dis′in kum′bər) *vt.* to
relieve of a burden; free from a hindrance
or annoyance

disengage (dis′in gāj′) *vt., vi.* **-gaged′,
-gag′ing** to release or loosen from
something that binds, holds, etc. —**dis′en-
gage′ment** *n.*

disengaged *adj.* **1.** at leisure **2.** set
loose; detached **3.** out of gear

disentangle (dis′in tan′g′l) *vt.* **-gled,
-gling** to free from something that
entangles, confuses, etc.; extricate;
untangle —**dis′entan′glement** *n.*

disequilibrium (dis ek′wə lib′rē əm) *n.,
pl.* **-riums, -ria** lack or destruction of
equilibrium

disestablish (dis′ə stab′lish) *vt.* to deprive
(a state church) of support by the
government —**dis′estab′lishment** *n.*

disfavour (dis fā′vər) *n.* **1.** an
unfavourable opinion; dislike **2.** the state
of being disliked or disapproved of —*vt.*
to regard or treat unfavourably

disfigure (dis fig′ər) *vt.* **-ured, -uring** to

hurt the appearance of; deface —**disfig′ure-
ment, disfig′ura′tion** *n.*

disfranchise (dis fran′chīz) *vt.* **-chised,
-chising** to deprive of a right or privilege,
esp. of the right to vote —**disfran′chise-
ment** *n.*

disgorge (dis gôrj′) *vt., vi.* **-gorged′,
-gorg′ing** [< OFr.: see DIS- & GORGE]
1. to vomit **2.** to pour forth (its contents)

disgrace (dis grās′) *n.* [< It. *dis-*, not
+ *grazia*, favour] **1.** a being in disfavour
2. loss of respect; shame **3.** a person
or thing that brings shame —*vt.* **-graced′,
-grac′ing** to bring shame or dishonour
upon

disgraceful *adj.* causing or characterized
by disgrace; shameful —**disgrace′fully** *adv.*

disgruntle (dis grun′t′l) *vt.* **-tled, -tling**
[ult. < DIS- + GRUNT] to make peevishly
discontented —**disgrun′tlement** *n.*

disguise (dis gīz′) *vt.* **-guised′, -guis′ing**
[< OFr.: see DIS- & GUISE] **1.** to make
appear, sound, etc. different so as to be
unrecognizable **2.** to hide the real nature
of —*n.* **1.** any clothes, manner, etc. used
for disguising **2.** the state of being disguised
3. the act or practice of disguising

disgust (dis gust′) *n.* [< DIS- + L. *gustus,
taste*] a sickening distaste or dislike;
repugnance —*vt.* to cause to feel disgust
—**disgust′ed** *adj.* —**disgust′ing** *adj.*

dish (dish) *n.* [< L. *discus*, DISCUS] **1.**
a) a shallow, concave container for food
b) [*pl.*] plates, bowls, cups, etc., collectively
2. a particular kind of food **3.** a dishful
4. a dish-shaped object **5.** [Slang] a pretty
girl or woman —*vt.* **1.** to serve (food)
in a dish (with *up* or *out*) **2.** to make
concave **3.** [Slang] to ruin —**dish out**
to distribute, esp. carelessly

dishabille (dis′ə bēl′) *n.* [< Fr. *dés-*, DIS-
+ *habiller*, to dress] the state of being
dressed only partially

disharmony (dis här′mə nē) *n.* lack of
harmony; discord —**dis′harmo′nious**
(-mō′nē əs) *adj.*

dishcloth (dish′kloth′) *n.* a cloth for
washing dishes

dishearten (dis här′t′n) *vt.* to discourage;
depress —**dishear′tening** *adj.* —**disheart′-
eningly** *adv.*

dishevel (di shev′′l) *vt.* **-elled, -elling** [<
OFr. *des-*, DIS- + *chevel*, hair] to cause
(hair, clothing, etc.) to become disarranged
and untidy; rumple —**dishev′elled** *adj.*
—**dishev′elment** *n.*

dishonest (dis on′ist) *adj.* not honest;
lying, cheating, etc. —**dishon′estly** *adv.*
—**dishon′esty** *n.*

dishonour (dis on′ər) *n.* **1.** *a)* loss of
honour, respect, etc. *b)* shame; disgrace
2. a cause of dishonour —*vt.* **1.** to treat
disrespectfully **2.** to disgrace **3.** to refuse
or fail to pay (a cheque, etc.)

dishonourable *adj.* causing or deserving
dishonour; shameful; disgraceful —**dis-
hon′ourably** *adv.*

dishwasher (dish′wosh′ər) *n.* **1.** a
machine for washing dishes **2.** a person
whose job is to wash dishes **3.** the water
wagtail

dishwater *n.* 1. water in which dishes, etc. have been washed 2. something resembling this

dishy *adj.* [Slang] good-looking; attractive

disillusion (dis′i lōō′zhən) *vt.* 1. to free from illusion or false ideas 2. to make bitter, etc. —*n.* a disillusioning or being disillusioned

disincentive (dis′in sen′tiv) *n.* a thing or factor that keeps one from doing something; deterrent

disincline (dis′in klīn′) *vt.* -clined′, -clin′-ing to make unwilling —disin′clina′tion (-klə nā′) *n.*

disinfect (dis′in fekt′) *vt.* to destroy with harmful bacteria, viruses, etc. in or on —dis′infec′tion *n.*

disinfectant *n.* anything that disinfects —*adj.* disinfecting

disingenuous (dis′in jen′yōō wəs) *adj.* not straightforward; not candid; insincere —dis′ingen′uously *adv.*

disinherit (dis′in her′it) *vt.* to deprive of an inheritance —dis′inher′itance *n.*

disintegrate (dis in′tə grāt′) *vt., vi.* -grat′-ed, -grat′ing to separate into parts or fragments; break up —disin′tegra′tion *n.* —disin′tegra′tor *n.*

disinter (dis′in tʉr′) *vt.* -terred′, -ter′ring 1. to dig up; exhume 2. to bring to light —dis′inter′ment *n.*

disinterest (dis in′trist) *n.* 1. lack of personal or selfish interest 2. lack of interest

disinterested *adj.* 1. impartial 2. [Colloq.] uninterested —disin′terestedly *adv.*

disjoint (dis joint′) *vt.* 1. to dislocate 2. to dismember 3. to destroy the connections or orderliness of

disjointed *adj.* 1. incoherent: said esp. of speech 2. out of joint 3. dismembered —disjoint′edly *adv.*

disjunctive (dis juŋk′tiv) *adj.* 1. disjoin-ing; separating or causing to separate 2. *Gram.* indicating an alternative between words, clauses, etc. ["or" and "but" are *disjunctive* conjunctions] —*n. Gram.* a disjunctive conjunction —disjunc′tively *adv.*

disk (disk) *n.* var. sp. of DISC

dislike (dis līk′) *vt.* -liked′, -lik′ing to have a feeling of not liking —*n.* distaste; aversion

dislocate (dis′lō kāt′) *vt.* -cat′ed, -cat′-ing 1. to displace (a bone) from its proper position at a joint 2. to disarrange —dis′loca′tion *n.*

dislodge (dis loj′) *vt., vi.* -lodged′, -lodg′-ing to force from a place where hiding, etc. —dislodg′ment *n.*

disloyal (dis loi′əl) *adj.* not loyal or faithful; faithless —disloy′ally *adv.* —disloy′alty *n.*

dismal (diz′m′l) *adj.* [< ML. *dies mali*, evil days] 1. causing or showing gloom or misery 2. dark and gloomy —dis′-mally *adv.*

dismantle (dis man′t′l) *vt.* -tled, -tling [see DIS- & MANTLE] 1. to strip of covering 2. to strip (a house, etc.) of furniture 3. to take apart —disman′tlement *n.*

dismay (dis mā′) *vt.* [< OFr. *des-*, intens. + *esmayer*, deprive of power] to fill with alarm; daunt —*n.* a loss of courage

dismember (dis mem′bər) *vt.* [see DIS- & MEMBER] 1. to remove the limbs of by cutting or tearing 2. to pull or cut to pieces; divide up or mutilate —dismem′-berment *n.*

dismiss (dis mis′) *vt.* [< L. *dis-*, from + *mittere*, send] 1. to cause or allow to leave 2. to discharge from an office, employment, etc. 3. to put out of one's mind 4. *Cricket* to put (a batsman) out, as by catching 5. *Law* to reject (a claim or action) —dismiss′al *n.* —dismis′sive *adj.*

dismount (dis′mount′) *vi.* to get off, as from a horse or bicycle —*vt.* 1. to remove (a thing) from its mounting 2. to cause to dismount 3. to take apart

disobedience (dis′ə bē′dē əns) *n.* refusal to obey; insubordination —dis′obe′dient *adj.*

disobey (dis′ə bā′) *vt., vi.* to refuse or fail to obey

disoblige (dis′ə blīj′) *vt.* -bliged′, -blig′-ing 1. to refuse to oblige 2. to slight; offend —dis′oblig′ing *adj.*

disorder (dis ôr′dər) *n.* 1. a lack of order; confusion 2. a breach of public peace; riot 3. irregularity 4. an upset of normal function —*vt.* 1. to throw into disorder 2. to upset the normal functions of —disor′-dered *adj.*

disorderly *adj.* 1. not orderly; untidy 2. unruly; riotous —disor′derliness *n.*

disorganize (dis ôr′gə nīz′) *vt.* -ized′, -iz′-ing to break up the order or system of —disor′ganiza′tion *n.*

disorient (dis ôr′ē ent′) *vt.* 1. to cause to lose one's bearings 2. to confuse mentally Also **diso′rientate**′(-ən tāt′)-tat′-ed, -tat′ing —diso′rienta′tion *n.*

disown (dis ōn′) *vt.* to refuse to acknowledge as one's own

disparage (dis par′ij) *vt.* -aged, -aging [< OFr. *des-*, DIS- + *parage*, rank] 1. to speak slightingly of 2. to lower in esteem —dispar′agement *n.* —dispar′ag-ing *adj.*

disparate (dis′pər it) *adj.* [< L. *dis-*, apart, not + *parare*, make equal] distinct or different in kind —dis′parately *adv.* —dis-par′ity (-par′ə tē) *n.*

dispassionate (dis pash′ən it) *adj.* free from passion, emotion, or bias; impartial —dispas′sionately *adv.*

dispatch (dis pach′) *vt.* [ult. < L. *dis-*, not + LL. *impedicare*, entangle] 1. to send promptly on an errand 2. to kill 3. to finish quickly —*n.* 1. a sending off 2. a killing 3. speed; promptness 4. a message, esp. an official message 5. a news story sent to a newspaper, etc., as by a reporter —mentioned in dispatches to be commended for bravery in action —dispatch′er *n.*

dispatch rider a soldier, originally on horseback, now on a motorcycle, who carries dispatches

dispel (dis pel') *vt.* **-pelled'**, **-pel'ling** [< L. *dis-*, away + *pellere*, drive] to scatter and drive away

dispensable (dis pen'sə b'l) *adj.* **1.** that can be dispensed with **2.** that can be dealt out —**dispen'sabil'ity** *n.*

dispensary (dis pen'sər ē) *n., pl.* **-ries** a room, as in a school or factory, where medicines are available

dispensation (dis'pen sā'shən) *n.* **1.** a dispensing **2.** anything distributed **3.** an administrative system **4.** a release from an obligation **5.** *R.C.Ch.* an exemption from a specific church law **6.** *Theol.* the ordering of events under divine authority —**dis'pensa'tional** *adj.*

dispense (dis pens') *vt.* **-pensed'**, **-pens'ing** [< L. *dis-*, out + *pendere*, weigh] **1.** to give out; distribute **2.** to prepare and give out (medicines, etc.) **3.** to administer **4.** to exempt; excuse —**dispense with 1.** to get rid of **2.** to do without —**dispen'ser** *n.*

disperse (dis purs') *vt.* **-persed'**, **-pers'-ing** [< L. *dis-*, out + *spargere*, strew] **1.** to break up and scatter **2.** to dispel (mist, etc.) **3.** to break up (light) into its component coloured rays —*vi.* to move in different directions —**disper'sal** *n.* —**dis-pers'er** *n.* —**disper'sion** *n.*

dispirit (di spir'it) *vt.* to deject —**dispir'-ited** *adj.*

displace (dis plās') *vt.* **-placed'**, **-plac'-ing 1.** to move from its usual place **2.** to discharge **3.** to replace

displaced person a person forced from his country, esp. in war, and left homeless elsewhere

displacement *n.* **1.** a displacing or being displaced **2.** the volume of a fluid displaced by a floating object

display (dis plā') *vt.* [< L. *dis-*, apart + *plicare*, to fold] **1.** to exhibit **2.** to disclose; reveal **3.** to unfold; spread out —*n.* **1.** an exhibition **2.** anything displayed **3.** ostentation; show —**display'er** *n.*

displease (dis plēz') *vt., vi.* **-pleased'**, **-pleas'ing** to fail to please; offend —**dis-pleas'ing** *adj.* —**displeas'ingly** *adv.*

displeasure (dis plezh'ər) *n.* a being displeased; dissatisfaction, annoyance, etc.

disport (dis pôrt') *vi.* [< OFr. *des-*, DIS-+ *porter*, carry] to play; frolic —*vt.* to amuse (oneself)

disposable (dis pō'zə b'l) *adj.* that can be discarded —*n.* something that is designed for disposal

disposal (dis pō'z'l) *n.* **1.** a disposing; specif., *a)* arrangement *b)* a settling of affairs *c)* a giving away; transfer *d)* a getting rid of **2.** the power to dispose —**at one's disposal** available to be used as one wishes

dispose (dis pōz') *vt.* **-posed'**, **-pos'ing** [see DIS- & POSITION] **1.** to place in a certain order; arrange **2.** to settle (affairs) **3.** to make willing —*vi.* to have the power to settle affairs —**dispose of 1.** to deal with; settle **2.** to give away or sell **3.** to get rid of

disposed *adj.* having an inclination as

specified [to feel *well-disposed* towards someone]

disposition (dis'pə zish'ən) *n.* **1.** one's temperament **2.** an inclination or tendency **3.** orderly arrangement **4.** management of affairs **5.** a selling or giving away **6.** the power to dispose

dispossess (dis'pə zes') *vt.* to deprive of the possession of land etc. —**dis'posses'-sion** *n.* —**dis'posses'sor** *n.*

disproportion (dis'prə pôr'shən) *n.* lack of proportion

disproportionate *adj.* not propor-tionate; not in proportion —**dis'propor'-tionately** *adv.*

disprove (dis prōōv') *vt.* **-proved'**, **-prov'-ing** to prove to be false or in error —**dis-prov'able** *adj.*

disputant (dis pyōōt''nt) *n.* one who disputes

disputation (dis'pyōō tā'shən) *n.* **1.** a disputing; dispute **2.** a debatelike dis-cussion

disputatious *adj.* fond of arguing : also **dispu'tative** —**dis'puta'tiously** *adv.*

dispute (dis pyōōt') *vi.* **-put'ed**, **-put'ing** [< L. *dis-*, apart + *putare*, to think] **1.** to argue; debate **2.** to quarrel —*vt.* **1.** to argue or debate (a question) **2.** to doubt **3.** to oppose in any way —*n.* **1.** a disputing; argument **2.** a quarrel —**beyond dispute 1.** settled **2.** indis-putably —**in dispute** not settled —**dispu'-table** *adj.*

disqualify (dis kwol'ə fī') *vt.* **-fied'**, **-fy'-ing 1.** to make unfit or unqualified **2.** to make or declare ineligible —**disqual'ifi-ca'tion** *n.*

disquiet (dis kwī'ət) *vt.* to make anxious or restless; disturb —*n.* restlessness; anxiety —**disqui'eting** *adj.*

disquietude (dis kwī'ə tyōōd') *n.* rest-lessness; anxiety

disquisition (dis'kwə zish'ən) *n.* [< L. *dis-*, apart + *quaerere*, seek] a formal discussion of some subject

disregard (dis'ri gärd') *vt.* **1.** to pay little or no attention to **2.** to treat without due respect —*n.* **1.** lack of attention **2.** lack of due regard or respect

disrepair (dis'ri pâer') *n.* the condition of needing repairs; state of neglect; dilapidation

disreputable (dis rep'yoo tə b'l) *adj.* **1.** having or causing a bad reputation **2.** not fit to be seen

disrepute (dis'ri pyōōt') *n.* lack or loss of repute; bad reputation; disgrace; disfavour

disrespect (dis'ri spekt') *n.* lack of respect; discourtesy —**dis'respect'ful** *adj.* —**dis'respect'fully** *adv.*

disrobe (dis rōb') *vt., vi.* **-robed'**, **-rob'-ing** to undress

disrupt (dis rupt') *vt., vi.* [< L. *dis-*, apart + *rumpere*, to break] **1.** to interrupt the orderly course of (a meeting, etc.) **2.** to break apart —**disrup'tion** *n.* —**disrup'-tive** *adj.*

dissatisfy (dis sat'is fī') *vt.* **-fied'**, **-fy'-**

ing to fail to satisfy; discontent —**dissat'is-fac'tion** n.

dissect (di sekt') vt. [< L. dis-, apart + secare, to cut] 1. to cut apart piece by piece, as a body for purposes of study 2. to analyse closely —**dissec'tion** n. —**dissec'tor** n.

disselboom (dis'əlbooəm) n. [S Afr.] the single shaft of a wagon esp. an ox wagon

dissemble (di sem'b'l) vt. -bled, -bling [< OFr. des-, DIS- + sembler, simulate] 1. to conceal under a false appearance 2. to make a false show of —vi. to conceal the truth, one's true feelings, etc., by pretence —**dissem'blance** n. —**dissem'bler** n.

disseminate (di sem'ə nāt') vt. -nat'ed, -nat'ing [< L. dis-, apart + seminare, sow] to scatter far and wide; spread abroad —**dissem'ina'tion** n. —**dissem'ina'tor** n.

dissension (di sen'shən) n. a dissenting in opinion; disagreement or, esp., violent quarrelling or wrangling

dissent (di sent') vi. [< L. dis-, apart + sentire, feel] 1. to disagree 2. to reject the doctrines of an established church —n. a dissenting —**dissent'ing** adj.

Dissenter n. a Protestant who refuses to conform to the established church

dissentient (di sen'shē ənt) adj. dissenting, esp. from the majority opinion —n. one who dissents

dissertation (dis'ər tā'shən) n. [< L. dis-, apart + serere, to join] a formal discourse or treatise; thesis

disservice (dis sur'vis) n. harmful action; injury

dissidence (dis'ə dəns) n. [< L. dis-, apart + sidere, sit] dissent, esp. from a government —**dis'sident** adj., n.

dissimilar (di sim'ə lər) adj. not similar or alike; different —**dissim'ilar'ity** (-lar'ə tē) n. —**dissim'ilarly** adv. —**dissimilitude** (dis'si mil'ə tyood) n.

dissimulate (di sim'yoo lāt') vt., vi. -lat'ed, -lat'ing [see DIS- & SIMULATE] to hide (one's feelings, etc.); dissemble —**dissim'ula'tion** n.

dissipate (dis'ə pāt') vt. -pat'ed, -pat'ing [< L. dis-, apart + supare, to throw] 1. to scatter 2. to make disappear 3. to waste or squander —vi. 1. to vanish 2. to indulge in pleasure to the point of harming oneself

dissipated adj. 1. squandered 2. debauched

dissipation (dis'ə pā'shən) n. a dissipating or being dissipated; dispersion, squandering, dissoluteness, etc.

dissociate (di sō'shē āt') vt., vi. -at'ed, -at'ing [< L. dis-, apart + sociare, join] 1. to sever association with; disunite 2. to undergo or cause to undergo dissociation —**dissociate oneself from** to repudiate any connection with —**disso'cia'tion** n.

dissoluble (di sol'yoo b'l) adj. that can be dissolved —**dissol'ubil'ity** n.

dissolute (dis'ə loot') adj. [see DISSOLVE] dissipated and immoral; debauched —**dis'solute'ly** adv.

dissolution (dis'ə loo'shən) n. a dissolving or being dissolved; specif., a) a breaking up or into parts b) termination c) death d) the dismissal of parliament before a general election

dissolve (di zolv') vt., vi. -solved', -solv'-ing [< L. dis-, apart + solvere, loosen] 1. to make or become liquid; melt 2. to pass or make pass into solution 3. to break up; decompose 4. to end as by breaking up; terminate 5. to disappear or make disappear —**dissolved in tears** weeping —**dissolv'able** adj.

dissonance (dis'ə nəns) n. [< L. dis-, apart + sonare, to sound] 1. an inharmonious combination of sounds 2. any lack of harmony or agreement —**dis'sonant** adj.

dissuade (di swād') vt. -suad'ed, -suad'-ing [< L. dis-, away + suadere, persuade] to turn (a person) aside (from a course, etc.) by persuasion —**dissua'sion** n. —**dissua'sive** adj.

dissyllable (dis'sil'ə b'l) n. same as DISYLLABLE

DISTAFF

distaff (dis'tăf) n. [< OE. dis-, flax + stæf, staff] a staff on which flax, wool, etc. is wound for use in spinning —adj. female

distance (dis'təns) n. [< L. dis-, apart + stare, stand] 1. a being separated in space or time; remoteness 2. an interval between two points in time 3. the length of a line between two points 4. a remote point in space or time —vt. -tanced, -tanc-ing to leave behind; outdistance —**keep at a distance** to treat aloofly —**keep one's distance** to be aloof

distant adj. 1. far apart in space or time 2. away [ten kilometres distant] 3. far apart in relationship 4. cool in manner; aloof 5. from or at a distance —**dis'tantly** adv.

distaste (dis tāst') n. dislike or aversion (for)

distasteful adj. unpleasant; disagreeable —**distaste'fully** adv. —**distaste'fulness** n.

distemper¹ (dis tem'pər) n. [< L. dis-, apart + temperare, mix in proportion] 1. an infectious virus disease of young dogs 2. a mental or physical disorder; disease —vt. to derange; disorder

distemper² n. [< L. dis-, intens. + temperare: see prec.] any of various water-based paints, as for walls, etc. —*vt.* to paint (walls, etc.) with distemper

distend (dis tend′) *vt., vi.* [< L. *dis-*, apart + *tendere*, stretch] 1. to make or become swollen 2. to stretch out —**disten′sible** *adj.* —**disten′tion, disten′sion** *n.*

distich (dis′tik) *n.* [< Gr. *di-*, two + *stichos*, row] two lines of verse regarded as a unit; couplet

distil (dis til′) *vt., vi.* -tilled′, -till′ing [< L. *de-*, down + *stillare*, to drip] 1. to undergo, subject to, or produce by, distillation 2. to let fall or fall in drops

distillate (dis′tə lət) *n.* a liquid obtained by distilling

distillation (dis′tə lā′shən) *n.* 1. a distilling 2. the process of heating a mixture and condensing the resulting vapour to produce a more nearly pure substance 3. a distillate

distiller (dis til′ər) *n.* a person, company, etc. in the business of distilling whisky, gin, etc. —**distill′ery** *n.*

distinct (dis tiŋkt′) *adj.* [see DISTINGUISH] 1. not alike; different 2. separate 3. clearly marked off; plain 4. unmistakable —**distinct′ly** *adv.* —**distinct′ness** *n.*

distinction *n.* 1. the act of making or keeping distinct 2. difference 3. a quality or feature that differentiates 4. fame; eminence 5. the quality that makes one seem superior 6. a mark of honour

distinctive *adj.* distinguishing from others; characteristic —**distinc′tively** *adv.* —**distinc′tiveness** *n.*

distingué (dis taŋ′gā) *adj.* [Fr.] having an air of distinction; distinguished

distinguish (dis tiŋ′gwish) *vt.* [< L. *dis-*, apart + *stinguere*, prick] 1. to perceive or show the difference in 2. to characterize 3. to recognize plainly 4. to classify 5. to make famous or eminent —*vi.* to make a distinction (*between* or *among*) —**distin′guishable** *adj.*

distinguished *adj.* 1. celebrated; famous 2. having an air of distinction

distort (dis tôrt′) *vt.* [< L. *dis-*, intens. + *torquere*, twist] 1. to twist out of shape 2. to misrepresent —**distort′er** *n.* —**distor′tion** *n.* —**distor′tionless** *adj.*

distract (dis trakt′) *vt.* [< L. *dis-*, apart + *trahere*, draw] 1. to draw (the mind, etc.) away in another direction; divert 2. to create conflict and confusion in —**distract′ed** *adj.* —**distract′ible** *adj.* —**distract′ing** *adj.*

distraction *n.* 1. a distracting or being distracted; confusion 2. anything that distracts; diversion 3. great mental distress —**to distraction** almost insanely —**distrac′tive** *adj.*

distrain (dis trān′) *vt., vi.* [< L. *dis-*, apart + *stringere*, draw tight] *Law* to seize and hold (property) as security for a debt —**distrain′able** *adj.* —**distrain′er, distrai′nor** *n.* —**distraint′** *n.*

distrait (dis trā′) *adj.* [see DISTRACT] absent-minded

distraught (dis trôt′) *adj.* [var. of prec.] 1. very troubled or confused 2. driven mad; crazed

distress (dis tres′) *vt.* [see DISTRAIN] to cause misery or suffering to —*n.* 1. pain, suffering, etc. 2. an affliction 3. a state of danger or trouble 4. *Law* distraint —**distress′ful** *adj.* —**distress′ing** *adj.*

distressed *adj.* 1. full of distress 2. designating an area in which there is much poverty, unemployment, etc. 3. in financial straits; poor

distribute (dis trib′yōot) *vt.* -uted, -uting [< L. *dis-*, apart + *tribuere*, allot] 1. to give out in shares 2. to scatter or spread out 3. to classify 4. to put (things) in various distinct places —**distrib′utable** *adj.*

distribution (dis′trə byōo′shən) *n.* 1. a distributing or being distributed 2. the process by which commodities get to consumers 3. anything distributed —**dis′tribu′tional** *adj.*

distributive (dis trib′yōo tiv) *adj.* 1. distributing or tending to distribute 2. *Gram.* referring to each member of a group regarded individually ["each" is a *distributive* word] 3. *Math.* of the principle in multiplication that allows the multiplier to be used separately with each term of the multiplicand

distributor (dis trib′yōo tər) *n.* 1. an agent or business firm that distributes goods to consumers 2. a device for distributing electric current to sparking plugs

district (dis′trikt) *n.* [see DISTRAIN] 1. a geographical or political division made for a specific purpose 2. any region

district nurse a nurse appointed by a local authority to attend patients within a district

distrust (dis trust′) *n.* a lack of trust or of confidence —*vt.* to have no trust or confidence in —**distrust′ful** *adj.* —**distrust′fully** *adv.*

disturb (dis turb′) *vt.* [< L. *dis-*, intens. + *turbare*, to disorder] 1. to break up the quiet or calm of 2. to make uneasy 3. to break up the settled order of 4. to interrupt —**disturb′er** *n.*

disturbance *n.* 1. a disturbing or being disturbed 2. anything that disturbs 3. commotion

disunion (dis yōon′yən) *n.* 1. the ending of union; separation 2. lack of unity; discord

disunite (dis′yōo nīt′) *vt.* -nit′ed, -nit′ing to destroy the unity of —*vi.* to become separated —**disu′nity** *n.*

disuse (dis yōoz′; *for n.* -yōos′) *vt.* -used′, -us′ing to stop using —*n.* lack of use

disyllable (di sil′ə b′l) *n.* [< Gr. *di-*, two + *syllabē*, syllable] a word of two syllables —**disyllabic** (di′si lab′ik) *adj.*

ditch (dich) *n.* [OE. *dic*] a long, narrow channel dug into the earth, as for drainage —*vt.* 1. to make a ditch in 2. to set (a disabled aircraft) down on water 3. [Slang] to get rid of —*vi.* 1. to dig a ditch 2. to ditch a disabled aircraft

dither (dith′ər) *vi.* [prob. akin to ME. *daderen*, DODDER] to be nervously excited or confused —*n.* an excited state

dithyramb (dith′ə ram′) *n.* [< Gr.

dithyrambos] 1. in ancient Greece, a wild choric hymn in honour of Dionysus 2. any wildly emotional speech or writing —**dith′yram′bic** *adj.*, *n.*

dittany (dit′ə nē) *n.*, *pl.* **-nies** [< Gr. *diktamnon* < ? *Dikte*, Mount Dicte, in Crete] a creeping, woolly herb native to Greece

ditto (dit′ō) *n.*, *pl.* **-tos** [< L. *dictum*, a saying] 1. the same (as above or before) 2. *same as* DITTO MARK —*adv.* as said before —*vt.* **-toed, -toing** 1. to duplicate 2. to repeat

ditto mark a mark (″) used in lists or tables to show that the item above is to be repeated

ditty (dit′ē) *n.*, *pl.* **-ties** [see DICTATE] a short, simple song

diuretic (dī′yoo ret′ik) *adj.* [< Gr. *dia-*, through + *ourein*, urinate] increasing the flow of urine —*n.* a diuretic drug or substance

diurnal (dī ur′n'l) *adj.* [< L. *dies*, day] 1. daily 2. of or in the daytime —**diur′- nally** *adv.*

divalent (dī vā′lənt) *adj.* *Chem.* same as BIVALENT

divan (di van′) *n.* [< Turk. *dīwān*] 1. a large, low couch, usually without armrests 2. a bed resembling such a couch

dive (dīv) *vi.* **dived, div′ing** [OE. *dyfan*] 1. to plunge headfirst into water 2. to submerge 3. to plunge suddenly into something 4. to make a steep, sudden descent, as an aircraft —*n.* 1. a plunge into water 2. any sudden plunge 3. a sharp descent, as of an aircraft 4. [Colloq.] a cheap, disreputable bar, nightclub, etc.

dive bomber an aircraft designed to release bombs while diving at a target —**dive′bomb′** *vt.*, *vi.*

diver *n.* 1. one who works or explores under water 2. a diving water bird

diverge (di vurj′) *vi.* **-verged′, -verg′ing** [< L. *dis-*, apart + *vergere*, turn] 1. to branch off or go in different directions 2. to take on gradually a different form [*customs diverge*] 3. to differ —**diver′- gence** *n.* —**diver′gent** *adj.*

divers (dī′vərz) *adj.* [OFr.: see ff.] [Archaic] various

diverse (dī vurs′) *adj.* [< L. *dis-*, apart + *vertere*, to turn] 1. different 2. varied —**diverse′ly** *adv.*

diversify (dī vur′sə fī′) *vt.* **-fied′, -fy′ing** [see prec.] 1. to make diverse; vary 2. to divide up (investments) among different securities, etc. 3. to expand (a company, etc.), as by varying products —**diver′sifi- ca′tion** *n.*

diversion (dī vur′shən) *n.* 1. a diverting, or turning aside, esp. an official detour used by traffic when a main road is closed 2. distraction of attention 3. a pastime —**diver′sionary** *adj.*

diversity (dī vur′sə tē) *n.*, *pl.* **-ties** 1. a being diverse; difference 2. variety

divert (dī vurt′) *vt.* [see DIVERSE] 1. to turn aside 2. to amuse 3. to distract —**divert′ing** *adj.*

‡**divertissement** (dē vertēs män′) *n.* [Fr.] 1. a diversion 2. a short ballet, etc.

divest (dī vest′) *vt.* [ult. < L. *dis-*, from + *vestire*, to dress] 1. to strip (of clothing, etc.) 2. to deprive (of rank, rights, etc.) 3. to rid (of something)

divide (də vīd′) *vt.* **-vid′ed, -vid′ing** [< L. *dividere*] 1. to separate into parts; split up 2. to classify 3. to make or keep separate 4. to apportion 5. to cause to disagree 6. *Math.* to separate into equal parts by a divisor —*vi.* 1. to be or become separate 2. to disagree 3. to separate into groups in voting 4. to share 5. *Math.* to do division —*n.* [Chiefly U.S.] a watershed —**divid′able** *adj.*

dividend (div′ə dend′) *n.* [< L.] 1. the quantity to be divided 2. *a)* a sum to be divided among stockholders, etc. *b)* a single share of this 3. a bonus

divider (də vīd′ər) *n.* 1. [*pl.*] an instrument for dividing lines, etc.; compasses 2. a set of shelves, etc. used to separate a room into distinct areas

divination (div′ə nā′shən) *n.* [see ff.] 1. the act of trying to foretell the future by occult means 2. a prophecy 3. a clever guess —**divinatory** (də vin′ə tər ē) *adj.*

divine (də vīn′) *adj.* [< L. *divus*, a god] 1. of or like God or a god 2. devoted to God; religious 3. supremely great, good, etc. —*n.* a clergyman —*vt.* **-vined′, -vin′- ing** 1. to prophesy 2. to guess 3. to find out by intuition —*vi.* to engage in divination —**divine′ly** *adv.* —**divin′er** *n.*

diving bell a large, hollow, air-filled apparatus in which divers can work under water

diving board a springboard projecting over a swimming pool, lake, etc., for use in diving

diving suit a heavy, waterproof garment worn by divers working under water

divining rod a forked stick alleged to reveal hidden water or minerals by dipping downwards

divinity (də vin′ə tē) *n.*, *pl.* **-ties** 1. a being divine 2. a god 3. the study of religion —**the Divinity** God

divisible (də viz′ə b'l) *adj.* that can be divided, esp. without leaving a remainder —**divis′ibil′ity** *n.*

division *n.* 1. a dividing or being divided 2. a sharing 3. a difference of opinion 4. a separation into groups in voting, esp. in the House of Commons 5. anything that divides; partition 6. a section, group, rank, segment, etc. [*Chancery Division*] 7. *Math.* the process of finding how many times a number (the *divisor*) is contained in another (the *dividend*) 8. *Mil.* a tactical unit under one command —**divi′sional** *adj.*

division sign the symbol (÷), indicating that the preceding number is to be divided by the following number (Ex.: 8 ÷ 4 = 2)

divisive (də vī′siv) *adj.* causing division —**divi′sively** *adv.* —**divi′siveness** *n.*

divisor (də vī′zər) *n.* [L.] the number

or quantity by which the dividend is divided to produce the quotient

divorce (də vôrs′) *n.* [see DIVERSE] 1. legal dissolution of a marriage 2. any complete separation —*vt.* -vorced′,-vorc′-ing 1. to dissolve legally a marriage between 2. to separate from (one's spouse) by divorce 3. to separate; disunite

divorcée (-vôr′sē′) *n.* [Fr.] a divorced woman

divot (div′ət) *n.* [< Scot.] a piece of turf dug out of a grass surface, esp. by a golf club

divulge (dī vulj′) *vt.* -vulged′, -vulg′ing [< L. *dis-*, apart + *vulgare*, make public] to make known; disclose —**divul′gence** *n.* —**divulg′er** *n.*

divvy (div′ē) *vt., vi.* -vied, -vying [< DIVIDE] [Colloq.] to share (*up*) —*n.* a dividend

dixie (dik′sē) *n.* [Hindi] a camp cooking-pot

DIY Do-It-Yourself

dizzy (diz′ē) *adj.* -zier, -ziest [OE. *dysig*, foolish] 1. feeling giddy or unsteady 2. causing giddiness 3. confused 4. [Colloq.] silly —*vt.* -zied, -zying to make dizzy —**diz′zily** *adv.* —**diz′ziness** *n.*

D.J., DJ 1. disc jockey 2. dinner jacket

djellaba (jə lä′bə) *n.* *same as* JELLABA

djinni (ji nē′) *n., pl.* **djinn** *same as* JINNI

dl decilitre(s)

D layer the lowest layer of the ionosphere

D.Lit., D.Litt. [L. *Doctor Lit(t)erarum*] Doctor of Letters

dm decimetre(s)

D.Mus. Doctor of Music

DNA deoxyribonucleic acid

D-notice [< *Defence Notice*] an official notice sent to newspapers, etc. prohibiting publication of certain material

do¹ (dōō) *vt.* did, done, do′ing [OE. *don*] 1. to perform (an action, etc.) [*do* great deeds] 2. to finish [dinner has been *done* for an hour] 3. to cause [it *does* no harm] 4. to exert [*do* your best] 5. to deal with as is required [*do* the ironing] 6. to have as one's occupation; work at 7. to work out; solve [*do* a sum] 8. to produce (a play, etc.) [we *did* Hamlet] 9. to cover (distance) [to *do* 30 miles] 10. to be convenient to; suit [this will *do* me very well] 11. [Colloq.] to provide; serve [this pub *does* lunches] 12. [Colloq.] to sightsee 13. [Colloq.] to cheat 14. [Colloq.] to serve (a jail term) 15. [Colloq.] to improve esp. in the phrase **do something to** or **for** —*vi.* 1. to behave [he *does* well when praised] 2. to be active; work [*do; don't* talk] 3. to get along [the patient is *doing* well] 4. to be adequate 5. [Colloq.] to take place [anything *doing* tonight?] Auxiliary uses of *do:* 1. to give emphasis [please *do* stay] 2. to ask a question [*did* you write?] 3. to serve as a substitute verb [love me as I *do* (love) you] —*n., pl.* **do's** or **dos** 1. [Colloq.] a party or social event 2. [*pl.*] share, esp. in **fair dos** —**do away with** 1. to kill 2. to throw away —**do for** 1. to act as a housekeeper

for 2. to be sufficient 3. [Colloq.] to ruin —**do in** [Slang] 1. to kill 2. to exhaust —**do over** 1. [Colloq.] to redecorate 2. [Slang] to beat up —**dos and don'ts** rules of conduct —**do up** 1. to wrap up (a parcel, etc.) 2. to redecorate 3. to fasten (a dress, etc.) —**do with** 1. to make use of 2. [Colloq.] to appreciate having —**have to do with** 1. to be related to 2. to deal with —**make do** to get along with what is available

do² (dō) *n.* [It.: see GAMUT] *Music* a syllable representing the first or last tone of the diatonic scale

dobbin (dob′in) *n.* [< *Dobbin*, nickname for *Robin*] a horse, esp. a patient, plodding one

Doberman pinscher (dō′bər mən-pin′shər) [< G.] a breed of large dog, with smooth, dark hair

doc (dok) *n.* [Slang] doctor

docile (dō′sīl) *adj.* [< L. *docere*, teach] easy to manage or discipline; tractable —**doc′ilely** *adv.* —**docility** (dō sil′ə tē) *n.*

dock¹ (dok) *n.* [< MDu. *docke*, channel] 1. a large excavated basin for receiving ships between voyages 2. [*pl.*] a dockyard 3. a landing pier; wharf —*vt.* 1. to pilot (a ship) into a dock 2. to join (vehicles) together in outer space —*vi.* 1. to come into a dock —**in dock** [Colloq.] 1. in the garage for repair: said of a motor vehicle 2. in hospital: said of a person

dock² *n.* [< Fl. *dok*, cage] the place where the accused stands or sits in court —**in the dock** on trial

dock³ *n.* [OE. *docce*] any of various coarse weeds with large leaves and tap roots

dock⁴ *n.* [< ON. *dockr*] the solid part of an animal's tail —*vt.* 1. to cut off the end of (a tail) 2. to deduct from (wages, etc.)

docker *n.* a man employed to load and unload ships

docket *n.* [earlier *doggette*, register] 1. a piece of paper accompanying a package, etc., stating contents and often used as a receipt 2. a customs certificate declaring that duty has been paid 3. a list of cases to be tried by a law court 4. a summary, as of legal decisions —*vt.* to put a docket on; label

dockyard *n.* a place with docks, machinery, etc. for repairing or building ships

doctor (dok′tər) *n.* [< L., teacher] 1. a medical practitioner 2. a person on whom a university has conferred a high degree [*Doctor* of Philosophy] 3. [Colloq.] a person who carries out repairs [tree *doctor*] 4. orig., a teacher —*vt.* [Colloq.] 1. to try to heal 2. to mend 3. to tamper with 4. to castrate; said esp. of dogs and cats —**doc′toral** *adj.*

doctorate *n.* the degree or status of doctor conferred by a university

doctrinaire (dok′tri nãer′) *n.* [Fr.] one who tries to apply theories regardless of the practical problems —*adj.* adhering to a doctrine in an unyielding, dogmatic way

doctrine (dok′trən) *n.* [see DOCTOR] 1.

something taught **2.** something taught as the principles of a religion, political party, etc. —**doctrinal** (dok trī′nəl) *adj.*

document (dok′yoo mənt; *for v.* -ment′) *n.* [< L. *documentum*, proof] anything printed, written, etc., relied upon to record or prove something —*vt.* to provide with, or support by reference to, documents —**doc′umen′tal** *adj.*

documentary (dok′yoo men′tə rē) *adj.* **1.** of or supported by documents **2.** dramatically showing or analysing news events, etc., with no fictionalization —*n.*, *pl.* -**ries** a documentary film, etc.

documentation (-men tā′shən) *n.* **1.** the collecting, abstracting, etc. of printed or written information for future reference **2.** the documents collected

dodder (dod′ər) *vi.* [ME. *daderen*] to shake or tremble, as from old age —**dod′derer** *n.* —**dod′dery** *adj.*

doddle (dod′'l) *n.* [< ?] [Colloq.] a simple task

dodecagon (dō dek′ə gən) *n.* [< Gr. *dōdeka*, twelve & -GON] a plane figure with twelve sides

dodecahedron (dō′dek ə hē′drən) *n.*, *pl.* -**drons, -dra** [< Gr. *dōdeka*, twelve & -HEDRON] a solid figure with twelve plane faces —**do′decahe′dral** *adj.*

dodge (doj) *vi.* **dodged, dodg′ing** [< ?] **1.** to move or twist quickly aside **2.** to use tricks or evasions —*vt.* **1.** to avoid by moving quickly aside **2.** to evade —*n.* **1.** a dodging **2.** a trick used in evading or cheating

dodgem (doj′əm) *n.* [DODG(E) + (TH)EM] an electrically powered vehicle that moves erratically within an enclosure, bumping other vehicles: found at funfairs, etc.

dodger *n.* a shifty, dishonest person

dodgy *adj.* -**ier, -iest** [Colloq.] **1.** risky; difficult; dangerous **2.** uncertain; tricky

DODO (60 cm high)

dodo (dō′dō) *n.*, *pl.* -**dos, -does** [Port. *doudo*, foolish] **1.** a large, flightless bird, now extinct: formerly found on Mauritius

doe (dō) *n.* [OE. *da*] the female of the deer, or of the antelope, rabbit, etc.

D.O.E. Department of the Environment

doek (dook) *n.* [< Afrik.] [S Afr. Colloq.] a head cloth worn esp. by African women

does (duz) *3rd pers. sing., pres. indic., of* DO[1]

doeskin (dō′skin′) *n.* **1.** the skin of a female deer **2.** leather made from this

doff (dof) *vt.* [see DO[1] & OFF] to take off (clothes, etc.); esp., to remove or raise (one's hat)

dog (dog) *n.* [OE. *docga*] **1.** a domesticated animal related to the fox, wolf, etc. **2.** the male of this **3.** a mean, contemptible fellow **4.** an andiron **5.** [Colloq.] a boy or man [*lucky dog*] **6.** [*pl.*] [Slang] feet **7.** [*pl.*] [Colloq.] greyhound racing **8.** [D-] *Astron.* either of the constellations Great Dog or Little Dog **9.** *Mech.* a device for grappling —*vt.* **dogged, dog′ging 1.** to follow or hunt like a dog **2.** to trouble; plague —*adv.* very; completely [*dog*-tired] —**a dog's age** [Colloq.] a long time —**a dog's life** a wretched existence —**dog in the manger** a person who keeps others from using something which he cannot use —**go to the dogs** [Colloq.] to deteriorate —**like a dog's dinner** [Colloq.] **1.** flashily: said of someone's style of dressing **2.** messy; jumbled

dogcart *n.* **1.** a small cart drawn by dogs **2.** an open carriage having two seats arranged back to back

dog collar 1. a collar for a dog **2.** [Colloq.] the stiff, white collar worn by many clergymen

dog days the hot, humid days in July and August

doge (dōj) *n.* [It. < L. *dux*, leader] the chief magistrate of either of the former republics of Venice and Genoa

dogear (dog′ēər′) *n.* a turned-down corner of the leaf of a book —*vt.* to turn down the corner or corners of (a leaf in a book) —**dog′eared′** *adj.*

dog end [Slang] a cigarette end

dogfight *n. Mil.* combat between fighter planes at close quarters

dogfish *n.* any of various small sharks

dogged (dog′id) *adj.* [see DOG] not giving in readily; persistent; stubborn —**dog′gedly** *adv.* —**dog′gedness** *n.*

doggerel (dog′ər əl) *n.* [< ?] trivial, poorly constructed verse, usually comic: also **dog′grel**

doggo *adv.* [Colloq.] out of sight: esp. in the phrase **lie doggo**, to lie low

doggy, doggie *n., pl.* -**gies** a little dog: a child's word —*adj.* -**gier, -giest** of or like a dog

doghouse *n.* [U.S.] a kennel —**in the doghouse** [Colloq.] in disfavour

dogie, dogy, dogey (dō′gē) *n., pl.* -**gies** or -**geys** [<?] [U.S. & Canad.] a motherless calf

dogma (dog′mə) *n., pl.* -**mas, -mata** [< Gr. *dokein*, think] **1.** a doctrine; belief **2.** a positive, arrogant assertion of opinion **3.** *Theol.* a body of doctrines authoritatively affirmed

dogmatic (dog mat′ik) *adj.* **1.** stating opinion in a positive or arrogant manner **2.** of or like dogma **3.** asserted without proof —**dogmat′ically** *adv.*

dogmatism (dog′mə tiz'm) *n.* dogmatic assertion of opinion, usually without evidence —**dog′matist** *n.*

do-gooder (doo′good′ər) *n.* [Colloq.] a person who seeks to correct social ills in an impractical way

dog paddle a swimming stroke in which the swimmer paddles his hands and beats his legs up and down

dog rose a European wild rose with single, pink flowers

dogsbody (dogz′bod′ē) *n.* [Colloq.] a drudge

Dog Star 1. the brightest star in the constellation Canis Major; Sirius 2. Procyon

dog-tired *adj.* extremely tired; exhausted

dog train [Canad.] a sleigh drawn by a team of dogs

dogtooth violet 1. a N American plant with yellow flowers 2. a European plant with purple flowers

dogwatch *n. Naut.* a duty period, either from 4 to 6 P.M. or from 6 to 8 P.M.

dogwood *n.* 1. a tree found in Europe with greenish-white flowers and black berries 2. a Canadian flowering shrub, the floral emblem of British Columbia

doh (dō) *n.* same as DO²

doily (doi′lē) *n., pl.* -lies [< 17th-c. London draper] a small mat, as of lace or paper, used to protect or decorate a surface: also **doy′ley**

do-it-yourself *n.* the practice of constructing, repairing, redecorating, etc. by oneself

doldrums (dol′dramz) *n.pl.* [< ? DULL] 1. low spirits 2. sluggishness 3. equatorial ocean regions noted for dead calms

dole (dōl) *n.* [OE. *dal*] 1. money or food given to those in need 2. anything given out sparingly 3. a form of payment by a government to the unemployed —*vt.* **doled, dol′ing** to give sparingly or as dole (often with *out*) —**on the dole** receiving a dole (sense 3)

doleful (dōl′fool) *adj.* [ult. < L. *dolere*, suffer] full of sorrow or sadness —**dole′-fully** *adv.* —**dole′fulness** *n.*

doll (dol) *n.* [< nickname for *Dorothy*] 1. a child's toy made to resemble a human being 2. a pretty but silly young woman 3. [Slang] any lovable person —*vt.,vi.* [Colloq.] to dress stylishly (with *up*)

dollar (dol′ər) *n.* [< G. *Thaler*] 1. the monetary unit of Canada, U.S., Australia, Ethiopia, etc. 2. [Colloq.] formerly, five shillings (25p)

dollop (dol′əp) *n.* [< ?] 1. a soft mass 2. a measure [a *dollop* of wit] —*vt.* to serve (*out*) in dollops

dolly (dol′ē) *n., pl.* -lies 1. a doll: child's word 2. a low, flat, wheeled frame for moving heavy objects —*adj.* [Colloq.] attractive [a *dolly* bird]

dolman sleeve (dol′mən) [< Turk. *dolama*, long robe] a kind of sleeve tapering from a wide opening at the armhole to a narrow one at the wrist

dolmen (dol′mən) *n.* [< ? Breton *taol*, table + *men*, stone] a prehistoric monument formed by a large, flat stone laid across upright stones

dolomite (do′lə mīt′) *n.* [< Fr. geologist *Dolomieu*] a common rock-forming mineral of calcium magnesium carbonate

dolos (dol′os) *n., pl.* **dolosse** [S Afr.] a knucklebone of a sheep, buck, etc. used esp. by diviners

dolour (do′lər) *n.* [< L. *dolere*, suffer] [Poet.] sorrow —**do′lorous** *adj.*

dolphin (dol′fən) *n.* [< Gr. *delphis, delphinos*] 1. any of several water-dwelling mammals, often with a beaklike snout 2. either of two game fishes that change to bright colours out of water

dolphinarium (-âar′ē əm) *n.* [< prec. + (AQU)ARIUM] an aquarium for dolphins

dolt (dōlt) *n.* [< ME. *dullen*, to dull] a stupid, slow-witted person —**dolt′ish** *adj.* —**dolt′ishness** *n.*

-dom (dəm) [OE. *dom*, state] a suffix meaning: 1. the rank, position, or dominion of [*kingdom*] 2. a total of all who are [*officialdom*]

domain (dō mān′) *n.* [< L. *dominus*, lord] 1. territory under one government or ruler 2. land belonging to one person 3. sphere of activity

dome (dōm) *n.* [< Gr. *dōma*, housetop] 1. a hemispherical roof 2. any dome-shaped structure 3. [Slang] the head —*vt.* **domed, dom′ing** 1. to cover as with a dome 2. to form into a dome

Domesday Book (dōōmz′dā′) [said to be so named because it judged all men without bias, like the Last Judgment] the record of a land survey of England made under William the Conqueror

domestic (dō mes′tik) *adj.* [< L. *domus*, house] 1. of the home or family [*domestic joys*] 2. of one's own country or the country referred to 3. tame: said of animals 4. devoted to home life —*n.* a servant for the home, as a maid —**domes′tically** *adv.*

domesticate *vt.* **-cat′ed, -cat′ing** 1. to accustom to home life 2. to tame for man's use —**domes′tica′tion** *n.*

domesticity (dō′mes tis′ə tē) *n., pl.* -ties 1. home life; family life 2. devotion to home and family life

domestic science same as HOME ECONOMICS

domicile (dom′ə sīl′) *n.* [< L. *domus*, house] a home; residence, esp. a person's legal residence —*vt.* **-ciled′, -cil′ing** to establish (oneself) in a domicile

dominant (dom′ə nənt) *adj.* 1. dominating; ruling; prevailing 2. *Genetics* designating or of that one of any pair of characters which, when both are present in the germ plasm, dominates the other and appears in the organism —*n. Music* the fifth note of a diatonic scale —**dom′i-nance** *n.* —**dom′inantly** *adv.*

dominate *vt., vi.* **-nat′ed, -nat′ing** [< L. *dominus*, master] 1. to rule or control by superior power 2. to rise high above (the surroundings, etc.) —**dom′ina′tion** *n.* —**dom′ina′tor** *n.*

dominee *n.* [S Afr.] a minister of the Dutch Reformed Church

domineer (dom′ə nēar′) *vi., vt.* [< Du.: see prec.] to rule (*over*) in a harsh or arrogant way; tyrannize —**dom′ineer′ing** *adj.*

Dominican (də min′i kən) *adj.* of Saint Dominic or of a mendicant order founded by him —*n.* a friar or nun of one of the Dominican orders

dominion (də min′yən) *n.* [< L. *dominus*, lord] 1. rule or power to rule 2. a governed territory 3. [D-] formerly, any of certain self-governing member nations of the British Commonwealth

Dominion Day *same as* CANADA DAY

DOMINOES

domino (dom′ə nō′) *n., pl.* -noes′[Fr. & It. < L. *dominus*, lord] 1. a small, oblong piece of wood, etc. marked with dots 2. [*pl., with sing. v.*] a game played with such pieces 3. a loose cloak with a hood and mask, worn at masquerades 4. a small mask for the eyes

domino theory the theory that an event, as a political takeover, in one place or context can precipitate similar events elsewhere

domkop (dom′kop) *n.* [< Afrik. *dom*, stupid + *kop*, head] [S Afr. Slang] a fool; dunderhead

don[1] (don) *n.* [Sp.] 1. a tutor of any college of Oxford or Cambridge 2. [D-] Sir; Mr.: a Spanish title of respect 3. a Spanish nobleman or gentleman 4. [Canad.] the head of a student dormitory at certain universities and colleges

don[2] *vt.* donned, don′ning [contr. of *do on*] to put on (a garment, etc.)

‡**Doña** (dō′nyä) *n.* [Sp.] 1. Lady; Madam: a Spanish title of respect 2. [d-] a Spanish lady

donate (dō nāt′) *vt., vi.* -nat′ed, -nat′ing [prob. < DONATION] to give or contribute —**dona′tor** *n.*

donation (dō nā′shən) *n.* [< L. *donum*, gift] 1. the act of donating 2. a gift or contribution

donder (don′ər) *vt.* [S Afr. Slang] to beat someone up —*n.* [S Afr. Slang] a wretch, swine, etc.

done (dun) *pp. of* DO[1] —*adj.* 1. completed 2. sufficiently cooked 3. socially acceptable —**done (for)** [Colloq.] dead, ruined, etc. —**done in** (or **up**) [Colloq.] exhausted

dong (doŋ) *n.* [echoic] a sound of a large bell

donga (doŋ′gə) *n.* [< Afrik.] [S Afr.] a deep gully created by soil erosion

donjon (don′jən) *n.* [old sp. of DUNGEON] the heavily fortified inner tower of a castle

Don Juan (don′jōō′ən; *Sp.* dôn Hwän′) 1. *Sp. Legend* a dissolute nobleman and seducer of women 2. any man who seduces women; libertine

donkey (doŋ′kē) *n., pl.* -keys [< ? *Duncan*] 1. a domesticated ass 2. a

stupid or stubborn person 3. a small steam engine: in full, **donkey engine**

donkey jacket a workman's jacket of thick woollen cloth

donkey's years [Colloq.] a very long time

‡**Donna** (dôn′ä) *n.* [It.] 1. Lady; Madam: an Italian title of respect 2. [d-] an Italian lady

donnish (don′ish) *adj.* of or like a university don

donor (dō′nər) *n.* [< L. *donator*] 1.a giver 2. one from whom blood for transfusion, etc. is taken

Don Quixote (don′kwik′sət, don′-kē hōt′ē) 1. a satirical romance by Cervantes 2. the chivalrous, unrealistic hero of this romance

doodle (dōōd′′l) *vi.* -dled, -dling [< ? Low G. *dudeltopf*, simpleton] to scribble or draw aimlessly —*n.* a mark, design, etc. made in doodling —**doo′dler** *n.*

doodlebug *n.* [Colloq.] a flying bomb

doom (dōōm) *n.* [OE. *dom*] 1. a judgment; esp., a sentence of condemnation 2. fate 3. ruin or death —*vt.* to condemn

doomsday (dōōmz′dā′) *n.* judgement Day

door (dôr) *n.* [OE. *dor, duru*] 1. a movable structure for opening or closing an entrance 2. *same as* DOORWAY 1. —**lay at the door of** to blame (a person) for —**out of doors** outdoors —**show (someone) the door** to command (someone) to leave

doorjamb *n.* a vertical piece of wood, etc. forming the side of a doorway: also **door′post′**

doorknob *n.* a small knob or lever on a door, usually for releasing the latch

doorman *n.* a man whose work is opening the door of a building for those who enter or leave, etc.

doormat *n.* a mat to wipe the shoes on before entering a house, room, etc.

doorstep *n.* 1. a step that leads from an outer door to a path, etc. 2. [Colloq.] a thick slice of bread

doorstop *n.* any device for controlling or stopping the closing of a door

door-to-door *adj., adv.* from one home to the next, calling on each in turn

doorway *n.* 1. an opening in a wall that can be closed by a door 2. any means of access

dop (dop) *n.* [S Afr. Slang] 1. Cape brandy 2. a tot of this

dope (dōp) *n.* [Du. *doop*, sauce] 1. any thick liquid or paste used as a lubricant, etc. 2. a varnish for protecting the cloth covering of aeroplane wings 3. [Slang] any drug or narcotic 4. [Slang] a slow-witted or stupid person 5. [Slang] information —*vt.* doped, dop′ing to drug —**dop′er** *n.*

dopey, dopy *adj.* -ier, -iest [Slang] 1. under the influence of a narcotic 2. stupid —**dop′iness** *n.*

doppelgänger (dop′′l gaŋ′ər) *n.* [G. < *Doppel,* double + *Gänger,* goer] the ghostly double of a living person

Doppler effect (dop′lər) *n.* [< C. *Doppler*] the apparent change in frequency of sound or light waves caused by relative motion between the source of radiation and the observer

dorado (dǝ rä′dō) *n.* [Sp., gilded] *same as* DOLPHIN (sense 2)

DORIC CAPITAL

Doric (dôr′ik) *adj.* [< Gr. *Dōris*, an ancient region of Greece] designating or of the simplest of the classic orders of architecture: cf. CORINTHIAN, IONIC —*n.* any rustic dialect of English with broad vowels, esp. that spoken in Scotland

dormant (dôr′mǝnt) *adj.* [< L. *dormire*, to sleep] **1.** sleeping **2.** quiet; still **3.** inactive, as some animals or plants in winter —**dor′mancy** *n.*

DORMER

dormer (dôr′mǝr) *n.* [see ff.] **1.** a window set upright in a sloping roof **2.** the roofed projection in which this window is set Also **dormer window**

dormitory (dôr′mǝ trē) *n.*, *pl.* **-ries** [< L. *dormire*, to sleep] **1.** a room with sleeping accommodation for a number of people **2.** a suburb of a large city where people live but do not work: in full **dormitory town**

Dormobile (dôr′mō bēl′) *Trademark* a vanlike vehicle, often equipped with eating and sleeping facilities

dormouse (dôr′mous′) *n.*, *pl.* **-mice**′ [< ? OFr. *dormeuse*, sleepy] a small rodent that resembles the squirrel, found in Europe and Asia

dorp (dôrp) *n.* [< Du.] [S Afr.] a small town or village

dorsal (dôr′s'l) *adj.* [< L. *dorsum*, back] of, on, or near the back —**dor′sally** *adv.*

dory (dôr′ē) *n.* [< MFr. *dorée*, gilt] any of various spiny-finned food fishes, as the John Dory

dose (dōs) *n.* [< Gr. *dosis*, a giving] **1.** an amount of medicine to be taken at one time **2.** amount of a punishment or other unpleasant experience undergone at one time —*vt.* dosed, dos′ing to give doses of medicine to —**like a dose of salts** [Colloq.] very quickly —**dos′age** *n.*

doss (dos) *n.* [< ?] [Slang] a bed, esp. in a cheap lodging house —*vi.* to sleep (with *down*) —**dos′ser** *n.*

doss house [Slang] a place where a night's lodging can be had very cheaply

dossier (dos′ē ā′) *n.* [Fr.] a collection of documents about some person or matter

dot (dot) *n.* [OE. *dott*, head of boil] **1.** a tiny spot, speck, or mark; point **2.** any small, round spot **3.** a short sound or click in Morse code —*vt.* dot′ted, dot′-ting **1.** to mark with a dot or dots **2.** to cover as with dots **3.** [Slang] to hit —**dot one's i's and cross one's t's** to be minutely correct —**on the dot** [Colloq.] at the exact time —**dot′ter** *n.*

dotage (dōt′ij) *n.* [ME. < *doten*, dote] **1.** feeble and childish state of old age **2.** excessive affection

dotard (dōt′ǝrd) *n.* [ME. < *doten*, dote] a foolish and doddering old person

dote (dōt) *vi.* dot′ed, dot′ing [ME. *doten*] **1.** to be excessively fond (with *on* or *upon*) **2.** to be weak-minded, esp. because of old age —**dot′ing** *adj.*

dotterel (dot′rǝl) *n.* [< DOTE] a European and Asian plover with a short bill

dottle (dot′'l) *n.* [< ME. *dosel*, plug] the tobacco plug left in a pipe after it has been smoked

dotty (dot′ē) *adj.* dottier, dottiest **1.** [Colloq.] feeble-minded or crazy **2.** [Colloq.] extremely fond of **3.** covered with dots —**dot′tiness** *n.*

double (dub′'l) *adj.* [< L. *duplus*, twofold] **1.** twofold; duplex **2.** having two layers **3.** having two of one kind; repeated **4.** being of two kinds [a *double* standard] **5.** having two meanings **6.** twice as much, as many, as large, etc. **7.** of extra size, value, etc. **8.** made for two [a *double* bed] **9.** two-faced; deceiving **10.** having a tone an octave lower [*double* bass] **11.** *Bot.* having more than one set of petals —*adv.* **1.** twofold **2.** two together; in pairs —*n.* **1.** anything twice as much, as many, etc. as normal **2.** a duplicate; counterpart **3.** a stand-in, as in films **4.** [*pl.*] a game of tennis, etc. with two players on each side **5.** [Colloq.] a double measure of whisky, etc. **6.** *Bridge* the doubling of an opponent's bid —*vt.* **-bled**, **-bling 1.** to make twice as much or many **2.** to fold **3.** to repeat or duplicate **4.** to be the double of **5.** *Bridge* to increase the point value or penalty of (an opponent's bid) **6.** *Naut.* to sail around —*vi.* **1.** to become double **2.** to turn sharply **3.** to serve as a double **4.** to serve an additional purpose or function —**double back 1.** to turn back in the direction from which one came **2.** to fold back —**double up 1.** to bend over, as in laughter or pain **2.** to share a room, etc. with someone —**at the double** [Colloq.] **1.** in double time **2.** quickly

double agent a spy who infiltrates an enemy espionage organization in order to betray it

double-barrelled *adj.* **1.** having two barrels, as a kind of shotgun **2.** having a double purpose **3.** having hyphenated parts: said of surnames

DOUBLE BASS

double bass (bās) the largest and deepest-toned instrument of the violin family

double-breasted (dub′'l bres′tid) *adj.* overlapping across the breast, as a coat

double-check (dub′'l chek′) *vt., vi.* to check again; verify

double chin a fold of flesh beneath the chin

double cream cream with a high fat content

double-cross (dub′'l krôs′) *vt.* [Colloq.] to betray (a person) by intentionally failing to do what one has promised —**dou′-ble-cross′er** *n.*

double-dealing (dub′'l dēl′iŋ) *n.* duplicity —*adj.* deceitful; treacherous —**dou′-ble-deal′er** *n.*

double-decker (dub′'l dek′ər) *n.* any structure or vehicle with two levels

double dutch nonsense; gibberish

double-dyed *adj.* 1. thoroughly infamous 2. staunch

double-edged *adj.* 1. having two cutting edges 2. applicable both ways, as an argument

double-entendre (dōō′blän tän′dr'a) *n.* [Fr. (now obs.), double meaning] a word or phrase with two meanings, esp. when one of them is risqué or indecorous

double entry a system of bookkeeping in which each transaction is entered as a debit and a credit

double glazing two panes of glass in a window with a space between them, to reduce the transmission of heat, sound etc.

double-jointed (dub′'l join′tid) *adj.* having joints that permit limbs, fingers, etc. to bend at other than the usual angles

double-knit (dub′'l nit′) *adj.* knitted with a double stitch

double pneumonia pneumonia of both lungs

double-quick (dub′'l kwik′) *adj.* very quick

double standard a system, code, etc. applied unequally; specif., one that is stricter for women than for men

doublet (dub′lit) *n.* [< OFr. *double,* something folded] 1. a man's short, closefitting jacket of the 14th to the 16th cent. 2. either of a pair 3. a pair

double take a delayed reaction to some remark, situation, etc., following unthinking acceptance

double talk ambiguous and deceptive talk

double time a rate of payment twice as high as usual

doubloon (du blōōn′) *n.* [< L. *duplus,* double] an obsolete Spanish gold coin

doubly (dub′le) *adv.* 1. twice 2. two at a time

doubt (dout) *vi.* [< L. *dubitare*] to be uncertain or undecided —*vt.* 1. to be uncertain about 2. to be inclined to disbelieve —*n.* 1. a lack of conviction or trust 2. a condition of uncertainty 3. an unsettled point or matter —**beyond** (or **without**) **doubt** certainly —**no doubt** 1. certainly 2. probably —**doubt′er** *n.* —**doubt′ingly** *adv.*

doubtful *adj.* 1. uncertain 2. giving rise to doubt 3. feeling doubt; unsettled —**doubt′fully** *adv.*

doubtless *adv.* 1. certainly 2. probably —**doubt′lessly** *adv.*

douche (dōōsh) *n.* [ult. < L. *ducere,* lead] 1. a jet of liquid applied externally or internally to some part of the body 2. a bath or treatment of this kind 3. a device for douching —*vt., vi.* **douched, douch′ing** to apply a douche (to)

dough (dō) *n.* [OE. *dag*] 1. a mixture of flour, liquid, etc. worked into a soft, thick mass for baking 2. any pasty mass like this 3. [Chiefly U.S. Slang] money —**dough′y** *adj.*

doughnut *n.* a small cake, fried in deep fat

doughty (dout′ē) *adj.* **-tier, -tiest** [< OE. *dugan,* to avail] valiant; brave —**dough′-tily** *adv.*

Doukhobor, Dukhobor (dōō′kō bôr′) *n.* [< Russ. *dukhoborets,* spirit wrestlers] any of a Russian Christian sect, many of whom migrated to W Canada in the late 19th cent.

dour (dooər) *adj.* [< L. *durus,* hard] 1. [Scot.] stern; severe 2. [Scot.] obstinate —**dour′ness** *n.*

douse[1] (dous) *vt.* **doused, dous′ing** [< ?] [Colloq.] to put out (a light or fire) quickly

douse[2] *vt.* **doused, dous′ing** [< ? prec.] 1. to plunge or thrust suddenly into liquid 2. to drench

dove (duv) *n.* [< ? ON. *dūfa*] 1. a bird with a full-breasted body and short legs: a symbol of peace 2. an advocate of peaceful international relationships 3. a person regarded as gentle or innocent —**dov′ish** *adj.*

dovecote *n.* [DOVE + COTE] a small box with compartments for nesting pigeons: also **dove′cot′**

DOVETAIL

dovetail *n.* a projecting, wedge-shaped part that fits into a corresponding indentation to form a joint —*vt., vi.* to join or fit together closely or by means of dovetails

dowager (dou'ə jər) *n.* [ult. < L. *dos, dowry*] 1. a widow with a title or property derived from her dead husband 2. an elderly woman of wealth and dignity

dowdy (dou'dē) *adj.* **-dier, -diest** [< ?] not smart in dress; dull; shabby —**dow'-dily** *adv.* —**dow'diness** *n.*

dowel (dou'əl) *n.* [ME. *doule*] a peg or pin of wood, etc., usually fitted into corresponding holes in two pieces to fasten them together

dower (dou'ər) *n.* [< OFr. < L. *dos, dowry*] 1. that part of a man's property which his widow inherits for life 2. a dowry —*vt.* to endow (*with*)

dower house formerly, a house set apart for the use of a widow, esp. on her deceased husband's estate

down[1] (doun) *adv.* [< OE. *dune*, hill] 1. from a higher to a lower place 2. in or on a lower position or level 3. in or to a place thought of as lower; often, specif., southwards, or away from a capital or a university 4. from an earlier to a later period 5. into a low physical or emotional condition 6. in an inferior position or condition 7. to a lower amount or bulk 8. into a quiet state 9. in cash —*adj.* 1. directed towards a lower position 2. in a lower place 3. gone, pulled, etc. down 4. dejected; discouraged 5. completed [*four down*, six to go] 6. in cash [a *down* payment] —*prep.* down towards, along, through, into, or upon —*vt.* to put or throw down —*n.* 1. a depressed condition [*ups and downs*] 2. in Canadian football, any of a series of three attempts to advance the ball ten yards *Down* is also used with some verbs to indicate intensity or completion [*calm down*] —**down and out** penniless, friendless, ill, etc. —**down on** [Colloq.] hostile to —**down tools** to cease work and go on strike —**down to the ground** thoroughly —**down with!** do away with! —**have a down on** to have a grudge against someone

down[2] *n.* [< ON. *dūnn*] 1. soft, fine feathers 2. soft, fine hair or hairy growth —**down'y** *adj.*

down[3] *n.* [OE. *dun*, hill] an expanse of open, high, grassy land: *usually used in pl.* —**the Downs** either of two ranges of low, grassy hills in SE England

downcast *adj.* 1. directed downwards 2. dejected

downfall *n.* 1. *a*) a sudden fall, as from power *b*) the cause of this 2. a sudden, heavy fall, as of rain

downgrade *vt.* **-grad'ed, -grad'ing** 1. to demote 2. to belittle —*n.* [Chiefly U.S.] a downward slope

downhearted (doun'här'tid) *adj.* discouraged; dejected

downhill *adv.* 1. towards the bottom of a hill 2. to a poorer condition, status, etc.

Downing Street (doun'iŋ) [< Sir G. *Downing*] 1. street in the West End of

London, location of some important government offices 2. the British government

down payment the deposit paid on an item being bought on hire purchase, etc.

downpour *n.* a heavy rain

downright *adv.* thoroughly; utterly —*adj.* 1. absolute; utter 2. plain; frank

Down's syndrome (dounz) [< J.L.H. *Down*] a congenital disease in which there is mental deficiency and a characteristic broad face, with slanting eyes, etc.

downstairs *adv.* 1. down the stairs 2. on or to a lower floor —*adj.* situated on a lower floor: also **downstair** —*n.* a lower floor or floors

downstream *adv., adj.* in the direction of the current of a stream

down-to-earth *adj.* realistic or practical

downtrodden *adj.* 1. oppressed; tyrannized over 2. trampled on or down

down under [Colloq.] Australia or New Zealand

downward *adv., adj.* towards a lower place, state, etc. Also **down'wards** *adv.* —**down'wardly** *adv.*

downwind *adv., adj.* in the direction in which the wind is blowing or usually blows

dowry (dou₁'rē) *n., pl.* **-ries** [see DOWER] the property that a woman brings to her husband at marriage

dowse[1] (dous) *vt.* **dowsed, dows'ing** *same as* DOUSE[1]

dowse[2] (douz) *vi.* **dowsed, dows'ing** [< ?] to search for a source of water or minerals with a divining rod (**dowsing rod**) —**dows'er** *n.*

doxology (dok sol'ə jē) *n., pl.* **-gies** [< Gr. *doxa*, praise + *-logia*, -LOGY] a hymn of praise to God

doyen (doi'ən) *n.* [Fr.: see DEAN[1]] the senior member of a group, profession, or society —**doyenne'** (-en') *n. fem.*

doz. dozen; dozens

doze (dōz) *vi.* **dozed, doz'ing** [prob. < Scand.] to sleep fitfully —*n.* a light sleep; nap

dozen (duz''n) *n., pl.* **-ens** or, esp. after a number, **-en** [< L. *duo*, two + *decem*, ten] a set of twelve

dozy (dō'zē) *adj.* **doz'ier, doz'iest** 1. sleepy; drowsy 2. [Colloq.] stupid; dull —**doz'ily** *adv.* —**doz'iness** *n.*

D.Phil. Doctor of Philosophy

DPP, D.P.P. Director of Public Prosecutions

Dr. 1. Doctor 2. Drive

drab[1] (drab) *n.* [< LL. *drappus*, cloth] a dull yellowish brown —*adj.* **drab'ber, drab'best** 1. of a dull yellowish-brown colour 2. dull; monotonous —**drab'ness** *n.*

drab[2] *n.* [< Celt.] a prostitute

drachma (drak'mə) *n., pl.* **-mas, -mae** (-mē), **-mai** (-mī) [< Gr. *drachmē*, a handful] 1. an ancient Greek silver coin 2. the monetary unit of modern Greece

Draconian (drə kō'nē ən) *adj.* [< *Draco*, 7th cent. B.C. Athenian statesman] 1. of the very harsh laws attributed to Draco 2. very severe or cruel

draft (dräft) *n.* [< OE. *dragan,* to draw]
1. a rough sketch of a piece of writing
2. a plan or drawing of a work to be
done 3. a written order for payment of
money 4. a demand made on something
5. the taking of persons, animals, etc.
for a special purpose, esp. [U.S.]
compulsory military service —*vt.* 1. to
make a preliminary sketch of 2. to draw
off or away 3. to take from a group
for a special purpose, esp. [U.S.] for
compulsory military service —*adj.* in a
preliminary or rough form —**draft′able**
adj. —**draft′er** *n.*

drag (drag) *vt.* **dragged, drag′ging** [OE.
dragan] 1. to pull, or move with effort,
esp. along the ground 2. to pull a grapnel,
net, etc. over the bottom of (a river, etc.)
in searching for something 3. to draw
(something) out over a period of time
—*vi.* 1. to be dragged 2. to move or
pass too slowly 3. to search a body of
water with a grapnel, net, etc. —*n.* 1.
something dragged along the ground, as
a harrow 2. a grapnel, dragnet, etc. 3.
anything that hinders 4. a dragging 5.
[Slang] a puff of a cigarette, etc. 6.
[Slang] a dull or boring person, situation,
etc. 7. [Slang] women's clothes worn
by a man —**drag on** (or **out**) to prolong
or be prolonged tediously —**drag one's
feet** (or **heels**) to be uncooperative —**drag
up** 1. to introduce unpleasantly 2.
[Colloq.] to rear (children) carelessly
—**drag′gy** *adj.*

draggle *vt., vi.* **-gled, -gling** [< DRAG]
to make or become wet or dirty by dragging
in mud or water

dragnet *n.* 1. a net dragged along the
bottom of a river, etc. for catching fish
2. an organized network for catching
criminals

dragoman (drag′ōmən) *n., pl.* **-mans,
-men** [< Ar. *targumān*] in the Near East,
an interpreter or guide

dragon (drag′ən) *n.* [< Gr. *drakōn*] 1.
a mythical monster, usually represented
as a large reptile with wings, breathing
out fire and smoke 2. a fierce person

dragonfly *n., pl.* **-flies′** a large, harmless
insect having narrow, transparent, net-
veined wings

dragoon (drəgōōn′) *n.* [Fr.: see DRAGON]
a heavily armed cavalryman —*vt.* to force
(*into* doing)

drag race a race between motor cars
to test their rates of acceleration from
a complete stop on a short, straight course
—**drag′-race′** *vi.*

drain (drān) *vt.* [< OE. *dryge,* dry] 1.
to draw off (liquid) gradually 2. to draw
liquid from gradually 3. to drink all the
liquid from (a cup, etc.) 4. to exhaust
(strength or resources) gradually —*vi.* 1.
to flow off gradually 2. to become dry
by the flowing off of liquid 3. to discharge
its waters [central Europe *drains* into the
Danube] —*n.* 1. a channel, pipe, tube,
etc. for carrying off water, sewage, pus,
etc. 2. that which gradually exhausts
strength, etc. —**down the drain** lost in
a wasteful, heedless way —**drain′er** *n.*

drainage *n.* 1. a draining 2. a system
of pipes, etc. for carrying off waste matter
3. that which is drained off 4. an area
drained, as by a river

draining board a sloping board attached
to a sink on which dishes, etc. are placed
after being washed up

drainpipe *n.* 1. a large pipe used to
carry off water, sewage, etc. 2. [*pl.*]
very narrow trousers

drake (drāk) *n.* [< ?] a male duck

dram (dram) *n.* [see DRACHMA] 1.
Apothecaries' Weight a unit equal to 1/8
ounce 2. *Avoirdupois Weight* a unit equal
to 1/16 ounce 3. a small drink of spirits

drama (drä′mə) *n.* [< Gr. *dran,* do] 1.
a literary composition to be performed
by actors; play 2. the art of writing,
acting, or producing plays 3. plays
collectively 4. a series of events as
interesting, vivid, etc. as a play 5. the
quality of being dramatic

dramatic (drəmat′ik) *adj.* 1. of or
connected with drama 2. like a play 3.
vivid, exciting, etc. —**dramat′ically** *adv.*

dramatics *n.pl.* 1. [*usually with sing.
v.*] the art of performing or producing
plays 2. plays presented by amateurs
3. histrionic or hysterical behaviour

dramatis personae (dräm′ətis pursō′-
nī) [ModL.] the characters in a play

dramatist (dram′ətist) *n.* a playwright

dramatize (dram′ə-tized′, -tiz′ing 1. to make
into a drama 2. to regard or present
in a dramatic manner —**dram′atiza′tion** *n.*

drank (draŋk) *pt.* of DRINK

drape (drāp) *vt.* **draped, drap′ing** [< OFr.
drap, cloth] 1. to cover or hang with
cloth in loose folds 2. to arrange (a
garment, etc.) in folds —*n.* [Chiefly U.S.]
[*pl.*] curtains

draper *n.* a dealer in fabrics, etc.

drapery *n., pl.* **-peries** 1. hangings, etc.
arranged in loose folds 2. [Chiefly U.S.]
[*pl.*] curtains of heavy material

drastic (dras′tik) *adj.* [< Gr. *dran,* do]
having a violent effect; severe; harsh
—**dras′tically** *adv.*

draught (dräft) *n.* [< OE. *dragan,* draw]
1. a current of air, as in a room 2.
a drawing, as of a vehicle or load 3.
a drink; specif. a dose of medicine 4.
a) drinking *b)* the amount taken at one
drink 5. *a)* a drawing in of a fish net
b) the amount of fish caught in one draw
6. *Naut.* the depth of water that a ship
displaces —*adj.* 1. used for pulling loads
[*draught* animals] 2. drawn from a cask
on order [*draught* beer] —**feel the draught**
to suffer financial losses

draughtboard *n.* a board with 64 squares
of two alternating colours, used in draughts
and chess

draught horse a strong horse capable
of pulling heavy loads

draughts *n.pl.* [*with sing. v.*] a game
played on a draughtboard by two players,
each with twelve round, flat pieces to move

draughtsman *n.* 1. a person who draws
plans of structures or machinery 2.

Draughts any of the pieces used in playing draughts —**draughts′manship′** *n.*

draughty *adj.* **-ier, -iest** letting in, having, or exposed to a draught or draughts of air —**draught′ily** *adv.* —**draught′iness** *n.*

Dravidian (drə vid′ē ən) *n.* any of a group of intermixed races chiefly in S India and N Ceylon —*adj.* of the Dravidians or their languages

draw (drô) *vt.* **drew, drawn, draw′ing** [< OE. *dragan*] **1.** to make move towards one; pull; drag **2.** to pull up, down, in, across, back, etc. **3.** to make (lines, pictures, objects, etc.) as with a pencil, pen, brush, etc. **4.** to attract; charm **5.** to breathe in **6.** to bring forth; elicit **7.** to bring on; provoke **8.** to reach (a conclusion, etc.); deduce **9.** to bring (a game or contest) to a tie **10.** to get from some source [to *draw* a salary] **11.** to withdraw (money) held in an account **12.** to write (a cheque or draft) **13.** to stretch to full length **14.** to extract (a cork, sword, etc.) **15.** *a)* to remove (liquid) by draining, etc. *b)* to cause (liquid) to flow [to *draw* blood] **16.** to disembowel **17.** to need (a specified depth of water) to float in: said of a ship —*vi.* **1.** to draw (in various senses of the *vt.*) **2.** to be drawn or have a drawing effect **3.** to come; move [to *draw* near] **4.** to shrink; contract **5.** to allow a draught, as of smoke, to move through **6.** to become stronger by infusion; said of tea —*n.* **1.** a drawing or being drawn (in various senses) **2.** the result of drawing **3.** a thing drawn **4.** a tie; stalemate **5.** a thing that attracts interest, audiences, etc. —**draw away** to move away or ahead —**draw in 1.** to grow shorter: said esp. of days **2.** to entice; lure —**draw on** (or **nigh**) to approach —**draw out 1.** to extend **2.** to take out **3.** to get (a person) to talk **4.** to grow longer: said esp. of days —**draw up 1.** to arrange in order **2.** to compose (a document) in proper form **3.** to stop

drawback *n.* anything that prevents or lessens full satisfaction; shortcoming

drawbridge *n.* a bridge that can be raised, lowered, or drawn aside

drawer (drô′ər; *for 3* drôr) *n.* **1.** a person or thing that draws **2.** one who draws an order for the payment of money **3.** a sliding box in a table, chest, bureau, etc.

drawers *n.pl.* a form of undergarments with legs

drawing *n.* **1.** the art of representing something by lines made on a surface with a pencil, pen, etc. **2.** a picture, design, etc. thus made

drawing pin a pin with a wide, flat head, that can be pressed into a board, etc. to support maps, notices, etc.

drawing room [< earlier *withdrawing room*] a room where guests are received or entertained; sitting room

drawl (drôl) *vt., vi.* [prob. < DRAW] to speak slowly, prolonging the vowels —*n.* a manner of speaking thus —**drawl′er** *n.* —**drawl′ingly** *adv.*

drawn (drôn) *pp.* of DRAW —*adj.* **1.**

pulled out of the sheath **2.** even; tied **3.** eviscerated **4.** tense; haggard

draw sheet a sheet that can be removed from the bed while the bed is occupied

drawstring *n.* a string that tightens or closes an opening, as of a bag, when drawn

dray (drā) *n.* [< OE. *dragan*, to draw] a low, sturdy cart with detachable sides, for carrying heavy loads

dread (dred) *vt.* [OE. *drædan*] to anticipate with great fear, misgiving, or distaste —*n.* **1.** intense fear **2.** fear mixed with awe —*adj.* **1.** dreaded or dreadful **2.** inspiring awe

dreadful *adj.* **1.** [Colloq.] very bad, offensive, etc. **2.** inspiring dread; terrible or awesome —**dread′fully** *adj.*

dreadnought *n.* a large, heavily armoured battleship with big guns

dream (drēm) *n.* [< OE. *dream*, joy] **1.** a sequence of images, thoughts, etc. passing through a sleeping person's mind **2.** a daydream; reverie **3.** a fond hope **4.** anything so lovely, transitory, etc. as to seem dreamlike —*vi.* **dreamed** (drēmd, dremt) or **dreamt** (dremt), **dream′ing 1.** to have dreams **2.** to think (of) as at all possible, etc. —*vt.* **1.** to have a dream of **2.** to imagine as possible —*adj.* ideal [her *dream* house] —**dream up** [Colloq.] to conceive of or devise —**dream′er** *n.* —**dream′less** *adj.* —**dream′like′** *adj.*

dreamy *adj.* **-ier, -iest 1.** filled with dreams **2.** visionary; impractical **3.** misty, vague, etc. **4.** soothing [*dreamy* music] —**dream′ily** *adv.* —**dream′iness** *n.*

dreary (drēr′ē) *adj.* **-ier, -iest** [< OE. *dreorig*, sad, orig., bloody] gloomy; depressing —**drear′iness** *n.*

dredge¹ (drej) *n.* [prob. < MDu. *dregge*] **1.** a net on a frame, dragged along the bottom of a river, bay, etc. to gather shellfish, etc. **2.** an apparatus for scooping up mud, etc., as in deepening harbours, etc. —*vt., vi.* **dredged, dredg′ing 1.** to gather (*up*) or search (*for*) as with a dredge **2.** to enlarge or clean out with a dredge —**dredg′er** *n.*

dredge² *vt.* **dredged, dredg′ing** [< ME. *dragge*, sweetmeat] to coat (food) with flour etc., as by sprinkling —**dredg′er** *n.*

dregs (dregz) *n.pl.* [< ON. *dregg*] **1.** the particles that settle at the bottom of a liquid **2.** the most worthless part —**dreg′giness** *n.* —**dreg′gy** *adj.*

drench (drench) *vt.* [< OE. *drincan*, drink] **1.** to make wet all over; soak **2.** to make (a horse, etc.) swallow a medicinal liquid —*n.* **1.** a soaking **2.** a large liquid dose, esp. for a sick animal

Dresden (drez′dən) *n.* [< *Dresden*, in East Germany] a type of fine, elaborately decorated porcelain

dress (dres) *vt.* **dressed, dress′ing** [ult. < L.] **1.** to put clothes on; clothe **2.** to provide with clothing **3.** to trim; adorn **4.** to arrange (the hair, a shop window, etc.) **5.** to arrange (troops, etc.) in straight lines **6.** to apply medicines and bandages to (a wound, etc.) **7.** to prepare for use, esp. for cooking **8.** to smooth or finish (leather, stone, etc.) —*vi.* 1. to put on or wear clothes 2. to get into a straight line —*n.* 1. clothes 2. a woman's one-piece garment with a skirt 3. external covering or appearance —*adj.* 1. of or for dresses *[dress* material *]* 2. worn on formal occasions *[a dress* suit *]* —**dress down** to scold severely —**dress up** 1. to dress in formal clothes 2. to improve the appearance *[to dress up* the facts *]*

dressage (dres′äzh) *n.* [Fr.] training of a horse through set piece exercises

dress circle a section of seats in a theatre, usually the first gallery, where formal dress was orig. customary

dresser[1] *n.* a person who dresses people, as actors in their costumes, or things, as shop windows

dresser[2] *n.* [< OFr. *dreceur*] 1. a kitchen cupboard with shelves above 2. [U.S.] a chest of drawers or dressing table

dressing *n.* 1. a sauce for salads, etc. 2. a stuffing for poultry, etc. 3. that which is used to dress something (as manure applied to soil, bandages applied to a wound, etc.) 4. the act of one that dresses

dressing-down (-doun′) *n.* a sound scolding

dressing gown a loose robe for wear when one is undressed or lounging

dressing station a military first aid station

dressing table a low table or chest of drawers with a mirror, for use while putting on cosmetics, etc.

dress rehearsal a final rehearsal, as of a play, performed exactly as it is to take place

dress suit a man's formal suit for evening wear

dressy *adj.* **-ier, -iest** 1. showy in dress or appearance 2. stylish, elegant, etc. —**dress′iness** *n.*

drew (droo) *pt. of* DRAW

drey (drā) *n.* [< ?] a squirrel's nest

dribble (drib′'l) *vi., vt.* **-bled, -bling** [freq. of obs. *drib*] 1. to flow, or let flow, in drops; trickle 2. to slaver; drool 3. in certain games, to move (the ball) along by rapid, repeated bounces, short kicks, or light taps —*n.* 1. a dribbling 2. a very small amount —**drib′bler** *n.*

dried (drīd) *pt. & pp. of* DRY

drier (drī′ər) *n.* 1. a substance added to paint, etc. to make it dry fast 2. *same as* DRYER —*adj. compar. of* DRY

driest *adj. superl. of* DRY

drift (drift) *vi.* [< OE. *drifan,* to drive] 1. to be carried along as by a current 2. to go along aimlessly 3. to pile up in heaps by force of wind —*vt.* to cause to drift —*n.* 1. a heap of snow, sand, etc. piled up by the wind 2. a being driven along, as by a current of water 3. the course on which something is directed 4. a tendency or trend 5. general meaning; tenor 6. the deviation of a ship, etc. from its course, caused by side currents or winds 7. a slow ocean current 8. a controlled four-wheel skid used for cornering at high speed 9. [S.Afr.] a ford

drifter *n.* a small fishing vessel that drifts with the tide

driftwood *n.* wood that is drifting in the water, or has been washed ashore

drill[1] (dril) *n.* [Du. < *drillen,* to bore] 1. a tool for boring holes in wood, metal, etc. 2. military or physical training, esp. of a group 3. [Colloq.] the correct procedure for performing a task —*vt.* 1. to bore (a hole) in (something) with or as with a drill 2. to train in military or physical exercises 3. to teach by having do repeated exercises 4. to instil (ideas, etc. *into*) by repetition —**drill′er** *n.*

drill[2] *n.* [< ?] 1. a furrow in which seeds are planted 2. a row of planted seeds 3. a machine for making holes or furrows and dropping seeds into them —*vt.* to sow (seeds) in rows

drill[3] *n.* [ult. < L. *tri-,* three + *licium,* thread] a coarse linen or cotton twill, used for work clothes, linings, etc.

drill[4] *n.* [< ?] a bright-cheeked monkey native to W Africa

drily (drī′lē) *adv. same as* DRYLY

drink (driŋk) *vt.* **drank, drunk, drink′ing** [OE. *drincan*] 1. to swallow (liquid) 2. to absorb (liquid or moisture) 3. to swallow the contents of 4. to bring (oneself) into a specified condition by drinking 5. to join in (a toast) —*vi.* 1. to swallow liquid 2. to absorb anything as if in drinking 3. to drink beer, etc. to excess —*n.* 1. any liquid for drinking 2. alcoholic liquor —**drink in** to take in eagerly with the senses or the mind —**drink to** to drink a toast to —**the drink** [Colloq.] the sea —**drink′able** *adj.* —**drink′er** *n.*

drip (drip) *vi., vt.* **dripped, drip′ping** [OE. *dryppan*] to fall or let fall in drops —*n.* 1. a falling in drops 2. the sound made by this 3. [Slang] a person regarded as dull, insipid, etc.

drip-dry *adj.* designating or of fabrics or garments that dry quickly and require little or no ironing —*vi.* **-dried′, -dry′ing** to launder as a drip-dry fabric does

drip-feed *vt.* to feed (someone) a liquid drop by drop, esp. intravenously —*n.* an apparatus for feeding thus: also **drip**

dripping *n.* the fat and juices that drip from roasting meat —*adv.* so as to drip; soaking

drive (drīv) *vt.* **drove, driv′en, driv′ing** [OE. *drifan*] 1. to force to go 2. to control the movement of (a vehicle) 3. to transport in a vehicle 4. to force to work, usually to excess 5. to hit (a ball) hard 6. to force into or from a state or act 7. to make penetrate 8. to produce by penetrating 9. to chase (game) from cover —*vi.* 1. to advance violently 2. to try hard 3. to drive a blow, ball, etc. 4. to be driven; operate: said of a motor vehicle 5. to operate, or go in, a motor vehicle —*n.* 1. a driving 2. a journey in a vehicle 3. *a)* a road for motor vehicles *b)* a driveway 4. [U.S.] a rounding up of animals 5. a hard, swift blow, thrust, etc. 6. an organized campaign 7. aggressive vigour; energy 8. an urge or impulse **9.** the propelling mechanism of a motor vehicle, machine, etc. **10.** a systematic chasing of game towards waiting guns —**drive at 1.** to aim at **2.** to mean; intend

drive-in *adj.* designating a restaurant, cinema, etc. designed to serve people seated in their cars

drivel (driv''l) *vi.* **-elled, -elling** [< OE. *dreflian*] **1.** to let saliva flow from one's mouth **2.** to speak in a silly or stupid manner —*n.* silly, stupid talk

driven (driv''n) *pp. of* DRIVE —*adj.* moved along and piled up by the wind [*driven* snow]

driver (dri'vər) *n.* **1.** a person who drives; specif., *a)* one who drives a motor car, etc. *b)* one who herds cattle **2.** a golf club used in hitting the ball from the tee —**the driver's seat** the position of control or dominance

driveway *n.* a path for cars, leading from the street to a garage, house, etc.

driving licence an official document authorizing a person to drive a motor vehicle

drizzle (driz''l) *vi., vt.* **-zled, -zling** [< OE. *drēosan,* fall] to fall in fine, mistlike drops —*n.* a fine, mistlike rain —**driz'-zly** *adj.*

droll (drōl) *adj.* [< MDu. *drol,* stout fellow] amusing in an odd or wry way —**droll'-ery** *n.* —**droll'ness** *n.* —**drol'ly** *adv.*

dromedary (drom'ə dər ē) *n., pl.* **-daries** [< Gr. *dramein,* run] the one-humped camel

drone[1] (drōn) *n.* [< OE. *dran*] **1.** a male honeybee, which does no work **2.** an idle parasite or loafer

drone[2] *vi.* droned, dron'ing [< prec.] **1.** to make a continuous humming sound **2.** to talk in a monotonous way —*vt.* to utter in a monotonous tone —*n.* **1.** a droning sound **2.** a pipe of fixed tone in a bagpipe

drool (drōol) *vi.* [< DRIVEL] **1.** to let saliva flow from one's mouth **2.** to flow from the mouth, as saliva —*n.* saliva running from the mouth

droop (drōop) *vi.* [< ON. *drūpa*] **1.** to sink, hang, or bend down **2.** to lose vitality **3.** to become dejected —*vt.* to let hang down —*n.* a drooping —**droop'y** *adj.*

drop (drop) *n.* [OE. *dropa*] **1.** a small, rounded quantity of liquid, esp. as when falling **2.** [*pl.*] liquid medicine taken in drops **3.** a very small quantity of anything **4.** a thing like a drop in shape, size, etc. **5.** a sudden fall, descent, slump, etc. **6.** anything that drops, as a drop curtain, etc. **7.** the distance between a higher and lower level —*vi.* **dropped, drop'-ping 1.** to fall in drops **2.** to fall; come down **3.** to fall exhausted, wounded, or dead **4.** to pass into a specified state [*to drop* off to sleep] **5.** to come to an end [let the matter *drop*] **6.** to become lower or less, as prices, etc. —*vt.* **1.** to let or make fall **2.** to give birth to: said of animals **3.** to utter (a hint, etc.) casually **4.** to send (a letter) **5.** to cause to fall, as by killing, etc. **6.** to have

done with; dismiss [*drop* the subject] **7.** to lower **8.** to omit (a letter or sound) in a word **9.** [Colloq.] to leave (a person or thing) at a specified place —**at the drop of a hat** immediately —**drop back** to be outdistanced : also **drop behind** —**drop in** (or **over, by,** etc.) to pay a casual or unexpected visit —**drop off 1.** to decline **2.** [Colloq.] to fall asleep —**drop out** to stop being a participant

drop curtain a theatre curtain that is lowered and raised rather than drawn

dropout *n.* a person who withdraws esp. from university, college, society, etc.

dropper *n.* a small tube with a hollow rubber bulb at one end, used to release a liquid in drops

droppings *n.pl.* dung, esp. of sheep, birds, etc.

dropsy (drop'sē) *n.* [< Gr. *hydōr,* water] *an earlier term for* OEDEMA —**drop'sical, drop'sied** *adj.*

droshky (drosh'kē) *n., pl.* **-kies** [Russ. *drozhki*] a low, open, four-wheeled Russian carriage: also **dros'ky**

dross (dros) *n.* [OE. *dros,* dregs] **1.** a scum formed on the surface of molten metal **2.** waste matter; rubbish

drought (drout) *n.* [< OE. *drugian,* dry up] prolonged dry weather —**drought'y** *adj.*

drove[1] (drōv) *n.* [< OE. *drifan,* drive] **1.** a flock or herd driven or moving as a group **2.** a crowd of people

drove[2] *pt. of* DRIVE

drover *n.* a person who herds droves of animals

drown (droun) *vi.* [< ON. *drukna*] to die by suffocation in water or other liquid —*vt.* **1.** to kill by such suffocation **2.** to flood **3.** to overpower another sound, etc.: usually with *out* **4.** to get rid of

drowse (drouz) *vi.* drowsed, drows'ing [< OE. *drusian,* become sluggish] to sleep lightly; doze —*n.* a doze

drowsy *adj.* **-sier, -siest 1.** sleepy or half asleep **2.** brought on by sleepiness —**drow'sily** *adv.* —**drow'siness** *n.*

drub (drub) *vt.* drubbed, drub'bing [< ? Ar. *darb,* a beating] **1.** to beat as with a stick **2.** to defeat soundly in a fight, contest, etc. —**drub'ber** *n.*

drubbing *n.* a thorough beating or defeat

drudge (druj) *n.* [prob. < OE. *dreogan,* suffer] a person who does hard, menial, or tedious work —*vi.* drudged, drudg'ing to do such work

drudgery *n., pl.* **-eries** work that is hard or tiresome

drug (drug) *n.* [< OFr. *drogue*] **1.** any substance used as or in a medicine **2.** a narcotic, hallucinogen, etc. —*vt.* **drugged, drug'ging 1.** to put a harmful drug in (a drink, etc.) **2.** to stupefy as with a drug —*vi.* to take narcotics, etc. —**drug on the market** something for which there is little demand

drug addict a person who uses narcotics

drugget (drug'it) *n.* [< Fr. *drogue,* trash] a coarse fabric used as a floor covering

drugstore *n.* [Chiefly U.S.] a shop where drugs, sweets, cosmetics, etc. are sold

druid (droo̅'id) *n.* [< Celt.] [*often* D-] 1. a member of a Celtic religious order in ancient Britain, Ireland, and France 2. an officer concerned with the Welsh eisteddfod —**druid'ic, druid'ical** *adj.* —**dru'idism** *n.*

drum (drum) *n.* [< Du. *trom*] 1. a percussion instrument consisting of a hollow cylinder or hemisphere with a membrane stretched tightly over the end or ends 2. the sound produced by beating a drum 3. any drumlike cylindrical object, as a metal container for oil, etc. 4. *Anat.* the eardrum —*vi.* **drummed, drum'ming** 1. to beat a drum 2. to tap continually, as with the fingers —*vt.* 1. to beat out (a tune, etc.) as on a drum 2. to instil (ideas, etc. *into*) by continued repetition —**beat the drum for** [Colloq.] to try to arouse enthusiasm for —**drum out of** to expel from in disgrace —**drum up** to get (business) by soliciting

drumhead *n.* the membrane stretched over the open end or ends of a drum

drum major a person who leads or precedes a marching band, often twirling a baton —**drum majorette** *fem.*

drummer *n.* a drum player

drumstick *n.* 1. a stick for beating a drum 2. the lower half of the leg of a cooked fowl

drunk (druŋk) *pp. & archaic pt. of* DRINK —*adj.* 1. intoxicated 2. overcome by any powerful emotion —*n.* [Slang] a drunken person

drunkard *n.* a person who often gets drunk

drunken *archaic pp. of* DRINK —*adj.* 1. intoxicated 2. caused by or occurring during intoxication —**drunk'enly** *adv.* —**drunk'enness** *n.*

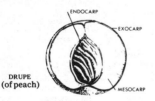

DRUPE
(of peach)

ENDOCARP

EXOCARP

MESOCARP

drupe (droo̅p) *n.* [< Gr. *dryppa*, olive] any fruit with a soft, fleshy part around an inner stone that contains the seed, as an apricot, plum, etc.

dry (drī) *adj.* **dri'er, dri'est** [OE. *dryge*] 1. not under water [*dry* land] 2. not wet or damp 3. lacking rain; arid 4. empty of water or other liquid 5. thirsty 6. not yielding milk [a *dry* cow] 7. without butter, jam, etc. [*dry* toast] 8. solid; not liquid 9. not sweet [*dry* wine] 10. prohibiting or opposed to the sale of wine, spirits, etc. 11. plain or sober [*dry* facts] 12. funny in a quiet but sharp way 13. dull or boring —*vt., vi.* **dried, dry'ing** to make or become dry —**dry out** 1. to make or become thoroughly dry 2.

to withdraw from addiction to alcohol or drugs —**dry up** 1. to make or become thoroughly dry 2. to become unproductive, uncreative, etc. 3. to dry washed plates, etc. 4. [Colloq.] to stop talking, esp. in public, as an actor —**dry'ness** *n.*

dryad (drī'əd) *n.* [< Gr. *drys*, an oak] [*also* D-] *Gr. & Rom. Myth.* a wood nymph

dry battery 1. an electric battery made up of several connected dry cells 2. a dry cell

dry cell a voltaic cell containing an absorbent so that its contents cannot spill

dry-clean (drī'klēn') *vt.* to clean (garments, etc.) with a solvent other than water —**dry cleaner** —**dry cleaning**

dry dock a dock from which the water can be emptied, used for building and repairing ships

dryer *n.* 1. a person or thing that dries; specif., an appliance for drying hair by heating and blowing air 2. *same as* DRIER

dry fly *Angling* an artificial fly designed to float on the water

dry ice carbon dioxide solidified and compressed into snowlike cakes, used as a refrigerant

dryly *adv.* in a dry manner; matter-of-factly

dry measure a system of measuring the volume of dry things, as grain, etc. in which 2 pints = 1 quart, 8 quarts = 1 peck, and 4 pecks = 1 bushel

dry rot a fungous decay causing seasoned timber to crumble to powder

dry run 1. [Mil. Slang] practice in firing without using live ammunition 2. [Slang] a rehearsal

dry-stone *adj.* made without mortar : said of walls, etc.

D.S., D.Sc. Doctor of Science

D.S.C., DSC Distinguished Service Cross

D.S.M., DSM Distinguished Service Medal

D.S.O., DSO Distinguished Service Order

D.T.'s, d.t.'s (dē'tēz') [Colloq.] *same as* DELIRIUM TREMENS

Du. Dutch

dual (dyoo̅'əl) *adj.* [< L. *duo*, two] 1. of two 2. double; twofold —**dual'ity** (-al'ə tē) *n.* —**du'ally** *adv.*

dual carriageway a road with a central reservation separating traffic travelling in opposite directions

dualism *n.* 1. the state of being dual 2. any theory based on a twofold distinction, as that the world is composed of mind and matter —**du'alist** *n.*

dual number in some languages, a grammatical number indicating *two, a pair*

dub¹ (dub) *vt.* **dubbed, dub'bing** [< OE. *dubbian*, strike] 1. to confer a title or name upon 2. to make smooth, as by hammering or scraping —**dub'ber** *n.*

dub² *vt.* **dubbed, dub'bing** [< DOUBLE] to produce a film with a new soundtrack in a different language —**dub'ber** *n.*

dubbin *n.* [see DUB¹] a greasy preparation for softening and waterproofing leather : also **dub'bing**

dubiety (dyoo̅ bī'ə tē) *n.* [LL. *dubietas*]

1. a being dubious 2. *pl.* -ties a doubtful thing

dubious (dyoo′bē əs) *adj.* [< L. *dubius*, uncertain] 1. causing doubt 2. feeling doubt 3. questionable —**du′biously** *adv.* —**du′biousness** *n.*

ducal (dyoo′k'l) *adj.* [see DUKE] of a duke or dukedom

ducat (duk′ət) *n.* [< LL. *ducatus*, duchy] any of several former European coins of gold or silver

duchess (duch′is) *n.* 1. the wife or widow of a duke 2. a woman who, like a duke, rules a duchy

duchy *n.*, *pl.* **duch′ies** [< L. *dux*, duke] the territory ruled by a duke or duchess; dukedom

duck[1] (duk) *n.* [< OE. *duce*, diver < ff.] 1. a swimming bird with a flat bill, short neck and legs, and webbed feet 2. a female duck: opposed to DRAKE 3. the flesh of a duck as food 4. [Colloq.] dear or darling 5. *Cricket* a score of zero by a batsman —**like a (dying) duck in a thunderstorm** looking forlorn or bedraggled —**like water off a duck's back** with no effect

duck[2] *vt., vi.* [ME. *douken*] 1. to lower or move (the head, body, etc.) suddenly, as in avoiding a blow 2. to plunge or dip under water for a moment 3. [Colloq.] to avoid (a task, person, etc.) —*n.* a ducking

duck[3] *n.* [Du. *doek*] 1. a cloth like canvas but lighter 2. [*pl.*] [Colloq.] trousers made of this cloth

duckbill *n.* same as PLATYPUS

duckling *n.* a young duck

ducks and drakes the game of throwing a flat stone so that it skims the surface of the water —**play ducks and drakes with** to deal with recklessly or squander

duct (dukt) *n.* [< L. *ducere*, to lead] 1. a tube or channel through which a fluid moves 2. a tube in the body for the passage of excretions or secretions 3. a pipe or conduit enclosing wires —*vt.* to convey through a duct —**duct′less** *adj.*

ductile (duk′t'l) *adj.* [see prec.] 1. that can be drawn or hammered thin without breaking: said of metals 2. easily moulded 3. easily led —**ductil′ity** (-til′ə tē) *n.*

ductless gland an endocrine gland

dud (dud) *n.* [< ?] [Colloq.] a person or thing that fails

dude (dyood) *n.* [< ?] [Chiefly U.S.] 1. a dandy; fop 2. [Slang] a city fellow or tourist

dudgeon (duj′ən) *n.* [< Anglo-Fr. *en digeon*, at the dagger hilt] anger or resentment: now chiefly in **in high dudgeon**, very angry, offended, or resentful

duds (dudz) *n.pl.* [prob. < ON. *dutha*, wrap up] [Colloq.] clothes, esp. old clothes

due (dyoo) *adj.* [< L. *debere*, owe] 1. owed or owing as a debt, etc.; payable 2. suitable; proper 3. enough [*due* care] 4. expected or scheduled to arrive —*adv.* exactly [*due* west] —*n.* anything due; specif., [*pl.*] fees or other charges [membership *dues*] —**become (or fall) due**

to become payable as previously arranged —**due to** 1. caused by 2. [Colloq.] because of

duel (dyoo′əl) *n.* [< L. *duellum*, war] 1. a formal, prearranged fight between two persons armed with deadly weapons 2. any contest like this —*vi., vt.* **-elled**, **-elling** to fight a duel (with) —**du′ellist**, **du′eller** *n.*

duenna (dyoo en′ə) *n.* [Sp. < L. *domina*, mistress] an elderly woman who has charge of the young unmarried women of a Spanish or Portuguese family

duet (dyoo et′) *n.* [< L. *duo*, two] *Music* 1. a composition for two voices or instruments 2. the two performers of such a composition

duff (duf) *vt.* [? < DUFFER] 1. to bungle 2. [Colloq.] to beat (*up*) —*adj.* bad or useless [a *duff* car]

duffel, duffle (duf′'l) *n.* [Du. < *Duffel*, in N Belgium] a coarse woollen cloth

duffel (or duffle) bag a large, cylindrical cloth bag for carrying clothing and personal belongings

duffel (or duffle) coat a knee-length coat made of duffel or other wool cloth, usually with a hood

duffer (duf′ər) *n.* [< thieves' slang *duff*, to fake] [Slang] an incompetent or stupid person

dug[1] (dug) *pt. & pp. of* DIG

dug[2] *n.* [< Dan. *dægge*, suckle] a nipple or udder

dugong (doo′goŋ) *n.* [Malay *dūyung*] a large, whalelike mammal of tropical seas

dugout (dug′out′) *n.* 1. a boat or canoe hollowed out of a log 2. a shelter, as in warfare, dug in the ground 3. in the Canadian prairies, a reservoir dug on a farm in which water from rain and snow is collected

duiker (dī′kər) *n.* [< Du.] [S Afr.] 1. a small antelope 2. a long-tailed cormorant or shag

duke (dyook) *n.* [< L. *ducere*, to lead] 1. the ruler of an independent duchy 2. a nobleman next in rank to a prince —**duke′-dom** *n.*

dulcet (dul′sit) *adj.* [< L. *dulcis*, sweet] soothing or pleasant to hear; melodious

DULCIMER

dulcimer (dul′sə mər) *n.* [< L. *dulce*, sweet + Gr. *melos*, song] a musical instrument with metal strings, which are struck with two small hammers

dull (dul) *adj.* [OE. *dol*, stupid] 1. mentally slow; stupid 2. lacking sensitivity 3. physically slow 4. lacking spirit; listless

5. causing boredom; tedious **6.** not sharp; blunt **7.** not felt keenly **8.** not vivid **9.** not glossy **10.** not distinct **11.** cloudy —*vt., vi.* to make or become dull —**dull′-ness** *n.* —**dul′ly** *adv.*

dullard *n.* a stupid person

duly (dyo͞o′lē) *adv.* in due manner; specif., *a)* as due; rightfully *b)* when due; at the right time *c)* as required

dumb (dum) *adj.* [OE.] **1.** lacking the power of speech **2.** silent **3.** [Colloq.] stupid —**dumb′ly** *adv.* —**dumb′ness** *n.*

dumbbell *n.* a device usually used in pairs for muscular exercise: it has round weights joined by a short bar

dumbfound, dumfound (dum′found′) *vt.* [DUMB + (CON)FOUND] to make speechless, esp. by shocking

dumb show gestures without speech

dumbwaiter (dum′wāt′ər) *n.* **1.** a small, portable stand for serving food **2.** [Chiefly U.S.] a small lift for food, rubbish, etc.

dumdum (**bullet**) (dum′dum′) [< *Dumdum*, arsenal near Calcutta, India] a soft-nosed bullet that expands when it hits, inflicting a large wound

dummy (dum′ē) *n., pl.* **-mies 1.** a figure made in human form, as for displaying clothing **2.** an imitation **3.** a baby's rubber comforter or teat **4.** [Slang] a stupid person **5.** a person unable to talk **6.** *Bridge*, etc. *a)* the declarer's partner, whose hand is exposed on the board and played by the declarer *b)* such a hand —*adj.* imitation; sham

dummy run a practice, rehearsal, or trial of some event

dump (dump) *vt.* [prob. < ON.] **1.** to unload in a heap or mass **2.** *a)* to throw away (rubbish, etc.) *b)* to get rid of abruptly **3.** to sell (a commodity) in a large quantity at a low price, esp. abroad —*n.* **1.** a rubbish pile or a place for dumping **2.** *Mil.* a temporary storage centre, as for ammunition **3.** [Slang] a place that is unpleasant, ugly, etc. —**dump′er** *n.*

dumpling (dump′liŋ) *n.* [< *dump*, lump] **1.** a small piece of dough, steamed or boiled and served with meat or soup **2.** [Colloq.] a short, plump person

dumps *n.pl.* a state of depression, esp. in **down in the dumps**

dumpy *adj.* **-ier, -iest** short and stout

dun¹ (dun) *adj., n.* [OE.] dull greyish-brown

dun² *vt., vi.* **dunned, dun′ning** [? < DIN] to ask (a debtor) repeatedly for payment —*n.* an insistent demand for payment of a debt

dunce (duns) *n.* [< *Duns Scotus*] **1.** a dull, ignorant person **2.** a person slow at learning

dunderhead (dun′dər hed′) *n.* [? < Du. *donder*, thunder] a stupid person; dunce

dune (dyo͞on) *n.* [Fr. < ODu. *duna*] a rounded hill or ridge of sand heaped up by the wind

dung (duŋ) *n.* [OE.] animal excrement; manure —*vt.* to spread with dung, as in fertilizing —**dung′y** *adj.*

dungaree (duŋ′gə rē′) *n.* [Hindi *dungrī*]

1. a coarse cotton cloth; specif., blue denim **2.** [*pl.*] work trousers or overalls of this cloth

dungeon (dun′jən) *n.* [< OFr. *donjon*] a dark, underground cell or prison

dunghill (duŋ′hil′) *n.* **1.** a heap of dung **2.** anything filthy

dunk (duŋk) *vt.* [G. *tunken*] **1.** to dip (bread, etc.) into coffee, etc. before eating it **2.** to immerse briefly

dunlin (dun′lin) *n.* [< DUN¹] a small sandpiper with a reddish back

dunnock (dun′ək) *n.* [< DUN¹] *same as* HEDGE SPARROW

duo (dyo͞o′ō) *n., pl.* **du′os, du′i** (-ē) [It.] **1.** *same as* DUET (esp. sense 2) **2.** a pair; couple

duodecimal (dyo͞o′ō des′ə m'l) *adj.* [< L. *duo*, two + *decem*, ten] relating to twelve or twelfths —*n.* **1.** one twelfth **2.** [*pl.*] *Math.* a system of numeration with twelve as its base

duodenum (dyo͞o′ō dē′nəm) *n., pl.* **-de′-na, -de′nums** [< L. *duodeni*, twelve each] the first section of the small intestine, below the stomach —**du′ode′nal** *adj.*

duologue (dyo͞o′ə log′) *n.* [< L. *duo*, two + (MONO)LOGUE] a conversation between two people

dupe (dyo͞op) *n.* [< ? L. *upupa*, stupid bird] a person easily tricked or fooled —*vt.* **duped, dup′ing** to deceive or cheat —**dup′er** *n.* —**dup′ery** *n.*

duple (dyo͞o′p'l) *adj.* [see DOUBLE] **1.** double **2.** *Music* having two beats to the bar

duplex (dyo͞o′pleks) *adj.* [L. < *duo*, two + *-plex*, -fold] **1.** double **2.** having two units operating in the same way —**duplex′-ity** *n.*

duplicate (dyo͞o′plə kət; *for v.* -kāt′) *adj.* [< L. *duplicare*, to double] **1.** double **2.** corresponding exactly **3.** designating a game of bridge, etc. in which the same hands are played again by other players to compare scores —*n.* **1.** an exact copy; facsimile **2.** a counterpart or double —*vt.* **-cat′ed, -cat′ing 1.** to make an exact copy of **2.** to cause to happen again —**in duplicate** in two precisely similar forms —**du′plica′tion** *n.*

duplicating machine a machine for making exact copies of a letter, photograph, drawing, etc.: also **du′plica′tor**

duplicity (dyo͞o plis′ə tē) *n., pl.* **-ties** [< LL. *duplicitas*] hypocritical cunning or deception

durable (dyoor′ə b'l) *adj.* [< L. *durare*, to last] **1.** lasting in spite of hard wear or frequent use **2.** stable —**du′rabil′ity** *n.* —**du′rably** *adv.*

durable goods goods usable for a relatively long time, as machinery, cars, or home appliances

durance (dyoor′əns) *n.* [see DURABLE] imprisonment: mainly in phrase **in durance vile**

duration (dyoo rā′shən) *n.* [< L. *durare*, to last] the time that a thing continues or lasts

durbar (dur′bär) *n.* [< Per. *dar*, portal + *bār*, court] formerly in India, a reception or audience held by a native prince or British governor

duress (dyoores′) *n.* [< L. *durus*, hard] 1. imprisonment 2. the use of force or threats

during (dyoor′iŋ) *prep.* [< ME. *duren*, to last] 1. throughout the entire time of 2. in the course of

durst (durst) *archaic pt. of* DARE

dusk (dusk) *n.* [< OE. *dox*, dark-coloured] 1. the dim part of twilight 2. gloom; dusky quality

dusky *adj.* **-ier, -iest** 1. somewhat dark in colour 2. dim 3. gloomy —**dusk′ily** *adv.* —**dusk′iness** *n.*

dust (dust) *n.* [OE.] 1. powdery earth or any finely powdered matter 2. confusion; turmoil 3. earth 4. disintegrated mortal remains 5. a humble condition —*vt.* 1. to sprinkle with dust, powder, etc. 2. to rid of dust, as by wiping —*vi.* to remove dust, as from furniture —**bite the dust** to be killed, esp. in battle —**shake the dust off one's feet** to leave with disdain —**throw dust in (someone's) eyes** to mislead (someone)

dustbin *n.* a container for household rubbish

dust bowl a region where eroded topsoil is blown away by winds during droughts

dust cart a vehicle used for removing household rubbish

dust cover 1. *same as* DUST JACKET 2. a cover for furniture, as a sheet, etc.

duster *n.* a cloth for removing dust from furniture, etc.

dust jacket a detachable paper cover for protecting the binding of a book

dustman *n.* a man whose work is removing rubbish

dustpan *n.* a shovellike receptacle into which dust or debris is swept from a floor

dustup *n.* [Colloq.] a commotion or fight

dusty *adj.* **-ier, -iest** 1. covered with or full of dust 2. like dust —**not so dusty** [Colloq.] quite good —**dust′ily** *adv.*

Dutch (duch) *adj.* of the Netherlands, its people, language, or culture —*n.* the language of the Netherlands —**go Dutch** [Colloq.] to have each pay his own expenses —**in Dutch** [Colloq.] in trouble or disfavour —**the Dutch** the people of the Netherlands

Dutch auction an auction at which the upset price is very high, and is gradually lowered till a purchaser is found

Dutch barn a farm building consisting of a roof and its supports : used for storing hay, etc.

Dutch cap a contraceptive diaphragm

Dutch courage bravery induced by spirits, wine, etc.

Dutch elm disease [from its first appearance in the Netherlands] a widespread fungous disease of elms

Dutchman *n.* 1. an inhabitant of the Netherlands 2. a Dutch ship 3. [S Afr. Derog.] an Afrikaner —**I'm a Dutchman** [Colloq.] a phrase used to imply disbelief

Dutch medicine [S Afr.] patent medicines, esp. made of herbs

Dutch nail [S Afr. Slang] a rock or other weight for securing roofs, etc.

Dutch oven 1. a heavy metal pot with a high, arched lid 2. a metal container for roasting meats, etc., with an open side placed towards the fire

Dutch treat [Colloq.] any entertainment, etc. at which each participant pays his own expenses

Dutch uncle [Colloq.] a person who bluntly and sternly lectures or scolds someone else

duteous (dyoot′ē əs) *adj.* dutiful; obedient —**du′teously** *adv.* —**du′teousness** *n.*

dutiable (dyoot′ē ə b′l) *adj.* necessitating payment of a duty or tax, as imported goods

dutiful (-ə fəl) *adj.* 1. showing, or resulting from, a sense of duty 2. obedient —**du′tifully** *adv.*

duty (dyoot′ē) *n., pl.* **-ties** [< Anglo-Fr. *dueté*, what is due] 1. obedience or respect to parents, older people, etc. 2. conduct based on moral or legal obligation 3. any action required by one's position 4. a sense of obligation 5. service, esp. military service 6. a tax imposed on imports, exports, etc. —**on** (or **off**) **duty** at (or having time off from) one's work or duty

duty-bound *adj.* obliged; beholden

duty-free shop a shop, usually at an airport, port, etc., where goods can be bought with no payment of tax

duvet (dyoo′vā) *n.* [Fr.] a quilt filled with eiderdown or a mixture of terylene and eiderdown

dwaal (dwäl) *n.* [S Afr.] a state of befuddlement; daze

dwarf (dwôrf) *n., pl.* **dwarfs, dwarves** (dwôrvz) [OE. *dweorg*] 1. a person, animal, or plant much smaller than usual for its species 2. *Folklore* an ugly little being with supposed magic powers —*vt.* 1. to stunt the growth of 2. to make seem small or insignificant —*adj.* undersized —**dwarf′ish** *adj.* —**dwarf′ishness** *n.*

dwell (dwel) *vi.* **dwelt, dwell′ing** [OE. *dwellan*, lead astray] to make one's home —**dwell on** to linger over in thought or speech —**dwell′er** *n.*

dwelling *n.* a residence; abode

dwindle (dwin′d′l) *vi., vt.* **-dled, -dling** [< OE. *dwinan*, wither] to become less; shrink

Dy *Chem.* dysprosium

dye (dī) *n.* [OE. *deag*] 1. colour produced by a colouring agent; tint; hue 2. any such colouring agent —*vt.* **dyed, dye′ing** to colour as with a dye —**of (the) deepest dye** of the worst sort —**dy′er** *n.*

dyed-in-the-wool *adj.* thoroughgoing; unchanging

dyeing (dī′iŋ) *n.* the process or work of colouring fabrics, hair, etc. with dyes

dying (dī′iŋ) *prp. of* DIE¹ —*adj.* 1. about to die or end 2. of or at the time of death —*n.* a ceasing to live or exist

dyke (dīk) *n., vt. same as* DIKE

dynamic (dīnam′ik) *adj.* [< Gr. *dynasthai,* to be able] 1. relating to energy or physical force in motion **2.** relating to dynamics **3.** energetic; vigorous; forceful —**dynam′ically** *adv.*

dynamics *n.pl.* [*with sing. v. for 1 & 3*] **1.** the branch of mechanics dealing with the motions of material bodies under the action of forces **2.** the various forces operating in any field **3.** the effect of varying degrees of loudness in musical performance

dynamism (dī′nə miz'm) *n.* a dynamic quality

dynamite (dī′nə mīt′) *n.* [< Gr. *dynamis,* power] **1.** a powerful explosive made with nitroglycerin **2.** a person or thing that is potentially dangerous —*vt.* -mit′-ed, -mit′ing to destroy with dynamite

dynamo (dī′nə mō′) *n., pl.* -mos′ [< *dynamoelectric machine*] a machine that generates electricity

dynamo- [see DYNAMIC] *a combining form meaning* power

dynamoelectric (dī′nə mō i lek′trik) *adj.* having to do with the production of electrical energy from mechanical energy

dynamometer (dī′nə mom′ə tər) *n.* an apparatus for measuring force or power

dynast (dī′nəst) *n.* [< Gr. *dynasthai,* to be strong] a ruler, esp. a hereditary ruler

dynasty *n., pl.* -ties a succession of rulers who are members of the same family —**dynastic** (di nas′tik), **dynas′tical** *adj.* —**dynas′tically** *adv.*

dyne (dīn) *n.* [< Gr. *dynamis,* power] the amount of force that imparts to a mass of one gram an acceleration of one centimetre per second per second

dys- [Gr.] *a prefix meaning* bad, ill, abnormal, etc.

dysentery (dis′'n trē) *n.* [< Gr. *dys-,* bad + *entera,* bowels] a painful intestinal inflammation characterized by diarrhoea with bloody, mucous faeces —**dys′enter′-ic** (-ter′ik) *adj.*

dyslexia (dis lek′sē ə) *n.* [< Gr. *dys-,* bad + *lexis,* speech] impairment of the ability to read —**dyslex′ic** *adj.*

dyspepsia (dis pep′sē ə) *n.* [< Gr. *dys-,* bad + *peptein,* digest] indigestion —**dyspep′tic** *adj.*

dysprosium (dis prō′sē əm) *n.* [< Gr. *dysprositos,* difficult of access] a chemical element of the rare-earth group : symbol, Dy

dystrophy (dis′trə fē) *n.* [see DYS- & -TROPHY] **1.** *short for* MUSCULAR DYSTROPHY **2.** degeneration or wasting of tissues, etc.

dz. dozen; dozens

E

E, e (ē) *n., pl.* **E's, e's** the fifth letter of the English alphabet

E (ē) *n. Music* the third tone in the ascending scale of C major

e *Math.* the number used as the base of a system of logarithms, approximately 2.71828: written *e*

e- *a prefix meaning* out, from, etc.: see EX-

E, E., e, e. 1. east 2. eastern

E. 1. Earl 2. Easter 3. English

E., e. 1. earth 2. engineer(ing)

each (ēch) *adj., pron.* [< OE. *ælc*] every one of two or more considered separately —*adv.* apiece [ten pence *each*] —**each other** one another —**each way** in betting, to back a horse, etc. to either win or be placed

eager (ē′gər) *adj.* [< L. *acer*, keen] feeling or showing keen desire —**ea′gerly** *adv.* —**ea′gerness** *n.*

eager beaver [Colloq.] a hardworking person

eagle (ē′g'l) *n.* [< L. *aquila*] 1. a large, strong bird of prey having sharp vision and powerful wings 2. a representation of the eagle, esp., as the national emblem of the U.S. 3. the standard of a Roman Legion, or French army

eagle-eyed *adj.* 1. having keen vision 2. [Colloq.] very observant, esp. in a critical way

eaglet (ē′glit) *n.* a young eagle

-ean (ē′ən) [< L. & Gr.] *a suffix meaning* of, belonging to, like [*European*]

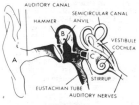

AUDITORY CANAL
SEMICIRCULAR CANAL
HAMMER   ANVIL
VESTIBULE
COCHLEA
STIRRUP
EUSTACHIAN TUBE
AUDITORY NERVES

HUMAN EAR
(A, external ear; B, middle ear; C, inner ear)

ear¹ (ēər) *n.* [OE. *eare*] 1. the part of the body that perceives sound; organ of hearing 2. the external part of the ear 3. the sense of hearing 4. the ability to recognize slight differences in sound, esp. in musical tones —**be all ears** to listen attentively —**fall on deaf ears** to be ignored —**give one's ears** to be prepared to make any sacrifice —**have** (or **keep**) **an ear to the ground** to pay attention

to the trends of public opinion —**lend an ear** to listen —**play it by ear** [Colloq.] to act as the situation demands —**turn a deaf ear** to be unwilling to listen

ear² *n.* [< OE. *ær*] the grain-bearing spike of a cereal plant [an *ear* of corn] —*vi.* to sprout ears

earache *n.* an ache or pain in the ear

eardrum *n.* *same as:* 1. TYMPANIC MEMBRANE 2. MIDDLE EAR

earl (url) *n.* [OE. *eorl*, warrior] a British nobleman ranking below a marquess —**earl′dom** *n.*

Earl Marshal the marshal at certain state ceremonies and head of the Heralds' College

early (ur′lē) *adv., adj.* **-lier, -liest** [< OE. *ær*, before] 1. near the beginning of a given period or of a series of events 2. before the expected or usual time 3. in the far distant past 4. in the near future —**ear′liness** *n.*

early bird [Colloq.] one who arrives or rises early

Early English a style of architecture used in England in the 12th and 13th cent. with lancet arches and plate tracery

Early Modern English English from c.1450 to c.1750

earmark (ēər′märk′) *n.* 1. an identifying feature 2. an identification mark put on the ear of an animal —*vt.* 1. to set aside for a special purpose 2. to mark the ears of (livestock) for identification

earmuffs *n.pl.* cloth or fur coverings for the ears

earn (urn) *vt.* [OE. *earnian*] 1. to receive (wages, etc.) for one's labour 2. to get or deserve as a result of something done 3. to gain (interest, etc.) as profit —**earn′er** *n.*

earnest¹ (ur′nist) *adj.* [OE. *eornoste*] serious and intense; not joking —**in earnest** 1. serious 2. in a determined manner —**ear′nestly** *adv.* —**ear′nestness** *n.*

earnest² *n.* [< OFr. *erres*] money given as a pledge in binding a bargain; token

earnings *n.pl.* 1. wages 2. profits, interest, etc.

earphone (ēər′fōn′) *n.* a receiver for radio, telephone, etc. held to or put into the ear

ear-piercing *adj.* shrill; deafening

earring *n.* an ornament for the lobe of the ear

earshot *n.* the distance within which a sound, esp. that of the unaided human voice, can be heard

earth (urth) *n.* [OE. *eorthe*] 1. the planet that we live on, the third in distance from the sun **2.** this world, as distinguished from heaven and hell **3.** land, as distinguished from sea or sky **4.** soil; ground **5.** the hole of a burrowing animal **6.** *Elec.* the connection of an electrical conductor with the earth —*vt.* **1.** to cover (*up*) with soil for protection, as plants **2.** *Elec.* to connect a circuit, etc. with the earth —**come back** (or **down**) **to earth** to return to reality —**down to earth** practical; realistic —**on earth** of all things [*what on earth* is that?] —**run to earth** to hunt down

earthbound *adj.* **1.** confined to or by the earth or earthly things **2.** headed for the earth

earth closet a privy in which earth is applied to the excreta as a deodorant

earthen *adj.* made of earth or of baked clay

earthenware *n.* tableware, etc. made of baked clay

earthly *adj.* **1.** terrestrial **2.** worldly **3.** temporal or secular **4.** possible [no earthly reason] —**not an earthly** [Colloq.] no chance whatever —**earth'liness** *n.*

earthnut *n.* the root, tuber, or underground pod of various plants, as the peanut

earthquake *n.* a shaking of the crust of the earth, caused by underground shifting of rock

earth sciences those sciences concerned with the structure, age, etc. of the earth, as geology, geography, etc.

earthward *adv., adj.* towards the earth: also **earth'wards** *adv.*

earthwork *n.* a defensive embankment made by piling up earth

earthworm *n.* a round, segmented worm that burrows in the soil

earthy *adj.* **-ier, -iest 1.** of or like earth **2.** *a)* coarse; unrefined *b)* simple and natural —**earth'iness** *n.*

ear trumpet a trumpet-shaped tube formerly used as a hearing aid by the partially deaf

earwig (êar'wig') *n.* [< OE. *eare*, ear + *wicga*, beetle] an insect with a pair of forceps at the tail end

ease (ēz) *n.* [< OFr. *aise*] **1.** freedom from pain or trouble; comfort **2.** natural manner; poise **3.** freedom from difficulty **4.** leisure; relaxation —*vt.* **eased, eas'ing 1.** to free from pain or trouble; comfort **2.** to lessen (pain, anxiety, etc.) **3.** to make easier **4.** to reduce the strain or pressure of **5.** to move by careful shifting, etc. —*vi.* **1.** to move or be moved by careful shifting, etc. **2.** to lessen in tension, speed, pain, etc. —**at ease** *Mil.* relaxed, but keeping silent and staying in place —**take one's ease** to relax —**ease'ful** *adj.*

easel (ē'z'l) *n.* [< Du. *ezel*, ass] an upright frame to hold an artist's canvas, a picture on display, etc.

easement *n.* **1.** a relief or convenience **2.** *Law* a right that one may have in another's land, as a right of way

easily (ē'zəl ē) *adv.* **1.** in an easy way **2.** by far [*easily* the best] **3.** very likely [it may *easily* rain]

easiness (ē'zi nis) *n.* the quality or state of being easy

east (ēst) *n.* [OE. *east*] **1.** the direction in which sunrise occurs (90° on the compass, opposite west) **2.** a region in this direction **3.** [E-] Asia and the nearby islands; the Orient —*adj.* **1.** in, of, to, or towards the east **2.** from the east —*adv.* in or towards the east —**back east** [Canad.] in or to E Canada, esp. east of Quebec

eastbound *adj.* going eastwards

Easter (ēs'tər) *n.* [< OE. *Eastre*, dawn goddess] an annual, movable Christian festival celebrating the resurrection of Jesus, held on a Sunday in Spring

Easter egg a coloured egg or an egg-shaped sweet, esp. made of chocolate, used as an Easter gift

easterly *adj., adv.* towards, or from, the east

eastern *adj.* **1.** in, of, or towards the east **2.** from the east **3.** [E-] of the East —**east'ernmost'** *adj.*

Eastern Church same as ORTHODOX EASTERN CHURCH: also **Eastern Orthodox Church**

Eastern Hemisphere that half of the earth that includes Europe, Africa, Asia, and Australia

Eastertide (ēs'tər tīd') *n.* the period after Easter

east-northeast *n.* the direction halfway between due east and northeast

east-southeast *n.* the direction halfway between due east and southeast

eastward (ēst'wərd) *adj., adv.* towards the east: also **east'wards** *adv.* —*n.* an eastward direction or region

eastwardly *adv., adj.* towards, or from, the east

easy (ē'zē) *adj.* **eas'ier, eas'iest** [see EASE] **1.** not difficult **2.** free from anxiety, pain, etc. **3.** providing comfort or rest **4.** not stiff or awkward **5.** lenient **6.** compliant **7.** *a)* unhurried *b)* gradual —*adv.* [Colloq.] slowly and carefully —**easy on the eye** [Colloq.] pleasant to look at —**go easy on** (or **with**) [Colloq.] **1.** to use with restraint **2.** to treat leniently —**on easy street** [Colloq.] well-to-do —**take it easy** [Colloq.] **1.** to refrain from anger, haste, etc. **2.** to relax; rest

easy chair a stuffed or padded armchair

easygoing *adj.* lenient or lackadaisical

eat (ēt) *vt.* **ate** (et, āt), **eaten** (ēt'ən), **eat'ing** [OE. *etan*] **1.** to chew and swallow (food) **2.** to consume or ravage (*away* or *up*) **3.** to corrode **4.** to make by eating [acid *ate* holes in the cloth] **5.** [Slang] to worry [what's *eating* him?] —*vi.* **1.** to eat food **2.** to destroy or use up (*into*) —**eat one's words** to retract something said earlier —**eat out** to eat a meal at a restaurant —**eat'er** *n.*

eatable *adj.* fit to be eaten; edible —*n.* [*pl.*] food

eating *n.* the edible quality of food —*adj.* **1.** good for eating uncooked [*eating* apples] **2.** of or for eating

eats *n.pl.* [Colloq.] food; meals

eau de Cologne (ō′də kə lōn′) [Fr., water of Cologne] a perfumed toilet water made of alcohol and aromatic oils

‡**eau de vie** (ō də vē′) [Fr., water of life] brandy

eaves (ēvz) *n.pl.*, *sing.* **eave** [OE. *efes*] the projecting lower edge or edges of a roof

eavesdrop *vi.* -**dropped**′, -**drop**′**ping** [prob. < *eavesdropper* < OE. *yfesdrype*, water from the eaves] to listen secretly to a private conversation —**eaves**′**drop**′**per** *n.*

ebb (eb) *n.* [OE. *ebba*] 1. the flow of water back towards the sea, as the tide falls 2. a weakening; decline —*vi.* 1. to recede, as the tide 2. to weaken; decline

ebony (eb′ən ē) *n.*, *pl.* -**onies** [< Gr. *ebenos*] the hard, heavy, dark wood of certain tropical trees —*adj.* 1. made of ebony 2. like ebony, esp. in colour; dark

ebullient (i bul′yənt) *adj.* [< L. *e-*, out + *bullire*, boil] 1. overflowing with enthusiasm; exuberant 2. boiling —**ebul**′**lience, ebul**′**liency** *n.* —**ebul**′**liently** *adv.*

ebullition (eb′ə lish′ən) *n.* 1. a boiling or bubbling up 2. a sudden outburst, as of emotion

E.C. East Central

eccentric (ik sen′trik) *adj.* [< Gr. *ek-*, out of + *kentron*, centre] 1. odd; unconventional 2. not having the axis exactly in the centre 3. not having the same centre, as two circles 4. not exactly circular —*n.* 1. an eccentric person 2. a disc off centre on a shaft, for converting circular motion into back-and-forth motion —**eccen**′**trically** *adv.*

eccentricity (ek′sen tris′ə tē) *n.*, *pl.* -**ties** 1. oddity 2. the state, quality, or degree of being eccentric

Eccles., Eccl. Ecclesiastes

ecclesiastic (i klē′zē as′tik) *adj.* [< Gr. *ekklēsia*, assembly] *same as* ECCLESIASTICAL —*n.* a clergyman

ecclesiastical *adj.* of the church or the clergy

ECG electrocardiogram

echelon (esh′ə lon′) *n.* [< Fr. < L. *scala*, ladder] 1. a steplike formation of ships, aircraft, or troops 2. *a)* an organizational level, as of responsibility *b)* persons at such a level

echidna (e kid′nə) *n.* [< Gr. *echidna*, adder] a small, egg-laying Australasian mammal with a spiny coat

echinoderm (i kī′nə durm′) *n.* [< Gr. *echinos*, sea urchin + *derma*, skin] a marine animal with a hard, spiny skeleton and radial body, as a starfish

echo (ek′ō) *n.*, *pl.* -**oes** [< Gr. *ēchō*] 1. *a)* the repetition of a sound by reflection of sound waves from a surface *b)* a sound so made 2. any repetition or imitation of words, ideas, etc. of another 3. a radar wave reflected from an object, appearing as a spot of light on a radarscope —*vi.* -**oed, -oing** 1. to resound 2. to be repeated as an echo —*vt.* to repeat (the words, etc.) of

echo chamber a room used in recording and broadcasting to increase resonance, produce echo effects, etc.

echoic (e kō′ik) *adj.* 1. like an echo 2. imitative in sound; onomatopoeic, as the word *clash* —**ech**′**oism** *n.*

echolocation (ek′ō lō kā′shən) *n.* the location of an object by reflected sound, as by a bat

echo sounding determination of water depth or of underwater distances by a device (**echo sounder**) that measures the time it takes for a sound wave to be reflected

éclair (ā klāər′) *n.* [Fr., lightning] a small, oblong pastry shell filled with cream and covered with icing

éclat (ā klä′) *n.* [Fr. < *éclater*, burst (out)] 1. brilliant success 2. dazzling display 3. acclaim; renown

eclectic (i klek′tik) *adj.* [< Gr. *ek-*, out + *legein*, pick] 1. selecting from various systems, doctrines, or sources 2. composed of material selected thus —*n.* one who uses eclectic methods —**eclec**′**tically** *adv.* —**eclec**′**ticism** *n.*

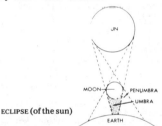

ECLIPSE (of the sun)

eclipse (i klips′) *n.* [< Gr. *ek-*, out + *leipein*, leave] 1. an obscuring of the sun when the moon comes between it and the earth (**solar eclipse**), or of the moon when the earth's shadow is cast upon it (**lunar eclipse**) 2. a dimming or extinction, as of fame —*vt.* **eclipsed**′, **eclips**′**ing** 1. to cause an eclipse of 2. to overshadow or surpass

ecliptic *n.* the apparent annual path of the sun; great circle on the celestial sphere —*adj.* of eclipses or the ecliptic

eclogue (ek′log) *n.* [see ECLECTIC] a short pastoral poem

eco- [< Gr. *oikos*, house] a combining form meaning environment or habitat [*ecosystem*]

ecology (ē kol′ə jē) *n.* [< Gr. *oikos*, house + *-logia*, -LOGY] the interrelationship of organisms and their environment, or the study of this —**ecological** (ēk′ə loj′i k′l) *adj.* —**ecol**′**ogist** *n.*

econ. 1. economic 2. economics 3. economy

economic (ē′kə nom′ik, ek′ə-) *adj.* 1. of the management of the income, expenditures, etc. of a business, community, etc. 2. of economics 3. of the satisfaction of the material needs of people 4. capable of being used, operated, etc. for profit; profitable

economical *adj.* 1. not wasting money, time, etc. 2. of economics —e'**conom'i-cally** *adv.*

economics *n.pl.* [*with sing. v.*] 1. the science dealing with the production, distribution, and consumption of wealth 2. economic factors

economist (i kon'ə mist) *n.* a specialist in economics

economize (i kon'ə mīz') *vi.* -mized', -miz'ing to reduce waste or expenses —*vt.* to manage or use with thrift (*on*)

economy (i kon'ə mē) *n., pl.* -mies [< Gr. *oikos,* house + *nomos,* managing] 1. management of income, expenditures, etc. 2. *a)* careful management of wealth, resources, etc.; thrift *b)* an instance of this 3. an economic system of a specified kind, place, era, or condition

ecosystem (ē'kō sis'təm, ek'ō-) *n.* [see ECO-] a given community of animals, plants, and bacteria and its interrelated physical and chemical environment

ecru (ā'krōō) *adj., n.* [Fr.] light tan; beige

ecstasy (ek'stə sē) *n., pl.* -sies [< Gr. *ek-,* out + *histanai,* to place] an overpowering feeling of joy; state of rapture —**ecstatic** (ek stat'ik) *adj.*

E.C.T. Electroconvulsive Therapy

ecto- [< Gr. *ektos,* outside] *a combining form meaning* outside, external

-ectomy (ek'tə mē) [< Gr. *ek-,* out + *temnein,* cut] *a combining form meaning* a surgical excision of

ectoplasm (ek'tə plaz'm) *n.* [ECTO- + -PLASM] a luminous substance believed by spiritualists to emanate from the medium in a trance —**ec'toplas'mic** *adj.*

ecumenical (ek'yoo men'i k'l) *adj.* [< Gr. *oikoumenē* (*gē*), the inhabited (world)] 1. general, or universal; esp., of the Christian church as a whole 2. furthering the unity of Christian churches Also **ec'umen'ic** —**ec'umen'icalism** *n.* —**ec'umen'ically** *adv.*

ecumenism (ē kyōō'mə niz'm) *n.* any ecumenical movement: also **ec'umenic'ity** —**ecu'menist** *n.*

eczema (ek'sə mə) *n.* [< Gr. *ek-,* out of + *zein,* boil] a disorder of the skin in which it becomes inflamed, scaly, and itchy —**eczematous** (ek sem'ə təs) *adj.*

-ed (id, əd; d, t) [< OE.] *a suffix used:* a) to form the past tense and past participle of weak verbs [*wanted*] b) to form adjectives from nouns or verbs [*cultured*]

ed. 1. edited 2. edition 3. editor 4. education

Edam (cheese) (ē'dam) [< Du. town of *Edam*] a round, mild, yellow cheese, usually coated with red paraffin

E.D.C. European Defence Community

eddy (ed'ē) *n., pl.* -dies [? < ON. *itha*] 1. a current of air, water, etc. moving with a circular motion against the main current 2. a contrary movement or trend —*vi.* -died, -dying to move in an eddy; whirl

edelweiss (ā'd'l vīs') *n.* [G. < *edel,* noble + *weiss,* white] a small, flowering plant of the Alps

Eden (ē'd'n) *n.* [< Heb. *'ēdhen,* delight] any delightful place: after the garden where Adam and Eve lived

edentate (ē den'tāt) *adj.* [< L. *e-,* out + *dens,* tooth] without teeth —*n.* any of an order of mammals with molars only or no teeth at all, as sloths and anteaters

edge (ej) *n.* [OE. *ecg*] 1. the sharp, cutting part of a blade 2. sharpness; keenness 3. a projecting ledge, as of a cliff 4. a border; margin; brink 5. [Colloq.] advantage [you have the *edge* on me] —*vt.* **edged, edg'ing** 1. *a)* to put an edge on *b)* to trim the edge of 2. to make (one's way) sideways 3. to move gradually or cautiously —*vi.* to move sideways or gradually —**on edge** nervously irritable or impatient —**set one's teeth on edge** 1. to give a sensation of tingling discomfort 2. to irritate —**take the edge off** to dull the intensity or pleasure (of) —**edg'er** *n.*

edgeways *adv.* with the edge foremost: also **edge'wise** —**get a word in edgeways** to manage to say something in a conversation monopolized by others

edging *n.* something forming an edge

edgy *adj.* -ier, -iest 1. irritable; on edge 2. having an edge; sharp —**edg'ily** *adv.* —**edg'iness** *n.*

edible (ed'ə b'l) *adj.* [< L. *edere,* eat] fit to be eaten —*n.* anything fit to be eaten —**ed'ibil'ity** (-bil'ə tē) *n.*

edict (ē'dikt) *n.* [< L. *e-,* out + *dicere,* say] a public proclamation issued by authority; decree

edifice (ed'ə fis) *n.* [see ff.] 1. a building, esp. a large, imposing one 2. any complicated organization

edify (ed'ə fī') *vt.* -fied', -fy'ing [< L. *aedificare,* build] to instruct so as to improve morally or spiritually —**ed'ifica'tion** (-fi kā'shən) *n.* —**ed'ifi'er** *n.*

edit (ed'it) *vt., vi.* [< EDITOR] 1. to prepare (a manuscript, etc.) for publication by selecting, revising, etc. 2. to govern the policy (of a newspaper or periodical) 3. to prepare (a film, tape, etc.) for presentation by cutting, rearranging, etc. 4. to alter written or recorded material, esp. for propaganda purposes

edit. 1. edited 2. edition 3. editor

edition (i dish'ən) *n.* [see ff.] 1. a form in which a book is published 2. the total number of copies of a book published at the same time 3. another version of something already existing [a younger *edition* of her mother]

editor (ed'i tər) *n.* [< L. *e-,* out + *dare,* give] 1. a person who edits 2. a writer of editorials 3. the head of a newspaper, or of a department of a newspaper, magazine, etc. —**ed'itorship'** *n.*

editorial (ed'ə tôr'ē əl) *adj.* of or by an editor —*n.* a statement of opinion in a newspaper —**ed'ito'rially** *adv.*

EDP electronic data processing

E.D.T. [US & Canad.] Eastern Daylight Time

educable (ed'yoo kə b'l) *adj.* that can be educated or trained —**ed'ucabil'ity** *n.*

educate (ed'yoo kāt') *vt.* **-cat'ed, -cat'-ing** [< L. *e-*, out + *ducere*, lead] to train, teach, instruct, or develop, esp. by formal schooling —**ed'uca'tor** *n.*

educated *adj.* 1. having education 2. based on experience

education (ed'yoo kā'shən) *n.* 1. an educating or a being educated 2. knowledge, etc. thus developed 3. a particular kind of instruction [a university *education*] 4. study of the methods of teaching and learning —**ed'uca'tional, ed'-ucative** *adj.* —**ed'uca'tionally** *adv.*

educe (ē dyoōs') *vt.* **-duced', -duc'ing** [see EDUCATE] 1. to draw out; elicit 2. to infer from data; deduce

Edwardian (ed wôr'dē ən) *adj.* of the reign of any of the English kings named Edward, esp. Edward VII

-ee (ē) [< OFr.] *a n.-forming suffix designating:* 1. the recipient of a specified action [*appointee*] 2. a person in a specified condition [*employee*]

E.E.C. European Economic Community

EEG electroencephalogram

eel (ēl) *n.* [OE. æl] a snakelike fish with a long, slippery body and no pelvic fins —**eel'like', eel'y** *adj.*

e'en (ēn) *adv.* [Poet.] even —*n.* [Poet.] even(ing)

e'er (âər) *adv.* [Poet.] ever

-eer (ēər) [< L.] *a suffix meaning* one that has to do with, or an action involving [*mountaineer, electioneer*]

eerie, eery (ēər'ē) *adj.* **-rier, -riest** [< OE. *earg*, timid] weird or uncanny —**ee'-rily** *adv.* —**ee'riness** *n.*

efface (i fās') *vt.* **-faced', -fac'ing** [< L. *ex*, out + *facies*, face] 1. to wipe out; erase [to *efface* a memory] 2. to make (oneself) inconspicuous —**efface'a-ble** *adj.* —**efface'ment** *n.* —**effac'er** *n.*

effect (ə fekt') *n.* [< L. *ex-*, out + *facere*, do] 1. anything brought about by a cause; result 2. the power to produce results 3. influence or action [a cathartic *effect*] 4. general meaning; purport [he spoke to this *effect*] 5. the impression produced, as by artistic design 6. the condition of being in force [a law now in *effect*] 7. [*pl.*] belongings —*vt.* to bring about; cause —**in effect** 1. in result; actually 2. in essence; virtually —**take effect** to begin to produce results —**effect'er** *n.*

effective *adj.* 1. producing a desired effect 2. operative 3. actual, not theoretical 4. making a striking impression 5. equipped and ready for combat —**effec'tively** *adv.* —**effec'tiveness** *n.*

effectual (ə fek'choo wəl) *adj.* 1.

producing the desired effect 2. having legal force; valid —**effec'tually** *adv.*

effeminate (i fem'ə nət) *adj.* [< L. *ex-*, out + *femina*, woman] having the appearance or qualities attributed to women; unmanly —**effem'inacy** *n.*

efferent (ef'ər ənt) *adj.* [< L. *ex-*, out + *ferre*, bear] *Physiol.* carrying away, specif., designating nerves that carry impulses away from a nerve centre

effervesce (ef'ər ves') *vi.* **-vesced', -vesc'ing** [< L. *ex-*, out + *fervere*, boil] 1. to give off gas bubbles, as lemonade 2. to be lively —**ef'ferves'cence, ef'fer-ves'cency** *n.* —**ef'ferves'cent** *adj.* —**ef'fer-ves'cently** *adv.*

effete (i fēt') *adj.* [L. *effetus*, exhausted by bearing] 1. decadent, soft, etc. 2. no longer able to produce; sterile —**effete'-ly** *adv.* —**effete'ness** *n.*

efficacious (ef'ə kā'shəs) *adj.* [see EFFECT] producing or capable of produc-ing the desired effect; effective —**ef'fica'-ciously** *adv.* —**efficacy** (ef'i kə sē) *n.*

efficient (ə fish'ənt) *adj.* [see EFFECT] producing a desired effect with the least effort or waste —**effi'ciency** *n.*

effigy (ef'ə jē) *n.,* *pl.* **-gies** [< L. *ex-*, out + *fingere*, to form] a statue or likeness —**burn** (or **hang**) **in effigy** to burn (or hang) a despised person's effigy in public

effloresce (ef'lô res') *vi.* **-resced', -resc'-ing** [< L. *ex-*, out + *florescere*, to blossom] 1. to blossom out; flower 2. *Chem.* to develop a powdery crust by evaporation or chemical change —**ef'flores'cence** *n.*

effluence (ef'loo wəns) *n.* [< L. *ex-*, out + *fluere*, flow] 1. a flowing out 2. a thing that flows out —**ef'fluent** *adj., n.*

effluvium (i floo'vē əm) *n.,* *pl.* **-via** [see prec.] an emanation; esp., a disagreeable or foul vapour or odour

effort (ef'ərt) *n.* [< L. *ex-*, intens. + *fortis*, strong] 1. physical or mental exertion 2. a try; attempt 3. a result of trying; achievement —**ef'fortless** *adj.* —**ef'fortlessly** *adv.* —**ef'fortlessness** *n.*

effrontery (i frun'tər ē) *n.,* *pl.* **-teries** [< L. *ex-*, from + *frons*, forehead] unashamed boldness; impudence

effulgence (i ful'jəns) *n.* [< L. *ex-*, forth + *fulgere*, shine] great brightness; radi-ance —**efful'gent** *adj.*

effuse (i fyooz') *vt., vi.* **-fused', -fus'ing** [< L. *ex-*, out + *fundere*, pour] to pour, or spread, out or forth

effusion *n.* 1. unrestrained expression in words 2. a pouring forth

effusive (i fyoo'siv) *adj.* too demonstra-tive gushing —**effu'sively** *adv.* —**effu'sive-ness** *n.*

eft (eft) *n.* [OE. *efeta*] same as NEWT

EFTA European Free Trade Association

e.g. [L. *exempli gratia*] for example

egad (ē gad') *interj.* [prob. < *oh God*] [Obs.] a softened or euphemistic oath

egalitarian (i gal'ə tãər'ē ən) *adj.* [< Fr. *égalité*, equality] of or for equal rights for all —*n.* an advocate of equal rights —**egal'itar'ianism** *n.*

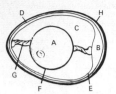

HEN'S EGG
(A, yolk; B, air space; C, white; D,
outer shell membrane; E, inner shell
membrane; F, chalaza-bearing
membrane; G, chalaza; H, shell)

egg¹ (eg) *n.* [ON.] 1. an oval body laid by a female bird, fish, etc. containing the germ of a new individual 2. a female reproductive cell; ovum 3. a hen's egg, raw or cooked 4. [Colloq.] a person [a bad *egg*] —**egg′y** *adj.*

egg² *vt.* [< ON. *eggja*, lit., to give edge to] to urge or incite (*on*)

egghead *n.* [Slang] an intellectual

eggnog *n.* [*egg* + *nog*, strong ale] a drink of beaten eggs, milk, sugar, and nutmeg, often with rum, brandy, etc.

eggplant *n.* 1. a plant with a large, ovoid, purple-skinned fruit eaten as a vegetable 2. the fruit: also called **aubergine**

eggshell *n.* the shell of an egg —*adj.* 1. fragile and thin 2. having a slight gloss: said of paint

eglantine (eg′lən tīn′) *n.* [< L. *aculeus*, a sting] a wild rose with hooked spines and sweet-scented leaves

ego (ē′gō, eg′ō) *n., pl.* **e′gos** [L., I] 1. the self; the individual as aware of himself 2. egotism; conceit 3. *Psychoanalysis* the part of the psyche which governs action rationally

egocentric (eg′ō sen′trik) *adj.* self-centred

egoism (eg′ō iz′m) *n.* 1. the tendency to be self-centred 2. self-conceit; egotism 3. the doctrine that self-interest is the proper goal of all human actions —**e′goist** *n.* —**e′gois′tic, e′gois′tical** *adj.*

egotism (eg′ə tiz′m) *n.* 1. constant, excessive reference to oneself in speaking or writing 2. self-conceit —**e′gotist** *n.* —**e′gotis′tic, e′gotis′tical** *adj.*

ego trip [Colloq.] an act, project, etc. undertaken to boost one's own image or devoted entirely to one's own interests

egregious (i grē′jəs) *adj.* [L. *egregius* outstanding < *e-*, out + *grex*, a herd] remarkably bad; flagrant —**egre′giously** *adv.* —**egre′giousness** *n.*

egress (ē′gres) *n.* [< L. *e-*, out + *gradi*, go] 1. a going out 2. the right to go out 3. a way out; exit

egret (ē′gret) *n.* [< OFr. *aigrette*] a heronlike wading bird, usually with long, white plumes

Egypt. Egyptian

Egyptian (i jip′shən) *adj.* of Egypt —*n.*

1. a native of Egypt 2. the language of the ancient Egyptians

Egyptology (ē′jip tol′ə jē) *n.* the study of ancient Egyptian culture, language, etc. —**E′gyptol′ogist** *n.*

eh (ā, e, en) *interj.* a sound expressing surprise or inquiry

EHF extremely high frequency

eider (ī′dər) *n.* [< ON. *æthr*] a large sea duck of northern regions: often **eider duck**

eiderdown *n.* 1. the soft, fine breast feathers of the eider duck, used to stuff quilts, etc. 2. a quilt so stuffed

eight (āt) *adj.* [OE. *eahta*] totalling one more than seven —*n.* 1. the cardinal number between seven and nine; 8; VIII 2. anything having eight units or members, specif., the crew of a racing rowing boat; —**have one over the eight** [Colloq.] to be intoxicated

eighteen (ā′tēn′) *adj., n.* [OE. *eahtatiene*] eight more than ten; 18; XVIII —**eight′-eenth′** *adj., n.*

eightfold (āt′fōld′) *adj.* 1. having eight parts 2. having eight times as much or as many —*adv.* eight times as much or as many

eighth (ātth) *adj.* 1. preceded by seven others in a series; 8th 2. designating any of eight equal parts —*n.* 1. the one following the seventh 2. any of the eight equal parts of something; 1/8 —**eighth′-ly** *adv.*

eightsome (reel) a Scottish reel for eight dancers

eighty *adj., n.* [OE. *(hund)eahtatig*] eight times ten; 80; LXXX —**the eighties** from the numbers or years, as of a century, from eighty to eighty-nine —**eight′ieth** *adj., n.*

einsteinium (īn stī′nē əm) *n.* [< A. *Einstein*] a radioactive chemical element: symbol, Es

eisteddfod (ī steth′vod) *n.* [W., a sitting < *eistedd*, sit] a yearly meeting in Wales of poets, musicians, etc., at which prizes are given

either (ī′thər) [OE. *æghwæther*] 1. one or the other (of two) [use *either* hand] 2. each (of two) [*either* end of the room] —*pron.* one or the other (of two) —*conj.* a correlative used with *or*, implying a choice of alternatives [*either* go or stay] —*adv.* any more than the other; also (after negatives) [if he won't, she won't *either*]

ejaculate (i jak′yōo lāt′) *vt., vi.* -**lat′ed,** -**lat′ing** [< L. *e-*, out + *jacere*, throw] 1. to eject (esp. semen) 2. to utter suddenly; exclaim —**ejac′ula′tion** *n.* —**ejac′ulatory** *adj.*

eject (ē jekt′) *vt.* [< L. *e-*, out + *jacere*, throw] 1. to throw out; expel; discharge 2. to drive out; evict —**eject′able** *adj.* —**ejec′tion** *n.* —**ejec′tive** *adj.* —**ejec′tor** *n.*

ejection seat a seat, esp. as fitted in military aircraft, that ejects the occupant in an emergency: also **ejector seat**

eke (ēk) *vt.* **eked, ek′ing** [OE. *eacan*, to increase] 1. to supplement 2. to make (a living) with difficulty **3.** to use (a supply) frugally (with *out*)

EKG electrocardiogram

elaborate (i lab'ər ət; *for v.* -ərāt') *adj.* [< L. e-, out + *laborare*, labour] developed in great detail; complicated —*vt.* -rat'ed, -rat'ing **1.** to produce by effort **2.** to work out in careful detail —*vi.* to state in detail or add details (*on* or *upon*) —elab'orately *adv.* —elab'orateness *n.* —elab'o-ra'tion *n.*

élan (ā län') *n.* [Fr.] spirited self-assurance; dash

eland (ē'lənd) *n.* [Du., elk] either of two large, oxlike African antelopes with spirally twisted horns

elapse (i laps') *vi.* elapsed', elaps'ing [< L. e-, out + *labi*, glide] to slip by; pass: said of time

elastic (i las'tik) *adj.* [< Gr. *elaunein*, to drive] **1.** able to return to its original size, shape, or position after being stretched, squeezed, etc. **2.** able to recover easily from dejection; buoyant **3.** adaptable —*n.* an elastic fabric with strands of rubber, etc. running through it —elas'tically *adv.* —elasticity (e'las'-tis'ə tē) *n.*

elasticate (-kāt') *vt.* -cat'ed, -cat'ing to make (a fabric or part of a garment) elastic by inserting elastic sections or thread —elas'tica'tion *n.*

elastic band *same as* RUBBER BAND

elate (i lāt') *vt.* -lat'ed, -lat'ing [< L. *elatus*, < *ex-*, out + *ferre*, bear] to raise the spirits of; make very proud, happy, etc. —elat'edly *adv.* —ela'tion *n.*

ELBOW (sense 2)

elbow (el'bō) *n.* [OE. *elboga*] **1.** the joint between the upper and lower arm; esp., the outer angle made by a bent arm **2.** anything bent like an elbow, as a pipe fitting —*vt., vi.* to shove with the elbow —**bend** (or **lift**) **one's elbow** to drink alcoholic liquor, esp. to excess —**out at (the) elbows** shabby or poor

elbow grease [Colloq.] vigorous physical effort

elbowroom *n.* sufficient space or scope

elder¹ (el'dər) *adj.* [OE. *ald*, old] born or brought forth earlier than another; senior; older —*n.* **1.** an older person, esp. one with authority in a community **2.** an ancestor **3.** an officer in an early Christian church and in some Protestant churches —**eld'ership**'*n.*

elder² *n.* [OE. *ellern*] a shrub or tree with clusters of white flowers and red or purple berries

elderberry *n.*, *pl.* -ries **1.** *same as* ELDER² **2.** its berry, or drupe, used in wines, etc.

elderly *adj.* somewhat old; approaching old age

eldest *adj.* oldest; esp., first-born or oldest surviving

El Dorado, Eldorado (el'də rä'dō) *pl.* -dos [Sp., the gilded] **1.** a legendary country rich in gold and jewels **2.** any place supposed to be rich in opportunity, etc.

eldritch (el'drich) *adj.* [< ?] eerie; unearthly

elec., elect. 1. electric **2.** electrical **3.** electricity

elect (i lekt') *adj.* [< L. e-, out + *legere*, choose] **1.** chosen **2.** elected but not yet installed in office [the mayor-*elect*] **3.** *Theol.* chosen by God for salvation —*vt., vi.* **1.** to select for some office by voting **2.** to choose —**the elect** *Theol.* those who are elect

election (i lek'shən) *n.* **1.** a choosing or being chosen for office by vote **2.** a choosing or choice

electioneer (i lek'shə nēr') *vi.* to canvass votes for a candidate, party, etc. in an election —elec'tioneer'ing *n.*

elective (i lek'tiv) *adj.* **1.** filled by election [an *elective* office] **2.** chosen by election **3.** having the power to choose **4.** optional —elec'tively *adv.*

elector *n.* **1.** one who elects; specif., a qualified voter **2.** [*usually* E-] any of the German princes of the Holy Roman Empire who elected the emperor —elec'-toral *adj.*

electorate *n.* all those qualified to vote in an election

electric (i lek'trik) *adj.* [< Gr. *ēlektron*, amber (orig., produced from amber by rubbing)] **1.** of, charged with, or conducting electricity **2.** producing or produced by electricity **3.** operated by electricity **4.** exciting; electrifying —*n.* **1.** a train, car, etc. operated by electricity **2.** [*pl.*] electrical equipment, esp. the wiring of a house, office, etc.

electrical *adj.* **1.** *same as* ELECTRIC **2.** connected with the science of electricity —elec'trically *adv.*

electric blanket a blanket containing an element that is heated electrically

electric chair 1. a chair used in electrocuting persons sentenced to death **2.** the death sentence by electrocution

electric eel a large, eel-shaped fish of N S. America, with special organs that can give electric shocks

electric eye *same as* PHOTOELECTRIC CELL

electric fire a domestic appliance that supplies heat by means of an electrically operated metal coil

electrician (i lek'trish'ən) *n.* a person whose work is the repair or installation of electric apparatus

electricity (i lek'tris'ə tē) *n.* **1.** a form of energy occurring in certain fundamental particles of all matter, as electrons (negative charges) and protons or positrons (positive charges) **2.** an electric current **3.** the branch of physics dealing with electricity **4.** electric current used for lighting, heating, etc. **5.** strong emotional tension, excitement, etc.

electric shock the effect of an electric current passing through the body

electrify (i lek′trə fī′) *vt.* **-fied′**, **-fy′ing** 1. to equip for the use of electricity 2. to charge with electricity 3. to give an electric shock to 4. to excite; thrill —**elec′**-**trifi′able** *adj.* —**elec′trifica′tion** *n.* —**elec′**-**trifi′er** *n.*

electro- *a combining form meaning* electric, electricity

electrocardiogram (i lek′trō kär′dē ə-gram′) *n.* [ELECTRO- + CARDIO- + -GRAM] a tracing showing the changes in electric potential produced by contractions of the heart

electrocardiograph (-kär′dē ə gräf′) *n.* an instrument for making an electro-cardiogram

electroconvulsive therapy (i lek′-trō kən vul′siv) *see* SHOCK THERAPY

electrocute (i lek′trə kyōōt′) *vt.* **-cut′ed**, **-cut′ing** [ELECTRO- + (EXE)CUTE] to kill or execute with a charge of electricity —**elec′trocu′tion** *n.*

electrode (i lek′trōd) *n.* [ELECTR(O-) + Gr. *hodos*, way] any terminal that conducts an electric current into or away from a battery, etc., or that controls the flow of electrons in an electron tube

electrodynamics (i lek′trō dī nam′iks) *n.pl.* [*with sing. v.*] the branch of physics dealing with the phenomena of electric currents and associated magnetic forces

electroencephalogram (i lek′trō en-sef′ə ləgram′) *n.* [< ELECTRO- + Gr. *enkephalos*, brain + -GRAM] a tracing showing the changes in electric potential produced by the brain

electroencephalograph (-en sef′ə lə-gräf′) *n.* an instrument for making electro-encephalograms

electrolyse (i lek′trō līz′) *vt.* **-lysed′**, **-lys′ing** to subject to electrolysis

electrolysis (i lek′trol′ə sis) *n.* [ELECTRO- + -LYSIS] 1. the decomposition of an electrolyte by the action of an electric current passing through it 2. the removal of unwanted hair with an electrified needle

electrolyte (i lek′trō līt′) *n.* [ELECTRO- + -LYTE] any substance which in solution can conduct an electric current by the movement of its dissociated ions to electrodes, where the ions are deposited as a coating, liberated as a gas, etc. —**elec′**-**trolyt′ic** *adj.*

electromagnet (i lek′trō mag′nit) *n.* a soft iron core surrounded by a coil of wire, that temporarily becomes a magnet when an electric current flows through the wire

electromagnetism *n.* 1. magnetism produced by an electric current 2. the branch of physics dealing with the relations between electricity and magnetism

electromotive (i lek′trō mōt′iv) *adj.* producing an electric current through differences in potential

electromotive force the force that causes a current to flow in a circuit, equivalent to the potential difference between the terminals

electron (i lek′tron) *n.* [< ELECTR(IC) + -ON] any of the negatively charged particles that form a part of all atoms

electronic (i lek′tron′ik) *adj.* 1. of electrons 2. operating, produced, or done by the action of electrons —**elec′tron′i**-**cally** *adv.*

electronic brain [Colloq.] an electronic computer

electronic data processing data processing by means of electronic equipment, esp. computers

electronic music music in which the sounds are originated by electronic devices and recorded on tape

electronic organ a musical instrument producing tones by means of electronic devices instead of organ pipes

electronics *n.pl.* [*with sing. v.*] the science that deals with the behaviour and control of electrons and with the use of electron tubes, transistors, etc.

electron microscope an instrument for focusing a beam of electrons to form an enlarged image of an object on a fluorescent screen or photographic plate

electron tube a sealed glass or metal tube completely evacuated or filled with gas and having two or more electrodes, used to control the flow of electrons

electron-volt *n.* a unit of energy equal to that attained by an electron falling unimpeded through a potential difference of one volt

electroplate (i lek′trō plāt′) *vt.* **-plat′ed**, **-plat′ing** to deposit a coating of metal on by electrolysis —*n.* anything so plated

electroshock therapy *see* SHOCK THERAPY

electrostatics (i lek′trō stat′iks) *n.pl.* [*with sing. v.*] the branch of physics dealing with the phenomena accompanying electric charges at rest, or static electricity —**elec′**-**trostat′ic** *adj.* —**elec′trostat′ically** *adv.*

electrotherapy (i lek′trō ther′ə pē) *n.* the treatment of disease by electricity, as by diathermy —**elec′trother′apist** *n.*

electrotype (i lek′trō tīp′) *n. Printing* a facsimile plate made by electroplating a wax or plastic impression of the surface to be reproduced

electrum (i lek′trəm) *n.* [< Gr. *ēlektron*: see ELECTRIC] a light-yellow alloy of gold and silver

elegant (el′ə gənt) *adj.* [L. *elegans* < e-, out + *legere*, choose] 1. characterized by dignified richness and grace; tastefully luxurious 2. refined in manners and tastes —**el′egance** *n.* —**el′egantly** *adv.*

elegiac (el′ə jī′ak) *adj.* 1. of or like an elegy 2. sad; mournful 3. *Prosody* of or composed in dactylic hexameter couplets Also **el′egi′acal** —*n.* 1. an elegiac couplet 2. [*pl.*] a poem written in such couplets

elegy (el′ə jē) *n., pl.* **-gies** [< Gr. *elegos*, a lament] 1. a mournful poem or song, esp. of lament and praise for the dead 2. any poem in elegiac verse —**el′egist** *n.*

element (el′ə mənt) *n.* [< L. *elementum*] 1. *Chem.* any substance that cannot be separated into different substances by ordinary chemical methods **2.** *a)* a component part or quality, often one that is basic or essential *b)* a constituent group of a specified kind *[the criminal element]* **3.** the natural or suitable environment for a person or thing **4.** *Elec.* the wire coil, etc. that becomes glowing hot, as in an electric oven **5.** any of the four substances (earth, air, fire, water) formerly believed to constitute all physical matter **6.** *[pl.]* *Eccles.* the bread and wine of Communion —**in one's element** in the surroundings most pleasing and natural for one —**the elements 1.** the first or basic principles; rudiments **2.** wind, rain, etc.; forces of the atmosphere

elemental (el′ə men′t'l) *adj.* **1.** basic and powerful; primal *[hunger is an elemental drive]* **2.** of or like the forces of nature **3.** of the four elements —**el′emen′talism** *n.*

elementary (el′ə men′tər ē) *adj.* of first principles; introductory; basic —**el′emen′tarily** *adv.* —**el′emen′tariness** *n.*

elementary particle a subatomic particle that is capable of independent existence, as a neutron, proton, etc.

elementary school same as PRIMARY SCHOOL

AFRICAN

INDIAN

ELEPHANTS
(shoulder height:
African, 3-4 m; Indian 2.5-3 m)

elephant (el′ə fənt) *n.* [< Gr. *elephas*] the largest of extant four-footed animals, with a long, flexible snout (*trunk*) and, usually, two ivory tusks: the **African elephant** has a flatter head and larger ears than the **Indian elephant**

elephantiasis (el′ə fan tī′ə sis) *n.* a chronic disease of the skin characterized by the enlargement of the legs etc., and by the hardening of the skin

elephantine (el′ə fan′tīn) *adj.* **1.** of an elephant **2.** like an elephant; huge, heavy, slow, etc.

elevate (el′ə vāt′) *vt.* **-vat′ed, -vat′ing** [< L. *e-*, out + *levare*, lift] **1.** to lift up **2.** to raise in rank or position **3.** to raise to a higher intellectual or moral level **4.** to raise the spirits of; exhilarate

elevation (el′ə vā′shən) *n.* **1.** an elevating or being elevated **2.** a high position **3.** a

height above the surface of the earth **4.** a flat scale drawing of the front, rear, or side of a building **5.** *Astron.* altitude **6.** *Geog.* height above sea level **7.** *Mil.* the angle of a gun with the horizontal

elevator (el′ə vāt′ər) *n.* **1.** [U.S.] a lift **2.** a machine for hoisting grain **3.** [Chiefly U.S.] a warehouse for storing and discharging grain **4.** a movable aerofoil for making an aircraft go up or down

eleven (i lev′ən) *adj.* [OE. *endleofan*] totalling one more than ten —*n.* **1.** the cardinal number between ten and twelve; 11; XI **2.** a football or cricket team —**elev′-enth** *adj., n.*

eleven-plus *n.* an examination used, esp. formerly, to determine the form of secondary education: taken by children about eleven years old

elevenses (-ən ziz) *n.pl.* [Colloq.] a light snack, usually with tea or coffee, taken in the middle of the morning

elf (elf) *n., pl.* **elves** (elvz) [OE. *ælf*] **1.** *Folklore* a tiny, often prankish fairy **2.** a mischievous, small child or being —**elf′-ish** *adj.* —**elf′ishly** *adv.* —**elf′ishness** *n.*

elfin *adj.* of or like an elf; fairylike

elicit (i lis′it) *vt.* [< L. *elicere*] to draw forth; evoke (a reply, the truth, etc.) —**elic′ita′tion** *n.* —**elic′itor** *n.*

elide (i līd′) *vt.* **elid′ed, elid′ing** [< L. *e-*, out + *laedere*, strike] to leave out or slur over (a vowel, syllable, etc.) in pronunciation —**elid′ible** *adj.*

eligible (el′i jə b'l) *adj.* [see ELECT] **1.** fit to be chosen; qualified **2.** desirable, esp. for marriage —**el′igibil′ity** *n.* —**el′igibly** *adv.*

eliminate (i lim′ə nāt′) *vt.* **-nat′ed, -nat′-ing** [< L. *e-*, out + *limen*, threshold] **1.** to get rid of **2.** to leave out of consideration; omit **3.** to drop (a team, etc. losing a round) from further competition **4.** *Algebra* to get rid of (an unknown quantity) by combining equations **5.** *Physiol.* to excrete —**elim′i-na′tion** *n.* —**elim′inative** *adj.* —**elim′ina′-tor** *n.* —**elim′inatory** *adj.*

elision (i lizh′ən) *n.* the eliding of a vowel, syllable, etc. in pronunciation (Ex.: it's, they'd, we've)

élite (ā lēt′) *n.* [< Fr.: see ELECT] **1.** the group or part of a group selected or regarded as the best, most powerful, etc. **2.** a size of type for typewriters, measuring 12 characters to the inch

élitism *n.* government or control by an élite —**élit′ist** *adj., n.*

elixir (i lik′sər) *n.* [< ML. < Ar.] **1.** a hypothetical substance sought for by medieval alchemists to change base metals into gold or (**elixir of life**) to prolong life indefinitely **2.** a cure-all **3.** a medicine made of drugs in alcoholic solution, usually sweetened

Elizabethan (i liz′ə bē′thən) *adj.* of or characteristic of the reign of Elizabeth I —*n.* an English person, esp. a writer, of the time of Elizabeth I

elk (elk) *n.* [OE. *eolh*] a large, mooselike

deer of N Europe and Asia, with broad antlers

ell (el) *n.* [OE. *eln*] *Hist.* a measure equal to 115 cm

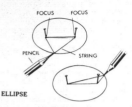

ELLIPSE

ellipse (i lips') *n.,* *pl.* **-lip′ses** [< Gr. *elleipein,* fall short (of a circle)] *Geom.* the path of a point that moves so that the sum of its distances from two fixed points is constant

ellipsis (i lip′sis) *n.,* *pl.* **-ses** (-sēz) [see prec.] **1.** *Gram.* the omission of a word or words understood in the context (Ex.: "if possible" for "if it is possible") **2.** a mark (. . .) indicating an omission of words or letters

ellipsoid *n.* *Geom.* a solid whose plane sections are all ellipses or circles —*adj.* shaped like an ellipsoid

elliptical (i lip′ti k′l) *adj.* **1.** of, or having the form of, an ellipse **2.** of or characterized by ellipsis; with a word or words omitted Also **ellip′tic** —**ellip′tically** *adv.*

elm (elm) *n.* [OE.] **1.** a tall, hardy tree **2.** the hard, heavy wood of this tree

elocution (el′ə kyoo′shən) *n.* [see ELOQUENT] **1.** style of speaking or reading in public **2.** the art of public speaking —**el′ocu′tionary** *adj.* —**el′ocu′tionist** *n.*

elongate (ē′loŋ gāt) *vt., vi.* **-gated, -gat-ing** [< L. *e-,* out + *longus,* long] to make or become longer; stretch —**e′lon-gated** *adj.* —**elongation** (ē loŋ′gā′shən) *n.*

elope (i lōp′) *vi.* **eloped′, elop′ing** [Anglo-Fr. *aloper*] to run away secretly, esp. in order to get married —**elope′ment** *n.* —**elop′er** *n.*

eloquence (el′ə kwəns) *n.* **1.** speech or writing that is forceful, fluent, etc. **2.** the art of such speech or writing

eloquent *adj.* [< L. *e-,* out + *loqui,* speak] **1.** having eloquence **2.** vividly expressive —**el′oquently** *adv.*

Elsan (el′san) *Trademark* a type of chemical lavatory

else (els) *adj.* [OE. *elles*] **1.** different; other [somebody *else*] **2.** in addition [is there anything *else?*] —*adv.* **1.** differently; otherwise [where *else* can I go?] **2.** if not [study, (or) *else* you will fail]

elsewhere *adv.* in or to some other place

elucidate (i loo′sə dāt′) *vt., vi.* **-dat′ed, -dat′ing** [< L. *e-,* out + *lucidus,* clear] to make clear; explain —**elu′cida′tion** *n.* —**elu′cida′tive** *adj.* —**elu′cida′tor** *n.*

elude (i lood′) *vt.* **elud′ed, elud′ing** [< L. *e-,* out + *ludere,* play] **1.** to avoid or escape from by quickness, cunning,

etc. **2.** to escape detection, notice, or understanding by **3.** to slip away from [his name *eludes* me] —**elud′er** *n.* —**elu′-sion** *n.*

elusive *adj.* **1.** tending to elude **2.** hard to grasp; baffling Also **elu′sory** —**elu′-sively** *adv.* —**elu′siveness** *n.*

elver (el′vər) *n.* [for *eelfare,* migration of eels] a young eel

elves (elvz) *n.* *pl.* of ELF

elvish (el′vish) *adj.* of or like an elf —**elv′-ishly** *adv.*

Elysium (i liz′ē əm) *n.* [L. < Gr.] any condition of complete happiness: after the dwelling place of virtuous people after death in Greek mythology: also **Elysian Fields**

em (em) *n.* **1.** the letter M, m **2.** *Printing* a square of any type body, used as a unit of measure

'em (əm, 'm) *pron.* [Colloq.] them

emaciate (i mā′shē āt′, -sē-) *vt.* **-at′ed, -at′ing** [< L. *e-,* out + *macies,* leanness] to cause to become abnormally lean, as by starvation —**ema′cia′tion** *n.*

emanate (em′ə nāt′) *vi.* **-nat′ed, -nat′ing** [< L. *e-,* out + *manare,* flow] to come forth; issue —**em′ana′tion** *n.*

emancipate (i man′sə pāt′) *vt.* **-pat′ed, -pat′ing** [< L. *e-,* out + *manus,* hand + *capere,* take] **1.** to free from restraint or restriction, esp. to remove social or legal disadvantages from **2.** to set free (a slave, etc.) —**eman′cipa′tion** *n.* —**eman′cipatory** *adj.* —**eman′cipa′tor** *n.*

emasculate (i mas′kyə lāt′; *for adj.,* -lit) *vt.* **-lat′ed, -lat′ing** [< L. *e-,* out + *masculus,* masculine] **1.** to deprive (a male) of the power to reproduce; castrate **2.** to destroy the strength or force of —*adj.* deprived of virility or vigour —**emas′cula′tion** *n.* —**emas′culatory** *adj.* —**emas′cula′tor** *n.*

embalm (im bäm′) *vt.* [see EN- & BALM] **1.** to preserve (a dead body) with various chemicals **2.** to preserve in memory **3.** to perfume —**embalm′er** *n.*

embankment (im baŋk′mənt) *n.* a bank of earth or rubble to keep back water, hold up a road, railway, etc.

embargo (em bär′gō) *n.,* *pl.* **-goes** [Sp., ult. < L. *in-,* on + ML. *barra,* bar] **1.** a government order prohibiting the entry or departure of commercial ships at its ports **2.** any restraint, or prohibition, esp. one imposed on commerce by law —*vt.* **-goed, -going** to put an embargo on

embark (im bärk′) *vt.* [< L. *in,* in + *barca,* small boat] to put or take aboard a ship, aeroplane, etc. —*vi.* **1.** to go aboard a ship, aeroplane, etc. **2.** to begin a journey, enterprise, etc. —**em′barka′tion** *n.*

embarrass (im bar′əs) *vt.* [< Fr. < It. *in-* + *barra,* bar] **1.** to cause to feel self-conscious; disconcert **2.** to hinder **3.** to cause to be in debt **4.** to complicate —**embar′rassing** *adj.* —**embar′rassment** *n.*

embassy (em′bə sē) *n.,* *pl.* **-sies** [see AMBASSADOR] **1.** the official residence or offices of an ambassador **2.** the position or functions of an ambassador **3.** any important or official mission

embattle (im bat′′l) *vt.* **-tled, -tling** to prepare or set in line for battle

embed (im bed′) *vt.* **-bed′ded, -bed′ding 1.** to fix firmly in a surrounding mass **2.** to fix in the mind, etc.

embellish (im bel′ish) *vt.* [< OFr. *em-*, in + *bel,* beautiful] **1.** to decorate; adorn **2.** to improve (a story, etc.) by adding details, often fictitious —**embel′lishment** *n.*

ember¹ (em′bər) *n.* [< OE. *æmerge*] **1.** a glowing piece of coal, wood, etc. from a fire **2.** [*pl.*] the smouldering remains of a fire

ember² *adj.* [< OE. *ymbryne,* a circuit] [*often* E-] designating or of three days set aside for prayer and fasting in a specified week of each season of the year

embezzle (im bez′′l) *vt.* **-zled, -zling** [< OFr. < *en-* + *besillier,* destroy] to steal (money, etc. entrusted to one's care) —**embez′zlement** *n.* —**embez′zler** *n.*

embitter (im bit′ər) *vt.* to cause to have bitter or more bitter feelings —**embit′terment** *n.*

emblazon (im blā′z′n) *vt.* [see BLAZON] **1.** to decorate (*with* coats of arms, etc.) **2.** to display brilliantly **3.** to praise —**embla′zonment** *n.*

emblem (em′bləm) *n.* [< Gr. *emblēma,* insertion < *en-,* in + *ballein,* throw] **1.** an object that stands for or suggests something else **2.** a sign; badge —**em′blemat′ic** *adj.*

embodiment (im bod′ē mənt) *n.* that in which some idea, quality, etc. is embodied [she is the *embodiment* of virtue]

embody (im bod′ē) *vt.* **-bod′ied, -bod′ying 1.** to give bodily form to **2.** to give definite form to **3.** to bring together into a whole; incorporate [the latest findings *embodied* in the new book]

embolden (im bōl′d′n) *vt.* to cause to be bold or bolder

embolism (em′bə liz′m) *n.* *Med.* the obstruction of a blood vessel by an embolus

embolus (em′bə ləs) *n., pl.* **-li′** (-lī′) [< Gr. *en-,* in + *ballein,* throw] any foreign matter, as a blood clot, carried in the bloodstream —**embol′ic** (-bol′ik) *adj.*

emboss (em bos′) *vt.* [see EN- & BOSS²] **1.** to decorate with raised designs **2.** to raise (a design, etc.) in relief —**emboss′er** *n.* —**emboss′ment** *n.*

embrace (em brās′) *vt.* **-braced′, -brac′ing** [< L. *im-,* in + *brachium,* arm] **1.** to clasp in the arms lovingly; hug **2.** to accept readily [to *embrace* an opportunity] **3.** to take up [to *embrace* a profession] **4.** to encircle **5.** to include **6.** to perceive —*vi.* to clasp each other in the arms —*n.* an embracing; hug —**embrace′able** *adj.* —**embrac′er** *n.*

embrasure (im brā′zhər) *n.* [Fr. < *embraser,* widen an opening] **1.** an opening (for a window, etc.) with the sides slanted so that it is wider on the inside than on the outside **2.** an opening in a parapet with the sides slanting outwards to increase the angle of fire of a gun

embrocate (em′brō kāt′) *vt.* **-cat′ed, -cat′ing** [< Gr. *en-,* in + *brechein,* to wet] to moisten and rub (a part of the body) with an oil, liniment, etc. —**em′broca′tion** *n.*

embroider (im broi′dər) *vt., vi.* [< OFr. *embroder*] **1.** to ornament (fabric) with a design in needlework **2.** to embellish (a story, etc.) —**embroi′derer** *n.*

embroidery *n., pl.* **-deries 1.** the art of embroidering **2.** embroidered work or fabric **3.** embellishment, as of a story

embroil (im broil′) *vt.* [see EN- & BROIL²] **1.** to confuse (affairs, etc.); mix up; muddle **2.** to draw into a conflict or fight; involve in trouble —**embroil′ment** *n.*

embryo (em′brē ō′) *n., pl.* **-os′** [< Gr. *en-,* in + *bryein,* swell] **1.** an animal in the earliest stages of development in the uterus **2.** *a)* an early stage of something *b)* anything in such an early stage **3.** the rudimentary plant contained in a seed —*adj.* embryonic

embryonic (-on′ik) *adj.* **1.** of or like an embryo **2.** in an early stage; rudimentary

emeer (e mēər′) *n.* same as EMIR —**emeer′ate** *n.*

emend (ē mend′) *vt.* [< L. *e-,* out + *mendum,* a fault] to make scholarly corrections or improvements in (a text) —**e′menda′tion** *n.*

emerald (em′ər əld) *n.* [< Gr. *smaragdos*] **1.** a bright-green precious stone; variety of beryl **2.** bright green —*adj.* bright-green

Emerald Isle [< its green landscape] Ireland

emerge (i murj′) *vi.* **emerged′, emerg′ing** [< L. *e-,* out + *mergere,* dip] **1.** to rise as from a fluid **2.** to become visible, apparent or known **3.** to develop as something new, improved, etc. [a strong breed *emerged*] —**emer′gence** *n.* —**emer′gent** *adj.*

emergency (i mur′jən sē) *n., pl.* **-cies** [orig. sense, an emerging] an unexpected occurrence or situation demanding immediate action —*adj.* for use in case of sudden necessity [an *emergency* exit]

emeritus (ē mer′ə təs) *adj.* [L. *e-,* out + *mereri,* serve] retired from active service, but retaining one's rank or title [professor *emeritus*]

emersion (ē mur′shən) *n.* an emerging

emery (em′ər ē) *n.* [< Gr. *smyris*] a dark variety of corundum used for grinding, polishing, etc.

emery board a strip of cardboard or wood with a rough surface of crushed emery used for filing the nails

emetic (i met′ik) *adj.* [< Gr. *emein,* to vomit] causing vomiting —*n.* an emetic substance

E.M.F., e.m.f., EMF, emf electromotive force

emigrate (em′ə grāt′) *vi.* **-grat′ed, -grat′ing** [< L. *e-,* out + *migrare,* move] to leave one country or region to settle in another —**em′igrant** *adj., n.* —**em′igra′tion** *n.*

émigré, emigré (em′ə grā′) *n.* [Fr.] **1.**

an emigrant **2.** a person forced to flee his country for political reasons

eminence (em'ənəns) *n.* [< L. *eminere*, stand out] **1.** a high place, thing, etc. **2.** superiority in rank, position, etc. **3.** [E-] *R.C.Ch.* a title of honour used of a cardinal

‡**éminence grise** (ā mē näns grēz') [Fr., grey eminence] a person who wields great power and influence unofficially

eminent (em'ənənt) *adj.* standing high by comparison with others; exalted; distinguished; noteworthy —**em'inently** *adv.*

emir (e mēər') *n.* [Ar. *amīr*, commander] in certain Moslem countries, a ruler —**emir'ate** *n.*

emissary (em'ə sər ē) *n.*, *pl.* -**saries** [see EMIT] a person, esp. a secret agent, sent on a specific mission

emission (i mish'ən) *n.* **1.** an emitting; issuance **2.** something emitted; discharge —**emis'sive** *adj.*

emit (i mit') *vt.* **emit'ted, emit'ting** [< L. *e-*, out + *mittere*, send] **1.** to give forth **2.** to utter (sounds) —**emit'ter** *n.*

Emmenthal (em'ən täl') *n.* [< valley in Switzerland] a hard Swiss cheese full of holes

emollient (i mol'yənt) *adj.* [< L. *e-*, out + *mollire*, soften] softening; soothing —*n.* an emollient preparation, esp. for the surface tissues of the body

emolument (i mol'yoo mənt) *n.* [< L. *e-*, out + *molere*, grind] gain from employment; salary, fees, etc.

emote (i mōt') *vi.* **emot'ed, emot'ing** [Colloq.] to express emotion in a showy or theatrical manner

emotion (i mō'shən) *n.* [< L. *e-*, out + *movere*, move] **1.** strong feeling; excitement **2.** any specific feeling, as love, hate, fear, anger, etc.

emotional *adj.* **1.** of the emotions **2.** showing emotion **3.** easily aroused to emotion **4.** appealing to or arousing the emotions —**emo'tionally** *adv.*

emotive (i mōt'iv) *adj.* **1.** expressing or producing emotion **2.** relating to the emotions —**emo'tively** *adv.*

Emp. 1. Emperor **2.** Empire **3.** Empress

empanel (im pan'']) *vt.* -**elled, -elling** to enter the name of on a jury list

empathy (em'pə thē) *n.* [< Gr. *en-*, in + *pathos*, feeling] Intellectual or emotional identification with another —**empathetic** (em'pə thet'ik) *adj.*

emperor (em'pər ər) *n.* [< L. *imperator* < *imperare*, to command] the supreme ruler of an empire

emperor penguin the largest penguin, growing to 1.3 m

emphasis (em'fə sis) *n.*, *pl.* -**ses'** (-sēz') [< Gr. *en-*, in + *phainein*, show] **1.** force of expression, action, etc. **2.** stress given to a syllable, word, etc. in speaking **3.** importance given to something; stress

emphasize *vt.* -**sized', -siz'ing** to give emphasis, or special force, to; stress

emphatic (im fat'ik) *adj.* **1.** expressed or done with emphasis **2.** using emphasis

in speaking, etc. **3.** forcible; definite [an *emphatic* defeat] —**emphat'ically** *adv.*

empire (em'pīər) *n.* [see EMPEROR] **1.** a) a group of states under the sovereignty of an emperor or empress *b*) a state uniting many territories under one ruler *c*) [E-] the British Empire **2.** government by an emperor or empress **3.** supreme rule; absolute power **4.** an extensive economic organization under the control of a single person

empire builder a person who ruthlessly seeks to extend the scope and power of his authority

empirical (em pir'i k'l) *adj.* [< Gr. *en-*, in + *peira*, trial] **1.** relying on experiment and observation rather than theory **2.** relying on practical experience without reference to scientific principles —**empir'ically** *adv.*

empiricism *n.* **1.** the search for knowledge by observation and experiment **2.** *Philos.* the theory that experience is the only source of knowledge —**empir'icist** *n.*

emplacement (im plās'mənt) *n.* **1.** placement **2.** the position in which something is placed; specif., *Mil.* the prepared position from which guns are fired

emplane (em plān') *vi.* -**planed', -plan'-ing** same as ENPLANE

employ (im ploi') *vt.* [< L. *implicare*, enfold] **1.** to engage the services or labour of for pay; hire **2.** to provide work and pay for **3.** to keep occupied **4.** to use —*n.* the state of being employed; employment —**employ'able** *adj.*

employee (im ploi'ē, em'ploi ē') *n.* a person hired to work for wages or salary

employer (im ploi'ər) *n.* one who employs others to work for wages or salary

employment *n.* **1.** an employing or being employed **2.** work; occupation; job

emporium (em pôr'ē əm) *n.*, *pl.* -**riums, -ria** [< Gr. *en-*, in + *poros*, way] **1.** a trading centre; marketplace **2.** a large store or shop

empower (im pou'ər) *vt.* to authorize; enable

empress (em'pris) *n.* **1.** the wife of an emperor **2.** a woman ruler of an empire

empty (emp'tē) *adj.* -**tier, -tiest** [< OE. *æmettig*, unoccupied] **1.** having nothing or no one in it; unoccupied **2.** worthless [*empty* pleasures] **3.** insincere [*empty* promises] **4.** [Colloq.] hungry —*vt.* -**tied, -tying 1.** to make empty **2.** to remove (the contents) of something **3.** to discharge (oneself or itself) —*vi.* **1.** to become empty **2.** to discharge —*n.*, *pl.* -**ties** an empty container, esp. a bottle —**empty of** lacking; without —**emp'tily** *adv.* —**emp'tiness** *n.*

empty-handed (emp'tē han'did) *adj.* bringing or carrying away nothing

empty-headed (emp'tē hed'id) *adj.* silly and ignorant

empyrean (em'pī rē'ən) *n.* [< Gr. *en-*, in + *pyr*, fire] **1.** the highest heaven **2.** the sky —**empyr'eal** *adj.*

EMS European Monetary System

EMU (to 1.5 m high)

emu (ē′myōō) *n.* [< Port.] a large, flightless Australian bird

emulate (em′yoolāt′) *vt.* -lat′ed, -lat′ing [< L. *aemulus*, trying to equal] 1. to try to equal or surpass 2. to imitate (a person admired) 3. to rival successfully —em′ula′tion *n.* —em′ulative *adj.* —em′-ula′tor *n.*

emulous *adj.* 1. desirous of equalling or surpassing 2. caused by emulation —em′ulously *adv.*

emulsify (imul′safī′) *vt., vi.* -fied′, -fy′-ing to form into an emulsion —emul′sifi-ca′tion *n.*

emulsion (imul′shən) *n.* [< L. *e-*, out + *mulgere*, to milk] 1. a fluid, as milk, formed by the suspension of one liquid in another 2. a medicine or paint in this form 3. *Photog.* a suspension of a salt of silver in gelatin, used to coat film —emul′sive *adj.*

en (en) *n.* 1. the letter N, n 2. *Printing* a space half the width of an em

en- (in, en) [< L.] *a prefix meaning:* 1. to put or get into or on [*entrain*] 2. to make, cause to be [*endanger, enfeeble*] 3. in or into [*enclose*]

-en (ən, ′n) [< OE.] *a suffix:* 1. *meaning:* a) to become or cause to be [*weaken*] b) to cause to have [*strengthen*] c) made of [*woollen*] 2. *used to form plurals* [*children*] 3. *used to form diminutives* [*chicken*]

enable (inā′b′l) *vt.* -bled, -bling to make able; provide with means, opportunity, power, etc. (*to* do something)

enabling act a bill or act giving power to take action

enact (in akt′) *vt.* 1. to decree; ordain 2. to perform in or as in a play —enac′-tive *adj.* —enac′tor *n.*

enactment *n.* 1. an enacting or being enacted 2. something enacted, as a law

enamel (inam′′l) *n.* [< OFr. *esmail*] 1. a glassy, opaque substance fused to metals, etc., as an ornamental or protective coating 2. the hard, white coating of a tooth 3. anything enamelled 4. paint or varnish with a hard, glossy surface when it dries —*vt.* -elled, -elling to inlay, cover, or decorate with enamel —enam′eller, enam′-ellist *n.*

enamour (in am′ər) *vt.* [< OFr. *en-*, + *amour*, love] to fill with love and desire; charm; captivate: now mainly in the passive voice, with *of* [much *enamoured* of her]

en bloc (on blok′) [Fr., in a block] in one lump; as a whole; all together

enc., encl. enclosure

encamp (in kamp′) *vt., vi.* to set up or put in a camp —encamp′ment *n.*

encapsulate (in kap′syoolāt′) *vt.* -lat′ed, -lat′ing 1. to enclose in a capsule 2. to condense; abridge Also **encap′sule** —encap′sula′tion *n.*

encase (in kās′) *vt.* -cased′, -cas′ing 1. to enclose 2. to put into a case —encase′-ment *n.*

encaustic (en kôs′tik) *adj.* [< Gr. *en-*, in + *kaiein*, burn] done by burning in or applying heat —*n.* a method of painting in which colours in wax are fused to a surface with hot irons —encaus′tically *adv.*

-ence (əns, ′ns) [< OFr. & L.] *a suffix meaning* act, quality, state, result, or degree [*conference, excellence*]

‡**enceinte** (änsant′) *adj.* [Fr.] pregnant

encephalitis (en′sef ə līt′is) *n.* [< ENCEPHALO- + -ITIS] inflammation of the brain —enceph′alit′ic (-lit′ik) *adj.*

encephalo- [< Gr. *enkephalos*, brain] *a combining form meaning* of the brain

encephalogram (en sef′ō lō gram′) *n.* same as ELECTROENCEPHALOGRAM

enchain (in chān′) *vt.* 1. to fetter 2. to captivate

enchant (in chänt′) *vt.* [see INCANTATION] 1. to cast a spell over; bewitch 2. to charm greatly; delight —enchant′er *n.* —enchant′ing *adj.* —enchant′ment *n.* —enchant′ress *n.fem.*

encircle (in sur′k′l) *vt.* -cled, -cling 1. to surround 2. to move in a circle around —encir′clement *n.*

enclave (en′klāv) *n.* [< L. *in*, in + *clavis*, key] a territory surrounded by the territory of a foreign country

enclose (in klōz′) *vt.* -closed′, -clos′ing 1. to shut in all around; surround 2. to insert in an envelope, wrapper, etc., often together with something else

enclosure *n.* 1. an enclosing or being enclosed 2. something that encloses 3. something enclosed; specif., a) an enclosed place b) a document, money, etc. enclosed as with a letter

encomium (en kō′mē əm) *n.,* pl. -miums, -mia [< Gr. *en-*, in + *kōmos*, a revel] a formal expression of high praise; eulogy; panegyric

encompass (in kum′pəs) *vt.* 1. to surround 2. to contain; include —encom′-passment *n.*

encore (oŋ′kôr, on kôr′) *interj.* [Fr.] again —*n.* 1. a demand by the audience for further performance 2. the performance in answer to such a demand —*vt.* -cored, -coring to demand further performance of or by

encounter (in koun′tər) *vt.* [< L. *in*, in + *contra*, against] 1. to meet unexpectedly 2. to meet in conflict —*n.* 1. an unexpected meeting 2. a meeting in conflict

encourage (in kur′ij) *vt.* -aged, -aging 1.

to give courage, hope, or confidence to
2. to give support to; help —**encour′age-
ment** *n.* —**encour′aging** *adj.*

encroach (in krōch′) *vi.* [< OFr. *en-*, in
+ *croc*, a hook] to trespass or intrude
(*on* or *upon*) —**encroach′ment** *n.*

encrust (in krust′) *vt., vi.* same as
INCRUST

encumber (in kum′bər) *vt.* [see EN- &
CUMBER] **1.** to hold back the motion
or action of; hinder **2.** to weigh down;
burden —**encum′berment** *n.*

encumbrance *n.* a hindrance; burden

-ency (ən sē, ′n sē) [< L.] a suffix meaning
act, quality, state, result, or degree
[*dependency, emergency*]

encyclical (in sik′li k′l) *adj.* [< Gr. *en-*,
in + *kyklos*, circle] for general circulation:
also **encyc′lic** —*n.* R.C.Ch. a letter from
the Pope to the bishops

encyclopedia, encyclopaedia (in sī′-
klō pē′dē ə) *n.* [< Gr. *enkyklios*, general
+ *paideia*, education] a book or set of
books giving information on one or on
many branches of knowledge, generally
alphabetically arranged —**ency′clope′dic,
ency′clopae′dic** *adj.* —**ency′clope′dically,
ency′clopae′dically** *adv.*

encyclopedist, encyclopaedist *n.* **1.**
a person who compiles an encyclopedia
2. [E-] [*pl.*] the writers of the French
Encyclopedia, edited by Diderot and
d'Alembert

end (end) *n.* [OE. *ende*] **1.** a limit; boundary
2. the last part of anything; conclusion
3. a ceasing to exist; death or destruction
4. the part at or near an extremity **5.**
a purpose; object **6.** an outcome; result
7. a remnant [odds and ends] **8.** the
limit of endurance, etc. —*vt., vi.* to bring
or come to an end; finish; stop —*adj.*
at the end; final [end product] —**end
it all** [Colloq.] to commit suicide —**end
of steel** [Canad.] **1.** a point up to which
railway tracks have been laid **2.** a town
at such a point —**ends of the earth** remote
regions —**make (both) ends meet** to keep
one's expenses within one's income —**no
end** [Colloq.] extremely —**on end 1.**
in an upright position **2.** without
interruption [for days on end] —**put an
end to 1.** to stop **2.** to do away with
—**the end** [Colloq.] the worst, esp.
something beyond the limits of endurance

endanger (in dān′jər) *vt.* to expose to
danger or loss

endear (in dēar′) *vt.* to make dear or
beloved

endearing *adj.* **1.** that makes dear or
well liked **2.** expressing affection
[*endearing* tones]

endearment *n.* **1.** a word or act
expressing affection **2.** warm liking;
affection

endeavour (in dev′ər) *vi.* [< EN- + OFr.
deveir, duty] to make an earnest attempt
—*vt.* to try (*to* do something) —*n.* an
earnest attempt or effort Also, U.S. sp.,
endeav′or

endemic (en dem′ik) *adj.* [< Gr. *en-*, in
+ *dēmos*, the people] **1.** native to a

particular country, region, etc. **2.** restricted
to and present in a particular locality:
said of a disease —*n.* an endemic plant,
animal, or disease —**endem′ically** *adv.*
—**endemicity** (en′də mis′ə tē) *n.*

ending (en′diŋ) *n.* **1.** *a)* the last part;
finish *b)* death **2.** Gram. the final letter
or letters added to a word base

endive (en′div) *n.* [< Gr. *entybon*] a
plant with curled, narrow leaves used in
salads

endless *adj.* **1.** having no end; eternal
2. lasting too long [an endless speech]
3. continual [endless interruptions] **4.**
with the ends joined to form a unit that
can move continuously over wheels, etc.
[an endless belt] —**end′lessly** *adv.* —**end′-
lessness** *n.*

endmost *adj.* at the end; farthest; last

endocrine (en′dō krīn) *adj.* [< Gr. *endon,*
within + *krinein*, to separate] designating
or of any gland producing a secretion
carried in the blood to other parts of
the body whose functions it regulates —*n.*
any such gland or its secretion, as the
thyroid, adrenal, and pituitary glands

endogenous (en doj′ə nəs) *adj.* [< Gr.
endon, within + -GENOUS] developing
from within

endorsation (en′dôr sā′shən) *n.*
[Canad.] approval; support

endorse (in dôrs′) *vt.* -**dorsed′,** -**dors′ing**
[< L. *in,* on + *dorsum,* the back] **1.**
to give approval to; sanction **2.** to write
on the back of (a document); specif., to
sign (one's name) as payee on the back
of (a cheque, etc.) **3.** to record an offence
on a driving licence, etc. —**endorse′ment**
n. —**endors′er** *n.*

endow (in dou′) *vt.* [< OFr. *en-,* in +
douer < L. *dotare,* endow] **1.** to give
money or property so as to provide an
income for the support of (a college,
hospital, etc.) **2.** to provide with some
talent, quality, etc. [endowed with courage]

endowment *n.* **1.** an endowing **2.** that
with which something is endowed; bequest
3. a talent, ability, etc.

endowment assurance an insurance
policy by which a stated amount is paid
to the assured after the period specified
or to the beneficiaries if the assured dies
within the time specified: also **endowment
insurance**

end paper the stout paper used in book
binding to cover the inner sides of the
cover and provide fly leaves

end product the final result of any series
of changes, processes, or chemical reactions

endue (in dyōō′) *vt.* -**dued′,** -**du′ing** [see
INDUCE] to provide (*with* qualities, talents,
etc.)

endurance (in dyooər′əns) *n.* **1.** an
enduring **2.** ability to last or remain **3.**
ability to stand pain, fatigue, etc.; fortitude

endure (in dyooər′) *vt.* -**dured′,** -**dur′ing**
[< L. *in-,* in + *durus,* hard] **1.** to bear
(pain, fatigue, etc.) **2.** to put up with;
tolerate —*vi.* **1.** to last; remain **2.** to
bear pain, etc. without flinching —**endur′-
able** *adj.*

enduring adj. lasting; permanent; durable

endways adv. 1. on end; upright 2. with the end foremost 3. lengthways 4. end to end Also **end′wise′**

enema (en′ə mə) n. [< Gr. en-, in + hienai, send] 1. a liquid injected into the colon through the anus, as a purgative, medicine, etc. 2. such an injection

enemy (en′ə mē) n., pl. -mies [< L. in-, not + amicus, friend] 1. a person who hates another and wishes to injure him 2. a) a nation hostile to another b) a soldier, citizen, etc. of a hostile nation 3. one hostile to an idea, cause, etc. 4. anything opposing —adj. of an enemy

energetic (en′ər jet′ik) adj. of, having, or showing energy; vigorous; forceful —en′erget′ically adv.

energize (en′ər jīz′) vt. -gized′, -giz′ing to give energy to; invigorate; activate —en′ergiz′er n.

energy (en′ər jē) n., pl. -gies [< Gr. en-, in + ergon, work] 1. force of expression 2. capacity for action 3. effective power 4. Physics the capacity for doing work and overcoming resistance

enervate (en′ər vāt′) vt. -vat′ed, -vat′ing [< L. e-, out + nervus, nerve] to deprive of strength, force, vigour, etc. —en′erva′tion n. —en′erva′tor n.

‡enfant terrible (än fän te rē′bl′) [Fr.] 1. a person who causes trouble or embarrassment by his imprudent remarks or actions 2. an unmanageable child

enfeeble (in fē′bl) vt. -bled, -bling to make feeble —enfee′blement n.

enfilade (en′fə lād′) n. [Fr. < enfiler, to thread] gunfire directed from either flank along the length of a line of troops —vt. -lad′ed, -lad′ing to direct such gunfire at (a column, etc.)

enfold (in fōld′) vt. 1. to wrap in folds; envelop 2. to embrace —enfold′ment n.

enforce (in fôrs′) vt. -forced′, -forc′ing 1. to compel observance of (a law, etc.) 2. to impose by force [to enforce one's will on a child] 3. to give force to —enforce′able adj. —enforce′ment n. —enforc′er n.

enfranchise (in fran′chīz) vt. -chised, -chising 1. to admit to citizenship, esp. to the right to vote 2. to free from slavery 3. to give (a town) the right to be represented in parliament —enfran′chisement (-chiz mənt) n.

Eng. 1. England 2. English

eng. 1. engineer(ing) 2. engraved 3. engraving

engage (in gāj′) vt. -gaged′, -gag′ing [see EN- & GAGE] 1. to pledge (oneself); specif. (now only in the passive), to bind by a promise of marriage 2. to hire 3. to reserve [to engage a hotel room] 4. to involve, as in conversation 5. to attract and hold (the attention, etc.) 6. to keep busy; occupy 7. to enter into conflict with (the enemy) 8. to interlock [engage the gears] —vi. 1. to pledge oneself; promise 2. to involve oneself [to engage in dramatics] 3. to enter into conflict 4. to interlock

engaged adj. 1. pledged, esp. betrothed 2. occupied, busy, or in use 3. involved in combat 4. in gear

engagement n. an engaging; specif., a) a betrothal b) an appointment or commitment c) employment, esp. in the performing arts d) a battle e) state of being in gear

engaging adj. attractive; winning; charming —engag′ingly adv.

engender (in jen′dər) vt. [< L. in-, in + generare, generate] to bring into being; cause; produce

engine (en′jən) n. [< L. ingenium, genius < in-, in & gignere, produce] 1. any machine that uses energy to develop mechanical power; esp., one for starting motion in some other machine 2. a railway locomotive 3. any instrument or apparatus [engines of torture] 4. same as FIRE ENGINE

engineer (en′jə nēar′) n. 1. a person skilled in some branch of engineering 2. an operator of technical equipment [a radio engineer] 3. Mil. a member of the armed forces concerned with the construction and demolition of bridges, roads, etc. —vt. 1. to plan, construct, or manage as an engineer 2. to direct skilfully [to engineer a business merger]

engineering n. 1. the science concerned with putting scientific knowledge to practical uses 2. the planning, designing, or construction of machinery, roads, buildings, etc.

English (iŋ′glish) adj. [OE. Englisc, of the Angles] 1. of England 2. of the English language —n. the language of the people of England, the official language of Britain, the British Commonwealth, the U.S., etc. —the English the people of England

English horn same as COR ANGLAIS

Englishman n. a native or inhabitant of England —Eng′lishwom′an n.fem.

engorge (in gôrj′) vt., vi. -gorged′, -gorg′ing 1. to eat gluttonously 2. Med. to congest with blood or other fluid

engraft (in gräft′) vt. 1. to graft (a shoot, etc.) from one plant onto another 2. to implant

engrave (in grāv′) vt. -graved′, -grav′ing [< Fr. en-, in + graver, incise] 1. to cut or etch (letters, designs, etc.) in or on (a metal plate, wooden block, etc.) for printing 2. to impress deeply on the mind or memory —engrav′er n.

engraving n. 1. the act, process, or art of one who engraves 2. a print made from an engraved surface

engross (in grōs′) vt. [see EN- & GROSS] 1. to occupy the attention of; absorb 2. to write in the large letters once used for legal documents 3. to express in legal form —engross′er n. —engross′ing adj., n. —engross′ment n.

engulf (in gulf′) vt. to swallow up; overwhelm

enhance (in häns′) vt. -hanced′, -hanc′ing [ult. < L. in, in + altus, high] to make greater; heighten —**enhance'ment** n. —**enhanc'er** n.

enigma (ə nig'mə) n., pl. **-mas** [< Gr. *ainigma*] 1. a riddle 2. a perplexing or baffling matter, person, etc. —**enigmatic** (en'ig mat'ik) adj. —e'nigmat'ically adv.

enjoin (in join') vt. [< L. in-, + jungere, join] 1. to order; enforce 2. to prohibit, esp. by legal injunction

enjoy (in joi') vt. [< OFr. enjoir] 1. to have or experience with joy or pleasure 2. to have the use of 3. to experience [to enjoy good health] —**enjoy oneself** to have a good time —**enjoy'able** adj. —**enjoy'ableness** n. —**enjoy'ably** adv. —**enjoy'ment** n.

enkindle (in kin'd'l) vt. **-dled, -dling** 1. to set on fire; make blaze up 2. to stir up; arouse

enlarge (in lärj') vt. **-larged', -larg'ing** 1. to make larger; increase in size, volume, extent, etc.; expand 2. Photog. to reproduce on a larger scale —vi. 1. to become larger; increase 2. to discuss at greater length (with on or upon) —**enlarge'ment** n. —**enlarg'er** n.

enlighten (in līt''n) vt. 1. to give clarification to (a person); inform 2. to free from ignorance, prejudice, or superstition

enlightenment n. an enlightening —**the Enlightenment** an 18th-cent. European philosophical and social movement characterized by rationalism

enlist (in list') vt., vi. 1. to enrol in some branch of the armed forces 2. to engage in a cause or movement (with in) —**enlist'ee'** n. —**enlist'ment** n.

enliven (in lī'v'n) vt. to make active, vivacious, interesting, or cheerful —**enliv'ener** n. —**enliv'enment** n.

en masse (on mas') [Fr.] in a group; all together

enmesh (en mesh') vt. to catch in or as in the meshes of a net; entangle

enmity (en'mə tē) n., pl. **-ties** [see ENEMY] the attitude or feelings of an enemy; hostility

ennoble (i nō'b'l) vt. **-bled, -bling** 1. to raise to the rank of nobleman 2. to dignify —**enno'blement** n.

ennui (on'wē) n. [Fr.] weariness and dissatisfaction resulting from inactivity or lack of interest; boredom —**ennuyé** (on wē'yā) adj.

enormity (i nôr'mə tē) n., pl. **-ties** [< L. e-, out + norma, rule] 1. great wickedness [the enormity of a crime] 2. a very wicked crime 3. enormous size or extent

enormous (i nôr'məs) adj. very much exceeding the usual size, number, or degree; huge; vast —**enor'mously** adv. —**enor'mousness** n.

enough (i nuf') adj. [OE. genoh] as much or as many as necessary; sufficient —n. the amount or number needed —adv. 1. sufficiently 2. fully; quite [oddly enough] 3. just adequately; fairly [he played well enough]

enow (i nou') adj., n., adv. [Archaic] enough

‡**en passant** (än på sän') [Fr.] in passing; by the way

enplane (en plān') vi. **-planed', -plan'ing** to board an aeroplane

enquire (in kwīr') vt., vi. **-quired', -quir'ing** same as INQUIRE —**enquir'y** n., pl. **-quir'ies**

enrage (in rāj') vt. **-raged', -rag'ing** to put into a rage

enrapture (in rap'chər) vt. **-tured, -turing** to fill with great pleasure or delight

enrich (in rich') vt. to make richer; specif., a) to give more wealth to b) to give greater value to c) to decorate d) to fertilize (soil) e) to add vitamins, minerals, etc. to (bread, etc.) f) Physics to increase the concentration of an isotope in a mixture —**enrich'ment** n.

enrol (in rōl') vt. **-rolled', -roll'ing** 1. to record in a list 2. to enlist 3. to accept as a member —vi. to enrol oneself; become a member —**enrol'ment** n.

en route (on root') [Fr.] on or along the way

ensconce (in skons') vt. **-sconced', -sconc'ing** [EN- + SCONCE²] to place or settle snugly

ensemble (on som'b'l) n. [< L. in-, in + simul, at the same time] 1. all the parts considered as a whole; total effect 2. a whole costume of complementary articles of dress 3. a company of actors, dancers, etc. 4. Music a small group of musicians performing together

enshrine (in shrīn') vt. **-shrined', -shrin'ing** 1. to enclose in or as in a shrine 2. to hold sacred; cherish

enshroud (in shroud') vt. to cover as if with a shroud; hide; veil; obscure

ensign (en'sīn; for 4 always, -s'n) n. [see INSIGNIA] 1. a badge or symbol 2. a banner; specif., a national flag 3. Brit. Army formerly, a commissioned officer who served as standard-bearer 4. U.S. Navy a commissioned officer of the lowest rank —**en'signship', en'signcy** n.

ensilage (en'sil ij) n. [Fr.] 1. the preserving of green fodder by storage in a silo 2. green fodder so preserved; silage

enslave (in slāv') vt. **-slaved', -slav'ing** 1. to make a slave of 2. to dominate —**enslave'ment** n. —**enslav'er** n.

ensnare (in snâr') vt. **-snared', -snar'ing** to catch in or as in a snare; trap —**ensnare'ment** n.

ensue (in syōō') vi. **-sued', -su'ing** [< L. in-, in + sequi, follow] 1. to follow immediately 2. to happen as a consequence; result

‡**en suite** (än swēt') [Fr., in sequence] forming a set, or single unit [with bathroom en suite]

ensure (in shooər') vt. **-sured', -sur'ing** 1. to make sure; guarantee 2. to make safe; protect

E.N.T. Med. Ear, Nose and Throat

-ent (ənt, 'nt) [< L.] 1. a suffix meaning that has, shows, or does [insistent] 2. a suffix meaning a person or thing that [superintendent, solvent].

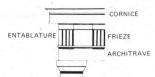

CORNICE
ENTABLATURE
FRIEZE
ARCHITRAVE

entablature (en tab'lə chər) *n.* [< It. *in-*, in + *tavola*, table] *Archit.* a horizontal superstructure supported by columns and composed of architrave, frieze, and cornice

entail (in tāl') *vt.* [< ME. *en-*, in + *taile*, agreement] **1.** to cause as a necessary consequence [the plan *entails* work] **2.** *Law* to limit the inheritance of (property) to a specific line of heirs —*n.* **1.** an entailed inheritance **2.** the order of descent for an entailed inheritance

entangle (in taŋ'g'l) *vt.* -**gled**, -**gling** **1.** to involve in a tangle **2.** to involve in difficulty **3.** to confuse **4.** to complicate —**entan'glement** *n.*

entente (on tänt') *n.* [Fr.] an understanding or agreement, as between nations

entente cordiale (kôr dyäl') [Fr., cordial understanding] a treaty of friendship between nations

enter (en'tər) *vt.* [< L. *intrare*] **1.** to come or go in or into **2.** to force a way into **3.** to insert **4.** to write down in a record, list, etc. **5.** to become a participant in or member of **6.** to get (someone) admitted **7.** to begin (a career, etc.) **8.** to submit [to *enter* a protest] **9.** *Law* to place on record before a court —*vi.* **1.** to come or go into a place **2.** to penetrate —**enter into 1.** to engage in **2.** to form a component of **3.** to deal with; discuss —**enter on** (or **upon**) **1.** to begin **2.** to begin to possess or enjoy

enteric (en ter'ik) *adj.* [< Gr. *enteron,* intestine] intestinal: also **enteral** (en'-tər əl)

enteritis (en'tə rīt'is) *n.* inflammation of the intestine

enterprise (en'tər prīz') *n.* [< OFr. *entreprendre,* undertake] **1.** an undertaking; project, esp. a bold, difficult, dangerous or important undertaking **2.** a business venture **3.** energy and initiative —**en'terpris'er** *n.*

enterprising *adj.* showing enterprise; full of energy and initiative; adventurous —**en'terpris'ingly** *adv.*

entertain (en'tər tān') *vt.* [ult. < L. *inter,* between + *tenere,* hold] **1.** to divert; amuse **2.** to have as a guest **3.** to have in mind; consider —*vi.* to have guests

entertainer *n.* a person who entertains; esp., a popular singer, dancer, comedian, etc.

entertaining *adj.* interesting and pleasurable; amusing —**en'tertain'ingly** *adv.*

entertainment *n.* something that entertains; interesting or amusing thing; esp., a show or performance

enthral (in thrôl') *vt.* -**thralled**, -**thrall'ing** [see EN- & THRALL] to captivate; fascinate —**enthral'ment** *n.*

enthrone (in thrōn') *vt.* -**throned**, -**thron'ing 1.** to place on a throne **2.** to exalt —**enthrone'ment** *n.*

enthuse (in thyo͞oz') *vi.* -**thused'**, -**thus'ing** [back-formation < ff.] [Colloq.] to express enthusiasm —*vt.* [Colloq.] to make enthusiastic

enthusiasm (in thyo͞o'zē az'm) *n.* [< Gr. *enthous,* possessed by a god] intense or eager interest; fervour

enthusiast *n.* a person full of enthusiasm; an ardent supporter, a devotee, etc.

enthusiastic (in thyo͞o'zē as'tik) *adj.* of, having, or showing enthusiasm; ardent —**enthu'sias'tically** *adv.*

entice (in tīs') *vt.* -**ticed'**, -**tic'ing** [< OFr. prob. ult. < L. *in,* in + *titio,* firebrand] to attract by offering hope of reward or pleasure —**entice'ment** *n.*

entire (in tīər') *adj.* [< L. *integer,* whole] **1.** a) not lacking any parts; whole b) complete; absolute **2.** unbroken; intact **3.** being wholly of one piece **4.** not castrated —**entire'ly** *adv.* —**entire'ness** *n.*

entirety (in tīər'tē) *n., pl.* -**ties 1.** wholeness; completeness **2.** an entire thing —**in its entirety** as a whole

entitle (in tīt''l) *vt.* -**tled**, -**tling 1.** to give a right to **2.** to give a title or name to —**enti'tlement** *n.*

entity (en'tə tē) *n., pl.* -**ties** [ult. < L. *esse,* be] **1.** being; existence **2.** a thing that has definite, individual existence in reality or in the mind

entomb (in to͞om') *vt.* to place in a tomb or grave; bury —**entomb'ment** *n.*

entomology (en'tə mol'ə jē) *n.* [< Gr. *entomon,* insect & -LOGY] the branch of zoology that deals with insects —**en'tomolog'ical** (-mə loj'i k'l) *adj.* —**en'tomol'ogist** *n.*

entourage (on'to͞o räzh') *n.* [Fr. < *entourer,* surround] a group of accompanying attendants; retinue

entr'acte (on'trakt) *n.* [Fr. < *entre-,* between + *acte,* an act] **1.** the interval between acts of a play, etc. **2.** music, a dance, etc. performed during this interval

entrails (en'trālz) *n.pl.* [< L. *interaneus,* internal < *inter,* between] **1.** the inner organs of men or animals; specif., the intestines **2.** the inner parts of a thing

entrain (in trān') *vt.* to put aboard a train, esp. troops —*vi.* to go aboard a train —**entrain'ment** *n.*

entrance¹ (en'trəns) *n.* **1.** the act or point of entering **2.** a place for entering; door, gate, etc. **3.** permission or right to enter; admission

entrance² (in träns') *vt.* -**tranced'**, -**tranc'ing 1.** to enchant; charm; enrapture **2.** to put into a trance —**entrance'ment** *n.* —**entranc'ing** *adj.*

entrant (en'trənt) *n.* **1.** a person who enters **2.** one who enters an examination, contest, profession, etc.

entrap (in trap′) *vt.* **-trapped′, -trap′ping**
1. to catch as in a trap **2.** to trick into
difficulty —**entrap′ment** *n.*

entreat (in trēt′) *vt., vi.* [< OFr. see TREAT]
to ask earnestly; beg; implore —**entreat′-
ingly** *adv.*

entreaty (–ē) *n., pl.* **-ies** an earnest
request; plea

entrecôte (on′trə kōt) *n.* [Fr.] a steak
cut from between the ribs

entrée (on′trā) *n.* [Fr.] **1.** the right to
enter **2.** *a)* the main course of a meal
b) formerly, a dish served before the roast

entrench (in trench′) *vt.* **1.** to establish
securely *[entrenched* in office *]* **2.** to
surround or fortify with a trench —*vi.*
to encroach (*on* or *upon*) —**entrench′-
ment** *n.*

entrepreneur (on′trə prə nur′) *n.* [Fr.:
see ENTERPRISE] a person who organizes
a business undertaking, assuming the risk
for the sake of profit

entropy (en′trə pē) *n.* [G. < Gr. *entropē,*
a turning towards] **1.** a measure of the
amount of energy unavailable for work
in a thermodynamic system **2.** a measure
of the degree of disorder in a system,
esp. the universe

entrust (in trust′) *vt.* **1.** to charge with
a trust or duty **2.** to assign the care
of —**entrust′ment** *n.*

entry (en′trē) *n., pl.* **-tries** [see ENTER]
1. *a)* the act of entering *b)* the right
to enter **2.** a way or passage by which
to enter; door, hall, etc. **3.** *a)* the recording
of an item in a list, journal, etc. *b)* an
item thus recorded **4.** one entered in
a race, competition, etc. **5.** *Law* the taking
possession of buildings, etc. by entering

entwine (in twīn′) *vt., vi.* **-twined′, -twin′-
ing** to twine or twist together or around

enumerate (i nyōō′mə rāt′) *vt.* **-at′ed,
-at′ing** [< L. *e-,* out + *numerare,* count]
1. to count **2.** to name one by one; specify,
as in a list —**enu′mera′ble** *adj.* —**enu′mer-
a′tion** *n.* —**enu′merative** *adj.*

enumerator *n.* [Canad.] one who
compiles the voting list for an area

enunciate (i nun′sē āt′) *vi.* **-at′ed, -at′-
ing** [< L. *e-,* out + *nuntiare,* announce]
to pronounce words clearly —*vt.* **1.** to
pronounce (words) **2.** to announce **3.**
to state definitely —**enun′cia′tion** *n.*

enuresis (en′yoo rē′sis) *n.* [< Gr.
enourein, urinate in] bed-wetting —**en′u-
ret′ic** (-ret′ik) *adj.*

envelop (in vel′əp) *vt.* [< OFr. *envoluper*]
1. to wrap up **2.** to surround **3.** to
hide —**envel′opment** *n.*

envelope (en′və lōp′) *n.* [see prec.] **1.**
a folded paper container for letters, etc.
2. a wrapper; covering **3.** the bag that
contains the gas in a dirigible or balloon

enviable (en′vē ə b'l) *adj.* worthy to be
envied or desired —**en′viableness** *n.* —**en′-
viably** *adv.*

envious (en′vē əs) *adj.* [< L. *invidia,* envy]
feeling or showing envy —**en′viously** *adv.*
—**en′viousness** *n.*

environment (in vīə′rən mənt) *n.* [see
ENVIRONS] **1.** surroundings, esp. those

in which people live or work **2.** all the
conditions and influences affecting the
development of an organism —**envi′ron-
men′tal** (-men′t'l) *adj.* —**envi′ronmen′-
tally** *adv.*

environmentalist (in vīə′rən men′t'l ist)
one working to solve environmental
problems, such as pollution

environs (in vīə′rəns) *n.pl.* [< OFr. *en-,*
in + *viron,* circuit] the districts surrounding a city etc.; outskirts

envisage (en viz′ij) *vt.* **-aged, -aging** [<
Fr.: see EN- & VISAGE] **1.** to form an
image of in the mind **2.** to conceive of
as a future possibility; foresee

envoy[1] (en′voi) *n.* [< Fr. < L. *in,* in
+ *via,* way] **1.** a messenger **2.** a diplomatic
agent: an **envoy extraordinary** ranks just
below an ambassador

envoy[2] *n.* [< OFr. see prec.] a postscript
to a poem, essay, or book, containing
a dedication, etc.; also **en′voi**

envy (en′vē) *n., pl.* **-vies** [< L. *invidia*
< *in-,* upon + *videre,* look] **1.** discontent
and ill will because of another's advantages,
possessions, etc. **2.** desire for something
that another has **3.** an object of envious
feeling —*vt.* **-vied, -vying** to feel envy
towards or because of —**en′vyingly** *adv.*

enzyme (en′zīm) *n.* [< G. < Gr. *en-,*
in + *zymē,* leaven] a proteinlike substance
in plant and animal cells, that acts as
an organic catalyst in chemical reactions
—**en′zymat′ic** (-zī mat′ik), **enzy′mic** *adj.*

Eocene (ē′ō sēn′) *adj.* [< Gr. *ēōs,* dawn
+ *kainos,* new] designating or of the
second and longest epoch of the Tertiary
Period in the Cainozoic Era

eolithic (ē′ō lith′ik) *adj.* [< Gr. *ēōs,* dawn
+ *lithos,* stone] designating or of the
early part of the Stone Age

-eous (ēəs) [< L.] *a suffix meaning*
like *[beauteous]*

EP Extended Play

EPAULETS

epaulet, epaulette (ep′ə let′) *n.* [< Fr.
épaule, shoulder] a shoulder ornament,
as on military uniforms

épée (ā pā′) *n.* [Fr. < Gr. *spathē,* blade]
a thin, pointed sword without a cutting
edge, used in fencing

epergne (i purn′) *n.* [Fr.] an ornamental
branched centrepiece for a table

Eph. Ephesians: also **Ephes.**

ephedrine (i fed′rin) *n.* [< Gr. *ephedra,*
horsetail] an alkaloid used to relieve nasal
congestion and asthma

ephemeral (i fem′ər əl) *adj.* [< Gr. *epi-,*
upon + *hēmera,* day] **1.** lasting only
one day **2.** short-lived; transitory
—**ephem′erally** *adv.*

epi- [< Gr. *epi*, at, on] *a prefix meaning* on, upon, over, beside *[epiglottis, epidemic, epidermis]*

epic (ep'ik) *n.* [< Gr. *epos*, word] **1.** a long narrative poem about the deeds of a traditional or historical hero, as the *Iliad* and *Odyssey* **2.** a play, etc. having the qualities of an epic —*adj.* of or like an epic; heroic; majestic: also **ep'ical** —**ep'ically** *adv.*

epicene (ep'əsēn') *adj.* [< Gr. *epi-*, to + *koinos*, common] **1.** belonging to one sex but having characteristics of the other; hermaphroditic **2.** sexless **3.** effeminate, effete —*n.* an epicene person

epicentre (ep'əsen'tər) *n.* **1.** the area of the earth's surface directly above the place of origin of an earthquake **2.** a focal point —**ep'icen'tral** *adj.*

epicure (ep'ikyooər') *n.* [< *Epicurus*] a person who enjoys and has a discriminating taste for fine foods and drinks —**ep'icurism** *n.*

Epicurean (ep'ikyoorē'ən) *adj.* **1.** of Epicurus or his philosophy **2.** [e-] fond of luxury and sensuous pleasure —*n.* **1.** a follower of Epicurus or his philosophy **2.** [e-] an epicure —**Ep'icure'anism,** ep'i**cure'anism** *n.*

epidemic (ep'ədem'ik) *adj.* [< Gr. *epi-*, among + *dēmos*, people] prevalent and spreading rapidly among a community, as a contagious disease: also **ep'idem'ical** —*n.* **1.** an epidemic disease **2.** the epidemic spreading of a disease —**ep'idem'ically** *adv.*

epidemiology (ep'ədē'mēol'əgē) *n.* the science concerned with the control of epidemic diseases —**ep'ide'miol'ogist** *n.*

epidermis (ep'ədur'mis) *n.* [< Gr. *epi-*, upon + *derma*, skin] **1.** the outermost layer of skin **2.** the outermost layer of cells covering plants —**ep'ider'mal** *adj.*

epidiascope (ep'ədī'əskōp') *n.* [EPI- + DIA- + -SCOPE] an optical device for projecting on a screen a magnified image of an opaque or transparent object

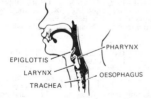

PHARYNX
EPIGLOTTIS
LARYNX   OESOPHAGUS
TRACHEA

epiglottis (ep'əglot'is) *n.* [see EPI- & GLOTTIS] the thin piece of cartilage that folds back over the opening of the windpipe during swallowing —**ep'iglot'tal** *adj.*

epigram (ep'əgram') *n.* [< Gr. *epi-*, upon + *graphein*, write] **1.** a short poem with a witty point **2.** any terse, witty, statement —**epigrammatic** (ep'igrəmat'ik) *adj.*

epigraph (ep'əgräf') *n.* [see EPIGRAM] **1.** an inscription on a building, monument, etc. **2.** a quotation at the beginning of a book, etc.

epilepsy (ep'əlep'sē) *n.* [< Gr. *epi-*, upon + *lambanein*, seize] a chronic disease of the nervous system, characterized by convulsions and, often, unconsciousness

epileptic (ep'əlep'tik) *adj.* of or having epilepsy —*n.* a person who has epilepsy

epilogue (ep'əlog') *n.* [< Gr. *epi-*, upon + *legein*, say] **1.** a closing section of a novel, play, etc., providing further comment **2.** a short speech to the audience by one of the actors at the end of a play

Epiphany (ipif'ənē) *n., pl.* **-nies** [< Gr. *epi-*, upon + *phainein*, show] a Christian festival (January 6) commemorating the revealing of Christ to the Magi

Epis. Epistle

episcopacy (ipis'kəpəsē) *n., pl.* **-cies** [< Gr. *episkopos*, overseer] **1.** church government by bishops **2.** same as EPISCOPATE

episcopal *adj.* **1.** of or governed by bishops **2.** [E-] designating or of any of various churches so governed, as the Anglican Church —**epis'copally** *adv.*

Episcopalian (ipis'kōpāl'yən) *adj.* same as EPISCOPAL —*n.* [*sometimes* e-] a member of an episcopal church —**Epis'copa'lianism** *n.*

episcopate (ipis'kōpət) *n.* **1.** the rank or term of office of a bishop **2.** a bishop's see **3.** bishops collectively

episode (ep'əsōd') *n.* [< Gr. *epi-*, upon + *eis-*, into + *hodos*, way] **1.** any part of a novel, poem, etc. that is complete in itself **2.** any event complete in itself but forming part of a larger one **3.** any instalment of a serial

episodic (ep'əsod'ik) *adj.* **1.** incidental **2.** sporadic Also **ep'isod'ical** —**ep'isod'ically** *adv.*

epistemology (epis'tēmol'əjē) *n., pl.* **-gies** [< Gr. *epistēmē*, knowledge + -LOGY] the study or theory of knowledge —**epis'temolog'ical** (-məloj'ik'l) *adj.*

epistle (ipis'l) *n.* [< Gr. *epi-*, to + *stellein*, to send] **1.** a letter: now used humorously **2.** [E-] *a)* any of the letters of the Apostles in the New Testament *b)* a selection from these, read as part of Mass, Communion, etc. in various churches —**epis'tler** *n.*

epistolary (ipis'tələrē) *adj.* **1.** of or suitable to letters **2.** conducted by letters

epitaph (ep'itäf') *n.* [< Gr. *epi-*, upon + *taphos*, tomb] an inscription on a tomb —**ep'itaph'ic,** ep'itaph'ial *adj.*

epithelium (ep'əthē'lēəm) *n., pl.* **-liums, -lia** [< Gr. *epi-*, upon + *thēlē*, nipple] tissue covering surfaces and lining most cavities of the body —**ep'ithe'lial** *adj.*

epithet (ep'ithet') *n.* [< Gr. *epi-*, on + *tithenai*, put] a word or phrase used to characterize some person or thing (Ex.: Philip the Fair) —**ep'ithet'ical,** ep'ithet'ic *adj.*

epitome (ipit'əmē) *n., pl.* **-mes** [< Gr. *epi-*, upon + *temnein*, cut] **1.** a typical example of a characteristic or class; embodiment **2.** a summary

epitomize vt. **-mized′**, **-miz′ing** to make or be an epitome of —**epit′omiz′er** n.

EPNS Electroplated Nickel Silver

epoch (ē′pok) n. [< Gr. epochē, a pause] 1. the beginning of a new and important period in the history of anything 2. a period considered in terms of noteworthy events, developments, etc. [an epoch of social revolution] 3. Geol. a subdivision of a geologic period —**ep′ochal** adj. —**ep′ochally** adv.

eponym (ep′ō nim′) n. [< Gr. epi-, upon + onyma, a name] a person from whose name the name of a nation, race, etc. is derived [William Penn is the eponym of Pennsylvania] —**eponymous** (i pon′ə-məs) adj.

epoxy (e pok′sē) adj. [EP(I)- + OXY(GEN)] designating or of a compound in which an oxygen atom is joined to two carbon atoms in a chain to form a bridge —n., pl. **-oxies** an epoxy resin

epsilon (ep si′lən) n. the fifth letter of the Greek alphabet (E, ϵ)

Epsom salts (ep′səm) [< Epsom, in Surrey] a white salt, magnesium sulphate, used as a cathartic

equable (ek′wə b'l) adj. [see ff.] 1. not varying much; steady [an equable temperature] 2. serene [an equable temperament] —**eq′uabil′ity** n. —**eq′uably** adv.

equal (ē′kwəl) adj. [< L. aequus, even] 1. of the same quantity, size, value, etc. 2. having the same rights, ability, rank, etc. 3. evenly proportioned 4. having the necessary ability, courage, etc. (to) —n. any thing or person that is equal —vt. **e′qualled**, **e′qualling** 1. to be equal to 2. to do or make something equal to [to equal a record] —**e′qually** adv.

equalitarian (i kwol′ə tãər′ē ən) adj., n. same as EGALITARIAN —**equal′itar′ianism** n.

equality (i kwol′ə tē) n., pl. **-ties** state of being equal

equalize (ē′kwə līz′) vt. **-ized′**, **-iz′ing** to make equal —vi. to become equal, esp., in football, to reach the same score as one's opponents —**e′qualiz′er** n.

equanimity (ek′wə nim′ə tē) n. [< L. aequus, even + animus, mind] calmness of mind; composure

equate (i kwāt′) vt. **equat′ed**, **equat′ing** 1. to make equal or equivalent 2. to treat, regard, or express as equal or equivalent —**equat′able** adj.

equation (i kwā′zhən) n. 1. an equating or being equated 2. a statement of equality between two quantities, as shown by the equal sign (=) 3. an expression in which symbols and formulas are used to represent a chemical reaction (Ex.: $SO_3 + H_2O = H_2SO_4$)

equator (i kwāt′ər) n. [see EQUATE] 1. an imaginary circle around the earth, equally distant from the North Pole and the South Pole 2. same as CELESTIAL EQUATOR

equatorial (e′kwə tôr′ē əl) adj. 1. of or near the equator 2. characteristic of

conditions near the equator [equatorial heat]

equerry (ek′wər ē, i kwer′i) n., pl. **-ries** [< OFr. escuerie, status of a squire] an officer who is a personal attendant on some member of a royal family

equestrian (i kwes′trē ən) adj. [< L. equus, horse] 1. of horses or horsemanship 2. on horseback [an equestrian statue] —n. a rider on horseback —**eques′trianism** n. —**eques′trienne′** (-trē en′) n. fem.

equi- [< L.] a combining form meaning equal

equiangular (ē′kwə aŋ′gyoo lər) adj. having all angles equal

equidistant (ē′kwə dis′tənt) adj. equally distant —**e′quidis′tance** n.

equilateral (ē′kwə lat′ər əl) adj. [< L. aequus, equal + latus, side] having all sides equal [an equilateral triangle] —n. a figure having equal sides

equilibrate (ē′kwə li′brāt) vt., vi. **-brated**, **-brating** to bring into or be in equilibrium —**equil′ibra′tion** n.

equilibrium (ē′kwə lib′rē əm) n., pl. **-riums**, **-ria** [< L. aequus, equal + libra, a balance] 1. a state of balance between opposing forces 2. bodily or mental stability

equine (ek′wīn) adj. [< L. equus, horse] of, like, or characteristic of a horse —n. a horse

equinoctial (ē′kwə nok′shəl) adj. relating to or occurring at the time of an equinox —n. 1. same as CELESTIAL EQUATOR 2. an equinoctial storm

equinoctial circle (or **line**) same as CELESTIAL EQUATOR

equinox (ē′kwə noks′) n. [< L. aequus, equal + nox, night] the time when the sun crosses the equator, making night and day equal in all parts of the earth: the **vernal equinox** occurs about March 21, the **autumnal equinox** about September 22

equip (i kwip′) vt. **equipped′**, **equip′ping** [< OFr. esquiper, embark] 1. to provide with what is needed 2. to prepare by training, instruction, etc. —**equip′per** n.

equipage (ek′wə pij) n. 1. the equipment of a ship, army, etc. 2. a carriage with horses and liveried servants

equipment (i kwip′mənt) n. whatever one is equipped with; supplies, resources, etc.

equipoise (ek′wə poiz′) n. [EQUI- + POISE[1]] 1. equal distribution of weight 2. a weight that balances another

equitable (ek′wit ə b'l) adj. 1. fair; just 2. Law having to do with equity, as distinguished from law —**eq′uitableness** n. —**eq′uitably** adv.

equitation (ek′wə tā′shən) n. [< L. equitare, ride] the art of riding on horseback; horsemanship

equity (ek′wət ē) n., pl. **-ties** [< L. aequus, equal] 1. fairness; justice 2. [pl.] the ordinary shares of a limited company 3. [E-] the Actors' Trade Union 4. Law a system of rules as in Britain, supplementing common and statute law

equiv. equivalent

equivalent (i kwiv′ə lənt) *adj.* [< L. *aequus*, equal + *valere*, be strong] 1. equal in quantity, value, meaning, etc. 2. *Chem.* having the same valence —*n.* an equivalent thing —**equiv′alence** *n.* —**equiv′alently** *adv.*

equivocal (i kwiv′ə k'l) *adj.* 1. having two or more meanings; purposely vague 2. uncertain; doubtful 3. questionable [*equivocal* conduct] —**equiv′ocally** *adv.*

equivocate (-kāt′) *vi.* -cat′ed, -cat′ing [< L. *aequus*, equal + *vox*, voice] to use equivocal terms in order to deceive —**equiv′oca′tion** *n.* —**equiv′oca′tor** *n.*

er (u, ə, ä, *etc.*) *interj.* a representation of a sound made by a speaker when hesitating briefly

-er (ər) [< OE.] *a suffix meaning:* 1. a) a person or thing having to do with [*hatter*] b) a person living in [*Londoner*] c) a person or thing that [*roller*] 2. more: *added to form the comparative degree* [*greater*]

Er *Chem.* erbium

E.R. 1. [L. *Elizabetha Regina*] Queen Elizabeth 2. [L. *Edwardus Rex*] King Edward

era (ēr′ə) *n.* [LL. *aera*] 1. a date that marks the beginning of a new period in the history of something 2. a period of time measured from some important occurrence 3. a period of time considered in terms of noteworthy events, men, etc. 4. any of the main divisions of geologic time

eradicate (i rad′ə kāt′) *vt.* -cat′ed, -cat′ing [< L. e-, out + *radix*, root] to uproot; wipe out; destroy —**erad′icable** *adj.* —**erad′ica′tion** *n.* —**erad′icative** *adj.* —**erad′ica′tor** *n.*

erase (i rās′) *vt.* erased′, eras′ing [< L. e-, out + *radere*, scrape] 1. to rub, scrape, or wipe out; efface 2. to remove (something recorded) from (magnetic tape) 3. to obliterate, as from the mind —**eras′able** *adj.*

eraser *n.* a thing that erases; specif., a pad of felt or cloth for removing chalk marks from a blackboard

erasure (i rā′zhər) *n.* 1. an erasing 2. an erased word, mark, etc. 3. the place where something has been erased

erbium (ur′bē əm) *n.* [< (*Ytt*)*erby*, Sw. town] a metallic chemical element of the rare-earth group: symbol, Er

ere (āer) *prep.* [< OE. *ær*] [Archaic or Poet.] before —*conj.* [Archaic or Poet.] 1. before 2. rather than

erect (i rekt′) *adj.* [< L. e-, up + *regere*, make straight] 1. upright; vertical 2. bristling; stiff 3. of penis, etc., enlarged and rigid through sexual stimulation —*vt.* 1. construct (a building, etc.) 2. to set up [to *erect* social barriers] 3. to set in an upright position 4. to put together —**erec′tion** *n.* —**erect′ly** *adv.* —**erect′ness** *n.*

erectile *adj.* that can become erect: used esp. of tissue that becomes swollen and rigid when filled with blood

erelong (āer′lôn′) *adv.* [Archaic or Poet.] soon

eremite (er′ə mīt′) *n.* [see HERMIT] a religious recluse; hermit —**er′emit′ic** (-mit′ik), **er′emit′ical** *adj.*

erf (urf) *n.*, *pl.* **er′ven** [S Afr.] a plot of land, usually urban

erg (urg) *n.* [< Gr. *ergon*, work] *Physics* the unit of work or energy in the cgs (metric) system

ergo (ur′gō) *conj.*, *adv.* [L.] therefore

ergonomics (ur′gō nom′iks) *n.pl.* [*with sing. v.*] [ERG + (EC)ONOMICS] the study of the relationships between workers and their working environment

ergot (ur′gət) *n.* [Fr.] 1. a fungous disease that attacks the kernels of rye, or of other cereal plants 2. an extract of the dried rye fungus, used as a drug

Erin (ēar′in) [Olr.] [Chiefly Poet.] Ireland

ermine (ur′min) *n.* [OFr.] 1. a weasel of northern regions whose fur is brown in summer but white with a black-tipped tail in winter 2. the soft, white fur of this animal, used for state robes —**er′mined** *adj.*

-ern (ərn) *a suffix meaning* from, concerning [*Southern*]

erne, ern (urn) *n.* [OE. *earn*] the European white-tailed eagle, which lives near the sea

Ernie (ur′nē) *n.* [*e*(*lectronic*) *r*(*andom*) *n*(*umber*) *i*(*ndicator*) *e*(*quipment*)] the machine used to pick winning numbers of Premium Bonds

erode (i rōd′) *vt.* erod′ed, erod′ing [< L. e-, out + *rodere*, gnaw] 1. to eat into; wear away 2. to form by wearing away gradually [the stream *eroded* a gully] —**erod′ible** *adj.*

erogenous (i roj′ə nəs) *adj.* [< Gr. *erōs*, love + -GENOUS] designating of or those areas of the body that are particularly sensitive to sexual stimulation

erosion (i rō′zhən) *n.* an eroding or being eroded —**ero′sional** *adj.* —**ero′sive** *adj.*

erotic (i rot′ik) *adj.* [< Gr. *erōs*, love] of, having, or arousing sexual feelings or desires —**erot′ically** *adv.*

erotica *n.pl.* [*often with sing. v.*] erotic books, pictures, etc.

eroticism *n.* 1. erotic quality or character 2. sexual excitement or behaviour 3. preoccupation with sex

err (ur) *vi.* [< L. *errare*, wander] 1. to be wrong or mistaken 2. to deviate from the established moral code

errand (er′ənd) *n.* [OE. *ærende*] 1. a short journey to do a definite thing, often for someone else 2. the thing to be done on such a journey

errant (er′ənt) *adj.* [ult. < L. *iter*, journey] 1. wandering, esp. in search of adventure [a knight-*errant*] 2. a) erring or straying from what is right b) shifting about [an *errant* wind] —**er′rantly** *adv.* —**er′rantry** *n.*

erratic (i rat′ik) *adj.* [< L. *errare*, wander] 1. having no fixed course; irregular 2. inconsistent; unpredictable 3. *Geol.* designating a boulder transported some distance from its source, as by a glacier —**errat′ically** *adv.*

erratum (e rät′əm) *n., pl.* **-ta** [L., *errare,* wander] an error in printing or writing

erroneous (i rō′nē əs) *adj.* containing or based on error; mistaken; wrong **—erro′neously** *adv.*

error (er′ər) *n.* [< L. *errare,* wander] 1. something incorrect or wrong; mistake 2. the state of believing what is untrue 3. a wrong belief 4. wrongdoing; sin 5. the amount by which something deviates from what is correct

ersatz (ãr′zats) *n., adj.* [G.] substitute or synthetic: the word usually suggests inferior quality

Erse (urs) *adj., n.* [ME. *Erish,* var. of *Irisc,* Irish] Gaelic

erst (urst) *adv.* [< OE. ær, ere] [Archaic] formerly

erstwhile *adv.* [Archaic] formerly **—adj.** former

eruct (i rukt′) *vt., vi.* [< L. e-, out + *ructare,* belch] to belch: also **eruc′tate** **—e′ructa′tion** (ē′ruk-) *n.*

erudite (er′ōō dīt′) *adj.* [< L. *erudire,* instruct < e-, out + *rudis,* rude] learned; scholarly **—er′udite′ly** *adv.*

erudition (er′ōō dish′en) *n.* learning acquired by reading and study; scholarship

erupt (i rupt′) *vt.* [< L. e-, out + *rumpere,* break] 1. to burst forth or out, as from restraint 2. to throw forth lava, steam, etc., as a volcano 3. to break out in a rash **—erupt′ible** *adj.*

eruption *n.* 1. a bursting forth or out 2. a throwing forth of lava, water, etc. 3. *Med. a)* a breaking out in a rash *b)* a rash **—erup′tive** *adj.* **—erup′tively** *adv.*

-ery (ər ē) [< LL.] *a suffix meaning:* 1. a place to [*tannery*] 2. a place for [*nunnery*] 3. the practice of [*cookery*] 4. the product of [*pottery*] 5. a collection of [*crockery*] 6. the state of [*drudgery*] 7. the qualities of [*tomfoolery*]

erythrocyte (i rith′rə sīt′) *n.* [< Gr. *erythros,* red + -CYTE] a red blood corpuscle **—eryth′rocyt′ic** (-sit′ik) *adj.*

-es (iz, əz, z) [< OE.] *a suffix used:* 1. to form the plural of some nouns, as *fishes* 2. to form the third person singular, present indicative, of verbs, as *kisses*

Es *Chem.* einsteinium

escalate (es′kə lāt′) *vi.* **-lat′ed, -lat′ing** [< ff.] 1. to expand, as from a limited conflict into a general war 2. to increase rapidly, as prices 3. to rise as on an escalator **—vt.** to cause to escalate **—es′cala′tion** *n.*

escalator *n.* [< L. *scala,* ladder] a moving stairway consisting of treads linked in an endless belt

escalator clause a clause in a contract by which wages, etc. are adjusted to cost of living, etc.

escallop (i skol′əp) *n., vt.* same as SCALLOP

escalope (es′kə lop′) *n.* [< OFr. shell] a thin slice of meat, usually veal, cut from the leg

escapade (es′kə pād′) *n.* [see ff.] a reckless adventure or prank

escape (i skāp′) *vi.* **-caped′, -cap′ing** [< L. ex-, out of + *cappa,* cloak (i.e., leave one's cloak)] 1. to get free; get away 2. to avoid an illness, accident, etc. 3. to leak away [gas *escaping* from a pipe] 4. to slip away; disappear **—vt.** 1. to get away from; flee 2. to avoid [to *escape* punishment] 3. to come from involuntarily [a scream *escaped* her lips] 4. to be missed or forgotten by [his name *escapes* me] **—n.** 1. an escaping 2. a means of escape 3. leakage 4. a temporary mental release from reality 5. *Bot.* a garden plant growing wild **—adj.** 1. giving temporary mental release from reality 2. *a)* making escape possible [an *escape* hatch] *b)* giving a basis for evading a claim, responsibility, etc. [an *escape* clause] **—escap′able** *adj.* **—escap′er** *n.*

ESCAPEMENT

escapement *n.* the part in a clock or watch that controls the speed and regularity of the balance wheel or pendulum, by means of a notched wheel (**escape wheel**), one tooth of which is allowed to escape from the detaining catch at a time

escape road a side road or track affording space for vehicles to stop, as on a hill

escape velocity the minimum speed required for a particle, space vehicle, etc. to escape permanently from the gravitational field of a planet, star, etc.

escapism *n.* a tendency to escape from reality, responsibilities, etc. through the imagination **—escap′ist** *adj., n.*

escapologist (es′kə pol′ə jist) *n.* a performer who specializes in freeing himself from chains, ropes, etc.

escarpment (i skärp′mənt) *n.* [see SCARP] 1. a steep slope or cliff 2. ground formed into a steep slope on the exterior of a fortification

-escence (es′′ns) *a n.-forming suffix corresponding to the adjective suffix* -ESCENT [*obsolescence*]

-escent (es′′nt) [< L.] *an adj.-forming suffix meaning:* 1. being or becoming [*convalescent*] 2. giving off light or colour [*phosphorescent*]

eschatology (es′kə tol′ə jē) *n.* [< Gr. *eschatos,* furthest + -LOGY] the doctrines, etc. dealing with the end of the world **—eschatological** (es′kə tə loj′ik′l) *n.*

escheat (is chēt′) *n.* [< OFr. < L. ex-, out + *cadere,* fall] *Law* 1. the reverting of property to the lord of the manor, to the crown, or to the government when there are no legal heirs 2. property so reverting **—vt., vi.** to confiscate or revert by escheat **—escheat′able** *adj.*

eschew (is chōō′) *vt.* [< OFr. < OHG.] to keep away from; shun **—eschew′al** *n.*

escort (es′kôrt; *for v.* i skôrt′) *n.* [< L.

ex-, out + *corrigere*, to correct] **1.** one or more persons (or cars, ships, etc.) accompanying another to give protection or show honour **2.** a person accompanying another, as to a party —*vt.* to go with as an escort

escritoire (es'krē twär') *n.* [< L. *scribere*, write] a writing desk or table; secretary

esculent (es'kyōō lənt) *adj.* [< L. *esca*, food] fit for food; eatable; edible —*n.* something fit for food

escutcheon (i skuch'ən) *n.* [< L. *scutum*, shield] a shield on which a coat of arms is displayed —**a blot on one's escutcheon** a stain on one's honour

-ese (ēz, ēs) [< L.] *a suffix meaning:* **1.** (a native or inhabitant) of [*Javanese*] **2.** (in) the language of [*Cantonese*] **3.** (in) the style of [*journalese*]

Eskimo (es'kə mō') *n.* [< Fr. < AmInd.] **1.** *pl.* **-mos', -mo'** a member of a group of people living in Greenland, N Canada, Alaska, etc.: the Eskimos are more properly referred to as the Inuit **2.** either of the two languages of the Eskimos —*adj.* of the Eskimos, their language, or their culture —**Es'kimo'an** *adj.*

Eskimo dog a strong breed of dog with greyish, shaggy fur, used by the Eskimos to pull sledges

E.S.N. Educationally Subnormal

esoteric (es'ō ter'ik) *adj.* [< Gr. *esōteros*, inner] understood by only a chosen few, as an inner group of initiates; beyond the understanding of most people; abstruse —**es'oter'ically** *adv.* —**es'oter'icism** *n.*

ESP extrasensory perception

esp., espec. especially

espadrille (es'pə dril') *n.* [Fr. < Sp. *esparto*, coarse grass] a canvas shoe with a sole of twisted rope, etc.

ESPALIER

espalier (is pal'yər) *n.* [Fr. < It.] **1.** a lattice on which trees and shrubs are trained to grow flat **2.** a tree, etc. so trained

esparto (es pär'tō) *n.* [Sp. < Gr. *sparton*] a long, coarse grass of Spain and N Africa, used to make paper, rope, etc.: also **esparto grass**

especial (i spesh'əl) *adj.* special; particular —**espe'cially** *adv.*

Esperanto (es'pə ran'tō) *n.* [< pseudonym of its inventor] an artificial language for international use

espionage (es'pē ə näzh') *n.* [< Fr. *espion*, a spy] **1.** the act of spying **2.** the use of spies by a government

esplanade (es'plə nād') *n.* [Fr. < It. <

L. *explanare*, to level] level, open ground; esp., *a)* a public walk; promenade, as by the sea *b)* an open space in front of a fortified place

espousal (i spou'z'l) *n.* **1.** [*often pl.*] *a)* a betrothal *b)* a wedding **2.** an espousing (of some idea, etc.)

espouse (i spouz') *vt.* **-poused', -pous'-ing** [see SPOUSE] **1.** to marry **2.** to advocate (an idea, etc.) —**espous'er** *n.*

espresso (es pres'ō) *n., pl.* **-sos** [It., pressed-out (coffee)] coffee prepared in a special machine by forcing steam through finely ground coffee beans

esprit (es'prē) *n.* [Fr.] **1.** spirit **2.** wit

esprit de corps (-də kôr') [Fr.] pride, honour, etc. shared by those in the same group or undertaking

espy (ə spī') *vt.* **-pied', -py'ing** to catch sight of; spy

Esq. Esquire

-esque (esk) [Fr. < It.] *a suffix meaning:* **1.** in the style of [*Romanesque*] **2.** like [*picturesque*]

esquire (i skwīr') *n.* [< L. *scutum*, a shield] **1.** [E-] a title of courtesy, usually abbrev. *Esq.*, placed after a man's surname **2.** a member of the gentry ranking below a knight **3.** formerly, an attendant for a knight

ESRO European Space Research Organization

ess (es) *n., pl.* **ess'es** **1.** the letter S, s **2.** something shaped like an S

-ess (is, əs, es) [< Gr.] *a suffix meaning* female [*lioness*]

essay (ə spī'; *for v.* e sā') *n.* [< L. *ex-*, out of + *agere*, do] **1.** a short, personal literary composition **2.** an attempt —*vt.* to try; attempt

essayist (es'ā ist) *n.* a writer of essays

essence (es''ns) *n.* [< L. *esse*, be] **1.** that which makes something what it is; fundamental nature **2.** *a)* a substance that keeps, in concentrated form, the flavour, fragrance, etc. of the plant, food, etc. from which it is extracted *b)* a perfume —**of the essence** essential; indispensable

essential (i sen'shəl) *adj.* **1.** absolutely necessary; indispensable **2.** of or constituting the essence of something; basic —*n.* [*sometimes pl.*] something fundamental or indispensable —**essentiality** (i sen'shē al'ə tē) *n.* —**essen'tially** *adv.* —**essen'tialness** *n.*

essential oil any volatile oil that gives distinctive odour, flavour, etc. to a plant, flower, or fruit

E.S.T. [U.S. & Canad.] Eastern Standard Time

-est (ist, əst) [< OE.] *a suffix used to form* the superlative degree of adjectives and adverbs [*greatest*]

est. **1.** established **2.** estimate **3.** estimated

establish (i stab'lish) *vt.* [< L. *stabilis*, firm] **1.** to found (a nation, business, etc.) **2.** to settle in an office, or set up in business **3.** to prove; demonstrate **4.** to cause (a precedent, theory, etc.) to be accepted **5.** to bring about [to *establish* good relations *]* **6.** to order, ordain, or enact (a law, etc.) permanently **7.** to make a state institution of (a church) —**estab′lisher** *n.*

establishment *n.* **1.** an establishing or being established **2.** a thing established, as a business, household, etc. —**the Establishment** those in authority within a nation, institution, etc.

estate (i stāt′) *n.* [< OFr. *estat*] **1.** landed property containing a residence **2.** a large area of new property development, esp. of houses or of industrial premises **3.** property; possessions **4.** a large area growing rubber, tea, grapes, etc. **5.** formerly, any of the three classes having specific powers: the clergy (**first estate**), nobility (**second estate**), and commons (**third estate**) **6.** *a)* a stage of life *[*man's *estate] b)* status or rank

estate agent 1. an agent responsible for the valuation, advertisement, and sale of property, esp. houses **2.** the administrator of a landed estate; estate manager

estate car a motor car with folding or removable rear seats and rear door for loading and unloading luggage

estate duty *same as* DEATH DUTY

esteem (i stēm′) *vt.* [< L. *aestimare*, to value] **1.** to have great regard for; value highly; respect **2.** to hold to be; consider —*n.* favourable opinion; high regard

ester (es′tər) *n.* [G.] an organic compound, comparable to an inorganic salt, formed by the reaction of an acid and an alcohol, or a phenol

estimable (es′tə mə b'l) *adj.* worthy of esteem

estimate (es′tə māt′; *for n.* -mət) *vt.* -**mat′-ed,** -**mat′ing** [see ESTEEM] **1.** to calculate approximately (size, cost, etc.) **2.** to form an opinion about —*n.* **1.** a general calculation of size, value, etc.; esp., of the cost of a piece of work made by a person undertaking to do the work **2.** an opinion or guess —**es′timative** *adj.* —**es′tima′-tor** *n.*

estimation (es′tə mā′shən) *n.* **1.** an estimating **2.** an opinion or judgment **3.** esteem; regard

estrange (i strānj′) *vt.* -**tranged***!*, -**trang′-ing** [< L. *extraneus*, strange] **1.** to turn (a person) from a friendly attitude to a hostile one; alienate **2.** to keep apart or away —**estranged** *adj.* —**estrange′-ment** *n.*

estuary (es′tyoo wə rē) *n., pl.* -**aries** [< L. *aestus*, tide] the wide mouth of a river, where the tide meets the current —**es′tuar′ial, es′tuarine** *adj.*

-**et** (it, ət) [< OFr.] *a suffix meaning* little *[islet]*

eta (ēt′ə) *n.* the seventh letter of the Greek alphabet (H, η): it is shown as ē in the etymologies of this dictionary

ETA, E.T.A. estimated time of arrival

et al. 1. [L. *et alibi*] and elsewhere **2.** [L. *et alii*] and others

etc. et cetera

et cetera (et set′ər ə) [L.] and others; and the like

etceteras *n.pl.* customary extras

etch (ech) *vt.* [< Du. < G.] **1.** to make (a design) on metal, glass, etc. by the action of an acid **2.** to engrave (metal, glass, etc.) in this way for use in printing such designs **3.** to impress sharply —**etch′-er** *n.*

etching *n.* **1.** an etched plate **2.** a print made from an etched plate **3.** the art of making such drawings, etc.

eternal (i tur′n'l) *adj.* [< L. *aevum*, age] **1.** without beginning or end; everlasting **2.** unchanging **3.** [Colloq.] continual *[eternal* bickering *]* **4.** timeless —**the Eternal** God —**eter′nally** *adv.* —**eter′nalness** *n.*

eternal triangle an emotional or sexual relationship in which there are conflicts involving a man and two women or a woman and two men

eternity *n., pl.* -**ties 1.** continuance without end **2.** time without beginning or end **3.** a long time that seems endless **4.** the endless time after death

eternity ring a ring set all around with stones, symbolizing continuity: given by a husband to his wife

ethane (eth′ān) *n.* [< ETHYL] an odourless, colourless hydrocarbon, found in natural gas and used as a fuel

ether (ē′thər) *n.* [< Gr. *aithēr* < *aithein*, to burn] **1.** *Chem.* a colourless, flammable liquid, used as an anaesthetic and solvent **2.** *Physics* an invisible substance postulated (in older theory) as pervading space and transmitting radiant energy **3.** the upper regions of space; clear sky

ethereal (i thēər′ē əl) *adj.* **1.** light; airy; delicate **2.** heavenly —**ethe′real′ity** (-al′ə tē) *n.* —**ethe′really** *adv.*

etherealize *vt.* -**ized′,** -**iz′ing** to make, or treat as being, ethereal —**ethe′realiza′-tion** *n.*

etherize (ē′thə rīz′) *vt.* -**ized′,** -**iz′ing** to anaesthetize as by causing to inhale ether fumes —**e′theriza′tion** *n.*

ethic (eth′ik) *n.* [see ff.] ethics or a system of ethics *[*the humanist *ethic]* —*adj. same as* ETHICAL

ethical *adj.* [< Gr. *ēthos*, character] **1.** having to do with ethics or morality **2.** conforming to professional standards of conduct **3.** of a drug available only on a doctor's prescription —**eth′ical′ity** (-kal′ə tē) *n.,* **eth′icalness** *n.* —**eth′ically** *adv.*

ethics *n.pl.* [*with sing. v.* in 1 and occas. 2] [see prec.] **1.** the study of standards of conduct and moral judgment **2.** the code of morals of a particular person, religion, group, profession, etc.

Ethiopian (ē′thē ō′pē ən) *adj.* **1.** of Ethiopia **2.** [Obs.] negro —*n.* **1.** a native of Ethiopia **2.** [Obs.] a negro

ethnic (eth′nik) *adj.* [< Gr. *ethnos*, nation] **1.** of a human group having racial, religious, etc., traits in common **2.** designating or of any of the basic divisions of mankind; ethnological: also **eth′nical 3.** resembling, or intended to resemble, peasant styles; said of clothes, etc. —**eth′nically** *adv.* —**eth-nic′ity** (-nis′-) *n.*

ethnology (eth nol′ə jē) *n*. [< Gr. *ethnos*, nation + -LOGY] the science that deals with the comparative cultures of various peoples —**ethnological** (eth′nə loj′i k'l), **eth′nolog′ic** *adj.* —**eth′nolog′ically** *adv.* —**ethnol′ogist** *n*.

ethos (ē′thos) *n*. [Gr. *ēthos*, character] the characteristic attitudes, beliefs, etc. of an individual or group

ethyl (eth′'l) *n*. [< ETHER] the hydrocarbon radical which forms the base of common alcohol, ether, etc.

ethyl alcohol *same as* ALCOHOL (sense 1): also **ethanol**

ethylene (eth′ə lēn′) *n*. [< ETHYL] a flammable, gaseous hydrocarbon used as a fuel, anaesthetic, etc.

etiolate (ēt′ē ō lāt′) *vt.* -lat′ed, -lat′ing [< Fr. *éteule*, straw] 1. to cause to be weak or unhealthy 2. *Bot.* to blanch by depriving of sunlight —**e′tiola′tion** *n*.

etiquette (et′i ket) *n*. [Fr. *étiquette*, ticket] 1. the manners and ceremonies established by convention as acceptable or required in social relations 2. conventional practice in certain professions [medical *etiquette*]

Eton collar (ē′tən) [< *Eton* College] a broad, white linen collar worn with an Eton jacket

Eton crop a women's short hair style of the 1920's

Eton jacket a black waist-length jacket with broad lapels, left open in front, as that worn by students at Eton

Etruscan (i trus′kən) *adj.* of Etruria —*n*. 1. a native of Etruria 2. the language of the ancient Etruscans Also **Etrurian** (i trooʻə ən)

et seq. [L. *et sequens*] and the following

-ette (et) [Fr.] *a suffix meaning:* 1. little [*statuette*] 2. female [*usherette*] 3. substitute [*leatherette*]

étude (ā tyōōd′) *n*. [Fr., study] a musical composition for a solo instrument, designed to give practice in some special point of technique

ety., etym., etymol. 1. etymological 2. etymology

etymology (et′ə mol′ə jē) *n., pl.* -gies [< Gr. *etymos*, true + -LOGY] the origin and development of a word, affix, etc., or the branch of linguistics dealing with this —et′ymolog′ical (-mə loj′ə k'l) *adj.* —et′ymolog′ically *adv.* —et′ymol′ogist *n*.

Eu *Chem.* europium

eucalyptus (yōō′kə lip′təs) *n*. [< Gr. *eu,* well + *kalyptos,* covered] any of a genus of tall, chiefly Australian evergreen trees, valued for their timber, gum, and oil: also **eu′calypt′**

Eucharist (yōō′kə rist) *n*. [< Gr. *eucharistia,* gratitude] 1. *same as* HOLY COMMUNION 2. the consecrated bread and wine used in Holy Communion —**Eu′charis′tic** *adj.*

Euclidean, Euclidian (yōō klid′ē ən) *adj.* relating to Euclid, 5th cent. B.C. Greek philosopher

eugenic (yōō jen′ik) *adj.* [< Gr. *eu,* well + GENESIS] 1. relating to the bearing of sound offspring 2. of, relating to, or improved by eugenics —**eugen′ically** *adv.*

eugenics *n.pl.* [*with sing. v.*] the movement devoted to improving the human species by control of hereditary factors in mating —**eugen′icist** *n*.

eulogize (yōō′lə jīz′) *vt.* -gized′, -giz′ing to praise

eulogy (yōō′lə jē) *n., pl.* -gies [< Gr. *eulegein,* speak well of] 1. speech or writing in praise of a person, event, or thing; esp., a funeral oration 2. high praise

eunuch (yōō′nək) *n*. [< Gr. *eunē,* bed + *echein,* keep] a castrated man; esp., one in charge of a harem

euphemism (yōō′fə miz′m) *n*. [< Gr. *eu-,* good + *phēmē,* voice] 1. the use of a word or phrase that is less direct but considered less offensive than another 2. a word or phrase so substituted (Ex.: *remains* for *corpse*) —**eu′phemis′tic, eu′-phemis′tical** *adj.* —**eu′phemis′tically** *adv.*

euphonious (yōō fō′nē əs) *adj.* having a pleasant sound; harmonious —**eupho′niously** *adv.*

euphonium (yōō fō′nē əm) *n*. a brass instrument with a mellow tone

euphony (yōō′fə nē) *n., pl.* -nies [< Gr. *eu-,* well + *phōnē,* voice] the quality of having a pleasing sound; pleasant combination of agreeable sounds, esp. words

euphoria (yōō fôr′ē ə) *n*. [< Gr. *eu-,* well + *pherein,* bear] a feeling of well-being or high spirits, specif. one without cause —**euphor′ic** (-for′ik) *adj.*

euphuism (yōō′fyōō wiz′m) *n*. [< *Euphues,* character in works by J. *Lyly*] 1. an artificial, high-flown style of writing 2. an instance of this —**eu′phuis′tic, eu′-phuis′tical** *adj.* —**eu′phuis′tically** *adv.*

Eur. 1. Europe 2. European

Eurasian (yōō rā′zhən) *adj.* 1. of Europe and Asia 2. of mixed European and Asian descent —*n*. a person of mixed European and Asian descent

Euratom (yōōə ra′təm) European Atomic Energy Community

eureka (yōō rē′kə) *interj.* [Gr. *heurēka*] I have found (it): an exclamation of triumphant achievement

eurhythmics (yōō rith′miks) *n.pl.* *same as* EURYTHMICS

Euro- (yōōər′ō) *a combining form meaning:* 1. Europe, European [*Eurocrat*] 2. Europe and [*Euro-American*]

Eurodollars *n.pl.* U.S. dollars used by banks, etc. outside the U.S. to finance short-term loans

European (yōōər′ə pē′ən) *adj.* 1. of or relating to Europe 2. native to Europe 3. concerned with the unity of Europe —*n*. 1. a native or inhabitant of Europe 2. a person who regards Europe as an essential whole 3. [S Afr.] any white person —**Europe′anism** *n*.

European Economic Community the European common market formed in 1958

europium (yōō rō′pē əm) *n*. [ModL. <

Europe] a chemical element of the rare-earth group: symbol, Eu

eurythmics (yoo rith'miks) *n.pl.* [*with sing. v.*] [< Gr. *eu-*, well + *rhythmos*, rhythm] the art of performing bodily movements in rhythm —**euryth'mic** *adj.*

Eustachian tube (yoo stā'shən) [< B. *Eustachio*] a slender tube between the middle ear and the pharynx, which equalizes air pressure on both sides of the eardrum

euthanasia (yoo'thə nā'zhə) *n.* [< Gr. *eu-*, well + *thanatos*, death] 1. the act of causing death painlessly to end suffering, esp. in cases of incurable, painful diseases 2. an easy and painless death

ev, EV electron-volt

evacuate (i vak'yoo wāt) *vt.* -ated, -ating [< L. *e-*, out + *vacuare*, make empty] 1. to remove (inhabitants, etc.) from (a place), as for protective purposes 2. to make empty; specif., to remove the air from 3. to discharge (bodily waste) —**evac'ua'tion** *n.* —**evac'uative** *adj.* —**evac'ua'tor** *n.* —**evac'uee'** *n.*

evade (i vād') *vt.* evad'ed, evad'ing [< L. *e-*, out + *vadere*, go] 1. to avoid or escape from by deceit or cleverness 2. to avoid doing or answering directly [to *evade* income tax] —**evad'able** *adj.* —**evad'er** *n.*

evaluate (i val'yoo wāt) *vt.* -at'ed, -at'-ing [see VALUE] 1. to find the value or amount of 2. to judge the quality of; appraise —**eval'ua'tion** *n.*

evanesce (ēv'ə nes') *vi.* -nesced', -nesc'-ing [< L. *e-*, out + *vanescere*, vanish] to fade from sight; vanish

evanescent *adj.* vanishing; fleeting —**ev'anes'cence** *n.*

evangel (i van'jəl) *n.* [< Gr. *eu-*, well + *angelos*, messenger] [Archaic] 1. the gospel 2. [E-] any of the four Gospels 3. an evangelist

evangelical (ē'van jel'i k'l) *adj.* 1. of or according to the Gospels or the New Testament 2. of those Protestant churches that emphasize salvation by faith in the atonement of Jesus 3. evangelistic Also **e'vangel'ic** —*n.* a member of an evangelical church —**e'vangel'icalism** *n.* —**e'vangel'ically** *adv.*

evangelism (i van'jə liz'm) *n.* a preaching of, or zealous effort to spread the gospel —**evan'gelis'tic** *adj.*

evangelist *n.* 1. [E-] any of the four writers of the Gospels; Matthew, Mark, Luke, or John 2. anyone who evangelizes; esp., a travelling preacher

evangelize *vt.* -ized', -iz'ing 1. to preach the gospel to 2. to convert to Christianity —**evan'geliza'tion** *n.*

evaporate (i vap'ə rāt') *vt.* -rat'ed, -rat'-ing [< L. *e-*, out + *vapor*, vapour] 1. to change (a liquid or solid) into vapour 2. to remove moisture from (vegetables, etc.), as by heating, so as to get a concentrated product —*vi.* 1. to become vapour 2. to give off vapour 3. to disappear —**evap'orabil'ity** *n.* —**evap'ora-**

ble *adj.* —**evap'ora'tion** *n.* —**evap'ora'-tor** *n.*

evaporated milk unsweetened milk thickened by evaporation to about half its weight, and then tinned

evasion (i vā'zhən) *n.* 1. an evading; specif., an avoiding of a duty, question, etc. by deceit or cleverness 2. a way of doing this; subterfuge

evasive *adj.* 1. tending or seeking to evade; not straightforward 2. hard to catch etc.; elusive

eve (ēv) *n.* [< OE. *æfen*, evening] 1. [*often* E-] the evening or day before a holiday 2. the period immediately before some event 3. [Poet.] evening

even[1] (ē'vən) *adj.* [OE. *efne*, *efen*] 1. flat; level; smooth 2. not varying; constant [an *even* tempo] 3. calm; tranquil [an *even* disposition] 4. in the same plane or line [*even* with the rim] 5. equally balanced 6. owing and being owed nothing 7. revenged 8. just; fair [an *even* exchange] 9. equal in number, quantity, etc. 10. exactly divisible by two 11. exact [an *even* mile] —*adv.* 1. however improbable; indeed [*even* a fool could do it] 2. exactly; just [*even* as I expected] 3. just as; while [*even* as he spoke] 4. still; yet [*even* worse] —*vt.*, *vi.* to make, become, or be even —**break even** [Colloq.] to finish with neither a profit nor a loss —**even if** despite the fact that —**even so** nevertheless —**e'venly** *adv.* —**e'venness** *n.*

even[2] *n.* [see EVE] [Poet.] evening

evenhanded (ē'vən han'did) *adj.* impartial; fair —**e'venhand'edly** *adv.* —**e'venhand'edness** *n.*

evening (ēv'niŋ) *n.* [< OE. *æfen*, evening] 1. the last part of the day and early part of night 2. the last period, as of life —*adj.* in or for the evening

evening dress clothes for wearing at a formal evening occasion, esp. a dinner jacket or long dress

evening primrose a plant having yellow flowers that open in the evening

evenings *adv.* [Colloq.] during the evenings

evening star a bright planet, esp. Venus, seen in the western sky soon after sunset

even money equal stakes in betting, with no odds: also **evens**

evensong *n.* Eccles. the service assigned to the evening

event (i vent') *n.* [< L. *e-*, out + *venire*, come] 1. a happening, esp. when important 2. a result; outcome 3. a particular item in a programme of sports —**in any event** no matter what happens: also **at all events** —**in the event of** in case of —**in the event that** if

eventful *adj.* 1. full of outstanding events 2. having an important outcome —**event'-fully** *adv.*

eventide (ē'vən tīd') *n.* [Archaic] evening

eventual (i ven'choo wəl) *adj.* happening in the end; ultimate —**even'tually** *adv.*

eventuality (i ven'choo wal'ə tē) *n.*, *pl.*

-ties a possible event, outcome, or condition;

eventuate (i ven'choo wāt') *vi.* **-at'ed, -at'ing** to happen in the end; result (often with *in*)

ever (ev'ər) *adv.* [< OE. *æfre*] 1. always [*ever* after] 2. at any time [have you *ever* seen her?] 3. at all; in any way [how can I *ever* repay you?] —**did you ever?** [Colloq.] have you ever heard or seen such a thing? —**ever so** [Colloq.] very —**for ever and a day** always: also **for ever and ever**

evergreen *adj.* having green leaves throughout the year —*n.* an evergreen plant or tree

everlasting (ev'ər lās'tiŋ) *adj.* 1. lasting forever; eternal 2. seeming never to stop —*n.* 1. eternity 2. a plant whose blossoms keep their colour and shape when dried —**the Everlasting** God —**ev'erlast'ingly** *adv.*

evermore (ev'ər môr') *adv.* forever; constantly

every (ev'rē) *adj.* [< OE. *æfre ælc*, ever each] 1. each, individually and separately [*every* man among you] 2. the fullest possible [given *every* chance] 3. each interval of [a pill *every* three hours] —**every last** [Slang] all —**every now and then** from time to time: also [Colloq.] **every so often** —**every other** each alternate, as the first, third, fifth, etc.

everybody *pron.* every person; everyone

everyday *adj.* 1. daily 2. suitable for regular or daily use or wear [*everyday* shoes] 3. usual; common

Everyman *n.* [< 15th-c. morality play] [*often* e-] the ordinary person; the man in the street

everyone *pron.* every person; everybody

everything *pron.* 1. every thing; all 2. all things pertinent to a specified matter 3. the most important thing [money isn't *everything*]

everywhere *adv.* in or every place

evict (i vikt') *vt.* [see EVINCE] to remove (a tenant) from leased premises by legal procedure —**evic'tion** *n.*

evidence (ev'ə dəns) *n.* 1. something that tends to prove 2. something that makes another thing evident; sign 3. *Law* a statement of a witness, an object, etc., which bears on or establishes the point in question 4. the condition of being evident —*vt.* **-denced, -dencing** to make evident; show —**in evidence** visible or perceptible

evident (i [< L. *e-*, from + *videre*, see] easy to see or perceive; clear; obvious; plain —**ev'idently** *adv.*

evidential (ev'ə den'shəl) *adj.* of, serving as, or providing evidence —**ev'iden'tially** *adv.*

evil (ē'v'l) *adj.* [OE. *yfel*] 1. morally wrong; wicked 2. harmful 3. unlucky; disastrous —*n.* 1. wickedness; sin 2. anything that causes harm, pain, etc. —**the Evil One** the Devil —**e'villy** *adv.* —**e'vilness** *n.*

evildoer *n.* a person who does evil, esp. habitually —**e'vildo'ing** *n.*

evil eye a look which, in superstitious belief, is able to harm or bewitch the one stared at

evince (i vins') *vt.* **evinced', evinc'ing** [< L. *e-*, intens. + *vincere*, conquer] to show plainly (a specified quality, feeling, etc.) —**evin'cible** *adj.* —**evin'cive** *adj.*

eviscerate (i vis'ə rāt') *vt.* **-at'ed, -at'ing** [< L. *e-*, out + *viscera*, viscera] to remove the entrails from —**evis'cera'tion** *n.*

evocation (ev'ō kā'shən) *n.* an evoking —**evocative** (i vok'ə tiv) *adj.* —**ev'oca'tor** *n.*

evoke (i vōk') *vt.* **evoked', evok'ing** [< L. *e-*, out + *vocare*, call] to draw forth or elicit (a mental image, reaction, etc.) —**evok'er** *n.*

evolution (ē'və loo'shən) *n.* [see EVOLVE] 1. *Biol.* a) the development of a species, organism, etc. from its original to its present state b) a theory that all species of plants and animals developed from earlier forms 2. an unfolding; process of development 3. a movement that is part of a series 4. a giving off, as of gas in a chemical reaction 5. *Mil.* any manoeuvre by which troops, ships, etc. change formation —**ev'olu'tionary** *adj.*

evolutionist *n.* a person who accepts the principles of evolution —*adj.* of this theory

evolve (i volv') *vt.* **evolved', evolv'ing** [< L. *e-*, out + *volvere*, roll] 1. to develop by gradual changes; unfold 2. to give off (gas, etc.) 3. to produce by evolution —*vi.* 1. to develop gradually 2. to become disclosed

ewe (yoo) *n.* [OE. *eowu*] a female sheep

EWER

ewer (yoo'ər) *n.* [ult. < L. *aqua*, water] a large water jug with a wide mouth

ex (eks) *prep.* [L.] without; exclusive of [*ex* interest] —*n.*, *pl.* **ex'es** [Colloq.] one's divorced husband or wife

ex- [< OFr. or L.] a prefix meaning: 1. from, out [*expel*] 2. beyond [*excess*] 3. out of [*expatriate*] 4. thoroughly [*exterminate*] 5. upwards [*exalt*] 6. former [*ex-convict*]

Ex. Exodus

ex. 1. example 2. except(ed) 3. extra

exacerbate (eks sas'ər bāt') *vt.* **-bat'ed, -bat'ing** [< L. *ex-*, intens. + *acerbus*, harsh] 1. to make more intense; aggravate (pain, etc.) 2. to irritate —**exac'erba'tion** *n.*

exact (ig zakt') *adj.* [< L. *ex-*, out + *agere*, drive] 1. characterized by or requiring accuracy; methodical; correct 2. without variation; precise [an *exact* replica] —*vt.* 1. to extort 2. to demand

and get by authority **3.** to require —**exact′**-
ness n. —**exac′tor** n.

exacting adj. **1.** making severe demands;
strict **2.** demanding great care, effort,
etc.; arduous

exaction n. **1.** an exacting **2.** an extortion
3. an exacted fee, tax, etc.

exactitude n. precision; accuracy

exactly adv. accurately; precisely: also
used as an affirmative reply, equivalent
to "I agree," "quite true"

exaggerate (ig zaj′ə rāt′) vt. -**at′ed**, -**at′**-
ing [< L. ex-, out + agger, a heap] **1.**
to think, speak, or write of as greater
than is really so; overstate **2.** to increase
to an abnormal degree —**exag′gerat′edly**
adv. —**exag′gera′tion** n.

exalt (ig zôlt′) vt. [< L. ex-, out + altus,
high] **1.** to raise in status, power, etc.
2. to praise; glorify **3.** to fill with joy,
pride, etc. —**ex′alta′tion** n. —**exalt′edly**
adv.

exam (ig zam′) n. [Colloq.] examination

examination (ig zam′ə nā′shən) n. **1.** an
investigation; inquiry **2.** a test of
knowledge, written or oral —**exam′ina′**-
tional adj. —**exam′inato′rial** (-nə tôr′ē əl)
adj.

examine (ig zam′ən) vt. -**ined**, -**ining** [<
L. examen, tongue of a balance] **1.** to
look at or into to find out the facts, condition,
etc. of; investigate **2.** to test to find out
the knowledge, skill, etc. of —**exam′ina-
ble** adj. —**exam′inee′** n. —**exam′iner** n.

example (ig zam′p'l) n. [< L. exemplum
< eximere, take out] **1.** something selected
to show the character of the rest; sample
2. a case that serves as a warning **3.**
a person or thing to be imitated; model
4. a problem, as in mathematics, that
illustrates a principle or method —**set an
example** to behave so as to be a model
for others —**without example** having no
precedent

exasperate (ig zas′pə rāt′) vt.-**at′ed**, -**at′**-
ing [< L. ex-, out + asper, rough] to
irritate or annoy very much; vex —**exas′-
perat′ingly** adv. —**exas′pera′tion** n.

ex cathedra (eks′kə thē′drə) [ModL.,
from the chair] with the authority that
comes from one's rank or office: often
used of papal pronouncements on faith
or morals

excavate (eks′kə vāt′) vt. -**vat′ed**, -**vat′**-
ing [< L. ex-, out + cavus, hollow] **1.**
to make a hole or cavity in **2.** to form
by hollowing out [to excavate a tunnel]
3. to unearth **4.** to dig out (earth, etc.) —**ex′-
cava′tion** n.

exceed (ik sēd′) vt. [< L. ex-, out +
cedere, go] **1.** to go beyond (a limit,
measure, etc.) **2.** to be greater than; surpass

exceeding adj. surpassing; extraordinary; extreme —adv. [Archaic] extremely
—**exceed′ingly** adv.

excel (ik sel′) vi., vt. -**celled′**, -**cel′ling**
[< L. excellere, rise] to be better or
greater than (others)

excellence (ek′səl əns) n. **1.** the fact
or condition of excelling; superiority **2.**
[E-] same as EXCELLENCY

excellency n., pl. -**cies** **1.** [E-] a title
of honour applied to various dignitaries
2. same as EXCELLENCE

excellent adj. outstandingly good of its
kind

except (ik sept′) vt. [< L. ex-, out +
capere, take] to leave out or take out;
exclude —prep. other than [everyone
except me] —conj. **1.** [Archaic] unless
2. [Colloq.] were it not that [I'd quit
except I need the money] —**except for**
if it were not for

excepting prep., conj. same as EXCEPT

exception n. **1.** an excepting **2.** anything
that is excepted; specif., a) a case to
which a rule does not apply b) a person
or thing different from others of the same
class —**take exception** **1.** to object **2.**
to resent; feel offended —**with the exception
of** except —**excep′tionless** adj.

exceptionable adj. liable or open to
exception

exceptional adj. not ordinary or average;
esp., above average in quality, ability, etc.
—**excep′tionally** adv.

excerpt (ek surpt′; for n. ek′surpt′) vt.
[< L. ex-, out + carpere, pick] to select
(passages from a book, etc.); extract —n.
a passage selected or quoted from a book,
etc.; extract —**excerp′tion** n.

excess (ik ses′; for adj. ek′ses′) n. [see
EXCEED] **1.** action that goes beyond a
reasonable limit **2.** intemperance; overindulgence **3.** an amount greater than is
necessary, desirable, etc. **4.** the amount
by which one thing exceeds another —adj.
extra or surplus —**in excess of** more
than —**exces′sive** adj.

excess luggage luggage that is more
than is allowed in weight, pieces, etc.:
also **excess baggage**

exchange (iks chānj′) vt., vi. -**changed′**,
-**chang′ing** [see EX- & CHANGE] **1.** to
give or receive (something) for another
2. to give up for a substitute [to exchange
honour for wealth] —n. **1.** a giving or
taking of one thing for another **2.** a
thing given or received in exchange **3.**
a place where trade is carried on by brokers,
merchants, etc. [a stock exchange] **4.**
a central office in a telephone system,
serving a certain area **5.** a quarrel **6.**
a) the payment of debts by negotiable
drafts or bills of exchange b) an exchanging
of a sum of money of one country for
the equivalent in the money of another
country c) the rate of exchange —**ex-
change′able** adj. —**exchang′er** n.

exchange rate the ratio of the value
of one currency in relation to the value
of another

exchequer (iks chek′ər) n. [< OFr.
eschekier: see CHEQUER] **1.** [often E-]
the British state department in charge
of the national revenue **2.** the funds in
the British treasury **3.** a treasury **4.**
money in one's possession

excise¹ (ek′sīz, for v. ek sīz′) n. [ult. <
L. assidere, assist (in office)] a tax
on the manufacture of various commodities
within a country, as wines, tobacco, etc.

2. the section of the government service responsible for the collection of excise —vt. **-cised', -cis'ing** to put an excise on

excise² (ek sīz') vt. **-cised', -cis'ing** [< L. ex-, out + caedere, cut] to remove (a tumour, etc.) by cutting out or away —**exci'sion** (-sizh'ən) n.

exciseman (ek'sīz mən) n. an official who collects excises

excitable (ik sīt'ə b'l) adj. that is easily excited —**excit'abil'ity** n. —**excit'ably** adv.

excite (ik sīt') vt. **-cit'ed, -cit'ing** [< L. ex-, out + ciere, call] **1.** to arouse the feelings of **2.** to arouse [to excite pity] **3.** to put into motion; stir up **4.** Physics to raise (a nucleus, atom, etc.) to a higher energy state —**excit'ative excit'atory** adj.

excited adj. aroused; stirred up —**excit'edly** adv.

excitement n. **1.** an exciting or being excited; agitation **2.** something that excites

exciting adj. causing excitement; thrilling, etc.

exclaim (iks klām') vi., vt. [< L. ex-, out + clamare, shout] to cry out; speak suddenly and excitedly, as in surprise, etc.—**exclaim'er** n.

exclamation (eks'klə mā'shən) n. **1.** the act of exclaiming **2.** something exclaimed; interjection —**exclamatory** (iks klam'ə tər ē) adj.

exclamation mark a mark (!) used after a word or sentence to express surprise, strong feeling, etc.

exclude (iks klōōd') vt. **-clud'ed, -clud'ing** [< L. ex-, out + claudere, close] **1.** to refuse to admit, consider, include, etc. **2.** to put out; expel —**exclud'er** n.

exclusion n. **1.** an excluding **2.** a thing excluded —**to the exclusion of** so as to keep out

exclusive adj. **1.** excluding all others **2.** not shared or divided [an exclusive right] **3.** excluding certain people or groups, as for social reasons **4.** dealing only in costly items [an exclusive shop] —**exclusive of** not including or allowing for —**exclu'siveness, ex'clusiv'ity** n.

excommunicate (eks'kə myōō'nə kāt'; for adj. and n., usually -kət) vt. **-cat'ed, -cat'ing** to exclude from communion with a church —adj. excommunicated —n. an excommunicated person —**ex'commu'nica'tion** n. —**ex'commu'nicative** adj. —**ex'commu'nica'tor** n.

excoriate (ik skôr'ē āt') vt. **-at'ed, -at'ing** [< L. ex-, out + corium, skin] **1.** to rub off the skin of **2.** to denounce harshly —**exco'ria'tion** n.

excrement (eks'krə mənt) n. [see EXCRETE] waste matter from the bowels —**ex'cremen'tal** (-men't'l) adj.

excrescence (iks kres'əns) n. [< L. ex-, out + crescere, grow] an abnormal or disfiguring outgrowth, as a bunion —**excres'cent** adj.

excreta (eks krēt'ə) n.pl. waste matter excreted from the body, esp. sweat, faeces, or urine —**excre'tal** adj.

excrete (eks krēt') vt., vi. **-cret'ed, -cret'ing** [< L. ex-, out of + cernere, sift] to discharge (waste matter) from the body —**excre'tion** n. —**excre'tory** adj.

excruciating (iks krōō'shē āt'iŋ) adj. [< L. ex-, intens. + cruciare, crucify] **1.** causing intense pain **2.** so bad as to be painful [an excruciating pun] —**excru'ciat'ingly** adv.

exculpate (eks'kul pāt') vt. **-pat'ed, -pat'ing** [< L. ex, out + culpa, fault] to free from blame; prove guiltless —**ex'cul pa'tion** n. —**excul'patory** adj.

excursion (ik skur'shən) n. [< L. ex-, out + currere, run] **1.** a short trip or journey, as for pleasure **2.** a round trip (on a train, bus, etc.) at special rates **3.** a digression [an excursion into politics] —adj. of or for an excursion —**excur'sionary** adj. —**excur'sionist** n.

excursive adj. rambling; digressive

excuse (ik skyōōz'; for n. -skyōōs') vt. **-cused', -cus'ing** [< L. ex-, from + causa, a charge] **1.** to try to free (a person) of blame **2.** to apologize or give reasons for **3.** to overlook (an offence or fault) **4.** to release from an obligation **5.** to permit to leave **6.** to justify —n. **1.** a defence of some action; apology **2.** a release from obligation **3.** something that excuses **4.** a pretended reason; pretext —**a poor** (or **bad,** etc.) **excuse for** a very inferior example of —**excuse oneself** **1.** to apologize **2.** to ask for permission to leave —**excus'able** adj.

ex-directory (eks'də rek'tə rē) adj. not in a directory, by request of the subscriber: said of a telephone number

exeat (eks'ē ət) n. [L., let him go out] a formal leave of absence granted as to a student

exec. **1.** executive **2.** executor

execrable (ek'si krə b'l) adj. [L. execrabilis] abominable; detestable —**ex'ecrably** adv.

execrate (-krāt') vt., vi. **-crat'ed, -crat'ing** [< L. ex-, out + sacrare, consecrate] **1.** to curse **2.** to denounce scathingly **3.** to loathe; detest —**ex'ecra'tion** n. —**ex'ecra'tive, ex'ecra'tory** adj. —**ex'ecra'tor** n.

execute (ek'sə kyōōt') vt. **-cut'ed, -cut'ing** [< L. ex-, intens. + sequi, follow] **1.** to carry out; do **2.** to administer (laws, etc.) **3.** to put to death in accordance with a legal sentence **4.** to create in accordance with an idea, plan, etc. **5.** Law to make valid (a deed, etc.) as by signing, sealing, etc. —**ex'ecut'er** n.

execution (ek'sə kyōō'shən) n. **1.** a carrying out, doing, etc. **2.** a putting to death in accordance with a legal sentence **3.** the manner of doing something, as of performing music —**ex'ecu'tionary** adj.

executioner n. one who carries out the death penalty

executive (ig zek'yōo tiv) adj. **1.** of or concerned with carrying out duties, functions, etc., as in business **2.** empowered to administer (laws, government affairs, etc.) **3.** of managerial personnel or functions —*n.* **1.** a branch of government empowered to administer the laws and affairs of a nation **2.** a person whose function is to administer or manage affairs, as of a company

executor *n.* a person appointed by a testator to carry out the provisions in his will —**exec′uto′rial, exec′utory** *adj.* —**exec′utrix** *n.fem.*

exegesis (ek′sə jē′sis) *n.,* pl. **-ge′ses** (-sēz) [< Gr. *ex-*, out + *hēgeisthai,* to guide] interpretation of a word, passage, etc., esp. of the Bible —**ex′eget′ic** (-jet′-ik) *adj.*

exemplar (ig zem′plər) *n.* [< L. *exemplum,* example] **1.** a model; pattern **2.** a typical specimen

exemplary *adj.* **1.** serving as a model [*exemplary* behaviour] **2.** serving as a warning [*exemplary* punishment] **3.** serving as a sample —**exem′plarily** *adv.*

exemplify (ig zem′plə fī′) *vt.* -**fied′,** -**fy′-ing** [< L. *exemplum,* example + *facere,* make] to serve as an example of —**exem′-plifica′tion** *n.*

exempt (ig zempt′) *vt.* [< L. *eximere:* see EXAMPLE] to free from a rule or obligation which applies to others —*adj.* not subject to a rule, obligation, etc. applying to others —**exempt′ible** *adj.* —**exemp′tion** *n.*

exequies (ek′sə kwēz) *n.pl.* [< L. *exequi,* follow up] funeral rites; obsequies

exercise (ek′sər sīz′) *n.* [< L. *exercere,* to put to work] **1.** activity for developing the body or mind **2.** [*pl.*] movements to strengthen or develop some part of the body **3.** a problem to be worked out for developing some skill **4.** active use or operation **5.** performance (of duties, etc.) **6.** *Mil.* manoeuvre or drill designed to train troops and increase efficiency —*vt.* -**cised′,** -**cis′ing** **1.** to use; employ [to *exercise* self-control] **2.** to put into use so as to develop or train **3.** to worry; perplex **4.** to exert (influence, etc.) —*vi.* to take exercise; do exercises —**ex′ercis′a-ble** *adj.* —**ex′ercis′er** *n.*

exert (ig zurt′) *vt.* [< L. *exserere,* to stretch out] **1.** to put into action or use [*exert* your will] **2.** to apply (oneself) with energy —**exer′tion** *n.* —**exer′tive** *adj.*

exeunt (ek′sē ənt) [L.] they (two or more characters) leave the theatre: a stage direction

exeunt omnes (om′nēz, -nās) [L.] all (of the characters who are on stage) leave: a stage direction

ex gratia (grā′shə) [L., out of kindness] given or granted as a favour, esp. where no legal obligation exists

exhale (eks hāl′) *vt., vi.* -**haled′,** -**hal′-ing** [< L. *ex-*, out + *halare,* breathe] **1.** to expel air; breathe out **2.** to give off (vapour, etc.) —**exhalation** (eks′-.hə lā′shən) *n.*

exhaust (ig zôst′) *vt.* [< L. *ex-*, out + *haurire,* draw] **1.** to tire out **2.** to use up **3.** to empty completely; drain **4.** to draw off or let out (air, gas, etc.), as from a container **5.** to deal with or

study thoroughly —*n.* **1.** the discharge of used steam, gas, etc. from an engine **2.** the pipe through which such steam, gas, etc. is released **3.** something given off, as fumes from an engine —**exhaust′i-bil′ity** *n.* —**exhaust′ible** *adj.* —**exhaust′-less** *adj.*

exhaustion *n.* the state of being exhausted; esp., *a)* great fatigue or weariness *b)* complete consumption

exhaustive *adj.* leaving nothing out; covering every detail —**exhaus′tively** *adv.* —**exhaus′tiveness** *n.*

exhibit (ig zib′it) *vt.* [< L. *ex-*, out + *habere,* hold] **1.** to show; display **2.** to present to public view —*n.* **1.** a show; display **2.** an object or objects displayed publicly **3.** *Law* an object produced as evidence in a court —**exhib′itor, exhib′-iter** *n.*

exhibition (ek′sə bish′ən) *n.* **1.** a public display, as of art **2.** the act of exhibiting **3.** the things exhibited **4.** a scholarship awarded at some universities

exhibitioner *n.* a student who receives an exhibition

exhibitionism *n.* **1.** a tendency to call attention to oneself or show off **2.** *Psychol.* a tendency to expose parts of the body that are conventionally concealed —**ex′hi-bi′tionist** *n.* —**ex′hibi′tionis′tic** *adj.*

exhilarate (ig zil′ə rāt′) *vt.* -**rat′ed,** -**rat′-ing** [< L. *ex-*, intens. + *hilaris,* glad] to make merry or lively —**exhil′arative** *adj.* —**exhil′ara′tion** *n.*

exhort (ig zôrt′) *vt., vi.* [< L. *ex-*, out + *hortari,* urge] to urge earnestly; entreat —**ex′horta′tion** (eg′-) *n.* —**exhor′tatory, exhor′tative** *adj.*

exhume (eks hyōōm′) *vt.* -**humed′,** -**hum′-ing** [< L. *ex,* out + *humus,* ground] to dig out of the earth; disinter —**exhuma-tion** (eks′hyōō mā′shən) *n.*

ex hypothesi (hī poth′ə sī) [L.] hypothetically

exigency (ek′sə jən sē) *n.,* pl. **-cies** [see EXACT] **1.** urgency **2.** a situation calling for immediate attention **3.** [*pl.*] pressing needs; demands Also **ex′igence** —**ex′i-gent** *adj.*

exiguous (eg zig′yōō wəs) *adj.* [see EXACT] scanty; little; small; meagre —**exi-guity** (ek′sə gyōo′ə tē) *n.*

exile (eg′sīl) *n.* [< L. *exilium,* banishment] **1.** a prolonged, often enforced, living away from one's country, etc. **2.** a person in exile —*vt.* -**iled, -iling** to force (a person) to leave his country, etc.; banish

exist (ig zist′) *vi.* [< L. *ex-*, forth + *sistere,* cause to stand] **1.** to have reality or being; be **2.** to be present (*in*) **3.** to continue being; live —**exist′ent** *adj.*

existence *n.* **1.** the state or fact of being **2.** continuance of being; life **3.** occurrence **4.** a manner of existing **5.** a thing that exists

existential (eg′zis ten′shəl) *adj.* **1.** of or based on existence **2.** of or relating to existentialism

existentialism *n.* a theory which holds that man is free and responsible for his acts —**ex′isten′tialist** *n.*

exit (ek′sit) *n.* [< L. *ex-*, out + *ire*, go]
1. a way out 2. a going out; departure
3. an actor's departure from the stage
4. he leaves: a stage direction —*vi.* to
leave a place; depart

‡**ex libris** (eks lī′bris, lī′-) [L.] from the
library of

exo- [< Gr.] *a prefix meaning* outside,
outer

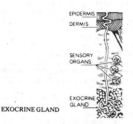

EPIDERMIS

DERMIS

SENSORY ORGANS

EXOCRINE GLAND

EXOCRINE GLAND

exocrine (ek′sə krin) *adj.* [EXO- +
(ENDO)CRINE] designating or of a gland
secreting externally, either directly or
through a duct —*n.* any such gland

Exod. Exodus

exodus (ek′sə dəs) *n.* [< Gr. *ex-*, out
+ *hodos*, way] a going out or forth —[E-]
1. the departure of the Israelites from
Egypt (with *the*) 2. the second book of
the Pentateuch, which describes this

ex officio (eks′ ə fish′ē ō′) [L., from office]
by virtue of one's office, or position

exonerate (ig zon′ə rāt′) *vt.* -at′ed, -at′-
ing [< L. *ex-*, out + *onus*, a burden]
to declare or prove blameless —**exon′era′-
tion** *n.*

exorbitant (ig zôr′bə tənt) *adj.* [< L. *ex-*,
out + *orbita*, track] going beyond what
is reasonable, fair, etc., excessive —**exor′-
bitance** *n.* —**exor′bitantly** *adv.*

exorcise, exorcize (ek′sôr siz′) *vt.*
-cised′ or -cized′, -cis′ing or -ciz′ing [<
Gr. *ex-*, out + *horkos*, oath] 1. to drive
(an evil spirit) out or away by prayers,
etc. 2. to free from such a spirit —**ex′or-
cis′er, ex′orciz′er** *n.*

exorcism *n.* 1. the act of exorcising
2. a formula or ritual used in exorcising
—**ex′orcist** *n.*

exordium (eks ôr′dē əm) *n.,* *pl.* -diums,
-dia [< L. *ex-*, from + *ordiri*, begin]
the opening part of a speech, treatise, etc.

exotic (ig zot′ik) *adj.* [< Gr. *exō*, outside]
1. not native 2. strangely beautiful, enticing, etc. —*n.* a plant that is not native
—**exot′ically** *adv.* —**exot′icism** *n.*

exotica *n.pl.* foreign or unfamiliar things,
as curious or rare art objects, strange
customs, etc.

exp. 1. expenses 2. export 3. express

expand (ik spand′) *vt.* [< L. *ex-*, out
+ *pandere*, spread] 1. to spread out;
unfold 2. to make greater in size, scope,
etc. 3. to enlarge upon (a topic, etc.)
in detail —*vi.* 1. to spread out; enlarge

2. to become increasingly relaxed, friendly,
or talkative —**expand′able** *adj.*

expanse *n.* a large, open area; wide extent

expansible *adj.* that can be expanded

expansion *n.* 1. an enlargement 2. an
expanded thing or part 3. the extent
of expansion 4. a development, as of
a topic 5. an increase, enlargement, etc.,
as in the activities of a company

expansionism *n.* the policy of expanding
a nation's territory or sphere of influence
—**expan′sionist** *adj., n.* —**expan′sionis′-
tic** *adj.*

expansive *adj.* 1. tending to expand 2.
broad; comprehensive 3. sympathetic;
demonstrative —**expan′sively** *adv.*
—**expan′siveness** *n.*

expatiate (ik spā′shē āt′) *vi.* -at′ed, -at′-
ing [< L. *ex-*, out + *spatiari*, walk] to
speak or write in detail (*on* or *upon*)
—**expa′tia′tion** *n.* —**expa′tiatory** *adj.*

expatriate (eks pa′trē āt′; *for adj. & n.,*
-it) *vt.* -at′ed, -at′ing [< L. *ex*, out of
+ *patria*, fatherland] 1. to exile 2. to
withdraw (oneself) from one's native land
—*adj.* expatriated —*n.* an expatriated
person —**expa′tria′tion** *n.*

expect (ik spekt′) *vt.* [< L. *ex-*, out +
spectare, look] 1. to look for as likely
to occur or appear 2. to look for as
proper or necessary 3. [Colloq.] to
presume; guess —**be expecting** [Colloq.]
to be pregnant

expectancy (ik spek′tən sē) *n.,* *pl.* -cies
1. expectation 2. that which is expected,
esp. on a statistical basis Also **expect′ance**

expectant *adj.* expecting; specif., *a)*
showing expectation *b)* waiting, as for
the birth of a child

expectation (ek′spek tā′shən) *n.* 1. a
looking forward to 2. a looking for as
due or necessary 3. [*also pl.*] prospect
of future success, prosperity, etc. —**in
expectation** in the state of being looked for

expectorant (ek spek′tər ənt) *adj.* causing or easing the bringing up of phlegm,
mucus, etc. from the respiratory tract —*n.*
an expectorant medicine

expectorate *vt., vi.* -rat′ed, -rat′ing [<
L. *ex-*, out + *pectus*, breast] 1. to cough
up and spit out (phlegm, mucus, etc.) 2.
to spit —**expec′tora′tion** *n.*

expediency (ik spē′ən sē) *n.,* *pl.* -cies
1. suitability for a given purpose 2. the
doing of what is of use or advantage
rather than what is right; self-interest
Also **expe′dience**

expedient *adj.* [see ff.] 1. useful for
effecting a desired result; convenient 2.
based on what is of use or advantage
rather than what is right; guided by self-
interest —*n.* an expedient thing —**expe′di-
ently** *adv.*

expedite (ek′spə dīt′) *vt.* -dit′ed, -dit′ing
[< L. *expedire*, lit., to free the feet] 1.
to speed up or make easy the progress
of; facilitate 2. to do quickly

expedition (ek′spə dish′ən) *n.* [<
EXPEDITE] 1. *a)* a journey, voyage, etc.,
as for exploration or battle *b)* the people,

ships, etc. on such a journey **2.** efficient speed; dispatch —**ex·pe'di·tion·ary** *adj.*

expeditious (ek'spə·dish'əs) *adj.* efficient and speedy

expel (ik·spel') *vt.* **-pelled', -pel'ling** [< L. *ex-*, out + *pellere*, thrust] **1.** to drive out by force; eject **2.** to dismiss or send away by authority —**expel'lable** *adj.*

expend (ik·spend') *vt.* [< L. *ex-*, out + *pendere*, weigh] **1.** to spend **2.** to use up —**expend'er** *n.*

expendable *adj.* **1.** that can be expended **2.** *Mil.* designating equipment (and men) expected to be used up (or sacrificed) in service —*n.* a person or thing considered expendable —**expend'abil'ity** *n.*

expenditure *n.* **1.** a spending of money, time, etc. **2.** the amount of money, time, etc. expended

expense (ik·spens') *n.* [see EXPEND] **1.** financial cost **2.** any cost or sacrifice **3.** [*pl.*] *a)* charges met with in doing one's work *b)* money to pay for these **4.** a cause of spending —**at the expense of** with the payment, loss, discredit, etc. borne by

expense account 1. an arrangement whereby certain expenses of an employee related to his work are paid for by his employer **2.** a record of these

expensive *adj.* involving much expense; high-priced —**expen'sively** *adv.* —**expen'siveness** *n.*

experience (ik·spēr'ē·əns) *n.* [< L. *experiri*, to try] **1.** the act of living through an event **2.** anything or everything observed or lived through **3.** *a)* training and personal participation *b)* knowledge or skill resulting from this —*vt.* **-enced, -enc·ing** to have experience of

experienced *adj.* **1.** having had much experience **2.** made wise, competent, etc. by experience

experiential (ik·spēr'ē·en'shəl) *adj.* of or based on experience —**expe'rien'tial·ist** *n.* —**expe'rien'tial·ly** *adv.*

experiment (ik·sper'ə·mənt, *for v., also* -ment') *n.* [see EXPERIENCE] any action or process undertaken to discover or test something —*vi.* to make an experiment —**exper'imenta'tion** *n.* —**exper'iment'er** *n.*

experimental (ik·sper'ə·men't'l) *adj.* **1.** based on, tested by, or having the nature of, experiment **2.** used for experiments —**exper'imen'tal·ism** *n.*

expert (ek'spərt) *n.* [see EXPERIENCE] a person who is skilful or highly trained and informed in some special field —*adj.* **1.** very skilful **2.** of or from an expert [*expert* opinion] —**ex'pertly** *adv.* —**ex'pertness** *n.*

expertise (ek'spər·tēz') *n.* [Fr.] the skill, knowledge, judgment, etc. of an expert

expiate (ek'spē·āt') *vt.* **-at'ed, -at'ing** [< L. *ex-*, out + *piare*, appease] **1.** to make amends for (wrongdoing) **2.** to suffer for —**ex'piable** *adj.* —**ex'pia'tion** *n.* —**ex'pia'tor** *n.*

expiatory (ek'spē·ə·tər·ē) *adj.* that expiates

expire (ik·spīr') *vi.* [< L. *ex-*, out + *spirare*, breathe] **1.** to come to an end **2.** to breathe out air **3.** to die —*vt.* **-pired', -pir'ing** to breathe out (air from the lungs) —**expiration** (ek'spə·rā'shən) *n.*

expiry (ik·spīr·ē) *n., pl.* **-ries** a coming to an end; termination [the *expiry* of the lease]

explain (ik·splān') *vt.* [< L. *ex-*, out + *planus*, level] **1.** to make plain or understandable **2.** to give the meaning of; expound **3.** to account for —*vi.* to give an explanation —**explain away** to state reasons for so as to justify —**explain oneself 1.** to make clear what one means **2.** to give reasons justifying one's conduct

explanation (eks'plə·nā'shən) *n.* **1.** an explaining **2.** something that explains **3.** the interpretation, meaning, etc. given in explaining

explanatory (ik·splan'ə·tər·ē) *adj.* explaining or intended to explain: also **explan'ative**

expletive (eks·plē'tiv) *n.* [< L. *ex-*, out + *plere*, fill] **1.** an oath or exclamation **2.** a word, phrase, etc. used to fill out a sentence or metrical line —*adj.* used to fill out a sentence, line, etc.: also **exple'tory**

explicable (iks·plik'·ə·b'l) *adj.* that can be explained

explicate (eks·pli·kāt') *vt.* **-cat'ed, -cat'ing** [< L. *ex-*, out + *plicare*, fold] to make clear or explicit; explain fully —**ex'plica'tion** *n.* —**ex'plica'tor** *n.*

explicit (ik·splis'it) *adj.* [see prec.] **1.** clearly stated or expressed, with nothing implied **2.** saying what is meant; outspoken —**explic'itly** *adv.* —**explic'itness** *n.*

explode (ik·splōd') *vt.* **-plod'ed, -plod'ing** [orig., drive off the stage < L. *ex-*, off + *plaudere*, applaud] **1.** to make burst with a loud noise **2.** to cause a rapid, violent change in by chemical reaction or by nuclear fission or fusion **3.** to expose as false; discredit —*vi.* **1.** to burst noisily **2.** to break forth noisily [to *explode* with anger] **3.** to increase rapidly [an *exploding* population]

exploit (eks'ploit; *for v.,* ik·sploit') *n.* [see EXPLICATE] an act of brilliance or daring; bold deed —*vt.* **1.** to utilize productively **2.** to profit from the labour of (others) in an unethical way; use selfishly —**exploit'able** *adj.* —**ex'ploita'tion** *n.* —**exploit'er** *n.*

explore (ik·splôr') *vt., vi.* **-plored', -plor'ing** [L. *explorare*, search out] **1.** to look into closely; investigate **2.** to travel in (a region previously little known) for discovery —**ex'plora'tion** *n.* —**explor'atory** *adj.* —**explor'er** *n.*

explosion (ik·splō'zhən) *n.* **1.** an exploding; detonation **2.** the noise made by exploding **3.** a noisy outburst **4.** a sudden, rapid, and widespread increase

explosive *adj.* **1.** of, causing, or like an explosion **2.** tending to explode —*n.* a substance that can explode —**explo'sively** *adv.* —**explo'siveness** *n.*

exponent (ik·spō'nənt) *n.* [see EXPOUND]

1. a person who expounds or promotes (principles, etc.) **2.** a person or thing that is an example (*of* something) **3.** *Algebra* a small figure at the upper right of another figure to show how many times the latter is to be multiplied by itself (Ex.: b^2 = b x b) —**exponential** (eks'-pō nen'shəl) *adj.* —**ex'ponen'tially** *adv.*

export (ik spôrt'; *for n. & adj.* eks'pôrt) *vt.* [< L. *ex-*, out + *portare*, carry] to send (goods, etc.) to other countries, esp. for sale —*n.* **1.** something exported **2.** an exporting Also **ex'porta'tion** —*adj.* of or for exporting or exports —**export'able** *adj.* —**export'er** *n.*

expose (ik spōz') *vt.* **-posed'**, **-pos'ing** [see EXPOUND] **1.** to reveal; display; make known **2.** to make known the crimes, etc. of **3.** *a)* to lay open (*to* danger, attack, ridicule, etc.) *b)* to subject (*to* an influence) **4.** *Hist.* to leave out in the open to die **5.** *Photog.* to subject (a film or plate) to radiation as of light rays —**expose oneself** to display one's sexual organs in public —**expos'er** *n.*

exposé (eks pō'zā) *n.* [Fr.] a public disclosure of a scandal, crime, etc.

exposed (ik spōzd') *adj.* **1.** not concealed **2.** left in the open; open to the weather **3.** vulnerable

exposition (eks'pə zish'ən) *n.* [see EXPOUND] **1.** a detailed explanation **2.** writing or speaking that explains **3.** a large public exhibition **4.** the first section of certain musical forms, introducing the main theme

expository (ek spoz'ə tə rē) *adj.* explanatory

ex post facto (eks pōst fak'tō) [L., from (the thing) done afterwards] done afterwards, esp. when retroactive

expostulate (ik spos'choo lāt') *vi.* **-lat'ed**, **-lat'ing** [< L. *ex-*, intens. + *postulare*, demand] to reason with a person, objecting to his actions or intentions (*with*) —**expos'tula'tion** *n.* —**expos'tula'tor** *n.* —**expos'tulatory** *adj.*

exposure (ik spō'zhər) *n.* **1.** an exposing or being exposed **2.** location in relation to the sun, winds, etc. [*an eastern exposure*] **3.** the disclosure of doubtful transactions **4.** a being exposed, when helpless, to the elements **5.** *Photog.* *a)* a film section for making one picture *b)* the time during which film is exposed

expound (ik spound') *vt.* [< L. *ex-*, out + *ponere*, put] **1.** to set forth in detail **2.** to explain

express (ik spres') *vt.* [< L. *ex-*, out + *premere*, press] **1.** to put into words; state **2.** to make known; show **3.** to represent; symbolize **4.** to press out (juice, etc.) —*adj.* **1.** *a)* expressed and not implied; explicit *b)* specific [his *express* reason] **2.** exact [the *express* image] **3.** fast and direct [an *express* train] —*adv.* by express —*n.* **1.** an express train, bus, etc. **2.** [Chiefly U.S.] a service for transporting goods rapidly —**express oneself 1.** to state one's thoughts **2.** to give expression to one's feelings, talents, etc. —**express'er** *n.* —**express'ible** *adj.*

expression *n.* **1.** a look, intonation, etc. that conveys meaning **2.** a showing of feeling, character, etc. [an *expression* of joy] **3.** a putting into words **4.** a particular word or phrase **5.** a manner of expressing; esp., with eloquence **6.** a representing in art, music, etc. **7.** a symbol or symbols expressing some mathematical fact —**expres'sionless** *adj.* —**expres'sionlessly** *adv.*

expressionism *n.* an early 20th-cent. movement in art, drama, etc., using symbols, stylization, etc. to give expression to inner experience —**expres'sionist** *adj.,n.*

expressive *adj.* **1.** that expresses; indicative (*of*) **2.** full of meaning [an *expressive* nod] —**expres'sively** *adv.* —**expres'siveness** *n.*

expressly *adv.* **1.** plainly; definitely **2.** particularly

expresso (ek spres'ō) *n.* same as ESPRESSO

expressway *n.* [U.S.] a divided road for high-speed, through traffic

expropriate (eks prō'prē āt') *vt.* **-at'ed**, **-at'ing** [< L. *ex-*, out + *proprius*, one's own] to take (property, etc.) from its owner —**expro'pria'tion** *n.* —**expro'pria'tor** *n.*

expulsion (ik spul'shən) *n.* an expelling, or forcing out, or the condition of being expelled —**expul'sive** *adj.*

expunge (ek spunj') *vt.* **-punged'**, **-pung'ing** [< L. *ex-*, out + *pungere*, prick] to erase or remove completely; delete —**expunc'tion** (-spuŋk'shən) *n.*

expurgate (eks'pər gāt') *vt.* **-gat'ed**, **-gat'ing** [< L. *ex-*, out + *purgare*, cleanse] to remove passages considered objectionable from (a book, etc.) —**ex'purga'tion** *n.*

exquisite (eks'kwi zit) *adj.* [< L. *ex-*, out + *quaerere*, ask] **1.** carefully or elaborately made **2.** very beautiful, esp. in a delicate way **3.** of highest quality **4.** intense; keen [*exquisite* pain] —*n.* one who is refined and fastidious in his tastes —**ex'quisitely** *adv.* —**ex'quisiteness** *n.*

ex-serviceman *n.* someone who has served in the Armed Forces —**ex-servicewoman** *n. fem.*

ext. 1. exterior **2.** external **3.** extra

extant (ek stant') *adj.* [< L. *ex-*, out + *stare*, stand] still existing

extemporaneous (ik stem'pə rā'nē əs) *adj.* [see EXTEMPORE] done or spoken without any preparation; impromptu: also **extemporary** (ik stem'pə rər ē) —**extem'-pora'neously** *adv.*

extempore (ek stem'pə rē) *adv., adj.* [L. < *ex*, out of + *tempus*, time] without preparation; impromptu

extemporize *vi., vt.* **-rized'**, **-riz'ing 1.** to speak, perform, or compose extempore; improvise **2.** to contrive as a makeshift —**extem'poriza'tion** *n.* —**extem'poriz'er** *n.*

extend (ik stend') *vt.* [< L. *ex-*, out + *tendere*, stretch] **1.** to stretch out; lengthen; prolong **2.** to enlarge in area, scope, etc.; expand **3.** to stretch forth **4.** to offer; grant **5.** to make (oneself) work or try hard —*vi.* **1.** to be extended **2.** to reach or stretch —**extend'ed** *adj.* —**extend'er** *n.* —**extend'ibil'ity** *n.*

extended family a social unit in which parents, grandparents, children, etc. live as a family unit

extended player a record containing three or four tracks instead of two : also **maxi single**

extensible (ik sten'sə b'l) *adj.* that can be extended

extension (ik sten'shən) *n.* **1.** an extending or being extended **2.** range; extent **3.** a part that forms a continuation or addition **4.** a service by which some of the facilities of an educational establishment are offered to outsiders **5.** an extra telephone on the same line as the main telephone **6.** *Physics* that property of a body by which it occupies space —*adj.* designating a device that can extend *[extension* ladder *]* —**exten'sional** *adj.*

extensive *adj.* **1.** of great extent; vast **2.** far-reaching —**exten'sively** *adv.* —**exten'siveness** *n.*

extensor *n.* a muscle that extends or straightens some part of the body, esp. a flexed arm or leg

extent (ik stent') *n.* **1.** the space, amount, or degree to which a thing extends; size; length; breadth **2.** range or limits; scope; coverage **3.** an extended space; vast area

extenuate (ik sten'yōō wāt') *vt.* -at'ed, -at'ing [< L. *ex-*, out + *tenuis*, thin] to lessen or seem to lessen the seriousness of (an offence, etc.) by giving excuses or serving as an excuse —**exten'ua'tion** *n.* —**exten'uatory, exten'uative** *adj.*

exterior (ik stēər'ē ər) *adj.* [see EXTERNAL] **1.** *a)* on the outside; outer *b)* for use on the outside **2.** coming from without *[exterior* forces *]* —*n.* **1.** an outside or outside surface **2.** an outward appearance **3.** a picture, etc. of an outdoor scene —**exte'riorly** *adv.*

exterior angle any of the four angles formed on the outside of two straight lines by a straight line cutting across them

exterminate (ik stur'mə nāt') *vt.* -nat'ed, -nat'ing [< L. *ex-*, out + *terminus*, boundary] to destroy entirely, as by killing; annihilate —**exter'mina'tion** *n.* —**exter'mina'tor** *n.*

external (ik stur'n'l) *adj.* [< L. *externus*] **1.** on the outside; exterior **2.** coming from without **3.** foreign **4.** for use on the outside of the body *[a* medicine for *external* use *]* **5.** existing apart from the mind; material **6.** for outward show; superficial **7.** of an examination, etc. taken by a student who is not resident at the university awarding the degree —*n.* [*pl.*] outward appearance or behaviour —**externality** (eks'tər nal'ə tē) *n.,* *pl.* -ties —**exter'nally** *adv.*

externalize *vt.* -ized', -iz'ing to make external; embody —**exter'naliza'tion** *n.*

extinct (ik stiŋkt') *adj.* [see EXTINGUISH] **1.** no longer in existence *[an extinct* species *]* **2.** having died down **3.** no longer active *[an extinct* volcano *]*

extinction *n.* **1.** the fact or state of being or becoming extinct **2.** a putting out or being put out, as of a fire **3.** a destroying or being destroyed

extinguish (ik stiŋ'gwish) *vt.* [< L. *ex-*, out + *stinguere*, extinguish] **1.** to put out (a fire, etc.) **2.** to destroy **3.** to eclipse; obscure —**extin'guishable** *adj.* —**extin'guisher** *n.* —**extin'guishment** *n.*

extirpate (ek'stur pāt') *vt.* -pat'ed, -pat'-ing [< L. *ex-*, out + *stirps*, root] **1.** to pull up by the roots **2.** to destroy completely; abolish —**ex'tirpa'tion** *n.*

extol (ik stōl') *vt.* -tolled', -tol'ling [< L. *ex-*, up + *tollere*, raise] to praise highly —**extol'ler** *n.* —**extol'ment** *n.*

extort (ik stôrt') *vt.* [< L. *ex-*, out + *torquere*, twist] to get (money, etc.) by violence, threats, misuse of authority, etc.; exact (*from*) —**extort'er** *n.*

extortion *n.* **1.** an extorting : sometimes applied to the exaction of too high a price **2.** something extorted —**extor'tionate, extor'tionary** *adj.*

extortioner *n.* a person guilty of extortion : also **extor'tionist**

extra (eks'trə) *adj.* [prob. < EXTRAORDINARY] **1.** more, larger, or better than is normal, expected, necessary, etc. **2.** to be paid for by an added charge —*n.* an extra person or thing; specif., *a)* an additional charge *b)* formerly, a special newspaper edition for important news *c)* an extra benefit *d) Cinema* an actor hired by the day to play a minor part *e) Cricket* a run that is not scored from the bat, as a bye —*adv.* more than usually *[extra* hot *]*

extra- [L. < *extern*(*us*), from outside] *a prefix meaning* outside, beyond, beside *[extramural, extramarital]*

extra cover *Cricket* a fielding position between cover and mid-off

extract (ik strakt'; *for n.* eks'trakt) *vt.* [< L. *ex-*, out + *trahere*, draw] **1.** to draw out by effort *[to extract* teeth, to *extract* a promise *]* **2.** to separate (metal) from ore **3.** to obtain by pressing, distilling, etc. *[to extract* juice from fruit *]* **4.** to derive, or elicit **5.** to copy out (a passage from a book, etc.) **6.** *Math.* to compute (the root of a quantity) —*n.* something extracted; specif., *a)* a concentrated form of a food, etc. *[beef extract] b)* a quotation from a book, etc. —**extrac'tive** *adj.* —**extrac'tor** *n.*

extraction *n.* **1.** an extracting; specif., the extracting of a tooth **2.** lineage; descent

extractor fan a device for extracting stale air and other gases from a room, building, etc.: also **extrac'tor**

extracurricular (eks'trə kə rik'yə lər) *adj.* not part of the required curriculum

extradite (eks'trə dīt') *vt.* -dit'ed, -dit'-ing [< L. *ex*, out + *traditio*, a surrender] **1.** to turn over (an alleged criminal, etc.) to the jurisdiction of another state **2.** to obtain the extradition of —**ex'tradit'a-ble** *adj.* —**ex'tradi'tion** (-dish'ən) *n.*

extramural (eks'trə myōōər'əl) *adj.* [EXTRA- + MURAL] connected with but outside the normal courses of a university, college, etc.

extraneous (ik strā′nē əs) *adj.* [< L. *extraneus*, foreign] 1. not essential 2. not pertinent 3. coming from outside; foreign —**extra′neousness** *n.*

extraordinary (ik strôr′d'n ər ē) *adj.* [< L. *extra ordinem*, out of the usual order] 1. very unusual; remarkable 2. not according to the usual custom 3. sent on a special errand [an envoy *extraordinary*] —**extraor′dinarily** *adv.* —**extraor′dinariness** *n.*

extrapolate (ik strap′ō lāt′) *vt., vi.* -**lated, -lating** [see EXTRA- + INTERPOLATE] to estimate (a value, quantity, etc. beyond the known range) on the basis of certain known facts —**extrap′ola′tion** *n.*

extrasensory (eks′trə sen′sər ē) *adj.* designating of or perception that seems to occur apart from the normal function of the senses

extravagance (ik strav′ə gəns) *n.* 1. a spending of more than is reasonable or necessary 2. a going beyond reasonable or proper limits; excess 3. an instance of excess in spending, behaviour, or speech Also **extrav′agancy**

extravagant *adj.* [< L. *extra*, beyond + *vagari*, wander] 1. costing or spending too much 2. going beyond reasonable limits; excessive 3. too ornate —**extrav′agantly** *adv.*

extravaganza (ik strav′ə gan′zə) *n.* [< It. *estravaganza*, extravagance] 1. a literary, musical, or dramatic fantasy 2. a spectacular theatrical show

extravasate (ik strav′ə sāt′) *vt.* [< EXTRA- + L. *vas*, vessel] to force (blood, etc.) out from its proper vessel

extreme (ik strēm′) *adj.* [< L. *exterus*, outer] 1. to an excessive degree 2. unconventional 3. deviating from a moderate view; specif., furthest to the right or left in politics 4. severe; drastic 5. at the outermost point; farthest away —*n.* 1. either of two things that are as different as possible from each other 2. an extreme degree, act, expedient, etc. —**go to extremes** to be immoderate in speech or action —**in the extreme** to the utmost degree —**extreme′ly** *adv.*

Extreme Unction *same as* ANOINTING OF THE SICK

extremism *n.* a being extreme, esp. in politics —**extrem′ist** *adj., n.*

extremity (ik strem′ə tē) *n., pl.* -**ties** 1. the utmost point; end 2. the greatest degree 3. a state of extreme necessity, danger, etc. 4. the end of life; dying 5. an extreme measure 6. [*pl.*] the hands and feet

extricate (eks′trə kāt′) *vt.* -**cated, -cating** [< L. *ex-*, out + *tricae*, hindrances] to set free; disentangle (*from* a net, embarrassment, etc.) —**ex′trica′tion** *n.*

extrinsic (ek strin′sik) *adj.* [< L. *exter*, without + *secus*, following] not belonging to the real nature of a thing; not inherent; extraneous —**extrin′sically** *adv.*

extroversion (eks′trō vur′shən) *n.* [<

EXTRA- + ML. *versio*, a turning] *Psychol.* an attitude in which a person directs his interest to things outside himself rather than to his own experiences and feelings

extrovert (eks′trə vurt′) *n. Psychol.* a person characterized by extroversion —*adj.* characterized by extroversion: usually **ex′trovert′ed**

extrude (ek strōōd′) *vt.* -**truded, -truding** [< L. *ex-*, out + *trudere*, thrust] 1. to push out 2. to force (metal, etc.) through a die to give it a certain shape —*vi.* to protrude —**extrud′er** *n.* —**extru′sion** *n.* —**extru′sive** *adj.*

exuberance (ig zyōō′bər əns) *n.* [< L. *ex-*, intens. + *uberare*, bear abundantly] 1. the state or quality of being exuberant 2. an instance of this; esp., action or speech showing high spirits Also **exu′berancy**

exuberant *adj.* 1. full of life, vitality, or high spirits 2. luxuriant —**exu′berantly** *adv.*

exude (ig zyōōd′) *vt., vi.* -**uded, -uding** [< L. *ex-*, out + *sudare*, sweat] 1. to pass out in drops through pores, etc.; ooze 2. to seem to radiate [to *exude* joy] —**exudation** (eks′yə dā′shən) *n.*

exult (ig zult′) *vi.* [< L. *ex-*, intens. + *salire*, to leap] to rejoice greatly; be jubilant; glory —**ex′ulta′tion** *n.*

exultant *adj.* exulting; triumphant; jubilant

-ey (ē, i) *same as* -Y²: used esp. after words ending in *y*

eye (ī) *n.* [OE. *eage*] 1. the organ of sight in man and animals 2. *a)* the eyeball *b)* the iris 3. the area around the eye [a black *eye*] 4. [*often pl.*] sight; vision 5. a look; glance 6. attention; observation 7. the power of judging by eyesight 8. [*often pl.*] judgment; opinion [in the *eyes* of the law] 9. a thing like an eye in shape or function, as a bud of a potato 10. *Meteorol.* the low-pressure centre (of a hurricane), around which the winds whirl —*vt.* **eyed, eye′ing** or **ey′ing** to look at —**all eyes** extremely attentive —**all my eye** [Slang] nonsense: also **all my eye and Betty Martin** —**an eye for an eye** punishment equivalent to the injury suffered —**catch one's eye** to attract one's attention —**easy on the eyes** [Slang] attractive —**feast one's eyes on** to look at with pleasure —**get one's eye in** to accustom oneself to one's surroundings: said esp. of sportsmen —**have an eye for** to have a keen appreciation of —**have an eye to** to attend to —**have eyes for** [Colloq.] to be interested in and want —**in the public eye** often brought to public attention —**keep an eye on** to look after —**keep an eye out for** to be watchful for —**keep one's eyes open** (or **peeled** or **skinned**) to be watchful —**lay** (or **set** or **clap**) **eyes on** to see —**make sheep's eyes at** to look at flirtatiously; ogle —**one in the eye** a rebuff; discomfiture —**open one's eyes** to make one aware of the facts —**see eye to eye** to agree —**shut one's eyes to** to refuse to see or think about: also **turn a blind eye to** —**up to the eyes in** deeply engaged in —**with**

an eye to 1. regarding 2. with the intention of —**with one's eyes shut** 1. without noticing 2. with great ease

eyeball *n.* the part of the eye enclosed by the socket and eyelids —**eyeball to eyeball** confronting closely; face to face [an *eyeball to eyeball* meeting]

eye-bright *n.* a small plant formerly used in treating eye disorders

eyebrow *n.* the the bony arch over each eye or the hair growing on this —**raise an eyebrow** to appear sceptical, etc.

eye-catching *adj.* tending to attract attention

eyed *adj.* having eyes (of a specified kind) [blue-eyed]

eyedropper *n.* *same as* DROPPER

eyeful *n.* 1. a full look at something 2. [Slang] a person or thing that looks striking

eyeglass *n.* 1. a lens to help faulty vision; monocle 2. [Chiefly U.S.] [*pl.*] spectacles

eyehole *n.* 1. the socket for the eyeball 2. a peephole

eyelash *n.* any of the hairs on the edge of the eyelid

eyelet *n.* 1. a small hole for receiving a cord, etc. 2. a metal ring for lining such a hole

eyelid *n.* either of the two folds of skin that cover and uncover the front of the eyeball

eye liner a cosmetic applied in a thin line on the eyelid

eye-opener *n.* a sudden realization

eyepiece *n.* in a telescope, microscope, etc., the lens or lenses nearest the viewer's eye

eye shadow a coloured cosmetic applied to the eyelids

eyeshot *n.* range of vision

eyesight *n.* 1. the power of seeing; sight; vision 2. the range of vision

eyesore *n.* a thing that is unpleasant to look at

eyestrain *n.* a strained condition of the eye muscles, caused by too much use of the eyes

eyetooth *n.,* *pl.* -teeth' a canine tooth of the upper jaw —**cut one's eyeteeth** to become experienced

eyewash *n.* 1. a lotion for the eyes 2. [Slang] *a*) nonsense *b*) flattery *c*) something done only to impress

eyewitness *n.* a person who sees something happen, as an accident, crime, etc.

eyrie, eyry (āər'ē, ēər'ē) *n.,* *pl.* -ries [ML. *aeria,* area: infl. by L. *aer,* air & ME. *ei,* egg] 1. the nest of an eagle or other bird of prey that builds in a high place 2. a house or stronghold on a high place

F

F, f (ef) *n., pl.* **F's, f's** the sixth letter of the English alphabet

F (ef) *n. Music* the fourth tone in the ascending scale of C major

F *Physics the symbol for* farad

F 1. Fahrenheit 2. fathom 3. *Chem.* fluorine

F/, f/, f:, f. f-number

F. 1. Fahrenheit 2. Fellow 3. France 4. Friday

F., f. 1. feminine 2. folio(s) 3. following 4. *Music* forte

fa (fä) *n.* [< ML.] *Music* a syllable representing the fourth tone of the diatonic scale

F.A. 1. Football Association 2. Fanny Adams

Fabian (fä'bē ən) *adj.* [< *Fabius*, Roman general] 1. using a cautious strategy of delay and avoidance of battle 2. of a socialist organization (**Fabian Society**) advocating gradual reforms —*n.* a member of the Fabian Society

fable (fä'b'l) *n.* [< L. *fabula*, story] 1. a fictitious story meant to teach a moral lesson: the characters are usually talking animals 2. a myth or legend 3. a falsehood or fiction

fabled *adj.* 1. legendary 2. fictitious

fabric (fab'rik) *n.* [< L. *fabrica*, a workshop < *faber*, workman] 1. any woven, knitted, or felted material 2. a framework or structure

fabricate (fab'rə kāt') *vt.* **-cat'ed, -cat'-ing** [see prec.] 1. to make, construct, etc.; manufacture 2. to make up (a story, lie, etc.) —**fab'rica'tion** *n.* —**fab'rica'tor** *n.*

fabulous (fab'yoo ləs) *adj.* [see FABLE] 1. incredible 2. [Colloq.] wonderful 3. of or like a fable; imaginary; fictitious —**fab'ulously** *adv.*

façade (fə säd') *n.* [Fr. < It.: see ff.] 1. the front of a building 2. an outer appearance, esp. one that is deceptive

face (fās) *n.* [< L. *facies*, the face] 1. the front of the head 2. the expression of the countenance 3. the main or front surface 4. any of the surfaces of a crystal 5. the surface that is marked, as of a clock, playing card, etc. 6. the appearance; outward aspect 7. dignity; self-respect: in **lose** (or **save**) **face** 8. [Colloq.] effrontery 9. *Typography* a) the printing surface of a letter or plate b) the design of type —*vt.* **faced, fac'ing** 1. to turn, or have the face turned, towards 2. to meet face to face 3. to confront with courage, etc. 4. to put another material on the surface of 5. to sew a facing to (a collar, etc.) —*vi.* 1. to turn, or have the face turned, in a specified direction 2. *Mil.* to pivot in a specified direction [*right face!*] —**face to face** 1. confronting one another 2.

in the presence of: followed by *with* —**face up to** to confront with courage —**in the face of** in spite of —**make a face** to grimace —**on the face of it** apparently —**set one's face against** to be determinedly against —**show one's face** to come and be seen —**to one's face** openly —**faced** *adj.*

face card *same as* COURT CARD

faceless *adj.* without individuality or identity

face lifting 1. plastic surgery for removing wrinkles, etc. from the face 2. an altering, cleaning, etc., as of the exterior of a building Also **face lift**

facer (fā'sər) *n.* [Colloq.] 1. a sudden blow in the face 2. any sudden, unexpected difficulty or defeat

face-saving *adj.* preserving or intended to preserve one's dignity or self-respect

facet (fas'it) *n.* [see FACE] 1. any of the small, polished plane surfaces of a cut gem 2. any of the sides or aspects, as of a personality —**fac'eted** *adj.*

facetious (fə sē'shəs) *adj.* [< L. *facetus*, witty] joking, or intended to be jocular, esp. at an inappropriate time

face value 1. the value shown on a bank note, bond, etc. 2. the seeming value [to take a promise at *face value*]

facia (fā'shē ə) *n.* [var. of FASCIA] 1. an instrument panel, as of a motor car 2. a board over a shop front with the proprietor's name

facial (fā'shəl) *adj.* of or for the face —*n.* a cosmetic treatment intended to improve facial appearance

-facient (fā'shənt) [< L.] *a suffix meaning* making or causing to become [*liquefacient*]

facile (fas'īl') *adj.* [< L. *facere*, do] 1. easy 2. done quickly and smoothly; fluent 3. not sincere or profound —**fac'ilely** *adv.* —**fac'ileness** *n.*

facilitate (fə sil'ə tāt') *vt.* **-tat'ed, -tat'-ing** [see prec.] to make easy or easier —**facili'ta'tion** *n.*

facility (fə sil'ə tē) *n., pl.* **-ties** 1. absence of difficulty 2. a ready ability; skill 3. [usually *pl.*] the means to do something 4. a room, etc. for some activity

facing (fās'iŋ) *n.* 1. a lining sewn on a collar, cuff, etc. 2. a covering of contrasting material, as for decorating or protecting a building

facsimile (fak sim'ə lē) *n.* [< L. *facere*, make + *simile*, like] (an) exact reproduction or copy

fact (fakt) *n.* [< L. *facere*, do] 1. a thing that has happened or is true 2. reality; truth 3. something supposed to be true 4. a deed; act: now esp. a criminal deed [an accessory after the *fact*] —**as a matter of fact** really: also **in fact, in**

point of fact —**facts and figures** exact details —**the facts of life 1.** basic information about sexual reproduction **2.** the unpleasant facts one must face in life

faction (fak′shən) *n*. [< L. *facere*, do] **1.** a group of people in a political party, club, etc. working in a common cause against the main body **2.** partisan conflict within an organization; dissension

faction fight [S Afr.] a fight, often serious, between blacks of different tribes

factious (fak′shəs) *adj.* characterized by, or producing faction —**fac′tiously** *adv.* —**fac′tiousness** *n*.

factitious (fak tish′əs) *adj.* [< L. *facere*, do] forced or artificial —**facti′tiously** *adv.*

factor (fak′tər) *n*. [< L. *facere*, do] **1.** any of the circumstances, conditions, etc. that bring about a result **2.** *Math.* any of the quantities which form a product when multiplied together **3.** a person who carries on business transactions for another —*vt*. *Math.* to resolve into factors: also **fac′torize′**

factorial (fak tôr′ē əl) *n*. *Math.* the product of all the whole numbers from 1 up to and including a given number [the *factorial* of 4 is $1 \times 2 \times 3 \times 4$, or 24]

factory (fak′tə rē) *n*., *pl.* **-ries** [see FACTOR] a building or buildings in which things are manufactured

factory farm a farm using industrial methods to promote maximum growth rate in animals

factory ship the vessel in a fishing fleet on which the catch is processed

factotum (fak tōt′əm) *n*. [< L. *facere*, do + *totum*, all] a person hired to do all sorts of work; handyman

factual (fak′choo wəl) *adj.* of facts; real; actual —**fac′tually** *adv.*

faculty (fak′əl tē) *n*., *pl.* **-ties** [see FACILE] **1.** any natural or specialized power of a living organism **2.** any mental power such as will, reason, etc. **3.** special aptitude **4.** *a)* a university department *b)* its teaching staff **5.** [U.S.] all the teachers of a school, college, etc. **6.** an authorization

fad (fad) *n*. [< Dial.] a custom, style, etc. that many people are interested in for a short time; craze —**fad′dish, fad′dy** *adj.* —**fad′dist** *n*.

fade (fād) *vi.* [< OFr. *fade*, pale] **1.** to lose colour, intensity, power, etc. **2.** to wane, wither away, or die out —*vt*. to cause to fade —**fade in** (or **out**) *Cinema, Radio & TV* to appear (or disappear) gradually or cause to do so

faeces (fē′sēz) *n.pl.* [L., dregs] waste matter expelled from the bowels; excrement —**fae′cal** (-k′l) *adj.*

faerie, faery (fāər′ē) *n*. [Archaic] **1.** fairyland **2.** *pl.* **-ies** a fairy Also written **faërie, faëry**

Faeroese (fãr′ō wēz′) *adj.* of the Faeroe Islands —*n*. **1.** *pl.* **Faer′oese′** a native of the Faeroe Islands **2.** their language Also sp. **Faroese**

faff (faf) *vi.* [< ?] [Colloq.] to dither; be flustered

fag[1] (fag) *vi.* **fagged, fag′ging** [< ?] **1.** to work hard and become very tired **2.** [Colloq.] to serve as a fag —*vt*. to make tired by hard work —*n*. **1.** [Colloq.] *a)* drudgery *b)* a schoolboy who acts as a servant for an older boy **2.** [U.S. Slang] a homosexual

fag[2] *n*. [< ff.] [Slang] a cigarette

fag end 1. the last and worst part of anything, esp. of a cigarette **2.** the frayed end of a cloth or rope

faggot (fag′ət) *n*. [ult. < Gr. *phakelos*, a bundle] **1.** a bundle of sticks, esp. for use as fuel **2.** a savoury roll made of liver, etc. **3.** a stack of iron or steel pieces **4.** [Derog.] an old woman

fah (fä) *n*. same as FA

Fah., Fahr. Fahrenheit

Fahrenheit (far′ən hīt′) *adj.* [< G. D. *Fahrenheit*] of a thermometer on which 32° is the freezing point and 212° the boiling point of water: abbrev. F

faience (fī äns′) *n*. [Fr. < *Faenza*, Italy] earthenware having a colourful, opaque glaze

fail (fāl) *vi.* [< L. *fallere*, deceive] **1.** to be unsuccessful in obtaining a desired end **2.** to stop functioning **3.** *Educ.* to be unsuccessful in an examination **4.** to be lacking or insufficient **5.** to weaken; die away **6.** to become bankrupt —*vt*. **1.** to be of no help to **2.** to abandon [his courage *failed* him] **3.** to miss or omit [to *fail* to go] **4.** *Educ.* *a)* to refuse to pass a candidate under examination *b)* to be unsuccessful in an examination —*n*. failure —**without fail** without failing (to occur, do, etc.) —**failed** *adj.*

failing *n*. a slight fault or defect; weakness —*prep.* without; lacking

fail-safe (fāl′sāf′) *adj.* of a procedure designed to prevent malfunctioning or unintentional operation

failure (fāl′yər) *n*. **1.** the act or fact of failing, or losing strength, breaking down, going bankrupt, not doing or succeeding, etc. **2.** a person or thing that fails

fain (fān) *adj.* [OE. *fægen*, glad] [Archaic] **1.** glad; ready **2.** compelled —*adv.* [Archaic] gladly

faint (fānt) *adj.* [see FEIGN] **1.** weak; feeble **2.** timid **3.** done without enthusiasm **4.** feeling weak and dizzy **5.** dim; indistinct —*n*. a condition of temporary loss of consciousness —*vi*. to fall into a faint; swoon

fainthearted *adj.* cowardly; timid

fair[1] (fãər) *adj.* [OE. *fæger*] **1.** just; impartial **2.** according to the rules **3.** light in colour; blond **4.** beautiful **5.** neither very bad nor very good **6.** of moderately good size **7.** unblemished; clean **8.** favourable [a *fair* wind] **9.** clear and sunny **10.** easy to read; clear [a *fair* hand] **11.** likely [in a *fair* way to benefit] —*adv.* **1.** in a fair manner [play *fair*] **2.** squarely [struck *fair* in the face] **3.** [Colloq.] extremely [I'm *fair* flummoxed] —**a fair treat** [Colloq.] a person or thing that is very pleasant —**fair and square** [Colloq.] with justice and honesty —**fair to middling** [Colloq.] moderately good —**fair'ish** adj. —**fair'-ness** n.

fair² n. [< L. *feriae*, festivals] 1. a regular gathering of people for the sale of goods 2. a collection of sideshows and amusements; funfair 3. an exhibition to promote trade [a world *fair*]

fairground n. an open space where fairs are held

fair-haired adj. 1. having blond hair 2. [Colloq.] favourite [mother's *fair-haired* boy]

fairing n. a structure added to an aircraft, etc., to streamline the shape and thus reduce drag

Fair Isle [< island in the Shetlands] a type of complex knitting pattern using coloured wools

fairly adv. 1. justly 2. moderately 3. distinctly 4. completely or really [his voice *fairly* rang]

fair play an abiding by the rules or by decency and honour in sports, business, etc.

fair sex women collectively: used with *the*

fairway n. 1. a navigable channel 2. the mowed part of a golf course between a tee and a green

fair-weather adj. dependable only in easy circumstances [*fair-weather* friends]

fairy (fāər'ē) n., pl. **fair'ies** [< OFr. *faerie*] 1. a tiny, graceful, imaginary being with magic powers 2. [Slang] a male homosexual

fairy-cycle n. a child's bicycle

fairy godmother n. a benefactress

fairyland n. 1. the imaginary land where the fairies live 2. a lovely, enchanting place

fairy lights small, coloured, decorative lights used esp. outdoors and on Christmas trees

fairy ring a circle of dark grass caused by fungus

fairy tale 1. a story about fairies, magic deeds, etc. 2. an unbelievable or untrue story; lie: also **fairy story**

fait accompli (fā'tə kom'plē) [Fr.] a thing already done, so that opposition or argument is useless

faith (fāth) n. [< L. *fidere*, to trust] 1. unquestioning belief esp. in God, religious tenets, etc. 2. a particular religion 3. anything believed 4. complete trust or confidence 5. loyalty —**bad faith** insincerity; duplicity —**good faith** sincerity; honesty

faithful adj. 1. loyal 2. conscientious 3. accurate —**the faithful** the true believers or loyal followers —**faith'fully** adv. —**faith'fulness** n.

faith healing a method of treating illness by religious faith, praying, etc.: also **faith curing** —**faith healer**

faithless adj. 1. dishonest; disloyal 2. unreliable —**faith'lessly** adv. —**faith'lessness** n.

fake (fāk) vt., vi. **faked, fak'ing** [< ? G. *fegen*, to clean] to practise deception by giving a false indication or appearance of (something); feign —n. anything or

anyone not genuine; fraud —adj. fraudulent; false

fakir (fā'kēər') n. [Ar. *faqīr*, poor] 1. a member of a Moslem holy sect who lives by begging 2. a Hindu ascetic

Falange (fəlanj') n. [Sp., phalanx] a fascist political party in Spain —**Falang'-ist** n.

falchion (fôl'chən) n. [< L. *falx*, sickle] a medieval sword with a broad, slightly curved blade

falcon (fôl'kən) n. [< L. *falx*, sickle] 1. any hawk trained to hunt and kill small game 2. a long-winged hawk with a short, curved beak

falconry n. 1. the art of training falcons to hunt game 2. the sport of hunting with falcons —**fal'coner** n.

falderal (fal'də ral') n. [nonsense syllables] 1. nonsense 2. a refrain in some old songs

fall (fôl) vi. **fell, fall'en, fall'ing** [OE. *feallan*] 1. to come down by gravity, as when dropped 2. to come down suddenly from an upright position; tumble 3. to be wounded or killed in battle 4. to collapse 5. to hang down 6. to strike; hit [to *fall* wide of the mark] 7. to take a downward direction 8. to become lower, less, weaker, etc. 9. to lose power, status, etc. 10. to do wrong; sin 11. to be captured or conquered 12. to take on a dejected look [his face *fell*] 13. to take place; occur 14. to come by lot, inheritance, etc. 15. to pass into a specified condition [to *fall* ill] 16. to be directed, esp. by chance —n. 1. a dropping; descending 2. a coming down suddenly from an upright position 3. a downward direction or slope 4. a becoming lower or less 5. a capture; overthrow; ruin 6. a loss of status, reputation, etc. 7. something fallen, as snow, or the amount of this 8. [U.S.] autumn 9. the distance something falls 10. [usually pl.] water falling over a cliff, etc. 11. a) the throwing of an opponent in wrestling b) a wrestling match —**fall about** [Colloq.] be helpless with laughter —**fall (all) over oneself** [Colloq.] to behave in too eager a manner —**fall away** to become less in size, strength, etc. —**fall back** to retreat —**fall back on** (or **upon**) to turn to for help —**fall down on** [Colloq.] to fail in —**fall flat** to fail to have the desired effect —**fall for** [Colloq.] 1. to fall in love with 2. to be tricked by —**fall foul of** to come into conflict or collision with —**fall in** 1. to give way 2. to line up in proper formation —**fall in with** 1. to meet accidentally 2. to agree to —**fall off** to become smaller, less, worse, etc. —**fall on** (or **upon**) 1. to attack 2. to be the duty of —**fall out** 1. to quarrel 2. to happen 3. to leave one's place in a formation —**fall short** to fail to meet a standard or goal (with *of*) —**fall through** to come to nothing —**fall to** to begin —**fall under** to be classified as —**the Fall (of Man)** Theol. Adam's sin of yielding to temptation in eating the forbidden fruit

fallacy (fal'ə sē) n., pl. **-cies** [< L. *fallere*,

deceive] 1. aptness to mislead 2. a mistaken idea; error 3. an error in reasoning —**fallacious** (fə lā'shəs) *adj.*

fallen (fôl'ən) *adj.* 1. dropped 2. prostrate 3. degraded 4. over-thrown 5. ruined 6. dead

fall guy [U.S. Slang] a person left to face the consequences, as of a scheme that has miscarried

fallible (fal'ə b'l) *adj.* [< L. *fallere*, deceive] 1. liable to be mistaken or deceived 2. liable to be inaccurate —**fal'libil'ity** *n.* —**fal'libly** *adv.*

falling sickness *former name for* EPILEPSY

falling star *same as* METEOR

Fallopian tube (fə lō'pē ən) [< G. *Fallopio*] either of two slender tubes that carry ova from the ovaries to the uterus

fallout (fôl'out') *n.* 1. the descent to earth of radioactive particles, as after a nuclear explosion 2. these particles

fallow (fal'ō) *n.* [< OE. *fealh*] land ploughed but not seeded for one or more seasons —*adj.* left uncultivated or unplanted —**lie fallow** to remain uncultivated, unused, etc. for a time —**fal'lowness** *n.*

fallow deer a small European deer having a yellowish coat spotted with white in summer

false (fôls) *adj.* **fals'er, fals'est** [< L. *fallere, deceive*] 1. not true; wrong 2. untruthful 3. disloyal; unfaithful 4. misleading 5. not real; artificial 6. not properly so named [*false* acacia] 7. based on mistaken ideas 8. nonessential, or added on for protection, disguise, etc. [a *false* drawer] —**play (a person) false** to deceive or betray (a person) —**false'ly** *adv.* —**false'ness** *n.*

falsehood *n.* 1. lack of accuracy or truth 2. a lie or the telling of lies 3. a false belief, theory, idea, etc.

false pretences misrepresentation of the facts to gain advantage

falsetto (fôl set'ō) *n., pl.* **-tos** [see FALSE] an artificially high vocal register —*adj., adv.* in falsetto

falsies (fôl'sēz) *n.pl.* [Colloq.] pads worn with a brassiere to make the breasts look fuller

falsify (fôl'sə fī') *vt.* **-fied', -fy'ing** [< L. *falsus*, false + *facere*, make] 1. to make false, as by lying or altering 2. to prove to be unfounded —*vi.* to lie —**fal'sifica'tion** *n.* —**fal'sifi'er** *n.*

falsity *n., pl.* **-ties** 1. the condition or quality of being false 2. a lie

falter (fôl'tər) *vi.* [ME. *faltren*] 1. to move uncertainly or unsteadily 2. to stumble in speech 3. to show uncertainty; waver —*vt.* to say hesitatingly or timidly

fame (fām) *n.* [< L. *fama*, fame] 1. reputation, esp. for good 2. the state of being well known or much talked about; renown

famed *adj.* famous; renowned (*for* something)

familial (fə mil'ē əl) *adj.* of a family

familiar (fə mil'ē ər) *adj.* [see FAMILY] 1. well-known; common [a *familiar* sight] 2. closely acquainted (*with*) 3. friendly; intimate 4. too friendly; unduly intimate —*n.* 1. a close friend 2. a spirit supposed to act as servant to a witch —**famil'iarly** *adv.* —**familiarity** (fə mil'ē ar'ə tē) *n.*

familiarize (fə mil'yə rīz') *vt.* **-ized', -iz'ing** 1. to make commonly known 2. to make fully acquainted —**famil'iariza'tion** *n.*

family (fam'ə lē) *n., pl.* **-lies** [< L. *familia*, household] 1. *a)* a social unit consisting of parents and their children *b)* the children of the same parents 2. a group of people related by ancestry or marriage 3. all the people living in the same house 4. a group of things having a common source or similar features; specif., *Biol.* a taxonomic category, ranking above a genus and below an order —**in the family way** [Colloq.] pregnant

Family Allowance in Canada, and formerly in Britain, a payment made by the government to families with dependent children : in Britain, now replaced by CHILD BENEFIT

family man 1. a man who has a wife and children 2. a man devoted to his family and home

family name a surname

family planning *same as* BIRTH CONTROL

family tree 1. all the ancestors and descendants in a family 2. a chart showing their relationship

famine (fam'in) *n.* [< L. *fames*, hunger] an acute and general shortage, specif. of food

famish (fam'ish) *vt., vi.* [< L. *ad*, to + *fames*, hunger] to make or be very hungry —**to be famished** (or **famishing**) [Colloq.] to feel very hungry

famous (fā'məs) *adj.* [< L. *fama*, fame] 1. having fame; renowned 2. [Colloq.] excellent —**fa'mously** *adv.*

fan¹ (fan) *n.* [< L. *vannus*, basket for winnowing grain] 1. a device used to set up a current of air for ventilating or cooling, esp. *a)* a folding device of paper, cloth, etc. that opens as a sector of a circle *b)* a motor-driven device with revolving blades 2. anything in the shape of a fan —*vt.* **fanned, fan'ning** 1. to move (air) as with a fan 2. to direct air (towards) as with a fan 3. to stir up; excite 4. to spread out into the shape of a fan —**fan out** to spread out like a fan

fan² *n.* [< ff.] [Colloq.] a person enthusiastic about a sport, performer, etc.; devotee [a football *fan*]

Fanagalo (fan'ə gə lō) *n.* in South Africa, a Zulu-based pidgin language with English and Afrikaans components, used esp. on the mines

fanatic (fə nat'ik) *adj.* [< L. *fanum*, temple] unreasonably enthusiastic; excessively zealous: also **fanat'ical** —*n.* a zealot —**fanat'icism** *n.*

fan belt in a motor vehicle, the belt driving the radiator cooling fan

fancier (fan'sē ər) *n.* a person with a

special interest in and knowledge of something [a dog *fancier*]

fanciful (fan′si fəl) *adj.* 1. full of fancy; having or showing a playful imagination 2. not real; imaginary —**fan′cifully** *adv.* —**fan′cifulness** *n.*

fancy (fan′sē) *n., pl.* **-cies** [< *fantasy*] 1. imagination, now esp. when light or whimsical 2. a mental image 3. a caprice; whim 4. an inclination or fondness —*adj.* **-cier, -ciest** 1. capricious; whimsical 2. extravagant [a *fancy* price] 3. not plain; decorated, elaborate, etc. 4. intricate 5. bred for some special feature —*vt.* **-cied, -cying** 1. to imagine 2. to have a liking for 3. to suppose 4. [Colloq.] to have a conceited opinion of (oneself) —**fancy (that)!** can you imagine (that)!

fancy dress a costume representing a historical character, an animal, etc., worn at a dance, carnival, etc.

fancy-free *adj.* 1. free to fall in love; not married, engaged, etc. 2. carefree

fancy goods small, decorative articles; knickknacks

fancy man [Slang] 1. a woman's lover 2. a man supported by a woman; esp., a pimp

fancy woman [Slang] 1. a mistress 2. a prostitute

fancywork *n.* ornamental needlework

fandango (fan daŋ′gō) *n., pl.* **-gos** [Sp.] a lively Spanish dance

fanfare (fan′fãr′) *n.* [Fr.] a loud flourish of trumpets

fang (faŋ) *n.* [OE. < *fon*, seize] 1. one of the long, pointed teeth of meat-eating animals 2. one of the long teeth through which poisonous snakes inject their venom

fanjet (fan′jet) *n.* same as TURBOFAN

fanlight (fan′līt′) *n.* a semicircular window, fanlike in shape, as over a door

fanny (fan′ē) *n.* [< ?] 1. [Vulg. Slang] the female genitals 2. [U.S. Slang] the buttocks

Fanny Adams [< C19 murder victim] [Slang] nothing at all: also **sweet Fanny Adams**

fantail (fan′tāl′) *n.* a pigeon or goldfish with a fanlike tail

fantasia (fan tā′zē ə) *n.* [see FANTASY] 1. a musical composition of no fixed form 2. a medley of familiar tunes

fantasize (fan′tə sīz′) *vt., vi.* **-sized′, -siz′-ing** to create (something) in a fantasy; daydream (about)

fantastic (fan tas′tik) *adj.* 1. imaginary; unreal 2. grotesque; odd 3. capricious; eccentric 4. [Colloq.] incredible [fantastic progress] Also **fantas′tical** *adj.* —**fantas′-tically** *adv.*

fantasy (fan′tə sē) *n., pl.* **-sies** [< Gr. *phainein*, to show] 1. imagination or fancy; esp., wild, visionary fancy 2. a mental image 3. a whim; caprice 4. a highly imaginative poem, play, etc. 5. same as FANTASIA 6. a daydream, esp. about an unfulfilled desire

fan vaulting *Archit.* vaulting having ribs that radiate, like those of a fan, from the top of a capital

FAO Food and Agriculture Organization (of the UN)

far (fär) *adj.* **far′ther, far′thest** [OE. *feorr*] 1. distant in space or time 2. extending a long way 3. more distant [the *far* side of the room] 4. very different in quality or nature [far from poor] —*adv.* 1. very distant in space, time, or degree 2. to or from a great distance in time or position 3. very much [far better] —**a far cry from** very different from —**as far as** 1. to the distance, extent, or degree that 2. [Colloq.] with reference to; as for —**by far** very much: also **far and away** —**far gone** in an advanced state of deterioration —**few and far between** scarce; rare —**go far** 1. to be sufficient or last long 2. to accomplish much —**go too far** to behave in a manner exceeding reasonable limits —**in so far as** to the extent or degree that —**so far** up to this place, time, or degree —**so far as** to the extent or point that —**so far, so good** up to this point everything is all right

farad (far′əd) *n.* [< M. *Faraday*] the SI unit of capacitance

faraway (fär′ə wä′) *adj.* 1. distant in time or place 2. dreamy; abstracted [a *faraway* look]

farce (färs) *n.* [< L. *farcire*, to stuff: early farces were used between acts] 1. an exaggerated comedy based on highly unlikely situations 2. a ridiculous display, pretence, etc. —**far′cical** *adj.*

fare (fãr) *n.* [OE. *faran*, go] 1. money paid for a trip in a train, taxi, plane, etc. 2. a passenger who pays a fare 3. a) food b) the usual diet —*vi.* **fared, far′-ing** 1. to get on [he *fared* well on his trip] 2. [Poet.] to travel; go

Far Eastern designating or of those countries east of India

fare stage 1. a section of a route, as a bus route, for which a set charge is imposed 2. the stop marking the end of such a section

farewell (fãr′wel′; *for adj.* -wel′) *interj.* goodbye —*n.* 1. good wishes at parting 2. a leaving or going away —*adj.* parting; final [a *farewell* gesture]

far-fetched *adj.* resulting or introduced in a forced, or unnatural, way; strained

far-flung *adj.* extending over a wide area

farina (fə rē′nə) *n.* [L., meal] flour or meal made from cereal grains, potatoes, nuts, etc.

farinaceous (far′ə nā′shəs) *adj.* [see prec.] 1. of or like flour or meal 2. containing starch

farm (färm) *n.* [< ML. *firma*, fixed payment] 1. a piece of land (with house, barns, etc.) on which crops or animals are raised 2. any place where certain things are raised [a fish *farm*] —*vt.* 1. a) to cultivate (land) b) to raise animals, etc. 2. to collect (taxes, etc.) for a fixed amount 3. to turn over to another for a fee —*vi.* to work on or operate a farm —**farm out** 1. to rent (land, a business, etc.) for a fixed payment 2. to send (work) from a shop, office, etc. to workers on the outside

farmer *n.* one who manages or works on a farm

farmhand *n.* a hired farm labourer

farmhouse *n.* the main dwelling house on a farm

farming *n.* the business of operating a farm

farmstead (färm'sted') *n.* the land and buildings of a farm

farmyard *n.* the yard surrounding or enclosed by the farm buildings

Far North the arctic and subarctic regions of the world

faro (fãar'ō) *n.* [Fr. *pharaon*] a gambling game played with cards

far-off (fär'of') *adj.* distant; remote

far-out *adj.* [Colloq.] very advanced, experimental or nonconformist; esp., avant-garde

far-reaching *adj.* having a wide range or effect

farrier (far'ē ər) *n.* [< L. *ferrum*, iron] a blacksmith who shoes horses —**far'ri-ery** *n.*

farrow (far'ō) *n.* [< OE. *fearh*, young pig] a litter of pigs —*vt., vi.* to give birth to (a litter of pigs)

farseeing (fär'sē'iŋ) *adj.* same as FARSIGHTED (senses 1 & 2)

farsighted *adj.* 1. prudent in judgment and foresight 2. longsighted

fart (färt) *vi.* [< OE. hyp. *feortan*] [Vulg.] to pass wind from the anus —*n.* such a passing of wind

farther (fär'thər) *compar.* of FAR —*adj.* 1. more distant 2. additional —*adv.* 1. at or to a greater distance 2. to a greater degree 3. in addition

farthermost *adj.* most distant; farthest

farthest *superl.* of FAR —*adj.* most distant —*adv.* 1. at or to the greatest distance 2. to the greatest degree

farthing (fär'thiŋ) *n.* [OE. *feorthing*, fourth part] 1. a former small British coin, equal to one quarter of an old penny 2. a thing of little value

farthingale (fär'thiŋ gäl') *n.* [< Sp. *verdugo*, rod] a hoop petticoat worn in the 16th and 17th centuries

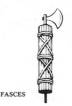

FASCES

fasces (fas'ēz) *n.pl.* [L., pl. of *fascis*, a bundle] a bundle of rods bound about an axe, carried before ancient Roman magistrates as a symbol of authority

fascia (fā'shē ə) *n.* [L., a band] same as FACIA

fascinate (fas'ə nāt') *vt.* -nat'ed, -nat'-

ing [< L. *fascinare*, bewitch] 1. to hold the attention of by being very interesting or delightful 2. to hold motionless, as by inspiring terror —**fas'cina'tion** *n.*

fascism (fash'iz'm) *n.* [< L.: see FASCES] [*also* F-] a system of government characterized by dictatorship, belligerent nationalism, racism, militarism, etc.: first instituted in Italy in 1922 —**fas'cist** *n., adj.*

fashion (fash'ən) *n.* [< L. *facere*, make] 1. current style, as of dress 2. way; manner 3. form or shape —*vt.* 1. to make; form 2. to fit, accommodate (*to* or *in*) **a fashion** to some extent

fashionable *adj.* 1. in fashion; stylish 2. of or used by people who follow fashion —**fash'ionably** *adv.*

fast[1] (fäst) *adj.* [OE. *fæst*] 1. swift; quick 2. ahead of the correct time [his watch is *fast*] 3. *a*) reckless; wild *b*) sexually promiscuous 4. firm, fixed 5. firmly fastened 6. loyal; devoted 7. that will not fade [*fast* colours] 8. *Photog.* adapted to very short exposure time —*adv.* 1. rapidly; swiftly 2. soundly [*fast* asleep] 3. firmly; fixedly 4. ahead of time 5. in a reckless way 6. [Obs.] near [*fast* by the river] —**a fast one** [Slang] a deceptive act [to pull a *fast one*] —**play fast and loose** to behave with duplicity

fast[2] *vi.* [OE. *fæstan*] 1. to abstain from all or certain foods, as in observing a holy day 2. to eat very little or nothing —*n.* the act or period of fasting

fastback *n.* a car with a back that forms a continuous slope from roof to rear

fast breeder reactor a breeder reactor that uses high energy neutrons to produce fissionable material

fasten (fäs''n) *vt.* [OE. *fæstnian*] 1. to join (one thing to another); attach 2. to make secure, as by locking, buttoning, etc. 3. to hold or direct (the attention, etc.) steadily (*on*) —*vi.* to become fastened —**fas'tener** *n.*

fastening *n.* anything used to fasten; bolt, clasp, hook, lock, button, etc.

fastidious (fas tid'ē əs) *adj.* [< L. *fastidium*, loathing] 1. not easy to please 2. daintily refined; easily disgusted —**fastid'iously** *adv.* —**fastid'iousness** *n.*

fat (fat) *adj.* **fat'ter, fat'test** [OE. *fæt*, fatted] 1. containing fat; oily; greasy 2. *a*) fleshy; plump *b*) obese 3. thick; broad 4. fertile [*fat* land] 5. profitable [a *fat* job] —*n.* 1. an oily material in animal tissue and plant seeds 2. fleshiness; corpulence 3. the richest part of anything —*vt., vi.* **fat'ted, fat'ting** to fatten —**a fat chance** [Slang] very little chance —**a fat lot** [Slang] very little or nothing —**kill the fatted calf for** to celebrate someone's return —**the fat is in the fire** an action has been taken from which trouble is bound to result —**the fat of the land** the best obtainable; great luxury —**fat'ly** *adv.* —**fat'ness** *n.*

fatal (fāt''l) *adj.* 1. resulting in death 2. disastrous 3. fateful; decisive —**fa'tally** *adv.*

fatalism *n.* the belief that all events

are determined by fate and are hence inevitable —**fa′talist** *n.* —**fa′talis′tic** *adj.*

fatality (fə tal′ə tē) *n., pl.* -**ties** 1. a death caused by a disaster, as in an accident, war, etc. 2. a fatal quality; deadliness 3. an inevitable liability to disaster 4. subjection to fate

fate (fāt) *n.* [< L. *fatum*, oracle] 1. the power supposed to determine the outcome of events; destiny 2. a) something supposedly so determined b) a person's lot or fortune 3. final outcome 4. death; destruction —*vt.* **fat′ed, fat′ing** to destine: usually in the passive —**the Fates** *Gr. & Rom. Myth.* the three goddesses who control human destiny

fated (fāt′id) *adj.* 1. destined 2. doomed

fateful *adj.* 1. having important consequences; decisive 2. bringing death or destruction 3. controlled as if by fate 4. prophetic —**fate′fully** *adv.*

fathead (fat′hed′) *n.* [Slang] a stupid person

father (fä′thər) *n.* [OE. *fæder*] 1. a male parent 2. a male guardian or protector 3. [F-] God 4. a forefather; ancestor 5. an originator; founder; inventor 6. any of the leaders of a city, assembly, etc. 7. [*often* F-] a) any of the important early Christian religious writers b) a Christian priest —*vt.* 1. to be the father of 2. to care for as a father does —**fa′therhood′** *n.*

father-in-law *n., pl.* **fa′thers-in-law′** the father of one's wife or husband

fatherland *n.* a person's native land

fatherly *adj.* of or like a father; kindly; protective

Father's Day the third Sunday in June, a day set aside in honour of fathers

fathom (fath′əm) *n.* [OE. *fæthm*] a nautical unit of depth or length, equal to 6 feet (1.8 m) —*vt.* 1. to measure the depth of 2. to understand thoroughly —**fath′omless** *adj.*

fatigue (fə tēg′) *n.* [< L. *fatigare*, to weary] 1. exhaustion; weariness 2. a) labour, other than drill or instruction, assigned to soldiers: in full, **fatigue duty** b) [*pl.*] clothing worn on fatigue duty 3. the tendency of a metal or other material to crack under stress —*vt., vi.* -**tigued′**, -**tigu′ing** to tire; weary

fatstock (fat′stok′) *n.* animals fattened for sale as meat

fatten (fat′'n) *vt., vi.* to make or become fat

fatty *adj.* **fattier, fattiest** 1. of or containing fat 2. like fat; greasy; oily —*n.* [Colloq.] a fat person

fatty acid any of a series of saturated organic carboxylic acids

fatuity (fə tyōō′ə tē) *n., pl.* -**ties** 1. complacent stupidity 2. a fatuous remark, act, etc. —**fatu′itous** *adj.*

fatuous (fat′yōō wəs) *adj.* [L. *fatuus*, foolish] complacently stupid; foolish —**fat′uously** *adv.*

faucet (fô′sit) *n.* [< OFr.] 1. a device to regulate the flow of liquid from a barrel 2. [U.S.] a tap

FAULT
(sense 4)

fault (fôlt) *n.* [see FALSE] 1. something that mars; flaw; defect 2. a misdeed or mistake 3. responsibility for something wrong; blame 4. *Geol.* a fracture and displacement of rock strata 5. *Tennis, Squash,* etc. an error in service —*vt.* 1. to blame 2. *Geol.* to cause a fault in —*vi.* 1. to commit a fault in tennis, etc. 2. *Geol.* to develop a fault —**at fault** guilty of error —**find fault (with)** to seek and point out faults (of) —**to a fault** excessively —**fault′less** *adj.*

faultfinding *n., adj.* calling attention to defects

faulty *adj.* -**ier**, -**iest** having a fault or faults; imperfect —**fault′ily** *adv.* —**fault′iness** *n.*

faun (fôn) *n.* [< L. *Faunus*, a Roman nature god] a Roman deity, half man and half goat

fauna (fô′nə) *n., pl.* -**nas**, -**nae** (-nē) [< LL. *Fauna*, Roman goddess] the animals of a specified region or time

faux pas (fō′pä′) *pl.* **faux pas** (fō′päz′) [Fr.] a social blunder; error in etiquette

favour (fā′vər) *n.* [< L. *favere*, to favour] 1. friendly regard 2. unfair partiality 3. a kind or obliging act 4. a small gift or token —*vt.* 1. to approve or like 2. to prefer unfairly 3. to support; advocate 4. to make easier; help 5. to do a kindness for 6. to resemble —**in favour of** 1. approving; supporting 2. to the advantage of 3. payable to U.S. sp. **favor**

favourable *adj.* 1. approving 2. helpful 3. pleasing —**fa′vourably** *adv.*

favoured *adj.* 1. treated with favour 2. having (specified) features [*ill-favoured*]

favourite (fā′vər it) *n.* 1. a person or thing regarded with special liking; specif., a person granted special privileges, as by a king, etc. 2. a contestant regarded as most likely to win —*adj.* best liked; preferred

favouritism *n.* 1. the act of being unfairly partial 2. the condition of being a favourite

fawn[1] (fôn) *vi.* [< OE. *fægen*, fain] 1. to cringe and flatter 2. to show friendliness by wagging its tail, etc.: said of a dog —**fawn′ing** *adj.*

fawn[2] *n.* [< L. *fetus*, offspring] 1. a deer less than one year old 2. a pale, yellowish brown —*adj.* of this colour —*vi., vt.* to bring forth (young): said of deer

fay (fā) *n.* [< L. *fatum*, fate] a fairy

FBI, F.B.I. [U.S.] Federal Bureau of Investigation

F.D. [L.; see FIDEI DEFENSOR] Defender of the Faith

Fe [L. *ferrum*] *Chem.* iron

fealty (fē′əl tē) *n., pl.* **-ties** [< L. *fidelitas*, fidelity] loyalty, esp. as owed by a vassal to his feudal lord

fear (fēər) *n.* [OE. *fær*, danger] 1. anxiety caused by the presence of danger, pain, etc.; fright 2. awe; reverence 3. apprehension; concern 4. a cause for fear —*vt.* 1. to be afraid of 2. to feel reverence or awe for 3. to expect with misgiving —*vi.* 1. to feel fear 2. to be uneasy or anxious —**never fear** do not worry; there is no danger of that —**no fear** [Colloq.] by no means —**fear′less** *adj.*

fearful *adj.* 1. causing, feeling, or showing fear 2. [Colloq.] very bad, great, etc. [*a fearful* liar] —**fear′fully** *adv.*

fearsome *adj.* 1. causing fear 2. frightened

feasible (fē′zə b'l) *adj.* [< L. *facere*, do] 1. practicable; possible 2. likely; probable 3. suitable —**fea′sibil′ity** *n.* —**fea′sibly** *adv.*

feast (fēst) *n.* [< L. *festus*, festal] 1. a rich and elaborate meal 2. a festival; esp., a religious festival 3. anything that gives pleasure by its abundance or richness —*vi.* to eat a rich, elaborate meal —*vt.* 1. to entertain at a feast 2. to delight [*to feast* one's eyes on a sight]

feat (fēt) *n.* [< L. *factum*, a deed] an act or deed showing unusual daring, skill, etc.

feather (feth′ər) *n.* [OE. *fether*] 1. any of the growths covering the body of a bird 2. [*pl.*] *a)* plumage *b)* attire 3. class; kind [*birds of a feather*] —*vt.* 1. to provide or adorn as with feathers 2. to turn the edge of (an oar or propeller) towards the line of movement —**feather in one's cap** an achievement worthy of pride —**feather one's (own) nest** to provide for one's own comfort or security —**in fine feather** in very good humour, health, or form —**feath′ered** *adj.* —**feath′ery** *adj.*

featherbed *vt.* to pamper; spoil

feather bed a mattress filled with feathers

featherbrain *n.* a foolish or frivolous person

featherweight *n.* 1. a very light person or thing 2. *see* BOXING AND WRESTLING WEIGHTS, table

feature (fē′chər) *n.* [< L. *facere*, make] 1. *a)* [*pl.*] the form or look of the face *b)* any of the parts of the face 2. an outstanding part or quality of something 3. a prominently displayed or publicized attraction at an entertainment, sale, etc. 4. a special story, article, etc. in a newspaper or magazine 5. a full-length film —*vt.* -tured, -turing 1. to give prominence to 2. to be a feature of —*vi.* to have a prominent part —**fea′tured** *adj.* —**fea′tureless** *adj.*

Feb. February

febrile (fē′brīl) *adj.* [< L. *febris*, fever] of or characterized by fever; feverish

February (feb′roo wər ē) *n.* [< L. *februa*, Roman festival of purification] the second month of the year, having 28 days (29 in leap years): abbrev. **Feb.**

feckless (fek′lis) *adj.* [Scot. < *feck*, effect + -LESS] 1. weak; ineffective 2. careless; irresponsible

fecund (fē′kənd) *adj.* [< L. *fecundus*] fruitful or fertile; productive —**fecundity** (fi kun′də tē) *n.*

fecundate (fē′kən dāt′) *vt.* -dat′ed, -dat′ing 1. to make fecund 2. to fertilize —**fe′cunda′tion** *n.*

fed (fed) *pt. & pp. of* FEED —**fed up** [Colloq.] having had enough to become disgusted, bored, etc.

Fed. 1. Federal 2. Federated 3. Federation

federal (fed′ər əl) *adj.* [< L. *foedus*, league] 1. designating or of a union of states, groups, etc. in which each member subordinates its power to a central authority in certain common affairs 2. designating or of a central government in such a union 3. [U.S.] [F-] of or supporting the northern states in the American Civil War —**fed′eralism** *n.* —**fed′eralist** *n.* —**fed′erally** *adv.*

Federal Government in Canada, the national government, located in Ottawa

federalize *vt.* -ized′, -iz′ing 1. to unite (states, etc.) in a federal union 2. to put under the authority of a federal government —**fed′eraliza′tion** *n.*

federate (fed′ə rāt′) *vt., vi.* -at′ed, -at′ing to unite in a federation

federation (fed′ə rā′shən) *n.* 1. the act of forming a union of states, groups, etc. by agreement of each member to subordinate its power to a central authority in common affairs 2. a federal union, as of states —**fed′erative** *adj.*

fee (fē) *n.* [< Anglo-Fr. *fee* & < OE. *feoh*, cattle] 1. a charge for professional services, admissions, licences, tuition, etc. 2. a sum paid for the transfer of a footballer to another club 3. *Law* an inheritance in land: an estate can be held with unrestricted rights of disposition (**fee simple**) or with restrictions (**fee tail**)

feeble (fē′b'l) *adj.* **-bler, -blest** [< L. *flere*, weep] weak; not strong; specif., *a)* infirm *b)* without force or effectiveness *c)* easily broken —**fee′bly** *adv.*

feebleminded *adj.* mentally retarded

feed (fēd) *vt.* fed, feed′ing [< OE. *fedan*] 1. to give food to; provide food for 2. to provide as food [*to feed* oats to horses] 3. to supply with what maintains or furthers growth, development, operation, etc. —*vi.* 1. to eat: said chiefly of animals 2. to flow steadily, as into a machine for use, processing, etc. —*n.* 1. *a)* fodder *b)* the amount of fodder given at one time 2. *a)* the material fed into a machine *b)* the part of the machine supplying this 3. a meal, esp. for babies —**feed on** (or **upon**) to be nourished or gratified by —**off one's feed** [Slang] lacking appetite

feedback *n.* 1. *Elec.* the transfer of part of the output back to the input 2. a process in which the result modifies the factors producing the result 3. the reaction in response to a process

feeder *n.* 1. a device that feeds material

into a machine **2.** a child's bib **3.** anything that supplies or leads into something else

feel (fēl) **vt. felt, feel′ing** [OE. *felan*] **1.** to examine by touching or handling **2.** to be aware of through physical sensation **3.** a) to experience (an emotion or condition) b) to be emotionally moved by **4.** to be aware of mentally **5.** to think or believe, often for emotional reasons —**vi. 1.** to have physical sensation **2.** to appear to be to the senses, esp. to the sense of touch **3.** to have the indicated effect [it *feels* good to be home] **4.** to grope **5.** to be aware of being [to *feel* sad] **6.** to be moved to sympathy, pity, etc. (for) —**n. 1.** the act of feeling **2.** the sense of touch **3.** the nature of a thing perceived through touch **4.** an emotional sensation **5.** instinctive ability or appreciation [a *feel* for design] —**feel like** [Colloq.] to have a desire for —**feel one's way** to move cautiously —**feel up to** [Colloq.] to feel capable of

feeler *n.* **1.** a specialized organ of touch in an animal or insect, as an antenna **2.** a remark, question, offer, etc. made to sound out another

feeling *n.* **1.** the sense of touch **2.** ability to experience physical sensation **3.** awareness **4.** emotion **5.** [pl.] sensibilities **6.** sympathy or pity **7.** an opinion or sentiment **8.** air; atmosphere **9.** a natural ability or sensitive appreciation

feet (fēt) *n. pl. of* FOOT —**have feet of clay** to reveal weaknesses —**have one's feet on the ground** to be practical, realistic, etc. —**sit at the feet of** to be an admiring disciple of —**stand on one's own feet** to be independent —**sweep** (or **carry**) **off one's feet** **1.** to fill with enthusiasm **2.** to impress deeply

feign (fān) **vt., vi.** [< L. *fingere*, to shape] **1.** to pretend **2.** to make up (a story, excuse, etc.) —**feigned** *adj.*

feint¹ (fānt) *n.* [see prec.] **1.** a pretended blow or attack intended to take the opponent off his guard **2.** a false show —**vi., vt.** to make (a feint)

feint² *adj.* with lines ruled across the width of the page

feldspar (feld′spär′) *n.* [< G. *Feld*, field + *Spat(h)*, spar] any of several crystalline and usually glassy minerals made up of aluminium silicates with sodium, potassium, or calcium —**feldspath′ic** (-spa′thik) *adj.*

felicitate (fə lis′ə tāt′) **vt. -tat′ed, -tat′ing** [< L. *felix*, happy] to wish happiness to —**felic′ita′tion** *n.*

felicity *n., pl.* **-ties** [< L. *felix*, happy] **1.** happiness **2.** anything producing happiness **3.** appropriate and pleasing expression in writing, speaking, etc. —**felic′itous** *adj.*

feline (fē′līn) *adj.* [< L. *felēs*, cat] **1.** of a cat or the cat family **2.** catlike; esp., a) sly b) graceful —*n.* any animal of the cat family —**felinity** (fi lin′ə tē) *n.*

fell¹ (fel) *pt. of* FALL

fell² *vt.* [OE. *fellan*] **1.** to knock down

2. to cut down (a tree) **3.** to turn over (the edge of a seam) and sew down

fell³ *adj.* [< ML. *fello*] fierce; terrible; cruel —**at one fell swoop** with one hasty and destructive action

fell⁴ *n.* [OE. *fel*] an animal's hide or skin

fell⁵ *n.* [< Scand.] a moor; down

fellatio (fe lāt′ē ō) *n.* [< L. *fellare*, suck] stimulation of the penis by the partner's mouth

fellow (fel′ō) *n.* [< OE. *feolaga*, partner] **1.** a companion; associate **2.** one of the same class or rank; equal **3.** either of a pair; mate **4.** a graduate student holding a fellowship in a university **5.** a member of a learned society **6.** [Colloq.] a man —*adj.* having the same ideas, position, work, etc.

fellow feeling **1.** sympathy for others, usually arising from a common experience **2.** a sense of common interest

fellowship *n.* **1.** companionship **2.** mutual sharing **3.** a group of people with the same interests **4.** an endowment for the support of a graduate student, scholar, etc., doing advanced study **5.** the rank or position of a fellow in a university or college

fellow traveller a person who espouses the cause of a party without being a member

felon (fel′ən) *n.* [< ML. *felo*] *Law* a person guilty of a major crime; criminal

felony *n., pl.* **-nies** a serious crime, as murder, arson, rape, etc. —**felonious** (fə lō′nē əs) *adj.*

felspar (fel′spär′) *n.* same as FELDSPAR

felt¹ (felt) *n.* [OE.] a fabric of wool, often mixed with fur, cotton, etc., the fibres being worked together as by pressure or heat —*adj.* of felt —*vt.* **1.** a) to make into felt b) to cover with felt **2.** to mat (fibres) together —*vi.* to become matted together

felt² *pt. and pp. of* FEEL

fem. feminine

female (fē′māl) *adj.* [< L. *femina*, woman] **1.** designating or of the sex that bears offspring **2.** of or suitable to members of this sex **3.** having a hollow part shaped to receive a corresponding inserted part, as an electric socket **4.** *Bot.* having a pistil and no stamen —*n.* a female person, animal, or plant

feminine (fem′ə nin) *adj.* [< L. *femina*, woman] **1.** of women **2.** having qualities regarded as characteristic of or suitable to women **3.** *Gram.* of gender referring to females **4.** *Prosody* of a rhyme of two or three syllables with only the first stressed (Ex.: danger, stranger) —*n. Gram.* **1.** the feminine gender **2.** a word in this gender —**fem′inin′ity** *n.*

feminism (fem′ə niz′m) *n.* the movement to win political, economic, and social equality for women —**fem′inist** *n., adj.*

‡**femme fatale** (fàm fà tàl′) [Fr., deadly woman] an alluring woman, esp. one who leads men to their ruin

femur (fē′mər) *n., pl.* **fe′murs, femora** (fem′ərə) [L.] same as THIGHBONE —**fem′oral** (fem′-) *adj.*

fen (fen) *n.* [OE.] an area of low, flat, marshy land —**the Fens** the flat, low-lying land around the Wash

fence (fens) *n.* [ME. < *defens*, defence] 1. a barrier of posts, wire, rails, etc., used as a means of protection or confinement 2. *a)* one who buys and sells stolen goods *b)* a place for such dealings —*vt.* **fenced, fenc′ing** 1. to enclose as with a fence (with *in, off*, etc.) 2. to keep (*out*) as by a fence —*vi.* 1. to practise the art of fencing 2. to be evasive 3. to buy or sell stolen goods —**sit on the fence** to avoid taking sides —**fenc′er** *n.*

fencing *n.* 1. the art of fighting with a foil or other sword 2. *a)* material for fences *b)* a system of fences

fend (fend) *vi.* [< ME. *defenden*, defend] to resist; parry —**fend for oneself** to get along without help from others —**fend off** to ward off; turn aside

fender *n.* anything that fends off or protects something else, as a low metal divider placed in front of a fireplace to confine falling coal

Fenian (fē′nē ən) *n.* [< Gael. *Fiann*, name of ancient people of Ireland] a member of a secret Irish revolutionary group formed about 1858 to free Ireland from British rule —*adj.* of the Fenians —**Fe′nianism** *n.*

fennel (fen′ʼl) *n.* [< L. *fenum*, hay] a tall herb with yellow flowers: its aromatic seeds are used as a seasoning and in medicine

fenugreek (fen′yoo grēk) *n.* [< L. *faenum Graecum*, Greek hay] a heavily scented, leguminous plant

feoff (fef) *n.* [< OFr. *fieu*] a fief

-fer (fər) [< L.] a suffix meaning bearer [*conifer*]

feral (fēər′əl) *adj.* [< L. *ferus*, fierce] 1. untamed; wild 2. savage; brutal

fermata (fər mät′ə) *n.* [It. < *fermare*, to stop] *Music* the holding of a tone or rest beyond its written value

ferment (fur′ment; *for v.* fər ment′) *n.* [< L. *fervere*, to boil] 1. a substance or organism causing fermentation, as yeast, bacteria, etc. 2. excitement; agitation —*vt.* 1. to cause fermentation in 2. to excite; agitate —*vi.* 1. to undergo fermentation 2. to be excited or agitated

fermentation (fur′mən tā′shən) *n.* 1. the breakdown of complex molecules in organic compounds, caused by a ferment [bacteria curdle milk by *fermentation*] 2. excitement; agitation —**fermentative** (fər men′tə tiv) *adj.*

fermium (fur′mē əm) *n.* [< E. *Fermi*] a radioactive chemical element: symbol Fm

fern (furn) *n.* [OE. *fearn*] a nonflowering plant having roots, stems, and fronds: it reproduces by spores —**fern′y** *adj.*

ferocious (fə rō′shəs) *adj.* [< L. *ferox*] fierce; savage; violently cruel —**ferocity** (fə ros′ə tē) *n.*

-ferous (fər əs) [< L.] a suffix meaning bearing, producing [*coniferous*]

ferret (fer′it) *n.* [< L. *fur*, thief] a weasellike animal, tamed for hunting rabbits, rats, etc. —*vt.* 1. to force out of hiding as with a ferret 2. to search (*out*) —*vi.* 1. to hunt with ferrets 2. to search around

Ferris wheel (fer′is) [< G. *Ferris*] a large, upright wheel revolving on a fixed axle and having seats hanging from the frame: used in fairgrounds, etc.

ferro- [< L.] a combining form meaning iron

ferroconcrete (fer′ō kon′krēt) *n.* reinforced concrete

ferrous (fer′əs) *adj.* [< L. *ferrum*, iron] of, containing, or derived from iron: also **fer′ric**

ferrule (fer′ool) *n.* [< L. *viriae*, bracelets] a metal ring or cap put around the end of a cane, tool handle, etc. to give added strength

ferry (fer′ē) *vt., vi.* **-ried, -rying** [OE. *ferian*, carry] 1. to take across or cross (a river, etc.) in a boat 2. to deliver (aeroplanes) by flying to the destination 3. to convey (passengers, goods, etc.) from one place to another —*n., pl.* **-ries** 1. a system for carrying people, cars, etc. across a river, etc. by boat 2. a boat (**ferryboat**) used for this, or the place where it docks —**fer′ryman** *n.*

fertile (fur′til) *adj.* [< L. *ferre*, to bear] 1. producing abundantly; fruitful 2. able to produce young, seeds, fruit, etc. 3. fertilized —**fertility** (fər til′ə tē) *n.*

fertilize (fur′til īz′) *vt.* **-ized′, -iz′ing** 1. to make fertile 2. to spread fertilizer on 3. to make (the female cell or female) fruitful by introducing the male germ cell; impregnate —**fer′tiliza′tion** *n.*

fertilizer *n.* manure, chemicals, etc. put in soil to improve plant growth

ferule (fer′ool) *n.* [L. *ferula*, rod] a flat stick or ruler used for punishing children

fervent (fur′vənt) *adj.* [< L. *fervere*, to glow] 1. showing great warmth of feeling; intensely earnest 2. hot; burning —**fer′vency** *n.*

fervid (fur′vid) *adj.* [see prec.] 1. impassioned; fervent 2. hot; glowing

fervour (fur′vər) *n.* [see FERVENT] 1. great warmth of emotion; ardour 2. intense heat U.S. sp. **fer′vor**

fess, fesse (tes) *n.* [< L. *fascia*, band] *Heraldry* a horizontal band across the middle of an escutcheon

festal (fes′t′l) *adj.* [< L. *festum*, feast] of or like a joyous celebration; festive —**fes′tally** *adv.*

fester (fes′tər) *vi.* [< L. *fistula*, ulcer] 1. to form pus 2. to cause irritation; rankle 3. to decay

festival (fes′tə v′l) *n.* [see ff.] 1. a time or day of feasting or celebration 2. a celebration or series of performances [a Bach *festival*] 3. merrymaking —*adj.* of, for, or fit for a festival

festive (fes′tiv) *adj.* [< L. *festum*, feast] of or for a feast or festival; merry; joyous —**fes′tively** *adv.*

festivity (fes tiv′ə tē) *n., pl.* **-ties** 1. merrymaking; gaiety 2. *a)* a festival *b)* [*pl.*] festive proceedings

festoon (fes tōōn´) *n.* [< It. *festa*, feast]
1. a garland of flowers, etc. hanging in
a loop or curve 2. any decoration like
this —*vt.* to adorn with or form into
festoons

fetch[1] (fech) *vt.* [OE. *feccan*] 1. to go
after and bring back 2. to cause to come
3. to draw (a breath) or heave (a sigh)
4. to sell for 5. [Colloq.] to deliver (a
blow) —*vi.* to go after things and bring
them back —*n.* 1. a fetching 2. a trick;
dodge —**fetch and carry** to perform menial
tasks —**fetch up** 1. [Colloq.] to reach;
stop 2. [Colloq.] to vomit

fetch[2] *n.* [< ?] the double or apparition
of a living person

fetching *adj.* attractive; charming
—**fetch´ingly** *adv.*

fête (fāt) *n.* [see FEAST] a festival;
entertainment, esp. one held outdoors, with
stalls, etc., to raise money —*vt.* **fêt´ed, fêt´-
ing** to honour with a fête; entertain

fetid (fet´id, fēt´-) *adj.* [< L. *foetere*,
to stink] having a bad smell, as of decay;
stinking —**fet´idly** *adv.*

fetish (fet´ish) *n.* [< Port. *feitiço*, a charm]
1. any object believed to have magical
power 2. anything to which one is
irrationally devoted 3. any nonsexual
object that abnormally excites erotic
feelings —**fet´ishism** *n.*

fetlock (fet´lok´) *n.* [ME. *fitlok*] 1. a
tuft of hair on the back of the leg of
a horse, donkey, etc., just above the hoof
2. the joint bearing this tuft

fetter (fet´ər) *n.* [OE. *feter*] 1. a shackle
or chain for the feet 2. anything that
holds in check; restraint —*vt.* 1. to bind
with fetters 2. to restrain

fettle (fet´'l) *n.* [ME. *fetlen*, make ready]
condition of body and mind [in fine *fettle*]

fetus (fēt´əs) *n.* *U.S. var. sp. of* FOETUS

feud (fyōōd) *n.* [OFr. *faide*] a long-
continued, deadly quarrel, esp. between
clans or families —*vi.* to carry on a
feud; quarrel

feudal (fyōōd´'l) *adj.* [< ML. *feodum*,
fief] of or like feudalism

feudalism *n.* the economic and social
system (**feudal system**) in medieval Europe,
in which land, worked by serfs, was held
by vassals in exchange for military and
other services to overlords —**feu´dalist** *n.*

fever (fē´vər) *n.* [< L. *febris*] 1. an
abnormally increased body temperature,
often accompanied by a quickened pulse,
delirium, etc. 2. any disease characterized
by a high fever 3. a condition of nervousness —*vt.* to cause fever in —**fe´vered** *adj.*

feverfew (fē´vər fyōō´) *n.* [< L. *febris*,
fever + *fugare*, drive away] a bushy
plant with small, white heads of flowers

feverish *adj.* 1. having fever, esp. slight
fever 2. of, like, or caused by fever 3.
causing fever 4. greatly excited Also **fe´-
verous** —**fe´verishly** *adv.*

fever pitch a condition of intense
excitement

few (fyōō) *adj.* [OE. *feawe*, pl.] not many
—*pron., n.* a small number —**a good**
few, quite a few [Colloq.] a rather large
number —**the few** a small select group

fey (fā) *adj.* [OE. *fæge*, fated] 1. [Scot.]
fated 2. strange, as in being eccentric,
visionary, etc.

FEZ

fez (fez) *n.*, *pl.* **fez´zes** [< *Fez*, city in
Morocco] a conical felt hat, usually red,
with a black tassel: worn, esp. formerly,
by Turkish men

ff *Music* fortissimo

ff. 1. folios 2. following (pages, etc.)

fiancé (fē än´sā) *n.* [Fr.] the man to
whom a woman is engaged to be married

fiancée (fē än´sā) *n.* [Fr.] the woman
to whom a man is engaged to be married

fiasco (fē as´kō) *n.*, *pl.* **-coes, -cos** [<
It. *fiasco*, bottle] a complete, ridiculous
failure

fiat (fī´at) *n.* [L., let it be done] 1. an
order issued by legal authority; decree
2. a sanction

fib (fib) *n.* [? < *fable*] a lie about something
unimportant —*vi.* **fibbed, fib´bing** to tell
such a lie —**fib´ber** *n.*

fibre (fī´bər) *n.* [< L. *fibra*] 1. a threadlike
structure that combines with others to
form animal or vegetable tissue 2. any
substance that can be separated into
threadlike structures for weaving, etc. 3.
texture 4. character [a man of strong
moral *fibre*] —**fi´brous** *adj.*

fibreboard *n.* a flexible boardlike material
made from pressed fibres of wood, etc.,
used in building

fibreglass *n.* a material made of finespun
filaments of glass, and used for textiles,
insulation, etc.

fibre optics the use of bundles of long,
transparent, glass fibres in transmitting
light, esp. optical images

fibril (fī´brəl) *n.* a small fibre

fibroid (fī´broid) *adj.* like or composed
of fibrous tissue —*n.* a benign fibroid
tumour in the uterus

fibrosis (fī brō´sis) *n.* an abnormal
increase in the amount of fibrous tissue

fibrositis (fī´brə sīt´is) *n.* a rheumatic
condition caused by the inflammation of
the fibrous tissues

fibula (fib´yoo lə) *n.*, *pl.* **-lae** (-lē´), **-las**
[L., a clasp] the long, thin, outer bone
of the lower leg —**fib´ular** *adj.*

-fic (fik) [< L.] *a suffix meaning* making
[*terrific*]

-fication (fi kā´shən) [< L.] *a suffix*
meaning a making, creating, causing
[*glorification*]

fickle (fik´'l) *adj.* [OE. *ficol*] changeable

or unstable in affection, interest, etc.
—**fick′leness** *n.*

fiction (fik′shən) *n.* [< L. *fingere*, to form]
1. anything made up or imagined, as a
statement, story, etc. **2.** *a*) any literary
work portraying imaginary characters and
events, as a novel, story, or play *b*) such
works collectively **3.** *Law* something
accepted as fact for convenience, although
not necessarily true —**fic′tional** *adj.*

fictionalize *vt.* -**ized′**, -**iz′ing** to deal
with (historical events, etc.) as fiction

fictitious (fik tish′əs) *adj.* **1.** assumed
for disguise [a *fictitious* name] **2.**
imaginary **3.** pretended

fiddle (fid′'l) *n.* [OE. *fithele*] **1.** any
stringed instrument played with a bow,
esp. the violin **2.** [Colloq.] a dishonest
arrangement —*vt.* -**dled, -dling** [Colloq.]
to make a dishonest arrangement; cheat
—*vi.* **1.** [Colloq.] to play on a fiddle
2. to tinker (*with*), esp. in a nervous way
—**fit as a fiddle** in excellent health —**play
second fiddle** to take a subordinate position
—**fid′dler** *n.*

fiddle-faddle (fid′'l fad′'l) *n.* a triviality
—*interj.* nonsense! —*vi.* to fuss; waste
time

fiddler (crab) a small, burrowing crab

fiddlesticks *interj.* nonsense!

fiddling *adj.* trifling; futile

fiddly *adj.* troublesome and time consuming

Fidei Defensor (fi dā′ē dā fen′sôr) [L.,
Defender of the Faith] title given to Henry
VIII by the pope: it appears on British
coins as *F.D.*

fidelity (fə del′ə tē) *n.*, *pl.* -**ties** [< L.
fides, faith] **1.** faithful devotion to duty
2. accuracy of description, sound
reproduction, etc.

fidget (fij′it) *n.* [< ? ON. *fikja*] **1.** a
being restless, nervous, or uneasy **2.** a
fidgety person —*vi.* to move about in
a restless, nervous, or uneasy way —**the
fidgets** restless, uneasy feelings or
movements —**fidg′ety** *adj.*

fiduciary (fi dyōō′shē ər ē) *adj.* [< L.
fidere, to trust] **1.** holding or held in
trust **2.** valuable only because of public
confidence: said of paper money —*n.*,
pl. -**aries** a trustee

fie (fi) *interj.* [< OFr.] for shame!

fief (fēf) *n.* [Fr.: see FEE] under feudalism,
heritable land held from a lord in return
for service

field (fēld) *n.* [OE. *feld*] **1.** a wide stretch
of open land **2.** a piece of cleared land
for crops or pasture **3.** a piece of land
for some particular purpose [a landing
field] **4.** an area producing some natural
resource **5.** any wide, unbroken expanse
[a *field* of ice] **6.** a battlefield **7.** *a*)
an area where practical work is done,
away from the office, laboratory, etc. *b*)
a realm of knowledge or work **8.** an
area of observation, as in a microscope
9. the background, as on a flag **10.** an
area where athletic events are held **11.**
all the entrants in a contest **12.** *Physics*
a space within which magnetic or electrical

lines of force are active: in full, **field
of force** —*adj.* of, in, on, or growing
in a field —*vt. Cricket*, etc. **1.** to stop
or catch and return (a ball) in play **2.**
to put (a player) into a field position
—*vi. Cricket*, etc. to play as a fielder
—**play the field** to explore every
opportunity —**take** (or **leave**) **the field** to
begin (or withdraw from) activity in a
game, military operation, etc.

field day 1. a day of military exercises
and display **2.** a day of enjoyably exciting
events or successful activity

fielder *n. Cricket*, etc. a player who is
fielding

field event *Athletics* any event, as the
high jump, that takes place on a field
rather than a running track

fieldfare (fēld′fāər) *n.* [< ?] a species
of N European thrush

field glass a small, portable, binocular
telescope: *usually used in pl.* **(field glasses)**

field hockey [U.S. & Canad.] hockey
played on a field, as distinguished from
ice hockey

field marshal *see* MILITARY RANKS, table

field officer a colonel, lieutenant colonel,
or major in the army

fieldsman *n.* a fielder in cricket

fieldsports *n.pl.* outdoor sports such as
hunting, racing, etc.

fieldwork *n.* **1.** a temporary fortification
2. practical work done away from an office
or laboratory, as by a scientist, social
worker, etc. —**field′work′er** *n.*

fiend (fēnd) *n.* [OE. *feond*] **1.** an evil
spirit; devil **2.** an inhumanly wicked person
3. [Colloq.] an addict [a fresh-air *fiend*]
—**the Fiend** the Devil —**fiend′ish** *adj.*

fierce (fēərs) *adj.* **fierc′er, fierc′est** [<
L. *ferus*, wild] **1.** violently cruel; savage
2. violent; uncontrolled **3.** intensely eager
[a *fierce* effort] **4.** vehement; intense
—**fierce′ly** *adv.* —**fierce′ness** *n.*

fiery (fi′ər ē) *adj.* -**erier, -eriest** **1.**
containing or consisting of fire **2.** like
fire; glaring, hot, etc. **3.** ardent **4.** excitable
—**fi′erily** *adv.* —**fi′eriness** *n.*

fiesta (fē es′tə) *n.* [Sp.] **1.** a religious
festival **2.** any gala celebration; holiday

FIFA (fē′fə) [< Fr. *F(édération) I(nter-
nationale) de F(ootball) A(ssociation)*] the
international organization of association
football

fife (fif) *n.* [< G. or Fr.] a small, shrill-
toned musical instrument resembling a flute
—**fif′er** *n.*

fifteen (fif′tēn′) *adj., n.* [OE. *fiftene*]
five more than ten; 15; XV —**fif′-
teenth′** *adj., n.*

fifth (fifth) *adj.* [< OE. *fif*, five] **1.** preceded
by four others in a series; 5th **2.** designating
any of five equal parts —*n.* **1.** the one
following the fourth **2.** any of the five
equal parts of something; 1/5

fifth column [orig. (1936) applied to
Franco sympathizers inside Madrid, then
besieged by four of his columns on the
outside] a group of people who give
aid to the enemy from within their own
country —**fifth columnist**

fifty (fif′tē) *adj., n., pl.* **-ties** [OE. *fiftig*] five times ten; 50; L. —**fif′tieth** *adj., n.*
fifty-fifty *adj.* [Colloq.] equal; even —*adv.* [Colloq.] equally
fig (fig) *n.* [< L. *ficus*] **1.** a small, hollow, pear-shaped fruit with sweet, seed-filled flesh **2.** a tree bearing this fruit **3.** a trifle [not worth a *fig*]
fig. **1.** figurative(ly) **2.** figure(s)
fight (fīt) *vi.* **fought, fight′ing** [OE. *feohtan*] **1.** to take part in a physical struggle or battle **2.** to struggle in trying to overcome; contend —*vt.* **1.** to oppose physically or in battle **2.** to struggle against **3.** to engage in (a war, etc.) **4.** to gain by struggle [he *fought* his way up] —*n.* **1.** any struggle, contest, or quarrel **2.** power or readiness to fight —**fight it out** to fight until one side is defeated —**fight off** to struggle to avoid —**fight shy of** keep aloof from; avoid
fighter *n.* **1.** one that fights; esp., a prizefighter **2.** a fast, highly manoeuvrable aircraft for aerial combat
fighting chance a chance of success dependent on a struggle
fig leaf a device intended to hide anything regarded as shameful, esp. the genitals
figment (fig′mənt) *n.* [< L. *fingere*, make] something merely imagined or made up in the mind
figuration (fig′yoo rā′shən) *n.* **1.** a forming; shaping **2.** form; appearance **3.** ornamentation
figurative (fig′yoor ə tiv) *adj.* **1.** representing by means of a figure or symbol **2.** not in its usual, literal, or exact sense; metaphorical **3.** using figures of speech —**fig′uratively** *adv.* —**fig′urativeness** *n.*
figure (fig′ər) *n.* [< L. *fingere*, to form] **1.** the outline or shape of something; form **2.** the human form **3.** a person thought of in a specified way [a great social *figure*] **4.** a likeness of a person or thing **5.** an illustration; diagram **6.** a design; pattern **7.** *a)* the symbol for a number [the figure 5] *b)* [*pl.*] arithmetic **8.** a sum of money **9.** *Dancing & Skating* a series or pattern of steps or movements **10.** *Geom.* a surface or space bounded by lines or planes **11.** *same as* FIGURE OF SPEECH —*vt.* **-ured, -uring** **1.** to represent in definite form **2.** to imagine **3.** to ornament with a design **4.** to compute with figures —*vi.* **1.** to be conspicuous **2.** to do arithmetic **3.** [U.S. Colloq.] to be as expected —**figure out** **1.** to solve **2.** [U.S. Colloq.] understand
figurehead *n.* **1.** a carved figure on a ship's bow **2.** one holding a high position but having no real power
figure of speech an expression using words in a nonliteral sense to add vividness, etc. to what is said
figurine (fig′yoo rēn′) *n.* [< It. *figurina*] a small sculptured or moulded figure; statuette
figwort (fig′wurt′) *adj.* designating a large family of plants including the foxglove, snapdragon, etc.
filament (fil′ə mənt) *n.* [< L. *filum*, thread]

1. a very slender thread or threadlike part; specif., the fine wire in a light bulb or thermionic valve **2.** the stalk of a stamen bearing the anther —**fil′amen′tary** (-men′tər ē) *adj.*
filbert (fil′bərt) *n.* [< St. *Philibert*, whose feast came in the nutting season] **1.** the edible nut of a cultivated hazel tree **2.** a tree bearing this nut
filch (filch) *vt.* [ME. *filchen*] to steal (esp. something small or petty); pilfer —**filch′er** *n.*
file¹ (fil) *vt.* **filed, fil′ing** [< L. *filum*, a thread] **1.** to arrange (papers, etc.) in order for future reference **2.** to dispatch (a news story) **3.** to register (an application, etc.) **4.** to put on public record **5.** to initiate (a legal action) —*vi.* to move in a line —*n.* **1.** a folder, etc. for keeping papers in order **2.** an orderly arrangement of papers, cards, etc. **3.** a line of persons or things, one behind another —**on file** kept as in a file for reference —**fil′er** *n.*
file² *n.* [OE. *feol*] a steel tool with a rough, ridged surface for smoothing or grinding —*vt.* **filed, fil′ing** to smooth or grind down with a file —**fil′er** *n.*
filial (fil′ē əl) *adj.* [< L. *filius*, son] of, suitable to, or due from a son or daughter —**fil′ially** *adv.*
filibuster (fil′ə bus′tər) *n.* [< MDu. *vrijbuiter*, freebooter] **1.** an adventurer who engages in unauthorized warfare against another country **2.** [U.S.] a member of a legislative body who obstructs a bill by making long speeches **3.** [U.S.] the use of such methods to obstruct a bill —*vi., vt.* [Chiefly U.S.] to obstruct (legislation) with delaying tactics
filigree (fil′ə grē′) *n.* [< L. *filum*, thread + *granum*, grain] **1.** lacelike ornamental work of intertwined wire of gold, silver, etc. **2.** any delicate work like this —*adj.* like or made of filigree
filing (fil′ing) *n.* a small piece, as of metal, scraped off with a file: *usually used in pl.*
Filipino (fil′ə pē′nō) *n. pl.* **-nos** [Sp.] a native or citizen of the Philippines —*adj.* Philippine
fill (fil) *vt.* [OE. *fyllan*] **1.** to put as much as possible into **2.** to occupy wholly **3.** *a)* to occupy (a position, etc.) *b)* to put a person into (a position, etc.) **4.** to satisfy (a need, etc.) **5.** to close or plug (holes, cracks, etc.) **6.** to satisfy the hunger of —*vi.* to become full —*n.* all that is needed to make full or satisfy —**fill in** **1.** to complete (a document, etc.) by inserting information **2.** to be a substitute **3.** to fill with some substance **4.** to complete by supplying (something) —**fill one in on** [Colloq.] to provide one with additional details about —**fill out** to make or become rounder, shapelier, etc. —**fill up** to make or become completely full
filler *n.* a person or thing that fills; specif., *a)* matter added to increase bulk *b)* a preparation used to fill in cracks, etc. *c)* a space-filling item in a newspaper
fillet (fil′it) *n.* [< L. *filum*, thread] **1.** a boneless piece of meat or fish **2.** a

thin strip or band, as a headband for the hair —*vt.* to bone and slice (meat or fish)

filling *n.* a substance used to fill something; specif., *a)* the metal, plastic, etc. inserted into a prepared cavity in a tooth *b)* the foodstuff used in a pastry shell, etc.

filling station *same as* SERVICE STATION

fillip (fil'ip) *n.* [< FLIP¹] 1. anything that stimulates or livens up 2. the snap made by a finger held down by the thumb and then suddenly released —*vt.* 1. to stimulate or liven up 2. to strike with a fillip

filly (fil'ē) *n., pl.* **-lies** [ON. *fylja*] 1. a young female horse 2. [Colloq.] a vivacious girl

film (film) *n.* [OE. *filmen*] 1. *a)* a sequence of photographs or drawings projected on a screen in such rapid succession as to create the illusion of moving persons and objects *b)* a play, story, etc. photographed as a film 2. a flexible cellulose material covered with a substance sensitive to light and used in photography 3. a fine, thin skin or coating 4. a haze or blur —*vt., vi.* 1. to make a film (of) 2. to cover or be covered as with a film

filmstrip *n.* a length of film containing still photographs arranged in sequence for projection separately

filmy *adj.* **-ier, -iest** 1. hazy, gauzy, etc. 2. covered as with a film —**film′iness** *n.*

filter (fil'tər) *n.* [< ML. *filtrum*, felt] 1. a device or substance for straining out solid particles, impurities, etc. from a liquid or gas passed through it 2. *a)* a device that passes electric currents of certain frequencies only *b)* a device that absorbs certain light rays *[a colour filter for a camera lens]* 3. a traffic signal that permits one line of vehicles to move, even when the main signals are red. —*vt.* 1. to pass through a filter 2. to remove with a filter —*vi.* 1. to pass through a filter 2. to pass slowly *[the news filtered through town]*

filter paper porous paper for filtering liquids

filter tip a mouthpiece attached to a cigarette to trap and absorb impurities

filth (filth) *n.* [OE. *fylthe*] 1. disgustingly offensive dirt 2. obscenity 3. corruption —**filth′y** *adj.*

filthy lucre [Colloq.] money

filtrate (fil'trāt) *vt.* **-trated, -trating** to filter —*n.* a filtered liquid —**filtra′tion** *n.*

fin (fin) *n.* [OE. *finn*] 1. any of several winglike organs on the body of a fish, dolphin, etc., used in swimming 2. anything like a fin in shape or use

fin. 1. finance 2. financial 3. finis

finagle (fənā'g'l) *vi., vt.* **-gled, -gling** [< ?] to use, or get by, craftiness or trickery —**fina′gler** *n.*

final (fī'n'l) *adj.* [< L. *finis*, end] 1. of or coming at the end; last 2. deciding; conclusive 3. having to do with the ultimate purpose *[a final cause]* —*n.* 1. anything final 2. *[pl.]* the last of a series of contests

3. a final examination —**final′ity** (-nal'ə tē) *n.* —**fi′nally** *adv.*

finale (fənä'lē) *n.* [It.] 1. the concluding part of a musical composition, etc. 2. the conclusion; end

finalist (fī'nəlist) *n.* a contestant who participates in the final, deciding contest of a series

finalize (fī'nəlīz') *vt.* **-ized, -iz′ing** to make final —**fi′naliza′tion** *n.*

finance (fīnans') *n.* [< OFr. *finer*, to settle accounts < L. *finis*, end] 1. *[pl.]* money resources, income, etc. 2. the science of managing money matters —*vt.* **-nanced′, -nanc′ing** to supply or obtain money for

financial (fīnan'shəl) *adj.* of finance, finances, or financiers —**finan′cially** *adv.*

financial year the twelve-month period between settlements of financial accounts : the British government financial year ends April 5

financier (fīnan'sē ər) *n.* [Fr.] 1. a person skilled in finance 2. a person who engages in financial operations on a large scale

finch (finch) *n.* [OE. *finc*] any of a group of small songbirds, including the bunting, canary, and linnet

find (fīnd) *vt.* **found, find′ing** [OE. *findan*] 1. to happen on; discover by chance 2. to get by searching 3. to perceive; learn 4. to experience or feel 5. to recover (something lost) 6. to consider; think 7. to reach 8. to declare after deliberation *[to find him guilty]* 9. to supply; furnish —*vi.* to announce a decision *[the jury found for the accused]* —*n.* 1. a finding 2. something found —**find oneself** to learn what one's real talents are and begin to apply them —**find one's feet** to become capable or confident —**find out** to discover; learn

finder *n.* 1. one that finds 2. a camera device that shows what will appear in the photograph 3. a small telescope attached to a larger one, and used to locate objects

finding *n.* 1. discovery 2. something found 3. *[often pl.]* the verdict of a judge, scholar, etc.

fine¹ (fīn) *adj.* **fin′er, fin′est** [< L. *finis*, an end] 1. superior in quality; excellent 2. *a)* good-looking *b)* elegant; refined 3. with no impurities; refined 4. containing a specified proportion of pure metal 5. clear and bright : said of the weather 6. not heavy or coarse 7. very thin or small 8. sharp *[a fine edge]* 9. subtle *[fine distinctions]* 10. delicate *[fine china]* 11. involving precision *[a fine adjustment]* 12. affectedly refined 13. [Colloq.] terrible *[this is a fine mess]* —*adv.* 1. finely 2. [Colloq.] very well —*vt., vi.* **fined, fin′ing** to make or become fine or finer —**cut** (or **run**) **it fine** 1. to arrive at the last minute 2. to leave only a very small reserve of something —**fine′ly** *adv.*

fine² *n.* [< L. *finis*, an end] a sum of money paid as a penalty —*vt.* **fined, fin′ing** to order to pay a fine —**in fine** in conclusion

fine art any of the art forms that appeal to the senses, as painting, sculpture, etc. or, occasionally, architecture, literature, music, etc.: *usually used in pl.*

fine-drawn *adj.* 1. drawn out until very fine, as wire 2. very subtle: said of reasoning, arguments, etc.

finery (fīn′ər ē) *n., pl.* **-eries** showy, gay, elaborate decoration, esp. clothes, jewellery, etc.

fines herbes (*Fr.*, fēn zãərb′) a mixture of fresh, finely-chopped herbs used to flavour omelettes, etc.

finespun (fīn′spun′) *adj.* 1. delicate; fragile 2. extremely or excessively subtle

finesse (fi nes′) *n.* [< OFr. *fin*, FINE¹] 1. adroitness or skill 2. the ability to handle difficult situations diplomatically 3. cunning 4. *Cards* an attempt to take a trick with a lower card while holding a higher card —*vt., vi.* **-nessed′, -ness′-ing** 1. to manage by or use finesse 2. *Cards* to make a finesse

fine-toothed comb a comb with fine, closely set teeth: also **fine-tooth comb** —**go over with a fine-toothed comb** to examine very thoroughly

finger (fiŋ′gər) *n.* [OE.] 1. any of the five parts at the end of the hand, esp. any of these other than the thumb 2. the part of a glove covering a finger 3. anything like a finger in shape or use 4. an approximate measurement based on the breadth of a finger —*vt.* 1. to touch with the fingers 2. to play (an instrument) by using the fingers —**get** (or **pull**) **one's finger out** [Colloq.] to begin or speed up activity —**put one's finger on** to ascertain exactly —**twist** (or **wrap**) **around one's little finger** to have complete control or influence over

fingerboard *n.* a strip of hard wood in the neck of a violin, cello, etc., against which the strings are pressed with the fingers to produce the desired tones

finger bowl a small bowl to hold water for rinsing the fingers at table after a meal

fingering *n. Music* 1. technique of using the fingers 2. directions on a score for using the fingers

fingernail *n.* the horny substance on the upper part of the end joint of a finger

finger plate an ornamental plate fixed above a doorhandle to prevent finger marks

FINGERPRINT

fingerprint *n.* 1. an impression of the lines and whorls on a fingertip, used to

identify a person 2. a characteristic mark, trait, etc. —*vt.* to take the fingerprints of

fingerstall *n.* a protective covering for an injured finger

finger tip the tip of a finger —**have at one's finger tips** to be completely familiar with —**to one's finger tips** entirely; altogether

finicky (fin′i kē′) *adj.* [< FINE¹] too particular; fussy: also **fin′icking**

finis (fin′is) *n., pl.* **-nises** [L.] the end, as of a book

finish (fin′ish) *vt.* [< L. *finis*, an end] 1. *a*) to bring to an end *b*) to come to the end of 2. to use up 3. to give (wood, etc.) a desired surface effect 4. *a*) to cause the defeat, death, etc. of *b*) to render worthless —*vi.* to come to an end —*n.* 1. the last part; end 2. anything used to give a desired surface effect, as varnish 3. completeness 4. the manner or method of completion 5. the way in which the surface, as of furniture, is finished 6. refinement in manners, speech, etc. 7. defeat, collapse, etc. or that which brings it about —**finish off** 1. to end 2. to kill or destroy —**finish up** 1. to end 2. to consume all of —**finish with** to end relations with

finishing school a private school for girls that specializes in imparting social poise and polish

finite (fī′nīt) *adj.* [< L. *finire*, finish] 1. having definable limits; not infinite 2. *Gram.* having limits of person, number, and tense: said of a verb —**fi′nitely** *adv.*

Finn. Finnish

finnan haddie (fin′ən had′ē) [prob. < *Findhorn* (Scot. fishing port)] smoked haddock: also **finnan haddock**

Finnish (fin′ish) *adj.* of Finland, its people, their language, etc. —*n.* the language of the Finns

FIORD

fiord (fyôrd) *n.* [< ON. *fjörthr*] a narrow inlet of the sea bordered by steep cliffs

fipple flute (fip′′l) [< ?] a vertical flute, as the recorder, in which a plug (**fipple**) near the mouthpiece diverts the breath in producing the tones

fir (fur) *n.* [< OE. *fyrh*] a cone-bearing evergreen tree of the pine family

fire (fīər) *n.* [OE. *fyr*] 1. the heat and light of combustion 2. something burning, as fuel in a furnace 3. a destructive burning [a forest *fire*] 4. anything like fire in heat, brilliance, etc. 5. tribulation [go through *fire* and water] 6. strong feeling;

fervour **7.** vivid imagination **8.** *a)* a discharge of firearms *b)* anything like this *[a fire of criticism]* —*vt.* **fired, fir′ing 1.** to shoot (a gun, bullet, etc.) **2.** to hurl or direct with force *[to fire questions]* **3.** to dismiss from a job **4.** to bake (bricks, etc.) in a kiln **5.** to ignite **6.** to supply with fuel **7.** to inspire, excite, etc. —*vi.* **1.** to shoot a firearm **2.** to discharge a projectile **3.** to start burning **4.** to become excited —**catch fire** to begin burning —**miss fire** *same as* MISFIRE —**on fire 1.** burning **2.** greatly excited —**open fire 1.** to begin to shoot **2.** to begin; start —**play with fire** to do something risky —**set fire to** to make burn; ignite —**set the Thames on fire** to do something outstanding —**under fire** under attack

fire alarm a signal to announce the outbreak of a fire

firearm *n.* any hand weapon from which a shot is fired by explosive force, as a rifle

fireball *n.* **1.** ball-shaped lightning **2.** a very bright ball of gas at the centre of a nuclear explosion **3.** a large, very bright meteor **4.** [Slang] an energetic person

firebomb *n.* an incendiary bomb

firebox *n.* the place for the fire in a furnace, etc.

firebrand *n.* **1.** a piece of burning wood **2.** a person who stirs up strife, etc.

firebreak *n.* a strip of land cleared to stop the spread of fire, as in a forest

firebrick *n.* a brick made to withstand great heat, used to line furnaces, etc.

fire brigade an organized body of firemen

fireclay *n.* a clay used to make firebricks, etc.

firecracker *n.* [U.S.] a roll of paper containing an explosive, set off at celebrations, etc.

firecrest *n.* a small bird related to the goldcrest

firedamp *n.* a gas, largely methane, formed in coal mines, which is explosive when mixed with air

firedog *n.* *same as* ANDIRON

fire-eater *n.* **1.** an entertainer who pretends to eat fire **2.** a belligerent person

fire engine a heavy road vehicle that carries firemen and firefighting equipment

fire escape a stairway, ladder, etc. down an outside wall, for escape from a burning building

fire extinguisher a portable device containing chemicals for spraying on a fire to put it out

firefly *n.*, *pl.* **-flies′** a winged beetle whose abdomen glows with a luminescent light

fire guard *n.* a meshed frame put before an open fire to protect against sparks, etc.

fire hall [Canad.] a fire station

fire irons the poker, shovel and tongs used for tending a fire

firelight *n.* light from an open fire

firelighter *n.* a composition of highly combustible material for kindling a domestic fire

fireman *n.* **1.** a member of a fire brigade **2.** a man who tends a furnace; stoker

fireplace *n.* a place for a fire, esp. an open place built in a wall, at a chimney base

fireplug *n.* [Chiefly U.S.] a street hydrant to which a hose can be attached for fighting fires

firepower *n.* *Mil.* **1.** the effectiveness of a weapon **2.** the capacity of a given unit to deliver fire

fire-raising *n.* arson

fire ship a ship filled with combustible materials, set on fire and floated among an enemy's ships to destroy them

fireside *n.* **1.** the part of a room near a fireplace; hearth **2.** home or home life

fire station the place where fire engines are kept and where firemen stay when on duty

firetrap *n.* a building unsafe in case of fire

firewater *n.* alcoholic spirits: now humorous

fireworks *n.pl.* **1.** devices in which combustible materials and explosives are ignited and produce coloured flames, sparks and smoke **2.** a display of fireworks **3.** [Colloq.] a burst of temper, etc.

firing *n.* **1.** the process of baking ceramics, etc. in a kiln **2.** the act of stoking a furnace, etc. **3.** the discharge of a firearm **4.** something used as fuel

firing line 1. the line from which gunfire is directed against the enemy **2.** any vulnerable front position

firm¹ (furm) *adj.* [< L. *firmus*] **1.** not yielding under pressure; solid **2.** not moved easily; fixed **3.** remaining the same; steady **4.** resolute; constant **5.** showing determination, strength, etc. **6.** definite; final *[a firm contract]* —*vt.*, *vi.* to make or become firm —**firm′ly** *adv.* —**firm′-ness** *n.*

firm² *n.* [< L. *firmus*, FIRM¹] a business company or partnership

firmament (fur′mə mənt) *n.* [< L. *firmus*, firm] the sky, viewed poetically as a solid arch or vault

first (furst) *adj.* [< OE. *fyrst*] **1.** before any others; 1st **2.** earliest **3.** foremost in importance, etc. **4.** *Music* playing or singing the highest or leading part —*adv.* **1.** *a)* before any other person or thing *b)* before doing anything else **2.** for the first time **3.** sooner; preferably —*n.* **1.** the first person, thing, place, etc. **2.** the beginning **3.** the winning place, as in a race

first aid emergency treatment for injury or illness, before medical care is available —**first′-aid′** *adj.*

firstborn *adj.* born first in a family; oldest —*n.* the firstborn child

first-class *adj.* **1.** of the highest class, quality, etc. **2.** of the most expensive accommodation on a ship, seats on a train, etc. **3.** of letters handled faster than second-class letters —*adv.* by first-class post, means of transport, etc.

first cousin the son or daughter of one's aunt or uncle

first-day cover an envelope postmarked on the first day of the issue of its stamps

first finger   the finger next to the thumb

first-foot (furst'foot') [Scot.] *n., vi.* (to be) the first person to enter a household in the New Year —**first'-foot'ing** *n.*

first fruits   1. the earliest produce of the season   2. the first products, results, or profits of any activity

firsthand *adj., adv.*   from the original producer or source; direct

first lady   [U.S.] [*often* F- L-] the wife of the U.S. president

firstly *adv.*   in the first place; first

first mate   a merchant ship's officer next in rank below the master : also **first officer**

first night   the opening night of a play, opera, etc.

first offender   a person convicted for the first time of an offence against the law

first person   that form of a pronoun (as *I* or *we*) or verb (as *do*) which refers to the speaker or speakers

first-rate *adj.*   of the highest class, rank, or quality; excellent —*adv.* [Colloq.] very well

first water   the best quality and purest lustre

firth (furth) *n.* [< ON. *fjörthr*]   a narrow arm of the sea; estuary

fiscal (fis'kəl) *adj.* [< L. *fiscus*, money basket]   1. having to do with the public treasury or revenues   2. financial —*n.* in some countries, a public prosecutor

fiscal year   *same as* FINANCIAL YEAR

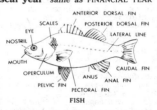

FISH

fish (fish) *n., pl.* **fish**; in referring to different species, **fish'es** [OE. *fisc*]   1. a coldblooded animal living in water and having a backbone, gills for breathing, and fins   2. the flesh of a fish used as food   3. [Colloq.] a person like a fish in being easily lured, lacking emotion, etc. —[F-] the constellation Pisces —*vi.* 1. to try to catch fish   2. to try to get something indirectly (often with *for*) —*vt.* 1. to fish in (a stream, etc.)   2. to grope for, find, and bring to view [he *fished* a coin out of his pocket] —**drink like a fish** to drink heavily —**fish in troubled waters** to turn a disturbed situation to one's own advantage —**like a fish out of water** in surroundings not suited to one —**neither fish, flesh, nor fowl** (or **nor good red herring**) not anything definite or recognizable —**other fish to fry** other, more important things to attend to

fish cake   a fried cake of flaked fish and mashed potatoes

fisher *n.*   1. a fisherman   2. a flesh-eating animal related to the marten

fisherman *n.*   1. a person who fishes for sport or for a living   2. a ship used in fishing

fishery *n., pl.* **-eries**   1. the business of catching fish   2. a place where fish are caught or bred

fish-eye lens   a camera lens designed to record a 180-degree field of vision

fish finger   a small, oblong-shaped portion of fish covered in breadcrumbs or batter

fishing *n.*   the catching of fish for sport or for a living

fishing rod   a slender pole with an attached line, hook, and usually a reel, used in fishing

fish-kettle *n.*   an oval pot in which fish are cooked

fish meal   ground, dried fish, used as fertilizer or fodder

fishmonger (fish'muŋ'gər) *n.*   a dealer in fish

fishplate *n.*   a flat piece of metal joining one rail or beam to another, esp. on railway tracks

fish slice   1. a fish carver   2. a flat-bladed utensil for serving fish

fishtail *n.*   anything shaped like a fish's tail, specif., a nozzle with a narrow slot placed over a Bunsen burner to produce a fanlike flame

fishwife *n.*   1. a woman who sells fish   2. a coarse, scolding woman

fishy *adj.* **-ier, -iest**   1. like a fish in odour, taste, etc.   2. dull or expressionless   3. [Colloq.] questionable; odd —**fish'ily** *adv.* —**fish'iness** *n.*

fissile (fis'il) *adj.* [< L. *findere*, to split]   1. that can be split   2. that can undergo fission

fission (fish'ən) *n.* [see prec.]   1. a splitting apart   2. *same as* NUCLEAR FISSION   3. *Biol.* a form of asexual reproduction in which the parent organism divides into two or more parts, each becoming an independent individual —**fis'sionable** *adj.*

fissure (fish'ər) *n.* [see FISSILE]   1. a cleft or crack   2. a dividing or breaking into parts —*vt., vi.* **-sured, -suring** to crack or split apart

fist (fist) *n.* [< OE. *fyst*]   a hand with the fingers closed tightly into the palm

fisticuffs (fis'ti kufs') *n.pl.*   1. a fight with the fists   2. the science of boxing

fistula (fis'tyoo lə) *n., pl.* **-las, -lae'** (-lē') [L.]   an abnormal passage, as from an abscess, cavity, or hollow organ to the skin —**fis'tulous, fis'tular** *adj.*

fit[1] (fit) *vt.* **fit'ted** or **fit, fit'ted, fit'ting** [ME. *fitten*]   1. to be suitable to   2. to be the proper size, shape, etc. for   3. to make or alter so as to fit   4. to make suitable or qualified   5. *a)* to insert, as into a receptacle *b)* to make a place for (with *in* or *into*)   6. to equip; outfit (often with *out*) —*vi.* 1. to be suitable or proper   2. to be in accord or harmony (often with *in* or *into*)   3. to have the proper size or shape —*adj.* **fit'ter, fit'test**   1. suited to some purpose, function, etc.   2. proper; right   3. healthy —*n.* the manner of fitting [a tight *fit*] —**fit′ly** *adv.* —**fit′-ness** *n.*

fit² *n.* [OE. *fitt*, conflict] 1. any sudden, uncontrollable attack [a *fit* of coughing] 2. a sharp, brief display of feeling 3. a burst of activity 4. a seizure involving loss of consciousness or convulsions —**by fits and starts** in an irregular way —**have** (or **throw**) **a fit** [Colloq.] to become very angry or upset

fitful *adj.* characterized by intermittent activity, impulses, etc.; spasmodic —**fit′-fully** *adv.* —**fit′fulness** *n.*

fitment *n.* 1. an added part, as to a machine 2. [*often pl.*] furnishings or equipment attached to a building but not a structural part of it

fitted *adj.* designed to conform to the contours of that which it covers

fitter *n.* 1. a person who alters garments to fit 2. a person who installs or adjusts machinery, etc.

fitting *adj.* suitable; proper —*n.* 1. an adjustment or trying on of clothes, etc. for fit 2. a part used to join or adapt other parts 3. [*pl.*] fixtures, furnishings, etc.

five (fīv) *adj., n.* [< OE. *fīf*] one more than four; 5; V

fivefold *adj.* 1. having five parts 2. having five times as much or as many —*adv.* five times as much or as many

fivepins *n. pl.* [*with sing. v.*] a bowling game played esp. in Canada

fiver *n.* [Slang] a five-pound note

fives *n.* [< ?] a game of handball played against a wall

five-year plan a government plan for intensive economic development over a five-year period

fix (fiks) *vt.* [< L. *figere*, fasten] 1. to fasten firmly 2. to set firmly in the mind 3. to direct steadily [to *fix* the eyes on a spot] 4. to make rigid 5. to make permanent 6. to establish definitely; determine 7. to set in order; adjust 8. to repair 9. [Colloq.] to influence the result or action of (a race, etc) by bribery, trickery, etc. 10. [Colloq.] to punish 11. to combine (atmospheric nitrogen) in the form of compounds, as nitrates, ammonia, etc. 12. *Photog.* to make (a film, print, etc.) permanent —*vi.* to become fixed —*n.* 1. [Colloq.] a predicament 2. the position of a ship or aircraft determined as from the bearings of two known points 3. [Slang] an injection of a narcotic —**fix on** (or **upon**) to choose —**fix up** [Colloq.] 1. to set in order; arrange 2. to repair —**fix′er** *n.*

fixation (fik sā′shən) *n.* 1. a fixing or being fixed 2. popularly, an exaggerated preoccupation; obsession 3. attachment to objects of an earlier stage of psychosexual development [a father *fixation*]

fixative (fik′sə tiv) *adj.* that is able or tends to make permanent, prevent fading, etc. —*n.* a fixative substance

fixed (fikst) *adj.* 1. firmly placed or attached 2. established; set 3. steady;

resolute 4. obsessive [a *fixed* idea] 5. [Colloq.] supplied with something, specif., money 6. [Slang] with the outcome dishonestly prearranged —**fixedly** (fik′sid lē) *adv.*

fixed star a star that appears to keep the same position in relation to other stars

fixity *n.* 1. stability; permanence 2. *pl.* **-ties** something fixed

fixture (fiks′chər) *n.* 1. anything firmly in place 2. any of the fittings or furnishings attached to a building [bathroom *fixtures*] 3. a sporting event fixed for a certain date 4. [Colloq.] a person long-established in a place or job

fizz (fiz) *n.* [echoic] 1. a hissing, sputtering sound 2. an effervescent drink —*vi.* 1. to make a hissing or bubbling sound 2. to give off gas bubbles; effervesce

fizzle (fiz′'l) *vi.* **-zled, -zling** [ME. *fesilen*, to break wind silently] 1. to make a hissing or sputtering sound 2. [Colloq.] to fail, esp. after a successful beginning (often with *out*) —*n.* a hissing or sputtering sound

fizzy *adj.* **-ier, -iest** fizzing; effervescent

fjord (fyôrd) *n.* *same as* FIORD

fl. 1. [L. *floruit*] (he or she) flourished 2. fluid

flab (flab) *n.* [Colloq.] soft, sagging flesh

flabbergast (flab′ər gäst′) *vt.* [< ? ff. + AGHAST] to dumbfound; amaze

flabby *adj.* **-ier, -iest** [< FLAP] 1. limp and soft 2. lacking force; weak

flaccid (flak′sid) *adj.* [< L. *flaccus*, flabby] 1. flabby 2. weak; feeble —**flaccid′ity** *n.* —**flac′cidly** *adv.*

flag¹ (flag) *n.* [< ?] a cloth with colours, patterns, or devices, used as a symbol of a country, organization, etc., or as a signal —*vt.* **flagged, flag′ging** 1. to mark with flags 2. to signal with or as with a flag; esp., to signal to stop (often with *down*) —**flag′ger** *n.*

flag² *n.* [ON. *flaga*, slab of stone] *same as* FLAGSTONE —*vt.* **flagged, flag′ging** to pave with flagstones

flag³ *n.* [ME. *flagge*, akin ? to ff.] any of various irises, with flowers of blue, purple, white, yellow, etc.

flag⁴ *vi.* **flagged, flag′ging** [< ? ON. *flakka*, flutter] to lose strength; grow weak or tired

flag day a day on which miniature flags are given in return for donations to a charity fund

flagellant (flaj′ə lənt) *n.* a person who whips; specif., one who whips himself or has himself whipped as for religious discipline —*adj.* engaging in flagellation

flagellate (flaj′ə lāt′) *vt.* **-lat′ed, -lat′ing** [< L. *flagellum*, a whip] to whip; flog —*adj.* having flagella or shaped like a flagellum —**flag′ella′tion** *n.*

flagellum (flə jel′əm) *n., pl.* **-la, -lums** [L.: see prec.] *Biol.* a whiplike part serving as an organ of locomotion in certain cells, bacteria, etc.

flageolet (flaj′ō let′) *n.* [Fr.] a small fipple flute similar to the recorder

flagging[1] (flag'iŋ) *adj.* weakening or drooping

flagging[2] *n.* flagstones

flag of convenience a foreign flag under which a company registers a ship to avoid the regulations, taxes, etc. of its own state

flag of truce a white flag shown to an enemy to indicate a desire to confer or parley

flagon (flag'ən) *n.* [< LL. *flasca*, flask] a container for liquids, with a handle, a spout, and, often, a lid

flagpole *n.* a pole on which a flag is flown: also **flag'staff'**

flagrant (flā'grənt) *adj.* [< L. *flagrare*, blaze] glaringly bad; notorious; outrageous —**fla'grancy** *n.*

flagship (flag'ship) *n.* the ship carrying the commander of a fleet or squadron and displaying his flag

flagstone *n.* a flat piece of hard stone used to pave walks, terraces, etc.

flag-waving *n.* an emotional appeal calculated to arouse intense patriotic feelings —**flag'-wav'er** *n.*

FLAIL

flail (flāl) *n.* [< L. *flagellum*, a whip] a farm tool having a free-swinging stick attached to a handle, used to thresh grain —*vt., vi.* 1. to thresh with a flail 2. to beat 3. to move (one's arms) about like flails

flair (flāər) *n.* [< L. *fragare*, to smell] 1. keen, natural discernment or aptitude; knack 3. [Colloq.] smartness in style; dash

flak (flak) *n.* [G. *Fl(ieger)a(bwehr)-k(anone)*, antiaircraft gun] the fire of anti-aircraft guns

flake (flāk) *n.* [prob. < Scand.] 1. a small, thin mass [a *flake* of snow] 2. a thin piece split off from anything; chip —*vt., vi.* **flaked, flak'ing** 1. to form into flakes 2. to chip off in flakes —**flake out** [Slang] to collapse or become unconscious, as through exhaustion —**flak'y** *adj.*

‡**flambé** (flän'bā) *adj.* [Fr., flaming] served with a flaming sauce containing brandy, rum, etc.

flamboyant (flam boi'ənt) *adj.* [see FLAME] 1. characterized by florid decoration 2. flamelike or brilliant 3. too showy or ornate 4. exuberant or ostentatious —**flamboy'ance** *n.*

flame (flām) *n.* [< L. *flagrare*, burn] 1. the burning gas of a fire, seen as a tongue of light 2. the state of burning with a blaze of light 3. a thing like a flame 4. an intense emotion 5. a sweetheart: now humorous —*vi.* **flamed, flam'ing** 1. to burst into flame 2. to grow red or hot 3. to become excited —**flame up** (or **out**) to burst out as in flames

flamenco (flə men'kō) *n.* [Sp.] 1. the energetic, emotional style of dance or music of Spanish gypsies 2. *pl.* **-cos** a song or dance in this style

flame thrower a military weapon for shooting a stream of flaming petrol, oil, etc.

flaming (flā'miŋ) *adj.* 1. burning with flames; blazing 2. like a flame in brilliance or heat 3. ardent; passionate 4. [Colloq.] damned [that *flaming* idiot]

flamingo (flə miŋ'gō) *n.*, *pl.* **-gos, -goes** [Port. < Sp. *flama*, flame] a tropical wading bird with long legs, a long neck, and bright pink or red feathers

flammable (flam'əb'l) *adj.* easily set on fire

flan (flan) *n.* [Fr.] an open case made of pastry or sponge cake and filled with custard, fruit, cheese, etc.

flange (flanj) *n.* [< ?] a projecting rim or collar on a wheel, pipe, etc., to hold it in place, give strength, etc.,

flank (flaŋk) *n.* [< OFr. *flanc*] 1. the fleshy side of an animal between the ribs and the hip 2. the side of anything 3. *Mil.* the right or left side of a formation —*vt.* 1. to be at the side of 2. to place at the side of 3. to attack, or pass around, the side of (an enemy unit)

flannel (flan'l) *n.* [< W. *gwlan*, wool] 1. a soft, loosely woven woollen cloth 2. a small cloth, usually of towelling, used in washing 3. [*pl.*] trousers, etc. made of flannel 4. [Colloq.] evasive talk; flattery —*vt.* **-nelled, -nelling** to wash with a flannel 2. [Colloq.] to flatter —**flan'nelly** *adj.*

flannelette (flan'ə let') *n.* a soft cotton cloth resembling flannel

flap (flap) *n.* [ME. *flappe*] 1. anything flat and broad that is attached at one end and hangs loose 2. the motion or sound of a swinging flap 3. a hinged section of an aeroplane wing 4. [Colloq.] a commotion; fuss —*vt.* **flapped, flap'ping** 1. to move back and forth or up and down, as wings 2. to slap —*vi.* 1. to flutter 2. [Colloq.] to be excited or confused —**flap'py** *adj.*

flapdoodle (flap'dōōd'l) *n.* [< ?] [Colloq.] nonsense

flapjack (flap'jak') *n.* a chewy biscuit made from rolled oats, sugar and butter

flapper *n.* 1. one that flaps 2. [Colloq.] in the 1920's, a young woman considered bold or unconventional

flare (flāər) *vi.* **flared, flar'ing** [ME. *fleare*] 1. to blaze up brightly or burn unsteadily 2. to burst out suddenly in anger, etc. (often with *up* or *out*) 3. to curve outwards, as the bell of a trumpet —*vt.* to make flare —*n.* 1. a bright, unsteady blaze 2. a very bright light used as a distress signal, etc. 3. an outburst, as of emotion 4. a curving outwards

flare-path n. an area lit up to facilitate the landing or take-off of an aircraft

flare-up n. a sudden outburst of anger, trouble, etc.

flash (flash) vi. [echoic] 1. to send out a sudden, brief light 2. to sparkle 3. to speak abruptly, esp. in anger (usually with *out*) 4. to come or pass suddenly —vt. 1. to cause to flash 2. to send (news, etc.) swiftly 3. [Colloq.] to show briefly or ostentatiously [to *flash* a roll of money] —n. 1. a sudden, brief light 2. a brief moment 3. a sudden, brief display [a *flash* of wit] 4. a brief item of news sent by telegraph or radio 5. same as FLASHLIGHT 6. anything that flashes (usually *a flash* flood) 2. [Colloq.] a) ostentatious; showy b) of or relating to the criminal underworld —**flash in the pan** [orig. of priming in pan of a flintlock] a sudden, apparently brilliant effort that fails

flashback n. an interruption in the continuity of a story, etc. by the presentation of some earlier episode

flashbulb n. Photog. an electric light bulb giving a brief, dazzling light

flashcube n. a small, rotating cube containing a flashbulb in each of four sides

flashgun n. Photog. a device that simultaneously sets off a flashbulb and works the camera shutter

flashing n. sheets of metal, etc. used to weatherproof joints, edges, etc., esp. of a roof

flashlight n. 1. a brief, dazzling light for taking photographs at night or indoors 2. [U.S.] a torch

flash point 1. the lowest temperature at which the vapour of a volatile oil will ignite 2. a critical moment beyond which violence is inevitable

flashy adj. -ier, -iest gaudy; showy

flask (fläsk) n. [< LL. *flasca*] 1. a bottle with a narrow neck, used in laboratories, etc. 2. a small, flat pocket container for spirits, etc. 3. same as THERMOS

flat¹ (flat) adj. flat′ter, flat′test [< ON. *flatr*] 1. having a smooth, level surface 2. lying spread out 3. broad, even, and thin 4. almost straight or level 5. absolute [a *flat* denial] 6. not fluctuating [a *flat* rate] 7. having little or no sparkle or taste 8. monotonous; dull 9. completely discharged; dead [a *flat* battery] 10. emptied of air [a *flat* tyre] 11. without gloss [*flat* paint] 12. lacking relief or perspective 13. Music below the true pitch —adv. 1. in a flat manner 2. in a flat position 3. a) exactly [ten seconds *flat*] b) bluntly; abruptly [she left him *flat*] 4. Music below the true pitch —n. 1. a flat surface or part 2. an expanse of level land 3. a low-lying marsh 4. a piece of theatrical scenery on a flat frame 5. a deflated tyre 6. Music a note or tone one semitone below another b) the symbol (♭) indicating such a note —fall flat to arouse no response —flat′-ly adv. —flat′ness n. —flat′tish adj.

flat² n. [< obs. *flet*, a floor] living accommodation on one floor of a building

flatboat n. a flat-bottomed boat for carrying cargo in shallow waters or on rivers

flatfish n. a fish with a flat body and both eyes on the uppermost side, as the flounder, halibut, etc.

flatfoot n. 1. a condition in which the instep arch of the foot has been flattened 2. [Slang] a policeman

flat-footed (flat′foot′id) adj. 1. having flatfoot 2. [Colloq.] uninspired —flat′-foot′edly adv.

flatiron n. an iron for pressing clothes

flatlet n. a small flat

flat race a horse race over a level course

flat spin 1. Aero. a spiral dive where an aircraft rotates in a plane more horizontal than vertical 2. [Colloq.] a state of confusion

flatten vt., vi. to make or become flat or flatter

flatter (flat′ər) vt. [< OFr. *flater*, to smooth] 1. to praise insincerely 2. to try to please, as by praise 3. to make seem more attractive than is so [his portrait *flatters* him] 4. to make feel pleased or honoured —vi. to use flattery —flatter oneself to be smug or deluded in thinking (that) —flat′terer n.

flattery n., pl. -teries excessive or insincere praise

flatulent (flat′yoo lənt) adj. [< L. *flare*, blow] 1. of, having, or producing gas in the stomach or intestines 2. windy in speech; pompous —flat′ulence, flat′u-lency n.

flatworm n. a flattened worm with a soft, unsegmented body, as the tape worm

flaunt (flônt) vi., vt. [< ? dial. *flant*, to strut] to show off proudly or impudently —flaunt′ingly adv.

flautist (flôt′ist) n. [< It. *flauto*, flute] a flute player

flavour (flā′vər) n. [< OFr. *flaur*] 1. a) the combined taste and smell of something b) taste in general 2. characteristic quality —vt. to give flavour to U.S. sp. fla′vor —fla′vourful adj. —fla′vour-less adj.

flavouring n. an essence, extract, etc. added to a food or drink to give it a certain taste

flaw¹ (flô) n. [prob. < Scand.] 1. a break, scratch, crack, etc. that spoils something; blemish 2. a defect; fault —vt., vi. to make or become faulty —flaw′-less adj. —flaw′lessly adv. —flaw′less-ness n.

flaw² n. [prob. < ON.] a sudden gust of wind; squall

flax (flaks) n. [OE. *fleax*] 1. a slender, erect plant with blue flowers: the seed (flax′seed′) yields linseed oil, and the fibres of the stem are spun into linen thread 2. these fibres

flaxen adj. 1. of flax 2. pale-yellow

flay (flā) vt. [OE. *flean*] 1. to strip off the skin of, as by whipping 2. to criticize mercilessly —flay′er n.

flea (flē) n. [< OE. *fleah*] a small, wingless,

jumping insect that is parasitic and sucks blood —**a flea in one's ear** an annoying rebuff

fleabite *n.* 1. the bite of a flea 2. a slight annoyance or inconvenience

flea-bitten *adj.* 1. bitten by or infested with fleas 2. wretched; shabby

flea market an outdoor bazaar dealing mainly in cheap, secondhand goods

fleapit *n.* [Colloq.] a small, shabby and dirty cinema or theatre

fleck (flek) *n.* [ON. *flekkr*] 1. a spot, speck, or flake —*vt.* to cover or sprinkle with flecks

fled (fled) *pt. & pp.* of FLEE

fledge (flej) *vi.* **fledged, fledg′ing** [< OE. *(un)flycge*, (un)fledged] to grow the feathers needed for flying —*vt.* 1. to rear (a young bird) until it can fly 2. to supply with feathers

fledgling *n.* 1. a young bird just fledged 2. a young, inexperienced person Also **fledge′ling**

flee (flē) *vi., vt.* **fled, flee′ing** [OE. *fleon*] 1. to run away or escape, as from danger 2. to vanish —**fle′er** *n.*

fleece (flēs) *n.* [OE. *fleos*] 1. the wool covering a sheep or similar animal 2. the wool cut from a sheep in one shearing 3. a fabric with a soft, warm pile —*vt.* **fleeced, fleec′ing** 1. to swindle 2. to shear fleece from —**fleec′y** *adj.*

fleet[1] (flēt) *n.* [OE. *fleot*] 1. *a)* a number of warships under one command *b)* an entire navy 2. any group of vehicles under one control

fleet[2] *vi.* [OE. *fleotan*, float] to move swiftly; fly —*adj.* swift; rapid —**fleet′-ly** *adv.* —**fleet′ness** *n.*

fleet chief petty officer *see* MILITARY RANKS, table

fleeting *adj.* passing swiftly; not lasting

Fleet Street [after the street in London where many newspaper offices are situated] British journalism or journalists collectively

Fleming (flem′iŋ) *n.* a native of Flanders

Flemish *adj.* of Flanders —**the Flemish** the language of the Flemings —**the Flemish** the people of Flanders

flesh (flesh) *n.* [OE. *flæsc*] 1. *a)* the soft substance of the body; esp., the muscular tissue *b)* the skin 2. meat 3. the pulpy part of fruits and vegetables 4. the body, as distinguished from the soul 5. human nature, esp. in its sensual aspect 6. all mankind 7. kindred: now mainly in **one's (own) flesh and blood**, one's close relatives —**flesh and blood** the human body —**in the flesh** 1. alive 2. in person

flesh-coloured *adj.* yellowish-pink

flesher *n.* [Scot.] a butcher

fleshly *adj.* **-lier, -liest** 1. of the body 2. sensual

fleshpots *n.pl.* 1. bodily comfort and pleasures; luxuries 2. a place where such pleasures are provided

flesh wound a wound that does not reach the bones or vital organs

fleshy *adj.* **-ier, -iest** 1. plump 2. of

or like flesh 3. having a firm pulp: said of fruits —**flesh′iness** *n.*

FLEUR-DE-LIS

fleur-de-lis (flur′də lē′) *n.*, *pl.* **fleurs-de-lis** (flur′də lēs′) [< OFr., flower of the lily] 1. *same as* IRIS (sense 2) 2. the coat of arms of the former French royal family 3. *Heraldry* a lilylike emblem: the unofficial floral emblem of Quebec Also sp. **fleur-de-lys**

flew (flōō) *pt.* of FLY[1]

flews (flōōz) *n.pl.* [< ?] the loose, hanging lip of a hound or other dog

flex[1] (fleks) *vt., vi.* [< L. *flectere*, bend] 1. to bend (an arm, knee, etc.) 2. to contract (a muscle)

flex[2] *n.* [< FLEXIBLE] flexible, insulated electric wire

flexible (flek′sə b'l) *adj.* 1. able to bend without breaking 2. easily influenced 3. adjustable to change —**flex′ibil′ity** *n.* —**flex′ibly** *adv.*

flextime *n.* [< FLEXIBLE] an arrangement whereby employees must complete a set total of working hours but are able to vary their starting and finishing times Also **flex′itime**

flibbertigibbet (flib′ər tē jib′it) *n.* [< ?] an irresponsible, flighty person

flick[1] (flik) *n.* [echoic] a light, quick stroke —*vt.* to strike, remove, etc. with a light, quick stroke

flick[2] *n.* [< ff.] [Slang] a cinema film —**the flicks** [Slang] a cinema showing of an entire performance

flicker (flik′ər) *vi.* [OE. *flicorian*] 1. to move with a quick, light, wavering motion 2. to burn or shine unsteadily —*n.* 1. a flickering 2. a flame or light that flickers 3. a quick, passing look or feeling

flick knife a knife with a retractable blade that springs out when a button on the handle is pressed

flier (flī′ər) *n.* *same as* FLYER

flight[1] (flīt) *n.* [OE. *flyht*] 1. the act, manner, or power of flying 2. distance flown 3. a group of birds, arrows, etc. flying together 4. a subdivision of a squadron in an air force 5. an aeroplane scheduled to fly a certain trip 6. a trip by aeroplane 7. a soaring above the ordinary [a *flight* of fancy] 8. a set of stairs, as between floors —**in the first (or top) flight** of the best quality

flight[2] *n.* [< OE. *fleon*, flee] a fleeing, as from danger —**put to flight** to force to flee

flight deck 1. the compartment in an airliner in which the pilots and crew sit

2. the upper deck of an aircraft carrier where aircraft take off and land

flightless *adj.* not able to fly

flight lieutenant *see* MILITARY RANKS, table

flight recorder a device fitted to an aircraft to monitor its performance in flight, and used to determine the cause of an accident: also called **black box**

flight sergeant *see* MILITARY RANKS, table

flighty *adj.* **-ier, -iest** frivolous or irresponsible —**flight′ily** *adv.* —**flight′iness** *n.*

flimsy (flim′zē) *adj.* **-sier, -siest** [< ?] **1.** easily broken or damaged; fragile **2.** weak or inadequate —*n.* a sheet of thin paper

flinch (flinch) *vi.* [< OFr. *flenchir*] **1.** to draw back, as from a blow, difficulty, etc. **2.** to wince

fling (fling) *vt.* **flung, fling′ing** [< ON. *flengja*, to whip] **1.** to throw, esp. with force; hurl **2.** to put abruptly or violently **3.** to move (one's limbs, head, etc.) suddenly —*n.* **1.** a flinging **2.** a brief time of self-indulgence **3.** a spirited dance [the Highland *fling*] **4.** [Colloq.] a trial effort —**fling′er** *n.*

flint (flint) *n.* [OE.] **1.** a very hard, siliceous rock that makes sparks when struck with steel **2.** a piece of this, used to start a fire, for primitive tools, etc. **3.** anything like flint in hardness, use, etc. [a heart of *flint*] —**flint′y** *adj.*

flintlock *n.* **1.** a gunlock using a flint to strike sparks **2.** a gun with such a lock

flip[1] (flip) *vt.* **flipped, flip′ping** [echoic] **1.** to move with a quick jerk **2.** to snap (a coin) into the air with the thumb **3.** to turn (a card, etc.) over quickly —*vi.* **1.** to make a quick, light stroke or move **2.** [Slang] to lose self-control: also **flip one's lid** (or **wig**) —*n.* a flipping

flip[2] *n.* [prob. < prec.] a sweetened mixed drink of wine or spirits with egg, spices, etc.

flip[3] *adj.* **flip′per, flip′pest** [< *flippant*] [Colloq.] flippant; saucy; impertinent

flippant (flip′ənt) *adj.* [prob. < FLIP[1]] frivolous and disrespectful; impertinent —**flip′pancy** *n.*

flipper *n.* **1.** a broad, flat limb, as of a seal, adapted for swimming **2.** a paddlelike rubber piece worn on each foot as a help in swimming **3.** [Slang] a hand

flip side [Colloq.] the reverse side (of a gramophone record), esp. the less important side

flirt (flurt) *vi.* [< ?] **1.** to woo someone lightly or frivolously **2.** to toy, as with an idea **3.** to move jerkily —*n.* a person who plays at love —**flirt′y** *adj.*

flirtation (flur tā′shən) *n.* a flirting, or playing at love

flirtatious *adj.* flirting or inclined to flirt

flit (flit) *vi.* **flit′ted, flit′ting** [< ON. *flytja*] **1.** to dart; flutter **2.** to move house —*n.* a flitting —**flit′ter** *n.*

flitch (flich) *n.* [OE. *flicce*] the cured and salted side of a pig; side of bacon —*vt.* to cut into flitches

flitter (flit′ər) *vi., vt.* [< FLIT] *same as* FLUTTER

flittermouse *n.* *same as* BAT[2]

float (flōt) *n.* [< OE. *fleotan*, to float] **1.** anything that stays on or at a liquid's surface; specif., *a)* a fishing-line cork *b)* a floating ball, etc. that regulates liquid level, as in a tank *c)* a buoyant device on an aircraft for landing on water **2.** a very low, flat lorry, esp. one that carries a display in a parade **3.** a sum of money used: *a)* to provide change *b)* to cover small expenses —*vi.* **1.** to stay on or at a liquid's surface **2.** to drift gently **3.** to move about aimlessly —*vt.* **1.** to make float **2.** to flood **3.** *a)* to put into circulation [*float* a bond issue] *b)* to allow the rate of exchange (of a currency) to vary *c)* to start (a business, etc.)

floatation (flō tā′shən) *n.* *same as* FLOTATION

floating *adj.* **1.** that floats **2.** not fixed; moving about **3.** designating an unfunded, short-time debt **4.** *Med.* displaced and more movable [a *floating* kidney]

floating ribs the eleventh and twelfth pairs of ribs, not attached to the breastbone or to other ribs

floating voter a voter of no fixed political allegiance

floats (flōts) *n.pl.* *same as* FOOTLIGHTS

flocculent (flok′yoo lənt) *adj.* [< L. *floccus*, lock of wool] woolly; fluffy —**floc′culence** *n.*

flock[1] (flok) *n.* [OE. *flocc*, a troop] **1.** a group of animals, as sheep, or of birds, living, feeding, etc. together **2.** any group, as of church members —*vi.* to assemble or travel in a flock

flock[2] *n.* [< L. *floccus*] **1.** a tuft of wool, cotton, etc. **2.** wool or cotton waste used to stuff furniture, etc. **3.** tiny fibres put on wallpaper, etc. to form a velvety surface

floe (flō) *n.* [prob. < Norw. *flo*, layer] *same as* ICE FLOE

flog (flog) *vt.* **flogged, flog′ging** [< ? L. *flagellare*, to whip] **1.** to beat with a stick, whip, etc. **2.** [Slang] to sell —**flog′ger** *n.*

flood (flud) *n.* [OE. *flod*] **1.** an overflowing of water on an area normally dry; deluge **2.** the rising of the tide **3.** a great outpouring, as of words —*vt.* **1.** to cover or fill with or as with a flood **2.** to put too much liquid on or in —*vi.* **1.** to gush out in a flood **2.** to become flooded —**the Flood** *Bible* the great flood in Noah's time

floodgate *n.* **1.** a gate to control water height and flow **2.** anything like this in controlling an outburst

floodlight *n.* **1.** a lamp that casts a broad beam of bright light **2.** such light —*vt.* **-light′ed** or **-lit′, -light′ing** to illuminate by a floodlight

flood tide the incoming or rising tide

floor (flôr) *n.* [OE. *flor*] **1.** the inside bottom surface of a room **2.** any bottom surface [the ocean *floor*] **3.** a storey in a building **4.** the part of a legislative chamber, stock exchange, etc. occupied by members **5.** the right to speak in an assembly **6.** a lower limit set on anything —*vt.* **1.** to furnish with a floor **2.** to knock down **3.** [Colloq.] *a)* to defeat *b)* to shock, confuse, etc.

floorboard *n.* a board in a floor

flooring *n.* **1.** material for making a floor **2.** a floor **3.** floors collectively

floor plan a scale drawing of the layout of rooms, halls, etc. on one floor of a building

floor show a show presenting singers, dancers, etc. in a restaurant, nightclub, etc.

floozy, floozie (floo'zē) *n., pl.* -zies [< ?] [Slang] a loose, disreputable woman: also sp. **floo'sy, floo'sie**

flop (flop) *vt.* **flopped, flop'ping** [var. of FLAP] to flap or throw noisily and clumsily —*vi.* **1.** to move, drop, or flap around loosely or clumsily **2.** [Colloq.] to be a failure —*n.* **1.** the act or sound of flopping **2.** [Colloq.] a failure —**flop'py** *adj.*

flora (flôr'ə) *n.* [< L. *flos*, flower] the plants of a specified region or time

floral (flôr'əl) *adj.* of, made of, or like flowers

Florentine (flor'ən tēn') *adj.* of Florence, Italy, or its people, culture, or art —*n.* a native of Florence

floret (flôr'it) *n.* [< L. *flos*, flower] **1.** a small flower **2.** any of the small flowers making up the head of a composite plant

floribunda (flor'ə bun'də) *n.* [< Mod.L. *floribundus*, flowering freely] a cultivated rose with clusters of flowers produced in profusion

florid (flor'id) *adj.* [< L. *flos*, flower] **1.** flushed; ruddy **2.** showy; ornate —**florid'ity** *n.*

florin (flor'in) *n.* [< L. *flos*, flower] **1.** any of various European or South African silver or gold coins **2.** a former British coin worth two shillings

florist (flor'ist) *n.* [< L. *flos*, flower] a person who cultivates or sells flowers —**flo'ristry** *n.*

floss (flos) *n.* [prob. < Fr.] **1.** the rough silk covering a cocoon **2.** short, downy waste fibres of silk **3.** a soft thread or yarn, as of silk, used in embroidery **4.** *same as* DENTAL FLOSS —**floss'y** *adj.*

flotation (flō tā'shən) *n.* the starting or financing of a business, etc., as by selling an entire issue of stock

flotilla (flō til'ə) *n.* [Sp.] a small fleet, or a fleet of small ships

flotsam (flot'səm) *n.* [< OFr.] the wreckage of a ship or its cargo floating at sea: chiefly in **flotsam and jetsam**, *a)* such wreckage *b)* miscellaneous trifles *c)* transient, unemployed people

flounce¹ (flouns) *vi.* **flounced, flounc'ing** [prob. < Scand.] to move with quick, flinging motions of the body, as in anger —*n.* the act of flouncing

flounce² *n.* [< OFr. *froncir*, to wrinkle] a wide, ornamental ruffle, as on a skirt —*vt.* **flounced, flounc'ing** to trim with flounces —**flounc'y** *adj.*

flounder¹ (floun'dər) *vi.* [< ? FOUNDER¹]

1. to struggle awkwardly, as in deep mud **2.** to speak or act in an awkward, confused way

flounder² *n.* [< Scand.] a flatfish caught for food, as the halibut

flour (flour) *n.* [orig. flower (i.e., best) of meal] **1.** a fine, powdery substance produced by grinding and sifting grain etc. **2.** any finely powdered substance —*vt.* to put flour on or in —**flour'y** *adj.*

flourish (flur'ish) *vi.* [< L. *flos*, flower] **1.** to grow vigorously; thrive; prosper **2.** to be at the peak of development, etc. **3.** to make showy, wavy motions —*vt.* to brandish (a sword, etc.) —*n.* **1.** anything done in a showy way **2.** a brandishing **3.** decorative lines in writing **4.** a fanfare —**flour'ishing** *adj.*

flout (flout) *vt., vi.* [prob. < ME. *flouten*, play the flute] to show scorn or contempt (for) —**flout'er** *n.*

flow (flō) *vi.* [OE. *flowan*] **1.** to move as a liquid does **2.** to move gently and smoothly **3.** to pour out **4.** to be derived; proceed **5.** to hang loose [*flowing hair*] **6.** to rise, as the tide **7.** to be plentiful —*n.* **1.** a flowing, or the manner or rate of this **2.** anything that flows **3.** a continuous production

flow chart a diagram showing the progress of work through a sequence of operations: also **flow sheet**

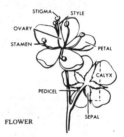

FLOWER

flower (flou'ər) *n.* [< L. *flos*, flower] **1.** the structure of many plants that produces seeds, typically with brightly coloured petals; blossom **2.** a plant cultivated for its blossoms **3.** the best or finest part **4.** [*pl.*] *Chem.* a powder made from condensed vapours —*vi.* **1.** to produce blossoms **2.** to reach the best period —**in flower** in a state of flowering

flowered *adj.* **1.** bearing or containing flowers **2.** having a floral design

flowerpot *n.* a container in which to grow plants

flowery *adj.* **-erier, -eriest** **1.** covered or decorated with flowers **2.** full of ornate expressions and fine words —**flow'eriness** *n.*

flown (flōn) *pp. of* FLY¹

fl. oz. fluid ounce; fluid ounces

flu (floo) *n.* **1.** *short for* INFLUENZA **2.**

popularly, a respiratory or intestinal infection caused by a virus

fluctuate (fluk′tyōo wāt′) *vi.* **-at′ed, -at′-ing** [< L. *fluctus*, a wave] **1.** to vary irregularly **2.** to move back and forth or up and down —**fluc′tua′tion** *n.*

flue (flōo) *n.* [< ?] a tube or shaft for the passage of smoke, hot air, etc., as in a chimney

fluent (flōo′ənt) *adj.* [< L. *fluere*, flow] **1.** able to write or speak easily, smoothly, and expressively **2.** flowing smoothly —**flu′ency** *n.*

fluff (fluf) *n.* [? blend of *flue*, downy mass + *puff*] **1.** soft, light down **2.** a loose, soft mass, as of dust **3.** *Theatre, Radio, TV* an error in speaking a line —*vt.* **1.** to shake or pat until loose, soft, and light **2.** *Theatre, Radio, TV* to make an error in speaking (one's lines, etc.) **3.** to bungle —**fluff′y** *adj.*

fluid (flōo′id) *adj.* [< L. *fluere*, flow] **1.** that can flow; not solid **2.** not settled or fixed **3.** available for investment or as cash [*fluid* assets] —*n.* a liquid or gas —**fluid′ity, flu′idness** *n.* —**flu′idly** *adv.*

fluid ounce a liquid measure equal to 1/20 pint, or 28.4 cm³: also **flu′idounce′** *n.*

fluke¹ (flōok) *n.* [OE. *floc*] **1.** a flatfish; esp. a flounder **2.** a flatworm parasitic in internal organs of vertebrates

fluke² *n.* [prob. < prec.] **1.** the triangular, pointed end of an anchor arm **2.** a barb or barbed head of an arrow, harpoon, etc. **3.** either of the lobes of a whale's tail

fluke³ *n.* [< ?] [Colloq.] a chance outcome, esp. a lucky one —*vt.* **fluked, fluk′ing** [Colloq.] to hit or get by a fluke

flummery (flum′ər ē) *n., pl.* **-meries** [W. *llymru*, soured oatmeal] **1.** a creamy pudding **2.** meaningless talk

flummox (flum′əks) *vt.* [< ?] [Slang] to confuse; perplex

flung (fluŋ) *pt. & pp. of* FLING

flunk (fluŋk) *vt., vi.* [< ?] [Chiefly U.S. Colloq.] to fail; esp. in an examination

flunkey (fluŋ′kē) *n., pl.* **-kies** [< ? Fr. *flanquer*, to flank] **1.** a footman **2.** one who obeys superiors in a servile way —**flun′keyism** *n.*

fluor (flōo′ôr) *n.* [< L. *fluere*, to flow] *same as* FLUORITE

fluoresce (flōo′ə res′) *vi.* **-resced′, -resc′-ing** to show or undergo fluorescence

fluorescence *n.* [ult. < L. *fluor*, flux] **1.** the property of a substance, as fluorite, of producing light when acted upon by radiant energy **2.** light so produced —**flu′o-res′cent** *adj.*

fluorescent lamp (or **tube**) a glass tube coated inside with a fluorescent substance giving off light (**fluorescent light**) when mercury vapour in the tube is acted upon by electrons from the cathode

fluoridate (flōoər′i dāt′) *vt.* **-dat′ed, -dat′-ing** to add fluorides to (a water supply) so as to reduce the incidence of tooth decay —**fluor′ida′tion** *n.*

fluoride (flōoər′īd) *n.* a compound of fluorine and another element or radical

fluorinate (flōoər′i nāt′) *vt.* **-nat′ed, -nat′-ing** *same as* FLUORIDATE —**fluor′ina′-tion** *n.*

fluorine (flōoər′ēn) *n.* a corrosive, poisonous, greenish-yellow, gaseous chemical element: symbol, F

fluorite (flōoər′īt) *n.* calcium fluoride, a transparent, crystalline mineral of various colours

fluor spar *same as* FLUORITE: also **flu′or-spar′** *n.*

flurry (flur′ē) *n., pl.* **-ries** [< ?] **1.** a sudden, brief rush of wind or fall of snow **2.** a sudden commotion —*vt.* **-ried, -rying** to confuse; agitate

flush¹ (flush) *vi.* [< ME. *flusschen*, fly up suddenly] **1.** to flow and spread suddenly **2.** to blush or glow **3.** to become cleaned or emptied with a sudden flow of water **4.** to start up from cover: said of birds —*vt.* **1.** to make flow **2.** to clean or empty with a sudden flow of water **3.** to make blush or glow **4.** to excite; exhilarate **5.** to drive (birds) from cover **6.** to make level —*n.* **1.** a rapid flow, as of water **2.** a sudden, vigorous growth [the first *flush* of youth] **3.** sudden excitement or exhilaration **4.** a blush or glow **5.** a sudden feeling of heat, as in a fever —*adj.* **1.** well supplied, esp. with money **2.** level or even (*with*)

flush² *n.* [see FLUX] a hand of cards all in the same suit

fluster (flus′tər) *vt., vi.* [prob. < Scand.] to get confused or nervous —*n.* a flustered state

flute (flōot) *n.* [< OFr.] **1.** a high-pitched wind instrument consisting of a long, slender tube with finger holes and keys **2.** an ornamental groove —*vt., vi.* **flut′-ed, flut′ing** **1.** to sing, speak, etc. in a flutelike tone **2.** to play on the flute **3.** to make grooves (in)

fluting *n.* **1.** a series of ornamental grooves, as in a column **2.** the act of one that flutes

flutter (flut′ər) *vi.* [< OE. *fleotan*, to float] **1.** to flap the wings rapidly **2.** to wave, move, or vibrate rapidly and irregularly **3.** to tremble **4.** to move about in a restless, fussy way —*vt.* to make flutter —*n.* **1.** a fluttering **2.** a state of excitement or confusion **3.** [Colloq.] a modest bet

fluty (flōot′ē) *adj.* **-ier, -iest** flutelike in tone

fluvial (flōo′vē əl) *adj.* [< L. *fluere*, to flow] of, found in, or produced by a river: also **flu′viatile** (-ə til)

flux (fluks) *n.* [< L. *fluere*, to flow] **1.** a flowing **2.** a coming in of the tide **3.** continual change **4.** any abnormal discharge from the body **5.** a substance used to help fuse metals together, as in soldering

fly¹ (flī) *vi.* **flew, flown, fly′ing** [OE. *fleogan*] **1.** to move through the air by using wings **2.** to travel in an aircraft **3.** to be propelled through the air or through space, as a missile **4.** to operate an aircraft **5.** to wave or float in the air **6.** to move or go swiftly **7.** to flee —*vt.* **1.** to cause to float in the air **2.** to operate (an aircraft)

3. to travel over in an aircraft **4.** to carry in an aircraft **5.** to flee from —*n., pl.* **flies** **1.** a flap concealing the zipper, buttons, etc. in a garment **2.** a flap serving as a tent door **3.** the length of a flag from the staff outwards **4.** [*pl.*] *Theatre* the space above the proscenium arch —**fly a kite** to obtain an indication beforehand of the real state of affairs —**fly at** to attack by or as by springing towards —**fly high** [Colloq.] to be ambitious —**let fly (at)** **1.** to shoot or throw (at) **2.** to unleash a verbal attack (at)

fly² ** *n., pl.* **flies [OE. *fleoge*] **1.** any of a large group of insects with two transparent wings, as the housefly **2.** a hooked lure for fishing, made to resemble an insect —**fly in the ointment** a tiny flaw that destroys the value of a thing —**there are no flies on him** [Slang] he is very alert; not easily hoaxed

**fly³ ** *adj.* [< ?] [Slang] alert and knowing; sharp

flyaway *adj.* **1.** streaming [*flyaway* hair] **2.** capricious

flyblown *adj.* **1.** full of flies' eggs **2.** spoiled; tainted **3.** [Colloq.] shabby; dingy

fly-by-night *adj.* not trustworthy, esp. financially —*n.* a fly-by-night person

flycatcher *n.* a bird that catches insects in flight

flyer *n.* **1.** a person or thing that flies or moves very fast **2.** an aviator

fly-fish *vi.* to fish by casting artificial flies

flying *adj.* **1.** that flies or can fly **2.** moving as if flying; fast **3.** hasty and brief **4.** organized to act quickly —*n.* the action of one that flies

flying boat an aeroplane with a hull that permits it to land on and take off from water

FLYING BUTTRESS

flying buttress a buttress connected to a wall by an arch, serving to resist outward pressure

flying colours notable victory or success

flying doctor a doctor who covers a wide area and visits his patients by aeroplane

flying fish a fish with winglike pectoral fins that enable it to glide through the air

flying fox a fruit-eating bat with a foxlike head

flying officer *see* MILITARY RANKS, table

flying saucer *same as* UFO

flying start **1.** the start of a race in which the contestants are already moving as they pass the starting line **2.** any rapid beginning

flying wing in Canadian football, the twelfth player, who has a variable position behind the scrimmage line

flyleaf (flī'lēf') *n., pl.* **-leaves'** a blank leaf at the beginning or end of a book

flyover *n.* an intersection of two roads at which one is carried over the other by a bridge

flypaper *n.* a sticky or poisonous paper set out to catch or kill flies

fly-past *n.* a ceremonial flight of aircraft over a given area

flysheet *n.* a piece of canvas drawn over the ridgepole of a tent to form an outer roof

fly-spray *n.* a liquid squirted from an aerosol can to kill flies

flytrap *n.* a plant that catches insects

flyweight *n.* *see* BOXING AND WRESTLING WEIGHTS, table

flywheel *n.* a heavy wheel attached to a machine so as to regulate its speed and motion

Fm *Chem.* fermium

FM frequency modulation

F.M. Field Marshal

fm. **1.** fathom **2.** from

f-number (ef'num'bər) *n.* *Photog.* the ratio of a lens diameter to its focal length

fo. folio

F.O. **1.** Flying Officer **2.** [obs.] Foreign Office

foal (fōl) *n.* [OE. *fola*] a young horse, mule, donkey, etc.; colt or filly —*vt., vi.* to give birth to (a foal)

foam (fōm) *n.* [OE. *fam*] **1.** the whitish mass of bubbles formed on or in liquids by agitation, fermentation, etc. **2.** something like foam, as frothy saliva **3.** a rigid or spongy cellular mass made from liquid rubber, plastic, etc. —*vi.* to produce foam; froth —**foam at the mouth** to rage **foam'y** *adj.*

foam rubber rubber treated to form a firm, spongy foam

fob¹ (fob) *n.* [prob. < dial. G. *fuppe*, pocket] **1.** a watch pocket in the front of a man's trousers **2.** a chain hanging from a watch in such a pocket

fob² *vt.* **fobbed, fob'bing** [< ME. *fobben*, cheat] [Obs.] to deceive —**fob off** to trick or put off (a person) with second-rate articles, lies, excuses, etc.

F.O.B., f.o.b. free on board

focal (fō'k'l) *adj.* of or at a focus —**fo'-cally** *adv.*

focal length the distance from the optical centre of a lens to the point where the light rays converge

fo'c's'le (fōk's'l) *n.* phonetic spelling of FORECASTLE

focus (fō'kəs) *n., pl.* **fo'cuses, fo'ci** (-sī) [L., hearth] **1.** the point where rays of light, heat, etc. come together; specif., the point where reflected or refracted light rays meet **2.** *same as* FOCAL LENGTH **3.** adjustment of focal length to make a clear image **4.** any centre of activity, attention, etc. —*vt.* **-cused** or **-cussed, -cusing** or **-cussing** **1.** to bring into focus **2.** to adjust the focal length of (the eye, a lens, etc.) so as to make a clear image **3.** to concentrate *[focus* one's attention *]* —*vi.* to come to a focus —**in focus** clear; distinct —**out of focus** blurred

fodder (fod′ər) *n.* [OE. *fodor*] coarse food for cattle, horses, etc., as hay and straw

foe (fō) *n.* [OE. *fah,* hostile] *same as* ENEMY

foetid (fēt′id) *adj.* *same as* FETID

foetus (fēt′əs) *n.,* *pl.* **-tuses** [< L. *fetus,* a bringing forth] the unborn young of an animal while still in the uterus or egg, esp. in its later stages : cf. EMBRYO —**foe′-tal** *adj.*

fog (fog) *n.* [prob. < Scand.] **1.** a large mass of water vapour condensed to fine particles, just above the earth's surface **2.** a similar mass of smoke, dust, etc. **3.** a state of mental confusion **4.** a blur on a photograph or film —*vt., vi.* **fogged, fog′ging** to make or become foggy, blurred, etc. —**fog′gy** *adj.*

fog bank a dense mass of fog

fogbound *adj.* **1.** surrounded or covered by fog **2.** prevented from sailing, flying, etc. because of fog

foghorn *n.* a horn blown to give warning to ships in a fog

fogy (fō′gē) *n.,* *pl.* **-gies** [< ?] a person who is oldfashioned or highly conservative : also **fo′gey,** *pl.* **-geys**

foible (foi′b'l) *n.* [< Fr. *faible,* feeble] a small weakness in character; frailty

foil[1] (foil) *vt.* [< OFr. *fuler,* trample] to thwart

foil[2] *n.* [< L. *folium,* leaf] **1.** a very thin sheet of metal **2.** one that sets off or enhances another by contrast **3.** [etym. unc.] a long, thin, blunted fencing sword **4.** a leaflike, rounded space or design, as in windows, etc. in Gothic architecture

foist (foist) *vt.* [prob. < dial. Du. *vuisten,* hide in the hand] to put in slyly; palm off *(on* or *upon)*

fold[1] (fōld) *vt.* [OE. *faldan*] **1.** to bend or press (something) so that one part is over another **2.** to draw together and intertwine *[to fold* the arms *]* **3.** to embrace **4.** to wrap up; envelop —*vi.* **1.** to be or become folded **2.** [Colloq.] *a)* to fail, as a business *b)* to succumb, as to exhaustion —*n.* **1.** a folded part **2.** a hollow or crease made by folding **3.** *Geol.* a rock layer folded by pressure —**fold in** to blend (an ingredient) into a mixture, using gentle, cutting strokes

fold[2] *n.* [OE. *fald*] **1.** a pen in which to keep sheep **2.** a flock of sheep **3.** a group with common aims, faith, etc., as a church —*vt.* to confine in a pen

-fold (fōld) [OE. *-feald*] a suffix meaning: **1.** having (a specified number of) parts *[tenfold]* **2.** (a specified number of) times as many or as much

foldaway *adj.* that can be folded for easy storage

folder *n.* **1.** a sheet of heavy paper folded as a holder for papers **2.** an unstitched, folded booklet

folderol (fol′də rol′) *n.* *same as* FALDERAL

folding door a door with hinged leaves or accordion pleats that can be folded back

foliaceous (fō′lē ā′shəs) *adj.* [< L. *folium,* leaf] **1.** of, like, or having leaves **2.** consisting of thin layers

foliage (fō′lē ij) *n.* [< L. *folium,* leaf] leaves, as of a plant or tree —**fo′liaged** *adj.*

foliation (fō′lē ā′shən) *n.* **1.** a growing of or developing into a leaf or leaves **2.** the state of being in leaf **3.** the act of beating metal into layers **4.** a leaflike decoration

folio (fō′lē ō′) *n.,* *pl.* **-lios**′ [< L. *folium,* leaf] **1.** a large sheet of paper folded once **2.** a book made of sheets so folded **3.** a leaf of a book, etc. numbered on only one side **4.** the number of a page in a book, etc. —*adj.* of folio size —**in folio** in the form of a folio

folk (fōk) *n.,* *pl.* **folk, folks** [OE. *folc*] **1.** *a)* a people; nation *b)* the common people of a nation **2.** [Colloq.] [*pl.*] people; persons —*adj.* of the common people —(one's) **folks** [Colloq.] (one's) family

folk dance **1.** a traditional dance of the common people of a country **2.** music for this

folk etymology the change that occurs in the form of a word over a period of prolonged usage so as to give it an apparent connection with some other word, as *Welsh rabbit* becomes *Welsh rarebit*

folklore (fōk′lôr′) *n.* the traditional beliefs, legends, sayings, etc. of a people —**folk′lor′ic** *adj.*

folk music music made and handed down among the common people

folk song **1.** a song made and handed down among the common people **2.** a song like this —**folk singer**

folksy *adj.* **-sier, -siest** **1.** affectedly simple **2.** [Colloq.] friendly or sociable

follicle (fol′i k'l) *n.* [< L. *follis,* bellows] any small sac, cavity, or gland *[a* hair *follicle]* —**follicular** (fə lik′yoo lər) *adj.*

follow (fol′ō) *vt.* [< OE. *folgian*] **1.** to come or go after **2.** to chase; pursue **3.** to go along *[follow* the road *]* **4.** to take up; engage in (a trade, etc.) **5.** to result from **6.** to take as a model; imitate **7.** to obey **8.** to listen to or observe closely **9.** to understand the continuity or logic of —*vi.* **1.** to come, go, or happen after something else in place, sequence, or time **2.** to result —*n.* the act of following —**follow out** to carry out fully —**follow through** to continue and complete a stroke or action —**follow up** **1.** to pursue or investigate closely **2.** to make more effective by doing something more

follower *n.* one that follows; esp. a person who follows another's teachings; disciple

following *adj.* that follows; next after —*n.* a group of followers —*prep.* after —**the following** **1.** the one or ones to be mentioned immediately **2.** what follows

follow-on *n.* *Cricket* an immediate second innings forced on a team scoring a prescribed number of runs fewer than its opponents in the first innings

follow-up *n.* a letter, visit, etc. that follows as a review or addition

folly (fol′ē) *n., pl.* **-lies** [see FOOL] **1.** a lack of sense; foolishness **2.** any foolish action or belief **3.** any foolish but expensive undertaking, esp. a useless and needlessly extravagant structure

foment (fō ment′) *vt.* [< L. *fovere*, keep warm] to stir up; incite *[to foment a riot]* **—fo′menta′tion** *n.*

fond (fond) *adj.* [< ME. *fonnen*, be foolish] **1.** tender and affectionate **2.** foolishly credulous or trusting **—fond of** having a liking for **—fond′ness** *n.*

fondant (fon′dənt) *n.* [Fr. < *fondre*, melt] **1.** a soft, creamy paste made of sugar **2.** a sweet made of this

fondle (fon′d'l) *vt.* **-dled, -dling** [< obs. *fond, v.*] to stroke lovingly; caress **—fon′dler** *n.*

fondue, fondu (fon′dyo͞o) *n.* [Fr. < *fondre*, melt] **1.** cheese melted in wine, used as a dip for cubes of bread, etc. **2.** any of various other dishes of hot, liquid ingredients, as hot oil into which cubes of meat are dipped

font (font) *n.* [< L. *fons*, fountain] **1.** a bowl to hold the water used in baptismal services **2.** a basin for holy water **3.** any source; origin **—font′al** *adj.*

FONTANELLES

fontanelle (fon′tə nel′) *n.* [< OFr. *fontaine*, fountain] any of the soft, boneless areas in the skull of a baby: also sp. **fon′tanel′**

food (fo͞od) *n.* [OE. *foda*] **1.** any substance taken into and assimilated by a plant or animal to keep it alive and enable it to grow **2.** solid substances of this sort: distinguished from *drink* **3.** anything that nourishes or stimulates

food poisoning sickness from eating food contaminated by bacteria, chemicals, etc.

foodstuff *n.* any material made into or used as food

fool[1] (fo͞ol) *n.* [< L. *follis*, windbag] **1.** a silly person; simpleton **2.** a man formerly kept by a nobleman or king to entertain as a clown; jester **3.** a dupe **—vi. 1.** to act like a fool; be silly **2.** to joke **—vt.** to trick; deceive **—be no** (or **nobody's**) **fool** to be shrewd and capable **—fool about** (or **around**) [Colloq.] **1.** to behave irresponsibly or aimlessly **2.** to

meddle (*with*) **—fool away** [Colloq.] to squander

fool[2] *n.* [< ? prec.] crushed stewed fruit mixed with cream

foolery *n., pl.* **-eries** (a) foolish action

foolhardy *adj.* **-dier, -diest** foolishly daring; rash **—fool′har′dily** *adv.* **—fool′har′diness** *n.*

foolish *adj.* **1.** silly; unwise **2.** absurd **—fool′ishly** *adv.* **—fool′ishness** *n.*

foolproof *adj.* so harmless, simple, etc. as not to be mishandled, damaged, etc. even by a fool

foolscap (fo͞olz′kap′) *n.* [from former watermark] a large size of writing paper

fool's errand a fruitless errand

fool's paradise a state of illusory happiness

fool's-parsley *n.* a poisonous plant resembling parsley

foot (fo͞ot) *n., pl.* **feet** [OE. *fot*] **1.** the end part of the leg, on which one stands **2.** the base or bottom *[the foot of a page]* **3.** the last of a series **4.** the end, as of a bed, towards which the feet are directed **5.** the part of a stocking, etc. covering the foot **6.** a measure of length, equal to 12 inches (c. 30cm) **7.** infantry **8.** a group of syllables serving as a unit of metre in verse **—vt.** [Colloq.] to pay (costs, etc.) **—foot it** [Colloq.] to dance, walk, or run **—have one foot in the grave** [Colloq.] to be near to death **—on foot 1.** walking **2.** in process **—put one's best foot forward** [Colloq.] **1.** to hurry **2.** to do one's best **3.** to try to appear at one's best **—put one's foot down** [Colloq.] to act decisively **—put one's foot in it** [Colloq.] to make an embarrassing blunder

footage (fo͞ot′ij) *n.* length expressed in feet

foot-and-mouth disease an acute, contagious disease of cattle, deer, etc. characterized by fever and blisters in the mouth and around the feet

football *n.* **1.** a field game played with an inflated leather ball by two teams **2.** the ball used in playing this **—foot′baller** *n.*

football pools *same as* POOLS

footboard *n.* **1.** a board or platform for supporting the feet **2.** a vertical piece across the foot of a bed

footbridge *n.* a narrow bridge for pedestrians

footfall *n.* the sound of a footstep

foothill *n.* a low hill at or near the foot of a mountain or mountain range

foothold *n.* **1.** a place to put a foot down securely, as in climbing **2.** a secure position

footing *n.* **1.** a secure position or basis **2.** a basis for relationship **3.** a secure placing of the feet **4.** a foothold

footle (fo͞ot′'l) *vi.* [< ?] [Colloq.] to act or talk foolishly or aimlessly **—foot′ling** *adj.*

footlights (fo͞ot′līts′) *n.pl.* a row of lights along the front of a stage at the actors' foot level

footloose *adj.* free to go where or do as one likes

footman *n.* a male servant who assists the butler in a household

footnote *n.* a note of comment or reference at the bottom of a page

footpad *n.* [see PAD³] formerly, a highway robber

footpath *n.* a narrow path for pedestrians

footplate *n.* the platform in a locomotive cab on which the crew stand to operate the controls

foot-pound (fo͝ot′po͝und′) *n.* the amount of energy required to raise a weight of one pound a distance of one foot

footprint *n.* a mark left by a foot

footrace *n.* a race run on foot

footrest *n.* a support to rest the feet on

footsie, footsy *n., pl.* **-sies** the foot : a child's term —**play footsie** (**with**) to flirt or have surreptitious dealings (with)

footsore *adj.* having sore feet, as from walking

footstep *n.* **1.** the distance covered in a step **2.** the sound of a step **3.** a footprint —**follow in** (**someone's**) **footsteps** to follow (someone's) example, vocation, etc.

footstool *n.* a low stool for supporting the feet of a seated person

footwear *n.* shoes, boots, slippers, etc.

footwork *n.* the act or manner of moving the feet, as in walking, boxing, dancing, etc.

fop (fop) *n.* [< ? ME. *foppe*, fool] a vain, affected man who pays too much attention to his clothes, appearance, etc. —**fop′pery** *n.* —**fop′pish** *adj.*

for (fôr; *unstressed* fər) *prep.* [OE.] **1.** in place of **2.** in the interest of [his agent acted *for* him] **3.** in defence of; in favour of **4.** in honour of **5.** with the aim or purpose of **6.** with the purpose of going to [to leave *for* home] **7.** in order to be, become, get, have, keep, etc. [to walk *for* exercise] **8.** in search of **9.** meant to be received by a specified person or thing, or to be used in a specified way [money *for* paying bills] **10.** suitable to [a room *for* sleeping] **11.** with regard to [need *for* improvement] **12.** as being [know *for* a fact] **13.** considering the nature of [cool *for* July] **14.** because of [to cry *for* pain] **15.** in spite of **16.** in proportion to [a pound tax *for* every four earned] **17.** at the price of [sold *for* £10] **18.** to the length, amount, duration, etc. of **19.** at (a specified time) [an appointment *for* two o'clock] —*conj.* because —**O! for** I wish that I had

for- [OE.] a prefix meaning away, apart, off, etc. [forbid, forget, forgo]

forage (fôr′ij) *n.* [< OFr.] **1.** food for domestic animals; fodder **2.** a search for food or provisions —*vi.* **-aged, -aging** to search for food, provisions, etc. —*vt.* to get or take food or provisions from

foramen (fo rā′mən) *n., pl.* **-ram′ina** (-ram′ə nə), **-ra′mens** [L. < *forare*, to bore] a small opening, esp. in a bone

forasmuch (fôr′əz much′) *conj.* inasmuch (as)

foray (fôr′ā) *vt., vi.* [< OFr. *forrer*] to plunder —*n.* a sudden raid, as for spoils

forbade, forbad (fər bad′) *pt. of* FORBID

forbear¹ (fôr bãr′) *vt.* **-bore′, -borne′, -bear′ing** [see FOR- & BEAR¹] to refrain from (doing, saying, etc.) —*vi.* **1.** to refrain or abstain **2.** to control oneself —**forbear′ance** *n.*

forbear² (fôr′bãr′) *n.* same as FOREBEAR

forbid (fər bid′) *vt.* **-bade′** or **-bad′, -bid′-den, -bid′ding** [see FOR- & BID] **1.** to rule against; prohibit **2.** to bar from **3.** to prevent —**forbid′dance** *n.*

forbidding *adj.* looking dangerous, threatening, or disagreeable; repellent —**forbid′dingly** *adv.*

forbore (fôr bôr′) *pt. of* FORBEAR¹

forborne (-bôrn′) *pp. of* FORBEAR¹

force¹ (fôrs) *n.* [< L. *fortis*, strong] **1.** strength; power **2.** impetus **3.** physical coercion **4.** the power to control, persuade, etc. **5.** a) military power b) any organized group of soldiers, sailors, police, etc. **6.** any group of people organized for some activity [a sales *force*] **7.** *Law* binding power; validity **8.** *Physics* the cause that puts an object at rest into motion or alters the motion of a moving object —*vt.* **forced, forc′ing 1.** to cause to do something by force; compel **2.** to break open, into, or through by force **3.** to take by force **4.** to drive as by force; impel **5.** to impose as by force (with *on* or *upon*) **6.** to produce as by force [to *force* a smile] **7.** to strain **8.** to cause (plants, etc.) to develop faster by artificial means —**in force 1.** in full strength **2.** in effect; valid

force² *n.* [< ON *fors*] [Dial.] a waterfall

forced *adj.* **1.** compulsory [*forced* labour] **2.** produced by unusual effort; strained [a *forced* smile] **3.** due to an emergency [a *forced* landing] **4.** at a pace faster than usual [a *forced* march]

force-feed (fôrs′fēd′) *vt.* **-fed′, -feed′-ing** to feed as by a tube through the throat to the stomach

forceful *adj.* full of force; powerful, vigorous, effective, etc. —**force′fully** *adv.* —**force′fulness** *n.*

forcemeat (fôrs′mēt) *n.* [< *farce* (obs.), to stuff] meat chopped up and seasoned, usually for stuffing

forceps (fôr′seps) *n., pl.* **for′ceps** [< L. *formus*, hot + *capere*, take] tongs or pincers for grasping, pulling, etc. used esp. by surgeons and dentists

forcible (fôr′sə b'l) *adj.* **1.** done or effected by force **2.** having force; forceful —**for′cibly** *adv.*

ford (fôrd) *n.* [OE.] a shallow place in a stream, river, etc. that can be crossed by wading, on horseback, in a car, etc. —*vt.* to cross (a stream) in this way —**ford′able** *adj.*

fore (fôr) *adv.* [OE.] at, in, or towards the front : now only of a ship —*adj.* situated in front —*n.* the front —*interj. Golf* a warning that one is about to hit the ball —**to the fore** to the front; active

'fore (fôr) *prep.* [Poet.] before

fore- [OE.] a prefix meaning : **1.** before in time, place, etc. [forenoon] **2.** the front part of [forearm]

forearm¹ (fôr′ärm′) *n.* the part of the arm between the elbow and the wrist

forearm² (fôr ärm′) *vt.* to arm in advance; prepare

forebear (fôr′bâer′) *n.* [< FORE + BE + -ER] an ancestor

forebode (fôr bōd′) *vt., vi.* -bod′ed, -bod′-ing [see FORE- & BODE¹] 1. to be an omen or warning of (esp. something bad or harmful) 2. to have a presentiment of (something bad or harmful) —**forebod′-ing** *n., adj.*

forecast (fôr′kast′) *vt.* -cast′ or -cast′-ed, -cast′ing 1. to predict (weather, etc.) 2. to serve as a prediction of —*n.* a prediction —**fore′cast′er** *n.*

forecastle (fōk′s'l) *n.* [fore + castle] the front part of a ship, where the sailors' quarters are located

foreclose (fôr klōz′) *vt.* -closed′, -clos′-ing [< OFr. fors, outside + clore, CLOSE²] 1. to take away the right to redeem (a mortgage, etc.) 2. to exclude; bar —**fore-clo′sure** *n.*

forecourt (fôr′kôrt′) *n.* a court at the front of a building, esp. a service station

forefather *n.* an ancestor

forefinger *n.* the finger nearest the thumb

forefoot *n., pl.* **-feet′** either of the front feet of an animal with four or more feet

forefront *n.* 1. the extreme front 2. the position of most activity, importance, etc.

foregather (fôr gath′ər) *vi.* same as FORGATHER

forego¹ (fôr gō′) *vt., vi.* -went′, -gone′, -go′ing to go before in place, time, or degree

forego² *vt.* same as FORGO

foregoing (fôr′gō′iŋ) *adj.* previously said, written, etc.

foregone (fôr′gon) *adj.* 1. previous 2. a) previously determined b) inevitable : said of a conclusion

foreground *n.* 1. the part of a scene, etc. nearest the viewer 2. the most conspicuous position

forehand *n.* a kind of stroke, as in tennis, made with the palm of the hand turned forwards —*adj.* done as with a forehand: also **forehand′ed**

forehead (fôr′id, fôr′hed) *n.* the part of the face between the eyebrows and the hairline

foreign (fôr′ən) *adj.* [< L. foras, out-of-doors] 1. situated outside one's own country, locality, etc. 2. of, from, or characteristic of another country 3. concerning the relations of one country to another [foreign affairs] 4. not characteristic or belonging

foreigner *n.* a person from another country; alien

foreign minister in some countries, a member of a governmental cabinet in charge of foreign affairs

foreign office in some countries, the office of government in charge of foreign affairs

foreign secretary the minister in the British government in charge of foreign affairs

foreknow (fôr nō′) *vt.* -knew′, -known′, -know′ing to know beforehand —**fore′-knowl′edge** *n.*

foreland (fôr′lənd) *n.* a headland; promontory

foreleg *n.* either of the front legs of an animal with four or more legs

forelimb *n.* a front limb, as an arm, wing, etc.

forelock *n.* a lock of hair growing just above the forehead —**take time by the forelock** to seize a chance

foreman *n.* 1. a man in charge of a group of workers in a factory, etc. 2. the chairman of a jury —**fore′wom′an** *n. fem.*

foremast *n.* the mast nearest the bow of a ship

foremost *adj.* 1. first in place or time 2. first in rank or importance —*adv.* first

forenoon *n.* the time from sunrise to noon; morning

forensic (fəren′sik) *adj.* [< L. forum, marketplace] of, or suitable for, a law court or public debate —**foren′sically** *adv.*

forensic medicine the application of medical knowledge to questions of law, as in determining cause of death

foreordain (fôr′ôr dān′) *vt.* to ordain beforehand —**fore′ordina′tion** *n.*

forepaw *n.* an animal's front paw

forerunner *n.* 1. a messenger sent or going before; herald 2. a predecessor

foresail (fôr′sāl′, -səl) *n.* the main sail on the foremast

foresee (fôr sē′) *vt.* -saw′, -seen′, -see′-ing to see or know beforehand —**foresee′a-ble** *adj.* —**foresee′er** *n.*

foreshadow (fôr shad′ō) *vt.* to indicate or suggest beforehand; presage —**fore-shad′ower** *n.*

foreshore *n.* the part of a shore between high-water mark and low-water mark

foreshorten (fôr shôr′t'n) *vt.* Drawing, Painting, etc. to shorten some lines of (an object) to give the illusion of proper relative size

foresight *n.* 1. prudent regard or provision for the future 2. a) a foreseeing b) the power to foresee

foreskin *n.* the fold of skin that covers the end of the penis; prepuce

forest (fôr′ist) *n.* [< L. foris, out-of-doors] 1. a thick growth of trees and underbrush covering an extensive tract of land 2. formerly, a tract of woodland or wasteland, preserved for game —*adj.* of or in a forest —*vt.* to cover with trees or woods —**for′ested** *adj.*

forestall (fôr stôl′) *vt.* [OE. foresteall, ambush] 1. to prevent by doing something ahead of time 2. to act in advance of; anticipate —**forestall′er** *n.*

forestation (for′is tā′shən) *n.* the plant-ing or care of forests

forester *n.* a person trained in forestry or charged with the care of a forest

forestry *n.* the science of planting and taking care of forests

foretaste (fôr'tāst') *n.* a taste or sample of what can be expected

foretell (fôr tel') *vt.* **-told', -tell'ing** to tell or indicate beforehand; predict —**foretell'er** *n.*

forethought (fôr'thôt') *n.* 1. a thinking or planning beforehand 2. foresight; prudence

foretoken (fôr'tō'kən; *for v.* fôr tō'kən) *n.* a prophetic sign; omen —*vt.* to foreshadow

foretop (fôr'top', -təp) *n.* the platform at the top of a ship's foremast

forever (fər ev'ər) *adv.* 1. for eternity; for always 2. at all times; always

forewarn (fôr wôrn') *vt.* to warn beforehand

foreword (fôr'wurd') *n.* an introductory remark, preface, or prefatory note

forfeit (fôr'fit) *n.* [< L. *foris*, beyond + *facere*, do] 1. a fine or penalty for some crime, fault, or neglect 2. the act of forfeiting —*adj.* lost or taken away as a forfeit —*vt.* to lose or be deprived of as a forfeit

forfeiture (fôr'fə chər) *n.* 1. a forfeiting 2. anything forfeited; penalty or fine

forgather (fôr gath'ər) *vi.* to come together; assemble

forgave (fôr gāv') *pt.* of FORGIVE

forge[1] (fôrj) *n.* [< L. *faber*, workman] 1. a furnace for heating metal to be wrought 2. a place where metal is heated and wrought; smithy —*vt., vi.* **forged, forg'ing** 1. to shape (metal) by blows or pressure, usually after heating 2. to form; shape 3. to imitate for purposes of fraud; esp., to counterfeit (a cheque, etc.) —**forg'er** *n.*

forge[2] *vt., vi.* **forged, forg'ing** [prob. altered < FORCE] 1. to move forward steadily, as if against difficulties 2. to move in a sudden spurt Often with *ahead*

forgery *n., pl.* **-geries** 1. the act of forging documents, signatures, etc. 2. anything forged

forget (fər get') *vt., vi.* **-got', -got'ten, -get'ting** [OE. *forgietan*] 1. to be unable to remember 2. to overlook or neglect —**forget it** don't trouble to think about it —**forget oneself** 1. to think only of others 2. to behave in an unseemly manner

forgetful *adj.* 1. apt to forget; having a poor memory 2. negligent —**forget'fully** *adv.*

forget-me-not *n.* a plant with small blue flowers, symbolic of friendship

forgive (fər giv') *vt., vi.* **-gave', -giv'en, -giv'ing** [OE. *forgiefan*] 1. to give up resentment against or the desire to punish; pardon 2. to cancel (a debt)

forgiveness *n.* 1. a forgiving; pardon 2. inclination to forgive

forgiving *adj.* inclined to forgive

forgo (fôr gō') *vt.* **-went', -gone', -go'ing** [OE. *forgan*] to do without; abstain from —**forgo'er** *n.*

forgot (fər got') *pt. & archaic pp.* of FORGET

forgotten *pp.* of FORGET

fork (fôrk) *n.* [< L. *furca*] 1. an instrument

with a handle and two or more prongs, used as an eating utensil or for pitching hay, etc. 2. something resembling a fork in shape 3. the point where a river, road, etc. divides into branches 4. any of these branches —*vi.* to divide into branches —*vt.* to pick up, spear, or pitch with a fork —**fork over** (or **out, up**) [Colloq.] to pay out; hand over —**fork'ful** *n.*

forked *adj.* 1. having a fork or forks; cleft [*forked* lightning] 2. having prongs [five-*forked*]

forklift *n.* a device with projecting prongs, as on a vehicle, for lifting heavy objects

forlorn (fər lôrn') *adj.* [< OE. *forleosan*, lose utterly] 1. abandoned or deserted 2. wretched; miserable

forlorn hope [< Du *verloren hoop*, lost group] 1. an undertaking with very little chance of success 2. a faint hope

form (fôrm) *n.* [< L. *forma*] 1. the shape; structure 2. the figure of a person or animal 3. a mould 4. the mode of existence a thing has or takes [water in the *form* of vapour] 5. arrangement; style 6. a way of doing something 7. a customary way of behaving 8. a fixed order of words; formula 9. a printed document with blank spaces to be filled in 10. a particular kind or type 11. condition of mind or body 12. what can be expected, based on past performances 13. a long, wooden bench 14. a class in school 15. the place where a hare sleeps 16. *Gram.* any of the different appearances of a word in changes of inflection, spelling, etc. —*vt.* 1. to shape; fashion 2. to train; instruct 3. to develop (habits) 4. to think of; conceive 5. to organize into 6. to make up —*vi.* 1. to be formed 2. to take form —**good** (or **bad**) **form** conduct in (or not in) accord with social custom

-form (fôrm) [< L.] a suffix meaning having the form of [*cuneiform*]

formal (fôr'məl) *adj.* 1. of external form or structure, rather than nature or content 2. according to fixed customs, rules, etc. 3. stiff in manner 4. designed for wear at ceremonies, etc. [*formal* dress] 5. methodical 6. rigidly symmetrical [a *formal* garden] 7. done or made in explicit, definite form [a *formal* contract] 8. designating or of that level of language usage characterized by expanded vocabulary, complex sentences, etc. —**for'mally** *adv.*

formaldehyde (fôr mal'də hīd') *n.* [FORM(IC) + ALDEHYDE] a colourless, pungent gas, used in solution as a disinfectant and preservative

formalism (fôr'məl iz'm) *n.* strict attention to outward forms and customs —**for'malist** *n., adj.*

formality (fôr mal'ə tē) *n., pl.* **-ties** 1. *a)* an observing of customs, rules, etc. *b)* too careful attention to convention; stiffness 2. a formal act; ceremony 3. something done merely for the sake of form

formalize (fôr'mə līz') *vt.* **-ized', -iz'ing** 1. to make formal or official 2. to give definite form to

format (fôr'mat) *n.* [< L. *formare*, to

form] 1. the shape, size, and general makeup of a book, magazine, etc. 2. general arrangement, as of a television programme

formation (fôr mā' shən) *n.* 1. a forming 2. a thing formed 3. the way something is arranged; structure 4. an arrangement, as of troops, a team, etc. 5. *Geol.* a rock unit having some common character, as origin

formative (fôr'mə tiv) *adj.* 1. helping to develop or mould *[a formative* influence *]* 2. of formation or development *[one's formative* years *]*

former (fôr'mər) *adj.* [< ME. *forme,* first] 1. preceding in time; earlier; past 2. first mentioned of two: often a noun (with *the*)

formerly *adv.* at or in a former or earlier time; in the past

formic (fôr'mik) *adj.* [< L. *formica,* ant] designating a colourless acid found in ants

Formica (fôr mīk'ə) *Trademark* a laminated, heat-resistant plastic used for table tops, etc.

formidable (fôr'mə də b'l) *adj.* [< L. *formidare,* to dread] 1. causing fear, dread, or awe 2. hard to handle or overcome —**for'midably** *adv.*

formless *adj.* having no regular form or plan

formula (fôr'myoo lə) *n., pl.* **-las,** **-lae** (-lē') [< L. *forma,* form] 1. a fixed form of words, esp. a conventional expression 2. a conventional rule for doing something 3. an exact statement of religious faith 4. a form of words that allows an agreement to be reached 5. a prescription for a medicine, etc. 6. a set of symbols expressing a mathematical rule 7. categorization of racing cars, usually according to engine capacity 8. *Chem.* an expression of the composition, as of a compound, using symbols and figures

formulary (fôr'myoo lər ē) *n., pl.* **-laries** 1. a collection of prescribed forms, as of prayers 2. a formula 3. a list of medicines with their formulas

formulate (fôr'myoo lāt') *vt.* **-lat'ed, -lat'-ing** 1. to express in or reduce to a formula 2. to express (a theory, plan, etc.) in a systematic way —**for'mula'tion.** —**for'-mula'tor** *n.*

fornicate (fôr'nə kāt') *vi.* **-cat'ed, -cat'-ing** [< L. *fornix,* brothel] to commit fornication —**for'nica'tor** *n.*

fornication (fôr'nə kā'shən) *n.* voluntary sexual intercourse between unmarried persons

forsake (fər sāk') *vt.* **-sook'** (-sook'), **-sak'en, -sak'ing** [< OE. *forsacan*] 1. to leave; abandon 2. to give up (a habit, etc.) —**forsak'en** *adj.*

forsooth (fər sooth') *adv.* [OE. *forsoth*] [Archaic] in truth; no doubt; indeed

forswear (fôr swâer') *vt.* **-swore', -sworn', -swear'ing** 1. to swear to give up 2. to deny earnestly or on oath —**forswear oneself** to perjure oneself

forsythia (fôr sith'ē ə) *n.* [< W. *Forsyth*] a shrub with yellow flowers in early spring

fort (fôrt) *n.* [< L. *fortis,* strong] a fortified place for military defence —**hold the fort** [Colloq.] to keep things in operation; remain on duty, etc.

forte¹ (fôr'tā) *n.* [see FORT] that which one does particularly well; one's strong point

forte² (fôr'tē) *adj., adv.* [It. < L. *fortis,* strong] *Music* loud —*n.* a forte note or passage

forth (fôrth) *adv.* [OE.] 1. forwards; onwards 2. out into view, as from hiding —**and so forth** and so on

forthcoming *adj.* 1. about to appear; approaching 2. ready when needed 3. friendly; communicative

forthright *adj.* straightforward; direct; frank

forthwith (fôrth'with') *adv.* immediately

fortification (fôr'tə fi kā'shən) *n.* 1. the act of fortifying 2. a fort or defensive earthwork, wall, etc.

fortify (fôr'tə fī') *vt.* **-fied', -fy'ing** [< L. *fortis,* strong + *facere,* make] 1. to strengthen physically, emotionally, etc. 2. to strengthen against attack, as by building forts, etc. 3. to support; corroborate 4. to strengthen (wine, etc.) by adding alcohol 5. to add vitamins, minerals, etc. (to food, etc.) —*vi.* to build military defences —**for'-tifi'able** *adj.* —**for'tifi'er** *n.*

fortissimo (fôr tis'ə mō') *adj., adv.* [It.] *Music* very loud

fortitude (fôr'tə tyood') *n.* [< L. *fortis,* strong] patient endurance of misfortune, pain, etc.; firm courage

fortnight (fôrt'nīt') *n.* [lit., fourteen nights] two weeks

fortnightly *adv., adj.* (happening or appearing) once every fortnight —*n., pl.* **-lies** a fortnightly periodical

FORTRAN (fôr'tran) *n.* [for(mula) tran(slation)] a digital computer language similar to algebra

fortress (fôr'tras) *n.* [< L. *fortis,* strong] a fortified place; fort

fortuitous (fôr tyoo'ə təs') *adj.* [< L. *fors,* luck] 1. happening by chance; accidental 2. bringing, or happening by, good luck; fortunate —**fortu'itously** *adv.*

fortuity (fôr tyoo'ə tē) *n., pl.* **-ties** chance or chance occurrence

fortunate (fôr'chə nət) *adj.* 1. having good luck 2. coming by good luck —**for'tu-nately** *adv.*

fortune (fôr'choon) *n.* [< L. *fors,* luck] 1. wealth; riches 2. luck; chance; fate 3. good luck; success 4. one's future lot, good or bad

fortuneteller *n.* one who professes to foretell events in other people's lives —**for'-tunetell'ing** *n., adj.*

forty (fôr'tē) *adj., n., pl.* **-ties** [OE. *feowertig*] four times ten; 40; XL —**the forties** the numbers or years from forty to forty-nine —**for'tieth** *adj., n.*

forty winks [Colloq.] a short sleep; nap

forum (fôr'əm) *n.* [L.] 1. an assembly for the discussion of public matters 2. a law court; tribunal 3. the public square or marketplace of an ancient Roman city

forward (fôr′wərd) *adj.* [OE. *foreweard*]
1. at, towards, or of the front 2. advanced
3. onward 4. ready; prompt 5. bold;
presumptuous 6. of or for the future
[*forward* buying] —*adv.* 1. towards the
front; ahead 2. towards the future 3.
into view or prominence —*n.* Football,
Hockey, etc. any of the players in a front
position —*vt.* 1. to send on; transmit
2. to promote

forwards *adv.* *same as* FORWARD

fosse, foss (fos) *n.* [< L. *fossa*, ditch]
a ditch or moat, esp. in fortifications

fossil (fos′'l) *n.* [< L. *fossilis*, dug up
< *fodere*, dig up] 1. any hardened remains
or traces of plant or animal life of some
previous geological age, preserved in the
earth's crust 2. a person who has
outmoded, fixed ideas —*adj.* 1. of, like,
or forming a fossil [coal is a *fossil* fuel]
3. antiquated

fossilize *vt., vi.* -ized′, -iz′ing to change
or be changed into a fossil —*fos′siliza′-
tion n.*

foster (fos′tər) *vt.* [OE. *fostrian*, nourish]
1. to bring up; rear 2. to help to develop;
promote 3. to cherish —*adj.* 1. having
the standing of a specified member of
the family but not by birth or adoption
[a *foster* child] 2. of or relating to the
care of such a person [*foster* home] —*fos′-
terer n.*

fought (fôt) *pt. & pp. of* FIGHT

foul (foul) *adj.* [OE. *ful*] 1. stinking;
loathsome 2. extremely dirty 3. clogged
with dirt, etc. 4. not decent; obscene
5. abominable 6. stormy [*foul* weather]
7. tangled [a *foul* rope] 8. not according
to the rules of a game; unfair 9. dishonest
10. [Colloq.] unpleasant, disagreeable, etc.
—*adv.* in a foul way —*n.* anything foul;
specif., *a)* a collision of boats, contestants,
etc. *b)* an infraction of rules, as of a
game —*vt.* 1. to make foul; dirty 2.
to dishonour or disgrace 3. to obstruct
4. to entangle 5. to collide with 6. to
make a foul against, as in a game —*vi.*
1. to be or become fouled 2. to break
the rules of a game —**foul up** [Colloq.]
to entangle or bungle —**run** (or **fall** or
go) **foul of** to get into trouble with —**foul′-
ly** *adv.* —**foul′ness n.**

foulard (fōō lärd′) *n.* [Fr.] 1. a lightweight
material of silk, rayon, etc. 2. a necktie,
scarf, etc. of this material

foul play 1. unfair play; action that breaks
the rules of the game 2. treacherous action
or violence

found¹ (found) *pt. & pp. of* FIND

found² *vt.* [< L. *fundus*, bottom] 1.
to base 2. to begin to build or organize;
establish —**found′er n.**

found³ *vt.* [< L. *fundere*, pour] 1. to
melt and pour (metal) into a mould 2.
to make by pouring molten metal into
a mould; cast

foundation (foun dā′shən) *n.* 1. a
founding; establishment 2. *a)* an endowment to maintain an institution *b)* an
institution so endowed 3. the base on
which something rests; specif., the suppor-

ting part of a wall, house, etc. 4. basis
5. a woman's corset or girdle : also
foundation garment

founder (foun′dər) *vi.* [see FOUND²] 1.
to stumble, fall, or go lame 2. to become
stuck as in soft ground 3. to fill with
water and sink : said of a ship 4. to
break down

foundling (found′lin) *n.* an infant of
unknown parents that has been found
abandoned

foundry (foun′drē) *n., pl.* -ries 1. a
place where metal is cast 2. the work
of founding metals; casting

fount¹ (fount) *n.* [< L. *fons*, FOUNTAIN]
1. [Poet.] a fountain or spring 2. a source

fount² *n.* [< OFr. *fondre:* see FOUND³]
Printing a complete assortment of type
in one size and style

fountain (foun′tən) *n.* [< L. *fons*, spring]
1. a natural spring of water 2. a source
3. *a)* an artificial jet of water *b)* the basin,
pipes, etc. where this flows 4. a reservoir,
as for ink

fountainhead *n.* the source, as of a stream

fountain pen a pen which is fed ink
from a supply in a reservoir or cartridge

four (fôr) *adj., n.* [OE. *feower*] one more
than three; 4; IV —**on all fours** on hands
and knees

fourfold *adj.* 1. having four parts 2.
having four times as much or as many
—*adv.* four times as much or as many

four-footed *adj.* having four feet

four-in-hand *n.* a coach drawn by a
team of four horses driven by one man

four-leaf clover a clover with four
leaves, popularly supposed to bring good
luck to the finder

four-letter word any short word
having to do with sex or excrement and
generally regarded as offensive

four-poster (fôr′pōs′tər) *n.* a bedstead
with tall corner posts often supporting
a canopy or curtains

fourscore (fôr′skôr′) *adj., n.* four times
twenty; eighty

foursome *n.* 1. a group of four people
2. *Golf* a game involving four players

foursquare (fôr′skwâr′) *adj.* 1.
unyielding; firm 2. forthright 3. square
—*adv.* squarely

four-stroke *adj.* firing once to every
four strokes of the piston : said of an
internal combustion engine

fourteen (fôr′tēn′) *adj., n.* [OE.
feowertyne] four more than ten; 14;
XIV —**four′teenth′ adj., n.**

fourth (fôrth) *adj.* [< OE.] 1. preceded
by three others in a series; 4th 2.
designating any of four equal parts —*n.*
1. the one following the third 2. any
of the four equal parts of something; 1/4
—**fourth′ly adv.**

fourth dimension a dimension in
addition to those of length, width, and
depth : in the theory of relativity, time
is regarded as this dimension —**fourth′-di-
men′sional adj.**

fourth estate [*often* F- E-] journalism
or journalists

fowl (foul) *n.* [OE. *fugol*] 1. any bird [wild*fowl*] 2. any of the domestic birds used as food, as the chicken, duck, etc. 3. the flesh of these birds used for food —*vi.* to hunt wild birds for food or sport —**fowl'er** *n.* —**fowl'ing** *n., adj.*

FOX
(average length 107cm,
including tail)

fox (foks) *n.* [OE.] 1. a small, wild mammal of the dog family, with a bushy tail : thought of as sly and crafty 2. its fur 3. a sly, crafty person —*vt.* 1. to baffle 2. to trick by slyness 3. to stain. (book leaves, etc.) with brownish discolourations —**foxed** *adj.*

foxglove *n.* same as DIGITALIS

foxhole *n.* a hole dug in the ground as a protection against enemy gunfire or tanks

foxhound *n.* a strong, swift hound with a keen scent, bred and trained to hunt foxes

fox hunt a sport in which hunters on horses ride after hounds in pursuit of a fox —**fox hunting**

fox trot a ballroom dance in 4/4 time, or music for it —**fox'-trot'** *vi.* -**trot'ted**, -**trot'ting**

foxy *adj.* -**ier**, -**iest** 1. foxlike; crafty; sly 2. covered with brownish stains —**fox'ily** *adv.*

foyer (foi'ā) *n.* [< L. *focus*, hearth] an entrance hall or a lobby, as in a theatre or hotel

F.P., f.p., fp foot-pound(s)

f.p., fp, fp. freezing point

F.P.A. Family Planning Association

fps, f.p.s. feet per second

Fr *Chem.* francium

Fr. 1. Father 2. France 3. French 4. Friday

fr. franc; francs

fracas (frak'ä) *n., pl.* **fracas** (frak'äz) [Fr. < It. *fracassare*, to smash] a noisy fight or loud quarrel; brawl

fraction (frak'shən) *n.* [< L. *frangere*, to break] 1. *Math.* any quantity expressed in terms of a numerator and denominator, as 1/2, 2x/xy, etc. 2. a small part, amount, etc.; fragment 3. *Chem.* a part separated, as by distillation, from a mixture —**frac'tional** *adj.* —**frac'tionally** *adv.*

fractious (frak'shəs) *adj.* [< ?] 1. peevish; irritable 2. unruly; rebellious —**frac'tiously** *adv.*

fracture (frak'chər) *n.* [< L. *frangere*, to break] a breaking or break, esp. of a bone —*vt., vi.* -**tured**, -**turing** to break, crack, or split —**frac'tural** *adj.*

frae (frā) *prep.* [Scot.] from

fragile (fraj'īl) *adj.* [< L. *frangere*, break] easily broken or damaged; frail —**fragility** (frə jil'ə tē) *n.*

fragment (frag'mənt; *for v.* frag ment') *n.* [< L. *frangere*, to break] 1. a part broken away 2. an incomplete part [a *fragment* of a song, etc.] —*vt., vi.* to break into fragments —**fragment'ed** *adj.*

fragmentary (frag'mən tər ē) *adj.* consisting of fragments or bits; not complete; disconnected

fragrance (frā'grəns) *n.* a fragrant smell; pleasant odour : also [Now Rare] **fra'-grancy**

fragrant (frā'grənt) *adj.* [< L. *fragrare*, emit a (sweet) smell] having a pleasant odour; sweet-smelling

frail (frāl) *adj.* [< L. *fragilis*, fragile] 1. slender and delicate 2. easily broken; fragile 3. easily tempted; morally weak —**frail'ly** *adv.* —**frail'ness** *n.*

frailty *n.* 1. a being frail 2. a moral weakness 3. *pl.* -**ties** a fault arising from such weakness

frame (frām) *vt.* **framed**, **fram'ing** [< OE. *framian*, be helpful] 1. to form according to a pattern [to *frame* a constitution] 2. to construct 3. to put into words; compose 4. to adjust; fit 5. to enclose (a picture, etc.) in a border 6. [Colloq.] to falsify evidence, etc. so as to make (an innocent person) appear guilty —*n.* 1. body structure; build 2. skeletal or basic, supporting structure; framework, as of a house 3. the framework supporting the chassis of a motor vehicle 4. the structural case into which a window, door, etc. is set 5. a border, as of a picture 6. [*pl.*] the framework for a pair of spectacles 7. the way that anything is constructed; form 8. setting or background circumstances 9. mood; temper [a bad *frame* of mind] 10. an established order or system 11. *Bowling*, etc. a division of a game 12. *Cinematography* each of the small exposures composing a strip of film 13. *Snooker*, etc. a) the wooden triangle used to set up the balls b) the balls when set up c) a single game —*adj.* having a wooden framework [a *frame* house] —**fram'er** *n.*

frame of reference 1. *Math.* the fixed points, lines, or planes from which coordinates are measured 2. the set of ideas or standards that determine and sanction a person's behaviour

frame-up *n.* [Colloq.] 1. a falsifying of evidence to make a person seem guilty 2. a secret, deceitful scheme

framework *n.* 1. a structure to hold together or to support something 2. a basic structure or system

franc (fraŋk) *n.* [< L. *Francorum rex*, king of the French, device on the coin in 1360] the monetary unit of France, Belgium, Switzerland, Luxembourg, etc.

franchise (fran'chīz) *n.* [< OFr. *franc*, free] 1. the right to vote; suffrage 2. any special right or privilege granted by a government 3. the right to market a product or provide a service in an area

Franciscan (fran sis'kən) *adj.* of Saint

Francis of Assisi or the religious order founded by him in 1209 —*n.* any member of this order

francium (fran′sē əm) *n.* [< *France*] a radioactive, metallic chemical element: symbol, Fr

Franco- [< LL.] *a combining form meaning:* **1.** French **2.** French and [*Franco*-German]

‡**Franglais** (frän glä′) *n.* [Fr. < *Fran(çais)*, French +(*An)glais*, English] informal French containing a high proportion of words of English origin

Frank (fraŋk) *n.* a member of the Germanic tribes that settled in Gaul in the 5th cent.

frank (fraŋk) *adj.* [< OFr. *franc*, free] **1.** open and honest in expressing oneself; candid **2.** free from disguise or guile —*vt.* to mark letters, etc., with an official stamp, other than a postage stamp, indicating payment of postage —**frank′ly** *adv.* —**frank′ness** *n.*

Frankenstein (fraŋ′kən stīn′) **1.** the title character in a novel by Mary Shelley: he creates a monster that destroys him **2.** popularly, the monster —*n.* anything that becomes dangerous to its creator

frankfurter, frankforter (fraŋk′fur tər) *n.* [G. < *Frankfurt*] a smoked sausage of beef or pork

frankincense (fraŋ′kin sens′) *n.* [< OFr. *franc encens*, pure incense] a gum resin burned as incense

franking machine a machine that prints marks on letters, etc., indicating that postage has been paid

Frankish *n.* the West Germanic language of the Franks

frantic (fran′tik) *adj.* [see PHRENETIC] **1.** wild with anger, worry, etc. **2.** marked by frenzy [*frantic* efforts] —**fran′tically** *adv.*

frappé (fra′pā) *adj.* [Fr.] iced; cooled —*n.* **1.** a dessert made of partly frozen fruit juices, etc. **2.** a beverage poured over crushed ice

fraternal (frə tur′n'l) *adj.* [< L. *frater*, brother] **1.** of brothers; brotherly **2.** of or like a fraternity **3.** designating twins developed from separately fertilized ova —**frater′nally** *adv.*

fraternity (frə tur′nə tē) *n.*, *pl.* -**ties** **1.** a group of people with the same beliefs, interests, work, etc. **2.** brotherliness **3.** [U.S.] a male students′ society

fraternize (frat′ər nīz′) *vi.* -**nized′**, -**niz′-ing** to associate in a brotherly manner; be friendly —**frat′erniza′tion** *n.*

fratricide (frat′rə sīd′) *n.* [< L. *frater*, brother + *caedere*, kill] **1.** the act of killing one′s brother or sister **2.** one who kills his brother or sister —**frat′rici′dal** *adj.*

‡**Frau** (frou) *n.*, *pl.* **Frau′en** [G.] a married woman: in Germany, a title corresponding to *Mrs.*

fraud (frôd) *n.* [< L. *fraus*] **1.** deceit; trickery **2.** intentional deception **3.** a person who deceives or is not what he pretends to be

fraudulent (frô′dyŏŏ lənt) *adj.* **1.** based

on or using fraud **2.** done or obtained by fraud —**fraud′ulence** *n.*

fraught (frôt) *adj.* [< MDu. *vracht*, a load] filled, charged, or loaded (*with*) [a life *fraught* with hardship]

‡**Fräulein** (froi′līn) *n.*, *pl.* -**lein** [G.] an unmarried woman: in Germany, a title corresponding to *Miss*

fray[1] (frā) *n.* [< AFFRAY] a noisy quarrel or fight; brawl

fray[2] *vt.*, *vi.* [< L. *fricare*, rub] **1.** to make or become worn, ragged, etc. by rubbing **2.** to make or become weakened or strained

frazil (frā′zil) *n.* [< Fr. *fraisil*, cinders] spikes of ice that form in water moving turbulently enough to prevent the formation of a sheet of ice

frazzle (fraz′'l) *vt.*, *vi.* -**zled**, [prob. < dial. *fazle*] [Colloq.] **1.** to tire out **2.** to wear to tatters; fray —*n.* [Colloq.] a being frazzled

freak (frēk) *n.* [< ? OE. *frician*, to dance] **1.** any abnormal animal, person, or plant **2.** an unusual happening **3.** a sudden fancy; whim **4.** [Slang] as a user of a specified narcotic, etc. [an acid *freak*] *b)* a devotee *c) same as* HIPPIE —*adj.* oddly different from what is normal —**freak out** [Slang] **1.** to experience extreme reactions, as from a psychedelic drug **2.** to make or become very excited, distressed, etc. **3.** to adopt an unconventional way of life —**freak′ish** *adj.*

freckle (frek′'l) *n.* [< Scand.] a small, brownish spot on the skin, esp. as a result of exposure to the sun —*vt.*, *vi.* -**led**, -**ling** to make or become spotted with freckles

free (frē) *adj.* **fre′er**, **fre′est** [OE. *freo*] **1.** not under the control or power of another; having liberty; independent **2.** having civil liberties **3.** able to move in any direction; loose **4.** not confined **5.** not burdened by obligations, discomforts, etc. **6.** at liberty; allowed [*free* to leave] **7.** not confined to the usual rules [*free* verse] **8.** not exact [a *free* translation] **9.** not busy or in use **10.** not stilted [a *free* gait] **11.** generous; profuse **12.** frank; straightforward **13.** too frank or familiar **14.** with no charge or cost **15.** exempt from taxes, duties, etc. **16.** clear of obstructions **17.** open to all [a *free* market] **18.** not fastened **19.** not combined [*free* oxygen] —*adv.* **1.** without cost **2.** in a free manner —*vt.* **freed**, **free′ing** to make free; specif., *a)* to release from bondage or arbitrary power, obligation, etc. *b)* to clear of obstruction, etc. —**free and easy** informal —**free from** (or **of**) without —**make free with** to take liberties with —**set free** to release; liberate —**free′-ly** *adv.*

freeboard *n.* the height of a ship′s side from the main deck or gunwale to the waterline

freebooter *n.* [< Du. *vrij*, free + *buit*, plunder] a pirate; buccaneer —**free′-boot′** *vi.*

freeborn *adj.* born free, not in slavery

Free Church a nonconformist church

freedman *n.* a man legally freed from bondage

freedom (frē′dəm) *n.* 1. a being free; esp., *a)* exemption from the control of some arbitrary power; independence *b)* civil or political liberty [*freedom* of speech] *c)* exemption from a specified obligation, discomfort, etc. *d)* a being able to act, move, use, etc. without hindrance *e)* ease of movement *f)* a being free from the usual rules, conventions, etc. *g)* frankness *h)* excessive frankness or familiarity 2. a right or privilege —**freedom of the city** honorary citizenship

free enterprise the economic doctrine of permitting private industry to operate under freely competitive conditions with a minimum of governmental control

free fall the unchecked fall of a body through the air; esp. before a parachute is opened

free fight a confused fight in which anyone may join

free flight the flight of a rocket after the fuel supply has been used up or shut off —**free′-flight′** *adj.*

free-for-all *n.* a disorganized, general fight; brawl —*adj.* open to anyone

freehand *adj.* drawn by hand without the use of instruments, measurements, etc.

freehanded *adj.* generous; liberal

freehold *n.* 1. an estate in land held for life or with the right to pass it on through inheritance 2. the holding of an estate in this way —*adj.* of or held by freehold —**free′hold′er** *n.*

free house a public house which is not owned by any brewery and therefore sells various brands of beer

free kick *Soccer* a kick allowed as compensation for an opponent's breach of the rules

free-lance *adj.* of or acting as a free lance —*vi.* **-lanced, -lancing** to work as a free lance

free lance a writer, artist, etc. who sells his services to individual buyers: also **free′-lanc′er** *n.*

free-living *adj.* 1. freely indulging one's appetites, desires, etc. 2. *Biol.* not parasitic

freeloader *n.* [U.S. Colloq.] a person who habitually imposes on others for free food, lodging, etc.

free love the principle or practice of sexual relations unrestricted by marriage or other legal obligations

freeman *n.* 1. a person not in slavery or bondage 2. one who holds a right, such as the freedom of a city

free market any market where trade can be carried on without restrictions as to price, etc.

Freemason (frē′mās′′n) *n.* a member of a secret society based on brotherliness, charity, and mutual aid; Mason —**Free′-ma′sonry** *n.*

free on board delivered (by the seller) aboard the train, ship, etc. at the point of shipment, without charge

free-range *adj.* kept or produced in natural nonintensive conditions [*free-range* eggs]

freesia (frē′zē ə) *n.* [< F. *Freese*] a South African bulbous plant with fragrant, funnel-shaped flowers

free-spoken *adj.* frank; outspoken

free-standing *adj.* resting on its own support, without attachment

Free State coal [S Afr. Slang] dried dung used as fuel

freestyle *n.* 1. *Swimming* a race in which competitors may choose any style 2. *Wrestling* a form of wrestling in which any type of hold or throw is allowed —*adj.* of or using freestyle

freethinker (frē′thin′kər) *n.* a person who forms his opinions about religion independently —**free′think′ing** *n., adj.*

free trade trade conducted without quotas on imports or exports, protective tariffs, etc.

free verse poetry not following regular metrical, rhyming, or stanzaic forms

freeway *n.* [U.S.] an expressway with interchanges for fully controlled access

freewheel (frē′wēl′) *n.* in a bicycle, a device that permits the rear wheel to go on turning when the pedals are stopped —*vi.* to coast

free-will *adj.* voluntary; spontaneous

free will one's freedom of decision or choice

Free World [sometimes f- w-] the non-Communist countries collectively

freeze (frēz) *vi.* **froze, fro′zen, freez′ing** [OE. *freosan*] 1. to be formed into, or become covered or clogged with ice 2. to become very cold 3. to become attached by freezing 4. to die or be damaged by cold 5. to become motionless 6. to be made speechless by fright, etc. 7. to become formal or unfriendly —*vt.* 1. to change into, or cover or clog with ice 2. to make very cold 3. to remove sensation from, as with a local anaesthetic 4. to preserve (food) by rapid refrigeration 5. to make fixed or attached by freezing 6. to kill or damage by cold 7. to make motionless 8. to make formal or unfriendly 9. *a)* to fix (prices, wages, etc.) at a given level *b)* to make (funds, etc.) unavailable —*n.* 1. a freezing or being frozen 2. a period of freezing weather —**freeze out** [Colloq.] to force out by a cold manner, competition, etc.

freeze-dry *vt.* **-dried′, -dry′ing** to subject (food, vaccines, etc.) to freezing followed by drying under high vacuum at a low temperature —**freeze′-dry′er** *n.*

freezer *n.* a refrigerator, compartment, or room for freezing and storing frozen foods

freezing point the temperature at which a liquid freezes: for water, it is 32°F or 0°C

freight (frāt) *n.* [< MDu. *vracht*, a load] 1. a method or service for transporting goods by water or air 2. the cost for such transportation 3. the goods transported —*vt.* 1. to load with freight 2. to transport by freight

freighter *n.* a ship or aircraft for carrying freight

French (french) *adj.* **1.** of France, its people, language, etc. **2.** [Canad.] of French Canadians —*n.* the language of the French —**the French** the people of France —**French'man** *n.* —**French'wom'-an** *n.*

French bread a long, slender loaf of crisp, white bread

French Canadian a Canadian of French ancestry

French chalk a very soft chalk used for marking lines on cloth or removing grease spots

French dressing a salad dressing made of vinegar, oil, and various seasonings

French fried potatoes *U.S. name for* potato chips: also **French fries**

FRENCH HORN

French horn a brass instrument with a long, coiled tube ending in a wide, flaring bell

Frenchify (french'ə fī') *vt., vi.* **-fied'**, **-fy'-ing** to make or become French or like the French

French leave an unauthorized departure; act of leaving secretly

French letter [Slang] a condom

French polish a shellac polish applied to furniture for a glossy finish

French windows two adjoining doors with long glass panes, opening onto a garden, etc.

frenetic (frə net'ik) *adj.* [see PHRENETIC] frantic; frenzied: also **frenet'ical** —**frenet'-ically** *adv.*

frenzy (fren'zē) *n., pl.* **-zies** [< Gr. *phrenitis*, madness] a wild outburst; brief delirium —*vt.* **-zied, -zying** to make frantic; drive mad —**fren'zied** *adj.* —**fren'ziedly** *adv.*

frequency (frē'kwən sē) *n., pl.* **-cies** **1.** frequent occurrence **2.** the number of times any event, value, etc. is repeated in a given period or group **3.** *Physics* the number of vibrations, waves, etc. per unit of time

frequency modulation the variation of the frequency of a carrier wave in accordance with the signal to be transmitted

frequent (frē'kwənt; *for v.*, frē kwent') *adj.* [< L. *frequens*, crowded] **1.** occurring often **2.** constant; habitual —*vt.* to go to or be in habitually

frequentative (frē kwen'tə tiv) *adj.*

Gram. expressing frequent and repeated action —*n. Gram.* a frequentative verb: *sparkle* is a frequentative of *spark*

fresco (fres'kō) *n., pl.* **-coes, -cos** [It., fresh] **1.** the art of painting with water colours on wet plaster **2.** a painting or design so made —*vt.* to paint in fresco

fresh (fresh) *adj.* [< OE. *fersc*] **1.** recently made, grown, etc. [*fresh* coffee] **2.** not salted, preserved, etc. **3.** not spoiled **4.** not tired; lively **5.** not worn, soiled, etc. **6.** healthy in appearance **7.** new; recent **8.** additional **9.** inexperienced **10.** having just arrived **11.** original and stimulating [*fresh* ideas] **12.** refreshing [a *fresh* day] **13.** brisk; said of wind **14.** not salt: said of water **15.** [Slang] saucy; impudent —*adv.* recently [*fresh*-painted] —**fresh'-ly** *adv.*

freshen *vt., vi.* to make or become fresh —**freshen up** to bath oneself, change, etc. —**fresh'ener** *n.*

fresher *n.* same as FRESHMAN

freshet (fresh'it) *n.* **1.** a rush of fresh water flowing into the sea **2.** a flooding of a stream

freshman *n.* a first year student at university

freshwater *adj.* **1.** of or living in water that is not salty **2.** sailing only on inland waters **3.** unskilled

fret¹ (fret) *vt., vi.* **fret'ted, fret'ting** [OE. *fretan*, eat up] **1.** to irritate or be irritated; worry **2.** to wear away, gnaw, chafe, etc. **3.** to make or become rough —*n.* irritation; worry

fret² *n.* [OFr. *frete*] an ornamental pattern of straight bars joining one another at right angles to form a design —*vt.* **fret'-ted, fret'ting** to ornament with a fret

FRETS

fret³ *n.* [OFr. *frette*, band] a ridge across the fingerboard of a banjo, guitar, etc. to regulate the fingering

fretful *adj.* tending to fret; peevish —**fret'-fully** *adv.*

fret saw a saw with a long, narrow, fine-toothed blade, for cutting curved patterns in thin boards or metal plates

fretwork *n.* decorative openwork

Freudian (froi'dē ən) *adj.* of Freud or his theories —*n.* a follower of Freud or his theories of psychoanalysis

Freudian slip a mistake made in speaking which seems to reveal one's true motives, desires, etc.

Fri. Friday

friable (frī'ə b'l) *adj.* [< L. *friare*, rub] easily crumbled into powder —**fri'abil'-ity, fri'ableness** *n.*

friar (frī′ər) *n.* [< L. *frater*, brother] *R.C.Ch.* a member of any of several mendicant orders; esp., an Augustinian, Carmelite, Dominican, or Franciscan

friar's balsam tincture of benzoin used as an inhalant

friary *n.*, *pl.* **-aries** a monastery of friars

fricassee (frik′ə sē′) *n.* [< Fr.] meat cut into pieces, stewed or fried, and served in its own gravy

fricative (frik′ə tiv) *adj.* [< L. *fricare*, rub] pronounced by forcing the breath through a narrow slit formed in the mouth, as *f*, *v*, *z* —*n.* a fricative consonant

friction (frik′shən) *n.* [< L. *fricare*, rub] 1. the resistance to motion of surfaces that touch 2. a rubbing of one object against another 3. conflict because of differences of opinion, etc. —**fric′tional** *adj.*

Friday (frī′dē) *n.* [OE. *frigedaeg*, day of the goddess *Frigg*] 1. the sixth day of the week 2. [< servant of ROBINSON CRUSOE] a faithful follower or efficient helper: usually **man** (or **girl**) **Friday**

Fridays *adv.* [Colloq.] on or during every Friday

fridge (frij) *n.* [Colloq.] a refrigerator

fried (frīd) *pt. & pp.* of FRY[1]

friend (frend) *n.* [OE. *freond*] 1. a person whom one knows well and is fond of 2. an ally, supporter or sympathizer 3. [F-] a member of the Society of Friends; Quaker —**friend at court** an influential acquaintance who can promote one's interests —**friend′less** *adj.*

friendly *adj.* **-lier, -liest** 1. of or like a friend; kindly 2. not hostile; amicable 3. supporting —*adv.* in a friendly manner —**friend′lily** *adv.* —**friend′liness** *n.*

friendly society an association of people who pay regular dues in return for life insurance, sickness benefits, etc.

friendship *n.* 1. the state of being friends 2. friendly feeling or attitude

frier (frī′ər) *n.* same as FRYER

frieze (frēz) *n.* [< ML. *frisium*] 1. a decoration forming an ornamental band around a room, mantel, etc. 2. a horizontal band, often decorated with sculpture, between the architrave and cornice of a building

frigate (frig′it) *n.* [< Fr. < It.] 1. *Hist.* a fast, medium-sized sailing warship 2. a British warship larger than a corvette and smaller than a destroyer

fright (frīt) *n.* [OE. *fyrhto, fryhto*] 1. sudden fear; alarm 2. an ugly, ridiculous, or startling person or thing

frighten *vt.* 1. to make suddenly afraid; scare 2. to force (*away, off*, etc.) by frightening

frightful *adj.* 1. causing fright; alarming 2. shocking 3. [Colloq.] *a)* unpleasant; annoying *b)* great [in a *frightful* hurry] —**fright′fully** *adv.*

frigid (frij′id) *adj.* [< L. *frigus*, coldness] 1. without warmth of feeling or manner 2. unaroused sexually: said of a woman 3. extremely cold —**frigid′ity** *n.*

Frigid Zone either of two zones (**North** or **South Frigid Zone**) between the polar circles and the poles

frill (fril) *n.* [< ?] 1. a gathered or pleated strip of cloth, etc. for trimming 2. an unnecessary ornament —*vt.* to decorate with a frill —**frill′y** *adj.*

fringe (frinj) *n.* [< L. *frimbria*] 1. a border of cords or threads, hanging loose or tied in bunches 2. a section of the hair cut short over the forehead 3. an outer edge; border 4. a peripheral or minor part —*vt.* **fringed, fring′ing** to be or make a fringe for —*adj.* 1. at the outer edge 2. additional 3. less important —**fring′y** *adj.*

fringe benefit an employee's benefit other than wages or salary, such as a pension or insurance

frippery (frip′ər ē) *n.*, *pl.* **-peries** [< OFr. *frepe*, a rag] 1. cheap, gaudy clothes 2. showy display in dress, manners, speech, etc.

Frisbee (friz′bē) [U.S.] *Trademark* a plastic disc tossed back and forth in a game

Frisian (frē′zhən) *adj.* of Friesland, a province of the Netherlands —*n.* 1. a native of Friesland 2. the language of the Frisians

frisk (frisk) *vi.* [OFr. *frisque*] to frolic —*vt.* to search (a person) for concealed weapons, etc. by passing the hands quickly over his clothing

frisky *adj.* **-ier, -iest** lively; frolicsome

frith (frith) *n.* var. of FIRTH

fritter[1] (frit′ər) *vt.* [< L. *frangere*, to break] to waste (money, time, etc.) bit by bit on petty things (often with *away*) —**frit′terer** *n.*

fritter[2] *n.* [< L. *frigere*, fry] a small cake of fried batter, usually containing meat, fruit, etc.

frivolous (friv′ə ləs) *adj.* [L. *frivolus*] 1. trifling; trivial 2. silly and light-minded —**frivolity** (fri vol′ə tē) *n.*

frizz (friz) *vt., vi.* frizzed, friz′zing [Fr. *friser*] to form into small, tight curls —*n.* hair, etc. that is frizzed

frizzle[1] (friz′′l) *vt., vi.* -zled, -zling [< FRY[1]] 1. to make or cause to make a sputtering, hissing noise, as in frying 2. to make or become crisp by grilling or frying

frizzle[2] *n., vt., vi.* -zled, -zling same as FRIZZ

frizzly *adj.* -zlier, -zliest full of or covered with small, tight curls: also **friz′zy**

fro (frō) *adv.* [< ON. *frā*] backwards; back: now only in **to and fro** back and forth —*prep.* [Scot.] from

frock (frok) *n.* [OFr. *froc*] 1. a woman's dress 2. a smock 3. a robe worn by friars, monks, etc. —*vt.* to ordain as a priest

frock coat a man's double-breasted dress coat with a full skirt reaching to the knees, worn chiefly in the 19th cent.

METAMORPHOSIS OF FROG

frog (frog) *n.* [OE. *frogga*] 1. a tailless, leaping, four-legged amphibian with webbed feet 2. a horny pad in the sole of a horse's foot 3. a braided loop used as a fastener on clothing 4. a device for keeping trains on the proper rails at junctions 5. [F-] [Slang] a Frenchman: also **Frog'gy** —**frog in the throat** a hoarseness

frogman *n.* a person trained and equipped, as with scuba gear, for underwater work

frogmarch *n.* a method of carrying a troublesome prisoner, face downwards, each limb being held —*vt.* 1. to carry in a frogmarch 2. to make someone move forward unwillingly

frolic (frol'ik) *n.* [< MDu. *vrō*, merry] 1. a playful trick; prank 2. a lively party 3. merriment; fun —*vi.* -**icked, -icking** 1. to make merry 2. to play or romp —**frol'-icker** *n.*

frolicsome *adj.* playful; merry: also **frol'icky**

from (from: *unstressed* frəm) *prep.* [OE.] 1. beginning at [to walk *from* the door] 2. starting with [*from* noon] 3. out of [*from* his pocket] 4. originating with [facts learned *from* reading] 5. at a place not near to 6. out of the whole of [take two *from* four] 7. out of the possibility or use of [kept *from* going] 8. out of the possession or control of [released *from* jail] 9. as not being like [to tell one *from* another] 10. because of [to tremble *from* fear]

frond (frond) *n.* [< L. *frons*, leafy branch] the leaf of a fern or palm

front (frunt) *n.* [< L. *frons*, forehead] 1. the part facing forward 2. the first part; beginning 3. the place or position directly before a person or thing 4. a forward or leading position 5. land along a seashore or large lake, esp. a promenade 6. *a)* the foremost position of troops *b)* the battle zone 7. a specified area of activity [the home *front*] 8. outward behaviour [put on a bold *front*] 9. a broad movement in which different groups are united for the achievement of common aims 10. a person or group used to cover the activity of another really in control 11. a face of a building 12. *Meteorol.* the boundary between two masses of air that are different, as in density —*adj.* at, to, in, on, or of the front —*vt., vi.* 1. to face 2. to serve as a front (*for*) —**in front of** before; ahead of

frontage *n.* 1. the front part of a building

2. the land between the front of a building and the street 3. the front boundary line of a building plot or the length of this line 4. land bordering a street, river, lake, etc.

frontal *adj.* 1. of, in, on, at, or against the front 2. of or for the forehead

front bench *n.* the leadership group of the government or opposition in the House of Commons —**front'bench'er** *n.*

frontier (frun'tēər) *n.* [see FRONT] 1. the border between two countries 2. that part of a country which lies next to an unexplored region 3. any new field or area of learning, etc. [the *frontiers* of medicine] —*adj.* of, on, or near a frontier

frontispiece (frun'tis pēs') *n.* [< L. *frons*, front + *specere*, to look] an illustration facing the first page or title page of a book

front-runner *n.* one who is leading in a race or contest

frost (frost) *n.* [OE. *freosan*, freeze] 1. a freezing or being frozen 2. a temperature low enough to cause freezing 3. frozen dew or vapour —*vt.* 1. to cover with frost 2. to damage or kill by freezing 3. to give a frostlike surface to (glass)

frostbite *vt.* -**bit', -bit'ten, -bit'ing** to injure the tissues of (a part of the body) by exposure to intense cold —*n.* tissue damage caused by such exposure

frosting *n.* *U.S. name for* ICING (sense 1)

frosty *adj.* -**ier, -iest** 1. cold enough to produce frost; freezing 2. covered as with frost 3. unfriendly —**frost'ily** *adv.* —**frost'iness** *n.*

froth (froth) *n.* [ON. *frotha*] 1. foam 2. foaming saliva 3. light, trifling talk, ideas, etc. —*vi., vt.* to foam or cause to foam —**froth'y** *adj.*

froward (frō'ərd) *adj.* [ME., unruly] [Now Rare] not easily controlled; wilful —**fro'wardness** *n.*

frown (froun) *vi.* [< OFr. *froigne*, sullen face] 1. to contract the brows, as in displeasure or concentration 2. to show disapproval (with *on* or *upon*) —*n.* 1. a contracting of the brows in sternness, thought, etc. 2. any expression of disapproval —**frown'ingly** *adv.*

frowsty (froust'ē) *adj.* [prob. < ff.] musty or stuffy

frowzy (frou'zē) *adj.* -**zier, -ziest** [< ?] dirty and untidy; slovenly: also sp. **frow'-sy** —**frow'zily** *adv.*

froze (frōz) *pt. of* FREEZE

frozen (frō'z'n) *pp. of* FREEZE —*adj.* 1. turned into or covered with ice 2. damaged or killed by freezing 3. preserved by freezing, as food 4. as if turned into ice [*frozen* with terror] 5. without warmth or affection 6. kept at a fixed level 7. not readily converted into cash [*frozen* assets]

F.R.S. Fellow of the Royal Society

fructify (fruk'tə fī') *vi., vt.* -**fied', -fy'-ing** [< L. *fructificare*] to bear or cause to bear fruit

fructose (fruk'tōs) *n.* [< L. *fructus*, fruit] a crystalline sugar found in sweet fruits and in honey

frugal (froo′g'l) *adj.* [L. *frugalis*] **1.** not wasteful; thrifty **2.** inexpensive or meagre [a *frugal* meal] —**frugal′ity** (-gal′ə tē) *n.* —**fru′gally** *adv.*

fruit (froot) *n.* [< L. *fructus*] **1.** any plant product, as grain, vegetables, etc.: *usually used in pl.* **2.** a sweet and edible plant structure, consisting of a fruit (sense 4), usually eaten raw or as a dessert **3.** the result or product of any action **4.** *Bot.* the mature ovary of a flowering plant, with its contents, as the whole peach —*vi.,* *vt.* to bear or cause to bear fruit

fruiterer *n.* a person who deals in fruit

fruitful *adj.* **1.** bearing much fruit **2.** productive; prolific **3.** profitable —**fruit′-fully** *adv.*

fruition (frooish′ən) *n.* [see FRUIT] **1.** the bearing of fruit **2.** fulfilment; realization

fruitless *adj.* **1.** without results; unsuccessful; vain **2.** bearing no fruit; sterile —**fruit′lessly** *adv.*

fruit machine a slot machine that pays out when certain combinations of diagrams, often representing fruit, appear

fruit sugar *same as* FRUCTOSE

fruity *adj.* **-ier, -iest** **1.** like fruit in taste or smell **2.** rich or mellow in tone, as a voice **3.** [Slang] full of coarse humour; salacious —**fruit′ily** *adv.* —**fruit′iness** *n.*

frump (frump) *n.* [< ? Du. *rompelen,* rumple] a dowdy, unattractive woman —**frump′ish, frump′y** *adj.*

frustrate (frus trāt′) *vt.* **-trat′ed, -trat′-ing** [< L. *frustra,* in vain] **1.** to cause to have no effect; nullify **2.** to keep from an objective or from gratifying certain desires —**frustra′tion** *n.*

FRUSTUM

frustum (frus′təm) *n., pl.* **-tums, -ta** [L., a piece] the solid figure formed when the top of a cone or pyramid is cut off by a plane parallel to the base

fry¹ (frī) *vt., vi.* **fried, fry′ing** [< L. *frigere*] to cook or be cooked, usually in hot fat or oil, over direct heat —*n., pl.* **fries** a fried food, esp. offal [pig's *fry*]

fry² *n., pl.* **fry** [< ON. *frjo,* seed & Anglo-Fr. *frei,* spawn] **1.** young fish **2.** offspring —**small fry** **1.** trivial people or things **2.** children

fryer *n.* **1.** one that fries **2.** a utensil for deep-frying foods

frying pan a shallow pan for frying food —**out of the frying pan into the fire** from a bad situation into a worse one

fry-up *n.* [Colloq.] a dish of several mixed, fried foods

f-stop (ef′stop′) *n.* any of the settings for the f-number of a camera

ft. **1.** foot; feet **2.** fort

fth., fthm. fathom

fuchsia (fyoo′shə) *n.* [< L. *Fuchs*] **1.** a shrub with drooping pink, red, or purple flowers **2.** purplish red

fuck (fuk) *vi., vt.* [< ?] [Vulg.] **1.** to have sexual intercourse **2.** *used to express disgust, annoyance, etc., as in* **fuck off** go away —*n.* [Vulg.] **1.** an act of sexual intercourse **2.** a partner in sexual intercourse **3.** a damn [don't give a *fuck*] —**fuck′ing** *adj., adv.*

fuddle (fud′'l) *vt.* **-dled, -dling** [< ?] to confuse or stupefy as with alcohol —*n.* a fuddled condition

fuddy-duddy (fud′ē dud′ē) *n., pl.* **-dies** [Slang] **1.** a fussy, critical person **2.** an old-fashioned person

fudge (fuj) *n.* [< ?] **1.** nonsense **2.** a soft sweet made of butter, milk, sugar, flavouring, etc. —*vt.* **fudged, fudg′ing** to make dishonestly or carelessly; fake

fuel (fyooəl) *n.* [ult. < L. *focus,* fireplace] **1.** coal, oil, gas, wood, etc. burned to supply heat or power **2.** fissionable material, as in a nuclear reactor **3.** anything that intensifies strong feeling, etc. —*vt., vi.* **-elled, -elling** to supply with or get fuel

fuel cell any of various devices that convert chemical energy directly into electrical energy

fug (fug) *n.* [< ?] the heavy air in a closed room —**fug′gy** *adj.*

fugitive (fyoo′jə tiv) *adj.* [< L. *fugere,* flee] **1.** fleeing or having fled, as from danger, justice, etc. **2.** passing quickly; fleeting **3.** roaming; shifting —*n.* a person who flees or has fled from danger, justice, etc.

fugue (fyoog) *n.* [< L. *fugere,* flee] a musical composition in which a subject is announced by one voice and then developed contrapuntally by each of usually two or three other voices —**fu′gal** *adj.* —**fugu′ist** *n.*

‡Führer, Fuehrer (fyooər′ər) *n.* [G.] leader

-ful (fəl, f'l, fool) [OE.] *a suffix meaning:* **1.** full of, having [joyful] **2.** having the qualities of or tendency to [helpful] **3.** the quantity that fills [handful]

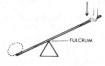

FULCRUM

fulcrum (ful′krəm) *n., pl.* **-crums, -cra** [L. < *fulcire,* to prop] the support on which a lever turns in raising something

fulfil, fulfill (fool fil′) *vt.* **-filled′, -fill′ing** [OE. *fullfyllan*] **1.** to carry out (something promised, etc.) **2.** to do (something required) **3.** to satisfy (a condition) **4.** to complete —**fulfil oneself** to realize completely one's ambitions, potentialities, etc. —**fulfil′ment** *n.*

full¹ (fool) *adj.* [OE.] **1.** having in it

all there is space for; filled **2.** having eaten all that one wants **3.** occupying all of a given space [a full load] **4.** well supplied (with of) [a tank full of petrol] **5.** complete [a full dozen] **6.** absolute [come to a full stop] **7.** having reached the greatest development, size, etc. **8.** having the same parents [full brothers] **9.** having clearness, volume, and depth [a full tone] **10.** plump; round **11.** with loose, wide folds; ample [a full skirt] **12.** engrossed —*adv.* **1.** completely **2.** directly **3.** very [full well] —**full time** as a full-time employee, student, etc. —**in full 1.** to, for, or with the full amount, etc. **2.** not abbreviated —**full′ness, ful′-ness** *n.*

full² *vt., vi.* [< L. *fullo*, cloth fuller] to shrink and thicken (cloth, esp. of wool) —**full′er** *n.*

fullback *n.* Football, etc. a defender in a team

full-blooded *adj.* **1.** of unmixed breed or race; purebred: also **full′-blood′ 2.** vigorous **3.** rich and full

full-blown *adj.* **1.** in full bloom; open: said of flowers **2.** fully developed; mature

full-bodied *adj.* having much strength, flavour, etc.

fuller's earth (fool′ərz) a highly absorbent clay used to remove grease from cloth in fulling, to clarify oils, etc.

full-fledged *adj.* completely developed or trained; of full rank or status

full house 1. a poker hand containing three of a kind and a pair **2.** in bingo, the complete set of numbers needed to win **3.** a theatre, etc., filled to capacity

full-length *adj.* **1.** showing the whole length [a full-length portrait] **2.** not shortened [a full-length novel]

full moon the phase of the moon when its entire illuminated hemisphere is seen as a full disc

full pitch *same as* FULL TOSS

full-scale *adj.* **1.** according to the original or standard scale **2.** to the utmost degree [full-scale war]

full stop 1. a punctuation mark (.) used at the end of a sentence **2.** the dot (.) following many abbreviations

full-time *adj.* on a complete regular schedule

full toss Cricket a bowled ball that reaches the batsman without bouncing

fully *adv.* **1.** to the full; completely; entirely **2.** abundantly; amply **3.** at least [fully two hours later]

fully fashioned shaped to conform to body contours, as stockings, knitwear, etc.

fulmar (fool′mər) *n.* [ON. < *full*, foul + *mār*, seagull] a grey sea bird, common in arctic regions

fulminate (ful′mənāt′) *vi., vt.* -nat′ed, -nat′ing [< L. *fulmen*, lightning] **1.** to explode with violence; detonate **2.** to shout forth (denunciations, etc.) —*n.* any highly explosive compound —**ful′mina′tion** *n.* —**ful′mina′tor** *n.*

fulsome (fool′səm) *adj.* [< FULL¹ + -som,

like] disgusting, esp. because excessive or insincere

fumble (fum′b'l) *vi., vt.* -bled, -bling [prob. < ON. *famla*, grope] **1.** to grope clumsily **2.** to handle (a thing) clumsily —*n.* the act of fumbling —**fum′bler** *n.*

fume (fyoom) *n.* [< L. *fumus*] [often *pl.*] a gas, smoke, or vapour, esp. if offensive or suffocating —*vi.* fumed, fum′ing **1.** to show anger **2.** to give off fumes —*vt.* to expose to fumes to darken colours, as oak

fumigate (fyoo′məgāt′) *vt.* -gat′ed, -gat′-ing [< L. *fumus*, smoke + *agere*, make] to expose to the action of fumes, esp. in order to disinfect or kill the vermin in —**fu′miga′tion** *n.* —**fu′miga′tor** *n.* —**fu′migant** *n.*

fun (fun) *n.* [< ME. *fonne*, fool] **1.** *a)* lively, gay play or playfulness *b)* pleasure **2.** a source of amusement —**for** (or in) **fun** playfully —**make fun of** to ridicule

function (funk′shən) *n.* [< L. *fungi*, perform] **1.** the normal or characteristic action of anything **2.** a specific duty required for a particular activity [the function of an auditor] **3.** a formal ceremony or social occasion **4.** a thing that depends on and varies with something else **5.** Math. a quantity whose value depends on that of another quantity or quantities —*vi.* **1.** to act in a required manner; work **2.** to be used (as)

functional *adj.* **1.** of a function **2.** designed with regard to usefulness rather than aesthetic appeal **3.** Med. affecting a function of some organ without apparent organic changes —**func′tionally** *adv.*

functionalism *n.* emphasis on adapting the structure of anything to its function —**func′tionalist** *n., adj.*

functionary *n., pl.* -aries a person who performs a certain function; esp., an official

fund (fund) *n.* [L. *fundus*, bottom] **1.** a supply that can be drawn on; store [a fund of good humour] **2.** *a)* a sum of money set aside for a purpose *b)* [pl.] ready money —*vt.* **1.** to put or convert into a long-term debt that bears interest **2.** to provide with a fund

fundamental (fun′dəmen′t'l) *adj.* [see FUND] **1.** of or forming a foundation or basis; basic **2.** primary **3.** most important —*n.* a principle, law, etc. serving as a basis; essential part —**fun′da-men′tally** *adv.*

fundamentalism *n.* religious beliefs based on a literal interpretation of the Bible —**fun′damen′talist** *n., adj.*

fundamental particle *same as* ELEMENTARY PARTICLE

funeral (fyoo′nərəl) *adj.* [< L. *funus*, funeral] of or for a funeral —*n.* **1.** the ceremonies connected with burial or cremation of the dead **2.** [Colloq.] concern; affair [that's your funeral] —**fu′nerary** *adj.*

funeral director *same as* UNDERTAKER

funeral home a place where bodies are prepared for burial or cremation; undertaker's establishment: also **funeral parlour**

funereal (fyo͞o nēr′ē əl) *adj.* suitable for a funeral; sad and solemn; gloomy : also **fune′brial** —**fune′really** *adv.*

funfair (fun′fār) *n.* a collection of amusements and sideshows; amusement park

fungicide (fun′jə sīd′) *n.* [< FUNGUS & -CIDE] any substance that kills fungi —**fun′gici′dal** *adj.*

fungoid (fun′goid) *adj.* like a fungus —*n.* a fungus

fungous (fun′gəs) *adj.* of, like, or caused by fungi

fungus (fun′gəs) *n., pl.* **fungi** (fun′gī), **fun′guses** [L.] 1. any of a group of plants, as moulds, mildews, mushrooms, etc., that lack chlorophyll and leaves and reproduce by spores 2. something that grows rapidly like a fungus —*adj.* of or like a fungus —**fun′gal** *adj.*

funicular (fyo͞o nik′yo͞o lər) *n.* [< L. *funis,* rope] a mountain railway on which counterbalanced cars ascend and descend by cables: also **funicular railway**

funk (funk) *n.* [< ?] [Colloq.] 1. a cowering through fear; panic: also **blue funk** 2. a coward —*vi.* [Colloq.] to be in a funk or panic —*vt.* [Colloq.] 1. to be afraid of 2. to shrink from in fear

funnel (fun′'l) *n.* [< L. *in-,* in + *fundere,* pour] 1. a slender tube with a cone-shaped mouth, for pouring liquids and powders into containers with small openings 2. a cylindrical smokestack, as of a steamship —*vi., vt.* **-nelled, -nelling** to move or pour as through a funnel

funny (fun′ē) *adj.* **-nier, -niest** 1. causing laughter; humorous 2. [Colloq.] *a)* strange; queer *b)* puzzling *c)* slightly ill; queasy —**fun′nily** *adv.* —**fun′niness** *n.*

funny bone [prob. a pun on *humerus*] a place on the elbow where a sharp impact on the nerve causes a strange, tingling sensation

fur (fur) *n.* [< OFr. *fuerre,* sheath] 1. the soft, thick hair covering many mammals 2. a skin bearing such hair, processed for making garments 3. any garment made of such skins 4. any furry deposit, specif., *a)* diseased matter on the tongue *b)* the deposit on the inside of kettles, etc., left by water containing lime —*adj.* of fur —*vt.* **furred, fur′ring** 1. to line, cover, or trim with fur 2. to coat with a furry deposit —*vi.* to become furred with a deposit —**make the fur fly** to cause dissension or fighting —**furred** *adj.*

fur. furlong

furbelow (fur′bə lō′) *n.* [< Fr. *falbala*] 1. a flounce or ruffle 2. [*usually pl.*] showy trimming

furbish (fur′bish) *vt.* [< OFr. *forbir*] 1. to polish 2. to renovate (often with *up*) —**fur′bisher** *n.*

fur brigade *Canad. Hist.* a convoy of canoes, horses, or dog sleighs that transported furs, etc. between trading posts

furcate (fur′kāt) *adj.* [< L. *furca,* fork] forked —*vi.* **-cated, -cating** to branch; fork —**furca′tion** *n.*

Furies (fyo͞or′ēz) *Gr. & Rom. Myth.* three

female spirits who punished doers of unavenged crimes

furious (fyo͞or′ē əs) *adj.* [< L. *furiosus*] 1. full of fury 2. violently overpowering 3. very great; intense —**fu′riously** *adv.* —**fu′riousness** *n.*

furl (furl) *vt.* [< OFr. *ferlier*] to roll up tightly and make secure, as a flag —*vi.* to become furled

furlong (fur′lon) *n.* [< OE. *furh,* furrow + *lang,* long] a measure of distance equal to 1/8 of a mile (c. 20 m)

furlough (fur′lō) *n.* [< Du. *verlof*] a leave of absence; esp., a leave granted to military enlisted personnel

furnace (fur′nəs) *n.* [< L. *fornus,* oven] 1. an enclosed structure in which heat is produced for destroying refuse, reducing ores, etc. 2. any extremely hot place

furnish (fur′nish) *vt.* [< OFr. *furnir*] 1. to supply with furniture, etc. 2. to supply; provide

furnishings *n.pl.* the furniture, carpets, etc. as for a room

furniture (fur′ni chər) *n.* [Fr. *fourniture*] 1. the movable things in a room which equip it for living, as chairs, beds, etc. 2. the necessary equipment of a ship

furore (fyo͞o rôr′ē) *n.* [< L. *furor*] *a)* a commotion or uproar *b)* widespread enthusiasm 2. fury; rage

furrier (fur′ē ər) *n.* 1. a dealer in furs 2. one who processes furs or makes and repairs fur garments

furrow (fur′ō) *n.* [OE. *furh*] 1. a narrow groove made in the ground by a plough 2. anything like this, as a wrinkle —*vt.* to make furrows in —*vi.* to become wrinkled

furry (fur′ē) *adj.* **-rier, -riest** 1. of or like fur 2. covered with fur 3. having a furlike coating

further (fur′thər) *adj.* [OE. *furthra*] 1. additional; more 2. more distant; farther —*adv.* 1. to a greater degree or extent 2. in addition 3. at or to a greater distance in space or time —*vt.* to give aid to; promote —**fur′therance** *n.* —**fur′therer** *n.*

further education education, usually full-time, for students above school age

furthermore *adv.* besides; moreover; in addition

furthest (fur′thist) *adj.* most distant; farthest —*adv.* at or to the greatest distance or degree

furtive (fur′tiv) *adj.* [< L. *fur,* thief] done or acting in a stealthy manner; surreptitious —**fur′tively** *adv.*

fury (fyo͞or′ē) *n., pl.* **-ries** 1. violent anger; wild rage 2. violence; vehemence 3. a violent, vengeful person 4. [F-] one of the Furies —**like fury** [Colloq.] violently, swiftly, etc.

furze (furz) *n.* [OE. *fyrs*] a prickly evergreen shrub with yellow flowers, esp. on wastelands —**fur′zy** *adj.*

fuse¹ (fyo͞oz) *vt., vi.* **fused, fus′ing** [< L. *fundere,* shed] 1. to melt or to join by melting, as metals 2. to unite or blend together

fuse² *n.* [< L. *fusus,* spindle] 1. a tube

or wick filled with combustible material for setting off an explosive charge **2.** *Elec.* a strip of easily melted metal placed in a circuit as a safeguard: if the current becomes too strong, the metal melts, thus breaking the circuit —*vt.* **fused, fus′ing** to connect a fuse to —*vi.* to fail as the result of the blowing of a fuse —**blow a fuse 1.** to cause an electrical fuse to melt **2.** [Colloq.] to become very angry

fuselage (fyo͞o′zə läzh′) *n.* [Fr. < L. *fuselé*, tapering] the body of an aircraft

fusible (fyo͞o′zə b′l) *adj.* that can be melted

fusil (fyo͞o′z′l) *n.* [Fr. < L. *focus*, hearth] a light flintlock musket

fusilier (fyo͞o′zə lēär′) *n.* formerly, a soldier armed with a fusil: a term still applied to certain British regiments

fusillade (fyo͞o′zə läd′) *n.* [Fr. < *fusiller*, to shoot] **1.** a simultaneous discharge of many firearms **2.** something like this [a *fusillade* of questions]

fusion (fyo͞o′zhən) *n.* **1.** a fusing or melting together **2.** a blending; coalition **3.** *same as* NUCLEAR FUSION

fuss (fus) *n.* [< ?] **1.** nervous, excited activity **2.** nervousness, agitation, etc. **3.** [Colloq.] a protest or objection **4.** [Colloq.] a showy display of delight, etc. —*vi.* to bustle about or worry over trifles —*vt.* [Colloq.] to bother unnecessarily

fusspot *n.* [Colloq.] a fussy person

fussy *adj.* **-ier, -iest 1.** bustling about or worrying over trifles **2.** hard to please **3.** full of unnecessary details —**fuss′ily** *adv.* —**fuss′iness** *n.*

fustian (fus′tē ən) *n.* [< OFr.] **1.** formerly, a coarse cloth of cotton and linen **2.** pompous, pretentious talk or writing —*adj.* pompous; pretentious

fusty (fus′tē) *adj.* **-tier, -tiest** [< OFr.

fust, a cask] **1.** musty; mouldy **2.** old-fashioned —**fus′tiness** *n.*

futile (fyo͞o′til) *adj.* [< L. *futilis*, that easily pours out] **1.** useless; vain **2.** trifling or unimportant —**fu′tilely** *adv.* —**futility** (fyo͞o til′ə tē) *n.*

future (fyo͞o′chər) *adj.* [< L. *futurus*, about to be] **1.** that is to be or come **2.** indicating time to come [*future* tense] —*n.* **1.** the time that is to come **2.** what is going to be **3.** prospective condition **4.** [*pl.*] commodities sold for delivery at a later date **5.** *Gram.* the future tense

future perfect a tense indicating an action or state as completed in relation to a specified time in the future (Ex.: will have gone)

futurism *n.* a movement in the arts which opposed traditionalism and stressed the dynamic movement of the machine age —**fu′turist** *n., adj.*

futuristic (fyo͞o′chər is′tik) *adj.* of or having to do with the future or futurism —**fu′turis′tically** *adv.*

futurity (fyo͞o tyooar′ə tē) *n.,* pl. **-ties 1.** a) the future b) a future event **2.** the quality of being future

futurology (fyo͞o′chər ol′ə jē) *n.* a system of stating the probable form of future conditions by making assumptions based on known facts and observations

fuzz (fuz) *n.* [< ?] loose, light particles of down, wool, etc.; fine hairs or fibres —**the fuzz** [Slang] a policeman or the police

fuzzy *adj.* **-ier, -iest 1.** of, like, or covered with fuzz **2.** not clear or precise; blurred —**fuzz′iness** *n.*

fwd. forward

-fy (fī) [< L.] *a suffix meaning:* **1.** to make [*liquefy*] **2.** to cause to have [*glorify*] **3.** to become [*putrefy*]

G

G, g (jē) *n., pl.* **G's, g's** 1. the seventh letter of the English alphabet 2. *Physics* gravity

G (jē) *n. Music* the fifth tone in the ascending scale of C major

g gram(me)(s)

Ga *Chem.* gallium

gab (gab) *vi.* **gabbed, gab'bing** [< ON. *gabba,* mock] [Colloq.] to talk idly; chatter —*n.* [Colloq.] idle talk —**gift of the gab** [Colloq.] the ability to speak glibly

gabble (gab''l) *vi., vt.* **-bled, -bling** [< GAB] to talk rapidly and incoherently —*n.* rapid, incoherent talk —**gab'bler** *n.*

gaberdine, gabardine (gab'ər dēn') *n.* [< OFr. *gaverdine,* kind of cloak < ?] 1. a twilled cloth of wool, cotton, etc., with a diagonal weave 2. *Hist.* a loose coat worn esp. by Jews

GABLE (sense 1)

gable (gā'b'l) *n.* [< ON. *gafl,* gable] 1. the triangular wall enclosed by the sloping ends of a ridged roof 2. an end wall having a gable at the top

gad (gad) *vi.* **gad'ded, gad'ding** [? < OE. *gædeling,* companion] to wander about in a restless way, as in seeking amusement —**gad'der** *n.*

gadabout (gad'ə bout') *n.* [Colloq.] a restless seeker after fun, excitement, etc.

gadfly *n., pl.* **-flies'** [< ON. *gaddr,* a spike] 1. a large fly that bites livestock 2. an annoying person

gadget (gaj'it) *n.* [< ?] 1. any small mechanical contrivance 2. any small object

gadoid (gā'doid) *adj.* [< Gr. *gados,* fish] of or like the cod family of fishes —*n.* any fish of this family

gadolinium (gad'ə lin'ē əm) *n.* [< J. *Gadolin*] a metallic chemical element of the rare-earth group: symbol, Gd

gadwall (gad'wôl) *n.* [< ?] a greyish-brown duck

gadzooks (gad'zōōks') *interj.* [< ?] [Obs.] a mild oath

Gael (gāl) *n.* [< Gael. *Gaidheal*] a Celt of Scotland (esp. the Highlands), Ireland, or the Isle of Man

Gaelic (gāl'ik, gal'-) *adj.* of the Gaels

or any of their Celtic languages —*n.* one of the Gaelic languages; esp., Scottish or Irish Gaelic: abbrev. **Gael.**

gaff¹ (gaf) *n.* [< Pr. *gaf* or Sp. *gafa*] 1. a large hook on a pole for landing large fish 2. a spar supporting a fore-and-aft sail —*vt.* to land (a fish) with a gaff

gaff² *n.* [< ?] [Slang] nonsense —**blow the gaff** to reveal a secret

gaffe (gaf) *n.* [Fr.] a blunder; faux pas

gaffer (gaf'ər) *n.* [< *godfather*] 1. an old man: now usually humorous 2. [Colloq.] a foreman

gag (gag) *vt.* **gagged, gag'ging** [echoic] 1. to cover the mouth of, so as to keep from talking 2. to keep from expressing oneself, as by intimidation 3. to cause to retch —*vi.* to retch —*n.* 1. something put into or over the mouth to prevent talking, etc. 2. any restraint of free speech 3. in parliament, a closure 4. [Slang] a comical remark or act; joke —**gag'ger** *n.*

gaga (gä'gä) *adj.* [Fr.] senile; doting; crazy

gage¹ (gāj) *n.* [< OFr., a pledge] 1. something pledged; security 2. a glove thrown down by a challenging knight 3. a challenge

gage² *n., vt.* same as GAUGE

gaggle (gag''l) *n.* [< ME. *gagelen,* to cackle] 1. a flock of geese 2. [Derog.] any group or cluster

gaiety (gā'ə tē) *n., pl.* **-ties** 1. the quality of being gay; cheerfulness 2. merrymaking 3. colourful brightness

gaily (gā'lē) *adv.* 1. happily; merrily 2. brightly

gain (gān) *n.* [< OFr. *gaaignier,* earn] 1. an increase; specif., *a)* [often *pl.*] profit *b)* an increase in advantage; improvement 2. acquisition —*vt.* 1. to get by labour; earn 2. to get by merit; win 3. to attract 4. to get as an addition, profit, or advantage 5. to make an increase 6. to reach —*vi.* 1. to make progress; advance 2. to acquire profit 3. to become heavier 4. to be fast: said of a clock, etc. —**gain on** to draw nearer to (an opponent)

gainful *adj.* profitable —**gain'fully** *adv.*

gainsay (gān'sā') *vt.* **-said'** (-sād'), **-say'ing** [< OE. *gegn,* against + *seggan,* say] 1. to deny 2. to contradict 3. to oppose —**gain'say'er** *n.*

gait (gāt) *n.* [< ON. *gata,* path] 1. manner of walking 2. any of various foot movements of a horse, as a trot

gaiter (gāt'ər) *n.* [< Fr. *guêtre*] a cloth or leather covering for the instep, ankle and, sometimes, the calf

Gal. Galatians

gal. gallon; gallons

gala (gä'lə) *n.* [< OFr. *gale,* enjoyment]

1. a festival   **2.** a competitive sporting occasion —*adj.* festive

galactic (gə lak′tik) *adj.* [< Gr. *gala*, milk] *Astron.* of the Milky Way or some other galaxy

galantine (gal′ən tēn′) *n.* [< L. *gelare*, congeal] a mould of boned white meat served in its own jelly

galaxy (gal′ək sē) [< Gr. *gala*, milk] [*often* G-] *same as* MILKY WAY —*n.*, *pl.* **-axies** **1.** any of innumerable vast groupings of stars **2.** an assembly of illustrious people

gale (gāl) *n.* [< ?] **1.** a strong wind; specif., one of c. 45-90 km per hour **2.** an outburst [*a gale* of laughter]

galena (gə lē′nə) *n.* [L., lead ore] native lead sulphide, a lustrous, lead-grey mineral: also **gale′nite**

gall[1] (gôl) *n.* [OE. *galla*] **1.** [Colloq.] impudence **2.** bitter feeling **3.** something distasteful **4.** the bitter, greenish fluid secreted by the liver

gall[2] *n.* [OE. *gealla* < L. *galla*: see ff.] **1.** a sore caused by chafing **2.** irritation, or a cause of this —*vt.* **1.** to make sore by rubbing **2.** to irritate

gall[3] *n.* [< OFr. < L. *galla*, gallnut] a tumour on plant tissue caused by fungi, insects, or bacteria

gallant (gal′ənt; *for n., also* gə lant′) *adj.* [*see* GALA] **1.** stately; imposing **2.** brave and noble **3.** polite and attentive to women —*n.* [Rare] **1.** a high-spirited, stylish man **2.** a man attentive to women **3.** a lover —**gal′lantly** *adv.*

gallantry *n.*, *pl.* **-ries** **1.** nobility; heroic courage **2.** the courtly manner of a gallant **3.** an act or speech characteristic of a gallant **4.** amorous intrigue

gallbladder (gôl′blad′ər) *n.* a membranous sac attached to the liver, in which excess gall, or bile, is stored

GALLEON

galleon (gal′ē ən) *n.* [*see* GALLEY] a large Spanish ship of the 15th and 16th cent., with three or four decks at the stern

gallery (gal′ə rē) *n.*, *pl.* **-leries** [< ML. *galeria*] **1.** a covered walk open at one side **2.** a long, narrow balcony on the outside of a building **3.** *a)* a platform or projecting upper floor in a church, theatre, etc.; esp., the highest platform in a theatre *b)* the people occupying this *c)* a group of spectators, as at a sporting event **4.** a long, narrow corridor or room **5.** a room or establishment for showing art works **6.** an underground passage, as one used in mining —**play to the gallery** to try to win the approval of the public, esp. in a showy way

galley (gal′ē) *n.*, *pl.* **-leys** [< MGr. *galaia*, kind of ship] **1.** *Hist.* a long, low, usually single-decked ship propelled by oars and sails **2.** a ship's or aircraft's kitchen **3.** *Printing a)* a shallow, oblong tray for holding composed type *b)* *same as* GALLEY PROOF

galley proof printer's proof taken from type in a galley to permit correction before the type is made up in pages

galley slave **1.** a slave or convict sentenced or compelled to pull an oar on a galley **2.** a drudge

galliard (gal′yärd) *n.* [< OFr. *gaillard*, brave] **1.** a lively French dance **2.** music for this

Gallic (gal′ik) *adj.* **1.** of ancient Gaul **2.** French

Gallicism (gal′ə siz'm) *n.* a French idiom, trait, etc.

gallinaceous (gal′ə nā′shəs) *adj.* [< L. *gallus*, a cock] of an order of birds having a heavy rounded body, including poultry, pheasants, etc.

galling (gôl′iŋ) *adj.* that galls; very annoying; vexing

gallium (gal′ē əm) *n.* [< L. *Gallia*, Gaul] a bluish-white, metallic chemical element: symbol, Ga

gallivant (gal′ə vant′) *vi.* [< GALLANT] to go about in search of amusement

gallnut (gôl′nut′) *n.* a nutlike gall, esp. on oaks

Gallo- (gal′ō) [L.] *a combining form meaning* French

gallon (gal′ən) *n.* [< ML. *galo*, jug] a measure of capacity equal to 277.42 cubic inches (4.55 litres)

gallop (gal′əp) *vi.* [< OFr. *galoper*] **1.** to go at a gallop **2.** to hurry —*vt.* to cause to gallop —*n.* **1.** the fastest gait of a horse, etc., consisting of leaping strides with all the feet off the ground at one time **2.** a ride on a galloping animal —**gal′loper** *n.*

gallows (gal′ōz) *n.*, *pl.* **-lowses, -lows** [OE. *galga*] **1.** an upright frame with a crossbeam and a rope, for hanging condemned persons **2.** the death sentence by hanging

gallows bird [Colloq.] a person who deserves hanging

gallstone (gôl′stōn′) *n.* a small, solid mass sometimes formed in the gallbladder or bile duct

Gallup poll (gal′əp) [< G. *Gallup*] a method of assessing public opinion by putting questions to a cross-section of the population

galop (gal′əp) *n.* [*see* GALLOP] **1.** a lively round dance in 2/4 time **2.** music for this

galore (gə lôr′) *adv.* [Ir. *go leór*, enough] in abundance

galoshes (gə losh′iz) *n.* [< OFr. *galoche*] a pair of waterproof overshoes

galumph (gə lumf′) *vi.* [coined by Lewis Carroll < GAL(LOP) + (TRI)UMPH] to march or bound along in a self-satisfied, triumphant, or clumsy manner

galvanic (gal van′ik) *adj.* 1. of or producing an electric current, esp. from a battery 2. stimulating

galvanism (gal′və niz′m) *n.* [< L. *Galvani*] formerly, electricity produced by chemical action

galvanize (gal′və nīz′) *vt.* -nized′, -niz′-ing 1. to stimulate; excite 2. to plate (metal) with zinc 3. to apply an electric current to —**gal′vaniza′tion** *n.*

galvanometer (gal′və nom′ə tər) *n.* an instrument for detecting and measuring a small electric current

gambit (gam′bit) *n.* [< Sp. *gambito*, a tripping] 1. *Chess* an opening in which a pawn or other piece is sacrificed to get an advantage in position 2. a manoeuvre intended to gain an advantage

gamble (gam′b'l) *vi.* -bled, -bling [OE. *gamenian*, to play] 1. to play games of chance for money, etc. 2. to take a risk in order to gain some advantage —*vt.* to bet; wager —*n.* an undertaking involving risk of a loss —**gamble away** to squander or lose in gambling —**gam′-bler** *n.*

gamboge (gam boozh′) *n.* [< *Cambodia*] a gum resin obtained from a tropical tree, used as a yellow pigment

gambol (gam′b'l) *n.* [< It. *gamba*, leg] a gambolling; frolic —*vi.* -bolled, -bolling to jump and skip about in play; frolic

game¹ (gām) *n.* [OE. *gamen*] 1. any form of play; amusement 2. *a)* an amusement or sport involving competition under specific rules *b)* a single contest in such a competition 3. the number of points required for winning 4. a victory 5. a set of equipment for a competitive amusement 6. quality of playing [to play a good *game*] 7. [Colloq.] *a)* a project *b)* a trick; strategy 8. any activity undertaken in a lighthearted spirit 9. *a)* wild birds or animals hunted for sport *b)* their flesh used as food 10. any object of pursuit: usually in **fair game** —*vi.* **gamed, gam′ing** to play cards, etc. for stakes; gamble —*adj.* 1. designating wild birds or animals hunted for sport or food 2. *a)* plucky *b)* ready (for) —**a game that two can play** any ploy that can be imitated to the disadvantage of its initiator —**give the game away** to reveal a secret —**make game of** to ridicule —**on the game** [Slang] engaged in prostitution —**play the game** [Colloq.] to behave as fairness requires —**the game is up** failure is certain —**game′-ly** *adv.* —**game′ness** *n.*

game² *adj.* [< ?] [Colloq.] lame: said esp. of a leg

gamecock *n.* a cock trained for cock-fighting

gamekeeper *n.* a person employed to breed and take care of game birds and animals on estates

game laws laws regulating hunting and fishing

gamesmanship *n.* skill in using ploys to gain a victory or advantage over another person

gamesome *adj.* playful; frolicsome

gamester *n.* a gambler

gamete (gam′ēt) *n.* [< Gr. *gamos*, marriage] a cell that can unite with another in sexual reproduction —**gametic** (gə met′ik) *adj.*

gamin (gam′in) *n.* [Fr.] a neglected child left to roam the streets

gamine (gam′ēn′) *n.* [Fr., fem. of prec.] a girl with a roguish, saucy charm

gaming (gā′miŋ) *n.* the practice of gambling

gamma (gam′ə) *n.* 1. the third letter of the Greek alphabet (Γ, γ) 2. the third of a group or series

gamma ray an electromagnetic radiation from a radioactive substance, of shorter wavelength and higher energy than an X-ray

gammer (gam′ər) *n.* [< godmother] an old woman

gammon¹ (gam′ən) *n.* [< ONormFr. *gambe*, leg] 1. the bottom end of a side of bacon 2. a smoked or cured ham or side of bacon

gammon² *n., interj.* [< ?] [Colloq.] humbug —*vt., vi.* [Colloq.] 1. to talk humbug (to) 2. to deceive

gammy (gam′ē) *adj.* [< ? GAME²] [Colloq.] *same as* GAME²

gamp (gamp) *n.* [< Mrs. *Gamp* in Dickens' *Martin Chuzzlewit*] [Colloq.] a large, bulky umbrella

gamut (gam′ət) *n.* [< *gamma*, Gr. letter for the lowest note of the medieval scale] 1. the entire range, as of emotions 2. *a)* the entire series of recognized notes in music *b)* any complete musical scale, esp. the major scale

gamy (gā′mē) *adj.* -ier, -iest having a strong flavour, like game kept uncooked until it is high

gander (gan′dər) *n.* [OE. *gan(d)ra*] 1. a male goose 2. a fool 3. [Slang] a look: chiefly in **take a gander**

gang¹ (gaŋ) *n.* [< OE. *gangan* (see ff.)] 1. a group of people associated in some way; specif., *a)* workers directed by a foreman *b)* organized criminals *c)* youths from one neighbourhood banded together; often, specif., juvenile delinquents 2. a set of tools, etc. designed to work together —*vi.* to form a gang (with *up*) —**gang up on** [Colloq.] to attack as a group

gang² *vi.* [OE. *gangan*, go] [Scot.] to go or walk

ganger *n.* a foreman of a gang of workers

gangling (gaŋ′gliŋ) *adj.* [? < dial.] tall,

thin, and awkward; of loose, lanky build: also **gan′gly**

ganglion (gaŋ′glē ən) *n.*, *pl.* **-glia, -glions** [< Ḡr. *ganglion*, tumour] a mass of nerve cells from which impulses are transmitted **—gan′glion′ic** (-on′ik) *adj.*

gangplank (gaŋ′plaŋk′) *n.* a narrow, movable platform by which to board or leave a ship

gangrene (gaŋ′grēn) *n.* [< Gr. *gran*, gnaw] decay of body tissue when the blood supply is obstructed by injury, disease, etc. **—gan′grenous** (-grə nəs) *adj.*

gangster (gan′stər) *n.* a member of a gang of violent criminals

gangue (gaŋ) *n.* [Fr. < G. *Gang*, lode] the commercially worthless mineral matter found with ores in a deposit

gangway (gaŋ′wā′) *n.* [OE. *gangweg*] 1. a passageway; specif., *a)* an opening in a ship's side *b)* a gangplank 2. a passageway between rows of seats

gannet (gan′it) *n.* [OE. *ganot*] 1. a large, web-footed seabird that breeds on cliffs 2. a person who is greedy

ganoid (gan′oid) *adj.* [< Gr. *ganos*, brightness] of a group of fishes covered by rows of hard, glossy scales or plates, as the sturgeons

gantry (gan′trē) *n.*, *pl.* **-tries** [< L. *canterius*, beast of burden] 1. a bridgelike framework to support signs or signals as over a motorway, railway, etc. 2. a framework that spans a distance, as one on wheels that carries a travelling crane 3. a wheeled framework used to position and service a rocket at its launching site

gaol (jāl) *n.* *var. sp.* of JAIL **—gaol′er** *n.*

gap (gap) *n.* [< ON. *gapa*, gape] 1. a hole or opening made by breaking or parting 2. a mountain pass or ravine 3. an interruption of continuity 4. a disparity between ideas, natures, etc.

gape (gāp) *vi.* **gaped, gap′ing** [< ON. *gapa*] 1. to stare with the mouth open, as in wonder 2. to open the mouth wide, as in yawning 3. to open wide, as a chasm **—n.** 1. an open-mouthed stare 2. a yawn 3. a wide opening **—gap′-er** *n.* **—gap′ingly** *adv.*

gar (gär) *n.* [< ME. *gare*, spear] a fish with a long beaklike snout and sharp teeth: also **gar′fish**

garage (gar′äj, -ij) *n.* [Fr. < *garer*, protect] 1. a closed shelter for motor vehicles 2. an establishment where motor vehicles are repaired, serviced, bought and sold, and which usually also sells petrol, etc. **—vt.** **-raged, -raging** to put or keep in a garage

garb (gärb) *n.* [< It. *garbo*, elegance] 1. clothing; manner of dress 2. external form **—vt.** to clothe

garbage (gär′bij) *n.* [ME., entrails of fowls] worthless, useless or unwanted matter

garble (gär′b'l) *vt.* **-bled, -bling** [< It. < Ar. *ghirbāl* < L., a sieve] 1. to select, distort, etc. parts of (a story, etc.) so

as to mislead or misrepresent 2. to confuse (a story, etc.) unintentionally **—gar′bler** *n.*

‡**garçon** (gàrson′) *n.*, *pl.* **-çons′**(-son′) [Fr.] a waiter

garden (gär′d'n) *n.* [< ONormFr. *gardin*] 1. a piece of ground, usually close to a house, for the growing of fruits, flowers, or vegetables 2. [*often pl.*] a parklike place for public enjoyment, sometimes having displays of animals or plants **—vi.** to work in a garden **—adj.** of, for, or grown in a garden **—common or garden** ordinary; commonplace **—lead (someone) up the garden path** to mislead or deceive (someone) **—the Garden of England** Kent **—gar′dener** *n.*

garden centre an establishment selling plants, equipment and furniture for the garden

garden city a town with many open spaces, designed to harmonize residential and industrial needs

gardenia (gär dēn′yə) *n.* [< A. *Garden*] a plant with fragrant, white or yellow, waxy flowers

gargantuan (gär gan′tyoo wən) *adj.* [< giant king in Rabelais' *Gargantua and Pantagruel*] huge; enormous

gargle (gär′g'l) *vt.*, *vi.* **-gled, -gling** [< Fr. *gargouille*, throat] to rinse (the throat) with a liquid kept in motion by the slow expulsion of air from the lungs **—n.** 1. a liquid used for gargling 2. a gargling sound

GARGOYLE

gargoyle (gär′goil) *n.* [see prec.] a waterspout, usually grotesquely carved, projecting from the gutter of a building

garish (gāər′ish) *adj.* [< ME. *gauren*, stare] too bright or gaudy; showy **—gar′-ishly** *adv.*

garland (gär′lənd) *n.* [< OFr. *garlande*] a wreath of flowers, leaves, etc. **—vt.** to decorate with garlands

garlic (gär′lik) *n.* [< OE. *gar*, spear + *leac*, leek] a plant with a strong-smelling bulb, used as a seasoning **—gar′licky** *adj.*

garment (gär′mənt) *n.* [see GARNISH] 1. any article of clothing 2. a covering **—vt.** to clothe

garner (gär′nər) *n.* [< L. *granum*, grain] 1. a granary 2. a store of something **—vt.** to gather up and store

garnet (gär′nit) *n.* [< ML. *granatum*, garnet, lit., pomegranate] any of a group of hard silicate minerals: red varieties are used as gems

garnish (gär′nish) *vt.* [< OFr. *garnir*, furnish] 1. to decorate; trim 2. to decorate (food) with something that adds colour or flavour —*n.* a decoration, esp. something used to garnish food, as parsley

garret (gar'it) *n.* [< OFr. *garir*, to watch] the space or rooms just below the sloping roof of a house; attic

garrison (gar'ə s'n) *n.* [see GARRET] 1. troops stationed in a fort 2. a military post —*vt.* to station troops in (a fortified place) for its defence

garrotte (gə rot') *n.* [Sp.] 1. a method of execution, as formerly in Spain, by strangling with an iron collar 2. a cord, length of wire, etc. for strangling a person —*vt.* -rot'ted, -rot'ting to execute with a garrotte or by strangling Also sp. **garotte'**, [U.S.] **garrote'** —**garrot'ter** *n.*

garrulous (gar'ōō ləs) *adj.* [< L. *garrire*, to chatter] talking much or too much; loquacious —**garrulity** (gə rōō'lə tē), **gar'-rulousness** *n.* —**gar'rulously** *adv.*

garter (gär'tər) *n.* [< OFr. *garet*, back of the knee] 1. an elastic band for holding a sock in position 2. [G-] the Order of the Garter, the highest order of British knighthood

garter stitch knitting with all the rows in plain stitch

garth (gärth) *n.* [< ON, *garthr*, court] [Archaic] an enclosed yard or garden

gas (gas) *n.* [coined < Gr. *chaos*, chaos] 1. the fluid form of a substance in which it can expand indefinitely; vapour 2. any mixture of flammable gases used for lighting, heating, or cooking 3. any gas used as an anaesthetic 4. any poisonous substance dispersed through the atmosphere, as in war 5. [U.S. Colloq.] petrol 6. [Slang] idle or boastful talk 7. *Mining* a mixture of firedamp with air that explodes if ignited —*vt.* **gassed, gas'-sing** 1. to subject to the action of gas 2. to injure or kill by gas, as in war —*vi.* [Slang] to talk idly —*adj.* of or using gas —**step on the gas** [Colloq.] to accelerate a motor vehicle

gasbag *n.* [Slang] a person who talks too much

gas chamber a room in which people are put to be killed with poisonous gas

gaseous (gas'yəs) *adj.* of, like, or in the form of gas

gas gangrene a gangrene in which bacilli multiply in dirty wounds, producing gas, muscle destruction and toxaemia

gash (gash) *vt.* [ult. < Gr. *charassein*, to cut] to make a long, deep cut in; slash —*n.* a long, deep cut

gasholder (gas'hōld'ər) *n.* a large, usually cylindrical container for storing gas; gasometer

gasify (gas'ə fī) *vt., vi.* -**fied'**, -**fy'ing** to change into gas —**gas'ifica'tion** *n.*

gasket (gas'kit) *n.* [prob. < OFr. *garcette*, small cord] a piece of metal, rubber, etc., sandwiched between the faces of a joint to seal it

gaslight *n.* the light produced by burning gas —*adj.* characteristic of the period of gaslight illumination [*gaslight* melodrama]

gasman *n.* a man employed to read household gas meters, supervise gas fittings, etc.

gas mask a filtering device worn over the face to protect against breathing in poisonous gases

gas meter an instrument for measuring the quantity of a gas, esp. of gas consumed as a fuel

gasoline, gasolene (gas'ō lēn') *n.* [< GAS] *U.S. name for* PETROL

gasometer (gas om'ə tər) *n.* *same as* GAS HOLDER

gasp (gäsp) *vi.* [< ON. *geispa*, to yawn] to inhale suddenly, as in surprise, or breathe with effort, as in choking —*vt.* to say with gasps —*n.* a gasping

Gaspesian (ga spā'zhən) *n.* a native or inhabitant of the Gaspé Peninsula, in Canada —*adj.* of the Gaspé Peninsula or Gaspesians

gas ring a tubular metal ring, perforated to form a circle of gas jets and used for cooking

gassy (gas'ē) *adj.* -**sier**, -**siest** 1. like, full of, or producing gas 2. [Colloq.] full of talk —**gas'siness** *n.*

gastric (gas'trik) *adj.* [< GASTRO-] of the stomach

gastric juice the acid digestive fluid produced by glands in the mucous membrane lining the stomach

gastric ulcer an ulcer of the stomach lining

gastro- [< Gr. *gastēr*] *a combining form meaning* the stomach (and): also **gastr-**

gastroenteritis (gas'trō en'tə rīt'is) *n.* [< GASTRO- + Gr. *enteron*, intestine + -ITIS] an inflammation of the stomach and the intestines

gastronome (gas'trə nōm') *n.* a person who enjoys and has a discriminating taste for foods

gastronomy (gas tron'ə mē) *n.* [< Gr. *gastēr*, stomach + *nomos*, rule] the art of good eating —**gas'tronom'ic** (-trənom'-ik), **gas'tronom'ical** *adj.*

gastropod (gas'trə pod') *n.* [GASTRO- + -POD] any of a large class of molluscs having a single shell, as snails, etc., or no shell, as certain slugs: most gastropods move by means of a broad, muscular, ventral foot: also **gas'teropod** —**gas'tropod'ous** *adj.*

gasworks *n.pl.* [with sing. v.] a plant where gas, esp. coal gas, is made for distribution as a fuel

gate (gāt) *n.* [< OE. *geat*] 1. a movable structure controlling entrance or exit through an opening in a fence or wall 2. a gateway 3. a movable barrier, as at a level crossing 4. a structure controlling the flow of water, as in a canal 5. *a)* the total admission money paid by spectators at a performance *b)* the total number of such spectators 6. the slatted metal frame that controls the positions of the gear lever in a motor vehicle —*vt.* to restrict (a student) to the school or college grounds as a punishment

gateau (gat'ō) *n., pl.* **-eaux** (-ō, -ōz) [Fr.] a rich, layered, elaborately-decorated cake

gate-crasher *n.* [Colloq.] a person who attends a social affair without an invitation —**gate'-crash'** *vt., vi.*

gatehouse *n.* a dwelling beside or over a gateway

GATELEG
TABLE

gateleg table a table with drop leaves supported by gatelike legs that swing back to let the leaves drop

gateway *n.* 1. an entrance in a wall, etc. fitted with a gate 2. a means of access

gather (gath'ər) *vt.* [< OE. gad(e)rian] 1. to bring together in one place or group 2. to get gradually; accumulate 3. to bring close 4. to pick; harvest 5. to infer 6. to prepare to meet a situation 7. to gain gradually [gather speed] 8. to draw (cloth) into folds 9. to wrinkle (one's brow) —*vi.* 1. to assemble 2. to form pus, as a boil 3. to increase 4. to become wrinkled: said of the brow —*n.* a pleat —**gath'erer** *n.*

gathering *n.* 1. a meeting; crowd 2. a series of pleats 3. a boil or abscess

G.A.T.T. General Agreement on Tariffs and Trade

gauche (gōsh) *adj.* [< MFr. gauchir, become warped] lacking social grace; awkward; tactless —**gau'cherie** *n.*

gaucho (gou'chō) *n., pl.* **-chos** [AmSp.] a cowboy of the S American pampas

gaud (gôd) *n.* [ME. gaude, trinket] a cheap, showy ornament

gaudy (gôd'ē) *adj.* **-ier, -iest** [see prec.] bright and showy, but in bad taste —**gaud'ily** *adv.* —**gaud'iness** *n.*

gauge (gāj) *n.* [< ONormFr. gaugier, to gauge] 1. a standard measure or scale of measurement 2. dimensions, capacity, thickness, etc. 3. any device for measuring something, as rainfall, the thickness of wire, steam pressure, etc. 4. any means of estimating 5. the distance between railway lines or parallel wheels 6. the size of the bore of a shotgun 7. the thickness of sheet metal, diameter of wire, etc. 8. the fineness of a knitted or woven fabric, usually expressed as the number of loops per centimetre —*vt.* **gauged, gaug'ing** 1. to measure the size, amount, or capacity of 2. to estimate; judge —**gauge'able** *adj.* —**gaug'er** *n.*

Gaul (gôl) *n.* 1. any of the Celtic-speaking people of Gaul 2. a Frenchman —**Gaul'ish** *adj.*

gaunt (gônt) *adj.* [< ?] 1. thin and bony; haggard 2. grim or desolate —**gaunt'ly** *adv.* —**gaunt'ness** *n.*

gauntlet[1] (gônt'lit) *n.* [< OFr. gant, glove] 1. a medieval armoured glove 2. a long glove with a flaring cuff —**take up the gauntlet** to accept a challenge —**throw down the gauntlet** to challenge, as to combat

gauntlet[2] *n.* [< Sw. < gata, lane + lopp, a run] a former military punishment in which the offender ran between two rows of men who struck him —**run the gauntlet** 1. to be punished by means of the gauntlet 2. to proceed while under attack from both sides, as by criticism or gossip

gauntry (gôn'trē) *n., pl.* **-tries** same as GANTRY

gauze (gôz) *n.* [Fr. gaze] any very thin, transparent, loosely woven material, as of cotton or silk —**gauz'y** *adj.*

gave (gāv) *pt.* of GIVE

gavel (gav''l) *n.* [< ?] a small mallet rapped on the table by a chairman, auctioneer, etc. to call for attention

gavotte (gəvot') *n.* [Fr.] 1. a 17th-cent. dance like the minuet, but livelier 2. the music for this

gawk (gôk) *n.* [prob. < gowk, simpleton] a clumsy, stupid fellow; simpleton —*vi.* to stare in a stupid way

gawky (gô'kē) *adj.* **-ier, -iest** awkward; clumsy; ungainly —**gawk'ily** *adv.* —**gawk'iness** *n.*

gawp (gôp) *vi.* [< ME. galpen, gape] [Slang] to stare open-mouthed; gape

gay (gā) *adj.* [< OFr.] 1. lively; merry 2. bright [gay colours] 3. licentious [a gay dog] 4. [Colloq.] homosexual —**gay'ness** *n.*

gaze (gāz) *vi.* **gazed, gaz'ing** [< Scand.] to look intently and steadily —*n.* a steady look —**gaz'er** *n.*

gazebo (gəzē'bō) *n., pl.* **-bos, -boes** [< ?] a turret, balcony, or summerhouse with an extensive view

gazelle (gəzel') *n.* [Fr. < Ar. ghazāl] a small, swift, graceful antelope with large, lustrous eyes

gazette (gəzet') *n.* [Fr. < It.] 1. a newspaper 2. an official publication containing announcements —*vt.* **-zet'ted, -zet'ting** to announce in a gazette

gazetteer (gaz'ətēər') *n.* a dictionary or index of geographical names

gazump (gəzump') *vt.* [< ?] to raise the price of something, esp. a house, in the period between a verbal agreement and the signing of the contract

G.B. Great Britain

G.B.E. Grand Cross of the British Empire

g.b.h. grievous bodily harm

G.C. George Cross

G.C.B. Grand Cross of the Bath

G.C.E. General Certificate of Education

G clef same as TREBLE CLEF

G.C.M.G. Grand Cross of St. Michael and St. George

G.C.V.O. Grand Cross of the Victorian Order

Gd *Chem.* gadolinium

Gdns. Gardens

GDR German Democratic Republic

Ge *Chem.* germanium

GEARS

gear (gēar) *n.* [prob. < ON. *gervi*, preparation] **1.** *a)* a toothed wheel, disc, etc. designed to mesh with another *b)* [*often pl.*] a system of gears meshed together so that the motion of one is passed on to the others *c)* a specific adjustment of such a system: in motor-vehicle transmissions, *high* or *top gear* provides greatest speed and *bottom* or *first gear* greatest power *d)* any part of a mechanism performing a specific function [the steering *gear*] **2.** equipment for some particular task, as a workman's tools **3.** clothing, esp. up-to-date clothes and accessories —*vt.* **1.** to furnish with, or connect by, **gears 2.** to adapt (one thing) to conform with another [to *gear* production to demand] —**in** (or **out of**) **gear 1.** (not) connected to the motor **2.** (not) in working order —**change gears 1.** to switch from one gear arrangement to another **2.** to alter one's approach

gearbox *n.* the case enclosing the transmission gears in a machine or vehicle

gearing *n.* a system of gears or other parts for transmitting motion

gearlever *n.* a device for connecting or disconnecting any of the transmission gears to a motor, etc.

gearwheel *n.* a toothed wheel in a system of gears

gecko (gek'ō) *n., pl.* **-os, -oes** [Malay *gekok*, echoic of its cry] a soft-skinned, insect-eating, tropical lizard

gee (jē) *interj., n.* [< ?] a word of command to a horse, etc. meaning "turn right!" or "go on!" (with *up*)

geelbek (khēl'bek) *n.* [< Afrik. *geel*, yellow + *bek*, mouth] [S Afr.] a yellow-jawed edible marine fish

geese (gēs) *n. pl. of* GOOSE

geezer (gē'zər) *n.* [< GUISE] [Slang] an eccentric old man

Geiger counter (gi'gər) [< H. *Geiger*] an instrument for detecting and measuring radioactivity

geisha (gā'shə) *n.* [Jap.] a Japanese girl entertainer trained to serve as a hired companion to men

gel (jel) *n.* [< ff.] a jellylike colloid in which a liquid is dispersed in a solid —*vi.* **gelled, gel'ling** to form a gel

gelatin (jel'ət in) *n.* [< L. *gelare*, freeze] the tasteless substance extracted by boiling bones, hoofs, etc.: dissolved and cooled, it forms a jellylike substance used in foods, photographic film, etc.: also **gel'atine** (-tēn)

gelatinize (jəlat'ən īz') *vt., vi.* **-nized', -niz'ing** to change or be changed into gelatin —**gelat'iniza'tion** *n.*

gelatinous (jəlat'ənəs) *adj.* **1.** of or containing gelatin **2.** like gelatin or jelly —**gelat'inously** *adv.*

geld (geld) *vt.* **geld'ed** or **gelt, geld'ing** [< ON. *geldr*, barren] to castrate (esp. a horse)

gelding (gel'diŋ) *n.* a gelded animal; esp., a horse

gelignite (jel'ig nīt') *n.* [GELATIN + L. *lignum*, wood] a blasting explosive containing nitroglycerin

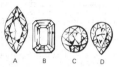

CUTS OF GEM

(A, marquise; B, emerald; C, round; D, pear-shaped)

gem (jem) *n.* [< L. *gemma*] **1.** a precious stone, cut and polished as a jewel **2.** a highly valued person or thing —*vt.* **gemmed, gem'ming** to adorn as with gems —**gem'my** *adj.*

geminate (jem'ə nāt') *adj.* [< L. *geminus*, twin] combined in pairs —*vt., vi.* **-nat'-ed, -nat'ing** to arrange or be arranged in pairs —**gem'ina'tion** *n.*

Gemini (jem'ə nī') [L., twins] **1.** a N constellation containing the stars Castor and Pollux **2.** the third sign of the zodiac

gemma (jem'ə) *n., pl.* **-mae** (-ē) [< L.] *Biol.* a budlike outgrowth which becomes detached and develops into a new organism

gemmate (jem'āt) *adj.* [< L. *gemma*, bud] having, or reproducing by, gemmae —**gemma'tion** *n.*

gemsbok (gemz'buk) *n.* [< Afrik.] a S African oryx with a large black band along its flanks

gen (jen) *n.* [*gen(eral)* information] [Colloq.] information —*vt., vi.* to make oneself fully informed (with *up*)

-gen (jən, jen) [< Gr. *gignesthai*, be born] a suffix meaning: **1.** something that produces [*oxygen*] **2.** something produced (in a specified way) [*zymogen*]

Gen. 1. General **2.** Genesis

gen. 1. gender **2.** general **3.** genitive **4.** genus

gendarme (zhän'därm) *n.* [Fr., men of arms] in France, a soldier serving as an armed policeman

gender (jen'dər) *n.* [< L. *genus*, origin] **1.** *Gram.* the classification of words as masculine, feminine, or neuter **2.** [Colloq.] sex

gene (jēn) *n.* [see -GEN] *Genetics* any of the units occurring at specific points on the chromosomes, by which hereditary characters are transmitted and determined

genealogy (jē'nē al'ə jē) *n.*, *pl.* **-gies** [< Gr. *genea*, race + -LOGY] **1.** a history of the ancestry of a person **2.** the study of family descent **3.** pedigree; lineage —**ge'nealog'ical** (-ə loj'i k'l) *adj.* —**ge'neal'ogist** *n.*

general (jen'ər əl) *adj.* [< L. *genus*, class] **1.** of, for, or from all; not particular or localized **2.** of or for a whole kind, class, etc. **3.** widespread [*general* unrest] **4.** most common; usual **5.** concerned with the main or overall features **6.** not precise; vague [*in general* terms] **7.** highest in rank [*general* manager] —*n.* **1.** the head of a religious order **2.** *see* MILITARY RANKS, table —**in general 1.** usually **2.** without specific details —**gen'eralness** *n.*

General Certificate of Education a public examination for which certificates are awarded at ordinary, advanced, or scholarship level

general election 1. in Britain, an election in which every constituency chooses a representative **2.** [U.S. & Canad.] a national, state, or provincial election, as distinguished from a local election

generalissimo (jen'ər ə lis'ə mō') *n.*, *pl.* **-mos'** [It.] the commander in chief of all the armed forces, or of several armies in the field

generality (jen'ə ral'ə tē) *n.*, *pl.* **-ties 1.** a nonspecific statement, rule, etc. **2.** the quality of being general **3.** the bulk; main body

generalization (jen'ər ə lī zā'shən) *n.* **1.** a generalizing **2.** a general idea, etc. resulting from this

generalize (jen'ər ə līz') *vt.* **-ized'**, **-iz'-ing 1.** to state in terms of a general law **2.** to infer (a general law) from (particular instances) **3.** to emphasize the general character rather than details of **4.** to cause to be widely known —*vi.* **1.** to formulate general principles from particulars **2.** to talk in generalities **3.** to become general or spread

generally *adv.* **1.** popularly; extensively **2.** usually **3.** in a general way; not specifically

general practitioner a practising doctor who does not specialize in any particular field of medicine

general-purpose *adj.* having a variety of uses

general staff *Mil.* a group of officers who assist the commander in planning and supervising operations

general strike a strike by all, or most, of the workers of a country, province, etc.

generate (jen'ə rāt') *vt.* **-at'ed**, **-at'ing** [< L. *genus*, race] to bring into being; produce

generation (jen'ə rā'shən) *n.* **1.** the producing of offspring **2.** production **3.** a single stage in the succession of descent **4.** the average period (c. 30 years) between the birth of successive generations **5.** all the people born at about the same time

generation gap the difference in outlook, resulting in lack of understanding, between people of different generations

generative (jen'ər ə tiv) *adj.* of, or having the power of, generation —**gen'eratively** *adv.*

generator (jen'ə rāt'ər) *n.* **1.** a machine for changing mechanical energy into electrical energy; dynamo **2.** a machine for producing gas or steam

generic (jə ner'ik) *adj.* [see GENUS] **1.** referring to a whole kind, class, or group; inclusive or general **2.** *Biol.* of a genus —**gener'ically** *adv.*

generosity (jen'ə ros'ə tē) *n.* **1.** the quality of being generous **2.** *pl.* **-ties** a generous act

generous (jen'ər əs) *adj.* [L. *generosus*, of noble birth < GENUS] **1.** noble-minded; magnanimous **2.** willing to give or share; unselfish **3.** large; ample [*generous* portions] —**gen'erously** *adv.* —**gen'erousness** *n.*

genesis (jen'ə sis) *n.*, *pl.* **-ses'** (-sēz') [< Gr. *gignesthai*, be born] a beginning; origin —[G-] the first book of the Bible, giving an account of the Creation

-genesis (jen'ə sis) a combining form meaning origination, creation, evolution (of something specified)

genetic (jə net'ik) *adj.* [< GENESIS] **1.** of the origin of something **2.** of genetics —**genet'ically** *adv.*

genetic code the order in which four chemical constituents are arranged in DNA molecules for transmitting genetic information to the cells

genetics *n.pl.* [with *sing. v.*] the branch of biology that deals with heredity and variation in animals and plants —**genet'icist** *n.*

Geneva Convention (jə nē'və) an international agreement (1864) establishing a code for the care in wartime of the sick, wounded, and prisoners of war

genial (jēn'yəl) *adj.* [see GENIUS] **1.** cheerful, friendly, and sympathetic **2.** promoting life and growth; warm and mild [a genial climate] —**geniality** (jē'nē al'ə tē) *n.* —**ge'nially** *adv.*

genie (jē'nē) *n.* [Fr. *génie*] same as JINNI

genital (jen'ə t'l) *adj.* [< L. *genere*, beget] of reproduction or the sexual organs

genitals *n.pl.* the reproductive organs; esp., the external sex organs : also **gen'ita'-lia** (-tāl'yə)

genitive (jen'ə tiv) *adj.* [< L. (*casus*) *genitivus*, case of origin] *Gram.* designating, of, or in a case expressing possession, source, etc. —*n.* **1.** the genitive case **2.** a word in the genitive case

genius (jēn'yəs) *n.*, *pl.* **gen'niuses** for 1, 2, 3; **genii** (jē'nē ī') for 4 [L., guardian spirit] **1.** *a)* great mental and inventive ability *b)* a person having this *c)* popularly, any person with a very high intelligence quotient **2.** a great natural ability or strong inclination (*for*) **3.** particular spirit of a nation, place, age, etc. **4.** *a)* [often G-] the guardian spirit of a person, place, etc. *b)* either of two spirits, one good and one evil, supposed to influence one's destiny *c)* a person considered as having strong influence over another

genocide (jen′ō sīd′) **n.** [< Gr. *genos*, race + -CIDE] the systematic killing of a whole national or ethnic group —**gen′o·ci′dal** (-sī′d′l) **adj.**

-genous (jə nəs) [see -GEN] *a suffix meaning:* 1. producing [*nitrogenous*] 2. produced by [*autogenous*]

genre (zhän′rə) **n.** [Fr. < L. *genus*, kind] 1. a kind or type of literature, art, etc. 2. painting in which subjects from everyday life are treated realistically

gent (jent) **n.** [Colloq.] a gentleman; man

genteel (jen tēl′) **adj.** [< Fr. *gentil*] 1. excessively or affectedly refined, polite, etc. 2. formerly, elegant or fashionable —**genteel′ly adv.** —**genteel′ness n.**

gentian (jen′shən) **n.** [< L. *gentiana*] a plant with blue, white, red, or yellow flowers

gentian violet a violet dye used as an antiseptic, etc.

gentile (jen′tīl) **n.** [< L. *gentilis*, of the same clan] [*also* G-] 1. any person not a Jew 2. a heathen —**adj.** [*also* G-] 1. not Jewish 2. heathen

gentility (jen til′ə tē) **n.,** *pl.* **-ties** [see ff.] 1. the condition of belonging by birth to the upper classes 2. the quality of being genteel

gentle (jent′′l) **adj.** **-tler, -tlest** [< L. *gentilis*, of the same clan] 1. kindly; patient 2. not violent [*a gentle tap*] 3. generous; kind 4. gradual [*a gentle slope*] 5. easily handled; tame 6. of the upper classes 7. polite; refined 8. [Archaic] noble; chivalrous —**n.** a maggot used for fishing bait —**gen′tleness n.** —**gen′tly adv.**

gentlefolk n.pl. people of high social standing

gentleman n. 1. orig. *a)* a man born into a family of high social standing *b)* any man of independent means [*country gentleman*] 2. a courteous, gracious man 3. any man: polite term, as (chiefly in pl.) of address —**gen′tlewom′an n.fem.**

gentlemanly adj. of, characteristic of, or fit for a gentleman; well-mannered: also **gen′tlemanlike′**

gentlemen's (or gentleman's) agreement an unwritten agreement secured only by the parties' pledge of honour

gentry (jen′trē) **n.** [see GENTLE] 1. people of high social standing; esp., the landowning people ranking below the nobility 2. [Derog.] people of a particular class

gents n.pl. [*with sing. v.*] [Colloq.] a men's lavatory

genuflect (jen′yōō flekt′) **vi.** [< L. *genu*, knee + *flectere*, bend] to bend the knee in reverence or worship —**gen′uflec′tion, gen′uflex′ion n.** —**gen′uflec′tor n.**

genuine (jen′yōō win) **adj.** [< L. *gignere*, be born] 1. really being what it is said to be; authentic 2. sincere; honest —**gen′u·inely adv.** —**gen′uineness n.**

genus (jē′nəs) **n.,** *pl.* **genera** (jen′ər ə) [L., race, kind] 1. a class; kind 2. *Biol.* a classification of plants or animals: a genus is the main subdivision of a family and includes one or more species 3. *Logic*

a class of things made up of subordinate species

geo- [< Gr. *gē*] *a combining form meaning:* earth, of the earth [*geocentric*]

geocentric (jē′ō sen′trik) **adj.** 1. viewed as from the centre of the earth 2. having the earth as a centre Also **ge′ocen′trical** —**ge′ocen′trically adv.**

geode (jē′ōd) **n.** [< Gr. *geoeidēs*, earthlike] 1. a globular stone having a cavity lined with inward-growing crystals 2. such a cavity —**geod′ic** (-od′ik) **adj.**

geodesic (jē′ə des′ik) **adj.** designating the shortest line between two points on a surface, esp. a curved surface

geodesy (jē od′ə sē) **n.** [< Gr. *gē*, earth + *daiein*, divide] the branch of mathematics concerned with measuring, or determining the shape of, the earth —**geod′esist n.**

geog. 1. geographic(al) 2. geography

geographical (jē′ə graf′i k'l) **adj.** of or according to geography: also **ge′ograph′ic** —**ge′ograph′ically adv.**

geographical mile *same as* NAUTICAL MILE

geography (jē og′rə fē) **n.,** *pl.* **-phies** [< Gr. *gē*, earth + *graphein*, write] 1. the science dealing with the earth, its continents and countries, climate, resources, people, etc. 2. the physical features of a region —**geog′rapher n.**

geoid (jē′oid) **n.** [< Gr. *geoeidēs*, earthlike] the earth viewed as a hypothetical ellipsoid with the surface represented as a mean sea level

geol. 1. geologic(al) 2. geologist 3. geology

geology (jē ol′ə jē) **n.,** *pl.* **-gies** [see GEO- & -LOGY] 1. the science dealing with the earth's structure and development, types of rocks, etc. 2. the structure of the earth's crust in a given region —**ge′olog′ical adj.** —**geol′ogist n.**

geometric (jē′ō met′rik) **adj.** 1. of geometry 2. characterized by straight lines, triangles, etc., as a pattern Also **ge′omet′rical** —**ge′omet′rically adv.**

geometric progression a sequence in which the ratio of each term to the preceding one is the same (Ex.: 1, 2, 4, 8)

geometry (jē om′ə trē) **n.,** *pl.* **-tries** [< Gr. *gē*, earth + *metrein*, measure] the branch of mathematics that deals with the properties of points, lines, surfaces, and solids —**geom′etri′cian, geom′eter n.**

Geordie (jôr′dē) **n.** [< *George*] a native of Tyneside

George Cross (jôrj) an award for bravery, esp. of civilians

georgette (jôr jet′) **n.** [< *Georgette* de la Plante] a kind of thin crepe fabric: also **georgette crepe**

Georgian (jôr′jən) **adj.** 1. of the reigns of George I, II, III, and IV, or of George V and VI, of Britain 2. of the Georgian S.S.R. 3. of the state of Georgia, U.S. —**n.** 1. *a)* a native of the Georgian S.S.R. *b)* the language of the Georgians 2. a native of Georgia, U.S.

geotropism (jē ot′rə piz′m) **n.** [GEO- +

Gr. *tropos,* a turning] movement or growth in response to the force of gravity

Ger. 1. German 2. Germany

geranium (jərān′yəm) *n.* [L. < Gr. *geranion,* cranesbill] 1. a plant with pink or purple flowers and seed pods like a crane's bill 2. pop. name for a pelargonium

gerbil, gerbille (jur′b'l) *n.* [< Fr. < ModL. *gerbo,* JERBOA] a burrowing rodent related to the mouse, with long hind legs and tail

gerfalcon (jur′fôl′k'n) *n.* same as GYRFALCON

geriatrics (jer′ē at′riks) *n.pl.* [with sing. v.] [< Gr. *gēras,* old age] the branch of medicine that deals with the diseases and hygiene of old age —**ger′iat′ric** adj.

germ (jurm) *n.* [< L. *germen,* bud] 1. any microscopic organism, esp. one that can cause disease 2. that from which something can develop [the *germ* of an idea] 3. the rudimentary form from which a new organism is developed; seed —**germ′less** adj.

German (jur′mən) adj. [< L. *Germanus*] of Germany, its people, language, or culture —*n.* 1. a native of Germany 2. the German language

german (jur′mən) adj. [< L. *germanus*] 1. having the same parents [a brother-*german*] 2. being a first cousin [a cousin-*german*]

germander (jur man′dər) *n.* [< Gr. *chamai,* on the ground + *drys,* tree] any of a genus of plants with spikes of flowers that lack an upper lip

germane (jur mān′) adj. [var. of GERMAN] truly relevant

Germanic (jur man′ik) adj. 1. German 2. designating the original language of the German peoples or the languages descended from it —*n.* 1. the original language of the Germanic peoples 2. a branch of the Indo-European family of languages, comprising this language and the languages descended from it

germanium (jur mā′nē əm) *n.* [< L. *Germania,* Germany] a rare, greyish-white, metallic chemical element that can be a semiconductor : symbol, Ge

German measles same as RUBELLA

German silver same as NICKEL SILVER

germ cell a cell from which a new organism can develop

germicide (jur′mə sīd′) *n.* [< GERM + -CIDE] anything used to destroy germs —**ger′mici′dal** adj.

germinal (jur′mə n'l) adj. 1. of or like germs or germ cells 2. in the first stage of development

germinate (jur′mə nāt′) *vi., vt.* -nat′ed, -nat′ing [see GERM] 1. to sprout or cause to sprout, as from a seed 2. to start developing —**ger′mina′tion** *n.* —**ger′minative** adj.

germ warfare the deliberate contamination of enemy territory with disease germs in warfare

gerontology (jer′on tol′ə jē) *n.* [< Gr. *gerōn,* old man + -LOGY] the scientific study of aging and of the problems of aged people —**ger′ontol′ogist** *n.*

gerrymander (jer′i man′dər) *vt.* [< E. *Gerry,* governor of Massachusetts, U.S. (1812) + SALAMANDER (the shape of the redrawn electoral district)] to divide (a voting area) so as to give one political party a majority in as many electoral districts as possible —*n.* the act or result of gerrymandering —**ger′ryman′derer** *n.*

gerund (jer′ənd) *n.* [< L. *gerere,* do] Gram. a verbal noun ending in -ing (Ex.: "Playing golf is this only exercise")

gerundive (jə run′div) *n.* a Latin verbal adjective with a typical gerund stem form, expressing duty, necessity, etc.

gesso (jes′ō) *n.* [It., gypsum, chalk] plaster of Paris prepared for use in sculpture, or as a surface for painting

Gestapo (ge stä′pō) *n.* [< G. *Ge*(*heime*) *Sta*(*ats*)*po*(*lizei*)] the secret police force of the German Nazi state

gestate (jes tāt′) *vt.* -tat′ed, -tat′ing [< L. *gerere,* to bear] to carry in the uterus during pregnancy —**gesta′tion** *n.*

gesticulate (jes tik′yoo lāt′) *vi.* -lat′ed, -lat′ing [< L. *gesticulari,* ult. < *gerere,* do] to make gestures, esp. with the hands, in adding force to one's speech —*vt.* to express by gesticulating —**gestic′ula′tion** *n.*

gesture (jes′chər) *n.* [< L. *gerere,* do] 1. a movement of the body, or of part of the body, to express or emphasize ideas, emotions, etc. 2. anything said or done to convey a state of mind or intention, sometimes something said or done only for effect —*vi.* -tured, -turing to use gestures —**ges′turer** *n.*

get (get) *vt.* got or archaic gat, got or archaic and U.S. got′ten, get′ting [< ON. *geta*] 1. to come into the state of having; receive, win, etc. 2. to reach [to *get* home] 3. to set up communication with, as by radio 4. to go and bring 5. to capture 6. to commit to memory 7. to persuade (a person) [*get* him to leave] 8. to cause to be [he *got* his hands dirty] 9. to prepare [to *get* lunch] 10. to give birth to; beget : said of animals 11. [Colloq.] to be obliged to (with *have* or *has*) 12. [Colloq.] to possess (with *have* or *has*) 13. [Colloq.] *a*) to overpower [his illness finally *got* him] *b*) to baffle [this problem *gets* me] *c*) to wound or kill 14. [Colloq.] to hit [the blow *got* him in the eye] 15. [Colloq.] to understand 16. [Slang] to cause an emotional response in —*vi.* 1. to arrive [to *get* to work] 2. to come to be [he *got* caught in the rain] 3. to contrive [to *get* to do something] —**get about** 1. to move from place to place 2. to go to many social events, places, etc. 3. to circulate, as news —**get across** [Colloq.] to succeed in making oneself understood —**get at** 1. to approach or reach 2. to apply oneself to [let's *get* at the work] 3. [Colloq.] to imply 4. [Colloq.] to bribe or intimidate 5. [Colloq.] to criticise, esp. in an indirect manner —**get away with** [Slang] to succeed in doing without being punished

—**get back** 1. to return 2. to recover 3. [Slang] to get revenge (usually with *at*) —**get by** 1. to be just acceptable 2. [Colloq.] to survive; manage —**get down to** to begin to consider or act on —**get off** 1. to come off, down, or out of 2. to take off 3. to escape punishment 4. to start, as in a race —**get off with** [Colloq.] to establish a friendly or sexual relationship with —**get on** 1. to go on or into 2. to put on 3. to proceed 4. to grow older 5. to succeed 6. to agree —**get out** 1. to go out or away 2. to take out 3. to become no longer a secret —**get over** 1. to recover from 2. to overcome —**get round** 1. to circumvent 2. to gain favour with by cajolery, flattery, etc. —**get round to** to find time for —**get somewhere** to succeed —**get through** 1. to finish 2. to survive 3. to pass (an examination, etc.) 4. to make oneself clear (*to*) —**get up** 1. to rise (from sleep, etc.) 2. to organize 3. to dress elaborately. 4. to intensify [*the wind got up*] 5. [Colloq.] work at [*I must get up* my maths for the exam*] —**get′ter** *n.*

getaway *n.* 1. the act of escaping, as from police 2. the act of starting, as in a race

get-together *n.* an informal social gathering

get-up *n.* [Colloq.] 1. outfit; dress 2. general arrangement

get-up-and-go *n.* [Colloq.] energy; drive

geum (jē′əm) *n.* [< L.] a perennial plant, having yellow, red or white flowers

geyser (gi′zər; *for 2,* gē′-) *n.* [< ON. *gjosa,* gush] 1. a spring from which columns of boiling water and steam gush into the air at intervals 2. a small, domestic, gas water heater

ghastly (gäst′lē) *adj.* -lier, -liest [< OE. *gast,* ghost] 1. [Colloq.] unpleasant 2. ghostlike; pale 3. frightful —*adv.* in a ghastly manner —**ghast′liness** *n.*

ghat, ghaut (gôt) *n.* [Hindi *ghāt*] in India, 1. a mountain pass 2. a flight of steps leading down to a river

ghee (gē) *n.* [Hindi *ghī*] in India, a liquid butter specially made from cow's milk or buffalo milk

gherkin (gur′kin) *n.* [< LowG. *gurken*] a small pickled cucumber

ghetto (get′ō) *n., pl.* -tos, -toes [It.] 1. any section of a city in which many members of some minority group live 2. in certain European cities, a section to which Jews were formerly restricted

ghost (gōst) *n.* [OE. *gast*] 1. the supposed disembodied spirit of a dead person; apparition 2. a slight trace [*not a ghost of a chance*] 3. [Colloq.] *same as* GHOST-WRITER 4. *Optics & TV* an unwanted secondary image —*vt., vi.* [Colloq.] to work as a ghostwriter (*for*) —**ghost′like** *adj.* —**ghost′liness** *n.* —**ghost′ly** *adj.*

ghost town the remains of a town that has been permanently abandoned, esp. for economic reasons

ghost word a word created through a misprint, etc.

ghostwriter *n.* a person who writes speeches, articles, etc. for another who professes to be the author

ghoul (gōōl) *n.* [< Ar. *ghāla,* seize] 1. one who enjoys things that disgust most people 2. *Oriental Folklore* an evil spirit that robs graves and feeds on the dead —**ghoul′ish** *adj.* —**ghoul′ishly** *adv.* —**ghoul′ishness** *n.*

GHQ, G.H.Q. General Headquarters

ghyll (gil) *n.* var. of GILL[3]

GI (jē′ī′) *adj.* [G(*overnment*) I(*ssue*)] [Colloq.] of or characteristic of the U.S. armed forces —*n., pl.* **GI's, GIs** [Colloq.] any member of the U.S. armed forces

giant (jī′ənt) *n.* [< Gr. *gigas*] 1. any imaginary being of human form but of superhuman size and strength 2. a person or thing of great size, intellect, etc. —*adj.* of great size, strength, etc. —**gi′antess** *n.fem.*

GIANT PANDA (1.2 m high at shoulder)

giant panda a large, black-and-white, bearlike mammal of China and Tibet

giaour (jouər) *n.* [< Ar. *kāfir,* infidel] in Moslem usage, a non-Moslem; esp., a Christian

gib (jib) *n.* [< ?] an adjustable piece of metal, etc., for keeping moving parts of a machine in place or for reducing friction

Gib. [Colloq.] Gibraltar

gibber (jib′ər) *vi., vt.* [echoic] to speak or utter rapidly and incoherently —*n.* gibberish

gibberish *n.* rapid, incoherent talk

gibbet (jib′it) *n.* [< Frank. *gibb,* forked stick] 1. a gallows 2. a structure like a gallows, from which bodies of criminals were hung and exposed to public scorn —*vt.* 1. to hang on a gibbet 2. to expose to public scorn

gibbon (gib′ən) *n.* [Fr.] a small, slender, long-armed ape

gibbous (gib′əs) *adj.* [< L. *gibba,* hump] 1. rounded and bulging 2. designating the moon when more than half of the disc is illuminated 3. humpbacked

gibe (jīb) *vi., vt.* **gibed, gib′ing** [< ? OFr. *giber,* handle roughly] to jeer; scoff (at) —*n.* a jeer; taunt —**gib′er** *n.*

giblet (jib′lit) *n.* [< OFr. *gibelet,* stew made of game] any of the parts of a fowl, as the heart, gizzard, neck, etc., usually cooked separately

giddy (gid′ē) *adj.* -dier, -diest [OE. *gydig,* insane] 1. having or causing a whirling, dazed sensation; dizzy 2. frivolous; flighty —**gid′dily** *adv.* —**gid′diness** *n.*

gie (gē) *vt., vi.* **gied, glen** (gē′ən), **gie′-ing** [Scot.] to give

gift (gift) *n.* [< OE. < *giefan,* give] 1.

something given; present **2.** the act, power, or right of giving [in the *gift* of] **3.** a talent —*vt.* to present with or as a gift —**look a gift horse in the mouth** to be critical of a gift

gift coupon a voucher given on purchase of certain articles; a specified number may be collected and exchanged for a gift

gifted *adj.* having a natural ability; talented

gift token a voucher given as a present which the recipient can exchange for a gift of a certain value

gift-wrap *vt.* **-wrapped′, -wrap′ping** to wrap as a gift, with decorative paper, ribbon, etc.

gig¹ (gig) *n.* [prob. < Scand.] **1.** a two-wheeled, open carriage drawn by one horse **2.** a long, light ship's boat

gig² *n.* [< ?] [Colloq.] a job, esp. a single booking, to play or sing jazz, rock, etc.

giga- (gig′ə) [< Gr. *gigas*, giant] a combining form meaning one thousand million; 10⁹

gigantic (jī gan′tik) *adj.* [see GIANT] **1.** huge; enormous; immense **2.** of, like, or fit for a giant —**gigan′tically** *adv.*

giggle (gig′'l) *vi.* **-gled, -gling** [prob. < Du. *giggelen*] to laugh with rapid, high-pitched sounds, suggestive of nervousness, etc. —*n.* such a laugh —**gig′gly** *adj.*

gigolo (zhig′ə lō) *n., pl.* **-los** [Fr.] a man paid by a woman to be her escort

gigot (jig′ət) *n.* [Fr.] a leg of mutton, lamb, etc.

gild¹ (gild) *vt.* **gild′ed** or **gilt, gild′ing** [OE. *gyldan*] **1.** to overlay or coat with a layer of gold **2.** to make (something) seem more attractive than it is —**gild′-er** *n.* —**gild′ing** *n.*

gild² *n.* same as GUILD

gill¹ (gil) *n.* [prob. < Anglo-N.] **1.** the organ for breathing of most animals that live in water, as fish **2.** [*pl.*] a) the wattle of a fowl b) the jowl of a person **3.** a thin, leaflike plate on the undersurface of a mushroom —**gilled** *adj.*

gill² (jil) *n.* [< LL. *gillo*, cooling vessel] a liquid measure, equal to 1/4 pint (0.142 litres)

gill³ (gil) *n.* [< ON. *gil*] **1.** a wooded ravine or glen **2.** a narrow stream; brook

gillie, gilly (gil′ē) *n., pl.* **-lies** [< Gael. *gille*, boy] in the Scottish Highlands, a sportsman's attendant

gilliflower (jil′ē flou′ər) *n.* [< Gr. *karyon*, nut + *phyllon*, leaf] any of several plants with clove-scented flowers, as the clove pink: also sp. **gil′lyflow′er**

gilt¹ (gilt) *alt. pt. & pp. of* GILD¹ —*adj.* overlaid with a thin layer of gold —*n.* gold leaf

gilt² *n.* [< ON. *gyltr*] a young female pig

gilt-edged (gilt′ejd′) *adj.* **1.** of the highest reliability or value [*gilt-edged securities*] **2.** having gilded edges

gimbals (gim′b'lz) *n.pl.* [with sing. *v.*] [< L. *geminus*, twin] a pair of rings pivoted so that one is free to swing within the other: a ship's compass will keep a horizontal position when suspended in gimbals

gimcrack (jim′krak) *adj.* [< ME. *gibbecrak*, an ornament] showy but cheap and useless —*n.* a cheap, showy, useless thing; knickknack —**gim′crack′ery** *n.*

gimlet (gim′lit) *n.* [< MDu. *wimmel, auger*] a small boring tool with a spiral, pointed cutting edge

gimlet-eyed *adj.* having a piercing glance

gimmick (gim′ik) *n.* [< ?] any superficial feature designed to attract attention, interest or publicity —**gim′-mickry, gim′mickery** *n.* —**gim′micky** *adj.*

gimp (gimp) *n.* [< ?] a ribbonlike braided fabric

gin¹ (jin) *n.* [< L. *juniperus*, juniper] a spirit distilled from grain and flavoured with juniper berries

gin² *n.* [< OFr. *engin*, engine] **1.** a snare or trap **2.** a machine in which a vertical shaft is turned to drive a horizontal beam in a circle **3.** same as COTTON GIN —*vt.* **ginned, gin′ning 1.** to catch in a trap **2.** to remove seeds from (cotton) with a gin —**gin′ner** *n.*

ginger (jin′jər) *n.* [< L. *zingiber*] **1.** an Asiatic plant grown for its aromatic rootstalk, used as a spice **2.** a reddish-brown colour **3.** [Colloq.] vigour —**gin′-gery** *adj.*

ginger ale a carbonated soft drink flavoured with ginger

ginger beer a drink like ginger ale but with a stronger flavour

gingerbread *n.* **1.** a cake flavoured with ginger and treacle **2.** showy ornamentation —*adj.* cheap and showy: also **gin′ger-bread′y** —**take the gilt off the gingerbread** to destroy the illusion

ginger group a group within a party, association, etc., that enlivens or radicalizes its parent body

gingerly *adv.* very carefully or cautiously —*adj.* very careful; cautious —**gin′gerliness** *n.*

gingersnap *n.* a crisp, spicy biscuit flavoured with ginger and treacle: also **ginger nut**

gingham (giŋ′əm) *n.* [< Malay *ginggang*, striped] a cotton cloth, usually woven in stripes or checks

gingivitis (jin′jə vīt′əs) *n.* [< L. *gingiva*, gum + -ITIS] inflammation of the gums

ginkgo (giŋ′kō) *n., pl.* **gink′goes** [Jap. < Chin.] an Asiatic tree with yellow seeds enclosing an edible kernel

gin-palace (jin′pal′is) *n.* formerly, a public house

gin rummy a variety of the card game rummy

ginseng (jin′seŋ) *n.* [Chin.] **1.** a perennial plant with a thick, forked, aromatic root: found in China and N. America **2.** the root of this plant, used medicinally

gip (jip) *n., vt., vi.* same as GYP¹

Gipsy (jip′sē) *n.* same as GYPSY

giraffe (jə räf′) *n.* [Fr. < Ar. *zarāfa*] a large, cud-chewing animal of Africa, with a very long neck and legs

gird¹ (gurd) *vt.* **gird′ed** or **girt, gird′ing** [OE. *gyrdan*] **1.** to encircle or fasten with a belt **2.** to enclose **3.** to endow **4.** to prepare (oneself) for action

gird² *vi., n.* [ME. *girden*, to strike] gibe; taunt

girder *n.* [< GIRD¹] a large beam of timber or steel, for supporting joists, a framework, etc.

girdle¹ (gur'd'l) *n.* [OE. *gyrdel*] **1.** a woman's elasticized undergarment for supporting the waist and hips **2.** anything that encircles **3.** a belt for the waist —*vt.* **-dled, -dling** to surround, as with a girdle —**gir'dler** *n.*

girdle² *n.* *same as* GRIDDLE

girl (gurl) *n.* [ME. *girle*, youngster] **1.** a female child **2.** a young, unmarried woman **3.** a female servant **4.** [Colloq.] a woman of any age **5.** [Colloq.] a sweetheart **6.** [S Afr. Derog.] a black female servant —**girl'ish** *adj.* —**girl'ish-ness** *n.*

girl Friday a female employee with a wide range of secretarial and clerical duties

girlfriend *n.* [Colloq.] **1.** a sweetheart of a boy or man **2.** a girl who is one's friend

girl guide a member of the Girl Guides' Association, an organisation founded to provide character-building activities

girlie, girly *n., pl.* **girl'ies** [Slang] a girl or woman —*adj.* [Slang] featuring nude women [a *girlie* magazine]

giro (ji'rō) *n., pl.* **-ros** [< Gr. *gyros*, circuit] a banking system, operated by post offices and banks, which provides for the transfer of money between accounts or by giro cheque

girt¹ (gurt) *alt. pt. & pp. of* GIRD¹

girt² *vt.* [var. of GIRD¹] **1.** to gird; girdle **2.** to fasten with a girth

girth (gurth) *n.* [< ON. *gjörth*] **1.** the circumference, as of a tree trunk or person's waist **2.** a band put around the belly of a horse, etc. to hold a saddle or pack

gist (jist) *n.* [< OFr. *gesir*, to lie < L. *jacere*] the essence or main point, as of an article or argument

git (git) *n.* [< GET] [Slang] a contemptible person

give (giv) *vt.* **gave, giv'en, giv'ing** [OE. *giefan*] **1.** to bestow; make a gift of **2.** to hand over [he *gave* the porter his bag] **3.** to pay (a price) for **4.** to relay [*give* my regards] **5.** to impart **6.** to confer **7.** to act as host of (a party, etc.) **8.** to produce; supply [cows give milk] **9.** *a)* to sacrifice [he *gave* his life] *b)* to devote [he *gives* all his time to his work] **10.** to concede **11.** to show; exhibit **12.** to offer; proffer **13.** to perform [to *give* a concert] **14.** to make (a gesture, movement, etc.) **15.** to inflict (punishment, etc.) —*vi.* **1.** to bend, sink, etc. from force or pressure **2.** to be resilient **3.** to provide a view of or access to [the window *gives* onto the park] —*n.* resiliency —**give and take** to exchange on an even basis —**give away 1.** to make a gift of **2.** to present (the bride) ritually to the bridegroom **3.** [Colloq.] to reveal —**give back** to return —**give forth** (or **off**) to send forth; emit —**give in 1.**

to hand in **2.** to yield —**give it to** [Colloq.] to beat or scold —**give or take** plus or minus —**give out 1.** to emit **2.** to make public **3.** to distribute **4.** to become worn out or used up —**give over 1.** to transfer **2.** to assign (the day was *given over* to pleasure] **3.** [Colloq.] to cease —**give to understand** (or **believe,** etc.) to cause to understand (or believe, etc.) —**give up 1.** to hand over **2.** to stop **3.** to admit failure **4.** to lose hope for **5.** to devote wholly —**giv'er** *n.*

give-and-take *n.* **1.** a mutual yielding **2.** a fair exchange of remarks or retorts

giveaway *n.* [Colloq.] **1.** an unintentional revelation **2.** something that betrays or reveals —*adj.* very cheap

given *pp. of* GIVE —*adj.* **1.** bestowed **2.** inclined [*given* to lying] **3.** specified **4.** assumed; granted

gizzard (giz'ərd) *n.* [< L. *gigeria*, cooked entrails of poultry] the second stomach of a bird —**stick in one's gizzard** to be intolerable

glacé (gla'sā) *adj.* [Fr.] **1.** having a smooth, glossy surface **2.** candied or glazed, as fruits

glacial (glā'shəl) *adj.* **1.** of ice or glaciers **2.** of or produced by a glacial epoch **3.** freezing; frigid **4.** cold and unfriendly —**gla'cially** *adv.*

glacial epoch any extent of geologic time when large parts of the earth were covered with glaciers

glaciate (glā'sē āt') *vt.* **-at'ed, -at'ing 1.** to cover with ice or a glacier **2.** to expose to or change by glacial action —**gla'cia'ted** *adj.* —**gla'cia'tion** *n.*

glacier (gla'sē ər) *n.* [< L. *glacies*, ice] a large mass of ice and snow that forms in areas where the rate of snowfall exceeds the melting rate: it moves slowly down a mountain, along a valley, etc. until it melts

glad¹ (glad) *adj.* **glad'der, glad'dest** [OE. *glæd*] **1.** happy; pleased **2.** causing pleasure **3.** willing [I'm *glad* to help] **4.** bright —**glad'ly** *adv.* —**glad'ness** *n.*

glad² *n.* [Colloq.] *same as* GLADIOLUS

gladden *vt., vi.* to make or become glad

glade (glād) *n.* [ME. < ?] an open space in a wood

glad eye [Slang] an inviting or flirtatious glance : usually in **give** (or **get**) **the glad eye**

gladiator (glad'ē āt'ər) *n.* [L. < *gladius*, sword] in ancient Rome, a man who fought other men or animals as a public show —**glad'iato'rial** (-ə tôr'ē əl) *adj.*

gladiolus (glad'ē ō'ləs) *n., pl.* **-luses, -li** (-lī) [< L. *gladius*, sword] a plant with swordlike leaves and tall spikes of funnel-shaped flowers

glad rags [Slang] fine or dressy clothes

gladsome (glad'səm) *adj.* joyful or cheerful

Gladstone (bag) (glad'stən) [< W.E. *Gladstone*] a travelling bag hinged so that it can open flat

glair (glãər) *n.* [< L. *clarus*, clear] **1.** raw white of egg, used in sizing **2.** a size or glaze made from this

Glam. Glamorgan

glamour (glam′ər) n. [Scot. var. of *grammar*] seemingly mysterious and elusive fascination or allure; bewitching charm —**glam′orous** adj.

glance (gläns) vi. **glanced, glanc′ing** [< ?] 1. to take a quick look 2. to make an indirect or passing reference 3. to gleam 4. to strike obliquely and go off at an angle —n. 1. a quick look 2. a flash 3. a glancing off

gland (gland) n. [< L. *glans*, acorn] any organ that separates certain elements from the blood and secretes them for the body to use or expel

glanders (glan′dərz) n.pl. [with sing. v.] [OFr. *glandres*, glands] a contagious disease of horses, etc. characterized by fever, swelling of glands beneath the jaw, etc.

glandular (glan′dyoo lər) adj. 1. of, like, or having a gland or glands 2. derived from or affected by glands

glandular fever same as INFECTIOUS MONONUCLEOSIS

glare (glãar) vi. **glared, glar′ing** [ME. *glaren*] 1. to stare fiercely or angrily 2. to shine with a steady, dazzling light 3. to be too bright —vt. to express with a glare —n. 1. a fierce or angry stare 2. a steady, dazzling light 3. a dazzling display

glaring adj. 1. flagrant [a glaring mistake] 2. dazzlingly bright 3. too bright 4. staring fiercely —**glar′ingly** adv.

glass (gläs) n. [OE. *glæs*] 1. a hard, brittle substance, usually transparent, made by fusing silicates with soda, lime, etc. 2. glass objects; glassware 3. a) an article made of glass, as a drinking container, mirror, etc. b) [pl.] spectacles c) [pl.] binoculars 4. the quantity contained in a drinking glass —vt. to equip with glass; glaze —adj. of, made of, or like glass

glass blowing the shaping of molten glass by blowing air into a mass of it at the end of a tube —**glass blower**

glasshouse n. 1. same as GREENHOUSE 2. [Slang] a military prison

glass-paper n. paper coated with pulverized glass for polishing

glass wool fine fibres of glass intertwined in a woolly mass, used in filters and as insulation

glassy adj. **-ier, -iest** 1. like glass, as in smoothness 2. expressionless [a glassy stare]

Glaswegian (glaz wē′jən) adj. of Glasgow —n. a native of Glasgow

glaucoma (glô kō′mə) n. [see ff.] a disease of the eye caused by increased pressure in the eyeball: it leads to a gradual loss of sight —**glauco′matous** adj.

glaucous (glô′kəs) adj. [< Gr. *glaukos*, gleaming] 1. bluish-green or yellowish-green 2. Bot. covered with a whitish bloom that can be rubbed off, as grapes

glaze (glāz) vt. **glazed, glaz′ing** [< ME. *glas*, glass] 1. to fit (windows, etc.) with glass 2. a) to overlay (pottery, etc.) with a substance that gives a glassy finish when fused b) to cover (foods) with a coating

of sugar syrup, etc. —vi. to become glassy or glossy —n. 1. a) a glassy finish, as on pottery b) any substance used to form this 2. a film or coating —**glaz′er** n. —**glaz′ing** n.

glazier n. a person whose work is fitting glass in windows, etc. —**gla′ziery** n.

G.L.C. Greater London Council

gleam (glēm) n. [OE. *glæm*] 1. a faint light 2. a reflected brightness, as from a polished surface 3. a faint manifestation, as of hope, etc. —vi. 1. to shine with a gleam 2. to appear suddenly

glean (glēn) vt., vi. [< Celt.] 1. to collect (facts, etc.) bit by bit 2. to collect (grain left by reapers) —**glean′er** n.

gleanings n.pl. that which is gleaned

glebe (glēb) n. [< L. *gleba*, clod] 1. church land forming part or all of a benefice 2. [Poet.] earth; land; field

glee (glē) n. [OE. *gleo*] 1. lively joy; merriment 2. a part song for three or more voices, usually unaccompanied

gleeful adj. full of glee; merry : also **glee′-some**

gleeman n. [ME. *gleman*] a medieval minstrel

glen (glen) n. [< ScotGael.] a narrow, secluded valley

Glengarry (glen gar′ē) n., pl. **-ries** [< *Glengarry*, in Scotland] [sometimes g-] a Scottish cap for men, creased lengthwise across the top

glib (glib) adj. **glib′ber, glib′best** [< or akin to Du. *glibberig*, slippery] speaking or spoken in a smooth, fluent manner, often too smooth and easy to be convincing —**glib′ly** adv. —**glib′ness** n.

glide (glīd) vi. **glid′ed, glid′ing** [OE. *glidan*] 1. to move smoothly and easily 2. to pass gradually and unnoticed 3. *Aeron.* a) to fly in a glider b) to descend at a normal angle without engine power —vt. to cause to glide —n. the act of gliding

glider n. an aircraft that has no engine and is carried along by air currents

glimmer (glim′ər) vi. [< OE. *glæm*, gleam] 1. to give a faint, flickering light 2. to appear dimly —n. 1. a faint, flickering light 2. a faint manifestation

glimpse (glimps) vt. **glimpsed, glimps′ing** [see GLIMMER] to catch a brief view of —n. 1. a flash 2. a faint, fleeting appearance 3. a brief view

glint (glint) vi., n. [prob. < Scand.] gleam; flash

glissade (gli säd′) n. [Fr.] 1. an intentional slide by a mountain climber down a snow-covered slope 2. *Ballet* a gliding step —vi. **-sad′ed, -sad′ing** to make a glissade

glisten (glis′′n) vi. [OE. *glisnian*] to shine or sparkle with reflected light —n. a glistening

glister (glis′tər) vi., n. archaic var. of GLISTEN

glitter (glit′ər) vi. [prob. < ON. *glitra*] 1. to shine with a sparkling light 2. to be brilliant, showy, or attractive —n. 1. a bright, sparkling light 2. showy brilliance

glitter ice [Canad.] ice formed from freezing rain

gloaming (glō′miṇ) *n.* [< OE. *glom*] dusk; twilight

gloat (glōt) *vi.* [prob. < ON. *glotta*, grin scornfully] to gaze or think with malicious pleasure —**gloat′er** *n.*

glob (glob) *n.* [prob. < globule] a rounded mass

global (glō′b'l) *adj.* 1. worldwide [global war] 2. complete 3. globe-shaped —**glob′ally** *adv.*

globe (glōb) *n.* [< L. *globus*] 1. any ball-shaped thing; sphere; specif., *a)* the earth *b)* a spherical model of the earth 2. anything shaped like a globe, as a glass cover for a lamp —**globate** (glō′bāt) *adj.*

globefish *n.* any of several tropical fishes that can puff themselves into a globular form

globeflower *n.* any of a genus of plants with white, orange, or yellow globe-shaped flowers

globe-trotter *n.* a person who travels widely, esp. for pleasure or sightseeing —**globe′-trot′ting** *n., adj.*

globigerina ooze (glō bij′ə rī′nə) [ModL.] a fine, deep-sea sediment, formed mainly of fossilized shells

globular (glob′yoo lər) *adj.* 1. shaped like a globe or ball; spherical 2. made up of globules —**glob′ularly** *adv.*

globule (glob′yool) *n.* [< L. *globus*, ball] a tiny ball or globe; esp., a drop of liquid

globulin (glob′yoo lin) *n.* [see prec.] any of a group of proteins in animal and vegetable tissue

GLOCKENSPIEL

glockenspiel (glok′ən spēl′) *n.* [G. < *Glocke*, a bell + *Spiel*, play] a percussion instrument with flat metal bars set in a frame, that are struck with small hammers

glomerate (glom′ər it) *adj.* [< L. *glomus*, ball] formed into a rounded mass —**glom′- era′tion** *n.*

gloom (gloom) *vi., vt.* [< ?] to be, become, or make dark, dismal, dejected, etc. —*n.* 1. dimness; obscurity 2. deep sadness; dejection 3. a dark place

gloomy *adj.* -ier, -iest 1. enveloped in darkness or dimness 2. melancholy or sullen 3. causing gloom; depressing —**gloom′ily** *adv.* —**gloom′iness** *n.*

glorify (glôr′ə fī′) *vt.* -fied′, -fy′ing [< L. *gloria*, glory + *facere*, make] 1. to give glory to 2. to exalt in worship 3. to honour 4. to make seem better, larger, etc. —**glo′rifica′tion** *n.* —**glo′rifi′er** *n.*

glorious (glôr′ē əs) *adj.* 1. full of glory; illustrious 2. receiving or deserving glory 3. splendid 4. [Colloq.] very delightful —**glo′riously** *adv.* —**glo′riousness** *n.*

glory (glôr′ē) *n., pl.* -ries [< L. *gloria*] 1. *a)* great honour and admiration *b)* anything bringing this 2. worshipful adoration 3. the condition of highest achievement, prosperity, splendour, etc. 4. heaven or the bliss of heaven 5. . a halo —*vi.* -ried, -rying to exult (with *in*) —**in one's glory** at one's best, happiest, etc.

glory-hole *n.* [Colloq.] any room, cupboard, etc., used for storage, esp. one which is very untidy

Glos. Gloucestershire

gloss[1] (glos) *n.* [prob. < Scand.] 1. the lustre of a polished surface 2. a deceptively pleasant appearance 3. paint with a shiny finish —*vt.* 1. to make lustrous 2. to cover up (an error, etc.) by minimizing (often with *over*) —**gloss′er** *n.*

gloss[2] *n.* [< Gr. *glōssa*, tongue] a note of comment or explanation, as in a footnote —*vt., vi.* to furnish (a text) with glosses —**gloss′er** *n.*

glossary (glos′ə rē) *n., pl.* -ries [< Gr. *glōssa*, tongue] a list of difficult, technical, or foreign terms with definitions or translations, for a particular book, etc.

glossy *adj.* -ier, -iest having a smooth, shiny appearance —*n., pl.* **gloss′ies** [Colloq.] a magazine printed on glossy paper —**gloss′ily** *adv.* —**gloss′iness** *n.*

glottis (glot′is) *n.* [< Gr. *glōtta*, tongue] the opening between the vocal cords in the larynx —**glot′tal** *adj.*

glove (gluv) *n.* [< OE. *glof*] 1. a covering for the hand, with a separate sheath for each finger and the thumb 2. a boxing glove —*vt.* **gloved, glov′ing** to cover as with a glove —**with the gloves off** with no restraint; ruthlessly : said of quarrels, etc.

glover *n.* one who makes or sells gloves

glow (glō) *vi.* [OE. *glowan*] 1. to give off a bright light as a result of great heat 2. to give out a steady light without flame 3. to be or feel hot 4. to be enlivened by emotion 5. to be bright with colour —*n.* 1. a light given off as the result of great heat 2. steady, even light without flame 3. brilliance of colour 4. brightness of skin colour 5. a sensation of warmth and well-being 6. warmth of emotion —**glow′ing** *adj.* —**glow′ingly** *adv.*

glower (glou′ər) *vi.* [prob. < ON.] to stare with sullen anger; scowl —*n.* a sullen, angry stare; scowl

glow-worm (glō′wurm′) *n.* a wingless insect or insect larva that gives off a luminescent light

gloxinia (glok sin′ē ə) *n.* [< B. P. *Gloxin*] a cultivated tropical plant with bell-shaped flowers

glucose (gloo′kōs) *n.* [< Gr. *gleúkos*, sweet wine] a crystalline sugar occurring naturally in fruits, honey, etc.

glue (gloo) *n.* [< LL. *glus*] 1. a sticky substance made from animal skins, bones, etc. and used to stick things together 2. any similar adhesive made from resin, etc. —*vt.* **glued, glu′ing** to make stick as with glue

gluey *adj.* **glu′ier, glu′iest 1.** like glue; sticky **2.** covered with or full of glue

glum (glum) *adj.* **glum′mer, glum′mest** [prob. < ME. *gloum(b)en,* to look morose] gloomy; sullen; morose

glut (glut) *vi.* **glut′ted, glut′ting** [< L. *gluttire,* to swallow] to eat like a glutton —*vt.* **1.** to feed, fill, etc. to excess **2.** to flood (the market) with certain goods so that supply is greater than demand —*n.* **1.** a supply that is greater than the demand **2.** a glutting or being glutted

gluten (glōōt′'n) *n.* [L., glue] a grey, sticky substance found in wheat, etc.; the protein part of flour

glutinous (glōōt′'n əs) *adj.* [< L. *gluten,* glue] gluey; sticky —**glu′tinously** *adv.*

glutton (glut′'n) *n.* [< L. *glutire,* devour] **1.** a person who greedily eats too much **2.** a person with a great capacity for something **3.** an animal of the weasel family: wolverine —**glut′tonous** *adj.*

gluttony *n., pl.* **-tonies** the habit or act of eating too much

glyceride (glis′ər īd′) *n.* an ester of glycerol

glycerin (glis′ər in) *n.* [< Gr. *glykeros,* sweet] *commercial term for* GLYCEROL: also sp. **glyc′erine** (-ēn)

glycerol (glis′ər ol′) *n.* [< prec.] a colourless, syrupy liquid made from fats and oils: used as a solvent, skin lotion, etc., and in explosives, etc.

glycogen (gli′kə jən) *n.* [prec. + -GEN] a starchlike substance produced in animal tissues and changed into sugar as the body needs it —**gly′cogen′ic** (-jen′ik) *adj.*

gm gram(me)(s)

GM 1. General Manager **2.** George Medal

G-man (jē′man′) *n.* [*g(overnment) man*] [U.S. Colloq.] an agent of the Federal Bureau of Investigation

G.M.T. Greenwich Mean Time

gnarled (närld) *adj.* [ult. < ME. *knur,* a knot] knotty and twisted [a *gnarled* tree, *gnarled* hands]: also **gnarl′y**

gnash (nash) *vt., vi.* [prob. < ON.] to grind (the teeth) together, as in anger —*n.* the act of gnashing

gnat (nat) *n.* [OE. *gnæt*] any of a number of small, two-winged insects some of which can bite or sting

gnaw (nô) *vt., vi.* [OE. *gnagen*] **1.** to bite and wear away bit by bit **2.** to consume; corrode **3.** to torment, as by pain, fear, etc. —**gnaw′ing** *n., adj.*

gneiss (nīs) *n.* [< OHG. *gneisto,* spark] a granitelike rock formed of layers of feldspar, quartz, mica, etc.

gnome (nōm) *n.* [< Gr. *gnōmē,* thought] **1.** *Folklore* a dwarf supposed to dwell in the earth and guard its treasures **2.** [Colloq.] an influential international financier —**gnom′ish** *adj.*

gnomic (nō′mik) *adj.* [< Gr. *gnōmē,* thought] wise and pithy; full of aphorisms —**gno′mically** *adv.*

gnomon (nō′mon) *n.* [L. < Gr. *gignōskein,* know] a column, pin, etc. on a sundial, that casts a shadow indicating the time of day —**gnomon′ic** *adj.*

gnostic (nos′tik) *adj.* [< Gr. *gnōsis,* knowledge] **1.** of or having knowledge **2.** [G-] of the Gnostics or Gnosticism —*n.* [G-] a believer in Gnosticism

Gnosticism (nos′tə siz′m) *n.* a system of belief combining ideas derived from Greek philosophy, Oriental mysticism, and, ultimately, Christianity

GNP gross national product

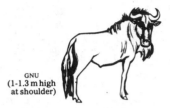

GNU
(1-1.3 m high
at shoulder)

gnu (nōō) *n.* [< Bushman *nqu*] either of two heavily built S African antelopes; wildebeest

go (gō) *vi.* **went, gone, go′ing** [OE. *gan*] **1.** to move along; travel; proceed **2.** to be in operation; work [the clock won't *go*] **3.** to gesture, act, etc., as specified **4.** to result; turn out [the war *went* badly] **5.** to pass **6.** to be in a certain state [he *goes* in rags] **7.** to become [to *go* mad] **8.** to be expressed, sung, etc. [as the saying *goes*] **9.** to be in harmony; fit in **10.** to tend; help [facts that *go* to prove a case] **11.** to have force, acceptance, etc. [what he says *goes*] **12.** to depart; pass away **13.** to die **14.** to be removed **15.** to fail; give way [his sight is *going*] **16.** to be given [the prize *goes* to you] **17.** to be sold [it *went* for £10] **18.** to extend; reach **19.** to turn to or participate in [to *go* to college] **20.** to pass (*through*), fit (*into*), etc. **21.** to be a divisor (*into*) **22.** to last **23.** to continue (unpunished, etc.) **24.** to have a regular place [pencils *go* on the desk] —*vt.* **1.** *a)* to bet *b)* to bid at cards **2.** [Colloq.] to furnish (bail) —*n., pl.* **goes 1.** a success **2.** [Colloq.] energy **3.** [Colloq.] an agreement [is it a *go*?] **4.** [Colloq.] a try —*adj.* [Slang] functioning properly —**as people** (or **things**) **go** in comparison with others —**go about 1.** to be busy at **2.** to circulate **3.** *Naut.* to change direction —**go after** [Colloq.] to try to catch or get —**go against** to be in opposition to —**go along with 1.** to agree **2.** to accompany —**go back on** [Colloq.] to break (a promise, etc.) —**go by 1.** to pass **2.** to be guided by **3.** to be known by (the name of) —**go down 1.** to sink; set **2.** to suffer defeat **3.** to be perpetuated in history **4.** to leave university —**go down with** to catch (a disease) —**go for 1.** to be taken as **2.** to try to get **3.** [Colloq.] to attack **4.** [Colloq.] to be attracted by —**go hard**

with to cause trouble to —**go in for** [Colloq.] to engage in —**go into** 1. to inquire into 2. to take up as a study —**go off** 1. to leave, esp. suddenly 2. to explode 3. to deteriorate 4. to happen 5. to lessen *[the pain's going off]* 6. [Colloq.] to develop a dislike of —**go on** 1. to continue 2. to happen —**go out** 1. to be extinguished, become outdated, etc. 2. to attend social affairs, the theatre, etc. 3. to go on strike 4. to be transmitted on radio, etc. —**go over** 1. to examine thoroughly 2. to review 3. to be received in a specified manner —**go round** 1. to circulate 2. to be sufficient *[enough to go round]* 3. to be long enough to surround —**go slow** to work slowly or deliberately curtail output as part of an industrial campaign —**go through** 1. to perform 2. to endure; experience 3. to search 4. to get acceptance 5. to spend —**go through with** to complete —**go to the country** to hold a general election —**go under** to fail —**go up** to rise in price, etc.; increase —**go without** to do without —**let oneself go** 1. to be unrestrained in emotion, etc. 2. to stop taking care of one's appearance —**no go** [Colloq.] not possible —**on the go** [Colloq.] in constant motion or action

goad (gōd) *n.* [OE. *gad*] 1. a sharp-pointed stick for driving oxen 2. any driving impulse; spur —*vt.* to drive as with a goad; prod into action

go-ahead *adj.* enterprising; pushing —*n.* permission or a signal to proceed: usually with *the*

goal (gōl) *n.* [ME. *gol*, boundary] 1. the place where a race, etc. is ended 2. an end that one strives to attain 3. *Sport a)* the line, net, etc. over or into which the ball must go to score *b)* the act of so scoring *c)* the score made

goalkeeper *n.* *Sport* a player stationed at a goal to prevent the ball from entering it: also **goal'ie**

goal line *Sport* the line marking each end of the pitch, on which the goals stand

goat (gōt) *n.* [OE. *gat*] 1. a cud-chewing mammal with hollow horns 2. a lecherous man 3. [Colloq.] a stupid person —[G-] the constellation Capricorn —**get one's goat** [Colloq.] to annoy one —**goat'-ish** *adj.*

goatee (gō tē′) *n.* a pointed beard on a man's chin

goatherd *n.* one who herds goats

goatskin *n.* 1. the skin of a goat 2. leather made from this 3. a container for wine, etc., made of this leather

goatsucker *n.* any of various large-mouthed, nocturnal birds that feed on insects, as the nightjar

gob[1] (gob) *n.* [see GOBBET] a soft lump or mass

gob[2] *n.* [< ?] [Slang] the mouth

gobbet (gob′it) *n.* [OFr. *gobet*, mouthful]

1. [Archaic] a fragment or bit, esp. of raw flesh 2. a literary extract

gobble[1] (gob′'l) *n.* [echoic] the throaty sound made by a male turkey —*vi.* **-bled, -bling** to make this sound

gobble[2] *vt., vi.* **-bled, -bling** [prob. < OFr. *gobe*, mouthful] to eat quickly

gobbledygook (gob′'l dē gook′) *n.* [Slang] pompous and wordy talk or writing: also **gob'bledegook'**

gobbler *n.* a male turkey

Gobelin (gō′bə lin) *adj.* of or like a kind of tapestry made at the Gobelin works in Paris —*n.* a Gobelin tapestry

go-between (gō′bi twēn′) *n.* one who makes arrangements between two sides; intermediary

goblet (gob′lit) *n.* [< OFr. *gobel*] a drinking glass with a base and stem

goblin (gob′lin) *n.* [< ML. *gobelinus*] *Folklore* an evil or mischievous sprite, ugly or misshapen in form

goby (gō′bē) *n.* [< Gr. *kōbios*] a small, spiny-finned fish: the ventral fins are modified into a suction disc

go-by (gō′bī′) *n.* [Colloq.] an intentional disregard: chiefly in **give** (or **get**) **the go-by** to slight (or be slighted)

go-cart *n.* *same as* KART

god (god) *n.* [OE.] 1. any of various beings conceived of as supernatural, immortal, and having power over people and nature; deity, esp. a male one 2. an idol 3. a person or thing deified or excessively honoured 4. [*pl.*] the gallery of a theatre —[G-] in monotheistic religions, the creator and ruler of the universe —**on the knees** (or **in the lap**) **of the gods** beyond human control —**god'-dess** *n. fem.* —**god'like** *adj.*

godchild *n.* the person for whom a godparent is sponsor

goddaughter *n.* a female godchild

godetia (gō dē′sha) *n.* [< C.H. *Godet*] a plant cultivated for its showy flowers

godfather *n.* 1. a male godparent 2. [Chiefly U.S. Slang] a head of a criminal enterprise

God-fearing *adj.* [*occas.* g-] devout; pious

Godforsaken *adj.* [*occas.* g-] desolate; forlorn

godhead *n.* 1. godhood 2. [G-] God

godless *adj.* 1. denying the existence of God; irreligious 2. wicked —**god'lessly** *adv.* —**god'lessness** *n.*

godly *adj.* **-lier, -liest** pious; devout; religious

godmother *n.* a female godparent

godown (gō′doun′) *n.* [Anglo-Ind. < Malay *gedong*] in the Far East, a warehouse

godparent (god′pāar′ənt) *n.* a person who sponsors a child and assumes responsibility for its faith

God's acre a burial ground, esp. in a churchyard

godsend *n.* anything unexpected and

needed or desired that comes at the opportune moment, as if sent by God

godson n. a male godchild

Godspeed n. [< *God speed you*] success; good fortune: a wish made for travellers

godwit (god′wit) n. [? echoic] a brownish wading bird, with a long bill that curves up at the tip

goer (gō′ər) n. one that goes

goffer (gŏf′ər) vt. [Fr. *gaufrer*, crimp] to pleat, crimp, or flute (cloth, paper, etc.) —n. the act of pleating or fluting: also **gof′-fering**

go-getter (gō′get′ər) n. [Colloq.] an enterprising and aggressive person

gogga (khokh′ə) n. [< Hottentot *xoxon*, insects] [S Afr. Colloq.] any small creature that crawls or flies, esp. an insect; creepy-crawly

goggle (gog′'l) vi. -gled, -gling [ME. *gogelen*] 1. to stare with bulging eyes 2. to bulge or roll: said of the eyes —n. 1. a staring with bulging eyes 2. [pl.] large spectacles to protect the eyes against dust, water, etc. —adj. bulging: said of the eyes —**gog′gle-eyed**′ adj.

gogglebox n. [Slang] a television set

go-go dancer (gō′gō′) adj. [< Fr. *à gogo*, ad lib.] an entertainer who performs lively erotic dances in nightclubs, etc.

Goidelic (goi del′ik) adj. [< OIr. *Góidel*] of the Gaels —n. *see* CELTIC

going (gō′in) n. 1. a departure 2. the condition of the ground as it affects travelling 3. circumstances affecting progress —adj. 1. moving; working 2. operating successfully [a *going* concern] 3. in existence or available 4. current —**be going to** to be intending to —**get going** [Colloq.] to start —**going on** [Colloq.] nearing (a specified time) —**going strong** continuing to function strongly, successfully, etc.

going-over n. [Colloq.] 1. an inspection, esp. a thorough one 2. a severe scolding or beating

goings-on n.pl. [Colloq.] actions or events, esp. when regarded with disapproval

goitre (goit′ər) n. [< L. *guttur*, throat] an enlarged thyroid gland, often visible as a swelling in the neck

gold (gōld) n. [OE.] 1. a heavy, yellow, metallic chemical element: it is a precious metal and is used in coins, jewellery, etc.: symbol, Au 2. money; riches 3. bright yellow —adj. 1. of, made of, or like gold 2. having the colour of gold

gold bloc the states which adhere to the GOLD STANDARD

goldcrest n. a small warbler with a yellow crown

gold digger 1. one who digs for gold 2. [Slang] a woman who tries to get money from her men friends

gold dust gold in very small bits or as a powder

golden adj. 1. of or containing gold 2.

bright yellow 3. precious; excellent 4. prosperous and joyful 5. marking the 50th anniversary —**gold′enness** n.

golden age a period of great progress, culture, etc.

golden eagle a large, strong eagle found in mountainous districts of the N Hemisphere

Golden Fleece Gr. Myth. the fleece of gold guarded by a dragon until captured by Jason

golden hamster *see* HAMSTER

golden handshake [Colloq.] money given to an employee on retirement or for loss of employment

golden mean the safe, prudent way between extremes

golden retriever a breed of dog with a golden coat

goldenrod n. a plant with long stalks bearing clusters of small, yellow flowers

golden rule 1. the precept that one should do as one would be done by 2. any important principle

golden syrup a light golden-coloured treacle used to flavour puddings, cakes, etc.

golden wedding a 50th wedding anniversary

goldfinch n. a songbird with yellow-streaked wings

goldfish n. a small, golden-yellow fish of the carp family, often kept in fishbowls

gold foil gold beaten into thin sheets slightly thicker than gold leaf —**gold′-foil**′ adj.

gold leaf gold beaten into very thin sheets, used for gilding —**gold′-leaf**′ adj.

gold medal a medal awarded to an entrant who is placed first in a competition

gold mine 1. a place where gold is mined 2. any source of wealth, profit, etc.

gold plate tableware made of gold

gold rush a rush of people to territory where gold has recently been discovered

goldsmith n. a skilled worker in gold

gold standard a monetary standard in which the basic unit equals a specified quantity of gold

golf (golf) n. [< ?] an outdoor game played on a golf course with a small, hard ball and a set of clubs, the object being to hit the ball into each of 9 or 18 holes in turn, with the fewest possible strokes —vi. to play golf —**golf′er** n.

golf club 1. any of a set of clubs used in golf 2. an organization operating a golf course

golf course (or **links**) a tract of land for playing golf

Goliath (gə lī′əth) n. [see 1 Samuel 17] a giant

golliwog (gol′ē wog′) n. [< ?] a soft doll with a black face, usually made of cloth

golly (gol′ē) interj. an exclamation of surprise, etc.

goloshes (gə losh′iz) n. var. of GALOSHES

-gon (gon, gən) [< Gr. *gōnia*, angle] a combining form meaning a figure having (a specified number of) angles

gonad (gō′nad) n. [< Gr. *gonē*, seed]

GONDOLA

an animal organ producing reproductive cells; ovary or testis

gondola (gon′də lə) *n.* [It.] **1.** a long, narrow boat used on the canals of Venice **2.** the car of an airship or balloon

gondolier (gon′də lēər′) *n.* a man who propels a gondola

gone (gon) *pp. of* GO —*adj.* **1.** moved away **2.** ruined **3.** lost **4.** dead **5.** consumed **6.** ago; past —**far gone** deeply involved —**gone on** [Colloq.] in love with

goner *n.* [Colloq.] one seemingly sure to die soon, be ruined, etc.

gonfalon (gon′fə lən) *n.* [< Frank. *gund*, battle + *fano*, banner] a flag hanging from a crosspiece and ending in streamers —**gon′falonier** *n.*

gong (goŋ) *n.* [Malay: echoic] a slightly convex metallic disc that gives a loud, resonant tone when struck

gonorrhoea (gon′ə rē′ə) *n.* [< Gr. *gonos*, semen + *rhein*, flow] a venereal disease marked by inflammation of the genital organs

goo (go͞o) *n.* [Slang] **1.** anything sticky, as glue **2.** anything sticky and sweet **3.** sentimentality

good (good) *adj.* **bet′ter, best** [OE. *god*] **1.** suitable to a purpose **2.** beneficial [*good exercise*] **3.** unspoiled [*good eggs*] **4.** valid; genuine [*good money*] **5.** healthy **6.** financially sound **7.** honourable; worthy [*one's good name*] **8.** enjoyable, happy, etc. **9.** dependable; reliable **10.** thorough [*did a good job*] **11.** not for everyday use [*her good china*] **12.** virtuous, pious, kind, generous, etc. **13.** correct [*good manners*] **14.** able; skilled **15.** considerable [*a good many*] **16.** complete [*a good six hours*] —*n.* **1.** something good; specif., *a*) worth; virtue *b*) benefit; advantage *c*) something desirable See also GOODS —*interj.* an exclamation of satisfaction, pleasure, etc. —**a good question** one which is difficult to answer —**as good as** virtually —**for good (and all)** permanently —**good and** [Colloq.] very or altogether —**good for 1.** able to endure or be used for (a period of time) **2.** worth **3.** able to pay or give —**good on you** [Aust. & N.Z.] well-done —**make good 1.** to repay or replace **2.** to fulfil **3.** to succeed —**to the good** as a profit or advantage

Good Book the Bible (usually with *the*)

goodbye, good-bye *interj., n., pl.* **-byes** [contr. of *God be with ye*] farewell: term used in parting

good day a salutation of greeting or farewell

good-for-nothing *adj.* useless or worthless —*n.* such a person

Good Friday the Friday before Easter Sunday, commemorating the crucifixion of Jesus

good-hearted *adj.* kind and generous

good humour a cheerful, agreeable, or pleasant mood —**good′-hu′moured** *adj.* —**good′-hu′mouredly** *adv.*

goodish *adj.* fairly good or fairly large

good looks attractive appearance —**good′-look′ing** *adj.*

goodly *adj.* **-lier, -liest 1.** of good appearance or quality **2.** rather large; ample —**good′liness** *n.*

good morning a salutation of greeting or farewell used in the morning

good nature a pleasant, agreeable, or kindly disposition —**good′-na′tured** *adj.* —**good′-na′turedly** *adv.*

goodness *n.* the state or quality of being good; virtue, kindness, etc. —*interj.* an exclamation of surprise

good night a salutation of parting used at night

goods *n.pl.* **1.** movable personal property **2.** merchandise; wares **3.** freight, esp. rail freight —**deliver the goods** [Colloq.] to do or produce the thing required —**get (or have) the goods on** [Slang] to discover (or know) something incriminating about

good Samaritan one who pities and unselfishly helps another or others: Luke 10:30-37

Good Shepherd an epithet for JESUS: John 10:11

good-tempered *adj.* not easily angered or annoyed —**good′-tem′peredly** *adv.*

good turn a good deed; friendly, helpful act

good will 1. a kindly attitude **2.** willingness **3.** the value of a business in patronage, reputation, etc., beyond its tangible assets Also **good′will′** *n.*

goody *n., pl.* **good′ies** [Colloq.] **1.** something good to eat, as a sweet **2.** [Colloq.] a hero —*interj.* a child's exclamation of delight

goody-goody *adj.* [Colloq.] moral or pious in a smug way —*n.* [Colloq.] a goody-goody person

gooey (go͞o′ē) *adj.* **goo′ier, goo′iest** [Colloq.] **1.** sticky **2.** sticky and sweet **3.** sentimental

goof (go͞of) *n.* [prob. ult. < It. *goffo*, clumsy] [Slang] **1.** a stupid person **2.** a mistake —*vt., vi.* [Slang] to bungle; botch —**goof′y** *adj.*

googly (go͞o′glē) *n.* [< ?] *Cricket* a ball which changes direction on the bounce in an unexpected way

goon (go͞on) *n.* [Slang] [< ?] **1.** one who is awkward, grotesque, stupid, etc. **2.** a ruffian or thug

goosander (go͞o san′dər) *n.* [prob. < GOOSE] a large, fish-eating, diving duck with a serrated red bill

goose (go͞os) *n., pl.* **geese**; for 4 **goos′-es** [OE. *gos*] **1.** a long-necked, web-footed bird like a duck but larger, esp. the female **2.** its flesh, used for food **3.** a silly person **4.** a tailor's pressing iron, with a long, curved handle —**cook one's goose** [Colloq.] to spoil one's chances —**the goose that lays the golden eggs** the source of one's present and future benefits

gooseberry (gōōz′bər ē) n., pl. **-ries 1.** a small, round, sour berry **2.** the shrub it grows on —**play gooseberry** to be an unwanted third person

goose flesh (or **pimples**) a roughened condition of the skin caused by cold, fear, etc.

goosegog (gōōz′gog) n. [Colloq.] a gooseberry

goose step a marching step in which the legs are raised high and kept unbent —**goose′-step′** vi.

gopher (gō′fər) n. [< ? Fr. gaufre, honeycomb] **1.** a burrowing rodent with wide cheek pouches **2.** a striped ground squirrel of N American prairies

Gordian knot (gôr′dē ən) Gr. Legend a knot tied by King Gordius of Phrygia: Alexander the Great cut the knot with his sword —**cut the Gordian knot** to find a quick, bold solution for a problem

gore[1] (gôr) n. [OE. gor, filth] blood shed from a wound; esp., clotted blood

gore[2] vt. gored, gor′ing [< OE. gar, spear] to pierce as with a horn or tusk

gore[3] n. [OE. gara, corner < gar, spear] a tapering piece of cloth in a skirt, sail, etc. to give it fullness —vt. gored, gor′-ing to make or insert a gore or gores in

gorge (gôrj) n. [< L. gurges, whirlpool] **1.** a deep, narrow pass between steep heights **2.** the food filling the stomach **3.** the throat —vi., vt. gorged, gorg′ing to stuff (oneself) with food —**make one's gorge rise** to make one disgusted, angry, etc.

gorgeous (gôr′jəs) adj. [< OFr. gorgias] **1.** brilliantly coloured **2.** [Slang] beautiful, delightful, etc. —**gor′geously** adv.

gorgon (gôr′gən) n. [from the three sisters in Gr. Myth., so horrible that the beholder was turned to stone] any ugly, terrifying, or repulsive woman

Gorgonzola (gôr′gən zō′lə) n. [< Gorgonzola, in Italy] a white Italian cheese with blue-green veins

gorilla (gə ril′ə) n. [< W Afr.] **1.** the largest and most powerful manlike ape, native to Africa **2.** [Slang] a person regarded as like a gorilla in strength, etc.

gormandize (gôr′mən dīz′) vi., vt. -ized′, -iz′ing [< Fr. gourmandise, gluttony] to eat or devour like a glutton

gormless (gôrm′lis) adj. [< ME. gome, care] [Colloq.] slowwitted; stupid

gorse (gôrs) n. [OE. gorst] furze —**gors′y** adj.

gory (gôr′ē) adj. -ier, -iest **1.** full of bloodshed **2.** covered with gore; bloody —**gor′iness** n.

gosh (gosh) interj. an exclamation of surprise, etc.

goshawk (gos′hôk′) n. [< OE.: see GOOSE & HAWK[1]] a large, swift hawk with short wings

gosling (goz′liŋ) n. [< ON.] a young goose

go-slow (gō′slō′) n. a deliberate slackening of the rate of production by workers as a tactic in industrial conflict

gospel (gos′p'l) n. [OE. gōdspel, good news] **1.** [often G-] the teachings of Jesus and the Apostles **2.** [G-] any of the first four books of the New Testament (Matthew, Mark, Luke, or John) **3.** anything regarded as the absolute truth: also **gospel truth 4.** any doctrine widely maintained —adj. of the gospel

gossamer (gos′ə mər) n. [ME. gosesomer, goose summer] **1.** a filmy cobweb on bushes, etc. **2.** a very thin, filmy cloth —adj. light, thin, and filmy

gossip (gos′ip) n. [< OE. godsibbe, godparent] **1.** one who chatters or repeats idle talk, esp. about others' private affairs **2.** such talk or rumours —vi. to indulge in idle talk —**gos′siper** n. —**gos′sipy** adj.

gossip column a part of a newspaper which is devoted to gossip about well-known people

got (got) pt. & pp. of GET

Goth (goth) n. an uncouth, uncivilized person: after the Germanic people that invaded the Roman Empire in the 3rd-5th cent. A.D.

Gothic adj. **1.** of the Goths or their language **2.** designating or of a style of architecture developed in W Europe from the 12th to 16th cent., with flying buttresses, pointed arches, etc. **3.** barbarous **4.** of a style of literature using a macabre atmosphere, etc., to suggest horror —n. **1.** the language of the Goths **2.** Gothic style in architecture **3.** Printing [often g-] a plain type face —**Goth′ically** adv.

gotten (got′'n) Archaic and U.S. pp. of GET

gouache (gōō äsh′) n. [Fr. < It. < L. aqua, water] **1.** a way of painting with opaque water colours mixed with gum **2.** such a pigment or a painting made thus

Gouda (cheese) (gou′də) [< Gouda, in Netherlands] a mild cheese, usually coated with wax

gouge (gouj) n. [< LL. gulbia] a chisel for cutting grooves or holes in wood —vt. gouged, goug′ing **1.** to make grooves or holes in as with a gouge **2.** in fighting, to push one's thumb into the eye of

goulash (gōō′lash) n. [< Hung. gulyás, herdsman] a stew of beef or veal seasoned with paprika: also **Hungarian goulash**

gourd (gooərd) n. [< L. cucurbita] **1.** any of various trailing or climbing plants, as the melon **2.** the ornamental, inedible fruit of certain related plants **3.** the dried, hollowed-out shell of such a fruit, used as a dipper, etc.

gourmand (gooər′mənd) n. [< OFr.] a person who likes good food and drink, sometimes to excess

gourmandise n. [Fr.] a love of and taste for good food

gourmet (gooər′mā) n. [< OFr., wine

taster] one who likes and is an excellent judge of fine foods and drinks

gout (gout) *n.* [< L. *gutta*, drop] a disease characterized by swelling and great pain, esp. in the big toe —**gout'ily** *adv.* —**gout'iness** *n.* —**gout'y** *adj.*

gov., Gov. 1. government 2. governor

govern (guv'ərn) *vt.* [< Gr. *kybernan*, steer] 1. to rule, control, manage, etc. 2. to influence the action or conduct of 3. to hold in check; curb 4. to be a rule or law for 5. *Gram.* to require (a word) to be in a particular case or mood —*vi.* to govern someone or something; rule —**gov'ernable** *adj.*

governance *n.* control or rule

governess *n.* a woman employed in a private home to train and teach the children

government (guv'ər mənt) *n.* 1. the exercise of authority over a state, district, group, etc.; control; rule 2. an established system of political administration by which a nation, state, etc. is governed 3. all the people that administer the affairs of a nation 4. [*often* G-] the administrative branch of government of a particular nation —**gov'ernmen'tal** *adj.*

governor (guv'ə nər) *n.* 1. a person who governs; esp., *a)* one appointed to govern a province, etc. *b)* the representative of the Crown in a Commonwealth country *c)* the elected head of any state of the U.S. 2. the administrator in charge of a prison 3. a device automatically controlling the speed of an engine 4. [Colloq.] one's father or employer —**gov'ernorship'** *n.*

governor general *pl.* **governors general, governor generals** 1. the representative of the Crown in a dominion of the Commonwealth 2. a governor with deputy governers under him Also **gov'ernorgen'eral** *n.*

govt., Govt. government

gown (goun) *n.* [< LL. *gunna*] 1. a woman's long, usually formal dress 2. a surgeon's smock 3. a long, flowing robe worn by clergymen, professors, etc. 4. the members of a college, etc. collectively

goy (goi) *n., pl.* **goy'im, goys** [< Heb. *gōi*, tribe] a Jewish name for a person who is not a Jew

G.P., g.p. general practitioner

GPO, G.P.O. General Post Office

Gr. 1. Grecian 2. Greece 3. Greek

gr. 1. grain(s) 2. gram(me)(s) 3. gross

grab (grab) *vt.* **grabbed, grab'bing** [prob. < MDu. *grabben*] 1. to snatch suddenly 2. to get by unscrupulous methods 3. [Slang] to impress —*vi.* to grab or try to grab something (often with *for, at,* etc.) —*n.* 1. a grabbing 2. a device for clutching something to be hoisted —**grab'ber** *n.*

grace (grās) *n.* [< L. *gratus*, pleasing] 1. beauty or charm of form, movement, or expression 2. an attractive quality, manner, etc. 3. decency 4. good will; favour 5. a delay granted beyond the date set for the payment of an obligation 6. a short prayer of thanks for a meal

7. [G-] a title of an archbishop, duke, or duchess 8. *Theol.* the unmerited love and favour of God towards man —*vt.* **graced, grac'ing** 1. to give or add grace or graces to 2. to dignify —**in the good** (or **bad**) **graces of** in favour (or disfavour) with —**with good** (or **bad**) **grace** in a willing (or unwilling) way

grace-and-favour *adj.* granted rent-free by the sovereign of Britain [a *grace-and-favour* house]

graceful *adj.* having grace (sense 1) —**grace'fully** *adv.* —**grace'fulness** *n.*

graceless *adj.* 1. lacking any sense of what is proper 2. clumsy —**grace'lessly** *adv.* —**grace'lessness** *n.*

grace note *Music* a merely ornamental note

Graces *Gr. Myth.* three sister goddesses who controlled pleasure, charm, elegance, and beauty

gracious (grā'shəs) *adj.* 1. having or showing kindness, courtesy, charm, etc. 2. compassionate 3. polite to those held to be inferiors 4. marked by luxury, ease, etc. [*gracious* living] —*interj.* an expression of surprise —**gra'ciously** *adv.* —**gra'ciousness** *n.*

gradation (grā dā'shən) *n.* 1. an arranging in grades, stages, or steps 2. a gradual change by stages 3. a step, stage, or degree in a graded series —**gradate'** *vt.,* *vi.* —**grada'tional** *adj.* —**grada'tionally** *adv.*

grade (grād) *n.* [< L. *gradus*, a step] 1. any of the stages in a systematic progression 2. *a)* a degree in a scale of quality, rank, etc. *b)* a group of the same rank, merit, etc. 3. a mark on an examination, in a school course, etc. —*vt.* **grad'ed, grad'ing** 1. to classify by grades of quality, rank, etc. 2. to give a grade (sense 3) to —*vi.* to change by gradation —**make the grade** to succeed

gradient (grā'dē ənt) *adj.* [< L. *gradi,* to step] ascending or descending with a uniform slope —*n.* 1. a slope, as of a road 2. the degree of such slope

gradual (graj'oo wəl) *adj.* [see GRADE] taking place little by little —*n.* *Eccles.* a set of verses, esp. from the Psalms, following the Epistle at Mass —**grad'ually** *adv.* —**grad'ualness** *n.*

gradualism *n.* the principle of seeking only gradual social or political change —**grad'ualist** *n., adj.*

graduate (grad'yoo wət; *for v.* -wāt') *n.* [see GRADE] a person who has completed a course of study at a university or college and has received a degree or diploma —*vt.* -at'ed, -at'ing 1. to mark with degrees for measuring 2. to grade by size, quality, etc. —*vi.* 1. to become a graduate of a university, etc. 2. to change by degrees —*adj.* 1. graduated from a university 2. of or for studies leading to degrees above the bachelor's

graduation (gra'dyoo wā'shən) *n.* 1. a graduating or being graduated from a university 2. the ceremony connected with this

Graeco- *a combining form meaning* **1.** Greek or Greeks **2.** Greek and or Greece and
Graeco-Roman (grē′kō rō′mən) *adj.* of or influenced by both Greece and Rome
graffiti (grə fēt′ō) *n.,* *pl.* **-fi′ti** [It., scribbling] an inscription or drawing scribbled on a wall, etc.
graft (gräft) *n.* [< Gr. *grapheion,* stylus] **1.** a shoot or bud of a plant or tree inserted into another where it grows permanently **2.** the inserting of such a shoot **3.** [Chiefly U.S.] a taking advantage of one's position to gain money, etc. **4.** *Surgery* a piece of skin, bone, etc. transplanted from one body, or place on a body, to another **5.** [Slang] work —*vt.* **1.** to insert as a graft **2.** to join as if by grafting **3.** *Surgery* to transplant as a graft —*vi.* **1.** to be grafted **2.** [Chiefly U.S.] to obtain money, etc. by graft —**graft′er** *n.*
Grail (grāl) [< ML. *gradalis,* cup] *Medieval Legend* the cup or platter used by Jesus at the Last Supper: also called **Holy Grail**
grain (grān) *n.* [< L. *granum*] **1.** a small, hard seed or seedlike fruit, esp. of a cereal plant, as wheat, rice, etc. **2.** cereal plants **3.** a tiny, solid particle, as of salt or sand **4.** a tiny bit **5.** the smallest unit in certain systems of weights **6.** *a)* the arrangement of fibres or particles of wood, leather, etc. *b)* the markings or texture due to this **7.** disposition; nature —*vt.* **1.** to form into grains; granulate **2.** to paint in imitation of the grain of wood, marble, etc. —**against the** (or **one's**) **grain** contrary to one's feelings, nature, etc. —**grained** *adj.*
grallatorial (gral′ə tôr′ē əl) *adj.* [L. *grallator,* stilt-walker] of long-legged wading birds
gram, gramme (gram) *n.* [< Gr. *gramma,* a small weight] the basic unit of weight in the metric system, equal to one thousandth of a kilogram
-gram (gram) [Gr.] *a combining form meaning* something written or recorded [*telegram*]
gram. **1.** grammar **2.** grammatical
gramineous (grə min′ē əs) *adj.* [< L. *gramen,* grass] of or like grass; grassy
graminivorous (gram′ə niv′ər əs) *adj.* [< L. *gramen,* grass + -VOROUS] feeding on grasses; grass-eating
grammar (gram′ər) *n.* [< Gr. *gramma,* writing] **1.** language study dealing with word forms and word order in sentences **2.** a body of rules for speaking or writing a given language **3.** a book of such rules **4.** one's manner of speaking or writing, as judged by rules
grammarian (grə mãar′ē ən) *n.* a specialist in grammar
grammar school **1.** a secondary school providing an academic education **2.** orig. an endowed secondary school teaching Latin and Greek
grammatical (grə mat′ik′l) *adj.* **1.** of grammar **2.** conforming to the rules of grammar
gramophone (gram′ə fōn′) *n.* [<

phonogram] an instrument for reproducing sound that has been transcribed in a special groove on a disc —**gram′-ophon′ic** *adj.*
grampus (gram′pəs) *n.,* *pl.* **-puses** [< L. *crassus,* fat + *piscis,* fish] **1.** a small, black, fierce whale related to the dolphin **2.** [Colloq.] a person who is breathing hard
gran (gran) *n.* [Colloq.] grandmother
granary (gran′ər ē) *n.,* *pl.* **-ries** [< L. *granum,* grain] a building for storing threshed grain
grand (grand) *adj.* [< L. *grandis,* large] **1.** imposing in size, beauty, and extent **2.** distinguished; illustrious **3.** pretentious **4.** lofty and dignified **5.** overall [the *grand* total] **6.** [Colloq.] excellent **7.** most important; main [the *grand* ballroom] **8.** higher in rank than others —*n.* a grand piano —**grand′ly** *adv.*
grand- *a combining form meaning* of the generation older (or younger) than [*grandfather, grandson*]
grandam (gran′dam) *n.* [see GRAND & DAME] [Archaic] **1.** a grandmother **2.** an old woman
grandchild (gran′chīld) *n.* a child of one's son or daughter
granddad, grand-dad, grandad *n.* [Colloq.] grandfather
granddaughter *n.* a daughter of one's son or daughter
grand duke **1.** the sovereign ruler of a territory (**grand duchy**), ranking just below a king **2.** in czarist Russia, a prince of the royal family —**grand duchess**
grande dame (gränd däm) [Fr., great lady] a woman, esp. an older one, of great dignity or prestige
grandee (gran dē′) *n.* [Sp. & Port.: see GRAND] **1.** a Spanish or Portuguese nobleman of the highest rank **2.** a man of high rank
grandeur (gran′jər) *n.* [see GRAND] **1.** splendour; magnificence **2.** dignity; nobility
grandfather *n.* the father of one's father or mother
grandfather clock a long-pendulum clock in a tall free-standing wooden case
grandiloquent (gran dil′ə kwənt) *adj.* [< L. *grandis,* grand + *loqui,* speak] using pompous, bombastic words —**grandil′o-quence** *n.*
grandiose (gran′dē ōs′) *adj.* [< L. *grandis,* great] **1.** having grandeur; imposing **2.** pompous and showy —**gran′-diose′ly** *adv.* —**gran′dios′ity** (-os′ə tē) *n.*
grand jury *Law* in the U.S., and formerly in Britain, a jury that investigates accusations against persons charged with crime and indicts them for trial if there is sufficient evidence
grandma (gran′mä) *n.* [Colloq.] grandmother
grand mal (gran mäl′) [Fr., great ailment] a type of epilepsy with convulsions and loss of consciousness
grandmother *n.* (gran′muth′ər) the mother of one's father or mother

Grand National an annual steeplechase run at Aintree, Liverpool

grand opera opera, generally on a serious theme, in which the whole text is set to music

grandpa *n.* [Colloq.] grandfather

grandparent *n.* a grandfather or grandmother

grand piano a large piano with strings set horizontally

Grand Prix (grän prē´) [Fr., great prize] any of various international formula motor races

grandsire (gran´sīər) *n.* [Archaic] 1. a grandfather 2. a male ancestor

grandson *n.* a son of one's son or daughter

grandstand *n.* the main seating structure for spectators at a sporting event, etc.

grand tour a tour of continental Europe

grange (grānj) *n.* [< L. *granum*, grain] a farm with its dwelling house, barns, etc.

granite (gran´it) *n.* [< It. < L. *granum*, grain] a very hard, crystalline rock consisting of feldspar and quartz

granivorous (grə niv´ər əs) *adj.* [< L. *granum*, grain + -VOROUS] feeding on grain and seeds

granny, grannie (gran´ē) *n.*, *pl.* **-nies** [Colloq.] 1. a grandmother 2. an old woman

granny knot a knot like a reef knot but with the ends crossed the wrong way: also **granny's knot**

grant (gränt) *vt.* [< L. *credere*, believe] 1. to give (what is requested, as permission, etc.) 2. to give or transfer according to legal procedure 3. to admit as true —*n.* something granted, as money to an individual or organization for a specific purpose —**take for granted** to accept as a matter of course —**grant´er**, *Law* **grant´or** *n.*

Granth (grunt) *n.* [< Hindi < Sans. *grantha*, tying together, book] the sacred scripture of the Sikhs

grant-in-aid *n.*, *pl.* **grants-in-aid** a grant of funds, as by a foundation, to support a specific programme

granular (gran´yoo lər) *adj.* 1. like, containing, or consisting of grains or granules 2. having a grainy surface —**gran´ular´ity** (-lar´ə tē) *n.* —**gran´ularly** *adv.*

granulate *vt.*, *vi.* **-lat´ed, -lat´ing** to form into grains or granules —**gran´ula´tion** *n.* —**gran´ula´tor** *n.*

granule (gran´yōōl) *n.* [< L. *granum*, a grain] 1. a small grain 2. a small, grainlike particle or spot

grape (grāp) *n.* [< OFr. *graper*, gather with a hook] 1. a small, round, juicy berry, growing in clusters on woody vines 2. a dark purplish red

grapefruit *n.* a large, round, edible citrus fruit with a pale-yellow rind and a somewhat sour, juicy pulp

grape hyacinth a small plant with clusters of blue flowers resembling grapes

grapeshot *n.* a cluster of small iron balls formerly fired as a cannon charge

grapevine *n.* 1. a woody vine bearing grapes 2. a secret means of spreading information 3. a rumour

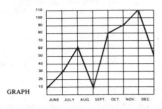

GRAPH

graph (graf) *n.* [short for *graphic formula*] 1. a diagram that shows the relationship between certain sets of numbers 2. *Math.* a picture showing the values taken on by a function —*vt.* to represent by a graph

-graph (gräf) [< Gr. *graphein*, write] *a combining form meaning:* 1. something that writes or records [*telegraph*] 2. something written

-grapher (grə fər) *a combining form meaning* a person who writes, records, etc. [*stenographer*]

graphic (graf´ik) *adj.* [< Gr. *graphein*, write] 1. described in realistic detail 2. written or inscribed Also **graph´ical** —**graph´ically** *adv.* —**graph´icness** *n.*

graphic arts any form of visual artistic representation, esp. painting, drawing, etching, etc.

graphics *n.pl.* [*with sing. v.*] the art of making drawings, as in architecture or engineering, in accordance with mathematical rules

graphite (graf´īt) *n.* [< Gr. *graphein*, write] a soft, black, form of carbon used in pencils, lubricants, etc.

graphology (grə fol´ə jē) *n.* [< Gr. *graphein*, write + -LOGY] the study of handwriting, esp. as a clue to character, etc. —**graphol´ogist** *n.*

graph paper paper with small ruled squares on which to make graphs, diagrams, etc.

-graphy (grə fē) [< Gr. *graphein*, write] *a combining form meaning:* 1. a process or method of writing, or representing [*lithography*] 2. a descriptive science [*geography*]

GRAPNEL

grapnel (grap´n'l) *n.* [< Pr. *grapa*, a hook] 1. a small anchor with several flukes 2. an iron bar with claws at one end for grasping things

grapple (grap′'l) *n.* [see GRAPNEL] 1. *same as* GRAPNEL (sense 2) 2. a coming to grips —*vt.* **grap′pled, grap′pling** to grip and hold —*vi.* 1. to struggle in hand-to-hand combat 2. to try to cope (*with*) 3. to use a grapnel (sense 2) —**grap′pler** *n.*

grappling iron (or **hook**) *same as* GRAPNEL (sense 2)

grasp (gräsp) *vt.* [ME. *graspen*] 1. to take hold of firmly, as with the hand 2. to take hold of eagerly 3. to understand —*vi.* 1. to try to seize (with *at*) 2. to accept eagerly (with *at*) —*n.* 1. control; possession 2. the power to hold or seize 3. comprehension —**grasp the nettle** tackle a difficult task —**grasp′able** *adj.* —**grasp′er** *n.*

grasping *adj.* eager for gain; avaricious

grass (gräs) *n.* [OE. *græs*] 1. any of a family of plants with long, narrow leaves and jointed stems, as wheat, rye, oats, etc. 2. any of various green plants with long, narrow leaves that are eaten by grazing animals 3. pasture land or lawn 4. [Slang] marijuana —*vt.* to grow grass over —*vi.* 1. to become covered with grass 2. [Slang] to inform on someone (with *on*) —**let the grass grow under one's feet** to neglect one's opportunities —**grass′like′** *adj.* —**grass′y** *adj.*

grass hockey [Canad.] in W Canada, hockey (or *field hockey*) as contrasted with ice hockey

grasshopper *n.* a plant-eating insect with two pairs of wings and powerful hind legs for jumping

grassland *n.* pasture land

grass parrot any of several small, bright, Australian parrots, esp. the budgerigar

grass roots [Colloq.] fundamentals —**grass′-roots′** *adj.* coming from the rank-and-file

grass widow a woman temporarily separated from her husband

grate[1] (grāt) *vt.* **grat′ed, grat′ing** [< OFr. *grater*] 1. to grind into particles by scraping 2. to rub against (an object) with a harsh sound 3. to grind (the teeth) 4. to irritate; annoy —*vi.* 1. to rub with or make a rasping sound 2. to cause irritation —**grat′er** *n.*

grate[2] *n.* [< L. *cratis*, hurdle] 1. a frame of metal bars for holding fuel in a fireplace, etc. 2. a fireplace

grateful (grāt′fəl) *adj.* [obs. *grate* (< L. *gratus*), pleasing] 1. feeling or expressing gratitude 2. causing gratitude; welcome —**grate′fully** *adv.*

gratify (grat′ə fī′) *vt.* **-fied′, -fy′ing** [< L. *gratus*, pleasing + *facere*, make] 1. to give pleasure or satisfaction to 2. to indulge; humour —**grat′ifica′tion** *n.*

grating[1] (grāt′iŋ) *n.* a framework of parallel or latticed bars set in a window, door, etc.

grating[2] *adj.* 1. harsh and rasping 2. irritating or annoying —**grat′ingly** *adv.*

gratis (grāt′is) *adv., adj.* [L. < *gratia*, favour] without charge or payment; free

gratitude (grat′ə tyōod) *n.* [< L. *gratus*, thankful] a feeling of thankfulness for favours received

gratuitous (grə tyōō′ə təs) *adj.* [< L. *gratus*, pleasing] 1. given or received without charge 2. uncalled-for —**gratu′itously** *adv.* —**gratu′itousness** *n.*

gratuity *n., pl.* **-ties** a gift of money, etc., esp. one given for a service rendered; tip

gravamen (grə vā′mən) *n., pl.* **-mens, gravam′ina** [< L. *gravis*, heavy] 1. a grievance 2. *Law* the gist of an accusation

grave[1] (grāv) *adj.* [< L. *gravis*, heavy] 1. important 2. threatening; ominous [*a grave illness*] 3. solemn 4. sombre; dull —**grave′ly** *adv.* —**grave′ness** *n.*

grave[2] *n.* [< OE. *grafan*, dig] 1. *a*) a hole in the ground in which to bury a dead body *b*) any place of burial 2. death —*vt.* **graved, grav′en** or **graved, grav′ing** 1. to carve out 2. [Archaic] to engrave 3. to impress sharply —**make a person turn in his grave** to be or do something that would have shocked a person now dead

grave accent (grāv) a mark (`) used to indicate the quality of a vowel, full pronunciation of a syllable, etc.

gravel (grav′'l) *n.* [< OFr. *grave*, coarse sand] 1. a loose mixture of pebbles and rock fragments coarser than sand 2. *Med.* a deposit in the kidneys, etc. —*vt.* **-elled, -elling** 1. to cover (a walk, etc.) with gravel 2. to perplex

gravelly *adj.* 1. full of, like, or consisting of gravel 2. sounding harsh [*a gravelly voice*]

graven (grāv′'n) *alt. pp. of* GRAVE[2]

graven image an idol made from stone, wood, etc.

Graves (grāv) *n.* a light wine from Graves in France

gravestone (grāv′stōn′) *n.* an engraved stone marking a grave; tombstone

graveyard *n.* a burial ground; cemetery

gravid (grav′id) *adj.* [< L. *gravis*, heavy] pregnant

gravimeter (grə vim′ə tər) *n.* [< L. *gravis*, heavy + -METER] 1. a device used to determine specific gravity 2. an instrument used to measure the force of gravity

gravimetry *n.* the measurement of weight or density —**grav′imet′ric** (grav′ə met′rik) *adj.*

gravitate (grav′ə tāt′) *vi.* **-tat′ed, -tat′ing** 1. to move or tend to move in accordance with the force of gravity 2. to be attracted or tend to move (*towards*)

gravitation (grav′ə tā′shən) *n.* 1. a gravitating 2. *Physics* the force by which every mass or particle of matter attracts and is attracted by every other mass or particle of matter —**grav′ita′tional** *adj.*

gravity (grav′ə tē) *n., pl.* **-ties** [< L. *gravis*, heavy] 1. the state or condition of being grave or serious 2. weight [*specific gravity*] 3. gravitation; esp., the force that tends to draw all bodies in the earth's sphere towards the centre of the earth

gravy (grā′vē) *n., pl.* **-vies** [< ?] 1. the juice given off by meat in cooking

2. a sauce made with this juice and flour, seasoning, etc. **3.** [Chiefly U.S. Slang] money easily obtained

gravy boat a boat-shaped dish for serving gravy

gray (grā) *adj.* var., now chiefly U.S., *sp. of* GREY

grayling *n.* a freshwater game fish related to the salmon

graze[1] (grāz) *vt.* grazed, graz'ing [< OE. *græs*, grass] **1.** to feed on (growing grass, herbage, etc.) **2.** to put livestock to feed on (a pasture, etc.) —*vi.* to feed on growing grass, etc. —**graz'er** *n.*

graze[2] *vt., vi.* grazed, graz'ing [prob. < prec.] to touch or rub lightly in passing; scrape —*n.* a grazing, or a scratch or scrape caused by it

grazier *n.* **1.** a person who grazes beef cattle for sale **2.** [Aust.] *a)* a cattle raiser *b)* a sheep farmer

grazing *n.* land to graze on; pasture

grease (grēs; *for v. also* grēz) *n.* [< L. *crassus*, fat] **1.** melted animal fat **2.** any thick, oily substance or lubricant —*vt.* greased, greas'ing **1.** to smear or lubricate with grease **2.** [Colloq.] to bribe : in **grease the palm** (or **hand**) **of**

greasepaint *n.* a mixture of grease and colouring matter used by performers in making up

greasy *adj.* -ier, -iest **1.** smeared with grease **2.** containing or like grease **3.** unctuous : said of a person's manner —**greas'ily** *adv.* —**greas'iness** *n.*

great (grāt) *adj.* [OE.] **1.** of much more than ordinary size, extent, number, etc. **2.** much above the ordinary or average; esp., *a)* intense [great pain] *b)* very much of a [a great reader] *c)* eminent [a great playwright] *d)* very impressive [great ceremony] *e)* noble [a great man] **3.** of most importance; main [great seal] **4.** designating a relationship one generation removed [great-grandmother] **5.** [Colloq.] excellent, splendid, fine, etc. —*n.* a great or distinguished person: *usually pl.* —**great'ly** *adv.* —**great'ness** *n.*

great-aunt *n.* a sister of any of one's grandparents

Great Bear the constellation URSA MAJOR

great circle any circle described on the surface of the earth or other sphere by a plane which passes through the centre of the sphere

greatcoat *n.* a heavy overcoat

Great Dane a breed of large dog with short hair

great-grandchild *n.* a child of any of one's grandchildren —**great'-grand'-daugh'ter** *n.* —**great'-grand'son'** *n.*

great-grandparent *n.* a parent of any of one's grandparents —**great'-grand'fa'-ther** *n.* —**great'-grand'moth'er** *n.*

great-great- *a combining form used with nouns of relationship to indicate two degrees of removal*

Great Russian 1. a member of the chief East Slavonic people of Russia **2.** their language

Greats *n.pl.* **1.** the B.A. course, esp. in classics and philosophy, at the University of Oxford **2.** the final examination of this course

great seal the chief seal of a nation, state, etc., with which official papers are stamped

great-uncle *n.* a brother of any of one's grandparents

Great War World War I (1914-18)

greaves (grēvz) *n.pl.* [< OFr. *greve*, shin] armour for the legs from the ankle to the knee

grebe (grēb) *n.* [Fr. *grèbe*] a diving and swimming bird with partially webbed feet

Grecian (grē'shən) *adj., n.* Greek

Grecian profile a profile in which the nose and forehead form an almost straight line

Greco- *same as* GRAECO-

greed (grēd) *n.* excessive desire, esp. for wealth or food

greedy *adj.* -ier, -iest [OE. *grædig*] **1.** wanting or taking all that one can get; avaricious **2.** gluttonous **3.** intensely eager —**greed'ily** *adv.* —**greed'iness** *n.*

Greek (grēk) *n.* **1.** a native or inhabitant of ancient or modern Greece **2.** the language of Greece, ancient or modern —*adj.* of ancient or modern Greece, its people, language, or culture —**be Greek to one** to be incomprehensible to one

Greek cross a cross with four equal arms at right angles

Greek fire an incendiary material used in ancient warfare, described as able to burn in water

Greek (Orthodox) Church *popular name for* ORTHODOX EASTERN CHURCH

green (grēn) *adj.* [OE. *grene*] **1.** of the colour of growing grass **2.** overspread with green foliage [a green field] **3.** sickly or bilious **4.** not mature; unripe **5.** not trained; inexperienced **6.** naive **7.** not dried, seasoned, or cured **8.** fresh; new **9.** flourishing; vigorous **10.** [Colloq.] jealous —*n.* **1.** the colour of growing grass **2.** any green pigment **3.** anything coloured green **4.** [pl.] green leafy plants or vegetables, as spinach, cabbage, etc. **5.** an area of smooth turf set aside for special purposes [a village green] **6.** *Golf* a putting green —*vt., vi.* to make or become green —**the Green** Ireland's national colour —**green'ish** *adj.*

green bean any of various bean plants, as the French bean, that have narrow, green, edible pods

greenbelt *n.* an area round a city, preserved by official authority as open or agricultural land

green card an insurance document for motorists travelling abroad

Green Cross Code a code for children giving rules for road safety

greenery *n., pl.* -eries green vegetation

green-eyed *adj.* very jealous

greenfinch *n.* a finch with olive-green and yellow feathers, native to Europe

green fingers talent in growing plants

greenfly *n.* a garden pest attacking rose bushes, etc.

greengage n. [< Sir William *Gage*] a large plum with golden-green skin and flesh

greengrocer n. a retail dealer in fresh vegetables and fruit —**green′gro′cery** n.

greenhorn n. an inexperienced person; novice

greenhouse n. a building made mainly of glass, with heat and humidity regulated for growing plants

greenkeeper n. a person in charge of maintaining a golf course

green light [after the green ("go") signal of a traffic light] [Colloq.] permission to proceed with some undertaking

green paper a report containing policy proposals to be discussed, esp. by parliament

green pepper the green, immature fruit of the sweet red pepper, eaten as a vegetable

green pound the value of the pound paid to farmers as fixed by the EEC

greenroom n. a room in theatres used by performers

greenshank n. a wading bird with pale green legs

green-stick fracture a partial fracture in which the bone is broken on only one side

greensward n. green, grassy ground

green tea tea prepared from leaves not fermented before drying

Greenwich (mean) time (grin′ij) the time on longitude 0 which passes through Greenwich : used as the basis for standard time throughout the world

greet[1] (grēt) vt. [OE. *gretan*] 1. to address with expressions of friendliness, respect, etc. 2. to meet, receive, or acknowledge (a person, event, etc.) in a specified way 3. to come or appear to —**greet′er** n.

greet[2] vi. [< OE. *grætan*] [Scot] to weep; lament

greeting n. 1. the act or words of a person who greets 2. [often pl.] a message of regards

greetings card a decorated card bearing a greeting for some occasion, as a birthday

gregarious (grə gãar′ē əs) adj. [< L. *grex*, *gregis*, a flock] 1. fond of the company of others 2. living in herds or flocks —**gregar′iousness** n.

Gregorian calendar (gri gôr′ē ən) a widely used calendar, introduced by Pope Gregory XIII in 1582

Gregorian chant the ritual plainsong of the Roman Catholic Church, introduced under Pope Gregory I

gremlin (grem′lən) n. [prob. < Dan. hyp. *græmling*, imp] an imaginary small creature humorously blamed for the faulty operation of aircraft, etc.

grenade (grə nād′) n. [ult. < L. *granum*, a seed] a small bomb detonated by a fuse and usually thrown by hand

grenadier (gren′ə dēər′) n. [Fr. < *grenade*] 1. orig., an infantry soldier who threw grenades 2. a member of the Grenadier Guards

grew (grōō) pt. of GROW

grey (grā) adj. [< OE. *græg*] 1. of the colour grey 2. a) darkish b) dismal 3. a) having hair that is grey b) old 4. designating an intermediate area between morality and immorality —n. 1. a colour made by mixing black and white 2. a grey animal or thing —vt., vi. to make or become grey —**grey′ly** adv. —**grey′ness** n.

Grey Cup [< Earl *Grey*] the annual championship game of the Canadian Football League or the trophy awarded to the winner

Grey Friar a Franciscan friar

greyhound n. a breed of tall, slender, swift hound with a narrow, pointed head

greylag n. [from its colour and its late migration] a wild grey goose of Europe and C Asia

grey matter 1. greyish nerve tissue of the brain and spinal cord 2. [Colloq] intelligence

grey squirrel a large, grey squirrel with a bushy tail, native to E N America; now common in Europe

grid (grid) n. [< GRIDIRON] 1. a gridiron; grating 2. a network of crossing parallel lines, as on graph paper 3. a network of transmission lines, pipes, etc. 4. a metallic plate in a storage cell 5. an electrode, as of wire mesh, for controlling the passage of electrons in an electron tube

griddle (grid′′l) n. [< L. *cratis*, wickerwork] a flat, metal plate or pan for cooking pancakes, etc.

gridiron (grid′ī′ərn) n. [see GRIDDLE] 1. a framework of metal bars or wires on which to cook meat or fish; grill 2. any framework resembling a gridiron

grief (grēf) n. [see GRIEVE] 1. intense emotional suffering caused by loss, disaster, etc. 2. a cause of such suffering —**come to grief** to fail or be ruined

grief-stricken adj. stricken with grief; sorrowful

grievance (grē′vəns) n. 1. a circumstance thought to be unjust and ground for complaint 2. complaint against a real or imagined wrong

grieve (grēv) vt., vi. grieved, griev′ing [< L. *gravis*, heavy] to feel or cause to feel grief —**griev′er** n.

grievous (grē′vəs) adj. 1. severe 2. deplorable; atrocious 3. showing or full of grief 4. causing grief —**griev′ously** adv. —**griev′ousness** n.

griffin (grif′ən) n. [< Gr. *grypos*, hooked] a mythical animal, part eagle and part lion

griffon (grif′ən) n. [Fr., griffin] 1. same as GRIFFIN 2. a wire-haired breed of dog 3. a large vulture

grill (gril) n. [see GRIDDLE] 1. a gridiron 2. a device on a cooker to radiate heat downwards 3. grilled food 4. short for GRILLROOM —vt. 1. to cook on a grill 2. to question relentlessly —**grilled** adj. —**grill′er** n.

grille (gril) n. [see GRIDDLE] an open grating forming a screen to a door, window, etc.

grillroom n. a restaurant that makes a speciality of grilled foods

grilse (grils) n. [< ?] a young salmon on its first return from the sea

grim (grim) *adj.* **grim′mer, grim′mest** [OE. *grimm*] **1.** hard and unyielding; stern **2.** appearing forbidding, harsh, etc. **3.** repellent; ghastly **4.** fierce; cruel —**grim′ly** *adv.*

grimace (gri mās′) *n.* [< OFr. *grimuche*] a distortion of the face, as in expressing pain, contempt, etc. —*vi.* **-maced′, -mac′ing** to make grimaces

grimalkin (gri mal′kin) *n.* [earlier *gray malkin* (cat)] **1.** an old female cat **2.** a malicious old woman

grime (grīm) *n.* [prob. < Fl. *grijm*] sooty dirt rubbed into or covering a surface, as of the skin —*vt.* **grimed, grim′ing** to make very dirty —**grim′y** *adj.*

grin (grin) *vi.* **grinned, grin′ning** [OE. *grennian*] to draw back the lips and show the teeth in amusement, pain, scorn, etc. —*vt.* to express by grinning —*n.* a broad smile —**grin and bear it** to accept philosophically something painful —**grin′ner** *n.*

grind (grīnd) *vt.* **ground, grind′ing** [OE. *grindan*] **1.** to crush into fine particles **2.** to oppress **3.** to sharpen or smooth by friction **4.** to press down or rub together harshly or gratingly **5.** to operate by turning the crank of —*vi.* **1.** to perform the act of grinding **2.** to undergo grinding **3.** to grate —*n.* **1.** [Colloq.] long, difficult work or study **2.** the degree of fineness of something ground into particles **3.** a grinding —**grind out** to produce by laborious effort —**grind′ingly** *adv.*

grinder *n.* **1.** any of various machines for crushing or sharpening **2.** a molar tooth

grindstone *n.* a revolving stone disc for sharpening tools or shaping and polishing things —**keep** (or **have** or **put**) **one's nose to the grindstone** to work steadily

grip (grip) *n.* [< OE. *gripan*, seize] **1.** a firm hold **2.** any special manner of clasping hands **3.** the power of grasping firmly **4.** mental grasp **5.** control; mastery **6.** a handle **7.** [Chiefly U.S.] a small travelling bag —*vt.* **gripped, gripp′ing 1.** to take firmly and hold fast with the hand, teeth, etc. **2.** *a*) to get and hold the attention of *b*) to have a strong emotional impact on —**come to grips** to cope (*with*) —**grip′per** *n.*

gripe (grīp) *vt.* **griped, grip′ing** [OE. *gripan*, seize] **1.** formerly, to clutch or afflict **2.** to cause sudden, sharp pain in the bowels of —*vi.* [Slang] to complain —*n.* **1.** [*pl.*] a sudden, sharp pain in the bowels **2.** [Slang] a complaint —**grip′er** *n.*

grippe (grip) *n.* [Fr., seizure] *earlier term for* INFLUENZA

grisly (griz′lē) *adj.* **-lier, -liest** [OE. *grislic*] terrifying; ghastly —**gris′liness** *n.*

grist (grist) *n.* [OE.] grain that is to be or has been ground —**grist to** (or **for**) **one's mill** anything one can use profitably

gristle (gris′'l) *n.* [OE.] cartilage, now esp. as found in meat —**gris′tliness** *n.* —**gristly** (gris′lē) *adj.*

grit (grit) *n.* [OE. *greot*] **1.** rough, hard particles of sand, stone, etc. **2.** a sandstone with sharp grains **3.** stubborn courage —*vt.* **grit′ted, grit′ting 1.** to grind (the teeth) in anger or determination **2.** to cover a surface, as icy roads, with grit —**grit′ty** *adj.*

Grit (grit) *n., adj.* [Canad. Colloq.] Liberal

grizzle (griz′'l) *vi.* [< ?] [Colloq.] to whine; whimper

grizzled *adj.* [< OFr. *gris*, grey] **1.** grey or streaked with grey **2.** having grey hair

grizzly *adj.* **-zlier, -zliest** greyish; grizzled —*n., pl.* **-zlies** *short for* GRIZZLY BEAR

grizzly bear a large, ferocious bear of western N America, with brown, grey, or yellow fur

groan (grōn) *vi.* [OE. *granian*] **1.** to utter a deep sound expressing pain, distress, etc. **2.** to make a creaking sound, as from strain **3.** to be weighed down —*n.* a groaning sound

groat (grōt) *n.* [< MDu. *grote*] an obsolete English silver coin worth four old pence

groats *n.pl.* [< OE. *grotan*] any grain that is hulled, or hulled and coarsely cracked

grocer (grō′sər) *n.* [< OFr. *gros*, GROSS] a shopkeeper who sells food and various household supplies

grocery *n., pl.* **-ceries 1.** a grocer's shop **2.** [*pl.*] the food and supplies sold by a grocer

grog (grog) *n.* [< nickname of E. Vernon, Brit. admiral] any alcoholic drink as rum diluted with water

groggy *adj.* **-gier, -giest** shaky or dizzy —**grog′gily** *adv.* —**grog′giness** *n.*

grogram (grog′rəm) *n.* [< OFr. *grosgrain*, coarse grain] formerly, a coarse fabric of silk and mohair

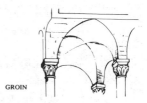

GROIN

groin¹ (groin) *n.* [< OE. *grynde*, abyss] **1.** the hollow or fold where the abdomen joins either thigh **2.** *Archit.* the sharp, curved edge at the junction of two intersecting vaults —**groined** *adj.*

groin² *n. var., esp. US.*, *sp. of* GROYNE

groom (grōōm) *n.* [ME. *grom*, boy] **1.** one whose work is tending horses **2.** any of various officials of the British royal household **3.** *same as* BRIDEGROOM —*vt.* **1.** to clean and curry (a horse, dog, etc.) **2.** to make neat and tidy **3.** to train for a particular purpose

groomsman *n.* a man who attends a bridegroom at the wedding

groove (grōōv) *n.* [< ON. *grof*, pit] **1.** a long, narrow furrow cut or formed in a surface with a tool **2.** a habitual way of doing something **3.** [Slang] an exciting place, experience, etc. —*vt.* **grooved,**

groov'ing to make a groove or grooves in —**in the groove** [Slang] performed with smooth, effortless skill: orig. of jazz

groovy *adj.* **-ier, -iest** [Slang] very pleasing

grope (grōp) *vi.* **groped, grop'ing** [OE. *grapian*, seize] to feel or search about blindly or uncertainly —*vt.* to seek or find (one's way) by groping —**grop'er** *n.*

grosbeak (grōs'bēk') *n.* [< Fr.: see GROSS & BEAK] any of various finchlike birds, with a thick, strong, conical bill

grosgrain (grō'grān') *n.* [Fr., lit., coarse grain] a ribbed silk or rayon fabric used for ribbons, etc.

‡**gros point** (grō'pwản) *n.* [Fr., large stitch] **1.** a cross-stitch in embroidery **2.** embroidery using this stitch

gross (grōs) *adj.* [< LL. *grossus*, thick] **1.** fat and coarse-looking **2.** flagrant; very bad **3.** dense; thick **4.** insensitive or unrefined **5.** vulgar; obscene **6.** total; with no deductions —*n.* **1.** *pl.* **gross'es** overall total **2.** *pl.* **gross** twelve dozen —*vt., vi.* [Colloq.] to earn (a specified total amount) before expenses are deducted —**in the gross 1.** in bulk **2.** wholesale: also **by the gross** —**gross'ly** *adv.* —**gross'ness** *n.*

gross national product the total value of a nation's annual output of goods and services

grotesque (grō tesk') *adj.* [< It. *grotta*, grotto] **1.** distorted; bizarre **2.** of painting, etc. in which forms of fantastic persons and animals are intermingled with foliage **3.** ludicrously eccentric; absurd —*n.* **1.** a grotesque painting, design, etc. **2.** a grotesque thing

grotto (grot'ō) *n., pl.* **-toes, -tos** [< It. < L. *crypta*, crypt] **1.** a cave **2.** a cave-like summerhouse, etc.

grotty (grot'ē) *adj.* [< GROTESQUE] [Slang] **1.** ugly; unpleasant **2.** unwell; miserable

grouch (grauch) *vi.* [< ME. *grucchen*, grudge] to grumble in a sulky way —*n.* **1.** one who grouches continually **2.** a sulky mood **3.** a complaint —**grouch'y** *adj.*

ground¹ (graund) *n.* [OE. *grund*, bottom] **1.** the solid surface of the earth **2.** the soil of the earth; land **3.** [*pl.*] land attached to a building; esp., the lawns, gardens, etc. of an estate **4.** any area of discussion, etc.; subject **5.** [*often pl.*] basis; foundation **6.** [*often pl.*] valid reason **7.** the underlying surface of a painting, coloured pattern, etc. **8.** [*pl.*] dregs [coffee *grounds*] **9.** *Elec.* [U.S.] earth —*adj.* **1.** of, on, or near the ground **2.** growing or living in or on the ground —*vt.* **1.** to set on the ground **2.** to cause (a ship, etc.) to run aground **3.** to found on a firm basis **4.** to base (a claim, etc.) on something specified **5.** to instruct (a person) in the elements of **6.** to keep (an aircraft or pilot) from flying —*vi.* to strike the bottom: said of a ship —**break new ground** to do something that has not been done before —**cover ground 1.** to move a certain distance **2.** to make progress —**cut the**

ground from under one's feet to deprive one of effective defence or argument —**gain ground 1.** to make progress **2.** to gain in strength, popularity, etc. —**get off the ground** to get (something) started —**give ground** to yield —**hold** (or **stand**) **one's ground** to keep one's position against opposition —**lose ground 1.** to drop back **2.** to lose in strength, popularity, etc. —**shift one's ground** to change one's argument or defence —**suit down to the ground** [Colloq.] to suit completely

ground² *pt. & pp. of* GRIND

ground bass *Music* a short phrase played repeatedly in the bass against the harmonies of the upper parts

ground control personnel, electronic equipment, etc. on the ground for guiding aircraft or spacecraft in takeoff, flight, and landing operations

ground cover any of various dense, low-growing plants used instead of grass for covering the ground

ground crew a group of people in charge of the maintenance and repair of aircraft: also **ground staff**

ground floor that floor of a building which is on or near the ground level —**in on the ground floor** [Colloq.] in at the beginning of an enterprise

grounding *n.* basic general knowledge of a subject

ground ivy a creeping plant with round, toothed leaves

groundless *adj.* without reason or cause

groundnut *n.* **1.** any of various N. American plants with edible tubers, as the peanut **2.** a peanut

groundsel (graun's'l) *n.* [< OE., ? < *gund*, pus + *swelgan*, swallow: from use in poultices] a plant with yellow flowers used to feed cage birds

groundsheet (graund'shēt) *n.* a water-proof cover placed on the ground, as in a tent

groundsman *n.* a person who tends the grounds of a playing field, estate, cemetery, etc.

groundswell *n.* **1.** a rolling of the ocean, caused by a distant storm **2.** a rapidly growing wave of public opinion, etc. Also **ground swell**

groundwork *n.* a foundation; basis

group (grōop) *n.* [< It. *gruppo*] **1.** a number of persons or things gathered or classified together **2.** *same as* POP GROUP **3.** *Mil.* a unit of two or more squadrons —*vt., vi.* to form into a group or groups —*adj.* of a group —**group'ing** *n.*

group captain *see* MILITARY RANKS, table

grouse¹ (graus) *n., pl.* **grouse** [< ?] a game bird with a round, plump body

grouse² *vi.* **groused, grous'ing** [< ?] [Colloq.] to complain; grumble —*n.* [Colloq.] a complaint —**grous'er** *n.*

grout (graut) *n.* [OE. *grut*] a thin mortar used to fill chinks, as between tiles —*vt.* to fill or finish with grout —**grout'er** *n.*

grove (grōv) *n.* [< OE. *graf*] **1.** a small

wood or group of trees 2. an orchard of fruit or nut trees

grovel (grov'l) *vi.* **-elled, -elling** [< ON.] 1. to behave humbly or abjectly 2. to lie or crawl in a prostrate position, esp. abjectly —**grov'eller** *n.*

grow (grō) *vi.* grew, grown, grow'ing [OE. *growan*] 1. to come into being; spring up 2. to exist as living vegetation 3. to increase in size, quantity, or degree 4. to come to be; become [to *grow* weary] —*vt.* 1. to cause to grow 2. to allow to grow [to *grow* a beard] 3. to develop —**grow on** to become gradually more acceptable, likable, etc. —**grow out of** 1. to develop from 2. to outgrow —**grow up** to become adult —**grow'er** *n.*

growing pains 1. recurrent pains in the joints and muscles of growing children 2. difficulties experienced in the early development of any enterprise

growl (groul) *vi.* [< ?] to make a low, rumbling, menacing sound in the throat, as a dog does —*vt.* to express by growling —*n.* the act or sound of growling —**growl'er** *n.*

grown (grōn) *pp.* of GROW —*adj.* 1. mature 2. cultivated as specified [home-grown]

grown-up *adj.* 1. adult 2. of or for adults —*n.* an adult: also **grown'up'**

growth (grōth) *n.* 1. a growing or developing 2. degree or extent of increase in size, weight, etc. 3. something that grows or has grown 4. a tumour or other abnormal mass of tissue

groyne (groin) *n.* [< ? OFr. *groign*, snout or GROIN] a breakwater to control erosion

grub (grub) *vi.* grubbed, grub'bing [ME. *grubben*] 1. to dig in the ground 2. to work hard, esp. at menial or tedious jobs —*vt.* to uproot (often with *up*) —*n.* 1. the short, fat, wormlike larva of an insect, esp. of a beetle 2. [Slang] food —**grub'ber** *n.*

grubby *adj.* **-bier, -biest** dirty; messy; untidy

grudge (gruj) *vt.* grudged, grudg'ing [OFr. *grouchier*] 1. to envy (someone) because of his possession of (something) 2. to give with reluctance —*n.* a strong feeling of ill will against someone —**grudg'ing** *adj.*

gruel (grōō'əl) *n.* [OFr., coarse meal] thin, easily digested porridge made by cooking meal in water or milk

gruelling *adj.* [prp. of obs. v. *gruel*, to punish] extremely trying; exhausting

gruesome (grōō'səm) *adj.* [< dial. *grue*, to shudder] causing horror or loathing; grisly —**grue'someness** *n.*

gruff (gruf) *adj.* [Du. *grof*] 1. rough or surly; rude 2. harsh and throaty; hoarse —**gruff'ly** *adv.* —**gruff'ness** *n.*

grumble (grum'b'l) *vi.* **-bled, -bling** [prob. < Du. *grommelen*] 1. to mutter or complain in a surly way 2. to growl or rumble —*vt.* to express by grumbling —*n.* a grumbling, esp. in complaint —**grum'bler** *n.*

grumpy *adj.* **-ier, -iest** [echoic] grouchy; peevish; bad-tempered —**grump'ily** *adv.* —**grump'iness** *n.*

Grundy, Mrs. (grun'dē) [busybody in an 18th-c. play] a personification of conventional social disapproval

grunt (grunt) *vi.* [OE. *grunnettan*] to make the short, deep, hoarse sound of a pig or a sound like this —*vt.* to express by grunting —*n.* the sound of grunting —**grunt'er** *n.*

Gruyère (cheese) (grōō yâər') [< *Gruyère*, Switzerland] a light-yellow Swiss cheese, rich in butterfat

gryphon (grif'ən) *n.* *same as* GRIFFIN

G.S., g.s. 1. general secretary 2. general staff

G-string (jē'striŋ') *n.* 1. a narrow loincloth 2. a similar band, worn by striptease dancers 3. *Music* a string tuned to G

G-suit *n.* [G for *gravity*] a pressurized garment for pilots or astronauts

G.T. [It. *gran turismo*] *Motoring* sports tourer capable of high speeds

GUANACO

guanaco (gwä nä'kō) *n.*, *pl.* **-cos** [Sp. < SAmInd.] a woolly, reddish-brown, wild animal of the Andes, related to the camel and llama

guano (gwä'nō) *n.*, *pl.* **-nos** [Sp. < SAmInd.] the manure of sea birds, used as a fertilizer

guarantee (gar'ən tē') *n.* [< GUARANTY] 1. *same as* GUARANTY 2. *a)* a pledge that something will be replaced if it is not as represented *b)* a positive assurance that something will be done in the manner specified 3. a guarantor —*vt.* **-teed', -teeing** 1. to give a guarantee or guaranty for 2. to promise

guarantor *n.* one who makes a guaranty or guarantee

guaranty *n.*, *pl.* **-ties** [< OFr. *garant*, a warrant] 1. a pledge or security for another's debt or obligation 2. an agreement that secures the existence or maintenance of something

guard (gärd) *vt.* [< OFr. *garder*, protect] 1. to watch over and protect; defend 2. *a)* to keep from escape or trouble *b)* to hold in check; control *c) Sports* to keep (an opponent) from making a gain or scoring —*vi.* 1. to keep watch (*against*) 2. to act as a guard —*n.* 1. a person or group that guards; specif., *a)* a sentinel or sentry *b)* the official in general charge of a railway train *c)* [*pl.*] [*often* **G-**] a special unit of troops assigned to the British royal household 2. any device that protects against injury or loss **3.** defence; protection **4.** a posture of defence, as in boxing, fencing, etc. —**off** (one's) **guard** not alert for defence —**on** (one's) **guard** alert for defence —**stand guard** to do sentry duty

guarded *adj.* **1.** watched over **2.** cautious; noncommittal —**guard'edly** *adv.*

guardhouse *n. Mil.* **1.** a building used by the members of a guard when not on duty: also **guard room 2.** a jail for temporary confinement

guardian *n.* **1.** a person who guards or takes care of another person, property, etc. **2.** a person legally placed in charge of the affairs of a minor or of someone incapable of managing his own affairs —*adj.* protecting —**guard'ianship'** *n.*

guardsman *n.* a member of The Guards or of any military guard

guava (gwä'və) *n.* [< Sp. < native name] **1.** a tropical American tree bearing a yellow, edible fruit **2.** the fruit

gubernatorial (gōō'bər nə tôr'ē əl) *adj.* [L. *gubernator*, governor] [Chiefly U.S.] of a governor or his office

gudgeon[1] (guj'ən) *n.* [< Gr. *kōbios*] **1.** a small freshwater fish, easily caught, and used for bait **2.** a person easily tricked

gudgeon[2] [< OFr. *gojon*, pivot] **1.** a metal pin or shaft at the pivot of an axle **2.** the socket of a hinge, into which the pin is fitted

guelder-rose (gel'dər rōz') *n.* [< *Gelderland*, in the Netherlands] a shrub bearing clusters of white flowers

Guernsey (gʉrn'zē) *n., pl.* **-seys** [< one of the Channel Islands] any of a breed of dairy cattle, usually fawn-coloured with white markings

guerrilla, guerilla (gə ril'ə) *n.* [Sp. dim. of *guerra*, war] any member of a small force of irregular soldiers, usually politically motivated, making surprise raids on regular forces

guess (ges) *vt., vi.* [prob. < MDu. *gessen*] **1.** to form a judgment or estimate of (something) without actual knowledge; surmise **2.** to judge correctly by doing this **3.** [U.S.] to think or suppose —*n.* **1.** a guessing **2.** something guessed; surmise —**guess'er** *n.*

guesswork *n.* **1.** the act of guessing **2.** a judgment, result, etc. arrived at by guessing

guest (gest) *n.* [ON. *gestr*] **1.** a person entertained at the home of another or at a restaurant, theatre, etc. **2.** any paying customer of a hotel, restaurant, etc. **3.** a person who appears on a programme by special invitation —*adj.* **1.** for guests **2.** performing by special invitation [a *guest* artist]

guest house a boarding house

guff (guf) *n.* [echoic] [Slang] foolish talk; nonsense

guffaw (gu fô') *n.* [echoic] a loud, coarse burst of laughter —*vi.* to laugh in this way

guidance (gīd'əns) *n.* **1.** the act of guiding; direction; leadership **2.** advice or assistance

guide (gīd) *vt.* **guid'ed, guid'ing** [< OFr. *guier*] **1.** to point out the way for; lead **2.** to direct the course of **3.** to direct in (policies, actions, work, etc.) —*n.* **1.** one who leads others on a trip or tour **2.** one who directs, or serves as the model for, another in his conduct, career, etc. **3.** a guidebook **4.** a book giving instruction in the elements of some subject **5.** *same as* GIRL GUIDE —**guid'able** *adj.*

guidebook *n.* a book containing directions and information for tourists

guided missile a military missile whose course is controlled by radio signals, radar devices, etc.

guide dog a dog trained to lead a blind person

guideline *n.* a standard or principle by which to determine a policy or action: also **guide line**

guider *n.* the adult leader of a company of girl guides

guidon (gīd''n) *n.* [Fr. < It.] the identification flag of a military unit

guild (gild) *n.* [< OE. *gyld* and ON. *gildi*] **1.** any association for mutual aid and the promotion of common interests **2.** in medieval times, a union of men in the same craft or trade

guilder (gil'dər) *n.* [< MDu.] **1.** the monetary unit of the Netherlands **2.** a former coin of the Netherlands, Germany, or Austria

guildhall *n.* **1.** a hall where a guild meets **2.** a town hall

guile (gīl) *n.* [OFr.] slyness and cunning in dealing with others —**guile'ful** *adj.* —**guile'less** *adj.*

guillemot (gil'ə mot') *n.* [Fr., dim. of *Guillaume*, William] any of various narrow-billed, northern diving birds

GUILLOTINE

guillotine (gil'ə tēn'; *for n. also* gil'ə tēn') *n.* [Fr., < J. I. *Guillotin*] **1.** an instrument for beheading by means of a heavy blade dropped between two grooved uprights **2.** a device with a long, rigid, blade for cutting or trimming paper, metal, etc. **3.** in Parliament, a form of closure under which a bill is divided into compartments, certain groups of which must be dealt with each day —*vt.* **-tined', -tin'ing 1.** to behead or cut with a guillotine **2.** in Parliament, to limit debate by means of a guillotine

guilt (gilt) *n.* [OE. *gylt*, sin] 1. the act or state of having done a wrong or committed an offence 2. a feeling of self-reproach resulting from a belief that one has done something wrong

guiltless *adj.* 1. innocent 2. having no knowledge (with *of*) —**guilt'lessly** *adv.*

guilty *adj.* **-ier, -iest** 1. having guilt 2. legally judged an offender 3. showing or conscious of guilt 4. involving guilt —**guilt'ily** *adv.* —**guilt'iness** *n.*

guinea (gin'ē) *n.* 1. [first coined of gold from *Guinea*] a former British gold coin equal to 21 shillings 2. formerly, the sum of 21 shillings

guinea fowl [orig. imported from *Guinea*] a domestic fowl with a rounded body and speckled feathers

guinea pig [prob. orig. brought to England by ships plying between England, *Guinea*, and S. America] 1. a small, fat rodent kept as a pet or used in biological experiments 2. any person or thing used in an experiment

guipure (gē pyoor') *n.* [Fr.] lace with the patterns held together by connecting threads

guise (gīz) *n.* [OFr. < OHG. *wisa*, manner] 1. a false appearance 2. outward aspect 3. manner of dress

guiser *n.* [< prec.] [Scot. and N Eng.] a mummer

guitar (gi tär') *n.* [< Sp. < Gr. *kithara*, lyre] a musical instrument usually with six strings that are plucked with the fingers or a plectrum —**guitar'ist** *n.*

Gulag (goo'lag) *n.* [Russ.] the central administrative department of the Soviet security service, responsible for prisons, labour camps, etc.

gulch (gulch) *n.* [prob. < dial. *gulch*, swallow greedily] a deep, narrow ravine

gulf (gulf) *n.* [ult. < Gr. *kolpos*, bosom] 1. an area of sea, larger than a bay, reaching into land 2. a wide, deep chasm 3. a wide separation

Gulf Stream a warm ocean current flowing from the Gulf of Mexico and around the British Isles

gulfweed *n.* a seaweed found in the Gulf Stream and the Sargasso Sea: also **sargasso weed**

gull¹ (gul) *n.* [< Celt.] a water bird with large wings, webbed feet, and white and grey feathers

gull² *n.* [< ?] [Archaic] a person easily tricked; dupe —*vt.* to cheat; trick

gullet (gul'ət) *n.* [< L. *gula*, throat] 1. the oesophagus 2. the throat or neck

gullible (gul'əb'l) *adj.* easily tricked; credulous —**gul'libil'ity** *n.* —**gul'libly** *adv.*

gully (gul'ē) *n.*, *pl.* **-lies** [see GULLET] 1. a channel worn by running water; small, narrow ravine 2. *Cricket* a close fielding position on the off side behind the wicket

gulp (gulp) *vt.* [prob. < Du. *gulpen*] 1. to swallow hastily or greedily 2. to choke back as if swallowing —*vi.* to catch the breath as in swallowing —*n.* 1. a gulping 2. the amount swallowed at one time

gum¹ (gum) *n.* [< L. *gumma* < Egypt.

kemai] 1. a sticky substance found in certain trees and plants, which dries into a brittle mass that swells in water 2. any similar plant secretion, as resin 3. an adhesive, as on the back of a postage stamp 4. any of various sticky substances or deposits 5. same as CHEWING GUM —*vt.* **gummed, gum'ming** to coat, unite, or stiffen with gum —*vi.* to become sticky or clogged —**gum up** [Colloq.] to put out of working order

gum² *n.* [OE. *goma*] [often *pl.*] the firm flesh surrounding the base of the teeth

gum arabic a gum obtained from several African acacias, used in medicine and sweets, for stabilizing emulsions, etc.

gumboil *n.* an abscess on the gum

gum boot same as WELLINGTON BOOT

gummy¹ *adj.* **-mier, -miest** 1. having the nature of gum; sticky 2. covered with gum 3. yielding gum

gummy² *adj.* toothless

gump (gump) *n.* [Colloq.] gumption

gumption (gump'shan) *n.* [< Scot. dial.] [Colloq.] 1. orig., common sense 2. courage and initiative

gum resin a mixture of gum and resin, given off by certain trees and plants

gum tree any of various trees that yield gum, as the eucalyptus —**up a gum tree** [Colloq.] to be in difficulties

gun (gun) *n.* [< ME. *gonne* < ?] 1. any of various weapons, as a cannon, rifle, etc., consisting of a metal tube from which a projectile is discharged by the force of an explosive 2. a discharge of a gun in signalling or saluting 3. anything like a gun in shape or use [air gun, spray gun] 4. a member of a shooting party —*vi.* **gunned, gun'ning** to shoot or hunt with a gun —*vt.* 1. [Colloq.] to shoot (a person) (often with *down*) 2. [Slang] to advance the throttle of (an engine) so as to increase the speed —**go great guns** [Slang] to act with speed and efficiency —**gun for** 1. to hunt for with a gun 2. [Slang] to be ambitious for —**jump the gun** [Slang] to begin before the proper time —**stick to one's guns** to be firm under attack

gunboat *n.* a small armed ship of shallow draught, used to patrol rivers, etc.

gunboat diplomacy diplomacy reinforced with the threat of military action

guncotton *n.* nitrocellulose in a highly nitrated form, used as an explosive

gun dog a dog trained to find or retrieve game

gunfire *n.* the firing of a gun or guns

gunman *n.* a man armed with a gun, esp. an armed gangster or hired killer

gunmetal *n.* 1. a kind of bronze formerly used for making cannons 2. the dark grey colour (**gunmetal grey**) of tarnished gunmetal —*adj.* dark grey

gunnel (gun'l) *n.* same as GUNWALE

gunner *n.* 1. a soldier etc. who helps fire artillery 2. an artilleryman 3. a naval warrant officer in charge of a ship's guns

gunnery *n.* the science of making and using heavy guns

gunny (gun′ē) *n.,* *pl.* **-nies** [< Sans. *gōnī,* sack] a coarse, heavy fabric of jute or hemp, used for sacks

gunpoint *n.* the muzzle of a gun —**at gunpoint** under threat of being shot with a gun

gunpowder *n.* an explosive powder used in cartridges, shells, etc., for blasting, etc.

gunrunning *n.* the smuggling of guns and ammunition into a country —**gun′run′-ner** *n.*

gunshot *n.* 1. shot fired from a gun 2. the range of a gun —*adj.* caused by a shot from a gun

gunslinger *n.* [Chiefly U.S. Slang] a gunman

gunstock *n.* the wooden handle or butt to which the barrel of a gun is attached

gunwale (gun′′l) *n.* [first applied to bulwarks supporting a ship's guns] the upper edge of the side of a ship or boat

guppy (gup′ē) *n.,* *pl.* **-pies** [< R. *Guppy,* of Trinidad] a tiny, brightly coloured tropical fish

gurgle (gur′g′l) *vi.* **-gled, -gling** [prob. echoic] 1. to flow with a bubbling sound 2. to make such a sound in the throat —*n.* the sound of gurgling

Gurkha (gur′kə) *n.* 1. any of a warlike people living in Nepal. 2. a member of this people serving as a soldier in the British army

gurnard (gur′nərd) *n.* [< OFr. *grogner,* to grunt] a sea fish with winglike fins for gliding short distances

guru (goor′oo) *n.* [< Sans. *guru-h,* venerable] in Hinduism, one's spiritual adviser

gush (gush) *vi.* [prob. akin to ON. *gjosa*] 1. to flow out suddenly and plentifully 2. to have a sudden flow 3. to express exaggerated enthusiasm or feeling —*vt.* to cause to flow out suddenly —*n.* 1. a sudden, plentiful outflow 2. gushing talk or writing —**gush′ing** *adj.*

gusher *n.* 1. a person who gushes 2. an oil well from which oil spouts without being pumped

gusset (gus′it) *n.* [< OFr. *gousset*] a triangular or diamond-shaped piece inserted in a garment to make it stronger or roomier —**gus′seted** *adj.*

gust (gust) *n.* [< OE. *gustr*] 1. a sudden, strong rush of air, rain, or wind 2. a sudden outburst of laughter, rage, etc. —*vi.* to blow in gusts —**gust′y** *adj.*

gustatory (gus′tə tər ē) *adj.* of or having to do with tasting or the sense of taste: also **gus′tative**

gusto (gus′tō) *n.* [< L. *gustus,* taste] 1. great vigour 2. zest; relish 3. [Obs.] taste; liking

gut (gut) *n.* [OE. *guttas,* pl.] 1. [*pl.*] the bowels; entrails 2. the intestine 3. tough cord made from animal intestines, used for violin strings, etc. 4. [*pl.*] [Colloq.] the basic or inner parts 5. [*pl.*] [Colloq.] daring, courage, etc. —*vt.* **gut′ted, gut′ting** 1. to remove the intestines from 2. to destroy the interior of, as by fire —*adj.* [Colloq.] 1. urgent and basic 2. instinctive

gutless *adj.* [Slang] lacking courage

gutsy *adj.* **-ier, -iest** [Slang] 1. greedy 2. courageous, forceful, etc. —**guts′iness** *n.*

gutta-percha (gut′ə pur′chə) *n.* [< Malay] a rubberlike gum produced from various SE Asian trees, used in insulation, dentistry, etc.

gutter (gut′ər) *n.* [< L. *gutta,* drop] 1. a trough to carry off water, as under the eaves of a roof, along the side of a street, etc. 2. a way of living characterized by squalor, poverty, etc. (with *the*) —*vt.* to furnish with gutters —*vi.* to melt rapidly so that the wax runs down in channels: said of a candle

gutter press journalism that seeks sensationalism

guttersnipe *n.* a child living in the slums, for the most part in the streets: contemptuous term

guttural (gut′ər əl) *adj.* [< L. *guttur,* throat] 1. of the throat 2. produced in the throat; rasping 3. formed with the back of the tongue close to the palate, as the *k* in *keen* —**gut′turally** *adv.* —**gut′-turalness** *n.*

guy¹ (gī) *n.* [< OFr. *guier,* to guide] a rope, chain, etc. attached to something to steady or guide it —*vt.* to guide or steady with a guy

guy² *n.* [< *Guy Fawkes*] 1. [Colloq.] any person, esp. a man or boy 2. an effigy of Guy Fawkes 3. a person dressed oddly —*vt.* to make fun of

guzzle (guz′′l) *vi., vt.* **-zled, -zling** [< ? OFr. *gosier,* throat] to drink or eat greedily —**guz′zler** *n.*

gybe (jīb) *n., vi., vt.* **gybed, gyb′ing** same as JIBE¹

gym (jim) *n.* [Colloq.] same as: 1. GYMNA-SIUM 2. PHYSICAL EDUCATION

gymkhana (jim kä′nə) *n.* [< Hindi & Urdu *gend-khāna,* racket court] 1. an event in which horses and riders display skill in races and contests 2. the place where such an event is held

gymnasium (jim nā′zē əm) *n., pl.* **-siums, -sia** [< Gr. *gymnos,* naked] a room or building equipped for physical training and athletic sports —**gymna′sial** *adj.*

gymnast (jim′nast) *n.* an expert in gymnastics

gymnastics (jim nas′tiks) *n.pl.* 1. [*with sing v.*] the practice of exercises that develop physical strength and agility 2. such exercises —**gymnas′tic** *adj.*

gymnosperm (jim′nə spurm′) *n.* [< Gr. *gymnos,* naked + *sperma,* seed] a plant having the ovules borne on open scales, usually in cones, as pines and cedars

gymp (gimp) *n.* same as GIMP

gym shoe a plimsoll

gymslip (jim′slip′) *n.* a tunic or pinafore

dress worn, esp. formerly, by schoolgirls, often as part of school uniform

gynaecology (gī′nəkol′əjē) *n.* [< Gr. *gynē,* woman + -LOGY] the branch of medicine dealing with the specific functions, diseases, etc. of women —**gyn′-aecolog′ic** (-kəloj′ik), **gyn′aeco·log′ical** *adj.* —**gyn′ae·col′ogist** *n.*

gyp[1] (jip) *n.* [< ? GYPSY] a male servant at a college, esp. at Cambridge

gyp[2] *n.* [< ?] [Slang] severe pain *[his arthritis gave him gyp]*

gypsum (jip′səm) *n.* [< Gr. *gypsos,* chalk] a hydrated sulphate of calcium used for making plaster of Paris, in treating soil, etc. —**gyp′seous** *adj.*

Gypsy (jip′sē) *n., pl.* -**sies** [< *Egipcien,* Egyptian] [*also* g-] a member of a wandering Caucasoid people with dark skin and black hair, believed to have originated in India

gyrate (jī rāt′; *for adj.* jī′rāt) *vi.* -**rat′ed, -rat′ing** [< Gr. *gyros,* circle] to move in a circular or spiral path —*adj.* spiral or circular —**gyra′tion** *n.* —**gy′ra′tor** *n.*

gyrfalcon (jur′fôl′kən) *n.* [< OFr. *girfaucon*] a large, fierce, strong falcon of N Europe, Asia and N America

gyro (jī′rō) *n., pl.* -**ros** *short for:* **1.** GYROSCOPE **2.** GYROCOMPASS

gyro- [< Gr. *gyros,* a circle] *a combining form meaning:* **1.** gyrating [*gyroscope*] **2.** gyroscope [*gyrocompass*]

gyrocompass *n.* a compass consisting of a motor-operated gyroscope whose rotating axis points to the geographic north pole

gyropilot *n.* *same as* AUTOMATIC PILOT

GYROSCOPE

gyroscope *n.* [GYRO- + -SCOPE] a wheel mounted in a ring so that its axis is free to turn in any direction: when the wheel is spun rapidly, it will keep its original plane of rotation —**gy′roscop′ic** (-skop′ik) *adj.*

gyrostabilizer *n.* a device consisting of a gyroscope spinning in a vertical plane, used to stabilize the side-to-side rolling of a ship

gyve (jīv) *n., vt.* gyved, gyv′ing [< Anglo-Fr. *gyves,* pl.] [Archaic or Poet.] fetter; shackle

H

H, h (āch) *n., pl.* **H's, h's** the eighth letter of the English alphabet

H *Chem.* hydrogen

H., h. 1. hard(ness) 2. height 3. high 4. hour(s)

ha¹ (hä) *interj.* [echoic] an exclamation variously expressing surprise, anger, triumph, etc.

ha² hectare(s)

habeas corpus (hā'bē əs kôr'pəs) [L., (that) you have the body] *Law* a writ requiring that a detained person be brought before a court to decide the legality of his detention or imprisonment

haberdasher (hab'ər dash'ər) *n.* [prob. < Anglo-Fr.] a dealer in various small articles, such as ribbons, thread, etc. —**hab'erdash'ery** *n.*

habiliment (hə bil'ə mənt) *n.* [< MFr. *habiller,* clothe] [*usually pl.*] clothing; dress

habit (hab'it) *n.* [< L. *habere,* have] 1. an acquired pattern of action that is difficult to break 2. a thing done often and, hence, easily; custom 3. tendency, disposition, etc. 4. an addiction, esp. to narcotics 5. a distinctive costume, as of a religious order —*vt.* to dress

habitable *adj.* fit to be lived in —**hab'ita·bil'ity** *n.*

habitant (hab'ə tənt) *n.* [Canad.] 1. one of the original French settlers in Canada or Louisiana 2. a descendant of these, esp. a farmer

habitat (hab'ə tat') *n.* [L., it inhabits] the natural environment, esp. of a plant or animal

habitation (hab'ə tā'shən) *n.* 1. an inhabiting; occupancy 2. a dwelling; home

habit-forming *adj.* resulting in the formation of a habit or in addiction

habitual (hə bit'yoo wəl) *adj.* 1. done or fixed as a habit; customary 2. being or doing by habit; steady [*a habitual* smoker] 3. much seen, done, or used; usual —**habit'ually** *adv.* —**habit'ualness** *n.*

habituate *vt.* **-at'ed, -at'ing** [see HABIT] to make used (*to*); accustom —**habit'ua'tion** *n.*

habitué (hə bit'yoo wā') *n.* [Fr.] a person who frequents a certain place or places

hachure (ha shyoo ər') *n.* [< OFr. *hacher,* chop] any of a series of short parallel lines used, esp. in map making, to represent a sloping or elevated surface

hacienda (ha'sē en'də) *n.* [Sp.] in Latin America, 1. a large estate 2. the main dwelling on such an estate

hack¹ (hak) *vt.* [OE. *haccian*] 1. to chop or cut roughly 2. in some sports, to foul by kicking an opponent's shin —*vi.* 1. to make rough or irregular cuts 2. to give harsh, dry coughs —*n.* 1. a tool for hacking 2. a slash, gash or notch 3. a kick on the shin —**hack'er** *n.*

hack² *n.* [< HACKNEY] 1. *a)* a horse kept for riding *b)* a horse for hire 2. an old, worn-out horse 3. one who does uninspired, routine writing 4. [U.S.] a devoted, unquestioning worker for a political party —*vi.* to ride a horse at a gentle pace —*adj.* 1. employed as or done by a hack 2. stale; trite

hackle (hak''l) *n.* [ME. *hechele*] 1. any of the long feathers at the neck of a cock 2. *Fishing* parts of an artificial fly made of feathers from a cock's neck 3. [*pl.*] the bristling hairs on a dog's neck and back 4. a comb for separating the fibres of flax, etc. —**get one's hackles up** to become tense with anger; bristle

hackney (hak'nē) *n., pl.* **-neys** [? < village where horses were formerly raised] 1. a horse for ordinary driving or riding 2. a carriage for hire

hackney carriage a taxi

hackneyed (hak'nēd') *adj.* made trite by overuse

HACKSAW

hacksaw (hak'sô') *n.* a saw for cutting metal, consisting of a narrow, fine-toothed blade held in a frame

had (had; *unstressed* həd, əd) *pt. & pp. of* HAVE

haddock (had'ək) *n.* [< ? OFr. *hadot*] a food fish related to the cod

hadedah (hä'di dä') *n.* [echoic] a large, grey-green S African ibis

Hades (hā'dēz) *Gr. Myth.* 1. the home of the dead 2. the ruler of the underworld

hadj (haj) *n. same as* HAJJ

hadji (haj'ē) *n. same as* HAJJI

haemal (hē'məl) *adj.* [< Gr. *haima,* blood] of the blood or blood vessels: also **hae'matal**

haematic (hi mat'ik) *adj.* of or filled with blood

haematite (hem'ə tīt') *n.* [< Gr. *haimatitēs,* bloodlike] ferric oxide, an important iron ore, brownish red or black —**haem'atit'ic** (-tit'ik) *adj.*

haemato- [< Gr.] *a combining form meaning* blood

haematology (hē'mə tol'ə jē) *n.* the study of blood and its diseases —**hae'mato-**

log'ic (-tə loj'ik), **hae'matolog'ical** adj. —**hae'matol'ogist** n.

haemo- [< Gr.] a combining form meaning blood [haemoglobin]: also [Chiefly U.S.] **hemo-**

haemoglobin (hē'mō glō'bin) n. [see HAEMATO + GLOBULIN] the red colouring matter of the red blood corpuscles: it carries oxygen from the lungs to the tissues

haemophilia (hē'mō fil'ē ə) n. [see HAEMO- & -PHILE] a hereditary condition in which one of the normal blood-clotting factors is absent, causing prolonged bleeding from even minor cuts —**hae'mophil'iac** (-fil'ē ak) n. —**hae'mophil'ic** adj.

haemorrhage (hem'ər ij) n. [< Gr. haima, blood + rhēgnynai, break] the escape of blood from a blood vessel; heavy bleeding —vi. **-rhaged, -rhaging** to have a haemorrhage —**haem'orrhag'ic** (-ə raj'ik) adj.

haemorrhoid (hem'ə roid') n. [< Gr. haima, blood + rhein, to flow] a painful swelling of a vein in the region of the anus, often with bleeding: usually used in pl.

hafnium (haf'nē əm) n. [< L. Hafnia, Roman name of Copenhagen] a metallic chemical element found with zirconium and somewhat resembling it: symbol, Hf

haft (häft) n. [OE. hæft] a handle of a knife, etc.

hag (hag) n. [< OE. hægtesse, witch] 1. a witch 2. an ugly, often vicious old woman —**hag'gish** adj.

haggard (hag'ərd) adj. [MFr. hagard, untamed] having a wild, worn look, as from grief —n. Falconry a hawk captured after reaching maturity

haggis (hag'is) n. [< ?] a Scottish dish made of offal, mixed with suet, seasoning, and oatmeal and boiled in a sheep's stomach

haggle (hag''l) vi. **-gled, -gling** [< Scot. hag, chop] to argue about terms, price, etc.; wrangle —n. a haggling

hagio- [< Gr.] a prefix meaning saintly, sacred

hagiography (hag'ē og'rə fē) n., pl. **-phies** [HAGIO- + -GRAPHY] the writing or study of lives of the saints

hagiology (hag'ē ol'ə jē) n., pl. **-gies** [HAGIO- -LOGY] literature about the saints' lives and legends

hagridden (hag'rid''n) adj. obsessed by fears

hah (hä) interj., n. same as HA[1]

ha-ha (hä'hä') n. [Fr. haha] a fence set in a ditch round a garden so as not to hide the view from within

haiku (hī'kōō) n. pl. **-ku** [Jap.] a Japanese poem of three unrhymed lines of 5, 7, and 5 syllables respectively

hail[1] (hāl) vt. [< ON. heill, sound] 1. to greet with cheers; acclaim 2. to salute as [they hailed him their leader] 3. to summon [hail a taxi] —vi. Naut. to signal to a ship —n. 1. a hailing 2. the distance a shout will carry [within hail] —interj. an exclamation of greeting, etc. —**hail fellow well met** very friendly to everyone —**hail from** to come from —**hail'er** n.

hail[2] n. [OE. hægel] 1. pellets of ice

that fall during thunderstorms 2. a showering of or like hail [a hail of bullets] —vi. to pour down hail [it is hailing] —vt. to shower, hurl, etc. violently like hail (on or upon)

Hail Mary pl. **Hail Marys** same as AVE MARIA

hailstone n. a pellet of hail

hailstorm n. a storm during which hail falls

hair (häər) n. [OE. hær] 1. any of the fine, threadlike outgrowths from the skin of an animal or human 2. a growth of these; esp. that covering the human head 3. an extremely small space, degree, etc. 4. a threadlike growth on a plant —adj. 1. made of hair 2. for the care of the hair —**get in one's hair** [Colloq.] to annoy one —**keep one's hair on** [Colloq.] to stay calm —**let one's hair down** [Colloq.] to behave without reserve —**make one's hair stand on end** to horrify one —**not turn a hair** to show no fear, surprise, etc. —**split hairs** to quibble —**to a hair** exactly

hairbreadth n. an extremely small space or amount: also **hairs'breadth'**, **hair's'-breadth'**

haircloth n. cloth woven from horsehair, camel's hair, etc.

hairdo n., pl. **-dos'** the style in which (a woman's) hair is arranged; coiffure

hairdresser n. a person whose work is cutting, styling, etc. (women's) hair —**hair'dress'ing** n., adj.

hair-grip n. a small metal clip for holding hair in place

hairline n. 1. a very thin line or stripe 2. the outline of the hair on the head, esp. above the forehead

hairpiece n. 1. a toupee 2. a section of extra hair attached to one's real hair to give greater body or length

hairpin n. a small, usually U-shaped, piece of wire, etc., for keeping the hair in place —adj. U-shaped

hair-raising adj. [Colloq.] terrifying —**hair'-rais'er** n.

hair shirt a shirt or girdle of haircloth, worn for self-punishment by religious ascetics

hair-slide n. an ornamental hinged clasp for holding hair in place

hairsplitting adj., n. making petty distinctions; quibbling —**hair'split'ter** n.

hairspring n. a slender, hairlike coil that controls the balance wheel in a watch or clock

hair trigger a trigger so delicately adjusted that slight pressure on it discharges the firearm

hairy adj. **-ier, -iest** 1. covered with, of, or like hair 2. [Slang] difficult —**hair'iness** n.

hairy-back n. [S Afr. Derog. Slang] an Afrikaner

hajj (haj) n. [Ar. ḥajj, pilgrimage] the pilgrimage to Mecca that every Moslem is expected to take at least once

hajji, haji (haj'ē) n. [see prec.] a Moslem who has made a pilgrimage to Mecca

hake (hāk) *n.* [prob. < ON. *haki,* hook] any of various marine food fishes related to the cod

halberd (hal′bərd) *n.* [ult. < MHG. *helm,* handle + *barte,* axe] *Hist.* a combination spear and battle-axe: also **hal′bert —hal′-berdier′** *n.*

halcyon (hal′sē ən) *adj.* [< Gr. *alkyōn,* kingfisher, supposed to calm the sea at the winter solstice] tranquil, happy, idyllic, etc.: esp. in **halcyon days**

hale¹ (hāl) *adj.* **hal′er, hal′est** [OE. *hal*] sound in body; vigorous and healthy —**hale′ness** *n.*

hale² *vt.* **haled, hal′ing** [< OFr. *haler*] to force (one) to go [*haled* him into court]

half (häf) *n., pl.* **halves** [OE. *healf*] **1.** either of the two equal parts of something **2.** *Sport* either of the two equal periods of a game **3.** [Colloq.] half a pint of beer —*adj.* **1.** being a half **2.** incomplete; partial —*adv.* **1.** to the extent of a half **2.** [Colloq.] to some extent [*half* convinced*] **3.** [Colloq.] at all: used with *not* [*not half* bad] —**by half** considerably [*too busy by half*] —**in half** into halves —**not the half of** only a small part of

half-and-half *n.* something that is half one thing and half another; a mixture of beer and stout —*adj.* combining two things equally

halfback *n.* Football, Hockey, etc. a player positioned behind the forwards

half-baked *adj.* **1.** not completely planned **2.** having or showing little intelligence

half binding a style of book binding in which leather, etc., is used to surround the spine and cover the corners

half blood kinship through one parent only [sisters of the *half blood*] —**half′-blood′ed** *adj.*

half-breed *n.* a person whose parents are of different races

half brother a brother through one parent only

half-caste *n.* a half-breed

half cock the halfway position of the hammer of a firearm, when the trigger is locked —**go off at half cock 1.** to fail because of inadequate preparation or premature starting **2.** to go off too soon: said of a firearm

half crown a former British coin worth two shillings and sixpence (12.5 new pence): also **half a crown**

halfhearted *adj.* with little enthusiasm, determination, interest, etc. —**half′heart′-edly** *adv.*

half hitch a knot made by passing the end of the rope around the rope and then through the loop thus made

half-hour *n.* **1.** half of an hour; thirty minutes **2.** the point thirty minutes after any given hour —**half′-hour′ly** *adj., adv.*

half-inch (häf′inch′) *vt., vi.* [< *pinch*] [Slang] to steal

half-life *n.* the period required for the disintegration of half of the atoms in a sample of some radioactive substance: also **half life**

half-mast (häf′mäst′) *n.* the position

of a flag lowered about halfway down its staff, as in public mourning

half measures inadequate means or actions

half-moon (häf′mōon′) *n.* **1.** the moon when only half its disc is seen **2.** anything shaped like a half-moon

halfpenny (hāp′nē) *n., pl.* **-pence** (-pəns), **-pennies** a coin worth half of one penny

half sister a sister through one parent only

half size any of a series of sizes in clothing, shoes, etc. that is halfway between two sizes

half sovereign a former British coin worth ten shillings (50 new pence)

half term a short holiday midway through an academic term

half-timbered (häf′tim′bərd) *adj.* *Archit.* made of a wooden framework having the spaces filled with plaster, etc.

half time the rest period between halves of a game

half title the title of a book appearing on the odd-numbered page preceding the main title page

halftone *n.* **1.** *Art* a shading between light and dark **2.** *Photoengraving* a) a technique of shading by use of dots b) a photoengraving so made

halftrack *n.* an army truck, armoured vehicle, etc. with tractor treads instead of rear wheels

half-truth *n.* a statement containing only some of the facts, often made with the intention of deceiving

halfway *adj.* **1.** equally distant between two points, etc. **2.** incomplete —*adv.* **1.** to the midway point **2.** incompletely —**meet halfway** to be willing to compromise with

halfway house 1. a place to rest midway on a journey **2.** the halfway point in any progression

half-wit *n.* a fool —**half′-wit′ted** *adj.*

halibut (hal′ə bət) *n.* [< ME. *hali,* holy + *butt,* flounder] a large, edible flatfish found in northern seas

halitosis (hal′ə tō′sis) *n.* [< L. *halitus,* breath + -OSIS] bad-smelling breath

hall (hôl) *n.* [OE. *heall*] **1.** a passageway or room between the entrance and the interior of a building **2.** a large public room for entertainments, etc. **3.** the dwelling of a baron, squire, etc. **4.** a residential building in a university **5.** *a)* in some colleges, a dining-room *b)* a dinner eaten there **6.** the large, main living-room in a castle or manor house **7.** the headquarters of a guild, etc. **8.** a passageway onto which rooms open

hallelujah, halleluiah (hal′ə lōō′yə) *interj.* [< Heb. *hallelū,* praise + *yāh,* Jehovah] praise (ye) the Lord! —*n.* a hymn of praise to God

halliard (hal′yərd) *n.* same as HALYARD

hallmark (hôl′märk′) *n.* **1.** an official mark stamped on British gold and silver articles orig. at Goldsmiths' Hall in London, as a guarantee of genuineness **2.** any mark of high quality —*vt.* to put a hallmark on

hallo (hə lō′) *interj.* [< HALLOO] an exclamation *a)* of greeting *b)* to attract attention *c)* of surprise —*n., pl.* **-los** a saying of 'hallo'

halloo (hə lōō′) *vi., vt.* **-looed′, -loo′ing** 1. to call out in order to attract attention 2. to urge on (hounds) by shouting 3. to shout —*interj., n.* a shout

hallow (hal′ō) *vt.* [OE. *halgian*] to make or regard as holy —**hal′lowed** *adj.*

Halloween, Hallowe'en (hal′ō wēn′) *n.* [< *all hallow even*] the evening of October 31st, which is followed by All Saints' Day

hallucinate (hə lōō′sə nāt′) *vi., vt.* **-nat′-ed, -nat′ing** [< L. *hallucinari*, wander mentally] to have or cause to have hallucinations —**hallu′cinant** *adj., n.*

hallucination (hə lōō′sə nā′shən) *n.* 1. the apparent perception of sights, sounds, etc. that are not actually present 2. the imaginary thing apparently seen, heard, etc. —**hallu′cinative, hallu′cinatory** *adj.*

hallucinogen (hə lōō′sə nə jen) *n.* a drug that produces hallucinations —**hallu′cino-gen′ic** *adj.*

hallway (hôl′wā′) *n.* a passageway; corridor; hall

halm (häm) *n. same as* HAULM

halo (hā′lō) *n., pl.* **-los, -loes** [< Gr. *halōs*, circular threshing floor] 1. a symbolic ring of light around the head of a saint, etc. 2. the glory with which a revered person or thing is invested 3. a ring of light that seems to encircle the sun, moon, etc.

halogen (hal′ə jən) *n.* [< Gr. *hals*, salt + -GEN] any of the five very active, nonmetallic chemical elements, fluorine, chlorine, bromine, astatine, and iodine

halt[1] (hôlt) *vi., vt.* [< G. *halten*, to hold] stop —*n.* 1. a stop 2. a minor railway station, without permanent buildings —**call a halt** to order a stop

halt[2] *vi.* [< OE. *healtian*] 1. to be uncertain; hesitate *[to halt in one's speech]* 2. to have defects in flow, as of rhythm or logic —*adj.* [Archaic] lame —**the halt** those who are lame —**halt′ingly** *adv.*

halter (hôl′tər) *n.* [OE. *hælftre*] 1. a rope, etc. for tying or leading an animal 2. a rope for hanging a person; noose 3. a woman's garment held up by a loop around the neck —*vt.* to put a halter on (an animal)

halve (häv) *vt.* **halved, halv′ing** 1. to divide into two equal parts 2. to share equally (*with* someone) 3. to reduce to half 4. *Golf* to draw (a hole, match, etc.)

halves *n. pl. of* HALF —**by halves** 1. incompletely; imperfectly 2. halfheartedly —**go halves** to share expenses, etc. equally

halyard (hal′yərd) *n.* [< ME. *halier*] a rope or tackle for raising or lowering a flag, sail, etc.

ham (ham) *n.* [OE. *hamm*] 1. *a)* the upper part of a pig's hind leg, salted, smoked, etc. *b)* meat from this 2. the back of the thigh 3. the thigh and the buttock together 4. [Slang] an incompetent actor, esp. one who overacts

5. [Colloq.] an amateur radio operator —*vi.* **hammed, ham′ming** to overact

hamadryad (ham′ə drī′əd) *n.* [< Gr. *Hamadryas*] *Gr. Myth.* a wood nymph whose life was bound up with that of the tree in which she lived

hamba (ham′bə) *interj.* [< Bantu -*hamba*, walk, travel] [S Afr.] go away; be off

hamburger (ham′bur gər) *n.* [< *Hamburg*, W. Germany] a fried or baked cake of minced meat, often eaten as a sandwich in a round bun

ham-fisted (ham′fist′id) *adj.* [Colloq.] clumsy: also **ham-handed**

Hamitic (ha mit′ik) *adj.* designating a group of African languages, including ancient Egyptian and Berber

hamlet (ham′lit) *n.* [< OFr. *hamel*] a very small village

hammer (ham′ər) *n.* [OE. *hamor*] 1. a tool for pounding, with a metal head and a handle 2. a thing like this in shape or use; specif., *a)* the mechanism that strikes the firing pin in a firearm *b)* any of the felted mallets that strike the strings of a piano 3. *a)* a heavy metal ball attached to a wire and thrown for distance *b)* this event 4. an auctioneer's gavel —*vt.* 1. to strike repeatedly as with a hammer 2. to drive, force, or shape as with hammer blows 3. [Colloq.] to defeat, esp. in a game —*vi.* to strike repeated blows as with a hammer —**come** (or **go**) **under the hammer** to be offered for sale by an auctioneer —**hammer and tongs** noisily and with much energy —**hammer** (**away**) **at** to keep emphasizing

hammer and sickle the emblem on the flag of the U.S.S.R., representing the industrial workers and the peasants

hammerhead *n.* a shark that has a mallet-shaped head

hammertoe *n.* a toe that is permanently bent downwards in a clawlike deformity

hammock (ham′ək) *n.* [Sp. *hamaca* < WInd.] a bed of canvas, etc. swung from ropes at both ends

hammy (ham′ē) *adj.* **-mier, -miest** [Slang] like or characteristic of a ham (actor); overacting

hamper[1] (ham′pər) *vt.* [ME. *hampren*] to hinder

hamper[2] *n.* [< OFr. *hanap*, cup] 1. a large basket, usually with a cover 2. its contents, usually food

hamster (ham′stər) *n.* [G.] a rodent with large cheek pouches: it is often kept as a pet

hamstring (ham′striŋ′) *n.* 1. a tendon at the back of the human knee 2. the great tendon at the back of the hock in a four-legged animal —*vt.* **-strung′, -string′ing** 1. to disable by cutting a hamstring 2. to make powerless

hand (hand) *n.* [OE.] 1. the part of the human arm below the wrist, used for grasping 2. the corresponding part in apes, etc. 3. a side or position *[* at one's right *hand]* 4. possession or care *[* the papers are in my *hands]* 5. control; power *[* to strengthen one's *hand]* 6. an active part *[take a hand* in this work*]* **7.** *a)* a pledge *b)* a promise to marry **8.** skill; ability *[a master's hand]* **9.** *a)* handwriting *b)* a signature **10.** applause *[they gave the singer a hand]* **11.** help *[lend a hand]* **12.** a person whose chief work is with his hands, as a labourer **13.** a member of a ship's crew **14.** a person having some special skill *[quite a hand at sewing]* **15.** a source *[get a story at second hand]* **16.** anything like a hand, as the pointer on a clock **17.** the breadth of a hand, about 10 centimetres, used in measuring the height of horses **18.** *Card Games a)* the cards held by a player at one time *b)* a player *c)* a round of play —*adj.* of, for, made by, or controlled by the hand —*vt.* **1.** to give as with the hand; transfer **2.** to help, steady, etc. with the hand *[to hand* a lady into her car*]* —**(at) first hand** from the original source —**at hand 1.** near **2.** imminent —**(at) second hand 1.** not from the original source **2.** previously used —**by hand** not by machines but with the hands —**change hands** to pass from one owner to another —**from hand to mouth** with just enough for immediate needs —**hand down 1.** to bequeath **2.** to announce (a verdict, etc.) —**hand in** to give; submit —**hand in (or and) glove** in intimate association —**hand it to** *[Colloq.]* to give deserved credit to —**hand on** to pass along —**hand out** to distribute —**hand over** to give up —**hand over fist** *[Colloq.]* easily and in large amounts —**hands down** without effort —**hand to hand** at close quarters: said of fighting —**have one's hands full** to be extremely busy —**in hand 1.** in control **2.** in possession **3.** in process —**keep one's hand in** to keep in practice in order to retain one's skill —**lay hands on 1.** to attack physically **2.** to seize **3.** to touch with the hands in blessing —**off one's hands** no longer in one's care —**on every hand** on all sides: also **on all hands** —**on hand 1.** near **2.** available **3.** present —**on one's hands** in one's care; as one's responsibility —**on the one hand** from one point of view —**on the other hand** from the opposed point of view —**out of hand 1.** out of control **2.** immediately; without reservation or close examination *[to condemn out of hand]* —**show one's hand** to disclose one's intentions —**turn one's hand to** to undertake —**wash one's hands of** to refuse to take responsibility for —**with a high hand** with arrogance —**hand′less** *adj.*

handbag *n.* **1.** a small container for money, toilet articles, etc., carried by women **2.** a small suitcase

handball *n.* a game in which a ball is thrown by hand from player to player

handbill *n.* a small printed notice, advertisement, etc. to be passed out by hand

handbook *n.* **1.** a compact reference book on some subject; manual **2.** a guidebook

handbreadth *n.* the breadth of the human palm, c. 10 cm

h. & **c.** hot and cold

handcart *n.* a small cart, often with only two wheels, pulled or pushed by hand

handcraft *n.* same as HANDICRAFT

handcuff *vt.* to put handcuffs on —*n.pl.* a pair of connected metal rings that can be locked about the wrists, as in fastening a prisoner to a policeman

handful *n.*, *pl.* **-fuls** **1.** as much or as many as the hand will hold **2.** a relatively small number or amount **3.** *[Colloq.]* someone or something hard to manage

handicap (han′dĕ kap′) *n.* [< *hand in cap,* former kind of lottery] **1.** *a)* a race or competition in which difficulties are imposed on, or advantages given to, the contestants to make their chances equal *b)* such a difficulty or advantage **2.** something that hampers, disables, etc. **3.** *Golf* the average number of strokes above par which a player takes to complete a course —*vt.* **-capped′**, **-cap′ping 1.** to give a handicap to **2.** to hinder —**the handicapped** those who are physically disabled or mentally retarded

handicraft (han′dĕ kräft′) *n.* **1.** expertness with the hands **2.** an occupation or art calling for skilful use of the hands, as weaving —**hand′icrafts′man** *n.*

handiwork *n.* **1.** same as HANDWORK **2.** anything made or done by a particular person

handkerchief (haŋ′kər chif) *n.*, *pl.* **-chiefs, -chieves** (-chēvz′) **1.** a small piece of cloth for wiping the nose, eyes, or face **2.** a kerchief

handle (han′d'l) *n.* [OE., < *hand*] **1.** that part of a utensil, tool, etc. which is to be held **2.** *[Colloq.]* a person's title *[a handle* to one's name*]* **3.** an opportunity or excuse *[his failure served as a handle* to his enemies*]* —*vt.* **-dled, -dling 1.** to touch, lift, etc. with the hand **2.** to operate with the hands *[he handles* the reins well*]* **3.** to manage, control, etc. **4.** to deal with **5.** to sell or deal in **6.** to behave towards; treat —*vi.* **1.** to respond to control *[the car handles* well*]* —**fly off the handle** *[Colloq.]* to become violently angry

handlebar *n.* **1.** a curved metal bar with handles on the ends, for steering a bicycle, etc. **2.** a moustache with long curved ends: in full, **handlebar moustache**

handler *n.* one that handles; specif., *a)* a boxer's trainer *b)* a person who trains and manages an animal

handmade *adj.* not made by machine

handmaiden *n.* [Archaic] a woman or girl servant Also **hand′maid′**

hand-me-down *n.* *[Colloq.]* a used article of clothing, etc. which is passed along to someone else

handout *n.* **1.** food, etc. given to a needy person **2.** a leaflet, statement, etc. handed out for publicity

handpick (hand′pik′) *vt.* **1.** to pick (fruit, etc.) by hand **2.** to choose with care —**hand′picked′** *adj.*

handrail *n.* a rail serving as a guard or hand support, as along a stairway

HANDSET

handset *n.* a telephone mouthpiece and receiver in a single unit, held in one hand

handshake *n.* a gripping of each other's hand in greeting, etc.

handsome (han′səm) *adj.* [orig., easily handled] 1. good-looking, esp. in a manly way 2. large [*a handsome* sum] 3. generous [*a handsome* gesture] —**hand′somely** *adv.*

handspring *n.* a gymnastic feat in which the performer turns over in midair with one or both hands touching the ground

handstand *n.* a gymnastic feat of supporting oneself upright on the hands with the arms outstretched

hand-to-hand (han′tə hand′) *adj.* in close contact; at close quarters: said of fighting

hand-to-mouth (-mouth′) *adj.* barely subsisting

handwork *n.* work done or an article made by hand, not by machine —**hand′worked′** *adj.*

handwriting *n.* 1. writing done by hand, with pen, pencil, etc. 2. a style of such writing —**hand′writ′ten** *adj.*

handy *adj.* -ier, -iest 1. close at hand 2. easily used or managed 3. useful 4. clever with the hands —**hand′ily** *adv.* —**hand′iness** *n.*

handyman *n.* a man who does odd jobs

hanepoot (han′ə pôt′) *n.* [< Du.] [S Afr.] a kind of grape eaten as a dessert or used in wine-making

hang (han) *vt.* **hung, hang′ing;** for *vt.* 3 & *vi.* 4 **hanged** is preferred *pt.* & *pp.* [OE. *hangian*] 1. to attach to something above; suspend 2. to attach so as to permit free motion [to *hang* a door on its hinges] 3. to put to death by suspending from a rope about the neck 4. to fasten (pictures, etc.) to a wall 5. to ornament [to *hang* a room with pictures] 6. to paste (wallpaper) to walls 7. [Chiefly U.S.] to deadlock (a jury) 8. to suspend (game) till it becomes slightly decomposed —*vi.* 1. to be suspended 2. to swing, as on a hinge 3. to fall in folds as cloth 4. to die by hanging 5. to droop 6. to be doubtful [*hang* in the balance] —*n.* the way a thing hangs —**get the hang of** [Colloq.] 1. to learn the knack of 2. to understand —**hang around** (or **about**) [Colloq.] to loiter —**hang back** (or **off**) to be reluctant to advance —**hang fire** to be undecided —**hang heavily** (or **heavy**) pass slowly (of time) —**hang on** 1. to keep hold 2. to persevere 3. to depend on 4. to listen attentively to 5. [Colloq.] to wait —**hang out** 1. to lean out 2. [Slang] to frequent —**hang together** 1. to stick together 2. to make sense —**hang up** 1. to put on a hanger, etc. 2. to end a telephone conversation by replacing the receiver 3. to delay

hangar (han′ər) *n.* [Fr., a shed] a repair shed or shelter for aircraft

hangdog *adj.* 1. contemptible or abject 2. ashamed and cringing [a *hangdog* expression]

hanger *n.* 1. a person or thing that hangs 2. a thing on which objects, as garments, are hung

hanger-on (han′ər on′) *n., pl.* **hang′ers-on′** a follower or dependant; specif., one not wanted

hang gliding the sport of gliding while suspended by a harness from a large type of kite (**hang glider**)

hanging *adj.* 1. suspended 2. leaning over 3. located on a steep slope 4. deserving or imposing the death penalty —*n.* 1. a putting to death by hanging 2. something hung, as a tapestry

hangman *n.* an executioner who hangs criminals

hangnail *n.* [OE. *angnægl*, a corn] a bit of torn skin hanging at the side or base of a fingernail

hangover *n.* 1. headache, etc. occurring as an aftereffect of drinking too much alcohol 2. something remaining

hang-up *n.* [Slang] an emotional problem

hank (hank) *n.* [prob. < Scand.] 1. a coil of something flexible 2. a standard length of coiled yarn

hanker (han′kər) *vi.* [prob. < Du. or LowG.] to crave or long (*after, for*) —**hank′ering** *n.*

hankie, hanky (han′kē) *n., pl.* -**kies** [Colloq.] a handkerchief

hanky-panky (han′kē pan′kē) *n.* [< ? HOCUS-POCUS] [Colloq.] 1. trickery or deception 2. *a)* foolish behaviour *b)* illicit sexual behaviour

Hansard (han′särd) *n.* [< L. *Hansard*] the official record of proceedings in *a)* the British parliament *b)* the Canadian parliament

Hanse (hans) *n.* [< OHG.] a medieval league of free towns in N Germany and adjoining countries, for economic advancement: also **Hanseatic League**

hansom (cab) (han′səm) *n.* [< J. A. *Hansom*] a two-wheeled covered carriage for two passengers, pulled by one horse: the driver's seat is above and behind the cab

Hants. Hampshire

hap (hap) *n.* [< ON. *happ*] [Archaic] chance; luck —*vi.* **happed, hap′ping** to occur by chance; happen

haphazard (hap′haz′ərd) *adj.* [prec. + HAZARD] 1. not planned; casual 2. careless —*adv.* by chance; casually —**hap′haz′ardly** *adv.* —**hap′haz′ardness** *n.*

hapless (hap'lis) *adj.* unlucky —**hap'-lessly** *adv.*

happen (hap''n) *vi.* [< HAP] 1. to occur 2. to be or occur by chance 3. to have the luck or occasion; chance [I *happened* to see it] —**happen on** (or **upon**) to meet or find by chance —**happen to** to be done to; befall

happening *n.* 1. an event 2. an entertainment, etc., which is spontaneous or improvised, and usually involves its spectators

happy (hap'ē) *adj.* **-pier, -piest** [< HAP] 1. favoured by circumstances; lucky 2. having, showing, or causing pleasure 3. clever; apt [a *happy* suggestion] —**hap'-pily** *adv.* —**hap'piness** *n.*

happy event [Colloq.] the birth of a baby

happy-go-lucky *adj.* easygoing; trusting to luck

hara-kiri (har'ə kir'ē) *n.* [Jap. *hara*, belly + *kiri*, a cutting] ritual suicide by disembowelment: it was practised by high-ranking Japanese to avoid facing disgrace

harangue (hə raŋ') *n.* [< OIt. *aringo*, site for public assemblies] a long, blustering or scolding speech; tirade —*vi.*, *vt.* **-rangued', -rangu'ing** to speak or address in a harangue —**harangu'er** *n.*

harass (har'əs) *vt.* [< OFr. *harer*, set a dog on] 1. to worry, as with cares, debts, etc. 2. to trouble by repeated raids or attacks —**har'asser** *n.* —**har'assment** *n.*

harbinger (här'bin jər) *n.* [< OFr. *herberge*, a shelter] a person or thing that comes before to indicate what follows

harbour (här'bər) *n.* [< OE. *here*, army + *beorg*, a shelter] 1. a protected inlet for anchoring ships 2. a refuge; shelter —*vt.* 1. to serve as, or provide, shelter 2. to cling to [to *harbour* a grudge] —*vi.* to take shelter in a harbour —**har'bourer** *n.* —**har'bourless** *adj.*

harbour master the official in charge of enforcing the regulations governing the use of a harbour

hard (härd) *adj.* [OE. *heard*] 1. firm to the touch; solid and compact 2. powerful [a *hard* blow] 3. difficult to do, understand, deal with, or explain 4. a) unfeeling [a *hard* heart] b) unfriendly [*hard* feelings] 5. practical and shrewd [a *hard* customer] 6. a) firm, esp. in an aggressive way [a *hard* line] b) undeniable [*hard* facts] 7. harsh; severe 8. sharp or too sharp [*hard* outlines, a *hard* red] 9. having mineral salts that interfere with the lathering: said of water 10. energetic [a *hard* worker] 11. strongly alcoholic 12. [Colloq.] designating any drug, as heroin, that is addictive and very damaging 13. popularly, designating the letters *c* and *g* sounded as in *can* or *gun* 14. high; extreme —*adv.* 1. energetically [*work hard*] 2. with strength or severity [*hit hard*] 3. with difficulty [*hard*-earned] 4. so as to withstand much use [*hard*-wearing] 5. firmly [*secure hard* and fast] 6. close [*we live hard* by] 7. so as to be solid [to freeze *hard*] 8. to the fullest extent [*turn hard* right] —**be hard on** 1. to treat severely 2. to be difficult or unpleasant for —**hard and fast** invariable —**hard of hearing** partially deaf —**hard put to it** having considerable difficulty —**hard up** [Colloq.] in great need of something, esp. money —**hard'ness** *n.*

hardback *n.* a hard-cover book

hard-bitten *adj.* tough; dogged

hardboard *n.* a material made in sheets by subjecting fibres from wood chips to pressure and heat

hard-boiled *adj.* 1. boiled until the white and the yolk solidify: said of an egg 2. [Colloq.] not affected by sentiment, pity, etc.; tough

hard case [Colloq.] a person who is difficult to deal with, or impossible to reform

hard copy computer output that can be read by eye: as contrasted with output that is machine-readable only

hard-core *adj.* absolute; complete

hard-cover *adj.* designating any book bound in a relatively stiff cover: also **hard'-bound'**

harden *vt.*, *vi.* to make or become hard

hardened *adj.* 1. made hard or harder 2. confirmed or inveterate in a callous way

hardheaded *adj.* shrewd and unsentimental; practical —**hard'head'edly** *adv.* —**hard'head'edness** *n.*

hardhearted *adj.* unfeeling; pitiless

hard labour formerly, compulsory physical labour imposed, with imprisonment, as a punishment

hard-line *adj.* characterized by an aggressive, unyielding position in politics, foreign policy, etc.

hardly *adv.* 1. only just; scarcely: often used ironically to mean "not at all" [*hardly* the person to ask] 2. probably not 3. with difficulty 4. harshly

hard pad a disease in dogs, similar to distemper

hard palate the bony part of the roof of the mouth

hard-pressed *adj.* in difficulties; harassed

hard sell high-pressure salesmanship —**hard'-sell'** *adj.*

hardship *n.* 1. hard circumstances of life 2. a thing hard to bear

hard shoulder a surfaced verge along a motorway for emergency stops

hardtack *n.* [< *tack*, food] unleavened, very hard, large biscuits: traditionally part of army and navy rations

hardware *n.* 1. articles made of metal, as nails, utensils, etc. 2. heavy military equipment 3. the mechanical, magnetic, and electronic components of a computer 4. [Colloq.] weapons

hardwood *n.* 1. any tough timber with a compact texture 2. *Forestry* wood other than that from a conifer

hardy *adj.* **-dier, -diest** [< OFr. *hardir*, make bold] 1. bold and resolute 2. able to withstand fatigue, privation, etc. 3. able to survive the winter without special care : said of plants —**har′di ly** *adv.* —**har′-diness** *n.*

hare (hãer) *n.* [OE. *hara*] a swift mammal related to the rabbit, with long ears, a cleft upper lip, and long, powerful hind legs

hare and hounds a game in which some players chase others who have left a trail of paper scraps

harebell *n.* a plant with clusters of blue, bell-shaped flowers

harebrained *adj.* reckless, giddy, rash, etc.

harelip *n.* a congenital deformity consisting of a harelike cleft of the lip —**hare′lipped′** *adj.*

harem (hä rēm′) *n.* [Ar. *harīm,* prohibited (place)] 1. that part of a Moslem's household in which the women live 2. the women in a harem Also **hareem′**

haricot (har′ə kō′) *n.* [Fr.] 1. *same as* KIDNEY BEAN 2. the pod or seed of other edible beans

hari-kari (har′ə kir′ē) *n.* *same as* HARA-KIRI

hark (härk) *vi.* [< ? OE. *heorcnian,* hearken] to listen carefully : usually in the imperative —**hark back** to go back; revert

HARLEQUIN

Harlequin (här′lə kwin) [< OFr. *hierlekin,* demon] a traditional comic character in pantomime, who wears a mask and gay, spangled tights —*n.* [h-] a clown —*adj.* [h-] of many colours

harlequinade (här′lə kwi nād′) *n.* 1. that part of a pantomime in which the Harlequin and the clown play leading parts 2. buffoonery

Harley Street (här′lē) 1. a street in London famous for its large number of medical specialists' consulting rooms 2. medical specialists collectively

harlot (här′lət) *n.* [OFr., rogue] a prostitute —**har′lotry** *n.*

harm (härm) *n.* [OE. *hearm*] 1. hurt; injury; damage 2. moral wrong —*vt.* to hurt, damage, etc.

harmful *adj.* causing or able to cause harm; hurtful

harmless *adj.* causing no harm; inoffensive

harmonic (här mon′ik) *adj.* *Music a)* of or in harmony *b)* pertaining to an overtone —*n.* *same as* OVERTONE (sense 2) —**harmon′i cally** *adv.*

harmonica (här mon′i kə) *n.* a small wind instrument played with the mouth; mouth organ : it has a series of graduated metal reeds that produce tones when air is blown or sucked across them

harmonics *n.pl.* [*with sing. v.*] the physical science dealing with musical sounds

harmonious (här mō′nē əs) *adj.* 1. having parts combined in an orderly or pleasing arrangement 2. having similar feelings, ideas, interests, etc. 3. having musical tones combined to give a pleasing effect

harmonium (här mō′nē əm) *n.* a small reed organ

harmonize (här′mə nīz′) *vi.* -**nized′**, -**niz′-ing** to be or sing in harmony —*vt.* 1. to make harmonious 2. to add chords to (a melody) so as to form a harmony —**har′moniza′tion** *n.* —**har′moniz′er** *n.*

harmony (här′mə nē) *n.,* *pl.* -**nies** [< Gr. *harmos,* a fitting] 1. a combination of parts into a pleasing or orderly whole 2. agreement in feeling, ideas, etc.; peaceable or friendly relations 3. agreeable sounds; music 4. *Music a)* the simultaneous sounding of two or more tones, esp. when satisfying to the ear *b)* structure in the arrangement of chords

harness (här′nis) *n.* [< OFr. *harneis,* armour] 1. the leather straps and metal pieces by which a horse is fastened to a vehicle 2. any trappings similar to this —*vt.* 1. to put harness on (a horse, etc.) 2. to control so as to use the power of —**in harness** in or at one's routine work

harp (härp) *n.* [OE. *hearpe*] a musical instrument with strings stretched across an open, triangular frame, held upright and played by plucking with the fingers —*vi.* to persist in talking or writing tediously (on or upon) —**harp′ist** *n.*

harpoon (här pōōn′) *n.* [< MFr. < *harper,* to claw] a barbed missile attached to a cord and hurled or fired from a gun when hunting whales, etc. —*vt.* to strike or kill with a harpoon —**harpoon′er** *n.*

harpsichord (härp′si kôrd′) *n.* [see HARP & CORD] a stringed musical instrument with a keyboard, predecessor of the piano —**harp′sichord′ist** *n.*

harpy (här′pē) *n.,* *pl.* -**pies** [< Gr. *harpazein,* seize] a greedy or grasping person : after the hideous, winged monsters in Greek mythology

harquebus (här′kwi bəs) *n.* [ult. < Du. *haak,* hook + *bus,* gun] an early type of portable gun

harridan (har′i d'n) *n.* [prob. < Fr. *haridelle,* worn-out horse] a disreputable, shrewish old woman

harrier[1] (har′ē ər) *n.* [< HARE] 1. a hound used for hunting hares and rabbits 2. a cross-country runner

harrier[2] *n.* 1. one who harries 2. a

hawk that preys on small mammals, reptiles, etc.

harrow (har′ō) *n.* [prob. < ON. *harfr*] a heavy frame with spikes or discs, used for breaking up ploughed ground, etc. —*vt.* 1. to draw a harrow over (land) 2. to torment; vex —**har′rowing** *adj.*

harry (har′ē) *vt.* -ried, -rying [< OE. *here*, army] 1. to raid and ravage or rob 2. to torment; harass

harsh (härsh) *adj.* [ME. *harsk*] 1. unpleasantly sharp or rough to the ear, eye, taste, or touch 2. excessively severe; cruel —**harsh′en** *vt., vi.* —**harsh′ly** *adv.*

hart (härt) *n.* [OE. *heorot*] a male of the red deer, esp. after its fifth year; stag

hartal (här′tal) *n.* [Hindī] in India, a suspension of work, esp. as an expression of political protest

hartebeest (här′tə bēst′) *n.* [obs. Afrik.] a large, swift S African antelope having lyre-shaped horns

hartshorn (härts′hôrn′) *n.* ammonium carbonate, used in smelling salts: orig. obtained from deer's antlers

harum-scarum (häar′əm skäar′əm) *adj.* [< ? HARE + SCARE] reckless or rash —*n.* a harum-scarum person

harvest (här′vist) *n.* [OE. *hærfest*] 1. the time of the year when grain, fruit, etc. is gathered in 2. a season's crop 3. the gathering in of a crop 4. the outcome of any effort —*vt., vi.* 1. to gather in (a crop, etc.) 2. to gather the crop from (a field) 3. to get (something) as the result of an action or effort —**har′vestable** *adj.*

harvester *n.* 1. a person who gathers in a crop 2. any of various farm machines for harvesting crops

harvest festival a religious thanksgiving service in autumn

harvest home 1. the bringing home of the last harvest load 2. a festival celebrating this

harvest moon the full moon at or about the time of the autumnal equinox, September 22nd or 23rd

harvest mouse a small mouse inhabiting cornfields, etc.

has (haz, həz, əz) *3rd pers. sing., pres. indic., of* HAVE

has-been *n.* [Colloq.] a person or thing whose popularity or effectiveness is past

hash¹ (hash) [Fr. *hacher*, chop] 1. a dish of diced, cooked meat reheated in a sauce 2. a jumble 3. a reuse of old material —**make a hash of** [Colloq.] to mess up —**settle one's hash** [Colloq.] to subdue

hash² *n.* [Slang] hashish

hashish (hash′ēsh) *n.* [Ar. *hashīsh*] a drug formed from the resin in the flowering tops of Indian hemp, chewed or smoked for its intoxicating effects

haslet (häz′lit) *n.* [ME. *hastelet*] a dish made from heart, liver, etc., fried and made into a loaf eaten cold

HASP

hasp (häsp) *n.* [OE. *hæpse*] a hinged fastening for a door, etc.; esp., a metal piece fitted over a staple and fastened by a padlock

hassle (has′'l) *n.* [< ?] [Colloq.] 1. a heated argument 2. a troublesome situation —*vi.* -sled, -sling [Colloq.] to have a heated argument —*vt.* [Chiefly U.S. Colloq.] to harass

hassock (has′ək) *n.* [OE. *hassuc*] 1. a thick clump of grass 2. a firmly stuffed cushion for kneeling on, etc.

haste (hāst) *n.* [OFr. *haste*] quickness of motion; hurrying; urgency —*vt., vi.* **hast′ed, hast′ing** *same as* HASTEN —**in haste** 1. in a hurry 2. in too great a hurry —**make haste** to hasten

hasten (hās′'n) *vt.* to cause to be or come faster; speed up —*vi.* to move swiftly; hurry

hasty (hās′tē) *adj.* -ier, -iest 1. done with haste; hurried 2. done with too little thought; rash 3. short tempered —**hast′ily** *adv.* —**hast′iness** *n.*

hat (hat) *n.* [OE. *hætt*] a covering for the head, usually with a brim and crown —**pass the hat** to take up a collection —**take one's hat off to** to congratulate —**talk through one's hat** [Colloq.] to talk nonsense —**under one's hat** [Colloq.] secret —**hat′less** *adj.*

hatband *n.* a band of cloth around the crown of a hat

hatch¹ (hach) *vt.* [ME. *hacchen*] 1. to bring forth (young) from (an egg or eggs) 2. to bring (a plan, plot, etc.) into existence —*vi.* 1. to bring forth young: said of eggs 2. to come forth from the egg —*n.* 1. the process of hatching 2. the brood hatched —**hatch′ling** *n.*

hatch² *n.* [OE. *hæcc*, grating] 1. an opening in a wall for serving food 2. *same as* HATCHWAY 3. a covering for a hatchway

hatch³ *vt.* [< OFr. *hache*, axe] to shade with fine parallel lines —**hatch′ing** *n.*

hatchback *n.* [< HATCH²] 1. a car with a single lifting door in the rear 2. the door itself

hatchet (hach′it) *n.* [< OFr. *hache*, axe] a small axe with a short handle —**bury the hatchet** to make peace

hatchet man [Colloq.] 1. a man hired to commit murder 2. any person assigned to carry out unscrupulous tasks

hatchway *n.* a covered opening in a ship's deck

hate (hāt) vt. **hat′ed, hat′ing** [OE. *hatian*] 1. to have strong dislike or ill will for 2. to shrink from [to *hate* arguments] —vi. to feel hatred —n. 1. strong dislike or ill will 2. a person or thing hated —**hate′able, hat′able** adj. —**hat′er** n.

hateful adj. causing or deserving hate —**hate′fulness** n.

hatrack (hat′rak′) n. a rack, set of pegs, etc. to hold hats

hatred (hā′trid) n. strong dislike or ill will

hatter (hat′ər) n. one who makes or sells hats

hat trick 1. in cricket, the taking of three wickets by one bowler with three successive balls 2. any achievement of three successive points or goals in other games

hauberk (hô′bərk) n. [ult. < Frank. *hals*, neck + *bergan*, protect] a medieval coat of armour, usually of chain mail

haughty (hôt′ē) adj. **-tier, -tiest** [< OFr. *haut*, high] having or showing great pride in oneself and contempt for others —**haugh′tily** adv. —**haugh′tiness** n.

haul (hôl) vt., vi. [< ODu. *halen*, fetch] 1. to move by pulling; drag 2. to transport by wagon, truck, etc. 3. *same as* HALE² 4. Naut. to change the course of (a ship) —n. 1. the act of hauling 2. the amount amassed, earned, caught, etc. at one time 3. the distance covered in transporting or travelling —**haul up** 1. to sail nearer the direction of the wind 2. [Colloq.] to call to account —**haul′er** n.

haulage n. 1. the act or process of hauling 2. the charge made for hauling, as by a railway

haulier (hôl′yər) n. 1. a mine worker who hauls coal to the foot of the shaft 2. a person or organization that transports goods by road

haulm (hôm) n. [< OE. *healm*, straw] the stalks of beans, peas, etc., esp. after the crop has been gathered

haunch (hônch) n. [< OFr. *hanche*] 1. the part of the body including the hip, buttock, and thickest part of the thigh 2. an animal's loin and leg together

haunt (hônt) vt. [< OFr. *hanter*, to frequent] 1. to visit in the form of a ghost 2. to visit (a place) often 3. to persistently force one's company on 4. to recur repeatedly to [memories *haunted* her] 5. to pervade [a house *haunted* by sorrow] —n. a place frequented [to make the library one's *haunt*]

haunted adj. supposedly frequented by ghosts

haunting adj. often recurring to the mind

hautboy (ō′boi′) n. [< Fr. *haut*, high + *bois*, wood] earlier name for OBOE

‡**haute couture** (ōt ko͞o tyooər′) [Fr.] the leading designers in women's clothing, or their creations

‡**haute cuisine** (ōt kwē zēn′) [Fr.] the preparation of fine food by highly skilled chefs, or the food so prepared

hauteur (ō tur′) n. [Fr.] disdainful pride; haughtiness

Havana (hə van′ə) n. [< *Havana*, Cuba] a type of cigar

have (hav; həv, əv; *before* 'to' haf) vt. **had, hav′ing** [OE. *habban*] 1. to hold; own; possess 2. to possess as a part, characteristic, etc. [the week *has* seven days] 3. to experience; undergo 4. to know [to *have* a little Spanish] 5. to hold in the mind [to *have* an idea] 6. to state [gossip *has* it] 7. a) to get, take, or obtain b) to eat or drink 8. to bear or beget 9. to engage in [to *have* an argument] 10. to cause to or cause to be 11. to be in a certain relation to [to *have* a wife] 12. to feel and show [*have* pity] 13. to permit [I won't *have* this] 14. [Colloq.] a) to hold at a disadvantage b) to cheat c) to engage in sexual intercourse with *Have* is used as an auxiliary expressing completed action, as in the perfect tenses (Ex.: I *had* left), and with infinitives to express necessity (Ex.: we *have* to go) *Have got* often replaces *have Have* is conjugated in the present indicative: (I) *have*, (he, she, it) *has*, (we, you, they) *have;* in the past indicative (I, he, she, it, we, you, they) *had* —n. a person or nation with relatively much wealth —**have had it** [Colloq.] to be defeated, etc. or no longer popular, useful, etc.—**have it both ways** to adopt either of contradictory alternatives to suit different moods or occasions —**have it out** to settle a disagreement by fighting or discussion —**have on** 1. to be wearing 2. to have an engagement 3. to deceive playfully —**the haves and the have-nots** those persons or nations who have wealth and those who do not

haven (hā′vən) n. [OE. *hæfen*] 1. a port; harbour 2. any sheltered, safe place; refuge

haver (hā′vər) vi. [< ?] to talk foolishly or waste time

haversack (hav′ər sak′) n. [< G. Dial. *habersack*, sack of oats] a canvas bag for rations, worn on the back or over one shoulder, as by soldiers and hikers

havoc (hav′ək) n. [< OFr. *havot*, plunder] great destruction and devastation —**play havoc with** to disorder, confuse

haw¹ (hô) n. [OE. *haga*] the berry of the hawthorn

haw² vi. [echoic] to hesitate in speaking —n. a sound made by a speaker when hesitating briefly

hawfinch (hô′finch′) n. [HAW¹ + FINCH] a small, brown bird with brightly-coloured wings

hawk¹ (hôk) n. [OE. *hafoc*] 1. a bird of prey with short, rounded wings, a long tail and legs, and a hooked beak and claws 2. an advocate of war or open hostilities —vi. to hunt birds with hawks —**hawk′er** n. —**hawk′ing** n.

hawk² vt., vi. [< HAWKER] to advertise or peddle (goods) in the street by shouting

hawk³ vi. [echoic] to clear the throat

audibly —*vt.* to bring up (phlegm) by coughing

hawker *n.* [ult. < MLowG. *hoken,* peddle] a person who hawks goods in the street

hawk-eyed *adj.* keen-sighted like a hawk

hawkmoth *n.* a moth with a thick, tapering body and a long feeding tube used for sucking nectar

hawser (hô'zər) *n.* [ult. < L. *altus,* high] a large rope or small cable, by which a ship is anchored or towed

hawthorn (hô'thôrn') *n.* [< OE. *haga,* hedge + *thorn*] a thorny shrub with white or pink flowers and small, red fruits

hay (hā) *n.* [OE. *hieg*] grass, clover, etc. cut and dried for fodder —**hit the hay** [Slang] to go to bed —**make hay of** to turn into confusion —**make hay while the sun shines** to make the most of an opportunity

haybox *n.* a box filled with hay in which heated food is left to continue cooking

hay fever an acute allergic inflammation of the eyes and upper respiratory tract, caused by pollen

haymaker *n.* a person who cuts hay and spreads it out to dry —**hay'mak'- ing** *n.*

hayride *n.* a pleasure ride taken by a group in a wagon partly filled with hay

haystack *n.* a large heap of hay piled up outdoors: also **hay'rick'**

haywire *adj.* [Colloq.] 1. out of order; confused 2. crazy: usually in **go haywire,** to become crazy

hazard (haz'ərd) *n.* [< OFr. < Ar.] 1. risk; danger 2. chance 3. an obstacle on a golf course 4. an early game of chance played with dice —*vt.* to risk or venture

hazardous *adj.* risky; dangerous —**haz'- ardously** *adv.*

haze (hāz) *n.* [prob. < HAZY] 1. a thin vapour of fog, smoke, etc. in the air 2. slight vagueness of mind —*vi., vt.* hazed, **haz'ing** to make or become hazy (often with *over*)

hazel (hā'z'l) *n.* [OE. *hæsel*] 1. a shrub bearing edible nuts 2. a light brown —*adj.* light-brown

hazelnut *n.* the small, roundish nut of the hazel

hazy (hā'zē) *adj.* -zier, -ziest [< ? OE. *hasu,* dusky] 1. somewhat foggy or smoky 2. vague, obscure, or indefinite [*hazy* thinking] —**ha'zily** *adv.* —**ha'ziness** *n.*

HB hard black (of pencil lead)

H.B.C. Hudson's Bay Company

H-bomb *n.* same as HYDROGEN BOMB

H.C. 1. Holy Communion 2. House of Commons

H.C.F., h.c.f. highest common factor

he (hē; *unstressed* hi, ē, i) *pron. for pl. see* THEY [OE.] 1. the man, boy, or male animal previously mentioned 2. anyone [*he* who laughs last laughs best] —*n.,*

pl. **hes** a man, boy, or male animal —*adj.* male

He *Chem.* helium

H.E. 1. high explosive 2. His Eminence 3. His (or Her) Excellency

head (hed) *n.* [OE. *heafod*] 1. the top part of the body in man, or the front part in most other animals containing the brain, eyes, ears, nose, and mouth 2. *a)* intelligence *b)* ability [to have a *head* for figures] 3. [Colloq.] a headache 4. a person [dinner at five pounds a *head*] 5. *pl.* **head** a unit of counting [fifty *head* of cattle] 6. the obverse of a coin: often **heads** 7. the highest or uppermost part or thing; specif., *a)* the top of a page, etc. *b)* a title *c)* a chief point of discussion *d)* froth floating on newly poured beer, etc. 8. the foremost part; front; specif., *a)* a part associated with the human head [the *head* of a bed] *b)* the front part of a ship *c) Naut.* a lavatory 9. the part designed for holding, striking, etc. [the *head* of a pin] 10. a headland 11. a projecting place in a boil, where pus is about to break through 12. the part of a tape recorder that records or plays back the magnetic signals on the tape 13. the membrane stretched across the end of a drum, etc. 14. the source of a river, stream, etc. 15. a source of water kept at some height to supply a mill, etc. 16. the pressure in an enclosed fluid, as steam 17. a position of leadership 18. a leader, director, etc. 19. a headmaster 20. a large, compact bud 21. [Slang] a habitual user of marijuana, LSD, etc. —*adj.* 1. most important; principal 2. at the top or front 3. striking against the front [*head* current] —*vt.* 1. to be in charge of 2. to lead; precede 3. to supply with a head or heading 4. to cause to go in a specified direction 5. *Soccer* to hit (the ball) with one's head —*vi.* to travel [to *head* eastwards] —**by a head** by a small margin —**come to a head** 1. to be about to suppurate, as a boil 2. to culminate —**give someone his head** to let someone do as he likes —**go to one's head** 1. to confuse or intoxicate one 2. to make one vain —**head off** 1. to intercept 2. to prevent; forestall —**head over heels** deeply; completely —**keep** (or **lose**) **one's head** to keep (or lose) one's poise, self-control, etc. —**make head or tail of** to understand —**off the top of one's head** [Colloq.] at random; extempore —**on** (or **upon**) **one's head** as one's responsibility —**off one's head** [Colloq.] crazy —**over one's head** 1. too difficult to understand 2. to a higher authority —**put heads together** to consult together —**turn one's head** to make one vain

headache *n.* 1. a continuous pain in the head 2. [Colloq.] a cause of worry, trouble, etc.

headboard *n.* a board that forms the head of a bed, etc.

headdress *n.* a covering or decoration for the head

headed *adj.* 1. formed into a head, as cabbage 2. having a heading

header *n.* 1. [Colloq.] a headlong fall or dive 2. a brick, etc. laid at right angles to the thickness of a wall 3. *Soccer* the act of heading the ball

headfirst (hed'furst') *adv.* 1. with the head in front 2. rashly; impetuously Also **head'fore'most**'

headgear *n.* a hat, cap, headdress, etc.

headhunter *n.* a member of any of certain primitive tribes who preserve the heads of slain enemies

heading *n.* 1. an inscription at the top of a chapter, page, etc., giving the title 2. a topic or category 3. the direction in which a plane, ship, etc. is moving: usually expressed as a compass reading

headland *n.* a point of land reaching out into the water

headlight *n.* a light with a reflector and lens, at the front of a car, locomotive, etc.: also **head'lamp**'

headline *n.* 1. a line or lines at the top of a newspaper article, giving its topic 2. an important news item —*vt.* -lined', -lin'ing 1. to provide with a headline 2. to give featured billing to

headlong *adj., adv.* 1. with the head first 2. with uncontrolled speed and force 3. reckless(ly); impetuous(ly)

headmaster (hed'mäs'tər) *n.* the principal of a school —**head'mas'ter-ship'** *n.* —**head'mis'tress** *n. fem.*

head of steel [Canad.] the furthest point to which railway tracks have been laid; end of steel

head-on *adj., adv.* head or front foremost [a *head-on* collision, meet problems *head-on]*

headphone *n.* a telephone or radio receiver held to the ear by a band over the head

headquarters *n.pl.* [often with *sing. v.*] 1. the centre of operations of one in command, as in an army 2. the main office in any organization —**head'quar'-ter** *vt.*

headroom *n.* space or clearance overhead

headship *n.* 1. the position or authority of a chief or leader 2. the position of a headmaster or headmistress

headshrinker *n.* 1. [Slang] a psychiatrist 2. a headhunter who shrinks his victims' heads

headstall *n.* the part of a bridle or halter that fits over a horse's head

head start an early start or initial advantage

headstone *n.* a stone marker at the head of a grave

headstrong *adj.* determined to do as one pleases

headwaters *n.pl.* the small streams that are the sources of a river

headway *n.* 1. forward motion, esp. of a ship 2. progress in work, etc. 3. *same as* HEADROOM

head wind a wind blowing in the direction directly against the course of a ship, aircraft, etc.

headword *n.* a key word at the beginning of a line, paragraph, etc., as the word defined in a dictionary entry

heady *adj.* -ier, -iest 1. impetuous; rash 2. intoxicating —**head'ily** *adv.* —**head'i-ness** *n.*

heal (hēl) *vt., vi.* [< OE. *hal,* healthy] 1. to make or become well or healthy again 2. to cure (a disease) or mend, as a wound, sore, etc. —**heal'er** *n.*

health (helth) *n.* [OE. *hælth*] 1. physical and mental well-being 2. condition of body or mind [good *health*] 3. a wish for a person's health and happiness, as in a toast 4. soundness or vitality, as of a society —*adj.* 1. relating to health [*health* service] 2. relating to foods, etc., beneficial to the health

health centre headquarters for administration of medical welfare in a district

healthful *adj.* helping to produce or maintain health

Health Service *same as* NATIONAL HEALTH SERVICE

health visitor a nurse who visits people's homes chiefly in connection with the health of babies and children

healthy *adj.* -ier, -iest having, showing, producing, or resulting from good health —**health'ily** *adv.* —**health'iness** *n.*

heap (hēp) *n.* [OE. *heap,* troop] 1. a pile or mass of things jumbled together 2. [Colloq.] a large amount —*vt.* 1. to make a heap of 2. to give in large amounts 3. to fill (a plate, etc.) full or to overflowing

hear (hēar) *vt.* **heard** (hurd), **hear'ing** [OE. *hieran*] 1. to perceive or sense (sounds) by the ear 2. to listen to 3. to conduct a hearing of (a law case, etc.); try 4. to grant [*hear* my plea] 5. to be informed of —*vi.* 1. to be able to hear sounds 2. to listen 3. to be told (of or about) —**hear from** to get a letter, etc. from —**not hear of** to forbid —**hear'er** *n.*

hearing *n.* 1. the act or process of perceiving sounds 2. the sense by which sounds are perceived 3. opportunity to speak, etc.; audience 4. a court appearance before a judge, other than a trial 5. a formal meeting of an official body for hearing testimony, etc. 6. the distance a sound will carry [within *hearing*]

hearing aid a device, usually a small electronic amplifier, worn to assist the hearing of a partially deaf person

hearken (här'kən) *vi.* [OE. *heorcnean*] [Archaic] to pay careful attention; listen carefully

hearsay (hēar'sā') *n.* rumour; gossip —*adj.* based on hearsay

hearse (hurs) *n.* [< L. *hirpex,* a harrow]

a vehicle used in a funeral for carrying the corpse

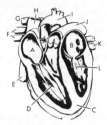

HUMAN HEART
(A, right atrium; B, left atrium, C myocardium; D, right ventricle; E, inferior vena cava; F, pulmonary veins; G, pulmonary artery; H, superior vena cava; I, aorta; J, pulmonary artery; K, pulmonary veins; L, left ventricle)

heart (härt) *n.* [OE. *heorte*] 1. the hollow, muscular organ that circulates the blood by alternate dilation and contraction 2. any place or part centrally located 3. the central, vital, or main part; essence 4. the human heart considered as the centre of emotions, etc.; specif., *a*) inmost thought and feeling *b*) one's disposition *c*) love, sympathy, etc. *d*) mood; feeling *e*) spirit or courage 5. a conventionalized design of a heart (♥) 6. the innermost, usually best, part of a vegetable 7. *a*) any of a suit of playing cards marked with such symbols in red *b*) [*pl.*] this suit of cards 8. a fertile condition in land [a field in good *heart*] —**at heart** in one's innermost nature —**break one's heart** to overwhelm one with grief or disappointment —**by heart** from memory —**change of heart** a change of mind, affections, etc. —**eat one's heart out** to brood over; regret —**have one's heart in one's mouth** (or **boots**) to be full of nervous anticipation —**have one's heart in the right place** to be well-meaning —**set one's heart on** to have a fixed desire for —**take heart** to cheer up —**take to heart** 1. to consider seriously 2. to be troubled by —**wear one's heart on one's sleeve** to show one's feelings plainly

heartache *n.* sorrow or grief

heart attack any sudden instance of heart failure, esp., a CORONARY THROMBOSIS

heartbeat *n.* one pulsation, or full contraction and dilation, of the heart

heartbreak *n.* overwhelming sorrow, grief, or disappointment —**heart′break′ing** *adj.* —**heart′bro′ken** *adj.*

heartburn *n.* a burning acid sensation beneath the breastbone

hearted *adj.* having a (specified kind of) heart: used in compounds [*stouthearted*]

hearten *vt.* to cheer up; encourage

heart failure the inability of the heart to pump enough blood through the body

heartfelt *adj.* sincere

hearth (härth) *n.* [OE. *heorth*] 1. the stone or brick floor of a fireplace 2. *a*) the fireside *b*) the home

heartless *adj.* lacking kindness; hard and pitiless

heart-rending *adj.* causing much grief or mental anguish —**heart′-rend′ingly** *adv.*

heart-searching *n.* honest and thorough investigation of one's own feelings

heartstrings *n.pl.* deepest feelings or affections

heart-throb *n.* 1. the object of one's romantic admiration 2. a heartbeat

heart-to-heart *adj.* intimate and candid —*n.* an intimate, confidential talk

heartwarming *adj.* such as to kindle a warm glow of genial feelings

heartwood *n.* the hard wood at the core of a tree trunk

hearty *adj.* -ier, -iest [see HEART] 1. warm and friendly; cordial 2. enthusiastic; wholehearted 3. strongly felt or expressed 4. strong and healthy 5. nourishing and plentiful [a *hearty* meal] —**heart′ily** *adv.* —**heart′iness** *n.*

heat (hēt) *n.* [OE. *hætu*] 1. the quality of being hot; hotness 2. much hotness; great warmth 3. degree of hotness or warmth 4. a feeling of hotness 5. hot weather or climate 6. the warming of a room, house, etc., as by a boiler: also **heating** 7. *a*) strong feeling; excitement, anger, etc. *b*) the period of such feeling 8. a single bout or trial; esp., a preliminary round of a race, etc. 9. *a*) sexual excitement *b*) the period of this in animals; esp., the oestrus of females 10. [Slang] great pressure, as in criminal investigation —*vt., vi.* 1. to make or become warm or hot 2. to make or become excited

heated *adj.* 1. hot 2. vehement, or angry —**heat′edly** *adv.*

heater *n.* a stove, radiator, etc. for heating a room, car, water, etc.

heath (hēth) *n.* [OE. *hæth*] 1. a tract of open wasteland, covered with heather, low shrubs, etc. 2. any of various plants that grow on heaths, as heather —**heath′y** *adj.*

heathen (hē′thən) *n.,* *pl.* -thens, -then [OE. *hæthen*] 1. one who believes in a god different from one's own, esp., anyone not a Jew, Christian, or Moslem 2. a person regarded as uncivilized, etc. —*adj.* 1. pagan 2. uncivilized, etc. —**hea′thendom** *n.* —**hea′thenish** *adj.* —**hea′thenism** *n.*

heather (heth′ər) *n.* [< ME. *haddyr*] a low-growing plant with stalks of small, bell-shaped, purplish-pink flowers —**heath′ery** *adj.*

Heath Robinson [W. *Heath Robinson*] of such fantastically impracticable design that it is unlikely to work

heatstroke *n.* a condition resulting from exposure to intense heat, characterized by fever and collapse

heat wave a period of unusually hot weather

heave (hēv) *vt.* **heaved** or (esp. *Naut.*) **hove, heav′ing** [< OE. *hebban*] 1. to lift, esp. with effort **2.** to lift in this way and throw **3.** to make rise or swell **4.** to utter (a sigh, etc.) with great effort **5.** *Naut.* to raise, haul, etc. by pulling with a rope —*vi.* **1.** to swell up **2.** to rise and fall rhythmically **3.** to retch or vomit **4.** *Naut. a)* to haul (*on* or at a rope, etc.) *b)* to move *[a ship hove into sight]* —*n.* the act or effort of heaving —**heave ho!** pull hard! —**heave to** *Naut.* to stop —**heav′er** *n.*

heaven (hev′'n) *n.* [OE. *heofon*] **1.** [*usually pl.*] the space surrounding the earth; firmament **2.** *Theol. a)* [*often* H-] the place where God and his angels are and where the blessed go after death *b)* [H-] God **3.** any place or state of great happiness —**move heaven and earth** to do all that can be done —**heav′enward** *adj., adv.*

heavenly *adj.* **1.** of or in the heavens *[the sun is a heavenly body]* **2.** *a)* causing or marked by great happiness, beauty, etc. *b)* [Colloq.] very pleasing **3.** *Theol.* of or in heaven; holy —**heav′enliness** *n.*

heavy (hev′ē) *adj.* -ier, -iest [< OE. *hebban*, *heave*] **1.** hard to lift because of great weight **2.** of concentrated weight for the size **3.** above the usual or a defined weight **4.** greater, more intense, etc. than usual *[a heavy vote, heavy thunder]* **5.** to an unusual extent *[a heavy drinker]* **6.** serious *[a heavy responsibility]* **7.** hard to endure *[heavy demands]* **8.** hard to do *[heavy work]* **9.** sorrowful *[a heavy heart]* **10.** burdened with fatigue *[heavy eyelids]* **11.** hard to digest *[a heavy meal]* **12.** not leavened properly *[a heavy cake]* **13.** cloudy **14.** dull; tedious **15.** clumsy *[a heavy gait]* **16.** designating any basic industry that uses massive machinery **17.** heavily armed **18.** *Theatre* serious, tragic, or villainous **19.** *Literature a)* grandiose *b)* not easily understood —*adv.* heavily —*n., pl.* **heav′ies** *Theatre a)* a serious, tragic, or villainous role *b)* an actor who plays such roles —**heav′ily** *adv.* —**heav′iness** *n.*

heavy-duty *adj.* made to withstand great strain, bad weather, etc.

heavy-handed *adj.* **1.** clumsy or tactless **2.** cruel; tyrannical —**heav′y-hand′ed-ness** *n.*

heavy-hearted *adj.* sad; depressed

heavy hydrogen *same as* DEUTERIUM

heavy water water containing atoms of deuterium

heavyweight *n.* **1.** a person or animal weighing much more than average **2.** *see* BOXING AND WRESTLING WEIGHTS, table **3.** [Colloq.] a very intelligent or influential person

Heb. **1.** Hebrew **2.** Hebrews

hebdomadal (heb dom′ə dəl) *adj.* [< Gr. *hepta*, seven] weekly —**hebdom′adally** *adv.*

Hebraic (hē brā′ik) *adj.* of or characteristic of the Hebrews, their language, culture, etc. —**He′braist** *n.*

Hebrew (hē′brōō) *n.* [< Heb. *'ibhri*, one from across (the river)] **1.** any member

of an ancient Semitic people; Israelite: in modern, but not recent, usage, a Jew **2.** *a)* the ancient Semitic language of the Israelites *b)* its modern form, the language of Israel —*adj.* **1.** of Hebrew or the Hebrews **2.** Jewish

heck (hek) *interj., n.* [Colloq.] *euphemism for* HELL

heckle (hek′'l) *vt.* -led, -ling [< ME. *hechele*] to harass (a speaker) by interrupting with questions or taunts —**heck′ler** *n.*

hectare (hek′tär) *n.* [Fr.] a metric measure of surface, equal to 10 000 square metres (100 ares or 2.471 acres)

hectic (hek′tik) *adj.* [< Gr. *hektikos*, habitual] **1.** full of confusion, rush, excitement, etc. **2.** feverish or flushed —**hec′tically** *adv.*

hecto- [< Gr.] *a combining form meaning* a hundred

hector (hek′tər) *n.* [< *Hector*, Trojan hero] a swaggering fellow; bully —*vt., vi.* to browbeat; bully

he'd (hēd) **1.** he had **2.** he would

hedge (hej) *n.* [OE. *hecg*] **1.** a row of closely planted shrubs, bushes, etc. forming a boundary **2.** any barrier or protection —*vt.* **hedged, hedg′ing 1.** to place a hedge around **2.** to hem in **3.** to try to avoid loss in (a bet, etc.) by making counterbalancing bets, etc. —*vi.* **1.** to make or trim hedges **2.** to refuse to commit oneself; avoid direct answers —**hedg′er** *n.*

hedgehog *n.* a small, insect-eating mammal, with sharp spines on the back, which bristle and form a defence when the animal curls up

hedgehop *vi.* -hopped′, -hop′ping [Colloq.] to fly an aircraft very close to the ground

hedgerow *n.* a row of bushes, etc., forming a hedge

hedge sparrow a small European bird with a brown back and wings and a grey breast: also called **dunnock**

hedonic (hē don′ik) *adj.* [< Gr. *hēdonē*, pleasure] having to do with pleasure

hedonism (hēd′ən iz'm) *n.* [< Gr. *hēdonē*, pleasure] the doctrine that pleasure is the principal good —**he′donist** *n.* —**he′donis′tic** *adj.* —**he′donis′tically** *adv.*

-hedron (hē′drən) [< Gr.] *a combining form meaning* a figure or crystal with (a specified number of) surfaces

heed (hēd) *vt., vi.* [OE. *hedan*] to take careful notice (of) —*n.* close attention —**heed′ful** *adj.*

heedless *adj.* careless; unmindful —**heed′lessly** *adv.*

heehaw (hē′hô′) *n., vi.* [echoic] *same as* BRAY

heel[1] (hēl) *n.* [OE. *hela*] **1.** the back part of the foot, under the ankle **2.** that part of a stocking, etc. which covers the heel **3.** the built-up part of a shoe, supporting the heel **4.** anything like the heel in location, shape, or function, as the end of a loaf **5.** [Colloq.] a cad —*vt.* **1.** to furnish with a heel **2.** to touch or move as with the heel —**at heel**

just behind —**cool one's heels** [Colloq.] to be kept waiting —**down at heel 1.** with the heels of one's shoes worn down **2.** shabby; seedy —**kick up one's heels** to have fun —**on** (or **upon**) **the heels of** —**take to one's heels** to run away: also **show a clean pair of heels** —**turn on one's heel** to turn around abruptly —**heel′er** n.

heel² vi. [OE. *hieldan*] to lean to one side; list —vt. to make (a ship) list —n. the act or extent of heeling

heelball n. [orig. used by shoemakers in polishing the edges of heels and soles] beeswax mixed with lampblack and used in making rubbings of brasses, etc.

heeled adj. **1.** [Colloq.] having money [*well-heeled*] **2.** [Colloq.] armed, esp. with a gun

hefty (hef′tē) adj. **-ier, -iest** [< HEAVE] [Colloq.] **1.** heavy **2.** large and powerful —**heft′ily** adv. —**heft′iness** n.

hegemony (hi gem′ə nē) n., pl. **-nies** [< Gr. *hēgemōn*, leader] leadership or dominance, esp. of one nation over others —**hegemonic** (hej′ə mon′ik) adj.

hegira (hej′ə rə) n. [< Ar. *hijrah*, flight] **1.** [often H-] the forced journey of Mohammed from Mecca to Medina in 622 A.D. **2.** any flight

heifer (hef′ər) n. [OE. *heahfore*] a young cow that has not borne a calf

heigh (hā) interj. an exclamation of pleasure, surprise, etc.

height (hīt) n. [< OE. *heah*, high] **1.** the distance from the bottom to the top **2.** elevation above a given level, as above the sea **3.** a relatively great distance above a given level or from bottom to top **4.** the topmost point **5.** the highest limit; extreme **6.** [often pl.] a high place

heighten vt., vi. to make or become higher, larger, greater, etc.; increase —**height′ener** n.

height of land [U.S. & Canad.] a watershed

heinous (hā′nəs) adj. [< OFr. *haine*, hatred] outrageously evil or wicked —**hei′nousness** n.

heir (âr) n. [< L. *heres*] **1.** one who inherits or is entitled to inherit another's property or title **2.** one who appears to get some trait from a predecessor or to carry on in his tradition —**heir′ess** n.fem.

heir apparent pl. **heirs apparent** the heir whose right to a property or title cannot be denied

heirloom n. [HEIR + LOOM¹] **1.** a piece of personal property that goes to an heir **2.** any treasured possession handed down from generation to generation

heir presumptive pl. **heirs presumptive** an heir whose right to a property or title will be lost if someone more closely related is born before the ancestor dies

hejira (hej′ə rə) n. same as HEGIRA

held (held) pt. & pp. of HOLD¹

hele (hēl) vt. [< OE. *hellan*, hide] to insert (cuttings, etc.) into the soil to keep them moist before planting them permanently (with *in*)

helical (hel′i kəl) adj. of, or having the form of, a helix; spiral —**hel′ically** adv.

helicopter (hel′ə kop′tər) n. [< Gr. *helix*, spiral + *pteron*, wing] a kind of aircraft moved, or kept hovering, by rotary blades mounted horizontally

helio- [< Gr.] a combining form meaning the sun

heliocentric (hē′lē ō sen′trik) adj. [HELIO- + -CENTRIC] having or regarding the sun as the centre

heliograph (hē′lē ə gräf′) n. [HELIO- + -GRAPH] a device for signalling by flashing the sun's rays from a mirror —vt., vi. to signal thus —**hel′iog′rapher** (-og′-rə fər) n.

heliotrope (hē′lē ə trōp′) n. [< Gr. *hēlios*, sun + *trepein*, turn] **1.** a plant with fragrant clusters of small, reddish-purple flowers **2.** reddish purple —adj. reddish-purple

heliotropism (hē′lē ot′rə piz′m) n. the tendency of plants or other organisms to turn towards or from light

heliport (hel′ə pôrt′) n. [HELI(COPTER) + (AIR)PORT] a flat place where helicopters land and take off

helium (hē′lē əm) n. [< Gr. *hēlios*, sun] a light, inert, colourless gas: used for inflating balloons, etc.: symbol, He

helix (hē′liks) n., pl. **-lixes, -lices′** (hel′ə sēz′) [< Gr., a spiral] **1.** any spiral, as a screw thread **2.** the folded rim of cartilage around the outer ear

hell (hel) n. [OE. *hel*] **1.** [often H-] a) Christianity the place to which sinners and unbelievers go after death for punishment b) the powers of evil **2.** any place or condition of evil, cruelty, etc. **3.** [Colloq.] any very disagreeable experience —interj. an exclamation of anger, emphasis, etc. —**get hell** [Slang] to receive a scolding, punishment, etc. —**come hell or high water** no matter what difficulties may arise —**hell for leather** at full speed

he'll (hēl; unstressed hil, il) **1.** he will **2.** he shall

hellbent (hel′bent′) adj. [Slang] firmly or recklessly determined (with *on*)

hellebore (hel′ə bôr′) n. [< Gr. *helleboros*] **1.** any of a group of winter-blooming plants with flowers like buttercups but of various colours **2.** any of a group of plants of the lily family **3.** the poisonous rhizomes of certain of these plants that have been used in medicine

Hellene (hel′ēn) n. [< Gr.] a Greek —**Hellenic** (hə len′ik) adj.

Hellenism (hel′ən iz′m) n. **1.** a Greek phrase, idiom, or custom **2.** the thought, culture, or ethics of ancient Greece —**Hel′lenist** n.

Hellenistic (hel′ə nis′tik) adj. of Greek history, culture, etc. after the death of Alexander the Great (323 B.C.) —**Hel′lenis′tically** adv.

hellfire (hel′fīər′) n. the fire or torment of hell

hellish adj. **1.** of, from, or like hell **2.**

fiendish **3.** [Colloq.] detestable —**hell'-
ishly** *adv.* —**hell'ishness** *n.*

hello (hə lō', hel'ō) *interj.* var. sp. of HALLO

hell's angel a member of a motorcycling
gang of violent youths

helm[1] (helm) *n., vt.* [OE.] archaic var.
of HELMET

helm[2] *n.* [OE. helma] **1.** the wheel or
tiller with which a ship is steered **2.**
the control or leadership, as of an organization

HELMETS

helmet (hel'mət) *n.* [< OFr. helme] a
hard, protective head covering, variously
designed for use in combat, certain sports,
etc. —**hel'meted** *adj.*

helminth (hel'minth) *n.* [Gr. helmins]
a worm, esp., a parasite of the intestine
—**helmin'thic** *adj.*

helmsman (helmz'mən) *n.* the person
who steers a ship

Helot (hel'ət) *n.* [< Gr. Heilōtes, serfs]
a member of the lowest class of serfs
in ancient Sparta

help (help) *vt.* [OE. helpan] **1.** to make
things easier or better for; specif., a) to
give money, etc. b) to share the burden
of c) to aid in getting (up, into, out of,
etc.) **2.** to make it easier for (something)
to exist, happen, etc. **3.** to relieve [this
will *help* your cough] **4.** a) to keep from;
avoid [she can't *help* crying] b) to stop,
change, etc. [faults that can't be *helped*]
5. to serve (a customer) —*vi.* **1.** to give
assistance; be useful **2.** to act as a waiter,
etc. —*n.* **1.** assistance **2.** relief; remedy
3. a) a hired helper, as a servant b)
employees —**cannot help but** to be obliged
to —**cannot help oneself** to be the victim
of circumstances, etc. —**help oneself to**
1. to serve oneself with (food, etc.) **2.**
to steal —**help'er** *n.*

helpful *adj.* giving help; useful —**help'-
fully** *adv.*

helping *n.* **1.** a giving of aid; assisting
2. a portion of food served to one person

helpless *adj.* **1.** not able to help oneself;
weak **2.** lacking help or protection **3.**
incompetent; ineffective

helpmate *n.* [< ff.] a helpful companion;
specif., a wife or husband

helpmeet *n.* [misreading of "an *help meet*
for him" (Gen. 2:18)] same as HELPMATE

helter-skelter (hel'tər skel'tər) *adv.*
[arbitrary formation] in haste and confusion —*adj.* disorderly —*n.* a high, spiral
slide, as at a fairground

helve (helv) *n.* [OE. helfe] the handle
of a tool

hem[1] (hem) *n.* [OE.] the border on a
garment, usually made by folding the edge
and sewing it down —*vt.* **hemmed, hem'-
ming** to fold back the edge of and sew
down —**hem in** (or **around** or **about**) **1.**
to surround **2.** to confine —**hem'mer** *n.*

hem[2] *interj., n.* the sound made in clearing
the throat —*vi.* **hemmed, hem'ming 1.**
to make this sound, as to get attention
2. to grope about in speech for the right
words: usually in **hem and haw**

he-man (hē'man') *n.* [Colloq.] a strong,
virile man

hemi- [Gr. hēmi-] a prefix meaning half

hemipteran (hi mip'tər ən) *n.* [see HEMI-
& Gr. pteron, wing] any of a group
of insects, including lice, aphids, etc., with
piercing and sucking mouthparts

hemisphere (hem'ə sfēər') *n.* [see HEMI-
& SPHERE] **1.** half of a sphere **2.** any
of the halves of the earth: the Northern,
Southern, Eastern, or Western Hemisphere
—**hem'ispher'ical** (-sfer'i kəl), **hem'i-
spher'ic** *adj.*

hemline (hem'līn') *n.* the bottom edge
of a dress, etc.

hemlock (hem'lok') *n.* [OE. hymlic] **1.**
a poisonous plant with small white flowers
2. a poison made from this plant

hemp (hemp) *n.* [OE. hænep] **1.** a tall
Asiatic plant having tough fibre in its
stem **2.** the fibre used to make rope,
etc. **3.** a substance, such as marijuana,
hashish, etc., made from its leaves and
flowers —**hemp'en** *adj.*

hemstitch (hem'stich') *n.* an ornamental
stitch made by pulling out several parallel
threads and tying the cross threads into
small bunches —*vt.* to put hemstitches on

hen (hen) *n.* [< OE. henn] **1.** the female
of the chicken (the domestic fowl) **2.**
the female of various other birds

henbane *n.* a coarse, hairy, foul-smelling,
poisonous plant, used in medicine

hence (hens) *adv.* [< OE. heonan] **1.**
from this place **2.** a) from this time b)
thereafter **3.** therefore —*interj.* [Archa-
ic] go away!

henceforth *adv.* from this time on: also
hence'for'ward

henchman (hench'mən) *n.* [OE. hengest,
male horse + man] a trusted helper
or follower

henge (henj) *n.* [back-formation <
Stonehenge] a circular monument, usually
with an outer bank or ditch

hen harrier the common harrier, of moors
and marshes

henna (hen'ə) *n.* [Ar. hinnā'] **1.** a tropical
plant **2.** a dye extracted from its leaves,
often used to tint the hair auburn —*vt.*
-naed, -naing to tint with henna

henpeck (hen'pek') *vt.* to nag and
domineer over (one's husband) —**hen'-
pecked'** *adj.*

henry (hen'rē) *n., pl.* **-rys, -ries** [< J.
Henry] Elec. the SI unit of inductance

hep (hep) *adj.* [< ?] [Slang] earlier form
of HIP[3]

hepatic (hi pat'ik) *adj.* [< Gr. hēpar, liver]
1. of or affecting the liver **2.** like the
liver in colour or shape

hepatitis (hep′ə tīt′is) *n.* [< Gr. *hēpar*, liver + -ITIS] inflammation of the liver

hepta- [< Gr.] *a combining form meaning* seven

heptagon (hep′tə gon′) *n.* [see HEPTA & -GON] a plane figure with seven angles and seven sides —**heptag′onal** (-tag′ə n'l) *adj.*

her (hur; *unstressed* ər) *pron.* [OE. *hire*] *objective case of* SHE —*possessive pronominal adj.* of, belonging to, made, or done by her

herald (her′əld) *n.* [< OFr. *heralt*] 1. a forerunner 2. a person who announces significant news 3. in Britain, an official in charge of genealogies, heraldic arms, etc. 4. formerly, an official who made proclamations, carried state messages, etc. —*vt.* to announce the approach of —**heraldic** (hə ral′dik) *adj.*

heraldry *n., pl.* **-ries** 1. the science of coats of arms, genealogies, etc. 2. heraldic devices 3. heraldic pomp

herb (hurb) *n.* [< L. *herba*] 1. any seed plant whose stem withers away annually 2. any plant used as a medicine, seasoning, or flavouring —**herbif′erous** *adj.*

herbaceous (hur bā′shəs) *adj.* of or like a herb

herbaceous border a flower bed that contains perennials rather than annuals, esp. one forming a border

herbage *n.* herbs collectively, esp. those used as pasturage

herbal *adj.* of herbs —*n.* formerly, a book about herbs

herbalist *n.* one who grows, collects, or deals in herbs

herbicide (hur′bə sīd′) *n.* [< L. *herba*, herb + -CIDE] any chemical substance used to destroy plants, esp. weeds

herbivorous (hur biv′ər əs) *adj.* [< L. *herba*, herb + -VOROUS] feeding on plants —**her′bivore** *n.*

Herculean (hur′kyoo lē′ən) *adj.* [< *Hercules*, hero in L. Myth.] 1. calling for great strength or courage, as a task 2. [*also* **h-**] having the great size and strength of Hercules

herd¹ (hurd) *n.* [OE. *heord*] 1. a number of cattle or other animals feeding or being driven together 2. [Derog.] the common people; masses —*vt., vi.* to form into or move as a herd

herd² *n.* [OE. *hierde*] a herdsman [*cowherd*] —*vt.* to tend or drive as a herdsman

herd instinct a tendency to associate in groups and to be uneasy when apart from the group

herdsman *n.* a person who keeps or tends a herd

here (hēar) *adv.* [OE. *her*] 1. at or in this place 2. towards, to, or into this place 3. at this point in action, speech, etc. —*interj.* an exclamation used to call attention, answer a roll call, etc. —*n.* this place or point —**here and there** in, at, or to various places —**neither here nor there** beside the point; irrelevant

hereabout *adv.* about or near here: *also* **here′abouts′**

hereafter (hēar àf′tər) *adv.* 1. in the future 2. following this, as in a writing 3. in the life after death —*n.* 1. the future 2. life after death

hereby (hēar′bī′) *adv.* by this means

hereditable (hə red′it ə b'l) *adj.* same as HERITABLE

hereditary (hə red′ə tər ē) *adj.* 1. of, or passed down by, heredity 2. a) of, or passed down by, inheritance from an ancestor *b*) having title, etc. by inheritance

heredity (hə red′ə tē) *n., pl.* **-ties** [< L. *heres*, heir] 1. the transmission of characteristics from parents to offspring by means of genes 2. all the characteristics that one inherits genetically

Hereford (her′ə ford) *n.* [< *Hereford-shire*] a breed of beef cattle having white and red markings

herein (hēar in′) *adv.* [Archaic] in this place, writing, etc.

hereinafter (hēar′in àf′tər) *adv.* [Archaic] in the following part (of this document, speech, etc.)

hereof (hēar′ov′) *adv.* [Archaic] of this

here's (hēarz) here is

here's to! here's a toast to! I wish joy, etc. to!

heresy (her′ə sē) *n., pl.* **-sies** [< Gr. *hairein*, take] 1. a religious belief opposed to the orthodox doctrines of a church 2. any opinion opposed to established views

heretic (her′ə tik) *n.* a person who professes a heresy —**heretical** (hə ret′i k'l) *adj.* —**heret′ically** *adv.*

hereto (hēar′tōō′) *adv.* [Archaic] to this (document, etc.)

heretofore (hēar′tə fôr′) *adv.* [Archaic] up to now; until the present; before this

hereupon (hēar′ə pon′) *adv.* 1. immediately following this 2. concerning this

herewith (hēar with′) *adv.* along with this

heritable (her′it ə b'l) *adj.* 1. that can be inherited 2. that can inherit —**her′itabil′ity** *n.*

heritage (her′ət ij) *n.* [see HEREDITY] 1. something handed down from one's ancestors or the past, as a characteristic, a tradition, etc. 2. property that is or can be inherited

hermaphrodite (hur maf′rə dīt′) *n.* [< Gr. *Hermaphroditos*, son of Hermes and Aphrodite, united in a single body with a nymph] a person, animal, or plant with the sexual organs of both the male and the female —*adj.* having the characteristics of a hermaphrodite —**hermaph′rodit′ic** (-dit′ik) *adj.* —**hermaph′rodit′ism, hermaph′rodism** *n.*

hermetic (hur met′ik) *adj.* [< Gr. *Hermēs* (reputed founder of alchemy)] airtight: *also* **hermet′ical** —**hermet′ically** *adv.*

hermit (hur′mit) *n.* [< Gr. *erēmos*, solitary] a person who lives by himself in a secluded spot, often from religious motives; recluse —**hermit′ic, hermit′ical** *adj.*

hermitage *n.* 1. the place where a hermit

lives **2.** a place away from other people; secluded retreat

hermit crab any of various soft-bellied crabs that live in the empty shells of certain molluscs, as snails

hernia (hur′nē ə) *n., pl.* **-nias, -niae′** (-ē′) [L.] the protrusion of an organ, esp. a part of the intestine, through a tear in the wall of the surrounding structure; rupture

hero (hēar′ō) *n., pl.* **-roes** [< Gr. *hērōs*] **1.** a man of great strength and courage, or one admired for his exploits **2.** any man regarded as an ideal **3.** the central male character in a novel, play, etc.

heroic (hi rō′ik) *adj.* **1.** like or characteristic of a hero or his deeds **2.** of or about heroes and their deeds; epic **3.** exalted; eloquent **4.** *Art* larger than life-size [a heroic statue] Also **hero′ical** —*n.* **1.** [*pl.*] *same as* HEROIC VERSE **2.** [*pl.*] extravagant or melodramatic talk or action —**hero′ically** *adv.*

heroic verse the verse form in which epic poetry is traditionally written, as iambic pentameter

heroin (her′ō win) *n.* [G., orig. a trademark] a very powerful, habit-forming narcotic, a derivative of morphine

heroine (her′ō win) *n.* a girl or woman hero

heroism (her′ō wiz′m) *n.* heroic qualities and actions

heron (her′ən) *n.* [< OFr. *hairon*] a wading bird with a long neck, long legs, and a long, tapered bill

heronry *n., pl.* **-ries** a place where herons breed

hero worship great or exaggerated admiration for heroes —**he′ro-wor′ship** *vt.* —**he′ro-wor′shipper** *n.*

herpes (hur′pēz) *n.* [< Gr. *herpein*, creep] a virus disease characterized by the eruption of small blisters

herpes simplex (sim′pleks) a form of herpes principally involving the mouth, lips, and face

herpes zoster (zos′tər) [< Gr. *zōstēr*, girdle] an infection of certain sensory nerves, causing pain and blisters

‡**Herr** (hãər) *n., pl.* **Her′ren** in Germany, a man; gentleman: also used as a title corresponding to *Mr.* or *Sir*

herring (her′iŋ) *n.* [OE. *hæring*] a small food fish of the N Atlantic: eaten dried, salted, or smoked

herringbone *n.* **1.** the spine of a herring, with the ribs extending in rows of parallel, slanting lines **2.** a pattern with such a design —*adj.* having the pattern of a herringbone

herring choker [Canad. Slang] a New Brunswicker

herring gull a common gull that has white plumage with black-tipped wings and pink legs

hers (hurz) *pron.* that or those belonging to her [that book is *hers*, *hers* are better, a friend of *hers*] —*possessive pronominal adj.* of, belonging to, or done by her

herself (hur self′) *pron.* a form of the 3rd pers. sing., fem. pronoun, used: *a)* as an intensive [she went *herself*] *b)* as a reflexive [she hurt *herself*] *c)* as a quasi-noun meaning "her true self" [she is not *herself* today]

Herts. Hertfordshire

hertz (hurts) *n., pl.* **hertz** [< H. R. *Hertz*] the SI unit of frequency

he's (hēz) **1.** he is **2.** he has

hesitant (hez′ə tənt) *adj.* hesitating or undecided —**hes′itancy** *n.* —**hes′itantly** *adv.*

hesitate *vi.* **-tat′ed, -tat′ing** [< L. *haerere*, stick] **1.** to stop in indecision **2.** to stop momentarily **3.** to be reluctant [I *hesitate* to ask] —**hes′itat′er, hes′ita′tor** *n.* —**hes′itat′ingly** *adv.* —**hes′ita′tion** *n.*

Hesperus (hes′pər əs) *n.* [L.] the evening star, esp. Venus: also **Hes′per**

hessian (hes′ē ən) *n.* a coarse cloth of jute or hemp

hest (hest) *n.* [< OE. *hæs*, command] [Archaic] behest

hetaera (hi tiər′ə) *n., pl.* **-rae** (-ē), **-ras** [< Gr. *hetairos*, companion] in ancient Greece, a courtesan

hetero- [< Gr.] *a combining form meaning* other, another, different [*heterosexual*]

heterodox (het′ər ō doks′) *adj.* [< HETERO- + Gr. *doxa*, opinion] opposed to the usual beliefs or established doctrines, esp. in religion; unorthodox —**het′ero-dox′y** *n.*

heterodyne (het′ər ō dīn′) *adj.* [HETERO- + DYNE] designating or of the combination of two different radio frequencies to produce beats with new frequencies

heterogeneous (het′ər ō jē′nē əs) *adj.* [< HETERO- + Gr. *genos*, a kind] **1.** differing in structure, quality, etc.; dissimilar **2.** composed of unlike parts; varied —**het′erogene′ity** (-jə nē′ə tē) *n.* —**het′eroge′neously** *adv.*

heteromorphic (het′ər ō môr′fik) *adj.* [< HETERO- + Gr. *morphē*, form] **1.** differing from the standard **2.** having different forms at various stages —**het′eromor′phism** *n.*

heterosexual (het′ər ō sek′shoo wəl) *adj.* of or characterized by sexual desire for those of the opposite sex —*n.* a heterosexual individual —**het′erosex′ual′ity** *n.*

het up (het) [*het*, dial. pt. & pp. of *heat*] [Colloq.] excited or angry

heuristic (hyoo ris′tik) *adj.* [< Gr. *heuriskein*, discover] helping to discover or learn

hew (hyoo) *vt.* **hewed, hewed** or **hewn, hew′ing** [OE. *heawan*] **1.** to chop or cut with an axe, knife, etc. **2.** to make or shape thus —**hew′er** *n.*

hexa- [< Gr.] *a combining form meaning* six

hexagon (hek′sə gon′) *n.* [< Gr. *hex*, six + *gōnia*, corner] a plane figure with six angles and six sides —**hexag′onal** (-sag′ə n′l) *adj.* —**hexag′onally** *adv.*

hexagram (hek′sə gram′) *n.* [HEXA- +

-GRAM] a six-pointed star formed by extending all sides of a regular hexagon to points of intersection

hexameter (hek sam′ə tər) *n.* [see HEXA- & -METER] a line of verse containing six metrical feet

hexapod (hek′sə pod′) *n.* [see HEXA- & -POD] an insect

hey (hā) *interj.* [echoic] an exclamation used to attract attention, express surprise, etc.

heyday *n.* the time of greatest vigour, success, etc.; prime

hey presto a conjuror's phrase announcing the surprise moment in a trick

Hf *Chem.* hafnium

HF, H.F., hf, h.f. high frequency

Hg [L. *hydrargyrum*] *Chem.* mercury

HG., H.G. High German

H.G.V. heavy goods vehicle

HH double hard (of pencil lead)

H.H. 1. His (or Her) Highness 2. His Holiness

hi (hī) *interj.* [< HEY] [Chiefly U.S.] an exclamation of greeting

hiatus (hī āt′əs) *n., pl.* -tuses, -tus [< L. *hiare*, gape] 1. a break or gap where a part is missing 2. a slight pause between two vowel sounds, as between the *e*'s in *reentry*

hibernate (hī′bər nāt′) *vi.* -nat′ed, -nat′- ing [< L. *hibernus*, wintry] to spend the winter in a dormant state —hi′berna′- tion *n.* —hi′berna′tor *n.*

Hibernia (hī bur′nē ə) [L.] *poet.* name of Ireland —Hiber′nian *adj., n.*

hibiscus (hī bis′kəs) *n.* [< Gr. *hibiskos*, marshmallow] a shrub or small tree with large, colourful flowers

hiccup (hik′up) *n.* [echoic] an involuntary contraction of the diaphragm that closes the glottis at the moment of breathing, making a sharp, quick sound —vi., vt. -cuped, -cuping to make or utter with a hiccup Also **hiccough**

hick (hik) *n.* [< *Richard*] [Chiefly U.S. Colloq.] an awkward, unsophisticated person regarded as typical of rural areas —adj. [Colloq.] like a hick

HICKORY
(leaf, nut & tree)

hickory (hik′ər ē) *n., pl.* -ries [< AmInd. *pawcohiccora*] 1. a N. American tree related to the walnut 2. the hard wood of the hickory 3. its nut

hidalgo (hi dal′gō) *n., pl.* -gos [Sp.] a Spanish nobleman of secondary rank, below that of a grandee

hidden (hid′n) *alt. pp. of* HIDE[1] —adj. concealed; secret

hide[1] (hīd) *vt.* hid, hid′den or hid, hid′- ing [OE. *hydan*] 1. to put or keep out of sight; conceal 2. to keep secret 3. to keep from being seen by covering up, obscuring, etc. —vi. 1. to be concealed 2. to conceal oneself —n. a place of concealment, as for a bird watcher —hid′- er *n.*

hide[2] *n.* [OE. *hid*] 1. an animal skin or pelt, either raw or tanned 2. [Colloq.] the skin of a person —neither hide nor hair nothing whatsoever

hide-and-seek *n.* a children's game in which one player tries to find the other players, who have hidden

hideaway *n.* [Colloq.] a hidden or secluded place

hidebound *adj.* obstinately conservative and narrow-minded

hideous (hid′ē əs) *adj.* [< OFr. *hide*, fright] very ugly or revolting; dreadful —hid′eously *adv.* —hid′eousness *n.*

hide-out *n.* [Colloq.] a hiding place

hiding[1] *n.* the condition of being hidden: usually in the phrase **in hiding**

hiding[2] *n.* [Colloq.] a severe beating

hie (hī) *vi., vt.* hied, hie′ing or hy′ing [OE. *higian*] [Archaic or Poet.] to hurry or hasten: usually reflexive

hierarchy (hī′ə rär′kē) *n., pl.* -chies [< Gr. *hieros*, sacred + *archos*, ruler] 1. a group arranged in order of rank, grade, etc. 2. church government by clergy in graded ranks 3. the officials in such a system —hi′erar′chical, hi′erar′chic *adj.*

hieratic (hī′ə rat′ik) *adj.* [< Gr. *hieros*, sacred] 1. of or used by priests 2. designating the abridged form of cursive hieroglyphic writing once used by Egyptian priests

hieroglyph (hī′ər ō glif′) *n.* same as HIEROGLYPHIC

hieroglyphic (hī′ər ō glif′ik) *adj.* [< Gr. *hieros*, sacred + *glyphein*, carve] of, like, or written in hieroglyphics —n. 1. a picture or symbol representing a word, syllable, or sound, used by the ancient Egyptians and others 2. [*usually pl.*] a method of writing using hieroglyphics 3. [*pl.*] writing hard to decipher —hi′eroglyph′i- cally *adv.*

hi-fi (hī′fī′) *n.* 1. same as HIGH FIDELITY 2. a radio, etc. having high fidelity —adj. of or having high fidelity

higgledy-piggledy (hig′′l dē pig′′l dē) *adv.* [prob. < *pig*] in jumbled confusion —adj. disorderly; jumbled

high (hī) *adj.* [OE. *heah*] 1. lofty; tall 2. extending upwards a (specified) distance 3. situated at, reaching to, or done from a height 4. above others in rank, position, quality, etc.; superior 5. very serious [*high* treason] 6. greater in size, amount, degree, power, etc. than usual 7. advanced to its acme or fullness [*high* noon] 8. noble; virtuous 9. expensive; luxurious [*high* living] 10. haughty; overbearing 11. shrill

12. slightly tainted: said of meat, esp. game **13.** extremely formal in matters of ceremony, doctrine, etc. **14.** elated [*high* spirits] **15.** designating that gear ratio of a motor vehicle transmission which produces the highest speed **16.** [Slang] *a*) drunk *b*) under the influence of a drug —*adv.* in or to a high level, degree, rank, etc. —*n.* **1.** a high level, place, etc. **2.** an area of high barometric pressure **3.** [Slang] a condition of euphoria induced as by drugs —**high and dry** stranded —**high and low** everywhere —**high and mighty** [Colloq.] arrogant —**on high 1.** high above **2.** in heaven

highball *n.* [U.S.] an alcoholic drink, usually whisky, served with ice in a tall glass

highbred *adj.* showing good breeding; cultivated

highbrow *n.* [Colloq.] a person who is or tries to be intellectual —*adj.* [Colloq.] of or for a highbrow

highchair *n.* a baby's chair with an attached tray, mounted on long legs

High Church that party of the Anglican Church which emphasizes the importance of the priesthood and of traditional rituals and doctrines —**High'-Church'** *adj.*

high commissioner the chief representative of the British government to one of the Commonwealth countries or from one of these countries to the British government

higher education education beyond secondary school, usually at colleges and universities

higher-up *n.* [Colloq.] a person of higher rank

high explosive any explosive in which the combustion of the particles is very rapid, producing great shattering effect

highfalutin, highfaluting (hī'fə loot'in) *adj.* [Colloq.] ridiculously pretentious or pompous

high fidelity in radio, sound recording, etc., a nearly exact reproduction of a wide range of sound frequencies

highflier, highflyer (hī'flī'ər) *n.* **1.** an ambitious person **2.** a person who achieves, or is capable of achieving, success

high frequency any radio frequency between 3 and 30 megahertz

High German 1. the West Germanic dialects spoken in C and S Germany **2.** the official and literary form of the German language

highhanded *adj.* overbearing or arbitrary —**high'hand'edly** *adv.* —**high'-hand'edness** *n.*

highjack *vt.* [Colloq.] *same as* HIJACK

high jump 1. an athletic event in which the contestants jump over a horizontal bar **2.** [Colloq.] severe punishment [he's for the *high jump*]

highland *n.* a region containing many hills or mountains —*adj.* of, in, or from such a region —**the Highlands** mountainous region occupying nearly all of N Scotland —**high'lander, High'lander** *n.*

Highland cattle a breed of cattle with shaggy hair, usually reddish-brown, and long horns

highlight *n.* **1.** a part on which light is, or is represented as, brightest: also **high light 2.** the most important or interesting part, scene, etc. —*vt.* **1.** to give highlights to **2.** to give prominence to

highliner *n.* [Canad.] in the Maritimes, the fishing boat or fisherman bringing in the most fish

highly *adv.* **1.** extremely **2.** favourably **3.** in a high rank **4.** at a high wage, salary, etc.

highly strung nervous and tense; highly sensitive

High Mass *R.C.Ch.* a sung Mass, usually celebrated with the complete ritual: also **Solemn High Mass, Solemn Mass**

high-minded *adj.* having high ideals, principles, etc. —**high'-mind'edness** *n.*

highness *n.* **1.** height **2.** [H-] a title used in speaking to or of a member of a royal family (with *His, Her,* or *Your*)

high-pitched *adj.* **1.** shrill **2.** steep: said of roofs

high-powered *adj.* **1.** very powerful **2.** of a high intellectual standard **3.** forceful; dynamic

high-pressure *adj.* **1.** having, using, or withstanding high pressure **2.** using forcefully persuasive or insistent methods —*vt.* **-sured, -suring** [Colloq.] to urge with such methods

high priest a chief priest

high-rise *adj.* designating a block of flats, offices, etc. of many storeys

high school a secondary school, esp. a grammar school

high seas open ocean waters outside the territorial limits of any single nation

high-sounding *adj.* pretentious or impressive

high-spirited (hī'spir'i tid) *adj.* **1.** courageous or noble **2.** spirited; lively —**high'-spir'itedly** *adv.*

high street the main street of a town, usually containing the principal shops (often preceded by *the*)

high table the table in a college dining hall, at a public function, etc., at which the most important guests, members of staff, etc., sit

high-tension *adj.* having, carrying, or operating under a high voltage

high tide 1. the highest level to which the tide rises **2.** the time when the tide is at this level **3.** any culminating point or time

high time 1. none too soon **2.** [Colloq.] a gay, exciting time: also **high old time**

high treason treason against the ruler or government

highveld (hī'felt') *n.* in South Africa, the high grasslands of the Transvaal province

high-water mark 1. the highest level reached by a body of water **2.** a culminating point

highway *n.* **1.** a public road **2.** a main road; thoroughfare Now chiefly a legal and U.S. usage

Highway Code a booklet of rules and advice compiled by the Ministry of the Environment for road users

highwayman n. formerly, a man who robbed travellers

hijack (hī′jak′) vt. [< ?] **1.** to steal (goods in transit, a lorry and its contents, etc.) by force **2.** to force the pilot (of an aircraft) to go to a nonscheduled destination —n. the act of hijacking —**hi′jack′er** n.

hike (hīk) vi. hiked, hik′ing [< dial. heik] to take a long, vigorous walk —n. a long, vigorous walk —**hik′er** n.

hilarious (hi lāar′ē əs) adj. [< Gr. hilaros, cheerful] **1.** noisily merry **2.** provoking laughter; funny —**hilar′iously** adv. —**hilar′iousness, hilarity** (hi lar′ə tē) n.

hill (hil) n. [OE. hyll] **1.** a natural raised part of the earth's surface, smaller than a mountain **2.** a small heap or mound [an anthill]

hillbilly (hil′bil′ē) n., pl. -lies [hill + Billy] [U.S. Colloq.] a person who lives in the mountains or backwoods —adj. **1.** [U.S. Colloq.] of hillbillies **2.** designating folk music originating from certain mountainous regions of the U.S.

hillock (hil′ək) n. a small hill; mound —**hill′ocky** adj.

hillside n. the side or slope of a hill

hilly adj. -ier, -iest **1.** full of hills **2.** like a hill; steep —**hill′iness** n.

hilt (hilt) n. [OE.] the handle of a sword, dagger, tool, etc. —(up) to the hilt thoroughly; entirely

HILUM

hilum (hī′ləm) n., pl. hi′la [< L., little thing] Bot. a scar on a seed, marking the place where it was attached to the seed stalk

him (him; unstressed im, əm) pron. [OE.] objective case of HE

himself (him self′) pron. a form of the 3rd pers. sing., masc. pronoun, used: a) as an intensive [he went himself] b) as a reflexive [he hurt himself] c) as a quasi-noun meaning "his true self" [he is not himself today]

hind¹ (hīnd) adj. hind′er, hind′most′ or hind′ermost′ [prob. < HINDER²] back; rear; posterior

hind² n. [OE.] the female of a deer, esp. the red deer

hinder¹ (hin′dər) vt. [OE. hindrian] to restrain; stop; thwart —vi. to be a hindrance

hinder² (hīn′dər) adj. [OE. hinder, behind] hind; rear

Hindi (hin′dē) n. [see HINDU] an Indo-Iranian language, the main, now official, language of India

hindmost (hīnd′mōst′) adj. superl. of HIND¹; farthest back; last: also hind′ermost′ (hīn′dər-)

hindquarters (hīnd′kwôr′tərz) n. pl. the hind part of a four-legged animal

hindrance (hin′drəns) n. **1.** the act of hindering **2.** any person or thing that hinders; obstacle

hindsight (hīnd′sīt′) n. an understanding, after the event, of what should have been done

Hindu (hin′dōō′) n. [ult. < Sans. sindhu, river, the Indus] a follower of Hinduism —adj. of the Hindus or Hinduism

Hinduism (hin′dōō wiz'm) n. the religion and social system of India, comprising many loosely-related sects

Hindustani (hin′dōō stä′nē) n. an important dialect of Western Hindi, used as a trade language in N India

hinge (hinj) n. [< ME. hengen, hang] **1.** a joint on which a door, lid, etc. swings **2.** anything on which matters depend —vt. hinged, hing′ing to attach by a hinge —vi. to be contingent (on)

hinny¹ (hin′ē) n., pl. -nies [< Gr. innos] the offspring of a male horse and a female donkey

hinny² n. [< honey] [Dial.] a term of endearment

hint (hint) n. [< OE. henten, to seize] a slight indication; indirect suggestion —vt., vi. to give a hint (of) —hint at to suggest indirectly —take a hint to perceive and act on a hint —hint′er n.

hinterland (hin′tər land′) n. [G. < hinter, back + Land, land] **1.** the district behind that bordering a coast or river **2.** an area near and dependent on a large city, esp. a port

hip¹ (hip) n. [OE. hype] the part of the body surrounding the joint formed by each thighbone and the pelvis

hip² n. [OE. heope] the fleshy fruit of the rose

hip³ adj. hip′per, hip′pest [< ? hep] [Slang] **1.** a) sophisticated b) fashionable **2.** of hippies —hip′ness n.

hip-bath n. a portable bath for sitting in immersed to the hips

hipbone n. the projecting, bony part of the hip

hip joint the junction between the thighbone and its socket in the pelvis

hipped adj. having hips of a specified kind [broad-hipped]

hippie n. [< HIP³] [Slang] a young person alienated from conventional society, who has turned to mysticism, drugs, communal living, etc.

hippo (hip′ō) n., pl. -pos [Colloq.] a hippopotamus

Hippocratic oath (hip′ə krat′ik) [< Hippocrates] the oath generally taken by medical graduates: it sets forth an ethical code for the medical profession

hippodrome (hip′ə drōm′) n. [< Gr. hippos, horse + dromos, course] **1.** a music hall, variety theatre, or circus **2.**

in ancient Greece and Rome, an oval course for horse races and chariot races

hippopotamus (hip'ə pot'ə məs) *n.*, *pl.* **-muses, -mi** (-mī') [< Gr. *hippos*, horse + *potamos*, river] a large, plant-eating mammal with a heavy, thick-skinned, almost hairless body and short legs: it lives chiefly in or near rivers in Africa

hippy *n.*, *pl.* **-pies** [Slang] *same as* HIPPIE

hipster *adj.* designating trousers, etc., cut with a low waist so that the top encircles the hips

hire (hīər) *n.* [OE. *hyr*] 1. the amount paid for the services of a person or the use of a thing 2. a hiring —*vt.* hired, hir'ing 1. to pay for the services of (a person) or the use of (a thing) 2. to give the use of for payment (often with *out*) —**for hire** available for use, for payment: also **on hire** —hir'er *n.*

hireling *n.* a person who will follow anyone's orders for pay

hire-purchase *n.* a system by which a hired article becomes the property of the hirer after a stipulated number of payments: also **hire-purchase system**

hirsute (hur'syōōt) *adj.* [L. *hirsutus*] hairy; shaggy

his (hiz) *pron.* [OE.] that or those belonging to him [that book is *his*, *his* are better] —*possessive pronominal adj.* of, belonging to, or done by him

Hispanic (his pan'ik) *adj.* Spanish or Spanish and Portuguese —Hispan'icism *n.*

hiss (his) *vi., vt.* [echoic] 1. to make, or utter with, a sound like that of a prolonged *s* 2. to show dislike or disapproval (of) by hissing —*n.* the sound of hissing —hiss'er *n.*

hist (st; hist) *interj.* be quiet! listen!

hist. 1. historian 2. historical 3. history

histamine (his'tə mēn') *n.* [see HISTO- & AMINE] an amine released by the tissues in allergic reactions

histo- [< Gr.] a combining form meaning tissue

histogram (his'tə gram') *n.* [HISTO(RY) + -GRAM] a graph using vertical columns to illustrate frequency distribution

histology (his tol'ə je) *n.* [see HISTO- + -LOGY] the branch of biology concerned with the structure of tissue

historian (his tôr'ē ən) *n.* 1. a writer of history 2. an authority on or specialist in history

historic (his tor'ik) *adj.* famous in history

historical *adj.* 1. of or concerned with history 2. providing evidence for a fact of history 3. based on people or events of the past 4. established by history; factual 5. in chronological order —histor'ically *adv.*

historicism (his tor'i siz''m) *n.* a theory of history holding that the course of events is determined by unchangeable laws or cyclic patterns

historicity (his'tə ris'ə tē) *n.* the condition of having actually occurred in history

historiographer (his tor'ē og'rə fər) *n.*

[< Gr. *historia*, history + *graphein*, write] a historian; esp., one appointed to write the history of some institution, country, etc. —histo'riog'raphy *n.*

history (his'tə rē) *n.*, *pl.* **-ries** [< Gr. *histōr*, learned] 1. an account of what has happened, esp. in the life of a people, country, etc. 2. all recorded events of the past 3. the branch of knowledge that deals systematically with the recording, analysing, etc. of past events 4. a known past [this coat has a *history*] —make history to be or do something important enough to be recorded

histrionic (his'trē on'ik) *adj.* [< L. *histrio*, actor] 1. overacted or overacting 2. of acting or actors

histrionics *n.pl.* [sometimes with sing. v.] 1. an artificial or affected manner or outburst 2. theatricals

hit (hit) *vt.* hit, hit'ting [< ON. *hitta*, meet with] 1. to come against with force; strike 2. to give a blow to; strike 3. to strike with a missile [to *hit* the target] 4. to cause to bump or strike, as in falling, moving, etc. 5. to propel or cause to move by striking 6. to affect strongly or adversely [a town *hit* by floods] 7. to come upon by accident or after search [to *hit* the right answer] 8. to reach; attain 9. [Slang] to apply oneself to frequently [to *hit* the bottle] —*vi.* 1. to strike 2. to attack suddenly 3. to come by accident or after search (with *on* or *upon*) —*n.* 1. a blow that strikes its mark 2. an effectively witty remark 3. a popular song, play, etc. —hit it off to get along well together —hit or miss in a haphazard way —hit the (right) nail on the head 1. to guess correctly 2. to express a point exactly —hit the road [Slang] to leave —make a hit to be a success

hit-and-run (hit''n run') *adj.* hitting and then fleeing [a *hit-and-run* driver]

hitch (hich) *vi.* [< ?] 1. to move jerkily; 2. to become fastened or caught 3. [Colloq.] to hitchhike —*vt.* 1. to move, pull, or shift with jerks 2. to fasten with a hook, knot etc. 3. [Colloq.] to marry: usually in the passive 4. [Colloq.] to hitchhike —*n.* 1. a hindrance; obstacle 2. [Colloq.] a ride obtained by hitchhiking 3. a tug; jerk 4. *Naut.* a kind of knot that can be easily undone 5. a hobble —without a hitch smoothly and successfully

hitchhike *vi.* -hiked', -hik'ing to travel by asking for free rides from motorists along the way —*vt.* to get (a ride) or make (one's way) by hitchhiking —hitch'hik'er *n.*

hither (hith'ər) *adv.* [OE. *hider*] to this place; here —*adj.* on or towards this side; nearer

hitherto (hith'ər tōō') *adv.* until this time; to now

hitman *n.* a hired assassin

hit parade the list of currently most popular records

Hittite (hit′īt) *n.* any of an ancient people of Asia Minor and Syria —*adj.* of the Hittites, their culture, etc.

hive (hīv) *n.* [OE. *hyf*] 1. a shelter for a colony of honey-bees 2. a colony of bees living in a hive 3. a place with many busy people —*vt.* hived, hiv′ing to gather (bees) into a hive —*vi.* to enter a hive —**hive off** 1. to withdraw in a group, as bees 2. to assign work to a subsidiary department, etc. 3. to transfer (assets etc.) of a company to another group

hives *n.* [orig. Scot. dial.] an allergic skin condition

H.L. House of Lords

H.M. 1. Her Majesty 2. His Majesty

H.M.A.S. His (or Her) Majesty's Australian Ship

H.M.C.S. His (or Her) Majesty's Canadian Ship

H.M.I. His (or Her) Majesty's Inspector (of Schools)

H.M.N.Z.S. His (or Her) Majesty's New Zealand Ship

H.M.S. 1. His (or Her) Majesty's Service 2. His (or Her) Majesty's Ship or Steamer

H.M.S.O. His (or Her) Majesty's Stationery Office

H.N.C. Higher National Certificate

H.N.D. Higher National Diploma

ho (hō) *interj.* an exclamation of surprise, derision, etc.

Ho *Chem.* holmium

hoar (hôr) *adj.* [OE. *hār*] *same as* HOARY

hoard (hôrd) *n.* [OE. *hord*] a supply stored up and hidden or kept in reserve —*vt., vi.* to accumulate and store away (money, goods, etc.) —**hoard′er** *n.* —**hoard′ing** *n.*

hoarding (hôr′diŋ) *n.* [< Frank. *hurda,* a fold] 1. a temporary wooden fence, as around a building site 2. a large board for displaying advertisements

hoarfrost (hôr′frost′) *n.* white, frozen dew on the ground, leaves, etc.; rime

hoarse (hôrs) *adj.* hoars′er, hoars′est [OE. *hās*] 1. sounding harsh and grating, etc. 2. having a rough, husky voice —**hoarse′-ly** *adv.* —**hoarse′ness** *n.*

hoary (hôr′ē) *adj.* -ier, -iest 1. white or grey 2. having white or grey hair because old 3. very old

hoax (hōks) *n.* [< ? HOCUS-POCUS] a trick or fraud, esp. a practical joke —*vt.* to deceive with a hoax —**hoax′er** *n.*

hob[1] (hob) *n.* [? < HUB] 1. the flat top part of a cooking stove, or a separate flat surface, containing hotplates or burners 2. a projecting ledge at the back or side of a fireplace, for keeping a kettle, etc. warm

hob[2] *n.* [< *Robin* Goodfellow] an elf; goblin

hobble (hob′′l) *vi.* -bled, -bling [ME. *hobelen*] to go unsteadily, haltingly, etc.; limp —*vt.* 1. to cause to limp 2. to hamper the movement of (a horse, etc.) by tying two legs together —*n.* 1. a halting walk; limp 2. a rope, strap, etc. used to hobble a horse —**hob′bler** *n.*

hobby (hob′ē) *n., pl.* -bies [ME. *hoby*] 1. something that a person likes to work at, collect, etc. in his spare time 2. a hobbyhorse —**hob′byist** *n.*

hobbyhorse *n.* 1. a toy consisting of a horse's head on a stick that one pretends to ride 2. a rocking horse 3. a favourite topic or fixed idea

hobgoblin (hob′gob′lin) *n.* [HOB[2] + GOBLIN] 1. an elf; goblin 2. a bogy; bugbear

hobnail *n.* [HOB[1] + NAIL] a nail with a broad head, put on the soles of shoes to prevent wear —**hob′nailed′** *adj.*

hobnob (hob′nob′) *vi.* -nobbed′, -nob′-bing [< ME. *habben,* have + *nabben,* not have] to be on close terms (*with*)

hobo (hō′bō) *n., pl.* -bos, -boes [U.S.] 1. a vagrant; tramp 2. esp. formerly, a migratory worker

Hobson's choice (hob′sənz) [< T. *Hobson,* liveryman, who let horses in order according to their position near the door] a choice of taking what is offered or nothing

hock[1] (hok) *n.* [OE. *hoh,* heel] the joint bending backwards in the hind leg of a horse, ox, etc., but corresponding to the human ankle

hock[2] *n.* [< *Hochheim,* Germany] a white Rhine wine

hock[3] *vt., n.* [< Du. *hok,* prison] [U.S. Slang] *same as* PAWN[1]

hockey (hok′ē) *n.* [prob. < OFr. *hoquet,* bent stick] 1. a team game played on a field, using curved sticks (**hockey sticks**) and a ball 2. [U.S. & Canad.] *same as* ICE HOCKEY

hocus-pocus (hō′kəs pō′kəs) *n.* [imitation L.] 1. trickery; deception 2. meaningless words used as a formula by conjurers 3. sleight of hand; legerdemain

hod (hod) *n.* [prob. < MDu. *hodde*] 1. a long-handled wooden trough, used for carrying bricks, mortar, etc. on the shoulder 2. a coal scuttle

hodgepodge (hoj′poj′) *n. same as* HOTCHPOTCH

hodometer (ho dom′i tər) *n. same as* ODOMETER

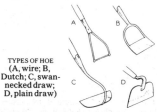

TYPES OF HOE
(A, wire; B, Dutch; C, swan-necked draw; D, plain draw)

hoe (hō) *n.* [< OHG. < *houwan,* hew] a tool with a flat blade set across the end of a long handle, used for weeding, loosening soil, etc. —*vt., vi.* hoed, hoe′ing to cultivate etc. with a hoe —**ho′er** *n.*

hog (hog) *n.* [OE. *hogg*] 1. a pig; esp., a castrated male pig 2. [Colloq.] a selfish, greedy, or filthy person —vt. **hogged, hog'-ging** [Colloq.] to take all of or an unfair share of —**go the whole hog** [Colloq.] to go all the way —**hog'gish** adj.

hogback n. a sharp ridge of land: also **hog's back**

hogmanay (hog'mə nā) n. [< ?] [Scot.] (Also H-) New Year's Eve

hogshead n. [ME. hoggeshede] 1. a large barrel of varying capacity 2. any of various liquid measures, esp. one of c 50 gallons

hogwash n. 1. nonsense 2. pig swill

hoick (hoik) vt. [< ?] [Slang] to raise abruptly

hoi polloi (hoi'pə loi') [Gr., the many] the common people; the masses: usually patronizing

hoist (hoist) vt. [< Du. hijschen] to raise aloft, esp. with a pulley, crane, etc. —n. 1. a hoisting 2. an apparatus for raising heavy things —**hoist with one's own petard** caught in one's own trap

hoity-toity (hoit'ē toit'ē) adj. [< obs. hoit, to be noisily mirthful] haughty or petulant

hokum (hōk'əm) n. [< HOCUS-POCUS] [Slang] 1. crudely comic or mawkishly sentimental elements in a play, story, etc. 2. nonsense; humbug

hold[1] (hōld) vt. **held, hold'ing** [OE. haldan] 1. to take and keep with the hands, arms, or other means; grasp 2. to keep in a certain position or condition 3. to restrain or control 4. to get and keep [to hold our attention] 5. to keep against an enemy; defend 6. to occupy [he holds the office of mayor] 7. to have or conduct (a meeting, conversation, etc.) 8. to have room for [this can holds a litre] 9. to regard; consider 10. to keep a telephone line open by not replacing the receiver 11. to possess [to hold a mortgage] 12. to bind [hold him to his word] —vi. 1. to retain a contact [hold tight] 2. to go on being firm, loyal, etc. [he held to his resolve] 3. to remain unbroken or unyielding [the rope held] 4. to be valid [a rule which still holds] 5. to continue [the wind held steady] —n. 1. a grip; specif., a way of gripping an opponent in wrestling 2. a thing to hold on by 3. a controlling force [to have a hold over someone] —**catch hold of** to seize —**get hold of** 1. to seize; 2. to acquire 3. [Colloq.] to make contact with (a person) —**hold back** 1. to restrain 2. to refrain 3. to retain —**hold down** 1. to restrain 2. [Colloq.] to have and keep (a job) —**hold forth** to preach; lecture —**hold off** 1. to keep at a distance 2. to keep from attacking or doing something —**hold on** 1. to retain one's hold 2. to persist 3. [Colloq.] wait! 4. [Colloq.] to wait, esp. during a telephone call, until a person, information, etc. is found —**hold one's own** to persist in spite of obstacles —**hold out** 1. to last 2. to stand firm —**hold out for** [Colloq.] to stand firm

in demanding —**hold out on** [Colloq.] to keep something from someone —**hold up** 1. to delay 2. to prop up 3. to stop forcibly and rob 4. to last; endure —**hold with** to approve of —**with no holds barred** [Colloq.] with no set rules or limits —**hold'er** n.

hold[2] n. [< HOLE] an area below the decks, as in a ship, for carrying cargo

holdall n. a large travelling bag or case

holdfast n. a specialized organ or part by which certain animals and plants attach themselves to an object

holding n. 1. land, esp. a farm, rented from another 2. [usually pl.] property owned, esp. stocks or bonds

holding company a corporation organized to hold bonds or stocks of other corporations, which it usually controls

holdup n. 1. a stoppage; delay 2. the act of stopping forcibly and robbing

hole (hōl) n. [OE. hol] 1. a hollow place; cavity 2. an animal's burrow 3. a small, dingy, squalid place 4. an opening in anything; gap, tear or rent 5. a flaw; defect [holes in an argument] 6. [Colloq.] an embarrassing situation; predicament 7. Golf a) a cup sunk into a green, into which the ball is to be hit b) any of the sections of a course —vt. **holed, hol'-ing** 1. to make a hole in 2. to put or drive into a hole —**hole up** [Colloq.] 1. to hibernate, usually in a hole 2. to shut oneself in —**pick holes in** to pick out errors or flaws in —**hole'y** adj.

hole-and-corner adj. [Colloq.] secretive; shady

holiday (hol'ə dā) n. [see HOLY + DAY] 1. [often pl.] a period in which a break is taken from work for rest or recreation 2. a day on which work is suspended by law or custom 3. a religious festival —adj. of or suited to a holiday; joyous —vi. to spend one's holidays

holier-than-thou adj. annoyingly self-righteous

holiness (hō'lē nis) n. 1. a being holy 2. [H-] a title of the Pope (with His or Your)

holland (hol'ənd) n. [< Holland, where first made] a linen or cotton cloth used for clothing, window blinds, etc.

Hollands (hol'əndz) n. [Du.] gin made in the Netherlands

holler (hol'ər) vi., vt., n. [< HOLLO] [Colloq.] yell

hollo (hol'ō) interj., n., pl. **-los** a shout or call, as to attract attention or urge on hounds —vi., vt. **-loed, -loing** to shout (at)

hollow (hol'ō) adj. [OE. holh] 1. having a cavity within it; not solid 2. shaped like a bowl; concave 3. sunken [hollow cheeks] 4. worthless [hollow praise] 5. hungry 6. deep-toned and muffled —n. 1. a cavity; hole 2. a valley —vt., vi. to make or become hollow —**beat (someone) hollow** [Colloq.] to surpass by far —**hollow out** to make by hollowing —**hol'lowly** adv. —**hol'lowness** n.

holly (hol'ē) n., pl. **-lies** [OE. holegn]

a small tree or shrub with glossy, sharp-pointed leaves and bright-red berries, used as Christmas ornaments

HOLLYHOCK

hollyhock (hol′ē hok′) *n.* [< OE. *halig*, holy + *hoc*, mallow] a tall, biennial plant with large flowers of various colours

holmium (hŏl′mē əm) *n.* [ModL. < *Holmia*, Latinized form of *Stockholm*] a metallic chemical element of the rare-earth group: symbol, Ho

holm oak (hōm) [< OE. *holegn*, holly] an evergreen oak with hollylike leaves

holo- [< Gr.] *a combining form meaning* whole, entire

holocaust (hol′ə kôst′) *n.* [< Gr. *holos*, whole + *kaustos*, burnt] great destruction of life

hologram (hol′ō gram′) *n.* a photographic plate containing the record of the interference pattern produced by means of holography

holograph (hol′ō gräf′) *adj.* [< Gr. *holos*, whole + *graphein*, write] written in the handwriting of the person under whose name it appears —*n.* a holograph document

holography (hə log′rə fē) *n.* [HOLO- + -GRAPHY] a method used to produce three-dimensional images by laser light and to record on a photographic plate the interference patterns from which an image can be reconstructed

hols (holz) *n.pl.* [Colloq.] holidays

holster (hōl′stər) *n.* [Du.] a pistol case, usually of leather and attached to a belt or saddle

holy (hō′lē) *adj.* -lier, -liest [< OE. *hal*, sound, whole] 1. dedicated to religious use 2. spiritually pure; sinless 3. deserving deep respect or reverence —*n.*, *pl.* -lies a holy thing or place

Holy Communion a Christian rite in which bread and wine are consecrated and received as the body and blood of Jesus or as symbols of them

Holy Ghost the third person of the Trinity

Holy Grail *see* GRAIL

Holy Land Palestine

holy of holies 1. the innermost part of the Jewish Temple 2. any most sacred place

holy orders 1. the position of being

an ordained Christian priest 2. the ranks of the Christian ministry

Holy See the position, authority, or court of the Pope

Holy Spirit the spirit of God; specif., the third person of the Trinity

Holy Week the week before Easter

homage (hom′ij) *n.* [< L. *homo*, man] 1. anything given or done to show reverence, honour, etc.: usually with *do* or *pay* [to pay *homage* to a hero] 2. orig., a public avowal of allegiance by a vassal to his lord

homburg (hom′bʉrg) *n.* [< *Homburg*, Prussia] a man's hat with a crown dented front to back and a stiff brim

home (hōm) *n.* [OE. *ham*] 1. the place where a person lives 2. the region or country where one was born or reared 3. a household and its affairs 4. an institution for the care of orphans, the aged, etc. 5. the natural environment of an animal, plant, etc. 6. the place of origin, development, etc. 7. in many games, the base or goal —*adj.* 1. of one's home or country; domestic 2. of or at the centre of operations 3. played in the city, etc. where the team originates —*adv.* 1. at, to, or in the direction of home 2. to the point aimed at 3. to the heart of a matter —*vi.* homed, hom′ing to return home accurately from a distance: said of birds and animals —**at home** 1. in one's own house, city, or country 2. comfortable; at ease 3. willing to receive visitors —**bring (something) home to** to impress upon —**home and dry** [Colloq.] safe; successful —**home (in) on** to be directed as by radar to —**home′less** *adj.* —**home′like′** *adj.*

home-brew (hōm′brōō′) *n.* an alcoholic beverage, esp. beer, made at home

Home Counties the counties surrounding London

home economics the science of managing a home

home farm a farm near or attached to the house of a landed proprietor who has other farms on his estate

Home Guard a volunteer, part-time force recruited for the defence of the United Kingdom in World War 2

home help a woman employed, esp. by a local authority, to do housework

homeland *n.* 1. the country in which one was born or makes one's home 2. [S Afr.] *official term for* BANTUSTAN

homely *adj.* -lier, -liest 1. plain or simple [*homely* virtues] 2. not elegant; crude 3. [U.S.] plain or unattractive —**home′li-ness** *n.*

homemade *adj.* 1. made at home 2. as if made at home; esp., plain, simple, or crude

homeo-, homoeo- [< Gr.] *a combining form meaning* like, the same, similar

Home Office the department of the British government responsible for law and order, immigration control, and other internal affairs

homeopathy, homoeopathy (hō′-mē op′ə thē) *n.* [see HOMEO- & -PATHY] treatment of a disease with small doses of drugs which in a healthy person and in large doses would produce its symptoms —ho′meopath′ic, ho′moeopath′ic (-ə-path′ik) adj.

homeowner n. a person who owns the house he lives in

Homeric (hō mer′ik) adj. of the poet Homer, his poems, or the Greek civilization that they describe

home rule the administration of the affairs of a country, colony, city, etc. granted to the citizens who live in it

Home Secretary in Britain, the Secretary of State for Home Affairs; the head of the Home Office

homesick adj. longing for home —home′sick′ness n.

homespun n. 1. cloth made of yarn spun at home 2. coarse, loosely woven cloth like this —adj. 1. spun at home 2. made of homespun 3. plain; homely

homestead n. 1. a place, esp. a farm, where a family makes its home, including the land, house, and outbuildings 2. [U.S. & Canad.] a house and adjoining land occupied by the owner and exempt from seizure and forced sale for debts —home′steader n.

homestead law [U.S. & Canad.] any of various laws conferring certain privileges on owners of homesteads

homeward adv., adj. towards home : also home′wards adv.

homework n. 1. schoolwork to be done outside the classroom 2. preparatory or introductory study

homicide (hom′ə sīd′) n. [< L. homo, man + caedere, kill] 1. any killing of one human being by another 2. a person who kills another —hom′ici′dal adj.

homily (hom′ə lē) n., pl. -lies [< Gr. homilos, assembly] 1. a sermon 2. a solemn, moralizing talk or writing

homing (hō′miŋ) adj. 1. homeward bound 2. having to do with guidance to a goal, target, etc.

homing pigeon a pigeon trained to find its way home

hominid (hom′ə nid) n. [< ModL. Hominidae (family name)] any form of man, extinct or living

hominoid (-noid′) n. [< ModL. Hominoidea (superfamily name)] any form of man or the great apes, extinct or living —adj. manlike

homo[1] (hō′mō) n., pl. homines (hom′ə nēz′) [L., a man] any of a genus of primates including modern man

homo[2] n., pl. -mos [Colloq.] a homosexual person —adj. [Colloq.] homosexual

homo- [< Gr.] a combining form meaning same, like

homogeneous (hō′mō jē′nē əs) adj. [< Gr. homos, same + genos, kind] 1. the same in structure, quality, etc. 2. composed of similar or identical parts —ho′moge′neity (-jə nē′ə tē) n. —ho′moge′neously adv.

homogenize (hə moj′ə niz′) vt. -nized, -niz′ing 1. to process (milk) so that the fat particles are finely divided and the cream does not separate on standing 2. to make homogeneous Also homog′enise

homograph (hom′ō graf′) n. [HOMO- + -GRAPH] a word with the same spelling as another but a different meaning and origin (Ex.: bow, part of a ship, bow, to bend)

homologous (ho mol′ə gəs) adj. [< Gr. homos, same + legein, say] 1. matching in structure, position, character, etc. 2. Biol. corresponding in structure and deriving from a common origin, as the wing of a bat and the foreleg of a mouse —hom′ologue n.

homology (ho mol′ə jē) n., pl. -gies 1. the state of being homologous 2. a homologous relationship

homonym (hom′ō nim) n. [< Gr. homos, same + onyma, name] a word with the same pronunciation as another but with a different meaning, origin, and, usually, spelling (Ex.: bore and boar)

Homo sapiens (hō′mō sap′ē ənz) [see HOMO[1] & SAPIENT] modern man; mankind

homosexual (hō′mō sek′shoo wal) adj. of or having sexual desire for those of the same sex as oneself —n. a homosexual person —ho′mosex′ual′ity n.

homy (hō′mē) adj. -ier, -iest having qualities usually associated with home; comfortable, familiar, etc.

Hon., hon. 1. honourable 2. honorary

hone (hōn) n. [< OE. han, stone] a whetstone used to sharpen tools —vt. honed, hon′ing to sharpen as with a hone

honest (on′əst) adj. [< L. honor, honour] 1. that will not lie, cheat, or steal; trustworthy 2. a) showing fairness and sincerity [an honest effort] b) gained by fair methods [an honest living] 3. frank and open [an honest face] —adv. [Colloq.] truly

honestly adv. 1. in an honest manner 2. truly

honesty n. 1. the state or quality of being honest: sincerity; straightforwardness 2. a plant with purple flowers and semi-transparent, silvery seedpods

honey (hun′ē) n., pl. -eys [OE. hunig] 1. a thick, sweet, syrupy substance that bees make as food from the nectar of flowers 2. sweetness 3. darling 4. [U.S. Colloq.] something pleasing

honeybee n. a bee that makes honey

honeycomb n. 1. the structure of six-sided wax cells made by bees to hold their honey, eggs, etc. 2. anything like this —vt. 1. to fill with holes like a honeycomb 2. to permeate or undermine —adj. of or like a honeycomb : also hon′ey-combed′

honeydew n. a sweet fluid exuded from various plants or secreted by some juice-sucking plant insects

honeyed adj. 1. sweetened with honey 2. flattering or affectionate [honeyed words] Also honied

honeymoon n. [< ?] 1. the holiday spent together by a newly married couple 2. a brief period of apparent agreement

—vi. to spend a honeymoon **—hon'ey-moon'er** n.

honeysuckle n. a woody plant with small, fragrant flowers of red, yellow, or white

honk (hoŋk) n. [echoic] **1.** the call of a wild goose **2.** any similar sound, as of a car horn **—vi., vt.** to make or cause to make such a sound **—honk'er** n.

honky-tonk (hoŋ'kē toŋk') n. [< ?] **1.** [Colloq.] a cheap, disreputable nightclub **2.** a style of ragtime piano-playing

honorarium (on'ə rāər'ē əm) n., pl. **-riums, -ria** [L. honorarium (donum), honorary (gift)] a payment as to a professional person for services for which no fee is set

honorary (on'ə rə rē) adj. [L. honorarius, of or conferring honour] **1.** given as an honour only [an honorary degree] **2.** a) designating an office held as an honour only, without service or pay b) holding such an office

honorific (on'ə rif'ik) adj. [< L. honor, honour + facere, make] conferring honour; showing respect

honour (on'ər) n. [< L. honor] **1.** high regard or respect; esp. a) glory; fame b) good reputation **2.** adherence to principles considered right **3.** chastity **4.** high rank; distinction [the honour of the presidency] **5.** [H-] a title given to judges (preceded by His, Her, or Your) **6.** something done or given as a token of respect; specif., a) a social courtesy b) [pl.] public ceremonies of respect [funeral honours] c) [pl.] special distinction given to students for high achievement d) [pl.] a specialized degree course **7.** one that brings respect and fame to a school, country, etc. **8.** Card Games [pl.] the four or five highest cards of the trump suit **—vt. 1.** to treat greatly **2.** to do something in honour of **3.** to accept and pay when due [to honour a cheque] **—do honour to 1.** to show great respect for **2.** to bring honour to **—do the honours** to act as host or hostess, esp. by making introductions, etc. **—on** (or **upon**) **one's honour** staking one's good name on one's truthfulness or reliability U.S. sp. **honor**

honourable adj. **1.** worthy of being honoured **2.** [H-] of high rank: used as a title of courtesy **3.** having or showing a sense of right and wrong **4.** bringing honour [honourable mention] **5.** accompanied with marks of respect [honourable burial] **—hon'ourably** adv.

hooch (hōōch) n. [< Alaskan] [Slang] alcoholic liquor

hood¹ (hood) n. [OE. hod] **1.** a covering for the head and neck, often part of a cloak **2.** an appendage to an academic gown, showing the type of degree **3.** anything like a hood, as the folding roof of a convertible car or the canopy of a pram **—vt.** to cover as with a hood **—hood'ed** adj. **—hood'less** adj.

hood² n. [Slang] short for HOODLUM

-hood [< OE.] a suffix meaning: **1.** state, quality [childhood] **2.** the whole group of [priesthood]

hooded crow a common crow with a grey body and black head, wings and tail: also called **hoodie-crow**

hoodlum (hood'ləm) n. [< ?] a wild, lawless person, often a member of a gang of criminals

hoodoo (hōō'dōō) n., pl. **-doos** [var. of VOODOO] [Chiefly U.S.] **1.** same as VOODOO **2.** [Colloq.] a) a person or thing that causes bad luck b) bad luck

hoodwink (hood'wiŋk') vt. [HOOD¹ + WINK] to deceive

hooey (hōō'ē) interj., n. [echoic] [Slang] nonsense

hoof (hoof) n., pl. **hoofs, hooves** (hōōvz) [OE. hof] the horny covering on the feet of cattle, deer, horses, etc., or the entire foot **—vt., vi.** [Colloq.] to walk

hoo-ha (hōō'hä') n. [echoic] [Colloq.] a noisy fuss

hook (hook) n. [< OE. hoc] **1.** a bent piece of metal, etc. used to catch, hold, or pull something; specif., a) a curved piece of wire for catching fish b) a curved piece of metal, etc. used to hang things on c) a small metal catch inserted in a loop, or eye, to fasten clothes **2.** a curved implement for cutting grain, etc. **3.** something shaped like a hook, as a curving headland **4.** Boxing a short blow delivered with the arm bent **5.** Sport a curved shot **—vt. 1.** to fasten or catch as with a hook **2.** [Colloq.] to steal **3.** Boxing to hit with a hook **4.** Sport to hit in a curve **—vi. 1.** to curve **2.** to be fastened or caught by a hook **—by hook or by crook** by any means **—hook, line and sinker** completely **—off the hook** [Colloq.] out of trouble **—sling one's hook** [Slang] to depart

HOOKAH

hookah, hooka (hook'ə) n. [Ar. huqqah] an Oriental tobacco pipe with a long tube by means of which the smoke is drawn through water and cooled

hooked adj. **1.** curved like a hook **2.** [Slang] addicted as to a drug (with on) **3.** [Slang] married

hooker¹ n. **1.** [U.S. Slang] a prostitute **2.** Rugby the centre forward in the front row of a scrum

hooker² n. [Du. hoeker] **1.** a small Dutch sailing ship **2.** a fishing smack

hookup n. **1.** the connection of parts, circuits, etc., as in (a) radio **2.** [Colloq.] a connection

hookworm *n.* a small, parasitic roundworm with hooks around the mouth, infesting the small intestine and causing **hookworm disease**

hooligan (hōō′li gən) *n.* [< ? *Hooligan*, family name] [Slang] a hoodlum —**hoo′li-ganism** *n.*

hoop (hōōp) *n.* [OE. *hop*] 1. a circular band for holding together the staves of a barrel 2. anything like a hoop; specif., *a)* any of the rings forming the framework of a hoop skirt *b)* a large ring, often with paper stretched over it, for circus performers or animals to jump through *c)* a toy shaped like a hoop and rolled along —*vt.* to bind or fasten as with a hoop —**go** (or **be put**) **through the hoop** to undergo an ordeal

hoopla (hōōp′lä) *n.* a game in which rings are thrown to encircle, and so win, prizes

hoopoe (hōō′pōō) *n.* [< L. *upupa*, prob. echoic] a bird with a long, curved bill and an erectile crest

hooray (hoo rā′) *interj., n., vi., vt.* same *as* HURRAH

hoot (hōōt) *vi.* [echoic] 1. to shout, esp. in scorn or disapproval 2. to utter its characteristic hollow sound: said of an owl 3. to utter a sound like this 4. to sound a horn 5. [Colloq.] to laugh loudly —*vt.* 1. to express scorn or disapproval (of) by hooting 2. to chase away by hooting —*n.* 1. the sound that an owl makes 2. any sound like this 3. a shout of scorn or disapproval 4. [Colloq.] an amusing or ridiculous person or thing

hooter *n.* 1. a person or thing that hoots, specif., *a)* a car horn *b)* a factory siren 2. [Colloq.] a nose

hoots *interj.* [< ? HOOT] [Scot.] an exclamation of objection, irritation or impatience

Hoover (hōō′vər) *Trademark* a type of vacuum cleaner —*n.* [h-] popularly, any vacuum cleaner —*vt.* [h-] to clean with a vacuum cleaner

hooves (hōōvz) *n.* alt. pl. of HOOF

hop[1] (hop) *vi.* **hopped, hop′ping** [OE. *hoppian*] 1. to make a short leap on one foot 2. to move by springing on both (or all) feet at once 3. [Colloq.] to go or move briskly —*n.* 1. a hopping 2. [Colloq.] a dance, esp. an informal one 3. [Colloq.] a short flight in an aircraft —**hop it** [Slang] go away —**on the hop** [Colloq.] 1. busy 2. unprepared *[caught on the hop]*

hop[2] *n.* [< MDu. *hoppe*] 1. a climbing plant with the flowers borne in cones 2. [*pl.*] the dried cones, used for flavouring beer —*vt.* **hopped, hop′ping** to flavour with hops

hop-bind *n.* the stalk on which hops grow: also **hop-bine**

hope (hōp) *n.* [OE. *hopa*] 1. a feeling that what is wanted will happen 2. the thing that one has a hope for 3. a reason for hope 4. a person or thing on which one may base some hope —*vt.* **hoped, hop′-**

ing 1. to want and expect 2. to want very much —*vi.* to have hope (*for*) —**hope against hope** to continue having hope though it seems baseless —**hop′er** *n.*

hopeful *adj.* feeling or giving hope —*n.* a person who hopes, or seems likely, to succeed —**hope′fulness** *n.*

hopefully *adv.* 1. in a hopeful manner 2. [Colloq.] it is to be hoped: regarded by some as a loose usage

hopeless *adj.* 1. without hope 2. impossible to solve, deal with, etc. 3. [Colloq.] incompetent —**hope′lessly** *adv.* —**hope′lessness** *n.*

hopper (hop′ər) *n.* 1. one that hops 2. a container from which the contents can be emptied slowly and evenly 3. [S Afr.] *same as* COCOPAN

hopscotch (hop′skoch′) *n.* [HOP[1] + SCOTCH] a children's game in which each player hops from one compartment to another of a figure drawn on the ground

horde (hôrd) *n.* [< Turk. *ordū*] 1. a large, moving crowd; swarm 2. a nomadic tribe or clan of Mongols

horehound (hôr′hound′) *n.* [< OE. *harhune*] a plant with a bitter juice used in cough medicine

horizon (hə rī′z'n) *n.* [< Gr. *horizōn* (*kyklos*), the bounding (circle)] 1. the line where the sky seems to meet the earth 2. [*usually pl.*] the limit of one's experience, interest, knowledge, etc.

horizontal (hor′ə zon′t'l) *adj.* 1. parallel to the plane of the horizon; not vertical 2. at, or made up of elements at the same level or status —*n.* a horizontal line, plane, etc. —**hor′izon′tally** *adv.*

hormone (hôr′mōn) *n.* [< Gr. *hormē*, impulse] a substance formed in some organ of the body, as the adrenal glands, and carried to another organ where it has a specific effect —**hormo′nal** *adj.*

horn (hôrn) *n.* [OE.] 1. *a)* a hard, permanent projection on the head of cattle, sheep, etc. *b)* the antler of a deer, shed annually 2. anything that protrudes from the head of an animal, as a tentacle of a snail 3. the substance that horns are made of 4. a container made by hollowing out a horn 5. anything shaped like a horn; specif., either end of a crescent 6. *a)* an instrument made of horn and sounded by blowing *b)* any brass instrument; specif., the French horn *c)* a device sounded to give a warning —*vt.* to furnish with horns —*adj.* made of horn —**horn in** (**on**) [Colloq.] to meddle (in) —**draw in one's horns** 1. to withdraw; recant 2. to economize —**horned** *adj.*

hornbeam *n.* any of various small, hardy trees with very hard, white wood

hornbill *n.* any of a family of large, tropical birds of Asia and Africa with a huge, curved bill

hornblende (hôrn′blend′) *n.* [G.] a black, rock-forming mineral, common in some granitic rocks

hornbook *n.* a parchment sheet with the alphabet, numbers, etc. on it, mounted on a small board under a thin, clear plate of horn: formerly a child's primer

hornet (hôr′nit) *n.* [OE. *hyrnet*] a large, yellow-and-black social wasp —**hornets′ nest** trouble

horn of plenty *same as* CORNUCOPIA

hornpipe *n.* a lively dance formerly popular with sailors

horny *adj.* **-ier, -iest** 1. of or like horn 2. having horns 3. toughened and calloused 4. [Slang] lustful —**horn′iness** *n.*

horology (ho rol′ə jē) *n.* [< Gr. *hōra*, hour + -LOGY] the science or art of measuring time or making timepieces —**hor′olog′ical** *adj.* —**horol′ogist** *n.*

horoscope (hôr′ə skōp′) *n.* [< Gr. *hōra*, hour + *skopos*, watcher] 1. one's future as predicted by an astrologer using a chart of the positions of the planets, etc. 2. this chart 3. the position of the planets and stars at a given time, esp. at a person's birth —**hor′oscop′ic** (-skop′ik) *adj.*

horrendous (ho ren′dəs) *adj.* [< L. *horrere*, to bristle] horrible; frightful —**horren′dously** *adv.*

horrible (hôr′ə b'l) *adj.* 1. causing a feeling of horror; terrible 2. [Colloq.] very bad —**hor′ribly** *adv.*

horrid (hôr′id) *adj.* 1. causing horror; revolting 2. very bad, ugly, unpleasant, etc. —**hor′ridly** *adv.*

horrific (ho rif′ik) *adj.* horrifying

horrify (hôr′ə fī′) *vt.* **-fied′, -fy′ing** 1. to cause to feel horror 2. [Colloq.] to shock —**hor′rifica′tion** *n.*

horror (hôr′ər) *n.* [< L. *horrere*, bristle] 1. the strong feeling caused by something frightful or shocking 2. strong dislike 3. the quality of causing horror 4. something that causes horror 5. [Colloq.] something very bad, ugly, etc. —*adj.* intended to cause horror —**the horrors** [Colloq.] a fit of extreme nervousness

hors d'oeuvre (ôr′ duvr′) *pl.* **hors′-d'oeuvres′** (durvrz′) [Fr.] an appetizer, served usually before a meal

horse (hôrs) *n.* [OE. *hors*] 1. a large, strong animal with solid hoofs, and flowing mane and tail, domesticated for drawing loads, carrying riders, etc. 2. the full-grown male of the horse 3. a frame on legs to support something 4. *Gym* a padded block on legs, used for vaulting 5. *Mil.* [with *pl.* v.] cavalry —*adj.* of or on horses —**from the horse's mouth** [Colloq.] from the original or authoritative source of information —**hold one's horses** [Colloq.] to curb one's impatience —**horse around** [Colloq.] to engage in horseplay —**on one's high horse** [Colloq.] acting in an arrogant manner

horseback *n.* the back of a horse —*adv.* on horseback

horse block a block of stone or wood used when mounting, or dismounting from, a horse

horse brass a brass ornament, usually circular, originally attached to a horse's harness

horse chestnut 1. a tree with large, palm-shaped leaves, clusters of pink or white

flowers, and glossy brown seeds 2. its seed —**horse′-chest′nut** *adj.*

horseflesh *n.* 1. horses collectively 2. the flesh of the horse, esp. as food

horsefly *n., pl.* **-flies′** any of various large flies, the female of which sucks the blood of horses, cattle, etc.

horsehair *n.* hair from the mane or tail of a horse —*adj.* 1. of horsehair 2. stuffed with horsehair

horselaugh *n.* a loud, usually derisive laugh; guffaw

horseless *adj.* 1. without a horse 2. self-propelled

horseman *n.* 1. a man who rides on horseback 2. a man skilled in the riding or care of horses —**horse′manship′** *n.* —**horse′wom′an** *n.fem.*

horseplay *n.* rough, boisterous fun

horsepower *n.* a unit for measuring the power of motors or engines, equal to 746 watts

horseradish *n.* 1. a plant of the cabbage family, grown for its pungent root 2. a relish made by grating this

horse sense [Colloq.] ordinary common sense

horseshoe (hôr′shoo′) *n.* 1. a flat, U-shaped, protective metal plate nailed to a horse's hoof 2. anything shaped like this —**horse′sho′er** *n.*

horsetail *n.* 1. a horse's tail 2. a rushlike plant

horsewhip *n.* a whip for driving horses —*vt.* **-whipped′, -whip′ping** to lash with a horsewhip

horsy *adj.* **-ier, -iest** 1. of, like, or suggesting a horse; esp., having large features 2. of, like, or characteristic of people who are fond of horses, fox hunting, or horse racing Also **hors′ey** —**hors′ily** *adv.*

hortatory (hôr′tə tər ē) *adj.* [< L. *hortari*, to urge] urging; exhorting Also **hor′ta-tive** —**horta′tion** *n.*

horticulture (hôr′tə kul′chər) *n.* [< L. *hortus*, garden + *cultura*, culture] the art or science of growing flowers, vegetables, etc. —**hor′ticul′tural** *adj.*

Hos. Hosea

hosanna (hō zan′ə) *n., interj.* [< Heb. *hōshī′āh nnā*, save, we pray] an exclamation of praise to God

hose (hōz) *n., pl.* **hose** or, for 1, usually **hos′es** [OE. *hosa*] 1. a flexible tube, used to convey fluids, esp. water from a tap 2. [*pl.*] stockings 3. orig., a man's tightfitting garment covering the hips, legs, and feet —*vt.* **hosed, hos′ing** to water with a hose

hosier (hō′zyər) *n.* a person who makes or sells hosiery

hosiery (hō′zyər ē) *n.* 1. hose; stockings and socks 2. similar knitted or woven goods

hospice (hos′pis) *n.* [< L. *hospes*, host, guest] a place of shelter for travellers, esp. one maintained by monks

hospitable (hos′pi tə b'l) *adj.* [see prec.] 1. showing friendliness, kindness, and solicitude towards guests 2. favouring health, growth, etc. [a *hospitable* climate] —**hos′pitably** *adv.*

hospital (hos′pi t'l) *n.* [see HOSPICE] **1.** an institution where the ill or injured may receive medical or surgical treatment, nursing care, lodging, etc. **2.** [Archaic] a charitable institution [a foundling *hospital*]

hospitality (hos′pə tal′ə tē) *n., pl.* **-ties** the act, practice, or quality of being hospitable

hospitalize (hos′pi t'l īz′) *vt.* **-ized′, -iz′-ing** to send to, put in, or admit to a hospital **—hos′pitaliza′tion** *n.*

hospitaller (hos′pi təl ər) *n.* a member of certain religious orders, dedicated to the care of the sick or poor in hospitals

host[1] (hōst) *n.* [< L. *hostia,* sacrifice] a wafer of the Eucharist; esp., [H-] a consecrated wafer

host[2] *n.* [see HOSPICE] **1.** a man who entertains guests **2.** any organism on or in which another (called a *parasite*) lives **3.** a man who keeps an inn —*vi., vt.* to act as host or hostess (to)

host[3] *n.* [< L. *hostis,* army] **1.** a multitude **2.** an army

hostage (hos′tij) *n.* [< OFr.] a person given or held as a pledge until certain conditions are met

hostel (hos′t'l) *n.* [see HOSPICE] **1.** *same as* YOUTH HOSTEL **2.** a residential establishment for students, homeless, etc.

hostel school in N Canada, a government boarding school for Indian and Eskimo students

hostess (hōs′tis) *n.* **1.** a woman who entertains guests **2.** *a)* a stewardess, as on an aeroplane *b)* a woman employed in a club, restaurant, etc. to receive and serve patrons

hostile (hos′tīl) *adj.* [< L. *hostis,* enemy] **1.** of an enemy **2.** antagonistic **3.** not hospitable; adverse

hostility (hos til′ə tē) *n., pl.* **-ties 1.** a feeling of enmity, ill will, unfriendliness, etc. **2.** *a)* an expression of enmity; hostile act *b)* [*pl.*] acts of war; warfare

hot (hot) *adj.* **hot′ter, hot′test** [OE. *hat*] **1.** *a)* having a temperature higher than that of the human body *b)* having a relatively or abnormally high temperature **2.** producing a burning sensation [*hot* pepper] **3.** full of intense feeling or activity, as *a)* impetuous; excitable [a *hot* temper] *b)* violent; angry [*hot* words] *c)* full of enthusiasm *d)* lustful *e)* very controversial **4.** *a)* electrically charged [a *hot* wire] *b)* [Colloq.] highly radioactive **5.** designating a colour that suggests heat, as red **6.** [Colloq.] *a)* recent; new [*hot* news] *b)* clear; strong [a *hot* scent] *c)* from an inside source [a *hot* tip] **7.** [Slang] *a)* recently stolen *b)* sought by the police **8.** [Slang] excellent **9.** Jazz of music or playing having exciting rhythmic effects, etc. **—hot under the collar** [Colloq.] embarrassed; annoyed **—make it hot for** [Colloq.] to make things uncomfortable for **—hot′ly** *adv.* **—hot′-ness** *n.*

hot air [Slang] empty or pretentious talk

hotbed *n.* **1.** a bed of earth covered with glass and heated by manure, for forcing plants **2.** any place that fosters rapid growth [a *hotbed* of vice]

hot-blooded *adj.* excitable, ardent, etc.

hotchpotch (hoch′poch′) *n.* [ME. *hochepot*] **1.** any jumbled mixture; mess **2.** a thick stew

hot dog [Colloq.] a hot sausage served in a soft roll

hotel (hō tel′) *n.* [< OFr. *hostel,* hostel] an establishment providing lodging and meals for guests

hotelier (hō tel′yā) *n.* [Fr.] an owner or manager of a hotel

hotfoot *adv.* [Colloq.] in great haste

hotheaded *adj.* **1.** quick-tempered; easily made angry **2.** hasty; impetuous **—hot′-head′edness** *n.*

hothouse *n.* a greenhouse **—***adj.* **1.** grown in a hothouse **2.** needing careful treatment; delicate

hot line a telephone line for direct, instant communication in an emergency, esp. between heads of state

hot money capital transferred from one commercial centre to another to take advantage of the highest interest rates

hotplate *n.* **1.** an electrically heated plate on a cooker **2.** a portable device on which food can be kept warm

hotpot *n.* meat and vegetables cooked together in a tightly covered pot

hot rod [Chiefly U.S. Slang] **1.** an old car adjusted or rebuilt for quick acceleration and high speed **2.** a driver of hot rods

hot seat [Slang] **1.** any position of embarrassment, difficulty, etc. **2.** [U.S.] *same as* ELECTRIC CHAIR

hot stuff [Colloq.] any person or thing considered important, exciting, sexually attractive, etc.

hot-tempered *adj.* easily made angry

Hottentot (hot′′n tot′) *n.* [echoic] **1.** a member of a race of people of South Africa of short stature and yellowish-brown complexion, now virtually extinct **2.** any language of these people **3.** [S Afr. Derog.] a nonwhite person

hot water [Colloq.] trouble: preceded by *in* or *into*

hot-water bottle a container, usually made of rubber, filled with hot water and used to provide warmth

hound (hound) *n.* [OE. *hund,* dog] **1.** any of several breeds of hunting dogs **2.** any dog **3.** a contemptible person **—***vt.* **1.** to hunt with or as with hounds [to *hound* a debtor] **2.** to urge on; incite **—follow the** (or **ride to**) **hounds** to hunt (a fox, etc.) with hounds

hour (our) *n.* [< Gr. *hōra,* hour] **1.** a division of time, one of the twenty-four parts of a day; sixty minutes **2.** a fixed point or period for a particular activity [the dinner *hour,* office *hours*] **3.** an indefinite period of a specified kind [his finest *hour*] **4.** the time of day **5.** a measure of distance set by the time it takes to travel it **6.** *Eccles. a) same as* CANONICAL HOUR *b)* the prayers said at a canonical hour **—after hours** after the regular hours for business, etc. —**of the hour** prominent at this time —**the small hours** the hours just after midnight

HOURGLASS

hourglass *n.* an instrument for measuring time by the trickling of sand, mercury, etc. from one glass bulb to another below it

houri (hoo͞ər′ē) *n., pl.* **-ris** [ult. < Ar. *ḥawira*, be dark-eyed] a beautiful nymph of the Moslem Paradise

hourly (ouər′lē) *adj.* **1.** done every hour **2.** reckoned by the hour [*hourly* wage] **3.** continual —*adv.* **1.** at every hour **2.** continually

house (hous; *for v.* houz) *n., pl.* **houses** (hou′ziz) [OE. *hus*] **1.** a building for human beings to live in; specif., *a*) a building occupied by one family *b*) a monastery or convent **2.** the people who live in a house; household **3.** a royal family; dynasty **4.** any of the divisions in a school to which pupils are assigned for competitive activities, etc. **5.** something regarded as a house, in providing shelter; specif., *a*) the habitation of an animal *b*) a building where things are stored **6.** *a*) a theatrical performance *b*) the audience in a theatre **7.** a business firm **8.** the management of a hotel, bar, etc. **9.** [*often* H-] *a*) the building where a legislative assembly meets *b*) a legislative assembly —*vt.* **housed** (houzd), **hous′ing 1.** to provide a house for **2.** to store, shelter, etc. —**keep house** to take care of the affairs of a home —**like a house on fire** very well, quickly, etc. —**on the house** given free —**set** (or **put**) **one's house in order** to put one's affairs in order

house arrest detention of an arrested person in his own house, often under guard

houseboat *n.* a boat designed for use as a dwelling place

housebound *adj.* confined to one's home, as by illness

housebreaking *n.* the act of breaking into another's house to commit theft —**house′break′er** *n.*

housecoat *n.* a woman's long, loose garment for casual wear at home

housefly *n., pl.* **-flies′** a two-winged fly found in and around houses: it feeds on rubbish, manure, and food

household *n.* **1.** all those living in one house; family, or family and servants **2.** the home and its affairs —*adj.* **1.** of a household **2.** ordinary

householder *n.* **1.** one who owns or

maintains a house **2.** the head of a household

household word a very familiar word or saying

housekeeper *n.* a woman who manages a home, esp. one hired to do so

housekeeping *n.* **1.** the management of domestic affairs **2.** the amount of money available for this

housemaid *n.* a woman servant who does housework

housemaid's knee an inflammation of the kneecap

houseman *n.* a recently qualified doctor who holds a resident post in a hospital

house martin a bird that builds its nest under the eaves of a house

House of Commons the lower branch of the legislature of Great Britain or Canada

House of Keys the elective branch of the legislature of the Isle of Man

House of Lords the upper house of the British Parliament, consisting of the Lords temporal and spiritual

house party the entertainment of guests overnight or over a few days, usually in a country house

house-proud *adj.* concerned, sometimes excessively, to keep one's home clean, tidy and attractive

housetop *n.* the top of a house; roof —**from the housetops** publicly and widely

house-trained *adj.* trained to void outdoors or in a special place: said of a dog, cat, etc. —**house′-train** *vt.*

housewarming *n.* a party given by or for someone moving into a new home

housewife *n., pl.* **-wives′ 1.** a woman, esp. a married woman, who manages a household **2.** (huz′if) a small sewing kit —**house′wife′ly** *adj.*

housework *n.* the work involved in housekeeping; cleaning, etc.

housing (hou′zin) *n.* **1.** the act of providing shelter or lodging **2.** houses collectively **3.** a shelter; covering **4.** *Mech.* a frame, box, etc. for containing some part

hove (hōv) *alt. pt. & pp.* of HEAVE

hovel (hov′l) *n.* [< ?] **1.** any small, miserable dwelling **2.** a low, open shed for sheltering animals, etc.

hover (hov′ər) *vi.* [< ME. *hoven*, stay] **1.** to stay suspended or flutter in the air near one place **2.** to linger close by **3.** to waver —*n.* a hovering —**hov′erer** *n.*

hovercraft *n.* [HOVER + (AIR)CRAFT] a vehicle which travels across land or water supported by a cushion of air and driven forwards by propellers

how (hou) *adv.* [OE. *hu*] **1.** in what manner or way **2.** in what state or condition **3.** for what reason **4.** to what extent, amount, etc. *How* is also used as an intensive —**how about** what is your thought concerning

howbeit (hou bē′it) *adv.* [Archaic] nevertheless

howdah (hou′də) *n.* [< Ar. *haudaj*] a canopied seat for riding on the back of an elephant or camel

however (hou ev′ər) *adv.* **1.** in whatever

manner **2.** to whatever degree **3.** nevertheless Also [Poet.] **howe'er'**

howitzer (hou'it sər) **n.** [< Czech *hauf-nice*, a sling] a short cannon, firing shells in a relatively high trajectory

howl (houl) **vi.** [echoic] **1.** to utter the long, wailing cry of wolves, dogs, etc. **2.** to utter a similar cry of pain, anger, etc. **3.** to make a sound like this [the wind *howls*] —**vt.** to utter with a howl —**n. 1.** the long, wailing cry of a wolf, dog, etc. **2.** any similar sound —**howl down** to drown out with shouts of scorn, etc.

howler n. [Colloq.] a ludicrous blunder

howling adj. [Colloq.] great [a *howling* success]

howsoever (hou'sō ev'ər) **adv. 1.** to whatever degree or extent **2.** by whatever means

how's that? 1. What do you think of that? **2.** *Cricket* a phrase used in appealing to the umpire to declare a batsman out: also **howzat?** (hou zat')

hoyden (hoid''n) **n.** [< Du. *heiden*, heathen] a bold, boisterous girl; tomboy

H.P. Houses of Parliament

HP, H.P., hp, h.p. 1. high pressure **2.** hire purchase **3.** horsepower

HQ, H.Q., hq, h.q. headquarters

hr. *pl.* **hrs.** hour; hours

H.R.H. His (or Her) Royal Highness

HT high tension

hub (hub) **n.** [? akin to HOB[1]] **1.** the centre part of a wheel, etc. **2.** a centre of interest, importance, or activity

hubble-bubble (hub''l bub''l) **n.** [echoic] **1.** a tobacco pipe in which the smoke is drawn through water, causing a bubbling sound **2.** a bubbling sound **3.** uproar

hubbub (hub'ub') **n.** [< Celt.] a confused uproar

hubby (hub'ē) **n.,** *pl.* **-bies** [Colloq.] a husband

hubris (hyoo'bris) **n.** [Gr. *hybris*] arrogance resulting from excessive pride —**hubris'tic adj.**

huckaback (huk'ə bak') **n.** [< ?] a coarse linen or cotton cloth with a rough surface, used for towelling

huckster (huk'stər) **n.** [< MDu.] **1.** a haggling merchant **2.** a pedlar —**vt.** to sell; peddle —**huck'sterism n.**

huddle (hud''l) **vi.** -**dled,** -**dling** [< ?] **1.** to crowd close together **2.** to hunch oneself up, as from cold —**vt. 1.** to crowd close together **2.** to hunch (oneself) up **3.** to do, put, or make hastily and carelessly —**n. 1.** a confused crowd or heap **2.** [Colloq.] a private conference

hue[1] (hyoo) **n.** [OE. *heow*] **1.** colour **2.** a particular shade or tint of a given colour —**hued adj.**

hue[2] n. [< OFr. *hu*, a warning cry] a shouting: now only in **hue and cry,** any loud outcry

huff[1] (huf) **n.** [echoic] a condition of smouldering anger or resentment —**vi.** to blow, puff

huff[2] vt. *Draughts* to remove (an opponent's man) from the board as a penalty for not effecting a capture

huffy adj. -**ier,** -**iest 1.** easily offended; touchy **2.** angered or offended —**huff'-ily adv.** —**huff'iness n.**

hug (hug) **vt. hugged, hug'ging** [prob. < ON. *hugga*, to comfort] **1.** to put the arms around and hold closely, esp. affectionately **2.** to squeeze tightly with the forelegs, as a bear does **3.** to keep close to [the bus *hugged* the kerb] —**vi.** to embrace one another closely —**n. 1.** a close, fond embrace **2.** a tight hold in wrestling **3.** a bear's squeeze

huge (hyooj) **adj.** [OFr. *ahuge*] very large; gigantic; immense —**huge'ly adv.** —**huge'-ness n.**

huggermugger (hug'ər mug'ər) **n.** [< ?] **1.** confusion **2.** [Archaic] secrecy

Huguenot (hyoo'gə not, -nō) **n.** [< G. *Eidgenosse*, confederate] *Hist.* a French Protestant

huh (hu) **interj.** an exclamation of contempt, surprise, etc.

hula (hoo'lə) **n.** [Haw.] a native Hawaiian dance marked by flowing gestures: also **hu'la-hu'la**

hulk (hulk) **n.** [OE. *hulc*] **1.** the body of a ship, esp. if old and dismantled **2.** a big, clumsy person or thing **3.** *Hist.* [*usually pl.*] a dismantled ship used as a prison

hulking adj. large, heavy, and unwieldy

hull[1] (hul) **n.** [OE. *hulu*] **1.** the outer covering of a seed or fruit **2.** the calyx of some fruits, as the strawberry —**vt.** to take the hulls off —**hull'er n.**

hull[2] n. [< ? prec. & Du. *hol*, ship's hold] the frame or body of a ship, hydrofoil, etc. —**vt.** to pierce the hull of

hullabaloo (hul'ə bə loo') **n.** [echoic] a hubbub

hullo (hə lō') **interj., n., vt., vi.** same as HALLO

hum (hum) **vi. hummed, hum'ming** [echoic] **1.** to make the low, murmuring sound of a bee, a motor, etc. **2.** to sing with the lips closed, not producing words **3.** [Colloq.] to be full of activity **4.** [Colloq.] to stink —**vt.** to sing (a tune, etc.) with the lips closed —**n.** the act or sound of humming —**hum'mer n.**

human (hyoo'mən) **adj.** [< L. *humanus*] of, typical of, or produced by mankind —**n.** a person: also **human being**

humane (hyoo mān') **adj.** [see prec.] **1.** kind, tender, merciful, sympathetic, etc. **2.** civilizing; humanizing [*humane* learning] —**humane'ly adv.**

humanism (hyoo'mə niz'm) **n. 1.** a rationalist movement that holds that man can be ethical, find self-fulfilment, etc. without recourse to supernaturalism **2.** the study of the humanities **3.** [H-] the movement that stemmed from the study of classical Greek and Roman culture and helped give rise to the Renaissance —**hu'-manist n., adj.** —**hu'manis'tic adj.**

humanitarian (hyoo man'ə tâer'ē ən) **n.** one devoted to promoting the welfare of

humanity —*adj.* helping humanity —**human'itar'ianism** *n.*

humanity (hyōō man'ə tē) *n., pl.* -**ties** 1. the fact or quality of being human 2. mankind; people 3. the fact or quality of being humane; kindness, mercy, etc. —**the humanities** 1. languages and literature, esp. classical Greek and Latin 2. the branches of learning concerned with human thought and relations; esp., literature, philosophy, the fine arts, history, etc.

humanize (hyōō'mə nīz') *vt., vi.* -**ized'**, -**iz'ing** to make or become human or humane —**hu'maniz'er** *n.*

humankind (hyōō'mən kīnd') *n.* the human race

humanly (hyōō'mən lē) *adv.* 1. in a human manner 2. by human means 3. from a human viewpoint

humanoid *adj.* nearly human —*n.* a nearly human creature

humble (hum'b'l) *adj.* -**bler**, -**blest** [< L. *humilis*, low] 1. having or showing a consciousness of one's defects 2. low in condition or rank; unpretentious —*vt.* -**bled**, -**bling** 1. to lower in condition or rank 2. to make modest or humble in mind —**hum'bleness** *n.* —**hum'bly** *adv.*

humble pie [< *umbles*, entrails of a deer] formerly, a pie made of the offal of a deer —**eat humble pie** to undergo humiliation, as by admitting one's error

humbug (hum'bug') *n.* [< ?] 1. an imposter 2. *a*) a fraud *b*) misleading or empty talk 3. a peppermint boiled sweet, usually striped —*vt.* -**bugged'**, -**bug'ging** to deceive; hoax —*interj.* nonsense! —**hum'bug'ger** *n.*

humdinger (hum'diŋ'ər) *n.* [Slang] a person or thing considered excellent of its kind

humdrum (hum'drum') *adj.* dull; routine

humerus (hyōō'mər əs) *n., pl.* -**meri** (-ī') [L., upper arm] the bone of the upper arm or forelimb, extending from the shoulder to the elbow —**hu'meral** *adj.*

humid (hyōō'mid) *adj.* [< L. *umere*, to be moist] full of water vapour; damp; moist —**hu'midly** *adv.*

humidex (hyōō'mi deks) *n.* [Canad.] an index of discomfort showing the combined effect of humidity and temperature

humidify (hyōō'mid'ə fī') *vt.* -**fied'**, -**fy'ing** to make humid —**humid'ifica'tion** *n.* —**humid'ifi'er** *n.*

humidity (hyōō'mid'ə tē) *n., pl.* -**ties** 1. moistness; dampness 2. the amount of moisture in the air

humiliate (hyōō'mil'ē āt') *vt.* -**at'ed**, -**at'ing** [< L. *humilis*, humble] to hurt the pride or dignity of by causing to seem foolish, etc.; mortify —**humil'ia'tion** *n.*

humility (hyōō'mil'ə tē) *n.* [< L. *humilitas*] the state or quality of being humble

hummingbird (hum'iŋ burd') *n.* any of a family of very small, brightly coloured birds with narrow wings that vibrate rapidly with a humming sound

hummock (hum'ək) *n.* [orig. naut. < ?] a low, rounded hill; knoll —**hum'mocky** *adj.*

humoresque (hyōō'mə resk') *n.* [G. *Humoreske*] a light, fanciful, or playful musical composition

humorist (hyōō'mər ist) *n.* a writer or teller of amusing stories, jokes, etc.

humorous (hyōō'mər əs) *adj.* having or expressing humour; amusing —**hu'morously** *adv.* —**hu'morousness** *n.*

humour (hyōō'mər) *n.* [< L. *humor*, moisture] 1. comic or amusing quality 2. *a*) the ability to appreciate or express what is amusing *b*) the expression of this in speech, writing, or action 3. a mood; state of mind 4. whim; fancy 5. any fluid of the body [the aqueous *humour*] 6. formerly, any of the four fluids considered responsible for one's disposition; blood, phlegm, choler, or melancholy —*vt.* to comply with the mood or whim of; indulge U.S. sp. **humor** —**out of humour** cross; disagreeable —**hu'mourless** *adj.*

hump (hump) *n.* [< LowG. *humpe*, thick piece] 1. a rounded, protruding lump, as on the back of a camel 2. a hummock; mound 3. [Colloq.] a fit of depression or sulks [he's got the *hump*] —*vt.* 1. to hunch; arch 2. [Colloq.] to carry, esp. heavy objects; heave —**over the hump** [Colloq.] over the worst part —**humped** *adj.* —**hump'y** *adj.*

humpback *n.* 1. a humped, deformed back 2. a person having a humped back 3. a whale having a dorsal fin resembling a humpback —**hump'backed'** *adj.*

humph (hmf) *interj., n.* a snorting or grunting sound expressing doubt, surprise, disdain, disgust, etc.

humus (hyōō'məs) *n.* [L., earth] the brown or black organic part of the soil, resulting from the partial decay of plant and animal matter

Hun (hun) *n.* [< *Huns*, a warlike asiatic people who invaded Europe in the 4th and 5th centuries A.D.] 1. [Slang] a German 2. [often h-] any savage or destructive person; vandal —**Hun'nish** *adj.*

hunch (hunch) *n.* [< ?] 1. [Colloq.] a premonition or suspicion 2. a hump 3. a chunk; hunk —*vt.* to draw (one's body) up so as to form a hump —*vi.* to push oneself forward jerkily

hunchback *n.* same as HUMPBACK (senses 1, 2)

hundred (hun'drəd) *n.* [OE.] 1. ten times ten; 100; C 2. [Obs.] a division of an English county —*adj.* ten times ten —**hun'dredth** *adj., n.*

hundredfold *adj., adv.* a hundred times as much or as many

hundreds and thousands tiny beads of coloured sugar used in decorating cakes, etc.

hundredweight *n.* 1. a unit of weight equal to 112 pounds (c. 50kg) or [U.S.] 100 pounds (c. 45kg) 2. a metric unit of weight equal to 50kg

hung (huŋ) *pt. & pp. of* HANG

Hung. 1. Hungarian 2. Hungary

Hungarian (huŋ gãer'ē ən) *adj.* of Hungary, its people, their language, or culture —*n.* 1. a native or inhabitant of Hungary 2. the language of the Hungarians

hunger (huŋ'gər) *n.* [OE. *hungor*] 1. a) the discomfort caused by a need for food b) famine; starvation 2. a need or appetite for food 3. any strong desire —*vi.* 1. to be hungry 2. to crave; long (with *for* or *after*)

hunger strike a voluntary fast undertaken, usually by a prisoner, as a means of protest

hung parliament a parliament in which no party has an absolute majority

hungry (huŋ'grē) *adj.* -grier, -griest 1. wanting or needing food 2. eager [*hungry* for praise] 3. barren: said of soil —**hun'grily** *adv.* —**hun'griness** *n.*

hunk (huŋk) *n.* [Fl. *hunke*, hunk] [Colloq.] a large piece, lump, or slice of bread, meat, etc.

hunkers (huŋ'kərz) *n.pl.* [prob. < ON. *hokra*, creep] haunches

hunt (hunt) *vt.* [OE. *huntian*] 1. to chase (game) for food or sport 2. to search for 3. to chase; harry —*vi.* 1. to go out after game 2. to search —*n.* 1. a hunting 2. a group of people who hunt together 3. a district covered in hunting 4. a search —**hunting** *n., adj.* —**hunt'ress** *n. fem.*

hunter *n.* 1. one who hunts 2. a horse trained for hunting 3. a watch with a hinged case to protect the glass

hunter's moon the full moon following the harvest moon

hunting-box *n.* a lodge used during the hunting season

huntsman *n.* 1. a hunter 2. a person who trains and looks after hounds

HURDLES

hurdle (hur'd'l) *n.* [OE. *hyrdel*] 1. a portable frame of interlaced twigs, etc., used as a temporary fence 2. any of a series of framelike barriers over which horses or runners must leap in a race (the **hurdles**) 3. a difficulty; obstacle —*vt.*

-**dled**, -**dling** 1. to fence off with hurdles 2. to jump over; overcome —**hur'dler** *n.*

hurdy-gurdy (hur'dē gur'dē) *n., pl.* -**gur'dies** [prob. echoic] *same as* BARREL ORGAN

hurl (hurl) *vt., vi.* [prob. < ON.] 1. to throw or move with force or violence 2. to utter with force —*n.* a violent throw —**hurl'er** *n.*

hurling *n.* [< prec.] an Irish game resembling hockey: also **hurley**

hurly-burly (hur'lē bur'lē) *n., pl.* -**burl'ies** turmoil

hurrah (hərä') *interj., n.* [echoic] a shout of joy, approval, etc. —*vi., vt.* to cheer; shout "hurrah" Also **hurray'** (-rä')

hurricane (hur'ə kən) *n.* [< WInd. *huracan*] a violent tropical cyclone, often with torrential rains

hurricane deck the upper deck of a passenger ship

hurricane lamp an oil lamp or candlestick with a tall glass chimney to keep the flame from being blown out

hurried (hur'id) *adj.* in a hurry; rushed or rushing —**hur'riedly** *adv.* —**hur'riedness** *n.*

hurry (hur'ē) *vt.* -**ried**, -**rying** [prob. akin to HURL] 1. to move or send with haste 2. to cause to occur more rapidly or too rapidly 3. to cause to act soon or too soon —*vi.* to move or act with haste —*n.* 1. a rush; urgency 2. eagerness to do, act, go, etc. —**hur'rier** *n.*

hurry-scurry, hurry-skurry (hur'ē-skur'ē) *n.* a disorderly confusion —*adj., adv.* with hurried confusion

hurst (hurst) *n.* [< OE. *hyrst*, hillock] 1. a hillock 2. a grove or wooded hillock

hurt (hurt) *vt.* **hurt**, **hurt'ing** [OFr. *hurter*, to push] 1. to cause pain or injury to 2. to harm or damage 3. to offend or distress —*vi.* 1. to cause injury, damage, or pain 2. to have pain —*n.* 1. a pain or injury 2. harm or damage 3. something that wounds the feelings —*adj.* damaged; injured —**hurt'er** *n.* —**hurt'ful** *adj.*

hurtle (hurt''l) *vi., vt.* -**tled**, -**tling** [< ME. *hurten*, hurt] to move swiftly and with great force

husband (huz'bənd) *n.* [< ON. *hūs*, house + *bondi*, freeholder] a woman's partner in marriage —*vt.* to manage economically

husbandry *n.* 1. farming 2. thrifty management

hush (hush) *vt., vi.* [< ME. *huscht*, quiet] 1. to make or become quiet 2. to calm —*n.* quiet; silence —*interj.* silence! —**hush up** to keep secret; suppress

hush-hush *adj.* [Colloq.] very secret; most confidential

husk (husk) *n.* [prob. < MDu. *huus*, house] 1. the dry outer covering of various fruits or seeds 2. the useless covering of anything —*vt.* to remove the husk from

husky¹ (hus'kē) *n., pl.* -**kies** [< ? ESKIMO] 1. [*sometimes* H-] a hardy dog used for pulling sledges in the Arctic 2. [H-] [Canad. Slang] a) a member of the Inuit b) their language

husky² *adj.* -**ier**, -**iest** 1. sounding deep

and hoarse **2.** full of or like husks **3.** big and strong —**husk′ily** adv. —**husk′i-ness** n.

hussar (hoo zär′) n. [< Serbian *husar*] a member of any European regiment of light-armed cavalry, usually with brilliant dress uniforms

hussy (hus′ē) n., pl. **-sies** [< ME. *huswife*, housewife] **1.** a woman of low morals **2.** a bold, saucy girl; minx

hustings (hus′tinz) n.pl. [usually with sing. v.] [< ON. *hūs*, house + *thing*, assembly] **1.** [Obs.] the platform where candidates for parliament stood and delivered speeches **2.** the proceedings at an election

hustle (hus′'l) vt. **-tled, -tling** [Du. *hutseln*, shake up] **1.** to jostle **2.** to force in a rough, hurried manner **3.** [Colloq.] to hurry (a person, a job, etc.) **4.** [Slang] to get, victimize, etc. by aggressive tactics —vi. **1.** to move hurriedly **2.** [Colloq.] to act rapidly or energetically **3.** [Slang] to obtain money by aggressive or dishonest means —n. a hustling —**hus′tler** n.

hut (hut) n. [< OHG. *hutta*] **1.** a little house or shed of the plainest kind **2.** a temporary structure, as at an army camp, etc. —vt., vi. **hut′ted, hut′ting** to shelter or be sheltered as in a hut

hutch (huch) n. [< ML. *hutica*, chest] a pen or coop for small animals

huzzah, huzza (hə zä′) interj., n., vi., vt. [echoic] former var. of HURRAH

hyacinth (hī′ə sinth) n. [< Gr. *hyakinthos*] **1.** a plant with spikes of fragrant, bell-shaped flowers **2.** a bluish purple —**hy′a-cin′thine** (-sin′thin) adj.

Hyades (hī′ə dēz) n. pl. [< Gr.] an open cluster of more than 200 stars in the constellation Taurus

hybrid (hī′brid) n. [L. *hybrida*] **1.** the offspring of two animals or plants of different species, etc. **2.** anything of mixed origin —adj. of or being a hybrid —**hy′-bridism, hybrid′ity** n.

hybridize vi., vt. **-ized′, -iz′ing** to produce or cause to produce hybrids —**hy′bridiza′-tion** n.

hydra (hī′drə) n., pl. **-dras, -drae** (-drē) [Gr. *hydra*, the nine-headed serpent of Gr. myth] **1.** a small freshwater polyp with a tubelike body and a mouth surrounded with tentacles **2.** any persistent or ever-increasing evil

hydrangea (hī drān′jə) n. [< HYDRO- + Gr. *angeion*, vessel] a shrubby plant, with large clusters of white, blue, or pink flowers

hydrant (hī′drənt) n. [< Gr. *hydōr*, water] an outlet from a water main from which water can be drawn for fighting fires, etc.

hydrate (hī′drāt) n. [< HYDRO-] a compound formed by the chemical combination of water and some other substance —vi., vt. **-drated, -drating 1.** to become or cause to become a hydrate **2.** to combine with water —**hydra′tion** n.

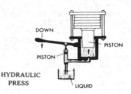

DOWN   PISTON   PISTON   HYDRAULIC PRESS   LIQUID

hydraulic (hī drô′lik) adj. [< Gr. *hydōr*, water + *aulos*, tube] **1.** of hydraulics **2.** operated by the movement and pressure of liquid [hydraulic brakes] —**hydrau′li-cally** adv.

hydraulics n.pl. [with sing. v.] the science dealing with the mechanical properties of water and other liquids in motion and their application in engineering

hydride (hī′drīd) n. [< HYDRO-] a compound of hydrogen with another element or a radical

Hydro (hī′drō) n., pl. **-dros** a Canadian hydroelectric power company [Ontario *Hydro*]

hydro (hī′drō) n., pl. **-dros** a hotel, resort, etc., where people go to get hydropathic treatment

hydro- [< Gr. *hydōr*, water] a combining form meaning: **1.** water **2.** containing hydrogen

hydrocarbon (hī′drō kär′bən) n. any compound, as benzene, containing only hydrogen and carbon

hydrocephalus (hī′drō sef′ə ləs) n. [< Gr. *hydōr*, water + *kephalē*, head] a condition characterized by an abnormal amount of fluid in the cranium, causing enlargement of the head : also **hy′droceph′-aly**

hydrochloric acid (hī′drō klor′ik) [HYDRO- + CHLORIC] a strong, corrosive acid that is a solution of the gas hydrogen chloride in water

hydrocyanic acid (hī′drō sī an′ik) [HYDRO- + CYANIC] a weak, highly poisonous acid, a colourless liquid with the odour of bitter almonds

hydrodynamics n.pl. [with sing. v.] the branch of physics dealing with the motion and action of water and other liquids —**hy′drodynam′ic** adj.

hydroelectric adj. producing, or relating to the production of, electricity by water power —**hy′droelec′tric′ity** n.

hydrofoil (hī′drō foil′) n. [HYDRO- + (AERO)FOIL] **1.** a winglike structure on the hull of some watercraft : at high speeds the craft skims along on the hydrofoils **2.** a craft with hydrofoils

hydrogen (hī′drə jən) n. [< Fr.: see HYDRO- + -GEN] a flammable, colourless, odourless, gaseous chemical element, the lightest of all known substances: symbol, H —**hydrogenous** (hī droj′ə nəs) adj.

hydrogenate (hī′drə jə nāt′, hī droj′ə-) vt. **-at′ed, -at′ing** to combine or treat with hydrogen —**hy′drogena′tion** n.

hydrogen bomb a highly destructive nuclear bomb, in which the atoms of heavy hydrogen are fused by explosion of a nuclear-fission unit in the bomb

hydrogen peroxide an unstable liquid often used, diluted, as a bleach or disinfectant

hydrogen sulphide a gaseous compound with the characteristic odour of rotten eggs

hydrography (hī drog′rə fē) *n.* [< Fr.: see HYDRO- & -GRAPHY] the study, description, and mapping of seas, lakes, and rivers —**hydrog′rapher** *n.*

hydrology (hī drol′ə jē) *n.* [see HYDRO- & -LOGY] the study of the distribution, use, etc., of water

hydrolysis (hī drol′ə sis) *n.,* *pl.* **-ses′**(-sēz′) [HYDRO- + -LYSIS] the breaking up of a substance into other substances by reaction with water —**hy′-drolyse** *vt.,* *vi.*

hydrometer (hī drom′ə tər) *n.* [HYDRO- + -METER] an instrument for measuring the specific gravity of liquids —**hydromet′ric** (hī′drə met′rik) *adj.* —**hydrom′etry** *n.*

hydropathy (hī drop′ə thē) *n.* [HYDRO- + -PATHY] a system of treating all diseases by the external or internal use of water —**hydropathic** (hī′drə path′ik) *adj.*

hydrophilic (hī′drō fil′ik) *adj.* [HYDRO- + Gr. *philos,* loving] capable of uniting with or taking up water

hydrophobia (hī′drō fō′bē ə) *n.* [see HYDRO- & -PHOBIA] 1. rabies 2. an abnormal fear of drinking water, esp. as a symptom of rabies —**hy′dropho′bic** *adj.*

hydroplane (hī′drō plān′) *n.* [HYDRO- + PLANE[1]] 1. a small, light motorboat with hydrofoils or with a flat bottom that can skim along the water at high speeds 2. a horizontal vane on the hull of a submarine for controlling its vertical motion

hydroponics (hī′drō pon′iks) *n.pl.* [with *sing. v.*] [< HYDRO- + Gr. *ponos,* labour] the cultivation of plants in solutions, or moist inert material, containing minerals, instead of in soil —**hy′dropon′ic** *adj.*

hydrosphere (hī′drō sfēər′) *n.* [HYDRO- + SPHERE] all the water on the surface of the earth or in its atmosphere

hydrostatics (hī′drō stat′iks) *n.pl.* [with *sing. v.*] [see HYDRO- & STATIC] the science dealing with the pressure and equilibrium of water and other liquids —**hy′drostat′ic** *adj.*

hydrotropism (hī drot′rə piz′m) *n.* [HYDRO- + -TROPISM] movement, as of a root, in response to moisture

hydrous (hī′drəs) *adj.* [see HYDRO-] containing water, as certain chemical compounds

hydroxide (hī drok′sīd) *n.* [HYDRO- + OXIDE] a compound of an element or radical with hydroxyl

hydroxyl (hī drok′sil) *n.* the monovalent radical OH, present in all hydroxides

hydrozoan (hī′drə zō′ən) *adj.* [< HYDRA + ZOO-] of a class of coelenterate animals having a saclike body and a mouth that opens directly into the body cavity

hyena (hī ē′nə) *n.* [< Gr. *hys,* pig] a wolflike animal of Africa and Asia, with a shrill cry

hygiene (hī′jēn) *n.* [< Gr. *hygiēs,* healthy] 1. principles for preserving health and preventing disease 2. hygienic practices —**hygien′ic** *adj.* —**hy′gienist** *n.*

hygro- [< Gr.] *a combining form meaning* moisture

hygrometer (hī grom′ə tər) *n.* [see prec. & -METER] an instrument for measuring moisture in the air

hygroscope (hī′grə skōp′) *n.* [HYGRO- + -SCOPE] an instrument that indicates, without actually measuring, changes in atmospheric humidity

hygroscopic (hī′grə skop′ik) *adj.* 1. *a)* absorbing moisture from the air *b)* changed by the absorption of moisture 2. of or according to a hygroscope

hying (hī′iŋ) *alt. prp. of* HIE

hymen (hī′men) *n.* [Gr. *hymēn,* membrane] the thin membrane that usually closes part of the opening of the vagina in a virgin —**hy′menal** *adj.*

hymenopteran (hī′mə nop′tər ən) *n.* [< Gr. *hymēn,* membrane + *pteron,* wing] any of a large order of insects, including wasps, bees, ants, etc., which have four membranous wings —**hy′menop′terous** *adj.*

hymn (him) *n.* [< Gr. *hymnos*] a song of praise, esp. in honour of God —*vt.* to praise in a hymn

hymnal (him′nəl) *n.* a collection of religious hymns: also **hymn′book′**, **hym′-nary** —*adj.* of hymns

hymnody (him′nə dē) *n.* 1. the singing of hymns 2. *same as* HYMNOLOGY —**hym′-nodist** *n.*

hymnology (him nol′ə jē) *n.* the study of or composition of hymns —**hymnol′o-gist** *n.*

hyoscyamine (hī′ə sī′ə mēn′) *n.* [< Gr. *hyoskamas,* henbane] a colourless, poisonous alkaloid obtained from henbane and used in medicine

hyper- [< Gr.] *a prefix meaning* over, above, more than normal, excessive [*hypercritical*]

hyperactive (hī′pər ak′tiv) *adj.* extremely or abnormally active —**hy′perac-tiv′ity** (-tiv′ə tē) *n.*

HYPERBOLA

hyperbola (hī pur′bə lə) *n.,* *pl.* **-las,** **-lae′** (-lē′) [< Gr. *hyper-,* over + *ballein,* throw] a curve formed by the section of a cone cut by a plane more steeply inclined to the base than to the side

hyperbole (hī pur′bə lē) *n.* [see prec.]

exaggeration for effect (Ex.: He's as strong as an ox)

hyperbolic (hī′pər bol′ik) *adj.* 1. of or using hyperbole 2. of a hyperbola

hyperborean (hī′pər bô rē′ən) *adj.* [< Gr. *hyperboreos*, beyond the north wind] 1. of the far north 2. very cold

hypercritical (hī′pər krit′i k'l) *adj.* too critical —**hy′percrit′ically** *adv.*

hyperglycaemia (hī pər glī sē′mē ə) *n.* [< HYPER- + Gr. *glykys*, sweet + -AEMIA] an abnormally high concentration of sugar in the blood

hypermarket (hī′pər mär′kit) *n.* a huge store, larger than a supermarket, usually on the outskirts of a town

hypermetropia (hī′pər mi trō′pē ə) *n.* [< Gr. *hypermetros*, excessive + -OPIA] abnormal vision in which distant objects are seen more clearly than near ones

hyperon (hī′pər on′) *n.* [HYPER- + (BARY)ON] any of a class of baryons which are heavier than the nucleons

hypersensitive (hī′pər sen′sə tiv) *adj.* abnormally or excessively sensitive —**hy′persen′sitiv′ity** *n.*

hypersonic (hī′pər son′ik) *adj.* of or moving at a speed equal to about five times the speed of sound or greater

hypertension (hī′pər ten′shən) *n.* abnormally high blood pressure, or a disease of which this is the chief sign

hypertrophy (hī pur′trō fē) *n.* [see HYPER- & -TROPHY] an abnormal increase in the size of an organ or tissue —**hypertrophic** (hī′pər trof′ik) *adj.*

hyperventilation (hī′pər ven′tə lā′shən) *n.* very rapid or deep breathing causing dizziness, fainting, etc. —**hy′perven′tilate′** *vi.*, *vt.*

hyphen (hī′f'n) *n.* [< Gr. *hypo-*, under + *heis*, one] a mark (-) used between the parts of a compound word or the syllables of a divided word, as at the end of a line —*vt.* same as HYPHENATE

hyphenate *vt.* -at′ed, -at′ing 1. to connect by a hyphen 2. to write with a hyphen —**hy′phena′tion** *n.*

hypno- [< Gr.] *a combining form meaning*: 1. sleep 2. hypnotism

hypnosis (hip nō′sis) *n.*, *pl.* -ses (-sēz) [see HYPNO-] a sleeplike condition psychically induced, in which the subject is in a state of altered consciousness and responds to the suggestions of the hypnotist

hypnotherapy (hip′nō ther′ə pē) *n.* [HYPNO- + THERAPY] the treatment of disease by hypnotism

hypnotic (hip not′ik) *adj.* [< Gr. *hypnos*, sleep] 1. causing sleep; soporific 2. of or inducing hypnosis —*n.* any agent causing sleep —**hypnot′ically** *adv.*

hypnotism (hip′nə tiz′m) *n.* the act or practice of inducing hypnosis —**hyp′notist** *n.*

hypnotize *vt.* -tized′, -tiz′ing 1. to induce hypnosis in 2. to spellbind as if by hypnotism

hypo (hī′pō) *n.*, *pl.* -pos *short for* HYPODERMIC

hypo- [Gr. < *hypo*, less than] a prefix

meaning: 1. under [*hypodermic*] 2. deficient in [*hypothyroid*]

hypocaust (hī′pō kôst′) *n.* [< Gr. *hypokaiein*, to heat from below] a space below the floor in some ancient Roman buildings, into which hot air was piped to warm the rooms

hypochondria (hī′pō kon′drē ə) *n.* [< Gr. *hypo-*, under + *chondros*, cartilage of the sternum] abnormal anxiety over one's health, often with imaginary illnesses

hypochondriac *n.* a person who has hypochondria —*adj.* of or having hypochondria

hypocrisy (hi pok′rə sē) *n.*, *pl.* -ries [< G. *hypo-*, under + *krinesthai*, to dispute] a pretending to be what one is not, or to feel what one does not feel; esp., a pretence of virtue

hypocrite (hip′ə krit) *n.* [see prec.] a person who pretends to be pious, virtuous, etc. without really being so —**hyp′ocrit′ical** *adj.* —**hyp′ocrit′ically** *adv.*

hypodermic (hī′pō dur′mik) *adj.* [see HYPO- + DERMA] 1. of the parts under the skin 2. injected under the skin —*n.* a hypodermic injection or syringe

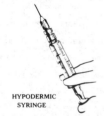

HYPODERMIC
SYRINGE

hypodermic syringe a piston syringe attached to a hollow needle (**hypodermic needle**), used for giving hypodermic injections

hypostasis (hī pos′tə sis) *n.*, *pl.* -ses′ (-sēz) [Gr. *hypostasis*, foundation] 1. the essential nature of anything 2. the substance of each of the three divisions of the Godhead

hypotension (hī′pō ten′shən) *n.* abnormally low blood pressure

hypotenuse (hī pot′ ən yōōz′) *n.* [< Gr. *hypo-*, under + *teinein*, stretch] the side of a right-angled triangle opposite the right angle

hypothecate (hī poth′ə kāt′) *vt.* -cat′ed, -cat′ing [< Gr. *hypotithenai*, to pledge] to pledge (property) to another as security

hypothermia (hī′pō thur′mē ə) *n.* [<

HYPO- + Gr. *thermē*, heat] the condition of having a subnormal body temperature

hypothesis (hī poth'ə sis) *n.,* *pl.* **-ses'** (-sēz') [Gr. < *hypo-*, under + *tithenai*, to place] an unproved theory, etc. tentatively accepted to explain certain facts

hypothesize *vi.* **-sized'**, **-siz'ing** to make a hypothesis —*vt.* to assume; suppose

hypothetical (hī'pə thet'i k'l) *adj.* based on a hypothesis; assumed; supposed —**hy'pothet'ically** *adv.*

hyssop (his'əp) *n.* [< Heb. *ēzōbh*] **1.** a fragrant, blue-flowered plant, used in folk medicine as a tonic, etc. **2.** *Bible* a plant whose twigs were used for sprinkling in certain ancient Jewish rites

hysterectomy (his'tə rek'tə mē) *n.,* *pl.* **-mies** [< Gr. *hystera*, uterus + -ECTOMY] surgical removal of all or part of the uterus

hysteresis (his'tə rē'sis) *n.* [Gr., deficiency] *Physics* a lag of effect, as in magnetization, when the forces acting on a body are changed

hysteria (his tēr'ē ə) *n.* [< ff.] **1.** a psychiatric condition characterized by excitability, sensory and motor disturbances, etc. **2.** any outbreak of wild, uncontrolled excitement, such as fits of laughing and crying

hysteric (his ter'ik) *n.* [< Gr. *hystera*, uterus: the ancients thought it was caused by disturbances of the uterus] **1.** [*usually pl., occas. with sing. v.*] a hysterical fit **2.** a person subject to hysteria —*adj.* same *as* HYSTERICAL

hysterical *adj.* **1.** of hysteria **2.** having or subject to hysteria —**hyster'ically** *adv.*

Hz *Physics the symbol for* hertz

I

I, i (ī) *n.,* *pl.* **I's, i's** the ninth letter of the English alphabet

I¹ (ī) *n.* a Roman numeral for 1 —*adj.* shaped like *I*

I² (ī) *pron.* for pl. see WE [OE. *ic*] the person speaking or writing —*n., pl.* **I's** the ego

i (ī) *n.* a Roman numeral for 1 [page *i*]

I *Chem.* iodine

I., i. 1. island(s) 2. isle(s)

-ia (ē ə, yə) [L. & Gr.] a suffix used in: 1. names of certain diseases 2. names of some plants and animals

I.A.E.A. International Atomic Energy Agency

-ial (ē əl, yəl, əl) [L.] same as -AL

iamb (ī'amb) *n.* [< Gr. *iambos*] a metrical foot of two syllables, the first unaccented and the other accented (Ex.: "Tŏ bé, ŏr nŏt tŏ bé"): also **iam'bus**

iambic (ī am'bik) *adj.* of or made up of iambs —*n.* 1. an iamb 2. an iambic verse

-ian (ē ən, yən, ən) [< L.] same as -AN [reptilian]

-iatry (ī'ə trē) [< Gr. *iatreia*, healing] a combining form meaning medical treatment [psychiatry]

I.B.A. Independent Broadcasting Authority

Iberian (ī bēar'ē ən) *adj.* of Spain and Portugal —*n.* an inhabitant of Spain or Portugal

ibex (ī'beks) *n., pl.* **i'bexes, ibices** (ī'bə sēz') [L.] a wild goat of Europe, Asia, or Africa: the male has backward-curved horns

ibid. [L. *ibidem*] in the same place: used in citing again the book, page, etc. cited just before

-ibility (ə bil'ə tē) *pl.* **-ties** [< L.] a suffix used to form nouns from adjectives ending in -IBLE [sensibility]

ibis (ī'bis) *n.* [< Egypt. *hīb*] a large wading bird related to the heron, as the sacred ibis of the Nile

-ible (i b'l, ə b'l) [L. *-ibilis*] same as -ABLE [legible]

Ibo (ē'bō) *n.* [< the native name] *pl.* **I'bos, I'bo** any member of an African people of SE Nigeria

-ic (ik) [< Gr.] a suffix meaning: a) of, having to do with [volcanic] b) like [angelic] c) produced by [photographic] d) having, affected by [lethargic] e) Chem. of a higher valence than the compound ending in -ous [nitric] Also **-ical**

i/c 1. in charge 2. internal combustion

I.C.A. Institute of Chartered Accountants in England and Wales

ICBM Intercontinental ballistic missile

ice (īs) *n.* [OE. *is*] 1. a) water frozen solid by cold b) a sheet or layer of this 2. anything like frozen water in appearance, etc. 3. a helping of a) water ice b) ice cream 4. icing —*vt.* **iced, ic'ing** 1. to freeze 2. to cover with ice 3. to cool by putting ice on, in, or around 4. to cover with icing —*vi.* to freeze (with *up* or *over*) —**break the ice** to make a start, as in getting acquainted —**cut no ice** [Colloq.] to have no effect —**on ice** [Slang] 1. in readiness or reserve 2. with success assured —**on thin ice** [Colloq.] in a risky situation

-ice (is, əs) [< L.] a suffix meaning condition or quality of [justice]

Ice. 1. Iceland 2. Icelandic

I.C.E. Institution of Civil Engineers

ice age same as GLACIAL EPOCH

iceberg (īs'bʉrg) *n.* [prob. < Du. *ijsberg*, ice mountain] a great mass of ice broken off from a glacier and floating in the sea

icebound *adj.* 1. held fast by ice, as a boat 2. made inaccessible by ice, as a port

icebox *n.* 1. a compartment in a refrigerator for storing or making ice 2. a cabinet with ice in it for keeping foods, etc. cold 3. [U.S.] a refrigerator

icebreaker *n.* a ship for breaking through ice

icecap *n.* a mass of glacial ice that spreads slowly out from a centre

ice cream a sweet, frozen food made from flavoured cream or milk —**ice'-cream'** *adj.*

ice field an extensive area of floating sea ice

ice floe a single piece, large or small, of floating sea ice

ice hockey a team game played on ice, in which the players, using curved sticks and wearing skates, try to drive a rubber disc (*puck*) into their opponents' goal

Icelandic (īs lan'dik) *adj.* of Iceland, its people, etc. —*n.* the Germanic language of the Icelanders

ice lolly frozen ice cream or water ice on a stick

ice pack 1. a bag, etc. filled with crushed ice and applied to the body, as to reduce a swelling 2. a large, floating expanse of ice masses frozen together

ice skate a skate for skating on ice: see SKATE¹ (sense 1) —**ice'-skate'** *vi.* **-skat'ed, -skat'ing** —**ice skater**

I.Chem.E. Institution of Chemical Engineers

ichor (ī'kôr) *n.* [Gr. *ichōr*] 1. *Gr. Myth.*

the fluid flowing in the veins of the gods
2. a watery discharge from a wound or sore

ichthyology (ik'thē ol'ə jē) *n.* [< Gr. *ichthys*, fish & -LOGY] the branch of zoology dealing with fishes —**ich'thyol'o-gist** *n.*

I.C.I. Imperial Chemical Industries

-ician (ish'ən) [< Fr.] *a suffix meaning* a person engaged in, practising, or specializing in [*physician*]

icicle (ī'si k'l) *n.* [< OE. *is*, ice + *gicel*, piece of ice] a hanging piece of ice, formed by the freezing of dripping water —**i'cicled** *adj.*

icing (ī'siŋ) *n.* **1.** a mixture, as of sugar, etc., for covering a cake **2.** the formation of ice, as on an aircraft

icing sugar granulated sugar ground to a powder

I.C.M.A. Institute of Cost and Management Accountants

icon (ī'kon) *n.* [< Gr. *eikōn*, image] **1.** Orthodox Eastern Ch. an image or picture of Jesus, Mary, a saint, etc. venerated as sacred **2.** an image —**icon'ic** *adj.*

icono- [< Gr. *eikōn*, image] *a combining form meaning* image, figure

iconoclast (ī kon'ō klast') *n.* [< Gr. *eikōn*, image + *klaein*, break] **1.** a person who attacks or ridicules traditional or venerated institutions or ideas **2.** anyone who deliberately destroys religious images —**icon'oclasm** *n.* —**icon'oclas'tic** *adj.*

icosahedron (ī'ko sə hē'drən) *n.*, *pl.* **-he'-dra, -drons** [< Gr. *eikosi*, twenty + -HEDRON] a solid figure with twenty plane surfaces

ictus (ik'təs) *n.*, *pl.* **-tuses, -tus** [< L. *icere*, to hit] rhythmical or metrical stress, or accent

icy (ī'sē) *adj.* **i'cier, i'ciest 1.** full of or covered with ice **2.** of ice **3.** like ice; slippery or very cold **4.** cold in manner; unfriendly —**i'cily** *adv.* —**i'ciness** *n.*

id (id) *n.* [L., it] *Psychoanalysis* that part of the psyche which is the source of the instinctual drives

-id (id, əd) [ult. < L. or Gr.] *a suffix meaning* a thing belonging to or connected with [*Aeneid, arachnid*]

ID, I.D. [U.S.] identification

id. [L. *idem*] the same

I'd (īd) **1.** I had **2.** I would **3.** I should

-idae (i dē') [ModL.] *a suffix used to form the name of a zoological family* [*Canidae* (the dog family)]

idea (ī dē'ə) *n.* [< Gr. *idea*, appearance of a thing] **1.** a mental conception or image **2.** an opinion or belief **3.** a plan; scheme **4.** a vague impression **5.** meaning or significance **6.** *Philos.* according to Plato, a model of which all real things are but imperfect imitations

ideal (ī dē'əl) *adj.* [see prec.] **1.** existing as an idea **2.** thought of as perfect **3.** existing only in the mind; imaginary —*n.* **1.** a conception of something in its most excellent form **2.** a perfect model **3.** a goal or principle

idealism *n.* **1.** behaviour or thought based on a conception of things as one thinks

they should be **2.** a striving to achieve one's ideals **3.** *Philos.* any theory which holds that things exist only as ideas in the mind or that things are really imperfect imitations of unchanging models

idealist *n.* **1.** a person whose behaviour or thought is based on ideals **2.** a visionary or impractical dreamer —*adj.* same as IDEALISTIC

idealistic (ī'dē ə lis'tik) *adj.* **1.** of or characteristic of an idealist **2.** of or based on idealism

idealize (ī dē'ə līz') *vt.* **-ized', -iz'ing** to regard or show as perfect or more nearly perfect than is true —**ide'aliza'tion** *n.*

ideally *adv.* **1.** in an ideal manner **2.** in theory

‡**idée fixe** (ē dā fēks') [Fr.] a fixed idea; obsession

‡**idem** (ī'dem) *pron.* [L.] the same as that previously mentioned

identical (ī den'ti k'l) *adj.* [see IDENTITY] **1.** the very same **2.** exactly alike **3.** designating twins developed from a single fertilized ovum and very much alike —**iden'tically** *adv.*

identification (ī den'tə fi kā'shən) *n.* **1.** an identifying or being identified **2.** anything by which a person or thing can be identified

identification parade a line of people from which a suspected criminal may be recognized

identify (ī den'tə fī') *vt.* **-fied', -fy'ing 1.** to show to be the very person or thing known, described, or claimed **2.** to connect or associate closely **3.** to make identical; treat as the same —*vi.* to understand and share another's feelings (*with*) —**iden'-tifi'able** *adj.*

Identikit (ī den'tə kit) [IDENTI(FICATION) + KIT] *Trademark* a composite picture, formed from descriptions given, of a person of whom no actual photograph is available

identity *n.*, *pl.* **-ties** [< L. *idem*, the same] **1.** *a)* the condition or fact of being a specific person or thing *b)* the condition of being as described **2.** the condition or fact of being the same

ideo- [< Gr.] *a combining form meaning* idea

ideogram (id'ē ō gram') *n.* [prec. + -GRAM] a graphic symbol representing an object or idea without expressing the sounds that form its name: also **id'eograph'**

ideographic (id'ē ə graf'ik) *adj.* of, or having the nature of, an ideogram: also **id'e-ograph'ical**

ideological (ī'dē ə loj'i k'l) *adj.* of or concerned with ideology: also **i'deolog'-ic** —**i'deolog'ically** *adv.*

ideology (ī'dē ol'ə jē) *n.*, *pl.* **-gies** [see IDEO- & -LOGY] **1.** the doctrines, opinions, or way of thinking of an individual, class, etc. **2.** the study of ideas, their nature and source —**i'deol'ogist** *n.*

ides (īdz) *n.pl.* [*often with sing. v.*] [< L. *idus*] in the ancient Roman calendar, the 15th day of March, May, July, or October, or the 13th of the other months

‡**id est** (id est) [L.] that is (to say)

idiocy (id′ē ə sē) *n.*, *pl.* **-cies 1.** the state of being an idiot **2.** great foolishness or stupidity

idiom (id′ē əm) *n.* [< Gr. *idios*, one's own] **1.** an accepted phrase having a meaning different from the literal **2.** the usual way in which the words of a particular language are joined together to express thought **3.** the language of a people, region, etc. **4.** a characteristic style, as in art or music

idiomatic (id′ē ə mat′ik) *adj.* **1.** characteristic of a particular language **2.** of, like, or having many idioms —**id′iomat′ically** *adv.*

idiosyncrasy (id′ē ə siŋ′krə sē) *n.*, *pl.* **-sies** [< Gr. *idio-*, one's own + *syn-*, together + *kerannynai*, mix] any personal peculiarity, mannerism, reaction, etc. —**id′iosyncrat′ic** (-sin krat′ik) *adj.*

idiot (id′ē ət) *n.* [< Gr. *idiōtēs*, ignorant person] **1.** a person having severe mental retardation **2.** a stupid person

idiotic (id′ē ot′ik) *adj.* of or like an idiot; very foolish or stupid —**id′iot′ically** *adv.*

idle (ī′d'l) *adj.* **i′dler**, **i′dlest** [OE. *idel*, empty] **1.** *a*) unemployed *b*) not in use **2.** lazy **3.** worthless; futile **4.** unfounded [*idle* rumours] —*vi.* **i′dled**, **i′dling 1.** to move slowly or aimlessly **2.** to be unemployed or inactive **3.** to operate without transmitting any power, esp. with disengaged gears —*vt.* **1.** to waste; squander **2.** to make (a motor, etc.) idle —**i′dleness** *n.* —**i′dly** *adv.*

idler *n.* **1.** one who loafs **2.** a gearwheel placed between two others to transfer motion from one to the other without changing their direction or speed

idol (ī′d'l) *n.* [< Gr. *eidōlon*, image] **1.** an image of a god, used as an object of worship **2.** an object of excessive devotion or admiration

idolater (ī dol′ə tər) *n.* [< Gr. *eidōlon*, image + *latris*, servant] **1.** a worshipper of idols **2.** a devoted admirer

idolatry *n.*, *pl.* **-tries 1.** worship of idols **2.** excessive devotion or reverence —**idol′atrous** *adj.*

idolize (ī′dəl īz′) *vt.* **-ized′**, **-iz′ing 1.** to love or admire excessively **2.** to make an idol of —**i′doliza′tion** *n.*

idyll, idyl (id′′l) *n.* [< Gr. *eidos*, a form] **1.** a short poem or prose work describing a simple, pleasant scene of rural or pastoral life **2.** a scene or incident suitable for such a work —**i′dyllist** *n.*

idyllic (i dil′ik) *adj.* **1.** of, or relating to an idyll **2.** peaceful; contented; happy

i.e. [L. *id est*] that is (to say)

I.E.E. Institution of Electrical Engineers

-ier (ēər, ər, yər) [< L.] *a suffix meaning* one concerned with (a specified action or thing) [*bombardier*]

if (if) *conj.* [OE. *gif*] **1.** on condition that [*if* I come, I'll see him] **2.** granting that [*if* he was there, I didn't see him] **3.** whether [ask him if he knows her] —*n.* **1.** a supposition **2.** a condition [too many *ifs* and buts] —**as if** as the situation would be if

iffy (if′ē) *adj.* [Colloq.] full of uncertainty

igloo (ig′l ōō) *n.*, *pl.* **-loos** [Eskimo *iglu*, snow house] an Eskimo hut, usually dome-shaped and built of snow

igneous (ig′nē əs) *adj.* [< L. *ignis*, fire] **1.** formed by volcanic action [*igneous* rock] **2.** of, or like fire

ignis fatuus (ig′nis fat′yoo wəs) *pl.* **ignes fatui** (ig′nēz fat′yoo wī′) [< L. *ignis*, fire + *fatuus*, foolish] a light seen at night moving over swamps, etc.: popularly called **will-o'-the-wisp**, **jack-o'-lantern**

ignite (ig nīt′) *vt.*, *vi.* **-nit′ed**, **-nit′ing** [< L. *ignis*, fire] to start burning —**ignit′able**, **ignit′ible** *adj.*

ignition (ig nish′ən) *n.* **1.** an igniting or means of igniting **2.** in an internal-combustion engine, the system for igniting the explosive mixture in the cylinder

ignoble (ig nō′b'l) *adj.* [< L. *in-*, not + *nobilis*, known] not noble; dishonourable; base —**igno′bly** *adv.*

ignominious (ig′nō min′ē əs) *adj.* **1.** disgraceful **2.** despicable **3.** degrading —**ig′nomin′iously** *adv.*

ignominy (ig′nə min′ē) *n.*, *pl.* **-min′ies** [< L. *in-*, without + *nomen*, name] **1.** loss of one's reputation; shame and dishonour **2.** shameful quality or action

ignoramus (ig′nə rā′məs) *n.*, *pl.* **-muses** [< L., lit., we are ignorant of] an ignorant person

ignorance (ig′nər əns) *n.* the condition or quality of being ignorant; lack of knowledge

ignorant *adj.* [see ff.] **1.** lacking knowledge or experience **2.** caused by or showing lack of these **3.** unaware (of) **4.** rude, sometimes because of lack of knowledge of good manners —**ig′norantly** *adv.*

ignore (ig nôr′) *vt.* **-nored′**, **-nor′ing** [< L. *in-*, not + *gnarus*, knowing] to disregard deliberately; pay no attention to —**ignor′er** *n.*

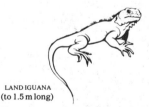

LAND IGUANA
(to 1.5 m long)

iguana (i gwä′nə) *n.* [< S. AmInd. *iuana*] a large tropical American lizard

IHS a contraction misread from the Greek word IHΣΟΥΣ, Jesus, used as a symbol or monogram

ikebana (ē′ke bä′nə) *n.* [Jap.] the Japanese art of arranging flowers

ikon (ī′kon) *n.* *var.* of ICON

il- *see* IN-[1], IN-[2]

ileum (il′ē əm) *n.*, *pl.* **il′ea** [< L., flank,

groin (var. of *ilium*)] the lowest part of the small intestine

ilex (ī'leks) *n.* [L.] *same as:* 1. HOLLY 2. HOLM OAK

ilium (il'ē əm) *n., pl.* **il′ia** [see ILEUM] the flat, uppermost section of the hipbone

ilk (ilk) *adj.* [< OE. *ilca*, same] [Obs.] same —*n.* kind; sort : only in **of that** (or **his, her,** etc.) **ilk**

ill (il) *adj.* **worse, worst** [< ON. *illr*] 1. not healthy, normal, or well 2. bad [*ill* repute, *ill* fortune, *ill* will] 3. improper [with an *ill* grace] —*n.* anything causing harm, trouble, pain, etc.; evil —*adv.* **worse, worst** 1. badly 2. with difficulty [he can *ill* afford it] —**ill at ease** uncomfortable

I'll (īl) 1. I shall 2. I will

ill. 1. illustrated 2. illustration

ill-advised (il'əd vīzd') *adj.* resulting from a lack of sound advice; unwise —**ill′-advis′edly** *adv.*

ill-bred *adj.* badly brought up; rude

ill-considered *adj.* not suitable or wise

ill-disposed *adj.* 1. malicious or malevolent 2. unfriendly or unfavourable (*towards*)

illegal (i lē'gəl) *adj.* not lawful; against the law —**illegality** (il'ē gal'ə tē) *n.* —**ille′- gally** *adv.*

illegible (i lej'ə b'l) *adj.* difficult or impossible to read, as because badly written or printed —**illeg′ibil′ity** *n.* —**illeg′ibly** *adv.*

illegitimate (il'ə jit'ə mət) *adj.* 1. born of parents not married to each other 2. not lawful 3. unsanctioned —**il′legit′i- macy** *n.* —**il′legit′imately** *adv.*

ill fame bad reputation —**house of ill fame** a brothel

ill-fated (il'fāt'id) *adj.* 1. having or sure to have an evil fate or unlucky end 2. unlucky

ill-favoured *adj.* 1. unpleasant 2. offensive

ill-founded *adj.* not supported by facts

ill-gotten *adj.* obtained by evil, unlawful, or dishonest means [*ill-gotten* gains]

ill humour a disagreeable, cross, or sullen mood or state of mind —**ill′-hu′moured** *adj.* —**ill′-hu′mouredly** *adv.*

illiberal (i lib'ər əl) *adj.* 1. intolerant; narrow-minded 2. miserly —**illib′eral′ity** (-ə ral'ə tē) *n.*

illicit (i lis'it) *adj.* not allowed by law, custom, etc.; unlawful —**illic′itly** *adv.* —**illic′itness** *n.*

illiterate (i lit'ə ət) *adj.* [L. *illiteratus*, unlettered] uneducated; esp., not knowing how to read or write —*n.* an illiterate person —**illit′eracy** *n.* —**illit′er- ately** *adv.*

ill-mannered (il'man'ərd) *adj.* rude; impolite

ill nature an unpleasant, disagreeable disposition —**ill′-na′tured** *adj.* —**ill′-na′- turedly** *adv.*

illness *n.* the condition of being ill; sickness; disease

illogical (i loj'i k'l) *adj.* not logical; using or based on faulty reasoning —**illog′ical′- ity** (-i kal'ə tē) *n.* —**illog′ically** *adv.*

ill-starred *adj.* unlucky; doomed

ill-timed *adj.* coming or done at the wrong time

ill-treat (il'trēt') *vt.* to treat unkindly, cruelly, or unfairly; abuse —**ill′-treat′- ment** *n.*

illuminant (i lyōō'mə nənt) *adj.* giving light; illuminating —*n.* something that gives light

illuminate (i lyōō'mə nāt') *vt.* **-nat′ed, -nat′ing** [< L. *in-*, in + *luminare*, to light] 1. to give light to; light up 2. *a*) to make clear; explain *b*) to inform 3. to decorate with lights 4. to decorate (an initial letter, a page border, etc.) with designs of gold, etc. —**illu′minative** *adj.*

illumination (i lyōō'mə nā'shən) *n.* 1. an illuminating or being illuminated 2. the designs used in illuminating manuscripts 3. [*pl.*] lights used as decorations, as at a seaside resort

illumine (i lyōō'min) *vt.* **-mined, -mining** *same as* ILLUMINATE —**illu′minable** *adj.*

illus., illust. 1. illustrated 2. illustration

ill-usage (il'yōō'zij) *n.* unfair, unkind, or cruel treatment; abuse : also **ill usage**

ill-use (-yōōz'; *for n.* -yōōs') *vt.* **-used′, -us′ing** to subject to ill-usage —*n.* same as ILL-USAGE

illusion (i lōō'zhən) *n.* [< L. *illudere*, mock] 1. a false idea or conception 2. an unreal or misleading appearance or image 3. a false perception or interpretation of what one sees —**illu′sive, illu′sory** *adj.*

illusionist *n.* an entertainer who performs sleight-of-hand tricks

illustrate (il'ə strāt') *vt.* **-trat′ed, -trat′- ing** [< L. *in-*, in + *lustrare*, illuminate] 1. to make clear or explain, as by examples or comparisons 2. to furnish (books, etc.) with explanatory or decorative drawings, pictures, etc. —**il′lustra′tor** *n.*

illustration (il'ə strā'shən) *n.* 1. an illustrating or being illustrated 2. an explanatory example, story, etc. 3. an explanatory or decorative picture, diagram, etc.

illustrative (il'ə strə tiv) *adj.* serving to illustrate

illustrious (i lus'trē əs) *adj.* [< L. *illustris*, bright] very distinguished; famous; eminent —**illus′triously** *adv.*

ill will unfriendly feeling; hostility; hate

ILO, I.L.O. International Labour Organization

I.L.P. Independent Labour Party

I'm (īm) I am

im- *see* IN-[1], IN-[2]

image (im'ij) *n.* [L. *imago*] 1. a representation of a person or thing, esp., a statue 2. the visual impression of something produced by a mirror, lens, etc. 3. a copy; likeness 4. *a*) a mental picture *b*) the public conception of a person, product, etc. 5. a type; embodiment 6. a metaphor or simile —*vt.* **-aged, -aging** 1. to picture in the mind 2. to reflect 3. to portray; delineate

imagery *n., pl.* **-ries** 1. descriptions and figures of speech 2. mental images

imaginary (i maj'ə nər ē) *adj.* existing only

in the imagination; unreal —**imag'inarily** *adv.*

imagination (i maj'ə nā'shən) *n.* **1.** a) the act or power of forming mental images of what is not actually present b) the act or power of creating new images by combining previous experiences **2.** responsiveness to the imaginative creations of others **3.** resourcefulness in dealing with new experiences

imaginative (i maj'ə nə tiv) *adj.* **1.** having or showing imagination **2.** of or resulting from imagination

imagine (i maj'in) *vt., vi.* -ined, -ining [< L. *imago*, image] **1.** to make a mental image (of) **2.** to suppose; think —**imag'inable** *adj.*

imago (i mā'gō) *n., pl.* -gos, imagines (i maj'ə nēz') [L.] an insect in its final, adult stage

imam (i mäm') *n.* [Ar. *imām*] **1.** the prayer leader in a Moslem mosque **2.** [*often* I-] title for a Moslem ruler

imbalance (im bal'əns) *n.* lack of balance, as in emphasis, proportion, etc.

imbecile (im'bə sēl) *n.* [< L. *imbecilis*, feeble] **1.** a person having moderate mental retardation **2.** a foolish or stupid person —*adj.* foolish or stupid —**im'becil'ity** (-sil'ə tē) *n.*

imbed (im bed') *vt. same as* EMBED

imbibe (im bīb') *vt.* -bibed', -bib'ing [< L. *in-*, in + *bibere*, drink] **1.** a) to drink (esp. alcoholic liquor) b) to drink in **2.** to absorb (moisture) —**imbib'er** *n.*

imbroglio (im brōl'yō) *n., pl.* -glios [It. < *imbrogliare*, embroil] an involved and confusing situation

imbue (im byoo') *vt.* -bued', -bu'ing [< L. *imbuere*] **1.** to permeate or inspire (*with* principles, ideas, etc.) **2.** to fill with colour; dye

I.Mech.E. Institution of Mechanical Engineers

I.M.F. International Monetary Fund

imitate (im'ə tāt') *vt.* -tat'ed, -tat'ing [< L. *imitari*, imitate] **1.** to follow the example of **2.** to mimic **3.** to copy the form, colour, etc. of **4.** to resemble —**im'itable** *adj.* —**im'ita'tor** *n.*

imitation (im'ə tā'shən) *n.* **1.** an imitating **2.** the result of imitating —*adj.* made to resemble something that is usually superior or genuine [*imitation* leather]

imitative (im'ə tā tiv) *adj.* **1.** formed from a model **2.** given to imitating

immaculate (i mak'yoo lət) *adj.* [< L. *in-*, not + *macula*, spot] **1.** perfectly clean **2.** without flaw **3.** pure; innocent **4.** [Colloq.] faultless —**immac'ulately** *adv.* —**immac'ulateness** *n.*

immanent (im'ə nənt) *adj.* [< L. *in-*, in + *manere*, remain] **1.** remaining or operating within **2.** present throughout the universe: said of God —**im'manence** *n.* —**im'manently** *adv.*

immaterial (im'ə tēər'ē əl) *adj.* **1.** not pertinent; unimportant **2.** spiritual —**im'mate'rial'ity** (-al'ə tē) *n.*

immature (im'ə tyooər') *adj.* **1.** not mature or ripe; not completely developed

2. not finished or perfected —**im'matu'rity** *n.*

immeasurable (i mezh'ər ə b'l) *adj.* not measurable; boundless —**immeas'urably** *adv.*

immediacy (i mē'dē ə sē) *n.* the quality or condition of being immediate

immediate (i mē'dē ət) *adj.* [see IN-.[2] & MEDIATE] **1.** without delay **2.** directly or closely related **3.** directly affecting; direct **4.** not separated in space; closest **5.** next in order, succession, etc. —**imme'diately** *adj.*

immemorial (im'ə môr'ē əl) *adj.* extending back beyond memory or record —**im'memo'rially** *adv.*

immense (i mens') *adj.* [< L. in-, not + *metiri*, measure] **1.** very large; vast; huge **2.** [Slang] very good —**immense'ly** *adv.* —**immense'ness** *n.* —**immen'sity** *n.*

immerse (i murs') *vt.* -mersed', -mers'ing [< L. *immergere*, plunge] **1.** to plunge or dip into or as if into a liquid **2.** to baptize by dipping under water **3.** to absorb deeply; engross —**immer'sion** *n.*

immersion heater an electric coil or rod that heats water while directly immersed in it

immigrant (im'ə grənt) *n.* one that immigrates —*adj.* immigrating

immigrate (im'ə grāt') *vi.*-grat'ed, -grat'ing [see IN-.[1] & MIGRATE] to come into a new country, esp. in order to settle there —**im'migra'tion** *n.*

imminent (im'ə nənt) *adj.* [< L. *in-*, in + *minere*, project] likely to happen soon : said of danger, events, etc. —**im'minence** *n.* —**im'minently** *adv.*

immiscible (i mis'ə b'l) *adj.* [< IN-.[2] + MISCIBLE] that cannot be mixed, as oil and water —**immis'cibil'ity** *n.*

immobile (i mō'bīl) *adj.* not movable or moving; stable; motionless —**im'mobil'ity** *n.*

immobilize (i mō'bə līz') *vt.* -lized', -liz'ing **1.** to make immobile **2.** to prevent the movement of (a limb or joint) with splints or a cast —**immo'biliza'tion** *n.*

immoderate (i mod'ər ət) *adj.* not moderate; without restraint; excessive —**immod'erately** *adv.*

immodest (i mod'ist) *adj.* **1.** indecent; improper **2.** bold; forward —**immod'estly** *adv.* —**immod'esty** *n.*

immolate (im'ō lāt') *vt.* -lat'ed, -lat'ing [< L. *immolare*, sprinkle with sacrificial meal] to sacrifice —**im'mola'tion** *n.* —**im'mola'tor** *n.*

immoral (i mor'əl) *adj.* morally wrong; sometimes, specif., unchaste —**immor'ally** *adv.* —**im'moral'ity** *n.*

immortal (i môr't'l) *adj.* **1.** living or lasting forever **2.** enduring **3.** having lasting fame —*n.* an immortal being; specif., a) [*pl.*] the ancient Greek or Roman gods b) a person of lasting fame —**im'mor'tal'ity** (-tal'ə tē) *n.*

immortalize *vt.* -ized', -iz'ing to make immortal; esp., to give lasting fame to —**immor'taliza'tion** *n.*

immovable (i moov'ə b'l) *adj.* **1.** firmly

fixed **2.** motionless **3.** unyielding; steadfast **4.** unemotional; impassive —*n.* [*pl.*] *Law* immovable objects or property, as land, etc. —**immov′ably** *adv.*

immune (i myōōn′) *adj.* [< L. *in*-, without + *munia*, duties] **1.** not susceptible to a specified disease **2.** exempt from or protected against something disagreeable or harmful

immunity *n., pl.* **-ties 1.** resistance to or protection against a specified disease **2.** exemption or freedom from something burdensome

immunize (im′yoo nīz′) *vt.* **-nized′, -niz′- ing** to give immunity to —**im′muniza′- tion** *n.*

immunology (im′yoo nol′ə jē) *n.* the branch of medicine dealing with immunity to disease or with allergic reactions —**im′- munol′ogist** *n.*

immure (i myoor′) *vt.* **-mured′, -mur′- ing** [< L. *im*-, in + *murus*, wall] to shut up as within walls

immutable (i myoot′ə b'l) *adj.* never changing or varying —**immu′tabil′ity, immu′tableness** *n.*

imp (imp) *n.* [< Gr. *em*-, in + *phyton*, a plant] **1.** a young demon **2.** a mischievous child

imp. 1. imperative **2.** imperfect **3.** imprimatur

impact (im pakt′; *for n.* im′pakt) *vt.* [< L. *impingere*, press firmly together] to force tightly together —*n.* **1.** a striking together **2.** the force of a collision; shock **3.** an effect, esp. a shock —**impac′tion** *n.*

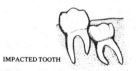

IMPACTED TOOTH

impacted *adj.* firmly lodged in the jaw: said of a tooth unable to erupt

impair (im pâer′) *vt.* [< L. *in*-, intens. + *pejor*, worse] to make worse, less, etc.; damage —**impair′ment** *n.*

impala (im pä′lə) *n.* [Zulu] a small African antelope with lyre-shaped horns, capable of moving with great leaps

impale (im pāl′) *vt.* **-paled′, -pal′ing** [< L. *in*-, on + *palus*, pole] **1.** to pierce through with, or fix on, something pointed **2.** to torture by fixing on a stake **3.** to make helpless, as if fixed on a stake —**impale′ment** *n.*

impalpable (im pal′pə b'l) *adj.* **1.** not perceptible to the touch **2.** too subtle to be grasped easily by the mind

impanel (im pan′'l) *vt.* **-elled, -elling** *same as* EMPANEL

impart (im pärt′) *vt.* [see IN-¹ & PART] **1.** to tell; reveal **2.** to give a share of; give —**impart′able** *adj.*

impartial (im pär′shəl) *adj.* without bias; fair —**impar′tial′ity** (-shē al′ə tē) *n.* —**impar′tially** *adv.*

impassable (im päs′ə b'l) *adj.* that cannot be passed, crossed, or travelled over —**impass′abil′ity** *n.*

impasse (am päs′) *n.* [Fr.] a situation offering no escape; deadlock

impassible (im pas′ə b'l) *adj.* [< L. *im*-, not + *pati*, suffer] **1.** that cannot feel pain or be injured **2.** that cannot be moved emotionally —**impas′sibil′ity** *n.*

impassioned (im pash′ənd) *adj.* filled with passion; passionate; fiery; ardent —**impas′sionedly** *adv.*

impassive (im pas′iv) *adj.* **1.** not feeling pain **2.** not feeling or showing emotion; calm —**impas′sively** *adv.* —**impassivity** (im′pə siv′ə tē) *n.*

impasto (im pas′tō) *n.* [< It. *impastare*, to paste over] painting with the paint laid on thickly

impatience (im pā′shəns) *n.* **1.** annoyance because of delay, etc. **2.** restless eagerness to do something

impatient *adj.* feeling or showing impatience —**impa′tiently** *adv.*

impeach (im pēch′) *vt.* [< L. *in*-, in + *pedica*, a fetter] **1.** to bring (a public official) before the proper tribunal on a charge of wrongdoing **2.** to discredit (a person's honour, etc.) —**impeach′able** *adj.* —**impeach′ment** *n.*

impeccable (im pek′ə b'l) *adj.* [< L. *in*-, not + *peccare*, sin] **1.** flawless **2.** not liable to sin —**impec′cabil′ity** *n.* —**impec′- cably** *adv.*

impecunious (im′pi kyōō′nē əs) *adj.* [< L. *in*-, not + *pecunia*, money] having no money; penniless —**im′pecu′nios′ity** (-əs′ə tē), **im′pecu′niousness** *n.*

impedance (im pēd′əns) *n.* [< IMPEDE] the total opposition in an electric circuit to the flow of an alternating current of a single frequency

impede (im pēd′) *vt.* **-ped′ed, -ped′ing** [< L. *in*-, in + *pes*, foot] to bar or hinder the progress of

impediment (im ped′ə mənt) *n.* [< L. *impedimentum*, hindrance] anything that impedes; specif., a speech defect —**impedi- men′tal** *adj.*

impedimenta (im ped′ə men′tə) *n.pl.* [see prec.] things hindering progress, as on a trip; esp., baggage

impel (im pel′) *vt.* **-pelled′, -pel′ling** [< L. *in*-, on + *pellere*, to drive] **1.** to force, compel, or urge **2.** to push, drive, or move forwards

impend (im pend′) *vi.* [< L. *in*-, in + *pendere*, to hang] to be about to happen —**impending** *adj.*

impenetrable (im pen′i trə b'l) *adj.* **1.** that cannot be penetrated or passed through **2.** that cannot be solved or understood **3.** unreceptive to ideas, influences, etc. —**impen′etrabil′ity** *n.* —**impen′etrably** *adv.*

impenitent (im pen′ə tənt) *adj.* without regret, shame, or remorse —**impen′itence** *n.* —**impen′itently** *adv.*

imper. imperative

imperative (im per′ə tiv) *adj.* [< L. *imperare*, to order] **1.** absolutely necessary; urgent **2.** of or indicating power or authority **3.** *Gram.* designating or of a verb mood expressing a command, etc. —*n.* **1.** a command **2.** *Gram.* the imperative mood —**imper'atively** *adv.* —**imper'ativeness** *n.*

imperator (im'pə rāt'ôr) *n.* [< L. *imperare*, to command] in ancient Rome, a title of honour for generals and, later, emperors —**imperatorial** (im per'ə tôr'- ē əl) *adj.*

imperceptible (im'pər sep'tə b'l) *adj.* not easily perceived; very slight, gradual, etc. —**im'percep'tibil'ity** *n.* —**im'percep'- tibly** *adv.*

imperf. 1. imperfect **2.** imperforate

imperfect (im pur'fikt) *adj.* **1.** having a defect or error **2.** not complete **3.** *Gram.* designating or of a verb tense indicating an incomplete or continuous past action: "was writing" is a form like the imperfect tense —*n.* *Gram.* the imperfect tense —**imper'fectly** *adv.*

imperfection (im'pər fek'shən) *n.* **1.** a being imperfect **2.** a shortcoming; defect; blemish

imperial (im pēar'ē əl) *adj.* [< L. *imperium*, empire] **1.** of an empire, emperor, or empress **2.** of a country having control over other countries or colonies **3.** having supreme authority **4.** majestic; august **5.** a) formerly, of the British Empire b) of a system of weights and measures, formerly official in Britain —*n.* a pointed tuft of beard on the lower lip and chin —**impe'rially** *adv.*

imperialism *n.* **1.** imperial state, authority, or government **2.** the policy of forming and maintaining an empire by conquest, colonization, economic domination, etc. —**impe'rialist** *n., adj.*

imperil (im per'əl) *vt.* **-iled, -illing** to put in peril —**imper'ilment** *n.*

imperious (im pēar'ē əs) *adj.* [< L. *imperium*, empire] **1.** arrogant; domineering **2.** urgent —**impe'riously** *adv.*

impermanent (im pur'mə nənt) *adj.* not lasting; temporary —**imper'manence, imper'manency** *n.*

impermeable (im pur'mē ə b'l) *adj.* not permeable; not permitting passage, esp. of fluids —**imper'meably** *adv.*

impermissible (im'pər mis'ə b'l) *adj.* not allowed

impersonal (im pur's'n əl) *adj.* **1.** without reference to any particular person **2.** not existing as a person [an *impersonal* force] **3.** *Gram.* designating of a verb occurring only in the third person singular (Ex.: "it is snowing") —**imper'sonal'ity** (-al'ə tē) *n.* —**imper'sonally** *adv.*

impersonate (im pur'sə nāt') *vt.* **-at'ed, -at'ing 1.** to act the part of **2.** a) to mimic (a person) for entertainment b) to pretend to be (an officer, etc.) with fraudulent intent —**imper'sona'tion** *n.* —**imper'sona'tor** *n.*

impertinent (im pur'tin ənt) *adj.* [L. *impertinens*] **1.** insolent **2.** not pertinent; irrelevant —**imper'tinently** *adv.* —**imper'- tinence, imper'tinency** *n.*

imperturbable (im'pər tur'bə b'l) *adj.* that cannot be perturbed or excited —**im'- perturb'abil'ity** *n.*

impervious (im pur'vē əs) *adj.* **1.** impermeable **2.** not affected by (with *to*) —**imper'viously** *adv.*

impetigo (im'pə tī'gō) *n.* [L.: see IMPETUS] a skin disease with eruption of pustules

impetuous (im pet'yōō wəs) *adj.* [see ff.] **1.** acting or done suddenly with little thought; impulsive **2.** rushing —**impet'u- ously** *adv.* —**impet'uos'ity** (-os'ə tē), **impet'uousness** *n.*

impetus (im'pə təs) *n., pl.* **-tuses** [< L. *in-*, in + *petere*, rush at] **1.** a stimulus to action; incentive **2.** the force with which a body moves against resistance

impi (im'pi) *n.* [< Zulu] [S Afr.] a Zulu regiment

impiety (im pī'ə tē) *n.* **1.** lack of piety, esp. towards God **2.** *pl.* **-ties** an impious act or remark

impinge (im pinj') *vi.* **-pinged', -ping'ing** [< L. *in-*, in + *pangere*, to strike] **1.** to encroach (*on* or *upon*) **2.** to strike or hit (*on, upon,* or *against*) —**impinge'- ment** *n.*

impious (im'pē əs) *adj.* not pious; specif., lacking reverence for God —**im'piously** *adv.* —**im'piousness** *n.*

impish (im'pish) *adj.* of or like an imp; mischievous —**imp'ishly** *adv.* —**imp'ish- ness** *n.*

implacable (im plak'ə b'l) *adj.* that cannot be appeased or pacified —**implac'abil'- ity** *n.*

implant (im plänt'; *for n.* im'plänt') *vt.* **1.** to plant firmly **2.** to fix firmly in the mind **3.** *Med.* to insert (an organ, tissue, etc.) within the body —*n.* *Med.* an implanted organ, etc. —**im'planta'- tion** *n.*

implausible (im plô'zə b'l) *adj.* not plausible —**implau'sibil'ity** *n.* —**implau'si- bly** *adv.*

implement (im'plə mənt; *for v.* -ment') *n.* [< L. *in-*, in + *plere*, fill] any tool, instrument, etc. used or needed in a given activity —*vt.* **1.** to carry into effect **2.** to accomplish —**im'plemen'tal** *adj.* —**im'- plementa'tion** *n.*

implicate (im'plə kāt') *vt.* **-cat'ed, -cat'- ing** [see IMPLY] **1.** to cause to be involved in or associated with a crime, etc. **2.** to imply —**im'plica'tion** *n.*

implicit (im plis'it) *adj.* [see IMPLY] **1.** suggested though not plainly expressed; implied **2.** necessarily involved though not apparent; inherent **3.** without reservation; absolute —**implic'itly** *adv.*

implied (im plīd') *adj.* involved, suggested, or understood without being directly expressed

implode (im plōd') *vt., vi.* **-plod'ed, -plod'- ing** [< IN-¹ + (EX)PLODE] to burst inwards —**implo'sion** (-plō'zhən) *n.*

implore (im plôr') *vt.* **-plored', -plor'ing** [< L. *in-*, intens. + *plorare*, cry out] **1.** to beg (a person) to do something **2.** to ask earnestly for —**implor'ingly** *adv.*

imply (im plī') *vt.* **-plied', -ply'ing** [< L. *in-*, in + *plicare*, to fold] **1.** to have as a necessary part, condition, or effect **2.** to indicate indirectly; suggest

impolite (im'pə līt') *adj.* not polite; discourteous; rude —**im'polite'ly** *adv.* —**im'polite'ness** *n.*

impolitic (im pol'ə tik) *adj.* unwise; injudicious

imponderable (im pon'dər ə b'l) *adj.* [see IN-[2] & PONDER] **1.** that cannot be weighed or measured **2.** that cannot be conclusively determined —*n.* anything imponderable —**impon'derabil'ity** *n.*

import (im pôrt'; *also, and for n. always*, im'pôrt) *vt.* [< L. *in-*, in + *portare*, carry] **1.** to bring in from the outside, esp. (goods) from another country **2.** to mean; signify —*n.* **1.** the importing of goods **2.** [*often pl.*] something imported **3.** meaning **4.** importance **5.** [Canad. Slang] a sportsman who is not native to the area where he plays —**import'er** *n.*

importance (im pôr'təns) *n.* the state or quality of being important; significance; consequence

important *adj.* [see IMPORT] **1.** having much significance or consequence **2.** having, or acting as if having, power, authority, etc. —**impor'tantly** *adv.*

importation (im'pôr tā'shən) *n.* **1.** an importing or being imported **2.** something imported

importunate (im pôr'tyoo nət) *adj.* persistent in asking or demanding —**impor'tunately** *adv.*

importune (im pôr'tyoon) *vt.* **-tuned, -tuning** [< L. *importunus*, troublesome] to trouble with requests or demands; entreat persistently —**im'por'tunely** *adv.* —**im'portu'nity** *n.*

impose (im pōz') *vt.* **-posed', -pos'ing** [< L. *in-*, on + *ponere*, to place] **1.** to put (a burden, tax, etc. *on* or *upon*) **2.** to force (oneself) on another **3.** to pass off by deception **4.** to arrange (pages of type) for printing —**impose on** (or **upon**) **1.** to put to some trouble or use unfairly for one's own benefit **2.** to cheat; defraud

imposing *adj.* impressive in size, dignity, etc.

imposition (im'pə zish'ən) *n.* **1.** a taking advantage of friendship, etc. **2.** something imposed, as a tax, burden, etc. **3.** an essay, etc. set as a punishment at school **4.** the laying on of hands as at ordination

impossibility (im pos'ə bil'ə tē) *n.* **1.** a being impossible **2.** *pl.* **-ties** something that is impossible

impossible (im pos'ə b'l) *adj.* **1.** not capable of being, being done, or happening **2.** not capable of being endured, used, etc. because disagreeable or unsuitable —**impos'sibly** *adv.*

impost[1] (im'pōst) *n.* [see IMPOSE] a tax; esp., a duty on imported goods

impost[2] *n.* [ult. < L.: see IMPOSE] the top part of a pillar, pier, etc. supporting an arch

impostor (im pos'tər) *n.* [see IMPOSE] one who deceives by pretending to be what he is not

imposture *n.* fraud; deception

impotent (im'pə tənt) *adj.* [see IN-[2] & POTENT] **1.** lacking physical strength **2.** ineffective; powerless **3.** unable to engage in sexual intercourse : said of males —**im'potence** *n.* —**im'potently** *adv.*

impound (im pound') *vt.* **1.** to shut up (an animal) in a pound **2.** to take into legal custody; confiscate —**impound'ment** *n.*

impoverish (im pov'ər ish) *vt.* [< L. *in-*, in + *pauper*, poor] **1.** to make poor **2.** to deprive of strength, resources, etc. —**impov'erishment** *n.*

impracticable (im prak'ti kə b'l) *adj.* not capable of being carried out in practice or of being used —**imprac'ticabil'ity, imprac'ticableness** *n.*

impractical *adj.* not practical —**imprac'tical'ity** *n.*

imprecate (im'prə kāt') *vt.* **-cat'ed, -cat'ing** [< L. *in-*, on + *precari*, pray] to invoke (evil, a curse, etc.) —**im'preca'tion** *n.* —**im'precatory** *adj.*

imprecise (im'prə sīs') *adj.* not precise or definite —**im'precise'ly** *adv.* —**im'preci'sion** *n.*

impregnable (im preg'nə b'l) *adj.* **1.** not capable of being captured or entered by force **2.** unshakable —**impreg'nabil'ity** *n.*

impregnate (im'preg nāt) *vt.* **-nated, -nating** [< L. *in-*, in + *praegnans*, pregnant] **1.** to fill; saturate **2.** to imbue (*with* ideas, etc.) **3.** to fertilize; make pregnant —**im'pregna'tion** *n.* —**impreg'nator** *n.*

impresario (im'prə sär'ē ō) *n.*, *pl.* **-rios** [It.] the manager of an opera company, concert series, etc.

impress[1] (im pres') *vt.* [< IN-[1] + PRESS[2]] to force (men) into public service, esp. into a navy

impress[2] (im pres'; *for n.* im'pres) *vt.* [see IN-[1] & PRESS[1]] **1.** to affect strongly the mind or emotions of **2.** to arouse the interest or approval of **3.** to fix in the memory **4.** to stamp; imprint —*n.* **1.** any mark, imprint, etc. **2.** an effect produced by some strong influence —**impress'ible** *adj.*

impression (im presh'ən) *n.* **1.** an impressing **2.** *a)* a mark, imprint, etc. *b)* an effect produced, as on the mind **3.** a vague notion **4.** an amusing impersonation **5.** *Printing* all the copies printed at one time from a set of type or plates —**impres'sional** *adj.*

impressionable *adj.* easily impressed or influenced; sensitive —**impres'sionably** *adv.*

impressionism *n.* a theory of art, music, etc. whose aim is to reproduce the immediate impression or mood —**impres'sionist** *n.*, *adj.* —**impres'sionis'tic** *adj.* —**impres'sionis'tically** *adv.*

impressive (im pres'iv) *adj.* tending to impress the mind or emotions; striking —**impres'sively** *adv.*

imprimatur (im'pri māt'ər) *n.* [ModL., let it be printed] licence to publish or print a book, article, etc.; esp. given by the Roman Catholic Church

imprint (im print´; *for n.* im´print) *vt.* [< L. *in-*, on + *premere*, to press] 1. to mark by pressing or stamping 2. to fix in the memory —*n.* 1. a mark made by imprinting 2. a characteristic result 3. a note in a book, giving facts of publication

imprison (im priz´'n) *vt.* 1. to put or keep in prison 2. to confine —**impris´onment** *n.*

improbable (im prob´ə b'l) *adj.* unlikely to happen or be true —**im´probabil´ity** *n.* —**improb´ably** *adv.*

improbity (im prō´bə tē) *n., pl.* dishonesty

impromptu (im promp´tyōō) *adj., adv.* [< *in promptu*, in readiness] without preparation; spontaneous —*n.* an impromptu speech, etc.

improper (im prop´ər) *adj.* 1. not suitable; unfit 2. incorrect 3. not in good taste; indecent —**improp´erly** *adv.* —**improp´erness** *n.*

improper fraction a fraction in which the denominator is less than the numerator (Ex.: 5/3)

impropriate (im prō´prē āt) *vt.* -at´ed, -at´ing [< ML. *impropriare*, take as one's own] to transfer (church income or property) to private individuals —**impro´pria´tion** *n.* —**impro´pria´tor** *n.*

impropriety (im´prə prī´ə tē) *n.* 1. a being improper 2. *pl.* -ties improper action, usage, etc.

improve (im prōōv´) *vt.* -proved´, -prov´ing [< L. *in-*, in + *prodesse*, to be of advantage] 1. to make better 2. to add value to by cultivation, etc. 3. to use profitably or to advantage —*vi.* to become better —**improve on** (or **upon**) to do or make better than —**improv´abil´ity** *n.* —**improv´able** *adj.* —**improv´er** *n.*

improvement *n.* 1. an improving or being improved 2. a change that improves something or adds to its value

improvident (im prov´ə dənt) *adj.* failing to provide for the future; lacking foresight or thrift —**improv´idence** *n.*

improvise (im´prə vīz´) *vt., vi.* -vised´, -vis´ing [< L. *in-*, not + *providere*, foresee] 1. to compose and perform without preparation 2. to make or do with whatever is at hand —**im´provisa´tion** *n.* —**improv´isa´tional** *adj.*

imprudent (im prōōd´ənt) *adj.* not prudent; rash; indiscreet —**impru´dence** *n.* —**impru´dently** *adv.*

impudent (im´pyōō dənt) *adj.* [< L. *in-*, not + *pudere*, feel shame] shamelessly bold; insolent —**im´pudence** *n.* —**im´pudently** *adv.*

impugn (im pyōōn´) *vt.* [< L. *in-*, against + *pugnare*, fight] to oppose or challenge as false —**impugn´able** *adj.* —**impugn´er** *n.*

impulse (im´puls) *n.* [see IMPEL] 1. *a)* an impelling force; impetus *b)* the motion or effect caused by such a force 2. *a)* incitement to action arising from a state of mind or an external stimulus *b)* a sudden inclination to act, without conscious

thought 3. *Physiol.* a stimulus transmitted in a muscle or nerve

impulsive (im pul´siv) *adj.* 1. *a)* likely to act on impulse *b)* resulting from impulse [an *impulsive* remark] 2. driving forwards —**impul´sively** *adv.* —**impul´siveness** *n.*

impundulu (im´pōōn dōō´lōō) *n.* [< Bantu] [S Afr.] a mythical bird often associated with witchcraft

impunity (im pyōō´nə tē) *n.* [< L. *in-*, without + *poena*, punishment] exemption from punishment or harm

impure (im pyōōər´) *adj.* 1. mixed with foreign matter; adulterated 2. unclean; dirty 3. immoral; obscene —**impure´ly** *adv.* —**impure´ness** *n.*

impurity *n.* 1. a being impure 2. *pl.* -ties an impure thing or element

impute (im pyōōt´) *vt.* -put´ed, -put´ing [< L. *in-*, + *putare*, to estimate] to attribute (esp. a fault or misconduct) to another —**im´puta´tion** *n.*

I.Mun.E. Institution of Municipal Engineers

in (in, ən, 'n) *prep.* [OE.] 1. contained by [in the room] 2. wearing [a lady in red] 3. during [done in a day] 4. at the end of [return in an hour] 5. perceptible to [in sight] 6. out of a group of [one in ten] 7. amidst [in a storm] 8. affected by [in trouble] 9. employed at [in business] 10. with regard to [in my opinion] 11. using [speak in French] 12. made of [done in wood] 13. because of [to cry in pain] 14. by way of [in recompense] 15. belonging to [not in his nature] 16. into [come in the house] 17. (of animals) pregnant with —*adv.* 1. from a point outside to one inside 2. so as to be contained by a certain space, condition, or position 3. so as to be agreeing [he fell in with our plans] 4. so as to form a part 5. in some games, so as to take a turn at something 6. at, inside one's home, etc. 7. alight [to keep the fire in] —*adj.* 1. [Colloq.] currently smart, popular, etc. 2. that is successful or in power [the in group] 3. ingoing [the in door] 4. inner; inside —*n.* 1. a person, group, etc. in power: *usually used in pl.* 2. [Colloq.] special influence, favour, etc. —**have it in for** [Colloq.] to hold a grudge against —**in for** certain to have —**in on** having a share of —**ins and outs** all the parts, details, and intricacies —**in that** because; since —**in with** associated with

in-¹ [< L.] *a prefix meaning* in, into, within, on, towards [inbreed, induct]: also used as an intensive [inflame]

in-² [< L.] *a prefix meaning* no, not, without, non-

The following list includes some common compounds formed with *in-* that do not have special meanings; they will be understood if *not* or *lack of* is used with the meaning of the base word:

inability	inactive
inaccuracy	inactivity
inaccurate	inadequacy
inaction	inadequate

inadmissible
inadvisable
inapplicable
inappreciative
inappropriate
inaudible
inauspicious
incapable
incautious
incertitude
incivility
incombustible
incommunicable
incommunicative
incomprehensible
incomprehension
inconceivable
inconclusive
inconsonant
incontrovertible
incorrect
incurious
indecipherable
indecorous
indefinable
indehiscent
indemonstrable
indiscernible
indiscipline
indisputable

indistinguishable
indivisible
inedible
ineffaceable
ineffective
ineffectual
inefficacious
inefficacy
inelastic
inelegant
ineligible
ineradicable
inessential
inexact
inexhaustible
inexpedient
inexpressive
inextinguishable
inharmonic
inharmonious
inhospitable
injudicious
inopportune
insanitary
insensitive
inseparable
insolvable
insufficiency
insufficient
insurmountable
insusceptible

In *Chem.* indium

in. inch; inches

-ina (ē′nə) [< L.] *a suffix used to form feminine names, titles, etc.* [Christina, czarina]

in absentia (in ab sen′tē ə) [L., in absence] although not present

inaccessible (in′ək ses′ə b'l) *adj.* **1.** impossible to reach or enter **2.** that cannot be seen, talked to, etc. **3.** not obtainable —**in′acces′sibil′ity** *n.*

inadvertent (in′əd vur′tənt) *adj.* **1.** not attentive or observant **2.** due to oversight; unintentional —**in′advert′ence** *n.* —**in′advert′ently** *adv.*

inalienable (in āl′yən ə b'l) *adj.* that may not be taken away or transferred —**inal′ienabil′ity** *n.*

inamorata (in am′ə rät′ə) *n.* [It.] one's sweetheart or mistress

inane (in ān′) *adj.* [L. *inanis*] **1.** empty **2.** lacking sense; silly —**inane′ly** *adv.* —**inan′ity** (-an′ə tē) *n.*

inanimate (in an′ə mət) *adj.* **1.** without (animal) life **2.** not animated; dull —**inan′imately** *adv.*

inanition (in′ə nish′ən) *n.* [< L. *inanitus*, empty] weakness, esp. exhaustion from lack of food

inapposite (in ap′ə zit) *adj.* not apposite; irrelevant —**inap′positely** *adv.* —**inap′positeness** *n.*

inapt (in apt′) *adj.* **1.** inappropriate **2.** lacking skill or aptitude —**inapt′itude′** (-ap′tə tyōōd′) *n.*

inarticulate (in′är tik′yoo lət) *adj.* **1.** not able to speak coherently **2.** without the articulation of normal speech [an inarticulate cry] **3.** unable to speak; mute

4. *Zool.* without joints —**in′artic′ulately** *adv.*

inasmuch as (in′əz much′əz) **1.** seeing that; since; because **2.** to the extent that

inattention (in′ə ten′shən) *n.* failure to pay attention; heedlessness; negligence —**in′atten′tive** *adj.*

inaugural (in ô′gyoo rəl) *adj.* [Fr.] of an inauguration —*n.* an inaugural ceremony or address

inaugurate (in ô′gyoo rāt′) *vt.* -**rat′ed**, -**rat′ing** [< L. *inaugurare*, practise augury] **1.** to induct into office with a formal ceremony **2.** to make a formal beginning of **3.** to celebrate formally the first public use of —**inau′gura′tion** *n.* —**inau′gura′tor** *n.*

inboard (in′bôrd′) *adv.*, *adj.* **1.** inside the hull of a ship or boat **2.** close to the fuselage of an aircraft —*n.* a marine motor mounted inboard

inborn *adj.* present in the organism at birth

inbred *adj.* **1.** innate or deeply instilled **2.** resulting from inbreeding

inbreed (in′brēd′) *vt.* -**bred′**, -**breed′ing** to breed by mating of individuals of closely related stocks

inc. **1.** inclusive **2.** incorporated **3.** increase

incalculable (in kal′kyoo lə b'l) *adj.* **1.** too great or too many to be counted **2.** unpredictable; uncertain —**incal′culabil′ity** *n.* —**incal′culably** *adv.*

incandescent (in′kən des′ənt) *adj.* [see IN-[1] & L. *kandere*, to shine] **1.** glowing with intense heat; red-hot or, esp., white-hot **2.** very bright —**in′candes′cence** *n.*

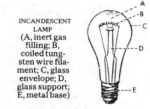

INCANDESCENT LAMP (A, inert gas filling; B, coiled tungsten wire filament; C, glass envelope; D, glass support; E, metal base)

incandescent lamp a lamp having a filament contained in a vacuum and heated to incandescence by an electric current

incantation (in′kan tā′shən) *n.* [< L. *in-*, IN-[1] + *cantare*, to chant] **1.** the chanting of special words in magic spells **2.** words so chanted —**in′canta′tional** *adj.* —**incan′tatory** *adj.*

incapacitate (in′kə pas′ə tāt′) *vt.* -**tat′ed**, -**tat′ing** **1.** to make unable or unfit; disable **2.** *Law* to disqualify —**in′capac′ita′tion** *n.*

incapacity (in′kə pas′ə tē) *n.*, *pl.* -**ties** **1.** lack of capacity, power, or fitness; disability **2.** legal ineligibility

incarcerate (in kär′sə rāt′) *vt.* -**at′ed**, -**at′ing** [< L. *in*, in + *carcer*, prison] **1.** to imprison **2.** to confine —**incar′cera′tion** *n.*

incarnadine 428 include

incarnadine (in kär′nə dīn′) *adj., n.* [see ff.] (of) the colour of either flesh or blood —*vt.* -dined′, -din′ing to make incarnadine

incarnate (in kär′nāt) *adj.* [< L. *in-*, in + *caro*, flesh] endowed with a human body; personified —*vt.* -nated, -nating 1. to give bodily form to 2. to make real 3. to be the type or embodiment of

incarnation (in′kär nā′shən) *n.* 1. endowment with a human body 2. [I-] the taking on of human form and nature by Jesus as the Son of God 3. any person or thing serving as the embodiment of a quality, spirit, etc.

incendiary (in sen′dē ər ē) *adj.* [see ff.] 1. relating to the wilful destruction of property by fire 2. designed to cause fires, as certain bombs 3. wilfully stirring up strife, riot, etc. —*n., pl.* **-aries** 1. one who wilfully destroys property by fire 2. one who wilfully stirs up strife, riot, etc. 3. an incendiary bomb, etc. —**incen′diarism** *n.*

incense[1] (in′sens) *n.* [< L. *in-*, in + *candere*, burn] 1. any substance burned for its pleasant odour, esp. in a church 2. the odour or smoke so produced —*vt.* -censed, -censing to burn or offer incense to

incense[2] (in sens′) *vt.* -censed′, -cens′ing [see prec.] to make very angry; enrage —**incense′ment** *n.*

incentive (in sen′tiv) *n.* [< L. *in-*, on + *canere*, sing] a stimulus; motive —*adj.* stimulating to action

inception (in sep′shən) *n.* [see INCIPIENT] a beginning

inceptive *adj.* [see INCIPIENT] 1. beginning; introductory 2. *Gram.* expressing the beginning of an action —*n.* an inceptive verb —**incep′tively** *adv.*

incessant (in ses′ənt) *adj.* [< L. *in-*, not + *cessare*, cease] continuing or repeated endlessly; constant

incest (in′sest) *n.* [< L. *in-*, not + *castus*, chaste] sexual intercourse between persons too closely related to marry legally —**inces′tuous** (in ses′tyoo wəs) *adj.*

inch[1] (inch) *n.* [< L. *uncia*, a twelfth] 1. a measure of length equal to 1/12 foot (2.54 cm); abbrev. **in.** 2. a very small amount, degree, or distance —*vt., vi.* to move very slowly —**every inch** in all respects —**inch by inch** slowly: also **by inches** —**within an inch of** very close to —**within an inch of one's life** almost to one's death

inch[2] *n.* [< Gael. *innis*, island] [Scot.] a small island

inchmeal (inch′mēl′) *adv.* [INCH[1] + ME. *mele*, a measure] gradually; inch by inch: also **by inchmeal**

inchoate (in kō′āt) *adj.* [< L. *inchoare*, begin] 1. just begun 2. not yet clearly formed —**incho′ately** *adv.* —**incho′ateness** *n.* —**in′choa′tion** *n.*

inchoative *adj., n. Gram. same as* INCEPTIVE

incidence (in′si dəns) *n.* 1. the degree or range of occurrence or effect; extent

of influence 2. the act, fact, or manner of falling upon or influencing

incident *n.* [< L. *in-*, on + *cadere*, fall] 1. something that happens; occurrence 2. a minor episode, esp. one in a play, etc. 3. an apparently minor conflict, etc. that may have serious results —*adj.* 1. likely to happen in connection with 2. falling upon or affecting

incidental (in′si den′t'l) *adj.* 1. happening in connection with something important 2. secondary or minor —*n. pl.* miscellaneous items

incidental music music included in the presentation of a play, film, etc. to heighten mood or effect on the audience

incinerate (in sin′ə rāt) *vt., vi.* -at′ed, -at′ing [< L. *in*, to + *cinis*, ashes] to burn to ashes —**incin′era′tion** *n.*

incinerator *n.* a furnace or other device for incinerating rubbish

incipient (in sip′ē ənt) *adj.* [< L. *in-*, on + *capere*, take] just beginning to exist or appear —**incip′ience, incip′iency** *n.* —**incip′iently** *adv.*

incise (in sīz′) *vt.* -cised′, -cis′ing [< L. *in-*, into + *caedere*, cut] to cut into with a sharp tool; engrave

incision (-sizh′ən) *n.* 1. a cut 2. *Surgery* a cut made into a tissue or organ 3. incisive quality

incisive (in sī′siv) *adj.* 1. cutting into 2. sharp; keen; penetrating; acute —**inci′sively** *adv.*

incisor (in sī′zər) *n.* any of the front cutting teeth between the canines in either jaw

incite (in sīt′) *vt.* -cit′ed, -cit′ing [< L. *in-*, in, on + *citare*, arouse] to urge to action; stir up —**incite′ment, in′cita′tion** *n.* —**incit′er** *n.*

incl. 1. inclosure 2. including 3. inclusive

inclement (in klem′ənt) *adj.* [see IN-[2] & CLEMENT] 1. rough; severe; stormy 2. lacking mercy or leniency; harsh —**inclem′ency** *n.* —**inclem′ently** *adv.*

inclination (in′klə nā′shən) *n.* 1. *a)* a tendency *b)* a liking or preference 2. the degree of incline from the horizontal or vertical 3. a slope; slant 4. an inclining, leaning, etc. 5. the angle made by two lines or planes

incline (in klīn′; *for n., usually* in′klīn) *vi.* -clined′, -clin′ing [< L. *in-*, on + *clinare*, lean] 1. to lean; slope 2. to bow the body or head 3. to have a tendency 4. to have a preference —*vt.* 1. to cause to lean, slope, etc. 2. to make willing; influence —*n.* an inclined plane or surface —**incline one's ear** to listen willingly —**inclin′able** *adj.* —**inclined′** *adj.* —**inclin′er** *n.*

inclined plane a plane surface set at any angle other than a right angle against a horizontal surface

inclose (in klōz′) *vt.* -closed′, -clos′ing *same as* ENCLOSE

include (in klōōd′) *vt.* -clud′ed, -clud′ing [< L. *in-*, in + *claudere*, to close] 1. to enclose 2. to have as part of a whole;

contain **3.** to put in a total, category, etc. —**includ'able, includ'ible** *adj.*

inclusion *n.* **1.** an including or being included **2.** something included

inclusive *adj.* **1.** taking everything into account **2.** including the terms, limits, or extremes mentioned [the first to the tenth *inclusive*] —**inclu'sively** *adv.* —**inclu'siveness** *n.*

incognito (in kog'ni tō, in'kog nēt'ō) *adv., adj.* [< L. *in-*, not + *cognoscere*, to know] disguised under an assumed name, rank, etc. —*n., pl.* **-tos 1.** a person who is incognito **2.** *a)* the state of being incognito *b)* the disguise assumed

incognizant (in kog'nə zənt) *adj.* unaware of —**incog'nizance** *n.*

incoherent (in'kō hēər'ənt) *adj.* **1.** not logically connected; disjointed **2.** characterized by incoherent speech, thought, etc. —**in'coher'ence** *n.* —**in'coher'ently** *adv.*

income (in'kum') *n.* the money or other gain received, for labour or services, or from property, investments, etc.

income tax a tax on annual income subject to certain deductions

incoming *adj.* **1.** coming in or about to come in **2.** about to come into office; succeeding

incommensurable (in'kə men'shər ə b'l) *adj.* **1.** that cannot be measured or compared **2.** having no common divisor —*n.* an incommensurable thing, quantity, etc. —**in'commen'surabil'ity** *n.*

incommensurate *adj.* not proportionate; not adequate —**in'commen'surately** *adv.*

incommode (in'kə mōd') *vt.* **-mod'ed, -mod'ing** [< L. *in-*, not + *commodus*, convenient] to inconvenience; bother

incommodious *adj.* **1.** causing inconvenience **2.** inconveniently small, etc. —**in'commo'diously** *adv.*

incommunicado (in'kə myōō'nə kä'dō) *adj.* [Sp.] unable or not allowed to communicate

incomparable (in kom'pər ə b'l) *adj.* **1.** having no basis of comparison **2.** beyond comparison; unequalled —**incom'parabil'ity** *n.* —**incom'parably** *adv.*

incompatible (in'kəm pat'ə b'l) *adj.* **1.** not able to exist in harmony **2.** logically contradictory **3.** not suitable for being used together —**in'compat'ibil'ity** *n.* —**in'compat'ibly** *adv.*

incompetent (in kom'pə tənt) *adj.* **1.** without adequate ability, fitness, etc. **2.** not legally qualified —*n.* an incompetent person —**incom'petence** *n.* —**incom'petently** *adv.*

incomplete (in'kəm plēt') *adj.* **1.** lacking a part or parts **2.** unfinished; not concluded **3.** not perfect —**in'complete'ly** *adv.* —**in'complete'ness, in'comple'tion** *n.*

incongruity (in'kon grōō'ə tē) *n.* **1.** lack of harmony or agreement **2.** lack of appropriateness **3.** *pl.* **-ties** something incongruous

incongruous (in kon'groo wəs) *adj.* **1.** lacking harmony or agreement of parts,

etc. **2.** unsuitable; inappropriate —**incon'gruously** *adv.* —**incon'gruousness** *n.*

inconnu (in'kən yōō) *n.* [Canad.] a whitefish of Far Northern waters

inconsequent (in kon'sə kwənt) *adj.* **1.** not following as a result **2.** irrelevant **3.** not proceeding in logical sequence —**incon'sequence** *n.* —**incon'sequent'ly** *adv.*

inconsequential (in kon'sə kwen'shəl) *adj.* **1.** illogical **2.** of no consequence; unimportant —**in'consequen'tial'ity** *n.* —**incon'sequen'tially** *adv.*

inconsiderable (in'kən sid'ər ə b'l) *adj.* not worth consideration; trivial; small —**in'consid'erably** *adv.*

inconsiderate *adj.* without thought or consideration for others —**in'consid'erately** *adv.* —**in'consid'erateness** *n.*

inconsistent (in'kən sis'tənt) *adj.* **1.** not in agreement or harmony **2.** self-contradictory **3.** changeable —**in'consis'tency** *n.* —**in'consis'tently** *adv.*

inconsolable (in'kən sōl'ə b'l) *adj.* that cannot be consoled —**in'consol'ably** *adv.*

inconspicuous (in'kən spik'yoo wəs) *adj.* attracting little attention —**in'conspic'uously** *adv.*

inconstant (in kon'stənt) *adj.* **1.** not remaining firm in mind or purpose **2.** fickle **3.** not uniform; irregular —**incon'stancy** *n.* —**incon'stantly** *adv.*

incontestable (in'kən tes'tə b'l) *adj.* not to be contested; unquestionable —**in'contest'ably** *adv.*

incontinent (in kont'n ənt) *adj.* [see IN-² & CONTINENT] **1.** without self-restraint, esp. in regard to sexual activity **2.** unable to restrain a natural discharge, as of urine —**incon'tinence** *n.* —**incon'tinently** *adv.*

inconvenience (in'kən vēn'yəns) *n.* **1.** a lack of comfort, ease, etc. **2.** anything inconvenient Also **in'conven'iency** —*vt.* **-ienced, -iencing** to trouble; bother

inconvenient *adj.* not favourable to one's comfort; causing trouble, bother, etc. —**in'conven'iently** *adv.*

inconvertible (in'kən vur'tə b'l) *adj.* that cannot be changed or exchanged —**in'convert'ibil'ity** *n.*

incorporate (in kôr'pər ət; *for v.* -pə rāt') *adj.* [see IN-¹ & CORPORATE] incorporated —*vt.* **-rat'ed, -rat'ing 1.** to combine with something already formed **2.** to bring together into a single whole **3.** to form into a corporation **4.** to give material form to —*vi.* **1.** to unite into a single whole **2.** [Chiefly U.S.] to form a corporation —**incor'pora'tion** *n.* —**incor'pora'tor** *n.*

incorporeal (in'kôr pôr'ē əl) *adj.* without material body or substance —**incorporeal'ity** *n.*

incorrigible (in kor'i jəb'l) *adj.* that cannot be corrected, improved, or reformed, esp. because set in bad habits *n.* —**incor'rigibly** *adv.*

incorrupt (in'kə rupt') *adj.* sound, pure, upright, honest, etc. —**in'corrupt'ly** *adv.* —**in'corrupt'ness** *n.*

incorruptible *adj.* that cannot be

corrupted, esp. morally —**in'corrupt'ibil'-
ity** n.

increase (in krēs'; *also for n.*, in'krēs) *vi.*, *vt.* **-creased'**, **-creas'ing** [< L. *in-*, in + *crescere*, grow] to become or cause to become greater in size, amount, numbers, etc. —*n.* 1. an increasing or becoming increased 2. the result or amount of an increasing —**on the increase** increasing —**increas'able** *adj.* —**increas'er** n.

increasingly *adv.* more and more

incredible (in kred'ə b'l) *adj.* 1. unbelievable 2. so great, unusual, etc. as to seem impossible —**incred'ibil'ity** n. —**incred'ibly** *adv.*

incredulity (in'krə dyōō'lə tē) n. unwillingness or inability to believe; doubt

incredulous (in kred'yoo ləs) *adj.* 1. unwilling or unable to believe 2. showing doubt or disbelief

increment (in'krə mənt) n. [< L. *increscere*, increase] 1. amount of increase 2. a becoming greater or larger; increase —**in'cremen'tal** (-men't'l) *adj.*

incriminate (in krim'ə nāt') *vt.* **-nat'ed**, **-nat'ing** [< IN-¹ & L. *crimen*, offence] 1. to involve in, or make appear guilty of, a crime or fault 2. to charge with a crime —**incrim'ina'tion** n. —**incrim'ina-tory** *adj.*

incrust (in krust') *vt.* 1. to cover as with a crust 2. to decorate, as with gems —**in'-crusta'tion** n.

incubate (in'kyoo bāt') *vt.* **-bat'ed**, **-bat'-ing** [< L. *in-*, on + *cubare*, to lie] 1. to sit on and hatch (eggs) 2. to keep (eggs, embryos, etc.) in a favourable environment for hatching or developing —*vi.* to undergo incubation

incubation (in'kyoo bā'shən) n. 1. an incubating or being incubated 2. the phase in the development of a disease before the first appearance of symptoms —**in'cu-bational** *adj.* —**in'cubative, in'cubatory** *adj.*

incubator (in'kyoo bā'tər) n. 1. an artificially heated container for hatching eggs 2. a similar apparatus for the care of premature babies

incubus (iŋ'kyoo bəs) n., *pl.* **-buses, -bi'** (-bī') [< LL., nightmare < L. *incubare*, lie on] 1. a spirit or demon thought in medieval times to have sexual intercourse with sleeping women 2. a nightmare

inculcate (in'kul kāt') *vt.* **-cat'ed**, **-cat'-ing** [< L. *in-*, in + *calcare*, trample underfoot] to impress upon the mind by repetition —**in'culca'tion** n.

inculpate (in'kul pāt') *vt.* **-pat'ed**, **-pat'-ing** [< L. *in*, on + *culpa*, a fault] *same as* INCRIMINATE —**in'culpa'tion** n. —**incul'patory** *adj.*

incumbency (in kum'bən sē) n., *pl.* **-cies** 1. a duty or obligation 2. *a)* the holding and administering of a position *b)* tenure of office

incumbent *adj.* [< L. *in-*, on + *cubare*, lie down] 1. lying or pressing with its weight on something else 2. currently in office —*n.* the holder of an office

or benefice —**incumbent on** (or **upon**) resting upon as a duty

incunabula (in'kyōō nab'yoo lə) *n.pl.*, *sing.* **-ulum** [< L. *in-*, in + *cunabula*, cradle] 1. the very first stages of anything 2. early printed books; esp., books printed before 1500

incur (in kur') *vt.* **-curred'**, **-cur'ring** [< L. *in-*, in + *currere*, run] 1. to acquire (something undesirable) 2. to bring upon oneself through one's own actions

incurable (in kyoor'ə b'l) *adj.* that cannot be remedied or corrected [*an incurable* romantic] —*n.* a person having an incurable disease —**incur'ably** *adv.*

incursion (in kur'shən) n. [*see* INCUR] 1. an inroad 2. a sudden, brief invasion or raid —**incur'sive** *adj.*

Ind. 1. India 2. Indian 3. Indies

ind. 1. independent 2. index 3. industrial 4. indicative

indaba (in dä'bə) n. [< Zulu] [S Afr.] 1. a meeting convened for a serious discussion 2. [Colloq.] a matter for discussion; problem

indebted (in det'id) *adj.* 1. obliged 2. in debt

indebtedness n. 1. a being indebted 2. the amount owed; all one's debts

indecency (in dē'sən sē) n. 1. a being indecent 2. *pl.* **-cies** an indecent act, statement, etc.

indecent *adj.* 1. obscene 2. not proper and fitting; unseemly —**inde'cently** *adv.*

indecision (in'di sizh'ən) n. inability to decide or a tendency to change the mind frequently

indecisive (-sī'siv) *adj.* 1. not decisive 2. showing indecision —**in'deci'sively** *adv.* —**in'deci'siveness** n.

indeclinable (in'di klīn'ə b'l) *adj. Gram.* having no case inflections; not declinable

indeed (in dēd') *adv.* [*see* IN & DEED] certainly; truly —*interj.* an exclamation of surprise, doubt, etc.

indef. indefinite

indefatigable (in'di fat'i gə b'l) *adj.* [< L. *in-*, not + *defatigare*, tire out] that cannot be tired out; untiring —**in'defat'iga-bil'ity** n. —**in'defat'igably** *adv.*

indefeasible (in'di fē'zə b'l) *adj.* that cannot be undone or made void —**in'defea'-sibly** *adv.*

indefensible (in'di fen'sə b'l) *adj.* 1. that cannot be justified 2. that cannot be defended —**in'defen'sibil'ity** n. —**in'defen'sibly** *adv.*

indefinite (in def'ə nət) *adj.* 1. having no exact limits 2. not precise in meaning; vague 3. not sure; uncertain 4. *Gram.* not limiting or specifying [*a* and *an* are *indefinite* articles] —**indef'initely** *adv.* —**indef'initeness** n.

indelible (in del'ə b'l) *adj.* [< L. *in-*, not + *delere*, destroy] 1. that cannot be erased, blotted out, etc. 2. leaving an indelible mark —**indel'ibil'ity** n. —**indel'ibly** *adv.*

indelicate (in del'i kət) *adj.* embarrassing; coarse; esp., lacking propriety or modesty —**indel'icately** *adv.* —**indel'i-cacy** n.

indemnify (in dem'nə fī') *vt.* **-fied'**, **-fy'-ing** [< L. *indemnis*, unhurt] **1.** to protect against loss, etc. **2.** to repay for loss or damage —**indem'nifica'tion** *n.*

indemnity *n.*, *pl.* **-ties** **1.** insurance against loss, damage, etc. **2.** legal exemption from penalties incurred by one's actions **3.** repayment for loss, damage, etc. **4.** in Canada, the annual salary paid by the government to a member of Parliament or of a provincial legislature

indent[1] (in dent'; *for n., usually* in'dent) *vt.* [< L. *in*, in + *dens*, tooth] **1.** to space (the first line of a paragraph, etc.) in from the usual margin **2.** to write out (a contract, etc.) in duplicate **3.** to order by an indent **4.** to notch **5.** to make jagged in outline —*vi.* **1.** to space in from the margin **2.** to draw up an order or requisition in duplicate —*n.* **1.** an order form, esp. one used in foreign trade **2.** an official order or requisition for goods **3.** an indenture **4.** a notch or cut in an edge **5.** an indented line, etc.

indent[2] *vt.* [IN-[1] + DENT] **1.** to make a dent in **2.** to press (a mark, etc.) in —*n.* a dent, or slight hollow

indentation (in'den tā'shən) *n.* **1.** an indenting or being indented **2.** a notch, cut, or inlet on a coastline, etc. **3.** a dent, or slight hollow **4.** space in from a margin

indention (in den'shən) *n.* **1.** a spacing in from the margin **2.** *a)* a dent *b)* the making of a dent

indenture (in den'chər) *n.* [< INDENT[1]] **1.** a written contract or agreement **2.** [*often pl.*] a contract binding a person to work for another, as an apprentice to a master —*vt.* **-tured, -turing** to bind by indenture

independence (in'di pen'dəns) *n.* a being independent; freedom from the control of another

independent *adj.* **1.** free from the influence or control of others; specif., *a)* self-governing *b)* objective [an *independent* observer] *c)* self-confident; self-reliant *d)* not adhering to any political party *e)* not connected with others **2.** *a)* not depending on another, esp. for financial support *b)* of, or having an income large enough to enable one to live without working —*n.* a person who is independent in thinking, action, etc., esp. in politics —**independent of** apart from —**in'depend'ently** *adv.*

independent clause *Gram.* same as MAIN CLAUSE

independent school a school which does not receive financial support from the government or local authorities

in-depth (in'depth') *adj.* carefully worked out, detailed, thorough, etc. [an *in-depth* study]

indescribable (in'di skrī'bə b'l) *adj.* beyond the power of description —**in'describ'ably** *adv.*

indestructible (in'di struk'tə b'l) *adj.* that cannot be destroyed —**in'destruct'ibly** *adv.*

indeterminable (in'di tur'mi nə b'l) *adj.* **1.** that cannot be decided **2.** that cannot be ascertained —**in'deter'minableness** *n.* —**in'deter'minably** *adv.*

indeterminate *adj.* **1.** inexact in its limits, nature, etc.; vague **2.** not yet settled; inconclusive —**in'deter'minacy, in'deter'mina'tion** *n.*

index (in'deks) *n.*, *pl.* **-dexes**, **-dices'** (-də sēz') [L. < *indicare*, indicate] **1.** *a)* an alphabetical list of names, subjects, etc. together with the page numbers where they appear in the text *b)* a catalogue [a library *index*] **2.** an indication [an *index* of ability] **3.** a pointer, as the needle on a dial **4.** *Math.* an exponent **5.** *a)* the relation or ratio of one amount or dimension to another *b)* a number used to measure changes in prices, wages, etc. : in full, **index number 6.** *short for* INDEX FINGER **7.** [I-] *R.C.Ch.* formerly, a list of books forbidden to be read —*vt.* **1.** to make an index of or for **2.** to include in an index —**in'dexer** *n.* —**index'ical** *adj.*

index finger the finger next to the thumb

index-linked *adj.* related to the change in prices : said of pensions, wages, etc.

Indiaman (in'dē ə mən) *n.* formerly, a large merchant ship engaged in trade with India or the East Indies

Indian (in'dē ən) *adj.* **1.** of India or the East Indies, their people, or culture **2.** of any of the aboriginal peoples (**American Indians**) of N. America, S. America, or the West Indies, or of their cultures **3.** of a type used or made by Indians —*n.* **1.** a native of India or the East Indies **2.** a member of any of the aboriginal peoples of N. America, S. America, or the West Indies

Indian club a club of wood, metal, etc. shaped like a tenpin and swung in the hand for exercise

Indian corn same as MAIZE (sense 1)

Indian file same as SINGLE FILE

Indian ink 1. a black pigment of lampblack **2.** a liquid ink made from this

Indian list [Canad. Colloq.] a list of persons to whom spirits may not be sold

Indian summer a period of mild, warm, hazy weather following the first frosts of late autumn

India paper a thin, strong, opaque printing paper, used for some Bibles, dictionaries, etc.

India (or **india**) **rubber** crude, natural rubber obtained from latex —**In'dia-rub'ber** *adj.*

Indic (in'dik) *adj.* **1.** of India **2.** of a branch of the Indo-European language family, including many of the languages of India

indic. indicative

indicate (in'də kāt') *vt.* **-cat'ed, -cat'ing** [< L. *in-*, in + *dicare*, declare] **1.** to direct attention to; point out **2.** to be a sign of; signify **3.** to show the need for **4.** to state briefly

indication (in'də kā'shən) *n.* **1.** an indicating **2.** something that indicates **3.** the amount registered by an indicator

indicative (in dik′ə tiv) *adj.* 1. giving an indication or intimation: also **indic′atory** 2. *Gram.* of that mood of a verb used to express an act, state, etc. as actual, or to ask a question —*n.* the indicative mood —**indic′atively** *adv.*

indicator (in′də kāt′ər) *n.* 1. a person or thing that indicates; specif., a gauge, dial, etc. that measures something 2. a device for showing that a motor vehicle is about to turn left or right

indices (in′də sēz′) *n. alt. pl.* of INDEX

indict (in dīt′) *vt.* [< L. *in*, against + *dictare*, declare] to charge with a crime; esp., to make formal accusation against on the basis of positive legal evidence —**indict′able** *adj.*

indictment *n.* a charge; specif., a formal accusation charging someone with a crime

indifference (in dif′ər əns) *n.* 1. lack of concern or interest 2. lack of importance or meaning

indifferent *adj.* 1. having or showing no preference 2. uninterested or unmoved 3. of no importance 4. not particularly good or bad, etc.; average 5. not really good 6. not very good; poor: said esp. of health —**indif′ferently** *adv.*

indigenous (in dij′ə nəs) *adj.* [< OL. *indu*, in + *gignere*, be born] born or growing naturally in a region or country; native (*to*)

indigent (in′di jənt) *adj.* [< OL. *indu*, in + *egere*, need] poor; needy —**in′digence** *n.* —**in′digently** *adv.*

indigestible (in′di jes′tə b′l) *adj.* not digestible; not easily digested —**in′digest′ibil′ity** *n.*

indigestion (in′di jes′chən) *n.* 1. difficulty in digesting food 2. the discomfort caused by this

indignant (in dig′nənt) *adj.* [< L. *in-*, not + *dignus*, worthy] feeling or expressing indignation —**indig′nantly** *adv.*

indignation (in′dig nā′shən) *n.* anger or scorn that is a reaction to something felt to be unfair, unworthy, or wrong

indignity (in dig′nə tē) *n.,* pl. **-ties** something that humiliates, insults, or injures the dignity or self-respect

indigo (in′di gō′) *n.,* pl. **-gos**, **-goes** [Sp. < Gr. *Indikos,* Indian] 1. a blue dye obtained from certain plants or made synthetically 2. a deep violet blue: also **indigo blue** —*adj.* of a deep violet-blue: also **in′digo′-blue′**

indirect (in′di rekt′) *adj.* 1. not straight 2. not straight to the point 3. dishonest 4. not immediate; secondary —**in′direct′ly** *adv.* —**in′direct′ness** *n.*

indirect lighting lighting reflected, as from a ceiling, or diffused so as to avoid glare

indirect object *Gram.* the person or thing indirectly affected by the action of the verb (Ex.: *him* in "do *him* a favour")

indirect speech *same as* REPORTED SPEECH

indirect tax a tax on manufactured goods, imports, etc. paid indirectly when included in the price

indiscreet (in′dis krēt′) *adj.* not discreet;

lacking prudence; unwise —**in′discreet′ly** *adv.*

indiscrete (in′dis krēt′) *adj.* [L. *indiscretus,* unseparated] not separated into distinct parts

indiscretion (in′dis kresh′ən) *n.* 1. lack of discretion 2. an indiscreet act or remark

indiscriminate (in′dis krim′ə nət) *adj.* 1. random or promiscuous 2. not making careful choices or distinctions —**in′discrim′inately** *adv.* —**in′discrim′inateness, in′discrim′ina′tion** *n.*

indispensable (in′dis pen′sə b′l) *adj.* 1. that cannot be dispensed with 2. absolutely necessary —**in′dispen′sabil′ity** *n.* —**in′dispen′sably** *adv.*

indisposed (in′dis pōzd′) *adj.* 1. slightly ill 2. unwilling; disinclined —**in′disposi′tion** *n.*

indissoluble (in′di sol′yoo b′l) *adj.* that cannot be dissolved or destroyed; lasting —**in′dissol′ubly** *adv.*

indistinct (in′dis tiŋkt′) *adj.* 1. not seen, heard, or perceived clearly 2. not plainly defined —**in′distinct′ly** *adv.* —**in′distinct′ness** *n.*

indite (in dīt′) *vt.* **-dit′ed, -dit′ing** [see INDICT] to compose and write —**indite′ment** *n.* —**indit′er** *n.*

indium (in′dē əm) *n.* [< L. *indicum,* indigo] a rare metallic chemical element, ductile and silver-white: symbol, In

individual (in′di vid′yoo wəl) *adj.* [< L. *individuus,* not divisible] 1. existing as a separate thing or being; single 2. of, for, by, or characteristic of a single person or thing 3. unique or striking —*n.* 1. a single thing or being 2. [Colloq.] a person

individualism *n.* 1. individuality 2. the doctrine that the state exists to serve the individual 3. egoism 4. the leading of one's life in one's own way —**in′divid′ualist** *n., adj.* —**in′divid′ualis′tic** *adj.*

individuality (in′di vid′yoo wal′ə tē) *n.,* pl. **-ties** 1. the sum of the characteristics that set one person or thing apart 2. separate existence

individualize (in′di vid′yoo wə līz) *vt.* **-ized′, -iz′ing** 1. to mark as different from others 2. to consider individually —**in′divid′ualiza′tion** *n.*

individually *adv.* 1. one at a time 2. as an individual 3. distinctively

Indo- (in′dō) *a combining form meaning* 1. Indian 2. India and; Indian and [*Indo-*European]

indoctrinate (in dok′trə nāt′) *vt.* **-nat′ed, -nat′ing** [see IN-[1] & DOCTRINE] 1. to instruct systematically in doctrines, theories, or beliefs 2. to teach —**indoc′trina′tion** *n.*

Indo-European (in′dō yooər′ə pē′ən) *adj.* designating or of a family of languages that includes most of those of Europe and some of those of Asia —*n.* this family of languages

indolent (in′də lənt) *adj.* [< L. *in-*, not + *dolere,* feel pain] avoiding work; idle; lazy —**in′dolence** *n.* —**in′dolently** *adv.*

indomitable (in dom′it ə b′l) *adj.* [< L. *in-*, not + *domare,* tame] not easily discouraged or defeated —**indom′itably** *adv.*

Indonesian (in′də nē′zhən) *adj.* 1. of Indonesia, its people, etc. 2. of a large group of languages spoken in Indonesia, Java, etc. —*n.* 1. a member of a race of people of Indonesia, Java, etc. 2. an inhabitant of Indonesia 3. the Indonesian languages

indoor (in′dôr′) *adj.* living, belonging, or carried on within a house or building

indoors *adv.* in or into a building

indorse (in dôrs′) *vt.* -dorsed′, -dors′ing *same as* ENDORSE

indrawn (in′drôn′) *adj.* 1. drawn in 2. [Chiefly U.S.] introspective

indubitable (in dyōō′bi tə b'l) *adj.* that cannot be doubted; unquestionable —**indu′bitably** *adv.*

induce (in dyōōs′) *vt.* -duced′, -duc′ing [< L. *in-*, in + *ducere*, lead] 1. to persuade 2. *a)* to bring on *[to induce* vomiting *] b)* to cause labour to begin 3. to draw (a conclusion) from particular facts 4. *Physics* to bring about (an electric or magnetic effect) in a body by placing it in a field of force —**induc′er** *n.* —**induc′ible** *adj.*

inducement *n.* 1. an inducing or being induced 2. anything that induces; incentive

induct (in dukt′) *vt.* [see INDUCE] to place formally in a benefice or an official position

inductance *n.* the property of an electric circuit by which a varying current in it induces voltages in the same circuit or in one nearby

induction *n.* 1. an inducting or being inducted 2. reasoning from particular facts to a general conclusion 3. *Physics* the act or process by which an electric or magnetic effect is produced in an electrical conductor or magnetizable body when it is exposed to the influence of a field of force

induction coil an apparatus made up of two magnetically coupled coils in a circuit in which interruptions of the direct-current supply to one coil produce an alternating current of high potential in the other

inductive *adj.* 1. of or using induction *[inductive* reasoning] 2. produced by induction —**induc′tively** *adv.*

inductor *n.* a device designed to introduce inductance into an electric circuit

indue (in dyōō′) *vt.* -dued′, -du′ing *same as* ENDUE

indulge (in dulj′) *vt.* -dulged′, -dulg′ing [L. *indulgere*, be kind to] 1. to satisfy (a desire) 2. to gratify the wishes of; humour —*vi.* to give way to one's own desires

indulgence *n.* 1. an indulging or being indulgent 2. a thing indulged in 3. a favour or privilege 4. *R.C.Ch.* a remission of punishment still due for a sin after the guilt has been forgiven

indulgent *adj.* indulging or inclined to indulge; kind or lenient, often to excess —**indul′gently** *adv.*

induna (in dōōn′ə) *n.* [< Zulu] [S Afr.] in South Africa, a powerful black male, as a headman or overseer

indurate (in′dyooə rāt′) *vt.*, *vi.* -rat′ed, -rat′ing [< L. *in-*, in + *durare*, harden] 1. to harden 2. to make or become callous or unfeeling —**in′dura′tion** *n.* —**in′dura-tive** *adj.*

industrial (in dus′trē əl) *adj.* 1. of, connected with, or resulting from industries 2. working in industries 3. of or concerned with people working in industries 4. for use by industries : said of products —**indus′-trially** *adv.*

industrial estate an area set aside for industrial and business use, usually on the outskirts of a city

industrialism *n.* social and economic organization characterized by large industries, etc.

industrialist *n.* a person who owns or manages an industrial enterprise

industrialize *vt.* -ized′, -iz′ing 1. to develop industrialism in 2. to organize as an industry —**indus′trializa′tion** *n.*

industrious *adj.* characterized by earnest, steady effort —**indus′triously** *adv.* —**indus′triousness** *n.*

industry (in′dəs trē) *n.*, *pl.* -tries [< L. *industrius*, active] 1. any branch of production, esp. manufacturing, or all of these collectively 2. the owners and managers of industry 3. systematic work 4. earnest, steady effort

-ine (īn, in, ēn, ən) [< L.] *a suffix meaning* of, having the nature of, like *[divine, marine, crystalline]*

inebriate (in ē′brē āt′; *for adj.& n., usually* -ət) *vt.* -at′ed, -at′ing [< L. *in-*, intens. + *ebrius*, drunk] 1. to make drunk 2. to excite; exhilarate —*adj.* drunk —*n.* a drunken person —**ine′briat′ed** *adj.* —**ine′bria′tion, inebriety** (in′ē bri′ə tē) *n.*

ineducable (in ed′yoo kə b'l) *adj.* thought to be incapable of being educated —**ined′-ucabil′ity** *n.*

ineffable (in ef′ə b'l) *adj.* [< L. *in-*, not + *effabilis*, utterable] 1. too overwhelming to be expressed in words 2. too sacred to be spoken —**in′effabil′ity, inef′fable-ness** *n.* —**inef′fably** *adv.*

inefficient (in′ə fish′ənt) *adj.* 1. not producing the desired effect with a minimum use of energy, time, etc. 2. incapable —**in′effi′ciency** *n.* —**in′effi′-ciently** *adv.*

inelegance (in el′ə gəns) *n.* 1. lack of elegance 2. something inelegant Also **inel′egancy**

ineluctable (in′i luk′tə b'l) *adj.* [< L. *in-*, not + *eluctari*, struggle] not to be avoided or escaped

inept (in ept′) *adj.* [< L. *in-*, not + *aptus*, fit] 1. unsuitable; unfit 2. absurd; foolish 3. clumsy; inefficient —**inept′ly** *adv.* —**inept′ness** *n.*

ineptitude (in ep′tə tyōōd′) *n.* 1. the quality or condition of being inept 2. an inept act, remark, etc.

inequable (in ek′wə b'l) *adj.* [IN-² +

EQUABLE] 1. unfairly distributed 2. not uniform 3. changeable

inequality (in′i kwol′ə tē) *n., pl.* **-ties** 1. lack of equality 2. *a)* a difference in size, quality, etc. *b)* an unevenness *c)* unequal distribution

inequitable (in ek′wit ə b′l) *adj.* not equitable; unfair; unjust —**ineq′uitably** *adv.*

inert (in urt′) *adj.* [< L. *in-*, not + *ars, art*] 1. without power to move or act 2. dull; slow 3. having few or no active properties —**inert′ly** *adv.*

inertia (in ur′shə) *n.* [see prec.] 1. *Physics* the tendency of matter to remain at rest (or to keep moving in the same direction) unless affected by an outside force 2. disinclination to move or act —**iner′tial** *adj.*

inertia reel a reel holding a seat belt and enabling it to adjust itself automatically

inertia selling the sending of unrequested goods to householders, relying on their not taking the trouble to return them

inescapable (in′ə skāp′ə b′l) *adj.* that cannot be escaped or avoided; inevitable —**in′escap′ably** *adv.*

inestimable (in es′tə mə b′l) *adj.* too great or valuable to be properly measured or estimated —**ines′timably** *adv.*

inevitable (in ev′ə tə b′l) *adj.* [< L. *in-*, not + *evitabilis,* avoidable] that cannot be avoided; certain to happen —**inev′itabil′ity** *n.* —**inev′itably** *adv.*

inexcusable (in′ik skyoo′zə b′l) *adj.* that cannot or should not be excused —**in′excus′ably** *adv.*

inexorable (in ek′sər ə b′l) *adj.* [< L. *in-*, not + *exorare,* move by entreaty] 1. that cannot be influenced by entreaty 2. that cannot be altered —**inex′orabil′ity** *n.* —**inex′orably** *adv.*

inexpensive (in′ik spen′siv) *adj.* costing relatively little; cheap —**in′expen′sively** *adv.*

inexperience (in′ik spēr′ē əns) *n.* lack of experience or of the knowledge or skill resulting from experience —**in′expe′rienced** *adj.*

inexpert (in ek′spurt) *adj.* not expert; unskilful; amateurish —**inex′pertly** *adv.* —**inex′pertness** *n.*

inexpiable (in ek′spē ə b′l) *adj.* that cannot be expiated or atoned for [an *inexpiable* sin]

inexplicable (in′iks plik′ə b′l) *adj.* that cannot be explained —**inexpli′cably** *adv.*

inexplicit (in′ik splis′it) *adj.* vague; indefinite; not clearly stated —**in′explic′itly** *adv.* —**in′explic′itness** *n.*

inexpressible (in′ik spres′ə b′l) *adj.* that cannot be expressed —**in′express′ibly** *adv.*

‡**in extenso** (in ik sten′sō) [L.] at full length

‡**in extremis** (in′ik strē′mis) [L., in extremity] at the point of death

inextricable (in eks′tri kə b′l) *adj.* 1. that one cannot extricate oneself from 2. that cannot be disentangled or untied 3. insolvable —**inex′tricably** *adv.*

inf. 1. [L. *infra*] below 2. infantry: also **Inf.** 3. infinitive

infallible (in fal′ə b′l) *adj.* [see IN-² & FALLIBLE] 1. incapable of error 2. not liable to fail, go wrong, etc. 3. *R.C.Ch.* incapable of error in setting forth doctrine on faith and morals —**infal′libil′ity** *n.* —**infal′libly** *adv.*

infamous (in′fə məs) *adj.* 1. notorious 2. causing a bad reputation —**in′famously** *adv.*

infamy *n., pl.* **-mies** [see IN-² & FAMOUS] 1. very bad reputation; disgrace 2. great wickedness 3. an infamous act

infancy (in′fən sē) *n., pl.* **-cies** 1. the state or period of being an infant 2. the earliest stage of anything 3. *Law* the state of being a minor

infant *n.* [< L. *in-*, not + *fari,* speak] 1. a very young child; baby 2. *Law* a minor —*adj.* 1. of or for infants 2. in a very early stage

infanta (in fan′tə) *n.* [Sp. & Port.] 1. any daughter of a king of Spain or Portugal 2. the wife of an infante

infante (-tē) *n.* [Sp. & Port.: see INFANT] any son of a king of Spain or Portugal, except the heir to the throne

infanticide (in fan′tə sīd′) *n.* [see INFANT & -CIDE] 1. the murder of a baby 2. a person guilty of this

infantile (in′fən tīl′) *adj.* 1. of infants or infancy 2. like an infant; babyish

infantile paralysis *same as* POLIOMYELITIS

infantry (in′fən trē) *n., pl.* **-tries** [< It. *infante,* foot soldier] that branch of an army consisting of soldiers trained to fight on foot —**in′fantryman** *n.*

infant school a school for children aged between four or five and seven

infatuate (in fat′yoo wāt′) *vt.* -**at′ed,** -**at′ing** [< L. *in-*, intens. + *fatuus,* foolish] 1. to inspire with shallow love 2. to make foolish —**infat′ua′tion** *n.*

infatuated *adj.* completely carried away by shallow love

infect (in fekt′) *vt.* [< L. *inficere,* stain] 1. to contaminate or cause to become diseased by bringing into contact with a germ or virus 2. to imbue with one's feelings or beliefs —**infec′tor** *n.*

infection *n.* 1. an infecting or being infected 2. a disease resulting from infection 3. anything that infects

infectious *adj.* 1. likely to cause infection 2. designating a disease communicated by infection 3. tending to spread to others —**infec′tiously** *adv.*

infectious hepatitis a viral disease causing inflammation of the liver

infectious mononucleosis an acute disease characterized by fever, swollen lymph nodes, etc.

infelicitous (in′fə lis′ə təs) *adj.* not felicitous; unfortunate or unsuitable —**in′felic′itously** *adv.*

infelicity *n.* 1. a being infelicitous 2.

pl. **-ties**   unsuitable or inapt remark, action, etc.

infer (in fur′) vt. **-ferred′, -fer′ring** [< L. *in-*, in + *ferre*, bring] **1.** to conclude by reasoning from something known or assumed **2.** [Colloq.] to imply: a loose usage —**infer′able, inferr′able** adj. —**infer′ably** adv.

inference (in′fər əns) n. **1.** the deriving of a conclusion by induction or deduction **2.** conclusion

inferential (in′fə ren′shəl) adj. of or based on inference —**in′feren′tially** adv.

inferior (in fēar′ē ər) adj. [< L. *inferus*, low] **1.** poor in quality; below average **2.** lower in order, status, quality, etc. (with to) **3.** lower in space —n. an inferior person or thing —**infe′rior′ity** (-or′ə tē) n.

inferiority complex Psychol. a neurotic condition resulting from various feelings of inferiority or inadequacy

infernal (in fur′n'l) adj. [see INFERIOR] **1.** of hell **2.** hellish; fiendish **3.** [Colloq.] hateful; outrageous —**infer′nally** adv.

infernal machine formerly, a booby trap or time bomb

inferno (in fur′nō) n., pl. **-nos** [It. < L.: see INFERIOR] hell or any place suggesting hell

infertile (in fur′tīl) adj. not fertile; barren; sterile —**infertility** (in′fər til′ə tē) n.

infest (in fest′) vt. [< L. *infestus*, hostile] **1.** to overrun in large numbers, usually so as to be harmful **2.** to be parasitic in or on —**in′festa′tion** n.

infidel (in′fə d'l) n. [< L. *in-*, not + *fidelis*, faithful] **1.** a person who does not believe in a particular, esp. the prevailing, religion **2.** a person who holds no religious belief —adj. **1.** that is an infidel **2.** of infidels

infidelity (in′fə del′ə tē) n., pl. **-ties 1.** unfaithfulness to another; esp., in marriage **2.** the fact or state of being an infidel **3.** an unfaithful or disloyal act

infield (in′fēld′) n. Cricket a) the area of ground near the wicket b) the fieldsmen stationed there

infighting (in′fīt′iŋ) n. **1.** fighting, esp. boxing, at close range **2.** intense personal conflict within a group

infiltrate (in′fil trāt) vi., vt. **-trat′ed, -trat′ing 1.** to pass into or through (a substance), as in filtering **2.** to penetrate, or cause to penetrate (enemy lines, a region, etc.) gradually, so as to gain influence or control —**in′filtra′tion** n. —**in′filtra′-tor** n.

infin. infinitive

infinite (in′fə nit) adj. [see IN-[2] & FINITE] **1.** lacking limits; endless **2.** very great; vast **3.** Math. greater than any finite number —n. something infinite —the **Infinite (Being)** God —**in′finitely** adv. —**in′finiteness** n.

infinitesimal (in′fin ə tes′ə məl) adj. [< L. *infinitus*, infinite] too small to be measured —n. **1.** an infinitesimal quantity **2.** Math. a number which is understood to be smaller than any preassigned number —**in′finites′imally** adv.

infinitive (in fin′ə tiv) n. [< L. *infinitus (modus)*, unlimited (mood)] Gram. the form of the verb without reference to person or tense: usually following to (to go) or another verb form (let him try) —**infin′iti′val** (-tī′vəl) adj.

infinitude (in fin′ə tyōod′) n. **1.** a being infinite **2.** an infinite quantity or extent

infinity (in fin′ə tē) n., pl. **-ties 1.** the quality of being infinite **2.** unlimited space, time, etc. **3.** an indefinitely large amount

infirm (in furm′) adj. **1.** weak; feeble **2.** not firm; unstable; frail —**infirm′ly** adv. —**infirm′ness** n.

infirmary n., pl. **-ries** a place for the care of the sick, injured, or infirm; hospital

infirmity n., pl. **-ties 1.** a physical weakness or defect **2.** a moral weakness

infix (in fiks′) vt. **1.** to fasten or set firmly in or on **2.** to instil

‡**in flagrante delicto** (in flə grän′-tē di lik′tō) [L.] in the very act of committing the offence

inflame (in flām′) vt., vi. **-flamed′, -flam′-ing** [see IN-[1] & FLAME] **1.** to arouse, excite, etc. or become aroused, excited, etc. **2.** to undergo, or cause inflammation

inflammable (in flam′ə b'l) adj. **1.** same as FLAMMABLE **2.** easily excited —**inflam′-mably** adv.

inflammation (in′flə mā′shən) n. **1.** an inflaming or being inflamed **2.** redness, pain, heat, etc. in some part of the body, caused by injury or disease

inflammatory (in flam′ə tər ē) adj. **1.** rousing or likely to rouse excitement, anger, etc. **2.** of inflammation

inflatable (in flāt′ə b'l) adj. capable of being inflated —n. any object made of strong, inflatable plastic

inflate (in flāt′) vt. **-flat′ed, -flat′ing** [< L. *in-*, in + *flare*, blow] **1.** to blow full with air or gas **2.** to raise in spirits; make proud **3.** to increase beyond what is normal; specif., to cause inflation of (money, credit, etc.)

inflation (in flā′shən) n. **1.** an inflating or being inflated **2.** an increase in the amount of money in circulation, resulting in a rise in prices —**infla′tionary** adj.

inflect (in flekt′) vt. [< L. *in-*, in + *flectere*, bend] **1.** Gram. to change the form of (a word) by inflection, as in conjugating or declining **2.** to vary the tone of (the voice) **3.** to bend

inflection, inflexion n. **1.** a change in tone of the voice **2.** Gram. the change of form by some words to indicate number, case, gender, tense, etc. **3.** a bend —**inflec′-tional, inflex′ional** adj.

inflexible (in flek′sə b'l) adj. **1.** rigid **2.** firm in mind or purpose; stubborn **3.** unalterable —**inflex′ibil′ity** n. —**inflex′i-bly** adv.

inflict (in flikt′) vt. [< L. *in-*, against + *fligere*, strike] **1.** to cause (pain, wounds, etc.) as by striking **2.** to impose (a punishment, etc.) on or upon —**inflic′tion** n. —**inflic′tive** adj. —**inflic′tor** n.

in-flight (in′flīt′) *adj.* done, occurring, shown, etc. while an aircraft is in flight

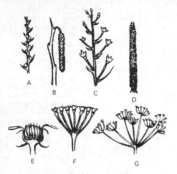

TYPES OF INFLORESCENCE
(A, spike; B, catkin; C, raceme;
D, spadix; E, head with disc,
flowers and ray flowers; F, umbel;
G, compound umbel)

inflorescence (in′flô res′əns) *n.* [see IN-¹ & L. *florere*, to bloom] *Bot.* **1.** a flowering **2.** the arrangement of flowers on a stem **3.** a single flower cluster **4.** flowers collectively

inflow (in′flō′) *n.* **1.** a flowing in or into **2.** anything that flows in

influence (in′floo wəns) *n.* [< L. *in-*, in + *fluere*, to flow] **1.** *a)* the power to affect others *b)* the effect of such power **2.** the ability to produce effects because of wealth, high position, etc. **3.** one that has influence —*vt.* -enced, -encing to have influence on —**under the influence** [Colloq.] drunk

influential (in′floo wen′shəl) *adj.* exerting influence, esp. great influence —**in′fluen′tially** *adv.*

influenza (in′floo wen′zə) *n.* [It., an influence] an acute, contagious, disease characterized by inflammation of the respiratory tract, fever, and muscular pain

influx (in′fluks′) *n.* [see INFLUENCE] a flowing in; inflow

info (in′fō) *n.* [Colloq.] information

infold (in fōld′) *vt.* same as ENFOLD

inform (in fôrm′) *vt.* [see IN-¹ & FORM] to give knowledge of something to; tell —*vi.* to give information, esp. in accusing another·

informal (in fôr′məl) *adj.* **1.** not according to fixed customs, rules, etc. **2.** casual, easy, or relaxed **3.** not requiring formal dress —**in′formal′ity** *n.* —**infor′mally** *adv.*

informal vote (Aust. & N.Z.] a spoilt ballot paper

informant (in fôr′mənt) *n.* a person who gives, or serves as a source of, information

information (in′fər mā′shən) *n.* **1.** an informing or being informed **2.** knowledge acquired in any manner; facts; news **3.** any data stored in a computer —**in′forma′tional** *adj.*

information theory the study of processes of communication and the transmission of messages

informative (in fôr′mə tiv) *adj.* giving information; instructive —**inform′atively** *adv.*

informer *n.* one who secretly accuses another, often for a reward

infra- (in′frə-) [< L.] a prefix meaning below

infraction (in frak′shən) *n.* [see INFRINGE] a violation of a law, pact, etc.

infra dig [L. *infra dig(nitatem)*] [Colloq.] beneath one's dignity

infrangible (in fran′jə b'l) *adj.* that cannot be broken or violated —**infran′gibil′ity, infran′gibleness** *n.*

infrared (in′frə red′) *adj.* designating or of those invisible rays just beyond the red of the visible spectrum

infrasonic (in′frə son′ik) *adj.* designating or of a frequency of sound below the range audible to the human ear

infrastructure (in′frə struk′chər) *n.* the basic requirements of a developed economy, as roads, power, education, etc. —**in′frastruc′tural** *adj.*

infrequent (in frē′kwənt) *adj.* not frequent; rare —**infre′quency, infre′quence** *n.* —**infre′quently** *adv.*

infringe (in frinj′) *vt.* -fringed′, -fring′-ing [< L. *in-*, in + *frangere*, reak] to break (a law or agreement) —**infringe on** (or **upon**) to encroach on (the rights, etc. of others) —**infringe′ment** *n.*

infuriate (in fyoor′ē āt′) *vt.* -at′ed, -at′-ing [< L. *in-*, in + *furia*, rage] to cause to become very angry —**infu′riat′ingly** *adv.* —**infu′ria′tion** *n.*

infuse (in fyooz′) *vt.* -fused′, -fus′ing [< L. *in-*, in + *fundere*, pour] **1.** to instil or impart (qualities, etc.) **2.** to imbue (with a quality, etc.) **3.** to steep (tea leaves, etc.) to extract flavour —**infus′-er** *n.*

infusible (in fyoo′zə b'l) *adj.* that cannot be fused or melted —**infu′sibil′ity, infu′si-bleness** *n.*

infusion (in fyoo′zhən) *n.* **1.** the liquid extract that results from steeping a substance in water **2.** an addition which revitalizes

-ing (iŋ) [< OE.] **1.** a suffix used to form the present participle [*hearing*] **2.** a suffix used to form verbal nouns [*talking*]

ingenious (in jēn′ē əs) *adj.* [< L. *in-*, in + *gignere*, produce] **1.** clever, resourceful, etc. **2.** cleverly or originally made or done —**ingen′iously** *adv.*

ingénue (an′zhā nyoo′) *n.* [Fr.] **1.** an innocent, inexperienced young woman **2.** the role of such a character or an actress playing it

ingenuity (in′jə nyoo′ə tē) *n.* [see ff.: associated with INGENIOUS] cleverness, originality, etc.

ingenuous (in jen′yoo wəs) *adj.* [< L. *in-*, in + *gignere*, produce] **1.** frank; candid **2.** artless; naive —**ingen′uously** *adv.*

ingest (in jest') *vt.* [< L. *in*-, into + *gerere*, carry] to take (food, drugs, etc.) into the body, as by swallowing —**inges'tion** *n.* —**inges'tive** *adj.*

ingle (in'g'l) *n.* [< Gael. *aingeal*, fire] [Dial.] 1. a fire or blaze 2. a fireplace

inglenook *n.* a corner by a fireplace

inglorious (in glôr'ē əs) *adj.* shameful; disgraceful —**inglo'riously** *adv.* —**inglo'riousness** *n.*

ingoing (in'gō'in) *adj.* going in; entering

ingot (in'gət) *n.* [? < MFr. *lingot*] a mass of metal cast into a bar or other convenient shape

ingraft (in gräft') *vt.* same as ENGRAFT

ingrain (in'grān) *adj.* [< OFr. *engrainer*, dye scarlet] dyed in the fibre, before manufacture

ingrained (in grānd') *adj.* 1. firmly fixed or established 2. inveterate; thoroughgoing

ingrate (in'grāt) *n.* [< L. *in*-, not + *gratus*, grateful] [Now Rare] an ungrateful person

ingratiate (in grā'shē āt') *vt.* -at'ed, -at'ing [< L. *in*, in + *gratia*, favour] to act so as to bring (oneself) into another's favour or good graces —**ingra'tiat'ingly** *adv.*

ingratitude (in grat'ə tyōod') *n.* ungratefulness

ingredient (in grē'dē ənt) *n.* [see INGRESS] any of the things that a mixture is made of; component

ingress (in'gres) *n.* [<, L. *in*-, into + *gradi*, go] 1. the act of entering: also **ingres'sion** 2. the right to enter 3. an entrance —**ingres'sive** *adj.*

ingrowing (in'grō'in) *adj.* growing within, inwards, or into; esp., growing into the flesh —**in'growth** *n.*

ingrown *adj.* grown within, inwards, or into; esp., grown into the flesh, as a toenail

inguinal (in'gwə n'l) *adj.* [< L. *inguen*, groin] of or near the groin

inhabit (in hab'it) *vt.* [< L. *in*-, in + *habitare*, dwell] to live in; occupy —**inhab'itable** *adj.* —**inhab'iter** *n.*

inhabitant *n.* a person or animal that inhabits some specified region, house, etc.

inhalant (in hāl'ənt) *adj.* used in inhalation —*n.* a medicine to be inhaled as a vapour

inhale (in hāl') *vt., vi.* -haled', -hal'ing [< L. *in*-, in + *halare*, breathe] to breathe in (air, smoke, etc.) —**in'hala'tion** (in'-hə lā'shən) *n.*

inhaler *n.* 1. same as RESPIRATOR 2. an apparatus for administering medicinal vapours in inhalation

inhere (in hēar') *vi.* -hered', -her'ing [< L. *in*-, in + *haerere*, to stick] to be inherent

inherent *adj.* [see prec.] existing in someone or something as a natural and inseparable quality or right —**inher'ence, inher'ency** *n.* —**inher'ently** *adv.*

inherit (in her'it) *vt.* [< L. *in*, in + *heres*, heir] 1. to receive (property, etc.) as an heir 2. to have (certain characteristics) by heredity —**inher'itor** *n.* —**inher'itress, inher'itrix** *n.fem.*

inheritable *adj.* 1. capable of being

transmitted by heredity 2. that can be inherited —**inher'itabil'ity** *n.*

inheritance *n.* 1. the action of inheriting 2. something inherited or to be inherited 3. the right to inherit

inhibit (in hib'it) *vt.* [< L. *in*-, in + *habere*, hold] to hold back or keep from some action, etc. —**inhib'itive, inhib'itory** *adj.* —**inhib'itor, inhib'iter** *n.*

inhibition (in'hi bish'ən) *n.* 1. an inhibiting or being inhibited 2. a mental or psychological process that restrains an action, emotion, or thought

inhuman (in hyōo'mən) *adj.* not having normal human characteristics; unfeeling, cruel, etc. —**inhu'manly** *adv.*

inhumane (in'hyōo mān') *adj.* unmoved by the suffering of others; cruel, brutal, etc. —**in'humane'ly** *adv.*

inhumanity (in'hyōo man'ə tē) *n.* 1. a being inhuman or inhumane 2. *pl.* -ties an inhuman or inhumane act

inhume (in hyōom') *vt.* -humed', -hum'-ing [< L. *inhumare*, bury] to bury (a dead body)

inimical (in im'i k'l) *adj.* [< L. *inimicus*, enemy] 1. unfriendly 2. in opposition —**inim'ically** *adv.*

inimitable (in im'ə tə b'l) *adj.* that cannot be imitated or matched —**inim'itably** *adv.*

iniquity (in ik'wə tē) *n.* [< L. *in*-, not + *aequus*, equal] 1. lack of righteousness or justice 2. *pl.* -ties a wicked, unjust, or unrighteous act —**iniq'uitous** *adj.*

initial (i nish'əl) *adj.* [< L. *in*-, in + *ire*, go] of or at the beginning —*n.* the first letter of a name —*vt.* -tialled, -tial-ling to mark with an initial or initials

initially *adv.* at the beginning; first

initial teaching alphabet an alphabet of 44 characters for teaching beginners to read English

initiate (i nish'ē āt'; *for adj. & n., usually* -ət) *vt.* -at'ed, -at'ing [see INITIAL] 1. to bring into practice or use 2. to teach the fundamentals of some subject to 3. to admit as a member into a society, etc., esp. with a ceremony —*adj.* initiated —*n.* a person who is about to be initiated —**ini'tia'tion** *n.* —**ini'tia'tor** *n.*

initiative (i nish'ē ə tiv) *n.* 1. the action of taking the first step or move 2. the characteristic of originating new ideas or methods; enterprise —*adj.* of, or having the nature of, initiation

initiatory *adj.* 1. beginning; introductory 2. of or used in an initiation

inject (in jekt') *vt.* [< L. *in*-, in + *jacere*, throw] 1. to force (a fluid) into a vein, tissue etc. by means of a syringe 2. to introduce (a missing quality, etc.) —**inject'-able** *adj.* —**injec'tion** *n.* —**injec'tor** *n.*

injunction (in junk'shən) *n.* [< LL. *injungere*, enjoin] 1. a court order prohibiting a person or group from carrying out a given action, or ordering a given action to be done 2. a command; order

injure (in'jər) *vt.* -jured, -juring [see INJURY] 1. to do physical harm to 2. to offend (one's feelings, etc.) 3. to weaken (a reputation, etc.) —**in'jurer** *n.*

injured *adj.* 1. hurt; wronged 2. feeling or displaying a sense of injury *[an injured expression]*

injurious (in jooәr′ē әs) *adj.* 1. harmful 2. offensive or abusive —**inju′riously** *adv.* —**inju′riousness** *n.*

injury (in′jәr ē) *n., pl.* **-ries** [< L. *in-*, not + *jus*, right] 1. physical harm to a person, etc. 2. an injurious act

injury time *Football* extra time allowed at the end of a match to compensate for time lost through a player's injury

injustice (in jus′tis) *n.* 1. the quality of being unjust or unfair 2. an unjust act; injury

ink (iŋk) *n.* [< Gr. *enkaiein*, to burn in] 1. a coloured liquid used for writing, printing, etc. 2. a liquid secretion squirted out by cuttlefish, etc. for protection —*vt.* 1. to cover with ink 2. to mark with ink

inkling *n.* 1. a suggestion; hint 2. a vague idea

inkosi (iŋ kôs′i) *n.* [< Bantu] [S Afr.] a chief; leader

inkstand *n.* a small stand holding an inkwell, pens, etc.

inkwell *n.* a container for holding ink

inky *adj.* **-ier, -iest** 1. like ink in colour; black 2. covered with ink —**ink′iness** *n.*

inlaid *adj.* 1. set into a surface by inlaying 2. decorated with such a surface

inland (in′lәnd; *for n. & adv., usually* -land′) *adj.* 1. of or in the interior of a country 2. within a country —*n.* inland areas —*adv.* towards the interior

Inland Revenue a department of the British government that collects major direct taxes, such as income tax

in-law (in′lô′) *n.* [Colloq.] a relative by marriage

inlay (in′lā′; *for v., also* in lā′) *vt.* **-laid′, -lay′ing** 1. to set (pieces of wood, metal, etc.) into, and level with, a surface to make a design 2. to decorate thus —*n., pl.* **-lays′** 1. inlaid decoration or material 2. a filling for a tooth made from a mould and cemented in

inlet (in′let) *n.* 1. a narrow strip of water extending into a body of land, or between islands 2. an entrance, as to a culvert

‡**in loco parentis** (in lō′kō pә ren′tis) [L.] in the place of a parent

inly (in′lē) *adv.* [Poet.] 1. inwardly 2. intimately

inmate (in′māt′) *n.* a person living with others in the same building, esp. a prison

‡**in memoriam** (in mә môr′ē әm) [L.] in memory (of)

inmost (in′mōst′) *adj.* 1. located farthest within 2. most intimate or secret *[inmost thoughts]*

inn (in) *n.* [OE.] 1. an establishment providing food and lodging for travellers 2. a tavern

innards (in′әrdz) *n.pl.* [< INWARDS] [Colloq.] the inner organs or parts

innate (i nāt′) *adj.* [< L. *in-*, in + *nasci*, be born] existing naturally rather than acquired; inborn; inherent —**innate′ly** *adv.* —**innate′ness** *n.*

inner (in′әr) *adj.* 1. located farther within

2. of the mind or spirit —*n. a)* the part of a target next to the bull's-eye *b)* a shot which hits this

inner city the sections of a large city in or near its centre, esp. when crowded or blighted

inner man 1. one's mind or soul 2. one's stomach

innermost *adj.* 1. located farthest within 2. most intimate or secret

inner tube an inflatable rubber tube that fits inside a pneumatic tyre casing

innings (in′iŋz) *n.pl.* [with *sing. v.*] [OE. *innung*, getting in] 1. *Cricket*, etc. *a)* the period of play in which a team has a turn at batting *b)* a numbered round of play in which both teams have a turn at batting 2. the period of action, exercise of authority, etc.

innkeeper (in′kē′pәr) *n.* the proprietor of an inn

innocence (in′ә sәns) *n.* 1. freedom from sin or guilt 2. guilelessness; simplicity 3. naiveté 4. harmlessness

innocent (in′ә sәnt) *adj.* [< L. *in-*, not + *nocere*, do wrong to] 1. free from sin, evil, or guilt; specif., not guilty of a crime 2. harmless 3. knowing no evil 4. without guile or cunning 5. naive —*n.* a person knowing no evil or sin, as a child —**in′no-cently** *adv.*

innocuous (i nok′yoo wәs) *adj.* [< L. *in-*, not + *nocere*, harm] harmless —**innoc′u-ously** *adv.*

innovate (in′ō vāt′) *vi.* **-vat′ed, -vat′ing** [< L. *in-*, in + *novus*, new] to introduce new methods, devices, etc. —**in′nova′tive** *adj.* —**in′nova′tor** *n.*

innovation (in′ō vā′shәn) *n.* 1. an innovating 2. a new method, practice, device, etc.

innuendo (in′yoo wen′dō) *n., pl.* **-does, -dos** [< L. *innuere*, nod to] an indirect remark, hint, etc., usually derogatory; insinuation

Innuit (in′yoo it) *n.* same as INUIT

innumerable (i nyoo′mәr ә b'l) *adj.* too numerous to be counted —**innu′merably** *adv.*

innumerate *adj.* lacking the knowledge needed to deal with scientific, esp. mathematical, concepts —**innu′meracy** *n.*

inoculate (i nok′yoo lāt′) *vt.* **-lat′ed, -lat′ing** [< L. *in-*, in + *oculus*, eye] to inject a serum, vaccine, etc. into, esp. in order to create immunity —**inoc′ula-ble** *adj.* —**inoc′ula′tion** *n.* —**inoc′ula′tor** *n.*

inoffensive (in′ә fen′siv) *adj.* not offensive; unobjectionable; causing no harm or annoyance —**in′offen′sively** *adv.* —**in′offen′siveness** *n.*

inoperable (in op′әr ә b'l) *adj.* not operable; specif., that will not practicably allow of surgical operation

inoperative (in op′әr ә tiv) *adj.* not operative; without effect —**inop′erative-ness** *n.*

inordinate (in ôr′din әt) *adj.* [see IN-[2] ORDINATE] immoderate; excessive —**inor′-dinately** *adv.*

inorganic (in′ôr gan′ik) *adj.* not organic;

specif., *a*) designating or composed of matter that is not animal or vegetable; not living *b*) designating any chemical compound not organic —**in′organ′ically** *adv.*

in patient a patient who lives in hospital while receiving treatment

‡**in perpetuum** (in′pər pet′yoo wəm) [L.] forever

input (in′poot) *n.* what is put in, as power into a machine, information into a computer, etc. —*vt.* to feed data into a computer

inquest (in′kwest) *n.* [see INQUIRE] 1. a judicial inquiry, as a coroner's investigation of a death 2. the jury or group holding such an inquiry

inquietude (in kwī′ə tyood′) *n.* restlessness; uneasiness

inquire (in kwīr′) *vi.* -quired′, -quir′ing [< L. *in*, into + *quaerere*, seek] 1. to ask a question or questions 2. to carry out an investigation —*vt.* to seek information about —**inquire after** to pay respects by asking about the health of —**inquir′er** *n.* —**inquir′ingly** *adv.*

inquiry *n.*, *pl.* -quir′ies 1. the act of inquiring 2. an investigation 3. a query

inquisition (in′kwə zish′ən) *n.* 1. an investigation 2. any harsh suppression of nonconformity 3. *Law* any judicial inquiry 4. [I-] *R.C.Ch.* formerly, the tribunal established to suppress heresy —**in′quisi′tional** *adj.*

inquisitive (in kwiz′ə tiv) *adj.* [see INQUIRE] 1. inclined to ask many questions 2. unnecessarily curious; prying —**inquis′i-tively** *adv.* —**inquis′itiveness** *n.*

inquisitor *n.* 1. an investigator 2. [I-] an official of the Inquisition

inquisitorial (in kwiz′ə tôr′ē əl) *adj.* of, or having the nature of, an inquisitor —**inquis′ito′rially** *adv.*

in re (in rē) [L.] in the matter (of); concerning

I.N.R.I. [L. *Iesus Nazarenus, Rex Iudaeorum*] Jesus of Nazareth, King of the Jews

inroad (in′rōd′) *n.* 1. a sudden invasion or raid 2. [*usually pl.*] any injurious encroachment

inrush *n.* a rushing in; inflow; influx

ins. 1. inches 2. insulated 3. insurance

insalubrious (in′sə loo′brē əs) *adj.* [< L. *insalubris*] unhealthy; unwholesome —**in′-salu′brity** *n.*

insane (in sān′) *adj.* 1. mentally ill or deranged; mad 2. of or for insane people 3. very foolish —**insane′ly** *adv.*

insanity (in san′ə tē) *n.*, *pl.* -ties 1. mental illness or derangement 2. great folly

insatiable (in sā′shə b'l) *adj.* that cannot be satisfied; very greedy —**insa′tiably** *adv.*

inscribe (in skrīb′) *vt.* -scribed′, -scrib′-ing [see -IN.¹ & SCRIBE] 1. to mark or engrave (words, symbols, etc.) on (a surface) 2. to add the name of (someone) to a list 3. *a*) to dedicate (a book, etc.) informally *b*) to write a short, signed message in (a book, etc.) 4. to fix in the mind 5. *Geom.* to draw (a figure) inside another figure so that their

boundaries touch at as many points as possible —**inscrib′er** *n.*

inscription (in skrip′shən) *n.* 1. an inscribing 2. something inscribed 3. an informal dedication in a book, etc. —**inscrip′tive, inscrip′tional** *adj.*

inscrutable (in skroot′ə b'l) *adj.* [< L. *in-*, not + *scrutari*, examine] that cannot be easily understood; enigmatic —**inscru′-tabil′ity, inscru′tableness** *n.*

insect (in′sekt) *n.* [< L. *insectum*, notched] 1. any of a large class of small arthropod animals, including beetles, flies, wasps, etc., having three pairs of legs, and, usually, two pairs of wings 2. popularly, any of a group of small animals, usually wingless, including spiders, centipedes, ticks, mites, etc.

insecticide (in sek′tə sīd′) *n.* any substance used to kill insects —**insec′tici′-dal** *adj.*

insectivore (in sek′tə vôr′) *n.* [see INSECT & -VOROUS] any animal or plant that feeds on insects —**insectivorous** (in′-sek tiv′ər əs) *adj.*

insecure (in′si kyooər′) *adj.* 1. not safe from danger 2. filled with anxieties 3. not firm or dependable —**in′secure′ly** *adv.* —**in′secu′rity** *n.*

inseminate (in sem′ə nāt′) *vt.* -nat′ed, -nat′ing [< L. *in-*, in + *semen*, seed] 1. to impregnate with semen 2. to implant (ideas, etc.) in (the mind, etc.) —**insem′ina′-tion** *n.*

insensate (in sen′sāt) *adj.* 1. lacking sensation 2. stupid 3. without feeling for others

insensible (in sen′sə b'l) *adj.* 1. unable to perceive with the senses 2. unconscious 3. unaware; indifferent 4. so slight as to be virtually imperceptible —**insen′sibil′-ity** *n.* —**insen′sibly** *adv.*

insert (in surt′; *for n.* in′surt) *vt.* [< L. *in-*, in + *serere*, join] to put or fit (something) into something else —*n.* anything inserted or for insertion —**insert′-er** *n.*

insertion (in sur′shən) *n.* 1. an inserting or being inserted 2. something inserted, as a single placement of an advertisement in a newspaper

in-service (in′sur′vis) *adj.* of training given to employees in connection with their work

inset (in set′; *for n. always*, in′set) *vt.* -set′, -set′ting to set into something; insert —*n.* something set in

inshore (in′shôr′) *adv., adj.* 1. in towards the shore 2. near the shore

inside (in′sīd′) *n.* 1. the inner side, surface, or part 2. the part closest to something implied, as the part of a pavement closest to the buildings 3. [*often pl.*] [Colloq.] the internal organs of the body —*adj.* 1. on or in the inside 2. secret or private [the *inside* story] 3. in some games, designating a forward who plays in the midfield area —*adv.* 1. on or to the inside 2. indoors 3. [Slang] in prison —*prep.* in; within; in less than —**inside out** 1.

with the inside where the outside should
be 2. [Colloq.] thoroughly

inside job [Colloq.] a crime committed
by, or with the aid of, a person employed
or trusted by the victim

insider n. 1. a person inside a given
place or group 2. a person having secret
or confidential information

insidious (in sid′ē əs) adj. [< L. insidiae,
an ambush] 1. characterized by treachery
or slyness 2. more dangerous than seems
evident —**insid′iously** adv.

insight (in′sīt′) n. 1. the ability to see
and understand clearly the inner nature
of things, esp. by intuition 2. an instance
of such understanding

insignia (in sig′nē ə) n.pl., sing. -sig′nia,
-sig′ne [ult. < L. in, in + signum, mark]
distinguishing marks, as emblems of rank,
membership, etc.

insignificant (in′sig nif′ə kənt) adj. 1.
having little or no meaning 2. trivial
3. small; unimposing —**in′signif′icance** n.
—**in′signif′icantly** adv.

insincere (in′sin sēr′) adj. deceptive or
hypocritical —**in′sincere′ly** adv. —**in′sin-
cer′ity** (-ser′ə tē) n.

insinuate (in sin′yoo wāt′) vt. -at′ed, -at′-
ing [< L. in-, in + sinus, a curve] 1.
to hint indirectly; imply 2. to introduce
or work into gradually, indirectly, etc.
—**insin′uat′ingly** adv. —**insin′ua′tor** n.

insinuation (in sin′yoo wā′shən) n. 1. an
insinuating 2. something insinuated;
specif., a) a sly hint b) an act or remark
intended to win favour

insipid (in sip′id) adj. [< L in-, not +
sapere, taste] 1. without flavour; tasteless
2. not exciting; dull —**in′sipid′ity, insip′id-
ness** n. —**insip′idly** adv.

insist (in sist′) vi. [< L. in-, in + sistere,
stand] to take and maintain a stand
(often with on or upon) —vt. 1. to demand
strongly 2. to declare firmly —**insist′er**
n. —**insist′ingly** adv.

insistent adj. 1. insisting or demanding
2. compelling the attention —**insist′ence**
n. —**insist′ently** adv.

‡**in situ** (in sī′tyōō) [L.] in position

insobriety (in′sō brī′ə tē) n. lack of
sobriety; intemperance, esp. in drinking

insofar (in′sə fär′) adv. to such a degree
or extent (usually with as)

insole (in′sōl′) n. 1. the inside sole of
a shoe 2. an extra, removable inside sole
for comfort

insolent (in′sə lənt) adj. [< L. in-, not
+ solere, be accustomed] boldly disrespectful; impertinent —**in′solence** n. —**in′-
solently** adv.

insoluble (in sol′yoo b′l) adj. 1.
unsolvable 2. that cannot be dissolved
—**insol′ubly** adv.

insolvent (in sol′vənt) adj. unable to pay
debts; bankrupt —n. an insolvent person
—**insol′vency** n.

insomnia (in som′nē ə) n. [< L. in-,
without + somnus, sleep] abnormal
inability to sleep —**insom′niac′** (-ak′)
n., adj.

insomuch (in′sō much′) adv. 1. to such

a degree or extent; so (with that) 2.
inasmuch (as)

insouciant (in sōō′sē ənt) adj. [Fr.] calm
and untroubled; carefree; indifferent
—**insou′ciance** n.

inspan (in span′) vt. -spanned′, -span′-
ning [< Afrik.] [S Afr.] 1. to harness
animals; yoke 2. to press (people) into
service

inspect (in spekt′) vt. [< L. in-, at +
specere, look] 1. to look at carefully
2. to examine or review officially —**inspec′-
tion** n. —**inspec′tive** adj.

inspector n. 1. one who inspects; official
examiner 2. an officer in a police force,
ranking next below a superintendent
—**inspec′torship′** n.

inspectorate n. 1. the position or duties
of an inspector 2. inspectors collectively

inspiration (in′spə rā′shən) n. 1. an
inspiring or being inspired mentally or
emotionally 2. a) any stimulus to creative
thought or action b) an inspired idea, action,
etc. 3. an inhaling —**in′spira′tional** adj.

inspire (in spīər′) vt. -spired′, -spir′ing
[< L. in-, in + spirare, breathe] 1. to
arouse (a thought or feeling) 2. to stimulate
or impel, as to some creative effort 3.
to cause to be written or said 4. to
motivate by divine influence 5. to inhale
—vi. to inhale —**inspir′able** adj.
—**inspired′** adj. —**inspir′er** n. —**inspir′-
ingly** adv.

instability (in′stə bil′ə tē) n. unstable
condition; lack of firmness, steadiness, etc.

install (in stôl′) vt. -stalled′, -stall′ing
[< ML. in-, in + stallum, place] 1. to
place in an office, rank, etc. with formality
2. to establish in a place 3. to fix in
position for use —**in′stalla′tion** (in′-
stə lā′shən) n. —**install′er** n.

installment plan U.S. name for HIRE-
PURCHASE

instalment (in stôl′mənt) n. [see INSTALL]
1. any of the parts of a sum of money
to be paid at regular times 2. any of
several parts, as of a serial story

instance (in′stəns) n. [see ff.] 1. an
example; case 2. a step in proceeding;
occasion [in the first instance] —vt.
-stanced, -stancing to use as an example;
cite —**at the instance of** at the suggestion
of —**for instance** as an example

instant (in′stənt) adj. [< L. in-, upon
+ stare, stand] 1. immediate 2. urgent;
pressing 3. imminent 4. designating a
food or beverage that can be prepared
quickly 5. of the current month [your
letter of the 13th instant] —n. 1. a moment
2. a particular moment —**the instant** as
soon as

instantaneous (in′stən tā′nē əs) adj.
done or happening in an instant; immediate
—**in′stanta′neously** adv.

instantly (in′stənt lē) adv. without delay;
immediately —conj. as soon as

instead (in sted′) adv. [IN + STEAD] in
place of the person or thing mentioned
—**instead of** in place of

INSTEP

instep (in'step') *n.* 1. the upper part of the arch of the foot, between the ankle and the toes 2. the part of a shoe or stocking covering this

instigate (in'stəgāt') *vt.* -gat'ed, -gat'ing [< L. *instigare*, incite] 1. to cause by inciting; foment 2. to urge on to some action —in'stiga'tion *n.* —in'stiga'tor *n.*

instil (in stil') *vt.* -stilled', -still'ing [< L. *in-*, in + *stilla*, drop] 1. to put (an idea, feeling, etc.) *in* or *into* gradually 2. to put in drop by drop —in'stilla'tion *n.* —instill'er *n.*

instinct (in'stiŋkt; *for adj.* in stiŋkt') *n.* [< L. *instinguere*, impel] 1. an inborn tendency to behave in a way characteristic of a species 2. a natural or acquired tendency; knack —*adj.* filled or charged (*with*) —instinc'tive *adj.* —instinctual (in stiŋk'choo wəl) *adj.*

institute (in'stətyoot') *vt.* -tut'ed, -tut'ing [< L. *in-*, in + *statuere*, set up] 1. to set up; establish 2. to start; initiate 3. to install in office —*n.* something instituted; specif., *a)* an organization for the promotion of art, science, etc. *b)* a building used by such an organization *c)* a school specializing in art, technical subjects, etc. *d)* an established principle

institution (in'stətyoo'shən) *n.* 1. an instituting or being instituted 2. an established law, practice, etc. 3. *a)* an organization having a social, educational, or religious purpose *b)* the building housing it 4. [Colloq.] a well-established person or thing

institutional *adj.* 1. of, or having the nature of, an institution 2. of or to institutions, rather than individuals 3. dull [*institutional* meals] —in'stitu'tionalism *n.* —in'stitu'tionalize *vt.*

instruct (in strukt') *vt.* [< L. *in-*, in + *struere*, pile up] 1. to teach 2. to inform or guide 3. to order or direct

instruction *n.* 1. [*often pl.*] orders; directions 2. an instructing; education 3. something taught —instruc'tional *adj.*

instructive *adj.* giving knowledge or information —instruc'tively *adv.* —instruc'tiveness *n.*

instructor *n.* 1. a teacher 2. [U.S.] a college teacher —instruc'tress *n.fem.*

instrument (in'strooment) *n.* [see INSTRUCT] 1. a tool or implement 2. any of various devices producing musical sound 3. a thing by means of which something is done; means 4. a device for indicating, measuring or controlling

instrumental (in'strəmen't'l) *adj.* 1. serving as a means; helpful 2. of or performed with an instrument or tool 3. performed on or written for a musical instrument or instruments —*n.* a piece of music for instruments —in'strumen'tally *adv.*

instrumentalist *n.* a person who performs on a musical instrument

instrumentality (in strə men tal'ə tē) *n.*, *pl.* -ties 1. a being instrumental 2. a means or agency

instrumentation (in strə mən tā'shən) *n.* 1. the arrangement of music for instruments 2. a using or equipping with instruments, esp. scientific instruments

instrument panel (or **board**) a panel or board with instruments, gauges, etc. mounted on it, as in a car

insubordinate (in'sə bôr'din ət) *adj.* not submitting to authority; disobedient —in'subor'dina'tion *n.*

insubstantial (in'səb stan'shəl) *adj.* not substantial; specif., *a)* not real *b)* not solid or firm

insufferable (in suf'ər ə b'l) *adj.* not sufferable; intolerable; unbearable —insuf'ferably *adv.*

insular (in'syoo lər) *adj.* [< L. *insula*, island] 1. of or like an island or islanders 2. narrow-minded, illiberal, etc. —in'sular'ity (-lar'ə tē), in'sularism *n.*

insulate (in'syoo lāt') *vt.* -lat'ed, -lat'ing [< L. *insula*, island] 1. to separate or cover with a nonconducting material in order to prevent the leakage of electricity, heat, etc. 2. to set apart; isolate —in'sula'tor *n.*

insulation (in'syoo lā'shən) *n.* 1. an insulating or being insulated 2. any material used to insulate

insulin (in'syoo lin) *n.* [< L. *insula*, island: referring to islands of tissue in the pancreas] 1. a secretion of the pancreas, which helps the body use carbohydrates 2. an extract from the pancreas of sheep, etc., used in the treatment of diabetes

insult (in sult'; *for n.* in'sult) *vt.* [< L. *in-*, in, on + *salire*, leap] to treat or speak to with scorn, insolence, or disrespect —*n.* an insulting act, remark, etc. —insult'er *n.* —insult'ing *adj.* —insult'ingly *adv.*

insuperable (in syoo'pər ə b'l) *adj.* that cannot be overcome —insu'perabil'ity *n.* —insu'perably *adv.*

insupportable (in'sə pôrt'ə b'l) *adj.* 1. intolerable 2. incapable of being upheld —in'support'ably *adv.*

insurance (in shoor'əns) *n.* 1. an insuring or being insured 2. a contract (**insurance policy**) whereby the insurer guarantees the insured that a certain sum will be paid for a specified loss 3. the amount for which life, property, etc. is insured 4. the business of insuring against loss 5. the amount paid in compensation

insure (in shoor') *vt.* -sured', -sur'ing [see ENSURE] 1. to take out or issue insurance on (something or someone) 2. *same as* ENSURE —*vi.* to give or take out insurance —insur'abil'ity *n.* —insur'able *adj.*

insured *n.* a person whose life, property, etc. is insured against loss

insurer *n.* a person or company that insures others against loss or damage

insurgence (in sur′jəns) *n.* a rising in revolt

insurgent *adj.* [< L. *in-*, upon + *surgere*, rise] rising up against established authority —*n.* one engaged in insurgent activity —**insur′gently** *adv.*

insurrection (in′sə rek′shən) *n.* [see INSURGENT] a rising up against established authority —**in′surrec′tional** *adj.* —**in′surrec′tionist** *n.*

int. 1. interest 2. interior 3. internal 4. international

intact (in takt′) *adj.* [< L. *in-*, not + *tangere*, touch] with nothing missing or injured —**intact′ness** *n.*

intaglio (in tal′yō) *n., pl.* **-ios** [It. *in-*, in + *tagliare*, cut] 1. a design or figure carved or engraved below the surface 2. a gem ornamented in this way

intake (in′tāk′) *n.* 1. a taking in 2. the amount, or body of people, taken in 3. the place at which a fluid is taken into a pipe, etc.

intangible (in tan′jə b'l) *adj.* 1. that cannot be touched 2. representing value that is neither intrinsic nor material 3. hard to define —*n.* something intangible —**intan′gibil′ity** *n.* —**intan′gibly** *adv.*

integer (in′tə jər) *n.* [L., whole] 1. any whole number or zero 2. anything complete in itself; entity

integral (in′tə grəl) *adj.* [< prec.] 1. necessary for completeness 2. whole or complete 3. made up of parts forming a whole 4. *Math.* of or having to do with integers —*n.* 1. the sum of a large number of minute quantities 2. a whole

integral calculus the branch of mathematics dealing with the determination of integrals

integrate (in′tə grāt′) *vt.* **-grat′ed, -grat′ing** [< L. *integer*, whole] 1. to make whole or complete 2. to bring (parts) together into a whole 3. to remove barriers imposing segregation upon (racial groups) —*vi.* to become integrated —**in′tegra′tion** *n.* —**in′tegra′tor** *n.*

integrated circuit an electronic circuit containing interconnected devices formed on a single chip of semiconductor material

integrity (in teg′rə tē) *n.* [see INTEGER] 1. honesty 2. soundness 3. wholeness

integument (in teg′yoo mənt) *n.* [< L. *in-*, upon + *tegere*, cover] an outer covering; skin, shell, etc.

intellect (in′tə lekt′) *n.* [< L. *inter-*, between + *legere*, choose] 1. the ability to reason or understand 2. high intelligence 3. a person of high intelligence

intellectual (in′tə lek′tyoo wəl) *adj.* 1. of, pertaining to, or appealing to the intellect 2. requiring the intellect 3. showing high intelligence —*n.* a person having intellectual tastes or work —**in′tellec′tual′ity** *n.* —**in′tellec′tually** *adv.*

intelligence (in tel′ə jəns) *n.* [see INTELLECT] 1. *a)* the ability to learn or

understand *b)* the ability to respond to a new situation 2. news or information 3. *a)* the gathering of secret information, as for military purposes *b)* the persons employed at this

intelligence quotient a number indicating a person's level of intelligence : it is the mental age multiplied by 100 and divided by the chronological age

intelligent *adj.* having or showing intelligence; bright, clever, etc. —**intel′ligently** *adv.*

intelligentsia (in tel′ə jent′sē ə) *n.pl.* [*also with sing. v.*] [< Russ.] intellectuals collectively

intelligible (in tel′i jə b'l) *adj.* [see INTELLECT] that can be understood; clear —**intel′ligibil′ity** *n.*

intemperate (in tem′pər ət) *adj.* 1. not moderate; excessive 2. drinking too much alcoholic liquor —**intem′perance** *n.* —**intem′perately** *adv.*

intend (in tend′) *vt.* [< L. *in-*, at + *tendere*, stretch] 1. to plan; purpose 2. to mean (something) to be or be used (*for*) 3. to mean or signify —*vi.* to have a purpose —**intend′er** *n.*

intended *adj.* 1. planned; purposed 2. prospective —*n.* [Colloq.] the person whom one has agreed to marry

intense (in tens′) *adj.* [see INTEND] 1. very strong [*an intense light*] 2. strained to the utmost; earnest [*intense thought*] 3. characterized by much action, emotion, etc. —**intense′ly** *adv.* —**intense′ness** *n.*

intensify *vt., vi.* **-fied′, -fy′ing** to make or become intense or more intense —**inten′sifica′tion** *n.* —**inten′sifi′er** *n.*

intensity *n., pl.* **-ties** 1. a being intense 2. great energy or vehemence, as of emotion 3. the amount of force or energy of heat, light, sound, etc.

intensive *adj.* 1. of or characterized by intensity; thorough 2. designating very attentive hospital care given to patients, as after surgery 3. *Agric.* designating a system of farming which aims at an increase of crops 4. *Gram.* giving force or emphasis (Ex.: "the very same") —*n.* an intensive word, prefix, etc. —**inten′sively** *adv.*

intent (in tent′) *adj.* [see INTEND] 1. firmly directed; earnest 2. *a)* having the attention firmly fixed *b)* strongly resolved —*n.* something intended; purpose; meaning —**to all intents and purposes** in almost every respect —**intent′ly** *adv.* —**intent′ness** *n.*

intention (in ten′shən) *n.* 1. determination to act in a specified way 2. *a)* anything intended; purpose *b)* [*pl.*] purpose in regard to marriage

intentional *adj.* done purposely —**inten′tionally** *adv.*

inter (in tur′) *vt.* **-terred′, -ter′ring** [< L. *in*, in + *terra*, earth] to put (a dead body) into a grave or tomb

inter- [L. *inter*] a combining form meaning: 1. between or among [*interdepartmental*] 2. with or on each other (or one another); mutual [*interact*]

interact (in′tər akt′) *vi.* to act on one

another —**in′terac′tion** *n.* —**in′terac′tive** *adj.*

‡**inter alia** (in′tər ā′lē ə) [L.] among other things

interbreed (in′tər brēd′) *vt., vi.* **-bred′, -breed′ing** *same as* HYBRIDIZE

intercede (in′tər sēd′) *vi.* **-ced′ed, -ced′-ing** [< L. *inter-*, between + *cedere*, go] **1.** to plead on behalf of another **2.** to intervene for the purpose of producing agreement —**in′terced′er** *n.*

intercept (in′tər sept′; *for n.* in′tər sept′) *vt.* [< L. *inter-*, between + *capere*, take] **1.** to seize, stop, or interrupt on the way [to *intercept* a message] **2.** *Math.* to mark off between two points, lines, or planes —*n.* *Math.* the part of a line, plane, etc. intercepted —**in′tercep′tion** *n.* —**in′tercep′tive** *adj.* —**in′tercep′tor, in′-tercep′ter** *n.*

intercession (in′tər sesh′ən) *n.* mediation or prayer on behalf of another —**in′terces′sor** *n.*

interchange (in′tər chānj′; *for n.* in′tər chānj′) *vt.* **-changed′, -chang′ing 1.** to give and take mutually; exchange **2.** to put (each of two things) in the other's place **3.** to alternate —*n.* **1.** an interchanging **2.** a motorway junction with interconnecting roads and bridges —**in′terchange′able** *adj.* —**in′terchange′ably** *adv.*

inter-city (in′tər sit′ē) *adj.* between cities

intercollegiate (in′tər kə lē′jē ət) *adj.* between colleges

intercom (in′tər kom′) *n.* a radio or telephone intercommunication system, within a building, aircraft, etc.

intercommunicate (in′tər kə myoo′-nə kāt′) *vt., vi.* **-cat′ed, -cat′ing** to communicate with or to each other or one another —**in′tercommu′nica′tion** *n.*

intercommunion (in′tər kə myoon′yən) *n.* mutual communion, as among religious groups

interconnect (in′tər kə nekt′) *vt., vi.* to connect with one another —**in′terconnec′-tion** *n.*

intercourse (in′tər kôrs′) *n.* [see INTER- & COURSE] **1.** communication or dealings between people, countries, etc. **2.** the sexual joining of two individuals: in full, **sexual intercourse**

interdenominational (in′tər di nom′ə-nā′shən′l) *adj.* among or involving different religious denominations

interdepartmental (in′tər di pärt′men′-t′l) *adj.* between or among departments

interdependence (in′tər di pen′dəns) *n.* mutual dependence: also **in′terdepend′-ency** —**in′terdepend′ent** *adj.*

interdict (in′tər dikt′; *for n.* in′tər dikt′) *vt.* [< L. *inter-*, between + *dicere*, speak] **1.** to prohibit (an action) **2.** to restrain from doing or using something **3.** *R.C.Ch.* to exclude (a person, parish, etc.) from certain acts or privileges —*n.* an official prohibition or restraint; specif., *R.C.Ch.* an interdicting of a person, parish, etc. —**in′terdic′tion** *n.* —**in′terdic′tory, in′ter-dic′tive** *adj.*

interdisciplinary (in′tər dis′ə pli nər ē)

adj. involving two or more disciplines, or branches of learning

interest (in′trist′) *n.* [< L. *inter-*, between + *esse*, be] **1.** *a)* a feeling of curiosity about something *b)* the power of causing this feeling *c)* something causing this feeling **2.** [*often pl.*] welfare; benefit **3.** a right to, or share in, something **4.** anything in which one has a share **5.** importance **6.** *a)* money paid for the use of money *b)* the rate of such payment **7.** [*usually pl.*] a group of people having a common concern in some industry, cause, etc. —*vt.* **1.** to excite the curiosity of **2.** to involve the interest of **3.** to cause to have an interest in —**in the interest** (or **interests**) **of** for the sake of

interested *adj.* **1.** feeling or showing curiosity **2.** influenced by personal interest **3.** having an interest

interesting *adj.* exciting interest, curiosity, or attention —**in′teres t in gly** *adv.*

interface (in′tər fās′) *n.* **1.** a plane forming the common boundary between two parts **2.** a point of communication as between disciplines

interfacing *n.* a piece of fabric sewn between the facing and the garment to give shape and firmness

interfere (in′tər fēr′) *vi.* **-fered′, -fer′-ing** [< L. *inter-*, between + *ferire*, strike] **1.** to come between; intervene; meddle **2.** to clash; conflict **3.** *Physics* to affect each other by interference: said of vibrating waves —**interfere with 1.** to hinder **2.** to molest, esp. sexually —**in′terfer′ingly** *adv.*

interference *n.* **1.** an interfering **2.** something that interferes **3.** *Physics* the mutual action of two waves of vibration, as of sound, light, etc., in reinforcing or neutralizing each other **4.** *Radio & TV* static, unwanted signals, etc., producing distortion

interfuse (in′tər fyooz′) *vt.* **-fused′, -fus′-ing 1.** to combine by fusing together **2.** to spread itself through —*vi.* to fuse

intergalactic (in′tər gə lak′tik) *adj.* existing or occurring between or among galaxies

interim (in′tər im) *n.* [< L. *inter*, between] the period of time between —*adj.* provisional

interior (in tēr′ē ər) *adj.* [< L. *inter*, between] **1.** situated within **2.** away from the coast, border, etc.; inland **3.** of the domestic affairs of a country —*n.* **1.** the interior part as of a room, country, etc. **2.** a picture of the inside of a room **3.** the domestic affairs of a country

interior angle any of the four angles formed on the inside of two straight lines by a straight line cutting them

interior decoration the decorating and furnishing of the interior of a room, house, etc.

interj. interjection

interject (in′tər jekt′) *vt.* [< L. *inter-*, between + *jacere*, throw] to insert; interpose —**in′terjec′tor** *n.*

interjection *n.* **1.** an interjecting **2.**

something interjected, as a word or phrase **3.** *Gram.* an exclamatory word or phrase (Ex.: ah! well!)

interlace (in'tər lās') *vt., vi.* **-laced', -lac'ing** [< OFr.: see INTER- & LACE] **1.** to weave together **2.** to connect intricately —**in'terlace'ment** *n.*

interlard (in'tər lärd') *vt.* [< Fr.: see INTER-& LARD] **1.** to intersperse; diversify **2.** to be intermixed in

interlay (in'tər lā') *vt.* **-laid', -lay'ing** to put between

interleaf (in'tər lēf') *n.*, *pl.* **-leaves'** a leaf, usually blank, bound between the other leaves of a book, for notes, etc. —**in'terleave'** *vt.* **-leaved', -leav'ing**

interline (in'tər līn') *vt.* **-lined', -lin'ing** to write (something) between the lines of (a text, document, etc.)

interlining *n.* a lining between the outer cloth and the ordinary lining

interlink (in'tər liŋk') *vt.* to link together

interlock (in'tər lok'; *for adj.*, in'-) *vt., vi.* to lock together; join with one another —*adj.* closely knitted

interlocutor (in'tər lok'yoo tər) *n.* [< L. *inter*, between + *loqui*, talk] a person taking part in a conversation

interlocutory *adj.* **1.** conversational **2.** *Law* pronounced during the course of a suit

interloper (in'tər lō'pər) *n.* [prob. < INTER- + LOPE] a person who intrudes in others' affairs

interlude (in'tər lood') *n.* [< L. *inter*, between + *ludus*, play] **1.** a period of different activity between two events **2.** an interval **3.** music played between the parts of a song, play, etc. **4.** any performance between the acts of a play **5.** a short play formerly presented between the parts of a miracle play

intermarry (in'tər mar'ē) *vi.* **-ried, -rying** to become connected by marriage —**in'termar'riage** *n.*

intermediary (in'tər mē'dē ər ē) *n.*, *pl.* **-aries** a go-between —*adj.* **1.** acting as a mediator **2.** intermediate

intermediate (in'tər mē'dē ət; *for v.* -āt') *adj.* [< L. *inter-*, between + *medius*, middle] being or happening between; in the middle —*n.* **1.** anything intermediate **2.** same as INTERMEDIARY —*vi.* **-at'ed, -at'ing** to mediate —**in'terme'diately** *adv.* —**in'terme'dia'tion** *n.*

interment (in tur'mənt) *n.* an interring; burial

intermezzo (in'tər met'sō) *n.*, *pl.* **-zos, -zi** (-sē) [It.] **1.** a short musical entertainment between the acts of a play or opera **2.** *Music* a short movement connecting the main parts of a composition

interminable (in tur'mi nə b'l) *adj.* lasting, or seeming to last, forever; endless —**inter'minably** *adv.*

intermingle (in'tər miŋ'g'l) *vt., vi.* **-gled, -gling** to mix together; mingle; blend

intermission (in'tər mish'ən) *n.* an interval of time between periods of activity, as between acts of a play

intermittent (in'tər mit'ənt) *adj.* stop-

ping and starting again at intervals —**in'termit'tently** *adv.*

intern (in'turn; *for vt. usually* in turn') *n.* [< L. *internus*, internal] [U.S.] a doctor serving as an assistant resident in a hospital, generally just after graduation from medical school —*vt.* to detain and confine within an area —**intern'ment** *n.*

internal (in tur'n'l) *adj.* [< L. *internus*] **1.** of or on the inside; inner **2.** to be taken inside the body **3.** intrinsic [*internal evidence*] **4.** of a person's inner nature **5.** domestic —**in'ternal'ity** (-nal'ə tē) *n.* —**inter'nally** *adv.*

internal-combustion engine an engine, as in a car, in which the power is produced by the combustion of a fuel-and-air mixture within the cylinders

international (in'tər nash'ən'l) *adj.* **1.** between or among nations **2.** concerned with the relations between nations **3.** for the use of all nations **4.** carried on by people in various nations —*n.* **1.** *a)* a contest between national teams *b)* a member of these teams **2.** [I-] any of several international socialist organizations —**in'terna'tional'ity** *n.* —**in'terna'tionally** *adv.*

internationalism *n.* the principle of international cooperation for the common good

International Phonetic Alphabet a set of phonetic symbols for international use: each symbol represents a single sound

internecine (in'tər nē'sin) *adj.* [< L. *inter-*, between + *necare*, kill] mutually destructive or harmful

internee (in'tur nē') *n.* a person interned as a prisoner of war, enemy alien, political dissident, etc.

internist (in tur'nist) *n.* a doctor who specializes in internal medicine

interpenetrate (in'tər pen'ə trāt') *vt.* **-trat'ed, -trat'ing** to penetrate thoroughly —**in'terpen'etra'tion** *n.*

interpersonal (in'tər pur'sən'l) *adj.* **1.** between persons **2.** of or involving relations between persons

interplanetary (in'tər plan'ə tər ē) *adj.* **1.** between planets **2.** within the solar system but outside the atmosphere of any planet or the sun

interplay (in'tər plā') *n.* action or effect on one another

Interpol (in'tər pol) *n.* [*inter*(national) *pol*(ice)] an international police organization: full name, *International Criminal Police Commission*

interpolate (in tur'pō lāt') *vt.* **-lat'ed, -lat'ing** [< L. *inter-*, between + *polire*, polish] **1.** to insert between or among others **2.** to change (a text, etc.) by putting in new material **3.** *Math.* to estimate a missing value by taking an average of known values at neighbouring points —**inter'pola'tion** *n.* —**inter'polative** *adj.*

interpose (in'tər pōz') *vt., vi.* **-posed', -pos'ing** [< L. *interponere*, set between] **1.** to place or come between **2.** to intervene (with) **3.** to interrupt (with) —**in'terpos'al** *n.* —**in'terposi'tion** *n.*

interpret (in tur′prit) *vt.* [< L. *interpres*, negotiator] **1.** to explain or translate **2.** to construe [to *interpret* a laugh as derisive] **3.** to give one's own conception of, as in performing a play —*vi.* to act as an interpreter; translate —**inter′pretable** *adj.* —**inter′pretive, inter′pretative** *adj.*

interpretation (in tur′prə tā′shən) *n.* **1.** an interpreting; explanation, translation, etc. **2.** the expression of a person's conception of a work of art, subject, etc. through acting, writing, etc.

interpreter (in tur′prə tər) *n.* a person whose work is translating a foreign language orally

interracial (in′tər rā′shəl) *adj.* between, among, or for persons of different races

interregnum (in′tər reg′nəm) *n., pl.* **-reg′nums, -reg′na** [L. < *inter-*, between + *regnum*, reign] **1.** an interval between two successive reigns, when the country has no sovereign **2.** any period without the usual ruler

interrelate (in′tər ri lāt′) *vt., vi.* **-lat′ed, -lat′ing** to make, be, or become mutually related —**in′terrela′tion** *n.*

interrogate (in ter′ō gāt′) *vt.* **-gat′ed, -gat′ing** [< L. *inter-*, between + *rogare*, ask] to ask questions of formally in examining —**inter′roga′tion** *n.* —**inter′roga′tor** *n.*

interrogation mark (or **point**) *same as* QUESTION MARK

interrogative (in′tə rog′ə tiv) *adj.* asking a question —*n.* an interrogative word, etc.

interrogatory *adj.* expressing a question —*n., pl.* **-ries** a formal set of questions

interrupt (in′tə rupt′) *vt.* [< L. *inter-*, between + *rumpere*, break] **1.** to make a break in the continuity of **2.** *a)* to break into (a discussion, etc.) *b)* to break in upon (a person) while he is speaking, working, etc. —**in′terrupt′er** *n.* —**in′terrup′tive** *adj.*

interrupter, interruptor *n. Elec.* a mechanism used to intermittently open and close a circuit

interruption (in′tə rup′shən) *n.* **1.** an interrupting **2.** anything that interrupts **3.** an intermission

interscholastic (in′tər skə las′tik) *adj.* between or among schools [an *interscholastic* debate]

intersect (in′tər sekt′) *vt.* [< L. *inter-*, between + *secare*, cut] to divide into two parts by passing through or across

intersection *n.* **1.** an intersecting **2.** the point or line where two lines, surfaces, or roads meet or cross

interspace (in′tər spās′) *n.* a space between —*vt.* **-spaced′, -spac′ing** to make spaces between

intersperse (in′tər spurs′) *vt.* **-spersed′, -spers′ing** [< L. *inter-*, among + *spargere*, scatter] **1.** to scatter among other things **2.** to diversify with things scattered here and there —**in′tersper′sion** (-spur′shən) *n.*

interstellar (in′tər stel′ər) *adj.* [INTER- + STELLAR] between or among the stars

interstice (in tur′stis) *n., pl.* **-stices**

(-stə sēz′) [Fr. < L. *inter-*, between + *sistere*, set] a crevice; crack —**interstitial** (in′tər stish′əl) *adj.*

intertwine (in′tər twīn′) *vt., vi.* **-twined′, -twin′ing** to twine together

interval (in′tər v'l) *n.* [< L. *inter-*, between + *vallum*, wall] **1.** a period of time between two events **2.** a space between two things **3.** *Music* the difference in pitch between two tones —**at intervals 1.** now and then **2.** here and there

intervene (in′tər vēn′) *vi.* **-vened′, -ven′-ing** [< L. *inter-*, between + *venire*, come] **1.** to come between as an influencing force **2.** to come or be between **3.** to occur between two events, etc. —**in′terven′er** *n.*

intervention (in′tər ven′shən) *n.* **1.** an intervening **2.** any interference in the affairs of others, esp. of one state in the affairs of another —**in′terven′tionist** *n., adj.*

interview (in′tər vyōō′) *n.* [< Fr.: see INTER- & VIEW] **1.** a meeting of people face to face, as for evaluating a job applicant **2.** *a)* a meeting in which a person is asked about his views, etc., as by a reporter *b)* a published account of this —*vt.* to have an interview with —**in′terviewee′** *n.* —**in′terview′er** *n.*

interweave (in′tər wēv′) *vt., vi.* **-wove′, -wo′ven, -weav′ing 1.** to weave together **2.** to connect closely

intestate (in tes′tāt) *adj.* [< L. *in-*, not + *testari*, make a will] having made no will —*n.* a person who has died intestate —**intes′tacy** *n.*

INTESTINES
(A, stomach; B, pancreas; C, descending colon; D, rectum; E, appendix; F, ileum; G, jejunum; H, ascending colon; I, transverse colon; J, duodenum; K, liver)

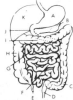

intestine (in tes′tin) *n.* [< L. *intus*, within] [*usually pl.*] the lower part of the alimentary canal, extending from the stomach to the anus and consisting of a convoluted upper part (**small intestine**) and a lower part of greater diameter (**large intestine**); bowel(s) —**intes′tinal** *adj.*

intimacy (in′tə mə sē) *n., pl.* **-cies 1.** familiarity **2.** an intimate act; esp., [*usually pl.*] sexual intercourse

intimate (in′tə mat; *for v.* -māt′) *adj.* [< L. *intus*, within] **1.** closely associated; very familiar **2.** most private or personal **3.** having sexual relations **4.** resulting from careful study **5.** fundamental; essential —*n.* an intimate friend or companion —*vt.* **-mat′ed, -mat′ing** to hint or imply —**in′timately** *adv.* —**in′timateness** *n.*

intimation (in′tə mā′shən) *n.* **1.** a hint **2.** a formal announcement

intimidate (in tim'ə dāt') *vt.* -dat'ed, -dat'ing [< L. *in-*, in + *timidus*, afraid] 1. to make afraid 2. to force or deter with threats —**intim'ida'tion** *n.*

into (in'tŏŏ, -tə) *prep.* [OE.] 1. towards and within 2. advancing to the midst of [dancing far *into* the night] 3. to the form, substance, etc. of 4. so as to strike [to bump *into* a door] 5. *Math.* used to indicate division

intolerable (in tol'ər ə b'l) *adj.* unbearable; too severe, painful, etc. to be endured —**intol'erably** *adv.*

intolerant *adj.* unwilling to tolerate others' opinions, beliefs, etc. or persons of other races, etc.; bigoted —**intolerant of** not able or willing to tolerate —**intol'erance** *n.* —**intol'erantly** *adv.*

intonation (in'tō nā'shən) *n.* 1. variations in pitch in speaking 2. an intoning 3. the manner of singing or playing tones with regard to accuracy of pitch

intone (in tōn') *vt., vi.* -toned', -ton'ing [see IN-[1] & TONE] to utter or recite in a singing tone; chant: also **intonate**

in toto (in tō'tō) [L.] as a whole; entirely

intoxicant (in tok'sə kənt) *n.* something that intoxicates; esp., alcoholic liquor —*adj.* intoxicating

intoxicate *vt.* -cat'ed, -cat'ing [< L. *in-*, in + *toxicum*, poison] 1. to make drunk 2. to excite to a point beyond self-control

intoxication (in tok'sə kā'shən) *n.* 1. a making or becoming drunk 2. a feeling of wild excitement

intr. intransitive

intra- [L.] *a combining form meaning* within, inside

intractable (in trak'tə b'l) *adj.* 1. unruly or stubborn 2. hard to work, cure, etc. —**intrac'tabil'ity, intrac'tableness** *n.* —**intrac'tably** *adv.*

intrados (in trā'dos) *n.* [Fr. < L. *intra*, within + Fr. *dos*, the back] the inside curve of an arch or vault

intramural (in'trə myŏŏar'əl) *adj.* [INTRA- + MURAL] within the walls or limits of a college, etc.

intrans. intransitive

intransigent (in tran'sə jənt) *adj.* [< L. *in-*, not + *transigere*, settle] refusing to compromise —*n.* one who is intransigent, esp. in politics —**intran'sigence, intran'sigency** *n.*

intransitive (in tran'sə tiv) *adj.* designating a verb that does not require a direct object to complete its meaning —*n.* an intransitive verb —**intran'sitively** *adv.*

intrauterine (in'trə yŏŏ'tə rīn') *adj.* within the uterus

intrauterine (contraceptive) device any of various devices inserted in the uterus as a contraceptive

intravenous (in'trə vē'nəs) *adj.* [INTRA- + VENOUS] in, or directly into, a vein or veins —**in'trave'nously** *adv.*

intray (in'trā') *n.* a receptacle for incoming papers, etc.

intrepid (in trep'id) *adj.* [< L. *in-*, not + *trepidus*, alarmed] bold; fearless; very

brave —**in'trepid'ity** (-trə pid'ə tē) *n.* —**in trep'idly** *adv.*

intricate (in'tri kət) *adj.* [< L. *in-*, in + *tricae*, perplexities] 1. hard to follow or understand because full of puzzling parts, details, etc. 2. full of elaborate detail —**in'tricacy** *n.* —**in'tricately** *adv.*

intrigue (in trēg'; *for n., also* in'trēg) *vi.* -trigued', -trigu'ing [see prec.] to plot or scheme secretly or underhandedly —*vt.* 1. to excite the interest or curiosity of 2. to get by secret plotting —*n.* 1. secret or underhanded plotting 2. a secret plot or scheme 3. a secret love affair —**intrigu'ingly** *adv.*

intrinsic (in trin'sik) *adj.* [< L. *intra-*, within + *secus*, close] belonging to the real nature of a thing; inherent —**intrin'sically** *adv.*

intro (in'trō) *n.* [Colloq.] introduction

intro- [< L.] *a combining form meaning* into, within

introduce (in'trə dyŏŏs') *vt.* -duced', -duc'ing [< L. *intro-*, within + *ducere*, lead] 1. *a*) to make acquainted; present (*to*) *b*) to give knowledge or experience of [they *introduced* him to music] 2. to present for consideration or approval [*introduce* a bill in parliament] 3. to add as a new feature 4. to begin 5. to bring into use or fashion 6. to put in; insert —**in'troduc'ible** *adj.*

introduction (-duk'shən) *n.* 1. an introducing or being introduced 2. the formal presentation of one person to another 3. anything that introduces, as the preliminary section of a book, speech, etc.

introductory *adj.* used as an introduction; preliminary: also **in'troduc'tive** —**in'troduc'torily** *adv.*

introit (in'troit) *n.* [< L. *intro-*, within + *ire*, go] 1. a psalm or hymn at the opening of a Christian worship service 2. [I-] R.C.Ch. the first variable part of the Mass

introspection (in'trō spek'shən) *n.* [< L. *intro-*, within + *specere*, look] a looking into one's own mind, feelings, etc. —**in'trospec'tive** *adj.*

introvert (in'trō vurt'; *for v., also* in'-trō vurt') *vt.* [< L. *intro-*, within + *vertere*, turn] to direct (one's interest, mind, etc.) upon oneself —*n.* *Psychol.* one who is more interested in his own feelings, etc. than in other people —**in'trover'sion** *n.* —**in'trovert'ed** *adj.*

intrude (in trŏŏd') *vt.* -trud'ed, -trud'ing [< L. *in-*, in + *trudere*, thrust] 1. to push or force (something *in* or *upon*) 2. to force (oneself) upon others without being asked or welcomed —**intrud'er** *n.*

intrusion (in trŏŏ'zhən) *n.* 1. an intruding 2. *Geol.* the invasion of liquid magma, etc. into or between solid rock —**intru'sive** *adj.*

intrust (in trust') *vt.* same as ENTRUST

intuition (in'tyŏŏ wish'ən) *n.* [< L. *in-*, in + *tueri*, look at] the direct knowing or learning of something without conscious reasoning —**in'tui'tional** *adj.*

intuitive (in tyo͞o′i tiv) *adj.* 1. having to do with, having, or perceiving by intuition 2. perceived by intuition —**intu′itively** *adv.* —**intu′itiveness** *n.*

Inuit (in′yo͞o it) *n., pl.* **-it, -its** an Eskimo of N America or Greenland

inundate (in′un dāt′) *vt.* **-dat′ed, -dat′-ing** [< L. *in-*, in + *undare*, flood] 1. to cover completely with water; flood 2. to overwhelm —**in′unda′tion** *n.*

inure (in yoͻar′) *vt.* **-ured′, -ur′ing** [< ME. *in*, in + *ure*, work] to make accustomed to something difficult, painful, etc. —*vi.* *Law* to take effect —**inure′-ment** *n.*

‡**in vacuo** (in vak′yo͞o ō′) [L.] in a vacuum

invade (in vād′) *vt.* **-vad′ed, -vad′ing** [< L. *in-*, in + *vadere*, go] 1. to enter forcibly, as to conquer 2. to crowd into; throng 3. to intrude upon; violate —*vi.* to make an invasion —**invad′er** *n.*

invalid[1] (in′və lid) *n.* [see IN.[2] + VALID] one who is chronically ill or disabled —*adj.* 1. of or for invalids 2. weak and sickly —*vt.* (in′və lēd′) 1. to disable or weaken 2. to remove (a soldier, etc.) from active duty because of illness —**in′validism** *n.*

invalid[2] (in val′id) *adj.* not valid; having no force; null or void —**invalidity** (in′-və lid′ə tē) *n.* —**inval′idly** *adv.*

invalidate (in val′ə dāt′) *vt.* **-dat′ed, -dat′-ing** to deprive of legal force —**inval′ida′-tion** *n.*

invaluable (in val′yoo wə b′l) *adj.* too valuable to be measured; priceless —**inval′-uableness** *n.*

invariable (in vāar′ē ə b′l) *adj.* unchang-ing; constant —**invar′iableness** *n.* —**invar′-iably** *adv.*

invasion (in vā′zhən) *n.* 1. an invading, as by an army 2. an intruding upon others —**inva′sive** *adj.*

invective (in vek′tiv) *n.* [see ff.] a violent verbal attack; insults, curses, etc. —*adj.* vituperative —**invec′tively** *adv.* —**invec′-tiveness** *n.*

inveigh (in vā′) *vi.* [< L. *in-*, in + *vehere*, carry] to make a violent verbal attack; rail (*against*)

inveigle (in vā′g′l) *vt.* **-gled, -gling** [< L. *ab*, from + *oculus*, eye] to entice or trick into doing something, etc. —**invei′-glement** *n.* —**invei′gler** *n.*

invent (in vent′) *vt.* [< L. *in-*, on + *venire*, come] 1. to think up 2. to think out or produce (a new device, etc.) —**inven′-tor** *n.*

invention *n.* 1. an inventing 2. something invented; specif., *a*) a new device or contrivance *b*) a falsehood 3. ingenuity

inventive *adj.* 1. of or characterized by invention 2. skilled in inventing; creative —**inven′tively** *adv.*

inventory (in′vən trē) *n., pl.* **-ries** [see INVENT] a detailed list of articles, goods, etc., as the effects of a house —*vt.* **-ried, -rying** 1. to make an inventory 2. to place on an inventory

inverse (in vurs′) *adj.* inverted; reversed in order or relation; directly opposite [an *inverse* ratio] —*n.* any inverse thing; direct opposite —**inverse′ly** *adv.*

inversion *n.* 1. an inverting or being inverted 2. something inverted; reversal 3. *Gram.* a reversal of the normal order of words in a sentence (Ex.: "said he" for "he said") —**inver′sive** *adj.*

invert (in vurt′; *for n.* in′vurt′) *vt.* [< L. *in-*, to + *vertere*, to turn] 1. to turn upside down 2. to reverse the order, position, direction, etc. of —*n.* 1. anything inverted 2. a homosexual —**invert′ible** *adj.*

invertebrate (in vur′tə brət) *adj.* 1. having no backbone, or spinal column 2. of invertebrates —*n.* any animal without a backbone

inverted comma *same as* QUOTATION MARK

invest (in vest′) *vt.* [< L. *in-*, in + *vestis*, clothing] 1. to put (money) into business, shares, etc. for the purpose of obtaining a profit 2. to install in office with ceremony 3. to furnish with power, privilege, or authority 4. to endow with qualities, attributes, etc. 5. to clothe 6. to cover or surround 7. *Mil.* to besiege (a town, etc.) —*vi.* 1. to invest money 2. [Colloq.] to buy —**inves′tor** *n.*

investigate (in ves′tə gāt′) *vt., vi.* **-gat′-ed, -gat′ing** [< L. *investigare*, trace out] to search into; inquire —**inves′tigable** *adj.* —**inves′tigative, inves′tigatory** *adj.* —**inves′tiga′tor** *n.*

investigation (in ves′tə gā′shən) *n.* 1. an investigating 2. a careful examination —**inves′tiga′tional** *adj.*

investiture (in ves′ti chər) *n.* a formal investing with an office, power, author-ity, etc.

investment (in vest′mənt) *n.* 1. an investing or being invested 2. *a*) the investing of money, time, etc. *b*) anything in which money may be invested *c*) the amount invested

investment trust an organization that invests its members' capital in a wide range of securities to provide profit and reduce the risk of depreciation

inveterate (in vet′ər ət) *adj.* [< L. *in-*, in + *vetus*, old] 1. firmly established over a long period 2. settled in a habit, practice, etc. —**invet′eracy** *n.* —**invet′er-ately** *adv.*

invidious (in vid′ē əs) *adj.* [< L. *invidia*, envy] such as to excite ill will or envy; giving offence —**invid′iously** *adv.* —**invid′-iousness** *n.*

invigilate (in vij′ə lāt′) *vi.* **-lat′ed, -lat′-ing** [< L. *invigilare*, watch over] to supervise, esp. candidates during an examination —**invig′ila′tor** *n.*

invigorate (in vig′ə rāt′) *vt.* **-at′ed, -at′-ing** [IN-[1] + VIGOUR] to give vigour to; fill with energy —**invig′orative** *adj.* —**invig′ora′tor** *n.*

invincible (in vin′sə b′l) *adj.* [see IN-[2] & VINCIBLE] that cannot be overcome; unconquerable —**invin′cibil′ity, invin′ci-bleness** *n.* —**invin′cibly** *adv.*

inviolable (in vī′ə lə b′l) *adj.* 1. not to

be violated; sacred **2.** indestructible —**invi′olabil′ity** *n.* —**invi′olably** *adv.*

inviolate (in vī′ə lət) *adj.* not violated; kept sacred or unbroken —**invi′olately** *adv.*

invisible (in viz′ə b'l) *adj.* **1.** that cannot be seen **2.** out of sight **3.** imperceptible **4.** kept hidden **5.** *Econ.* relating to services, as banking, insurance, etc., rather than goods —**the Invisible 1.** God **2.** the unseen world —**invis′ibil′ity** *n.* —**invis′ibly** *adv.*

invitation (in′və tā′shən) *n.* **1.** an inviting **2.** the message or note used in inviting

invite (in vīt′; *for n.* in′vīt) *vt.* **-vit′ed, -vit′- ing** [< L. *invitare*] **1.** to ask courteously to come somewhere or do something **2.** to make a request for [*to invite questions*] **3.** to give occasion for **4.** to entice —*n.* [Colloq.] an invitation

inviting *adj.* tempting; enticing

invocation (in′vō kā′shən) *n.* **1.** an invoking of God, the Muses, etc. for blessing, help, etc. **2.** a formal prayer used in invoking **3.** an incantation —**in′vo- ca′tional** *adj.* —**invoc′atory** (-vok′ə tər ē) *adj.*

invoice (in′vois) *n.* [prob. < ME. *envoie*, a message] an itemized list of goods sent or shipped to a buyer, stating quantities, prices, etc. —*vt.* **-voiced, -voic- ing** to present an invoice for or to

invoke (in vōk′) *vt.* **-voked′, -vok′ing** [< L. *in-*, on + *vocare*, call] **1.** to call on (God, the Muses, etc.) for blessing, help, etc. **2.** to put into use (a law, penalty, etc.) as pertinent **3.** to call forth **4.** to conjure up spirits, etc. **5.** to ask solemnly for —**invok′er** *n.*

involuntary (in vol′ən tər ē) *adj.* **1.** not done of one's own free will **2.** unintentional **3.** not consciously controlled [*sneezing is involuntary*]

involute (in′və lōōt′) *adj.* [< L. *involvere*, involve] **1.** intricate; involved **2.** rolled up or curled in a spiral **3.** *Bot.* rolled inwards at the edges —*n.* *Math.* the curve traced by any point of a taut string when it is wound upon or unwound from a fixed curve on the same plane with it —*vi.* **-lut′ed, -lut′ing** to become involute —**in′volu′tion** *n.*

involve (in volv′) *vt.* **-volved′, -volv′ing** [< L. *in-*, in + *volvere*, roll] **1.** to include by necessity; entail **2.** to entangle in difficulty, danger, etc. **3.** to include **4.** to relate to or affect [*his honour is involved*] **5.** to make busy; occupy **6.** to make intricate or complicated —**involve′ment** *n.*

invulnerable (in vul′nər ə b'l) *adj.* **1.** that cannot be wounded or injured **2.** incapable of being damaged or captured —**invul′nera- bil′ity** *n.* —**invul′nerably** *adv.*

inward (in′wərd) *adj.* **1.** situated within **2.** mental or spiritual **3.** directed towards the inside —*adv.* **1.** towards the inside or centre **2.** into the mind or spirit Also **in′- wards** *adv.*

inwardly *adv.* **1.** in or on the inside; internally **2.** in the mind or spirit **3.** towards the inside or centre

inwardness *n.* **1.** the inner nature or meaning **2.** spirituality **3.** introspection

inwrought (in rôt′) *adj.* **1.** worked or woven into a fabric **2.** closely blended with other things

iodide (ī′ō dīd′) *n.* a compound of iodine with another element or with a radical

iodine (ī′ō dēn′) *n.* [< Gr. *ion*, violet + *eidos*, a form] **1.** a nonmetallic chemical element consisting of greyish-black crystals that volatilize into a violet-coloured vapour: used as an antiseptic, etc.: symbol, I **2.** tincture of iodine, used as an antiseptic

iodize (ī′ō dīz′) *vt.* **-dized′, -diz′ing** to treat with iodine

I.O.M. Isle of Man

ion (ī′ən) *n.* [< Gr. *ienai*, go] an electrically charged atom or group of atoms, the electrical charge of which results from a neutral atom or group of atoms losing or gaining one or more electrons —**ionic** (ī on′ik) *adj.*

-ion [< L.] *a suffix meaning* the act, condition, or result of

ion exchange a chemical process whereby ions are reversibly transferred between an insoluble solid and a fluid mixture: used in water softening, etc.

IONIC
CAPITAL

Ionic (ī on′ik) *adj.* designating or of that one of the three orders of Greek architecture distinguished by ornamental scrolls on the capitals

ionize (ī′ə nīz′) *vt., vi.* **-ized′, -iz′ing** to dissociate into ions, as a salt dissolved in water, or become electrically charged, as a gas under radiation —**i′oniza′tion** *n.*

ionosphere (ī on′ə sfēar′) *n.* the outer part of the earth's atmosphere, with an appreciable electron and ion content —**ion′- ospher′ic** *adj.*

iota (ī ōt′ə) *n.* **1.** the ninth letter of the Greek alphabet (I, ι) **2.** a very small quantity; jot

IOU, I.O.U. (ī′ō′yōō′) **1.** I owe you **2.** a signed note bearing these letters, acknowledging a debt

-ious (ē əs, yəs, əs) *a suffix used to form adjectives meaning* having, characterized by [*furious*]

I.O.W. Isle of Wight

IPA International Phonetic Alphabet

ipecac (ip′ə kak′) *n.* [< Tupi] **1.** a tropical S. American plant **2.** a preparation from the dried roots, used to induce vomiting

ipso facto (ip′sō fak′tō) [L.] by that very fact

IQ, I.Q. intelligence quotient

ir- *see* IN-¹ & IN-²

Ir *Chem.* iridium

IR, ir, i-r infrared

Ir. 1. Ireland **2.** Irish

I.R.A. Irish Republican Army

Iranian (i rā′nē ən) *adj.* of Iran, its people,

their language, or culture —*n.* one of the people of Iran; Persian

irascible (i ras′ə b'l) *adj.* [see ff.] easily angered; quick-tempered —**iras′cibil′ity** *n.* —**iras′cibly** *adv.*

irate (ī rāt′) *adj.* [< L. *ira*, ire] angry; wrathful; incensed

ire (īər) *n.* [L. *ira*] anger; wrath —**ire′ful** *adj.*

iridaceous (ir′ə dā′shəs) *adj.* [ModL. *iridaceus*] belonging to the iris family

iridescent (ir′ə des′ənt) *adj.* [< Gr. *iris*, rainbow + -ESCENT] having or showing an interplay of rainbowlike colours —**ir′i-des′cence** *n.* —**ir′ides′cently** *adv.*

iridium (ī rid′ē əm) *n.* [< Gr. *iris*, rainbow] a white, brittle, metallic chemical element found in platinum ores : symbol, Ir

IRIS

iris (ī′ris) *n.*, *pl.* **i′rises** [< Gr. *iris*, rainbow] 1. the round, pigmented membrane surrounding the pupil of the eye 2. a plant with sword-shaped leaves and showy flowers

Irish (ī′rish) *adj.* of Ireland, its people, their language, or culture —*n.* same as IRISH GAELIC —**the Irish** the people of Ireland —**I′rishman** *n.* —**I′rishwom′an** *n.fem.*

Irish bull same as BULL³

Irish coffee coffee made with Irish whiskey and cream

Irish Gaelic the Celtic language of Ireland

Irish stew a stew of mutton, potatoes, and onions

irk (ʉrk) *vt.* [ME. *irken*, be weary of] to annoy, disgust, irritate, tire out, etc.

irksome *adj.* tiresome or annoying —**irk′-somely** *adv.* —**irk′someness** *n.*

I.R.O. Inland Revenue Office

iron (ī′ərn) *n.* [OE. *iren*] 1. a white, malleable, ductile, metallic chemical element : it is the most common of all metals : symbol, Fe 2. any tool, device, etc. made of iron, as a device with a handle and flat undersurface, used, when heated, for pressing clothes 3. [*pl.*] iron shackles 4. firm strength; power 5. *Golf* any of a set of clubs with metal heads 6. a leg-support for a malformed or paralysed limb —*adj.* 1. of or consisting of iron 2. like iron; strong 3. cruel; merciless —*vt.*, *vi.* to press (clothes or cloth) with a hot iron —**have many** (or **several,** etc.) **irons in the fire** to be engaged in many (or several, etc.) activities —**iron**

out to smooth out —**strike while the iron is hot** to act at the opportune time

Iron Age a phase of human culture characterized by the use of iron tools, weapons, etc.

ironclad *adj.* covered or protected with iron —*n.* formerly, a warship armoured with thick iron plates

Iron Curtain a barrier of secrecy and censorship regarded as isolating the Soviet Union, etc.

iron hand firm, rigorous control —**i′ron-hand′ed** *adj.*

iron horse [Old Colloq.] a railway engine

ironical (ī ron′i k'l) *adj.* [see IRONY] 1. meaning the contrary of what is expressed 2. using irony 3. opposite to what might be expected Also **iron′ic**

ironing board (or **table**) a cloth-covered board or stand on which clothes are ironed

iron lung a large metal respirator enclosing all the body but the head, used for maintaining artificial respiration

Iron Maiden a former instrument of torture consisting of a case in the form of a woman, with spikes inside

ironmaster *n.* a manufacturer of iron

ironmonger *n.* a dealer in hardware —**i′-ronmon′gery** *n.*

iron pyrites same as PYRITE

iron rations emergency food supplies

ironsides *n.pl.* [with *sing. v.*] same as IRONCLAD

ironstone *n.* 1. any rock rich in iron 2. a hard variety of white ceramic ware

ironware *n.* things made of iron

iron-wood *n.* a name for the exceptionally hard wood of various S African trees, or the trees themselves

ironwork *n.* articles or parts made of iron

ironworks *n.pl.* [often with *sing. v.*] a place where iron is smelted or heavy iron goods are made

irony¹ (ī′ə rə nē) *n.*, *pl.* **-nies** [< Gr. *eirōn*, dissembler in speech] 1. expression in which the intended meaning of the words is the opposite of their usual sense 2. an event or a result that is the opposite of what might be expected

irony² (ī′ər nē) *adj.* of, like, or containing iron

irradiate (i rā′dē āt′) *vt.* -at′ed, -at′ing [see IN-¹ & RADIATE] 1. to shine upon; light up 2. to expose to X-rays, ultraviolet rays, etc. 3. to enlighten 4. to radiate —**irra′diance, irra′diancy** *n.* —**irra′dia′-tion** *n.*

irrational (i rash′ən 'l) *adj.* 1. lacking the power to reason 2. senseless; absurd 3. *Math.* designating a real number not expressible as an integer or a quotient of two integers —**irra′tional′ity** (-ə nal′ə tē) *n.*

irreconcilable (i rek′ən sīl′ə b'l) *adj.* that cannot be brought into agreement; incompatible —**irrec′oncil′abil′ity** *n.* —**irrec′oncil′ably** *adv.*

irrecoverable (ir′i kuv′ər ə b'l) *adj.* that cannot be recovered, rectified, or remedied —**ir′recov′erably** *adv.*

irredeemable (ir′i dēm′ə b'l) *adj.* 1. that

cannot be bought back **2.** that cannot be converted into coin, as certain paper money **3.** that cannot be reformed

irredentist (ir´i den´tist) *n.* [< It. (*Italia*) *irredenta*, unredeemed (Italy)] a person who advocates a policy of recovering territory formerly a part of his country

irreducible (ir´i dyōōs´ə b'l) *adj.* that cannot be reduced —**ir´reduc´ibil´ity** *n.* —**ir´reduc´ibly** *adv.*

irrefutable (i ref´yoo tə b'l) *adj.* that cannot be refuted or disproved —**irref´utably** *adv.*

irreg. **1.** irregular **2.** irregularly

irregular (i reg´yoo lər) *adj.* **1.** not straight or even; not uniform in shape, design, etc. **2.** uneven in occurrence; variable **3.** not conforming to established rule, standard, etc. **4.** *Gram.* not inflected in the usual way [*go* is an *irregular* verb] **5.** *Mil.* not belonging to the regularly established army —*n.* a person or thing that is irregular —**irreg´ular´ity** (-lar´ə tē) *n.* —**irreg´ularly** *adv.*

irrelevant (i rel´ə vənt) *adj.* not pertinent; not to the point —**irrel´evance, irrel´evancy** *n.*

irreligious (ir´i lij´əs) *adj.* **1.** not religious **2.** indifferent or hostile to religion **3.** profane; impious —**ir´reli´gion n.** —**ir´reli´gionist** *n.* —**ir´reli´giously** *adv.*

irremediable (ir´i mē´dē ə b'l) *adj.* that cannot be remedied; incurable —**ir´reme´diably** *adv.*

irremissible (ir´i mis´ə b'l) *adj.* that cannot be excused, pardoned, or shirked —**ir´remis´sibly** *adv.*

irremovable (ir´i mōō´və b'l) *adj.* not removable —**ir´remov´abil´ity** *n.* —**ir´remov´ably** *adv.*

irreparable (i rep´ər ə b'l) *adj.* that cannot be repaired, mended, remedied, etc. —**irrep´arably** *adv.*

irreplaceable (ir´i plās´ə b'l) *adj.* not replaceable

irrepressible (ir´i pres´ə b'l) *adj.* that cannot be repressed —**ir´repress´ibil´ity** *n.* —**ir´repress´ibly** *adv.*

irreproachable (ir´i prō´chə b'l) *adj.* blameless; faultless —**ir´reproach´abil´ity** *n.* —**ir´reproach´ably** *adv.*

irresistible (ir´i zis´tə b'l) *adj.* that cannot be resisted; too strong, fascinating, etc. to be withstood —**ir´resist´ibil´ity, ir´-resist´ibleness** *n.* —**ir´resist´ibiy** *adv.*

irresolute (i rez´ə lōōt´) *adj.* wavering in decision or purpose —**irres´olute´iy** *adv.* —**irres´olu´tion** *n.*

irrespective (ir´i spek´tiv) *adj.* regardless (*of*) —**ir´respec´tively** *adv.*

irresponsible (ir´i spon´sə b'l) *adj.* **1.** showing the lack of a sense of responsibility **2.** not accountable for actions —**ir´respon´-sibly** *adv.*

irretrievable (ir´i trēv´ə b'l) *adj.* that cannot be retrieved, recovered, restored, or recalled —**ir´retriev´ably** *adv.*

irreverence (i rev´ər əns) *n.* **1.** lack of reverence **2.** an act or statement showing this —**irrev´erent** *adj.* —**irrev´erently** *adv.*

irreversible (ir´i vur´sə b'l) *adj.* **1.** that

cannot be repealed or annulled **2.** that cannot be run backwards, etc. —**ir´revers´i-bil´ity** *n.* —**ir´revers´ibly** *adv.*

irrevocable (i rev´ə kə b'l) *adj.* that cannot be revoked or undone —**irrev´oca-bil´ity, irrev´ocableness** *n.*

irrigable (ir´i gə b'l) *adj.* that can be irrigated

irrigate (ir´ə gāt´) *vt.* **-gat´ed, -gat´ing** [< L. *in-*, in + *rigare*, water] **1.** to supply (land) with water by means of artificial ditches, etc. **2.** *Med.* to wash out continually —**ir´riga´tion** *n.* —**ir´riga´-tor** *n.*

irritable (ir´i tə b'l) *adj.* **1.** easily annoyed or provoked **2.** *Med.* excessively sensitive to a stimulus **3.** *Physiol.* able to respond to a stimulus —**ir´ritabil´ity, ir´ritable-ness** *n.*

irritant *adj.* causing irritation —*n.* something causing irritation —**ir´ritancy** *n.*

irritate (ir´ə tāt´) *vt.* **-tat´ed, -tat´ing** [< L. *irritare*, excite] **1.** to provoke to impatience or anger **2.** to make (a part of the body) inflamed or sore **3.** *Physiol.* to excite (an organ, muscle, etc.) —**ir´rita´tion** *n.* —**ir´rita´tive** *adj.*

irrupt (i rupt´) *vi.* [< L. *in-*, in + *rumpere*, break] to burst violently (*into*) —**irrup´-tion** *n.* —**irrup´tive** *adj.*

is (iz) [OE.] *3rd pers. sing., pres. indic.,* of BE

is. **1.** island(s) **2.** isle(s)

Isa., Is. Isaiah

I.S.B.N. International Standard Book Number

-ise (īz) *var. of* -IZE

-ish (ish) [OE. *-isc*] *a suffix meaning:* a) of (a specified people) [*Spanish*] b) like [*devilish*] c) tending to [*bookish*] d) somewhat, rather [*tallish*] e) [Colloq.] approximately [*thirtyish*]

isinglass (ī´ziŋ glas´) *n.* [prob. < MDu. *huizen*, sturgeon + *blas*, bladder] **1.** a form of gelatin prepared from fish bladders **2.** mica, esp. in thin sheets

isl. *pl.* **isls.** **1.** island **2.** isle

Islam (iz´läm) *n.* [Ar. *islām*, submission (to God)] **1.** the Moslem religion, a monotheistic religion whose founder is Mohammed **2.** Moslems collectively **3.** all the lands in which the Moslem religion predominates —**Islam´ic** (-lam´-) *adj.* —**Is´lamism** (iz´ləm iz´m) *n.*

island (ī´lənd) *n.* [< OE. *igland*, lit., island land] **1.** a land mass not as large as a continent, surrounded by water **2.** anything like an island in position or isolation

island authority a local government administrative area of Scotland

islander *n.* a native or inhabitant of an island

isle (īl) *n.* [L. *insula*] an island, esp. a small one

islet (ī´lit) *n.* a very small island

ism (iz´m) *n.* a doctrine, theory, system, etc., esp. one whose name ends in *-ism*

-ism (iz´m; iz əm) [< Gr. *-ismos*] *a suffix meaning:* **1.** the act or result of [*terrorism*] **2.** the condition, conduct, or qualities characteristic of [*patriotism*] **3.** the theory of [*socialism*] **4.** devotion to [*nationalism*] **5.** an instance of [*witticism*] **6.** an abnormal condition caused by [*alcoholism*]

iso- [< Gr.] *a combining form meaning* equal, similar

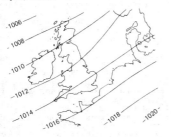

ISOBARS

isobar (ī′sō bär′) *n.* [< prec. + Gr. *baros*, weight] a line on a map connecting points having equal barometric pressure

isochronal (ī sok′rə n'l) *adj.* [< Gr. *isos*, equal + *chronos*, time] **1.** equal in length of time **2.** occurring at equal intervals of time Also **isoch′ronous —isoch′ro-nism** *n.*

isolate (ī′sə lāt′) *vt.* **-lat′ed, -lat′ing** [< It. *isola* (< L. *insula*), island] **1.** to set apart from others **2.** *Chem.* to separate (an element or compound) in pure form from another compound or mixture **3.** *Med.* to place (a patient with a contagious disease) apart from others **—i′solable** *adj.* **—i′sola′tion** *n.* **—i′sola′tor** *n.*

isolationist (ī′sə lā′shən ist) *n.* one who opposes the involvement of his country in international agreements, etc. **—adj.** of isolationists

isomer (ī′sō mər) *n.* [< Gr. *isos*, equal + *meros*, part] any of two or more chemical compounds having the same elements in the same proportion by weight but differing in properties because of differences in the structure of their molecules **—i′somer′ic** (-mer′ik) *adj.* **—isomerism** (ī som′ər iz'm) *n.*

isometric (ī′sō met′rik) *adj.* [< Gr. *isos*, equal + *metron*, measure] **1.** having equality of measure **2.** of isometrics **—n.** [*pl.*] exercises in which one set of muscles is briefly tensed in opposition to another set of muscles or to an immovable object **—i′somet′rically** *adv.*

isomorphic (ī′sō môr′fik) *adj.* [ISO- + Gr. *morphē*, form] having similar or identical structure: also **i′somor′phous**

isomorphism *n.* [ISO- + Gr. *morphē*, form] **1.** *Biol.* a similarity in organisms belonging to different species **2.** *Chem.* an identity or similarity in the crystalline form of substances of different elements **—i′somorph′n.**

ISOSCELES TRIANGLES

isosceles (ī sos′ə lēz′) *adj.* [< Gr. *isos*, equal + *skelos*, leg] designating a triangle with two equal sides

isotherm (ī′sō thurm′) *n.* [< ISO- + Gr. *thermē*, heat] a line on a map connecting points having the same mean temperature or the same temperature at a given time **—i′sother′mal** *adj.*

isotope (ī′sō tōp′) *n.* [< ISO- + Gr. *topos*, place] any of two or more forms of an element having the same atomic number but different atomic weights [*uranium isotopes* U 235, U 238, U 239] **—i′sotop′-ic** (-top′ik) *adj.*

isotropic (ī′sō trop′ik) *adj.* [ISO- + Gr. *trepein*, to turn] having physical properties, as conductivity, elasticity, etc., that are the same regardless of the direction of measurement **—isot′ropy** *n.*

I spy a children's guessing game **—I spy strangers** a demand for all but members and officials of the House of Commons to leave

Israel (iz′rā əl) *n.* [< Heb. *yisrā'ēl*, contender with God] **1.** the modern Jewish state **2.** the Jewish people, as descendants of Jacob **3.** their ancient land

Israelite (iz′rēə əlīt′) *n.* any of the people of ancient Israel or their descendants; Jew; Hebrew **—adj.** of ancient Israel or the Israelites

issue (ish′$\overline{oo}$) *n.* [< L. *ex-*, out + *ire*, go] **1.** a sending or giving out **2.** *a)* all that is put forth and circulated at one time [*an issue* of shares] *b)* an edition [the May *issue*] **3.** an outgoing; outflow **4.** an exit; outlet **5.** offspring **6.** a point or matter under dispute **7.** a result; consequence **8.** *Med.* a discharge of blood, etc. **—vi. -sued, -suing 1.** to go or flow out; emerge **2.** to result (*from*) or end (*in*) **3.** to be published **—vt. 1.** to let out; discharge **2.** to give or deal out [to *issue* supplies] **3.** to publish **—at** (or in) **issue** in dispute **—join issue** to meet in conflict, etc. **—take issue** to disagree **—is′suable** *adj.* **—is′suer** *n.*

-ist (ist, əst) [< Gr.] *a suffix meaning:* **1.** one who does, makes, or practises [*satirist*] **2.** one occupied with [*chemist, violinist*] **3.** an adherent of [*anarchist*]

isthmus (is′məs) *n., pl.* **-muses, -mi** (-mī) [< Gr. *isthmos*, neck] a narrow strip of land having water at each side and connecting two bodies of land **—isth′mian** *adj.*

-istic (is′tik) [< Gr.] *a suffix used to form adjectives from nouns ending in* -ISM *and* -IST

it[1] (it) *pron.* for *pl.* see THEY [OE. *hit*]

the animal or thing under discussion *It* is used as : *a)* the subject of an impersonal verb *[it* is snowing *] b)* the subject of a clause of which the actual subject is a following clause, etc. *[it* is settled that he will go *] c)* a subject or object of indefinite sense *[it's* all right, to lord *it* over someone *] d)* the antecedent to a relative pronoun from which it is separated by a predicate *[it* is your car that I want *] e)* [Colloq.] an emphatic predicate pronoun referring to something ultimate or perfect *[this* is *it] —n.* the player, as in the game of tag, who must do some specific thing —**that's it** [Colloq.] that is : *a)* the difficulty *b)* the end *[that's it* for today *] c)* exactly what is required —**with it** [Slang] alert, informed, or hip

it² *n.* [contr. < *Italian*] [Colloq.] Italian vermouth

It., Ital. 1. Italian 2. Italic 3. Italy

I.T.A. Independent Television Authority

i.t.a. initial teaching alphabet

ital. italic (type)

Italian (i tal'yən) *adj.* of Italy, its people, their language, etc. —*n.* 1. a native or inhabitant of Italy 2. the language of the Italians

Italianate *adj.* of Italian form or character

Italic (i tal'ik) *adj.* of ancient Italy, its people, etc.

italic (i tal'ik) *adj.* [< its first use in *Italy*] designating or of a type in which the characters slant upwards to the right *[this* is *italic type] —n.* [usually *pl.*] italic type or print

italicize (i tal'ə sīz') *vt.* **-cized', -ciz'ing** to print in italics

itch (ich) *vi.* [OE. *giccan*] 1. to feel an irritating sensation on the skin 2. to have a restless desire —*n.* 1. an itching on the skin 2. a restless desire —**itching palm** greediness for money —**the itch** a skin disorder accompanied by severe irritation of the skin —**itch'y** *adj.*

-ite (īt) [< Gr.] *a suffix meaning :* 1. an inhabitant of *[suburbanite]* 2. a descendant from *[Israelite]* 3. an adherent of *[Luddite]* 4. a manufactured product *[dynamite]* 5. a (specified) mineral or rock *[anthracite]*

item (īt'əm) *n.* [< L. *ita,* so, thus] i. an article; unit; separate thing 2. a bit of news or information —*adv.* also : used before each article in a series being enumerated

itemize *vt.* **-ized', -iz'ing** to specify the items of; set down by items *[itemize* the bill *] —i'temiza'tion* *n.*

iterate (it'ə rāt') *vt.* **-at'ed, -at'ing** [< L. *iterum,* again *]* to utter or do repeatedly —**it'era'tion** *n.* —**it'era'tive** *adj.*

itinerant (ī tin'ər ənt) *adj.* [< L. *iter,* a walk *]* travelling from place to place or on a circuit —*n.* a person who travels from place to place —**itin'erantly** *adv.*

itinerary (ī tin'ə rər ē) *n., pl.* **-aries** [see prec.] 1. a route 2. a record of a journey 3. a detailed plan for a journey —*adj.* of travelling, routes, or roads

-ition (ish'ən) [< L.] *var.* of -ATION *[nutrition]*

-itis (īt'əs, -is) [< Gr.] *a suffix meaning* inflammation of

it'll (it''l) 1. it will 2. it shall

its (its) *pron.* that or those belonging to it —*possessive pronominal adj.* of, belonging to, or done by it

it's (its) 1. it is 2. it has

itself (it self') *pron.* a form of the 3rd pers. sing., neuter pronoun, used : *a)* as an intensive *[the* work *itself* is easy *] b)* as a reflexive *[the* dog bit *itself] c)* as a quasi-noun meaning "its true self" *[the* bird is not *itself* today *]*

ITV Independent Television

-ity (ə tē, i-) [< L.] *a suffix meaning* state, condition

IUD intrauterine (contraceptive) device : also **IUCD**

I've (īv) I have

-ive (iv) [< L.] *a suffix meaning :* 1. of, relating to, having the nature of *[substantive]* 2. tending to *[creative]*

ivory (ī'vər ē) *n., pl.* **-ries** [< L. *ebur,* ivory *]* 1. the hard, white substance forming the tusks of elephants, walruses, etc. 2. any substance like ivory 3. creamy white 4. [*pl.*] [Slang] *a)* piano keys *b)* teeth *c)* dice —*adj.* 1. of or like ivory 2. creamy-white

ivory tower figuratively, a place of mental withdrawal from reality and action

ivy (ī'vē) *n., pl.* **i'vies** [OE. *ifig]* 1. a climbing plant with a woody stem and evergreen leaves 2. any of various similar plants, as ground ivy, poison ivy, etc.

ixia (ik'sē ə) *n.* [< Gr. *ixos,* birdlime *]* a South African plant related to the iris

-ization (ə zā'shən, ī-) *a suffix used to form nouns from verbs ending in* -IZE *[realization]*

-ize (īz) [< Gr.] *a suffix meaning :* 1. to cause to be; make *[democratize]* 2. to become like *[crystallize]* 3. to treat or combine with *[oxidize]* 4. to engage in *[theorize]*

J

J, j (jā) *n.*, *pl.* **J's, j's** the tenth letter of the English alphabet

J *Physics the symbol for* joule

jab (jab) *vt.*, *vi.* **jabbed, jab′bing** [< ME. *jobben*, peck] to poke or thrust, as with a sharp instrument —*n.* **1.** a quick thrust, blow, or punch **2.** [Colloq.] an injection

jabber (jab′ər) *vi.*, *vt.* [prob. echoic] to speak or say quickly, incoherently, or nonsensically; chatter —*n.* fast, incoherent, nonsensical talk —**jab′berer** *n.*

jabot (zha′bō) *n.* [Fr., bird's crop] a frill, as of lace, attached to the front of a blouse or shirt

jacinth (jas′inth) *n.* [see HYACINTH] a reddish-orange or brownish gem

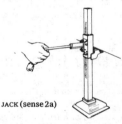

JACK (sense 2a)

jack (jak) *n.* [< name] **1.** [often J-] a man or boy **2.** *a)* any of various devices used to lift something heavy a short distance *b)* a device for turning a spit **3.** any of various fishes, as the pickerel, pike, etc. **4.** *Elec.* a socket for receiving a plug (**jack plug**) **5.** *Games a)* a playing card with a pageboy's picture on it *b)* any of the small pebbles or metal pieces used in playing jacks *c)* in the game of bowls, the target ball **6.** *Naut.* a small flag flown on a ship's bow as a signal or to show nationality —*vt.* to raise by means of a jack —**before you could say Jack Robinson** suddenly; very quickly —**every man jack** everyone —**jack in** [Colloq.] to abandon (an activity) —**jack up 1.** to raise by means of a jack **2.** [Colloq.] to raise (prices, etc.)

jack- [see prec.] *a combining form meaning:* **1.** male [*jackass*] **2.** large or strong [*jackboot*] **3.** boy; fellow

jackal (jak′ôl) *n.* [< Per. *shagāl*] **1.** a yellowish-grey wild dog of Asia and N Africa **2.** one who does dishonest or humiliating tasks for another

jackanapes (jak′ə nāps′) *n.* [< nickname of a Duke of Suffolk] a conceited, insolent fellow

jackaroo, jackeroo (jak′ə rōō′) *n.* [JACK- + (KANG)AROO] [Aust.] a novice on a sheep station

jackass (jak′as′) *n.* [JACK- + ASS] **1.** a male donkey **2.** a stupid or foolish person; nitwit

jackboot *n.* [JACK- + BOOT¹] **1.** a sturdy boot that reaches above the knee **2.** oppressive behaviour

jackdaw (jak′dô′) *n.* [JACK- + ME. *dawe*] a European black bird related to the crow, but smaller

jacket (jak′it) *n.* [< OFr. < proper name *Jacques*] **1.** a short coat **2.** an outer covering; specif., *a) same as* DUST JACKET *b)* the insulating casing on a boiler, etc. *c)* the skin of a potato, etc.

Jack Frost frost or cold weather personified

jack-in-office *n.*, *pl.* **jacks-** an official with a high opinion of his own importance

jack-in-the-box *pl.* **-box′es** a box from which a toy figure on a spring jumps up when the lid is lifted

jackknife *n.*, *pl.* **-knives** [JACK- + KNIFE] **1.** a large pocketknife **2.** a dive in which the diver keeps his knees unbent, touches his feet, and then straightens out; forward pike dive —*vi.* **-knifed′, -knif′ing 1.** to turn on the coupling so as to form a sharp angle: said of a vehicle and its trailer **2.** to bend at the middle as in a jackknife dive

jack-of-all-trades *n.*, *pl.* **jacks-** [often J-] a person who can do many kinds of work acceptably; handyman

jack-o'-lantern *n.*, *pl.* **-terns 1.** a shifting, elusive light seen over marshes at night **2.** a hollow pumpkin used as a lantern

jackpot (jak′pot′) *n.* [JACK + POT] cumulative stakes, as in a poker game, slot machine, etc. —**hit the jackpot** [Slang] **1.** to win the jackpot **2.** to attain the highest success

jack rabbit a large hare of W N America, with long ears and strong hind legs

jacks (jaks) *n.pl.* [< JACKSTONE] [*with sing. v.*] a game in which pebbles or small metal pieces are tossed and picked up, esp. while bouncing a small ball

jackstone *n.* [for dial. *checkstone*, pebble] **1.** *same as* JACK (*n.* 5 *b*) **2.** [*pl.*, *with sing. v.*] *same as* JACKS

jack-tar *n.* [JACK + TAR²] [often J-] a sailor

Jacobean (jak′ə bē′ən) *adj.* [< *Jacobus*, Latinized form of *James*] of the period when James I was king of England (1603-1625) —*n.* a person of this period

Jacobin (jak′ə bin) *n.* [< the Church of

St. *Jacques* in Paris] **1.** any member of a society of radical democrats in France during the Revolution of 1789 **2.** a political radical

Jacobite (jak′ə bīt′) *n.* [see JACOBEAN] a supporter of James II of England after his abdication, or of his descendants' claims to the throne —**Jac′obitism** *n.*

Jacquard (ja′kärd′) *n.* [< J. M. *Jacquard*] a loom having an endless belt of cards punched with holes arranged to produce a figured weave (**Jacquard weave**)

jade[1] (jād) *n.* [Fr. < Sp. *ijada*, side: from the belief that it cured pains in the side] **1.** a hard, ornamental stone, usually green **2.** a green colour of medium hue

jade[2] *n.* [< ON. *jalda*, a mare] **1.** a horse, esp. a worn-out, worthless one **2.** a disreputable woman

jaded (jā′did) *adj.* **1.** tired; worn-out **2.** satiated

Jaffa (jaf′ə) *n.* [< *Jaffa*, in Israel] a kind of large orange or grapefruit with a thick skin, grown in Israel

jag[1] (jag) *n.* [ME. *jagge*] a sharp, toothlike projection —*vt.* **jagged, jag′ging** to notch or prick (cloth, etc.)

jag[2] *n.* [< ?] [Slang] **1.** a drunken spree **2.** a period of uncontrolled activity [a crying *jag*]

jagged (jag′id) *adj.* having sharp projecting points or notches —**jag′gedly** *adv.* —**jag′gedness** *n.*

jaguar (jag′yoo wər) *n.* [Port. < Tupi] a large cat, yellowish with black spots, found from SW U.S. to Argentina: it is similar to the leopard, but larger

jail (jāl) *n.* [ult. < L. *cavea*, cage] **1.** a prison **2.** imprisonment —*vt.* to put or keep in jail

jailbird *n.* [Colloq.] a person who has often been in jail

jailer, jailor *n.* a person in charge of a jail or of prisoners

jail fever typhus, formerly common in jails

jalap (jal′əp) *n.* [< Sp. *Jalapa*, in Mexico] the dried root of a Mexican plant, formerly used as a purgative

jalopy (jə lop′ē) *n.*, *pl.* **-lop′ies** [< ?] [Slang] an old, ramshackle motor car

jalousie (zhal′oo zē′) *n.* [see JEALOUS] a window, blind, or door formed of adjustable, horizontal slats

jam[1] (jam) *vt.* **jammed, jam′ming** [< ?] **1.** to squeeze into a confined space **2.** to crush **3.** to crowd **4.** to fill or block (a passageway, etc.) by crowding in **5.** to wedge so that it cannot move **6.** to make (radio or radar signals) unintelligible, as by sending out others on the same wavelength —*vi.* **1.** to become wedged or stuck fast, esp. so as to become unworkable **2.** to push against one another in a confined space **3.** [Slang] *Jazz* to improvise —*n.* **1.** a jamming or being jammed **2.** a group of persons or things blocking a passageway, etc. [a traffic *jam*] **3.** [Colloq.] a difficult situation —**jam on** to apply suddenly [to *jam* on the brakes]

jam[2] *n.* [< ? prec.] a food made by boiling fruit with sugar to a thick mixture

—**jam tomorrow** a promise of some pleasant future event that often does not occur

jamb (jam) *n.* [< LL. *gamba*, leg] a side post of an opening for a door, window, etc.

jamboree (jam′bə rē′) *n.* [< ?] **1.** a large assembly of boy scouts **2.** [Colloq.] a boisterous party or revel

jammy (jam′ē) *adj.* **1.** of, like, or smeared with jam **2.** [Slang] lucky; excellent [*jammy* beggar]

jampacked (jam′pakt′) *adj.* tightly packed

jam session an informal gathering of jazz musicians to play improvisations

Jan. January

jangle (jaŋ′g'l) *vi.* **-gled, -gling** [< OFr. *jangler*] to make a harsh, inharmonious sound —*vt.* **1.** to cause to make a harsh sound **2.** to irritate [to *jangle* one's nerves] —*n.* a harsh sound —**jan′gler** *n.*

janitor (jan′i tər) *n.* [L., doorkeeper] the caretaker of a building —**jan′ito′rial** (-ə tôr′ē əl) *adj.*

janizary (jan′i zar ē) *n.*, *pl.* **-zaries** [< Turk. *yeni*, new + *cheri*, soldiery] [often J-] a Turkish soldier, orig. one in the former sultan's guard: also **jan′issary**

January (jan′yoo wər ē) *n.*, *pl.* **-aries** [< L. *Januarius* (*mensis*), (the month) of Janus] the first month of the year, having 31 days: abbrev. **Jan.**

japan (jə pan′) *n.* [orig. from Japan] a varnish giving a hard, glossy finish —*vt.* **-panned′, -pan′ning** to varnish with japan

Japanese (jap′ə nēz′) *adj.* of Japan, its people, language, culture, etc. —*n.*, *pl.* **-nese** a native of Japan **2.** the language of Japan

jape (jāp) *vi.* **japed, jap′ing** [ME. *japen*] **1.** to joke **2.** to play tricks —*n.* **1.** a joke **2.** a trick —**jap′ery** *n.*

japonica (jə pon′i kə) *n.* [< Fr. *Japon*, Japan] an ornamental variety of quince used as a garden shrub

jar[1] (jär) *vi.* **jarred, jar′ring** [ult. echoic] **1.** to vibrate from a sudden impact **2.** to make a harsh sound; grate **3.** to have a harsh, irritating effect (*on* one) **4.** to clash or quarrel —*vt.* to jolt or shock —*n.* **1.** a jolt or shock **2.** a vibration due to a sudden impact **3.** a harsh, grating sound **4.** a sharp clash or quarrel

jar[2] *n.* [< Ar. *jarrah*, earthen container] **1.** a container made of glass, stone, or earthenware, with a large opening and no spout **2.** as much as a jar will hold: also **jar′ful** **3.** [Colloq.] a glass of beer, etc.

jar[3] *n.* [see AJAR[1]] only in **on the jar**, ajar

jardinière (jär′di nyâer′) *n.* [< Fr. *jardin*, garden] **1.** an ornamental bowl or stand for flowers or plants **2.** a garnish of several vegetables cooked separately

jargon (jär′gən) *n.* [MFr., a chattering] **1.** the specialized vocabulary and idioms of those in the same work, profession, etc. **2.** incoherent speech; gibberish

Jas. James

jasmine, jasmin (jas′min) *n.* [< Per.

yásamín] a tropical and subtropical plant with fragrant flowers of yellow, red, or white

jasper (jas′pər) *n.* [< Gr. *iaspis*] an opaque variety of coloured quartz, usually reddish, yellow, or brown

jaundice (jôn′dis) *n.* [ult. < L. *galbus,* yellow] **1.** a diseased condition in which the eyeballs, skin, and urine become abnormally yellow as a result of bile in the blood **2.** bitterness or prejudice caused by envy, etc. —*vt.* **-diced, -dicing 1.** to make bitter or prejudiced through envy, etc. **2.** to cause to have jaundice

jaunt (jônt) *vi.* [< ?] to take a short trip for pleasure —*n.* such a trip; excursion

jaunting car a light, two-wheeled cart used in Ireland

jaunty *adj.* **-tier, -tiest** [< Fr. *gentil,* genteel] **1.** fashionable; chic **2.** gay and carefree; sprightly —**jaun′tily** *adv.* —**jaun′tiness** *n.*

Javanese (jäv′ənēz′) *adj.* of Java —*n.* **1.** *pl.* **-nese′** a native of Java **2.** the language of Java

javelin (jav′lin) *n.* [< MFr. *javelot,* a spear] a light spear, esp. one thrown in athletics

jaw (jô) *n.* [< ? OFr. *joue,* cheek] **1.** either of the two bony parts that hold the teeth and frame the mouth **2.** either of two parts that grip or crush something, as in a vice **3.** [*pl.*] the mouth *b)* the entrance of a canyon, valley, etc. **4.** [*pl.*] something grasping [the *jaws* of death] **5.** [Slang] talk; esp., boring talk —*vi.* [Slang] to talk, esp. in a boring way —*vt.* [Slang] to scold

jawbone *n.* a bone of a jaw, esp. of the lower jaw

jay (jā) *n.* [< LL. *gaius,* jay] **1.** a noisy bird with gay blue and black plumage **2.** [Colloq.] a stupid or foolish person

jaywalk *vi.* [JAY + WALK] [Colloq.] to walk in or across a street carelessly without obeying traffic rules and signals —**jay′walk′er** *n.* —**jay′walk′ing** *n.*

jazz (jaz) *n.* [< ? Creole patois *jass,* sexual term] **1.** a kind of music characterized by syncopation, melodic variations, and unusual tonal effects **2.** [Slang] rigmarole; paraphernalia [all that *jazz*] —*adj.* of, in, or like jazz —*vt.* **1.** to play as jazz **2.** [Slang] to enliven or embellish (usually with *up*)

jazzy *adj.* **-ier, -iest** [Colloq.] **1.** of or like jazz music **2.** gaudy or flashy

jealous (jel′əs) *adj.* [< ML. *zelosus,* zeal] **1.** *a)* resentfully suspicious, as of a rival *b)* resentfully envious *c)* resulting from such feelings [a *jealous* rage] **2.** watchful in guarding [*jealous* of one's rights] **3.** [Now Rare] requiring exclusive loyalty [a *jealous* God] —**jeal′ously** *adv.* —**jeal′ousness** *n.*

jealousy *n., pl.* **-ousies 1.** the quality or condition of being jealous **2.** an instance of this; jealous feeling

jean (jēn) *n.* [< L. *Genua,* Genoa] **1.** a twilled cotton cloth **2.** [*pl.*] trousers of this material or of denim

Jean Baptiste (zhȧn bap tēst′) [Canad. Slang] a French Canadian

jeep (jēp) *n.* [< creature in a comic strip by E. C. Segar] a small, rugged vehicle with a four-wheel drive

jeer (jēər) *vt., vi.* [< ? CHEER] to make fun of in a rude, sarcastic manner; scoff (at) —*n.* a sarcastic or derisive comment —**jeer′er** *n.* —**jeer′ingly** *adv.*

Jehovah (ji hō′və) [< Heb.] God; (the) Lord

Jehovah's Witnesses a proselytizing Christian sect founded by Charles T. Russell (1852–1916)

jejune (ji jōōn′) *adj.* [L. *jejunus,* empty] **1.** not mature; childish **2.** not interesting or satisfying

Jekyll and Hyde (jek′l′n hīd′) [< novel by R. L. Stevenson] a person with two distinct personalities, esp. one good and one evil

jell (jel) *vi.* [< JELLY] **1.** to become jelly **2.** [Colloq.] to take definite form; crystallize [the plans didn't *jell*]

jellaba (jə la′bə) *n.* [Ar. *jallabah*] a long, loose, outer garment worn by many Arab men

jellify (jel′ə fī′) *vt., vi.* **-fied′, -fy′ing** to change into jelly

jelly (jel′ē) *n., pl.* **-lies** [< L. *gelare,* freeze] **1.** a soft, gelatinous food made from cooked fruit syrup or meat juice **2.** any substance like this —*vt.* **-lied, -lying 1.** to make into jelly **2.** to coat or serve with jelly —*vi.* to become jelly

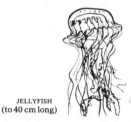

JELLYFISH
(to 40 cm long)

jellyfish *n.* an invertebrate sea animal with an umbrella-shaped body of jellylike substance and long tentacles with stinging cells on them

jemmy (jem′ē) *n., pl.* **-mies** [< James] a short crowbar, used by burglars to pry open windows, etc.

jenny (jen′ē) *n., pl.* **-nies** [< Jenny] **1.** *short for* SPINNING JENNY **2.** *a)* the female of some birds [a *jenny* wren] *b)* a female donkey

jeopardize (jep′ər dīz′) *vt.* **-ized′, -iz′ing** to put in jeopardy; endanger

jeopardy (jep′ər dē) *n., pl.* **-ies** [< OFr. *jeu parti,* a game with even chances] great danger; peril

Jer. Jeremiah

jerbil (jur′b′l) *n.* *same as* GERBIL

jerboa (jur bō′ə) *n.* [Ar. *yarbū*′] a small,

nocturnal, leaping rodent of Africa and Asia, with long hind legs

jeremiad (jer′ə mī′əd) *n.* a lamentation or tale of woe: in allusion to the *Lamentations of Jeremiah*

jerepigo (jer′ə pig ō) *n.* [S Afr.] a sweet, sherry-type wine, white or red

jerk¹ (jurk) *vt.* [< ?] to pull, twist, push, or throw with a sudden, sharp movement —*vi.* 1. to move with a jerk 2. to twitch —*n.* 1. a sharp, abrupt pull, twist, etc. 2. a sudden muscular contraction 3. [Slang] a person regarded as stupid, foolish, etc.

jerk² *vt.* [< Sp. *charqui*] to preserve (meat) by slicing into strips and drying in the sun

jerkin (jur′kin) *n.* [< ?] a sleeveless jacket

jerky *adj.* **-ier, -iest** making sudden starts and stops; spasmodic —**jerk′ily** *adv.* —**jerk′iness** *n.*

Jerry (jer′ē) *n.* [< GERMAN] [Slang] 1. a German, esp. a German soldier 2. the Germans collectively

jerrybuilt (jer′ē bilt′) *adj.* [prob. < name *Jerry,* infl. by JURY²] built poorly, of cheap materials

Jersey (jur′zē) *n., pl.* **-seys** [< *Jersey,* in the Channel Islands] 1. any of a breed of small, reddish-brown dairy cattle, originally from Jersey 2. [j-] a) a soft, elastic, knitted cloth b) any closefitting, knitted upper garment

Jerusalem artichoke (jə rōō′sə ləm) [altered after *Jerusalem*) < It. *girasole,* sunflower] a tall N American sunflower with edible potatolike tubers

jest (jest) *n.* [< L. *gerere,* perform] 1. a joke 2. fun; joking [said in *jest*] 3. something to be laughed at —*vi.* to joke

jester *n.* one who jests; esp., a professional fool employed by a medieval ruler to amuse him

Jesuit (jez′yoo wit) *n.* a member of the Society of Jesus, a Roman Catholic religious order for men founded by Ignatius Loyola in 1534 —**Jes′uit′ical** *adj.*

Jesus (jē′zəs) *n.* [< Heb. *yēhōshu'a,* help of Jehovah] the founder of the Christian religion: also called **Jesus Christ, Jesus of Nazareth**

jet¹ (jet) *vt., vi.* **jet′ted, jet′ting** [< L. *jacere,* throw] 1. to gush out in a stream 2. to travel or convey by jet aircraft —*n.* 1. a stream of liquid or gas emitted, as from a spout 2. a spout for emitting a jet 3. a jet-propelled aeroplane: in full, **jet (aero)plane** —*adj.* 1. jet-propelled 2. of jet propulsion or jet-propelled aircraft

jet² *n.* [< Gr. *Gagas,* town in Asia Minor] 1. a hard, black variety of lignite, used in jewellery 2. a lustrous black —*adj.* 1. made of jet 2. black like jet

jet-black *adj.* glossy black, like jet

jet lag a disruption of the body's natural rhythms, associated with high-speed travel by jet aircraft

jet propulsion a method of propelling aircraft, boats, etc. by the discharge of gases under pressure through a rear vent —**jet′propelled′** *adj.*

jetsam (jet′səm) *n.* [var. of JETTISON] 1. cargo thrown overboard to lighten a ship in danger 2. such cargo washed ashore 3. discarded things

jet set a social set of rich, fashionable people who travel widely in pursuit of pleasure

jettison (jet′ə s'n) *vt.* [< L. *jactare,* throw] 1. to throw (goods) overboard 2. to discard —*n.* a throwing overboard of goods to lighten a ship, etc. in an emergency

jetty (jet′ē) *n., pl.* **-ties** [see JET¹] 1. a wall built out into the water to restrain currents, protect a harbour, etc. 2. a landing pier

Jew (jōō) *n.* [< Heb. *yehūdī,* member of the tribe of Judah] 1. a person descended from the ancient Hebrews 2. a person whose religion is Judaism —**Jew′ess** *n.fem.*

jewel (jōō′əl) *n.* [ult. < L. *jocus,* a joke] 1. a precious stone; gem 2. any person or thing that is very precious 3. a small gem used as one of the bearings in a watch 4. a valuable ring, necklace, etc., esp. one set with gems —*vt.* **-elled, -elling** to decorate or set with jewels

jeweller *n.* a person who makes, deals in, or repairs jewellery, watches, etc.

jewellery (jōō′əl rē) *n.* jewels collectively

Jewish *adj.* of Jews or Judaism

Jewry (jooə′rē) *n., pl.* **-ries** Jewish people collectively

JEW'S-HARP

jew's-harp, jews'-harp (jōōz′härp′) *n.* a small, metal musical instrument, held between the teeth and played by plucking a projecting piece with the finger

Jezebel (jez′ə b'l) *n.* [< *Jezebel,* in Bible] [also j-] a shameless, wicked woman

jib¹ (jib) *n.* [prob. < GIBBET] 1. the projecting arm of a crane 2. the boom of a derrick

jib² *n.* [< Dan. *gibbe,* to jibe] a triangular sail projecting ahead of the foremast —**cut of one's jib** [Colloq.] one's appearance

jib³ *vi.* **jibbed, jib′bing** [? < prec.] 1. to obstinately refuse to do something (usually with *at*) 2. to start or shy (*at* something) 3. to refuse to go forwards

jib boom a spar fixed to and extending beyond the bowsprit of a ship: the jib is attached to it

jibe¹ (jīb) *vi.* **jibed, jib′ing** [< Du. *gijpen*] 1. to shift from one side of a ship to the other, as a sail 2. to change the course of a ship so that the sails shift thus

jibe² *vi., n.* same as GIBE —**jib′er** *n.*

jiffy (jif′ē) *n., pl.* **-fies** [< ?] [Colloq.] a very short time; instant [done in a *jiffy*]: also **jiff**

jig (jig) *n.* [prob. < MFr. *gigue,* a fiddle] 1. *a)* a fast, springy dance in triple time *b)* the music for such a dance 2. a device

used as a guide for a tool —*vi., vt.* **jigged,**
jig′ging 1. to dance (a jig) **2.** to move
jerkily up and down or to and fro —**the**
jig is up [Slang] all chances for success
are gone

jigger (jig′ər) *n.* **1.** [U.S.] *a)* a small
glass used to measure whisky, gin, etc.
b) the quantity in a jigger **2.** *Billiards*
a support for the cue

jiggered (jig′ərd) *adj.* [< ?] [Colloq.]
amazed; confounded: often used instead
of damned [I'll be *jiggered*]

jiggery-pokery (jig′ər ē pō′kər ē) *n.* [<
Scot. *jouk,* a trick] [Colloq.] trickery
or deception

jiggle (jig′'l) *vt., vi.* **-gled, -gling** [< *jig*]
to move in quick, slight jerks —*n.* a
jiggling movement

JIGSAW

jigsaw (jig′sô′) *n.* a saw with a narrow
blade set in a frame, that moves with
an up-and-down motion for cutting along
curved or irregular lines

jigsaw puzzle a puzzle made by cutting
up a picture into irregular pieces, which
must be put together again to re-form
the picture

jilt (jilt) *vt.* [< *Jill*] to reject or cast
off (a previously accepted lover or
sweetheart)

Jim Crow [< Negro minstrel song] [*also*
j- c-] [U.S. Colloq.] discrimination against
Negroes

jimjams (jim′jamz′) *n.pl.* [echoic]
[Slang] **1.** delirium tremens **2.** a nervous
feeling; jitters

jingle (jiŋ′g'l) *vi.* **-gled, -gling** [echoic]
1. to make light, ringing sounds, as small
bells **2.** to have obvious, easy rhythm,
simple repetitions of sound, etc., as some
poetry and music —*vt.* to cause to jingle
—*n.* **1.** a jingling sound **2.** a verse that
jingles [advertising *jingles*] —**jin′gly** *adj.*

jingo (jiŋ′gō) *n., pl.* **-goes** [< phr. *by*
jingo in a patriotic Brit. song] one who
boasts of his patriotism and favours an
aggressive, warlike foreign policy —**jin′go-**
ism *n.* —**jin′goist** *n.* —**jin′gois′tic** *adj.*

jink (jiŋk) *vi.* [< ?] to move swiftly
or with sudden turns, as in dodging a
pursuer —*n.* an eluding, as by a quick
sudden turn —**high jinks** lively pranks

jinn (jin) *n., pl. of* JINNI: popularly regarded
as a singular, with the pl. **jinns**

jinni (ji nē′) *n., pl.* **jinn** [< Ar.] *Moslem*
Legend a supernatural being that can take
human or animal form

jinx (jiŋks) *n.* [< Gr. *iynx,* the wryneck
(bird used in black magic)] [Colloq.]
a person or thing supposed to bring bad luck

jitter (jit′ər) *vi.* [? echoic] [Colloq.] to
be nervous —**the jitters** [Colloq.] an
uneasy, nervous feeling —**jit′tery** *adj.*

jitterbug *n.* [prec. + BUG] a fast, acrobatic
dance for couples, esp. in the early 1940's
—*vi.* **-bugged′, -bug′ging** to dance the
jitterbug

jiujitsu, jiujutsu (jōō jit′sōō) *n.* var. of
JUJITSU

jive (jīv) *vi.* **jived, jiv′ing** [< ?] to play,
or dance to, jazz music —*n.* a style of
lively and jerky dance

job (job) *n.* [< ?] **1.** a piece of work
done for pay **2.** a task; duty **3.** the
thing or material being worked on **4.**
employment; work **5.** [Colloq.] a criminal
act, as a theft, etc. **6.** [Colloq.] any
happening, affair, etc. [*bad job*] —*adj.*
hired or done by the job —*vi.* **jobbed, job′-**
bing 1. to do odd jobs **2.** to act as
a jobber **3.** to engage in jobbery —*vt.*
1. to buy and sell (goods) as a wholesaler
2. to sublet (work, etc.) —**just the job**
[Colloq.] exactly what is needed —**odd**
jobs miscellaneous pieces of work —**job′-**
less *adj.*

jobber (job′ər) *n.* **1.** a wholesaler;
middleman, esp. dealing in stocks **2.** a
person who does piecework

jobbery *n.* public business done dishonestly for gain

jobbing *adj.* not regularly employed;
working by the piece [*jobbing* gardener]

jobcentre *n.* a government office in which
advertisements giving details of jobs
available are displayed

job lot 1. an assortment of goods for
sale as one quantity **2.** any random
assortment

Job's comforter (jōbz) a person who
aggravates one's misery while attempting
to comfort: see Job 16

Jock (jok) *n.* [Scot. form of *Jack*] [Slang]
a Scot

jockey (jok′ē) *n., pl.* **-eys** [< Scot. dim.
of *Jack*] a person whose work is riding
horses in races —*vt., vi.* **-eyed, -eying**
1. to manoeuvre for position or advantage
2. to cheat; swindle

jockstrap (jok′strap′) *n.* [*jock,* penis +
STRAP] a belt with a pouch to support
the genitals, worn by men

jocose (jō kōs′) *adj.* [< L. *jocus,* a joke]
joking or playful; humorous —**jocos′ity**
(-kos′ə tē) *n.*

jocular (jok′yə lər) *adj.* [< L. *jocus,* a
joke] joking; full of fun —**joc′ular′ity**
(-lar′ə tē) *n.*

jocund (jok′ənd) *adj.* [< L. *jucundus,*
pleasant] cheerful; gay —**jocundity**
(jō kun′də tē) *n.*

jodhpurs (jod′pərz) *n. pl.* [< *Jodhpur,*
former state in India] riding breeches
made loose and full above the knees and
tight from knees to ankles

jog (jog) *vt.* **jogged, jog′ging** [ME. *joggen,*
to spur] **1.** *a)* to give a little shake to
b) to nudge **2.** to shake up or revive
(a person's memory) —*vi.* to move along

at a slow, steady, jolting pace —*n.* **1.** a little shake or nudge **2.** a slow, steady, jolting motion; trot —**jog′ger** *n.*

jogging *n.* a slow jolting run or trot, esp. as a keep-fit exercise

joggle (jog′′l) *vt., vi.* **-gled, -gling** [< JOG] to shake or jolt slightly —*n.* a slight jolt

jogtrot *n.* a slow, steady trot

john (jon) *n.* [Chiefly U.S. Slang] a toilet

John Bull England, or an Englishman, personified

Johnny Canuck (jon′ē kə nuk′) [Canad.] **1.** [Colloq.] a Canadian **2.** a personification of Canada

Johnny Raw a novice; new recruit

Johnsonian (jon sō′nē ən) *adj.* [< S. *Johnson*] **1.** of or like Samuel Johnson or his style **2.** written in a formal or pompous style, full of Latinate constructions

‡joie de vivre (zhwäd vē′vr′) [Fr.] joy of living

join (join) *vt., vi.* [< L. *jungere*] **1.** to bring or come together (with); combine; unite **2.** to become a part or member of (a club, etc.) **3.** [Colloq.] to adjoin **4.** to participate (*in*) —*n.* a place of joining, as a seam —**join battle** to start fighting

joiner *n.* a workman trained and skilled in making finished woodwork, as doors, stairs, etc.

joinery *n.* the work or skill of a joiner

joint (joint) *n.* [< L. *jungere*, join] **1.** a place where, or way in which, two things are joined **2.** one of the parts of a jointed whole **3.** *Anat.* a place where two bones, etc. are joined, usually so that they can move **4.** a large cut of meat, often with the bones still in it **5.** [Slang] *a)* a cheap bar, restaurant, etc. *b)* any building **6.** [Slang] a marijuana cigarette —*adj.* **1.** common to two or more *[joint property]* **2.** sharing with someone else *[a joint owner]* —*vt.* **1.** to fasten together by a joint **2.** to cut (meat) into joints —**out of joint 1.** dislocated **2.** disordered —**joint′ed** *adj.*

jointly *adv.* in common; together

joint-stock company a business firm owned by the stockholders in shares which each may sell or transfer

jointure (join′chər) *n.* [< L. *jungere*, join] property settled on a wife for use after her husband's death

JOISTS

joist (joist) *n.* [< OFr. *giste*, a bed] any of the parallel beams that hold up the planks of a floor or the laths of a ceiling

joke (jōk) *n.* [L. *jocus*] **1.** anything said or done to arouse laughter; a funny anecdote **2.** a thing done or said merely in fun **3.** a person or thing to be laughed at —*vi.* joked, jok′ing to tell or play jokes —**jok′ingly** *adv.*

joker *n.* **1.** a person who jokes **2.** an extra playing card used in some games

jollify (jol′ə fī′) *vt., vi.* **-fied′, -fy′ing** [Colloq.] to make or be merry —**jol′lifica′- tion** *n.*

jollity *n.* a being jolly; fun; gaiety

jolly (jol′ē) *adj.* **-lier, -liest** [< OFr. *joli*] **1.** full of high spirits and good humour **2.** [Colloq.] enjoyable; pleasant —*adv.* [Colloq.] very —*vt., vi.* **-lied, -lying** [Colloq.] to try to make (a person) feel good by coaxing, flattering, etc. (often with *along*) —*n., pl.* **-lies** [Colloq.] a British marine —**jol′lily** *adv.* —**jol′liness** *n.*

Jolly Roger a black flag of pirates, with white skull and crossbones

jolt (jōlt) *vt.* [< earlier *jot*, to jog] **1.** to shake up or jar, as with a bumpy ride **2.** to shock or surprise —*vi.* to move along in a bumpy manner —*n.* **1.** a sudden jerk, bump, etc. **2.** a shock or surprise —**jolt′ingly** *adv.* —**jolt′y** *adj.*

Jonah (jō′nə) *n.* [< *Jonah*, Hebrew prophet] any person said to bring bad luck by his presence

jonquil (jon′kwəl) *n.* [< L. *juncus*, a rush] a species of narcissus having yellow flowers and long, slender leaves

josh (josh) *vt., vi.* [< ?] [U.S. Colloq.] to ridicule in a good humoured way; banter

joss (jos) *n.* [PidE. < Port. *deos* < L. *deus*, a god] a figure of a Chinese god

joss stick a thin stick of dried, fragrant wood dust, burned by the Chinese as incense

jostle (jos′′l) *vt., vi.* **-tled, -tling** [see JOUST] **1.** to bump or push, as in a crowd **2.** to contend (*with* someone *for* something) —*n.* a jostling —**jos′tler** *n.*

jot (jot) *n.* [< Gr. *iōta*, the smallest letter] a trifling amount; the smallest bit —*vt.* jot′- ted, jot′ting to make a brief note of (usually with *down*)

jotter *n.* a small notebook for rough notes

jotting *n.* a short note jotted down

joual (zhwäl) *n.* [< pronunciation of Fr. *cheval*, horse] a nonstandard Canadian French dialect

joule (jōōl) *n.* [< J. P. *Joule*] *Physics* the SI unit of energy, work, and quantity of heat

journal (jur′n'l) *n.* [< L. *diurnalis*, daily] **1.** a newspaper, magazine, etc. **2.** a daily record of happenings, as a diary **3.** a logbook **4.** *Bookkeeping* a book of original entry for recording transactions **5.** *Mech.* the part of a rotatory axle or shaft that turns in a bearing

journalese (jur′n'l ēz′) *n.* a superficial style of newspaper writing with many clichés

journalism (jur′n'l iz'm) *n.* the work of gathering, writing, and publishing news, as through newspapers, etc. or by radio and TV —**jour′nalist** *n.*

journey (jur′nē) *n., pl.* **-neys** [< L.

diurnus, daily] 1. a travelling from one place to another; trip 2. distance of, or time taken for, a journey —*vi.* -neyed, -ney-ing to travel

journeyman *n.* [ME. < *journee,* day's work] 1. a worker who has learned his trade 2. an experienced craftsman of average ability

joust (joust) *n.* [< L. *juxta,* beside] a combat with lances between two knights on horseback —*vi.* to engage in a joust —**joust′er** *n.*

Jove (jōv) *same as* JUPITER —**by Jove!** an exclamation of astonishment, emphasis, etc. —**Jo′vian** (jō′vē ən) *adj.*

jovial (jō′vē əl) *adj.* [< LL. *Jovialis,* of Jupiter] full of good humour; genial —**jo′vial′ity** (-al′ə tē) *n.*

jowl[1] (joul) *n.* [< OE. *ceafl,* jaw] 1. a jaw; esp., the lower jaw with the chin and cheeks 2. the cheek

jowl[2] *n.* [< OE. *ceole,* throat] [*often pl.*] the fleshy, hanging part under the lower jaw —**jowl′y** *adj.*

joy (joi) *n.* [< L. *gaudium,* joy] 1. a very glad feeling; happiness; delight 2. anything causing such feeling 3. [Colloq.] success or luck [to get no *joy*]

joyful *adj.* feeling, expressing, or causing joy; glad; happy —**joy′fully** *adv.* —**joy′fulness** *n.*

joyless *adj.* without joy; unhappy; sad

joyous *adj.* full of joy; happy —**joy′-ously** *adv.*

joy ride [Colloq.] a motor car ride merely for pleasure, often with reckless speed and, sometimes, in a stolen car

joy stick [Slang] the control stick of an aircraft

J.P. justice of the peace

Jr., jr. junior

jubilant (jōō′bil ənt) *adj.* [see ff.] joyful and triumphant; elated —**ju′bilance** *n.* —**ju′bilantly** *adv.*

jubilate (jōō′bi lāt′) *vi.* -lat′ed, -lat′ing [< L. *jubilare,* to shout for joy] to rejoice, as in triumph; exult —**ju′bila′tion** *n.*

jubilee (jōō′bi lē′) *n.* [< Heb. *yōbēl,* a horn (trumpet)] 1. a 50th or 25th anniver-sary 2. a time or occasion of rejoicing 3. jubilation

Jud. Judges

Judaic (jōō dā′ik) *adj.* of the Jews or Judaism

Judaism (jōō′dā iz'm) *n.* the Jewish religion, a monotheistic religion based on the laws and teachings of the Holy Scripture and the Talmud

Judas (jōō′dəs) *n.* [< *Judas Iscariot,* the disciple who betrayed Jesus] a traitor or betrayer

judder (jud′ər) *n.* [< ? SHUDDER] vibration or shaking motion —*vi.* to shake, wobble, or vibrate

Judg. Judges

judge (juj) *n.* [< L. *jus,* law + *dicere,* say] 1. a public official with authority to hear and decide cases in a court of law 2. a person designated to determine the winner, settle a controversy, etc. 3. a person qualified to decide on the relative

worth of anything [a good *judge* of music] —*vt., vi.* **judged, judg′ing** 1. to hear and pass judgment (*on*) in a court of law 2. to determine the winner of (a contest) or settle (a controversy) 3. to form an opinion about 4. to criticize or censure

judgment *n.* 1. power of comparing and deciding; understanding 2. a legal decision; order given by a judge or law court 3. a judging; deciding 4. an opinion 5. criticism or censure 6. [J-] *short for* LAST JUDGMENT Also sp. **judge′ment**

Judgment Day *Theol.* the time of God's final judgment

judicature (jōō′di kə chər) *n.* 1. the administering of justice 2. jurisdiction of a judge or court of law 3. judges or courts of law collectively

judicial (jōō dish′əl) *adj.* [< L. *judex, judge*] 1. of judges, law courts, or their functions 2. allowed, enforced, or set by order of a judge or law court 3. befitting a judge 4. fair; unbiased —**judi′cially** *adv.*

judiciary (jōō dish′ēər ē) *adj.* of judges or law courts —*n., pl.* -aries 1. the part of government that administers justice 2. judges collectively

judicious (jōō dish′əs) *adj.* [see JUDGE] having, applying, or showing sound judgment; wise

judo (jōō′dō) *n.* [Jap. < *jū,* soft + *dō,* art] a form of jujitsu, esp. as a means of self-defence

jug (jug) *n.* [< ?] 1. a container, usually with a handle and lip, for holding and pouring liquids 2. [Slang] a jail —*vt.* **jugged, jug′ging** 1. to stew in a covered earthenware container 2. [Slang] to put in jail

juggernaut (jug′ər nôt′) *n.* [after Hindi *Jagannath,* an incarnation of the Hindu god Vishnu] 1. any terrible, irresistible force 2. a large, heavy lorry

juggins (jug′inz) *n.* [? < surname] [Slang] a dupe

juggle (jug′'l) *vt.* -gled, -gling [< L. *jocus,* a joke] 1. to perform skilful tricks of sleight of hand with (balls, etc.) 2. to use trickery to deceive or cheat [to *juggle* figures to show a profit] —*vi.* to toss up a number of balls, etc. and keep them in the air —*n.* 1. a juggling 2. a trick or deception —**jug′gler** *n.*

jugular (jug′yoo lər) *adj.* [< L. *jugum,* a yoke] of the neck or throat —*n.* either of two large veins in the neck carrying blood back from the head to the heart : in full, **jugular vein**

juice (jōōs) *n.* [< L. *jus,* broth] 1. the liquid part of a plant, fruit, or vegetable 2. a liquid in or from animal tissue [gastric *juice*] 3. [Colloq.] energy; vitality 4. [Slang] a) electricity b) petrol

juicy *adj.* -ier, -iest 1. full of juice 2. [Colloq.] full of interest; spicy 3. [Colloq.] highly profitable

jujitsu (jōō jit′sōō) *n.* [< Jap. *jū,* soft + *jutsu,* art] a Japanese system of wrest-ling in which the strength and weight of an opponent are used against him: also **jujutsu**

ju-ju (jōō′jōō) n. [Hausa] 1. a magic charm or fetish used by some West African tribes 2. its magic

jujube (jōō′jōōb) n. [< Gr. zizyphon] 1. a tree with an edible, datelike fruit 2. a gelatinous, fruit-flavoured lozenge

jukebox (jōōk′boks) n. [< Negro juke, wicked] a coin-operated electric gramophone: also **juke box**

jukskei (jook′skā) n. a S African game in which a peg (skey) is thrown over a fixed distance at a stake driven into the ground

Julian calendar (jōō′lē ən) the calendar introduced by Julius Caesar in 46 B.C., in which every fourth year had 366 days: replaced by the Gregorian calendar

julienne (jōō′lē en′) n. [Fr.] a clear soup containing vegetables cut into strips or bits —adj. Cooking cut into strips: said of vegetables

July (jōō lī′) n., pl. **-lies**′ [< L. < Julius Caesar] the seventh month of the year, having 31 days: abbrev. **Jul.**

jumble (jum′b'l) vt. **-bled, -bling** [< ?] 1. to mix in a confused heap 2. to confuse mentally —vi. to be jumbled —n. 1. a confused heap; muddle 2. goods for a jumble sale

jumble sale a sale of second-hand goods, often in aid of a charity or other worthy cause

jumbo (jum′bō) n., pl. **-bos** [< Negro jamba, elephant] a very large person, animal, or thing —adj. very large

jumbo jet a large, jet-propelled passenger aircraft

jump (jump) vi. [< ?] 1. to move oneself suddenly from the ground, etc. by using the leg muscles; leap; spring 2. to jerk; bob 3. to start in surprise 4. to act or react eagerly (often with at) 5. to pass suddenly as from one topic to another 6. to rise suddenly, as prices 7. to arrive at prematurely, as a conclusion, etc. —vt. 1. a) to leap over b) to pass over; skip 2. to cause to leap 3. to cause (prices, etc.) to rise 4. to attack suddenly 5. [Colloq.] to react to prematurely, in anticipation —n. 1. a jumping; leap 2. a distance or height jumped 3. a thing to be jumped over 4. a sudden transition 5. a sudden rise, as in prices 6. a sudden, nervous start —**get** (or **have**) **the jump on** [Slang] to get (or have) an advantage over —**jump a claim** to seize land claimed by someone else —**jump bail** to forfeit one's bail by running away —**jump down someone's throat** [Slang] to address someone sharply; to scold —**jump the queue** to move ahead of others waiting for transport, jobs, etc. —**jump the rails** (or **track**) to go suddenly off the rails —**one jump ahead** one step ahead of a rival

jumped-up adj. upstart

jumper[1] n. 1. a short wire used to make an electrical connection 2. one that jumps

jumper[2] n. [< dial. jump, short coat]

1. a pullover 2. a loose jacket worn as part of a sailor's outfit

jump jet a fixed-wing jet aircraft that can land and take off vertically

jump leads electric cables with crocodile clips at each end: used to start a vehicle with a flat battery

jump suit 1. overalls 2. any one-piece garment like this

jumpy adj. **-ier, -iest** 1. easily startled 2. moving in jumps, jerks, etc. —**jump′iness** n.

Jun., jun. junior

junction (junk′shən) n. [< L. jungere, to join] 1. a joining or being joined 2. a place or point of joining or crossing, as of roads or railways —**junc′tional** adj.

juncture (junk′chər) n. 1. a point of time, esp. a crisis 2. a state of affairs 3. a joining or being joined 4. a point of joining or connection

June (jōōn) n. [< L. Junius, of Juno] the sixth month of the year, having 30 days: abbrev. **Jun.**

jungle (jun′g'l) n. [< Sans. jangala, desert] 1. land with a dense growth of trees, vines, etc., as in the tropics 2. any tangled growth 3. [Slang] a place where people compete ruthlessly —**jun′gly** adj.

junior (jōōn′yər) adj. [< L. juvenis, young] 1. of more recent position or lower status [a junior partner] 2. made up of younger members 3. the younger: written Jr. after the name of a son who bears the same name as his father —n. 1. a younger person 2. a person of lower standing or rank —**one's junior** a person younger than oneself

junior school a school for children aged between 7 and 12

juniper (jōō′nə pər) n. [L. juniperus] a small evergreen shrub or tree with scalelike foliage and berrylike cones

junk[1] (junk) n. [< ?] 1. old metal, paper, rags, etc. 2. [Colloq.] useless stuff; rubbish 3. [Slang] a narcotic drug; esp., heroin —**junk′y** adj.

JUNK

junk[2] n. [< Jav. joṅ] a Chinese flat-bottomed ship

Junker (yoong′kər) n. [G.] a Prussian of the militaristic, landowning class

junket (jun′kit) n. [ult. < L. juncus, a rush: orig. sold in reed baskets] 1. milk sweetened, flavoured, and thickened into curd with rennet 2. a feast or picnic 3. an excursion for pleasure 4. an excursion by an official, paid for out of public funds —*vi.* to go on a junket —**jun′keting** *n.*

junk food food with a low nutritional content, often not forming part of a balanced diet

junkie, junky (juŋ′kē) *n., pl.* **junk′ies** [Slang] a drug addict, esp. one addicted to heroin

junta (jun′tə) *n.* [< L. *jungere,* to join] a group of political intriguers, esp. military men in power after a coup d'état: also **junto** (jun′tō), *pl.* **-tos**

Jupiter (jōō′pə tər) **1.** the chief Roman god **2.** the largest planet of the solar system

Jurassic (joo ras′ik) *adj., n.* [< *Jura* (Mountains)] (of) the second period of the Mesozoic Era

juridical (joo͞ə rid′i k'l) *adj.* [< L. *jus,* law + *dicere,* declare] of judicial proceedings or of law

jurisdiction (jōō͞ər′is dik′shən) *n.* [< L. *jus,* law + *dicere,* declare] **1.** the administering of justice; authority to hear and decide cases **2.** authority **3.** the range of authority —**ju′risdic′tional** *adj.*

jurisprudence (jōō͞ər is prōō′dəns) *n.* [< L. *jus,* law + *prudentia,* a foreseeing] **1.** the science or philosophy of law **2.** a division of law

jurist (jōō͞ər′ist) *n.* [< L. *jus,* law] an expert in law

juror (jōō͞ər′ər) *n.* **1.** a member of a jury; juryman **2.** a person taking an oath, as of allegiance

jury¹ (jōō͞ər′ē) *n., pl.* **-ries** [< L. *jurare,* swear < *jus,* law] **1.** a group of people sworn to hear evidence in a law case and to give a decision **2.** a group selected to decide the winners in a contest

jury² *adj.* [< ?] *Naut.* for temporary use; makeshift [a *jury* mast]

jury-rigged *adj.* [see JURY²] *Naut.* rigged for temporary use

just (just) *adj.* [< L. *jus,* law] **1.** right or fair [a *just* decision] **2.** righteous [a *just* man] **3.** deserved [*just* praise] **4.** lawful **5.** proper, fitting, etc. **6.** well-founded [a *just* suspicion] **7.** correct or true **8.** exact —*adv.* **1.** a very short time ago **2.** almost at the point of **3.** only [*just* a taste] **4.** exactly [*just* one o'clock] **5.** immediately [*just* to my right] **6.** barely [*just* missed the train] **7.**

[Colloq.] quite; really [looks *just* right] —**just now** a moment ago —**just the same** [Colloq.] nevertheless —**just′ly** *adv.*

justice (jus′tis) *n.* **1.** a being righteous **2.** fairness **3.** rightfulness **4.** reward or penalty as deserved **5.** the use of authority to uphold what is just **6.** the administration of law **7.** *same as:* a) JUDGE b) JUSTICE OF THE PEACE —**bring to justice** to cause (a wrongdoer) to be tried in court and duly punished —**do justice to 1.** show to advantage **2.** to treat fairly **3.** to enjoy properly —**do oneself justice** to do something in a manner worthy of one's abilities —**jus′ticeship′** *n.*

justice of the peace a local magistrate, authorized to decide minor cases, etc.

justiciary (jus ti′shə rē) *n., pl.* **-aries** [< L. *jus,* law] an officer of justice —**the Justiciary** judges collectively

justifiable (jus′tə fī′ə b'l) *adj.* that can be justified or defended as correct —**jus′tifi′ably** *adv.*

justify (jus′tə fī′) *vt.* **-fied′, -fy′ing** [< L. *justus,* just + *facere,* make] **1.** to show to be just, right, or reasonable **2.** *Theol.* to free from blame **3.** to supply good grounds for **4.** to space (type) to make the lines correct in length —**jus′tifi ca′tion** *n.*

justle (jus′'l) *vt., vi., n.* same as JOSTLE

jut (jut) *vi.*₁ *vt.* **jut′ted, jut′ting** [prob. var. of JET¹] to stick out; project —*n.* a part that juts

jute (jōōt) *n.* [< Sans. *jūta,* matted hair] **1.** a strong fibre used for making burlap, sacks, rope, etc. **2.** either of two East Indian plants yielding this fibre

juvenile (jōō′və nīl) *adj.* [< L. *juvenis,* young] **1.** a) young b) immature; childish **2.** of or suitable for young persons —*n.* **1.** a young person **2.** an actor who plays youthful roles —**ju′venil′ity** (-nil′ə tē) *n.*

juvenile delinquency antisocial or unlawful behaviour by minors —**juvenile delinquent**

juvenilia (jōō′və nil′yə) *n. pl.* [< L. *juvenilis,* juvenile] writings, paintings, etc. done in childhood or youth

juxtapose (juk′stə pōz′) *vt.* **-posed′, -pos′ing** [< Fr. < L. *juxta,* near + POSE¹] to put side by side or close together —**jux′tapo si′tion** *n.*

K

K, k (kā) *n., pl.* **K's, k's** the eleventh letter of the English alphabet

K 1. *Physics the symbol for* kelvin 2. *Chess* king 3. knit 4. [ModL. *kalium*] potassium 5. 1000 (strictly, 1024)

k kilo

K., k. 1. *Elec.* capacity 2. *Music* Köchel (in numbering Mozart's works)

Kaffir (kaf′ər) *n.* [Ar. *kāfir*, infidel] [Obs. Derog.] 1. in South Africa, any black African 2. a former name for the Xhosa language

Kaffir beer [S Afr.] a sorghum beer

Kaffirboom (kaf′ər bō○əm) *n.* [< KAFFIR + Afrik. *boom*, tree] a deciduous flowering tree

Kaffir corn a S African variety of sorghum

Kaffir sheeting [S Afr.] a coarsely woven cloth

kaftan (kaf′tan) *n. same as* CAFTAN

kaiser (kī′zər) *n.* [< L. *Caesar*] emperor: the title [**K-**] of the former rulers of Austria and of Germany

kaie (kāl) *n.* [Scot. var. of COLE] a hardy cabbage with loose, spreading, curled leaves

kaleidoscope (kə lī′də skōp′) *n.* [< Gr. *kalos*, beautiful + *eidos*, form + -SCOPE] 1. a small tube containing loose bits of coloured glass, plastic, etc. reflected by mirrors so that various symmetrical patterns appear when the tube is rotated 2. anything that constantly changes —**kalei′doscop′ic** (-skop′ik) *adj.* —**kalei′-doscop′ically** *adv.*

kaleyard (kāl′yärd) *n.* [Scot.] a kitchen garden

Kamasutra (kä′mə sō○′trə) [Sans. < *kāma*, love + *sūtra*, manual] a Hindu love manual

kamikaze (ka′mi kä′zē) *n.* [Jap., divine wind] 1. a suicide attack by a Japanese aircraft pilot in World War II 2. the aircraft or pilot in such an attack

Kamloops trout (kam′lōops) a variety of rainbow trout common in British Columbia

kangaroo (kaŋ′gə rō○′) *n.* [< ? native name] a leaping, plant-eating, Australian mammal with short forelegs and strong, large hind legs: the female has a pouch in front, in which she carries her young

kangaroo closure the confinement of discussion, esp. in Parliament, to selected amendments

kangaroo court [Colloq.] a mock court illegally passing and executing judgment, as among prison inmates

KANU Kenya African National Union

kaolin (kā′ə lin) *n.* [Fr. < Chin., name of hill] a fine white clay used in making porcelain

kapok (kā′pok) *n.* [Malay *kapoq*] the silky fibres from a tropical tree: used for stuffing sleeping bags, etc.

kappa (kap′ə) *n.* the tenth letter of the Greek alphabet (K, κ)

kaput (kə pō○t′) *adj.* [G. *kaputt*] [Slang] ruined, destroyed, defeated, etc.

karakul (kar′ə kəl) *n.* [< *Kara Kul*, lake in U.S.S.R.] 1. a sheep of C Asia 2. the wavy pelt of the karakul lamb

karate (kə rät′ē) *n.* [Jap. < *kara*, empty + *te*, hand] a Japanese system of self-defence in which blows are struck with the side of the open hand

karma (kär′mə) *n.* [Sans., deed] *Buddhism & Hinduism* a person's actions in one reincarnation thought of as determining his fate in the next

karroo (kə rō○′) *n.* [< Afrik. *karo*] [S Afr.] a high, arid plateau

kaross (kə ros′) *n., pl.* -**oss′es** [< Afrik. *karos*] [S Afr.] a cloak or mantle made of skins

kart (kärt) *n.* [< CART] a small, flat, 4-wheeled, motorized vehicle for one person, used in racing (**karting**): also **go-kart, go-cart**

katydid (kāt′ē did′) *n.* [echoic] a large, green, American tree insect resembling the grasshopper

kauri (kou′rē) *n.* [Maori] a New Zealand pine that yields a resin (**kauri gum**) used in varnishes, etc.

KAYAK

kayak (kī′ak) *n.* [Eskimo] an Eskimo canoe made of skins covering a wooden frame

kayo (kā′ō′) *vt.* -**oed′**, -**o′ing** [< KO] [Slang] to knock out —*n.* [Slang] a knockout

kazoo (kə zō○′) *n.* [echoic] a toy musical instrument that gives a buzzing quality to tones hummed through a small tube

K.B.E. Knight Commander of the British Empire

kc, kc. kilocycle; kilocycles

K.C. King's Counsel

kcal. kilocalorie; kilocalories

K.C.B. Knight Commander of the Bath

K.C.M.G. Knight Commander of St. Michael and St. George

kea (kā'ə) *n.* [Maori] a large, green parrot of New Zealand that sometimes kills sheep

kebab (kə bab') *n.* [Ar. *kabāb*] [*often pl*] a dish consisting of small pieces of meat cooked on a skewer, often with alternating pieces of onion, tomato, etc.

kedge (kej) *vt., vi.* kedged, kedg'ing [< ME. *caggen*, fasten] to move (a ship) by hauling on a rope fastened to an anchor —*n.* a light anchor: also **kedge anchor**

kedgeree (kej'ə rē) *n.* [Hindi *khicarī*] 1. an Indian dish of rice boiled with onions, pulse, and butter 2. a British breakfast dish of fish, boiled rice, and eggs

keek (kēk) *n., vi.* [prob. < MDu. *kīken*, to look] [Scot.] *same as* PEEP²

keel (kēl) *n.* [< ON. *kjolr*] the chief timber or steel piece along the length of the bottom of a ship or boat —*vt., vi.* to turn over so as to turn up the keel —**keel over** 1. to turn over 2. to fall in a faint, etc. —**on an even keel** upright and level, steady, stable, etc.

keelhaul *vt.* 1. to haul (a person) under the keel of a ship as a punishment 2. to scold or rebuke harshly

keelson (kel's'n) *n.* [prob. < Dan. *kjøl*, keel + *sville*, sill] a beam or set of timbers or metal plates fastened inside a ship's hull along the keel for added strength

keen¹ (kēn) *adj.* [OE. *cene*, wise] 1. eager 2. sharp; acute: said of the senses 3. having a sharp edge or point 4. piercing [a *keen* wind] 5. strong or intense 6. extremely competitive: said of prices —**keen on** fond of —**keen'ly** *adv.* —**keen'ness** *n.*

keen² *n.* [< Ir. *caoinim*, I wail] [Irish] a wailing for the dead —*vt., vi.* [Irish] to wail for (the dead)

keep (kēp) *vt.* kept, keep'ing [< OE. *cepan*, behold] 1. to continue to have or hold 2. to fulfil (a promise, etc.) 3. to go on maintaining [*keep* pace] 4. to protect; guard; take care of; tend 5. to raise (livestock) 6. to preserve 7. to provide for; support 8. to make regular entries in [to *keep* books, a diary, etc.] 9. to conduct; manage 10. to make stay in a specified condition, position, etc. [to *keep* an engine running] 11. to hold for future use or a long time 12. to have regularly in stock 13. to hold in custody 14. to detain 15. to restrain from action 16. to withhold 17. to conceal (a secret) 18. to observe; celebrate [*keep* the Sabbath] 19. to stay in or at (a path, course, or place) —*vi.* 1. to stay in a specified condition, position, etc. 2. to continue; go on; (often with *on*) 3. to refrain [to *keep* from telling someone] 4. to stay fresh —*n.* 1. food and shelter; support 2. a) a donjon b) a fort; castle —**for keeps** [Colloq.] forever —**keep at** to continue doing; persist in —**keep**

back 1. to refuse to reveal 2. to stay at a distance —**keep to** 1. to persevere in 2. to adhere to 3. to remain in —**keep to oneself** 1. to avoid others 2. to refrain from telling —**keep track of** [Colloq.] to continue to be informed about —**keep up** 1. to continue 2. to maintain the pace 3. to maintain in good condition 4. to remain informed about (with *on* or *with*) —**keep up with the Joneses** to try to obtain the same material goods as one's neighbours

keeper *n.* 1. a guard, as of prisoners, animals, etc. 2. a guardian or protector 3. a caretaker

keeping *n.* 1. observance (of a rule, etc.) 2. care; charge —**in keeping with** in conformity or accord with

keepsake *n.* something kept, in memory of the giver

keg (keg) *n.* [< ON. *kaggi*] a small barrel

kelp (kelp) *n.* [ME. *culp*] large coarse, brown seaweed, rich in iodine

kelpie¹, kelpy¹ (kel'pē) *n., pl.* -pies [Scot. < ?] *Gaelic Folklore* a water spirit in the form of a horse

kelpie², kelpy² *n., pl.* -pies [< ?] a breed of Australian sheepdog

kelson (kel's'n) *n.* *same as* KEELSON

Kelt (kelt) *n.* *same as* CELT —**Kelt'ic** *adj., n.*

kelt (kelt) *n.* [ME.] [Scot.] a salmon that has spawned

kelvin (kel'vin) *n.* the SI unit of thermodynamic temperature

Kelvin scale [< 1st Baron *Kelvin*] a scale of temperature measured from absolute zero (-273.15°C)

ken (ken) *vt., vi.* kenned, ken'ning [OE. *cennan*, cause to know] [Scot.] to know —*n.* range of knowledge

kennel (ken'l) *n.* [< L. *canis*, dog] 1. a shelter for dogs 2. [*often pl.*] a place where dogs are bred or kept 3. a pack of dogs —*vt.* -nelled, -nelling to place or keep in a kennel

kepi (kā'pē) *n., pl.* kep'is [Fr. *képi*] a visored cap with a flat, round top, worn by French soldiers

kept (kept) *pt. & pp.* of KEEP —*adj.* maintained as a mistress [a *kept* woman]

kerb (kurb) *n.* [var. of CURB] the stone or concrete edging forming a gutter along a street

kerbstone *n.* any of the stones making up a kerb

kerchief (kur'chif) *n.* [< OFr. *covrir*, to cover + *chef*, head] 1. a piece of cloth worn over the head or around the neck 2. a handkerchief —**ker'chiefed** *adj.*

kerel (kāar'əl) *n.* [< Afrik.] [S Afr.] a young man

kerfuffle (kər fuf'l) *n.* [< ?] [Colloq.] a commotion

kermes (kur'mēz) *n.* [< Ar. & Per. *qirmiz*, crimson] 1. the dried bodies of certain Mediterranean insects, used to make a purple-red dye 2. the dye

kernel (kur'n'l) *n.* [< OE. *corn*, seed] 1. the inner, softer part of a nut, etc.

2. a grain or seed, as of corn **3.** the central, most important part; essence

kerosene (ker'ə sēn') *n.* [< Gr. *kēros*, wax] a thin oil distilled from petroleum or shale oil, used as a fuel, solvent, etc.: also sp. **kerosine**

kestrel (kes'trəl) *n.* [echoic] a small falcon that can hover in the air against the wind

ketch (kech) *n.* [< ME. *cacchen*, to catch] a small two-masted sailing vessel

ketchup (kech'əp) *n.* [Malay *kēchap*, < Chin.] a sauce for meat, fish, etc.; esp., a thick sauce (**tomato ketchup**) of tomatoes flavoured with onion and spices

ketone (kē'tōn) *n.* [< G. *Keton*] an organic chemical compound containing the bivalent radical CO in combination with two hydrocarbon radicals

kettle (ket''l) *n.* [< L. *catinus*, bowl] a metal container with a handle and a spout, used for boiling water

kettledrum *n.* a percussion instrument consisting of a hollow hemisphere and a top made of parchment, etc. that can be tightened or loosened to change the pitch

kettle of fish set of circumstances; situation

key[1] (kē) *n., pl.* **keys** [OE. *cæge*] **1.** an instrument for moving the bolt of a lock and thus locking or unlocking something **2.** anything like this; specif., *a)* a device to turn a bolt, etc. [a skate key] *b)* a pin, bolt, etc. used to hold parts together *c)* any of the levers, pressed down to operate a piano, typewriter, etc. *d)* a device for opening or closing an electric circuit *e)* an implement for winding up a clock **3.** a thing that explains or solves, as a book of answers **4.** a controlling or essential person or thing **5.** tone of thought or expression **6.** a dry, winged fruit of various trees **7.** *Music* a system of notes forming a given scale —*adj.* controlling; essential; important —*vt.* **keyed, key'ing 1.** to bring into harmony **2.** to fasten or lock with a key **3.** to furnish with a key **4.** *same as* KEYBOARD **5.** to set the tone or pitch of **6.** to roughen a surface, as for plastering, etc. —**key up** to make tense or excited

key[2] *n., pl.* **keys** [Sp. *cayo*] a reef or low island

keyboard *n.* the row(s) of keys of a piano, typewriter, linotype, etc.—*vt.* to set (a text) in type using a composing machine having a keyboard

keyhole *n.* an opening (in a lock) into which a key is inserted

key money a sum of money demanded from a new tenant as a condition of granting a lease: now illegal in the U.K.

keynote *n.* **1.** the basic idea or ruling principle, as of a speech, policy, etc. **2.** the lowest, basic note or tone of a musical scale

key punch a keyboard machine that records data by punching holes in cards

key signature *Music* the sharps or flats after the clef on the staff, showing the key

KEYSTONE

keystone *n.* **1.** the central, topmost stone of an arch **2.** the main part or principle

kg kilogram(s)

K.G. Knight of (the Order of) the Garter

KGB, K.G.B. [Russ., Committee of State Security] the security police, or intelligence agency, of the Soviet Union

khaki (kä'kē) *adj.* [< Per. *khāk*, dust] dull yellowish-brown —*n., pl.* **-kis** a strong, twilled cloth of this colour, used esp. for uniforms

khan (kän) *n.* [< Turki *khān*, lord] **1.** *Hist.* a title of Turkish, Tatar, and Mongol rulers **2.** a title of honour in Iran, Afghanistan, etc. —**khan'ate** *n.*

khedive (kə dēv') *n.* [< Per. *khidīw*, prince] the title of the Turkish viceroys of Egypt, from 1867 to 1914

kHz kilohertz

kibbutz (kē bŏŏts') *n., pl.* **kibbutzim** (kē'-bŏŏ tsēm') [ModHeb.] an Israeli collective settlement, esp. a collective farm

kibosh (kī'bosh) *n.* [< ?] [Slang] orig., nonsense —**put the kibosh on** to put an end to; veto

kick (kik) *vi.* [ME. *kiken*] **1.** to strike out with the foot or feet **2.** to spring back suddenly, as a gun when fired **3.** [Colloq.] to complain **4.** *Football* to kick the ball —*vt.* **1.** to strike suddenly with the foot or feet **2.** to drive, force, etc. as by kicking **3.** to score (a goal) by kicking **4.** [Slang] to get rid of (a habit) —*n.* **1.** a blow with the foot **2.** a kicking **3.** a sudden recoil **4.** [Colloq.] a stimulating effect **5.** [Colloq.] [often *pl.*] pleasure; thrill **6.** [Slang] a temporary enthusiasm —**kick around** (or **about**) [Colloq.] **1.** to treat roughly **2.** to move from place to place **3.** to lie about unnoticed **4.** to discuss —**kick off** **1.** to put a football into play with a kick **2.** to start (a campaign, etc.) —**kick out** [Colloq.] to get rid of; expel —**kick up** [Colloq.] to cause (trouble, etc.) —**kick upstairs** [Colloq.] to promote to an effectively powerless position

kickback *n.* **1.** [Colloq.] a sharp reaction **2.** [Chiefly U.S. Slang] a sum paid in return for an opportunity to make a profit, often illegally

kickoff *n.* **1.** the act of kicking off in football **2.** the start of a campaign, etc.

kickstand *n.* a short metal bar that can be kicked down to hold a stationary cycle upright

kick starter a foot-operated lever used for starting motorcycle engines —**kick'-start** *vt., vi.*

kid (kid) *n.* [ME. *kide*] **1.** a young goat **2.** leather from the skin of young goats **3.** [Colloq.] a child —*adj.* **1.** made of kidskin **2.** [Colloq.] younger [my **kid** sister] —**vt., vi. kid'ded, kid'ding 1.** [Colloq.] to deceive or tease playfully **2.** to give birth to (a kid) : said of goats —**kid'der** n. —**kid'like', kid'dish** adj.

kiddy, kiddie n., pl. **-dies** [Colloq.] a child

kid gloves soft, smooth gloves made of kidskin —**handle with kid gloves** [Colloq.] to treat with care, tact, etc.

kidnap (kid'nap') vt. **-napped', -nap'ping** [KID + dial. nap, nab] **1.** to seize and hold (a person) against his will, often for ransom **2.** to steal (a child) —**kid'nap'per** n.

KIDNEYS
(A, right kidney; B, left kidney;
C, vena cava; D, aorta; E, ureter;
F, renal vein; G, renal artery;
left kidney shown in cross section)

kidney (kid'nē) n., pl. **-neys** [ME. kidenei] **1.** either of a pair of glandular organs which separate waste products from the blood and excrete them as urine **2.** an animal kidney, used as food **3.** a) temperament b) kind

kidney bean the kidney-shaped seed of the common garden bean

kidney machine a machine which takes over the function of damaged human kidneys

kidney stone a hard mineral deposit formed in the kidney

kill (kil) vt. [ME. killen] **1.** to cause the death of **2.** to destroy; put an end to **3.** to defeat or veto (legislation) **4.** turn off (a light, etc.) **5.** to prevent publication of **6.** [Colloq.] to overcome with laughter, chagrin, etc. **7.** [Colloq.] to make feel great pain or exhaustion —**vi.** to destroy life —**n. 1.** an act of killing **2.** an animal or animals killed **3.** an enemy plane, ship, etc. destroyed —**in at the kill** present at the end of some action —**kill time** to waste time while waiting for an event, appointment, etc. —**kill'er** n.

killer whale any of several small whales that hunt in packs and prey on large fish, seals, and other whales

killing adj. **1.** causing death; deadly **2.** exhausting **3.** [Colloq.] very comical —**n. 1.** slaughter; murder **2.** [Colloq.] a sudden, great profit or success

kill-joy n. a person who destroys or lessens other people's enjoyment : also **kill'-joy'**

kiln (kiln) n. [< L. culina, kitchen] a furnace or oven for drying, burning, or baking something, as bricks, pottery, or grain

kilo (kē'lō) n., pl. **-los** [Fr.] short for: **1.** KILOGRAM **2.** KILOMETRE

kilo- [< Gr.] a combining form meaning a thousand

kilocycle (kil'ə sī'k'l) n. former name for KILOHERTZ

kilogram, kilogramme (kil'ə gram') n. the SI unit of mass

kilohertz (kil'ə hurts') n., pl. **-hertz'** 1000 hertz

kilolitre (kil'ə lēt'ər) n. a unit of capacity equal to 1000 litres, or one cubic metre: also U.S. **kil'oli'ter**

kilometre (kil'ə mēt'ər) n. a unit of length or distance, equal to 1000 metres: also U.S. **kilo'meter** —**kilometric** (kil'ə met'rik) adj.

kiloton (kil'ə tun') n. the explosive force of 1000 tons of TNT

kilowatt (kil'ə wot') n. a unit of electrical power, equal to 1000 watts

kilowatt-hour n. a unit of electrical energy or work, equal to one kilowatt acting for one hour

kilt (kilt) n. [prob. < Scand.] a pleated skirt reaching to the knees; esp., the tartan skirt worn sometimes by men of the Scottish Highlands —**vt. 1.** [Scot.] to tuck up (a skirt, etc.) **2.** to pleat —**kilt'ed** adj.

kimono (kə mō'nō) n., pl. **-nos** [Jap.] **1.** a loose outer garment with a sash, a traditional Japanese costume **2.** a woman's dressing gown like this

kin (kin) n. [< OE. cynn] relatives; family; kindred —**adj.** related, as by blood

-kin (kin) [< MDu.] a suffix meaning little [lambkin]

kind (kīnd) n. [< OE. cynd] **1.** sort; class **2.** essential character **3.** a natural group or division —**adj. 1.** sympathetic, gentle, generous, etc. **2.** cordial [kind regards] —**in kind 1.** in goods or produce instead of money **2.** with something like that received —**kind of** somewhat; rather —**of a kind 1.** alike **2.** inferior

kindergarten (kin'dər gär't'n) n. [G., garden of children] a school for young children in which teaching is by means of games, music, simple handicrafts, etc.

kindhearted (kīnd'här'tid) adj. sympathetic; kindly

kindle (kin'd'l) vt. **-dled, -dling** [< ON. kynda] **1.** to set on fire; ignite **2.** to excite (interest, feelings, etc.) —**vi. 1.** to catch fire **2.** to become excited

kindling (kin'dlin) n. bits of dry wood or other easily lighted material for starting a fire

kindly (kīnd'lē) adj. **-lier, -liest 1.** kind **2.** agreeable; pleasant —**adv. 1.** in a kind way **2.** agreeably **3.** please [kindly reply] —**take kindly to 1.** to be naturally attracted to **2.** to accept willingly —**kind'liness** n.

kindness (kīnd'nis) n. **1.** the state, quality, or habit of being kind **2.** kind act or treatment

kindred (kin'drid) adj. [< OE. cynn, kin + ræden, condition] of like nature *[kindred* spirits *] —n.* **1.** formerly, family relationship **2.** relatives or family; kin

kine (kīn) *n.pl.* [< OE. *cy*] [Archaic] cows; cattle

kinematics (kin′ə mat′iks) *n.pl.* [*with sing. v.*] [< Gr. *kinēma,* motion] the branch of mechanics dealing with abstract motion, without reference to force or mass —**kin′emat′ic, kin′emat′ical** *adj.*

kinetic (ki net′ik) *adj.* [< Gr. *kinein,* to move] **1.** of or resulting from motion **2.** energetic or dynamic

kinetic art sculpture or assemblage involving the use of moving parts, sounds, shifting lights, etc.

kinetics *n.pl.* *same as* DYNAMICS (sense 1)

kinfolk (kin′fōk′) *n.pl.* [Chiefly U.S.] relatives; kin

king (kiŋ) *n.* [OE. *cyning*] **1.** the male ruler of a monarchy **2.** *a)* a man who is supreme in some field *[an oil king]* *b)* something supreme in its class **3.** a playing card with a picture of a king on it **4.** *Chess* the chief piece **5.** *Draughts* a piece crowned upon reaching the opponent's base —*adj.* chief (in size, importance, etc.) —**king′ly** *adj.* —**king′-ship** *n.*

King Charles spaniel a toy breed of spaniel with very long ears and a wavy coat

kingcup *n.* **1.** a buttercup **2.** a marsh marigold

kingdom *n.* **1.** a country headed by a king or queen; monarchy **2.** a realm; domain *[the kingdom of poetry]* **3.** any of the three great divisions of things in nature (the animal, vegetable, and mineral kingdoms)

kingfisher *n.* a brightly-coloured bird with a crested head, a large, strong beak, and a short tail

kingklip (kiŋ′klip) *n.* [< Du.] an edible, eellike marine fish

king-of-arms *n.* in Great Britain, any of the chief officers who decide questions of heraldry

king of beasts *an epithet for* a lion

king of birds *an epithet for* an eagle

kingpin *n.* **1.** the metal rod upon which the steering stub axle of a motorcar is pivoted **2.** [Colloq.] the main or essential person or thing

King's (or **Queen's**) **Bench** *Law* one of the three divisions of the High Court of Justice

King's (or **Queen's**) **Counsel** **1.** in England, an eminent barrister selected to serve as counsel to the Crown **2.** in Canada, an honorary title which may be bestowed by the government on lawyers with long experience

King's (or **Queen's**) **English, the** standard (esp. British) English

king's (or **queen's**) **evidence** *Law* evidence given for the Crown by a person against his former associates in crime

king's (or **queen's**) **highway** **1.** any public road or right of way **2.** [Canad.] a main road maintained by the provincial government

king-size *adj.* bigger than normal: also **king′-sized′**

king's post *Canad. Hist.* any of the fur-trading and fishing posts in Quebec

kink (kiŋk) *n.* [< Scand.] **1.** a twist or curl in a rope, hair, etc. **2.** an eccentricity; quirk **3.** a defect, as in a plan —*vi., vt.* to form or cause to form a kink

kinky *adj.* **-ier, -iest** **1.** [Slang] weird, bizarre, etc.; specif., sexually abnormal **2.** full of kinks; tightly curled

kinsfolk (kinz′fōk′) *n.pl.* *var. of* KINFOLK

kinsman (kinz′mən) *n.* a relative; esp., a male relative —**kins′wom′an** *n.fem.*

kiosk (kē′osk) *n.* [< Fr. < Per. *kūshk,* palace] **1.** a small booth from which newspapers, cigarettes, etc. are sold **2.** a telephone box

kip (kip) *n.* [< Dan. *kippe,* low alehouse] [Slang] **1.** sleep **2.** a bed —*vi.* **kipped, kip′ping** [Slang] to sleep

kipper (kip′ər) *n.* [< ?] **1.** a kippered herring, salmon, etc. **2.** a male salmon during the spawning season —*vt.* to cure (herring, salmon, etc.) by cleaning, salting, and drying or smoking

kirk (kurk) *n.* [Scot. & North Eng.] a church

kirschwasser (kēərsh′väs′ər) *n.* [G.] an alcoholic drink distilled from the fermented juice of black cherries: often **kirsch**

kismet (kis′met) *n.* [< Ar. *qismah*] fate; destiny

kiss (kis) *vt., vi.* [OE. *cyssan*] **1.** to touch or caress with the lips in affection, greeting, etc. **2.** to touch lightly —*n.* a kissing —**kiss′able** *adj.*

kiss curl a circular curl of hair on the forehead or cheek

kisser *n.* **1.** one who kisses **2.** [Slang] *a)* the mouth *b)* the face

kiss of life artificial resuscitation whereby air is blown into the victim's lungs through his mouth by the rescuer

kist (kist) *n.* [< Afrik.] [S Afr.] a wooden chest, usually large

kit (kit) *n.* [prob. < MDu. *kitte,* a tub] **1.** a set of tools, articles for special use, parts to be assembled, etc. **2.** a container for such equipment, tools, etc. **3.** personal equipment, esp. as packed for travel —*vt., vi.* **kit′ted, kit′ting** to fit out or be fitted out with kit —**the whole kit and caboodle** everybody or everything

kitbag *n.* a bag, usually canvas, that holds kit

kitchen (kich′ən) *n.* [< L. *coquere,* to cook] a room or place for preparing and cooking food

kitchen Dutch [S Afr.] an impoverished form of Afrikaans often mixed with words from other languages, as English

kitchenette (kich′ə net′) *n.* a small, compact kitchen

kitchen garden a garden in which vegetables, and sometimes fruit, are grown, usually for home use

kitchen Kaffir [S Afr. Derog.] Fanagalo

kite (kīt) *n.* [OE. *cyta*] **1.** a light wooden frame covered with paper or cloth, to be flown in the wind at the end of a string **2.** a bird of the hawk family, with long, pointed wings

kitemark the kite-shaped mark on goods approved by the British Standards Institution

kith (kith) *n.* [OE. *cyth*] only in **kith and kin,** friends and relatives

kitsch (kĭch) *n.* [G.] pretentious but shallow art, writing, etc., designed for popular appeal —**kitsch′y** *adj.*

kitten (kit′'n) *n.* [< OFr. dim. of *chat,* cat] a young cat —**to have kittens** [Colloq.] to react with anxiety, shock, etc.

kittenish *adj.* playful; frisky; often, playfully coy

kittiwake (kit′iwāk′) *n.* [echoic] any of several sea gulls of the Arctic and North Atlantic

kitty (kit′ē) *n., pl.* -ties [prob. < KIT] **1.** in poker, etc., the stakes **2.** any money pooled for some special use

kiwi (kē′wē) *n., pl.* -wis [Maori] **1.** a tailless New Zealand bird with undeveloped wings, hairlike feathers, and a long bill **2.** [Colloq.] a New Zealander

kl, kl. kilolitre; kilolitres

klaar (klär) *n.* [< Afrik.] [S Afr.] finish, esp. in the phrase **finish and klaar**

klaxon (klak′s'n) *n.* a kind of electric horn with a loud, shrill sound

kleptomania (klep′tə mā′nē ə) *n.* [< Gr. *kleptēs,* thief + -MANIA] an abnormal, persistent impulse to steal —**klep′toma′niac′** *n.*

klipspringer (klip′spriŋ′ər) *n.* [< Afrik. *klip,* rock + *spring,* jump] a small S African antelope inhabiting rocky areas

kloof (klo͞of) *n.* [< Afrik.] [S Afr.] a mountain pass or valley

km, km. kilometre; kilometres

knack (nak) *n.* [ME. *knak,* sharp blow] **1.** a clever way of doing something **2.** ability to do something easily

knacker (nak′ər) *n.* [< ?] **1.** a person who buys and slaughters worn-out horses **2.** a person who buys and wrecks old houses, etc. and sells their materials —*vt.* [Slang] to exhaust [he was *knackered*]

knapsack (nap′sak′) *n.* [< Du. *knappen,* eat + *zak,* a sack] a leather or canvas bag for carrying equipment or supplies on the back

knapweed (nap′wēd′) *n.* [< ME. *knoppe,* knob + *weed*] a hardy perennial with heads of rose-purple flowers

knave (nāv) *n.* [OE. *cnafa,* boy] **1.** a deceitful rascal; rogue **2.** a jack (the playing card) —**knav′ish** *adj.*

knavery *n., pl.* -eries behaviour characteristic of a knave; rascality

knead (nēd) *vt.* [OE. *cnedan*] **1.** to work (dough, clay, etc.) into a pliable mass by pressing and squeezing **2.** to massage with similar movements —**knead′er** *n.*

knee (nē) *n.* [OE. *cneow*] **1.** the joint between the thigh and the lower leg **2.** the area between this and the thigh, when sitting **3.** anything like a knee, esp. like a bent knee **4.** the part of a stocking,

trouser leg, etc. covering the knee —*vt.* **kneed, knee′ing** to hit or touch with the knee —**bring to one's knees** to force to submit

kneecap *n.* a movable bone at the front of the knee —*vt.* to shoot through the kneecap as a punishment

knee-deep *adj.* **1.** sunk to the knees, as in water **2.** so deep as to reach the knees

knee-high *adj.* so high or tall as to reach to the knees

kneel (nēl) *vi.* **knelt, kneel′ing** [< OE. *cneow,* knee] to bend or rest on a knee or the knees —**kneel′er** *n.*

knell (nel) *vi.* [OE. *cnyllan*] to ring in a slow, solemn way; toll —*n.* **1.** the sound of a tolling bell **2.** an omen of death, failure, etc.

knelt (nelt) *pt. and pp.* of KNEEL

knew (nyo͞o) *pt.* of KNOW

knickerbockers (nik′ər bok′ərz) *n.pl.* [< fictitious author of W. Irving's *History of New York*] short, loose trousers gathered just below the knees

knickers (nik′ərz) *n.pl.* [contr. < prec.] a woman's undergarment covering the lower trunk

knickknack (nik′nak′) *n.* [< KNACK] a small ornamental article or contrivance

knife (nīf) *n., pl.* **knives** [OE. *cnif*] **1.** a cutting or stabbing instrument with a sharp blade set in a handle **2.** a cutting blade, as in a machine —*vt.* **knifed, knif′-ing** to cut or stab with a knife —**have one's knife into someone** to have a grudge against or victimize someone —**under the knife** [Colloq.] undergoing surgery

knife-edge *n.* a metal wedge whose fine edge serves as the fulcrum for a scale beam, pendulum, etc.

knight (nīt) *n.* [OE. *cniht,* boy] **1.** *Hist.* a man formally raised to honourable military rank and pledged to chivalrous conduct **2.** in Britain, a man who for some achievement is given honorary nonhereditary rank next below a baronet, entitling him to use *Sir* before his Christian name **3.** [*usually* K-] a member of any society that officially calls its members *knights* **4.** [Poet.] a lady's devoted champion or attendant **5.** *Chess* a piece typically shaped like a horse's head —*vt.* to make (a man) a knight

knight-errant (nīt′er′ənt) *n., pl.* **knights′-er′rant 1.** a medieval knight wandering in search of adventure **2.** a chivalrous or quixotic person —**knight′-er′rantry** *n.*

knighthood *n.* **1.** the rank or vocation of a knight **2.** knightly conduct **3.** knights collectively

knightly *adj.* like a knight; chivalrous, brave, etc.

knit (nit) *vt., vi.* **knit′ted** or **knit, knit′-ting** [< OE. *cnotta,* knot] **1.** to make (cloth or clothing) by looping yarn or thread together with special needles **2.** to join closely and firmly **3.** to draw (the brows) together —**knit′ter** *n.*

knitting *n.* knitted work

knitting needle an eyeless, long needle used in pairs, etc. in knitting by hand

knitwear *n.* knitted clothing

knives (nīvz) *n.* *pl. of* KNIFE

knob (nob) *n.* [< MLowG. *knobbe*, knot] 1. a rounded lump or protuberance 2. a handle, usually round, of a door, drawer, etc. —**with knobs on** [Slang] that, and more: usually ironic —**knob′by** *adj.*

knobkierie (nob′ker′ē) *n.* [< Afrik. *knopkierie*] [S Afr.] a stick with a knob at one end used as a club or missile

knock (nok) *vi.* [OE. *cnocian*] 1. to strike a blow, as with the fist; esp., to rap on a door 2. to bump; collide 3. to make a thumping noise, as an engine —*vt.* 1. to hit; strike 2. to make by hitting 3. [Colloq.] to find fault with —*n.* 1. a knocking 2. a sharp blow; rap, as on a door 3. a thumping noise, as in an engine 4. [Colloq.] a misfortune or trouble —**knock about** (or **around**) [Colloq.] 1. to wander about 2. to treat roughly —**knock back** [Slang] to drink or eat —**knock down** 1. to strike down 2. to take apart 3. to indicate the sale of at an auction 4. [Colloq.] to reduce (a price) —**knock off** 1. [Colloq.] to stop working 2. [Colloq.] to deduct 3. [Colloq.] to make or do hastily or easily 4. [Slang] to kill 5. [Slang] to steal —**knock on** *Rugby* to play the ball forward with the hand or arm —**knock out** 1. to make unconscious or exhausted 2. to defeat, destroy, etc. —**knock sideways** [Colloq.] to disconcert sharply —**knock together** to make or compose hastily or crudely —**knock up** 1. to wake (someone) as by knocking at the door 2. [U.S. Slang] to make pregnant

knockabout *adj.* rough; noisy; boisterous

knockdown *adj.* 1. overwhelming 2. made so as to be easily taken apart 3. very low: said of prices

knocker *n.* a small metal ring, knob, etc. on a door, for knocking

knock-knee *n.* a condition in which the legs bend inward at the knees —**knock′-kneed′** *adj.*

knockout *adj.* that knocks out, as a blow —*n.* 1. a competition in which various competitors are eliminated progressively 2. *Boxing* a victory won when the opponent is knocked down and cannot rise before an official count of ten 3. [Slang] a very attractive or striking person or thing

knoll (nōl) *n.* [OE. *cnoll*] a hillock; mound

knot[1] (not) *n.* [OE. *cnotta*] 1. a lump in a thread, etc., as formed by a tangle 2. a fastening made by tying together pieces of string, rope, etc. 3. an ornamental bow of ribbon, etc. 4. a small group or cluster 5. something that ties closely; esp., the bond of marriage 6. a problem; difficulty 7. a hard lump on a tree where a branch grows out, or a cross section of such a lump in a board 8. *Naut.* a unit of speed of one nautical mile (1852 m) an hour —*vt.* **knot′ted, knot′ting** 1. to tie with a knot 2. to entangle —*vi.* 1. to form a knot or knots 2. to make knots for fringe —**get knotted** [Slang] an expression of disapproval or rejection —**tie the knot** [Colloq.] to get married —**knot′ted** *adj.*

knot[2] *n.* [< ?] a small grey northern sandpiper

knotgrass *n.* a common weed with slender stems and narrow leaves: also **knot′weed′**

knothole *n.* a hole in a board, etc. where a knot has fallen out

knotty *adj.* **-tier, -tiest** 1. full of knots 2. hard to solve; puzzling [a *knotty* problem] —**knot′tiness** *n.*

know (nō) *vt.* **knew, known, know′ing** [OE. *cnawan*] 1. to be well informed about 2. to be aware of [to *know* that one is loved] 3. to have securely in the memory [the actor *knows* his lines] 4. to be acquainted with 5. to have understanding of or skill in [to *know* music] 6. to recognize [I'd *know* that face anywhere] 7. to distinguish [to *know* right from wrong] —*vi.* 1. to have knowledge 2. to be sure or aware —**in the know** [Colloq.] having confidential information —**know what's what** to be very shrewd and wide-awake

know-all *n.* [Colloq.] a conceited person who thinks he knows everything

know-how *n.* knowledge of how to do something well; technical skill

knowing *adj.* 1. having knowledge 2. shrewd; clever 3. implying shrewd understanding or secret knowledge [a *knowing* look] 4. deliberate —**know′ingly** *adv.*

knowledge (nol′ij) *n.* 1. the body of facts, principles, etc. accumulated by mankind 2. the fact or state of knowing 3. range of information or understanding 4. what is known; learning —**to (the best of) one's knowledge** as far as one knows

knowledgeable *adj.* having or showing knowledge or intelligence —**knowl′edgeably** *adv.*

known (nōn) *pp. of* KNOW

knuckle (nuk′'l) *n.* [< MDu. & MLowG. *knokel*, little bone] 1. a joint of the finger; esp., the joint connecting a finger to the rest of the hand 2. the knee or hock joint of an animal, used as food —*vt.* **-led, -ling** to strike or touch with the knuckles —**knuckle down** to work energetically or seriously —**knuckle under** to yield; give in —**near the knuckle** [Colloq.] almost indecent

knuckle-duster *n.* linked metal rings or a metal bar with finger holes, worn for rough fighting

knurl (nurl) *n.* [prob. < ME. *knur*, knot + GNARL] any of a series of small beads or ridges, as along the edge of a coin —**knurled** *adj.*

KO (kā′ō′) *vt.* **KO'd, KO'ing** [Slang] *Boxing* to knock out —*n., pl.* **KO's** [Slang] *Boxing* a knockout Also **K.O., k.o.**

KOALA
(70-90 cm long)

koala (kō ä′lə) *n.* [< Abor.] an Australian, tree-dwelling marsupial with thick, grey fur

koeksister (kook′sist′ər) *n.* [< Afrik.] [S Afr.] a small cake of sweetened dough, usually dipped in syrup

kohl (kōl) *n.* [Ar. *kuhl*] a cosmetic preparation used, esp. in Eastern countries, for eye makeup

kohlrabi (kōl′rä′bē) *n., pl.* **-bies** [G. < It. *cavolo rapa*] a garden vegetable with an edible bulbous stem

kokanee (kō kan′ē) *n.* [< *Kokanee* Creek, British Columbia] a landlocked salmon of N American lakes

kola (kō′lə) *n.* alt. sp. of COLA

kolinsky (kə lin′skē) *n., pl.* **-skies** [< Russ.] 1. any of several weasels of Asia 2. the golden-brown fur of such a weasel

kolkhoz (kol hôz′) *n.* [Russ.] a collective farm in the Soviet Union

komatik (kō′mat ik) *n.* [< Eskimo] a sledge with wooden runners, used by Eskimos

kook (kook) *n.* [< ? *cuckoo*] [U.S. Slang] a person regarded as eccentric, crazy, etc. —**kook′y, kook′ie** *adj.*

kookaburra (kook′ə bur′ə) *n.* [< Abor.] an Australian kingfisher with an abrupt, harsh cry suggestive of loud laughter: also **laughing jackass**

kopeck, kopek (kō′pek) *n.* [< Russ.] a monetary unit of U.S.S.R.: equal to 1/100 of a ruble

kopje (kop′ē) *n.* [Afrik.] in South Africa, a small hill: also **koppie**

Koran (kō rän′) *n.* [< Ar. *qur'ān*, book] the sacred book of the Moslems: its contents are reported revelations made to Mohammed by Allah

Korean (kə rē′ən) *adj.* of Korea, its people, etc. —*n.* 1. a native of Korea 2. the language of the Koreans

kosher (kō′shər) *adj.* [Heb. *kāshēr*, proper] 1. *Judaism* a) clean or fit to eat according to the dietary laws b) dealing in such food 2. [Slang] all right, proper, etc. —*n.* kosher food

kowtow (kou′tou′) *n.* [Chin. *k'o-t'ou*, knock head] the act of kneeling and touching the ground with the forehead to show great deference, etc. —*vi.* 1. to make a kowtow 2. to show submissive respect (*to*)

Kr *Chem.* krypton

kraal (kräl) *n.* [Afrik. < Port. *curral*] in South Africa: 1. a village, usually surrounded by a stockade 2. a fenced enclosure for cattle or sheep

krans (kräns) *n.* [< Afrik.] [S Afr.] a cliff

kremlin (krem′lin) *n.* [< Russ. *kreml′*] in Russia, the citadel of a city, esp. of Moscow —**the Kremlin** the government of the Soviet Union

krill (kril) *n., pl.* **krill** [Norw. *kril*, young fry (of fish)] a small, shrimplike crustacean

kris (krēs) *n.* [Malay] a Malay dagger with a wavy blade

krona (krō′nə) *n., pl.* **-nor** (-nôr) [Sw. < L. *corona*, crown] the monetary unit of Sweden

krone (krō′nə) *n., pl.* **-ner** [Dan. < L. *corona*, crown] the monetary unit of Denmark or Norway

krypton (krip′ton) *n.* [< Gr. *kryptein*, to hide] a rare, inert, gaseous chemical element: symbol, Kr

Kt *Chess* knight

kudos (kyoo′dos) *n.* [Gr. *kydos*, glory] praise for an achievement; glory; fame

kudu (koo′doo) *n.* [< Afrik.] a spiral-horned African antelope

Ku Klux Klan (kyoo′kluks′klan) [< Gr. *kyklos*, circle] [U.S.] a secret, terrorist society that is anti-Negro, anti-Semitic, anti-Catholic, etc.

kukri (koo′kri) *n.* [Hindi] a short, curved, Gurkha knife

kulak (koo′läk) *n.* [< Russ., fist] a well-to-do farmer in Russia who opposed the Soviet collectivization of the land

kümmel (koom′'l) *n.* [G., caraway] a colourless liqueur flavoured with caraway seeds, anise, cumin, etc.

kumquat (kum′kwot) *n.* [< Chin. *chin-chü*, golden orange] a small, orange-coloured, oval fruit, with a sour pulp and a sweet rind, used in preserves

kung fu (kun′foo′) [< Chin.] a Chinese system of self-defence, like karate but emphasizing circular movements

KW kilowatt; kilowatts

kwashiorkor (kwa′shē ôr′kər) *n.* [< name in Ghana] a severe disease of young children, caused by a deficient diet

kwedien (kwe′dēn′) *n.* [< Xhosa] [S Afr.] a young African boy

kwh, K.W.H., kw.-hr., kw-hr kilowatt-hour

kyle (kīl) *n.* [Gael. *caol*] a narrow strait

L

L, l (el) *n., pl.* **L's, l's** the twelfth letter of the English alphabet

L (el) *n., pl.* **L's 1.** an object shaped like L **2.** a Roman numeral for 50

L. 1. Latin **2.** Learner (driver)

L., l. 1. lake **2.** left **3.** *pl.* **LL., ll.** line **4.** [L. *libra*, pl. *librae*] pound(s)

l litre

£ pounds (sterling)

la (lä) *n.* [see GAMUT] *Music* a syllable representing the sixth tone of the diatonic scale

La *Chem.* lanthanum

laager (lä′gər) *n.* [< Afrik.] [S Afr.] an encampment surrounded by wagons for defence

lab (lab) *n.* [Colloq.] a laboratory

Lab. 1. Labour **2.** Labrador

label (lä′b'l) *n.* [OFr., a rag] **1.** a card, paper, etc. marked and attached to an object to indicate its contents, ownership, etc. **2.** a convenient generalized classification for a person, group, etc. —*vt.* **-belled, -belling 1.** to attach a label to **2.** to classify as; describe

labial (lä′bē əl) *adj.* [< L. *labium*, lip] **1.** of the lips **2.** *Phonet.* formed mainly with the lips, as *b*, *m*, and *p* —*n.* a labial sound —**la′bially** *adv.*

labiate (lä′bē it) *adj.* [< L. *labium*, lip] **1.** formed like a lip **2.** having a lip or lips

labium (lä′bē əm) *n., pl.* **-bia** [L., a lip] *Anat., Bot.,* etc. a lip or liplike organ

laboratory (lə bor′ə tər ē) *n., pl.* **-ries** [see LABOUR] **1.** a room or building for scientific experimentation or research **2.** a place for preparing chemicals, drugs, etc.

laborious (lə bôr′ē əs) *adj.* **1.** involving much hard work; difficult **2.** hard-working —**labo′riously** *adv.*

labour (lä′bər) *n.* [< L. *labor*] **1.** physical or mental exertion; work **2.** a specific task **3.** *a)* all wage-earning workers as a group *b)* all manual workers **4.** trade unions collectively **5.** [L-] *same as* LABOUR PARTY **6.** *Med.* the process of giving birth to a child —*vi.* **1.** to work **2.** to work hard **3.** to move slowly and with difficulty **4.** to be burdened (with *under*) —*vt.* to develop in too great detail U.S. sp. **la′bor**

Labour Day a public holiday in honour of labour, held in many countries on May 1st, but in US and Canada on the first Monday in September

laboured *adj.* made or done with great effort; strained

labourer *n.* one who labours; esp., a wage-earning worker whose work involves physical exertion

Labour Exchange formerly, a government office set up locally to help the unemployed find work: also **employment exchange**

labour party 1. a political party organized to protect and further the rights of workers **2.** [L- P-] such a party in Great Britain

labour-saving *adj.* eliminating or lessening physical labour [*labour-saving appliances*]

Labrador retriever (lab′rə dôr′) a breed of dog having a black or yellow coat of short, thick hair

laburnum (lə bur′nəm) *n.* [L.] a small, poisonous tree or shrub with drooping racemes of yellow flowers

LABYRINTH

labyrinth (lab′ə rinth′) *n.* [< Gr. *labyrinthos*] **1.** a structure containing an intricate network of winding passages hard to follow without losing one's way; maze **2.** a complicated arrangement, condition, etc. **3.** *Anat.* the inner ear —**lab′yrin′thine** (-rin′thīn) *adj.*

lac (lak) *n.* [< Hindi < Sans. *lākṣā*] **1.** a resinous substance secreted on various trees in S Asia by a scale insect: source of shellac **2.** *same as* LAKH

lace (lās) *n.* [< L. *laqueus*, noose] **1.** a string, etc. used to draw together and fasten the parts of a shoe, corset, etc. **2.** an openwork fabric of linen, silk, etc., woven in ornamental designs —*vt.* **laced, lac′ing 1.** to fasten with a lace **2.** to weave together; intertwine **3.** to ornament with lace **4.** to thrash; beat **5.** to add a dash of brandy, etc. to —*vi.* **1.** to be fastened with a lace **2.** to attack (with *into*)

lacerate (las′ə rāt′) *vt.* **-at′ed, -at′ing** [< L. *lacer*, mangled] **1.** to tear jaggedly; mangle **2.** to hurt (one's feelings, etc.) deeply —**lac′era′tion** *n.*

lacework (lās′wurk′) *n.* lace, or any openwork decoration like lace

lachrymal (lak′rə məl) *adj.* [< L. *lacrima*, TEAR[2]] **1.** of or producing tears **2.** *same as* LACRIMAL (sense 1)

lachrymose (lak′rə mōs′) *adj.* [< L.

lacrima, TEAR[2]] **1.** inclined to shed tears **2.** causing tears

lacing (lās′iŋ) *n.* **1.** the act of a person who laces **2.** a beating **3.** gold or silver braid used to trim a uniform

lack (lak) *n.* [< MDu. *lak*] **1.** the fact or condition of not having enough or not having any **2.** the thing that is needed —*vi.* to be wanting or missing —*vt.* to be deficient in or entirely without

lackadaisical (lak′ə dā′zi k′l) *adj.* [ult. < *alack the day*] showing lack of interest or spirit; listless

lackey (lak′ē) *n.,* pl. **-eys** [< Sp. *lacayo*] **1.** a servile follower **2.** a male servant of low rank —*vt., vi.* **-eyed, -eying** to serve as a lackey

lacklustre (lak′lus′tər) *adj.* lacking brightness; dull

laconic (lə kon′ik) *adj.* [< Gr. *Lakōn*, a Spartan] terse in expression; using few words —**lacon′ically** *adv.*

lacquer (lak′ər) *n.* [< Port. *laca*, gum lac] **1.** a coating substance of natural or synthetic resins, dissolved in a solvent that evaporates rapidly **2.** a natural resin varnish obtained from certain trees in China and Japan, or woodenware coated with it —*vt.* to coat with or as with lacquer —**lac′querer** *n.*

lacrimal (lak′rə məl) *adj.* **1.** *Anat.* of or near the glands that secrete tears **2.** *same as* LACHRYMAL (sense 1)

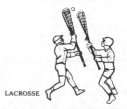

LACROSSE

lacrosse (lə kros′) *n.* [< Fr. *la*, the + *crosse*, a crutch] a ball game in which two teams use long-handled, pouched rackets, or **lacrosse sticks**

lactate (lak′tāt) *vi.* **-tated, -tating** [< L. *lac*, milk] to secrete milk —*n.* any salt or ester of lactic acid

lactation (lak tā′shən) *n.* **1.** the secretion of milk by a mammary gland **2.** the period during which milk is secreted

lacteal (lak′tē əl) *adj.* [< L. *lac*, milk] **1.** of or like milk; milky **2.** containing or carrying chyle —*n.* any of the lymphatic vessels that carry chyle from the small intestine to the blood

lactic (lak′tik) *adj.* [see LACTATE] of or obtained from milk

lactic acid a clear, syrupy acid formed when milk sours

lactose (lak′tōs) *n.* [see LACTATE] a white, crystalline sugar found in milk

lacuna (lə kyōō′nə) *n.,* pl. **-nas, -nae** (-nē) [L., a ditch] a space where something

has been omitted or has come out; missing part; gap; hiatus

lacy (lā′sē) *adj.* **-ier, -iest** of or like lace

lad (lad) *n.* [ME. *ladde*] **1.** a boy or youth **2.** [Colloq.] any man; fellow: familiar term

ladder (lad′ər) *n.* [OE. *hlæder*] **1.** a framework of two parallel sidepieces connected by rungs for use in climbing up or down **2.** any means of climbing [the *ladder* of success] **3.** a vertical break in a knitted fabric, esp. in a stocking —*vt.* to cause to have a ladder (*n.* 3)

ladder back a type of chair in which the back is constructed of horizontal slats between two uprights

laddie (lad′ē) *n.* [Chiefly Scot.] a young lad

lade (lād) *vt., vi.* **lad′ed, lad′ed** or **lad′en, lad′ing** [OE. *hladan*] **1.** to load **2.** to bail; ladle

laden *alt. pp.* of LADE —*adj.* **1.** loaded **2.** burdened; afflicted [*laden* with sorrow]

la-di-da, la-de-da (lä′dē dä′) *adj.* [Colloq.] affected in speech, manners, etc.; pretentiously refined

Ladies (lā′dēz) *n.pl.* [with *sing. v.*] a women's public toilet

lading (lā′diŋ) *n.* a load; cargo; freight

ladle (lā′d′l) *n.* [OE. *hlædel*] a long-handled, cuplike spoon for dipping out or carrying with or as with a ladle —*vt.* **-dled, -dling** to dip out or carry with or as with a ladle —**ladle out** to distribute lavishly

lady (lā′dē) *n.,* pl. **-dies** [< OE. *hlaf*, loaf + base of *dæge*, kneader] **1.** a) a woman of high social position b) a woman who is polite, refined, etc. **2.** any woman **3.** [L-] the Virgin Mary (usually with *Our*) **4.** [L-] in Great Britain, the title given to women of certain ranks —*adj.* female

ladybird *n.* a small, roundish beetle with a spotted back, that feeds chiefly on insect pests

Lady Day *same as* ANNUNCIATION (sense 2b)

lady-in-waiting *n.,* pl. **la′dies-in-wait′-ing** a woman attending, or waiting upon, a queen or princess

lady-killer *n.* a man who behaves towards women as if he were irresistible to them

ladylike *adj.* like or suitable for a lady; refined

lady's finger *another name for* BHINDI

ladyship *n.* the rank or position of a lady: used in speaking to or of a woman having the title of *Lady*, always preceded by *your* or *her*

lady's-slipper *n.* an orchid with reddish or purple flowers: the pink variety, or moccasin flower, is the floral emblem of Prince Edward Island

laevo- (lē′vō) [< L. *laevus*, left] a combining form meaning towards or on the left-hand side

lag[1] (lag) *vi.* **lagged, lag′ging** [? akin to MDan. *lakke*, go slowly] **1.** to fall, move, or stay behind **2.** to wane —*n.* **1.** a falling behind or being retarded **2.** the amount of this —**lag′ger** *n.*

lag² vt. **lagged, lag'ging** [prob. < Scand.] to cover a boiler, cylinder, etc., with insulating material —n. a narrow strip of insulating material

lag³ n. [< ?] [Colloq.] a convict or ex-convict

lager (beer) (lä'gər) [G. *Lagerbier*, storehouse beer] a beer which is stored for several months for aging after it has been brewed

laggard (lag'ərd) n. [< LAG¹] a slow person, esp. one who is always falling behind —adj. slow or late in doing things —**lag'gardly** adv., adj.

lagging (lag'iŋ) n. [< LAG²] insulating material wrapped around pipes, etc., to prevent loss of heat

lagoon (lə gōōn') n. [< L. *lacuna*, lake] 1. the water enclosed by a coral reef or separated from the sea by dunes 2. a shallow lake or pond, esp. one connected with a larger body of water

lah (lä) n. same as LA

laid (lād) pt. & pp. of LAY¹

laid paper paper having evenly spaced parallel lines water-marked in it

lain (lān) pp. of LIE¹

lair (lāər) n. [OE. *leger*] the resting place of a wild animal

laird (lāərd) n. [Scot. form of LORD] in Scotland, a landowner, esp. a wealthy one

lairiness (lāər'i nis) n. [Aust.] crude behaviour

laissez faire (les'ā fāər') [Fr., let do] noninterference; specif., the policy of letting industry and business operate without governmental regulation

laity (lā'ət ē) n., pl. -ties [< LAY³] all the people not included among the clergy; laymen collectively

lake¹ (lāk) n. [< L. *lacus*, lake] a large, inland body of water, usually fresh water

lake² n. [see LAC] 1. a dark-red pigment prepared from cochineal 2. its colour

Lake District (or **Country**) lake & mountain region in NW England: also called the **Lakes, Lake'land'**

lake trout a yellow-spotted char of the Great Lakes region of Canada

lakh (läk) n. [< Hindi] in India and Pakistan, the sum of 100 000: said specifically of rupees

lam (lam) vt., vi. **lammed, lam'ming** [< Scand.] [Slang] to beat; thrash; flog

Lam. Lamentations

lama (lä'mə) n. [Tibetan *blama*] a Buddhist priest or monk in Lamaism

Lamaism n. a form of Buddhism found in C Asia —**La'maist** adj., n. —**La'mais'-tic** adj.

lamb (lam) n. [OE.] 1. a young sheep 2. its flesh used as food 3. lambskin 4. a gentle, innocent, or gullible person —vi. to give birth: said of a ewe —**the Lamb** Jesus

lambaste (lam bāst') vt. **-bast'ed, -bast'-ing** [LAM + BASTE³] 1. to beat soundly 2. to scold severely

lambda (lam'də) n. the eleventh letter of the Greek alphabet (Λ, λ)

lambent (lam'bənt) adj. [< L. *lambere*, to lick] 1. playing lightly over a surface 2. softly glowing 3. light and graceful —**lam'bency** n. —**lam'bently** adv.

lambkin (lam'kin) n. a little lamb

lambskin (lam'skin') n. 1. the skin of a lamb, esp. with the fleece left on it 2. leather made from this

lamb's tail another name for CATKIN

lamb's wool soft, fine wool: also **lambs'-wool**

lame (lām) adj. [OE. *lama*] 1. crippled; esp., having an injured leg or foot that causes a limp 2. stiff and painful 3. poor, ineffectual, etc. [a lame excuse] —vt. **lamed, lam'ing** to make lame —**lame'ly** adv.

lamé (lä'mā) n. [< Fr. *lame*, metal plate] a cloth interwoven with metallic threads

lame duck a disabled, ineffectual, or helpless person or thing

lament (lə ment') vi., vt. [< L. *lamentum*, wailing] to feel or express deep sorrow (for); mourn —n. 1. a lamentation; wail 2. an elegy or dirge —**lam'entable** (lam'-) adj. —**lam'enta'tion** n.

lamented adj. mourned for: usually said of someone dead —**lament'edly** adv.

lamina (lam'ə nə) n., pl. **-nae'** (-nē') , **-nas** [L.] a thin flake, scale, or layer —**lam'i-nar** adj.

laminate (lam'ə nāt') vt. **-nat'ed, -nat'-ing** 1. to press into a thin sheet 2. to separate into or cover with thin layers 3. to make by building up in layers —n. something made by laminating —**lam'ina-ble** adj. —**lam'ina'tion** n.

laminated adj. composed of or built in thin sheets or layers, as of fabric, wood, plastic, etc., that have been bonded or pressed together

Lammas (lam'əs) n. [< OE. *hlammæsse*, bread feast] 1. a harvest festival formerly held on August 1 2. this day (**Lammas Day**) or this time (**Lam'mastide'**) of the year

lamp (lamp) n. [< Gr. *lampein*, shine] 1. any device for producing light or therapeutic rays 2. a container with a wick for burning oil, etc. to produce light or heat

lampblack n. fine soot used as a pigment in paint, ink, etc.

lamplighter n. formerly, a person who lit and extinguished gas street lamps

lampoon (lam pōōn') n. [< Fr. *lampons*, let us drink (refrain in a drinking song)] a piece of strongly satirical writing, usually attacking or ridiculing someone —vt. to attack in a lampoon —**lampoon'er, lampoon'ist** n.

lamppost n. a post supporting a street lamp

lamprey (lam'prē) n., pl. **-preys** [ML. *lampreda*] an eellike parasitic fish with a funnel-shaped, jawless, sucking mouth: it preys on other fish

lampshade n. an ornamental covering for an electric, gas, or oil lamp, made of glass, fabric, etc.

Lancastrian (laŋ kas'trē ən) adj. of Lancashire or Lancaster —n. a supporter of the house of Lancaster during the Wars of the Roses

lance (läns) *n.* [< L. *lancea*] 1. a thrusting weapon consisting of a long wooden shaft with a sharp metal head 2. a lancer 3. any sharp instrument like a lance 4. a surgical lancet —*vt.* **lanced, lanc'ing** 1. to cut open as with a lancet 2. to attack with a lance

lance corporal *see* MILITARY RANKS, table

lanceolate (län'sē ə lət) *adj.* [< LL. *lanceola*, little lance] tapering like the head of a lance, as certain leaves

lancer (län'sər) *n.* a cavalry soldier armed with a lance

lancers *n.pl.* [*with sing. v.*] [< LANCE] 1. a 19th-cent. quadrille 2. music for this

lancet (län'sit) *n.* [< OFr. dim. of *lance*, lance] a small, pointed surgical knife, usually two-edged

Lancs. Lancashire

land (land) *n.* [OE.] 1. the solid part of the earth's surface not covered by water 2. a country, region, or nation 3. ground or soil 4. ground considered as property 5. rural regions —*vt.* 1. to set on shore from a ship 2. to bring into a particular place 3. to set (an aircraft) down on land or water 4. to catch (a fish, etc.) 5. [Colloq.] to get or win [to *land* a job] 6. [Colloq.] to deliver (a blow) —*vi.* 1. to leave a ship and go on shore 2. to come to a port: said of a ship 3. to arrive at a specified place [to *land* up at home] 4. to alight or come to rest, as after a flight, jump, or fall 5. in Canada, to be legally admitted to the country as an immigrant, or **landed immigrant**

land agent a person employed by an estate-owner to collect rents, let farms, etc.

landau (lan'dô) *n.* [< *Landau*, Germany] a four-wheeled carriage with the top in two sections

landed (lan'did) *adj.* 1. owning land [*landed* gentry] 2. consisting of land or real estate [a *landed* estate]

landfall *n.* 1. a sighting of land from a ship at sea 2. the land sighted 3. a landing by ship or aircraft

land-girl *n.* a member of the Women's Land Army recruited to replace agricultural workers in wartime

landgrave (land'grāv') *n.* [< G. *Land*, land + *Graf*, a count] in medieval Germany, a count

landholder *n.* an owner or occupant of land

landing *n.* 1. the act of coming to shore 2. a platform at the end of a flight of stairs 3. the act of alighting, as after a flight, jump, or fall

landing field a field with a smooth surface to enable aircraft to land and take off easily

landing gear the undercarriage of an aircraft, including wheels, pontoons, etc.

landlady *n., pl.* **-dies** a woman landlord

landless *adj.* not owning land

landlocked *adj.* entirely or almost entirely surrounded by land, as a bay or a country

landlord *n.* 1. one who rents or leases land, houses, etc. to others 2. a man who keeps an inn, etc.

landlubber (land'lub'ər) *n.* a person who has had little experience at sea, and is awkward aboard a ship

landmark *n.* 1. any prominent feature of the landscape marking a locality 2. an important event in the development of something 3. an object used to mark the boundary of a piece of land

landmass *n.* a very large area of land

land mine an explosive charge hidden under the surface of the ground and detonated by pressure upon it

landowner *n.* one who owns land —**land'own'ership'** *n.* —**land'own'ing** *adj., n.*

Landrost (lan'drost, lant'-) *n.* [< Afrik. *landros*] *S Afr. Hist.* the chief magistrate of a district

landscape (land'skāp') *n.* [< Du. *land*, land + *-schap*, -SHIP] 1. an expanse of natural scenery seen in one view 2. a picture representing natural, inland scenery —*vt.* **-scaped'**, **-scap'ing** to change the natural features of (a plot of ground) so as to make it more attractive

landscape gardening the art or work of arranging lawns, trees, etc. on a plot of ground to make it more attractive —**landscape gardener**

landslide *n.* 1. the sliding of a mass of rocks or earth down a slope 2. the mass sliding down 3. an overwhelming victory in an election

landslip *n.* same as LANDSLIDE (senses 1 & 2)

landward (land'wərd) *adv.* towards the land: also **land'wards** —*adj.* situated or facing towards the land

lane (lān) *n.* [OE. *lanu*] 1. a narrow country road or city street 2. any narrow way, as an opening in a crowd 3. a marked strip of road wide enough for a single line of cars, etc. 4. any of the parallel courses marked off for contestants in a race 5. a designated path for ships and aircraft

lang. language

language (lan'gwij) *n.* [< L. *lingua*, tongue] 1. *a)* human speech *b)* the vocal sounds used in speech, or the written symbols for them 2. *a)* any means of communicating *b)* a special set of symbols, rules, etc. used for transmitting information, as in a computer 3. the speech of a particular nation, tribe, etc.

language laboratory a room equipped with tape recorders, etc., where language skills are developed

languid (lan'gwid) *adj.* [< L. *languere*, be faint] 1. without vigour or vitality; weak 2. listless 3. sluggish; slow —**lan'-guidly** *adv.*

languish (lan'gwish) *vi.* [see prec.] 1. to become weak; droop 2. to live under distressing conditions 3. to become slack or dull 4. to pine 5. to put on a wistful air —**lan'guisher** *n.* —**lan'guishing** *adj.*

languor (lan'gər) *n.* [see LANGUID] 1.

a lack of vigour or vitality **2.** listlessness **3.** tenderness of mood or feeling —**lan'guorous** *adj.*

lank (laŋk) *adj.* [OE. *hlanc*] **1.** long and slender; lean **2.** straight and limp: said of hair —**lank'ness** *n.*

lanky *adj.* **-ier, -iest** awkwardly tall and lean or long and slender —**lank'iness** *n.*

lanolin (lan'ō lin) *n.* [< L. *lana*, wool + *oleum*, oil] a fatty substance obtained from sheep wool and used in ointments, cosmetics, etc.

lantern (lan'tərn) *n.* [< Gr. *lampein*, to shine] **1.** a transparent case holding a light and protecting it from wind and weather **2.** the room containing the lamp at the top of a lighthouse

lantern jaws long, thin jaws, with sunken cheeks, that give the face a gaunt look —**lan'tern-jawed'** *adj.*

lanthanide series (lan'thə nīd') [< ff.] the rare-earth group of chemical elements from element 57 (lanthanum) to element 71 (lutetium)

lanthanum (lan'thə nəm) *n.* [< Gr. *lanthanein*, be concealed] a silvery, metallic chemical element of the rare-earth group: symbol, La

lanyard (lan'yərd) *n.* [< OFr. *lasne*, noose: altered after YARD¹] **1.** a short rope used on board ship for holding or fastening something **2.** a cord used esp. by sailors to hang a knife, whistle, etc. around the neck

laodicean (lā'ō də sē'ən) *adj.* [< *Laodicea*: see Rev. 3: 14-16] lukewarm; indifferent

lap¹ (lap) *n.* [OE. *læppa*] **1.** *a)* the front part from the waist to the knees of a sitting person *b)* the part of the clothing covering this **2.** that in which one is cared for, sheltered, etc. **3.** *a)* an overlapping *b)* amount or place of this **4.** one complete circuit around a race track **5.** a lapping —*vt.* **lapped, lap'ping 1.** to fold (*over* or *on*) **2.** to wrap; enfold **3.** to envelop **4.** to place partly upon something else **5.** to get a lap ahead of (an opponent) in a race —*vi.* **1.** to overlap **2.** to extend beyond something in space or time (with *over*) —**drop** (or **dump,** etc.) **into someone's lap** to cause to be someone's responsibility

lap² *vi., vt.* **lapped, lap'ping** [OE. *lapian*] **1.** to drink (a liquid) by dipping it up with the tongue as a dog does **2.** to strike gently with a light splash, as waves —*n.* the sound of lapping —**lap up 1.** to take up (liquid) by lapping **2.** [Colloq.] to take in eagerly

lap dog a pet dog small enough to hold in the lap

lapel (lə pel') *n.* [dim. of LAP¹] either of the front parts of a coat, etc. folded back and forming a continuation of the collar

lapful (lap'fool') *n., pl.* **-fuls'** as much as a lap can hold

lapidary (lap'ə dər ē) *n., pl.* **-daries** [< L. *lapis*, stone] a workman who cuts, polishes, and engraves precious stones

—*adj.* of or connected with the art of cutting precious stones

lapis lazuli (lap'is laz'yoo lī') [< L. *lapis*, a stone + ML. *lazulus*, azure] **1.** an azure-blue, opaque stone **2.** a blue pigment obtained from it **3.** its colour

LAP JOINT

lap joint a joint made by overlapping parts

lap of honour a circuit of the field or track by the winner(s) in a race or football game, etc.

Lapp (lap) *n.* **1.** a member of a people living in Lapland: also **Lap'land'er 2.** their language

lappet (lap'it) *n.* [dim. of LAP¹] a small fold or flap, as of a garment or flesh

lapse (laps) *n.* [< L. *labi*, to slip] **1.** a slip or small error **2.** *a)* a moral slip *b)* a falling into a lower condition **3.** a passing away, as of time **4.** *Law* the termination of a right or privilege through disuse, etc. —*vi.* **lapsed, laps'ing 1.** to slip into a specified state **2.** to backslide **3.** to pass away: said of time **4.** to become void because of failure to meet requirements —**laps'able, laps'ible** *adj.*

lapwing (lap'wiŋ') *n.* [< OE. *hleapan*, to leap + *wincian*, wink] a crested plover noted for its irregular, wavering flight: also called **peewit**

larboard (lär'bərd) *n., adj.* [< OE. *hladan*, to lade + *bord*, side] port; left

larceny (lär'sə nē) *n., pl.* **-nies** [< L. *latro*, robber] *Law* the unlawful taking of another's property; theft —**lar'cenist** *n.* —**lar'cenous** *adj.*

larch (lärch) *n.* [< L. *larix*] **1.** a coniferous tree bearing needlelike leaves that are shed annually **2.** the tough wood of this tree

lard (lärd) *n.* [< L. *lardum*] the fat of pigs, melted down and clarified —*vt.* **1.** to put strips of bacon, etc. on (meat or poultry) before cooking **2.** to add to; embellish

larder (lär'dər) *n.* a place where the food supplies of a household are kept; pantry

lardy cake (lär'd'ē) a rich, sweet cake made of bread dough, lard, sugar, and dried fruit

lares and penates (lāər'ēz ənd pi nāt'ēz) the household gods of the ancient Romans

large (lärj) *adj.* **larg'er, larg'est** [< L. *largus*] **1.** big; great; bulky, spacious, of great extent or amount, etc. **2.** big as compared with others of its kind **3.** operating on a big scale [a *large* manufacturer] —**at large 1.** free; not confined **2.** fully; in complete detail **3.** in general —**large'ness** *n.*

largely *adv.* **1.** for the most part; mainly **2.** much; in great amounts

large-scale *adj.* **1.** drawn to a large scale **2.** of wide scope; extensive

largess, largesse (lär jes') *n.* [see LARGE]
1. generous giving 2. a gift or gifts generously given

largish (lär'jish) *adj.* rather large

largo (lär'gō) *adj., adv.* [It.] *Music* slow and stately

lariat (lar'ē ət) *n.* [Sp. *la reata*, the rope]
1. a rope used for tethering grazing horses, etc. 2. a lasso

lark[1] (lärk) *n.* [OE. *læwerce*] any of a large family of songbirds; esp., the skylark

lark[2] *vi.* [? altered after prec. < ? ON. *leika*] to play or frolic (with *about* or *around*) —*n.* a frolic or spree —**lark'y** *adj.*

larkspur (lärk'spur') *n.* a common garden plant with spurred flowers, related to the delphinium

larrigan (lar'i gən) *n.* [< ?] a knee-high, oiled leather moccasin boot worn by trappers, etc.

larrikin (lar'ə kin) *n.* [< ?] [Aust.] a rough; a disorderly person —*adj.* rowdy

larva (lär'və) *n., pl.* **-vae** (-vē), **-vas** [L., ghost] the early, immature form of an animal that changes when it becomes an adult, as the caterpillar

laryngeal (lar'ən jē'əl) *adj.* of, in, or near the larynx

laryngitis (lar'ən jīt'əs) *n.* [ff. + -ITIS] inflammation of the larynx, often with a temporary loss of voice

larynx (lar'iŋks) *n., pl.* **lar'ynxes, laryn-ges** (lə rin'jēz) [< Gr.] the structure at the upper end of the human trachea, containing the vocal cords

lascar (las'kər) *n.* [< Hindi < Per. *lashkar*, army] an Oriental sailor, esp. one who is a native of India

lascivious (lə siv'ē əs) *adj.* [< L. *lascivus*, wanton] 1. characterized by or expressing lust 2. tending to excite lust —**lasciv'i-ously** *adv.* —**lasciv'iousness** *n.*

laser (lā'zər) *n.* [*l(ight) a(mplification by) s(timulated) e(mission of) r(adiation)*] a device that amplifies focused coherent light waves and concentrates them in a narrow, very intense beam

lash[1] (lash) *n.* [< ?] 1. a stroke as with a whip 2. the flexible part of a whip 3. an eyelash —*vt.* 1. to strike or drive as with a lash 2. to switch [the cat *lashed* her tail] 3. to strike with great force 4. to censure or rebuke —*vi.* 1. to make strokes as with a whip —**lash out** 1. to strike out violently 2. to speak angrily —**lash'er** *n.*

lash[2] *vt.* [see LACE] to fasten or tie with a rope, etc.

lashing[1] *n.* 1. a whipping 2. a strong rebuke

lashing[2] *n.* 1. the act of fastening or tying with a rope, etc. 2. a rope, etc. so used

lashings *n.pl.* [Colloq.] large amounts (often with *of*)

lash-up *n.* [Colloq.] an improvised contrivance

lass (las) *n.* [prob. < ON.] a young woman

Lassa fever (las'ə) [< *Lassa*, village in E Nigeria] an acute virus disease endemic to western Africa, characterized by high fever

lassie (las'ē) *n.* [dim. of LASS] [Scot.] a young girl

lassitude (las'ə tyōod') *n.* [< L. *lassus*, faint] a state or feeling of being tired and listless; weariness

lasso (la sōo') *n., pl.* **-sos, -soes** [Sp. < L. *laqueus*, noose] a long rope with a sliding noose at one end, used to catch cattle —*vt.* **-soed', -so'ing** to catch with a lasso

last[1] (lāst) *adj. alt. superl.* of LATE [see LATE] 1. being or coming after all others in place or time 2. only remaining 3. most recent [last month] 4. least likely 5. utmost 6. lowest in rank, as a prize 7. conclusive —*adv.* 1. after all others 2. most recently 3. finally —*n.* 1. someone or something which comes last 2. end [friends to the *last*] —**at (long) last** finally —**see the last of** to see for the last time

last[2] *vi.* [< OE. *læstan*] 1. to remain in existence or operation 2. to remain in good condition 3. to be enough (for) —*vt.* to continue or endure throughout: often with *out* —**last'er** *n.*

last[3] *n.* [< OE. *last*, footstep] a form shaped like a foot, on which shoes are made or repaired —**stick to one's last** to mind one's own business —**last'er** *n.*

last-ditch *adj.* made, done, etc. in a final, often desperate effort to resist or oppose

lasting *adj.* that lasts a long time; durable

Last Judgment *Theol.* the final judgment of mankind at the end of the world

lastly *adv.* in conclusion; finally

last name a surname or family name

last rites final rites for a dead person

last straw [from the last straw that broke the camel's back in the fable] a final trouble or annoyance that results in a breakdown, loss of patience, etc.

last word 1. a) the final word or speech, regarded as settling the argument b) final authority 2. something regarded as perfect 3. [Colloq.] the very latest style

lat. latitude

latch (lach) *n.* [< OE. *læccan*, to catch] a fastening for a door, gate, or window; esp. a bar that falls into a notch —*vt., vi.* to fasten with a latch —**latch onto** [Colloq.] 1. to attach (oneself) to 2. to understand

latchkey child a child who regularly arrives home to an empty house because his parents are at work

late (lāt) *adj.* **lat'er** or **lat'ter, lat'est** or **last** [OE. *læt*] 1. happening, coming, etc. after the usual or expected time 2. a) happening, continuing, etc. far on in the day, night, a period, etc. [the *late* Middle Ages] 3. recent [of *late* years] 4. former [my *late* employer] 5. having recently died —*adv.* **lat'er, lat'est** or **last** 1. after the expected time 2. at or until an advanced time of the day, night, etc. 3. towards the end of a period 4. recently —**late in the day** [Colloq.] at some late point in the proceedings, etc. —**of late** lately —**late′ness** n.

lateen (lə tēn′) adj. [< Fr. (voile) latine, Latin (sail)] designating or of a triangular sail attached to a long yard suspended from a short mast —n. a vessel with such a sail: also **lateen′er**

Late Greek the Greek language of the period after classical Greek, c.200 to c.600 A.D.

Late Latin the Latin language of the period after classical Latin, seen chiefly in writings from c.200 to c.600 A.D.

lately (lāt′lē) adv. recently; a short while ago

latent (lāt′ənt) adj. [< L. latere, to lurk] lying hidden and undeveloped within a person or thing

later (lāt′ər) adj. alt. compar. of LATE —adv. compar. of LATE at a later time —**later on** subsequently

lateral (lat′ər əl) adj. [< L. latus, a side] of, at, from, or towards the side; sideways —n. any lateral part, growth, etc. —**lat′erally** adv.

lateral thinking a way of solving problems by finding unorthodox solutions

latest (lāt′ist) alt. superl. of LATE —**at the latest** no later than (the time specified)

latex (lā′teks) n., pl. **latices** (lat′ə sēz′), **la′texes** [L., a fluid] a milky liquid in certain plants and trees: used esp. as the basis of rubber

lath (lāth) n., pl. **laths** (lāths) [< OE. lætt] any of the thin, narrow strips of wood nailed to studs, rafters, etc. as a groundwork for plastering, tiling, etc. —vt. to cover with laths

lathe (lāth) n. [prob. < MDu. lade] a machine for shaping wood, metal, etc. by holding and turning it rapidly against the edge of a cutting tool

lather (lāth′ər) n. [OE. leathor, soap] 1. the foam formed by soap and water 2. foamy sweat, as on a horse 3. [Slang] an agitated state —vt., vi. to cover with, or form lather —**lath′ery** adj.

Latin (lat′in) adj. 1. of ancient Rome, its people, their language, etc. 2. designating or of the languages derived from Latin, the peoples who speak them, their countries, etc. —n. 1. the language of ancient Rome 2. a person, as a Spaniard or Italian, whose language is derived from Latin 3. a native or inhabitant of ancient Rome

Latinate adj. of, derived from, or similar to Latin

latish (lāt′ish) adj., adv. somewhat late

latitude (lat′i tyōōd′) n. [< L. latus, wide] 1. Geog. a) distance, measured in degrees, north or south from the equator b) a region in relation to its latitude 2. extent; scope 3. freedom from narrow restrictions —**lat′itu′dinal** adj.

latitudinarian (lat′i tyōō′də nãär′ē ən) adj. [see prec. & -ARIAN] liberal in one's views, esp. in religious matters —n. one who is very liberal in his views, esp. in religion

latrine (lə trēn′) n. [< L. lavare, wash]

a toilet for the use of many people, as in an army camp

latter (lat′ər) adj. alt. compar. of LATE [OE. læt, late] 1. last mentioned of two: often a noun (with the) 2. a) nearer the end or close b) later; more recent

latter-day adj. of recent or present time

latterly adv. lately; recently

LATTICE

lattice (lat′is) n. [< MHG. latte, lath] 1. an openwork structure of crossed strips of wood or metal used as a screen, support, etc. 2. a door, shutter, etc. formed of such a structure 3. Physics a pattern of points in space, as of atoms in a crystal —vt. **-ticed, -ticing** 1. to arrange like a lattice 2. to furnish with a lattice

latticework n. 1. a lattice 2. lattices collectively

laud (lôd) n. [< L. laus, praise] 1. praise 2. [pl.] Eccles. [often L-] the first service at dawn —vt. to praise; extol

laudable adj. praiseworthy —**laud′ability, laud′ableness** n. —**laud′ably** adv.

laudanum (lod′'n əm) n. [< L. ladanum, mastic] a solution of opium in alcohol

laudatory (lôd′ə tər ē) adj. expressing praise

laugh (läf) vi. [< OE. hleahhan] to make the sounds and facial movements that express mirth, ridicule, etc. —vt. to cause to be by means of laughter [to laugh oneself hoarse] —n. 1. the act or sound of laughing 2. a cause of laughter 3. [pl.] [Colloq.] mere diversion —**have the last laugh** to win after apparent defeat —**laugh at** 1. to be amused by 2. to make fun of —**laugh in (or up) one's sleeve** to laugh secretly —**laugh off** to scorn or reject by laughter or ridicule —**no laughing matter** a serious matter —**laugh′er** n.

laughable adj. amusing or ridiculous —**laugh′ableness** n. —**laugh′ably** adv.

laughing gas nitrous oxide used as an anaesthetic: it may cause laughter and exhilaration

laughingstock n. an object of ridicule

laughter n. the action or sound of laughing

launch[1] (lônch) vt. [< L. lancea, lance] 1. to cause (a newly built vessel) to slide into the water 2. to start [to launch an attack] 3. to start (a person) on some course 4. to hurl, or send off (a weapon, blow, rocket, etc.) —vi. 1. to put to sea 2. to start on some new course or enterprise **3.** to plunge (*into*) —*n.* the launching of a ship, spacecraft, etc. —**launch′er** *n.*

launch² *n.* [Sp. or Port. *lancha*] **1.** an open motorboat **2.** formerly, the largest boat carried by a warship

launching pad the platform from which a rocket, guided missile, etc. is launched: also **launch pad**

launder (lôn′dər) *vt.* [< L. *lavare*, to wash] to wash, or wash and iron, (clothes, etc.) —*vi.* **1.** to withstand washing [this fabric *launders* well] **2.** to do laundry —**laun′derer** *n.*

Launderette (lôn′də ret′) *n.* a self-service laundry: also **Laundrette′**

laundress (lôn′dris) *n.* a woman whose work is washing clothes, ironing, etc.: also **laundrywoman**

laundry (lôn′drē) *n.,* pl. **-dries 1.** a place for laundering **2.** clothes, etc. laundered or to be laundered

laureate (lôr′ē ət) *adj.* [< L. *laurus*, laurel] crowned with a laurel wreath as a mark of honour —*n.* **1.** *same as* POET LAUREATE **2.** one on whom honour is conferred

laurel (lor′əl) *n.* [< L. *laurus*] **1.** an evergreen tree or shrub, native to S Europe, with large, glossy leaves; bay **2.** Its foliage, esp. as woven into wreaths used by the ancient Greeks to crown victors in contests **3.** [*pl.*] a) fame; honour b) victory —**look to one's laurels** to beware of having one's achievements surpassed —**rest on one's laurels** to be satisfied with what one has already achieved

Laurentian (lôr en′shən) *adj.* [Canad.] of or near the St. Lawrence river

Laurentian Shield *same as* CANADIAN SHIELD

lav *n.* [Colloq.] lavatory

lava (lä′və) *n.* [It. < L. *labi*, slide] **1.** melted rock issuing from a volcano **2.** such rock when cool and solid

lavatory (lav′ə tər ē) *n.,* pl. **-ries** [< L. *lavare*, wash] **1.** a room equipped with a washbowl, flush toilet, etc. **2.** the flush toilet itself

lave (lāv) *vt., vi.* **laved, lav′ing** [< L. *lavare*, wash] [Poet.] to wash or bathe

lavender (lav′ən dər) *n.* [< ML. *lavandria*] **1.** a fragrant plant having spikes of pale-purplish flowers and yielding an aromatic oil (**oil of lavender**) **2.** its dried flowers, leaves, and stalks used to perfume clothes, linens, etc. **3.** a pale purple —*adj.* pale-purple

lavender water a perfume or toilet water made from flowers of the lavender plant

lavish (lav′ish) *adj.* [< OFr. *lavasse*, torrent of rain] **1.** very generous in giving or spending **2.** very abundant —*vt.* to give or spend liberally —**lav′ishly** *adv.* —**lav′ishness** *n.*

law (lô) *n.* [OE. *lagu*] **1.** a) all the rules of conduct established by the authority or custom of a given community b) any one of such rules **2.** obedience to such rules **3.** jurisprudence **4.** the system of courts in which such rules are referred to in securing justice **5.** all such rules dealing with a particular activity **6.** the profession of lawyers, judges, etc. (often with *the*) **7.** a) a sequence of events in nature occurring with unvarying uniformity: often **law of nature** b) the formulation in words of such a sequence **8.** any rule expected to be observed [the *laws* of hygiene] **9.** *Eccles.* a divine commandment **10.** *Math., Logic,* etc. a general principle —**in** (or **at**) **law** according to the laws —**lay down the law 1.** to give orders in an authoritative manner **2.** to give a scolding (*to*) —**read law** to study to become a lawyer —**the Law 1.** [l-] [Colloq.] a policeman or the police **2.** the Mosaic law, or the part of the Hebrew Scriptures containing it

law-abiding *adj.* obeying the law

law agent in Scotland, a solicitor

lawbreaker *n.* a person who violates the law

lawful *adj.* **1.** in conformity with the law **2.** recognized by law; just —**law′-fully** *adv.*

lawgiver *n.* one who draws up a code of laws for a nation or people; lawmaker —**law′giv′ing** *n., adj.*

lawless *adj.* **1.** not regulated by the authority of law **2.** illegal **3.** not obeying the law; unruly —**law′lessness** *n.*

Law Lord a member of the House of Lords qualified to participate in the legal work of the House

lawmaker *n.* one who makes or helps to make laws; esp., a legislator —**law′mak′-ing** *adj., n.*

lawn¹ (lôn) *n.* [< OFr. *launde*, heath] land covered with grass kept closely mown, esp. around a house

lawn² *n.* [< *Laon*, city in France] a fine, sheer cloth of linen or cotton

lawn mower a hand-propelled or power-driven machine for cutting the grass of a lawn

lawn tennis *see* TENNIS

lawrencium (lo ren′sē əm) *n.* [< E. O. *Lawrence*] a radioactive chemical element produced by nuclear bombardment of californium: symbol, Lr

lawsuit (lô′soot′) *n.* a suit at law between two parties

law term a period in the year when the law courts sit

lawyer (lô′yər) *n.* a person whose profession is advising others in matters of law or representing others in lawsuits

lax (laks) *adj.* [< L. *laxus*;] **1.** not strict or exact; careless **2.** loose; slack —**lax′-ly** *adv.* —**lax′ness** *n.*

laxative (lak′sə tiv) *adj.* [< L. *laxus*, loose] making the bowels loose and relieving constipation —*n.* any laxative medicine

laxity (lak′sə tē) *n.* lax quality or condition

lay¹ (lā) *vt.* **laid, lay′ing** [< OE. *lecgan*] **1.** to place or put so as to rest, lie, etc. **2.** to cause to fall with force; knock down **3.** a) to put down (bricks, carpeting, etc.) in the correct position b) to situate [the scene is *laid* in France] **4.** to place; put [to *lay* emphasis on accuracy] **5.** to produce (an egg or eggs) **6.** to allay, overcome, or appease **7.** to smooth down **8.** to wager **9.** to impose (a tax, etc. *on* or *upon*) **10.** to devise *[to lay plans]* **11.** to set (a table) with plates, etc. **12.** to place fuel in a grate for lighting **13.** to present or assert *[to lay claim to property]* **14.** to attribute *[to lay the blame on Tom]* —*vi.* **1.** to lay an egg or eggs **2.** *Naut.* to go *[all hands lay aft]* —*n.* the way in which something is situated or arranged *[the lay of the land]* —**lay aside** to set aside for the future: also **lay by** —**lay bare** to disclose —**lay in** to get and store away —**lay into** [Slang] to attack —**lay it on** (thick) [Colloq.] **1.** to exaggerate **2.** to flatter effusively —**lay off 1.** to discharge (an employee), esp. temporarily **2.** [Slang] to cease —**lay on 1.** to spread on **2.** to attack with force —**lay oneself open** to expose oneself to attack, blame, etc. —**lay open 1.** to cut open **2.** to expose —**lay out 1.** to spread out (clothes, etc.) **2.** to make (a dead body) ready for burial **3.** to arrange according to a plan **4.** to spend —**lay up 1.** to store for future use **2.** to confine to bed —**lay up in lavender** to preserve for future use —**lay waste** to devastate

lay² *pt. of* LIE¹

lay³ *adj.* [< Gr. *lāos*, the people] **1.** of the laity, as distinguished from the clergy **2.** not belonging to a given profession

lay⁴ *n.* [OFr. *lai*] **1.** a short poem, esp. a narrative poem, for singing **2.** [Archaic or Poet.] a song or melody

layabout *n.* [Colloq.] a lazy idler or loafer

lay-by *n.* a widened section along a road allowing vehicles to park

layer (lā′ər) *n.* **1.** a single thickness, coat, fold, or stratum **2.** a person or thing that lays —**lay′ered** *adj.*

layette (lā et′) *n.* [Fr. < MDu. *lade*, chest] a complete outfit for a newborn baby, including bedding, clothes, etc.

lay figure [earlier *layman* < Du. *led*, limb + *man*, man] **1.** an artist's jointed model of the human form **2.** a person who is a nonentity

Lay Lord a peer in the British House of Lords other than a Law Lord

layman *n.* **1.** a person not a clergyman **2.** a person not belonging to a given profession

layoff *n.* the act of laying off; esp., temporary unemployment, or the period of this

layout *n.* **1.** the manner in which anything is laid out; arrangement; specif., the makeup of a newspaper, advertisement, etc. **2.** the thing laid out

lay reader a church member licensed to take some services, though not ordained

laze (lāz) *vi.* lazed, laz′ing to be idle —*vt.* to spend (time, etc.) in idleness —*n.* an instance of lazing

lazy *adj.* -zier, -ziest [prob. < MLowG.] **1.** not eager or willing to work or exert oneself **2.** slow and heavy; sluggish —**la′zily** *adv.* —**la′ziness** *n.*

lazybones *n.* [Colloq.] a lazy person

lb. [L. *libra*, pl. *librae*] pound; pounds

l.b.w. *Cricket* leg before wicket

l.c. 1. [L. *loco citato*] in the place cited **2.** *Printing* lower case

L.C.C. (formerly) London County Council

L.C.D., l.c.d. least (or lowest) common denominator

L.C.J. Lord Chief Justice

L.C.M., l.c.m. least (or lowest) common multiple

L/Cpl. lance corporal

L.D.S. Licentiate in Dental Surgery

lea (lē) *n.* [OE. *leah*] [Chiefly Poet.] a meadow, grassy field, or pasture; grassland

L.E.A. Local Education Authority

leach (lēch) *vt.* [prob. < OE. *leccan*, to water] **1.** to cause (a liquid) to filter down through some material, as wood ashes **2.** to extract (a soluble substance) from some material —*vi.* **1.** to lose soluble matter through a filtering liquid **2.** to dissolve and be washed away

lead¹ (lēd) *vt.* **led**, **lead′ing** [OE. *lǣdan*] **1.** to direct the course of by going before or along with, by physical contact, pulling a rope, etc.; guide **2.** to conduct (water, steam, etc.) in a certain direction, channel, etc. **3.** to direct by influence, etc. to a course of action or thought **4.** to be the head or leader of (an expedition, orchestra, etc.) **5.** to be at the head of *[to lead the world]* **6.** to live; spend *[to lead a hard life]* **7.** *Card Games* to begin the play with (a card or suit) —*vi.* **1.** to show the way by going before or along **2.** to be or form a way (*to, from, under,* etc.); go **3.** to bring as a result (with *to*) *[one thing led to another]* **4.** to be or go first **5.** *Card Games* to play the first card —*n.* **1.** *a)* first or front place *b)* the amount or distance ahead **2.** example *[follow his lead]* **3.** leadership **4.** the strap by which a dog is held in check **5.** anything that leads, as a clue **6.** *Card Games* the right of playing first, or the card or suit played **7.** *Elec.* a wire carrying current in a circuit **8.** *Theatre a)* a main role *b)* an actor or actress playing such a role —*adj.* acting as leader *[the lead horse]* —**lead a person a dog's life** to torment someone constantly —**lead off** to begin —**lead on** to lure —**lead up to** to prepare the way for

lead² (led) *n.* [OE.] **1.** a heavy, soft, bluish-grey metallic chemical element used for piping: symbol, Pb **2.** anything made of this metal; specif., *a)* a weight for sounding depths at sea, etc. *b)* *Printing* a thin strip of metal inserted to increase the space between lines **3.** bullets **4.** a thin stick of graphite, used in pencils —*adj.* made of or containing lead —*vt.* to cover, line, or weight with lead

leaden (led′'n) *adj.* **1.** heavy **2.** sluggish **3.** gloomy **4.** made of lead **5.** of a dull grey

leader (lē′dər) *n.* **1.** a person or thing that leads; guiding head **2.** a horse harnessed before all others **3.** a pipe for carrying fluid **4.** a section of blank film or recording tape at the beginning of a reel **5.** *Bot.* the central stem of a plant **6.** *Journalism* the editorial in a newspaper **7.** *Music* the leader of the first violins, often an assistant to the conductor: in full **leader of the orchestra** —**lead′erless** *adj.* —**lead′ership′** *n.*

leading (lē′diŋ) *adj.* **1.** that leads; guiding **2.** principal; chief —*n.* guidance; direction

leading aircraftman *see* MILITARY RANKS, table

leading light an important or influential member of a club, community, etc.

leading note *Music* the note a semitone below the keynote

leading question a question put in such a way as to suggest the answer sought

leading rating *see* MILITARY RANKS, table

leading rein 1. a rein used to lead a horse, esp. for someone learning to ride **2.** [*usually pl.*] straps used to control a child who is learning to walk

leading strings *same as* LEADING REIN (sense 2)

lead pencil (led) a pencil consisting of a slender stick of graphite encased in wood, etc.

lead poisoning (led) an acute or chronic poisoning caused by the absorption of lead into the body

lead time (lēd) the period of time from the decision to make a product to its actual production

leaf (lēf) *n., pl.* **leaves** [OE.] **1.** any of the flat, thin, expanded organs, usually green, growing from the stem of a plant **2.** leaves collectively [*choice tobacco leaf*] **3.** a sheet of paper **4.** a thin sheet of metal **5.** a hinged section of a table top —*vi.* **1.** to turn the pages of a book, etc. (with *through*) **2.** to bear leaves —**in leaf** with foliage —**take a leaf from someone's book** to follow someone's example —**turn over a new leaf** to make a new start —**leaf′less** *adj.*

leafage *n.* leaves collectively; foliage

leaflet *n.* **1.** a young leaf **2.** a separate sheet of printed matter, often folded but not stitched

leaf mould a rich soil consisting of decayed leaves

leafy *adj.* **-ier, -iest 1.** of, consisting of, or like a leaf or leaves **2.** having many leaves

league[1] (lēg) *n.* [< L. *ligare*, bind] **1.** an association of nations, groups, or individuals for promoting common interests, etc. **2.** *Sports* a group of teams organized to compete against one another **3.** [Colloq.] a group or class —*vt., vi.* **leagued, leagu′ing** to form into a league —**in league** allied —**leagu′er** *n.*

league[2] *n.* [ult. < Celt.] a measure of distance varying in different countries: usually about 5 kilometres

leak (lēk) *vi.* [< ON. *leka*, to drip] **1.** to let a fluid out or in accidentally **2.** to enter or escape in this way, as a fluid **3.** to become known little by little [the truth *leaked* out] —*vt.* to allow to leak —*n.* **1.** an accidental hole or crack that

lets something out or in **2.** any accidental means of escape for something **3.** leakage **4.** an intentional disclosure **5.** *a*) a loss of electrical charge through faulty insulation *b*) the point where this occurs —**leak′y** *adj.*

leakage *n.* **1.** a leaking; leak **2.** something that leaks in or out **3.** the amount that leaks

lean[1] (lēn) *vi.* **leaned** or **leant, lean′ing** [OE. *hlinian*] **1.** to bend or deviate from an upright position **2.** to bend the body so as to rest part of one's weight upon something **3.** to rely (on or upon) **4.** to tend (towards or to) —*vt.* to cause to lean —*n.* an inclination; slant —**lean′er** *n.*

lean[2] *adj.* [OE. *hlæne*] **1.** with little flesh or fat; thin **2.** containing little or no fat: said of meat **3.** meagre —*n.* meat containing little or no fat —**lean′ness** *n.*

leaning *n.* **1.** the act of a person or thing that leans **2.** tendency; inclination

leant (lent) *alt. pt. & pp. of* LEAN[1]

lean-to *n., pl.* **lean′-tos** a structure whose sloping roof abuts a wall or building

leap (lēp) *vi.* **leaped** (lept) or **leapt** (lept), **leap′ing** [OE. *hleapan*] **1.** to jump; spring;, bound **2.** to accept eagerly something offered (with *at*) —*vt.* **1.** to pass over by a jump **2.** to cause to leap —*n.* **1.** a jump; spring **2.** the distance covered in a jump —**by leaps and bounds** very rapidly —**leap in the dark** a risky act whose consequences cannot be foreseen —**leap′er** *n.*

leapfrog *n.* a game in which each player in turn jumps over the bent back of each of the other players —*vi.* **-frogged′, -frog′-ging 1.** to skip (over) **2.** to progress in jumps or stages —*vt.* to jump or skip over

leap year a year of 366 days, occurring every fourth year: the additional day is February 29

learn (lurn) *vt.* **learned** or **learnt** (lurnt), **learn′ing** [OE. *leornian*] **1.** to get knowledge of or skill in (an art, trade, etc.) by study, experience, etc. **2.** to come to know **3.** to memorize **4.** to acquire as a habit or attitude —*vi.* **1.** to gain knowledge or skill **2.** to be informed; hear (of or about) —**learn′able** *adj.* —**learn′er** *n.*

learned (lur′nid; *for 3* lurnd) *adj.* **1.** having or showing much learning **2.** of or characterized by study and learning **3.** acquired by study, experience, etc.

learner driver someone who is learning to drive a motor vehicle but who has not yet passed a driving test

learning *n.* **1.** the acquiring of knowledge or skill **2.** acquired knowledge or skill

lease (lēs) *n.* [< L. *laxus*, loose] a contract by which a landlord gives to a tenant the use of lands, buildings, etc. for a specified time and for fixed payments —*vt.* **leased, leas′ing** to give or get by a lease

leash (lēsh) *n.* [< L. *laxus*, loose] a cord, strap, etc. by which a dog or other animal is held in check —*vt.* to control as by a leash —**hold in leash** to control —**strain at the leash** to be impatient

least (lēst) *adj.* *alt. superl.* of LITTLE [OE. *læst*] smallest in size, degree, etc. —*adv.* in the smallest degree —*n.* the smallest in size, importance, etc. —**at (the) least** 1. with no less 2. at any rate

leastways *adv.* [Colloq.] at least; anyway

leather (*leth'*ər) *n.* [OE. *lether*] animal skin prepared for use by removing the hair and tanning —*adj.* of or made of leather —*vt.* [Colloq.] to whip

leathering *n.* [Colloq.] a beating

leatherjacket *n.* the tough-skinned larva of certain craneflies

leathery *adj.* like leather; tough and flexible

leave[1] (lēv) *vt.* **left**, **leav'ing** [OE. *læfan*, let remain] 1. to go away from 2. to allow to remain 3. to cause to remain [*to leave* footprints] 4. to have remaining after one [the deceased *leaves* a widow] 5. to bequeath 6. to entrust (with *to* or *up to*) 7. to cause to be in a certain condition [the flood *left* them homeless] 8. to abandon 9. to stop living in, working for, or belonging to —*vi.* to go away or set out —**leave off** 1. to stop 2. to stop doing or using —**leave out** 1. to omit 2. to fail to consider —**leave (someone) alone** to refrain from bothering (someone)

leave[2] *n.* [OE. *leaf*] 1. permission 2. *a*) permission to be absent from duty *b*) the period for which this is granted —**on leave** absent from duty with permission —**take leave** to say goodbye to

leave[3] *vi.* **leaved**, **leav'ing** [see LEAF] to put forth, or bear, leaves; leaf

leaven (lev'n) *n.* [< L. *levare*, raise] 1. a small piece of fermenting dough used for producing fermentation in a fresh batch of dough 2. *same as* LEAVENING —*vt.* 1. to make (batter or dough) rise with a leavening agent 2. to spread through, causing a gradual change

leavening *n.* 1. a substance, such as yeast, used to make dough rise by the formation of gas 2. any influence working to bring about a gradual change

leave of absence a leave from work or duty, esp. for a long time; also, the period of time

leaves (lēvz) *n.* *pl.* of LEAF

leave-taking *n.* the act of saying goodbye

leavings *n.pl.* things left over; leftovers, remnants, etc.

lecher (lech'ər) *n.* [< OFr. *lechier*, to be debauched, lit., lick] a lewd, grossly sensual man —**lech'erous** *adj.* —**lech'ery** *n.*

lectern (lek'tərn) *n.* [< L. *legere*, read] 1. a reading desk in a church 2. a stand for holding the notes, speech, etc., as of a lecturer

lecture (lek'chər) *n.* [< L. *legere*, read] 1. an informative talk given before an audience, class, etc., and usually prepared beforehand 2. a lengthy scolding —*vt.*, *vi.* **-tured**, **-turing** to give a lecture (to) —**lec'turer** *n.*

LED light-emitting diode

led (led) *pt.* & *pp.* of LEAD[1]

ledge (lej) *n.* [see ff.] 1. a shelf or shelflike projection 2. a projecting ridge of rocks

ledger (lej'ər) *n.* [prob. < ME. *leggen*, lay] 1. *Bookkeeping* the book of final entry, in which a record of debits, credits, etc. is kept 2. *Angling* a wire trace that allows the weight to rest on the bottom and the bait to float freely

lee (lē) *n.* [OE. *hleo*, shelter] 1. shelter 2. *Naut.* the side or part away from the wind —*adj.* of or on the side away from the wind

LEECH (to 8 cm long)

leech (lēch) *n.* [OE. *læce*] 1. an annelid worm with suckers, living in water and formerly used to bleed patients 2. a person who is a parasite —*vt.* to bleed with leeches

leek (lēk) *n.* [OE. *leac*] an onionlike vegetable: a Welsh national emblem

leer (lēər) *n.* [OE. *hleor*, cheek] a sly, sidelong look showing salaciousness, malicious triumph, etc. —*vi.* to look with a leer —**leer'ingly** *adv.*

leery *adj.* **-ier**, **-iest** wary

lees (lēz) *n.pl.* [< ML. *lia*] dregs, as of wine

lee shore the shore towards which the wind is blowing

leeward (lē'wərd; *naut.* loo'ərd) *adj.* in the direction towards which the wind blows —*n.* the lee part or side —*adv.* towards the lee

leeway (lē'wā') *n.* 1. [Colloq.] *a*) margin of time, money, etc. *b*) room for freedom of action 2. the leeward drift of a ship or aircraft from course

left[1] (left) *adj.* [< OE. *lyft*, weak] 1. designating that side of one's body which is towards the west when one faces north 2. closer to the left side of one facing the thing mentioned 3. of the bank of a river on the left of a person facing downstream 4. of the political left —*n.* 1. the left side 2. *Boxing* a blow delivered with the left hand 3. [often L-] *Politics* a radical or liberal position, party, etc. (often with *the*) —*adv.* on or towards the left hand or left side —**have two left feet** to be very clumsy

left[2] *pt.* & *pp.* of LEAVE[1]

left-hand *adj.* 1. on or directed towards the left 2. of, for, or with the left hand

left-handed (left'hand'-) *adj.* 1. using the left hand more skilfully than the right 2. done with the left hand 3. clumsy; awkward 4. insincere or ambiguous —*adv.* with the left hand [to write *left-handed*] —**left'-hand'edly** *adv.* —**left'-hand'edness** *n.* —**left'-hand'er** *n.*

leftist *n.* a person whose political position

is radical or liberal —*adj.* radical or liberal —**left'ism** *n.*

leftover *n.* [*usually pl.*] something left over, as from a meal —*adj.* remaining unused, etc.

leftward *adv., adj.* on or towards the left: also **left'wards** *adv.*

left wing the more radical or liberal section of a political party, group, etc. —**left'-wing'** *adj.* —**left'-wing'er** *n.*

lefty *n., pl.* **left'ies** [Slang] 1. a left-handed person 2. a left-winger in politics

leg (leg) *n.* [ON. *leggr*] 1. one of the parts of the body by means of which men and animals stand and walk 2. the part of a garment covering the leg 3. anything resembling a leg in shape or use, as one of the supports of a piece of furniture 4. any of the stages of a journey 5. a single stage, lap, or game in a race or competition 6. *Cricket* that part of the field to the left of, and behind, the batsman —*vi.* **legged, leg'ging** [Colloq.] to walk or run: used chiefly in **leg it** —**not have a leg to stand on** [Colloq.] to have absolutely no excuse —**on one's** (or its) **last legs** [Colloq.] not far from death, breakdown, etc. —**shake a leg** [Slang] to hurry —**stretch one's legs** to walk, esp. after sitting a long time —**leg'gy** *adj.*

legacy (leg'ə sē) *n., pl.* **-cies** [< L. *legatus,* leave by will] 1. money or property left to someone by a will 2. anything handed down, as from an ancestor

legal (lē'gəl) *adj.* [< L. *lex,* law] 1. of, based on, or authorized by law 2. permitted by law 3. of or applicable to lawyers —**le'gally** *adv.*

legal aid financial assistance available to people unable to meet their legal costs

legalese (lē'gə lēz') *n.* the special vocabulary of legal forms, documents, etc.

legalism (lē'gəl iz'm) *n.* strict, often too strict and literal, adherence to law —**le'galist** *n.* —**le'galis'tic** *adj.*

legality (lē gal'ə tē) *n., pl.* **-ties** quality, condition, or instance of being legal or lawful

legalize (lē'gə līz') *vt.* **-ized', -iz'ing** to make legal or lawful —**le'galiza'tion** *n.*

legal tender money that may be legally offered in payment of an obligation and that a creditor must accept

legate (leg'it) *n.* [< L. *legare,* to send as ambassador] an envoy, esp. one officially representing the Pope

legation (li gā'shən) *n.* 1. a diplomatic minister and his staff, representing their government in a foreign country and ranking just below an embassy 2. their headquarters

legato (lə gät'ō) *adj., adv.* [It.] *Music* in a smooth, even style

leg before wicket *Cricket* a dismissal because the ball, if it had not hit part of the batsman's body (except his hand) would, in the umpire's opinion, have hit the wicket

legend (lej'ənd) *n.* [< L. *legere,* read] 1. a story handed down for generations and popularly believed to have a historical basis 2. a notable person much talked about in his own time 3. an inscription on a coin, medal, etc. 4. a title, key, etc., as under an illustration

legendary *adj.* 1. of, based on, or presented in legends 2. worthy of being considered in legend

legerdemain (lej'ər di măn') *n.* [< MFr. *leger de main,* light of hand] 1. sleight of hand 2. deceit

leger line (lej'ər) [< *ledger line*] *Music* a short line written above or below the staff, for notes beyond the range of the staff

legged (leg'id, legd) *adj.* having (a specified number or kind of) legs *[long-legged]*

legging (leg'iŋ) *n.* [*often pl.*] a covering of canvas, leather, etc. for protecting the leg below the knee

leghorn (leg'hôrn', li gôrn') *n.* [< *Leghorn,* in Italy] 1. [*sometimes* L-] any of a breed of small chicken 2. *a)* a plaiting made of Italian wheat straw *b)* a broad-brimmed hat of this straw

legible (lej'ə b'l) *adj.* [< L. *legere,* read] that can be read, esp. easily —**leg'ibil'ity** *n.*

legion (lē'jən) *n.* [< L. *legere,* to select] 1. *Rom. History* a military division varying at times from 3000 to 6000 foot soldiers, with additional cavalrymen 2. a large group of soldiers 3. a large number —**le'gionary** *adj.*

legionnaire (lē'jə nāer') *n.* a member of a legion

Legionnaire's disease [after the outbreak at a meeting of the American Legion] a disease caused by viruses and having symptoms similar to those of pneumonia

legislate (lej'is lāt') *vi.* **-lat'ed, -lat'ing** to make or pass a law or laws —*vt.* to cause to be, go, etc. by making laws —**leg'isla'tor** *n.*

legislation (lej'is lā'shən) *n.* [< L. *lex,* law + *latio,* a proposing] 1. the making of laws 2. the laws made

legislative (lej'is lətiv) *adj.* 1. of legislation or a legislature 2. having the power to make laws

legislative assembly the single-chamber legislature in most Canadian provinces

legislature (lej'is lā'chər) *n.* a body of persons given the power to make laws for a country, state, etc.

legitimate (lə jit'i mət) *adj.* [ult. < L. *lex,* law] 1. born of parents legally married to each other 2. lawful 3. ruling by the rights of heredity 4. *a)* logically correct *b)* justifiable 5. conforming to established rules, standards, etc. 6. *Theatre* designating or of stage plays, as distinguished from films, etc. —**legit'imacy** *n.* —**legit'imately** *adv.*

legitimatize (lə jit'ə mə tīz') *vt.* **-tized', -tiz'ing** *same as* LEGITIMIZE

legitimize (lə jit'ə mīz') *vt.* **-mized', -miz'ing** 1. to make or declare legitimate 2. to make seem just, right, etc.

leg-pull *n.* a practical joke

legroom *n.* room to move one's legs comfortably, as in a car

leguan (leg′ oō än′) *n.* [< Du. *leguaan*] a large amphibious S African lizard

legume (leg′ yoōm) *n.* [< L. *legere*, gather] **1.** any of a large family of plants, including the peas, beans, clovers, etc., with fruit that is a pod **2.** the pod or seed of such a plant

leguminous (le gyoō′ min əs) *adj.* of, having the nature of, or bearing legumes

lei (lā′ē) *n., pl.* **leis** [Haw.] in Hawaii, a wreath of flowers and leaves

Leics. Leicestershire

leisure (lezh′ ər) *n.* [< L. *licere*, be permitted] free time that can be used for rest, recreation, etc. —*adj.* **1.** free and unoccupied **2.** having much leisure —**at leisure 1.** having free time **2.** with no hurry **3.** not occupied —**at one's leisure** when one has the time —**lei′ sured** *adj.*

leisurely *adj.* without haste; slow —*adv.* in an unhurried manner —**lei′ sureliness** *n.*

leitmotif, leitmotiv (līt′ mō tēf′) *n.* [< G. *leiten*, to lead + *Motiv*, motive] **1.** a short musical phrase representing and recurring with a given character, situation, etc. **2.** a dominant theme

lekker (lek′ ər) *adj.* [< Afrik.] [S Afr. Slang] pleasing; nice

LEM (lem) Lunar Excursion Module

lemming (lem′ iŋ) *n.* [Dan. < ON.] a small arctic rodent resembling the mouse

lemon (lem′ ən) *n.* [< Per. *līmūn*] **1.** a small, sour, pale-yellow citrus fruit **2.** the spiny, semitropical tree bearing this fruit **3.** pale yellow **4.** [Slang] something that is defective —*adj.* **1.** pale-yellow **2.** made with or flavoured like lemon —**lem′ ony** *adj.*

lemonade (lem′ ə nād′) *n.* a drink made of lemon juice and water, usually sweetened, often effervescent

lemon curd a paste made from lemons, eggs, and butter, used as a spread or a filling: also **lemon cheese**

lemon sole a flatfish, like the sole, valued as food

lemon squash 1. a drink made from a sweetened lemon concentrate and water **2.** the lemon concentrate

lemur (lē′ mər) *n.* [< L. *lemures*, ghosts] a small primate related to the monkey, with large eyes and soft, woolly fur

lend (lend) *vt.* **lent, lend′ ing** [< OE. *læn*, a loan] **1.** to let another use or have (a thing) temporarily **2.** to let out (money) at interest **3.** to give [to lend an air of mystery] —**lend an ear** (or **ears**) to listen —**lend itself** (or **oneself**) **to** to be useful for or open to —**lend′ er** *n.*

length (leŋth) *n.* [< OE. *lang*, long] **1.** the measure of how long a thing is from end to end **2.** extent in space or time **3.** a long stretch or extent **4.** the state or fact of being long **5.** a piece of a certain length **6.** a unit of measure consisting of the length of an object or animal in a race —**at full length** completely extended —**at length 1.** finally **2.** in full

lengthen *vt., vi.* to make or become longer

lengthways *adv., adj.* in the direction of the length: also [U.S.] **length′ wise**′

lengthy *adj.* **-ier, -iest** long; esp., too long —**length′ ily** *adv.* —**length′ iness** *n.*

lenient (lē′ nē ənt) *adj.* [< L. *lenis*, soft] not harsh or severe in disciplining, judging, etc.; mild; merciful —**le′ niency** *n.* —**le′ niently** *adv.*

lenitive (len′ ə tiv) *adj.* [< L. *lenire*, soften] soothing; lessening pain

lenity *n.* [see LENIENT] **1.** a being lenient; mildness **2.** *pl.* **-ties** a lenient act

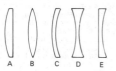

LENS
(A, plano-convex; B, double-convex; C, divergent meniscus; D, double-concave; E, plano-concave)

lens (lenz) *n.* [L., lentil < its shape] **1.** a piece of glass, plastic, etc. for bringing together or spreading rays of light passing through it: used in optical instruments **2.** a transparent body of the eye: it focuses upon the retina light rays entering the pupil

Lent (lent) *n.* [OE. *lengten*, the spring] the period of forty weekdays from Ash Wednesday to Easter, observed in Christian churches by fasting and penitence —**Lent′ en** *adj.*

lent (lent) *pt. & pp. of* LEND

lentil (lent′ il) *n.* [< L. *lens*] **1.** a leguminous plant with small, edible seeds **2.** the seed of this plant —**lenticular** (len tik′ yoo lər) *adj.*

lento (len′ tō) *adv., adj.* [It.] *Music* slow

Leo (lē′ ō) [L.: see LION] **1.** a N constellation between Cancer and Virgo **2.** the fifth sign of the zodiac

leonine (lē′ ō nīn′) *adj.* [< L. *leo*, lion] of or like a lion : said esp. of thick, tawny hair

leopard (lep′ ərd) *n.* [< Gr. *leōn*, lion + *pardos*, panther] a large, ferocious animal of the cat family, with a black-spotted tawny coat, found in Africa and Asia

leotard (lē′ ō tärd′) *n.* [< J. *Léotard*] a tightfitting garment for the torso, worn by acrobats, etc.

leper (lep′ ər) *n.* [< Gr. *lepros*, scaly] a person having leprosy

lepidopteran (lep′ ə dop′ tər ən) *n.* [< Gr. *lepis*, scale + PTERO-] an order of insects, including the butterflies and moths, characterized by four membranous wings covered with very fine scales —**lep′ idop′-terous** *adj.*

lepidopterist *n.* a person who studies or collects moths and butterflies

leprechaun (lep′ rə kôn′) *n.* [< OIr. *lu*, little + *corp*, body] *Irish Folklore* a fairy in the form of a little old man

leprosy (lep′ rə sē) *n.* [see LEPER] a

chronic, infectious disease that attacks the skin, flesh, nerves, etc., characterized by ulcers, white scaly scabs, deformities, etc.

leprous *adj.* **1.** of or like leprosy **2.** having leprosy

lepton (lep′ton) *n., pl.* **-ta** [< Gr. *leptos,* thin] *Physics* one of a group of primary particles which do not interact strongly with other particles

lesbian (lez′bē ən) *adj.* [< *Lesbos*] [*sometimes* L-] of homosexuality between women —*n.* [*sometimes* L-] a homosexual woman —**les′bianism** *n.*

lese majesty (lēz′maj′es tā) [< Fr.] **1.** treason **2.** any insolence towards one to whom deference is due

lesion (lē′zhən) *n.* [< L. *laedere,* harm] an injury of an organ or tissue resulting in impairment of function

less (les) *adj.* *alt. compar. of* LITTLE [OE. *læssa*] not so much, so great, etc.; smaller; fewer —*adv.* *compar. of* LITTLE to a smaller extent —*n.* a smaller amount —*prep.* minus —**less and less** decreasingly

-less (lis, ləs) [OE.] *a suffix meaning:* **1.** without, lacking [*valueless*] **2.** that cannot be [*dauntless*]

lessee (les ē′) *n.* [see LEASE] a person to whom property is leased; tenant

lessen (les′'n) *vt., vi.* to make or become less; decrease

lesser (les′ər) *adj.* *alt. compar. of* LITTLE [< LESS] smaller, less, or less important —*adv.* less

lesson (les′'n) *n.* [< L. *legere,* to read] **1.** a teaching session **2.** an exercise that a student is to prepare or learn **3.** something from which useful knowledge can be learned; example **4.** [*pl.*] course of instruction **5.** a selection read from the Bible **6.** a rebuke; reproof

lessor (les ôr′) *n.* [see LEASE] one who gives a lease; landlord

lest (lest) *conj.* [< OE. *thy læs the,* by the less that] **1.** for fear that; in case **2.** that: used after expressions denoting fear

let[1] (let) *vt.* let, let′ting [< OE. *lætan,* leave behind] **1.** to allow; permit [*let me help*] **2.** to rent; hire out **3.** to allow to pass, come, or go **4.** to allow or cause to escape **5.** to leave: now only in **let alone** (or **let be**), to refrain from bothering, etc. When used in commands, suggestions, or dares, *let* serves as an auxiliary [*let us go*] —*vi.* to be rented [*house to let*] —**let down 1.** to lower **2.** to deflate **3.** to disappoint —**let drop** (or **fall**) to drop accidentally or on purpose a word or hint —**let go** to release —**let off 1.** to give forth (steam, etc.) **2.** to deal leniently with —**let on** [Colloq.] to indicate one's awareness of a fact —**let out 1.** to release **2.** to rent out **3.** to reveal (a secret, etc.) **4.** to make a garment larger by reducing (the seam, etc.) —**let up 1.** to relax **2.** to cease

let[2] *n.* [< OE. *lettan,* make late] **1.** an obstacle or impediment: used in **without let or hindrance 2.** in tennis, etc., an

interference with the ball making it necessary to play the point over again

-let (lit, lət) [< MFr.] *a suffix meaning:* **1.** small [*ringlet*] **2.** a small object worn as a band on [*anklet*]

letdown *n.* a disappointment or disillusionment

lethal (lē′thəl) *adj.* [< L. *letum,* death] **1.** causing death; fatal **2.** of or suggestive of death

lethargy (leth′ər jē) *n., pl.* **-gies** [< Gr. *lēthē,* oblivion + *argos,* idle] **1.** sluggishness, apathy, etc. **2.** a condition of abnormal drowsiness —**lethargic** (li thär′jik) *adj.*

Lethe (lē′thē) [< Gr. *lēthē,* oblivion] *Gr. & Rom. Myth.* the river of forgetfulness, in Hades —*n.* oblivion; forgetfulness

letter (let′ər) *n.* [< L. *littera*] **1.** any of the characters of the alphabet **2.** a written or printed message, usually sent by post **3.** [*usually pl.*] an official document authorizing someone or something **4.** [*pl.*] a) literature b) learning; knowledge **5.** literal meaning —*vt.* to mark with letters —**to the letter** just as written or directed —**let′terer** *n.*

letter bomb an explosive device in an envelope that detonates when the envelope is opened

letter box 1. a box for receiving letters, as on the inside of a house door **2.** same as PILLAR BOX

lettered *adj.* **1.** literate **2.** well educated

letterhead *n.* **1.** the name, address, etc. of a person or firm printed as a heading on sheets of letter paper **2.** such a sheet

letter of credit a letter from a bank asking that the holder be allowed to draw sums of money from other banks

letterpress *n.* **1.** the method of printing from raised surfaces, as set type **2.** matter so printed

letters (or **letter**) **of marque** formerly, a government document authorizing an individual to arm a ship and capture enemy merchant ships

letters patent a document granting a patent

lettuce (let′is) *n.* [< L. *lac,* milk: from its milky juice] **1.** a hardy, annual plant, grown for its crisp, green leaves **2.** the leaves, much used for salads

letup (let′up′) *n.* [< phr. *let up*] [Colloq.] **1.** a slackening or lessening **2.** a stop or pause

leuco- [< Gr.] *a combining form meaning* white

leucocyte (lyoo′kō sīt′) *n.* [see prec. & -CYTE] any of the small, colourless cells in the blood, lymph, and tissues, which are important in the body's defences against infection; white blood corpuscle

leukaemia (lyoo kē′mē ə) *n.* [< Gr. *leukos,* white + -AEMIA] a disease of the blood-forming organs, resulting in an abnormal increase in the production of leucocytes: also sp. **leukemia** —**leukae′mic** *adj.*

Lev. Leviticus

Levant (lə vant′) [< L. *levare,* to raise, applied to the East, where the sun "rises"] coastal region on the E Mediterranean, between Greece & Egypt —**Levantine** (lev'ən tīn') *adj., n.*

levanter (lə van'tər) *n.* [< LEVANT] a strong wind that blows over the Mediterranean area from the east

levee[1] (lev'ē) *n.* [< Fr. < L. *levare*, to raise] [U.S.] **1.** an embankment built alongside a river to prevent high water from flooding land bordering land **2.** a quay

levee[2] *n.* [< Fr. *se lever*, to rise] formerly, a morning reception held by a sovereign

level (lev''l) *n.* [< L. *libra*, balance] **1.** a horizontal plane or line [*sea level*] **2.** an instrument for determining whether a surface is horizontal **3.** position, rank, etc. in a scale of values [*levels of income*] **4.** normal position [*water seeks its level*] **5.** a horizontal area —*adj.* **1.** perfectly flat and even **2.** not sloping **3.** even in height (*with*) **4.** even with the top of the container **5.** equal in importance, rank, degree, etc. **6.** *a*) well-balanced; equable *b*) calm or steady —*vt., vi.* **-elled, -elling 1.** to make or become level, even, flat, equal (as in rank), etc. **2.** to demolish **3.** to raise and aim (a gun, etc.) —**level off 1.** to give a flat surface to **2.** *Aeron.* to come or bring to a horizontal line of flight: also **level out 3.** to become stable or constant —**one's level best** [Colloq.] the best one can do —**on the level** [Slang] honest(ly) and fair(ly) —**lev'eller** *n.*

level crossing the place where one railway intersects another railway or a road on the same level

levelheaded *adj.* having or showing an even temper and sound judgment —**lev'el-head'edly** *adv.*

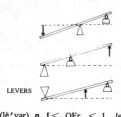

LEVERS

lever (lē'vər) *n.* [< OFr. < L. *levare*, raise] **1.** *Mech.* a device consisting of a bar turning about a fixed point, using force at a second point to lift a weight at a third **2.** a bar used to open by force, as a crowbar **3.** a means to an end —*vt.* to move, lift, etc. with a lever

leverage *n.* **1.** the action of a lever **2.** the mechanical power resulting from this **3.** increased means of accomplishing some purpose

leveret (lev'ər it) *n.* [< L. *lepus*, hare] a hare during its first year

leviathan (lə vī'ə thən) *n.* [< Heb. *liwyāthān*] **1.** *Bible* a sea monster **2.** any huge thing

Levi's (lē'vīz) [< *Levi* Strauss] *Trademark* closefitting trousers of denim,

reinforced at the seams, etc. with small copper rivets

levitate (lev'ə tāt') *vt.* **-tat'ed, -tat'ing** [< L. *levis*, light] to cause to rise and float in the air supposedly, often by using supernatural powers —**lev'ita'tion** *n.*

levity (lev'ə tē) *n., pl.* **-ties** [< L. *levis*, light] **1.** lightness of disposition, conduct, etc. **2.** fickleness

levy (lev'ē) *n., pl.* **lev'ies** [< MFr.: see LEVER] **1.** an imposing and collecting of a tax, fine, etc. **2.** the amount levied **3.** *a*) compulsory enlistment for military service *b*) a group so enlisted —*vt.* **lev'ied, lev'ying 1.** to impose (a tax, fine, etc.) **2.** to enlist (troops) for military service **3.** to wage (war)

lewd (lōōd) *adj.* [< OE. *læwede*, unlearned] showing, or intended to excite, lust or sexual desire; obscene

lexical (lek'si k'l) *adj.* [< Gr. *lexikon*, lexicon] **1.** of items of vocabulary in a language **2.** of a lexicon

lexicographer (lek'sə kog'rə fər) *n.* [< Gr. *lexikon*, lexicon + *graphein*, write] a person who writes or compiles a dictionary —**lex'icog'raphy** *n.*

lexicon (lek'si kən) *n.* [< Gr. *legein*, to say] **1.** a dictionary, esp. of an ancient language **2.** a special vocabulary, as a of a particular author

ley (lā) *n.* [< LEA] farmland temporarily under grass

Leyden jar (or **vial**) (līd''n) [< *Leiden*, Netherlands] a condenser for static electricity, consisting of a glass jar with a coat of tinfoil outside and inside and a metallic rod connecting with the inner lining and passing through the lid

LF, L.F., lf, l.f. low frequency

LGr., L.Gr. Late Greek

l.h., L.H., LH left hand

Li *Chem.* lithium

liability (lī'ə bil'ə tē) *n., pl.* **-ties 1.** the state of being liable **2.** anything for which a person is liable **3.** [*pl.*] *Accounting* the debts of a person or business **4.** something that works to one's disadvantage

liable (lī'ə b'l) *adj.* [< L. *ligare*, bind] **1.** legally bound; responsible **2.** subject to [*liable* to heart attacks] **3.** likely (*to*) [*liable* to cause hard feelings]

liaise (li āz') *vi.* **-aised', -ais'ing** [< ff.] to establish liaison (usually with *with*)

liaison (lē ā'zon) *n.* [< L. *ligare*, to bind] **1.** a connecting of the parts of a whole, as of military units, in order to bring about proper coordination of activities **2.** an illicit love affair

liana (li än'ə) *n.* [NormFr. *liane*] any luxuriantly growing, tropical vine that roots in the ground and climbs, as around tree trunks

liar (lī'ər) *n.* a person who tells lies

lib (lib) *n. short for* liberation

Lib. Liberal

lib. 1. [L. *liber*] book **2.** librarian **3.** library

libation (lī bā'shən) *n.* [< L. *libare*, pour out] **1.** the ritual of pouring out wine or oil upon the ground as a sacrifice to a god **2.** the liquid so poured out

libel (lī′b'l) *n.* [< L. *liber*, book] **1.** any written or printed matter tending to injure a person's reputation unjustly **2.** the act of publishing such a thing **3.** anything that gives a damaging picture of the subject —*vt.* **-belled, -belling** to make a libel against — **li′beller** *n.*

libellous *adj.* **1.** of or involving a libel **2.** given to writing and publishing libels — **li′bellously** *adv.*

liberal (lib′ər əl) *adj.* [< L. *liber*, free] **1.** favouring reform or progress; specif., favouring political reforms **2.** broad-minded **3.** giving freely; generous **4.** ample; abundant **5.** not restricted to the literal meaning **6.** [L-] designating a political party upholding liberal principles, as in Great Britain or Canada —*n.* **1.** a person favouring reform **2.** [L-] a member of a liberal political party — **lib′eralism** *n.* — **lib′erally** *adv.*

liberality (lib′ə ral′ə tē) *n.,* pl. **-ties** **1.** generosity; broad-mindedness

liberalize (lib′ər ə līz′) *vt., vi.* **-ized′, -iz′ing** to make or become liberal — **lib′eraliza′tion** *n.*

liberate (lib′ə rāt′) *vt.* **-at′ed, -at′ing** [< L. *liber*, free] to release from slavery, enemy occupation, etc. — **lib′era′tion** *n.* — **lib′era′tor** *n.*

libertine (lib′ər tēn′) *n.* [< L. *liber*, free] a man who leads an unrestrained, sexually immoral life; rake —*adj.* licentious — **lib′ertinism, lib′ertinage** *n.*

liberty (lib′ər tē) *n.,* pl. **-ties** [< L. *liber*, free] **1.** freedom from slavery, captivity, etc. **2.** a particular right, franchise, freedom, etc. **3.** a too free, too familiar, or impertinent attitude — **at liberty 1.** not confined; free **2.** allowed (to do or say something) **3.** not busy or in use — **take liberties 1.** to be impertinent in action or speech **2.** to deal (*with* facts, etc.) in a distorting way

libidinous (li bid′ə nəs) *adj.* [see ff.] lustful; lewd; lascivious — **libid′inously** *adv.*

libido (li bē′dō) *n.* [L., desire] the sexual urge or instinct — **libid′inal** (-bid′′n əl) *adj.*

Libra (lī′brə) [L., a balance] **1.** a S constellation between Virgo and Scorpio **2.** the seventh sign of the zodiac

librarian (lī brāar′ē ən) *n.* **1.** a person in charge of a library **2.** a qualified library worker — **librar′ianship′** *n.*

library (lī′brə rē) *n.,* pl. **-braries** [< L. *liber*, book] **1.** a room or building where a collection of books, periodicals, etc. is kept **2.** an institution in charge of the care and circulation of such a collection **3.** a collection of books, periodicals, etc.

libretto (li bret′ō) *n.,* pl. **-tos, -ti** [It. < L. *liber*, book] the words, or text, of an opera, oratorio, etc. — **libret′tist** *n.*

lice (līs) *n.* pl. of LOUSE

licence (līs′′ns) *n.* [< L. *licere*, be permitted] **1.** formal or legal permission to do something specified **2.** a document indicating such permission **3.** freedom to deviate from strict conduct, rule, or

practice [poetic *licence*] **4.** excessive, undisciplined freedom Also, U.S. sp., **license**

license (līs′′ns) *vt.* **-censed, censing** [< prec.] to permit formally — **li′censable** *adj.*

licensee (līs′′n sē′) *n.* a person to whom a licence is granted, esp. one to sell alcoholic drink

licentiate (lī sen′shē it) *n.* a person licensed to practise a specified profession — **licen′tiateship′** *n.*

licentious (lī sen′shəs) *adj.* [see LICENCE] morally unrestrained, esp. in sexual activity; lascivious — **licen′tiously** *adv.* — **licen′tiousness** *n.*

lichee (lī′chē′) *n.* same as LITCHI

lichen (lī′kən) *n.* [< Gr. *leichein*, to lick] a mosslike plant growing in patches on rocks, wood, soil, etc.

lich gate (lich) [< OE. *lic-*, akin to G. *Leiche*, corpse + gate] a roofed gate at the entrance to a churchyard, where a coffin awaits the arrival of the clergyman

licit (lis′it) *adj.* [< L. *licere*, be permitted] permitted; lawful — **lic′itly** *adv.* — **lic′itness** *n.*

lick (lik) *vt.* [OE. *liccian*] **1.** to pass the tongue over **2.** to bring into a certain condition by passing the tongue over **3.** to pass lightly over like a tongue [flames *licking* the logs] **4.** [Colloq.] *a)* to whip *b)* to vanquish —*n.* **1.** a licking with the tongue **2.** [Colloq.] *a)* a sharp blow *b)* a short, rapid burst of activity *c)* a fast pace — **lick and a promise** a hasty, superficial effort in cleaning, etc. — **lick into shape** [Colloq.] to bring into proper condition — **lick one's chops** to anticipate eagerly — **lick one's wounds** to retire after a severe defeat — **lick up** to consume as by licking

lick-spittle *n.* a servile flatterer: also **lick′spit′**

licorice (lik′ər is) *n.* same as LIQUORICE

lid (lid) *n.* [OE. *hlid*] **1.** a movable cover, as for a box, pot, etc. **2.** short for EYELID **3.** [Colloq.] a curb or restraint — **lid′ded** *adj.* — **lid′less** *adj.*

lido (lē′dō) *n.* [< *Lido,* NE Italy] **1.** a pleasure resort **2.** a public swimming pool

lie[1] (lī) *vi.* lay, lain, ly′ing [OE. *licgan*] **1.** to be or put oneself in a horizontal or reclining position (often with *down*) **2.** to rest on a support in a horizontal position **3.** to be in a specified condition **4.** to be situated [Scotland *lies* to the north of England] **5.** to extend [the road that *lies* before us] **6.** to exist [the love that *lies* in her eyes] **7.** [Archaic] to stay overnight —*n.* the way in which something is situated or arranged; lay — **lie down on the job** [Colloq.] to put forth less than one's best efforts — **lie in 1.** to stay in bed in the morning **2.** to be in confinement for childbirth — **lie over** to wait until some future time — **take lying down** to submit to (a wrong, etc.) without protest — **li′er** *n.*

lie[2] *vi.* lied, ly′ing [OE. *leogan*] to make a statement that one knows to be false —*n.* **1.** a thing said in lying **2.** anything that gives a false impression —**give the lie to** 1. to prove to be false 2. to charge with telling a lie

lied (lēd) *n., pl.* **lied'er** [G.] a German lyrical song

lief (lēf) *adv.* [OE. *leof*] willingly; gladly: only in **would** (or **had**) **as lief**

liege (lēj) *adj.* [< OFr.] 1. *Feudal law* a) entitled to the allegiance of his vassals b) bound to give allegiance to the lord 2. loyal; faithful —*n. Feudal Law* 1. a lord or sovereign 2. a subject or vassal

lien (li'ən) *n.* [< L. *ligare*, bind] *Law* a claim on the property of another as security for the payment of a debt

lieu (lyōō) *n.* [< L. *locus*, place] place: now chiefly in **in lieu of,** in place of; instead of

lieutenant (lef ten'ənt) *n.* [< MFr. *lieu*, place + *tenant*, holding] 1. one who acts for a superior 2. *see* MILITARY RANKS, table —**lieuten'ancy** *n.*

lieutenant colonel *see* MILITARY RANKS, table

lieutenant commander *see* MILITARY RANKS, table

lieutenant general *see* MILITARY RANKS, table

lieutenant governor the official head of government of a Canadian province, appointed by the governor general: also **lieuten'ant-gov'ernor** *n.*

life (līf) *n., pl.* **lives** [OE. *lif*] 1. that property of plants and animals (ending at death) which makes it possible for them to take in food, get energy from it, grow, etc. 2. the state of possessing this property 3. a human being *[the lives lost in wars]* 4. living things collectively *[plant life]* 5. the time a person or thing is alive 6. one's manner of living *[a life of ease]* 7. the people and activities of a given time, setting, or class *[military life]* 8. human existence *[to learn from life]* 9. a) an individual's lifetime experiences b) an account of this 10. the existence of the soul *[eternal life]* 11. something essential to the continued existence of something else *[freedom of speech is the life of democracy]* 12. the source of liveliness *[the life of the party]* 13. vigour; liveliness —*adj.* of, in, or for life —a **matter of life and death** a matter of extreme importance —**as large as life** 1. life-size 2. in actual fact —**for dear life** with a desperate intensity —**for life** for the duration of one's life —**from life** from a living model —**not on your life** certainly not —**take one's (own) life** to commit suicide —**to the life** exactly —**true to life** true to reality

lifeblood *n.* 1. the blood necessary to life 2. a vital element or animating influence

lifeboat *n.* 1. a small boat carried by a ship for use if the ship must be abandoned 2. a boat launched from the shore to help ships in distress

life buoy a buoyant device for saving a person from drowning by keeping his body afloat

life-giving *adj.* 1. that gives life 2. refreshing

lifeguard *n.* an expert swimmer employed at a beach, a pool, etc. to prevent drownings

life insurance insurance in which a stipulated sum is paid to the beneficiary at the death of the insured

LIFE JACKET

life jacket (or **vest**) a life buoy in the form of a sleeveless jacket

lifeless *adj.* 1. a) inanimate b) dead 2. dull; listless —**life'lessly** *adv.*

lifelike *adj.* resembling actual life or a real person or thing

lifeline *n.* 1. a rope for saving life 2. the rope used to raise or lower a diver 3. a vital line of access or communication

lifelong *adj.* lasting or not changing during one's whole life

life peer a peer whose title lapses at his death

life preserver 1. a club kept for self-defence 2. [U.S.] a life jacket

lifer *n.* [Slang] one sentenced to imprisonment for life

life raft a small, inflatable raft or boat

lifesaver *n.* 1. a lifeguard 2. [Colloq.] a person or thing that is of great timely help —**life'sav'ing** *adj., n.*

life-size *adj.* of the same size as the person or thing represented: also **life'-sized'**

life style one's way of life

lifetime *n.* the length of time that one lives, or that something lasts —*adj.* lasting for such a period

lift (lift) *vt.* [< ON. *lopt*, air] 1. to bring up to a higher position; raise 2. to raise in rank, condition, etc. 3. to end (a siege, etc.) by withdrawing forces 4. to revoke (a ban or order) 5. to subject to FACE LIFTING 6. [Colloq.] to plagiarize 7. [Colloq.] to steal —*vi.* 1. to exert strength in raising something 2. to rise and vanish 3. to become raised; go up —*n.* 1. a lifting, raising, or rising 2. the amount lifted 3. the distance something is lifted 4. lifting force, power, or influence 5. elevation of mood 6. elevated position or carriage 7. a ride in a car or bus in the direction one is going 8. help of any kind 9. a cage or car for hoisting or lowering people or things, attached by cables to a machine that moves it in a shaft 10. a device used to transport people up or down a slope

liftoff *n.* the vertical thrust and rise of a spacecraft, missile, etc. as it is launched

ligament (lig'ə mənt) *n.* [< L. *ligare*, to

bind] 1. *Anat.* a band of tough tissue connecting bones or holding organs in place 2. a bond or tie

ligature (lig'ə chōoər) *n.* [< L. *ligare*, to bind] 1. a tying or binding together 2. a tie, bond, etc. 3. two or more letters united, as *ff, th* 4. *Music* a curved line indicating a slur 5. *Surgery* a thread used to tie up an artery, etc.

light[1] (līt) *n.* [OE. *leoht*] 1. *a*) the form of electromagnetic radiation that acts upon the retina of the eye making sight possible *b*) ultraviolet and infrared radiation 2. brightness; illumination, often of a specified kind 3. a source of light, as the sun, a lamp, etc. 4. *same as* TRAFFIC LIGHT 5. daylight or dawn 6. a thing by means of which something can be started burning 7. the means by which light is let in; window 8. knowledge; enlightenment 9. spiritual inspiration 10. the way in which something is seen; aspect 11. facial expression 12. an outstanding figure —*adj.* 1. having light; bright 2. pale in colour; whitish —*adv.* palely [a *light* blue colour] —*vt.* light'ed or lit, light'ing 1. to set on fire; ignite 2. to cause to give off light 3. to furnish with light 4. to brighten; animate —*vi.* 1. to catch fire 2. to brighten (usually with *up*) —**according to one's lights** as one's opinions, standards, etc. may direct —**in the light of** considering —**see the light (of day)** 1. to come into existence 2. to come into public view 3. to understand —**strike a light** 1. to make a flame, as with a match 2. [Colloq.] an exclamation of surprise

light[2] *adj.* [OE. *leoht*] 1. having little weight; not heavy, esp. for its size 2. less than usual in weight, amount, extent, force, intensity, etc. [a *light* blow] 3. of little importance 4. easy to bear [a *light* duty] 5. easy to do; not difficult [*light* work] 6. gay; happy [*light* spirits] 7. loose in morals; wanton 8. dizzy; giddy 9. of an amusing or entertaining nature [*light* reading] 10. containing little alcohol [*light* wine] 11. not as full as usual [a *light* meal] 12. soft and spongy [a *light* cake] 13. loose in consistency 14. moving with ease [*light* on one's feet] 15. carrying little weight 16. designating industry equipped with relatively light machinery and producing small products 17. equipped with light weapons, armour, etc. —*adv.* lightly —*vi.* light'ed or lit, light'ing 1. to come to rest after travelling through the air 2. to come or happen (*on* or *upon*) by chance 3. to strike suddenly, as a blow —**light into** [Colloq.] 1. to attack 2. to scold —**light out** [Colloq.] to depart suddenly —**make light of** to treat as unimportant —**light'ish** *adj.*

lighten[1] *vt.* 1. to illuminate 2. to make light or pale —*vi.* 1. to grow brighter 2. to shine brightly

lighten[2] *vt., vi.* 1. to make or become lighter in weight 2. to make or become more cheerful

lighter[1] *n.* a small device for lighting a cigarette, etc.

lighter[2] *n.* [< MDu. *licht*, light] a large barge used in loading or unloading ships

light-fingered *adj.* 1. having a light touch 2. skilful at stealing, esp. by picking pockets

light flyweight *see* BOXING AND WRESTLING WEIGHTS, table

light-footed *adj.* stepping lightly and gracefully: also [Poet.] **light'foot'** —**light'-foot'edly** *adv.*

lightheaded *adj.* 1. giddy; dizzy 2. flighty; frivolous —**light'head'edly** *adv.* —**light'head'edness** *n.*

lighthearted *adj.* free from care; gay —**light'heart'edly** *adv.* —**light'heart'edness** *n.*

light heavyweight *see* BOXING AND WRESTLING WEIGHTS, table

lighthouse *n.* a tower with a bright light at the top by which ships are guided and warned

lighting *n.* 1. a giving light or being lighted; illumination 2. the distribution of light and shade

lighting-up time the time after which vehicles on the road must show lights: usually half an hour after sunset

lightly *adv.* 1. with little weight or pressure; gently 2. to a small degree or amount 3. nimbly; deftly 4. cheerfully 5. with indifference or neglect

light middleweight *see* BOXING AND WRESTLING WEIGHTS, table

lightness[1] *n.* 1. the quality or intensity of lighting; brightness 2. paleness

lightness[2] *n.* 1. the state of being light, not heavy 2. nimbleness, cheerfulness, lack of seriousness, etc.

lightning *n.* [< ME. *lightnen*, to lighten] a flash of light in the sky caused by the discharge of atmospheric electricity from one cloud to another or between a cloud and the earth —*adj.* like lightning; very fast —**like (greased) lightning** like a flash

lights[1] *n.pl.* [from their light weight] the lungs of animals, used as food

lights[2] *n.pl.* *same as* TRAFFIC LIGHT

lightweight *n.* 1. one below normal weight 2. *see* BOXING AND WRESTLING WEIGHTS, table 3. a person of limited influence, intelligence, etc. —*adj.* 1. light in weight 2. not serious

light welterweight *see* BOXING AND WRESTLING WEIGHTS, table

light-year *n.* the distance that light travels in a vacuum in one year, approximately 10^{16} metres

ligneous (lig'nē əs) *adj.* [< L. *lignum*, wood] of, or having the nature of, wood; woody

lignite (lig'nīt) *n.* [< Fr.: see LIGNEOUS] a soft, brownish-black coal with the texture of the original wood

lignum vitae (lig'nəm vīt'ē) [< L., wood of life] *commercial name for* the very hard wood of the guaiacum

likable (līk'ə b'l) *adj.* having qualities that

inspire liking; attractive, genial, etc.: also **likeable**

like[1] (līk) *adj.* [OE. *gelic*] having the same characteristics; similar; equal —*adv.* [Colloq.] likely [*like* as not, he's there] —*prep.* 1. similar to [she sings *like* a bird] 2. characteristic of [not *like* her to cry] 3. in the mood for [to feel *like* sleeping] 5. indicative of [it looks *like* rain] —*conj.* [Colloq.] 1. as [it was just *like* you said] 2. [Chiefly U.S.] as if —*n.* an equal or counterpart [the *like* of it] —**and the like** and others of the same kind —**like anything** [Colloq.] very much —**like blazes** (or **crazy, the devil, mad,** etc.) [Colloq.] with furious energy, speed, etc. —**nothing like** not at all like —**something like** 1. almost like; about 2. [Colloq.] exactly what is desired or needed —**the like** (or **likes**) **of** [Colloq.] any person or thing like

like[2] *vi.* liked, lik'ing [OE. *lician*] to be so inclined [do as you *like*] —*vt.* 1. to be pleased with; enjoy 2. to wish [I would *like* to go] —*n.* [*pl.*] preferences or tastes

-like (līk) [see LIKE[1]] *a suffix meaning* like, characteristic of, suitable for [*doglike, homelike*]

likelihood (līk'lē hood') *n.* (a) probability

likely *adj.* **-lier, -liest** [< OE. *geliclic*] 1. credible; probable 2. reasonably to be expected [a *likely* man] 3. suitable [a *likely* man] 4. promising [a *likely* lad] —*adv.* probably —**not likely** [Colloq.] there is no chance

like-minded (līk'mīn'did) *adj.* having the same ideas, tastes, etc. —**like'-mind'edly** *adv.* —**like'-mind'edness** *n.*

liken *vt.* to describe as being similar; compare

likeness *n.* 1. a being like; similarity 2. (the same) form or shape 3. a copy, portrait, etc.

likewise *adv.* [short for *in like wise*] 1. in the same manner 2. also; too; moreover

liking *n.* 1. fondness; affection 2. preference; taste; pleasure [not to my *liking*]

lilac (lī'lak) *n.* [Fr. < Per. *nīlak*, bluish] 1. a shrub with large clusters of tiny, fragrant flowers ranging from white to lavender 2. a pale-purple colour —*adj.* pale-purple

Lilliputian (lil'ə pyōō'shən) *adj.* [< *Lilliput*, in Swift's *Gulliver's Travels*] very small; tiny —*n.* a very small person

lilt (lilt) *vt., vi.* [ME. *lilten*] to sing, speak, or play with a light, graceful rhythm —*n.* a light, swingy, and graceful rhythm —**lilt'ing** *adj.*

lily (lil'ē) *n., pl.* **lil'ies** [< L. *lilium*] 1. a plant grown from a bulb and having trumpet-shaped flowers, white or coloured 2. the flower 3. any of several similar plants, as the waterlily —*adj.* like a lily, as in whiteness, purity, etc. —**gild the lily** to attempt vain improvements on something that is already perfect

lily-livered *adj.* cowardly; timid

LILY OF THE VALLEY

lily of the valley *pl.* **lilies of the valley** a plant with a spike of fragrant, small, white, bell-shaped flowers

limb[1] (lim) *n.* [OE. *lim*] 1. an arm, leg, or wing 2. a large branch of a tree 3. a person or thing regarded as a part or agent —**out on a limb** [Colloq.] 1. in a precarious position 2. isolated, esp. because of unpopular opinions —**limb'less** *adj.*

limb[2] *n.* [< L. *limbus*, edge] *Astron.* the apparent outer edge of a heavenly body

limbed *adj.* having (a specified number or kind of) limbs [*four-limbed*]

limber[1] (lim'bər) *adj.* [< ? LIMB[1]] 1. easily bent; flexible 2. able to bend the body easily —*vt., vi.* to make or become limber (usually with *up*)

limber[2] *n.* [< ?] the two-wheeled, detachable front part of a gun carriage —*vt.* to attach the limber to (a gun carriage)

limbo[1] (lim'bō) *n., pl.* **-bos** [< L. (*in*) *limbo*, (on) the border] 1. [*often* **L-**] in some Christian theologies, a region bordering on hell, the abode after death of unbaptized children and righteous people who lived before Jesus 2. a place of oblivion 3. an indeterminate state

limbo[2] *n., pl.* **-bos** [< ?] a West Indian dance in which the dancers pass, while leaning backwards, under a low bar

lime[1] (līm) *n.* [OE. *lim*] a white substance, calcium oxide, obtained by the action of heat on limestone and used in making mortar and cement and in neutralizing acid soil —*vt.* **limed, lim'ing** 1. to smear or catch with birdlime 2. to treat with lime

lime[2] *n.* [Fr. < Ar. *līma*] 1. a small, lemon-shaped, greenish-yellow citrus fruit with a juicy, sour pulp 2. the small, semitropical tree that it grows on

lime[3] *n.* [< ME. *lind*: see LINDEN] a tree with dense, heart-shaped leaves

limekiln *n.* a furnace in which limestone, shells, etc. are burned to make lime

limelight *n.* 1. a prominent position before the public 2. a brilliant light created by the incandescence of lime, formerly used in theatres

limerick (lim'ər ik) *n.* [prob. < *Limerick*, Ireland] a rhymed, nonsense poem of five lines

limestone (līm'stōn') *n.* rock consisting mainly of calcium carbonate

limey (lī'mē) *n.* [from the LIME[2] juice

formerly served to British sailors to prevent scurvy] [U.S. Slang] **1.** a British sailor **2.** any Briton

limit (lim′it) *n.* [< L. *limes*] **1.** the point, line, or edge where something ends or must end; boundary **2.** [*pl.*] bounds **3.** the greatest amount allowed —*vt.* to restrict; curb —**lim′itable** *adj.* —**lim′iter** *n.*

limitation (lim′ə tā′shən) *n.* **1.** a limiting or being limited **2.** qualification; restriction

limited *adj.* **1.** confined within bounds; restricted **2.** exercising governmental powers under constitutional restrictions [a *limited* monarch] **3.** restricting the liability of each partner or shareholder [a *limited* company] —**lim′itedly** *adv.* —**lim′itedness** *n.*

limited liability of a company in which the liability of the shareholder is in proportion to the amount of his stock

limitless *adj.* without limits; unbounded; vast

limn (lim) *vt.* **limned, limn′ing** [< L. *illuminare*, make light] [Obs.] **1.** to paint or draw **2.** to describe

Limoges (lē mōzh′) *n.* [< *Limoges*, in France] a fine porcelain: also **Limoges ware**

limousine (lim′ə zēn′) *n.* [Fr., lit., a hood] any large, luxurious motor car, esp. one driven by a chauffeur

limp[1] (limp) *vi.* [< OE. *lemphealt*, lame] **1.** to walk with or as with a lame leg **2.** to move jerkily, laboriously, etc. —*n.* a halt or lameness in walking —**limp′ing** *adj.*

limp[2] *adj.* [? < prec.] **1.** lacking stiffness; drooping **2.** lacking firmness —**limp′ly** *adv.*

limpet (lim′pit) *n.* [< ML. *lempreda*] a mollusc which clings to rocks, etc. by means of a thick, fleshy foot

limpid (lim′pid) *adj.* [< L. *limpidus*] **1.** perfectly clear; transparent **2.** clear and simple —**limpid′ity, lim′pidness** *n.*

limy (lī′mē) *adj.* **-ier, -iest** **1.** covered with or like birdlime; sticky **2.** of, like, or containing lime

linage (lī′nij) *n.* the number of written or printed lines on a page

linchpin (linch′pin′) *n.* [< OE. *lynis*] **1.** a pin that goes through the end of an axle to keep the wheel from coming off **2.** a person or thing on which the success of a project, organization, etc. depends

Lincs. Lincolnshire

linctus (liŋk′təs) *n.* [< L. *lingere*, to lick] a soothing, syrupy cough mixture

linden (lin′dən) *n.* [< OE. *lind*] *same as* LIME[3]

line[1] (līn) *n.* [< L. *linea*, linen thread] **1.** a very thin, threadlike mark; specif., a) made by a pencil, pen, etc. b) a thin crease on the face **2.** a cord, rope, wire, etc. **3.** a wire or system of wires connecting stations in a telephone system **4.** any wire pipe, etc., or system of these, for conducting gas, water, electricity etc. **5.** a limit **6.** outline; contour **7.** [*usually pl.*] a plan of making or doing **8.** a

row or series of persons or things, as written or printed characters across a page **9.** *same as* LINEAGE[1] **10.** the descendants of a common ancestor or of a particular breed **11.** a) a transport system consisting of regular trips by buses, ships, etc. between points b) a company operating such a system c) a single track of a railway **12.** the course anything moving takes **13.** course of conduct, action, explanation, etc. **14.** a person's trade or occupation **15.** a stock of goods **16.** the field of one's special knowledge or interest **17.** a short letter, note, or card **18.** a verse of poetry **19.** [*pl.*] all the speeches of any one character in a play **20.** [*pl.*] a marriage certificate: in full **marriage lines 21.** [*pl.*] in schools, a punishment consisting of copying out some passage of literature, etc. **22.** [L-] the regular regiments of the army **23.** [Colloq.] flattering talk **24.** *Math.* the path of a moving point **25.** *Mil.* a) a formation of ships, troops, etc. abreast of each other b) the area or position in closest contact with the enemy during combat c) the troops in this area **26.** *Music* any of the long parallel marks forming the staff **27.** *T.V.* any of a number of narrow horizontal bands forming a television picture —*vt.* **lined, lin′ing 1.** to mark with lines **2.** to bring into alignment (often with *up*) **3.** to form a line along —*vi.* **1.** to form a line (usually with *up*) —**all along the line 1.** everywhere **2.** at every turn of events —**bring** (or **come, get**) **into line** to bring (or come) into alignment —**down the line** completely —**draw the** (or a) **line** to set a limit —**hard lines** [Colloq.] bad luck —**in** (or **out of**) **line** in (or not in) alignment, agreement, or conformity —**lay** (or **put**) **it on the line** to speak frankly —**line up** to bring into or take a specified position —**read between the lines** to discover a hidden meaning in something written, said, or done

line[2] *vt.* **lined, lin′ing** [ult. < L. *linum*, flax] **1.** to put a layer of a different material on the inside of **2.** to be used as a lining in **3.** to fill: now chiefly in **line one's pockets,** to make money

lineage (lin′ē ij) *n.* [< OFr. *ligne*: see LINE[1]] **1.** direct descent from an ancestor **2.** ancestry; family

lineal (lin′ē əl) *adj.* **1.** in the direct line of descent from an ancestor **2.** hereditary **3.** linear

lineament (lin′ē ə mənt) *n.* [< L. *linea*, line] a distinctive feature, esp. of the face *Usually used in pl.*

linear (lin′ē ər) *adj.* **1.** of or relating to a line or lines **2.** made of or using lines —**lin′ear′ity** (-ē ar′ə tē) *n.* —**lin′early** *adv.*

linear measure a system of measuring length, esp. the system in which 100 centimetres = 1 metre or in which 12 inches = 1 foot

lineation (lin′ē ā′shən) *n.* **1.** marking with lines **2.** a system or series of lines

line drawing a drawing done entirely in lines, from which a cut (**line cut**) can be photoengraved for printing

linen (lin′ən) *n.* [< OE. *lin*, flax] 1. thread or cloth made of flax 2. things orig. made of linen, as tablecloths, sheets, shirts, etc., collectively —*adj.* made of, or for, linen

linen draper a retailer who deals in linen, cloth, etc.

line of fire 1. the course of a bullet, shell, etc. 2. a position open to attack of any kind

liner (līˈnər) *n.* 1. a steamship, aircraft, etc. in regular service on a specific route 2. a cosmetic applied in a fine line, as along the eyelid

linesman (līnzˈmən) *n.* *Football, Tennis* an official who reports whether the ball is inside or outside the lines

lineup (līnˈup′) *n.* an arrangement of persons or things in or as in a line, as the list of a team's players arranged according to playing position, etc.

ling[1] (liŋ) *n.* [akin to MDu. *lange*] an edible fish related to the cod, found in the North Atlantic

ling[2] *n.* [ON. *lyng*] *same as* HEATHER

-ling (liŋ) [OE.] *a suffix added to nouns, meaning:* 1. small [*duckling*] 2. unimportant or contemptible [*hireling*]

linger (liŋˈgər) *vi.* [< OE. *lang*, long] 1. to continue to stay, esp. through reluctance to leave 2. to continue to live although very close to death 3. to loiter —**lin′gerer** *n.* —**lin′gering** *adj.*

lingerie (lanˈzhə rē′) *n.* [Fr.] women's underwear and night clothes of silk, nylon, lace, etc.

lingo (liŋˈgō) *n., pl.* -goes [< L. *lingua*, tongue] language; esp., a dialect, jargon, etc. that one is not familiar with: a humorous or disparaging term

lingua franca (liŋˈgwə fraŋˈkə) *pl.* **lin′-gua fran′cas, linguae francae** (liŋˈ-gwē franˈsē) [It., lit., Frankish language] a hybrid language used for communication between different peoples, as pidgin English

lingual (liŋˈgwəl) *adj.* [< L. *lingua*, the tongue] 1. of the tongue 2. of language or languages 3. articulated with the tongue —**lin′gually** *adv.*

linguist (liŋˈgwist) *n.* [< L. *lingua*, the tongue] 1. a specialist in linguistics 2. *same as* POLYGLOT (sense 1)

linguistic (liŋ gwisˈtik) *adj.* 1. of language 2. of linguistics —**linguis′tically** *adv.*

linguistics *n.pl.* [with sing. v.] 1. the science of language, including morphology, syntax, etc. 2. the study of a particular language

liniment (linˈə mənt) *n.* [< L. *linere*, to smear] a medicated liquid to be rubbed on the skin to soothe sore, sprained, or inflamed areas

lining (līˈniŋ) *n.* [see LINE[2]] the material covering an inner surface

link (liŋk) *n.* [< Scand.] 1. any of the series of rings or loops making up a chain 2. *a)* a section of something resembling a chain *b)* an element in a series [a weak link in the evidence] 3. anything serving to connect or tie 4. one division (1/100)

of a surveyor's chain —*vt., vi.* to join together with a link or links —**link′er** *n.*

linkage *n.* 1. a linking or being linked 2. a series or system of links

linkman *n.* 1. someone who links various parts of TV and radio broadcasts 2. formerly, someone who carried a torch for pedestrians

links *n.pl.* [< OE. *hlinc*, a slope] *same as* GOLF COURSE

Linnaean, Linnean (li nēˈən) *adj.* [< C. *Linnaeus*] designating a system of classifying plants and animals by using a double name

linnet (linˈit) *n.* [< L. *linum*, flax: it feeds on flaxseed] a small finch found in Europe, Asia, and Africa

lino (līˈnō) *n., pl.* -nos linoleum

linocut *n.* [< ff.] 1. a design cut into the surface of a linoleum block 2. a print made from this

linoleum (li nōˈlē əm) *n.* [< L. *linum*, flax + *oleum*, oil] a hard, washable floor covering made of a mixture of ground cork and linseed oil with a canvas backing

Linotype (līnˈō tīp′) [< *line of type*] *Trademark* a typesetting machine that casts an entire line of type in one bar, or slug —*vt., vi.* [l-] -typed′, -typ′ing to set (matter) with this machine —**lin′otyp′ist, lin′otyp′er** *n.*

linseed (linˈsēd′) *n.* [OE. *linsæd*] the seed of flax

linseed oil a yellowish oil extracted from flaxseed, used in oil paints, etc.

linsey-woolsey (linˈzē woolˈzē) *n., pl.* -wool′seys [ME. < *lin*, flax + *wolle*, wool] a coarse cloth made of linen (or cotton) and wool: also **lin′sey**

lint (lint) *n.* [prob. < OE. *lin*, linen] 1. scraped and softened linen used as a dressing for wounds 2. bits of thread or fluff from cloth or yarn

LINTEL

lintel (linˈt'l) *n.* [ult. < L. *limen*, threshold] the horizontal crosspiece over a door, window, etc.

lion (līˈən) *n.* [< Gr. *leōn*] 1. a large, powerful mammal of the cat family, found in Africa and SW Asia 2. a person of great courage or strength 3. a celebrity —**liˈoness** *n.fem.*

lionhearted *adj.* very brave

lionize *vt.* -ized′, -izˈing to treat as a celebrity —**liˈoniza′tion** *n.*

lion's share the biggest portion

lip (lip) *n.* [OE. *lippa*] 1. either of the two fleshy folds forming the edges of the mouth 2. anything like a lip, as the rim of a jug, cup, etc. 3. [Slang] insolent talk —*vt.* lipped, lip′ping 1. to touch with the lips 2. to utter softly —*adj.*

spoken, but insincere —**bite one's lip** to keep back one's anger, annoyance, etc. —**curl one's lip** to display one's scorn —**keep a stiff upper lip** [Colloq.] to avoid becoming frightened or discouraged —**lip'less** adj.

lipped (lipt) adj. having a lip or lips [tight-lipped]

lip-read vt., vi. -read', -read'ing to recognize (a speaker's words) by lip reading —**lip reader**

lip reading recognition of a speaker's words by watching the movement of his lips, as by the deaf

lip service insincere expression of respect, loyalty, etc.

lipstick n. a small stick of cosmetic paste, set in a case, for colouring the lips

liquefy (lik'wəfī') vt., vi. -fied', -fy'ing [< L. liquere, be liquid + facere, make] to change into a liquid —**liq'uefac'tion** n. —**liq'uefi'er** n.

liqueur (li kyoo'ər) n. [Fr.] any of certain sweet, syrupy alcoholic liquors, variously flavoured

liquid (lik'wid) adj. [< L. liquidus] 1. readily flowing; fluid 2. clear; limpid 3. flowing smoothly and gracefully [liquid verse] 4. readily convertible into cash 5. like a vowel, as the consonants l and r —n. a liquid substance —**liquid'ity, liq'-uidness** n.

liquidate (lik'wədāt') vt. -dat'ed, -dat'ing [< ML. liquidare, to make clear] 1. to settle the accounts of (a bankrupt business, etc.) by apportioning assets and debts 2. to pay (a debt) 3. to convert (assets) into cash 4. to get rid of, as by killing —**liq'uida'tor** n.

liquidation (lik'wədā'shən) n. a liquidating or being liquidated —**go into liquidation** to close one's business by collecting assets and settling all debts

liquidize (lik'wədīz') vt. -ized', -iz'ing to cause to have a liquid quality

liquidizer n. a kitchen appliance used to make purées, etc.

liquid measure a system of measuring liquids; esp., the system in which 1000 millilitres = 1 litre or in which 2 pints = 1 quart, etc.

liquor (lik'ər) n. [L.] 1. an alcoholic drink, esp. one made by distillation, as whisky or rum 2. any liquid

liquorice (lik'ər is) n. [ult. < Gr. glykys, sweet + rhiza, root] 1. a European plant 2. its dried root or the black flavouring extract made from this 3. a sweet flavoured with this extract

lira (lēar'ə) n., pl. -re (-ā), for 2 -ras [It. < L. libra, balance] the monetary unit of 1. Italy 2. Turkey

lisle (līl) n. [< Lille, in France] 1. a fine, hard, extra-strong cotton thread 2. a fabric, or stockings, gloves, etc., woven of lisle —adj. made of lisle

lisp (lisp) vi. [< OE. wlisp, a lisping] 1. to substitute the sounds (th) and (t͡h) for the sounds of s and z 2. to speak imperfectly —vt. to utter with a lisp

—n. the act, speech defect, or sound of lisping —**lisp'ing** adj.

lissome, lissom (lis'əm) adj. [< lithesome] moving gracefully or with ease and lightness —**lis'someness, lis'somness** n.

list¹ (list) n. [merging of OE. liste & Anglo-Fr. liste] 1. a series of names, words, numbers, etc. set forth in order; catalogue, roll, etc. 2. the selvage of cloth 3. formerly, a narrow strip or border See also LISTS —vt. to set forth or enter in a list, directory, catalogue, etc. —**list'er** n. —**list'ing** n.

list² vt. [< OE. lust, desire] [Archaic] to be pleasing to; suit —vi. [Archaic] to wish; choose

list³ vt., vi. [prob. < prec.] to tilt to one side, as a ship —n. a tilting or inclining to one side

list⁴ vt., vi. [< OE. hlyst, hearing] [Archaic] to listen (to)

listed building a building listed as being of historical or architectural importance

listen (lis''n) vi. [OE. hlysnan] 1. to make a conscious effort to hear 2. to give heed; take advice —n. a listening —**listen in** 1. to eavesdrop 2. to listen to a broadcast —**lis'tener** n.

listless adj. [LIST² + -LESS] lacking energy or enthusiasm —**list'lessly** adv.

list price retail price as given in a list or catalogue, discounted in sales to dealers, etc.

lists n.pl. [< ME. liste, border] 1. the fenced area where knights held tournaments 2. any place of combat —**enter the lists** to enter a struggle

lit (lit) alt. pt. & pp. of LIGHT¹

litany (lit'ən ē) n., pl. -nies [< Gr. litē, a request] a prayer in which the congregation recites responses

litchi (lī'chē') n. [Chin. li-chih] 1. a Chinese evergreen tree 2. the dried fruit of this tree (**litchi nut**), with a single seed, a sweet pulp, and a papery shell

-lite (līt) [Fr.] a combining form meaning stone: used in the names of minerals, rocks, and fossils

literacy (lit'ər ə sē) n. the ability to read and write

literal (lit'ər əl) adj. [< L. littera, a letter] 1. following the exact words of the original 2. in a basic or strict sense [the literal meaning] 3. matter-of-fact [a literal mind] 4. real; not going beyond the actual facts [the literal truth] —**lit'erally** adv. —**lit'eralness** n.

literalism n. the tendency to take words, statements, etc. in their literal sense

literary (lit'ər ə rē) adj. 1. of or dealing with literature 2. of the relatively formal language of literature 3. versed in literature 4. making literature a profession —**lit'erariness** n.

literate (lit'ər ət) adj. [< L. littera, letter] 1. able to read and write 2. well-educated —n. a literate person

literati (lit'ə rät'ē) n.pl. [It. < L.] men of letters

literature (lit'ər ə chər) n. [< L. littera, letter] 1. a) all the writings of a particular time, country, etc., esp. those valued for excellence of form and expression *b*) all the writings on a particular subject **2.** [Colloq.] printed matter **3.** the profession of an author

lithe (lī*th*) *adj.* **lith′er, lith′est** [OE. soft] bending easily; supple; limber: also **lithe′-some —lithe′ly** *adv.*

lithium (lith′ē əm) *n.* [< LITHO-] a soft, metallic chemical element, the lightest known metal: symbol, Li

litho (līth′ō) *n., pl.* **-os;** *vt., vi.* **-oed, -oing** *short for* LITHOGRAPH

litho- [< Gr.] *a combining form meaning* stone, rock

lithograph (lith′ə gräf′) *n.* a print made by lithography —*vi., vt.* to make (prints or copies) by lithography —**lithographer** (li thog′rə fər) *n.*

lithography (li thog′rə fē) *n.* [LITHO- + -GRAPHY] printing from a flat stone or metal plate parts of which absorb the ink —**lithographic** (lith′ə graf′ik) *adj.*

litigant (lit′ə gant) *n.* a party to a lawsuit

litigate *vt., vi.* **-gat′ed, -gat′ing** [< L. *lis,* dispute + *agere,* do] to contest in a lawsuit —**lit′iga′tor** *n.*

litigation (lit′ə gā′shən) *n.* **1.** the carrying on of a lawsuit **2.** a lawsuit

litmus (lit′məs) *n.* [< ON. *litr,* colour + *mosi,* moss] a purple colouring matter obtained from various lichens: it turns blue in bases and red in acids

litre (lēt′ər) *n.* [Fr. < Gr. *litra,* a pound] a unit of capacity in the metric system, now defined as equal to 1000 cubic centimetres

Litt.D. [L. *Lit(t)erarum Doctor*] Doctor of Letters

litter (lit′ər) *n.* [< L. *lectus,* a couch] **1.** things lying about in disorder; esp., bits of scattered rubbish **2.** the young borne at one time by a dog, cat, etc. **3.** straw, hay, etc. used as bedding for animals **4.** a framework enclosing a couch on which a person can be carried **5.** a stretcher for carrying the sick or wounded —*vt.* **1.** to bring forth (a number of young) at one time **2.** to make untidy **3.** to scatter about carelessly —*vi.* to bear a litter of young

litterlout (lit′ər lout′) *n.* a person who litters a public place with rubbish, bits of paper, etc.

little (lit′′l) *adj.* **less** or **less′er, least** [OE. *lytel*] **1.** small in size, amount, number, or degree **2.** short in duration; brief **3.** small in importance or power [the *little* man] **4.** trivial; trifling **5.** narrow-minded **6.** young: said of children or animals *Little* is sometimes used to express endearment [bless your *little* heart] —*adv.* **less, least 1.** in a small degree; not much **2.** not in the least [he *little* suspects] —*n.* **1.** a small amount, degree, etc. **2.** a short time or distance —**little by little** gradually —**make little of** to treat as unimportant —**not a little** very much; very —**lit′tleness** *n.*

Little Bear the constellation URSA MINOR

little people the fairies

little woman [Colloq.] one's wife

liturgy (lit′ər jē) *n., pl.* **-gies** [< Gr. *leōs,* people + *ergon,* work] prescribed forms or ritual for public worship —**litur′gical** (li tur′jə k'l) *adj.*

livable (liv′əb'l) *adj.* **1.** fit to live in, as a house **2.** endurable **3.** agreeable to live with Also sp. **liveable**

live¹ (liv) *vi.* **lived, liv′ing** [OE. *libban*] **1.** to have life **2.** *a*) to remain alive *b*) to endure **3.** to pass one's life in a specified manner **4.** to enjoy a full life **5.** to maintain life [to *live* on a pension] **6.** to feed [to *live* on fruit] **7.** to make one's dwelling; reside —*vt.* **1.** to carry out in one's life [to *live* one's faith] **2.** to spend; pass [to *live* a useful life] —**live and let live** to be tolerant —**live down** to live in such a way as to wipe out the shame of (some misdeed, etc.) —**live it up** [Colloq.] to indulge in pleasures, etc. that one usually forgoes —**live on air** to appear to take little or no food —**live together 1.** to share a house, etc. **2.** to have a permanent sexual relationship outside marriage: also **live in sin** —**live up to** to act in accordance with (ideals, promises, etc.) —**live well** to live in luxury

live² (līv) *adj.* [< ALIVE] **1.** having life **2.** of the living state or living beings **3.** having qualities of warmth, vigour, vitality, brilliance, etc. **4.** of present interest [a *live* issue] **5.** *a*) still burning [a *live* spark] *b*) not extinct [a *live* volcano] **6.** unexploded [a *live* shell] **7.** unused; unexpended [*live* steam] **8.** carrying electrical current [a *live* wire] **9.** involving a performance in person, not one on film, tape, etc.

-lived (livd) *a combining form meaning* having (a specified kind or duration of) life [short-*lived*]

livelihood (līv′lē hood′) *n.* [< OE. *lif,* life + *-lad,* course] means of supporting life; subsistence

livelong (liv′lon′) *adj.* [ME. *lefe longe, lief* long; *lief* is merely intens.] whole; entire [the *livelong* day]

lively (līv′lē) *adj.* **-lier, -liest** [OE. *liflic*] **1.** full of life; vigorous **2.** full of spirit; exciting **3.** gay; cheerful **4.** vivid; keen —**live′liness** *n.*

liven (lī′vən) *vt., vi.* to make or become lively; cheer (*up*)

LIVER
(A, liver; B, stomach; C, small intestine; D, large intestine)

liver¹ (liv′ər) *n.* [OE. *lifer*] **1.** the largest glandular organ in vertebrate animals: it

secretes bile and is important in metabolism
2. the liver of cattle, etc. used as food

liver² *n.* a person who lives (in a specified way or place) [a clean *liver*]

liveried (liv′ər ēd) *adj.* wearing a livery

liverish (liv′ər ish) *adj.* [Colloq.] **1.** bilious **2.** peevish; cross

liversausage *n.* a sausage containing minced liver

liverwort (liv′ər wurt′) *n.* a plant, often forming dense, mosslike mats on rocks, etc. in moist places

livery (liv′ər ē) *n.,* *pl.* **-eries** [< OFr. *livree,* gift of clothes to a servant] **1.** an identifying uniform such as is worn by servants **2.** characteristic dress or appearance **3.** a) the keeping and feeding of horses for a fixed charge b) a stable providing these services: also **livery stable**

lives (līvz) *n.* *pl. of* LIFE

livestock (līv′stok′) *n.* domestic animals kept for use on a farm or raised for sale and profit

live wire 1. a wire carrying an electric current **2.** [Colloq.] an energetic and enterprising person

livid (liv′id) *adj.* [< L. *lividus*] **1.** discoloured by a bruise; black-and-blue **2.** greyish-blue; lead-coloured [livid with rage] **3.** [Colloq.] furious

living (liv′iŋ) *adj.* **1.** alive; having life **2.** in active operation or use **3.** of persons alive [within living memory] **4.** true to reality; lifelike [the living image] **5.** of life or the sustaining of life [living conditions] **6.** very [the living daylights] —*n.* **1.** the state of being alive **2.** livelihood **3.** manner of existence [the standard of living] **4.** a church benefice —**the living** those that are still alive

living wage a wage sufficient to maintain a person and his family in reasonable comfort

lizard (liz′ərd) *n.* [< L. *lacerta*] **1.** a reptile with a long slender body and tail, a scaly skin, and four legs (sometimes vestigial), as the slow worm, chameleon, and iguana **2.** loosely, any similar animal, as the alligator

L.J. Lord Justice

'll *contraction of* will or shall [I'll go]

LL., L.L. Late Latin

L.L. Lord Lieutenant

llama (lä′mə) *n.* [Sp. < S AmInd] a S American animal related to the camel but smaller and without humps

LL.B. [L. *Legum Baccalaureus*] Bachelor of Laws

LL.D. [L. *Legum Doctor*] Doctor of Laws

LL.M. [L. *Legum Magister*] Master of Laws

Lloyd's (loidz) *n.* [< *Lloyd's* coffeehouse, meeting place of the original associates] an association dealing with insurance: it publishes an annual list (**Lloyd's Register**) of the seagoing vessels of all countries

lo (lō) *interj.* [OE. *la*] look! see!

loach (lōch) *n.* [< OFr. *loche*] a small freshwater fish

load (lōd) *n.* [< OE. *lad,* a course] **1.** something carried at one time; burden

2. the amount that can be carried **3.** a) a heavy burden or weight b) a great mental burden [a *load* off one's mind] **4.** the weight that a structure bears **5.** [often pl.] [Colloq.] a great number [loads of friends] **6.** *Elec.* the amount of power carried by a circuit —*vt.* **1.** to put something to be carried into or upon **2.** to put into or upon a carrier **3.** to burden; oppress **4.** to supply in abundance [loaded with money] **5.** to put ammunition into (a gun or firearm), film into (a camera), etc. **6.** to weight (dice) unevenly **7.** to phrase (a question, etc.) so as to elicit a desired response —*vi.* to put on or take on a load —**get a load of** [Slang] **1.** to listen to or hear **2.** to look at or see —**load′er** *n.* —**load′ing** *n.*

loaded *adj.* [Slang] **1.** rich; well-endowed **2.** intoxicated

loadstar *n.* *same as* LODESTAR

loadstone *n.* *same as* LODESTONE

loaf¹ (lōf) *n.,* *pl.* **loaves** (lōvz) [OE. *hlaf*] **1.** a portion of bread baked in one piece, commonly of oblong shape **2.** any mass of food shaped somewhat like a loaf of bread

loaf² *vi.* [prob. < ff.] to loiter or lounge about; idle

loafer *n.* [< G. *Landläufer,* vagabond] one who loafs

loam (lōm) *n.* [OE. *lam*] a rich soil of clay, sand, and organic matter —**loam′y** *adj.*

loan (lōn) *n.* [< ON. *lān*] **1.** the act of lending **2.** something lent; esp., a sum of money lent, often at interest —*vt.,* *vi.* to lend —**on loan** lent for temporary use

loath (lōth) *adj.* [< OE. *lath,* hostile] unwilling; reluctant [to be *loath* to depart] —**nothing loath** willing(ly)

loathe (lōth) *vt.* loathed, loath′ing [< OE. *lathian,* be hateful] to feel intense dislike for —**loath′er** *n.*

loathing (lōth′iŋ) *n.* intense dislike, disgust, or hatred

loathsome (lōth′səm) *adj.* causing loathing; disgusting —**loath′somely** *adv.* —**loath′someness** *n.*

loaves (lōvz) *n.* *pl. of* LOAF¹

lob (lob) *n.* [prob. < Du.] *Tennis* a stroke in which the ball is sent high into the air, dropping into the back of the opponent's court —*vt.,* *vi.* **lobbed, lob′bing** to send (a ball) in a lob —**lob′ber** *n.*

lobar (lō′bər) *adj.* of a lobe or lobes

lobate (lō′bāt) *adj.* having a lobe or lobes

lobby (lob′ē) *n.,* *pl.* **-bies** [see LODGE] **1.** a hall or large anteroom, as a waiting room of a hotel, theatre, etc. **2.** a group of people who try to influence M.P.s, officials, etc. **3.** the corridor in the House of Commons to which members retire to vote on a division: also called **division lobby** —*vi.* **-bied, -bying** to frequent the lobby, as of the House of Commons, to influence members —*vt.* to try to get legislators to vote for or against (a measure) by lobbying

lobby correspondent a reporter who frequents the lobby (n. 3) to gain parliamentary news

lobbyist *n.* [Chiefly U.S.] a person who tries to influence the voting on legislation

lobe (lōb) *n.* [< Gr. *lobos*] a rounded projecting part, as the lower end of the human ear or any of the divisions of the brain, lung, or liver —**lobed** *adj.*

lobelia (lō bēl′ yə) *n.* [< Matthias de *L'Obel*] a low-growing plant with white, blue, or red flowers

lobola (lə bō′ lə) *n.* [< Zulu] in South Africa, a custom among Africans of making payment in cattle or money to a prospective bride's family; bride price

lobotomy (lō bot′ə mē) *n., pl.* **-mies** [< LOBE] an operation in which a lobe of the brain is cut across

lobscouse (lob′ skous′) *n.* [< ?] a sailor's stew of meat, vegetables, and hardtack

LOBSTER
(to 60 cm long)

lobster (lob′ stər) *n.* [< L. *locusta*] a large, edible sea crustacean with long antennae, and five pairs of legs, the first pair of which are modified into large pincers

local (lō′ k'l) *adj.* [< L. *locus*, a place] **1.** relating to place **2.** of, characteristic of, or confined to a particular place **3.** of or for a particular part of the body **4.** making all stops along its run [a local bus] —*n.* **1.** a local train, bus, etc. **2.** [often L-] [Colloq.] the local public house —**lo′cally** *adv.*

local authority the governing body of a county, district, or other locality

local colour behaviour, speech, etc. characteristic of a certain region or time, introduced into a novel, play, etc. to supply realism

locale (lō kāl′) *n.* [Fr. *local*] a place or locality, esp. with reference to events, etc. connected with it

local improvement district in Canada, a district that is directly governed by the province because it is too thinly populated to have its own municipality

locality (lō kal′ə tē) *n., pl.* **-ties 1.** position with regard to surrounding objects, landmarks, etc. **2.** a place; district

localize (lō′ kə līz′) *vt.* **-ized′, -iz′ing** to limit, confine, or trace to a particular place or locality

locate (lō kāt′) *vt.* **-cat′ed, -cat′ing** [< L. *locus*, a place] **1.** to establish in a certain place [located in the Town Hall] **2.** to discover the position of after a search **3.** to show the position of **4.** to assign to a particular place, etc.

location (lō kā′ shən) *n.* **1.** a locating or being located **2.** position; place **3.** an area marked off for a specific purpose **4.** *Cinema* an outdoor setting, where scenes

are photographed: in **on location 5.** in South Africa, a black African or coloured township —**loca′tional** *adj.*

locative (lok′ə tiv) *adj.* [see LOCATE] *Linguis.* expressing place where —*n.* the locative case (in Latin, Greek, etc.)

loc. cit. [L. *loco citato*] in the place cited

loch (lok, lokh) *n.* [< Gael.] [Scot.] **1.** a lake **2.** an arm of the sea

loci (lō′ sī) *n. pl. of* LOCUS

lock¹ (lok) *n.* [OE. *loc*, a bolt] **1.** a mechanical device for fastening a door, strongbox, etc. by means of a key or combination **2.** an enclosed part of a canal, waterway, etc. equipped with gates so that the level of the water can be changed **3.** the mechanism of a firearm used to explode the charge **4.** the extent to which a vehicle's front wheels will turn **5.** *Rugby* a player in the second row of the scrum: also **lock forward 6.** *Wrestling* a hold in which a part of the opponent's body is firmly gripped —*vt.* **1.** to fasten (a door, case, etc.) by means of a lock **2.** to shut (*up, in,* or *out*); confine **3.** to fit closely; link **4.** to embrace tightly **5.** to jam together so as to make immovable —*vi.* **1.** to become locked **2.** to interlock —**lock out** to keep (workers) from a place of employment in seeking to force terms upon them —**lock, stock, and barrel** [Colloq.] completely

lock² (lok) *n.* [OE. *loc*] **1.** a ringlet of hair **2.** [*pl.*] [Poet.] the hair of the head **3.** a tuft of wool, etc.

locker *n.* a chest, cupboard, drawer, etc. which can be locked, esp. one for individual use

locket (lok′ it) *n.* [< OFr. *loc*, latch] a small, hinged case of gold, silver, etc., for holding a picture, lock of hair, etc.: it is usually worn on a necklace

lockjaw *n.* same as TETANUS

lock keeper one in charge of a canal lock

locksmith *n.* a person whose work is making or repairing locks and keys

lockup *n.* **1.** a jail **2.** a shop or private garage that is separate from living accommodation

loco¹ (lō′ kō) *n.* [Colloq.] a locomotive

loco² *adj.* [Sp., mad] [U.S. Slang] crazy; demented

loco- [< L. *locus*, a place] a combining form meaning from place to place [*locomotion*]

‡**loco citato** (lō′ kō si tät′ō) [L.] in the place cited

locomotion (lō′ kə mō′ shən) *n.* [LOCO- + MOTION] motion, or the power of moving, from one place to another

locomotive (lō′ kə mōt′ iv) *n.* an engine that can move about by its own power; esp., an engine on wheels, designed to pull a railway train —*adj.* **1.** of locomotion **2.** moving or capable of moving from one place to another

locum tenens (lō′ kəm tē′ nənz) [< L. *locum,* place + *tenens,* holding] a temporary substitute, as for a doctor or clergyman: also **locum**

locus (lō′ kəs) *n., pl.* **loci** (-sī) [L.] *Math.*

locust (lō′kəst) *n.* [< L. *locusta*] a large grasshopper often travelling in swarms destroying vegetation

locust tree 1. a spiny tree found in the U.S. 2. the carob

locution (lō kyōō′shən) *n.* [< L. *loqui*, speak] 1. a word, phrase, or expression 2. a particular style of speech

lode (lōd) *n.* [< OE. *lad*, course] *Mining* a vein or deposit of metallic ore

lodestar *n.* 1. a star by which a person directs his course; esp., the North Star 2. a guiding principle

lodestone *n.* 1. a strongly magnetic variety of the mineral magnetite 2. something that attracts

lodge (loj) *n.* [< OFr. *loge*, arbour] 1. a small house at the entrance to the grounds of a country mansion 2. a small house for special or seasonal use [a hunting *lodge*] 3. the meeting place of a local chapter, as of freemasons, etc. 4. the den of certain animals, esp. beavers 5. the hut or tent of an American Indian —*vt.* **lodged, lodg′ing** 1. to house, esp. temporarily 2. to rent rooms to 3. to deposit or place 4. to bring (a complaint, etc.) before legal authorities 5. to confer (powers) upon (with *in*) —*vi.* 1. to live in a place for a time 2. to live (*with* or *in*) as a paying guest 3. to come to rest (*in*); become embedded

lodger *n.* one who rents a room in another's home

lodging *n.* 1. a place to live in, esp. temporarily 2. [*pl.*] a room or rooms rented in a private home

lodgment *n.* 1. a lodging or being lodged 2. a lodging place 3. an accumulation of deposited material Also sp. **lodge′ment**

loft (loft) *n.* [< ON. *lopt*, upper room] 1. the space just below the roof of a house, barn, etc. 2. a gallery [the choir *loft*] 3. *a*) the slope of the face of a golf club *b*) the height of a ball hit in a high curve —*vt.* to hit or throw (a golf ball, etc.) into the air in a high curve

lofty *adj.* **-ier, -iest** 1. very high 2. elevated; noble 3. haughty; arrogant —**loft′ily** *adv.* —**loft′iness** *n.*

log¹ (log) *n.* [ME. *logge*] 1. a section of the trunk of a felled tree 2. a device for measuring the speed of a ship 3. a daily record of a ship's speed, progress, etc.; logbook 4. a record of an aircraft's flight, a pilot's flying time, experience, etc. 5. any similar record —*adj.* made of a log or logs —*vt.* **logged, log′ging** 1. to saw (trees) into logs 2. to enter or record in a log —**like a log** inert; heavy [she slept *like a log*]

log² *n.* short for LOGARITHM

logan (lō′gən) *n.* [Canad.] *same as* BOGAN

loganberry (lō′gən ber ē) *n., pl.* **-ries** [< J. H. *Logan*] 1. a hybrid bramble developed from the blackberry and the red raspberry 2. its purplish-red fruit

logarithm (log′ə rith′m) *n.* [< Gr. *logos*, ratio + *arithmos*, number] *Math.* the exponent of the power to which a fixed number (the *base*) must be raised in order to produce a given number (the *antilogarithm*) —**log′arith′mic** *adj.* —**log′arith′mically** *adv.*

logbook (log′book′) *n.* 1. *same as* LOG¹ (senses 3, 4, & 5) 2. a book showing the registration details of a motor vehicle

logger *n.* [U.S.] a lumberjack

loggerhead (log′ər hed′) *n.* [< LOG¹ + HEAD] a sea turtle with a large head: also **loggerhead turtle** —**at loggerheads** quarrelling

LOGGIA

loggia (lō′jə) *n., pl.* **-gias** [It.] a roofed gallery projecting from the side of a building, often one overlooking an open court

logging (log′iŋ) *n.* the occupation of cutting down trees, cutting them into logs, and transporting them to the sawmill

logic (loj′ik) *n.* [ult. < Gr. *logos*, word] 1. the science of correct reasoning 2. a book on this science 3. correct reasoning 4. way of reasoning [poor *logic*] 5. the systematized interconnections in an electronic digital computer

logical *adj.* 1. of or used in the science of logic 2. according to the principles of logic 3. expected because of what has gone before 4. using correct reasoning —**log′ical′ity** (-kal′ə tē) *n.* —**log′ically** *adv.*

logician (lō jish′ən) *n.* an expert in logic

logistics (lō jis′tiks) *n.pl.* [with sing. v.] [< Fr. *loger*, to quarter] the branch of military science having to do with maintaining and transporting personnel —**logis′tic, logis′tical** *adj.*

logjam (log′jam′) *n.* 1. logs jammed together in a stream 2. an accumulation of many items to deal with

logo (lōg′ō) *n.* [< Gr. *logos*, word] a letter, symbol, etc. used to represent an entire word, esp. the name of a company

-logue (log) [see LOGIC] *a combining form meaning* a (specified kind of) speaking or writing [monologue] .

-logy (lə jē) [ult. < Gr. *logos*, word] *a combining form meaning:* 1. a (specified kind of) speaking [eulogy] 2. science, doctrine, or theory of [biology, theology]

loin (loin) *n.* [ult. < L. *lumbus*] 1. [usually *pl.*] the lower part of the back between the hipbones and the ribs 2. the front part of the hindquarters of beef, lamb, veal, etc. 3. [*pl.*] the hips and the lower abdomen regarded as the region of strength and procreative power —**gird (up) one's loins** to prepare to do something difficult

loincloth *n.* a cloth worn about the loins, as by some tribes in warm climates

loiter (loit′ər) *vi.* [< MDu. *loteren*] 1. to spend time idly; linger 2. to move slowly and lazily —**loi′terer** *n.*

loll (lol) *vi.* [< MDu. *lollen*] 1. to lean or lounge about in a lazy manner 2. to droop —*vt.* to let droop

Lollard (lol′ərd) *n.* [< MDu., a mutterer] any of the followers of John Wycliffe in 15th-cent. England

lollipop, lollypop (lol′ē pop′) *n.* [prob. < dial. *lolly*, the tongue] a boiled sweet fixed to the end of a small stick

lollipop man [Colloq.] someone, usually carrying a pole with a circular sign on top, employed to stop traffic so children may cross the road —**lollipop lady** *fem.*

lollop (lol′əp) *vi.* [< LOLL] 1. to lounge about 2. to move in a clumsy, bobbing way

lolly (lol′ē) *n., pl.* **-lies** [see LOLLIPOP] 1. [Colloq.] *same as* LOLLIPOP 2. [Slang] money

Lombard Street (lom′bərd) [< the *Lombard* merchants who settled there] street in London where many banks are located

London pride (lun′dən) a saxifrage, with pink flowers

lone (lōn) *adj.* [< ALONE] 1. by oneself; solitary 2. lonely 3. isolated —**lone′ness** *n.*

lonely (lōn′lē) *adj.* **-lier, -liest** 1. unhappy at being alone 2. *a)* isolated *b)* unfrequented 3. alone —**lone′lily** *adv.* —**lone′liness** *n.*

loner *n.* [Colloq.] one who avoids the company of others

lonesome *adj.* having or causing a lonely feeling

long[1] (loŋ) *adj.* [OE. *long, lang*] 1. measuring much from one end to the other in space or time 2. of a specified extent in length [a metre *long*] 3. of greater than usual length, quantity, etc. [a *long* list] 4. tedious; slow 5. far-reaching [a *long* view of the matter] 6. well supplied [*long* on excuses] 7. holding a supply of a commodity in anticipation of a rise in price 8. requiring a long time to pronounce: said of a speech sound —*adv.* 1. for a long time 2. for the duration of [all day *long*] 3. at a remote time —*n.* 1. a signal, syllable, etc. of long duration 2. a long time [it won't take *long*] —**as (or so) long as** 1. during the time that 2. since 3. provided that —**before long** soon —**in the long run** eventually —**the long and (the) short of it** the whole story of in a few words

long[2] *vi.* [OE. *langian*] to feel a strong yearning; wish earnestly [to *long* to go home]

long. longitude

longbow *n.* a large bow drawn by hand and shooting a long, feathered arrow

long-distance *adj.* 1. covering long distances 2. connecting points that are far apart

long division the process of dividing

one number by another and putting the steps down in full

long-drawn *adj.* prolonged: also **long′-drawn′-out′**

longevity (lon jev′ə tē) *n.* [< L. *longus*, long + *aevum*, age] long life

longhair *adj.* [Colloq.] of intellectuals or their tastes; specif., preferring classical music to jazz, etc.: also **long′haired′**

longhand *n.* ordinary handwriting

long-headed, longheaded *adj.* having much foresight; shrewd —**long′-head′edness** *n.*

longing *n.* a yearning —*adj.* feeling a yearning

longitude (lon′jə tyōod′) *n.* [< L. *longus*, long] angular distance east or west on the earth's surface, measured in degrees from the prime meridian passing through Greenwich

longitudinal (lon′jə tyōod′ən əl) *adj.* 1. of or in length 2. running or placed lengthways 3. of longitude

long johns [Colloq.] long underwear

long jump an athletic event that is a jump for distance rather than height

long-lived *adj.* having or tending to have a long life span or existence

long-playing *adj.* of a gramophone record for playing at 33 1/3 revolutions per minute

long-range *adj.* 1. having a range of great distance 2. taking the future into consideration

long shot [Colloq.] a betting choice that has little chance of winning —**not by a long shot** [Colloq.] not at all

longsighted (loŋ′sīt′id) *adj.* having better vision for distant objects than for near ones —**long′sight′edly** *adv.* —**long′-sight′edness** *n.*

longstanding *adj.* having continued for a long time

long-suffering (loŋ′suf′ər iŋ) *adj.* bearing trouble patiently for a long time —*n.* long and patient endurance

long-term *adj.* for or extending over a long time

longtime *adj.* over a long period of time

long ton *same as* TON (sense 1)

long wave a radio wave more than 1000 metres in length

longways *adv.* *same as* LENGTHWAYS: also **long′wise′**

long-winded (loŋ′win′did) *adj.* 1. tiresomely long 2. not easily winded by exertion —**long′-wind′edly** *adv.* —**long′-wind′edness** *n.*

loo (lōo) *n.* [< ? Fr. *l'eau*, water] [Colloq.] a toilet

loofah (lōo′fə) *n.* [Ar. *lūfah*] the fibrous interior of a plant of the gourd type, used as a bath sponge

look (look) *vi.* [OE. *locian*] 1. to direct one's eyes in order to see 2. to search 3. to appear; seem 4. to be facing in a specified direction 5. to direct one's attention —*vt.* 1. to direct one's eyes on 2. to express by one's looks 3. to appear as having attained (some age) —*n.* 1. the act of looking; glance 2. outward aspect **3.** [Colloq.] *a)* [*usually pl.*] appearance [*from the looks of things*] *b)* [*pl.*] personal appearance —*interj.* **1.** see! **2.** pay attention! —**look after** to take care of —**look down on** (or **upon**) to regard with contempt —**look for** **1.** to search for **2.** to expect —**look forward to** to anticipate, esp. eagerly —**look in** (**on**) to pay a brief visit (to) —**look on** **1.** to be an observer or spectator **2.** to consider —**look** (**like**) **oneself** to seem in normal health, spirits, etc. —**look out** **1.** to be careful **2.** to select by inspection —**look out for** **1.** to be wary about **2.** to take care of —**look over** to examine —**look to** **1.** to take care of **2.** to rely upon **3.** to expect —**look up** **1.** to search for in a reference book, etc. **2.** [Colloq.] to visit **3.** [Colloq.] to improve —**look up to** to admire —**look'er** *n.*

looker-on (look'ər on') *n.*, *pl.* **look'ers-on'** an observer or spectator; onlooker

looking glass a (glass) mirror

lookout *n.* **1.** a careful watching **2.** a place for keeping watch **3.** a person detailed to watch **4.** outlook; prospect **5.** [Colloq.] concern; business

look-see *n.* [< PidE.] [Slang] a quick look

loom¹ (lōōm) *n.* [< OE. (*ge*)*loma*, tool] a machine for weaving thread or yarn into cloth

loom² *vi.* [< ?] to come in sight indistinctly, esp. in a large or threatening form

loon (lōōn) *n.* [< ON. *lomr*] a name given to several fish-eating diving birds

loony (lōō'nē) *adj.* **-ier, -iest** [< LUNATIC] [Slang] crazy —*n.*, *pl.* **loon'ies** [Slang] a loony person

loop (lōōp) *n.* [< ?] **1.** the figure formed by a line, thread, etc. that curves back to cross itself **2.** anything forming this figure **3.** a ring-shaped fastening or ornament **4.** a plastic intrauterine contraceptive device **5.** *Aeron.* a manoeuvre in which an aeroplane describes a closed curve in the vertical plane —*vt.* **1.** to make a loop or loops in or of **2.** to wrap around one or more times **3.** to fasten with a loop —*vi.* to form a loop or loops —**loop the loop** to make a vertical loop in the air, as in an aeroplane

loophole *n.* [prob. < MDu. *lupen*, to peer + HOLE] **1.** a means of evading a law, etc. **2.** a hole or narrow slit in the wall of a fort, etc. for looking or shooting through

loopy *adj.* **-ier, -iest** [Slang] crazy; foolish

loose (lōōs) *adj.* [< ON. *lauss*] **1.** not confined or restrained; free **2.** not put into a package **3.** not firmly fastened down or in **4.** not tight or compact **5.** not restrained [*loose talk*] **6.** not precise; inexact [*a loose translation*] **7.** sexually immoral **8.** moving freely [*loose bowels*] —*vt.* **loosed, loos'ing** **1.** to set free; unbind **2.** to make less tight, compact, etc. **3.** to release [*he loosed the arrow*] —*vi.* to become loose —**break loose** to free oneself —**let loose** (**with**) to release; let go —**on the loose** **1.** free **2.** [Colloq.] having fun in a free, unrestrained manner

—**set** (or **turn**) **loose** to release —**loose'-ly** *adv.*

loose-jointed (lōōs'join'tid) *adj.* **1.** having loose joints **2.** moving freely; limber —**loose'joint'edly** *adv.*

loose-leaf *adj.* having leaves, or sheets, that can easily be removed or replaced

loosen *vt.*, *vi.* to make or become loose or looser

loot (lōōt) *n.* [Hindi *lūt*] **1.** goods stolen or taken by force **2.** [Slang] money —*vt.*, *vi.* to plunder —**loot'er** *n.*

lop¹ (lop) *vt.* **lopped, lop'ping** [OE. *loppian*] **1.** to trim (a tree, etc.) by cutting off branches or twigs **2.** to remove by or as by cutting off

lop² *vi.* **lopped, lop'ping** [prob. akin to LOB] **1.** to hang down loosely **2.** to move in a halting way

lope (lōp) *vi.* **loped, lop'ing** [< ON. *hlaupa*, leap] to move with a long, swinging stride —*n.* a loping stride

lop-eared *adj.* having ears that droop or hang down

lopsided (lop'sīd'id) *adj.* noticeably heavier, bigger, or lower on one side —**lop'-sid'edly** *adv.*

loquacious (lō kwā'shəs) *adj.* [< L. *loqui*, to speak] very talkative; fond of talking —**loqua'ciously** *adv.* —**loquac'ity** (-kwas'ə tē)

lor (lôr) *interj.* [< LORD] an expression of surprise

Loran (lôr'an) *n.* [< *Lo*(*ng*) *Ra*(*nge*) *N*(*avigation*)] [*also* l-] a form of radar by which a ship or aircraft can determine its position

lord (lôrd) *n.* [< OE. *hlaf*, loaf + *weard*, keeper] **1.** a ruler; master **2.** the head of a feudal estate **3.** [L-] *a)* God *b)* Jesus Christ **4.** *a)* a member of the House of Lords *b)* a man who by courtesy is given the title of Lord **5.** [L-] [*pl.*] the House of Lords in the British Parliament **6.** [L-] in Great Britain, the title of a lord —*interj.* [*often* L-] an exclamation of surprise or irritation —**lord it** (**over**) to domineer (over)

Lord Chief Justice the president of one division of the High Court of Justice, second only to the Lord Chancellor

Lord (High) Chancellor the highest officer of state of Great Britain

Lord Lieutenant **1.** the representative of the Crown in a county **2.** formerly, the British viceroy in Ireland

lordly *adj.* **-lier, -liest** **1.** noble; grand **2.** haughty; overbearing —**lord'liness** *n.*

Lord Mayor the title of the mayor of the City of London and of the mayor of several other British cities

Lord of Misrule formerly, a person who presided over revels and games at Christmas

Lord President of the Council the cabinet minister who presides over meetings of the Privy Council

Lord Privy Seal a senior cabinet minister who has no official duties

Lord's *n.* [< Thomas *Lord*, founder] Lord's

cricket ground, now headquarters of the M.C.C.

Lord's day Sunday

lordship (lôrd′ship′) *n.* **1.** the rank or authority of a lord **2.** rule; dominion **3.** [*also* L-] a title used in speaking of or to a lord: with *his* or *your*

Lord's Prayer the prayer beginning *Our Father*, which Jesus taught his disciples: Matt. 6:9-13

lords spiritual the archbishops and bishops who are members of the House of Lords

Lord's Supper Holy Communion; Eucharist

lords temporal those members of the House of Lords who are not clergymen

lore (lôr) *n.* [OE. *lar*] knowledge or learning; specif., all the knowledge concerning a particular subject, esp. that of a traditional nature

lorgnette (lôr nyet′) *n.* [< OFr. *lorgne*, squinting] a pair of glasses, or an opera glass, attached to a handle

lorry (lôr′ē) *n., pl.* **-ries** [< ?] **1.** a motor vehicle used to transport heavy loads along motorways, roads, etc. **2.** a low, flat wagon without sides

lose (lōōz) *vt.* **lost, los′ing** [< OE. *losian*, be lost] **1.** to become unable to find **2.** to have taken from one by accident, death, removal, etc. **3.** to get rid of **4.** to fail to keep [*to lose* one's temper] **5.** *a)* to fail to see, hear, or understand *b)* to fail to keep in sight, mind, etc. **6.** to fail to have, get, take, etc. **7.** to fail to win **8.** to cause the loss of [*it lost* him his job] **9.** to wander from (one's way, etc.) **10.** to waste; squander [*to lose* time] **11.** to engross or preoccupy [*to be lost* in reverie] **12.** to go slower by [*my watch lost* a minute] —*vi.* **1.** to suffer loss **2.** to be defeated in a contest, etc. **3.** to be slow: said of a timepiece —**lose oneself 1.** to go astray **2.** to become engrossed —**lose out** [Colloq.] to fail —**lose out on** [Colloq.] to fail to take advantage of

loser *n.* **1.** [Colloq.] one that seems doomed to lose **2.** a person who reacts to loss as specified [*a poor loser*]

losing *adj.* **1.** that loses **2.** resulting in loss —*n.* [*pl.*] losses by gambling

loss (los) *n.* [< ? OE. *los*, ruin] **1.** a losing or being lost **2.** the damage, disadvantage, etc. caused by losing something **3.** the person, thing, or amount lost —**at a loss (to)** puzzled or uncertain (how to)

loss leader any article that a shop sells cheaply or below cost to attract customers

lost (lost) *pt. & pp. of* LOSE —*adj.* **1.** not to be found; missing **2.** having wandered from the way **3.** bewildered **4.** wasted **5.** no longer held, seen, heard, etc. **6.** not gained or won **7.** destroyed; ruined —**lost in** engrossed in —**lost on** without effect on

lot (lot) *n.* [OE. *hlot*] **1.** [*often pl.*] [Colloq.] a great number or amount **2.** a number of persons or things regarded as a group **3.** fortune [*her unhappy lot*] **4.** any of

a number of counters, etc. drawn from at random to decide a matter by chance **5.** the use of such a method **6.** the decision arrived at by this means **7.** one's share by lot **8.** a plot of ground **9.** [Colloq.] sort (of person) [he's a bad *lot*] —*adv.* very much [*a lot* richer]: also **lots** —**cast** (or **throw**) **in one's lot with** to share the fortunes of —**draw** (or **cast**) **lots** to decide an issue by using lots

loth (lōth) *adj.* *alt. sp. of* LOATH

Lothario (lō thār′ē ō′) *n., pl.* **ios′** [< the young rake in a play] [*often* l-] a lighthearted seducer of women

lotion (lō′shən) *n.* [< L. *lavare*, wash] a liquid preparation used on the skin for washing, healing, etc.

lottery (lot′ər ē) *n., pl.* **-teries** [< MDu. *lot*, lot] **1.** a game of chance in which people buy numbered chances on prizes, the winning numbers being drawn by lot **2.** any undertaking involving chance selection

lotto (lot′ō) *n.* [< MDu. *lot*, lot] a game of chance played with cards having squares numbered in rows: counters are placed on those numbers drawn by lot

lotus, lotos (lōt′əs) *n.* [< Gr. *lōtos*] **1.** *Gr. Legend* a plant whose fruit was supposed to induce a dreamy languor and forgetfulness **2.** any of several tropical waterlilies **3.** a plant with yellow, purple, or white flowers

lotus-eater *n.* one who becomes indolent, dreamy, etc.

loud (loud) *adj.* [OE. *hlud*] **1.** strongly audible: said of sound **2.** sounding with great intensity **3.** noisy **4.** emphatic [*loud* denials] **5.** [Colloq.] flashy **6.** [Colloq.] vulgar —*adv.* in a loud manner —**loud′-ly** *adv.* —**loud′ness** *n.*

loudmouthed *adj.* **1.** gossipy or tactless **2.** talking in a loud, irritating voice

loudspeaker (loud′spē′kər) *n.* a device for converting electric current into sound and amplifying it

lough (lok, lokh) *n.* [< Gaelic & OIr. *loch*, loch] [Ir.] **1.** a lake **2.** an arm of the sea

lounge (lounj) *vi.* **lounged, loung′ing** [< ?] **1.** to stand, move, sit, etc. in a relaxed or lazy way **2.** to spend time in idleness —*n.* **1.** a room, as in a hotel or theatre, with comfortable furniture **2.** a living room in a private house **3.** a time of lounging —**loung′er** *n.*

lounge suit a man's suit for daytime wear

lour (louər) *vi., n.* *same as* LOWER²

lourie (lou′rē) *n.* an African bird with bright plumage

louse (lous) *n., pl.* **lice** [OE. *lus*] **1.** a small, wingless, parasitic insect that infests the hair or skin of man and some other mammals **2.** any similar insect, arachnid, etc., as the wood louse **3.** *pl.* **lous′es** [Slang] a person regarded as mean, contemptible, etc. —**louse up** [Slang] to spoil; ruin

lousy (lou′zē) *adj.* **-ier, -iest 1.** [Slang] disgusting **2.** [Slang] poor; inferior **3.**

infested with lice 4. [Slang] oversupplied (*with*)

lout (lout) *n.* [prob. < OE. *lutan*, to stoop] a clumsy, stupid person; boor —**lout'ish** *adj.*

louvre (loo'vər) *n.* [< OFr. *lover*, skylight] 1. an opening fitted with sloping slats so as to admit light and air but shed rain 2. any of these slats Also esp. U.S. **lou'ver** —**lou'vred** *adj.*

lovage (luv'ij) *n.* [< L. *ligusticum*, the plant of Liguria] an umbelliferous plant, sometimes used as a flavouring

love (luv) *n.* [OE. *lufu*] 1. a deep affection for or attachment to someone or something 2. *a*) a passionate affection of one person for another *b*) the object of this; sweetheart 3. sexual passion or intercourse 4. [L-] Cupid 5. *Tennis* a score of zero —*vt.*, *vi.* **loved**, **lov'ing** to feel love (for) —**fall in love (with)** to begin to feel love (for) —**for the love of** for the sake of —**in love** feeling love —**make love** 1. to have sexual intercourse 2. to woo or embrace, kiss, etc. —**not for love or money** not under any conditions —**lov'able**, **love'able** *adj.* —**love'less** *adj.*

lovebird *n.* a small parrot: the mates appear to be greatly attached to each other

love child a euphemism for an illegitimate child; bastard

love-lies-bleeding (luv'līz'blēd'iŋ) *n.* a cultivated amaranth with spikes of small, red flowers

lovelorn *adj.* pining from love

lovely *adj.* **-lier**, **-liest** 1. beautiful 2. morally or spiritually attractive 3. [Colloq.] highly enjoyable —*n.*, *pl.* **-lies** [Colloq.] a beautiful young woman —**love'-liness** *n.*

lover *n.* 1. a partner, esp. the male partner, in a love affair 2. [*pl.*] a couple in love with each other 3. a sweetheart 4. a person who greatly enjoys some (specified) thing [a *lover* of jazz] —**lov'erly** *adj.*, *adv.*

lovesick *adj.* so much in love as to be unable to act normally —**love'sick'ness** *n.*

lovey-dovey (luv'ē duv'ē) *adj.* [LOVE + DOVE] [Slang] very affectionate, amorous, or sentimental

loving *adj.* feeling or expressing love —**lov'ingly** *adv.* —**lov'ingness** *n.*

loving cup a large drinking cup with two handles, formerly passed among guests at banquets

low¹ (lō) *adj.* [< ON. *lagr*] 1. not high or tall 2. depressed below the surrounding surface 3. shallow 4. of little quantity, degree, value, etc. 5. of less than normal height, depth, degree, etc. 6. below others in order, position, etc. 7. near the horizon [the sun is *low*] 8. near the equator [*low* latitudes] 9. exposing the neck and shoulders 10. in hiding 11. deep [a *low* bow] 12. depressed; melancholy 13. not of high rank 14. vulgar; coarse 15. contemptible [a *low* trick] 16. unfavourable 17. *a*) not well supplied with [*low* on fuel] *b*) [Colloq.] short of ready cash 18. *a*) not loud *b*) deep in pitch —*adv.* 1. in, to, or towards a low position,

level, etc. 2. quietly; softly 3. with a deep pitch —*n.* 1. a low level, point, degree, etc. 2. *Meteorol.* an area of low barometric pressure —**lay low** to overcome or kill —**lie low** 1. to keep oneself hidden 2. to wait patiently —**low'ness** *n.*

low² *vi.* [OE. *hlowan*] to make the characteristic sound of a cow; moo —*n.* this sound

lowborn *adj.* of humble birth

lowbred *adj.* ill-mannered; vulgar

lowbrow *n.* [Colloq.] one regarded as lacking intellectual tastes —*adj.* [Colloq.] of or for a lowbrow

Low Church that party of the Anglican Church which attaches little importance to the priesthood or to traditional rituals, doctrines, etc. —**Low'-Church'** *adj.*

low comedy comedy that gets its effect mainly from action and situation, as burlesque, farce, etc.

lowdown *n.* [Slang] the pertinent facts (with *the*) —*adj.* [Colloq.] mean; contemptible

lower¹ *adj.* *compar.* of LOW¹ 1. below or farther down in place, rank, dignity, etc. 2. [L-] *Geol.* earlier: used of a division of a period —*vt.* 1. to let or put down [*lower* the window] 2. to reduce in height, amount, value, etc. 3. to weaken or lessen 4. to demean 5. to reduce (a sound) in volume or in pitch —*vi.* to become lower; sink; fall

lower² (lou'ər) *vi.* [ME. *louren*] 1. to scowl 2. to appear dark and threatening —*n.* a threatening look

Lower Canada the official name of the present-day province of Quebec

lower case small-letter type used in printing, as distinguished from capital letters (*upper case*)

lower class the working class, or proletariat

Lower House [often l- h-] the larger and more representative branch of a legislature having two branches, as the House of Commons

lowering (lou'ər iŋ) *adj.* 1. scowling; frowning darkly 2. dark, as if about to rain or snow —**low'eringly** *adv.*

low frequency any radio frequency between 30 and 300 kilohertz

Low German the West Germanic languages, other than High German, including English, Dutch, etc.

low-grade *adj.* of inferior quality

low-key *adj.* of low intensity, tone, etc.; subdued or restrained: also **low'-keyed'**

lowland (lō'lənd) *n.* land that is below the level of the surrounding land —**the Lowlands** lowland region in SC Scotland —**low'lander**, **Low'lander** *n.*

Low Latin nonclassical, esp. medieval, Latin

lowly *adj.* **-lier**, **-liest** 1. of low position or rank 2. humble; meek —*adv.* 1. humbly 2. in a low manner, position, etc. 3. softly; gently —**low'liness** *n.*

Low Mass a Mass said, not sung, less ceremonial than High Mass, and offered by one priest

low-minded *adj.* having or showing a coarse, vulgar mind —**low'-mind'edness** *n.*

low-pitched *adj.* 1. low in pitch 2. having little slope, as a roof

low-pressure *adj.* 1. using a relatively low pressure 2. having a low barometric pressure

low profile an unobtrusive presence, or concealed activity

low-spirited (lō'spir'i tid) *adj.* in low spirits; sad; depressed —**low'-spir'itedly** *adv.*

low tide 1. the lowest level reached by the ebbing tide 2. the time when the tide is at this level

lowveld (lō'felt) *n.* in South Africa, the low grasslands of the Transvaal province

low water 1. same as LOW TIDE 2. water at its lowest level, as in a stream

lox (loks) *n.* [l(iquid) ox(ygen)] oxygen in a liquid state, used in a fuel mixture for rockets

loyal (loi'əl) *adj.* [Fr.: see LEGAL] 1. faithful to one's country, friends, ideals, etc. 2. of or indicating loyalty —**loy'-ally** *adv.*

loyalist *n.* 1. a person who supports the established government of his country during times of revolt 2. a supporter of the Stuart cause in the 17th cent. 3. in Northern Ireland, a protestant opposing the unification of Ireland 4. [L-] a United Empire Loyalist —**loy'alism** *n.*

loyal toast the toast drunk in pledging allegiance to the Sovereign, usually after a meal

loyalty *n.*, *pl.* **-ties** quality, state, or instance of being loyal; faithful adherence, etc.

lozenge (loz'inj) *n.* [< OFr. *losenge*] 1. a cough drop, sweet, etc. 2. a diamond-shaped figure

LP *n.* [L(ong) P(laying)] a long-playing record

L-plate a letter L attached to the front and back of a motor vehicle indicating that the driver is a learner

Lr *Chem.* lawrencium

LSD [l(y)s(ergic acid) d(iethylamide)] a psychedelic drug that produces hallucinations, delusions, etc.

L.S.D., £.s.d., l.s.d. [L. *librae, solidi, denarii*] pounds, shillings, pence

L.S.E. London School of Economics

Lt. Lieutenant

LTA Lawn Tennis Association

Ltd., ltd. limited

Lu *Chem.* lutetium

lubber (lub'ər) *n.* [< ME. *lobbe-*, heavy] 1. a big, slow, clumsy person 2. a landlubber —**lub'berliness** *n.*

lubricant (lōō'bri kənt) *adj.* reducing friction by providing a smooth film as a covering over parts that move against each other —*n.* a lubricant oil, grease, etc.

lubricate *vt.* **-cat'ed, -cat'ing** [< L. *lubricus*, smooth] 1. to apply a lubricant to 2. to make slippery or smooth —**lu'brica'tion** *n.* —**lu'brica'tor** *n.*

lubricity (lōō bris'ə tē) *n.* 1. lewdness 2. shiftiness 3. slipperiness; smoothness

lucerne, lucern (lōō surn') *n.* [< Fr. *luzerne*] same as ALFALFA

lucid (lōō'sid) *adj.* [< L. *lucere*, shine] 1. readily understood 2. shining 3. transparent 4. sane 5. rational —**lucid'-ity, lu'cidness** *n.* —**lu'cidly** *adv.*

Lucifer (lōō'si fər) *n.* [< L. *lux*, light + *ferre*, to bear] 1. [Poet.] the planet Venus when it is the morning star 2. *Theol.* Satan —*n.* [l-] an early type of friction match

luck (luk) *n.* [prob. < MDu. *luk*] 1. the seemingly chance happening of events which affect one; fortune 2. good fortune, success, etc. —**down on one's luck** unlucky —**in luck** lucky —**out of luck** unlucky —**push one's luck** [Colloq.] to take superfluous risks —**worse luck** unfortunately —**luck'less** *adj.*

lucky *adj.* **-ier, -iest** 1. having good luck 2. resulting fortunately 3. believed to bring good luck —**luck'ily** *adv.*

lucky dip a receptacle from which one chooses from among a number of unseen articles

lucrative (lōō'krə tiv) *adj.* [see ff.] profitable —**lu'cratively** *adv.*

lucre (lōō'kər) *n.* [< L. *lucrum*, gain, riches] riches; money: chiefly derogatory, as in **filthy lucre**

Luddite (lud'it) *n.* [< ? Ned *Ludd*, who destroyed industrial machinery] 1. any of the textile workers who organized machine breaking 2. any opponent of industrial change or innovation

ludicrous (lōō'di krəs) *adj.* [< L. *ludus*, game] causing laughter because absurd or ridiculous —**lu'dicrously** *adv.* —**lu'dicrousness** *n.*

ludo (lōō'dō) *n.* [L., I play] a children's game played with counters and a special board

luff (luf) *n.* [< ODu. *loef*, weather side (of a ship)] a sailing close to the wind —*vi.* to turn the bow of a ship towards the wind

lug (lug) *vt.* **lugged, lug'ging** [prob. < Scand.] to carry or drag with effort —*n.* 1. an earlike projection by which a thing is held or supported 2. [Colloq.] an ear

luggage (lug'ij) *n.* [< LUG] suitcases, bags, trunks, etc.

lugger (lug'ər) *n.* a small vessel equipped with a lugsail

lugsail (lug's'l) *n.* [< ? LUG] a four-sided sail attached to an upper yard that hangs obliquely on the mast

lugubrious (lōō gōō'brē əs) *adj.* [< L. *lugere*, mourn] very sad or mournful, esp. in a way that seems exaggerated or ridiculous —**lugu'briously** *adv.*

lugworm (lug'wurm') *n.* [< ?] a worm that burrows in sand along the shore and is used for bait

lukewarm (lōōk'wôrm') *adj.* [ME. *luke*, tepid + *warm*, warm] 1. barely warm: said of liquids 2. not very enthusiastic —**luke'warm'ness** *n.*

lull (lul) *vt.* [ME. *lullen*] 1. to calm by gentle sound or motion 2. to bring into a specified condition by soothing and reassuring **3.** to allay —*vi.* to become calm —*n.* a short period of comparative calm

lullaby (lul'ə bī') *n., pl.* **-bies'** a song for lulling a baby to sleep —*vt.* **-bied'**, **-by'-ing** to lull as with a lullaby

lumbago (lum bā'gō) *n.* [< L. *lumbus*, loin] backache, esp. in the lower back

lumbar (lum'bər) *adj.* [< L. *lumbus*, loin] of or near the loins

lumber¹ (lum'bər) *n.* [< ? orig., pawnshop in *Lombardy*, Italy] **1.** discarded household articles, furniture, etc. stored away or taking up room **2.** [Chiefly Canad.] timber sawn into beams, boards, etc. —*vt.* **1.** to clutter with useless articles or rubbish **2.** [Colloq.] to burden with something unpleasant, tedious, etc. —*vi.* to cut down timber and saw it into lumber —**lum'bering** *n.*

lumber² *vi.* [< ? Scand.] to move heavily, clumsily, and, often, noisily —**lum'bering** *adj.*

lumberjack *n.* one who cuts down and removes trees

luminary (lōō'mi nər ē) *n., pl.* **-naries** [< L. *lumen*, light] **1.** a body that gives off light, such as the sun or moon **2.** any notable person

luminescence (lōō'mi nes'əns) *n.* [< L. *lumen*, a light + -ESCENCE] any giving off of light caused by the absorption of radiant energy, etc. —**lu'mines'cent** *adj.*

luminous (lōō'mi nəs) *adj.* [< L. *lumen*, a light] **1.** giving off light **2.** glowing in the dark **3.** enlightened or enlightening —**lu'minos'ity** (-nos'ə tē) *n.* —**lu'minously** *adv.*

lumme (lum'ē) *interj.* [contr. < *Lord love me*] an expression of surprise

lump¹ (lump) *n.* [ME. *lumpe*] **1.** a solid mass of no special shape **2.** a small cube, as of sugar **3.** a swelling; bulge **4.** a large amount **5.** a clodlike person **6.** [*usually* L-] a system of employment, esp. in the building industry, under which workers are paid as sub-contractors —*adj.* in lumps [*lump sugar*] —*vt.* **1.** to put together in a lump or lumps **2.** to treat or deal with in a mass —*vi.* to become lumpy —**in the lump** all together —**lump in one's throat** a tight feeling in the throat, as from emotion

lump² *vt.* [< ?] [Colloq.] to put up with (something disagreeable) [if you don't like it, you can *lump it*]

lumpish *adj.* **1.** like a lump **2.** clumsy, dull, etc. —**lump'ishly** *adv.* —**lump'ishness** *n.*

lump sum a gross, or total, sum paid at one time

lumpy *adj.* **-ier, -iest 1.** full of lumps **2.** covered with lumps **3.** rough: said of water —**lump'iness** *n.*

lunacy (lōō'nə sē) *n., pl.* **-cies** [< LUNATIC] **1.** insanity **2.** utter foolishness

lunar (lōō'nər) *adj.* [< L. *luna*, moon] of, on, or like the moon

lunar (excursion) module the module used to go between the orbiting spacecraft and the moon

lunatic (lōō'nə tik) *adj.* [< L. *luna*, moon] **1.** [Rare] *a)* insane *b)* of or for insane persons **2.** utterly foolish —*n.* an insane person

lunatic asylum [Rare] a mental hospital

lunatic fringe the minority considered fanatical in any political, social, or other movement

lunch (lunch) *n.* [? < Sp. *lonja*, slice of ham] the light midday meal between breakfast and dinner —*vi.* to eat lunch

luncheon (lun'chən) *n.* [< prec.] a lunch; esp., a formal lunch with others

luncheon voucher a voucher issued to employees and redeemable at a restaurant for food: also **L.V.**

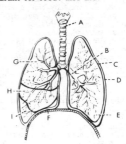

LUNGS
(A, trachea; B, bronchus; C, visceral pleura; D, parietal pleura; E, bronchiole; F, diaphragm; G, upper lobe; H, middle lobe; I, lower lobe)

lung (luŋ) *n.* [OE. *lungen*] either of the two spongelike respiratory organs in the thorax of vertebrates —**at the top of one's lungs** in one's loudest voice

lunge (lunj) *n.* [< Fr. *allonger*, to lengthen] **1.** a sudden thrust, as with a sword **2.** a sudden plunge forward —*vi., vt.* **lunged, lung'ing** to move, or cause to move, with a lunge

lungfish (luŋ'fish') *n.* any of various fishes having lungs as well as gills

lupin, lupine (lōō'pin) *n.* [< L. *lupus*, wolf] **1.** a plant with racemes of white, rose, yellow, or blue flowers and pods containing beanlike seeds **2.** the seed of this plant

lupine (lōō'pīn) *adj.* [< L. *lupus*, wolf] **1.** of a wolf or wolves **2.** fierce

lupus (lōō'pəs) *n.* [< L., wolf] any of various diseases with skin lesions, esp. tuberculosis of the skin

lurch¹ (lurch) *vi.* [< ?] **1.** to pitch or sway suddenly to one side **2.** to stagger —*n.* a lurching movement

lurch² *n.* [prob. < OFr. *lourche*, duped] only in **leave in the lurch** to leave in a difficult situation

lurcher *n.* a crossbred dog trained to hunt silently, used by poachers

lure (lyŏŏər) *vt.* **lured, lur'ing** [< OFr. *loirre*] to entice —*n.* 1. *a*) the power of attracting *b*) anything having this power 2. a feathered device on the end of a long cord, used in falconry to recall the hawk

lurid (lyŏŏər'id) *adj.* [< L. *luridus*, ghastly] 1. startling; sensational; horrifying 2. gaudy; garish 3. [Rare] deathly pale —**lu'ridly** *adv.* —**lu'ridness** *n.*

lurk (lurk) *vi.* [ME. *lurken*] 1. to stay hidden, ready to attack, etc. 2. to be present as a latent threat, etc. 3. to move furtively —**lurk'er** *n.*

luscious (lush'əs) *adj.* [ME. *lucius*, infl. by ff.] 1. very pleasing to taste or smell 2. delighting any of the senses —**lus'ciously** *adv.*

lush (lush) *adj.* [< OFr. *lasche*, lax] 1. of or characterized by rich growth 2. tender and full of juice 3. rich, abundant, extravagant, etc. —**lush'ly** *adv.*

lust (lust) *n.* [OE., pleasure] 1. strong sexual desire 2. excessive desire [a lust for power] —*vi.* to feel an intense desire, esp. sexual desire —**lust'ful** *adj.* —**lust'fully** *adv.* —**lust'fulness** *n.*

lustre (lus'tər) *n.* [< L. *lustrare*, illumine] 1. gloss; sheen 2. brightness; radiance 3. *a*) radiant beauty *b*) fame; glory 4. the iridescent appearance of glazed pottery

lustrous *adj.* shining; bright —**lus'trously** *adv.*

lusty (lus'tē) *adj.* **-ier, -iest** full of vigour; strong, robust, hearty, etc. —**lust'ily** *adv.* —**lust'iness** *n.*

lutanist, lutenist (lōōt'ən ist) *n.* a lute player

LUTE

lute¹ (lōōt) *n.* [< Ar. *al'ūd*, lit., the wood] an early stringed instrument with a rounded back and a long, fretted neck

lute² *n.* [< L. *lutum*, mud] a clayey cement used as a sealing agent for the joints of pipes, etc.

lutetium (lōō tē'shē əm) *n.* [< L. *Lutetia*, Paris] a metallic chemical element of the rare-earth group: symbol, Lu

Lutheran (lōō'thər ən) *adj.* of the Protestant denomination founded by Luther, or of its doctrines, etc. —*n.* a member of a Lutheran church

lutist (lōōt'ist) *n.* a lute player

luxe (luks) *n.* [Fr. < L. *luxus*] luxury: see also DELUXE

luxuriant (lug zhōōər'ē ənt) *adj.* [see ff.] 1. growing with vigour and in abundance 2. richly varied, elaborate, etc. —**luxu'riance, luxu'riancy** *n.*

luxuriate *vi.* **-at'ed, -at'ing** [< L. *luxuria*, luxury] 1. to revel (*in*) 2. to grow in great abundance 3. to live in great luxury etc. —**luxu'riously** *adv.*

luxurious *adj.* 1. splendid, rich, comfortable, etc. 2. fond of or indulging in luxury —**luxu'riously** *adv.*

luxury (luk'shə rē) *n.*, *pl.* **-ries** [< L. *luxus*] 1. the enjoyment of the best and most costly things 2. anything giving such enjoyment, usually something considered unnecessary to life and health —*adj.* characterized by luxury

L.V. Luncheon Voucher

-ly¹ (lē) [OE. *-lic*] a suffix meaning: 1. like, characteristic of [manly] 2. happening (once) every (specified period of time) [monthly]

-ly² [OE. *-lic*] a suffix meaning: 1. in a (specified) manner, to a (specified) extent or direction, in or at a (specified) time or place [harshly, outwardly, hourly] 2. in the (specified) order of sequence [secondly]

lyceum (lī sē'əm) *n.* [< Gr. *Lykeion*, grove at Athens where Aristotle taught] [Chiefly U.S.] a lecture hall

lychee (lī'chē') *n.* same as LITCHI

lych gate same as LICH GATE

lye (lī) *n.* [OE. *leag*] any strongly alkaline substance: lye is used in cleaning and in making soap

lying¹ (lī'iŋ) *prp.* of LIE¹

lying² *prp.* of LIE² —*adj.* false; not truthful —*n.* the telling of a lie or lies

lying-in (lī'iŋ in') *n.* confinement in childbirth —*adj.* of or for childbirth [a lying-in hospital]

lymph (limf) *n.* [< L. *lympha*, spring water] a yellowish fluid resembling blood plasma, found in vertebrates

lymphatic (lim fat'ik) *adj.* 1. of, containing, or conveying lymph 2. sluggish; without energy

lymph node any of many small, compact structures lying in groups along the course of the lymphatic vessels

lynch (linch) *vt.* [< W. *Lynch*, vigilante in 18th-cent. Virginia] to murder (an accused person) by mob action and without lawful trial, as by hanging —**lynch'ing** *n.*

lynx (liŋks) *n.* [< Gr. *lynx*] a wildcat characterized by a short tail, long, tufted ears, and keen vision

lynx-eyed *adj.* having very keen sight

Lyon King of Arms (lī'ən) the chief herald of Scotland

Lyra (līə'rə) a N constellation: it contains Vega

LYRE

lyre (līər) *n.* [< Gr. *lyra*] a small stringed instrument played by the ancient Greeks

lyrebird *n.* an Australian songbird: the long tail feathers of the male when spread resemble a lyre

lyric (lir′ik) *adj.* [< Gr. *lyrikos*] 1. suitable for singing; specif., designating poetry expressing the poet's emotions and thoughts 2. *same as* LYRICAL 3. having a relatively high voice with a light, flexible quality [*a lyric tenor*] —*n.* 1. a lyric poem 2. [*usually pl.*] the words of a song

lyrical *adj.* 1. *same as* LYRIC 2. expressing rapture or enthusiasm —**lyr′ically** *adv.*

lyricist *n.* a writer of lyrics, esp. lyrics for popular songs

-lyse (līz) *a combining form used to form verbs corresponding to nouns ending in* -LYSIS [*electrolyse*]

-lysis (lə sis) [see ff.] *a combining form meaning* a loosing, dissolution, destruction [*paralysis*]

-lyte (līt) [< Gr. *lyein,* to loose] *a combining form meaning* a substance subjected to a process of decomposition [*hydrolyte*]

-lytic (lit′ik) *a combining form used to form adjectives corresponding to nouns ending in* -LYSIS [*catalytic*]

M

M, m (em) *n., pl.* **M's, m's** the thirteenth
letter of the English alphabet
M (em) *n.* the Roman numeral for 1000
M. 1. Medieval 2. *Music* mezzo 3.
Monday 4. *pl.* **MM.** Monsieur 5.
Motorway
M., m. 1. majesty 2. male 3. married
4. masculine 5. meridian 6. mile(s) 7.
minute(s) 8. month
m metre; metres
ma (mä) *n.* [Colloq.] mamma; mother
M.A. [L. *Magister Artium*] Master of Arts
ma'am (mam, mäm, məm) *n.* madam
Mac (mak) *n.* [< MAC-, MC-] [Colloq.]
a Scotsman
mac (mak) *n. see* MACK
Mac- (mak, mək, mə) [< Ir. & Gael. *mac*,
son] *a prefix meaning* son of: also **Mc-**,
Mᶜ-, **M'-**
macabre (məkäb'rə) *adj.* [Fr.] gruesome;
horrible
macadam (məkad'əm) *n.* [< J. L.
McAdam] small broken stones used in
making roads, usually combined with tar
or asphalt —**macad'amize** *vt.*
macaroni (mak'ərō'nē) *n.* [It. *maccaroni*,
pl.] 1. pasta in the form of tubes 2.
pl. **-nies** an 18th-cent. dandy
macaroon (mak'ərōōn') *n.* [< prec.] a
small biscuit made of egg white, crushed
almonds, and sugar
macaw (məkô') *n.* [prob. < Braz. native
name] a large, brightly-coloured, harsh-
voiced parrot of C and S America
Macc. Maccabees
mace¹ (mās) *n.* [< OFr. *masse*] 1. *Hist.*
a heavy, spiked club 2. a staff used as
a symbol of authority by certain officials,
esp. as carried before the Speaker of the
House of Commons —**mace'bear'er** *n.*
mace² *n.* [< L. *makir*, a fragrant resin]
a spice made from the dried outer covering
of the nutmeg
macerate (mas'ərāt') *vt.* **-at'ed, -at'ing**
[< L. *macerare*, soften] 1. to soften
and break down the parts of by soaking
in liquid 2. to cause to waste away —*vi.*
to waste away —**mac'era'tion** *n.* —**mac'er-
a'tor** *n.*
Mach (mak) *n. short for* MACH NUMBER
machete (məchet'ē, məshet'ē) *n.* [Sp.]
a large, heavy-bladed knife used for cutting
sugar cane, etc. in the W Indies and S
America
Machiavellian (mak'ēəvel'ēən) *adj.* of
or like Machiavelli, the 15th cent. Florentine
statesman, or the political principles of
craftiness and duplicity advocated by him
machicolation (məchik'ōlä'shən) *n.*
[prob. < L. *masticare*, grind + *col*, neck]
an opening through which hot liquids, etc.
could be dropped by the defenders of a
fortress
machinate (mak'ənāt') *vi., vt.* **-nat'ed,
-nat'ing** [< L. *machinari*, to plot] to
plan or plot, esp. to do evil —**mach'ina'-
tion** *n.* —**mach'ina'tor** *n.*
machine (məshēn') *n.* [Fr. < Gr. *mēchos*,
contrivance] 1. a structure consisting of
a framework and various moving parts,
for doing some kind of work 2. a vehicle:
old-fashioned term 3. a person or
organization regarded as acting like a
machine; esp., a smoothly functioning
complex organization —*adj.* 1. of
machines 2. made or done by machinery
—*vt.* **-chined', -chin'ing** to make, shape,
etc. by machinery —**machin'able** *adj.*
machine gun an automatic gun firing
a rapid stream of bullets —**machine'-
gun'** *vt.* **-gunned', -gun'ning**
machinery *n., pl.* **-eries** 1. machines
collectively 2. the working parts of a
machine 3. any means by which something
is kept in action [the *machinery of
government*]
machine shop a factory for making
or repairing machines or machine parts
machine tool a power-driven tool, as
an electric lathe
machinist *n.* 1. a person who makes
or repairs machinery 2. a worker who
operates a machine
‡**machismo** (ma kiz'mō) *n.* [< Sp. *macho*,
masculine] strong or aggressive mascu-
linity; virility
Mach number (mak) [< Ernst *Mach*]
[*also* m-] a number representing the ratio
of the speed of an object to the speed
of sound through the same medium, as air
mack (mak) *n. short for* MACKINTOSH
mackerel (mak'rəl) *n.* [< OFr. *makerel*
< ?] an edible fish with a greenish, blue-
striped back and a silvery belly
mackintosh, macintosh (mak'intosh')
n. [< C. *Macintosh*] a waterproof
raincoat, or the fabric for it
macramé (məkrä'mē) *n.* [ult. < Ar.
miqramah, a veil] 1. a coarse fringe or
lace of thread or cord knotted in designs
2. the craft of making these fringes
macro- [< Gr. *makros*, long] *a combining
form meaning* long, large, enlarged, or
elongated
macrobiotics (mak'rōbīot'iks) *n.pl.*
[*with sing. v.*] [< prec. + Gr. *bios*, life]
the art of prolonging life, as by a special
diet —**mac'robiot'ic** *adj.*
macrocosm (mak'rōkoz'm) *n.* [see
MACRO- & COSMOS¹] 1. the universe 2.
any large, complex entity

macron (ma′kron) *n.* [< Gr. *makros*, long] a short, straight mark (‾) placed horizontally over a vowel to indicate that it is long or is to be pronounced in a certain way

macroscopic (mak′rō skop′ik) *adj.* [MACRO- + -SCOPE] 1. visible to the naked eye 2. to do with large units

macula (mak′yoo lə) *n., pl.* **-lae** (-lē′) [L.] a spot; esp., *a*) a discoloured spot on the skin *b*) a sunspot

mad (mad) *adj.* **mad′der, mad′dest** [< OE. (*ge*)*mædan*, drive mad] 1. insane 2. frenzied; frantic 3. foolish and rash 4. foolishly enthusiastic [*mad* about clothes] 5. wildly amusing 6. having rabies [*a mad dog*] 7. [Colloq.] angry (often with *at*) —**mad′ness** *n.*

madam (mad′əm) *n., pl.* **mad′ams**; for 1, usually **mesdames** (mā dam′) [Fr.] 1. a woman: a polite term of address 2. a woman in charge of a brothel 3. [Slang] a precocious or pert girl

madame (mad′əm) *n., pl.* **mesdames** (mā dam′) [Fr.] a married woman: French title equivalent to *Mrs.*: abbrev. Mme.

madcap (mad′kap′) *n.* [MAD + CAP, fig. for head] a reckless, impulsive person —*adj.* reckless and impulsive

madden (mad′'n) *vt., vi.* to make or become insane, angry, or wildly excited —**mad′dening** *adj.*

madder (mad′ər) *n.* [OE. *mædere*] 1. a plant with small, yellow flowers 2. *a*) its red root *b*) a red dye made from this

made (mād) *pt. & pp.* of MAKE —*adj.* 1. formed 2. prepared from various ingredients [*a made dish*] 3. sure of success [*a made man*] —**be made for** to be ideally suited —**have it made** [Slang] to be assured of success

Madeira (mə dēər′ə) *n.* [< *Madeira*, the island off NW Africa] [also m-] a fortified wine

mademoiselle (mad′ə mə zel′) *n.,* Fr. *pl.* **mesdemoiselles** (mād mwä zel′) [Fr. < *ma*, my + *demoiselle*, young lady] an unmarried woman or girl: French title equivalent to *Miss*: abbrev. Mlle.

made-up (mād′up′) *adj.* 1. put together 2. invented; false 3. with cosmetics applied 4. of road, surfaced with tarmac, etc.

madhouse (mad′hous′) *n.* 1. [Archaic] a place of confinement for the mentally ill 2. any place of turmoil

madly *adv.* 1. foolishly 2. wildly; furiously 3. insanely 4. extremely

madman *n.* an insane person —**mad′-wom′an** *n.fem.*

Madonna (mə don′ə) *n.* [It. < *ma*, my + *donna*, lady] 1. Mary, mother of Jesus 2. a picture or statue of Mary

madrigal (mad′ri gəl) *n.* [< It.] a part song, without accompaniment —**mad′rigalist** *n.*

maelstrom (māl′strom) *n.* [Early ModDu. < *malen*, grind + *stroom*, stream] 1. any large or violent whirlpool 2. a violently agitated state

maenad (mē′nad) *n.* [< Gr. *mainesthai*, to rave] 1. [often M-] a female worshipper of Dionysus; bacchante 2. a frenzied woman —**maenadic** (mi nad′ik) *adj.*

maestro (mä es′trō) *n., pl.* **-tros, -tri** (-trē) [It. < L. *magister*, master] a master in any art; esp., a great composer, conductor, or teacher of music

Mae West (mā′west′) [< U.S. actress] an inflatable life-jacket

Mafia, Maffia (ma′fē ə) *n.* [It. *maffia*, hostility to law] an alleged secret society of criminals, esp. in the U.S.

magazine (mag′ə zēn′) *n.* [< Fr. < Ar. *makhzan*, granary] 1. a publication that appears at regular intervals and contains stories, articles, etc. 2. a supply chamber, as the space in a rifle from which the cartridges are fed 3. a warehouse or military supply depot 4. a space in which explosives are stored, as in a fort

magenta (mə jen′tə) *n.* [< *Magenta*, town in Italy] purplish red —*adj.* purplish-red

maggot (mag′ət) *n.* [ME. *magotte*] 1. a wormlike insect larva, esp. of the housefly 2. a whim —**mag′goty** *adj.*

Magi (mā′jī) *n.pl.* [< OPer. *magus*] 1. the priestly caste in ancient Persia 2. the wise men from the East who brought gifts to the infant Jesus: Matt. 2:1-13

magic (maj′ik) *n.* [< Gr. *magikos*, of the Magi] 1. the use of charms, spells, etc. in seeking or pretending to control events or forces 2. any power that seems mysterious 3. the art of producing illusions by sleight of hand, etc. —*adj.* 1. of, produced by, or using magic 2. producing extraordinary results, as if by magic —**magic away** to bring about the disappearance of, as if by magic —**mag′ical** *adj.* —**mag′ically** *adv.*

magician (mə jish′ən) *n.* an expert in magic; specif., *a*) a wizard *b*) a performer skilled in magic

magic lantern an early type of slide projector

magisterial (maj′is tēər′ē əl) *adj.* [< L. *magister*, master] 1. authoritative 2. domineering 3. of a magistrate

magistracy (maj′is trə sē) *n., pl.* **-cies** 1. the office of a magistrate 2. magistrates collectively

magistrate *n.* [< L. *magister*, master] 1. a civil officer empowered to administer the law 2. a justice of the peace

magistrate's court a court dealing with minor crimes

magma (mag′mə) *n.* [L.] molten rock deep in the earth, from which igneous rock is formed

Magna Charta (or **Carta**) (mag′nə kär′-tə) [ML., great charter] 1. the charter that King John was forced to grant in 1215, interpreted as guaranteeing certain liberties 2. any constitution guaranteeing certain liberties

magnanimous (mag nan′ə məs) *adj.* [< L. *magnus*, great + *animus*, soul] generous in overlooking injury or insult; rising above pettiness —**magnanimity** (mag′-nə nim′ə tē) *n.* —**magnan′imously** *adv.*

magnate (mag′nāt) *n.* [< L. *magnus*,

great] a very influential person, esp. in business

magnesia (mag nē′shə) n. [ult. < Gr. *Magnésia*, in Thessaly] magnesium oxide, a white, tasteless powder used as a laxative and antacid

magnesium (mag nē′zē əm) n. [< prec.] a light, silver-white, metallic chemical element : symbol, Mg

magnet (mag′nit) n. [< Gr. *Magnétis* (*lithos*), (stone) of Magnesia: see MAGNESIA] 1. any piece of iron, steel, or lodestone that has the property of attracting iron, steel, etc. 2. a person or thing that attracts

magnetic (mag net′ik) adj. 1. having the properties of a magnet 2. of, producing, or caused by magnetism 3. of the earth's magnetism 4. that can be magnetized 5. powerfully attractive —**magnet′ically** adv.

magnetic field a region of space in which there is an appreciable magnetic force

magnetic mine a mine exploded when the metal hull of a ship deflects a magnetic needle, thus detonating the charge

magnetic needle a bar of magnetized steel which, when swinging freely, points towards the magnetic poles

magnetic north the direction towards which a magnetic needle points, usually not true north

magnetic pole 1. either pole of a magnet 2. either point on the earth's surface towards which a magnetic needle points: the magnetic poles differ from the geographical poles

magnetic recording the recording of electrical signals by means of changes of magnetization on a tape or disc

magnetic storm a worldwide disturbance of the earth's magnetic field, believed to be caused by sunspot activity

magnetic tape a thin plastic ribbon coated with iron oxide particles, used for magnetic recording

magnetism (mag′nə tiz′m) n. 1. the property or quality of being magnetic 2. the force to which this is due 3. the branch of physics dealing with magnetic phenomena 4. personal charm

magnetite n. a black iron oxide, an important iron ore: called *lodestone* when magnetic

magnetize vt. -ized′, -iz′ing 1. to give magnetic properties to 2. to charm (a person) —**mag′netiza′tion** n.

magneto (mag nēt′ō) n., pl. -tos a dynamo in which one or more magnets produce the magnetic field

magnetron (mag′nə tron′) n. [MAGNE(T) + (ELEC)TRON] an electron tube in which the electrons are acted upon by a magnetic field to produce microwave frequencies

Magnificat (mag nif′i kat′) n. [L.] 1. the hymn of the Virgin Mary in Luke 1 :46–55 2. any musical setting for this

magnification (mag′nə fi kā′shən) n. 1. a magnifying or being magnified 2. the power of magnifying 3. a magnified image or model

magnificent (mag nif′i sənt) adj. [< L. *magnus*, great + *facere*, do] 1. beautiful and stately; sumptuous, as in construction, decoration, etc. 2. exalted: said of ideas, etc. 3. [Colloq.] very good —**magnif′icence** n. —**magnif′icently** adv.

magnify (mag′nə fī′) vt. -fied′, -fy′ing [see MAGNIFICENT] 1. to increase the apparent size of, esp. by means of a lens 2. to exaggerate 3. [Archaic] to praise —vi. to have the power of increasing the apparent size of an object

magnifying glass a lens that increases the apparent size of an object seen through it

magniloquent (mag nil′ō kwənt) adj. [< L. *magnus*, great + *loqui*, speak] 1. pompous or grandiose in speech or style 2. boastful —**magnil′oquence** n.

magnitude (mag′nə tood′) n. [< L. *magnus*, great] 1. greatness 2. size 3. importance 4. *Astron.* the degree of brightness of a fixed star —**of the first magnitude** of the greatest importance

magnolia (mag nōl′yə) n. [< P. *Magnol*] a tree or shrub with large, fragrant flowers of white, pink, or purple

magnum (mag′nəm) n. [L. < *magnus*, great] a wine bottle holding about 2 quarts or 2.3 litres

‡**magnum opus** (mag′nəm ō′pəs) [L.] 1. a great work; masterpiece 2. a person's greatest work

magpie (mag′pī′) n. [< *Mag*, dim. of *Margaret* + PIE[3]] 1. a noisy bird related to the crows, with black-and-white colouring and a long, tapering tail 2. one who chatters 3. one who collects odds and ends

Magyar (mag′yär) n. [Hung.] 1. a member of the main ethnic group in Hungary 2. their language; Hungarian —adj. of the Magyars, their language, etc.

maharajah, maharaja (mä′hə rä′jə) n. [< Hindi *mahā*, great + *rājā*, king] formerly in India, a prince

maharani, maharanee (-nē) n. [< Hindi *mahā*, great + *rānī*, queen] the wife of a maharajah

maharishi (mä′hä rish′ē) n. [Hindi] a Hindu teacher of mysticism and transcendental meditation

mahatma (mə hät′mə) n. [< Sans. *mahā*, great + *ātman*, soul] *Theosophy & Buddhism* any of a class of wise and holy persons held in special reverence

mah-jongg, mahjong (mä joŋ′) n. [< Chin. *ma-ch'iao*, house sparrow] a game played with 136 or 144 small tiles

mahogany (mə hog′ə nē) n., pl. -nies [< ?] 1. any of various tropical trees with hard, reddish-brown wood valued for furniture 2. reddish brown

mahout (mə hout′) n. [< Hindi] in India and the East Indies, an elephant driver or elephant keeper

maid (mād) n. [< ME. *maiden*] 1. a) a girl or young unmarried woman b) a virgin 2. a female servant

maiden (mād′'n) n. [OE. *mægden*] 1.

a) a girl or young unmarried woman b) a virgin **2.** a racehorse that has never won a race —*adj.* **1.** a) unmarried b) virgin **2.** untried; new; fresh **3.** first or earliest [*a maiden voyage*]

maidenhair *n.* any of various ferns with delicate fronds and slender stalks : also **maidenhair fern**

maidenhead *n.* **1.** virginity **2.** the hymen

maiden name the surname that a woman had when not yet married

maiden over *Cricket* an over in which no runs are scored

maid of all work 1. a woman employed for doing general housework **2.** someone doing a variety of work

maid of honour 1. a tartlet **2.** an unmarried woman attending a queen or princess

maidservant *n.* a girl or woman servant

mail[1] (māl) *n.* [< OHG. *malaha*, wallet] **1.** letters, packages, etc. transported and delivered by the post office **2.** a vehicle that carries mail —*vt.* to send by mail

MAIL

mail[2] *n.* [< L. *macula*, mesh of a net] **1.** a flexible body armour made of small metal rings or scales **2.** armour in general —**mailed** *adj.*

mailbag *n.* a bag in which mail is transported : also **mail sack**

mailing list a list of names and addresses used by an organization in sending out its literature, advertising matter, etc.

mail-order firm a business that takes mail orders and sends goods by post

maim (mām) *vt.* [OFr. *mahaigner*] to cripple; mutilate; disable

main[1] (mān) *adj.* [OE. *mægen*, strength] chief in size, importance, etc. —*n.* **1.** a principal pipe or line in a distributing system for water, gas, etc. **2.** strength : only in **with might and main**, with all one's strength **3.** [Poet.] the sea **4.** [Archaic] the mainland —**by main force** by sheer force —**in the main** chiefly

main[2] *n.* [prob. < prec.] a match in cockfighting

main chance self-interest : usually in **have an eye to the main chance**

main clause in a complex sentence, a clause that can function as a complete sentence by itself

mainland *n.* the main land mass of a continent, as distinguished from nearby islands —**main'land'er** *n.*

mainline *n.* the major railway line between two points —*adj.* designating a railway station on a mainline —*vt.* **-lined'**, **-lin'ing** [Slang] to inject (a narcotic drug) directly into a large vein —**main'lin'er** *n.*

mainly *adv.* chiefly; principally; in the main

mainmast (-məst, -mäst') *n.* the principal mast of a vessel

MAINMAST
MAINSTAY
MAINSAIL
MIZZENMAST
JIB
MAINSHEET
MIZZEN
BOW
STERN

mainsail (-s'l, -sāl') *n.* the principal sail of a ship, set from the mainmast

mainspring *n.* **1.** the driving spring in a clock, watch, etc. **2.** the chief motive or incentive

mainstay *n.* **1.** the supporting line run forward from the mainmast **2.** a chief support

mainstream *n.* the prevailing trend of thought, action, etc.

maintain (mān tān') *vt.* [< L. *manu tenere*, to hold in the hand] **1.** to keep or keep up; carry on **2.** to keep in continuance or in a certain condition, as of repair **3.** a) to uphold or defend b) to declare positively; assert **4.** to support by aid, influence, etc. **5.** to provide the means of existence for —**maintain'able** *adj.* —**maintain'er** *n.*

maintenance (mān'tən əns) *n.* **1.** a maintaining or being maintained **2.** means of support; livelihood

maintop *n.* a platform at the head of the lower section of the mainmast

maisonette, maisonnette (mā'zə net') *n.* [Fr., dim. of *maison*, house] a flat, usually on more than one floor

‡**maître d'hôtel** (me'tr'dō tel') [Fr., master of the house] **1.** a butler or steward **2.** a headwaiter

maize (māz) *n.* [Sp. < WInd. *mahiz*] **1.** a cultivated cereal plant, with the grain borne on cobs; Indian corn **2.** the colour of ripe maize; yellow

Maj. Major

majesty (maj'əs tē) *n.*, *pl.* **-ties** [< L. *magnus*, great] **1.** sovereign power **2.** [M-] a title used in speaking to or of a sovereign **3.** stateliness —**majestic** (mə jes'tik) *adj.*

majolica (mə jol'i kə) *n.* [< It. *Maiolica*, Majorca] a variety of Italian pottery, enamelled, glazed, and richly decorated

major (mā'jər) *adj.* [L., compar. of *magnus*, great] **1.** greater in size, amount, importance, etc. **2.** of full legal age **3.** *Music* a) designating an interval greater than the corresponding minor by a semitone b) characterized by major intervals, scales, etc. *[the major key] c)* based on the major scale —*n.* **1.** see MILITARY RANKS, table **2.** [U.S.] *Educ.* major field of study **3.** *Law* a person of full legal age

major-domo (mā′jər dō′mō) *n.*, *pl.* -mos [< Sp. or It. < L. *major*, greater + *domus*, house] a man in charge of a great or royal household; chief steward

major general *pl.* **major generals** see MILITARY RANKS, table

majority (mə jôr′ə tē) *n.*, *pl.* -ties [see MAJOR] **1.** the greater number; more than half **2.** the excess of the larger number of votes cast for one candidate, bill, etc. over the rest of the votes **3.** the party with the majority of votes **4.** the state of being legally an adult **5.** *Mil.* the rank of a major

major scale a musical scale, with semitones instead of whole tones after the third and seventh notes

make (māk) *vt.* **made**, **mak′ing** [OE. *macian*] **1.** to bring into being; build, create, devise, etc. **2.** to cause to be, become, or seem **3.** to prepare *[make the beds]* **4.** to amount to *[1000 grammes make a kilo]* **5.** to have the qualities of *[to make a fine leader]* **6.** to establish *[to make rules]* **7.** to acquire; earn **8.** to cause the success of *[that venture made him]* **9.** to understand *[what do you make of that?]* **10.** to estimate *[I make the distance about 500 miles]* **11.** to do, accomplish, engage in, etc. **12.** to deliver (a speech) **13.** to force *[make him behave]* **14.** to reach *[the ship made port]* **15.** to travel *[to make 500 miles]* **16.** [Colloq.] to succeed in getting a position on, etc. *[to make the team]* —*vi.* **1.** to start (to do something) *[she made to go]* **2.** to tend; move *(to, towards,* etc.) **3.** to behave in a specified manner *[make merry]* **4.** to cause something to be in a specified condition *[make ready]* —*n.* **1.** style; build **2.** type or brand —**make after** to chase —**make a meal of** **1.** to eat **2.** to do something laboriously or fussily —**make away with** **1.** to steal **2.** to get rid of **3.** to kill —**make believe** to pretend —**make do** to manage with whatever means available —**make for** **1.** to head for **2.** to attack **3.** to help effect —**make it** [Colloq.] to achieve a certain thing —**make off with** to steal —**make or break** to cause the success or failure of —**make out** **1.** to see with some difficulty **2.** to understand **3.** to write out **4.** to fill in (a blank form, etc.) **5.** to (try to) prove to be **6.** to succeed —**make over** **1.** to change; renovate **2.** to transfer the ownership of —**make up** **1.** to compose **2.** to form **3.** to invent **4.** to complete by providing what is lacking **5.** to compensate *(for)* **6.** to become friendly again after a quarrel **7.** to put cosmetics on **8.** to decide —**make up to** to try to ingratiate oneself with —**on the make**

[Colloq.] trying to succeed financially, socially, etc.

make-believe *n.* pretence —*adj.* pretended

maker *n.* **1.** one that makes **2.** [M-] God

makeshift *n.* a temporary expedient —*adj.* that will do for a while as a substitute

makeup, **make-up** *n.* **1.** cosmetics generally **2.** the cosmetics, costumes, etc. put on for theatrical roles **3.** the way in which something is put together **4.** nature; disposition —*adj.* of or for making-up

makeweight *n.* **1.** anything added to a scale to complete the required weight **2.** an unimportant person or thing added to make up some lack

making *n.* **1.** the process of being made **2.** the cause of success *[that will be the making of him]* **3.** [*pl.*] potential; qualities needed *[the makings of a lawyer]*

mal- [< L. *malus*, bad] *a prefix meaning* bad or badly, wrong, ill *[maladjustment]*

Mal. **1.** Malachi **2.** Malay

malachite (mal′ə kīt′) *n.* [< Gr. *malachē*, mallow] copper carbonate, a green mineral used for table tops, etc.

maladjusted (mal′ə jus′tid) *adj.* poorly adjusted, esp. to the circumstances of one's life —**mal′adjust′ment** *n.*

maladminister (mal′əd min′ə stər) *vt.* to administer badly or corruptly —**mal′admin′istra′tion** *n.*

maladroit (mal′ə droit′) *adj.* [see MAL- & ADROIT] awkward; clumsy —**mal′adroit′ly** *adv.*

malady (mal′ə dē) *n.*, *pl.* -dies [< L. *male habitus*, out of condition] a disease; illness; sickness

malaise (ma lāz′) *n.* [Fr. < *mal*, bad + *aise*, ease] a vague feeling of discomfort or uneasiness

malapropism (mal′ə prop iz′m) *n.* [< Mrs. *Malaprop*, a character in Sheridan's *The Rivals*] ludicrous misuse of words, esp. of words that sound somewhat alike

malaria (mə lãr′ē ə) *n.* [It. < *mala aria*, bad air] an infectious disease transmitted to man by the bite of an infected mosquito: it is characterized by severe chills and fever —**malar′ial** *adj.*

malarkey, malarky (mə lär′kē) *n.* [< ? Irish surname] [Slang] insincere talk; nonsense

malathion (mal′ə thī′on) *n.* an organic phosphate, used as an insecticide

Malay (mə lā′) *n.* **1.** a member of a group of peoples living in the Malay Peninsula, and the Malay Archipelago **2.** their Indonesian language —*adj.* of the Malays, their country, language, culture, etc. Also **Malay′an**

malcontent (mal′kən tent′) *adj.* [see MAL- & CONTENT[1]] dissatisfied or rebellious —*n.* a dissatisfied or rebellious person

male (māl) *adj.* [< L. *mas*, a male] **1.** designating or of the sex that fertilizes the ovum of the female **2.** of, like, or suitable for members of this sex **3.** having a part shaped to fit into a corresponding hollow part **4.** *Bot.* designating or of fertilizing bodies, organs, etc. —n. a male person, animal, or plant —male'ness n.

malediction (mal′ə dik′shən) n. [see MAL-& DICTION] a calling down of evil on someone; curse

malefactor (mal′ə fak′tər) n. [< L. male, evil + facere, do] an evildoer or criminal —mal′efac′tion n.

malevolent (mə lev′ə lənt) adj. [< L. male, evil + velle, to wish] wishing evil or harm to others; malicious —malev′olence n. —malev′olently adv.

malfeasance (mal fē′zəns) n. [< Fr. mal, evil + faire, do] wrongdoing or misconduct, esp. by a public official

malformation (mal′fôr mā′shən) n. faulty, irregular, or abnormal formation —malformed′ adj.

malfunction (mal′fuŋk′shən) vi. to fail to function as it should —n. the act or an instance of malfunctioning

malice (mal′is) n. [< L. malus, bad] 1. active ill will; desire to harm another 2. Law evil intent —malice aforethought a deliberate plan to do something unlawful —malicious (mə lish′əs) adj.

malign (mə līn′) vt. [< L. male, ill + genus, born] to speak evil of; slander —adj. 1. showing ill will; malicious 2. evil; sinister 3. very harmful —malign′er n.

malignant (mə lig′nənt) adj. [see MALIGN] 1. having an evil influence 2. wishing evil; malevolent 3. very harmful 4. causing or likely to cause death [a malignant growth] —malig′nancy n.

malignity n. 1. intense ill will 2. the quality of being very harmful 3. pl. -ties a malignant act or feeling

malinger (mə liŋ′gər) vi. [< Fr. malingre, sickly] to pretend to be ill in order to escape duty or work; shirk —malin′gerer n.

mall (môl) n. [var. of MAUL] 1. a shaded walk or public promenade 2. a street for pedestrians only

mallard (mal′ərd) n. [< OFr. malart] the common wild duck : the male has a green head

malleable (mal′ē ə b′l) adj. [< L. malleus, a hammer] 1. that can be hammered, pounded, or pressed into various shapes without breaking 2. adaptable —mal′leabil′ity, mal′leableness n.

mallet (mal′it) n. [see MAUL] 1. a hammer with a wooden head and a short handle 2. a long-handled hammer used in playing croquet or polo

mallow (mal′ō) n. [< L. malva] any of a group of plants, with downy leaves

malmsey (mäm′zē) n. [< Gr. Monembasia, Greek town] a strong, full-flavoured, sweet white wine

malnutrition (mal′nyoo trish′ən) n. faulty or inadequate nutrition; poor nourishment

malodorous (mal ō′dər əs) adj. stinking

malpractice (mal′prak′tis) n. 1. unprofessional treatment of a patient by a physician 2. misconduct in any professional or official position

malt (môlt) n. [OE. mealt] 1. barley or other grain softened by soaking and germination and then kiln-dried : used for brewing and distilling certain alcoholic liquors 2. such liquor, esp. beer —adj. made with malt —vt., vi. to change (barley, etc.) into malt —malt′y adj.

Maltese (môl tēz′) adj. of Malta, its inhabitants, etc. —n. 1. pl. -tese′ a native of Malta 2. the Arabic language of Malta 3. a cat with bluish-grey fur

Maltese cross a cross whose arms look like arrowheads pointing inwards

Malthusian (mal thyoo′zhən) adj. [< R. Malthus] designating a theory that the population of the world tends to increase faster than its food supplies, etc.

maltose (môl′tōs) n. a white, crystalline sugar obtained by the action of the diastase of malt on starch

maltreat (mal′trēt′) vt. [see MAL- & TREAT] to treat roughly, unkindly, or brutally —maltreat′ment n.

malversation (mal′vər sā′shən) n. [Fr. < L. male, badly + versari, occupy oneself] corrupt conduct in public office or other position of trust

mam (mam) n. [Colloq.] mother

mamba (mam′bə) n. [Zulu imamba] any of several extremely poisonous African tree snakes

mambo (mam′bō) n. [AmSp.] a rhythmic ballroom dance to music of Cuban Negro origin in 4/4 time

Mameluke (mam′ə look′) n. [obs. Fr. < Ar. mamlick, slave] a member of a military caste, orig. made up of slaves, that dominated Egypt from 1250-1811

mamilla (ma mil′ə) n. pl. -lae (-ē) [L. : see MAMMA²] 1. a nipple 2. any nipple-shaped protuberance —mam′illary adj.

mamma¹ (mə mä′) n. [< baby talk] mother : a child's word : also ma′ma

mamma² (mam′ə) n., pl. -mae (-ē) [L., breast] a gland for secreting milk —mam′mary adj.

mammal (mam′əl) n. [see prec.] any of a large class of warmblooded vertebrates whose offspring are fed with milk secreted by the female mammary glands —mammalian (mə mā′lē ən) adj., n.

mammon (mam′ən) n. [< Aram. māmōnā, riches] [often M-] riches regarded as an object of worship and greed

mammoth (mam′əth) n. [Russ. mamont] an extinct elephant with a hairy skin and long tusks —adj. huge

man (man) n., pl. men (men) [OE. mann] 1. an adult male human being 2. a human being; person 3. the human race; mankind 4. an adult male servant, employee, etc. 5. a husband or a lover 6. any of the pieces used in chess, draughts, etc. 7. [Colloq.] fellow; chap 8. [S Afr. Slang] any person —vt. manned, man′ning 1. to furnish with men for work, defence etc. [to man a ship] 2. to take assigned

places in or at [*man* the guns!*] —*adj.*
male —**as a** (or **one**) **man** in unison
—**he is your man** he can accommodate
you —**to a man** with no one as an exception

Man. Manitoba

manacle (man'ə k'l) *n.* [< L. *manus*, hand]
1. a handcuff; fetter for the hand 2.
any restraint —*vt.* **-cled, -cling** to fetter

manage (man'ij) *vt.* **-aged, -aging** [It.
maneggiare < L. *manus*, hand] 1. to
have charge of; direct 2. to succeed in
accomplishing 3. to get (a person) to
do what one wishes by tact, flattery, etc.
4. to control the movement or behaviour
of 5. to handle or use —*vi.* 1. to direct
affairs 2. to contrive to get along —**man'-
ageable** *adj.*

management *n.* 1. the persons managing
a business, institution, etc. 2. executive
ability 3. skilful managing 4. the art
or manner of managing

manager *n.* a person who manages the
affairs of a business, client, team, etc.
—**managerial** (man'ə jēər'ē əl) *adj.*

‡**mañana** (ma nyä'nə) *n.* [Sp.] tomorrow
—*adv.* 1. tomorrow 2. at some indefinite
future time

man-at-arms *n.,* pl. **men'-at-
arms'** formerly, a soldier

manatee (man'ə tē') *n.* [Sp. *manatí* <
native (Carib) name] a large, plant-eating
aquatic mammal living in shallow tropical
waters; sea cow

Manchu (man choo') *n.* pl. **-chus',
-chu'** a member of a Mongolian people
of Manchuria: the Manchus conquered
China in 1643-44 and ruled until 1912

Mancunian (man kyoo'nē ən) *adj.* [< ML.
Mancunium, Manchester] of Manchester
—*n.* a native or inhabitant of Manchester

mandala (man'də lə) *n.* [Sans. *maṇḍala*]
a circular design of concentric geometric
forms symbolizing the universe or
wholeness in Hinduism and Buddhism

mandamus (man dā'məs) *n.* [L., we
command] *Law* a writ commanding that
a specified thing be done, issued by a
higher court to a lower one, or to an
official, etc.

mandarin (man'də rin) *n.* [< Port. <
Sans. *mantra*, counsel] 1. a high official
of China under the Empire 2. a member
of any elite group 3. [M-] the main
dialect of Chinese 4. a small, sweet orange

mandate (man'dāt) *n.* [< L. *mandare*,
to command] 1. an authoritative order
2. the wishes of constituents expressed
to a representative, party, etc. 3. *a)*
formerly, a commission from the League
of Nations to a country to administer
some region, etc. *b)* the area so administered
—*vt.* **-dated, -dating** to assign (a region,
etc.) as a mandate —**man'da'tor** *n.*

mandatory (man'də tər ē) *adj.*
authoritatively commanded or required;
obligatory —**man'datorily** *adv.*

mandible (man'də b'l) *n.* [< L. *mandere*,
chew] the jaw; specif., a) the lower jaw
of a vertebrate *b)* either of the biting
jaws of an insect *c)* either jaw of a beaked
animal

MANDOLIN

mandolin (man'də lin) *n.* [< LGr.
pandoura, kind of lute] a musical
instrument with strings and a deep, rounded
sound box: it is played with a plectrum

mandrake (man'drāk) *n.* [< Gr.
mandragoras] a poisonous plant with a
short stem and a thick root, formerly
used as a narcotic: also **mandragora**
(man drag'ər ə)

mandrel, mandril (man'drəl) *n.* [prob.
< Fr. *mandrin*] 1. a bar inserted into
something to hold it while it is being
machined 2. a metal bar used as a core
around which metal, glass, etc. is cast
or shaped

mandrill (man'dril) *n.* [MAN + DRILL⁴]
a large, fierce, strong baboon of W Africa

mane (mān) *n.* [OE. *manu*] the long
hair growing from the top or sides of
the neck of certain animals

manège, manege (ma näzh') *n.* [Fr.:
see MANAGE] 1. the art of riding and
training horses 2. a school teaching this
art 3. the paces of a trained horse

man Friday see FRIDAY

manful (man'fəl) *adj.* manly; brave
—**man'fully** *adv.*

manganese (man'gə nēz') *n.* [< Fr. <
It. < ML. *magnesia*, magnesia] a greyish-
white, metallic chemical element, usually
hard and brittle: symbol, Mn

mange (mānj) *n.* [see MANGER] a skin
disease of mammals characterized by
itching, loss of hair, etc.

mangel-wurzel (maŋ'g'l wur'z'l) *n.* [G.
< *Mangold*, beet + *Wurzel*, root] a variety
of large beet, used as cattle food

manger (mān'jər) *n.* [ult. < L. *mandere*,
chew] a box or trough to hold hay, etc.
for horses or cattle to eat

mangle¹ (maŋ'g'l) *vt.* **-gled, -gling** [<
OFr. *mehaigner*, maim] 1. to mutilate
by roughly cutting, hacking, etc. 2. to
spoil; botch —**man'gler** *n.*

mangle² *n.* [Du. *mangel* < Gr. *manganon*,
war machine] a machine for pressing
and smoothing cloth between heavy rollers
to remove water —*vt.* **-gled, -gling** to
press in a mangle —**man'gler** *n.*

mango (maŋ'gō) *n.,* pl. **-goes, -gos** [<
Port. < Tamil *mān-kāy*] 1. a yellow-red,
somewhat acid tropical fruit with a juicy
pulp 2. the tree on which it grows

mangrove (maŋ'grōv) *n.* [altered (after
GROVE) < Port. < ?] a tropical tree
with branches that spread and send down
roots, thus forming more trunks

mangy (mān'jē) *adj.* **-gier, -giest** 1. having
or caused by the mange 2. shabby and

filthy **3.** mean and low; despicable —**man'-gily** *adv.* —**man'giness** *n.*

manhandle (man'han'd'l) *vt.* **-dled, -dling**
1. to handle roughly **2.** [Rare] to move by human strength only

manhole *n.* a hole through which a man can get into a sewer, conduit, etc. for repair work or inspection

man-hour *n.* an industrial time unit equal to one hour of work done by one person

manhunt *n.* a hunt for a fugitive : also **man hunt**

mania (mā'nē ə) *n.* [< Gr. *mainesthai*, to rage] **1.** wild or violent mental disorder **2.** an excessive, persistent enthusiasm; obsession; craze —**manic** (man'ik) *adj.*

-mania (mā'nē ə) [see prec.] *a combining form meaning:* **1.** a (specified) type of mental disorder [*kleptomania*] **2.** intense enthusiasm for [*bibliomania*]

maniac (mā'nē ak') *n.* **1.** [Colloq.] an enthusiast [a car *maniac*] **2.** a violently insane person —*adj.* wildly insane —**maniacal** (mə nī'ə k'l) *adj.* —**mani'acally** *adv.*

manic-depressive *adj.* of or having a psychosis characterized by alternating periods of mania and mental depression —*n.* a person who has this psychosis

manicure (man'ə kyoor') *n.* [< L. *manus*, hand + *cura*, care] the care of the hands and fingernails —*vt.* **-cured', -cur'ing** to trim, polish, etc. (the fingernails)

manifest (man'ə fest) *adj.* [< L. *manifestus*, struck by the hand] apparent to the senses or to the mind; evident; obvious —*vt.* **1.** to reveal **2.** to be evidence of —*n.* **1.** an itemized list of a ship's cargo, to be shown to customs officials **2.** a list of passengers and cargo on an aircraft —**man'ifesta'tion** *n.*

manifesto (man'ə fes'tō) *n., pl.* **-toes, -tos** [It.: see MANIFEST] a public declaration of intentions by a government or by an important person or group

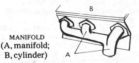

MANIFOLD
(A, manifold;
B, cylinder)

manifold (man'ə fōld') *adj.* [see MANY & -FOLD] **1.** having many forms, parts, etc. **2.** of many sorts [*manifold* duties] **3.** being such in many ways [a *manifold* villain] —*n.* **1.** something that is manifold **2.** a pipe with several outlets for connecting with other pipes, as the cylinder exhaust system in a motor car —**man'ifold'ly** *adv.* —**man'ifold'ness** *n.*

manikin (man'ə kin) *n.* [Du. *manneken*] a little man; dwarf

Manila hemp (mə nil'ə) [*often* m-] a strong fibre from the leafstalks of a Philippine plant, used in making rope, etc.

Manila paper [*often* m-] strong, buff or brownish paper orig. made of Manila hemp, now of various fibres

man in the street the average person

manipulate (mə nip'yoo lāt') *vt.* **-lat'ed, -lat'ing** [< L. *manus*, hand + *plere*, fill] **1.** to operate, or handle with skill **2.** to manage artfully, often in an unfair way —**manip'ula'tion** *n.* —**manip'ula'tor** *n.*

Manitoban (man'itō'bən) *n.* a native or inhabitant of Manitoba —*adj.* of Manitoba or Manitobans

mankind (man'kīnd'; *also, & for 2 always,* man'kīnd') *n.* **1.** the human race **2.** the male sex

manly *adj.* **-lier, -liest 1.** having qualities generally regarded as befitting a man; strong, brave, etc. **2.** fit for a man [*manly* sports] —**man'liness** *n.*

man-made *adj.* made by man; synthetic

manna (man'ə) *n.* [< Heb. *mān*, gift] **1.** *Bible* food miraculously provided for the Israelites in the wilderness **2.** anything badly needed that comes unexpectedly

mannequin (man'ə kin) *n.* [see MANIKIN] **1.** a model of the human body, used by window dressers, artists, etc. **2.** a woman whose work is modelling clothes

manner (man'ər) *n.* [< L. *manus*, a hand] **1.** a way in which something is done or happens **2.** behaviour or bearing **3.** [*pl.*] *a)* ways of social life [a *comedy* of *manners*] *b)* ways of social behaviour [good *manners*] *c)* polite ways of social behaviour [the child lacks *manners*] **4.** characteristic style in art, etc. **5.** kind; sort —**by no manner of means** definitely not —**in a manner of speaking** in a certain sense —**to the manner born** as if accustomed from birth —**man'nerless** *n.*

mannered *adj.* **1.** having manners of a specified sort [ill-*mannered*] **2.** artificial, stylized, or affected

mannerism *n.* **1.** a peculiarity of manner in behaviour, speech, etc. that has become a habit **2.** excessive use of some distinctive manner in art, literature, etc.

mannerly *adj.* polite —*adv.* politely —**man'nerliness** *n.*

manoeuvre (mə noo'vər) *n.* [Fr. < L. *manu operare*, to work by hand] **1.** a strategem; scheme **2.** any skilful change of movement or direction **3.** a planned and controlled movement of troops, aircraft, etc. **4.** [*pl.*] practice movements of troops, etc. —*vi., vt.* **1.** to move, get, etc. by some strategem U.S. sp. **maneuver 2.** to manage skilfully; scheme **3.** to perform or cause to perform manoeuvres —**manoeu'vrabil'ity** *n.* —**manoeu'vrable** *adj.*

man of letters a writer; scholar

man of the world a man familiar with and tolerant of various sorts of people and their ways

man-of-war *n., pl.* **men'-of-war'** a warship

manor (man'ər) *n.* [< L. *manere*, remain] **1.** a mansion, as on an estate : also **manor house 2.** a landed estate, orig. of a feudal lord and subject to the jurisdiction of his court **3.** [Colloq.] a police district —**manorial** (mə nôr'ē əl) *adj.*

manpower *n.* **1.** power furnished by

human physical strength **2.** the collective strength or availability for work of the people in a given area Also **man power**

‡**manqué** (män´kā) *adj.* [Fr.] unfulfilled; would-be Placed after a noun [a scholar *manqué*] —**manquée** *adj. fem.*

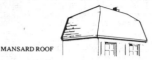

MANSARD ROOF

mansard (roof) (man´särd) [< F. *Mansard*] a roof with two slopes on each of the four sides, the lower steeper than the upper

manse (mans) *n.* [< L. *manere*, dwell] a parsonage

manservant *n.*, *pl.* **menservants** a male servant : also **man servant**

mansion (man´shən) *n.* [< L. *manere*, dwell] a large, imposing house

Mansion House the official residence of the Lord Mayor of London

manslaughter *n.* the unlawful killing of a human being without malice aforethought

mantel (man´t'l) *n.* [see MANTLE] **1.** the facing about a fireplace, including a shelf above it **2.** the shelf

mantelpiece (man´t'l pēs´) *n.* a mantel shelf, or this shelf and the side elements framing the fireplace

mantic (man´tik) *adj.* [< Gr. *mantis*, seer] of, or having powers of, divination; prophetic

mantilla (mantil´ə) *n.* [Sp. < L. *mantellum*, mantle] a woman's scarf, as of lace, worn over the hair and shoulders

mantis (man´tis) *n.* [< Gr. *mantis*, seer] a slender insect that grasps its prey with spiny forelegs often held up together as if praying

mantissa (mantis´ə) *n.* [L., (useless) addition] the decimal part of a logarithm

mantle (man´t'l) *n.* [< L. *mantellum*] **1.** a loose, sleeveless cloak **2.** anything that cloaks or envelops **3.** a small, mesh hood which becomes white-hot over a flame and gives off light —*vt.* **-tled, -tling** to cover as with a mantle —*vi.* **1.** to be or become covered, as a surface with froth **2.** to blush

mantra (man´trə) *n.* [Sans.] Hinduism a hymn or text, esp. from the Veda, chanted as an incantation or prayer

manual (man´yŏŏ wəl) *adj.* [< L. *manus*, hand] **1.** of the hands **2.** made, done, worked, or used by the hands **3.** involving or doing hard physical work —*n.* **1.** a handy book of instructions, etc. **2.** a keyboard of an organ console or harpsichord —**man´ually** *adv.*

manual alphabet the finger alphabet used by the deaf and dumb

manufactory (man´yŏŏ fak´tər ē) *n.*, *pl.* **-ries** same as FACTORY

manufacture (man´yŏŏ fak´chər) *n.* [<

L. *manus*, hand + *facere*, make] **1.** the making of goods, esp. by machinery on a large scale **2.** anything so made **3.** the making of something in a way regarded as mechanical —*vt.* **-tured, -turing 1.** to make, esp. by machinery **2.** to produce (something) in a way regarded as mechanical **3.** to make up (excuses, evidence, etc.) —**man´ufac´turer** *n.*

manumit (man´yŏŏ mit´) *vt.* **-mit´ted, -mit´ting** [< L. *manus*, hand + *mittere*, send] to free from slavery —**man´umis´- sion** *n.*

manure (mənyŏŏr´) *vt.* **-nured´, -nur´- ing** [< OFr. *manouvrer*, to work with the hands] to put manure on or into (soil) —*n.* animal excrement or other substance used to fertilize soil —**manur´- er** *n.*

manuscript (man´yŏŏ skript´) *n.* [< L. *manus*, hand + *scribere*, write] **1.** a written or typewritten book, etc.; esp., an author's copy of his work, as submitted to a publisher **2.** writing as distinguished from print —*adj.* written by hand or with a typewriter

Manx (maŋks) *adj.* of the Isle of Man —*n.* the Celtic language of the Isle of Man —**the Manx** the people of the Isle of Man

Manx cat [*also* m-] a domestic cat that has no tail

many (men´ē) *adj.* **more, most** [OE. *manig*] **1.** numerous **2.** relatively numerous (preceded by *as, too*, etc.) —*n.* a large number (of persons or things) —*pron.* many persons or things —**a good many** [*with pl. v.*] a relatively large number —**many's the time** often —**the many** the people; the masses

Maoism (mou´iz'm) *n.* the communist theories and policies of Mao Tse-tung —**Mao´ist** *adj.*, *n.*

Maori (mou´rē) *n.* **1.** *pl.* **-ris, -ri** any of a people native to New Zealand, of Polynesian origin **2.** their Polynesian language —*adj.* of the Maoris

map (map) *n.* [< L. *mappa*, napkin] **1.** a representation, usually flat, of all or part of the earth's surface, showing countries, bodies of water, cities, roads, etc. **2.** a similar representation of the sky, showing stars, etc. —*vt.* **mapped, map´ping 1.** to make a map of **2.** to plan [to *map* out a project] **3.** *Math.* to link the elements of one set with the elements of another —**put on the map** to make well known —**wipe off the map** to put out of existence

maple (mā´p'l) *n.* [OE. *mapel(treo)*] **1.** any of a large group of trees grown for wood, sap, or shade **2.** the light-coloured wood **3.** the flavour of maple syrup

maple leaf the leaf of the maple, emblem of Canada

maple syrup syrup made by boiling down the sap of the sugar maple

Maquis (ma´kē) *n.* [Fr. < It. *macchia*, thicket] **1.** a member of the French underground fighting against the Nazis in World War II **2.** this organization

mar (mär) *vt.* **marred, mar´ring** [OE.

mierran, to hinder]   to hurt or spoil the looks, value, perfection, etc. of

Mar. March

marabou (mar′ə bōō′) *n.* [Fr. < Ar. *murābit,* hermit] 1. any of certain large storks 2. soft feathers from the marabou Also **mar′about′** (-bōō′)

maraca (mə ra′kə) *n.* [Port.] a percussion instrument consisting of a dried gourd or rattle with pebbles in it, shaken to beat out a rhythm

maraschino (mar′ə skē′nō) *n.* [It.] a sweet liqueur made from a kind of black wild cherry

marathon (mar′ə thən) *n.* 1. a footrace of 26 miles, 385 yards (42.2 km): so called in allusion to the Greek runner who carried word of the victory at Marathon to Athens 2. any long-distance or endurance contest

maraud (mə rôd′) *vi., vt.* [< Fr. *maraud,* vagabond] to raid; plunder —**maraud′-er** *n.*

marble (mär′b′l) *n.* [< Gr. *marmaros,* white stone] 1. a hard limestone, which can take a high polish 2. a monument, sculpture, etc. in marble 3. *a)* a little ball of glass, etc. used in games *b)* [*pl.,* with *sing.* v.] a children's game using marbles —*adj.* of or like marble —*vt.* **-bled, -bling** to stain (book edges) to look mottled like marble

marbled *adj.* [< prec.] with fat evenly distributed in streaks throughout: said of meat

marc (märk) *n.* [Fr.] 1. refuse of grapes, seeds, fruits, etc. after pressing 2. a brandy distilled from this

marcasite (mär′kə sīt′) *n.* [< Fr. < Ar.] 1. a pale, crystallized pyrite 2. this mineral or polished steel cut and used like brilliants

March (märch) *n.* [< L. *Martius,* of Mars] the third month of the year, having 31 days: abbrev. **Mar.**

march¹ (märch) *vi.* [Fr. *marcher*] 1. to walk with regular steps, as in a military formation 2. to walk in a grave, stately way 3. to progress steadily —*vt.* to make march or go —*n.* 1. a marching 2. a steady advance 3. a regular, steady step 4. the distance covered in marching 5. a piece of music for marching 6. an organized walk by people demonstrating on a public issue —**on the march** marching —**steal a march on** to get an advantage over secretly —**march′er** *n.*

march² *n.* [OFr. *marche* < Frank. *marka*] a boundary or frontier —**the Marches** borderlands between England and Scotland and between England and Wales

March hare a hare in breeding time, proverbially regarded as an example of madness

marching orders orders to march, go, or leave

marchioness (mär′shə nis) *n.* [< ML. *marchio,* prefect of the marches] 1. the wife of a marquis 2. a lady whose own rank equals that of a marquis

marchpane (märch′pān′) *n.* former name *for* MARZIPAN

march-past *n.* a review of troops as they march past a saluting point

Mardi gras (mär′di grä′) [Fr., lit., fat Tuesday] Shrove Tuesday, the last day before Lent : a day of carnival

mare¹ (mâər) *n.* [OE. *mere*] a female horse, donkey, etc.

mare² (mär′ē) *n., pl.* **-ria** (-ē ə) [L., sea] a large, dark area on the surface of the moon or of Mars

mare's-nest (mâərz′nest′) *n.* a hoax; delusion

margarine (mär′jə rēn′) *n.* [Fr.] a spread or cooking fat of refined vegetable oils

marge (märj) *n.* [Colloq.] *short for* MARGARINE

margin (mär′jin) *n.* [L. *margo*] 1. a border or brink 2. the blank border of a printed or written page 3. a limit to what is desirable or possible 4. *a)* an amount beyond what is needed *b)* provision for increase, or advance 5. the amount by which something is higher or lower 6. *Econ.* the minimum return of profit needed to continue activities —*vt.* to provide with a margin

marginal *adj.* 1. written in the margin 2. slight 3. yielding little profit because it is difficult to cultivate: said of land —**mar′ginally** *adv.*

marginal seat *Politics* a constituency in which a political party cannot be sure of retaining a majority

margrave (mär′grāv) *n.* [< OHG.] the title of certain princes of Germany —**mar′-gravine′** (-grə vēn′) *n.fem.*

marguerite (mär′gə rēt′) *n.* [Fr., pearl] 1. a large daisy 2. a cultivated chrysanthemum with a single flower

marigold (mar′ə gōld′) *n.* [< *Marie* (prob. the Virgin Mary) + *gold,* gold] a plant of the composite family, with red, yellow, or orange flowers

marijuana, marihuana (mar′ə hwä′nə) *n.* [AmSp.] 1. the dried leaves and flowers of hemp, smoked for the psychological effects 2. *same as* HEMP (sense 1 *a*)

marimba (mə rim′bə) *n.* [< Afr.] a kind of xylophone, usually with resonators under the wooden bars

marina (mə rē′nə) *n.* [It. & Sp., seacoast: see MARINE] a harbour with dockage, services, etc. for small pleasure craft

marinade (mar′ə nād′) *n.* [Fr. < Sp. *marinar,* to pickle] 1. a spiced pickling solution, esp. with oil and wine or vinegar, in which meat, etc. is steeped 2. meat, etc. so steeped —*vt.* **-nad′ed, -nad′ing** *same as* MARINATE

marinate (mar′ə nāt′) *vt.* **-nat′ed, -nat′-ing** [< It. *marinare,* to pickle] to steep (meat, etc.) in a marinade

marine (mə rēn′) *adj.* [< L. *mare,* sea] 1. of or found in the sea 2. *a)* of navigation; nautical; maritime *b)* naval 3. used, or to be used, at sea —*n.* 1. *a)* see MILITARY RANKS, table *b)* a member of the Royal Marines 2. naval or merchant ships collectively [the merchant *marine*]

mariner (mar′ə nər) *n.* a sailor; seaman

marionette (mar′ē ə net′) *n.* [Fr. *Marion*, name] a puppet moved by strings or wires from above

marital (mar′ət'l) *adj.* [< L. *maritus*, husband] of marriage —**mar′itally** *adv.*

maritime (mar′ə tīm′) *adj.* [< L. *mare*, sea] 1. on or near the sea 2. of sea navigation, shipping, etc.

Maritime Provinces certain of the Canadian provinces facing the Atlantic, esp. New Brunswick, Nova Scotia, and Prince Edward Island : also called **Maritimes**

Maritimer *n.* [Canad.] a native or inhabitant of the Maritime Provinces

marjoram (mär′jər əm) *n.* [ult. < Gr. *amarakos*] any of various perennial plants having aromatic leaves used in cooking

mark[1] (märk) *n.* [OE. *mearc*, orig., boundary] 1. a spot, scratch, etc. on a surface 2. a printed or written sign [punctuation marks] 3. a brand, label, etc. put on an article to show the maker 4. a sign of some quality [courtesy is the *mark* of a gentleman] 5. a numerical assessment of proficiency, as in an examination 6. a cross, etc. made by a person unable to write his signature 7. a standard of quality, etc. [up to the *mark*] 8. distinction [a man of *mark*] 9. impression [left his *mark* in history] 10. a visible object of known position, serving as a guide 11. a line, dot, etc. used to indicate position, as on a graduated scale 12. a target; goal 13. *Sports* the starting line of a race —*vt.* 1. to put or make a mark or marks on 2. to identify or indicate as by a mark 3. to draw, write, record, etc. 4. to show plainly 5. to characterize 6. to take notice of 7. to grade; rate 8. to put price labels on 9. to keep (score, etc.); record 10. *Sport* to follow closely the movements of a player in the opposing team, so as to hinder his play —*vi.* 1. to make a mark or marks 2. to observe —**make one's mark** to achieve fame —**mark down** 1. to write down; record 2. to mark for sale at a reduced price —**mark off** (or **out**) to mark the limits of —**mark time** 1. to keep time while at a halt by lifting the feet as if marching 2. to suspend progress —**wide of the mark** 1. not striking the point aimed at 2. irrelevant —**mark′er** *n.*

mark[2] *n.* [< ON. *mork*, a half pound of silver] 1. the monetary unit of East Germany 2. *same as* DEUTSCHE MARK

marked (märkt) *adj.* 1. having a mark or marks 2. singled out as an object of hostility, etc. [a marked man] 3. noticeable; distinct [a marked change] —**mark′edly** (mär′kid lē) *adv.* —**mark′edness** *n.*

market (mär′kit) *n.* [< L. *merx*, merchandise] 1. a gathering of people for buying and selling things 2. an open space or a building with goods for sale from stalls, etc. 3. a region where goods can be bought and sold [the European *market*] 4. the trading or selling opportunities provided by a particular group of people 5. trade [an active *market*] 6. *short for* STOCK MARKET 7. demand (for goods or services) —*vt.* 1. to offer for sale 2. to sell —*vi.* to buy or sell —**be in the market for** to be seeking to buy —**be on the market** to be offered for sale —**put on the market** to offer for sale —**mar′ketabil′ity** *n.* —**mar′ketable** *adj.*

market garden an establishment where fruit and vegetables are grown and sold —**market gardener**

marketing *n.* the business of moving goods from the producer to the consumer

market research the study of the demands or needs of consumers in relation to particular goods or services

market town a town that holds a public market

marking *n.* 1. the act of making marks 2. the characteristic arrangement of marks, as on fur or feathers

marksman *n.* a person who shoots, esp. with skill —**marks′manship′** *n.*

marl (märl) *n.* [< L. *marga*] a crumbly mixture of clay, sand, and limestone —*vt.* to fertilize with marl —**marl′y** *adj.*

marlinespike, marlinspike (mär′-lin spīk′) *n.* [< Du. *marlijn*, small cord] a pointed iron instrument for separating rope strands, as in splicing : also **mar′ling-spike′**

marmalade (mär′mə lād′) *n.* [< Gr. *meli*, honey + *mēlon*, apple] a jam made of oranges or other citrus fruits and sugar

marmoreal (mär môr′ē əl) *adj.* [< L. *marmor*, marble] of or like marble : also **marmo′rean**

marmoset (mär′mō zet′) *n.* [< OFr. *marmouset*, grotesque figure] a very small American monkey

marmot (mär′mət) *n.* [< Fr. prob. < L. *mus montanus*, mountain mouse] a thick-bodied, burrowing rodent

maroon[1] (mə rōōn′) *n., adj.* [Fr. *marron*, chestnut] dark brownish red

maroon[2] *vt.* [< Fr. < AmSp. *cimarrón*, wild] 1. to put (a person) ashore in some desolate place and abandon him there 2. to leave abandoned, helpless, etc.

marque (märk) *n.* [Fr.] an identifying emblem on a car

marquee (mär kē′) *n.* [< Fr. *marquise*] a large tent, as for an outdoor entertainment

marquess (mär′kwis) *n.* *same as* MARQUIS

marquetry, marqueterie (mär′kə trē) *n.* [< Fr. *marque*, mark] decorative inlaid work, as in furniture

marquis (mär′kwis) *n., pl.* -**quises** [< ML. *marchisus*] a nobleman ranking above an earl or count and below a duke

marquise (mär kēz′) *n.* 1. the wife of a marquis 2. a lady whose rank in her own right equals that of a marquis 3. a gem cut as a pointed oval

marriage (mar′ij) *n.* [see MARRY[1]] 1. the state of being married; relation between husband and wife 2. the act or rite of marrying; wedding 3. any close union

marriageable *adj.* old enough or suitable for marriage

marriage bureau a business concern set up to introduce people wishing to get married

marriage certificate a document giving the place and date of the wedding ceremony and the names of the couple

marriage guidance advice given by a counsellor to couples who experience difficulties in their marriages

marriage lines *same as* MARRIAGE CERTIFICATE

married *adj.* 1. living together as husband and wife 2. having a husband or wife 3. of marriage —*n.* a married person: chiefly in **young marrieds**

marrow (mar'ō) *n.* [OE. *mearg*] 1. the soft, fatty tissue that fills the cavities of bones 2. the innermost, essential, or choicest part 3. *same as* VEGETABLE MARROW

marrowfat *n.* a variety of large, rich pea

marry[1] (mar'ē) *vt.* -ried, -rying [< L. *maritus*, husband] 1. to join as husband and wife 2. to take as husband or wife 3. to join closely —*vi.* to get married

marry[2] *interj.* [< (the Virgin) *Mary*] [Archaic] an exclamation of surprise, anger, etc.

Mars (märz) 1. a planet, fourth in distance from the sun 2. *Rom. Myth.* the god of war 3. war

Marsala (mär sä'lə) *n.* [< *Marsala*, in Sicily] a light, fortified, sweet wine

Marseillaise (mär sā yāz') [Fr., of Marseille] the French national anthem

marsh (märsh) *n.* [OE. *merisc*] a tract of low, wet, soft land; swamp; bog; morass —**marsh'y** *adj.*

marshal (mär'shəl) *n.* [< OHG. *marah*, horse + *scalh*, servant] 1. a military commander; specif., *same as* FIELD MARSHAL 2. [U.S.] a Federal officer appointed to a judicial district to perform functions like those of a sheriff 3. an official in charge of ceremonies, processions, etc. 4. a high state official [Earl *Marshal*] —*vt.* -shalled, -shalling 1. to arrange (troops, ideas, etc.) in order 2. to guide ceremoniously —**mar'shalcy, mar'shalship'** *n.*

marshalling yard a railway depot for goods trains

Marshal of the Royal Air Force *see* MILITARY RANKS, table

marsh gas a gaseous product, chiefly methane, formed from decomposing vegetable matter

marshmallow *n.* [orig. made from the root of the marsh mallow] a soft, spongy confection

marsh mallow a pink-flowered, perennial plant

marsh marigold a marsh plant with yellow flowers

marsh tit a greyish-brown European tit that lives in woods, hedges, etc.

marsupial (mär syōō'pē əl) *adj.* of an order of mammals whose young are carried by the female for several months after birth in an external pouch of the abdomen —*n.* an animal of this kind, as a kangaroo

marsupium *n.*, *pl.* -pia [< Gr. *marsypos*, pouch] the pouch on the abdomen of a female marsupial

mart (märt) *n.* [MDu.] a market

martello tower (mär tel'ō) [< *Mortello*, Corsica, where such a tower was attacked by Brit. fleet in 1794] [*occas.* M-] a circular fort of masonry, formerly built on coasts to protect against invaders: also **martel'lo** *n.*

marten (mär'tin) *n.* [< OFr. *martre*] a small, flesh-eating mammal like a weasel but larger, with soft, valuable fur

martial (mär'shəl) *adj.* [< L. *martialis*, of Mars] 1. of or connected with war, soldiers, etc.; military [*martial music*] 2. warlike; militaristic [*martial spirit*] —**mar'tialism** *n.*

martial law temporary rule by the military authorities over the civilians, as in time of war

Martian (mär'shən) *adj.* of Mars (god or planet) —*n.* an imagined inhabitant of the planet Mars

martin (mär'tin) *n.* [Fr.] a stout-billed bird related to the swallow, as the house martin

martinet (mär'tin et') *n.* [< Gen. J. *Martinet*] a very strict disciplinarian or stickler for rigid regulations

martingale (mär'tin gāl') *n.* [Fr.] 1. the strap of a horse's harness passing from the noseband to the girth between the forelegs, to keep the horse from rearing 2. a lower stay for the jib boom of a sailing vessel

martini (mär tē'nē) *n.*, *pl.* -nis [< ?] a cocktail of gin and dry vermouth

Martinmas (mär'tin məs) *n.* [see -MAS] Saint Martin's Day, a church festival held on November 11

martyr (mär'tər) *n.* [< Gr., a witness] 1. a person tortured or killed because of his beliefs 2. a person suffering great pain or misery for a long time [he was a *martyr* to catarrh] —*vt.* to make a martyr of —**mar'tyrdom** *n.*

marvel (mär'v'l) *n.* [< L. *mirari*, admire] a wonderful or astonishing thing —*vi.* -velled, -velling to be amazed —*vt.* to wonder at or about (followed by a clause)

marvellous *adj.* 1. causing wonder; astonishing 2. [Colloq.] splendid —**mar'vellously** *adv.*

Marxism (märk'siz'm) *n.* the system of thought developed by Karl Marx, his co-worker Friedrich Engels, and their followers —**Marx'ist, Marx'ian** *adj., n.*

marzipan (mär'zi pan') *n.* [G. < It.] a paste of ground almonds, sugar, and egg white

-mas (məs) a combining form for MASS meaning a (specified) church festival [*Martinmas*]

Masai (mä'sī) *n. pl.* -sai', -sais' any member of a pastoral people of Kenya and Tanzania

masc., mas. masculine

mascara (mas kär'ə) *n.* [see MASK] a cosmetic for colouring the eyelashes

mascot (mas'kət) *n.* [< Fr. < Pr. *masco*,

masculine 516 mast

sorcerer] any person, animal, or thing supposed to bring good luck

masculine (mas′kyoo lin) *adj.* [< L. *mas, male*] 1. male 2. having qualities regarded as characteristic of men and boys 3. suitable for a man 4. *Gram.* designating or of the gender of words referring to males or things conventionally regarded as male 5. *Prosody* designating a rhyme of stressed final syllables (Ex.: enjoy, destroy) —*n. Gram.* 1. the masculine gender 2. a word in this gender —**mas′culinely** *adv.* —**mas′culin′ity** *n.*

maser (mā′zər) *n.* [*m*(icrowave) *a*(mplification by) *s*(timulated) *e*(mission of) *r*(adiation)] a device which emits a narrow beam of microwave radiation formed by raising atoms in a crystal or gas to a higher energy level

mash (mash) *n.* [< OE. *mascwyrt*] 1. any soft mixture 2. a mixture of bran, etc. in water for feeding horses 3. crushed malt soaked in hot water for making wort, used in brewing 4. [Colloq.] mashed potatoes —*vt.* 1. to change into a soft mass by beating, crushing, etc. 2. to mix (crushed malt, etc.) in hot water for making wort

mashie (mash′ē) *n.* [< ? Fr. *massue*, club] a golf club with a metal head used for lofting

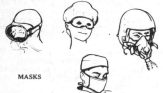

MASKS

mask (mask) *n.* [Fr. *masque* < It.] 1. a covering to conceal or disguise the face 2. anything that conceals or disguises 3. *a)* a moulded likeness of the face *b)* a grotesque or comic representation of a face, worn to amuse or frighten 4. a protective covering for the face [a gas *mask*] 5. a covering for the mouth and nose, as for administering an anaesthetic, etc. 6. the face of a dog, fox, etc. —*vt.* to conceal, cover, disguise, etc. with or as with a mask —**masked** *adj.* —**mask′er** *n.*

masking tape an adhesive tape for covering borders, etc., as during painting

maskinonge (mas′kə nonj′) *n. same as* MUSKELLUNGE

masochism (mas′ō kiz′m) *n.* [< L. von Sacher-*Masoch*] the getting of pleasure, specif. sexual pleasure, from being dominated or hurt —**mas′ochist** *n.* —**mas′ochis′tic** *adj.*

mason (mā′s′n) *n.* [< ML. *matio*] 1. one whose work is building with stone 2. [M-] *same as* FREEMASON

Masonic (mə son′ik) *adj.* [*also* m-] of Masons (Freemasons) or Masonry (Freemasonry)

masonry (mā′s′n rē) *n., pl.* **-ries** 1. the trade or art of a mason 2. brickwork or stonework 3. [*usually* M-] *same as* FREEMASONRY

masque (mask) *n.* [see MASK] 1. a masquerade 2. a former kind of dramatic entertainment with lavish costumes, music, etc. —**masqu′er** *n.*

masquerade (mas′kə rād′) *n.* [see MASK] 1. a masquerade in which masks are worn 2. a disguise; pretence —*vi.* **-ad′ed, -ad′ing** 1. to take part in a masquerade 2. to act under false pretences —**mas′querad′er** *n.*

Mass (mas) *n.* [< *missa* in L. *ite, missa est* (*contio*), go, (the meeting) is dismissed] [*also* m-] 1. the service of the Eucharist in the Roman Catholic Church and some other churches 2. a musical setting for certain parts of this service

mass (mas) *n.* [< Gr. *maza*, barley cake] 1. a piece or amount of indefinite shape or size [a *mass* of clay, a *mass* of cold air] 2. a large quantity or number 3. bulk; size 4. the main part 5. *Physics* the quantity of matter in a body as measured in its relation to inertia —*adj.* 1. of a large number [*mass* production] 2. of or for the masses [*mass* education] —*vt., vi.* to gather or form into a mass —**in the mass** collectively —**the masses** the common people

massacre (mas′ə kər) *n.* [Fr. < OFr. *maçacre*, shambles] an indiscriminate, merciless, and large-scale slaughter —*vt.* **-cred, -cring** to kill indiscriminately and mercilessly —**mas′sacrer** *n.*

massage (mə säzh′) *n.* [Fr.] a rubbing, kneading, etc. of part of the body, as to stimulate circulation —*vt.* **-saged′, -sag′ing** to give a massage to —**massag′er** *n.*

massasauga (mas′ə sô′gə) *n.* [< *Missisauga* River, Ontario] a N American venomous rattlesnake

masseur (ma sur′) *n.* [Fr.] a man whose work is giving massages —**masseuse′** (-surz′) *n.fem.*

mass hysteria the irrational behaviour evidenced in large crowds

massif (mas′ēf) *n.* [Fr., solid] *Geol.* a distinctive, compact group of mountains

massive (mas′iv) *adj.* 1. *a)* big and solid; bulky *b)* larger than normal [a *massive* dose] 2. large and imposing 3. large-scale; extensive —**mas′sively** *adv.*

mass media those means of communication that reach and influence large numbers of people, as television

mass production quantity production of goods, esp. by machinery and division of labour —**mass′-produce′** *vt.*

mass spectrometer an instrument which, by passing ionized particles through electric and magnetic fields, separates and counts isotopes according to their mass

mast[1] (mast) *n.* [OE. *mæst*] 1. a tall spar rising vertically from the deck of a vessel and used to support the sails, radar equipment, etc. 2. any vertical pole, as in a crane

mast[2] *n.* [OE. *mæst*] beechnuts, acorns, chestnuts, etc., esp. as food for pigs

mastaba (mas′tə bə) *n.* [< Ar.] an oblong tomb with a flat roof and sloping sides, built in ancient Egypt

mastectomy (mas tek′tə mē) *n., pl.* **-mies** [< Gr. *mastos*, breast + -ECTOMY] the surgical removal of a breast

master (mäs′tər) *n.* [< L. *magister*] 1. a man who rules others; specif., *a)* a man who is head of a household or institution *b)* an employer *c)* an owner of an animal or slave *d)* the captain of a merchant ship *e)* a victor *f)* a male schoolteacher *g)* a person whose teachings one follows *h)* [M-] Jesus Christ 2. *a)* a highly skilled workman *b)* an artist regarded as great 3. [M-] a title applied to *a)* a boy regarded as too young to be addressed as *Mr.* *b)* a man who heads some institution, group, etc. *c)* a person who is a MASTER OF ARTS (or SCIENCE, etc.) 4. an original copy from which duplicates are made 5. *Chess* a player who has won a specified number of tournament games —*adj.* 1. being a master 2. chief; main 3. controlling; specif., designating a mechanism that controls others *[a master switch]* —*vt.* 1. to become an expert in 2. to conquer

masterful *adj.* 1. expert; skilful 2. acting the part of a master; imperious —**mas′terfully** *adv.*

master key a key that will open a set of locks

masterly *adj.* showing the skill of a master; expert

mastermind *n.* 1. a very intelligent person, esp. one with the ability to plan a group project 2. [M-] *Trademark* a game requiring logical thinking —*vt.* to be the mastermind of (a project)

Master of Arts (or **Science,** etc.) 1. a degree given by a university to a person who has completed a course of postgraduate study 2. a person who has this degree

master of ceremonies 1. a person who supervises a ceremony 2. a person who presides over an entertainment, introducing the participants, etc.

Master of the Rolls the Court of Appeal judge who acts as head of the Public Record Office

masterpiece *n.* 1. a thing done with masterly skill 2. the greatest work of a person or group: also **mas′terwork′**

masterstroke *n.* a masterly move or achievement

mastery *n., pl.* **-teries** 1. expert skill or knowledge 2. ascendancy or victory

masthead *n.* 1. the top part of a ship's mast 2. that part of a newspaper stating its address, publishers, etc.

mastic (mas′tik) *n.* [< Gr. *mastichē*] a resin obtained from a Mediterranean tree, used in making varnish, adhesives, etc.

masticate (mas′tə kāt′) *vt.* -cat′ed, -cat′ing [< Gr. *mastax*, mouth] to chew

up (food, etc.) —**mas′tica′tion** *n.* —**mas′ticatory** *adj.*

mastiff (mas′tif) *n.* [< L. *mansuetus*, tame] a large, powerful, smooth-coated dog with hanging lips

mastitis (mas tīt′is) *n.* [< Gr. *mastos*, breast + -ITIS] inflammation of the breast or udder

mastodon (mas′tə don′) *n.* [< Gr. *mastos*, breast + *odous*, tooth] a large, extinct animal resembling the elephant but larger

mastoid (mas′toid) *adj.* [< Gr. *mastos*, a breast + *eidos*, form] 1. shaped like a breast 2. designating a projection of the temporal bone behind the ear —*n.* 1. the mastoid projection 2. [Colloq.] inflammation of the mastoid projection

masturbate (mas′tər bāt′) *vi., vt.* -bat′ed, -bat′ing [< L. *masturbari*] to manipulate one's own genitals, or the genitals of (another) —**mas′turba′tion** *n.*

mat[1] (mat) *n.* [< LL. *matta*] 1. a flat, coarse fabric of woven hemp, straw, etc. 2. a piece of this or of rubber, etc., used as a doormat, etc. 3. a flat piece of cloth, etc. put under a vase, etc. 4. a thickly padded floor covering, as in a gymnasium 5. anything growing or interwoven in a thick tangle —*vt., vi.* mat′ted, mat′ting to make or become thickly tangled —**on the mat** [Colloq.] in trouble

mat[2] *adj.* [Fr.] same as MATT

matador (mat′ə dôr′) *n.* [Sp. < *matar*, kill] the bullfighter who kills the bull with a sword

match[1] (mach) *n.* [< OFr. *mesche*] 1. a slender piece of wood, cardboard, etc. tipped with a composition that catches fire by friction 2. orig., a cord prepared to burn at a uniform rate, used for firing guns

match[2] *n.* [OE. (ge)mæcca, a mate] 1. any person or thing equal or similar to another; specif., *a)* one able to cope with another as an equal *b)* a counterpart 2. two or more persons or things that go together in appearance, size, etc. 3. a contest or game 4. a marriage or mating 5. a suitable mate —*vt.* 1. to be equal, similar, or suitable to 2. to put in opposition 3. to join in marriage; mate 4. to suit or fit (one thing) to another 5. to make or get a competitor or equivalent to *[match this cloth]* —*vi.* to be equal, similar, suitable, etc. —**match′able** *adj.* —**match′er** *n.*

matchless *adj.* having no equal; peerless

matchlock *n.* 1. a gunlock in which the powder was ignited by a slow-burning match 2. a musket with such a gunlock

matchmaking *n.* the arranging of marriages for others —**match′mak′er** *n.*

match play *Golf* a form of play in which the score is calculated by counting holes won rather than strokes taken

matchstick *n.* same as MATCH[1] (sense 1)

matchwood *n.* 1. wood for making matches 2. very small pieces: splinters

mate[1] (māt) *n.* [MDu.] 1. *a)* the male or female of paired animals *b)* a husband or wife **2.** a companion or fellow worker **3.** one of a matched pair **4.** *Naut.* an officer of a merchant ship, ranking below the captain **5.** an assistant [a carpenter's *mate*] —*vt., vi.* **mat′ed, mat′ing 1.** to pair **2.** to couple in marriage or sexual union

mate² *n., interj., vt.* **mat′ed, mat′ing** *same as* CHECKMATE

matelot (mat′lō) *n.* [Fr.] a sailor: also **matlow, matlo**

mater (māt′ər) *n.* [L.] mother

material (mətēər′ē əl) *adj.* [< L. *materia*, matter] **1.** of matter; physical **2.** *a)* of the body or bodily needs, etc. [*material* pleasures] *b)* of comfort, wealth, etc. [*material* success] **3.** important, essential, etc. (*to*) —*n.* **1.** what a thing is made of; elements or parts **2.** ideas, notes, etc. that may be developed **3.** cloth or other fabric **4.** [*pl.*] tools, articles, etc. for a specified use —**mate′rial′ity** (-al′ə tē) *n.*

materialism *n.* **1.** the tendency to be more concerned with material than with spiritual values **2.** the doctrine that everything can be explained only in terms of matter —**mate′rialist** *adj., n.* —**mate′rialis′tic** *adj.*

materialize *vi.* **-ized′, -iz′ing 1.** to become fact [a plan that never *materialized*] **2.** to take on bodily form: said of spirits, etc. **3.** to appear suddenly —*vt.* to represent in material form —**mate′rializa′tion** *n.*

materially *adv.* **1.** to a great extent **2.** physically **3.** with regard to the content and not the form

matériel (mətēər′ē el′) *n.* [Fr.] the necessary materials; specif., weapons, supplies, etc. of armed forces

maternal (mətur′n'l) *adj.* [< L. *mater*, mother] **1.** of or like a mother; motherly **2.** derived from a mother **3.** related through the mother's side of the family [*maternal* grandparents] —**mater′nally** *adv.*

maternity (mətur′nə tē) *n.* motherhood —*adj.* for pregnant women

matey (māt′ē) *adj.* [< MATE¹] [Colloq.] friendly

math. **1.** mathematical **2.** mathematician

mathematical (math′ə mat′i k'l) *adj.* [< Gr. *manthanein*, learn] **1.** of or concerned with mathematics **2.** rigorously precise —**math′emat′ically** *adv.*

mathematician (math′ə mə tish′ən) *n.* an expert or specialist in mathematics

mathematics (math′ə mat′iks) *n.pl.* [with *sing. v.*] [see MATHEMATICAL] the sciences (arithmetic, geometry, etc.) dealing with quantities, magnitudes, and forms by the use of numbers and symbols

maths (maths) *n.* *short for* MATHEMATICS

matinée (mat′i nā′) *n.* [< Fr.: see MATINS] a performance, as of a play, in the afternoon

matinée coat a baby's short coat, usually knitted

matins (mat′inz) *n.pl.* [< L. *matutinus*,

of the morning] a service of morning prayer

matriarch (mā′trē ärk′) *n.* [< L. *mater*, mother + -ARCH] a mother who rules her family or tribe —**ma′triar′chal** (-är′k'l) *adj.*

matriarchy *n., pl.* **-chies** a form of social organization in which the mother is head of the family or tribe, descent being through the female line —**ma′triar′chic** *adj.*

matricide (māt′rə sīd′) *n.* [< L. *mater*, mother + *caedere*, kill] **1.** the act of killing one's mother **2.** a person who kills his mother —**mat′rici′dal** *adj.*

matriculate (mə trik′yoo lāt′) *vt., vi.* **-lat′ed, -lat′ing** [< ML. *matriculare*, to register] to enrol, esp. as a student in a university —**matric′ula′tion** *n.*

matrimony (mat′ri mə nē) *n., pl.* **-nies** [< L. *mater*, mother] **1.** the rite of marriage **2.** married life —**mat′rimo′nial** *adj.* —**mat′rimo′nially** *adv.*

matrix (mā′triks) *n., pl.* **-trices** (-trə sēz′), **-trixes** [ult. < L. *mater*, mother] **1.** that within which something originates, takes form, etc.; specif., a die or mould for casting or shaping **2.** *Math.* a regular array of quantities or symbols

matron (mā′trən) *n.* [< L. *mater*, mother] **1.** a wife or widow, esp. one with a mature manner **2.** *a)* a woman manager of the domestic arrangements of a school or other institution *b)* formerly, a woman in charge of the nursing staff of a hospital; senior nursing officer —**ma′tronly** *adj.*

matron of honour a married woman acting as principal attendant to the bride at a wedding

Matt. Matthew

matt (mat) *adj.* [see MAT²] not shiny or glossy; dull

matted *adj.* **1.** closely tangled together in a dense mass **2.** covered with matting or mats

matter (mat′ər) *n.* [< L. *materia*, material] **1.** what a thing is made of; constituent material **2.** whatever occupies space and is perceptible to the senses **3.** any specified sort of substance [colouring *matter*] **4.** content of thought or expression, as distinguished from style or form **5.** an amount or quantity [a *matter* of a few days] **6.** *a)* a thing or affair [business *matters*] *b)* cause or occasion [no laughing *matter*] **7.** importance [it's of no *matter*] **8.** trouble [what's the *matter*?] **9.** pus —*vi.* to have significance —**as a matter of fact** really —**for that matter 1.** as far as that is concerned **2.** indeed on consideration —**no matter 1.** it is of no importance **2.** regardless of [no *matter* what you say]

matter-of-fact *adj.* sticking strictly to facts; literal, unimaginative, etc. —**mat′ter-of-fact′ness** *n.*

matting (mat′in) *n.* **1.** a fabric of fibre, as straw for mats, floor covering, etc. **2.** mats collectively

mattins (mat′inz) *n.pl.* *var. of* MATTINS

MATTOCK

mattock (mat′ək) *n.* [OE. *mattuc*] a tool like a pickaxe but with at least one flat blade, for loosening the soil, digging up roots, etc.

mattress (mat′ris) *n.* [< Ar. *matrah,* cushion] a casing of strong cloth filled with cotton, foam rubber, etc., and usually coiled springs, and used on or as a bed

maturate (mat′yoo rāt′) *vi.* -rat′ed, -rat′-ing [< MATURE] 1. to mature 2. to discharge pus

mature (mə tyooər′) *adj.* [< L. *maturus,* ripe] 1. full-grown, ripe, fully developed, perfected, etc. 2. due: said of a note, bond, etc. —*vt., vi.* -tured′, -tur′ing to make or become mature —**matu′rity** *n.*

matutinal (ma tyoo tī′n′l) *adj.* [see MATINS] of or in the morning; early —**matuti′nally** *adv.*

maudlin (môd′lin) *adj.* [< ME. *Maudeleyne,* (Mary) Magdalene] foolishly and tearfully or weakly sentimental

maul (môl) *vt.* [< L. *malleus,* hammer] 1. to handle roughly 2. to bruise —*n.* 1. a heavy hammer or mallet 2. *Rugby* a scrimmage —**maul′er** *n.*

maunder (môn′dər) *vi.* [prob. < obs. *maund,* beg] to talk, move, or act in a vague, rambling way

Maundy money (môn′dē) specially minted coins given by the British sovereign to poor people on Maundy Thursday

Maundy Thursday [< L. *mandatum,* commandment: from use in a prayer] the Thursday before Easter

mausoleum (mô′sə lē′əm) *n., pl.* -le′ums, -le′a [< the tomb of *Mausolus,* king of an ancient land in Asia Minor] a large, imposing tomb —**mau′sole′an** *adj.*

mauve (mōv) *n.* [Fr. < L. *malva,* mallow] a delicate purple —*adj.* of such a colour

maverick (mav′ər ik) *n.* [< S. *Maverick,* 19th-c. Texas rancher who did not brand his cattle] a person who acts independently of his political party or group

maw (mô) *n.* [OE. *maga*] 1. the throat, gullet, jaws, etc. of a voracious animal 2. the stomach

mawkish (mô′kish) *adj.* [< ON. *mathkr,* maggot] sentimental in a weak, insipid way —**mawk′ishly** *adv.*

max. maximum

maxi- [< MAXI(MUM)] *a combining form meaning* maximum, very large, very long [*maxicoat*]

maxilla (mak sil′ə) *n., pl.* -lae (-ē) [L.] a jaw; in vertebrates, the upper jaw —**max-il′lary** *adj.*

maxim (mak′sim) *n.* [< LL. *maxima (propositio),* greatest (premise)] a concisely expressed rule of conduct; precept

maximize (mak′sə mīz′) *vt.* -mized′, -miz′ing to increase to the maximum —**max′imiza′tion** *n.*

maximum *n., pl.* -ma [L., superl. of *magnus,* great] 1. the greatest quantity, number, etc. possible or permissible 2. the highest degree or point reached or recorded —*adj.* 1. greatest possible, permissible, or reached 2. of, marking or setting a maximum

maxwell (maks′wel) *n.* [< James Clark *Maxwell*] a unit of magnetic flux

May (mā) *n.* [< L. *Maia,* goddess of increase] the fifth month of the year, having 31 days

may (mā) *v.aux., pt.* **might** [OE. *mæg*] an auxiliary verb expressing: 1. possibility [it may rain] 2. permission [you may go] 3. purpose, result, etc. [they died that we may be free] 4. wish or hope [may he rest in peace]

Maya (mī′yə) *n.* 1. a member of a tribe of Indians in Central America 2. their language —**Ma′yan** *adj., n.*

maybe (mā′bē) *adv.* [ME. (for *it may be*)] perhaps

Mayday (mā′dā′) *n.* [< Fr. (*venez*) *m′aider,* (come) help me] the international radiotelephone signal for help, used by ships and aircraft in distress

May Day May 1: as a traditional spring festival, often celebrated by dancing, etc.; as an international labour holiday, observed by parades, etc.

mayfly *n., pl.* -flies′ a slender insect with gauzy wings held vertically when at rest

mayhap *adv.* [< *it may hap(pen)*] [Archaic] perhaps

mayhem (mā′hem) *n.* [see MAIM] 1. *Law* the offence of maiming a person 2. any deliberate destruction or violence

mayn't (mā′′nt) may not

mayonnaise (mā′ə nāz′) *n.* [Fr.] a salad dressing made of egg yolks, oil, vinegar, etc.

mayor (mā′ər) *n.* [< L. *major,* greater] the chief administrative official of a city, town, or other municipality —**may′oral** *adj.* —**may′oress** *n.* **fem.**

mayoralty *n., pl.* -ties the office or term of office of a mayor

Maypole (mā′pōl′) *n.* a high pole decorated with ribbons, around which merrymakers dance on May Day

May queen a girl chosen to be queen of the merrymakers on May Day

may tree the hawthorn

maze (māz) *n.* [< OE. *amasian,* amaze] 1. a confusing, intricate network of winding pathways; labyrinth 2. a state of confusion —**ma′zy** *adj.* —**ma′zily** *adv.*

mazurka, mazourka (mə zur′kə) *n.* [Pol.] 1. a lively Polish dance like the polka 2. music for this

M.B. [L. *Medicinae Baccalaureus*] Bachelor of Medicine

M.B.E. Member of the Order of the British Empire

M.C. 1. Master of Ceremonies 2. Military Cross

M.C.C. Marylebone Cricket Club

McCoy (mə koi'), **the** (**real**) [Slang] the real person or thing, not a substitute

M.Ch(ir). [L. *Magister Chirurgiae*] Master of Surgery

Md *Chem.* mendelevium

M.D. [L. *Medicinae Doctor*] Doctor of Medicine

M.D.T. [U.S. & Canad.] Mountain Daylight Time

MDu. Middle Dutch

me[1] (mē) *pron.* [OE.] *objective case of* I

me[2] *same as* MI

ME. Middle English

‡**mea culpa** (mā'ə kool'pə) [L.] (by) my fault

mead[1] (mēd) *n.* [OE. *meodu*] an alcoholic drink made with fermented honey and water, often with spices added

mead[2] *n.* [OE. *mæd*] [Poet.] a meadow

meadow (med'ō) *n.* [< OE. *mæd*] 1. a piece of grassland, esp. one whose grass is grown for use as hay 2. low, level grassland near a stream —**mead'owy** *adj.*

meadowsweet *n.* a fragrant plant with feathery flowers

meagre (mē'gər) *adj.* [< L. *macer*, lean] 1, of poor quality or small amount 2. lean; emaciated Also U.S., **mea'ger**

meal[1] (mēl) *n.* [OE. *mæl*] 1. any of the times for eating; breakfast, lunch, etc. 2. the food served or eaten

meal[2] *n.* [OE. *melu*] any edible grain, coarsely ground and unbolted [oatmeal] —**meal'y** *adj.*

mealie (mēl'ē) *n.* [Afrik. *milie*] in South Africa, maize

mealie-meal *n.* in South Africa, meal made from maize

mealie-pap *n.* [< MEALIE + Afrik. *pap*, porridge] in South Africa, porridge made from maize

meals-on-wheels *n.* a service taking hot meals to the infirm and elderly, run as a branch of the social services

meal ticket 1. [U.S.] a luncheon voucher 2. a person, job, skill, etc. depended on as one's means of support

mealy-mouthed *adj.* evasive, euphemistic, insincere, etc.

mean[1] (mēn) *vt.* **meant** (ment), **mean'ing** [OE. *mænan*] 1. to intend to express 2. *a)* to intend for [a gift meant for you] *b)* to destine [he was meant to be a doctor] 3. to have in mind; intend 4. to signify; denote 5. to entail [it means getting up early] —*vi.* 1. to have a purpose in mind 2. to have a (specified) degree of importance [she means little to him] —**mean well (by)** to have good intentions (towards)

mean[2] *adj.* [OE. (ge)mæne] 1. stingy; miserly 2. bad-tempered, selfish, etc. 3. ignoble; petty 4. poor in appearance 5. low in quality, value, or importance 6. [U.S.] bad-tempered: said of a horse, etc.

7. [Colloq.] secretly guilty; disturbed —**mean'ness** *n.*

mean[3] *adj.* [< L. *medius*, middle] 1. halfway between extremes 2. average —*n.* 1. what is between extremes; intermediate state, quality, etc. 2. *Math.* a number between the smallest and largest values of a set of quantities

meander (mē an'dər) *n.* [< Gr. *Maiandros*, a winding river in Asia Minor] 1. [*pl.*] windings, as of a stream 2. an aimless wandering —*vi.* 1. to take a winding course : said of a stream 2. to wander aimlessly

meanie, meany *n.,* *pl.* **mean'ies** [Colloq.] a person who is mean, selfish, cruel, etc.

meaning *n.* what is meant; significance —*adj.* that has meaning; significant

meaningful *adj.* full of meaning; having significance

meaningless *adj.* without significance

means *n.pl.* [< MEAN[3], *n.*] 1. [*with sing. or pl. v.*] that by which something is done or obtained 2. resources [a person of means] —**by all means** 1. without fail 2. certainly —**by any means** in any way possible —**by means of** with the aid of —**by no (manner of) means** certainly not —**means to an end** a method of getting what one wants

mean (solar) time time having exactly equal divisions

means test a financial investigation of a person's eligibility for financial or social help

meant (ment) *pt.* & *pp. of* MEAN[1]

meantime *adv.* 1. in or during the intervening time 2. at the same time —*n.* the intervening time Also, and for adv. usually, **mean'while'**

measles (mē'z'lz) *n.pl.* [*with sing. v.*] [ME. *maseles*] 1. an infectious virus disease, characterized by small red spots, high fever, etc. 2. any of various similar but milder diseases; esp., rubella

measly (mēz'lē) *adj.* **-slier, -sliest** 1. [Colloq.] contemptibly slight or skimpy 2. infected with measles

measure (mezh'ər) *n.* [< L. *metiri*, to measure] 1. the extent, dimensions, capacity, etc. of anything 2. a determining of extent, dimensions, etc.; measurement 3. *a)* a unit of measurement, as a litre *b)* any criterion 4. a system of measurement [dry measure] 5. an instrument or container for measuring 6. a definite quantity measured out 7. an extent or degree not to be exceeded [within measure] 8. quantity or degree [in large measure] 9. course of action 10. a law 11. *a)* rhythm in verse; metre *b)* a metrical unit 12. [Obs.] a dance 13. [*pl.*] *Geol.* strata : chiefly in **coal measures** 14. *Music* *a)* a bar *b)* musical time —*vt.* **-ured, -uring** 1. to find out the extent, dimensions, etc. of 2. to mark off by measuring (often with *off* or *out*) 3. to make a judgment of by comparing 4. to bring into comparison or rivalry (*against*) —*vi.* 1. to take measurements 2. to be of specified measurements —**a measure of** some degree of —**beyond measure** exceedingly —**for good measure** extra —**made to measure** custom-made: said of clothes —**measure up to** to meet (expectations, etc.) —**take someone's measure** to estimate someone's ability, character, etc. —**meas′urable** *adj.*

measured *adj.* 1. regular 2. rhythmical 3. calculated, deliberate, etc., as speech —**meas′uredly** *adv.*

measurement *n.* 1. a measuring or being measured 2. extent or quantity determined by measuring 3. a system of measuring

meat (mēt) *n.* [OE. *mete*] 1. the flesh of animals used as food 2. [Archaic] food 3. the substance or essence

meat safe a cupboard of perforated zinc or gauze-covered wooden frame for storing meat, esp. in hot weather

meaty *adj.* -ier, -iest 1. of, like, or full of meat 2. full of substance; thought-provoking

Mecca (mek′ə) *n.* [< the holy city of Islam] [often m-] any place that many people feel drawn to

meccano (mə kä′nō) *Trademark* small-scale fitments used to make engineering models

mech. 1. mechanical 2. mechanics

mechanic (mə kan′ik) *n.* [< Gr. *mēchanē*, machine] a worker skilled in using tools or in making, operating, and repairing machines

mechanical *adj.* 1. involving or having skill in the use of machinery or tools 2. produced or operated by machinery 3. of the science of mechanics 4. automatic, as if from habit 5. lacking feeling [her acting is *mechanical*] —**mechan′ically** *adv.*

mechanical drawing same as TECHNICAL DRAWING

mechanics *n.pl.* [with *sing. v.*] 1. the branch of physics that deals with the motion of bodies and the action of forces on bodies 2. knowledge of machinery 3. the mechanical aspect [the *mechanics* of writing]

mechanism (mek′ə niz′m) *n.* [< Gr. *mēchanē*, machine] 1. the working parts of a machine 2. a system whose parts work together as in a machine 3. the mechanical aspect —**mech′anis′tic** *adj.* —**mech′anis′tically** *adv.*

mechanize (mek′ə nīz′) *vt.* -nized′, -niz′-ing 1. to do or operate by machinery, not by hand 2. to bring about the use of machinery in (an industry, etc.) 3. to equip (an army, etc.) with motor vehicles, tanks, etc. —**mech′aniza′tion** *n.* —**mech′a-niz′er** *n.*

Mechlin (mek′lin) *n.* [< E. name of *Mechelen*, in Belgium] a fine lace, with the design outlined by a thread

Med *short for* MEDITERRANEAN

med. 1. medical 2. medicine 3. medieval 4. medium

M.Ed. Master of Education

medal (med′'l) *n.* [< L. *metallum*, metal] a small, flat piece of metal with a design or inscription on it, made to commemorate some event, or awarded for some distinguished action, merit, etc. —**med′al-ist** *n.*

medallion (mə dal′yən) *n.* [see MEDAL] 1. a large medal 2. any of various designs, carvings, etc. like a medal in shape, used decoratively, as in architecture

medal play *Golf* a form of competitive play in which the score is calculated by counting the total number of strokes taken to play the designated number of holes

meddle (med′'l) *vi.* -dled, -dling [< L. *miscere*, mix] 1. to concern oneself with other people's affairs without being asked or needed; interfere (*in* or *with*) 2. to tamper (*with*) —**med′dler** *n.* —**med′dlesome** *adj.*

media (mē′dē ə) *n.* *alt. pl. of* MEDIUM: see MEDIUM (*n.* 3)

mediaeval (med′ē ē′v'l) *adj.* same as MEDIEVAL

medial (mē′dē əl) *adj.* [< L. *medius*, middle] 1. of or in the middle 2. average —**me′dially** *adv.*

median *adj.* [< L. *medius*, middle] 1. middle; intermediate 2. designating a line from a vertex of a triangle to the middle of the opposite side 3. designating the middle number in a series —*n.* a median number, point, or line

mediate (mē′dē āt′; *for adj.* -ət) *vi.* -at′-ed, -at′ing [< L. *medius*, middle] to be an intermediary between persons or sides —*vt.* to settle through efforts as an intermediary —*adj.* acting by or connected through some intervening agency —**me′dia′tion** *n.* —**me′dia′tor** *n.*

medic (med′ik) *n.* [Colloq.] 1. a physician or surgeon 2. a medical student or intern

medical (med′i k'l) *adj.* [< Fr. < L. *medicus*, physician] of or connected with medicine —*n.* [Colloq.] a medical examination —**med′ically** *adv.*

medical certificate a certificate issued by a doctor to a worker who is unfit, in order that he may claim sick leave

medicate (med′ə kāt′) *vt.* -cat′ed, -cat′-ing [< L. *medicari*, heal] 1. to treat with medicine 2. to add a medicinal substance to —**med′icative** *adj.*

medication (med′ə kā′shən) *n.* 1. a medicating 2. a medicine; substance for healing, or for relieving pain

medicinal (mə dis′in 'l) *adj.* of, or having the properties of, medicine; healing or relieving —**medic′inally** *adv.*

medicine (med′sin) *n.* [< L. *medicus*, physician] 1. the science of diagnosing, treating, and preventing disease 2. the branch of this science that makes use of drugs, diet, etc., as distinguished esp. from surgery 3. any substance used in treating disease, relieving pain, etc. —**take one's medicine** to endure just punishment, etc.

medicine man among primitive peoples, a man supposed to have supernatural powers of curing disease

medico (med′i kō′) *n.,* *pl.* -cos′ [It.] [Colloq.] 1. a doctor 2. a medical student

medieval (med′ē ē′v'l) *adj.* [< L. *medius*,

middle + *aevum*, age] of, like, or suggestive of the Middle Ages —**me′die′- valist** *n.* —**me′die′vally** *adv.*

Medieval Greek the Greek language c.600–c.1500 A.D.

Medieval Latin the Latin language c.600–c.1500 A.D.

mediocre (mē′dē ō′kər) *adj.* [< L. *medius*, middle + *ocris*, peak] 1. neither very good nor very bad; ordinary 2. not good enough —**me′dioc′rity** (-ok′rə tē) *n.*

meditate (med′ə tāt′) *vt.* -tat′ed, -tat′ing [< L. *meditari*] to plan or intend —*vi.* to think deeply; reflect —**med′itative** *adj.* —**med′itatively** *adv.* —**med′ita′tor** *n.*

meditation (med′ə tā′shən) *n.* deep reflection, esp. on sacred matters as a devotional act

Mediterranean (med′i tə rā′nē ən) *adj.* [< L. *medius*, middle + *terra*, land] of the Mediterranean Sea or nearby regions

medium (mē′dē əm) *n.*, *pl.* -diums; also (except sense 5), for sense 3 usually, -dia [L. < *medius*, middle] 1. *a)* something intermediate *b)* a middle state or degree 2. an intervening thing through which a force acts 3. any means, agency, etc.; specif., a means of communication that reaches the general public 4. any surrounding substance or environment 5. a person through whom communications are supposedly sent from the spirits of the dead 6. any material or technique as used in art —*adj.* intermediate in quality, amount, etc.

medium wave any radio frequency between 200 kilohertz and 2 megahertz (100 to 2000 metres)

medlar (med′lər) *n.* [< Gr. *mespilon*] a tree with a small, brown, applelike fruit, eaten when partly decayed

medley (med′lē) *n.*, *pl.* -leys [see MEDDLE] 1. a mixture of things not usually placed together 2. a musical piece made up of tunes or passages from various works

medulla (me dul′ə) *n.*, *pl.* -dul′las, -dul′- lae (-ē) [L., marrow] 1. *Anat. a)* the inner substance of an organ *b)* bone marrow 2. *Bot.* same as PITH —**medul′lary** *adj.*

medusa (mə dyoo͞′zə) *n.*, *pl.* -sas, -sae (-zē) [< *Medusa*, Gorgon slain by Perseus] *Zool.* same as JELLYFISH

meek (mēk) *adj.* [< ON. *miukr*, gentle] patient and mild; submissive —**meek′ly** *adv.* —**meek′ness** *n.*

meerkat (mēər′kat′) *n.* [< Du.] [S Afr.] a mongoose

meerschaum (mēər′shəm) *n.* [G., sea foam] 1. a soft, white, claylike mineral used for tobacco pipes, etc. because heat-resistant 2. a pipe made of this

meet[1] (mēt) *vt.* met, meet′ing [OE. *metan*] 1. to come upon; esp., to come face to face with 2. to be present at the arrival of [to *meet* a bus] 3. to come into contact with 4. *a)* to get acquainted with *b)* to keep an appointment with 5. *a)* to face [to *meet* angry words with a laugh] *b)* to deal with effectively [to *meet* an

objection] 6. to experience [to *meet* disaster] 7. to come within the perception of (the eye, ear, etc.) 8. *a)* to satisfy (a demand, etc.) *b)* to pay (a bill, etc.) —*vi.* 1. to come together 2. to come into contact, etc. 3. to become acquainted 4. to assemble 5. to come together for discussion, etc. (with) —*n.* 1. a meeting, gathering, etc. 2. the people who meet —**meet a person half-way** to be willing to compromise —**meet with** 1. to experience 2. to receive 3. to encounter: also [Colloq.] **meet up with**

meet[2] *adj.* [< OE. (ge)mǣte] [Archaic] suitable; proper

meeting *n.* 1. an assembly 2. an assembly for worship 3. a series of horse or dog races 4. a point of contact; junction

mega- (meg′ə) [Gr.] à combining form meaning: 1. large, powerful [*megaphone*] 2. a million (of) [*megaton*]

megahertz (meg′ə hurts′) *n.*, *pl.* -hertz′[see MEGA-] one million hertz: formerly **meg′acy′cle** (-sī′k′l)

megalith (meg′ə lith′) *n.* [MEGA- + Gr. *lithos*, stone] a huge stone, esp. one used in prehistoric monuments —**meg′alith′ic** *adj.*

megalomania (meg′ə lō mān′yə) *n.* [< Gr. *megas*, large & MANIA] a mental disorder characterized by delusions of grandeur, power, etc. —**meg′aloma′- niac′** (-ak′) *adj.*, *n.*

megalopolis (meg′ə lop′ə lis) *n.* [Gr., great city] a vast, heavily populated urban area, including many cities

megaphone (meg′ə fōn′) *n.* [see MEGA- + -PHONE] a large, funnel-shaped device for increasing the volume of the voice and directing it

megaton (meg′ə tun′) *n.* [see MEGA-] the explosive force of a million tons of TNT —**meg′aton′nage** *n.*

meiosis (mī ō′sis) *n.* [< Gr. *meioun*, make smaller] the process of nuclear division in the formation of germ cells that halves the number of chromosomes present

melamine (mel′ə mēn′) *n.* [G. *Melamin*] a white, crystalline compound used in making synthetic resins

melancholia (mel′ən kōl′yə) *n.* [see ff.] a mental disorder characterized by extreme depression, brooding, etc. —**mel′ancho′- liac**′ (-kō′lē ak′) *adj.*, *n.*

melancholy (mel′ən kəl ē) *n.*, *pl.* -cholies [< Gr. *melas*, black + *cholē*, bile] 1. sadness and depression of spirits 2. pensiveness —*adj.* 1. sad and depressed 2. causing sadness or depression 3. pensive —**mel′anchol′ic** (-kol′ik) *adj.*

Melanesian (mel ə nē′zhən) *adj.* of Melanesia —*n.* a member of the native people of Melanesia

mélange (mā länzh′) *n.* [Fr.] a mixture or medley

melanin (mel′ə nin) *n.* [< Gr. *melas*, black] a brownish-black pigment found in skin, hair, etc.

mêlée (me′lā) *n.* [Fr.] a noisy, confused,

hand-to-hand fight among a number of people

meliorate (mēl′yə rāt′) *vt., vi.* -rat′ed, -rat′ing [< L. *melior*, better] to improve

melliferous (mə lif′ər əs) *adj.* [< L. *mel*, honey + *ferre*, bear] producing honey

mellifluous (mə lif′loo wəs) *adj.* [< L. *mel*, honey + *fluere*, to flow] sounding sweet and smooth : also **mellif′luent** —**mellif′luously** *adv.*

mellow (mel′ō) *adj.* [prob. < OE. *melu*, meal] 1. sweet and juicy because ripe : said of fruit 2. full-flavoured : said of wine, etc. 3. rich, soft, and pure : said of sound, light, etc. 4. moist and rich : said of soil 5. made gentle and understanding by experience 6. slightly intoxicated —*vt., vi.* to make or become mellow

melodeon (mə lō′dē ən) *n.* [< G. *Melodie*, melody] a small keyboard organ

melodic (mə lod′ik) *adj.* 1. of melody 2. melodious

melodious (mə lō′dē əs) *adj.* 1. containing or producing melody 2. tuneful —**melo′diousness** *n.*

melodrama (mel′ō drä′mə) *n.* [< Fr. < Gr. *melos*, song + *drama*, drama] 1. a drama with exaggerated conflicts and emotions, stereotyped characters, etc. 2. any sensational, highly emotional speech, utterance, etc.

melodramatic (mel′ō drə mat′ik) *adj.* sensational, violent, and extravagantly emotional —**mel′odramat′ically** *adv.* —**mel′odramat′ics** *n.pl.*

melody (mel′ə dē) *n., pl.* -dies [< Gr. *melos*, song + *aeidein*, sing] 1. pleasing sounds or arrangement of sounds in sequence 2. *Music* a) a tune, song, etc. b) the leading part in a harmonic composition

melon (mel′ən) *n.* [< Gr. *mēlon*, apple] the large, juicy, many-seeded fruit of certain trailing plants

Melpomene (mel pom′ə nē′) *Gr. Myth.* the Muse of tragedy

melt (melt) *vt., vi.* [OE. *m(i)eltan*] 1. to change from a solid to a liquid state, generally by heat 2. to dissolve 3. to disappear or cause to disappear gradually 4. to merge gradually [the sea *melts* into the sky] 5. to soften [a story to *melt* our hearts] —**melt down** to melt (metal) so that it can be cast or moulded again —**melt′er** *n.*

melting point the temperature at which a specified solid becomes liquid : abbrev. **melt. pt.**

meltwater *n.* water produced by the melting of snow or ice

mem. 1. member 2. memorandum

member (mem′bər) *n.* [< L. *membrum*] 1. a person belonging to an organization 2. a limb or organ of a person, animal, or plant 3. a distinct part of a whole

member of parliament a member of the House of Commons or similar legislative body

membership *n.* 1. the state of being a member 2. all the members of a group 3. the number of members

membrane (mem′brān) *n.* [< L. *membrum*, member] a thin, soft, pliable layer of animal or plant tissue that covers or lines an organ or part —**mem′braned** *adj.*

memento (mi men′tō) *n., pl.* -tos, -toes [< L. *meminisse*, remember] anything serving as a reminder; souvenir

‡**memento mori** (mō′rī, -rē) [L., remember you must die] any reminder of death

memo (mem′ō) *n., pl.* -os short for MEMORANDUM

memoir (mem′wär) *n.* [< Fr. < L. *memoria*, memory] 1. a biography 2. [*pl.*] an autobiography 3. [*pl.*] a record of events based on the writer's personal observation or knowledge 4. a scholarly report

memorabilia (mem′ər ə bil′ē ə) *n.pl.* [L.] things worth remembering or recording and collecting

memorable (mem′ər ə b'l) *adj.* worth remembering; notable —**mem′orabil′ity** *n.*

memorandum (mem′ə ran′dəm) *n., pl.* -dums, -da [L.] 1. a note written to help one remember something 2. an informal written communication, as in a business office 3. a short written statement of the terms of an agreement, contract, or transaction

memorial (mə môr′ē əl) *adj.* serving to help people remember some person or event —*n.* anything meant to help people remember some person or event, as a statue, holiday, etc.

memorize (mem′ə rīz′) *vt.* -rized′, -riz′ing to commit to memory —**mem′oriza′tion** *n.*

memory (mem′ər ē) *n., pl.* -ries [< L. *memor*, mindful] 1. the power or process of recalling facts or experiences 2. the total of what one remembers 3. a person, thing, etc. remembered 4. the period over which remembering extends [within *memory*] 5. commemoration [in *memory* of his son] 6. reputation after death 7. the components of a computer that retain information

memsahib (mem′sä ib) *n.* [Anglo-Ind.] in India formerly, a term of address for a European married woman

men (men) *n. pl.* of MAN

menace (men′is) *n.* [< L. *minari*, threaten] 1. a threat 2. anything threatening harm 3. [Colloq.] an annoying person —*vt., vi.* -aced, -acing to threaten —**men′acingly** *adv.*

ménage (me näzh′) *n.* [Fr. < L. *mansio*, dwelling] a household

‡**ménage à trois** (me näzh′ ä trwä′) [Fr., household of three] an arrangement by which a married couple and the lover of one of them live together

menagerie (mə naj′ər ē) *n.* [< Fr. : see MENAGE] 1. a collection of wild animals kept in cages for exhibition **2.** a place where such animals are kept

mend (mend) *vt.* [ME. < *amenden*, amend] **1.** to repair; restore to good condition **2.** to improve [*mend* your manners] —*vi.* to heal, as a fracture —*n.* a mended place —**on the mend** improving, esp. in health —**mend′er** *n.*

mendacious (men dā′shəs) *adj.* [< L. *mendax*] not truthful; lying; false —**mendac′ity** (-das′ə tē) *n.*

mendelevium (men′də lē′vē əm) *n.* [< D.I. *Mendeleev*] a radioactive chemical element of the actinide series: symbol, Md

Mendels laws (men′d'lz) the principles of hereditary phenomena formulated by Gregor Mendel (1822-84)

mendicant (men′di kənt) *adj.* [< L. *mendicare*, beg] asking for alms —*n.* **1.** a beggar **2.** a mendicant friar

menhir (men′hēər′) *n.* [Fr. < Breton *men*, stone + *hir*, long] a tall, upright stone erected probably as a monument in prehistoric times

menial (mēn′yəl) *adj.* [see MANSION] **1.** of or fit for servants **2.** servile; low —*n.* **1.** a servant **2.** a servile, low person —**me′nially** *adv.*

meninges (mə nin′jēz) *n.pl.* [< Gr. *mēninx*, membrane] the three membranes that envelop the brain and spinal cord —**menin′geal** (-jē əl) *adj.*

meningitis (men′in jīt′is) *n.* inflammation of the meninges, esp. as the result of infection

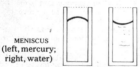

MENISCUS
(left, mercury;
right, water)

meniscus (mi nis′kəs) *n.,* pl. **-nis′ci** (-nis′ī) [< Gr. *mēnē*, moon] **1.** the curved upper surface of a column of liquid **2.** a lens convex on one side and concave on the other

menopause (men′ə pôz′) *n.* [< Gr. *mēn*, month + *pauein*, to make cease] the permanent cessation of menstruation —**men′opaus′al** *adj.*

menorah (mə nôr′ə) *n.* [Heb., lamp stand] a candelabrum with seven branches, a symbol of Judaism

menses (men′sēz) *n.pl.* [L., months] the periodic flow of blood from the uterus: normally every four weeks

menstruate (men′stroo wāt′) *vi.* **-at′ed, -at′ing** [< L. *mensis*, month] to have a discharge of the menses —**men′strual** *adj.* —**men′strua′tion** *n.*

mensuration (men′shyoo rā′shən) *n.* [< L. *mensura*, measure] **1.** a measuring **2.** the branch of mathematics dealing with the determination of length, area, or volume

menswear *n.* clothing for men

-ment (mənt) [< L.] a suffix meaning: **1.** result [*improvement*] **2.** means [*adornment*] **3.** act [*movement*] **4.** state [*disappointment*]

mental (men′t'l) *adj.* [< L. *mens*, mind] **1.** of, for, done by, or in the mind **2.** [Colloq.] mentally ill **3.** for the mentally ill [a *mental* hospital] —**men′tally** *adv.*

mentality (men tal′ə tē) *n.,* pl. **-ties** mental capacity

mental retardation congenital subnormality of intelligence

menthol (men′thol) *n.* [G. < L. *mentha*, mint] a white, waxy, crystalline alcohol obtained from oil of peppermint and used in medicine, cosmetics, etc.

mention (men′shən) *n.* [< L. *mens*, mind] **1.** a brief reference **2.** a citing for honour —*vt.* **1.** to refer to briefly or incidentally **2.** to cite for honour —**men′tionable** *adj.*

mentor (men′tôr) *n.* [< *Mentor* adviser of Odysseus] a wise, loyal adviser

menu (men′yoo) *n.,* pl. **men′us** [Fr. < L. *minutus*, small] **1.** a detailed list of the foods served at a meal or available at a restaurant **2.** the foods served

meow, meou (mē ou′) *n.* [echoic] the characteristic vocal sound made by a cat —*vi.* to make such a sound

MEP Member of European Parliament

Mephistopheles (mef′ə stof′ə lēz′) *n.* [the devil to whom Faust sold his soul] a powerful, sardonic person —**Mephistophelean, Mephistophelian** (mef′is tə fē′-lē ən) *adj.*

mercantile (mur′kən tīl) *adj.* [see MERCHANT] **1.** of merchants or trade; commercial **2.** of mercantilism

mercantilism *n.* the doctrine that the economic interests of a nation could be strengthened by the government through protective tariffs, etc. —**mer′cantilist** *n., adj.*

Mercator projection (mur kāt′ôr) [< G. *Mercator*] a method of making maps on which the meridians are equally spaced parallel straight lines and the parallels of latitude are parallel straight lines spaced farther apart as they get farther from the equator

mercenary (mur′sə nər ē) *adj.* [< L. *merces*, wages] **1.** working or done for payment only **2.** designating a soldier serving for pay in a foreign army —*n.,* pl. **-naries** a mercenary soldier —**mer′cenarily** *adv.*

mercer (mur′sər) *n.* [< L. *merx*, wares] a dealer in textiles

mercerize (mur′sə rīz′) *vt.* **-ized′, -iz′ing** [< J. *Mercer*] to treat (cotton) with a caustic soda solution in order to strengthen it and give it a silky lustre

merchandise (mur′chən dīz′) *n.* [see ff.] things bought and sold; goods —*vt., vi.* **-dised′, -dis′ing** **1.** to trade in (some kind of goods) **2.** to promote and organize the sale of (a product) —**mer′chandis′er** *n.*

merchant (mur′chənt) *n.* [< L. *merx*,

wares] **1.** a person whose business is buying and selling goods for profit **2.** [Scot. & U.S.] a shopkeeper **3.** [Colloq.] someone well-known for something [a speed *merchant*] —*adj.* **1.** of or used in trade **2.** of the merchant navy

merchant bank a financial institution dealing in commercial investment and credit for manufacturers, etc.

merchantman *n.* a ship used in commerce

merchant navy 1. all the ships of a nation that are used in commerce **2.** their personnel

merciful (mur′si fəl) *adj.* having, feeling, or showing mercy —**mer′cifully** *adv.* —**mer′cifulness** *n.*

merciless *adj.* showing no mercy; pitiless; cruel —**mer′cilessly** *adv.* —**mer′cilessness** *n.*

mercurial (mur kyoor′ē əl) *adj.* **1.** of or containing mercury **2.** quick, quick-witted, changeable, fickle, etc.

mercuric (mur kyoor′ik) *adj.* of or containing mercury, esp. with a valence of two

mercurous (mur′kyoo rəs) *adj.* of or containing mercury, esp. with a valence of one

Mercury (mur′kyoo rē) **1.** *Rom. Myth.* the messenger of the gods **2.** the smallest planet in the solar system and the one nearest to the sun —*n.* [m-] a heavy, silver-white metallic chemical element, liquid at ordinary temperatures; quicksilver: it is used in thermometers, dentistry, etc.: symbol, Hg

mercy (mur′sē) *n.,* pl. **-cies** [< L. *merces*, payment] **1.** a refraining from harming or punishing offenders, enemies, etc.; kindness in excess of what may be expected **2.** a disposition to forgive; clemency **3.** kind or compassionate treatment **4.** a fortunate thing —**at the mercy of** completely in the power of

mercy flight an aircraft flight to bring a seriously ill or injured person to hospital from an isolated community

mercy killing *same as* EUTHANASIA

mere[1] (mēər) *adj.* *superl.* **mer′est** [< L. *merus*, pure] nothing more or other than [a *mere* boy] —**mere′ly** *adv.*

mere[2] *n.* [OE.] [Poet.] a lake

meretricious (mer′ə trish′əs) *adj.* [< L. *meretrix*, prostitute] **1.** alluring by false, showy charms; tawdry **2.** specious —**mer′etri′ciously** *adv.*

merganser (mur gan′sər) *n.* [< L. *mergus*, diver + *anser*, goose] *same as* GOOSANDER

merge (murj) *vi., vt.* **merged, merg′ing** [< L. *mergere*, to dip] **1.** to lose or cause to lose identity by being absorbed, swallowed up, or combined **2.** to unite; combine

merger *n.* a merging; specif., the combination of several companies, etc. in one

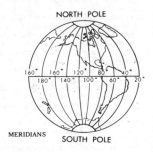

MERIDIANS

meridian (mə rid′ē ən) *n.* [< L. *medius*, middle + *dies*, day] **1.** *a)* a great circle of the earth passing through the geographical poles and any given point on the earth's surface *b)* any of the lines of longitude **2.** orig., the highest point reached by a heavenly body in its course **3.** the highest point of power, prosperity, etc.; zenith

meridional *adj.* [< LL. *meridionalis*, southern] **1.** of a meridian **2.** southern **3.** of the people living in the south, esp. of France

meringue (mə raŋ′) *n.* [Fr.] **1.** egg whites beaten stiff and mixed with sugar **2.** a baked cake or shell made of this

merino (mə rē′nō) *n.,* pl. **-nos** [Sp.] **1.** a breed of sheep with long, fine wool **2.** the wool **3.** a fine, soft yarn or cloth made from this wool

merit (mer′it) *n.* [< L. *mereri*, earn] **1.** worth; value; excellence **2.** something deserving reward, praise, etc. **3.** a mark, badge, etc. awarded for excellence **4.** [pl.] essential rightness or wrongness —*vt.* to deserve

meritocracy (mer′ə tok′rə sē) *n.* control by an intellectual elite —**mer′itocrat′** *n.*

meritorious (mer′ə tôr′ē əs) *adj.* having merit; deserving reward, praise, etc. —**mer′ito′riously** *adv.*

merl, merle (murl) *n.* [< L. *merula*] [Poet.] the blackbird

merlin (mur′lin) *n.* [< OFr. *esmerillon*] a small, black and white falcon

mermaid (mur′mād′) *n.* [see MERE[2] & MAID] an imaginary sea creature with the body of a beautiful woman and the tail of a fish —**mer′man′** *n.masc.*

merry (mer′ē) *adj.* **-rier, -riest** [OE. *myrge*] **1.** full of fun and laughter; gay **2.** [Colloq.] slightly drunk —**make merry** to have fun —**mer′rily** *adv.* —**mer′riment** *n.*

merry-andrew *n.* a buffoon; clown

merry-go-round *n.* **1.** *same as* ROUNDABOUT **2.** a whirl or busy round, as of pleasure

merrymaking *n.* **1.** festivity **2.** a merry festival or entertainment —**mer′rymak′er** *n.*

mésalliance (me zal′ē əns) *n.* [Fr.] a

marriage with a person of a lower social status

mescaline (mes'kə lēn') *n.* [< Mex. Ind.] a psychedelic drug obtained from mescal buttons, the tops of a Mexican cactus

mesdames (mā'dam) *n.*, *pl. of* MADAME, MADAM (sense 1), or MRS.: abbrev. **Mmes.**

mesdemoiselles (mā'd'mwə zel') *n. pl. of* MADEMOISELLE: abbrev. **Mlles.**

mesh (mesh) *n.* [prob. < MDu. *maesche*] 1. a net or network 2. any of the open spaces of a net, screen, etc. 3. [*pl.*] the threads, cords, etc. forming these openings 4. a netlike material, as for stockings 5. a structure of interlocking metal links 6. anything that entangles or snares —*vt.*, *vi.* 1. to entangle or become entangled 2. to engage or become engaged: said of gears 3. to interlock 4. to coordinate (*with*) —**mesh'y** *adj.*

mesmerize (mez'mər īz') *vt.* -**ized'**, -**iz'**-**ing** [< F.A. *Mesmer*] to hypnotize or fascinate —**mes'merism** *n.* —**mes'meriz'**-**er** *n.*

meso- [< Gr.] a combining form meaning in the middle, intermediate

Mesolithic (mes'ō lith'ik) *adj.* [MESO- + Gr. *lithos*, stone] designating a period between the Paleolithic and Neolithic, during which certain animals were domesticated

mesomorphic (mes'ō môr'fik) *adj.* [MESO- + Gr. *morphē*, form] designating the muscular type of human body

meson (mē'zon) *n.* [MES(O)- + (ELEC-TR)ON] an unstable particle between the electron and proton in mass, first observed in cosmic rays —**meson'ic** *adj.*

mesosphere (mes'ō sfēar') *n.* [MESO- + SPHERE] an atmospheric zone above the stratosphere

Mesozoic (mes'ō zō'ik) *adj.* [MESO- + ZO(O)-] designating a geologic era after the Paleozoic and before the Cainozoic

mess (mes) *n.* [< L. *missus*, a course (at a meal)] 1. *a*) a state of trouble or difficulty *b*) a state of being untidy or dirty *c*) [Colloq.] a person in either of these states 2. a jumble; hotchpotch 3. *a*) a group of people who regularly have their meals together, as in the army *b*) the meal eaten by such a group *c*) the place where such a group eats —*vt.* 1. to make dirty or untidy 2. to bungle; botch Often with *up* —*vi.* 1. to eat as one of a mess 2. to make a mess —**mess around** (or **about**) 1. to potter around 2. to play the fool

message (mes'ij) *n.* [< L. *mittere*, send] 1. a report, request, etc. sent between persons 2. the chief idea that an artist, writer, etc. seeks to communicate in a work —**get the message** [Colloq.] to understand a hint, etc.

messenger (mes'ən jər) *n.* [see MESSAGE] 1. a person who carries a message or is sent on an errand 2. [Archaic] a harbinger

Messiah (mə sī'ə) [< Heb. *māshīah*, anointed] 1. *Judaism* the expected deliverer of the Jews 2. *Christianity* Jesus —*n.* [m-] any expected saviour

messieurs (mes'ərz) *n. pl. of* MONSIEUR: abbrev. **MM.**

mess jacket a man's short, closefitting jacket, as that worn by officers in the mess for formal dinners

mess kit the compactly arranged metal or plastic plates and eating utensils carried by a soldier or camper

Messrs. (mes'ərz) Messieurs: used as the pl. of MR.

mess tin a soldier's cooking-vessel, the lid of which can be used as a plate and the lower part as a cup or bowl

messy *adj.* -**ier**, -**iest** in or like a mess; untidy, disordered, dirty, etc. —**mess'i**-**ness** *n.*

Met (met) *n.* [Colloq.] short for METEOROLOGICAL

met (met) *pt. & pp. of* MEET[1]

met. metropolitan

meta- [< Gr. *meta*, with, after] a prefix meaning: 1. changed [*metamorphosis*] 2. after, beyond [*metaphysics*]

metabolism (mə tab'ə liz'm) *n.* [< Gr. *meta*, beyond + *ballein*, throw] the processes in organisms by which food is built up into protoplasm and protoplasm is broken down into simpler substances or waste matter, with the release of energy —**metabolic** (met'ə bol'ik) *adj.*

metacarpus (met'ə kär'pəs) *n.* [< Gr. *meta*, beyond + *karpos*, wrist] the five bones between the wrist and the fingers

metal (met''l) *n.* [< Gr. *metallon*, mine] 1. *a*) any of a class of chemical elements, as iron, gold, etc., characterized by ductility, lustre, and conductivity of heat *b*) an alloy of such elements, as brass 2. any substance consisting of metal 3. broken stones, etc. used as in making roads —*adj.* made of metal —*vt.* -**alled**, -**alling** to cover with metal

metal., metall. 1. metallurgical 2. metallurgy

metallic (mə tal'ik) *adj.* 1. of, like, or producing metal 2. suggestive of metal [a *metallic* sound] —**metal'lically** *adv.*

metalliferous (met'ə lif'ər əs) *adj.* [< L. *metallum*, metal + *ferre*, bear] containing, yielding, or producing metal or ore

metallography (met'əl og'rə fē) *n.* [see METAL & -GRAPHY] the study of the structure and physical properties of metals —**metallographic** (mə tal'ə graf'ik) *adj.*

metalloid (met'əl oid') *n.* an element having some of, but not all, the properties of metals, as arsenic or silicon

metallurgy (me tal'ur jē) *n.* [< Gr. *metallon*, metal + *ergon*, work] the science of separating metals from their ores and preparing them for use, by smelting, refining, etc., and of their structure and chemical suitability for particular functions —**metal'lurgist** *n.*

metalwork (met''l wurk') *n.* 1. things made of metal 2. the making of such things —**met'alwork'er** *n.*

metamorphic (met'ə môr'fik) *adj.* of,

characterized by, or formed by metamorphism or metamorphosis

metamorphism (-môr′fiz′m) *n.* **1.** *same as* METAMORPHOSIS **2.** change in the structure of rocks under pressure, heat, etc.

metamorphosis (-môr′fə sis) *n., pl.* **-ses** (-sēz) [< Gr. *meta*, over + *morphē*, form] **1.** change of form, as, in myths, by magic **2.** a marked change of character, appearance, etc. **3.** *Biol.* a change in form or function, specif., that undergone by various animals after the embryonic state, as of the tadpole to the frog —**met′amor′phose** *vt., vi.* **-phosed, -phosing**

metaphor (met′ə far) *n.* [< Gr. *meta*, over + *pherein*, carry] a figure of speech that suggests a likeness by speaking of one thing as if it were another (Ex.: "all the world's a stage") —**mix metaphors** to use inconsistent metaphors in a single expression (Ex.: the storm of protest was nipped in the bud) —**met′aphor′ical** *adj.* —**met′aphor′ically** *adv.*

metaphysical (met′ə fiz′i k'l) *adj.* **1.** of metaphysics **2.** so subtle as to be hard to understand **3.** designating the 17th-cent. English poets whose verse is characterized by subtle and fanciful images

metaphysics (met′ə fiz′iks) *n.pl.* [*with sing. v.*] [< Gr. *(ta) meta (ta) physika*, (that) after (the) *Physics* (in Aristotle's works)] **1.** the branch of philosophy that seeks to explain the nature of being and of the origin of the world **2.** speculative philosophy in general

metastasis (mə tas′tə sis) *n., pl.* **-ses′** (-sēz′) [< Gr. *meta*, after + *histanai*, to place] the spread of disease from one part of the body to another unrelated to it, as of cancer cells by way of the bloodstream

metatarsus (met′ə tär′səs) *n., pl.* **-tar′si** (-sī) [< Gr. *meta-*, after + *tarsus*, sole] the five bones between the ankle and toes —**met′atar′sal** *adj., n.*

metazoan (met′ə zō′ən) *n.* [META- & Gr. *zōion*, animal] any of the very large zoological division made up of all animals whose bodies are composed of many cells arranged into organs —*adj.* of the metazoans

mete (mēt) *vt.* **met′ed, met′ing** [OE. *metan*] **1.** to allot; distribute (usually *with out*) **2.** [Archaic] to measure

metempsychosis (me temp′si kō′sis) *n., pl.* **-ses** (-sēz) [< Gr. *meta*, over + *en*, in + *psyche*, soul] the supposed passing of the soul at death into another body; transmigration

meteor (mēt′ē ər) *n.* [< Gr. *meta*, beyond + *eōra*, a hovering] **1.** loosely, a meteoroid or meteorite **2.** the streak of light, the ionized trail, etc. occurring when a meteoroid enters the earth's atmosphere

meteoric (mēt′ē ôr′ik) *adj.* **1.** of a meteor **2.** like a meteor; momentarily brilliant, flashing, or swift

meteorite (mēt′ē ə rīt′) *n.* that part of a meteoroid that falls to earth as a mass of metal or stone

meteoroid (mēt′ē ə roid′) *n.* any of the many small, solid bodies travelling through space, which are seen as meteors when they enter the earth's atmosphere

Meteorological Office a department of the Civil Service responsible for collecting meteorological data from all over the world, and for providing weather forecasts

meteorology (mēt′ē ə rol′ə jē) *n.* [see METEOR & -LOGY] the science of the atmosphere; study of weather and climate —**me′teorolog′ical** *adj.* —**me′teorol′ogist** *n.*

meter (mēt′ər) *n.* [< ff.] **1.** an instrument for measuring and recording the quantity or rate of flow of gas, water, etc. passing through it **2.** *same as* PARKING METER —*vt.* to measure with a meter

-meter (mēt′ər, mi tər) [< Gr. *metron*, a measure] a suffix meaning: **1.** a device for measuring [*barometer*] **2.** having (a specified number of) metrical feet [*pentameter*]

meterage *n.* measurement as by a meter, or the charge for this

Meth. Methodist

methane (mēth′ān) *n.* [< METHYL] a colourless, odourless, flammable gas present in firedamp and natural gas

methanol (meth′ə nol′) *n.* [< METHANE] a poisonous liquid, obtained by the destructive distillation of wood and used as a fuel, etc.

methinks (mi thinks′) *v.impersonal pt.* **methought′** [< OE. *me*, to me + *thyncth*, it seems] [Archaic] it seems to me

method (meth′əd) *n.* [< Gr. *meta*, after + *hodos*, a way] **1.** a way of doing anything; esp., a regular, orderly procedure **2.** system in doing things **3.** orderly habits

methodical (mə thod′i k'l) *adj.* characterized by method; orderly; systematic —**method′ically** *adv.*

Methodist *n.* a member of a Protestant denomination that developed from the evangelistic teachings of Wesley —*adj.* of Methodists or Methodism : also **Meth′odis′tic** —**Meth′odism** *n.*

methodology (meth′ə dol′ə jē) *n., pl.* **-gies** [see METHOD & -LOGY] **1.** the science of method, or orderly arrangement **2.** a system of methods, as in any particular science

meths (meths) *n.* [Colloq.] *short for* METHYLATED SPIRITS

methyl (meth′əl) *n.* [< Gr. *methy*, wine + *hylē*, wood] the monovalent hydrocarbon radical CH_3, normally existing only in combination

methylate (meth′ə lāt′) *vt.* **-at′ed, -at′ing** to mix with methanol, often in order to make undrinkable

methylated spirits ethyl alcohol made unfit to drink by the addition of methanol

meticulous (mə tik′yoo ləs) *adj.* [< L. *metus*, fear] extremely or excessively careful about details; scrupulous or finicky —**metic′ulously** *adv.* —**metic′ulousness** *n.*

métier (mā′tyā) *n.* [Fr.] a trade,

profession, or occupation, esp., the work that one is particularly suited for

Métis (metès') *n., pl.* **-tis'** (-tès') [< Fr.] [Canad.] a person of mixed parentage, esp. the offspring of a French Canadian and a N American Indian

metonymy (mətonʹ'əmē) *n., pl.* **-mies** [< Gr. *meta*, change + *onyma*, name] use of the name of one thing for that of another associated with it (Ex.: "the press" for "journalists") —**metonymic** (met'ənim'ik) *adj.*

metre (mēʹtər) *n.* [< Gr. *metron*, measure] **1.** the SI unit of length; 1.094 yards **2.** *a)* rhythm in verse; arrangement according to stress and length *b)* the specific rhythmic pattern of a stanza **3.** rhythm in music

metric (metʹrik) *adj.* **1.** *same as* METRICAL **2.** of the system of measurement based on the metre: see METRIC SYSTEM —**go metric** [Colloq.] to change to the metric system —**metʹricize** *vt.* **-cized'**, **-ciz'ing**

metrical *adj.* **1.** of, involving, or used in measurement; metric **2.** of or composed in metre or verse

metrication (met'rəkāʹshən) *n.* the process of changing to the metric system —**metʹricate** *vt.* **-cat'ed**, **-cat'ing**

metric system a decimal system of weights and measures in which the gram, the metre, and the litre are the basic units of weight, length, and capacity, respectively

metric ton *same as* TONNE

Metro (metʹrō) *n.* [Canad.] a metropolitan city administration, esp. Metropolitan Toronto

METRONOME

metronome (metʹrənōm') *n.* [< Gr. *metron*, measure + *nomos*, law] a clockwork device with an inverted pendulum that beats time, as in setting a musical tempo

metropolis (mətropʹəlis) *n., pl.* **-lises** [< Gr. *mētēr*, mother + *polis*, city] the main city, often the capital, of a country, esp. [M-] London

metropolitan (met'rəpolʹət'n) *adj.* **1.** of a metropolis or metropolitan **2.** constituting a city and its suburbs —*n.* an archbishop having authority over a church province

-metry (mətrē) [< Gr.] a terminal combining form meaning measuring [geometry]

mettle (metʹ'l) *n.* [var. of METAL] quality

of character; spirit; courage; ardour —**on one's mettle** prepared to do one's best —**metʹtlesome** *adj.*

mev, MeV [M(ILLION) E(LECTRON-) V(OLTS)] a unit of energy equal to one million (10^6) electron-volts

mew¹ (myōō) *n.* [echoic] the characteristic vocal sound made by a cat —*vi.* to make this sound

mew² *n.* [OE. *mæw*] a sea gull

mews (myōōz) *n.pl.* [*usually with sing. v.*] [< L. *mutare*, to change] a row of stables or carriage houses, now often converted into dwellings

Mex. 1. Mexican **2.** Mexico

Mexican (mekʹsikən) *adj.* of Mexico, its people, their language, or their culture —*n.* a native of Mexico

mezzanine (metʹsənēn') *n.* [< It. *mezzano*, middle] a storey between two main storeys in a building, usually in the form of a balcony projecting partly over the main floor

mezzo (medʹzō) *adj., adv.* [It. < L. *medius*, middle] *Music* moderate(ly); half

mezzo-soprano *n., pl.* **-nos, -ni** (-nē) [It.] a voice or singer between soprano and contralto

mezzotint *n.* [see MEZZO & TINT] **1.** a method of engraving by scraping or polishing parts of a roughened surface to produce impressions of light and shade **2.** an engraving so produced

MF, M.F., mf, m.f. medium frequency

mf *Music* mezzo forte

MFr. Middle French

Mg *Chem.* magnesium

mg, mg. milligram(me)(s)

MGr. Medieval (or Middle) Greek

Mgr. 1. Manager **2.** Monseigneur **3.** Monsignor

MHG. Middle High German

MHz, Mhz megahertz

mi (mē) *n.* [ML.: see GAMUT] *Music* a syllable representing the third tone of the diatonic scale

M.I. Military Intelligence

M.I.5 Military Intelligence, section 5, dealing with counterintelligence

miaow, miaou (mēou') *n., vi.* *same as* MEOW

miasma (mīazʹmə) *n., pl.* **-mas, -mata** [< Gr. *miainein*, pollute] an unwholesome atmosphere, vapour, etc.

Mic. Micah

mica (mīʹkə) *n.* [< L., crumb] any of a group of minerals that crystallize in thin, somewhat flexible, easily separated layers, resistant to heat and electricity

mice (mīs) *n. pl. of* MOUSE

M.I.C.E. Member of the Institution of Civil Engineers

Michaelmas (mikʹ'lməs) *n.* [see -MAS] the feast of the archangel Michael, celebrated on September 29

Michaelmas daisy a perennial aster that blooms in the autumn

M.I.Ch.E. Member of the Institution of Chemical Engineers

mickey (mikʹē) *n.* [prob. < *Mickey*,

nickname for *Michael*] 1. [Slang] an Irishman: also **mick** 2. [Slang] spirit; pride: chiefly in **take the mickey** to make fun; mock

Mickey Finn [*also* m- f-] [Slang] an alcoholic drink to which a powerful narcotic has been secretly added

mickle (mik′′l) *adj., adv., n.* [OE. *micel*] [Archaic or Scot.] much

micro- [< Gr.] *a combining form* meaning: 1. small; minute [*microfilm*] 2. enlarging [*microscope*] 3. microscopic [*microchemistry*] 4. one millionth [*microgram*]

microbe (mī′krōb) *n.* [< Gr. *mikros*, small + *bios*, life] a microscopic organism; esp., any of the bacteria that cause disease; germ —**micro′bic, micro′bial** *adj.*

microbiology (mī′krō bī ol′ə jē) *n.* the branch of biology that deals with microorganisms

microchemistry (mī′krō kem′is trē) *n.* the chemistry of microscopic or submicroscopic quantities or objects

microchip (mī′krō chip) *n.* same as CHIP (*n.* 6)

microcopy (mī′krō kop′ē) *n., pl.* **-cop′-ies** a copy produced in greatly reduced size, as by microfilming

microcosm (mī′krō koz′m) *n.* a miniature universe; specif., man, a community, etc. regarded as a miniature of the world —**mi′crocos′mic** *adj.*

microdot (mī′krō dot′) *n.* a copy, as of written matter, reduced by microphotography to the size of a pinhead

microelectronics (mī′krō i′lek tron′iks) *n.pl.* [*with sing. v.*] the science dealing with the theory and applications of small circuits (**microcircuits**) used in computers, etc.

microfiche (mī′krō fēsh′) *n.* [Fr. < micro-, micro- + *fiche*, small card] a small sheet of microfilm, containing a number of pages of microcopy

microfilm *n.* film on which documents, etc. are photographed in a reduced size —*vt., vi.* to photograph on microfilm

microgram *n.* one millionth of a gram

microgroove *n.* a very narrow needle groove, as for a long-playing gramophone record

micrometer (mī krom′ə tər) *n.* [see MICRO- & -METER] an instrument for measuring small distances, angles, etc.

microminiaturize (mī′krō min′ə-chə rīz′) *vt.* **-ized′, -iz′ing** to provide with electronic equipment of extremely small size —**mi′cromin′iaturiza′tion** *n.*

micron (mī′kron) *n., pl.* **-crons, -cra** [< Gr. *mikros*, small] one millionth of a metre

microorganism (mī′krō ôr′gə niz′m) *n.* any microscopic organism; esp., a bacterium, virus, etc.

microphone (mī′krə fōn′) *n.* [MICRO- + -PHONE] an instrument that converts the mechanical energy of sound waves into an electric signal, as for radio

microprint (mī′krō print′) *n.* a photographic copy so greatly reduced that it can be read only through a magnifying device

microprocessor (mī′krō prō′ses ər) *n.* a single integrated circuit performing the basic functions of the central processing unit in a small computer

microscope (mī′krə skōp′) *n.* [see MICRO- & -SCOPE] an instrument consisting of a lens for making very small objects, as microorganisms, look larger

microscopic (mī′krə skop′ik) *adj.* 1. so small as to be invisible or obscure except through a microscope 2. of or with a microscope —**mi′croscop′ically** *adv.*

microstructure (mī′krō struk′chər) *n.* the structure as of a metal or alloy, seen under a microscope

microwave (mī′krō wāv′) *n.* an electromagnetic wave between 300 000 and 300 megahertz in frequency

microwave oven an oven which cooks food very rapidly by use of microwaves

micturate (mik′tyoo rāt′) *vi.* **-rat′ed, -rat′ing** [< L. *mingere*] to urinate —**mic′-turi′tion** *n.*

mid[1] (mid) *adj.* [OE. *midd*] same as MIDDLE

mid[2] *prep.* [Poet.] amid: also **'mid**

midair *n.* any point in space, not in contact with the ground or other surface

midday *n.* [OE. *middæg*] the middle part of the day; noon —*adj.* of midday

middelskot (mid′′l skot′) *n.* in South Africa, an intermediate payment to a farmers' cooperative for a crop or wool clip

midden (mid′′n) *n.* [prob. < Scand.] a dunghill or refuse heap

middle (mid′′l) *adj.* [OE. *middel*] 1. halfway between two given points, times, limits, etc. 2. in between; intermediate 3. [M-] *Geol.* designating a division, as of a period, between *Upper* and *Lower* 4. [M-] *Linguis.* in a stage in language development intermediate between *Old* and *Modern* —*n.* 1. a point or part halfway between extremes; middle point, time, etc. 2. the waist

middle age the time of life between youth and old age: now from about 40 to about 65 —**mid′dle-aged′** *adj.*

Middle Ages the period of European history between ancient and modern times

middle C the musical note of the first leger line below the treble staff and the first above the bass staff

middle class the social class between the aristocracy and the working class —**mid′dle-class′** *adj.*

middle ear the eardrum and the adjacent cavity containing the hammer, the anvil, and the stirrup bones

Middle East the area from Afghanistan to Egypt, including Arabia, Cyprus, and Asiatic Turkey

Middle English the English language c. 1100 to c. 1500

Middle French the French language c. 1300 to c. 1500

Middle Greek same as MEDIEVAL GREEK

Middle High German the High German language c. 1100 to c. 1500

Middle Latin *same as* MEDIEVAL LATIN

Middle Low German the Low German language c. 1100 to c. 1500

middleman *n.* 1. a trader who buys from the producer and sells to the retailer or, sometimes, the consumer 2. an intermediary

middle name 1. the name between a Christian name and a surname 2. the characteristic, peculiarity, or character of a person [modesty was his *middle name*]

middle-of-the-road *adj.* avoiding extremes

middle school a school for children between 10 and 14

middleweight *n.* *see* BOXING AND WRESTLING WEIGHTS, table

middling *adj.* of middle size, quality, grade, state, etc.; medium —*adv.* [Colloq.] moderately

Middx. Middlesex

midfield *n.* *Soccer* the area of the pitch between the penalty areas —*adj.* of the midfield

midge (mij) *n.* [OE. *mycg*] 1. a small, two-winged, gnatlike insect 2. a very small person

midget (mij′it) *n.* 1. a very small person 2. anything very small of its kind —*adj.* very small of its kind

mid heavyweight *see* BOXING AND WRESTLING WEIGHTS, table

midi (mid′ē) *adj.* [< MID[1], after MINI-] [Colloq.] of clothing reaching to below the knee or midcalf

midland *n.* the middle region of a country —*adj.* 1. of or in the midland 2. [M-] of the Midlands —**the Midlands** region in WC England, around Birmingham

midnight *n.* twelve o'clock at night —*adj.* of or at midnight —**burn the midnight oil** to study or work very late at night

midnight sun the sun visible at midnight in the arctic or antarctic regions during the summer

mid-off *n.* *Cricket* the fielding position close to and on the bowler's left, when the batsman is right-handed

mid-on *n.* *Cricket* the fielding position close to and on the bowler's right, when the batsman is right-handed

midriff (mid′rif) *n.* [< OE. *midd*, mid + *hrif*, belly] 1. the middle part of the torso 2. *same as* DIAPHRAGM

midshipman *n.* *see* MILITARY RANKS, table

midships *adv.* *same as* AMIDSHIPS

midst (midst) *n.* the middle; central part —**in our** (or **your, their**) **midst** among us (or you, them) —**in the midst of** 1. in the middle of 2. during

midsummer *n.* the middle of summer, about June 21 —*adj.* of, in, or like midsummer

Midsummer's Day June 24, feast of St. John the Baptist

midway *adj., adv.* in the middle

midweek *n., adj.* (in) the middle of the week

mid-wicket *n.* *Cricket* the fielding

position opposite the middle of the wicket and usually near the boundary

midwife (mid′wīf′) *n., pl.* **-wives'** (-wīvz′) [OE. *mid*, with + *wif*, woman] a woman who is trained to help women in childbirth —**mid′wif′ery** (-wif′ə rē) *n.*

midwinter *n.* the middle of the winter, about December 22 —*adj.* of, in, or like midwinter

M.I.E.E. Member of the Institution of Electrical Engineers

mien (mēn) *n.* [< DEMEANOUR] 1. a way of conducting oneself; manner 2. a way of looking; appearance

might[1] (mīt) *v.* [OE. *mihte*] 1. *pt. of* MAY 2. an auxiliary generally equivalent to *may* [it *might* rain]

might[2] *n.* [OE. *miht*] great strength, power, force, or vigour

might-have-been *n.* a past possibility, esp., a person who might have achieved more in his field or profession

mighty *adj.* [OE. *mihtig*] **-ier, -iest** 1. powerful; strong 2. remarkably large, extensive, etc. —*adv.* [Colloq.] very —**might′ily** *adv.* —**might′iness** *n.*

mignonette (min′yə net′) *n.* [Fr.] a plant bearing spikes of small, fragrant flowers

migraine (mē′grān) *n.* [< Gr. *hēmi-*, half + *kranion*, skull] a type of intense, periodically returning headache

migrant (mī′grənt) *adj.* migrating —*n.* a person, bird, or animal that migrates

migrate (mī grāt′) *vi.* **-grat′ed, -grat′ing** [< L. *migrare*] 1. to move from one place to another, esp. to another country 2. to move from one region to another with the change in seasons, as many birds —**migra′tion** *n.* —**migratory** (mī′grə tər ē) *adj.*

mikado (mi kä′dō) *n., pl.* **-dos** [Jap.] [*often* M-] the emperor of Japan: title no longer used

mike (mīk) *n.* [Colloq.] a microphone

mil (mil) *n.* [< L. *mille*, thousand] a unit of length, 1/1000 inch, used in measuring the diameter of wire

milady (mi lā′dē) *n.* [*my lady*] an English noblewoman

milage (mīl′ij) *n.* *alt. sp. of* MILEAGE

milch (milch) *adj.* [OE. *-milce*] giving milk; kept for milking

mild (mīld) *adj.* [OE. *milde*] 1. a) gentle or kind in disposition, action, or effect b) not extreme; moderate [a *mild* winter] 2. having a pleasant flavour; not strong, bitter, etc. —*n.* mild ale

mildew (mil′dyōo′) *n.* [OE. *meledeaw*, lit., honeydew] a fungus that attacks plants or appears on damp cloth, etc. as a furry, whitish coating —*vt., vi.* to affect or become affected with mildew —**mil′dew′y** *adj.*

mild steel malleable steel with a low carbon content

mile (mīl) *n.* [< L. *milia* (*passuum*), thousand (paces)] a unit of linear measure, equal to 1760 yards (1609.35 metres): in full, **statute mile**

mileage *n.* **1.** a distance expressed in miles **2.** total number of miles travelled **3.** an allowance per mile for travelling expenses **4.** the number of miles a vehicle will go on one gallon of fuel **5.** [Colloq.] the amount of use one can get from something

milepost *n.* a signpost showing the distance in miles from a specified place

miler *n.* one who competes in mile races

milestone *n.* **1.** a stone set up as a milepost **2.** a significant event in history, in one's career, etc.

milfoil (mil′foil′) *n.* [< L. *millefolium*, thousand-leaved] *same as* YARROW

milieu (mēl′yur) *n.*, *pl.* **-lieus′** [Fr.] environment; esp., social setting

militant (mil′i tənt) *adj.* [< L. *miles*, a soldier] **1.** ready to fight; vigorous in support of a cause **2.** fighting —*n.* a militant person —**mil′itancy** *n.* —**mil′itantly** *adv.*

militarism (mil′ə tər iz′m) *n.* **1.** military spirit **2.** the policy of maintaining a strong military organization in aggressive preparedness for war —**mil′itaris′tic** *adj.*

militarize *vt.* **-rized′**, **-riz′ing 1.** to equip for war **2.** to fill with warlike spirit —**mil′itariza′tion** *n.*

military (mil′ə tər ē) *adj.* [see MILITANT] **1.** of, for, or by soldiers or the armed forces **2.** of, for, or fit for war —**the military** the army or the armed forces —**mil′itarily** *adv.*

militate (mil′ə tāt′) *vi.* **-tat′ed**, **-tat′ing** [see MILITANT] to be directed (*against*); operate (*against* or, rarely, *for*)

militia (mə lish′ə) *n.* [L.: see MILITANT] any army composed of civilians rather than professional soldiers, called up in time of emergency —**mili′tiaman** *n.*

milk (milk) *n.* [OE. *meolc*] **1.** a white liquid secreted by the mammary glands of female mammals for suckling their young **2.** cow's milk, etc. drunk by humans **3.** any liquid like this [*coconut milk*] —*vt.* **1.** to draw milk from the mammary glands of (a cow, etc.) **2.** to extract (something) or extract something (from) as if by milking [*to milk a rich uncle for his money*] —**milk′er** *n.* —**milk′ing** *n.*

milk and honey being prosperous; easy circumstances

milk-and-water *adj.* insipid; weak

milk float a shallow cart usually powered by batteries and used for delivering milk

milkmaid *n.* a woman who milks cows or works in a dairy

MILITARY RANKS

NAVY	ARMY	MARINES	AIR FORCE
Commissioned			
Admiral of the Fleet	Field Marshal		Marshal of the Royal Air Force
Admiral	General	General	Air Chief Marshal
Vice-Admiral	Lieutenant-General	Lieutenant-General	Air Marshal
Rear-Admiral	Major-General	Major-General	Air Vice-Marshal
Commodore	Brigadier	Brigadier	Air Commodore
Captain	Colonel	Colonel	Group Captain
Commander	Lieutenant-Colonel	Lieutenant-Colonel	Wing Commander
Lieutenant-Commander	Major	Major	Squadron Leader
Lieutenant	Captain	Captain	Flight Lieutenant
Sub-Lieutenant Acting Sub-Lieutenant [1]	Lieutenant	Lieutenant	Flying Officer
Midshipman [2]	Second-Lieutenant	Acting Lieutenant [3] Second-Lieutenant	Pilot Officer Acting Pilot Officer [4]
Noncommissioned			
Fleet Chief Petty Officer	Warrant Officer I Warrant Officer II [5]	Warrant Officer I Warrant Officer II [5]	Master Aircrew } Warrant Officer
Chief Petty Officer	Staff Corporal Staff Sergeant	Colour Sergeant	Flight Sergeant Chief Technician
Petty Officer	Corporal of Horse Sergeant	Sergeant	Sergeant
	Corporal	Corporal	Corporal
Leading Rating [6]	Bombardier Lance Corporal [7]		
Able Rating Ordinary Rating	Private Trooper Gunner etc	Marine	Junior Technician Senior Aircraftman Leading Aircraftman

[1] But Junior to Lieutenant and Flying Officer
[2] But Junior to Army and Air Force Ranks
[3] But Senior to Second-Lieutenant and Pilot Officer
[4] But Junior to Second-Lieutenant

[5] But Junior to Navy and Air Force Ranks
[6] But Junior to Corporal
[7] But Junior to Corporal and Leading Rating

milkman *n.* a man who sells or delivers milk

milk of magnesia a milky-white suspension of magnesium hydroxide, in water, used as an antacid

milk run [Slang] a routine mission, as of a bomber aircraft, not expected to be dangerous

milkshake *n.* a drink made of milk, flavouring, and, usually, ice cream, mixed until frothy

milksop *n.* an unmanly man or boy; sissy

milk tooth any of the temporary, first set of teeth

milkweed *n.* any of a group of plants with a milky juice

milky *adj.* -ier, -iest 1. like milk; esp., white as milk 2. of or containing milk 3. cloudy; not clear : said of liquids —**milk'i-ness** *n.*

Milky Way a broad, faint band of light seen as an arch across the sky at night, created by billions of distant stars

mill (mil) *n.* [< L. *mola*, millstone] 1. a factory *[a textile mill]* 2. any of various machines for cutting, stamping, shaping, etc. 3. a machine for grinding any solid material 4. *a*) a building with machinery for grinding corn *b*) a machine for grinding corn —*vt.* 1. grind, work, form, etc. by or in a mill 2. to raise and ridge the edge of (a coin) —*vi.* to move slowly in a circle, as cattle, or aimlessly, as a confused crowd (*around* or *about*) —**through the mill** [Colloq.] through a hard, painful, instructive experience —**milled** *adj.*

milldam *n.* a dam built across a stream to raise its level enough to provide water power for turning a mill wheel

millennium (mi len'ē əm) *n., pl.* -niums, -nia [< L. *mille*, thousand + *annus*, year] 1. a period of 1000 years 2. [*also* M-] *Theol.* the period of a thousand years during which some believe Christ will reign on earth 3. a future period of peace and happiness —**millen'nial** *adj.*

millepede (mil'ə pēd') *n.* same as MILLIPEDE

miller (mil'ər) *n.* 1. a person who owns or operates a mill, esp. a corn mill 2. a tool used for milling

miller's-thumb *n.* any of several small freshwater fishes with spiny fins and a broad, flat head

millesimal (mi les'ə m'l) *adj.* [L. *millesimus*] 1. thousandth 2. consisting of thousandths —*n.* a thousandth

millet (mil'it) *n.* [< L. *milium*] a cereal grass whose small grain is used for food in Europe and Asia

mill hand a person employed in a factory or mill

milli- [< L.] *a combining form meaning* a 1000th part of

milliard (mil'yärd') *n.* [Fr. < prec.] 1000 millions

milligram *n.* one thousandth of a gram

millilitre *n.* one thousandth of a litre

millimetre *n.* one thousandth of a metre

milliner (mil'ə nər) *n.* [< *Milaner*, importer of dress wares from Milan] a person who designs, makes, trims, or sells women's hats —**mil'linery** *n.*

milling *prp. of* MILL —*n.* 1. the process or business of grinding corn 2. the grinding, cutting, or processing of metal, cloth, etc. in a mill

million (mil'yən) *n., adj.* [< L. *mille*, thousand] 1. a thousand thousands; 10^6; over 1000000 2. very many —**mil'lionth** *adj., n.*

millionaire (mil'yə nãar') *n.* [< Fr.] a person worth at least a million pounds, francs, dollars etc.

millipede (mil'ə pēd') *n.* [< L. *mille*, thousand + *pes*, foot] a many-legged arthropod

millpond *n.* a pond from which water flows for driving a mill wheel

millrace *n.* the current of water that drives a mill wheel

millstone *n.* 1. either of a pair of large, flat, round stones between which grain is ground 2. a heavy burden

mill wheel the wheel, usually a water wheel, that drives the machinery in a mill

milometer (mīl'om'ə tər) *n.* an instrument used to determine how many miles a vehicle has travelled

milord (mi lôrd') *n.* [*my lord*] an English nobleman

milt (milt) *n.* [prob. < Scand.] the reproductive glands or sperm of male fishes

mime (mīm) *n.* [< Gr. *mimos*] the representation of an action, character, mood, etc. by gestures rather than words —*vt.* mimed, mim'ing to mimic or act as a mime —**mim'er** *n.*

M.I.Mech.E. Member of the Institution of Mechanical Engineers

mimeograph (mim'ē ə gräf') *n.* [< Gr. *mimeomai*, I imitate + -GRAPH] a machine for making copies of written or typewritten matter by means of a stencil —*vt.* to make (copies) on such a machine

mimetic (mi met'ik) *adj.* [< Gr. *mimeisthai*, imitate] 1. imitative 2. characterized by mimicry

mimic (mim'ik) *n.* [< Gr. *mimos*, a mime] a person or thing that imitates —*vt.* mim'-icked, mim'icking 1. to imitate in speech or action, as in ridicule 2. to copy closely 3. to take on the appearance of —**mim'-icker** *n.* —**mim'icry**

M.I.Min.E. Member of the Institution of Mining Engineers

mimosa (mi mō'zə) *n.* [< L. *mimus*, mime] a tree or shrub growing in warm regions, with heads of small, round flowers

Min. 1. Minister 2. Ministry

min. 1. minim(s) 2. minimum 3. minute(s)

mina (mī'nə) *n.* same as MYNA: also sp. **mi'nah**

MINARET

minaret (min'əret') *n.* [Fr. < Ar. *manārah*, lighthouse] a high tower attached to a mosque from which a muezzin calls the people to prayer

minatory (min'ətər ē) *adj.* [< L. *minari*, threaten] menacing; threatening

mince (mins) *vt.* minced, minc'ing [ult. < L. *minutus*, small] 1. to cut up into very small pieces 2. to lessen the force of [to *mince* words] —*vi.* to speak, act, or walk in an affected, dainty manner —*n.* minced meat —**not mince matters** to speak frankly —**minc'er** *n.*

mincemeat *n.* a mixture of chopped apples, spices, suet, raisins, etc. —**make mincemeat of** to defeat or refute completely

mince pie a pie with a filling of mincemeat

mincing *adj.* 1. affectedly elegant or dainty 2. with short steps or affected daintiness [a *mincing* walk]

mind (mīnd) *n.* [OE. (ge)*mynd*] 1. that which thinks, perceives, feels, etc.; the seat of consciousness 2. memory or remembrance [to bring to *mind*] 3. opinion [speak your *mind*] 4. reason; sanity [to lose one's *mind*] 5. a person having intelligence [great *minds*] 6. way of thinking and feeling [the reactionary *mind*] —*vt.* 1. to pay attention to; heed 2. [Chiefly U.S.] to obey 3. to look after [*mind* the baby] 4. to be careful about [*mind* those stairs] 5. a) to care about; feel concern about b) to object to; dislike [to *mind* the cold] —*vi.* 1. to pay attention 2. to be careful 3. a) to care b) to object —**bear** (or **keep**) **in mind** to remember —**be in one's right mind** to be sane —**be in two minds** to be undecided or irresolute —**change one's mind** to change one's opinion or intention —**come to mind** 1. to occur to 2. to be remembered —**do you mind?** 1. do you object? 2. [Colloq.] please stop that —**give (someone) a piece of one's mind** to rebuke sharply —**have a (good) mind to** to feel (strongly) inclined to —**have in mind** 1. to intend 2. to think of 3. to remember —**know one's own mind** to know one's own real desires, etc. —**make up one's mind** to form a decision —**mind out** 1. to be careful 2. to pay attention —**mind your backs** give way —**never mind** it doesn't matter —**on one's mind** 1. occupying one's thoughts 2. worrying one —**out of one's mind** 1.

insane 2. frantic (*with* worry, grief, etc.) —**take one's mind off** to turn one's thoughts or attention from —**mind'er** *n.*

minded *adj.* 1. having a (specified kind of) mind [high-*minded*] 2. inclined; disposed

mindful *adj.* aware or careful (*of*) —**mind'fully** *adv.*

mindless *adj.* 1. showing little or no intelligence; thoughtless 2. heedless (*of*) —**mind'lessly** *adv.*

mind reader one who professes to be able to perceive another's thoughts —**mind reading**

mind's eye the imagination

mine¹ (mīn) *pron.* [OE. *min*] that or those belonging to me [this is *mine*, *mine* are better] —**possessive pronominal adj.** [Mainly Archaic] my [*mine* eyes, daughter *mine*]

mine² *n.* [< MFr.] 1. a) a large excavation made in the earth, from which to extract ores, coal, etc. b) a deposit of ore, coal, etc. 2. any great source of supply [a *mine* of information] 3. Mil. a) a tunnel dug under an enemy's fort, etc., in which an explosive is placed b) an explosive charge in a container, buried in the ground or placed in the sea for destroying enemy troops, ships, etc. —*vt.*, *vi.* mined, min'ing 1. to dig (ores, coal, etc.) from (the earth) 2. to place explosive mines in or under (a place)

mine detector an electromagnetic device for locating the position of hidden explosive mines

mine-dump *n.* [S Afr.] large mounds of residue esp. from gold mining operations

mine field an area where explosive mines have been set

minelayer *n.* a ship equipped to lay explosive mines

miner *n.* a person whose work is digging coal, ore, etc. in a mine

mineral (min'ər əl) *n.* [< ML. *minera*, a mine] 1. an inorganic substance occurring naturally in the earth: sometimes applied to organic substances in the earth, such as coal 2. an ore 3. any substance that is neither vegetable nor animal 4. any of certain elements, as iron, vital to animals and plants —*adj.* of, like, or containing minerals

mineralogy (min'ə ral'ə jē) *n.* the scientific study of minerals —**min'eral'ogist** *n.*

mineral water water naturally or artificially impregnated with mineral salts or gases

minestrone (min'i strō'nē) *n.* [It.] a thick vegetable soup containing vermicelli, barley, etc. in a meat broth

mine sweeper a ship for destroying enemy mines

Ming (miŋ) Chin. dynasty (1368-1644): period noted for scholarly achievements and artistic works, esp. porcelain

mingle (miŋ'g'l) *vt.* -gled, -gling [< OE. *mengan*, mix] to mix together; blend —*vi.* 1. to become mixed, blended, etc. 2. to join with others —**min'gler** *n.*

mingy (min′jē) *adj.* **-gier, -giest** [< MEAN² & STINGY] [Colloq.] mean and stingy; miserly

mini- [< MINI(ATURE)] *a combining form meaning:* **1.** very small [*miniskirt*] **2.** less than usual [*mini-crisis*]

miniature (min′ə chər) *n.* [< L. *minium*, red lead] **1.** a copy or model on a very small scale **2.** a very small painting, esp. a portrait **3.** on or done on a very small scale **—in miniature** greatly reduced **—min′iaturist** *n.*

miniaturize *vt.* **-ized′, -iz′ing** to make in a small and compact form **—min′iatur′iza′tion** *n.*

minibus (min′ē bus′) *n.* a small bus for about ten passengers

minicab (min′ē kab′) *n.* a small saloon car used as a taxi

minim (min′im) *n.* [see MINIMUM] **1.** the smallest liquid measure, 1/60 fluid dram, or about a drop **2.** *Music* a note having one half the duration of a semibreve

minimize (min′ə mīz′) *vt.* **-mized′, -miz′ing 1.** to reduce to or estimate at the least possible amount, degree, etc. **2.** to depreciate; undervalue

minimum (min′ə məm) *n., pl.* **-ma** [L. < *minimus*, least] **1.** the smallest quantity, number, or degree possible or permissible **2.** the lowest degree or point reached or recorded **—adj. 1.** smallest possible, permissible, or reached **2.** of, marking, or setting a minimum **—min′imal** *adj.* **—min′imally** *adv.*

minimum lending rate the minimum rate at which the Bank of England lends money: it influences other lending rates

minimum wage a wage established by contract or by law as the lowest that may be paid to employees doing a specified type of work

mining (mī′niŋ) *n.* the act, process, or work of removing ores, coal, etc. from a mine

minion (min′yən) *n.* [< Fr. *mignon*, darling] **1.** a subordinate official **2.** [Derog.] a favourite, esp. a servile follower

miniskirt (min′ē skurt′) *n.* [MINI- + SKIRT] a very short skirt ending well above the knee

minister (min′is tər) *n.* [< L. *minister*, servant] **1.** a person in charge of some governmental department **2.** a diplomatic officer sent to a foreign nation to represent his government **3.** a clergyman, esp. of the Presbyterian and Nonconformist Churches **4.** any person or thing thought of as the agent of some power, force, etc. [a *minister* of evil] **—vi.** to give help (*to*)

ministerial (min′is tēər′ē əl) *adj.* of a minister or (the) ministry **—min′iste′rially** *adv.*

Minister of State 1. a government minister other than a cabinet minister **2.** any government minister

Minister of the Crown a cabinet minister

ministrant *adj.* serving as a minister;

ministering **—n.** a person who ministers, or serves

ministration (min′is trā′shən) *n.* **1.** help or care **2.** the act of serving as a minister or clergyman

ministry (min′is trē) *n., pl.* **-tries 1.** the act of ministering **2.** a) the office or function of a minister of religion b) such ministers collectively; clergy **3.** a) the department under a minister of government b) his term of office c) his headquarters d) such ministers collectively

miniver (min′i vər) *n.* [< OFr. *menu*, small + *vair*, fur] a white fur used for trimming ceremonial robes

MINK (43-70 cm long, including tail)

mink (miŋk) *n.* [< Scand.] **1.** a small, stoatlike mammal **2.** its valuable fur

minnow (min′ō) *n.* [< OE. *myne*] a small freshwater fish

Minoan (mi nō′ən) *adj.* [< *Minos*, a king of Crete, in Greek Mythology] designating an advanced prehistoric culture in Crete from c. 2800 to c. 1100 B.C.

minor (mī′nər) *adj.* [L.] **1.** lesser in size, amount, importance, or rank **2.** under full legal age **3.** *Music* a) designating an interval smaller than the corresponding major by a semitone b) characterized by minor intervals, scales, etc. c) based on the minor scale **—vi.** [U.S.] *Educ.* to pursue a secondary specialization **—n. 1.** a person under full legal age **2.** [U.S.] *Educ.* a minor field of study

minority (mī nor′ə tē) *n., pl.* **-ties 1.** the smaller number; less than half **2.** a racial, religious, or political group smaller than and differing from the larger, controlling group **3.** the period of being under full legal age

minor scale one of the two standard diatonic scales, with semi tones instead of whole tones, after the second and seventh notes (**melodic minor scale**) or after the second, fifth, and seventh notes (**harmonic minor scale**), in ascending order

minster (min′stər) *n.* [< L. *monasterium*, monastery] **1.** the church of a monastery **2.** any of various large churches or cathedrals

minstrel (min′strəl) *n.* [< L. *ministerium*, ministry] **1.** a travelling singer of the Middle Ages **2.** a member of a comic variety show, in which the performers blacken their faces

minstrelsy *n., pl.* **-sies 1.** the art of a minstrel **2.** a group of minstrels **3.** a collection of minstrels' songs

mint¹ (mint) *n.* [< L. *Moneta*, epithet of Juno, in whose temple money was coined] **1.** a place where money is coined by the government **2.** a large amount [a *mint* of ideas] **—adj.** new, as if freshly minted *[in mint condition]* —*vt.* **1.** to coin (money) **2.** to create —**mint′er** *n.*

mint² *n.* [OE. *minte*] **1.** a plant with leaves used for flavouring **2.** a sweet flavoured with mint

minuend (min′yōō wend′) *n.* [see MINUTE²] *Arith.* the number from which another is to be subtracted

minuet (min′yōō wet′) *n.* [< Fr. *menu*, small: from the small steps taken] **1.** a slow, stately dance of the 17th and 18th cent. **2.** the music for this, in 3/4 time

minus (mī′nəs) *prep.* [< L. *minor*, less] **1.** less *[four minus two]* **2.** [Colloq.] without *[minus a toe]* —*adj.* **1.** indicating subtraction *[a minus sign]* **2.** negative *[a minus quantity]* **3.** somewhat less than *[a mark of A minus]* **4.** *Elec.* same as NEGATIVE *[the minus terminal]* —*n.* **1.** a minus sign **2.** a negative quantity

minuscule (min′ə skyōōl′) *adj.* [< L. *minusculus*] very small

minus sign *Math.* a sign (–) indicating subtraction or negative quantity

minute¹ (min′it) *n.* [< L. (*pars*) *minuta* (*prima*), (first) small (part)] **1.** the sixtieth part of an hour or of a degree of an arc **2.** a moment **3.** a specific point in time **4.** a measure of the distance covered in a minute *[ten minutes from the centre]* **5.** *[pl.]* an official record of what was said at a meeting —*vt.* **-uted, -uting** to make minutes of; record —**up to the minute** in the latest fashion

minute² (mī nyōōt′) *adj.* [< L. *minuere*, lessen] **1.** very small **2.** trifling **3.** attentive to tiny details; precise

minute hand (min′it) the longer hand of a clock or watch, which indicates the minutes

minute steak (min′it) a small, thin steak that can be cooked quickly

minutiae (mī nyōō′shi ē′) *n.pl., sing.* **-tia** [L.: see MINUTE²] small or relatively unimportant details

minx (miŋks) *n.* [< ?] a pert, saucy young woman

Miocene (mī′ō sēn′) *adj.* [< Gr. *meiōn*, less + *kainos*, recent] designating the fourth epoch of the Tertiary Period in the Cainozoic Era

miracle (mir′ə k'l) *n.* [< L. *mirus*, wonderful] **1.** an event or action that apparently contradicts known scientific laws *[the miracles in the Bible]* **2.** a remarkable thing **3.** a wonderful example *[a miracle of tact]*

miracle play a medieval religious drama dealing with events in the lives of the saints

miraculous (mi rak′yōō ləs) *adj.* **1.** like a miracle; marvellous **2.** supernatural —**mirac′ulously** *adv.*

mirage (mi′räzh) *n.* [< L. *mirari*, wonder at] **1.** an optical illusion in which a distant object is made to appear nearby: it is caused by the refraction of light through layers of air of different temperatures **2.** something that falsely appears to be real

mire (mīər) *n.* [< ON. *myrr*] **1.** an area of wet, soggy ground **2.** deep mud —*vt.* **mired, mir′ing 1.** to cause to get stuck in or as in mire **2.** to soil with mud or dirt

mirror (mir′ər) *n.* [< L. *mirari*, wonder at] **1.** a smooth surface that reflects images; esp., a looking glass **2.** anything that truly pictures or describes *[a play that is a mirror of life]* —*vt.* to reflect as in a mirror

mirror image an image as seen in a mirror, i.e., with the right side as though it were the left, and vice versa

mirth (murth) *n.* [< OE. *myrig*, pleasant] joyfulness or gaiety, esp. when characterized by laughter —**mirth′ful** *adj.*

miry (mīər′ē) *adj.* **-ier, -iest 1.** swampy **2.** muddy

mis- [< OE. or OFr.] a prefix meaning: **1.** wrong(ly), bad(ly) *[misplace, misrule]* **2.** no, not *[mistrust, misfire]*

misadventure (mis′əd ven′chər) *n.* an unlucky accident; bad luck; mishap

misalliance (mis′ə lī′əns) *n.* an improper alliance; esp., an unsuitable marriage

misanthrope (miz′ən thrōp′) *n.* [< Gr. *misein*, to hate + *anthrōpos*, man] one who hates or distrusts all people: also **mizanthropist** (miz an′thrə pist) —**mis′anthrop′ic** (-throp′ik) *adj.* —**mis′anthrop′ically** *adv.*

misanthropy (miz an′thrə pē) *n.* hatred or distrust of all people

misapply (mis′ə plī′) *vt.* **-plied′, -ply′ing** to apply or use badly or improperly —**mis′applica′tion** *n.*

misappropriate (mis′ə prō′prē āt′) *vt.* **-at′ed, -at′ing** to appropriate to a bad or dishonest use —**mis′appro′pria′tion** *n.*

misbegotten (mis′bi got′'n) *adj.* wrongly or unlawfully begotten; specif., born out of wedlock: also **mis′begot′**

misbehave (mis′bi hāv′) *vt., vi.* **-haved′, -hav′ing** to behave (oneself) improperly —**mis′behav′iour** *n.*

miscalculate (mis kal′kyōō lāt′) *vt., vi.* **-lat′ed, -lat′ing** to calculate incorrectly; misjudge —**mis′calcula′tion** *n.*

miscarriage (mis′kar′ij) *n.* **1.** the expulsion of a foetus from the womb before it is sufficiently developed to survive **2.** failure to carry out what was intended *[a miscarriage of justice]* **3.** failure of post, etc. to reach its destination

miscarry (mis′kar′ē) *vi.* **-ried, -rying 1.** to suffer a miscarriage of a foetus **2.** a) to go wrong; fail: said of a plan, project, etc. b) to go astray: said of post

miscegenation (mis′i jə nā′shən) *n.* [< L. *miscere*, mix + *genus*, race] sexual relations between a man and a woman of different races, esp. between a white and a black

miscellaneous (mis′ə lā′nē əs) *adj.* [< L. *miscere*, mix] consisting of various kinds; varied; mixed

miscellany (mi sel′ə nē) *n., pl.* **-nies** [see prec.] a miscellaneous collection, esp. of literary works

mischance (mis′chäns′) *n.* bad luck; misadventure

mischief (mis′chif) *n.* [< OFr. *mes-*, *mis-* + *chief*, end] **1.** a) a prank; playful, annoying trick *b*) playful teasing **2.** a tendency to annoy with playful tricks **3.** an action or a person causing damage or annoyance **4.** harm or damage, esp. that done by a person —**do (someone) a mischief** to injure, wound or kill

mischief-maker *n.* a person who causes mischief; esp. by gossiping —**mis′chief-mak′ing** *n., adj.*

mischievous (mis′chi vəs) *adj.* **1.** inclined to annoy with playful tricks **2.** prankish; teasing **3.** causing mischief; harmful —**mis′chievously** *adv.*

miscible (mis′ə b'l) *adj.* [< L. *miscere*, mix] that can be mixed —**mis′cibil′ity** *n.*

misconceive (mis′kən sēv′) *vt., vi.* -ceived′, -ceiv′ing to misunderstand —**mis′concep′tion** (-sep′shən) *n.*

misconduct (mis kon′dukt) *n.* **1.** bad or dishonest management **2.** improper behaviour

misconstrue (mis′kən strōō′) *vt.* -strued′,-stru′ing to misinterpret —**mis′-construc′tion** (-struk′shən) *n.*

miscount (mis kount′; *for n. usually* mis′-kount) *vt., vi.* to count incorrectly —*n.* an incorrect count

miscreant (mis′krē ənt) *adj.* [< OFr. *mes-, mis-* + *croire*, believe] villainous; evil —*n.* a criminal; villain

misdeal (mis′dēl′) *vt., vi.* -dealt′, -deal′-ing to deal (playing cards) wrongly —*n.* a wrong deal —**mis′deal′er** *n.*

misdeed (mis′dēd′) *n.* a wrong or wicked act

misdemeanour (mis′di mēn′ər) *n.* **1.** a misbehaving **2.** *Law* any minor offence for which, formerly, statute provided a lesser punishment than for a felony

misdirect (mis′də rekt′) *vt.* to direct wrongly

misdoubt (mis′dout′) *vt., vi.* [Archaic] to distrust; fear

‡**mise en scène** (mē zän sān′) [Fr.] **1.** the setting of a play, film, etc. **2.** surroundings; environment

miser (mī′zər) *n.* [L., wretched] a stingy person who hoards money for its own sake —**mi′serly** *adj.*

miserable (miz′ər ə b'l) *adj.* **1.** in misery; wretched **2.** causing misery, discomfort, etc. [*miserable* weather] **3.** bad [a *miserable* performance] **4.** pitiable **5.** shameful —**mis′erableness** *n.* —**mis′era-bly** *adv.*

misericord, misericorde (miz er′ə kôrd′) *n.* [< L. *misere*, pity + *cor*, heart] a narrow ledge on the underside of a hinged seat in a choir stall offering support to the occupant when standing

misery (miz′ər ē) *n., pl.* -eries [< L. *miser*, wretched] **1.** a condition of great suffering; distress **2.** a cause of such suffering; pain, sorrow, poverty, squalor, etc.

misfeasance (mis fē′zəns) *n.* [< OFr. *mes-, mis-* + *faire*, do] *Law* wrongdoing; specif., the doing of a lawful act in an unlawful manner

misfire (mis′fīər′) *vi.* -fired′, -fir′ing **1.** to fail to ignite properly : said of an internal-combustion engine **2.** to fail to be discharged : said of a firearm, missile, etc. **3.** to fail to achieve the desired effect —*n.* a misfiring

misfit (mis′fit′) *n.* **1.** a person not suited to his position, associates, etc. **2.** a garment, etc. that fits badly

misfortune (mis fôr′chən) *n.* **1.** bad luck; trouble; adversity **2.** an instance of this

misgive (mis′giv′) *vt.* -gave′, -giv′en, -giv′ing to cause fear, doubt, or suspicion in [his heart *misgave* him]

misgiving *n.* [*often pl.*] a disturbed feeling of fear, doubt, apprehension, etc.

misgovern (mis′guv′ərn) *vt.* to govern or administer badly

misguide (mis′gīd′) *vt.* -guid′ed, -guid′-ing to lead into error or misconduct; mislead —**misguid′ed** *adj.*

mishandle (mis′han′d'l) *vt.* -dled, -dling to handle badly or roughly; abuse, mismanage, etc.

mishap (mis′hap′) *n.* an unlucky accident

mishit (mis′hit′) *n. Sport* a faulty shot or stroke —*vt.* (mis′hit′) -hit′ting, -hit′ to hit a ball with a faulty stroke

mishmash (mish′mash′) *n.* a hotchpotch; jumble

misinform (mis′in fôrm′) *vt.* to supply with false or misleading information —**mis′informa′tion** *n.*

misinterpret (mis′in tur′prit) *vt.* to understand or explain incorrectly —**mis′in-ter′preta′tion** *n.*

misjudge (mis′juj′) *vt., vi.* -judged′, -judg′ing to judge wrongly or unfairly —**misjudg′ment, misjudge′ment** *n.*

mislay (mis′lā′) *vt.* -laid′, -lay′ing to put in a place afterwards forgotten

mislead (mis′lēd′) *vt.* -led′, -lead′ing **1.** to lead in a wrong direction **2.** to deceive or delude **3.** to lead into wrongdoing —**mis-lead′ing** *adj.* —**mislead′ingly** *adv.*

mismanage (mis′man′ij) *vt.* -aged, -aging to manage or administer badly —**misman′agement** *n.*

misnomer (mis nō′mər) *n.* [< OFr. *mes-, mis-* + *nomer*, to name] a name or epithet wrongly used

misogamy (mi sog′ə mē) *n.* [< Gr. *misein*, to hate + *gamos*, marriage] hatred of marriage —**misog′amist** *n.*

misogyny (mi soj′ə nē) *n.* [< Gr. *misein*, to hate + *gynē*, woman] hatred of women —**misog′ynist** *n.*

misplace (mis′plās′) *vt.* -placed′, -plac′-ing **1.** to put in a wrong place **2.** to bestow (one's trust, affection, etc.) unwisely **3.** *same as* MISLAY —**mis′place′ment** *n.*

misprint (mis′print′; *for n. usually* mis′-print′) *vt.* to print incorrectly —*n.* an error in printing

misprision (mis′prizh′ən) *n.* [< OFr. *mesprendre*, take wrongly] *Law* misconduct or neglect of duty, esp. by a public official

misprision of felony (or **treason**) *Law* the offence of concealing knowledge of another's felony (or treason)

mispronounce (mis′prə nouns′) *vt., vi.* -nounced′, -nounc′ing to give (a word) a pronunciation different from the accepted pronunciations —**mis'pronun'cia'tion** (-nun'sē ā'shən) *n.*

misquote (mis'kwōt') *vt., vi.* **-quot'ed, -quot'ing** to quote incorrectly —**mis'quo-ta'tion** *n.*

misread (mis'rēd') *vt., vi.* **-read'** (-red'), **-read'ing** to read wrongly; misunderstand

misrepresent (mis'rep ri zent') *vt.* to represent falsely; give an untrue idea of

misrule (mis'rōōl') *vt.* **-ruled', -rul'ing** to rule badly or unjustly; misgovern —*n.* 1. misgovernment 2. disorder

miss[1] (mis) *vt.* [OE. *missan*] 1. to fail to hit, meet, catch, do, see, hear, etc. 2. to let (an opportunity, etc.) go by 3. to avoid *[he missed being hit]* 4. to fail or forget to do, attend, etc. *[he missed his appointment]* 5. to regret the absence or loss of —*vi.* 1. to fail to hit 2. to fail to be successful 3. to misfire, as an engine —*n.* a failure to hit, obtain, etc. —**miss the boat** [Colloq.] to fail to seize an opportunity

miss[2] *n., pl.* **miss'es** [contr. of MISTRESS] 1. [M-] a title for an unmarried woman, placed before the name 2. a young unmarried woman 3. a size in clothing for young women

missal (mis'l) *n.* [< LL. *missa,* Mass] R.C.Ch. a book containing all the prayers, rites, etc. for the Mass throughout the year

misshapen (mis'shāp''n) *adj.* badly shaped; deformed

missile (mis'il) *n.* [< L. *mittere,* send] a weapon or other object, as a rocket, designed to be thrown or launched towards a target; often, specif., a guided missile

missing *adj.* 1. absent; lost 2. not able to be traced and not known to be dead

missing link something necessary for completing a series; specif. the hypothetical animal supposed to bridge the gap between anthropoid apes and man in evolution

mission (mish'ən) *n.* [< L. *mittere,* send] 1. a sending out or being sent out to perform a special duty 2. *a)* a group of missionaries *b)* its headquarters 3. a special embassy sent to a foreign country for a specific purpose 4. the special duty for which someone is sent 5. a vocation; calling 6. any charitable or religious organization doing welfare work 7. *Mil.* an assigned combat operation; esp., a single combat flight by an aeroplane

missionary *adj.* of religious missions or missionaries —*n., pl.* **-aries** a person sent on a mission; specif., a person sent out by his church to preach, teach, and proselytize

missis (mis'iz) *n.* [altered < MISTRESS] [Colloq.] one's wife: also used with *the:* also **mis'sus**

missive (mis'iv) *n.* [Fr. < L. *mittere,* send] a letter or written message

misspell (mis'spel') *vt., vi.* **-spelled'** or **-spelt', -spell'ing** to spell incorrectly

misspend (mis'spend') *vt.* **-spent', -spend'ing** to spend improperly or wastefully

misstate (mis'stāt') *vt.* **-stat'ed, -stat'-**

ing to state incorrectly or falsely —**mis-state'ment** *n.*

mist (mist) *n.* [OE.] 1. a large mass of water vapour like a light fog 2. a cloud of dust, gas, etc. 3. a fine spray, as of perfume 4. a film before the eyes *[a mist of tears]* 5. anything that obscures the understanding, etc. —*vt., vi.* to obscure as with a mist

mistake (mi stāk') *vt.* **-took', -tak'en, -tak'ing** [< ON. *mistaka,* to take wrongly] 1. to understand or perceive wrongly 2. to take to be another —*vi.* to make a mistake —*n.* a fault in understanding, etc.; blunder; error

mistaken *adj.* 1. wrong; having an incorrect understanding 2. incorrect: said of ideas, etc. —**mistak'enly** *adv.*

mister (mis'tər) *n.* [< MASTER] 1. [M-] a title used for a man, placed before his name and usually written Mr. 2. [Colloq.] sir: in direct address, not followed by a name

mistime (mis'tīm') *vt.* **-timed', -tim'ing** 1. to do at an inappropriate time 2. to judge incorrectly the time of

mistle thrush (mis''l) a large thrush supposed to like mistletoe berries: also **missel thrush**

mistletoe (mis''l tō') *n.* [< OE. *mistel,* mistletoe + *tan,* twig] an evergreen plant with yellowish-green leaves and waxy white, poisonous berries, parasitic on trees

mistook (mi stook') *pt. & obs. pp.* of MISTAKE

mistral (mis'trəl, mi strāl') *n.* [Fr. < Pr., master-wind] a cold, dry, north wind that blows over the Mediterranean coast of France and nearby regions

mistreat (mis'trēt') *vt.* to treat wrongly or badly

mistress (mis'tris) *n.* [< OFr. fem. of *maistre,* master] 1. a woman who has sexual relations with a man to whom she is not married 2. a woman who rules others or controls something; specif., *a)* a woman head of a household or institution *b)* a woman schoolteacher 3. [Archaic] a sweetheart

mistress of the robes the title of the lady in charge of the Queen's wardrobe

mistrial (mis trī'əl) *n.* *Law* a trial made void because of an error in the proceedings

mistrust (mis'trust') *n.* lack of trust or confidence; suspicion —*vt., vi.* to have no trust or confidence in; doubt —**mistrust'-ful** *adj.* —**mistrust'fully** *adv.*

misty (mis'tē) *adj.* **-ier, -iest** 1. of, like, or covered with mist 2. *a)* blurred, as by mist *b)* obscure or vague —**mist'ily** *adv.* —**mist'iness** *n.*

misunderstand (mis'un dər stand') *vt.* **-stood', -stand'ing** to fail to understand correctly

misunderstanding *n.* 1. a failure to understand correctly 2. a quarrel; disagreement

misunderstood *adj.* 1. not properly understood 2. not properly appreciated

misusage (mis yōō'zij) *n.* 1. incorrect

usage, as of words **2.** bad or harsh treatment

misuse (mis yōz'; *for n.* -yōs') *vt.* -used', -us'ing **1.** to use improperly; misapply **2.** to treat badly or harshly —*n.* incorrect or improper use —**misus'er** *n.*

mite¹ (mīt) *n.* [OE.] any of a large number of tiny arachnids, often parasitic upon animals or plants

mite² *n.* [< MDu.] **1.** a very small child or animal **2.** a very small sum of money **3.** a bit; a little [*a mite slow*]

mitigate (mit'ə gāt') *vt., vi.* -gat'ed, -gat'-ing [< L. *mitis*, mild + *agere*, drive] to make or become milder, less severe, or less painful —**mit'iga'tion** *n.* —**mit'igatory** *adj.*

mitigating circumstances circumstances which lessen the culpability of an offender

mitosis (mī tō'sis) *n.*, *pl.* -ses (-sēz) [< Gr. *mitos*, thread] the process by which a cell divides into two so that the nucleus of each new cell has the full number of chromosomes

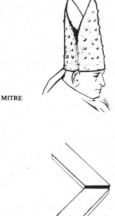

MITRE

MITRE JOINT

mitre (mīt'ər) *n.* [< Gr. *mitra*, headband] **1.** a tall, ornamented cap worn by bishops and abbots as a mark of office **2.** a diagonal joint made by fitting together two pieces of wood, material, etc. to form a corner —*vt.* to fit together in a mitre

mitt (mit) *n.* [contr. < MITTEN] **1.** a woman's glove covering part of the arm, the hand, and sometimes part of the fingers **2.** *same as* MITTEN **3.** [Slang] a hand **4.** a boxing glove

mitten (mit''n) *n.* [< OFr. *mitaine*] a glove with a thumb but no separately divided fingers

mix (miks) *vt.* mixed, mix'ing [< L. *miscere*] **1.** to blend together in a single

mass **2.** to make by blending ingredients [*to mix a cake*] **3.** to combine [*to mix work and play*] —*vi.* **1.** to be mixed; mingle **2.** to associate or get along —*n.* **1.** a mixing or being mixed **2.** a mixture, as of ingredients for making something —**mix up 1.** to mix thoroughly **2.** to confuse —**mix'able** *adj.*

mixed *adj.* **1.** blended **2.** made up of different parts, elements, races, sexes, etc. **3.** confused

mixed bag a random assortment of diverse elements, types of people, etc.

mixed blessing an event or situation that has advantages and disadvantages

mixed doubles *Sport* a doubles game in which each pair is composed of one man and one woman

mixed farming combined arable and livestock farming

mixed grill a dish of grilled sausages, bacon, etc.

mixed marriage marriage between persons of different religions or races

mixed-up *adj.* in a state of mental confusion

mixer *n.* **1.** a person with reference to his sociability **2.** a machine or an electric appliance for mixing **3.** a drink, as ginger ale, added to an alcoholic drink

mixture (miks'chər) *n.* **1.** a mixing or being mixed **2.** something mixed **3.** *Chem.* a substance containing two or more ingredients not chemically united —**the mixture as before** a repeat of various elements

mix-up *n.* a condition or instance of confusion

mizzenmast (miz''n mäst') *n.* [< L. *medius*, middle] the mast nearest the stern in a ship with two or three masts

mizzle (miz''l) *vi.* -zled, -zling [< prob. LowG. *miseln*] to rain in a fine mist —*n.* a misty rain; drizzle

ML. Medieval (or Middle) Latin

ml. **1.** mile **2.** millilitre(s): also **ml**

MLA, M.L.A. [Canad.] Member of the Legislative Assembly

M.Litt. [L. *Magister Litterarum*] Master of Letters

Mlle. *pl.* **Mlles.** Mademoiselle

MLowG. Middle Low German

MLR minimum lending rate

mm millimetre(s)

M.M. Military Medal

Mme. Madame

M.Mus. Master of Music

Mn *Chem.* manganese

MNA, M.N.A. [Canad.] Member of the National Assembly (of Quebec)

mnemonic (nē mon'ik) *adj.* [< Gr. *mnēmōn*, mindful] helping the memory —*n.* a verse, rhyme, etc. to aid the memory —**mnemon'ically** *adv.*

mo (mō) *n.* [Colloq.] *short for* MOMENT

Mo *Chem.* molybdenum

M.O., MO 1. Medical Officer **2.** money order

moa (mō'ə) *n.* [< Maori] any of an extinct group of very large, flightless birds of New Zealand

moan (mōn) *n.* [< OE. *mænan*, complain]
1. a low, mournful sound of sorrow or
pain 2. any similar sound, as of the wind
3. a complaint —*vi.* 1. to make a moan
2. to complain —*vt.* 1. to say with a
moan 2. to bewail

moat (mōt) *n.* [< OFr. *mote*] a deep,
broad ditch dug around a castle, and often
filled with water, for protection —*vt.* to
surround with a moat

mob (mob) *n.* [< L. *mobile* (*vulgus*),
excitable (crowd)] 1. a disorderly and
lawless crowd 2. [Derog.] the common
people 3. [Slang] a gang of criminals
—*vt.* **mobbed**, **mob'bing** 1. to crowd
around and jostle, annoy, etc. 2. to throng

mobcap *n.* [< MDu. *mop*, woman's cap]
formerly, a woman's cap, worn indoors,
with a high, puffy crown

mobile (mō'bil) *adj.* [< L. *movere*, move]
1. a) moving, or able to move, from place
to place b) movable by means of a motor
vehicle 2. that can change rapidly or
easily, as to suit moods or needs; flexible,
adaptable, etc. —*n.* an abstract sculpture
with parts that can move, as a suspended
arrangement —**mobility** (mō bil'ə tē) *n.*

mobilize (mō'bə līz') *vt., vi.* **-lized'**, **-liz'-
ing** to make or become ready for immediate
service or use, as for war —**mo'biliz'a-
ble** *adj.* —**mo'biliza'tion** *n.*

mobster (mob'stər) *n.* [Slang] a gangster

MOCCASINS

moccasin (mok'ə sin) *n.* [< Algonquian]
a heelless shoe of soft, flexible leather,
worn orig. by N American Indians

mocha (mok'ə) *n.* [< *Mocha*, seaport
in Yemen] a choice coffee grown orig.
in Arabia —*adj.* flavoured with coffee
or coffee and chocolate

mock (mok) *vt.* [< OFr. *mocquer*] 1.
to ridicule 2. to mimic, as in fun or
derision 3. to lead on and disappoint;
deceive 4. to defy and make futile —*vi.*
to express scorn, ridicule, etc. —*adj.* 1.
sham; imitation 2. practice [*mock* 'O'
levels] —**mock'ingly** *adv.*

mockery *n.*, *pl.* **-eries** 1. a mocking
2. an object of ridicule 3. a false, derisive,
or impertinent imitation 4. vain effort;
futility

mock-heroic *adj.* mocking, or
burlesquing, heroic manner, action, or
character —**mock'-hero'ically** *adv.*

mockingbird *n.* an American songbird
able to imitate many birdcalls

mock orange a shrub with fragrant
white flowers like those of the orange:
also called **syringa**

mock turtle soup a soup made from
calf's head, veal, etc., spiced to taste like
green turtle soup

mock-up *n.* a scale model or replica,
used for instructional or experimental
purposes

mod (mod) *n.* [< MOD(ERN)] [*also* M-]
[Colloq.] a member of a youth cult in
the mid-60's

mod. 1. moderate 2. modern

modal (mōd''l) *adj.* of a mode or mood;
specif., *Gram.* of or expressing mood
—**modality** (mō dal'ə tē) *n.*

mod cons *short for* modern conveniences

mode (mōd) *n.* [L. *modus*, measure,
manner] 1. a way of acting, doing, or
being 2. customary usage or current
fashion 3. *Music* the arrangement of tones
and semitones in a scale

model (mod''l) *n.* [see MODE] 1. *a*) a
small representation of an existing or
planned object *b*) same *as* ARCHETYPE
(sense 1) 2. a person or thing considered
as a standard of excellence to be imitated
3. a style or design [a 1972 *model*] 4.
a) a person who poses for an artist or
photographer *b*) a person employed to
display clothes by wearing them —*adj.*
serving as a standard of excellence —*vt.*
-elled, **-elling** 1. *a*) to make a model
of *b*) to plan or form after a model 2.
to form in clay, wax, etc. 3. to display
(a dress, etc.) by wearing —*vi.* to serve
as a model (sense 4) —**mod'eller** *n.*

moderate (mod'ər ət; *for v.* -ə rāt') *adj.*
[< L. *moderare*, to restrain] 1. within
reasonable limits; avoiding extremes 2.
mild [*moderate* weather] 3. of average
or medium quality, range, etc. —*n.* a
person holding moderate views, as in
politics —*vt.*, *vi.* -at'ed, -at'ing 1. to
make or become moderate 2. to preside
over (a meeting, etc.) —**mod'erately** *adv.*
—**mod'erateness** *n.*

moderation (mod'ə rā'shən) *n.* 1. a
moderating 2. avoidance of extremes 3.
absence of violence —**in moderation** to
a moderate degree

moderato (mod'ə rät'ō) *adj.*, *adv.* [It.]
Music with moderation in tempo

moderator (mod'ə rāt'ər) *n.* 1. a person
or thing that moderates; specif., a person
who presides at a meeting, etc. 2. a
substance used to slow down high-energy
neutrons in a nuclear reactor —**mod'era'-
torship'** *n.*

modern (mod'ərn) *adj.* [< Fr. < L. *modo*,
just now] 1. of the present or recent
times; specif., *a*) up-to-date *b*) designating
contemporary trends in art, literature, etc.
2. of the period of history from c.1450
A.D. 3. [*often* M-] designating the most
recent stage of a language —*n.* a person
living in modern times or with modern
ideas, etc. —**moder'nity** (mo dur'na tē) *n.*

Modern English the English language
since about the mid-15th cent.

modernism *n.* modern practices, ideas,
etc., or sympathy with these —**mod'ern-
ist** *n.*, *adj.* —**mod'ernis'tic** *adj.*

modernize *vt.*, *vi.* **-ized'**, **-iz'ing** to make
or become modern in design, methods,
etc. —**mod'erniza'tion** *n.*

modern languages the current European languages as a subject of study

Modern Latin the Latin used since c. 1500

modest (mod'ist) *adj.* [< L. *modus*, measure] 1. having or showing a moderate opinion of one's own abilities, etc. 2. not forward; unassuming 3. behaving, dressing, etc. decorously or decently 4. reasonable; not extreme [a *modest* request] 5. quiet and humble in appearance, style, etc. —mod'estly *adv.* —mod'esty *n.*

ModGr. Modern Greek

modicum (mod'i kəm) *n.* [L., moderate] a small amount

modification (mod'ə fi kā'shən) *n.* 1. a slight change in form 2. a product of this 3. a slight reduction 4. a qualification or limitation of meaning

modifier (mod'ə fi'ər) *n.* a word, phrase, or clause that limits the meaning of another word or phrase [adjectives and adverbs are *modifiers*]

modify (mod'ə fi') *vt.* -fied', -fy'ing [< L. *modus*, measure + *facere*, make] 1. to change or alter slightly or partially 2. to limit or lessen slightly 3. *Gram.* to limit the meaning of; qualify ["old" *modifies* "man" in *old man*] —mod'ifi'able *adj.*

modish (mōd'ish) *adj.* in the latest style; fashionable

modiste (mō dēst') *n.* [Fr.] a woman who makes or deals in fashionable clothes, hats, etc. for women

ModL. Modern Latin

modular (mod'yoo lər) *adj.* 1. of a module 2. designating units of standardized size, design, etc. that can be arranged or fitted together in various ways

modulate (mod'yoo lāt') *vt.* -lat'ed, -lat'ing [< L. *modus*, measure] 1. to regulate or adjust 2. to vary the pitch, intensity, etc. of (the voice) 3. *Radio* to vary the amplitude, frequency, etc. of (a radio wave) in accordance with some signal —*vi.* to shift from one key to another within a musical composition —mod'ula'tion *n.*

module (mod'yōōl) *n.* [< L. *modus*, measure] 1. any of a set of units, as cabinets, designed to be arranged in various ways 2. a detachable section with a specific function, as in a spacecraft 3. *Electronics* a compact assembly functioning as a component of a larger unit

modulus (mod'yoo ləs) *n.,* pl. -uli' (-lī') [see prec.] 1. *Math.* the value of a number regardless of a prefixed plus or minus sign 2. *Physics* a constant expressing the measure of some property, as elasticity

‡**modus operandi** (mō'dəs op'ə ran'dē) [L.] mode of operation; procedure

‡**modus vivendi** (vi ven'dē) [L.] 1. mode of living 2. a temporary compromise in a dispute

mog (mog) *n.* [< ?] [Slang] a cat: also **mog'gie**

Mogul (mō'gul) *n.* [Per. *Mughul*] 1. a Mongolian; esp., any of the Mongolian conquerors of India 2. [m-] a powerful or important person

M.O.H. Medical Officer of Health

mohair (mō'hâer) *n.* [< Ar. *mukhayyar*] 1. the hair of the Angora goat 2. yarn or a fabric made from this

Mohammedan (mō ham'id'n) *adj.* of Mohammed or the Moslem religion —*n. same as* MOSLEM

Mohammedanism *n. same as* ISLAM

moiety (moi'ə tē) *n.,* pl. -ties [< L. *medius*, middle] 1. a half 2. an indefinite part

moil (moil) *vi.* [< L. *mollis*, soft] to toil —*n.* 1. toil 2. turmoil

moire (mwär) *n.* [Fr.] a fabric, as silk or rayon, having a watered, or wavy, pattern

moiré (mwä'rā) *adj.* [Fr.] having a watered, or wavy, pattern —*n.* 1. a watered pattern pressed into cloth, etc. with engraved rollers 2. *same as* MOIRE

moist (moist) *adj.* [< L. *mucus*, mucus] 1. slightly wet; damp 2. tearful —moist'ly *adv.* —moist'ness *n.*

moisten (mois''n) *vt., vi.* to make or become moist

moisture *n.* water, etc. causing a slight wetness or dampness —mois'tureless *adj.*

moisturize *vt., vi.* -ized', -iz'ing to add or restore moisture to (the skin, air, etc.) —mois'turiz'er *n.*

moke (mōk) *n.* [< ?] [Slang] a donkey

mol mole

mol. 1. molecular 2. molecule

molar (mō'lər) *adj.* [< L. *mola*, millstone] 1. designating a tooth adapted for grinding 2. used for or capable of grinding —*n.* a molar tooth

molasses (mō las'iz) *n.* [< L. *mel*, honey] [Chiefly U.S.] treacle

mole¹ (mōl) *n.* [OE. *mal*] a small, congenital spot on the human skin, usually dark-coloured and raised

mole² *n.* [< ME. *molle*] a small, burrowing, insect-eating mammal with soft fur

mole³ *n.* [< Fr. < L. *moles*, mass] 1. a breakwater 2. a harbour formed by a breakwater

mole⁴ *n.* [< G. *Mol*] the SI unit of substance; the quantity of a substance having a weight in grams numerically equal to its molecular weight —mo'lar *adj.*

molecular (mō lek'yoo lər) *adj.* produced by or existing between molecules —molec'ular'ity (-lar'ə tē) *n.*

molecular weight the sum of the atomic weights of all atoms in a given molecule

molecule (mol'ə kyōōl') *n.* [< L. *moles*, mass] 1. the smallest particle of an element or compound that can exist in the free state and still retain the characteristics of the element or compound 2. a small particle

molehill (mōl'hil') *n.* a small ridge or mound of earth, formed by a burrowing mole

molest (mō lest') *vt.* [< L. *moles*, a burden] 1. to annoy so as to trouble or harm 2. to make improper sexual advances to (esp. a child) —molesta'tion *n.*

moll (mol) *n.* [< var. of name *Molly*] [Slang] 1. a gangster's mistress 2. a prostitute

mollify (mol'ə fi') *vt.* -fied', -fy'ing [< L. *mollis*, soft + *facere*, make] 1. to soothe, pacify, or appease **2.** to make less severe or violent —**mol′lifica′tion** *n.*

mollusc (mol′əsk) *n.* [< L. *mollis*, soft] any of a group of invertebrate animals, including oysters, snails, etc., having a soft body often enclosed in a hard shell

mollycoddle (mol′ē kod ′′l) *vt.* **-dled, -dling** [< *Molly* + CODDLE] to pamper; coddle —*n.* one used to being coddled or pampered, etc. —**mol′lycod′dler** *n.*

Molotov cocktail (mō′lə tof) [< V.M. *Molotov*] [Slang] a bottle filled with an inflammable liquid, plugged with a rag, ignited, and hurled as a grenade

molten (mōl′t'n) *archaic pp. of* MELT —*adj.* **1.** melted by heat **2.** made by being melted and cast in a mould

molto (mōl′tō) *adv.* [It.] *Music* very; much

molybdenum (mə lib′də nəm) *n.* [< Gr. *molybdos*, lead] a soft, lustrous, silver-white metallic chemical element, used in alloys, etc.: symbol, Mo

moment (mō′mənt) *n.* [< L. *momentum*, movement] **1.** a brief period of time; instant **2.** a definite point in time **3.** a brief time of being important **4.** importance [news of great *moment*] **5.** *Mech.* a) the tendency to cause rotation about a point or axis b) a measure of this —**at the moment** now

momentarily *adv.* **1.** for a moment or short time **2.** in an instant **3.** from moment to moment

momentary *adj.* **1.** lasting for only a moment; passing **2.** [U.S.] likely to occur at any moment

momently *adv.* **1.** every moment **2.** at any moment **3.** for a single moment

moment of truth 1. a crucial moment **2.** the point in a bullfight when the matador faces the bull for the kill

momentous (mō men′təs) *adj.* very important [a *momentous* decision] —**momen′tousness** *n.*

momentum (mō men′təm) *n.*, *pl.* **-tums, -ta** [see MOMENT] **1.** the impetus of a moving object **2.** *Physics & Mech.* the quantity of motion of a moving body, equal to the product of its mass and its velocity

Mon. 1. Monastery **2.** Monday **3.** Monsignor

monad (mon′ad) *n.* [< Gr. *monos*, alone] **1.** a unit; something simple and indivisible **2.** *Chem.* an atom, element, or radical with a valence of one

monandrous (mə nan′drəs) *adj.* [Gr. *monandros*, having one husband] **1.** having only one husband **2.** *Bot.* having only one stamen —**monan′dry** *n.*

monarch (mon′ərk) *n.* [< Gr. *monos*, alone + *archein*, to rule] **1.** a supreme ruler; king, queen, etc. **2.** a person or thing surpassing others of the same kind

monarchical (mə när′ki k'l) *adj.* **1.** of a monarch or monarchy **2.** favouring a monarchy Also **monar′chic**

monarchism (mon′ər kiz′m) *n.* monarchical principles or the advocacy of these —**mon′archist** *n., adj.*

monarchy *n., pl.* **-archies** a government or state headed by a monarch

monastery (mon′ə stər ē) *n., pl.* **-teries** [< LGr. *monos*, alone] the residence of a group of people, esp. monks, retired from the world under religious vows

monastic (mə nas′tik) *adj.* **1.** of or characteristic of monasteries **2.** of or characteristic of monks or nuns; ascetic; self-denying

monasticism *n.* the monastic state or way of life

monaural (mon ôr′′l) *adj.* [MON(O)- + AURAL] designating or of sound reproduction that uses only one source of sound, giving a monophonic effect

Monday (mun′dē) *n.* [OE. *monandæg*, moon's day] the second day of the week; the first day of the working week

Mondays *adv.* [Colloq.] on or during every Monday

monetarist (mun′ə tər ist) *n.* one who advocates regulation of the money supply as a method of controlling the economy of a country —**mon′etarism** *n.*

monetary (mun′ə tər ē) *adj.* **1.** of the coinage or currency of a country **2.** of money —**mon′etarily** *adv.*

money (mun′ē) *n., pl.* **-eys, -ies** [< L. *moneta*, MINT¹] **1.** a) pieces of gold, silver, copper, etc., stamped by government authority and used as a medium of exchange b) any paper note authorized to be so used **2.** anything used as a medium of exchange **3.** any sum of money **4.** wealth —**for one's money** [Colloq.] in one's opinion —**in the money** [Slang] wealthy —**money for jam** money obtained with very little trouble —**one's money's worth** full value —**place** (or put) **money on** to bet on —**put money into** to invest money in

moneybag *n.* **1.** a bag for money **2.** [pl., with sing. v.] [Colloq.] a rich person

money-box *n.* a box with a slit, for holding savings

money-changing *n.* the exchanging of currency, usually of different countries, esp. at an established or official rate —**mon′ey-chang′er** *n.*

moneyed (mun′ēd) *adj.* wealthy; rich

money-grubber *n.* a person who is greedily intent on accumulating money —**mon′ey-grub′bing** *adj., n.*

moneylender *n.* a person whose business is lending money at interest

moneymaker *n.* one that makes money or a profit

money of account a monetary denomination used in keeping accounts, etc., esp. one not issued in coin or in paper money, as, formerly in Britain, the guinea

money-spinner *n.* **1.** a source of wealth **2.** a small spider supposed to bring good luck: also **money spider**

monger (muŋ′gər) *n.* [< L. *mango*] a dealer or trader: usually in compounds [fishmonger]

Mongol (moŋ′gol) *adj., n.* same as MONGOLIAN

Mongolian (moŋ gō′lē ən) *adj.* **1.** of

Mongolia **2.** *same as* MONGOLOID —*n.*
1. a native of Mongolia **2.** *same as*
MONGOLOID **3.** the language of Mongolia
mongolism (moŋ'gəliz'm) *n.* *same as*
DOWN'S SYNDROME
Mongoloid (moŋ'gəloid') *adj.* **1.** of the
natives of Mongolia **2.** designating one
of the major groups of mankind: it includes
most of the peoples of Asia **3.** [*often*
m-] of or having Down's syndrome —*n.*
1. a member of the Mongoloid group **2.**
a person having Down's syndrome

MONGOOSE
(body 22-65 cm long;
tail 22-50 cm long)

mongoose (moŋ'gōōs) *n., pl.* **-gooses** [<
native name] a ferretlike mammal found
in Africa and Asia, noted for its ability
to kill snakes
mongrel (muŋ'grəl) *n.* [< OE. *mengan,*
mix] **1.** an animal or plant produced
by crossing breeds or varieties; esp., a
dog of this kind **2.** anything produced
by indiscriminate mixture —*adj.* of mixed
breed, race, etc. Often Derog.
monism (mon'iz'm) *n.* [< Gr. *monos,*
single] *Philos.* the doctrine that there
is only one ultimate substance or principle
monition (mō nish'ən) *n.* [< L. *monere,*
warn] **1.** warning; caution **2.** an official
or legal notice
monitor (mon'ə tər) *n.* [L. < *monere,*
warn] **1.** a device or instrument used
for monitoring **2.** in some schools, a
student chosen to help keep order, record
attendance, etc. **3.** a person who monitors
4. *Radio & TV* a receiver for checking
the quality of transmission —*vt., vi.* **1.**
to watch or check on (a person or thing)
2. to regulate the performance of (a
machine, aircraft, etc.) **3.** to listen to
(a broadcast, telephone conversation, etc.)
to gather some specified type of information
4. *Radio & TV* to check with a monitor
—**mon'itress** *n.fem.* —**mon'ito'rial**
(-tôr'ē əl) *adj.*
monitory (mon'ə tər ē) *adj.* admonishing
monk (muŋk) *n.* [< Gr. *monos,* alone]
a member of certain male religious orders,
generally under vows, as of poverty,
obedience, and chastity —**monk'ish** *adj.*
monkey (muŋ'kē) *n., pl.* **-keys** [prob.
< MLowG. *Moneke,* son of Martin the
Ape in *Reynard the Fox*] **1.** any of the
primates except man and the lemurs;
specif., any of the smaller, long-tailed
primates **2.** a person regarded as like
a monkey, as a mischievous child —*vi.*
[Colloq.] to play or meddle
monkey business [Colloq.] foolish,
mischievous, or deceitful tricks or behaviour
monkey nut *another name for* PEANUT
monkey puzzle a tall, prickly, coniferous
tree

monkey's wedding [S Afr. Colloq.]
a combination of rain and sunshine
monkeytrick *n.* [Colloq.] a mischievous
trick
monkey wrench a wrench with one
movable jaw
monkshood (muŋks'hŏŏd') *n.* *same as*
ACONITE
mono (mon'ō) *adj.* *short for* MONOPHONIC
mono- [< Gr.] *a prefix meaning* one,
alone, single
monochromatic (mon'ō krō mat'ik) *adj.*
[see ff.] of or having one colour
monochrome (mon'ə krōm') *n.* [< Gr.
monos, single + *chrōma,* colour] a
painting, drawing, etc. in one colour or
shades of one colour —**mon'ochro'mic** *adj.*
monocle (mon'ə k'l) *n.* [Fr. < Gr. *monos,*
single + L. *oculus,* eye] an eyeglass for
one eye only
monocotyledon (mon'ō kot'il ē'dən) *n.*
a flowering plant with one seed leaf
(cotyledon)
monody (mon'ə dē) *n., pl.* **-dies** [< Gr.
monos, alone + *aeidein,* sing] **1.** a solo
lament, as in ancient Greek tragedy **2.**
Music a style of composition in which
the melody is carried by one part, or voice
monogamy (mo nog'ə mē) *n.* [MONO- +
Gr. *gamos,* marriage] the practice of being
married to only one person at a time
—**monog'amous** *adj.*
monogram (mon'ə gram') *n.* [< Gr.
monos, single + *gramma,* letter] the
initials of a name, combined in a single
design —*vt.* **-grammed', -gram'ming** to
put a monogram on —**mon'ogrammat'ic**
(-grə mat'ik) *adj.*
monograph (mon'ə gräf') *n.* [MONO- +
-GRAPH] a writing, esp. a scholarly one,
on a single subject or aspect of a subject
—**monog'rapher** *n.*
monogyny (mə noj'ə nē) *n.* [MONO- + Gr.
gynē, woman] the practice of being
married to only one woman at a time
monolith (mon'ō lith') *n.* [< Gr. *monos,*
single + *lithos,* stone] **1.** a single large
block of stone **2.** something made of
this, as an obelisk **3.** something like a
monolith in size, unity of structure, etc.
—**mon'olith'ic** *adj.*
monologue (mon'ə log') *n.* [< Gr. *monos,*
alone + *legein,* speak] **1.** a long speech,
esp. one monopolizing a conversation **2.**
a soliloquy **3.** a play, skit, or recitation
for one actor only
monomania (mon'ō mā'nē ə) *n.* an
excessive enthusiasm for one thing —**mon'-
oma'niac** *n.*
monomial (mo nō'mē əl) *n.* [MO(NO)- +
(BI)NOMIAL] consisting of one term
mononucleosis (mon'ə nyŏŏ'klē ō'sis) *n.*
[MO(NO)- + NUCLE(US)] **1.** *same as*
INFECTIOUS MONONUCLEOSIS **2.** presence
in the blood of too many cells with a
single nucleus
monophonic (mon'ō fon'ik) *adj.*
designating or of sound reproduction using
a single channel
Monophysite (mə nof'ə sīt') *n.* [< Gr.
monos, single + *physis,* nature] *Theol.*

one who believes that Christ had only one nature, part human and part divine

monoplane (mon′ō plān′) *n.* an aircraft with only one pair of wings

monopolist (mə nop′ə list) *n.* a person who has a monopoly or who favours monopoly —**monop′olis′tic** *adj.*

monopolize *vt.* -lized′, -liz′ing 1. to have a monopoly of 2. to dominate completely —**monop′oliza′tion** *n.*

monopoly *n.,* *pl.* -lies [< Gr. *monos,* single + *pōlein,* sell] 1. exclusive control of a commodity or service in a given market 2. such control granted by a government 3. any exclusive possession or control 4. something held as a monopoly 5. [M-] *Trademark* a board game in which players move tokens to acquire squares representing property

monorail (mon′ō rāl′) *n.* a single rail serving as a track for cars suspended from it or balanced on it

monosodium glutamate (mon′ō sō′-dē əm glōō′tə māt′) a white powder used in foods to enhance flavour

monosyllabic (mon′ō si lab′ik) *adj.* 1. having only one syllable 2. using or speaking in monosyllables

monosyllable (mon′ə sil′ə b'l) *n.* a word of one syllable

monotheism (mon′ō thē iz′m) *n.* [MONO- + THEISM] the doctrine or belief that there is only one God —**mon′otheist** *n.* —**mon′otheis′tic, mon′otheis′tical** *adj.*

monotone (mon′ə tōn′) *n.* 1. utterance of successive words without change of pitch or key 2. monotony of tone, colour, etc. 3. a single, unchanging musical tone 4. recitation, singing, etc. in such a tone

monotonous (mə not′'n əs) *adj.* [see MONO- & TONE] 1. having little or no variety 2. tiresome because unvarying —**monot′onously** *adv.* —**monot′onousness** *n.*

monotony *n.* 1. lack of variety 2. tiresome sameness

monotype (mon′ō tīp′) *n.* [MONO- + -TYPE] *Printing* type produced by Monotype —[M-] *Trademark* either of a pair of machines for casting and setting up type in separate characters

monovalent (mon′ə vā′lənt) *adj.* *Chem.* same as UNIVALENT —**mon′ova′lence, mon′ova′lency** *n.*

monoxide (mon ok′sīd) *n.* an oxide with one atom of oxygen in each molecule

Monseigneur (mon′ sen yur′) *n.,* *pl.* **Messeigneurs** (mes′ en yurz′) [Fr.] a French title of honour given to persons of high birth or rank, as princes, bishops, etc.

monsieur (mə syur′) *n.,* *pl.* **messieurs** (mes′ərz) [Fr.] a man; gentleman: French title [M-], equivalent to *Mr.* or *Sir:* abbrev. **M., Mons.**

Monsignor (mon sēn′yər) *n.,* *pl.* -**gnors** [It.] a title of certain Roman Catholic prelates

monsoon (mon sōōn′) *n.* [< Ar. *mausim,* a season] 1. a seasonal wind of the Indian Ocean and S Asia, blowing from the southwest from April to October, and from the northeast the rest of the year 2. the rainy season, when this wind blows from the southwest

monster (mon′stər) *n.* [< L. *monere,* warn] 1. any huge animal or thing 2. any very cruel or wicked person 3. any imaginary creature with striking incongruities in form, as a centaur 4. any plant or animal greatly malformed, lacking parts, etc. —*adj.* huge; monstrous

monstrance (mon′strəns) *n.* [< L. *monstrare,* show] *R.C.Ch.* a receptacle in which the consecrated Host is exposed for adoration

monstrosity (mon stros′ə tē) *n.* 1. the state of being monstrous 2. *pl.* -**ties** a monstrous thing

monstrous (mon′strəs) *adj.* 1. abnormally large; enormous 2. very unnatural in shape or character 3. like a monster 4. horrible; hideous 5. hideously wrong or evil —**mon′strously** *adv.* —**mon′strousness** *n.*

montage (mon täzh′) *n.* [Fr. < *monter,* MOUNT²] 1. *a)* the process of making a composite picture from a number of different pictures *b)* a picture so made 2. *Cinema & T.V.* a sequence of abruptly alternating or superimposed scenes or images

Montessori method (or **system**) (mon′te sôr′ē) [< Maria *Montessori*] a system of teaching young children which emphasizes training of the senses and guidance intended to encourage self-education

month (munth) *n.* [OE. *monath*] 1. any of the twelve parts into which the calendar year is divided 2. *a)* the time from any day of one month to the corresponding day of the next *b)* a period of four weeks or 30 days

monthly *adj.* 1. lasting for a month 2. done, happening, payable, etc. every month —*n.,* *pl.* -**lies** a periodical published once a month —*adv.* every month

monument (mon′yoo mənt) *n.* [< L. *monere,* remind] 1. something set up to keep alive the memory of a person or event, as a tablet, statue, building, etc. 2. a work of enduring significance 3. [Obs.] a tomb

monumental (mon′yoo men′t'l) *adj.* 1. of or serving as a monument 2. like a monument; massive, enduring, etc. 3. of lasting importance 4. colossal [*monumental* pride]

monumental mason a maker and engraver of tombstones

moo (mōō) *n.,* *pl.* **moos** [echoic] the vocal sound made by a cow —*vi.* mooed, moo′ing to make this sound; low

mooch (mōōch) *vi., vt.* [ult. < OFr. *muchier,* to hide] to loaf, loiter or walk aimlessly or idly —**mooch′er** *n.*

mood¹ (mōōd) *n.* [OE. *mod,* mind] 1. a particular state of mind or feeling 2. a prevailing feeling, spirit, or tone 3. [*sometimes pl.*] a fit of sullen or uncertain temper —**in the mood** in a favourable state of mind

mood² *n.* [< MODE, altered after prec.]
Gram. that aspect of verbs which indicates
whether the action or state expressed is
a fact (*indicative mood*), supposition,
desire, etc. (*subjunctive mood*), or
command (*imperative mood*)

moody *adj.* **-ier, -iest** subject to or
characterized by gloomy, sullen, or
changing moods —**mood'ily** *adv.* —**mood'-
iness** *n.*

Moog Synthesizer (mōog) [< Robert
Moog] *Trademark* an electronic instrument
capable of producing a wide range of
musical sounds

mooi (moi) *adj.* [< Afrik.] [S Afr. Slang]
pleasing; nice

PHASES OF THE MOON

moon (mōon) *n.* [OE. *mona*] 1. the satellite
of the earth, that revolves around it once
in 29½ days and shines at night by
reflecting the sun's light 2. this body
as it appears at a particular time of the
month 3. a month 4. any satellite
of a planet —*vi.* to behave in an idle,
dreamy, or abstracted way —**over the
moon** elated; very excited

moonbeam *n.* a ray of moonlight

mooncalf *n.* 1. an idiot 2. a youth
who moons about

moon-faced *adj.* round-faced

moonlight *n.* the light of the moon —*adj.*
1. of moonlight 2. lighted by the moon
3. done or occurring by moonlight, or
at night

moonlight flit a hurried departure by
night to escape one's creditors

moonlighting *n.* [< the usual night hours
of such jobs] the practice of holding
a second regular job in addition to one's
main job

moonlit *adj.* lighted by the moon

moonscape *n.* [MOON + (LAND)SCAPE]
the surface of the moon or a representation
of it

moonshine *n.* 1. moonlight 2. foolish
or empty talk, etc. 3. [U.S. Colloq.] whisky
unlawfully made or smuggled

moonshot *n.* the launching of a rocket
to the moon

moonstone *n.* a translucent feldspar with
a pearly lustre, used as a gem

moonstruck *adj.* 1. crazed 2. romantically dreamy 3. dazed or distracted Also
moon'strick'en

moony *adj.* **-ier, -iest** mooning; listless;
dreamy

Moor (mooər) *n.* [< Gr. *Mauros*] a
member of a Moslem people of NW Africa :
they invaded and occupied Spain in the
8th cent. A.D. —**Moor'ish** *adj.*

moor¹ (mooər) *n.* [OE. *mor*] a tract of
open, rolling wasteland, usually covered
with heather and often marshy

moor² *vt.* [< ? MDu. *maren*, to tie] to

secure (a ship, etc.) or be secured in place
by cables or chains as to a pier or buoy
—*vi.* to moor a ship, etc. —**moor'age** *n.*

moorhen *n.* a common bird inhabiting
ponds, lakes, etc.

mooring *n.* 1. [often *pl.*] the cables,
etc. by which a ship is moored 2. [*pl.*]
a place where a ship is moored

moorland *n.* same as MOOR¹

moose (mōos) *n.,* *pl.* **moose** [<
Algonquian] 1. the largest animal of the
deer family, native to the N U.S. and
Canada 2. same as ELK

moot (mōot) *n.* [OE. *mot, gemot,* meeting]
an early English assembly of freemen to
administer justice, etc. —*adj.* debatable
—*vt.* 1. to debate 2. to propose for debate

mop (mop) *n.* [ult. < ? L. *mappa,* napkin]
1. a bundle of rags or a sponge, etc.,
fastened to the end of a stick, as for
washing floors 2. anything suggestive of
this, as a thick head of hair —*vt.* **mopped,
mop'ping** to wash or remove as with
a mop —**mop up** [Colloq.] to finish

mope (mōp) *vi.* **moped, mop'ing** [akin
to MDu. *mopen*] to be gloomy and
apathetic —*n.* 1. a person who mopes
2. [*pl.*] low spirits —**mop'er** *n.* —**mop'-
ish** *adj.*

moped (mō'ped') *n.* [< MO(TOR) +
PED(AL)] a two-wheel vehicle propelled
by a small motor

moppet (mop'it) *n.* [< ?] [Colloq.] a
little child : a term of affection

moquette (mo ket') *n.* [Fr.] a thick,
velvety fabric used for carpets, etc.

moraine (mo rān') *n.* [Fr. < *morre,* a
muzzle] a mass of rocks, gravel, sand,
etc. deposited by a glacier

moral (mor'əl) *adj.* [< L. *mos,* pl. *mores,*
morals] 1. dealing with, or capable of
distinguishing between, right and wrong
in conduct 2. of, teaching, or in accordance
with, the principles of right and wrong
3. good in conduct or character; sometimes,
specif., sexually virtuous 4. having
psychological rather than tangible effects
[*moral* support, a *moral* victory] 5. based
on a sense of right and wrong according
to conscience [a *moral* obligation] —*n.*
1. a moral lesson taught by a fable, etc.
2. [*pl.*] principles or habits with respect
to right or wrong in conduct —**mor'ally** *adv.*

morale (mo räl') *n.* [Fr. : see prec.]
mental condition with respect to courage,
discipline, confidence, etc.

moralist (mor'əl ist) *n.* 1. one who
moralizes 2. one who adheres to a system
of moral teaching —**mor'alis'tic** *adj.*

morality (məral'ətē) *n.,* *pl.* **-ties** 1.
rightness or wrongness, as of an action
2. a being in accord with the principles
or standards of right conduct; virtue 3.
principles of right and wrong in conduct;
ethics 4. moral instruction

morality play *Hist.* an allegorical drama
whose characters were personifications,
as Everyman, Vice, etc.

moralize (mor′ə līz′) *vi.* **-ized**′, **-iz**′**ing** to consider or discuss matters of right and wrong, often in a self-righteous way —*vt.* **1.** *a)* to explain in terms of right and wrong *b)* to draw a moral from **2.** to improve the morals of —**mor**′**aliza**′**tion** *n.* —**mor**′**aliz**′**er** *n.*

moral philosophy *same as* ETHICS

morass (mə ras′) *n.* [< Du. < Frank. *marisk*] a tract of low, soft, watery ground; swamp: often used figuratively of a difficult or troublesome state of affairs

moratorium (mor′ə tôr′ē əm) *n.*, *pl.* **-riums**, **-ria** [< L. *mora*, a delay] **1.** a legal authorization to delay payment of money due **2.** the effective period of such an authorization **3.** any authorized delay or stopping

moray (mo rā′) *n.* [< Port. < Gr. *myraina*] a voracious, brilliantly coloured eel, found esp. among coral reefs

morbid (môr′bid) *adj.* [< L. *morbus*, disease] **1.** having or showing an interest in gruesome matters **2.** gruesome; horrible **3.** of, having, or caused by disease; diseased —**morbid**′**ity**, **mor**′**bidness** *n.* —**mor**′**bidly** *adv.*

mordant (môr′d′nt) *adj.* [< L. *mordere*, to bite] **1.** biting, caustic, or sarcastic **2.** acting as a mordant —*n.* **1.** a substance used in dyeing to fix the colours **2.** an acid, etc. used in etching to bite lines, areas, etc. into the surface—**mor**′**dancy** *n.* —**mor**′**dantly** *adv.*

more (môr) *adj.* *superl.* MOST [OE. *mara*] **1.** greater in amount or degree: the comparative of MUCH **2.** greater in number: the comparative of MANY **3.** additional [take *more* tea] —*n.* **1.** a greater amount or degree **2.** [*with pl. v.*] a greater number (*of*) **3.** something additional [*more* can be said] —*adv.* *superl.* MOST **1.** in or to a greater degree or extent: used with many adjectives and adverbs (esp. those of three or more syllables) to form comparatives **2.** in addition —**more and more 1.** increasingly **2.** a constantly increasing amount, quantity, etc. —**more or less 1.** somewhat **2.** approximately

morel (mo rel′) *n.* [< OHG. *morhila*, carrot] an edible mushroom that looks like a sponge on a stalk

morello (mə rel′ō) *n.*, *pl.* **-los** [It.] a variety of small sour cherry with dark-red skin and juice

moreover (môr ō′vər) *adv.* in addition to what has been said; besides; further; also

mores (môr′ēz) *n.pl.* [L., customs] folkways that, through general observance, develop the force of law

morganatic (môr′gə nat′ik) *adj.* [< OHG. *morgengeba*, morning gift given to one's bride] designating or of a form of marriage in which a man of royalty or nobility marries a woman of inferior social status with the provision that neither she nor their offspring may lay claim to his rank or property —**mor**′**ganat**′**ically** *adv.*

morgen (môr′gən) *n.* [< Du. *morgen*, morning] [S Afr.] a unit of area approximately two acres or 0.8 hectare

morgue (môrg) *n.* [Fr.] **1.** a place where the bodies of dead persons are kept **2.** a newspaper office's reference library of back numbers, clippings, etc.

moribund (mor′ə bund′) *adj.* [< L. *mori*, die] **1.** dying **2.** coming to an end —**mor**′**i-bund**′**ity** *n.*

morion (môr′ē ən) *n.* [Fr.] *Hist.* a crested helmet with a curved brim coming to a peak in front and behind

Morisco (mə ris′kō) *adj.* Moorish —*n.*, *pl.* **-cos**, **-coes** a Moor; esp., one of the Moors of Spain

Mormon (môr′mən) *n.* a member of the Church of Jesus Christ of Latter-day Saints founded in the U.S. in 1830 by Joseph Smith —**Mor**′**monism** *n.*

morn (môrn) *n.* [OE. *morne*] [Poet.] morning

mornay (môr′nā′) *adj.* [? < Phillipe de *Mornay*] denoting a white sauce to which cheese is added

morning (môr′niŋ) *n.* [OE. *morgen*] **1.** the first or early part of the day, from midnight, or esp. dawn, to noon **2.** dawn; daybreak —*adj.* of, for, or in the morning

morning after [Colloq.] a hangover, or painful awakening

morning dress formal daytime dress for men, including a cutaway frock coat (**morning coat**)

morning glory a twining annual plant with trumpet-shaped flowers of lavender, blue, pink, or white

mornings *adv.* [Colloq.] during every morning

morning sickness nausea and vomiting occurring in the morning during the first months of pregnancy

morning star a planet, esp. Venus, visible in the eastern sky before sunrise

morocco (mə ro′kō) *n.* [< *Morocco*] a fine, soft leather made, orig. in Morocco, from goatskins

moron (môr′on) *n.* [< Gr. *mōros*, foolish] **1.** [Colloq.] a very stupid person **2.** a person having mild mental retardation —**moron**′**ic** *adj.* —**moron**′**ically** *adv.*

morose (mə rōs′) *adj.* [< L. *mos*, manner] ill-tempered; gloomy, sullen, etc. —**morose**′**ly** *adv.* —**morose**′**ness** *n.*

morpheme (môr′fēm) *n.* [< Gr. *morphē*, form] the smallest meaningful unit in a language, as an affix, a base, or an inflectional form —**morphe**′**mic** *adj.*

morphine (môr′fēn) *n.* [< L. *Morpheus*, god of sleep and dreams] a bitter, white or colourless alkaloid derived from opium and used to relieve pain: also **mor**′**phia**

morphology (môr fol′ə jē) *n.* [< Gr. *morphē*, form + -LOGY] **1.** the branch of biology dealing with the form and structure of animals and plants **2.** the branch of linguistics dealing with the structure and forms of words —**mor′pho-log′ical** (-fə loj′i k′l), **mor′pholog′ic** *adj.*

morris (mor′is) *adj.* [< ME. *morys*, *moorish*] of an old folk dance performed esp. on May Day, in which fancy costumes are worn —*n.* this dance

morris man a dancer in a morris dance: also **morris dancer**

morrow (mor′ō) *n.* [< OE. *morgen*, *morning*] [Poet.] 1. morning 2. the next day

Morse (môrs) *adj.* [< Samuel *Morse*] [*often* m-] designating a code, or alphabet, consisting of dots and dashes, or short and long sounds —*n.* the Morse code

morsel (môr′s'l) *n.* [< L. *morsum*, a bite] 1. a small bite or portion of food 2. a small amount; bit

mortal (môr′t'l) *adj.* [< L. *mors*, death] 1. that must eventually die 2. of man as a being who must eventually die 3. of this world 4. of death 5. causing death 6. to the death [*mortal* combat] 7. not to be pacified [a *mortal* enemy] 8. very intense [*mortal* terror] 9. [Colloq.] a) extreme b) long and tedious c) possible [no *mortal* good to anyone] —*n.* a being who must eventually die; esp., a human being —**mor′tally** *adv.*

mortality (môr tal′ə tē) *n.* 1. the mortal nature of man 2. death on a large scale, as from war 3. the proportion of deaths to population; death rate 4. human beings collectively

mortar (môr′tər) *n.* [< L. *mortarium*] 1. a bowl in which substances are ground to a powder with a pestle 2. a short-barrelled cannon which hurls shells in a high trajectory 3. a mixture of cement or lime with sand and water, used between bricks, etc. —*vt.* to plaster together with mortar

mortarboard *n.* 1. a square board with a handle beneath, on which mortar is carried 2. an academic cap with a square, flat top

mortgage (môr′gij) *n.* [< OFr. *mort*, dead + *gage*, GAGE¹] *Law* 1. the pledging of property to a creditor as security for the payment of a debt 2. a) the deed by which this pledge is made b) the sum of money borrowed —*vt.* -gaged, -gaging 1. *Law* to pledge (property) by a mortgage 2. to put an advance liability on [he *mortgaged* his future] —**mort′gagor**, **mort′gager′** *n.*

mortgagee (môr′gə jē′) *n.* a person to whom property is mortgaged

mortice (môr′tis) *n.*, *vt.* alt. sp. of MORTISE

mortification (môr′tə fi kā′shən) *n.* 1. shame, humiliation, etc. 2. something causing shame, humiliation, etc. 3. the control of physical desires by self-denial, fasting, etc. 4. *old term for* GANGRENE

mortify (môr′tə fī′) *vt.* -fied, -fy′ing [< L. *mors*, death + *facere*, make] 1. to shame, humiliate, etc. 2. to punish (one's body) or control (one's physical desires) by self-denial, fasting, etc. —*vi.* [Rare] to become gangrenous

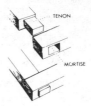

TENON

MORTISE

mortise (môr′tis) *n.* [< Ar. *murtazza*, joined] a notch or hole cut, as in a piece of wood, to receive a projecting part (*tenon*) shaped to fit —*vt.* -tised, -tising 1. to join securely, esp. with a mortise and tenon 2. to cut a mortise in

mortise lock a lock set into a mortise in a door so that the mechanism is enclosed by the door

mortmain (môrt′mān′) *n.* [< L. *mori*, die + *manus*, hand] *Law* a transfer of property to a corporate body for perpetual ownership

mortuary (môr′tyoo wər ē) *n.*, *pl.* -aries [< L. *mortuus*, dead] a place where dead bodies are kept before burial or cremation

Mosaic (mō zā′ik) *adj.* of Moses or the writings, principles, etc. attributed to him

mosaic (mō zā′ik) *n.* [< L. *musa*, MUSE] 1. the making of designs by inlaying small bits of coloured stone, glass, etc. in mortar 2. a picture or design so made 3. anything resembling this —*adj.* of or resembling mosaic

Moselle (mō zel′) *n.* a white wine from the Rhine valley

Moslem (moz′lem) *n.* [< Ar. *aslama*, to resign oneself (to God)] an adherent of Islam —*adj.* of Islam or the Moslems: also **Moslem′ic** —**Mos′lemism** *n.*

mosque (mosk) *n.* [< Ar. *sajada*, pray] a Moslem temple or place of worship

mosquito (mə skēt′ō) *n.*, *pl.* -toes, -tos [Sp. & Port. < L. *musca*, fly] a two-winged insect, the female of which has skin-piercing, bloodsucking mouthparts: some varieties transmit diseases, as malaria or yellow fever

mosquito net (or **netting**) a fine mesh curtain for keeping out mosquitoes

moss (mos) *n.* [OE. *mos*, swamp] 1. a very small, green plant growing in velvety clusters on rocks, trees, etc. 2. [Chiefly Scot.] a peat bog or swamp —*vt.* to cover with a growth of moss —**moss′y** *adj.*

moss hag a portion of a peat moor from which the peat has been cut

mossie (mos′ē) *n.* see CAPE SPARROW

moss rose a variety of the cabbage rose with a roughened, mossy flower stalk and calyx

moss stitch *Knitting* rows alternating plain and purl stitches yielding a knobbly pattern

mosstrooper *n.* 1. *Hist.* any of the raiders

who infested the borderland between England and Scotland **2.** a raider

most (mōst) *adj. compar.* MORE [OE. *mæst*] **1.** greatest in amount or degree: the superlative of MUCH **2.** greatest in number: the superlative of MANY **3.** in the greatest number of instances —*n.* **1.** the greatest amount or degree **2.** [*with pl. v.*] the greatest number (*of*) —*adv. compar.* MORE in or to the greatest degree or extent: used with many adjectives and adverbs (esp. those of three or more syllables) to form superlatives —**at (the) most** not more than —**make the most of** to take the fullest advantage of

mostly *adv.* **1.** for the most part **2.** chiefly **3.** usually

Most Reverend the form of address used for archbishops or Irish Roman Catholic bishops

mot (mō) *n.* [Fr., word] a witticism or pithy remark

M.O.T. Ministry of Transport —*n.* [Colloq.] *same as* M.O.T. TEST

mote (mōt) *n.* [OE. *mot*] a speck, as of dust

motel (mō tel′) *n.* [MO(TORIST) + (HO)TEL] a hotel for those travelling by car, with accessible parking

motet (mō tet′) *n.* [OFr., dim. of *mōt*, word] a contrapuntal song of a sacred nature for several voices

moth (moth) *n., pl.* **moths** [OE. *moththe*] a four-winged, chiefly night-flying insect related to the butterfly but generally smaller and less brightly coloured; specif., a small moth (**clothes moth**) whose larvae eat holes in woollens, furs, etc.

mothball *n.* a small ball of naphthalene, the fumes of which repel moths —**in (or out of) mothballs** put into (or taken from) storage

moth-eaten *adj.* **1.** gnawed away in patches by moths, as cloth **2.** worn-out **3.** outdated

mother (muth′ər) *n.* [OE. *modor*] **1.** a female parent **2.** that which is the origin of something **3.** a woman who is the head (**mother superior**) of a religious establishment **4.** an elderly woman: used as a title of affectionate respect —*adj.* **1.** of or like a mother **2.** native [*mother tongue*] —*vt.* **1.** to be the mother of **2.** to care for as a mother does —**moth′er-less** *adj.*

Mother Carey's chicken (kāər′ēz) [< ?] any of various sea petrels; esp., *same as* STORMY PETREL (sense 1)

mother country *same as* MOTHERLAND

mother earth **1.** the earth as a mother, particularly in its fertility **2.** soil; ground

motherhood *n.* **1.** the state of being a mother **2.** the qualities of a mother **3.** mothers collectively

mother-in-law *n., pl.* **moth′ers-in-law′** the mother of one's husband or wife

motherland *n.* a person's native land

motherly *adj.* of, like, or befitting a mother; maternal —**moth′erliness** *n.*

mother-naked *adj.* completely naked

mother-of-pearl *n.* the hard, pearly

internal layer of certain marine shells, as of the pearl oyster

Mother's Day **1.** in Britain, a Sunday in Lent set aside in honour of mothers: also **Mothering Sunday** **2.** in the US and Canada, the second Sunday in May, observed as a day in honour of mothers

mother's meeting **1.** a parish meeting of mothers **2.** any meeting where gossip is exchanged

mother tongue one's native language

mothproof (moth′proof′) *adj.* treated chemically so as to repel moths —*vt.* to make mothproof

motif (mō tēf′) *n.* [Fr.: see MOTIVE] **1.** a theme or subject that is repeated with various changes, as in a piece of music, a book, etc. **2.** a repeated figure in a design

motion (mō′shən) *n.* [< L. *movere*, move] **1.** a moving from one place to another **2.** a meaningful movement of the hand, etc.; gesture **3.** *a*) the capacity for movement *b*) a manner of movement; gait **4.** a proposal formally made in an assembly **5.** *a*) the evacuation of the bowels *b*) faeces —*vi.* to make a meaningful movement of the hand, head, etc. —*vt.* to command by a meaningful gesture —**go through the motions** to do something in a mechanical way —**in motion** moving —**mo′tionless** *adj.*

motivate (mō′tə vāt′) *vt.* **-vat′ed, -vat′-ing** to provide with, or affect as, a motive —**mo′tiva′tion** *n.*

motive (mō′tiv) *n.* [< L. *movere*, to move] **1.** some inner drive, impulse, etc. that causes one to act in a certain way **2.** *same as* MOTIF —*adj.* of or causing motion

-motive [see prec.] *a suffix meaning* of motion, moving

motive power **1.** any power, as steam, electricity, etc., used to impart motion **2.** an impelling force

‡**mot juste** (mō zhüst′) *pl.* **mots justes** (mō zhüst′) [Fr.] the right word; exact, appropriate word or phrase

motley (mot′lē) *adj.* [< ?] **1.** of many colours **2.** of many different elements [*a motley group*] —*n. Hist.* a garment of various colours, worn by a jester

motocross (mō′tə kros′) *n.* [MOTO(R) + CROSS(-COUNTRY)] a cross-country race for lightweight motorcycles

motor (mō′tər) *n.* [< L. *movere*, to move] **1.** anything that produces motion **2.** an engine; esp., an internal-combustion engine **3.** *short for* MOTOR CAR **4.** a machine for converting electrical energy into mechanical energy —*adj.* **1.** producing motion **2.** of or powered by a motor **3.** of, by, or for motor vehicles —*vi.* to travel by motor car

motor bicycle a bicycle driven by a motor; a moped

motorbike *n.* [Colloq.] a motorcycle

motorboat *n.* a boat propelled by a motor

motorcade (mō′tər kād′) *n.* [MOTOR + (CAVAL)CADE] [U.S.] a procession of motor cars

motor car a passenger car propelled

by an engine, and used for travelling on roads: also **motorcar**

motorcycle *n.* a two-wheeled vehicle, like a bicycle, propelled by an internal-combustion engine —*vi.* **-cled, -cling** to ride a motorcycle —**mo′torcy′clist** *n.*

motorist *n.* a person who drives a motor car

motorize *vt.* **-ized′, -iz′ing** 1. to equip with motor-driven vehicles 2. to equip (a vehicle, etc.) with a motor

motorman *n.* 1. a person who drives an electric locomotive 2. a person who operates a motor

motor nerve a nerve which controls muscular movement

motor vehicle a vehicle on wheels having its own motor for use on roads, as a motor car

motorway *n.* a main road for fast moving traffic with separate carriageways for vehicles travelling in opposite directions

M.O.T. test a compulsory annual test of the roadworthiness of motor vehicles over a certain age

mottle (mot′′l) *vt.* **-tled, -tling** [< MOTLEY] to mark with blotches or streaks of different colours —**mot′tled** *adj.*

motto (mot′ō) *n., pl.* **-toes, -tos** [It., word] 1. a word, phrase, or sentence chosen as expressive of the ideals of a nation, group, etc. and inscribed on something 2. a maxim adopted as a principle of behaviour

‡**moue** (moo) *n., pl.* **moues** (moo) [Fr.] a pouting grimace

mould[1] (mōld) *n.* [see MODULE] 1. a hollow form for shaping something plastic or molten 2. a frame on which something is modelled 3. a pattern or model 4. something formed in or on a mould 5. distinctive character —*vt.* 1. to make or shape in or on, or as if in or on, a mould 2. to influence (opinion, etc.) strongly 3. to fit closely to the contours of —**mould′er** *n.*

mould[2] *n.* [ME. *moul*] a downy fungous growth on organic matter, esp. in the presence of dampness or decay

mould[3] *n.* [OE. *molde*, earth] loose, soft soil, esp. when rich with decayed organic matter

mouldboard *n.* a curved iron plate on a ploughshare, for turning over the soil

moulder *vt. vi.* [see MOULD[3]] to crumble into dust; decay

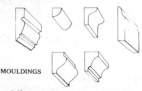

MOULDINGS

moulding *n.* something moulded, esp. a shaped strip of wood, etc., for finishing or decorating walls (esp. near the ceiling), furniture, etc.

mouldy *adj.* **-ier, -iest** 1. covered with mould 2. musty, as from age or decay 3. [Colloq.] miserable, dull, etc. —**mould′iness** *n.*

moult (mōlt) *vi.* [< L. *mutare*, to change] to shed skin, feathers, etc. prior to replacement by a new growth: said of reptiles, birds, etc. —*vt.* to shed thus —*n.* a moulting —**moulter** *n.*

mound (mound) *n.* [< ?] a heap or bank of earth, sand, etc.; small hill —*vt.* to heap up in a mound

mount[1] (mount) *n.* [< L. *mons*] a mountain or hill: now poetic or [M-] before a proper name [*Mount* Everest]

mount[2] *vi.* [see prec.] 1. to climb; ascend 2. to climb up on something; esp. a horse 3. to increase in amount —*vt.* 1. to go up; ascend [*to* mount stairs] 2. a) to get up on (a horse, platform, etc.) b) to provide with a horse 3. to place or fix on or in the proper support, backing, etc., as a gem in a setting 4. to arrange (a skeleton, dead animal, etc.) for exhibition 5. to prepare for and undertake (an expedition, etc.) 6. *Mil.* a) to place (a gun) in position for use b) to post (a guard) on sentry duty c) to go on (guard) as a sentry —*n.* 1. a horse for riding 2. the support, setting, etc. on or in which something is mounted —**mount′able** *adj.* —**mount′er** *n.*

mountain (moun′tin) *n.* [< L. *mons,* MOUNT[1]] 1. a natural raised part of the earth's surface, larger than a hill 2. [*pl.*] a chain or group of such elevations: also **mountain chain, mountain range** 3. a large heap or mound 4. a very large amount —*adj.* of or in mountains

mountain ash the rowan tree

mountain dew [Colloq.] 1. orig., Scotch whisky 2. any whisky esp. when illegally distilled

mountaineer (moun′tin ēr′) *n.* a mountain climber —*vi.* to climb mountains, as for sport —**moun′taineer′ing** *n.*

mountain goat *same as* ROCKY MOUNTAIN GOAT

mountain lion *same as* PUMA

mountainous (moun′tin əs) *adj.* 1. full of mountains 2. like a mountain; esp., very large

mountain sickness a feeling of weakness, nausea, etc. brought on at high altitudes by the rarefied air

mountebank (moun′tə baŋk) *n.* [< It. *montare*, to mount + *banco*, bench] 1. orig., a person who sold quack medicines in a public place 2. any charlatan, or quack —*vi.* to act as a mountebank

mounted *adj.* provided with a mount, or horse, vehicle, support, etc. [*mounted* police]

Mountie, Mounty *n., pl.* **-ies** [Colloq.] a member of the Royal Canadian Mounted Police

mounting block a slab of stone or wooden block used to facilitate mounting of a horse

mourn (môrn) *vi., vt.* [OE. *murnan*] 1. to grieve for (someone who has died)

2. to feel or express sorrow for (something regrettable) —**mourn'er** n.

mournful adj. **1.** feeling or expressing grief **2.** causing sorrow; melancholy —**mourn'fully** adv.

mourning n. **1.** a sorrowing; specif., the expression of grief at someone's death, or the period of this **2.** black clothes worn as a sign of grief

mourning band a strip of black cloth or crêpe worn, usually around the arm, to show mourning

mouse (mous; for v., usually mouz) n., pl. **mice** [OE. mus] **1.** any of numerous small rodents, esp., the **house mouse**, which infests human dwellings **2.** a timid or spiritless person —vi. moused, mous'- ing to hunt for mice

mouse-coloured adj. of an indeterminate greyish-brown

mousetrap n. **1.** a trap for catching mice **2.** [Colloq.] cheese of an inferior quality

mousey adj. same as MOUSY

moussaka (moo sä'ka) n. [ModGr.] a Greek dish of mutton, aubergines, etc., topped with a cheese sauce

mousse (moos) n. [Fr., foam] **1.** a light dessert made with egg white, gelatin, fruit, etc. **2.** a similar preparation made from fish, ham, etc.

moustache (ma stäsh') n. [< Fr. < Gr. mystax, upper lip] the hair on the upper lip of men

moustache cup a drinking cup partly covered on top, to keep the moustache dry

mousy (mou'sē) adj. -ier, -iest **1.** same as MOUSE-COLOURED **2.** of or like a mouse; quiet, timid, etc. **3.** infested with mice —mous'iness n.

mouth (mouth; for v. mouth) n., pl. **mouths** (mouthz) [OE. muth] **1.** the opening through which an animal takes in food and through which sounds are uttered **2.** any opening regarded as like the mouth [the mouth of a river, of a jar, etc.] **3.** [Colloq.] boastful or rude talk [he is all mouth] —vt. **1.** to say, esp. in an affected manner **2.** to form (a word) with the mouth soundlessly —vi. to declaim —**down in** (or **at**) **the mouth** [Colloq.] depressed; unhappy —**mouth'- er** (mouth'ar) n.

mouthful n., pl. -fuls' **1.** as much as the mouth can hold **2.** the usual amount taken into the mouth **3.** a small amount

mouth organ same as HARMONICA

mouthpiece n. **1.** the part of a musical instrument, telephone, etc., held in or to the mouth **2.** a person, periodical, etc. used by others to express their views

mouthwash n. a flavoured liquid used for rinsing the mouth or gargling

movable (moo'va b'l) adj. **1.** that can be moved **2.** changing in date from one year to the next [movable holidays] —n. Law personal property, as furniture: usually used in pl. Also **move'able** —**mov'a-bly** adv.

move (moov) vt. moved, mov'ing [< L. movere] **1.** to change the place or position

of **2.** to set or keep in motion **3.** to cause (to act, do, say, etc.) **4.** to arouse the emotions, etc. of **5.** to propose formally, as in a meeting **6.** to cause (the bowels) to evacuate —vi. **1.** to change place or position **2.** to change one's residence **3.** to be active [to move in artistic circles] **4.** to make progress **5.** to take action **6.** to be, or be set, in motion **7.** to make a formal application (for) **8.** to evacuate: said of the bowels **9.** [Colloq.] to depart [time to be moving on] **10.** Chess, Draughts, etc. to change the position of a piece **11.** Commerce to be disposed of by sale: said of goods —n. **1.** a movement **2.** an action towards some goal **3.** a trend **4.** a change of residence **5.** Chess, Draughts, etc. the act of moving or one's turn to move —**get a move on** [Colloq.] to hurry —**move house** to change one's residence —**move in on** [Slang] to draw near to and try to gain control of —**move up** to promote or be promoted —**move a muscle** to be completely still —**on the move** [Colloq.] moving from place to place —mov'er n.

movement n. **1.** the act or manner of moving **2.** a) organized action by people working together towards some goal b) those active in this way **3.** a trend **4.** the moving parts of a mechanism [the movement of a clock] **5.** the progress of events in a literary work **6.** the effect of motion in painting, sculpture, etc. **7.** an evacuation (of the bowels) **8.** Music any of the principal divisions of a symphony or other extended composition

movie n. [< moving picture] [Chiefly U.S.] a cinema film

moving adj. **1.** that moves **2.** stirring the emotions —mov'ingly adv.

moving staircase (or **stairway**) same as ESCALATOR

mow (mō) vt., vi. mowed, mowed or mown, mow'ing [OE. mawan] to cut down (grass or grain) with a sickle, lawn mower, etc. from (a lawn, field, etc.) —**mow down** to kill or destroy at random or in great numbers —mow'er n.

mown alt. pp. of MOW

mp [It. mezzo piano] Music moderately soft

M.P. **1.** Member of Parliament **2.** Mounted Police

mpg, m.p.g. miles per gallon

mph, m.p.h. miles per hour

M.Phil. Master of Philosophy

M.P.P. [Canad.] Member of Provincial Parliament

Mr. (mis'tar) pl. **Messrs.** (mes'arz) mister: used before the name or title of a man

Mrs. (mis'iz) pl. **Mmes.** (mā dam') mistress: now used as a title before the name of a married woman

Mrs. Mopp a charwoman

MS., ms., ms pl. **MSS., mss., mss** manuscript

Ms. (miz) a title used for both married and unmarried women; the feminine of Mr.

M.S., M.Sc. Master of Science

M.S.T. [U.S. & Canad.] Mountain Standard Time

Mt., mt. *pl.* **mts.** 1. mount 2. mountain

M.Tech. Master of Technology

mu (myōō) *n.* the twelfth letter of the Greek alphabet (M, μ)

much (much) *adj.* more, most [OE. *mycel*] great in amount, degree, etc. —*adv.* 1. to a great degree or extent [*much* happier] 2. nearly [*much* the same] 3. often [do you dine out *much?*] —*n.* 1. a great amount [*much* to be done] 2. something great, outstanding, etc. [not *much* to look at] —**a bit much** [Colloq.] somewhat extreme —**make much of** to treat as of great importance —**much as** 1. almost as 2. though —**much of a muchness** very much alike

mucilage (myōō'sə lij) *n.* [< L. *mucere*, be mouldy] 1. a thick, sticky substance produced in certain plants 2. any watery gum, glue, etc. used as an adhesive

muck (muk) *n.* [< or akin to ON. *myki, dung*] 1. farmyard manure 2. dirt; filth —*vt.* 1. to fertilize with muck 2. [Colloq.] to dirty as with muck 3. [Slang] to bungle (often with *up*) —**muck about (or around)** [Slang] 1. to waste time 2. to interfere (with) —**muck in** to share something, such as duties, expenses, etc. —**muck'y** *adj.*

muckrake *vi.* **-raked', -rak'ing** to search for and publicize corruption by public officials, etc. —**muck'rak'er** *n.*

mucksweat *n.* a profuse or copious sweat

mucous (myōō'kəs) *adj.* 1. of, containing, or secreting mucus 2. slimy —**mucos'ity** (-kos'ə tē) *n.*

mucous membrane a mucus-secreting membrane lining body cavities, as the mouth, connecting with the air

mucus (myōō'kəs) *n.* [L.] the slimy secretion that moistens and protects the mucous membranes

mud (mud) *n.* [prob. < LowG.] wet, soft, sticky earth —*vt.* **mud'ded, mud'ding** to cover or soil with or as with mud —**throw (or sling) mud at** [Colloq.] to slander or defame

muddle (mud'l) *vt.* **-dled, -dling** [< MUD] 1. to mix up; jumble 2. to confuse; befuddle —*vi.* to act or think in a confused way —*n.* mess, confusion, etc. —**muddle through** to succeed in spite of confusion

muddle-headed *adj.* stupid; blundering; confused

muddy *adj.* **-dier, -diest** 1. full of or spattered with mud 2. cloudy [*muddy* coffee] 3. confused, obscure, etc. —*vt., vi.* **-died, -dying** to make or become muddy —**mud'dily** *adv.* —**mud'diness** *n.*

mudguard *n.* a metal frame over the wheels of a bicycle, etc., to protect against splashing mud

mudlark *n.* 1. formerly, one who made a living by picking up odds and ends in the mud of tidal rivers 2. [Colloq.] a street urchin

mudpack *n.* a paste made up of fuller's earth, astringents, etc., used as a facial

mudslinging *n.* unscrupulous attacks against an opponent, as in a political campaign —**mud'sling'er** *n.*

muesli (myōō'zlē) *n.* [SwissG.] a mixture of uncooked cereals, usually mixed with nuts, fruits, etc.

muezzin (mōō ez'in) *n.* [< Ar. *adhana*, proclaim] a Moslem crier who calls the people to prayer

muff¹ (muf) *n.* [Du. *mof* < Fr. *moufle*, mitten] a cylindrical covering of fur, etc. into which the hands are placed for warmth

muff² *vt., vi.* [< ?] to do (something) badly or awkwardly; specif., to bungle (a catch)

muffin (muf'in) *n.* [< ?] a thick, plain, yeast roll, usually served hot and buttered

muffin man a man who used to sell muffins in the street

muffle (muf''l) *vt.* **-fled, -fling** [< ? OFr. *moufle*, mitten] 1. to wrap up so as to hide, keep warm, etc. 2. to cover in order to deaden sound 3. to deaden (a sound)

muffler *n.* 1. a scarf worn around the throat, as for warmth 2. [U.S.] a silencer

mufti (muf'tē) *n.* [Ar. < *āftā*, to judge] ordinary clothes, esp. when worn by one who usually wears a uniform

mug (mug) *n.* [prob. < Scand.] 1. a large drinking cup with a handle but no saucer 2. as much as a mug will hold 3. [Slang] *a*) the face *b*) the mouth 4. [Colloq.] a stupid or gullible person —*vt.* **mugged, mug'ging** 1. to assault and rob 2. [Colloq.] to learn by studying (with *up*) —*vi.* to assault someone —**a mug's game** something only a gullible or simple person would do —**mug'ger** *n.*

muggins (mug'inz) *n.* [< personal name] [Slang] a dupe; fool

muggy (mug'ē) *adj.* **-gier, -giest** [< ? ON. *mugga*, a drizzle] hot, damp, and close —**mug'giness** *n.*

mukluk (muk'luk) *n.* [< Eskimo] a soft, usually sealskin boot worn by Eskimos

mulatto (myōō lat'ō) *n., pl.* **-toes** [Sp. & Port. *mulato*, of mixed breed] a person who has one Negro parent and one white parent

mulberry (mul'bər ē) *n., pl.* **-ries** [OE. *morberie*] 1. any of several trees that bear edible fruits resembling the raspberry 2. purplish red

mulch (mulch) *n.* [ME. *molsh*, soft] leaves, peat etc., spread on the ground around plants to retain moisture, protect roots, etc. —*vt.* to apply mulch to

mulct (mulkt) *vt.* [< L. *multa*, a fine] 1. to fine 2. to extract (money) from (someone), as by fraud —*n.* a fine

mule¹ (myōōl) *n.* [< L. *mulus*] 1. the offspring of a donkey and a horse, esp. of a jackass and a mare 2. a machine that spins cotton fibres into yarn

mule² *n.* [Fr. < L. *mulleus*, red shoe] a slipper that does not cover the heel

muleteer (myōō'lə tēər') *n.* [< OFr.] a driver of mules

mulish *adj.* stubborn; obstinate —**mul'ishly** *adv.*

mull¹ (mul) *vt., vi.* [< ?] [Colloq.] to cogitate or ponder (usually with *over*)

mull² *vt.* [< ?] to heat, sweeten, and flavour with spices

mull³ *n.* [< ON. *muli*, snout] [Scot.] a headland

mullah, mulla (mul'ə) *n.* [< Ar. *mawlā*] a Moslem teacher of the religious law: used as a title of respect

mullet (mul'it) *n.* [< L. *mullus*] any of a group of edible, spiny-rayed fishes found in fresh and salt waters

mulligatawny (mul'i gə tô'nē) *n.* [Tamil *milagutannir*, pepper water] a soup flavoured with curry

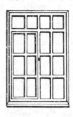

MULLIONS

mullion (mul'ē ən) *n.* [prob. < L. *medianus*, middle] a slender, vertical dividing bar between the panes of windows, panels, etc. **—mul'lioned** *adj.*

multangular (mul taŋ'gyoo lər) *adj.* having many angles

multi- [L. < *multus*, much, many] *a combining form meaning:* **1.** having many **2.** more than two **3.** many times more than The meanings of the following words can be determined by combining the meanings of their component elements: multicoloured, multilingual, multipurpose, multiracial, multistorey

multifarious (mul'tə fāar'ē əs) *adj.* [L. *multifarius*] having many kinds of parts or elements **—mul'tifar'iously** *adv.*

multiflora rose (mul'tə fiôr'ə) a rose with thick clusters of small flowers

multiform (mul'tə fôrm') *adj.* having many forms, shapes, etc.

multilateral (mul'ti lat'ər əl) *adj.* **1.** involving more than two nations, etc. **2.** many-sided

multimillionaire (mul'ti mil'yə nāar') *n.* one whose wealth amounts to many millions of pounds, etc.

multinational (mul'ti nash'ə n'l) *adj.* designating a company with branches in a number of countries **—n.** a multinational company

multiple (mul'tə p'l) *adj.* [< L. *multus*, many + -*plex*, -fold] having or consisting of many parts, elements, etc. **—n.** a number that is a product of some specified number and another number [10 is a *multiple* of 5]

multiple-choice *adj.* designating a question for which one of several proposed answers is to be selected

multiple sclerosis a disease in which

there is damage to the central nervous system, marked by speech defects, etc.

multiplex (mul'tə pleks') *adj.* multiple

multipliable (mul'tə plī'ə b'l) *adj.* that can be multiplied: also **mul'tiplic'able** (-plik'ə b'l)

multiplicand (mul'tə pli kand') *n.* Math. the number that is, or is to be, multiplied by another (the *multiplier*)

multiplication (mul'tə pli kā'shən) *n.* a multiplying or being multiplied; specif., Math. a method used to find the result of adding a specified quantity repeated a specified number of times: indicated in arithmetic by the symbol ×

multiplication table a table for memorization showing the results of multiplying each number of a series, usually 1 to 12, by each of the numbers in succession

multiplicity (mul'tə plis'ə tē) *n.* [< MULTIPLE] **1.** a being manifold or various **2.** a great number

multiplier (mul'tə pli'ər) *n.* Math. the number by which another number (the *multiplicand*) is, or is to be, multiplied

multiply (mul'tə plī') *vt., vi.* **-plied'**, **-ply'ing** [see MULTIPLE] **1.** to increase in number, amount, degree, etc. **2.** Math. to find the product (of) by multiplication

multitude (mul'tə tyōōd') *n.* [< L. *multus*, many] **1.** a large number; host **2.** the masses (preceded by *the*)

multitudinous (mul'tə tyōōd'in əs) *adj.* **1.** very numerous **2.** consisting of many parts, elements, etc.

mum¹ (mum) *vi.* **mummed**, **mum'ming** [< OFr. *momer*, grimace] to wear a mask or costume in fun; specif., to act as a mummer at Christmas time

mum² *n.* [Colloq.] mother

mum³ *adj.* [ME. *momme*] silent **—mum's the word** say nothing

mumble (mum'b'l) *vt., vi.* **-bled**, **-bling** [ME. *momelen*] **1.** to speak or say indistinctly **2.** [Rare] to chew gently **—n.** a mumbled utterance **—mum'blingly** *adv.*

mumbo jumbo (mum'bō jum'bō) [of Afr. orig.] **1.** meaningless ritual, gibberish, etc. **2.** an idol or fetish

mummer (mum'ər) *n.* [see MUM¹] any of the masked and costumed persons who travel from house to house acting folk plays at Christmas time

mummery *n., pl.* **-meries** **1.** performance by mummers **2.** any pretentious or hypocritical show

mummify (mum'ə fī) *vt.* **-fied'**, **-fy'ing** to make into a mummy **—vi.** to shrivel up **—mum'mifica'tion** *n.*

mummy¹ (mum'ē) *n., pl.* **-mies** [ult. < Per. *mum*, wax] a dead body preserved by embalming, as by the ancient Egyptians

mummy² *n., pl.* **-mies** [< MUM²] [Colloq.] mother

mumps (mumps) *n.pl.* [with sing. v.] [pl. of obs. *mump*, a grimace] an acute communicable disease, caused by a virus and characterized by swelling of the salivary glands

mun. municipal

munch (munch) *vt., vi.* [echoic] to chew steadily, often with a crunching sound

mundane (mun dān') *adj.* [< L. *mundus*, world] 1. commonplace; everyday 2. worldly, as distinguished from heavenly

municipal (myo͞o nis'əp'l) *adj.* [< L. *munia*, official duties + *capere*, take] of or having to do with a city, town, etc. or its local government —**munic'ipally** *adv.*

municipality (myo͞o nis'ə pal'ə tē) *n., pl.* **-ties** a city, town, etc. having its own government

munificent (myo͞o nif'ə sənt) *adj.* [< L. *munus*, gift + *facere*, make] 1. very generous in giving 2. given with great generosity —**munif'icence** *n.*

munitions (myo͞o nish'ənz) *n.pl.* [< L. *munire*, fortify] war supplies; esp., weapons and ammunition

muon (myo͞o'on) *n.* [MU + (MES)ON] a subatomic particle with a mass 207 times that of an electron

mural (myo͞oər'əl) *adj.* [< L. *murus*, wall] of, on, in, or like a wall —*n.* a picture, esp. a large one, painted or applied directly on a wall —**mu'ralist** *n.*

murder (mur'dər) *n.* [OE. *morthor*] the unlawful and malicious or premeditated killing of one human being by another —*vt.* 1. to kill unlawfully and with malice 2. to spoil, as in performance —*vi.* to commit murder —**cry** (or **scream**) **blue murder** to make a scene —**get away with murder** [Colloq.] to escape censure; do as one pleases —**mur'derer** *n.* —**mur'deress** *n.fem.*

murderous *adj.* 1. of or characteristic of murder; brutal 2. capable or guilty of, or intending, murder —**mur'derously** *adv.*

muriatic acid (myo͞oər'ē at'ik) [< L. *muria*, brine] hydrochloric acid: a commercial term

murk (murk) *n.* [< ON. *myrkr*, dark] darkness; gloom

murky *adj.* **-ier, -iest** 1. dark or gloomy 2. heavy and obscure with smoke, mist, etc.

murmur (mur'mər) *n.* [< L.: echoic] 1. a low, indistinct, continuous sound, as of a stream, far-off voices, etc. 2. a mumbled complaint 3. *Med.* any abnormal sound, esp. in the region of the heart —*vi.* 1. to make a murmur 2. to mumble a complaint —*vt.* to say in a murmur —**mur'murous** *adj.*

murphy (mur'fē) *n., pl.* **-phies** [< Ir. surname] [Slang] a potato

murrain (mur'in) *n.* [< L. *mori*, die] 1. any of various infectious diseases of cattle 2. [Archaic] a plague

mus. 1. museum 2. music 3. musical

Mus.B., Mus. Bac. [L. *Musicae Baccalaureus*] Bachelor of Music

muscat (mus'kət) *n.* [< LL. *muscus*, musk] 1. a variety of sweet grape from which muscatel and raisins are made 2. *same as* MUSCATEL

muscatel (mus'kə tel') *n.* [< It. *moscato*, MUSCAT] 1. a rich, sweet wine made

from the muscat 2. *same as* MUSCAT Also **mus'cadel'**

muscle (mus''l) *n.* [< L. *mus*, mouse] 1. any of the body organs consisting of bundles of fibres that can be contracted and expanded to produce bodily movements 2. the tissue making up such an organ 3. muscular strength 4. [Colloq.] power based on force —*vi.* **-cled, -cling** [U.S. Colloq.] to impose one's presence or will (with *in*)

muscle-bound *adj.* having some of the muscles enlarged and less elastic, as from too much exercise

muscleman *n.* 1. a man with highly developed muscles 2. a henchman employed by a gangster to intimidate victims or opponents

Muscovite (mus'kō vīt') *n.* a Russian, esp. of Moscow —*adj.* of Russia or of Moscow

Muscovy duck (mus'kō vē) a common domesticated duck with a large crest

muscular (mus'kyo͞o lər) *adj.* 1. of or accomplished by muscles 2. having well-developed muscles; strong —**mus'cular'-ity** (-lar'ə tē) *n.* —**mus'cularly** *adv.*

muscular dystrophy a chronic disease characterized by a progressive wasting of the muscles

musculature (mus'kyə lə chər) *n.* [Fr.] the arrangement of the muscles; muscular system

Mus.D., Mus.Doc., Mus.Dr. [L. *Musicae Doctor*] Doctor of Music

Muse (myo͞oz) *n.* [< Gr. *mousa*] 1. Gr. Myth. any of the nine goddesses who presided over literature, arts, and sciences 2. [m-] the spirit regarded as inspiring a poet or artist

muse (myo͞oz) *vi.* **mused, mus'ing** [< OFr. *muser*, loiter] to meditate —*vt.* to think or say meditatively

museum (myo͞o zē'əm) *n.* [< Gr. *mousa*, Muse] a building, room, etc. for preserving and exhibiting artistic, historical, or scientific objects

museum piece 1. an object of sufficient age or interest to be kept in a museum 2. [Colloq.] a person or thing regarded as antiquated or decrepit

mush¹ (mush) *n.* [prob. var. of MASH] 1. any thick, soft mass 2. [Colloq.] maudlin sentimentality

mush² *interj.* [< ? Fr. *marchons*, let's go] a shout urging on sledge dogs —*vi.* to travel on foot over snow, usually with a dog sledge —*n.* a journey by mushing

mushroom (mush'room') *n.* [< LL. *mussirio*] any of various rapid-growing, fleshy fungi having an umbrellalike top, esp., any edible variety —*adj.* 1. of or like a mushroom —*vi.* 1. to grow or spread rapidly 2. to flatten out at the end so as to resemble a mushroom

mushroom cloud the large mushroom-shaped cloud of smoke, debris, etc. produced by a nuclear explosion

mushy *adj.* **-ier, -iest** 1. like mush; thick

and soft **2.** [Colloq.] maudlin and sentimental —**mush'ily** adv.

music (myōō'zik) n. [< Gr. mousa, Muse] **1.** the art of combining tones in varying melody, harmony, etc., to form complete and expressive compositions **2.** a musical composition or its written or printed score **3.** any rhythmic sequence of pleasing sounds, as of birds —**face the music** [Colloq.] to accept the consequences, however unpleasant —**set to music** to compose music for

musical adj. **1.** of or for music **2.** melodious or harmonious **3.** fond of or skilled in music **4.** set to music —n. a theatrical or film production with dialogue, songs, and dances : often, **musical comedy** —**mu'sical'ity** (-kal'ə tē) n. —**mu'sically** adv.

musical box a mechanical musical instrument containing a bar with tuned steel teeth that are struck by pins on a revolving cylinder to produce a certain tune

musical chairs a game in which the players march to music around empty chairs (one fewer than the number of players) and rush to sit down each time the music stops : the player with no seat drops out

music centre a single hi-fi unit containing a turntable, amplifier, radio, and cassette player

music hall 1. a variety entertainment consisting of songs, comic tunes, etc., esp. in the Edwardian period **2.** the theatre where such entertainments are staged

musician (myōō zish'ən) n. a person skilled in music; esp., a professional performer of music —**musi'cianship'** n.

musicology (myōō'zi kol'ə jē) n. [see MUSIC & -LOGY] the systematized study of the science, history, and methods of music —**mu'sicol'ogist** n.

music-stool n. **1.** an adjustable stool for a pianist **2.** a hollow stool for storing sheet music

musk (musk) n. [< Sans. muska, testicle] a substance with a strong odour, obtained from the male musk deer or produced synthetically, and used as the basis of perfumes —**musk'like'**, **musk'y** adj.

musk deer a small, hornless deer of C Asia

muskeg (mus'keg') n. [< AmInd] [Canad.] an undrained boggy hollow

muskellunge (mus'kə lunj') n. [< AmInd.] a large N American freshwater game fish : also [Colloq.] **muskie, musky**

musket (mus'kit) n. [< L. musca, a fly] a smooth-bore, long-barrelled firearm used before the invention of the rifle

musketeer (mus'kə tēər') n. a soldier armed with a musket

muskmelon n. any of several sweet, juicy fruits, as the cantaloupe

musk ox a hardy ox of arctic America and Greenland, with a long coat, curved horns, and a musklike odour

muskrat n. **1.** a N American rodent with glossy brown fur and a musklike odour **2.** its fur

musk rose a rose with fragrant white flowers

Muslim (mooz'ləm) n., adj. same as MOSLEM

muslin (muz'lin) n. [< Fr. < Mosul, city in Iraq] a fine, plain-weave cotton fabric

musquash (mus'kwosh) n. [< Algonquian] another name for MUSKRAT, esp. the fur

mussel (mus''l) n. [ult. < L. musculus] any of various bivalve molluscs

Mussulman (mus''l mən) n., pl. -mans [< Ar. muslim] [Now Rare] a Moslem

must¹ (must; unstressed məst) v.aux. pt. **must** [< OE. moste] an auxiliary used to express : **1.** necessity [I must pay her] **2.** probability [you must be my cousin] **3.** certainty [all men must die] —n. [Colloq.] something that must be done, had, etc.

must² (must) n. [< L. mustum, new wine] the juice pressed from grapes or other fruit before it has fermented

mustachio (məs tä'shē ō') n., pl. -chios [< Sp. or It.] a moustache, esp. a large, bushy one —**musta'chioed** adj.

mustang (mus'tan) n. [< Sp. mesteño, wild] a small wild or half-wild horse of the SW plains of the U.S.

mustard (mus'tərd) n. [< OFr.] **1.** any of several plants with yellow flowers and slender pods **2.** the powdered seeds from these pods, used as a pungent seasoning **3.** a dark yellow

mustard gas a volatile liquid used as a poison gas in war

mustard plaster a plaster made with powdered mustard, applied to the skin as a counterirritant

muster (mus'tər) vt. [< L. monere, warn] **1.** to assemble (troops, etc.) **2.** to collect; summon [to muster up strength] —vi. to assemble as for inspection —n. **1.** an assembling, as of troops for inspection **2.** the persons or things assembled —**pass muster** to measure up to the required standards

musty (mus'tē) adj. -tier, -tiest [ult. < ? MOIST] **1.** having a stale, mouldy smell or taste **2.** trite or antiquated [musty ideas] —**mus'tily** adv. —**mus'tiness** n.

mutable (myōōt'ə b'l) adj. [< L. mutare, to change] **1.** that can be changed **2.** inconstant —**mu'tabil'ity** n.

mutant (myōōt''nt) adj. [< L. mutare, to change] undergoing mutation —n. an animal or plant with inheritable characters that differ from those of the parents

mutate (myōō tāt') vi., vt. -tat'ed, -tat'-ing [< L. mutare, to change] to change; specif., to undergo or cause to undergo mutation

mutation n. **1.** a change, as in form, nature, etc. **2.** Biol. a) a sudden variation in some inheritable character of an animal or plant b) a mutant —**muta'tional** adj.

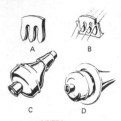

MUTES
(A, violin mute; B, on violin bridge;
C, trumpet mute; D, in bell of trumpet)

mute (myōōt) *adj.* [< L. *mutus*] 1. voluntarily silent 2. unable to speak 3. not spoken [a *mute* appeal] 4. not pronounced, as the *e* in mouse —*n.* 1. a person who does not speak; specif., one who cannot speak because deaf; deaf-mute 2. *Music* a device to soften the tone of an instrument —*vt.* mut′ed, mut′-ing 1. to soften the sound of 2. to tone down (a colour) —mute′ly *adv.*

mute swan a common swan with an orange-red beak

muti (mōō′tē) *n.* [< Zulu *umuthi*] [S Afr.] medicine, esp. herbal

mutilate (myōō′ə lāt′) *vt.* -lat′ed, -lat′-ing [< L. *mutilus*, maimed] 1. to cut off or damage a limb, etc. of (a person or animal) 2. to damage or otherwise make imperfect —mu′tila′tion *n.*

mutineer (myōōt′ə nēər′) *n.* one guilty of mutiny

mutiny (myōōt′ə nē) *n.,* pl. -nies [ult. < L. *movere*, to move] revolt against constituted authority; esp., rebellion of soldiers or sailors against their officers —*vi.* -nied, -nying to take part in a mutiny —mu′tinous *adj.*

mutt (mut) *n.* [prob. < *muttonhead*, a dolt] [Slang] 1. a stupid person; blockhead 2. a mongrel dog; cur

mutter (mut′ər) *vi., vt.* [ME. *moteren*] 1. to speak or say in low, indistinct tones 2. to grumble —*n.* 1. a muttering 2. something muttered —mut′terer *n.*

mutton (mut′'n) *n.* [< ML. *multo*, sheep] the flesh of sheep, used as food —**mutton dressed up as lamb** an older person, thing, or idea dressed up or presented so as to look young or new —mut′tony *adj.*

mutton chop 1. a piece cut from the rib of a sheep for grilling or frying 2. [pl.] side whiskers shaped like mutton chops

muttonhead *n.* [Slang] a stupid person

mutual (myōō′choo wəl) *adj.* [< L. *mutuus*, reciprocal] 1. a) done, felt, etc. by each of two or more for or towards the other or others; reciprocal [mutual admiration] b) of each other [mutual enemies] 2. [Colloq.] shared in common [our mutual friend] —mu′tual′ity (-wal′ə tē) *n.* —mu′tually *adv.*

mutual insurance company a company in which policy holders share in the profits

Muzak (myōō′zak) *Trademark* a system of transmitting recorded music to restaurants, factories, etc.

muzzle (muz′'l) *n.* [< ML. *musum*] 1. the part of the head of a dog, horse, etc. including the mouth, nose, and jaws 2. a device fastened over the mouth of an animal to prevent its biting or eating 3. the front end of the barrel of a firearm —*vt.* -zled, -zling 1. to put a muzzle on (an animal) 2. to prevent from expressing an opinion

muzzy (muz′ē) *adj.* -zier, -ziest [prob. < MU(DDY) + (FU)ZZY] [Colloq.] 1. confused; befuddled 2. blurred —muz′-zily *adv.* —muz′ziness *n.*

M.V.O. Member of the Royal Victorian Order

MW 1. medium wave 2. megawatt; megawatts

mW milliwatt; milliwatts

Mx 1. maxwell 2. Middlesex

my (mī; *unstressed* mə) *possessive pronominal adj.* [OE. *min*] of, belonging to, or done by me —*interj.* an exclamation of surprise, dismay, etc.

mycelium (mī sē′lē əm) *n.,* pl. -lia [< Gr. *mykēs*, mushroom] the vegetative part of a fungus

Mycenaean (mī′sə nē′ən) *adj.* of a civilization that existed in Greece, Asia Minor, etc. from 1500 to 1100 B.C.

mycology (mī kol′ə jē) *n.* [< Gr. *mykes*, fungus & -LOGY] the branch of botany dealing with fungi —mycol′ogist *n.*

myna, mynah (mī′nə) *n.* [Hindi *mainā*] a tropical bird of SE Asia that can mimic speech

Mynheer (mī nēər′) *n.* [Du.] Sir; Mr.: a Dutch title of address

myope (mī′ōp) *n.* a person having myopia

myopia (mī ō′pē ə) *n.* [< Gr. *myein*, to close + *ōps*, eye] abnormal vision in which light rays from distant objects focus in front of the retina, so that the objects are not seen distinctly; shortsightedness —myop′ic (-op′ik) *adj.*

myosotis (mī′ō sōt′is) *n.* [< Gr. *myosōtis*, mouse ear] any of a family of plants, including the forget-me-not

myriad (mir′ē əd) *n.* [< Gr. *myrias*, ten thousand] an indefinitely large number —*adj.* countless

myriapod (mir′ē ə pod′) *n.* [see prec. & -POD] an arthropod having many pairs of jointed legs, as the centipede

myrmidon (mur′mə dən) *n.,* pl. -dons [< tribe of Thessalian warriors who fought under Achilles] an unquestioning follower or subordinate

myrrh (mur) *n.* [< Ar. *murr*] a fragrant, bitter-tasting gum resin from Arabia and E Africa, used in making incense, perfume, etc.

myrtle (mur′t'l) *n.* [< Gr. *myrtos*] a shrub with evergreen leaves, white flowers, and dark berries

myself (mī self′, mə-) *pron.* a form of

the 1st pers. sing. pronoun, used: *a*) as an intensive [I went *myself*] *b*) as a reflexive [I hurt *myself*] *c*) as a quasi-noun meaning "my real or true self" [I am not *myself* today]

mysterious (mis tēər′ē əs) *adj.* of, containing, implying, or characterized by mystery —**myste′riously** *adv.*

mystery[1] (mis′tə rē) *n., pl.* **-teries** [< Gr. *mystērion,* secret rite] **1.** something unexplained, unknown, or kept secret **2.** a novel, play, etc. about a crime and its solution **3.** obscurity or secrecy **4.** [*pl.*] secret rites known only to the initiated [the Eleusinian *mysteries*]

mystery[2] *n., pl.* **-teries** [< L. *ministerium,* office, by confusion with prec.] [Archaic] a craft or craft guild

mystery play any of a class of medieval dramatic representations of Biblical events

mystery tour a bus tour, the itinerary of which is not known beforehand by the passengers

mystic (mis′tik) *adj.* [< Gr. *mystēs,* one initiated] **1.** *same as* MYSTICAL **2.** mysterious, secret, occult, etc. [*mystic* rites, *mystic* powers] —*n.* one who professes to undergo profound spiritual experiences

mystical *adj.* **1.** of mystics or mysticism **2.** spiritually symbolic **3.** *same as* MYSTIC (sense 2) —**mys′tically** *adv.*

mysticism *n.* **1.** the beliefs or practices of mystics **2.** the doctrine that knowledge of spiritual truths can be acquired by intuition and meditation

mystify (mis′tə fī′) *vt.* **-fied′, -fy′ing 1.** *a*) to puzzle *b*) to bewilder deliberately **2.** to make obscure —**mys′tifica′tion** *n.*

mystique (mis tēk′) *n.* [Fr., mystic] an aura of mystery, power, and awe surrounding some person, activity, etc.

myth (mith) *n.* [< Gr. *mythos*] **1.** a traditional story of unknown authorship, serving usually to explain some phenomenon, custom, etc. **2.** such stories collectively **3.** any fictitious story **4.** any imaginary person or thing

mythical *adj.* **1.** of myths **2.** existing only in myth **3.** imaginary or fictitious Also **myth′ic** —**myth′ically** *adv.*

mythologize (mi thol′ə jīz′) *vi.* **-gized′, -giz′ing** to relate or explain myths —*vt.* to make into a myth: also **myth′icize**

mythology (mi thol′ə jē) *n., pl.* **-gies** [< Gr. *mythos,* myth + -LOGY] **1.** the study of myths **2.** myths collectively; esp., the myths of a specific people —**mythological** (mith′ə loj′i k'l) *adj.* —**myth′olog′ically** *adv.*

myxomatosis (mik′sō mə tō′sis) *n.* [< Gr. *myxa,* mucus] an infectious virus disease in rabbits, characterized by tumorous growths

N

N, n (en) *n.*, *pl.* **N's, n's** the fourteenth letter of the English alphabet

n (en) *n.* 1. *Math.* the symbol for an indefinite number 2. *Physics* the symbol for neutron

N 1. *Chem.* nitrogen 2. *Physics* the symbol for newton

N, N., n, n. 1. north 2. northern 3. *Chess* knight

n. 1. net 2. neuter 3. noon 4. noun 5. number

Na [L. *natrium*] *Chem.* sodium

N.A.A.F.I. (naf′ē) 1. Navy, Army and Air Force Institutes 2. a shop or canteen run by this organization for servicemen

naartjie (när′chē) *n.* [< Afrik.] [S Afr.] a tangerine

nab (nab) *vt.* **nabbed, nab′bing** [< ?] [Colloq.] 1. to seize suddenly 2. to arrest or catch (a wrongdoer)

nabob (nā′bob) *n.* [< Ar. *nā′ib*, deputy] *Hist.* 1. a very rich man, esp. one who obtained his fortune in India 2. a governor of the old Mogul Empire in India

nacre (nā′kər) *n.* [Fr. < Ar.] mother-of-pearl —**na′creous** (-krē əs) *adj.*

nadir (nā′dēər′) *n.* [< Ar. *nazīr*, opposite] 1. the point opposite to the zenith and directly below the observer 2. the lowest point

nae (nā) *adv.* [Scot.] no; not —*adj.* no

naevus (nē′vəs) *n.*, *pl.* **nae′vi** (-vī) [L.] a birthmark or mole —**nae′void** *adj.*

nag[1] (nag) *vt.*, *vi.* **nagged, nag′ging** [< Scand.] 1. to annoy by continual scolding, etc. 2. to keep troubling —*n.* one who nags: also **nag′ger** —**nag′gingly** *adv.*

nag[2] *n.* [< ?] 1. a horse that is worn-out, old, etc. 2. a small riding horse

naiad (nī′ad) *n.* [< Gr. *naein*, to flow] [*also* N-] *Gr. & Rom. Myth.* any of the nymphs living in springs, fountains, rivers, etc.

naif, naïf (nä ēf′) *adj.* [Fr.] same as NAIVE

NAILS
(A, common wire; B, flooring;
C, finishing; D, oval; E, screw)

nail (nāl) *n.* [OE. *nægl*] 1. *a*) the thin, horny substance growing out at the ends of the fingers and toes *b*) a claw 2. a tapered piece of metal driven with a hammer to hold pieces of wood together —*vt.* 1. to attach, fasten, etc. with nails 2. to fix (the eyes, etc.) steadily on an object 3. to discover or expose (a lie, etc.) 4. [Colloq.] to catch, capture, etc. —**hit the nail on the head** to do whatever is exactly right —**nail down** to settle definitely —**on the nail** at once, esp. where payment is concerned

nail file a small, flat file for trimming the fingernails

nail set a tool for sinking a nail so that it is below the surface of the wood: also **nail punch**

naive, naïve (nä ēv′) *adj.* [Fr. < L. *nativus*, natural] unaffectedly simple; artless; unsophisticated —**naive′ly, naïve′ly** *adv.*

naiveté, naïveté (nä ēv′tā) *n.* [Fr.] 1. a being naive 2. a naive action or remark

naked (nā′kid) *adj.* [OE. *nacod*] 1. completely unclothed; nude 2. without protection or defence 3. without its usual covering [a naked sword] 4. without additions, etc. [the naked truth] 5. not aided by a microscope, etc. [the naked eye] —**na′kedly** *adv.* —**na′kedness** *n.*

naked ape a human being

NALGO (nal′gō) National and Local Government Officers' Association

namby-pamby (nam′bē pam′bē) *adj.* [< Ambrose Philips] insipidly pretty or nice —*n.*, *pl.* **-bies** a namby-pamby person

name (nām) *n.* [OE. *nama*] 1. a word or phrase by which a person, thing, or class of things is known; title 2. a word or phrase considered descriptive; epithet 3. *a*) reputation *b*) good reputation 4. a family 5. appearance only [in name only] 6. a famous person —*vt.* **named, nam′ing** 1. to give a name to 2. to designate by name 3. to identify by the right name [name the oceans] 4. to appoint to an office, etc. 5. to specify (a day, price, etc.) —**call names** to swear at —**in the name of** 1. in appeal to 2. by the authority of —**name names** to identify specific persons, esp. as doing wrong —**name the day** to decide on a date, esp. for a wedding —**to one's name** belonging to one —**name′able** *adj.*

name day the feast of the saint after whom one is named

name-dropper *n.* one who tries to impress others by mentioning famous persons in a familiar way

nameless *adj.* 1. without a name 2. left unnamed 3. not well known 4.

indescribable **5.** too horrible to specify —**name′lessly** *adv.*

namely *adv.* that is to say; to wit

nameplate *n.* a piece of metal, etc. on which a name is inscribed

namesake *n.* one with the same name as another

nankeen, nankin (naŋ kēn′) *n.* [< *Nanking*, in China] a buff-coloured cotton cloth, orig. from China

nanny (nan′ē) *n. pl.* **-nies** [< *Nan*, dim. of Ann(a)] **1.** a child's nurse **2.** [Colloq.] grandmother

nanny goat [see prec.] a female goat

nano- [< Gr. *nanos*, dwarf] *a combining form meaning* one thousand-millionth part of [*nanosecond*]

nap[1] (nap) *vi.* **napped, nap′ping** [OE. *hnappian*] **1.** to sleep lightly for a short time **2.** to be careless or unprepared —*n.* a brief, light sleep

nap[2] *n.* [< MLowG. *noppe*] the downy surface of cloth formed by short hairs or fibres, raised by brushing, etc.

nap[3] *n.* [< NAPOLEON] **1.** a card game for two or more players, similar to whist **2.** *Racing* a tip, supposed to be a certainty to win —*vt.* **napped, nap′ping** to name a horse as a winner —**go nap 1.** a bid in the game of nap to win all the tricks **2.** to risk all

napalm (nā′päm) *n.* [*na*(*phthene*) + *palm*(*itate*)] a jellylike substance with petrol or oil in it, used in flame throwers and bombs

nape (nāp) *n.* [ME.] the back of the neck

naphtha (naf′thə) *n.* [< Per. *neft*, pitch] a flammable liquid made by distilling petroleum

naphthalene (naf′thə lēn′) *n.* [< prec.] a white, crystalline hydrocarbon made by distilling coal tar and used in moth repellents, etc.

napkin (nap′kin) *n.* [< L. *mappa*, cloth] **1.** a small, usually square cloth or paper used while eating for protecting the clothes, etc. **2.** *same as* NAPPY

napkin ring a ring, often ornate, for holding a table napkin

napoleon (nə pō′lē ən) *n.* [< *Napoleon I*] **1.** a former gold coin of France **2.** *original name of* NAP[3]

nappy (nap′ē) *n., pl.* **-pies** [< NAPKIN] a soft, absorbent cloth arranged between the legs and around the waist of a baby

narcissism (när sis′iz′m) *n.* [< *Narcissus*] self-love —**narcis′sist** *n., adj.* —**nar′cissis′tic** *adj.*

narcissus (när sis′əs) *n., pl.* **-cis′suses, -cis′si** (-ī) [< L. < Gr. *narkissos*] any of a genus of bulb plants with yellow or orange flowers, including the daffodils

narcosis (när kō′sis) *n.* unconsciousness caused by a narcotic

narcotic (när kot′ik) *n.* [< Gr. *narkē*, numbness] **1.** a drug, as opium, used to relieve pain and induce sleep **2.** anything with a soothing, lulling, or dulling effect —*adj.* **1.** of, like, or producing narcosis **2.** of, by, or for narcotic addicts

nard (närd) *n.* [< Gr. *nardos*] spikenard

nark (närk) *n.* [< Romany *nak*, nose] [Slang] an informer or spy —*vt., vi.* [Slang] **1.** to make, be, or become annoyed, etc. **2.** to inform on (a person) —**nark′y** *adj.*

narrate (nə rāt′) *vt., vi.* **-rat′ed, -rat′ing** [< L. *narrare*, relate] **1.** to tell (a story) **2.** to give an account of (events) —**narra′tor** *n.*

narration (nə rā′shən) *n.* **1.** a narrating **2.** *same as* NARRATIVE **3.** writing or speaking that narrates

narrative (nar′ə tiv) *adj.* in story form —*n.* **1.** a story; tale **2.** the art or practice of relating stories

narrow (nar′ō) *adj.* [OE. *nearu*] **1.** small in width; not wide **2.** limited in meaning, size, amount, or extent **3.** limited in outlook; not liberal **4.** close; careful [a *narrow* inspection] **5.** with barely enough space, time, etc. **6.** limited in means —*vi., vt.* to decrease or limit in width, extent, or scope —*n.* [*usually pl.*] a narrow passage; strait —**nar′rowly** *adv.* —**nar′rowness** *n.*

narrow boat a long, narrow canal boat

narrow gauge a width (between railway lines) less than the standard of 56$\frac{1}{2}$ in. —**nar′row-gauge′** *adj.*

narrow-minded (nar′ō mīn′dəd) *adj.* limited in outlook; not liberal; prejudiced —**nar′row-mind′edness** *n.*

narrow seas the seas separating Britain and Europe

narwhal (när′wəl) *n.* [< Scand. *narhval*] an arctic whale valued for its oil and ivory: the male has a long, spiral tusk: also **nar′wal, nar′whale′**

N.A.S. National Association of Schoolmasters

NASA (nas′ə) [U.S.] National Aeronautics and Space Administration

nasal (nā′z'l) *adj.* [< L. *nasus*, nose] **1.** of the nose **2.** produced by making breath go through the nose **3.** characterized by such sounds [a *nasal* voice] —*n.* a nasal sound —**na′sally** *adv.*

nasalize (nā′zə līz′) *vt., vi.* **-ized′, -iz′ing** to pronounce or speak with a nasal sound or sounds —**na′saliza′tion** *n.*

nascent (nas′'nt) *adj.* [< L. *nasci*, be born] **1.** coming into being **2.** beginning to form, or develop —**nas′cence, nas′cency** *n.*

nasturtium (nə stur′shəm) *n.* [< L. *nasus*, nose + *torquere*, to twist] **1.** a plant with shield-shaped leaves and red, yellow, or orange flowers **2.** the flower

nasty (näs′tē) *adj.* **-tier, -tiest** [< ?] **1.** unpleasant **2.** offensive **3.** painful; dangerous [a *nasty* wound] **4.** spiteful; abusive, etc. —**a nasty piece of work** [Colloq.] an unpleasant person —**nas′tily** *adv.* —**nas′tiness** *n.*

nat. 1. national **2.** native **3.** natural

natal (nāt′'l) *adj.* [< L. *nasci*, be born] of or connected with one's birth

natatorial (nāt′ə tôr′ē əl) *adj.* [< L. *natator*, swimmer] characterized by swimming: also **na′tatory**

nation (nā′shən) *n.* [< L. *nasci*, be born]

1. a community of people with a territory, economic life, language, etc. in common **2.** a country **3.** a people or tribe —**na′tion-hood′** n.

national (nash′ən'l) adj. of or affecting a nation as a whole —n. **1.** a citizen of a nation **2.** [N-] same as GRAND NATIONAL —**na′tionally** adv.

national an̶them a patriotic hymn or song commonly sung by the people of a nation at public gatherings

National Assistance a former name for various social security benefits

National Debt the total debt of central government

National Front a political organization opposing immigration and advocating extreme nationalism

national grid 1. the system connecting electric power stations by a network of high-voltage power lines **2.** the metric coordinate system used in Ordnance Survey maps

National Guard [U.S.] a state military force that can be called into federal service by the president

National Health Service a system introduced in Britain in 1948 by which medical services are funded mainly by taxation rather than payments by individuals

National Insurance an insurance scheme operated by the British government, based on contributions from employers and employees and providing State aid for the sick, jobless, retired, etc.

nationalism n. **1.** the advocacy of national independence **2.** patriotism **3.** the putting of national interests above international considerations —**na′tionalist** n., adj. —**na′-tionalis′tic** adj.

nationality (nash′ə nal′ə tē) n., pl. **-ties 1.** the status of belonging to a particular nation by birth or naturalization **2.** a national group, esp. of immigrants from some other country **3.** national character

nationalize (nash′ə nə līz′) vt. **-ized′, -iz′-ing 1.** to transfer ownership or control of (land, industries, etc.) to the nation **2.** to make national —**na′tionaliza′tion** n.

national park an area of great scenic beauty set aside for the use of the public

national service compulsory military service, usually for a fixed period of time; conscription

National Trust a society founded to preserve and administer places of historic interest or natural beauty

nationwide (nā′shən wīd′) adj. by or throughout the whole nation

native (nāt′iv) adj. [< L. nasci, be born] **1.** inborn; natural **2.** belonging to a locality or country by birth, production, or growth **3.** being, or associated with, the place of one's birth [one's native land] **4.** as found in nature **5.** of or characteristic of the people born in a certain place —n. **1.** a person born in the region indicated **2.** an original inhabitant, esp. as distinguished from colonists, etc. **3.** an indigenous plant or animal **4.** a permanent

resident, not a mere visitor —**go native** to adopt the simpler way of life found in the country one is visiting, etc. —**na′-tively** adv. —**na′tiveness** n.

nativity (nə tiv′ə tē) n., pl. **-ties** [see NATIVE] birth —**the Nativity 1.** the birth of Jesus **2.** Christmas Day

NATO (nā′tō) North Atlantic Treaty Organization

NATSOPA (nat sō′pə) National Society of Operative Printers, Graphical & Media Personnel

natter (nat′ər) vi. [< dial.] [Colloq.] **1.** to chatter idly **2.** to grumble —n. [Colloq.] a chat

natterjack toad (nat′ər jak′) [< ? echoic] a small toad

natty (nat′ē) adj. **-tier, -tiest** [< ?] trim and smart in appearance or dress —**nat′-tily** adv. —**nat′tiness** n.

natural (nach′rəl) adj. [< L. naturalis, by birth] **1.** of or arising from nature **2.** produced or existing in nature; not artificial **3.** innate; inborn [natural abilities] **4.** based on instinctive moral feeling [natural rights] **5.** true to nature; lifelike **6.** normal [a natural outcome] **7.** customarily expected [a natural courtesy] **8.** free from affectation **9.** a) illegitimate b) not adoptive **10.** Music neither sharpened nor flattened —n. **1.** [Colloq.] a person who is naturally expert **2.** [Colloq.] a sure success **3.** a yellowish-grey colour **4.** Music a) the sign (♮) cancelling a preceding sharp or flat: in full, **natural sign** b) the note affected: in full, **natural note 5.** an idiot —**nat′ural-ness** n.

natural gas a mixture of gaseous hydrocarbons occurring naturally in the earth and used as a fuel

natural history the study of the animal, vegetable, and mineral world, esp. in a popular way

naturalism n. **1.** Literature, Art, etc. faithful adherence to nature; realism **2.** action or thought based on natural desires or instincts

naturalist n. **1.** a person who studies animals and plants **2.** a person who believes in or practises naturalism —**nat′u-ralis′tic** adj.

naturalize vt. **-ized′, -iz′ing 1.** to confer citizenship upon (someone of foreign birth) **2.** to adopt and make common (a custom, word, etc.) from another place **3.** to adapt (a plant or animal) to a new environment —**nat′uraliza′tion** n.

naturally adv. **1.** in a natural manner **2.** by nature; innately **3.** as one might expect; of course

natural number any positive integer, as 1, 2, etc.

natural philosophy earlier name for physics

natural resources the forms of wealth supplied by nature, as coal, oil, water power, etc.

natural science the systematized knowledge of nature, including biology, chemistry, physics, etc.

natural selection the process in evolution by which those individuals (of a species) with characters that help them to become adapted to their specific environment tend to transmit their characters

nature (nā′chər) *n.* [< L. *nasci*, be born] **1.** the quality or qualities that make something what it is; essence **2.** inborn character, disposition, or tendencies **3.** kind; sort **4.** the basic biological functions, instincts, drives, etc. **5.** the physical universe **6.** [*sometimes* N-] the power, force, etc. that seems to regulate this **7.** the primitive state of man **8.** natural scenery —**by nature** inherently —**call of nature** [Colloq.] the desire or need to urinate or defecate —**in a state of nature 1.** completely naked **2.** not cultivated **3.** uncivilized

-natured (nā′chərd) *a combining form meaning* having or showing a (specified kind of) temperament

nature trail a path set out in woods, etc., so as to facilitate the study of nature by its users

naught (nôt) *n.* [< OE. *na*, no + *wiht*, person] **1.** nothing **2.** *Arith.* the figure zero (0) —*adj.* [Archaic] worthless Also **nought** —**set at naught** to defy

naughty (nôt′ē) *adj.* **-tier, -tiest** [< obs. *naught*, wicked] **1.** not behaving properly; disobedient **2.** improper or obscene —**naugh′tily** *adv.* —**naugh′tiness** *n.*

nausea (nô′sē ə) *n.* [< Gr. *nausia*, seasickness] **1.** a feeling of sickness in the stomach, with an urge to vomit **2.** disgust

nauseate *vt., vi.* **-at′ed, -at′ing** to feel or cause to feel nausea

nauseous (nô′sē əs) *adj.* causing nausea; sickening —**nau′seously** *adv.* —**nau′-seousness** *n.*

naut. nautical

nautch (nôch) *n.* [< Sans. *nṛt*, to dance] in India, a performance by professional dancing girls (**nautch girls**)

nautical (nôt′i k'l) *adj.* [< Gr. *naus*, ship] of or relating to sailors, ships, or navigation —**nau′tically** *adv.*

nautical mile an international unit of distance for sea and air navigation, equal to 6076.11549 feet (1852 metres)

NAUTILUS
(shown in
cross section)

nautilus (nôt′il əs) *n., pl.* **-luses, -li′** (-ī′) [< Gr. *naus*, ship] a tropical mollusc with a many-chambered, spiral shell having a pearly interior

naval (nā′v'l) *adj.* [< L. *navis*, ship] of, having, characteristic of, or for a navy, its ships, etc.

nave[1] (nāv) *n.* [< L. *navis*, ship] the main part of a church, extending from the chancel to the principal entrance

nave[2] *n.* [OE. *nafu*] the hub of a wheel

navel (nā′v'l) *n.* [OE. *nafela*] the small depression in the middle of the abdomen, where the umbilical cord was attached

navel orange a seedless orange having a navellike depression containing a small, secondary fruit

navigable (nav′i gə b'l) *adj.* [see ff.] **1.** wide or deep enough for ships, etc. to go through **2.** that can be steered —**nav′i-gabil′ity** *n.* —**nav′igably** *adv.*

navigate (nav′ə gāt′) *vt., vi.* **-gat′ed, -gat′-ing** [< L. *navis*, ship + *agere*, lead] **1.** to steer or direct (a ship or aircraft) **2.** [Colloq.] to make one's way **3.** to travel through or over (water, air, or land) in a ship or aircraft —**nav′iga′tor** *n.*

navigation (nav′ə gā′shən) *n.* the act or practice of locating the position and plotting the course of ships and aircraft —**nav′iga′tional** *adj.*

navvy (nav′ē) *n., pl.* **-vies** [< NAVIGATE] an unskilled labourer, as on canals, roads, etc.

navy (nā′vē) *n., pl.* **-vies** [< L. *navis*, ship] **1.** all the warships of a nation **2.** [*often* N-] the entire sea force of a nation, including vessels, personnel, stores, yards, etc. **3.** *same as* NAVY BLUE

navy blue very dark, purplish blue

nawab (nə wäb′) *n.* [Hindi *navāb*] *same as* NABOB

nay (nā) *adv.* [< ON. *ne*, not + *ei*, ever] not that only, but also [*he* is well-off, *nay*, *rich*] —*n.* **1.** a refusal or denial **2.** a negative vote or voter

Nazarene (naz′ə rēn′) *adj.* of Nazareth or the Nazarenes —*n.* a native or inhabitant of Nazareth —**the Nazarene** Jesus

Nazi (nät′sē) *adj.* [G., contr. of party name] designating or of the German fascist political party that ruled Germany under Hitler (1933–45) —*n.* **1.** a member of this party **2.** [*often* n-] a supporter of this party or its ideology; fascist —**Na′-zism, Na′ziism** *n.*

Nb *Chem.* niobium

N.B. New Brunswick

N.B., n.b. [L. *nota bene*] note well

N.C.B. National Coal Board

NCO, N.C.O. noncommissioned officer

NCR no carbon required

Nd *Chem.* neodymium

N.D., n.d. no date

N.D.P. [Canad.] New Democratic Party

N.D.T. [Canad.] Newfoundland Daylight Time

Ne *Chem.* neon

NE, N.E., n.e. **1.** northeast **2.** northeastern

Neanderthal (nē an′dər täl′) *adj.* [< German valley where remains were found] designating or of a form of primitive man of the paleolithic period

neap (nēp) *adj.* [< OE. *nepflod*, neap

tide] designating either of the two lowest monthly tides

Neapolitan (nē'ə pol'ə t'n) *adj.* of Naples —*n.* a native or inhabitant of Naples

near (nēar) *adv.* [< OE. *neah*, nigh] **1.** at a short distance in space or time **2.** [Colloq.] almost —*adj.* **1.** close in distance or time **2.** close in relationship; akin **3.** close in friendship **4.** close in degree [a *near* escape] **5.** on the left side, facing forward: said of an animal, car wheel, etc. **6.** stingy —*prep.* close to in space, time, degree, etc. —*vt., vi.* to draw near (to) —**near at hand** very close in time or space —**near'ness** *n.*

nearby *adj., adv.* near; close at hand

Near Eastern of or designating those countries near the E end of the Mediterranean

nearly *adv.* almost —**not nearly** not at all

nearsighted (nēar'sīt'id) *adj.* short sighted —**near'sight'edness** *n.*

neat (nēt) *adj.* [< L. *nitere*, shine] **1.** *a)* clean and orderly; trim; tidy *b)* skilful and precise *c)* simple **2.** unmixed [to drink whisky *neat*] **3.** well-proportioned **4.** cleverly phrased or done —**neat'ly** *adv.* —**neat'ness** *n.*

neaten *vt.* to make neat

'neath, neath (nēth) *prep.* [Poet.] beneath

N.E.B. National Enterprise Board

nebula (neb'yoo lə) *n., pl.* **-lae'** (-lē'), **-las** [< L., fog] a vast cloudlike patch seen in the night sky, consisting of very distant groups of stars, etc. —**neb'ular** *adj.*

nebulous (neb'yoo ləs) *adj.* **1.** unclear; vague; indefinite **2.** of or like a nebula —**neb'ulously** *adv.*

necessarily (nes'ə sər ə lē) *adv.* **1.** because of necessity **2.** as a necessary result

necessary (nes'ə sər ē) *adj.* [< L. *ne-*, not + *cedere*, give way] **1.** essential; indispensable **2.** inevitable **3.** that must be done **4.** that follows logically —*n., pl.* **-saries** a thing necessary to life, to some purpose, etc.

necessitarianism (nə ses'ə tāər'ē ən iz'm) *n.* the theory that there is no free will, but that human behaviour is causally determined —**neces'sitar'ian** *n., adj.*

necessitate (nə ses'ə tāt') *vt.* **-tat'ed, -tat'ing** **1.** to make (something) necessary **2.** to compel

necessitous *adj.* needy; destitute

necessity (nə ses'ə tē) *n., pl.* **-ties** [see NECESSARY] **1.** something that cannot be done without **2.** what is required by circumstances, custom, law, etc. **3.** great need **4.** poverty **5.** natural causation; fate —**of necessity** necessarily

neck (nek) *n.* [OE. *hnecca*] **1.** that part of man or animal joining the head to the body **2.** a narrow part between the head and the body of any object, as of a violin **3.** that part of a garment nearest the neck **4.** a narrow, necklike part; specif., *a)* a narrow strip of land *b)* the narrowest part of a bottle, vase, etc. *c)* a strait—*vt.,*

vi. [Slang] to kiss and caress in making love —**get it in the neck** [Slang] to be severely reprimanded —**neck and neck** very close, as in a race —**neck or nothing** risking all —**risk one's neck** to put one's life, career, etc. in danger —**stick one's neck out** to expose oneself to possible failure, etc. —**neck'er** *n.* —**neck'ing** *n.*

neckband *n.* the part of a garment that encircles the neck

neckerchief (nek'ər chif) *n.* a kerchief worn around the neck

necklace *n.* [NECK + LACE] a string of beads, jewels, etc. worn as an ornament around the neck

neckline *n.* the line formed by the edge of a garment around or nearest the neck

necktie *n.* same as TIE (*n.* 4)

necro- [< Gr.] *a combining form meaning* death, corpse

necromancy (nek'rō man'sē) *n.* [< Gr. *nekros*, corpse + *manteia*, divination] **1.** divination by alleged communication with the dead **2.** sorcery —**nec'roman'cer** *n.*

necrophilia (nek'rō fil'ē ə) *n.* [< NECRO- + Gr. *philos*, loving] an abnormal, often erotic, fascination with death and the dead —**nec'rophile'** (-fil') *n.* —**nec'rophil'iac** *adj.*

necropolis (ne krop'ə lis) *n., pl.* **-lises** [< Gr. *nekros*, dead body + *polis*, city] a cemetery

necrosis (ne krō'sis) *n., pl.* **-ses** (-sēz) [< Gr. *nekros*, dead body] the death or decay of tissue in a part of a living body or plant, as from disease —**necrose** (ne krōs') *vt., vi.* **-crosed'**, **-cros'ing**

nectar (nek'tər) *n.* [< Gr. *nektar*, that overcomes death] **1.** *Bot.* the sweetish liquid in many flowers, made into honey by bees **2.** *Gr. Myth.* the drink of the gods **3.** any delicious beverage —**nec'tarous** *adj.*

nectarine (nek'tə rin) *n.* [< prec.] a variety of peach having a smooth skin without down

N.E.D.C. National Economic Development Council

neddy¹ (ne'dē) *n., pl.* **-dies** [< *Edward*] a child's word for donkey

neddy² *n.* [< N.E.D.C.] [Colloq.] the National Economic Development Council

née (nā) *adj.* [Fr.] born: used to indicate the maiden name of a married woman

need (nēd) *n.* [OE. *nied*] **1.** necessity **2.** lack of something required or desired **3.** something required or desired [one's daily *needs*] **4.** *a)* a condition of deficiency, or one requiring relief or supply *b)* extreme want —*vt.* to have need of; require *Need* is often used as an auxiliary followed by an infinitive with or without *to*, meaning "to be obliged", "must" [he *need* not come] —*vi.* **1.** to be in need —**have need to** to be compelled to —**if need be** if it is required

needful *adj.* necessary —*n.* [Colloq.] ready money

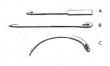

NEEDLES
(A, sewing machine;
B, straight; C,
surgical)

needle (nēd′′l) *n.* [OE. *nædl*] **1.** a slender, sharp-pointed piece of steel with a hole for thread, used for sewing **2.** *a)* a slender, hooked rod of steel, bone, etc., for crocheting *b)* a similar but hookless rod, for knitting **3.** a short, pointed piece of metal, etc. that moves in gramophone record grooves to transmit vibrations **4.** the pointer of a compass, gauge, etc. **5.** the thin, short, pointed leaf of the pine, spruce, etc. **6.** the sharp, very slender metal tube at the end of a hypodermic syringe **7.** a needlelike structure or part **8.** [Colloq.] a spur **9.** [Slang] an attack of nerves —*vt.* **-dled, -dling** [Colloq.] *a)* to goad *b)* to tease **2.** to sew, puncture, etc. with a needle —**look for a needle in a haystack** to search for something that is almost impossible to find —**nee′dle-like′** *adj.*

needlecord *n.* a fine corduroy fabric

needle game a game which is fiercely contested and in which there is personal antagonism between the players

needlepoint *n.* **1.** an embroidery of woollen threads on canvas **2.** lace made on a paper pattern

needless (nēd′lis) *adj.* unnecessary —**need′lessly** *adv.*

needle time *Radio* the amount of programme time during which recorded music is played

needlewoman *n.* a seamstress

needlework *n.* work done with a needle; sewing or embroidery —**nee′dlework′er** *n.*

needs (nēdz) *adv.* [OE. *nedes*] [Now Rare] of necessity; necessarily (with *must*) [he must *needs* obey]

needy (nēd′ē) *adj.* **-ier, -iest** very poor; destitute

ne'er (nāər) *adv.* [Poet.] never

ne'er-do-well *n.* a shiftless, irresponsible person —*adj.* lazy, worthless, etc.

nefarious (ni fāər′ē əs) *adj.* [< L. *ne-*, not + *fas*, lawful] very wicked —**nefar′iously** *adv.*

neg. 1. negative **2.** negatively

negate (ni gāt′) *vt.* **-gat′ed, -gat′ing** [see ff.] **1.** to make ineffective **2.** to deny the existence or truth of

negation (ni gā′shən) *n.* [< L. *negare*, deny] **1.** a denial **2.** the lack or opposite of something positive

negative (neg′ə tiv) *adj.* [see prec.] **1.** expressing denial or refusal; saying "no" **2.** opposite to or lacking what is positive [a *negative* personality] **3.** *Elec.* having an excess of electrons **4.** *Math.* less than zero **5.** *Med.* not indicating the presence of symptoms, bacteria, etc. **6.** *Photog.* reversing the relation of light and shade of the original subject —*n.* **1.** a word, phrase, etc. expressing denial, rejection, or refusal **2.** the point of view opposing the affirmative **3.** the plate in a voltaic battery where the lower potential is **4.** *Math.* a negative quantity **5.** *Photog.* an exposed and developed negative film from which positive prints are made —*vt.* **-tived, -tiving 1.** to veto **2.** to contradict **3.** to disprove **4.** to neutralize —**in the negative 1.** in refusal or denial of a plan, etc. **2.** with a negative answer —**neg′atively** *adv.*

negativism (neg′ə tiv iz′m) *n.* *Psychol.* an attitude characterized by ignoring or resisting suggestions or orders from others —**neg′ativist** *n., adj.* —**neg′ativis′tic** *adj.*

neglect (ni glekt′) *vt.* [< L. *neg-*, not + *legere*, gather] **1.** to fail to attend to properly **2.** to leave undone **3.** to ignore or disregard —*n.* **1.** a neglecting or being neglected **2.** lack of proper care

neglectful *adj.* negligent (often with *of*)

négligé (neg′lē zhā′) *n.* [< Fr. *négliger*, to neglect] a woman's loosely fitting dressing gown

negligent (neg′li jənt) *adj.* [see NEGLECT] **1.** habitually failing to do the required thing **2.** careless, inattentive, etc. —**neg′ligence** *n.* —**neg′ligently** *adv.*

negligible (neg′li jə b'l) *adj.* that can be neglected or disregarded, esp. because small —**neg′ligibly** *adv.*

negotiable (ni gō′shē ə b'l) *adj.* **1.** that can be passed, crossed, etc. **2.** legally transferable, as a promissory note —**nego′tiabil′ity** *n.*

negotiate (ni gō′shē āt′) *vi.* **-at′ed, -at′ing** [< L. *negotium*, business] to confer or discuss with a view to reaching agreement —*vt.* **1.** to succeed in crossing, moving through, etc. **2.** to settle (a transaction, treaty, etc.) **3.** to transfer or sell (negotiable paper) —**nego′tia′tor** *n.*

negotiation (ni gō′shē ā′shən) *n.* [often *pl.*] a conferring or bargaining to reach agreement —**nego′tiatory** *adj.*

Negress (nē′gris) *n.* a Negro woman or girl

Negrito (ne grēt′ō) *n., pl.* **-tos, -toes** [Sp., < *negro*, NEGRO] a member of any of various dwarfish Negroid peoples of the East Indies, the Philippines, and Africa

negritude (nē′grə tyōōd′) *n.* [Fr. *négritude*] [*also* N-] the affirmation by Negroes of their cultural heritage

Negro (nē′grō) *n., pl.* **-groes** [Sp. < L. *niger*, black] **1.** a member of the Negroid peoples of Africa **2.** *same as* NEGROID **3.** any person with Negro ancestors —*adj.* of Negroes

Negroid (nē′groid) *adj.* designating or of a major group of mankind that includes the dark-skinned peoples of Africa —*n.* a Negroid person

negus (nē′gəs) *n.* [< Col. Francis *Negus*] a beverage of hot water, wine, and lemon juice

neigh (nā) *vi.* [OE. *hnægan*] to utter the characteristic cry of a horse; whinny —*n.* this cry

neighbour (nā′bər) *n.* [< OE. *neah*, nigh + *gebur*, farmer] 1. one who lives near another 2. a person or thing situated near another 3. a fellow man —*adj.* nearby; adjacent —*vt.*, *vi.* to live or be situated near U.S. sp., **neighbor**

neighbourhood *n.* 1. a district, esp. with regard to some characteristic 2. people living near one another —**in the neighbourhood of** 1. near (a place) 2. [Colloq.] approximately

neighbourly *adj.* friendly —**neigh′bourliness** *n.*

neither (nī′thər) *adj.*, *pron.* [OE. *nahwæther*, not whether] not either [*neither* of them sings] —*conj.* 1. not either [*can neither* laugh *nor* cry] 2. nor [*neither* does he drink]

nelly (nel′ē) *n.* [< rhyming slang] life: only in **not on your nelly**

nelson (nel′s'n) *n.* [< name] a wrestling hold in which one arm is placed under the opponent's arm from behind with the hand pressing the back of his neck

nematode (nem′ətōd′) *n.* [< Gr. *nēma*, thread] a long, cylindrical worm, as the hookworm

Nemesis (nem′əsis) *n.*, *pl.* **-ses** (-sēz′) [< Gr. *nemein*, deal out] 1. *a)* just punishment *b)* one who imposes this 2. anyone or anything that it seems will surely defeat or thwart one After the goddess of retribution in Greek myth

neo- [< Gr.] *a combining form meaning* new [*neolithic, neocolonialism*]

neoclassic (nē′ōklas′ik) *adj.* designating or of a revival of classic style in art, literature, etc.: also **ne′oclas′sical** —**ne′oclas′sicism** *n.* —**ne′oclas′sicist** *n.*

neodymium (nē′ōdim′ēəm) *n.* [< NEO- + Gr. *didymos*, twin] a metallic chemical element of the rare-earth group: symbol, Nd

Neolithic (nē′ōlith′ik) *adj.* [NEO- + Gr. *lithos*, stone] designating or of the later part of the Stone Age

neologism (nēol′əjiz′m) *n.* [see NEO- & -LOGY] a new word or a new meaning for an established word

neon (nē′on) *n.* [< Gr. *neos*, new] a rare, colourless, and inert gaseous chemical element: symbol, Ne

neon lamp a tube containing neon, which glows red when an electric current is sent through it

neophyte (nē′ōfīt′) *n.* [< Gr. *neos*, new + *phyein*, produce] 1. a new convert 2. any beginner

Nepali (nipôl′ē) *n.* 1. the Indic language of Nepal 2. an inhabitant of Nepal

nephew (nev′yoo) *n.* [< L. *nepos*] 1. the son of one's brother or sister 2. the son of one's brother-in-law or sister-in-law

nephritis (nefrīt′əs) *n.* [see ff. & -ITIS] disease of the kidneys, characterized by inflammation, fibrosis, etc.

nephro- [< Gr.] *a combining form meaning* kidney

ne plus ultra (nā′plus ul′trə) [L., no more beyond] the highest point of perfection

nepotism (nep′ətiz′m) *n.* [< L. *nepos*, nephew] favouritism shown to relatives, esp. in appointment to desirable positions

Neptune (nep′tyoon) 1. *Rom. Myth.* the god of the sea 2. a planet of the solar system, eighth in distance from the sun

neptunium (neptyoo′nēəm) *n.* a radioactive chemical element produced by irradiating uranium atoms with neutrons: symbol, Np

N.E.R.C. National Environment Research Council

nervate (nur′vāt) *adj. Bot.* having nerves, or veins

nerve (nurv) *n.* [< L. *nervus*] 1. any of the cordlike fibres carrying impulses between the body organs and the central nervous system 2. courage 3. strength; vigour 4. [*pl.*] nervousness 5. [Colloq.] audacity 6. a tendon: now chiefly in **strain every nerve**, to try as hard as possible 7. *Biol.* a vein in a leaf or insect's wing —*vt.* **nerved, nerv′ing** 1. to give strength or courage to 2. to brace (oneself) —**bundle of nerves** a very nervous person —**get on one's nerves** [Colloq.] to make one irritable

nerve cell *same as* NEURON

nerve centre 1. any group of nerve cells that function together 2. a control centre; headquarters

nerve gas a gas which can paralyse the respiratory and central nervous systems

nerveless *adj.* 1. without strength, courage, etc.; weak 2. controlled 3. *Biol.* without nerves —**nerve′lessly** *adv.*

nerve-racking *adj.* very trying to one's patience or equanimity

nervous (nur′vəs) *adj.* 1. characterized by or having a disordered state of the nerves 2. emotionally tense, restless, agitated, etc. 3. fearful 4. of or made up of nerves 5. vigorous in expression —**nerv′ously** *adv.* —**nerv′ousness** *n.*

nervous breakdown a psychotic or neurotic disorder that impairs the ability to function normally

nervous system all the nerve cells and nervous tissues in an organism, including, in the vertebrates, the brain, spinal cord, nerves, etc.

nervy *adj.* **-ier, -iest** nervous; excitable —**nerv′ily** *adv.*

nescient (nes′ēənt) *adj.* [< L. *ne-*, not + *scire*, know] ignorant —**nes′cience** *n.*

ness (nes) *n.* [< OE. *næs*] a headland: chiefly in place names [*Inverness*]

-ness (nis, nəs) [OE. *-nes(s)*] *a suffix meaning* state, quality, or instance of being [*sadness, weakness*]

nest (nest) *n.* [OE.] 1. the structure or place where a bird lays its eggs and shelters its young 2. the place used by hornets, fish, etc. for spawning or breeding 3. a cosy place; retreat 4. a resort, haunt,

or den or its frequenters [a *nest* of thieves]
5. a swarm or colony of birds, insects,
etc. **6.** a set of similar things, each fitting
within the one next larger —*vi.*, *vt.* **1.**
to build or live in (a nest) **2.** to fit (an
object) closely within another —**nest′able**
adj. —**nest′er** *n.*

nest egg money, etc. put aside as a
reserve or to set up a fund

nestle (nes′'l) *vi.* -tled, -tling [OE. *nestlian*]
1. to settle down comfortably and snugly
2. to press close for comfort or in affection
3. to lie sheltered, as a house among
trees —*vt.* **1.** to rest or press snugly
2. to house as in a nest

nestling (nest′liŋ) *n.* a young bird still
in the nest

net[1] (net) *n.* [OE. *nett*] **1.** an openwork
fabric of string, cord, etc., used to snare
birds, fish, etc. **2.** a trap; snare **3.** a
meshed fabric used to hold, protect, or
mark off something [a hairnet] **4.** a fine,
meshed, lacelike cloth —*vt.* **net′ted, net′-
ting 1.** to snare or acquire, as with a
net **2.** to shelter or enclose as with a
net —*vi.* **1.** to make a net out of rope,
etc. —**net′like′** *adj.*

net[2] *adj.* [Fr.: see NEAT] **1.** remaining
after certain deductions or allowances have
been made, as for expenses **2.** final [net
result] —*vt.* **net′ted, net′ting** to gain
as profit

netball *n.* a team game played mainly
by women, in which a ball is thrown
through a netted ring attached to a post
—**net′baller** *n.*

nether (neth′ər) *adj.* [OE. *neothera*]
lower or under

nether garments [Archaic] same as
TROUSERS

nethermost *adj.* lowest

nether world Theol. & Myth. the world
of the dead or of punishment after death;
hell: also **nether regions**

net profit the profit remaining after all
operating expenses have been deducted
from the gross or total profit

nett *n.* var. sp. of NET[2]

netting *n.* netted material

nettle (net′'l) *n.* [OE. *netele*] any of
a number of related weeds with stinging
hairs —*vt.* -tled, -tling **1.** to irritate; annoy;
vex **2.** to sting with or as with nettles

nettle rash same as HIVES

network (net′wurk′) *n.* **1.** any
arrangement of parallel wires, threads, etc.
crossed at regular intervals by others so
as to leave open spaces **2.** a) a system
of connecting roads, canals, etc. b) Radio
& TV a chain of transmitting stations c)
a system, etc. of cooperating individuals

neural (nyoor′əl) *adj.* [< NEURO-] of
a nerve, nerves, or the nervous system

neuralgia (nyoo ral′jə) *n.* [see NEURO-
& -ALGIA] severe pain along the course
of a nerve —**neural′gic** *adj.*

neurasthenia (nyoor′as thē′nē ə) *n.* [<
NEURO- + Gr. *astheneia*, weakness] a
type of neurosis characterized by
irritability, fatigue, etc. —**neu′rasthen′ic**
(-then′ik) *adj.*, *n.*

neuritis (nyoo rīt′əs) *n.* [see ff. & -ITIS]
inflammation of a nerve or nerves,
accompanied by pain

neuro- [< Gr.] a combining form meaning
of a nerve, nerves, or the nervous system
[neuropathy]

neurology (nyoo rol′ə jē) *n.* [see prec.
& -LOGY] the branch of medicine dealing
with the nervous system and its diseases
—**neurol′ogist** *n.*

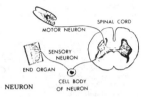

neuron (nyoor′on) *n.* [< Gr. *neuron*,
nerve] the nerve cell body and all its
processes: also **neu′rone** (-ōn) —**neu′ro-
nal** *adj.*

neuropteran (nyoo rop′tər ən) *n.* [<
NEURO- + Gr. *pteron*, wing] any of a
group of insects with four membranous
wings and biting mouthparts

neurosis (nyoo rō′sis) *n.*, *pl.* -ses (-sēz)
[see NEURO-] a mental disorder
characterized by anxiety, compulsions and
obsessions, depression, etc.

neurosurgery (nyoor′ō sur′jər ē) *n.* the
branch of surgery involving the brain and
spinal cord

neurotic (nyoo rot′ik) *adj.* of or having
a neurosis —*n.* a neurotic person —**neu-
rot′ically** *adv.*

neut. neuter

neuter (nyoot′ər) *adj.* [< L. *ne-*, not +
uter, either] **1.** Biol. a) having no sexual
organs b) having undeveloped sexual
organs in the adult, as the worker bee
2. Gram. designating or of the gender
that refers to things regarded as neither
masculine nor feminine —*n.* **1.** a castrated
or spayed animal **2.** Biol. a neuter plant
or animal **3.** Gram. a) the neuter gender
b) a neuter word —*vt.* to castrate or
spay (an animal)

neutral (nyoo′trəl) *adj.* [see prec.] **1.**
not taking part in either side of a quarrel
or war **2.** not one thing or the other;
indifferent **3.** having little or no decided
colour **4.** Biol. same as NEUTER **5.** Chem.
neither acid nor alkaline **6.** Elec. neither
negative nor positive —*n.* **1.** a nation
not taking part in a war **2.** a neutral
person **3.** a neutral colour **4.** Mech. a
disengaged position of gears: also called
neutral gear —**neu′trally** *adv.*

neutrality (nyoo tral′ə tē) *n.* **1.** a being
neutral **2.** the status or policy of a neutral
nation

neutralize (nyoo′trə līz′) *vt.* -ized′, -iz′-
ing **1.** to destroy the effectiveness, etc.
of **2.** Chem. to destroy the active properties
of **3.** Elec. to make electrically neutral

4. to declare (a nation, etc.) neutral —**neu′-traliza′tion** *n.*

neutrino (nyōō trē′nō) *n.,* pl. **-nos** [It.] *Physics* a neutral particle having a mass approaching zero

neutron (nyōō′tron) *n.* [NEUTER + (ELECTR)ON] an uncharged fundamental particle in the nucleus of an atom

never (nev′ər) *adv.* [< OE. *ne,* not + *æfre,* ever] **1.** not ever; at no time **2.** not at all; in no case

nevermore *adv.* never again

never-never *n.* [Colloq.] the hire purchase system of buying

never-never land [< *Peter Pan*] an unreal or unrealistic place or situation

nevertheless (nev′ar tha les′) *adv.* in spite of that; nonetheless; however

new (nyōō) *adj.* [OE. *niwe*] **1.** appearing, thought of, discovered, made, etc. for the first time **2.** a) different [a *new* hairdo] b) strange; unfamiliar **3.** more or most recent of two or more things of the same class [the *new* library] **4.** recently grown [*new* potatoes] **5.** not previously used or worn **6.** modern; recent **7.** more; additional **8.** starting as a repetition of a cycle, series, etc. [the *new* year] **9.** having just reached a position, rank, place, etc. [a *new* arrival] **10.** refreshed [a *new* man] —*n.* something new (with *the*) —*adv.* **1.** again **2.** newly; recently —**new wine in old bottles** new ideas, institutions, etc. added to an established order

New Brunswicker (brunz′wik ər) a native or inhabitant of New Brunswick

New Canadian a recent immigrant to Canada

newcomer *n.* a person who has come recently

newel (nyōō′al) *n.* [< L. *nux,* nut] **1.** the upright pillar around which the steps of a winding staircase turn **2.** the post at the top or bottom of a flight of stairs, supporting the handrail: also **newel post**

newfangled (nyōō′faŋ′g′ld) *adj.* [< ME. *newe,* new + OE. *fon,* take] new; novel: a humorously derogatory term

New High German see GERMAN, HIGH GERMAN

New Jerusalem *Bible* heaven: Rev. 21 :2

new-laid *adj.* freshly laid: said of eggs

newly *adv.* **1.** recently; lately **2.** anew; afresh

newlywed *n.* a recently married person

new maths a system for teaching basic mathematics based on the use of sets

new moon the moon when it is between the earth and the sun, with its dark side towards the earth

news (nyōōz) *n.pl.* [with *sing. v.*] **1.** reports of recent happenings, esp. those broadcast, printed in a newspaper, etc. **2.** new information; information previously unknown —**in the news** much talked about

newsagent *n.* a person who sells newspapers, magazines, etc., esp. as a retailer

news bulletin the latest news, esp. as broadcast by radio and television

newscast *n.* a programme of news broadcast over radio or TV —**news′-caster** *n.*

news conference *same as* PRESS CONFERENCE

newsflash *n.* a brief item of urgent or important news, esp. one that interrupts a radio or TV programme

newsletter *n.* a news bulletin issued at regular intervals to a special group

newspaper *n.* a regular publication, usually a daily or weekly, containing news, advertisements, etc. —**news′pa′per-man′** *n.* —**news′pa′perwom′an** *n.fem.*

Newspeak *n.* [coined by *G. Orwell*] the use of ambiguous and deceptive talk, as by government officials seeking to mould public opinion

newsprint (nyōōz′print′) *n.* a cheap paper, made mainly from wood pulp, for newspapers, etc.

newsreel *n.* a short film of news events

news room 1. the room where newscasts and newspapers are prepared **2.** the room in a library where newspapers can be read

newsstand *n.* a stand at which newspapers, magazines, etc. are sold

new star *same as* NOVA

newsworthy *adj.* timely and important

newsy *adj.* **news′ier, news′iest** [Colloq.] containing much news

NEWT
(7-10 cm long)

newt (nyōōt) *n.* [< OE. *efeta,* eft] any of various small amphibians

New Testament the part of the Bible containing the life and teachings of Jesus and his followers

newton (nyōōt′′n) *n.* [< Sir Isaac *Newton*] the SI unit of force

New Town any of a number of planned communities built in Great Britain since World War II

New World the Western Hemisphere; the Americas

new year [also N- Y-] **1.** the year just about to begin or just begun (usually with *the*) **2.** the first day of the new year

New Year′s Day January 1, the first day of a calendar year, usually a public holiday

New Year′s Eve the evening before New Year′s Day

next (nekst) *adj.* [OE. *neahst,* superl. of *neah, nigh*] nearest; immediately preceding or following —*adv.* **1.** in the time, place, degree, or rank immediately preceding or following **2.** on the first subsequent occasion —*prep.* beside; nearest to [sit *next* the tree] —*n.* the one immediately following

next-door *adj.* in or at the next house, building, etc.

next of kin one's relative(s) most nearly related

nexus (nek'səs) *n.* [L.] a connection, tie, or link between individuals, members of a series, etc.

N.F., Nfld., Nfd. Newfoundland

n.f. *Banking* no funds

N.F.U. National Farmers' Union

N.G. New Guinea

N.G., n.g. [Slang] no good

N.G.A. National Graphical Association

N.H.S. National Health Service

Ni *Chem.* nickel

N.I. 1. National Insurance 2. Northern Ireland

niacin (nī'ə sin) *n.* [< NICOTINE] a white, odourless substance, found in protein foods: it is a member of the vitamin B complex

nib (nib) *n.* [< OE. *nebb*] 1. the point of a pen 2. a point; sharp prong 3. the bill or beak of a bird

nibble (nib''l) *vt., vi.* **-bled, -bling** [< ?] 1. to eat (food) with quick, small bites 2. to bite at with small, gentle bites —*n.* 1. a small bite or morsel 2. a nibbling

nibs (nibz) *n.* [< ?] [Colloq.] an important, or self-important, person (with *his*)

nice (nīs) *adj.* **nic'er, nic'est** [< L. *nescius*, ignorant] 1. *a*) agreeable *b*) attractive *c*) kind *d*) respectable *e*) good 2. delicate; precise; subtle [a nice distinction] 3. calling for care, tact, etc. [a nice problem] 4. *a*) finely discriminating *b*) minutely accurate 5. difficult to please; fastidious —**nice and** [Colloq.] altogether; very —**nice work** a phrase used to signify approval of a task, etc. —**nice'ly** *adv.* —**nice'ness** *n.*

nicety (nī'sə tē) *n., pl.* **-ties** 1. a subtle or minute detail, distinction, etc. 2. something choice or dainty 3. precision; accuracy 4. fastidiousness; refinement —**to a nicety** exactly

niche (nich) *n.* [Fr., ult. < L. *nidus*, nest] 1. a recess in a wall for a statue, bust, or vase 2. a place or position particularly suitable to the person or thing in it

nick (nik) *n.* [< ?] 1. small cut, chip, etc. made on a surface; notch 2. [Slang] prison —*vt.* 1. to make a nick or nicks in 2. *a*) to wound slightly *b*) to strike glancingly 3. [Slang] *a*) to steal *b*) to arrest —**in good nick** [Colloq.] in good condition —**in the nick of time** just before it is too late

nickel (nik''l) *n.* [Sw. < G. *Kupfernickel*, copper demon: the copperlike ore contains no copper] 1. a hard, silver-white, malleable metallic chemical element, used in alloys and for plating: symbol, Ni 2. a U.S. or Canadian coin equal to five cents

nickelodeon (nik'ə lō'dē ən) *n.* [< NICKEL + MELODEON] [U.S.] an early type of jukebox operated by a nickel

nickel plate a thin layer of nickel deposited by electrolysis on metallic objects to prevent rust —**nick'el-plate'** *vt.* **-plat'-ed, -plat'ing**

nickel silver a hard, tough, ductile, malleable alloy composed essentially of nickel, copper, and zinc

nicker[1] (nik'ər) *vi.* [? < NEIGH] to utter a whinnying sound: said of a horse

nicker[2] *n., pl.* **-er** [< ?] [Colloq.] a pound sterling

nicknack (nik'nak') *n.* same as KNICK-KNACK

nickname (nik'nām') *n.* [< ME. *an ekename*, a surname] 1. a substitute, often descriptive name given in fun, affection, etc., as "Doc," "Shorty," etc. 2. a familiar form of a name, as "Dick" for "Richard" —*vt.* **-named', -nam'ing** to give a nickname to

nicotine (nik'ə tēn') *n.* [< J. *Nicot*] a poisonous alkaloid, found in tobacco leaves and used as an insecticide

nictitate (nik'tə tāt') *vi.* **-tat'ed, -tat'ing** [< L. *nictare*, wink] to wink or blink rapidly, as some birds and animals

nictitating membrane a transparent third eyelid hinged at the inner side or lower lid of the eye of various animals

niece (nēs) *n.* [< L. *neptis*] 1. the daughter of one's brother or sister 2. the daughter of one's brother-in-law or sister-in-law

niff (nif') *vi.* [< ?] to smell, usually unpleasantly

nifty (nif'tē) *adj.* **-tier, -tiest** [prob. < MAGNIFICENT] [Slang] attractive, smart, stylish, enjoyable, etc.

niggard (nig'ərd) *n.* [prob. < Scand.] a stingy person

niggardly *adj.* 1. stingy; miserly 2. small, few, or scanty —*adv.* stingily —**nig'gardli-ness** *n.*

nigger (nig'ər) *n.* [< Fr. *nègre*, black] a derogatory term for a negro or any dark-skinned person —**nigger in the woodpile** a hidden snag

nigger brown a very dark, chocolate brown

niggle (nig''l) *vi.* **-gled, -gling** [? akin to Norw. *nigla*] to be finicky —*vt.* to annoy —**nig'gling** *adj., n.*

nigh (nī) *adj., adv. prep.* [OE. *neah*] [Archaic or Dial.] near

night (nīt) *n.* [OE. *niht*] 1. the period of darkness between sunset and sunrise 2. the darkness of night 3. any period or condition of darkness or gloom —*adj.* 1. of, for, or at night 2. active or working at night —**make a night of it** to celebrate all night —**night and day** continuously

night blindness imperfect vision in the dark or in dim light: a symptom of vitamin A deficiency

nightcap *n.* 1. [Colloq.] a drink taken at bedtime, esp. an alcoholic one 2. a cap worn in bed

nightclub *n.* a place of entertainment open at night for eating, drinking, dancing, etc.

nightdress *n.* a loose dress worn in bed by women

nightfall *n.* the close of day; dusk

nightgown *n.* 1. same as NIGHTDRESS 2. same as NIGHTSHIRT

nightie *n.* *colloq. dim. of* NIGHTDRESS

nightingale (nīt′′iŋ gāl′) *n.* [< OE. *niht*, night + *galan*, sing] a small thrush known for the melodious singing of the male, esp. at night

nightjar (nīt′jär′) *n.* [NIGHT + JAR¹] a a nocturnal insect-eating bird with a sustained trilling callnote

night light a small, dim light kept on all night, as in a hallway, bathroom, sickroom, etc.

nightlong *adj.* lasting the entire night —*adv.* during the entire night

nightly *adj.* 1. done or occurring every night 2. of or like the night —*adv.* 1. at night 2. every night

nightmare *n.* [< ME. *niht*, night + *mare*, demon] 1. a frightening dream 2. any frightening experience —**night′mar′ish** *adj.*

nights *adv.* [Colloq.] on every night or most nights

night safe a safety-deposit box set in the wall of a bank to receive money, etc. after the bank closes

night school a school held in the evening, as for adults unable to attend by day

nightshade (nīt′shād′) *n.* [OE. *nihtscada*] 1. a flowering plant related to the potato, tomato, etc. 2. *same as* BELLADONNA

nightshirt *n.* a long, loose, shirtlike garment, worn in bed, esp. formerly, by men or boys

nightspot *n.* *colloq. var. of* NIGHTCLUB

nighttime *n.* the period of darkness from sunset to sunrise

night watch 1. a guarding during the night 2. [*pl.*] any of the periods into which the night was formerly divided for such guarding 3. the person or persons doing such guarding

night watchman 1. a watchman hired for duty at night 2. *Cricket* a batsman sent in to play out time when a wicket has fallen near the end of a day's play

nighty *n.*, *pl.* **night′ies** *alt. sp. of* NIGHTIE

nihilism (nī′i liz′m) *n.* [< L. *nihil*, nothing] 1. *Philos.* a) the denial of the existence of any basis for knowledge b) the general rejection of customary beliefs in morality, religion, etc. 2. a) the doctrine that all social, political, and economic institutions must be destroyed b) loosely, any terroristic revolutionary movement —**ni′hilist** *n.* —**ni′hilis′tic** *adj.*

nil (nil) *n.* [L., contr. of *nihil*] nothing

nilgai (nil′gī) *n.* [< Per. *nīlgāw*, blue cow] a large, grey Indian antelope

nimble (nim′b′l) *adj.* -**bler**, -**blest** [< OE. *niman*, take] 1. quick-witted; alert 2. moving quickly and lightly —**nim′bleness** *n.* —**nim′bly** *adv.*

nimbus (nim′bəs) *n.*, *pl.* -**bi** (-bī), -**buses** [L.]. 1. orig., any rain-producing cloud 2. a halo surrounding the heads of saints, etc., as in pictures

nincompoop (nin′kəm po͞op′) *n.* [< ?] a fool; simpleton

nine (nīn) *adj., n.* [OE. *nigon*] one more

than eight; 9; IX —**999** the telephone number for emergency services in Britain —**the Nine** the nine Muses —**to the nines** in the most elaborate manner [*dressed to the nines*]

nine days' wonder anything that arouses great excitement or interest, but only for a short time

ninefold *adj.* 1. having nine parts 2. having nine times as much or as many —*adv.* nine times as much or as many

ninepins *n.* 1. [*pl. with sing. v.*] another name *for* skittles 2. any of the pins used in this game

nineteen (nīn′tēn′) *adj., n.* [OE. *nigontyne*] nine more than ten; 19; XIX —**talk** (or **chatter**, etc.) **nineteen to the dozen** to talk or chatter very animatedly —**nine′teenth′** *adj., n.*

nineteenth hole [Colloq.] in golf, the bar of the clubhouse

ninety (nīn′tē) *adj., n.,* *pl.* -**ties** [OE. *nigontig*] nine times ten; 90; XC (or LXXXX) —**the nineties** the numbers or years, as of a century, from ninety to ninety-nine —**nine′tieth** *adj., n.*

ninny (nin′ē) *n.,* *pl.* -**nies** [? < *an innocent*] a fool

ninth (nīnth) *adj.* [OE. *nigonthe*] 1. preceded by eight others in a series; 9th 2. designating any of nine equal parts —*n.* 1. the one following the eighth 2. any of the nine equal parts of something; 1/9

niobium (nī ō′bē əm) *n.* [< L. *Niobe*, the Queen of Thebes] a grey or white metallic chemical element used in chromium steels etc.: symbol, Nb

nip¹ (nip) *vt.* **nipped**, **nip′ping** [prob. < MLowG. *nippen*] 1. to pinch or squeeze; bite 2. to sever (shoots, etc.) as by pinching 3. to check the growth of [*to nip in the bud*] 4. to have a painful or injurious effect on because of cold —*vi.* 1. to give a nip or nips 2. to move quickly (with *along*) —*n.* 1. a nipping; pinch; bite 2. a stinging quality, as in cold air 3. stinging cold; frost

nip² *n.* [prob. < Du. *nippen*, sip] a small drink of liquor —*vt., vi.* to drink (liquor) in nips

nipper *n.* 1. anything that nips 2. [*pl.*] pliers, pincers, etc. 3. the claw of a crab, etc. 4. [Colloq.] a small boy

nipple (nip′'l) *n.* [< OE. *nebb*, beak] 1. the part of a breast or udder through which a baby or young animal sucks milk from its mother; teat 2. a teatlike part, as of rubber, for a baby's bottle 3. any projection or thing resembling a nipple in shape or function

nippy *adj.* -**pier**, -**piest** 1. tending to nip 2. cold in a stinging way 3. [Colloq.] quick; nimble

nirvana (nēər′vä′nə) *n.* [< Sans.] *Buddhism* the state of blessedness achieved by the extinction of the self

Nissen hut (nis′'n) [< P.N. *Nissen*] a military shelter made of corrugated steel, having a semicircular cross section

nit[1] (nit) *n.* [OE. *hnitu*] 1. the egg of a louse or similar insect 2. a young louse, etc.

nit[2] *n.* [Colloq.] *short for* NITWIT

nit-picking *adj., n.* paying too much attention to petty details —**nit'-pick'er** *n.*

nitrate (nī'trāt) *n.* [Fr. < *nitre*, NITRE] 1. a salt or ester of nitric acid 2. potassium nitrate or sodium nitrate, used as a fertilizer —*vt.* -**trated**, -**trating** to treat or combine with nitric acid —**nitra'tion** *n.*

nitre (nīt'ər) *n.* [< Gr. *nitron*] *same as* POTASSIUM NITRATE

nitric (nī'trik) *adj.* of or containing nitrogen, esp. of a higher valence than in the corresponding nitrous compounds

nitric acid a colourless, corrosive acid

nitrify (nī'trə fī') *vt.* -**fied**, -**fy'ing** [see NITRE] 1. to impregnate (soil, etc.) with nitrates 2. to cause the oxidation of (ammonium salts, etc.) to nitrates, as by the action of soil bacteria, etc. —**ni'trifica'tion** *n.*

nitrogen (nī'trə jən) *n.* [see NITRE & -GEN] a colourless, odourless, gaseous chemical element forming nearly four fifths of the atmosphere: symbol, N —**nitrogenous** (nī troj'i nəs) *adj.*

nitrogen cycle the cycle through which atmospheric nitrogen is converted into compounds used by plants and animals in the formation of proteins and is eventually returned by decay to its original state

nitrogen fixation the conversion of atmospheric nitrogen into nitrates by soil bacteria

nitroglycerin, nitroglycerine (nī'trō glis'ər ēn) *n.* a thick, explosive oil used in medicine and in making dynamite

nitrous (nī'trəs) *adj.* 1. of, like, or containing nitre 2. of compounds in which nitrogen has a lower valence than in the corresponding nitric compounds

nitrous oxide a colourless, non-flammable gas used as an anaesthetic and in aerosols

nitty (nit'ē) *adj.* -**tier**, -**tiest** full of nits

nitty-gritty *n.* [Slang] the actual, basic facts, issues, etc.

nitwit (nit'wit') *n.* [? NIT[1] + WIT[1]] a stupid person

NNE, N.N.E., n.n.e. north-northeast

NNW, N.N.W., n.n.w. north-north-west

no[1] (nō) *adv.* [< OE. *ne a, not ever*] 1. not in any degree 2. nay; not so: the opposite of YES —*adj.* not any; not a [*no errors*] —*n., pl.* **noes, nos** 1. refusal or denial 2. a negative vote or voter

no[2] *n., pl.* **no** [Jap. *nō*] [*often* N-] a classic form of Japanese drama with music and dancing: also **noh**

No *Chem.* nobelium

No. 1. north 2. northern 3. number: also **no.**

n.o. *Cricket* not out

nob[1] (nob) *n.* [later form of KNOB] [Slang] the head

nob[2] *n.* [< ?] [Slang] a person of high social status

no-ball (nō'bôl') *n.* *Cricket* an improperly bowled ball for which one run is scored by the batting side

nobble (nob''l) *vt.* -**bled**, -**bling** [? freq. of NAB] [Slang] 1. to disable (a horse), as by drugging, to prevent it winning a race 2. to cheat or swindle 3. to get hold of; grab

nobby (nob'ē) *adj.* -**bier**, -**biest** [< ?] [Slang] stylish

nobelium (nō bel'ē əm) *n.* [< *Nobel* Institute] a radioactive chemical element produced by the nuclear bombardment of curium: symbol, No

Nobel prize (nō bel') [< A.B. *Nobel*] annual prizes given for distinction in physics, chemistry, physiology, medicine, literature, and work for peace

nobility (nō bil'ə tē) *n., pl.* -**ties** 1. a being noble 2. high rank in society 3. the class of people of noble rank

noble (nō'b'l) *adj.* -**bler**, -**blest** [< L. *nobilis*, well-known] 1. of high rank or title 2. having high moral qualities 3. grand; stately [*a noble view*] 4. excellent 5. famous or renowned —*n.* a person having hereditary rank or title —**no'bleness** *n.* —**no'bly** *adv.*

nobleman *n.* a member of the nobility; peer —**no'blewom'an** *n.fem.*

noblesse oblige (nō bles'ō blēzh') [Fr., nobility obliges] the obligation of people of high rank to be kind and generous

nobody (nō'bəd ē) *pron.* not anybody; no one —*n., pl.* -**bodies** a person of no importance

nock (nok) *n.* [< Scand.] 1. a notch for holding the string at either end of a bow 2. the notch in the end of an arrow, for the bowstring

no-claim bonus a refund of part of the premium paid to the holder of an insurance policy, esp. on a motor vehicle, if no claims are made within a specified period: also **no-claims bonus**

nocturnal (nok tʉr'n'l) *adj.* [< L. *nox, night*] 1. of or happening in the night 2. active during the night

nocturne (nok'tʉrn) *n.* [Fr.] 1. a painting of a night scene 2. a romantic, dreamy musical composition

nod (nod) *vi.* **nod'ded, nod'ding** [ME. *nodden*] 1. to bend the head forward quickly, as in agreement, greeting, etc. 2. to let the head fall forward because of drowsiness 3. to be careless 4. to sway back and forth, as plumes —*vt.* 1. to bend (the head) forward quickly 2. to signify (assent, etc.) by doing this —*n.* 1. a nodding 2. [N-] the imaginary realm of sleep and dreams: usually **land of Nod** —**nod off** to fall asleep

nodding acquaintance a slight acquaintance

noddle (nod'l) *n.* [< ?] [Colloq.] the head or brains

noddy (nod'ē) *n., pl.* -**dies** [< ? NOD] 1. a simpleton 2. a tropical sea bird

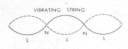

VIBRATING STRING

NODES

(N, nodes formed when vibrating string
is stopped at intervals along its length;
L, loops between nodes)

node (nōd) *n.* [L. *nodus,* knot] **1.** a knot;
knob **2.** *Astron.* either of the two points
at which the orbit of a heavenly body
intersects a fundamental plane **3.** *Bot.*
that part of a stem from which a leaf
starts to grow **4.** *Physics* the point, line,
or surface of a vibrating object where
there is comparatively no vibration —**nod′-
al** *adj.*

nodule (noj′ōōl) *n.* [L. *nodulus*] **1.** a
small knot or rounded lump **2.** *Bot.* a
small knot or joint on a stem or root —**nod′-
ular, nod′ulose, nod′ulous** *adj.*

noel, noël (nō el′) *n.* [< L. *natalis,* natal]
1. a Christmas carol **2.** [N-] Christmas

nog, nogg (nog) *n.* [< dial.] **1.** a strong
ale **2.** eggnog

noggin (nog′in) *n.* [prob. < prec.] **1.**
a small cup or mug **2.** one fourth of
a pint **3.** [Colloq.] the head

no-go (nō′gō′) *adj.* [Slang] **1.** not
functioning properly **2.** hopeless

no-go area a district in a town separated
by barricades, esp. in Northern Ireland

noise (noiz) *n.* [OFr.] **1.** *a)* loud shouting;
clamour *b)* any loud, disagreeable sound
2. sound —*vt.* noised, nois′ing to spread
(a rumour, etc.)

noiseless *adj.* with little or no noise
—**noise′lessly** *adv.*

noisome (noi′səm) *adj.* [see ANNOY] **1.**
injurious to health **2.** foul-smelling —**noi′-
somely** *adv.*

noisy (noi′zē) *adj.* **-ier, -iest** **1.** making
noise **2.** full of noise —**nois′ily** *adv.*
—**nois′iness** *n.*

nom. nominative

nomad (nō′mad) *n.* [< Gr. *nemein,* to
pasture] **1.** a member of a tribe or people
moving about constantly in search of food,
pasture, etc. **2.** a wanderer —*adj.*
wandering: also **nomad′ic** —**no′madism** *n.*

no man's land **1.** a piece of land to
which no one has a recognized title **2.**
the area on a battlefield separating the
combatants

nom de plume (nom′də plōōm′) *pl.*
noms de plume′ [Fr.] a pen name;
pseudonym

nomenclature (nō men′klə chər) *n.* [<
L. *nomen,* name + *calare,* call] the system
of names used in a branch of learning

nominal (nom′in'l) *adj.* [< L. *nomen,*
name] **1.** of or like a name **2.** in name
only, not in fact **3.** relatively very small
—**nom′inally** *adv.*

nominalism *n.* [see prec.] the
philosophical doctrine that general nouns

such as "triangle" do not stand for an
object but are merely names —**nom′inal-
ist** *n., adj.*

nominal value *same as* PAR VALUE

nominate (nom′ə nāt′) *vt.* **-nat′ed, -nat′-
ing** [< L. *nomen,* name] **1.** to appoint
to an office or position **2.** to name as
a candidate for election, an award, etc.
—**nom′ina′tion** *n.* —**nom′ina′tor** *n.*

nominative (nom′ə nə tiv) *adj.* **1.** *Gram.*
designating the case of the subject
of a finite verb and the words that agree
with it **2.** named to a position or office
—*n.* **1.** the nominative case **2.** a word
in this case

nominee (nom′ə nē′) *n.* [< NOMINATE]
a person who is nominated, esp. a candidate
for election

non- [< L. *non,* not] *a prefix meaning*
not : less emphatic than *in-* and *un-,* which
often give a word an opposite meaning
(Ex.: *nonhuman, inhuman*) The list below
includes the more common compounds
formed with *non-* that do not have special
meanings; they will be understood if *not*
is used before the meaning of the base word

nonacademic	nonconfidential
nonadjustable	nonconflicting
nonaffiliated	nonconforming
nonaggression	nonconnective
nonalcoholic	nonconscious
nonallergic	nonconstitutional
nonappearance	nonconstructive
nonapplicable	noncontagious
nonaristocratic	noncontemporary
nonassertive	noncontinuous
nonassessable	noncontradictory
nonassignable	noncontributory
nonassimilable	noncontroversial
nonathletic	nonconviction
nonattendance	noncorresponding
nonattributive	noncreative
nonbeliever	noncritical
nonbelligerent	noncumulative
nonbreakable	nòndeceptive
noncarnivorous	nondeciduous
noncertified	nondeductible
nonchargeable	nondefensive
nonchemical	nondenominational
nonclassifiable	nondependence
nonclerical	nonderivative
nonclinical	nondestructive
noncohesive	nondetachable
noncollapsable	nondevelopment
noncollapsible	nondictatorial
noncollectable	nondifferentiation
noncollectible	nondiffusible
noncombat	nondiplomatic
noncombustible	nondisciplinary
noncommunicable	nondiscrimination
noncommunicating	nondisposal
noncompensating	nondivergent
noncompetent	nondivisible
noncompeting	nondrinker
noncompletion	nondriver
noncompliance	nonecclesiastical
nóncompressible	noneconomic
noncompulsory	noneducational
nonconducive	nonefficient
nonconducting	nonelective

nonenforceable
nonexchangeable
nonexclusive
nonexcusable
nonexempt
nonexpendable
nonexperimental
nonexpert
nonextensive
nonfactual
nonfading
nonfat
nonfatal
nonfederated
nonfiction
nonfigurative
nonfissionable
nonflammable
nonforfeiture
nonfreezing
nonhabitable
nonhazardous
nonhereditary
nonhistoric
nonimaginary
nonimitative
nonimmunized
nonimpregnated
noninclusive
nonindustrial
noninfected
noninflammable
noninflationary
noninformative
nonintegrated
nonintellectual
noninterference
nonintoxicating
nonintuitive
noninvolvement
nonjudicial
nonlethal
nonlicensed
nonliterate
nonmalignant
nonmalleable
nonmaterial
nonmechanical
nonmember
nonmilitant
nonnegotiable
nonnutritious
nonobservance
nonoccupational
nonofficial
nonoperational
nonoperative
nonparental
nonpaying
nonpayment
nonperforated
nonperishable
nonpermanent
nonpermeable
nonpermissible
nonpersistent
nonporous
nonpredictable
nonpreferential
nonprescriptive

nonprofessional
nonprofitable
nonprogressive
nonprohibitive
nonprolific
nonprotective
nonpunishable
nonreader
nonrealistic
nonreciprocating
nonrecoverable
nonrecurrent
nonregistered
nonrelative
nonremovable
nonrenewable
nonrepayable
nonrepresentative
nonrestricted
nonretiring
nonreturnable
nonreversible
nonrigid
nonsalable
nonsalaried
nonsaturated
nonscholastic
nonscientific
nonsecular
nonseditious
nonsegregated
nonselective
nonsensitized
nonsensory
nonshrinkable
nonsinkable
nonsmoker
nonspeaking
nonspecialist
nonspecialized
nonspecific
nonstandard
nonstandardized
nonstarting
nonstationary
nonstatutory
nonstriker
nonstructural
nonsubscriber
nonsupporting
nonsymptomatic
nontaxable
nonteachable
nontechnical
nontheatrical
nonthinking
nontoxic
nontransferable
nontransparent
nontributary
nontypical
nonuniform
nonusable
nonutilitarian
nonverbal
nonviable
nonviolation
nonvocal
nonwhite
nonworker

nonage (nō′nij) *n.* [< OFr.: see NON-

& AGE] **1.** *Law* the state of being under full legal age **2.** immaturity

nonagenarian (nō′nə ji nãer′ē ən) *adj.* [< L. *nonaginta*, ninety] ninety years old, or between the ages of ninety and one hundred —*n.* a person of this age

nonaggression pact (non′ə gresh′ən) an agreement between two nations not to attack each other

nonagon (non′ə gon′) *n.* [< L. *nonus*, ninth + -GON] a polygon with nine angles and nine sides

nonaligned (non′ə līnd′) *adj.* not aligned with either side in a conflict —**non′align′**-ment *n.*

nonce (nons) *n.* [by merging of *for then ones*, for the once] the present use, occasion etc.: chiefly in **for the nonce**

nonce word a word used for a single occasion

nonchalant (non′shə lənt)' [< L. *non*, not + *calere*, be warm] **1.** casually indifferent **2.** without warmth or enthusiasm —**non′-chalance′** *n.*

noncom (non′kom′) *n. colloq. form of* NONCOMMISSIONED OFFICER

noncombatant (non′kom′bə tənt) *n.* **1.** a member of the armed forces not engaged in actual combat **2.** any civilian in wartime —*adj.* of noncombatants

noncommissioned officer (non′-kə mish′ənd) an enlisted person of any of various ranks in the armed forces: see MILITARY RANKS, table

noncommittal (non′kə mit′'l) *adj.* not committing one to any point of view —**non′-commit′tally** *adv.*

non compos mentis (non′kom′-pəs men′tis) [L.] *Law* not of sound mind: often **non compos**

nonconductor (non′kən duk′tər) *n.* a substance that does not readily transmit electricity, heat, etc.

nonconformist (non′kən fôr′mist) *adj.* not following established customs, beliefs, etc. —*n.* one who is nonconformist; esp. [N-], a Protestant who is not a member of the Anglican Church —**non′conform′**-ity *n.*

noncooperation (non′kō op′ə rā′shən) *n.* **1.** failure to work together **2.** refusal to cooperate with a government, as by nonpayment of taxes —**non′coop′erative** *adj.*

nondescript (non′di skript′) *adj.* [< L. *non*, not + *describere*, describe] **1.** having no outstanding features **2.** belonging to no definite class or type

none (nun) *pron.* [< OE. *ne*, not + *an*, one] **1.** no one; not anyone **2.** [*usually with pl. v.*] not any —*n.* no part; nothing [I want *none* of it] —*adv.* not at all [*none* the worse for wear]

nonentity (non en′tə tē) *n., pl.* **-ties 1.** a person of no importance **2.** the state of not existing

nones (nōnz) *n.pl.* [< L. *novem*, nine] in the Roman calendar, the ninth day before the ides of a month

nonessential (non′i sen′shəl) *adj.* not

essential; unnecessary —*n.* a nonessential person or thing

nonesuch (nun′such′) *n.* a person or thing unrivalled or unequalled; nonpareil

nonetheless (nun′*th*ə les′) *adv.* nevertheless

nonevent (non′i vent′) *n.* an event that fails to attract attention or otherwise take on significance

nonferrous (non′fer′əs) *adj.* 1. not made of or containing iron 2. designating or of metals other than iron

nonintervention (non′in tər ven′shən) *n.* a refraining by one nation from interference in the affairs of another —**non′interven′tionist** *adj., n.*

noniron (non′ī′ərn) *adj.* not requiring ironing

nonmetal (non′met′'l) *n.* an element lacking the characteristics of a metal, as oxygen, carbon, nitrogen, fluorine —**non′metal′lic** *adj.*

nonmoral (non′mor′əl) *adj.* not moral and not immoral

nonnuclear (non′nyōō′klē ər) *adj.* not operated by or using nuclear energy

nonpareil (non′pə rəl) *adj.* [Fr. < *non*, not + *pareil*, equal] unequalled; peerless —*n.* someone or something unequalled or unrivalled

nonpartisan (non′pär ti zan′) *adj.* not supporting any single political party : also **non′partizan′**

nonplus (non′plus′) *vt.* -plussed′, -plus′-sing [L. *non*, not + *plus*, more] to bewilder

nonproductive (non′prə duk′tiv) *adj.* 1. not productive 2. not directly related to the production of goods —**non′produc′tively** *adv.* —**non′produc′tiveness** *n.*

nonprofit (non prof′it) *adj.* not intended to earn a profit

nonproliferation (non′prō lif′ə rā′shən) *n.* the limitation of production, esp. of nuclear weapons

nonrepresentational (non′rep ri zən-tā′shən 'l) *adj.* designating or of art that does not attempt to represent in recognizable form any object in nature; abstract

nonresident (non rez′i dənt) *adj.* not residing in the locality where one works, attends school, etc. —*n.* a nonresident person —**nonres′idence, nonres′idency** *n.*

nonresistant (non′ri zis′tənt) *adj.* not resistant; submitting to force or arbitrary authority —*n.* a person who believes that force and violence should not be used to oppose arbitrary authority, however unjust

nonscheduled (non shed′yōold) *adj.* of an airline, aircraft, etc. making commercial flights on demand

nonsectarian (non′sek tãr′ē ən) *adj.* not sectarian; not confined to any specific religion

nonsense (non′səns) *n.* [NON- + SENSE] 1. words or actions that are absurd or meaningless 2. things of relatively no importance or value —*interj.* how foolish! how absurd! —**nonsen′sical** (-sen′si k'l) *adj.*

non sequitur (non′sek′wi tər) [L., it does not follow] 1. a conclusion that does not follow from the premises 2. a remark having no bearing on what has just been said

nonskid (non′skid′) *adj.* so constructed as to reduce skidding: said of a tyre tread, etc.

nonstarter (non′stärt′ər) *n.* 1. a competitor who fails to run in a race for which he has entered 2. a person, idea, etc. with little or no chance of success

nonstick (non′stik′) *adj.* coated with a substance that prevents food adhering : said of saucepans, etc.

nonstop (non′stop′) *adj., adv.* without a stop

nonsuch (nun′such′) *n.* same as NONE-SUCH

nonsuit (non′sōōt′) *n.* [< Anglo-Fr.] *Law* a judgment against a plaintiff due to his failure to establish a valid case —*vt.* to bring a nonsuit against (a plaintiff)

non-U (non′yōō′) *adj.* [Colloq.] not characteristic of the upper classes : said of language, table manners, etc.

nonunion (non yōōn′yən) *adj.* 1. not belonging to a trade union 2. not made or serviced under conditions required by a trade union 3. refusing to recognize a trade union

nonviolence (non′vī′ə ləns) *n.* an abstaining from violence or physical force —**nonvi′olent** *adj.*

nonvoter (non vōt′ər) *n.* a person who does not vote or is not permitted to vote —**nonvot′ing** *adj.*

noodle[1] (nōō′d'l) *n.* [< *noddle*, head] a fool

noodle[2] *n.* [G. *Nudel*] a flat, narrow strip of dry dough, usually made with egg and served in soup, etc.

nook (nook) *n.* [ME. *nok*] 1. a corner, esp. of a room 2. a small recess or secluded spot

noon (nōōn) *n.* [< L. *nona* (*hora*), ninth (hour)] 1. twelve o'clock in the daytime; midday 2. the highest point —*adj.* of or occurring at noon Also **noon′day′, noon′time′**

no one no person; not anybody; nobody

noose (nōōs) *n.* [< L. *nodus*, knot] 1. a loop formed in a rope, cord, etc. by means of a slipknot so that the loop tightens as the rope is pulled 2. anything that restricts one's freedom —**the noose** death by hanging

no-par (nō′pär′) *adj.* having no stated par value

nor (nôr; *unstressed* nər) *conj.* [ME., contr. of *nother*, neither] and not; and not either [I can *neither* go *nor* stay]

nor′, nor (nôr) north : used especially in compounds

Nor. North

Nordic (nôr′dik) *adj.* [< OE. *north*, north] designating a physical type of the Caucasoid peoples exemplified by the long-headed, tall, blond people of Scandinavia

Norfolk jacket (or **coat**) (nôr′fək) *n.* a loose-fitting, single-breasted, belted jacket with box pleats

norm (nôrm) *n.* [< L. *norma*, carpenter's square] a standard, model, or pattern; esp., the standard of achievement of a large group

normal (nôr′m'l) *adj.* **1.** conforming with an accepted standard or norm; natural; usual **2.** *Med., Psychol. a)* free from disease, disorder, etc. *b)* mentally sound **3.** *Math.* perpendicular; at right angles —*n.* **1.** anything normal **2.** the usual state, amount, etc. **3.** *Math.* a perpendicular —**nor′malcy, normal′ity** (-mal′ə tē) *n.*

normalize *vt., vi.* -**ized′**, -**iz′ing 1.** to bring or come to the normal state **2.** to bring or come into conformity with a standard —**nor′maliza′tion** *n.*

normally *adv.* **1.** in a normal manner **2.** under normal circumstances; ordinarily

Norman (nôr′mən) *n.* [< OFr.] **1.** any of the Scandinavians who occupied Normandy in the 10th cent. A.D. **2.** a descendant of the Normans and French who conquered England in 1066 **3.** same as NORMAN FRENCH **4.** a native of Normandy —*adj.* of Normandy, the Normans, their language, or culture

Norman French the French spoken in England by the Norman conquerors; Anglo-French —**Nor′man-French′** *adj.*

Norman style a style of architecture with rounded arches, used in Britain in the 11th and 12th cent.

normative (nôr′mə tiv) *adj.* of or establishing a norm, or standard —**norm′atively** *adv.*

norn (nôrn) *n.* [ON. *norn*] *Norse Myth.* any of three goddesses who determine the destiny of gods and men

Norse (nôrs) *adj.* [prob. < Du. *noord*, north] Scandinavian —*n.* the Scandinavian group of languages

Norseman *n.* a member of the ancient Scandinavian people; Northman

north (nôrth) *n.* [OE.] **1.** the direction to the right of a person facing the sunset (0° or 360° on the compass, opposite south) **2.** a region or district in or towards this direction **3.** [*often* N-] the northern part of the earth —*adj.* **1.** in, or towards the north **2.** from the north —*adv.* in or towards the north —**the North** that part of England north of the Humber

Northants. Northamptonshire

north country the northern part of England, esp. Yorkshire, Northumbria & Cumbria —**north-coun′tryman** *n.*

northeast (nôrth′ēst′; *nautical,* nôr-) *n.* **1.** the direction halfway between north and east **2.** a region in or towards this direction —*adj.* **1.** in, of, to, or towards the northeast **2.** from the northeast —*adv.* in, towards, or from the northeast —**north′east′erly** *adj., adv.* —**north′east′ern** *adj.* —**north′east′ward** *adv., adj.* —**north′east′wards** *adj.*

northeaster (nôrth′ēs′tər; *nautical,* nôr-) *n.* a storm or strong wind from the northeast

northerly (nôr′thə lē) *adj., adv.* **1.** towards the north **2.** from the north

northern (nôr′thərn) *adj.* **1.** in, of, or towards the north **2.** from the north **3.** [N-] of or characteristic of the North

northerner *n.* a native or inhabitant of the north, specif. [N-] *a)* of the North of England *b)* [Canad.] of the Far North

Northern Hemisphere that half of the earth north of the equator

northern lights same as AURORA BOREALIS

Northman same as NORSEMAN

north-northeast *n.* the direction halfway between north and northeast

north-northwest *n.* the direction halfway between north and northwest

North Pole the northern end of the earth's axis

North-Sea gas natural gas obtained from deposits beneath the North Sea

North Star Polaris, the bright star almost directly above the North Pole; polestar

Northum. Northumbria

northward (nôrth′wərd) *adv., adj.* towards the north : also **north′wards** *adv.* —*n.* a northward direction, point, etc.

northwest (nôrth′west′; *nautical,* nôr-) *n.* **1.** the direction halfway between north and west **2.** a district or region in or towards this direction —*adj.* **1.** in, of, or towards the northwest **2.** from the northwest —*adv.* in, towards, or from the northwest —**north′west′erly** *adj., adv.* —**north′west′ern** *adj.* —**north′west′ward** *adv., adj.* —**north′west′wards** *adv.*

northwester (nôrth′wes′tər; *nautical,* nôr-) *n.* a storm or strong wind from the northwest

Norw. 1. Norway **2.** Norwegian

Norwegian (nôr wē′jən) *adj.* of Norway, its people, their language, etc. —*n.* **1.** a native or inhabitant of Norway **2.** the language of the Norwegians

Nos., nos. numbers

nose (nōz) *n.* [OE. *nosu*] **1.** the part of the human face between the mouth and the eyes, having two openings for breathing and smelling **2.** the corresponding part in animals **3.** the sense of smell **4.** power to perceive as by scent [*a nose* for news] **5.** anything noselike in shape or position —*vt.* **nosed, nos′ing 1.** to discover as by smell **2.** to rub with the nose **3.** to push with the nose (with *aside,* etc.) **4.** to push (a way, etc.) with the front forward —*vi.* **1.** to pry inquisitively **2.** to advance; move forwards —**by a nose** by a very small margin —**lead by the nose** to dominate completely —**look down one's nose at** [Colloq.] to be disdainful of —**pay through the nose** to pay an unreasonable price —**turn up one's nose at** to sneer at —**under one's nose** in plain view

nose bag a bag filled with grain, fastened over a horse's muzzle for feeding

noseband *n.* that part of a bridle or halter which passes over the animal's nose

nosebleed *n.* a bleeding from the nose

nose cone the cone-shaped foremost part of a spacecraft, missile, etc.

nose dive 1. a swift, downward plunge of an aircraft, nose first **2.** any sudden, sharp drop —**nose′-dive** vi. **-dived′, -div′-ing**

nosegay (nōz′gā′) n. [NOSE + GAY (in obs. sense of "gay object")] a small bouquet

nosey adj. **nos′ier, nos′iest** same as NOSY

nosh (nosh) vt., vi. [< Yid.] [Slang] to eat (a snack) —n. [Slang] food

nosh-up n. [Slang] a meal, esp. a large one

nostalgia (nos tal′jē ə) n. [< Gr. nostos, return] 1. a longing for former times 2. a longing for home —**nostal′gic** adj.

nostril (nos′trəl) n. [< OE. nosu, nose + thyrel, hole] either of the openings into the nose

no-strings (nō′striŋs′) adj. free of conditions

nostrum (nos′trəm) n. [L., ours] 1. a quack medicine 2. a pet scheme for solving some problem

nosy (nō′zē) adj. **-ier, -iest** [Colloq.] prying; inquisitive —**nos′ily** adv. —**nos′iness** n.

Nosy Parker [also n- p-] [Colloq.] a nosy person

not (not) adv. [< ME. nought] in no manner; to no degree: a term of negation —**not half** [Colloq.] very much —**not quite** 1. nearly 2. obviously not [not quite proper]

‡**nota bene** (nō′tə bē′nē) [L.] note well

notable (nōt′ə b'l) adj. [< L. notare, to note] worthy of notice; remarkable —n. a well-known person —**no′tabil′ity** n. —**no′tably** adv.

notary (nōt′ər ē) n., pl. **-ries** [< L. notare, to note] someone, usually a solicitor, who attests deeds and writings: also **notary public** —**notar′ial** (-tāər′-) adj.

notation (nō tā′shən) n. [< L. notare, to note] 1. the use of a system of signs or symbols for words, quantities, etc. 2. any such system used in algebra, music, etc.

notch (noch) n. [by merging of ME. an oche, a notch] 1. a V-shaped cut in an edge or surface 2. [Colloq.] a step; degree —vt. 1. to cut a notch or notches in 2. to record, as by notches —**notched** adj.

NOTES
(A, semibreve; B, minim; C, crotchet; D, quaver; E, semiquaver; F, demisemiquaver; G, hemidemisemiquaver)

note (nōt) n. [< L. nota, mark] 1. a brief, written statement, as to aid memory 2. a) a short, informal letter b) a formal diplomatic communication 3. a comment or explanation, as at the foot of a page 4. a distinguishing feature [a note of joy] 5. importance or distinction [a man of note] 6. notice; heed [worthy of note] 7. any of certain commercial papers relating to debts or payment of money [a promissory note] 8. a cry or call, as of a bird 9.

a signal [a note of warning] 10. Music a) a tone of definite pitch b) a symbol for a tone, indicating pitch and duration —vt. **not′ed, not′ing** 1. to heed; observe 2. to put in writing 3. to mention specially —**compare notes** to exchange views —**strike** (or **hit**) **the right note** to behave in a manner appropriate to the occasion

notebook n. a book for memorandums

noted adj. distinguished; renowned; eminent

notelets (nōt′ləts) n.pl. small cards of folded paper used for short letters, etc.

note paper paper for writing notes, or letters

noteworthy adj. worthy of note; remarkable

nothing (nuth′iŋ) n. [OE. na thing] 1. no thing; not anything 2. nothingness 3. a thing that does not exist 4. a person or thing considered of no value or importance 5. a nought; zero —adv. not at all —**for nothing** 1. at no cost; free 2. in vain 3. without reason —**have nothing on** 1. to be naked 2. to have no appointments [he has nothing on tonight] 3. not to be a match for (someone) —**make nothing of** 1. to treat as of little importance 2. to fail to understand —**nothing but** nothing other than —**nothing doing** [Colloq.] 1. no: used in refusal 2. no result, etc. —**nothing less than** no less than: also **nothing short of** —**think nothing of** 1. to attach no importance to 2. to regard as easy to do

nothingness n. 1. nonexistence 2. lack of value, meaning, etc. 3. unconsciousness

notice (nōt′is) n. [see NOTE] 1. attention; heed 2. an announcement or warning 3. a sign giving some public information, warning, or rule 4. a formal warning of intention to end an agreement or contract at a certain time [to give an employee notice] 5. a brief mention or review of a book, play, etc. —vt. **-ticed, -ticing** 1. to observe; pay attention to 2. to refer to or comment on —**at short notice** with little warning —**serve notice** to give formal warning —**take notice** to pay attention

noticeable adj. 1. readily noticed; conspicuous 2. significant —**no′ticeably** adv.

notice board a board or wall area on which bulletins, notices or displays are put up

notifiable (nōt′ə fī′ə b'l) adj. that must be reported to the health authorities [notifiable diseases]

notification (nōt′ə fi kā′shən) n. 1. a notifying or being notified 2. the notice given or received 3. the letter, form, etc. notifying

notify (nōt′ə fī′) vt. **-fied′, -fy′ing** [< L. notus, known + facere, make] 1. to give notice to 2. to announce

notion (nō′shən) n. [see NOTE] 1. a) a mental image b) a vague thought 2. a belief; opinion; view 3. an inclination; whim 4. an intention

notional adj. 1. of or expressing notions, or concepts 2. imaginary 3. fanciful

notoriety (nōt′ə rī′ə tē) *n.* a being notorious

notorious (nō tôr′ē əs) *adj.* [see NOTE] widely but unfavourably known

not proven *Scots Law* a verdict given when the evidence is insufficient to warrant a conviction

no-trump (nō′trump′) *adj. Cards* with no suit being trumps —*n. Cards* a no-trump bid or hand

Notts. Nottinghamshire

notwithstanding (not′with stan′diŋ) *prep.* in spite of —*adv.* nevertheless —*conj.* although

nougat (nōō′gä) *n.* [Fr. < L. *nux*, nut] a confection of sugar paste with nuts

nought (nôt) *n.* [< OE. *ne*, not + *awiht*, aught] 1. *Arith.* the figure zero (0) 2. nothing —**set at nought** to defy; scorn Also **naught**

noughts and crosses a game for two, each marking either X's or O's in an open block of nine squares, the object being to complete a line of three

noun (noun) *n.* [< L. *nomen*, a name] *Gram.* 1. any of a class of words naming or denoting a person, thing, action, quality, etc. 2. any word, phrase, or clause so used

nourish (nur′ish) *vt.* [< L. *nutrire*] 1. to feed or sustain with substances necessary to life and growth 2. to foster; promote —**nour′ishing** *adj.*

nourishment *n.* 1. a nourishing or being nourished 2. something that nourishes

nous (nous) *n.* [Gr. *nous, noos*] 1. [Colloq.] common sense 2. *Philos.* mind; reason

nouveau riche (nōō′vō rēsh′) [Fr.] a newly rich person

Nov. November

nova (nō′və) *n., pl.* **-vae** (-vē), **-vas** [< L. *nova* (*stella*), new (star)] *Astron.* a star that suddenly becomes vastly brighter and then gradually dims

novel (nov′'l) *adj.* [< L. *novus*, new] new and unusual —*n.* a relatively long fictional prose narrative with a complex plot; book-length story

novelette (nov′ə let′) *n.* a short novel

novelist (nov′'l ist) *n.* a person who writes novels

novella (nō vel′ə) *n.* [It.] 1. a short prose narrative, as a tale by Boccaccio 2. a short novel

novelty (nov′'l tē) *n., pl.* **-ties** 1. the quality of being novel 2. an innovation 3. [*pl.*] a small, often cheap, cleverly made article, as a toy or ornament

November (nō vem′bər) *n.* [< L. *novem*, nine] the eleventh month of the year, having 30 days: abbrev. **Nov.**

novena (nō vē′nə) *n.* [< L. *novem*, nine] *R.C.Ch.* a nine-day period of devotions

novice (nov′is) *n.* [< L. *novus*, new] 1. a beginner 2. a person on probation in a religious group before taking vows

novitiate (nō vish′ē ət) *n.* 1. the period or state of being a novice 2. the quarters of religious novices

now (nou) *adv.* [OE. *nu*] 1. *a*) at the present time *b*) at once 2. at the time referred to; then; next 3. very recently

[he left just *now*] 4. with things as they are [*now* I'll never know] —*conj.* since; seeing that —*n.* the present time —*adj.* of the present time —*interj.* an exclamation of warning, reproach, etc. —**now and then** sometimes: also **now and again**

nowadays *adv.* in these days; at the present time —*n.* the present time

noway (nō′wā′) *adv.* by no means; not at all

nowel, nowell (nō el′) *n. alt. sp.* of NOEL

nowhere (nō′wãar′) *adv.* not in, at, or to any place —**get nowhere** [Colloq.] to fail to make progress —**nowhere near** not nearly

nowise *adv.* in no manner

nowt (nout) *n.* [Dial.] nothing

noxious (nok′shəs) *adj.* [< L. *nocere*, to hurt] harmful to health or morals —**nox′iously** *adv.*

nozzle (noz′'l) *n.* [dim. of NOSE] a spout at the end of a hose, etc. for controlling a stream of liquid or gas

Np *Chem.* neptunium

nr. near

N.S. 1. New Style 2. Nova Scotia

N.S.B. National Savings Bank

N.S.P.C.C. National Society for the Prevention of Cruelty to Children

N.S.T. [Canad.] Newfoundland Standard Time

N.S.W. New South Wales

NT., NT, N.T. New Testament

N.T. 1. Northern Territory 2. National Trust

nth (enth) *adj.* of the indefinitely large or small quantity represented by *n* —**to the nth degree** (or **power**) 1. to an indefinite degree or power 2. to an extreme

nt. wt. net weight

nu (nyōō) *n.* the thirteenth letter of the Greek alphabet (N, ν)

nuance (nyōō′äns′) *n.* [Fr. < L. *nubes*, cloud] a slight or delicate variation in colour, meaning, etc.

nub (nub) *n.* [var. of *knub*, knob] 1. a lump or small piece 2. [Colloq.] the main point; gist

nubble (nub′'l) *n.* [< NUB] a small knob —**nub′bly** *adj.*

nubby *adj.* **-bier, -biest** having a rough, knotted surface —**nub′biness** *n.*

nubile (nyōō′bil) *adj.* [< L. *nubere*, marry] marriageable: said of a young woman

nuclear (nyōō′klē ər) *adj.* 1. of or involving atomic nuclei, atomic energy, or nuclear weapons 2. of, like, or forming a nucleus

nuclear bomb an atomic bomb or a hydrogen bomb

nuclear disarmament the attempted elimination of nuclear weapons from a country's armament

nuclear energy *same as* ATOMIC ENERGY

nuclear family a basic social unit consisting of parents and their children living in one household

nuclear fission the splitting of the nuclei of atoms, as in an atomic bomb

nuclear fusion the fusion of atomic

nuclei into a nucleus of heavier mass, as in a hydrogen bomb

nuclear physics the branch of physics dealing with the structure of atomic nuclei and their interactions

nuclear reactor a device for initiating a controlled nuclear chain reaction for the production of energy

nucleate adj. having a nucleus —vt., vi. -at'ed, -at'ing to form into a nucleus —nu'clea'tion n.

nuclei (nyōō'klē ī') n. pl. of NUCLEUS

nucleic acid (nyōō klē'ik) any of a group of complex organic acids found in all living cells

nucleonics (nyōō'klē on'iks) n.pl. [with sing. v.] the branch of physics dealing with the practical applications of atomic energy

nucleus (nyōō'klē əs) n., pl. -clei', -cle-uses [L., kernel] 1. a central thing or part around which other things or parts are grouped 2. any centre of growth or development 3. Biol. the central mass of protoplasm in most plant and animal cells, necessary to growth, etc. 4. Chem., Physics the central part of an atom, the fundamental particles of which are the proton and neutron

nude (nyōōd) adj. [L. nudus] naked; bare —n. 1. the condition of being nude [in the nude] 2. a nude figure, as in painting, sculpture, etc. —nude'ly adv. —nu'dity n.

nudge (nuj) vt. nudged, nudg'ing [< ?] to push gently, esp. with the elbow, so as to get attention, etc. —n. a gentle push with the elbow, etc.

nudism (nyōō'diz'm) n. the practice or cult of going nude in the belief that it benefits health —nud'ist n., adj.

nugatory (nyōō'gə tər ē) adj. [< L. nugari, to trifle] 1. trifling; worthless 2. inoperative; invalid

nugget (nug'it) n. [prob. < dial. nug, lump] a lump, esp. of native gold

nuisance (nyōō's'ns) n. [< L. nocere, annoy] an act, thing, person, etc. causing trouble, annoyance, or inconvenience

nuisance value the value of a person or thing because of its ability to irritate

N.U.J. National Union of Journalists

null (nul) adj. [< L. nullus, none] 1. without legal force: usually in null and void 2. amounting to nought 3. of no value, effect, etc.

nullify (nul'ə fī') vt. -fied', -fy'ing [< L. nullus, none + facere, make] 1. to make legally null 2. to make valueless 3. to cancel out —nul'lifica'tion n.

nullity (nul'ə tē) n. 1. a being null 2. pl. -ties anything that is null

null set Math. a set having no members: also empty set

Num. (the book of) Numbers

num. 1. number 2. numeral(s)

N.U.M. National Union of Mineworkers

numb (num) adj. [< ME. nimen, take] deadened; insensible —vt. to make numb —numb'ly adv. —numb'ness n.

number (num'bər) n. [< L. numerus] 1. a symbol or word showing how many,

or which one in a series 2. the sum or total of persons or units 3. a collection of persons or things 4. a) [often pl.] a large group b) [pl.] numerical superiority 5. quantity 6. a) a single issue of a periodical b) a single song, skit, etc. in a programme 7. [Colloq.] a person or thing singled out 8. Gram. a) the differentiation in form to show whether one or more than one is meant b) the form itself 9. [pl.] metrical form or lines —vt. 1. to give a number to 2. to comprise 3. to count; enumerate 4. to include as one of a group (among) 5. to limit the number of —a number of several or many —beyond (or without) number too many to be counted —get (or have) one's number [U.S. Slang] to discover (or know) one's true character or motives —one's number is up [Slang] one's time to die, etc. has arrived —num'berer n.

numberless adj. 1. countless 2. without a number

number one [Colloq.] n. oneself —adj. first in importance, urgency, etc. [number one priority]

number plate a plate mounted on the front and back of a motor vehicle bearing the registration number

Number Ten the official residence of the British Prime Minister in Downing Street

numbskull (num'skul') n. same as NUMSKULL

numerable (nyōō'mər ə b'l) adj. that can be counted

numeracy (nyōō'mər ə sē) n. the ability to handle numbers

numeral (nyōō'mər əl) n. [< L. numerus, number] a figure, letter, or word expressing a number —adj. of or denoting a number or numbers

numerate adj. able to do basic arithmetic

numeration (nyōō'mə rā'shən) n. 1. a numbering or counting 2. a system of numbering

numerator (nyōō'mə rāt'ər) n. Math. the term above the line in a fraction, indicating how many of the specified parts of a unit are taken

numerical (nyōō mer'i k'l) adj. 1. of, or having the nature of, number 2. in or by numbers 3. expressed by numbers

numerology (nyōō'mə rol'ə jē) n. divination based on assigning meanings to numbers

numerous (nyōō'mər əs) adj. 1. consisting of many 2. very many —nu'-merously adv.

numismatic (nyōō'miz mat'ik) adj. [< L. numisma, a coin] 1. of coins or medals 2. of currency 3. of numismatics —nu'mis-mat'ically adv.

numismatics n.pl. [with sing. v.] the study or collection of coins, medals, etc. —numis'matist n.

numskull (num'skul') n. [NUM(B) + SKULL] a stupid person; dolt; dunce

nun (nun) n. [< LL. nonna] a woman devoted to a religious life, esp. in a convent

nuncio (nun'shē ō') n., pl. -cios' [It. <

L. *nuntius,* messenger] an ambassador of the Pope

nunnery (nun′ər ē) *n., pl.* **-neries** *a former name for* CONVENT

nunny bag (nun′ē) [prob. < Scots. *noony,* lunch] [Canad.] a small sealskin haversack

NUPE (nyoo′pē) National Union of Public Employees

nuptial (nup′shəl) *adj.* [< L. *nubere,* marry] 1. of marriage 2. of mating —*n.* [*pl.*] a wedding

N.U.R. National Union of Railwaymen

nurse (nʉrs) *n.* [< L. *nutrire,* nourish] 1. a person trained to take care of the sick or aged, assist doctors, etc. 2. a woman hired to take care of another's children —*vt.* **nursed, nurs′ing** 1. to take care of (a child, invalid, etc.) 2. to give milk from the breast to (an infant) 3. to suck milk from the breast of 4. to try to cure [to *nurse* a cold] 5. to use, handle, hold, etc. carefully, so as to protect or conserve 6. to bring up; rear 7. to nourish or foster —*vi.* 1. to tend the sick, etc. as a nurse 2. to feed at the breast 3. to suckle a child —**nurs′er** *n.*

nursemaid *n.* a woman hired to take care of a child or children: also **nurs′ery-maid′**

nursery (nʉrs′rē) *n., pl.* **-eries** 1. a room in a home, set aside for the children 2. *same as* NURSERY SCHOOL 3. a place where young plants are raised for sale, etc.

nurseryman *n.* one who owns, operates, or works for a nursery (sense 3)

nursery rhyme a short poem for children

nursery school a school for young children

nursery slopes gentle slopes used by beginners in skiing

nursery stakes a horse race for two-year-olds

nursing home a residence providing care for the infirm, chronically ill, disabled, etc.

nurture (nʉr′chər) *n.* [< L. *nutrire,* nourish] 1. training, upbringing, fostering, etc. 2. food —*vt.* **-tured, -turing** 1. to nourish 2. to train, rear, foster, etc.

N.U.S. National Union of Students

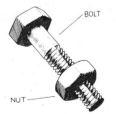

BOLT

NUT

nut (nut) *n.* [OE. *hnutu*] 1. a dry, one-seeded fruit, consisting of a kernel, often edible, in a woody shell, as the walnut 2. the kernel itself 3. loosely, any hard-shelled fruit keeping more or less indefinitely, as a peanut 4. a small, usually

metal block with a centre threaded hole for screwing onto a bolt, etc. 5. [Slang] a crazy person 6. [Slang] the head 7. a small piece of coal See also NUTS —*vi.* **nut′ted, nut′ting** to hunt for or gather nuts —**do one's nut** [Slang] to be extremely angry —**hard** (or **tough**) **nut to crack** a person or thing hard to deal with —**off one's nut** [Slang] crazy

N.U.T. National Union of Teachers

nut case [Slang] an eccentric or insane person

nutcracker *n.* a device, usually hinged, for cracking the shells of nuts

nuthatch *n.* a small, nut-eating bird with a sharp beak and short tail

nutmeg (nut′meg′) *n.* [< L. *nux,* nut + *muscus,* musk] the hard, aromatic seed of an East Indian tree: it is grated and used as a spice

nutria (nyoo′trē ə) *n.* [Sp. < L. *lutra,* otter] 1. a S American water-dwelling rodent with webbed feet 2. its soft, brown fur

nutrient (nyoo′trē ənt) *adj.* [< L. *nutrire,* nourish] nutritious; nourishing —*n.* anything nutritious

nutriment *n.* anything that nourishes; food

nutrition (nyoo trish′ən) *n.* [< L. *nutrire,* nourish] 1. a nourishing or being nourished; esp., the processes by which an organism takes in and assimilates food 2. nourishment 3. the science or study of proper diet —**nutri′tional** *adj.* —**nutri′-tionist** *n.*

nutritious *adj.* nourishing; of value as food —**nutri′tiously** *adv.* —**nutri′tious-ness** *n.*

nutritive (nyoo′trə tiv) *adj.* 1. having to do with nutrition 2. nutritious —**nu′tri-tively** *adv.*

nuts (nuts) *adj.* [see NUT] [Slang] crazy —*interj.* [Slang] an exclamation of disgust, scorn, etc.: often in the phrase **nuts to** (**someone** or **something**) —**be nuts about** [Slang] to like very much

nuts and bolts the practical, basic elements or mechanics of a situation or thing

nutshell *n.* the shell enclosing the kernel of a nut —**in a nutshell** concisely

nutter *n.* [< NUT] [Slang] an eccentric person

nutty *adj.* **-tier, -tiest** 1. containing or producing nuts 2. nutlike in flavour 3. [Slang] *a*) very enthusiastic *b*) crazy —**nut′tily** *adv.* —**nut′tiness** *n.*

nux vomica (nuks′vom′i kə) [< L. *nux,* nut + *vomere,* vomit] the poisonous seed of an Asiatic tree, containing strychnine

nuzzle (nuz′'l) *vt., vi.* **-zled, -zling** [< NOSE] 1. to push (against) or rub with the nose, snout, etc. 2. to nestle; snuggle —**nuz′zler** *n.*

NW, N.W., n.w. 1. northwest 2. northwestern

N.W.M.P. [Canad.] North West Mounted Police

N.W.T. Northwest Territories

nylon (nī′lon) *n.* [arbitrary coinage] 1. a synthetic polymeric amide made into fibre, bristles, etc. of great strength and elasticity **2.** [*pl.*] stockings made of this

nymph (nimf) *n.* [< Gr. *nymphē*] **1.** *Gr. & Rom. Myth.* any of a group of minor nature goddesses, represented as beautiful maidens living in rivers, trees, etc. **2.** a lovely young woman **3.** *Entomology* the young of an insect with incomplete metamorphosis

nympho (nim′fō) *n., pl.* **-phos** [contr. < *nymphomaniac*] [Colloq.] a woman who suffers from nymphomania

nymphomania (nim′fō mā′nē ə) *n.* [< Gr. *nymphē*, bride, nymph + -MANIA] abnormal and uncontrollable desire by a woman for sexual intercourse —**nym′pho-ma′niac′** *adj., n.*

N.Z., N.Zeal. New Zealand

O

O, o (ō) *n., pl.* **O's, o's 1.** the fifteenth letter of the English alphabet **2.** the numeral zero

O (ō) *interj.* an exclamation used: **1.** in direct address [O Lord!] **2.** to express surprise, fear, etc.: now usually *oh*

o' (ə, ō) *prep. an abbreviated form of:* **1.** of [o'clock] **2.** [Archaic or Dial.] on

O 1. Linguis. Old [OFr.] on

O 1. Chem. oxygen

Ω *Physics* the symbol for ohm

O. 1. Ocean **2.** Ontario

O., o. 1. octavo **2.** old

oaf (ōf) *n. pl.* **oafs, oaves** (-vz) [< ON. *alfr*, elf] a stupid, clumsy lout —**oaf′-ish** *adj.* —**oaf′ishness** *n.*

oak (ōk) *n.* [OE. *ac*] **1.** a large hardwood tree bearing nuts called *acorns* **2.** its wood —*adj.* of oak: also **oak′en**

oak apple an applelike gall on oak trees

Oaks (ōks) *n.* an annual race for fillies held at Epsom

oakum (ō′kəm) *n.* [< OE. a-, out + *camb*, a comb] loose, stringy, hemp fibre got by taking apart old ropes: used in caulking

OAP, O.A.P. 1. old age pensioner **2.** old age pension

oar (ōr) *n.* [OE. *ar*] **1.** a pole with a broad blade at one end, used in rowing **2.** a rower —**put one's oar in** to meddle —**rest on one's oars** to stop or relax —**oared** *adj.*

oarsman *n.* a man who rows —**oars′man-ship′** *n.* —**oars′woman** *n. fem.*

OAS, O.A.S. Organization of American States

oasis (ō ā′sis) *n., pl.* **-ses** (-sēz) [< Gr. *ōasis*] **1.** a fertile place in a desert **2.** anything offering relief in the midst of difficulty, dullness, etc.

oast (ōst) *n.* [< OE. *ast*] a kiln for drying hops or malt —**oast′house** *n.*

oat (ōt) *n.* [OE. *ate*] **1.** a hardy cereal grass **2.** [*usually pl.*] its edible grain —**oat′en** *adj.*

oath (ōth) *n., pl.* **oaths** (ōthz) [OE. *ath*] **1.** a) a ritualistic declaration, as by appeal to God, that one will speak the truth, keep a promise, etc. b) the thing declared **2.** the profane use of the name of God, as in anger **3.** a swearword —**take oath** to promise with an oath

oatmeal (ōt′mēl′) *n.* **1.** oats ground or rolled into meal or flakes **2.** a greyish-yellow colour

O.A.U. Organization of African Unity

ob- [< L. *ob*] a prefix meaning: **1.** to, towards, before [*object*] **2.** against [*obnoxious*] **3.** upon, over [*obfuscate*] **4.** completely [*obsolete*] In words of Latin

origin, *ob-* assimilates to *o-* before *m*, *oc-* before *c*, *of-* before *f*, and *op-* before *p*

OB, O.B. 1. obstetrician **2.** obstetrics

ob. [L. *obiit*] he (or she) died

O.B. Outside Broadcast

obbligato (ob′lə gät′ō) *adj.* [It.] *Music* indispensable: said of a required accompaniment —*n., pl.* **-tos, -ti** (-ē) such an accompaniment

obdurate (ob′dyoor ət) *adj.* [< L. *ob-*, intens. + *durare*, harden] **1.** hardhearted **2.** hardened and unrepenting **3.** stubborn —**ob′duracy** *n.*

O.B.E. Officer (of the Order of the) British Empire

obedient (ō bē′dē ənt) *adj.* [< OBEY] obeying or willing to obey; submissive —**obe′dience** *n.* —**obe′diently** *adv.*

obeisance (ō bā′səns) *n.* [< OFr. *obeir*, OBEY] **1.** homage **2.** a gesture of respect, as a bow —**obei′sant** *adj.*

QBELISK

obelisk (ob′əlisk) *n.* [< Gr. *obelos*, a spit] a four-sided stone pillar tapering towards its pyramidal top

obese (ō bēs′) *adj.* [< L. *ob-*, OB- + *edere*, eat] very fat —**obe′sity** *n.*

obey (ə bā′) *vt.* [< L. *ob-*, OB- + *audire*, hear] **1.** to carry out the orders of **2.** to carry out (an order) **3.** to be guided by [to *obey* one's conscience] —*vi.* to be obedient —**obey′er** *n.*

obfuscate (ob′fus kāt′) *vt.* **-cat′ed, -cat′-ing** [< L. *ob-*, OB- + *fuscus*, dark] **1.** to darken; obscure **2.** to muddle; confuse —**ob′fusca′tion** *n.*

obituary (ə bi′tyoo wər ē) *n., pl.* **-aries** [< L. *obire*, die] a notice of someone's death, usually with a brief biography —*adj.* of or recording a death

obj. 1. object **2.** objection **3.** objective

object (ob′jikt; *for v.* əb jekt′) *n.* [< L. *ob-*, OB- + *jacere*, throw] **1.** a thing that can be seen or touched **2.** a person or thing to which action, thought, etc. is directed **3.** aim; purpose **4.** *Gram.* a noun or substantive receiving the action of a verb or governed by a preposition **5.** *Philos.* anything that can be perceived by the mind —*vt.* to state in opposition or disapproval —*vi.* to feel or express opposition or disapproval —**no object** not a hindrance [*money is no object*] —**objec'-tor** *n.*

objectify (ob jek'tə fī') *vt.* -**fied'**, -**fy'ing** to make objective —**objec'tifica'tion** *n.*

objection (əb jek'shən) *n.* **1.** a feeling or expression of opposition or disapproval **2.** a reason for objecting

objectionable *adj.* causing objection; disagreeable; offensive —**objec'tionably** *adv.*

objective (əb jek'tiv) *adj.* **1.** having existence independent of the mind; real **2.** concerned with the actual features of the thing dealt with rather than the thoughts, feelings, etc. of the artist, writer, or speaker [*an objective description*] **3.** without bias or prejudice **4.** *Gram.* designating or of the case of an object —*n.* **1.** an aim; goal **2.** *Gram. a)* the objective case *b)* a word in this case **3.** *Optics* the lens nearest the object observed, as in a telescope —**objec'tively** *adv.* —**objectivity** (ob'jek tiv'ə tē) *n.*

object lesson an actual or practical demonstration or exemplification of some principle

objet d'art (ob'zhä där') *pl.* **objets d'art** (ob'zhä-) [Fr.] a small object of artistic value, as a figurine

objurgate (ob'jur gāt') *vt.* -**gat'ed**, -**gat'-ing** [< L. *ob-*, OB- + *jurgare*, chide] to upbraid sharply; berate —**ob'jurga'tion** *n.*

oblate (ob'lāt) *adj.* [< OB- + (PRO)LATE] *Geom.* flattened at the poles [*an oblate spheroid*]

oblation (ō blā'shən) *n.* [see OFFER] an offering made to God or a god —**obla'-tional** *adj.*

obligate (ob'lə gāt') *vt.* -**gat'ed**, -**gat'ing** [see OBLIGE] to bind by a contract, promise, sense of duty, etc.

obligation (ob'lə gā'shən) *n.* **1.** *a)* a legal or moral responsibility *b)* the thing that such a responsibility binds one to do **2.** binding power of a contract, promise, etc. **3.** indebtedness for a favour, service, etc.

obligato (ob'lə gät'ō) *adj., n., pl.* -**tos**, -**ti** (-ē) *same as* OBBLIGATO

obligatory (ə blig'ə tər ē) *adj.* legally or morally binding; required —**oblig'atorily** *adv.*

oblige (ə blīj') *vt.* **obliged'**, **oblig'ing** [< L. *ob-*, OB- + *ligare*, bind] **1.** to compel by moral, legal, or physical force **2.** to make indebted for a kindness or favour —*vi.* to do a favour —**much obliged** thank you —**oblig'er** *n.*

obliging *adj.* helpful; accommodating —**oblig'ingly** *adv.*

oblique (ə blēk') *adj.* [< L. *ob-*, OB- + *liquis*, awry] **1.** neither perpendicular nor horizontal; slanting **2.** indirect; evasive **3.** *Gram.* designating any case but the nominative and vocative —*n.* an oblique angle, muscle, line, etc. —**oblique'ly** *adv.* —**obliquity** (ə blik'wə tē), **oblique'ness** *n.*

oblique angle an acute or obtuse angle

obliterate (ə blit'ə rāt') *vt.* -**at'ed**, -**at'ing** [< L. *ob-*, OB- + *litera*, letter] **1.** to blot out; efface **2.** to destroy —**oblit'era'-tion** *n.* —**oblit'era'tor** *n.*

oblivion (ə bliv'ē ən) *n.* [< L. *oblivisci*, forget] **1.** forgetfulness **2.** the state of being forgotten

oblivious *adj.* forgetful or unmindful (usually *with* of or to) —**obliv'iously** *adv.* —**obliv'iousness** *n.*

oblong (ob'lon) *adj.* [< L. *ob-*, OB- + *longus*, long] longer than broad; specif., rectangular and longer in one direction than in the other —*n.* an oblong figure

obloquy (ob'lə kwē) *n., pl.* -**quies** [< LL. *obloqui*, speak against] **1.** verbal abuse; esp., widespread censure **2.** disgrace or infamy resulting from this

obnoxious (əb nok'shəs) *adj.* [< L. *ob-*, OB- + *noxa*, a harm] very unpleasant; offensive —**obnox'iousness** *n.*

oboe (ō'bō) *n.* [It. < Fr.: see HAUTBOY] a double-reed woodwind instrument having a high, penetrating, melancholy tone —**o'boist** *n.*

Obs., obs. obsolete

obscene (əb sēn') *adj.* [< L. *obscenus*, filthy] **1.** offensive to modesty or decency; lewd **2.** disgusting; repulsive —**obscene'-ly** *adv.* —**obscen'ity** (əb sen'-) *n.*

obscure (əb skyoor') *adj.* [< L. *obscurus*, covered over] **1.** not easily understood; vague; ambiguous **2.** not easily perceived; not distinct **3.** inconspicuous; hidden **4.** not well-known [*an obscure scientist*] **5.** dim; dark —*vt.* -**scured'**, -**scur'ing** to make obscure; darken; conceal; overshadow; confuse, etc. —**obscu'rity** *n.*

obsequies (ob'sə kwēz) *n.pl.* [< L. *obsequium:* see ff.), substituted for L. *exsequiae*, funeral] funeral rites

obsequious (əb sē'kwē əs) *adj.* [< L. *obsequium*, compliance] showing too great a willingness to serve or obey; fawning

observable (əb zur'və b'l) *adj.* that can be observed

observance (əb zur'vəns) *n.* **1.** the observing of a law, duty, custom, etc. **2.** a customary act, rite, etc.

observant *adj.* **1.** paying careful attention **2.** perceptive or alert —**observ'antly** *adv.*

observation (ob'zər vā'shən) *n.* **1.** *a)* the act or power of noticing *b)* something noticed **2.** a being noticed **3.** *a)* a noting and recording of facts, as for some scientific study *b)* the data so noted **4.** a comment —**ob'serva'tional** *adj.*

observatory (əb zur'və trē) *n., pl.* -**ries** a building or institution equipped for scientific observation, esp. one with a large telescope for astronomical research

observe (əb zurv') *vt.* -**served'**, -**serv'ing** [< L. *ob-*, OB- + *servare*, keep] **1.** *a)* to notice (something) *b)* to pay special attention to **2.** to examine scientifically **3.** to conclude after study **4.** to remark **5.** to keep (a law, custom, etc.) **6.** to celebrate (a holiday, etc.) —*vi.* **1.** to take notice **2.** to comment (*on* or *upon*) —**observ'er** *n.*

obsess (əb ses′) *vt.* [< L. *obsidere*, besiege] to haunt or trouble in mind; preoccupy greatly —**obses′sive** *adj.*

obsession *n.* 1. a being obsessed with an idea, desire, etc. 2. such an idea, desire, etc. —**obses′sional** *adj.*

obsidian (ob sid′ē ən) *n.* [< *Obsius*, who discovered it] a hard, dark volcanic glass, used as a gemstone

obsolescent (ob′sə les′ənt) *adj.* in the process of becoming obsolete —**ob′soles′cence** *n.*

obsolete (ob′sə lēt′) *adj.* [< L. *obsolescere*, to decay] no longer in use; discarded; out-of-date —**ob′solete′ly** *adv.*

obstacle (ob′stə k'l) *n.* [< L. *ob-*, OB- + *stare*, to stand] anything that gets in the way or hinders; obstruction

obstetrician (ob′ste trish′ən) *n.* a medical doctor who specializes in obstetrics

obstetrics (ob stet′riks) *n.pl.* [with sing. v.] the branch of medicine concerned with the care and treatment of women in pregnancy and childbirth

obstinate (ob′stə nət) *adj.* [< L. *obstinare*, resolve on] 1. unreasonably determined to have one's own way; stubborn 2. resisting treatment [an *obstinate* fever] —**ob′stinacy** *n.*

obstreperous (əb strep′ər əs) *adj.* [< L. *ob-*, *struere*, pile up] 1. to block (a passage); clog 2. to hinder (progress, etc.); impede 3. to block (the view) —**obstruc′tive** *adj.*

obstruct (əb strukt′) *vt.* [< L. *ob-*, OB- + *struere*, pile up] 1. to block (a passage); clog 2. to hinder (progress, etc.); impede 3. to block (the view) —**obstruc′tive** *adj.*

obstruction *n.* 1. an obstructing or being obstructed 2. anything that obstructs; hindrance

obstructionist *n.* anyone who obstructs progress; esp., a member of a legislature who hinders legislation by technical manoeuvres —*adj.* of obstructionists

obtain (əb tān′) *vt.* [< L. *ob-*, OB- + *tenere*, hold] to get possession of by effort; procure —*vi.* to be in force; prevail [peace will *obtain*] —**obtain′able** *adj.*

obtrude (əb trood′) *vt.* -**trud′ed**, -**trud′ing** [< L. *ob-*, OB- + *trudere*, thrust] 1. to thrust forward 2. to force (oneself, one's opinions, etc.) upon others —*vi.* to obtrude oneself (on or upon) —**obtru′sion** *n.*

obtrusive *adj.* 1. inclined to obtrude 2. obtruding itself —**obtru′sively** *adv.* —**obtru′siveness** *n.*

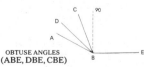

OBTUSE ANGLES
(ABE, DBE, CBE)

obtuse (əb tyoos′) *adj.* [< L. *ob-*, OB- + *tundere*, strike] 1. slow to understand; dull or insensitive 2. greater than 90 degrees and less than 180 degrees [an *obtuse* angle] 3. not sharp or pointed; blunt —**obtuse′ly** *adv.* —**obtuse′ness** *n.*

obverse (ob′vurs) *adj.* [< L. *ob-*, OB- + *vertere*, turn] 1. turned towards the observer 2. forming a counterpart —*n.* 1. a counterpart 2. the side, as of a coin, bearing the main design 3. the main surface of anything

obviate (ob′vē āt′) *vt.* -**at′ed**, -**at′ing** [see OBVIOUS] to make unnecessary —**ob′via′tion** *n.*

obvious (ob′vē əs) *adj.* [L. *obvius*, in the way: see OB- & VIA] easy to see or understand; evident —**ob′viously** *adv.* —**ob′viousness** *n.*

o/c overcharge

O.C. Officer Commanding

ocarina (ok′ə rē′nə) *n.* [It. < LL. *auca*, goose] a small, rounded wind instrument with finger holes and a mouthpiece

occasion (ə kā′zhən) *n.* [< L. *ob-*, OB- + *cadere*, fall] 1. a) a happening b) a particular time 2. need; reason 3. a fact or event that makes something else possible 4. a favourable time; opportunity 5. a special time or event —*vt.* to cause —**on occasion** sometimes —**rise to the occasion** to meet the demands of a situation

occasional *adj.* 1. happening now and then; infrequent 2. on, of, or for a special occasion —**occa′sionally** *adv.*

occident (ok′sə dənt) *n.* [< L. *occidens*, direction of the setting sun: see OCCASION] the west: now rare, except [O-] the part of the world west of Asia, esp. Europe and the Americas —**oc′ciden′tal, Oc′ciden′tal** *adj., n.*

occiput (ok′si put′) *n., pl.* **occip′ita** (-sip′ə tə), -**puts′** [< L. *ob-*, OB- + *caput*, head] the back part of the skull or head —**occipital** (ok sip′ə t'l) *adj.*

occlude (o klood′) *vt.* -**clud′ed**, -**clud′ing** [< L. *ob-*, OB- + *claudere*, shut] 1. to close or block (a passage) 2. to shut in or out 3. *Chem.* to retain or absorb (a gas, etc.) —**occlu′sion** *n.*

occluded front *Meteorol.* the front formed when a warm front is overtaken by a cold front and the warm air is forced up away from ground level

occult (o kult′) *adj.* [< L. *occulere*, conceal] 1. of alleged supernatural powers, manifestations, etc. 2. beyond human understanding 3. hidden 4. secret; esoteric —**the occult** the occult arts —**occult′ism** *n.*

occupancy (ok′yoo pən sē) *n., pl.* -**cies** an occupying; a taking or keeping in possession

occupant *n.* one who occupies a house, post, etc.

occupation (ok′yoo pā′shən) *n.* 1. (one's) trade, profession, or business 2. an occupying or being occupied; specif., the seizure and control of a country or area by military forces —**oc′cupa′tional** *adj.* —**oc′cupa′tionally** *adv.*

occupational disease a disease commonly acquired by people in a particular occupation

occupational therapy therapy by means of work designed to divert the mind or to correct a physical defect

occupier (ok′yŏŏ pī′ər) *n.* the person in possession; an occupant; a tenant

occupy (ok′yŏŏ pī′) *vt.* **-pied′**, **-py′ing** [< L. *ob-*, OB- + *capere*, seize] **1.** to hold possession of by tenure; specif., a) to dwell in b) to hold (a position or office) **2.** to employ or busy (oneself, one's mind, etc.) **3.** to take up or fill up (space, time, etc.) **4.** to take possession of by settlement or seizure

occur (ə kur′) *vi.* **-curred′**, **-cur′ring** [< L. *ob-*, OB- + *currere*, run] **1.** to happen **2.** to be found; exist **3.** to present itself; come to mind

occurrence (ə kur′əns) *n.* **1.** the act or fact of occurring **2.** something that occurs; event; incident —**occur′rent** *adj.*

ocean (ō′shən) *n.* [< Gr. *Ōkeanos*] **1.** the great body of salt water that covers about 71 % of the earth's surface **2.** any of its five principal divisions : the Atlantic, Pacific, Indian, Arctic, or Antarctic Ocean **3.** any great expanse or quantity —**oce-anic** (ō′shē an′ik) *adj.*

oceangoing *adj.* of or for travel on the ocean

oceanography (ō′shyə nog′rə fē) *n.* the study of the environment in the oceans —**o′ceanog′rapher** *n.*

ocelot (ō′sə lot′) *n.* [Fr. < SAmInd. *ocelotl*, jaguar] a large cat of N and S America, with a yellow or grey coat marked with black spots

och (okh) *interj.* [Scot. & Ir.] an expression of regret, impatience, surprise, etc.

ochre (ō′kər) *n.* [< Gr. *ōchros*, pale yellow] **1.** a yellow or reddish-brown clay used as a pigment **2.** the colour of ochre, esp., dark yellow —**o′chreous** *adj.*

-ock (ək) [< OE.] *a suffix used orig. to form the diminutive* [*hillock*]

o'clock (ə klok′) *adv.* of or according to the clock

OCR *Data Processing* optical character recognition

oct- *same as :* **1.** OCTA- **2.** OCTO- Used before a vowel

Oct. October

oct. octavo

octa- [< Gr.] *a combining form meaning* eight

octagon (ok′tə gən) *n.* [see OCTA- & -GON] a plane figure with eight angles and eight sides —**octag′onal** (-tag′ə n'l) *adj.* —**octag′onally** *adv.*

octahedron (ok′tə hē′drən) *n.*, *pl.* **-drons, -dra** [see OCTA- & -HEDRON] a solid figure with eight plane surfaces

octane (ok′tān) *n.* [< OCTO-] an oily paraffin hydrocarbon found in petroleum

octane number (or **rating**) a number representing the antiknock quality of a fuel : the higher the number, the greater this quality

octave (ok′tiv) *n.* [< L. *octo*, eight] **1.** *Music* a) the eighth full tone above or below a given tone b) the interval of eight diatonic degrees between a tone and either of its octaves c) the series of tones (a full scale) within this interval, or the keys of an instrument producing such a series d) a tone and either of its octaves sounded together **2.** the first eight lines of a sonnet

octavo (ok tā′vō) *n.*, *pl.* **-vos** [< L. (*in*) *octavo*, (in) eight] **1.** the page size (c. 15 x 23 cm) of a book made from folding a sheet of paper to form eight leaves **2.** a book with pages of this size Also written **8vo** or **8°**

octet, octette (ok tet′) *n.* [< OCT(O)- + (DU)ET] **1.** any group of eight **2.** *Music* a) a composition for eight voices or instruments b) the performers of this

octo- [< Gr.] *a combining form meaning* eight

October (ok tō′bər) *n.* [< L. *octo*, eight : eighth month of the Roman year] the tenth month of the year, having 31 days : abbrev. **Oct.**

octogenarian (ok′tō ji näər′ē ən) *adj.* [< L. *octoginta*, eighty] eighty years old, or between the ages of eighty and ninety —*n.* a person of this age

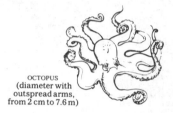

OCTOPUS
(diameter of body
with
outspread arms,
from 2 cm to 7.6 m)

octopus (ok′tə pəs) *n.*, *pl.* **-puses** [< Gr. *oktō*, eight + *pous*, foot] a mollusc with a soft body and eight arms covered with suckers

O.C.T.U. Officer Cadets Training Unit

ocular (ok′yŏŏ lər) *adj.* [< L. *oculus*, eye] **1.** of, for, or like the eye **2.** by eyesight —*n.* the eyepiece of an optical instrument

oculist *n.* [< L. *oculus*, eye] formerly, a specialist in eye diseases

OD, O.D. **1.** Officer of the Day **2.** outside diameter **3.** overdose

O.D. ordnance datum

odalisque, odalisk (ōd′ə lisk) *n.* [Fr. < Turk. *ōdalik*, chambermaid] a female slave in an Oriental harem

odd (od) *adj.* [< ON. *oddi*, triangle, hence odd number] **1.** a) peculiar b) eccentric **2.** occasional; incidental [*odd* jobs] **3.** having a remainder of one when divided by two **4.** numbered with an odd number [the *odd* months] **5.** a) remaining or separated from a pair, set, etc. [an *odd* glove] b) remaining after the others are paired, taken, etc. **6.** a) in addition to a round number [ten pounds and some *odd* change] b) with a small number over [thirty *odd* years ago] **7.** out-of-the-way [in *odd* corners] —**odd man out** from a person or thing different or excluded from others forming a group —**odd′ly** *adv.* —**odd′ness** *n.*

oddity *n.* 1. queerness; peculiarity 2. *pl.* **-ties** an odd person or thing

oddment *n.* something odd or left over

odds *n.pl.* 1. an equalizing advantage given by a bettor or competitor in proportion to the assumed chances in his favour 2. difference in favour of one side over the other; advantage 3. difference [it makes no *odds*] —**against all odds** despite all difficulties —**at odds** in disagreement —**over the odds** more than is expected, necessary, etc. —**the odds are** the likelihood is

odds and ends scraps; remnants; oddments

odds-on *adj.* having better than an even chance of winning [an *odds-on* favourite]

ode (ōd) *n.* [< Gr. *ōidē*, song] a lyric poem typically addressed to some person or thing and characterized by lofty feeling and dignified style

odious (ō′dē əs) *adj.* [see ff.] arousing or deserving hatred or loathing; disgusting —**o′diously** *adv.*

odium *n.* [< L. *odi*, I hate] 1. hatred 2. the disgrace brought on by hateful action; opprobrium

odometer (ō dom′ə tər) *n.* [< Gr. *hodos*, way + *metron*, a measure] an instrument for measuring the distance travelled by a vehicle

-odont (ə dont′) [< Gr.] a combining form meaning tooth

odonto- [see prec.] a combining form meaning tooth or teeth

odontology (o′don tol′ə jē) *n.* [see prec. & -LOGY] the science dealing with the structure and diseases of the teeth —**odon′tolog′ical** (-tə loj′i k'l) *adj.*

odoriferous (ō′də rif′ər əs) *adj.* giving off an odour, often, specif., a fragrant one —**o′dorif′erously** *adv.*

odour (ō′dər) *n.* [< L. *odor*] a smell, whether pleasant or unpleasant U.S. sp. **odor** —**be in bad** (or **ill**) **odour** to be in ill repute —**o′dorous** *adj.*

Odyssey (od′ə sē) *n.*, *pl.* **-seys** [< the Greek epic poem] any extended wandering

oe- a variant spelling for many words of Gr. and L. origin now sometimes written with *e-*

OE., OE, O.E. Old English

O.E.C.D. Organization for Economic Co-operation and Development

oedema (ē dē′mə) *n.*, *pl.* **-mas, -mata** [< Gr. *oidēma*, swelling] an abnormal accumulation of fluid in tissues of the body, causing swelling

Oedipus complex (ē′də pəs) *Psycho-analysis* the unconscious tendency of a child to be attached to the parent of the opposite sex

o′er (ōər) *prep., adv.* chiefly poet. contr. of OVER

oesophagus (ē sof′ə gəs) *n.*, *pl.* **-agi′** (-gī′) [< Gr. *oisophagos*, gullet] the tube through which food passes from the pharynx to the stomach

oestrogen (ēs′trō jən) *n.* [< Gr. *oistros*, frenzy + -GEN] any of several female sex hormones

of (ov; *unstressed* əv, ə) *prep.* [OE.] 1. from; specif., a) coming from [men *of* Harlech] b) as relates to [how wise *of* her] c) resulting from [to die *of* fever] d) at a distance from [east *of* the city] e) by [the poems *of* Poe] f) separated from [robbed *of* his money] g) from the whole [part *of* the time] h) made from [a sheet *of* paper] 2. belonging to 3. a) possessing [a man *of* property] b) containing [a bag *of* nuts] 4. specified as [a height *of* two metres] 5. with (something specified) as object, goal, etc. [a reader *of* books] 6. characterized by [a man *of* honour] 7. about [think *of* me] 8. set aside for [a day *of* rest] 9. during [*of* late years] 10. [Colloq.] indicating a time when some activity habitually occurs [I go to the pub *of* an evening]

off (of) *adv.* [LME. variant of *of*, OF] 1. so as to be away or at a distance [to move *off*] 2. so as to be measured, divided, etc. [to mark *off*] 3. so as to be no longer on, attached, etc. [take *off* your hat] 4. (a specified distance) away in space or time [two weeks *off*] 5. so as to be no longer in operation [turn the motor *off*] 6. so as to be less, smaller, etc. [5 % *off* for cash] 7. so as to lose consciousness [to doze *off*] 8. away from one's work [take a day *off*] —*prep.* 1. no longer (or not) on, attached, etc. [the car is *off* the road] 2. away from [to live *off* the beaten track] 3. a) from the substance of [to live *off* the land] b) at the expense of 4. branching out from [a road *off* the High Street] 5. relieved from [*off* duty] 6. not up to the usual standard, etc. of [*off* one's game] 7. [Colloq.] no longer using, supporting, etc. [to be *off* a diet] —*adj.* 1. not on, attached, etc. 2. not in operation [the motor is *off*] 3. on the way [be *off* to bed] 4. away from work, etc. 5. not up to what is usual [an *off* day] 6. more remote [on the *off* chance] 7. designating the horse on the right in double harness, etc. 8. in (specified) circumstances [to be well *off*] 9. sour, rotten, etc. 10. postponed or cancelled [the game's *off*] 11. *Cricket* designating the side of the field facing the batsman —*n.* 1. *Cricket* the off side 2. *Horse Racing* the beginning of a race —*interj.* go away! stay away! —**a bit off** [Colloq.] irritating; unjust —**off and on** now and then

off. 1. office 2. officer 3. official

offal (of′'l) *n.* [ME. *ofall*, lit., off-fall] 1. [with sing. or pl. v.] the entrails, etc. of a butchered animal 2. refuse

offbeat (of′bēt′) *adj.* [< a rhythm in jazz music] [Colloq.] unconventional, unusual, etc.

off-chance *n.* a slight possibility

off-colour *adj.* 1. slightly ill; unwell 2. not quite proper; risqué

off cut a piece of plywood, etc. remaining after the main pieces have been cut

offence (ə fens′) *n.* **l.** a breaking of the law; sin or crime **2.** a feeling of resentment or anger **3.** something that causes resentment, anger, etc. **4.** the act of attacking **5.** the person, army, etc. that is attacking U.S. sp. **offense** —**give offence** to anger, insult, etc. —**take offence** to feel hurt, angry, etc. —**offence′less** *adj.*

offend (ə fend′) *vi.* [< L. *ob-* (see OB-) + *fendere*, hit] **l.** to commit a sin or crime **2.** to create resentment, anger, etc. —*vt.* **l.** to hurt the feelings of; make resentful, angry, etc. **2.** to be displeasing to (the taste, sense, etc.) —**offend′er** *n.* —**offend′edly** *adv.*

offensive (ə fen′siv) *adj.* **l.** unpleasant; disgusting **2.** causing resentment, anger, etc.; insulting **3.** attacking, or for attack —*n.* **l.** attitude or position of attack **2.** an attack or hostile action —**offen′siveness** *n.*

offer (of′ər) *vt.* [< L. *ob-* (see OB-) + *ferre*, bring] **l.** to present for acceptance or consideration [to *offer* one's services] **2.** to express willingness or intention [to *offer* to go] **3.** a) to present for sale b) to bid (a price, etc.) **4.** to present in an act of worship [to *offer* prayers] **5.** to show or give signs of [to *offer* resistance] —*vi.* **l.** to occur; present itself —*n.* the act of offering or thing offered —**of′ferer, of′feror** *n.*

offering *n.* something offered; a contribution

offertory (of′ər tər ē) *n., pl.* **-ries** [< LL. *offere*, OFFER] [*often* O-] **l.** that part of Holy Communion during which the Eucharistic bread and wine are offered to God **2.** any collection of money at a church service

offhand *adv.* without prior preparation —*adj.* **l.** said or done offhand **2.** casual, curt, etc. Also **off′hand′ed** —**off′hand′edly** *adv.* —**off′hand′edness** *n.*

office (of′is) *n.* [< L. *opus*, a work + *facere*, do] **l.** a place where work that is clerical, administrative, professional, etc. is carried on **2.** a governmental department [the Foreign *Office*] **3.** a position of authority or trust, esp. in a government **4.** a duty, esp. one that is part of one's work **5.** something done for another [done through his good (or ill) *offices*] **6.** a place where tickets, information, etc. can be obtained **7.** a religious rite **8.** [*pl*] the rooms or buildings of a house or estate in which servants carry out their duties

officer (of′ə sər) *n.* **l.** a person holding a position of authority, esp. by commission, in the armed forces **2.** a policeman **3.** the captain or any of the mates of a nonnaval ship **4.** anyone holding an office or position of authority in a government, business, society, etc.

official (ə fish′əl) *adj.* **l.** of or holding an office, or position of authority **2.** authorized or authoritative [an *official*

request] **3.** formal or ceremonious —*n.* a person holding office —**offi′cially** *adv.*

officialdom *n.* **l.** officials collectively **2.** the domain or position of officials

officialese (ə fish′ə lēz′) *n.* the pompous, wordy, and involved language typical of official communications

Official Receiver a public official charged with certain duties in bankruptcy cases

officiate (ə fish′ē āt′) *vi.* **-at′ed, -at′ing** **l.** to perform the duties of an office **2.** to perform the functions of a priest, minister, etc. **3.** *Sports* to act as referee, umpire, etc.

officious (ə fish′əs) *adj.* [< L. *officium*, OFFICE] offering unwanted advice or services; meddlesome —**offi′ciously** *adv.* —**offi′ciousness** *n.*

offing (of′iŋ) *n.* [< OFF] the distant part of the sea visible from the shore —**in the offing l.** at some distance but in sight **2.** at some indefinite future time

offish (of′ish) *adj.* [Colloq.] aloof; standoffish

off-key *adj.* **l.** not on the right note; flat or sharp **2.** not quite in accord with what is normal, fitting, etc.

off-licence *n.* **l.** a shop, etc. where alcohol is sold in unopened containers for consumption elsewhere **2.** a licence permitting such sales

off-line *adj.* designating equipment not directly controlled by the central processor of a computer

off-peak *adj.* of services used at times other than those of the highest demand

off-putting *adj.* [Colloq.] distracting, annoying, etc.

offset *n.* **l.** an offshoot **2.** a) same as OFFSET PRINTING b) an impression made by this process —*vt.* **-set′, -set′ting** **l.** to balance, compensate for, etc. **2.** to make (an impression) by offset printing

offset printing a printing process in which the inked impression is first made on a rubber-covered roller, then transferred to paper

offshoot *n.* **l.** a shoot growing from the main stem of a plant **2.** anything that derives from a main source

offshore (of′shôr′) *adj.* **l.** moving away from the shore **2.** at some distance from shore —*adv.* away from the shore

offside (of′sīd′) *adj.* **l.** designating the side of a motor vehicle nearest the centre of the road [the *offside* headlight] **2.** *Sports* in a position illegally ahead of the ball when it is played

offspring *n.* **l.** a child or animal as related to its parent **2.** progeny **3.** a result

off-the-peg *adj.* ready-to-wear, as opposed to made-to-measure: said of clothing

OFr. Old French

oft (oft) *adv.* [OE.] *chiefly poet. var. of* OFTEN

often (of′'n) *adv.* [ME. var. of prec.] many times; frequently —**every so often** occasionally

OGEE ARCH

ogee (ō′jē) *n.* [< OFr. *ogive*] 1. an S-shaped curve, moulding, etc. 2. a pointed arch formed with the curve of an ogee on each side: also **ogee arch**

ogle (ō′g'l) *vi., vt.* o′gled, o′gling [prob. < LowG. *oog*, the eye] to keep looking (at) boldly and with obvious desire —**o′gler** *n.*

ogre (ō′gər) *n.* [Fr.] 1. in fairy tales and folklore, a man-eating giant 2. a hideous or cruel man —**o′gress** *n.fem.*

oh (ō) *interj., n.* an exclamation of surprise, fear, wonder, pain, etc.

OHG, OHG., O.HG. Old High German

ohm (ōm) *n.* [< G. S. *Ohm*] the SI unit of electrical resistance —**ohm′ic** *adj.*

O.H.M.S. On Her (or His) Majesty's Service

-oid (oid) [< Gr. *eidos*, a form] *a suffix meaning* like, resembling [*crystalloid*]

oil (oil) *n.* [< Gr. *elaion*, (olive) oil] 1. any of various greasy, combustible, normally liquid substances obtained from animal, vegetable, and mineral sources: oils are not soluble in water 2. *same as* PETROLEUM 3. *same as:* a) OIL COLOUR b) OIL PAINTING —*vt.* 1. to lubricate or supply with oil 2. to bribe [*to oil* someone's palm] —*adj.* of, from, or like oil, or having to do with the production or use of oil —**oil the wheels** to make things go more smoothly —**oil′er** *n.*

oil cake a mass of crushed linseed, etc. from which the oil has been extracted, used as livestock feed

oilcloth *n.* cloth made waterproof with oil

oil colour paint made by grinding a pigment in oil

oiled *adj.* 1. treated with oil 2. drunk, esp. in the phrase **well oiled**

oil field a place where oil deposits of value are found

oil-fired *adj.* using oil as a fuel

oil painting 1. a picture painted in oil colours 2. the art of painting in oil colours

oil rig *see* RIG

oilskin *n.* 1. cloth made waterproof by treatment with oil 2. [*often pl.*] a garment or outfit made of this

oil slick a film of oil, esp. from a ship, covering an area of water

oil well a well bored through layers of rock, etc. to a supply of petroleum

oily *adj.* oil′ier, oil′iest 1. of, like, or containing oil 2. covered with oil; greasy 3. unctuous —**oil′iness** *n.*

oink (oiŋk) *n.* the grunt of a pig, or a sound imitating it

ointment (oint′mənt) *n.* [see UNGUENT] a fatty substance applied to the skin as a salve or cosmetic

OK, O.K. (ō′kā′; *also, & for v. & n. usually,* ō′kā′) *adj., adv., interj.* [abbrev. for "oll korrect," jocular misspelling of *all correct*] all right; correct —*n., pl.* **OK's, O.K.'s** approval —*vt.* **OK'd, O.K.'d, OK'ing, O.K.'ing** to put an OK on; approve Also **okay**

okapi (ō kä′pē) *n.* [native Afr. name] an African animal related to the giraffe, but having a shorter neck

okra (ō′krə) *n.* [< WAfr. name] a tall plant with pods that are used as a food

-ol (ol) [< (ALCOH)OL] *a suffix used in chemistry to mean* an alcohol or phenol [*menthol*]

old (ōld) *adj.* old′er or eld′er, old′est or eld′est [OE. *ald*] 1. having lived or existed for a long time; aged 2. of aged people 3. of a certain age [*ten years old*] 4. not new 5. [*often* O-] designating the earliest stage of a language [*Old English*] 6. worn out by age or use 7. former 8. having had long experience [*an old hand*] 9. having existed long ago [*an old joke*] 10. of long standing [*an old joke*] 11. [Colloq.] dear: a term of affection [*old boy*] Also **used as a** colloquial intensive [*a fine old time*] —*n.* 1. time long past [*days of old*] 2. something old (with *the*) —**old′ish** *adj.* —**old′ness** *n.*

old age the advanced years of life

old age pension *former name for* RETIREMENT PENSION —**old age pensioner**

Old Bailey popular name for the Central Criminal Court, London

Old Boy [*often* o- b-] [Colloq.] 1. a male ex-pupil of a school 2. *a)* a familiar name used to refer to a man *b)* an old man Also **old girl** *fem.*

Old Contemptibles the British Expeditionary Force of 1914

old country the country from which an immigrant came

olden *adj.* [Poet.] (of) old; ancient

Old English the Germanic language of the Anglo-Saxons, spoken in England from c. 400 to c. 1100 A.D.

old-fashioned *adj.* suited to or favouring the styles, ideas, etc. of past times; out-of-date

old fogy, old fogey *see* FOGY

Old French the French language c. 800 to c. 1550 A.D.

old guard [< Napoleon's imperial guard] 1. any group that has long defended a cause 2. the conservative element of a group, party, etc.

old hat [Slang] 1. old-fashioned 2. trite

Old High German the High German language from the 8th to the 12th century

oldie, oldy *n.,* pl. old′ies [Colloq.] an old joke, song, film, etc.

old lady [Slang] 1. one's mother 2. one's wife

Old Lady of Threadneedle Street the Bank of England

old maid 1. a woman, esp. an older woman, who has never married; spinster 2. a prim, fussy person

old man [Slang] 1. one's father 2. one's husband 3. [*usually* O- M-] any man in authority

old master 1. any great European painter before the 18th cent. 2. a painting by such a painter

old moon the moon in its last quarter, when it appears as a crescent curving to the left

Old Nick the Devil; Satan : also **Old Harry**

old rose greyish or purplish red —**old'-rose'** *adj.*

old school a group of people who cling to traditional or conservative ideas, methods, etc.

old school tie 1. a necktie in the distinctive colours of any of the British public schools 2. the system of mutual aid supposed to operate among their former pupils

old style the old method of reckoning time according to the Julian calendar —**old'-style'** *adj.*

Old Testament the Holy Scriptures of Judaism, the first of the two general divisions of the Christian Bible

old-time *adj.* 1. of or like past times 2. of long standing or experience

old wives' tale a silly story or superstition

Old World the Eastern Hemisphere, often esp. Europe

oleaginous (ō'lē aj'i nəs) *adj.* [< L. *olea*, olive tree] oily; unctuous —**o'leag'inousness** *n.*

oleander (ō'lē an'dər) *n.* [ML.] a poisonous evergreen shrub with fragrant white, pink, or red flowers

oleo- (ō'lē ō) [< L. *oleum*, oil] *a combining form meaning* oil [*oleomargarine*]

'O' level *short for* ORDINARY LEVEL

olfactory (ol fak'tər ē) *adj.* [< L. *olere*, have a smell + *facere*, make] of the sense of smell : also **olfac'tive**

oligarch (ol'ə gärk') *n.* any of the rulers of an oligarchy

oligarchy (ol'ə gär'kē) *n.*, *pl.* -**chies** [see OLIGO- & -ARCHY] 1. a form of government with the ruling power belonging to a few 2. a state so governed 3. those ruling such a state —**ol'igar'chic, ol'igar'chical** *adj.*

oligo- [Gr. < *oligos*, small] *a combining form meaning* few, small, a deficiency of

Oligocene (o lig'ō sēn') *adj.* [< prec. + Gr. *kainos*, new] designating or of the third epoch of the Tertiary Period in the Cainozoic Era

olio (ō'lē ō') *n.*, *pl.* **o'lios'** [< Sp.] 1. a spicy stew 2. a medley or miscellany

olive (ol'iv) *n.* [< Gr. *elaia*] 1. a) an evergreen tree of S Europe and the Near East b) its small, oval fruit, eaten green or ripe, or pressed to extract its oil 2. the dull, yellowish-green colour of the unripe fruit —*adj.* olive-coloured

olive branch 1. the branch of the olive tree, a symbol of peace 2. any peace offering

olive oil a light-yellow oil pressed from ripe olives

olivine (ol'ə vēn') *n.* [< OLIVE] a green silicate of magnesium and iron

Olympiad (ō lim'pē ad') *n.* [after the plain in Greece where the first Olympic Games were held] 1. a celebration of the modern Olympic games 2. an international contest in chess, etc. 3. in ancient Greece, a four-year period between Olympic games

Olympian (ō lim'pē ən) *n.* Gr. Myth. any of the gods on Mount Olympus —*adj.* 1. of Olympia or Mount Olympus 2. exalted; majestic

Olympic (ō lim'pik) *adj.* same as OLYMPIAN —*n.* [*pl.*] the Olympic games (preceded by *the*)

Olympic games 1. an ancient Greek festival with contests in athletics, poetry, and music, held every four years at Olympia to honour Zeus 2. a modern international athletic competition held every four years

O.M. Order of Merit

-oma (ō'mə) [< Gr.] *a suffix meaning* tumour [*sarcoma*]

ombudsman (om'boodz mən) *n.*, *pl.* -**men** [Sw.] a public official appointed to investigate citizens' complaints against government officials, etc.

omega (ō'mə gə) *n.* 1. the twenty-fourth and final letter of the Greek alphabet (Ω, ω) 2. the last (of any series)

omelette, omelet (om'lit) *n.* [< Fr., ult. < L. *lamella*, small plate] eggs beaten up, cooked as a pancake in a frying pan and served usually folded over and with a filling

omen (ō'men) *n.* [L.] a thing or happening supposed to foretell a future event; augury —*vt.* to augur

omicron, omikron (ō mī'krən) *n.* the fifteenth letter of the Greek alphabet (O, o)

ominous (om'ə nəs) *adj.* [L. *ominosus*] of or serving as an evil omen; threatening —**om'inously** *adv.*

omission (ə mish'ən) *n.* [< LL. *omissio*] 1. an omitting or being omitted 2. anything omitted

omit (ə mit') *vt.* **omit'ted, omit'ting** [< L. *ob*- (see OB-) + *mittere*, send] 1. to fail to include; leave out 2. to fail to do; neglect —**omit'ter** *n.*

omni- [L. < *omnis*, all] *a combining form meaning* all, everywhere [*omniscient*]

omnibus (om'nə bəs) *n.*, *pl.* -**buses** [L., for all] 1. same as BUS 2. a one-volume collection of previously published works —*adj.* providing for many things at once

omnifarious (om'nə fãar'ē əs) *adj.* [< L. *omnis*, all + *fari*, speak] of all kinds, varieties, or forms

omnipotent (om nip'ə tənt) *adj.* [< L. *omnis*, all + *potens*, able] all-powerful —**omnip'otence** *n.*

omnipresent (om'ni prez'ənt) *adj.* [< L. *omnis*, all + *praesens*, present] present in all places at once

omniscient (om nis'ē ənt) *adj.* [< L. *omnis*, all + *scire*, know] knowing all things —**omnis'cience** *n.*

omnivorous (om niv'ər əs) *adj.* [see OMNI- & -VOROUS] 1. eating any sort of food

2. taking in everything indiscriminately [an *omnivorous* reader]

on (on) *prep.* [OE.] **1.** in contact with, supported by, covering, or attached **2.** in the surface of **3.** near to [a cottage *on* the lake] **4.** at the time of [*on* entering] **5.** with (something specified) as the basis [*on* purpose] **6.** connected with, as a part [*on* the committee] **7.** engaged in [*on* a trip] **8.** in a state of [*on* parole] **9.** as a result of [a profit *on* the sale] **10.** in the direction of [a light shone *on* us] **11.** through the use of [to live *on* bread] **12.** concerning [an essay *on* war] **13.** coming after [insult *on* insult] **14.** chargeable to [a drink *on* the house] **15.** [Colloq.] using [*on* drugs] —*adv.* **1.** in a situation of contacting, being supported by, or covering [put your shoes *on*] **2.** towards [looked *on*] **3.** forward [move *on*] **4.** continuously [she sang *on*] **5.** into operation or action [turn the light *on*] **6.** *Theatre* on stage —*adj.* **1.** in action or operation **2.** possible [his getting the post is *on*] **3.** *Cricket* designating the side of the field to the left of a right-handed batsman —*n.* *Cricket* the on side —**and so on** and more like the preceding —**be on at** [Colloq.] to nag —**on and off** intermittently —**on and on** continuously —**on time** punctually

-on (on) [< -*on* in *ion*] *a suffix designating:* **1.** an inert gas [*radon*] **2.** a subatomic particle [*electron*]

onager (on′ə gər) *n.,* *pl.* **-gri**′ (-grī′), **-gers** [< Gr. *onagros,* wild ass] a wild ass of C Asia

onanism (ō′nə niz′m) *n.* [< *Onan* (Gen. 38:9)] **1.** withdrawal in coition before ejaculation **2.** masturbation

O.N.C. Ordinary National Certificate

once (wuns) *adv.* [< ME. *on,* one] **1.** one time only **2.** at any time; ever **3.** formerly **4.** by one degree [a cousin *once* removed] —*conj.* as soon as —*n.* one time [go this *once*] —**all at once 1.** all the same time **2.** suddenly —**at once 1.** immediately **2.** at the same time —**for once** for at least one time —**once and again** repeatedly —**once (and) for all** finally; decisively —**once in a while** occasionally —**once upon a time** long ago

once-over (wuns′ō′vər) *n.* [Colloq.] **1.** a swiftly appraising glance **2.** a quick cleaning or going-over

oncoming (on′kum′iŋ) *adj.* approaching [*oncoming* traffic] —*n.* approach

O.N.D. Ordinary National Diploma

one (wun) *adj.* [OE. *an*] **1.** being a single thing **2.** united **3.** designating a person or thing as contrasted with another [from *one* day to another] **4.** being uniquely such [the *one* solution] **5.** the same [all of *one* mind] **6.** a certain but unspecified [*one* day last week] —*n.* **1.** the first and lowest cardinal number; 1; I **2.** a single person or thing **3.** anything consisting of a single unit or numbered one **4.** [Colloq.] a joke; story [the *one* about the man and the gorilla] —*pron.* **1.** some or a certain person or thing **2.** any person or thing **3.** the person or

thing previously mentioned —**all one** making no difference —**at one** in accord —**one another** each one the other; each other

one-armed bandit [Colloq.] a term for a slot machine used for gambling

one-horse *adj.* [Colloq.] small, unimportant, etc.

oneness *n.* **1.** singleness; unity **2.** unity of mind, feeling, etc. **3.** sameness; identity

one-night stand a performance given only once at any one place

one-off *n.* something that is carried out or made only once —*adj.* of something done only once

onerous (on′ər əs) *adj.* [< L. *onus,* a load] burdensome; oppressive —**on′erously** *adv.*

oneself (wun self′) *pron.* a person's own self: also **one's self** —**by oneself** alone —**come to oneself** to recover one's senses

one-sided (wun′sīd′id) *adj.* **1.** favouring one side; unfair **2.** unequal [a *one-sided* race] **3.** larger, heavier, etc. on one side; lopsided —**one′sid′edness** *n.*

one-time *adj.* at a past time; former

one-to-one *adj.* permitting the pairing of an element of one group uniquely with a corresponding element of another group

one-track *adj.* **1.** [Colloq.] able or willing to deal with only one thing at a time **2.** having a single track

one-up (wun′up′) *adj.* [Colloq.] having an advantage (over another): often in **be one-up** on —**one′-up′manship′** *n.*

one-way *adj.* **1.** moving, or allowing movement, in one direction only **2.** without reciprocal action

ongoing (on′gō′iŋ) *adj.* going on; in process

onion (un′yən) *n.* [< L. *unio,* a kind of single onion] **1.** a plant with an edible bulb of strong, sharp smell and taste **2.** the bulb —**know one's onions** [Colloq.] to be fully acquainted with a subject

onionskin *n.* a tough, thin, translucent paper

on-line (on′līn′) *adj.* of equipment directly controlled by the computer unit that interprets and executes instructions

onlooker *n.* one who watches without taking part; spectator —**on′look′ing** *adj., n.*

only (ōn′lē) *adj.* [< OE.] **1.** alone of its or their kind **2.** alone in superiority; best —*adv.* **1.** and no other; and no (or nothing) more [drink water *only*] **2.** (but) in the end [to meet one crisis, *only* to face another] **3.** as recently as [*only* last autumn] —*conj.* [Colloq.] except that; but [I'd go, *only* it's late] —**if . . . only** I wish that —**only too** very

o.n.o. or nearest offer

onomatopoeia (on′ō mat′ō pē′ə) *n.* [< Gr. *onoma,* a name + *poiein,* make] formation of a word by imitating the sound associated with an object or action (Ex.: *buzz*) —**on′omat′opoe′ic** *adj.*

onrush (on′rush′) *n.* a strong onward rush

onset *n.* **1.** an attack **2.** a beginning

onshore *adj.* **1.** moving towards the shore

2. on land *[an onshore* patrol *] —adv.* landward

onslaught (on′slôt′) *n.* [< Du. *slagen,* to strike] a violent, intense attack

Ont. Ontario

Ontarian (on tär′ē ən) *n.* a native or inhabitant of Ontario *—adj.* of Ontario or Ontarians Also **Ontar′io′an** (-ō′ən)

onto (on′tōō, -tə) *prep.* **1.** to a position on **2.** [Slang] aware of *[he's onto* our schemes] Also **on to**

onto- [< Gr. *einai,* to be] *a combining form meaning:* **1.** being; existence **2.** organism

ontology (on tol′ə jē) *n.* the study of the nature of being **—ontological** (on′-tə loj′i k'l) *adj.*

onus (ō′nəs) *n.* [L.] **1.** a hard or unpleasant task, duty, etc.; burden **2.** responsibility

onward (on′wərd) *adv.* ahead; forward: also **on′wards** *—adj.* advancing

onyx (on′iks) *n.* [< Gr. *onyx,* fingernail] **1.** a variety of chalcedony with alternate coloured layers **2.** a variety of calcite used as an ornamental stone: also **onyx marble**

oodles (ōō′d'lz) *n.pl.* [< ?] [Colloq.] a great amount

Ookpik (ōōk′pik) *Trademark* a model of an "Arctic owl" made by an Inuit artist, now a promotional symbol for Canadian handicrafts

oolite (ō′ə līt′) *n.* [< Gr. *ōion,* egg & -LITE] a limestone made of tiny calcium carbonate particles, formed in the sea **—oolitic** (-lit′ik) *adj.*

oomiak (ōō′mē ak′) *n.* *same as* UMIAK

oompah, oom-pah (ōōm′pä′) *n.* [echoic] the sound of a repeated, rhythmic bass figure played in a brass band

oomph (ōōmf) *n.* [< ?] [Slang] **1.** sex appeal **2.** vigour; energy

oops (ōōps) *interj.* *same as* WHOOPS

ooze[1] (ōōz) *n.* [< OE. *wos,* sap] an oozing *—vi.* **oozed, ooz′ing 1.** to flow or leak out slowly; seep **2.** to give forth moisture, as through pores *—vt.* to exude

ooze[2] *n.* [OE. *wase*] soft mud or slime; esp., the sediment at the bottom of a lake, etc. **—ooz′zy** *adj.*

op. 1. opera **2.** operation **3.** opposite **4.** opus

O.P. Order of Preachers (Dominicans)

O.P., OP, o.p., op 1. out of print **2.** *Philately* over-print

opacity (ō pas′ə tē) *n.* opaque state or quality

opal (ō′p'l) *n.* [< Sans. *upala,* precious stone] various coloured forms of silica, esp. an iridescent semiprecious stone

opalescent (ō′pə les′ənt) *adj.* iridescent like opal **—o′pales′cence** *n.*

opaline (ō′pə līn′) *adj.* of or like opal *—n.* a translucent, milky glass

opaque (ō pāk′) *adj.* [< L. *opacus,* shady] **1.** not letting light through **2.** not reflecting light **3.** obscure

op. cit. [L. *opere citato*] in the work cited

OPEC (ō′pek′) Organization of Petroleum Exporting Countries: also **O.P.E.C.**

open (ō′p'n) *adj.* [OE.] **1.** not closed, covered, or shut **2.** unenclosed or unobstructed **3.** unsealed; unwrapped **4.** unprotected **5.** spread out; unfolded **6.** having spaces, gaps, etc. *[open* texture] **7.** *a)* not excluding anyone *b)* ready to admit customers, etc. **8.** free to be argued *[an open* question] **9.** *a)* not prejudiced or narrow-minded *b)* generous **10.** socially mobile, politically free, etc. *[an open* society] **11.** in operation **12.** not already taken *[the job is open]* **13.** accessible; available **14.** not secret; public **15.** frank; candid *—vt., vi.* **1.** to make or become open **2.** to spread out; expand; unfold **3.** to make or become available without restriction **4.** to begin; start **5.** to start operating, going, etc. **6.** to open ceremonially or formally *—n.* [usually **O-**] any of various golf tournaments for both professionals and amateurs **—be open with** to communicate frankly with **—open onto** (or **on**) to give access (to) or a view of **—open out 1.** to expand **2.** to develop **3.** to reveal **—open to 1.** willing to receive, discuss, etc. **2.** liable to **3.** available or accessible to or for **—open up 1.** to make or become open **2.** to unfold **3.** to start; begin **4.** [Colloq.] to begin firing a gun or guns **5.** [Colloq.] to speak freely **6.** [Colloq.] to go or make go faster **—the open 1.** any open, unobstructed area **2.** the outdoors **3.** public knowledge **—o′pened** *adj.* **—o′pener** *n.* **—o′penly** *adv.* **—o′penness** *n.*

open air the outdoors **—o′pen-air′** *adj.*

open-and-shut *adj.* easily decided; obvious

open-cast mining mining by excavating from the surface

open-ended *adj.* **1.** unrestricted **2.** allowing for a freely formulated answer: said of a question **—o′pen-end′edness** *n.*

open-eyed *adj.* with the eyes wide open, as in amazement

openhanded *adj.* generous **—o′pen-hand′edness** *n.*

openhearted *adj.* **1.** kindly; generous **2.** not reserved; frank **—o′penheart′edness** *n.*

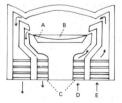

OPEN-HEARTH FURNACE
(A, lining; B, metal; C, heater
ports; D, gas; E, air; fired alternately from either end)

open-hearth (ō′pən härth′) *adj.* designating a furnace with a wide, saucer-shaped hearth for making steel

open-heart surgery heart surgery with

the chest opened and the blood recirculated by mechanical means

opening *n.* **1.** a becoming or making open **2.** a hole; gap **3.** *a)* a beginning *b)* a first performance **4.** an opportunity —*adj.* first

opening time the time at which public houses legally start selling alcoholic drinks

open letter a letter written as to a specific person but published in a newspaper, etc. for all to read

open-minded (ō'pən mīn'did) *adj.* open to new ideas; not biased

open-mouthed (ō'pən mouthd') *adj.* gaping, as in astonishment

open-plan *adj.* designating accommodation in which there are few dividing walls or partitions

open prison a prison allowing prisoners considerable freedom

open sandwich a sandwich made from a slice of bread and meat, fish, etc., but no top slice

open sea **1.** the expanse of sea away from coastlines, bays, inlets, etc. **2.** *same as* HIGH SEAS

open secret something supposed to be secret but known to almost everyone

open sesame **1.** magic words spoken to open the door of the thieves' den in the story of Ali Baba **2.** any sure means of achieving an end

Open University a university teaching by radio, television, correspondence courses, etc.

opera[1] (op'ər ə) *n.* [It. < L., a work] **1.** a play with most or all the text sung to orchestral accompaniment **2.** the art of such plays

opera[2] *n.* *pl. of* OPUS

operable (op'ər ə b'l) *adj.* [see OPERATE] **1.** treatable surgically **2.** practicable —**op'erabil'ity** *n.*

opera glasses a small binocular telescope used at the opera, in theatres, etc.

opera hat a man's tall, collapsible silk hat

operate (op'ə rāt') *vi.* **-at'ed, -at'ing** [< L. *operari,* to work] **1.** to be in action; work **2.** to perform a surgical operation **3.** to produce a certain effect **4.** to carry on military movements —*vt.* **1.** to put or keep in action **2.** to manage

operatic (op'ə rat'ik) *adj.* of or like the opera —**op'erat'ically** *adv.*

operating theatre a room for surgical operations

operation (op'ə rā'shən) *n.* **1.** the act or method of operating **2.** the condition of being in action **3.** a procedure that is part of a series in some work **4.** any strategic military movement **5.** any specific plan, project, etc. *[Operation Overlord]* **6.** any surgical procedure to remedy a physical ailment or defect —**in operation** **1.** in action **2.** in force

operational *adj.* **1.** of the operation of a system, process, etc. **2.** *a)* that can be operated *b)* in use; operating **3.** ready for use in a military operation

operations research systematic

analysis of problems, as in business operations : also **operations analysis**

operative (op'ər ə tiv) *adj.* **1.** capable of or in operation **2.** effective **3.** of or resulting from a surgical operation —*n.* a worker, esp. a skilled industrial worker

operator (op'ə rāt'ər) *n.* **1.** one who operates; specif., *a)* one who connects lines at a telephone exchange *b)* a person who works a machine *c)* a person engaged in commercial or industrial operations or enterprises **2.** [Slang] a clever person who generally manages to achieve his ends

operculum (ō pur'kyoo ləm) *n., pl.* **-la, -lums** [< L. *operire,* to close] any of various covering flaps or lidlike structures in plants and animals, as the bony covering protecting the gills of fishes —**oper'cular** *adj.*

operetta (op'ə ret'ə) *n.* [It. < OPERA[1]] a light, amusing opera with spoken dialogue

ophthalmia (of thal'mē ə) *n.* [< Gr. *ophthalmos,* eye] inflammation of the eyeball or conjunctiva

ophthalmic *adj.* of the eye; ocular

ophthalmic optician an optician who tests eyes, prescribes, and dispenses glasses

ophthalmology (of'thal mol'ə jē) *n.* the branch of medicine dealing with the structure, functions, and diseases of the eye —**oph'thalmol'ogist** *n.*

-opia (ō'pē ə) [< Gr. *ōps,* eye] *a combining form meaning* a (specified kind of) eye defect

opiate (ō'pē ət) *n.* **1.** any medicine containing opium or any of its derivatives, and acting as a sedative and narcotic **2.** anything quieting, soothing, etc.

opine (ō pīn') *vt., vi.* **opined', opin'ing** [< L. *opinari,* think] to hold or express (some opinion)

opinion (ə pin'yən) *n.* [< L. *opinari,* think] **1.** a belief not based on certainty but on what seems true or probable **2.** an evaluation, estimation, etc. **3.** an expert's formal judgment

opinionated *adj.* holding unreasonably or obstinately to one's own opinions —**opin'ionat'edly** *adv.*

opinionative *adj.* **1.** of, or of the nature of, opinion **2.** opinionated

opium (ō'pē əm) *n.* [L. < Gr. *opos,* vegetable juice] a narcotic drug made from the juice of the seed capsules of the **opium poppy,** used to relieve pain and produce sleep

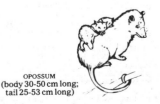

OPOSSUM
(body 30–50 cm long;
tail 25–53 cm long)

opossum (ə pos'əm) *n.* [< Algonquian]

1. a small, tree-dwelling, American mammal: it pretends to be dead when trapped 2. any of various Australian phalangers

opp. 1. opposed 2. opposite

opponent (ə pō′nənt) *n.* [< L. *ob-* (see OB-) + *ponere*, to set] one who opposes, as in a fight, game, etc.; adversary

opportune (op′ər tyōō n′) *adj.* [< L. *ob-* (see OB-) + *portus*, port] 1. right for the purpose: said of time 2. happening or done at the right time; timely —**op′portune′ly** *adv.*

opportunism *n.* the adapting of one's actions, judgments, etc. to circumstances, without regard for principles —**op′portun′ist** *n.*

opportunity (op′ər tyōō′nə tē) *n., pl.* -**ties** 1. a combination of circumstances favourable for the purpose 2. a good chance or occasion

opposable (ə pō′zə b'l) *adj.* 1. that can be resisted 2. that can be placed opposite something else

oppose (ə pōz′) *vt.* -**posed′**, -**pos′ing** [see OB- & POSITION] 1. to contend with in speech or action; resist 2. to place opposite, in balance or contrast —**oppos′er** *n.*

opposite (op′ə zit) *adj.* [see OB- + POSITION] 1. set against, facing, or back to back 2. entirely different; exactly contrary 3. *Bot.* growing in pairs, but separated by a stem —*n.* anything opposed or opposite —*adv.* in an opposite position —*prep.* facing; across from —**op′positely** *adv.*

opposite number a person holding an equivalent position in another organization or group

opposition (op′ə zish′ən) *n.* 1. an opposing 2. resistance, contrast, etc. 3. [O-] a political party opposing the party in power 4. *Astrol., Astron.* the position of two heavenly bodies 180° apart in longitude

oppress (ə pres′) *vt.* [< L. *ob-* (see OB-) + *premere*, PRESS¹] 1. to keep down by the cruel or unjust use of power; tyrannize over 2. to weigh heavily on the mind, spirits, or senses of —**oppres′sion** *n.* —**oppres′sor** *n.*

oppressive *adj.* 1. tyrannical 2. weighing heavily on the mind 3. hard to put up with 4. very hot and close [the day was oppressive] —**oppres′sively** *adv.*

opprobrious (ə prō′brē əs) *adj.* expressing opprobrium; abusive

opprobrium (ə prō′brē əm) *n.* [< L. *opprobrare*, to reproach] 1. the disgrace or infamy attached to conduct viewed as grossly shameful 2. anything bringing shame or disgrace

oppugn (o pyōō n′) *vt.* [< L. *ob-* (see OB-) + *pugnare*, to fight] to oppose with argument; controvert

opsit-bank (op′sit) *n.* [S Afr.] a bench for two people, formerly used for courting couples

opt (opt) *vi.* [< L. *optare*] to make a choice (often with *for*) —**opt out (of)** to choose not to be or continue in

opt. 1. optical 2. optician 3. optional

optative (op′tə tiv) *adj.* [< Fr. < L. *optare*, to desire] expressing wish or desire, as a mood in Greek grammar —*n.* the optative mood, or a verb in this mood

optic (op′tik) *adj.* [< Gr. *optikos*] of the eye or sense of sight

optical *adj.* 1. of the sense of sight; visual 2. of optics 3. for aiding vision —**op′tically** *adv.*

optician (op tish′ən) *n.* a person who makes or deals in optical instruments, esp. one who dispenses spectacles

optics *n.pl.* [*with sing. v.*] [< OPTIC] the branch of physics dealing with the nature and properties of light and vision

optimism (op′tə miz'm) *n.* [< L. *optimus*, best] 1. the tendency to take the most hopeful view of matters 2. *Philos.* a) the doctrine that the existing world is the best possible b) the belief that good ultimately prevails over evil —**op′timist** *n.* —**op′timis′tic** *adj.* —**op′timis′tically** *adv.*

optimum (op′tə məm) *n., pl.* -**mums**, -**ma** [L. *optimus*, best] the best or most favourable degree, condition, etc. —*adj.* most favourable or desirable: also **op′timal**

option (op′shən) *n.* [< L. *optare*, to wish] 1. a choosing; choice 2. the right or liberty of choosing 3. something that is or can be chosen 4. the right to buy, sell, or lease at a fixed price within a specified time —**keep (or leave) one's options open** to be uncommitted

optional *adj.* left to one's option, or choice

opulent (op′yoo lənt) *adj.* [< L. *ops*, wealth] 1. wealthy; rich 2. abundant; profuse —**op′ulence** *n.*

opus (ō′pəs) *n., pl.* **opera** (op′ər ə) [L., a work] a composition; esp., any of the musical works of a composer numbered in order of composition or publication

or¹ (ôr; *unstressed* ər) *conj.* [< OE. *oththe*] a coordinating conjunction introducing: a) an alternative [beer or wine] b) a synonymous term [ill, or sick]

or² (ôr) *n.* [< L. *aurum*, gold] *Heraldry* gold

-or (ər; *occas.* ôr) [< L. *-or*] a suffix meaning: 1. a person or thing that [inventor] 2. quality or condition [error]: see also -OUR

O.R. operations research

Oracle (or′ək'l) *Trademark* the ITV teletext service

oracle (or′ək'l) *n.* [< L. *orare*, pray] 1. in ancient Greece and Rome, a) the place where, or medium by which, deities were consulted b) the revelation of a medium or priest 2. a) any person of great wisdom b) the statements of any such oracle

oracular (o rak′yoo lər) *adj.* of or like an oracle; wise, mysterious, etc. —**orac′ularly** *adv.*

oral (ôr′əl) *adj.* [< L. *os, oris*, mouth] 1. spoken 2. of or using speech 3. of, at, or near the mouth 4. done or taken by the mouth —*n.* a spoken examination —**o′rally** *adv.*

orange (or′inj) *n.* [ult. < Ar. < Per.

< Sans. *naranga*] **1.** a reddish-yellow, round, juicy citrus fruit **2.** the evergreen tree it grows on **3.** reddish yellow —*adj.* reddish-yellow —**or'angy** *adj.*

orangeade *n.* an effervescent orange-flavoured drink

orange blossom the flowers of the orange tree, traditionally worn by brides

Orangeman *n.* [< the Prince of *Orange*] a member of a secret society organized in Ulster in 1795 to support Protestantism

orangery (or'inj ə rē) *n., pl.* **-ries** a hothouse or other sheltered place for growing orange trees in cooler climates

orangewood *n.* the wood of the orange tree

orangutan (ô raŋ' $\overline{oo}$ tan') *n.* [< Malay *oraṅ*, man + *utan*, forest] an ape of Borneo and Sumatra, with shaggy, reddish-brown hair, very long arms, small ears, and a hairless face: also sp. **orang'ou-tang'** (-taŋ')

oration (ô rā'shən) *n.* [< L. *orare*, speak] a formal speech, as at a ceremony

orator (or'ət ər) *n.* **1.** a person who delivers an oration **2.** an eloquent public speaker

oratorical (or'ə tor'i k'l) *adj.* **1.** of orators or oratory **2.** given to oratory —**or'ator'i-cally** *adv.*

oratorio (or'ə tôr'ē ō') *n., pl.* **-os'** [It., small chapel] a long, dramatic musical work, usually on a religious theme, consisting of arias, recitatives, etc. with orchestral accompaniment

oratory (or'ə tə rē) *n., pl.* **-ries** [L. *oratoria*] **1.** skill in public speaking **2.** [< L. *orare*, pray] a small chapel, esp. for private prayer

orb (ôrb) *n.* [< L. *orbis*, a circle] **1.** a small globe with a cross on top, as a royal symbol **2.** a globe; sphere **3.** [Poet.] the eye **4.** any heavenly sphere, as the sun —**orbed** *adj.*

orbicular (ôr bik'yoo lər) *adj.* [< L. *orbis*, a circle] spherical or circular

orbit (ôr'bit) *n.* [< L. *orbis*, a circle] **1.** the path of a heavenly body, artificial satellite, or spacecraft around another body **2.** the range of one's activity **3.** the eye socket —*vi., vt.* to go or put into an orbit in space —**or'bital** *adj.* —**or'biter** *n.*

Orcadian (ôr kā'dē ən) *n.* [< L. *Orcades*, Orkney Islands] a native of the Orkneys —*adj.* of the Orkneys

orchard (ôr'chərd) *n.* [< L. *hortus*, garden + OE. *geard*, enclosure] **1.** an area where fruit trees are grown **2.** such trees

orchestra (ôr'kis trə) *n.* [< Gr. *orchēstra*, space for the chorus] **1.** a large group of musicians playing together **2.** the space in front of and below the stage, where the musicians sit: in full, **orchestra pit** —**orches'tral** (-kes'trəl) *adj.* —**orches'trally** *adv.*

orchestrate (ôr'kis trāt') *vt., vi.* **-trat-ed, -trat'ing 1.** to compose or arrange (music) for an orchestra **2.** to furnish (a ballet, etc.) with an orchestral score **3.** to combine or arrange harmoniously —**or'chestra'tion** *n.*

orchid (ôr'kid) *n.* [< Gr. *orchis*, testicle:

from the shape of its roots] **1.** any of a family of plants having bulbous roots and flowers with three petals, one lip-shaped **2.** the flower

ordain (ôr dān') *vt.* [< L. *ordo*, an order] **1.** to invest with the office of a minister, priest, or rabbi **2.** to decree; order; enact —**ordain'er** *n.* —**ordain'ment** *n.*

ordeal (ôr dēl') *n.* [OE. *ordal*] **1.** a painful or severe experience **2.** an old method of trial exposing the accused to physical dangers from which he was supposedly protected if innocent

order (ôr'dər) *n.* [< L. *ordo*, straight row] **1.** a condition in which everything is in its right place and functioning properly **2.** condition in general [in working *order*] **3.** arrangement of things or events; series **4.** a state of peace; orderly conduct **5.** social position **6.** a definite plan; system **7.** a group of persons organized for military, monastic, or social purposes **8.** *a)* a group of persons distinguished by having received a certain award *b)* the group's insignia **9.** a command, direction, etc. **10.** kind; sort [sentiments of a high *order*] **11.** an established method, as of conduct in meetings **12.** *a)* a request to supply something *b)* the goods supplied **13.** *Archit.* any of several classical styles of structure, determined chiefly by the type of column **14.** *Biol.* a classification ranking above a family and below a class **15.** *Finance* written instructions to pay money or surrender property **16.** *Theol. a)* any rank in the Christian clergy *b)* [pl.] the position of ordained minister —*vt., vi.* **1.** to put or keep (things) in order; arrange **2.** to command **3.** to request (something to be supplied) —**call to order** to request to be quiet —**in** (or **out of**) **order 1.** in (or not in) proper sequence or position **2.** in (or not in) good condition **3.** in (or not in) accordance with the rules **4.** being (or not being) suitable to the occasion —**in order that** so that —**in order to** as a means to —**on order** ordered but not yet supplied —**to order 1.** as specified by the buyer **2.** when called upon —**or'derer** *n.*

order in council an order issued by a British sovereign with the advice of the Privy Council

orderly *adj.* **1.** *a)* neatly arranged *b)* systematic **2.** well-behaved; law-abiding —*n., pl.* **-lies 1.** *Mil.* a soldier assigned as a personal attendant or given a specific task **2.** a male hospital attendant —**or'der-liness** *n.*

Order of Merit a limited order awarded for outstanding achievement in any sphere, civil or military

order paper a list indicating the order of business in Parliament

ordinal (ôr'dən əl) *adj.* [< L. *ordo*, an order] expressing order in a series —*n. same as* ORDINAL NUMBER

ordinal number a number used to indicate order (e.g., ninth, 25th, etc.) in a series

ordinance (ôr'dən əns) *n.* [see ORDAIN]

1. an authoritative command **2.** an established practice, rite, etc.

ordinarily (ôr′d′n rə lē) *adv.* usually; as a rule

ordinary (ôr′d′n rē) *adj.* [< L. *ordo*, an order] **1.** customary; usual **2.** *a)* unexceptional; common *b)* relatively inferior —*n.*, *pl.* **-naries** *Eccles.* [often **O-**] the unvarying part of the Mass —**out of the ordinary** unusual —**or′dinariness** *n.*

Ordinary Level 1. the basic standard of the General Certificate of Education **2.** a pass in a particular subject at this standard

ordinary rating *see* MILITARY RANKS, table

ordinate (ôr′din ət) *n.* [< ORDAIN] *Math.* in a system of coordinates, the distance of a point from the horizontal axis as measured along a line parallel to the vertical axis: cf. ABSCISSA

ordination (ôr′din ā′shən) *n.* an ordaining or being ordained

ordnance (ôrd′nəns) *n.* [contr. < ORDINANCE] **1.** artillery **2.** all military weapons, ammunition, equipment, etc. **3.** a military unit supplying and storing ordnance

ordnance datum mean sea level, as at Newlyn, Cornwall, used as basis for height on Ordnance Survey maps

Ordnance Survey the official map-making body of the British or Irish government

Ordovician (ôr′də vish′ən) *adj.* [< L. *Ordovices*, a tribe in Wales] designating or of the second period of the Palaeozoic Era

ordure (ôr′dyooər) *n.* [< L. *horridus*, horrid] dung; excrement

ore (ôr) *n.* [OE. *ar*, brass, copper] any natural combination of minerals from which a metal or other valuable constituent can be profitably extracted

oregano (o re gä′nō) *n.* [< Gr. *origanon*] a plant with fragrant leaves used for seasoning

organ (ôr′gən) *n.* [< Gr. *organon*, instrument] **1.** a keyboard musical instrument with sets of graduated pipes through which compressed air is passed, causing sound by vibration **2.** in animals and plants, a part adapted to perform a specific function or functions **3.** a means for performing some action **4.** a means of communicating ideas, as a periodical

organdie, organdy (ôr′gən dē) *n.*, *pl.* **-dies** [Fr.] a very sheer, crisp cotton fabric

organic (ôr gan′ik) *adj.* **1.** of, like, or derived from living organisms **2.** of or having to do with an organ **3.** *a)* designating or of any chemical compound containing carbon *b)* designating the branch of chemistry dealing with carbon compounds **4.** inherent; constitutional **5.** systematically arranged; organized **6.** grown with only animal or vegetable fertilizers **7.** *Med.* producing or involving alteration in the structure of an organ —**organ′ically** *adv.*

organism (ôr′gə niz′m) *n.* **1.** any animal

or plant with organs and parts that function together **2.** anything like a living thing in its complexity of structure or functions

organist (ôr′gə nist) *n.* one who plays the organ

organization (ôr′gə nī zā′shən) *n.* **1.** an organizing or being organized **2.** the way in which the parts of a thing are organized **3.** any unified group, as a club, union, etc. **4.** the administrative or executive structure of a business or political party —**or′ganiza′tional** *adj.* —**or′ganiza′tionally** *adv.*

organize (ôr′gə nīz′) *vt.* **-ized′, -iz′ing 1.** to provide with an organic structure; esp., *a)* to arrange in an orderly way *b)* to make plans and arrange for **2.** to establish **3.** to enlist in, or cause to form, a trade union —**or′ganiz′er** *n.*

organ loft the gallery in a church, etc. for an organ

organza (ôr gan′zə) *n.* [< ?] a stiff, sheer fabric of rayon, silk, etc.

orgasm (ôr′gaz′m) *n.* [< Gr. *organ*, to swell] the climax of a sexual act —**orgas′mic, orgas′tic** *adj.*

orgy (ôr′jē) *n.*, *pl.* **-gies** [< Gr. *orgia*, secret rites] **1.** any wild, licentious merrymaking **2.** unrestrained indulgence in any activity **3.** [usually *pl.*] in ancient Greece and Rome, wild celebration in worship of certain gods —**or′gias′tic** *adj.* —**or′gias′tically** *adv.*

ORIEL

oriel (ôr′ē əl) *n.* [< ?] a large window built out from ə wall

orient (ôr′ē ənt, *for v.,* -ent′) *n.* [< L. *oriri*, arise] [**O-**] the East, or Asia; esp., the Far East —*vt.* **1.** to adjust to a particular situation (often used reflexively) **2.** to set (a map or chart) in agreement with the points of the compass **3.** to arrange with reference to the east

oriental (ôr′ē en′t′l) *adj.* **1.** [Poet.] eastern **2.** [**O-**] of the Orient, its people, or their culture —*n.* [usually **O-**] a member of a people native to the Orient

orientate (ôr′ē en tāt′) *vt.* **-tat′ed, -tat′ing** *same as* ORIENT

orientation (ôr′ē en tā′shən) *n.* **1.** an orienting or being oriented **2.** awareness of one′s environment as to time, space, objects, and persons

orienteering (ôr′ē en tēər′iŋ) *n.* [< Sw.] a sport in which competitors race on foot over a course, usually rough country, with the aid of a map and compass

orifice (or′ə fis) *n.* [< L. *os*, mouth +

facere, make] an opening or mouth, as of a cavity

orig. 1. origin 2. original 3. originally

origami (ôr'əgä'mē) *n.* [Jap.] a traditional Japanese art of folding paper to form flowers, animal figures, etc.

origin (ôr'əjin) *n.* [< L. *oriri*, to rise] 1. source; root 2. a coming into existence or use; beginning 3. birth; lineage 4. *Math.* the point at which coordinate axes intersect

original (ərij'ən'l) *adj.* 1. first; earliest 2. never having been before; new 3. thinking or acting in an independent, fresh way; inventive 4. coming from someone as the maker, author, etc. 5. being that from which copies, translations, etc. have been made —*n.* 1. a primary type that has given rise to varieties 2. an original work of art, writing, etc. 3. the person or thing depicted in a painting, etc. —**origi-nal'ity** *n.* —**orig'inally** *adv.*

original sin *Christian Theology* sinfulness regarded as innate in man as a direct result of Adam's sin

originate (ərij'ənāt') *vt.* -nat'ed, -nat'-ing to bring into being; esp., to create; invent —*vi.* to come into being; begin —**orig'ina'tion** *n.* —**orig'ina'tor** *n.*

oriole (ôr'ēōl') *n.* [< L. *aurum*, gold] any of a family of yellow and black birds found from Europe to Australia

Orion (əri'ən) an equatorial constellation near Taurus, containing the bright star Rigel

orison (or'iz'n) *n.* [see ORATION] a prayer

Orlon (ôr'lon) *Trademark* a synthetic acrylic fibre somewhat like nylon, or a fabric made from this fibre

ormolu (ôr'mōlo̅o̅') *n.* [< Fr. *or moulu*, ground gold] an imitation gold consisting of an alloy of copper and tin, used as decoration, etc.

ornament (ôr'nəmənt; *for v.* -ment') *n.* [< L. *ornare*, adorn] 1. anything that adorns; decoration 2. a person whose character or talent adds lustre to society, etc. 3. mere external display —*vt.* to furnish with ornaments or be an ornament to; decorate —**ornamen'tal** *adj.* —**orna-menta'tion** *n.*

ornate (ôr nāt') *adj.* [< L. *ornare*, adorn] 1. heavily ornamented; overadorned 2. showy or flowery, as some literary styles —**ornate'ly** *adv.* —**ornate'ness** *n.*

ornithology (ôr'nəthol'əjē) *n.* [< Gr. *ornis*, bird + -LOGY] the branch of zoology dealing with birds —**ornithological** (ôr'-nithəlog'ik'l) *adj.* —**or'nithol'ogist** *n.*

orotund (ôr'ōtund') *adj.* [< L. *ore rotundo*, lit., with round mouth] 1. clear, strong, and deep: said of the voice 2. bombastic or pompous, as speech

orphan (ôr'fən) *n.* [< Gr. *orphanos*] a child whose parents are dead —*adj.* 1. being an orphan 2. of, or for orphans —*vt.* to cause to become an orphan

orphanage *n.* an institution housing orphans

Orphic (ôr'fik) *adj.* 1. of or characteristic of Orpheus 2. [*also* o-] mystic; occult Also **or'phean** (ôr'fē ən)

orrery (or'ərē) *n.*, *pl.* -reries [< Charles Boyle, Earl of *Orrery*] a mechanical apparatus which illustrates with balls of various sizes the relative motions and positions of the bodies in the solar system

orris (or'is) *n.* [prob. < L. *iris*, iris] an iris whose rootstocks yield orrisroot

orrisroot *n.* the rootstock of the orris, ground and used in perfumery, tooth powders, etc.

ortho- [< Gr. *orthos*, straight] a combining form meaning: 1. straight [*orthodontics*] 2. correct [*orthography*] 3. *Med.* correction of deformities [*ortho-paedics*]

orthodontics (ôr'thōdon'tiks) *n.pl.* [*with sing. v.*] [see ORTHO- & -ODONT] the branch of dentistry concerned with correcting irregularities of the teeth

orthodox (ôr'thədoks') *adj.* [< Gr. *orthos*, correct + *doxa*, opinion] 1. conforming to the usual beliefs or established doctrines, esp. in religion 2. [O-] strictly observing the rites and traditions of Judaism 3. [O-] designating or of any church in the Orthodox Eastern Church —**or'thodox'y** *n.*

Orthodox Eastern Church the Christian church dominant in E Europe, W Asia, and N Africa, including the autonomous churches of the Soviet Union, Greece, Romania, Bulgaria, etc.

orthography (ôr thog'rəfē) *n.*, *pl.* -phies [see ORTHO- & -GRAPHY] 1. spelling in accord with accepted usage 2. spelling as a subject for study —**orthog'rapher** *n.*

orthopaedics (ôr'thō pē'diks) *n.pl.* [*with sing. v.*] [< Gr. *orthos*, straight + *pais*, child] the branch of surgery dealing with the treatment of deformities, diseases, and injuries of the bones, joints, etc.: also U.S. sp. **orthopedics** —**or'thopae'dic** *adj.* —**or'thopae'dist** *n.*

orthopteran (ôr thop'tər ən) *n.* [< ORTHO- + Gr. *pteron*, wing] any of an order of insects, including grasshoppers, having chewing mouthparts and hard forewings covering membranous hind wings —**orthop'terous** *adj.*

ortolan (ôr'tə lən) *n.* [Fr. < L. *hortus*, garden] a European bunting, prized as food

-ory (ərē) [< L.] a suffix meaning: 1. of, having the nature of [*contradictory*] 2. a place or thing for [*laboratory*]

Os *Chem.* osmium

OS, O.S. 1. Old Style 2. outsize

oscillate (os'əlāt') *vi.* -lat'ed, -lat'ing [< L. *oscillare*, to swing] 1. to swing back and forth 2. to vacillate 3. *Physics* to vary between maximum and minimum values, as electric current —*vt.* to cause to oscillate —**oscilla'tion** *n.* —**os'cilla'-tor** *n.*

oscilloscope (o sil'ə skōp') *n.* [< L. *oscillare*, to swing + -SCOPE] an instrument that visually displays an oscillating electrical wave on a fluorescent screen, as of a cathode-ray tube —**oscil'lo-scop'ic** (-skop'ik) *adj.*

oscular (os'kyoo lər) *adj.* [see ff.] of the mouth or kissing

osculate (os'kyŏŏ lāt') *vt., vi.* -**lat'ed,** -**lat'-** **ing** [< L. *osculum*, kiss] to kiss: a jocular usage —**os'cula'tion** *n.*

-**ose¹** (ōs) [Fr. < (*gluc*)*ose*] *a suffix designating:* **1.** a carbohydrate [*sucrose*] **2.** the product of a protein hydrolysis [*proteose*]

-**ose²** [L. -*osus*] *a suffix meaning* full of, having the qualities of, like [*verbose*]

osier (ō'zhər) *n.* [< ML. *ausaria*, bed of willows] **1.** a willow whose stems are used for baskets and furniture **2.** a willow branch used for wickerwork

-**osis** (ō'sis) [< Gr.] *a suffix meaning:* **1.** state, action [*osmosis*] **2.** an abnormal or diseased condition [*neurosis*]

-**osity** (os'ətē) [< L.] *a suffix used to form nouns from adjectives ending in* -OSE² *or* -OUS

Osmanli (oz man'lē) *n., pl.* -**lis** [Turk. < *Osman*, founder of Ottoman Empire] an Ottoman Turk —*adj.* Turkish

osmium (oz'mē əm) *n.* [< Gr. *osmē*, odour] a bluish-white, metallic chemical element that occurs as an alloy with platinum and iridium: symbol, Os

osmosis (oz mō'sis) *n.* [< Gr. *ōsmos*, impulse] the tendency of a solvent to pass through a semipermeable membrane, so as to equalize concentrations on both sides —**osmot'ic** (-mot'ik) *adj.* —**osmot'i- cally** *adv.*

OSPREY
(51-61 cm long)

osprey (os'prē) *n., pl.* -**preys** [< L. *os*, bone + *frangere*, break] a large bird of prey of the hawk family that feeds on fish

osseous (os'ē əs) *adj.* [< L. *os*, bone] of, containing, or like bone

ossify (os'əfī') *vt., vi.* -**fied',** -**fy'ing** [< L. *os*, a bone] **1.** to change into bone **2.** to settle or fix rigidly in a practice, custom, etc. —**os'sifica'tion** (-fi kā'-) *n.*

ostensible (os ten'səb'l) *adj.* [< L. *ostendere*, to show] apparent; seeming —**osten'sibly** *adv.*

ostensive (os ten'siv) *adj.* directly pointing out

ostentation (os'tən tā'shən) *n.* [see OSTENSIBLE] showy display, as of wealth, knowledge, etc.; pretentiousness —**os'ten- ta'tious** *adj.* —**os'tenta'tiousness** *n.*

osteo- (os'tē ō') [< Gr.] *a combining form meaning* a bone or bones [*osteopath*]

osteomyelitis (os'tē ō mī'ə līt'əs) *n.* [see OSTEO- & Gr. *myelos*, marrow] infection of bone marrow or structures

osteopathy (os'tē op'ə thē) *n.* [see OSTEO- & -PATHY] a school of medicine and surgery that seeks to cure ailments by manipulation of joints, esp. the spine —**os'-**

teopath' (os'tē ə path') *n.* —**os'teopath'ic** *adj.*

ostler (os'lər) *n.* [< HOSTEL] one who takes care of horses at an inn, stable, etc.

ostracism (os'trə siz'm) *n.* [see ff.] **1.** an exclusion by general consent, as from society **2.** in ancient Greece, the temporary banishment of a citizen by popular vote

ostracize (os'trə sīz') *vt.* -**cized',** -**ciz'- ing** [< Gr. *ostrakon*, potsherd] to banish, exclude, etc. by ostracism

OSTRICH
(to 2.5 m high)

ostrich (os'trich) [< L. *avis*, bird + *struthio*, ostrich] **1.** a swift-running, nonflying bird of Africa : the largest living bird **2.** a person who refuses to recognize the truth

OT., OT, O.T. Old Testament

O.T.C. Officers' Training Corps

other (*uth*'ər) *adj.* [OE.] **1.** being the remaining one or ones of two or more [Bill and the *other* boy(s)] **2.** different or distinct from that or those. implied [some *other* girl] **3.** additional [no *other* coat] **4.** former [in *other* times] —*pron.* **1.** the other one **2.** some other person or thing [do as others do] —*adv.* otherwise [he can't do *other* than go] —**the other day** (or **night, etc.**) not long ago

otherwise *adv.* **1.** differently [to believe *otherwise*] **2.** in all other respects [an *otherwise* intelligent man] **3.** in other circumstances —*adj.* different [his answer could not be *otherwise*]

otherworldly (*uth*'ər wurld'lē) *adj.* concerned with life in a future world —**oth'- erworld'liness** *n.*

otic (ōt'ik) *adj.* [< Gr. *ous*, EAR¹] of or connected with the ear

otiose (ō'shē ōs') *adj.* [< L. *otium*, leisure] **1.** ineffective **2.** useless **3.** idle —**o'tios'- ity** (-os'ətē) *n.*

otitis (ō tīt'əs) *n.* [< Gr. *ous, ōtos,* ear & -ITIS] inflammation of the ear

otter (ot'ər) *n.* [OE. *otor*] a furry, flesh- eating, aquatic mammal with webbed feet and a long tail

Ottoman (ot'ə mən) *adj.* [see OSMANLI] Turkish —*n., pl.* -**mans** **1.** a Turk **2.** [o-] *a)* a low, cushioned couch without a back or arms *b)* a container for blankets, often with a cushioned seat

ou (ō) *n.* [< Afrik.] [S Afr. Slang] a man

O.U. **1.** Open University **2.** Oxford University

oubaas (ō′bäs′) *n.* [< Afrik.] [S Afr.] a man in authority

oubliette (ōō′blē et′) *n.* [Fr. < *oublier,* forget] a concealed dungeon having a trap door in the ceiling as its only opening

ouch (ouch) *interj.* an exclamation of pain

ought[1] (ôt) *v.aux.* [< OE. *agan,* owe] an auxiliary used with infinitives to express obligation or duty [he *ought* to pay his debts] or desirability [you *ought* to eat more] or probability [it *ought* to be over soon] or advisibility [you *ought* to wear a hat]

ought[2] *n.* [var. of AUGHT] anything whatever; aught

ought[3] *n.* [< a *nought*] a nought; the figure zero (0)

Ouija (wē′jä) [Fr. *oui,* yes + G. *ja,* yes] *Trademark* a device consisting of a planchette and a board bearing the alphabet and other symbols, used in spiritualistic séances, etc.

ouma (ō′mä) *n.* [< Afrik.] in S Africa, 1. grandmother, esp. in titular use with surname 2. [Slang] any elderly woman

ounce (ouns) *n.* [< L. *uncia,* a twelfth] 1. a unit of weight equal to 1/16 pound avoirdupois (28.35gm) 2. any small amount Abbrev. oz.

O.U.P. Oxford University Press

oupa (ō′pä) *n.* [< Afrik.] in S Africa, 1. grandfather, esp. in titular use with surname 2. [Slang] any elderly man

our (ouər) *possessive pronominal adj.* [OE. *ure*] of, belonging to, made, or done by us

-our (ər) [< L.] a suffix meaning state or activity [*behaviour, labour*]: in U.S. usage, often **-or**

ours (ouərz) *pron.* that or those belonging to us: used without a following noun [*ours* are better, a friend of *ours*]

ourself (ouər self′) *pron.* a form corresponding to OURSELVES, used, as in royal proclamations, by one person

ourselves (ouər selvz′) *pron.* a form of the 1st pers. pl. pronoun, used: *a)* as an intensive [we went *ourselves*] *b)* as a reflexive [we hurt *ourselves*] *c)* as a quasi-noun meaning "our true selves" [we are not *ourselves* today]

-ous (əs) [< L.] a suffix meaning: 1. having, characterized by [*dangerous*] 2. *Chem.* having a lower valence than is indicated by the suffix *-ic* [*nitrous*]

ousel (ōō′z′l) *n.* same as OUZEL

oust (oust) *vt.* [< OFr. *ouster*] to force or drive out; expel, dispossess, etc.

out (out) *adv.* [OE. *ut*] 1. *a)* away or forth from a place, position, etc. *b)* away from home *c)* away from shore *d)* on strike 2. into the open air 3. into existence or activity [disease broke *out*] 4. *a)* to a conclusion [fight it *out*] *b)* completely [tired *out*] *c)* in bloom, or in leaf 5. into sight or notice [the moon came *out*] 6. into or in circulation or society 7. from existence or activity [fade *out*] 8. so as to remove from power or office [vote them *out*] 9. aloud [sing *out*] 10. beyond a regular surface, condition, etc. [stand *out*] 11. away from the interior or midst [spread *out*] 12. into disuse [long skirts went *out*] 13. from a number or stock [pick *out*] 14. [Colloq.] into unconsciousness [to pass *out*] —*adj.* 1. not possible 2. [Colloq.] outmoded 3. *a)* not in operation, use, etc. *b)* turned off; extinguished 4. away from home, etc. 5. deviating from what is accurate 6. not in power 7. external: usually in combination [*outpost*] 8. outlying 9. beyond regular limits —*prep.* out of; through to the outside —*n.* [Slang] a way out; means of avoiding —*vi.* to come out; esp., to become known —*vt.* to put out —*interj.* get out! —**out and away** by far —**out and out** completely —**out for** making a determined effort to get or do —**out of** 1. from inside 2. from the number of 3. beyond 4. from (material, etc.) [made *out of* stone] 5. because of [*out of* spite] 6. having no [*out of* breath] 7. not in a condition of [*out of* order] 8. so as to deprive [cheat *out of* money] —**out to** making a determined effort to

out- [< OUT] a combining form meaning: 1. at or from a point away, outside [*outbuilding*] 2. going away or forth, outward [*outbound*] 3. better, greater, or more than [*outact, outdo, outfight, outscore*]

outage *n.* an accidental suspension of operation, as of electric power

out-and-out (out′′n out′) *adj.* complete; thorough

outback *n.* [also O-] the sparsely settled, flat, arid inland region of Australia

outbid (out′bid′) *vt.* -bid′, -bid′ding to bid or offer more than

outboard *adj., adv.* 1. outside the hull of a ship 2. away from the fuselage of an aircraft

outboard motor a portable petrol engine mounted outboard on a boat to propel it

outbreak *n.* a breaking out; sudden occurrence

outbuilding *n.* a structure, as a garage, separate from the main building

outburst *n.* a sudden release, as of feeling, etc.

outcast *adj.* driven out; rejected —*n.* a person or thing cast out or rejected

outcaste *n.* in India, a person expelled from his caste, or one who belongs to no caste

outclass (out′kläs′) *vt.* to surpass; excel

outcome *n.* result; consequence

outcrop *n.* 1. the emergence of a mineral or a rock formation from the earth so as to be exposed on the surface 2. the mineral

outcry *n.,* pl. -cries 1. a crying out 2. a strong protest

outdated (out′dāt′id) *adj.* no longer popular

outdistance (out′dis′təns) *vt.* -tanced, -tancing to leave behind, as in a race

outdo (out′dōō′) *vt.* -did′, -done′, -do′ing to surpass

outdoor *adj.* 1. being, taking place, or used outdoors 2. fond of the outdoors

outdoors (out'dôrz') *adv.* in or into the open; outside —*n.* 1. any area outside a building 2. the countryside

outer *adj.* farther out; exterior

outermost *adj.* located furthest without

outer space 1. space beyond the atmosphere of the earth 2. space outside the solar system

outface (out'fās') *vt.* -faced', -fac'ing to subdue with a look or stare

outfall *n.* the outlet of a river, sewer, etc.

outfield *n.* the playing area beyond the infield in cricket

outfit *n.* 1. the equipment used in any craft or activity 2. articles of clothing worn together 3. a group of people associated in some activity —**out'fit'ter** *n.*

outflank (out'flaŋk') *vt.* 1. to go around and beyond the flank of (enemy troops) 2. to thwart; outwit

outflow *n.* 1. that which flows out 2. amount flowing out

outfox (out'foks') *vt.* to outwit; outsmart

outgoing *adj.* 1. leaving 2. sociable, friendly, etc. —*n.* [*pl.*] expenses

outgrow (out'grō') *vt.* -grew', -grown', -grow'ing 1. to grow faster or larger than 2. to lose or get rid of by becoming mature 3. to grow too large for

outgrowth *n.* 1. an offshoot 2. a result; development

outguess (out'ges') *vt.* to outwit; anticipate

outhouse *n.* an outbuilding

outing *n.* a pleasure trip or excursion

outlandish (out lan'dish) *adj.* 1. very odd; fantastic 2. remote; out-of-the-way —**out-land'ishly** *adv.*

outlast (out'läst') *vt.* to endure longer than; outlive

outlaw *n.* 1. orig., a person deprived of legal rights and protection 2. a notorious criminal who is a fugitive from the law —*vt.* 1. orig., to declare to be an outlaw 2. to declare illegal 3. to bar

outlay *n.* 1. a spending (of money, energy, etc.) 2. money, etc. spent

outlet *n.* 1. a passage for letting something out 2. a means of expression [an *outlet* for rage] 3. a market for goods

outline *n.* 1. [*also pl.*] an undetailed general plan 2. a systematic listing of the important points of a subject 3. a line bounding the limits of an object 4. a sketch showing the contours of an object —*adj.* not detailed [an *outline* proposal] —*vt.* -lined', -lin'ing 1. to draw in outline 2. to list the main points of

outlive (out'liv') *vt.* -lived', -liv'ing 1. to live or endure longer than 2. to live through; outlast

outlook *n.* 1. viewpoint 2. prospect; probable result 3. the view from a place

outlying *adj.* far out from a centre; remote

outmanoeuvre (out'mə nōō'vər) *vt.* -vred, -vring to manoeuvre with better effect than; outwit

outmatch (out'mach') *vt.* to surpass; outdo

outmoded (out'mōd'id) *adj.* no longer in fashion or accepted; obsolete

outnumber (out'num'bər) *vt.* to exceed in number

out-of-date *adj.* outmoded; old-fashioned

out-of-doors *adv., n.* same as OUTDOORS

out-of-pocket *adj.* 1. having lost money 2. unbudgeted [out-of-pocket expenses]

out-of-the-way *adj.* 1. secluded 2. unusual

outpace (out'pās') *vt.* -paced', -pac'ing to exceed

outpatient *n.* a patient, not an inmate, receiving treatment at a hospital

outport *n.* [Canad.] a small fishing village of Newfoundland —**out'porter** *n.*

outpost *n.* 1. *Mil.* a) a small group stationed at a distance from the main force b) the station so occupied 2. a) a settlement on a frontier b) a place considered remote from the centre of an activity [outpost of learning]

output *n.* 1. the work done or amount produced 2. in computers, a) information transferred or delivered b) the act or process of transferring or delivering this information 3. *Elec.* the useful current delivered by amplifiers, generators, etc.

outrage (out'rāj') *n.* [ult. < L. *ultra*, beyond] 1. an extremely vicious or violent act 2. a deep insult or offence 3. great anger, indignation, etc. aroused by such an act —*vt.* -raged', -rag'ing 1. to cause great anger, etc. in 2. to commit an outrage upon

outrageous (out rā'jəs) *adj.* 1. involving or doing great injury or wrong 2. very offensive or shocking

outrank (out'raŋk') *vt.* to exceed in rank

outré (ōō'trā) *adj.* [Fr.] eccentric; bizarre

outreach (out'rēch') *vt., vi* 1. to surpass 2. to extend

outrider (out'rīd'ər) *n.* 1. a motorcyclist, who rides ahead of or beside a car 2. an attendant on horseback who rides ahead of or beside a carriage

OUTRIGGER

outrigger *n.* 1. any framework extended beyond the rail of a ship 2. a timber rigged out from the side of a canoe to prevent tipping; also, a canoe of this type

outright (out'rīt'; *for adv.* out'rīt') *adj.* 1. downright 2. straightforward 3. complete —*adv.* 1. entirely 2. openly 3. at once

outrun (out'run') *vt.* -ran', -run', -run'-ning 1. to run faster or further than 2. to exceed

outsell (out'sel') *vt.* -sold', -sell'ing 1. to sell in greater amounts than 2. to excel in salesmanship

outset *n.* a setting out; beginning

outshine (out'shīn') *vt.* **-shone', -shin'-ing** 1. to shine brighter or longer than (another) 2. to surpass; excel

outside *n.* 1. the outer side; exterior 2. *a)* outward aspect *b)* that which is obvious or superficial 3. any place or area not inside 4. [Canad.] the settled parts of Canada —*adj.* 1. outer 2. coming from or situated beyond given limits [*outside* help] 3. extreme [an *outside* estimate] 4. slight [an *outside* chance] —*adv.* 1. on or to the outside 2. beyond certain limits 3. outdoors —*prep.* 1. on or to the outer side of 2. beyond the limits of —**at the outside** at the very most

outside broadcast *Radio & T.V.* a broadcast taking place away from the studio

outsider (out'sīd'ər) *n.* 1. one who is not included; esp., one not a member of or in sympathy with a given group 2. [Canad.] one who does not live in the arctic regions

outsize *n.* 1. an unusually large size 2. a garment, etc. of such a size —*adj.* unusually large: also **out'sized'**

outskirts *n.pl.* the outer areas, as of a city

outsmart (out'smärt') *vt.* [Colloq.] to outwit

outspan (out'span') *n.* [< Afrik. *uit*, out + *spannen*, to stretch] in South Africa, 1. the act of unyoking oxen, etc. 2. an area set aside for rest

outspoken (out'spō'kən) *adj.* 1. unrestrained in speech; frank 2. spoken candidly —**out'spo'kenness** *n.*

outspread (out'spred'; *for adj.* out'-spred') *vt., vi.* **-spread', -spread'ing** to spread out; extend —*adj.* spread out; extended; expanded

outstanding (out'stand'iŋ) *adj.* 1. prominent; distinguished 2. unsettled 3. unpaid 4. projecting

outstretch (out'strech') *vt.* 1. to extend 2. to stretch beyond —**out'stretched'** *adj.*

outstrip (out'strip') *vt.* **-stripped', -strip'-ping** 1. to go at a faster pace than 2. to surpass; excel

outtalk (out'tôk') *vt.* to talk more skilfully, loudly, or forcibly than

outthink (out'think') *vt.* **-thought', -think'ing** 1. to think faster or more cunningly than 2. to outwit thus

outvote (out'vōt') *vt.* **-vot'ed, -vot'ing** to defeat or surpass in voting

outward *adj.* 1. having to do with the outside; outer 2. visible 3. to or towards the outside 4. superficial or external —*adv.* towards the outside; away: also **out'wards** —**out'wardly** *adv.* —**out'wardness** *n.*

outward bound 1. travelling away from home, as a ship 2. [O- B-] a scheme to provide adventure training, such as mountaineering, for young people

outweigh (out'wā') *vt.* 1. to be more important than 2. to weigh more than

outwit (out'wit') *vt.* **-wit'ted, -wit'ting** to get the better of by cunning or cleverness

outwork *n.* a lesser fortification built out beyond the main defences

ouzel (oo'z'l) *n.* [OE. *osle*] any of several perching birds including the dippers

ouzo (oo'zō) *n.* [< Mod Gr. *ouzon*] a colourless Greek spirit flavoured with aniseed

ova (ō'və) *n.* *pl. of* OVUM

oval (ō'v'l) *adj.* [< L. *ovum*, egg] 1. shaped like the cross section of an egg lengthways; elliptical 2. having the form of an egg —*n.* anything oval —**o'vally** *adv.*

ovary (ō'vər ē) *n.,* *pl.* **-ries** [< L. *ovum*, egg] 1. *Anat., Zool.* either of the female reproductive glands producing eggs 2. *Bot.* the enlarged hollow part of the pistil, containing ovules —**ovarian** (ō vāar'ē ən) *adj.*

ovate (ō'vāt) *adj.* [< L. *ovum*, egg] egg-shaped, esp. with the broader end at the base, as some leaves

ovation (ō vā'shən) *n.* [< L. *ovare*, celebrate a triumph] an enthusiastic outburst of applause

oven (uv'ən) *n.* [OE. *ofen*] a compartment or receptacle for baking or roasting food or for heating or drying things

over (ō'vər) *prep.* [OE. *ofer*] 1. *a)* in, at, or to a position above *b)* across and down from [*over* a cliff] 2. while engaged in [discuss it *over* dinner] 3. upon the surface of 4. so as to cover 5. upon, as an effect or influence 6. with care for [watch *over* the flock] 7. above in authority, power, etc. 8. along or across, or above and to the other side of [fly *over* the lake] 9. through all or many parts of 10. during [*over* a decade] 11. more than 12. up to and including [stay *over* Easter] 13. concerning; about 14. through the medium of [*over* the radio] —*adv.* 1. *a)* above, across, or to the other side *b)* across the edge 2. more; beyond 3. covering the entire area [the wound healed *over*] 4. from start to finish [count the money *over*] 5. *a)* from an upright position *b)* upside down [turn the cup *over*] 6. from one side, person, etc. to another —*adj.* 1. upper, outer, superior, excessive, or extra 2. finished; past 3. having reached the other side 4. [Colloq.] surplus; extra —*n. Cricket* 1. a set of six (or eight) balls bowled by one bowler from one end of the wicket 2. the time during which this takes place —**all over** 1. finished 2. over one's entire body 3. typical [that's men *all over*] 4. [Colloq.] extremely attentive or affectionate towards —**over again** once more —**over against** opposite; in front of; in contrast to —**over all** from end to end —**over and above** in addition —**over and over (again)** repeatedly

over- *a combining form meaning:* 1. above in position, outer, upper, superior [*overhead, overlord*] 2. passing across or beyond [*overrun*] 3. downward from above [*overflow*] 4. excessive(ly) [*overload, oversell*]: the list below includes some common compounds formed with *over-* that can be understood if *too* or *too much* is added to the meaning of the base word

overabundance
overabundant
overactive
overambitious
overanxious
overattentive
overbid
overbook
overburden
overcareful
overcautious
overcompensate
overconfident
overcook
overcrowd
overeager
overeat
overemotional
overemphasize
overenthusiastic
overexert
overexpose

overfed
overfond
overheat
overindulge
overindulgence
overinflate
overladen
overman
overpay
overpopulate
overpraise
overprotect
overripe
oversell
oversew
oversexed
overstock
overstretch
overstuff
oversupply
overtire
overuse

long —**overdo** it (or **things**) to overtax one's strength, etc.

overdose *n.* too large a dose, esp. one causing death

overdraft *n.* 1. an overdrawing of money from a bank 2. the amount overdrawn

overdraw (ō′vər drô′) *vt.* **-drew′**, **-drawn′**, **-draw′ing** 1. to draw on in excess of the amount credited to the drawer 2. to spoil the effect of by exaggeration

overdress (ō′vər dres′) *vt., vi.* to dress too warmly, too showily, or too formally for the occasion

overdrive *n.* a gear that automatically reduces an engine's power output without reducing its driving speed

overdue *adj.* past or delayed beyond the time set for payment, arrival, etc.

overestimate (ō′vər es′tə māt′; *for n.* -mit) *vt.* **-mat′ed, -mat′ing** to set too high an estimate on or for —*n.* an estimate that is too high

overflow (ō′vər flō′; *for n.* ō′vər flō′) *vt.* 1. to flow across; flood 2. to flow over the brim of 3. to fill beyond capacity —*vi.* 1. to run over 2. to be superabundant —*n.* 1. an overflowing 2. the amount that overflows 3. an outlet for overflowing liquids

overgrow (ō′vər grō′) *vt.* **-grew′**, **-grown′**, **-grow′ing** to overspread with growth or foliage —*vi.* to grow too large or too fast —o′ver**grown′** *adj.*

overhang (ō′vər haŋ′; *for n.* ō′vər haŋ′) *vt.* **-hung′, -hang′ing** 1. to hang or project over or beyond 2. to impend; threaten —*vi.* to project out over something —*n.* an overhanging part

overhaul (ō′vər hôl′; *for n.* ō′vər hôl′) *vt.* 1. a) to check thoroughly for needed repairs, adjustments, etc. b) to make such repairs 2. to overtake —*n.* an overhauling

overhead (ō′vər hed′; *for adv.* ō′vər hed′) *adj.* 1. above the level of the head 2. in the sky 3. on a higher level —*n.* [*pl.*] the general, continuing costs of running a business, as rent, taxes, etc. —*adv.* above the head; aloft

overhear (ō′vər hēr′) *vt.* **-heard′, -hear′-ing** to hear without the speaker's knowledge or intention

overjoy (ō′vər joi′) *vt.* to give great joy to; delight

overland *adv., adj.* by, on, or across land

overlap (ō′vər lap′; *for n.* ō′vər lap′) *vt., vi.* **-lapped′, -lap′ping** to extend over (something or each other) so as to coincide in part —*n.* 1. an overlapping 2. a part that overlaps

overlay (ō′vər lā′; *for n.* ō′vər lā′) *vt.* **-laid′, -lay′ing** 1. to lay or spread over 2. to cover, as with a decorative layer —*n.* 1. a covering 2. a decorative layer

overleaf (ō′vər lēf′) *adj., adv.* on the other side of the page or sheet

overleap (ō′vər lēp′) *vt.* 1. to leap over or across 2. to leap too far

overlie (ō′vər lī′) *vt.* **-lay′, -lain′, -ly′-ing** 1. to lie on or over 2. to smother by lying on, esp. a newborn baby or animal

overload (ō′vər lōd′; *for n.* ō′vər lōd′) *vt.*

overact (ō′vər akt′) *vt., vi.* to act with exaggeration

overage (ō′vər āj′) *adj.* over the age fixed as a standard

overall (ō′vər ôl′; *for adv.* -ôl′) *adj.* 1. from end to end 2. including everything; total —*adv.* in general —*n.* a garment worn over the ordinary clothing as a protection against dirt

overalls *n.pl.* loose-fitting trousers with an attached upper part, worn to protect against dirt and wear

overarm *adj.* performed by raising the arm above the shoulder, as in swimming or cricket

overawe (ō′vər ô′) *vt.* **-awed′, -aw′ing** to overcome or subdue by inspiring awe

overbalance (ō′vər bal′əns) *vi., vt.* **-anced, -ancing** to lose, or cause to lose, balance and fall over

overbear (ō′vər bãar′) *vt.* **-bore′, -borne′, -bear′ing** 1. to dominate 2. to press down by weight or physical power

overbearing *adj.* arrogant or domineering

overblown (ō′vər blōn′) *adj.* 1. pompous; bombastic 2. past the stage of full bloom

overboard *adv.* 1. over a ship's side 2. from a ship into the water —**go overboard** [Colloq.] to go to extremes

overcast *adj.* 1. cloudy 2. *Sewing* made with long, loose stitches to prevent unravelling: said of edges

overcharge (ō′vər chärj′) *vt., vi.* **-charged′, -charg′ing** 1. to charge too high a price 2. to overload —*n.* an excessive charge

overcloud (ō′vər kloud′) *vt., vi.* to make or become cloudy, gloomy, etc.

overcoat *n.* a coat, esp. a heavy coat, worn over the usual clothing for warmth

overcome (ō′vər kum′) *vt.* **-came′, -come′, -com′ing** 1. to get the better of in competition, etc. 2. to prevail over, overwhelm, etc.

overdo (ō′vər doo′) *vt.* **-did′, -done′, -do′-ing** 1. to do too much 2. to spoil the effect of by exaggeration 3. to cook too to put too great a load in or on —*n.* too great a load

overlook (ō′vər look′) *vt.* 1. *a)* to look beyond and not see *b)* to ignore; neglect 2. to excuse 3. to rise above 4. to give a view of from above 5. to supervise

overmuch *adj., adv., n.* too much

overnight (ō′vər nīt′; *for adj.* ō′vər nīt′) *adv.* 1. during the night 2. on the previous evening 3. suddenly —*adj.* 1. during the night 2. for one night [*an overnight* guest *]* 3. for a brief trip [*an overnight* bag *]*

overpass *n.* a bridge or other passageway over a road, railway, etc.

overplay (ō′vər plā′) *vt.* 1. to overdo or overemphasize 2. *Card Games* to overestimate the strength of (one's hand)

overpower (ō′vər pou′ər) *vt.* to subdue; overwhelm —**o′verpow′ering** *adj.*

overprint (ō′vər print′; *for n.* ō′vər print′) *vt.* to print over —*n.* anything overprinted, as (on) a stamp

overproduce (ō′vər prə dyōōs′) *vt., vi.* -**duced′,** -**duc′ing** to produce in a quantity that exceeds the need or demand —**o′ver produc′tion** *n.*

overrate (ō′vər rāt′) *vt.* -**rat′ed,** -**rat′ing** to estimate too highly

overreach (ō′vər rēch′) *vt.* 1. to outwit 2. to reach beyond —**overreach oneself** to fail because of trying more than one can do or because of being too crafty

overreact (ō′vər rē akt′) *vi.* to react in an extreme, highly emotional way

override (ō′vər rīd′) *vt.* -**rode′,** -**rid′den,** -**rid′ing** 1. to disregard, overrule, or nullify 2. to prevail over

overrule (ō′vər rōōl′) *vt.* -**ruled′,** -**rul′ing** 1. to set aside or decide against, as by higher authority 2. to prevail over

overrun (ō′vər run′) *vt.* -**ran′,** -**run′,** -**run′ning** 1. to swarm over, as vermin, or ravage, as an army 2. to conquer by a rapid advance 3. to spread swiftly throughout, as ideas 4. to run beyond (certain limits)

overseas *adv.* over or beyond the sea —*adj.* 1. foreign 2. over or across the sea

oversee (ō′vər sē′) *vt.* -**saw′,** -**seen′,** -**see′ing** to supervise; superintend —**o′ver see′er** (-sē′ər) *n.*

overset (ō′vər set′) *vt.* -**set′,** -**set′ting** 1. to upset 2. to overturn

overshadow (ō′vər shad′ō) *vt.* 1. to be, or appear to be, more important than by comparison 2. *a)* to cast a shadow over *b)* to darken

overshoe *n.* a kind of boot of rubber, etc. worn over the regular shoe to protect against cold or dampness

overshoot (ō′vər shōōt′) *vt.* -**shot′,** -**shoot′ing** 1. to shoot or pass over or beyond (a target, mark, etc.) 2. to go farther than (an intended or normal limit)

overshot *adj.* 1. with the upper part extending past the lower [*an overshot* jaw *]* 2. driven by water flowing onto the upper part [*an overshot* water wheel *]*

oversight *n.* a careless mistake or omission

oversimplify (ō′vər sim′plə fī′) *vt., vi.*

-**fied′,** -**fy′ing** to simplify to an extent that distorts, as by ignoring essential details —**o′versim′plifica′tion** *n.*

oversleep (ō′vər slēp′) *vi.* -**slept′,** -**sleep′ ing** to sleep past the intended time for getting up

overspend (ō′vər spend′) *vi.* -**spent′,** **spend′ing** to spend more than one can afford

overspill *n.* something that spills over or is in excess, esp. a surplus population

overstate (ō′vər stāt′) *vt.* -**stat′ed,** -**stat′ ing** to exaggerate (facts, truth, etc.) —**over state′ment** *n.*

overstay (ō′vər stā′) *vt.* to stay beyond the limits of

overstep (ō′vər step′) *vt.* -**stepped′,** -**step′ping** to go beyond the limits of; exceed

overstrung (ō′vər struŋ′) *adj.* too highly strung; tense

oversubscribe (ō′vər səb skrīb′) *vt., vi.* -**scribed′,** -**scrib′ing** to subscribe for more (of) than is available or asked

overt (ō′vurt) *adj.* [< L. *aperire*, to open] not hidden; open —**overt′ly** *adv.* —**overt′ ness** *n.*

overtake (ō′vər tāk′) *vt.* -**took′,** -**tak′en,** -**tak′ing** 1. to catch up with and go beyond 2. to come upon suddenly

overtax (ō′vər taks′) *vt.* 1. to tax too heavily 2. to make excessive demands on

overthrow (ō′vər thrō′; *for n.* ō′vər thrō′) *vt.* -**threw′,** -**thrown′,** -**throw′ing** 1. to conquer; end 2. to upset 3. to throw a ball, etc. beyond (the intended receiver) —*n.* 1. an overthrowing 2. destruction; end

overtime *n.* 1. time beyond the established limit, as of working hours 2. pay for work done in such time —*adj., adv.* of, for, or during overtime

overtone *n.* 1. an implication; nuance : *usually used in pl.* 2. any of the attendant higher tones heard with a fundamental musical tone

overture (ō′vər tyōōər) *n.* [< L. *apertura*, APERTURE] 1. a musical introduction to an opera, oratorio, etc. 2. an introductory proposal or offer

overturn (ō′vər turn′) *vt.* 1. to turn over; upset 2. to conquer —*vi.* to tip over; capsize

overweening (ō′vər wē′niŋ) *adj.* [< OE. *oferwenan*] arrogant; presumptious; exaggerated

overweight (ō′vər wāt′; *for n.* ō′vər wāt′) *adj.* above the normal, desirable, or allowed weight —*n.* extra or surplus weight

overwhelm (ō′vər welm′) *vt.* [see OVER- & WHELM] 1. to crush; overpower 2. to pour down on and bury beneath —**o′ver whelm′ing** *adj.*

overwork (ō′vər wurk′) *vt.* to work or use to excess —*vi.* to work too hard or too long

overwrought (ō′vər rôt′) *adj.* very nervous or excited

ovi- [< L. *ovum*, an egg] *a combining*

form meaning egg *or* ovum [*oviduct, oviform*]

oviduct (ō′vi dukt′) *n.* [see OVI- & DUCT] a tube through which the ovum passes from an ovary

oviform (ō′vi fôrm′) *adj.* [OVI- & -FORM] egg-shaped

ovine (ō′vīn) *adj.* [< L. *ovis*, sheep] of sheep

oviparous (ō vip′ər əs) *adj.* [< L.: see OVI- & -PAROUS] producing eggs which hatch after leaving the body —**ovip′arously** *adv.*

ovoid (ō′void) *adj.* [see OVI-] egg-shaped

ovulate (ov′yoo lāt′) *vi.* -**lat′ed**, -**lat′ing** to produce and discharge ova from the ovary —**o′vula′tion** *n.*

ovule (ō′vyōōl) *n.* [< L. *ovum*, egg] 1. *Bot.* the part of a plant which develops into a seed 2. *Zool.* the immature ovum —**o′vular** *adj.*

ovum (ō′vəm) *n., pl.* **ova** [L., egg] *Biol.* a mature female germ cell

owe (ō) *vt.* **owed**, **ow′ing** [< OE. *agan*, to own] 1. to be indebted to (someone) for (a specified amount or thing) 2. to feel the need to do, give, etc. 3. to cherish (a feeling) towards another : only in **owe a grudge**

owing *adj.* 1. that owes 2. due; unpaid —**owing to** because of

owl (oul) *n.* [OE. *ule*] a nocturnal bird of prey having large eyes, a short, hooked beak, and feathered legs: applied figuratively to a person who looks solemn, dull, etc. —**owl′ish** *adj.* —**owl′ishly** *adv.* —**owl′like′** *adj.*

own (ōn) *adj.* [< OE. *agan*, possess] belonging or relating to oneself or itself [*his own book*] —*n.* that which belongs to oneself [*the car is his own*] —*vt.* 1. to possess; have 2. to admit —*vi.* to confess (*to*) —**come into one's own** to receive what properly belongs to one, esp. recognition —**on one's own** [Colloq.] by one's own efforts; independent(ly) —**own up (to)** to confess (to) —**own′er** *n.* —**own′ership** *n.*

owner occupier someone who both occupies and owns a house

ox (oks) *n., pl.* **ox′en** [OE. *oxa*] 1. any of several bovine mammals, as the buffalo, bison, yak, etc. 2. a castrated bull, used as a draught animal

oxalic acid (ok sal′ik) [< Gr. *oxys*, acid] a colourless, poisonous, crystalline acid, found in many plants and used in dyeing, bleaching, etc.

oxblood (oks′blud′) *n.* a deep red colour

oxbow *n.* 1. the U-shaped part of an ox yoke which passes under and around the animal's neck 2. something shaped like this, as a bend in a river

Oxbridge (oks′brij) *n.* [*Ox(ford)* + *(Cam)bridge*] the universities of Oxford and Cambridge, esp. considered as influencing political, intellectual, and social life —*adj.* of Oxbridge [an *Oxbridge* accent]

oxen (ok′s'n) *n. pl. of* OX

oxeye *n.* any of several composite plants

Oxfam (oks′fam′) *n.* Oxford Famine Relief Fund

Oxford movement (oks′fərd) a High-Church movement within the Anglican Church, begun at Oxford University in 1833

oxidation (ok′sə dā′shən) *n.* an oxidizing or being oxidized —**oxidant** (ok′sə dənt) *n.* —**ox′idative** *adj.*

oxide (ok′sīd) *n.* [< Gr. *oxys*, sour + Fr. (ac)*ide*, acid] a binary compound of oxygen with another element or a radical

oxidize (ok′sə dīz′) *vt.* -**dized′**, -**diz′ing** [< prec.] 1. to unite with oxygen, as in burning or rusting 2. to increase the positive valence or decrease the negative valence of (an element or ion) —*vi.* to become oxidized

Oxon. 1. Oxfordshire 2. of Oxford (University)

Oxonian (ok sō′nē ən) *adj.* of Oxford or Oxford University —*n.* 1. a student of Oxford University 2. a native of Oxford

oxtail (oks′tāl′) *n.* the tail of an ox, esp. when skinned and used in soup or stew

oxtongue *n.* 1. any of a number of plants with rough, tongue-shaped leaves 2. the tongue of an ox, braised or boiled as food: also **tongue**

oxy- [< Gr. *oxys*, sharp] *a combining form meaning*: 1. sharp, acid 2. oxygen

oxyacetylene (ok′sē ə set′əl ēn′) *adj.* of or using a mixture of oxygen and acetylene, as for producing an extremely hot flame used in welding

oxygen (ok′si jən) *n.* [see OXY- & -GEN] a colourless, odourless, tasteless, gaseous chemical element, the most abundant of all elements: it is essential to life processes and to combustion: symbol, O

oxygenate (ok′si jə nāt′) *vt.* -**at′ed**, -**at′ing** to mix, treat, or combine with oxygen: also **ox′ygenize′**

oxygen tent a transparent enclosure into which oxygen is released, fitted around a bed-ridden patient to help him breathe

oxyhaemoglobin (ok′si hē′mə glō′bin) *n.* [OXY- + HAEMOGLOBIN] the bright-red substance found in the arterial blood, formed in the lungs by the union of oxygen with haemoglobin

oxymoron (ok′si môr′on) *n., pl.* -**mo′ra** [< Gr. *oxys*, sharp + *moros*, dull] a figure of speech in which contradictory ideas are combined (Ex.: sweet sorrow)

oyez, oyes (ō yes′) *interj.* [ult. < L. *audire*, hear] hear ye! attention!: cried out by an official to command silence before a proclamation is made

oyster (oi′stər) *n.* [< Gr. *ostreon*] a marine mollusc with an irregular, bivalve shell, found esp. on the sea floor and widely used as food

oyster catcher a wading bird with stout legs

oz. *pl.* **oz., ozs.** ounce

ozone (ō′zōn) *n.* [< Gr. *ozein*, to smell] 1. a pale-blue gas with a strong odour: it is an allotropic form of oxygen 2. [Colloq.] pure, fresh air

P

P, p (pē) *n., pl.* **P's, p's** the sixteenth letter of the English alphabet —**mind one's p's and q's** to be careful what one says or does

P 1. *Chess* pawn 2. *Chem.* phosphorus 3. *Physics* pressure

p penny; pence

p. 1. *pl.* **pp.** page 2. penny 3. per 4. piano

pa (pä) *n.* [Colloq.] father; papa

Pa *Chem.* protactinium

PA Personal Assistant

P.A. public address (system)

pabulum (pab'y͞o lәm) *n.* [L.] 1. food 2. nourishment for the mind

pace¹ (pās) *n.* [< L. *passus,* step] 1. a step in walking, running, etc. 2. the length of a step or stride 3. speed in walking, etc. 4. rate of progress, development, etc. 5. a particular way of walking, etc. 6. the gait of a horse in which both legs on the same side are raised together —*vt.* **paced, pac'ing** 1. to walk back and forth across 2. to measure by paces 3. to set the pace for (a runner, etc.) —*vi.* 1. to walk with regular steps 2. to raise both legs on the same side at the same time: said of a horse —**change of pace** variation in tempo or mood —**keep pace (with)** to maintain the same rate of progress (as) —**put through one's paces** to test one's abilities, etc. —**set the pace** 1. to go at a speed that others try to equal 2. to do or be something for others to emulate —**pac'er** *n.*

†pace² (pā'sē) *prep.* [< L. *pax,* peace] with all due respect to: used in polite disagreement

pacemaker (pās'mā'kәr) *n.* 1. a runner, horse, etc. that sets the pace, as in a race: also **pace'set'ter** 2. *Med.* an electronic device implanted in the body to regulate the heartbeat —**pace'mak'ing** *n.*

pachyderm (pak'әdurm') *n.* [< Gr. *pachys,* thick + *derma,* skin] a large, thick-skinned, hoofed animal, as the elephant, rhinoceros, or hippopotamus —**pach'y-der'matous** *adj.*

pacific (pә sif'ik) *adj.* [< PACIFY] 1. making or tending to make peace 2. peaceful; calm —**pacif'ically** *adv.*

pacificate (pas'ә fi kāt') *vt.* **-cat'ed, -cat'ing** *same as* PACIFY —**pac'i'fication** *n.* —**pacif'icatory** *adj.*

pacifier (pas'ә fī'әr) *n.* [U.S.] a baby's dummy

pacifism (pas'ә fiz'm) *n.* [see PACIFY] opposition to the use of force under any circumstances; specif., refusal to participate in war —**pac'ifist** *n., adj.*

pacify (pas'ә fī') *vt.* **-fied', -fy'ing** [<

Fr. < L. *pax,* peace + *facere,* make] 1. to make peaceful or calm; appease 2. to secure peace in (a nation, etc.) —**pac'ifi'-able** *adj.*

pack¹ (pak) *n.* [< MFl. *pac*] 1. a bundle of things tied up for carrying 2. a group or set [a *pack* of lies] 3. a package of a standard number [a *pack* of cards] 4. a set of hunting hounds 5. a group of wild animals living and hunting together 6. *Rugby* the forwards of a team 7. the organizational unit of Brownies and Cub Scouts 8. *same as* PACK ICE 9. a cosmetic paste applied to the skin and left to dry [mudpack] 10. a method of packing or bottling —*vt.* 1. to make a pack of 2. *a)* to put together in a box, trunk, etc. *b)* to fill (a box, etc.) 3. to crowd; cram [the hall was *packed*] 4. to press together firmly [*packed* earth] 5. to send (*off*) 6. [Slang] to carry (a gun, etc.) 7. [Slang] *a)* to deliver (a punch, etc.) with force *b)* to contain [a play that *packs* a message] —*vi.* 1. to make up packs 2. to put one's clothes, etc. into luggage for a trip 3. to crowd together 4. to admit of being folded compactly [this suit *packs* well] 5. to settle into a compact mass —**pack it in** [Colloq.] to stop doing something —**pack up** [Colloq.] 1. to stop working: said esp. of a machine 2. to retire from a contest, activity, etc. —**send packing** to dismiss (a person) abruptly —**pack'-able** *adj.* —**pack'er** *n.*

pack² *vt.* to choose (a jury, court, etc.) dishonestly so as to get desired results

package *n.* 1. a wrapped or boxed thing; parcel 2. a number of items, plans, etc. offered as an inseparable unit —*vt.* **-aged, -aging** to put into a package

package holiday a holiday with a fixed itinerary and at a price inclusive of travel and lodging

packet *n.* 1. a small package 2. a container in which a commodity is packed for sale 3. *same as* PACKET BOAT 4. [Colloq.] a large sum of money

packet boat a boat that travels on a regular route carrying passengers, freight, and mail

packhorse *n.* a horse used to transport goods, equipment, etc.

pack ice a large, floating expanse of ice masses

packing *n.* 1. the act or process of a person or thing that packs 2. any material used to pack

packsaddle *n.* a saddle with fastenings to secure the load carried by a **pack animal**

packthread *n.* strong, thick thread for tying bundles

pact (pakt) *n.* [< L. *pax,* peace] an agreement between persons, groups, or nations

pad¹ (pad) *n.* [echoic] the dull sound made, as by a footstep, on the ground

pad² *n.* [? var. of POD] 1. anything made of or stuffed with soft material to fill out a shape, protect from friction, jarring, blows, etc. 2. folded gauze, etc. used as a dressing on a wound, etc. 3. the cushionlike sole of an animal's paw 4. the floating leaf of a water lily 5. a tablet of paper for writing on 6. a small cushion soaked with ink for inking a rubber stamp: in full, **stamp pad** or **ink pad** 7. *same as* LAUNCHING PAD 8. [Slang] the room, flat, etc. where one lives —*vt.* **pad′ded, pad′ding** 1. to stuff or cover with padding 2. to lengthen (a speech, etc.) with unnecessary material

pad³ *vi.* **pad′ded, pad′ding** [< Du. *pad,* path] to walk or run with a soft step

padded cell a room in a mental hospital, with padded surfaces, in which violent inmates are placed

padding *n.* any material used to pad

paddle¹ (pad′'l) *n.* [< ?] 1. a short oar with a wide blade, used without a rowlock 2. any of various implements shaped like this 3. any of the propelling boards in a water wheel or paddle wheel —*vt., vi.* **-dled, -dling** to propel (a canoe, etc.) with a paddle —**paddle one's own canoe** to depend entirely on oneself

paddle² *vi.* **-dled, -dling** [prob. < PAD³] to move the hands or feet about in the water; dabble

PADDLE WHEEL

paddle wheel a wheel with paddles around it for propelling a steamboat

paddock (pad′ək) *n.* [< OE. *pearruc,* enclosure] 1. a small enclosure near a stable, in which horses are exercised 2. an enclosure at a race track, where horses are assembled before a race

paddy¹ (pad′ē) *n., pl.* **-dies** [Malay *padi*] 1. a rice field: often **rice paddy** 2. rice 3. rice in the husk

paddy² *n., pl.* **-dies** [< *Paddy,* a nickname for an Irishman] [Colloq.] a fit of temper; also **pad′dywhack′**

padlock (pad′lok′) *n.* [< ME.] a removable lock with a hinged link to be passed through a staple, chain, or eye —*vt.* to fasten or keep shut as with a padlock

padre (pä′drē) *n., pl.* **-dres** (-drēz) [Sp., It., Port. < L. *pater,* father] 1. father:

the title of a priest in Italy, Spain, Portugal, etc. 2. [Colloq.] a chaplain, esp. in the army

paean (pē′ən) *n.* [< Gr. *Paian,* epithet of Apollo] a song of joy, triumph, praise, etc.

paediatrician (pē′dē ə trish′ən) *n.* a specialist in paediatrics : also **pae′diat′rist** (-at′rist)

paediatrics (pē′dē at′riks) *n.pl.* [with *sing. v.*] [< PAEDO-] the branch of medicine dealing with the care and diseases of infants and children —**pae′diat′ric** *adj.*

paedo- [< Gr.] *a combining form meaning* child, children

paedophilia (pē′də fil′ē ə) *n.* [< PAEDO- + -PHILE] a sexual desire in an adult for children

paella (pä yel′ə) *n.* [Catalan < L. *patella,* small pan] a Spanish dish of rice cooked with chicken, seafood, etc.

pagan (pā′gən) *n.* [< L. *paganus,* a peasant] 1. anyone not a Christian, Moslem, or Jew; heathen 2. a person who has no religion —*adj.* 1. of pagans 2. not religious —**pa′ganish** *adj.* —**pa′ganism** *n.*

page¹ (pāj) *n.* [< L. *pangere,* fasten] 1. *a)* one side of a leaf of a book, newspaper, etc. *b)* the writing on it [*the sports pages*] *c)* an entire leaf 2. [*often pl.*] a record of events 3. an event that might fill a page —*vt.* **paged, pag′ing** to number the pages of

page² *n.* [< It. *paggio*] 1. a boy or girl who runs errands, as in a hotel, etc. 2. a boy attendant, esp. one serving a person of high rank 3. formerly, a boy training for knighthood —*vt.* **paged, pag′ing** to try to find (a person) by calling his name, esp. using a loudspeaker

pageant (paj′ənt) *n.* [Anglo-L. *pagina,* stage < L., PAGE¹] 1. a spectacular exhibition, parade, etc., as a procession with floats 2. an outdoor drama celebrating a historical event

pageantry *n., pl.* **-ries** 1. grand spectacle; gorgeous display 2. empty show or display

pageboy (pāj′boi′) *n.* 1. a medium-length hair style with the ends of the hair curled under 2. *same as* PAGE²

paginate (paj′ə nāt′) *vt.* **-nat′ed, -nat′ing** to number the pages of (a book, etc.) —**pag′ina′tion** *n.*

pagoda (pə gō′də) *n.* [? < Per. *but,* idol + *kadah,* house] in the Orient, a temple that is a tapering tower with rooflike projections between its several storeys

paid (pād) *pt. & pp.* of PAY¹ —**put paid to** [Colloq.] to end or destroy (chances, hopes, etc.)

paid-up *adj.* having made all necessary payments

pail (pāl) *n.* [OE. *pægel,* small measure] 1. a cylindrical container, usually with a handle, for carrying liquids, etc.; bucket 2. the amount held by a pail: also **pail′ful′**

pain (pān) *n.* [< Gr. *poinē,* penalty] 1. suffering caused by injury, disease, etc. 2. the suffering caused by anxiety, grief, disappointment, etc. 3. [*pl.*] the labour of childbirth 4. [*pl.*] great care [to take *pains* with one's work *]* **5.** [Colloq.] an annoyance —*vt.* to cause pain to —**on** (or **upon** or **under**) **pain of** at the risk of bringing upon oneself (punishment, death, etc.) —**pain'less** *adj.* —**pain'lessly** *adv.*

pained *adj.* **1.** hurt or distressed; offended **2.** showing hurt feelings or resentment

painful *adj.* **1.** causing pain; hurting **2.** having pain; aching **3.** exacting **4.** irritating —**pain'fully** *adv.*

painkiller *n.* a medicine that relieves pain

painstaking (pānz'tā'kiŋ) *adj.* **1.** very careful **2.** characterized by great care —**pains'tak'ingly** *adv.*

paint (pānt) *vt.* [< L. *pingere*] **1.** *a)* to make (a picture, etc.) in colours applied to a surface *b)* to depict with paints **2.** to describe colourfully **3.** to cover or decorate with paint **4.** to apply cosmetics to **5.** to apply (a medicine, etc.) with a brush —*vi.* to paint pictures —*n.* **1.** a mixture of pigment with oil, water, etc. used as a covering or colouring **2.** colouring matter, as lipstick, rouge, etc., used as a cosmetic —**paint out** to cover up as with a coat of paint —**paint the town (red)** [Colloq.] to go on a boisterous spree —**paint'able** *adj.*

paintbrush *n.* a brush used for applying paint

painter[1] *n.* **1.** an artist who paints pictures **2.** one whose work is covering surfaces, as walls, with paint

painter[2] *n.* [ult. < L. *pendere*, hang] a rope attached to the bow of a boat for tying it to a dock, etc.

painting *n.* **1.** the work or art of one who paints **2.** a picture made with paints

pair (pãer) *n.,* *pl.* **pairs**; sometimes, after a number, **pair** [< L. *par*, equal] **1.** two corresponding things associated or used together *[a pair* of shoes *]* **2.** a single thing with two joined corresponding parts *[a pair* of trousers *]* **3.** two persons or animals regarded as a unit *[a pair* of oxen *]* **4.** two legislators on opposing sides who agree to withhold their vote so as to offset each other **5.** two playing cards of the same denomination —*vt.,* *vi.* **1.** to form a pair or pairs (of); match **2.** to mate —**pair off** to join (two people or things) in a pair

PAISLEY
PATTERN

paisley (pāz'lē) *adj.* [< *Paisley*, Scotland where orig. made] [*also* P-] **1.** having an elaborate, colourful pattern of intricate,

curved figures **2.** made of cloth having such a pattern

pajamas (pəjä'məz) *n.pl.* U.S. sp. of PYJAMAS

Pak (pak) *n.* [Derog. Slang] a Pakistani immigrant residing in Britain: also **Pak'i**

Pakistani (pä'ki stä'nē) *adj.* of Pakistan or its people —*n.* a native of Pakistan

pal (pal) *n.* [< Romany] [Colloq.] an intimate friend; comrade —*vi.* **palled, pal'ling** [Colloq.] to associate as pals (with *up*)

palace (pal'is) *n.* [< L. *Palatium,* a hill in Rome, where Augustus lived] **1.** the official residence of a king, etc. **2.** any large house or building

paladin (pal'ə din) *n.* [see prec.] **1.** any of the twelve peers of Charlemagne's court **2.** a heroic champion

palaeo- same as PALEO-

palanquin, palankeen (pal'ən kēn') *n.* [< Port. < Sans.] formerly in eastern Asia, a covered litter for one person, carried by poles on men's shoulders

palatable (pal'it ə b'l) *adj.* [PALAT(E) + -ABLE] **1.** pleasant or acceptable to the taste **2.** acceptable to the mind —**pal'atabil'ity, pal'atableness** *n.*

palatal (pal'ət 'l) *adj.* **1.** of the palate **2.** pronounced with the tongue near the hard palate, as *y* in *yes*

palate (pal'ət) *n.* [L. *palatum*] **1.** the roof of the mouth, consisting of a hard, bony forward part (the *hard palate*) and a soft, fleshy back part (the *soft palate*) **2.** taste

palatial (pə lā'shəl) *adj.* [see PALACE] **1.** of, suitable for, or like a palace **2.** magnificent —**pala'tially** *adv.*

palatine (pal'ə tīn') *adj.* [< L. *palatium,* palace] having royal privileges *[a count palatine]* —*n.* a medieval vassal lord having the rights of royalty in his own territory, or palatinate —**palatinate** (pə lat'ən at') *n.*

palaver (pə läv'ər) *n.* [Port. < LL. *parabola,* parable] **1.** fuss; bother **2.** talk; esp., idle chatter **3.** a conference, as orig. between African natives and European explorers **4.** flattery —*vi.* to talk, esp. idly

pale[1] (pāl) *adj.* [< L. *pallere,* to be pale] **1.** of a whitish or colourless complexion **2.** lacking intensity, as colour, light, etc. —*vi., vt.* **paled, pal'ing** to make or become pale —**pale'ly** *adv.* —**pale'ness** *n.*

pale[2] *n.* [< L. *palus,* stake] **1.** a pointed stake used in fences **2.** a fence; enclosure; boundary —**beyond the pale** outside the limits of social convention

paleface *n.* a white person: a term allegedly first used by N American Indians

paleo- [< Gr.] *a combining form meaning* ancient, prehistoric, etc. *[paleolithic]*

Paleocene (pal'ē ō sēn') *adj.* [< prec. + Gr. *kainos,* recent] of the first epoch of the Tertiary Period in the Cainozoic Era

paleography (pal'ē og'rə fē) *n.* **1.** ancient forms of writing **2.** the study of ancient writings —**pa'leog'rapher** *n.*

paleolithic (pal'ē ō lith'ik) *adj.* [< PALEO-

+ Gr. *lithos*, stone] of the middle part of the early Stone Age

paleontology (pal′ē on tol′ə jē) *n*. [< Fr.: see PALE(O)- & ONTO- & -LOGY] the branch of geology that deals with prehistoric life through the study of fossils —**pa′leontol′o·gist** *n*.

Paleozoic (pal′ē ō zō′ik) *adj*. [< PALEO- + Gr. *zōion*, animal] of the era between the Precambrian and the Mesozoic

Palestinian (pal′əs tin′ē ən) *adj*. of the region on the E coast of the Mediterranean —*n*. an inhabitant, esp. an Arab, of this area

palette (pal′ət) *n*. [< L. *pala*, shovel] 1. a thin board with a hole for the thumb at one end, on which an artist arranges and mixes his paints 2. the colours used, as by a particular artist

palette knife a round-ended spatula with a thin flexible blade, used esp. in painting and cookery

palfrey (pôl′frē) *n.*, *pl.* **-freys** [ult. < Gr. *para*, beside + L. *veredus*, horse] [Archaic] a saddle horse

palindrome (pal′in drōm′) *n*. [< Gr. *palin*, again + *dramein*, run] a word, phrase, or sentence that reads the same backwards or forwards (Ex.: madam) —**pal′indrom′ic** (-drom′ik) *adj*.

paling (pāl′iŋ) *n*. 1. a fence made of pales 2. a pale, or pales collectively

palisade (pal′ə sād′) *n*. [< L. *palus*, stake] 1. any of a row of large pointed stakes set in the ground to form a fence as for fortification 2. such a fence —*vt*. **-sad′-ed**, **-sad′ing** to fortify with a palisade

pall¹ (pôl) *vi*. **palled**, **pall′ing** [ME. *pallen*] 1. to become cloying, insipid, etc. 2. to become satiated or bored

pall² *n*. [< L. *pallium*, cover] 1. a piece of velvet, etc. used to cover a coffin, hearse, or tomb 2. a dark or gloomy covering [a *pall* of smoke]

palladium (pə lā′dē əm) *n*. [< Gr. *Pallas* (*Athene*), the goddess] a rare, silvery-white, metallic chemical element: it is used in jewellery: symbol, Pd

pallbearer (pôl′bâar′ər) *n*. [PALL² + BEARER] one of the persons who bear the coffin at a funeral

pallet¹ (pal′it) *n*. [see PALETTE] 1. a wooden tool consisting of a flat blade with a handle, as used for smoothing pottery 2. a palette 3. a low, portable platform for storing goods in warehouses, etc.

pallet² *n*. [< L. *palea*, chaff] a small, inferior bed or a mattress filled as with straw and used on the floor

palliasse (pal′ē as) *n*. [< L. *palea*, chaff] a mattress filled with straw, sawdust, etc.

palliate (pal′ē āt′) *vt*. **-at′ed**, **-at′ing** [< L. *pallium*, a cloak] 1. to lessen the severity of without curing 2. to make appear less serious or offensive; excuse —**pal′liative** *adj., n*.

pallid (pal′id) *adj*. [< L. *pallidus*, pale] faint in colour

pall-mall (pal′mal′) *n*. [< It. *palla*, ball + *maglio*, hammer] an old game in which a boxwood ball was struck by a mallet through an iron ring

pallor (pal′ər) *n*. [see PALE¹] unnatural paleness, as of the face

pally (pal′ē) *adj*. [PAL] [Colloq.] friendly

palm¹ (päm) *n*. [< L. *palma*: from its handlike fronds] 1. a tropical or subtropical tree with a tall, branchless trunk and a bunch of large leaves at the top 2. a leaf of this tree carried as a symbol of victory 3. victory; triumph —**bear** (or **carry off**) **the palm** to be the winner —**palmaceous** (pal mā′shəs) *adj*.

palm² *n*. [< L. *palma*] 1. the inner surface of the hand between the fingers and wrist 2. the part of a glove, etc. that covers the palm —*vt*. to hide (something) in the palm or between the fingers, as in a sleight-of-hand trick —**have an itching palm** [Colloq.] to desire money greedily —**palm off** 1. to pass off by deceit 2. [Colloq.] to get rid of —**palmar** (pal′mər) *adj*.

palmate (pal′mit) *adj*. [see PALM²] shaped like a hand with the fingers spread —**pal′mately** *adv*.

palmetto (pal met′ō) *n.*, *pl.* **-tos**, **-toes** [Sp. < L.] a small new-world palm

palmistry (päm′is trē) *n*. [< ME., prob. < *paume*, palm + *maistrie*, mastery] the pretended art of telling a person's fortune by the lines, etc. on the palm of his hand —**palm′ist** *n*.

palm oil an oil obtained from the fruit of certain palms

Palm Sunday the Sunday before Easter, commemorating Jesus' triumphal entry into Jerusalem

palmy *adj*. **-ier**, **-iest** 1. prosperous 2. of or like a palm 3. abounding in palm trees

palomino (pal′ə mē′nō) *n.*, *pl.* **-nos** [AmSp. < L. *palumbes*, pigeon] a cream, golden, or light-chestnut horse with white mane and tail

palpable (pal′pə b′l) *adj*. [< L. *palpare*, touch] 1. easily perceived by the senses 2. obvious 3. that can be touched, felt, etc. —**pal′pabil′ity** *n*. —**pal′pably** *adv*.

palpate (pal′pāt) *vt*. **-pated**, **-pating** [< L. *palpare*, touch] *Med.* to examine by touching —**palpa′tion** *n*.

palpitate (pal′pə tāt′) *vi*. **-tat′ed**, **-tat′ing** [< L. *palpare*, to feel] 1. to beat rapidly or flutter: said of the heart 2. to throb; quiver —**pal′pita′tion** *n*.

palsy (pôl′zē) *n.*, *pl.* **-sies** [< PARALYSIS] paralysis of any voluntary muscle, sometimes accompanied by uncontrollable tremors —*vt*. **-sied**, **-sying** to afflict with palsy

paltry (pôl′trē) *adj*. **-trier**, **-triest** [prob. < LowG. *palte*, rag] worthless; trifling; petty —**pal′triness** *n*.

pampas (pam′pəz; *for adj.*, -pəs) *n.pl.* [< SAmInd.] the extensive treeless plains of S America —*adj*. —of the pampas

pampas grass any of several S American grasses grown for their large, feathery flower branches

pamper (pam′pər) *vt*. [< LowG.] to be overindulgent with; coddle [to *pamper* a child] —**pam′perer** *n*.

pamphlet (pam′flit) *n.* [< OFr. *Pamphilet*, a ML. poem] a small, unbound booklet, often on some topic of current interest

pamphleteer (pam′flə tēer′) *n.* a writer of pamphlets, esp. those dealing with political or social issues

pan¹ (pan) *n.* [OE. *panne*] **1.** any broad, shallow container, used in cooking, etc. **2.** a pan-shaped part or object, as either receptacle in a pair of scales **3.** the part holding the powder in a flintlock **4.** the bowl of a lavatory —*vt.* **panned, pan′ning 1.** [Colloq.] to criticize unfavourably, as in reviewing **2.** *Mining* to wash (gold-bearing gravel) in a pan —*vi.* *Mining* to wash gravel in a pan —**pan out** [Colloq.] to turn out; esp., to turn out well

pan² *vt., vi.* **panned, pan′ning** [< PAN(ORAMA)] to move (a film or television camera) so as to get a panoramic effect or to follow a moving object —*n.* the act of panning

pan³ *n.* [< Afrik. < Du.] [S Afr.] a shallow, natural basin in which water collects

pan- [< Gr.] *a combining form meaning:* **1.** all [*pantheism*] **2.** [P-] of, comprising, or common to every [*Pan*-American] In sense 2, usually with a hyphen, as in: Pan-African, Pan-Slavic

panacea (pan′ə sē′ə) *n.* [< Gr. *pan*, all + *akeisthai*, cure] a supposed remedy for all ills; cure-all

panache (pə nash′) *n.* [< LL. *pinnaculum*, plume] carefree self-confidence; flamboyance

Panama (hat) (pan′ə mä′) [< *Panama* (city)] a fine, hand-plaited hat made from leaves of a South American plant

Pan-American (pan′ə mer′ə kən) *adj.* of North, Central, and South America, collectively

panatela, panatella (pan′ə tel′ə) *n.* [AmSp.] a long, slender cigar

pancake (pan′kāk′) *n.* **1.** a thin, flat cake of batter fried on both sides in a pan **2.** a landing in which the plane drops almost vertically: in full, **pancake landing**

Pancake Day *same as* Shrove Tuesday (*see* SHROVETIDE)

pancreas (paŋ′krē əs) *n.* [< Gr. *pan*, all + *kreas*, flesh] a large gland that secretes a digestive juice (**pancreatic juice**) into the small intestine: the pancreas of animals, used as food, is called *sweetbread* —**pan′-creat′ic** (-at′ik) *adj.*

panda (pan′də) *n.* [Fr. < native name] *short for* GIANT PANDA

panda car a police patrol car, usually with a white stripe

pandemic (pan dem′ik) *adj.* [< Gr. *pan*, all + *dēmos*, people] epidemic over a large region

pandemonium (pan′də mō′nē əm) *n.* [< Gr. *pan*, all + *daimon*, demon] disorder or confusion, or a place where this exists: after the capital of Hell in *Paradise Lost*

pander (pan′dər) *n.* [< L. *Pandarus*, in the story of Troilus and Cressida] **1.** one who provides the means of helping to satisfy the ambitions, vices, etc. of another **2.** a go-between in a sexual intrigue —*vi.* to act as a pander (*to*)

pandit (pun′dit) *n.* [var. of PUNDIT] in India, a learned man: used [P-] as a title of respect

P & L profit and loss

P and O Peninsular and Oriental (Steamship Company)

p. & p. postage and packing

pane (pān) *n.* [< L. *pannus*, piece of cloth] **1.** a single division of a window, etc., consisting of a sheet of glass in a frame **2.** such a sheet of glass

panegyric (pan′ə jir′ik) *n.* [< Gr. *panēgyris*, public meeting] **1.** a formal speech or writing praising a person or event **2.** high praise —**pan′egyr′ical** *adj.*

panel (pan′′l) *n.* [< L. *pannus*, piece of cloth] **1.** *a)* a flat piece, usually rectangular, forming a part of the surface of a wall, door, etc., often recessed *b)* a board for instruments or controls **2.** *a)* a list of persons summoned for jury duty *b)* *Scots Law* the accused **3.** a group of persons selected for a specific purpose, as for judging a contest **4.** a lengthwise strip, as of contrasting material, as in a skirt —*vt.* **-elled, -elling** to provide with panels

panel game a quiz, etc. played by a group of people, esp. on TV

panelling panels collectively; a series of panels in a wall, etc.

panellist *n.* a member of a panel (*n.* 3.)

pang (paŋ) *n.* [< ?] a sudden, sharp, brief pain

pangolin (paŋ gō′lin) *n.* [Malay *pĕngulin*, roller] a scaly mammal able to roll into a ball when attacked

panic (pan′ik) *n.* [< Gr. *panikos*, of Pan] **1.** a sudden, unreasoning, hysterical fear **2.** a widespread fear of financial collapse —*adj.* like, showing, or resulting from, panic —*vt.* **-icked, -icking** to affect with panic —*vi.* to give way to panic —**pan′-icky** *adj.*

PANICLE
OF OATS

panicle (pan′i k′l) *n.* [< L. *panus*, a swelling] a loose, irregularly branched flower cluster —**pan′icled** *adj.*

panic-stricken *adj.* badly frightened: also **panic-struck**

panjandrum (pan jan′drəm) *n.* [arbitrary

coinage] a self-important, pompous official

pannier (pan′ē ər) *n.* [< L. *panis*, bread] 1. a large basket for carrying loads on the back 2. either of a pair of baskets hung across the back of a donkey, etc. 3. a large bag, often one of a pair, as on the back of a bicycle

panoply (pan′ə plē) *n.*, *pl.* -**plies** [< Gr. *pan*, all + *hopla*, arms] 1. any magnificent covering or array 2. a complete suit of armour —**pan′oplied** *adj.*

panorama (pan′ə räm′ə) *n.* [< PAN-+ Gr. *horama*, view] 1. an open view in all directions 2. a picture unrolled in such a way as to give the impression of a continuous view 3. a constantly changing scene —**pan′oram′ic** (pan′ə-ram′ik) *adj.*

panpipe (pan′pīp′) *n.* [*also* P-] a primitive musical instrument made of a row of tubes of graduated lengths, played by blowing across the open ends

pansy (pan′zē) *n.*, *pl.* -**sies** [Fr. *pensée*, thought] 1. a small, flowering plant with velvety petals in many colours 2. [Colloq.] a male homosexual

pant[1] (pant) *vi.* [ult. < L. *phantasia*, nightmare] 1. to breathe rapidly and heavily, as from running fast 2. to throb 3. to yearn eagerly (with *for* or *after*) —*vt.* to gasp out —*n.* 1. a gasp 2. a throb, as of the heart

pant[2] *n.*, *adj. see* PANTS

pantaloon (pan′tə lōōn′) *n.* [< It., ult. after saint *Pantalone*] [P-] a foolish old man in early Italian comedy —*n.* [*pl.*] [Chiefly U.S.] trousers

pantechnicon (pan tek′ni kən) *n.* [PAN-+ Gr. *technikon*, of the arts] 1. a furniture removal van 2. orig., a bazaar where all kinds of things were sold

pantheism (pan′thē iz′m) *n.* 1. the belief that God is not a personality but the sum of all beings, things, forces, etc. in the universe 2. the worship of all gods —**pan′theist** *n.*

pantheon (pan′thē ən) *n.* [< Gr. *pan*, all + *theos*, a god] 1. a temple for all the gods; esp., [P-] a temple built in Rome in 27 B.C. 2. all the gods of a people 3. [*often* P-] a building in which the famous dead of a nation are entombed

panther (pan′thər) *n.* [< Gr. *panthēr*] 1. a leopard 2. [U.S.] a) a puma b) a jaguar

panties (pan′tēz) *n.pl.* women's or children's short undergarments

pantihose (pan′tē hōz) *n.pl.* tights

pantile (pan′tīl′) *n.* [PAN[1] + TILE] a roofing tile having an S curve

panto (pan′tō) *n.* [Colloq.] a pantomime

panto- [< Gr.] *a combining form meaning* all or every

pantograph (pan′tō gräf′) *n.* [< Fr.: see *prec.* & -GRAPH] a mechanical device for reproducing a drawing

pantomime (pan′tə mīm′) *n.* [< PANTO-+ Gr. *mimos*, a mimic] 1. a spectacular entertainment based usually on a fairy tale and performed at Christmas 2. a

play, skit, etc. performed without words 3. actions and gestures without words —*vt.*, *vi.* -**mimed′**, -**mim′ing** to express or act in pantomime —**pan′tomim′ic** (-mim′ik) *adj.*

pantry (pan′trē) *n.*, *pl.* -**tries** [< L. *panis*, bread] a small room off the kitchen where cooking ingredients and utensils, china, etc. are kept

pants (pants) *n.pl.* [< PANTALOON(S)] 1. [U.S.] trousers 2. panties —**with one's pants down** [Colloq.] unprepared

panzer (pan′zər) *adj.* [G., armour] armoured

pap[1] (pap) *n.* [? < baby talk] [Archaic] a nipple

pap[2] *n.* [< baby talk] 1. any soft food for babies 2. any oversimplified writing, etc. 3. [< Afrik.] [S Afr.] maize porridge

papa (pə pä′) *n.* [< baby talk] father: a child's word

papacy (pā′pə sē) *n.*, *pl.* -**cies** [< ML. *papa*, pope] 1. the position or authority of the Pope 2. the period during which a Pope rules 3. [*also* P-] the government of the Roman Catholic Church

papal (pā′pəl) *adj.* [< ML.: see POPE] of the Pope or the papacy —**pa′pally** *adv.*

papaw (pə pôr′) *n.* [prob. < ff.] 1. *same as* PAPAYA 2. a tree of the U.S. having a yellowish, edible fruit

papaya (pə pī′yə) *n.* [Sp.] 1. a palmlike tropical American tree bearing a large, yellowish-orange fruit like a melon 2. its fruit

paper (pā′pər) *n.* [< L. *papyrus*, papyrus] 1. a thin, flexible material usually in sheets, made from wood pulp, rags, etc., and used for writing or printing on 2. a single sheet of this 3. an official document 4. an essay, dissertation, etc. 5. a written examination, report, etc. 6. *same as* PAPER MONEY 7. a) a newspaper b) wallpaper 8. a small wrapper of paper 9. [*pl.*] documents identifying a person —*adj.* 1. made of paper 2. like paper 3. theoretical [*paper* profits] —*vt.* to cover with paper, esp. wallpaper —**on paper** 1. in written or printed form 2. in theory —**pa′perer** *n.* —**pa′perlike′**, **pa′pery** *adj.*

paperback *n.* a book bound in flexible card —**pa′perbacked′**, **pa′perbound′** *adj.*

paperboy *n.* a boy or man who sells or delivers newspapers —**pa′pergirl** *n. fem.*

paperchase *n.* a cross-country race in which runners follow a trail of torn-up pieces of paper

paper clip a flexible clasp of metal wire for holding loose sheets of paper together

paperhanger *n.* a person whose work is covering walls with wallpaper —**pa′per-hang′ing** *n.*

paper knife a knifelike blade, as of metal, used to slit sealed envelopes and uncut book pages

paper money noninterest-bearing notes issued by a government or its banks, circulating as legal tender

paperweight *n.* any small, heavy object set on papers

paper work the keeping of records, filing

of reports, etc. incidental to some work or task

papier-mâché (pap′yä ma′shã) *n.* [< Fr. *papier,* paper + *mâcher,* chew] a material made of paper pulp mixed with glue, etc. that is easily moulded when moist

papilla (pə pil′ə) *n., pl.* **-lae** (-ē) [L. < *papula,* pimple] a small bulge of flesh, as at the root of a hair —**papil′lary** *adj.*

papist (pā′pist) *n.* [< LL. *papa,* pope] 1. one who believes in papal supremacy 2. [Derog] a Roman Catholic

papoose (pə p⊙⊙s′) *n.* [< AmInd. *papoos*] a North American Indian baby

paprika (pap′ri kə) *n.* [Hung. < Gr. *peperi,* pepper] a mild, red condiment ground from the fruit of certain peppers

Pap test (pap) [< G. *Papanicolaou*] the examination of a smear (**Pap smear**) taken from the cervix of a woman: a test for uterine cancer

papyrus (pə pī′rəs) *n., pl.* **-ri** (-rī), **-ruses** [< Gr. *papyros*] 1. a tall water plant abundant in the Nile region 2. a writing material made from this plant by the ancient Egyptians 3. any ancient document on papyrus

par (pär) *n.* [L., an equal] 1. the average state, condition, etc. [work that is above *par*] 2. an equal status, footing, level, etc.: usually in **on a par (with)** 3. the established value of a currency in foreign-exchange rates 4. *Commerce* the face value of shares, etc. 5. *Golf* the number of strokes established as a skilful score for a hole or course —*adj.* 1. of or at par 2. average; normal

par. 1. paragraph 2. parallel 3. parenthesis

para- [< Gr.] a prefix meaning: 1. by or at the side of, beyond, [*paramilitary*] 2. *Med.* in a secondary capacity

parable (par′ə b'l) *n.* [< Gr. *para-,* beside + *ballein,* throw] a simple story teaching a moral or religious lesson

PARABOLA

parabola (pə rab′ə lə) *n.* [see prec.] *Geom.* a plane curve formed by the intersection of a cone with a plane parallel to its side

parabolic (par′ə bol′ik) *adj.* 1. of, like, or expressed by a parable 2. of or like a parabola —**par′abol′ically** *adv.*

paracetamol (par′ə sēt′ə mol′) *n.* [< *para-acetamidophenol*] a mild analgesic drug

parachute (par′ə sh⊙⊙t′) *n.* [Fr. < *para-* (< It. *parare,* ward off) + *chute,* fall] a large cloth contrivance shaped like an umbrella, used to retard the speed of a person or thing dropping from an aircraft, etc. —*vt., vi.* **-chut′ed, -chut′ing** to drop or descend by parachute —**par′achut′ist** *n.*

parade (pə rād′) *n.* [< L. *parare,* to prepare] 1. any organized procession or march, as for display 2. *a*) a review of troops *b*) a place where troops assemble for parade 3. ostentatious display 4. a public walk or promenade —*vt.* - **rad′-ed, -rad′ing** 1. to march or walk through (the streets, etc.), as for display 2. to show off —*vi.* 1. to march in a parade 2. to walk about ostentatiously 3. to assemble in military formation for review —**on parade** on display

paradigm (par′ə dīm) *n.* [< Gr. *para,* beside + *deigma,* example] 1. a pattern, example, or model 2. *Gram.* an example of a declension or conjugation, giving all the inflectional forms —**par′adigmat′ic** (-dig mat′ik) *adj.*

paradise (par′ə dīs′) *n.* [< Gr. *paradeisos,* garden] 1. [P-] the garden of Eden 2. heaven 3. any place or state of perfection, happiness, etc. —**par′adisi′acal** (-di sī′-ə k'l) *adj.*

paradox (par′ə doks′) *n.* [< Gr. *para-,* beyond + *doxa,* opinion] 1. a statement that seems contradictory, absurd, etc. but may be true in fact 2. a statement that contradicts itself and is false 3. a person, situation, etc. that seems inconsistent —**par′adox′ical** *adj.* —**par′adox′ically** *adv.*

paraffin (par′ə fin) *n.* [< L. *parum,* too little + *affinis,* akin: from its inertness] 1. a liquid mixture of hydrocarbons used as a fuel in domestic heaters, etc. 2. *Chem.* a saturated hydrocarbon 3. a white, waxy substance distilled from petroleum and used for making candles, sealing jars, etc.

paragon (par′ə gən) *n.* [< It. *paragone,* touchstone] a model of perfection or excellence

paragraph (par′ə gräf′) *n.* [< Gr. *para-,* beside + *graphein,* write] 1. a distinct section of a chapter, letter, etc., begun on a new line and often indented 2. a mark (¶) used to indicate the beginning of a paragraph 3. a brief item in a newspaper —*vt.* to arrange in paragraphs —**par′agraph′ic** (par′ə graf′ik) *adj.*

parakeet (par′ə kēt′) *n.* [prob. < MFr. *perrot,* parrot] a small, slender parrot with a long, tapering tail

parallax (par′ə laks′) *n.* [< Gr. *para-,* beyond + *allassein,* change] 1. the apparent change in the position of an object resulting from a change in the viewer's position 2. the amount of such change —**par′allac′tic** *adj.*

parallel (par′ə lel′) *adj.* [< Gr. *para-,* side by side + *allēlos,* one another] 1. extending in the same direction and at a constant distance apart, so as never to meet, as lines, planes, etc. 2. similar or corresponding, as in purpose, time, or essential parts 3. *Elec.* designating a circuit in parallel —*n.* 1. a parallel line, surface, etc. **2.** any person or thing similar to another **3.** any comparison showing likeness **4.** *a)* any of the imaginary lines parallel to the equator and representing degrees of latitude *b)* such a line drawn on a map or globe: in full, **parallel of latitude 5.** [*pl.*] a sign (‖) used as a reference mark **6.** *Elec.* a circuit connection in which the negative terminals are joined to one conductor and the positive to another: usually in phrase, **in parallel** —*vt.* **-alleled'**, **-allel'ing 1.** to make parallel **2.** to be parallel to **3.** to compare (things) **4.** to match

parallel bars two parallel, horizontal bars set on adjustable upright posts : used in gymnastics

parallelepiped (par'ə lel'ə pipid) *n.* [< Gr. *parallēlos*, parallel + *epipedos*, plane] a solid with six faces, each of which is a parallelogram

parallelism (par'ə lel iz'm) *n.* **1.** the state of being parallel **2.** close resemblance; similarity

parallelogram (par'ə lel'ō gram') *n.* [< Gr. *parallēlos*, parallel + *grammē*, line] a plane figure with four sides, having the opposite sides parallel and equal

paralyse (par'ə liz') *vt.* **-lysed', -lys'ing 1.** to cause paralysis or to make ineffective or powerless

paralysis (pə ral'ə sis) *n., pl.* **-ses'** (-sēz') [< Gr. *para-*, beside + *lyein*, to loose] **1.** partial or complete loss of the power of motion or sensation, esp. voluntary motion **2.** a condition of helpless inactivity

paralytic (par'ə lit'ik) *adj.* **1.** relating to paralysis **2.** [Slang] drunk —*n.* a person affected with paralysis

paramedical (par'ə med'i k'l) *adj.* [PARA- + MEDICAL] of auxiliary medical personnel, as midwives, nurses' aides, etc. —**par'amed'ic** *n.*

parameter (pə ram'i tər) *n.* [< Gr. *para-*, alongside + *metron*, measure] **1.** *Math.* a quantity whose value varies with the circumstances of its application **2.** any constant, with variable values, used as a reference for other variables

paramilitary (par'ə mil'ə tər ē) *adj.* [PARA- + MILITARY] of forces working along with, or in place of, a regular military organization

paramount (par'ə mount') *adj.* [< OFr. *par*, by + *amont*, uphill] ranking higher than any other; chief —**par'amount'ly** *adv.*

paramour (par'ə mooor') *n.* [< OFr. *par amour*, with love] a lover; esp., the illicit sexual partner of a married person

paranoia (par'ə noi'ə) *n.* [< Gr. *para-*, beside + *nous*, the mind] a mental disorder characterized by delusions, as of grandeur —**par'anoid', par'anoi'ac** *adj., n.*

parapet (par'ə pit) *n.* [< It. *parare*, guard + *petto*, breast] **1.** a low wall or railing, as on a balcony **2.** a wall or bank for screening troops from enemy fire

paraphernalia (par'ə fər nāl'ē ə) *n.pl.* [*often with sing. v.*] [< Gr. *para-*, beyond + *phernē*, dowry] miscellaneous articles or equipment

paraphrase (par'ə frāz') *n.* [< Gr. *para-*, beyond + *phrazein*, tell] a rewording of the meaning of something spoken or written —*vt., vi.* **-phrased', -phras'ing** to express in a paraphrase —**par'aphras'tic** *adj.*

paraplegia (par'ə plē'jə) *n.* [< Gr. *paraplēgia*, a stroke at one side] paralysis of the entire lower half of the body —**par'aple'gic** *adj., n.*

parapsychology (par'ə sī kol'ə jē) *n.* [PARA- + PSYCHOLOGY] the study of psychic phenomena, as telepathy

paraquat (par'ə kwat') *n.* [PARA- + QUAT(ERNARY)] *Trademark* a quick-acting, extremely poisonous weedkiller

parasite (par'ə sīt') *n.* [< Gr. *para-*, beside + *sitos*, food] **1.** one who lives at others' expense without making any useful return **2.** a plant or animal that lives on or within another from which it derives sustenance —**par'asit'ic** (-sit'ik) *adj.* —**par'asit'ically** *adv.* —**par'asit'ism** *n.*

parasol (par'ə sol') *n.* [< It. *parare*, ward off + *sole*, sun] a light umbrella carried as a sunshade

parathion (par'ə thī'on) *n.* [< Gr. *para-*, alongside + *theion*, sulphur] a poisonous insecticide

paratroops (par'ə troops) *n.pl.* [< PARA(CHUTE) + TROOP] troops trained and equipped to parachute into a combat area —**par'atroop'er** *n.*

paratyphoid (par'ə tī'foid) *n.* [PARA-+ TYPHOID] a disease similar to typhoid fever but milder

‡**par avion** (pår á vyôn') [Fr.] by air mail

parboil (pär'boil') *vt.* [< L. *per*, through + *bullire*, to boil: meaning infl. by Eng. *part*] **1.** to boil until partly cooked, as before roasting **2.** to make hot

parcel (pär's'l) *n.* [see PARTICLE] **1.** a small, wrapped bundle; package **2.** a quantity of items put up for sale **3.** a piece, as of land —*vt.* **-celled, -celling 1.** to separate into parts and distribute (with *out*) **2.** to make up in or as a parcel

parcel post a postal service for delivering parcels

parch (pärch) *vt.* [< ?] **1.** to make hot and dry **2.** to make very thirsty **3.** to expose (corn, etc.) to great heat, so as to dry or roast —*vi.* to become very hot, dry, thirsty, etc.

parchment (pärch'mənt) *n.* [< *Pergamum*, in Asia Minor] **1.** an animal skin, as of a sheep or goat, prepared as a surface for writing **2.** paper treated to resemble this

pardon (pär'd'n) *vt.* [< L. *per-*, through + *donare*, give] **1.** to release (a person) from punishment **2.** to cancel a penalty for (an offence) **3.** to excuse (a person) for (a minor fault, discourtesy, etc.) —*n.* **1.** forgiveness **2.** an official document granting a pardon —(**I beg your**) **pardon 1.** excuse me: a polite form of apology, disagreement, etc. **2.** a request to repeat what has just been said —**par'donable** *adj.* —**par'donably** *adv.*

pardoner *n.* in the Middle Ages, a person

authorized to sell ecclesiastical pardons, or indulgences

pare (pãar) *vt.* **pared, par'ing** [< L. *parare*, prepare] **1.** to cut or trim away (the rind, skin, etc.) of **2.** to reduce gradually —**par'er** *n.*

paregoric (par'ə gor'ik) *n.* [< Gr. *parēgoros*, consoling] a camphorated tincture of opium, used to relieve diarrhoea

parent (pãar'ənt) *n.* [< L. *parere*, beget] **1.** a father or mother **2.** an ancestor **3.** any organism in relation to its offspring **4.** a source; origin —**parental** (pə ren't'l) *adj.* —**paren'tally** *adv.* —**par'enthood'** *n.*

parentage *n.* descent from parents or ancestors; lineage

parenthesis (pə ren'thə sis) *n.*, *pl.* **-ses'** (-sēz') [< Gr. *para-*, beside + *entithenai*, insert] **1.** a word, clause, etc. added as an explanation or comment within a complete sentence and usually marked off by curved lines, commas, etc. **2.** either or both of the curved lines ( ) so used —**parenthetical** (par'ən thet'i k'l), **par'enthet'ic** *adj.* —**par'enthet'ically** *adv.*

parenthesize *vt.* **-sized', -siz'ing 1.** to insert (a word, etc.) as a parenthesis **2.** to put into parentheses

parent teacher association an organization formed by the parents of schoolchildren and their teachers to advance better relations between them

par excellence (pär ek'sə läns') [Fr.] in the greatest degree of excellence; beyond comparison

parfait (pär'fã) *n.* [Fr., perfect] a frozen dessert of cream, eggs, syrup, etc. in a tall glass

pariah (par'ē ə, pə rī'ə) *n.* [< Tamil *paraiyan*] **1.** an outcast **2.** a member of one of the lowest social castes in India

parietal (pə rī'ə t'l) *adj.* [< L. *paries*, wall] *Anat.* of the walls of a cavity, etc.; esp., designating either of two bones forming part of the top and sides of the skull

parimutuel (par'ə myo͞o'cho͞o wəl) *n.* [Fr., mutual bet] a system of betting on races in which the winning bettors share the total amount bet, minus a percentage for the track operators, taxes, etc.

paring (pãar'iŋ) *n.* a thin piece or strip pared off

parish (par'ish) *n.* [< LGr. *paroikia*, diocese] **1.** a part of a diocese, under the charge of a priest or minister **2.** *a)* the members of a church congregation *b)* the area they live in **3.** a district of British local government **4.** in some provinces in Canada, a subdivision of a county

parish clerk an official appointed by a clergyman to perform certain duties in a parish

parish council a body elected to administer the affairs of a parish

parishioner (pə rish'ə nər) *n.* a member of a parish

parish register a book in which all the births, baptisms, marriages and deaths in a particular parish are recorded

parity (par'ə tē) *n.*, *pl.* **-ties** [< L. *par*,

equal] **1.** equality in power, value, etc. **2.** resemblance; similarity **3.** equivalence in value of a currency in terms of another country's currency

park (pärk) *n.* [< ML. *parricus*] **1.** a national park **2.** an area of public land for public recreation, usually with walks, playgrounds, etc. **3.** land with woods, lakes, etc., held as part of a private estate **4.** *Mil.* an area for storing and servicing vehicles, etc. —*vt.* **1.** to leave (a vehicle) in a certain place temporarily **2.** to manoeuvre (a vehicle) into a space for parking **3.** [Colloq.] to deposit in a certain place **4.** to enclose as in a park —**park oneself** [Colloq.] to sit down

parka (pär'kə) *n.* [Aleutian] a hip-length, hooded jacket

parkin (pär'kin) *n.* [< ?] a moist, spicy ginger cake

parking meter a coin-operated timing device at a parking space to show the length of time that a parked vehicle may occupy that space

parking ticket the notice of a fine incurred by a motorist in violation of parking laws

Parkinson's disease (pär'kin sənz) [< J. *Parkinson*] a brain disease characterized by a tremor and muscular rigidity

Parkinson's Law [< C. *Parkinson*] the idea, expressed facetiously as a law of economics, that work expands to fill the time allotted to it

parkland (pärk'land') *n.* **1.** an open expanse of grass with trees dotted about in it **2.** in the Prairie Provinces of Canada, the belt of land with rich soil lying between the open prairie and the northern forests

parky (pärk'ē) *adj.* **-ier, -iest** [Colloq.] chilly; cold: used esp. of the weather

Parl. 1. Parliament **2.** Parliamentary

parlance (pär'ləns) *n.* [< OFr. *parler*, speak] a style of speaking or writing

parley (pär'lē) *vi.* [< Fr. *parler*, speak] to confer, esp. with an enemy —*n.*, *pl.* **-leys** a conference; specif., with an enemy

parliament (pär'lə mənt) *n.* [see prec.] **1.** an official government council **2.** [P-] the national legislative body of Great Britain, composed of the House of Commons and the House of Lords **3.** [P-] a similar body in other countries

parliamentarian (pär'lə men täar'ē ən) *n.* a person skilled in parliamentary rules or debate

parliamentary (pär'lə men'tə rē) *adj.* **1.** of, like, or established by a parliament **2.** conforming to the rules of a parliament **3.** governed by a parliament

Parliamentary Private Secretary a member of parliament who helps the head of a government department

parlour (pär'lər) *n.* [see PARLEY] **1.** a living room **2.** a small, semi-private room in a hotel, etc. **3.** [Chiefly U.S.] a business establishment *[a billiard parlour]* U.S. sp. **parlor**

parlous (pär'ləs) *adj.* [ME., contr. of *perilous*] [Chiefly Archaic] perilous; full of danger

Parmesan (cheese) (pär′mə zan′) [< *Parma*, in Italy] a hard, dry Italian cheese usually grated for sprinkling on spaghetti, etc.

parochial (pə rō′kē əl) *adj.* [see PARISH] 1. of or in a parish 2. narrow; provincial —**paro′chialism** *n.*

parody (par′ə dē) *n.*, *pl.* **-dies** [< Gr. *para-*, beside + *ōidē*, song] 1. a literary or musical composition imitating the style of a writer or composer 2. a weak imitation —*vt.* **-died**, **-dying** to make a parody of —**par′odist** *n.*

parole (pə rōl′) *n.* [< LL. *parabola*, parable] 1. *a*) the release of a prisoner before his sentence has expired, on condition of future good behaviour *b*) the freedom thus granted 2. the condition of being on parole 3. word of honour —*vt.* **-roled′**, **-rol′ing** to release on parole —**on parole** at liberty under conditions of parole

parotid (pə rot′id) *adj.* [< Gr. *para-*, beside + *ous*, ear] designating or of either of the salivary glands below and in front of each ear

parotitis (par′ə tīt′əs) *n.* [< prec. & -ITIS] mumps

-parous (pər əs) [< L.] *a combining form meaning* bringing forth, bearing [*viviparous*]

paroxysm (par′ək siz′m) *n.* [< Gr. *para-*, beyond + *oxys*, sharp] 1. a sudden attack 2. a sudden outburst of laughter, rage, etc. —**par′oxys′mal** (-siz′m′l) *adj.*

parquet (pär′kā) *n.* [Fr. < MFr. *parc*, a park] a flooring of parquetry —*vt.* **-queted** (-kād), **-queting** (-kā in) to decorate the floor of (a room) with parquetry

PARQUETRY

parquetry (pär′kə trē) *n.* inlaid woodwork in geometric forms: used esp. in flooring

parr (pär) *n.* [< ?] a young salmon

parrakeet (par′ə kēt′) *n.* *alt. sp. of* PARAKEET

parricide (par′ə sīd′) *n.* [Fr. < L. *parricida*, murderer of a relative] 1. a person who murders his parent or another near relative 2. the act of a parricide —**par′rici′dal** *adj.*

parrot (par′ət) *n.* [Fr. dial. *perrot*] 1. a bird with a hooked bill and brightly coloured feathers: some parrots can learn to imitate human speech 2. a person who mechanically repeats the words or acts of others —*vt.* to repeat, esp. without understanding

parrot fever *same as* PSITTACOSIS

parry (par′ē) *vt.* **-ried, -rying** [< L. *parare*, prepare] 1. to ward off (a blow, etc.) 2. to turn aside (a question, etc.) —*n.*, *pl.* **-ries** 1. a warding off 2. an evasive reply

parse (pärz) *vt., vi.* **parsed, pars′ing** [< L. *pars (orationis)*, part (of speech)] [Now Rare] to separate (a sentence) into its parts, explaining the grammatical form, function, etc. of each part

parsec (pär′sek′) *n.* [PAR(ALLAX) + SEC(OND)²] a unit of measure of astronomical distance

Parsee, Parsi (pär sē′) *n.* [Per., a Persian] a member of a Zoroastrian religious sect in India descended from Persian refugees —**Par′seeism, Par′siism** *n.*

parsimony (pär′sə mə nē) *n.* [< L. *parcere*, spare] a tendency to be very careful in spending —**par′simo′nious** (-si mō′nē əs) *adj.* —**par′simo′niously** *adv.*

parsley (pärs′lē) *n.* [< Gr. *petros*, rock + *selinon*, celery] an umbelliferous plant with aromatic, curled leaves used to flavour or garnish some foods

parsnip (pär′snip) *n.* [< L. *pastinare*, dig up] 1. an umbelliferous plant with a long, thick, sweet, white root used as a vegetable 2. its root

parson (pär′s′n) *n.* [see PERSON] 1. a clergyman in charge of a parish 2. any clergyman

parsonage *n.* the dwelling provided by a church for the use of its parson

parson's nose the rump of a fowl

part (pärt) *n.* [< L. *pars*] 1. a division or portion of a whole 2. an essential, separable element [radio *parts*] 3. a certain amount but not all 4. a segment or organ as of the body 5. a share assigned or given; specif., *a*) duty [to do one's *part*] *b*) [usually *pl.*] ability [a man of *parts*] *c*) a role in a play *d*) *Music* any voice or instrument in an ensemble, or the score for it 6. a region; esp., [usually *pl.*] district 7. one of the sides in a transaction, dispute, etc. —*vt.* 1. to break or hold apart 2. to comb (the hair) so as to leave a parting 3. to break or divide into parts —*vi.* 1. to separate and go different ways 2. to cease associating 3. to go away 4. to break or divide into parts —*adj.* partial —*adv.* not fully; partly —**for one's part** as far as one is concerned —**for the most part** mostly —**in good part** good- naturedly —**in part** to some extent —**on the part of one** 1. as far as one is concerned 2. by or coming from one Also **on one's part** —**part and parcel** an essential part —**part with** to give up —**take someone's part** to side with someone

part. 1. participial 2. participle

partake (pär tāk′) *vi.* **-took′, -tak′en, -tak′ing** [< *part taker*] 1. to take part (in an activity) 2. to eat or drink, esp. with others (usually with *of*) 3. to have some of the qualities (*of*) —**partak′er** *n.*

parterre (pär tãər′) *n.* [Fr. < *par*, on + *terre*, earth] 1. an ornamental garden area 2. the pit of a theatre

part exchange a transaction in which used goods are taken as partial payment

parthenogenesis (pär′thə nō jen′ə sis) *n.* [< Gr. *parthenos*, virgin + *genesis*, origin] reproduction by the development of an unfertilized ovum, seed, or spore, as in certain insects, algae, etc.

Parthian shot (pär′thē ən) any hostile gesture made in leaving: Parthian cavalrymen shot at the enemy while retreating

partial (pär′shəl) *adj.* [< L. *pars*, part] 1. favouring one person, faction, etc. more than another 2. not complete —**partial to** fond of —**par′tial′ity** (-shē al′ə tē) —**par′tially** *adv.*

participant (pär tis′ə pənt) *n.* one who participates

participate (pär tis′ə pāt′) *vi.* -**pat′ed,** -**pat′ing** [< L. *pars*, part + *capere*, to take] to have or take a share with others (*in* an activity, etc.) —**partic′ipa′tion** *n.* —**partic′ipa′tor** *n.* —**partic′ipatory** *adj.*

participle (pär′tə sip′ʼl) *n.* [< L. *pars*, part + *capere*, to take] a verbal form having the qualities of both verb and adjective [*the beaten* path, *raving* mad] —**par′ticip′ial** *adj.*

particle (pär′ti kʼl) *n.* [< L. *pars*, part] 1. a tiny fragment or trace 2. *Gram.* a short, uninflected part of speech, as an article, preposition, etc. 3. *Physics* a piece of matter so small as to be considered without magnitude

parti-coloured (pär′tē kul′ərd) *adj.* [see PARTY] 1. having different colours in different parts 2. diversified

particular (pər tik′yoo lər) *adj.* [< L. *particula*, PARTICLE] 1. of or belonging to a single person, group, or thing 2. regarded separately; specific 3. unusual 4. hard to please; exacting —*n.* 1. a distinct fact, item, or instance 2. [*pl.*] a detailed account —**in particular** especially

particularity (pər tik′yoo lar′ə tē) *n.,* *pl.* -**ties** 1. *a)* individuality *b)* attention to detail 2. *a)* a peculiarity *b)* a minute detail

particularize (pər tik′yoo lə rīz′) *vt.* -**ized′, -iz′ing** to specify; itemize —*vi.* to give particulars or details

particularly *adv.* 1. especially 2. specifically 3. in detail

parting (pärt′iŋ) *adj.* 1. given, spoken, etc. at parting 2. departing 3. dividing; separating —*n.* 1. the dividing line made by combing the hair in different directions 2. a breaking or separating 3. a leave-taking or departure

partisan (pärt′ə zən) *n.* [< L. *pars*, PART] 1. a strong supporter of a side, party, or person 2. a guerrilla fighter —*adj.* of or like a partisan Also sp. **par′ti-zan′** —**par′tisan′ship** *n.*

partition (pär tish′ən) *n.* [< L. *partitio*] 1. division into parts 2. something that divides, as a wall separating rooms 3. a part or section —*vt.* to divide into parts

partitive (pärt′ə tiv) *adj.* [see PART] 1. making a division 2. *Gram.* restricting to a part of a whole —*n.* a partitive word

partly (pärt′lē) *adv.* in part; not fully

partner (pärt′nər) *n.* [< *parcener*, joint inheritor] one who takes part in an activity with another or others; specif., *a)* one of two or more persons heading the same business enterprise *b)* a husband or wife *c)* either of two persons dancing together *d)* either of two players on the same side or team —*vt.* 1. to join (others) together as partners 2. to be a partner for

partnership *n.* 1. the relationship of partners 2. *a)* an association of partners in a business *b)* the contract for this

part of speech any of the traditional classes of words of a given language, variously based on form, function, meaning, etc.: in English, noun, verb, adjective, adverb, pronoun, preposition, conjunction, and interjection

partook (pär took′) *pt.* of PARTAKE

partridge (pär′trij) *n.* [< Gr. *perdix*] a quaillike game bird with an orange-brown head, greyish neck, and rust-coloured tail

part song a song for several voices singing in harmony, usually unaccompanied: also **part′-song**′ *n.*

part-time (pärt′tīm′) *adj.* of, or engaged in work, study, etc. for periods of less time than in a full schedule —**part′tim′-er** *n.*

part time as a part-time employee, student, etc.

parturient (pär tyoor′ē ənt) *adj.* [< L. *parturire*, to be in labour] 1. giving birth or about to give birth to young 2. of childbirth

parturition (pär′tyoo rish′ən) *n.* [< see prec.] a giving birth; childbirth

partway (pärt′wā′) *adv.* to some point, degree, etc.

party (pär′tē) *n.,* *pl.* -**ties** [< L. *pars,* part] 1. a gathering for social entertainment 2. any group acting together to accomplish something [a surveying *party*] 3. a group working to promote certain principles of government 4. a participant in an action, plan, etc. (often with *to*) [a *party* to the plan] 5. either of the persons concerned in a legal matter 6. [Colloq.] a person —*adj.* of, or for a party

party line 1. a single circuit connecting two or more telephone users with the exchange 2. the policies of a political party

party wall a wall separating and common to two buildings or properties

par value the value of a stock, bond, etc. fixed at the time of its issue; face value

parvenu (pär′və nyoo′) *n.* [Fr. < L. *parvenire*, arrive] a newly-rich person who is considered an upstart —*adj.* like a parvenu

pas (pä) *n.,* *pl.* **pas** (päz) [Fr. < L. *passus*, step] a step or series of steps in dancing: in ballet, a **pas de deux** is a dance for two

Pasch (pask) *n.* [< Heb. *pesach*, Passover] *same as:* 1. PASSOVER 2. EASTER —**pas′-chal** (pas′kʼl) *adj.*

pasha (pä′shə) *n.* [Turk. *pasha*] formerly,

in Turkey, a title of honour placed after the name

pas op (pas′op) *interj.* [< Afrik.] [S Afr.] beware

pasqueflower (pask′flou′ər) *n.* [< MFr. *passer*, pass + *fleur*, flower] a kind of anemone with large, purple flowers

pass[1] (päs) *n.* [see PACE[1]] a narrow passage or opening, esp. between mountains; gap; defile

pass[2] *vi.* [< L. *passus*, a step] 1. to go forward, through, or out 2. to extend; lead 3. to go or be conveyed from one place, condition, possession, etc. to another 4. *a*) to cease *b*) to go away; depart 5. to die (usually with *away*, *on*) 6. to go by or past 7. to elapse [*an hour passed*] 8. to make a way (with *through* or *by*) 9. to be accepted without question 10. to be approved, as by a legislative body 11. *a*) to go through an examination, etc. successfully *b*) to be barely acceptable as a substitute 12. to take place; happen 13. to give a judgment, sentence, etc. 14. to be pronounced [*the judgment passed against us*] 15. to decline a chance to bid, play, etc. 16. *Sports* to make a pass of the ball, etc. —*vt.* 1. to go by, beyond, past, over, or through; specif., *a*) to leave behind *b*) to undergo (usually with *through*) *c*) to go through (a test, course, etc.) successfully *d*) to surpass 2. to cause or allow to go or move; specif., *a*) to guide into position [*to pass a rope around a stake*] *b*) to ratify, enact, or approve *c*) to spend (time) *d*) to excrete 3. to make move from place to place or person to person; specif., *a*) to hand to another *b*) to put into circulation *c*) to throw or kick (a ball, etc.) from one player to another 4. to give (an opinion or judgment) —*n.* 1. an act of passing 2. the successful completion of a course in university, etc. esp. without honours 3. condition or situation [*a strange pass*] 4. *a*) a ticket, etc. giving one free entry or exit, reduced fares, etc. *b*) *Mil.* a written leave of absence for a brief period 5. a motion of the hands 6. a tentative attempt 7. [Slang] an overfamiliar attempt to embrace or kiss 8. *Sports a*) an intentional transfer of the ball, etc. to another player during play *b*) a thrust in fencing —**come** (or **bring**) **to pass** to (cause to) happen —**pass for** to be accepted or looked upon as [*it passes for the real thing*] —**pass off** 1. to cease 2. to take place 3. to be or cause to be accepted as genuine, etc., esp. through deceit —**pass out** 1. to faint 2. to complete a course of military training 3. to distribute —**pass over** to disregard; ignore —**pass up** [Colloq.] to refuse, or let go by an opportunity —**pass′er** *n.*

passable *adj.* 1. adequate; fair 2. that can be passed, travelled over, or crossed —**pass′ably** *adv.*

passage (pas′ij) *n.* [see PASS[2]] 1. a way or means of passing; road, passageway etc. 2. a portion of a book, etc. 3. a journey, esp. by water 4. passenger accommodation, esp. on a ship 5. the

act of passing; specif., *a*) migration *b*) transition *c*) the enactment of a law 6. permission, right, or a chance to pass 7. an interchange, as of blows or words

passageway *n.* a narrow way for passage, as a hall, corridor, or alley

passbook (päs′book′) *n.* a book recording deposits and withdrawals for a bank, building society, etc.

pass degree an ordinary degree awarded at a university, without honours

passé (pä′sā) *adj.* [Fr., past] 1. outof-date; old-fashioned 2. rather old

passenger (pas′ən jər) *n.* [< OFr. *passage*, PASSAGE] 1. a person travelling in a vehicle 2. one who does not participate as fully as others in the work of a team

passe-partout (pas′pär too′) *n.* [Fr., passes everywhere] 1. a picture mounting using gummed paper 2. that which allows passage everywhere 3. a passkey

passer-by (päs′ər bī′) *n., pl.* **pass′ers-by′** a person who passes by

passerine (pas′ə rīn′) *adj.* [< L. *passer*, a sparrow] of the order of perching songbirds to which many birds belong —*n.* a bird of this order

‡**passim** (pas′im) *adv.* [L.] in various parts (of a book, etc.)

passing (päs′iŋ) *adj.* 1. going by, beyond, etc. 2. momentary 3. incidental —*n.* the act of one that passes; specif., death —**in passing** 1. casually 2. incidentally

passion (pash′ən) *n.* [< L. *pati*, suffer] 1. any emotion, as hate, grief, love, etc. 2. extreme emotion as rage, fury, enthusiasm, lust, etc. 3. the object of strong desire or fondness 4. [P-] the suffering of Jesus during the Crucifixion or after the Last Supper —**pas′sionless** *adj.*

passionate *adj.* 1. readily aroused sexually 2. intense; ardent 3. having or showing strong emotions 4. hottempered —**pas′sionately** *adv.*

passionflower *n.* [< supposed resemblance of parts of the flowers to crown of thorns] any of a number of tropical plants with variously coloured flowers and egglike fruit (**passion fruit**)

Passion play a religious play representing the Passion of Jesus

passive (pas′iv) *adj.* [< L. *pati*, suffer] 1. inactive 2. not resisting; submissive 3. acted upon without acting in return 4. *Gram.* denoting the voice of a verb whose subject receives the action —*n.* *Gram.* the passive voice —**pas′sively** *adv.* —**passivity** (pa siv′ə tē) *n.*

passive resistance opposition, as to a government, by nonviolent acts as fasting, public demonstrations, etc.

passkey (päs′kē′) *n.* 1. *same as: a*) MASTER KEY *b*) SKELETON KEY 2. any private key

Passover (päs′ō′vər) *n.* a Jewish holiday commemorating the ancient Hebrews′ deliverance from slavery in Egypt

passport (päs′pôrt′) *n.* [< Fr. *passer*, pass & *port*, port] 1. a government document issued to a citizen for travel abroad, certifying his identity and citizenship **2.** anything making a person accepted

password *n.* a secret word that must be uttered by someone wishing to pass a guard

past (päst) *rare pp. of* PASS² —*adj.* **1.** gone by; ended **2.** of a former time **3.** just gone by [the *past* week] **4.** having served formerly [a *past* chairman] **5.** *Gram.* indicating a time gone by —*n.* **1.** time gone by **2.** the history or former life of a person, group, etc. **3.** *Gram.* the past tense —*prep.* **1.** beyond in amount or degree **2.** beyond the extent, power, etc. of [*past* belief] —*adv.* to and beyond —**not put it past someone** to believe someone is not unlikely (to do a certain thing) —**past it** [Colloq.] incompetent because of age, etc.

pasta (pas'tə) *n.* [It.] **1.** dough made as of semolina and dried in the form of spaghetti, macaroni, etc. **2.** spaghetti, macaroni, etc. cooked in some way

paste (päst) *n.* [< Gr. *pastē,* barley porridge] **1.** any soft, moist, smooth-textured substance [*toothpaste,* almond *paste*] **2.** a mixture of flour or starch, water, resin, etc., used as an adhesive **3.** dough for making rich pastry **4.** a hard, brilliant glass for making artificial gems **5.** the moistened clay used to make pottery —*vt.* **past'ed, past'ing** to fasten or make stick as with paste

pasteboard *n.* a stiff material made of layers of paper pasted together or of pressed paper pulp

pastel (pas't'l) *n.* [Fr. < LL. *pasta,* paste] **1.** a crayon of ground colouring matter **2.** a picture drawn with such crayons **3.** a soft, pale shade of any colour —*adj.* soft and pale: said of colours

PASTERN

pastern (pas'tərn) *n.* [< MFr. *pasture,* tether] the part of a horse's foot between the fetlock and the hoof

pasteurization (pas'tər ī zā'shən) *n.* a method of destroying bacteria in milk, etc. by heating the liquid to a specified temperature for a specified time

pasteurize (pas'tə rīz) *vt.* **-ized', -iz'ing** [< Louis *Pasteur*] to subject (milk, etc.) to pasteurization —**pas'teuriz'er** *n.*

pastiche (pas tēsh') *n.* [Fr.] **1.** an artistic composition made up of bits from various sources **2.** such a composition intended to imitate another artist's style

pastille (pas'təl) *n.* [< L. *pastillus,* lozenge] **1.** a lozenge containing medicine,

flavouring, etc. **2.** a pellet of aromatic paste, burned for fumigating Also **pas'til**

pastime (päs'tīm') *n.* a way of spending spare time pleasantly

past master 1. an expert **2.** a former master, as in a lodge or guild —**past mistress fem.**

pastor (päs'tər) *n.* [< L., a shepherd] a clergyman in charge of a congregation

pastoral *adj.* [< L. *pastor,* a shepherd] **1.** of rural life idealized as peaceful, simple, and natural **2.** of a pastor or his duties **3.** of shepherds or their work, etc. —*n.* **1.** a poem, play, etc. having an idealized pastoral setting **2.** a letter from a bishop to those in his charge —**pas'torally** *adv.*

pastorale (pas'tə rä'lē) *n.* [It.] *Music* a composition suggesting rural scenes or life

pastoralist (päs'tər ə list) *n.* [Aust.] a rancher; grazier

pastorate *n.* **1.** the position, rank, or term of office of a pastor **2.** a group of pastors

past participle à participle used: *a)* to indicate completed action or a time or state gone by *b)* as an adjective (as *grown* in "a grown man")

past perfect 1. a tense indicating an action as completed before a specified time in the past **2.** a verb form in this tense (Ex.: had gone)

pastry (pās'trē) *n., pl.* **-tries** [see PASTE] **1.** flour dough made with fat, for pie crust, etc. **2.** foods made with this

pasturage (päs'tyoor ij) *n.* same as PASTURE

pasture (päs'chər) *n.* [< L. *pascere,* to feed] **1.** grass or other growing plants used as food by grazing animals **2.** ground suitable for grazing —*vt.* **-tured, -turing** to put (cattle, etc.) out to graze in a pasture —**put out to pasture** to cause to retire from work

pasty¹ (päs'tē) *adj.* **-ier, -iest 1.** of or like paste **2.** unhealthy-looking [*pasty-faced*] —**past'iness** *n.*

pasty² (pas'tē) *n., pl.* **pas'ties** [< PASTE] pastry folded over a filling, often of meat and potatoes

pat¹ (pat) *adj.* [prob. < ff.] **1.** apt; timely **2.** exactly suitable **3.** so glibly plausible as to seem contrived —*adv.* in a pat manner —**have (down) pat** [Colloq.] to know or have memorized thoroughly —**stand pat** to stick to an opinion, etc.

pat² *n.* [prob. echoic] **1.** a gentle tap or stroke with a flat surface **2.** the sound made by this **3.** a small lump, as of butter —*vt.* **pat'ted, pat'ting 1.** to tap or stroke gently with the hand or a flat surface **2.** to shape, apply, etc. by patting

pat. 1. patent **2.** patented

patch (pach) *n.* [prob. < OFr. *pieche,* PIECE] **1.** a piece of material to cover or mend a hole or to strengthen a weak spot **2.** a dressing for a wound **3.** a shield worn over an injured eye **4.** a differing part of a surface area [*patches* of blue sky] **5.** a small plot of ground **6.** a scrap; remnant **7.** [Colloq.] the area patrolled by a policeman **8.** [Colloq.]

a stage; period, etc. [a bad *patch*] —*vt.*
1. to put a patch on 2. to put together
crudely (often with *up* or *together*) 3.
Electronics to connect electrical circuits
temporarily —**not a patch on** not nearly
as good as —**patch up** to end or settle
(differences, a quarrel, etc.) —**patch'er** *n.*

patchwork *n.* 1. anything made of odd,
miscellaneous parts 2. needlework, as a
quilt, made of odd patches of cloth

patchy *adj.* 1. irregular in quality,
occurrence, etc. 2. having patches

pate (pāt) *n.* [< ?] [Archaic Colloq.]
1. the head 2. the brain

pâté (pa'tā) *n.* [Fr.] 1. a meat paste
2. a pie

pâté de foie gras (pa tä'də fwä'grä')
[Fr.] a paste made of the livers of
fattened geese

patella (pətel'ə) *n., pl.* **-las, -lae** (-ē)
[L., a pan] kneecap —**patel'lar** *adj.*

paten (pat''n) *n.* [see prec.] a metal
plate, esp. for the Eucharistic bread

patent (pāt''nt) *adj.* [< L. *patere*, be
open] 1. open to public inspection 2.
obvious; evident [a *patent* lie] 3. *a*)
protected by a patent *b*) of or having
to do with patents *c*) made or sold under
a patent —*n.* 1. an official document
granting the exclusive right to produce
or sell an invention, process, etc. 2. *a*)
the right so granted *b*) the thing so protected
—*vt.* 1. to grant a patent to or for 2.
to get a patent for —**pat'entee'** *n.* —**pat'en-**
tor *n.*

patent leather leather with a hard, glossy
finish

patent medicine a trademarked medical
preparation obtainable without a prescription

patent office the government office
which grants letters patent

pater (pāt'ər) *n.* [L.] [Colloq.] father

paternal (pətur'n'l) *adj.* [< L. *pater*,
father] 1. of or like a father 2. inherited
from a father 3. on the father's side
of the family —**pater'nally** *adv.*

paternity *n.* 1. the state of being a father
2. male parentage 3. origin in general

paternoster (pat'ərnos'tər) *n.* [L., our
father] the Lord's Prayer, esp. in Latin

path (päth) *n.* [OE. *pæth*] 1. a way worn
by footsteps 2. a walk for use by people
on foot 3. a course along which something
moves 4. a course of conduct

pathetic (pəthet'ik) *adj.* [< Gr. *pathos*,
suffering] 1. arousing pity, sympathy,
etc.; pitiful 2. pitifully unsuccessful, etc.
—**pathet'ically** *adv.*

pathetic fallacy the ascribing of human
feelings, etc. to nonhuman things (Ex.:
the angry sea)

-pathic (path'ik) *a combining form used
to form adjectives from nouns ending in*
-PATHY

pathology (pəthol'əjē) *n., pl.* **-gies** [<
< Gr.: see ff. & -LOGY] 1. the branch
of medicine dealing with the nature of
disease, esp. with the structural and
functional changes 2. all the symptoms

of a particular disease —**pathological**
(path'əloj'ik'l) *adj.* —**pathol'ogist** *n.*

pathos (pā'thos) *n.* [Gr., suffering] the
quality in something experienced or
observed which arouses feelings of pity,
sorrow, sympathy, or compassion

pathway (päth'wā') *n.* same as PATH

-pathy (pəthē) [< Gr. *pathos*, suffering]
a combining form meaning: 1. feeling
[*antipathy*] 2. disease [*osteopathy*]

patience (pā'shəns) *n.* [< L. *pati*, suffer]
1. the state, quality, or fact of being patient
2. any of many card games, played by
one person

patient *adj.* [< L. *pati*, suffer] 1. enduring
pain, trouble, etc. without complaint 2.
calmly tolerating insult, delay, confusion,
etc. 3. showing calm endurance [a *patient*
face] 4. diligent; persevering —*n.* a
person receiving medical care —**pa'tiently**
adv.

patina (pat'in ə) *n.* [Fr. < It.] 1. a fine
greenish crust formed by oxidation on
bronze or copper 2. any surface change
due to age, as on old wood

patio (pat'ē ō',) *n., pl.* **-tios** [Sp.] 1. a
courtyard open to the sky, as in Spanish
and Spanish-American architecture 2. a
paved area, as one next to a house, for
outdoor lounging, dining, etc.

patois (pat'wä) *n., pl.* **-ois** (-wäz) [Fr.]
1. a form of a language differing from
the accepted standard, as a local dialect
2. jargon

pat. pend. patent pending

patrial (pā'trē əl) *n.* [< L. *patria*, native
land] a person who has the right of
residence in a given country because his
parents or grandparents were born there

patriarch (pā'trē ärk') *n.* [< Gr. *patēr*,
father + *archein*, to rule] 1. the father
and ruler of a family or tribe: in the
Bible, Abraham, Isaac, Jacob, and Jacob's
sons were patriarchs 2. a man of great
age and dignity 3. [*often* P-] *a*) R.C.Ch.
the Pope or any of certain Eastern bishops
b) *Orthodox Eastern Ch.* the highest-
ranking bishop at Constantinople, Jerusalem, Moscow, etc. —**pa'triar'chal** *adj.*

patriarchate *n.* the position, rank, etc.
of a patriarch

patriarchy *n., pl.* **-chies** a form of social
organization in which the father is the
head of the family, descent being traced
through the male line

patrician (pətrish'ən) *n.* [< L. *pater*,
father] 1. in ancient Rome, a member
of the nobility 2. an aristocrat —*adj.*
1. of or characteristic of patricians 2. noble

patricide (pat'rə sīd') *n.* [see PARRICIDE]
1. the act of killing one's father 2. one
who kills his father

patrimony (pat'rə mə nē) *n., pl.* **-nies** [<
L. *pater*, father] 1. property inherited
from one's father or ancestors 2. anything
inherited; heritage —**pat'rimo'nial** (-mō'-
nē əl) *adj.*

patriot (pat'rē ət) *n.* [< Fr. < Gr. *patris*,
fatherland] a person who loves and
zealously supports his own country —**pa'-**

triot′ic· (-ot′ik) *adj.* —pa′triot′ically *adv.*
—pa′triotism *n.*

patrol (pə trōl′) *vt., vi.* -trolled′, -trol′-
ling [< OFr. *patouiller*, paddle] to make
a regular, repeated circuit of, in guarding
—*n.* 1. a patrolling 2. a person or group
patrolling 3. a group of ships, aircraft,
etc. used in patrolling 4. a subdivision
of a troop of Boy Scouts or Girl Guides

patron (pā′trən) *n.* [< L. *pater*, father]
1. a protector; benefactor 2. one who
sponsors and supports some person,
activity, etc. 3. a regular customer —pa′-
troness *n.fem.*

patronage (pa′trən ij) *n.* 1. support,
sponsorship, etc. given by a patron 2.
condescension 3. *a)* clientele; customers
b) business; trade 4. *a)* the power to
appoint to office or grant political favours
b) the offices, etc. thus distributed 5.
the legal right to present a clergyman
to an Anglican benefice

patronize *vt.* -ized′, -iz′ing 1. to treat
kindly but as an inferior 2. to sponsor;
support 3. to be a regular customer of
(a shop, etc.)

patronizing *adj.* condescending

patron saint a saint looked upon as
the special guardian of a person, place,
institution, etc.

patronymic (pat′rə nim′ik) *n.* [< Gr.
patēr, father + *onyma*, name] a name
showing descent from a given person (e.g.,
Stevenson, son of Steven)

patter[1] (pat′ər) *vi.* [< PAT[2]] to make,
or move so as to make, a patter —*n.*
a series of quick, light taps

patter[2] *vt., vi.* [< PATERNOSTER] to speak
rapidly or glibly —*n.* 1. glib, rapid speech,
as of salesmen, comedians, etc. 2. language
peculiar to a group, class, etc.

pattern (pat′ərn) *n.* [< OFr. *patron*,
patron] 1. a design [*wallpaper patterns*]
2. a model, plan, etc. used in making
things 3. a regular way of acting
[*behaviour patterns*] 4. a person or thing
worthy of imitation 5. a sample —*vt.*
to make, do, or plan in imitation of a
model or pattern (with *on, upon,* or *after*)

patty (pat′ē) *n., pl.* -ties [Fr. *pâté*, pie]
1. a small pie 2. [U.S.] a small, flat
cake of minced meat, etc.

paucity (pô′sə tē) *n.* [< L. *paucus*, few]
1. fewness; small number 2. scarcity;
insufficiency

Pauline (pôl′īn) *adj.* of the Apostle Paul,
his writings, or doctrines

paunch (pônch) *n.* [< L. *pantex*, belly]
the abdomen, or belly; esp., a potbelly
—paunch′y *adj.*

pauper (pô′pər) *n.* [L.] 1. an extremely
poor person 2. one who lives on charity
—pau′perism *n.*

pause (pôz) *n.* [< Gr. *pauein*, to stop]
1. a temporary stop or rest 2. hesitation;
delay 3. *Music* a mark over a note showing
that it is lengthened —*vi.* paused, paus′-
ing 1. to make a pause; stop; hesitate
2. to linger (*on* or *upon*) —**give one pause**
to make one hesitant

pavane (pav′ən) *n.* [< It. *Pavana*, Paduan

(dance)] 1. a slow, stately court dance
performed by couples 2. the music for
this Also **pavan**

pave (pāv) *vt.* paved, pav′ing [< L. *pavire*,
beat] to cover the surface of (a road,
etc.), as with concrete, asphalt, etc. —**pave
the way (for)** to prepare the way (for)
—pav′er *n.*

pavement (pāv′mənt) *n.* a paved surface,
as of concrete, brick, etc.; specif., a paved
path for pedestrians

pavilion (pə vil′yən) *n.* [< L. *papilio*, tent]
1. a building attached to a sports ground
in which players change, etc. 2. a building,
often partly open, for exhibits, etc., as
at a fair or park 3. a large tent, usually
with a peaked top

paving (pā′viŋ) *n.* 1. a pavement 2.
material for a pavement

paw (pô) *n.* [< OFr. *poue*] 1. the foot
of a four-footed animal having claws 2.
[Colloq.] a hand —*vt., vi.* 1. to touch,
dig, strike, etc. with the paws or feet
2. to handle clumsily or overintimately

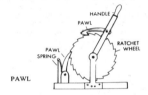

pawl (pôl) *n.* [akin ? to Du. *pal*, pole]
a device as a hinged tongue which engages
the notches of a ratchet wheel, preventing
backward motion

pawn[1] (pôn) *n.* [< MFr. *pan*] 1. anything
given as security, as for a debt; pledge
2. the state of being pledged —*vt.* 1.
to put in pawn 2. to stake or risk

pawn[2] *n.* [< ML. *pedo*, foot soldier] 1.
a chessman of the lowest value 2. one
used to advance another's purposes

pawnbroker *n.* one who lends money
at interest on personal belongings left with
him as security —pawn′bro′king *n.*

pawnshop *n.* a pawnbroker's shop

pawpaw (pô′pô′) *n.* same as PAPAW

pax (paks) *n.* [< L., peace] the kiss of
peace —*interj.* [Slang] a call signalling
a desire for an end to hostilities

pay (pā) *vt.* paid, pay′ing [< L. *pacare*,
pacify] 1. to give to (a person) what
is due, as for goods or services 2. to
give (what is due) in return, as for goods
or services 3. to settle (a debt, etc.)
4. *a)* to give (a compliment, etc.) *b)* to
make (a visit, etc.) 5. to yield [*this job
pays £50*] 6. to be profitable to [*it will
pay him to listen*] —*vi.* 1. to give due
compensation 2. to be profitable —*n.*
1. a paying or being paid 2. money paid;
esp., wages or salary —**in the pay of**
employed by —**pay back** 1. to repay
2. to get even with —**pay for** 1. to undergo
punishment because of 2. to atone for

—**pay off** 1. to pay all that is owed 2. to turn out to be profitable —**pay out** 1. to give out (money, etc.) 2. to let out a rope, cable, etc. gradually —**pay up** to pay in full —**pay′er** n.

payable adj. 1. that can be paid 2. that is to be paid (on a specified date); due

pay-as-you-earn a system by which income tax is paid by employers directly to the government: also **P.A.Y.E.**

pay-bed n. a hospital bed whose occupant is not treated under the National Health Service

paycheque n. a cheque in payment of wages, etc.

payee (pā ē′) n. the person to whom a cheque, note, money, etc. is payable

paying guest same as LODGER: also **P.G.**

payload n. 1. a cargo, or the part of a cargo, producing income: also **pay load** 2. the warhead of a ballistic missile, etc.

paymaster n. the official in charge of paying employees

Paymaster General the government official appointed to make payments on behalf of various government departments

payment n. 1. a paying or being paid 2. something paid 3. penalty or reward

payoff n. 1. payment, settlement, or reckoning 2. [Colloq.] a bribe 3. [Colloq.] an unexpected climax

payola (pā ō′lə) n. [Slang] the paying of bribes for commercial advantage, as to a disc jockey for promoting a song unfairly

pay packet 1. the envelope containing an employee's wages 2. the wages themselves

payroll n. a list of employees to be paid, with the amount due to each

Pb [L. plumbum] Chem. lead

P.C. 1. Police Constable 2. Privy Councillor 3. [Canad.] Progressive Conservative

p.c. 1. percent: also **pct.** 2. postcard

Pd Chem. palladium

pd. paid

P.D.S.A. People's Dispensary for Sick Animals

P.D.T. [U.S. & Canad.] Pacific Daylight Time

P.E. Physical Education

pea (pē) n., pl. **peas**, archaic **pease** [< ME. pese, a pea, taken as pl.: ult. < Gr. pison] 1. a climbing plant with green seedpods 2. its small, round seed, eaten as a vegetable —**as like as two peas (in a pod)** exactly alike

peace (pēs) n. [< L. pax] 1. freedom from war 2. a treaty or agreement to end war 3. freedom from public disturbance 4. harmony; concord 5. serenity; calm; quiet —**at peace** free from war, conflict, etc. —**hold (or keep) one's peace** to be silent —**keep the peace** to maintain law and order —**make peace** to end hostilities

peaceable adj. 1. fond of or promoting peace 2. peaceful —**peace′ably** adv.

peaceful adj. 1. not quarrelsome 2. free from disturbance; calm 3. of or characteristic of a time of peace —**peace′fully** adv.

peacemaker n. a person who makes peace, as by settling the quarrels of others —**peace′mak′ing** n., adj.

peace offering [Heb. shelem, thank-offering] 1. an offering made to bring about peace 2. an offering in thanksgiving to God

peace pipe same as CALUMET

peacetime n. a time of peace

peach¹ (pēch) n. [< L. Persicum (malum), Persian (apple)] 1. a tree with round, juicy, orange-yellow fruit with a fuzzy skin 2. its fruit 3. the colour of this fruit 4. [Slang] any person or thing well liked

peach² vi. [< IMPEACH] [Old Slang] to inform against another

peach brandy [S Afr.] a coarse brandy made from fermented peaches

peachy adj. -ier, -iest peachlike, as in colour or texture

peacock (pē′kok′) n. [< L. pavo, peacock] the male of a species of peafowls, with a long showy tail which can be spread out like a fan —**pea′hen′** n.fem.

pea green a light yellowish green

pea jacket [< Du. pijjekker] a hip-length, heavy woollen coat worn by seamen

peak¹ (pēk) n. [var. of pike (summit)] 1. a pointed end or top, as of a cap, roof, etc. 2. a) the summit of a mountain ending in a point b) a mountain with such a summit 3. the highest point or degree —adj. maximum [peak production] —vt., vi. to come or cause to come to a peak

peak² vi. [< ?] to become sickly; waste away; droop

peaked (pēkt) adj. 1. pointed 2. same as PEAKY

peak hour the time at which a maximum occurs, either in the amount of traffic or the demand for gas, electricity, etc.

peak load the maximum demand for electricity in a power station

peaky adj. -ier, -iest [< PEAK²] thin; sickly

peal (pēl) n. [< ME. apele, appeal] 1. the loud ringing of a bell or bells 2. a set of bells 3. any loud, prolonged sound, as of laughter —vt., vi. to resound; ring

PEANUT PLANT

peanut (pē′nut′) *n.* 1. a trailing plant with brittle pods ripening underground and containing edible seeds 2. the pod or its seed 3. [*pl.*] [Slang] a trifling sum
pear (pãər) *n.* [< L. *pirum*] 1. a tree with soft, juicy fruit 2. its fruit with a narrow top and rounded base
pearl (purl) *n.* [ult. < L. *perna*, a sea mussel] 1. a smooth, hard, usually white or bluish-grey, roundish growth formed around a foreign body within the shell of some oysters and other molluscs: it is used as a gem 2. *same as* MOTHER-OF-PEARL 3. anything pearllike in size, beauty, etc. —*vt.* 1. to decorate with pearls 2. to make round, esp. barley, etc. —*vi.* to fish for pearl-bearing molluscs —*adj.* 1. of or having pearls 2. like a pearl in shape or colour —**pearl′er** *n.* —**pearl′iness** *n.* —**pearl′y** *adj.*
pearl barley barley seed rubbed down into small, round grains, used esp. in soups and stews: also **pearled barley**
pearl diver (or **fisher**) a person who dives for pearl-bearing molluscs
pearl grey a pale, bluish grey
Pearly Gates [Colloq.] the gates of heaven: cf. Rev. 21:21
pearly king the London costermonger whose ceremonial clothes display many pearl buttons —**pearly queen**
peasant (pez′′nt) *n.* [< LL. *pagus*, district] any person of the class of small farmers or of farm labourers, as in Europe or Asia
peasantry *n.* peasants collectively
pease (pēz) *n.* 1. *pl.* **peas′es, peas′en** [Obs.] a pea 2. *archaic pl. of* PEA
peasecod, peascod (pēz′kod′) *n.* [Archaic] the pod of the pea plant
pease pudding a dish of boiled split peas
peasouper (pē′sōōp′ər) *n.* 1. [Colloq.] a very thick fog 2. [Canad. Derog.] a French Canadian
peat (pēt) *n.* [< ML. *peta*, piece of turf] 1. partly decayed plant matter found in ancient bogs 2. a dried block of this used as fuel —**peat′y** *adj.*
peat bog marshland whose foundation is peat
peat moss 1. *same as* SPHAGNUM 2. peat composed of residues of mosses, used as a mulch
pebble (peb′′l) *n.* [< OE. *papol(stan)*, pebble (stone)] a small stone worn smooth and round, as by the action of water —**peb′bly** *adj.*
pebble dash a mortar containing pebbles used for surfacing exterior walls
peccadillo (pek′ə dil′ō) *n., pl.* **-loes, -los** [< Sp. < L. *peccare*, to sin] a slight fault
peccary (pek′ər ē) *n.* [< AmSp. name] a greyish, piglike animal of N and S America
peck[1] (pek) *vt.* [< ME. *picken*, pick] 1. to strike with a pointed object, as a beak 2. to make by doing this 3. to pick up or get by pecking —*vi.* to make strokes as with a beak —*n.* 1. a stroke so made, as with the beak 2. a mark made, as by pecking 3. [Colloq.] a quick kiss —**peck at** [Colloq.] to eat very little of

peck[2] *n.* [< OFr. *pek*] 1. a unit of dry measure equal to 1/4 bushel, eight quarts or 9.09 litres 2. [Colloq.] a large amount
pecker *n.* in **keep one's pecker up** [Colloq.] do not become depressed or discouraged
peckish *adj.* [Colloq.] somewhat hungry
pectin (pek′tin) *n.* [< Gr. *pēktos*, congealed] a water-soluble carbohydrate obtained from certain ripe fruits, which yields a gel that is the basis of jams
pectoral (pek′tər əl) *adj.* [< L. *pectus*, breast] 1. of or located in or on the breast or chest 2. worn on the chest or breast —*n.* a pectoral fin or muscle
pectoral fin either of a pair of fins just behind the head of a fish
peculate (pek′yoo lāt′) *vt., vi.* **-lat′ed, -lat′ing** [< L. *peculari*] to embezzle (money, etc.) —**pec′ula′tion** *n.* —**pec′ula′tor** *n.*
peculiar (pi kyool′ē ər) *adj.* [< L. *peculium*, private property] 1. odd; strange 2. particular; special 3. of only one person, thing, group, etc. —**pecul′iarly** *adv.*
peculiarity (pi kyoo′lē ar′ə tē) *n.* 1. a being peculiar 2. *pl.* **-ties** something that is peculiar, as a trait
pecuniary (pi kyoo′nē ər ē) *adj.* [< L. *pecunia*, money] 1. of or involving money 2. involving a money penalty, or fine —**pecu′niarily** *adv.*
pedagogue (ped′ə gog′) *n.* [< Gr. *pais* child + *agein*, to lead] a teacher; often specif., a pedantic teacher
pedagogy (ped′ə goj′ē) *n.* the art or science of teaching; esp., instruction in teaching methods —**ped′agog′ic, ped′agog′ical** *adj.*
pedal (ped′′l) *n.* [< L. *pes*, foot] a lever operated by the foot to transmit motion, as in a bicycle, or to change the volume of an organ, etc. —*adj.* of the foot or feet —*vt., vi.* **-alled, -alling** to operate by a pedal or pedals
pedalo (ped′ə lō′) *n., pl.* **-os** a small watercraft with a paddle wheel propelled by foot pedals
pedant (ped′ənt) *n.* [see PEDAGOGUE] 1. a person who emphasizes trivial points of learning 2. a narrow-minded teacher who insists on exact adherence to rules —**pedantic** (pi dan′tik) *adj.* —**pedan′tically** *adv.*
pedantry (ped′ən trē) *n., pl.* **-ries** 1. the qualities, practices, etc. of a pedant 2. adherence to rules
peddle (ped′′l) *vi.* **-dled, -dling** [< ? ME. *ped*, basket] to go from place to place selling small articles —*vt.* to carry from place to place and offer for sale
-pede (pēd) [< L.] *a combining form meaning* foot or feet [centipede]
pederasty (ped′ə ras′tē) *n.* [< Gr. *pais*, boy + *eran*, to love] sodomy between males, esp. by a man with a boy: also sp. **paed′eras′ty** —**ped′erast′, paed′erast′n.**
pedestal (ped′is t′l) *n.* [< It. *piè*, a foot + *di*, of + *stal*, a rest] 1. the bottom

support of a column, statue, etc. **2.** any foundation

pedestrian (pi des'trē ən) *adj.* [< L. *pes*, foot] **1.** going or done on foot **2.** of or for pedestrians **3.** prosaic; dull —*n.* one who goes on foot —**pedes'trianism** *n.*

pedestrian crossing a path across a road marked as a crossing for pedestrians

pedestrianize *vt.* **-ized', -iz'ing** to convert a street, etc., into an area solely for the use of pedestrians —**pedes'trianiza'tion** *n.*

pedi- [< L.] *a combining form meaning* foot or feet [*pedicure*]

pediculosis (pi dik'yoo lō'sis) *n.* [< L. *pedis*, louse + -OSIS] infestation with lice —**pedic'ulous** *adj.*

pedicure (ped'i kyoor') *n.* [< Fr. < L. *pes*, foot + *cura*, care] **1.** a trimming, polishing, etc. of the toenails **2.** treatment of corns, bunions, etc.

pedigree (ped'ə grē') *n.* [< MFr. *piè de grue*, crane's foot : from the lines in the genealogical tree] **1.** a recorded line of descent, esp. of a purebred animal **2.** a family tree **3.** descent; lineage —**ped'igreed'** *adj.*

PEDIMENT

pediment (ped'i mənt) *n.* [< earlier *periment*, prob. < PYRAMID] **1.** a low-pitched gable on the front of some buildings **2.** any similar triangular piece, as over a doorway, etc. —**ped'imen'ted** *adj.*

pedlar (ped'lər) *n.* one who peddles; hawker

pedo- [< Gr. *pais*, a child] *same as* PAEDO-

pedometer (pi dom'i tər) *n.* [< L. *pes*, foot + Gr. *metron*, measure] an instrument which measures the distance covered in walking by recording the number of steps

peduncle (pi duŋ'k'l) *n.* [< L. *pes*, foot] **1.** *Anat., Med., Zool.* a stalklike part **2.** *Bot.* a stalk of a flower cluster or solitary flower —**pedun'cular** *adj.*

pee (pē) *vi., vt.* [orig. euphemistic use of P(ISS)] [Colloq.] to urinate —*n.* [Colloq.] **1.** urine **2.** the act of urinating

peek (pēk) *vi.* [< ?] to glance or look quickly and furtively, as through an opening —*n.* such a glance

peel[1] (pēl) *vt.* [< L. *pilare*, to make bald] to cut away or strip off (the rind, skin, etc.) —*vi.* **1.** to shed skin, bark, etc. **2.** to come off in layers or flakes, as old paint **3.** [Slang] to undress —*n.* the rind or skin of fruit

peel[2] *n.* [< OFr. a fort, stake] *Hist.* a fortified tower of a type built on the Scottish border

peeling *n.* a peeled-off strip, as of apple skin

peen (pēn) *n.* [prob. < Scand.] the part of certain hammer heads opposite to the flat striking surface

peep[1] (pēp) *vi.* [echoic] to make the short, high-pitched cry of a young bird —*n.* a short, high-pitched sound

peep[2] *vi.* [? akin to ME. *piken*, peek] **1.** to look through a small opening or from a place of hiding **2.** to appear gradually or partially —*n.* **1.** a brief look; furtive glimpse **2.** the first appearance, as of dawn

peepers *n.* [Slang] the eyes

peeping Tom [< the tailor who peeped at Lady Godiva] a person who gets sexual pleasure from furtively watching others undressing, etc.

peep show a pictured scene or group of objects, as in a box, viewed through a small opening

peer[1] (pēar) *n.* [< L. *par*, an equal] **1.** one that has the same rank, etc. as another; specif., an equal before the law **2.** a noble; esp., a British duke, earl, etc. —**peer of the realm** a peer in the House of Lords —**peer'ess** *n.fem.*

peer[2] *vi.* [< ? APPEAR] **1.** to look closely, as in trying to see more clearly **2.** to come partly into sight

peerage *n.* **1.** all the peers of a country **2.** the rank of a peer **3.** a list of peers

peer group a group of people of about the same age and status

peerless *adj.* without equal; unrivalled

peeve (pēv) *vt.* peeved, peev'ing [< ff.] [Colloq.] to irritate; vex; annoy —*n.* [Colloq.] **1.** an object of annoyance **2.** a peevish state

peevish *adj.* [< ?] irritable; fretful --**pee'vishly** *adv.* —**pee'vishness** *n.*

peewit (pē'wit) *n.* [echoic] *same as* LAPWING

peg (peg) *n.* [? < LowG.] **1.** a short pin or bolt used to hold parts together, hang things on, fasten ropes to, etc. **2.** a step or degree **3.** any of the pins that regulate the tension of the strings of a violin, etc. **4.** a point of reference, esp. an excuse or reason **5.** *short for* CLOTHESPEG **6.** a small drink of spirits —*vt.* pegged, peg'ging **1.** to put a peg or pegs into so as to fasten, mark, etc. **2.** to maintain (prices, etc.) at a fixed level **3.** [U.S. Colloq.] to categorize [*pegged* him as a scholar] —*vi.* to keep score with pegs, as in cribbage —**peg away (at)** to work steadily (at) —**round peg in a square hole** one in a position, etc. for which he is unfitted: also **square peg in a round hole** —**take down a peg** to lower the pride of

Pegasus (peg'ə səs) [< *Pegasus*, in Gr. mythology] a large northern constellation

pegboard (peg'bôrd') *n.* **1.** a board with holes in it for inserting pegs for cribbage **2.** a board with rows of holes for hooks to hold displays, tools, etc.

peg leg [Colloq.] **1.** a wooden leg **2.** a person with a wooden leg

P.E.I. Prince Edward Island

peignoir (pān′wär) *n.* [Fr. < L. *pecten*, comb] a négligé

pejorative (pi jor′ə tiv, pēj′ə rə tiv) *adj.* [< L. *pejor*, worse] disparaging or derogatory —*n.* a pejorative word

peke (pēk) *n. short for* PEKINGESE

Pekingese (pē′ka nēz′) *n., pl.* **Pekingese** a small dog with long, silky hair, short legs, and a pug nose: also **Pe′kinese′**

Peking man (pē′kiŋ) a type of early man known from fossil remains found near Peking

pekoe (pē′kō) *n.* [< Chin. *pek-ho*, white down (on the young leaves used)] a black, small-leaved tea

pelargonium (pel′ər gō′nē əm) *n.* [< Gr. *pelargos*, stork] a plant with showy flowers

pelf (pelf) *n.* [akin to MFr. *pelfre*, booty] wealth regarded with contempt

pelican (pel′i kən) *n.* [< Gr. *pelekan*] a large water bird with webbed feet and an expandable pouch in the lower bill for scooping up fish

pelican crossing a type of road crossing with pedestrian-operated traffic lights

pelisse (pe lēs′) *n.* [Fr. < L. *pellis*, a skin] a long cloak or outer coat, esp. one lined with fur

pellagra (pə lā′grə) *n.* [It. < *pelle*, skin + Gr. *agra*, seizure] a deficiency disease, characterized by skin eruptions

pellet (pel′it) *n.* [< L. *pila*, a ball] 1. a little ball, as of clay, paper, medicine, compressed food, etc. 2. a small lead shot

pell-mell, pellmell (pel′mel′) *adv., adj.* [< OFr. *mesler*, to mix] 1. in a jumbled, confused mass or manner 2. in reckless haste

pellucid (pe lyōō′sid) *adj.* [< L. *per*, through + *lucere*, shine] 1. transparent or translucent 2. clear and simple in style

pelmet (pel′mit) *n.* [? < Fr. *palmette*, a palm-leaf ornament] a board for concealing curtain fixtures

pelt¹ (pelt) *vt.* [? < L. *pillare*, drive] 1. to throw things at 2. to beat repeatedly —*vi.* 1. to strike heavily or steadily, as hard rain 2. to hurry —*n.* a blow —(at) full pelt at full speed

pelt² *n.* [< ? L. *pellis*, skin] 1. the skin of a fur-bearing animal 2. the human skin: a humorous usage

pelvis (pel′vis) *n., pl.* **-vises, -ves** (-vēz) [< L., a basin] *Anat., Zool.* 1. the basinlike cavity in the posterior part of the trunk of man and many other vertebrates 2. the bones forming this cavity: also **pelvic girdle** —**pel′vic** *adj.*

Pemb. Pembrokeshire

pen¹ (pen) *n.* [OE. *penn*] 1. a small enclosure for domestic animals 2. any small enclosure —*vt.* **penned** or **pent, pen′-ning** to confine or enclose as in a pen

pen² *n.* [< L. *penna*, a feather] 1. orig., a heavy quill trimmed to a split point, for writing with ink 2. any of various devices used in writing or drawing with ink, often with a metal point split into two nibs 3. the metal point 4. writing

as a profession —*vt.* **penned, pen′ning** to write as with a pen

pen³ *n.* [< ?] a female swan

Pen., pen. peninsula

penal (pē′n'l) *adj.* [< L. *poena*, punishment] of, for, or involving punishment

penal code a body of law dealing with various crimes or offences and their legal penalties

penalize (pē′nal īz′) *vt.* **-ized′, -iz′ing** to impose a penalty on, as for breaking some rule

penalty (pen′'l tē) *n., pl.* **-ties** 1. a punishment fixed by law, as for a crime 2. the handicap, fine, etc. imposed upon an offender 3. any unfortunate consequence 4. *Sports* a free shot at goal, etc. imposed for breaking a rule

penalty box *Ice Hockey* a bench for players serving time penalties

penance (pen′əns) *n.* [see PENITENT] 1. *R.C.Ch.* a sacrament involving the confession of sin, repentance, and submission to penalties imposed, followed by absolution 2. any voluntary suffering to show repentance for wrongdoing —**do penance** to perform an act of penance

pence (pens; in compounds, pəns) *n. pl. of* PENNY: used also in compounds [*twopence*]

penchant (pän shän′) *n.* [Fr. < L. *pendere*, hang] a strong liking or fondness

pencil (pen′s'l) *n.* [< L. *penis*, a tail] 1. a pointed, rod-shaped instrument with a core of graphite or crayon, used for writing, drawing, etc. 2. something shaped or used as a pencil [*a styptic pencil*] 3. a series of lines coming to or spreading out from a point —*vt.* **-cilled, -cilling** to write, draw, etc. as with a pencil

pend (pend) *vi.* [< L. *pendere*, hang] to await decision

pendant (pen′dənt) *n.* [< prec.] 1. an ornamental hanging object, as from an earring 2. anything hanging, as a chandelier —*adj.* same as PENDENT

pendent *adj.* [see PEND] 1. suspended 2. overhanging 3. undecided —*n.* same as PENDANT —**pend′ency** *n.*

pending *adj.* 1. not decided 2. impending —*prep.* 1. during 2. while awaiting; until

pendragon (pen drag′ən) *n.* [< W. *pen*, head + *dragon*, leader] leader: a title used in ancient Britain

pendulous (pen′dyoo ləs) *adj.* [< L. *pendere*, hang] 1. hanging freely 2. drooping —**pen′dulously** *adv.*

pendulum (pen′dyoo ləm) *n.* [see prec.] a body hung from a fixed point so as to swing freely to and fro: often used to regulate clock movements

peneplain, peneplane (pē′na plān′) *n.* [L. *pene, paene*, almost + PLAIN, PLANE²] land worn down by erosion almost to a level plain

penetrable (pen′i trə b'l) *adj.* that can be penetrated —**pen′etrabil′ity** *n.*

penetrate (pen′ə trāt′) *vt.* **-trat′ed, -trat′-ing** [< L. *penitus*, inward] 1. to find or force a way into or through 2. to see into the interior of **3.** to have an effect throughout **4.** to understand —*vi.* to make a way into or through something

penetrating *adj.* **1.** that can penetrate **2.** sharp; piercing **3.** discerning [a *penetrating* mind] Also **pen'etrative** —**pen'etrat'ingly** *adv.*

penetration (pen'ə trā'shən) *n.* **1.** act of penetrating **2.** the depth to which something penetrates **3.** insight

pen friend a person, esp. a stranger in another country with whom one arranges to exchange letters: also **pen pal**

penguin (peŋ'gwin) *n.* [prob. < W. *pen gwyn*, white head] a flightless bird of the S Hemisphere, having paddlelike flippers for swimming

penicillin (pen'ə sil'in) *n.* [< L. *penicillus*, brush] an antibiotic obtained from certain moulds

peninsula (pə nin'syoo lə) *n.* [< L. *paene*, almost + *insula*, isle] **1.** a land area almost surrounded by water **2.** any land area projecting into the water —**penin'sular** *adj.*

penis (pē'nis) *n.*, *pl.* **-nises, -nes** (-nēz) [L., a tail] the male organ of sexual intercourse: in mammals it is also the organ through which urine is ejected by the male

penitent (pen'i tənt) *adj.* [< L. *paenitere*, repent] sorry for having done wrong and willing to atone —*n.* a penitent person —**pen'itence** *n.* —**pen'iten'tial** (-ten'shəl) *adj.*

penitentiary (pen'i ten'shə rē) *adj.* **1.** of or for penance **2.** used in reforming —*n.*, *pl.* **-ries** [U.S.] a prison for persons convicted of serious crimes

penknife (pen'nīf') *n.*, *pl.* **-knives'** (-nīvz') a small pocketknife; orig., one used in making quill pens

penman *n.* **1.** a person skilled in penmanship **2.** an author

penmanship *n.* **1.** handwriting as an art or skill **2.** a style of handwriting

pen name a name used by an author in place of his true name; nom de plume

pennant (pen'ənt) *n.* [< PEN², altered after PENDANT] any long, narrow flag

penniless (pen'i lis) *adj.* extremely poor

pennon (pen'ən) *n.* [see PEN²] **1.** a long, narrow, triangular flag used as an ensign by knights **2.** any flag or pennant

penny (pen'ē) *n.*, *pl.* **-nies**; for **1** (esp. collectively), **pence** [< OE. *pening*] **1.** in the United Kingdom and certain Commonwealth countries, *a)* formerly, a unit of currency equal to one twelfth of a shilling *b)* a unit of currency equal to one 100th part of a pound **2.** a sum of money —**a pretty penny** [Colloq.] a large sum of money —**spend a penny** [Colloq.] to urinate —**the penny dropped** comprehension dawned

-penny (pen'ē, pə nē') *a combining form meaning* costing (a specified number of) pennies [*sixpenny*]

Penny Black the first postage stamp issued in Britain in 1840

penny-dreadful *n.*, *pl.* **-fuls** a cheap, often lurid book

penny-farthing *n.* an early type of bicycle with a large front wheel and a small rear wheel

penny pincher a person who is extremely frugal —**pen'ny-pinch'ing** *n.*, *adj.*

pennyroyal (pen'ē roi'əl) *n.* [< OFr. *poliol* + *real*, royal] a mint with lavender flowers

pennyweight *n.* a unit of weight, equal to 24 grains, 1/20 ounce troy weight or 1.55 gms

penny-wise *adj.* careful or thrifty in small matters —**penny-wise and pound-foolish** thrifty in small matters but wasteful in major ones

pennywort (pen'ē wurt') *n.* [ME. *penywort*] a plant with round leaves growing in crevices of rocks

pennyworth *n.* **1.** the amount that can be bought for one penny **2.** a small amount

penology (pē nol'ə jē) *n.* [Gr. *poinē*, penalty + -LOGY] the study of the rehabilitation of criminals and of prison management —**penol'ogist** *n.*

pen pusher a clerk involved with boring paperwork —**pen'-push'ing** *adj.*, *n.*

pension (pen'shən; *for 2* pän'syōn) *n.* [< L. *pendere*, to pay] **1.** a regular payment to one who is disabled, retired, etc. **2.** in France, etc., *a)* a boardinghouse *b)* room and board —*vt.* to grant a pension to —**pension off** to dismiss from service with a pension —**pen'sionable** *adj.* —**pen'-sionary** *adj.*, *n.* —**pen'sioner** *n.*

pensive (pen'siv) *adj.* [< L. *pensare*, consider] thinking deeply, often of sad or melancholy things —**pen'sively** *adv.* —**pen'siveness** *n.*

pent (pent) *alt. pt. & pp. of* PEN¹ —*adj.* held or kept in; penned (often with *up*)

penta- [< Gr.] *a combining form meaning* five

pentacle (pen'tə k'l) *n.* [< Gr. *penta-*, five] a symbol, usually a five-pointed star, formerly used in magic: also called **pen'ta-gram, pentan'gle**

pentagon (pen'tə gən') *n.* [< PENTA- & -GON] a plane figure with five angles and five sides —**the Pentagon** a five-sided building in the U.S.A., housing the Department of Defense —**pentag'onal** (-tag'ə n'l) *adj.*

pentameter (pen tam'ə tər) *n.* [see PENTA- & -METER] a line of verse containing five metrical feet

Pentateuch (pen'tə tyook') *n.* [< Gr. *penta-*, five + *teuchos*, book] the first five books of the Bible

pentathlon (pen tath'lon) *n.* [< Gr. *penta-*, five + *athlon*, contest] an athletic contest in which each contestant takes part in five events

pentatonic (pen tə ton'ik) *adj.* [see PENTA- & TONIC] designating a musical scale having only five tones

Pentecost (pen'tə kost') *n.* [< Gr. *pentēkostē (hēmera)*, the fiftieth (day) after Passover] a Christian festival on the seventh Sunday after Easter; Whitsunday

Pentecostal (pen'tə kost'əl) *adj.* of or relating to any of various charismatic Christian groups

penthouse (pent'hous') *n.* [< L. *appendere*, append] 1. a flat built on the roof of a building 2. a small structure with a sloping roof attached to the side of a building

pent-up (pent'up') *adj.* held in check; curbed; confined

penult (pi nult') *n.* [< L. *paene*, almost + *ultimus*, last] the one next to the last

penultimate (pi nul'ti mət) *adj.* next to the last —**penul'timately** *adv.*

penumbra (pi num'brə) *n.*, *pl.* -**brae** (-brē), -**bras** [< L. *paene*, almost + *umbra*, shade] 1. the partly lighted area surrounding the complete shadow of a body, as the moon, in full eclipse 2. a vague, borderline area

penurious (pə nyoor'ē əs) *adj.* 1. miserly; stingy 2. destitute —**penu'riously** *adv.*

penury (pen'yoo rē) *n.* [< L. *penuria*, want] lack of money, property, or necessities; destitution

peon (pē'on) *n.* [< Sp. < ML. *pedo*, foot soldier] 1. in Latin America, a person of the labouring class 2. (pyoon) in India, a messenger, esp. in an office —**pe'onage** *n.*

peony (pē'ə nē) *n.*, *pl.* -**nies** [< Gr. *Paiōn*, Apollo, god of medicine] 1. a plant with large pink, red, or yellow, showy flowers 2. the flower

people (pē'p'l) *n.*, *pl.* -**ple**; for 1, -**ples** [< L. *populus*, nation] 1. all the persons of a racial, national, religious, linguistic, or cultural group; nation; race, ethnic group, etc. 2. the persons belonging to a certain place, community, or class 3. the persons under the leadership or control of a particular person or body 4. one's relatives or ancestors 5. the electorate of a country, etc. 6. persons considered indefinitely [what will *people* say?] 7. human beings —*vt.* -**pled**, -**pling** to populate

pep (pep) *n.* [< PEPPER] [Colloq.] energy; vigour; liveliness —*vt.* **pepped**, **pep'ping** [Colloq.] to invigorate; stimulate (with up) —**pep'py** *adj.*

pepper (pep'ər) *n.* [< Gr. *peperi*] 1. *a)* a pungent condiment obtained from the small, dried fruits of an East Indian plant *b)* the plant itself 2. same as CAPSICUM 3. any of various pungent spices, as cayenne pepper —*vt.* 1. to season with ground pepper 2. to shower with many small objects [*peppered* with hailstones]

pepper-and-salt *adj.* speckled with contrasting colours, esp. black and white

peppercorn *n.* the dried berry of the black pepper

peppercorn rent rent, for a property, that is nominal

pepper mill a hand mill used to grind peppercorns

peppermint *n.* 1. a species of mint with lance-shaped leaves 2. the pungent oil it yields, used for flavouring 3. a sweet flavoured with this oil

peppery *adj.* 1. of, like, or highly seasoned with pepper 2. sharp or fiery 3. irritable

pep pill [Slang] a pill containing a stimulant

pepsin (pep'sin) *n.* [< Gr. *peptein*, digest] an enzyme secreted in the stomach, aiding in the digestion of proteins

pep talk a talk to instil enthusiasm, etc.

peptic (pep'tik) *adj.* [< Gr. *peptein*, digest] 1. of or aiding digestion 2. caused by digestive secretions [a *peptic* ulcer]

per (pur; *unstressed* pər) *prep.* [L.] 1. through; by means of 2. for each [fifty pence *per* metre] 3. according to [*per* his instructions]

per- [< L. *per*, through] a prefix meaning: 1. through; throughout [*percolate*] 2. thoroughly [*permeate*]

peradventure (pər ad ven'chər) *adv.* [< OFr. *par*, by + *aventure*, chance] [Archaic] 1. possibly 2. by chance —*n.* chance; doubt

perambulate (pər am'byoo lāt') *vt.* -**lat'ed**, -**lat'ing** [< L. *per*, through + *ambulare*, to walk] to walk through, over, around, etc. —*vi.* to stroll —**peram'bula'tion** *n.*

perambulator *n.* same as PRAM

per annum (pər an'əm) [L.] by the year; yearly

percale (pər kāl') *n.* [Fr. < Per. *pargāla*] closely woven cotton cloth, used for sheets, etc.

per capita (pər kap'ə tə) [ML., by heads] for each person

perceive (pər sēv') *vt.*, *vi.* -**ceived'**, -**ceiv'ing** [< L. *per*, through + *capere*, take] 1. to become aware (of) through the senses 2. to grasp or take in mentally —**perceiv'able** *adj.* —**perceiv'ably** *adv.*

percent (pər sent') *adv.*, *adj.* [< L. *per centum*] in or for every hundred [a 20 *percent* rate means 20 in every hundred]: symbol, % : also **per cent** —*n.* [Colloq.] percentage

percentage *n.* 1. a given part in every hundred 2. part; portion [a *percentage* of the audience] 3. [Colloq.] advantage

percentile (pər sen'tīl) *n.* Statistics any of 100 divisions of a series, each of equal frequency

perceptible (pər sep'tə b'l) *adj.* that can be perceived —**percep'tibil'ity** *n.* —**percep'tibly** *adv.*

perception (pər sep'shən) *n.* [see PERCEIVE] 1. *a)* the act of perceiving; awareness *b)* insight or intuition 2. the understanding, knowledge, etc., or a specific idea, etc. got by perceiving —**percep'tual** (-tyoo əl) *adj.*

perceptive *adj.* 1. of or capable of perception 2. able to perceive quickly and easily —**percep'tiveness** *n.*

perch[1] (purch) *n.* [< Gr. *perkē*] a small, spiny-finned, freshwater food fish

perch[2] *n.* [< L. *pertica*, a pole] 1. a horizontal pole, branch, etc. serving as a roost for birds 2. any high resting place 3. formerly, a measure of length (5m) —*vi.*, *vt.* to alight and rest on or as on a perch

perchance (pər chāns') *adv.* [< OFr. *par*,

by + *chance*, chance] [Archaic] 1. by chance 2. perhaps; possibly

percipient (pər sip'ē ənt) *adj.* perceiving, esp. keenly —*n.* one who perceives

percolate (pur'kə lāt') *vt.* -lat'ed, -lat'ing [< L. *per*, through + *colare*, strain] 1. to pass (a liquid) through a porous substance; filter 2. to ooze through (a porous substance) 3. to brew (coffee) in a percolator —*vi.* to ooze through a porous substance —**per'cola'tion** *n.*

percolator *n.* a coffeepot in which boiling water bubbles up through a tube and filters back down through the ground coffee

percussion (pər kush'ən) *n.* [< L. *percutere*, to strike] 1. the hitting of one body against another, as the hammer of a firearm against a powder cap 2. percussion instruments collectively 3. *Med.* the tapping of the chest, back, etc. to determine the condition of internal organs —**percus'sive** *adj.*

percussion cap a small paper or metal container holding a charge that explodes when struck

percussion instrument a musical instrument producing a tone when struck, as the drums, cymbals, xylophone, etc.

percussionist *n.* a musician who plays percussion instruments

perdition (pər dish'ən) *n.* [< L. *perdere*, to lose] *Theol.* 1. damnation 2. same as HELL

peregrinate (per'ə gri nāt') *vt., vi.* -nat'ed, -nat'ing [see PILGRIM] to travel, esp. walk (along or through) —**per'egrina'tion** *n.*

peregrine (falcon) (per'ə grin) [see PILGRIM] a very swift European falcon with a spotted breast

peremptory (pə remp'tər ē) *adj.* [< L. *perimere*, destroy] 1. that cannot be denied, delayed, etc., as a command 2. intolerantly positive; dogmatic —**peremp'torily** *adv.* —**peremp'toriness** *n.*

perennial (pə ren'ē əl) *adj.* [< L. *per*, through + *annus*, year] 1. lasting throughout the whole year 2. continuing for a long time 3. having a life cycle of more than two years: said of plants —*n.* a perennial plant —**peren'nially** *adv.*

perf. 1. perfect 2. perforated

perfect (pur'fikt; *for v.*, pər fekt') *adj.* [< L. *per*, through + *facere*, to do] 1. complete in all respects; flawless 2. excellent, as in skill or quality 3. completely accurate; exact 4. utter; absolute 5. *Gram.* expressing an action completed at the time of speaking or at the time indicated 6. *Music* designating an interval, as an octave, whose character is not altered by inversion —*vt.* 1. to bring to completion 2. to make perfect —*n.* 1. the perfect tense 2. a verb form in this tense —**perfect'er** *n.* —**per'fectly** *adv.*

perfectible (pər fek'tə b'l) *adj.* that can be made perfect or more nearly perfect —**perfect'ibil'ity** *n.*

perfection (pər fek'shən) *n.* 1. a being perfect 2. a person or thing that is the

perfect embodiment of some quality —**to perfection** completely; perfectly

perfectionism *n.* extreme or obsessive striving for perfection, as in one's work —**perfec'tionist** *n., adj.*

perfect participle same as PAST PARTICIPLE

perfidy (pur'fə dē) *n., pl.* -dies [< L. *per fidem* (*decipi*), (deceive) through faith] betrayal of trust; treachery —**perfidious** (pər fid'ē əs) *adj.*

perforate (pur'fə rāt'; *for adj.* -rit) *vt., vi.* -rat'ed, -rat'ing [< L. *per*, through + *forare*, bore] 1. to make a hole or holes through, as by boring 2. to pierce with holes in a row, as a pattern, computer tape, etc. —*adj.* pierced with holes; for easy tearing: also **per'forat'ed** —**per'fo-ra'tor** *n.*

perforation (pur'fə rā'shən) *n.* 1. a hole made by piercing, etc. 2. any of a series of punched holes, as those between postage stamps

perforce (pər fôrs') *adv.* [< OFr.: see PER & FORCE¹] by or through necessity; necessarily

perform (pər fôrm') *vt.* [< OFr. *par*, through + *fournir*, accomplish] 1. to act on so as to complete 2. to fulfil (a promise, etc.) 3. to render or enact (a piece of music, etc.) —*vi.* to act in a play, dance, etc. before an audience —**perform'able** *adj.* —**perform'er** *n.*

performance *n.* 1. the act of performing; execution, accomplishment, etc. 2. functional effectiveness, as of a machine 3. a deed or feat 4. *a*) a formal presentation before an audience, as a play *b*) one's part in this

perfume (pər fyōōm'; *for n.*, pur'fyōōm) *vt.* -fumed', -fum'ing [< L. *per-*, intens. + *fumare*, smoke] 1. to fill with a pleasing odour 2. to put perfume on —*n.* 1. a sweet scent; fragrance 2. a substance producing a pleasing odour

perfumer (pər fyōō'mər) *n.* one who makes or sells perfumes

perfumery *n., pl.* -eries 1. the art of a perfumer 2. perfumes collectively 3. a place where perfume is sold

perfunctory (pər funk'tər ē) *adj.* [< L. *per-*, intens. + *fungi*, perform] 1. done merely as a routine; superficial 2. without concern; indifferent —**perfunc'torily** *adv.*

pergola (pur'gə lə) *n.* [It. < L. *pergula*] an arbour, esp. one of trelliswork covered with climbing plants

perhaps (pər haps') *adv.* [PER- + HAP] possibly

peri- [< Gr.] *a prefix meaning:* 1. around, about [*periscope*] 2. near [*perigee*]

perianth (per'ē anth') *n.* [< Gr. *peri-*, around + *anthos*, flower] the outer envelope of a flower

pericardium (per'ē kär'dē əm) *n., pl.* -dia [< Gr. *peri-*, around + *kardia*, heart] in vertebrates, the thin, membranous sac around the heart

perigee (per'ə jē') *n.* [< Fr. < Gr. *peri-*, near + *gē*, earth] the point nearest to the earth, the moon, or another planet, in the orbit of a satellite around it

perihelion (per′ə hē′lē ən) *n.*, *pl.* **-lions, -lia** [< Gr. *peri-*, around + *hēlios*, sun] the point nearest the sun in the orbit around it of a planet, comet, or satellite

peril (per′əl) *n.* [< L. *periculum*, danger] **1.** exposure to harm or injury **2.** something that may cause harm —**at your peril** accept the consequences of your action, etc. —**per′ilous** *adj.*

perimeter (pə rim′ə tər) *n.* [< Gr. *peri-*, around + *metron*, measure] **1.** the outer boundary of a figure or area **2.** the total length of this

perineum (per′ə nē′əm) *n.*, *pl.* **-ne′a** [< Gr. *peri-*, around + *inein*, discharge] the small area between the anus and the vulva or the scrotum —**per′ine′al** *adj.*

period (pēar′ē əd) *n.* [< Gr. *periodos*, cycle] **1.** a portion of time distinguished by certain processes, conditions, etc.; stage **2.** the menses **3.** a subdivision of a geologic era **4.** any of the portions of time into which a school day, etc. is divided **5.** the interval between the successive occurrences of an astronomical event **6.** *Gram.* a) a sentence, esp. a well-balanced sentence b) *Chiefly U.S.* name for FULL STOP **7.** an end or conclusion —*adj.* of or like that of an earlier period or age

periodic (pēar′ē od′ik) *adj.* **1.** appearing or recurring at regular intervals **2.** occurring from time to time **3.** of or characterized by periods

periodical *adj.* **1.** same as PERIODIC **2.** published at regular intervals, as weekly, monthly, etc. —*n.* a periodical publication —**pe′riod′ically** *adv.*

periodicity (pēar′ē ə dis′ə tē) *n.*, *pl.* **-ties** the tendency or fact of recurring at regular intervals

periodic law the law that properties of chemical elements recur periodically when the elements are arranged in order of their atomic numbers

periodic table an arrangement of the chemical elements according to their atomic numbers, to exhibit the periodic law

periodontal (per′ē ə don′t'l) *adj.* [< PERI- + -ODONT] occurring around a tooth or affecting the gums

peripatetic (per′i pə tet′ik) *adj.* [< Gr. *peri-*, around + *patein*, walk] **1.** itinerant **2.** of a teacher employed in more than one school **3.** [P-] of the philosophy of Aristotle, who taught while walking about —*n.* [P-] a follower of Aristotle —**per′ipatet′ically** *adv.*

peripheral (pə rif′ər əl) *adj.* **1.** merely incidental; tangential **2.** of, belonging to, or forming a periphery

periphery *n.*, *pl.* **-eries** [< Gr. *peri-*, around + *pherein*, to bear] **1.** an outer boundary line, esp. of a rounded figure **2.** surrounding space or area

periphrasis (pə rif′rə sis) *n.*, *pl.* **-ses** (-sēz) [< Gr. *peri-*, around + *phrazein*, speak] the use of many words where a few would do —**per′iphras′tic** (per′ə fras′tik) *adj.*

PERISCOPE

periscope (per′ə skōp′) *n.* [PERI- + -SCOPE] an optical instrument consisting of a tube equipped with lenses and mirrors, so arranged that a person looking through one end can see objects reflected at the other: used on submarines, etc. —**per′iscop′ic** (-skop′ik) *adj.*

perish (per′ish) *vi.* [< L. *per-*, intens. + *ire*, go] **1.** to be destroyed, ruined, or wiped out **2.** to die **3.** to decay: said esp. of rubber —**perish the thought!** do not even consider such a possibility!

perishable *adj.* liable to spoil, as some foods —*n.* something, esp. a food, liable to spoil

perisher *n.* [Colloq.] one who is a pest, esp. a child

perishing *adj.* **1.** [Colloq.] extremely cold **2.** [Slang] confounded

peristalsis (per′ə stal′sis) *n.*, *pl.* **-ses** (-sēz) [< Gr. *peri-*, around + *stellein*, place] the wavelike muscular contractions and dilations of the walls of the alimentary canal —**per′istal′tic** *adj.*

peritoneum (per′i tō nē′əm) *n.*, *pl.* **-ne′a, -ne′ums** [< Gr. *peri-*, around + *teinein*, stretch] the serous membrane lining the abdominal cavity and covering the visceral organs —**per′itone′al** *adj.*

peritonitis *n.* inflammation of the peritoneum

periwig (per′ə wig′) *n.* [< Fr. *perruque*, peruke] a wig, formerly worn by men

periwinkle¹ (per′ə wiŋ′k'l) *n.* [< L. *pervinca*] a creeper with blue, white, or pink flowers

periwinkle² *n.* [OE. *pinewincle*] a saltwater snail having a thick, cone-shaped shell: also **winkle**

perjure (pur′jər) *vt.* **-jured, -juring** [< L. *per*, through + *jurare*, swear] to make (oneself) guilty of perjury —**per′jurer** *n.*

perjury *n.*, *pl.* **-ries** [< L. *perjurus*, false] the wilful telling of a lie while under oath

perk¹ (purk) *vt.* [< ?] **1.** to raise (the head, etc.) briskly (often with *up*) **2.** to make smart in appearance (often with *up*) **3.** to restore freshness to (with *up*) —*vi.* to become lively (with *up*)

perk² *n. colloq.* form of PERQUISITE

perky (pur′kē) *adj.* **-ier, -iest** **1.** self-confident **2.** gay or lively —**perk′ily** *adv.*

perm¹ (purm) *n. colloq. form of*

PERMANENT WAVE —vt. [Colloq.] to give a permanent wave to

perm² n. colloq. form of PERMUTATION (sense 2) —vt. [Colloq.] to make a permutation of

permafrost (pur'mə frost') n. [PERMA-(NENT) + FROST] permanently frozen subsoil

permanent (pur'mə nənt) adj. [< L. per, through + manere, remain] lasting or intended to last indefinitely —per'manence n. —per'manently adv.

permanent wave a hair wave, produced by applying heat or chemicals, that is relatively longlasting

permanent way the track of a railway, including the ballast, sleepers, rails, etc.

permanganate (pur man'gə nāt') n. a salt of an acid containing manganese, used as a disinfectant

permeable (pur'mē ə b'l) adj. that can be permeated, as by liquids —per'meabil'ity n. —per'meably adv.

permeate (pur'-at'ed, -at'ing [< L. per, through + meare, glide] to pass into and affect every part of —vi. to spread (with through or among) —per'mea'tion n.

Permian (pur'mē ən) adj. [< Perm, Russia] of the seventh and last period of the Paleozoic Era

permissible (pər mis'ə b'l) adj. allowable —permis'sibil'ity n.

permission (pər mish'ən) n. formal consent; leave

permissive adj. 1. allowing freedom 2. giving permission —permis'siveness n.

permit (pər mit'; for n., pur'mit) vt. -mit'-ted, -mit'ting [< L. per, through + mittere, send] 1. to allow; consent to 2. to give permission to; authorize 3. to give opportunity for —vi. to give opportunity [if time permits] —n. a document granting permission; licence

permutation (pur'myoo tā'shən) n. 1. Math. any one of the total number of groupings, or subsets, into which a group, or set, of elements can be arranged 2. any alteration 3. a fixed plan for selection of results on football pools

pernicious (pər nish'əs) adj. [< Fr. < L. per, thoroughly + necare, kill] causing great injury, destruction, or ruin —perni'ciously adv.

pernicious anaemia a form of anaemia characterized by a reduction of the red blood cells, nervous disturbances, etc.

pernickety (pər nik'ə tē) adj. [< Scot. dial] [Colloq.] too particular or precise; fussy

peroration (per'ə rā'shən) n. [< L. per, through + orare, speak] the concluding part of a speech, including a summing up

peroxide (pə rok'sīd) n. [< L. per, through + OXIDE] any oxide containing the oxygen (O₂) group linked by a single bond; specif., hydrogen peroxide —vt. -ided, -iding to bleach (hair, etc.) with hydrogen peroxide

perpendicular (pur'pən dik'yoo lər) adj. [< L. perpendiculum, plumb line] 1. at right angles to a given plane or line 2. exactly upright; vertical 3. very steep

4. [P-] of the style of English Gothic architecture characterized by vertical lines —n. 1. a line at right angles to another line or plane 2. a perpendicular position —per'pendic'ular'ity (-lar'ə tē) n.

perpetrate (pur'pə trāt') vt. -trat'ed, -trat'ing [< L. per, thoroughly + patrare, effect] 1. to do (something evil, criminal, etc.) 2. to commit (a blunder), impose (a hoax), etc. —per'petra'tion n. —per'petra'tor n.

perpetual (pər pech'oo wəl) adj. [< L. perpetuus, constant] 1. lasting forever or for a long time 2. continuing indefinitely without interruption; constant —perpet'-ually adv.

perpetual motion the motion of a hypothetical device which, once set in motion, would operate indefinitely

perpetuate vt. -at'ed, -at'ing to cause to continue or be remembered —perpet'u-a'tion n.

perpetuity (pur'pə tyoo'ə tē) n., pl. -ties 1. unlimited time; eternity 2. something perpetual, as a pension —in perpetuity forever

perplex (pər pleks') vt. [< L. per, through + plectere, twist] 1. to make (a person) uncertain, hesitant, etc. 2. to make complicated —perplexed' adj. —perplex'-ing adj.

perplexity n. 1. bewilderment 2. pl. -ties something that perplexes

perquisite (pur'kwə zit) n. [< L. per-, intens. + quaerere, seek] 1. something additional to regular pay 2. a tip or gratuity 3. a prerogative, by virtue of one's status, etc.

perry (per'ē) n. [< L. pirum, pear] a fermented drink like cider, made from pear juice

per se (pur'sā') [L.] by (or in) itself; intrinsically

persecute (pur'sə kyoot') vt. -cut'ed, -cut'ing [< L. per, through + sequi, follow] 1. to afflict constantly so as to injure or distress, esp. for reasons of religion, politics, or race 2. to annoy constantly —per'secu'tion n. —per'secu'tor n.

Perseus (pur'syoos) [< Perseus in Greek Myth.] a N constellation

perseverance (pur'sə vēar'əns) n. steadfastness

persevere vi. -vered', -ver'ing [< L. per-, intens. + severus, severe] to continue in some effort, course of action, etc. in spite of difficulty, opposition, etc.

Persian (pur'shən) adj. of Persia, its people, their language, etc.; Iranian —n. 1. a native of Persia 2. the language of Iran

Persian cat a variety of domestic cat with long silky hair

Persian lamb the black pelt of newborn karakul lambs, having small, tight curls

persiflage (pur'sə fläzh') n. [Fr. < persifler, to banter] light, frivolous talk or writing

persimmon (pər sim'ən) n. [< AmInd.] 1. a tree with white flowers and plumlike fruit 2. the fruit, sweet and edible when ripe

persist (pər sist′) *vi.* [< L. *per,* through + *sistere,* cause to stand] **1.** to refuse to give up, esp. when faced with opposition **2.** to continue insistently **3.** to endure; last

persistent *adj.* **1.** continuing, esp. in the face of opposition **2.** continuing to exist **3.** constantly repeated —**persist′ence** *n.*

person (pur′s′n) *n.* [< L. *persona*] **1.** a human being **2.** *a)* a living human body *b)* bodily appearance **3.** *Gram.* division into three sets of pronouns (**personal pronouns**), and, usually, corresponding verb forms, to identify the subject **4.** *Law* any individual or incorporated group having certain legal rights —**in person** actually present

-person (pur′s′n) *a combining form meaning* person (of either sex) in a specified activity [*chairperson*]

persona (pur sō′nə) *n., pl.* **-nae** (-nē), **-nas** [L., actor's mask] the personality presented to others by an individual

personable (pur′sən ə b'l) *adj.* having a pleasing appearance and personality

personage (pur′s'n ij) *n.* **1.** an important person **2.** any person

†**persona grata** (pər sō′nə grät′ə) [L.] a person who is acceptable or welcome

personal (pur′sən əl) *adj.* **1.** private; individual **2.** done in person **3.** involving human beings **4.** of the body or physical appearance **5.** *a)* having to do with the character, conduct, etc. of a certain person *b)* making critical or derogatory remarks about a person **6.** of or like a person or rational being **7.** *Gram.* indicating grammatical person **8.** *Law* of property (**personal property**) that is movable or not attached to the land

personal column a part of a newspaper devoted to births, marriages, deaths, personal messages, etc.

personality (pur′sən nal′ə tē) *n., pl.* **-ties** **1.** distinctive individual qualities of a person, considered collectively **2.** *a)* the sum of such qualities as impressing others *b)* personal attractiveness **3.** a notable person **4.** the quality of being a unique person **5.** [*pl.*] offensive remarks aimed at a person

personalize (pur′sən ə līz′) *vt.* **-ized′, -iz′- ing 1.** to personify **2.** to have marked with one's name or initials

personally *adv.* **1.** in person **2.** as a person [I dislike him *personally*] **3.** in one's own opinion **4.** as though directed at oneself

†**persona non grata** (pər sō′nə- non grät′ə) [L.] a person who is not acceptable

personate (pur′sə nāt′) *vt.* **-at′ed, -at′- ing** to assume the identity of, as with intent to defraud —**per′sona′tion** *n.* —**per′- sona′tor** *n.*

personify (pur son′ə fī′) *vt.* **-fied′, -fy′- ing 1.** to think or speak of (a thing) as a person **2.** to symbolize (an abstract idea) by a human figure, as in art **3.** to be a symbol or perfect example of; typify —**person′ifica′tion** *n.*

personnel (pur′sə nel′) *n.* [Fr.] **1.** persons employed in any work, service, etc. **2.** a department for hiring employees, etc. —*adj.* of or in charge of personnel

PERSPECTIVE

perspective (pər spek′tiv) *adj.* [< L. *per,* through + *specere,* look] of or in perspective —*n.* **1.** a specific point of view in judging things or events **2.** the ability to see things in a true relationship **3.** the appearance of objects as determined by their relative distance and positions **4.** the art of picturing objects so as to show relative distance or depth

perspex (pur′speks) *Trademark* a hard transparent plastic, an acrylic resin

perspicacious (pur′spə kā′shəs) *adj.* [see PERSPECTIVE] having keen judgment or understanding —**per′spicac′ity** (-kas′- ə tē) *n.*

perspicuous (pər spik′yoo wəs) *adj.* [see PERSPECTIVE] clear in statement or expression; easily understood —**perspicu- ity** (pur′spə kyoo′ə tē) *n.*

perspiration (pur′spə rā′shən) *n.* [Fr.] **1.** a perspiring; sweating **2.** sweat

perspire (pər spīr′) *vt., vi.* **-spired′, -spir′- ing** [< Fr. < L. *per,* through + *spirare,* breathe] to sweat

persuade (pər swād′) *vt.* **-suad′ed, -suad′- ing** [< L. *per-,* intens. + *suadere,* to urge] to cause to do something, esp. by reasoning, urging, etc. —**persua′sible** *adj.* —**persuad′- er** *n.*

persuasion (pər swā′zhən) *n.* **1.** the power of persuading **2.** a strong belief; conviction **3.** *a)* a particular religious belief *b)* a particular sect

persuasive *adj.* having the power, or tending, to persuade —**persua′sively** *adv.* —**persua′siveness** *n.*

pert (purt) *adj.* [< L. *apertus,* open] **1.** bold; impudent; saucy **2.** chic and jaunty —**pert′ly** *adv.* —**pert′ness** *n.*

pertain (pur tān′) *vi.* [< L. *per-,* intens. + *tenere,* hold] **1.** to belong; be connected or associated **2.** to be appropriate **3.** to have reference [*pertaining* to the case]

pertinacious (pur′tə nā′shəs) *adj.* [< L. *per-,* intens. + *tenere,* hold] **1.** holding firmly to some purpose, belief, or action **2.** hard to get rid of —**per′tinac′ity** (-nas′ə tē) *n.*

pertinent (pur′tin ənt) *adj.* [see PERTAIN] of or connected with the matter at hand; relevant —**per′tinence, per′tinency** *n.*

perturb (pər turb′) *vt.* [< L. *per-,* intens. + *turbare,* disturb] **1.** to cause to be alarmed, agitated, or upset **2.** to cause confusion in —**per'turba'tion** (pur'-tər bā'shən) *n.*

peruke (pə rōōk') *n.* [< Fr. *perruque*] *same as* PERIWIG

perusal (pə rōō'z'l) *n.* a perusing

peruse (pə rōōz') *vt.* -rused', -rus'ing [prob. < L. *per-*, intens. + ME. *usen*, to use] to read carefully; study

pervade (pər vād') *vt.* -vad'ed, -vad'ing [< L. *per*, through + *vadere*, go] to pass or be prevalent throughout —**perva'-sion** *n.* —**perva'sive** *adj.*

perverse (pər vurs') *adj.* [see PERVERT] 1. deviating from what is considered right or good 2. stubbornly contrary 3. obstinately disobedient —**perverse'ly** *adv.* —**perver'sity** *n.*

perversion *n.* 1. something perverted 2. any sexual act or practice considered abnormal

pervert (pər vurt'; *for n.,* pur'vərt) *vt.* [< L. *per-*, intens. + *vertere*, turn] 1. to misuse 2. to misinterpret; distort 3. to lead astray from what is right or good 4. to debase —*n.* one who practises sexual perversion —**pervert'ed** *adj.*

pervious (pur'vē əs) *adj.* [< L. *per*, through + *via*, way] 1. allowing passage through; permeable 2. having a mind open to influence, etc. —**per'viously** *adv.*

peseta (pə sāt'ə) *n.* [Sp.] the monetary unit of Spain and Equatorial Guinea

pesky (pes'kē) *adj.* -kier, -kiest [< PEST] [U.S. Colloq.] annoying; troublesome

peso (pā'sō) *n., pl.* -sos [Sp.] the monetary unit of Argentina, Colombia, Cuba, Mexico, the Philippines, etc.

pessary (pes'ər ē) *n., pl.* -ries [< Gr. *pessos*, pebble] a device worn in the vagina to support the uterus or prevent conception

pessimism (pes'ə miz'm) *n.* [< Fr. < L. *pejor*, worse] 1. the tendency to expect the worst outcome in any circumstance 2. the belief that the evil in life outweighs the good —**pes'simist** *n.* —**pes'simis'tic** *adj.* —**pes'simis'tically** *adv.*

pest (pest) *n.* [< L. *pestis*, plague] a person or thing that causes trouble, annoyance, etc.; specif., any destructive insect, small animal, weed, etc.

pester (pes'tər) *vt.* [< OFr. *empestrer*, entangle] to annoy repeatedly with petty irritations; bother

pesticide (pes'tə sīd') *n.* any chemical used for killing insects, weeds, etc. —**pes'ti-ci'dal** *adj.*

pestiferous (pes tif'ər əs) *adj.* [< L. *pestis*, plague + *ferre*, to bear] 1. annoying; bothersome 2. dangerous to society 3. orig., bringing or carrying disease

pestilence (pes'tə ləns) *n.* [see ff.] any very contagious or infectious disease, esp. bubonic plague —**pes'tilen'tial** (-tə len'shəl) *adj.* —**pes'tilen'tially** *adv.*

pestilent *adj.* [< L. *pestis*, plague] 1. annoying; troublesome 2. dangerous to society 3. likely to cause death

pestle (pes''l) *n.* [< L. *pinsere*, to pound] a tool used to pound or grind substances, as in a mortar

pestology (pest ol'ə jē) *n.* the branch of science dealing with pests, esp. insects harmful to animal and plant life

pet¹ (pet) *n.* [orig. Scot. dial.] 1. an animal that is domesticated and kept as a companion or treated with fondness 2. one who is a favourite —*adj.* 1. kept or treated as a pet 2. especially liked 3. particular [*one's pet hatred*] —*vt.* **pet'-ted, pet'ting** 1. to fondle; caress 2. to pamper —*vi.* [Colloq.] to fondle intimately, etc. in making love

pet² *n.* [< ?] a state of sulky peevishness or ill humour

Pet. *Bible* Peter

petal (pet''l) *n.* [< Gr. *petalos*, outspread] any of the leaflike parts of a blossom —**pet'-alled** *adj.*

petard (pi tärd') *n.* [< Fr. < L. *pedere*, to break wind] a metal cone filled with explosives: formerly fastened to walls and gates and exploded

peter (pē'tər) *vi.* [< ?] [Colloq.] to become gradually smaller, weaker, etc. and cease (with *out*)

Peter Pan [< character created by J.M. Barrie] a youthful or immature man

petersham (pēt'ər shəm) *n.* [< Lord *Petersham*] a thick, corded ribbon used for stiffening belts, etc.

pethidine (peth'i dēn') *n.* a soluble pain-relieving drug

petiole (pet'ē ōl') *n.* [< L. *pes*, a foot] *Bot.* the slender portion of a leaf that supports the blade

petit (pet'ē) *adj.* [< OFr.] *same as* PETTY (sense 4)

petite (pə tēt') *adj.* [Fr.] small and trim of figure: said of a woman —**petite'ness** *n.*

petit bourgeois (pet'ē) the section of the middle class with the lowest social status and least wealth, as small shopkeepers, etc.

petit four (pet'ē fôr') *pl.* **petits fours, petit fours** [Fr. < *petit*, small + *four*, oven] any of various small fancy cakes

petition (pə tish'ən) *n.* [< L. *petere*, ask] 1. a solemn, earnest request to a superior 2. a formal document making such a request, often signed by a number of persons 3. *Law* a written plea asking for specific court action —*vt.* 1. to address a petition to 2. to ask for —*vi.* to make a petition —**peti'tioner** *n.*

petit mal (pet'ē mal') [Fr., small ailment] a type of epilepsy in which there are attacks of momentary unconsciousness

petit point 1. a small diagonal needlepoint stitch used for fine detail 2. work done with such stitches

petrel (pet'rəl) *n.* [< ?] a small, dark, sea bird with long wings, as the stormy petrel

petrify (pet'rə fī') *vt.* -fied', -fy'ing [< L. *petra*, a rock + *facere*, make] 1. to re-form as a stony substance 2. to harden or deaden 3. to paralyse, as with fear —*vi.* to become petrified —**pet'rifica'-tion** *n.*

petrochemical (pet'rō kem'i k'l) *n.* [PETRO(LEUM) + CHEMICAL] a chemical derived ultimately from petroleum, as ethylene glycol, etc. —**pet′rochem′istry** *n.*

petrodollar (pet′rō dol′ər) *n.* [< PETROLEUM + DOLLAR] the dollars earned by a petroleum-exporting country

petrol (pet′rəl) *n.* [see PETROLEUM] a volatile liquid produced by the distillation of petroleum and used chiefly as a fuel in internal-combustion engines

petrolatum (pet′rəlāt′əm) *n.* [< ff.] a greasy, jellylike substance consisting of a mixture of hydrocarbons obtained from petroleum

petroleum (pətrō′lē əm) *n.* [< L. *petra*, rock + *oleum*, oil] an oily, liquid solution of hydrocarbons occurring naturally in certain rock strata: it yields paraffin, petrol, etc.

petroleum jelly *same as* PETROLATUM

petrol station a garage that sells petrol

petticoat (pet′i kōt′) *n.* [< PETTY + COAT] an underskirt, worn by women and girls —*adj.* of or by women

pettifogger (pet′ē fog′ər) *n.* [PETTY + obs. *fogger* < ?] 1. a lawyer who handles petty cases, esp. by using unethical methods 2. a quibbler —**pet′tifog′gery** *n.* —**pet′tifog′ging** *adj.*

pettish (pet′ish) *adj.* [< PET²] peevish; petulant; cross —**pet′tishly** *adv.* —**pet′tishness** *n.*

petty (pet′ē) *adj.* **-tier, -tiest** [OFr. *petit*] 1. relatively unimportant 2. narrow-minded, mean, etc. 3. relatively low in rank 4. insignificant: now used chiefly in law —**pet′tiness** *n.*

petty cash a cash fund for incidental expenses

petty jury a group of twelve citizens picked to weigh evidence in and decide the issues of a trial in court

petty officer *see* MILITARY RANKS, table

petulant (pet′yoo lənt) *adj.* [< L. *petere*, attack] impatient or irritable, esp. over a petty annoyance —**pet′ulance** *n.*

petunia (pətyoon′yə) *n.* [< Tupi *petun*, tobacco] a plant with variously coloured, funnel-shaped flowers

pew (pyoo) *n.* [< Gr. *pous*, a foot] 1. a benchlike seat with a back in a church 2. any of the boxlike enclosures with seats, in some churches 3. [Colloq.] a seat

pewter (pyoot′ər) *n.* [< OFr. *peautre*] 1. a dull, silvery-grey alloy of tin with lead 2. articles made of pewter —*adj.* made of pewter

peyote (pā ōt′ē) *n.* [< SAmInd *peyotl*, caterpillar] a Mexican cactus, source of mescaline

pf pianoforte

pH (pē′āch′) [< Fr. p(*ouvoir*) h(*ydrogène*), hydrogen power] a symbol for the degree of acidity or alkalinity

phaeton, phaëton (fā′t′n) *n.* [< the son of Helios in Greek Myth.] a light four-wheeled carriage with front and back seats

phalanger (fəlan′jər) *n.* [< Gr. *phalanx*, bone between two joints] any of various small Australian marsupials with a long, bushy tail

phalanx (fal′aŋks) *n., pl.* **-lanxes, phalan-**

ges (fəlan′jēz) [< Gr., line of battle] 1. an ancient military formation of infantry in close ranks 2. a massed group of individuals 3. a group united for a common purpose 4. *pl.* **-lan′ges** any of the bones of the fingers or toes

phallus (fal′əs) *n., pl.* **-li** (-ī), **-luses** [< Gr. *phallos*] an image of the penis as a symbol of generative power —**phal′lic** *adj.*

phantasm (fan′taz′m) *n.* [< Gr. *phantazein*, to show] 1. a figment of the mind; esp., a spectre, or ghost 2. a deceptive likeness

phantasmagoria (fan′taz məgor′ē ə) *n.* [< Gr. *phantasma*, phantasm + *ageirein*, assemble] a rapidly changing series of things seen or imagined —**phantas′mago′ric** *adj.*

phantasy (fan′tə sē) *n., pl.* **-sies** *same as* FANTASY

phantom (fan′təm) *n.* [see PHANTASM] 1. an apparition; spectre 2. an illusion 3. a person or thing that is something in appearance but not in fact 4. any mental image —*adj.* illusory

Pharaoh (fâər′ō) *n.* the title of the rulers of ancient Egypt

Pharisaic (far′ə sā′ik) *adj.* 1. of the Pharisees 2. [p-] hypocritical —**phar′isa′ically** *adv.*

Pharisee (far′ə sē′) *n.* 1. a member of an ancient Jewish party that observed the written and the oral law 2. [p-] a pharisaic person —**Phar′isee′ism** *n.*

pharmaceutical (fär′mə syoot′i k′l) *adj.* [< Gr. *pharmakon*, a medicine] 1. of pharmacy or pharmacists 2. of or by drugs

pharmaceutics *n.pl.* [with *sing. v.*] *same as* PHARMACY (sense 1)

pharmacist (fär′mə sist) *n.* a person licensed to practise pharmacy

pharmacology (fär′mə kol′ə jē) *n.* [< Gr. *pharmakon*, a drug] the science dealing with the effects of drugs —**phar′macolog′ical** (-kə loj′i k′l) *adj.* —**phar′macolog′ically** *adv.* —**phar′macol′ogist** *n.*

pharmacopoeia (fär′mə kə pē′ə) *n.* [< Gr. *pharmakon*, a drug + *poiein*, to make] a book containing a list of drugs and the lawful standards for their production, dispensation, etc.

pharmacy (fär′mə sē) *n., pl.* **-cies** [< Gr. *pharmakon*, a drug] 1. the profession of preparing and dispensing drugs and medicines 2. a place where this is done

pharyngitis (far′in jīt′əs) *n.* inflammation of the mucous membrane of the pharynx; sore throat

pharynx (far′iŋks) *n., pl.* **phar′ynxes, pharynges** (fərin′jēz) [Gr.] the cavity leading from the mouth and nasal passages to the larynx and oesophagus —**pharyngeal** (far′ən jē′əl) *adj.*

phase (fāz) *n.* [< Gr. *phasis*] 1. any stage in a series of changes, as in development 2. any stage in the illumination or appearance of the moon or a planet 3. aspect or side, as of a problem 4. a solid, liquid, or gaseous homogeneous form [ice is a *phase* of H₂O] 5. the part of a cycle through which a periodic wave of light or sound has advanced at any instant, with reference to a standard position —vt. **phased, phas'-ing** to introduce, carry out, etc. in phases (often with in, into, etc.) —**in** (or **out of**) **phase** in (or not in) synchronization —**phase out** to terminate (an activity) by stages

Ph.D. Doctor of Philosophy

PHEASANT
(to 89 cm long,
including beak
and tail)

pheasant (fez''nt) n. [< Gr. phasianos, (bird) of Phasis, river in Asia] a chickenlike game bird with a long tail and brilliant feathers

phen- [< Gr. phainein, to show] a combining form meaning of or derived from benzene

phenobarbital (fē'nə bär'bə təl) n. [PHEN- + BARBITURIC ACID] an odourless, white powder used as a sedative: also **phe'nobar'-bitone** (-bə tōn)

phenol (fē'nol) n. a white crystalline compound used in making explosives, etc.: its dilute aqueous solution is commonly called carbolic acid

phenomena (fi nom'ə nə) n. pl. of PHE-NOMENON

phenomenal adj. 1. of or constituting a phenomenon or phenomena 2. extraordinary —**phenom'enally** adv.

phenomenalism n. the philosophic theory that all knowledge comes from sense perceptions

phenomenon (fi nom'ə nən) n., pl. **-na;** also, esp. for 3 and 4, **-nons'** [< Gr. phainesthai, appear] 1. any observable fact that can be scientifically described 2. the appearance of something as distinguished from the thing in itself 3. anything extremely unusual 4. [Colloq.] a person who is extraordinary

phenyl (fē'nil) n. [< PHEN-] the monovalent radical, C_6H_5, forming the basis of phenol, benzene, etc.

phenylketonuria (fē nil kēt'ə nyooər'ē ə) n. [PHENYL + KETON(E) + -URIA] a genetic disorder which causes severe mental retardation in infants

phew (fyoo: conventionalized pronun.) interj. a breathy sound expressing disgust, surprise, etc.

phi (fī) n. the 21st letter of the Greek alphabet (Φ, φ)

phial (fī'əl) n. [< Gr. phialē, shallow bowl] a small glass bottle

Phil. 1. Philippians 2. Philippine

philadelphus (fil'ə del'fəs) n. [< Gr.] the mock orange

philander (fi lan'dər) vi. [< Gr. philos,

loving + anēr, a man] to make love insincerely: said of a man —**philan'derer** n.

philanthropy (fi lan'thrə pē) n. [< Gr. philein, to love + anthrōpos, man] 1. a desire to help mankind, as by gifts to charitable institutions 2. pl. **-pies** a philanthropic act, gift, etc. —**phil'anthrop'-ic** (-ən throp'ik) adj. —**philan'thropist** n.

philately (fi lat'əl ē) n. [< Gr. philos, loving + ateleia, exemption from (further) tax] the collection and study of postage stamps, postmarks, etc. —**philat'elist** n.

-phile (fīl) [< Gr.] a combining form meaning loving, liking [Anglophile]

philharmonic (fil'här mon'ik) adj. [< Gr. philos, loving + harmonia, harmony] loving or devoted to music —n. a specific choir, orchestra or society

philhellene (fil'hel'ēn) n. [see PHILO- & HELLENE] a friend or supporter of the Greeks or Greece

philippic (fi lip'ik) n. [< Philip of Macedon] any bitter verbal attack

Philippine (fil'ə pēn') adj. of the Philippine Islands or their people

Philistine (fil'is tīn') n. 1. [often p-] a person regarded as indifferent to cultural values 2. a member of a non-Semitic people who repeatedly warred with the Israelites —adj. [often p-] smugly conventional, lacking in culture, etc. —**Phil'istinism** (-tin-) n.

Phillips (fil'əps) [< H. Phillips] a screwdriver that can be used on a screw (**Phillips screw**) that has two slots crossing at the centre of the head

philo- [< Gr.] a combining form meaning loving, liking, having a predilection for [philology]

philology (fi lol'ə jē) n. [< Gr. philein, to love + logos, word] 1. the study of literary texts, etc. 2. earlier term for LINGUISTICS —**philological** (fil'ə loj'i k'l) adj. —**philol'ogist** n.

philos. philosophy

philosopher (fi los'ə fər) n. [< Gr. philos, loving + sophos, wise] 1. a person who studies or is learned in philosophy 2. a person who lives by a system of philosophy 3. a person who meets difficulties with calmness and composure

philosophers' (or **philosopher's**) **stone** an imaginary substance that alchemists believed would change base metals into gold or silver

philosophic (fil'ə sof'ik) adj. 1. of a philosophy or philosopher 2. devoted to or learned in philosophy 3. calm; rational Also **phil'osoph'ical** —**phil'osoph'ically** adv.

philosophize (fi los'ə fīz') vi. **-phized', -phiz'ing** 1. to reason like a philosopher 2. to moralize

philosophy (fi los'ə fē) n., pl. **-phies** [see PHILOSOPHER] 1. theory or analysis of the principles underlying conduct, thought, knowledge, and the nature of the universe 2. the general principles of a field of knowledge 3. a particular system of ethics

philtre (fil'tər) n. [< Gr. philein, to love]

a potion thought to arouse sexual love, esp. towards a specific person

phlebitis (fli bīt′is) *n.* [< Gr. *phleps*, vein + -ITIS] inflammation of a vein —**phlebit′ic** (-bit′ik) *adj.*

phlegm (flem) *n.* [< Gr. *phlegma*, inflammation] 1. thick mucus discharged from the throat, as during a cold 2. [Obs.] the humour believed to cause sluggishness 3. a) sluggishness b) calmness

phlegmatic (fleg mat′ik) *adj.* [see prec.] 1. sluggish; dull 2. calm; cool —**phlegmat′ically** *adv.*

phloem (flō′em) *n.* [< Gr. *phloos*, bark] the cell tissue serving as a path for the distribution of food material in a plant

phlogiston (flō jis′tən) *n.* [< Gr. *phlegein*, to burn] an imaginary element formerly believed to cause combustion

phlox (floks) *n.* [Gr., a flame] a plant with white, pink, red, or bluish flowers

-phobe (fōb) [< Gr. *phobos*, a fear] a *suffix* meaning one who fears or hates [*xenophobe*]

phobia (fō′bē ə) *n.* [< Gr. *phobos*, a fear] an irrational, persistent fear of some thing or situation —**pho′bic** *adj.*

-phobia (fō′bē ə) [see prec.] a *combining form* meaning fear, dread, hatred [*claustrophobia*]

Phoenician (fə nish′ən) *adj.* of Phoenicia, its people, their language, etc. —*n.* a native of Phoenicia

phoenix (fē′niks) *n.* [< Gr. *phoinix*] *Egyptian Myth.* a beautiful bird which consumed itself in fire, rising renewed from the ashes : a symbol of immortality

phone (fōn) *n., vt., vi.* **phoned, phon′ing** *colloq.* shortened form of TELEPHONE

-phone (fōn) [< Gr. *phōnē*, a sound] a *combining form* meaning : 1. a device transmitting sound 2. a telephone

phone-in *n.* *Radio & TV* a programme in which questions, comments, etc. are telephoned to the studio and broadcast live

phoneme (fō′nēm) *n.* [< Gr. *phōnē*, a voice] *Linguis.* a set of similar sounds in a language that are heard as the same sound and represented by the same symbol —**phonemic** (fō nē′mik) *adj.*

phonemics (fō nē′miks) *n.pl.* [with sing. v.] the study of phonemic systems and the phonemes of a language

phonetic (fō net′ik) *adj.* [< Gr. *phōnē*, a sound] 1. of speech sounds 2. of phonetics 3. conforming to pronunciation —**phonet′ically** *adv.*

phonetics *n.pl.* [with sing. v.] the study of speech sounds, their production and written representation —**phonetician** (fō′-nə tish′ən), **phonetist** (fō′nə tist) *n.*

phoney (fō′nē) *adj., n.* [Colloq.] same as PHONY

phonic (fō′nik) *adj.* [< Gr. *phōnē*, a sound] of, or having the nature of, sound —**phon′ically** *adv.*

phono- [< Gr.] a *combining form* meaning sound, speech

phonograph (fō′nə gräf′) *n.* [PHONO- + -GRAPH] 1. [U.S.] a gramophone 2. an early type of gramophone with an external horn —**pho′nograph′ic** (-graf′ik) *adj.*

phonology (fō nol′ə jē) *n.* [PHONO- + -LOGY] the study of the changes in speech sounds in a language —**phonological** (fō′-nə loj′i k′l) *adj.*

phony (fō′nē) *adj.* **-nier, -niest** [< ?] [Colloq.] not genuine; false —*n., pl.* **-nies** [Colloq.] 1. something not genuine; fake 2. a person who deceives, dissembles, is insincere, etc. —**pho′niness** *n.*

phooey (fōō′ē) *interj.* [echoic] an exclamation expressing contempt, scorn or disgust

phosphate (fos′fāt) *n.* [Fr.] 1. a salt of phosphoric acid 2. a fertilizer containing phosphates

phosphor (fos′fər) *n.* [see PHOSPHORUS] 1. same as PHOSPHORUS : now esp. in **phosphor bronze** 2. a fluorescent substance

phosphoresce (fos′fə res′) *vi.* **-resced′, -resc′ing** to show or undergo phosphorescence

phosphorescence *n.* [see PHOSPHORUS & -ESCENCE] 1. the property of giving off light after exposure to light, X-rays, etc. 2. such light —**phos′phores′cent** *adj.*

phosphoric (fos for′ik) *adj.* of, like, or containing phosphorus, esp. with a valence of five

phosphoric acid any of several oxygen acids of phosphorus

phosphorous (fos′fər əs) *adj.* of, like, or containing phosphorus, esp. with a valence of three

phosphorus (fos′fər əs) *n.* [< Gr. *phōs*, light + *pherein*, to bear] a nonmetallic chemical element, a white, phosphorescent, waxy solid that ignites spontaneously at room temperature : symbol, P

photo (fōt′ō) *n., pl.* **-tos** short form of PHOTOGRAPH

photo- (fōt′ō) [< Gr. *phos,* a light] a *combining form* meaning : 1. of or produced by light 2. of photography

photocopier *n.* a device which produces photographic copies

photocopy *n., pl.* **-cop′ies** a photographic copy of printed or other graphic material —*vt.* **-cop′ied, -cop′ying** to make a photocopy of

photoelectric *adj.* of or having to do with the electric effects produced by light or other radiation

photoelectric cell any device in which light controls an electric circuit which operates a mechanical device, as for opening doors, etc.; electric eye

photoengraving (fōt′ō in grā′viŋ) *n.* a photomechanical process by which photographs are reproduced in relief on printing plates

photo finish 1. a race so close that the winner can be determined only from a photograph at the finish line 2. any close finish of a contest

photoflash *adj.* *Photog.* designating a flashbulb, electrically synchronized with the shutter

photoflood *adj.* *Photog.* designating a

high-intensity electric lamp used for sustained illumination

photogenic (fōt′ō jen′ik) *adj.* [see PHOTO] 1. that looks attractive in photographs: said esp. of a person 2. giving off light —**pho′togen′ically** *adv.*

photograph (fōt′ə gräf′) *n.* a picture made by photography —*vt.* to take a photograph of —*vi.* to appear (as specified) in photographs [to *photograph* well] —**photographer** (fə tog′rə fər) *n.*

photographic (fōt′ə graf′ik) *adj.* 1. of or like a photograph or photography 2. used in photography 3. recalling in precise detail —**pho′tograph′ically** *adv.*

photography (fə tog′rə fē) *n.* [PHOTO- + -GRAPHY] the process of producing images of objects upon a photosensitive surface by the chemical action of light or other radiant energy

photogravure (fōt′ō grə vyōōər′) *n.* [Fr.] a photomechanical process by which photographs are reproduced on intaglio printing plates

photolithography (fōt′ō li thog′rə fē) *n.* a printing process combining photography and lithography

photometer (fō tom′ə tər) *n.* [PHOTO- + -METER] a device used to measure the intensity of light

photometry *n.* the measurement of the intensity of light —**photometric** (fōt′ə met′rik) *adj.*

photomontage (fōt′ō mon täzh′) *n.* montage done in or with photographs

photon (fō′ton) *n.* [PHOT(O)- (ELECTR)ON] a quantum of electromagnetic energy, as of light, X-rays, etc., having both particle and wave behaviour

photosensitive (fōt′ō sen′sə tiv) *adj.* reacting or sensitive to radiant energy, esp. to light

Photostat (fōt′ō stat′) [PHOTO- + -STAT] *Trademark* a device for making photographic copies of printed matter, drawings, etc. directly as positives upon special paper —*vt.* [p-] -**stat′ted, -stat′ting** to make a photostat of

photosynthesis (fōt′ə sin′thə sis) *n.* the formation in green plants of organic substances, chiefly sugars, from carbon dioxide and water in the presence of light and chlorophyll —**pho′tosyn′thesize′** *vt., vi.*

phototropism (fō′tō trop′iz′m) *n.* *Bot.* movement of a part of a plant towards or away from light sources

phrasal verb *Gram.* a phrase consisting of a verb and adverb whose meaning cannot be deduced from the constituents (Ex.: "take in" meaning "deceive")

phrase (frāz) *n.* [< Gr. *phrazein,* speak] 1. *Gram.* a sequence of two or more words conveying a single thought but not containing a subject and predicate 2. a short, colourful expression 3. a manner of expression 4. *Music* a short, distinct passage —*vt.* **phrased, phras′ing** 1. *Music* to mark off (notes) into phrases 2. to express in a phrase —**phras′al** *adj.*

phraseology (frā′zē ol′ə jē) *n., pl.* **-gies**

choice and pattern of words —**phra′seolog′ical** (-ə loj′i k'l) *adj.*

phrenetic (fri net′ik) *adj.* [< Gr. *phrenētikos,* mad] *earlier sp. of* FRENETIC

phrenology (fri nol′ə jē) *n.* [< Gr. *phrēn,* mind + -LOGY] a system, now rejected, by which character and mental faculties are analysed by studying the shape of the skull —**phrenol′ogist** *n.*

phthisis (thī′sis) [< Gr. *phthiein,* waste away] *old term for* any wasting disease, esp. tuberculosis of the lungs —**phthis′ical** *adj.*

phut (fut) *n.* [< Hind. *phatna,* to burst] 1. the sound made by a passing bullet 2. the sound of a bladder collapsing —**to go phut** [Colloq.] to collapse

PHYLACTERIES

phylactery (fi lak′tər ē) *n., pl.* **-teries** [< Gr. *phylassein,* to guard] a small leather case holding slips inscribed with Scripture passages worn by Orthodox Jewish men during morning prayer

phylum (fī′ləm) *n., pl.* **-la** [< Gr. *phylon,* tribe] any principal division of the plant or animal kingdom

phys. 1. physical 2. physician 3. physics

physic (fiz′ik) *n.* [< Gr. *physis,* nature] 1. [Archaic] medical science 2. a medicine —*vt.* **-icked, -icking** to dose with medicine

physical *adj.* [see prec.] 1. of the body 2. of nature and all matter; material 3. of or according to the laws of nature 4. of, or produced by the forces of, physics —**phys′ically** *adv.*

physical chemistry chemistry dealing with physical properties in relation to chemical properties

physical education instruction in the exercise, hygiene, etc. of the human body

physical geography the study of the features and nature of the earth's surface, atmosphere, climate, etc.

physical jerks [Colloq.] physical training

physical science any science dealing with inanimate matter or energy, as physics, chemistry, etc.

physical therapy *same as* PHYSIOTHERAPY

physical training a method of keeping fit by following a course of bodily exercises

physician (fə zish′ən) *n.* [see PHYSIC] 1. a person licensed to practise medicine 2. a medical doctor other than a surgeon 3. a healer

physicist (fiz′ə sist) *n.* a specialist in physics

physics (fiz′iks) *n.pl.* [< L. *physica*] 1. [*with sing. v.*] the science dealing with the properties, changes, etc. of matter and energy 2. physical properties or processes

physiognomy (fiz′ē on′ə mē) *n.* [< Gr. *physis*, nature + *gnōmōn*, one who knows] 1. facial features, esp. as supposedly indicative of character 2. the practice of trying to judge character by observation of bodily, esp. facial, features 3. outward features —**phys′iognom′ic** (-ə nom′ik), **phys′iognom′ical** *adj.* —**phys′iog′nomist** *n.*

physiography (fiz′ē og′rə fē) *n.* [< Gr. *physis*, nature + -GRAPHY] 1. a description of the features and phenomena of nature 2. physical geography —**phys′iog′rapher** *n.*

physiology (fiz′ē ol′ə jē) *n.* [< Gr. *physis*, nature + -LOGY] the study of the functions and vital processes of living organisms or their parts and organs —**phys′iolog′ical** (-ə loj′i k'l), **phys′iolog′ic** *adj.* —**phys′iol′ogist** *n.*

physiotherapy (fiz′ē ō ther′ə pē) *n.* therapy using exercise, massage, heat, etc. instead of drugs —**phys′iother′apist** *n.*

physique (fi zēk′) *n.* [Fr.] the structure, constitution, strength, or appearance of the body

pi[1] (pī) *n., pl.* **pies** [< PIE[1]] chiefly U.S. *sp. of* PIE[2]

pi[2] *n.* 1. the sixteenth letter of the Greek alphabet (Π, π) 2. the symbol (π) designating the ratio of the circumference of a circle to its diameter, about equal to 3.14

pia mater (pī′ə māt′ər) [ML., gentle mother] the vascular membrane that is the innermost of the three membranes around the brain and spinal cord

pianissimo (pya′nis′ə mō′) *adj., adv.* [It.] *Music* very soft

pianist (pē′ən ist) *n.* a person who plays the piano

piano[1] (pē an′ō) *n., pl.* **-os** [It., < *pianoforte*] a large, stringed percussion instrument played from a keyboard: each key operates a felt-covered hammer that strikes a steel wire or set of wires

piano[2] (pyä′nō) *adj., adv.* [It.] *Music* soft —*n., pl.* **-nos** a note or passage played softly

piano accordion an accordion in which the right hand plays a piano-like keyboard rather than studs or buttons

pianoforte (pyan′ə fôr′tē) *n.* [It. < *piano*, soft + *forte*, strong] same as PIANO[1]

Pianola (pē′ə nō′lə) *Trademark* a kind of mechanical piano

piazza (pi at′sə) *n.* [It.] 1. in Italy, an open public square 2. a covered arcade

pibroch (pē′brok) *n.* [< Gael. *piob*, bagpipe] a martial or dirgelike piece of music for the bagpipes

pica (pī′kə) *n.* [< ? ML., directory] 1. formerly, a size of type, approx. 12 point

2. the height of this type, about .42 cm or ¹/₆ inch 3. a type size of typewriters with 10 spaces to the inch

picador (pik′ə dôr′) *n.* [Sp. < *picar*, to prick] in bullfighting, a horseman who pricks the bull's neck with a lance

picaresque (pik′ə resk′) *adj.* [< Sp. *pícaro*, rascal] of or dealing with sharp-witted vagabonds and their adventures [a *picaresque* novel]

picayune (pik′ə yōōn′) *n.* [< Fr. *picaillon*, small coin] [U.S.] a coin of small value —*adj.* trivial; petty

piccalilli (pik′ə lil′ē) *n.* [prob. < PICKLE] a pickle of chopped vegetables, mustard, spices, etc.

piccanin (pik′ə nin) *n.* [See ff.] [S Afr. Colloq.] a male African child

piccaninny (pik′ə nin′ē) *n.* [? < Port. *pequenino*, tiny one] a small Negro or Aboriginal child

piccolo (pik′ə lō′) *n., pl.* **-los** [It., small] a small flute, pitched an octave above the ordinary flute —**pic′colo′ist** *n.*

pick[1] (pik) *n.* [var. of PIKE[4]] 1. a heavy tool with a long, pointed metal head set at a right angle to the handle, used for breaking up soil, rock, etc. 2. a pointed instrument for picking 3. same as PLECTRUM

pick[2] *vt.* [ME. *picken*] 1. to choose 2. to gather (flowers, berries, etc.) 3. to dig, probe, or scratch at in trying to remove or to clear something from 4. to eat sparingly or daintily 5. to break up, pierce, or dig up with something pointed 6. to pull (fibres, rags, etc.) apart 7. to open (a lock) with a wire, etc. instead of a key 8. to steal from (another's pocket, etc.) —*vi.* 1. to select, esp. in a fussy way 2. to gather growing berries, flowers, etc. 3. to use a pick 4. to eat sparingly or fussily 5. to thieve —*n.* 1. the act of choosing 2. the most desirable one(s) —**pick and choose** to select carefully —**pick apart** (or **to pieces**) to find flaws in by examining critically; also —**pick holes in** —**pick a quarrel** to provoke a dispute —**pick at** 1. to eat small portions of, esp. in a fussy way 2. [Colloq.] to find fault with —**pick off** 1. to pluck 2. to hit with a carefully aimed shot —**pick on** 1. to choose 2. [Colloq.] to single out for abuse, etc. —**pick one's way** to move cautiously —**pick out** 1. to choose 2. to single out from among a group 3. to play (a tune) note by note —**pick over** to sort out, item by item —**pick someone's brains** [Colloq.] to obtain information from someone —**pick up** 1. to grasp and lift 2. to learn, esp. by chance 3. to stop for and take along 4. to arrest 5. to gain (speed) 6. to regain (health, power, etc.); improve 7. to resume (an activity, etc.) after a pause 8. to bring into range of sight, hearing, etc. 9. [Colloq.] to get to know casually, esp. for lovemaking —**pick′er** *n.*

pickaback *n., adv., adj.* [< PACK[1]] *same as* PIGGYBACK

PICKAXE

pickaxe *n.* [< OFr. *picquois*] a pick with a point at one end of the head and a chisellike edge at the other

picked *adj.* [< PICK²] selected with care

picket (pik′it) *n.* [< Fr. *pic,* pickaxe] 1. a stake, usually pointed, used in a fence, etc. 2. a person stationed, as by a trade union, outside a factory, etc. to demonstrate, keep strikebreakers out, etc. 3. a soldier or soldiers stationed to guard troops from surprise attack —*vt.* 1. to place pickets, or serve as a picket, at (a factory, etc.) 2. to guard (troops) with a picket 3. to hitch (an animal) to a picket 4. to enclose with a picket fence —**pick′eting** *n.*

picket fence a fence made of upright stakes

picket line a line of people serving as pickets

pickings *n.pl.* 1. small scraps; leftovers 2. returns; profit 3. spoils

pickle (pik′'l) *n.* [< MDu. *pekel*] 1. [usually *pl.*] vegetables, such as onions, cucumbers, etc. so preserved 2. any brine, vinegar, etc. used to preserve or marinate food 3. [Colloq.] an awkward or difficult situation —*vt.* -led, -ling to treat or preserve in a pickle solution —**pick′ler** *n.*

pickled *adj.* [Slang] drunk

pick-me-up *n.* [Colloq.] a tonic, esp. an alcoholic drink, taken to raise one's spirits

pickpocket *n.* one who steals from people's pockets

pickup *n.* 1. in an electric gramophone, a device producing audio-frequency currents from the vibrations of a needle in a record groove 2. a small, open truck for light loads 3. [Colloq.] a casual acquaintance, as for lovemaking 4. a picking up 5. [Colloq.] improvement

picky (pik′ē) *adj.* **-ier, -iest** [U.S. Colloq.] very fastidious or exacting; fussy

picnic (pik′nik) *n.* [< Fr. *pique-nique*] 1. a pleasure outing, with an outdoor meal 2. [Slang] *a)* a pleasant experience *b)* an easy task —*vi.* **-nicked, -nicking** to hold or attend a picnic —**pic′nicker** *n.*

picot (pē′kō) *n.* [Fr. < *pic,* a point] any of the small loops in an ornamental edging on lace, ribbon, etc.

picric acid (pik′rik) [< Gr. *pikros,* bitter] a yellow, crystalline acid used in dyes, explosives, etc.

Pict (pikt) *n.* any of an ancient people of Great Britain —**Pict′ish** *adj., n.*

pictograph (pik′tō gräf′) *n.* [see PICTURE + -GRAPH] 1. a picture or picturelike symbol, as used in ancient writing 2. a diagram using pictures Also **pic′togram** —**pic′tograph′ic** (-graf′ik) *adj.*

pictorial (pik tôr′ē əl) *adj.* of, containing, or expressed in pictures —*n.* a periodical featuring many pictures —**picto′rializa′tion** *n.*

picture (pik′chər) *n.* [< L. *pingere,* to paint] 1. a likeness produced on a flat surface, as by painting or photography 2. anything resembling or typifying something else 3. anything regarded as like a painting, etc. 4. a film 5. a mental image; idea 5. a vivid description 6. all the facts of an event 7. a film 8. the image on a TV screen —*vt.* **-tured, -turing** 1. to imagine 2. to describe or explain 3. to make a picture of 4. to make visible —**in** (or **out of**) **the picture** considered as involved (or not involved) in a situation

picture card *same as* COURT CARD

picture moulding the rail near the ceiling from which framed pictures are hung: also **picture rail**

picture palace a cinema: also **picture house, picture theatre**

picture postcard a postcard with a picture on one side

pictures *n.pl.* [Colloq.] the cinema or a film performance

picturesque (pik′chə resk′) *adj.* 1. *a)* having a wild beauty, as mountain scenery *b)* quaint 2. vivid

picture window a large window, esp. in a living room

piddle (pid′'l) *vi.* **-dled, -dling** [< ?] 1. [Colloq.] to urinate 2. to trifle or deal in trifles —**pid′dler** *n.*

piddling (pid′liŋ) *adj.* [Colloq.] trifling; petty

pidgin (pij′in) *n.* [supposed Chin. pronun. of BUSINESS] a jargon incorporating the vocabulary of different languages

pidgin English a simplified form of English with a Chinese syntax, used as a trade language

pi-dog *same as* PYE-DOG

pie¹ (pī) *n.* [< ?] a baked dish consisting of fruit, meat, etc. with an under or upper crust, or both —**(as) easy as pie** [Colloq.] extremely easy

pie² *n.* [< ?] a disordered collection of printing type

pie³ *n.* [OFr. < L. *pica*] *same as* MAGPIE

piebald (pī′bôld′) *adj.* [PIE³ + BALD] covered with patches of two colours, esp. white and black —*n.* a piebald horse or other animal

piece (pēs) *n.* [OFr. *pece*] 1. a section of a whole, regarded as complete in itself 2. a part broken or separated from the whole 3. a single thing, as an artistic work, an action, a firearm, a coin, one of a set, etc. 4. an amount of work constituting a single job 5. *Chess* any

chessman other than a pawn —vt. **pieced,
piec′ing** 1. to add pieces to, as in repairing
2. to join (together) the pieces of, as in
mending —**a piece of one's mind** frank
criticism —**go to pieces** 1. to lose all self-
control 2. to fall apart —**nasty piece
of work** an unpleasant person —**of a**
(or one) **piece** alike —**piece of cake**
[Colloq.] something easily obtained or
achieved

‡**pièce de résistance** (pyes′də-
rä zēs täns′) [Fr. piece of resistance]
1. the main or most remarkable item 2.
the principal dish of a meal

piece goods textiles usually sold by the
metre, or yard

piecemeal (pēs′mēl′) adv. [< ME. pece,
piece + -mele, a measure] in small amounts
or degrees —adj. made or done in pieces
or one piece at a time

piece of eight the obsolete Spanish dollar

piecework n. work paid for at a fixed
rate (**piece rate**) per piece —**piece′work′-
er** n.

pie chart a graph in the form of a circle
divided into sectors in which relative
quantities are indicated by the
proportionately different sizes of the sectors

pled (plĕd) adj. covered with patches of
two or more colours

‡**pied-à-terre** (pye tä täar′) n., pl. **pieds-à-
terre** (pye tä-) [Fr. foot on the ground]
a lodging used only part of the time

pie-eyed (pī′id′) adj. [Slang] intoxicated;
drunk

pie in the sky [Slang] a promise of
benefits or a reward in an afterlife or
in the remote future

pier (pēar) n. [ML. pera] 1. a structure
supporting the spans of a bridge 2. a
structure built out over water and supported
by pillars: used as a landing place, pavilion,
etc. 3. Archit. a) a heavy supporting
column b) the part of a wall between
windows

pierce (pēars) vt. **pierced, pierc′ing** [<
L. per, through + tundere, strike] 1.
to pass into or through as a pointed
instrument does 2. to make a hole in;
bore 3. to break into or through 4.
to sound sharply through 5. to penetrate
with the sight or mind —vi. to penetrate
—**pierc′ingly** adv.

pier glass a mirror set in the pier between
windows

Pierrot (pēə′rō′) [Fr.] a stock comic
character in old French pantomime

pietism (pī′ə tiz′m) n. religious piety, esp.
when exaggerated —**pi′etis′tic, pi′etis′ti-
cal** adj.

piet-my-vrou (pit′mä frō′) n. [echoic]
[S Afr.] the red-breasted cuckoo

piety (pī′ətē) n., pl. **-ties** [< L. pius,
pious] 1. devotion to religious duties and
practices 2. devotion to parents, family,
etc. 3. a pious act, etc.

piezoelectric effect (pī ē′zō i lek′trik)
the property exhibited by certain crystals
of generating voltage when subjected to
pressure, and, conversely, undergoing

mechanical stress when subjected to
voltage

piezoelectricity (pī ē′zō i lek tris′ə tē) n.
[< Gr. piezein, to press + ELECTRICITY]
electricity resulting from the piezoelectric
effect

piffle (pif′′l) n. [< ?] [Colloq.] talk,
action, etc. regarded as nonsensical
—interj. nonsense! —vi. -fled, -fling to
talk in a silly manner —**pif′fling** adj.

pig (pig) n. [ME. pigge] 1. a domesticated
animal with a broad snout and a fat body
covered with bristles; swine 2. pork 3.
a person regarded as like a pig 4. an
oblong casting of iron, etc. poured from
the smelting furnace 5. [Derog. Slang]
a policeman —vi. **pigged, pig′ging** to
live like a pig, esp. in the phrase **pig
it** —**buy a pig in a poke** to buy an article
without prior sight or knowledge, usually
something of no value

pigeon[1] (pij′ən) n. [< L. pipire, to peep]
1. any of various related birds with a
small head, plump body, and short legs,
larger than doves 2. [Slang] a dupe

pigeon[2] n. same as PIDGIN —**one's pigeon**
[Slang] one's special concern

pigeonhole n. a small, open
compartment, as in a desk, for filing papers
—vt. **-holed′, -hol′ing** 1. to put in the
pigeonhole of a desk, etc. 2. to put aside
indefinitely 3. to classify

pigeon-toed adj. having the toes or feet
turned in

piggery (pig′ər ē) n., pl. **-geries** var.
of PIGSTY

piggish (pig′ish) adj. like a pig; gluttonous
or filthy —**pig′gishly** adv. —**pig′gishness** n.

piggy (pig′ē) n., pl. **-gies** a little pig
—adj. **-gier, -giest** same as PIGGISH

piggyback n. [< PACK[1]] a ride on the
back or shoulders of another —adv., adj.
on the back or shoulders of another

piggy bank any small money-box with
a slot for coins

pigheaded adj. stubborn; obstinate

pig iron [see PIG, n. 4] crude iron,
as it comes from the blast furnace

piglet (pig′lit) n. a little pig, esp. a suckling

pigment (pig′mənt) n. [< L. pigmentum]
1. colouring matter used to make paints
2. colouring matter in the cells and tissues
of plants or animals —vi., vt. to take
on pigment —**pig′mentary** adj.

pigmentation (pig′mən tā′shən) n.
colouration in plants or animals due to
pigment in the tissue

Pigmy (pig′mē) adj., n., pl. **-mies** same
as PYGMY

pignut (pig′nut′) n. same as EARTHNUT

pigpen n. [U.S.] same as PIGSTY

pigskin n. 1. the skin of a pig 2. leather
made from this

pigsty n., pl. **-sties′** a pen where pigs
are confined

pig swill kitchen or brewery swill given
to pigs: also **pig's wash, pig wash**

pigtail n. a plait of hair hanging at the
back of the head

pike[1] (pīk) n. [< Fr. pique] Hist. a

weapon with a metal spearhead on a long, wooden shaft

pike² *n.* [see ff.] a slender, voracious, freshwater game fish of northern waters, with a narrow, pointed head and sharp teeth

pike³ *n.* [OE. *pic,* a pickaxe] a spike or point, as the pointed tip of a spear

pike⁴ *n.* [see prec.] [Dial.] a peaked summit

pikestaff *n., pl.* **-staves** the shaft of a pike

pilaf, pilaff (pilaf´) *n.* [Pers. & Turk. *piláw*] rice boiled in a seasoned liquid, and usually containing meat or fish: also **pilau´**

PILASTER

pilaster (pilas´tər) *n.* [< It. < L. *pila,* a pile] a columnlike rectangular support projecting partially from a wall

pilchard (pil´chərd) *n.* [< ?] a small saltwater fish of the herring family, the commercial sardine of western Europe

pile¹ (pīl) *n.* [< L. *pila,* a pillar] 1. a mass of things heaped together 2. [Colloq.] a large amount 3. a heap of wood, etc. on which a corpse or sacrifice is burned 4. a large building 5. *Elec.* a series of alternate plates of unlike metals with acid-saturated cloth between them, for making an electric current 6. *an earlier name for* NUCLEAR REACTOR —*vt.* **piled, pil´ing** 1. to heap up 2. to load 3. to accumulate Often with *up* —*vi.* 1. to form a pile 2. to move confusedly in a mass (with *in, out, on,* etc.) —**pile it on** to exaggerate

pile² *n.* [< L. *pilus,* a hair] a soft, velvety, raised surface on a rug, fabric, etc.

pile³ *n.* [OE. *pil*] a long, heavy beam driven into the ground to support a bridge, dock, etc.

pile driver (or **engine**) a machine with a drop hammer for driving piles

piles *n.pl.* [< L. *pila,* ball] haemorrhoids

pileup *n.* [Colloq.] a collision involving several vehicles

pilfer (pil´fər) *vt., vi.* [< MFr. *pelfre,* booty] to steal (esp. small sums, petty objects, etc.) —**pil´ferage** *n.*

pilgrim (pil´grim) *n.* [< L. *peregrinus,* foreigner] 1. a traveller to a shrine or holy place 2. a wanderer 3. [P-] one of the English Puritans who founded Plymouth colony in Massachusetts, U.S. in 1620

pilgrimage *n.* 1. a pilgrim's journey,

esp. to a shrine, etc. 2. any similar long journey

Pilgrim Fathers the Pilgrims

pill (pil) *n.* [< L. *pila,* ball] 1. a small ball, tablet, etc. of medicine to be swallowed whole 2. a thing that is unpleasant but unavoidable 3. [Slang] a billiard ball, golf ball, etc. —**the pill** [Colloq.] a contraceptive taken as a pill by women

pillage (pil´ij) *n.* [< MFr. *piller,* rob] 1. a plundering 2. booty; loot —*vt., vi.* **-laged, -laging** 1. to loot; plunder

pillar (pil´ər) *n.* [< L. *pila,* column] 1. a slender, vertical structure used as a support; column 2. a person who is a main support of an institution, etc. —**from pillar to post** from one predicament, place of appeal, etc. to another

pillar box a pillar-shaped public letter box, usually red and often situated on a pavement

pillbox (pil´boks´) *n.* 1. a small box for pills 2. a low, enclosed gun emplacement of concrete

pillion (pil´yən) *n.* [< L. *pellis,* a skin] an extra saddle behind the driver on a motorcycle —**ride pillion** to travel on the pillion, esp. of a motorcycle

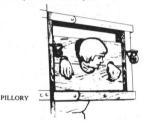

PILLORY

pillory (pil´ər ē) *n., pl.* **-ries** [OFr. *pilori*] *Hist.* a wooden board with holes for the head and hands, in which offenders were locked and exposed to public scorn —*vt.* **-ried, -rying** 1. to lay open to public ridicule, scorn, or abuse 2. to put in a pillory

pillow (pil´ō) *n.* [OE. *pyle*] a cloth case filled with feathers, etc. and used as a support for the head in sleeping —*vt.* 1. to rest as on a pillow 2. to be a pillow for

pillowcase *n.* a removable cloth case to cover a pillow: also **pil´lowslip´**

pilot (pī´lət) *n.* [< Gr. *pēdon,* oar blade] 1. a qualified operator of an aircraft 2. a steersman; specif., one licensed to steer ships into or out of a harbour 3. a guide 4. *same as* PILOT LIGHT —*vt.* 1. to act as a pilot of, on, in, or over 2. to guide —*adj.* 1. that guides or activates 2. that serves as a testing unit

pilothouse *n.* *same as* WHEELHOUSE

pilot lamp an electric lamp placed in an electric circuit to indicate when the current is on

pilot light a small gas burner kept lighted to rekindle a principal burner when needed

pilot officer *see* MILITARY RANKS, table

pilule (pil'yōōl) *n.* [see PILL] a small pill

pimento (pi men'tō) *n., pl.* **-tos** [< L. *pigmentum*, pigment] *same as* ALL-SPICE

pimiento (pi myen'tō) *n.* [var. of PIMENTO] a sweet variety of the capsicum pepper

pimp (pimp) *n.* [< ?] a man who is an agent for prostitutes —*vi.* to act as a pimp

pimpernel (pim'pər nəl) *n.* [< L. *piper*, pepper] any of certain related plants with clustered flowers and leafless stems; esp., the **scarlet pimpernel**, with starlike flowers which close in bad weather

pimple (pim'p'l) *n.* [? < OE. *piplian*, break out in pimples] any small, rounded, usually inflamed swelling of the skin —**pim'ply** *adj.*

pin (pin) *n.* [OE. *pinn*] 1. a little piece of stiff wire with a pointed end and a rounded head, for fastening things together 2. something worthless or insignificant 3. anything like a pin in form, use, etc. 4. *Bowling* any of the wooden clubs at which the ball is rolled 5. a peg for regulating the tension of a string in a piano, harp, etc. 6. *Golf* a pole with a flag attached, in and marking the hole of a green 7. a peg of wood, metal, etc., used as a fastening, support, etc. 8. [Colloq.] the leg: *usually used in pl.* —*vt.* **pinned, pin'ning** 1. to fasten as with a pin 2. to hold firmly in one position —**pin down** 1. to get (someone) to commit himself as to his opinion, plans, etc. 2. to confirm (a fact, details, etc.) —**pin (something) on someone** [Colloq.] to lay the blame for (something) on someone

pinafore (pin'ə fôr') *n.* [PIN + AFORE] 1. an apron, esp. a wraparound one or one with a bib 2. a sleeveless dress worn over a sweater or blouse : also **pinafore dress**

pinball machine a game machine with an inclined board having pins, holes, etc. marked with scores for a spring-driven ball to contact

pince-nez (pans'nā') *n., pl.* **pince'-nez'** (-nāz') [Fr., nose-pincher] spectacles without sidepieces, kept in place by a spring gripping the bridge of the nose

pincers (pin'sərz) *n.pl.* [occas. with sing. v.] [< OFr. *pincier*, to pinch] 1. a tool with two pivoted parts for gripping or nipping things 2. a grasping claw, as of a crab —**pin'cerlike'** *adj.*

pinch (pinch) *vt.* [< OFr. *pincier*] 1. to squeeze as between finger and thumb 2. to nip off the end of (a plant shoot) 3. to press painfully upon (a part of the body) 4. to cause distress or discomfort to 5. to make thin, cramped, etc., as by hunger or cold 6. to restrict closely; straiten 7. [Colloq.] a) to steal b) to arrest —*vi.* 1. to squeeze painfully 2. to be stingy or frugal —*n.* 1. a pinching; squeeze 2. a quantity graspable between finger and thumb 3. distress 4. an emergency

pinchbeck (pinch'bek') *n.* [< C. *Pinchbeck*] 1. an alloy of copper and zinc used to imitate gold in jewellery 2. anything cheap or imitation

pinch-hit (pinch'hit') *vi.* **-hit', -hit'ting** [U.S.] 1. *Baseball* to bat in place of the batter whose turn it is 2. to substitute (*for*) in an emergency —**pinch hitter**

pincushion (pin'kŏŏsh'ən) *n.* a small cushion to stick pins and needles in

pine¹ (pīn) *n.* [< L. *pinus*] 1. any of various evergreen trees with needlelike leaves and woody cones : pines are valuable for wood and for resin, from which turpentine, tar, etc. are obtained 2. the wood

pine² *vi.* **pined, pin'ing** [< L. *poena*, a pain] 1. to have an intense desire; yearn 2. to waste (*away*) with grief, longing, etc.

pineal body (pin'ē əl) [< Fr. < L. *pinea*, pine cone] a small, cone-shaped body in the brain of all vertebrates : its function is obscure

pineapple (pīn'ap''l) *n.* [< ME. *pinappel*, pine cone] 1. a juicy, edible tropical fruit somewhat resembling a pine cone 2. the plant it grows on

pine cone the cone of a pine tree

ping (piŋ) *n.* [echoic] a sharp sound, as of a bullet striking, an engine knocking, etc. —*vi., vt.* to make or cause to make such a sound

Ping-Pong (piŋ'poŋ) [echoic] *Trademark* table tennis equipment —*n.* [**p-p-**] *same as* TABLE TENNIS

pinhead (pin'hed') *n.* 1. anything tiny or trifling 2. [Slang] a stupid or silly person

pinhole *n.* 1. a tiny hole made as by a pin 2. a hole into which a pin or peg goes

pinion¹ (pin'yən) *n.* [< L. *pinna*, feather] a small cogwheel with teeth that fit into a gearwheel

pinion² *n.* [< L. *pinna*, feather] 1. the end joint of a bird's wing 2. a wing 3. any wing feather —*vt.* 1. to bind the arms of 2. to confine 3. to bind (the wings) 4. to cut off the pinions of (a bird)

pink¹ (piŋk) *n.* [< ?] 1. pale red 2. any of certain annual and perennial plants with brightly-coloured flowers 3. the finest example, degree, etc. —*adj.* 1. pale-red 2. [Colloq.] somewhat radical politically —**in the pink** [Colloq.] in good physical condition —**pink'ish** *adj.*

pink² *vt.* [ME. *pynken*] 1. to cut a saw-toothed edge on (cloth, etc.) to prevent unravelling or for decoration 2. to prick or stab

pink³ *vi.* [echoic] to make a metallic knocking sound : said of an internal-combustion engine —**pink'ing** *n.*

pinkie, pinky *n., pl.* **pink'ies** [prob. < Du. *pink*, little finger] [U.S. & Scot.] the smallest finger

pinking shears shears with notched blades, for pinking the edges of cloth, etc.

pin money 1. orig., an allowance given to a wife for small personal expenses 2. any small sum of money

pinnace (pin'is) *n.* [< Fr. < Sp. < L. *pinus*, pine] 1. a small sailing ship 2. a ship's boat

pinnacle (pin′ək'l) *n.* [< L. *pinna*, wing] 1. the highest point 2. a slender, pointed formation, as a mountain peak 3. a small turret or spire

pinnate (pin′it) *adj.* [< L. *pinna*, a feather] *Bot.* with leaflets on each side of a common axis

pinny (pin′ē) *n.* [Colloq.] a pinafore

pinpoint (pin′point′) *vt.* to locate, define, or focus on precisely —*n.* the point of a pin

pinprick *n.* a minor irritation or annoyance

pins and needles a prickling feeling as in a numb limb

pin stripe a very thin stripe, as in some suits

pint (pīnt) *n.* [< ML. *pinta*] 1. a measure of capacity (liquid or dry) equal to 1/2 quart (0.568 litre) 2. a pint container Abbrev. **pt., p.** 3. [Colloq.] a pint of beer

pinta (pin′tə) *n.* [< *pint of*] [Colloq.] a pint, esp. of milk

pintail (pin′tāl′) *n.* a duck or grouse with a long, pointed tail —**pin′tailed′** *adj.*

PINTLE

pintle (pin′t'l) *n.* [OE. *pintel*, penis] a pin or bolt upon which some other part pivots or turns

pinto (pin′tō) *n.*, *pl.* **-tos** [AmSp.] [U.S.] a horse marked with patches of white and another colour

pint-size (pīnt′sīz′) *adj.* [Colloq.] tiny: also **pint′-sized′**

pin tuck a very narrow, ornamental fold in the fabric of a shirt, dress, etc.

pinup (pin′up′) *adj.* [Colloq.] designating an attractive woman or man whose picture is often pinned up on walls —*n.* [Colloq.] a pinup woman or man, picture, etc.

pinwheel *n.* a firework that revolves when set off

pion (pī′on′) *n.* [PI² + (MES)ON] any of three mesons, positive, negative, or neutral

pioneer (pī′ə nēar′) *n.* [< Fr. see PEON] 1. one who goes before, preparing the way for others, as an early settler 2. an innovator or inventor —*adj.* of a pioneer —*vi.* to be a pioneer —*vt.* 1. to prepare or open (a way, etc.) 2. to be a pioneer in or of

pious (pī′əs) *adj.* [L. *pius*] 1. having or showing religious devotion 2. hypocritically virtuous —**pi′ously** *adv.*

pip¹ (pip) *n.* [< PIPPIN] a small seed, as of an apple

pip² *n.* [< ?] 1. any of the spots on playing cards, dice, etc. 2. the emblem worn by certain officers in the army indicating their rank

pip³ *n.* [< L. *pituita*, phlegm] 1. a contagious disease of fowl 2. [Slang] a bad temper or depression [he gives me the *pip*]

pip⁴ *vt.* **pipped, pip′ping** [< ?] [Colloq.] 1. to wound, esp. with a gun 2. to defeat someone, esp. when their victory seemed certain [to *pip* at the post]

pip⁵ *n.* [echoic] a high-pitched sound, of which a sequence (**the pips**) acts as a time signal, esp. on the radio

pipe (pīp) *n.* [< L. *pipare*, to chirp] 1. a long tube of concrete, metal, etc., for conveying water, gas, oil, etc. 2. a tubular part, organ, etc. 3. *a)* a tube with a small bowl at one end, in which tobacco, etc. is smoked *b)* enough tobacco, etc. to fill such a bowl 4. a tube into which air is blown to make musical sounds; specif., [*pl.*] *same as:* a) PANPIPE b) BAGPIPE 5. any of the tubes in an organ that produce the tones 6. a boatswain's whistle 7. a cask holding about 105 gallons (447 litres) —*vi.* **piped, pip′ing** 1. to play on a pipe 2. to utter shrill sounds —*vt.* 1. to play (a tune, etc.) on a pipe 2. to utter in a shrill voice 3. to bring, etc. by piping 4. to convey (water, etc.) by pipes 5. to provide with pipes 6. to transmit recorded music, etc. —**pipe down** [Slang] to become quiet —**pipe up** 1. to begin to play or sing (music) 2. to speak up or say, esp. in a piping voice

pipe clay a white clay used for making tobacco pipes, whitening leather, etc.

pipe cleaner a short length of wires twisted to hold tiny tufts of yarn, for cleaning pipestems

pipe dream [Colloq.] a fanciful idea or vain hope: alluding to dreams induced by smoking an opium pipe

pipeline *n.* 1. a line of pipes for conveying water, oil, etc. 2. any means whereby something is conveyed —**in the pipeline** in the process of being completed, delivered, etc.

pip emma [Colloq.] the army signallers term for P.M.

pipe organ an organ with pipes

piper *n.* a person who plays on a pipe; esp., a bagpiper

pipe rolls the record of Exchequer accounts kept between 1131 and 1833

pipestem *n.* the slender stem of a tobacco pipe

pipette (pi pet′) *n.* [< Fr. *pipe*, a pipe] a slender tube for measuring or transferring small amounts of liquids

piping (pīp′iŋ) *n.* 1. a system of pipes 2. material used for pipes 3. a narrow, rounded fold of material with which edges are trimmed —*adj.* shrill —**piping hot** so hot as to sizzle

pipit (pip′it) *n.* [echoic] a small songbird with a slender bill and streaked breast

pippin (pip′in) *n.* [OFr. *pepin*, seed] any of a number of varieties of apple

pipsqueak (pip′skwēk′) *n.* [< PEEP¹ +

SQUEAK] [Colloq.] a person, etc. regarded as small or insignificant

piquant (pē′kənt) *adj.* [Fr. < *piquer*, to prick] 1. pleasantly sharp or spicy to the taste 2. exciting interest; stimulating —**pi′quancy** *n.*

pique (pēk) *n.* [Fr. < *piquer*, to prick] resentment at being slighted —*vt.* **piqued**, **piqu′ing** 1. to arouse resentment in 2. to arouse (one's curiosity, etc.)

piqué (pē′kā) *n.* [Fr. < *piquer*, to prick] a firmly woven cotton fabric with ribbed wales

piquet (pi ket′) *n.* [Fr. < *pic*, orig., a sting] a game of cards for two, played with 32 cards

piracy (pīə′rə sē) *n.*, *pl.* **-cies** [see PIRATE] 1. robbery of ships on the high seas 2. the unauthorized use of copyrighted work

piranha (pi rän′yə) *n.* [< Tupi, toothed fish] a small, fiercely voracious freshwater fish of South America

pirate (pīə′rət) *n.* [< Gr. *peirān*, to attack] a person who practises piracy —*vt.*, **-rated**, **-rating** 1. to publish or reproduce without authorization (a book, etc.), esp. in violation of a copyright 2. to practise piracy (upon) 3. to take (something) by piracy —**piratical** (pī rat′i k'l) *adj.*

pirouette (pir′ŏŏ wet′) *n.* [Fr., spinning top] a whirling around on one foot or the point of the toe, esp. in ballet —*vi.* **-et′ted**, **-et′ting** to do a pirouette

piscatorial (pis′kə tôr′ē əl) *adj.* [< L. *piscator*, fisherman] of fishermen or fishing: also **pis′catory**

Pisces (pī′sēz) [L. *piscis*, fish] 1. a constellation south of Andromeda 2. the twelfth sign of the zodiac

pisciculture (pis′i kul′chər) *n.* [prec. + CULTURE] the breeding of fish as a science or industry

piscine[1] (pis′īn) *adj.* [< L. *piscis*, fish] of or resembling fish

piscine[2] (pis′ēn) *n.* [< prec.] a swimming pool

pish (psh, pish) *interj.*, *n.* an exclamation of disgust or impatience —*vi.*, *vt.* to make this exclamation (at)

piss (pis) *vi.* [prob. echoic] [Vulg.] to urinate —*vt.* to discharge as or with the urine —*n.* urine —**piss off** [Vulg. Slang] to go away; depart —**pissed off** [Vulg. Slang] annoyed

pissed (pist) *adj.* [Vulg. Slang] drunk, intoxicated

pistachio (pi stä′shē ō′) *n.*, *pl.* **-chios**′ [< OPer. *pistah*] 1. a small tree related to the cashew 2. its edible, greenish seed (**pistachio nut**)

pistil (pis′t'l) *n.* [< L. *pistillum*, pestle] the seedbearing organ of a flowering plant

pistillate (pis′tə lit) *adj.* having a pistil or pistils

pistol (pis′t'l) *n.* [< Czech *píšt'al*] a small firearm held and fired with one hand —*vt.* **-tolled**, **-tolling** to shoot with a pistol

pistol-whip *vt.* **-whipped**′, **-whip′ping** to beat with a pistol, esp. about the head

PISTON

piston (pis′t'n) *n.* [< L. *pinsere*, to pound] a short cylinder fitted in a hollow cylinder and moved back and forth by the pressure of a fluid so as to transmit motion to a rod (**piston rod**), or moved by the rod to exert pressure on the fluid

pit[1] (pit) *n.* [< MDu. *pitte*] [U.S.] the stone of various fruits

pit[2] *n.* [< L. *puteus*, a well] 1. a large, deep hole in the ground 2. an abyss 3. *hell*; used with *the* 4. a covered hole used to trap wild animals 5. any concealed danger 6. an enclosed area in which animals are kept or made to fight 7. *a*) a mine or excavation *b*) the shaft of a coal mine 8. a small hollow in a surface 9. the rear part of the ground floor of a theatre 10. the sunken section in front of the stage, where the orchestra sits 11. *a*) an area off the side of a motor racing circuit for servicing cars *b*) a sunken area in a garage for servicing cars —*vt.* **pit′ted**, **pit′ting** 1. to set in competition (*against*) 2. to make pits in 3. to put in a pit —**pit of the stomach** the hollow depression below the breastbone

pitapat (pit′ə pat′) *adv.* [echoic] with rapid beating —*n.* a rapid succession of beats

pitch[1] (pich) *n.* [< L. *pix*] 1. a black, sticky substance formed from coal tar and used for waterproofing, pavements, etc. 2. natural asphalt —*vt.* to cover or smear as with pitch

pitch[3] *vt.* [ME. *picchen*] 1. to set up [to pitch a tent] 2. to throw; toss 3. to fix at a particular point, level, etc. 4. *Cricket* to throw a cricket ball, esp. at some specified point 5. *Music* to set the key of (a tune, etc.) —*vi.* 1. to take up one's position 2. to toss anything, as hay, a ball, etc. 3. to fall or plunge forwards 4. to toss with the bow and stern rising and falling: said of a ship —*n.* 1. act or manner of pitching 2. a throw; toss 3. the pitching of a ship or aircraft in rough sea or air 4. a point or degree 5. the degree of slope 6. a vendor's station, esp. his position on a pavement 7. [Slang] a line of talk, such as a salesman uses 8. *Machinery* the distance between corresponding points or adjacent threads of a screw 9. *Music* that quality of a tone or sound determined by the frequency of vibration of the sound waves: the greater the frequency, the higher the pitch 10. *Sports* the field of play, esp. in football and cricket —**pitch in** [Colloq.] to set to work energetically —**pitch into** [Colloq.] to attack

pitch-black *adj.* very black

pitchblende *n.* [< G. *Pech*, pitch + *Blende*, blende] a brown mineral, the chief ore of uranium

pitch-dark *adj.* very dark

pitched battle 1. a battle in which positions are fixed before the action 2. a hard-fought battle

pitcher[1] *n.* [see BEAKER] a container, usually rounded with a narrow neck, used mainly as a water container

pitcher[2] *n.* [< PITCH[2]] [U.S.] *Baseball* the player who pitches the ball to opposing batters

pitcher plant a plant with pitcherlike leaves: floral emblem of Newfoundland and Labrador

pitchfork *n.* a large, long-handled fork used for tossing hay, etc. —*vt.* to toss as with a pitchfork

pitch pine a resinous pine from which pitch or turpentine is obtained

pitch pipe a small pipe which produces a fixed tone as a standard for tuning instruments, etc.

pitchy *adj.* **-ier, -iest** 1. thick and sticky like pitch 2. black

piteous (pit'ē əs) *adj.* arousing or deserving pity —**pit'eously** *adv.* —**pit'eousness** *n.*

pitfall (pit'fôl') *n.* [< ME. *pit*, pit + *falle*, trap] 1. any hidden difficulty 2. a covered pit to trap animals

pith (pith) *n.* [OE. *pitha*] 1. the fibrous tissue under the rind of an orange, etc. 2. the essential part 3. the soft, spongy tissue in the centre of certain plant stems

pit head the area at the top of a mine shaft

pith helmet a lightweight hat made of pith covered with white cotton and worn in hot climates

pithy (pith'ē) *adj.* **-ier, -iest** 1. terse and full of substance 2. of, like, or full of pith —**pith'ily** *adv.*

pitiable (pit'ē ə b'l) *adj.* arousing pity, sometimes mixed with scorn —**pit'iably** *adv.*

pitiful (pit'i fool) *adj.* 1. exciting or deserving pity 2. deserving contempt —**pit'ifully** *adv.* —**pit'ifulness** *n.*

pitiless (pit'i lis) *adj.* without pity; merciless

piton (pē'ton) *n., pl.* **-tons** (-tonz) [< MFr., a spike] a metal spike that is driven into rock or ice for support in mountain climbing

pittance (pit'əns) *n.* [ult. < L. *pietas*, piety] 1. a meagre allowance of money 2. a small amount

pitter-patter (pit'ər pat'ər) *n.* [echoic] a rapid succession of light tapping sounds, as of raindrops

pituitary (pi tyo͞o'ə tər ē) *adj.* [< L. *pituita*, phlegm] of the pituitary gland —*n., pl.* **-taries** *same as* PITUITARY GLAND

pituitary gland (or **body**) a small, oval endocrine gland at the base of the brain: it secretes hormones influencing body growth, metabolism, etc.

pity (pit'ē) *n., pl.* **pit'ies** [< L. *pietas*, piety] 1. sorrow for another's suffering 2. a cause for sorrow or regret —*vt., vi.* **pit'ied, pit'ying** to feel pity (for) —**have** (or **take**) **pity on** to show pity for —**pit'yingly** *adv.*

‡**più** (pyo͞o) *adv.* [It.] more: a direction in music

pivot (piv'ət) *n.* [Fr.] 1. a point, shaft, etc. on which something turns 2. a person or thing on which something depends —*vt.* to provide with a pivot —*vi.* to turn as on a pivot

pivotal *adj.* 1. of or acting as a pivot 2. on which something turns or depends; crucial

pix (piks) *n.pl.* [< PIC(TURE)S] [Slang] 1. films 2. photographs

pixie, pixy (pik'sē) *n., pl.* **pix'ies** [< ?] a fairy or sprite, esp. one that is puckish —**pix'ieish, pix'yish** *adj.*

pizza (pēt'sə) *n.* [It.] an Italian dish of dough covered with tomatoes, cheese, etc.

pizzicato (pit'sə kät'ō) *adj.* [It.] *Music* plucked: a direction to pluck the strings of a violin, viola, etc. —*adv.* in a pizzicato manner

pl. 1. place 2. plate 3. plural

PLA Port of London Authority

plaas (pläs) *n.* [< Afrik.] [S Afr.] a farm

placable (plak'ə b'l) *adj.* [< L. *placare*, to soothe] capable of being placated —**plac'abil'ity** *n.*

placard (plak'ärd) *n.* [< MDu. *placke*, a piece] a notice for display in a public place —*vt.* 1. to place placards on or in 2. to advertise by means of placards 3. to display as a placard

placate (plə kāt') *vt.* **-cat'ed, -cat'ing** [< L. *placare*, to soothe] to appease; pacify —**placa'tory** *adj.*

place (plās) *n.* [< Gr. *plateia*, street] 1. a) the part of space occupied by a person or thing b) situation or state 2. a city, town, or village 3. a square or court in a city 4. space; room 5. a region or locality 6. a residence; dwelling 7. a building or space devoted to a special purpose 8. a particular spot on or part of something 9. a particular passage or page in a book, etc. 10. position or standing 11. a step or point in a sequence 12. the customary or proper position, time, or character 13. a space reserved by a person, as a seat in a theatre, etc. 14. a job or position; employment 15. official position 16. one's duty or business 17. *Arith.* the position of an integer, as in noting decimals 18. *Racing* the first, second, or third position at the finish —*vt.* **placed, plac'ing** 1. a) to put in a particular place, condition, or relation b) to identify by associating with the correct place or circumstances 2. to offer for consideration, etc. 3. to repose (trust, etc.) in a person or thing 4. to finish in (a specified position) in a competition —**give place** to make room —**go places** [Colloq.] to achieve success —**How are you placed (for)?** [Colloq.] What are your present circumstances? —**in** (or **out of**) **place** 1. in (or out of) the customary or proper place 2. being (or not being) fitting —**in place of** instead of —**put someone in his place** to humble someone —**take place** to occur —**take the place of** to be a substitute for

placebo (plə sē′bō) *n.*, *pl.* **-bos, -boes** [L., I shall please] *Med.* a sugar pill given merely to humour a patient or used as a control during drug trials

place kick *Rugby* a kick made in which the ball is placed in position before it is kicked —**place′-kick′** *vi.*

place mat a small mat serving as an individual table cover for a person at a meal

placement (plās′mənt) *n.* a placing or being placed

placenta (plə sen′tə) *n.*, *pl.* **-tas, -tae** (-tē) [< Gr. *plax*, flat object] an organ developed within the uterus, connected by the umbilical cord to the foetus and supplying it with nourishment —**placen′-tal** *adj.*

placer (plas′ər) *n.* [AmSp., ult. < Gr. *plateia, street*] a deposit of gravel or sand containing particles of gold, platinum, etc. that can be washed out

place setting the china, cutlery, etc. for setting one place at a table for a meal

placid (plas′id) *adj.* [L. *placidus*] tranquil; calm —**placidity** (plə sid′ə tē), **plac′id-ness** *n.*

placket (plak′it) *n.* [prob. < PLACARD] a slit at the waist of a skirt or dress

plagiarize (plā′jə rīz′) *vt., vi.* **-rized′, -riz′-ing** [< L. *plagiarius*, kidnapper] to take (ideas, writings, etc.) from (another) and pass them off as one's own —**pla′giarism** *n.* —**pla′giarist** *n.*

plague (plāg) *n.* [< Gr. *plēgē*, misfortune] 1. any deadly epidemic disease 2. anything that afflicts or troubles 3. [Colloq.] a nuisance —*vt.* **plagued, plagu′ing** to vex; torment

plaguy (plā′gē) *adj.* [Dial. or Colloq.] vexatious

plaice (plās) *n.*, *pl.* **plaice** [< Gr. *platys*, broad] a kind of flatfish used as food

plaid (plad) *n.* [Gael. *plaide*, blanket] 1. a long woollen cloth with a crossbarred pattern, worn over the shoulder by Scottish Highlanders 2. any pattern of this kind —*adj.* having such a pattern

Plaid Cymru (plīd′kum′rē) the Welsh nationalist party

plain (plān) *adj.* [< L. *planus*, flat] 1. not obstructed; open [in *plain* view] 2. clearly understood [his meaning was *plain*] 3. direct; frank 4. not fancy; simple 5. not good-looking; homely 6. ordinary [a *plain* man] —*n.* 1. an extent of level country 2. a simple stitch in knitting —*adv.* clearly or simply —**as plain as a pikestaff** perfectly clear and obvious —**plain′ly** *adv.* —**plain′ness** *n.*

plain chocolate eating chocolate with a slightly bitter taste and a dark colour

plainclothes man a police detective who wears civilian clothes on duty: also **plain′clothes′man**

plain flour flour that contains no raising agent

plain sailing 1. smooth progress or advancement 2. *Naut.* sailing in a sea of water that is unobstructed

plainsong *n.* early Christian church music, in free rhythm and sung in unison: also **plain′chant′**

plain-spoken (plān′spō′k′n) *adj.* speaking or spoken plainly or frankly —**plain′-spo′kenness** *n.*

plaint (plānt) *n.* [< L. *plangere*, to lament] 1. [Poet.] lament 2. a complaint

plaintiff (plān′tif) *n.* [see prec.] a person who brings a suit into a court of law; complainant

plaintive (plān′tiv) *adj.* [see PLAINT] expressing sorrow or melancholy; sad —**plain′tively** *adv.*

plait (plat) *n.* [< L. *plicare*, to fold] 1. a length of plaited hair 2. *same as* PLEAT —*vt.* to interweave three or more strands of (hair, straw, etc.)

plan (plan) *n.* [Fr.] 1. a scheme for making, doing, or arranging something 2. a diagram showing the arrangement in horizontal section of a structure, piece of ground, etc. 3. any outline or sketch —*vt., vi.* **planned, plan′ning** to make or have in mind a plan of or for (something) —**plan on** [Colloq.] aim to do —**plan′ner** *n.*

planar (plā′nər) *adj.* 1. of or relating to a plane 2. lying in one plane; flat

planchette (plän shet′) *n.* [Fr.] a small device used on a Ouija board: it is believed to move without guidance to letters or words as the fingers rest on it

plane¹ (plān) *n.* [< Gr. *platys*, broad] any of several trees with broad leaves and dark bark that comes off in large patches: also **plane tree**

plane² *adj.* [L. *planus*] 1. flat; level 2. *Math.* a) on a surface that is a plane b) of such surfaces —*n.* 1. a surface that wholly contains a straight line joining any two points lying in it 2. a flat or level surface 3. a level of achievement, existence, etc. 4. *short for* AEROPLANE 5. an aerofoil

PLANE

plane³ *n.* [< L. *planus*, level] a carpenter's tool for smoothing or levelling wood —*vt.* **planed, plan′ing** 1. to make smooth or level with a plane 2. to remove with a plane (with *off* or *away*) —*vi.* 1. to work with a plane **2.** to do the work of a plane —**plan'er** *n.*

plane⁴ *vi.* **planed, plan'ing** [Fr. *planer*] **1.** to soar or glide **2.** to rise from the water, as a hydroplane does **3.** to travel by aircraft

planet (plan'it) *n.* [< Gr. *planan*, wander] any heavenly body revolving about a star, as the earth does about the sun, and shining by light reflected from the star: the major planets, in their order from the sun, are Mercury, Venus, Earth, Mars, Jupiter, Saturn, Uranus, Neptune, and Pluto —**plan'etary** *adj.*

planetarium (plan'ǝtãər'ēǝm) *n., pl.* **-iums, -ia** [< LL. *planeta*, planet + L. (*sol)arium*, solarium] **1.** an arrangement for projecting the images of the sun, moon, planets, and stars inside a large dome **2.** the room or building containing this

planetoid (plan'ǝtoid') *n.* same as ASTEROID (*n.* 1)

plank (plaŋk) *n.* [< LL. *planca*] **1.** a long, broad, thick board **2.** an article of principle in a political programme —*vt.* **1.** to cover, lay, etc. with planks **2.** [Colloq.] *a)* to lay or set (*down*) with force *b)* to pay (usually with *down* or *out*) —**walk the plank** to walk off a plank projecting out from a ship's side, as pirates' victims were forced to do

planking *n.* **1.** the act of laying planks **2.** planks collectively

plankton (plaŋk'tǝn) *n.* [G. < Gr. *planktos*, wandering] floating microscopic animal and plant life, source of food for fish

planning (plan'iŋ) *n.* the making of comprehensive plans to control the physical and social developments of an area

plant (plänt) *n.* [< L. *planta*, a sprout] **1.** a living organism that cannot move voluntarily, synthesizes food from carbon dioxide, and has no sense organs **2.** a soft-stemmed organism of this kind, as distinguished from a tree or shrub **3.** the machinery, buildings, etc. of a factory **4.** the apparatus for a certain mechanical operation [a ship's power *plant*] **5.** [Slang] a person placed, or thing used, to trick or trap —*vt.* **1.** *a)* to put into the ground to grow *b)* to set plants in (a piece of ground) **2.** to set firmly in position **3.** to fix in the mind **4.** to settle; establish **5.** [Slang] to deliver (a punch, etc.) with force **6.** [Slang] to place (a person or thing) in such a way as to trick, trap, etc. —**plant oneself** position oneself

plantain¹ (plan'tin) *n.* [< L. *plantago*] a plant with broad leaves and spikes of tiny, greenish flowers

plantain² *n.* [< L. *platanus*, plane] a tropical banana plant with a coarse fruit cooked as a vegetable

plantation (plan tā'shǝn) *n.* [< L. *plantare*, to plant] **1.** an estate cultivated by workers living on it **2.** an area growing cultivated crops **3.** a large, cultivated planting of trees **4.** formerly, a colony

planter (plan'tǝr) *n.* **1.** the owner of a plantation **2.** a container for house plants

plantigrade (plan'tǝgrād') *adj.* [< L. *planta*, sole + *gradi*, walk] walking on the whole sole of the foot, as a bear

plant louse same as APHID

plaque (plăk) *n.* [Fr. < MDu. *placke*, disc] **1.** a thin, flat, decorated or lettered piece of metal, wood, etc., placed on a wall **2.** a thin film on teeth

plash (plash) *vt., vi., n.* [echoic] same as SPLASH

-plasm (plaz'm) [see ff.] a combining form meaning: **1.** the fluid substances of a cell **2.** protoplasm

plasma (plaz'mǝ) *n.* [G. < Gr. *plassein*, to form] **1.** the fluid part of blood, without the corpuscles **2.** the fluid part of lymph, milk, or intramuscular liquid **3.** protoplasm **4.** a high-temperature, ionized, electrically neutral gas

plaster (plăs'tǝr) *n.* [< Gr. *emplassein*, to daub over] **1.** a pasty mixture of lime, sand, and water, hard when dry, for coating walls, etc. **2.** same as PLASTER OF PARIS **3.** a pasty preparation spread on cloth and applied to the body as a medicine **4.** a small prepared bandage of gauze and adhesive tape —*vt.* **1.** to cover as with plaster **2.** to apply like a plaster **3.** to make lie smooth and flat **4.** [Colloq.] to affect or strike with force —**plas'terer** *n.*

plasterboard *n.* a thin board formed of layers of plaster and paper, used in wide sheets

plastered *adj.* [Slang] intoxicated; drunk

plaster of Paris a white powder, calcined gypsum, which, when mixed with water, forms a thick paste that sets quickly: used for casts, statuary, etc.

plastic (plas'tik) *adj.* [< Gr. *plassein*, to form] **1.** made of a plastic **2.** *a)* that can be moulded or shaped *b)* impressionable **3.** dealing with moulding or modelling **4.** moulding or shaping matter; formative —*n.* any of various nonmetallic, synthetic compounds which can be moulded and hardened —**plastic'-ity** (-tis'ǝtē) *n.*

plastic bomb a bomb made from an adhesive puttylike substance

Plasticine (plas'tǝsēn') [< PLASTIC] *Trademark* an oil-based modelling paste, used like clay or wax

plasticize (plas'tǝsīz') *vt., vi.* **-cized', -ciz'ing** to make or become plastic

plasticizer *n.* any substance added to a plastic material to keep it soft and viscous

plastic surgery surgery dealing with the repair of injured, deformed, or destroyed parts of the body, as by skin transfer —**plastic surgeon**

plate (plāt) *n.* [< Gr. *platys*, flat] **1.** a shallow dish **2.** a plateful **3.** a container passed in churches, etc. for donations of money **4.** a smooth, flat, thin piece of metal, etc. **5.** dishes, utensils, etc. of, or plated with, gold or silver **6.** a full-page book illustration printed on special paper **7.** an impression taken from engraved metal **8.** a print of a woodcut, lithograph, etc. **9.** a horse race with a silver or gold cup as a prize **10.** *Anat., Zool.* a thin layer or scale, as of horny tissue, etc. **11.** *Dentistry a)* that part of a denture which fits to the mouth and holds the teeth *b)* [*often pl.*] loosely, a full set of false teeth **12.** *Photog.* a sheet of glass, metal, etc. coated with a film sensitive to light **13.** *Printing* a cast made from a mould of set type —*vt.* **plat′ed, plat′-ing 1.** to coat with gold, tin, etc. **2.** to cover with metal plates —**on a plate** acquired without trouble —**on one's plate** waiting to be dealt with —**put up one's plate** start practising as a doctor, etc.

plateau (pla′tō) *n., pl.* **-teaus, -teaux** (-tōz) [Fr.: see PLATE] **1.** an elevated tract of level land **2.** a period of little change following some upward progress

plated (plāt′id) *adj.* **1.** coated with a metal [*silver-plated*] **2.** protected with plates, as of armour

plateful *n.* as much as a plate will hold

plate glass polished, clear glass in thick sheets, used for shop windows, mirrors, etc.

platelayer *n.* one whose work is laying and repairing railway lines

platelet (plāt′lit) *n.* [< PLATE] a roundish disc found in the blood and associated with blood clotting

platen (plat′'n) *n.* [see PLATE] **1.** a flat metal plate, as that in a printing press which presses the paper against the inked type **2.** in a typewriter, the roller against which the keys strike

plate rack a kitchen device for holding plates that are draining or not in use

platform (plat′fôrm) *n.* [Fr. *plate-forme*, flat form] **1.** a raised horizontal surface; specif., *a)* a raised flooring beside a railway line, etc. *b)* a space at the entrance of a bus, etc. *c)* a raised stage for performers, speakers, etc. **2.** a statement of principles, as of a political party **3.** a shoe with a thick sole

platform ticket a ticket allowing entry to a railway platform but not allowing the holder to travel by train

plating (plāt′iŋ) *n.* **1.** an external layer of metal plates **2.** a thin coating of gold, silver, tin, etc.

platinum (plat′ə nəm) *n.* [< Sp. *plata*, silver] a steel-grey, metallic chemical element, resistant to corrosion: used as a chemical catalyst, for dental alloys, jewellery, etc.: symbol, Pt

platinum blonde 1. a girl or woman with very light, silvery blonde hair **2.** such a colour

platitude (plat′ə tyōōd) *n.* [Fr. < *plat*, flat] a trite remark, esp. one uttered as though it were fresh —**plat′itu′dinous** *adj.*

Platonic (plə ton′ik) *adj.* **1.** of Plato or his philosophy **2.** [*usually* p-] not sexual, but purely spiritual or intellectual [*platonic love*]

Platonism (plāt′ən iz′m) *n.* the philosophy of Plato or his school; Platonic idealism —**Pla′tonist** *n.*

platoon (plə tōōn′) *n.* [Fr. *peloton*, a ball, group] **1.** a military unit composed of two or more squads **2.** a group like this [*a platoon of police*]

platteland (plat′ə lant′) *n.* [< Afrik.] [S Afr.] a rural district

platter (plat′ər) *n.* [see PLATE] a large, shallow dish, usually oval, for serving food

PLATYPUS
(40-60 cm long,
including tail)

platypus (plat′ə pəs) *n., pl.* **-puses** [< Gr. *platys*, flat + *pous*, foot] a small, aquatic, egg-laying mammal of Australia, with webbed feet, a tail like a beaver's, and a bill like a duck's: in full, **duckbill platypus**

plaudit (plô′dit) *n.* [< L. *plaudere*, applaud] [*usually pl.*] **1.** applause **2.** any expression of approval

plausible (plô′zə b'l) *adj.* [< L. *plaudere*, applaud] seemingly true, trustworthy, etc.: often implying disbelief or distrust —**plau′sibil′ity** *n.* —**plau′sibly** *adv.*

play (plā) *vi.* [OE. *plegan*] **1.** to take part in a game or sport **2.** to have fun **3.** to trifle (*with*) **4.** to gamble **5.** to move lightly, rapidly, etc. [*sunlight playing on the waves*] **6.** to perform on a musical instrument **7.** to give out sounds, etc.: said of an instrument, gramophone record, etc. **8.** to act in a specified way [*to play fair*] **9.** to perform on the stage, etc. **10.** to impose (on another's feelings, etc.) —*vt.* **1.** *a)* to take part in (a game or sport) *b)* to be stationed at (a specified position) in a sport **2.** to oppose (a person, etc.) in a game **3.** to use (a player, etc.) in a game **4.** to do, as in fun [*to play tricks*] **5.** to bet (on) **6.** to cause to move, etc.; wield **7.** to put (a specified card) into play **8.** to cause [*to play havoc*] **9.** to perform (music, a drama, etc.) **10.** *a)* to perform on (an instrument) *b)* to put (a gramophone, etc.) into operation **11.** to act the part of [*to play Iago*] **12.** to imitate for amusement [*to play teacher*] **13.** to give performances in [*to play Newcastle*] **14.** to direct (a light, a stream of water, etc.) repeatedly or continuously (*on, over,* or *along*) **15.** to let (a fish) tire itself by tugging at the line —*n.* **1.** a dramatic composition or performance; drama **2.** sport, games, etc. **3.** the playing of a game **4.** gambling **5.** motion or activity, esp. when free and rapid **6.** freedom or looseness of movement in a mechanical part **7.** fun; joking —**in** (or **out of**) **play** *Sports* in (or not in) the condition for continuing play: said of a ball, etc. —**make a play for** [Colloq.] to employ one's arts or skills to obtain —**play along (with)** to cooperate (with), often just for expediency —**play around (or about)** 1. to behave in a frivolous way 2. to be sexually unfaithful or promiscuous —**play by ear** 1. to play an instrument without music 2. to follow one's instinct —**play down** to make seem not too important —**played out** 1. finished 2. exhausted —**play off** 1. to pit (one) against another 2. to break (a tie) by playing once more —**play up** 1. to give prominence 2. to behave irritatingly 3. to become painful, etc. —**play up to** [Colloq.] to try to please by flattery, etc.

playback n. the playing of a gramophone record or tape to listen to or check the sound recorded on it —vt. to play a tape, record, etc. that has just been recorded

playbill n. a poster or circular advertising a play

playboy n. a man of means who is given to pleasure-seeking, sexual promiscuity, etc.

player n. 1. a person who plays a game 2. an actor 3. a person who plays a musical instrument

player piano a piano that can play mechanically

playful adj. 1. fond of play or fun; frisky 2. said or done in fun —**play'fully** adv. —**play'fulness** n.

playgoer n. one who goes frequently to the theatre

playground n. a place, often part of a schoolground, for outdoor games and play

playgroup n. a group of preschool children who meet for periods of supervised play: also **play'school'**

playhouse n. a theatre

playing cards cards used in playing various games, arranged in four suits: a standard pack has 52 cards

playing field a field or open space used for sport

playmate n. a companion in games and recreation: also **play'fel'low**

play-off n. a game played to break a tie or to decide a championship

play on words a pun or punning

playpen n. a small, portable enclosure in which an infant can play, crawl, etc.

plaything n. a thing to play with; toy

playtime n. time for play or recreation

playwright n. a writer of plays; dramatist

plaza (plä′zə) n. [Sp. < L.: see PLACE] a public square

plea (plē) n. [< L. placere, please] 1. an appeal; entreaty 2. a statement in defence; excuse 3. Law a defendant's statement

plead (plēd) vi. **plead'ed** or **pled** or **plead** (pled), **plead'ing** [< OFr.: see PLEA] 1. to make an appeal; beg 2. to present a case or a plea in a law court —vt. 1. to offer as an excuse 2. to answer (guilty or not guilty) to a charge 3. to argue (a law case) —**plead'er** n.

pleadings n.pl. the statements setting

forth to the court the claims of the plaintiff and the answer of the defendant

pleasant (plez′ənt) adj. [< MFr. plaisir, please] 1. agreeable to the mind or senses; pleasing 2. having an agreeable manner, appearance, etc. —**pleas'antly** adv.

pleasantry n., pl. -ries 1. jocularity 2. a) a humorous remark b) a polite social remark

please (plēz) vt. **pleased**, **pleas'ing** [< L. placere] 1. to be agreeable to; satisfy 2. to be the wish of [it pleased him to remain] —vi. 1. to be agreeable; satisfy 2. to have the wish; like [to do as one pleases] Please is also used in polite requests [please sit down] —**if you please** if you wish or like

pleasing adj. giving pleasure; agreeable

pleasurable (plezh′ər ə b'l) adj. pleasant; enjoyable —**pleas'urableness** n. —**pleas'urably** adv.

pleasure (plezh′ər) n. 1. a pleased feeling; delight 2. one's wish, will, or choice 3. a thing that gives delight or satisfaction 4. sensual satisfaction 5. amusement; fun —**pleas'ureful** adj.

pleat (plēt) n. [< PLAIT] a flat double fold in cloth or other material, pressed or stitched in place —vt. to lay and press (cloth) in a pleat or pleats —**pleat'er** n.

pleb (pleb) n. [< ff.] [Colloq.] a common, vulgar person

plebeian (pli bē′ən) n. [< L. plebs, common people] 1. one of the common people 2. a member of the ancient Roman lower class 3. a vulgar, coarse person —adj. vulgar, coarse, or common

plebiscite (pleb′ə sit′) n. [< L. plebs, common people + scitum, decree] a direct vote of the people on a political issue

plectrum (plek′trəm) n., pl. -trums, -tra [< Gr. plēssein, to strike] a thin piece of metal, plastic, etc. for plucking the strings of a guitar, mandolin, etc.

pled (pled) [U.S. & Scot.] alt. pt. & pp. of PLEAD

pledge (plej) n. [? < OS. plegan, to guarantee] 1. a promise or agreement 2. the condition of being given or held as security for a contract, payment, etc. 3. a person or thing given or held as such security 4. a token 5. the drinking of a toast 6. something promised, esp. money —vt. **pledged**, **pledg'ing** 1. to promise to give 2. to bind by a promise 3. to present as security 4. to drink a toast to —**take the pledge** to vow not to drink alcohol —**pledg'er** n.

Pleiades (plī′ə dēz′) n.pl. Astron. a cluster of stars in the constellation Taurus

Pleiocene (plī′ō sēn′) adj. same as PLIOCENE

Pleistocene (plīs′tō sēn′) adj. [< Gr. pleistos, most + kainos, recent] designating or of the first epoch of the Quaternary Period in the Cainozoic Era

plenary (plē′nə rē) adj. [< L. plenus, full] 1. full; complete 2. for attendance by all members

plenipotentiary (plen′i pō ten′shər ē)

adj. [< L. *plenus*, full + *potens*, powerful] having full authority —*n.*, pl. **-aries** a diplomat given full authority

plenitude (plen'ə tyōōd') *n.* [< L. *plenus*, full] 1. fullness; completeness 2. abundance; plenty

plenteous (plen'tē əs) *adj.* plentiful; abundant

plentiful (plen'ti fool) *adj.* 1. having or yielding plenty 2. abundant —**plen'tifully** *adv.* —**plen'tifulness** *n.*

plenty (plen'tē) *n.*, *pl.* **-ties** [< L. *plenus*, full] 1. an ample supply 2. a large number 3. prosperity; opulence —*adv.* [Colloq.] fully

plenum (plē'nəm) *n.*, *pl.* **-nums, -na** [< L. *plenus*, full] 1. a full assembly 2. space filled with matter

pleonasm (plē'ō naz'm) *n.* [< Gr. *pleonazein*, be in excess] 1. the use of more words than are necessary for the meaning 2. a redundant expression —**ple'-onas'tic** *adj.*

plethora (pleth'ə rə) *n.* [< Gr. *plēthos*, fullness] an overabundance; excess —**plethoric** (ple thor'ik) *adj.*

pleura (plooər'ə) *n.*, *pl.* **-rae** (-ē) [< Gr. *pleura*, a rib] the thin membrane lining each half of the chest cavity and covering each lung —**pleu'ral** *adj.*

pleurisy (plooər'ə sē) *n.* inflammation of the pleura, characterized by painful breathing —**pleurit'ic** *adj.*

plexus (plek'səs) *n.*, *pl.* **-uses, -us** [< L. *plectere*, to twine] *Anat.* a network of blood vessels, nerves, etc.

pliable (plī'ə b'l) *adj.* [< L. *plicare*, to fold] 1. easily bent; flexible 2. easily influenced or persuaded 3. adaptable —**pli'abil'ity** *n.* —**pli'ably** *adv.*

pliant (plī'ənt) *adj.* [see prec.] 1. easily bent; pliable 2. compliant —**pli'ancy** *n.* —**pli'antly** *adv.*

pliers (plī'ərz) *n.pl.* [< PLY[1]] small pincers for gripping small objects, bending wire, etc.

plight[1] (plīt) *n.* [< OFr. *pleit*, a fold] a condition or state; esp., an awkward, sad, or dangerous situation

plight[2] *vt.* [< OE. *pliht*, danger] to pledge or promise —**plight one's troth** to promise to marry

Plimsoll mark (or **line**) (plim'səl) [< S. *Plimsoll*] a line on the outside of merchant ships, showing the water level to which they may legally be loaded

plimsolls (plim'səlz) *n.pl.* [? < resemblance to prec.] lightweight canvas sports shoes with rubber soles

plinth (plinth) *n.* [< Gr. *plinthos*, a brick] 1. the square block at the base of a column, pedestal, etc. 2. the base on which a statue rests

Pliocene (plī'ō sēn') *adj.* [< Gr. *pleōn*, more + *kainos*, new] designating one of the last epoch of the Tertiary Period in the Cainozoic Era

plissé (plē'sā) *n.* [Fr., pleated] 1. a crinkled finish given to cotton, nylon, etc. 2. a fabric with this finish

PLO Palestine Liberation Organization

plod (plod) *vi.* **plod'ded, plod'ding** [prob. echoic] 1. to move heavily and laboriously; trudge 2. to work steadily; drudge —*n.* 1. the act of plodding 2. the sound of a heavy step —**plod'der** *n.*

plonk[1] (plonk) *vt.*, *vi.*, *n.* same as PLUNK

plonk[2] (plonk) *n.* [< ?] alcohol, esp. inferior wine

plop (plop) *vt.*, *vi.* **plopped, plop'ping** [echoic] to drop with a sound like that of something flat falling into water —*n.* the sound of plopping —*adv.* with a plop

plosive (plō'siv) *adj.* [< (EX)PLOSIVE] produced by the sudden release of the breath, as the sounds of *k*, *p*, and *t* used initially —*n.* a plosive sound

plot (plot) *n.* [OE., piece of land] 1. a small area of ground 2. a secret, usually evil, scheme 3. the plan of action of a play, novel, etc. —*vt.* **plot'ted, plot'-ting** 1. to draw a plan, map, etc. of 2. to make secret plans for 3. to plan the action of (a story, etc.) 4. to form (a curve) on a graph —*vi.* to scheme

Plough (plou) the plough-shaped group of stars in the constellation Ursa Major (Great Bear)

plough (plou) *n.* [OE., *ploh*] 1. a farm implement used to cut and turn up the soil 2. anything like this; specif., a SNOWPLOUGH —*vt.* 1. to cut and turn up (soil) with a plough 2. to make as if by ploughing [*he ploughed* his way in] —*vi.* 1. to use a plough 2. to cut a way (*through* water, etc.) 3. to plod 4. to begin work vigorously (with *into*) 5. to collide forcefully (with *into*) —**plough a lonely furrow** to continue without assistance from others —**plough back** to reinvest (profits) in the same enterprise —**plough'er** *n.*

ploughman *n.* a man who guides a plough

ploughman's lunch a meal of cheese, bread, and, often, beer

ploughshare *n.* the cutting blade of a plough

plover (pluv'ər) *n.* [< L. *pluvia*, rain] a shore bird with a short tail, long, pointed wings, and a short beak

plow (plou) *n.*, *vt.*, *vi.* U.S. sp. of PLOUGH

ploy (ploi) *n.* [? < (EM)PLOY] an action or manoeuvre intended to outwit or disconcert another person

PLP Parliamentary Labour Party

PLR Public Lending Right

pluck (pluk) *vt.* [OE. *pluccian*] 1. to pull off or out; pick 2. to pull feathers or hair from [to *pluck* a chicken, *pluck* eyebrows] 3. to pull at (the strings of a musical instrument) and release quickly 4. [Slang] to rob or swindle —*vi.* to pull (*at*) —*n.* 1. courage 2. a pulling; tug 3. the heart, liver, and lungs, esp. of an animal used for food —**pluck up** to rouse one's (courage) —**pluck'er** *n.*

plucky *adj.* **-ier, -iest** brave; spirited; resolute —**pluck'ily** *adv.* —**pluck'iness** *n.*

plug (plug) *n.* [MDu. *plugge*] 1. an object used to stop up a hole, drain, etc. 2. a device, as with prongs, for fitting into an electric outlet, appliance, etc. to make electrical contact **3.** same as SPARKING PLUG **4.** a cake of tobacco **5.** a handle for the release of a water-closet flushing mechanism **6.** [Colloq.] an electric socket **7.** [Colloq.] a free boost, advertisement, etc. —**vt. plugged, plug′ging 1.** to stop up (a hole, etc.) with a plug **2.** to insert (something) as a plug **3.** [Colloq.] a) to promote (a song) by frequent performance b) to promote with a plug (n. 7) **4.** [Slang] to shoot a bullet into —**vi.** [Colloq.] to work hard and steadily —**plug in** to connect electrically by inserting a plug in a socket or jack

plum (plum) *n.* [OE. *plume*] **1.** a) a tree bearing a smooth-skinned, edible fruit with a flattened stone b) the fruit **2.** a raisin, when used in pudding or cake **3.** a dark bluish-red colour **4.** something choice or desirable

plumage (plo͞o′mij) *n.* [< L. *plumbe*, a feather] a bird's feathers

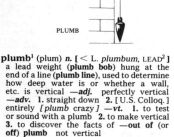

PLUMB

plumb[1] (plum) *n.* [< L. *plumbum*, LEAD[2]] a lead weight (**plumb bob**) hung at the end of a line (**plumb line**), used to determine how deep water is or whether a wall, etc. is vertical —**adj.** perfectly vertical —**adv. 1.** straight down **2.** [U.S. Colloq.] entirely [*plumb* crazy] —**vt. 1.** to test or sound with a plumb **2.** to make vertical **3.** to discover the facts of —**out of** (or **off**) **plumb** not vertical

plumb[2] *vt.* to fit as part of a plumbing system —**vi.** to work as a plumber

plumber *n.* [< L. *plumbum*, LEAD[2]] a skilled worker who installs and repairs pipes, fixtures, etc., as of water or gas systems in a building

plumbing *n.* **1.** the work of a plumber **2.** the pipes and fixtures with which a plumber works

plume (plo͞om) *n.* [< L. *pluma*] **1.** a) a feather, esp. a large, showy one b) a cluster of these **2.** an ornament made of feathers **3.** something like a plume in shape or lightness [a *plume* of smoke] —**vt. plumed, plum′ing 1.** to adorn with plumes **2.** to preen (its feathers): said of a bird **3.** to plume (oneself)

plummet (plum′it) *vi.* [see PLUMB[1]] to fall straight downwards —**n.** a plumb

plummy (plum′ē) *adj.* -mier, -miest **1.** full of or tasting of plums **2.** [Colloq.] good or desirable **3.** [Colloq.] rich, full, and mellow: said of a sound or voice

plump[1] (plump) *adj.* [< MDu. *plomp*, bulky] full and rounded in form; chubby —**vt., vi.** to fill out (sometimes with *up* or *out*) —**plump′ish** *adj.* —**plump′ness** *n.*

plump[2] *vi.* [echoic] **1.** to fall or bump (*against*) **2.** to choose (with *for*) —**vt.** to drop or put down heavily or all at once —**n.** a fall or the sound of this —**adv. 1.** suddenly or heavily **2.** straight down **3.** bluntly —**adj.** blunt; direct

plum pudding [orig. made with plums] a rich pudding made of raisins, currants, flour, suet, etc., boiled or steamed, as in a linen bag

plumy (plo͞o′mē) *adj.* -ier, -iest **1.** covered or adorned with plumes **2.** like a plume; feathery

plunder (plun′dər) *vt., vi.* [< G. *Plunder*, baggage] **1.** to rob by force, esp. in warfare **2.** to take (property) by force or fraud —**n. 1.** the act of plundering **2.** goods taken by force or fraud —**plun′derer** *n.*

plunge (plunj) *vt.* **plunged, plung′ing** [< L. *plumbum*, LEAD[2]] to thrust or throw suddenly (*into*) —**vi. 1.** to dive or rush **2.** to move violently and rapidly downwards or forwards **3.** to pitch, as a ship **4.** to extend down in a revealing way [a *plunging* neckline] **5.** [Colloq.] to gamble heavily —**n. 1.** a) a dive or downward leap b) a swim **2.** any plunging motion —**take the plunge** to start on some new and uncertain enterprise

plunger *n.* **1.** a large, rubber suction cup used to free clogged drains **2.** a device that operates with a plunging motion, as a piston **3.** a person who plunges

plunk (pluŋk) *vt.* [echoic] **1.** to strum (a guitar, etc.) **2.** to throw or put down heavily —**vi. 1.** to give out a twanging sound **2.** to fall heavily —**n.** the act or sound of plunking —**adv.** with a twang or thud

pluperfect (plo͞o pur′fikt) *adj.* [abbrev. of L. *plus quam perfectum*, more than perfect] designating a tense in certain languages corresponding to the past perfect in English —**n.** a pluperfect tense or form

plural (ploo͝ər′əl) *adj.* [< L. *plus*, more] **1.** of or including more than one **2.** of or involving a plurality of persons or things **3.** *Gram.* designating or of more than one —**n.** *Gram.* **1.** the plural number **2.** a plural form of a word (Ex.: *hands, men*) **3.** a word in plural form

pluralism *n.* **1.** the existence within a society of groups that differ ethnically, culturally, etc. **2.** the holding of more than one office at the same time —**plu′ralist** *n., adj.* —**plu′ralis′tic** *adj.*

plurality (ploo͝ə ral′ə tē) *n., pl.* -ties **1.** a being plural or numerous **2.** a multitude **3.** same as MAJORITY

pluralize (ploo͝ər′ə līz′) *vt., vi.* -ized′, -iz′ing to make or become plural —**plu′raliza′tion** *n.* —**plu′raliz′er** *n.*

plus (plus) *prep.* [L., more] **1.** added to [2 *plus* 2] **2.** in addition to —**adj. 1.** designating a sign indicating addition [+ is a *plus* sign] **2.** positive [a *plus* quantity] **3.** higher than [a mark of B *plus]* **4.** involving extra gain or advantage [a *plus* factor *]* **5.** [Colloq.] and more [personality *plus]* **6.** *Elec.* same as POSITIVE —*adv.* [Chiefly U.S. Colloq.] moreover [he has the time *plus* he has the money *]* —*n., pl.* **plus'ses, plus'es 1.** a plus sign **2.** something added or favourable

plus fours loose knickerbockers worn, esp. formerly, for active sports

plush (plush) *n.* [< L. *pilus*, hair] a fabric with a soft, thick pile —*adj.* [Slang] luxurious —**plush'y** *adj.*

Pluto (ploo͞o'tō) **1.** *Gr. & Rom. Myth.* the god ruling the lower world **2.** the outermost planet of the solar system

plutocracy (ploo͞otok'rə sē) *n., pl.* **-cies** [< Gr. *ploutos*, wealth + *kratein*, to rule] **1.** government by the wealthy **2.** a group of wealthy people who control a government

plutocrat (ploo͞ot'ō krat') *n.* **1.** a member of a wealthy ruling class **2.** a person whose wealth gives him control or great influence —**plu'tocrat'ic** *adj.*

plutonic (ploo͞oton'ik) *adj.* [< PLUTO] formed far below the earth's surface by intense heat, as some rocks

plutonium (ploo͞otō'nē əm) *n.* [< *Pluto* (planet)] a radioactive, metallic chemical element: symbol, Pu

pluvial (ploo͞o'vē əl) *adj.* [< L. *pluvia*, rain] **1.** *a)* of rain *b)* rainy **2.** *Geol.* formed by the action of rain

ply¹ (plī) *n., pl.* **plies** [< L. *plicare*, to fold] **1.** a thickness or layer, as of plywood, cloth, etc. **2.** one of the twisted strands in rope, yarn, etc. —*adj.* having (a specified number of) layers, strands, etc. [three-*ply*]

ply² *vt.* **plied, ply'ing** [contr. < APPLY] **1.** to work with (a tool, etc.) **2.** to work at (a trade) **3.** to address (someone) urgently (*with* questions, etc.) **4.** to keep supplying (*with* food, etc.) **5.** to sail back and forth across —*vi.* **1.** to keep busy or work **2.** to travel regularly (*between* places): said of ships, buses, etc.

Plymouth Brethren (plim'əth) a Calvinistic religious sect with no ordained ministry

plywood (plī'wood') *n.* [PLY¹ + WOOD] a material made of thin layers of wood glued and pressed together

Pm *Chem.* promethium

P.M. 1. Paymaster **2.** Postmaster **3.** Prime Minister

P.M., p.m., PM [L. *post meridiem*] after noon

p.m. post-mortem

PMG Postmaster General

pneumatic (nyoo͞omat'ik) *adj.* [< Gr. *pneuma*, breath] **1.** of or containing wind, air, or gases **2.** worked by or filled with compressed air [*pneumatic* drill] —**pneumat'ically** *adv.*

pneumatics *n.pl.* [with *sing. v.*] the branch of physics dealing with such properties of air and other gases as pressure, density, etc.

pneumonia (nyoo͞omō'nē ə) *n.* [< Gr. *pnein*, breathe] inflammation or infection of the lungs, caused by bacteria, viruses, etc. —**pneumon'ic** (-mon'ik) *adj.*

Po *Chem.* polonium

P.O., p.o. 1. petty officer: also **PO 2.** post office **3.** postal order

po (pō) *n., pl.* **pos** [< POT] [Colloq.] a chamber pot

poach¹ (pōch) *vt.* [< MFr. *poche*, pocket] to cook (fish, an egg without its shell, etc.) in water or other liquid near the boiling point

poach² *vt., vi.* [< MHG. *puchen*, to plunder] **1.** *a)* to trespass on (private property), esp. for shooting or fishing *b)* to hunt or catch (game or fish) illegally **2.** to steal —**poach'er** *n.*

pock (pok) *n.* [OE. *pocc*] **1.** a pustule, esp. one caused by smallpox **2.** same as POCKMARK —**pocked** *adj.*

pocket (pok'it) *n.* [< ONormFr. *poque*, a bag] **1.** *a)* a little bag or pouch sewn into or on clothing, for carrying small articles *b)* any usually small container, compartment, etc. **2.** a cavity for holding something **3.** a small area or group [a *pocket* of poverty] **4.** funds [a drain on one's *pocket*] **5.** *Aeron.* same as AIR POCKET **6.** *Geol.* a cavity filled with ore, oil, etc. **7.** [S Afr.] a bag or sack of vegetables or fruit —*adj.* **1.** that can be carried in a pocket **2.** smaller than standard —*vt.* **1.** to put into a pocket **2.** to envelop; enclose **3.** to take dishonestly; appropriate (money, etc.) **4.** to put up with (an insult, etc.) without showing anger **5.** to suppress [*pocket* one's pride] —**out of pocket** having made a loss after a transaction

pocket book [Chiefly U.S.] a case for carrying money and papers in one's pocket

pocket borough a borough whose representation in Parliament was controlled by one family or person

pocketful *n.* as much as a pocket will hold

pocket handkerchief 1. a handkerchief small enough for a pocket **2.** anything small, esp. a small lawn

pocketknife *n., pl.* **-knives'** a knife with blades that fold into the handle

pocket money cash for small expenses, esp. that given to children to buy sweets, etc.

pocket-size *adj.* of a size to fit in a pocket

pockmark (pok'märk') *n.* a scar or pit left by a pustule, as of smallpox —**pock'marked'** *adj.*

poco (pō'kō) *adv.* [It.] *Music* somewhat

pod (pod) *n.* [< ?] a dry fruit or seed vessel enclosing one or more seeds, as of a pea or bean —*vi.* **pod'ded, pod'ding 1.** to bear pods **2.** to remove the pods from

-pod (pod) [< Gr.] a combining form meaning foot: also **-pode** (pōd)

podgy (poj'ē) *adj.* **-ier, -iest** var. of PUDGY

podium (pō'dē əm) *n., pl.* **-diums, -dia** [see -POD] a low platform, esp. for the conductor of an orchestra

poem (pō'əm) *n.* [< Gr. *poiein*, to make] **1.** an arrangement of words written or spoken, traditionally a rhythmical or

metrical composition, sometimes rhymed
2. anything suggesting a poem in its effect
poesy (pō′ə zē′) *n.*, *pl.* **-sies** *old-fashioned var. of* POETRY

poet (pō′ət) *n.* **1.** one who writes poems **2.** one who expresses himself with beauty of thought and language

poet. 1. poetic **2.** poetry

poetaster (pō′ə tas′tər) *n.* [< POET + L. *-aster*, dim. suffix] a writer of mediocre verse; rhymester

poetic (pō et′ik) *adj.* **1.** of, like, or for poets or poetry **2.** written in verse **3.** having the beauty, imagination, etc. of poetry Also **poet′ical**

poetic justice justice, as in some plays, etc., in which good is rewarded and evil punished

poetic licence 1. disregard of strict fact or of rigid form, as by a poet, for artistic effect **2.** freedom to do this

poet laureate *pl.* **poets laureate, poet laureates** the official poet of a nation, appointed to write poems celebrating national events, etc.

poetry (pō′ə trē) *n.* [< L. *poeta*, poet] **1.** the art, theory, or structure of poems **2.** poems **3.** poetic qualities

Poets′ Corner that area of Westminster Abbey devoted to the graves and monuments of various poets

po-faced (pō′fāst) *adj.* wearing a disapproving, stern expression

pogey, pogy (pō′gē) *n.* [< obs. *pogie*, workhouse] [Canad. Slang] **1.** relief given by the government to the unemployed; dole **2.** the office where it is distributed **3.** unemployment insurance

pogo stick (pō′gō) [arbitrary coinage] a stilt with pedals and a spring at one end, used as a toy on which one can move along in a series of bounds

pogrom (po′grəm) *n.* [Russ., devastation] an organized persecution and massacre, as of Jews in Czarist Russia

poignant (poin′ənt) *adj.* [< L. *pungere*, to prick] **1.** sharply painful to the feelings **2.** biting [*poignant* wit] **3.** *a*) sharp to the smell *b*) keenly affecting the other senses [*poignant* beauty] —**poign′ancy** *n.*

poinsettia (poin set′ē ə) *n.* [< J. R. Poinsett] a plant with yellow flowers and petallike red leaves

point (point) *n.* [< L. *pungere*, to prick] **1.** a dot in writing etc., as a decimal point **2.** *a*) an element in geometry having definite position, but no size, shape, or extension *b*) a particular position, location, etc. [*points* on an itinerary] **3.** the position of certain players, as in cricket [*cover point*] **4.** the exact moment **5.** a condition, degree, etc. reached [boiling *point*] **6.** an item [explain it *point* by *point*] **7.** a distinguishing characteristic **8.** [often *pl.*] any of the extremities; as ears, feet, etc. of a domestic animal **9.** a unit, as of value, game scores, etc. **10.** a sharp end **11.** needlepoint lace **12.** a projecting piece of land; cape **13.** a branch of a deer's antler **14.** the essential fact or idea **15.** aim; purpose **16.** an impressive

argument or fact **17.** [often *pl.*] a movable section of railway line used in transferring a train from one line to another **18.** *Ballet* the position of being on the tips of the toes **19.** *Elec. a*) either of the contacts that make or break the circuit in a distributor *b*) [Colloq.] *same as* POWER POINT **20.** a mark showing direction on a compass **21.** a measuring unit for printing type, about $^1/_{72}$ of an inch —*vt.* **1.** to show (usually with *out*) [*point* the way] **2.** to give (a story, etc.) emphasis (sometimes with *up*) **3.** to aim **4.** to sharpen to a point **5.** to show the location of (game) by facing towards it: said of dogs **6.** *Masonry* to fill the joints of (brickwork) with fresh mortar —*vi.* **1.** to direct one's finger (*at* or *to*) **2.** to call attention (*to*); hint (*at*) **3.** to be directed (*to* or *towards*) **4.** to point game: said of a dog —**at the point of** very close to —**beside the point** not pertinent —**in point of** in the matter of —**make a point of 1.** to insist on **2.** to call special attention to —**on** (or **upon**) **the point of** on the verge of —**to the point** pertinent; apt: also **in point**

point-blank *adj.* [POINT + BLANK (white centre of the target)] **1.** aimed straight at a mark **2.** straightforward **3.** very close [*point-blank* range] —*adv.* **1.** straight **2.** bluntly [to refuse *point-blank*]

point duty the regulation of traffic by a policeman or traffic warden, stationed at a point, usually in the road

pointed (poin′tid) *adj.* **1.** having a sharp end **2.** sharp; incisive **3.** aimed at someone [a *pointed* remark] **4.** very evident —**point′edly** *adv.* —**point′edness** *n.*

POINTER
(66 cm high
at shoulder)

pointer *n.* **1.** an indicator on a clock, meter, etc. **2.** a long, tapered rod for pointing to things, as on a map **3.** a large, lean hunting dog with a smooth coat **4.** [Colloq.] a helpful hint —**the Pointers** *Astron.* the two stars in the Plough that are almost in a line with the North Star

pointillism (pwan′tē iz′m) *n.* [Fr. < L. *punctus*, point] the method of painting of certain impressionists, using dots of pure colour rather than mixing colours on the canvas

pointing (point′iŋ) *n.* **1.** the act of filling the crevices of walls with mortar **2.** the material used for this

pointless *adj.* **1.** without a point **2.** without meaning or force; senseless —**point′lessness** *n.*

point of no return a point at which

an irreversible commitment must be made to an action, stance, etc.

point of order a question as to whether the procedural rules of an assembly are being observed

point of view 1. the way in which, something is viewed; standpoint 2. a mental attitude

point-to-point *n.* a steeplechase organized by a hunt or some other body: usually restricted to amateurs

poise (poiz) *n.* [< L. *pendere*, weigh] 1. ease and dignity of manner 2. carriage, as of the body 3. balance; stability —*vt.* **poised, pois′ing** 1. to balance 2. to suspend —*vi.* to be suspended or balanced

poison (poi′z'n) *n.* [< L. *potio*, potion] 1. a substance causing illness or death when eaten, drunk, or absorbed in small quantities 2. anything harmful to happiness or welfare —*vt.* 1. to harm or destroy by means of poison 2. to put poison on or into 3. to influence wrongfully —*adj.* poisonous or poisoned

poison ivy an American plant having leaves of three leaflets: it can cause a severe rash on contact

poisonous *adj.* capable of injuring or killing by or as by poison —**poi′sonously** *adv.*

poisonpen (poi′z'n pen′) *adj.* [Colloq.] concerning an abusive letter written out of spite or malice, usually anonymously

poke[1] (pōk) *vt.* **poked, pok′ing** [MDu. or LowG. *poken*] 1. to jab with a stick, finger, etc. 2. to make (a hole, etc.) by poking 3. to stir up (a fire) 4. to thrust forwards [to *poke* one's head out of a window] —*vi.* 1. to jab (*at*) 2. to intrude; meddle 3. to search (*about* or *around*) 4. to stick out —*n.* a jab; thrust —**poke fun** (**at**) to ridicule

poke[2] *n.* [< Frank.] [Dial.] a sack or bag

pokelogan (pōk′′lo′gən) *n.* [Canad.] same as BOGAN

poker[1] (pō′kər) *n.* [< ?] a card game in which the players bet on the value of their hands

poker[2] *n.* a bar, as of iron, for stirring a fire

poker face [Colloq.] an expressionless face, as of a poker player hiding the nature of his hand

poker work same as PYROGRAPHY

poky (pō′kē) *adj.* **-ier, -iest** [< POKE[1]] 1. slow; dull 2. small; stuffy [a *poky* room] —**pok′ily** *adv.*

Pol. 1. Poland 2. Polish

polar (pō′lər) *adj.* [see POLE[2]] 1. of or near the North or South Pole 2. of a pole or poles 3. having polarity 4. opposite in character, direction, etc.

polar bear a large, white bear of the Arctic regions

polar circle same as : 1. ARCTIC CIRCLE 2. ANTARCTIC CIRCLE

Polaris (pō lär′is) [< ML. *polaris*, polar] 1. the North Star 2. a kind of U.S. ballistic missile, usually fired by a submarine

polarity (pō lar′ə tē) *n.*, *pl.* **-ties** 1. the tendency of bodies having opposite magnetic poles to become aligned so that they point to the two magnetic poles of the earth 2. any tendency to turn, feel, etc. in a certain way, as if magnetized 3. the having of two contrary qualities, powers, etc. 4. the condition of being positive or negative with respect to some reference point

polarization (pō′lər ī zā′shən) *n.* 1. the producing or acquiring of polarity 2. *Optics* a condition of light in which the vibrations of the waves are in one plane or direction only

polarize (pō′lə rīz′) *vt.* **-ized′, -iz′ing** [< Fr. *polaire*, polar] to give polarity to —*vi.* to acquire polarity; specif., to separate into opposed groups, etc.

Polaroid (pō′lə roid′) [POLE[2]] *Trademark:* 1. a transparent material capable of polarizing light 2. a camera that develops and prints snapshots

polder (pol′dər) *n.* [Du.] an area of low-lying land reclaimed from a sea, lake, or river

Pole (pōl) *n.* a native or inhabitant of Poland

pole[1] (pōl) *n.* [< L. *palus*, stake] 1. a long, slender piece of wood, metal, etc. 2. a unit of measure, equal to one rod or one square rod —*vt.*, *vi.* **poled, pol′ing** to propel (a boat or raft) with a pole —**up the pole** [Colloq.] 1. slightly mad 2. in a dilemma

pole[2] *n.* [< Gr. *polos*] 1. either end of any axis, as of the earth 2. the region around the North Pole or South Pole 3. either of two opposed forces, parts, etc., as the ends of a magnet, the terminals of a battery, etc. —**poles apart** widely separated, as in opinions, etc.

poleaxe *n.* [< POLL + AXE] 1. a long-handled battle-axe 2. any axe with a spike, hook, etc. opposite the blade —*vt.* **-axed′, -ax′ing** to attack or fell as if with a poleaxe

polecat *n.* [see PULLET & CAT] 1. a small, weasellike carnivore 2. [U.S.] same as SKUNK

polemic (po lem′ik) *adj.* [< Fr. < Gr. *polemos*, a war] of or involving dispute: also **polem′ical** —*n.* an argument or controversial discussion

polemics *n.pl.* [with sing. v.] the art or practice of disputation —**polem′icist** *n.*

polestar (pōl′stär′) *n.* 1. Polaris, the North Star 2. a guiding principle

pole vault *Athletics* a leap for height by vaulting over a bar with the aid of a long, flexible pole —**pole′-vault** *vi.* —**pole′-vault′er** *n.*

police (pə lēs′) *n.* [Fr. < Gr. *polis*, city] 1. the governmental department (of a city, county, etc.) for keeping order, enforcing the law, and investigating crime 2. [with pl. v.] the members of such a department, or of a private organization like this —*vt.* **-liced′, -lic′ing** to control, protect, etc. with police

police constable the lowest rank in the police force

police dog a dog specially trained to assist police

policeman *n.* a member of a police force —**police′wom′an** *n.fem.*

police state a government that uses a secret police force to suppress political opposition

police station the office or headquarters of the police force of a district

policy[1] (pol′ə sē) *n., pl.* **-cies** [see POLICE] 1. any governing principle, plan, etc. 2. wise management

policy[2] *n., pl.* **-cies** [< Gr. *apodeixis*, proof] a written insurance contract

polio (pō′lē ō′) *n.* *short for* POLIOMYELITIS

poliomyelitis (pō′lē ō mī′ə līt′əs) *n.* [< Gr. *polios*, grey + *myelos*, marrow] an infectious disease caused by a virus inflammation of the grey matter of the spinal cord, often resulting in muscular paralysis

Polish (pō′lish) *adj.* of Poland, its people, their language, or culture —*n.* the Slavic language of the Poles

polish (pol′ish) *vt.* [< L. *polire*] 1. to make smooth and glossy, as by rubbing 2. to refine (manners, etc.) 3. to complete or embellish —*vi.* to take a polish —*n.* 1. a surface gloss 2. refinement 3. a substance used for polishing —**polish off** [Colloq.] to finish or get rid of —**polish up** [Colloq.] to improve —**pol′ished** *adj.* —**pol′isher** *n.*

Politburo (pol′it byooər′ō) *n.* [< Russ.] the executive committee of a Communist Party

polite (pə līt′) *adj.* [< L. *polire*, polish] 1. cultured; refined 2. having good manners; courteous —**polite′ly** *adv.* —**polite′ness** *n.*

politic (pol′ə tik) *adj.* [see POLICE] 1. having practical wisdom; prudent 2. crafty 3. expedient [a *politic* plan] 4. [Rare] political: see BODY POLITIC —*vi.* **-ticked, -ticking** to engage in political campaigning

political (pə lit′i k′l) *adj.* 1. of, concerned with, or engaged in government, politics, etc. 2. of or characteristic of political parties or politicians —**polit′ically** *adv.*

political asylum refuge given to someone for political reasons

political prisoner someone imprisoned for political offences rather than criminal ones

political science the science of the principles, organization, and methods of government

politician (pol′ə tish′ən) *n.* a person actively engaged in politics, often one holding or seeking political office

politicize (pə lit′ə sīz′) *vi.* **-cized′, -ciz′ing** to talk about, engage in politics —*vt.* to make political in tone, character, etc. —**polit′iciza′tion** *n.*

politics (pol′ə tiks) *n.pl.* [with sing. or pl. v.] 1. political science 2. political affairs 3. participation in political affairs 4. political methods, etc. 5. political principles, etc. 6. factional scheming for power

polity (pol′ə tē) *n., pl.* **-ties** [see POLICE] 1. the government organization of a state, church, etc. 2. a society or institution with a government; state

polka (pōl′kə) *n.* [< Czech] 1. a fast dance for couples 2. music for this dance —*vi.* to dance the polka

polka dot one of the small round dots regularly spaced to form a pattern on cloth —**pol′ka-dot′** *adj.*

poll (pōl) *n.* [< or akin to MDu. *pol*, head] 1. a counting, listing, etc. of persons, esp. of voters 2. the number of votes recorded 3. a canvassing to collect information or to discover public opinion 4. the head —*vt.* 1. to receive (a certain number of votes) 2. to register the votes of 3. to canvass in a poll 4. to cast (a vote) 5. to trim the wool, branches, etc. of 6. to cut off or cut short

pollack (pol′ak) *n.* [< ?] a food fish of the cod family: also sp. **pol′lock**

pollen (pol′ən) *n.* [< L., dust] the yellow, powderlike male sex cells on the stamens of a flower

pollen count a measure of the pollen grains present in the air over a 24 hour period

pollinate (pol′ə nāt′) *vt.* **-nat′ed, -nat′ing** to transfer pollen from a stamen to a pistil of (a flower) —**pol′lina′tion** *n.* —**pol′lina′tor** *n.*

polling booth a voting place in a polling station

polling station a place where the voters of an area can cast their votes

pollster (pōl′stər) *n.* a person whose work is taking public opinion polls

pollutant (pə loot′′nt) *n.* something that pollutes, as a harmful chemical discharged into the air

pollute (pə loot′) *vt.* **-lut′ed, -lut′ing** [< L. *polluere*] to make unclean, impure, or corrupt —**pollu′tion** *n.*

polo (pō′lō) *n.* [prob. < Tibet. *pulu*, the ball] 1. a game played on horseback by two teams using a wooden ball and long-handled mallets 2. *same as* WATER POLO

polonaise (pol′ə nāz′) *n.* [Fr. < *polonais*, Polish] 1. a stately Polish dance in triple time 2. music for this

poloneck (pō′lō nek′) *n.* a high, snugly fitting, turnover collar on a pullover, shirt, etc.

polonium (pə lō′nē əm) *n.* [< ML. *Polonia*, Poland] a radioactive chemical element formed by the disintegration of radium: symbol, Po

poltergeist (pol′tər gīst′) *n.* [G. < *poltern*, make noise + *Geist*, GHOST] a ghost supposed to be responsible for rappings and other mysterious noisy disturbances

poltroon (pol troon′) *n.* [< Fr. < It. *poltrone*] a thorough coward —**poltroon′ery** *n.*

Poly (pol′ē) *n.* [Colloq.] *short for* POLYTECHNIC

poly- [< Gr.] *a combining form meaning much, many*

polyandry (pol′ē an′drē) *n.* [< Gr. *poly-*, many + *anēr*, man] the practice of having two or more husbands at the same time —**pol′yan′drous** *adj.*

polyanthus (pol′ē an′thəs) *n.* [< Gr. *poly-*, many + *anthos*, flower] any of various primroses with many flowers

polychromatic (pol′ē krō mat′ik) *adj.* [POLY- + CHROMATIC] having various or changing colours

polyester (pol′ē es′tər) *n.* [POLY(MER) + ESTER] a synthetic resin used in making plastics, fibres, etc.

polyethylene (pol′ē eth′ə lēn′) *n.* *U.S. var. of* POLYTHENE

polygamy (pə lig′ə mē) *n.* [< Gr. *poly-*, many + *gamos*, marriage] the practice of having two or more wives or husbands at the same time —**polyg′amist** *n.* —**polyg′- amous** *adj.*

polyglot (pol′i glot′) *adj.* [< Gr. *poly-*, many + *glōtta*, tongue] **1.** speaking or writing several languages **2.** written in several languages —*n.* a polyglot person

polygon (pol′i gən) *n.* [see POLY- & -GON] a closed plane figure, esp. one with more than four sides and angles —**polygonal** (pə lig′ə n′l) *adj.*

polygraph (pol′ē gräf′) *n.* an instrument for recording changes in blood pressure, pulse rate, etc.

polygyny (pə lij′ə nē) *n.* [< POLY- + Gr. *gynē*, woman] the practice of having two or more wives or concubines at the same time —**polyg′ynous** *adj.*

polyhedron (pol′i hē′drən) *n.*, *pl.* **-drons, -dra** [see POLY- & -HEDRON] a solid figure, esp. one with more than six plane surfaces —**pol′yhe′dral** *adj.*

polymath (pol′i math′) *n.* [< Gr. *poly-*, much + *manthanein*, to learn] a person of great and diversified learning

polymer (pol′i mər) *n.* [G. < Gr. *poly-*, many + *meros*, a part] a substance made up of giant molecules formed by polymerization

polymeric (pol′i mer′ik) *adj.* composed of the same chemical elements in the same proportions by weight, but differing in molecular weight —**pol′ymer′ically** *adv.*

polymerization (pə lim′ər ī zā′shən) *n.* the process of joining two or more like molecules to form a more complex molecule —**polym′erize′** *vt., vi.*

polymorphous (pol′i môr′fəs) *adj.* [< POLY + Gr. *morphē*, form] having, occurring in, or passing through several or various forms: also **pol′ymor′phic**

Polynesian (pol′ə nē′zhən) *adj.* of Polynesia, its people, their language, etc. —*n.* **1.** a member of the people of Polynesia **2.** the languages of Polynesia

polynomial (pol′i nō′mē əl) *n.* [POLY- + (BI)NOMIAL] **1.** *Algebra* an expression consisting of two or more terms (Ex. : $x^3 + 3x + 2$) **2.** *Biol.* a name having two or more terms —*adj.* consisting of polynomials

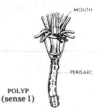

POLYP
(sense 1)

polyp (pol′ip) *n.* [< Gr. *poly-*, many + *pous*, foot] **1.** a coelenterate with a fringe of tentacles at the top of a tubelike body, as the sea anemone, hydra, etc. **2.** a projecting growth of mucous membrane

polyphonic (pol′i fon′ik) *adj.* [see POLY- & -PHONE] **1.** having or making many sounds **2.** *Music* of or characterized by polyphony

polyphony (pə lif′ə nē) *n.* **1.** multiplicity of sounds **2.** *Music* a combining of a number of harmonious melodies; counterpoint

polystyrene (pol′i stī′rēn) *n.* a tough plastic, a polymer of styrene

polysyllabic (pol′i si lab′ik) *adj.* **1.** having several, esp. four or more, syllables **2.** characterized by polysyllables

polysyllable (pol′i sil′ə b′l) *n.* a polysyllabic word

polytechnic (pol′i tek′nik) *adj.* [< Gr. *poly-*, many + *technē*, an art] of or providing instruction in many scientific and technical subjects —*n.* a polytechnic college, etc.

polytheism (pol′i thē iz′m) *n.* [< Gr. *poly-*, many + *theos*, god] belief in more than one god —**pol′ytheist** *adj., n.* —**pol′ythe- is′tic** *adj.*

polythene (pol′i thēn′) *n.* [POLY(MER) + (ETHYL)ENE] a thermoplastic resin used in making plastics, pipes, etc.

polyunsaturated (pol′i un sach′ə rāt′id) *adj.* designating a class of fats thought not to increase cholesterol in the blood stream

polyurethane (pol′i yoõr′ə thān′) *n.* [< POLY- & UREA & ETHER] a synthetic rubber polymer used in cushions, etc.

poly vinyl chloride a polymer of vinyl chloride that is tough and resistant, used for pipes, insulation, etc.

pomace (pum′is) *n.* [< L. *pomum*, fruit] the crushed pulp of apples or other fruit pressed for juice

pomade (pə mäd′) *n.* [< Fr. < L. *pomum*, fruit] a perfumed preparation, as for the hair

pomander (pō man′dər) *n.* [< OFr. *pome*, apple + *ambre*, amber] **1.** a mixture of aromatic substances compressed in a ball, used for perfuming drawers, etc. **2.** a case for this

pomegranate (pom′ə gran′it) *n.* [< OFr. *pome*, apple + L. *granatum*, having seeds]

1. a round fruit with a thick, red rind and many seeds covered with red, juicy, flesh 2. the bush or tree that bears it

Pomeranian (pom′ə rā′nē ən) *n.* a small dog with long, silky hair, pointed ears, and a bushy tail

pomfret cake (pum′frət) a small, cakelike sweet made of liquorice: also **pom′fret-cake, pontefract cake**

pommel (pum′′l; *also, for n.,* pom′′l) *n.* [< L. *pomum,* fruit] 1. the rounded, upward-projecting front part of a saddle 2. a round knob on the end of some sword hilts —*vt.* **-melled, -melling** *same as* PUMMEL

Pommy, Pommie (pom′ē) *n., pl.* **-mies** [< ?] [*also* p-] [Aust. Slang] a Briton —*adj.* [also p-] [Aust. Slang] British

pomp (pomp) *n.* [< Gr. *pompē,* solemn procession] 1. stately display 2. ostentatious show or display

pom-pom (pom′pom′) *n.* [echoic] 1. a rapid-firing automatic weapon 2. *same as* POMPON: also **pom′pom′**

pompon (pom′pon′) *n.* [Fr.] 1. an ornamental tuft as of silk or wool, worn as on hats, shoes, etc. 2. a chrysanthemum, dahlia, etc. with small, round flowers

pompous (pom′pəs) *adj.* 1. pretentious, as in speech or manner; self-important 2. full of pomp —**pompos′ity** (-pos′ə tē) *n.* —**pom′pously** *adv.*

ponce (pons) *n.* [< ?] [Slang] *same as* PIMP —*vi.* **ponced, ponc′ing** [Slang] 1. *same as* PIMP 2. to go around in a flashy or showy way [*he* ponced *around the room*]

poncho (pon′chō) *n., pl.* **-chos** [< SAmInd.] 1. a cloak like a blanket with a hole in the middle for the head 2. a garment, esp. a raincoat, like this

pond (pond) *n.* [< ME. POUND³] a body of standing water smaller than a lake, often man-made

ponder (pon′dər) *vt., vi.* [< L. *ponderare,* weigh] to think deeply (about); deliberate —**pon′derable** *adj.*

ponderous (pon′dər əs) *adj.* 1. very heavy; unwieldy 2. laboured; dull [*a* ponderous *style*]

pondok (pon′dok′) *n., pl.* **-doks** [< Malay, leaf house] [S Afr. Derog.] a crudely-made house or shelter: also **pondokie** (-kē)

pondweed (pond′wēd′) *n.* any of various related water plants, with submerged or floating leaves •

pong (poŋ) *vi., n.* [prob. < Romany *pan,* to stink] [Slang] *same as* STINK

pongee (pon jē′) *n.* [< Chin. dial. *pen-chi,* domestic loom] a soft, thin silk cloth, usually in natural tan

poniard (pon′yərd) *n.* [< L. *pugnus,* fist] a dagger

pons (ponz) *n., pl.* **pontes** (pon′tēz) [L., a bridge] *Anat., Zool.* a piece of connecting tissue

pontiff (pon′tif) *n.* [< L. *pontifex,* high priest] 1. a bishop; specif., [P-] the Pope 2. a high priest

pontifical (pon tif′i k'l) *adj.* 1. having

to do with a high priest 2. papal 3. pompous, dogmatic, or arrogant

pontificate (pon tif′i kit; *for v.,* -kāt′) *n.* the office or tenure of a pontiff —*vi.* **-cat′-ed, -cat′ing** 1. to be pompous or dogmatic 2. to officiate as a pontiff

pontoon¹ (pon tōōn′) *n.* *same as* VINGT-ET-UN

pontoon² *n.* [Fr. < L. *pons,* a bridge] 1. a flat-bottomed boat 2. any of a number of these, or of floating cylinders, etc., used to support a temporary bridge (**pontoon bridge**)

pony (pō′nē) *n., pl.* **-nies** [< Scot., prob. < L. *pullus,* foal] 1. a horse of any small breed 2. [Colloq.] in bookmaking, £25

ponytail *n.* a hair style in which long hair, tied high at the back of the head, hangs free

pony trekking the pastime of travelling through the countryside on horseback, usually in an organized group

poodle (pōō′d'l) *n.* [G. *Pudel*] a dog with a solid-coloured, curly coat

poof (poof, pōōf) *n.* [< Fr. *pouffe,* puff] [Colloq.] an effeminate man, esp. a male homosexual

pooh (pōō) *interj.* [prob. echoic] an exclamation of disdain, disbelief, or impatience

pooh-pooh (pōō′pōō′) *vt.* to make light of; belittle

pool¹ (pōōl) *n.* [OE. *pol*] 1. a small pond 2. a small, shallow body of any liquid 3. *same as* SWIMMING POOL 4. a deep, still spot in a river

pool² *n.* [< LL. *pulla,* hen] 1. a) a combination of resources, funds, etc. for some common purpose b) the parties forming it 2. a supply of equipment, personnel, etc. shared by a group 3. the total stakes played for, as in a single deal of a card game 4. a combination of business firms for creating a monopoly 5. a game of billiards played with numbered balls —*vt., vi.* to contribute to a common fund

pools *n.pl.* an organized postal gambling pool betting on the result of football matches: also **football pools**

poop (pōōp) *n.* [< L. *puppis,* stern] a raised deck at the stern of a sailing ship: also **poop deck**

poor (pooər) *adj.* [< L. *pauper,* poor] 1. a) having little or no means to support oneself; needy b) indicating or characterized by poverty 2. lacking in some quality or thing; specif., a) inadequate b) inferior or worthless c) contemptible d) lacking skill 3. worthy of pity; unfortunate —**poor′ness** *n.*

poorhouse *n.* formerly, an institution for paupers, supported from public funds

poor law formerly, a law providing for the relief or support of the poor from public, esp. parish, funds

poorly *adv.* in a poor way; badly —*adj.* [Colloq.] in poor health; unwell

poor man's weatherglass *same as* PIMPERNEL

poort (poort) *n.* [< Afrik.] a narrow mountain pass, usually following a river

poor white a poverty stricken white person, esp. in S US or South Africa

pop[1] (pop) *n.* [echoic] 1. a sudden, light explosive sound 2. any carbonated, nonalcoholic beverage —*vi.* **popped, pop'-ping** 1. to make, or burst with, a pop 2. to move, go, etc. suddenly or for a brief visit 3. to bulge: said of the eyes 4. to shoot a pistol, etc. —*vt.* 1. [U.S.] to cause (maize) to pop, as by roasting 2. to shoot 3. to put suddenly [to *pop* one's head in at the door] 4. to place in pawn —*adv.* with or like a pop —**pop off** [Slang] 1. to die suddenly 2. to leave hastily —**pop the question** [Colloq.] to propose marriage

pop[2] *n.* [< PAPA] [Slang] father

pop[3] *adj.* short for POPULAR

pop[4] *n.* [< POP(ULAR)] music popular among young people, characterized by strong rhythm and electronic amplification

pop. 1. popular 2. population

P.O.P. Post Office Preferred

pop (art) a realistic art style using techniques and subjects from commercial art, comic strips, etc.

popcorn *n.* the puffed, edible kernels of a variety of maize with small ears and hard grains which pop open when heated

pope (pōp) *n.* [< Gr. *pappas*, father] [usually **P-**] R.C.Ch. the bishop of Rome and head of the Church

popery (pōp'ər ē) *n.* the doctrines and rituals of the Roman Catholic Church: a hostile term

popeyed (pop'īd') *adj.* having protruding eyes

popgun *n.* a toy gun that shoots pellets by air compression, with a pop

popinjay (pop'in jā') *n.* [< Ar. *babaghā*, parrot] a talkative, conceited person

popish (pōp'ish) *adj.* of popery: a hostile term

poplar (pop'lər) *n.* [< L. *populus*, the people] a tall, fast-growing tree with alternate leaves and catkins

poplin (pop'lin) *n.* [< Fr. prob. < It. *papalina*, papal] a sturdy fabric of cotton, rayon, etc. with fine ribbing

popper (pop'ər) *n.* [Colloq.] same as PRESS STUD

poppet (pop'it) *n.* [var. of PUPPET] 1. [Colloq.] a little person: a term of endearment 2. a valve that moves into and from its seat: in full, **poppet valve**

popping crease Cricket the line 4 feet in front of the wicket at, or behind which, the batsman stands

poppy (pop'ē) *n.,* pl. **-pies** [< L. *papaver*] 1. a plant with a milky juice and showy, variously coloured flowers 2. an extract, as opium, made from poppy juice 3. yellowish red

poppycock (pop'ē kok') *n.* [Du. *pappekak,* dung] [Colloq.] nonsense

Poppy Day another name for Remembrance Day, because of the artificial poppies sold in aid of the Earl Haig Fund

pop shop [Colloq.] a pawnshop

popsy, popsie (pop'sē) *n.,* pl. **-sies** [< POPPET] [Colloq.] a young woman: a term of affection

populace (pop'yoo ləs) *n.* [< L. *populus*, people] the common people; the masses

popular (pop'yoo lər) *adj.* [< L. *populus*, people] 1. liked by many people 2. having many friends 3. common; prevalent 4. of or carried on by people generally 5. intended for the general public [*popular* music] 6. within the means of the ordinary person [*popular* prices] —**pop'ular'ity** (-lar'ə tē) *n.*

popular front a group of left wing political parties

popularize *vt.* **-ized', -iz'ing** 1. to make popular 2. to make understandable to the general public

populate (pop'yoo lāt') *vt.* **-lat'ed, -lat'-ing** [< L. *populus*, people] 1. to inhabit 2. to supply with inhabitants

population (pop'yoo lā'shən) *n.* 1. a) all the people in a country, region, etc. b) the number of these 2. a populating or being populated

populous (pop'yoo ləs) *adj.* thickly populated

porcelain (pôr's'l in) *n.* [< Fr. < It. *porcellana*, a kind of shell] 1. a hard, white, translucent ceramic ware, made of kaolin, feldspar, and quartz or flint 2. porcelain dishes or ornaments, collectively

porch (pôrch) *n.* [< L. *porta*, gate] a structure projecting from the doorway of a building and forming a covered entrance

porcine (pôr'sīn) *adj.* [< L. *porcus*, pig] of or like pigs

porcupine (pôr'kyoo pīn') *n.* [< L. *porcus*, pig + *spina*, spine] a rodent having coarse hair mixed with long, stiff, sharp spines

pore[1] (pôr) *vi.* **pored, por'ing** [< ?] 1. to study carefully [to *pore* over a book] 2. to ponder (with *over*)

pore[2] *n.* [< Gr. *poros*, passage] 1. a tiny opening, as in plant leaves, skin, etc., for absorbing or discharging fluids 2. a similar opening in rocks or other substances

pork (pôrk) *n.* [< L. *porcus*, pig] the flesh of a pig used, fresh or cured, as food

pork butcher a butcher who specializes in selling pork

porker *n.* a pig fattened for use as food

pork pie 1. a meat pie made with chopped pork 2. a man's soft hat with a round, flat crown

porky *adj.* **-ier, -iest** 1. of or like pork 2. fat

porn (pôrn) *n.* [Colloq.] short for PORNOGRAPHY

porno (pôrn'ō) *n., adj.* [Colloq.] short for: 1. PORNOGRAPHY 2. PORNOGRAPHIC

pornography (pôr nog'rə fē) *n.* [< Gr. *porne,* a prostitute + *graphein,* write] writings, pictures, etc. intended primarily to arouse sexual desire —**pornog'rapher** *n.* —**por'nograph'ic** (-nō graf'ik) *adj.*

porous (pôr'əs) *adj.* full of pores, through

which fluids, air, or light may pass —**poros-ity** (pô ros'ə tē) *n.*

porphyry (pôr'fər ē) *n., pl.* -**ries** [< Gr. *porphyros*, purple] **1.** orig., an Egyptian rock with large feldspar crystals in a purplish rock mass **2.** any igneous rock resembling this —**por'phyrit'ic** (-fə rit'ik) *adj.*

porpoise (pôr'pəs) *n.* [< L. *porcus*, pig + *piscis*, fish] a small whale with a blunt snout

porridge (por'ij) *n.* [altered < POTTAGE] **1.** a soft food made of cereal or oatmeal boiled in water or milk **2.** [Slang] imprisonment

porringer (por'in jər) *n.* [< Fr. *potager*, soup dish] a bowl for porridge, soup, etc., esp. one used by children

port[1] (pôrt) *n.* [< L. *portus*, haven] **1.** a harbour **2.** a city with a harbour where ships load and unload

port[2] *n.* [< *Oporto*, city in Portugal] a sweet, fortified, usually dark-red wine

port[3] *vt.* [< L. *portare*, carry] to hold (a rifle or sword) diagonally in front of one, as for inspection

port[4] *n.* [prob. < PORT[1]] the left-hand side of a ship or aircraft as one faces the bow —*adj.* of or on the port —*vt., vi.* to turn (the helm) to the port side

Port. **1.** Portugal **2.** Portuguese

portable (pôr'tə b'l) *adj.* [< L. *portare*, carry] **1.** that can be carried **2.** easily carried —*n.* something portable —**port'a-bil'ity** *n.*

portage (pôr'tij) *n.* [< L. *portare*, carry] **1.** a carrying of boats and supplies between rivers, lakes, etc. **2.** any route over which this is done —*vt., vi.* -**taged, -taging** to carry (boats, etc.) over a portage

portal (pôr't'l) *n.* [< L. *porta*, gate] a doorway, gate, or entrance, esp. a large or imposing one

portcullis (pôrt'kul'is) *n.* [< MFr. *porte*, gate + *coleïce*, sliding] a heavy iron grating lowered to bar the gateway of a castle or fortified town

portend (pôr tend') *vt.* [< L. *por-*, through + *tendere*, stretch] **1.** to be an omen of **2.** to signify

portent (pôr'tent) *n.* **1.** something that portends an event; omen **2.** significance **3.** a marvel

portentous (pôr ten'təs) *adj.* **1.** ominous **2.** amazing **3.** pompous —**porten'tous-ness** *n.*

porter[1] (pôr'tər) *n.* [< L. *porta*, gate] a doorman or gatekeeper —**port'ress** *n. fem.*

porter[2] *n.* [< L. *portare*, carry] **1.** a man whose work is to carry luggage, as at a railway station **2.** [abbrev. of *porter's ale*] a dark-brown beer

porterhouse *n.* a choice cut of beef from the loin just before the sirloin: in full, **porterhouse steak**

portfolio (pôrt'fō'lē ō') *n., pl.* -**lios** [< L. *portare*, carry + *folium*, leaf] **1.** a. flat, portable case for loose papers, etc. **2.** the office of a minister of state [a

minister without *portfolio*] **3.** a list of an investor's stocks, bonds, etc.

porthole (pôrt'hōl') *n.* an opening in a ship's side, as for admitting light and air

PORTICO

portico (pôr'tə kō') *n., pl.* -**coes**, -**cos** [It. < L. *porticus*] a porch or covered walk, consisting of a roof supported by columns

portion (pôr'shən) *n.* [< L. *portio*] **1.** a part, esp. as allotted to a person; share **2.** a helping of food **3.** a dowry **4.** one's lot; destiny —*vt.* **1.** to divide into portions **2.** to give as a portion to

portland cement (pôrt'lənd) [it resembles stone from the Isle of *Portland*] [*sometimes* P-] a kind of cement that hardens under water

portly (pôrt'lē) *adj.* -**lier, -liest** **1.** stout; corpulent **2.** large and heavy in a dignified way —**port'liness** *n.*

portmanteau (pôrt'man'tō) *n., pl.* -**teaus, -teaux** (-tōz) [< Fr. *porter*, carry + *manteau*, cloak] a stiff suitcase that opens like a book into two compartments

portmanteau word a word that is a combination of two others (Ex.: *smog*, from *smoke* and *fog*)

portrait (pôr'trit) *n.* [see PORTRAY] **1.** a painting, photograph, etc. of a person, esp. of his face **2.** a description, portrayal, etc. —**por'traitist** *n.*

portraiture (pôr'tri chər). *n.* **1.** the making of portraits **2.** a portrait

portray (pôr trā') *vt.* [< L. *pro-*, forth + *trahere*, draw] **1.** to make a portrait of **2.** to describe **3.** to play the part of in a play, film, etc. —**portray'al** *n.*

Portuguese (pôr'choo gēz') *adj.* of Portugal, its people, their language, etc. —*n.* **1.** *pl.* -**guese'** a native of Portugal **2.** the language of Portugal

Portuguese man-of-war a large, warm-sea animal having long, dangling tentacles that sting, and a large, bladderlike sac that enables it to float on water

pose[1] (pōz) *vt.* **posed, pos'ing** [< LL. *pausare*, to pause] **1.** to present (a question, problem, etc.) **2.** to put (a model, etc.) in a certain attitude —*vi.* **1.** to assume a certain attitude, as in modelling for an artist **2.** to strike attitudes for effect **3.** to pretend to be what one is not —*n.* **1.** a bodily attitude, esp. one held for an artist, etc. **2.** behaviour assumed for effect; pretence

pose[2] *vt.* **posed, pos'ing** [< APPOSE, OPPOSE] to baffle, as by a difficult question

poser *n.* a baffling question or problem

poseur (pō zur′) *n.* [Fr.] a person who assumes attitudes or manners merely for their effect upon others

posh (posh) *adj.* [prob. < obs. slang *posh*, a dandy] [Colloq.] luxurious and fashionable; elegant

position (pə zish′ən) *n.* [< L. *ponere*, to place] 1. the place where one is; location 2. the usual or proper place 3. the manner in which a person or thing is placed or arranged 4. one's attitude or opinion 5. rank or status 6. a place high in society, business, etc. [a man of *position*] 7. a post of employment; job; office —*vt.* to put in a particular position; place —**posi′tional** *adj.*

positive (poz′ə tiv) *adj.* [< L. *ponere*, to place] 1. *a)* definitely set; explicit *b)* allowing no doubt; certain 2. *a)* confident *b)* overconfident or dogmatic 3. showing agreement; affirmative 4. tending in the direction regarded as that of increase, progress, etc. 5. constructive [*positive* criticism] 6. absolute; unqualified 7. having real existence in itself [a *positive* good] 8. based on facts [*positive* proof] 9. concerned only with real things and experience; practical 10. [Colloq.] complete; downright [a *positive* fool] 11. *Elec.* a) of electricity predominating in a glass body after it has been rubbed with silk *b)* charged with positive electricity *c)* having a deficiency of electrons 12. *Gram.* of an adjective or adverb in its uninflected or unmodified form neither comparative nor superlative 13. *Math.* greater than zero; plus 14. *Med.* indicating the presence of a condition, bacteria, etc. 15. *Photog.* with the relation of light and shade the same as in the thing photographed 16. *Physics* having an opposite polarity to that of an electron; said of an electric charge —*n.* something positive, as a degree, quality, etc.; specif., *a)* the plate in a voltaic battery where the higher potential is *b)* *Math.* a positive quantity *c)* *Photog.* a positive print —**pos′itively** *adv.* —**pos′itiveness** *n.*

positivism *n.* a system of philosophy based solely on observable scientific facts —**pos′itivist** *n., adj.*

positron (poz′ə tron) *n.* [POSI(TIVE) + (ELEC)TRON] the positive antiparticle of an electron, with about the same mass and magnitude of charge

poss. 1. possession 2. possessive 3. possibly

posse (pos′ē) *n.* [< L., be able] 1. [Now Chiefly U.S.] a body of men summoned to assist a sheriff 2. in W Canada, a troop of trained horses and riders who perform at rodeos

possess (pə zes′) *vt.* [< L. *possidere*] 1. to have as something that belongs to one; own 2. to have as an attribute, quality, etc. 3. to gain control over; dominate [*possessed* by an idea] —**posses′sor** *n.*

possessed *adj.* 1. owned 2. controlled as by an evil spirit; crazed —**possessed of** having

possession (pə zesh′ən) *n.* 1. a possessing or being possessed; ownership 2. anything possessed 3. [pl.] property; wealth 4. territory ruled by an outside country

possessive (pə zes′iv) *adj.* 1. of possession 2. showing an excessive desire to possess, or retain possession or control of 3. *Gram.* designating or of a case, form, or construction expressing possession (Ex.: *men's, of men, her*) —*n.* *Gram.* a possessive case or form —**posses′siveness** *n.*

possible (pos′ə b'l) *adj.* [< L. *posse*, be able] 1. that can be 2. that may or may not happen 3. that can be done, chosen, etc. 4. permissible —*n.* 1. the highest attainable score, esp. in shooting 2. a candidate, etc. who has a good chance of winning, being chosen, etc. —**pos′sibil′ity** *n.*

possibly *adv.* 1. by any possible means [it can't *possibly* work] 2. perhaps; maybe

post¹ (pōst) *n.* [< L. *postis*] 1. a piece of wood, metal, etc., set upright to support a sign, fence, etc. 2. the starting point of a horse race 3. the finishing point of a race —*vt.* 1. to put up (a notice, etc.) on (a wall, etc.) 2. to announce or publicize thus 3. to put (a name) on a posted or published list

post² *n.* [ult. < L. *ponere*, to place] 1. an assigned or appointed position, job, or duty 2. the place where a soldier, guard, etc. is stationed 3. *a)* a place where troops are stationed *b)* the troops there; garrison 4. either of two military bugle calls (**first** and **last post**) giving notice of the time to retire for the night 5. short for TRADING POST —*vt.* to assign to a post

post³ *n.* [see prec.] 1. a single collection or delivery of mail 2. a post office 3. a postbox or pillar box 4. the system or organization for the collection, transport, and delivery of letters, etc. —*vt.* 1. to send by post 2. to inform [keep me *posted*] 3. *Bookkeeping a)* to transfer (an item) to the ledger *b)* to enter all necessary items in (a ledger, etc.)

post- [L.] *a prefix meaning:* 1. after in time, following [*postglacial*] 2. after in space, behind

postage (pōs′tij) *n.* the amount charged for delivering a letter, etc., esp. as represented by stamps

postage stamp a government stamp for a letter or package, showing postage paid

postal (pōs′t'l) *adj.* having to do with mail or post offices

postal code a code consisting of letters and numbers, added to the last line of an address to facilitate processing of mail

postal order a money order issued by one office authorizing payment at another post office

post bag a mailbag

postbox *n.* a box, as on a street, into which mail is put for collection

postcard *n.* a card, often a picture card, for posting when a postage stamp is affixed: also **post card**

post chaise a closed, four-wheeled coach

drawn by fast horses, formerly used to carry mail and passengers

post code a code used as part of a postal address to aid the sorting of mail: also **postal code**

postdate (pōst′dāt′) *vt.* **-dat′ed, -dat′-ing** 1. to assign a later date to than the actual date 2. to follow in time

poster (pōs′tər) *n.* 1. a large advertisement or notice, often illustrated, posted publicly 2. a large coloured picture, as of a pop star, used for decoration

poste restante (pōst′res′tänt) a department in a post office to which letters can be addressed to be kept till called for

posterior (pos tēar′ē ər) *adj.* [L. < *post*, after] 1. at or towards the rear 2. later; following —*n.* the buttocks —**poste′rior′-ity** (-or′ə tē) *n.*

posterity (pos ter′ə tē) *n.* [see prec.] 1. all future generations 2. all of a person's descendants

postern (pōs′tərn) *n.* [see POSTERIOR] a door or entrance at the side or rear

post-free *adj., adv.* 1. with the postage prepaid 2. free of postal charge

postgraduate (pōst′grad′yoo wət) *adj.* of or taking a course of study after graduation —*n.* a postgraduate student

posthaste (pōst′hāst′) *adv.* with great haste

posthumous (pos′tyoo məs) *adj.* [< L. *postumus*, last] 1. occurring after one's death 2. published after the author's death 3. born after the father's death —**post′hu-mously** *adv.*

posthypnotic (pōst′hip not′ik) *adj.* of, or carried out in, the period following a hypnotic trance

postilion, postillion (pos til′yən) *n.* [Fr. < It. *posta*, POST[3]] a person riding the left-hand horse of a team drawing a carriage

postimpressionism (pōst′im presh′-ən iz′m) *n.* the theory or practice of some late 19th-cent. painters reacting against impressionism and emphasizing what is subjective —**post′impres′sionist** *adj., n.*

postman (pōst′mən) *n.* one whose work is carrying and delivering the post

postman's knock a parlour game involving the exchange of kisses

postmark (pōst′märk′) *n.* a post-office mark stamped on mail, cancelling the postage stamp and recording the date and place —*vt.* to stamp with a postmark

postmaster *n.* a person in charge of a post office —**post′mis′tress** *n.fem.*

postmaster general *pl.* **postmasters general, postmaster generals** the head of a government's postal system

postmeridian (pōst′mə rid′ē ən) *adj.* [< L.: see POST- & MERIDIAN] of or in the afternoon

post meridiem (pōst′mə rid′ē əm) [L.] after noon

post-mortem (pōst′môr′təm) *adj.* [L.] after death —*n.* 1. an examination of a dead body to determine the cause of death 2. a detailed evaluation of some event just ended

postnatal (pōst′nāt′′l) *adj.* after birth

post-obit (pōst′ō′bit) *n.* [< L., after death] a bond pledging to pay a debt upon the death of a person from whom one expects to inherit money

post office 1. the governmental department in charge of postal and telecommunications services 2. a place where post is sorted, postage stamps are sold, etc.

postoperative (pōst′op′ər ə tiv) *adj.* of or in the period after surgery —**post′op′er-atively** *adv.*

postpaid (pōst′pād′) *adj.* with the postage prepaid

postpone (pōst′pōn′) *vt.* **-poned′, -pon′-ing** [< L. *post*, after + *ponere*, put] to put off until later; delay —**postpon′able** *adj.* —**postpone′ment** *n.*

postprandial (pōst′pran′dē əl) *adj.* [< POST- + L. *prandium*, noonday meal] after a meal

postscript (pōs′skript) *n.* [< L. *post*, after + *scribere*, write] a note, paragraph, etc. added below the signature of a letter

postulant (pos′choo lənt) *n.* [see ff.] a petitioner, esp. for admission into a religious order

postulate (pos′choo lāt′; *for n.* -lət) *vt.* **-lat′ed, -lat′ing** [< L. *postulare*, to demand] 1. to assume to be true, real, etc., esp. as a basis for argument 2. to take for granted 3. to demand; require —*n.* something postulated —**pos′tula′-tion** *n.*

posture (pos′chər) *n.* [< L. *ponere*, to place] 1. the position or carriage of the body 2. a position assumed as in posing 3. state; condition [the *posture* of foreign affairs] 4. a) frame of mind b) an attitude assumed merely for effect —*vt.* **-tured, -tur-ing** to place in a posture; pose —*vi.* to assume a bodily or mental posture, esp. for effect —**pos′tural** *adj.*

postwar (pōst′wôr′) *adj.* after the (or a) war

posy (pō′zē) *n., pl.* **-sies** [< POESY] a flower or bouquet: an old-fashioned usage

pot (pot) *n.* [OE. *pott*] 1. a round vessel for holding liquids, cooking, etc. 2. a pot with its contents 3. shortened form for FLOWERPOT, etc. 4. [Colloq.] *a)* all the money bet at a single time *b)* a large amount of money 5. [Colloq.] a cup or other prize 6. [Colloq.] a potbelly 7. [Slang] marijuana —*vt.* **pot′ted, pot′ting** 1. to put into a pot 2. to cook or preserve in a pot 3. to shoot 4. to hit or get as by a potshot 5. *Billiards* to pocket a ball —**go to pot** to go to ruin

potable (pōt′ə b'l) *adj.* [Fr. < L. *potare*, to drink] fit to drink; drinkable

‡**potage** (pо täzh′) *n.* [Fr.] soup or broth

potash (pot′ash′) *n.* [< Du. *pot*, pot + *asch*, ash] any substance containing potassium; esp., any potassium compound used in fertilizers

potassium (pə tas′ē əm) *n.* [see prec.] a soft, silver-white, metallic chemical element: symbol, K

potassium nitrate a crystalline

compound used in fertilizers, gunpowder, etc. and as an oxidizing agent

potation (pō tā'shən) *n.* [< L. *potare*, to drink] 1. the act of drinking 2. a drink, esp. of alcohol

potato (pə tāt'ō) *n., pl.* **-toes** [Sp. *patata* < WInd.] 1. the starchy tuber of a widely cultivated plant cooked as a vegetable 2. the plant

potato beetle (or **bug**) *same as* COLORADO BEETLE

potato crisp a very thin slice of potato fried crisp and often salted and flavoured: also, U.S., **potato chip**

potbelly (pot'bel'ē) *n., pl.* **-lies** a protruding belly

potboiler *n.* a piece of writing, etc., usually inferior, done quickly for money

pot-bound *adj.* of a plant whose roots are too great for their container

poteen (po tēn') *n.* [< Ir. *pota*, pot] illicitly distilled Irish whiskey: also **potheen**

potent (pōt'ənt) *adj.* [< L. *posse*, be able] 1. having authority or power 2. convincing; cogent 3. effective, as a drug 4. able to engage in sexual intercourse —**po'tency** *n.*

potentate (pōt''n tāt') *n.* a ruler; monarch

potential (pō ten'shəl) *adj.* [see POTENT] that can come into being; possible; latent —*n.* 1. something potential 2. unrealised ability or capacity 3. *Elec.* the relative voltage at a point in an electric circuit or field with respect to some reference point in the same circuit or field —**poten'tially** *adv.*

potential difference the difference in electrical potential between two points in an electric field; voltage

potentiality (pō ten'shē al'ə tē) *n.* possibility or capability of becoming, developing, etc.; latency

potful (pot'fool') *n.* as much as a pot will hold

pother (poth'ər) *n.* [< ?] a commotion or fuss

potherb (pot'hurb') *n.* any herb whose leaves and stems are boiled for food or used as a flavouring

pothole (pot'hōl') *n.* 1. a deep hole or pit 2. a rough hole in a road, made by wear and weathering

potholing *n.* the exploration of deep holes, esp. those with systems of passages occurring in limestone rocks —**pot'holer** *n.*

pothook (pot'hook') *n.* 1. an S-shaped hook for hanging a pot over a fire 2. a curved mark in writing

pothunter (pot'hun'tər) *n.* 1. a hunter who kills game indiscriminately 2. a person who enters competitions merely to win prizes

potion (pō'shən) *n.* [< L. *potare*, to drink] a drink or liquid dose, as of medicine or poison

potluck (pot'luk') *n.* whatever the family meal happens to be —**to take potluck**

to accept what is available without knowing much about it

pot plant a plant grown in a flowerpot

potpourri (pō poor'ē) *n.* [Fr. < *pot*, a pot + *pourrir*, to rot] 1. a fragrant mixture of dried flower petals 2. a medley, miscellany, or anthology

pot roast meat cooked in one piece by braising

potsherd (pot'shurd') *n.* [see POT & SHARD] a piece of broken pottery

potshot (pot'shot') *n.* 1. an easy shot 2. a random shot 3. a haphazard try

pottage (pot'ij) *n.* [< MFr. *pot*, a pot] a thick soup or stew of vegetables, or meat and vegetables

potted (pot'id) *adj.* 1. put into a pot 2. cooked or preserved in a pot 3. summarized or abridged

potter[1] (pot'ər) *n.* a maker of earthenware pots, dishes, etc.

potter[2] *vi.* [< OE. *potian*, to push] to busy oneself in an aimless way (often with *around*, etc.)

Potteries (pot'ər ēz) an area of W central England where china and earthenware are manufactured

POTTER'S WHEEL

potter's wheel a rotating horizontal disc upon which clay is moulded into bowls, etc.

pottery (pot'ər ē) *n., pl.* **-teries** 1. a potter's workshop or factory 2. the art of a potter 3. pots, bowls, etc. made of baked clay

potting shed a shed in the garden originally used to pot plants, now often used to store gardening equipment

potty[1] (pot'ē) *n., pl.* **-ties** a child's small chamber pot

potty[2] *adj.* **-tier, -tiest** [Colloq.] 1. trivial 2. slightly crazy

pouch (pouch) *n.* [MFr. *poche*, a poke] 1. a small bag or sack 2. any pouchlike cavity, part, etc. 3. a saclike structure, as that on the abdomen of the kangaroo, etc. for carrying young —*vt.* 1. to put into a pouch 2. to make into a pouch

pouf (poof) *n.* [Fr. echoic] a large, solid cushion used as a seat; hassock: also sp. **pouff, pouffe**

poulterer (pōl'tər ər) *n.* a dealer in poultry and game

poultice (pōl'tis) *n.* [ML. *pultes*, pap] a hot, moist mass, as of flour, mustard, etc., applied to a sore part of the body —*vt.* **-ticed, -ticing** to apply a poultice to

poultry (pōl'trē) *n.* [< OFr. *poulet*: see

PULLET] domestic fowls, as chickens, raised for meat or eggs

pounce (pauns) *vi.* **pounced, pounc'ing** [< ?] to swoop down, or leap (*on, upon,* or *at*) as in attacking —*n.* the act of pouncing

pound[1] (pound) *n.* [< L. *pondus,* weight] **1.** a unit of weight, equal to 16oz. avoirdupois (.454 kgm) or 12 oz. troy (.373 kgm): abbrev. **lb. 2.** the monetary unit of the United Kingdom: in full **pound sterling:** symbol £ **3.** the monetary unit of various other countries, as of Ireland, Israel, etc. —**pound of flesh** a literal, legal but unreasonable fulfilment of a bargain

pound[2] *vt.* [OE. *punian*] **1.** to beat to a pulp, powder, etc. **2.** to strike with repeated heavy blows —*vi.* **1.** to deliver repeated, heavy blows (*at* or *on*) **2.** to move with heavy steps **3.** to beat heavily —**pound out** to produce (musical notes, etc.) with a very heavy touch

pound[3] *n.* [< OE. *pund-*] **1.** an enclosure for confining stray animals **2.** an enclosure for keeping officially removed vehicles, etc.

poundage *n.* a tax, etc. per pound (sterling or weight)

pounder *n.* a person or thing that pounds

-pounder *a combining form meaning* something weighing or worth (a specified number of pounds)

pound-foolish *adj.* not handling large sums of money wisely: see PENNY-WISE

pound note a banknote valued at one pound sterling

pour (pôr) *vt.* [< ?] **1.** to make flow in a continuous stream **2.** to emit, utter, etc. profusely or steadily —*vi.* **1.** to flow freely, continuously, etc. **2.** to rain heavily **3.** to swarm **4.** to serve tea, coffee, etc. —**pour cold water on** to discourage; disparage —**pour'er** *n.*

‡**pourboire** (pōōrbwär´) *n.* [Fr.] a tip, or gratuity

pout (pout) *vi.* [ME. *pouten*] **1.** to thrust out the lips, as in sullenness **2.** to protrude: said of the lips —*vt.* to thrust out (the lips) —*n.* a pouting

pouter *n.* **1.** a person who pouts **2.** any of a breed of pigeon that can distend its crop: also **pouter pigeon**

poverty (pov´ər tē) *n.* [< L. *pauper,* poor] **1.** the condition or quality of being poor; need **2.** inferiority; inadequacy **3.** scarcity

poverty-stricken *adj.* very poor

poverty trap the situation of a family on social security where an increase in earned income means a decrease in total income, because of a decrease in State benefits

POW, P.O.W. prisoner of war

powder (pou´dər) *n.* [< L. *pulvis*] **1.** any dry substance in the form of fine, dustlike particles **2.** a specific kind of powder [*face powder*] **3.** *same as* GUNPOWDER —*vt.* **1.** to put powder on **2.** to make into powder —**pow'dery** *adj.*

powder horn a container made of an animal's horn, for carrying gunpowder

powder keg 1. a small barrel used to

hold gunpowder **2.** [Colloq.] an explosive situation

powder puff a soft pad for applying cosmetic powder

powder room [U.S.] a lavatory for women

power (pou´ər) *n.* [ult. < L. *posse,* be able] **1.** ability to do or act **2.** a specific ability or faculty **3.** vigour; force **4.** *a)* influence; authority *b)* legal authority **5.** physical force or energy [*water power*] **6.** a person or thing of great influence, force, or authority **7.** a nation, esp. one dominating others **8.** a spirit or divinity **9.** *Math.* the result of multiplying a quantity by itself [4 is the second *power* of 2 (2^2)] **10.** *Optics* the degree of magnification of a lens, telescope, etc. —*vt.* to supply with power —*adj.* **1.** operated by electricity, etc. [*power tools*] **2.** using an auxiliary, engine-powered system [*power steering*] **3.** carrying electricity —**in power 1.** in authority **2.** in office —**the powers that be** the persons in control

powerful *adj.* having much power; strong; influential —**pow'erfully** *adv.* —**pow'erfulness** *n.*

powerhouse *n.* **1.** *same as* POWER STATION **2.** [Colloq.] a powerful person, team, etc.

powerless *adj.* without power; weak, impotent, etc.

power of attorney a written statement legally authorizing a person to act for one

power point an electrical socket mounted on, or recessed into, a wall

power station a building where electric power is generated

powwow (pou´wou´) *n.* [< AmInd.] **1.** a conference of or with N American Indians **2.** [Colloq.] any conference or gathering —*vi.* [Colloq.] to confer

pox (poks) *n.* [see POCK] **1.** a disease characterized by skin eruptions, as smallpox **2.** [Colloq.] syphilis

pp, pp. 1. [L. *per procurationem*] by delegation to **2.** *Music* pianissimo

pp. 1. pages **2.** past participle

P.P., p.p. 1. past participle **2.** postpaid **3.** prepaid

ppd. 1. postpaid **2.** prepaid

ppr., p.pr. present participle

P.P.S., p.p.s. 1. [L. *post postscriptum*] an additional postscript **2.** Parliamentary Private Secretary

P.Q. 1. Province of Quebec **2.** [Canad.] Parti Québécois

Pr *Chem.* praseodymium

Pr. 1. Prince **2.** Provençal

pr. 1. pair(s) **2.** present **3.** price **4.** pronoun

PR Proportional Representation

P.R., PR 1. public relations **2.** Puerto Rico

P.R.A. President of the Royal Academy

practicable (prak´ti kə b'l) *adj.* [see PRACTICE] **1.** that can be put into practice; feasible **2.** that can be used —**prac'ticabil'ity** *n.* —**prac'ticably** *adv.*

practical (prak´ti k'l) *adj.* [see PRACTICE] **1.** concerned with application to useful

ends, rather than theory [*practical* science]
2. given to actual practice [a *practical*
farmer] **3.** realistic and sensible about
everyday activities, work, etc. **4.** useful
or designed for use **5.** of or from practice
or action **6.** that is so in practice; virtual
—*n.* a practical examination —**prac′tical′-
ity** (-kal′ə tē) *n.*

practical joke a trick played on someone
but meant in fun —**practical joker**

practically *adv.* **1.** in a practical way
2. virtually **3.** [Colloq.] nearly

practice (prak′tis) *n.* [< Gr. *prassein*,
do] **1.** a practising; habit, custom, etc.
2. a) repeated action for gaining skill b)
the resulting condition of being skilled
[out of *practice*] **3.** knowledge put into
action **4.** a) the exercise of a profession
b) a business based on this —*vt., vi.* **-ticed,
-ticing** *U.S. sp.* of PRACTISE

practise (prak′tis) *vt., vi.* **-tised, -tising**
[see PRACTICE] **1.** to do repeatedly so
as to gain skill **2.** to do or engage in
regularly; make a habit of **3.** a) to work
at, esp. as a profession [to *practise* law]
b) to observe (beliefs, ideals, etc.) —*vi.*
1. to do something repeatedly so as to
gain skill **2.** to work at a profession

practitioner (prak tish′ə nər) *n.* a person
who practises a profession, art, etc., esp.
medicine

praetor (prēt′ər) *n.* [L.] a magistrate
of ancient Rome, next below a consul
in rank

Praetorian Guard (prē tôr′ē ən) the
bodyguard of a Roman emperor

pragmatic (prag mat′ik) *adj.* [< Gr.
pragma, deed] **1.** concerned with practice,
not with theory **2.** dealing with historical
facts as causally related **3.** of pragmatism
—**pragmat′ically** *adv.*

pragmatism (prag′mə tiz′m) *n.* **1.** a
philosophy that tests all concepts by
practical results **2.** the quality or condition
of being pragmatic —**prag′matist** *n., adj.*

prairie (prâ ər′ē) *n.* [Fr. < L. *pratum*,
meadow] a large area of level or rolling
grassland, esp. in N America

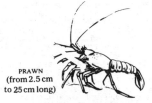

PRAIRIE DOG
(to 38 cm long,
including tail)

prairie dog a small, squirrellike,
burrowing rodent of N America, with a
barking cry

Prairie Provinces the Canadian
provinces of Manitoba, Saskatchewan, and
Alberta

praise (prāz) *vt.* **praised, prais′ing** [<
L. *pretium*, worth] **1.** to commend the
worth of **2.** to glorify (God, etc.), as

in song —*n.* a praising or being praised;
commendation —**sing someone's praise** (or
praises) to praise someone highly
—**prais′er** *n.*

praiseworthy *adj.* worthy of praise
—**praise′wor′thiness** *n.*

praline (prä′lēn) *n.* [Fr., < Marshal
Duplessis-*Praslin*] a crisp sweet made
of nuts browned in boiling sugar

pram (pram) *n.* a light carriage for
wheeling a baby about

prance (präns) *vi.* **pranced, pranc′ing** [<
?] **1.** to caper or strut **2.** to rise up,
or move along on the hind legs: said
of a horse —*n.* a prancing

prang (praŋ) *vt.* [echoic] [Slang] **1.**
to crash or damage (an aircraft, car, etc.)
2. to bomb heavily —*n.* [Slang] **1.** a
collision **2.** a bombing raid

prank (praŋk) *n.* [< ?] a playful trick,
often one causing some mischief —**prank′-
ster** *n.*

praseodymium (prā′zē ō dim′ē əm) *n.*
[< Gr. *prasios*, green + *didymos*, twin]
a metallic chemical element of the rare-
earth group: symbol, Pr

prate (prāt) *vi., vt.* **prat′ed, prat′ing** [<
MDu. *praten*] to talk on and on, foolishly;
chatter —*n.* chatter

prattle (prat′'l) *vi., vt.* **-tled, -tling**
[MLowG. *pratelen*] to speak childishly;
babble —*n.* chatter or babble

PRAWN
(from 2.5 cm
to 25 cm long)

prawn (prôn) *n.* [< ?] an edible,
shrimplike crustacean

praxis (prak′sis) *n.* [< Gr. *prassein*, do]
1. practice **2.** a set of examples or exercises

pray (prā) *vi.* [< L. *prex*, prayer] to
make supplication or offer prayers —*vt.*
1. to implore [(I) *pray* (you) tell me]
2. to ask for by prayer

prayer[1] (prâər) *n.* **1.** the act of praying
2. a) an earnest request to God, etc. b)
an utterance of praise, etc. to God c)
a set of words used in praying **3.** [often
pl.] a religious prayer service **4.** something
prayed for

prayer[2] (prā′ər) *n.* a person who prays

prayer mat the small carpet on which
a Muslim kneels while saying his prayers

prayer wheel a revolving drum with
written prayers, used by Tibetan Buddhists,
in counting prayers

praying mantis same as MANTIS

pre- [< L. *prae*, before] a prefix meaning
before in time, place, or rank [*prewar*]

preach (prēch) *vi.* [< L. *prae-*, before + *dicare*, proclaim] **1.** to give a sermon **2.** to give moral advice, esp. tediously —*vt.* **1.** to advocate or urge, as by preaching **2.** to deliver (a sermon)

preacher *n.* one who preaches; esp., a clergyman

preamble (prē am'b'l) *n.* [< L. *prae-*, before + *ambulare*, go] an introduction, esp. to a constitution, statute, etc., stating its reason and purpose

prearrange (prē'ə ränj') *vt.* **-ranged'**, **-rang'ing** to arrange beforehand —**pre'ar·range'ment** *n.*

prebend (preb'ənd) *n.* [< L. *praebere*, give] the amount paid a clergyman by his cathedral or collegiate church

prebendary *n.*, *pl.* **-ies** a person receiving a prebend

prec. preceding

Precambrian (prē kam'brē ən) *adj.* designating or of the geologic era covering all the time before the Cambrian Period

precarious (pri kāar'ē əs) *adj.* [see PRAYER[1]] dependent upon circumstances or chance; insecure; risky —**precar'iously** *adv.* —**precar'iousness** *n.*

precaution (pri kô'shən) *n.* [< L. *prae-*, before + *cavere*, take care] a measure taken beforehand against possible danger, failure, etc. —**precau'tionary** *adj.*

precede (pri sēd') *vt., vi.* **-ced'ed**, **-ced'-ing** [< L. *prae-*, before + *cedere*, go] to be, come, or go before in time, order, rank, importance, etc.

precedence (pres'i dəns, prē sēd'’ns) *n.* the act, right, or fact of preceding; priority in time, order, rank, etc.: also **prec'edency**

precedent (pres'i dənt; *for adj.* pri sēd''nt) *n.* an act, decision, etc. that may serve as an example or justification for a later one —*adj.* that precedes

precentor (prē sen'tər) *n.* [< L. *prae*, before + *canere*, sing] a person who directs church singing

precept (prē'sept) *n.* [< L. *prae-*, before + *capere*, take] **1.** a direction meant as a rule of conduct **2.** a rule of moral conduct —**precep'tive** *adj.*

preceptor (pri sep'tər) *n.* [see prec.] a teacher —**preceptorial** (prē'sep tôr'ē əl) *adj.*

precession (pri sesh'ən) *n.* **1.** a preceding **2.** *Mech.* a change in direction of the rotational axis of a spinning body, in which the axis describes a cone

precinct (prē'siŋkt) *n.* [< L. *prae-*, before + *cingere*, surround] **1.** a) [*usually pl.*] an enclosure between buildings, walls, etc. b) an area in a town where vehicles are not allowed **2.** [*pl.*] environs

preciosity (presh'ē os'ə tē) *n.*, *pl.* **-ties** [see PRECIOUS] great fastidiousness or affectation, esp. in language

precious (presh'əs) *adj.* [< L. *pretium*, a price] **1.** of great price or value; costly **2.** much loved or cherished **3.** overrefined or affected **4.** [Colloq.] very great [*a precious liar*] —*adv.* [Colloq.] very

precious metals any of gold, silver, or platinum

precious stone a rare and costly gem

precipice (pres'ə pis) *n.* [< L. *prae-*, before + *caput*, a head] a vertical or overhanging rock face

precipitant (pri sip'i tənt) *adj.* [see prec.] *same as* PRECIPITATE —*n.* a substance causing formation of a precipitate —**pre·cip'itancy, precip'itance** *n.*

precipitate (pri sip'i tāt'; *also, for adj. & n.,* -tit) *vt.* **-tat'ed**, **-tat'ing** [see PRECIPICE] **1.** to make happen before expected, needed, etc. **2.** to hurl downwards **3.** *Chem.* to separate (a dissolved substance) out from a solution —*vi.* **1.** *Chem.* to be precipitated **2.** *Meteorol.* to condense and fall as rain, snow, etc. —*adj.* **1.** falling steeply **2.** acting, happening, or done hastily or rashly **3.** very sudden; abrupt —*n.* a substance precipitated out from a solution —**precip'i·tately** *adv.* —**precip'itateness** *n.*

precipitation (pri sip'i tā'shən) *n.* **1.** *Meteorol.* a) rain, snow, etc. b) the amount of this **2.** a precipitating or being precipitated **3.** sudden or rash haste

precipitous (pri sip'i təs) *adj.* **1.** steep like a precipice **2.** rash; impetuous —**precip'itously** *adv.*

précis (prā'sē) *n.*, *pl.* **pré'cis** (-sēz) [Fr.: see ff.] a summary or abstract —*vt.* to make a précis of

precise (pri sīs') *adj.* [< L. *prae-*, before + *caedere*, to cut] **1.** accurately stated; definite **2.** minutely exact **3.** very careful or strict in following a procedure, rules, etc. —**precise'ly** *adv.* —**precise'ness** *n.*

precision (pri sizh'ən) *n.* **1.** the quality of being precise; exactness **2.** the degree of this —*adj.* characterized by precision, as in measurement, operation, etc.

preclude (pri klōōd') *vt.* **-clud'ed**, **-clud'-ing** [< L. *prae-*, before + *claudere*, to shut] to make impossible, esp. in advance; prevent —**preclu'sion** *n.*

precocious (pri kō'shəs) *adj.* [< L. *prae-*, before + *coquere*, to cook] **1.** matured beyond normal for one's age **2.** of or showing premature development —**preco'-ciousness, precoc'ity** (-kos'ə tē) *n.*

precognition (prē'kog nish'ən) *n.* supposed perception, esp. extrasensory, of something before it occurs —**precog'nitive** *adj.*

preconceive (prē'kən sēv') *vt.* **-ceived'**, **-ceiv'ing** to form a conception or opinion of beforehand —**pre'concep'tion** *n.*

precondition (prē'kən dish'ən) *n.* a condition required in advance for something to occur, be done, etc.

precursor (prē kur'sər) *n.* [< L. *praecurrere*, to run ahead] **1.** a forerunner **2.** a predecessor, as in office

precursory *adj.* **1.** serving as a precursor **2.** introductory; preliminary

pred. predicate

predacious (pri dā'shəs) *adj.* [< L. *praeda*, a prey] preying on other animals

predate (prē dāt') *vt.* **-dat'ed**, **-dat'ing** **1.** to date before the actual date **2.** to come before in date

predator (pred′ə tər) *n.* a predatory person or animal

predatory *adj.* [< L. *praeda,* a prey] 1. capturing and feeding upon other animals 2. plundering, robbing, or exploiting —**pred′atorily** *adv.*

predecease (prē′di sēs′) *vt., vi.* -ceased′, -ceas′ing to die before (someone else)

predecessor (prē′di ses′ər) *n.* [< L. *prae-,* before + *decedere,* go away] a person preceding another, as in office

predestinate (prē des′tə nāt′; *for adj.* -nit) *vt.* -nat′ed, -nat′ing *Theol.* to foreordain by divine decree —*adj.* predestined

predestination (prē des′tə nā′shən) *n.* *Theol.* divine foreordaining of everything, specif. of certain souls to salvation

predestine (prē des′tin) *vt.* -tined, -tining to foreordain

predetermine (prē′di tûr′min) *vt.* -mined, -mining 1. to determine or decide beforehand 2. to bias or prejudice

predicable (pred′i kə b'l) *adj.* that can be predicated —**pred′icably** *adv.*

predicament (pri dik′ə mənt) *n.* [see PREACH] a situation, esp. one that is difficult, embarrassing, or comical

predicant (pred′i kənt) *adj.* [< L. *praedicare,* to preach] preaching —*n.* a preacher, esp. a Dominican friar

predicate (pred′i kāt′; *for n.* -kət) *vt.* -cat′-ed, -cat′ing [see PREACH] 1. orig., to affirm 2. to affirm as a quality, attribute, etc. —*n.* 1. *Gram.* the verb or verbal phrase that makes a statement about the subject of a sentence or clause 2. *Logic* something that is affirmed or denied about the subject of a proposition (Ex.: *green* in "grass is green") —**pred′ica′tion** *n.* —**pred′icative** *adj.*

predict (pri dikt′) *vt., vi.* [< L. *prae-,* before + *dicere,* tell] to state (what one believes will happen) —**predict′able** *adj.* —**predict′ably** *adv.* —**predic′tor** *n.*

prediction (pri dik′shən) *n.* 1. a predicting or being predicted 2. something predicted

predikant (prēə′də kant′) *n.* [< L. *praedicare,* preach] in S Africa, a minister in the Dutch Reformed Church

predilection (prē′di lek′shən) *n.* [< L. *prae-,* before + *diligere,* prefer] a preconceived liking; partiality (*for*)

predispose (prē′dis pōz′) *vt.* -posed′, -pos′ing to make receptive beforehand —**pre′disposi′tion** (-pə zish′ən) *n.*

predominant (pri dom′i nənt) *adj.* 1. having authority over others 2. most frequent; prevailing —**predom′inance** *n.* —**predom′inantly** *adv.*

predominate (pri dom′i nāt′) *vi.* -nat′ed, -nat′ing 1. to have influence or authority (*over* others) 2. to prevail; preponderate —**predom′inately** *adv.*

preeminent, pre-eminent (prē em′-i nənt) *adj.* eminent above others; surpassing —**preem′inence, pre-em′i-nence** *n.* —**preem′inently, pre-em′inently** *adv.*

preempt, pre-empt (prē empt′) *vt.* [< ff.] 1. to seize before anyone else can 2. to acquire (public land) by preemption

—**preemp′tive, pre-emp′tive** *adj.* —**pre-emp′tor, pre-emp′tor** *n.*

preemption, pre-emption *n.* [< L. *prae-,* before + *emere,* buy] the act or right of buying land, etc. before, or in preference to, others

preen (prēn) *vt.* [< ME. *proinen,* to prune (a tree, etc.)] 1. to clean and trim (the feathers) with the beak: said of birds 2. to dress up or adorn (oneself) 3. to be proud of (oneself) —**preen′er** *n.*

preexist, pre-exist (prē′ig zist′) *vt., vi.* to exist previously or before (another person or thing) —**pre′exist′ence, pre′-exist′ence** *n.*

pref. 1. preface 2. preference 3. prefix

prefab (prē′fab) *n.* [Colloq.] a prefabricated building

prefabricate (prē fab′rə kāt′) *vt.* -cat′ed, -cat′ing to make (houses, etc.) in standardized sections for quick assembly —**pre′fabrica′tion** *n.*

preface (pref′is) *n.* [< L. *prae-,* before + *fari,* speak] an introductory statement to an article, book, etc. —*vt.* -aced, -acing 1. to introduce with a preface 2. to be as a preface to

prefatory (pref′ə tôr ē) *adj.* of, like, or serving as a preface —**pref′atorily** *adv.*

prefect (prē′fekt) *n.* [< L. *praeficere,* to set over] 1. any of various administrators; specif., the head of a department of France 2. in some schools, a pupil given certain powers in order to help maintain discipline

prefecture (prē′fek tyoor′) *n.* the office, authority, territory, or residence of a prefect —**prefec′tural** *adj.*

prefer (pri fur′) *vt.* -ferred′, -fer′ring [< L. *prae-,* before + *ferre,* bear] 1. to like better or value more highly 2. to put before a magistrate, court, etc. to be considered 3. to promote

preferable (pref′ər ə b'l) *adj.* to be preferred; more desirable —**pref′erably** *adv.*

preference (pref′ər əns) *n.* 1. a preferring or being preferred 2. something preferred 3. the right, power, etc. of prior choice or claim 4. a giving of advantage to one person, country, etc. over others

preference shares shares on which dividends are paid before dividends on ordinary shares

preferential (pref′ə ren′shəl) *adj.* of, giving, or receiving preference —**pref′eren′tially** *adv.*

preferment (pri fur′mənt) *n.* an advancement in rank or office; promotion

prefigure (prē fig′ər) *vt.* -ured, -uring [< L. *prae-,* before + *figurare,* to fashion] 1. to foreshadow (something that will appear later) 2. to imagine beforehand —**pre′figura′tion** *n.* —**prefig′urative** *adj.*

prefix (prē′fiks; *also, for v.,* prē fiks′) *n.* [< L. *prae-,* before + *figere,* to fix] a syllable or group of syllables joined to the beginning of a word to alter its meaning —*vt.* to fix to the beginning of a word, speech, book, etc.

preggers (preg'ərz) *adj.* [Colloq.] *same as* PREGNANT

pregnant (preg'nənt) *adj.* [< L. *pregnans*] 1. having (an) offspring developing in the uterus 2. full of meaning, significance, etc. 3. mentally fertile; inventive 4. fruitful —**preg'nancy** *n.* —**preg'nantly** *adv.*

prehensile (pri hen'sil) *adj.* [< Fr. < L. *prehendere*, take] adapted for grasping, esp. by wrapping itself around something, as a monkey's tail

prehistoric (prē'his tor'ik) *adj.* of the period before recorded history: also **pre'historical**

prejudge (prē juj') *vt.* -**judged'**, -**judg'ing** [see PRE- & JUDGE] to judge beforehand, or without all the evidence

prejudice (prej'oo dis) *n.* [< L. *prae-*, before + *judicium*, judgment] 1. a preconceived idea, usually one that is unfavourable 2. an opinion held in disregard of facts that contradict it 3. intolerance of other races, etc. 4. harm resulting as from some action of another —*vt.* -**diced**, -**dicing** 1. to harm, as by some judgment or action 2. to bias

prejudicial (prej'oo dish'əl) *adj.* causing prejudice, or harm; injurious

prelacy (prel'ə sē) *n.*, *pl.* -**cies** 1. a) the office or rank of a prelate b) prelates collectively 2. church government by prelates

prelate (prel'it) *n.* [< L. *praeferre*, to PREFER] a high-ranking ecclesiastic, as a bishop —**prel'ateship'** *n.* —**prelatic** (pri lat'ik) *adj.*

prelim (prē'lim) *n.* [Colloq.] *short for* PRELIMINARY

prelim. preliminary

preliminary (pri lim'ə nər ē) *adj.* [< L. *prae-*, before + *limen*, threshold] leading up to the main action, etc.; preparatory —*n.*, *pl.* -**naries** [often *pl.*] a preliminary step, examination, contest, etc. —**prelim'inarily** *adv.*

prelude (prel'yōōd) *n.* [< L. *prae-*, before + *ludere*, play] 1. something serving as an introduction; opening 2. *Music* a) an introductory section of a suite, fugue, etc. b) any short, romantic composition —*vt.*, *vi.* -**uded**, -**uding** to serve as or be a prelude (to)

premarital (prē mar'ət'l) *adj.* before marriage

premature (prem'ə tyōoər') *adj.* [< L.: see PRE- & MATURE] 1. happening or existing before the usual time; specif., born before the full period of gestation 2. impulsive or hasty —**pre'mature'ly** *adv.* —**pre'matu'rity** *n.*

premeditate (prē med'i tāt') *vt.* -**tat'ed**, -**tat'ing** to think out or plan beforehand —**premed'itat'ed** *adj.* —**premed'ita'tion** *n.*

premenstrual (prē men'strōo wəl) *adj.* of the period in the menstrual cycle just before menstruation

premier (prem'yər) *n.* [< L. *primus*, first] a chief official; specif., the prime minister in Britain and certain other countries —*adj.*

1. first in importance; chief 2. first in time —**premier'ship** *n.*

première (prem'ē âär') *n.* [Fr., fem. of *premier*] a first performance of a play, film, etc. —*vt.*, *vi.* -**mièred'**, -**mièr'ing** to exhibit (a play, film, etc.) for the first time

premise (prem'is) *n.* [< L. *prae-*, before + *mittere*, send] 1. a previous statement serving as a basis for an argument: also sp. **prem'iss** 2. [*pl.*] a piece of real estate [keep off the *premises*] 3. [*pl.*] the part of a deed or lease that states the parties and property involved, etc. —**on the premises** in the shop, business, etc., rather than elsewhere

premium (prē'mē əm) *n.*, *pl.* -**ums** [< L. *prae-*, before + *emere*, take] 1. a reward or prize, esp. as an inducement to buy or do something 2. a payment, as for an insurance policy 3. very high value [a *premium* on honesty] —**at a premium** 1. at a value or price higher than normal 2. very valuable, as because of scarcity

Premium Savings Bonds bonds issued by the Treasury that yield no interest but give one the opportunity of winning cash prizes: also **premium bonds**

premonition (prē'mə nish'ən) *n.* [< L. *prae-*, before + *monere*, warn] 1. a foreboding 2. a forewarning —**premonitory** (pri mon'ə tər ē) *adj.*

preoccupy (prē ok'yə pī') *vt.* -**pied'**, -**py'ing** [see PRE- & OCCUPY] to occupy completely the thoughts of; engross —**preoc'cupa'tion** *n.*

preordain (prē'ôr dān') *vt.* to ordain or decree beforehand —**pre'ordina'tion** (-dən ā'shən) *n.*

prep (prep) *n.* [Colloq.] *short for a)* PREPARATION b) PREPARATORY SCHOOL

prep. 1. preparation 2. preparatory 3. preposition

prepaid (prē'pād') *pt.* & *pp.* of PREPAY

preparation (prep'ə rā'shən) *n.* 1. a preparing or being prepared 2. something prepared for a special purpose 3. school homework

preparatory (pri par'ə tər ē) *adj.* that prepares or serves to prepare; introductory —**prepar'atorily** *adv.*

preparatory school a private school for children between the ages of 6 and 13, generally preparing them for public school

prepare (pri pâär') *vt.* -**pared'**, -**par'ing** [< L. *prae-*, before + *parare*, get ready] 1. to make ready or suitable 2. to equip or furnish 3. to put together; construct [to *prepare* a dinner] —*vi.* 1. to make things ready 2. to make oneself ready —**be prepared** to to be ready to

prepay (prē'pā') *vt.* -**paid'**, -**pay'ing** to pay or pay for in advance —**pre'pay'ment** *n.*

prepense (pri pens') *adj.* [< OFr. *pur-*, *pro-* + *penser*, think] planned beforehand

preponderate (pri pon'də rāt') *vi.* -**at'ed**, -**at'ing** [< L. *prae-*, before + *ponderare*, weigh] to be greater in amount, power, influence, etc. —**prepon′derance** *n.* —**prepon′derant** *adj.*

preposition (prep′ə zish′ən) *n.* [< L. *prae*-, before + *ponere*, to place] a word, as *in*, *by*, *for*, *with*, *to*, etc., that connects a noun or pronoun, or a noun phrase, to another element, as to another noun (Ex.: the sound *of* rain, he went *to* the shop) —**prep′osi′tional** *adj.*

prepossess (prē′pə zes′) *vt.* 1. to prejudice or bias 2. to impress favourably at once —**pre′posses′sion** *n.*

prepossessing *adj.* that impresses favourably; pleasing —**pre′possess′ingly** *adv.*

preposterous (pri pos′tər əs) *adj.* [< L. *prae*-, before + *posterus*, coming after] so contrary to nature, common sense, etc. as to be laughable; absurd

prep school *Colloq.* form of PREPARATORY SCHOOL

prepuce (prē′pyo͞os) *n.* [< L. *praeputium*] the fold of skin covering the end of the penis

Pre-Raphaelite (prē′raf′ē ə lit′) *n.* a member of a society of artists (**Pre-Raphaelite Brotherhood**) formed in Britain in 1848 to revive the qualities of Italian art before Raphael

prerequisite (prē rek′wə zit) *adj.* required beforehand as a necessary condition for something following —*n.* something prerequisite

prerogative (pri rog′ə tiv) *n.* [ult. < L. *prae*-, before + *rogare*, ask] a prior or exclusive privilege, esp. one peculiar to a rank, class, etc.

Pres. 1. Presbyterian: also **Presb.** 2. President

pres. 1. present 2. presidency

presage (pres′ij) *n.* [< L. *prae*-, before + *sagire*, perceive] 1. a sign or warning; portent 2. a foreboding —*vt.* -**aged**, -**aging** 1. to give a warning of; portend 2. to have a foreboding of 3. to predict

presbyter (prez′bi tər) *n.* [LL.: see PRIEST] 1. in the Presbyterian Church, an elder 2. in the Episcopal Church, a priest or minister

presbyterian (prez′bi tēər′ē ən) *adj.* 1. having to do with church government by presbyters 2. [P-] designating a church of a Calvinistic Protestant denomination governed by elders —*n.* [P-] a member of a Presbyterian church —**pres′byter′ianism** *n.*

presbytery (prez′bi tar ē) *n. pl.* -**teries** 1. in Presbyterian churches, a governing body made up of all the ministers and an equal number of elders in a district

preschool (prē′sko͞ol′) *adj.* of, or for a child between infancy and school age

prescience (pre′sē əns) *n.* [< L. *prae*-, before + *scire*, know] apparent knowledge of things before they happen —**pre′scient** *adj.*

prescribe (pri skrīb′) *vt.* -**scribed′**, -**scrib′ing** [< L. *prae*-, before + *scribere*, write] 1. to order or direct 2. to order or advise as a medicine or treatment: said of doctors, etc. —*vi.* 1. to set down

rules 2. to give medical advice or prescriptions

prescription (pri skrip′shən) *n.* 1. a prescribing 2. *a)* a doctor's direction for the preparation and use of a medicine *b)* a medicine so prescribed —*adj.* purchasable only with a doctor's prescription —**prescrip′tive** *adj.*

presence (prez′əns) *n.* 1. a being present 2. immediate surroundings [admitted to his *presence*] 3. one that is present, esp. a person of imposing appearance 4. *a)* a person's bearing, appearance, etc. *b)* poised and confident bearing

presence of mind the ability to think clearly and act quickly and intelligently in an emergency

present (prez′ənt; *for v.* pri zent′) *adj.* [< L. *prae*-, before + *esse*, be] 1. existing or happening now 2. being at the specified place 3. now being discussed, considered, etc. [the *present* writer] 4. *Gram.* indicating action as now taking place (Ex.: he *goes*), or state as now existing (Ex.: the plums *are* ripe), or action that is habitual (Ex.: he *speaks* softly) —*n.* 1. the present time 2. the present occasion 3. *Gram.* the present tense or a verb in it 4. [*pl.*] *Law* this very document [know by these *presents*] 5. something presented, or given; gift —*vt.* 1. to introduce (a person *to* someone) 2. to offer for viewing or notice 3. to offer for consideration 4. to give (a gift, etc.) to (someone) 5. to hand over, send, etc. (a bill, etc.) to 6. to point or aim (a weapon, etc.) —**present arms** *Mil.* to hold a rifle vertically in front of the body: a position of salute —**present′er** *n.*

presentable (pri zen′tə b'l) *adj.* 1. properly dressed for meeting people 2. fit to be shown, given, etc. to others —**present′abil′ity** *n.* —**present′ably** *adv.*

presentation (prez′ən tā′shən) *n.* 1. a presenting or being presented 2. something presented, as a theatrical performance, a gift, etc. —**pre′senta′tional** *adj.*

present-day (prez′ənt dā′) *adj.* of the present time

presentiment (pri zen′ti mənt) *n.* [see PRE- & SENTIMENT] a foreboding, esp. of approaching evil

presently (prez′ənt lē) *adv.* 1. soon 2. [Chiefly U.S. & Scot.] at present; now

present participle a participle used to express present or continuing action

present perfect a tense indicating an action or state as completed but not at any definite time in the past

preservative (pri zur′və tiv) *n.* anything that preserves; esp., a substance added to food to keep it from spoiling —*adj.* preserving

preserve (pri zurv′) *vt.* -**served′**, -**serv′ing** [< L. *prae*-, before + *servare*, keep] 1. to keep from harm, damage, etc. 2. to keep from spoiling or rotting 3. to prepare (food), as by bottling, for future use 4. to keep up; maintain —*n.* 1. [usually *pl.*] fruit preserved whole 2.

a place where game is reared for hunting, fishing, etc. **3.** the special domain of some person —**preservation** (prez′ər-vā′shən) **n.**

preside (pri zīd′) **vi.** **-sid′ed, -sid′ing** [< L. *prae-*, before + *sedere*, sit] **1.** to act as chairman **2.** to have authority, control, etc. (usually with *over*)

presidency (prez′i dən sē) **n.,** *pl.* **-cies** the office, function, or term of president

president (prez′i dənt) **n.** [see PRESIDE] **1.** [Chiefly U.S.] the highest executive officer of a company, university, etc. **2.** [*often* P-] the chief executive, or sometimes the formal head, of a republic **3.** a person who presides over a council, society, etc. —**pres′iden′tial** (-den′shəl) **adj.**

presidium (pri sid′ē əm) **n.,** *pl.* **-ia, -iums** [< L. *praesidium*, a presiding over] in the Soviet Union, **1.** any of a number of permanent administrative committees **2.** [P-] the permanent administrative committee of the Supreme Soviet

press[1] (pres) **vt.** [< L. *premere*] **1.** to act on with steady force or weight; push against **2.** to squeeze (juice, etc.) from **3.** *a*) to compress *b*) to iron (clothes, etc.) **4.** to mould or form using pressure **5.** to embrace closely **6.** to force; compel **7.** to urge persistently; entreat **8.** to try to force acceptance of **9.** to be troubled, inconvenienced by shortage of **10.** to urge on —**vi.** **1.** to weigh down **2.** to go forwards with determined effort **3.** to crowd; throng **4.** to be urgent or insistent **5.** to iron clothes, etc. —**n.** **1.** an instrument or machine by which something is crushed, stamped, smoothed, etc. **2.** *a*) *short for* PRINTING PRESS *b*) the art or business of printing *c*) newspapers, magazines, etc. or the persons who write for them *d*) publicity, criticism, etc., as in newspapers **3.** a crowd; throng **4.** pressure, urgency, etc. **5.** an upright cupboard for clothes, etc. —**go to press** to start to be printed

press[2] **vt.** [< L. *praes*, surety + *stare*, to stand] **1.** to force into service, esp. military or naval service **2.** to use in a different way, esp. in an emergency

press agent a person whose work is to get publicity for an individual, organization, etc. —**press′-a′gentry n.**

press conference a collective interview granted to journalists as by a celebrity or personage

press gallery a section set apart for journalists in a legislative chamber

press gang [see PRESS[2]] formerly, a group who rounded up and forced others into military or naval service

pressgang vt. **1.** formerly, to force (someone) to enlist for military service **2.** to induce (someone) to perform a duty, etc., by forceful persuasion

pressing adj. calling for immediate attention —**n.** something stamped, squeezed, etc. with a press, as gramophone records

press stud a fastening device, one part with a projecting knob that snaps into a hole on another part

press-up n. an exercise in which a person lying face down pushes the body up by straightening the arms

pressure (presh′ər) **n.** [< L. *premere*, to press] **1.** compression; squeezing **2.** a state of distress or strain **3.** a compelling influence *[social pressure]* **4.** pressing demands; urgency **5.** *Physics* the force pressing against a surface, expressed in units of force per unit of area —**vt.** **-sured, -suring** to exert pressure on

pressure cooker an airtight container for quick cooking by steam under pressure —**pres′sure-cook′ vt.**

pressure group any group exerting pressure on legislators and the public through lobbying, etc.

pressurize vt. **-ized′, -iz′ing** to keep nearly normal air pressure inside (an aircraft, etc.), as at high altitudes —**pres′-suriza′tion n.**

Prestel (pres′tel) *Trademark* the Post Office teletext service

prestidigitation (pres′tə dij′i tā′shən) **n.** [< It. *presto*, quick + L. *digitus*, a finger] sleight of hand; conjuring —**pres′tidig′ita′-tor n.**

prestige (pres tēzh′) **n.** [L. *praestigium*, illusion] **1.** reputation based on high achievement, character, etc. **2.** the power to impress or influence —**presti′gious** (-tij′əs) **adj.**

presto (pres′tō) **adv., adj.** [It.] *Music* in fast tempo

prestressed (prē strest′) **adj.** designating concrete that is strengthened by steel wires

presume (pri zyōōm′) **vt.** **-sumed′, -sum′-ing** [< L. *prae-*, before + *sumere*, take] **1.** to take for granted, lacking proof; suppose **2.** to dare (to say or do something) **3.** to constitute reasonable evidence for supposing —**vi.** **1.** to act presumptuously **2.** to rely too much (*on* or *upon*) —**presum′a-ble adj.** —**presum′ably adv.**

presumption (pri zump′shən) **n.** **1.** a presuming; specif., *a*) effrontery *b*) a taking of something for granted **2.** the thing presumed **3.** a reason for presuming —**pre-sump′tive adj.**

presumptuous (pri zump′tyōō wəs) **adj.** too bold or forward; showing presumption

presuppose (prē′sə pōz′) **vt.** **-posed′, -pos′ing** **1.** to suppose or assume beforehand **2.** to require or imply as a preceding condition

pretence (pri tens′) **n.** [see PRETEND] **1.** a false show of something **2.** a false claim or profession **3.** a pretending, as at play; make-believe **4.** a pretext **5.** a claim; pretension Also, U.S. sp., **pretense**

pretend (pri tend′) **vt.** [< L. *prae-*, before + *tendere*, to stretch] **1.** to claim; profess **2.** to claim or profess falsely **3.** to make believe, as in play —**vi.** **1.** to make believe **2.** to lay claim (with *to*) —**pretend′ed adj.**

pretender n. a claimant to a throne; specif., [P-] in British history, the son or grandson of James II

pretension (pri ten′shən) **n.** [see PRETEND] **1.** a claim, as to a title **2.**

the assertion of a claim **3.** a pretext **4.** pretentiousness

pretentious *adj.* [< Fr.] claiming or pretending to be more important, elegant, etc. than is really so

preterite (pret′ər it) *adj.* [< L. *praeter-*, beyond + *ire*, go] *Gram.* expressing past action or state —*n.* **1.** the past tense **2.** a verb in this

preternatural (prē′tər nach′ər əl) *adj.* [< L. *praeter-*, beyond + *naturalis*, natural] **1.** differing from or beyond what is natural; abnormal **2.** *same as* SUPERNATURAL

pretext (prē′tekst) *n.* [see PRE- & TEXT] a false reason or motive put forth to hide the real one

prettify ◂prit′ə fī′) *vt.* -fied′, -fy′ing to make pretty

pretty (prit′ē) *adj.* -tier, -tiest [< OE. *prættig*, crafty] **1.** pleasing or attractive, esp. in a dainty or graceful way **2.** fine; nice : often used ironically **3.** [Colloq.] considerable *[a pretty price]* —*adv.* fairly; somewhat *[pretty sure]* —**pretty much** very nearly —**sitting pretty** [Slang] in a favourable position —**pret′tily** *adv.* —**pret′tiness** *n.*

pretty-pretty *adj.* insipid; characterless; over pretty

pretzel (pret′s′l) *n.* [G. *Brezel*] a hard, brittle biscuit usually in the form of a knot

prev. previous

prevail (pri vāl′) *vi.* [< L. *prae-*, before + *valere*, be strong] **1.** to be victorious (*over* or *against*) **2.** to succeed **3.** to be or become stronger or more widespread; predominate —**prevail** (**up**)**on** to persuade; induce

prevailing *adj.* **1.** widely existing **2.** most frequent; predominant **3.** superior in strength, influence, etc.

prevalent (prev′ə lənt) *adj.* [see PREVAIL] widely existing, practised, or accepted; common —**prev′alence** *n.* —**prev′alently** *adv.*

prevaricate (pri var′ə kāt′) *vi.* -cat′ed, -cat′ing [< L. *prae-*, before + *varicare*, straddle] to speak or act falsely with intent to deceive; equivocate —**prevar′ica′- tion** *n.*

prevent (pri vent′) *vt.* [< L. *prae-*, before + *venire*, come] **1.** to stop or keep (*from* doing something) **2.** to keep from happening; hinder —**prevent′able, prevent′ible** *adj.* —**preven′tion** *n.*

preventive *adj.* preventing or serving to prevent; esp., preventing disease —*n.* anything that prevents Also **prevent′ative** —**preven′tively** *adv.*

preventive detention formerly, prolonged imprisonment for habitual offenders, with corrective training, etc.

Preventive Service the Customs department concerned with preventing smuggling

preview (prē′vyōō) *vt.* to view or show beforehand —*n.* a restricted showing, as of a film, before exhibition to the public generally

previous (prē′vē əs) *adj.* [< L. *prae-*, before + *via*, a way] **1.** occurring before;

prior **2.** [Colloq.] premature —**previous to** before —**pre′viously** *adv.*

prewar (prē′wôr′) *adj.* before a (or the) war

prey (prā) *n.* [< L. *praeda*] **1.** an animal hunted for food by another animal **2.** a victim of someone or something **3.** the mode of living by preying on other animals *[a bird of prey]* —*vi.* **1.** to hunt other animals for food **2.** to profit by swindling **3.** to have a wearing or destructive influence : generally used with *on* or *upon*

price (prīs) *n.* [< L. *pretium*] **1.** the amount of money, etc. asked or paid for something; cost **2.** the cost, as in life, labour, etc., of obtaining some benefit **3.** a reward for the capture or death of a person **4.** in gambling, odds —*vt.* **priced, pric′ing 1.** to fix the price of **2.** [Colloq.] to find out the price of —**at any price** no matter what the cost —**beyond** (or **without**) **price** invaluable —**what price...? 1.** what is the possibility of...? **2.** what do you think of...now?

price control the setting of price ceilings on basic commodities by a government, as to fight inflation

price fixing setting prices at a certain level, esp. by mutual agreement of competitors

priceless *adj.* **1.** too valuable to be measured by price **2.** [Colloq.] very amusing or absurd

price tag 1. a label on an item showing the cost **2.** the cost of an enterprise, etc.

pricey *adj.* [Colloq.] expensive; dear

prick (prik) *n.* [< OE. *prica*, a dot] **1.** a very small puncture made by a sharp point **2.** a sharp pain caused as by being pricked **3.** [Vulg. Slang] the penis **4.** [Derog. Slang] a man —*vt.* **1.** to make (a hole) in (something) with a sharp point **2.** to pain sharply **3.** to mark by dots, points, etc. **4.** to cause to stick up (with *up*) **5.** [Archaic] to goad —*vi.* **1.** to cause or feel a slight, sharp pain **2.** to point or stick up : said esp. of ears —**prick up one's ears** to listen closely —**prick′- er** *n.*

prickle (prik′′l) *n.* [< OE. *prica*, prick] a thornlike growth on a plant —*vt.,vi.* -led, -ling to tingle

prickly *adj.* -lier, -liest **1.** full of prickles **2.** stinging; tingling —**prick′liness** *n.*

prickly heat an itching skin disease with small eruptions caused by inflammation of the sweat glands

prickly pear 1. any of various cactus plants **2.** its pear-shaped, edible fruit

pride (prīd) *n.* [< OE. *prut*, proud] **1.** dignity; self-respect **2.** *a)* a high opinion of oneself *b)* arrogance **3.** satisfaction in one's achievements, etc. **4.** a person or thing that one is proud of **5.** the best part; prime *[the pride of manhood]* **6.** a group or family (of lions) —**pride oneself** on to be proud of —**pride′ful** *adj.*

prie-dieu (prē′dyur) *n.* [Fr. < *prier*, pray + *dieu*, God] an upright frame with a ledge for kneeling on at prayer

priest (prēst) *n.* [< Gr. *presbys,* old]
1. a person whose function is to perform
religious rites 2. in some Christian
churches, a clergyman authorized to
administer the sacraments 3. any
clergyman —**priest'hood'** *n.* —**priest'li-**
ness *n.* —**priest'ly** *adj.*

priestess *n.* a woman priest, esp. of
a pagan religion

prig (prig) *n.* [< ?] a person who is
excessively proper and smug —**prig'gery**
n. —**prig'gish** *adj.* —**prig'gishness** *n.*

prim (prim) *adj.* **prim'mer, prim'mest** [<
?] stiffly formal, precise, moral, etc.;
proper; demure —**prim'ly** *adv.* —**prim'-**
ness *n.*

prim. 1. primary 2. primitive

prima ballerina (prē'mə) [It.] the
principal woman dancer in a ballet company

primacy (prī'mə sē) *n., pl.* **-cies** [see
PRIMATE] 1. the state of being first in
time, order, rank, etc. 2. the rank or
authority of a primate

prima donna (prē'mə don'ə) *pl.* **pri'ma**
don'nas [It.] 1. the principal woman
singer, as in an opera 2. [Colloq.] a
temperamental person

prima facie (prī'mə fā'shē) [L.] at first
sight : used to designate legal evidence
that is enough to establish a fact unless
refuted

primal (prī'm'l) *adj.* [< L. *primus,* first]
1. first in time; original 2. first in
importance; chief

primarily (prī'mə rə lē) *adv.* 1. mainly;
principally 2. at first; originally

primary (prī'mer ē) *adj.* [< L. *primus,*
first] 1. first in importance; chief 2.
first in time or order; original 3. *a)* from
which others are derived; fundamental *b)*
designating colours regarded as basic, from
which all others may be derived 4. *Elec.*
designating an inducing current, input
circuit, or input coil in a transformer,
etc. 5. *Zool.* of the large feathers on
the end joint of a bird's wing —*n., pl.*
-ries 1. something first in order, quality,
etc. 2. in the U.S., a local meeting of
voters of a given political party to nominate
candidates for public office, etc. 3. *Zool.*
a primary feather

primary accent (or **stress**) the heavier
stress given to one syllable in a spoken word

primary education the education
obtained in an elementary school,
emphasizing reading, writing, etc.

primary school a school for children
below the age of 11, or 9 if there is
a middle school

primate (prī'māt; *also, for 1,* -mət) *n.*
[< L. *primus,* first] 1. an archbishop
2. any of an order of mammals, including
man, the apes, monkeys, etc.

prime (prīm) *adj.* [< L. *primus,* first]
1. first in quality 2. fundamental 3. first
in time; original 4. first in rank or
importance; chief; principal 5. *Math.* of
or being a prime number —*n.* 1. the
best part 2. the best or most vigorous
period 3. the first or earliest part 4.
Math. same as PRIME NUMBER 5. [often

P-] the first daylight canonical hour —*vt.*
primed, prim'ing 1. to make ready;
prepare 2. to prepare (a gun) for firing
or (a charge) for exploding by providing
with priming or a primer 3. to get (a
pump) into operation by pouring in water
or petrol 4. to undercoat, size, etc. (a
surface) for painting, etc. 5. to provide
(a person) beforehand with information,
answers, etc. 6. to ply (someone) with
spirits or other liquor

prime meridian the meridian from which
longitude is measured east and west; 0°
longitude : see GREENWICH TIME

prime minister [also P- M-] in
parliamentary governments, the chief
executive

prime number an integer that can be
evenly divided by no other whole number
than itself and 1, as 2, 3, 5, or 7

primer¹ (prī'mər) *n.* [< L. *primus,* first]
1. a simple book for first teaching children
to read 2. a textbook giving the first
principles of any subject

primer² *n.* 1. a small cap, tube, etc.
containing an explosive, used to set off
the main charge 2. a preliminary coat
of paint, etc.

primeval (prī mē'v'l) *adj.* [< L. *primus,*
first + *aevum,* age] of the earliest times
or ages; primordial

priming (prī'miŋ) *n.* 1. the explosive
used to set off the charge in a gun, etc.
2. paint, sizing, etc. used as a primer

primitive (prim'ə tiv) *adj.* [< L. *primus,*
first] 1. of the earliest times; original
2. crude, simple, etc. 3. primary; basic
—*n.* 1. a primitive person or thing · 2.
an artist or a work of art characterized
by lack of formal training

primogenitor (prī'mō jen'i tər) *n.* [< L.
primus, first + *genitor,* a father] 1. a
forefather 2. the earliest ancestor

primogeniture (prī'mō jen'i chər) *n.* [<
L. *primus,* first + *genitura,* a begetting]
1. being the firstborn of the same parents
2. *Law* the right of the eldest son to inherit

primordial (prī môr'dē əl) *adj.* [< L.
primus, first + *ordiri,* begin] existing
at or from the beginning; primitive

primp (primp) *vt., vi.* [prob. < PRIM]
to groom or dress up in a fussy way

primrose (prim'rōz') *n.* [< MFr. altered
(after *rose*) < ML. *primula*] 1. a spring-
blooming plant with light yellow flowers
2. the flower of this plant —*adj.* 1. of
the primrose 2. light yellow

primrose path [cf. *Hamlet* I, iii] the
path of pleasure, self-indulgence, etc.

primula (prim'yoo lə) *n.* [ML.] any of
a genus of plants including the primrose,
oxlip, etc. having variously coloured,
tubelike flowers with five petals

Primus (prī'məs) *Trademark* a small,
portable stove (**Primus stove**) fuelled with
propane or butane

prin. 1. principal 2. principle

prince (prins) *n.* [< L. *princeps,* chief]
1. in Great Britain, a son of the sovereign
2. a nonreigning male member of a royal
family 3. a ruler whose rank is below

that of a king 4. orig., any male monarch 5. a preeminent person in any class or group

princeling *n.* a young, small, or subordinate prince

princely *adj.* **-lier, -liest** 1. of a prince 2. characteristic or worthy of a prince

Prince of Wales *title conferred on* the oldest son and heir apparent of a British king or queen

princess (prin′ses) *n.* 1. in Great Britain, a daughter of the sovereign 2. a nonreigning female member of a royal family 3. the wife of a prince 4. orig., any female monarch

princess royal the eldest daughter of a king or queen

principal (prin′sə pəl) *adj.* [see PRINCE] first in rank, authority, importance, etc. —*n.* 1. a principal person or thing 2. the head of some educational institutions 3. a main actor or performer 4. *Finance* the amount of a debt, investment, etc. minus the interest 5. *Law a)* one who employs another to act as his agent *b)* the one primarily responsible for an obligation *c)* one who commits a crime —**prin′cipally** *adv.* —**prin′cipalship′** *n.*

principal boy the actress who plays the principal male part in a pantomime

principality (prin′si pal′ə tē) *n., pl.* **-ties** 1. the territory ruled by a prince 2. [P-] Wales

principal parts the principal inflected forms of a verb, from which the other forms may be derived : in English, they are the present infinitive, the past tense, and the past participle (Ex.: *drink, drank, drunk*)

principle (prin′sə pəl) *n.* [see PRINCE] 1. *a)* a rule of conduct *b)* adherence to such rules; integrity 2. a fundamental truth, law, etc., upon which others are based 3. an essential element or quality *[the* active *principle* of a medicine *]* 4. the ultimate source 5. the scientific law that explains a natural action —**in principle** theoretically or in essence

prink (priŋk) *vt., vi.* [prob. < LowG.] *same as* PRIMP

print (print) *n.* [< L. *premere*, to PRESS[1]] 1. printed material *[newsprint]* 2. a picture or design printed from a plate, block, etc. 3. printed lettering 4. a photograph, esp. one made from a negative 5. a cloth printed with a design 6. a mark made on a surface by pressing or stamping 7. the impression made by inked type —*vt.* 1. to produce (a book, etc.) by typesetting, etc. 2. to produce on (paper, etc.) the impression of inked type, plates, etc. by means of a printing press 3. to publish in print 4. to write in letters resembling printed ones 5. to stamp or draw, trace, etc. (a mark, letter, etc.) on or in a surface 6. to produce (a photograph) from (a negative) 7. to impress upon the mind, memory, etc. —*vi.* to practise the trade of a printer —**in** (or **out of**) **print** still (or no longer) for sale by the publisher : said of books, etc.

printed circuit an electrical circuit formed by applying conductive material in fine lines or other shapes to an insulating surface

printer *n.* 1. one whose work is printing 2. in computers, a device that produces information in printed form

printer's devil an apprentice in a printing shop

printing *n.* 1. the act of a person or thing that prints 2. an impression of a book 3. written letters made like printed ones

printing press a machine for printing from inked type, plates, or rolls

printout *n.* the output of a computer presented in printed or typewritten form

prior (prī′ər) *adj.* [L.] 1. preceding in time; earlier 2. preceding in order or importance —*n.* the head of a priory —**prior to** before in time —**pri′oress** *n.fem.*

priority (prī or′ə tē) *n., pl.* **-ties** 1. a being prior; precedence 2. a right to precedence over others in obtaining, buying, etc. 3. something given prior attention

priory (prī′ər ē) *n., pl.* **-ries** a monastery governed by a prior, or a convent governed by a prioress

prise (prīz) *vt.* **prised, pris′ing** *same as* PRIZE[2] (*vt.*)

TRIANGULAR PRISM

prism (priz′m) *n.* [< Gr. *prizein*, to saw] 1. a solid figure whose ends are equal and parallel polygons and whose sides are parallelograms 2. *Optics* a transparent body, as of glass, whose ends are triangles : used for dispersing light, as into the spectrum

prismatic (priz mat′ik) *adj.* 1. of or like a prism 2. that refracts light as a prism —**prismat′ically** *adv.*

prison (priz′n) *n.* [< L. *prehendere*, take] 1. a building, usually with cells, where persons convicted by trial or awaiting trial are confined 2. a place where persons are confined 3. imprisonment

prisoner *n.* 1. a person confined in prison, as for some crime 2. a person captured or held captive

prisoner of state one confined for political rather than criminal reasons : also **State prisoner**

prisoner of war a member of the armed forces of a nation at war held captive by the enemy

prissy (pris′ē) *adj.* **-sier, -siest** [prob. PR(IM) + (S)ISSY] [Colloq.] prim; fussy; prudish etc. —**pris′sily** *adv.*

pristine (pris′tīn) *adj.* [L. *pristinus*, former] 1. characteristic of the earliest period; original 2. still pure; unspoiled —**pris′tinely** *adv.*

privacy (prī′və sē) *n., pl.* **-cies** 1. withdrawal from public view; seclusion

2. secrecy 3. one's private life or personal affairs

private (prī'vit) *adj.* [< L. *privus*, separate] 1. secret; confidential 2. for an individual person or a group [*a private room*] 3. not open to or controlled by the public [*a private club*] 4. of or concerning a particular person or group 5. not holding public office [*a private citizen*] 6. dealing with clients or patients who pay directly for services rendered —*n. see* MILITARY RANKS, table —in **private** not publicly —**pri'vately** *adv.*

private bill a bill presented to Parliament that affects an individual or company only

private company a limited company that does not issue shares for public subscription

privateer (prī'və tēr') *n.* [< PRIVAT(E) + -EER] 1. a privately owned ship commissioned in a war to attack and capture enemy ships 2. a commander of a privateer

private eye [Colloq.] a private detective

private means an unearned income, as from investment

private member's bill a parliamentary bill sponsored by a member of parliament who is not a government minister

private parts the genitals

private school a school accepting pupils mostly on a feepaying basis

privation (prī vā'shən) *n.* [see PRIVATE] 1. lack of the ordinary necessities of life 2. the loss or absence of some quality or condition

privative (priv'ə tiv) *adj.* 1. depriving or tending to deprive 2. *Gram.* indicating negation, absence, or loss

privet (priv'it) *n.* [< ?] any of various shrubs with bluish-black berries and white flowers

privilege (priv'ə lij) *n.* [< L. *privus*, separate + *lex*, a law] a right, advantage, favour, etc. specially granted to a certain person, group, or class —*vt.* **-leged, -leging** to grant a privilege to

privileged *adj.* enjoying or granted as a privilege or privileges

privy (priv'ē) *adj.* [< L. *privatus*, private] [Archaic] hidden, secret, etc. —*n., pl.* **priv'ies** a toilet —**privy to** privately informed about —**priv'ily** *adv.*

privy council a body of advisers appointed by or serving a ruler —**privy councillor**

privy purse 1. an allowance from public revenue for the personal expenses of the monarch 2. the official responsible for dealing with the monarch's personal expenses: also **Keeper of the Privy Purse**

privy seal in Great Britain, the seal placed on documents which later received the great seal

prize¹ (prīz) *n.* [see PRICE] 1. something offered or given to the winner of a contest, lottery, etc. 2. anything worth striving for —*adj.* 1. that has received a prize 2. worthy of a prize —*vt.* **prized, priz'ing** to value highly; esteem

prize² *n.* [< L. *prehendere*, take]

something taken by force, esp., a captured enemy warship —*vt.* **prized, priz'ing** to open by force, as with a crowbar

prizefight *n.* a professional boxing match —**prize'fight'er** *n.* —**prize'fight'ing** *n.*

pro¹ (prō) *adv.* [L., for] on the affirmative side —*prep.* in favour of —*n., pl.* **pros** a reason, vote, etc. in favour of something [*the pros and cons of a matter*]

pro² *adj., n., pl.* **pros** *short form of* PROFESSIONAL

PRO, P.R.O. public relations officer

pro-¹ [< Gr.] a prefix meaning before in place or time

pro-² [L. < *pro*, forward] a prefix meaning: 1. forward or ahead [*progress*] 2. forth [*produce*] 3. substituting for [*pronoun*] 4. supporting, favouring

prob. 1. probable 2. probably 3. problem

probability (prob'ə bil'ə tē) *n., pl.* **-ties** 1. a being probable; likelihood 2. a probable thing or event 3. a measure of the relative frequency of the occurrence of something —**in all probability** very likely

probable (prob'ə b'l) *adj.* [< L. *probare*, prove] 1. likely to occur or be 2. reasonably so, as on the basis of evidence, but not proved —**prob'ably** *adv.*

probate (prō'bāt) *n.* [see PROBE] the act or process of establishing that a document submitted for official certification and registration, as a will, is genuine —*adj.* having to do with probate —*vt.* **-bated, -bating** [U.S.] to establish officially the validity of (a will) —**pro'bative** *adj.*

probation (prə bā'shən) *n.* [see PROBE] 1. the suspension of sentence of a person convicted but not imprisoned, on condition of continued good behaviour 2. the status of a person being tested or on trial 3. a testing or trial, as of a person's character, etc. —**proba'tionary** *adj.*

probationer *n.* a person on probation

probation officer an officer appointed by a court to supervise persons placed on probation

probe (prōb) *vt.* **probed, prob'ing** [< L. *probare*, to test] 1. to examine thoroughly 2. to explore (a wound, etc.) with a probe —*n.* 1. a blunt surgical instrument for exploring a wound 2. the act of probing 3. a searching investigation 4. an instrumented spacecraft for exploring outer space, another planet, etc. —**prob'er** *n.*

probity (prō'bə tē) *n.* [< L. *probus*, good] uprightness; honesty; integrity

problem (prob'ləm) *n.* [< Gr. *problēma*] 1. a question or matter to be worked out 2. a matter, person, etc. that is perplexing —*adj.* 1. depicting a social problem [*a problem play*] 2. very difficult to train or discipline

problematic (prob'lə mat'ik) *adj.* 1. hard to solve or deal with 2. uncertain Also **prob'lemat'ical**

proboscis (prō bos'is) *n., pl.* **-cises** [< Gr. *pro-*, before + *boskein*, to feed] 1. an elephant's trunk, or a long, flexible snout, as of a tapir 2. any tubular organ for sucking, as of some insects

procedure (prə sē′jər) *n.* 1. the act or method of proceeding in some action 2. a particular course of action 3. the established way of carrying on the business of a law court, etc. —**proce′dural** *adj.*

proceed (prə sēd′) *vi.* [< L. *pro-*, forward + *cedere*, go] 1. to go on, esp. after stopping 2. to carry on some action 3. to move along or be carried on 4. to take legal action (often with *against*) 5. to come forth or issue (*from*)

proceeding *n.* 1. a going on with what one has been doing 2. a course of action 3. [*pl.*] a record of the business transacted by a learned society, etc. 4. [*pl.*] legal action

proceeds (prō′sēdz) *n.pl.* the sum or profit derived from a sale, venture, etc.

process (prō′ses) *n.* [see PROCEED] 1. a series of changes by which something develops [*the process of growth*] 2. a method of doing something, in which there are a number of steps 3. *Biol.* a projecting part of a structure or organism 4. *Law* a written order, as a summons to appear in court —*vt.* to prepare by or subject to a special process —**in process** in the course of being done —**in (the) process of** during the course of

procession (prə sesh′ən) *n.* [see PROCEED] 1. the act of proceeding 2. a number of persons or things moving forwards, as in a parade, in an orderly way

processional *adj.* of or relating to a procession —*n.* a hymn sung at the beginning of a church service during the entrance of the clergy

process server *Law* a sheriff's officer who serves legal documents as writs, warrants, etc.

proclaim (prə klām′) *vt.* [< L. *pro-*, before + *clamare*, cry out] 1. to announce officially; announce to be 2. to show to be [*acts that proclaimed* him a friend *]*

proclamation (prok′lə mā′shən) *n.* 1. a proclaiming 2. something that is proclaimed

proclivity (prə kliv′ə tē) *n.,* pl. **-ties** [< L. *pro-*, before + *clivus*, a slope] a natural tendency or inclination

procrastinate (prō kras′tə nāt′) *vi., vt.* **-nat′ed, -nat′ing** [< L. *pro-*, forward + *cras*, tomorrow] to put off doing (something) until later —**procras′tina′tion** *n.*

procreate (prō′krē āt′) *vt., vi.* **-at′ed, -at′ing** [< L. *pro-*, before + *creare*, create] 1. to produce (young); beget 2. to produce —**pro′crea′tion** *n.* —**pro′crea′tive** *adj.*

Procrustean (prō krus′tē ən) *adj.* 1. of or like Procrustes in Greek Myth. who seized travellers, tied them to a bedstead, and either stretched them or cut off their legs to make them fit 2. securing conformity at any cost

proctor (prok′tər) *n.* [see PROCURE] a college or university official who maintains order, discipline, etc. among students —**proctorial** (prok tôr′ē əl) *adj.* —**proc′torship′** *n.*

procurator (prok′yooə rāt′ər) *n.* [see PROCURE] a person employed to manage another's affairs; agent

procurator fiscal a legal officer in Scotland who performs the functions of public prosecutor and coroner

procure (prə kyooər′) *vt.* **-cured′, -cur′-ing** [< L. *pro*, for + *curare*, to attend to] 1. to bring about by some effort; obtain 2. to obtain (women) for the purpose of prostitution —**procur′able** *adj.* —**procure′ment** *n.*

procurer *n.* a man who obtains women for the purpose of prostitution —**procur′ess** *n.fem.*

Procyon (prō′sē ən) [< Gr. *pro-*, before + *kyōn*, dog: it rises before the Dog Star] a bright star in Canis Minor

prod (prod) *vt.* **prod′ded, prod′ding** [< ?] 1. to jab or poke as with a pointed stick 2. to urge or stir into action —*n.* 1. a jab, poke, etc. 2. something that prods —**prod′der** *n.*

prodigal (prod′i gəl) *adj.* [< L. *pro-*, forth + *agere*, to drive] 1. wasteful in a reckless way 2. extremely generous; lavish —*n.* a person who recklessly wastes his wealth, etc. —**prod′igal′ity** (-gal′ə tē) *n.*

prodigal son *Bible* a wastrel son who repented and was welcomed home: Luke 15 : 11–32

prodigious (prə dij′əs) *adj.* [see ff.] 1. wonderful; amazing 2. enormous; huge —**prodi′giously** *adv.*

prodigy (prod′ə jē) *n.,* pl. **-gies** [L. *prodigium,* omen] a person or thing so extraordinary as to inspire wonder; specif., a child who is extremely talented

produce (prə dyo͞os′; *for n.* prod′yo͞os) *vt.* **-duced′, -duc′ing** [< L. *pro-,* forward + *ducere,* to lead] 1. to bring forth; bear; yield 2. to make or manufacture 3. to cause; give rise to 4. to offer for inspection 5. to get ready and present (a play, film, etc.) 6. *Econ.* to create (anything having exchange value) 7. *Geom.* to extend (a line or plane) —*n.* something produced; esp., fresh fruits and vegetables

producer (prə dyo͞os′ər) *n.* 1. one who produces goods and services 2. *a)* a person in charge of the artistic direction of a play *b)* a person in charge of the financing, etc. of a film

product (prod′əkt) *n.* 1. something produced by nature or by man 2. result; outgrowth 3. *Chem.* any substance resulting from a chemical change 4. *Math.* the quantity obtained by multiplying two or more quantities together

production (prə duk′shən) *n.* 1. the act or process of producing 2. the rate of producing 3. *a)* something produced *b)* a work of art, literature, etc. *c)* a show, film, etc. 4. the producing of goods and services

productive *adj.* 1. fertile 2. marked by abundant production 3. bringing as a result (with *of*) 4. of or engaged in the creating of economic value —**produc′tively** *adv.* —**productivity** (prō′-dək tiv′ə tē) *n.*

proem (prō′em) *n.* [< Gr. *pro-*, before + *oimē*, song] a brief introduction; preface

prof (prof) *n.* [Colloq.] shortened form of PROFESSOR

Prof. Professor

profanation (prof′ə nā′shən) *n.* a profaning or being profaned; desecration

profane (prə fān′) *adj.* [< L. *pro-*, before (i.e., outside) + *fanum*, temple] 1. showing disrespect or contempt for sacred things 2. not connected with religion; secular —*vt.* -**faned′**, -**fan′ing** 1. to treat (sacred things) with disrespect or contempt 2. to put to a base or improper use —**profane′**-**ness** *n.*

profanity (prə fan′ə tē) *n.* 1. a being profane 2. *pl.* -**ties** profane language; swearing

profess (prə fes′) *vt.* [< L. *pro-*, before + *fateri*, avow] 1. to make an open declaration of; affirm 2. to claim to have (some feeling, knowledge, etc.) 3. to declare one's belief in —**professed′** *adj.*

profession (prə fesh′ən) *n.* 1. *a)* an occupation requiring advanced education, as medicine, law, teaching, etc. *b)* the body of persons in any such occupation 2. an avowal, as of love, religious belief, etc. 3. the act of taking vows on entering a religious order —**the oldest profession** prostitution

professional *adj.* 1. of, engaged in, connected with, or worthy of the standards of, a profession 2. earning one's living from an activity, such as a sport, not normally thought of as an occupation 3. engaged in by professional players [*professional* boxing] 4. engaged in a specific occupation for pay —*n.* a person who is professional —**profes′sionalism** *n.*

professor (prə fes′ər) *n.* 1. a teacher holding a university chair 2. a person who professes something —**professorial** (prō′fə sôr′ē əl) *adj.*

proffer (prof′ər) *vt.* [< OFr. *por-*, PRO-[1] + *offrir*, to offer] to offer (advice, friendship, etc.)

proficient (prə fish′ənt) *adj.* [< L. *pro-*, forward + *facere*, make] highly competent; skilled —**profi′ciency** *n.* —**profi′ciently** *adv.*

profile (prō′fīl) *n.* [< L. *pro-*, before + *filum*, a thread] 1. *a)* a side view of the face *b)* a drawing of this 2. outline 3. a short, vivid biographical and character sketch —*vt.* -**filed**, -**filing** to sketch a profile of

profit (prof′it) *n.* [see PROFICIENT] 1. [*often pl.*] the sum remaining after all costs are deducted from the income of a business 2. advantage; gain; benefit —*vi.* 1. to make a profit 2. to benefit; gain —*vt.* to be of profit to —**prof′ita-ble** *adj.*

profiteer (prof′ə tēar′) *n.* one who makes an unfair profit by charging very high prices when there is a shortage —*vi.* to be a profiteer

profit sharing the practice of dividing a share of the profits of a business among

employees, in addition to paying them their wages —**prof′it-shar′ing** *adj.*

profligate (prof′li gət) *adj.* [< L. *pro-*, forward + *fligere*, to drive] 1. immoral and shameless; dissolute 2. recklessly extravagant —*n.* a profligate person —**prof′ligacy** *n.*

profound (prə found′) *adj.* [< L. *pro-*, forward + *fundus*, bottom] 1. marked by intellectual depth 2. very deep or low [a *profound* abyss] 3. deeply or intensely felt 4. thoroughgoing [*profound* changes] —**profun′dity** (-fun′-) *n.*

profuse (prə fyo͞os′) *adj.* [< L. *pro-*, forth + *fundere*, pour] giving or given freely and abundantly —**profuse′ly** *adv.* —**pro-fu′sion** *n.*

progenitor (prō jen′i tər) *n.* [< L. *pro-*, forth + *gignere*, beget] 1. a forefather; ancestor in direct line 2. an originator or precursor

progeny (proj′ə nē) *n.*, *pl.* -**nies** [see prec.] children, descendants, or offspring

progesterone (prō jes′tə rōn′) *n.* [< PRO-[1] & GESTATION & (CHOLE)STEROL] a steroid hormone that prepares the uterus for the fertilized ovum

prognosis (prog nō′sis) *n.*, *pl.* -**no′ses** (-sēz) [< Gr. *pro-*, before + *gignōskein*, know] a prediction of the probable course of a disease —**prognos′tic** (-nos′tik) *n.*

prognosticate (prog nos′tə kāt′) *vt.* -**cat′ed**, -**cat′ing** 1. to foretell or predict 2. to indicate beforehand —**prognos′tica′-tion** *n.* —**prognos′tica′tor** *n.*

program (prō′gram) *n.* 1. Chiefly U.S. *sp.* of PROGRAMME 2. *a)* a sequence of operations to be performed by a computer *b)* the coded instructions and data for this —*vt.* -**grammed** or -**gramed**, -**gram-ming** or -**graming** 1. Chiefly U.S. *sp.* of PROGRAMME 2. to furnish (a computer) with a program —**pro′grammer** *n.*

programmable, programable (prō-gram′ə b'l) *adj.* of a computer that can be programmed

programme (prō′gram) *n.* [< Gr. *pro-*, before + *graphein*, write] 1. *a)* the acts, speeches, musical pieces, etc. that make up an entertainment, ceremony, etc. *b)* a printed list of these 2. a scheduled broadcast on radio or television 3. a plan or procedure 4. a specially arranged selection of things to be done —*vt.* -**grammed**, -**gramming** to schedule in a programme —**programmatic** (prō′-grə mat′ik) *adj.* —**pro′grammer** *n.*

progress (prō′gres; for *v.* prō gres′) *n.* [< L. *pro-*, before + *gradi*, to step] 1. a moving forwards or onwards 2. development 3. advance; improvement —*vi.* 1. to move forwards 2. to advance towards perfection; improve —**in progress** going on

progression (prō gresh′ən) *n.* 1. a moving forwards 2. a succession, as of events 3. Math. a series of numbers increasing or decreasing by a constant difference between terms

progressive (prō gres′iv) *adj.* 1. moving forwards 2. continuing by successive steps

3. designating a tax whose rate increases as the base increases **4.** favouring or working for progress, reform, etc. **5.** of a dance in which partners dance one figure with each other before moving on **6.** *Gram.* indicating continuing action: said of certain verb forms **7.** *Med.* becoming more severe: said of a disease —*n.* one who favours political progress or reform —**progres′sively** *adv.*

prohibit (prə hib′it) *vt.* [< L. *pro-*, before + *habere*, have] **1.** to forbid by law or by an order **2.** to prevent; hinder —**prohib′itor** *n.*

prohibition (prō′ə bish′ən) *n.* **1.** a prohibiting **2.** an order that forbids **3.** the forbidding by law of the manufacture or sale of alcohol —**pro′hibi′tionist** *n.*

prohibitive (prə hib′i tiv) *adj.* **1.** prohibiting or tending to prohibit something **2.** such as to prevent purchase, use, etc. Also **prohib′itory**

project (proj′ekt; *for v.* prə jekt′) *n.* [< L. *pro-*, before + *jacere*, to throw] **1.** a proposal; plan **2.** an organized undertaking, as a special unit of work, research, etc. —*vt.* **1.** to propose (a plan of action) **2.** to throw forwards **3.** to cause (one's voice) to be heard clearly and at a distance **4.** to send forth in one's imagination **5.** to cause to jut out **6.** to cause (a shadow, image, etc.) to fall upon a surface **7.** *same as* EXTRAPOLATE —*vi.* **1.** to jut out **2.** to project one's voice, ideas, etc.

projectile (prō jek′til) *n.* an object designed to be shot forwards, as a cannon shell, bullet, or rocket —*adj.* **1.** designed to be hurled forwards, as a javelin **2.** hurling forwards

projection (prə jek′shən) *n.* **1.** a projecting or being projected **2.** something that projects, or juts out **3.** in map making, the representation on a plane of all or part of the earth's surface or of the celestial sphere **4.** *Photog.* the process of projecting an image, as from a transparent slide, upon a screen, etc. —**projec′tive** *adj.*

projectionist *n.* the operator of a film or slide projector

projector (prə jek′tər) *n.* a machine for throwing an image on a screen, as from a film

prolapse (prō′laps; *for v.* prō laps′) *n.* [< L. *pro-*, forward + *labi*, to fall] *Med.* the slipping out of place of an internal organ, as the uterus: also **prolap′sus** —*vi.* **-lapsed′, -laps′ing** *Med.* to slip out of place

prolate (prō′lāt) *adj.* [< L. *proferre*, bring forwards] extended or elongated at the poles

prole (prōl) *adj., n.* [Colloq.] proletarian

proletariat (prō′lə tāar′ē ət) *n.* [< L. *proletarius*, a citizen of the poorest class] the working class; esp., the industrial working class —**pro′letar′ian** *adj., n.*

proliferate (prō lif′ə rāt′) *vt., vi.* **-at′ed, -at′ing** [< L. *proles*, offspring + *ferre*, to bear] **1.** to reproduce (new parts) in quick succession **2.** to create in profusion; multiply rapidly —**prolif′era′tion** *n.*

prolific (prō lif′ik) *adj.* [< L. *proles*, offspring + *facere*, make] **1.** producing many young or much fruit **2.** creating many products of the mind **3.** fruitful; abounding (often with *in*) —**prolif′ically** *adv.*

prolix (prō′liks) *adj.* [< L. *prolixus*, extended] verbose; long-winded —**prolix′ity** *n.*

prologue (prō′log) *n.* [< Gr. *pro-*, before + *logos*, a discourse] **1.** an introduction to a poem, play, etc. **2.** any preliminary act, event, etc.

prolong (prō′long′) *vt.* [< L. *pro-*, forth + *longus*, long] to lengthen in time or space —**pro′longa′tion** *n.*

prom (prom) *n.* [contr. < ff.] **1.** *same as* PROMENADE (sense 2) **2.** *short for* PROMENADE CONCERT

promenade (prom′ə näd′) *n.* [< L. *pro-*, forth + *minare*, to herd] **1.** a public place for a walk, esp. a paved walk along the front at a seaside resort **2.** a leisurely walk taken for pleasure —*vi., vt.* **-nad′ed, -nad′ing** to take or perform a promenade (along or through); parade —**prom′enad′er** *n.*

promenade concert a musical performance at which some of the audience pay a low entrance fee to stand

promethium (prə mē′thē əm) *n.* [ModL. < *Prometheus*] a metallic chemical element of the rare-earth group: symbol Pm

prominent (prom′i nənt) *adj.* [< L. *prominere*, to project] **1.** sticking out; projecting **2.** conspicuous **3.** widely and favourably known —**prom′inence** *n.* —**prom′inently** *adv.*

promiscuous (prə mis′kyoo wəs) *adj.* [< L. *pro-*, forth + *miscere*, to mix] **1.** showing little taste in choosing; specif., engaging in sexual intercourse with many persons casually **2.** consisting of different elements mixed together without sorting —**promiscuity** (prom′is kyoo′ə tē) *n.* —**promis′cuously** *adv.*

promise (prom′is) *n.* [< L. *pro-*, forth + *mittere*, send] **1.** an agreement to do or not to do something **2.** a sign that gives reason for expecting success **3.** something promised —*vi.* **-ised, -ising 1.** to make a promise **2.** to give a basis for expectation —*vt.* **1.** to make a promise of (something) **2.** to engage or pledge [*to promise* to go] **3.** [Colloq.] to assure

promised land a place where one expects to have a better life: after Canaan, in the Bible

promising *adj.* showing promise of success, excellence, etc. —**prom′isingly** *adv.*

promissory note (prom′i sər ē) a written promise to pay a certain sum of money to a certain person

promontory (prom′ən tər ē) *n., pl.* **-ries** [prob. < L. *prominere*, to project] a peak of high land that juts out into a body of water

promote (prə mōt′) *vt.* **-mot′ed, -mot′-**

ing [< L. *pro-*, forward + *movere*, to move] 1. to raise or advance to a higher position or rank 2. to further the growth or establishment of 3. to further the popularity, sales, etc. of 4. to support the passage of a private bill in Parliament —**promot'able** *adj.* —**promo'tion** *n.*

promoter *n.* a person who begins, secures financing for, and helps to organize an undertaking

prompt (prompt) *adj.* [< L. *pro-*, forth + *emere*, take] 1. quick to act or to do what is required 2. done, spoken, etc. at once —*n.* a reminder, esp. one to an actor of forgotten lines —*vt.* 1. to urge into action 2. to remind (a person) of something he has forgotten; specif., to help (an actor, etc.) with a cue 3. to inspire —**prompt'ly** *adv.* —**promp'ti-tude'**, **prompt'ness** *n.*

prompter *n.* one who cues performers when they forget their lines

promulgate (prom'əl gāt') *vt.* -gat'ed, -gat'ing [< L. *promulgare*, to publish] 1. to make known officially (a decree, law, etc.) 2. to make widespread —**prom'-ulga'tion** *n.* —**prom'ulga'tor** *n.*

pron. 1. pronoun 2. pronunciation

prone (prōn) *adj.* [< L. *pronus*]. 1. lying or leaning face downwards 2. lying flat or prostrate 3. disposed or inclined (*to*) [*prone* to error] —**prone'ly** *adv.*

prong (prôṇ) *n.* [akin to MLowG. *prangen*, to pinch] 1. any of the pointed ends of a fork 2. any pointed projecting part —**pronged** *adj.*

pronominal (prō nom'in'l) *adj.* *Gram.* of, or having the function of, a pronoun —**pronom'inally** *adv.*

pronoun (prō'noun) *n.* [< L. *pro*, for + *nomen*, noun] *Gram.* a word that can assume the functions of a noun and be used in place of a noun (Ex.: *I, you, them, it, who, myself,* etc.)

pronounce (prə nouns') *vt.* -nounced', -nounc'ing [< L. *pro-*, before + *nuntiare*, announce] 1. *a)* to utter or articulate (a sound or word) *b)* to utter in the required or standard manner 2. to say officially, solemnly, etc. —*vi.* 1. to pronounce words, syllables, etc. 2. to make a pronouncement (*on*) —**pronounce'able** *adj.*

pronounced *adj.* 1. unmistakable; decided [a *pronounced* change] 2. spoken or uttered

pronouncement *n.* 1. a formal statement of a fact, opinion, or judgment 2. a pronouncing

pronto (pron'tō) *adv.* [Sp.: see PROMPT] [Chiefly U.S. Slang] at once; quickly; immediately

pronunciamento (prə nun'sē ə men'tō) *n., pl.* -tos [Sp. < L.: see PRONOUNCE] a proclamation

pronunciation (prə nun'sē ā'shən) *n.* 1. the act or manner of pronouncing words 2. any of the accepted or standard pronunciations of a word

proof (prōōf) *n.* [see PROBE] 1. anything serving to establish the truth of something 2. a proving, testing, or trying of something

3. a test or trial of the truth, quality, etc. of something 4. the state of having been tested or proved 5. the relative strength of an alcoholic liquor: see PROOF SPIRIT 6. *Photog.* a trial print of a negative 7. *Printing* an impression of composed type taken for checking errors and making changes —*adj.* 1. able to resist, withstand, etc. (with *against*) 2. of tested and proved strength —*vt.* 1. to make a proof of 2. to render proof against, esp. to make materials impervious to water

-proof (prōōf) *a combining form meaning:* 1. impervious to [*waterproof*] 2. protected from [*rustproof*] 3. resistant to [*fireproof*]

proofread (prōōf'rēd') *vt., vi.* to read and mark corrections on (printers' proofs, etc.) —**proof'read'er** *n.*

proof spirit an alcoholic liquor that is 100 proof and contains 57.10 of its volume of alcohol

prop[1] (prop) *n.* [MDu. *proppe*] 1. a support, as a pole, placed under or against a structure 2. a person or thing that gives support to a person, institution, etc. —*vt.* propped, prop'ping 1. to support, as with a prop (often with *up*) 2. to place or lean (something) *against* a support

prop[2] *n.* *Theatre* same as PROPERTY

prop[3] *n.* short for PROPELLER

prop. 1. proper(ly) 2. property 3. proposition

propaganda (prop'ə gan'də) *n.* [< ff.] 1. the systematic, widespread promotion of a certain set of ideas, doctrines, etc., esp. to further one's own cause 2. ideas, doctrines, or allegations so spread, esp. if regarded as spread by deception —**prop'-agan'dist** *n., adj.* —**prop'agan'dize** *vt., vi.*

propagate (prop'ə gāt') *vt.* -gat'ed, -gat'ing [< L. *propago*, slip (of a plant)] 1. to cause (a plant or animal) to reproduce itself 2. to reproduce (itself): said of a plant or animal 3. to spread (ideas, customs, etc.) 4. to extend or transmit (sound waves, etc.) —*vi.* to reproduce, as plants or animals —**prop'aga'tion** *n.* —**prop'aga'tor** *n.*

propane (prō'pān) *n.* [< PROPYLENE & (METH)ANE] a heavy, gaseous hydrocarbon used as a fuel, in refrigerants, etc.

propel (prə pel') *vt.* -pelled', -pel'ling [< L. *pro-*, forward + *pellere*, to drive] to drive forwards —**propel'lant** *n.* —**propel'-lent** *adj., n.*

propeller *n.* a device (**screw propeller**) consisting of blades twisted to move in a spiral as they rotate with the hub, to propel a ship or aircraft

propensity (prə pen'sə tē) *n., pl.* -ties [< L. *propendere*, to hang forward] a natural tendency

proper (prop'ər) *adj.* [< L. *proprius*, one's own] 1. specially adapted or suitable 2. naturally belonging or peculiar (*to*) 3. conforming to an accepted standard; correct 4. fitting; seemly; right 5. decent or decorous or exceedingly respectable 6. in its most restricted sense [the family *proper*] 7. real; genuine 8. [Colloq.] complete; thorough [a *proper* scoundrel]

9. *Gram.* designating a noun that names a specific individual, place, etc. —**prop'-erly** *adv.* —**prop'erness** *n.*

proper fraction *Math.* a fraction in which the numerator is less than the denominator (Ex.: 2/5)

propertied (prop'ər tēd) *adj.* owning property

property (prop'ər tē) *n., pl.* **-ties** [< L. *proprius*, one's own] **1.** a thing or things owned; possessions; esp., land or real estate owned **2.** ownership **3.** a specific piece of land **4.** any trait or attribute proper to a thing *[the properties* of a chemical compound *]* **5.** any of the movable articles used as part of a stage setting, except the costumes, backdrops, etc. —**prop'erty-less** *adj.*

prophecy (prof'ə sē) *n., pl.* **-cies** **1.** prediction of the future by a prophet, as supposedly under divine guidance **2.** any prediction **3.** something prophesied

prophesy (prof'ə sī') *vt., vi.* **-sied', -sy'-ing** **1.** to predict (something) by the influence of divine guidance **2.** to predict (a future event)

prophet (prof'it) *n.* [< Gr. *pro-*, before + *phanai*, speak] **1.** a person who claims to speak for God, or a religious leader who is thought to be divinely inspired **2.** a spokesman for some cause, group, etc. **3.** a person who predicts the future —**the Prophet** *a name used for* Mohammed (by Moslems) —**the Prophets** **1.** the prophetic books of the Bible that include Isaiah, Jeremiah, etc. **2.** the authors of these —**proph'etess** *n. fem.*

prophetic (prə fet'ik) *adj.* **1.** of, or like a prophet **2.** of or containing a prophecy —**proph'ically** *adv.*

prophylactic (prō'fi lak'tik) *adj.* [< Gr. *pro-*, before + *phylassein*, to guard] preventive; esp., preventing disease —*n.* a prophylactic medicine, device, etc.

propinquity (prə piŋ'kwə tē) *n.* [< L. *propinquus*, near] **1.** nearness in time or place **2.** nearness of relationship; kinship

propitiate (prə pish'ē āt') *vt.* **-at'ed, -at'-ing** [see ff.] to win or regain the good will of —**propi'tiable** *adj.* —**propi'tia'tion** *n.* —**propi'tia'tor** *n.* —**propi'tiatory** *adj.*

propitious (prə pish'əs) *adj.* [< L. *pro-*, before + *petere*, seek] **1.** favourable; auspicious **2.** favourably inclined —**propi'-tiously** *adv.* —**propi'tiousness** *n.*

propjet (prop'jet') *n.* same as TURBOPROP

proponent (prə pō'nənt) *n.* [< L. *pro-*, forth + *ponere*, to place] **1.** a person who makes a proposal **2.** a person who supports a cause, etc.

proportion (prə pôr'shən) *n.* [< L. *pro-* for + *portio*, a part] **1.** the comparative relation between things with respect to size, amount, etc.; ratio **2.** a part, share, etc., esp. in its relation to the whole **3.** balance or symmetry **4.** [*pl.*] dimensions **5.** *Math.* an equality between ratios: also called **geometrical proportion** —*vt.* **1.** to cause to be in proper relation, balance, etc. **2.** to arrange the parts of (a whole)

so as to be harmonious —**propor'tioned** *adj.* —**propor'tionment** *n.*

proportional *adj.* **1.** in proportion **2.** *Math.* having the same ratio **3.** relative —**propor'tionally** *adv.*

proportional representation representation of political parties in proportion to the number of votes they receive

proportionate (prə pôr'shə nət) *adj.* in proper proportion —**propor'tionately** *adv.*

proposal (prə pō'z'l) *n.* **1.** a proposing **2.** a plan or action proposed **3.** an offer of marriage

propose (prə pōz') *vt.* **-posed', -pos'ing** [see PROPONENT] **1.** to put forth for consideration or acceptance **2.** to plan or intend **3.** to present as a toast in drinking —*vi.* **1.** to make a proposal **2.** to offer marriage —**propos'er** *n.*

proposition (prop'ə zish'ən) *n.* **1.** something proposed; plan **2.** [Colloq.] a proposed deal, as in business **3.** [Colloq.] a person, problem, etc. to be dealt with **4.** a subject to be discussed **5.** a statement; assertion **6.** *Math.* a theorem to be demonstrated or a problem to be solved —*vt.* [Colloq.] to make a proposition, esp. an improper one, to

propound (prə paund') *vt.* [see PROPONENT] to put forth for consideration; propose —**propound'er** *n.*

proprietary (prə prī'ə tar ē) *adj.* [see PROPERTY] **1.** belonging to a proprietor **2.** holding property **3.** held under patent, trademark, or copyright *[a proprietary medicine]*

proprietor (prə prī'ə tər) *n.* [< PROPERTY] one who owns and operates a business establishment —**propri'etress** *n.fem.*

propriety (prə prī'ə tē) *n., pl.* **-ties** [see PROPERTY] **1.** the quality of being proper, fitting, etc. **2.** conformity with what is proper or fitting —**the proprieties** accepted standards of behaviour in polite society

propulsion (prə pul'shən) *n.* [see PROPEL] **1.** a propelling or being propelled **2.** a propelling force —**propul'sive** *adj.*

propylene (prō'pə lēn) *n.* [< PROTO- & Gr. *pion*, fat] a flammable, colourless gas, used in making polypropylene, etc.

pro rata (prō rāt'ə) [L.] in proportion

prorogue (prə rōg') *vt., vi.* **-rogued', -rogu'ing** [< L. *pro-*, for + *rogare*, ask] to discontinue or end a session of (a legislative assembly) —**pro'roga'tion** *n.*

prosaic (prō zā'ik) *adj.* [< L. *prosa*, PROSE] **1.** commonplace; dull **2.** of or like prose —**prosa'ically** *adv.*

proscenium (prō sē'nē əm) *n., pl.* **-niums, -nia** [< Gr. *pro-*, before + *skēnē*, a tent] the plane separating the stage proper from the audience and including the arch (**proscenium arch**) and its curtain

proscribe (prō skrīb') *vt.* **-scribed', -scrib'ing** [< L. *pro-*, before + *scribere*, write] **1.** to denounce or forbid the practice of **2.** to outlaw **3.** to banish; exile —**pro-scrip'tion** (-skrip'shən) *n.* —**proscrip'tive** *adj.*

prose (prōz) *n.* [< L. *provertere*, turn forwards] **1.** the ordinary form of language, without rhyme or metre **2.** dull, commonplace talk —*vt., vi.* prosed, pros'-ing to speak or write in prose

prosecute (pros'i kyoot') *vt.* -cut'ed, -cut'ing [< L. *pro-*, before + *sequi*, follow] **1.** *a)* to conduct legal proceedings against, esp. for a crime *b)* to try to get, enforce, etc. by legal process **2.** to carry on; engage in —*vi.* to institute and carry on a legal action —**pros'ecu'tor** *n.*

prosecution (pros'i kyoo'shən) *n.* **1.** the conducting of a lawsuit **2.** the lawyers acting for the Crown against the accused in criminal proceedings **3.** a prosecuting, or following up

proselyte (pros'ə līt') *n.* [< Gr. *prosēlytos*] a person who has been converted from one religion, belief, etc. to another —*vt., vi.* -lyt'ed, -lyt'ing to try to convert (a person), esp. to one's religion —**pros'elytism** (-lit iz'm) *n.*

proselytize (pros'ə li tīz') *vi., vt.* -ized', -iz'ing *same as* PROSELYTE —**pros'ely-tiz'er** *n.*

prosody (pros'ə dē) *n., pl.* -dies [< Gr. *prosōidia*, accent] the science of versification, including the study of metre, rhyme, etc. —**prosodic** (prə sod'ik) *adj.* —**prosod'ically** *adv.* —**pros'odist** *n.*

prospect (pros'pekt; *for v.* pros pekt') *n.* [< L. *pro-*, forward + *specere*, to look] **1.** *a)* something hoped for *b)* [*usually pl.*] apparent chance for success **2.** anticipation **3.** outlook **4.** *a)* a broad view; scene *b)* a place from which one can see such a view **5.** a mental view; survey **6.** a likely customer, candidate, etc. —*vt., vi.* to explore or search (*for*) [*to prospect for gold*] —**prospec'tor** *n.*

prospective (prə spek'tiv) *adj.* **1.** looking towards the future **2.** expected; likely —**prospec'tively** *adv.*

prospectus (prə spek'təs) *n.* [L. : see PROSPECT] **1.** a statement of the features of a new work, business, etc. **2.** a pamphlet giving details of courses, as at a university

prosper (pros'pər) *vi.* [< L. *prosperus*, favourable] to succeed, thrive, grow, etc. vigorously

prosperity (pro sper'ə tē) *n.* prosperous condition; wealth, success, etc.

prosperous (pros'pər əs) *adj.* **1.** flourishing **2.** well-to-do; well-off **3.** conducive to success —**pros'perously** *adv.*

prostate (pros'tāt) *adj.* [< Gr. *prostatēs*, one standing before] of or relating to the prostate gland: also **prostat'ic** (-tat'-ik) —*n.* the prostate gland

prostate gland a gland surrounding the urethra at the base of the bladder in most male mammals

prosthesis (pros'thə sis) *n., pl.* -the-ses' (-sēz') [< Gr. *pros*, to + *tithenai*, to place] *Med.* **1.** the replacement of a missing limb, etc. by an artificial substitute **2.** such a substitute —**prosthet'ic** (-thet'-ik) *adj.*

prostitute (pros'tə tyoot') *n.* [< L. *pro-*, before + *statuere*, make stand] a man or woman who engages in promiscuous sexual intercourse for pay —*vt.* -tut'ed, -tut'ing **1.** to sell the services of (oneself or another) for purposes of sexual intercourse **2.** to sell (oneself, one's integrity, etc.) for unworthy purposes —**pros'titu'tion** *n.*

prostrate (pros'trāt, *for v.* pros trāt') *adj.* [< L. *pro-*, before + *sternere*, to stretch out] **1.** lying face downwards in humility or submission **2.** lying flat, prone, or supine **3.** *a)* laid low; overcome *b)* physically weak or exhausted —*vt.* -trat'-ed, -trat'ing **1.** to lay flat on the ground **2.** to overcome or exhaust —**prostra'tion** *n.*

prosy (prō'zē) *adj.* -ier, -iest **1.** like prose **2.** prosaic, dull, etc. —**pros'ily** *adv.* —**pros'-iness** *n.*

Prot. Protestant

protactinium (prō'tak tin'ē əm) *n.* [ModL. : see PROTO- & ACTINIUM] a rare, radioactive, metallic chemical element: symbol, Pa

protagonist (prō tag'ə nist) *n.* [< Gr. *prōtos*, first + *agōnistēs*, actor] **1.** the main character in a drama, novel, or story **2.** a person playing a leading or active part

protea (prō'tēə) *n.* [< Gr. god *Proteus*] a small S African shrub or tree esp. prized for its showy flowers

protean (prōtē'ən) *adj.* **1.** [P-] of or like Proteus, in Gr. Myth. who could change shape at will **2.** readily taking on different shapes

protect (prə tekt') *vt.* [< L. *pro-*, before + *tegere*, to cover] **1.** to shield from injury, danger, or loss; defend **2.** *Econ.* to guard (domestic goods) by tariffs on imports

protection (prə tek'shən) *n.* **1.** a protecting **2.** a person or thing that protects **3.** [Colloq.] money extorted by racketeers threatening violence **4.** *Econ.* the system of protecting domestic goods by taxing imports

protectionism *n.* *Econ.* the system, theory, or policy of protection —**protec'-tionist** *n., adj.*

protective *adj.* protecting or intended to protect, esp. economically [*a protective tariff*] —**protec'tiveness** *n.*

protector (prə tek'tər) *n.* **1.** a guardian **2.** *a)* one ruling a kingdom during the minority, etc. of the sovereign *b)* [P-] the title (in full **Lord Protector**) held by Oliver Cromwell and his son Richard —**protec'torship'** *n.* —**protec'tress** *n.fem.*

protectorate *n.* **1.** a weak state under the control and protection of a stronger state **2.** government by a protector **3.** the office or term of a protector **4.** [P-] the government of England under the Protectors (1653–1659)

protégé (prō'te zhā') *n.* [Fr. : see PROTECT] a person guided and helped in his career by another —**pro'tégée'** *n.fem.*

protein (prō'tēn) *n.* [ult. < Gr. *prōtos*, first] any of a class of complex nitrogenous substances occurring in all living matter and essential to the diet of animals

pro tempore (prō tem'pə rē') [L.] for the time (being); temporary or temporarily: shortened to **pro tem**

protest (prə test'; *for n.* prō'test) *vt.* [< L. *pro-*, forth + *testari*, affirm] **1.** to state positively, esp. in contradiction, disapproval, etc. **2.** to make a written declaration of the nonpayment of (a cheque, etc.) —*vi.* to express disapproval; object —*n.* **1.** public disapproval or dissent, often organized, as a march **2.** an objection **3.** a document formally objecting to something **4.** *Law* a formal declaration that a bill or note has not been honoured by the drawer —**under protest** unwillingly —**protest'er, protes'tor** *n.*

Protestant (prŏt'is tənt) *n.* [see prec.] a member of any of the Christian churches deriving from the Reformation under the leadership of Luther, Calvin, etc. —*adj.* of Protestants or Protestant beliefs, practices, etc. —**Prot'estantism** *n.*

protestation (prō'tes tā'shən) *n.* **1.** a strong affirmation **2.** an objection

protium (prŏt'ē əm) *n.* [ModL.: see ff.] the most common isotope of hydrogen with mass number 1

proto- [< Gr. *prōtos*, first] *a combining form meaning:* **1.** first in time, original [*prototype*] **2.** first in importance, chief [*protagonist*]

protocol (prŏt'ə kol') *n.* [< LGr. *prōtokollon*, contents page] **1.** the code of ceremonial forms and courtesies used in official dealings, as between heads of state or diplomats **2.** an original draft of a document, negotiation, etc.

proton (prō'ton) *n.* [< Gr. *prōtos*, first] a fundamental particle in the nucleus of all atoms: it carries a unit positive charge of electricity

protoplasm (prŏt'ō plaz'm) *n.* [< G.: see PROTO- & PLASMA] a semifluid, colloidal substance that is the living matter of all animal and plant cells —**pro'toplas'-mic** *adj.*

prototype (prŏt'ō tīp') *n.* [see PROTO- & TYPE] **1.** the first of its kind; original **2.** a model for another of its kind

protozoan (prŏt'ō zō'ən) *n.* [see PROTO- & Gr. *zōion*, animal] a microscopic, one-celled animal living chiefly in water: also **pro'tozo'on,** *pl.* **-zo'a**

protract (prə trakt') *vt.* [< L. *pro-*, forward + *trahere*, to draw] **1.** to draw out in time; prolong **2.** to draw to scale, using a protractor and scale —**protract'-edly** *adv.* —**protrac'tion** *n.*

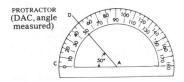

PROTRACTOR (DAC, angle measured)

protractor *n.* [ML.] a graduated, semicircular instrument for plotting and measuring angles

protrude (prə trōōd') *vt., vi.* **-trud'ed,** **-trud'ing** [< L. *pro-*, forth + *trudere,* to thrust] to thrust or jut out; project —**pro-tru'sion** *n.*

protrusive *adj.* jutting or bulging out —**protru'sively** *adv.*

protuberance (prə tyōō'bər əns) *n.* **1.** a being protuberant **2.** a part or thing that protrudes Also **protu'berancy**

protuberant *adj.* [< L. *pro-*, forth + *tuber,* a bump] bulging or swelling out; protruding; prominent —**protu'berantly** *adv.*

proud (proud) *adj.* [< LL. *prode,* beneficial] **1.** having or showing a proper pride in oneself **2.** haughty; arrogant **3.** feeling or causing great pride or joy **4.** caused by pride **5.** stately; splendid —**do oneself proud** [Colloq.] to do extremely well —**proud of** highly pleased with —**proud'-ly** *adv.*

proud flesh [< notion of swelling up] an abnormal growth of flesh around a healing wound

Prov. 1. Provençal **2.** Proverbs **3.** Province **4.** Provost

prove (prōōv) *vt.* **proved** or **prov'en, prov'-ing** [see PROBE] **1.** to establish as true **2.** to establish the validity of (a will, etc.) **3.** to test by experiment, a standard, etc.; try out **4.** to show (oneself) to be capable, etc. —*vi.* to turn out to be —**prov'able** *adj.* —**prov'ably** *adv.*

provenance (prov'ə nəns) *n.* [Fr. < L. *pro-*, forth + *venire,* come] origin; derivation; source

Provençal (prov'ən säl') *adj.* of Provence, its people, their language, etc. —*n.* the vernacular of S France, a Romance language which, in its medieval form, was an important literary language

provender (prov'ən dər) *n.* [see PREBEND] **1.** dry food for livestock **2.** [Colloq.] provisions; food

proverb (prov'urb) *n.* [< L. *pro-*, before + *verbum,* a word] **1.** a short, popular saying that expresses some obvious truth **2.** a person who has become commonly recognized as a type

proverbial (prə vur'bē əl) *adj.* **1.** of, or having the nature of, a proverb **2.** well-known because commonly referred to —**prover'bially** *adv.*

provide (prə vīd') *vt.* **-vid'ed, -vid'ing** [< L. *pro-*, before + *videre,* see] **1.** to make available; supply **2.** to supply (someone *with* something) **3.** to state as a condition; stipulate —*vi.* **1.** to prepare (*for* or *against*) a possible situation or event **2.** to furnish the means of support (*for*) —**provid'er** *n.*

provided (prə vīd'id) *conj.* on the condition or understanding; if (often with *that*)

providence (prov'i dəns) *n.* [see PROVIDE] **1.** the benevolent guidance of God or nature **2.** [P-] God **3.** a looking to, or preparation for, the future

provident *adj.* [see PROVIDE] **1.** providing for the future **2.** prudent or economical —**prov'idently** *adv.*

providential (prov'i den'shəl) *adj.* of,

by, or as if decreed by divine providence —**prov'iden'tially** *adv.*

providing (prə vīd'iŋ) *conj.* provided (often with *that*)

province (prov'ins) *n.* [< L. *provincia*] **1.** an administrative division of a country, esp. of Canada and New Zealand **2.** *a)* a district; territory *b)* [*pl.*] the parts of a country removed from the capital and major cities **3.** range of duties or functions **4.** a field of knowledge, activity, etc.

provincial (prə vin'shəl) *adj.* **1.** of a province **2.** having the ways, speech, etc. of a certain province **3.** countrified; rustic **4.** narrow or limited in outlook —*n.* **1.** a native of a province **2.** a provincial person —**provin'cialism** *n.*

proving ground a place for testing new equipment, new theories, etc.

provision (prə vizh'ən) *n.* [see PROVIDE] **1.** a providing or supplying **2.** something provided for the future; specif., [*pl.*] a stock of food **3.** a preparatory measure taken in advance **4.** a stipulation; proviso —*vt.* to supply with provisions

provisional *adj.* conditional or temporary, pending a permanent arrangement —*n.* [P-] a member of the Provisional IRA, advocating terrorism as a means to achieve Irish unity —**provi'sionally** *adv.*

proviso (prə vī'zō) *n., pl.* -**sos, -soes** [ML. *proviso* (*quod*), provided that] **1.** a conditional clause, as in a document **2.** a condition —**provi'sory** *adj.*

provocation (prov'ə kā'shən) *n.* **1.** a provoking **2.** something that provokes; esp., a cause of anger or irritation

provocative (prə vok'ə tiv) *adj.* provoking or tending to provoke —**provoc'atively** *adv.* —**provoc'ativeness** *n.*

provoke (prə vōk') *vt.* -**voked', -vok'ing** [< L. *pro-*, forth + *vocare*, to call] **1.** to excite to some action or feeling **2.** to anger or irritate **3.** to stir up (action or feeling)

provost (prov'əst) *n.* [< L. *praepositus*, chief] **1.** the chief administrative official of a Scottish burgh **2.** the head of some colleges

provost marshal (prə vō') the officer in charge of military police, in a camp, etc.

prow (prou) *n.* [ult. < Gr. *prōira*] **1.** the forward part of a ship **2.** anything like this

prowess (prou'is) *n.* [< OFr. *prouesse*] **1.** superior ability, skill, etc. **2.** bravery; valour

prowl (proul) *vi., vt.* [< ?] to roam about as in search of prey —*n.* a prowling —**on the prowl** prowling about —**prowl'er** *n.*

prox. proximo

proximate (prok'si mət) *adj.* [< L. *prope*, near] **1.** next or nearest in space, order, time, etc. **2.** approximate —**prox'imately** *adv.*

proximity (prok sim'ə tē) *n.* [see prec.] nearness in space, time, etc.

proximo (prok'si mō') *adv.* [L. *proximo* (*mense*)] in or of the next month

proxy (prok'sē) *n., pl.* **prox'ies** [< ME. *procuracie*, office of a procurator] **1.** the function of a deputy **2.** *a)* the authority to act for another, or a person given this authority *b)* a document giving this authority

P.R.S. President of the Royal Society

prude (prood) *n.* [Fr. < *prudefemme*, excellent woman] a person who is excessively modest or proper in behaviour, dress, speech, etc. —**prud'ish** *adj.*

prudence (prood'əns) *n.* **1.** a being prudent **2.** careful management; economy

prudent *adj.* [< L. *providens*, provident] **1.** exercising sound judgment in practical matters, esp. as concerns one's own interests **2.** cautious; not rash —**pru'dently** *adv.*

prudential (proo den'shəl) *adj.* characterized by or exercising prudence —**pruden'tially** *adv.*

prudery (prood'ər ē) *n.* a being prudish

prune[1] (proon) *n.* [< Gr. *proumnon*, plum] a plum dried for eating

prune[2] *vt.* pruned, prun'ing [< ?] **1.** to remove dead or living parts from (a plant) to encourage new growth **2.** to cut out as being unnecessary —**prun'er** *n.*

prurient (prooər'ē ənt) *adj.* [< L. *prurire*, to itch] **1.** having lustful ideas or desires **2.** full of or causing lust —**pru'rience** *n.*

pruritus (prooə rīt'əs) *n.* [< L. *prurire*, to itch] intense itching without a rash —**prurit'ic** (-rit'ik) *adj.*

prussic acid (prus'ik) same as HYDROCYANIC ACID

pry (prī) *vi.* pried, pry'ing [< ?] to look (*into*) closely or inquisitively

prying *adj.* improperly curious or inquisitive

Ps., Psa. Psalm; Psalms

P.S. **1.** Private Secretary **2.** Public School

P.S., p.s., PS postscript

psalm (säm) *n.* [< Gr. *psallein*, to pluck (a harp)] **1.** a sacred song or poem **2.** [P-] any of the songs in praise of God that make up the Book of Psalms in the Bible

psalmody (sal'mə dē) *n.* [< Gr. *psalmos*, psalm + *ōidē*, a song] **1.** the singing of psalms **2.** psalms collectively

Psalter (sôl'tər) [< Gr. *psallein*, to pluck] the Book of Psalms —*n.* [*also* p-] a version of the Psalms for use in religious services

psaltery (sôl'tər ē) *n., pl.* -**teries** an ancient stringed instrument with a shallow sound box, played by plucking the strings

psephology (se fol'ə jē) *n.* [< Gr. *psēphos*, pebble (used in voting) + -LOGY] the statistical evaluation of election returns or of political polls —**psephol'ogist** *n.*

pseud (syood) *n.* [< PSEUDO] [Colloq.] a false, artificial, or pretentious person; phoney

pseud. pseudonym

pseudo (syoo'dō) *adj.* [see ff.] sham; false; spurious; pretended; counterfeit

pseudo- [< Gr. *pseudēs*, false] a combining form meaning: **1.** fictitious [*pseudonym*] **2.** spurious **3.** deceptively similar to

pseudonym (syōō'də nim') *n.* [< Gr. *pseudēs*, false + *onyma*, a name] a fictitious name, esp. one assumed by an author —**pseu'donym'ity** *n.* —**pseudon'ymous** (-don'ə məs) *adj.*

pshaw (pshô) *interj., n.* an exclamation of impatience, disgust, contempt, etc.

psi (psī) *n.* the twenty-third letter of the Greek alphabet (Ψ, ψ)

psittacosis (psit'ə kō'sis) *n.* [< Gr. *psittakos*, parrot] an acute virus disease of parrots, often transmitted to man

psoriasis (sərī'ə sis) *n.* [< Gr. *psōra*, an itch] a skin disease in which scaly, reddish patches are formed

psst (pst) *interj.* a sound made to get someone's attention quickly and quietly

P.S.T. [U.S. & Canad.] Pacific Standard Time

P.S.V. Public Service Vehicle

psyche (sī'kē) *n.* [< Gr. *psychē*, the soul] 1. the human soul 2. the human mind

psychedelic (sī'kə del'ik) *adj.* [< PSYCHE + Gr. *delein*, make manifest] 1. of or causing extreme changes in the conscious mind, with hallucinations, etc. 2. of or like the intense, distorted sights, sounds, colours, etc. produced by such changes —*n.* a psychedelic drug

psychiatry (sī kī'ə trē) *n.* [see PSYCHO-] the branch of medicine dealing with disorders of the mind —**psychiatric** (sī'kē at'rik), **psy'chiat'rical** *adj.* —**psychi'atrist** *n.*

psychic (sī'kik) *adj.* [< Gr. *psychē*, the soul] 1. of the psyche, or mind 2. beyond physical processes 3. apparently sensitive to supernatural forces Also **psy'chical** —*n.* a person who is supposedly psychic —**psy'chically** *adv.*

psycho (sī'kō) *adj., n.* [Colloq] *short for* PSYCHOTIC, PSYCHOPATHIC, PSYCHOPATH

psycho- [< Gr. *psychē*, soul] *a combining form meaning* the mind or mental processes [*psychology*]

psychoanalyse (sī'kō an'ə līz') *vt.* -lysed', -lys'ing to treat by means of psychoanalysis

psychoanalysis (sī'kō ə nal'ə sis) *n.* [see PSYCHO- & ANALYSIS] a method of treating neuroses and other mental disorders by getting the patient to talk freely, analysing his dreams, etc. —**psy'choan'alyt'ic** (-an'ə lit'ik), **psy'choan'alyt'ical** *adj.*

psychoanalyst (sī'kō an'ə list) *n.* a specialist in psychoanalysis

psychogenic (sī'kō jen'ik) *adj.* [< PSYCHO-] caused by mental conflicts; psychic

psychokinesis (sī'kō ki nē'sis) *n.* [< PSYCHO- + Gr. *kinēsis*, motion] the supposed ability to influence physical objects or events by thought processes

psychological (sī'kə loj'i k'l) *adj.* 1. of psychology 2. of the mind 3. affecting the mind —**psy'cholog'ically** *adv.*

psychological moment 1. the moment when one is mentally ready for something 2. the critical moment

psychological warfare the use of psychological means to influence the thinking of an enemy

psychologize (sī kol'ə jīz') *vi.* -gized', -giz'ing to reason psychologically

psychology (sī kol'ə jē) *n., pl.* -gies [see PSYCHO- & -LOGY] 1. *a)* the science dealing with the mind and with mental and emotional processes *b)* the science of human and animal behaviour 2. a person's actions, thoughts, etc. —**psychol'ogist** *n.*

psychopath (sī'kō path) *n. same as* PSYCHOPATHIC PERSONALITY

psychopathic (sī'kō path'ik) *adj.* mentally ill

psychopathic personality a person with serious personality defects, whose behaviour is amoral, irresponsible, and often criminal

psychopathology (sī'kō pə thol'ə jē) *n.* the science dealing with mental disorders —**psy'chopath'olog'ical** (-path'ə loj'-i k'l) *adj.*

psychopathy (sī kop'ə thē) *n.* [PSYCHO- + -PATHY] mental disorder

psychosis (sī kō'sis) *n., pl.* -cho'ses (-sēz) [see PSYCHO- & -OSIS] a major mental disorder in which the personality is very seriously disorganized and one's sense of reality is usually altered —**psychot'ic** *adj., n.*

psychosomatic (sī'kō sō mat'ik) *adj.* [PSYCHO- + SOMATIC] designating or of a physical disorder originating in or aggravated by emotional processes —**psy'chosomat'ically** *adv.*

psychotherapy (sī'kō ther'ə pē) *n.* [PSYCHO- + THERAPY] treatment of mental disorder by counselling, psychoanalysis, etc. —**psy'chother'apist** *n.*

Pt *Chem.* platinum

P.T. 1. Physical Therapy 2. Physical Training

pt. *pl.* **pts.** 1. part 2. pint 3. point

p.t. 1. past tense 2. pro tempore

P.T.A. Parent/Teacher Association

ptarmigan (tär'mə gən) *n.* [< Scot. *tarmachan*] any of several varieties of northern or alpine grouse

ptero- [< Gr.] *a combining form meaning* feather, wing [*pterodactyl*]

PTERODACTYL
(wingspread to 6 m)

pterodactyl (ter'ō dak'til) *n.* [see prec. & DACTYL] an extinct flying reptile, having wings of skin stretched between the hind limb and a long digit of the forelimb

P.T.O., p.t.o. please turn over

Ptolemaic (tol'ə mā'ik) *adj.* of Ptolemy, the Greek astronomer, or his theory that the earth is the centre of the universe

ptomaine (tō'mān) *n.* [< Gr. *ptōma*, a corpse] any of a class of alkaloid substances, some of which are poisonous, formed in decaying animal or vegetable matter by bacteria

Pty. [Aust., N.Z., S.Afr.] Proprietary

Pu *Chem.* plutonium

pub (pub) *n.* [Colloq.] a public house

pub. 1. public 2. published 3. publisher

pub-crawl *n.* [Colloq.] a drinking tour of a number of pubs or bars : also **pub crawl**

puberty (pyoo'bər tē) *n.* [< L. *puber*, adult] the state of physical development when sexual reproduction first becomes possible —**pu'bertal** *adj.*

pubes[1] (pyoo'bēz) *n.* [L., pubic hair] 1. the body hair appearing at puberty surrounding the genitals 2. the region of the abdomen covered by such hair

pubes[2] *n.* *pl. of* PUBIS

pubescent (pyoo bes''nt) *adj.* [< L. *pubes*, adult] 1. reaching or having reached puberty 2. covered with a soft down, as many plants and insects —**pubes'cence** *n.*

pubic (pyoo'bik) *adj.* of or in the region of the pubes

pubis (pyoo'bis) *n.*, *pl.* **pu'bes** (-bēz) [see PUBES[1]] that part of the hipbone forming the front arch of the pelvis

public (pub'lik) *adj.* [< L. *populus*, people] 1. of the people as a whole 2. for the use or benefit of all [*public* transport] 3. acting in an official capacity for the people [the *public* prosecutor] 4. known by most people —*n.* 1. the people as a whole 2. a specific part of the people [the reading *public*] —**go public** *Finance* to offer company shares for sale to the public —**in public** openly —**pub'licly** *adv.*

public-address system an electronic system used to amplify sound at public gatherings

publican (pub'li kən) *n.* the licensee of a public house

publication (pub'li kā'shən) *n.* [see PUBLISH] 1. the printing and distribution, usually for sale, of books, magazines, etc. 2. something published 3. public notification

public company a limited company whose shares may be purchased by the public

public convenience a public lavatory, esp. one situated in a public park, on the street, etc.

public enemy a hardened criminal or other person who is a menace to society

public house an establishment where beer, spirits, etc. are served; bar

publicist (pub'li sist) *n.* 1. a journalist who writes about public affairs 2. a specialist in public relations

publicity (pub lis'ə tē) *n.* 1. a) any

information that makes a person, place, etc. known to the public b) the work of handling such information 2. a being noticed by the public 3. any act intended to gain public notice

publicize (pub'li sīz') *vt.* **-cized', -ciz'ing** to give publicity to; draw public attention to

public lending right the right for authors to receive payment when their books are loaned out by public libraries

public relations relations of an organization with the public through publicity seeking to form public opinion

public school 1. an independent fee-paying school 2. in Scotland, a state-maintained school 3. [U.S.] any school that is part of the local educational system 4. [Canad.] a public elementary school, as distinguished from a separate school

public servant an elected or appointed government official or a civil-service employee

public-spirited *adj.* having or showing zeal for the public welfare

public transport vehicles, such as trains, buses, etc. that have fixed routes and are available to the general public

public utility an organization that supplies water, electricity, transportation, etc. to the public

publish (pub'lish) *vt.* [< L. *publicus*, public] 1. to make publicly known; announce 2. to issue (a printed work, etc.) to the public, as for sale —*vi.* to write books, etc. that are published

publisher *n.* a person or firm that publishes books, newspapers, magazines, etc.

puce (pyoos) *n.* [Fr., lit., a flea] brownish purple

puck[1] (puk) *n.* [akin to POKE[1]] *Ice Hockey* a hard rubber disc which the players try to drive into the opponents' goal

puck[2] *n.* [OE. *puca*] a mischievous sprite or elf —**puck'ish** *adj.* —**puck'ishly** *adv.*

pucker (puk'ər) *vt.*, *vi.* [< POKE[2]] to draw up into wrinkles or small folds (with *up*) —*n.* such a wrinkle or fold

pud (pood) *n.* [Colloq.] a pudding; dessert

pudding (pood'iŋ) *n.* [< ?] 1. a sweetened dessert containing eggs, fruit, etc. 2. a soft, mushy food, of flour, cereal, etc., boiled or baked [Yorkshire *pudding*] 3. the dessert course in a meal, following the main dish 4. a kind of boiled sausage [black *pudding*] —**in the pudding club** [Slang] pregnant

puddle (pud''l) *n.* [< OE. *pudd*, a ditch] 1. a small pool of water, esp. dirty water 2. a thick mixture of clay with water —*vt.* **-dled, -dling** 1. to make muddy 2. to make a thick mixture of (wet clay and sand) 3. to treat (iron) by the puddling process —*vi.* to dabble in muddy water —**pud'dly** *adj.*

puddling *n.* the process of making wrought iron by heating and stirring it with oxidizing agents

pudendum (pyoo den'dəm) *n.*, *pl.* **-den'-da** [< L. *pudere*, to be ashamed] [*usually* *pl.*] the external human sex organs, esp. of the female

pudgy (puj′ē) *adj.* -ier, -iest [prob. < Scot. *pud*, belly] short and fat —**pudg′iness** *n.*

puerile (pyooər′il) *adj.* [< L. *puer*, boy] childish; silly; immature —**pu′eril′ity** (-ə ril′ə tē) *n.*

puerperal (pyoo ur′pər əl) *adj.* [< L. *puer*, boy + *parere*, to bear] of or connected with childbirth

puerperal fever septic poisoning occurring during childbirth: a term no longer used

puff (puf) *n.* [OE. [OE. *pyff*] 1. a short, sudden gust, as of wind, or an expulsion, as of breath 2. a drawing into the mouth of smoke from a cigarette, etc. 3. a swelling 4. a shell of light pastry filled with whipped cream, etc. 5. a soft roll of hair on the head 6. a soft pad for dabbing powder on the skin 7. exaggerated praise, as in a book review —*vi.* 1. to blow in puffs, as the wind 2. a) to give forth puffs of smoke, etc. b) to breathe rapidly 3. to fill, swell (*out* or *up*), as with air or pride 4. to take a puff or puffs on a cigarette, etc. —*vt.* 1. to blow, drive, etc, in or with a puff 2. to inflate; swell 3. to praise unduly 4. to smoke (a cigarette, etc.) —**puff′ily** *adv.* —**puff′iness** *n.* —**puff′y** *adj.*

puff adder a large, poisonous African snake which inflates its body when alarmed

puffball *n.* any of various round, white-fleshed fungi that burst at the touch when mature

puffed *adj.* 1. breathless; winded 2. swollen; puffy

puffin (puf′in) *n.* [< ?] a northern sea bird with a short neck, ducklike body, and brightly coloured beak

puff pastry a dough used for making a rich, flaky pastry for pies, pastries, etc.

puff-puff *n.* [echoic] a child's name for a train

pug (pug) *n.* [< ?] a small, short-haired dog with a wrinkled face, snub nose, and curled tail

pugilism (pyoo′jə liz′m) *n.* [< L. *pugil*, boxer] *same as* BOXING —**pu′gilist** *n.* —**pu′gilis′tic** *adj.*

pugnacious (pug nā′shəs) *adj.* [< L. *pugnare*, to fight] eager and ready to fight; quarrelsome —**pugna′ciously** *adv.* —**pugnac′ity** (-nas′ə tē) *n.*

pug nose a short, thick, turned-up nose —**pug′-nosed′** *adj.*

puissance (pwē′säns) *n.* in show-jumping, a competition testing a horse's ability to jump large obstacles

puissant (pyoo′i sənt) *adj.* [OFr.: see POWER] [Archaic] powerful; strong

puke (pyook) *n., vi., vt.* puked, puk′ing [< ?] [Slang] *same as* VOMIT

pukka (puk′ə) *adj.* [Hindi *pakkā*, ripe] [Anglo-Indian] 1. good or first-rate of its kind 2. genuine; real

pulchritude (pul′krə tyood′) *n.* [< L. *pulcher*, beautiful] physical beauty —**pul′chritu′dinous** *adj.*

pule (pyool) *vi.* puled, pul′ing [echoic] to whine or whimper, as a sick or fretful child

pull (pool) *vt.* [OE. *pullian*, to pluck] 1. to exert force or influence on so as to make move towards the source of the force 2. to pluck out (a tooth, etc.) 3. to draw apart; tear 4. to strain and injure [to *pull* a muscle] 5. [Colloq.] to restrain [to *pull* one's punches] 6. [Colloq.] to take out (a gun, etc.) 7. *Golf* to hit (the ball) so it goes to the left or, if left-handed, to the right 8. *Rowing* to work (an oar) by drawing it towards one —*vi.* 1. to exert force in dragging, tugging, etc. 2. to take a deep draught of a drink, etc. 3. to be capable of being pulled 4. to move or drive a vehicle (*away, ahead, out*, etc.) —*n.* 1. the act or force of pulling; specif., *a)* a dragging, tugging, attracting, etc. *b)* a drink, a puff on a cigarette, etc. *c)* a hard, steady effort 2. [Colloq.] *a)* influence or special advantage *b)* appeal —**pull apart** to find fault with —**pull down** 1. to tear down 2. to degrade; humble —**pull in** 1. to arrive 2. to draw in 3. to receive as payment 4. [Slang] to arrest —**pull off** [Colloq.] to accomplish —**pull oneself together** to regain one's poise, courage, etc. —**pull one's socks up** [Colloq.] to try harder —**pull one's weight** to do a fair share of a task —**pull out** 1. to depart 2. to withdraw 3. to escape from a responsibility, etc. 4. of vehicle, to move towards the centre of the road —**pull over** to drive (a vehicle) towards the kerb —**pull someone's leg** [Colloq.] to tease; make fun of; deceive good-humouredly —**pull through** to get over (an illness, etc.) —**pull up** 1. to uproot 2. to bring or come to a stop 3. to rebuke —**pull′er** *n.*

pullet (pool′it) *n.* [< L. *pullus*, chicken] a young hen, usually not more than a year old

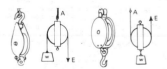

PULLEYS (A, anchor; E, energy; W, weight)

pulley (pool′ē) *n., pl.* -leys [< Gr. *polos*, axis] a small wheel with a grooved rim in which a rope or chain runs, as to raise a weight attached at one end by pulling on the other end

Pullman (pool′mən) *n.* [< G. M. *Pullman*] a railway carriage with private compartments or seats that can be made up into berths for sleeping

pullover (pool′ō′vər) *n.* a garment, esp.

a knitted sweater, put on by being pulled over the head

pulmonary (pul′mə nər ē) *adj.* [< L. *pulmo*, lung] of, like, or affecting the lungs

pulp (pulp) *n.* [< L. *pulpa*, flesh] 1. a soft, moist, formless mass 2. the soft, juicy part of a fruit 3. the soft pith of a plant stem 4. ground-up, moistened fibres of wood, rags, etc., from which paper is made 5. [Chiefly U.S.] a magazine printed on inferior paper, featuring shocking stories about sex, crime, etc. —*vt.* to reduce to pulp —*vi.* to become pulp —**pulp′ily** *adv.* —**pulp′iness** *n.* —**pulp′y** *adj.*

pulpit (pool′pit) *n.* [L. *pulpitum*, a stage] 1. a raised platform from which a clergyman preaches in a church 2. preachers as a group

pulpwood (pulp′wood′) *n.* 1. soft wood for making paper 2. wood ground to pulp for paper

pulsar (pul′sər) *n.* [PULS(E[1]) + -AR] any of several small heavenly objects in the Milky Way that emit radio pulses

pulsate (pul sāt′) *vi.* -sat′ed, -sat′ing [< L. *pulsare*, to beat] 1. to beat or throb rhythmically, as the heart 2. to vibrate; quiver —**pulsa′tion** *n.* —**pulsa′tor** *n.*

pulse[1] (puls) *n.* [< L. *pellere*, to beat] 1. the regular beating in the arteries, caused by the contractions of the heart 2. any regular beat 3. the underlying feelings of a group, the public, etc. 4. a brief surge of electric current —*vi.* **pulsed, puls′ing** to pulsate

pulse[2] *n.* [< L. *puls*, a pottage] the edible seeds of peas, beans, lentils, etc.

pulverize (pul′və rīz′) *vt.* -ized′, -iz′ing [< L. *pulvis*, dust] 1. to crush, grind, etc. into a powder or dust 2. to demolish —*vi.* to be crushed into a powder or dust —**pul′veriza′tion** *n.* —**pul′veriz′er** *n.*

puma (pyoo′mə) *n.* [SAmInd.] a large tawny-brown animal of the cat family

pumice (pum′is) *n.* [< L. *pumex*] a light, porous, volcanic rock used to scour, smooth, and polish: also **pumice stone**

pummel (pum′l) *vt.* -melled, -melling [< POMMEL] to beat or hit with repeated blows, esp. with the fist

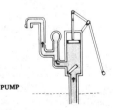

PUMP

pump[1] (pump) *n.* [echoic] any of various machines that force a liquid or gas into, or draw it out of, something —*vt.* 1.

to move (fluids) with a pump 2. to remove water, etc. from 3. to drive air into, as with a pump 4. to force in, draw out, move up and down, etc. like a pump 5. [Colloq.] to question closely and persistently —*vi.* 1. to work a pump 2. to move or go up and down like a pump handle —**pump up** to inflate the tyre of a bicycle, motor car, etc.

pump[2] *n.* [< ?] 1. a low-cut, low-heeled shoe worn esp. for dancing 2. a rubber-soled shoe used in tennis, etc.; plimsoll

pumpernickel (poom′pər nik′′l) *n.* [G.] a coarse, dark, sour bread made of unsifted rye

pumpkin (pump′kin) *n.* [< Gr. *pepōn*, ripe] 1. a large, edible, round, orange-yellow fruit with many seeds 2. the climbing plant on which it grows

pun (pun) *n.* [< ?] the humorous use of words that have the same sound, but have different meanings —*vi.* **punned, pun′ning** to make puns

Punch (punch) [< PUNCHINELLO] the hero of the puppet show **Punch and Judy**, a humpbacked figure with a hooked nose —**pleased as Punch** greatly pleased

punch[1] (punch) *n.* [< L. *pungere*, to prick] a tool driven or pressed against a surface that is to be pierced, shaped, or stamped —*vt.* 1. to pierce, stamp, etc. with a punch 2. to make (a hole, etc.) with a punch

punch[2] *vt.* [ME. *punchen*] to strike with the fist —*n.* 1. a thrusting blow with the fist 2. [Colloq.] effective force; vigour —**pull one's punches** [Colloq.] to deliver blows, criticisms, etc. intended to have little effect

punch[3] *n.* [< Hindi *pāc*, five] a sweet drink of fruit juices, etc., often mixed with wine or spirits, and served in cups from a large bowl (**punch bowl**)

punch ball a stuffed or inflated leather bag hung up in order to be punched for exercise or practice

punch card a card with holes or notches positioned in it, esp. by a key punch for data processing: also **punched card**

punch-drunk *adj.* dazed, unsteady in gait, etc., as because of many blows to the head in boxing

punchinello (pun′chə nel′ō) *n., pl.* -los [< a character in a Neapolitan puppet play] a buffoon; clown

punch line the line carrying the point of a joke

punch-up *n.* [Slang] a fight or violent argument

punchy *adj.* -ier, -iest [Colloq.] forceful; vigorous

punctilio (puŋk til′ē ō′) *n., pl.* -os′ [< L. *punctum*, point] a point of conduct, etc.

punctilious (puŋk til′ē əs) *adj.* 1. very careful about every detail of behaviour 2. very exact

punctual (puŋk′tyoo wəl) *adj.* [< L.

punctus, a point] on time; prompt **—punc´-tual´ity** (-wal´ə tē) *n.*

punctuate (puŋk´tyoo wāt´) *vt.* **-at´ed, -at´ing** [< L. *punctus,* a point] **1.** to insert punctuation marks in **2.** to break in on here and there *[punctuated* with applause *]* **3.** to emphasize

punctuation (puŋk´tyoo wā´shən) *n.* **1.** the use of standardized marks in writing and printing to make meaning clearer **2.** a punctuation mark or marks

punctuation mark any of the marks used in punctuation, as a full stop or comma

puncture (puŋk´chər) *n.* [< L. *pungere,* pierce] **1.** a perforating or piercing **2.** a hole made by a sharp point **—vt., vi. -tured, -turing** to perforate or pierce, as with a sharp point

pundit (pun´dit) *n.* [< Sans.] **1.** an acknowledged authority on some subject **2.** in India, a learned Brahman

pungent (pun´jənt) *adj.* [< L. *pungere,* to prick] **1.** producing a sharp sensation of taste or smell **2.** sharp to the mind; poignant **3.** biting **—pun´gency** *n.*

punish (pun´ish) *vt.* [< L. *punire,* to punish] **1.** to cause to undergo pain, loss, or suffering, as for a crime **2.** to impose a penalty for (an offence) **3.** to treat harshly **—pun´ishabil´ity** *n.* **—pun´-ishable** *adj.* **—pun´isher** *n.*

punishment *n.* **1.** a punishing or being punished **2.** the penalty imposed **3.** harsh treatment

punitive (pyoo´nə tiv) *adj.* inflicting or concerned with punishment **—pu´nitively** *adv.*

punk¹ (puŋk) *n.* [var. of SPUNK] any substance, as decayed wood, that smoulders when ignited, used as tinder

punk² *n.* [< ?] [Slang] **1.** anyone regarded as inexperienced, insignificant, etc. **2.** a follower of punk rock **3.** a young hoodlum **—adj.** [Slang] **1.** poor or bad in quality **2.** designating a form of rock music characterized by strong rhythm

punkah, punka (puŋ´kə) *n.* [Hindi *pankhā*] in India, a large, swinging fan hung from the ceiling

punnet (pun´it) *n.* [< ?] a small, shallow basket for fruit, esp. strawberries

punster (pun´stər) *n.* a person who is fond of making puns

punt¹ (punt) *n.* [< ?] *Sport* a kick in which the ball is dropped from the hands and then kicked before it strikes the ground **—vt., vi.** to kick (a ball) in this way

punt² *n.* [see PONTOON²] a flat-bottomed boat with square ends, usually propelled by a long pole **—vt., vi.** to propel (a boat) with a long pole **—punt´er** *n.*

punt³ *vi.* [< L. *punctum,* a point] **1.** in certain card games, to bet against the banker **2.** to gamble **—punt´er** *n.*

puny (pyoo´nē) *adj.* **-nier, -niest** [< OFr. *puis,* after + *né,* born] of inferior size, strength, etc. **—pu´niness** *n.*

pup (pup) *n.* **1.** a young dog; puppy **2.** a young seal, whale, etc. **—vi. pupped, pup´-ping** to give birth to pups

PUPA

pupa (pyoo´pə) *n., pl.* **-pae** (-pē), **-pas** [< L., a doll] an insect in the stage between the larval and adult forms **—pu´-pal** *adj.*

pupil¹ (pyoo´p'l) *n.* [< L. *pupillus,* ward] a person being taught by a teacher or tutor, as in a school **—pu´pillage, pu´pil-age** *n.*

pupil² *n.* [< L. *pupilla,* one's figure reflected in another's eye] the contractile circular opening in the centre of the iris of the eye

puppet (pup´it) *n.* [< L. *pupa,* a doll] **1.** a small, usually jointed figure, as of a human being, moved with the hands or by strings, usually in a **puppet show 2.** a person whose actions, ideas, etc. are controlled by another **—pup´petry** *n.*

puppeteer (pup´itēr´) *n.* a person who operates or designs puppets or produces puppet shows

puppet state an apparently independent country that, in reality, is controlled by another country

puppy (pup´ē) *n., pl.* **-pies** [see PUPPET] **1.** a young dog **2.** a conceited, or silly young man **—pup´pyish** *adj.*

puppy fat the chubbiness associated with adolescence that usually disappears in adulthood

purblind (pur´blīnd´) *adj.* [ME. *pur blind,* quite blind] **1.** partly blind **2.** slow in understanding

purchase (pur´chəs) *vt.* **-chased, -chasing** [< OFr. *pour,* for + *chacier,* to chase] **1.** to buy **2.** to get at a cost, as of suffering **—n. 1.** anything obtained by buying **2.** a buying **3.** a fast hold applied to move something mechanically or to keep from slipping **—pur´chasable** *adj.* **—pur´chaser** *n.*

purdah (pur´də) *n.* the practice of hiding women from strangers, esp. behind a curtain or veil

pure (pyooər) *adj.* [< L. *purus*] **1.** free from any adulterant or anything harmful **2.** simple; mere *[pure luck]* **3.** utter; absolute **4.** free from defects **5.** free from sin or guilt **6.** virgin or chaste **7.** of unmixed stock **8.** abstract or theoretical *[pure physics]* **—pure´ly** *adv.*

purebred *adj.* belonging to a recognized breed through generations of unmixed descent

purée (pyooər´ā) *n.* [< L. *purus,* pure] food prepared by putting cooked vegetables, fruits, etc. through a sieve or liquidizer **—vt. -réed, -réeing** to make a purée of Also sp. **puree**

purgative (pur´gə tiv) *adj.* **1.** that purges

2. causing bowel movement —*n.* a substance that purges; specif., a cathartic

purgatory (pur′gə tər ē) *n., pl.* **-ries** [see ff.] **1.** [*often* P-] in R.C. and other Christian doctrine, a state or place in which those who have died in the grace of God expiate their sins **2.** any state or place of temporary punishment

purge (purj) *vt.* **purged, purg′ing** [< L. *purus,* clean + *agere,* to do] **1.** to cleanse of impurities, etc. **2.** to cleanse of guilt, sin, etc. **3.** to remove by cleansing **4.** to rid (a nation, party, etc.) of individuals regarded as disloyal **5.** *Med.* to empty (the bowels) —*vi.* to become clean, clear, or pure —*n.* **1.** a purging **2.** that which purges; esp., a cathartic —**purga′tion** *n.* —**purg′er** *n.*

purify (pyoor′i fī′) *vt.* **-fied′, -fy′ing** [< L. *purus,* pure + *facere,* make] **1.** to rid of impurities, etc. **2.** to free from guilt, sin, etc. —**pu′rifica′tion** *n.* —**pu′rifica′-tory** *adj.*

purism (pyoor′iz′m) *n.* strict observance of precise usage or style, as in grammar or art —**pur′ist** *n.* —**puris′tic** *adj.*

Puritan (pyoor′i t'n) *n.* [see PURITY] **1.** a member of a Protestant group who, in the 16th and 17th centuries, wanted to make the Church of England simpler in its services **2.** [p-] a person regarded as excessively strict in morals and religion —*adj.* **1.** of the Puritans **2.** [p-] puritanical —**Pu′ritanism, pu′ritanism** *n.*

puritanical (pyoor′i tan′i k'l) *adj.* **1.** excessively strict in morals and religion **2.** [P-] of the Puritans —**pu′ritan′ically** *adv.*

purity (pyoor′ə tē) *n.* [< L. *purus,* pure] a being pure; specif., *a)* freedom from adulterating matter *b)* cleanness *c)* innocence or chastity

purl[1] (purl) *vi.* [< ?] to move in ripples or with a murmuring sound

purl[2] *vt., vi.* [< ?] **1.** to edge (lace) with small loops **2.** to invert (stitches) in knitting —*n.* **1.** a chain of loops on the edge of lace **2.** an inversion of knitting stitches

purlieu (purl′yōō) *n.* [< OFr. *pur-,* through + *aler,* to go] **1.** orig., an outlying part of a royal forest **2.** a place one visits often **3.** [*pl.*] bounds; limits **4.** an outlying part

purlin, purline (pur′lin) *n.* [< ?] a horizontal timber supporting rafters of a roof

purloin (pur loin′) *vt., vi.* [< OFr. *pur-,* for + *loin,* far] to steal; filch —**purloin′-er** *n.*

purple (pur′p'l) *n.* [< Gr. *porphyra,* shellfish yielding purple dye] **1.** a dark colour that is a blend of red and blue **2.** crimson cloth or clothing, esp. as an emblem of royalty or high rank —*adj.* **1.** of the colour purple **2.** imperial **3.** flowery [*purple* prose] —*vt., vi.* **-pled, -pling** to make or become purple —**born to** (or **in) the purple** of royal or high birth

purple heart [Colloq.] a heart-shaped tablet consisting mainly of amphetamine

purport (pər pôrt′; *for n.* pur′pôrt) *vt.* [< OFr. *por-,* forth + *porter,* to bear] **1.** to profess or claim as its meaning **2.** to give the appearance, often falsely, of being, intending, etc. —*n.* meaning; main idea —**purport′ed** *adj.*

purpose (pur′pəs) *n.* [< OFr. *proposer,* to propose] **1.** the reason or use for something **2.** what one plans to get or do; aim **3.** determination —*vt., vi.* **-posed, -posing** to plan, intend, or resolve —**on purpose** intentionally —**to little** (or **no) purpose** with little or no effect —**to the purpose** apt; relevant —**pur′poseful** *adj.* —**pur′poseless** *adj.*

purpose-built *adj.* made to serve a specific purpose

purposely *adv.* intentionally; deliberately

purposive (pur′pə siv) *adj.* **1.** serving a purpose **2.** having purpose —**pur′posively** *adv.*

purr (pur) *n.* [echoic] a low, vibratory sound made by a cat when it seems to be pleased —*vi., vt.* to make, or express by, such a sound

purse (purs) *n.* [< Gr. *brysa,* a hide] **1.** a small pouch for carrying money **2.** finances; money **3.** a sum of money given as a present or prize **4.** [U.S.] a handbag —*vt.* **pursed, purs′ing** to pucker (one's lips, etc.)

purser (pur′sər) *n.* [ME., purse bearer] a ship's officer in charge of accounts, freight, tickets, etc.

purse strings a drawstring for certain purses —**hold the purse strings** to be in control of the money

purslane (purs′lin) *n.* [< L. *portulaca*] an annual plant used as a potherb and in salads

pursuance (pər syoo′əns) *n.* a pursuing, or carrying out, as of a project, plan, etc.

pursuant *adj.* [Now Rare] pursuing —**pursuant to 1.** in accordance with **2.** following upon

pursue (pər syoo′) *vt.* **-sued′, -su′ing** [< L. *pro-,* forth + *sequi,* follow] **1.** to follow in order to overtake, capture, etc. **2.** to follow (a specified course, action, etc.) **3.** to strive for; seek after **4.** to have as one's occupation, profession, or study **5.** to keep on harassing —*vi.* **1.** to chase **2.** to go on; continue —**pursu′er** *n.*

pursuit (pər syoot′) *n.* **1.** a pursuing **2.** a career, interest, etc. to which one devotes oneself

pursuivant (pur′si vənt) *n.* [see PURSUE] in Britain, an officer ranking below a herald

pursy[1] (pur′sē) *adj.* **-sier, -siest** [< L. *pulsare,* to beat] **1.** short-winded, esp. from being too fat **2.** fat —**pur′siness** *n.*

pursy[2] *adj.* **-sier, -siest** pursed; puckered

purulent (pyoor′oo lənt) *adj.* [< L. *pus, pus*] of, like, or discharging pus —**pu′rulence** *n.*

purvey (pər vā′) *vt.* [see PROVIDE] to supply (esp. food or provisions) —**purvey′-or** *n.*

purview (pur′vyōō) *n.* [see PROVIDE] 1. extent of control, activity, concern, etc. 2. the scope of an act or bill

pus (pus) *n.* [L.] the yellowish liquid matter produced in infections, consisting of bacteria, white corpuscles, etc.

push (poosh) *vt.* [< L. *pulsare*, to beat] 1. a) to exert force against, esp. so as to move b) to move in this way 2. to urge on; impel 3. to bring into a critical state; press [be *pushed* for time] 4. [Colloq.] to urge or promote the use, sale, etc. of 5. [Colloq.] to be close to [*pushing* sixty years] —*vi.* 1. to press against a thing so as to move it 2. to try hard to advance, succeed, etc. 3. to move forwards against opposition —*n.* 1. a pushing 2. a vigorous effort, campaign, etc. 3. pressure of circumstances 4. [Colloq.] enterprise; drive —**push off** [Colloq.] to set out; depart —**push on** to proceed —**the push** [Colloq.] dismissal from employment

push bike [Colloq.] a pedal cycle

push button a small knob that is pushed to cause something to operate —**push′-but′ton** *adj.*

push chair a light, chairlike baby carriage

pusher *n.* [Slang] a person peddling drugs illegally

pushing *adj.* 1. aggressive 2. forward

pushover *n.* [Slang] 1. anything very easy to do 2. a person, etc. easily persuaded, seduced, etc.

push-start *n.* a way of starting a car engine by pushing it to turn the engine over —*vt.* -**start′ed, -start′ing** to start a motor car using this method

pushy *adj.* -ier, -iest [Colloq.] annoyingly aggressive and persistent

pusillanimous (pyōō′sə lan′ə məs) *adj.* [< L. *pusillus*, tiny + *animus*, the mind] timid or cowardly —**pu′sillanim′ity** (-ə nim′ə tē) *n.*

puss[1] (poos) *n.* [< ?] 1. a cat: pet name 2. a girl: term of affection

puss[2] *n.* [< ?] [Slang] 1. the face 2. the mouth

pussy[1] (pus′ē) *adj.* -sier, -siest containing or like pus

pussy[2] (poos′ē) *n., pl.* **puss′ies** [dim. of PUSS[1]] 1. a cat, esp. a kitten : also **puss′y-cat**[2] [Vulg. Slang] the female genitals

pussyfoot *vi.* [Chiefly U.S. Colloq.] 1. to move with stealth 2. to avoid committing oneself

pussy willow any of several willows bearing silvery, velvety catkins before the leaves appear

pustulate (pus′tyoo lāt′) *vt., vi.* -lat′ed, -lat′ing [< L. *pustula*, a pustule] to form into pustules

pustule (pus′tyool) *n.* [L. *pustula*] a small swelling in the skin, containing pus

put (poot) *vt.* put, put′ting [< OE. *potian*, to push] 1. to make be in a specified place, condition, relation, etc.; place [put her at ease] 2. to make undergo; subject 3. to impose (a burden, tax, etc.) 4. to bring about [put a stop to] 5. to attribute [put the blame on him] 6. to express; state 7. present for consideration, etc. [put the question] 8. to estimate as being (with *at*) [to put the cost at £25] 9. a) to bet (money) on b) to invest (money) in or into 10. a) to drive or send by a blow or thrust b) to throw with an overhand thrust from the shoulder [put the shot] —*vi.* to go (in, out, back, etc.) —*n.* a cast or thrust —*adj.* [Colloq.] fixed [stay put] —**put about** 1. to turn from one tack or direction to another 2. to make widely known —**put across** [Colloq.] to make understood or accepted —**put aside** (or **by**) to keep for later —**put away** 1. *same as* PUT ASIDE 2. to tidy up 3. [Colloq.] a) to put in a jail, etc. b) to consume (food or drink) —**put down** 1. to crush; repress 2. to write down; record 3. to attribute (to) 4. to consider as; classify 5. to kill (a pet) to prevent suffering 6. [Slang] to belittle or humiliate —**put in** 1. to enter a port or haven 2. to enter (a claim, etc.) 3. [Colloq.] to spend (time) —**put in for** to apply for —**put it** (or **something**) **across on someone** [Colloq.] to deceive; trick —**put off** 1. to delay 2. to evade 3. to cause to lose interest in or enjoyment of —**put on** 1. to clothe or cover oneself with 2. to take on; add 3. to assume or pretend 4. to apply (a brake, etc.) 5. to stage (a play) —**put out** 1. to expel 2. to extinguish (a fire or light) 3. to disconcert or vex 4. to inconvenience 5. *Sports* to cause (a batsman) to be out —**put over** [Colloq.] *same as* PUT ACROSS —**put through** 1. to carry out successfully 2. to connect (someone) by telephone with someone else —**put under** to render unconscious —**put up** 1. to erect; build 2. to lodge, or provide lodgings for 3. to offer, as for consideration, sale, etc. 4. to carry on [to put up a struggle] 5. to advance or provide (money) 6. to offer as a candidate 7. [Colloq.] to incite (a person) *to* some action —**put upon** to impose on —**put up with** to tolerate

putative (pyōōt′ə tiv) *adj.* [< L. *putare*, suppose] reputed; supposed —**pu′tatively** *adv.*

put-down (poot′doun′) *n.* [Slang] a crushing retort

putrefy (pyōō′trə fī′) *vt., vi.* -fied′, -fy′-ing [< L. *putris*, putrid + *facere*, make] to make or become putrid —**pu′trefac′-tion** *n.*

putrescent (pyōō tres′ənt) *adj.* rotting; putrefying —**putres′cence** *n.*

putrid (pyōō′trid) *adj.* [< L. *putrere*, be rotten] 1. rotten and smelling bad 2. corrupt or depraved 3. [Colloq.] very unpleasant —**putrid′ity** *n.* —**pu′tridly** *adv.*

‡**Putsch** (pooch) *n.* [G.] an attempted uprising

putt (put) *n.* [< PUT] *Golf* a light stroke

made on the putting green in trying to put the ball into the hole —*vt., vi.* to hit (the ball) thus

PUTTEES

puttee (put'ē) *n.* [< Sans. *patta*, a strip of cloth] a legging or a cloth strip wound spirally to cover the leg from ankle to knee

putter *n.* *Golf* a short, straight-faced club used in putting

putting green *Golf* the area of smooth, closely mowed turf in which the hole is sunk

putt-putt (put'put') *n.* [echoic] the chugging sounds of a motorboat engine, etc.

putty (put'ē) *n.* [< Fr. *potée*, lit., potful] a soft, plastic mixture of powdered chalk and linseed oil, used to hold glass panes in place, etc. —*vt.* **-tied, -tying** to cement, fill, etc. with putty

put-up (poot'up') *adj.* [Colloq.] dishonestly or craftily prearranged [a put-up job]

puzzle (puz''l) *vt.* **-zled, -zling** [< ?] to perplex; bewilder —*vi.* 1. to be perplexed, etc. 2. to exercise one's mind, as on a problem —*n.* 1. a puzzling problem, etc. 2. a toy or problem to test skill or ingenuity —**puzzle out** to solve by deep thought —**puzzle over** to give deep thought to —**puz'zlement** *n.* —**puz'zler** *n.*

P.V.C. Poly Vinyl Chloride

PW policewoman

pyaemia (pī ē'mē ə) *n.* [see PYO- & -AEMIA] blood poisoning caused by pus-producing organisms

pye-dog (pī'dog') *n.* [< *pariah dog*] an undomesticated Asian dog, often roaming in packs

Pygmy (pig'mē) *n., pl.* **-mies** [< Gr. *pygmaios*, of the length of the forearm] 1. a member of any of several African and Asian peoples of small stature 2. [p-] any abnormally undersized or insignificant person —*adj.* 1. of Pygmies 2. [p-] very small

pyjamas (pə jäm'əz) *n.pl.* [< Per. *pai*, leg + *jāma*, garment] a loosely fitting sleeping suit consisting of jacket and trousers

pylon (pī'lən) *n.* [Gr. *pylōn*, gateway] a towerlike structure, as for supporting electric lines

pyo- [< Gr.] *a combining form meaning* pus

pyorrhoea (pī'ə rē'ə) *n.* [see PYO- & -RRHOEA] a discharge of pus; specif., short for PYORRHOEA ALVEOLARIS

pyorrhoea alveolaris (al vē'ə lär'is) an infection of the gums and tooth sockets, in which pus forms and the teeth become loose

EGYPTIAN PYRAMID

pyramid (pir'ə mid) *n.* [Gr. *pyramis*] 1. any huge structure with a square base and four sloping, triangular sides meeting at the top, as those built in ancient Egypt 2. *Geom.* a solid figure the base of which is a polygon whose sides are the bases of triangular surfaces meeting at a common vertex —**pyramidal** (pi ram'ə d'l) *adj.* —**pyram'idally** *adv.*

pyramid selling a method of selling in which the right to sell certain goods is purchased by people who then sell this right to other people

pyre (pīər) *n.* [< Gr. *pyr*, a fire] a pile of wood for burning a corpse in a funeral rite

pyrethrum (pī rē'thrəm) *n.* [< Gr. *pyrethron*, feverfew] 1. a chrysanthemum with white, red, or purple flowers 2. an insecticide made from their dried flowers

pyretic (pī ret'ik) *adj.* [< Gr. *pyretos*, fever] of or causing fever

Pyrex (pī'reks) [arbitrary coinage] *Trademark* a heat-resistant glassware for cooking, etc.

pyrite (pī'rīt) *n., pl.* **pyrites** (pī rīt'ēz) [< Gr. *pyritēs*, flint] iron sulphide, an important ore of sulphur

pyrites (pī rīt'ēz) *n.* any of various native metallic sulphides, as pyrite

pyro- [< Gr.] *a combining form meaning* fire, heat

pyrography (pī rog'rə fē) *n.* [PYRO- + -GRAPHY] the art of burning designs on wood or leather with heated tools —**py'rograph'ic** (-rō graf'ik) *adj.*

pyromania (pī'rō mā'nē ə) *n.* [see PYRO- & -MANIA] an uncontrollable desire to start destructive fires —**py'roma'niac'** *n., adj.*

pyrotechnics (pī'rō tek'niks) *n.pl* [< PYRO- & Gr. *technē*, art] 1. [with sing. v.] the art of making and using fireworks 2. a display of fireworks 3. a dazzling display, as of eloquence —**py'rotech'nic** *adj.*

Pyrrhic victory (pir'ik) [< *Pyrrhus*, king of Epirus] a victory that is too costly

Pythagoras' Theorem (pī thag'ər əs) [< *Pythagoras*] the theorem that the square on the hypotenuse of a right-angled triangle is equal to the sum of the squares on the other two sides

python (pī'thən) *n.* [< Gr. *Pythōn*, a serpent slain by Apollo] any of a group of large, nonpoisonous snakes of Asia and Africa that crush their prey to death

pythoness (pī'thə nis) *n.* [< Gr. *Pythō*, Delphi] a priestess of Apollo at Delphi

pyx (piks) *n.* [< Gr. *pyxis*, a box] the container in which the consecrated wafer of the Eucharist is kept or carried

Q, q (kyōō) *n., pl.* **Q's, q's** the seventeenth
letter of the English alphabet
Q *Chess* queen
Q. 1. Quebec 2. Queen 3. Question
q. 1.quart 2.quarter 3.quarto 4.question
Q.A.R.A.N.C. Queen Alexandra's Royal
Army Nursing Corps
Q.A.R.N.N.S. Queen Alexandra's Royal
Naval Nursing Service
Q.B. Queen's Bench
Q-boat *n.* [< *Q,* Query + BOAT] a
boat with concealed guns used in anti-
submarine warfare in World War I
Q.C. Queen's Counsel
Q.E.D. [L. *quod erat demonstrandum*]
which was to be proved
Q'ld. Queensland
QM, Q.M. Quartermaster
Q.M.G. Quartermaster General
qr. *pl.* **qrs.** 1. quarter 2. quire
qt. 1. quart 2. quantity
Q.T., q.t. [Slang] quiet —**on the Q.T.**
(or **q.t.**) in secret
qua (kwā) *adv.* [L. < *qui,* who] in the
function or capacity of [the Queen *qua*
Head of the Commonwealth]
quack[1] (kwak) *vi.* [echoic] to utter the
sound of a duck, or a sound like it —*n.*
the sound made by it
quack[2] *n.* [< MDu. *quacken,* to brag]
1. a person who practises medicine without
having been trained, licensed, etc. 2. any
person who pretends to have knowledge
or skill that he does not have; charlatan
—*adj.* fraudulent —**quack'ery** *n.*
quad (kwod) *n.* same as: 1. QUADRANGLE
(of a college). 2. QUADRUPLET
Quadragesima (kwod'rə jes'i mə) *n.* [<
L. *quadragesimus,* fortieth] the first
Sunday in Lent
quadrangle (kwod'raŋ'g'l) *n.* [see
QUADRI- & ANGLE[1]] 1. a plane figure with
four angles and four sides 2. *a)* an area
surrounded on four sides by buildings *b)*
the buildings themselves —**quadran'gular**
adj.
quadrant (kwod'rənt) *n.* [< L. *quadrans,*
fourth part] 1. an arc of 90° 2. a quarter
section of a circle 3. an instrument for
measuring altitudes or angular elevations
in astronomy and navigation
quadraphonic (kwod'rə fon'ik) *adj.* [<
L. *quadra,* a square + PHONIC] using
four channels to record and reproduce
sounds
quadrate (kwo drāt'; *for adj.,* kwod'rət)
adj. [< L. *quadrare,* make square] square
or nearly square —*vi., vt.* **-rat'ed, -rat'-**
ing to square; agree or cause to agree (*with*)
quadratic (kwod rat'ik) *adj.* [< prec.]

Algebra involving a quantity or quantities
that are squared but none that are raised
to a higher power —*n. Algebra* a quadratic
term or equation —**quadrat'ically** *adv.*
quadratic equation *Algebra* an
equation in which the second power, or
square, is the highest to which the unknown
quantity is raised
quadrature (kwod'rə chər) *n.* [see
QUADRATE] 1. the act of squaring 2.
the determining of the dimensions of a
square equal in area to a given surface
3. *Astron.* the relative position of two
heavenly bodies when 90° distant from
each other
quadrennial (kwod ren'ē əl) *adj.* [< ff.
+ L. *annus,* a year] 1. lasting four years
2. occurring once every four years
quadri- [L. < *quattuor,* four] *a combining
form meaning* four times, fourfold

QUADRILATERALS

quadrilateral (kwod'rə lat'ər əl) *adj.* [see
QUADRI- & LATERAL] four-sided —*n.*
Geom. a plane figure having four sides
and four angles
quadrille (kwə dril') *n.* [Fr.] 1. a square
dance performed by four couples 2. music
for this dance
quadrillion (kwod ril'yən) *n.* [see QUADRI-
+ (MI)LLION] 1. in Great Britain and
Germany, the number represented by 1
followed by 24 zeros 2. in the U.S. and
France, the number represented by 1
followed by 15 zeros
quadriplegia (kwod'rə plē'jē ə) *n.* [see
QUADRI- & Gr. *plēgē,* a stroke] paralysis
of the body from the neck down —**quad'ri-**
ple'gic *adj., n.*
quadrivalent (kwod'rə vā'lənt) *adj.*
having four valences
quadruped (kwod'roo ped') *n.* [< L.
quadru-, four + *pes,* foot] an animal,
esp. a mammal, with four feet
quadruple (kwod'roo p'l) *vt., vi.* **-pled,**
-pling [< L. *quadru-,* four + *-plus,* -fold]
to make or become four times as much
or as many —*adj.* 1. four times as much
or as many 2. consisting of four 3.
Music having four beats to the bar —*n.*
an amount four times as much or as many
quadruplet (kwod'roo plit) *n.* [< prec.]
any of four offspring born at a single birth

quadruplicate (kwo drōō′plə kāt′; *for adj., usually* -kət) *vt.* **-cat′ed, -cat′ing** [< L. *quadru-*, four + *plicare*, to fold] to make four copies of —*adj.* **1.** fourfold **2.** designating the fourth of identical copies —**in quadruplicate** in four identical copies

quaestor (kwēs′tər) *n.* [L. < *quaerere*, inquire] in ancient Rome, **1.** orig., a judge in certain criminal cases **2.** later, any of certain state treasurers

quaff (kwof, kwäf) *vt., vi.* [< ?] to drink deeply in a hearty or thirsty way

quagga (kwag′ə) *n.* [Afrik.] an extinct wild ass of Africa

quagmire (kwag′mīr′) *n.* [< *quag*, bog + MIRE] wet, boggy ground, yielding under the feet

quail¹ (kwāl) *vi.* [< ?] to draw back in fear; cower

quail² *n.* [< OFr.: echoic] a small game bird resembling the partridge

quaint (kwānt) *adj.* [< L. *cognitus*, known] **1.** unusual or old-fashioned in a pleasing way **2.** fanciful; whimsical

quake (kwāk) *vi.* quaked, quak′ing [OE. *cwacian*] **1.** to tremble or shake **2.** to shudder or shiver, as from fear —*n.* **1.** a shaking or tremor **2.** an earthquake

Quaker (kwāk′ər) *n.* [< founder's admonition to "quake" at the word of the Lord] a member of the Society of Friends —**Quak′erism** *n.*

qualification (kwol′ə fi kā′shən) *n.* **1.** a qualifying or being qualified **2.** any skill, experience, etc. that fits a person for a position **3.** a condition that must be met, in order to be eligible **4.** a modification or restriction

qualified (kwol′ə fīd′) *adj.* **1.** having the necessary qualities; competent **2.** limited; modified [*qualified* approval] **3.** having met requirements set

qualify (kwol′ə fī′) *vt.* **-fied′, -fy′ing** [< L. *qualis*, of what kind + *facere*, make] **1.** to make fit for an office, position, etc. **2.** to modify; limit **3.** to make legally capable; license **4.** *Gram.* to modify the meaning of (a word) **5.** to describe (*as*) —*vi.* to be or become competent, eligible, etc. —**qual′ifi′able** *adj.* —**qual′ifi′er** *n.*

qualitative (kwol′ə tə tiv) *adj.* having to do with quality or qualities —**qual′itatively** *adv.*

qualitative analysis the branch of chemistry dealing with the determination of the elements of a mixture

quality (kwol′ə tē) *n., pl.* **-ties** [< L. *qualis*, of what kind] **1.** a characteristic; attribute **2.** basic nature; character **3.** degree of excellence **4.** excellence; superiority **5.** [Obs.] *a*) high social position *b*) people of such position

quality control a system for maintaining desired standards in a product, esp. by inspecting samples

qualm (kwäm) *n.* [OE. *cwealm*, disaster] **1.** a sudden feeling of faintness or nausea **2.** a sudden feeling of uneasiness or doubt; misgiving **3.** a twinge of conscience

quandary (kwon′dər ē) *n., pl.* **-ries** [< ?] a state of perplexity; dilemma

quango (kwaŋ′gō) *n.* [*qu(asi)* -*a(utonomous)* *n(ational)* or *n(on)* *g(overnment)* *o(rganization)*] a body set up by, and receiving financial support from, the government, but not controlled by it

quantify (kwon′tə fī′) *vt.* **-fied′, -fy′ing** [< L. *quantus*, how much + *facere*, make] to determine or express the quantity of; measure —**quan′tifica′tion** *n.*

quantitative (kwon′ti tə tiv) *adj.* **1.** having to do with quantity **2.** capable of being measured

quantitative analysis the branch of chemistry dealing with the measurement of the amounts or percentages of the components of a mixture

quantity (kwon′tə tē) *n., pl.* **-ties** [< L. *quantus*, how much] **1.** an amount; portion **2.** any bulk, weight, or number not definitely specified **3.** [*also pl.*] a great amount **4.** that property of anything which can be measured **5.** the relative length of a vowel, musical tone, etc. **6.** *Math. a)* a thing that has the property of being measurable *b)* a number or symbol expressing a quantity

quantity surveyor a person who estimates the costs of materials and labour for builders

quantum (kwon′təm) *n., pl.* **-ta** [L., how much] *Physics* an (or the) elemental unit, as of energy: the **quantum theory** states that energy is absorbed or radiated discontinuously, in quanta

quarantine (kwor′ən tēn′) *n.* [< L. *quadraginta*, forty] **1.** the period, orig. 40 days, during which a vessel suspected of carrying contagious disease is detained in a port in isolation **2.** any isolation or restriction on travel to keep contagious diseases, insect pests, etc. from spreading **3.** the state of being quarantined —*vt.* **-tined′, -tin′ing** to place under quarantine

quark (kwärk) *n.* [orig. a word in *Finnegans Wake*] any of three proposed particles thought of as the building blocks of baryons and mesons

quarrel (kwor′əl) *n.* [< L. *queri*, complain] **1.** a dispute, esp. one marked by anger and resentment **2.** a cause for dispute **3.** a breaking up of friendly relations —*vi.* **-relled, -relling** **1.** to find fault **2.** to dispute heatedly **3.** to have a breach in friendship

quarrelsome *adj.* inclined to quarrel

quarry¹ (kwor′ē) *n., pl.* **-ries** [< OFr. *curer*, eviscerate] **1.** an animal that is being hunted **2.** anything pursued

quarry² *n., pl.* **-ries** [< L. *quadrare*, to square] a place where building stone, marble, or slate is excavated —*vt.* **-ried, -rying** to excavate from a quarry

quarry tile a flooring tile that is unglazed

quart (kwôrt) *n.* [< L. *quartus*, fourth] a liquid measure, equal to ¹/₄ gallon (1.136 litres) —**put** (or **pour**) **a quart into a pint pot** to attempt to perform the impossible

quarter (kwôr′tər) *n.* [< L. *quartus*, fourth] **1.** any of the four equal parts of something; fourth **2.** one fourth of a year **3.** *a)* one fourth of an hour *b)* the moment marking the end of each fourth of an hour **4.** a coin of the U.S. and Canada equal to 25 cents **5.** any leg of a four-legged animal, with the adjoining parts **6.** any of the four main points of the compass **7.** a particular district in a city [the Latin *quarter*] **8.** [*pl.*] lodgings; place of abode **9.** mercy granted to a surrendering foe **10.** a particular source [news from the highest *quarters*] **11.** *a)* the period in which the moon makes one fourth of its revolution around the earth *b)* a phase of the moon when it is half lighted **12.** *Naut.* the after part of a ship's side —*vt.* **1.** to divide into four equal parts **2.** to dismember (the body of a person put to death) **3.** to provide lodgings for; specif., to assign (soldiers) to lodgings **4.** to pass over (an area) in many directions, as hounds do in searching for game **5.** *Heraldry* to place (different coats of arms) on the quarters of a shield —*vi.* to be lodged or stationed (*at* or *with*) —*adj.* constituting or equal to a quarter —**at close quarters** at close range —**cry quarter** to beg for mercy

quarter day any of the four days regarded as beginning a new quarter of the year, when quarterly payments on rents, etc. are due

quarter-deck, quarterdeck *n.* the after part of a ship's upper deck, usually reserved for officers

quarterfinal *n.* a match or round coming just before the semifinals —**quar′terfi′nalist** *n.*

quartering *n. Heraldry a)* the marshalling of several coats of arms on one shield, usually representing family intermarriages *b)* such a coat of arms

quarterlight *n.* a small pivoted window in the door of a car

quarterly *adj.* occurring regularly four times a year —*adv.* once every quarter of the year —*n., pl.* **-lies** a publication issued every three months

quartermaster *n.* **1.** *Mil.* an officer who provides troops with quarters, equipment, etc. **2.** a ship's petty officer who attends to navigation, signals, etc.

Quartermaster General *Mil.* an official in charge of supplies, etc. for the whole army

quartern (kwôr′tərn) *n.* [see QUART] one fourth of a pint, a peck, etc.

quarter sessions *Hist.* in Britain, a court that sat quarterly in civil proceedings, with limited criminal jurisdiction

quarterstaff *n., pl.* **-staves** a stout, iron-tipped wooden staff, six to eight feet long

quartet, quartette (kwôr tet′) *n.* [< Fr. < L. *quartus*, a fourth] **1.** *Music a)* a composition for four voices or instruments *b)* the four performers of this **2.** any group of four

quarto (kwôr′tō) *n., pl.* **-tos** [< L. (*in*) *quarto*, (in) a fourth] **1.** the page size of a book made up of sheets folded into four leaves **2.** a book with pages of this size

quartz (kwôrts) *n.* [G. *Quarz*] a brilliant, crystalline mineral, silicon dioxide, occurring most often in a colourless transparent form

quasar (kwā′zär) *n.* [< *quas*(*i-stell*)*ar* (*radio source*)] any of a number of extremely distant starlike objects that emit powerful radio waves

quash[1] (kwosh) *vt.* [< L. *cassus*, empty] *Law* to annul or set aside (an indictment)

quash[2] *vt.* [< L. *quatere*, to break] to put down or overcome as by force; suppress

quasi (kwā′zī) *adv.* [L. < *quam*, as + *si*, if] as if; seemingly —*adj.* seeming

quassia (kwosh′ə) *n.* [< Graman *Quassi*, who discovered its medicinal value] **1.** any of a group of tropical trees related to the ailanthus **2.** the wood of certain of these, or a drug extracted from it

quaternary (kwə tur′nər ē) *adj.* [< L. *quaterni*, four each] **1.** consisting of four **2.** [Q-] designating or of the geologic period following the Tertiary in the Cainozoic Era

quatrain (kwo′trān) *n.* [Fr. < L. *quattuor*, four] a stanza or poem of four lines

quatrefoil (kat′rə foil′) *n.* [< MFr. *quatre*, four + *feuille*, leaf] **1.** a flower with four petals or a leaf with four leaflets **2.** *Archit.* a circular design of four converging arcs

quattrocento (kwat′trō chen′tō) *n.* [It., four hundred] the 15th cent. as a period in Italian art and literature

quaver (kwā′vər) *vi.* [ME. *cwafien*] **1.** to shake or tremble **2.** to be tremulous : said of the voice **3.** to make a trill in singing or playing —*vt.* **1.** to utter in a tremulous voice **2.** to sing or play with a trill —*n.* **1.** *Music* a note having one eighth the duration of a semibreve **2.** a tremulous quality in a voice or tone —**qua′very** *adj.*

quay (kē) *n.* [MFr. *cai*] a wharf for loading and unloading ships

Que. Quebec

quean (kwēn) *n.* [OE. *cwene*] [Obs.] **1.** a hussy **2.** a prostitute

queasy (kwē′zē) *adj.* **-sier, -siest** [< ?] **1.** causing or feeling nausea **2.** squeamish; easily nauseated **3.** uncomfortable; uneasy —**quea′siness** *n.*

Quebec heater (kwi bek′) [Canad.] a kind of coal or wood burning stove for heating rooms

Quebecker, Quebecer (kwi bek′ər, ke-) *n.* a native or inhabitant of Quebec

Québécois (ke be kwä′) *n., pl.* **-cois′** (-kwä′) a native or inhabitant of the province of Quebec, esp. a French-speaking one

queen (kwēn) *n.* [OE. *cwen*] **1.** the wife of a king **2.** a woman who rules over a monarchy in her own right **3.** a woman, place, or thing regarded as the finest possible **4.** the fully developed, reproductive female in a colony of bees, ants, etc. **5.** a playing card with a picture of a queen on it **6.** *Chess* the most powerful piece —**queen it** to domineer —**queen'-ly** *adj.*

Queen Anne's lace *same as* WILD CARROT

Queen Anne Style a style of English design of the early 18th cent., characterized by simple, dignified curves

queen consort the wife of a reigning king

queen dowager the widow of a king

queen mother a queen dowager who is mother of a reigning sovereign

Queen of the May a young girl, crowned with flowers, who is the ruler of May Day celebrations

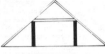

QUEEN POSTS

queen post either of two vertical posts set between the rafters and the base of a truss

Queensberry rules (kwēnz'bər ē) the rules for boxing formulated by the Marquis of Queensberry

Queen's Counsel see KING'S COUNSEL

queen's English see KING'S ENGLISH

queen's highway see KING'S HIGHWAY

queer (kwēər) *adj.* [< ?] **1.** odd; strange **2.** slightly ill; giddy, queasy, etc. **3.** [Colloq.] doubtful; suspicious **4.** [Colloq.] eccentric **5.** [Slang] homosexual —*n.* [Slang] a homosexual —*vt.* [Slang] to spoil the success of —**in queer street** in trouble or difficulty, esp. financially —**queer the pitch for** to spoil someone's chances, esp. by underhand means —**queer'ness** *n.*

quell (kwel) *vt.* [< OE. *cwellan*, to kill] **1.** to subdue [to *quell* a mutiny] **2.** to allay [to *quell* fears]

quench (kwench) *vt.* [OE. *cwencan*] **1.** to satisfy; slake [he *quenched* his thirst] **2.** to extinguish [water *quenched* the fire] **3.** to overcome; subdue **4.** to cool (hot steel, etc.) suddenly by plunging into water —**quench'less** *adj.*

quern (kwʉrn) *n.* [OE. *cweorn*] a primitive hand mill, esp. for grinding grain

querulous (kwer'ʊ ləs) *adj.* [< L. *queri*, complain] inclined to find fault; complaining; peevish —**quer'ulousness** *n.*

query (kwēər'ē) *n.*, *pl.* -ries [< L. *quaerere*, ask] **1.** a question; inquiry **2.** a doubt **3.** a question mark (?) —*vt.* -ried, -rying **1.** to question **2.** to question the accuracy of (written matter) by marking with a question mark

quest (kwest) *n.* [< L. *quaerere*, seek] a seeking; hunt; search —*vi.* to go in search or pursuit —*vt.* to seek —**quest'-er** *n.*

question (kwes'chən) *n.* [< L. *quaerere*, ask] **1.** something asked; interrogative sentence **2.** a matter open to discussion or inquiry **3.** doubt; uncertainty **4.** a matter of difficulty [not a *question* of money] **5.** an asking; inquiry **6.** a point being debated as before an assembly —*vt.* **1.** to ask questions of **2.** to express uncertainty about; doubt **3.** to dispute; challenge —*vi.* to ask questions —a **question of** (only) a matter of; all that is necessary is... —**beyond (all) question** without any doubt —**in question** being considered, debated, etc. —**out of the question** impossible; not to be considered —**ques'tioner** *n.* —**ques'tioning** *adj.*

questionable *adj.* **1.** open to doubt **2.** suspected with good reason of being dishonest, etc. **3.** uncertain [of *questionable* excellence]

question mark 1. a mark of punctuation (?) put after a sentence, word, etc. to indicate a direct question **2.** a doubt; uncertainty

question master the chairman of a quiz or panel game

questionnaire (kwes'chə nāər') *n.* [Fr.] a written list of questions used in gathering information from people

question time in the British parliament, the time set aside each day for ministers' oral answers to questions from members

queue (kyo͞o) *n.* [Fr. < L. *cauda*, tail] **1.** a line, as of persons waiting to be served **2.** a pigtail —*vi.* **queued, queu'-ing** to form in a line (often with *up*)

quibble (kwib'l) *n.* [< L. *qui*, who] **1.** a petty evasion; cavil **2.** a petty objection or criticism —*vi.* -bled, -bling to evade the truth of a point under discussion by cavilling —**quib'bler** *n.*

quiche (kēsh) *n.* [Fr.] a savoury tart with a rich filling of eggs, milk, etc.

quick (kwik) *adj.* [OE. *cwicu*, living] **1.** *a)* rapid in action [a *quick* worker] *b)* prompt [a *quick* reply] **2.** lasting a short time [a *quick* look] **3.** prompt to understand or learn **4.** easily stirred [a *quick* temper] —*adv.* quickly —*n.* **1.** the sensitive flesh under a fingernail or toenail **2.** the deepest feelings [cut to the *quick*] **3.** the living, esp. in **the quick and the dead** —**quick'ly** *adv.* —**quick'-ness** *n.*

quick-change artist an entertainer who undertakes several rapid costume changes during his performances

quicken *vt.* **1.** to move more rapidly; hasten **2.** to animate; enliven; arouse —*vi.* **1.** to speed up [the pulse *quickens* with fear] **2.** to revive **3.** *a)* to begin to show signs of life *b)* to enter the stage of pregnancy in which the movement of the foetus can be felt

quick-freeze *vt.* -froze', -froz'en, -freez'-ing to subject (food) to sudden freezing

quickie *n.* [Colloq.] anything done or made quickly

quicklime *n.* lime, or calcium oxide, which

gives off much heat in combining with water; unslaked lime

quick one [Colloq.] a speedily consumed alcoholic drink

quicksand *n.* a deep deposit of loose, wet sand in which a person or heavy object may be easily engulfed

quickset *n.* 1. a live cutting, as of hawthorn, planted, as for a hedge 2. a hedge of such plants

quicksilver *n.* the metal mercury —*adj.* rapid or unpredictable in movement or change

quickstep *n.* 1. a ballroom dance with a spirited step 2. music for such a dance

quick-tempered (kwik´tem´pərd) *adj.* easily angered

quick time the normal rate of marching: in the Army, 120 paces a minute

quick-witted (kwik´wit´id) *adj.* nimble of mind; alert —**quick´-wit´tedness** *n.*

quid[1] (kwid) *n.* [var. of cud] a piece, as of tobacco, to be chewed

quid[2] *n.*, *pl.* **quid** [Slang] one pound sterling

quiddity (kwid´ə tē) *n.*, *pl.* **-ties** [< L. *quid*, what] 1. essential quality 2. a quibble

quid pro quo (kwid´prō kwō´) [L.] one thing in return for another

quiescent (kwī es´ənt) *adj.* [< L. *quiescere*, become quiet] quiet; still; inactive —**qui·es´cence** *n.*

quiet (kwī´ət) *adj.* [< L. *quies*, rest] 1. a) not noisy; hushed b) not speaking; silent 2. still; calm; motionless 3. not agitated 4. not easily excited 5. not bright or showy 6. unobtrusive [a *quiet* manner] 7. secluded [a *quiet* glade] 8. peaceful; relaxing —*n.* 1. a quiet state; calmness, stillness, etc. 2. a quiet or peaceful quality —*vt.*, *vi.* to make or become quiet —**qui´etly** *adv.* —**qui´etness** *n.*

quieten *vt.*, *vi.* to make or become quiet

quietism (kwī´ət iz´m) *n.* [see QUIET] a form of religious mysticism originating in Spain in the 17th cent., requiring complete passivity of the will —**qui´etist** *n.*, *adj.*

quietude (kwī´ə tyoōd´) *n.* rest; calmness

quietus (kwī ēt´əs) *n.* [< ML. *quietus* (*est*), (he is) quiet] 1. discharge or release from debt, obligation, etc. 2. discharge or release from life; death

quiff (kwif) *n.* [< ?] a lock or tuft of hair, esp. one brushed up above the forehead

quill (kwil) *n.* [< ?] 1. any of the large, stiff wing or tail feathers of a bird 2. a) the hollow stem of a feather b) anything made from this, as a pen 3. any of the spines of a porcupine or hedgehog

quilt (kwilt) *n.* [< L. *culcita*, bed] a bedcover filled with down, wool, etc. and stitched together in lines or patterns —*vt.* to stitch as or like a quilt

quilting *n.* material for quilts

quin (kwin) *n.* shortened form of QUINTUPLET

quince (kwins) *n.* [< Gr. *kydōnion*] 1.

a greenish-yellow, hard, apple-shaped fruit used in preserves, etc. 2. the tree that bears this fruit

quincunx (kwin´kuŋks) *n.* [L. < *quinque*, five + *uncia*, a twelfth] an arrangement of five objects in a square, with one at each corner and one in the middle

quinine (kwi nēn´) *n.* [< Sp. *quina*, cinchona bark] a bitter, crystalline substance extracted from cinchona bark and used in medicine, esp. for treating malaria

Quinquagesima (kwiŋ´kwə jes´i mə) *n.* [LL. *quinquagesima* (*dies*), fiftieth (day)] the Sunday before Lent

quinquennial (kwiŋ kwen´ē əl) *adj.* [< L. *quinque*, five + *annus*, year] 1. lasting five years 2. taking place every five years

quinquereme (kwiŋ´kwə rēm´) *n.* [< L. *quinque*, five + *remus*, oared] an ancient galley having five tiers of rowers

quinsy (kwin´zē) *n.* [< Gr. *kyōn*, dog + *anchein*, choke] an earlier term for TONSILLITIS

quintal (kwin´t'l : for 3 also kan´t'l) *n.* [< Ar.] 1. a unit of weight equal to 100 pounds 2. a unit of weight equal to 100 kilograms 3. [Canad.] a) a unit of weight equal to 112 pounds b) a container which can hold this

quintessence (kwin tes´əns) *n.* [< ML. *quinta essentia*, fifth essence, or ultimate substance] 1. the perfect type or example of something 2. the essence of something in its purest form —**quin´tessen´tial** (-tə sen´shəl) *adj.*

quintet, quintette (kwin tet´) *n.* [< L. *quintus*, a fifth] 1. any group of five 2. *Music* a) a composition for five voices or instruments b) the five performers of this

quintillion (kwin til´yən) *n.* [< L. *quintus*, a fifth + (M)ILLION] 1. in Great Britain and Germany, the number represented by 1 followed by 30 zeros 2. in the U.S. and France, the number represented by 1 followed by 18 zeros

quintuple (kwin´tyoo p'l) *adj.* [< L. *quintus*, a fifth + *-plex*, -fold] 1. consisting of five 2. five times as much or as many —*n.* an amount five times as much or as many —*vt.*, *vi.* **-pled**, **-pling** to make or become five times as much or as many

quintuplet (kwin´tyoo plit) *n.* [dim. of prec.] any of five offspring born at a single birth

quip (kwip) *n.* [< L. *quippe*, indeed] a witty or sarcastic remark; jest —*vi.* **quipped**, **quip´ping** to utter quips

quire (kwīər) *n.* [< L. *quaterni*, four each] a set of 24 or 25 sheets of paper of the same size and stock

quirk (kwʉrk) *n.* [< ?] 1. a) a sudden twist, turn, etc. [a *quirk* of fate] b) a flourish in writing 2. a peculiar trait or mannerism —**quirk´y** *adj.*

quisling (kwiz´liŋ) *n.* [< Vidkun *Quisling*] a person who collaborates with enemy forces of occupation; traitor

quit (kwit) *vt.* **quit´ted**, **quit´ting** [< ML.

quietus, free] **1.** to stop, discontinue, or resign from **2.** to leave; depart from **3.** to give up —*vi.* [Colloq] **1.** to stop doing something **2.** to give up one's job; resign —*adj.* clear, free, or rid, as of an obligation

quitch (kwich) *n.* [< OE. *cwicu,* alive] *same as* COUCH GRASS

quite (kwīt) *adv.* [ME. form of QUIT, *adj.*] **1.** completely **2.** really; truly **3.** to a considerable degree —**quite a few** (or **bit,** etc.) [Colloq.] more than a few (or bit, etc.) —**quite (so)!** certainly! —**quite something** an unusual thing

quitrent (kwit′rent′) *n.* a rent paid in lieu of feudal services: also **quit rent**

quits (kwits) *adj.* [see QUIETUS] on even terms, as by paying a debt, retaliating, etc. —**call it quits** [Colloq.] **1.** to stop working, playing, etc. **2.** to declare oneself even with another; agree to stop competing

quittance (kwit′əns) *n.* [see QUIT] **1.** *a)* payment of a debt *b)* a document certifying this **2.** discharge; release

quitter (kwit′ər) *n.* [Colloq.] a person who gives up easily, without trying hard

quiver[1] (kwiv′ər) *vi.* [< ME. *cwiver,* quick] to shake with a tremulous motion; tremble —*n.* the act of quivering —**quiv′-ery** *adj.*

quiver[2] *n.* [OFr. *coivre*] a case for holding arrows

quixotic (kwik sot′ik) *adj.* [< Don *Quixote*] extravagantly chivalrous or romantically idealistic; impractical: also **quixot′ical** —**quixot′ically** *adv.* —**quix′ot-ism** *n.*

quiz (kwiz) *n., pl.* **quiz′zes** [prob. < L. *quis,* what?] **1.** *same as* QUIZ PROGRAMME **2.** a short examination to test one's knowledge —*vt.* **quizzed, quiz′-zing 1.** to ask questions of **2.** [Obs.] *a)* to stare at with curiosity *b)* to make fun of —**quiz′zer** *n.*

quiz programme a radio or TV programme in which a group of people compete in answering questions posed by a question master

quizzical (kwiz′i k'l) *adj.* **1.** odd; comical **2.** teasing **3.** perplexed —**quiz′zically** *adv.*

quod (kwod) *n.* [< ?] [Slang] prison; jail

quoin (koin) *n.* [var. of COIN] **1.** the external corner of a building; esp., any

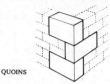

QUOINS

of the stones forming the corner **2.** a wedge-shaped block

quoit (koit) *n.* [< ?] a ring thrown at an upright peg to encircle it in the game of **quoits**

quondam (kwon′dəm) *adj.* [L.] former [a *quondam* pacifist]

quorum (kwôr′əm) *n.* [L. < *qui,* who] the minimum number of members required to be present at an assembly or meeting before it can validly transact business

quota (kwōt′ə) *n.* [< L. *quota pars,* how large a part] **1.** a share which each of a number is to contribute or receive **2.** the number or proportion that is allowed or admitted

quotation (kwō tā′shən) *n.* **1.** a quoting **2.** the words or passage quoted **3.** *Commerce* the current quoted price of a stock, bond, commodity, etc.

quotation mark either of a pair of punctuation marks (". . .") used to enclose a direct quotation

quote (kwōt) *vt.* **quot′ed, quot′ing** [< ML. *quotare,* to number (chapters, etc.)] **1.** to repeat a passage from or statement of **2.** to repeat (a passage, statement, etc.) **3.** to cite as an example or authority **4.** to state (the price of something) —*vi.* to make a quotation, as from a book —*n.* [Colloq.] *same as:* **1.** QUOTATION **2.** QUOTATION MARK —*interj.* I shall quote —**quot′able** *adj.*

quoth (kwōth) *vt.* [< OE. *cwethan,* speak] [Archaic] said

quotidian (kwō tid′ē ən) *adj.* [< L. *quot,* as many as + *dies,* day] **1.** daily **2.** everyday; ordinary —*n.* anything, esp. a fever, that recurs daily

quotient (kwō′shənt) *n.* [< L. *quot,* how many] *Arith.* the result obtained when one number is divided by another

q.v. [L. *quod vide*] which see (used to mean that the reader should look up the reference given)

R

R, r (är) *n.,* *pl.* **R's, r's** the eighteenth
letter of the English alphabet
R 1. *Chem.* radical 2. *Math.* ratio 3.
Elec. resistance 4. *Chess* rook —**the three
R's** reading, writing, and arithmetic,
regarded as the basic studies
r 1. *Math.* radius 2. roentgen(s)
R., r. 1. [L. *Rex*] king 2. [L. *Regina*]
queen 3. radius 4. railway 5. right 6.
river 7. road
Ra *Chem.* radium
R.A. 1. Rear Admiral 2. Royal
Academician 3. Royal Academy 4. Royal
Artillery
R.A.A.F. Royal Australian Air Force
rabbet (rab'it) *n.* [< OFr. *rabattre,* beat
down] a groove made in the edge of
a board so that another piece may be
fitted into it to form a joint (**rabbet joint**)
—*vt.* 1. to cut a rabbet in 2. to join
by a rabbet
rabbi (rab'ī) *n., pl.* **-bis, -bies** [< Heb.
rabbī, my master] a teacher of the Jewish
law, now usually the ordained head of
a congregation —**rabbin'ical** (-bin'-) *adj.*
rabbit (rab'it) *n.* [ME. *rabette*] 1. a
burrowing mammal that is smaller than
the hare, with long ears and a stubby
tail 2. [Colloq.] a poor performer at a
game —*vi.* 1. to hunt rabbits 2. [Colloq.]
to talk inconsequentially or in a rambling
way
rabbit punch a sharp blow to the back
of the neck
rabble (rab''l) *n.* [< ?] a noisy, disorderly
crowd; mob —**the rabble** [Derog.] the
common people
rabble-rouser *n.* a person who tries
to arouse people to violent action by appeals
to emotions, prejudices, etc.
Rabelaisian (rab'əlā'zē ən) *adj.* 1. of
Rabelais (1495?-1553) or his writings 2.
coarsely humorous
rabid (rab'id) *adj.* [< L. *rabere,* to rage]
1. of or having rabies 2. fanatical 3.
violent; raging —**rabid'ity** (rə bid'ə tē),
rab'idness *n.*
rabies (rā'bēz) *n.* [L., madness] an
infectious virus disease of mammals, passed
on to man by the bite of an infected animal
R.A.C. 1. Royal Armoured Corps 2. Royal
Automobile Club
raccoon (ra kōōn') *n.* [< Algonquian
äräkun, scratcher] a small, tree-climbing
mammal of N America, having yellowish-
grey fur and a black-ringed tail
race¹ (rās) *n.* [< ON. *rās,* a running]
1. a competition of speed in running, riding,
etc. 2. [*pl.*] a series of such competitions
for horses, cars, etc., on a regular course
3. a contest [the *race* for the moon] 4.

a) a swift current of water *b)* a channel
for this [a *millrace*] —*vi.* **raced, rac'ing**
1. to take part in a race 2. to go or
move fast or too fast —*vt.* 1. to compete
with in a race 2. to enter or run (a
horse, etc.) in a race 3. to make go
or operate fast or too fast
race² *n.* [< It. *razza*] 1. any of the
different varieties of mankind,
distinguished by kind of hair, colour of
skin, etc. 2. any geographical, national,
or tribal ethnic grouping 3. any group
of people having the same ancestry or
the same habits, ideas, etc. 4. a subspecies,
variety, or breed —**the (human) race**
mankind
racecourse *n.* a course prepared for
horse racing
racehorse *n.* a horse bred and trained
for racing

RACEME

raceme (rə sēm') *n.* [L. *racemus,* cluster
of grapes] a flower cluster with individual
flowers growing on small stems at intervals
along one central stem
race meeting a regularly organized
fixture for racing horses, dogs, etc.
race relations the relations between
members of two or more human races,
esp. within a single community
race riot violence and fighting in a
community, brought on by racial hostility
race track a circuit for motor racing, etc.
Rachmanism (rak'mə niz'm) *n.* [< Perec
Rachman] the practice of charging high
rents for slum property
racial (rā'shəl) *adj.* 1. of a race, or ethnic
group 2. of or between races —**ra'cially
adv.**
racialism *n.* a doctrine without scientific
support, that claims the superiority of some
one race: also **racism** —**ra'cialist** *n., adj.*
rack¹ (rak) *n.* [prob. < MDu. *recken,*
stretch] 1. a framework, stand, etc. for
holding things [clothes *rack*] 2. a toothed

bar that meshes with a cogwheel, etc.
3. formerly, a frame on which a victim was tortured by stretching his limbs out of place —*vt.* **1.** to put in or on a rack **2.** to torture on a rack **3.** to torment or afflict —**on the rack** in a very painful situation —**rack one's brains** (or **memory,** etc.) to try very hard to think of something

rack² *n.* [var. of WRACK] destruction: now only in **go to rack and ruin**

rack³ *n.* [prob. < Scand.] a broken mass of clouds blown by the wind

rack⁴ *vt.* [< Provençal *raca,* husks] to draw off (cider, wine, etc.) from the dregs

rack and pinion *adj.* designating a type of steering in motor cars with a track rod that can engage with a pinion attached to the steering column

racket¹ (rak′it) *n.* [prob. echoic] **1.** a noisy confusion; uproar **2.** *a)* an obtaining of money illegally *b)* [Colloq.] any dishonest scheme **3.** [Slang] any business, profession, etc. —*vi.* to make a racket, or uproar (with *about*) —**rack′ety** *adj.*

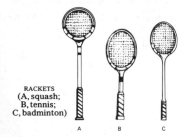

RACKETS
(A, squash;
B, tennis;
C, badminton)

A   B   C

racket² *n.* [< Ar. *rāhah,* palm of the hand] **1.** a light bat for tennis, etc., with a network of catgut, nylon, etc. in an oval or round frame **2.** [*pl.,* with *sing. v.*] the game of racquets

racketeer (rak′ə tēər′) *n.* [see RACKET¹] one who gets money illegally, as by fraud or extortion

rack railway a mountain railway having a middle rail fitted with a rack that engages a pinion on the locomotive

rack-rent *n.* [RACK¹ + RENT] an excessively high rent

raconteur (rak′on tur′) *n.* [Fr. < *raconter,* recount] a person skilled at telling anecdotes

racoon (rə kōōn′) *n.* same as RACCOON

racquet (rak′it) *n.* **1.** same as RACKET² **2.** [*pl.,* with *sing. v.*] a game similar to squash

racy (rā′sē) *adj.* **-ier, -iest** [< RACE²] **1.** lively; spirited **2.** having a characteristic or distinctive taste or quality **3.** risqué —**rac′ily** *adv.* —**rac′iness** *n.*

RADA (rä′də) Royal Academy of Dramatic Art

radar (rā′där) *n.* [*ra*(dio) *d*(etecting) *a*(nd) *r*(anging)] a system or device that transmits radio waves to a reflecting object,

as an aircraft, to determine its location, speed, etc. by the reflected waves

radar trap a device using radar to detect motorists who exceed the speed limit

raddle (rad′'l) *vt.* [< *rud,* red ochre] **1.** to colour with red ochre **2.** to paint (the face) with rouge, esp. heavily —**rad′-dled** *adj.*

radial (rā′dē əl) *adj.* [see RADIUS] **1.** of or like a ray or rays; branching out from a centre **2.** of or like a radius —*n.* a radial tyre

radial (ply) tyre a tyre with the ply cords almost at right angles to the centre line of the tread

radian (rā′dē ən) *n.* [< RADIUS] a unit of angular measurement equal to the angle formed at the centre of a circle by an arc whose length equals the radius of the circle

radiant (rā′dē ənt) *adj.* [see RADIUS] **1.** shining brightly **2.** filled with light **3.** showing joy, love, etc. **4.** issuing (from a source) in rays **5.** *a)* sent out by means of radiation [*radiant* heat] *b)* sending out (heat) by radiation —*n.* a source of heat or light rays —**ra′diance, ra′diancy** *n.*

radiant energy energy travelling in waves; esp., electromagnetic radiation, as heat, light, X-rays, etc.

radiate (rā′dē āt′) *vi.* **-at′ed, -at′ing** [see RADIUS] **1.** to send out rays of heat, light, etc. **2.** to spread out from a centre —*vt.* **1.** to send out (heat, light, etc.) in rays **2.** to give forth (happiness, love, etc.) —*adj.* having raylike parts

radiation (rā′dē ā′shən) *n.* **1.** a radiating; specif., the process in which radiant energy is sent out from atoms and molecules as they undergo internal change **2.** such radiant energy **3.** nuclear particles

radiation sickness sickness produced by overexposure to radiation from X-rays, nuclear explosions, etc.

radiator (rā′dē āt′ər) *n.* a device that radiates heat, as into a room, or, in a motor vehicle, away from the engine

radical (rad′i k'l) *adj.* [< L. *radix,* root] **1.** *a)* of or from the root; fundamental *b)* extreme; thorough **2.** favouring basic or extreme change, as in the social structure —*n.* **1.** a person having radical views **2.** *Chem.* a group of atoms that acts as a single atom and goes through a reaction unchanged, or is replaced by a single atom **3.** *Math.* a root of a number or quantity, such as ∛5 —**rad′ically** *adv.*

radical sign *Math.* the sign (√ or √) used before a quantity to show that its root is to be extracted

radicle (rad′i k'l) *n.* [< L. *radix,* root] *Bot.* the primary root of an embryo seedling; rootlet

radii (rā′dē ī′) *n.* *pl.* of RADIUS

radio (rā′dē ō′) *n., pl.* **-os′** [ult. < L. *radius,* ray] **1.** the transmission of sounds or signals by electromagnetic waves through space, without wires, to a receiving set **2.** such a receiving set **3.** broadcasting by radio as an industry, entertainment, etc. —*adj.* **1.** of, using, used in, or sent by radio **2.** of electromagnetic wave frequencies from c. 10 kilohertz to c. 300 000 megahertz —**vt., vi. -oed', -o'ing** to send (a message, etc.) or communicate with (a person, etc.) by radio

radio- [Fr. < L. *radius*, ray] *a combining form meaning:* **1.** ray **2.** by radio **3.** by means of radiant energy [*radiotherapy*] **4.** radioactive [*radioisotope*]

radioactive (rā'dē ō ak'tiv) *adj.* giving off radiant energy in particles or rays by the disintegration of the atomic nuclei —**ra'dioactiv'ity** (-ak tiv'ə tē) *n.*

radio astronomy astronomy dealing with radio waves in space in order to get data about the universe

radiocarbon *n.* *same as* CARBON 14: see CARBON

radiochemistry (rā'dē ō kem'is trē) *n.* the branch of chemistry dealing with radioactive phenomena

radio frequency any frequency between normally audible sound waves and infrared light, from c.10 kilohertz to c. 1,000 000 megahertz

radiogram (rā'dē ō gram') *n.* **1.** a single unit consisting of a radio and a gramophone **2.** a message sent by radio: also **ra'diotel'e-gram 3.** *same as* RADIOGRAPH

radiograph (rā'dē ō gräf') *n.* a picture made on a sensitized film or plate by X-rays —**ra'diog'rapher** (-og'rə fər) *n.* —**ra'diog'raphy** *n.*

radioisotope (rā'dē ō ī'sə tōp') *n.* a natural or artificial radioactive isotope of a chemical element

radiology (rā'dē ol'ə jē) *n.* [RADIO- + -LOGY] the science dealing with X-rays and other radiant energy, esp. as used in medicine —**ra'diol'ogist** *n.*

radioscopy (rā'dē os'kə pē) *n.* [RADIO- + Gr. *skopein*, to see] the direct examination of the inside structure of opaque objects by radiation, as by X-rays

radiosonde (rā'dē ō sond') *n.* [Fr. < *radio*, radio + *sonde*, sounding line] a compact radio transmitter with meteorological instruments sent into the upper atmosphere, by balloon, to radio back temperature, pressure, and humidity data

radiotelegraph (rā'dē ō tel'ə gräf') *n.* *same as* WIRELESS TELEGRAPHY: also **ra'-dioteleg'raphy** (-tə leg'rə fē)

radiotelephone (rā'dē ō tel'ə fōn') *n.* the equipment needed at one station for two-way voice communication by radio: also **ra'diophone' — ra'dioteleph'ony** (-tə lef'-ə nē) *n.*

radio telescope a radio antenna or array of antennas for use in radio astronomy

radiotherapy (rā'dē ō ther'ə pē) *n.* the treatment of disease by X-rays or by rays from a radioactive substance

radish (rad'ish) *n.* [< L. *radix*, root] an annual plant with a pungent root, eaten raw in a salad

radium (rā'dē əm) *n.* [< L. *radius*, ray] a radioactive metallic chemical element, found in uranium minerals, which

undergoes spontaneous atomic disintegration: symbol, Ra

radius (rā'dē əs) *n., pl.* **-dii'** (dē ī'), **-uses** [L., spoke, ray] **1.** *a)* a straight line from the centre to the periphery of a circle or sphere *b)* its length **2.** the area or distance within the sweep of such a line [no house within a *radius* of five miles] **3.** the shorter and thicker of the two bones of the forearm on the same side as the thumb

radon (rā'don) *n.* [RAD(IUM) + -ON] a radioactive gaseous chemical element formed in the atomic disintegration of radium: symbol, Rn

RAF, R.A.F. Royal Air Force

raffia (raf'ē ə) *n.* [< Malagasy name] **1.** a palm tree of Madagascar **2.** fibre from its leaves, woven into baskets, etc.

raffish (raf'ish) *adj.* [< (RIFF)RAFF] **1.** disreputable, rakish, etc. **2.** tawdry; vulgar

raffle (raf''l) *n.* [< MFr. *rafle*, dice game] a lottery in which chances to win a prize are bought —*vt.* **-fled, -fling** to offer as a prize in a raffle (often with *off*)

raft (räft) *n.* [< ON. *raptr*, log] **1.** a flat structure of logs, boards, etc. fastened together and floated **2.** a life raft

RAFTERS

rafter (räf'tər) *n.* [OE. *ræfter*] any of the beams that slope from the ridge of a roof to the eaves and serve to support the roof

rag¹ (rag) *n.* [ult. < ON. *rögg*, tuft of hair] **1.** a waste piece of cloth, esp. an old or torn one **2.** a small cloth for dusting, washing, etc. **3.** [*pl.*] old, worn clothes **4.** [Derog. Slang] newspaper —*adj.* made of rags —**rags to riches** poverty to prosperity

rag² *vt.* **ragged, rag'ging** [< ?] [Slang] **1.** to tease **2.** to play practical jokes on —*n.* **1.** [Slang] an instance of ragging **2.** an organized student procession of floats, etc., usually to raise money for charity

rag³ *n.* **1.** *short for* RAGTIME **2.** a composition in ragtime

ragamuffin (rag'ə muf'in) *n.* [< ?] a dirty, ragged person; esp., a poor, ragged child

rag-and-bone man a man who buys, collects, and sells discarded clothing, furniture, etc.

ragbag *n.* **1.** a bag for rags **2.** a collection of odds and ends

rage (rāj) *n.* [< L. *rabies*, madness] **1.** furious, uncontrolled anger **2.** violence or intensity —*vi.* **raged, rag'ing** 1. to show violent anger 2. to be violent, uncontrolled, etc. 3. to spread unchecked, as a disease —**(all) the rage** a fashion or craze

ragged (rag'id) *adj.* 1. shabby or torn from wear 2. wearing shabby or torn clothes 3. uneven; rough 4. imperfect —**run ragged** to make (someone) exhausted

raglan (rag'lən) *n.* [< Lord *Raglan*] a loose overcoat without shoulder seams, each sleeve (**raglan sleeve**) continuing in one piece to the collar

ragman (rag'man') *n.* a man who collects, buys, and sells rags, old paper, etc.

ragout (ra'gōō) *n.* [< Fr. *ragoûter*, revive the appetite of] a highly seasoned stew of meat and vegetables

ragtag (and bobtail) [RAG[1] + TAG] the lowest classes; the rabble : term of contempt

ragtime (rag'tīm') *n.* [prob. < *ragged time*] a type of strongly syncopated music in fast, even time

rag trade [Colloq.] the clothing business

ragwort (rag'wurt') *n.* [< its ragged-edged leaves] a common wild flower with bright-yellow flowers on a tall, erect stem

raid (rād) *n.* [< ROAD, in obs. sense "a riding"] 1. a sudden, hostile attack, as by aircraft, bandits, etc. 2. any sudden invasion by police, to discover violations of the law —*vt., vi.* to make a raid (on) —**raid'er** *n.*

rail[1] (rāl) *n.* [< L. *regula*, a rule] 1. a bar of wood, metal, etc. placed horizontally between posts as a barrier or support 2. a railing 3. any of a series of parallel metal bars laid to make a track for trains 4. a railway as a means of transport [travel by *rail*] —*vt.* to fence —**go off the rails** 1. to go off the proper course 2. to become insane 3. to start to behave in a manner considered unconventional, improper, etc.

rail[2] *vi.* [ult. < LL. *ragere*, to bellow] to complain violently (*against* or *at*)

rail[3] *n.* [< MFr. *raaler*, to screech] any of a number of small wading birds living in marshes and having a harsh cry

railhead (rāl'hed') *n.* the furthest point to which rails have been laid in a railway

railing *n.* a fence or balustrade

raillery (rāl'ərē) *n., pl.* **-leries** [Fr. *raillerie* : see RAIL[2]] 1. light ridicule; banter 2. a teasing act or remark

railroad *n.* [U.S.] a railway —*vt.* [Colloq.] to force (a person) into an action with haste or by unfair means

railway *n.* 1. a permanent way laid with parallel steel rails along which engines draw carriages in a train 2. a complete system of such tracks, including land, rolling stock, etc. 3. the company owning such a system

raiment (rā'mənt) *n.* [see ARRAY] [Archaic] clothing

rain (rān) *n.* [OE. *regn*] 1. water falling in drops condensed from the moisture in the atmosphere 2. the falling of such drops 3. *a)* rainy weather *b)* [*pl.*] the rainy season 4. a rapid falling of many small objects [a *rain* of ashes] —*vi.* 1. to fall : said of rain [it is *raining*] 2. to fall like rain —*vt.* 1. to pour down 2. to give in large quantities —**rain off** to cause (an event) to be postponed or cancelled because of rain —**rain'y** *adj.*

rainbow (-bō') *n.* an arc containing the colours of the spectrum in bands, formed in the sky by the refraction of the sun's rays in falling rain or in mist —*adj.* of many colours

raincoat *n.* a waterproof or water-repellent coat

raindrop *n.* a single drop of rain

rainfall *n.* 1. a falling of rain 2. the amount of water falling as rain, snow, etc. over a given area in a given time : measured in an instrument (**rain gauge**) into which the water falls

rain forest a dense, evergreen forest in a tropical region having abundant rainfall throughout the year

rain shadow a region of little rainfall on the lee slopes of mountains whose windward slopes receive the rain

rainwater *n.* water that falls or has fallen as rain and is soft and fairly free of mineral matter

rainwear *n.* rainproof clothing

rainy day a possible future time of difficulty or need

raise (rāz) *vt.* **raised, rais'ing** [< ON. *reisa*] 1. to make rise; lift 2. to construct (a building, etc.) 3. to stir up [to *raise* a revolt] 4. to increase in value, amount, degree, intensity, etc. [to *raise* prices, to *raise* one's voice] 5. to improve the rank of [to *raise* oneself from poverty] 6. to cause to arise, appear, or come [to *raise* the dead] 7. to produce [the joke *raised* a laugh] 8. to bring forward for consideration 9. to collect (an army, money, etc.) 10. to utter (a cry, etc.) 11. to end [to *raise* a siege] 12. to leaven (bread, etc.) 13. *a)* to make (vegetables, etc.) grow *b)* to breed (cattle, etc.) *c)* to bring up (children) —*n.* 1. a raising 2. [U.S.] a rise (in wages or salary) —**raise Cain** (or **the devil, hell,** etc.) [Colloq.] to create a disturbance; cause trouble —**raise the wind** obtain ready money

raisin (rā'z'n) *n.* [< L. *racemus*, cluster of grapes] a sweet, dried grape, usually seedless

raison d'être (rā'zōn det'rə) [Fr.] reason for being; justification for existence

raj (räj) *n.* [see ff.] in India, rule; sovereignty

rajah, raja (rä'jə) *n.* [< Sans. *rāj*, to rule] formerly, a prince or chief in India

rake[1] (rāk) *n.* [OE. *raca*] a long-handled tool with prongs at one end, used for gathering loose grass, etc. —*vt.* **raked, rak'ing** 1. *a)* to gather with or as with a rake *b)* to make (a lawn, etc.) tidy with a rake 2. to gather with great care 3. to scratch or smooth as with a rake 4. to search through carefully 5. to direct gunfire along (a line of troops, etc.) —*vi.* to use a rake —**rake in** to gather fast a great deal of —**rake up** to uncover (facts or gossip)

rake² *n.* [< *rakehell*] a man who leads a wild, dissolute life: also **rake'hell'**

rake³ *vi., vt.* **raked, rak'ing** [< ?] to be or make slightly inclined, as a ship's masts; slant —*n.* a slanting

rake-off *n.* [Slang] a commission or share, esp. one gained in a shady deal

rakish¹ (rā'kish) *adj.* [< RAKE³] 1. having a trim, neat appearance 2. dashing and gay; jaunty

rakish² *adj.* wild and dissolute

rallentando (ral'ən tan'dō) *adj., adv.* [It.] *Music* gradually slower: abbrev. **rall.**

rally¹ (ral'ē) *vt., vi.* **-lied, -lying** [< OFr. *re-*, again + *alier*, to join: see ALLY] 1. to gather together (retreating troops) and restore or come to a state of order 2. to bring or come together for a common purpose 3. to revive; recover —*n., pl.* **-lies** 1. a rallying or being rallied; specif., a mass meeting 2. an organized run, esp. of sports cars, over a course, designed to test driving skills 3. *Tennis,* etc. an exchange of several strokes before the point is won —**ral'lier** *n.*

rally² *vt., vi.* **-lied, -lying** [Fr. *rallier*, RAIL²] to tease or mock playfully

ram (ram) *n.* [OE. *ramm*] 1. a male sheep 2. *same as* BATTERING RAM 3. *a)* formerly, a sharp projection at a prow, for piercing enemy vessels *b)* a ship with this 4. a hydraulic device for raising a liquid 5. the striking part of a pile driver —[R-] Aries —*vt.* **rammed, ram'ming** 1. to strike against with great force 2. to force into place 3. to cram (*with*) —*vi.* to crash (*into*) —**ram'mer** *n.*

R.A.M. Royal Academy of Music

Ramadan (ram'ə dan') *n.* [Ar. *ramadān,* the hot month] the ninth month of the Moslem year, a period of daily fasting

ramble (ram'b'l) *vi.* **-bled, -bling** [< ME. *romblen,* roam] 1. to roam about 2. to walk for pleasure, sometimes without a planned route 3. to talk or write aimlessly, without sticking to any point 4. to wander or spread in all directions —*vt.* to roam through —*n.* a rambling, esp. a stroll

rambler *n.* 1. a person or thing that rambles 2. any of certain climbing roses

rambunctious (ram bunk'shəs) *adj.* [altered < *robust*] [U.S.] wild, boisterous, unruly, etc.

R.A.M.C. Royal Army Medical Corps

ramekin, ramequin (ram'ə kin) *n.* [< MDu. *rammeken,* cheese dish] a small, individual baking dish, or the food cooked in it

ramification (ram'ə fi kā'shən) *n.* 1. a branch or offshoot 2. a derived effect, consequence, or result

ramify (ram'ə fī') *vt., vi.* **-fied', -fy'ing** [< L. *ramus,* branch + *facere,* to make] to divide or spread out into branches or branchlike divisions

ramose (rā'mōs) *adj.* [< L. *ramus,* branch] branching

ramp¹ (ramp) *n.* [see ff.] 1. a sloping walk, plank, etc. joining different levels 2. a wheeled staircase rolled up to an aircraft for use in getting on or off

ramp² *vi.* [OFr. *ramper,* to climb] 1. to rear up on the hind legs 2. to rampage

rampage (ram pāj'; *also, for n.,* ram'pāj) *vi.* **-paged', -pag'ing** [prob. < RAMP²] to rush violently or wildly about; rage —*n.* a rampaging: chiefly in **on the rampage** —**rampa'geous** *adj.*

rampant (ram'pənt) *adj.* [see RAMP²] 1. growing unchecked; rife 2. violent and uncontrollable 3. standing up on the hind legs; specif., *Heraldry* shown so in profile, one forepaw above the other

rampart (ram'pärt) *n.* [< Fr. *re-,* again + *emparer,* fortify] 1. a defensive embankment round a castle, fort, etc., with a parapet at the top 2. any defence

rampike (ram'pīk) *n.* [Canad.] a tall tree that has been burned or is bare of branches

ramrod (ram'rod') *n.* a rod for ramming down the charge in a gun loaded through the muzzle

ramshackle (ram'shak''l) *adj.* [< RANSACK] rickety; likely to fall to pieces

ran (ran) *pt. of* RUN

RAN, R.A.N. Royal Australian Navy

ranch (ränch) *n.* [< Sp. *rancho,* small farm] 1. [Chiefly U.S.] a large farm for raising many cattle, horses, or sheep 2. any large farm for raising a particular livestock [a mink *ranch*] —*vi.* to work on a ranch —**ranch'er** *n.*

rancherie (rän'chər ē) *n.* [< Sp. *rancheria*] [Canad.] an Indian reservation

rancid (ran'sid) *adj.* [< L. *rancere,* to be rank] having the bad smell or taste of spoiled fats or oils —**rancid'ity** *n.*

rancour (raŋ'kər) *n.* [< L. *rancere,* to be rank] a continuing and bitter hate or ill will

rand (rand) *n., pl.* **rand** [Afrik., orig., shield] in South Africa, 1. the chief monetary unit, divided into 100 cents 2. *short for* the **Witwatersrand** in the Transvaal

R & B, r & b rhythm and blues

R & D, R. and D. research and development

random (ran'dəm) *adj.* [< OFr. *randir,* run violently] 1. made, done, etc. in a haphazard way 2. having an equal opportunity of occurring or of being chosen —**at random** without careful choice, aim, plan, etc.

randy (ran'dē) *adj.* **-dier, -diest** [prob. < RANT] [Slang] sexually aroused; lustful —**ran'diness** *n.*

ranee (rä nē') *n. alt. sp. of* RANI

rang (raŋ) *pt. of* RING¹

range (rānj) *n.* [< OFr. *renc,* a row] 1. the full extent over which something moves or is heard, seen, effective, etc.; scope 2. the limits within which there are differences in amount, degree, etc. [a wide *range* in price] 3. *a)* the firing distance of a weapon *b)* the flight path of a missile or rocket 4. the farthest distance a plane, etc. can go without refuelling **5.** *a)* a place for shooting practice *b)* a place for testing rockets in flight **6.** the full extent of pitch of a voice, instrument, etc. **7.** [Chiefly U.S.] a large, open area for grazing livestock **8.** a row, line, or series **9.** a chain or single system of mountains **10.** a cooking unit with an oven and surface heating units usually heated by solid fuel —*vt.* **ranged, rang'ing 1.** to put in a certain order, esp. in a row or rows **2.** to place with others in a cause, party, etc. **3.** to roam over or through —*vi.* **1.** to extend in a given direction **2.** to wander about; roam **3.** to vary between stated limits

range finder any of various instruments to determine the distance of a target or object from a gun, camera, etc.

ranger *n.* **1.** *a)* the chief official of a royal park, etc. *b)* a warden patrolling forests **2.** [R-] a member of the senior branch of the Girl Guides **3.** [U.S.] a member of a special military or police force that patrols a region **4.** a roamer

rangy (rān'jē) *adj.* **-ier, -iest** long-limbed and slender

rani (rä'nē') *n.* [see RAJAH] the wife of a rajah

rank[1] (raŋk) *n.* [< OFr. *renc*] **1.** an official grade [the *rank* of captain] **2.** a social class [all *ranks* of life] **3.** a high position in society **4.** a row, line, or series **5.** a relative position as measured by quality, etc. [of the first *rank*] **6.** a row of soldiers, etc., side by side **7.** [*pl.*] all those in an organization, as the army, who are not officers or leaders: also **rank and file** —*vt.* **1.** to place in a rank **2.** to assign a relative position to —*vi.* to hold a certain position —**pull (one's) rank** [Colloq.] to use one's higher rank to get others to obey, etc.

rank[2] *adj.* [OE. *ranc*, strong] **1.** growing too vigorously and coarsely **2.** producing a too luxuriant crop **3.** very bad in smell or taste **4.** indecent **5.** extreme [*rank* injustice]

rankle (raŋ'k'l) *vi.* **-kled, -kling** [< ML. *dracunculus*, a fester] to cause or fill with long-lasting rancour, resentment, etc.

ransack (ran'sak) *vt.* [< ON. *rann*, house + *sækja*, to search] **1.** to search through **2.** to plunder; pillage

ransom (ran'səm) *n.* [< L. *redemptio*, REDEMPTION] **1.** the securing of the release of a captive by paying money or meeting other demands **2.** the price so paid or demanded —*vt.* to get (a captive, etc.) released by paying the demanded price —**ran'somer** *n.*

rant (rant) *vi., vt.* [< obs. Du. *ranten*] to talk or say in a loud, wild, extravagant way; rave

R.A.O.C. Royal Army Ordnance Corps

rap[1] (rap) *vt.* **rapped, rap'ping** [prob. echoic] **1.** to strike quickly and sharply; tap **2.** [Colloq.] to criticize sharply —*vi.* to knock quickly and sharply —*n.* **1.** a quick, sharp knock; tap **2.** [Slang] blame or punishment: usually in **take the rap** take the blame, whether guilty or not —**rap out** to utter sharply

rap[2] *n.* [< ?] [Colloq.] the least bit: in **not care a rap**

rapacious (rə pā'shəs) *adj.* [< L. *rapere*, seize] **1.** plundering **2.** greedy; voracious **3.** predatory —**rapacity** (rə pas'ə tē) *n.*

R.A.P.C. Royal Army Pay Corps

rape[1] (rāp) *n.* [< L. *rapere*, seize] **1.** *a)* the crime of having sexual intercourse with a woman forcibly and without her consent *b)* any sexual assault **2.** any violent or outrageous assault —*vt., vi.* **raped, rap'ing** to commit rape (on) —**rap'ist** *n.*

rape[2] *n.* [L. *rapa*, turnip] a plant with seed (**rape'seed'**) yielding an oil (**rape oil, rapeseed oil**) and with leaves used for fodder

rapid (rap'id) *adj.* [< L. *rapere*, to rush] moving or acting with speed; swift —*n.* [usually *pl.*] a part of a river where the current is swift, as because of a narrowing of the river bed —**rapidity** (rə pid'ə tē) *n.*

rapier (rāp'yər) *n.* [Fr. *rapière*] a light, sharp-pointed sword used only for thrusting

rapine (rap'in) *n.* [< L. *rapere*, seize] plunder; pillage

rapport (ra pôr') *n.* [Fr. < L. *ad-*, to + *portare*, to carry] relationship, esp. of a sympathetic kind; harmony

rapprochement (ra prosh'mäṅ) *n.* [Fr.] an establishing or restoring of friendly relations

rapscallion (rap skal'yən) *n.* [< RASCAL] a rogue

rapt (rapt) *adj.* [< L. *rapere*, seize] **1.** absorbed (in) **2.** carried away with joy, love, etc.; full of rapture

raptorial (rap tôr'ē əl) *adj.* [< L. *rapere*, seize] **1.** predatory, as the eagle **2.** adapted for seizing prey [*raptorial* claws]

rapture (rap'chər) *n.* [< RAPT] **1.** the state of being carried away with joy, love, etc. **2.** an expression of great joy, pleasure, etc. —**rap'turous** *adj.*

rare[1] (râər) *adj.* **rar'er, rar'est** [< L. *rarus*] **1.** not often seen, done, found, etc.; uncommon **2.** unusually good; excellent **3.** not dense [*rare* atmosphere] —**rare'ly** *adv.*

rare[2] *adj.* **rar'er, rar'est** [OE. *hrere*] not fully cooked; partly raw: said esp. of meat

rarebit *n.* same as WELSH RABBIT

rare earth 1. any of the oxides of the rare-earth metals **2.** any of the rare-earth metals

rare-earth metals (or **elements**) a group of rare metallic chemical elements with consecutive atomic numbers of 57 to 71 inclusive

rarefy (râər'ə fī') *vt., vi.* **-fied', -fy'ing** [< L. *rarus*, rare + *facere*, to make] **1.** to make or become thin, or less dense **2.** to make or become more refined —**rar'e-fac'tion** (-fak'shən) *n.*

rarely *adv.* **1.** seldom **2.** beautifully **3.** unusually

raring (râər'iŋ) *adj.* [< *rare*, Dial. var. of REAR[2]] eager; enthusiastic [*raring* to go]

rarity (râər'ə tē) *n.* **1.** a being rare; uncommonness; scarcity **2.** *pl.* **-ties** a rare thing

rascal (räs'k'l) *n.* [OFr. *rascaille*,

scrapings]　a scoundrel; rogue; scamp
—**rascal′ity** (-kal′-) *n.*
rase (rāz) *vt.* rased, ras′ing *alt. sp. of* RAZE
rash[1] (rash) *adj.* [ME. *rasch*] too hasty
and careless; reckless —**rash′ly** *adv.*
—**rash′ness** *n.*
rash[2] *n.* [MFr. *rasche*] 1. a breaking
out of red spots on the skin 2. a sudden
appearance of a large number [a *rash*
of complaints]
rasher (rash′ər) *n.* [< ?] a thin slice
of bacon
rasp (rāsp) *vt.* [< OHG. *raspon*, scrape
together] 1. to scrape as with a file
2. to utter in a rough, grating tone 3.
to grate upon; irritate —*vi.* 1. to grate
2. to make a rough, grating sound —*n.*
1. a type of rough file with sharp, projecting
points 2. a rough, grating sound —**rasp′-**
ingly *adv.*
raspberry (raz′bər ē) *n., pl.* -**ries** [<
?] 1. a small, juicy, edible fruit, usually
red 2. the bramble bearing this 3. [Slang]
a jeering sound made by blowing out so
as to vibrate the tongue between the lips
Rastafarian (ras′tə fäär′ē ən) *n.* a member of a Jamaican cult that regards the
former emperor of Ethiopia, Haile Selassie,
as its spiritual leader
rat (rat) *n.* [OE. *ræt*] 1. *a)* a long-tailed
rodent resembling, but larger than, the
mouse *b)* any of various ratlike rodents
2. [Slang] an informer, traitor, etc. —*vi.*
rat′ted, rat′ting 1. [Slang] *a)* to betray
a cause, movement, etc. *b)* to act as an
informer 2. to hunt rats —**smell a rat**
to suspect a trick, plot, etc.
ratable (rāt′ə b'l) *adj.* 1. that can be
estimated, etc. 2. liable to payment of
rates Also *sp.* **rate′able**
ratable value the value of property for
rating purposes
ratafia (rat′ə fē′ə) *n.* [Fr.: < ?] 1. a
cordial flavoured with almond or fruit
kernels 2. a macaroon
ratan (rə tan′) *n. alt. sp. of* RATTAN
rat-a-tat (rat′ə tat′) *n.* [echoic] a series
of sharp, quick rapping sounds: also **rat′-a-**
tat′-tat′

RATCHET
WHEEL

ratchet (rach′it) *n.* [< Fr. < It. *rocca*,
distaff] 1. a toothed wheel (in full, **ratchet**
wheel) or bar that catches and holds a
pawl, preventing backward movement 2.
such a pawl 3. such a wheel (or bar)
and pawl as a unit
rate[1] (rāt) *n.* [< L. *reri*, reckon] 1. the
amount, degree, etc. of anything in relation
to units of something else [the *rate* of
pay per month] 2. a fixed ratio [the
rate of exchange] 3. a price; specif., the
cost per unit of some commodity, service,
etc. 4. speed 5. rank [of the first *rate*]
6. [*often pl.*] a tax on property levied
by a local authority —*vt.* **rat′ed, rat′ing**
1. to appraise 2. to assess the value
of property for taxation purposes 3. to
put into a particular class or rank 4.
to consider; esteem 5. [U.S. Colloq.] to
deserve —*vi.* to be classed or ranked
—**at any rate** 1. in any event 2. anyway
—**at this rate** this being so
rate[2] *vt., vi.* **rat′ed, rat′ing** [ME. *raten*]
to scold severely
ratepayer *n.* one who pays rates
rather (räth′ər; *for interj.* rä′thur′) *adv.*
[< OE. *hrathe*, quickly] 1. more willingly;
preferably 2. with more justice, reason,
etc. 3. more accurately 4. on the contrary
5. somewhat —*interj.* certainly —**had (or
would) rather** 1. would choose to 2.
would prefer that —**rather than** instead of
ratify (rat′ə fī′) *vt.* -**fied**, -**fy′ing** [see
RATE[1] + L. *facere*, make] to approve
or confirm; esp., to give official sanction
to —**rat′ifica′tion** *n.*
rating[1] (rāt′iŋ) *n.* 1. a placement in a
certain rank or class 2. a rank or grade,
as of naval personnel 3. an evaluation
of the credit or financial standing of a
businessman, firm, etc. 4. the assessment
of the value of a property for taxation
5. *Radio & TV* the relative popularity of
a programme, determined by polls
rating[2] *n.* [see RATE[2]] a scolding
ratio (rā′shē ō′) *n., pl.* -**tios** [L.: see
REASON] 1. a fixed relation in degree,
number, etc. between two similar things;
proportion 2. *Math.* the quotient of one
quantity divided by another of the same kind
ratiocinate (rat′ē os′ə nāt′) *vi.* -**nat′ed,**
-**nat′ing** [see REASON] to reason, esp.
using formal logic —**ra′tio′cina′tion** *n.*
ration (rash′ən) *n.* [see REASON] 1. a
fixed portion; share 2. a fixed allowance
of food, as a daily allowance for one
soldier, etc. 3. [*pl.*] food supply —*vt.*
1. to distribute (food, clothing, etc.) in
rations, as in times of scarcity 2. to
give rations to —**ra′tioning** *n.*
rational (rash′ən 'l) *adj.* [see REASON] 1.
of or based on reasoning 2. able to reason
3. sensible [a *rational* plan] 4. *Math.*
designating a number that can be expressed
as the quotient of two integers or as an
integer —**ra′tional′ity** (-ə nal′ə tē) *n.*
rationale (rash′ə näl′) *n.* [L.: see REASON]
1. the rational basis for something 2.
an explanation of reasons
rationalism (rash′ən ə liz'm) *n.* the
principle or practice of accepting reason
as the only basis for forming one's opinions
or course of action —**ra′tionalist** *n., adj.*
rationalize *vt.* -**ized**, -**iz′ing** 1. to think
of explanations for (one's acts, etc.) that
seem to make sense but do not truly
reveal one's motives 2. to make conform
to reason 3. to reorganize (an industry)
so as to eliminate uneconomic units and
increase productivity —*vi.* to rationalize
one's acts, beliefs, etc. —**ra′tionaliza′-**
tion *n.*

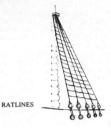

RATLINES

ratline (rat′lin) *n.* [< ?] any of the small ropes that join the shrouds of a ship and serve as a ladder: also sp. **rat′lin**

rat race [Colloq.] an intense competitive struggle, as in the business world

ratsbane *n.* rat poison

rattan (rə tan′) *n.* [< Malay *raut*, to strip] 1. a climbing palm with long, slender, tough stems 2. these stems, used in making wickerwork, etc.

ratter (rat′ər) *n.* a dog or cat skilled at catching rats

rattle (rat′'l) *vi.* -tled, -tling [prob. echoic] 1. to make a series of short, sharp sounds 2. to move with such sounds 3. to chatter (often with *on*) —*vt.* 1. to cause to rattle 2. to utter or perform rapidly (usually with *off*) 3. to confuse or upset —*n.* 1. a succession of short, sharp sounds 2. a device, as a baby's toy, intended to rattle when shaken 3. a rattling noise in the throat, as of a dying person

rattlesnake *n.* a poisonous American viper having horny rings at the end of the tail that rattle when shaken

rattletrap *n.* anything worn out, rickety, or rattling

rattling *adj.* 1. that rattles 2. [Colloq.] very fast, good, etc. —*adv.* [Colloq.] very

ratty (rat′ē) *adj.* -tier, -tiest [Slang] irritable; annoyed

raucous (rô′kəs) *adj.* [L. *raucus*] hoarse; rough-sounding

raunchy (rôn′chē) *adj.* -chier, -chiest [< ?] [U.S. Slang] 1. dirty, smelly, etc. 2. lecherous or risqué

ravage (rav′ij) *n.* [see RAVISH] ruin; devastating damage: *usually used in pl.* —*vt.* -aged, -aging to devastate; ruin

rave (rāv) *vi.* raved, rav′ing [prob. < OFr. *raver*] 1. to talk incoherently or wildly, as when delirious 2. to talk with excessive enthusiasm (*about*) —*n.* [Colloq.] an excessively enthusiastic commendation —**rav′er** *n.*

ravel (rav′'l) *vt., vi.* -elled, -elling [MDu. *ravelen*] 1. to tangle or become entangled 2. to separate into its parts, esp. threads; untwist; fray (*out*) —*n.* a ravelling

ravelling *n.* anything unravelled, as a thread unravelled from knitted or woven fabric

raven (rā′vən) *n.* [OE. *hræfn*] a large bird of the crow family, with shiny black feathers —*adj.* black and shiny

ravening (rav′ən iŋ) *adj.* [see RAVENOUS] greedily searching for prey

ravenous (rav′ə nəs) *adj.* [< L. *rapina*, RAPINE] 1. greedily hungry 2. greedy [*ravenous* for praise] 3. rapacious

rave-up (rāv′up) *n.* [Slang] an enjoyable social event, usually an energetic party

ravine (rə vēn′) *n.* [Fr., flood: see RAPINE] a long, deep hollow in the earth's surface, worn by a stream

raving (rā′viŋ) *adj.* 1. delirious 2. [Colloq.] exciting admiration [a *raving* beauty] —*adv.* so as to cause raving [*raving* mad] —*n.* incoherent speech

ravioli (rav′ē ō′lē) *n.pl.* [*with sing. v.*] [It.] small, square casings of pasta containing seasoned minced meat, cheese, etc., served usually in a savoury tomato sauce

ravish (rav′ish) *vt.* [< L. *rapere*, seize] 1. to enrapture 2. to rape 3. to seize and carry away forcibly

ravishing *adj.* causing great delight; entrancing

raw (rô) *adj.* [OE. *hreaw*] 1. not cooked 2. in its natural condition; not processed, etc. 3. inexperienced [a *raw* recruit] 4. with the skin rubbed off; sore and inflamed 5. cold and damp [a *raw* wind] 6. [Colloq.] harsh or unfair [a *raw* deal] —**in the raw** 1. in the natural state 2. naked

rawboned *adj.* having little fat; lean; gaunt

rawhide *n.* 1. an untanned hide 2. a whip made of this

ray[1] (rā) *n.* [see RADIUS] 1. any of the thin lines, or beams, of light that appear to come from a bright source 2. any of several lines coming out from a centre 3. a tiny amount [a *ray* of hope] 4. *Bot., Zool.* any part of a structure with parts coming like rays from a centre, as the petals of certain flowers 5. *Physics* a stream of radioactive particles, beam of radiant energy, etc.

ray[2] (rā) *n.* [< L. *raia*] a fish, as the stingray, skate, etc., having a flat body with both eyes on top

rayon (rā′on) *n.* [arbitrary coinage] 1. a synthetic textile fibre produced from cellulose solution 2. any fabric woven or knitted from such fibres

raze (rāz) *vt.* razed, raz′ing [< L. *radere*, to scrape] to tear down completely; demolish

razor (rā′zər) *n.* [see prec.] a sharp-edged cutting instrument for shaving off or cutting hair

razorbill *n.* a black and white auk with a black compressed bill

razor blade a sharp-edged cutting tool placed in a handle and used for shaving

razzle-dazzle (raz′'l daz′'l) *n.* [Slang] 1. a flashy display 2. a spree; frolic: also **razzle**

Rb *Chem.* rubidium

R.C. 1. Red Cross 2. Roman Catholic

R.C.A. Royal College of Art

R.C.A.F., RCAF Royal Canadian Air Force
R.C.M. Royal College of Music
R.C.M.P., RCMP Royal Canadian Mounted Police
R.C.N. Royal Canadian Navy
R.C.P. Royal College of Physicians
R.C.S. 1. Royal College of Science 2. Royal College of Surgeons 3. Royal Corps of Signals
Rd., rd. 1. road 2. rod 3. round
r.d., R/D return to drawer
re¹ (rā) *n.* [It.: see GAMUT] *Music* a syllable representing the second tone of the diatonic scale
re² (rē) *prep.* [< L. *res,* thing] as regards; about
re- [< Fr. < L.] *a prefix meaning:* 1. back [*repay*] 2. again, anew [*reappear*] It is used with a hyphen: 1) to distinguish between a word in which the prefix means *again* or *anew* and a word having a special meaning (Ex.: *re-sound, resound*) 2) usually, before words beginning with an *e* The following list contains some of the more common words in which *re-* means *again* or *anew*

reabsorb	recolour	repaint
reaccustom	recombine	repaper
reacquaint	recommence	rephotograph
reacquire	recompress	rephrase
re-act	recondense	replant
readapt	reconduct	replaster
readdress	reconfirm	replate
readjust	reconquer	replay
readmit	reconquest	repolish
readmittance	reconsecrate	repopularize
readopt	reconsign	repopulate
reaffiliate	reconsolidate	repot
reaffirm	recontaminate	re-press
reaffirmation	reconvene	reprice
realliance	reconvert	reprocess
reallocation	recook	republication
reallot	recopy	republish
reappearance	re-cover	repurchase
reapplication	recross	reread
reapply	recultivate	rerecord
reappoint	redecorate	resaddle
rearrest	redefine	reseal
reassemble	redeliver	resell
reassert	redescribe	reset
reassume	redesign	resettle
reattack	redetermine	resew
reattempt	redevelop	reshape
reawaken	redirect	resharpen
rebaptism	rediscover	reshuffle
rebaptize	rediscovery	resolder
rebind	redistribute	resolidify
reborn	redistribution	respace
rebroadcast	redraft	respell
rebuild	redraw	restabilize
rebury	re-edit	restage
recalculate	re-educate	restamp
recarry	re-elect	restart
recharge	re-election	restitch
rechargeable	re-embark	restock
recharter	re-emerge	restraighten
recheck	re-emphasize	restrengthen
recirculate	re-enact	restudy
reclassify	re-engage	resubmit
reclothe	re-enlist	resummon
	re-enter	resupply
	re-entrance	resurvey
	re-establish	reswallow
	re-examination	retack
	re-examine	retape
	re-exchange	retelevise
	re-experience	retell
	re-explain	rethread
	reface	retie
	refashion	retrain
	refasten	retranslate
	refloat	retrial
	refocus	retune
	refold	retype
	reformulate	reunite
	reframe	reusuable
	refurnish	revalue
	regather	revarnish
	reglorify	revisit
	regroup	rewaken
	rehang	reweigh
	reheat	
	rehire	
	rehouse	
	reimpose	
	reimprison	
	reincorporate	
	reinfect	
	reinflate	
	reinform	
	reinsert	
	reinspect	
	reinstall	
	reinstruct	
	reinsure	
	reinterpret	
	reinterrogate	
	reintroduce	
	reinvestigate	
	reinvigorate	
	reissue	
	rekindle	
	reknit	
	relabel	
	re-lay	
	relearn	
	relet	
	remarriage	
	remarry	
	remeasure	
	remerge	
	remix	
	remodel	
	remodify	
	remount	
	rename	
	renegotiate	
	renotify	
	renumber	
	reoccupy	
	reoccur	
	reoccurrence	
	reopen	
	reorient	
	repack	

Re *Chem.* rhenium
R.E. Royal Engineers
reach (rēch) *vt.* [OE. *ræcan*] 1. to go as far as; attain 2. to extend to, or touch, by thrusting out, etc. 3. to carry as far as [the news *reached* him] 4. to obtain and hand over [*reach* me the salt] 5.

to thrust out or extend (the hand, etc.) **6.** to get in touch with, as by telephone —*vi.* **1.** to thrust out the hand, etc. **2.** to stretch in influence, space, time, etc. **3.** to carry, as sound **4.** to try to obtain something —*n.* **1.** a stretching out **2.** the power of stretching, obtaining, etc. **3.** the distance or extent covered in stretching, obtaining, etc. **4.** a continuous extent of water

reach-me-downs *n.pl.* [Colloq.] second-hand clothing

react (rē akt´) *vi.* **1.** to respond to a stimulus, influence, etc. **2.** to act in return or reciprocally **3.** to act in opposition **4.** to go back to a former condition, stage, etc. **5.** *Chem.* to act with another substance in producing a chemical change

reactance *n.* *Elec.* opposition to the flow of alternating current, caused by inductance or capacitance

reaction (rē ak´shən) *n.* **1.** a response, as to a stimulus **2.** a returning or opposing action, etc. **3.** a movement back to a former or less advanced stage, etc.; esp. in politics **4.** *Chem. a)* the mutual action of substances undergoing chemical change *b)* a process that produces changes in an atomic nucleus **5.** *Med. a)* an action induced by resistance to another action *b)* depression or exhaustion following overstimulation, etc.

reactionary *adj.* showing or favouring reaction, esp. in politics —*n.*, *pl.* **-aries** a reactionary person

reactivate (rē ak´tə vāt´) *vt.* **-vat´ed, -vat´ing** to make active again —**reac´ti-va´tion** *n.*

reactor (rē ak´tər) *n.* same as NUCLEAR REACTOR

read (rēd) *vt.* **read** (red), **read´ing** (rēd´-ing) [OE. *rædan,* to counsel] **1.** to get the meaning of (something written or printed) by interpreting its characters **2.** to utter aloud (something written or printed) **3.** to know (a language) well enough to interpret its written form **4.** to understand the nature, significance, or thinking of **5.** to interpret (dreams, etc.) or foretell (the future) **6.** to interpret (a printed passage, etc.) as having a particular meaning **7.** to study [to read law] **8.** to register [the thermometer *reads* 25°C] **9.** to obtain (information) from (punch cards, tape, etc.): said of a computer **10.** [Slang] to hear and understand —*vi.* **1.** to read something written or printed **2.** to utter aloud the words of written or printed matter **3.** to learn by reading (*about* or *of*) **4.** to be drawn up in certain words **5.** to admit of being read [it *reads* well] —*n.* something for reading or a spell of reading —**read between the lines** to deduce a meaning that is implied —**read into** to interpret in a certain way —**read out** to display or record with a readout device —**read up (on)** to become well informed (about) by reading

readable *adj.* **1.** interesting or easy to read **2.** legible

reader *n.* **1.** a person who reads **2.** a person who reads lessons, etc. aloud

in church **3.** a schoolbook containing stories, poems, etc. for use in teaching how to read **4.** a lecturer in a university **5.** in publishing, *a)* a person who assesses the merit of manuscripts submitted *b)* a proofreader

readership *n.* all the people who read a particular publication, author, etc.

reading *adj.* of or for reading —*n.* **1.** the act or practice of one who reads **2.** the reciting of a literary work in public **3.** material read **4.** the extent to which a person has read **5.** the amount measured by a thermometer, etc. **6.** the way something is performed, understood, etc. [a superb *reading* of Hamlet] **7.** in Parliament, a formal recital of a bill

reading matter books, magazines, etc. collectively

reading room a room (in a club, library, etc.) for reading and writing

readout *n.* **1.** a retrieving of information from a computer **2.** this information, displayed visually or recorded, as by typewriter or on tape

ready (red´ē) *adj.* **-ier, -iest** [OE. *ræde*] **1.** prepared to act or be used immediately **2.** willing [a *ready* worker] **3.** *a)* liable [*ready* to cry] *b)* apt; inclined [always *ready* to blame others] **4.** prompt [a *ready* reply] **5.** available immediately [*ready* cash] —*vt.* **read´ied, read´ying** to make ready —**at the ready** prepared for immediate use —**make ready** to prepare —**read´ily** *adv.* —**read´iness** *n.*

ready-made *adj.* made so as to be ready for immediate use or sale: also, as applied to clothing, **read´y-to-wear´**

ready reckoner a book of tabulated calculations, providing a quick and easy method of finding the amounts of money involved in commercial transactions

reagent (rē ā´jənt) *n.* [RE- + AGENT] *Chem.* a substance used to detect, measure or react with another

real¹ (rē´əl) *adj.* [< L. *res,* thing] **1.** existing as or in fact; actual; true **2.** *a)* genuine *b)* sincere **3.** designating income as measured by purchasing power **4.** *Law* of or relating to permanent, immovable things [*real* property]

real² (rä äl´) *n.* [Sp. & Port., royal] a former silver coin of Spain

real estate land, including the buildings or improvements on it and its natural assets, as minerals, timber, etc.

realign (rē´ə līn´) *vt., vi.* to align again; specif., to readjust alliances (between) —**re´align´ment** *n.*

realism (rē´ə liz´m) *n.* **1.** a tendency to face facts and be practical **2.** the picturing in art and literature of people and things as they really appear to be **3.** *Philos.* the doctrine that universals are objectively actual —**re´alist** *n.* —**re´alis´tic** *adj.* —**re´-alis´tically** *adv.*

reality (rē al´ə tē) *n.,* *pl.* **-ties** **1.** the quality or fact of being real **2.** a person or thing that is real **3.** the quality of being true to life —**in reality** actually

realize (rē´ə līz´) *vt.* **-ized´, -iz´ing** **1.**

to understand fully 2. to make real; achieve 3. to be sold for (a specified sum) 4. to convert (assets, etc.) into money 5. to gain [to realize a profit] —re'aliza'tion n.

really (rē'ə lē) adv. 1. in reality; actually 2. truly [really hot] —interj. indeed

realm (relm) n. [< L. regimen, rule] 1. a kingdom 2. a region; sphere [the realm of imagination]

real tennis an ancient form of tennis played in a walled indoor court: also **royal tennis**

realty (rē'əl tē) n. [< REAL¹] same as REAL ESTATE

ream (rēm) n. [< Ar. rizma, bale] 1. 20 quires of paper 2. [pl.] [Colloq.] a great amount

reanimate (rē an'ə māt') vt. -mat'ed, -mat'ing to give new life, vigour, courage, etc. to —rean'ima'tion n.

reap (rēp) vt. [OE. ripan] 1. to cut (grain) with a scythe, machine, etc. 2. to gather (a harvest) 3. to get as the result of action, work, etc.

reaper n. 1. a person who reaps 2. a machine for reaping grain —the (Grim) Reaper death

reapportion (rē'ə pôr'shən) vt. to apportion again

reappraise (rē'ə prāz') vt. -praised', -prais'ing to reconsider —re'apprais'al n.

rear¹ (rēər) n. [< ARREAR(S)] 1. the back part 2. the position behind or at the back 3. [Slang] the buttocks: also **rear end** —adj. of, at, or in the rear —**bring up the rear** to come at the end

rear² vt. [OE. ræran] 1. to bring to maturity by educating, nourishing, etc. [to rear children] 2. to grow or breed 3. to put upright 4. to build; erect —vi. to rise on the hind legs, as a horse

rear admiral see MILITARY RANKS, table

rear guard a military detachment to protect the rear of a main force

rear light a light, usually red, at the rear of a vehicle to warn other vehicles coming from behind

rearm (rē ärm') vt., vi. 1. to arm again 2. to arm with new or more effective weapons —rear'mament n.

rearmost (rēər'mōst') adj. farthest in the rear

rearrange (rē'ə rānj') vt. -ranged', -rang'ing to arrange again or in a different manner —re'arrange'ment n.

rear-view mirror a mirror in a motor vehicle positioned so that the driver can see the traffic behind his vehicle

rearward adj. at, in, or towards the rear —adv. towards the rear: also **rear'wards**

reason (rē'z'n) n. [< L. reri, think] 1. an explanation or justification of an act, idea, etc. 2. a cause or motive 3. the ability to think, draw conclusions, etc. 4. good sense 5. sanity —vi. 1. to think logically; infer 2. to argue or talk in a logical way —vt. 1. to think logically about 2. to argue or infer [he reasoned that the method was too costly] 3. to

persuade by reasoning (into or out of) —**by reason of** because of —**in** (or **within**) **reason** in accord with what is reasonable —**stand to reason** to be logical —**with reason** justifiably

reasonable adj. 1. using or showing reason; sensible 2. not extreme or excessive 3. not expensive 4. fair; average —rea'sonableness n. —rea'sonably adv.

reasoning n. the drawing of inferences or conclusions from known or assumed facts

reassure (rē'ə shooər') vt. -sured', -sur'ing to restore to confidence —re'assur'ance n.

rebate (rē'bāt) n. [< OFr. re-, re- + abattre, beat down] 1. a return of part of the amount paid, as for goods 2. same as RABBET

rebec, rebeck (rē'bek) n. [< Ar. rabāb] a medieval pear-shaped instrument played with a bow

rebel (reb''l; for v. ri bel') n. [< L. re-, again + bellare, to war] 1. a person who takes up arms against the government of his country 2. a person who resists any authority —adj. 1. rebellious 2. of rebels —vi. -elled', -el'ling 1. to be a rebel against the government of one's country 2. to resist authority 3. to feel or show strong aversion

rebellion (ri bel'yən) n. [see prec.] 1. armed resistance to one's government 2. defiance of any authority

rebellious (ri bel'yəs) adj. 1. engaged in rebellion 2. of or like rebels or rebellion 3. defiant

rebid (rē bid'; for n., rē'bid') vt., vi. Cards to bid again, esp., in bridge, in the same suit as before —n. a rebidding

rebirth (rē burth') n. a reawakening; revival

rebound (ri bound'; also, for n., rē'bound') vi. 1. to spring back, as upon impact 2. to misfire, esp. so as to harm the perpetrator —n. a rebounding; recoil —**on the rebound** 1. after bouncing off the ground, etc. 2. while reacting to rejection, as in love

rebuff (ri buf') n. [< It. rabbuffo] 1. a blunt refusal of offered help, advice, etc. 2. any repulse —vt. 1. to refuse bluntly; snub 2. to repel

rebuke (ri byook') vt. -buked', -buk'ing [< OFr. re-, back + buchier, beat] to blame or scold in a sharp way; reprimand —n. a sharp reprimand —rebuk'ingly adv.

rebus (rē'bəs) n. [L., lit., by things] a puzzle consisting of pictures combined so as to suggest words [a picture of a bee plus the figure 4 is a rebus for "before"]

rebut (ri but') vt. -but'ted, -but'ting [< OFr. re-, back + buter, to push] to contradict or oppose, esp. in a formal manner by argument, proof, etc. —rebut'tal n.

rec (rek) n. shortened form of RECREATION

rec. 1. receipt 2. recipe 3. record(ed)

recalcitrant (ri kal'si trənt) adj. [< L. re-, back + calcitrare, to kick] refusing to obey authority, regulation, etc.; stubbornly defiant —recal'citrance n.

recall (ri kôl'; for n. also rē'kôl') vt. 1.

to remember 2. to order to return 3. to take back; revoke 4. to bring back in awareness, attention, etc. —*n.* 1. a recalling 2. the ability to remember; memory

recant (ri kant´) *vt., vi.* [< L. *re-*, back + *canere*, sing] to take back or confess being wrong about (former beliefs, etc.), esp. publicly —**recantation** (rē´kan tā´shən) *n.*

recap (rē´kap´) *vi., vt.* -**capped´**, -**cap´**-**ping** to recapitulate —*n.* a recapitulation, or summary

recapitulate (rē´kə pit´yoo lāt´) *vi., vt.* -**lat´ed**, -**lat´ing** [see RE- & CAPITULATE] to summarize —**re´capit´ula´tion** *n.*

recapture (rē kap´chər) *vt.* -**tured**, -**tur**-**ing** 1. to capture again 2. to remember —*n.* a recapturing or being recaptured

recast (rē kāst´; *for n.* rē´kāst´) *vt.* -**cast´**, -**cast´ing** 1. to cast again 2. to improve the form of by redoing; reconstruct —*n.* a recasting

recce (rek´ē) *n., vt., vi. Mil. colloq. var. of* RECONNAISSANCE or RECONNOITRE

recd., rec'd. received

recede (ri sēd´) *vi.* -**ced´ed**, -**ced´ing** [see RE- & CEDE] 1. to move back 2. to withdraw 3. to slope backwards [her chin *recedes*] 4. to lessen, dim, etc.

receipt (ri sēt´) *n.* [see RECEIPT] 1. a written acknowledgment that something has been received 2. a receiving or being received 3. [*pl.*] the money taken in by a business 4. *old-fashioned var. of* RECIPE —*vt.* to mark (a bill) paid

receive (ri sēv´) *vt.* -**ceived´**, -**ceiv´ing** [< L. *re-*, back + *capere*, take] 1. to take or get (something given, sent, etc.) 2. to experience; undergo [to *receive* acclaim] 3. to take the force of; bear 4. to react to [the song was well *received*] 5. to learn [to *receive* news] 6. to accept as authentic, valid, etc. 7. *a*) to let enter *b*) to have room for; contain 8. to greet (visitors, etc.) —*vi.* 1. to be a recipient 2. to greet guests 3. to buy and sell stolen goods 4. *Radio & TV* to convert incoming electromagnetic waves into sounds or images —**be on the receiving end** [Colloq.] to be the recipient of something unpleasant

Received Pronunciation the accent of standard British English as spoken by educated English people

receiver *n.* 1. one that receives; specif., *a*) *Law* a person appointed to administer or hold in trust property in bankruptcy or in a lawsuit *b*) a receptacle *c*) an apparatus that converts electrical signals, etc. into sound or light, as a radio receiving set, or that part of a telephone held to the ear 2. someone who receives stolen goods knowing that they are stolen

receiving set an apparatus for receiving radio or television signals

recent (rē´s'nt) *adj.* [< L. *recens*] 1. done, made, etc. just before the present time; new 2. of a time just before the present 3. [R-] designating the present

epoch, extending from the close of the Pleistocene —**re´cently** *adv.*

receptacle (ri sep´tə k'l) *n.* [see RECEIVE] 1. a container 2. *Bot.* the part of the stalk from which the flower grows

reception (ri sep´shən) *n.* [see RECEIVE] 1. *a*) a receiving or being received *b*) the manner of this [a friendly *reception*] 2. a social function for the receiving of guests 3. an area in an office, hotel, etc. where clients or visitors are received 4. *Radio & TV* the manner of receiving, with reference to quality

receptionist *n.* a person employed at a hotel, doctor's surgery, etc. to receive clients, etc.

reception room 1. a room for receiving visitors, clients, etc. 2. a living room in a house : term used chiefly by estate agents

receptive *adj.* able or ready to receive requests, suggestions, etc. —**recep´tiv´ity, recep´tiveness** *n.*

recess (rē´ses; *also, for v.,* ri ses´) *n.* [< L. *recedere*, recede] 1. a receding or hollow place, as in a wall 2. a secluded or inner place 3. a temporary halting of work, study, etc. [the parliamentary *recess*] —*vt.* 1. to place in a recess 2. to form a recess in

recession (ri sesh´ən) *n.* 1. a temporary falling off of business activity 2. a going backwards; withdrawal

recessional *n.* a hymn sung after a church service as the clergy and choir leave

recessive (ri ses´iv) *adj.* 1. receding 2. *Genetics* designating or of that one of any pair of genes which, when both are present in the germ plasm, remains latent

recherché (rə shāor´shā) *adj.* [Fr.]. 1. sought out with care; choice 2. having refinement or contrived elegance 3. too refined

recidivism (ri sid´ə viz'm) *n.* [< L. *re-*, back + *cadere*, to fall] relapse, or tendency to relapse, esp. into crime or antisocial behaviour —**recid´ivist** *n., adj.*

recipe (res´ə pē) *n.* [L.: see RECIPE] 1. a list of ingredients and directions for preparing a dish 2. any procedure for bringing about a desired result

recipient (ri sip´ē ənt) *n.* [see RECEIVE] a person or thing that receives

reciprocal (ri sip´rə k'l) *adj.* [< L. *reciprocus*, returning] 1. done, felt, given, etc. in return 2. mutual 3. equivalent or complementary 4. *Gram.* expressing mutual relation [*each other* is a *reciprocal* pronoun] —*n.* 1. anything that has a reciprocal relation to another; counterpart 2. *Math.* the quantity resulting from the division of 1 by the given quantity [the *reciprocal* of 7 is 1/7]

reciprocate (ri sip´rə kāt´) *vt., vi.* -**cat´**-**ed**, -**cat´ing** 1. *a*) to give and get reciprocally *b*) to give, do, feel, etc. (something similar) in return 2. to move alternately back and forth —**recip´roca´**-**tion** *n.*

reciprocity (res´ə pros´ə tē) *n., pl.* -**ties** 1. reciprocal relationship 2. mutual exchange; esp., exchange of special privileges between two countries

recital (ri sīt′′l) n. 1. a musical programme given by a soloist or a small ensemble 2. a) a telling in detail b) the account, story, etc. told

recitation (res′ə tā′shən) n. 1. a recital (sense 2) 2. a) the speaking aloud in public of something memorized b) the piece so presented

recitative (res′ə tə tēv′) n. [< It. < L. recitare, recite] Music a type of declamatory singing, free in rhythm and tempo, as in the dialogue of operas

recite (ri sīt′) vt., vi. -cit′ed, -cit′ing [see RE- & CITE] 1. to speak aloud, as from memory (a poem, etc.) 2. to tell in detail

reck (rek) vi., vt. [OE. reccan] [Archaic] 1. to have care or concern (for) or take heed (of) 2. to matter (to)

reckless (rek′lis) adj. [see prec. & -LESS] not regarding consequences; rash

reckon (rek′ən) vt. [OE. -recenian] 1. to count; compute 2. to regard as being 3. [Colloq.] to suppose —vi. 1. to count up 2. [Colloq.] to rely (with on) —reckon up to add a bill, etc. —reckon with to take into consideration

reckoner n. any device or table used to aid reckoning, esp., a ready reckoner

reckoning n. 1. counting or computation 2. a calculated guess 3. a settlement of an account 4. the giving of rewards or punishments [day of reckoning]

reclaim (ri klām′) vt. [see RE- & CLAIM] 1. to regain possession of 2. to make (marshland, etc.) capable of being cultivated or lived on 3. to recover (useful materials) from waste products 4. to rescue from error, vice, etc. —reclamation (rek′lə mā′shən) n.

recline (ri klīn′) vt., vi. -clined′, -clin′-ing [< L. re-, back + clinare, to lean] to lie or cause to lie back or down; lean back —reclin′er n.

recluse (ri kloos′) n. [< L. re-, back + claudere, to shut] a person who leads a secluded, solitary life —reclu′sive adj.

recognition (rek′əg nish′ən) n. [see ff.] 1. a recognizing or being recognized 2. approval, gratitude, etc. [in recognition of his services]

recognizance (ri kog′ni zəns) n. [< L. re-, again + cognoscere, know] Law 1. a bond binding a person to some act, as to appear in court 2. a sum of money that one must forfeit if this obligation is not fulfilled

recognize (rek′əg nīz′) vt. -nized′, -niz′-ing [see prec.] 1. to identify as known before 2. to know by some detail, as of appearance 3. to be aware of the significance of 4. to acknowledge the existence, validity, etc. of 5. to accept as a fact [to recognize defeat] 6. to acknowledge as worthy of appreciation or approval 7. to formally acknowledge the legal standing of (a government) 8. to show acquaintance with (a person) by greeting —rec′ogniz′able adj. —rec′og-niz′ably adv.

recoil (ri koil′; also for n., rē′koil′) vi. [< L. re-, back + culus, buttocks] 1. to draw back, as in fear, disgust, etc. 2. to spring or kick back, as a gun when fired 3. to react unfavourably upon the originator (with on or upon) —n. a recoiling

recollect (rek′ə lekt′) vt., vi. [see RE- & COLLECT[1]] to remember, esp. with some effort —rec′ollec′tion n.

recommend (rek′ə mend′) vt. [see RE- & COMMEND] 1. to advise 2. to suggest as suited for some function, position, etc. 3. to make acceptable or pleasing [his charm recommends him] 4. to entrust [recommended to his care] —rec′ommen-da′tion n.

recompense (rek′əm pens′) vt. -pensed′, -pens′ing [see RE- & COMPENSATE] 1. to repay; reward 2. to compensate (for) (a loss, etc.) —n. 1. compensation for a loss, injury, etc. 2. requital, reward, etc.

reconcile (rek′ən sīl′) vt. -ciled′, -cil′ing [see RE- & CONCILIATE] 1. to make content or acquiescent (to) 2. to make friendly again 3. to settle (a quarrel, etc.) 4. to make (facts, ideas, etc.) consistent —rec′oncil′able adj. —rec′oncil′ia′tion (-sil′ē ā′shən) n.

recondite (ri kon′dīt) adj. [< L. re-, back + condere, to hide] 1. beyond the grasp of ordinary understanding; profound 2. dealing with abstruse or difficult subjects

recondition (rē′kən dish′ən) vt. to put back in good condition by cleaning, repairing, etc.

reconnaissance (ri kon′ə səns) n. [Fr.: see RECOGNIZANCE] an exploratory survey or examination, as in seeking information about enemy positions

reconnoitre (rek′ə noit′ər) vt., vi. [< Fr.: see RECOGNIZANCE] to make a reconnaissance (of)

reconsider (rē′kən sid′ər) vt., vi. to think over, as with a view to changing a decision —re′consid′era′tion n.

reconstitute (rē kon′stə tyoot′) vt. -tut′-ed, -tut′ing to constitute again; specif., to restore (a dehydrated or condensed substance) to its full form by adding water

reconstruct (rē′kən strukt′) vt. 1. to construct again, as from remaining parts 2. to form a picture of (a crime, past event, etc.) by re-enacting it or piecing together the evidence —re′construc′tion n.

record (ri kôrd′; for n. & adj., rek′ôrd) vt. [< L. recordari, remember] 1. to put in writing for future use 2. to indicate, as on a graph or dial 3. to register (sound or visual images) in some permanent form, as on a magnetic tape, for reproduction —vi. 1. to record something 2. to admit of being recorded —n. 1. the condition of being recorded 2. a) an account of events b) anything that serves as evidence of an event, etc. c) an official report of public proceedings 3. a register, monument, etc. 4. a) the known facts about anyone or anything b) the recorded offences of a person who has been convicted one or more times 5. a thin, flat, grooved disc for playing on a gramophone 6.

the best performance, highest speed, greatest amount, etc. achieved —*adj.* establishing a record as the best, largest, etc. *[a record crop]* —**for the record** officially —**go on record** to state one's opinions publicly —**have a record** to have been convicted of criminal offences —**off the record** confidential(ly) —**on record** publicly declared

recorded delivery a post office service by which an official record of posting and delivery is obtained for a letter or package

recorder *n.* 1. one who keeps records 2. a machine or device that records; esp., *same as* TAPE RECORDER 3. a kind of flute 4. a barrister or solicitor who is appointed to act as a judge in certain courts

recording *n.* 1. the act of one that records 2. what is recorded, as on a disc or tape —*adj.* that records

Record Office the state department responsible for public and state records: also **Public Record Office**

record player a gramophone operated electrically or electronically

recount (ri kount′) *vt.* [see RE- & COUNT[1]] to tell in detail; narrate

re-count (rē′kount′; *for n.* rē′kount′) *vt.* to count again —*n.* a second count, as of votes: also **recount**

recoup (ri kōōp′) *vt.* [< Fr. *re-*, again + *couper*, to cut] 1. *a*) to make up for *[to recoup a loss]* *b*) to regain 2. to reimburse —*n.* a recouping —**recoup′ment** *n.*

recourse (ri kôrs′) *n.* [see RE- & COURSE] 1. a turning for aid, safety, etc. *[he had recourse to the law]* 2. that to which one turns seeking aid, safety, etc.

recover (ri kuv′ər) *vt.* [< L. *recuperare*] 1. *a*) to get back (something lost, stolen, etc.) *b*) to regain (health, etc.) 2. to compensate for *[to recover losses]* 3. to save (oneself) from a fall, loss of control, betrayal of feeling, etc. 4. *Law* to get or get back by final judgment in a court —*vi.* to regain health, balance, control, etc.

recovery *n.*, *pl.* **-eries** a recovering; specif., *a*) a regaining of something lost *b*) a return to health *c*) a regaining of balance, composure, etc.

recreant (rek′rē ənt) *adj.* [< OFr. *recreire*, surrender allegiance] 1. cowardly 2. disloyal; traitorous —*n.* 1. a coward 2. a traitor —**rec′reancy** *n.*

recreation (rek′rē ā′shən) *n.* [< L. *recreare*, refresh] any form of play, amusement, etc. used for refreshment of body or mind —**rec′rea′tional** *adj.*

recriminate (ri krim′ə nāt′) *vi.* -**nat′ed**, -**nat′ing** [see RE- & CRIME] to answer an accuser by accusing him in return —**recrim′ina′tion** *n.* —**recrim′inatory** (-nə tə rē), *adj.*

recrudesce (rē′krōō des′) *vi.* -**desced′**, -**desc′ing** [< L. *re-*, again + *crudus*, raw] to break out again after being relatively inactive —**re′crudes′cence** *n.*

recruit (ri krōōt′) *vt.* [< Fr. < L. *re-*, again + *crescere*, grow] 1. to enlist

(personnel) into an army or navy 2. to enlist (new members) for a party, organization, etc. —*vi.* to enlist new personnel, esp. for a military force —*n.* 1. a recently enlisted soldier, sailor, etc. 2. a new member of any group —**recruit′-ment** *n.*

rectal (rek′t'l) *adj.* of, for, or near the rectum

rectangle (rek′taŋ′g'l) *n.* [< L. *rectus*, straight + ANGLE[1]] any four-sided plane figure with four right angles —**rectan′gular** *adj.*

rectify (rek′tə fī′) *vt.* -**fied′**, -**fy′ing** [< L. *rectus*, straight + *facere*, make] 1. to put right; correct 2. *Chem.* to refine or purify (a liquid) by distillation 3. *Elec.* to convert (alternating current) to direct current —**rec′tifica′tion** *n.* —**rec′tifi′er** *n.*, *adj.*

rectilinear (rek′tə lin′ē ər) *adj.* [< LL. *rectus*, straight + *linea*, LINE[1]] 1. in or forming a straight line 2. bounded or formed by straight lines Also **rec′tilin′eal**

rectitude (rek′tə tyōōd′) *n.* [< L. *rectus*, straight] 1. honesty; uprightness of character 2. correctness of judgment or method

recto (rek′tō) *n.*, *pl.* -**tos** [< L. *recto*, to the right] *Printing* any right-hand page of a book

rector (rek′tər) *n.* [< L. *regere*, to rule] 1. *Anglican Ch.* a clergyman in charge of a parish in which the incumbent was formerly entitled to the whole of the tithes 2. *R.C.Ch.* the head priest of a parish, or of a college, etc. 3. in certain academic institutions, the principal or head

rectory *n.*, *pl.* -**ries** the residence of a clergyman who is a rector

rectum (rek′təm) *n.*, *pl.* -**tums**, -**ta** [< L. *rectum* (*intestinum*), straight (intestine)] the last segment of the large intestine, ending at the anus

recumbent (ri kum′bənt) *adj.* [< L. *re-*, back + *cumbere*, lie down] lying down; reclining

recuperate (ri kyōō′pə rāt′) *vt.*, *vi.* -**at′-ed**, -**at′ing** [< L. *recuperare*, recover] to recover (losses, health, etc.) —**recu′per-a′tion** *n.* —**recu′perative** *adj.*

recur (ri kur′) *vi.* -**curred′**, -**cur′ring** [< L. *re-*, back + *currere*, run] 1. to occur again or at intervals 2. to return in thought, talk, etc. *[to recur to a topic]* —**recur′-rence** (-kur′-) *n.* —**recur′rent** (-kur′-) *adj.*

recusant (rek′yōō zənt) *n.* [< L. *recusare*, to reject] a person who refuses to obey an established authority; specif., in England in the 16th to 18th cent., a Roman Catholic who refused to attend the services of the Church of England —**rec′usancy** *n.*

recycle (rē sī′k'l) *vt.*, *vi.* -**cled**, -**cling** 1. to pass through a cycle again 2. to use again and again, as a single supply of water 3. to change (waste substances) into a usable form

red (red) *n.* [OE. *read*] 1. a colour varying in hue from that of blood to pink 2. a pigment producing this colour 3. *[often* R-] a political radical; esp., a communist

4. anything coloured red, as a red draughts piece —*adj.* **red′der, red′dest** 1. of the colour red 2. auburn: said of hair 3. *a)* flushed or blushing *b)* bloodshot *c)* sore 4. [R-] radical; esp., communist —**in the red** in debt or losing money —**see red** [Colloq.] to become angry —**red′dish** *adj.* —**red′ness** *n.*

red blood cell *same as* ERYTHROCYTE

red-blooded *adj.*   vigorous, lusty, etc.

redbreast *n.*   the robin

redbrick, red-brick *adj.* [< the typical building material] of a British university of relatively recent foundation —*n.* a redbrick university

red carpet a very grand welcome and entertainment

redcoat *n.* 1. a British soldier in a uniform with a red coat 2. [Canad. Colloq.] a Mountie

Red Crescent a Moslem organization equivalent to the Red Cross

Red Cross an international society for the relief of suffering in time of war or disaster

red deer a deer native to Europe and Asia

redden *vt., vi.* to make or become red

redeem (ri dēm′) *vt.* [< L. *re(d)-* + *emere,* buy] 1. to get or buy back; recover 2. to pay off (a mortgage, etc.) 3. to convert (bonds, tokens, etc.) into cash 4. *a)* to ransom *b)* to deliver from sin 5. to fulfil (a promise) 6. *a)* to make amends or atone for *b)* to restore (oneself) to favour *c)* to make worthwhile —**redeem′er** *n.*

redemption (ri demp′shən) *n.* [see prec.] 1. a redeeming or being redeemed 2. something that redeems

Red Ensign the flag flown by the British merchant navy, having the Union Jack on a red background at the upper corner: the national flag of Canada until 1965

redeploy (rē′di ploi′) *vt., vi.* to move (troops, etc.) from one front or area to another —**re′deploy′ment** *n.*

redeye (red′ī) *n.* [Canad. Slang] a drink of beer and tomato juice

redfish *n.* [Canad.] *same as* KOKANEE

red flag 1. the emblem of revolution 2. a danger signal

red-handed (red′han′did) *adv., adj.* in the very act of committing a crime

red hat a wide-brimmed, flat, red hat: symbol of a cardinal's rank

redhead *n.* a person with red hair —**red′head′ed** *adj.*

red herring 1. something used to turn attention away from the basic issue 2. a smoked herring

red-hot *adj.* 1. hot enough to glow 2. very excited, angry, etc. 3. very new; up-to-the-minute

Rediffusion (rē′di fyōō′zhən) *Trademark* in Britain, a system by which radio or television programmes are relayed to subscribers from a receiver via cables

Red Indian a N American Indian

redistribution (rē′dis trə byōō′shən) *n.* a revision of the number of seats in the Canadian House of Commons allocated

to each province, made every ten years on the basis of a new census

red lead red oxide of lead, used in making paint, etc.

red-letter (red′let′ər) *adj.* designating a memorable or joyous day or event : from the custom of marking holidays on the calendar in red ink

red light 1. any warning signal 2. a red traffic light

red-light district a district containing many brothels

red meat meat that is red before cooking, as beef

redo (rē dōō′) *vt.* -**did′, -done′, -do′ing** 1. to do again 2. to redecorate

redolent (red′ō lənt) *adj.* [< L. *re(d)-,* intens. + *olere,* to smell] 1. fragrant 2. smelling (*of*) [*redolent* of tar] 3. suggestive (*of*) —**red′olence** *n.*

redouble (rē dub′'l) *vt., vi.* -**bled, -bling** 1. to make or become twice as great or twice as much 2. *Bridge* to double (a bid that an opponent has already doubled) —*n.* *Bridge* a redoubling

redoubt (ri dout′) *n.* [< Fr.: see REDUCE] 1. a breastwork outside or within a fortification 2. any stronghold

redoubtable (ri dout′a b'l) *adj.* [< L. *re-,* intens. + *dubitare,* to doubt] 1. inspiring fear 2. commanding respect —**redoubt′ably** *adv.*

redound (ri dound′) *vi.* [< L. *re(d)-,* intens. + *undare,* to surge] 1. to have a result (*to* the credit or discredit of) 2. to recoil (*upon*)

red pepper 1. a plant with a red, many-seeded fruit 2. the fruit 3. the ground fruit or seeds, used for seasoning

redpoll *n.* a finch, the male of which has a red crown

red rag [Colloq.] anything which excites one to fury

redress (ri dres′) *vt.* [see RE- & DRESS] to set right, as by making compensation for (a wrong, etc.) —*n.* 1. a redressing 2. compensation

Red River cart *Canad. Hist.* a strongly-built, two-wheeled ox or horse-drawn cart

Red River Rebellion the Métis uprising of 1869-70 against the Canadian government's takeover of their territory in the Red River region

red salmon any salmon having reddish flesh, esp. the sockeye salmon

redshank *n.* a sandpiper with red legs

red shift *Astron.* a shift towards longer wavelengths of the spectral lines of remote galaxies, thought to indicate an expanding universe

redskin *n.* [Colloq.] a North American Indian

red squirrel a squirrel with reddish fur

redstart (red′stärt′) *n.* [RED + obs. *start,* tail] a small warbler with a reddish tail

red tape [< the tape used to tie official papers] rigid adherence to routine and regulations, causing delay in getting business done

reduce (ri dyōōs′) *vt.* -**duced′, -duc′ing** [< L. *re-,* back + *ducere,* to lead] 1.

to lessen, as in size, price, etc. **2.** to bring into a certain order **3.** to change to a different form *[to reduce to ashes]* **4.** to lower, as in rank or circumstances **5.** to subdue or conquer **6.** to compel by need *[reduced to stealing]* **7.** to make thin **8.** to simplify; explain **9.** *Arith.* to change in denomination or form without changing in value *[to reduce 4/8 to 1/2]* **10.** *Chem.* a) to decrease the positive valence of (an atom or ion) b) to remove the oxygen from c) to combine with hydrogen d) to bring into the metallic state by removing nonmetallic elements —**vi.** **1.** to become reduced **2.** to diet —**reduc'ible** *adj.*

‡**reductio ad absurdum** (ri duk'tē ō'- ad ab sur'dəm) [L., reduction to absurdity] *Logic* the disproof of a proposition by showing the logical conclusions drawn from it to be absurd

reduction (ri duk'shən) *n.* **1.** a) a reducing or being reduced b) the amount of this **2.** anything made by reducing, as a smaller copy —**reduc'tive** *adj.*

redundancy payment a sum of money given to a worker who is made redundant by an employer

redundant (ri dun'dənt) *adj.* [see REDOUND] **1.** more than enough; superfluous **2.** unnecessary to the meaning: said of words **3.** of a worker deprived of a job because he is no longer needed —**redun'dance, redun'dancy** *n.* —**redun'- dantly** *adv.*

reduplicate (ri dyoo'plə kāt') *vt.* **-cat'ed, -cat'ing** **1.** to redouble, double, or repeat **2.** to double (a syllable or word) to form a new word (as *tom-tom*), sometimes with changes (as *chitchat*) —**redu'plica'tion** *n.* —**redu'plicative** *adj.*

redwing (red'wiŋ') *n.* a thrush with an orange-red patch on the underside of the wings

redwood *n.* a giant N American evergreen tree

re-echo (rē ek'ō) *vt., vi.* **-ech'oed, -ech'o- ing** to echo back or again; resound

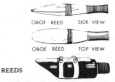

OBOE REED   SIDE VIEW

OBOE REED   TOP VIEW

REEDS

CLARINET REED   SIDE VIEW

reed (rēd) *n.* [OE. *hreod*] **1.** a tall, slender grass growing in wet or marshy land **2.** a musical pipe made from a hollow stem **3.** *Music* a) a thin strip of some flexible substance placed within the mouthpiece of certain wind instruments : when vibrated by the breath, it produces a musical tone b) an instrument with a reed c) in some organs, a similar device that vibrates in a current of air

reed bunting *same as* ORTOLAN

reedy *adj.* **-ier, -iest** **1.** full of reeds **2.**

made of reed **3.** slender, fragile, etc. **4.** thin; piping —**reed'ily** *adv.* —**reed'iness** *n.*

reef¹ (rēf) *n.* [prob. < ON. *rif*, rib] a ridge of rock, coral, or sand at or near the surface of the water

reef² *n.* [< or akin to prec.] a part of a sail which can be folded and tied down to reduce the area exposed to the wind —**vt.** to reduce (a sail) by taking in part of it

reefer *n.* **1.** a short, thick, double-breasted coat like a seaman's jacket **2.** [Slang] a marijuana cigarette

reef knot a double knot in which the free ends run parallel to the standing parts

reek (rēk) *vi.* [OE. *rec*] **1.** to have a strong, offensive smell **2.** to be permeated with —*n.* **1.** a strong, unpleasant smell **2.** [Chiefly Scot.] vapour; fume —**reek'y** *adj.*

reel¹ (rēl) *vi.* [< OE. *hreol*] **1.** to sway or stagger, as from dizziness or drunkenness **2.** to spin; whirl

reel² *n.* [prob. < REEL] **1.** any of various lively, esp. Scottish, dances **2.** music for these

reel³ *n.* [OE. *hreol*] **1.** a spool on which thread, wire, film, fishing line, etc. is wound **2.** the quantity of wire, thread, film, etc. usually wound on one reel —*vt., vi.* to wind on a reel —**reel off** to tell, write, etc. easily and quickly

re-entry (rē en'trē) *n., pl.* **-tries** a re-entering; specif., a coming back, as of a space vehicle, into the earth's atmosphere

reeve¹ (rēv) *n.* [OE. *gerefa*] **1.** *Hist.* the chief officer of a town or district **2.** *Hist.* the overseer of a manor; steward **3.** [Canad.] the president of a local council esp. in a rural area

reeve² *vt.* **reeved** or **rove, rove** or **rov'- en, reev'ing** [prob. < Du. *reven*] *Naut.* **1.** to slip (a rope) through a block, ring, etc. **2.** a) to pass in, through, or round something b) to fasten by so doing

ref (ref) *n., vt., vi.* [Colloq.] *same as* REFEREE

ref. 1. referee **2.** reference **3.** reformed

refection (ri fek'shən) *n.* [< L. *re-*, again + *facere*, make] a light meal

refectory (ri fek'tər ē) *n., pl.* **-ries** a dining hall in a monastery, convent, college, etc.

refectory table a long, narrow, rectangular table

refer (ri fur') *vt.* **-ferred', -fer'ring** [< L. *re-*, back + *ferre*, to bear] **1.** to direct (to someone or something) for aid, information, etc. **2.** to assign (to) as cause or origin **3.** to assign as belonging (to a kind, class, etc.) **4.** to submit (a quarrel, etc.) for settlement —*vi.* **1.** to relate or apply (to) **2.** to direct attention (to) **3.** to turn for information, aid, etc. (to) —**refer'able** *adj.* —**refer'ral** *n.*

referee (ref'ə rē') *n.* **1.** a person to whom something is referred for decision **2.** an official who enforces the rules in certain sports contests **3.** someone who testifies to the good character of another —*vt., vi.* **-eed', -ee'ing** to act as referee (in)

reference (ref'rəns) *n.* 1. a referring or being referred 2. *a)* an indication, as in a book, of some other work to be consulted *b)* the work so indicated 3. *a)* the direction of attention to a person or thing *b)* a mention 4. relation; regard; connection 5. *a)* the giving of the name of a person who can offer information or recommendation *b)* the person so indicated *c)* a written statement giving the qualifications, abilities, etc. of someone seeking a position, etc. —**make reference to** to mention —**with reference to** concerning —**ref′eren′tial** (-ə ren′shəl) *adj.*

reference book a book, such as an encyclopedia, from which information may be obtained

reference library a library where books may be consulted but not taken away by readers

referendum (ref′ə ren′dəm) *n.,* *pl.* **-dums** or **-da** [L.: see REFER] 1. the submission of a law, proposed or already in effect, to a direct vote of the people 2. the vote itself

refill (rē fil′; *for n.* rē′fil) *vt., vi.* to fill again —*n.* a new filling; esp., a unit to replace the used-up contents of a container —**refill′able** *adj.*

refine (ri fīn′) *vt., vi.* **-fined′, -fin′ing** [RE- + FINE¹, *v.*] 1. to free or become free from impurities, etc. 2. to make or become more polished or elegant —**refin′er** *n.*

refined *adj.* 1. cultivated; elegant 2. characterized by great subtlety, precision, etc. 3. purified

refinement *n.* 1. *a)* a refining or being refined *b)* the result of this 2. delicacy or elegance of speech, manners, etc. 3. a development; improvement 4. a subtlety

refinery *n., pl.* **-eries** a plant for refining such raw materials as oil, metal, sugar, etc.

refit (rē fit′; *also for n.* rē′fit′) *vt., vi.* **-fit′-ted, -fit′ting** to make or be made ready or fit for use again, as by repairing —*n.* a refitting

reflation (rē flā′shən) *n.* [RE- + (IN)FLATION] 1. an increase in money supply designed to cause an increase in economic activity 2. the increase in economic activity —**refla′tionary** *adj.*

reflect (ri flekt′) *vt.* [< L. *re-*, back + *flectere*, to bend] 1. to throw back (light, heat, or sound) 2. to give back an image of; mirror 3. to bring as a consequence (with *on*) [deeds that *reflect* honour on him] 4. to show [skills that *reflect* years of training] 5. to realize (*that*) —*vi.* 1. to be thrown back [light *reflecting* from the water] 2. to throw back light, heat, etc. 3. to give back an image 4. to think seriously (*on* or *upon*) 5. to cast blame or discredit (*on* or *upon*)

reflection, reflexion *n.* 1. a reflecting or being reflected 2. anything reflected; specif., an image 3. *a)* serious thought *b)* an idea, remark, etc. that comes from such thought 4. *a)* discredit *b)* a statement casting, or an action bringing, discredit

reflective *adj.* 1. reflecting 2. thoughtful

reflector *n.* 1. a surface, object, or device that reflects radiant energy, as light, sound, etc. 2. a reflecting telescope

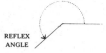

REFLEX
ANGLE

reflex (rē′fleks) *n.* [see REFLECT] 1. *a)* a reflex action *b)* any quick, automatic response *c)* [*pl.*] ability to react quickly and effectively 2. reflection 3. a reflected image —*adj.* 1. coming in reaction; esp., designating an involuntary action, as a sneeze, resulting when a stimulus is directly transmitted to the muscle or gland that responds 2. *Geom.* designating an angle greater than a straight angle (180°) 3. turned or bent back

reflexive (rē flek′siv) *adj.* 1. *Gram. a)* designating a verb whose subject and object refer to the same person or thing ("I *wash* myself") *b)* designating a pronoun used as the object of such a verb 2. reflex —*n.* a reflexive verb or pronoun

reform (ri fôrm′) *vt.* [see RE- & FORM] 1. to make better by stopping abuses, introducing better procedures, etc. 2. to cause (a person) to behave better —*vi.* to become better; give up bad ways —*n.* 1. a correction of faults or evils, as in government 2. an improvement in character and conduct —**reform′ative** *adj.*

reformation (ref′ər mā′shən) *n.* 1. a reforming or being reformed 2. [R-] the 16th-cent. religious movement that aimed at reforming the Roman Catholic Church and resulted in establishing the Protestant churches

reformatory (ri fôr′mə tər ē) *n., pl.* **-ries** formerly, an institution to which young offenders were sent for training —*adj.* reforming or aiming at reform

reformed *adj.* 1. improved or corrected 2. [R-] designating a Protestant church

reformer *n.* a person who seeks to bring about reform, esp. political or social reform

refract (ri frakt′) *vt.* [< L. *re-*, back + *frangere*, to break] to cause (a ray of light, heat, etc.) to undergo refraction —**refrac′tive** *adj.* —**refract′or** *n.*

refraction *n.* 1. the bending of a ray or wave of light, heat, or sound, as it passes obliquely from one medium to another 2. the ability of the eye to refract light entering it, so as to form an image on the retina

refractory *adj.* [see REFRACT] 1. hard to manage; stubborn 2. hard to melt or work: said of ores or metals 3. not yielding to treatment, as a disease

refrain¹ (ri frān′) *vi.* [< L. *re-*, back + *frenare,* to curb] to hold back; keep oneself (*from* doing something)

refrain² *n.* [see REFRACT] 1. a phrase or verse repeated at intervals in a song or poem 2. music for this

refrangible (ri fran′jə b'l) *adj.* [< REFRACT] that can be refracted, as light rays

refresh (ri fresh′) *vt.* [see RE- & FRESH] 1. to make (another or oneself) feel cooler, stronger, etc., as by food, drink, or sleep 2. to make fresh by cooling, wetting, etc. 3. to revive (the memory, etc.) 4. to replenish —*vi.* to revive —**refresh′er** *n.* —**refresh′ing** *adj.*

refreshment *n.* 1. a refreshing or being refreshed 2. something that refreshes 3. [*pl.*] food or drink or both

refrigerant (ri frij′ər ənt) *n.* any of various liquids that vaporize at a low temperature, used in mechanical refrigeration —*adj.* that refrigerates; cooling or freezing

refrigerate (ri frij′ə rāt′) *vt.* -at′ed, -at′-ing [< L. *re-*, intens. + *frigus*, cold] 1. to make or keep cool or cold 2. to preserve (food, etc.) by keeping cold or freezing —**refrig′era′tion** *n.*

refrigerator *n.* a box, cabinet, or room in which food, etc. is kept cool

reft (reft) *adj.* bereft

refuel (rē fyōō′əl) *vt.* -fu′elled, -fu′elling to supply again with fuel —*vi.* to take on a fresh supply of fuel

refuge (ref′yōōj) *n.* [< L. *re-*, back + *fugere*, flee] 1. shelter or protection from danger, difficulty, etc. 2. a place of safety; shelter

refugee (ref′yoo jē′) *n.* a person who flees from his home or country to seek refuge elsewhere

refulgent (ri ful′jənt) *adj.* [< L. *refulgere*, to reflect light] shining; radiant —**reful′-gence** *n.*

refund (ri fund′; *for n.* rē′fund′) *vt., vi.* [< L. *re-*, back + *fundere*, pour] to give back (money, etc.) —*n.* the act of refunding or the amount refunded

refurbish (ri fur′bish) *vt.* [RE- + FURBISH] to brighten, freshen, or polish up again

refusal (ri fyōō′z'l) *n.* 1. the act of refusing 2. the chance to accept or refuse something before it is offered to another

refuse[1] (ri fyōoz′) *vt.* -fused′, -fus′ing [see REFUND] 1. to decline to accept; reject 2. to decline to do, give, etc. 3. to stop short at (a fence, etc.) without jumping it: said of a horse —*vi.* to decline to accept, agree to, or do

refuse[2] (ref′yōos) *n.* [see REFUND] anything thrown away or rejected as worthless or useless; waste; rubbish

refute (ri fyōot′) *vt.* -fut′ed, -fut′ing [< L. *refutare*, repel] 1. to prove (a person) wrong 2. to prove (an argument or statement) to be false or wrong, by argument or evidence: sometimes incorrectly used to mean *deny* —**refut′a-bly** *adj.* —**refutation** (ref′yōō tā′shən) *n.*

regain (ri gān′) *vt.* 1. to get back again; recover 2. to get back to

regal (rē′gəl) *adj.* [< L. *rex*, king] of, like, or fit for a king; splendid, stately, etc. —**regality** (rē gal′ə tē) *n.*

regale (ri gāl′) *vt.* -galed′, -gal′ing [< Fr. *ré-*, RE- + OFr. *gale*, joy] 1. to

delight (*with*) 2. to entertain by providing a feast

regalia (ri gāl′yə) *n.pl.* [L.: see REGAL] 1. the insignia of kingship, as a crown, sceptre, etc. 2. the insignia or decorations of any rank, society, etc.

regard (ri gärd′) *n.* [see RE- & GUARD] 1. a firm, fixed look; gaze 2. consideration; concern 3. respect and affection 4. reference [*in regard* to your plan] 5. [*pl.*] good wishes [give my *regards* to Bill] —*vt.* 1. to look at with a firm, steady gaze 2. to take into account 3. to hold in affection and respect 4. to think of in a certain light [to *regard* taxes as a burden] 5. to concern [this *regards* your welfare] —**as regards** concerning —**without regard to** without considering —**regard′ful** *adj.*

regarding *prep.* concerning; about

regardless *adj.* without regard; heedless; careless —*adv.* [Colloq.] without regard for objections, difficulties, etc.; anyway —**regardless of** in spite of

regatta (ri gat′ə) *n.* [It.] a series of boat races

regency (rē′jən sē) *n., pl.* -cies 1. the position or authority of a regent or group of regents 2. a group of men serving as regents 3. the time during which a regent or regency governs; specif., [R-] in Britain, the period between 1811 and 1820

regenerate (rej′ər it; *for v.* -ə rāt′) *adj.* [see RE- & GENERATE] 1. spiritually reborn 2. renewed or restored —*vt.* -at′ed, -at′-ing 1. to cause to be spiritually reborn 2. to cause to be completely reformed 3. to bring into existence again 4. *Biol.* to grow anew (a part to replace one hurt or lost) 5. *Physics* to restore (a battery, etc.) to its original state —*vi.* 1. to form again 2. to be spiritually reborn —**regen′-era′tion** *n.* —**regen′erative** *adj.*

regent (rē′jənt) *n.* [< L. *regere*, to rule] a person appointed to rule a monarchy when the sovereign is absent, too young, or incapacitated —*adj.* acting in place of a king or ruler —**re′gentship′** *n.*

reggae (reg′ā) *n.* [< ?] a form of popular music of Jamaican origin, characterized by a strong rhythm and influenced by calypso and rock-and-roll

regicide (rej′ə sīd′) *n.* [see REGAL + -CIDE] 1. a person who kills a king 2. the killing of a king

regime, régime (rā zhēm′) *n.* [< Fr.: see ff.] 1. a form of government or rule 2. a social system 3. *same as* REGIMEN

regimen (rej′ə mən) *n.* [< L. *regere*, to rule] a system of diet, exercise, etc. for promoting health

regiment (rej′ə mənt; *for v.* -ment′) *n.* [< L. *regere*, to rule] 1. an army unit usually containing a number of subunits, such as batteries or squadrons 2. a large number —*vt.* 1. to organize in a rigid system under strict discipline and control 2. to form into regiments —**reg′imen′tal** *adj.* —**reg′imenta′tion** *n.*

regimentals (rej′ə men′t'lz) *n.pl.* 1. a

regiment's uniform and insignia **2.** military uniform

regimental sergeant major *see* WARRANT OFFICER

regina (ri jī'nə) *n.* [L.] [also **R-**] queen

region (rē'jən) *n.* [< L. *regere*, to rule] **1.** a part of the earth's surface, esp. a part having a specified feature [a coastal *region*] **2.** any area, place, etc. or sphere, realm, etc. [the upper *regions* of the air, a *region* of research] **3.** an administrative division of a country, as in Scotland, or of a Canadian province, such as Ontario **4.** a part of the body [the abdominal *region*] —**in the region of** approximately —**re'gional** *adj.*

register (rej'i stər) *n.* [< L. *regerere*, to record] **1.** *a)* a list of names, items, etc. *b)* a book in which this is kept **2.** a device for recording fares paid, money deposited, etc. [a cash *register*] **3.** an opening into a room by which the amount of air passing, as from a furnace, can be controlled **4.** *Music a)* a part of the range of a voice or instrument *b)* an organ stop, or the tone quality it produces **5.** *Printing* exact placing of lines, pages, etc. —*vt.* **1.** to enter in a record or list **2.** to indicate as on a scale **3.** to show [to *register* surprise] **4.** to safeguard (a letter, etc.) by having its committal to the postal system recorded, for a fee —*vi.* **1.** to enter one's name, as in a hotel register **2.** to make an impression

registered post a postal service, by which, for a fee, either delivery of post or compensation for its loss is guaranteed

registrar (rej'i strär') *n.* **1.** an official who keeps records, as of the students in a college **2.** a hospital doctor senior to a houseman and junior to a consultant

registration (rej'i strā'shən) *n.* **1.** a registering or being registered **2.** an entry in a register

registration plate *same as* NUMBER PLATE

registry (rej'is trē) *n., pl.* **-tries 1.** an office where registers are kept **2.** *same as* REGISTRATION

registry office a government office where civil marriages are performed and births, marriages, and deaths are recorded

regius (rē'jē əs) *adj.* [< L. *rex*, king] designating certain professors holding chairs founded by royal charter

regmaker (rekh'mä'kər) *n.* [< Afrik., right maker] [S Afr.] a drink to relieve symptoms of a hangover

regnant (reg'nənt) *adj.* [< L. *regnare*, to reign] **1.** reigning **2.** predominant **3.** prevalent

regress (ri gres') *vi.* [< L. *re-*, back + *gradi*, go] **1.** to move backwards **2.** to revert to an earlier form —**regres'sion** *n.* —**regres'sive** *adj.*

regret (ri gret') *vt.* **-gret'ted, -gret'ting** [< OFr. *regreter*, mourn] **1.** to feel troubled or remorseful over (one's acts, etc.) **2.** to be sorry about or mourn for (a person or thing gone, lost, etc.) —*n.* **1.** a troubled feeling or remorse, esp. over

one's acts or omissions **2.** sorrow over a person or thing gone, lost, etc. —**(one's) regrets** a polite expression of regret, as at declining an invitation —**regret'ful** *adj.* —**regret'table** *adj.* —**regret'tably** *adv.*

regular (reg'yoo lər) *adj.* [see RULE] **1.** usual; customary **2.** conforming to a rule, type, etc.; orderly; symmetrical **3.** consistent, steady, etc. [a *regular* customer] **4.** conforming to a fixed principle or procedure **5.** functioning in a normal way **6.** properly qualified [a *regular* doctor] **7.** [Colloq.] absolute [a *regular* nuisance] **8.** *Eccles.* belonging to a religious order and adhering to its rule **9.** *Gram.* conforming to the usual type as in inflection **10.** *Math.* having all angles and sides equal **11.** *Mil.* designating or of the permanent army of a country —*n.* **1.** a member of a regular army **2.** [Colloq.] a regular customer, visitor, etc. —**reg'ular'ity** (-lar'ə tē) *n.* —**reg'ularly** *adv.*

regulate (reg'yoo lāt') *vt.* **-lat'ed, -lat'ing** [see RULE] **1.** to adjust to a standard, rate, etc. [*regulate* price rises] **2.** to adjust (a clock, etc.) so as to make operate accurately **3.** to control or direct according to a rule, principle, etc.

regulation (reg'yoo lā'shən) *n.* **1.** a regulating or being regulated **2.** a rule by which conduct, etc. is regulated —*adj.* **1.** required by regulation [a *regulation* uniform] **2.** usual; normal

regulator (reg'yoo lāt'ər) *n.* a person or thing that regulates, esp. the device in a watch or clock by which its speed is adjusted

regurgitate (ri gur'jə tāt') *vi., vt.* **-tat'-ed, -tat'ing** [< ML. *re-*, back + LL. *gurgitare*, to surge] to surge or flow back; specif., to bring (partly digested food) from the stomach back to the mouth —**regur'gita'tion** *n.*

rehabilitate (rē'ə bil'ə tāt') *vt.* **-tat'ed, -tat'ing** [< ML. *rehabilitare*, to restore] **1.** to help (one who is ill or disabled, or has just been released from prison) to readjust to society, a new job, etc., as by therapy or special training **2.** to restore to rank, reputation, etc. which one has lost **3.** to put back in good condition —**re'habil'ita'tion** *n.*

rehash (rē hash'; *for n.*rē'hash) *vt.* [RE- + HASH[1]] to put something, as an idea, joke, etc. which has already been used, into a slightly different form, without significant improvement —*n.* the act or result of rehashing

rehearse (ri hurs') *vt.* **-hearsed', -hears'-ing** [< OFr. *re-*, again + *herser*, to harrow] **1.** to practise (a play, concert, etc.) in preparation for a public performance **2.** to recite **3.** to tell in detail **4.** to drill (a person) in what he is to do —*vi.* to rehearse a play, etc. —**rehears'al** *n.*

Reich (rīk) *n.* [G.] *Hist.* the German government; specif., the German fascist state under the Nazis from 1933 to 1945 (**Third Reich**)

reign (rān) *n.* [< L. *regere*, to rule] **1.** royal power **2.** dominance; prevalence

3. the period of rule, dominance, etc. —*vi.* **1.** to rule as a sovereign **2.** to prevail [peace *reigns*]

reimburse (rē'im burs') *vt.* **-bursed'**, **-burs'ing** [RE- + archaic *imburse*, to pay] **1.** to pay back (money spent) **2.** to compensate (a person) for expenses, losses, etc. —**re'imburse'ment** *n.*

rein (rān) *n.* [see RETAIN] **1.** a narrow strip of leather attached to each end of a horse's bit and held by the rider or driver to control the animal: *usually pl.* **2.** [*pl.*] a means of controlling [the *reins* of government] —*vt.* to guide, control, etc. as with reins —*vi.* to stop or slow down as with reins (with *in* or *up*) —**give (free) rein to** to allow to act without restraint

reincarnation (rē'inkär nā'shən) *n.* a rebirth of the soul in another body —**rein car'nate** *vt.*

reindeer (rān'dēr') *n.*, *pl.* **-deer**, occas. **-deers'** [< ON. *hreinn*, reindeer + *dyr*, deer] a large deer with branching antlers, found in northern regions and often domesticated

reinforce (rē'in fôrs') *vt.* **-forced'**, **-forc'ing** [RE- + var. of ENFORCE] **1.** to strengthen, as by propping, adding new material, etc. **2.** to strengthen (a military or naval force) with more troops, ships, etc.

reinforced concrete concrete containing steel bars or mesh to increase its strength

reinforcement *n.* **1.** a reinforcing or being reinforced **2.** anything that reinforces; specif., [*pl.*] additional troops, ships, etc.

reinstate (rē'in stāt') *vt.* **-stat'ed**, **-stat'-ing** to restore to a former condition, position, etc. —**re'instate'ment** *n.*

reiterate (rē it'ə rāt') *vt.* **-at'ed**, **-at'ing** [see RE- & ITERATE] to say or do again or repeatedly —**reit'era'tion** *n.*

reject (ri jekt'; *for n.* rē'jekt) *vt.* [< L. *re-*, back + *jacere*, to throw] **1.** to refuse to take, agree to, use, believe, etc. **2.** to deny love or acceptance to (someone) **3.** *Physiol.* to be incompatible with (a part or organ transplanted into the body) —*n.* a thing or person rejected as unsatisfactory, useless, etc. —**rejec'tion** *n.*

rejig (rē'jig') *vt.* **-jigged'**, **-jig'ging** [< RE- + JIG] **1.** to reequip a factory, etc. **2.** to change or rearrange, esp. in an unscrupulous way

rejoice (ri jois') *vi.*, *vt.* **-joiced'**, **-joic'ing** [< OFr. *rejoir*] to be or make glad or happy (often with *at* or *in*)

rejoin (ri join') *vt.*, *vi.* **1.** to join again **2.** to answer

rejoinder *n.* an answer; retort

rejuvenate (ri jōō'və nāt') *vt.* **-nat'ed**, **-nat'ing** [< RE- + L. *juvenis*, young] **1.** to make young again **2.** to make seem new or fresh again —**reju'vena'tion** *n.*

relapse (ri laps') *vi.* **-lapsed'**, **-laps'ing** [< L. *relabi*, to slip back] to slip back into a former condition, esp. into illness after apparent recovery —*n.* a relapsing

relate (ri lāt') *vt.* **-lat'ed**, **-lat'ing** [< L. *referre*, bring back] **1.** to tell the story

of; narrate **2.** to connect, as in thought or meaning; show a relation between —*vi.* **1.** to have reference or some connection (*to*) **2.** to show sympathy and understanding

related *adj.* **1.** connected **2.** of the same family

relation *n.* **1.** a narrating **2.** what is narrated **3.** connection, as in thought, meaning, etc. **4.** connection by blood or marriage; kinship **5.** a person related to others by kinship; relative **6.** [*pl.*] a) the connections between or among persons, groups, nations, etc. b) sexual intercourse —**in** (or **with**) **relation to** concerning —**rela'tionship** *n.*

relative (rel'ə tiv) *adj.* **1.** regarded in relation to something else; comparative [*relative* comfort] **2.** meaningful only in relationship ["cold" is a *relative* term] **3.** relevant **4.** related each to the other **5.** *Gram.* a) designating a word that introduces a subordinate clause and refers to an antecedent ["which" is a *relative* pronoun in "the hat which you bought"] b) introduced by such a word [a *relative* clause] —*n.* **1.** a person related to others by kinship **2.** a relative word —**relative to 1.** concerning **2.** in proportion to —**rel'atively** *adv.*

relativity (rel'ə tiv'ə tē) *n.* **1.** *Physics* the theory of the relative, rather than absolute, character of motion, velocity, mass, time, etc., as developed esp. by Albert Einstein **2.** a being relative

relax (ri laks') *vt.*, *vi.* [< L. *re-*, back + *laxare*, loosen] **1.** to make or become less firm, stiff, or tense **2.** to make or become less strict or intense, as discipline **3.** to rest or give rest to, from work, worry, etc. —**relaxed'** *adj.*

relaxation (rē'lak sā'shən) *n.* **1.** a relaxing or being relaxed **2.** a) a lessening of or rest from work, worry, etc. b) recreation

relay (rē'lā; *for v., also* ri lā') *n.* [< MFr. *re-*, back + *laier*, leave] **1.** a crew of workers relieving others; shift **2.** a fresh supply of horses, etc., as for a stage of a journey **3.** *same as* RELAY RACE **4.** *Elec.* a device activated by variations in conditions in one electric circuit and controlling a larger current or activating other devices in the same or another circuit —*vt.* **-layed**, **-laying** to convey as by relays [to *relay* news]

relay race (rē'lā) a race between teams, each runner going in turn only part of the total distance

release (ri lēs') *vt.* **-leased'**, **-leas'ing** [see RELAX] **1.** to set free, as from confinement, work, etc. **2.** to let (a missile) go **3.** to permit to be issued, published, etc. **4.** to give up to someone else (a claim, right, etc.) —*n.* **1.** a freeing, as from prison, pain, etc. **2.** a letting loose of something caught, held, etc. **3.** a device for releasing a catch, etc., as on a machine **4.** a) a releasing to the public, as of a book, news, etc. b) the book, news, etc. released

relegate (rel'ə gāt') *vt.* **-gat'ed**, **-gat'ing**

[< L. *re-*, away + *legare*, send] **1.** to consign or assign, esp. to an inferior position, specif., *Football* to demote (a team) to a lower division **2.** to exile or banish (*to*) —**rel′ega′tion** *n.*

relent (ri lent′) *vi.* [< L. *re-*, again + *lentus*, pliant] to become less severe, stern, or stubborn

relentless *adj.* **1.** harsh; pitiless **2.** persistent; unremitting

relevant (rel′ə vant) *adj.* [see RELIEVE] bearing upon or relating to the matter in hand —**rel′evance** *n.*

reliable (ri lī′ə b'l) *adj.* that can be relied on; dependable —**reli′abil′ity** *n.* —**reli′a-bly** *adv.*

reliance *n.* trust, dependence, or confidence —**reli′ant** *adj.*

relic (rel′ik) *n.* [< OFr.: see RELINQUISH] **1.** an object, custom, etc. that has survived from the past **2.** a souvenir **3.** [*pl.*] ruins **4.** the bodily remains of a saint, martyr, etc., or an object associated with him, reverenced as a memorial

relict (rel′ikt) *n.* [see RELINQUISH] [Archaic] a widow

relief (ri lēf′) *n.* [see ff.] **1.** an easing, as of pain, anxiety, a burden, etc. **2.** anything that lessens tension, or offers a pleasing change **3.** any aid given in times of need, danger, or disaster **4.** *a)* release from work or duty *b)* those bringing such release by taking over a post **5.** *a)* the projection of sculptured forms from a flat surface *b)* a work of art so made **6.** the differences in height, collectively, of land forms, shown by lines, colours, or raised areas on a map (**relief map**) **7.** the freeing of a besieged town, fortress, etc. **8.** *a) Painting* the apparent solidity or projection of objects *b)* distinctness of outline **9.** goods or money given formerly under the Poor Law —**in relief** carved so as to project from a surface

relieve (ri lēv′) *vt.* -**lieved′**, -**liev′ing** [< L. *re-*, again + *levare*, raise] **1.** *a)* to ease or reduce (pain, anxiety, etc.) *b)* to free from pain, distress, etc. **2.** to give or bring aid to [*to relieve* a besieged city*]* **3.** to set free from a burden **4.** to set free from duty or work by replacing [*to relieve* a nurse*]* **5.** to make less tedious, etc. by providing a pleasing change **6.** to set off by contrast **7.** to ease (oneself) by urinating or defecating —**relieve someone of** to take from —**reliev′able** *adj.* —**reliev′er** *n.*

relievo (ri lē′vō) *n.,* *pl.* -**vos** *same as* RELIEF (SENSE 5)

religion (ri lij′ən) *n.* [< L. *religio*] **1.** *a)* belief in a superhuman power or powers to be worshipped *b)* expression of this belief in conduct and ritual **2.** any specific system of belief, worship, etc., often involving a code of ethics **3.** the state or way of life of a person in a monastic order, etc. **4.** any object that is seriously pursued

religiosity (ri lij′ē os′ə tē) *n.* the quality of being excessively or mawkishly religious

religious (ri lij′əs) *adj.* **1.** that believes in a religion; devout **2.** of or concerned with religion **3.** belonging to a community of monks, nuns, etc. **4.** scrupulous —*n.,* *pl.* -**gious** a member of a community of monks, nuns, etc.

relinquish (ri liŋ′kwish) *vt.* [< L. *re-*, from + *linquere*, leave] **1.** to give up (a plan, etc.) **2.** to surrender (a right, etc.) **3.** to let go (a grasp, etc.) —**relin′-quishment** *n.*

reliquary (rel′ə kwər ē) *n.,* *pl.* -**quaries** [see prec.] a small box in which relics are kept and shown

relish (rel′ish) *n.* [< OFr. *relais*, something remaining] **1.** enjoyment **2.** pickles, olives, etc. served with a meal to add flavour **3.** an appetizing flavour **4.** anything that gives pleasure, zest, etc. **5.** a trace (*of* some quality) —*vt.* to enjoy

relive (rē liv′) *vt.* -**lived′**, -**liv′ing** to experience again (a past event) as in the imagination

relocate (rē lō kāt′) *vt., vi.* -**cat′ed**, -**cat′-ing** to move to a new location —**re′loca′-tion** *n.*

reluctance (ri luk′təns) *n.* **1.** unwillingness **2.** *Elec.* a measure of the opposition presented to the lines of force in a magnetic circuit

reluctant *adj.* [< L. *re-*, against + *luctari*, to struggle] **1.** unwilling or disinclined (*to* do something) **2.** marked by unwillingness [a *reluctant* answer]

rely (ri lī′) *vi.* -**lied′**, -**ly′ing** [< L. *re-*, back + *ligare*, to bind] to have confidence in; depend (with *on* or *upon*)

remain (ri mān′) *vi.* [< L. *re-*, back + *manere*, to stay] **1.** to be left over when the rest has been taken away, destroyed, etc. **2.** to stay **3.** to go on being [*to remain* a cynic] **4.** to continue [*hope remains*] **5.** to be left to be dealt with, done, etc.

remainder *n.* **1.** those remaining **2.** what is left when a part is taken away **3.** a copy of a book disposed of at a low price by the publisher when the sale has fallen off **4.** *Arith.* what is left when a smaller number is subtracted from a larger —*vt.* to sell (books, etc.) as remainders

remains *n.pl.* **1.** what is left after part has been used, destroyed, etc. **2.** a dead body **3.** relics from the past [Roman *remains*]

remand (ri mänd′) *vt.* [< L. *re-*, back + *mandare*, to order] *Law* **1.** to send (a prisoner or accused person) back into custody, as to await trial, etc. **2.** to send (a case) back to a lower court for further proceedings —*n.* a remanding or being remanded

remand home an institution to which juvenile offenders may be sent while waiting to appear before a court

remark (ri märk′) *vt.* [< Fr. *re-*, intens. + *marquer*, to mark] **1.** to say or write as an observation **2.** to notice; observe —*vi.* to make an observation (*on* or *upon*) —*n.* **1.** a comment **2.** a noticing or observing

remarkable *adj.* 1. worthy of remark or notice 2. unusual; extraordinary —**remark′ably** *adv.*

R.E.M.E. Royal Electrical and Mechanical Engineers

remedial (ri mē′dēəl) *adj.* 1. providing, or intended to provide, a remedy 2. *Educ.* of or for slow or backward learners

remedy (rem′ə dē) *n.,* pl. **-dies** [< L. re-, again + mederi, heal] 1. any medicine or treatment that cures or relieves a disease 2. something that corrects an evil or wrong —*vt.* **-died, -dying** to cure, correct, etc. —**reme′diable** (ri mē′-) *adj.*

remember (ri mem′bər) *vt.* [< L. re-, again + memorare, bring to mind] 1. to think of again 2. to bring back to mind by an effort; recall 3. to be careful not to forget 4. to keep (a person) in mind for a present, legacy, etc. 5. to mention as sending greetings (to) —*vi.* to bear in mind or call back to mind

remembrance *n.* 1. a remembering or being remembered 2. the power to remember 3. the extent of time over which one can remember 4. a souvenir or keepsake 5. [pl.] greetings

Remembrance Day the day commemorating those killed in World War I and World War II, celebrated in Britain on Armistice Day (November 11th) and the preceding Sunday (**Remembrance Sunday**), and in Canada, as a statutory holiday, on November 11th

remind (ri mīnd′) *vt.* to put (a person) in mind (of something); cause to remember —**remind′er** *n.*

reminisce (rem′ə nis′) *vi.* **-nisced′, -nis′cing** [< ff.] to talk or write about one's past experiences

reminiscence *n.* [< L. re-, again + memini, remember] 1. a remembering of past experiences 2. a memory 3. [pl.] an account, written or spoken, of remembered experiences

reminiscent *adj.* 1. suggestive (of) 2. characterized by reminiscence

remiss (ri mis′) *adj.* [see REMIT] careless in, or negligent about, carrying out a task

remission (ri mish′ən) *n.* 1. reduction of the term of prison sentence, as for good behaviour 2. lessening or leaving of pain or symptoms, etc. 3. forgiveness of sins, debts, etc.

remit (ri mit′) *vt.* **-mit′ted, -mit′ting** [< L. re-, back + mittere, send] 1. to send (money) in payment 2. to refer (a matter) for consideration, judgment, etc.; specif., Law same as REMAND 3. to free someone from (a debt, tax, penalty, etc.) 4. to lessen [without remitting one's efforts] 5. to forgive (sins, etc.) —*vi.* 1. to send money in payment 2. to moderate: said esp. of an illness —*n.* (rē′mit) area of authority or competence; scope

remittance *n.* 1. the sending of money 2. the money sent

remittent *adj.* abating at intervals, as a fever

remnant (rem′nənt) *n.* [see REMAIN]

what is left over, esp. a piece of cloth at the end of the bolt

remonstrance (ri mon′strəns) *n.* a remonstrating; protest, complaint, etc.

remonstrate (rem′ən strāt) *vi.* [< L. re-, again + monstrare, to show] to protest —*vt.* **-strated, -strating** to say in protest, objection, etc. —**remon′strant** (ri mon′-) *adj., n.* —**remonstration** (rem′ən strā′shən) *n.*

remorse (ri môrs′) *n.* [< L. re-, again + mordere, to bite] 1. a deep, torturing sense of guilt over a wrong one has done 2. pity: now only in **without remorse,** pitilessly —**remorse′ful** *adj.* —**remorse′less** *adj.*

remote (ri mōt′) *adj.* **-mot′er, -mot′est** [< L. removere, remove] 1. distant in space or time 2. secluded 3. distant in connection, relation, etc. 4. distantly related [a remote cousin] 5. distant in manner; aloof 6. slight [a remote chance] —**remote′ly** *adv.*

remote control control of aircraft, missiles, or other apparatus from a distance, as by radio waves

remould (rē′mōld′; for n. rē′mōld′) *vt.* **-mould′ed, -mould′ing** [RE- + MOULD¹] to cement, mould, and vulcanize a strip of rubber on the outer surface of (a worn tyre) —*n.* a remoulded tyre

removal (ri mōō′v′l) *n.* a removing or being removed; esp., a moving to somewhere else, as of a household

removal man a person whose work is packing and conveying furniture, etc. for those moving house

remove (ri mōōv′) *vt.* **-moved′, -mov′ing** [see RE- & MOVE] 1. to move (something) from where it is; take away or off 2. to dismiss, as from an office 3. to get rid of 4. to extract (from) —*vi.* to move away, as to another place of residence —*n.* 1. a removing 2. any step or degree [but one remove from war] 3. a move to another residence 4. a class in certain schools —**remov′able** *adj.* —**remov′er** *n.*

remunerate (ri myōō′rə rāt′) *vt.* **-at′ed, -at′ing** [< L. re-, again + munus, gift] to pay (a person) for (a service, loss, etc.); reward; recompense —**remu′nera′tion** *n.* —**remu′nerative** *adj.*

renaissance (ri nā′səns) *n.* [Fr. < re-, again + naître, be born] 1. a rebirth; revival 2. [R-] a) the great revival of art, literature, and learning in Europe in the 14th, 15th, and 16th centuries b) the period of this c) the style of art, literature, architecture, etc. of this period

renal (rē′n′l) *adj.* [< L. renes, kidneys] of or near the kidneys

renascent (ri nas′ənt) *adj.* [see RE- & NASCENT] having or showing new life, strength, or vigour —**renas′cence** *n.*

rend (rend) *vt.* **rent, rend′ing** [OE. rendan] to tear or split with violence

render (ren′dər) *vt.* [< L. re-, back + dare, give] 1. to submit, as for approval, payment, etc. [render an account of your actions] 2. to give in return or pay as due 3. to cause to be; make [to render one helpless *]* **4.** *a)* to give (aid) *b)* to do (a service) **5.** to represent; depict **6.** to play (music), act (a role), etc. **7.** to translate **8.** to melt down (fat) **9.** *Masonry* to cover (brickwork, etc.) directly with a coat of plaster —**ren′dering** *n.*

rendezvous (ron′dē vōō′) *n., pl.* **-vous** (-vōōz′) *[< Fr. rendez vous, betake yourself]* **1.** a meeting place **2.** *a)* an agreement to meet at a certain time or place *b)* the meeting itself —*vi., vt.* **-voused′** (-vōōd′), **-vous′ing** (-vōō′iŋ) to bring or come together at a rendezvous

rendition (ren dish′ən) *n.* a rendering; performance, translation, etc.

renegade (ren′ə gād′) *n.* [< Sp. < L. *re-*, again + *negare*, deny] a person who abandons his party, principles, etc. to join the other side

renege (ri nēg′) *vi.* **-neged′, -neg′ing** [see prec.] **1.** to go back on a promise (often with *on*) **2.** *Card Games* same as REVOKE

renew (ri nyōō′) *vt.* **1.** to reestablish **2.** to resume **3.** to repeat [*renew* a promise] **4.** to give or get an extension of [to *renew* a lease] **5.** to make new, fresh, or strong again **6.** to replace as by a fresh supply of —**renew′able** *adj.* —**renew′al** *n.*

rennet (ren′it) *n.* [< OE. *gerennan*, coagulate] **1.** the membrane lining the stomach of a calf **2.** an extract of this membrane, used to curdle milk, as in making junket **3.** any substance used to curdle milk

renounce (ri nouns′) *vt.* **-nounced′, -nounc′ing** [< L. *re-*, back + *nuntiare*, tell] **1.** to give up formally (a claim, right, etc.) **2.** to give up (a practice, belief, etc.) **3.** to disown

renovate (ren′ō vāt′) *vt.* **-vat′ed, -vat′ing** [< L. *re-*, again + *novus*, new] to make fresh or sound again, as though new; repair, rebuild, etc. —**ren′ova′tion** *n.* —**ren′ova′tor** *n.*

renown (ri noun′) *n.* [< OFr. *re-*, again + *nom(m)er*, to name] great fame or reputation —**renowned′** *adj.*

rent¹ (rent) *n.* [< L. *reddita*, paid] a stated payment at fixed intervals for the use of a house, land, etc. —*vt.* to get or give temporary possession or use of in return for rent —*vi.* to be leased or let for rent or a fee —**for rent** available to be rented

rent² *pt. & pp.* of REND

rent³ *n.* [< REND] a hole or gap made by tearing or splitting

rental *n.* an amount paid or received as rent

‡**rentier** (ron′tē ā) [Fr.] a person who has a fixed income from lands, bonds, etc.

renunciation (ri nun′sē ā′shən) *n.* [see RENOUNCE] a renouncing, as of a right, claim, pursuit, etc.

reorder (rē ôr′dər) *vt.* **1.** to order again **2.** to put in order again —*vi.* to order goods again

reorganize (rē ôr′gə nīz′) *vt., vi.* **-ized′, -iz′ing** to organize again or anew —**reor′ganiza′tion** *n.*

rep¹ (rep) *n.* [Fr. *reps* < Eng. *ribs*] a ribbed fabric of silk, wool, cotton, rayon, etc.: also **repp**

rep² *n. short for:* **1.** REPERTORY (THEATRE) **2.** REPRESENTATIVE

repaid (rē pād′) *pt. & pp.* of REPAY

repair¹ (ri pâar′) *vt.* [< L. *re-*, again + *parare*, prepare] **1.** to put back in good condition after damage, decay, etc.; mend **2.** to remedy (a mistake, etc.) **3.** to make amends for (a wrong, etc.) —*n.* **1.** a repairing **2.** [*usually pl.*] work done in repairing **3.** the state of being fit for use [a car kept in *repair*] **4.** state with respect to being repaired [in bad *repair*] —**repair′er** *n.*

repair² *vi.* [< L. *re-*, back + *patria*, one's native country] to go (*to* a place)

reparable (rep′ər ə b'l) *adj.* that can be repaired, remedied, etc. —**rep′arably** *adv.*

reparation (rep′ə rā′shən) *n.* [see REPAIR¹] **1.** a making up for a wrong or injury **2.** compensation; specif., [*usually pl.*] compensation by a defeated nation for damage done by it in a war

repartee (rep′är tē′) *n.* [< Fr. *re-*, back + *partir*, to part] **1.** a quick, witty reply **2.** a series of such retorts; banter **3.** skill in making witty replies

repast (ri pâst′) *n.* [< RE- + L. *pascere*, to feed] food and drink; a meal

repatriate (rē pa′trē āt′; *for n. usually* -it) *vt., vi.* **-at′ed, -at′ing** [see REPAIR²] to send back or return to the country of birth or citizenship —*n.* a person who has been repatriated —**repa′tria′tion** *n.*

repay (ri pā′) *vt.* **-paid′, -pay′ing** [OFr. *repaier*] **1.** *a)* to pay back **2.** to make some return for [*repay* a kindness] —**repay′able** *adj.* —**repay′ment** *n.*

repeal (ri pēl′) *vt.* [see RE- & APPEAL] to revoke; cancel [to *repeal* a law] —*n.* the act of repealing

repeat (ri pēt′) *vt.* [< L. *re-*, again + *petere*, seek] **1.** to say again **2.** to recite, as a poem **3.** to say (something) as said by someone else **4.** to tell to others [to *repeat* a secret] **5.** to do or make again —*vi.* **1.** to say or do again **2.** to recur **3.** to continue to be tasted, as because of belching: often with *on* —*n.* **1.** a repeating **2.** *a)* anything said or done again *b)* a rebroadcast of a radio or TV programme **3.** *Music a)* a passage repeated in playing *b)* a symbol for this —**repeat′edly** *adv.*

repeater *n.* **1.** a person or thing that repeats **2.** same as REPEATING FIREARM **3.** a watch that repeats the hour and the quarter just passed, when a spring is pressed

repeating firearm a firearm that can fire a number of shots without reloading

repel (ri pel′) *vt.* **-pelled′, -pel′ling** [< L. *re-*, back + *pellere*, drive] **1.** to drive or force back **2.** to spurn [she *repelled* his attentions] **3.** to disgust [the odour *repels* me] **4.** *a)* to be resistant to [plastic *repels* water] *b)* to fail to mix with [water *repels* oil] —**repel′lent** *adj., n.*

repent (ri pent′) *vi., vt.* [< L. *re-*, again

+ *paenitere,* repent] **1.** to feel sorry for (an error, omission, etc.) **2.** to feel such regret over (some past act, etc.) as to change one's mind —**repent′ance** *n.* —**repent′ant** *adj.*

repercussion (rē′pər kush′ən) *n.* [see RE- & PERCUSSION] **1.** a reaction to some event or action: *usually used in pl.* **2.** reflection, as of sound

repertoire (rep′ər twär′) *n.* [see ff.] the stock of plays, songs, etc. that a company, singer, etc. knows and is ready to perform

repertory (rep′ər tər ē) *n., pl.* **-ries** [< L. *reperire,* discover] **1.** a storehouse, or the things in it **2.** *same as* REPERTOIRE **3.** the system of play production used by a repertory theatre

repertory theatre a theatre with a repertoire of plays and a permanent company

repetition (rep′ə tish′ən) *n.* [< L. *repetitio*] **1.** a repeating **2.** something repeated **3.** a copy —**rep′e ti′tious, repet′- itive** (ri pet′ə tiv) *adj.*

repine (ri pīn′) *vi.* **-pined′, -pin′ing** [RE- + PINE[2]] to feel discontent; complain; fret

replace (ri plās′) *vt.* **-placed′, -plac′ing 1.** to put back in a former or the proper place **2.** to take the place of **3.** to provide an equivalent for **4.** to pay back; restore [*replace* stolen goods]

replacement *n.* **1.** a replacing or being replaced **2.** a person or thing that takes the place of another

replenish (ri plen′ish) *vt.* [< L. *re-,* again + *plenus,* full] **1.** to make full or complete again **2.** to supply again —**replen′ish- ment** *n.*

replete (ri plēt′) *adj.* [< L. *re-,* again + *plere,* fill] **1.** well-filled; plentifully supplied **2.** stuffed with food and drink —**reple′tion** *n.*

replica (rep′li kə) *n.* [It.: see REPLY] a close copy, esp. of a work of art

reply (ri plī′) *vt. & vi.* **-plied′, -ply′ing** [< L. *re-,* back + *plicare,* to fold] **1.** to answer in speech or writing **2.** to respond by some action —*vt.* to say in answer —*n., pl.* **-plies′** an answer or response

report (ri pôrt′) *vt.* [< L. *re-,* back + *portare,* carry] **1.** to give an account of; give information about **2.** to carry and repeat (a message, etc.) **3.** to write or broadcast an account of (news events) **4.** to give an official account of **5.** to make a charge about (an offence or offender) to a person in authority —*vi.* **1.** to make a report **2.** to present oneself [*to report* for duty] **3.** to be responsible (*to* a superior) —*n.* **1.** a statement or account **2.** rumour; gossip [*report* has it] **3.** a formal or official presentation of facts **4.** a statement of a child's progress in school sent to the parents **5.** reputation [of good *report*] **6.** a loud noise made by an explosion —**report progress** notify (someone) of the developments that have occurred

reported speech statement of what a person said, without quoting his exact words (Ex.: she said that she could not go)

reporter *n.* a person who reports; specif., a person who gathers information and writes reports for a newspaper, etc., or reports news on radio or TV

repose[1] (ri pōz′) *vt.* **-posed′, -pos′ing** [< L. *re-,* again + LL. *pausare,* to rest] to lay or place for rest —*vi.* **1.** to lie at rest **2.** to rest **3.** to rest in death **4.** to be supported [the shale *reposes* on limestone] —*n.* **1.** a) rest b) sleep **2.** composure **3.** calm; peace —**repose′ful** *adj.*

repose[2] *vt.* **-posed′, -pos′ing** [see ff.] to place (trust, etc.) in

repository (ri poz′ə tər ē) *n., pl.* **-ries** [< L. *re-,* back + *ponere,* to place] **1.** a box, room, etc. in which things may be placed for safekeeping **2.** a person to whom something is confided

repossess (rē′pə zes′) *vt.* to get possession of again; specif., to take back from a buyer who has failed to keep up payments —**re′posses′sion** *n.*

reprehend (rep′ri hend′) *vt.* [< L. *re-,* back + *prehendere,* take] **1.** to reprimand or rebuke **2.** to find fault with

reprehensible (-hen′sə b'l) *adj.* deserving to be reprehended —**rep′rehen′- sibly** *adv.*

represent (rep′ri zent′) *vt.* [see RE- & PRESENT, *v.*] **1.** to be the equivalent of [a cave *represents* home] **2.** to be a substitute for **3.** to speak and act for by conferred authority, as a legislator for his constituents **4.** a) to be a symbol for b) to express by symbols **5.** to serve as a specimen, type, etc. of **6.** to present a likeness of **7.** to present to the mind **8.** to describe or set forth, often in order to influence, persuade, etc. **9.** to act (a role), as in a play

representation (rep′ri zen tā′shən) *n.* **1.** a representing or being represented **2.** legislative representatives, collectively **3.** a likeness **4.** [*often pl.*] facts, arguments, etc. intended to influence action, etc.

representative (rep′rə zen′tə tiv) *n.* **1.** a person authorized to act or speak for others, as an elected legislator or a salesman, agent, etc. **2.** an example or type —*adj.* **1.** representing **2.** typical **3.** including examples from various groups, types, etc. [a *representative* collection] **4.** of or based on representation of the people by elected delegates —*n.* **1.** a person authorized to act or speak for others, as an elected legislator or a salesman, agent, etc. **2.** an example or type

repress (ri pres′) *vt.* [see RE- & PRESS[1]] **1.** to hold back; restrain **2.** to put down; subdue **3.** to control so strictly as to stifle natural behaviour **4.** *Psychiatry* to force (painful ideas, impulses, etc.) into the unconscious —**repres′sion** *n.* —**repres′sive** *adj.*

reprieve (ri prēv′) *vt.* **-prieved′, -priev′- ing** [ult. < Fr. *reprendre,* take back] **1.** to postpone the punishment of; esp., to postpone the execution of (a condemned person) **2.** to give temporary relief to —*n.* a reprieving or being reprieved

reprimand (rep'rə mänd') *n.* [< L. *reprimere*, repress] a severe or formal rebuke —*vt.* to rebuke severely or formally

reprint (rē print'; *for n.* rē'print') *vt.* to print again —*n.* something reprinted; specif., an additional impression or edition

reprisal (ri prī'z'l) *n.* [see REPREHEND] injury done in return for injury received, esp. in war

reproach (ri prōch') *vt.* [< L. *re-*, back + *prope*, near] to accuse of and blame for a fault; rebuke —*n.* 1. a rebuke 2. disgrace or blame, or a cause of this —**reproach'ful** *adj.*

reprobate (rep'rō bāt') *adj.* [< LL. *reprobare*, reprove] depraved; corrupt —*n.* a reprobate person —*vt.* -bat'ed, -bat'ing to disapprove of; condemn —**rep'roba'tion** *n.*

reproduce (rē'prə dyōōs') *vt.* -duced', -duc'ing to produce again; specif., *a)* to make a copy of (a picture, sound, etc.) *b)* to bring forth others of (its kind), esp. by sexual intercourse —*vi.* 1. to produce offspring, esp. by sexual intercourse 2. to undergo copying, duplication, etc. —**re'produc'ible** *adj.*

reproduction (rē'prə duk'shən) *n.* 1. the process by which animals and plants produce new individuals 2. a copy 3. a reproducing or being reproduced —*adj.* made in imitation of a style of the past [*reproduction* furniture] —**re'produc'tive** *adj.*

reproof (ri prōōf') *n.* a rebuke

reprove (ri prōōv') *vt.* -proved', -prov'ing [see RE- & PROVE] 1. to speak to in disapproval; rebuke 2. to express disapproval of —**reprov'ingly** *adv.*

reptile (rep'til) *n.* [< L. *repere*, creep] any of a group of coldblooded vertebrates having a body covered with scales or horny plates and including snakes, crocodiles, etc. —*adj.* of or like a reptile —**reptilian** (rep til'ē ən) *adj.*, *n.*

republic (ri pub'lik) *n.* [< L. *res*, thing + *publica*, public] 1. a nation or government in which the supreme power rests with all the citizens and is exercised by representatives elected by them 2. a nation with a president as its head

republican *adj.* 1. of or like a republic 2. favouring a republic —*n.* 1. a person who favours a republican form of government 2. [U.S.] [R-] a member of the Republican Party

repudiate (ri pyōō'dē āt') *vt.* -at'ed, -at'ing [< L. *repudium*, separation] 1. *a)* to refuse to accept or support (a belief, treaty, etc.) *b)* to deny (a charge, etc.) 2. to refuse to acknowledge or pay (a debt, etc.) 3. to disown —**repu'dia'tion** *n.*

repugnance (ri pug'nəns) *n.* [< L. *re-*, back + *pugnare*, to fight] 1. extreme dislike or distaste 2. inconsistency —**repug'nant** *adj.*

repulse (ri puls') *vt.* -pulsed', -puls'ing [< REPEL] 1. to drive back (an attack, etc.) 2. to repel with discourtesy, coldness, etc. —*n.* a refusal, rejection, or rebuff

repulsion *n.* 1. a repelling or being repelled 2. strong dislike or aversion 3. *Physics* the mutual action by which bodies tend to repel each other

repulsive *adj.* 1. causing strong dislike or aversion 2. tending to repel

reputable (rep'yōō tə b'l) *adj.* having a good reputation; respectable

reputation (rep'yōō tā'shən) *n.* [see ff.] 1. the regard, favourable or not, shown for a person or thing by the public 2. such regard when favourable 3. distinction

repute (ri pyōōt') *vt.* -put'ed, -put'ing [< L. *re-*, again + *putare*, think] to consider to be [he is *reputed* to be rich] —*n.* reputation

reputed *adj.* generally regarded as being such [the *reputed* owner]

request (ri kwest') *n.* [see REQUIRE] 1. an asking for something 2. something asked for 3. demand [a song much in *request*] —*vt.* 1. to ask for 2. to ask (a person) to do something —**by request** in response to a request

request stop a point on a route at which public transport will stop only if signalled to do so

Requiem (rek'wē əm) *n.* [L., < *requies*, rest] [*also* r-] 1. a Mass for the repose of the dead 2. a musical setting for this

‡**requiescat in pace** (rek'wē es'kät in pä'chä) [L.] may he (or she) rest in peace

require (ri kwīr') *vt.* -quired', -quir'ing [< L. *re-*, again + *quaerere*, ask] 1. to need 2. to call for as needed [the work *requires* skill] 3. to ask or insist upon, as by right; demand 4. to command

requirement *n.* 1. something required or demanded 2. something needed; necessity

requisite (rek'wə zit) *adj.* [see REQUIRE] required; necessary —*n.* something requisite

requisition (rek'wə zish'ən) *n.* 1. a requiring, as by authority 2. a formal request, as for equipment —*vt.* 1. to demand or take, as by authority [to *requisition* food for troops] 2. to submit a written request for (equipment, etc.)

requite (ri kwīt') *vt.* -quit'ed, -quit'ing [RE- + *quite*, obs. var. of QUIT] to repay or make return to for (a benefit, service, etc. or an injury, wrong, etc.) —**requit'al** *n.*

reredos (rēar'dos) *n.* [< OFr. *arere*, behind + *dos*, back] an ornamental screen behind an altar

reroute (rē rōōt') *vt.* -rout'ed, -rout'ing to send by a different route

rerun (rē run'; *for n.* rē'run') *vt.* -ran', -run'ning to run again —*n.* a rerunning; esp., a repeat showing of a film, TV programme, etc.

resale (rē'sāl') *n.* the act of selling again

rescind (ri sind') *vt.* [< L. *re-*, back + *scindere*, to cut] to revoke, repeal, or cancel (a law, etc.)

rescission (ri sizh'ən) *n.* a rescinding

rescript (rē'skript) *n.* [< L. *re-*, back + *scribere*, write] an official decree or order

rescue (res′kyōō) vt. **-cued, -cuing** [< L. re-, again + ex-, off + quatere, to shake] to free or save from danger, evil, etc. —n. a rescuing —res′cuer n.

research (ri surch′) n. [see RE- & SEARCH] [sometimes pl.] systematic investigation in a field of knowledge, to discover or establish facts or principles —vi., vt. to do research (on or in) —research′er n.

resemble (ri zem′b'l) vt. **-bled, -bling** [< OFr. re-, again + sembler, to feign] to be similar to —resem′blance n.

resent (ri zent′) vt. [< OFr. re-, again + sentir, feel] to feel or show hurt or indignation at (some act, etc.) or towards (a person), from a sense of being offended —resent′ful adj. —resent′ment n.

reservation (rez′ər vā′shən) n. 1. a reserving or the thing reserved; specif., a) an arrangement by which a hotel room, theatre ticket, etc. is set aside for use at a certain time or until called for b) (U.S. & Canada) public land set aside for some special use [an Indian reservation] 2. a limiting condition or qualification

reserve (ri zurv′) vt. **-served′, -serv′ing** [< L. re-, back + servare, to hold] 1. to keep back or set apart for later or special use 2. to set aside or have set aside (a theatre seat, etc.) for someone 3. to retain [to reserve the right to refuse] —n. 1. something reserved 2. a limitation [without reserve] 3. the practice of keeping one's thoughts, feelings, etc. to oneself; aloofness; reticence 4. a substitute member of a team 5. {pl.} a) manpower kept out of action and ready for replacing others b) military forces not on active duty but subject to call 6. cash or liquid assets kept aside by a bank, business, etc. to meet demands 7. land set apart for special use [a nature reserve] —adj. being, or having the nature of, a reserve —in reserve reserved for later use

reserved adj. 1. set apart for some purpose, person, etc. 2. showing reserve; reticent

reserve price the minimum price acceptable to the owner of property being auctioned

reservist n. a member of a country's military reserves

reservoir (rez′ər vwär′) n. [Fr.: see RESERVE] 1. a place where anything is collected and stored; esp., a natural or artificial lake in which water is stored for use 2. a receptacle (in an apparatus) for a fluid 3. a reserve supply

reshuffle (rē′shuf′'l) n. a reorganization, as in a reassignment of jobs within a government —vt. to carry out a reshuffle

reside (ri zīd′) vi. **-sid′ed, -sid′ing** [< L. re-, back + sedere, sit] 1. to dwell for a long time; live (in or at) 2. to be present (in): said of qualities, etc. 3. to be vested (in): said of rights, powers, etc.

residence (rez′i dəns) n. 1. a residing 2. the fact or status of living in a place while working or in training, etc. 3. the place where one resides; one's home 4.

the time during which a person resides in a place

residency n., pl. **-cies** 1. [U.S.] a period of advanced medical training at a hospital 2. formerly, the official residence of a governor-general at the court of an Indian prince

resident n. 1. a person who lives in a place and is not a visitor or transient 2. a junior houseman in a hospital —adj. 1. having a residence (in or at); residing 2. living at a place in order to discharge a duty 3. existing (in) 4. not migratory: said of birds, etc.

residential (rez′ə den′shəl) adj. 1. of or connected with residence 2. suitable for homes [a residential area] 3. chiefly for residents rather than transients [a residential hotel]

residual (ri zid′yōō wəl) adj. of or like a residue; remaining —n. something remaining, as at the end of a process

residuary (-yōō wər ē) adj. 1. residual 2. Law a) relating to the residue of an estate b) receiving such a residue [a residuary legatee]

residue (rez′ə dyōō′) n. [< L. residuus, remaining] 1. what is left after part is removed; remainder 2. Law that part of a testator's estate left after all claims and bequests have been satisfied

residuum (ri zid′yōō wəm) n., pl. **-ua** [L.] same as RESIDUE

resign (ri zīn′) vt., vi. [< L. re-, back + signare, sign] to give up or relinquish (a claim, office, position, etc.), esp. by formal notice (often with from) —resign oneself (to) to become reconciled (to)

resignation (rez′ig nā′shən) n. 1. a) a resigning b) formal notice of this 2. patient submission

resigned (ri zīnd′) adj. feeling or showing resignation —resign′edly (-zīn′id lē) adv.

resilient (ri zil′ē ənt) adj. [< L. re-, back + salire, to jump] 1. springing back into shape, position, etc. after being stretched, bent, or compressed 2. recovering strength, spirits, etc. quickly —resil′ience n.

resin (rez′in) n. [< L. resina] 1. a substance exuded from various plants and trees: natural resins are used in varnishes and lacquers 2. same as: a) SYNTHETIC RESIN b) ROSIN —vt. to treat or rub with resin —res′inous adj.

resist (ri zist′) vt. [< L. re-, back + sistere, to set] 1. to withstand; fend off 2. to oppose actively; fight against 3. to keep from yielding to or enjoying —vi. to offer resistance —n. a resistant substance, as a protective coating

resistance n. 1. a resisting 2. power to resist; specif., the ability of an organism to ward off disease 3. opposition of some force, thing, etc. to another 4. [often R-] an underground movement in a country fighting against a foreign occupying power 5. Elec. a) the property by which a conductor opposes current flow and thus generates heat b) same as RESISTOR —resist′ant adj., n.

resistor *n.* *Elec.* a device, as a wire coil, used to produce resistance in a circuit

resit (rē sit´) *vt.* to sit (an examination) again after previously failing it

resoluble (ri zol´yoo b'l) *adj.* that can be resolved or analysed

resolute (rez´ə loot´) *adj.* [see RE- & SOLVE] having or showing a fixed, firm purpose; determined

resolution (rez´ə loo´shən) *n.* 1. *a)* a resolving *b)* the result of this 2. a decision as to future action 3. a resolute quality of mind 4. a formal statement of opinion adopted by a group 5. a solving or answering; solution 6. *Music* the process in harmony where a dissonant note or chord is followed by a consonant one 7. *Physics* the ability of a lens to distinguish between adjoining points

resolve (ri zolv´) *vt.* **-solved´, -solv´ing** [see RE- & SOLVE] 1. to determine [to *resolve* to go] 2. *a)* to find an answer to; solve *b)* to make a decision about, esp. by vote or formally *c)* to remove (doubt, etc.) 3. to break up into separate parts; analyse 4. to change [the talk *resolved* itself into a dispute] 5. to cause to decide [this *resolved* him to go] 6. *Music* to make (a dissonant chord or tone) become consonant —*vi.* 1. to be resolved, as by analysis 2. to come to a decision —*n.* a fixed purpose or intention

resolved *adj.* firm in purpose; resolute

resonance (rez´ə nəns) *n.* 1. a being resonant 2. the reinforcing and prolonging of a sound or musical tone by reflection or vibration of other bodies 3. *Physics* the effect produced when the natural vibration frequency of a body is amplified by vibrations from another body

resonant *adj.* [< L. *resonare*, resound] 1. resounding or reechoing 2. producing resonance [*resonant* walls] 3. full of, or intensified by resonance [a *resonant* voice]

resonate *vi., vt.* **-nat´ed, -nat´ing** to be or make resonant

resort (ri zôrt´) *vi.* [< OFr. *re-*, again + *sortir*, go out] 1. to turn (*to*) for help, support, etc. 2. to go; esp., to go often —*n.* 1. a place people often go to for rest or recreation, as on a holiday 2. a person or thing one turns to for help, support, etc. 3. a turning for help, support, etc.; recourse —**as a last resort** as the last available means

resound (ri zound´) *vi.* [< L. *re-*, again + *sonare*, to sound] 1. to echo or be filled with sound 2. to make a loud, echoing or prolonged sound 3. to be celebrated [an act that *resounded* through the ages] —*vt.* 1. to give back (sound); echo 2. to give forth loudly

resounding *adj.* 1. reverberating 2. thoroughgoing; complete [a *resounding* victory]

resource (ri sôrs´) *n.* [< OFr. *re-*, again + *sourdre*, spring up] 1. something ready for use or available as needed 2. [*pl.*] wealth; assets 3. [*pl.*] something useful, as coal or oil, that a country, state, etc.

has 4. an expedient 5. [*pl.*] a source of strength or ability within oneself

resourceful *adj.* full of resource; able to deal promptly and effectively with difficulties, etc.

respect (ri spekt´) *vt.* [< L. *re-*, back + *specere*, look] 1. to hold in high regard; show honour or courtesy to 2. to show consideration for [*respect* others´ privacy] —*n.* 1. high regard; esteem 2. deference or dutiful regard [*respect* for law] 3. courteous consideration 4. a point or detail [right in every *respect*] 5. reference; relation [with *respect* to this] 6. [*pl.*] courteous expressions of regard: chiefly in **pay one's respects,** to show polite regard as by visiting and **pay one's last respects,** to attend someone's funeral

respectable *adj.* 1. worthy of respect or esteem 2. socially acceptable; proper 3. fairly good 4. good enough to be seen, worn, etc. —**respect´abil´ity** *n.* —**respect´-ably** *adv.*

respectful *adj.* full of or showing respect; polite

respecting *prep.* concerning; about

respective *adj.* as relates individually to each of two or more [their *respective* merits]

respectively *adv.* in regard to each in the order named [the first and second prizes went to Mary and George, *respectively*]

respiration (res´pə rā´shən) *n.* 1. breathing 2. the processes by which a living organism or cell takes in oxygen and gives off products, esp. carbon dioxide —**respiratory** (ri spīər´ə tə rē) *adj.*

respirator (res´pə rāt´ər) *n.* 1. a device worn over the mouth and nose, as to prevent the inhaling of harmful substances 2. an apparatus for giving artificial respiration

respire (ri spīər´) *vi., vt.* **-spired´, -spir´-ing** [< L. *re-*, back + *spirare*, breathe] to breathe

respite (res´pit) *n.* [see RESPECT] 1. a period of temporary relief, as from pain 2. a delay or postponement —*vt.* **-pited, -pit-ing** to give a respite to

resplendent (ri splen´dənt) *adj.* [< L. *re-*, again + *splendere*, shine] shining brightly; dazzling —**resplend´ence** *n.*

respond (ri spond´) *vi.* [< L. *re-*, back + *spondere*, to pledge] 1. to answer 2. to act as if in answer [to *respond* by issuing an invitation] 3. to react favourably, as to medical treatment

respondent *adj.* responding —*n.* 1. a person who responds 2. *Law* a defendant

response (ri spons´) *n.* 1. something said or done in answer; reply or reaction 2. a word, phrase, etc. sung or spoken by a congregation or choir in answer to an officiating clergyman 3. any reaction to a stimulus

responsibility (ri spon´sə bil´ə tē) *n., pl.* **-ties** 1. a being responsible; obligation 2. a person or thing that one is responsible for 3. the quality of being reliable or dependable

responsible (ri spon'sə b'l) *adj.* [see
RESPOND] 1. obliged to account (*for*
something, *to* someone); answerable 2.
involving obligation or duties [*a responsible
job*] 3. accountable as being the cause
of something 4. accountable for one's
behaviour 5. dependable or reliable
—**respon'sibly** *adv.*

responsive (ri spon'siv) *adj.* 1. answering 2. reacting readily [*a responsive
audience*] 3. containing responses

respray (rē sprā') *vt.* [RE- & SPRAY¹] to
spray again; specif., to spray a vehicle
with paint

MUSICAL RESTS
(A, semibreve; B, minim; C, crotchet
D, quaver; E, semiquaver)

rest¹ (rest) *n.* [OE.] 1. sleep or repose
2. refreshing inactivity after exertion, or
a period of this 3. *a)* relief from anything
distressing, tiring, etc. *b)* peace of mind
4. the repose of death 5. absence of
motion 6. a lodging place, as for travellers
7. a thing that supports [*a foot rest*]
8. *Music a)* a measured interval of silence
between tones *b)* a symbol for this —*vi.*
1. to become refreshed by sleeping, lying
down, ceasing work, etc. 2. *a)* to lie,
sit, or lean *b)* to be placed (*in, on,* etc.)
3. to be at ease 4. to be buried (in)
5. to be quiet or still 6. to remain unchanged
[*let the matter rest*] 7. to lie (where
specified) [*the fault rests with him*] 8.
to be fixed [*his eyes rested on her*] 9.
to rely; depend 10. *Law* to end voluntarily
the introduction of evidence in a case
—*vt.* 1. to refresh by rest 2. to put
for ease, support, etc. 3. to base [*to
rest an argument on facts*] 4. to fix
(the eyes, etc.) 5. *Law* to cause (a case)
to rest —**be resting** [Theatrical Colloq.]
to be out of work —**lay to rest** to bury
—**rest on one's oars** to slacken one's
efforts

rest² *n.* [< L. *re-*, back + *stare,* to stand]
1. what is left; remainder 2. [*with pl.
v.*] the others —*vi.* to go on being [*rest
assured*] —**for the rest** as regards all
other matters —**rest with** to be the
responsibility (of)

restaurant (res'tə rənt) *n.* [Fr.: see
RESTORE] a place where meals can be
bought and eaten

restaurant car *same as* DINING CAR

restaurateur (res'tor ə tur') *n.* [Fr.] a
person who owns or operates a restaurant

rest cure medical treatment consisting
of complete rest

restful (rest'fəl) *adj.* 1. full of or giving
rest 2. quiet; peaceful; soothing

restitution (res'tə tyōō'shən) *n.* [< L.
re-, again + *statuere,* set up] 1. restoration
to the rightful owner 2. a making good

for loss or damage 3. a return to a former
condition

restive (res'tiv) *adj.* [see REST²] 1. hard
to control; unruly 2. nervous or impatient
under restraint

restless (rest'lis) *adj.* 1. unable to rest
or relax 2. disturbed [*restless sleep*] 3.
always moving 4. seeking change;
discontented

restoration (res'tə rā'shən) *n.* 1. a
restoring or being restored 2. a
reconstruction of the original form of a
building, fossil animal, etc. —**the
Restoration** 1. reestablishment of the
monarchy in England in 1660 under Charles
II 2. the period of his reign (1660–85)

restorative (ri stor'ə tiv) *adj.* restoring
or able to restore health —*n.* a thing
that restores

restore (ri stôr') *vt.* -**stored', -stor'ing**
[< L. *restaurare,* rebuild] 1. to give back
(something taken away, lost, etc.) 2. to
bring back to a former condition, as by
repairing 3. to put (a person) back into
a position, rank, etc. 4. to bring back
to health, strength, etc. 5. to bring back
into being, use, etc. —**restor'er** *n.*

restrain (ri strān') *vt.* [< L. *re-*, back
+ *stringere,* raw tight] 1. to hold back
from action; check; curb 2. to keep under
control 3. to deprive of physical liberty,
as by shackling 4. to restrict

restraint (ri strānt') *n.* 1. a restraining
or being restrained 2. a restraining influence or action 3. a means of restraining
4. loss or limitation of liberty 5. control
of emotions; reserve

restrict (ri strikt') *vt.* [see RESTRAIN] to
limit; confine —**restric'tive** *adj.*

restriction *n.* 1. restricting or being
restricted 2. something that restricts;
limitation

restrictive practice any agreement or
work practice that hinders the most
efficient use of machinery, labour, etc.

restructure (rē struk'chər) *vt.* -**tured, -tur-
ing** to plan or provide a new structure
or organization for

result (ri zult') *vi.* [< L. *resultare,* to
rebound] 1. to follow as an effect (often
with *from*) 2. to end (*in* something) as
an effect —*n.* 1. *a)* a consequence; outcome
b) [*pl.*] desired effects 2. the number,
quantity, etc. obtained by mathematical
calculation 3. [*often pl.*] the score in
a match, game etc.

resultant *adj.* that results —*n. Physics*
a force, velocity, etc. with an effect equal
to that of two or more such forces, etc.
acting together

resume (ri zyōōm') *vt.* -**sumed', -sum'-
ing** [< L. *re-*, again + *sumere,* take]
1. to begin again after interruption 2.
to take or occupy again —*vi.* to begin
again or go on again

résumé (rez'yōō mā') *n.* [Fr.] a
summary

resumption (ri zump'shən) *n.* the act
of resuming

resurface (rē sur'fis) *vt.* -**faced, -facing**

to put a new surface on —*vi.* to come to the surface again

resurgent (rē sur′jənt) *adj.* rising again —**resur′gence** *n.*

resurrect (rez′ə rekt′) *vt.* [< ff.] 1. *Theol.* to bring back to life 2. to bring back into notice, use, etc.

resurrection (rez′ə rek′shən) *n.* [< L. *resurgere,* rise again] 1. *Theol.* a rising from the dead 2. a revival —**the Resurrection** *Theol.* 1. the rising of Jesus from the dead 2. the rising of all the dead at the Last Judgment

resuscitate (ri sus′ə tāt′) *vt., vi.* -tat′ed, -tat′ing [< L. *re-*, again + *suscitare,* revive] to revive (someone who is unconscious, apparently dead, etc.) —**resus′cita′tion** *n.*

ret (ret) *vt.* ret′ted, ret′ting [MDu. *reten*] to soak (flax, etc.) in water to separate the fibres from woody tissue

retail (rē′tāl; *for vt.* 2, *usually* ri tāl′) *n.* [< OFr. *re-*, again + *tailler,* to cut] the sale of goods in small quantities directly to the consumer —*adj.* having to do with the selling of goods in this way —*adv.* in small amounts or at a retail price —*vt.* 1. to sell as retail goods 2. to repeat (gossip, etc.) —*vi.* to be sold as retail goods —**re′tailer** *n.*

retain (ri tān′) *vt.* [< L. *re-*, back + *tenere,* to hold] 1. to keep in possession, use, etc. 2. to keep in a fixed state 3. to continue to hold (heat, etc.) 4. to keep in mind 5. to engage (a lawyer, etc.) by an advance fee

retainer *n.* 1. a person or thing that retains 2. a servant, attendant, etc., as of a person of rank or wealth 3. *Law* a fee paid in advance to make the services of a lawyer, etc. available when needed

retaining wall a wall built to hold back earth, water, loose rocks, etc.

retake (rē tāk′; *for n.* rē′tāk′) *vt.* -took′, -tak′en, -tak′ing 1. to take again or recapture 2. to photograph again —*n.* a film scene, etc. rephotographed

retaliate (ri tal′ē āt′) *vi.* -at′ed, -at′ing [< L. *re-*, back + *talio,* punishment in kind] to return like for like; esp., injury for injury —**retal′ia′tion** *n.* —**retal′iative, retal′iatory** *adj.*

retard (ri tärd′) *vt.* [< L. *re-*, back + *tardus,* slow] to hinder or slow the advance or progess of —**re′tarda′tion** *n.*

retarded *adj.* delayed in development or progress, esp. because of mental retardation

retch (rech) *vi.* [OE. *hræcan,* to spit] to undergo the straining action of vomiting, esp. without bringing anything up

retention (ri ten′shən) *n.* 1. a retaining or being retained 2. power of retaining 3. a) memory b) ability to remember —**reten′tive** *adj.*

rethink (rē think′) *vt.* -thought′, -think′-ing to reconsider esp., with a view to changing

reticent (ret′i ə sənt) *adj.* [< L. *re-*, again + *tacere,* be silent] not willing to say much; tending to keep one's thoughts, etc. to oneself; reserved —**ret′icence** *n.*

reticulate (ri tik′yoolit; *for v.,* -lāt′) *adj.* [see ff.] like a net or network —*vt., vi.* -lat′ed, -lat′ing to divide or mark so as to look like network —**retic′ula′-tion** *n.*

reticule (ret′ə kyool′) *n.* [< L. *rete,* net] formerly, a woman's drawstring handbag, orig. of net

retina (ret′in ə) *n., pl.* -nas, -nae′ (-ē′) [prob. < L. *rete,* net] the innermost coat of the back part of the eyeball, on which the image is formed —**ret′inal** *adj.*

retinue (ret′ə nyoo′) *n.* [see RETAIN] a body of assistants, servants, etc. attending a person of rank or importance

retire (ri tīər′) *vi.* -tired′, -tir′ing [< Fr. *re-*, back + *tirer,* draw] 1. to give up one's work, career, etc., esp. because of advanced age 2. to withdraw, as to a secluded place 3. to go to bed 4. *Cricket,* etc. to stop (batting) before one is out, as because of injury 5. to retreat, as in battle —*vt.* 1. to cause to retire from a job, etc. 2. to withdraw (troops) —**retire into oneself** to become uncommunicative —**retire′ment** *n.*

retired *adj.* having given up one's work, etc., esp. because of advanced age

retirement pension a state pension paid to people above a certain age

retiring *adj.* 1. reserved; shy 2. that retires

retook (rē took′) *pt. of* RETAKE

retort[1] (ri tôrt′) *vt., vi.* [< L. *re-*, back + *torquere,* to twist] 1. to return in kind (an insult, etc.) 2. to answer back, esp. in a sharp, quick, or clever way —*n.* a retorting or the response so made

RETORT

retort[2] *n.* [< ML. *retorta :* see prec.] 1. a container for distilling, usually of glass and with a long tube 2. a vessel for heating ore to extract metal

retouch (rē tuch′) *vt.* to touch up details in (a painting, photograph, etc.)

retrace (ri trās′) *vt.* -traced′, -trac′ing [see RE- & TRACE[1]] 1. to go back over again [*to retrace* one's steps] 2. to trace again the story of

retract (ri trakt′) *vt., vi.* [< L. *re-*, back + *trahere,* draw] 1. to draw back or in [*to retract* claws] 2. to withdraw (a statement, offer, etc.) —**retract′able** *adj.* —**retrac′tion** *n.* —**retrac′tive** *adj.*

retractile *adj.* [Fr.] that can be retracted

retread (rē tred′; *for n.* rē′tred′) *vt., n. same as* REMOULD

retreat (ri trēt′) *n.* [< L. *re-*, back + *trahere,* draw] 1. a withdrawal in the face of opposition, etc. 2. a safe, quiet, or secluded place 3. a period of seclusion, esp. for religious contemplation 4. *Mil.*

a) the forced withdrawal of troops under attack, or a signal for this *b*) a signal by bugle at sunset for lowering the flag, or this ceremony —*vi.* to withdraw —**beat a retreat** to withdraw in a hurry

retrench (rē trench´) *vt., vi.* [see RE- & TRENCH] to cut down or reduce (esp. expenses) —**retrench´ment** *n.*

retribution (ret´rə byo͞o´shən) *n.* [< L. *re-*, back + *tribuere*, to pay] deserved punishment for evil done

retrieve (ri trēv´) *vt.* -trieved´, -triev´ing [< OFr. *re-*, again + *trouver*, to find] 1. to get back; recover 2. to restore; revive 3. to save 4. to set right (a loss, error, etc.) 5. to recall to mind 6. to recover (information) from data stored in a computer 7. to find and bring back (game): said of dogs —*vi.* to retrieve game —*n.* a retrieving —**retriev´able** *adj.* —**retriev´al** *n.*

retriever *n.* a dog bred or trained to retrieve game

retro- [< L.] *a combining form meaning* backwards, back, behind

retroactive (ret´rō ak´tiv) *adj.* applying to the preceding period [*a retroactive pay increase*]

retrochoir (ret´rō kwīr) *n.* [RETRO-+ CHOIR] that part of a church which lies behind the choir and main altar

retrofire (ret´rō fīər) *vi., vt.* -fired´, -fir´ing to ignite: said of a retrorocket —*n.* a retrofiring

retrograde (ret´rō grād´) *adj.* [see RETRO- & GRADE] 1. moving backwards 2. going back to an earlier, esp. worse, condition —*vi.* -grad´ed, -grad´ing 1. to go backwards 2. to deteriorate

retrogress (ret´rō gres´) *vi.* [see prec.] to move backwards, esp. into an earlier or worse condition —**ret´rogres´sion** *n.* —**ret´rogres´sive** *adj.*

retrorocket, retro-rocket (ret´rō rok´-it) *n.* a small rocket on a larger rocket or spacecraft, used to produce thrust against flight direction so as to reduce speed

retrospect (ret´rō spekt´) *n.* [< L. *retro-*, back + *specere*, to look] a looking back on or thinking about things past —**in retrospect** in reviewing the past —**ret´rospec´tive** *adj.*

retroussé (rə tro͞o´sā) *adj.* [Fr.] turned up at the tip

retsina (ret sē´nə) *n.* [ModGr.] a wine of Greece, flavoured with pine resin

return (ri turn´) *vi.* [see RE- & TURN] 1. to go or come back 2. to answer; retort —*vt.* 1. to bring, send, or put back 2. to reciprocate [*to return* a compliment, etc.] 3. to produce (a profit); yield 4. to report officially or formally 5. to elect 6. to render (a verdict, etc.) 7. *Sports* to hit or throw back (a ball) —*n.* 1. a coming or going back 2. a bringing, sending, or putting back 3. something returned 4. repayment; requital 5. [*often pl.*] yield or profit 6. an answer; retort 7. *a*) an official or formal report [*election returns*] *b*) a form for reporting income tax due : in full, **(income) tax return**

—*adj.* 1. of or for returning [*a return* ticket *]* 2. given, sent, done, etc. in return [*a return* visit *]* —**in return** as an equivalent, response, etc.

returned man [Canad.] a war veteran

returning officer an official in charge of an election in a district

return ticket a ticket entitling a passenger to travel to his destination and back again

reunify (rē yo͞o´nə fī´) *vt., vi.* -fied´, -fy´-ing to unify again after being divided —**re´-unifica´tion** *n.*

reunion (rē yo͞on´yən) *n.* 1. a reuniting 2. a gathering of persons after separation

Reuters (roit´ərz) *n.* [< Baron Paul Julius von *Reuter*] a private British agency for gathering and distributing news among member newspapers

rev (rev) *n.* [Colloq.] a revolution, as of an engine —*vt., vi.* **revved, rev´ving** [Colloq.] to speed up (an engine)

Rev. 1. *Bible* Revelation 2. *pl.* **Revs.** Reverend

revamp (rē vamp´) *vt.* to renovate; revise —*n.* a revamping

Revd. Reverend

reveal (ri vēl´) *vt.* [< L. *re-*, back + *velum*, a veil] 1. to make known; disclose 2. to expose to view; show

reveille (ri val´ē) *n.* [< Fr. < L. *re-*, again + *vigilare*, to watch] *Mil.* a signal on a bugle, drum, etc. early in the morning to wake soldiers

revel (rev´'l) *vi.* -elled, -elling [see REBEL] 1. to take much pleasure (*in*) 2. to be noisily festive —*n.* merrymaking —**rev´eller** *n.* —**rev´elry** *n.*

revelation (rev´ə lā´shən) *n.* 1. a revealing 2. something disclosed, especially when it comes as a great surprise 3. *Theol.* God's revealing of himself to man —[R-] the last book of the New Testament (in full, **The Revelation of Saint John the Divine**): also **Revelations**

revenge (ri venj´) *vt.* -venged´, -veng´-ing [< OFr. *re-*, again + *vengier*, to take vengeance] 1. to inflict injury in return for (an injury, insult, etc.) 2. to avenge (a person, oneself, etc.) —*n.* 1. a revenging 2. what is done in revenging 3. desire to take vengeance 4. a chance to retaliate —**be revenged** to get revenge —**revenge´-ful** *adj.*

revenue (rev´ə nyo͞o´) *n.* [< OFr. *re-*, back + *venir*, come] 1. the income from property or investment 2. the income of a government from taxes, licences, etc.

reverberate (ri vur bə rāt´) *vi.* [< L. *re-*, again + *verberare*, beat] 1. to reecho or resound 2. to be reflected, as light or sound waves —*vt.* -at´ed, -at´ing 1. to cause (a sound) to reecho 2. to reflect (light, heat, etc.) —**rever´bera´tion** *n.*

revere (ri vēər´) *vt.* -vered´, -ver´ing [< L. *re-*, again + *vereri*, to fear] to regard with deep respect, love, and awe

reverence (rev´ər əns) *n.* 1. deep respect, love, and awe; veneration 2. a bow or curtsy 3. [R-] a title used in speaking to or of a clergyman —*vt.* **-enced, -enc-ing** to treat with reverence

reverend *adj.* [see REVERE] worthy of reverence: used [*usually the* **R-**] as a title of respect for a clergyman —*n. colloq. term for* CLERGYMAN

reverent *adj.* feeling or showing reverence

reverie (rev′ər ē) *n.* [< Fr. *rever*, to wander] dreamy thinking, esp. of agreeable things; daydreaming

revers (ri vēar′) *n., pl.* **-vers′** (-vēarz′) [Fr.] a part (of a garment) turned back to show the reverse side, as a lapel

reverse (ri vʉrs′) *vt.* **-versed′, -vers′ing** [see REVERT] 1. to turn in an opposite direction, upside down, or inside out 2. to change to the opposite 3. to cause to go in an opposite direction 4. to transfer (the charges for a telephone call) to the party being called 5. to annul (a decision, etc.) —*vi.* 1. to go in the opposite direction 2. to put a motor, engine, etc. in reverse —*n.* 1. the opposite or contrary 2. the back, as the side of a coin or medal that does not show the main design 3. a defeat; check 4. a mechanism for reversing, as a gear in a machine or motor vehicle —*adj.* 1. turned backwards; opposite or contrary 2. reversing the usual effect, as to show white letters on black 3. causing movement backwards or in the opposite direction —**the reverse of** far from —**rever′sal** *n.*

reversible *adj.* that can be reversed, as cloth, coats, etc. finished so that either side can be used as the outer side

reversing light a small light at the rear of a motor vehicle that is illuminated when the vehicle is reversed

revert (ri vʉrt′) *vi.* [< L. *re-*, back + *vertere*, to turn] 1. return, as to a former practice, subject, etc. 2. *Biol.* to return to an earlier type 3. *Law* to go back to a former owner or his heirs —**revert′i-ble** *adj.* —**rever′sion** *n.*

review (ri vyoo′) *n.* [< L. *re-*, again + *videre*, see] 1. a looking at or looking over again 2. a general survey or report 3. a looking back, as on past events 4. reexamination, as of the decision of a lower court 5. a critical evaluation of a book, play, etc. 6. a magazine containing articles of criticism and evaluation 7. a formal inspection, as of troops on parade —*vt.* 1. to look back on 2. to survey 3. to inspect (troops, etc.) formally 4. to give or write a critical report of (a book, play, etc.) 5. to reexamine (a lower court's decision) —*vi.* to review books, plays, etc.

reviewer *n.* one who reviews books, plays, etc. as for a newspaper

revile (ri vīl′) *vt., vi.* **-viled′, -vil′ing** [see RE- & VILE] to call bad names in talking (to or about) —**revil′er** *n.*

revise (ri vīz′) *vt.* **-vised′, -vis′ing** [< Fr. < L. *re-*, back + *visere*, to survey] 1. to change or amend 2. to go over (lessons, etc.) again 3. to read (a manuscript, etc.) carefully and correct and improve it —*n.* a revising —**revi′sion** (rē vizh′-) *n.*

Revised Standard Version a mid-20th-cent. revision of the Bible, made by U.S. scholars

Revised Version a late 19th-cent. revision of the Bible, made by British and U.S. scholars

revisory *adj.* of, or having the power of, revision

revitalize (rē vīt′ə līz′) *vt.* **-ized′, -iz′ing** to bring vitality, vigour, etc. back to after a decline

revival (ri vī′v′l) *n.* 1. a reviving or being revived 2. a bringing or coming back into use, being, etc. 3. a new presentation of an earlier play, etc. 4. restoration to vigour and activity 5. a stirring up of religious feelings by the preaching of evangelists at public meetings

revivalist *n.* a person who promotes or conducts religious revivals —**reviv′a-lism** *n.*

revive (ri vīv′) *vi., vt.* **-vived′, -viv′ing** [< L. *re-*, again + *vivere*, to live] 1. to return to life or consciousness 2. to return to health and vigour 3. to come or bring back into use, operation, or attention

revivify (ri viv′ə fī′) *vt., vi.* **-fied′, -fy′-ing** to give or acquire new life or vigour; revive —**reviv′ifica′tion** *n.*

revoke (ri vōk′) *vt.* **-voked′, -vok′ing** [< L. *re-*, back + *vocare*, to call] to withdraw, repeal, or cancel (a law, permit, etc.) —*vi. Card Games* to play a card of another suit, against the rules, when holding any of the suit called for —*n. Card Games* an act of revoking

revolt (ri vōlt′) *n.* [see REVOLVE] 1. a rebellion against the government or any authority 2. the state of revolting [*the slaves were in revolt*] —*vi.* 1. to rise up against authority; rebel 2. to be disgusted or shocked (*at* or *against*) —*vt.* to disgust

revolting *adj.* 1. rebellious 2. disgusting

revolution (rev′ə loo′shən) *n.* [see REVOLVE] 1. the overthrow of a government or social system, with another taking its place 2. complete or radical change 3. a turning motion round a centre or axis; rotation 4. a complete cycle 5. movement of a body in an orbit

revolutionary *adj.* 1. of, favouring, or causing a revolution in a government or social system 2. bringing about a very great change —*n., pl.* **-aries** one who favours or takes part in a revolution

revolution counter same as TACHOMETER: also **rev counter**

revolutionize *vt.* **-ized′, -iz′ing** to make a complete and basic change in

revolve (ri volv′) *vt.* **-volved′, -volv′ing** [< L. *re-*, back + *volvere*, to roll] 1. to cause to rotate 2. to cause to travel in a circle or orbit 3. to turn over in the mind —*vi.* 1. to move in a circle or orbit 2. to rotate 3. to seem to move (*around* or *about*)

revolver *n.* a handgun with a revolving cylinder holding several bullets which can be fired without reloading

revolving door a door consisting of four sections hung on a central axle, and turned by pushing

revue (ri vyo͞o′) *n.* [Fr.: see REVIEW] a musical show consisting of skits, songs, and dances, often satirical

revulsion (ri vul′shən) *n.* [< L. *re-*, back + *vellere*, to pull] a sudden, complete, and violent change of feeling, esp. one of extreme disgust

reward (ri wôrd′) *n.* [< OFr. *regarde*: see RE- + GUARD] 1. something given in return for good or, sometimes, evil 2. money offered, as for the capture of a criminal 3. compensation; profit —*vt.* 1. to give a reward for 2. to give a reward for (service, etc.)

rewarding *adj.* giving a sense of reward, or return

rewind (rē wīnd′) *vt.* -wound′, -wind′ing to wind (film, tape, etc.) back on the reel

rewire (rē wīər′) *vt., vi.* -wired′, -wir′-ing to put new electrical wires in or on (a house, etc.)

reword (rē wurd′) *vt.* to state again in other words

rewrite (rē rīt′; *for n.* rē′rīt′) *vt., vi.* -wrote′, -writ′ten, -writ′ing 1. to write again 2. to write (news turned in by a reporter) in a different form for publication —*n.* an article so written

rex (reks) *n.* [L.] [*also* R-] king

Rexine (rek′sēn) *Trademark* a kind of imitation leather

Reynard (ren′ərd) [< OHG.] the fox in the medieval beast epic *Reynard the Fox;* hence, a name for any fox

RF, R.F., r.f. 1. radio frequency 2. rapid-fire

R.F.C. Rugby Football Club

R.G.S. Royal Geographical Society

Rh 1. *see* RH FACTOR 2. *Chem.* rhodium

r.h., R.H., RH right hand

rhabdomancy (rab′də man′sē) *n.* [< Gr. *rhabdos*, rod + *manteia*, divination] divination of water, ores, etc. by means of a divining rod

Rhadamanthine (rad′ə man′thin) *adj.* [< *Rhadamanthus* in Gr. Myth.] judicially strict, impartial, and severe

rhapsodize (rap′sə dīz′) *vi., vt.* -dized′, -diz′ing to speak, write, or recite in a rhapsodic manner

rhapsody (rap′sə dē) *n., pl.* -dies [< Gr. *rhaptein*, stitch together + *ōidē*, song] 1. *Music* an instrumental composition of free, irregular form 2. great delight 3. any ecstatic or extravagantly enthusiastic speech or writing —**rhapsod′ic** (rap sod′-) *adj.*

rhea (rē′ə) *n.* [< *Rhea*, in Gr. Myth.] a large S American flightless bird

rhebuck (rē′buk′) *n.* [< Du. *ree*, roe + *bok*, buck] a S African antelope with brownish-grey hair

Rhenish (ren′ish) *adj.* of the Rhine or the regions around it

rhenium (rē′nē əm) *n.* [< L. *Rhenus*, Rhine] a rare metallic chemical element resembling manganese: symbol, Re

rheostat (rē′ō stat′) *n.* [< Gr. *rheos*, current + -STAT] a device for varying the resistance of an electric circuit without interrupting the circuit, used to dim or brighten electric lights

rhesus (rē′səs) *n.* [< Gr. proper name] a brownish-yellow macaque of India: in full, **rhesus monkey**

rhetoric (ret′ər ik) *n.* [< Gr. *rhētōr*, orator] 1. the art of using words effectively in speaking or writing 2. artificial eloquence; showiness in literary style —**rhetor′ical** *adj.*

rhetorical question a question asked only to produce an effect, no spoken answer being expected

rheum (ro͞om) *n.* [< Gr. *rheuma*, a flow] any watery discharge from the mucous membranes, as of the mouth, eyes, or nose —**rheum′y** *adj.*

rheumatic (ro͞o mat′ik) *adj.* of, caused by, or having rheumatism —*n.* [pl.] [Colloq.] rheumatism —**rheumat′ically** *adv.* —**rheumat′icky** *adj.*

rheumatic fever a disease in which there is fever, the joints ache and swell, and the heart becomes inflamed

rheumatism (ro͞o′mə tiz'm) *n.* [see RHEUM] *a popular term for* any of various painful conditions in which the joints and muscles become inflamed and stiff

rheumatoid *adj.* of or like rheumatism

rheumatoid arthritis a chronic disease in which the joints become inflamed, painful, and swollen

Rh factor (är′ ăch′) [RH(ESUS): first discovered in rhesus monkeys] a group of antigens, usually present in human blood, which may cause dangerous reactions during pregnancy or after transfusion of blood containing this factor into someone lacking it: people who have this factor are **Rh positive;** those who lack it are **Rh negative**

rhinal (rī′n'l) *adj.* [< Gr. *rhis, rhinos,* nose] of the nose

rhinestone (rīn′stōn′) *n.* [orig. made at Strasbourg (on the Rhine)] a bright, artificial gem made of colourless glass, often cut to imitate a diamond

rhino (rī′nō) *n., pl.* -nos, -no *shortened form of* RHINOCEROS

rhinoceros (rī nos′ər əs) *n.* [< Gr. *rhis,* nose + *keras,* horn] a large, thick-skinned, plant-eating mammal of Africa and Asia, with one or two upright horns on the snout

RHIZOME
OF GRASS

rhizome (rī′zōm) *n.* [< Gr. *rhiza,* root] a creeping stem lying horizontally at the surface of the soil: it bears leaves, and produces roots from its undersurface

rho (rō) *n.* the seventeenth letter of the Greek alphabet (P, ρ)

Rhodes scholarship (rōdz) a scholarship at Oxford University established by the will of C.J. Rhodes for selected students (**Rhodes scholars**) from the Commonwealth and the United States

rhodium (rō′dē əm) *n.* [< Gr. *rhodon*, rose : from the colour of its salts in solution] a hard, grey-white metallic chemical element : symbol, Rh

rhododendron (rō′də den′drən) *n.* [< Gr. *rhodon*, rose + *dendron*, tree] an evergreen shrub with flowers of pink, white, or purple

rhombohedron (rom′bə hē′drən) *n.*, *pl.* **-drons, -dra** [see RHOMBUS & -HEDRON] a six-sided prism each face of which is a rhombus

RHOMBOID

rhomboid (rom′boid) *n.* [see RHOMBUS] a parallelogram with oblique angles and only the opposite sides equal —**rhomboi′-dal** *adj.*

RHOMBUS

rhombus (rom′bəs) *n.*, *pl.* **-buses, -bi** (-bī) [< Gr. *rhombos*, turnable object] an equilateral parallelogram, esp. one with oblique angles

R.H.S. 1. Royal Historical Society 2. Royal Horticultural Society 3. Royal Humane Society

rhubarb (rōō′bärb) *n.* [< Gr. *rhēon*, rhubarb + *barbaron*, foreign] 1. a perennial plant having large leaves whose long, thick, sour stalks are cooked in pies, etc. 2. the roots of certain Asiatic varieties, used as a cathartic

rhumb (rum) *n.* [< Port. & Sp. *rumbo*] any of the points of a mariner's compass

rhumba (rum′bə) *n.* *alt. sp. of* RUMBA

rhyme (rīm) *n.* [prob. < L. *rhythmus*, rhythm] 1. likeness of sounds at the ends of words or lines of verse 2. a word that has the same end sound as another 3. a poem, or verse in general, using such end sounds —*vi.* **rhymed, rhym′-ing** 1. to make rhyming verse 2. to form a rhyme [“more” *rhymes* with “door”] 3. to be composed with rhymes : said of verse —*vt.* 1. to put into rhyme 2. to use as a rhyme —**rhyme or reason** order or sense : preceded by *without*, *no*, etc.

rhyme scheme the pattern of rhymes used in a piece of verse, usually indicated by letters

rhymester *n.* a maker of simple or inferior verse

rhyming slang a word or phrase that rhymes with, and is a slang term for, a particular word (Ex.: *bees and honey* for *money*)

rhythm (rith′əm) *n.* [< Fr. < Gr. *rhythmos*, measure] 1. flow or movement having a regularly repeated pattern of accents, beats, etc. 2. *Biol.* a periodic occurrence in living organisms of specific physiological changes 3. *Music* a) regular, repeated grouping of strong and weak beats b) the form or pattern of this [*waltz rhythm*] 4. *Prosody* the pattern of the regularly repeated stressed and unstressed syllables —**rhyth′mic** (rith′mik), **rhyth′mical** *adj.* —**rhyth′mically** *adv.*

rhythm and blues a form of popular music, influenced by the blues and having a strong beat

rhythm method a method of birth control by abstaining from sexual intercourse during the woman's probable monthly ovulation period

R.I. 1. [L. *Rex et Imperator*] King and Emperor 2. [L. *Regina et Imperatrix*] Queen and Empress

rialto (rē al′tō) *n.*, *pl.* **-tos** [< It.] a marketplace

rib (rib) *n.* [OE.] 1. any of the curved bones attached to the backbone and enclosing the chest cavity 2. a cut of meat having one or more ribs, as spareribs 3. a raised ridge in woven or knitted material 4. any riblike piece used to form a framework, or to shape or strengthen something 5. any of the main veins of a leaf —*vt.* **ribbed, rib′bing** 1. to provide or strengthen with ribs 2. [Slang] to tease playfully —**ribbed** *adj.*

R.I.B.A. Royal Institute of British Architects

ribald (rib′əld) *adj.* [< OFr. *ribaud*, debauchee] characterized by coarse joking; esp., dealing with sex in a humorously earthy way —*n.* a ribald person —**rib′aldry** *n.*

riband (rib′ənd) *n.* archaic var. of RIBBON

ribbing (rib′iŋ) *n.* an arrangement or series of ribs, as in knitted fabric, a ship's framework, etc.

ribbon (rib′ən) *n.* [MFr. *riban*] 1. a narrow strip as of silk or rayon, used for decorating or tying, for badges, etc. 2. anything suggesting such a strip 3. [*pl.*] shreds; tatters [torn to *ribbons*] 4. a narrow strip of cloth inked for use in a typewriter, etc. —**rib′bonlike′** *adj.*

ribbon development the siting of houses in a continuous row on one or both sides of a main road

riboflavin (rī′bə flā′vin) *n.* [< *ribose*, a sugar + L. *flavus*, yellow] a factor of the vitamin B complex, found in milk, eggs, liver, fruits, etc.

ribonucleic acid (rī′bə nyōō klē′ik) [< *ribose*, a sugar + NUCLEIC ACID] an essential component in the cytoplasm of all living cells : one form carries the genetic information needed for protein synthesis in the cell

rice (rīs) *n.* [< Gr. *oryza*: of Oriental origin] 1. a cereal grass of warm climates, planted in ground under water 2. its starchy seeds, used as food

rice paper 1. a thin, edible paper made from the straw of rice 2. a fine, delicate paper made by cutting and pressing the pith of **an** Asian plant

rich (rich) *adj.* [OE. *rice*, noble] 1. having much money or property; wealthy 2. having abundant natural resources 3. well-supplied (*with*); abounding (*in*) 4. valuable; sumptuous [*rich* gifts] 5. containing much butter, cream, sugar, etc. 6. *a)* full and mellow: said of sounds *b)* deep; vivid: said of colours *c)* very fragrant 7. abundant [a *rich* fund of stories] 8. yielding in abundance, as soil, etc. 9. [Colloq.] very amusing —**rich′ly** *adv.* —**rich′ness** *n.*

riches *n.pl.* valuable possessions; wealth

Richter scale (rik′tər) [< C. *Richter*] a scale for measuring the magnitude of earthquakes, with each of its 10 steps about 60 times greater than the preceding step

rick[1] (rik) *n.* [OE. *hreac*] a stack of hay, straw, etc.

rick[2] *vt., n.* [var. of WRICK] sprain or wrench

rickets (rik′its) *n.* [< ?] a disease, chiefly of children, characterized by a softening and, often, bending of the bones: it is caused by lack of vitamin D

rickettsia (ri ket′sē ə) *n., pl.* **-siae** (-ē′), **-sias** [< H. T. *Ricketts*] any of a genus of microorganisms that cause certain diseases, as typhus, and are transmitted by the bite of certain lice and ticks

rickety (rik′it ē) *adj.* 1. weak; shaky 2. of or having rickets

rickrack (rik′rak′) *n.* [redupl. of RACK[1]] flat, zigzag braid for trimming dresses, etc.

rickshaw, ricksha (rik′shô) *n.* [< Jap. *jinrikisha* < *jin*, man + *riki*, power + *sha*, carriage] a small, two-wheeled, hooded carriage pulled by one or two men and used, esp. formerly, in the Orient

ricochet (rik′ə shā′) *n.* [Fr.] 1. the rebound of a bullet, stone, etc. after striking a surface 2. a bullet, etc. that ricochets *vi.* **-cheted** (-shād′) or **-chet′ted** (-shet′-id), **-chet′ing** (-shā′iŋ) or **-chet′ting** (-shet′-iŋ) to move with such a motion

R.I.C.S. Royal Institute of Chartered Surveyors

rid (rid) *vt.* **rid, rid′ding** [< ON. *rythja*, to clear (land)] to free or relieve, as of something undesirable —**get rid of** to dispose of

riddance *n.* a ridding or being rid —**good riddance!** welcome relief or deliverance

ridden (rid′′n) *pp.* of RIDE

riddle[1] (rid′′l) *n.* [< OE. *rædan*, to guess] 1. a puzzle in the form of a question or statement with an ingenious meaning or answer that is hard to guess 2. any puzzling person or thing —*vi.* to utter riddles

riddle[2] *vt.* **-dled, -dling** [OE. *hriddel*] 1. *a)* to make many holes in, as with gun shot *b)* to affect every part of [*riddled* with errors] 2. to sift through a riddle —*n.* a coarse sieve

ride (rīd) *vi.* **rode, rid′den, rid′ing** [OE. *ridan*] 1. to sit on and control a horse or other animal in motion 2. to be carried along (*in* a vehicle, *on* a bicycle, etc.) 3. to be supported in motion (*on* or *upon*) 4. to move or float on water 5. [Colloq.] to continue undisturbed, with no action taken —*vt.* 1. to sit on or in so as to move along 2. to be carried or supported on [to *ride* the waves] 3. to move over, along, or through (a road, area, etc.) by horse, car, etc. 4. to cover (a specified distance) by riding 5. to engage in by riding [to *ride* a race] 6. to dominate or oppress [*ridden* by fear] —*n.* 1. a riding; journey by horse, car, etc. 2. a road, etc. for riding —**ride down** 1. to knock down by riding against 2. to overtake by riding —**ride out** to endure (a storm, crisis, etc.) successfully —**ride up** to move upwards out of place, as an article of clothing —**take for a ride** [Slang] 1. to cheat or swindle 2. to take somewhere, as in a car, and kill

rider *n.* 1. a person who rides 2. *a)* an amendment to a contract, jury verdict, etc. *b)* a clause added to a bill

ridge (rij) *n.* [OE. *hrycg*] 1. a long, narrow elevation of land or similar range of hills 2. any narrow, raised strip, as on fabric 3. the long, narrow top or crest of something, as of a wave 4. the horizontal line formed by the meeting of two sloping surfaces 5. *Meteorol.* an elongated area of high pressure —*vt., vi.* **ridged, ridg′-ing** to form into ridges —**ridg′y** *adj.*

RIDGEPOLE

ridgepole *n.* 1. the horizontal beam at the ridge of a roof 2. the horizontal pole forming the apex of a tent

ridicule (rid′i kyōōl′) *n.* [< L. *ridere*, to laugh] 1. the act of making someone or something the object of scornful laughter 2. words or actions used in doing this —*vt.* **-culed′, -cul′ing** to make fun of; deride; mock

ridiculous (ri dik′yōo ləs) *adj.* deserving ridicule; absurd

riding (rīd′iŋ) *n.* [OE. *-thrithing*, a third part] 1. any of the three former administrative divisions of Yorkshire 2. [Canad.] a parliamentary constituency

riding crop a short whip with a looped lash used when riding horses

riding-light *n.* a white light hung in the rigging of a vessel at anchor during the night, indicating its position

riempie (rim′pē) *n., pl.* **-ples** [< Afrik.]

[S Afr.] a leather thong used esp. to make chair seats

Riesling (rēz'liŋ) *n.* [< G.] [*also* r-] a dry, white wine made in the Rhine valley, Austria, etc.

rife (rif) *adj.* [OE. *ryfe*] 1. widespread [*gossip* was *rife*] 2. abounding; filled [*rife* with error]

riffle (rif''l) *vt., vi.* -fled, -fling [< ?] 1. to leaf rapidly (through) by releasing pages, etc. along their edge with the thumb 2. to shuffle (playing cards) by holding part of the pack in each hand and mixing the cards together with riffling motions —*n.* the act of riffling cards

riffraff (rif'raf') *n.* [< OFr. *rifler*, to scrape + *rafle*, a raking in] those people regarded as worthless, insignificant, etc.; rabble

rifle[1] (rī'f'l) *n.* [< Fr. *rifler*, to scrape] 1. a shoulder gun with a rifled barrel 2. [*pl.*] troops armed with rifles —*vt.* -fled, -fling to cut spiral grooves on the inside of (a gun barrel, etc.)

rifle[2] *vt.* -fled, -fling [< OFr. *rifler*] 1. to ransack and rob; plunder 2. to take as plunder; steal

rifling *n.* 1. the cutting of spiral grooves within a gun barrel, to make the projectile spin when fired 2. a system of such grooves

rift (rift) *n.* [< Dan. *rive*, to tear] 1. an opening caused by splitting; cleft 2. a break in friendly relations

rift valley a long, narrow, sunken area thought to result from the subsidence of land between two parallel faults

rig (rig) *vt.* **rigged, rig'ging** [< Scand.] 1. to fit (a ship, mast, etc.) with sails, shrouds, etc. 2. to fit (*out*); equip 3. to prepare for use, esp. in a hurry (often with *up*) 4. to arrange in a dishonest way [to *rig* a contest] 5. [Colloq.] to dress (with *out*) —*n.* 1. the arrangement of sails, masts, etc. on a vessel 2. equipment; gear 3. the installation used in drilling for and exploiting petroleum and natural gas deposits: also **oil rig**

Rigel (rī'g'l) [< Ar. *rijl*, foot] a bright, bluish star, brightest in the constellation Orion

rigging (rig'iŋ) *n.* the chains, ropes, etc. used for supporting and working the masts, sails, etc. of a vessel

right (rīt) *adj.* [OE. *riht*] 1. in accordance with accepted standards of moral behaviour, justice, etc. [*right* conduct] 2. correct; true 3. *a*) suitable *b*) most convenient or favourable 4. having sound physical or mental health 5. *a*) designating or of that side which is towards the east when one faces north *b*) closer to the right side of a person facing the thing mentioned 6. of the bank of a river on the right of a person facing downstream 7. of the political right; conservative or reactionary 8. formed with a straight line or axis perpendicular to a base [a *right* angle] 9. designating the side meant to be seen [the *right* side of cloth] 10. [Colloq.] real; utter [a *right* idiot] —*n.* 1. a power, privilege, etc. that a person

has by law, nature, etc. 2. what is just, lawful, proper, etc. 3. the true report (with *the*) 4. the right side 5. *Boxing a*) the right hand *b*) a blow with the right hand 6. [*often* R-] *Politics* a conservative or reactionary position, party, etc. (often with *the*) —*adv.* 1. in a way that is correct, proper, etc. 2. directly [go *right* home] 3. on or towards the right hand 4. completely [soaked *right* through] 5. [Colloq.] immediately [come *right* down] 6. [Colloq.] exactly [*right* here] 7. [Obs. or Dial] very [he knows *right* well] 8. most : used in certain titles [the *right* reverend] —*interj.* agreed! I understand! —*vt.* 1. to put upright [we *righted* the boat] 2. to correct 3. to put in order [she *righted* the room] 4. to make amends for —*vi.* to regain an upright position —**by right** (or **rights**) in justice —**in one's own right** through one's own status, ability, etc. —**in the right** on the side supported by truth, justice, etc. —**on the right side of** 1. to be approved of (by someone) 2. to be less than [on the *right* side of forty] —**right and left** on all sides —**right away** at once —**to rights** [Colloq.] into proper order

rightabout-face *n.* 1. a turning directly about so as to face the opposite direction 2. a complete reversal of belief, conduct, etc.

RIGHT ANGLE

right angle an angle of 90 degrees, made by the meeting of two straight lines perpendicular to each other —**right'-an'-gled** *adj.*

right-angled triangle a triangle with one right angle

right arm a reliable helper

righteous (rī'chəs) *adj.* 1. upright; virtuous [a *righteous* man] 2. morally right [*righteous* anger]

rightful *adj.* 1. fair; just 2. having a lawful claim [the *rightful* owner] 3. owned by lawful claim [a *rightful* rank]

right-hand *adj.* 1. on or towards the right 2. of, for, or with the right hand 3. most helpful or reliable [my *right-hand* man]

right-handed *adj.* 1. using the right hand more skilfully than the left 2. done with or made for use with the right hand —*adv.* with the right hand —**right'hand'er** *n.*

rightly *adv.* 1. fairly 2. suitably 3. correctly

right-minded *adj.* having correct views or sound principles

right of way 1. the right to move in front of others, as at a traffic intersection 2. *a*) the right to use a certain route, as over another's property *b*) a path marking such a route

Right Reverend the form of address used for bishops

rightward *adv., adj.* on or towards the right: also **right′wards** *adv.*

right whale a large-headed whalebone whale

right wing the more conservative or reactionary section of a political party, group, etc. —**right′-wing′** *adj.*

rigid (rij′id) *adj.* [< L. *rigere*, be stiff] 1. not bending or flexible 2. strict or rigorous —**rigidity** (ri jid′ə tē) *n.*

rigmarole (rig′mə rōl′) *n.* [< ME. *rageman rolle*, a document] 1. a fussy or time-wasting procedure 2. rambling talk; nonsense

rigor mortis (rig′ər môr′tis) [ModL., stiffness of death] the stiffening of the muscles after death

rigorous (rig′ər əs) *adj.* 1. very strict [*rigorous* rules] 2. very severe [a *rigorous* climate] 3. exactly precise [*rigorous* bookkeeping]

rigour (rig′ər) *n.* [< L. *rigere*, be rigid] 1. harshness or severity 2. precision or accuracy 3. a harsh or oppressive act, etc. 4. rigidity, esp. in the body tissues Also U.S. sp., **rig′or**

rig-out (rig′out′) *n.* [Colloq.] clothing or costume

rile (rīl) *vt.* riled, ril′ing [< *roil*, to disturb] [Colloq.] to anger

rill (ril) *n.* [< Du. *ril*] a little brook

rim (rim) *n.* [OE. *rima*, an edge] 1. an edge or margin, esp. of something circular 2. *a)* the outer part of a wheel *b)* the metal flange of a motor car wheel, on which the tyre is mounted —*vt.* rimmed, rim′ming to put a rim on

rime[1] (rīm) *n., vt., vi.* rimed, rim′ing same as RHYME

rime[2] *n.* [OE. *hrim*] hoarfrost —*vt.* rimed, rim′ing to coat with rime —**rim′y** *adj.*

rind (rīnd) *n.* [OE.] a thick or tough outer layer, as on fruit, cheese, bacon, etc.

rinderpest (rin′dər pest′) *n.* [< G. *Rinder*, cattle + *Pest*, plague] an acute infectious disease of cattle, etc.

ring[1] (riŋ) *vi.* rang, rung, ring′ing [OE. *hringan*] 1. to give forth the resonant sound of a bell 2. to produce a specified impression [to *ring* false] 3. to cause a bell to sound, esp. as a summons 4. to resound [the room *rang* with laughter] 5. to have a sensation of ringing: said of the ears —*vt.* 1. to cause (a bell, etc.) to ring 2. to signal, announce, etc. as by ringing 3. to call by telephone (often with *up*) —*n.* 1. the sound of a bell 2. any similar sound 3. an impression [the *ring* of sincerity] 4. the act of ringing a bell, etc. 5. [Colloq.] a telephone call: chiefly in **give (someone) a ring**, to telephone (someone) —**ring a bell** to stir up a memory —**ring down** (or **up**) **the curtain** 1. to signal for a theatre curtain to be lowered (or raised) 2. to end (or begin) something —**ring off** to terminate a telephone conversation —**ring up** 1. to record on a cash register 2. to telephone

ring[2] *n.* [OE. *hring*] 1. a circular band, esp. of precious metal, to be worn on the finger 2. any similar band [a key *ring*] 3. a circular line, mark, or figure 4. the outer edge or rim 5. a number of people or things grouped in a circle 6. a group working together to advance their own interests 7. an enclosed area, for contests, exhibitions, etc. [a circus *ring*] 8. prizefighting (with *the*) —*vt.* **ringed, ring′ing** 1. to encircle 2. to form into, or furnish with, a ring or rings 3. to cut a circle of bark from (a tree) 4. to mark a bird with a ring or clip for later identification —**run rings around** [Colloq.] to be so much better, more skilful, etc. as to expose someone else as inferior or foolish —**ringed** *adj.*

ringdove *n.* the wood pigeon

ring finger the finger next to the little finger, esp. of the left hand, on which a wedding ring is usually worn

ringleader *n.* a person who leads others, esp. in unlawful acts

ringlet *n.* a curl of hair, esp. a long one —**ring′leted** *adj.*

ring main a domestic electrical wiring system consisting of a ring circuit supplied by mains electricity

ringmaster *n.* a man who directs the performances in a circus ring

ring road a road bypassing a busy town centre

ringside *n.* 1. the place just outside the ring, as at a boxing match 2. any place that provides a close view

ringworm *n.* any contagious skin disease caused by a fungus that produces ring-shaped patches

rink (riŋk) *n.* [< Scot. < ?] 1. a smooth expanse of ice for ice skating or ice hockey 2. a smooth floor for roller-skating 3. a building enclosing either of such rinks 4. a section of the green or ice used for play in bowls and curling

rinkhals (riŋk′hous′) *n.* [< Afrik.] a S African ring-necked cobra

rink rat [Canad. Slang] a youth who helps with odd chores around an ice hockey rink in return for free admission to games, etc.

rinse (rins) *vt.* rinsed, rins′ing [ult. < L. *recens*, fresh] 1. to wash lightly, as by dipping into clear water 2. to remove (soap, etc.) by washing 3. to flush (the mouth or teeth), as with clear water 4. to use a rinse on (hair) —*n.* 1. a rinsing 2. a substance used to tint hair

riot (rī′ət) *n.* [< OFr. *rihoter*, make a disturbance] 1. a violent, public disturbance of the peace by a number of persons 2. wild or violent disorder, confusion, etc. 3. a brilliant display [a *riot* of colour] 4. [Colloq.] an extremely amusing person, thing, or event —*vi.* to take part in a riot —**run riot** 1. to act in a wild, unrestrained manner 2. to grow in profusion —**ri′oter** *n.*

riotous *adj.* 1. having the nature of a riot 2. engaging in rioting 3. disorderly or boisterous

rip[1] (rip) *vt.* ripped, rip′ping [< ?] 1. to cut or tear apart roughly 2. to remove as by cutting or tearing (with *off, out,* etc.) **3.** to make (a hole) in this way **4.** to slash with a sharp instrument —*vi.* **1.** to become torn or split apart **2.** [Colloq.] to move with speed or violence —*n.* a torn place or burst seam —**let rip** to act or speak without restraint or control —**rip off** [Slang] **1.** to steal **2.** to cheat, exploit, etc. —**rip′per** *n.*

rip² *n.* [< ?] [Colloq.] a debauched, dissipated person

R.I.P. *abbrev. of* REQUIESCAT IN PACE

riparian (ri pãar′ē ən) *adj.* [< L. *ripa,* bank] of or living on the bank of a river, etc.

rip cord a cord pulled to open a parachute during descent

ripe (rīp) *adj.* [OE.] **1.** ready to be harvested, as grain **2.** sufficiently processed to be ready for use [*ripe* cheese] **3.** highly developed; mature **4.** advanced in years [the *ripe* age of ninety] **5.** fully prepared [*ripe* for marriage] **6.** far enough along (*for*): said of time —**ripe′ness** *n.*

ripen *vi., vt.* to become or make ripe; mature

riposte, ripost (ri post′) *n.* [< Fr. < L.: see RESPOND] **1.** a sharp, swift retort **2.** *Fencing* a sharp, swift thrust made after parrying an opponent's lunge —*vi.* **-post′ed, -post′ing** to make a riposte

ripple (rip′'l) *vi.* **-pled, -pling** [< ?] **1.** to form or have little waves on the surface **2.** to give the effect of alternately rising and falling [laughter *rippling* through the hall] —*vt.* to cause to ripple —*n.* **1.** a small wave, as on the surface of water **2.** a movement like this **3.** a sound like that of rippling water —**rip′ply** *adj.*

rip-roaring (rip′rôr′iŋ) *adj.* [Slang] boisterous; uproarious

ripsaw *n.* [RIP¹ + SAW¹] a saw with coarse teeth, for cutting wood along the grain

rise (rīz) *vi.* **rose, risen** (riz′'n), **ris′ing** [OE. *risan*] **1.** to stand or assume an erect position after sitting, lying, etc. **2.** to get up after sleeping or resting **3.** to ascend **4.** to appear above the horizon [the moon *rose*] **5.** to attain a higher level, status, rank, etc. **6.** to become erect or rigid **7.** to extend upwards [hills *rising* steeply] **8.** to increase in amount, degree, etc. **9.** to become louder, shriller, etc. **10.** to become stronger, more vivid, etc. **11.** to become larger and puffier, as dough with yeast **12.** to originate; begin **13.** to happen; occur **14.** to become apparent [land *rising* ahead of the ship] **15.** to be built [the house *rose* quickly] **16.** to rebel **17.** to end an official assembly or meeting **18.** to return to life after dying —*n.* **1.** upward motion; ascent **2.** an advance in status, rank, etc. **3.** an increase in degree, amount, etc. **4.** an increase in wages **5.** a hill **6.** a slope upwards **7.** the vertical height of something, as a staircase **8.** a beginning, origin, etc. —**get a rise out of** [Slang] to draw a desired response from, as by

teasing —**give rise to** to bring about —**rise to** to prove oneself capable of coping with [to *rise* to the occasion]

riser *n.* a vertical piece between the steps in a stairway

risible (riz′ə b'l) *adj.* [< L. *ridere,* to laugh] **1.** inclined to laugh **2.** causing laughter; laughable —**ris′ibil′ity** *n.*

rising (rī′ziŋ) *adj.* **1.** that rises; ascending, advancing, etc. **2.** growing; maturing [the *rising* generation] **3.** [Colloq.] approaching [a man *rising* fifty] —*n.* **1.** an uprising; revolt **2.** something that rises

risk (risk) *n.* [< Fr. < It. *risco*] **1.** the chance or likelihood of injury, damage, or loss; hazard **2.** the person or thing exposed to such chance or likelihood —*vt.* **1.** to expose to risk; hazard [to *risk* one's life] **2.** to take the chance of [to *risk* a fight] —**at risk** in a dangerous position —**run** (or **take**) **a risk** to expose oneself to a risk —**risk′y** *adj.*

risqué (ris′kā) *adj.* [Fr. < *risquer,* to risk] very close to being improper or indecent; suggestive

rissole (ris′ōl) *n.* [Fr.] a small ball of minced meat mixed with breadcrumbs, eggs, etc., often fried

ritardando (rē′tär dan′dō) *adj., adv.* [It.] *Music* becoming gradually slower

rite (rīt) *n.* [L. *ritus*] **1.** a solemn or ceremonial act or observance, as in religious use **2.** a particular system of ceremonial procedure; ritual **3.** [*often* R-] liturgy

ritual (rich′ōō wəl) *n.* **1.** a system of rites, religious or otherwise **2.** the observance of set forms, as in worship **3.** a practice or procedure done as a rite —*adj.* of, like, or done as a rite —**rit′ually** *adv.*

ritualism *n.* **1.** observance of, or excessive devotion to, ritual **2.** the study of religious ritual —**rit′ualist** *n., adj.* —**rit′ualis′tic** *adj.* —**rit′ualis′tically** *adv.*

ritzy (rit′sē) *adj.* **ritz′ier, ritz′iest** [< the *Ritz* hotels] [Colloq.] luxurious, fashionable, elegant

rival (rī′v'l) *n.* [< L. *rivalis*] **1.** a person who tries to get the same thing as another, or to equal or surpass another; competitor **2.** a satisfactory substitute [plastics are *rivals* of many metals] —*adj.* acting as a rival; competing —*vt.* **-valled, -valling 1.** to try to equal or surpass **2.** to equal

rivalry *n., pl.* **-ries** the act of rivalling or the fact of being a rival; competition

rive (rīv) *vt., vi.* **rived, rived** or **riven** (riv′'n), **riv′ing** [ON. *rifa*] **1.** to tear apart **2.** to split; cleave

river (riv′ər) *n.* [see RIPARIAN] **1.** a large, natural flow of water emptying into a sea, lake, etc. **2.** any plentiful flow —**sell down the river** to betray, deceive, etc.

river basin the area drained by a river and its tributaries

riverbed *n.* the channel in which a river flows or has flowed

RIVETS

(A, rivet holding steel beams
together; B, C, D rivets)

rivet (riv′it) *n.* [< MFr. *river*, to clinch]
a metal bolt with a head on one end,
used to fasten beams, etc. together by
being inserted through holes: the plain
end is then hammered into a head —*vt.*
1. to fasten with rivets **2.** to hammer
the end of (a bolt, etc.) into a head **3.**
to fasten firmly **4.** to hold (the eyes,
etc.) firmly —**riv′eter** *n.*

rivulet (riv′yoo lit) *n.* [< It. < L. *rivus*,
a brook] a little stream

rly. railway

rm. *pl.* **rms.** **1.** ream **2.** room

R.M. **1.** Royal Mail **2.** Royal Marines
3. [Canad.] Rural Municipality

R.M.A. Royal Military Academy

Rn *Chem.* radon

R.N. **1.** [Canad.] registered nurse **2.**
Royal Navy

RNA ribonucleic acid

R.N.A.S. Royal Naval Air Service

R.N.L.I. Royal National Lifeboat
Institution

R.N.(V.)R. Royal Naval (Volunteer)
Reserve

R.N.Z.A.F. Royal New Zealand Air Force

R.N.Z.N. Royal New Zealand Navy

roach (rōch) *n.* [OFr. *roche*] a freshwater
fish of the carp family

road (rōd) *n.* [OE. *rad*, a ride] **1.** a
way made for travelling between places
by motor car, horseback, etc. **2.** a path;
course [the *road* to fortune] **3.** [often
pl.] a protected place near shore where
ships can ride at anchor —**one for the
road** [Colloq.] a last alcoholic drink before
leaving —**on the road 1.** travelling, as
a salesman **2.** on tour, as actors **3.**
leading a wandering life, as a tramp

road allowance [Canad.] land set aside
by a government for building a road

roadblock *n.* a blockade set up in a
road to prevent movement of vehicles

road fund formerly, the money from
motor licence fees, used for the
maintenance of roads and bridges

road fund licence a disc showing that
the tax to which a motor vehicle is subject
has been paid

road hog a selfish, dangerous, or
aggressive driver

road-holding *n.* the stability of a motor
vehicle under varied driving conditions

roadhouse *n.* a restaurant, hotel, etc.
situated on a country road

roadshow *n.* **1.** a show presented by
a theatrical company on tour **2.** a touring
discotheque, esp. one associated with a
radio station

roadside *n.* the side of a road —*adj.*
on or at the side of a road

roadstead *n.* *same as* ROAD (sense 3)

roadster *n.* an open motor car with front
seats only

road test a test of a vehicle, tyres, etc.
under operating conditions —**road′test′** *vt.*

roadway *n.* **1.** a road **2.** that part of
a road intended for vehicles to travel on

road works repairs to, and maintenance
of, the roads

roadworthy *adj.* mechanically sound; fit
for use on the roads: said of a vehicle

roam (rōm) *vi.* [ME. *romen*] to travel
with no special plan or purpose; wander
—*vt.* to wander over or through —*n.*
the act of roaming

roan (rōn) *adj.* [< OSp. *roano*] chestnut,
black, etc., with a thick sprinkling of white
hairs: said chiefly of horses —*n.* a roan
horse or other animal

roar (rôr) *vi.* [OE. *rarian*] **1.** to utter
a loud, deep, rumbling sound, as a lion
2. to talk or laugh boisterously **3.** to
operate with a loud noise —*vt.* to utter
with a roar —*n.* **1.** a loud, deep, rumbling
sound, as of a lion **2.** a loud noise, as
of waves, etc.

roaring *n.* the sound of a roar —*adj.*
[Colloq.] successful; brisk [a *roaring*
business] —*adv.* to the point of being
noisy, boisterous, etc. [*roaring* drunk]

roast (rōst) *vt.* [< OFr. *rostir*] **1.** to
cook (something) with little or no moisture,
as in an oven **2.** to process (coffee, etc.)
by exposure to heat **3.** to expose to great
heat **4.** [U.S. Colloq.] to criticize severely
—*vi.* **1.** to be cooked by being roasted
2. to be or become very hot —*n.* **1.**
roasted meat **2.** a cut of meat for roasting
—*adj.* roasted [*roast* pork] —**roast′ing**
adj.

roaster *n.* **1.** a pan, oven, etc. for roasting
meat **2.** a chicken, etc. suitable for roasting

rob (rob) *vt.* **robbed, rob′bing** [< OFr.
rober] **1.** to take property from unlawfully
by using or threatening force **2.** separately,
to steal something from in any way **3.**
to deprive [the accident *robbed* him of
his health] —*vi.* to commit robbery
—**rob′ber** *n.*

robbery *n.,* *pl.* **-beries** a robbing; specif.,
the taking of another's property by violence
or threat of violence

robe (rōb) *n.* [< OFr.] **1.** a long, loose
outer garment; specif., such a garment
worn to show rank or office **2.** [U.S.]
a dressing gown —*vt., vi.* **robed, rob′-
ing** to dress in a robe

robin (rob′in) *n.* [< Fr. dim. of *Robert*]
a small warbler with an orange-red breast:
also **robin redbreast**

Robin Goodfellow *Eng. Folklore* a mischievous elf

Robin Hood *Eng. Legend* an outlaw
of the 12th cent. who lived with his followers
in Sherwood Forest and robbed the rich
to help the poor

Robinson Crusoe (rob′in s'n krōō′sō)
the hero of Defoe's novel (1719) of the
same name, a sailor who is shipwrecked
on a tropical island

robot (rō′bot) *n.* [< Czech *robota*, forced
labour] **1.** *a)* any manlike mechanical

being b) any mechanical device operated automatically to perform in a seemingly human way 2. a person who acts or works mechanically 3. [S Afr.] traffic lights

robust (rō bust′) *adj.* [< L. *robur,* hard oak] 1. a) strong and healthy; hardy b) strongly built; muscular or sturdy 2. requiring physical strength [robust work] 3. rough; boisterous

robustious (rō bus′chəs) *adj.* [< prec.] rough; boisterous

roc (rok) *n.* [< Ar. < Per. *rukh*] Arabian & Persian Legend a bird, so huge and strong that it could carry off large animals

R.O.C. Royal Observer Corps

rochet (roch′it) *n.* [< OFr. < OHG. *roch*] a vestment like a surplice, worn by bishops

rock[1] (rok) *n.* [< OFr. *roche*] 1. mineral matter formed in masses in the earth's crust 2. a large mass of stone 3. a large stone detached from the mass; boulder 4. anything like a rock; esp., a firm support, etc. 5. a hard sweet made in sticks 6. [Slang] a diamond or other gem —**on the rocks** [Colloq.] 1. ruined 2. bankrupt 3. served undiluted over ice cubes: said of spirits —**the Rock** Gibraltar

rock[2] *vt., vi.* [OE. *roccian*] 1. to move backwards and forwards or from side to side 2. to sway strongly; shake —*n.* 1. a rocking motion 2. a) *same as* ROCK-AND-ROLL b) popular music evolved from rock-and-roll, containing elements of folk music, country music, etc. —**rock the boat** to upset a stable situation

rock-and-roll (rok′'n rōl′) *n.* 1. a form of popular music, having a strong rhythm, which evolved from jazz and the blues 2. dancing performed to such music Also **rock 'n' roll**

rock bottom the lowest level or point —**rock′-bot′tom** *adj.*

rock-bound *adj.* surrounded by rocks [a rock-bound coast]

rock cake a small fruit cake with a rough surface

rock crystal a transparent, esp. colourless, quartz

rock dove the wild ancestor of the domestic pigeons

rocker *n.* 1. any of various devices that work with a rocking motion 2. *same as* ROCKING CHAIR 3. either of the curved pieces on the bottom of a cradle, rocking chair, etc. —**off one's rocker** [Slang] crazy; insane

rockery *n., pl.* -**eries** rocks and soil arranged for growing a rock garden

rocket (rok′it) *n.* [< It. *rocchetta,* spool] 1. any device containing a combustible substance which when ignited produces gases that escape through a rear vent and drive the container forwards by the principle of reaction: rockets are used as fireworks, projectile weapons, etc. 2. a spacecraft, missile, etc. propelled by a rocket 3. [Colloq.] a severe reprimand —*vi.* to move in or like a rocket; soar

rocketry *n.* the science of designing, building, and launching rockets

rock garden a garden with plants growing among rocks variously arranged

rocking chair a chair mounted on rockers or springs, so as to allow a rocking movement

rocking horse a toy horse mounted on rockers or springs and big enough for a child to ride

rock plant a plant which thrives in dry exposed places among stones and rocks

rock rabbit [S Afr.] *same as* DASSIE

rock salmon the name used for dogfish by fishmongers

rock salt common salt in solid masses

rockspider *n.* [S Afr. Derog.] an Afrikaner

rocky[1] *adj.* -**ier, -iest** full of, consisting of, or like rock

rocky[2] *adj.* -**ier, -iest** shaky

Rocky Mountain goat a white, goatlike antelope of the mountains of northwest N America

rococo (rə kō′kō) *n.* [Fr. < *rocaille,* shell work] an elaborate style of architecture and decoration popular in the 18th cent. —*adj.* 1. of or in rococo 2. too elaborate; florid

rod (rod) *n.* [OE. *rodd*] 1. any straight bar of wood, metal, etc. 2. a stick for beating as punishment 3. a staff, sceptre, etc., carried as a symbol of office or rank 4. *same as* FISHING ROD 5. a measure of length equal to 5$^1/_2$ yards (5m) 6. [U.S. Slang] a pistol or revolver

rode (rōd) *pt. & archaic pp. of* RIDE

rodent (rōd′'nt) *n.* [< L. *rodere,* gnaw] any of various gnawing mammals, including rats, mice, beavers, etc.

rodent officer an official ratcatcher

rodeo (rō dā′ō) *n., pl.* -**deos** [Sp. < L. *rotare,* ROTATE] [U.S. & Canad.] a public exhibition of the skills of cowboys, as broncobusting, lassoing, etc.

rodomontade (rod′ə mon tād′) *n.* [Fr. < It.] arrogant or blustering talk

roe[1] (rō) *n.* [< ?] fish eggs, esp. when still massed in the ovarian membrane

roe[2] *n.* [OE. *ra*] a small, agile, graceful deer

rogation (rō gā′shən) *n.* [< L. *rogare,* ask] a supplication or prayer, esp. as chanted during Rogation days

Rogation days the three days before Ascension Day

Roger (roj′ər) *interj.* [< signal flag for R] [also r-] 1. received: term used in radiotelegraphy to indicate reception of a message 2. [Colloq.] right!; OK!

rogue (rōg) *n.* [< ?] 1. a scoundrel 2. a fun-loving, mischievous person 3. any inferior or defective specimen, esp. a plant that is of a different, unwanted variety from the main crop 4. formerly, a vagabond 5. an animal that wanders alone and is fierce and wild —**ro′guish** *adj.*

roguery (rō′gər ē) *n., pl.* -**gueries** the behaviour of a rogue; specif., a) cheating b) playful mischief

rogues' gallery a collection of photographs of criminals, as used by police in identification

roister (rois′tər) *vi.* [see RUSTIC] 1. to

boast or swagger **2.** to revel boisterously —**roist′ering** *n.*, *adj.*

role, rôle (rōl) *n.* [Fr.] **1.** a part that an actor plays **2.** a function assumed [an advisory *role*]

roll (rōl) *vi.* [< L. *rota*, wheel] **1.** to move by turning over and over **2.** to move on wheels **3.** to pass [the years *rolled* by] **4.** to flow in a full, sweeping motion **5.** to extend in gentle undulations **6.** to make a loud, rising and falling sound [thunder *rolls*] **7.** to trill **8.** to turn in a circular motion [with eyes *rolling*] **9.** to rock from side to side, as a ship **10.** to walk by swaying **11.** to become spread under a roller **12.** to make progress **13.** to start operating [the presses *rolled*] **14.** [Colloq.] to abound (*in*) —*vt.* **1.** to move by turning over and over **2.** to move on wheels or rollers **3.** to cause to start operating **4.** to beat (a drum) with light, rapid blows **5.** to utter with a full, flowing sound **6.** to say with a trill [to *roll* one's r's] **7.** to give a swaying motion to **8.** to move around or from side to side [to *roll* one's eyes] **9.** to wind into a ball or cylinder [to *roll* a cigarette] **10.** to enfold **11.** to make flat by using a roller, etc. —*n.* **1.** a rolling **2.** *a)* a scroll *b)* something that is rolled up **3.** *a)* a register *b)* the official list of solicitors **4.** a list of names **5.** a measure of something rolled into a cylinder [a *roll* of wallpaper] **6.** a cylindrical mass of something **7.** a small cake of bread **8.** a swaying motion **9.** a rapid succession of light blows on a drum **10.** a loud, reverberating sound, as of thunder **11.** a trill **12.** a slight swell on the surface of something, as land **13.** *Aeron.* a manoeuvre in which an aircraft makes one complete rotation about its longitudinal axis —**roll in** to arrive or appear in large numbers or amounts —**roll up 1.** to form into a cylinder **2.** [Colloq.] to arrive in or as if in a vehicle —**strike off the rolls** to expel from membership

roll call the reading aloud of a roll to find out who is absent

rolled gold brass or other base metal covered with a thin layer of gold

roller *n.* **1.** *a)* a cylinder on which something is rolled up [a hair *roller*] *b)* a rolling cylinder used to crush, smooth, or spread something **2.** a long, heavy wave that breaks on the shoreline **3.** a person or thing that rolls

roller coaster [U.S.] a switchback

roller skate a skate with wheels —**roll′-er-skate′** *vi.* —**roller skater**

roller towel a towel whose ends are sewn together and which is hung on a roller

rollick (rol′ik) *vi.* [< ?] to behave in a gay, carefree way —**rol′licking** *adj.*

rolling (rōl′iŋ) *adj.* **1.** that rolls; revolving, recurring, swaying, surging, etc. **2.** [Colloq.] wealthy —*n.* the action, motion, or sound of something that rolls

rolling mill 1. a factory in which metal bars, sheets, etc. are rolled out **2.** a machine used for such rolling

rolling pin a heavy, smooth cylinder with a handle at each end, used to roll out pastry, etc.

rolling stock all the vehicles of a railway or [U.S.] of a trucking company

rolling stone a person who is incapable of settling down in any one place

roll-mop (rōl′mop′) *n.* [G. < *rollen*, to ROLL + *Mops*, pug dog] a fillet of fresh herring rolled around an onion and marinated

roll-on (rōl′on) *n.* **1.** a liquid, esp. a deodorant, that is packed in a container having an applicator consisting of a revolving ball **2.** [Colloq.] a woman's foundation garment —*adj.* **1.** dispensed by rolling the applicator over the flesh or other surface **2.** designed to allow vehicles to be driven aboard: said of a ferry, etc.

Rolls-Royce (rōlz′rois′) *n.* [< Charles Stewart *Rolls* & Sir Frederick Henry *Royce*] a make of motor car, famed for its luxury

roll-top *adj.* made with a flexible top of parallel slats that slides back [a roll-top desk]

roly-poly (rō′lē pō′lē) *adj.* [redupl. of ROLL] short and plump; pudgy —*n.*, *pl.* **-lies 1.** a pudding made of rich dough spread with jam, rolled up, and boiled, steamed, etc. **2.** a roly-poly person

Rom. 1. Roman **2.** Romans (Epistle to the Romans)

Roman (rō′mən) *adj.* **1.** of ancient or modern Rome, its people, etc. **2.** of the Roman Catholic Church **3.** [*usually* r-] designating or of the usual upright style of printing types; not italic —*n.* **1.** a native or inhabitant of ancient or modern Rome **2.** [*usually* r-] roman type

Roman alphabet the alphabet of the ancient Romans, used with little change in most modern European languages

Roman candle a firework consisting of a long tube that sends out balls of fire, sparks, etc.

Roman Catholic 1. of the Roman Catholic Church **2.** a member of this church —**Roman Catholicism**

Roman Catholic Church the Christian church headed by the Pope

Romance (rō mans′) *adj.* [see ff.] designating or of any of the languages derived from Latin, as Italian, Spanish, French, etc. —*n.* these languages

romance (rō mans′) *n.* [ult. < L. *Romanicus*, Roman] **1.** a love affair **2.** a spirit of, or inclination for, excitement, mystery, etc. **3.** a long narrative, orig. written in one of the Romance languages, about knights and chivalric deeds, adventure, and love **4.** a novel of love, adventure, etc. **5.** an exaggeration or fabrication —*vi.* **-manced′**, **-manc′ing 1.** to write or tell romances **2.** to exaggerate or embroider the truth

Romanesque (rō′mə nesk′) *adj.* designating a style of European architecture of the 11th and 12th cent., using round arches, massive walls, etc. —*n.* this style of architecture

Roman nose a nose with a prominent bridge

Roman numerals the Roman letters which are used as numerals: I=1, V=5, X=10, L=50, C=100, D=500, M=1000

Romano- (rō mä′nō) *a combining form meaning* Roman

romantic (rō man′tik) *adj.* **1.** of, like, or characterized by romance **2.** full of thoughts, feelings, etc. of romance **3.** of romance, or lovemaking *[a romantic night]* **4.** not practical; visionary **5.** fanciful or fictitious **6.** *[often* R-*]* of the ROMANTIC MOVEMENT —*n.* a romantic person —**roman′tically** *adv.*

romanticism *n.* **1.** romantic spirit, outlook, etc. **2.** the spirit, style, etc. of, or adherence to, the Romantic Movement —**roman′ticist** *n.*

romanticize *vt.* **-cized′, -ciz′ing** to treat or regard romantically —*vi.* to have romantic ideas, attitudes, etc.

Romantic Movement the revolt in the 18th and 19th cent. against neoclassicism in literature, music, art, etc.: it emphasized freedom of form, full expression of feeling, etc.

Romany (rom′ə nē) *n.* [< Romany *rom*, man] **1.** *pl.* **-ny, -nies** a Gypsy **2.** the language of the Gypsies —*adj.* of the Gypsies, their language, etc. Also sp. **Rom′-many**

Romeo (rō′mē ō′) *n.*, *pl.* **-os** [< the hero of Shakespeare's *Romeo and Juliet]* a man who is an ardent lover

romp (romp) *n.* [prob. < RAMP²] boisterous, lively play —*vi.* **1.** to play in a boisterous, lively way **2.** to win with ease, etc. *[he romped home]*

rompers *n.pl.* a young child's loose-fitting, one-piece outer garment with bloomerlike pants

rondavel (ron′dä′vəl) *n.* [< ?] [S Afr.] a circular building, often thatched

rondeau (ron′dō) *n.*, *pl.* **-deaux** (-dōz) [Fr. < *rond*, round] a short lyrical poem of thirteen (or ten) lines and an unrhymed refrain that consists of the opening words and is used within the poem

rondo (ron′dō) *n.*, *pl.* **-dos** [It. < Fr.: see RONDEAU] *Music* a composition or movement having its principal theme stated three or more times

rood (rōōd) *n.* [OE. *rod*] **1.** a crucifix **2.** formerly, a measure of area usually equal to 1/4 acre

rood screen a screen, usually surmounted by a rood, dividing the choir or chancel of a church from its nave

roof (rōōf) *n.*, *pl.* **roofs** [OE. *hrof*] **1.** the outside top covering of a building **2.** figuratively, a home **3.** anything like a roof *[the roof of the mouth]* —*vt.* to cover as with a roof —**hit (or go through) the roof** to become extremely angry —**raise the roof** [Colloq.] to be very noisy

roof garden a garden on the flat roof of a building

roofing *n.* material for roofs

roof rack a rack attached to the roof of a motor vehicle and used to carry luggage, etc.

rooftop *n.* the roof of a building

rooftree *n.* the ridgepole of a roof

rooibos (roi′bos′) *n.* [< Afrik. *rooi*, red + *bos*, bush] any of various S African trees with red leaves

rooibostea (roi′bos tē′) *n.* [S Afr.] a tealike drink made from the leaves of rooibos

rooikat (roi′kat′) *n.* [< Afrik. *rooi*, red + *kat*, cat] a S African lynx

rooinek (roi′nek) *n.* [< Afrik. *rooi*, red + *nek*, neck] [S Afr. Derog.] an Englishman; red neck

rook¹ (rook) *n.* [OE. *hroc*] a crowlike bird —*vt.*, *vi.* to swindle; cheat

rook² *n.* [< Per. *rukh*] *Chess* either of the two corner pieces, usually shaped like a castle tower

rookery *n.*, *pl.* **-eries** a colony of rooks, or of seals, penguins, etc.

rookie (rook′ē) *n.* [< ?] [Slang] an inexperienced recruit

room (rōōm) *n.* [OE. *rum*] **1.** space to contain something **2.** opportunity *[room for doubt]* **3.** a space within a building enclosed by walls **4.** [*pl.*] lodgings **5.** the people in a room *[the whole room was silent]* —*vi.*, *vt.* [U.S.] to have, or provide with, lodgings

rooming house [U.S.] a lodging house

roommate *n.* a person with whom one shares a room

room service the service provided by hotels serving food, etc. in the guest's room

roomy *adj.* **-ier, -iest** spacious —**room′iness** *n.*

roost (rōōst) *n.* [OE. *hrost*] **1.** a perch on which birds, esp. domestic fowls, can rest or sleep **2.** a place with perches for birds —*vi.* **1.** to sit, sleep, etc. on a perch **2.** to settle down, as for the night —**come home to roost** to come back in an unfavourable way to the doer —**rule the roost** to be master

rooster *n.* [Chiefly U.S.] a cock

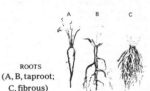

ROOTS
(A, B, taproot;
C, fibrous)

root¹ (rōōt) *n.* [< ON. *rot*] **1.** the part of a plant, usually below the ground, that holds the plant in place and draws water and food from the soil **2.** loosely, any underground part of a plant **3.** the embedded part of a tooth, hair, etc. **4.** a source or cause **5.** [*pl.*] the close ties one has with some place or people as through birth, long association, etc. **6.** an essential or basic part *[the root of* the matter *]* 7. *Math. a)* a quantity that, multiplied by itself a specified number of times, produces a given quantity *[4 is the square root (4 × 4) of 16]* *b)* a number that, when substituted for the unknown quantity in an equation, will satisfy the equation 8. *Linguis.* same as BASE[1] —*vi.* 1. to begin to grow by putting out roots 2. to become fixed, settled, etc. —*vt.* 1. to fix the roots of in the ground 2. to establish; settle —**root up** (or **out, away**) to pull out by the roots; remove completely —**take root** 1. to begin growing by putting out roots 2. to become settled

root[2] *vt.* [OE. *wrot,* snout] to dig (*up* or *out*) as with the snout —*vi.* 1. to search about; rummage 2. [U.S. Colloq.] to encourage a team by applauding and cheering: with *for*

root canal a small, tubular channel in the root of a tooth

root crop a crop, as turnips, grown for the edible roots

rootle (rōōt′′l) *vi.* [< ROOT[2]] to search out; burrow

rootless *adj.* having no roots or ties

root mean square the square root of the averages of a set of numbers

rootstock *n. Bot.* 1. same as RHIZOME 2. a plant onto which another is grafted

rope (rōp) *n.* [OE. *rap*] 1. a thick, strong cord made of intertwisted strands of fibre, wires, etc. 2. *a)* a noose for hanging a person *b)* death by hanging 3. a ropelike string *[a rope of pearls]* —*vt.* **roped, rop′-ing** 1. to fasten or tie with a rope 2. to connect by a rope 3. to mark off or enclose with a rope (with *in, off,* or *out*) —**know the ropes** [Colloq.] to know the details or procedures, as of a job —**rope in** to persuade someone to do something

ropewalk *n.* a long, narrow shed, etc. in which ropes are made

ropewalker *n.* a performer on a tightrope: also **rope′danc′er —rope′-walk′ing** *n.*

ropy *adj.* **-ier, -iest** inferior; inadequate

Roquefort (cheese) (rok′fôr) [< *Roquefort,* France] a cheese with a bluish mould, made from goats' and ewes' milk

rorqual (rôr′kwəl) *n.* [Fr. < Norw. *röyrkval,* red whale] any of the whalebone whales with a well-developed dorsal fin

Rorschach test (rôr′shäk) [< H. *Rorschach*] *Psychol.* a test for personality analysis, in which responses to a standard series of inkblots are interpreted

rosaceous (rō zā′shəs) *adj.* 1. of the rose family of plants, as the strawberry, plum, etc. 2. like a rose

rosary (rō′zər ē) *n., pl.* **-ries** [< L. *rosa,* rose] *R.C.Ch.* 1. a string of beads used to keep count in saying certain prayers 2. [*also* R-] the prayers said with these beads

rose[1] (rōz) *n.* [OE. < L. *rosa*] 1. a bush or shrub with prickly stems and usually fragrant flowers of red, pink, white, yellow, etc. 2. the flower 3. any of several

related plants 4. pinkish red 5. anything like a rose in form, as the perforated nozzle of a watering can —*adj.* 1. of or having to do with roses 2. rose-coloured

rose[2] *pt.* of RISE

rosé (rō′zā) *n.* [Fr.] a light, pink wine made by removing the grape husks after partial fermentation

roseate (rō′zē ət) *adj.* 1. rose-coloured 2. cheerful or optimistic

rose bay a willow herb with spikes of large purple flowers

rosebud (rōz′bud′) *n.* the bud of a rose

rosebush *n.* a shrub that bears roses

rose-coloured *adj.* pinkish-red —**through rose-coloured glasses** with excessive optimism

rosemary (rōz′mə rē) *n.* [ult. < L. *ros marinus,* dew of the sea] an evergreen plant with small, light-blue flowers and fragrant leaves

rose of Sharon 1. a plant with purplish, bell-shaped flowers 2. a shrub with large, yellow flowers

rose tree same as ROSE[1] (*n. 1*)

rosette (rō zet′) *n.* [Fr.] an ornament, arrangement, etc. resembling a rose, esp. one given as an award

rose water a perfume made of water and attar of roses

rose window a circular window with roselike tracery or mullions arranged like the spokes of a wheel

rosewood *n.* [< its odour] any of a number of valuable hard, reddish, black-streaked woods, used in making furniture, etc.

Rosh Hashana (rōsh′hə shä′nə) the Jewish New Year

Rosicrucian (rō′zə krōō′shən) *n.* [< Christian *Rosenkreuz*] 1. a member of a secret society in the 17th and 18th cent. said to have occult power 2. a member of any of several later groups supposed to be based on the original society —*adj.* of the Rosicrucians

rosin (roz′in) *n.* [< RESIN] the hard, brittle resin left after the distillation of crude turpentine —*vt.* to rub with rosin

ROSPA Royal Society for the Prevention of Accidents

roster (ros′tər) *n.* [< Du. *rooster,* orig., gridiron] a list, as of military personnel, showing assignments, duties, etc.

rostrum (ros′trəm) *n., pl.* **-trums, -tra** [L., (ship's) beak] a platform for public speaking

rosy (rō′zē) *adj.* **-ier, -iest** 1. rose-red or pink *[rosy cheeks]* 2. bright, promising, cheerful, etc. *[a rosy future]* —**ros′ily** *adv.* —**ros′iness** *n.*

rot (rot) *vi.* **rot′ted, rot′ting** [OE. *rotian*] 1. to decompose; decay 2. to become unhealthy, etc. *[to rot in prison]* —*vt.* to cause to rot —*n.* 1. a rotting or being rotten 2. something rotten 3. any of various plant and animal diseases causing decay 4. [Colloq.] nonsense

rota (rōt′ə) *n.* [L., wheel] a list of names, esp. one listing the rotation of duties

rotary (rōt′ər ē) *adj.* [< L. *rota,* wheel]

1. turning around a central point or axis
2. having a rotating part or parts —*n.*, *pl.* **-ries** a rotary machine
Rotary Club any local organization of an international club (**Rotary International**) of business and professional men, founded in 1905 to promote community welfare —**Rotarian** (rō tãr′ē ən) *n.*, *adj.*
rotate (rō tāt′) *vi.*, *vt.* **-tat′ed**, **-tat′ing** [< L. *rota*, wheel] 1. to move or turn around, as a wheel 2. to go or cause to go in a regular succession of changes [to *rotate* crops] —**rota′tion** *n.*
rotation of crops a system of rotating kinds of crops grown in the same field, to maintain soil fertility
rote (rōt) *n.* [< ?] a fixed, mechanical way of doing something —**by rote** by memory alone, without thought
rotgut (rot′gut′) *n.* [Slang] raw, low-grade whisky or other spirit
rotisserie (rō tis′ər ē) *n.* [< Fr., ROAST] a grill with a spit, often electrically turned
rotor (rōt′ər) *n.* [< ROTATE] 1. the rotating part of a motor, dynamo, etc. 2. a device, as on a helicopter, consisting of generally horizontal aerofoils with their hub
rotovator (rōt′ə vāt′ər) *n.* [< *rotavator* < ROTA(RY) + (CULTI)VATOR] a motorized cultivator with rotary blades —**ro′to-vate′** *vt.*
rotten (rot′'n) *adj.* [ON. *rotinn*] 1. decayed; spoiled 2. smelling of decay; putrid 3. breaking up, through age or long use 4. morally corrupt 5. unsound, as if decayed within 6. [Colloq.] very bad 7. [Colloq.] unwell
rotten borough before 1832, a borough with only a few voters but with the right to send a representative to Parliament
rotter *n.* [Colloq.] a despicable person
rotund (rō tund′) *adj.* [L. *rotundus*] 1. plump or stout 2. full-toned; sonorous [a *rotund* voice] —**rotun′dity** *n.*
rotunda (rō tun′da) *n.* [< It. < L. *rotundus*, rotund] a round building or room, esp. one with a dome
rouble (rōō′b'l) *n.* same as RUBLE
roué (rōō′ā) *n.* [Fr.] a dissipated man; debauchee; rake
rouge (rōōzh) *n.* [Fr., red] 1. a reddish cosmetic for colouring the cheeks 2. a reddish powder, mainly ferric oxide, for polishing metal, etc. 3. *Canad. Football* a score of one point that the attacking team gets when the defending team fails to run a kickoff or a punt back from their own end zone —*vi.*, *vt.* **rouged**, **roug′-ing** 1. to use cosmetic rouge (on) 2. *Canad. Football* to score a rouge
rough (ruf) *adj.* [OE. *ruh*] 1. a) not smooth or level; uneven b) overgrown, wild, etc. [*rough* country] 2. shaggy [a *rough* coat] 3. a) stormy [*rough* weather] b) boisterous or disorderly [*rough* play] 4. harsh, rude, etc. [a *rough* temper] 5. sounding, feeling, or tasting harsh 6. lacking comforts and conveniences 7. not refined or polished 8. not finished, perfected, etc. [a *rough* sketch] 9. needing

strength rather than skill [*rough* work] 10. approximate [a *rough* estimate] 11. [Colloq.] difficult, severe, etc. [a *rough* time] 12. [Colloq.] ill —*n.* 1. rough ground 2. rough material or condition 3. a rowdy person 4. *Golf* any part of the course where grass, weeds, etc. grow uncut —*adv.* in a rough manner —*vt.* 1. to make rough 2. to treat roughly (often with *up*) 3. to make or shape roughly (usually with *in* or *out*) [*rough* out a scheme] —**in the rough** in a rough or crude state —**rough edge of one's tongue** harsh words —**rough it** to live without comforts and conveniences —**rough up** [Slang] to attack someone violently
roughage *n.* coarse food or fodder, as bran, serving as a stimulus to peristalsis
rough-and-ready *adj.* 1. rough, or crude, rude, etc., but effective 2. characterized by rough vigour rather than refinement, formality, etc.
rough-and-tumble *adj.* violent and disorderly, with no concern for rules —*n.* a fight of this kind
roughcast *n.* a coarse plaster for covering outside surfaces, as walls —*vt.* **-cast′**, **-cast′ing** to cover (walls, etc.) with roughcast
rough diamond 1. a diamond in its natural state 2. a person or thing of fine quality but lacking polish
rough-dry (ruf′drī′) *vt.* **-dried′**, **-dry′-ing** to dry (washed laundry) without ironing: also **rough′dry′**
roughen *vt.*, *vi.* to make or become rough
rough-hew (ruf′hyōō′) *vt.* **-hewed′**, **-hewed′** or **-hewn′**, **-hew′ing** 1. to hew (stone, etc.) roughly, without finishing 2. to form roughly Also **rough′hew′**
roughhouse *n.* [Slang] rough or boisterous play, fighting, etc.
roughneck *n.* [U.S. Slang] a rough person; rowdy
roughrider *n.* 1. a person who breaks horses for riding 2. a person who does much hard, rough riding
roughshod *adj.* shod with horseshoes that have metal points to prevent slipping —**ride roughshod over** to treat in a harsh, arrogant, inconsiderate manner
roulette (rōō let′) *n.* [Fr. < L. *rota*, wheel] a gambling game played by rolling a small ball around a shallow bowl with a revolving inner disc (**roulette wheel**) with red and black numbered compartments
Roumanian (rōō mān′yən) same as RUMANIAN
round (round) *adj.* [< L. *rotundus*, rotund] 1. shaped like a ball, circle, or cylinder 2. plump 3. with a circular motion [a *round* dance] 4. full; complete [a *round* dozen] 5. expressed by a whole number, or in tens, hundreds, etc. 6. large in amount, size, etc. [a *round* sum] 7. mellow and full in tone 8. brisk [a *round* pace] 9. outspoken —*n.* 1. something round 2. a rung of a ladder 3. movement in a circular course 4. same as ROUND DANCE 5. a series or succession [a *round* of parties] 6. the complete extent 7. a regular,

customary circuit **8.** a single serving, as of drinks, for each in a group **9.** a single slice of bread **10.** *a*) a single shot from a rifle, etc. or from a number of rifles fired together *b*) ammunition for such a shot **11.** a single outburst, as of applause **12.** a single period or division of action in certain games, sports, and competitions **13.** the playing of all the holes on a golf course **14.** *Music* a short song for two or more persons or groups, in which the second starts when the first reaches the second phrase, etc. —*adv.* **1.** in a circle **2.** through a recurring period of time [to work the year *round*] **3.** from one person or place to another [the peddler came *round*] **4.** for each of several [not enough to go *round*] **5.** in circumference **6.** on all sides **7.** about; near **8.** in a roundabout way **9.** here and there **10.** with a rotating movement **11.** in or to the opposite direction or viewpoint —*prep.* **1.** so as to encircle **2.** on the circumference or border of **3.** on all sides of **4.** in the vicinity of **5.** in a circuit or course through **6.** here and there in —*vt.* **1.** to make round **2.** to make plump **3.** to express as a round number (usually with *off*) **4.** to complete; finish **5.** to make a circuit of **6.** to make a turn about [to *round* a corner] —*vi.* **1.** to turn **2.** to become round or plump —**go the rounds** to be circulated widely, as a rumour —**in the round 1.** with the audience, etc. seated all around a central stage, etc. **2.** in full and completely rounded form, not in relief: said of sculpture **3.** in full detail —**round down** (or **up**) to lower (or raise) a number or price to the nearest whole or convenient number —**round on** to attack, esp. verbally —**round up 1.** to drive together in a herd, group, etc. **2.** [Colloq.] to assemble

roundabout *n.* **1.** a road junction where traffic flows round a central island **2.** a circular, revolving platform with artificial animals, etc. on it, used in a funfair —*adj.* indirect [*roundabout* methods] —*adv.* approximately

round dance 1. a dance with the dancers moving in a circle **2.** any of several dances, as the waltz, polka, etc., in which the couples make circular movements

roundel (roun′d'l) *n.* [< OFr. *rond*, ROUND] **1.** a small circular window, panel, medallion, etc. **2.** a form of rondeau

roundelay (roun′də lā′) *n.* [< OFr. *rondel*, *rondel*] a simple song in which some phrase, line, etc. is continually repeated

rounder (roun′dər) *n.* **1.** a complete circuit of bases in the game of rounders **2.** [*pl. with sing. v.*] a bat-and-ball game in which players run between bases when the ball is hit, scoring if they run round all four bases

Roundhead *n.* a member of the Parliamentary party in England during the civil war (1642–52)

roundhouse *n.* [Obs.] a cabin on the after part of a ship's quarter-deck

roundly *adv.* vigorously, severely, etc.

round robin a petition, etc. with the

signatures written in a circle to conceal the order of signing

round-shouldered *adj.* stooped because the shoulders are bent forwards

Round Table 1. the table around which King Arthur and his knights sat **2.** an organization of clubs for business and professional men who seek to promote social and business activities and charitable work **3.** [r- t-] an informal discussion group or discussion

round-the-clock *adj., adv.* continuously

round trip a trip to a place and back again

roundup *n.* **1.** the act of driving cattle, etc. together and collecting them in a herd **2.** any similar collecting **3.** a summary, as of news

roundworm *n.* a species of nematode worms, living as parasites, esp. in the intestines of man and other mammals

rouse (rauz) *vt., vi.* **roused, rous′ing** [< ?] **1.** to stir up; excite or become excited **2.** to wake —**rous′ing** *adj.*

roustabout (roust′ə bout) *n.* [< ROUSE + ABOUT] an unskilled worker on an oil rig

rout[1] (rout) *n.* [see ROUTE] **1.** an overwhelming defeat **2.** a disorderly flight **3.** a disorderly crowd **4.** [Archaic] a large party —*vt.* **1.** to put to disorderly flight **2.** to defeat overwhelmingly

rout[2] *vi.* [< ROOT[2]] to poke or rummage about —*vt.* **1.** to dig up with the snout **2.** to force out —**rout out 1.** to expose to view **2.** to scoop, gouge, or hollow out **3.** to make (a person) get out, esp. of bed

route (root) *n.* [< L. *rupta* (*via*), broken (path)] a road, etc. for travelling, esp. any regularly followed course or way —*vt.* **rout′ed, rout′ing** to send by a specified route

route march a training march undertaken by troops

routine (roo tēn′) *n.* [Fr.: see ROUTE] **1.** a regular, unvarying procedure, prescribed or habitual **2.** a theatrical skit **3.** a series of dance steps **4.** a set of coded instructions for a computer —*adj.* like or using routine

roux (roo) *n.* [Fr.] a cooked mixture of butter and flour, used as a basis for sauces, etc.

rove[1] (rōv) *vi., vt.* **roved, rov′ing** [< ?] to wander about

rove[2] *alt. pt. & pp. of* REEVE[2]

roven *alt. pp. of* REEVE[2]

rover *n.* [< ROVE[1]] a person or thing that roves

row[1] (rō) *n.* [OE. *ræw*] **1.** a number of people or things in a line **2.** any of the lines of seats in a theatre, etc. **3.** a street with a line of buildings, as of a specified nature, on either side —**in a row** one after the other

row[2] *vt., vi.* [OE. *rowan*] **1.** to move (a boat, etc.) on water by using oars **2.** to carry in a rowing boat [*row* us across the lake] —*n.* a trip made by rowing boat —**row′er** *n.*

row[3] (rou) *n.* [< ?] a noisy quarrel,

dispute, or disturbance —*vi.* to take part in a row

rowan (rō′ən, rou′-) *n.* [< Scand.] 1. the mountain ash, a tree with white flowers and reddish berries 2. its fruit

rowdy (rou′dē) *adj.* [< ?] rough, quarrelsome, and disorderly —*n.*, *pl.* **-dies** a rowdy person —**row′dily** *adv.* —**row′diness** *n.* —**row′dyism** *n.*

ROWEL

rowel (rou′əl) *n.* [see ROULETTE] a small wheel with sharp projecting points, forming the end of a spur

rowing boat a boat made to be rowed: U.S. **row′boat**

rowlock (rol′ək) *n.* [altered (after ROW²) < *oarlock*] a device, often U-shaped, for holding the oar in place in rowing

royal (roi′əl) *adj.* [< L. *regalis*] 1. of a king or queen 2. having the rank of a king or queen 3. of a kingdom, its government, etc. [the *royal* fleet] 4. *a*) founded or supported by a king or queen *b*) in the service of the Crown 5. suitable for a king or queen; magnificent, stately, etc. —*n.* [Colloq.] a royal personage

Royal Air Force the airborne branch of the British armed forces

royal blue a deep, vivid blue

Royal British Legion, the an organization founded in 1921 to help former members of the armed forces

Royal Family the reigning monarch and his or her family

royalist *n.* a person who supports a king or a monarchy, esp. in times of revolution —**roy′alism** *n.*

royal jelly a highly nutritious food fed by worker bees to all very young larvae and continued to be fed to larvae chosen to be queens

Royal Marines a branch of the Armed Forces trained for land and sea combat

Royal Navy the seafaring branch of the British armed forces

royal palm a tall, ornamental palm tree

Royal prerogative the special privilege of a sovereign to act at his own unrestricted discretion

royalty *n.*, *pl.* **-ties** 1. the rank or power of a king or queen 2. a royal person or persons 3. *a*) a share of the proceeds paid to the owner of a right, as a patent, for its use *b*) a share paid to one who leases out lands rich in oil or minerals *c*) a share of the proceeds from his work paid to an author, composer, etc.

royal warrant the authorization for a tradesman to advertise that he supplies goods to a member of the royal family

rozzer (roz′ər) *n.* [< ?] [Slang] a policeman

rpm, r.p.m. revolutions per minute

R.R. 1. Right Reverend 2. [Canad.] rural route

-rrhoea (rē′ə) [< Gr. *rhein*, to flow] *a combining form meaning* a flow, discharge: also U.S. **-rrhea**

R.S. Royal Society

R.S.A. 1. Royal Scottish Academy 2. Royal Society of Arts

R.S.F.S.R., RSFSR Russian Soviet Federated Socialist Republic

R.S.P.C.A. Royal Society for the Prevention of Cruelty to Animals

RSV, R.S.V. Revised Standard Version (of the Bible)

R.S.V.P., r.s.v.p. [Fr. *répondez s'il vous plaît*] please reply

Rt. Hon. Right Honourable

Rt. Rev. Right Reverend

Ru *Chem.* ruthenium

RU Rugby Union

rub (rub) *vt.* **rubbed, rub′bing** [ME. *rubben*] 1. to move (one's hand, a cloth, etc.) back and forth over (something) firmly 2. to spread (polish, etc.) on a surface 3. to move (things) over each other with pressure and friction 4. to make sore by rubbing 5. to remove by rubbing (out, off, etc.) —*vi.* 1. to move with pressure and friction (on, against, etc.) 2. to rub something 3. to admit of being removed by rubbing (often with off, out, etc.) —*n.* 1. a rubbing 2. an obstacle or difficulty 3. something that irritates —**rub it in** [Colloq.] to keep reminding someone of his failure or mistake —**rub off on** to be left on as a mark, as by rubbing or, figuratively, by close contact —**rub shoulders with** to come into contact with socially —**rub up the wrong way** to annoy or irritate

rubato (rōō bät′ō) *adj., adv.* [It.] *Music* with some notes lengthened and others shortened in dropping strict tempo in a passage for effect

rubber¹ (rub′ər) *n.* 1. an elastic substance produced from the milky sap of various tropical plants or synthetically 2. a piece of rubber used for erasing writing, etc. *adj.* made of rubber —**rub′bery** *adj.*

rubber² *n.* [< ?] 1. *Bridge* a series limited to three games, two of which must be won to win the series 2. any game played to break a tie in games won

rubber band a narrow, continuous band of rubber for holding small objects together

rubberize *vt.* **-ized′, -iz′ing** to coat or impregnate with rubber

rubberneck *n.* [Colloq.] one who gazes about in curiosity, as a sightseer —*vi.* to gaze about in this way

rubber plant 1. any plant yielding latex 2. a house plant with large, glossy, leathery leaves

rubber stamp 1. a stamp of rubber, inked and used for printing signatures, dates, etc. 2. [Colloq.] *a*) a person, bureau, etc. that approves something in a routine way *b*) such approval —**rub′ber-stamp′** *vt., adj.*

rubbing *n.* an impression of a raised or incised design, etc. taken by placing a paper over it and rubbing with graphite, wax, etc.

rubbish (rub′ish) *n.* [< ?] 1. any material thrown away as worthless; waste food, etc. 2. worthless ideas, statements, etc.; nonsense —**rub′bishy** *adj.*

rubble (rub′'l) *n.* [< ?] rough, broken pieces of stone, brick, etc.

rubella (ro͞o bel′ə) *n.* [< L. *ruber*, red] a contagious virus disease, characterized by small red spots on the skin; German measles

Rubicon (ro͞o′bi kən) small river in N Italy crossed by Caesar to march on Rome (49 B.C.) —**cross the Rubicon** to make a decisive move that cannot be undone

rubicund (ro͞o′bi kənd) *adj.* [< L. *ruber*, red] reddish; ruddy

rubidium (ro͞o bid′ē əm) *n.* [< L. *rubidus*, red (from red lines in its spectrum)] a soft, silvery-white metallic chemical element : symbol, Rb

ruble (ro͞o′b'l) *n.* [Russ. *rubl'*] the monetary unit of the U.S.S.R.

rubric (ro͞o′brik) *n.* [< L. *ruber*, red] 1. a heading, title, etc. 2. an established rule of procedure 3. a note of comment; gloss 4. in early books and manuscripts, a chapter heading, initial letter, etc. written in red, decorative lettering, etc.

ruby (ro͞o′bē) *n.*, *pl.* **-bies** [< L. *rubeus*, red] 1. a clear, deep-red variety of corundum, valued as a precious stone 2. deep red —*adj.* deep-red

ruby wedding a fortieth wedding anniversary

ruche (ro͞osh) *n.* [Fr.] a fluting or pleating of lace, ribbon, etc. for trimming garments

ruck[1] (ruk) *n.* [< Scand.] a large quantity, mass or crowd, esp. of undistinguished people or things

ruck[2] *n.*, *vt.*, *vi* [< ON. *hrukka*] crease, wrinkle, or pucker

rucksack (ruk′sak′) *n.* [G. < *Rücken*, back + *Sack*, sack] a kind of knapsack

ruction (ruk′shən) *n.* [< ?] [Colloq.] noisy confusion; uproar; disturbance

RUDDER

rudder (rud′ər) *n.* [OE. *rother*, steering oar] 1. a broad, flat, movable piece of wood or metal hinged vertically at the stern of a ship, used for steering 2. a piece like this on an aircraft, etc. —**rud′derless** *adj.*

ruddy (rud′ē) *adj.* **-dier, -diest** [OE. *rudig*] 1. having a healthy red colour 2. reddish —**rud′diness** *n.*

rude (ro͞od) *adj.* **rud′er, rud′est** [< L. *rudis*] 1. impolite [a *rude* reply] 2. coarse, uncouth 3. crude or rough [a *rude* hut] 4. harsh [a *rude* awakening] 5. simple

or primitive 6. barbarous [*rude* savages] —**rude′ly** *adv.* —**rude′ness** *n.*

rudiment (ro͞o′də mənt) *n.* [< L. *rudis*, rude] 1. a first principle or element, as of a subject to be learned 2. a first slight beginning of something 3. *Biol.* an incompletely developed or vestigial part —**ru′dimen′tary** (-men′tər ē) *adj.*

rue[1] (ro͞o) *vt.*, *vi.* **rued, ru′ing** [OE. *hreowan*] to feel sorrow or remorse (for); regret; repent

rue[2] *n.* [< Gr. *rhytē*] a strong-scented herb with bitter-tasting leaves formerly used in medicine

rueful *adj.* feeling or showing sorrow or regret, esp. in a wry way

ruff[1] (ruf) *n.* [< of RUFFLE, *n.*] 1. a high, frilled, stiff collar worn in the 16th and 17th cents. 2. a ring of feathers or fur standing out about the neck of a bird or animal 3. a Eurasian sandpiper —**ruffed** *adj.*

ruff[2] *n.* [< OFr. *roffle*] *Card Games* the act of trumping —*vt.*, *vi.* *Card Games* to trump

ruffian (ruf′yən) *n.* [< It. *ruffiano*] a brutal, lawless person —**ruf′fianly** *adj.*

ruffle (ruf′'l) *vt.* **-fled, -fling** [< ?] 1. to disturb the smoothness of 2. to make (feathers, etc.) stand up as in a ruff 3. to disturb or annoy 4. to turn (pages, etc.) rapidly —*vi.* 1. to become uneven 2. to become disturbed, annoyed, etc. —*n.* a strip of cloth, lace, etc. gathered in pleats and used for trimming

rufous (ro͞o′fəs) *adj.* [L. *rufus*, red] brownish-red

rug (rug) *n.* [< Scand.] 1. a piece of thick fabric, an animal skin, etc. used as a floor covering 2. a heavy blanket, etc., laid over the lap and legs for warmth

Rugby (rug′bē) *n.* [< *Rugby* School] 1. a kind of football in which there are 15 (**Rugby Union**) or 13 (**Rugby League**) players on each side : the oval ball may be kicked, thrown, or run with : also **Rugby Football**, **rug′ger** 2. in Canada, football

rugged (rug′id) *adj.* [< Scand.] 1. uneven, rough, craggy, etc. 2. strong, irregular, and lined [a *rugged* face] 3. sounding harsh 4. severe; hard 5. not polished or refined

ruin (ro͞o′in) *n.* [< L. *ruere*, to fall] 1. [*pl.*] the remains of a building, city, etc., destroyed, decayed, etc. 2. anything destroyed, etc. 3. the state of being destroyed, dilapidated, etc. 4. downfall, destruction, etc., or the cause of this [*gambling* was his *ruin*] —*vt.* to bring to ruin; destroy, damage, bankrupt, seduce, etc.

ruination (ro͞o′ə nā′shən) *n.* 1. a ruining or being ruined 2. anything that ruins

ruinous (ro͞o′ə nəs) *adj.* 1. falling or fallen into ruin 2. bringing ruin; disastrous —**ru′inously** *adv.* —**ru′inousness** *n.*

rule (ro͞ol) *n.* [< L. *regere*, lead straight] 1. *a)* an authoritative regulation for conduct, procedure, etc. *b)* an established practice that serves as a guide [*rules* of grammar] 2. government; reign 3. customary course of events **4.** a custom **5.** a ruler **6.** *Printing* a thin strip of metal as high as type, used to print lines **7.** a set of regulations in a religious order **8.** *Law* a decision, order, etc. made by a judge in regard to a specific question —*vt.* **ruled, rul'ing 1.** to govern **2.** to have an influence over; guide **3.** to determine **4.** to mark (lines) on (paper, etc.) as with a ruler **5.** to keep under control —*vi.* **1.** to govern **2.** to prevail **3.** to issue a formal decree —**as a rule** usually —**rule out 1.** to leave out from consideration **2.** to make impossible; prevent —**rule the roost** to be in control

rule of thumb a rule, method, etc. based on experience or practice rather than on scientific knowledge

ruler *n.* **1.** a person or thing that governs **2.** a thin strip of wood, metal, etc. with a straight edge, used in drawing lines, measuring, etc.

ruling *adj.* governing; predominating —*n.* **1.** a decision made by a court **2.** a) the making of ruled lines b) the lines so made

rum[1] (rum) *n.* [< ?] a spirit distilled from fermented sugar cane, molasses, etc.

rum[2] *adj.* [< ?] [Colloq.] **1.** odd; strange **2.** bad, poor, etc. *[a rum joke]* —**rum'my** *adj.*

Rumanian (rōō mān'yən) *adj.* of Rumania —*n.* **1.** a native of Rumania **2.** the language of the Rumanians

rumba (rum'bə) *n.* [AmSp.] **1.** a dance of Cuban Negro origin **2.** music for this dance —*vi.* to dance the rumba

rumble[1] (rum'b'l) *vi., vt.* **-bled, -bling** [prob. < MDu. *rommelen*] **1.** to make or cause to make a deep, heavy rolling sound **2.** to move with such a sound —*n.* **1.** a rumbling sound **2.** [U.S. Slang] a gang fight

rumble[2] *vt.* [< ?] [Slang] to see through; understand

rumbustious (rum bus'tē əs) *adj.* [< ROBUSTIOUS] boisterous, unruly, etc.

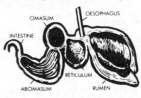

STOMACH OF A RUMINANT

ruminant (rōō'mə nənt) *n.* [< L. *ruminare*, ruminate] any of a group of four-footed, hoofed, cud-chewing mammals, as the cow, deer, etc. —*adj.* **1.** of the cud-chewing animals **2.** chewing the cud **3.** meditative

ruminate (rōō'mə nāt') *vt., vi.* **-nat'ed, -nat'ing** [see prec.] **1.** to chew (the cud), as a cow does **2.** to meditate (on) —**ru'mina'tion** *n.* —**ru'minative** *adj.*

rummage (rum'ij) *vt., vi.* **-maged, -mag-** ing [< MFr. *run*, ship's hold] to search through (a place, etc.) thoroughly by moving the contents about —*n.* a rummaging search

rummage sale a jumble sale

rummy (rum'ē) *adj.* **-mier, -miest** [< ?] [Colloq.] odd; strange —*n.* any of certain card games in which the object is to match cards into sets or sequences

rumour (rōō'mər) *n.* [< L. *rumor*, noise] **1.** general talk not based on definite knowledge **2.** an unconfirmed report, story, etc. in general circulation —*vt.* to tell or spread by rumour

rump (rump) *n.* [ON. *rumpr*] **1.** the hind part of an animal, where the legs and back join **2.** a cut of beef from this part **3.** the buttocks **4.** the last and unimportant part

rumple (rum'p'l) *n.* [< MDu. *rompe*, a wrinkle] an uneven crease; wrinkle —*vt., vi.* **-pled, -pling** to wrinkle; crumple

rumpus (rum'pəs) *n.* [< ?] [Colloq.] noisy disturbance

run (run) *vi.* **ran, run, run'ning** [ON. *rinna* & OE. *rinnan*] **1.** to go by moving the legs faster than in walking **2.** to move swiftly **3.** to go, move, etc. easily and freely **4.** to flee **5.** to make a quick trip (*up to, down to,* etc.) **6.** *a)* to take part in a contest or race *b)* to be a candidate in an election **7.** to swim in migration: said of fish **8.** to go, as on a schedule **9.** to pass lightly and rapidly *[his eyes ran over the page]* **10.** to circulate, as a rumour **11.** to climb or creep, as a vine **12.** to ladder *[her stocking ran]* **13.** to operate, as a machine **14.** to flow **15.** to melt and flow, as wax **16.** *a)* to spread over cloth, etc. when moistened, as colours *b)* to be subject to this spreading, as fabric **17.** to be wet with a flow *[her eyes ran with tears]* **18.** *a)* to discharge pus, mucus, etc. *b)* to leak **19.** *a)* to appear in print *b)* to appear continuously *[the play ran for a year]* **20.** to continue in effect or existence **21.** *a)* to extend in a continuous line *b)* to extend in scope **22.** to pass into a specified condition *[to run into trouble]* **23.** to be written, expressed, etc. in a specified way —*vt.* **1.** to travel over **2.** to perform as by running *[to run a race]* **3.** to bring or force into a specified condition **4.** to hunt; chase (game, etc.) **5.** to follow (a specified course) **6.** to incur (a risk) **7.** *a)* to convey, as in a vehicle *b)* to smuggle **8.** to drive or force (an object) into, against, etc. (something) **9.** to make pass, flow, etc., esp. rapidly, in a specified way, place, etc. **10.** to manage or conduct **11.** to mark or draw **12.** to undergo (a fever, etc.) **13.** to publish (a story, etc.) as in a newspaper **14.** to compete with, as in a race **15.** *a)* to make run, move, compete, etc. *b)* to cause (an engine, etc.) to idle for a while **16.** to get past *[to run a blockade]* **17.** *Cricket* to score (a run) by hitting the ball —*n.* **1.** *a)* an act or period of running *b)* a running pace **2.** the distance covered in running **3.** a trip; journey **4.** a continuous course or period **5.** a continuous course of performances, etc., as of a play **6.** a continued series of demands, as for specified goods **7.** a flow or rush of water, etc. **8.** *a)* a period of operation of a machine *b)* the output during this period **9.** a kind or class, esp. the average kind **10.** *a)* an inclined pathway or course *[a ski run] b)* an enclosed area for domestic animals **11.** freedom to move about at will *[the run of the house]* **12.** a large number of fish migrating together **13.** *Cricket* a score of one made by running from one wicket to the other after hitting the ball —*adj.* **1.** melted **2.** poured while in a melted state *[run metal]* —**a run for one's money 1.** powerful competition **2.** satisfaction for what one has expended —**in the long run** ultimately —**on the run 1.** running **2.** running away —**run across** to encounter by chance —**run away 1.** to flee **2.** to desert one's home or family **3.** to escape and run loose —**run down 1.** to stop operating **2.** to run or drive against so as to knock down **3.** to pursue and capture or kill **4.** to search out the source of **5.** to speak of with disapproval **6.** to make or become run-down **7.** to read through rapidly **8.** to reduce in numbers or size —**run for it** to run to escape something —**run in 1.** to run a car engine for a specified period of time **2.** *[Slang]* to arrest —**run in the family** to be a hereditary characteristic —**run into 1.** to encounter by chance **2.** to collide with **3.** to add up to (a large sum of money) —**run off 1.** to print, make copies of, etc. **2.** to cause to be run, played, etc. **3.** to drive (trespassers) away **4.** to drain **5.** *same as* RUN AWAY —**run out 1.** to come to an end **2.** to drive out **3.** *Cricket* to dismiss (a batsman) while he is running between the wickets —**run out of** to use up —**run out on** *[Colloq.]* to desert —**run over 1.** to ride or drive over **2.** to overflow **3.** to go beyond a limit **4.** to examine, rehearse, etc. rapidly: also **run through** —**run to 1.** to extend to **2.** to be able to afford **3.** to show inclination towards —**run up 1.** to let (bills, etc.) go without paying them **2.** sew with a rapid succession of stitches **3.** to raise or make rapidly

runabout *n.* **1.** a small car, esp. one for use in town **2.** a light motorboat

runaway *n.* **1.** a fugitive **2.** a horse, etc. that runs away —*adj.* **1.** fugitive **2.** easily won, as a race **3.** rising rapidly, as prices

run-down *adj.* **1.** in poor physical condition, as from overwork **2.** fallen into disrepair **3.** not wound and therefore not running, as a clock

rundown *n.* **1.** a concise summary **2.** a decrease in numbers, esp. of employees

rune (rōōn) *n.* [OE. *run*] **1.** any of the characters of an ancient Germanic alphabet **2.** any sign, poem, song, etc. that is mystical or obscure —**ru′nic** *adj.*

rung[1] (ruŋ) *n.* [OE. *hrung*, staff] **1.** a rod used as a crossbar, support, etc.; specif.,

a) any of the steps of a ladder *b)* a crosspiece between the legs of a chair, etc. **2.** a degree, as of social status, success, etc.

rung[2] *pp. & chiefly dial. pt. of* RING[1]

runnel (run′'l) *n.* [OE. *rinnan*, to run] a small stream

runner *n.* **1.** one that runs; specif., an athlete **2.** a messenger **3.** a smuggler **4.** a long, narrow cloth or rug **5.** a long, trailing stem, as of a strawberry, that puts out roots along the ground **6.** something on or in which something else moves **7.** either of the long, narrow pieces on which a sledge slides **8.** the blade of a skate

runner bean a bean that grows twining about supports

runner-up (run′ər up′) *n., pl.* -**ners-up′** a person or team that finishes second in a race, contest, etc.

running *n.* the act of one that runs; racing, managing, etc. —*adj.* **1.** continuous *[a running commentary]* **2.** simultaneous *[a running translation]* **3.** moving easily or smoothly **4.** done in or by a run *[a running jump]* **5.** discharging pus *[a running sore]* **6.** in operation, as machinery **7.** current *[a running account]* **8.** moving or advancing rapidly **9.** flowing **10.** cursive: said of handwriting **11.** melting —*adv.* in succession *[for ten days running]* —**in (or out of) the running** in (or out of) the competition

running board esp. formerly, a footboard along the lower part of the side of some motor cars

running fire a rapid succession of shots fired, questions asked, etc.

running head (or **title**) a heading or title printed at the top of every, or every other, page

running knot *same as* SLIPKNOT

running lights the lights that a ship or aircraft travelling at night is required to display

running repairs minor repairs

runny *adj.* -**nier**, -**niest 1.** that flows, esp. too freely **2.** that keeps on discharging mucus *[a runny nose]*

run-of-the-mill *adj.* ordinary

runt (runt) *n.* [< ?] **1.** the smallest animal of a litter **2.** a stunted animal, plant, thing, or *[Derog.]* person

run-up (run′up′) *n.* **1.** an approach run by an athlete for a long jump, etc. **2.** any preparatory period before some major event

runway *n.* a strip of levelled ground for use by aircraft in taking off and landing

rupee (rōō pē′) *n.* [< Hindi] the monetary unit of India, Pakistan, Sri Lanka, etc.

rupture (rup′chər) *n.* [< L. *rumpere*, to break] **1.** a breaking apart or being broken apart **2.** a breaking off of friendly relations **3.** a hernia —*vt., vi.* -**tured**, -**turing 1.** to burst **2.** to affect with or undergo a rupture

rural (rōōər′əl) *adj.* [< L. *rus*, the country] of, like, or living in the country

rural dean a senior clergyman having authority over a group of parishes

rural district formerly, an administrative district formed by a group of country parishes

rural route [Canad.] a mail service or route in a rural area, the mail being delivered by car or van

rusbank (roos'baŋk) *n.* [< Afrik.] [S Afr.] a wooden bench or settee without upholstery

ruse (rooz) *n.* [< OFr. *reuser,* deceive] a stratagem or trick

rush[1] (rush) *vt., vi.* [see prec.] **1.** to move, dash, etc. swiftly or impetuously **2.** to make a sudden attack (*on* or *upon*) **3.** to pass, come, go, etc. swiftly or suddenly **4.** to act, or force to act, hastily —*n.* **1.** a rushing **2.** an eager movement of many people to get to a place **3.** intense activity; haste **4.** a sudden attack **5.** great pressure, as of much business requiring attention **6.** [*usually pl.*] *Cinema* a first print of a scene or scenes of a film shown for the director, etc. to inspect —*adj.* necessitating haste [*rush* orders] —**rush one's fences** to act hastily, without due consideration

rush[2] *n.* [OE. *risc*] a grasslike plant usually growing in wet places and having, in some species, round stems and pliant leaves used in making baskets, mats, etc. —**rush'y** *adj.*

rush hour a time of the day when business, traffic, etc. are especially heavy —**rush'-hour'** *adj.*

rush light a primitive candle made from the pith of various types of rush dipped in tallow: also **rush candle**

rusk (rusk) *n.* [< Sp. *rosca,* twisted bread roll] bread toasted in an oven until crisp, usually after being sliced

Russ. 1. Russia **2.** Russian

russet (rus'it) *n.* [< L. *russus,* reddish] **1.** reddish brown **2.** a coarse, brownish cloth, formerly used for clothing by country folk **3.** a winter apple with a rough, mottled skin —*adj.* reddish-brown

Russian (rush'ən) *adj.* of Russia —*n.* **1.** a native or inhabitant of Russia **2.** the Slavic language of the Russians

Russian roulette a deadly game of chance in which a person spins the cylinder of a revolver holding only one bullet, aims at his head, and pulls the trigger

Russo- *a combining form meaning* Russia or Russian

rust (rust) *n.* [OE.] **1.** the reddish-brown coating (mainly ferric oxide) formed on iron or steel during exposure to air and moisture **2.** any similar coating or stain **3.** a reddish brown **4.** a plant disease caused by parasitic fungi that produce reddish spots on stems and leaves —*vi., vt.* **1.** to become or cause to be coated or affected with rust **2.** to spoil, as from lack of use —**rust'less** *adj.*

rustic (rus'tik) *adj.* [see RURAL] **1.** of or living in the country; rural **2.** not sophisticated; specif., *a*) plain or artless *b*) uncouth or boorish **3.** made of bark-covered branches [*rustic* furniture] —*n.* a country person, esp. one regarded as simple, uncouth, etc. —**rustic'ity** (-tis'ə tē) *n.*

rusticate (rus'ti kāt') *vi.* -cat'ed, -cat'-ing to go to or live in the country —*vt.* **1.** to suspend (a student) temporarily from a university **2.** to make rustic —**rus'tica'-tion** *n.*

rustle[1] (rus''l) *vi., vt.* -tled, -tling [ult. echoic] to make or cause to make soft sounds, as of leaves moved by a breeze —*n.* a series of such sounds

rustle[2] *vi., vt.* -tled, -tling [< ?] [U.S. Colloq.] to steal (cattle, etc.) —**rustle up** [Colloq.] to collect or get together —**rus'tler** *n.*

rustproof (rust'proof') *adj.* resistant to rust —*vt.* to make rustproof

rusty *adj.* -ier, -iest **1.** coated with rust, as a metal, or affected by rust, as a plant **2.** *a*) impaired by disuse, neglect, etc. *b*) having lost one's skill through lack of practice **3.** rust-coloured **4.** faded, old-looking, or shabby —**rust'ily** *adv.* —**rust'i-ness** *n.*

rut[1] (rut) *n.* [< ?] **1.** a track or furrow, esp. one made by wheeled vehicles **2.** a fixed, routine procedure, way of thinking, etc. —*vt.* **rut'ted, rut'ting** to make a rut or ruts in —**in a rut** to be fixed in a routine

rut[2] *n.* [< L. *rugire,* to roar] the periodic sexual excitement of certain mammals, esp. males —*vi.* **rut'ted, rut'ting** to be in rut

ruth (rooth) *n.* [ult. < OE. *hreowian,* to rue] [Now Rare] **1.** pity **2.** sorrow

ruthenium (roo thē'nē əm) *n.* [< ML. *Ruthenia,* Russia, where first found] a rare, very hard, silvery-grey metallic chemical element: symbol, Ru

ruthless (rooth'lis) *adj.* pitiless and relentless —**ruth'lessly** *adv.* —**ruth'less-ness** *n.*

R.V. Revised Version (of the Bible)

Rwy., Ry. Railway

-ry (rē) *shortened form of* -ERY [*dentistry*]

rye (rī) *n.* [OE. *ryge*] **1.** a hardy cereal grass **2.** the grain or seeds of this plant **3.** whisky distilled from this grain

rye bread bread made altogether or partly of rye flour

ryegrass *n.* any of various grasses that are annuals or that live for only a few years

RYT reference your telex (*or* telegram)

S

S, s (es) *n.,* *pl.* **S's, s's** the nineteenth letter of the English alphabet

S (es) *n.* something shaped like an *S*

S *Chem.* sulphur

-s [< -ES] **1.** the plural ending of most nouns [*hips*] **2.** the ending of the third person singular, present indicative, of verbs [*runs*]

-'s¹ [OE. *-es*] the ending of the possessive singular of nouns (and some pronouns) and of the possessive plural of nouns not ending in *s* [*boy's,* women's*]

-'s² the assimilated form of is, has, does or us [*he's* here, let's go]

S, S., s, s. **1.** south **2.** southern

S. **1.** Saturday **2.** September **3.** Sunday

S., s. **1.** *pl.* **SS., ss.** saint **2.** school

s. **1.** second(s) **2.** shilling(s) **3.** singular

S.A. **1.** Salvation Army **2.** [*Slang*] sex appeal

Sabbath (sab'əth) *n.* [< Heb. *shābath,* to rest] **1.** the seventh day of the week (Saturday), observed as a day of rest and worship by Jews **2.** Sunday as the usual Christian day of rest and worship

Sabbatical (səbat'ik'l) *adj.* [see prec.] **1.** of the Sabbath **2.** [**s-**] designating a period of absence for study, rest, or travel, given at intervals, as to some university teachers —*n.* [**s-**] a sabbatical year or leave

S.A.B.C. South African Broadcasting Corporation

Sabine (sa'bīn) *n.* a member of an ancient tribe living in central Italy, conquered by the Romans, 3rd century B.C.

sable (sā'b'l) *n.* [< Russ. *sobol'*] **1.** the marten; esp. the **European marten,** with light-coloured underfur **2.** the costly fur of the sable **3.** *Heraldry* the colour black —*adj.* black or dark brown

SABOT

sabot (sab'ō) *n.* [Fr., ult. < Ar. *sabbât,* sandal] a heavy leather shoe with a wooden sole

sabotage (sab'ətäzh') *n.* [Fr. < *sabot*] **1.** deliberate destruction, disruption, or damage of equipment, etc., as during labour disputes or by enemy agents **2.** deliberate obstruction of or damage to any cause, effort, etc. —*vt.* **-taged', -tag'ing** to destroy by sabotage —*vi.* to engage in sabotage

saboteur (sab'ətʉr') *n.* [Fr.] a person who sabotages

sabre (sā'bər) *n.* [< Fr. < G. *Sabel*] a cavalry sword with a curved blade U.S. sp. **saber**

sabre rattling a threatening of war, or a menacing show of armed force

sac (sak) *n.* [Fr.: see SACK¹] a pouchlike part in a plant or animal, esp. one filled with fluid

S.A.C. Senior Aircraftman

saccharin (sak'ərin) *n.* [< Gr. *sakcharon,* sugar] a white, crystalline coal-tar compound used as a sugar substitute

saccharine (sak'ərīn') *adj.* **1.** of or like sugar **2.** too sweet [a *saccharine* voice]

sacerdotal (sas'ərdōt''l) *adj.* [< L. *sacerdos,* priest] of priests or the office of priest

sachem (sā'chəm) *n.* [< AmInd.] the chief in some N American Indian tribes

sachet (sash'ā) *n.* [Fr.] **1.** a small, sealed envelope containing shampoo, cream, etc. **2.** a small bag, pad, etc. filled with perfumed powder and placed with stored clothing

sack¹ (sak) *n.* [ult. < Heb. *śaq*] **1.** *a)* a large bag of coarse cloth, for holding grain, foodstuffs, etc. *b)* the contents or capacity of a sack **2.** a loose-fitting dress **3.** [Colloq.] dismissal from a job (with the) **4.** [Slang] a bed —*vt.* **1.** [Colloq.] to dismiss from a job **2.** to put into sacks —**hit the sack** [Slang] to go to bed

sack² *n.* [< It. *sacco,* plunder, lit., bag] the plundering of a captured city, etc. —*vt.* to plunder (a city, etc.)

sack³ *n.* [< Fr. (vin) *sec,* dry (wine)] a dry white wine from Spain or the Canary Islands

sackbut (sak'but') *n.* [Fr. < OFr. *saquer,* to pull + *bouter,* to push] a medieval wind instrument, forerunner of the trombone

sackcloth *n.* **1.** same as SACKING **2.** a rough cloth worn as a symbol of mourning or penitence

sacking *n.* a cheap, coarse cloth of flax, hemp, jute, etc., used esp. for sacks

sacrament (sak'rəmənt) *n.* [< L. *sacer,* sacred] **1.** any of certain Christian rites, as baptism, Holy Communion, etc. **2.** [*sometimes* **S-**] the Eucharist, or Holy Communion **3.** something regarded as sacred —**sac'ramen'tal** (-men't'l) *adj.*

sacred (sā'krid) *adj.* [< L. *sacer,* holy] **1.** consecrated to a god or deity; holy **2.** having to do with religion **3.** given the respect accorded holy things; venerated **4.** dedicated to a person, place, etc. **5.** that must not be broken, etc.; inviolate [a *sacred* promise] —**sa′credly** *adv.* —**sa′-credness** *n.*

sacred cow any person or thing regarded as above criticism

sacrifice (sak′rə fīs′) *n.* [< L. *sacer,* sacred + *facere,* make] 1. a giving up, destroying, etc. of one thing for the sake of another 2. *a)* an offering, as of a life or object, to a deity *b)* the thing offered 3. a selling of a thing at less than its value —*vt.* **-ficed′, -fic′ing** 1. to give up, destroy, etc. for the sake of another thing 2. to offer as a sacrifice to a deity —*vi.* to make a sacrifice —**sac′rifi′cial** (-fish′-) *adj.* —**sac′rifi′cially** *adv.*

sacrilege (sak′rə lij) *n.* [< L. *sacer,* sacred + *legere,* take away] a desecrating of anything held sacred —**sac′rile′gious** *adj.*

sacristan (sak′ris tən) *n.* a person in charge of a sacristy: also **sac′rist**

sacristy *n., pl.* **-ties** [ult. < L. *sacer,* sacred] a room in a church where the sacred vessels, vestments, etc. are kept

sacrosanct (sak′rō saŋkt′) *adj.* [< L. *sacer,* sacred + *sanctus,* holy] very sacred, holy, or inviolable —**sac′rosanc′tity** *n.*

sacrum (sā′krəm) *n.* [< L. *(os) sacrum,* sacred (bone)] a thick, triangular bone at the lower end of the spinal column

sad (sad) *adj.* **sad′der, sad′dest** [OE. *sæd,* sated] 1. unhappy; sorrowful 2. causing sorrow, dejection, etc. 3. dark or dull in colour 4. [Colloq.] very bad; deplorable —**sad′ly** *adv.* —**sad′ness** *n.*

sadden *vt., vi.* to make or become sad

saddle (sad′′l) *n.* [OE. *sadol*] 1. a padded part of a harness worn over a horse's back 2. a seat, usually of padded leather, for a rider on a bicycle, etc. 3. anything like a saddle in form, position, etc., as a ridge between two peaks 4. a cut of lamb, etc. including the two loins —*vt.* **-dled, -dling** 1. to put a saddle upon 2. to burden (a person) with (a debt, etc.) —**in the saddle** 1. seated on a saddle 2. having control

saddle-backed *adj.* having a concave outline, as a ridge between peaks

saddlebag *n.* 1. a large bag, usually one of a pair, carried on either side of a horse, etc., just behind the saddle 2. a similar bag carried on a motorcycle, etc.

saddle horse a horse trained for riding

saddler (sad′lər) *n.* a person whose work is making, repairing, or selling saddles, harnesses, etc.

saddlery *n., pl.* **-dleries** 1. articles made by a saddler 2. a shop where these are sold

saddle soap a mild soap for cleaning and softening leather

saddletree *n.* [ME. *sadeltre*] the frame of a saddle

sad dog a reprobate, rake, or black sheep

Sadducee (sad′yoo sē′) *n.* a member of an ancient Jewish party accepting only the written law

sadhu (sä′doo) *n.* [Sans.] a Hindu holy man

sadism (sā′diz′m) *n.* [Fr. < Marquis de *Sade*] the getting of pleasure, specif. sexual pleasure, from hurting others —**sad′ist** *n.* —**sadistic** (sə dis′tik) *adj.* —**sadis′tically** *adv.*

sadomasochism (sā′dō mas′ə kiz′m) *n.* sadism and masochism in the same individual —**sad′omas′ochist** *n.* —**sad′o-mas′ochis′tic** *adj.*

s.a.e. stamped addressed envelope

safari (sə fär′ē) *n., pl.* **-ris** [< Ar. *safara,* to travel] a journey or hunting expedition, esp. in Africa

safari park an enclosed park where wild animals are kept in the open for viewing by the public

safe (sāf) *adj.* **saf′er, saf′est** [< L. *salvus*] 1. *a)* free from danger, etc. *b)* having escaped injury 2. *a)* giving protection *b)* trustworthy 3. unable to cause trouble 4. taking or involving no risks —*n.* 1. a strong, locking metal container for valuables 2. any compartment to store food, etc. —**on the safe side** allowing extra in case of error, etc. —**safe′ly** *adv.* —**safe′ness** *n.*

safe-conduct (sāf′kon′dukt) *n.* 1. permission to travel through a dangerous area, as in time of war 2. a written pass giving this

safecracking *n.* the breaking open and robbing of safes: also **safe′break′ing** —**safe′crack′er** *n.*

safe-deposit *adj.* of a box or vault, esp. in a bank, for storing valuables: also **safe′-ty-depos′it**

safeguard *n.* a precaution or protection —*vt.* to protect or guard

safety *n., pl.* **-ties** 1. a being safe; security 2. a device to prevent accident, as a locking device (also **safety catch, safety lock**) on a firearm —*adj.* giving safety

safety belt *same as* SEAT BELT

safety curtain a fire-resistant curtain between the stage and the auditorium

safety lamp a miner's oil lamp designed to prevent its igniting gases

safety match a match that will light only when it is struck on a prepared surface

safety pin a pin bent back on itself so as to form a spring, the point being held with a guard

safety razor a razor with guards for the blade to protect the skin from cuts

safety valve 1. an automatic valve for a boiler, etc., to release steam if the pressure is too great 2. any outlet for emotion, energy, etc.

saffron (saf′rən) *n.* [< Ar. *za′farān*] 1. a species of crocus with flowers having orange stigmas 2. the dried stigmas, used in flavouring 3. orange yellow —*adj.* orange-yellow

S. Afr. 1. South Africa 2. South African

sag (sag) *vi.* **sagged, sag′ging** [prob. < Scand.] 1. to sink, esp. in the middle, as from weight 2. to hang down unevenly 3. to lose firmness, strength, etc. 4. to decline in price, sales, etc. —*n.* 1. a sagging 2. a sunken place

saga (sä′gə) *n.* [ON., a tale] 1. a medieval

Scandinavian story of battles, etc. **2.** any long story relating complicated adventures

sagacious (sə gā′shəs) *adj.* [< L. *sagax*, wise] keenly perceptive, farsighted, etc. —**sagac′ity** (-gas′ə tē) *n.*

sage[1] (sāj) *n.* [ult. < L. *sapere*, know] a very wise man —*adj.* **sag′er, sag′est** having or showing wisdom or good judgment —**sage′ly** *adv.* —**sage′ness** *n.*

sage[2] *n.* [< L. *salvus*, safe] **1.** any of various plants, esp. the **garden sage,** with leaves dried for seasoning meats, etc. **2.** *same as* SAGEBRUSH

sagebrush *n.* any of certain plants common in dry, alkaline areas of the western U.S.

Sagittarius (saj′i tāər′ē əs) [L., archer] **1.** a large S constellation in the Milky Way **2.** the ninth sign of the zodiac

sago (sā′gō) *n.,* pl. **-gos** [Malay *sāgū*] **1.** an edible starch prepared from certain palm trees **2.** a milk pudding made from this

sahib (säb) *n.* [< Ar.] sir; master : title formerly used in India when speaking to or of a European

said (sed) *pt. & pp.* of SAY —*adj.* named before

sail (sāl) *n.* [OE. *segl*] **1.** any of the sheets of canvas, etc. spread to catch the wind and drive vessels forward **2.** sails collectively **3.** a sailing vessel **4.** a trip in a ship or boat **5.** anything like a sail, as an arm of a windmill —*vi.* **1.** to be moved forwards by means of sails or a propeller, etc. **2.** to travel on water **3.** to begin a trip by water **4.** to manage a sailing boat **5.** to glide or move smoothly **6.** [Colloq.] to attack or criticize someone severely (with *into*) —*vt.* **1.** to move upon (a body of water) in a boat **2.** to manage (a boat) —**sail close to the wind 1.** to sail a course almost directly into the wind **2.** to run great risks, esp. by nearly breaking a moral law —**set sail 1.** to hoist the sails for departure **2.** to begin a trip by water —**under sail** with sails set —**sail′ing** *n., adj.*

sailcloth *n.* canvas or other cloth used in making sails, tents, etc.

sailer *n.* a ship or boat, esp. one with sails, specif. with regard to its speed, etc.

sailfish *n.* a large, tropical marine fish with a large, saillike dorsal fin

sailor *n.* **1.** one who makes his living by sailing **2.** *a)* a man in the navy below the rank of officer *b)* anyone in the navy —**sail′orly** *adj.*

sainfoin (san′foin) *n.* [Fr. < L. *sanus,* healthy + *faenum,* hay] a Eurasian perennial plant cultivated as a cover crop

saint (sānt) *n.* [< L. *sanctus,* holy] **1.** in certain Christian churches, a deceased person officially recognized as having lived an exceptionally holy life **2.** a holy person **3.** a person who is unusually charitable, patient, etc. —*vt.* to make a saint of —**saint′hood′** *n.*

Saint Bernard (bur′nərd) a large dog of a breed formerly trained to rescue travellers

sainted *adj.* **1.** of or fit for a saint; saintly **2.** regarded as a saint **3.** holy; sacred

Saint James (jāmz) [< the palace in Pall Mall, London] the British court : also **St. James**

Saint Johnswort (jonz′wurt′) [< ?] a plant usually with yellow flowers and spotted leaves

Saint Leger (lej′ər) an annual horse race run at Doncaster : also **St. Leger**

saintly *adj.* **-lier, -liest** like or suitable for a saint —**saint′liness** *n.*

Saint Swithin's Day (swi′thinz) July 15; if it rains on this day it is commonly believed that it will rain for the next forty days

Saint Valentine's Day (val′ən tīnz′) February 14, observed as a day for sending valentines to sweethearts, etc.

Saint Vitus' dance (vi′təs) [< *St. Vitus,* patron saint of persons having convulsive fits] *same as* CHOREA

saithe (sāth) *n.* [ON. *seithr*] a food fish like cod: also called **coalfish**

sake[1] (sāk) *n.* [OE. *sacu,* suit at law] **1.** purpose or reason; motive **2.** behalf; benefit *[for my sake]* —**for heaven's (or Pete's) sake!** a mild exclamation of surprise, annoyance, etc.

sake[2] (sä′kē) *n.* [Jap.] a Japanese alcoholic beverage made from fermented rice : also sp. **sa′ki**

salaam (sə läm′) *n.* [Ar. *salām,* peace] **1.** an Oriental greeting made by bowing low with the palm of the right hand to the forehead **2.** a greeting showing respect

salacious (sə lā′shəs) *adj.* [< L. *salire,* to leap] **1.** lecherous; lustful **2.** obscene —**sala′ciously** *adv.*

salad (sal′əd) *n.* [< L. *sal,* salt] **1.** a dish, usually cold, of vegetables, usually raw, or fruits, often served with a dressing **2.** any green plant or herb used for a dish

salad days time of youth and inexperience

salad dressing a preparation of olive oil or other vegetable oil, vinegar, spices, etc. served with a salad

salamander (sal′ə man′dər) *n.* [< Gr. *salamandra*] **1.** a tailed amphibian with a soft, moist skin **2.** a mythological reptile that was said to live in fire

salami (sə lä′mē) *n.* [It., ult. < L. *sal,* salt] a highly spiced, salted sausage, orig. Italian

sal ammoniac ammonium chloride, used in dry batteries, etc.

salaried (sal′ə rēd) *adj.* **1.** receiving a salary **2.** yielding a salary *[a salaried position]*

salary (sal′ə rē) *n.,* pl. **-ries** [< L. *salarium,* salt money < *sal,* salt] a fixed payment at regular intervals for services, esp. when clerical or professional

sale (sāl) *n.* [< ON. *sala*] **1.** the exchange

of property for an agreed sum of money **2.** opportunity to sell **3.** an auction **4.** a selling at prices lower than usual **5.** [*pl.*] receipts in business **—for** (or **on**) **sale** to be sold **—sale or return** an arrangement whereby the retailer can return any goods left unsold to the wholesaler

saleable *adj.* fit for sale: also **salable**

sale of work a sale of articles, usually made by the contributors, to raise funds for some specific charity

saleroom *n.* a room in which goods are shown and offered for sale, esp. by auction

salesman *n.* **1.** a man who is employed to sell goods in a shop **2.** a travelling agent who sells goods or services

salesperson *n.* a man or woman who sells goods in a shop

sales talk any persuasion or argument used in trying to sell something or to persuade one to do something

saleswoman *n.* a woman who sells goods in a shop: also **sales'la'dy, sales'girl'**

Salic law (sal'ik) [< LL. *Salii*, a tribe of Franks] a law excluding women from succession to the throne in the French and Spanish monarchies

salicylic acid (sal'əsil'ik) [< L. *salix*, willow] a white, crystalline compound used in making aspirin, etc.

salient (sā'lēənt) *adj.* [< L. *salire*, to leap] **1.** noticeable; prominent **2.** projecting **—n. 1.** the part of a battle line, fort, etc. projecting farthest towards the enemy **2.** a projecting angle, part, etc. **—sa'liently** *adv.*

saline (sā'līn) *adj.* [< L. *sal*, salt] of, like, or containing salt; salty **—n. 1.** a salt lake, salt marsh, etc. **2.** a salt of an alkali metal **3.** a saline solution **—salinity** (səlin'ətē) *n.*

saliva (səli'və) *n.* [L.] the thin, watery fluid secreted by glands in the mouth: it aids digestion **—sali'vary** *adj.*

salivate (sal'əvāt') *vi.* -vat'ed, -vat'ing [< L. *salivare*] to secrete saliva **—sal'i-va'tion** *n.*

saliva test a test for drug use in athletes, racehorses, etc. made by sampling the saliva

Salk vaccine (sôlk) [< J.E. *Salk*] a vaccine for injection to prevent poliomyelitis

sallow[1] (sal'ō) *adj.* [OE. *salu*] of a sickly, pale-yellowish complexion **—vt.** to make sallow **—sal'lowness** *n.*

sallow[2] *n.* [OE. *saelh*] a type of small willow tree

sally (sal'ē) *n.,* pl. **-lies** [< L. *salire*, to leap] **1.** a sudden rushing forth, as of troops to attack besiegers **2.** a quick witticism; quip **3.** an excursion **—vi. -lied, -lying 1.** to make a sally **2.** to set out on a trip Used with *forth* or *out*

Sally Lunn (lun) [< 18th-c. Brit. woman] [*also* **s- l-**] a type of sweetened tea-cake, usually served hot

sally port a postern gate or underground

passage allowing the defenders to make a sally

salmagundi (sal'məgun'dē) *n.* [< ?] **1.** a dish of chopped meat, eggs, etc. flavoured with onions, anchovies, etc. **2.** any medley

salmon (sam'ən) *n.* [< L. *salmo*] **1.** a game and food fish of the N Hemisphere, with flesh that is pink when cooked: salmon spawn in fresh water but usually live in salt water **2.** yellowish pink: also **salmon pink**

salmonella (sal'mənel'ə) *n.* [< D. *Salmon*] any of certain rod-shaped bacteria that cause various diseases, as food poisoning

salmon ladder a series of steps to enable a salmon to move upstream to its breeding grounds: also **salmon leap**

salon (sal'on) *n.* [Fr.: see SALOON] **1.** a large reception hall **2.** a regular gathering of writers, artists, etc. in a celebrity's home **3.** an art exhibition **4.** a shop specially equipped for performing some personal service

saloon (səloon') *n.* [< Fr. < It. *sala*, hall] **1.** any large room or hall for receptions, etc.; specif., the main cabin of a passenger ship **2.** a room in a public house that is supposed to be quieter than the public bar: also **saloon bar 3.** [U.S.] a public bar **4.** an enclosed motor car with two or four doors: also **saloon car**

salsify (sal'səfē') *n.* [< It. *sassefrica*] a plant with white, edible, fleshy roots

SALT (sôlt) Strategic Arms Limitation Talks

salt (sôlt) *n.* [OE. *sealt*] **1.** sodium chloride, NaCl, a white, crystalline substance found in natural beds, in sea water, etc., and used for seasoning and preserving food, etc. **2.** a chemical compound derived from an acid by replacing hydrogen with a metal **3.** that which lends piquancy, as pungent wit **4.** *same as* SALTCELLAR **5.** [*pl.*] mineral salts used as a cathartic, a restorative, etc. **6.** [Colloq.] a sailor **—adj.** containing, preserved with, tasting, or smelling of salt **—vt. 1.** to sprinkle, season, or preserve with salt **2.** to treat or provide with salt **—salt away** (or **down**) [Colloq.] to store or save (money, etc.) **—the salt of the earth** [after Matt 5:13] any person or persons regarded as the finest, noblest, etc. **—with a grain** (or **pinch**) **of salt** with reserve; sceptically **—worth one's salt** worth one's wages, etc. **—salt'ish** *adj.* **—salt'like'** *adj.* **—salt'-ness** *n.*

saltcellar *n.* [< SALT + MFr. *salière*, saltcellar] a small dish or shaker for salt at the table

salt lick an exposed natural deposit of rock salt which animals come to lick

salt mine 1. a mine where rock salt is obtained **2.** any place where hard labour is necessary

saltpetre (sôlt'pēt'ər) *n.* [< L. *sal*, salt

+ *petra*, a rock] *same as* POTASSIUM NITRATE

saltshaker *n.* a container for salt, with a perforated top

saltwater *adj.* of, having to do with, or living in salt water or the sea

salty *adj.* **-ier, -iest** 1. of, tasting of, or containing salt 2. *a)* piquant *b)* coarse or earthy —**salt'iness** *n.*

salubrious (sə lōō'brē əs) *adj.* [< L. *salus*, health] healthful, wholesome, etc. —**salu'briously** *adv.* —**salu'brity, salu'briousness** *n.*

Saluki (sə lōō'kē) *n.* [Ar. *salūqīy*] an ancient breed of dog shaped like a greyhound

salutary (sal'yōō tər ē) *adj.* [< L. *salus*, health] 1. promoting some good purpose; beneficial 2. promoting health —**sal'utarily** *adv.*

salutation (sal'yōō tā'shən) *n.* [see SALUTE] 1. the act of greeting, addressing, etc. by gestures or words 2. a greeting, as "Dear Sir" —**salu'tatory** (sə lōōt'ə tər ē) *adj.*

salute (sə lōōt') *vt.* **-lut'ed, -lut'ing** [< L. *salus*, health] 1. to greet in a friendly way, as by bowing 2. to honour ceremonially and officially by firing cannon, raising the right hand to the forehead, etc. 3. to commend —*vi.* to make a salute —*n.* 1. an act, remark, or gesture made in saluting 2. *Mil.* the position of the hand, etc. assumed in saluting —**take the salute** to receive a formal salute, usually from a procession

salvage (sal'vij) *n.* [< MFr. *salver*, to save] 1. *a)* the rescue of a ship and cargo at sea from fire, shipwreck, etc. *b)* compensation paid for such rescue *c)* the ship or cargo so rescued 2. *a)* the saving of any goods, etc. from destruction or waste *b)* goods, etc. so saved —*vt.* **-vaged, -vaging** to save or rescue from shipwreck, destruction or loss —**sal'vageable** *adj.* —**sal'vager** *n.*

salvation (sal vā'shən) *n.* [< L. *salvare*, to save] 1. a saving or being saved 2. a person or thing that rescues 3. *Theol.* spiritual rescue from the consequences of sin

Salvation Army a Christian organization that works to bring religion and help to the very poor —**Salva'tionist** *n.*

salve[1] (salv) *n.* [OE. *sealf*] 1. any soothing or healing ointment for wounds, burns, etc. 2. anything that soothes or heals —*vt.* **salved, salv'ing** to soothe

salve[2] *vt.* **salved, salv'ing** *same as* SALVAGE

salver (sal'vər) *n.* [< L. *salvare*, to SAVE[1]] a tray on which something is served or presented

salvia (sal'vē ə) *n.* [L.] *same as* SAGE[2] (sense 1)

salvo (sal'vō) *n.*, *pl.* **-vos, -voes** [< L. *salve*, hail!] 1. a discharge of a number of guns in succession or at the same time, either in salute or at a target 2. the release of a load of bombs 3. a burst of applause

sal volatile (vō lat'əl ē') [ModL., volatile salt] ammonium carbonate, used in smelling salts

Sam. *Bible* Samuel

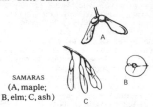

SAMARAS
(A, maple;
B, elm; C, ash)

samara (sam'ər ə, sə mä'rə) *n.* [< L., elm seed] a dry, winged, seeded fruit, as of the ash

Samaritan (sə mar'ət'n) *n.* 1. a native of Samaria 2. *see* GOOD SAMARITAN —*adj.* of Samaria or its people

samarium (sə māər'ē əm) *n.* [ult. < Col. *Samarski*] a metallic chemical element of the rare-earth group: symbol, Sm

samba (sam'bə) *n.* [Port.] 1. a Brazilian dance of African origin 2. music for this dance —*vi.* to dance the samba

same (sām) *adj.* [ON. *samr*] 1. being the very one; identical 2. alike in kind, quality, amount, etc. 3. unchanged [he looks the *same*] 4. before-mentioned; just spoken of —*pron.* the same person or thing —*adv.* in the same way —**all the same** 1. nevertheless: also **just the same** 2. immaterial —**same'ness** *n.*

samite (sam'īt) *n.* [< MGr. *hexamitos*, woven with six threads] a heavy silk fabric worn in the Middle Ages

‡**samizdat** (sam'iz dat') *n.* [Russ., self-published] a system by which manuscripts denied official publication in Russia are circulated clandestinely

samoosa (səmōō'sə) *n., pl.* **-sas** [prob. < Urdu] [S Afr.] a small, spiced meat pastie

SAMOVAR

samovar (sam'ō vär') *n.* [Russ., self-boiler] a Russian metal urn with an internal tube for heating water for tea

Samoyed, Samoyede (sam'ɔi ed'; *for* 2, *also* sə mɔi'ed) *n.* [Russ.] 1. any of a Uralic people of Siberia 2. a strong breed of Siberian dog, with a thick, white coat

samp (samp) *n.* [< AmInd.] [S Afr.] crushed maize used for porridge

sampan (sam'pan) *n.* [Chin. < *san*, three + *pan*, a plank] a small boat used in China and Japan, often having a sail and a small cabin formed of mats

samphire (sam'fiər') *n.* [< Fr. *(herbe de) Saint Pierre*, St. Peter's (herb)] a seashore plant with small clusters of yellowish flowers

sample (săm'p'l) *n.* [< OFr.: see EXAMPLE] a part, piece, or item that shows what the whole thing or group is like; specimen or example —*vt.* -pled, -pling to take or test a sample of —*adj.* being a sample; typical

sampler *n.* a cloth embroidered with designs, mottoes, etc. in different stitches

Samson (sam's'n) *n.* [< *Samson*: Judges 13-16] a man of outstanding strength

samurai (sam'oo rī') *n., pl.* -rai' [Jap.] 1. a member of a military class in feudal Japan 2. a Japanese army officer

sanatorium (san'ə tôr'ē əm) *n., pl.* -riums, -ria [< L. *sanare*, to heal] a nursing home, hospital, etc. for the treatment of invalids or convalescents

sanctify (saŋk'tə fī') *vt.* -fied', -fy'ing [< L. *sanctus*, holy + *facere*, make] 1. *a)* to set apart as holy; consecrate *b)* to make free from sin; purify 2. to make binding by sanction —**sanc'tifica'tion** *n.*

sanctimonious (saŋk'tə mō'nē əs) *adj.* pretending to be very pious —**sanc'timo'niousness** *n.*

sanctimony *n.* [< L. *sanctus*, holy] affected piety or righteousness

sanction (saŋk'shən) *n.* [< L. *sanctus*, holy] 1. the confirming of an action by authority; authorization 2. support; approval 3. something that gives binding force to a law, as the penalty for breaking it or a reward for carrying it out 4. [usually *pl.*] a boycott, blockade, or similar coercive measure, as against one nation by others to enforce international law —*vt.* 1. to ratify or confirm 2. to authorize or permit

sanctity (saŋk'tə tē) *n., pl.* -ties [< L. *sanctus*, holy] 1. saintliness or holiness 2. a being sacred or inviolable

sanctuary (saŋk'tyoo wər ē) *n., pl.* -aries [< L. *sanctus*, sacred] 1. a holy place, as a building set aside for worship 2. a place of refuge or protection 3. refuge; immunity from punishment 4. a reservation where animals or birds may not be hunted or trapped

sanctum (saŋk'təm) *n.* [L.] 1. a sacred place 2. a study or private room

sand (sand) *n.* [OE.] 1. loose, gritty grains of disintegrated rock, as on beaches, in deserts, etc. 2. [usually *pl.*] an area of sand; beach —*vt.* 1. to smooth with sandpaper 2. to sprinkle, fill, or mix with sand —**sand'ed** *adj.* —**sand'er** *n.*

sandal (san'd'l) *n.* [< Gr. *sandalon*] a kind of footwear consisting of a sole fastened in various ways to the foot by straps —**san'dalled** *adj.*

sandalwood (san'd'l wood') *n.* [ult. < Sans. *candana*] 1. the hard, sweet-smelling heartwood of an Asiatic tree, used for carving or burned as incense 2. any tree yielding such wood

sandbag (sand'bag') *n.* a bag filled with sand and used for ballast, in fortifications, etc. —*vt.* -bagged', -bag'ging to place sandbags in or around —**sand'bag'ger** *n.*

sand bar a ridge of sand formed in a river or along a shore: also **sandbank** *n.*

sandblast *n.* a current of air or steam carrying sand at a high velocity, used in cleaning surfaces as of metals, stone, etc. —*vt.* to engrave, clean, etc. with a sandblast —**sand'blast'er** *n.*

sandcastle *n.* the edifice resembling a castle constructed by children out of sand

sanderling (san'dər liŋ) *n.* a bird of the sandpiper family found on sandy beaches

sandman *n.* a mythical person supposed to make children sleepy by dusting sand in their eyes

sand martin a bird that nests in sand burrows in river banks, etc.

sandpaper *n.* a strong paper with sand glued on one side, used for smoothing and polishing—*vt.* to smooth or polish with sandpaper

sandpiper *n.* a small wading bird with a long, soft-tipped bill

sandpit *n.* a box containing sand for children to play in

sand-shoes *n.pl.* 1. light shoes suitable to be worn on the beach 2. [Scot.] same as PLIMSOLLS

sandstone *n.* a sedimentary rock much used for building, composed largely of sand grains

sandstorm *n.* a windstorm in which large quantities of sand are blown about

sandwich (san'wich) *n.* [< 4th Earl of *Sandwich*] two or more slices of bread with a filling of meat, cheese, etc. between them —*vt.* to place between other persons, things, materials, etc.

sandwich course a course of study in which academic study is alternated with practical experience

sandwich man a man who walks the street with two signboards, usually bearing advertisements, hung from his shoulders in front and behind

sandy (san'dē) *adj.* -ier, -iest 1. of, or like sand 2. yellowish-red [sandy hair] —**sand'iness** *n.*

sand yacht a vehicle mounted on wheels that uses sails to skim over stretches of firm sand

sane (sān) *adj.* [L. *sanus*, healthy] 1. having a healthy mind; rational 2. showing good sense; sensible —**sane'ly** *adv.*

sang (saŋ) *pt. of* SING

sang-froid (säŋ'frwä') *n.* [Fr., cold blood] cool self-possession

sangoma (saŋgō′mə) *n.*, *pl.* -mas [< Bantu] [S Afr.] a witchdoctor

Sangraal (san grāl′) *n.* [< OFr. *saint graal*, holy grail] *same as* GRAIL: also **Sangreal, Sangrail**

sangria (sän grē′ä) *n.* [Sp. lit., bleeding] a Spanish punch made with red wine and fruit

sanguinary (saŋ′gwi nər ē) *adj.* [see ff.] 1. with much bloodshed or killing 2. of or stained with blood 3. bloodthirsty

sanguine (saŋ′gwin) *adj.* [< L. *sanguis*, blood] 1. of the colour of blood; ruddy 2. [< medieval idea about humours] cheerful; confident —**san′guinely** *adv.*

Sanhedrin (san′ē drin) *n.* [Heb. < Gr. *syn-*, together + *hedra*, seat] the highest court and council of the ancient Jewish nation

sanitary (san′ə tər ē) *adj.* [< L. *sanitas*, health] 1. promoting health by getting rid of dirt and of things that bring disease 2. clean; hygienic —**san′itarily** *adv.* —**san′itariness** *n.*

sanitary towel an absorbent pad of cotton, etc. worn by women during menstruation

sanitation (san′ə tā′shən) *n.* 1. the science and work of bringing about hygienic conditions 2. drainage and disposal of sewage

sanity (san′ə tē) *n.* [< L. *sanitas*, health] 1. a being sane; soundness of mind 2. soundness of judgment

sank (saŋk) *pt.* of SINK

sans (sanz; *Fr.* sän) *prep.* [Fr. < L. *sine*] without; lacking

Sans. Sanskrit

sans-culotte (sanz′kyoo lot′) *n.* [Fr., without breeches] a revolutionary: after the republicans in the French Revolution, who wore pantaloons instead of knee breeches

Sanskrit (san′skrit) *n.* [< Sans. *samskrta*, well arranged] the classical literary language of ancient India; the oldest Indo-European language —*adj.* of or written in Sanskrit Also *sp.* **San′scrit** —**Sanskrit′ic** *adj.* —**San′skritist** *n.*

Santa (san′tə) *short for* SANTA CLAUS

Santa Claus (san′tə klôz′) *n.* [< Du. *Sant Nikolaas*, St. Nicholas] *Folklore* a fat, white-bearded, jolly old man in a red suit, who distributes gifts at Christmas: also called **Saint Nicholas**

sap[1] (sap) *n.* [OE. *sæp*] 1. the juice that circulates through a plant bearing water, food, etc. 2. vigour; energy 3. [Slang] a stupid person —*vt.* **sapped, sap′ping** to drain of sap

sap[2] *n.* [< MFr. < It. *zappe*, a spade] a trench for approaching or undermining an enemy position —*vt.* **sapped, sap′ping** 1. to undermine by digging away foundations 2. to weaken; exhaust —*vi.* to dig saps

sap green 1. a paint made from buckthorn berries 2. the light green colour of this paint

sapid (sap′id) *adj.* [< L. *sapere*, have a taste] 1. having a taste, esp. a pleasing one 2. interesting —**sapid′ity** (sə pid′-ə tē) *n.*

sapient (sā′pē ənt) *adj.* [< L. *sapere*, to taste, know] full of knowledge; wise —**sa′pience** *n.*

sapling (sap′liŋ) *n.* 1. a young tree 2. a youth

saponify (sə pon′ə fī′) *vt.* -fied′, -fy′ing [< L. *sapo*, soap + *facere*, make] to convert (a fat) into soap by reaction with an alkali —*vi.* to be made into soap —**sapon′ifica′tion** *n.*

sapper (sap′ər) *n.* 1. a soldier employed in digging saps, laying mines, etc., esp. a soldier in the Royal Engineers 2. a private of the Royal Engineers

Sapphic (saf′ik) *adj.* [< Gr. *Sapphō*] 1. of Sappho, 6th cent. B.C. Greek poetess, or her poetry 2. of a lesbian relationship

sapphire (saf′īər) *n.* [< Gr. *sappheiros*] 1. a hard, transparent precious stone of a clear, deep-blue corundum 2. its colour —*adj.* deep-blue

sappy (sap′ē) *adj.* -pier, -piest full of sap; juicy

saprophyte (sap′rō fīt′) *n.* [< Gr. *sapros*, rotten + *phyton*, plant] any organism that lives on dead or decaying organic matter, as some fungi

saraband (sar′ə band′) *n.* [< Sp.] 1. a stately, slow Spanish dance in triple time 2. music for this dance

Saracen (sar′ə s'n) *n.* any Arab or any Moslem, esp. at the time of the Crusades —*adj.* of the Saracens

sarcasm (sär′kaz′m) *n.* [< Gr. *sarkazein*, to tear flesh] 1. a taunting or sneering remark, generally ironical 2. the making of such remarks 3. sarcastic quality

sarcastic (sär kas′tik) *adj.* 1. of, like, or full of sarcasm; sneering 2. using sarcasm —**sarcas′tically** *adv.*

sarcoma (sär kō′mə) *n.*, *pl.* -mata [< Gr. *sarx*, flesh] any of various malignant tumours that begin in connective tissue

sarcophagus (sär kof′ə gəs) *n.*, *pl.* -gi′ (-gī′), -guses [< Gr. *sarx*, flesh + *phagein*, to eat] a stone coffin, esp. one on display, as in a monumental tomb

sard (särd) *n.* [L. *sarda*] a very hard, deep orange-red variety of chalcedony, used in jewellery, etc.

sardine (sär dēn′) *n.* [< L. *sarda*, kind of fish] a small ocean fish preserved in tightly packed tins for eating —**like sardines** crowded together

sardonic (sär don′ik) *adj.* [< Gr. *sardanios*, bitter] disdainfully or bitterly sneering or sarcastic [a *sardonic* smile] —**sardon′ically** *adv.*

sardonyx (sär′də niks) *n.* [< Gr. *sardios*, sard + *onyx*, onyx] a variety of onyx made up of layers of white chalcedony and sard, used as a gem

sargassum (sär gas′əm) *n.* [< Port. *sarga*, kind of grape] a brown seaweed having special branches with berrylike air sacs: also **sargas′so, sargasso weed**

sarge (särj) *n. colloq.* shortened form of SERGEANT

SARI

sari (sä′rē) *n.* [< Sans.] an outer garment of Hindu women, a long cloth wrapped around the body with one end over the shoulder

sarong (sə roŋ′) *n.* [Malay] a garment of men and women in the Malay Archipelago, consisting of a long cloth, often brightly coloured, worn like a skirt

sarsaparilla (sär′sə′pə ril′ə) *n.* [< Sp. *zarza*, bramble + *parra*, vine] 1. a tropical American plant with fragrant roots 2. a carbonated drink flavoured with sarsaparilla

sarsenet (särs′nit) *n.* [< Anglo-Fr. *sarzinett*] a soft, silk cloth, formerly used for linings, etc.

sartorial (sär tôr′ē əl) *adj.* [< LL. *sartor*, a tailor] 1. of tailors or their work 2. of men's clothing or dress

S.A.S.E., s.a.s.e. self-addressed stamped envelope

sash[1] (sash) *n.* [< Ar. *shāsh*, muslin] an ornamental scarf worn over the shoulder or around the waist

sash[2] *n.* [< Fr. *châssis*, a frame] a frame for holding the glass pane of a window or door, esp. a sliding frame as in a **sash window**

sash cord a cord attached to either side of a sliding sash, having balancing weights (**sash weights**) for raising or lowering the window easily

Sask. Saskatchewan

saskatoon (sas′kə tōōn′) *n.* [< AmInd.] a Canadian shrub with purplish berries

sasquatch (sas′kwat) *n. Canad. Folklore* in British Columbia, a hairy beast or manlike monster said to leave huge footprints

sassafras (sas′ə fras′) *n.* [Sp. *sasafras*] a small N American tree whose dried root bark is used as a flavouring

Sassenach (sas′ə nak′) *n.* [< Gael. *Sasunn*, Saxon] an Englishman: term used, often disparagingly, by Scots

sat (sat) *pt. & pp. of* SIT

Sat. 1. Saturday 2. Saturn

Satan (sāt′′n) [< Heb. *sātān*, to plot against] *Christian Theol.* the chief evil spirit; the Devil

satanic (sə tan′ik) *adj.* of or like Satan; devilish; wicked —**satan′ically** *adv.*

Satanism (sāt′′n iz′m) *n.* worship of Satan

S.A.T.B. *Music* Soprano, Alto, Tenor, Bass

satchel (sach′əl) *n.* [< L. *saccus*, a sack] a small bag for carrying books, etc., usually having a shoulder strap

sate (sāt) *vt.* sat′ed, sat′ing [prob. < L. *satiare*, to fill full] 1. to satisfy (an appetite, etc.) to the full 2. to satiate

sateen (sa tēn′) *n.* [< SATIN] a smooth, glossy cotton cloth, made to imitate satin

satellite (sat′əl īt′) *n.* [< L. *satelles*, an attendant] 1. *a)* a small planet revolving round a larger one *b)* a man-made object put into orbit round the earth, the moon, etc. 2. an attendant of some important person 3. a small state that is economically dependent on a larger state

satiable (sā′shə b'l) *adj.* that can be sated or satiated —**sa′tiabil′ity** *n.* —**sa′tiably** *adv.*

satiate (sā′shē āt′) *vt.* -at′ed, -at′ing [< L. *satis*, enough] to provide with more than enough, so as to weary or disgust —*adj.* having had enough or more than enough —**sa′tia′tion** *n.*

satiety (sə tī′ə tē) *n.* a being satiated; surfeit

satin (sat′in) *n.* [< Ar. *zaitūnī*] a fabric of silk, nylon, etc. with a smooth, glossy finish on one side —*adj.* of or like satin; smooth and glossy —**sat′iny** *adj.*

satinwood *n.* 1. a smooth, hard wood used in fine furniture, etc. 2. a tree yielding such wood

satire (sa′tīər) *n.* [Fr. < L. *satira*, a poetic medley] 1. a literary work in which vices, follies, etc. are held up to ridicule and contempt 2. the use of sarcasm, irony, etc. to attack or deride vices, follies, etc. —**satir′ical** (sə tir′i k'l) *adj.*

satirist (sat′ə rist) *n.* a writer of satires

satirize *vt.* -rized′, -riz′ing to attack, ridicule, or criticize with satire

satisfaction (sat′is fak′shən) *n.* 1. a satisfying or being satisfied 2. *a)* anything that brings pleasure or contentment *b)* settlement of debt *c)* reparation for insult or injury —**give satisfaction** 1. to satisfy 2. to accept a challenge to duel

satisfactory *adj.* satisfying; fulfilling a need, wish, etc. —**sat′isfac′torily** *adv.*

satisfy (sat′is fī′) *vt.* -fied′, -fy′ing [< L. *satis*, enough + *facere*, make] 1. to fulfil the needs or desires of; gratify 2. to fulfil the requirements of 3. to answer (a doubt, etc.) adequately 4. *a)* to give what is due to *b)* to discharge (a debt, etc.) 5. to make reparation to or for —*vi.* to be adequate, sufficient, etc. —**sat′isfi′able** *adj.*

satrap (sat′rəp) *n.* [< OPer.] the governor of a province in ancient Persia

Satsuma (sat′sōō mə, *for* 2 sat sōō′mə) *n.* [< Jap. *Satsuma* Peninsula] 1. a variety of Japanese pottery 2. [s-] a small, loose-skinned variety of orange

saturate (sach´ə rāt´) *vt.* **-rat´ed, -rat´ing** [< L. *satur*, full] **1.** to cause to be thoroughly soaked **2.** to cause to be so completely filled or supplied that no more can be taken up **3.** *Chem. a)* to cause (a substance) to combine to its full capacity with another *b)* to dissolve the maximum amount of (a gas, liquid, or solid) in a solution —**sat´ura´tion** *n.*

saturation point 1. the point at which the maximum amount of something has been absorbed **2.** the limit beyond which something cannot be continued, endured, etc.

Saturday (sat´ər dē) *n.* [OE. *Sæterdæg*, Saturn's day] the seventh and last day of the week

Saturdays *adv.* [Colloq.] on every Saturday

Saturn (sat´ərn) **1.** *Rom. Myth.* the god of agriculture **2.** the second largest planet in the solar system

Saturnalia (sat´ər nā´lē ə) *n.pl.* **1.** the ancient Roman festival of Saturn with general feasting and revelry **2.** [s-] [often with *sing. v.*] a period of unrestrained revelry

saturnine (sat´ər nīn´) *adj.* sluggish, grave, taciturn, etc. —**sat´urnine´ly** *adv.*

satyr (sat´ər) *n.* [< Gr. *satyros*] **1.** *Gr. Myth.* a lecherous woodland deity represented as having the head and body of a man, and the legs of a goat **2.** a lecherous man

sauce (sôs) *n.* [< L. *sal*, salt] **1.** a liquid or soft dressing served with food as a relish **2.** something that adds interest or zest **3.** [Colloq.] impudence —*vt.* **sauced, sauc´ing** [Colloq.] to be impudent or saucy to —**sauce for the goose is sauce for the gander** an appeal for consistency

saucepan *n.* a small pot with a projecting handle, used for cooking

saucer *n.* [< SAUCE] a small, round, shallow dish, esp. one with an indentation to hold a cup —**sau´cerful** *n.*

saucy *adj.* **-cier, -ciest** [< SAUC(E)] **1.** rude; impudent **2.** pert; sprightly **3.** stylish or smart —**sau´cily** *adv.*

sauerkraut (souər´krout´) *n.* [G. *sauer*, sour + *Kraut*, cabbage] chopped cabbage fermented in a brine of its own juice with salt

sault (sōō) *n.* [< Fr. *saut*, a leap] [Canad.] a waterfall or rapids

sauna (sô´nə) *n.* [Finn.] **1.** a Finnish bath, consisting of exposure to very hot, dry air **2.** the enclosure for this

saunter (sôn´tər) *vi.* [< ?] to walk about idly; stroll —*n.* a leisurely and aimless walk

saurian (sôr´ē ən) *n.* [< Gr. *sauros*, a lizard] any of those reptiles that are lizards —*adj.* of or like lizards

-saurus (sôr´əs) [see prec.] *a combining form meaning* lizard

sausage (sô´sij) *n.* [see SAUCE] pork or other meat, finely chopped, seasoned, and stuffed into membranous casings —**not a sausage** [Colloq.] nothing whatsoever

sausage roll a small roll of pastry filled with sausage meat

sauté (sō´tā) *adj.* [Fr. < *sauter*, to leap] fried quickly in a little fat —*vt.* **-téed´, -té´ing** to fry quickly in a pan with a little fat —*n.* a sautéed dish

sauterne (sōturn´) *n.* [< *Sauternes*, in France] a white, usually sweet table wine

savage (sav´ij) *adj.* [< L. *silva*, a wood] **1.** fierce; untamed **2.** cruel; pitiless **3.** without civilization; barbarous **4.** wild; uncultivated —*n.* **1.** a member of a primitive society **2.** a fierce, brutal person —*vt.* **-aged, -aging** to attack violently, either physically or verbally —**sav´agely** *adv.* —**sav´ageness** *n.*

savagery *n., pl.* **-ries 1.** the condition of being savage **2.** savage act or behaviour

savanna, savannah (sə van´ə) *n.* [< Sp. < native name] a treeless plain in or near the tropics

savant (sav´ənt) *n.* [< L. *sapere*, know] a learned person

save¹ (sāv) *vt.* **saved, sav´ing** [< L. *salvus*, safe] **1.** to rescue or preserve from harm or danger **2.** to preserve for future use (often with *up*) **3.** to prevent loss or waste of **4.** to avoid or lessen **5.** to treat carefully in order to preserve **6.** *Theol.* to deliver from sin —*vi.* **1.** to avoid expense, loss, waste, etc. **2.** to hoard money or goods **3.** *Theol.* to exercise power to redeem from sin —*n.* *Sports* an action that keeps an opponent from scoring —**sav´er** *n.*

save² *prep., conj.* [< OFr. *sauf*, safe] except; but

save-as-you-earn *n.* a way of saving by having regular deposits made into a savings account from a salary

saving¹ *adj.* that saves; specif., *a)* rescuing *b)* economical *c)* containing an exception *d)* redeeming —*n.* **1.** the act of one that saves **2.** [often *pl.* with *sing. v.*] any reduction in expense, time, etc. **3.** *a)* anything saved *b)* [*pl.*] sums of money saved

saving² *prep.* [Now Rare] **1.** with due respect for **2.** except; save

savings certificate a certificate, issued by the government to savers, that also pays interest on the deposit

saviour (sāv´yər) *n.* [< LL. *salvare*, to SAVE¹] one who saves —**the Saviour** Jesus Christ Also U.S. sp., **sav´ior**

savoir-faire (sav´wär fâar´) *n.* [Fr., to know (how) to do] ready knowledge of what to do or say

savory (sā´vər ē) *n.* [< L. *satureia*, savoury] a fragrant herb used in cooking

savour (sā´vər) *n.* [< L. *sapor*] **1.** the taste or smell of something **2.** characteristic quality **3.** noticeable trace —*vi.* **1.** to have the particular taste, smell, or quality (*of*) **2.** to show traces (*of*) —*vt.* **1.** to dwell on with delight; relish

2. to season or flavour   Also U.S. sp., savor —**sa'vourless** *adj.*

savoury (sā'vər ē) *adj.* **-vourier, -vouriest** **1.** pleasing to the taste or smell **2.** not sweet **3.** pleasant, agreeable, etc. —*n.,* *pl.* **-vouries** a small, highly seasoned portion of food served at the end of a meal or as an appetizer   Also, U.S. sp., savory —**sa'vouriness** *n.*

savoy (sə voi´) *n.* [Fr. *(chou de) Savoie,* (cabbage of) Savoy] a type of cabbage with a compact head

savvy (sav'ē) *vi.* **-vied, -vying** [< Sp. *sabe (usted),* do (you) know?] [Slang] to understand —*n.* [Slang] **1.** shrewd understanding **2.** skill or know-how

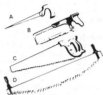

SAWS
(A, keyhole;
B, hacksaw;
C, handsaw;
D, crosscut)

saw[1] (sô) *n.* [OE. *sagu*] a cutting tool having a thin, metal blade with sharp teeth along the edge —*vt.* **sawed, sawed** or **sawn, saw'ing** **1.** to cut or shape with a saw **2.** to make sawlike cutting motions through or with (something) —*vi.* **1.** to cut with a saw or as a saw does **2.** to be cut with a saw **3.** to make sawlike cutting motions —**saw'er** *n.*

saw[2] *n.* [OE. *sagu*] an old saying

saw[3] *pt. of* SEE[1]

sawbones *n.* [Slang] a surgeon

sawdust *n.* tiny bits of wood formed in sawing

sawfish *n.* a tropical giant ray with a long, flat, sawlike snout edged with teeth

sawhorse *n.* a rack on which wood is placed while being sawed

sawmill *n.* a place where logs are sawed into boards

sawn (sôn) *pp. of* SAW[1]

sawn-off *adj.* designating a shotgun with the barrel cut off short: also **sawed-off**

saw-toothed (sô'tŏŏthd') *adj.* having notches like the teeth of a saw: also **saw'- tooth'**

sawyer (sô'yər) *n.* a person whose work is sawing wood, as into planks and boards

sax (saks) *n.* [Colloq.] a saxophone

saxe (saks) *n.* [< Fr. *Saxe,* Saxony] a light greyish-blue colour

saxifrage (sak'sə frij) *n.* [< L. *saxum,* a rock + *frangere,* to break] a plant with white, yellow, purple, or pinkish small flowers

Saxon (sak's'n) *n.* **1.** a member of an ancient Germanic people of northern Germany: some Saxons conquered parts of England in the 5th and 6th cent. A.D. **2.** *same as* ANGLO-SAXON —*adj.* of the Saxons, their language, etc.

SAXOPHONE

saxophone (sak'sə fōn') *n.* [Fr., < A. J. *Sax* & -PHONE] a single-reed wind instrument having a curved metal body —**saxoph'onist** (-sof'ə nist) *n.*

say (sā) *vt.* **said, say'ing;** 3rd pers. sing., pres. indic., **says** (sez) [OE. *secgan*] **1.** to utter; speak **2.** to express in words **3.** to state positively or as an opinion **4.** to indicate or show **5.** to recite; repeat **6.** to estimate [I'd *say,* forty] **7.** to allege; report **8.** to communicate (an idea, feeling, etc.) —*vi.* to make a statement; speak —*n.* **1.** a chance to speak **2.** authority, as to make a final decision —*adv.* **1.** for example [any fish, *say* perch] **2.** about; nearly [costing, *say,* £5] —**go without saying** to be obvious —**not to say** as well as; and indeed —**says you** [Colloq.] an exclamation of disagreement —**that is to say** in other words —**say'- er** *n.*

S.A.Y.E. Save As You Earn

saying *n.* something said; esp., an adage, proverb, or maxim

Sb [L. *stibium*] *Chem.* antimony

Sc *Chem.* scandium

Sc. **1.** Scotch **2.** Scots **3.** Scottish

S.C. [Canad.] Social Credit

s.c. *Printing* small capitals

scab (skab) *n.* [ON. *skabb*] **1.** a crust that forms over a sore as it is healing **2.** a mangy skin disease, esp. of sheep **3.** a plant disease **4.** [Derog.] a worker who refuses to strike, or who takes the place of a striking worker —*vi.* **scabbed, scab'bing** **1.** to become covered with a scab **2.** to work as a scab

scabbard (skab'ərd) *n.* [< Anglo-Fr. *escaubers* (pl.)] a sheath or case to hold the blade of a sword, dagger, etc.

scabby (skab'ē) *adj.* **-bier, -biest** **1.** covered with or consisting of scabs **2.** [Colloq.] lowly; mean

scabies (skā'bē ēz) *n.* [< L. *scabere,* to scratch] a contagious skin disease caused by mites and characterized by intense itching

scabiosa (skā'bē ō'sə) *n.* [see prec.: once considered a remedy for scabies] a plant having showy flowers in flattened heads: also **scabious**

scabrous (skā'brəs) *adj.* [< L. *scabere,*

to scratch] 1. rough, scaly, scabby, etc.
2. full of difficulties 3. indecent,
scandalous, etc.

scaffold (skaf''ld) *n.* [OFr. *escafalt*] 1.
a temporary framework for supporting
people working on a building, etc. 2.
a raised platform on which criminals are
executed, as by hanging 3. any raised
framework

scaffolding *n.* 1. the materials that form
a scaffold 2. a scaffold or scaffolds

scalar (skā'lər) *adj.* 1. in, on, or of a
scale 2. *Math.* designating or of a quantity
that has magnitude but no direction in
space —*n.* a scalar quantity

scalawag (skal'ə wag') *n.* [< ?] a
scamp; rascal; also sp. **scallawag**

scald (skôld) *vt.* [< L. *ex-*, intens. +
calidus, hot] 1. to burn with hot liquid
or steam 2. to heat almost to the boiling
point 3. to use boiling liquid on, as in
sterilizing, etc. —*n.* a burn caused by
scalding

scale[1] (skāl) *n.* [< L. *scala*, a ladder]
1. *a)* a series of marks along a line, used
in measuring [the *scale* of a thermometer]
b) any instrument so marked 2. the
proportion that a map, model, etc. bears
to the thing that it represents [a *scale*
of one centimetre to a kilometre] 3. a
series of degrees classified according to
relative size, amount, rank, etc. [a wage
scale] 4. *Math.* a number system [the
binary *scale*] 5. *Music* a sequence of
tones, rising or falling in pitch, in
accordance with a system of intervals —*vt.*
scaled, scal'ing 1. to climb up or over
2. to make according to a scale —*vi.*
to climb; go up —**in scale** in proportion
with —**on a large** (or **small**) **scale** to
a relatively large (or small) extent —**scale
down** (or **up**) to reduce (or increase)
according to a ratio —**to scale** to a
particular scale; of uniform reduction or
enlargement —**scal'er** *n.*

scale[2] *n.* [< OFr. *escaille*, shell < Gmc.]
1. any of the thin, flat, horny plates covering
many fishes and reptiles 2. any thin,
platelike layer or piece 3. a coating that
forms on metals when heated or rusted
—*vt.* **scaled, scal'ing** 1. to scrape scales
from 2. to remove in thin layers —*vi.*
to peel off in scales —**scales fell from
his eyes** he was no longer blinded to
a particular situation —**scale'less** *adj.*
—**scal'y** *adj.*

scale[3] *n.* [ON. *skāl*, bowl] 1. [*often pl.*]
a balance or other weighing device 2.
either of the pans of a balance —*vt.* **scaled,
scal'ing** to have a weight of —**the Scales**
same as LIBRA —**turn** (or **tip**) **the scales**
to decide

scalene (skā'lēn) *adj.* [< Gr. *skalēnos*,
uneven] *Geom.* having unequal sides and
angles: said of a triangle

scallion (skal'yən) *n.* [< L. (*caepa*)
Ascalonia, (onion of) Ascalon] 1. the
shallot 2. a green onion with an almost
bulbless root

SCALLOP (sense 1)

scallop (skol'əp) *n.* [OFr. *escalope*] 1.
a kind of mollusc with two deeply grooved,
curved shells 2. the large muscle of this
mollusc, used as food 3. a single shell
of such a mollusc 4. any of a series
of curves, etc. forming an ornamental edge
—*vt.* 1. to cut the border of in scallops
2. to bake with a milk sauce and bread
crumbs

scallywag (skal'ē wag') *n. same as*
SCALAWAG

scalp (skalp) *n.* [< Scand.] 1. the skin
on the top and back of the head, usually
covered with hair 2. a part of this, cut
off for a trophy as by some N American
Indians —*vt.* 1. to cut or tear the scalp
from 2. [Chiefly U.S. Colloq.] to buy
and sell in order to make small, quick
profits —**scalp'er** *n.*

scalpel (skal'pəl) *n.* [< L. *scalpere*, to
cut] a small, straight knife with a very
sharp blade, used by surgeons

scamp[1] (skamp) *n.* [< MFr. *escamper*,
to flee] a mischievous fellow; rascal

scamp[2] *vt.* [akin to or < ON. *skammr*,
short] to do in a careless, inadequate
way —**scamp'er** *n.*

scamper *vi.* [see SCAMP[1]] to run or go
hurriedly or quickly —*n.* the act of
scampering

scampi (skam'pē) *n.pl.* [It.] large prawns

scan (skan) *vt.* **scanned, scan'ning** [<
L. *scandere*, to climb] 1. to look at closely;
scrutinize 2. to glance at quickly 3. to
analyse (verse), as by marking off the
metrical feet and showing the rhythmic
structure 4. *Electronics* to traverse (a
surface) point by point with a beam of
electrons 5. to traverse (a region) with
a succession of transmitted radar or sonar
beams —*vi.* to be in a certain poetic
metre —*n.* a scanning

Scan., Scand. 1. Scandinavia 2.
Scandinavian

scandal (skan'd'l) *n.* [< Gr. *skandalor*,
a snare] 1. any act, person, or thing
that offends the moral feelings of people
2. shame, outrage, etc. caused by this
3. disgrace 4. wicked gossip

scandalize *vt.* **-ized', -iz'ing** to outrage
the moral feelings of by improper conduct

scandalmonger (skan'd'l muŋ'gər) *n.* a
person who gossips maliciously and
spreads scandal

scandalous *adj.* 1. causing scandal;
shameful 2. spreading slander; libellous
—**scan'dalously** *adv.*

Scandinavian (skan'də nā'vē ən) *adj.*
of Scandinavia, its people, their languages,
etc. —*n.* 1. any of the people of Scandinavia
2. the Germanic languages spoken by them

scandium (skan′dē əm) *n.* [< L. *Scandia*, N European lands] a rare metallic chemical element: symbol, Sc

scansion (skan′shən) ·*n.* the act of scanning verse

scant (skant) *adj.* [< ON. *skammr*, short] 1. inadequate; meagre 2. not quite up to full measure —*vt.* to limit; stint —*adv.* scarcely; barely

scanty *adj.* -ier, -iest 1. barely sufficient; meagre 2. not enough —**scant′ily** *adv.* —**scant′iness** *n.*

scape (skāp) *n., vt., vi.* scaped, scap′ing [Archaic] *same as* ESCAPE: also **'scape**

scapegoat *n.* [SCAPE + GOAT: see Lev. 16:7–26] a person, group, or thing that bears the blame for the mistakes of others

scapula (skap′yōō lə) *n., pl.* -lae′ (-lē′), -las [L.] *same as* SHOULDER BLADE

scapular *adj.* of the shoulder or scapula —*n.* a sleeveless outer garment worn by monks

scar[1] (skär) *n.* [< Gr. *eschara*, fireplace] 1. a mark left after a wound, burn, etc. has healed 2. any mark like this, as on a plant where a leaf was attached 3. the lasting emotional effects of suffering —*vt., vi.* scarred, scar′ring to mark with or form a scar

scar[2] *n.* [< ON. *sker*] a precipitous rocky place or cliff: also **scaur**

scarab (skar′əb) *n.* [< Fr. < L. *scarabaeus*] 1. a beetle, esp. the black, winged dung beetle, held sacred by the ancient Egyptians 2. an image of this beetle, cut from a gem

scarce (skäers) *adj.* [ult. < L. *excerpere*, to select] 1. not common; rarely seen 2. not plentiful; hard to get —*adv.* literary var. of SCARCELY —**make oneself scarce** [Colloq.] to go or stay away —**scarce′ness** *n.*

scarcely *adv.* 1. hardly; not quite 2. probably not

scarcity *n., pl.* -ties 1. the condition of being scarce; inadequate supply 2. rarity; uncommonness

scare (skäer) *vt.* scared, scar′ing [< ON. *skjarr*, timid] to fill with sudden fear or terror —*vi.* to become frightened, esp. suddenly —*n.* 1. a sudden fear or panic 2. a state of widespread fear or panic [a war *scare*]

scarecrow *n.* 1. a figure of a man made with sticks, old clothes, etc., put in a field to frighten birds away from crops 2. a person who is dressed like a scarecrow

scarf[1] (skärf) *n., pl.* scarfs, scarves [< ONormFr. *escarpe*, a purse hung from the neck] a long or broad piece of cloth worn about the neck, head, etc., as for warmth

scarf[2] *n., pl.* scarfs [prob. < Scand.] a joint made by notching, grooving, etc. the ends of two pieces and fastening them into one continuous piece: also **scarf joint** —*vt.* to join by a scarf

scarfpin *n.* an ornamental pin worn in a scarf

scarify (skäer′ə fī′) *vt.* -fied′, -fy′ing [< Gr. *skariphos*, a stylus] 1. to make a series of small cuts in (the skin), as in surgery 2. to criticize 3. *Agric.* to loosen (the topsoil) —**scar′ifica′tion** *n.* —**scar′ifi′er** *n.*

scarlatina (skär′lə tē′nə) *n.* [< ML. *(febris) scarlatina*] popular term for a mild form of SCARLET FEVER

scarlet (skär′lət) *n.* [< ML. *scarlatum*, scarlet cloth] 1. very bright red with a slightly orange tinge 2. clothing of this colour —*adj.* 1. of this colour 2. sinful [*scarlet* woman]

scarlet fever an acute contagious disease in which one has a sore throat, fever, and a scarlet rash

scarp (skärp) *n.* [< It. *scarpa*] 1. a steep slope; specif., an escarpment 2. the outer slope of a rampart —*vt.* to make into a steep slope

scarper (skär′pər) *vi.* [< It. *scappare*, escape] [Slang] to run away or depart; decamp

scarves (skärvz) *n.* alt. pl. of SCARF[1]

scary (skäər′ē) *adj.* -ier, -iest [Colloq.] 1. causing fear 2. easily frightened —**scar′iness** *n.*

scat[1] (skat) *vi.* scat′ted, scat′ting [< ?] [Colloq.] to go away: usually in the imperative

scat[2] *adj.* [< ?] *Jazz* of singing in which meaningless syllables are used —*n.* such singing —*vi.* scat′ted, scat′ting to engage in scat singing

scathe (skāth) *vt.* scathed, scath′ing [< ON. *skathi*, harm] 1. [Archaic] to injure 2. to denounce fiercely —*n.* [Archaic] injury or harm —**scathe′less** *adj.*

scathing *adj.* searing; harsh or caustic

scatology (skə tol′ə jē) *n.* [< Gr. *skōr*, excrement + -LOGY] obsession with the obscene, esp. with excrement, in literature —**scatological** (skat′ə loj′i k′l) *adj.*

scatter (skat′ər) *vt.* [ME. *skateren*] 1. to throw here and there; sprinkle 2. to separate and drive in many directions; disperse —*vi.* to separate and go off in several directions —*n.* 1. a scattering 2. what is scattered about

scatterbrain *n.* a person not able to think in a serious way —**scat′ter-brained′** *adj.*

scatty (skat′ē) *adj.* -tier, -tiest [< ?] [Colloq.] foolish or crazy

scavenge (skav′inj) *vt.* -enged, -enging [< ff.] 1. to salvage (usable goods) from rubbish or discarded material 2. to clean (streets, etc.) —*vi.* 1. to act as a scavenger 2. to look for food

scavenger *n.* [ult. < OFrank. *scouwon*, peer at] 1. one who gathers things that have been discarded by others 2. any animal that eats refuse and decaying matter

Sc.D. [L. *Scientiae Doctor*] Doctor of Science

S.C.E. Scottish Certificate of Education

scenario (si när′ē ō′) *n., pl.* -ios′ [It. < L. *scaena*, scene] 1. a synopsis of a play, opera, etc. 2. the script of a film 3. any sequence of events, esp. an imagined one

scene (sēn) *n.* [< Gr. *skēnē*, stage] 1.

the place in which any event occurs **2.** the setting of the action of a play, story, etc. **3.** a division of a play, usually part of an act **4.** a part of a play, story, etc. *[a deathbed scene]* **5.** *same as* SCENERY (sense 1) **6.** a view of people or places **7.** a public display of strong feeling, esp. one that embarrasses the onlookers **8.** an episode or event, real or imaginary **9.** [Colloq.] the environment for a specified activity *[the poetry scene]* **10.** [Colloq.] interest; way of life *[not my scene]* —**behind the scenes 1.** backstage **2.** in private —**set the scene** to describe the background of an event, etc.

scenery *n.*, *pl.* **-neries 1.** painted screens, backdrops, etc., used on the stage to represent places **2.** the features of a landscape

scene shifter the person responsible for moving scenery between scenes of a theatrical performance —**scene shifting**

scenic (sē'nik) *adj.* **1.** having beautiful scenery **2.** of the stage and its scenery, lighting, etc. —**sce'nically** *adv.*

scent (sent) *n.* [< L. *sentire*, to feel] **1.** a smell; odour **2.** the sense of smell **3.** a perfume **4.** an odour left by an animal, by which it is tracked **5.** any clue by which something is followed —*vt.* **1.** to smell **2.** to suspect **3.** to fill with an odour; perfume —**put (or throw) off the scent** to mislead wilfully —**scent'ed** *adj.*

sceptic (skep'tik) *n.* [< Gr. *skeptikos*, inquiring] **1.** one who habitually doubts or questions matters generally accepted **2.** one who doubts religious doctrines

sceptical *adj.* **1.** of or characteristic of sceptics or scepticism **2.** not easily convinced; doubting

scepticism *n.* **1.** doubt, esp. about religious doctrines **2.** the philosophical doctrine that the truth of all knowledge must always be in question

sceptre (sep'tər) *n.* [< Gr. *skēptron*, staff] a staff held by rulers as a symbol of sovereignty U.S. sp. **scepter**

schedule (shed'yōōl) *n.* [< L. *scheda*, a leaf of paper] **1.** a timed plan for a project **2.** a list of times of recurring events, etc.; timetable **3.** a list of details —*vt.* **-uled, -uling 1.** to place in a schedule **2.** to make a schedule of **3.** to plan for a certain time

schema (skē'mə) *n.*, *pl.* **-mata** [Gr.: see SCHEME] an outline, diagram, scheme, plan, etc.

schematic (skə mat'ik) *adj.* of, or having the nature of, a scheme, plan, etc. —*n.* a diagram, as of the wiring of an electric circuit —**schemat'ically** *adv.*

schematize (skē'mə tīz') *vi.*, *vt.* **-tized', -tiz'ing** [< Gr. *schēmatizein*, to form] to arrange according to a scheme

scheme (skēm) *n.* [< Gr. *schēma*, a form] **1.** a systematic programme for attaining some object **2.** an orderly combination of things on a definite plan *[a colour scheme]* **3.** a diagram; outline **4.** a plot

—*vt.*, *vi.* **schemed, schem'ing** to contrive; plot —**schem'er** *n.*

scheming *adj.* given to forming schemes or plots; crafty, underhand, etc. —**schem'ingly** *adv.*

scherzo (skāər'tsō) *n.*, *pl.* **-zos, -zi** (-tsē) [It.] a lively, playful movement, as of a sonata, in 3/4 time

schism (siz''m) *n.* [< Gr. *schizein*, to cleave] a split in an organized group, esp. a church, because of difference of doctrine, etc. —**schismat'ic** (-mat'ik) *adj.*

schist (shist) *n.* [< Gr. *schizein*, to cleave] a metamorphic rock that splits easily into thin leaves

schizo (skit'sō) *n.* [Colloq.] schizophrenic

schizo- [< Gr. *schizein*, to cleave] a combining form meaning split, division

schizoid (skit'soid) *adj.* of, like, or having schizophrenia —*n.* a schizoid person

schizophrenia (skit'sō frē'nē ə) *n.* [< SCHIZO- + Gr. *phrēn*, the mind] a major mental disorder characterized by bizarre behaviour, delusions, hallucinations, etc. —**schiz'ophren'ic** (-fren'ik) *adj.*, *n.*

schmaltz (shmalts) *n.* [< G. *schmalz*, melted fat] [Slang] banal sentimentalism —**schmaltz'y** *adj.*

schnapps (shnaps) *n.*, *pl.* **schnapps** [G., a dram] any strong spirit, esp. Hollands gin: also sp. **schnaps**

schnorkle (shnôr'k'l) *n.* *same as* SNORKEL

scholar (skol'ər) *n.* [< L. *schola*, a SCHOOL¹] **1.** a learned person **2.** a student given a scholarship **3.** any student or pupil —**schol'arly** *adj.*

scholarship *n.* **1.** the systematized knowledge of a scholar **2.** a gift of money or other aid to help a student

scholastic (skə las'tik) *adj.* [< SCHOOL¹] **1.** of schools, colleges, students, teachers, etc.; academic **2.** [also S-] of or relating to scholasticism —*n.* [also S-] *same as* SCHOOLMAN —**scholas'tically** *adv.*

scholasticism *n.* [often S-] a medieval system of Christian thought based on Aristotelian logic

school¹ (skōōl) *n.* [< Gr. *scholē*, leisure, school] **1.** a place or institution for teaching and learning, as a grammar school **2.** *a)* the building or buildings of a school *b)* all of its students and teachers *c)* a regular session of teaching at a school **3.** the process of being educated at a school **4.** any situation or experience through which one gains knowledge, training, etc. **5.** a division of an institution of learning, esp. of a university **6.** a group following the same beliefs, methods, etc. —*vt.* **1.** to teach; instruct **2.** to discipline or control —*adj.* of a school or schools —**at school** to be attending school

school² *n.* [Du., a crowd] a large number of fish, whales, etc. swimming or feeding together

school age the years during which attendance at school is required or customary —**school'-age'** *adj.*

schoolbag *n.* a bag, of vinyl, cloth, leather, etc., in which a pupil at a school carries his books, pens, etc.

schoolboy *n.* a boy attending school

schoolchild *n.* a child attending school

schoolgirl *n.* a girl attending school

schoolhouse *n.* a building, often attached to a school, where a schoolmaster or janitor lives

schooling *n.* 1. training or education; esp., formal instruction at school 2. cost of attending school

school leaver a pupil who has just left school, either at the minimum age possible or at any later stage

schoolman *n.* [*often* S-] any of the medieval teachers of scholasticism

schoolmarm *n.* [Chiefly U.S. Colloq] a woman schoolteacher: also **school'-ma'am'**

schoolmaster *n.* a man who teaches in a school —**school'mis'tress** *n.fem.*

schoolroom *n.* a classroom either in a school or private house

schoolteacher *n.* a person whose work is teaching in a school

school year the part of a year when schools are in session, usually from September to June

schooner (skōō'nər) *n.* [< ?] 1. a ship with two or more masts, rigged fore and aft 2. a large sherry glass

schottische (shot ēsh') *n.* [< G. (*der*) *schottische* (*Tanz*), (the) Scottish (dance)] 1. a round dance similar to the polka 2. music for this

schwa (shwä) *n.* [G. < Heb. *sh'wā*] 1. the neutral vowel sound of most unstressed syllables in English; sound of *a* in *ago* 2. the symbol (ə) for this

sci. 1. science 2. scientific

sciatic (sī at'ik) *adj.* [< Gr. *ischion*, hip] of, near, or affecting the hip or its nerves

sciatica (sī at'i kə) *n.* neuritis of the long nerve (**sciatic nerve**) passing down the back of the thigh

science (sī'əns) *n.* [< L. *scire*, know] 1. systematized knowledge derived from observation, study, and experimentation 2. a branch of knowledge, esp. one that systematizes facts, principles, and methods [the *science* of mathematics] 3. the systematized knowledge of nature: see NATURAL SCIENCE 4. skill; technique

science fiction highly imaginative fiction typically involving real or imagined scientific phenomena

scientific (sī'ən tif'ik) *adj.* 1. of, dealing with, or used in science 2. based on, or using, the principles and methods of science; systematic and exact 3. done according to methods gained by systematic training [*scientific* boxing] —**sci'entif'i-cally** *adv.*

scientist (sī'ən tist) *n.* a specialist in science

sci-fi (sī'fī') *adj., n. same as* SCIENCE FICTION

scilicet (sīl'i set') *adv.* [< L. *scire licet*, it is permitted to know] namely; that is to say

scimitar, scimiter (sim'ə tər) *n.* [< ?] a short, curved sword used chiefly by Turks, Arabs, etc.

scintilla (sin til'ə) *n.* [L.] 1. a spark 2. the least trace

scintillate (sin'til āt') *vi.* -lat'ed, -lat'ing [< L. *scintilla*, a spark] 1. to flash; sparkle 2. to twinkle, as a star 3. to sparkle with wit —**scin'tilla'tion** *n.*

scintillation counter an instrument for measuring the scintillations induced by ionizing radiation in a phosphor

sciolism (sī'ə liz'm) *n.* [< L. *scire*, know] the practice of giving opinions based on only a superficial knowledge —**sci'olist** *n.* —**sci'olis'tic** *adj.*

scion (sī'ən) *n.* [OFr. *cion*] 1. a descendant 2. a shoot of a plant, esp. one for grafting

scissors (siz'ərz) *n.pl.* [< LL. *cisorium*, cutting tool] a cutting instrument with two opposing blades pivoted together so that they work against each other: also **pair of scissors**

sclera (sklēər'ə) *n.* [< Gr. *sklēros*, hard] the tough, white membrane covering all of the eyeball except the cornea

sclerosis (sklē ə rō'sis) *n., pl.* -**ses** (-sēz) [< Gr. *sklēros*, hard] an abnormal hardening of body tissues, esp. of the nervous system or the walls of arteries —**sclerot'ic** (-rot'ik) *adj.*

scoff¹ (skof) *vt., vi.* [prob. < Scand.] to mock or jeer (*at*) —*n.* an expression of scorn or derision; jeer —**scoff'er** *n.*

scoff² *vt., vi.* [< ?] [Slang] to eat or devour —*n.* [Slang] food

scold (skōld) *vt.* [< ON. *skald*, poet] to find fault; rebuke —*vi.* 1. to find fault angrily 2. to use abusive language habitually —*n.* a person, esp. a woman, who habitually uses abusive language —**scold'er** *n.* —**scold'ing** *adj., n.*

scollop (skol'əp) *n., vt.* var. of SCALLOP

sconce¹ (skons) *n.* [ult. < L. *abscondere*, to hide] a bracket attached to a wall for holding a candle, etc.

sconce² *n.* [Du. *schans*, wickerwork] a small fort, bulwark, etc.

scone (skon, skōn) *n.* [Scot.] a sweet or savoury cake baked on a griddle

scoop (skōōp) *n.* [< MDu. *schope*, bailing vessel & *schoppe*, a shovel] 1. any of various small, shovellike utensils for taking up flour, ice cream, etc. 2. the deep shovel of a dredge or steam shovel 3. the act of taking up with a scoop 4. the amount taken up at one time by a scoop 5. a hollowed-out place 6. [Colloq.] a large profit made by speculation 7. [Colloq.] the publication of a news item before a rival newspaper —*vt.* 1. to take up or out as with a scoop 2. to hollow (*out*) 3. to gather (*in* or *up*) as if with a scoop 4. [Colloq.] to effect a scoop (*n.* 7) in competition with

scoot (skōōt) *vi., vt.* [< ?] [Colloq.] to go or move quickly

scooter *n.* 1. a child's toy for riding on, consisting of a footboard with wheels, and a raised handlebar for steering: it is moved by pushing one foot against the ground 2. a similar vehicle with a seat, propelled by a motor: in full, **motor scooter**

scope (skōp) *n.* [< Gr. *skopos,* watcher] **1.** room or opportunity for action or thought **2.** the extent of the mind's grasp **3.** the range or extent of action, content, etc., or of an activity, concept, etc. **4.** *short for* TELESCOPE, MICROSCOPE, etc.

-scope (skōp) [< Gr. *skopein,* see] *a combining form meaning* an instrument, etc. for seeing or observing

scopolamine (skō pol′ə mēn′) *n.* [< G. A. *Scopoli*] an alkaloid used in medicine as a sedative, hypnotic, etc.

scorbutic (skôr byōōt′ik) *adj.* [< ML. *scorbutus,* scurvy] of, like, or having scurvy: also **scorbu′tical**

scorch (skôrch) *vt.* [< ?] **1.** *a)* to burn slightly or on the surface *b)* to parch or shrivel by heat **2.** to criticize very sharply **3.** to burn and destroy everything in (an area) before yielding it to the enemy [a *scorched*-earth policy] —*vi.* **1.** to become scorched **2.** [Slang] to drive very fast —*n.* a superficial burn

scorcher *n.* [Colloq.] a very hot day

score (skôr) *n.* [< ON. *skor*] **1.** the number of points made in a game, contest, etc. **2.** [Colloq.] the way things are: chiefly in **know the score 3.** *a)* twenty people or things *b)* [*pl.*] very many **4.** *Music a)* a written copy of a composition, showing all parts *b)* the music for a stage production, film, etc. **5.** a scratch, mark, incision, etc. **6.** an amount due; debt **7.** a reason or ground **8.** a grievance one seeks to settle **9.** [Colloq.] a successful action, remark, etc. —*vt.* **scored, scor′ing 1.** *a)* to make (runs, goals, etc.) in a game *b)* to record the score of **2.** to mark or mark out with notches, lines, gashes, etc. **3.** *Music* to arrange in a score **4.** to gain [to *score* a success] —*vi.* **1.** to make points, as in a game **2.** to keep score in a game —**on that score** on that matter, etc. —**score out** to cross out —**score points off** to gain the advantage over: also **score off** —**scor′er** *n.*

scoreboard *n.* a large board for posting the score and other details of a game, as at a cricket ground

score card 1. a card for recording the score of a game, etc. **2.** a card printed with the names, positions, etc. of the players of competing teams

scoria (skôr′ē ə) *n., pl.* **-riae′** (-ē′) [< Gr. *skōr,* dung] **1.** the refuse left after metal has been smelted from ore **2.** cinderlike lava

scorn (skôrn) *n.* [< OFr. *escharnir,* to scorn] **1.** great contempt, often with some indignation **2.** expression of this feeling —*vt.* **1.** to regard with scorn; treat with contempt **2.** to refuse or reject as wrong or disgraceful —**scorn′ful** *adj.*

Scorpio (skôr′pē ō′) [L.] **1.** a S constellation **2.** the eighth sign of the zodiac

SCORPION
(to 25 cm long)

scorpion (skôr′pē ən) *n.* [< Gr. *skorpios*] an arachnid found in warm regions, with a long tail ending in a curved, poisonous sting —[S-] *same as* SCORPIO

Scot (skot) *n.* a native or inhabitant of Scotland

scot (skot) *n.* [ON. *skot,* tribute] money assessed or paid; tax

Scot. 1. Scotch **2.** Scotland **3.** Scottish

Scotch (skoch) *adj.* of Scotland, its people, their language, etc.: cf. SCOTTISH —*n. same as:* **1.** SCOTTISH **2.** SCOTCH WHISKY

scotch (skoch) *vt.* [< ?] **1.** to put an end to; stifle **2.** to wound without killing; maim

Scotch broth a broth of mutton and vegetables, thickened with barley

Scotch egg a hard-boiled egg enclosed in sausage meat

Scotch mist a thick, wetting haze

Scotch pine a hardy Eurasian pine, with yellow wood

Scotch whisky whisky distilled in Scotland from malted barley

scot-free (skot′frē′) *adj.* unharmed or unpunished

Scotland Yard 1. the headquarters of the London metropolitan police **2.** its Criminal Investigation Department

Scots (skots) *adj., n. same as* SCOTTISH

Scotsman (skots′mən) *n.* a native or inhabitant of Scotland, esp. a man —**Scots′ wom′an** *n.fem.*

Scottie, Scotty (skot′ē) *n., pl.* **-ties** *colloq.* name for SCOTTISH TERRIER

Scottish (skot′ish) *adj.* of Scotland, its people, etc. *Scottish* is preferred in formal usage, but with some words, *Scotch* is used (e.g., whisky), with others, *Scots* (e.g., law)

Scottish Certificate of Education the Scottish equivalent of the GENERAL CERTIFICATE OF EDUCATION

Scottish terrier a terrier with short legs, wiry hair, and pointed ears

scoundrel (skoun′drəl) *n.* [< ?] a mean, wicked person; villain —**scoun′drelly** *adj.*

scour[1] (skouər) *vt.* [< L. *ex-,* intens. + *curare,* to take care of] **1.** to clean by vigorous rubbing, as with abrasives **2.** to wash or clear as by a swift current of water; flush **3.** to clear of (something undesirable) —*n.* **1.** the act of scouring **2.** the place scoured, esp. by running water —**scour′er** *n.*

scour[2] *vt.* [< ?] to pass over quickly, or range over, as in search or pursuit —*vi.* to run about, as in search or pursuit —**scour′er** *n.*

scourge (skurj) *n.* [< L. *ex-,* off + *corrigia,*

a whip] 1. a whip 2. any means of severe punishment or any cause of great suffering *[the scourge of war]* —*vt.* **scourged, scourg'ing** 1. to whip 2. to punish severely —**scourg'er** *n.*

scouse (skaus) *n.* [< (LOB)SCOUSE] [sometimes S-] [Colloq.] 1. an inhabitant of Liverpool 2. the dialect of Liverpool —*adj.* [Colloq.] of or from Liverpool —**scous'er** *n.*

scout[1] (skaut) *n.* [< L. *auscultare*, listen] 1. a soldier, etc. sent to spy out the enemy's strength, etc. 2. a person sent out to search out new talent, etc. 3. a member of the Scouts, a worldwide boys' organization 4. the act of reconnoitring 5. [Colloq.] a fellow; person —*vt.* 1. to follow closely so as to spy upon 2. to look for; watch 3. to find by looking around (often with *out*, *up*) —*vi.* 1. to reconnoitre 2. to go in search of something —**scout'ing** *n.*

scout[2] *vt.* [? < ON. *skuti*, a taunt] to reject as absurd

scouter *n.* one of the adult leaders of a troop of Boy Scouts

scow (skau) *n.* [Du. *schouw*] a large, flat-bottomed boat used for carrying coal, sand, etc.

scowl (skaul) *vi.* [prob. < Scand.] 1. to look angry, sullen, etc. 2. to have a threatening look —*n.* the act of scowling; angry frown

scrabble (skrab''l) *vi.* **-bled, -bling** [< Du. *schrabben*, to scrape] 1. to scratch, scrape, etc. as though looking for something 2. to struggle 3. to scribble —*n.* a scrabbling; scramble, scribble, etc. —[**S-**] *Trademark* a word game played with lettered tiles —**scrab'bler** *n.*

scrag (skrag) *n.* [prob. < ON.] 1. a thin, scrawny person or animal 2. the neck of mutton, etc.: also **scrag end** —*vt.* **scragged, scrag'ging** [Slang] to choke or wring the neck of

scraggly *adj.* **-glier, -gliest** [see SCRAG] sparse, scrubby, ragged, or the like —**scrag'gliness** *n.*

scraggy *adj.* **-gier, -giest** [< SCRAG] lean; bony; skinny —**scrag'gily** *adv.*

scram (skram) *vi.* **scrammed, scram'ming** [< ff.] [Slang] to leave or get out, esp. in a hurry

scramble (skram'b'l) *vi.* **-bled, -bling** [< ?] 1. to climb, crawl, or clamber hurriedly 2. to struggle for something, esp. something highly prized 3. to get aircraft into the air quickly —*vt.* 1. *a)* to throw together haphazardly; jumble *b) Electronics* to modify (transmitted signals) so as to make unintelligible without special receiving equipment 2. to cook (eggs) while stirring the mixed whites and yolks —*n.* 1. a hard climb or advance, as over difficult ground 2. a disorderly struggle, as for something prized 3. a motorcycle race over rough country

scrambler *n. Electronics* a device for scrambling speech, etc. during transmission and unscrambling it in a receiving unit

scrap[1] (skrap) *n.* [< ON. *skrap*] 1. a small piece; fragment 2. *a)* discarded metal suitable only for reprocessing *b)* discarded articles of paper, etc. 3. [*pl.*] bits of leftover food —*adj.* in the form of pieces, leftovers, etc. —*vt.* **scrapped, scrap'ping** 1. to make into scrap 2. to discard

scrap[2] *n.* [< ?] [Colloq.] a fight or quarrel —*vi.* **scrapped, scrap'ping** [Colloq.] to fight or quarrel

scrapbook *n.* a book of blank pages for mounting newspaper cuttings, pictures, etc.

scrape (skrāp) *vt.* **scraped, scrap'ing** [< ON. *skrapa*] 1. to make smooth or clean by rubbing .with a tool or abrasive 2. to remove by rubbing (with *off*, *out*, etc.) 3. to scratch or abrade 4. to rub with a harsh, grating sound 5. to gather slowly and with difficulty —*vi.* 1. to rub against something harshly; grate 2. to give out a harsh, grating noise 3. to gather goods or money slowly and with difficulty 4. to manage to get by (with *through*, *along*, *by*) 5. to draw the foot back along the ground in bowing —*n.* 1. a scraping 2. a scraped place 3. a harsh, grating sound 4. a predicament 5. a fight —**scrape the bottom of the barrel** to use the last of one's resources —**scrap'er** *n.*

scrap merchant a dealer in scrap, esp. scrap metal

scrap metal discarded or waste pieces of iron, etc.

scrappy (skrap'ē) *adj.* **-pier, -piest** [< SCRAP[1]] 1. made of scraps 2. disconnected —**scrap'pily** *adv.*

scratch (skrach) *vt.* [< ?] 1. to mark or cut the surface of slightly with something sharp 2. to tear or dig with the nails or claws 3. to scrape lightly to relieve itching 4. to scrape with a grating noise 5. to write hurriedly 6. to strike out (writing, etc.) 7. to scrape (*together* or *up*) 8. [U.S.] *Politics* to strike out the name of (a candidate) on (a ballot) 9. *Sports* to withdraw (an entry) from a contest —*vi.* 1. to use nails in digging or wounding 2. to scrape the skin lightly to relieve itching 3. to make a harsh, scraping noise 4. to withdraw from a race or contest —*n.* 1. the act of scratching 2. a mark, tear, etc. made by scratching 3. a scraping sound 4. the starting line of a race 5. *Sports* the starting point or time of a contestant who receives no handicap —*adj.* 1. [Chiefly U.S.] used for hasty notes, etc. *[scratch paper]* 2. having no handicap in a contest 3. put together hastily, without selection —**from scratch** from nothing; without advantage —**scratch one's head** to be puzzled —**scratch the surface** to consider something superficially —**up to scratch** [Colloq.] up to a standard —**scratch'y** *adj.*

scrawl (skrôl) *vt., vi.* [< ?] to write hastily, carelessly, etc. —*n.* 1. sprawling handwriting, often hard to read 2. something scrawled —**scrawl'y** *adj.*

scrawny (skrô'nē) *adj.* **-nier, -niest** [prob. < Scand.] skinny and bony —**scraw'niness** *n.*

scream (skrēm) *vi.* [< ME. *screamen*]
1. to utter or make a shrill, piercing cry
2. to laugh loudly or hysterically 3. to
be obvious —*vt.* to utter with or as with
a scream —*n.* 1. a sharp, piercing cry
or sound 2. [Colloq.] a hilariously funny
person or thing

scree (skrē) *n.* [< ON. *skirtha*, a landslide]
a pile of rock debris at the foot of a
rock face

screech[1] (skrēch) *vi.* [ON. *skraekja*] to
utter or make a shrill, high-pitched sound
—*vt.* to utter with a screech —*n.* a
shrill, high-pitched sound —**screech′y** *adj.*

screech[2] *n.* [< ?] [Canad.] 1. a dark
rum 2. any cheap strong drink

screech owl *same as* BARN OWL

screed (skrēd) *n.* [< ME. *screde*, shred]
a long, tiresome speech or piece of writing

screen (skrēn) *n.* [< OFr. *escren*] 1.
a curtain or partition used to separate,
conceal, protect, etc. 2. anything that
shields, conceals, etc. [a smoke *screen*]
3. a coarse mesh of wire, etc. used as
a sieve. [Chiefly U.S.] a frame covered
with a wire mesh, used to keep insects
out 5. a) a white surface upon which
films, slides, etc. are projected b) the film
industry 6. the visual display surface of
a television or radar receiver —*vt.* 1.
to separate, conceal, or protect, as with
a screen 2. to provide with a screen
3. to sift through a screen 4. to interview
or test in order to separate according
to skills, personality, etc. 5. to project
(films, etc.) upon a screen —**screen off**
to hide from view by means of a screen

screenplay *n.* a story written, or adapted
from a novel, etc., for production as a film

screen printing *same as* SILK-SCREEN
printing

screw (skrōō) *n.* [< OFr. *escroue*, hole
in which a screw turns] 1. a) a piece
of metal for fastening things by being
turned: it is threaded evenly with an
advancing spiral ridge : **male** (or **external**)
screw b) the internal thread, as of a
nut, into which a male screw can be turned :
female (or **internal**) **screw** 2. any of various
devices operating or threaded like a screw
3. [Slang] a prison guard 4. [Colloq.]
a stingy person 5. [Colloq.] a salary
—*vt.* 1. to twist; turn 2. to fasten, tighten,
etc. as with a screw 3. to contort 4.
to make stronger (often with *up*) 5. to
force or compel, as if by using screws
6. [Slang] to cheat; swindle 7. [Vulg.
Slang] to have sexual intercourse with
—*vi.* 1. to go together or come apart
by being turned like a screw [a lid *screws*
on] 2. to be fitted for screws 3. to
twist; turn; wind —**have a screw loose**
[Colloq.] to be eccentric, odd, etc. —**put
the screws on** [Slang] to subject to force
or great pressure —**screw up** [Slang]
to make a mess of

screwball *n.* [U.S. Slang] an odd or
eccentric person

screwdriver *n.* a tool used for turning
screws, having an end that fits into the
slot in the head of a screw

screwed *adj.* 1. twisted 2. [Slang] drunk

screw top a bottle top that screws on
allowing a container to be resealed after
use —**screw′-top** *adj.*

screwy *adj.* **-ier, -iest** [Slang] 1. mentally
unbalanced 2. peculiar, odd, etc.

scribble (skrib′'l) *vt., vi.* **-bled, -bling** [<
L. *scribere*, write] 1. to write carelessly,
hastily, etc. 2. to make marks that are
meaningless or hard to read —*n.* scribbled
writing; scrawl —**scrib′bler** *n.*

scribe (skrīb) *n.* [< L. *scribere*, write]
1. a penman who copied manuscripts before
the invention of printing 2. a writer 3.
a person learned in the Jewish law —**scrib′-
al** *adj.*

scrim (skrim) *n.* [< ?] 1. a light, sheer,
loosely woven cotton or linen cloth, often
used for bookbinding

scrimmage (skrim′ij) *n.* [< SKIRMISH]
a tussle; confused struggle —*vi.* **-maged,
-maging** to take part in a scrimmage

scrimp (skrimp) *vt.* [prob. < Scand.]
1. to treat stingily; stint 2. to make too
small, short, etc. —*vi.* to be frugal
—**scrimp′er** *n.* —**scrimp′y** *adj.*

scrip (skrip) *n.* [< SCRIPT] a document
which acts as proof of ownership of a
holding in a joint stock company

script (skript) *n.* [< L. *scribere*, write]
1. handwriting 2. *Printing* a typeface that
looks like handwriting 3. an original
manuscript 4. a copy of the text of a
play, film, television show, etc. 5. the
written work of an examination candidate
—*vt.* to write the script for (a film, etc.)

scripture (skrip′chər) *n.* [see SCRIPT] 1.
[S-] [*often pl.*] a) the sacred writings
of the Jews, identical with the Old
Testament of the Christians b) the Christian
Bible 2. any sacred writing —**scrip′tural**
adj. —**scrip′turally** *adv.*

scriptwriter (skript′rīt′ər) *n.* a person
who writes scripts for films, television
shows, etc.

scrivener (skriv′nər) *n.* [< L. *scriba*,
a SCRIBE] [Archaic] 1. a scribe or clerk
2. a notary

scrofula (skrof′yōō lə) *n.* [< L. *scrofa*,
a sow] tuberculosis of the lymphatic
glands, esp. of the neck, in which the
glands become enlarged —**scrof′ulous** *adj.*

scroll (skrōl) *n.* [< ME. *scrowe*] 1. a
roll of parchment, paper, etc., usually with
writing on it 2. an ornamental design
in coiled or spiral form

Scrooge (skrōōj) *n.* [< *Scrooge*, in
Dickens' *A Christmas Carol*] [*also* s-]
a hard, miserly old man

scrotum (skrōt′əm) *n., pl.* **-ta, -tums** [L.]
in most male mammals, the pouch of skin
containing the testicles

scrounge (skraunj) *vt.* **scrounged,
scroung′ing** [< ?] [Colloq.] to get by
begging or sponging —*vi.* [Colloq.] to
search (*around*) for something —**scroung′-
er** *n.*

scrub[1] (skrub) *n.* [see SHRUB] 1. a) short,
stunted trees or bushes growing thickly
together b) land covered with such growth

2. any person, animal, or thing smaller than the usual, or considered inferior

scrub² vt. scrubbed, scrub'bing [prob. < Scand.] 1. to clean or wash by rubbing hard 2. to rub hard 3. to cleanse (a gas) of impurities 4. [Colloq.] to cancel or call off —vi. to clean something by rubbing, as with a brush —n. the act of scrubbing —scrub up the act of a surgeon in washing his hands and arms before an operation

scrubber¹ n. [Aust.] a bullock which has escaped into the scrub and becomes wild

scrubber² n. 1. a device for cleaning a gas 2. [Slang] a promiscuous girl

scrubby adj. -bier, -biest 1. stunted 2. covered with brushwood 3. paltry, shabby, etc.

scruff (skruf) n. [< ON. skrufr, tuft of hair] the back of the neck; nape

scruffy (skruf'ē) adj. -ier, -iest [< SCURF] shabby, unkempt, or untidy —scruff'ily adv. —scruff'iness n.

scrummage (skrum'ij) n. [< SKIRMISH] Rugby a play in which the two sets of forwards link together to support the hookers who try to pass the ball back to their teammates —vi. -maged, -maging to take part in a scrummage Also scrum

scrump (skrump) vi.,vt. [< SCRUMPY] to steal (apples) from an orchard or garden

scrumptious (skrump'shəs) adj. [? < SUMPTUOUS] [Colloq.] 1. very pleasing, attractive, etc. 2. delicious —scrump'tiously adv. —scrump'tiousness n.

scrumpy (skrum'pē) n. [< dial. scrump, withered apple] a rough cider, brewed mainly in the West Country

scrunch (skrunch) vt., vi. [see CRUNCH] to crush or crunch

scruple (skrōo'p'l) n. [< L. scrupulus, small sharp stone] 1. a doubt arising from difficulty in deciding what is right, proper, etc. 2. an apothecaries' weight equal to 1/3 dram (20 grains) —vt., vi. -pled, -pling to hesitate (at) from doubt

scrupulous (skrōo'pyoo ləs) adj. 1. conscientiously honest 2. demanding or using precision, care, and exactness —scru'pulos'ity (-los'e tē), scru'pulousness n.

scrutinize (skrōo'tin īz') vt. -nized', -niz'ing to look at carefully or examine closely —scru'tiniz'er n.

scrutiny (skrōo'tin ē) n., pl. -nies [< L. scrutari, to search into carefully] 1. a close examination 2. a lengthy, searching look

scuba (skōo'bə) n. [s(elf-)c(ontained) u(nderwater) b(reathing) a(pparatus)] a diver's apparatus with compressed-air tanks for breathing under water

scud (skud) vi. scud'ded, scud'ding [< ?] 1. to move swiftly 2. to be driven before the wind —n. 1. a scudding 2. spray, rain, or snow driven, by the wind

scuff (skuf) vt. [prob. < Scand.] 1. to wear a rough place on the surface of 2. to scrape (the ground, etc.) with the feet —vi. to walk without lifting the feet;

shuffle —n. 1. a scuffing 2. a worn or rough spot

scuffle (skuf''l) vi. -fled, -fling [< prec.] to struggle or fight in rough confusion —n. a rough, confused fight

scull (skul) n. [prob. < Scand.] 1. an oar worked from side to side to move a boat forward 2. either of a pair of light oars used by a single rower —vt., vi. to propel with a scull —scull'er n.

scullery (skul'ər ē) n., pl. -leries [< L. scutella, a tray] a room where pots and pans are cleaned, etc.

scullion (skul'yən) n. [< L. scopa, a broom] [Archaic] a servant doing the rough work in a kitchen

sculpt (skulpt) vt., vi. [see SCULPTURE] [Colloq.] to carve as a sculptor

sculptor (skulp'tər) n. [L. < sculpere, carve] an artist who carves figures of clay, stone, metal, wood, etc. —sculp'tress n. fem.

sculpture (skulp'chər) n. [< L. sculpere, carve] 1. the art of carving wood, chiselling stone, modelling clay, etc. into statues or figures 2. any work or works of sculpture —vt. -tured, -turing 1. to carve, chisel, etc. into statues, figures, etc. 2. to portray in sculpture —sculp'tural adj. —sculp'turally adv.

scum (skum) n. [< MDu. schum] 1. a thin layer of impurities which forms on the top of liquids 2. worthless parts or things 3. mean, despicable people —vi. scummed, scum'ming to form scum —scum'my adj.

scunner (skun'ər) vi. [< ?] to feel disgust —n. a strong dislike or disgust

scupper¹ (skup'ər) n. [< ?] an opening in a ship's side to allow water to run off the deck

scupper² vt. [< ?] [Colloq.] to annihilate or disable, as by a surprise attack

scurf (skurf) n. [< ON.] little, dry scales shed by the skin, as dandruff —scurf'y adj.

scurrilous (skur'ə ləs) adj. [< L. scurra, buffoon] using or containing coarse, vulgar, or abusive language —scurrility (sku ril'ə tē) n.

scurry (skur'ē) vi. -ried, -rying [< HURRY-SCURRY] to run hastily —n. a scurrying

scurvy (skur'vē) n. [< SCURF] a disease resulting from a deficiency of vitamin C in the body —adj. -vier, -viest mean; contemptible —scur'vily adv. —scur'viness n.

scut (skut) n. [< ?] a short tail, esp. of a rabbit or deer

scuttle¹ (skut''l) n. [< L. scutella, dish] a kind of bucket used for pouring coal on a fire: in full, coal scuttle

scuttle² vi. -tled, -tling [prob. < SCUD] to scurry, esp. away from trouble, etc. —n. a scurry

scuttle³ vt. -tled, -tling [< Sp. escotilla, a notch] 1. to make or open holes in the hull of (a ship) below the waterline; esp., to sink in this way 2. to abandon (a plan, undertaking, etc.) —n. a small, covered opening in the hull or deck of a ship

Scylla (sil′ə) a dangerous rock on the S Italian coast, opposite the whirlpool Charybdis —**between Scylla and Charybdis** facing danger or evil on either hand

SCYTHE

scythe (sīth) *n.* [OE. *sithe*] a tool with a long, single-edged blade on a bent wooden shaft, used in cutting grass, grain, etc. by hand —*vt.* **scythed, scyth′ing** to cut with a scythe

Se *Chem.* selenium

SE, S.E., s.e. 1. southeast 2. southeastern

sea (sē) *n.* [OE. *sæ*] 1. the ocean 2. a large body of salt water wholly or partly enclosed by land 3. a large body of fresh water 4. the condition of the ocean's surface 5. a large wave 6. a very great expanse —*adj.* of or for use at sea —**at sea** 1. on the open sea 2. uncertain; bewildered —**go to sea** to become a sailor —**put (out) to sea** to sail away from land

sea anchor a canvas-covered frame used to reduce drifting

sea anemone a sea polyp having a firm, gelatinous body topped with coloured, petallike tentacles

sea bird a bird living on or near the sea: also **sea fowl**

seaboard *n.* land or a coastal region bordering on the sea —*adj.* bordering on the sea

seaborne *adj.* carried on or by the sea

sea breeze a breeze blowing inland from the sea

seacoast *n.* land bordering on the sea

sea cow 1. any of several sea mammals, as the dugong or manatee 2. *earlier name for* WALRUS

sea dog 1. an experienced sailor 2. any of various seals

sea elephant a large seal that is hunted for oil

seafarer *n.* a traveller by sea; esp., a sailor

seafaring *adj.* of or engaged in life at sea

seafood *n.* food consisting of saltwater fish or shellfish

seagirt *adj.* surrounded by the sea

seagoing *adj.* 1. made for use on the open sea 2. *same as* SEAFARING

sea green a pale bluish green —**sea′-green′** *adj.*

sea gull *same as* GULL[1]

sea horse 1. a small fish with a head

like that of a horse 2. a mythical sea creature

sea kale a fleshy, coastal plant whose young shoots are eaten as a vegetable

seal[1] (sēl) *n.* [< L. *sigillum*] 1. a design, initials, etc. placed on a letter, document, etc. to prove it is authentic 2. a stamp or signet ring for making such an impression 3. a piece of paper, etc. bearing a design recognized as official 4. something that closes or fastens tightly or securely 5. anything that guarantees; pledge 6. a sign; token 7. an ornamental paper stamp [a Christmas *seal*] —*vt.* 1. to mark with a seal 2. to secure the contents of (a letter, etc.) by closing with a gummed flap, etc. 3. to confirm the truth of (a promise, etc.) by some action 4. to settle or determine finally [to *seal* one's fate] 5. *a)* to close, etc. with or as with a seal [to *seal* one's lips] *b)* to apply a nonpermeable coating to (a porous surface, as a wood) —**seal off** to close or isolate completely —**set one's seal to** to endorse —**the seals** symbols of office, esp. of public office —**seal′able** *adj.* —**seal′er** *n.*

seal[2] *n.* [OE. *seolh*] 1. a sea mammal with a sleek coat: it lives in cold waters and eats fish 2. the fur of a fur seal —*vi.* to hunt seals

sealant *n.* [< SEAL[1]] a substance, as a wax, plastic, silicone, etc., used for sealing

sea legs the ability to walk without loss of balance on board ship

sealery (sēl′ər ē) *n., pl.* **-eries** a place where seals are hunted

sea level the mean level of the sea between high and low tide

sealing wax a hard mixture of resin and turpentine used for sealing letters, dry cells, etc.

sea lion a large, eared seal of the N Pacific

Sea Lord a naval member of the Board of Admiralty

seal ring *same as* SIGNET RING

sealskin *n.* 1. the skin of the seal 2. a garment made of this —*adj.* made of sealskin

seam (sēm) *n.* [OE.] 1. the line formed by sewing together two pieces of material 2. any line marking joining edges, as of boards 3. a mark, line, etc. like this, as a scar 4. a stratum of ore, coal, etc. —*vt.* 1. to join so as to form a seam 2. to mark with a line, crack, etc. —**seam′less** *adj.*

seaman (sē′mən) *n.* 1. a sailor 2. a man ranking below a petty officer in the navy

seamanship *n.* skill in sailing, navigating, or working a ship

seam bowler *Cricket* a bowler who makes the ball swing during its flight and after it hits the ground

seamstress (sēm′stris) *n.* a woman who sews expertly or who makes her living by sewing

seamy (sē′mē) *adj.* **-ier, -iest** 1. unpleasant, or sordid 2. having or showing seams —**seam′iness** *n.*

séance (sā′äns) *n.* [< L. *sedere*, to sit]

a meeting at which spiritualists seek to communicate with the dead

sea pie 1. a sailor's pie made from salt meat, vegetables, etc. 2. the oystercatcher: also **sea pilot**

seaplane (sē′plān′) *n.* any aircraft designed to land on and take off from water

seaport *n.* 1. a port or harbour used by ocean ships 2. a town or city having such a port

sear (sēar) *vt.* [OE.] 1. to scorch the surface of 2. to wither 3. to make callous or unfeeling —*adj.* withered; sere —**sear′-ingly** *adv.*

search (surch) *vt.* [< LL. *circare,* to go about] 1. to go over and look through in order to find something 2. to examine (a person) for something concealed 3. to probe —*vi.* to make a search —*n.* a searching; examination —**in search of** trying to find —**search me** [Slang] I do not know —**search′er** *n.*

searching *adj.* keen; piercing —**search′-ingly** *adv.*

searchlight *n.* 1. an apparatus that projects a strong, far-reaching beam of light 2. such a beam

search warrant a legal document authorizing a police search, as for stolen goods, etc.

Sea Scout a member of the branch of the Boy Scouts that emphasizes seamanship

seashell (sē′shel′) *n.* the shell of any saltwater mollusc

seashore *n.* land along the sea; seacoast

seasickness *n.* nausea, dizziness, etc. caused by the rolling or pitching of a ship at sea —**sea′sick′** *adj.*

seaside *n.* seashore —*adj.* at or of the seaside

season (sē′z'n) *n.* [< L. *satio,* sowing time] 1. any of the four divisions into which the year is divided; spring, summer, autumn, or winter 2. the time of the year when something takes place, is popular, permitted, etc. 3. a period of time [the busy *season*] 4. the fitting or convenient time —*vt.* 1. to make (food) more tasty by adding salt, spices, etc. 2. to add zest to 3. to make more fit for use, as by aging 4. to accustom —*vi.* to become seasoned, as wood by drying —**in season** 1. available fresh for use as food 2. at the legal time for being hunted: said of game 3. in or at the proper time 4. early enough: also **in good season** 5. in heat: said of animals

seasonable *adj.* 1. suitable to the time of year 2. timely; opportune —**sea′sonably** *adv.*

seasonal *adj.* of or depending on a season or the seasons [*seasonal* work] —**sea′son-ally** *adv.*

seasoning *n.* any flavouring added to food

season ticket a ticket for a series of events or for transportation, for a given period of time

seat (sēt) *n.* [ON. *sæti*] 1. *a)* a place to sit *b)* a thing to sit on; chair, etc. 2. *a)* the buttocks *b)* the part of a chair, garment, etc. that one sits on 3. the

right to sit, as in a theatre 4. a surface on which another part rests 5. the centre [the *seat* of government] 6. a country house 7. a parliamentary constituency 8. the manner of sitting, as on horseback —*vt.* 1. to set in or on a seat 2. to have seats for [the car *seats* six] 3. to put in a certain place, position, etc. —*vi.* to stretch or sag as a result of wear: said of skirts, etc. —**be seated** 1. to sit down: also **take a seat** 2. to be located, settled, etc.

seat belt anchored straps buckled across the hips, to protect a seated passenger, as in a motor car or aircraft

SEATO (sē′tō) Southeast Asia Treaty Organization

sea urchin a small sea animal with a spiny shell

seaward (sē′wərd) *adj., adv.* towards the sea: also, for adv., **sea′wards** —*n.* a seaward direction or position

seaway *n.* 1. a route by sea 2. an inland waterway to the sea for ocean ships

seaweed *n.* any sea plant or plants; esp., any alga

seaworthy *adj.* fit to travel in on the open sea; sturdy: said of a ship —**sea′wor′-thiness** *n.*

sebaceous (si bā′shəs) *adj.* [< L. *sebum,* tallow] of, like, or secreting fat

Sec. Secretary

‡**sec** (sek) *adj.* [Fr.] dry; not sweet: said of wine

sec. 1. second(s) 2. secondary 3. secretary 4. section(s) 5. sector 6. security

secateurs (sek′ə turz′) *n.pl.* [< L. *secare,* to cut] shears used esp. for pruning

secede (si sēd′) *vi.* **-ced′ed, -ced′ing** [< L. *se-,* apart + *cedere,* to go] to withdraw formally from a larger body, as from a political union —**seced′er** *n.*

secession (si sesh′ən) *n.* a seceding —**seces′sionist** *n.*

seclude (si klōōd′) *vt.* **-clud′ed, -clud′ing** [< L. *se-,* apart + *claudere,* to shut] 1. to shut off from others; isolate 2. to make private or hidden

secluded *adj.* isolated; withdrawn

seclusion *n.* 1. retirement; isolation 2. a secluded spot —**seclu′sive** *adj.*

second[1] (sek′ənd) *adj.* [< L. *sequi,* to follow] 1. coming next after the first in order; 2nd 2. another of the same kind; additional [a *second* helping, a *second* Caesar] 3. next below the first in rank, value, merit, etc. —*n.* 1. the second person, thing, class, place, etc. 2. an article of merchandise that is not of the first quality 3. an aid or assistant, as to a duellist or boxer 4. [Colloq.] [*pl.*] a second helping of food —*vt.* 1. to assist 2. to indicate formal support of (a motion, etc.) so that it may be discussed or voted on —**second to none** unsurpassed —**sec′onder** *n.*

second[2] *n.* [< ML. *secunda*] 1. 1/60 of a minute of time 2. 1/60 of a minute of angular measurement 3. a very short time; instant 4. a specific point in time 5. the SI unit of time

second[3] (si kond′) *vt.* [see SECOND[1]] to

transfer (an official, etc.) from his regular work to a special assignment —**second'ment** *n.*

secondary (sek'ən dər ē) *adj.* 1. second, or below the first, in rank, importance, place, etc.; subordinate; minor 2. not primary; derivative 3. coming after the first in a series of processes, events, stages, etc. 4. *Zool.* designating or of the long flight feathers on the second joint of a bird's wing —*n., pl.* -**aries** a person or thing that is secondary, subordinate, etc. —**sec'ondarily** *adv.*

secondary accent (or **stress**) any accent, or stress, that is weaker than the full, or primary, accent

secondary education formal education that succeeds primary education and precedes a university education

secondary picketing a form of picketing intended to prevent a worker, in an industry, firm, etc. which is not on strike, from doing his own job

second best something of the quality next below the best —**sec'ond-best'** *adj.*

second chamber the higher body in a bicameral system of government

second-class *adj.* 1. of the class, rank, etc. next below the highest 2. designating a class of travel accommodation next below the best 3. designating a class of letters that is handled more slowly than first-class post 4. **inferior** —*adv.* as or by second-class post

Second Coming in the theology of some Christian sects, the expected return of Christ, at the Last Judgment

second cousin the child of one's parent's first cousin

secondhand *adj.* 1. used before; not new 2. not direct from the original source 3. of or dealing in merchandise that is not new —*adv.* not directly

second hand the hand (of a clock or watch) that indicates the seconds

second lieutenant *see* MILITARY RANKS, table

secondly *adv.* in the second place; second

second nature acquired habits, etc. fixed so deeply as to seem part of a person's nature

second person that form of a pronoun (as *you*) or verb (as *are*) which refers to the person(s) spoken to

second-rate *adj.* 1. inferior; mediocre 2. second in quality, rank, etc. —**sec'ond-rat'er** *n.*

second sight the supposed ability to see things not physically present, to foresee the future, etc.

second wind 1. the return of normal breathing following severe exertion 2. recovered capacity for continuing any effort

secrecy (sē'krə sē) *n., pl.* -**cies** 1. a being secret 2. the practice or habit of being secretive

secret (sē'krit) *adj.* [< L. *se-*, apart + *cernere*, sift] 1. kept from the knowledge of others 2. remote; secluded 3. secretive 4. concealed from sight or notice; hidden 5. acting in secret —*n.* 1. something known only to some and kept from the

knowledge of others 2. something not understood or explained 3. the true explanation [the *secret* of success] —**in secret** without the knowledge of others —**se'cretly** *adv.*

secret agent a person who engages in espionage, as for a government

secretaire (sek'rə tāer') *n.* same as ESCRITOIRE

secretariat (sek'rə tāar'ē ət) *n.* the office, or quarters of a secretary of high position in a government, etc.

secretary (sek'rə tər ē) *n., pl.* -**taries** [ML. *secretarius*, one entrusted with secrets] 1. *a)* one who keeps records, handles correspondence, etc. as in a business office *b)* an officer of a company, club, etc. having somewhat similar duties 2. an official in charge of a department of government —**sec'retar'ial** *adj.* —**sec'retaryship'** *n.*

secretary bird a large, greyish-blue and black African bird of prey

secretary-general *n., pl.* -**taries-gen'eral** the chief administrative officer of an organization

secretary of state 1. the head of any of several British government departments 2. [U.S.] the foreign minister

secrete (si krēt') *vt.* -**cret'ed**, -**cret'ing** [see SECRET] 1. to form and release (a specified secretion) as a gland, etc. does 2. to hide; conceal

secretion (si krē'shən) *n.* 1. *a)* the process by which a substance is formed from the blood or sap and then released *b)* such a substance 2. a hiding or concealing

secretive (sē'krə tiv) *adj.* [< SECRET] keeping one's affairs to oneself; reticent —**se'cretively** *adv.*

secretory (si krēt'ər ē) *adj.* of, or having the function of, secretion

secret police a police force that operates secretly, esp. in order to suppress opposition to the government

secret service a government service that carries on secret investigation

sect (sekt) *n.* [< L. *sequi*, to follow] 1. a religious denomination 2. a group of people having a common leadership, philosophy, etc.

sectarian (sek tāar'ē ən) *adj.* 1. of or devoted to some sect 2. narrow-minded —*n.* a member of any religious sect —**sectar'ianism** *n.*

section (sek'shən) *n.* [< L. *secare*, to cut] 1. a part cut off; slice 2. a division of a book, numbered paragraph of a law, etc. 3. any distinct or separate part 4. [U.S.] a division of public lands 5. a cutting; specif., an incision in surgery 6. a drawing, etc. of a thing as it would appear if cut straight through in a given plane 7. *Printing* a mark (§) used to indicate a section in a book, etc.: also **section mark** —*vt.* to divide into sections

sectional *adj.* 1. of or devoted to a given district 2. made up of sections —**sec'tionally** *adv.*

sector (sek'tər) *n.* [< L. *secare*, to cut] 1. a distinct part of a society, economy, etc. **2.** part of a circle bounded by any two radii and the included arc **3.** a mathematical instrument for measuring angles **4.** any of the districts into which an area is divided for military operations

secular (sek'yoo lər) *adj.* [< L. *saeculum*, an age] **1.** *a)* not related to church or religion; temporal; wordly *b)* of secularism **2.** not bound by a monastic vow **3.** occurring only once in an age or century —*n.* a member of the secular clergy —**sec'ularly** *adv.*

secularism *n.* **1.** a system of beliefs and practices that rejects any form of religious faith **2.** the belief that religion should be separated from the state, esp. from education —**sec'ularist** *n., adj.*

secularize *vt.* -**ized'**, -**iz'ing** to deprive of religious character, influence, etc. —**sec'ulariza'tion** *n.*

secure (si kyoor') *adj.* [< L. *se-*, free from + *cura*, care] **1.** free from fear, care, doubt, etc. **2.** free from danger **3.** firm; stable **4.** reliable; dependable —*vt.* -**cured'**, -**cur'ing** **1.** to make secure, or safe **2.** to guarantee, as with a pledge *[to secure a loan]* **3.** to make firm, fast, etc. **4.** to obtain; acquire *[to secure aid]* —**secur'able** *adj.* —**secure'ly** *adv.*

security *n., pl.* -**ties** **1.** a feeling free from fear, anxiety, danger, etc. **2.** protection or defence, as against attack, espionage, etc. **3.** something given as a pledge of repayment, etc. **4.** a stock certificate : *usually used in pl.*

Security Council the United Nations council responsible for maintaining international peace and security

security risk a person thought to be a threat to state security

SEDAN CHAIR

sedan chair (si dan') an enclosed chair for one person, carried on poles by two men : also **sedan**

sedate[1] (si dāt') *adj.* [< L. *sedare*, to settle] calm or composed; decorous —**sedate'ly** *adv.* —**sedate'ness** *n.*

sedate[2] *vt.* -**dat'ed**, -**dat'ing** [see prec.] to dose with a sedative

sedation (si dā'shən) *n. Med.* **1.** reduction of nervousness, esp. by sedatives **2.** the calm state produced by sedatives

sedative (sed'ə tiv) *adj.* [see SEDATE[1]] tending to soothe or quiet —*n.* a sedative medicine

sedentary (sed'ʼn tər ē) *adj.* [< L. *sedere*, sit] keeping one seated much of the time *[a sedentary job]* —**sed'entarily** *adv.*

sedge (sej) *n.* [OE. *secg*] a coarse, grasslike plant often found on wet ground or in water —**sedg'y** *adj.*

sedge warbler a common European songbird

sediment (sed'i mənt) *n.* [< L. *sedere*, sit] **1.** matter that settles to the bottom of a liquid **2.** *Geol.* matter deposited by water or wind —**sed'imen'tal** (-men'-t'l), **sed'imen'tary** *adj.* —**sed'imenta'tion** *n.*

sedition (si dish'ən) *n.* [< L. *sed-*, apart + *itio*, a going] a stirring up of rebellion against the government —**sedi'tious** *adj.*

seduce (si dyoos') *vt.* -**duced'**, -**duc'ing** [< L. *se-*, apart + *ducere*, to lead] **1.** to persuade to engage in sexual intercourse, esp. for the first time **2.** to tempt to wrongdoing; lead astray **3.** to entice —**seduc'er** *n.* —**seduc'ible** *adj.* —**seduc'tion** (-duk'shən) *n.*

seductive (si dukt'tiv)' *adj.* tending to seduce, or lead astray; enticing —**seduc'tively** *adv.* —**seduc'tiveness** *n.*

sedulous (sed'yoo ləs) *adj.* [< L. *se-*, apart + *dolus*, trickery] working hard and steadily; diligent and persistent —**sedulity** (si dyōol'ə tē) *n.*

sedum (sē'dəm) *n.* [L.] a plant found on rocks and walls, with fleshy stalks and leaves

see[1] (sē) *vt.* **saw**, **seen**, **see'ing** [OE. *seon*] **1.** *a)* to get knowledge of through the eyes; look at *b)* to picture mentally **2.** to grasp mentally; understand **3.** to find out; learn **4.** to know by experience **5.** to make sure *[see that he goes]* **6.** *a)* to escort *[to see someone home]* *b)* to date someone **7.** to meet **8.** to visit or consult **9.** to receive *[too ill to see anyone]* **10.** to view or attend *[see a show]* **11.** *Card Games* to meet (a bet) of (another) by staking an equal sum —*vi.* **1.** to have the power of sight **2.** to discern objects, colours, etc. by using the eyes **3.** to take a look **4.** to understand **5.** to reflect *[let's see, where is it?]* —*interj.* look! —**see about** **1.** to inquire into **2.** to attend to —**see after** to take care of —**see fit (to)** to think it is proper (to do something) —**see into** to look into —**see off** to go with and watch (another) leave —**see out** **1.** to go through with; finish **2.** to wait till the end of —**see through** **1.** to perceive the true meaning of **2.** to finish **3.** to help through a time of difficulty —**see to** to attend to

see[2] *n.* [< L. *sedes*, a seat] the official seat, or centre of authority, of a bishop

seed (sēd) *n.* [OE. *sæd*] **1.** the part of a plant that contains the embryo **2.** seeds used for sowing **3.** source; origin *[the seeds of revolt]* **4.** descendants; posterity **5.** seed-bearing condition *[in seed]* **6.** *same as* SPORE **7.** sperm or semen **8.** *Sports* a seeded player —*vt.* **1.** to plant with seeds **2.** to remove the seeds from **3.** to sprinkle particles of dry ice, silver iodide, etc. into (clouds), as in trying to produce rainfall **4.** *Sports* to distribute the names of contestants in (the draw for position in a tournament) so as to avoid matching the most skilled too early

—*vi.* 1. to produce seeds 2. to sow seeds —**go** (or **run**) **to seed** 1. to shed seeds after flowering 2. to become weak, useless, etc. —**seed′ed** *adj.* —**seed′er** *n.* —**seed′less** *adj.*

seedbed *n.* a bed of soil, usually covered with glass, in which seedlings are grown for transplanting

seedling *n.* 1. a plant grown from a seed, rather than from a cutting, etc. 2. any young plant

seed pearl a very small pearl, often imperfect

seedpod *n.* a carpel or pistil, enclosing ovules or seeds

seedsman (sēdz′mən) *n.* a dealer in seeds

seedtime *n.* the season for sowing seeds

seed vessel any dry, hollow fruit containing seed

seedy *adj.* **-ier, -iest** 1. shabby or run-down 2. full of seeds 3. gone to seed 4. feeling ill —**seed′ily** *adv.* —**seed′iness** *n.*

seeing (sē′iŋ) *n.* the power or use of sight —*adj.* having the sense of sight —*conj.* considering

seeing eye dog a guide dog for the blind

seek (sēk) *vt.* **sought, seek′ing** [OE. *secan*] 1. to try to find; look for 2. to try to get or find out, as by asking *[to seek* an answer *]* 3. to aim at 4. to try *[to seek* to please *]* —*vi.* to look for someone or something —**seek out** 1. to go to find 2. to look hard for —**seek′er** *n.*

seem (sēm) *vi.* [prob. < ON. *sæma,* to conform to] 1. *a)* to appear to be *b)* to appear *[he seems* to know *]* *c)* to have the impression *[I seem* to recall *]* 2. to appear to exist 3. to be apparently true

seeming *adj.* that seems real, true, etc.; apparent *[her seeming* anger *]* —**seem′ingly** *adv.*

seemly *adj.* **-lier, -liest** 1. suitable, proper, decorous, etc. 2. pleasing in appearance

seen (sēn) *pp.* of SEE¹

seep (sēp) *vi.* [OE. *sipian,* to soak] to leak; ooze —*n.* 1. a seeping 2. liquid that seeps —**seep′age** *n.*

seer (sē′ər *for 1;* sēər *for 2*) *n.* 1. a person who sees 2. a person with the supposed power to foretell the future

seersucker (sēar′suk′ər) *n.* [< Per. *shir u shakar,* milk and sugar] a light fabric of cotton, etc. woven with a crinkled surface

seesaw (sē′sô′) *n.* [< SAW¹] 1. a plank balanced at the middle, used by children, one end going up when the other comes down 2. any up-and-down or back-and-forth movement —*adj.* moving up and down or back and forth —*vt., vi.* to move on a seesaw or like a seesaw

seethe (sēth) *vi.* **seethed, seeth′ing** [OE. *sēothan*] 1. to boil 2. to be violently agitated —*vt.* to cook by boiling

segment (seg′mənt; *for v.* seg ment′) *n.* [< L. *secare,* to cut] 1. any of the parts into which something is separated; section 2. *Geom.* any part of a circle or sphere, cut off by a line or plane —*vt., vi.* to divide into segments —**seg′men′tally** *adv.* —**seg′menta′tion** *n.*

segregate (seg′rə gāt′) *vt.* **-gat′ed, -gat′-**

ing [< L. *se-,* apart + *grex,* a flock] to set apart from others; specif., to impose racial segregation on —*vi.* to become segregated

segregation (seg′rə gā′shən) *n.* the policy or practice of compelling racial groups to live apart, go to separate schools, etc. —**seg′rega′tionist** *n., adj.*

Seidlitz powder (sed′lits) [< Sedlčany (G. *Seidlitz*), Czechoslovakia] a laxative powder, dissolved in water and drunk while effervescing

seigneur (se nyur′) *n.* [see SENIOR] 1. a feudal lord 2. *Canad. Hist.* the landlord of an estate subdivided among peasants who held their plots by a form of feudal tenure

seigneury (sān′yər ē) *n., pl.* **-ries** the estate of a seigneur

seignior (sān′yər) *n.* [see SENIOR] a lord or noble

seigniorial, seignorial (sān yôr′ē əl) *adj.* of or relating to a seignior

seigniory (sān′yər ē) *n., pl.* **-gniories** 1. the estate of a seignior 2. the authority of a feudal lord

seine (sān) *n.* [< Gr. *sagēnē*] a large fishing net with floats along the top edge and weights along the bottom —*vt., vi.* **seined, sein′ing** to fish with a seine

seismic (sīz′mik) *adj.* [< Gr. *seiein,* to shake] of, relating to, or from an earthquake —**seis′mically** *adv.*

seismo- [see prec.] *a combining form meaning* earthquake

seismogram (sīz′mə gram′) *n.* the chart of an earthquake as recorded by a seismograph

seismograph (sīz′mə gräf′) *n.* an instrument that records the intensity and duration of earthquakes —**seismographer** (sīz mog′rə fər) *n.*

seismology (sīz mol′ə jē) *n.* [SEISMIC + -LOGY] a geophysical science dealing with earthquakes and related phenomena —**seismol′ogist** *n.*

seize (sēz) *vt.* **seized, seiz′ing** [< ML. *sacire*] 1. to take forcibly or quickly; grasp 2. to suddenly fill the mind of *[an idea seized* him *]* 3. to afflict suddenly *[seized* with tremors *]* 4. *a)* to take possession of by legal power; confiscate *b)* to capture and put into custody —**seized of** 1. to be in legal possession of : also **seised of** 2. to be aware of —**seize on** (or **upon**) to grasp or take eagerly —**seize up** to become jammed, esp. through overheating : usually said of a machine —**seiz′able** *adj.* —**seiz′er** *n.*

seizure (sē′zhər) *n.* 1. a seizing or being seized 2. a sudden attack, as of disease

seldom (sel′dəm) *adv.* [OE. *seldan*] not often; rarely

select (sə lekt′) *vt., vi.* [< L. *se-,* apart + *legere,* choose] to choose, as for excellence —*adj.* 1. chosen in preference to others 2. choice; excellent 3. careful in choosing; discriminating 4. exclusive —**selec′tor** *n.*

select committee a number of members

of parliament chosen to investigate a matter of public interest

selection (sə lek′shən) *n.* 1. a selecting or being selected 2. a thing, person, or group chosen 3. a range from which something may be selected 4. *Biol.* any process by which certain organisms survive rather than others

selective *adj.* 1. of or characterized by selection 2. having the power of selecting —**selec′tively** *adv.* —**selec′tiv′ity** *n.*

selenium (sə lē′nē əm) *n.* [< Gr. *selēnē*, the moon] a nonmetallic chemical element whose electrical conductivity varies with the intensity of light : symbol, Se

self (self) *n., pl.* **selves** [OE.] 1. the identity, character, or essential qualities of a person or thing 2. one's own person as apart from all others 3. one's own well-being or advantage —*pron.* [Colloq.] myself, himself, herself, or yourself —*adj.* 1. uniform throughout 2. of the same kind, colour, etc. as the rest

self- *a prefix used in hyphenated compounds, meaning :* 1. of oneself or itself 2. by oneself or itself 3. in oneself or itself 4. to, with, or for oneself or itself

self-abnegation (self′ab′nə gā′shən) *n.* lack of consideration for oneself; self-denial

self-absorption (self′əb sôrp′shən) *n.* absorption in one's own interests, affairs, etc. —**self′-absorbed′** *adj.*

self-abuse (self′ə byŏŏs′) *n.* a euphemism for masturbation

self-addressed (self′ə drest′) *adj.* addressed to oneself

self-aggrandizement (self′ə gran′-diz mənt) *n.* the act of making oneself powerful, wealthy, etc.

self-appointed (self′ə poin′tid) *adj.* acting as such on one's own, but not recognized as such by others

self-assertion (self′ə sur′shən) *n.* the act of demanding recognition for oneself or of insisting upon one's rights, claims, etc. —**self′-asser′tive** *adj.*

self-assurance (self′ə shooər′əns) *n.* confidence in oneself, one's own ability, etc. —**self′-assured′** *adj.*

self-centred (self′sen′tərd) *adj.* egocentric; selfish

self-complacent (self′kəm plā′s'nt) *adj.* self-satisfied, esp. in a smug way —**self′-compla′cency** *n.*

self-conceit (self′kən sēt′) *n.* too high an opinion of oneself; conceit —**self′-conceit′ed** *adj.*

self-confessed (self′kən fest′) *adj.* being such by one's own admission

self-confidence (self′kon′fə dəns) *n.* confidence in oneself, one's own abilities, etc. —**self′-con′fident** *adj.*

self-conscious (self′kon′shəs) *adj.* 1. embarrassed or. ill at ease 2. showing embarrassment —**self′-con′sciously** *adv.* —**self′-con′sciousness** *n.*

self-contained (self′kən tānd′) *adj.* 1. complete in itself; self-sufficient 2. (of a flat) having its own kitchen, bathroom, etc. 3. keeping one's affairs to oneself

4. showing self-control —**self′-contain′-ment** *n.*

self-contradiction (self′kon′trə dik′-shən) *n.* any statement or idea containing elements that contradict each other —**self′-con′tradic′tory** *adj.*

self-control (self′kən trōl′) *n.* control of oneself, or of one's own emotions, desires, actions, etc.

self-deception (self′di sep′shən) *n.* the deceiving of oneself as to one's true feelings, motives, etc.

self-defeating (self′di fēt′iŋ) *adj.* that unwittingly defeats its own purpose or interests

self-defence (self′di fens′) *n.* 1. defence of oneself, one's rights, etc. 2. boxing: usually in **manly art of self-defence**

self-denial (self′di nī′əl) *n.* denial or sacrifice of one's own desires or pleasures —**self′-deny′ing** *adj.*

self-destruction (self′di struk′shən) *n.* destruction of oneself or itself —**self′-de-struc′tive** *adj.*

self-determination (self′di tur′min ā′-shən) *n.* 1. determination according to one's own mind 2. the right of a people to decide upon its own form of government —**self′-deter′mined** *adj.*

self-discipline (self′dis′ə plin) *n.* the controlling of oneself, one's actions, etc. —**self′-dis′ciplined** *adj.*

self-educated (self′ed′jŏŏ kāt′id) *adj.* educated by oneself, with little or no formal teaching

self-effacement (self′i fās′mənt) *n.* modest, retiring behaviour —**self′-effac′-ing** *adj.*

self-employed (self′im ploid′) *adj.* working for oneself, with direct control over work, fees, etc.

self-esteem (self′ə stēm′) *n.* belief in oneself; self-respect

self-evident (self′ev′ə dənt) *adj.* evident without need of proof or explanation —**self′-ev′idently** *adv.*

self-examination (self′ig zam′ə nā′-shən) *n.* examination or analysis of oneself and one's conduct, motives, etc.

self-existent (self′ig zis′tənt) *adj.* existing or by itself without external cause —**self′-exist′ence** *n.*

self-explanatory (self′ik splan′ə tər ē) *adj.* explaining itself

self-expression (self′ik spresh′ən) *n.* expression of one's own personality or emotions, as in the arts

self-fulfilment (self′fəl fil′mənt) *n.* fulfilment of one's aspirations through one's own efforts

self-government (self′guv′ərn mənt) *n.* government of a group by its own members, as in electing representatives —**self′-gov′-erning** *adj.*

selfheal (self′hēl′) *n.* a plant supposed to have healing properties

self-help (self′help′) *n.* care or betterment of oneself by one's own efforts, as through study

self-hypnosis (self′hip nō′sis) *n.* a hypnotizing of oneself

self-important (self′im pôr′t'nt) *adj.* having an exaggerated opinion of one's own importance

self-imposed (self′im pōzd′) *adj.* imposed on oneself by oneself, as a duty

self-improvement (self′im prōōv′mənt) *n.* improvement of one's status, mind, etc. by one's own efforts

self-incrimination (self′in krim′ə nā′shən) *n.* incrimination of oneself by one's own statements

self-induced (self′in dyōōst′) *adj.* induced by oneself

self-indulgence (self′in dul′jəns) *n.* indulgence of one's own desires, impulses, etc. —**self′-indul′gent** *adj.*

self-inflicted (self′in flik′tid) *adj.* inflicted on oneself by oneself, as an injury

self-interest (self′in′trist) *n.* 1. one's own interest or advantage 2. an exaggerated regard for this

selfish (sel′fish) *adj.* too much concerned with one's own welfare or interests —**self′ishly** *adv.* —**self′ishness** *n.*

self-justification (self′jus′tə fi kā′shən) *n.* the explaining away of one's actions or motives

selfless (self′lis) *adj.* devoted to others' welfare or interests —**self′lessly** *adv.* —**self′lessness** *n.*

self-made *adj.* successful, rich, etc. through one's own efforts

self-opinionated (self′ə pin′yə nāt′id) *adj.* stubborn or conceited with regard to one's own opinions

self-pity (self′pit′ē) *n.* pity for oneself

self-portrait (self′pôr′trit) *n.* a painting, drawing, etc. of oneself, done by oneself

self-possession (self′pə zesh′ən) *n.* full control of one's feelings, actions, etc. —**self′possessed′** *adj.*

self-preservation (self′prez′ər vā′shən) *n.* instinctive preservation of oneself from danger, injury, or death

self-propelled (self′prə peld′) *adj.* propelled by its own motor or power: also **self′-propel′ling**

self-raising (self′rāz′iŋ) *adj.* rising by itself: said specif. of flour sold with a raising agent blended in

self-realization (self′rē′ə li zā′shən) *n.* fulfilment of oneself, one's capabilities, etc.

self-recording (self′ri kôr′diŋ) *adj.* recording its own operations automatically, as a seismograph

self-regard (self′ri gärd′) *n.* concern for oneself and one's own interests

self-regulating (self′reg′yə lāt′iŋ) *adj.* regulating oneself or itself automatically

self-reliance (self′ri lī′əns) *n.* reliance on oneself, one's abilities, etc. —**self′-reli′-ant** *adj.*

self-reproach (self′ri prōch′) *n.* blame of oneself; guilt feeling —**self′-reproach′-ful** *adj.*

self-respect (self′ri spekt′) *n.* proper respect for oneself and one's worth as a person —**self′-respect′ing** *adj.*

self-restraint (self′ri stränt′) *n.* self-control

self-revealing (self′ri vēl′iŋ) *adj.* revealing one's innermost thoughts, feelings, etc.

self-righteous (self′rī′chəs) *adj.* thinking oneself more righteous or moral than others —**self′-right′eousness** *n.*

self-sacrifice (self′sak′rə fis′) *n.* sacrifice of oneself or one's interests to benefit others —**self′-sac′rific′ing** *adj.*

selfsame (self′sām′) *adj.* identical; (the) very same

self-satisfied (self′sat′is fīd′) *adj.* excessively pleased with oneself or with what one has done —**self′-sat′isfac′tion** *n.*

self-satisfying *adj.* satisfying to oneself

self-sealing (self′sēl′iŋ) *adj.* 1. automatically sealing punctures, etc., as some tyres 2. sealable by pressure alone, as some envelopes

self-seeker (self′sē′kər) *n.* a person seeking only or mainly to further his own interests —**self′-seek′ing** *n., adj.*

self-service (self′sur′vis) *n.* the practice of serving oneself in a shop, cafeteria, etc. and then paying a cashier

self-serving (self′sur′viŋ) *adj.* serving one's own selfish interests

self-starter (self′stärt′ər) *n.* an electric motor used for automatically starting an internal-combustion engine

self-styled (self′stīld′) *adj.* so named by oneself

self-sufficient (self′sə fish′ənt) *adj.* able to get along without help; independent —**self′-suffi′ciency** *n.*

self-support (self′sə pôrt′) *n.* support of oneself or itself without aid or reinforcement —**self′-support′ing** *adj.*

self-sustaining (self′sə stān′iŋ) *adj.* supporting or able to support oneself or itself

self-taught (self′tôt′) *adj.* having taught oneself

selfward (self′wərd) *adv.* towards oneself: also **self′wards** —*adj.* directed towards oneself

self-willed (self′wild′) *adj.* stubborn about getting one's own way; wilful —**self′-will′** *n.*

self-winding *adj.* winding automatically, as certain wristwatches

sell (sel) *vt.* **sold, sell′ing** [OE. *sellan*, give] 1. to exchange (property, goods, etc.) for money 2. to offer for sale 3. to betray (a country, etc.), as for money 4. to promote the sale of [television *sells* many products] 5. [Colloq.] to establish confidence or belief in [to *sell* oneself to the public] —*vi.* 1. to sell something 2. to be a popular item on the market 3. to be sold (*for* or *at*) 4. [Colloq.] to be accepted, approved, etc. —*n.* [Slang] 1. a hoax 2. selling [hard *sell*] —**sell out** 1. to dispose of completely by selling 2. [Colloq.] to betray (someone, a cause, etc.) —**sell short** to disparage —**sell up** 1. to sell all of (the land or goods) of (a debtor) so as to satisfy his debts 2. to dispose of one's house, business, etc., on leaving —**sell′er** *n.*

selling race a horse race immediately after which the winner is auctioned and the losers may be claimed for prices previously set

Sellotape (sel'ō tāp) *Trademark* an adhesive tape, usually transparent —*vt.* [**s-**] to stick something with Sellotape

sellout (sel'out') *n.* [Colloq.] 1. a show, etc. for which all seats have been sold 2. a selling out, or betrayal

selvage, selvedge (sel'vij) *n.* [< SELF + EDGE] a specially woven edge to keep cloth from unravelling

selves (selvz) *n.*, *pl. of* SELF

Sem. 1. Seminary 2. Semitic

semantic (sə man'tik) *adj.* [< Gr. *sēma*, a sign] of meaning, esp. in language —**seman'tically** *adv.*

semantics *n.pl.* [with sing. v.] the branch of linguistics dealing with the meanings given to words and the changes that occur to these meanings

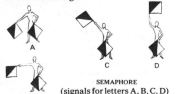

SEMAPHORE
(signals for letters A, B, C, D)

semaphore (sem'ə fôr') *n.* [< Gr. *sēma*, a sign + *pherein*, to bear] any device or system for signalling as by lights, flags, etc. —*vt.*, *vi.* **-phored'**, **-phor'ing** to signal by semaphore

semblance (sem'blans) *n.* [< L. *similis*, like] 1. outward look or show 2. a likeness 3. a false or deceiving appearance

semen (sē'mən) *n.* [< L., a seed] the fluid secreted by the male reproductive organs, containing the spermatozoa

semester (sə mes'tər) *n.* [< L. *sex*, six + *mensis*, month] [U.S.] either of the two divisions of the academic year

semi (sem'ē) *n.* [Colloq.] a semi-detached house

semi- (sem'i, -ē, -ə) [L.] *a prefix meaning*: 1. half 2. partly 3. twice in a (specified period)

semiannual (sem'ē an'yōō wəl) *adj.* happening every half year —**sem'ian'nually** *adv.*

semibreve (sem'i brēv') *n.* [It.] *Music* a note, the longest in current use: other notes are defined in terms of it

semicircle (sem'ē sur'k'l) *n.* a half circle —**sem'icir'cular** *adj.*

semicircular canal any of the three loop-shaped, tubular structures of the inner ear that serve to maintain balance

semicolon (sem'ē kō'lən) *n.* a mark of punctuation (;) showing more separation than that marked by the comma and less than that marked by the full stop

semiconductor (sem'ē kən duk'tər) *n.* a substance, as silicon, whose conductivity is improved by minute additions of certain substances: used in transistors, etc.

semiconscious (sem'i kon'shəs) *adj.* not fully conscious or awake —**sem'icon'-sciousness** *n.*

semidetached (sem'i di tacht') *adj.* partly separate, as two houses joined by a common wall

semifinal (sem'i fī'n'l) *adj.* coming just before the final match, as of a tournament —*n.* 1. a semifinal match 2. [*pl.*] a semifinal round —**sem'ifi'nalist** *n.*

seminal (sem'ə n'l) *adj.* [< L. *semen*, a seed] 1. being a source, esp. an important source; able to develop or be developed further 2. of or containing seed or semen 3. of reproduction

seminar (sem'ə när') *n.* [see ff.] 1. a group of students meeting for study and discussion 2. one such meeting 3. any similar group discussion

seminary (sem'ə nər ē) *n.*, *pl.* **-naries** [< L. *semen*, a seed] a school or college where priests, ministers, or rabbis are trained —**sem'inar'ian** (-när'ē ən) *n.*

semiofficial (sem'ē ə fish''l) *adj.* having some, but not full, official authority —**sem'i-offi'cially** *adv.*

semipermanent (sem'i pur'mə nənt) *adj.* not permanent but (esp. of buildings) expected to remain in use for some time

semipermeable (sem'i pur'mē ə b'l) *adj.* allowing some substances to pass

semiprecious (sem'i presh'əs) *adj.* designating gems, as garnets and opals, of lower value than precious gems

semiprofessional (sem'i prə fesh'ən 'l) *adj.* engaging in a sport, etc. for pay but not as a regular occupation —*n.* a semiprofessional player, etc.

semiquaver (sem'i kwā'vər) *n.* *Music* a note having one sixteenth the duration of a semibreve

semirigid (sem'i rij'id) *adj.* somewhat or partly rigid

semiskilled (sem'i skild') *adj.* 1. partly skilled 2. of or doing manual work that requires only limited training

semisolid (sem'i sol'id) *adj.* viscous and slowly flowing, as asphalt

semisweet (sem'i swēt') *adj.* only slightly sweetened

Semite (sē'mīt) *n.* [see ff.] a member of any people speaking a Semitic language, as a Hebrew, Arab, etc.

Semitic (sə mit'ik) *adj.* [< Heb. *Shēm*, Shem] 1. of or like the Semites 2. designating a major division of a family of languages including Hebrew, Arabic, etc.

semitone (sem'i tōn') *n.* *Music* the difference in pitch between any two immediately adjacent keys on the piano

semitrailer (sem'i trā'lər) *n.* a detachable trailer partly supported by the towing vehicle

semitropical (sem'i trop'i k'l) *adj.* somewhat like the tropics; nearly tropical

semivowel (sem'i vou'əl) *n.* *Phonet.* a glide at the beginning of a syllable, as the sound of w in *wall*

semolina (sem'ə lē'nə) *n.* [< It. *semola*, bran] 1. particles of coarsely ground durum, used in making macaroni **2.** a milk pudding made with this

sempiternal (sem′pi tur′n'l) *adj.* [< L. *semper*, always + *aeternus*, ETERNAL] everlasting —**sem′piter′nally** *adv.*

sempre (sem′prē) *adv.* [It.] *Music* throughout

sempstress (sem′stris) *n.* *var. of* SEAMSTRESS

sen. **1.** senate **2.** senator **3.** senior

S.E.N. State Enrolled Nurse

senate (sen′it) *n.* [< L. *senex*, old] **1.** a lawmaking assembly, esp. [S-] the upper branch of the legislature of the U.S., France, etc. **2.** a governing body in some universities

senator (sen′ə tər) *n.* a member of a senate —**sen′ato′rial** (-tôr′ē əl) *adj.*

send (send) *vt.* **sent, send′ing** [OE. *sendan*] **1.** *a)* to cause to go or be carried *b)* to dispatch **2.** to command to go **3.** to cause to happen, come, etc. *[joy sent by the gods]* **4.** [Slang] to excite; thrill —*vi.* to send a message, messenger, etc. *[to send for help]* —**send away** **1.** to dispatch or banish —**send down** **1.** to suspend or expel from a university **2.** to send to prison —**send for** **1.** to order to come; summon **2.** to request or order delivery of —**send forth** **1.** to give out or forth —**send in** **1.** to dispatch or send to one receiving **2.** to put (a player) in a game —**send off** **1.** to dispatch (a letter, gift, etc.) **2.** to dismiss, esp. in some sporting event as football **3.** to give a send-off to —**send on** **1.** to send in advance **2.** to redirect to another place —**send up** **1.** to cause to rise **2.** [Colloq.] to parody or satirize —**send′er** *n.*

send-off *n.* [Colloq.] **1.** a demonstration of friendly feeling towards someone starting out on a journey, career, etc. **2.** a start given to someone or something

send-up *n.* [Colloq.] a parody or imitation

senescent (sə nes′'nt) *adj.* [< L. *senescere*, grow old] growing old; aging —**senes′cence** *n.*

seneschal (sen′i shəl) *n.* [< Frank. *siniskalk*, oldest servant] a steward in a medieval household

senile (sē′nīl) *adj.* [< L. *senex*, old] **1.** of old age **2.** showing signs of old age, as memory loss —**senility** (si nil′ə tē) *n.*

senior (sēn′yər) *adj.* [< L. *senex*, old] **1.** of higher rank or longer service **2.** the older —*n.* **1.** a person of greater rank or longer service **2.** an older person —**one's senior** a person older than oneself

senior aircraftman *see* MILITARY RANKS, table

senior citizen an elderly person, esp. one who is retired

senior common room the room used by senior members of a college or university

seniority (sēn i or′ə tē) *n., pl.* **-ties** **1.** a being senior, as in age or rank **2.** status, priority, etc. achieved by length of service in a given job

senior service the Royal Navy

senna (sen′ə) *n.* [< Ar. *sanā*] **1.** a plant

of the legume family, with yellow flowers **2.** their dried leaflets used as a laxative

sennight, se'night (sen′īt) *n.* [< OE. *seofen nichta*, seven nights] [Archaic] a week

‡señor (se nyôr′) *n., pl.* **seño′res** (-nyô′res) [Sp.] **1.** [S-] Mr. **2.** a man; gentleman

‡señora (se nyô′rä) *n., pl.* **seño′ras** (-räs) [Sp.] **1.** [S-] Mrs. **2.** a married woman

‡señorita (se′nyô rē′tä) *n., pl.* **se′ñori′-tas** (-täs) [Sp.] **1.** [S-] Miss **2.** an unmarried woman or girl

sensation (sen sā′shən) *n.* [< L. *sensus, sense*] **1.** the receiving of sense impressions through hearing, seeing, etc. **2.** a conscious feeling *[a sensation of cold]* **3.** a generalized feeling, as of joy **4.** *a)* a state or feeling of general excitement *b)* the cause of this

sensational *adj.* **1.** intended to startle, shock, thrill, etc. **2.** [Colloq.] unusually good, fine, etc. **3.** of the senses or sensation —**sensa′tionalize′** *vt.* —**sensa′tionally** *adv.*

sensationalism *n.* the use of subject matter, etc. intended to shock, thrill, etc. —**sensa′tionalist** *n.*

sense (sens) *n.* [< L. *sentire*, to feel] **1.** ability to receive and react to stimuli, as light, sound, etc.; specif., sight, touch, taste, smell, and hearing **2.** *a)* perception through the senses *[a sense of warmth] b)* a generalized feeling *[a sense of longing]* **3.** an ability to judge external conditions, sounds, etc. **4.** an ability to feel, appreciate, or understand some quality *[a sense of humour]* **5.** *a)* sound thinking; judgment *b)* something wise or reasonable *[talk sense]* **6.** *[pl.]* normal ability to reason soundly *[to come to one's senses]* **7.** meaning, as of a word —*vt.* **sensed, sens′-ing** **1.** to be aware of; perceive **2.** to understand **3.** to detect, as by sensors —**in a sense** from one aspect —**make sense** to be intelligible —**take the sense of the meeting** to take a vote, etc.

senseless *adj.* **1.** meaningless **2.** unconscious **3.** stupid —**sense′lessly** *adv.* —**sense′lessness** *n.*

sense organ any organ, as an eye, that receives stimuli and transmits them as sensations to the brain

sensibility (sen′sə bil′ə tē) *n., pl.* **-ties** [see SENSE] **1.** the capacity for physical sensation **2.** [often *pl.*] the capacity for being affected emotionally or intellectually

sensible (sen′sə b'l) *adj.* [see SENSE] **1.** showing good sense or sound judgment; wise **2.** that can cause physical sensation **3.** capable of receiving sensation **4.** perceptible to the intellect **5.** having appreciation or understanding **6.** striking —**sen′sibly** *adv.*

sensitive (sen′sə tiv) *adj.* [see SENSE] **1.** keenly susceptible to stimuli *[a sensitive ear]* **2.** easily hurt; tender **3.** easily offended, shocked, etc. **4.** of the senses or sensation **5.** highly responsive as to light *[sensitive equipment]* **6.** highly responsive to whatever is stimulating intellectually, artistically, etc. **7.** of or dealing with secret or delicate government matters —**sen'sitiv'ity** n.

sensor (sen'sər) n. [< L. *sentire*, to feel] a device designed to detect, measure, or record physical phenomena, as radiation

sensory adj. of the senses or sensation

sensual (sen'shoo wəl) adj. [see SENSE] 1. of the body and the senses as distinguished from the intellect or spirit 2. a) connected or preoccupied with bodily or sexual pleasures b) lustful; lewd —**sen'-sually** adv.

sensualism n. frequent or excessive indulgence in sensual pleasures —**sen'sualist** n.

sensuality (sen'shoo wal'ə tē) n. 1. fondness for or indulgence in sensual pleasures 2. lewdness

sensuous (sen'shoo wəs) adj. 1. of, based on, or appealing to the senses 2. enjoying or readily affected by sense impressions —**sen'suously** adv. —**sen'suousness** n.

sent (sent) pt. & pp. of SEND

sentence (sen'təns) n. [< L. *sententia*, opinion] 1. *Gram.* a word or group of words stating, asking, commanding, or exclaiming something, usually having a subject and predicate 2. a) a decision, as of a court; esp., the determination by a court of a convicted person's punishment b) the punishment —vt. **-tenced, -tencing** to condemn (*to* a specified punishment) —**senten'tial** (-ten'shəl) adj.

sententious (sen ten'shəs) adj. [see prec.] 1. short and pithy 2. full of, or fond of using, maxims, proverbs, etc., often pompously trite or moralizing —**senten'-tiously** adv.

sentient (sen'shənt) adj. [< L. *sentire*, to feel] of, having, or capable of feeling —**sen'tience, sen'tiency** n.

sentiment (sen'tə mənt) n. [< L. *sentire*, to feel] 1. susceptibility to emotional appeal 2. an opinion, attitude, etc.: *often used in the pl.* 3. sentimentality; maudlin emotion 4. appeal to the emotions 5. a complex combination of feelings and opinions 6. a short sentence expressing some thought 7. the real meaning behind something

sentimental (sen'tə men't'l) adj. 1. having or showing tender or delicate feelings, often in an excessive way 2. influenced more by emotion than reason —**sen'timen'talism** n. —**sen'timen'talist** n. —**sen'timen'tally** adv.

sentimentality (sen'tə men tal'ə tē) n. the quality or condition of being sentimental

sentimentalize (sen'tə men'tə līz') vi., vt. **-ized', -iz'ing** to be or make sentimental

sentimental value the value of an object having no intrinsic worth but prized because of its associations

sentinel (sen'ti n'l) n. [< L. *sentire*, to feel] a person or animal set to guard a group; specif., a sentry

sentry (sen'trē) n., pl. **-tries** [< ?] a sentinel; esp., any member of a military guard posted to guard against, and warn of, danger

sentry box a small boxlike structure serving as a shelter for a sentry on duty during bad weather

SEPALS

sepal (sep''l) n. [< Gr. *skepē*, a covering + L. *petalum*, petal] *Bot.* any of the usually green, leaflike parts of the calyx —**se'palled** adj.

separable (sep'ər ə b'l) adj. that can be separated —**sep'arabil'ity** n.

separate (sep'ə rāt'; *for adj. & n.* sep'-rət) vt. **-rat'ed, -rat'ing** [< L. *se-*, apart + *parare*, arrange] 1. to keep apart by being between 2. to set apart from others 3. to take away (a part or ingredient) from a combination or mixture 4. to distinguish between 5. to set apart into groups, sets, units, etc. —vi. 1. to part, become disconnected, etc. 2. to withdraw or secede 3. to become distinct, as from a mixture 4. to go in different directions 5. to stop living together as man and wife but without getting a divorce —adj. 1. set apart from others 2. distinct; individual 3. not shared —n. [pl.] articles of dress designed to be worn as a set or separately —**sep'arately** adv. —**sep'ara-tive** (sep'ər ə tiv) adj. —**sep'ara'tor** n.

separate school [Canad.] a school for a large religious minority run by its own school board but under the authority of the provincial department of education

separation (sep'ə rā'shən) n. 1. a separating or being separated 2. an arrangement by which a man and wife live apart: also **judicial** (or **legal**) **separation**

separatism (sep'ər ə tiz'm) n. a movement for political, religious, or racial separation, specif., [S-] in Canada, the movement for the secession of Quebec —**sep'aratist** n., adj.

sepia (sē'pē ə) n. [< Gr., cuttlefish] 1. a dark reddish-brown colour 2. a photographic print in this colour —adj. dark reddish-brown

sepoy (sē'poi) n. [< Per. *sipāh*, army] formerly, a native of India serving in the British army

sepsis (sep'sis) n. [< Gr. *sēpein*, make putrid] poisoning caused by the absorption into the blood of certain microorganisms

sept (sept) n. [< SECT] a clan, as in Ireland

Sept. 1. September 2. Septuagint

September (sep tem'bər) n. [< L. *septem*, seven] the ninth month of the year, having 30 days

septennial (sep ten'ē əl) adj. [< L. *septum*, seven + *annus*, year] 1. lasting seven years **2.** coming, happening, etc. every seven years

septet, septette (sep tet′) *n.* [< L. *septem*, seven] **1.** a group of seven **2.** *Music a)* a composition for seven voices or instruments *b)* the performers of this

septic (sep′tik) *adj.* [< see SEPSIS] caused by or involving microorganisms that are infecting or putrefying —**sep′tically** *adv.*

septicemia (sep′tə sē′mē ə) *n.* [< Gr. *sēptikos*, putrefactive + *haima*, blood] a disease caused by certain microorganisms and their toxic products in the blood

septic tank an underground tank in which waste matter is putrefied and decomposed through bacterial action

septuagenarian (sep′tyоо wə ji nāar′ē ən) *adj.* [< L. *septuaginta*, seventy] seventy years old, or between the ages of seventy and eighty —*n.* a person of this age

Septuagint (sep′tyоо wə jint) [< L. *septuaginta*, seventy] a Greek translation of the Hebrew Scriptures made in the 3rd cent. B.C.

septum (sep′təm) *n.*, *pl.* **-tums, -ta** [< L. *saepes*, a hedge] *Biol.* a part that separates two cavities or masses of tissue, as in the nose —**sep′tal** *adj.*

septuple (sep tyоо′p'l) *adj.* [< L. *septem*, seven] **1.** consisting of seven **2.** seven times as much or as many —*vt.*, *vi.* **-pled, -pling** to multiply by seven

sepulchral (sə pul′krəl) *adj.* **1.** dismal; gloomy **2.** deep and melancholy: said of sound **3.** of sepulchres

sepulchre (sep′'l kər) *n.* [< L. *sepelire*, to bury] a vault for burial; grave; tomb —*vt.* to bury in a sepulchre U.S. sp. **sepulcher**

sepulture (sep′'l chər) *n.* burial; interment

sequel (sē′kwəl) *n.* [< L. *sequi*, follow] **1.** something that follows **2.** a result or consequence **3.** any literary work complete in itself but continuing an earlier story

sequence (sē′kwəns) *n.* [see prec.] **1.** *a)* the following of one thing after another *b)* the order in which this occurs **2.** a continuous or related series **3.** a consequence **4.** *Cinema* the series of shots forming a single, uninterrupted episode

sequential (si kwen′shəl) *adj.* characterized by or forming a regular sequence of parts —**sequen′tially** *adv.*

sequester (si kwes′tər) *vt.* [< LL. *sequestrare*, remove] **1.** to set apart; separate **2.** to take possession of (property) as security for a debt, etc. **3.** to confiscate **4.** to seclude —**seques′tered** *adj.* —**seques′tra′tion** *n.*

sequin (sē′kwin) *n.* [< Ar. *sikkah*, a stamp] a small, shiny spangle, as a metal disc, sewn on material for decoration —**se′quined, se′quinned** *adj.*

sequoia (si kwoi′ə) *n.* [< name of an Am. Indian] either of two giant N American evergreen trees

seraglio (si räl′ē ō) *n.*, *pl.* **-lios** [It. < L. *sera*, a lock] **1.** a harem **2.** the palace of a Turkish sultan

seraph (ser′əf) *n.*, *pl.* **-aphs,**

-aphim′ (-ə fim′) [< Heb.] *Bible* one of the heavenly beings surrounding the throne of God —**seraphic** (sə raf′ik) *adj.*

Serb (surb) *n.* **1.** a native or inhabitant of Serbia **2.** *same as* SERBIAN (*n.* 1) —*adj.* *same as* SERBIAN

Serbian *adj.* of Serbia, the Serbs, or their language —*n.* **1.** Serbo-Croatian as spoken in Serbia **2.** *same as* SERB (*n.* 1)

Serbo-Croatian (sur′bō krō ā′shən) *n.* the major South Slavic language of Yugoslavia —*adj.* of this language Also **Serbo-Croat**

sere (sēar) *adj.* [< SEAR] [Poet.] withered

serenade (ser′ə nād′) *n.* [< L. *serenus*, clear] **1.** the act of playing or singing music outdoors at night, esp. by a lover under the window of his sweetheart **2.** music suitable for this —*vt.*, *vi.* **-nad′ed, -nad′ing** to play or sing a serenade (to) —**ser′enad′er** *n.*

serendipity (ser′ən dip′ə tē) *n.* [< Per. fairy tale, *The Three Princes of Serendip*] a seeming gift for making fortunate discoveries accidentally

serene (sə rēn′) *adj.* [L. *serenus*] **1.** calm, peaceful, etc. **2.** clear; unclouded **3.** [S-] exalted *[His Serene Highness]* —**serene′ly** *adv.* —**seren′ity** (-ren′ə tē) *n.*

serf (surf) *n.* [< L. *servus*, a slave] a person in the feudal system, bound to his master's land and transferred with it —**serf′dom** *n.*

Serg., serg. sergeant

serge (surj) *n.* [< L. *sericus*, silken] a strong, twilled material made of wool, silk, rayon, etc.

sergeant (sär′jənt) *n.* [< L. *servire*, serve] **1.** *see* MILITARY RANKS, table **2.** a police officer ranking next below an inspector

sergeant-at-arms *n.*, *pl.* **ser′geants-at-arms′** an officer appointed to keep order in a legislative body, court, etc.

sergeant major *pl.* **sergeants major** the chief administrative noncommissioned officer of a military headquarters: see also note at WARRANT OFFICER

Sergt., sergt. sergeant

serial (sēar′ē əl) *n.* [< L. *series*, SERIES] a story presented in serial form —*adj.* **1.** of, in, or forming a series **2.** appearing in a series of continuing parts at regular intervals **3.** *Music same as* TWELVE-TONE —**se′rially** *adv.*

serialize *vt.* **-ized′, -iz′ing** to put or publish (a story, etc.) in serial form —**se′ri-aliza′tion** *n.*

series (sēar′ēz) *n.*, *pl.* **-ries** [< L. *serere*, to join] **1.** a number of similar things or people in a row, sequence, or related group **2.** *Elec.* a circuit connection in which the components form a single path for the current: usually in the phrase **in series 3.** *Geol.* a subdivision of a geologic system

serif (ser′if) *n.* [< ?] *Printing* a fine line projecting from a main stroke of a character

seriocomic (sēar′ē ō kom′ik) *adj.* partly serious and partly comic

serious (sēar′ē əs) *adj.* [< L. *serius*] **1.**

earnest, grave, or solemn **2.** *a)* meaning what one says *b)* meant in earnest **3.** concerned with important matters *[a serious novel]* **4.** requiring careful consideration **5.** giving cause for concern *[a serious wound]*

serious-minded *adj.* having or showing earnestness of purpose, etc.; not frivolous, jocular, etc.

serjeant (sär′jənt) *n.* *var. of* SERGEANT

sermon (sur′mən) *n.* [< L. *sermo*, discourse] **1.** a speech, esp. by a clergyman, on some religious topic or on morals **2.** any serious talk on one's behaviour, responsibilities, etc. —**ser′monize′** *vi., vt.*

Sermon on the Mount the sermon given by Jesus to his disciples: Matt. 5-7, Luke 6:20-49

serous (sēar′əs) *adj.* **1.** of or containing serum **2.** like serum; thin and watery

serpent (sur′pənt) *n.* [< L. *serpere*, creep] **1.** a snake, esp. a large one **2.** a sly, treacherous person

serpentine (sur′pəntīn′) *adj.* of or like a serpent; esp., *a)* treacherous *b)* coiled or winding —*n.* a green or brownish-red mineral, magnesium silicate

serrate (ser′āt; *for v.* se rāt′) *adj.* [< L. *serra*, a saw] having sawlike notches along the edge: also **serrat′ed** —*vt.* **-rat′-ed, -rat′ing** to make serrate

serration (se rā′shən) *n.* **1.** the condition of being serrate **2.** a single notch in a serrate edge

serried (ser′ēd) *adj.* [see SERAGLIO] placed close together; compact, as soldiers in ranks

serum (sēar′əm) *n., pl.* **-rums, -ra** [L., whey] **1.** any watery animal fluid, esp. the yellowish fluid that is left after blood clots: in full, **blood serum 2.** blood serum used as an antitoxin, taken from an animal made immune to a specific disease by inoculation

servant (sur′vənt) *n.* [< L. *servire*, serve] **1.** a person hired to work in another's home as a maid, cook, etc. **2.** a person who works for a government *[a civil servant]* **3.** a person who works earnestly for a cause, etc.

servants' hall formerly, the room in which the household servants ate, etc.

serve (surv) *vt.* **served, serv′ing** [< L. *servire*] **1.** to work for as a servant **2.** to do services for; aid; help **3.** to do military or naval service for **4.** to pass or spend (a term of imprisonment, military service, etc.) **5.** to carry out the duties of (a position, office, etc.) **6.** to provide (customers) with (goods or services) **7.** to prepare and offer (food, etc.) to **8.** *a)* to meet the needs of *[to serve many purposes]* *b)* to further *[to serve the national interest]* **9.** to function for *[my memory serves me well]* **10.** to treat *[she was cruelly served]* **11.** to deliver (a summons, subpoena, etc.) to **12.** to hit (a tennis ball, etc.) to one's opponent in order to start play **13.** to operate (a large gun) **14.** to copulate

with (a female): said of an animal —*vi.* **1.** to work as a servant **2.** to be in service *[to serve in the navy]* **3.** to carry out the duties of an office or position **4.** to function **5.** to satisfy requirements **6.** to wait at table **7.** to start play by hitting the ball, etc. —*n.* the act or manner of serving the ball in tennis, etc., or one's turn to serve —**serve (someone) right** to be what (someone) deserves, as for doing something wrong —**serve (one's) time 1.** to undergo imprisonment **2.** to serve an apprenticeship —**serv′er** *n.*

servery *n.* a pantry from which meals are served

service (sur′vis) *n.* [< L. *servus*, slave] **1.** *a)* an act of assistance *b)* benefit *c)* *[pl.]* friendly help; also, professional aid **2.** *[often pl.]* a system or method of providing people with water, transport, etc. **3.** installation, repairs, etc. provided to customers by a dealer, etc. **4.** *a)* employment, esp. public employment *b)* a branch of this, specif., the armed forces **5.** work done or duty performed for others **6.** the occupation or condition of a servant **7.** the serving of food **8.** a set of utensils used in serving *[a tea service]* **9.** a religious ceremony **10.** the act or manner of serving the ball in tennis, etc., or one's turn to serve —*adj.* **1.** of, for, or in service **2.** of, for, or used by servants, tradespeople, etc. *[a service entrance]* —*vt.* **-iced, -icing 1.** to furnish with a service **2.** to make fit for service, as by repairing, etc. —**has seen service 1.** to have been a member of the armed forces in wartime **2.** to have been put to long and usually hard use —**in service 1.** in use **2.** working as a servant —**of service** helpful; useful

serviceable *adj.* **1.** useful **2.** that will give good service; durable —**serv′iceabil′-ity** *n.*

service area a place on a motorway providing facilities for motorway users, as a restaurant, garage, etc.

service charge a percentage added to a bill in a restaurant etc. to pay for service

service flat a self-contained flat where the management provides certain services, as cleaning, washing, etc.

serviceman *n.* **1.** a member of the armed forces **2.** a person whose work is servicing or repairing something: also **service man**

service road a road, usually parallel to a main road, providing access to houses, shops, etc.

service station a place selling petrol and oil, for motor vehicles

service tree [ult. < L. *sorbus*] a tree resembling the mountain ash and having small, edible fruits

serviette (sur′vē et′) *n.* [Fr.] a table napkin

servile (sur′vīl) *adj.* [< L. *servus*, slave] **1.** humbly submissive; cringing **2.** of or suitable for a slave or slaves —**servility** (sər vil′ə tē) *n.*

serving *n.* a helping of food —*adj.* used for serving food *[a serving spoon]*

servitor (sur'və tər) *n.* a servant, attendant, etc.

servitude (sur'və tyōōd') *n.* [< L. *servus*, slave] **1.** slavery or bondage **2.** work imposed as punishment

servomechanism (sur'vō mek'ə niz'm) *n.* [ff. + MECHANISM] an automatic control system in which output is compared with input so that any error in control is corrected

servomotor (sur'vō mōt'ər) *n.* [< L. *servus*, slave + Fr. *moteur*, MOTOR] a device, as an electric motor, that is controlled by an amplified signal as from a servomechanism

sesame (ses'ə mē') *n.* [< Gr.] **1.** an East Indian plant whose flat seeds yield an edible oil **2.** its seeds, used for flavouring bread, etc.

sesqui- [< L. *semis*, half + *que*, and] *a combining form meaning* one and a half [*sesquicentennial*]

sessile (ses'il) *adj.* [< L. *sedere*, sit] *Anat., Bot., Zool.* attached directly by its base

session (sesh'ən) *n.* [< L. *sedere*, sit] **1.** *a)* a meeting of a court, council, etc. *b)* a series of such meetings *c)* the period a session lasts **2.** an academic year or period of study, classes, etc. **3.** the governing body of a Presbyterian church **4.** any period of activity [a *session* of golf] **—in session** meeting **—ses'sional** *adj.*

sessional indemnity in certain Canadian provinces, the indemnity paid each session to members of the legislature

sestet (ses tet') *n.* [It. < L. *sex*, six] **1.** *Music* same as SEXTET **2.** the final six lines of a sonnet

set (set) *vt.* **set, set'ting** [OE. *settan*] **1.** to put in a certain place, condition, etc. **2.** to bring (something) into contact with something else [to *set* a match to paper] **3.** to cause to be in some condition or relation **4.** to arrange; fix; specif., *a)* to fix (a net, trap, etc.) to catch animals *b)* to adjust; regulate [to *set* a clock] *c)* to arrange (a table) with tableware for a meal *d)* to put (a fractured bone) into normal position **5.** *a)* to make fixed, determined, firm, etc. [pectin *sets* jam] *b)* to make (a colour) fast in dyeing **6.** *a)* to mount (gems) in jewellery *b)* to decorate (jewellery) with gems *c)* to arrange (hair) in a certain style with lotion, hairpins, etc. **7.** to place (a scene, story, etc.) in a given locale **8.** to direct [he *set* his face towards home] **9.** to appoint, establish, determine, etc. **10.** to begin to apply (oneself) to a task **11.** to assign (a task etc.) **12.** to value or estimate [to *set* little store by someone] **13.** to point towards (game): said of dogs **14.** *Music* to write or fit (words *to* music or music *to* words) **15.** *Printing a)* to arrange (type) for printing *b)* to put (manuscript) into type **16.** *Theatre* to arrange the scenery and properties on (the stage) **17.** to cause to sit; seat **18.** *a)* to cause (a fowl) to sit on eggs to hatch them *b)* to put (eggs) under a fowl to hatch them **—vi.** **1.** to become firm,

hard, fixed, etc. [the cement *set*] **2.** *a)* to begin to move (with *out, off,* etc.) *b)* to get started [to *set* to work] **3.** to have a certain direction **4.** *a)* to sink below the horizon *b)* to wane; decline **5.** to grow together: said of a broken bone **6.** *Bot.* to begin to develop into a fruit **7.** to sit on eggs: said of a fowl **—adj.** **1.** fixed in advance [a *set* time] **2.** established, as by authority [a *set* book] **3.** deliberate **4.** conventional [a *set* speech] **5.** fixed; rigid **6.** *a)* resolute *b)* obstinate **7.** firm in consistency **8.** ready [get *set*] **9.** formed; built **—n.** **1.** a setting or being set; specif., the act of a dog in setting game **2.** the way in which a thing is set; specif., *a)* direction, as of a current *b)* tendency *c)* the position of a part of the body [the *set* of her head] **3.** something which is set; specif., *a)* a twig, young bulb, etc. for planting or grafting *b)* the constructed scenery for a play, film, etc. **4.** the act or a style of arranging hair **5.** a group of persons or things classed or belonging together **6.** equipment for radio or television reception **7.** *Math.* a collection of elements or objects that satisfy a given condition **8.** *Tennis* a group of games of which the winner must win a specified number **—all set** [Colloq.] ready **—set about** **1.** to begin **2.** to attack **—set against** **1.** to balance **2.** to compare **3.** to make hostile towards **—set aside** **1.** to reserve for a purpose: also **set apart** **2.** to discard; reject **3.** to annul **—set down** **1.** to put down **2.** to land (an aircraft) **3.** to put in writing or print **—set in** **1.** to begin **2.** to insert **3.** to become established **—set off** **1.** to start (a person) doing something **2.** to make begin **3.** to make prominent by contrast **4.** to enhance **5.** to cause to explode **—set on** **1.** to incite to attack **2.** to attack: also **set upon** **—set one's sights on** to train upon; determine upon **—set sail** **1.** to hoist the sails into position **2.** to begin a voyage **—set to** **1.** to get to work **2.** to begin fighting **—set up** **1.** to establish **2.** to begin **3.** to raise to power, a high position, etc. **4.** to make successful, etc. **5.** to put together or erect (a tent, machine, etc.) **6.** to make detailed plans for **7.** to place in an upright position **8.** to present as specified: also **set up as** **—set upon** to attack, esp. with violence

setback *n.* a reversal or check; relapse

set piece **1.** an artistic composition intended to impress others **2.** a scenic display of fireworks

setscrew *n.* a screw passing through one part and against or into another to prevent movement

set square a flat piece of plastic, metal, etc., in the shape of a right-angled triangle, used in technical drawing

sett (set) *n.* [see SET] **1.** a small rectangular paving block **2.** a badger's burrow

settee (se tē') *n.* [prob. < SETTLE¹] a seat with a back and, usually, arms, for two or more people

setter (set'ər) *n.* **1.** any of several breeds

of long-haired gun dogs trained to find game and point it out by standing rigid **2.** a person who sets or a thing used in setting

setting *n.* **1.** the position of something, as a dial, that has been set **2.** a thing in or on which something, as a gem, has been set **3.** time and place, environment, etc. of a story or play **4.** actual physical surroundings **5.** the music for a set of words **6.** *same as* PLACE SETTING

settle¹ (set′'l) *n.* [OE. *setl*] a long wooden bench with a back and armrests

settle² *vt.* **-tled, -tling** [< OE. *setl*, a seat] **1.** to put in order; arrange [to *settle* one's affairs] **2.** to set in place firmly or comfortably **3.** to establish as resident [he *settled* his family in London] **4.** to colonize **5.** to cause to sink and become more compact [the rain *settled* the dust] **6.** to clarify (a liquid) by causing the sediment to sink to the bottom **7.** to free (the mind, nerves, stomach, etc.) from disturbance **8.** to establish in business, marriage, etc. **9.** to decide (something in doubt) **10.** to end (a dispute) **11.** to pay (a bill, debt, etc.) **12.** to make over (property, etc.) to someone by legal action (with *on* or *upon*) **13.** to decide (a legal dispute) without court action —*vi.* **1.** to stop moving and stay in one place **2.** to cast itself, as fog over a landscape **3.** to become localized in a part of the body : said of pain or disease **4.** to take up permanent residence **5.** to sink [the car *settled* in the mud] **6.** to become more dense by sinking, as sediment **7.** to become clearer by the settling of dregs **8.** to become more stable **9.** to reach a decision (with *with, on,* or *upon*) **10.** to pay a bill or debt —**settle down 1.** to take up permanent residence, a regular job, etc. **2.** to become less nervous, erratic, etc. **3.** to apply oneself steadily —**settle for** to resign oneself to accepting —**settle up** to pay any outstanding amount

settlement *n.* **1.** a settling or being settled **2.** a new colony **3.** a village **4.** an agreement, adjustment, etc. **5.** *a*) the disposition of property for the benefit of a person *b*) this property **6.** an institution, usually in a depressed neighbourhood, offering social services, etc.: also **settlement house 7.** subsidence in all or part of a building

settler (set′lər) *n.* one who settles in a new country

set-to *n.*, *pl.* **-tos**′ [Colloq.] a fight or struggle

setup *n.* plan, makeup, etc., as of equipment, an organization, etc.

seven (sev′'n) *adj., n.* [OE. *seofon*] one more than six; 7; VII —**sev′enth** *adj., n.*

sevenfold *adj.* **1.** having seven parts **2.** having seven times as much or as many —*adv.* seven times as much or as many

seven seas all the oceans of the world

seventeen (sev′'n tēn′) *adj., n.* [OE. *seofentyne*] seven more than ten; 17; XVII —**sev′enteenth′ adj., n.**

seventh-day *adj.* **1.** of the seventh day (Saturday) **2.** [*often* S- D-] observing

the Sabbath on Saturday [*Seventh-Day Adventists*]

seventh heaven a state of perfect happiness

seventy *adj., n., pl.* **-ties** seven times ten; 70; LXX —**the seventies** the numbers or years, as of a century, from seventy to seventy-nine —**sev′entieth** *adj., n.*

sever (sev′ər) *vt., vi.* [< L. *separare*] to separate, divide, or break off —**sev′erance** *n.*

several (sev′rəl) *adj.* [< L. *separ, separate*] **1.** more than two but not many; few **2.** separate; distinct **3.** different; respective [went their *several* ways] —*n.* [*with pl. v.*] a small number (of persons or things) —*pron.* [*with pl. v.*] a few

severally *adv.* **1.** separately **2.** respectively

severance pay compensation paid by a firm to employees for loss of employment

severe (sə vēər′) *adj.* **-ver′er, -ver′est** [< L. *severus*] **1.** harsh or strict, as in treatment **2.** serious; grave **3.** rigidly accurate or demanding **4.** extremely plain [a *severe* style] **5.** intense [*severe* pain] **6.** difficult; rigorous [a *severe* test] —**sever′ity** (-ver′ə tē) *n.*

Seville orange (sə vil′) a bitter orange used esp. for making marmalade

Sèvres (sãv′rə) *n.* [< *Sèvres,* suburb of Paris] a type of fine French porcelain

sew (sō) *vt.* **sewed, sewn** or **sewed, sew′ing** [OE. *siwian*] **1.** to join with stitches made with needle and thread **2.** to make, mend, etc. by such means —*vi.* to work with needle and thread or at a sewing machine —**sew up 1.** to close together the edges of with stitches **2.** [Colloq.] to complete or negotiate successfully

sewage (syōō′ij) *n.* waste matter carried off by sewers

sewage farm a place where sewage is treated, esp. for use as manure

sewer (syōō′ər) *n.* [ult. < L. *ex,* out + *aqua,* water] a pipe or drain, usually underground, for carrying off water and waste matter

sewerage *n.* **1.** removal of surface water and waste matter by sewers **2.** a system of sewers **3.** *same as* SEWAGE

sewing (sō′iŋ) *n.* **1.** the act or occupation of a person who sews **2.** material for sewing; needlework

sewing machine a machine with a mechanically driven needle used for sewing and stitching

sewn (sōn) *alt. pp. of* SEW

sex (seks) *n.* [L. *sexus*] **1.** the character of being male or female **2.** either of the two divisions of male, female, of persons, animals, or plants **3.** sexual intercourse **4.** the attraction of one sex for the other —*adj.* [Colloq.] *same as* SEXUAL —*vt.* to ascertain the sex of

sex- [< L.] *a combining form meaning* six

sexagenarian (sek′sə ji nãar′ē ən) *adj.* [< L. *sexageni,* sixty each] sixty years old, or between the ages of sixty and seventy —*n.* a person of this age

sex appeal the physical attractiveness

and erotic charm that attracts members of the opposite sex

sex chromosome a sex-determining chromosome in the germ cells of most animals

sexed (sekst) *adj.* 1. having (a specified degree of) sexuality 2. of sex

sexism *n.* [SEX + (RAC)ISM] the economic exploitation and social domination of members of one sex by the other, specif. of women by men —**sex′ist** *adj., n.*

sexless *adj.* 1. lacking the characteristics of sex; asexual 2. lacking in normal sexual appetite or appeal

sex maniac someone who is considered to be oversexed and/or perverted

sexology (sek sol′ə jē) *n.* the science dealing with human sexual behaviour —**sex-ol′ogist** *n.*

sex-starved *adj.* of or relating to someone who is not obtaining sufficient sexual gratification

sext (sekst) *n.* [< L. *sexta*, sixth] [*often* S-] the fourth of the canonical hours

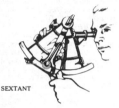

SEXTANT

sextant (seks′tənt) *n.* [< L. *sextans*, sixth part of a circle] an instrument used by navigators for measuring the angular distance of the sun, a star, etc. from the horizon, as in finding the position of a ship

sextet, sextette (seks tet′) *n.* [< SESTET] 1. any group of six 2. *Music a)* a composition for six voices or instruments *b)* the six performers of this

sexton (seks′tən) *n.* [see SACRISTY] a church official in charge of the maintenance of church property, who often acts as gravedigger, etc.

sextuple (seks′tyσσ p′l) *adj.* [< L. *sextus*, sixth] six times as much or as many

sextuplet (seks′tyσσ plit) *n.* any of six offspring born at a single birth

sexual (sek′syσσ wəl) *adj.* 1. of or involving sex, the sexes, the organs of sex, etc. 2. *Biol. a)* having sex *b)* designating or of reproduction by the union of male and female germ cells —**sex′ual′-ity** (-wal′ə tē) *n.*

sexy *adj.* **sex′ier, sex′iest** [Colloq.] exciting or intended to excite sexual desire —**sex′ily** *adv.*

sez (sez) *vi.* [Slang] says, esp. in **sez you**

s.f., sf, SF science fiction

S.F.A. Scottish Football Association

sforzando (sfôr tsan′dō) *adj., adv.* [It.] *Music* with emphasis: abbrev. **sf., sfz.**

Sgt. Sergeant

sh (sh: *a lengthened sound*) *interj.* hush!

shabby (shab′ē) *adj.* **-bier, -biest** [OE. *sceabb*] 1. dilapidated 2. *a)* worn; threadbare *b)* wearing worn clothing 3. unworthy; shameful [*shabby* treatment] —**shab′bily** *adv.* —**shab′biness** *n.*

shabby-genteel *adj.* shabby but trying to keep up a genteel appearance

shack (shak) *n.* [< ?] a small, crudely built cabin —**shack up with** [Slang] to share living quarters with

shackle (shak′′l) *n.* [OE. *sceacul*] 1. a metal fastening, usually in pairs, for the wrist or ankle of a prisoner; fetter 2. [*usually pl.*] anything that keeps one from acting, thinking, or developing freely 3. a device for fastening or coupling —*vt.* **-led, -ling** to bind, fasten, or hinder with or as with shackles

shad (shad) *n.* [OE. *sceadd*] a herringlike saltwater food fish

shade (shād) *n.* [OE. *sceadu*] 1. slight darkness caused by cutting off rays of light, as from the sun 2. an area less brightly lighted than its surroundings 3. [Archaic] a shadow 4. a representation of darkness in a painting, etc. 5. degree of darkness of a colour 6. *a)* a small difference [*shades* of opinion] *b)* a slight trace [a *shade* of humour in his voice] 7. [Chiefly Literary] a ghost 8. any device used to protect or screen from light, esp. a cover for a lamp: in full, **lamp shade** —*vt.* **shad′ed, shad′ing** 1. to screen from light or heat 2. to hide as with a shadow 3. to darken; dim 4. *a)* to represent shade in (a painting, etc.) *b)* to mark with gradations of light or colour —*vi.* to change slightly or by degrees —**in** (or **into**) **the shade** 1. in or into darkness or shadow 2. in comparative obscurity

shading *n.* 1. the representation of light or shade in a picture 2. any small variation, as in quality

shadow (shad′ō) *n.* [< OE. *sceadu*, shade] 1. the darkness or the dark shape cast upon a surface by something cutting off light from it 2. gloom, sadness, etc. or anything causing this 3. a shaded area, as in a picture 4. *a)* something imagined, not real *b)* a ghost 5. a vague indication 6. *a)* a faint suggestion [a *shadow* of hope] *b)* weakened remnant, vestige 7. a constant companion 8. a person who trails another closely, as a spy —*vt.* 1. to throw a shadow upon 2. to make dark or gloomy 3. to follow closely, esp. in secret —*adj.* designating a member of the parliamentary opposition in Britain who would be a minister if his party were in power —**shad′ower** *n.*

shadow cabinet members of the opposition party in the British Parliament selected to form a cabinet that is a counterpart of the one in power

shadowy *adj.* 1. *a)* without reality; illusory *b)* dim; indistinct 2. shaded or full of shadow

shady (shād′ē) *adj.* **-ier, -iest** 1. giving shade 2. shaded, as from the sun 3. [Colloq.] of questionable character or honesty —**shad′ily** *adv.* —**shad′iness** *n.*

shaft (shäft) *n.* [OE. *sceaft*] 1. *a)* an arrow or spear *b)* its long stem 2. a missile or something like a missile [*shafts* of light, wit, etc.] 3. a long, slender part or object; specif., *a)* the stem of a feather *b)* the main, usually cylindrical, part between the ends of a column *c)* a handle, as on some tools *d)* either of the two poles between which an animal is harnessed to a vehicle *e)* a bar transmitting motion to a mechanical part, as of an engine 4. a long, narrow opening sunk into the earth [a mine *shaft*] 5. a vertical opening through the floors of a building, as for a lift 6. a conduit for air

shag (shag) *n.* [OE. *sceacga*] 1. a heavy, rough nap, as on some woollen cloth 2. any disordered, tangled mass 3. coarse, shredded tobacco 4. a cormorant

shaggy (shag′ē) *adj.* -gier, -giest 1. covered with long, coarse hair 2. carelessly groomed; unkempt 3. of coarse growth; straggly —**shag′gily** *adv.* —**shag′giness** *n.*

shagreen (sha grēn′) *n.* [< Turk. *saghri*, hide] 1. rawhide with a rough, granular surface 2. the skin of the shark or dogfish

shah (shä) *n.* [Per. *shāh*] a title of the former ruler of Iran

Shak. Shakespeare

shake (shāk) *vt.* shook, shak′en, shak′ing [OE. *sceacan*] 1. to cause to move up and down, back and forth, etc. with short, quick movements 2. to bring, force, mix, scatter, etc. by abrupt, brisk movements 3. to cause to tremble 4. *a)* to cause to totter or become unsteady *b)* to unnerve; upset 5. to brandish; wave 6. to clasp (another's hand), as in greeting 7. [U.S. Colloq.] to get away from or rid of [to *shake* one's pursuers] —*vi.* 1. to move quickly up and down, back and forth, etc.; vibrate 2. to tremble, as from cold 3. to become unsteady; totter 4. to clasp each other's hand, as in greeting —*n.* 1. an act of shaking 2. an unsteady movement; tremor 3. [Colloq.] an earthquake 4. *short for* MILKSHAKE 5. [*pl.*] [Colloq.] a convulsive trembling (usually with *the*) 6. [Colloq.] a moment [be back in a *shake*] 7. *Music* *same as* TRILL —**no great shakes** [Colloq.] not outstanding —**shake down** 1. to cause to fall by shaking 2. to go to bed, esp. to a makeshift bed 3. to settle down —**shake hands** to clasp each other's hand as a token of agreement or friendship, or in parting or greeting —**shake off** to get away from or rid of —**shake up** 1. to shake, esp. so as to mix 2. to jar or shock 3. to reorganize

shakedown *n.* a makeshift bed —*adj.* for testing the performance [the *shakedown* cruise for a ship]

shaker *n.* 1. a person or thing that shakes 2. a device used in shaking [a cocktail *shaker*]

shako (shak′ō) *n.*, *pl.* shak′os [< Hung.] a stiff, cylindrical military dress hat, usually with a flat top and a plume

shaky (shā′kē) *adj.* -ier, -iest 1. weak, unsound, etc., as a structure, belief, etc.

2. *a)* trembling *b)* nervous 3. not reliable; questionable [*shaky* evidence]

shale (shāl) *n.* [OE. *scealu*, shell] a fine-grained rock formed by the hardening of clay: it splits easily into thin layers

shall (shal; *unstressed* shəl) *v.*, *pt.* **should** [OE. *sceal*] 1. an auxiliary sometimes used to express the simple future in the first person [I *shall* tell him] and determination, obligation, etc. in the second and third persons [you *shall* obey]: see also WILL² 2. an auxiliary used in questions in the first person asking for agreement

shallot (shə lot′) *n.* [< OFr. *eschaloigne*, scallion] a small onion whose clustered bulbs are used for flavouring

shallow (shal′ō) *adj.* [ME. *shalow*] 1. not deep 2. lacking depth of character or intellect; superficial —*n.* [*usually pl.*, *often with sing. v.*] a shallow place in water; shoal —**shal′lowness** *n.*

shalom (shə lom′) *n., interj.* [< Heb.] a word used as the traditional Jewish greeting or farewell

sham (sham) *n.* [< ?] 1. an imitation that is meant to deceive 2. one who falsely affects a certain character —*adj.* false; fake —*vt., vi.* to fake; pretend

shaman (sham′ən) *n., pl.* -mans [Russ.] a priest or medicine man of shamanism

shamanism *n.* a religion of northeast Asia, based on a belief in spirits who are influenced only by shamans

shamateur (sham′ə tər) *n.* [SHAM + (AM)ATEUR] a sports player who although technically an amateur makes gains from his sport

shamble (sham′b'l) *vi.* -bled, -bling [prob. < ff., in obs. sense of stool] to walk in a clumsy manner, barely lifting the feet —*n.* a shambling walk

shambles (sham′b'lz) *n.pl.* [with sing. v.] [ult. < L. *scamnum*, bench] 1. any scene of great destruction or disorder 2. a slaughterhouse 3. a scene of great slaughter

shambolic (sham bol′ik) *adj.* [< SHAMBLES] extremely disorderly or disorganized

shame (shām) *n.* [OE. *scamu*] 1. a painful feeling of having lost the respect of others because of improper behaviour, incompetence, etc. 2. a capacity for such feeling 3. dishonour or disgrace 4. a person or thing that brings dishonour or disgrace 5. something unfortunate or outrageous —*vt.* shamed, sham′ing 1. to cause to feel shame 2. to disgrace 3. to force by a sense of shame [shamed into apologizing] —*interj.* [S Afr. Slang] a general exclamation of delight, sympathy, etc. —**for shame!** you ought to be ashamed! —**put to shame** 1. to cause to feel shame 2. to surpass

shamefaced *adj.* 1. shy 2. showing a feeling of shame —**shamefac′edly** *adv.*

shameful *adj.* 1. bringing or causing shame or disgrace 2. not just, moral, or decent; offensive

shameless *adj.* having or showing no shame, modesty, or decency; brazen

shammy (sham′ē) *n.*, *pl.* **-mies; adj., vt. -mied, -mying** *same as* CHAMOIS

shampoo (sham pōō′) *n.* [< Hindi *chāmpnā*, to press] **1.** a special soap, or soaplike preparation, that produces suds **2.** a shampooing —*vt.* **-pooed′, -poo′ing 1.** to wash (the hair) **2.** to wash the hair of **3.** to wash (a rug, upholstery, etc.) with a shampoo

shamrock (sham′rok′) *n.* [< Ir. *seamar*, clover] a cloverlike plant with leaflets in groups of three: emblem of Ireland

shandy (shan′dē) *n.* [< ?] a drink of beer mixed with ginger beer or lemonade: also **shan′dy-gaff**

shanghai (shaŋ′hī′) *vt.* **-haied′, -hai′ing** [< *Shanghai*, seaport in E China] **1.** to kidnap, usually by drugging, for service aboard ship **2.** [Slang] to induce (another) to do something through force or underhanded methods

shank (shaŋk) *n.* [OE. *scanca*] **1.** the part of the leg between the knee and the ankle in man or a corresponding part in animals **2.** a cut of meat from the leg of an animal **3.** a straight, narrow part between other parts, as the part of a tool between the handle and the working part —**ride (or go) on shank's mare (or pony)** to walk

shantung (shan′tuŋ′) *n.* [< *Shantung*, province of China] a fabric of silk with an uneven surface

shanty[1] (shan′tē) *n.*, *pl.* **-ties** [< CanadFr. *chantier*, workshop] a small, shabby dwelling; hut

shanty[2] *n.*, *pl.* **-teys** [< ? Fr.: see CHANT] a song that sailors sing while working

shape (shāp) *n.* [< OE. (ge)*sceap*, form] **1.** the way a thing looks because of its outline; outer form **2.** the form of a particular person or thing **3.** the contour of the body; figure **4.** guise [a foe in the *shape* of a friend] **5.** a phantom **6.** a mould **7.** definite or regular form [to begin to take *shape*] **8.** [Colloq.] *a*) condition [in poor *shape*] *b*) good physical condition [exercises that keep one in *shape*] —*vt.* **shaped, shap′ing 1.** to give definite shape to; make **2.** to arrange, express, etc. in definite form **3.** to adapt [*shape* your plans to your abilities] **4.** to direct (one's life, the course of events, etc.) —*vi.* [Colloq.] to take shape —**shape up** [Colloq.] **1.** to develop to a definite form, condition, etc. **2.** to develop satisfactorily —**take shape** to begin to have definite form

SHAPE (shāp) Supreme Headquarters Allied Powers, Europe

shapeless *adj.* **1.** without distinct or regular form **2.** without a pleasing shape

shapely *adj.* **-lier, -liest** having a pleasing shape; well-proportioned: used esp. of a woman —**shape′liness** *n.*

shard (shärd) *n.* [OE. *sceard*] **1.** a fragment or broken piece, esp. of pottery **2.** *Zool.* a hard covering, as a shell or scale

share[1] (shãr) *n.* [OE. *scearu*] **1.** a portion that belongs to an individual **2.** a just or full part [to do one's *share* of work]

3. any of the equal parts of the capital stock of a company —*vt.* **shared, shar′-ing 1.** to distribute in shares **2.** to receive, use, etc. in common with others —*vi.* to have a share; participate (*in*) —**share and share alike** with each having an equal share

share[2] *n.* [OE. *scear*] the part of a plough or other agricultural tool that cuts the soil

shareholder *n.* a person who holds or owns shares in a company

SHARK
(13.5 m maximum length)

shark *n.* [< ?] **1.** a large marine fish with a tough, slate-grey skin: most sharks are fish-eaters and some will attack man **2.** a swindler

sharkskin *n.* **1.** leather made from the skin of a shark **2.** a cloth with a smooth, silky surface

sharp (shärp) *adj.* [OE. *scearp*] **1.** having a very thin edge or fine point for cutting or piercing **2.** having a point or edge; not rounded [a *sharp* ridge] **3.** abrupt [a *sharp* turn] **4.** clearly defined; distinct [a *sharp* contrast] **5.** quick in perception; clever **6.** vigilant [a *sharp* lookout] **7.** crafty; underhanded **8.** harsh or severe [*sharp* criticism] **9.** violent [a *sharp* attack] **10.** brisk; active [a *sharp* run] **11.** intense [a *sharp* pain] **12.** pungent, as in taste **13.** high-pitched; shrill **14.** cold and cutting [a *sharp* wind] **15.** [Colloq.] attractively dressed or groomed **16.** *Music* above true pitch —*adv.* **1.** in a sharp manner; specif., *a*) abruptly; briskly *b*) *Music* above true pitch **2.** precisely [one o'clock *sharp*] —*n.* **1.** *Music a*) a tone one semitone above another *b*) the symbol (♯) indicating this **2.** *same as* SHARPER —**sharp′ish** *adj.*

sharpen *vt.*, *vi.* to make or become sharp or sharper

sharper *n.* a person, esp. a gambler, who is dishonest in dealing with others; swindler

sharp practice unscrupulous, dishonest dealings

sharp-set *adj.* hungry; ravenous

sharp-tongued *adj.* using or characterized by harshly critical language

sharp-witted *adj.* having or showing keen intelligence

shatter (shat′ər) *vt.* [ME. *schateren*, scatter] **1.** to break into pieces suddenly **2.** to damage severely [to *shatter* one's health] **3.** to dumbfound; thoroughly upset —*vi.* to burst into pieces —**to be shattered** [Colloq.] to feel exhausted

shave (shāv) *vt.* **shaved, shaved** or **shav′-en, shav′ing** [OE. *sceafan*] **1.** *a*) to cut off (hair, esp. the beard) at the surface of the skin b) to cut the hair to the surface of [to shave the legs] c) to cut the beard of (a person) 2. to cut or scrape away thin slices from 3. to barely touch in passing; graze —vi. to cut off hair with a razor —n. 1. the act or an instance of shaving 2. a tool for cutting off thin slices

shaver n. 1. a razor 2. [Colloq.] a boy; lad

Shavian (shā'vē ən) adj. [< ModL. Shavius, Shaw] of or characteristic of George Bernard Shaw or his work —n. an admirer of Shaw

shaving n. 1. the act of one that shaves 2. a thin piece of wood, metal, etc. shaved off

shawl (shôl) n. [< Per. shāl] an oblong or square cloth worn by women as a covering for the head or shoulders, or used to wrap round a baby

she (shē; unstressed shi) pron. for pl. see THEY [< OE. seo] the woman, girl, or female animal (or the object regarded as female) previously mentioned —n., pl. **shes** a woman, girl, or female animal

sheaf (shēf) n., pl. **sheaves** [OE. sceaf] 1. a bunch of cut stalks of grain, etc. bound together 2. a collection, as of papers, bound in a bundle —vt. same as SHEAVE

shear (shēər) vt. sheared, sheared or shorn, shear'ing [OE. scieran] 1. to cut as with shears 2. a) to remove (wool, etc.) by cutting b) to cut the wool, etc. from 3. to tear (off) by shearing stress 4. to strip (of a power, right, etc.) —vi. 1. to use shears, etc. in cutting wool, metal, etc. 2. to break under a shearing stress 3. to move as if by cutting —shear'er n.

shearing stress the force causing two contacting parts to slide upon each other in opposite directions

shears n.pl. [also with sing. v.] 1. large scissors: also called **pair of shears** 2. any of several large tools or machines with two opposed blades, used to cut metal, etc.

shearwater (shēər'wôt'ər) n. a sea bird that flies low over water, with its wings sometimes touching the water

sheath (shēth) n., pl. **sheaths** (shēthz) [OE. sceath] 1. a case for the blade of a knife, sword, etc. 2. a covering resembling this, as the membrane round a muscle, etc. 3. a woman's closefitting dress 4. a condom —vt. same as SHEATHE

sheathe (shēth) vt. sheathed, sheath'ing 1. to put into a sheath or scabbard 2. to enclose in a case or covering

sheathing (shē'thiŋ) n. something that sheathes, as the inner covering of boards or waterproof material on a roof

sheave (shēv) vt. sheaved, sheav'ing [< SHEAF] to gather and fix (grain, papers, etc.) in a sheaf or sheaves

sheaves (shēvz) n. pl. of SHEAF

shebeen (shi bēn') n. [< Ir.] a house or establishment in Ireland, Scotland or South Africa where alcohol is sold without a licence

shebeen king in South Africa, the male proprietor of a shebeen —**shebeen queen** fem.

shed[1] (shed) n. [OE. scead] 1. a small building or lean-to, used for shelter or storage 2. a large, barnlike structure for storage

shed[2] vt. shed, shed'ding [OE. sceadan, to separate] 1. to pour out 2. to cause to flow [to shed tears] 3. to radiate [to shed light] 4. to cause to flow off [oilskin sheds water] 5. to cast off (a natural growth or covering, as leaves, hair, etc.) —**shed blood** to kill in a violent way

sheen (shēn) n. [< OE. sciene, beautiful] brightness; lustre

sheep (shēp) n., pl. **sheep** [OE. sceap] 1. a cud-chewing mammal with heavy wool; the edible flesh is called mutton 2. a person who is meek, stupid, timid, etc. 3. a member of a church's congregation —**make sheep's eyes at** to look shyly but amorously at

sheep-dip n. any chemical preparation used as a bath, as to free sheep from vermin or to clean the fleece

sheep dog any dog trained to herd and protect sheep, or of a breed used for this

sheepfold n. a pen or enclosure for sheep

sheepish adj. 1. embarrassed 2. awkwardly shy or bashful

sheep run in Australia, a farm raising sheep, smaller than a sheep station

sheepshank n. a knot used for shortening a rope

sheepskin n. 1. a) the skin of a sheep, esp. with the fleece left on b) a garment, rug, etc. made of this 2. leather made from the skin of a sheep

sheer[1] (shēər) vi., vt. [< SHEAR] to change or cause to change course suddenly

sheer[2] adj. [< ON. skærr, bright] 1. extremely steep, as the face of a cliff 2. very thin; transparent: said of textiles 3. absolute; downright [sheer persistence] —adv. 1. completely; utterly 2. very steeply

sheet[1] (shēt) n. [OE. sceat] 1. a large piece of cotton, linen, etc., used on a bed 2. a) a single piece of paper b) a large piece of paper with a number of pages printed on it, to be folded for binding into a book c) [Colloq.] a newspaper 3. a broad, continuous surface or layer, as of flame, water, etc. 4. a broad, thin piece of any material, as glass, metal, etc. —vt. to cover or provide with a sheet —adj. in the form of a sheet [sheet iron]

sheet[2] n. [< OE. sceatline] a rope for controlling the set of a sail, attached to a lower corner —**three sheets in the wind** [Slang] very drunk

sheet anchor 1. a large anchor used only in emergencies 2. a person or thing to be relied upon in emergency

sheeting n. 1. cotton or linen material used for making sheets 2. material used in covering or lining a surface [copper sheeting]

sheet music music printed on unbound sheets of paper

sheik, sheikh (shāk) *n.* [Ar. *shaikh*, old man] 1. the chief of an Arab family, tribe, or village 2. an official in the Moslem religious organization —**sheik′dom** *n.*

sheila (shē′lə) *n.* [< *Sheila*, name] [Aust. Colloq.] a girl or young woman

shekel (shek′′l) *n.* [< Heb. *shāqal*, weigh] 1. among the ancient Hebrews, etc., a unit of weight or a gold or silver coin 2. [*pl.*] [Slang] money

shelduck (shel′duk) *n.* [prob. < MDu. *schillede*, variegated] a large wild duck found in Europe, Asia, etc.: the plumage is variegated: also **shel′drake′**

shelf (shelf) *n., pl.* **shelves** [< MLowG. *schelf*] 1. a thin, flat length of wood, etc. fixed horizontally to a wall, or in a cupboard, etc., used for holding things 2. something like a shelf; specif., a) a flat ledge of rock b) a sand bar or reef —**on the shelf** 1. out of use, circulation, etc. 2. unmarried: said esp. of a woman

shelf life the length of time a packaged food, chemical, etc. will last without deteriorating

shell (shel) *n.* [OE. *sciel*] 1. a hard outer covering, as of a turtle, egg, nut, etc. 2. something like a shell in being hollow, empty, a covering, etc., as the framework of a building 3. a shy manner [to come out of one's *shell*] 4. a light, narrow racing boat rowed by a team of oarsmen 5. an explosive artillery projectile 6. a small-arms cartridge —*vt.* 1. to remove the shell or covering from 2. to fire shells at from large guns —**shell out** [Colloq.] to pay out (money) —**shell′-like′** *adj.*

she'll (shēl; *unstressed* shil) 1. she shall 2. she will

shellac (shə lak′) *n.* [SHEL(L) + LAC] 1. a resin usually produced in thin, flaky layers 2. a thin varnish containing this resin and alcohol —*vt.* **-lacked′, -lack′-ing** to apply shellac to

shellfire (shel′fīər′) *n.* the firing of large shells

shellfish *n.* any aquatic animal, esp. an edible one, with a shell, as the lobster, etc.

shellproof *adj.* proof against damage from shells or bombs

shell shock *an earlier term for* COMBAT FATIGUE —**shell′shocked′** *adj.*

shelta (shel′tə) *n.* [< ?] a jargon based on Gaelic and used by tinkers, etc.

shelter (shel′tər) *n.* [< ?] 1. something that covers or protects 2. a being covered, protected, etc. —*vt.* to provide shelter for; protect —*vi.* to find shelter

shelve (shelv) *vi.* **shelved, shelv′ing** [< SHELF] to slope gradually —*vt.* 1. to furnish with shelves 2. to put on a shelf or shelves 3. a) to lay aside [to *shelve* a discussion] b) to dismiss from active service

shelves *n. pl. of* SHELF

shelving *n.* 1. material for shelves 2. shelves collectively

shemozzle (shə moz′əl) *n.* [< Yiddish *shlimazel*, bad luck] [Slang] 1. a confused situation; muddle 2. a quarrel

shenanigan (shi nan′i gən) *n.* [< ?] [usually *pl.*] [Colloq.] nonsense; trickery; mischief

shepherd (shep′ərd) *n.* [see SHEEP & HERD²] 1. a person who herds sheep 2. a leader of a group; esp., a clergyman —*vt.* to herd, guard, lead, etc. as a shepherd —**shep′herdess** *n.fem.*

shepherd's pie a dish of minced meat with mashed potatoes on top

Sheraton (sher′ə tan) *adj.* [< T. *Sheraton*] designating a style of furniture of the late 18th cent.

sherbet (shur′bət) *n.* [< Ar. *sharbah*, a drink] 1. a beverage of watered fruit juice and sugar 2. a fruit-flavoured powder that effervesces when water is added

sherd (shurd) *n. same as* SHARD (sense 1)

sheriff (sher′if) *n.* [< OE. *scir*, shire + *gerefa*, reeve] 1. in England, esp. formerly, any of various officers of a shire, or county 2. in Scotland, a judge or chief magistrate 3. in the U.S., the chief law-enforcement officer of a county 4. in Canada, a municipal official who enforces court orders, escorts convicted criminals to prison, etc.

Sherpa (shur′pə) *n.* a member of a Tibetan people from the southern slopes of the Himalayas

sherry (sher′ē) *n., pl.* **-ries** [< *Xeres* (now Jerez), Spain] 1. a strong, yellow or brownish Spanish wine 2. any similar wine made elsewhere

she's (shēz) 1. she is 2. she has

Shetland pony (shet′lənd) any of a breed of sturdy ponies, orig. from the Shetland Islands

shew (shō) *n., vt., vi.* **shewed, shewn** or **shewed, shew′ing** *archaic sp. of* SHOW

shibboleth (shib′ə leth) *n.* [< Heb. *shibbōleth*, a stream] something said or done that is a sign or test of belonging to a certain group, class, or party: see Judg. 12:4-6

shied (shīd) *pt. & pp. of* SHY²

shield (shēld) *n.* [OE. *scield*] 1. a piece of armour carried in the hand or on the forearm to ward off blows or missiles 2. any person or thing that guards or protects 3. anything shaped like a triangular shield, as an escutcheon, badge, etc. or a trophy presented in a sports competition 4. a safety guard, as over the moving parts of machinery —*vt., vi.* to defend; protect —**the Shield** the Canadian Shield

shieling (shē′lig) *n.* [< Scot. *shiel*, hut] [Scot.] 1. a grazing ground; pasture 2. a rude hut

shift (shift) *vt.* [OE. *sciftan*, divide] 1. to move from one person, place, etc. to another 2. to replace by another or others 3. [U.S.] to change (gears) in driving a motor vehicle 4. [Colloq.] to move very quickly —*vi.* 1. to change position, direction, etc. 2. to get along [to *shift* for oneself] 3. [U.S.] to change gear 4. in typing, to change from small letters, etc. to capitals by depressing a key (**shift key**) —*n.* 1. a change [a *shift* in public opinion] 2. a group of people working in relay with other groups, or the work period involved *[the night shift]* **3.** a plan of conduct, esp. for an emergency; expedient **4.** a deceitful scheme; trick **5.** the displacement of a series or group *[a vowel shift]* **6.** a loose dress that hangs straight —**make shift** to do the best one can (*with*)

shiftless *adj.* lazy or careless

shifty *adj.* **-ier, -iest** not to be trusted; evasive —**shift'ily** *adv.* —**shift'iness** *n.*

shillelagh, shillalah (shi lā'lə) *n.* [< *Shillelagh,* Irish village] a club or cudgel: also sp. **shille'lah**

shilling (shil'iŋ) *n.* [OE. *scylling*] **1.** a former British coin, equal to 1/20 of a pound **2.** a monetary unit used in several countries

shilly-shally (shil'ē shal'ē) *vi.* **-lied, -lying** [< *shall I?*] to be unable to make up one's mind; vacillate

shim (shim) *n.* [< ?] a thin piece of wood, metal, etc. used for filling space, levelling, etc.

shimmer (shim'ər) *vi.* [OE. *scymrian*] **1.** to shine with an unsteady light **2.** to form a wavering image —*n.* a shimmering light

shimmy (shim'ē) *n.* [< CHEMISE] a jazz dance of the 1920's, with much shaking of the body

shin (shin) *n.* [OE. *scinu*] the front part of the leg between the knee and the ankle —*vt., vi.* **shinned, shin'ning** to climb (a rope, pole, etc.) by gripping with both hands and legs: often with *up*

shinbone *n.* same as TIBIA

shindig (shin'dig') *n.* [< SHINDY] [Colloq.] a noisy dance, party, etc.

shindy (shin'dē) *n., pl.* **-dies** [< ?] [Colloq.] a noisy disturbance; commotion

shine (shin) *vi.* **shone, shin'ing** [OE. *scinan*] **1.** to give off or reflect light; gleam; glow **2.** to excel; be eminent **3.** to show itself clearly —*vt.* **1.** to direct the light of **2.** to make shiny by polishing —*n.* **1.** brightness; radiance **2.** lustre; polish **3.** splendour; brilliance **4.** fair weather —**take a shine to** [Colloq.] take a liking to (someone)

shiner *n.* [Colloq.] a black eye

shingle[1] (shiŋ'g'l) *n.* [< ?] an area of coarse, waterworn gravel, as on a beach —**shin'gly** *adj.*

shingle[2] *n.* [< L. *scindula,* a shingle] **1.** a thin, wedge-shaped piece of wood, slate, etc. laid with others in overlapping rows as a covering for roofs, etc. **2.** a woman's short haircut tapered at the nape —*vt.* **-gled, -gling** **1.** to cover (a roof, etc.) with shingles **2.** to cut (hair) in shingle style

shingles (shiŋ'g'lz) *n.* [< L. *cingere,* gird] a viral disease, with inflammation and skin blisters

Shinto (shin'tō) *n.* [Jap. < Chin. *shin,* god + *tao,* way] a religion of Japan, emphasizing worship of nature and of ancestors —**Shin'toism** *n.* —**Shin'toist** *n., adj.*

shinty (shin'tē) *n., pl.* **-ties** [< ?] **1.**

a simple form of hockey **2.** the curved stick used in this game

shiny (shin'ē) *adj.* **-ier, -iest** **1.** bright; shining **2.** highly polished; glossy **3.** rubbed smooth and glossy, as clothing —**shin'iness** *n.*

ship (ship) *n.* [OE. *scip*] **1.** any large vessel navigating deep water **2.** [Chiefly U.S.] an aircraft —*vt.* **shipped, ship'ping 1.** to put or take on board a ship **2.** to send or transport by any carrier *[to ship coal by rail]* **3.** to take in (water) over the side, as in a heavy sea **4.** to put in its proper place on a vessel *[ship the oars]* **5.** to hire for work on a ship —*vi.* **1.** to embark **2.** to be hired to serve on a ship —**when** (or **if,** etc.) **one's ship comes in** (or **home**) when (or if, etc.) one's fortune is made

-ship (ship) [OE. *-scipe*] *a suffix meaning:* **1.** the quality or state of *[friendship]* **2.** *a)* the rank or office of *[governorship] b)* one having the rank of *[lordship]* **3.** ability as *[leadership]* **4.** all individuals (of the specified class) collectively *[readership]*

shipboard *n.* a ship: chiefly in **on shipboard,** aboard a ship —*adj.* done, happening, etc. on a ship

shipbuilder *n.* one whose business is building ships —**ship'build'ing** *n.*

ship canal a canal large enough for seagoing ships

shipmaster *n.* the officer in command of a merchant ship; captain

shipmate *n.* a fellow sailor on the same ship

shipment *n.* **1.** the shipping or transporting of goods **2.** goods shipped

ship money a former tax levied to provide money for warships

ship of the desert a camel

shipowner *n.* an owner of a ship or ships

shipper *n.* a person who ships goods

shipping *n.* **1.** the act or business of transporting goods **2.** ships collectively

shipping agent the person who arranges the shipment of goods or passengers

shipshape *adj.* having everything neatly in place —*adv.* in a neat and orderly manner

shipwreck *n.* **1.** the remains of a wrecked ship **2.** the loss of a ship through storm, etc. **3.** any ruin or destruction —*vt.* to cause to undergo shipwreck

shipwright *n.* a man, esp. a carpenter, whose work is the construction and repair of ships

shipyard *n.* a place where ships are built and repaired

shire (shīər) *n.* [OE. *scir,* office] a county —**the Shires** the Midland counties of England

shire horse a breed of large, powerful, draught horse

shirk (shurk) *vt., vi.* [< ?] to neglect or evade doing —**shirk'er** *n.*

shirring (shur'iŋ) *n.* [< ?] a gathering made in cloth by drawing the material up on parallel rows of short stitches

shirt (shurt) *n.* [OE. *scyrte*] **1.** the usual

sleeved garment worn by men on the upper part of the body, often under a suit jacket, typically having a collar and a buttoned opening down the front **2.** a similar garment for women —**keep one's shirt on** [Slang] to remain patient or calm —**put one's shirt on** [Slang] **1.** to bet all one has on **2.** to support to the fullest extent possible

shirting *n.* material for making shirts

shirttail *n.* the part of a shirt extending below the waist

shirtwaister a dress with a bodice like a shirt

shirty *adj.* **-ier, -iest** [< SHIRT] [Slang] ill-tempered, angry, etc.

shish kebab (shēsh′kə bab′) [< Ar. *shīsh*, skewer + *kabāb*, kebab] a dish of small chunks of meat, esp. lamb, placed on skewers alternately with tomatoes, onions, etc., and grilled

shit (shit) *vi.* **shat,** or **shit′ted, shit′ting** [OE. *scītan*, dung] [Vulg.] to defecate —*n.* [Vulg.] **1.** excrement **2.** [Slang] rubbish, nonsense **3.** [Slang] a contemptible person —**shit′ty** *adj.*

shiver¹ (shiv′ər) *n.* [ME. *schivere*] a fragment or splinter —*vt., vi.* to break into many fragments or splinters

shiver² *vi.* [ME. *cheveren*] to shake, tremble, etc., as from fear or cold —*n.* a shaking, trembling, etc. —**the shivers** a fit of shivering —**shiv′ery** *adj.*

shoal¹ (shōl) *n.* [OE. *scolu*] a large school of fish —*vi.* to move about as a shoal

shoal² *n.* [OE. *sceald,* shallow] **1.** a shallow place in a river, sea, etc. **2.** a sand bar, etc. forming a danger to navigation, esp. one visible at low water **3.** [*usually pl.*] hidden snags —*vt., vi.* to make or become shallow

shock¹ (shok) *n.* [< MFr. *choquer*] **1.** a sudden, powerful blow, shake, etc. **2.** *a)* a sudden emotional disturbance *b)* something causing this **3.** the violent effect on the body of an electric current passed through it **4.** *Med.* a disorder caused by severe injury, loss of blood, etc., and marked by rapid pulse, etc. —*vt.* **1.** to disturb emotionally; astonish, horrify, etc. **2.** to produce electric shock in —*vi.* to be shocked [one who does not *shock* easily] —**shock′er** *n.*

SHOCKS OF CORN

shock² *n.* [ME. *schokke*] a number of grain sheaves stacked together on end to dry —*vt., vi.* to gather in shocks

shock³ *n.* [< ?] a thick, bushy or tangled mass, as of hair

shock absorber a device, as on the springs of a car, that lessens or absorbs the force of shocks

shocking *adj.* **1.** causing shock, horror, etc. **2.** [Colloq] very bad **3.** garish [*shocking* pink]

shockproof *adj.* able to absorb shock without being damaged

shock therapy a method of treating certain psychotic conditions by injecting drugs or by applying electric current to the brain: also **shock treatment**

shod (shod) *alt. pt. & pp. of* SHOE

shodden (shod′'n) *alt. pp. of* SHOE

shoddy (shod′ē) *adj.* **shod′dier, shod′diest** [< ?] **1.** made of any inferior material **2.** poorly done or made **3.** sham **4.** contemptible; low [a *shoddy* trick] —*n., pl.* **shod′dies** an inferior woollen cloth made from fibres of used fabrics —**shod′dily** *adv.* —**shod′diness** *n.*

shoe (shōo) *n.* [OE. *sceoh*] **1.** an outer covering for the foot, made of leather, canvas, etc. **2.** something like a shoe in shape or use; specif., *short for* HORSESHOE, BRAKE SHOE —*vt.* **shod** or **shoed, shod, shoe′ing** to furnish with shoes —**in another's shoes** in another's position

shoehorn *n.* a curved implement inserted at the back of a shoe to help in slipping the heel in

shoelace *n.* a length of cord, leather, etc. used for fastening a shoe

shoe leather 1. leather suitable for the manufacture of shoes **2.** shoes, in general

shoemaker *n.* a person whose business is making or repairing shoes —**shoe′mak′ing** *n.*

shoestring *n.* **1.** *same as* SHOELACE **2.** a small amount of money as capital [the business was started on a *shoestring*] —*adj.* precarious; barely sufficient

shoe tree a block of wood, etc. put into a shoe to preserve its shape

shone (shon) *pt. & pp. of* SHINE

shoo (shōo) *interj.* [echoic] go away! get out! —*vt.* **shooed, shoo′ing** to drive away abruptly, as by crying "shoo"

shook (shook) *pt. of* SHAKE —**shook up** [Chiefly U.S. Slang] upset; disturbed

shoot (shōot) *vt.* **shot, shoot′ing** [OE. *sceotan*] **1.** to wound or kill with a bullet, arrow, etc. **2.** to discharge or fire (a bullet, gun, bow, etc.) **3.** to send forth swiftly or with force **4.** to hurl or thrust out [volcanoes *shooting* molten rock] **5.** to slide (a door bolt) into or out of its fastening **6.** to pour or empty out **7.** to move swiftly over, by, etc. [to *shoot* the rapids] **8.** to photograph or film **9.** to fleck (*with* another colour or substance) **10.** to put forth (a branch, etc.) **11.** *Games, Sports* to throw or drive (a ball, etc.) towards the objective **12.** [Slang] to inject, as with drugs —*vi.* **1.** to fire a missile, gun, etc. **2.** to move swiftly **3.** to be felt suddenly and keenly, as pain **4.** to use guns, etc., as in hunting **5.** to jut out **6.** to grow or sprout rapidly **7.** to start film cameras working **8.** *Sports* to propel a ball, etc. towards the objective **—n.** **1.** a new growth; sprout **2.** *a)* a party organized to hunt game *b)* the ground over which game is hunted **3.** a chute **—interj.** [Chiefly U.S.] begin talking! **—shoot one's mouth off** [Slang] to talk indiscreetly **—shoot'er n.**

shooting brake *same as* ESTATE CAR

shooting star *same as* METEOR

shooting stick a canelike stick with a spike at one end and a narrow, folding seat at the top

shop (shop) *n.* [OE. *sceoppa*, booth] **1.** *a)* a place where goods are offered for sale *b)* a specialized department in a large store **2.** a place where a particular kind of work is done [a printing *shop*] **—vi.** **shopped, shop'ping** to visit shops to examine or buy merchandise **—vt.** [Slang] to inform on to the police **—all over the shop** [Colloq.] **1.** everywhere **2.** in disorder **—set up shop** to start a business **—shop around 1.** to go from shop to shop, looking for bargains **2.** to search for a better job, idea, etc. **—talk shop** to discuss one's work

shop assistant someone who is employed to assist customers in a shop or store

shop floor 1. the part of a factory where goods are produced **2.** workers as opposed to management

shopkeeper *n.* a person who owns or operates a shop **—shop'keep'ing n.**

shoplifter *n.* a person who steals articles from a store during shopping hours **—shop'lift' vt., vi.**

shopping bag a bag used to carry purchases made while shopping: also **shop'per**

shopping centre a complex of stores, restaurants, etc. with an adjoining car park

shopping mall [Chiefly U.S. & Canad.] a large, enclosed shopping centre, often with central heating

shopping plaza [Chiefly U.S. & Canad.] a shopping centre, esp. a smaller group of stores built as a strip

shop-soiled *adj.* **1.** soiled, faded, etc. from having been displayed in a shop **2.** drab, dull, etc.

shop steward a trade-union official elected by his fellow workers to represent them in dealing with the employer

shoptalk *n.* conversation about one's work, esp. after hours

shore¹ (shôr) *n.* [< ME. *schore*] land at the edge of a body of water

shore² *n.* [akin to MDu. *schore*] a beam, etc. placed under or against something as a prop **—vt. shored, shor'ing** to support as with shores (usually with *up*)

shoreline *n.* the edge of a body of water

shoreward *adv.* towards the shore : also **shore'wards —adj.** moving towards the shore

shorn (shôrn) *alt. pp. of* SHEAR

short (shôrt) *adj.* [OE. *scort*] **1.** not extending far from end to end **2.** not great in range or scope **3.** low in height;

not tall **4.** brief **5.** not retentive [a *short* memory] **6.** condensed or concise **7.** brief to the point of rudeness; curt **8.** less than a sufficient or correct amount **9.** having a tendency to crumble, as pastry **10.** designating a sale of securities, etc. which the seller expects to buy later at a lower price **11.** *Phonet. & Prosody* comparatively brief in duration, as sounds, syllables, etc. **—n.** **1.** something short; specif., a short sound or syllable **2.** a drink of whisky, gin, etc. as opposed to beer **3.** [*pl.*] *a)* short trousers reaching partway to the knee *b)* [U.S.] a man's underpants **4.** *colloq. form of* SHORT CIRCUIT **—adv.** **1.** abruptly; suddenly **2.** briefly; concisely **3.** so as to be short **4.** unawares [caught *short*] **—vt., vi. colloq. form of** SHORT-CIRCUIT **—fall** (or **come**) **short 1.** to be insufficient **2.** to fail to reach **—in short** briefly **—run short** to have less than enough **—short for** being an abbreviation of **—short of 1.** less than **2.** lacking **3.** without actually resorting to **—short'ish adj. —short'ness n.**

shortage *n.* a deficiency in the amount needed or expected

shortbread *n.* a rich, crumbly biscuit made with a lot of butter : also **short'cake**

shortchange (shôrt'chānj') *vt., vi.* **-changed', -chang'ing** [Colloq.] **1.** to give less money than is due in change **2.** to cheat

short-circuit (shôrt'sur'kit) *vt.* **1.** *Elec.* to make a short circuit in **2.** to bypass (an obstruction, etc.) **—vi.** to develop a short circuit

short circuit 1. a low-resistance connection between two points in an electric circuit that deflects the current or causes excessive current flow **2.** popularly, a disrupted electric circuit resulting from this

shortcoming *n.* a fault, defect, or deficiency

shortcut *n.* **1.** a shorter way to get to the same place **2.** any way of saving time, effort, etc.

shorten *vt., vi.* to make or become short or shorter

shortening *n.* fat used to make pastry, etc. crisp or flaky

shortfall *n.* **1.** failure to meet a goal **2.** the amount of such a failure; deficiency

shorthand *n.* any system of special symbols for letters, words, etc. as for taking dictation rapidly **—adj.** written in or using shorthand

short-handed (shôrt'han'did) *adj.* short of workers or helpers

shorthorn *n.* a breed of cattle with short, curved horns

short list the candidates left for a position, etc. after preliminary tests, interviews, etc. **—short'-list vt.** to include on a short list

short-lived *adj.* having a short life span or existence

shortly *adv.* 1. soon 2. briefly 3. rudely; curtly

short-range *adj.* 1. having a range of short distance 2. not looking far into the future

short shrift very little care or attention, as from lack of patience or sympathy

shortsighted (shôrt′sīt′id) *adj.* 1. having better vision for near things than for far ones; myopic 2. having or showing a lack of foresight

short-tempered *adj.* easily or quickly angered

short-term *adj.* for or lasting a short time

short ton in the U.S., Canada, and S Africa, a ton that is 2000 pounds avoirdupois

shortwave *n.* a radio wave sixty metres or less

short-winded (shôrt′win′did) *adj.* easily put out of breath by exertion

shot[1] (shot) *n.* [OE. *sceot*] 1. the act of shooting; discharge of a missile, esp. from a gun 2. *a)* a projectile for a firearm *b)* such projectiles collectively 3. small pellets of lead for a shotgun 4. range; scope 5. a marksman *[a fair shot]* 6. an attempt to hit with a missile 7. an attempt 8. a guess 9. the path of an object thrown, etc. in various games 10. the ball used in the shot put 11. a blast 12. *a)* a single photograph *b)* a sequence or view taken by a single continuous run of a film 13. a hypodermic injection, as of vaccine 14. a drink of alcohol —**a shot in the arm** something that bolsters up, encourages, etc. —**have a shot at** [Colloq.] to make a try at —**like a shot** quickly or eagerly —**shot in the dark** a wild guess

shot[2] *pt. & pp. of* SHOOT —*adj.* variegated, streaked, etc. with another colour or substance

shotgun *n.* a smoothbore gun for firing a charge of small shot at short range

shot put (poot′) 1. a contest in which a heavy metal ball is propelled by an overhand thrust from the shoulder 2. a single put of the shot —**shot′-put′ting** *n.*

should (shood; *unstressed, often* shəd) *v.* [OE. *sceolde*] 1. *pt. of* SHALL 2. an auxiliary used to express: a) obligation, duty, etc. *[he should help her]* b) expectation or probability *[he should be here soon]* c) futurity in polite requests or in statements implying doubt *[I should think he'd like it]* d) a future condition *[if I should die tomorrow]*

shoulder (shōl′dər) *n.* [OE. *sculdor*] 1. *a)* the joint connecting the arm or forelimb with the body *b)* the part of the body including this joint 2. *[pl.]* the two shoulders and the part of the back between them 3. a cut of meat consisting of the upper foreleg and attached parts 4. the part of a garment that covers the shoulder 5. a shoulderlike projection 6. the strip along the edge of a paved road —*vt.* 1. to assume the burden of 2. to push through, as with the shoulder 3. to carry

upon the shoulder —**cry on someone's shoulder** to tell one's troubles to someone —**put one's shoulder to the wheel** to set to work vigorously —**shoulder to shoulder** 1. side by side 2. working together —**straight from the shoulder** 1. moving straight forward from the shoulder: said of a blow 2. frankly —**turn (or give) a cold shoulder to** to treat with disdain; avoid

shoulder blade either of two flat bones in the upper back

shoulder strap 1. a strap worn over the shoulder to support a garment 2. a strap worn over the shoulder for carrying an attached bag, camera, etc. 3. a flap of cloth on the shoulder of a uniform, etc.

shout (shout) *n.* [ME. *schoute*] 1. a loud, sudden cry or call 2. [Chiefly Aust. Colloq.] a turn to pay, esp. for a round of drinks —*vt., vi.* 1. to utter in a shout or cry out loudly 2. [Aust. Colloq.] to treat (someone), as to a drink —**shout down** to silence by loud shouting —**shout′-er** *n.*

shove (shuv) *vt., vi.* shoved, shov′ing [OE. *scufan*] 1. to push, as along a surface 2. to push roughly —*n.* a push —**shove off** 1. to push (a boat) away from shore 2. [Colloq.] to leave

shovel (shuv′'l) *n.* [OE. *scofl*] 1. a tool with a broad scoop or blade and a long handle: used in lifting and moving loose material 2. any machine with a shovellike device —*vt.* **-elled, -elling** 1. to lift and move with a shovel 2. to put in large quantities *[to shovel food in one's mouth]* —**shov′elful** *n.*

show (shō) *vt.* showed, shown *or* showed, show′ing [OE. *sceawian*, to look] 1. to reveal *[to show anger]* 2. to bring or put in sight; display 3. to conduct *[show him to his room]* 4. to point out *[we showed him the sights]* 5. to explain, prove, or demonstrate 6. to register *[a clock shows the time]* 7. to grant or bestow (favour, mercy, etc.) —*vi.* 1. to appear 2. to be noticeable *[the scratch won't show]* 3. [Colloq.] to come or arrive as expected —*n.* 1. a showing *[a show of passion]* 2. a public display or exhibition 3. a pompous display 4. something false; pretence 5. a presentation of entertainment, as a TV programme 6. a thing or affair, esp. in **good show, bad show** —**good show!** an exclamation of appreciation and congratulations —**show off** 1. to make a display of 2. to do something meant to attract attention —**show one's hand** 1. *Cards* to show opponents one's cards 2. to reveal one's intentions, plans, etc. —**show up** 1. to expose or be exposed 2. to come; arrive 3. to embarrass —**show willing** to appear cheerful, helpful, etc.

show business the theatre, cinema, television, etc. as a business or industry: also [Colloq.] **show biz**

showcase *n.* a glass-enclosed case for protecting things on display

showdown *n.* [Colloq.] any action that brings matters to a climax

shower (shou′ər) *n.* [OE. *scur*] **1.** a brief fall of rain, hail, sleet, or snow **2.** a sudden, abundant fall, as of sparks, **3.** *a*) a bath in which the body is sprayed with fine streams of water: in full, **shower bath** *b*) an apparatus, or a room or enclosure, for this **4.** [Slang] a disreputable group of people —*vt.* **1.** to make wet as with a spray of water **2.** to pour forth as in a shower —*vi.* **1.** to fall or come as a shower **2.** to bathe under a shower —**show′ery** *adj.*

showing (shō′iŋ) *n.* an exhibition or performance

showjumping *n.* a horse-riding competition in which skill in jumping is demonstrated

showman *n.* **1.** a person whose business is producing shows **2.** a person skilled at presenting anything in a striking manner —**show′manship′** *n.*

shown (shōn) *alt. pp. of* SHOW

show-off *n.* a person who shows off

showpiece *n.* **1.** something exhibited **2.** something that is a fine example of its kind

showplace *n.* **1.** a place that is exhibited to the public for its beauty, etc. **2.** any place that is beautiful, lavishly furnished, etc.

showroom *n.* a room where merchandise is displayed, as for advertising or sale

showy *adj.* **-ier, -iest** **1.** of striking appearance **2.** attracting attention in a gaudy or flashy way —**show′ily** *adv.* —**show′iness** *n.*

shrank (shraŋk) *alt. pt. of* SHRINK

shrapnel (shrap′n'l) *n.* [< H. *Shrapnel*] **1.** an artillery shell filled with an explosive charge and small metal balls, set to explode in the air **2.** these metal balls or the shell fragments scattered by any exploding shell

shred (shred) *n.* [OE. *screade*] **1.** a long, narrow strip cut or torn off **2.** a fragment [*not* a *shred* of truth] —*vt.* **shred′ded** or **shred, shred′ding** to cut or tear into shreds —**shred′der** *n.*

shrew (shrōō) *n.* [OE. *screawa*] **1.** a small, mouselike mammal with a long snout **2.** a nagging, bad-tempered woman —**shrew′ish** *adj.*

shrewd (shrōōd) *adj.* [< ME. *schrewe*, shrew] keen-witted or sharp in practical affairs; astute —**shrewd′ly** *adv.* —**shrewd′ness** *n.*

shriek (shrēk) *vi., vt.* [prob. < ON.] to make or utter with a loud, sharp, piercing cry or sound; screech —*n.* such a sound

shrift (shrift) *n.* [< OE. *scrifan*, shrive] [Archaic] confession and absolution by a priest: see also SHORT SHRIFT

shrike (shrīk) *n.* [OE. *scric*] a shrill-voiced bird with a hooked beak

shrill (shril) *adj.* [echoic] having or producing a high, thin, piercing tone; high-pitched —*vt., vi.* to utter with or make a shrill sound —**shrill′ness** *n.* —**shril′ly** *adv.*

SHRIMP (to 23 cm long)

shrimp (shrimp) *n.* [< OE. *scrimman*, shrink] **1.** a small, long-tailed crustacean, valued as food **2.** [Colloq.] a small, slight person —*vi.* to fish for shrimps —**shrimp′-er** *n.*

shrine (shrīn) *n.* [< L. *scrinium*, box] **1.** a place of worship, usually one whose centre is a sacred scene or object **2.** a container holding sacred relics **3.** the tomb of a saint **4.** a place or thing hallowed or honoured because of its history or associations

shrink (shriŋk) *vi.* **shrank** or **shrunk**, **shrunk** or **shrunk′en**, **shrink′ing** [OE. *scrincan*] **1.** to contract, as from heat, cold, wetness, etc. **2.** to lessen, as in amount, worth, etc. **3.** to draw back in fear, etc.; flinch —*vt.* to cause to shrink —*n.* **1.** a shrinking **2.** [< (*head*)-*shrink*(*er*)] [Slang] a psychiatrist

shrinkage *n.* **1.** the act of shrinking **2.** the amount of shrinking, decrease, etc.

shrinkwrap *vt.* **-wrapped′, -wrap′ping** to package (something) in a flexible plastic material which shrinks and encloses it tightly

shrive (shrīv) *vt., vi.* **shrived** or **shrove**, **shriv′en** (shriv′'n) or **shrived**, **shriv′ing** [< L. *scribere*, to write] [Archaic] **1.** to hear the confession of (a person) and give absolution **2.** to get absolution for (oneself) by confessing

shrivel (shriv′'l) *vt., vi.* **-elled, -elling** [< ?] to shrink and make or become wrinkled or withered

shroud (shroud) *n.* [OE. *scrud*] **1.** a cloth used to wrap a corpse for burial **2.** something that covers or screens **3.** any of the ropes stretched from a ship's side to a masthead to offset lateral strain on the mast —*vt.* **1.** to wrap (a corpse) in a shroud **2.** to cover; screen

shrove (shrōv) *alt. pt. of* SHRIVE

Shrovetide (shrōv′tīd′) *n.* the three days before Ash Wednesday (**Shrove Sunday, Monday,** and **Tuesday**), formerly a period of confession and festivity before Lent

shrub (shrub) *n.* [OE. *scrybb*, brushwood] a low, woody plant with several permanent stems; bush

shrubbery *n., pl.* **-beries** an area planted with shrubs

shrubby *adj.* **-bier, -biest** **1.** covered with shrubs **2.** like a shrub —**shrub′biness** *n.*

shrug (shrug) *vt., vi.* **shrugged, shrug′ging** [< ?] to draw up (the shoulders), as in indifference, doubt, etc. —*n.* the gesture so made —**shrug off** to dismiss in a carefree way

shrunk (shruŋk) alt. pt. & pp. of SHRINK

shrunken alt. pp. of SHRINK —adj. shrivelled

shudder (shud′ər) n. [ME. schoderen] **1.** to shake or tremble violently, as in horror **2.** to shake violently; vibrate —n. a shuddering

shuffle (shuf′'l) vt., vi. -fled, -fling [prob. < LowG. schuffeln] **1.** to move (the feet) with a dragging gait **2.** to mix (playing cards) so as to change their order **3.** to mix together in a jumbled mass **4.** to shift or keep shifting about from one place to another **5.** to bring, put, or thrust (into or out of) clumsily —n. **1.** the act of shuffling **2.** a) a shuffling of the feet b) a gait, dance, etc. characterized by this **3.** a) a shuffling of playing cards b) one's turn at this —**shuffle off** to get rid of

shun (shun) vt. shunned, shun′ning [OE. scunian] to avoid strictly

'shun (shun) interj. short form of ATTENTION

shunt (shunt) vt., vi. [< ?] **1.** to move or turn to one side **2.** to switch (a train, etc.) from one line to another —n. **1.** a shunting **2.** a railway switch **3.** [Slang] a collision between motor vehicles **4.** Elec. a conductor connecting two points in a circuit and diverting part of the current from the main circuit

shush (shush) interj. [echoic] hush! be quiet! —vt. to say "shush" to; tell (another) to be quiet

shut (shut) vt. shut, shut′ting [OE. scyttan] **1.** to move (a door, lid, etc.) into a position that covers the opening to which it is fitted **2.** to close (an opening, container, etc.) **3.** a) to prevent entrance to or exit from; bar b) to confine or enclose (in) **4.** to fold up or close the parts of (an umbrella, a book, etc.) **5.** to stop the operation of (a school, etc.) —vi. to be or become shut —adj. closed, fastened, etc. —**shut down** to close (a factory, etc.), usually temporarily —**shut off 1.** to prevent the passage of (water, electricity, etc.) **2.** to isolate —**shut out** to deny entrance to; exclude —**shut up 1.** to enclose or imprison **2.** [Colloq.] to stop or cause to stop talking

shut-eye n. [Slang] sleep

shutter n. **1.** a movable, usually hinged cover for a window **2.** a device for opening and closing the aperture of a camera lens to expose the film or plate —vt. to close or furnish with shutters —**put up the shutters** (of a shop) to close for the night or permanently

shuttle (shut′'l) n. [OE. scytel] **1.** a) a device used to pass the woof thread back and forth between the warp threads in weaving b) any similar device, as that which carries the lower thread back and forth on a sewing machine **2.** a bus, aircraft, etc. making frequent trips back and forth over a short route —vt., vi. -tled, -tling to move rapidly to and fro

shuttlecock n. a rounded piece of cork having a flat end stuck with feathers: it is struck back and forth across a net by players in badminton

shuttle service a transport service, esp. an airline, operating to and fro over a short distance

shy[1] (shī) adj. shy′er or shi′er, shy′est or shi′est [OE. sceoh] **1.** easily frightened; timid **2.** not at ease with other people; bashful **3.** distrustful; wary —vi. shied, shy′ing **1.** to move suddenly when startled; start **2.** to become cautious or unwilling (often with at or from) —n., pl. shies an act of shying —**fight shy of** to avoid or evade —**shy′ly** adv. —**shy′ness** n.

shy[2] vt., vi. shied, shy′ing [< ?] to fling, esp. sidewise with a jerk —n., pl. shies a shying; fling

Shylock (shī′lok′) n. [< Shylock, in Merchant of Venice] an exacting creditor

si (sē) n. Music same as TI

‡**si** (sē) adv. [Sp.] yes: also [It.] sì

Si Chem. silicon

Siamese (sī′ə mēz′) adj., n., pl. Si′a-mese′ same as THAI

Siamese cat a short-haired cat with blue eyes, a fawn coat, and dark ears, paws, and tail

Siamese twins [< such a pair born in Siam] any pair of twins born joined to each other

sibilant (sib′ə lənt) adj. [< L. sibilare, to hiss] having or making a hissing sound —n. Phonet. a consonant characterized by a hissing sound, as (s) —**sib′ilance, sib′-ilancy** n.

sibling (sib′liŋ) n. [< OE. sibling, a relative] one of two or more persons born of the same parents, or, sometimes, having one parent in common

sibyl (sib′əl) n. [< Gr. sibylla] a prophetess; fortuneteller —**sibyl′-line′** (si bil′in) adj.

‡**sic**[1] (sik) adv. [L.] thus; so: used within brackets, [sic], to show that a quoted passage, esp. one containing some error, is shown exactly as in the original

sic[2] vt. [< SEEK] sicked, sick′ing to urge to attack [to sic a dog on someone]: also **sick**

sick (sik) adj. [OE. seoc] **1.** suffering from disease; ill **2.** vomiting or about to vomit **3.** of or for sick people [sick leave] **4.** deeply disturbed, as by grief, failure, etc. **5.** disgusted by reason of excess [sick of his excuses]: often **sick and tired 6.** having a great longing (for) **7.** [Colloq.] sadistic, morbid, etc. [a sick joke] —vt. [Colloq.] to vomit (up) —**look sick** [Colloq.] to appear disconcerted, discomfited, upset, etc. —**take sick** to become ill —**the sick** sick people collectively

sick bay a room for treating the sick, as on a ship

sickbed n. the bed of a sick person

sicken vt. to nauseate, disgust, etc. —vi. **1.** to become nauseated, disgusted, etc. **2.** to show symptoms of (with for)

sickening *adj.* 1. causing nausea 2. disgusting

SICKLE

sickle (sik′'l) *n.* [ult. < L. *secare*, to cut] a tool consisting of a crescent-shaped blade with a short handle, for cutting tall grass, etc.

sick leave leave from work granted for illness, often with pay (**sick pay**)

sickle cell anaemia an inherited anaemia characterized by an abnormal red blood cell (**sickle cell**) containing a defective form of haemoglobin

sickly (sik′lē) *adj.* -lier, -liest 1. in poor health much of the time 2. of or produced by sickness 3. producing illness 4. sickening; nauseating 5. feeble [a *sickly* light] 6. weak [a *sickly* smile] —**sick′liness** *n.*

sickness *n.* 1. illness 2. a particular illness 3. nausea

sickroom *n.* the room to which a sick person is confined

side (sīd) *n.* [OE.] 1. *a)* any of the lines or surfaces that bound something *b)* either of the two bounding surfaces of an object that are not the front, back, top, or bottom 2. either of the two surfaces of paper, cloth, etc. 3. the right or left half of a human or animal body 4. a position beside one 5. a specified surface [the visible *side* of the moon] 6. a quality [his cruel *side*, the bright *side* of life] 7. the slope of a hill, bank, etc. 8. any location with reference to a central point 9. the ideas or position of one person or faction opposing another 10. one of the parties or teams in a contest, conflict, etc. 11. line of descent 12. [Slang] patronizing manner 13. *Billiards* a spinning motion given to a ball —*adj.* 1. of, at, or on a side 2. to or from one side [a *side* glance] 3. incidental [a *side* effect] 4. secondary [a *side* issue] —**let the side down** to do or say something that causes embarrassment or frustration among one's colleagues —**on the side** in addition to the main thing, part, etc. —**side by side** beside each other; together —**side with** to support (one of opposing factions, etc.) —**take sides** to support one of the parties in a dispute, etc.

side arms weapons of the kind that may be worn at the at the waist, as a sword, pistol, etc.

sideboard *n.* a piece of dining-room furniture for holding table linen, silver, china, etc.

sideboards *n.pl.* the hair growing on a man's face just in front of the ears

sideburns *n.pl. Chiefly U.S.* var. of SIDEBOARDS

sidecar *n.* a small car attached to the side of a motorcycle, for carrying a passenger, parcels, etc.

sided *adj.* having (a specified number of) sides [six-*sided*]

sidekick *n.* [U.S. Slang] 1. a close friend or follower 2. a partner

sidelight *n.* 1. a light at or coming from the side 2. either of two small lights on the front of a vehicle, used to indicate its presence rather than to aid the driver 3. a bit of incidental information on a subject

sideline *n.* 1. *a)* either of the two lines marking the side limits of a playing area, as in football *b)* [*pl.*] the areas just outside these lines 2. a line, as of merchandise or work, in addition to one's main activity —**sit on the sidelines** to be only passively involved

sidelong *adj.* directed to the side, as a glance —*adv.* towards the side

sidereal (sī dēər′ē əl) *adj.* [< L. *sidus*, star] of, or determined with reference to, the stars

sidesaddle (sīd′sad′'l) *n.* a saddle upon which the rider sits with both legs on the same side of the animal —*adv.* on or as if on a sidesaddle

sideshow *n.* 1. a small show apart from the main show, as of a circus 2. activity of minor importance

sideslip *vi.* -slipped′, -slip′ping 1. to slip sideways 2. *Aeron.* to move in a sideslip —*n.* 1. a slip to the side 2. *Aeron.* a sideways and downwards movement towards the inside of a turn by an aircraft in a sharp bank

sidesman *n., pl.* -men *Church of England* a man who helps the church warden, esp. in taking the collection

sidesplitting *adj.* causing hearty laughter

sidestep *vt.* -stepped′, -step′ping to avoid by or as by stepping aside; dodge [to *sidestep* a difficulty]

sideswipe *vt., vi.* -swiped′, -swip′ing [U.S.] to hit along the side in passing —*n.* [U.S.] a glancing blow of this kind

sidetrack *vt., vi.* 1. to turn away from the main issue 2. to switch (a train, etc.) to a siding

sidewalk *n.* [U.S.] a pavement

sideways *adv., adj.* 1. from the side 2. with one side forward

side whiskers whiskers at the side of the face

siding *n.* a short railway track connected with a main track and used for unloading, bypassing, etc.

sidle (sī′d'l) *vi.* -dled, -dling [< *sideling*, sideways] to move sideways, esp. in a shy or stealthy manner

SIDS sudden infant death syndrome

siege (sēj) *n.* [< L. *sedere*, sit] 1. the surrounding of a city, fort, etc. by an enemy army trying to capture it by continued blockade and attack 2. any continued effort to win or control something —**lay siege to** to subject to a siege

siemens (sē′mənz) *n.* [< Sir William

Siemens] the SI unit of electrical conductance

sienna (sē en'ə) *n.* [< It. city] 1. a yellowish-brown earth pigment 2. a reddish-brown pigment made by burning this; burnt sienna

sierra (sē âr'ə) *n.* [Sp. < L. *serra*, a saw] a range of mountains with a saw-toothed appearance

siesta (sē es'tə) *n.* [Sp. < L. *sexta* (*hora*), sixth (hour), noon] a rest taken after the noon meal, esp. in hot countries

sieve (siv) *n.* [OE. *sife*] a utensil having many small openings for straining or sifting —*vt., vi.* sieved, siev'ing to pass through a sieve

sift (sift) *vt.* [OE. *siftan*] 1. to pass through a sieve so as to separate the coarse from the fine particles, or to break up lumps, as of flour 2. to scatter by a sieve 3. to examine (evidence, etc.) with care 4. to separate; screen [to *sift* fact from fable] —*vi.* to pass through or as through a sieve —sift'er *n.*

sigh (sī) *vi.* [OE. *sican*] 1. to take in and let out a long, deep, sounded breath, as in sorrow, relief, etc. 2. to make a sound like a sigh [trees *sighing* in the wind] 3. to long or lament (for) —*vt.* to express with a sigh —*n.* the act or sound of sighing —sigh'er *n.*

sight (sīt) *n.* [< OE. *seon*, see] 1. the ability to see; eyesight 2. the act of seeing 3. range of vision 4. opinion [a hero in her *sight*] 5. a glimpse 6. *a*) something seen *b*) a thing worth seeing : *usually used in pl.* [the *sights* of the city] 7. [Colloq.] a person or thing not pleasant to look at 8. any device used to aid the eyes in aiming a gun, etc. 9. aim or an observation taken as with a sextant, gun, etc. 10. [Colloq. or Dial.] a large amount [a *sight* better than fighting] —*vt.* 1. to observe 2. to catch sight of 3. to adjust the sights of 4. to aim (a gun, etc.) at —a sight for sore eyes [Colloq.] a welcome sight —at first sight when seen or considered for the first time —at (or on) sight when or as soon as seen —by sight by recognizing but not through being acquainted —catch sight of to glimpse —lose sight of 1. to see no longer 2. to forget —sight unseen without seeing (the thing) beforehand

sighted *adj.* 1. having sight; not blind 2. having (a specified kind of) sight [longsighted]

sightless *adj.* blind

sightly *adj.* -lier, -liest pleasant to the sight

sight reading the skill of performing unfamiliar written music without previous study —sight'-read'vt., vi.

sightscreen *n.* Cricket a white screen placed near the boundary behind the bowler to help the batsman see the ball

sightseeing *n.* the act of visiting places and things of interest —sight'se'er *n.*

sigma (sig'mə) *n.* the eighteenth letter of the Greek alphabet (Σ, σ)

sign (sīn) *n.* [< L. *signum*] 1. something that indicates a fact, quality, etc. [black

is a *sign* of mourning] 2. a gesture that tells something specified [a nod is a *sign* of approval] 3. a mark or symbol having a specific meaning [the *sign* £ for pounds] 4. a publicly displayed board, placard, etc. bearing information, advertising, etc. 5. any visible indication [*signs* of spring] 6. an omen —*vt.* 1. to write (one's name) as a signature 2. to write one's name on, as in agreement, etc. 3. to mark with a sign, esp. of the cross as in blessing —*vi.* 1. to write one's signature 2. to make a sign; signal —sign away to transfer ownership of (something) by signing a document —sign in (or out) to sign a register on arrival (or departure) —sign off to stop broadcasting, as for the day —sign on to hire or be hired —sign'er *n.*

signal (sig'n'l) *n.* [< L. *signum*, a sign] 1. any sign, event, etc. that is a call to some kind of action 2. *a*) a sign given by gesture, a device, etc. to convey a direction, warning, etc. *b*) a device providing such a sign 3. Telegraphy, Radio & TV, etc. the electrical impulses, sound or picture elements, etc. transmitted or received —*adj.* not ordinary; notable —*vt., vi.* -nalled, -nalling 1. to make a signal or signals (to) 2. to communicate by signals —sig'naller *n.*

signal box a building from which railway signals are operated

signalize *vt.* -ized', -iz'ing to make notable

signally *adv.* notably; remarkably

signalman *n.* a person responsible for signalling or receiving signals, esp. on a railway

signatory (sig'nə tər ē) *n., pl.* -ries any of the persons, states, etc. that have signed a document —*adj.* that has or have joined in the signing of something

signature (sig'nə chər) *n.* [< L. *signare*, to sign] 1. a person's name written by himself 2. the act of signing one's name 3. Music a sign at the beginning of a staff to show key or time 4. Printing *a*) a large sheet on which pages are printed and which, when folded, forms one section of a book *b*) a letter or number on the first page of each sheet showing in what order that section is to be bound

signature tune an identifying song or melody used by a performer or for a radio or television series

signboard (sīn'bôrd') *n.* a board bearing a sign, esp. one advertising a business, product, etc.

signet (sig'nit) *n.* [MFr. < *signe*, a sign] a small seal used in marking documents as official, etc.

signet ring a finger ring containing a signet, often in the form of an initial

significance (sig nif'ə kəns) *n.* 1. meaning 2. importance; consequence

significant *adj.* [see SIGNIFY] 1. having or expressing a meaning 2. full of meaning 3. important; momentous

significant figure 1. a figure of a number that expresses a magnitude to a specified degree of accuracy **2.** the number of such figures [3.142 has four *significant figures*]

signify (sig′nəfī′) *vt.* **-fied′**, **-fy′ing** [< L. *signum*, a sign + *facere*, make] **1.** to be a sign or indication of; mean **2.** to make known by a sign, words, etc. —*vi.* to be significant; matter —**significa-tion** (sig′nəfi kā′shən) *n.*

sign language communication of thoughts or ideas by means of signs and gestures of the hands and arms

‡**signor** (sēn′yôr) *n., pl.* **signo′ri** (-nyô′rē) [It.] **1.** [S-] Mr. **2.** a gentleman

‡**signora** (sēn yôr′ə) *n., pl.* **signo′re** (-re); E. **signo′ras** [It.] **1.** [S-] Mrs. **2.** a married woman

‡**signorina** (sēn′yə rē′nə) *n., pl.* **-ri′ne** (-ne) [It.] **1.** [S-] Miss **2.** an unmarried woman

sign painter someone who paints signs for inns, shops, etc.

signpost (sīn′pōst′) *n.* **1.** a post with a sign on it, as for showing a direction **2.** a clear indication

Sikh (sēk) *n.* [Hindi, disciple] a member of a monotheistic Hindu religious sect

silage (sī′lij) *n.* [< ENSILAGE] green fodder stored in a silo

silence (sī′ləns) *n.* **1.** a keeping silent or still **2.** absence of any sound or noise; stillness **3.** a withholding of knowledge or omission of mention **4.** failure to communicate, write, etc. —*vt.* **-lenced, -lencing 1.** to make silent **2.** to repress —*interj.* be silent!

silencer *n.* **1.** a device for muffling the report of a firearm **2.** a device for silencing noises, as a section in the exhaust pipe of an internal-combustion engine

silent *adj.* [< L. *silere*, to be silent] **1.** making no vocal sound; mute **2.** not talkative **3.** free from noise; quiet; still **4.** not spoken, expressed, etc. [*silent* grief] **5.** making no mention, explanation, etc. **6.** designating films without synchronized sound

SILHOUETTE

silhouette (sil′ ∞ wet′) *n.* [< E. de *Silhouette*] **1.** any dark shape seen against a light background **2.** a solid, usually black, outline drawing, often a profile portrait —*vt.* **-et′ted, -et′ting** to show or project in silhouette

silica (sil′i kə) *n.* [see SILICON] a hard, glassy mineral found in various forms, as in quartz, sand, opal, etc.

siliceous (səlish′əs) *adj.* of, containing, or like silica

silicon (sil′ikən) *n.* [< L. *silex*, flint] a nonmetallic chemical element found always in combination, as in silica: symbol, Si

silicon chip *same as* CHIP (*n.* 6)

silicone (sil′ikōn′) *n.* [see SILICON] any of a group of organic silicon compounds resistant to heat, water, etc. and used in lubricants, polishes, etc.

silicosis (sil′əkō′sis) *n.* [see SILICON & -OSIS] a chronic lung disease caused in miners, etc. by inhaling silica dust

silk (silk) *n.* [OE. *seoluc*] **1.** the fine, soft, shiny fibre produced by silkworms **2.** thread or fabric made from this **3.** *a)* [*pl.*] a distinctive silk uniform, as of a jockey *b)* the silk gown worn by a King's or Queen's Counsel *c)* a King's or Queen's Counsel —*adj.* of or like silk —**take silk** to become a Queen's or King's Counsel

silken *adj.* **1.** made of silk **2.** like silk; soft, smooth, glossy, etc.

silk hat a tall, cylindrical hat covered with silk or satin, worn by men in formal dress

silk-screen (silk′ skrēn′) *adj.* designating a stencil process of printing a design through a screen of silk or other fine cloth, parts of the screen being blocked as with an impermeable film —*vt.* to print by this process

silkworm *n.* a caterpillar that produces cocoons of silk fibre

silky *adj.* **-ier, -iest** of or like silk; soft, smooth, lustrous, etc. —**silk′iness** *n.*

sill (sil) *n.* [OE. *syll*] a horizontal piece forming the bottom frame of the opening into which a window or door is set

sillabub (sil′əbub′) *n. var. of* SYLLABUB

silly (sil′ē) *adj.* **-lier, -liest** [OE. *sælig*, happy] **1.** having or showing little sense or judgment; foolish **2.** [Colloq.] dazed as from a blow **3.** *Cricket* a fielder standing close to a batsman [*silly* mid-on] —*n., pl.* **-lies** a silly person —**sil′li-ness** *n.*

silo (sī′lō) *n., pl.* **-los** [Sp. < Gr. *siros*] **1.** an airtight pit or tower in which grain or green fodder is stored **2.** an underground structure for storing and launching a long-range ballistic missile

silt (silt) *n.* [prob. < Scand.] earthy sediment made up of fine particles carried or laid down by moving water —*vt., vi.* to fill or choke up with silt —**silt′y** *adj.*

Silurian (sī lyoo or′ē ən) *adj.* [< L. *Silures*, ancient tribe in Wales] designating or of the geological period after the Ordovician in the Paleozoic Era

silvan (sil′vən) *adj., n. same as* SYLVAN

silver (sil′vər) *n.* [OE. *seolfor*] **1.** a white, precious metallic chemical element that is extremely ductile and malleable: symbol, Ag **2.** silver coin **3.** silverware **4.** the lustrous, greyish-white colour of silver **5.** something having this colour, as the coating for a mirror —*adj.* **1.** of or containing silver **2.** marking the 25th anniversary *[a silver wedding anniversary] —vt.* **1.** to cover with silver **2.** to make silvery in colour

silver birch a tree with a silvery-white, peeling bark

silverfish *n.* **1.** any of various unrelated fishes of silvery colour **2.** a wingless insect with silvery scales, found in damp, dark places

silver jubilee a 25th anniversary of an event, esp. the accession of a sovereign

silver lining anything seen as hopeful or comforting in the midst of despair, misfortune, etc.

silver medal a medal awarded to an entrant who is placed second in a competition

silver-plate (sil′vər plāt′) *vt.* **-plat′ed, -plat′ing** to coat with silver, esp. by electroplating

silver screen **1.** a screen onto which films are projected in cinemas **2.** films collectively

silverside *n.* a cut of beef from the upper round

silversmith *n.* one who makes articles of silver

silver thaw [Canad.] **1.** a freezing rainstorm **2.** *same as* GLITTER ICE

silverware *n.* articles, esp. tableware, made of or plated with silver

silvery *adj.* **1.** like silver, as in colour or lustre **2.** soft and clear, like the sound of a silver bell

silviculture (sil′vi kul′chər) *n.* [< L. *silva*, forest + *culta*, culture] the art of cultivating a forest; forestry

simian (sim′ē ən) *adj.* [< L. *simia*, ape] of or like an ape or monkey —*n.* an ape or monkey

similar (sim′ə lər) *adj.* [< L. *similis*] **1.** nearly but not exactly the same **2.** *Geom.* having the same shape, but not the same size or position —**sim′ilarly** *adv.*

similarity (sim′ə lar′ə tē) *n.* **1.** a being similar **2.** *pl.* **-ties** a point, feature, etc. in which things are similar

simile (sim′ə lē) *n.* [L., likeness] a figure of speech in which one thing is likened to another, dissimilar thing by using *like*, *as*, etc. (Ex.: a voice like thunder)

similitude (sə mil′ə tyōōd′) *n.* [< L. *similitudo*] similarity; likeness

simmer (sim′ər) *vi.* [echoic] **1.** to remain at or just below the boiling point **2.** to be about to break out, as in anger, revolt, etc. —*vt.* **1.** to make (a liquid) simmer **2.** to cook in such a liquid —*n.* a simmering —**simmer down** to become calm; cool off

simnel (sim′n'l) *n.* [ult. < L. *simila*, fine flour] a rich fruit cake eaten in mid-Lent or at Easter

simony (sī′mə nē) *n.* [< *Simon Magus*, a magician: Acts 8: 9-24] the buying or selling of sacred or spiritual things, as church offices

simoom (si mōōm′) *n.* [< Ar. *samm*, to poison] a hot, violent, sand-laden desert wind: also **simoon′**

simper (sim′pər) *vi.* [< ?] to smile in a silly or affected way —*vt.* to say with a simper —*n.* a silly or affected smile —**sim′peringly** *adv.*

simple (sim′p'l) *adj.* **-pler, -plest** [< L. *simplex*] **1.** easy to do, solve, or understand **2.** *a)* unadorned *[simple clothes] b)* not luxurious; plain *[simple tastes]* **3.** having only one or a few parts, features, etc.; not complicated **4.** not affected; natural **5.** of low rank or position **6.** *a)* stupid *b)* ignorant *c)* credulous; gullible **7.** without additions *[the simple facts]* **8.** insignificant; unimportant **9.** *Law* unconditional *[in fee simple]* —*n.* [Archaic] a medicinal plant or herb

simple fraction a fraction in which both numerator and denominator are whole numbers, as 1/2

simple fracture a bone fracture in which the broken ends of bone do not pierce the skin

simple interest interest computed on principal alone, not on principal plus interest

simple-minded *adj.* **1.** stupid **2.** mentally retarded **3.** artless; unsophisticated

simple sentence a sentence having one main clause and no subordinate clauses (Ex.: The boy ran home.)

simpleton *n.* a person who is stupid or easily deceived

simplicity (sim plis′ə tē) *n., pl.* **-ties** **1.** a being simple; freedom from complexity **2.** absence of luxury, elegance, etc. **3.** freedom from affectation **4.** lack of sense

simplify (sim′plə fī′) *vt.* **-fied′, -fy′ing** to make simpler, easier, less complex, etc. —**sim′plifica′tion** *n.*

simplistic (sim plis′tik) *adj.* oversimplifying or oversimplified —**simplis′tically** *adv.*

simply (sim′plē) *adv.* **1.** in a simple way **2.** merely; only *[simply trying to help]* **3.** absolutely; completely

simulacrum (sim′yōō lā′krəm) *n., pl.* **-cra** [L.] **1.** a likeness **2.** a false appearance; semblance

simulate (sim′yōō lāt′) *vt.* **-lat′ed, -lat′ing** [< L. *simulare*, feign] **1.** to give a false appearance of; feign **2.** to reproduce the conditions of (a situation), as in carrying out an experiment **3.** to look or act like —**sim′ula′tion** *n.*

simulator *n.* a training device that duplicates artificially the conditions likely to be encountered in some operation *[a flight simulator]*

simultaneous (sī′m'l tān′yəs) *adj.* [< L. *simul*, at the same time] occurring, done, existing, etc. together or at the same time

SIN [Canad.] Social Insurance Number

sin¹ (sin) *n.* [OE. *synne*] **1.** the breaking of religious or moral law, esp. through a wilful act **2.** any offence or fault —*vi.* **sinned, sin′ning** to commit a sin

sin² (sīn) sine

sin bin [Canad. Slang] the penalty box in ice hockey

since (sins) *adv.* [< OE. *sith*, after + *thæt*, that] **1.** from then until now *[he came on Monday and has been here ever *since]* **2.** at some or any time between then and now *[he was ill last week but has since recovered]* **3.** ago *[long since]* —*prep.* **1.** continuously from (the time given) until now *[out walking since noon]* **2.** during the period following *[he's written twice since May]* —*conj.* **1.** after the time that *[two years since he died]* **2.** continuously from the time when *[lonely ever since he left]* **3.** because *[since you're tired, let's go home]*

sincere (sin sēar') *adj.* **-cer'er, -cer'est** [< L. *sincerus*, clean] **1.** without deceit or pretence; honest **2.** genuine; real *[sincere grief]* —**sincere'ly** *adv.*

sincerity (sin ser'ə tē) *n.*, *pl.* **-ties** a being sincere; honesty, genuineness, etc.

sine (sīn) *n.* [< L. *sinus*, a curve] *Trigonometry* the ratio between the side opposite a given acute angle in a right-angled triangle and the hypotenuse

sinecure (sī'nə kyooər) *n.* [< L. *sine*, without + *cura*, care] a position that brings profit without involving much work, responsibility, etc.

sine die (sī'nē dī'ē, sin'ā dē'ā) [LL., without a day] for an indefinite period *[to adjourn an assembly sine die]*

sine qua non (sī'nē kwā non', sin'ā-kwä nōn') [L., without which not] something essential or indispensable

sinew (sin'yōō) *n.* [OE. *seonu*] **1.** a tendon **2.** muscular strength **3.** *[often pl.]* any source of power or strength

sinewy *adj.* **1.** of or like sinew; tough **2.** having good muscular development **3.** vigorous; powerful

sinful (sin'fəl) *adj.* full of or characterized by sin; wicked

sing (siŋ) *vi.* **sang, sung, sing'ing** [OE. *singan*] **1.** *a)* to produce musical sounds with the voice *b)* to perform musical selections vocally **2.** *a)* to make musical sounds, as a songbird *b)* to whistle, buzz, hum, etc., as a kettle, bee, etc. **3.** to have a sensation of ringing, etc., in the ears —*vt.* **1.** to render by singing **2.** to describe, proclaim, etc. in song **3.** to bring or put, as to sleep, by singing —**sing out** [Colloq.] to call out loudly —**sing'er** *n.*

singe (sinj) *vt.* **singed, singe'ing** [OE. *sengan*] **1.** to burn superficially or slightly **2.** to expose (a carcass) to flame in removing bristles or feathers —*n.* **1.** a singeing **2.** a slight burn

Singh (siŋ) *n.* [Sans. *sinhá*, lion] a title assumed by a Sikh after being initiated as a full member of the community

single (siŋ'g'l) *adj.* [< L. *singulus*] **1.** *a)* one only *b)* distinct from others of the same kind *[every single time]* *c)* designating a ticket valid for a journey in one direction only **2.** alone **3.** of or for one person or family **4.** between two persons only *[single combat]* **5.** unmarried **6.** having only one part; not compound, etc. **7.** the same for all; uniform **8.** unbroken **9.** having only one set of petals —*vt.* **-gled, -gling** to select from

others (with *out*) —*n.* **1.** a single person or thing; specif., *a)* a single ticket for a bus, train, etc. *b)* a gramophone record with one short piece of music on each side **2.** *Cricket* a hit by which one run is scored **3.** *[pl.]* *Tennis*, etc. a match with only one player on each side —**sin'gle-ness** *n.*

single-breasted (siŋ'g'l bres'tid) *adj.* overlapping over the breast just enough to be fastened with one button or one row of buttons

single entry a simple bookkeeping system in which transactions are entered in one account only

single file a single column of persons or things, one directly behind another

single-handed (siŋ'g'l han'did) *adj., adv.* **1.** done or working alone **2.** using or requiring the use of only one hand —**sin'gle-hand'edly** *adv.*

single-hearted *adj.* honest; sincere

single-minded *adj.* with only one aim or purpose

singlestick *n.* **1.** a swordlike stick formerly used for fencing **2.** the sport of fencing with such sticks

singlet (siŋ'glit) *n.* a man's sleeveless vest or top

singleton (siŋ'g'l tən) *n.* **1.** the only playing card held by a player in a given suit **2.** a single thing

singly (siŋ'glē) *adv.* **1.** one by one **2.** alone **3.** unaided

singsong (siŋ'soŋ') *n.* **1.** an unvarying rise and fall of tone **2.** speech, etc. marked by this **3.** [Colloq.] an informal session of singing —*adj.* monotonous because done in singsong

singular (siŋ'gyoo lər) *adj.* [< L. *singulus*, single] **1.** extraordinary; remarkable **2.** strange; odd **3.** being the only one of its kind **4.** *Gram.* designating only one —*n.* *Gram.* **1.** the singular number **2.** the singular form of a word **3.** a word in singular form —**sin'gular'ity** (-lar'-ə tē) *n.*

Sinhalese (siŋ'hə lēz') *adj.* of Sri Lanka, its principal people, their language, etc. —*n.* **1.** *pl.* **-lese'** any of the Sinhalese people **2.** their language

sinister (sin'is tər) *adj.* [< L., left] **1.** threatening harm, evil, etc.; ominous **2.** evil or dishonest *[a sinister plot]* **3.** on the left-hand side (on a coat of arms, the right of the viewer)

sink (siŋk) *vi.* **sank** or **sunk, sink'ing** [OE. *sincan*] **1.** to go beneath the surface of water, snow, etc. **2.** *a)* to go down slowly *b)* to seem to descend, as the sun **3.** to become lower, as in level, degree, volume, or strength **4.** to become less in value, as prices **5.** to become hollow, as the cheeks **6.** to pass gradually (*into* sleep, etc.) **7.** to approach death **8.** to stoop (*to* an unworthy action) **9.** to become absorbed; penetrate —*vt.* **1.** to cause to sink, go down, etc. **2.** to make (a well, design, etc.) by digging, or cutting **3.** to invest **4.** to defeat; ruin **5.** *Sports* to put (a basketball) through the basket or (a golf ball) into the hole, and so score —*n.* 1. a basin, as in a kitchen, with a drainpipe 2. *Geol.* an area of slightly sunken land 3. a cesspool or sewer 4. any place considered morally filthy —**sink in** [Colloq.] to be grasped mentally, esp. with difficulty

sinker *n.* a lead weight for fishing

sinking fund a fund made up of money set aside at intervals, to pay a debt

sinless (sin′lis) *adj.* without sin; innocent

sinner *n.* a person who sins; wrongdoer

Sinn Fein (shin′fān′) [Ir., we ourselves] a political movement for the unification of Ireland —**Sinn′Fein′er**

Sino- (sī′nō, sin′ō) [< Gr. *Sinai*] *a combining form meaning* Chinese

Sinology (sī nol′ə jē, si-) *n.* [SINO- + -LOGY] the study of Chinese languages, customs, etc. —**Sinol′ogist, Sinologue** (sī′-nə log′) *n.*

sinuous (sin′yoo wəs) *adj.* [< L. *sinus*, a bend] bending or winding in and out —**sin′uos′ity** (-wos′ə tē) *n.*

sinus (sī′nəs) *n.* [L., a bent surface] a cavity: specif., any air cavity in the skull opening into a nasal cavity

sinusitis (sī′nə sīt′əs) *n.* [see prec. & -ITIS] inflammation of a sinus

-sion (shən; *sometimes* zhən) [< L.] *a suffix meaning* act, quality, condition, or result of *[discussion, confusion]*

sip (sip) *vt., vi.* **sipped, sip′ping** [akin to LowG. *sippen*] to drink a little at a time —*n.* 1. a sipping 2. a small quantity sipped

SIPHON

siphon (sī′fən) *n.* [Fr. < Gr. *siphōn*, tube] 1. a bent tube for carrying liquid over the edge of a container to a lower level through the atmospheric pressure on the liquid 2. a sealed bottle from which carbonated water may be drawn off —*vt., vi.* to draw off, or pass, through a siphon

sir (sur) *n.* [see ff.] 1. a respectful term of address used to a man: not followed by the name 2. [S-] the title used before the name of a knight or baronet

sire (sīər) *n.* [< L. *senex*, old] 1. the male parent of an animal 2. a title of respect used in addressing a king 3. [Poet.] a father or forefather —*vt.* **sired, sir′ing** to beget: said esp. of animals

siren (sī′rən) *n.* [< Gr. *Seirēn*] 1. a device using steam or air to make a loud, wailing sound, esp. as a warning signal 2. *Gr. & Rom. Myth.* any of several sea nymphs who lured sailors to their death on rocky coasts by seductive singing 3. a seductive woman

Sirius (sir′ē əs) [< Gr. *Seirios*, the scorcher] *same as* DOG STAR

sirloin (sur′loin) *n.* [< OFr. *sur*, over + *loigne*, loin] a choice cut, esp. of beef, from the loin

sirocco (sə rok′ō) *n.*, *pl.* **-cos** [It. < Ar. *sharq*, the east] a hot, steady wind blowing from the Libyan deserts into S Europe

sirrah (sir′ə) *n.* [< SIRE] [Archaic] a contemptuous term of address used to a man

sis (sis) *n.* [U.S. Colloq.] sister

sisal (sī′s'l) *n.* [< *Sisal*, Yucatán] a strong fibre obtained from a Mexican agave used for making rope, insulation, etc.

siskin (sis′kin) *n.* [< G. *Zeischen*] a finch with green plumage and black and yellow markings

sissy (sis′ē) *n.*, *pl.* **-sies** [< SIS] [Colloq.] 1. an effeminate man or boy 2. a coward

sister (sis′tər) *n.* [ON. *systir*] 1. a female as she is related to other children of her parents 2. a close friend who is like a sister 3. a female fellow member of the same race, creed, profession, etc. 4. a nun 5. one of the same kind, model, etc. 6. a nurse, esp. a head nurse

sisterhood *n.* 1. the state of being sisters 2. an association of women united in a common work, creed, etc.

sister-in-law *n.*, *pl.* **sis′ters-in-law′** 1. the sister of one's husband or wife 2. the wife of one's brother 3. the wife of the brother of one's husband or wife

sisterly *adj.* 1. of or like a sister 2. friendly, kind, affectionate, etc. —**sis′terli-ness** *n.*

Sisyphean (sis′i fē′ən) *adj.* endless and laborious, like the task of Sisyphus, in Greek mythology, doomed to roll uphill a heavy stone which always rolled down again

sit (sit) *vi.* **sat, sit′ting** [OE. *sittan*] 1. *a*) to rest the body on the buttocks, as on a chair *b*) to rest on the haunches with forelegs braced, as a dog *c*) to perch, as a bird 2. to cover eggs for hatching 3. *a*) to occupy a seat as a judge, member of parliament, etc. *b*) to be in session, as a court 4. to pose, as for a portrait 5. to be inactive 6. to be located 7. to rest or lie as specified *[cares sit lightly on him]* 8. to take an examination (for a degree, etc.) 9. *same as* BABY-SIT —*vt.* 1. to cause to sit or be placed 2. to stay seated on (a horse, etc.) —**sit back** 1. to relax 2. to be passive —**sit down** to take a seat —**sit in** 1. to take part; attend (often with *on*) 2. to deputize (often with *for*) 3. to take part in a sit-in —**sit on** 1. to be on (a jury, committee, etc.) 2. [Colloq.] to suppress, check, etc. 3. [Colloq.] to rebuke; snub —**sit out** 1. to stay until the end of 2. to stay seated during or take no part in (a dance, game, etc.) or to refuse to move or be moved —**sit up** 1. to rise to a sitting position 2. to sit erect 3. to put off going to bed 4. [Colloq.] to become suddenly alert

SITAR

sitar (si·tär′) *n.* [< Hindi *sitār*] a lutelike instrument of India

sit-down (sit′doun′) *adj.* designating a form of civil disobedience in which demonstrators sit down in streets, etc. and resist being moved

sit-down strike a strike in which employees stop work but refuse to leave their place of employment

site (sīt) *n.* [< L. *situs*, position] 1. a piece of land considered for a certain purpose [a good *site* for a town] 2. a place where something is, or is intended to be, located [a *campsite*] 3. the place or scene of anything —*vt.* sit′ed, sit′ing to locate on a site

sit-in (sit′in′) *n.* a form of civil disobedience in which demonstrators occupy a public building and refuse to vacate it

sitkamer (sit′kä mər) *n.* [< Afrik.] [S Afr.] a sitting room

sitter *n.* one that sits; specif., *a*) short for BABY SITTER *b*) a person who is posing for a portrait

sitting *n.* 1. a session, as of a court 2. a period of being seated at some activity 3. one of two or more times at which a meal is served —*adj.* seated

sitting duck [Colloq.] a person or thing especially vulnerable to attack: also **sitting target**

sitting tenant a tenant already living in a house, flat, etc.

situate (sit′yoo wāt′) *vt.* -at′ed, -at′ing [< L. *situs*, site] to put in a certain place or position; place; locate

situation (sit′yoo wā′shən) *n.* 1. location; position 2. a place; locality 3. state of affairs; circumstances 4. a combination of circumstances at a given time 5. a position of employment

situation comedy a comedy in which the humour arises from the difficulties and misunderstandings in which the characters become involved

sit-up, situp (sit′up′) *n.* an exercise in which a person lying flat on the back rises to a sitting position without using the hands and keeping the legs straight

sit-upon *n.* [Colloq.] the backside or buttocks

SI Units [< Fr. *Système International*] the international system of units (based on the metre and kilogram) adopted as the metric system for Britain

six (siks) *adj., n.* [OE. *sex*] one more than five; 6; VI —**at sixes and sevens** [Colloq.] 1. in confusion 2. disagreeing —**hit** (or **knock**) **for six** to stun; overwhelm completely —**sixth** *adj., n.*

sixfold *adj.* 1. having six parts 2. having six times as much or as many —*adv.* six times as much or as many

sixpence *n.* 1. the sum of six British (old) pennies 2. a former British coin of this value

six-shooter *n.* [Colloq.] a revolver that fires six shots without reloading: also **six′-gun**

sixteen (siks′tēn′) *adj., n.* [OE. *syxtene*] six more than ten; 16; XVI —**six′-teenth′** *adj., n.*

sixth sense a supposed power to perceive by intuition

sixty (siks′tē) *adj., n.* [OE. *sixtig*] six times ten; 60; LX —**the sixties** the numbers or years, as of a century, from sixty to sixty-nine —**six′tieth** *adj., n.*

sizable (sī′zə b'l) *adj.* quite large: also **size′able**

size¹ (sīz) *n.* [ult. < L. *sedere*, sit] 1. that quality of a thing which determines how much space it occupies; dimensions 2. any of a series of graded classifications for goods [*size* ten shoes] 3. *a*) extent, amount, etc. *b*) sizable amount, dimensions, etc. —*vt.* sized, siz′ing to make or arrange according to size —**size up** [Colloq.] to estimate; judge —**that's the size of it** [Colloq.] that is a true account

size² *n.* [ME. *syse*] a thin, gluey substance used as a glaze or filler on porous materials, as paper: also **sizing** —*vt.* sized, siz′ing to apply size to

-sized *a combining form meaning* having (a specified) size [*small-sized*]: also **-size** [*life-size*]

sizzle (siz′'l) *vi.* -zled, -zling [echoic] 1. to make a hissing sound when in contact with heat 2. to simmer with suppressed emotion, esp. rage —*n.* a sizzling sound

S.J. Society of Jesus

S.J.A. Saint John's Ambulance (Brigade or Association)

sjambok (sham′buk, -bok) *n.* [< Urdu] [S Afr.] a heavy whip made of hippopotamus or rhinoceros hide

skaapsteker (skäp′stēə′kər) *n.* [< Afrik. *skaap*, sheep + *steek*, pierce] any of several back-fanged, venomous S African snakes

skate¹ (skāt) *n.* [< OFr. *eschace*, stilt] 1. *a*) a bladelike metal runner in a frame fastened to a shoe, for gliding on ice *b*) a shoe with this attached Also **ice skate** 2. a frame or shoe with two small wheels at the toe and two at the heel, for gliding on a pavement, etc.: also **roller skate** —*vi.* skat′ed, skat′ing to move along on skates —**skate on thin ice** to place oneself in a dangerous or delicate situation —**skat′er** *n.*

skate² *n.* [ON. *skata*] a fish with a broad, flat body and short, spineless tail

skateboard *n.* a short, oblong board with two wheels at each end, which one rides on, usually standing —*vi.* **-board'-ed, -board'ing** to ride on a skateboard

skean (skēn) *n.* [ScotGael. *sgian,* a knife] formerly, a dagger used in Ireland and Scotland —**skean-dhu** (skēan'dōō') the dagger worn in the stocking as part of Highland dress

skedaddle (ski dad''l) *vi.* **-dled, -dling** [< ?] [Colloq.] run off; leave fast

skein (skān) *n.* [< MFr. *escaigne*] a quantity of thread or yarn wound in a coil

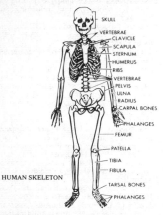

SKULL
VERTEBRAE
CLAVICLE
SCAPULA
STERNUM
HUMERUS
RIBS
VERTEBRAE
PELVIS
ULNA
RADIUS
CARPAL BONES
PHALANGES
FEMUR
PATELLA
TIBIA
FIBULA
TARSAL BONES
PHALANGES

HUMAN SKELETON

skeleton (skel'ət'n) *n.* [< Gr. *skeletos,* dried up] **1.** the hard framework of bones of a human being or other vertebrate **2.** a very thin person or animal **3.** a supporting framework, as of a ship **4.** an outline, as of a novel —*adj.* of or like a skeleton; greatly reduced *[a skeleton force]* —**skeleton in the cupboard** some fact kept secret because of shame —**skel'etal** *adj.*

skeleton key a key that can open any of various simple locks

skelm (skel'əm) *n.* [< Afrik.] [S Afr. Slang] a villain

skeptic (skep'tik) *adj., n. chiefly U.S. sp.* of SCEPTIC

sketch (skech) *n.* [< Gr. *schedios,* extempore] **1.** a rough drawing or design, done rapidly **2.** a brief outline **3.** a short, light, informal story, skit, etc. —*vt., vi.* to make a sketch (of)

sketchbook *n.* a book of drawing paper for making sketches

sketchy *adj.* **-ier, -iest** **1.** existing only in outline **2.** superficial; hasty

skew (skyōō) *vi.* [see ESCHEW] to swerve or twist —*vt.* **1.** to make slanting **2.** to bias or distort —*adj.* slanting; oblique —*n.* a slant or twist

skewbald (skyōō'bôld') *adj.* [< ?] having large patches of white and brown or any other colour except black —*n.* a skewbald horse

skewer (skyōō'ər) *n.* [< ON. *skifa,* a slice] a long pin used to hold meat together while cooking —*vt.* to fasten or pierce as with skewers

skewwhiff (skyōō'wif') *adj.* [Colloq.] askew; awry

ski (skē) *n., pl.* **skis, ski** [Norw. < ON. *skith,* snowshoe] either of a pair of long runners of wood, etc., fastened to the shoes for gliding over snow —*vi.* **skied** (skēd), **ski'ing** to glide on skis, as down snow-covered hills —**ski'er** *n.*

skid (skid) *vi.* **skid'ded, skid'ding** [see SKI] **1.** to slide without turning, as a wheel when brakes are applied on a slippery surface **2.** to slide, as a vehicle not gripping an icy road —*vt.* to cause (a vehicle, etc.) to skid —*n.* **1.** a skidding **2.** [Chiefly U.S.] a plank, log, etc. used as a track to slide a heavy object on **3.** a low, movable platform for holding loads **4.** a sliding wedge used to brake a vehicle **5.** [*pl.*] a wooden fender put against the side of a ship **6.** a runner in place of a wheel on some aircraft landing gear —**be on** (or **hit**) **the skids** [Slang] to be in decline —**on the skids** [Colloq.] to be ready for launching —**put the skids on** (or **under**) [Slang] to thwart or cause to fail

skidoo (skI d'ōō) *n.* [< *Ski-Doo,* Trademark] [Canad.] a snowmobile —*vt., vi.* to travel using a snowmobile

skidpan *n.* an area made slippery so that a vehicle driver can practise controlling skids

skid row [altered < *skid road,* a trail for dragging logs] [Chiefly U.S.] a section of a city where vagrants, derelicts, etc. gather

skiff (skif) *n.* [< It. *schifo*] a light rowing boat

ski jump a high ramp overhanging a slope from which skiers compete to make the longest jump

skilful (skil'fəl) *adj.* having or showing skill; expert —**skil'fully** *adv.* —**skil'fulness** *n.*

skill (skil) *n.* [ON. *skil,* distinction] **1.** great ability or expertness **2.** an art, craft, or science, esp. one involving the use of the hands —**skilled** *adj.*

skillet (skil'it) *n.* [< ?] **1.** a cooking pot with a long handle **2.** [U.S.] a frying pan

skim (skim) *vt., vi.* **skimmed, skim'ming** [prob. akin to SCUM] **1.** to remove (floating matter) from a liquid **2.** to look (*through* a book, etc.) hastily **3.** to glide swiftly or lightly over

skim milk milk from which the cream has been removed

skimp (skimp) *vi.* [prob. < SCRIMP] [Colloq.] to allow too little; be stingy —*vt.* [Colloq.] **1.** to do poorly or carelessly **2.** to be stingy in or towards; specif., to make too small, too short, etc.

skimpy *adj.* **-ier, -iest** [Colloq.] barely enough; scanty —**skimp'ily** *adv.* —**skimp'iness** *n.*

skin (skin) *n.* [ON. *skinn*] 1. the outer covering of the animal body 2. this covering removed and prepared for use; pelt 3. a skinlike outer layer, as fruit rind, a film or scum, etc. 4. a container made of animal skin, for holding liquids —*vt.* **skinned, skin′ning** 1. to remove skin from 2. to cover as with skin 3. [Colloq.] to swindle —**by the skin of one's teeth** by the tiniest margin —**get under one's skin** [Colloq.] to irritate one —**have a thick** (or **thin**) **skin** to be insensitive (or very sensitive) to criticism, etc. —**save one's skin** [Colloq.] to avoid death, injury, ruin, etc. —**skin′ner** *n.*

skin-deep *adj.* 1. penetrating no deeper than the skin 2. without real significance; superficial

skin diving underwater swimming in which the swimmer is equipped with a mask, a snorkel or scuba equipment, etc. —**skin′-dive′** (-dīv′) *vi.* **-dived′, -div′ing** —**skin diver**

skinflick *n.* [Slang] a pornographic film

skinflint *n.* a miser

skin grafting the surgical transplanting of skin (**skin graft**) to replace skin destroyed, as by burning

skinless *adj.* without a skin, casing, etc.

skinned *adj.* having skin (of a specified kind) [*dark-skinned*]

skinny *adj.* **-nier, -niest** emaciated; thin —**skin′niness** *n.*

skint (skint) *adj.* [< *skinned*, pp. of SKIN] [Slang] penniless; broke

skintight (skin′tīt′) *adj.* very tightfitting

skip[1] (skip) *vi.* **skipped, skip′ping** [ME. *skippen*] 1. to leap, jump, etc. lightly; specif., *a*) to move along by hopping lightly on one foot and then the other *b*) to jump over a skipping rope 2. to ricochet 3. to pass from one point to another, omitting what lies between 4. [Chiefly U.S. Colloq.] to leave hurriedly —*vt.* 1. to leap lightly over 2. to pass over or omit 3. to fail to attend a session of (school, etc.) 4. to cause to skip or ricochet 5. [Chiefly U.S. Colloq.] to leave (a town, etc.) hurriedly —*n.* 1. a small jump or leap 2. a skipping gait —**skip it!** [Colloq.] it doesn't matter!

skip[2] *n.* [< OE. *skeppa*, basket] 1. a large, open, metal container in which refuse is put 2. a cage used as a lift in mines, etc.

ski pole either of a pair of light poles with a sharp tip, used by skiers as a help in climbing, keeping balance, etc.

skipper (skip′ər) *n.* [< MDu. *schip*, ship] 1. the captain of a ship 2. any leader, director, or captain —*vt.* to act as skipper of

skipping rope a length of rope, often with handles, that is held in the hands and swung so that the holder, or another person, can jump over it

skirl (skurl) *vt., vi.* [prob. < Scand.] [Scot. & Dial.] to sound in shrill, piercing tones, as a bagpipe —*n.* a shrill sound, as of a bagpipe

skirmish (skur′mish) *n.* [< It. *schermire*, to fight < Gmc.] 1. a brief fight between small groups, usually an incident of a battle 2. any slight, unimportant conflict —*vi.* to take part in a skirmish —**skir′-misher** *n.*

skirt (skurt) *n.* [ON. *skyrt*, shirt] 1. a woman's garment that hangs down from the waist 2. that part of a dress, coat, etc. that hangs below the waist 3. something like a skirt, as a flap hanging from a hovercraft 4. a cut of beef from the flank 5. [Old Slang] a girl [a bit of *skirt*] —*vt.* 1. to lie along or form the edge of 2. to move along the edge of or miss narrowly 3. to avoid (a problem, etc.) —*vi.* to be on, or move along, the edge —**skirt′ed** *adj.*

skirting board a board or moulding covering the edge of a wall next to the floor

skit (skit) *n.* [prob. < ON. *skjota*, to shoot] a short, comic sketch, as in the theatre

skittish (skit′ish) *adj.* 1. lively or playful, esp. in a coy way 2. easily frightened; jumpy

skittle (skit′'l) *n.* [< ?] 1. [*pl. with sing.″ v.*] a bowling game in which a wooden disc or ball is used to knock down pins 2. any of these pins —(**not**) **all beer and skittles** (not) pure pleasure

skive (skīv) *vt.* **skived, skiv′ing** [ON. *skifa*, to slice] 1. to slice (leather, etc.) in thin layers 2. [Slang] to evade (work or responsibility) —*vi.* [Slang] to evade work —**skive off** [Slang] to depart, so as to evade work, etc. —**skiv′er** *n.*

skivvy (skiv′ē) *n., pl.* **-vies** [< ?] a servant, esp. a housemaid; a drudge —*vi.* to work as a skivvy

skokiaan (skô′ki än′) *n.* [< Afrik.] in South Africa, a potent alcoholic drink consumed esp. by black Africans

skolly (skol′ē) *n.* [< ?] [S Afr.] a Coloured hooligan, usually one of a gang: also **skollie**

skookum (skōō′kəm) *a.* [< AmInd.] [Canad.] large; big

skop skiet en donder (skop′-skit′ ən don′ə) [< Afrik.] [S Afr. Slang] blood and thunder: used to describe cowboy films, etc.

skua (skyōō′ə) *n.* [ult. < ON. *skúfr*, a tuft] any of several large, brown and white, rapacious sea gulls

skulduggery, skullduggery (skul dug′-ər ē) *n.* [< ?] [Colloq.] underhand, dishonest behaviour; trickery

skulk (skulk) *vi.* [< Scand.] 1. to move about in a stealthy or sinister manner 2. to shirk

skull (skul) *n.* [< Scand.] 1. the bony framework of the head, enclosing the brain 2. the head or mind

skull and crossbones a representation of two crossed bones under a human skull, a symbol of death or piracy

skullcap *n.* a light, closefitting, brimless cap

skunk (skuŋk) *n.* [< AmInd. *segonku*] 1. a bushy-tailed mammal having black fur with white stripes down its back:

it ejects a foul-smelling liquid when molested **2.** [Colloq.] a despicable, person

sky (skī) *n., pl.* **skies** [ON., a cloud] **1.** [*often pl.*] the upper atmosphere [*blue skies,* a cloudy *sky*] **2.** the heavens, apparently arching over the earth; firmament —*vt.* **skied** or **skyed, sky'ing** to hit high in the air —**out of a clear (blue) sky** without warning —**to the skies** without reserve

sky blue a blue colour like that of the sky on a clear day —**sky'-blue'** *adj.*

sky diving the sport of jumping from an aircraft and executing free-fall manoeuvres before opening the parachute —**sky'-dive'** *vi.* —**sky diver**

Skye terrier [< Isle of Skye] a breed of small terrier with long hair, a long body, and short legs

sky-high (skī'hī') *adj., adv.* very high

skyjack *vt.* [Colloq.] to hijack (an aircraft) —**sky'jack'er** *n.* —**sky'jack'-ing** *n.*

skylark *n.* a lark, famous for the song it utters as it soars towards the sky —*vi.* [SKY + LARK²] to play about boisterously

skylight *n.* a window in a roof or ceiling

skyline *n.* **1.** the line along which sky and earth seem to meet **2.** the outline, as of a city, seen against the sky

skyrocket *n.* a firework rocket that explodes in midair —*vi., vt.* to rise or cause to rise rapidly

skyscraper *n.* a very tall building

skyward *adv., adj.* towards the sky: also **sky'wards** *adv.*

slab (slab) *n.* [ME. *sclabbe*] a flat, broad, and fairly thick piece of something solid

slack¹ (slak) *adj.* [OE. *slæc*] **1.** loose; not taut **2.** careless or negligent [a *slack* workman] **3.** slow; sluggish **4.** not busy or active [a *slack* period] —*vt., vi.* to make or become slack; slacken —*n.* **1.** a part that is slack or hangs loose **2.** a dull period; lull —**slack off** to slacken —**slack up** to go more slowly —**slack'-ness** *n.*

slack² *n.* [< ME. *sleck*] a mixture of small pieces of coal, coal dust, and dirt left from the screening of coal

slacken *vt., vi.* **1.** to relax or loosen **2.** to make or become less active, intense, etc.

slacker *n.* a person who shirks his work or duty

slacks *n.pl.* informal trousers for men or women

slack water the period between tides when the water is still, esp. at low tide

slag (slag) *n.* [MLowG. *slagge*] the fused refuse separated from a metal in smelting —*vt., vi.* **slagged, slag'ging** to form into slag —**slag'gy** *adj.*

slag heap a large pile of waste matter from coal-mining or metal-smelting

slain (slān) *pp.* of SLAY

slake (slāk) *vt.* **slaked, slak'ing** [< OE. *slæc, slack*] less intense by satisfying **1.** to make (thirst, desire, etc.) **2.** to produce a chemical change in (lime) by combination with water

slalom (slä'ləm) *n.* [Norw., sloping trail] a downhill skiing race over a zigzag course —*vi.* to ski in a slalom

slam¹ (slam) *vt.* **slammed, slam'ming** [prob. < Scand.] **1.** to shut with force and noise **2.** to hit, put, etc. with force and noise [to *slam* a football over the fence] **3.** [Colloq.] to criticize severely —*vi.* to shut with force and noise —*n.* **1.** a heavy impact, shutting, etc. **2.** the noise made by this

slam² *n.* [< ?] *Bridge* a winning of all, or all but one, of the 13 tricks

slander (slän'dər) *n.* [see SCANDAL] **1.** the utterance of a falsehood damaging to a person's reputation **2.** such a spoken falsehood —*vt.* to utter such a falsehood about —**slan'derous** *adj.*

slang (slaŋ) *n.* [< ?] **1.** highly informal language, usually short-lived and of a colourful nature, that is avoided in formal speech and writing **2.** such language used by those in the same work, way of life, etc. —*vi.* to use abusive talk —*vt.* to abuse; criticize —**slang'y** *adj.*

slant (slänt) *vt., vi.* [< Scand.] **1.** to turn or lie in a direction that is not straight; slope **2.** to write or tell so as to express a particular bias —*n.* **1.** a slanting surface, line, etc.; slope **2.** a point of view, esp. one that shows bias —*adj.* oblique; sloping —**slant'ing** *adj.*

slap (slap) *n.* [echoic] **1.** a blow with something flat, as the palm of the hand **2.** the sound of this, or a sound like it —*vt.* **slapped, slap'ping** **1.** to strike with something flat **2.** to put, hit, etc. carelessly or with force **3.** [Colloq.] to apply in large quantities [she *slapped* some make-up on] —*vi.* to make a dull, sharp noise, as upon impact —*adv.* **1.** [Colloq.] straight; directly **2.** [Colloq.] abruptly —**slap down** [Colloq.] to rebuke sharply —**slap in the face** a snub or rebuff

slap and tickle [Colloq.] rowdy, boisterous behaviour, esp. of a sexual nature

slapdash *adv.* in a hasty, careless manner —*adj.* hasty, careless, impetuous, etc.

slap-happy *adj.* [Colloq.] silly or giddy

slapshot *n.* *Ice Hockey* a fast shot given by a short, powerful swing of the stick

slapstick *n.* crude comedy full of violent activity, horseplay etc. —*adj.* character-ized by such comedy

slap-up *adj.* [Colloq.] stylish; lavish; elegant

slash (slash) *vt.* [< ?] **1.** to cut with sweeping strokes, as of a knife **2.** to whip viciously **3.** to cut slits in (a fabric, etc.), esp. so as to expose underlying material **4.** to reduce drastically [to *slash* prices] **5.** to criticize severely —*vi.* to make a sweeping motion with something sharp —*n.* **1.** a slashing **2.** a cut made by such a stroke; gash **3.** [Vulg. Slang] an act of urinating

slat (slat) *n.* [OFr. *esclat,* fragment] a thin, narrow strip of wood, metal, etc. —**slat'ted** *adj.*

slate¹ (slāt) *n.* [see prec.] **1.** a hard rock that separates easily into thin, smooth layers **2.** its bluish-grey colour: also **slate blue 3.** a thin piece of slate, esp. one used as a roofing tile or as a tablet for writing on with chalk —*vt.* **slat′ed, slat′ing** to cover with slate —**a clean slate** a clean record without blemish —**slat′y** *adj.*

slate² *vt.* **slat′ed, slat′ing** [< ON. *sleita*] [Colloq.] to scold or criticize harshly —**slat′ing** *n.*

slattern (slat′ᵊrn) *n.* [< dial. *slatter*,·to slop] a woman who is careless and sloppy in her habits, appearance, etc. —**slat′ternliness** *n.* —**slat′ternly** *adj.*

slaughter (slôt′ᵊr) *n.* [ON. *slātr*, slain flesh] **1.** the killing of animals for food; butchering **2.** the brutal killing of a human being **3.** the killing of people in large numbers —*vt.* **1.** to kill (animals) for food; butcher **2.** to kill (people) brutally or in large numbers —**slaugh′terer** *n.*

slaughterhouse *n.* a place where animals are butchered for food; abattoir

Slav (släv) *n.* a member of any of a group of Slavic-speaking peoples of E, SE, and C Europe, including the Russians, Czechs, Poles, etc.

slave (släv) *n.* [< LGr. *Sklabos*: first applied to captive Slavs] **1.** a human being who is owned by another **2.** a person who is dominated by some influence, habit, etc. **3.** a person who slaves; drudge —*vi.* **slaved, slav′ing** to work like a slave; drudge

slave driver 1. a person who oversees the work of slaves **2.** any merciless taskmaster

slaver¹ (slav′ᵊr) *vi.* [< Scand.] to let saliva run from the mouth; drool —*n.* saliva drooling from the mouth

slaver² (slā′vᵊr) *n.* **1.** a ship used in the slave trade: also **slave ship 2.** a person who deals in slaves

slavery *n.* **1.** the owning of slaves as a practice or institution **2.** the condition of being a slave; bondage **3.** toil; drudgery

slavish *adj.* **1.** of or like slaves; servile **2.** blindly dependent [*slavish* imitation] —**slav′ishly** *adv.*

Slavonic (slᵊvon′ik) *adj.* of a group of languages including Russian, Polish, etc.: also **Slavic**

slay (slā) *vt.* **slew, slain, slay′ing** [OE. *slean*] to kill by violent means

sleazy (slē′zē) *adj.* **-zier, -ziest** [< ?] dirty, vulgar, sordid, etc. —**slea′zily** *adv.* —**slea′ziness** *n.*

sled (sled) *n.* [MLowG. or MDu. *sledde*] same as SLEDGE²

sledge¹ (slej) *n., vt., vi.* **sledged, sledg′-ing** [OE. *siecge*] same as SLEDGEHAMMER

sledge² *n.* [MDu. *sleedse*] a vehicle mounted on runners for carrying loads or people over snow or ice —*vt.* **sledged, sledg′ing** to carry or ride on a sledge

sledgehammer *n.* [see SLEDGE¹] a large, heavy hammer —*adj.* crushingly powerful

sleek (slēk) *adj.* [< SLICK] **1.** smooth and shiny; glossy **2.** having a healthy, well-groomed appearance —*vt.* to make sleek

sleep (slēp) *n.* [OE. *slæp*] **1.** *a)* a condition of rest for the body and mind at regular

times, during which the eyes stay closed and there is dreaming *b)* a period of sleeping **2.** any state like sleep, as a coma —*vi.* **slept, sleep′ing 1.** to be in the state of sleep **2.** to be in a state like sleep, as hibernation **3.** [Colloq.] to have sexual intercourse (*with*) —*vt.* **1.** to have (a specified kind of sleep) [*to sleep* the sleep of the just] **2.** to provide sleeping accommodation for —**last sleep** death —**put to sleep 1.** to anaesthetize **2.** to kill painlessly, esp. a pet animal —**sleep around** [Colloq.] to have promiscuous sexual relations —**sleep in** to sleep later than usual in the morning —**sleep off** to rid oneself of by sleeping —**sleep on it** to give extended consideration to, esp. overnight

sleeper *n.* **1.** one who sleeps **2.** any of the parallel crossbeams to which the rails of a railway are fastened **3.** *a)* same as SLEEPING CAR *b)* a compartment in a sleeping car **4.** a plain ring worn in a pierced ear to stop the hole from closing

sleeping bag a large bag with a warm lining, for sleeping in, esp. outdoors

sleeping car a railway coach with berths, compartments, etc. for passengers to sleep in: also **sleeping carriage**

sleeping partner a partner who shares in financing but not in managing a business, firm, etc.

sleeping sickness an infectious, usually fatal disease, esp. of tropical Africa, characterized by fever, lethargy, and coma

sleepless *adj.* **1.** with little or no sleep [a *sleepless* night] **2.** always alert or active

sleepwalking *n.* the act or practice of walking while asleep —**sleep′walk′er** *n.*

sleepy *adj.* **-ier, -iest 1.** likely to fall asleep; drowsy **2.** dull; quiet [a *sleepy* little town] **3.** causing drowsiness —**sleep′ily** *adv.* —**sleep′iness** *n.*

sleet (slēt) *n.* [ME. *slete*] **1.** rain that freezes as it falls **2.** a mixture of rain and snow —*vi.* to shower in the form of sleet —**sleet′y** *adj.*

sleeve (slēv) *n.* [OE. *sliefe*] **1.** that part of a garment that covers an arm **2.** a tubelike part fitting around another part **3.** an envelope for a gramophone record —**up one's sleeve** hidden but ready at hand —**sleeved** *adj.* —**sleeve′less** *adj.*

sleigh (slā) *n.* [Du. *slee*] a carriage with runners instead of wheels, for travel over snow and ice —*vi.* to ride in or drive a sleigh —**sleigh′ing** *n.*

sleight (slīt) *n.* [< ON. *slœgr*, crafty] **1.** cunning **2.** dexterity

sleight of hand 1. skill in using the hands so as to confuse those watching, as in doing magic tricks **2.** the performance of tricks that deceive in this way

slender (slen′dᵊr) *adj.* [< ?] **1.** long and thin **2.** having a slim figure **3.** small in amount, size, degree, etc.; [*slender* earnings] —**slen′derness** *n.*

slept (slept) *pt. & pp.* of SLEEP

sleuth (slo͞oth) *n.* [ON. *sloth*, a track] **1.** [Colloq.] a detective **2.** a bloodhound:

in full, **sleuth'hound'** —*vi.* to act as a detective

slew[1] (slōō) *vt., vi.* **slewed, slew'ing** [< ?] to turn or swing round, esp. awkwardly —*n.* the position to which a thing has been slewed

slew[2] *pt.* of SLAY

slice (slīs) *n.* [< Frank. *slizzan,* to slice] **1.** *a)* a thin, broad piece cut from something *b)* a wedge [a *slice* of cake] **2.** a share [a *slice* of the profits] **3.** a spatula or knife with a broad, flat blade **4.** a hit ball that curves away to the right from a right-handed player or to the left from a left-handed player —*vt.* **sliced, slic'ing 1.** to cut into slices **2.** to cut as a slice (with *off, from, away,* etc.) **3.** to hit (a ball) in a slice —*vi.* to cut (*through*) like a knife —**slic'er** *n.*

slick (slik) *adj.* [OE. *slician*] **1.** [Colloq.] smooth and clever, but superficial **2.** accomplished; adept **3.** sleek; smooth —*n.* a smooth area on the surface of water, as from a film of oil —*vt.* to make sleek or smooth

slide (slīd) *vi.* **slid** (slid), **slid'ing** [OE. *slidan*] **1.** to move along in constant contact with a smooth surface, as on ice **2.** to glide **3.** to slip [it *slid* from his hand] **4.** to pass gradually (*into* or *out of* some condition, habit, etc.) —*vt.* **1.** to cause to slide **2.** to move or slip quietly or stealthily (*in* or *into*) —*n.* **1.** an act of sliding **2.** a smooth, often sloping track, surface, or chute down or along which to slide **3.** something that works by sliding **4.** a piece of film with a photograph on it, mounted for use with a viewer or projector **5.** a small glass plate on which objects are mounted for microscopic study **6.** an ornamental clip to hold sections of hair in place —**let slide** to fail to take care of (some matter)

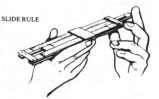

SLIDE RULE

slide rule an instrument for rapid calculations, consisting of a ruler with a central sliding piece, both marked with logarithmic scales

sliding scale a scale, as of costs, that varies with given conditions

slight (slīt) *adj.* [OE. *sliht*] **1.** small in amount or extent **2.** having little weight, strength, significance, etc. **3.** *a)* light in build; slender *b)* frail; fragile —*vt.* to treat with disrespect or indifference —*n.* a slighting or being slighted by pointedly discourteous treatment —**slight'ingly** *adv.* —**slight'ness** *n.*

slim (slim) *adj.* **slim'mer, slim'mest** [<

Du., crafty] **1.** small in girth in proportion to height or length **2.** slight; meagre —*vt., vi.* **slimmed, slim'ming 1.** to make or become slim, esp. by dieting **2.** to decrease in extent, numbers, costs, etc. [to slim an industry] —**slim'ness** *n.*

slime (slīm) *n.* [OE. *slim*] any soft, moist, slippery, often sticky matter; specif., any such matter considered disgusting

slimy *adj.* **-ier, -iest 1.** of, like or covered with slime **2.** disgusting; repulsive —**slim'ily** *adv.* —**slim'iness** *n.*

sling (sliŋ) *n.* [prob. < ON. *slyngva,* to throw] **1.** a primitive instrument for throwing stones, etc., consisting of a piece of leather tied to cords that are whirled for releasing the missile **2.** *a)* a looped or hanging band, used in raising or lowering a heavy object, etc. *b)* a wide piece of cloth looped from the neck under an injured arm for support —*vt.* **slung, sling'ing 1.** to throw (stones, etc.) with, or as if with, a sling **2.** to hang in a sling; suspend

slingback *n.* a shoe with a strap instead of a full covering for the heel

slink (sliŋk) *vi.* **slunk, slink'ing** [OE. *slincan,* to creep] to move in a fearful or stealthy way, or as if ashamed

slinky *adj.* **-ier, -iest 1.** sinuous and graceful in movement, line, etc. **2.** sneaky in movement

slip[1] (slip) *vi.* **slipped, slip'ping** [MLowG. *slippen*] **1.** to go quietly or secretly **2.** *a)* to move or pass smoothly, quickly, or easily *b)* to get (*into* or *out of* clothes) quickly **3.** to pass gradually into or out of some condition, habit, etc. **4.** to escape from one's mind, power, etc. [to let a chance *slip* by] **5.** to slide [the plate *slipped* from my hand] **6.** to slide accidentally, lose footing, etc. [to *slip* on ice] **7.** to make a mistake; err **8.** to become worse; weaken [my memory is *slipping*] —*vt.* **1.** to put or move smoothly, easily, or quickly **2.** to escape (one's mind) **3.** to get loose from [the dog *slipped* his lead] **4.** to transfer (a stitch) from one needle to another without knitting it **5.** to put out of joint; dislocate —*n.* **1.** a slipping or falling down **2.** an error or mistake **3.** a woman's sleeveless undergarment, full or half length **4.** an inclined plane leading down to water, on which ships are built or repaired: also **slip'-way 5.** *Cricket* a fielder placed behind the wicket on the off side —**give someone the slip** to escape from someone —**let slip** to say without intending to —**slip up** to make a mistake

slip[2] *n.* [< MDu. *slippen,* to cut] **1.** a small piece of paper, esp. one for a specific use [an order *slip*] **2.** a stem, root, twig, etc. cut off for planting or grafting **3.** a young, slim person

slip[3] *n.* [OE. *slypa,* paste] *Ceramics* clay thinned to a watery paste for decorating, etc.

slipknot *n.* a knot made so that it will slip along the rope, etc. around which it is tied

slip-on *adj.* easily put on or taken off, as shoes without laces —*n.* a slip-on shoe or garment

slipped disc a herniated disc between two vertebrae, esp. in the lumbar region, often causing sciatica

slipper *n.* a light, low shoe easily slipped on the foot, esp. one for indoor wear

slippery *adj.* slip′perier, slip′periest [OE. *slipor*] 1. liable to cause slipping, as a wet surface 2. tending to slip away, as from the grasp 3. untrustworthy —slip′periness *n.*

slippery elm a N American elm with sticky inner bark

slippy *adj.* [Colloq.] alert; sharp; quick

slip road a fairly narrow road used for joining and leaving a motorway

slipshod *adj.* [SLIP¹ + SHOD] 1. careless; slovenly 2. wearing shoes with worn-down heels

slip-slop *n.* [S. Afr.] a sandal with a single bifurcating thong

slipstream *n.* the current of air thrust backwards by a moving object, esp. the spinning propeller of an aircraft

slip-up *n.* [Colloq.] an error, oversight, or mishap

slipway *n.* a long, inclined ramp on which a ship is built or from which it is launched

slit (slit) *vt.* **slit, slit′ting** [OE. *slitan*] 1. to cut or split open, esp. by a straight, lengthwise incision 2. to cut into strips —*n.* a long, straight cut

slither (sli*th*′ər) *vi.* [< OE. *slidan,* to slide] 1. to slip or slide on a loose, broken surface, as a gravelly slope 2. to move along by gliding, as a snake —*n.* a slithering motion —slith′ery *adj.*

sliver (sliv′ər) *n.* [OE. *slifan,* to cut] a thin, sharp piece cut, split, or broken off; splinter —*vt., vi.* to cut or break into slivers

slob (slob) *n.* [Ir. *slab,* mud] [Colloq.] a sloppy, coarse, or gross person

slobber (slob′ər) *vi.* [prob. < LowG. *slubberen,* to swig] 1. to let saliva, etc. run from the mouth 2. to speak, write, etc. in a gushy or maudlin way —*vt.* to smear with saliva —*n.* saliva running from the mouth —slob′bery *adj.*

slob ice [Canad.] sludgy masses of floating ice

sloe (slō) *n.* [OE. *sla*] 1. the blackthorn 2. its small, blue-black, plumlike fruit

sloe-eyed *adj.* having dark, almond-shaped eyes

slog (slog) *vt., vi.* **slogged, slog′ging** [< ?] 1. to hit hard 2. to make (one's way) with great effort; plod 3. to work hard (at something) —*n.* 1. a tiring walk 2. long, exhausting work 3. a heavy blow

slogan (slō′gən) *n.* [< Gael. *sluagh,* a host + *gairm,* a call] 1. a catchword associated with a political party or other group 2. a catch phrase used to advertise a product

sloop (slōop) *n.* [Du. *sloep*] a fore-and-aft rigged, single-masted sailing vessel

sloot (slooət) *n.* [< Afrik.] [S Afr.] a ditch for irrigation or drainage

slop (slop) *n.* [OE. *sloppe*] 1. a splash or puddle of spilled liquid 2. liquid or semiliquid food that is unappetizing 3. [often *pl.*] a) liquid waste of any kind b) kitchen swill —*vi., vt.* **slopped, slop′-ping** to spill or splash —slop over 1. to overflow 2. [Colloq.] to display sentimentality; gush

slop bowl (or **basin**) a bowl into which the dregs from tea cups are emptied at table

slope (slōp) *n.* [< OE. *slupan,* to glide] 1. ground that slants, as a hillside 2. any inclined line, surface, etc.; slant 3. amount or degree of slant —*vi., vt.* **sloped, slop′ing** to slant or cause to slant —slope arms *Mil.* to hold a rifle resting on the shoulder with the butt in the hand —slope off [Colloq.] to leave furtively

sloppy (slop′ē) *adj.* slop′pier, slop′piest 1. wet and slushy 2. a) slovenly or messy b) careless; slipshod 3. [Colloq.] gushingly sentimental —slop′pily *adv.* —slop′piness *n.*

slosh (slosh) *vt.* [< SLUSH] 1. [Colloq.] to shake or agitate (a liquid) 2. [Colloq.] to apply (a liquid) carelessly 3. [Slang] to hit violently —*vi.* 1. to splash clumsily through water, mud, etc. 2. to splash about: said of a liquid —*n.* 1. a heavy blow 2. the sound of liquid splashing about —slosh′y *adj.*

sloshed *adj.* [Slang] drunk

slot (slot) *n.* [< OFr. *esclot,* hollow between the breasts] 1. a narrow notch or opening, as a slit for a coin in a vending machine 2. [Colloq.] a position in a group, series, etc. —*vt.* slot′ted, slot′ting 1. to make a slot in 2. [Colloq.] to place in a series, schedule, etc.

sloth (slōth) *n.* [< OE. *slaw,* slow] 1. the condition of not liking to work or be active; laziness 2. a slow-moving mammal of Central and South America that lives in trees

slothful *adj.* characterized by sloth; lazy —sloth′fully *adv.*

slot machine a machine, esp. a gambling device, worked by putting a coin in a slot

slouch (slouch) *n.* [< ON. *slōka,* to droop] 1. a drooping or slovenly posture 2. a drooping, as of a hat brim 3. [Colloq.] a person who lacks skill —*vi.* to sit, stand, walk, etc. in a slouch

slough¹ (sluf) *n.* [ME. *slouh*] any castoff layer, esp. the skin of a snake —*vi.* to be shed, cast off, etc. —*vt.* to shed or throw (*off*); get rid of

slough² (slou) *n.* [OE. *sloh*] 1. a place full of soft, deep mud 2. [< *Slough of Despond,* in Bunyan's *Pilgrim's Progress*] deep, hopeless discouragement 3. (slōō) [U.S. & Canada.] in the prairies, a) a large hole where water collects b) water in such a hole

sloven (sluv′ən) *n.* [prob. < MDu. *slof,* lax] a dirty or untidy person

slovenly (sluv′ənlē) *adj.* -lier, -liest careless in appearance, habits, work, etc.; untidy —*adv.* in a slovenly manner —slov′enliness *n.*

slow (slō) *adj.* [OE. *slaw*] 1. taking a longer time than is expected or usual 2. marked by low speed, etc.; not fast 3. making speed difficult [a slow track] 4. behind the correct time: said of a timepiece

5. lacking in energy; sluggish **6.** not quick in understanding **7.** passing tediously; dull **8.** not readily responsive or prone *to* **9.** slack *[slow* trading*]* **10.** giving off low heat *[a slow* fire*]* **11.** *Photog.* adapted to a relatively long exposure time —*vt.*, *vi.* to make or become slow or slower (often with *up* or *down*) —*adv.* in a slow manner —**slow′ly** *adv.* —**slow′ness** *n.*

slowcoach *n.* [Colloq.] one who acts or moves slowly

slow-motion *adj.* **1.** moving below usual speed **2.** designating a film in which the action is made to appear much slower than the actual action

slowworm *n.* [OE. *slawyrm*] a legless lizard: also called **blind′worm′**

sludge (sluj) *n.* [< *slutch*, mud] **1.** mud, mire, or ooze **2.** any heavy, slimy sediment, as the waste resulting from oil refining, the precipitate in a sewage tank, etc. —**sludg′y** *adj.*

slue (slṓo) *vt.*, *vi.* **slued, slu′ing** *same as* SLEW¹

slug¹ (slug) *n.* [< Scand.] a small mollusc resembling a land snail, but having only a rudimentary internal shell

slug² *n.* [prob. < prec.] **1.** a small piece of metal; specif., a bullet **2.** *Printing a)* a strip of nonprinting metal used to space between lines *b)* a line of type made in one piece, as by a linotype machine

slug³ *vt.* **slugged, slug′ging** [ON. *slag*] [Colloq.] to hit hard —*n.* [Colloq.] a hard blow

sluggard (slug′ərd) *n.* [< ME. *sluggen*, be lazy] a habitually lazy person —*adj.* lazy: also **slug′gardly**

sluggish (slug′ish) *adj.* [< SLUG¹] **1.** lacking energy or alertness; slothful **2.** slow or slow-moving

sluice (slṓos) *n.* [< L. *excludere*, EXCLUDE] **1.** an artificial channel for water, with a gate at its head to regulate the flow **2.** the water held back by such a gate **3.** such a gate: also **sluice gate 4.** any channel, esp. one for excess water **5.** a sloping trough for rinsing ore, etc. —*vt.* **sluiced, sluic′ing 1.** to draw off as by means of a sluice **2.** to wash with water from or as from a sluice —*vi.* to run or flow as in a sluice

slum (slum) *n.* [< ?] [*often pl.*] a heavily populated area of a city having much poverty, poor housing, etc. —*vi.* **slummed, slum′ming 1.** to visit slums in a condescending way **2.** to experience slum conditions: also **slum it —slum′my** *adj.*

slumber (slum′bər) *vi.* [< OE. *sluma*, slumber] **1.** to sleep **2.** to be inactive —*n.* **1.** sleep **2.** an inactive state —**slum′-berous, slum′brous** *adj.*

slump (slump) *vi.* [echoic] **1.** to fall or sink suddenly **2.** to have a drooping posture —*n.* **1.** a sudden or sharp decline, as in prices, demand, etc. **2.** a drooping posture

slung (slun) *pt. & pp. of* SLING

slunk (slunk) *pt. & pp. of* SLINK

slur (slur) *vt.* **slurred, slur′ring** [< ?] **1.** to pass (*over*) quickly and carelessly

2. to pronounce rapidly in an unclear way **3.** to discredit **4.** *Music* to sing or play (successive notes) by gliding from one to another without a break —*n.* **1.** a slurring **2.** a remark that is harmful to a person's reputation; aspersion **3.** *Music* a curved symbol connecting slurred notes

slurp (slurp) *vt.*, *vi.* [Du. *slurpen*, to sip] [Slang] to drink or eat noisily —*n.* [Slang] a loud sipping noise

slurry (slur′ē) *n.* [< ?] a thin, watery mixture, as of cement or mud

slush (slush) *n.* [prob. < Scand.] **1.** partly melted snow or ice **2.** soft mud **3.** excessively sentimental talk or writing —**slush′y** *adj.*

slush fund [Chiefly U.S.] money used for bribery, influencing politicians, or other corrupt purposes

slut (slut) *n.* [< ?] **1.** a dirty, slovenly woman **2.** a sexually promiscuous woman —**slut′tish** *adj.*

sly (slī) *adj.* **sli′er** or **sly′er, sli′est** or **sly′-est** [ON. *slœgr*] **1.** skilful at tricking others in an underhanded way **2.** teasing in a playful way —**on the sly** secretly —**sly′ly** *adv.* —**sly′ness** *n.*

Sm *Chem.* samarium

smack¹ (smak) *n.* [OE. *smæc*] a slight flavour or trace —*vi.* to have a smack (*of*)

smack² *vt.* [< ?] **1.** to slap loudly **2.** to part (the lips) suddenly so as to make a smack —*vi.* to make a loud, sharp noise —*n.* **1.** a sharp blow with a flat object; slap **2.** a loud kiss **3.** a sharp noise made by parting the lips suddenly —*adv.* **1.** directly: also [Colloq.] **smack′-dab′ 2.** with a smack —**smack in the eye** a snub or rebuff

smack³ *n.* [prob. < Du. *smak*] a small sailing boat, usually rigged as a sloop and used for fishing

smacker *n.* **1.** [Slang] a loud kiss **2.** [Slang] a pound note

small (smôl) *adj.* [OE. *smæl*] **1.** comparatively little in size; not large **2.** *a)* little in quantity, extent, value, duration, etc. *[a small* income*] b)* consisting of relatively few units; low in numbers *[a small* crowd*]* **3.** of little importance **4.** having relatively little investment, capital, etc. *[a small* business*]* **5.** small-minded; petty —*adv.* **1.** in small pieces **2.** in a small manner —*n.* **1.** the small or narrow part *[the small* of the back*]* **2.** [*pl.*] undercothes —**feel small** to feel shame or humiliation —**small′ish** *adj.* —**small′ness** *n.*

small beer [Colloq.] people or things of no importance

small change 1. coins, esp. those of low denomination **2.** something of little value

smallest room *a euphemism for* LAVATORY

smallholding *n.* a holding of agricultural land smaller than a farm, usually worked by one man —**small′holder** *n.*

small hours the first few hours after midnight

small-minded (smôl′mīn′did) *adj.* selfish, petty, prejudiced, narrow-minded, etc.

smallpox *n.* an acute, contagious disease causing fever and pustular eruptions that often leave pitted scars

small-scale *adj.* 1. drawn to a small scale 2. of limited scope [*small-scale* trading]

small talk light conversation about everyday things

small-time (smôl′tīm′) *adj.* [Colloq.] of little importance

smarm (smärm) *vt.* [< ?] [Colloq.] 1. to flatten the hair with grease 2. to ingratiate oneself —**smarm′y** *adj.*

smart (smärt) *adj.* [OE. *smeortan*] 1. *a)* intelligent, alert, witty, etc. *b)* shrewd or sharp 2. stylish 3. neat; trim 4. causing sharp pain [a *smart* slap] 5. sharp or stinging, as pain 6. brisk; lively [a *smart* pace] —*vi.* 1. *a)* to cause sharp, stinging pain, as a slap *b)* to feel such pain 2. to feel mental distress, as in resentment, remorse, etc. —*n.* a smarting sensation —*adv.* in a smart way

smart aleck, smart alec (al′ik) [< *Alexander*, name] [Colloq.] a conceited, cocky person

smarten *vt.* to make smart or smarter: usually with *up*

smash (smash) *vt.* [echoic] 1. to break into pieces with noise or violence 2. to hit (a tennis ball, etc.) with a hard overhand stroke 3. to hit with a hard, heavy blow 4. to ruin; destroy —*vi.* 1. to break into pieces 2. to be destroyed 3. to move or collide with force —*n.* 1. a hard, heavy hit 2. a violent, noisy breaking 3. a violent collision 4. total failure, esp. in business 5. an overwhelming popular success —*adj.* that is a great popular success

smash-and-grab raid robbery in which thieves smash a shopwindow and grab goods

smashing *adj.* [Colloq.] very good

smattering (smat′ər iŋ) *n.* [< ?] slight or superficial knowledge

smear (smēər) *vt.* [OE. *smerian*, anoint] 1. to cover or soil with something greasy, sticky, etc. 2. to apply (something greasy, etc.) 3. to smudge or obscure by rubbing 4. to harm the reputation of; slander —*vi.* to be or become smeared —*n.* 1. a mark made by smearing 2. a small quantity of some substance smeared on a slide for microscopic study, etc. 3. a slandering —**smear′y** *adj.*

smell (smel) *vt.* **smelled** or **smelt, smell′-ing** [ME. *smellen*] 1. to be aware of by means of the nose; detect the odour of 2. to sense [to *smell* trouble] 3. to test by the odour; sniff [*smell* the milk to tell if it's sour] —*vi.* 1. to use the sense of smell; sniff (often with *at* or *of*) 2. *a)* to have a scent *b)* to have an unpleasant odour 3. [Colloq.] to be foul, corrupt, etc. —*n.* 1. the sense by which a substance is perceived through the stimulation of nerves in the nasal cavity 2. odour; scent 3. an act of smelling —**smell out** to look for as by smelling

smelling salts carbonate of ammonium, inhaled to relieve faintness, headaches, etc.

smelly *adj.* **-ier, -iest** having an unpleasant smell —**smell′iness** *n.*

smelt[1] (smelt) *n.* [OE.] a small, silvery food fish

smelt[2] *vt.* [MDu. or MLowG. *smelten*] 1. to melt or fuse (ore, etc.) so as to separate impurities from pure metal 2. to refine or extract (metal) in this way

smelter *n.* 1. a person engaged in the work of smelting 2. a place where smelting is done: also **smelt′ery**

smew (smyōō) *n.* [< ?] a duck of N Europe and Asia related to the goosander

smilax (smī′laks) *n.* [L. < Gr. *smilax*, bindweed] 1. *same as* CAT BRIER. 2. a twining plant with bright green leaves

smile (smīl) *vi.* **smiled, smil′ing** [ME. *smilen*] 1. to show pleasure, amusement, affection, etc. by an upward curving of the corners of the mouth 2. to regard with favour (with *on* or *upon*) —*vt.* to express with a smile —*n.* the act or expression of smiling —**smil′ingly** *adv.*

smirch (smurch) *vt.* [< ?] 1. to soil or smear 2. to dishonour —*n.* 1. a smudge; smear 2. a stain on a reputation

smirk (smurk) *vi.* [OE. *smearcian*, to smile] to smile in a conceited or self-satisfied way —*n.* such a smile

smite (smīt) *vt.* **smote, smit′ten, smit′-ing** [OE. *smitan*] 1. [Now Rare] to hit or strike hard 2. to attack with disastrous effect 3. to affect strongly and suddenly (with) 4. to impress favourably [*smitten* with her charms]

smith (smith) *n.* [OE.] 1. a person who makes or repairs metal objects [*silversmith*] 2. *shortened form of* BLACKSMITH

smithereens (smith′ə rēnz′) *n.pl.* [Ir. *smidirín*] [Colloq.] small fragments; bits

smithy (smith′ē) *n., pl.* **smith′ies** 1. the workshop of a smith 2. *same as* BLACKSMITH

smitten (smit′′n) *pp.* of SMITE

smock (smok) *n.* [OE. *smoc*] 1. a loose, shirtlike, outer garment worn to protect the clothes 2. a woman's loose, blouselike garment —*vt.* to decorate with smocking

smocking *n.* decorative stitching used in gathering cloth

smog (smog) *n.* [SM(OKE) + (F)OG] a harmful mixture of fog and smoke —**smog′-gy** *adj.*

smoke (smōk) *n.* [OE. *smoca*] 1. the vaporous matter arising from something burning 2. *a)* an act of smoking tobacco, etc. [time for a *smoke*] *b)* something to smoke, as a cigarette —*vi.* **smoked, smok′ing** 1. to give off smoke 2. to discharge smoke excessively or improperly, as a fireplace, etc. 3. *a)* to draw the smoke of tobacco, etc. into the mouth and blow it out again *b)* to be habitual smoker —*vt.* 1. to use (tobacco, a pipe, etc.) in smoking 2. to force out with smoke [to *smoke* an animal from its lair]

3. to cure (meat, etc.) with smoke —**go up in smoke 1.** to burn vigorously **2.** to come to nothing **3.** to flare up in anger —**smoke out** to force out of hiding, secrecy, etc.

smokeless *adj.* having or making little or no smoke

smoker *n.* **1.** a person who habitually smokes tobacco **2.** a railway compartment reserved esp. for smoking

smoke screen 1. a cloud of smoke spread to screen the movements of troops, ships, etc. **2.** anything said or done to conceal or mislead

smokestack *n.* a pipe for the discharge of smoke from a steamship, factory, etc.

smoky *adj.* **-ier, -iest 1.** giving off smoke, esp. excessive smoke **2.** like smoke *[a smoky haze]* **3.** filled with smoke **4.** having the colour of smoke —**smok'ily** *adv.* —**smok'iness** *n.*

smolt (smōlt) *n.* [Scot] a young salmon when it first leaves fresh water and descends to the sea

smooch (smōōch) *n.* [echoic] [Slang] a kiss —*vi.* [Slang] to kiss or pet —**smooch'y** *adj.*

smooth (smōōth) *adj.* [OE. *smoth*] **1.** having an even surface with no roughness **2.** without lumps *[a smooth paste]* **3.** even or gentle in movement *[a smooth voyage]* **4.** free from interruptions, difficulties, etc. **5.** having an easy, flowing rhythm or sound **6.** suave, polished, or ingratiating, esp. in an insincere way —*vt.* **1.** to make level or even **2.** to remove the lumps from **3.** to free from interruptions, difficulties, etc. —*adv.* in a smooth manner —*n.* **1.** a smooth part **2.** an act of smoothing —**smooth over** to gloss over or make light of (an unpleasant situation) —**smooth'ly** *adv.* —**smooth'ness** *n.*

smoothing iron *same as as* IRON (n. sense 2)

smooth-shaven (smōōth'shā'v'n) *adj.* wearing no beard or moustache

smooth-spoken (smōōth'spō'k'n) *adj.* speaking in a pleasing, persuasive, or polished manner

smooth-tongued (smōōth'tuŋd') *adj.* smooth-spoken, esp. in a plausible or flattering way

smorgasbord, smörgåsbord (smôr'gəsbôrd') *n.* [Sw.] a wide variety of appetizers, cheeses, fishes, meats, salads, etc., served buffet style

smote (smōt) *pt. of* SMITE

smother (smuth'ər) *vt.* [< ME. *smorther*, dense smoke] **1.** to keep from getting air; suffocate; stifle **2.** to cover (a fire), causing it to go out **3.** to cover over thickly **4.** to suppress or stifle —*vi.* to be kept from getting air —*n.* dense, suffocating smoke, dust, etc.

smoulder (smōl'dər) *vi.* [ME. *smoldren*] **1.** to burn and smoke without flame **2.** to exist in a suppressed state **3.** to have suppressed anger or hate —*n.* the act of smouldering U.S. sp. **smolder**

smudge (smuj) *n.* [< ?] a stain, smear,

etc.; dirty spot —*vt., vi.* **smudged, smudg'-ing** to make or become dirty; smear —**smudg'y** *adj.*

smug (smug) *adj.* **smug'ger, smug'gest** [prob. < LowG. *smuk*, trim] so pleased with oneself, one's opinions, etc. as to be annoying to others; too self-satisfied —**smug'ness** *n.*

smuggle (smug''l) *vt.* **-gled, -gling** [< LowG. *smuggeln*] **1.** to bring into or take out of a country secretly or illegally **2.** to bring, take, etc. secretly —**smug'-gler** *n.*

smut (smut) *n.* [< LowG. *smutt*] **1.** sooty matter **2.** a soiled spot **3.** obscene talk, writing, etc. **4.** a plant disease in which certain fungi form masses of black spores that break up into a fine powder —*vt., vi.* **smut'ted, smut'ting** to make or become covered with smuts —**smut'ty** *adj.*

Sn [L. *stannum*] *Chem.* tin

snack (snak) *n.* [prob. < MDu. *snacken*, to snap] light refreshment taken between regular meals

snack bar a lunch counter, cafeteria, etc. serving snacks

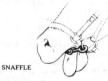

SNAFFLE

snaffle (snaf''l) *n.* [prob. < ODu. *snabbe*, bill of a bird] a bit, usually light and jointed, attached to a bridle and having no curb —*vt.* **-fled, -fling 1.** to fit with a snaffle **2.** [Colloq.] to steal

snag (snag) *n.* [< Scand.] **1.** an unexpected or hidden difficulty **2.** a sharp part, point, etc. that may catch on things **3.** a tear or a pulled thread in fabric, made by a snag **4.** an underwater tree stump dangerous to navigation —*vt.* **snagged, snag'ging** to catch, tear, etc. on a snag

snail (snāl) *n.* [OE. *snægl*] a slow-moving gastropod mollusc living on land or in water and having a spiral protective shell

snail's pace a very slow speed

snake (snāk) *n.* [OE. *snaca*] **1.** a limbless reptile with a long, scaly body, lidless eyes, and a tapering tail **2.** a treacherous person **3.** the band within which EEC currencies are allowed to fluctuate —*vi.* **snaked, snak'ing** to move, twist, etc. like a snake

snake charmer a person who, as an entertainer, appears to hypnotize snakes by body movements and music

snake in the grass a treacherous person or harmful thing that is seemingly harmless

snakes and ladders a children's board game in which tossed dice determine how far counters move either to climb ladders or slide down snakes

snaky *adj.* **-ier, -iest 1.** of or like a snake **2.** sinuous; winding **3.** cunningly treacherous **4.** infested with snakes

snap (snap) *vi., vt.* **snapped, snap'ping** [< MDu. *snappen*] **1.** to break or part suddenly, esp. with a sharp, cracking sound **2.** to make or cause to make a sharp, cracking sound [to *snap* one's fingers] **3.** to break down suddenly under strain **4.** to close, fasten, etc. with a sound like this **5.** to move or cause to move suddenly and smartly **6.** to grasp quickly or eagerly (often with *at* or *up*) **7.** to bite suddenly (often with *at*) **8.** to speak or say in a sharp, abrupt way **9.** to take a snapshot (of) —*n.* **1.** a sharp cracking sound **2.** any clasp that closes with a click **3.** a sudden bite, grasp, etc. **4.** a hard, thin biscuit [*gingersnaps*] **5.** *same as* SNAPSHOT **6.** a brief spell of cold weather **7.** a simple card game in which cards can be won by the first person to say snap on seeing two similar cards —*adj.* **1.** made or done quickly without deliberation [a *snap* decision] **2.** that fastens with a snap —*adv.* with a snap —**snap one's fingers at 1.** to dismiss with contempt **2.** to defy —**snap out of it** to recover quickly or regain one's senses

snapdragon *n.* [SNAP + DRAGON: from the mouth-shaped flowers] *same as* ANTIRRHINUM

snap fastener *same as* PRESS STUD

snappish *adj.* **1.** likely to snap or bite **2.** irritable; sharp-tongued

snappy *adj.* **snap'pier, snap'piest 1.** snappish; cross **2.** [Colloq.] a) brisk or lively [a *snappy* pace] b) chilly [*snappy* weather] c) smart; fashionable [a *snappy* dresser] —**make it snappy** [Slang] be quick

snapshot *n.* an informal photograph taken with a hand camera

snare (snãər) *n.* [< ON. *snara*] **1.** a trap for small animals, usually consisting of a noose which jerks tight **2.** anything dangerous, risky, etc. that tempts or attracts **3.** a length of spiralled wire or of gut strung across the bottom of a drum for added vibration —*vt.* **snared, snar'ing 1.** to catch in a trap or snare **2.** to lure into a situation that is risky, etc.

snare drum a small, double-headed drum with snares

snarl[1] (snärl) *vi.* [< *snar*, to growl] **1.** to growl fiercely, baring the teeth, as a dog **2.** to speak sharply, as in anger —*vt.* to utter with a snarl —*n.* **1.** a fierce growl **2.** a harsh utterance

snarl[2] *vt., vi.* [ME. *snarlen*] to make or become knotted or tangled —*n.* **1.** a tangle **2.** a confused, disordered situation

snatch (snach) *vt.* [< ?] **1.** to grasp or seize suddenly, eagerly, or without right, etc. **2.** to remove abruptly **3.** to take hastily or while there is a chance **4.** [U.S. Slang] to kidnap —*vi.* to grasp (*at* something) —*n.* **1.** the act of snatching **2.** a short time [to sleep in *snatches*] **3.** a fragment; bit [*snatches* of gossip]

snazzy (snaz'ē) *adj.* **snaz'zier, snaz'ziest** [< ?] [Slang] stylishly or showily attractive —**snaz'zily** *adv.*

sneak (snēk) *vi.* **sneaked, sneak'ing** [< ?] **1.** to move quietly and stealthily **2.** to act in an underhanded or cowardly manner **3.** [Slang] to tell tales, esp. in school —*vt.* to give, put, take, etc. secretly or in a sneaking manner —*n.* one who sneaks; underhanded person, esp. an informer —*adj.* without warning [a *sneak* attack] —**sneak'y** *adj.*

sneakers *n.pl.* [U.S.] soft-soled canvas shoes, worn for sports or informally

sneaking *adj.* **1.** cowardly, underhanded, or furtive **2.** not admitted; secret [a *sneaking* fondness for chocolate] —**sneaking suspicion** a slight or growing suspicion

sneak thief a person who commits thefts in a sneaking way, without the use of force or violence

sneer (snēər) *vi.* [ME. *sneren*] **1.** to look scornful as by curling the lip **2.** to express scorn, derision, etc. in speech or writing —*vt.* to utter in a sneering way —*n.* **1.** an act of sneering **2.** a sneering look, remark, etc.

sneeze (snēz) *vi.* **sneezed, sneez'ing** [< OE. *fneosan*] to exhale breath from the nose and mouth in a sudden, uncontrolled way, because the mucous membrane of the nose has been irritated —*n.* an act of sneezing —**not to be sneezed at** not to be disregarded

sneeze wood 1. a S African tree **2.** its exceptionally hard wood, used for furniture, gateposts, etc.

snick (snik) *n.* [< ?] **1.** a small cut or notch; nick **2.** *Cricket* a glancing blow —*vt.* **1.** to nick **2.** *Cricket* to hit the ball with a snick

snicker (snik'ər) *vi.* [echoic] to laugh in a sly or partly stifled manner —*n.* a snickering laugh

snide (snīd) *adj.* [< ?] slyly malicious or derisive [a *snide* remark] —**snid'ery** *n.*

sniff (snif) *vi., vt.* [echoic] **1.** to draw (air) up the nose with enough force to be heard **2.** to express (disdain, scepticism, etc.) by sniffing **3.** to smell (a substance) by sniffing —*n.* an act or sound of sniffing —**sniff at 1.** to smell **2.** to express contempt for

sniffle (snif'l) *vi.* **-fled, -fling** to sniff repeatedly, as in checking mucus running from the nose —*n.* an act or sound of sniffling —**the sniffles** [Colloq.] a head cold, etc. in which there is much sniffling

snifter (snif'tər) *n.* a small alcoholic drink

snigger (snig'ər) *vi., vt., n.* [echoic] *same as* SNICKER

snip (snip) *vt., vi.* **snipped, snip'ping** [Du. *snippen*] to cut or cut off with a short, quick stroke —*n.* **1.** a small cut made with scissors, etc. **2.** the sound of this **3.** a small piece cut off **4.** [*pl.*] heavy hand shears for cutting sheet metal, etc. **5.** [Colloq.] a bargain

snipe (snīp) *n.* [ON. *snipa*] a wading bird with a long, flexible bill —*vi.* **sniped, snip'-**

ing 1. to shoot from a hidden position at individuals of an enemy force 2. to direct an attack (*at* someone) in a sly or underhanded way —**snip′er** *n.*

snippet (snip′it) *n.* [< SNIP] a small scrap or fragment, specif. of information, a writing, etc.

snitch (snich) *vt.* [Slang] to steal; pilfer —*vi.* [Slang] to be an informer (*on*) —*n.* [Slang] an informer

snivel (sniv′'l) *vi.* -**elled**, -**elling** [< OE. *snofl,* mucus] 1. to cry and sniffle 2. to complain in a whining, tearful manner

snob (snob) *n.* [< ?] 1. a person who attaches great importance to wealth, social position, etc., having contempt for those he considers inferior 2. a person who feels smugly superior about his particular tastes or interests [an intellectual *snob*] —**snob′bery** *n.* —**snob′bish** *adj.*

snoek (snook) *n.* [Afrik.] a S African edible marine fish

snog (snog) *vi.* [< ?] [Slang] to kiss and cuddle —*n.* [Slang] the act of kissing and cuddling

snood (snood) *n.* [OE. *snod*] a baglike net worn, esp. formerly, at the back of a woman's head to hold the hair

snook (snook) *n.* [< ?] the gesture of thumbing one's nose in defiance or derision: used chiefly in the phrase **cock a snook at**

snooker (snook′ər) *n.* [< ?] 1. a variety of the game of billiards played with fifteen red balls and six other balls 2. a position in this game in which the object ball is masked by a ball of a different colour —*vt.* 1. to put (someone) into a snooker position 2. [Colloq.] to thwart; defeat

snoop (snoop) *vi.* [< Du. *snoepen,* to eat on the sly] [Colloq.] to look about in a furtive, prying way —*n.* [Colloq.] the act of snooping —**snoop′er** *n.* —**snoop′y** *adj.*

snoot (snoot) *n.* [see SNOUT] [Colloq.] the nose

snooty (snoot′ē) *adj.* -**ier,** -**iest** [Colloq.] haughty; snobbish —**snoot′ily** *adv.* —**snoot′iness** *n.*

snooze (snooz) *n.* [< ?] [Colloq.] a brief sleep; nap —*vi.* **snoozed, snooz′ing** [Colloq.] to take a brief sleep; nap

snore (snôr) *vi.* **snored, snor′ing** [echoic] to breathe, while asleep, with harsh sounds caused by vibration of the soft palate, usually with the mouth open —*n.* the act or sound of snoring

SNORKEL

snorkel (snôr′k'l) *n.* [G. *Schnörkel,* spiral]

1. a device for submarines, with air intake and exhaust tubes, permitting submergence for long periods 2. a breathing tube extending above the surface of the water, used in swimming just below the surface —*vi.* -**kelled, -kelling** to swim under water using a snorkel

snort (snôrt) *vi.* [echoic] 1. to force breath from the nose in a sudden and noisy way 2. to express anger, scorn, etc. by a snort 3. to make a noise like a snort —*vt.* to express or utter with a snort —*n.* 1. the act or sound of snorting 2. [U.S. Slang] a drink of spirits, taken in one gulp

snot (snot) *n.* [OE. (*ge*)*snot,* mucus] [Vulg.] 1. nasal mucus 2. [Slang] a contemptible person —**snot′ty** *adj.*

snot-en-trane (snot′ən trä′nə) *adj.* [< Afrik.] [S Afr. Slang] inducing a state of sentimental or maudlin misery: used of films, etc.

snout (snout) *n.* [MDu. *snute*] 1. the projecting nose and jaws, or muzzle, of an animal 2. [Colloq.] a human nose, esp. a large one

snow (snō) *n.* [OE. *snaw*] 1. frozen particles of water vapour which fall to earth as soft, white, crystalline flakes 2. a falling of snow 3. a mass of fallen snow 4. fluctuating spots appearing on a TV screen 5. [Slang] cocaine —*vi.* to fall as or like snow —*vt.* to cover, obstruct, etc. with or as with snow (usually with *in, under,* etc.) —**snow under** to overwhelm, as with work —**snow′y** *adj.*

snow apple [Canad.] a variety of red apple with white flesh like granulated snow

snowball *n.* 1. a mass of snow packed together into a ball 2. *same as* GUELDER-ROSE —*vi.* 1. to increase rapidly like a rolling ball of snow 2. to throw snowballs —*vt.* to throw snowballs at

snowberry *n.,* *pl.* -**ries** a hardy plant with small, pink flowers and soft, white berries

snow-blind *adj.* blinded temporarily by ultraviolet rays of the sun reflected from snow

snowblower *n.* [Canad.] a snow-clearing machine that draws the snow in and blows it away

snowbound *adj.* shut in or blocked off by snow

snow bunting a bunting of northern and arctic regions, having white plumage with dark markings

snowcap *n.* a cap of snow, as on a mountain

snowdrift *n.* a smooth heap of snow blown together by the wind

snowdrop *n.* a low-growing, bulbous plant with small, bell-shaped white flowers

snowfall *n.* the amount of snow that falls in a given time

snow fence [Canad.] a lath and wire fence put up in winter beside windy roads to prevent snow drifts

snowflake *n.* a single crystal of snow

snow goose a white goose that breeds

in the Arctic, having a red bill and black wing tips

snow lily [Canad.] *same as* DOGTOOTH VIOLET

snow line the lower boundary of a high region in which snow never melts

snowman *n.* a crude human figure made of packed snow

snowmobile (snō'mō bēl') *n.* a motor vehicle, usually with caterpillar tracks and front skis, for travelling on snow

snowplough *n.* any ploughlike machine used to clear snow off a road, railway, etc.

SNOWSHOES

snowshoe *n.* a racket-shaped frame of wood crisscrossed with strips of leather, etc., worn on the feet to prevent sinking in deep snow

snowstorm *n.* a storm with a heavy snowfall

SNP Scottish National Party

snub (snub) *vt.* **snubbed, snub′bing** [ON. *snubba*, chide] **1.** to treat with scorn, disregard, etc.; slight **2.** orig., to check with sharp words —*n.* **1.** scornful, slighting action or treatment **2.** a snubbing —*adj.* short and turned up : said of the nose —**snub′ber** *n.*

snub-nosed *adj.* having a snub nose

snuff[1] (snuf) *vt.* [< ?] **1.** to trim off the charred end of (a candle wick) **2.** to put out (a candle) —**snuff it** [Colloq.] to die —**snuff out** **1.** to put out (a candle, etc.) **2.** to cause to die suddenly

snuff[2] *n.* [MDu. *snuffen*] **1.** powdered tobacco taken up into the nose by sniffing or applied to the gums **2.** a sniff —*vt., vi.* to sniff or smell —**up to snuff** [Colloq.] up to the usual standard

snuffbox *n.* a small box for holding snuff

snuffer *n.* a device for putting out a burning candle

snuffle (snuf′'l) *vi.* **-fled, -fling** [< SNUFF[2]] **1.** to breathe audibly and with difficulty **2.** to speak or sing in a nasal tone —*vt.* to utter by snuffling —*n.* the act or sound of snuffling —**snuf′fler** *n.*

snug (snug) *adj.* **snug′ger, snug′gest** [prob. < Scand.] **1.** warm and cosy **2.** compact and convenient **3.** large enough to provide ease : said of an income **4.** tight in fit **5.** hidden —*n.* a bar in certain public houses —**snug′ly** *adv.* —**snug′ness** *n.*

snuggery *n., pl.* **-geries** a snug or comfortable room

snuggle *vi.* **-gled, -gling** [< SNUG] to cuddle, as for warmth, in affection, etc.

snye (snī) *n.* [< Fr. *chenal*, channel] [Canad.] a side channel of a river

so[1] (sō) *adv.* [OE. *swa*] · **1.** in the way shown, expressed, understood, etc. **2.** a) to such an extent [why are you *so* late?] b) very **3.** therefore **4.** approximately [fifty pounds or *so*] **5.** also; likewise **6.** then [and *so* to bed] —*conj.* **1.** in order that **2.** [Colloq.] with the result that —*pron.* that which has been specified or named —*interj.* an exclamation of surprise, approval, triumph, etc. —*adj.* **1.** true; in reality [that's *so*] **2.** in proper order [everything must be just *so*] —**and so on** (or **forth**) et cetera (etc.) —**so as** with the purpose or result —**so be it** an expression of acceptance or resignation —**so much** to an unspecified but limited degree, amount, etc. —**so much for** no more need be said about —**so to say** as it were —**so what?** [Colloq.] even if so, what then?

so[2] *n. Music same as* SOL[1]

So. **1.** south **2.** southern

soak (sōk) *vt.* [OE. *socian*] **1.** to make thoroughly wet **2.** to submerge in a liquid **3.** to take in; absorb (with *up*) —*vi.* **1.** to stay immersed in liquid **2.** to pass (*into* or *through*) as a liquid does —*n.* **1.** a soaking or being soaked **2.** [Slang] a drunkard

soakaway *n.* a depression in the ground where rainwater is drained away through the soil

so-and-so *n., pl.* **so′-and-sos′** [Colloq.] **1.** some person or thing whose name is not specified **2.** a disliked or difficult person or thing

soap (sōp) *n.* [OE. *sape*] a substance used with water to produce suds for washing : made by the action of an alkali, as potash, on fats —*vt.* to lather, scrub, etc. with soap

soapbox *n.* any improvised platform used by a person (**soapbox orator**) speaking to a street audience

soap flakes soap in the form of flakes used esp. for washing delicate clothes

soap opera [Colloq.] a radio or TV serial drama of a melodramatic, sentimental nature

soap powder a powder used for washing clothes, usually containing additives as well as soap

soapstone *n. same as* STEATITE

soapsuds *n.pl.* **1.** soapy water, esp. when stirred into a foam **2.** the foam on soapy water

soapy *adj.* **-ier, -iest** **1.** of, like, or containing soap **2.** [Slang] suave; oily —**soap′iness** *n.*

soar (sôr) *vi.* [< L. *ex-*, out + *aura*, air] **1.** to rise or fly high into the air **2.** to glide along high in the air, as a glider **3.** to rise above the ordinary level

sob (sob) *vi.* **sobbed, sob′bing** [ME. *sobben*] **1.** to weep aloud with short, gasping breaths **2.** to make a sound like this, as the wind

—*vt.* to utter with sobs —*n.* the act or sound of sobbing

sober (sō'bər) *adj.* [< L. *sobrius*] 1. not drunk 2. temperate, esp. in the use of alcohol 3. serious, solemn, sedate, etc. 4. quiet; plain: said of colour, clothes, etc. 5. not distorted [the *sober* truth] —*vt., vi.* to make or become sober (often with *up* or *down*)

sobriety (sō brī'ə tē) *n.* 1. temperance, esp. in the use of alcohol 2. seriousness; sedateness

sobriquet (sō'brə kā') *n.* [Fr.] a nickname

sob story [Colloq.] an account of personal troubles meant to arouse sympathy

sob-stuff *n.* [Colloq.] writing, narration, etc. presented in a sentimental manner in order to arouse sympathy or sorrow

Soc., soc. 1. social 2. socialist 3. society

so-called (sō'kôld') *adj.* 1. known by this term 2. inaccurately regarded as such [a *so-called* liberal]

soccer (sok'ər) *n.* [< (AS)SOC(IATION FOOTBALL)] *same as* ASSOCIATION FOOTBALL

sociable (sō'shə b'l) *adj.* [Fr.: see ff.] 1. friendly; affable 2. characterized by pleasant, informal conversation and companionship —**so'ciabil'ity** *n.* —**so'ciably** *adv.*

social (sō'shəl) *adj.* [< L. *socius*, companion] 1. of or having to do with human beings living together in groups 2. living in this way [man as a *social* being] 3. of or having to do with society, esp. fashionable society 4. getting along well with others 5. of or for companionship 6. of or engaged in welfare work [a *social* worker] 7. living in groups or communities —*n.* an informal gathering; party —**so'cially** *adv.*

social contract an agreement among individuals forfeiting some of their individual liberties for greater security

Social Credit in Canada, a right-wing political party, movement, or doctrine

Social Credit Rally a Canadian political party formed in 1963 from a splinter group of the Social Credit Party

Social Insurance Number an identification number issued to individuals by the Canadian government in connection with income tax and social assistance

socialism *n.* 1. any of various theories of the ownership and operation of the means of production and distribution by society rather than by private individuals 2. [often S-] a political movement for establishing such a system —**so'cialist** *n., adj.*

socialite (sō'shə līt') *n.* a person who is prominent in fashionable society

socialize (sō'shə līz') *vt.* -ized', -iz'ing 1. to make social or fit for cooperative group living 2. to put under government ownership 3. to cause to become socialist —*vi.* to take part in social activity —**so'cializa'tion** *n.*

social science any of several studies, as history, economics, civics, etc., dealing with society and the activity of its members —**social scientist**

social security a State system of old-age, unemployment, or disability insurance, financed by a fund maintained jointly by employees, employers, and the government

social service *same as* SOCIAL WORK

social services the welfare activities organized by the state

social studies a course of study, esp. in schools, including history, civics, geography, etc.

social welfare the welfare of society, esp. of those who are underprivileged or disadvantaged

social work the promotion of the welfare of the community and the individual, as through counselling services, aid for the needy and aged, etc. —**social worker**

society (sə sī'ə tē) *n., pl.* -ties [< L. *socius*, companion] 1. all people, collectively 2. a group of persons regarded as forming a single community 3. the system of living together in such a group 4. companionship 5. any organized group with work, interests, etc. in common 6. a group of persons regarded as a dominant class because of their wealth, birth, etc. —*adj.* of or involving society (*n.* 6) —**soci'etal** *adj.*

Society of Friends a Christian religious sect founded in England c. 1650 by George Fox: the Friends have no formal creed, rites, liturgy, or priesthood

Society of Jesus see JESUIT

socio- (sō'sē ō) [< L. *socius*, companion] a combining form meaning social, society, sociological

socioeconomic (sō'sē ō ē'kə nom'ik) *adj.* of or involving both social and economic factors

sociology (sō'sē ol'ə jē) *n.* [see SOCIO- & -LOGY] the science of human society and of social relations, organization, and change —**so'ciolog'ical** (-ə loj'i k'l) *adj.* —**so'ciolog'ically** *adv.* —**so'ciol'ogist** *n.*

sociopolitical (sō'sē ō pə lit'i k'l) *adj.* of or involving both social and political factors

sock[1] (sok) *n.* [< L. *soccus*, a light shoe] a short stocking reaching only part way to the knee —**put a sock in it** [Slang] to stop talking, complaining, etc.

sock[2] *vt.* [Slang] to hit with force, esp. with the fist —*n.* [Slang] a blow —**sock it to (someone)** to attack or assault (someone)

socket (sok'it) *n.* [< OFr. *soc*, ploughshare] a hollow part into which something fits [an eye *socket*, the *socket* for a light bulb]

Socratic (so krat'ik) *adj.* of or relating to Socrates (470?-399 B.C.), Athenian philosopher

Socratic method a method of teaching, as used by Socrates, in which a series of questions leads the answerer to a logical conclusion

Socred (sō'kred) *n.* [Canad.] a supporter or member of a Social Credit movement or party —*adj.* [Canad.] of or relating to Social Credit

sod¹ (sod) *n*. [prob. < MDu. *sode*] 1. a surface layer of earth containing grass; turf 2. a piece of this layer —**under the sod** dead and buried

sod² *n*. [see SODOMITE] [Vulg. Slang] 1. any obnoxious person 2. a person

soda (sō'də) *n*. [ult. < Ar.] 1. *same as*: a) SODIUM BICARBONATE b) SODIUM CARBONATE 2. *same as* SODA WATER

soda fountain 1. [U.S.] a counter serving soft drinks, sundaes, etc. 2. an apparatus for making soda water

sodality (sō dal'ə tē) *n*., *pl*. **-ties** [< L. *sodalis*, companion] an association or brotherhood

soda water water charged under pressure with carbon dioxide gas, used as a drink, with or without spirits

sodden (sod'n) *adj*. [obs. pp. of SEETHE] 1. soaked through 2. soggy from incomplete cooking 3. dull or stupefied, as from drunkenness —**sod'denness** *n*.

sodium (sō'dē əm) *n*. [< SODA] a silver-white, alkaline metallic chemical element: symbol, Na

sodium bicarbonate a white, crystalline compound used in baking powder, as an antacid, etc.

sodium carbonate 1. the anhydrous sodium salt of carbonic acid 2. any of the hydrated carbonates of sodium

sodium chloride common salt, NaCl

Sodom (sod'əm) *n*. any place that is notorious for vice and depravity: after the city described in the Bible: Gen. 18-19

sodomite *n*. a person who practises sodomy

sodomy *n*. [see SODOM] any sexual intercourse held to be abnormal, as between two persons of the same sex

soever (sō ev'ər) *adv*. 1. in any way 2. of any kind [no rest *soever*]

-soever (sō ev'ər) a combining form added for emphasis or generalization to who, what, when, where, how, etc.

sofa (sō'fə) *n*. [Fr. < Ar. *suffah*] an upholstered couch with fixed back and arms

S. of Sol. Song of Solomon

soft (soft) *adj*. [OE. *softe*] 1. giving way easily under pressure, as a feather pillow 2. easily cut, shaped, or worn away [a *soft* metal] 3. not as hard as is normal, desirable, etc. 4. smooth to the touch 5. easy to digest: said of a diet 6. nonalcoholic: said of drinks 7. having few of the mineral salts that interfere with the lathering of soap: said of water 8. a) mild, as a breeze b) rainy; drizzling; misty [*soft* weather] 9. weak; not strong or vigorous 10. requiring little effort; easy [a *soft* job] 11. kind or lenient; not severe 12. subdued: said of colour or light 13. showing little distinctness, as an etching 14. gentle; low: said of sound 15. not addictive: said of drugs 16. *Phonet*. sibilant: said of *c* and *g*, as in *cent* and *germ* —*adv*. gently; quietly —*interj*. [Archaic] hush! —**soft in the head** stupid or foolish —**soft'ly** *adv*. —**soft'ness** *n*.

softball *n*. [U.S.] a game like baseball played with a larger and softer ball

soft-boiled *adj*. boiled only a short time so that the yolk is still soft: said of an egg

soft coal *same as* BITUMINOUS COAL

soft drink a nonalcoholic, esp. carbonated drink

soften (sof'n) *vt.*, *vi*. 1. to make or become soft or softer 2. to make or become less resistant

soft furnishings fabrics for curtains, cushions, etc.

softhearted *adj*. 1. full of compassion or tenderness 2. not strict or severe, as in discipline

soft palate the soft, fleshy part at the rear of the roof of the mouth; velum

soft-pedal (soft'ped'l) *vt*. **-alled**, **-alling** 1. to soften the tone of (a piano, etc.) by use of a special pedal (**soft pedal**) 2. [Colloq.] to tone down; make less emphatic

soft sell selling that relies on subtle suggestion rather than high-pressure salesmanship

soft-shoe *adj*. designating a kind of tap dancing done without metal taps on the shoes

soft soap 1. soap in liquid form 2. [Colloq.] flattery or smooth talk —**soft'-soap'** *vt*.

soft-spoken *adj*. 1. speaking with a soft, low voice 2. smooth; suave

soft spot particular affection for someone or something

software *n*. the programs, data, etc. for a computer

softwood *n*. wood from a needle-bearing conifer

softy, softie *n*., *pl*. **soft'ies** [Colloq.] a person who is too sentimental or trusting

SOGAT (sō'gat) Society of Graphical and Allied Trades

soggy (sog'ē) *adj*. **-gier**, **-giest** [< ?] 1. saturated with moisture; soaked 2. moist and heavy —**sog'gily** *adv*. —**sog'giness** *n*.

soh (sō) *n*. *same as* SOL¹

soigné (swän'yā) *adj*. [Fr.] well groomed; elegant —**soi'gnée** *fem*.

soil¹ (soil) *n*. [< L. *solum*] 1. the surface layer of earth, supporting plant life 2. land; country 3. ground or earth

soil² *vt*. [ult. < L. *sus*, pig] 1. to make dirty; stain 2. to bring disgrace upon —*n*. 1. a soiled spot 2. excrement; sewage, etc.

soiree, soirée (swä'rā') *n*. [< Fr. *soir*, evening] a party or gathering in the evening

sojourn (so'jurn) *vi*. [< L. *sub-*, under + *diurnus*, of a day] to stay for a while —*n*. a brief stay; visit

sol¹ (sol) *n*. [see GAMUT] *Music* a syllable representing the fifth tone of the diatonic scale

sol² *n*. a liquid colloidal solution

sola (sō'lə) *n*. [< Hindi *shola*] an Indian plant, whose pith is used for making topees

solace (sol'əs) *n*. [< L. *solari*, to comfort] 1. an easing of grief, loneliness, etc. 2. something that relieves; comfort —*vt*. **-aced**, **-acing** to comfort

solan (sō′lən) *n.* [< ON. *sūla*, gannet] *same as* GANNET

solar (sō′lər) *adj.* [< L. *sol*, the sun] **1.** of or having to do with the sun **2.** produced by or coming from the sun **3.** depending upon the sun's light or energy [*solar* heating]

solar battery an assembly of devices (**solar cells**) that convert the energy of sunlight into electricity

solarium (sō lãar′ē əm) *n., pl.* **-ia** [L. < *sol*, the sun] a glassed-in porch, etc. where people sun themselves

solar plexus a network of nerves in the abdominal cavity behind the stomach

solar system the sun and all the heavenly bodies that revolve around it

sold (sōld) *pt. & pp.* of SELL —**be sold on** [Slang] to be uncritically attached to or interested in

solder (sold′ər) *n.* [< L. *solidare*, make firm] a metal alloy used when melted to join or patch metal parts or surfaces —*vt., vi.* to join (things) with solder

soldering iron a pointed metal tool heated for use in melting and applying solder

soldier (sōl′jər) *n.* [< LL. *solidus*, a coin] **1.** a member, or former member, of an army **2.** such a person as distinguished from an officer **3.** an ant or other social insect with powerful jaws adapted for defence of the colony —*vi.* to serve as a soldier —**soldier on** to carry on regardless of other events —**sol′dierly** *adj.*

soldier of fortune 1. a mercenary soldier **2.** any adventurer

sole[1] (sōl) *n.* [< L. *solum*, a base] **1.** the bottom surface of the foot **2.** the part of a shoe, etc. corresponding to this **3.** the bottom surface of various objects —*vt.* **soled, sol′ing** to furnish (a shoe, etc.) with a sole

sole[2] *adj.* [< L. *solus*] **1.** without another; single; one and only **2.** not shared; exclusive [*sole* rights]

sole[3] *n.* [< L. *solea*, sole of a shoe: from its shape] any of certain sea flatfishes, highly valued as food

solecism (sol′ə siz′m) *n.* [< Gr. *soloikos*, speaking incorrectly] **1.** a violation of the conventional usage, grammar, etc. of a language **2.** a mistake in etiquette —**sol′ecist** *n.* —**sol′ecis′tic** *adj.*

solely (sōl′lē) *adv.* **1.** only, exclusively, merely, or altogether **2.** without another or others; alone

solemn (sol′əm) *adj.* [< L. *sollus*, all + *annus*, year] **1.** serious; deeply earnest **2.** formal **3.** glum; sad **4.** awe-inspiring **5.** observed or done according to ritual, as religious rites, etc. —**sol′emnly** *adv.* —**sol′emnness** *n.*

solemnity (sə lem′nə tē) *n., pl.* **-ties 1.** seriousness **2.** solemn ceremony, ritual, etc.

solemnize (sol′əm nīz′) *vt.* **-nized′, -niz′-ing 1.** to perform the ceremony of (marriage, etc.) **2.** to make serious, grave, etc. —**sol′emniza′tion** *n.*

solenoid (sō′lə noid′) *n.* [< Gr. *sōlēn*, a channel + *eidos*, a form] a coil of wire carrying an electric current and acting like a magnet

sol-fa (sōl′fä′) *n.* [It.: see GAMUT] the syllables *do, re, mi, fa, sol, la, ti, do*, used for the tones of a scale, regardless of key

solicit (sə lis′it) *vt.* [see SOLICITOUS] **1.** to ask or seek earnestly for **2.** to approach for some immoral purpose, as a prostitute does —*vi.* to solicit someone or something —**solic′ita′tion** *n.*

solicitor *n.* a member of the legal profession who draws up legal documents, advises barristers, etc.

solicitor general *pl.* **solicitors general, solicitor generals** a law officer ranking next below the attorney general

solicitous *adj.* [< L. *sollus*, whole + *ciere*, set in motion] **1.** showing care, attention, or concern **2.** showing anxious desire; eager **3.** full of anxiety —**solic′itously** *adv.*

solicitude *n.* a being solicitous; care, concern, etc.

solid (sol′id) *adj.* [< L. *solidus*] **1.** tending to keep its form; relatively firm or compact **2.** not hollow **3.** having the three dimensions of length, breadth, and thickness **4.** firm and strong; substantial **5.** serious; not trivial **6.** complete [*solid* satisfaction] **7.** having no breaks or divisions **8.** with no pauses [to talk for a *solid* hour] **9.** of one or the same colour, material, etc. throughout **10.** showing unity; unanimous **11.** thick or dense, as a fog **12.** firm or dependable [a *solid* friendship] **13.** sound, but not brilliant **14.** financially sound **15.** [Colloq.] healthful and filling [a *solid* meal] —*n.* **1.** a substance that is solid, not a liquid or gas **2.** an object or figure having length, breadth, and thickness —**sol′idly** *adv.* —**sol′idness** *n.*

solidarity (sol′ə dar′ə tē) *n., pl.* **-ties** agreement of all elements or individuals, as of a group; complete unity

solid fuel fuel, as coal, coke, etc. that is solid, rather than oil or gas

solid geometry geometry dealing with solid figures

solidify (sə lid′ə fī′) *vt., vi.* **-fied′, -fy′ing** to make or become solid, firm, hard, etc. —**solid′ifica′tion** *n.*

solidity (sə lid′ə tē) *n.* a being solid; firmness, hardness, etc.

solid-state *adj.* of electronic devices, as semiconductors, that can control current without moving parts

solidus (sol′i dəs) *n., pl.* **-idi′** (-dī′) [L.] a slant line (/) used in a text to separate items (Ex.: and/or)

soliloquy (sə lil′ə kwē) *n., pl.* **-quies** [< L. *solus*, alone + *loqui*, speak] **1.** a talking to oneself **2.** lines in a drama spoken by a character as if to himself —**solil′o-quize** *vi., vi.*

solipsism (sol′ip siz′m) *n.* [< L. *solus*, alone + *ipse*, self] the theory that nothing exists but the self —**sol′ipsist** *n.* —**sol′ip-sis′tic** *adj.*

solitaire (sol′ə tãer′) *n.* [Fr.: see ff.] **1.**

a single gem, esp. a diamond, set by itself **2.** any of many games played by one person, as patience

solitary (sol′ə tər ē) *adj.* [< L. *solus*, alone] **1.** living or being alone **2.** single; only **3.** lacking companions **4.** with few or no people; remote —*n.*, *pl.* **-taries 1.** a hermit **2.** [Colloq.] *same as* SOLITARY CONFINEMENT —**sol′itarily** *adv.* —**sol′itariness** *n.*

solitary confinement confinement of a prisoner, usually as extra punishment, away from all others

solitude (sol′ə tyo͞od′) *n.* [< L. *solus*, alone] **1.** a being solitary **2.** a secluded place

solo (sō′lō) *n.*, *pl.* **-los** [It. < L. *solus*, alone] **1.** a musical piece or passage to be played or sung by one person **2.** an aircraft flight made by a pilot alone **3.** any performance by one person alone **4.** any card game in which there are no partners —*adj.* **1.** for or by a single performer **2.** performing a solo —*adv.* alone —**so′loist** *n.*

Solomon (sol′ə mən) *n.* [< *Solomon*, king of Israel] a very wise man

Solomon's seal a plant with broad, waxy leaves and blue or black berries

so long **1.** *colloq.* term for GOODBYE **2.** [S Afr. Slang] for the time being; meanwhile

solstice (sol′stis) *n.* [< L. *sol*, the sun + *stare*, to stand] the time when the sun is farthest from the equator: see SUMMER SOLSTICE, WINTER SOLSTICE

soluble (sol′yo͞o b'l) *adj.* [see SOLVE] **1.** that can be dissolved **2.** that can be solved —**sol′ubil′ity** *n.* —**sol′ubly** *adv.*

solute (sol′yo͞ot) *n.* the substance dissolved in a solution

solution (sə lo͞o′shən) *n.* [see SOLVE] **1.** a) the solving of a problem b) the answer to a problem c) an explanation, etc. **2.** a) the dispersion of one or more substances in another, usually a liquid, so as to form a homogeneous mixture b) the mixture so produced

solve (solv) *vt.* **solved, solv′ing** [< L. *se-*, apart + *luere*, let go] to find a satisfactory answer for (a problem, mystery, etc.) —**solv′abil′ity** *n.* —**solv′able** *adj.* —**solv′er** *n.*

solvent (sol′vənt) *adj.* [see SOLVE] **1.** able to pay all one's debts **2.** that can dissolve another substance —*n.* a substance that can dissolve another —**sol′vency** *n.*

Som. Somerset

somatic (sō mat′ik) *adj.* [< Gr. *sōma*, the body] of the body; corporeal; physical

sombre (som′bər) *adj.* [< L. *sub*, under + *umbra*, shade] **1.** dismal; melancholy **2.** solemn; grave **3.** dark and gloomy or dull Also U.S. sp., **som′ber** —**som′brely** *adv.*

sombrero (som brãər′ō) *n.*, *pl.* **-ros** [Sp.: see prec.] a broad-brimmed felt or straw hat, worn in Mexico, etc.

some (sum; *unstressed* səm) *adj.* [OE. *sum*] **1.** being a certain one or ones not specified or known **2.** being of a certain unspecified quantity, degree, etc. **3.** about [some ten of us] **4.** [Colloq.] remarkable; striking [it was some fight] —*pron.* **1.** a certain one or ones not specified or known **2.** a certain unspecified number, quantity, etc. —*adv.* about [some ten men]

somebody *pron.* some person; someone —*n.*, *pl.* **-bodies** a person of importance

someday *adv.* at some future time

somehow *adv.* in a way not known, stated, or understood [it was damaged somehow]

someone *pron.* *same as* SOMEBODY

someplace *adv.* [U.S.] somewhere

somersault (sum′ər sôlt′) *n.* [< L. *supra*, over + *saltus*, a leap] an acrobatic stunt done by turning the body one full revolution, heels over head: often used figuratively —*vi.* to do a somersault

something (sum′thiŋ) *n.* **1.** a thing not definitely known, understood, etc. [something went wrong] **2.** some thing or things, definite but unspecified **3.** a bit; a little **4.** [Colloq.] a remarkable person or thing —*adv.* somewhat —**make something of 1.** to find a use for **2.** to treat as of great importance **3.** [Colloq.] to treat as a point of dispute —**something like 1.** approximately **2.** [Colloq.] impressive

sometime *adv.* **1.** at some time not known or specified **2.** at some future time —*adj.* **1.** former **2.** occasional

sometimes *adv.* at times; occasionally

someway *adv.* in some way or manner

somewhat *adv.* to some extent, degree, etc. —*n.* [Obs.] some degree, amount, part, etc.

somewhere *adv.* in, to, or at some place not known or specified

somnambulate (som nam′byo͞o lāt′) *vt.* **-lat′ed, -lat′ing** [< L. *somnus*, sleep + *ambulare*, walk] to walk in a trancelike state while asleep —**somnam′bulant** *adj.*

somnambulism *n.* the act or practice of sleepwalking —**somnam′bulist** *n.* —**somnam′bulis′tic** *adj.*

somnolent (som′nə lənt) *adj.* [< L. *somnus*, sleep] **1.** sleepy; drowsy **2.** causing drowsiness —**som′nolence** *n.* —**som′nolently** *adv.*

son (sun) *n.* [OE. *sunu*] **1.** a boy or man as he is related to either or both parents **2.** a male descendant **3.** a male thought of as if in the relation of child to parent [a son of revolution] **4.** a familiar form of address to a boy —**the Son** Jesus Christ

sonar (sō′när) *n.* [so(und) n(avigation) a(nd) r(anging)] an apparatus that transmits high-frequency sound waves through water and registers the vibrations reflected back from an object: used to find depths, etc.

sonata (sə nät′ə) *n.* [It.] a musical composition for one or two instruments, usually in three or four movements in different tempos, etc.

son et lumière (soṇ'ä lyōō mē âar') [Fr., sound and light] a historical spectacle at night before a monument, etc., using special lighting effects, narration, music, etc.

song (soṇ) *n.* [OE. *sang*] 1. a piece of music sung or as if for singing 2. *a)* poetry *b)* a ballad or lyric set to music 3. a singing sound 4. the act or art of singing —**for a song** cheaply —**song and dance** [Colloq.] a fuss, esp. about something trivial

songbird *n.* a bird' that makes vocal sounds that are like music

songololo (soṇ'go lo'lo) *n.* [< Bantu] [S Afr.] a millipede

songster *n.* [OE. *sangestre*] 1. a singer 2. a songbird —**song'stress** *n.fem.*

song thrush a European songbird with brown wings

sonic (son'ik) *adj.* [< L. *sonus*, SOUND¹] 1. of or having to do with sound 2. designating or of a speed equal to the speed of sound

sonic barrier *same as* SOUND BARRIER

sonic boom an explosive sound made by an aircraft moving at or above the speed of sound

son-in-law (sun'in lô') *n., pl.* **sons'-in-law**' the husband of one's daughter

sonnet (son'it) *n.* [< L. *sonus*, SOUND¹] a poem normally of fourteen lines in any of several rhyme schemes, expressing a single theme

sonny (sun'ē) *n., pl.* **-nies** little son: used in addressing any young boy in a familiar way

sonorous (sə nôr'əs) *adj.* [< L. *sonor*, a sound] 1. producing sound; resonant 2. full, deep, or rich: said of sound 3. impressive [*sonorous prose*] —**sonor'ity** *n.*

Sons of Freedom [Canad.] a Doukhobor sect, esp. in British Columbia, formerly notorious for acts of terrorism in opposition to the government

sonsy, sonsie (son'sē) *adj.* [< Gael. *sonas*, good fortune] [Scot.] buxom; handsome

soon (sōōn) *adv.* [OE. *sona*, at once] 1. in a short time; shortly 2. promptly; quickly [*as soon as possible*] 3. ahead of time; early 4. readily; willingly —**had sooner** would rather —**sooner or later** eventually

soot (soot) *n.* [OE. *sot*] a black substance formed by the incomplete combustion of burning matter —*vt.* to cover with soot —**soot'y** *adj.*

sooth (sōōth) *adj.* [OE. *soth*] [Archaic] true —*n.* [Archaic] truth —**in sooth** [Archaic] in truth

soothe (sōōth) *vt.* **soothed, sooth'ing** [< OE. *soth*, truth] 1. to make calm or composed, as by gentleness, flattery, etc. 2. to relieve (pain, etc.) —*vi.* to have a soothing effect —**sooth'er** *n.* —**sooth'ing** *adj.*

soothsayer (sōōth'sā'ər) *n.* a person who claims to foretell the future —**sooth'-say'ing** *n.*

sop (sop) *n.* [OE. *sopp*] 1. a piece of food, as bread, soaked in milk, gravy, etc. 2. something given by way of appeasement, etc. —*vt.* **sopped, sop'ping** 1. to soak, steep, etc. 2. to take (*up*), as liquid, by absorption

sop. soprano

sophism (sof'iz'm) *n.* [< Gr. *sophos*, clever] clever and reasonable argument that is faulty or misleading

sophist *n.* 1. [*often* S-] in ancient Greece, any of a group of teachers of rhetoric, philosophy, etc. 2. any person practising clever, specious reasoning

sophisticate (sə fis'tə kāt') *vt.* **-cat'ed, -cat'ing** [< SOPHISM] 1. to change from being natural, naive, etc. to being artificial, worldly-wise, etc. 2. to bring to a more developed, complex, or refined form, level, etc. —*n.* a sophisticated person

sophisticated *adj.* 1. not simple, natural, or naive; wise in the ways of the world 2. appealing to sophisticated people 3. highly complex, refined, etc. —**sophis'ti-ca'tion** *n.*

sophistry (sof'is trē) *n., pl.* **-tries** unsound or misleading but subtle argument or reasoning

sophomore (sof'ə môr') *n.* [< obs. *sophumer*, sophist] [U.S.] a student in his second year in college —*adj.* of or for sophomores —**soph'omor'ic** *adj.*

-sophy (sə fē) [< Gr. *sophia*, skill, wisdom] a combining form meaning knowledge [*philosophy*]

soporific (sop'ə rif'ik) *adj.* [< L. *sopor*, sleep] 1. causing or tending to cause sleep 2. sleepy —*n.* a drug, etc. that causes sleep

sopping (sop'iṇ) *adj.* thoroughly wet

soppy (sop'ē) *adj.* **-pier, -piest** 1. very wet; sopping 2. [Colloq.] sentimental —**sop'piness** *n.*

soprano (sə prä'nō) *n., pl.* **-nos, -ni** (-nē) [It. < *sopra*, above] 1. the highest singing voice of women, girls, and young boys 2. *a)* a singer or instrument with this range *b)* a part for a soprano

sorbet (sôr'bət) *n.* [< Arab. *sharbah*, a drink] a mixture of crushed fruit, sugar, etc. frozen to make water ice

sorcerer (sôr'sər ər) *n.* a person who practises sorcery; wizard —**sor'ceress** *n.fem.*

sorcery (sôr'sər ē) *n., pl.* **-ceries** [< L. *sors*, lot] 1. the supposed use of magical power for an evil purpose; witchcraft 2. seemingly magical power, charm, etc.

sordid (sôr'did) *adj.* [< L. *sordes*, filth] 1. *a)* dirty; filthy *b)* squalid 2. meanly selfish or grasping —**sor'didly** *adv.* —**sor'-didness** *n.*

sore (sôr) *adj.* **sor'er, sor'est** [OE. *sar*] 1. giving or feeling pain; painful 2. *a)* filled with grief, etc. [*sore at heart*] *b)* causing sadness, grief, etc. **3.** provoking irritation **4.** [U.S. Colloq.] angry; offended —*n.* **1.** a sore spot on the body, as an ulcer **2.** a source of pain, distress, etc. —*adv.* [Archaic] sorely —**sore'ness** *n.*

sorely *adv.* **1.** grievously; painfully [*sorely* vexed *]* **2.** urgently; extremely [*sorely* needed *]*

sorghum (sôr'gəm) *n.* [< It. *sorgo*] a tropical cereal grass grown for grain, syrup, fodder, etc.

soroptimist (sô rop'tə mist) *n.* a member of one of an international association of women's clubs

sorority (sə ror'ə tē) *n., pl.* **-ties** [< L. *soror,* sister] [Chiefly U.S.] a group of women or girls joined together for social or professional reasons

sorrel[1] (sor'əl) *n.* [< Frank. *sur,* sour] a plant with sour, fleshy leaves

sorrel[2] *n.* [< Gmc.] **1.** light reddish brown **2.** a horse, etc. of this colour —*adj.* light reddish-brown

sorrow (sor'ō) *n.* [OE. *sorg*] **1.** mental suffering caused by loss, disappointment, etc. **2.** that which produces such suffering —*vi.* to feel sorrow; grieve —**sor'rowingly** *adv.*

sorrowful *adj.* feeling or causing sorrow

sorry (sor'ē) *adj.* **-rier, -riest** [< OE. *sar,* sore] **1.** full of sorrow, pity, sympathy, etc.: also used in apologizing **2.** *a)* inferior in worth or quality *b)* wretched —**sor'rily** *adv.* —**sor'riness** *n.*

sort (sôrt) *n.* [< L. *sors,* a lot] **1.** any group of related things; kind; class **2.** quality or type; nature —*vt.* to arrange according to class or kind (often with *out*) —**of sorts** of an inferior kind: also **of a sort** —**out of sorts** [Colloq.] cross, irritable, or ill —**sort of** [Colloq.] somewhat —**sort out 1.** to separate out **2.** to find a solution **3.** [Slang] to punish someone, esp. by beating them —**sort'er** *n.*

sortie (sôr'tē) *n.* [Fr. < *sortir,* to issue] **1.** a sudden attack by troops from a besieged place **2.** one mission by a single military plane

SOS (es'ō'es') **1.** a signal of distress in code (. . . - - - . . .) used internationally in wireless telegraphy **2.** [Colloq.] any urgent call for help

sosatie (sə sä'tē) *n.* [Afrik.] [S Afr.] curried meat on skewers

so-so (sō'sō') *adv.* indifferently; just passably —*adj.* neither too good nor too bad; just fair　Also **so so**

sostenuto (sos'tə nōōt'ō) *n., adj., adv.* [It.] *Music* sustained or prolonged in tempo

sot (sot) *n.* [< OFr. *sot,* a fool] a drunkard —**sot'tish** *n.*

sotted (sot'id) *adj.* besotted; stupefied

sotto voce (sot'ō vō'chē) [It.] in an undertone

sou (sōō) *n., pl.* **sous** (sōōz) [Fr. < L.

solidus, SOLIDUS] **1.** a former French coin **2.** a very small amount of money

soubrette (sōō bret') *n.* [Fr. ］　*Theatre* **1.** the role of a pert lady's maid **2.** an actress who plays such roles

soubriquet (sōō'brə kā') *n.* var. of SOBRIQUET

soufflé (sōō'flā) *n.* [Fr. < *souffler,* to blow] a baked food made light and puffy by adding beaten egg whites before baking —*adj.* made light and puffy in cooking

sough (sou) *n.* [< OE. *swogan,* to sound] a soft, murmuring or rustling sound —*vi.* to make a sough

sought (sôt) *pt. & pp.* of SEEK

souk (sōōk) *n.* [Ar. *sūq*] an open-air marketplace in North Africa and the Middle East

soul (sōl) *n.* [OE. *sawol*] **1.** the part of one's being that is thought of as the centre of feeling, thinking, will, etc., apart from the body **2.** the moral or emotional nature of man **3.** spiritual or emotional warmth, force, etc. **4.** vital or essential part, quality, etc. **5.** the central or leading figure **6.** embodiment; personification **7.** a person *[a* town of 1000 *souls]* **8.** [Colloq.] among U.S. Negroes, a sense of racial pride and social and cultural solidarity —*adj.* [Colloq.] of, for, or like, U.S. Negroes —**upon my soul!** an exclamation of surprise

soul-destroying *adj.* monotonous; dreary; tedious

soul food [Colloq.] items of food popular esp. among U.S. Negroes, as chitterlings, ham hocks, etc.

soulful *adj.* full of or showing deep feeling —**soul'fully** *adv.*

soulless *adj.* lacking sensitivity or deep feeling

soul mate [Colloq.] a person with whom one has a close relationship

soul music [Colloq.] *a form of* RHYTHM AND BLUES

soul-searching *n.* a close, honest examination of one's true feelings, motives, etc.

sound[1] (sound) *n.* [< L. *sonus*] **1.** *a)* vibrations in air, water, etc. that act on the nerves of the inner ear and produce the sensation of hearing *b)* the sensation that these vibrations stimulate in the ear **2.** any identifiable noise, tone, etc. **3.** the distance within which a sound may be heard **4.** the impression made by something said, etc. **5.** meaningless noise —*vi.* **1.** to make a sound **2.** to seem through sound *[to sound* troubled *]* —*vt.* **1.** *a)* to cause to sound *b)* to utter distinctly *[to sound* one's r's *]* **2.** to express, signal, proclaim, etc. **3.** to examine (the chest) by percussion, etc. —**sound off** [Slang] to give free voice to complaints, opinions, etc.

sound[2] *adj.* [OE. *(ge)sund*] **1.** free from defect, damage, or decay **2.** healthy *[a sound* body *]* **3.** firm and safe; stable [a *sound* bank] **4.** based on valid reasoning [*sound* advice] **5.** agreeing with established beliefs **6.** thorough, complete, etc. [a *sound* defeat] **7.** deep and undisturbed: said of sleep —*adv.* deeply [*sound* asleep] —**sound'ly** *adv.* —**sound'ness** *n.*

sound³ *n.* [< OE. & ON. *sund*] a wide channel linking two large bodies of water or separating an island from the mainland

sound⁴ *vt.* [< L. *sub*, under + *unda*, a wave] **1.** *a)* to measure the depth of (water), esp. with a weighted line (**sounding line**) *b)* to examine (the bottom of the sea, etc.) **2.** to try to find out the opinions of (a person): often with *out* —**sound'a ble** *adj.* —**sound'er** *n.*

sound barrier the large increase in resistance encountered by an aircraft approaching the speed of sound

sound effects sounds, as of thunder, animals, etc., produced artificially or by recording as for radio, TV, etc.

sounding *n.* **1.** *a)* the act of measuring the depth of water *b)* [*pl.*] a place where a sounding line will touch bottom **2.** [*pl.*] measurements or data learned by sounding **3.** [*often pl.*] a sampling, as of public opinion

sounding board **1.** any structure designed to reflect sound **2.** a person on whom one tests one's opinions, etc.

soundproof *adj.* able to keep sound from coming through —*vt.* to make soundproof

sound track the area along one side of a film, carrying the sound record of the film

sound wave *Physics* a pressure wave transported by an elastic medium, as air

soup (s̅o̅o̅p) *n.* [< OFr. *soupe*] a liquid food made by cooking meat, vegetables, etc. in water, milk, etc. —**in the soup** [Colloq.] in trouble —**soup up** [Slang] to increase the power, capacity for speed, etc. of (an engine, etc.) —**soup'y** *adj.*

soupçon (s̅o̅o̅p'sôn′) *n.* [Fr.] **1.** a suggestion or trace **2.** a tiny amount; bit

soup kitchen a place where hot soup or the like is given to people in dire need

sour (sour) *adj.* [OE. *sur*] **1.** having the sharp, acid taste of lemon juice, vinegar, etc. **2.** spoiled by fermentation [*sour* milk] **3.** cross, bad-tempered, etc. **4.** distasteful or unpleasant **5.** excessively acid: said of soil —*vt., vi.* to make or become sour —**sour'ish** *adj.* —**sour'ly** *adv.* —**sour'ness** *n.*

source (sôrs) *n.* [< L. *surgere*, to rise] **1.** that from which something originates, develops, etc. **2.** a spring, etc. from which a stream arises **3.** a person, book, etc. that provides information

sourcebook *n.* a collection of selections giving information about a subject to be studied or written about

sourdough (sour'dō′) *n.* [Chiefly U.S.] [Dial.] fermented dough saved from one baking to the next, for use as leaven

sour grapes a scorning or belittling of

something only because it cannot be had or done

sourpuss (sour'poos′) *n.* [Colloq.] a disagreeable person

sourveld (sour'felt′) *n.* [< Afrik. *suur*, sour + *veld*, grassland] in South Africa, a particular type of grazing

souse (sous) *vt., vi.* soused, sous'ing [< OHG. *sulza*, brine] **1.** to plunge in a liquid **2.** to pickle **3.** [Slang] to make or become intoxicated —*n.* **1.** liquid for pickling **2.** a pickled food, as the feet or ears of a pig **3.** a plunging into a liquid **4.** [Slang] a drunkard

soutane (s̅o̅o̅tan′) *n.* [< It.] *same as* CASSOCK

south (south) *n.* [OE. *suth*] **1.** the direction to the left of a person facing the sunset (180° on the compass, opposite north) **2.** a region or district in or towards this direction **3.** [*often* S-] the southern part of the earth —*adj.* **1.** in or towards the south **2.** from the south —*adv.* in or towards the south —**the South** that part of England south of the Humber

southeast (south'ēst′; *nautical* sou-) *n.* **1.** the direction halfway between south and east **2.** a region in or towards this direction —*adj.* **1.** in or towards the southeast **2.** from the southeast —*adv.* in, towards, or from the southeast —**south'east'erly** *adj., adv.* —**south'east'ern** *adj.* —**south'east'ward** *adv., adj.* —**south'east'wards** *adv.*

southeaster (south'ēs'tər; *nautical* sou-) *n.* a storm or strong wind from the southeast

southerly (suth'ər lē) *adj., adv.* **1.** towards the south **2.** from the south

southern (suth'ərn) *adj.* **1.** in, of, or towards the south **2.** from the south **3.** [S-] of the South —**south'ernmost′** *adj.*

Southern Cross a small constellation in the S hemisphere with four bright stars in the form of a cross

southerner (suth'ər nər) *n.* an inhabitant of the south

Southern Hemisphere that half of the earth south of the equator

southern lights *same as* AURORA AUSTRALIS

southpaw (south'pô′) *n.* [Colloq.] a person who is left-handed; esp., a boxer —*adj.* [Slang] left-handed

South Pole the southern end of the earth's axis

South Seas the South Pacific

south-southeast *n.* the direction halfway between due south and southeast

south-southwest *n.* the direction halfway between due south and southwest

southward (south'wərd; *nautical* suth'-ərd) *adv., adj.* towards the south: also **south'wards** *adv.* —*n.* a southward direction, point, or region

southwardly *adj., adv.* **1.** towards the south **2.** from the south

southwest (south'west′; *nautical* sou-) **1.** the direction halfway between south and west **2.** a region in or towards this direction —*adj.* **1.** in or towards the southwest **2.** from the southwest —*adv.* in, towards, or from the southwest —**south′wes′terly** *adj., adv.* —**south′-west′ern** *adj.* —**south′west′ward** *adv., adj.* —**south′west′wards** *adv.*

SOUTHWESTER

southwester (south′wes′tər; *nautical* sou-) *n.* **1.** a wind from the southwest **2.** a sailor's waterproof hat, having a broad brim at the back

souvenir (soo′və neər′) *n.* [Fr. < L. *subvenire,* come to mind] something kept as a reminder of a place, person, or occasion

sou'wester (sou wes′tər) *n.* same as SOUTHWESTER

sov. sovereign

sovereign (sov′rin) *n.* [< L. *super,* above] **1.** a person having sovereign authority; monarch **2.** formerly, a British gold coin valued at one pound sterling —*adj.* **1.** supreme in power, rank, etc. **2.** above all others; greatest **3.** of or being a ruler; reigning **4.** independent of all others **5.** very effectual, as a remedy

sovereignty *n., pl.* -**ties** **1.** a being sovereign **2.** the status, rule, power, etc. of a sovereign

soviet (sō′vē it) *n.* [Russ., council] in the Soviet Union, any of various elected governing councils —*adj.* **1.** of a soviet or soviets **2.** [S-] of or connected with the Soviet Union

sow[1] (sou) *n.* [OE. *sugu*] an adult female pig

sow[2] (sō) *vt.* **sowed, sown** (sōn) or **sowed, sow′ing** [OE. *sawan*] **1.** to scatter or plant (seed) for growing **2.** to plant (a field, etc.) with seed **3.** to spread or scatter —*vi.* to sow seed

soy (soi) *n.* [< Chin. *chiang,* salted bean + *yu,* oil] **1.** a dark, salty sauce made from fermented soyabeans: also **soy sauce 2.** the soyabean plant or its seeds Also **soya** (soi′ə)

soyabean (soi′ə bēn′) *n.* **1.** a plant of the legume family widely grown for its seeds, rich in protein and oil **2.** its seed

sozzled (soz′'ld) *adj.* [< dial. *sozzle*] [Colloq.] drunk; intoxicated

Sp. 1. Spain **2.** Spaniard **3.** Spanish

sp. 1. special **2.** *pl.* **spp.** species **3.** spelling

spa (spä) *n.* [< *Spa,* resort in Belgium] **1.** a spring of mineral water **2.** a place with such a spring

space (spās) *n.* [< L. *spatium*] **1.** a)

the boundless expanse extending in all directions, within which all things exist *b*) same as OUTER SPACE **2.** *a*) the distance, expanse, or area between or within things *b*) room for something **3.** a period of time **4.** *Music* the open area between any two lines of a staff **5.** *Printing* a blank piece of type metal used to separate characters, etc. —*adj.* of space —*vt.* **spaced, spac′ing** to arrange with spaces between —**spac′er** *n.*

Space Age [*also* s- a-] the period in which artificial satellites and manned space vehicles have been launched

spacecraft *n., pl.* -**craft′** a spaceship or satellite for use in outer space

spaceflight *n.* a flight through outer space

spaceman *n.* an astronaut

spaceship *n.* a rocket-propelled vehicle for travel in outer space

space shuttle a spacecraft designed to transport persons and equipment between earth and an orbiting space station

space station (or **platform**) a structure designed to orbit in space as a launching pad or as an observation centre

spacesuit *n.* same as G-SUIT

space-time (**continuum**) a continuum having the three dimensions of space and that of time

spacious (spä′shəs) *adj.* **1.** having more than enough space; vast **2.** not limited; large —**spa′ciousness** *n.*

spade[1] (spād) *n.* [OE. *spadu*] a long-handled digging tool with a flat blade that is pressed with the foot —**call a spade a spade** to use plain, blunt words —**spade′ful** *n.*

spade[2] *n.* [< L. *spatha,* SPATULA] **1.** the black figure (♠) marking one of the four suits of playing cards **2.** [*pl.*] this suit **3.** a card of this suit

spadework *n.* work done to get a project started, esp. when tiresome or difficult

spadix (spä′diks) *n., pl.* -**di′ces** (spä dī′-sēz) [< Gr., palm branch] a fleshy spike of tiny flowers

spaghetti (spə get′ē) *n.* [It.] long, thin strings of pasta, cooked by boiling and served with a sauce

spake (spāk) *archaic pt. of* SPEAK

Spam (spam) *Trademark* a kind of tinned meat, made chiefly from pork

span[1] (span) *n.* [OE. *sponn*] **1.** the full amount or extent between any two limits **2.** a part between two supports [a bridge of four *spans*] **3.** shortened form of WING-SPAN **4.** a measure of length, equal to nine inches (23 cm): the distance between the tips of the thumb and little finger —*vt.* **spanned, span′ning 1.** to extend, reach, or pass over or across **2.** to measure

span[2] *archaic pt. of* SPIN

Span. 1. Spaniard **2.** Spanish

spandrel (span′drəl) *n.* [< ?] the space between the exterior curve of an arch and a rectangular frame enclosing it

spangle (spaŋ′g'l) *n.* [< OE. *spang,* a

clasp] 1. a small piece of bright metal sewn on fabric for decoration 2. any small, glittering object —*vt.* **-gled, -gling** to cover with spangles —**span'gly** *adj.*

Spaniard (span'yərd) *n.* a native or inhabitant of Spain

spaniel (span'yəl) *n.* [< MFr. *espagnol*, Spanish] a breed of dog with a silky coat, drooping ears, and short legs and tail

Spanish (span'ish) *adj.* of Spain, its people, their language, etc. —*n.* its Romance language of Spain

Spanish fly a blister beetle of S Europe whose crushed bodies are used as an aphrodisiac, etc.

Spanish Main the coastal region of the Americas along the Caribbean Sea

spank (spaŋk) *vt.* [echoic] to strike with something flat, as the open hand, esp. on the buttocks —*vi.* to move along swiftly —*n.* a smack given in spanking

spanking *adj.* 1. [Colloq.] unusually fine, large, etc. 2. rapid 3. brisk: said of a breeze —*adv.* [Colloq.] completely [*spanking* new] —*n.* a series of smacks given by one who spanks

spanner (span'ər) *n.* a tool used to tighten nuts, bolts, etc.; wrench

spanspek (span'spek) *n.* [< Afrik.] [S Afr.] the sweet melon

spar[1] (spär) *n.* [< MDu.] any shiny, crystalline mineral that cleaves easily into flakes —**spar'ry** *adj.*

spar[2] *n.* [< ON. *sparri*] 1. any pole, as a mast, or boom, for supporting the sails on a ship 2. a lengthwise support for the ribs of an aircraft wing

spar[3] *vi.* **sparred, spar'ring** [< ?] 1. to box with jabbing or feinting movements, landing few heavy blows, as in practice matches 2. to dispute; argue

spare (spâər) *vt.* **spared, spar'ing** [OE. *sparian*] 1. to refrain from killing, hurting, etc. 2. to save or free (a person) from (something) [*spare* me the trouble] 3. to avoid using, or use frugally 4. to part with or give up (money, time, etc.) without trouble to oneself —*vi.* 1. to be frugal 2. to show mercy —*adj.* 1. not in regular use; extra 2. free [*spare* time] 3. meagre; scanty 4. not fleshy; lean —*n.* an extra or replacement part, thing, etc. —**go spare** [Colloq.] to become extremely angry, annoyed, etc. —**(something) to spare** a surplus of (something) —**spare'ly** *adv.* —**spare'ness** *n.*

spareribs *n.pl.* a cut of meat, esp. pork, consisting of the thin end of the ribs with most of the meat cut away

spare tyre [Colloq.] the roll of fat that many people have just above the waist

sparing *adj.* 1. that spares 2. frugal 3. scanty; meagre —**spar'ingly** *adv.*

spark[1] (spärk) *n.* [OE. *spearca*] 1. a glowing bit of matter, esp. one thrown off by a fire 2. any flash or sparkle 3. a particle or trace, as of life, interest, etc. 4. liveliness; vivacity 5. Elec. a very

brief flash of light accompanying an electric discharge —*vi.* to make or throw off sparks —**spark'er** *n.*

spark[2] *n.* [ON. *sparkr*, lively] a dashing, gallant young man

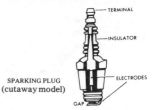

SPARKING PLUG (cutaway model)

TERMINAL
INSULATOR
ELECTRODES
GAP

sparking plug a piece fitted into a cylinder of an internal-combustion engine to make sparks that ignite the fuel mixture within: also **spark plug**

sparkle (spär'k'l) *vi.* **-kled, -kling** [see SPARK[1]] 1. to throw off sparks 2. to glitter, as jewels 3. to be brilliant and lively 4. to effervesce, as some wines —*n.* 1. a spark, or glowing particle 2. a glittering 3. brilliance; liveliness

sparkler *n.* 1. a pencil-shaped firework that burns with bright sparks 2. [Colloq.] a diamond

sparring partner 1. any person with whom a prizefighter boxes for practice 2. an opponent, usually a friend, in argument

sparrow (spar'ō) *n.* [OE. *spearwa*] a brownish-grey finch-like bird, as the house sparrow

sparrow hawk a small European hawk

sparse (spärs) *adj.* [< L. *spargere*, scatter] thinly spread or scattered —**sparse'ly** *adv.* —**sparsity** *n.*

Spartan (spär't'n) *adj.* 1. of ancient Sparta, its people, or their culture 2. brave, frugal, highly disciplined, etc. —*n.* a citizen of Sparta

spasm (spaz'm) *n.* [< Gr. *span*, to pull] 1. a convulsive, involuntary contraction of a muscle 2. any short, sudden burst of activity, feeling, etc.

spasmodic (spaz mod'ik) *adj.* [see prec.] of or like a spasm or spasms; fitful; intermittent —**spasmod'ically** *adv.*

spastic (spas'tik) *adj.* [see SPASM] of, marked by, or having spasm or spastic paralysis —*n.* a person with spastic paralysis —**spas'tically** *adv.*

spastic paralysis a condition, as in cerebral palsy, in which movements are more or less uncontrollable

spat[1] (spat) *n.* [echoic] [U.S. Colloq.] a brief, petty quarrel

spat[2] *n.* [contr. < SPATTER] a short gaiter for the instep and ankle

spat[3] *alt. pt. & pp. of* SPIT[2]

spat[4] *n.* [< ?] the spawn of the oyster or other bivalve shellfish

spate (spāt) *n.* [< ?] 1. a sudden flood or heavy rain 2. a large outpour, as of words

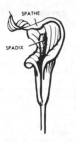

SPATHE
SPADIX

spathe (spāth) *n.* [< Gr. *spathē*, flat blade] a large, leaflike part or pair of such parts enclosing a flower cluster

spatial (spā′shəl) *adj.* [< L. *spatium*, space] 1. of space 2. happening or existing in space —**spa′tially** *adv.*

spatter (spat′ər) *vt., vi.* [< Fris. *spatten*, to splash] 1. to scatter or spurt out in drops or small blobs 2. to splash —*n.* 1. *a*) a spattering *b*) its sound 2. a mark made by spattering

spatula (spat′yoo lə) *n.* [L. < *spatha*, flat blade] an implement with a flat, flexible blade used for spreading or blending foods, paints, etc.

spavin (spav′in) *n.* [MFr. *esparvain*] a disease of horses affecting the hock joint and causing lameness —**spav′ined** *adj.*

spawn (spôn) *vt., vi.* [see EXPAND] 1. to produce or deposit (eggs, sperm, or young) 2. [Derog.] to bring into being (esp. in great quantity) —*n.* 1. the mass of eggs or young produced by fishes, amphibians, etc. 2. [Derog.] offspring or progeny

spay (spā) *vt.* [see SPATHE] to sterilize (a female animal) by removing the ovaries

speak (spēk) *vi.* spoke, spo′ken, speak′- ing [OE. *sp(r)ecan*] 1. to utter words; talk 2. to express opinions, feelings, ideas, etc. by or as by talking 3. to make a speech; discourse 4. to be a spokesman (*for*) 5. to converse 6. to give out sound —*vt.* 1. to make known as by speaking 2. to use (a given language) in speaking 3. to utter (words) orally —**so to speak** that is to say —**speak for itself** to be self- evident —**speak out** (or **up**) 1. to speak audibly or clearly 2. to speak freely —**speak volumes** to be significant —**speak well for** to indicate something favourable about —**to speak of** worthy of mention

speak-easy *n.*, *pl.* **-eas′ies** [U.S. Slang] a place selling alcoholic drinks illegally

speaker *n.* 1. a person who speaks or makes speeches 2. a person who serves as presiding officer of a lawmaking body; specif., [S-] the presiding officer in many legislative bodies, including the House of Commons in Britain and Canada: in full, **Speaker of the House**

speaking *adj.* expressive; vivid —*n.* the act or art of one who speaks —**generally** (**strictly**) **speaking** in the common (strict) sense of the words —**on speaking terms** friendly enough to carry on conversation

speaking clock a telephone service by which the correct time is given to the one who telephones

spear (spēər) *n.* [OE. *spere*] 1. a weapon with a long shaft and sharp head, for thrusting or throwing 2. any spearlike, often forked implement, as one used in fishing 3. [var. of SPIRE] a shoot, as of grass —*vt.* to pierce or stab as with a spear

spearhead *n.* 1. the pointed head of a spear 2. the person, group, unit, etc. leading an activity, esp. a military attack —*vt.* to lead (an attack, etc.)

spearmint *n.* [< its flower spikes] a fragrant plant used for flavouring

spec *n.* [Colloq.] speculation —**on spec** [Colloq.] as a speculation or gamble [all the tickets were sold, so I went to the theatre *on spec*]

spec. 1. special 2. specification

special (spesh′əl) *adj.* [< L. *species*, kind] 1. different, distinctive, or unique 2. exceptional; extraordinary 3. highly regarded 4. of or for a particular occasion, purpose, etc. [a *special* edition] 5. not general; specific —*n.* something special, as a featured item in a sale —**spe′cially** *adv.*

Special Branch the branch of the police force that deals with political offences and security

special constable someone who becomes a temporary member of the police force for special occasions

special delivery delivery of mail by special postal messenger, for an extra fee

specialist *n.* a person who specializes in a particular branch of study, professional work, etc.

speciality (spesh′ē al′ə tē) 1. a special quality, feature, etc. 2. a special field of study, branch of a profession, etc. 3. a product or service given special attention to make it attractive, superior, etc.

specialize (spesh′ə līz′) *vi.* **-ized′, -iz′ing** to take up a special study or work in a special branch of a profession —*vt.* 1. to direct towards a specific end 2. to make specific —**spe′cializa′tion** *n.*

special licence a licence that is issued to allow a marriage to take place although the banns have not been called

specie (spē′shē) *n.* [< L. *species*, kind] coin, as distinguished from paper money

species (spē′shēz) *n.*, *pl.* **-cies** [L., appearance, kind] 1. *Biol.* a group of highly similar plants or animals that is part of a genus 2. a distinctive kind; sort

specif. specifically

specific (spi sif′ik) *adj.* [< L. *species*, kind + *facere*, make] 1. definite; explicit 2. peculiar to or characteristic of something 3. of a particular sort 4. *Med.* specially indicated as a cure for a particular disease —*n.* 1. a distinct item or detail; particular 2. a specific cure or remedy —**specif′i- cally** *adv.* —**specificity** (spes′ə fis′ə tē) *n.*

specification (spes′ə fi kā′shən) *n.* 1. a detailed mention 2. [*usually pl.*] a statement of particulars as to size, materials, etc. **3.** something specified

specific gravity the ratio of the weight of a given volume of a substance to that of an equal volume of another substance (as water) used as a standard

specify (spes′ə fī′) *vt.* **-fied′, -fy′ing** [see SPECIFIC] **1.** to mention or describe in detail **2.** to include as an item in a set of specifications **—spec′ifi′able** *adj.*

specimen (spes′i min) *n.* [L. < *specere*, see] **1.** a part or one individual, used as a sample of the rest **2.** [Colloq.] a (specified kind of) individual **3.** *Med.* a sample, as of urine, for analysis

specious (spē′shəs) *adj.* [< L. *species*, appearance] seeming good, sound, etc., but not really so

speck (spek) *n.* [OE. *specca*] **1.** a small spot or mark **2.** a tiny bit; particle —*vt.* to mark with specks

speckle (spek′'l) *n.* a small speck —*vt.* **-led, -ling** to mark with speckles

specs (speks) *n.pl.* [Colloq.] **1.** spectacles **2.** specifications

spectacle (spek′tə k'l) *n.* [< L. *specere*, see] **1.** a remarkable sight **2.** a public show on a grand scale **3.** [*pl.*] a pair of lenses to correct faulty vision, placed in a frame **—spec′tacled** *adj.*

spectacular (spek tak′yə lər) *adj.* strikingly grand or unusual **—spectac′ularly** *adv.*

spectator (spek tāt′ər) *n.* [L. < *spectare*, behold] a person who watches something without taking part

spectra (spek′trə) *n.* alt. *pl.* of SPECTRUM

spectral (spek′trəl) *adj.* **1.** of or like a spectre; ghostly **2.** of a spectrum

spectre (spek′tər) *n.* [< L. *spectare*, behold] **1.** a ghost; apparition **2.** any object of dread   Also U.S. sp., **spec′ter**

spectroscope (spek′trə skōp′) *n.* an optical instrument for breaking up light into a spectrum so that it can be studied **—spec′troscop′ically** *adv.*

spectroscopy (spek tros′kə pē) *n.* the study of spectra by use of the spectroscope **—spectros′copist** *n.*

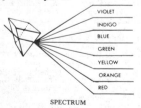

SPECTRUM

spectrum (spek′trəm) *n.,* *pl.* **-tra, -trums** [< L., appearance] **1.** the series of coloured bands into which white light is broken up by passing through a prism, etc.: it is arranged according to wavelength **2.** any like series of bands or lines formed from other kinds of radiant energy **3.** a range or extent, as of opinion

speculate (spek′yoo lāt′) *vi.* **-lat′ed, -lat′-ing** [< L. *specere*, see] **1.** to ponder; esp., to conjecture **2.** to engage in any risky venture for possible huge profits **—spec′ula′tion** *n.* **—spec′ulative** *adj.* **—spec′ula′tor** *n.*

sped (sped) *alt. pt. & pp.* of SPEED

speech (spēch) *n.* [< OE. *sp(r)ecan*, speak] **1.** the act of speaking **2.** the power or ability to speak **3.** the manner of speaking **4.** what is spoken **5.** a talk given to an audience **6.** the language used by a certain group of people

speech day an annual prize-giving event in most schools

speechify (spē′chə fī′) *vi.* **-fied′, -fy′ing** to make a speech: used humorously **—speech′ifi′er** *n.*

speechless *adj.* **1.** not able to speak **2.** silent, as from shock **—speech′lessly** *adv.*

speed (spēd) *n.* [OE. *spǣd*, success] **1.** rapid motion; swiftness **2.** *a*) the rate of movement; velocity *b*) the rate of any action **3.** an arrangement of gears for the drive of a bicycle **4.** [Slang] any of various amphetamine compounds **5.** [Archaic] success **—adj.** of speed —*vi.* **sped** or **speed′ed, speed′ing 1.** to go fast in a motor car, etc., esp. at a speed greater than the legal limit **2.** [Archaic] to prosper —*vt.* **1.** to cause to move swiftly **2.** to help succeed; aid **3.** to wish Godspeed to **—speed up** to go or make go faster **—speed′er** *n.*

speedboat *n.* a motorboat built for speed

speed limit the legal limit of speed of any vehicle on any given road

speedo (spēd′ō) *n.* [Colloq.] speedometer

speedometer (spi dom′ə tər) *n.* [< SPEED + -METER] a device attached to a motor vehicle, etc. to indicate speed

speedway (spēd′wā′) *n.* **1.** *a*) a track for racing cars or motorcycles *b*) this sport **2.** [U.S.] a road for high-speed traffic

speedwell *n.* a plant with spikes of bluish flowers

speedy *adj.* **-ier, -iest 1.** rapid **2.** without delay; prompt **—speed′ily** *adv.* **—speed′i-ness** *n.*

spek (spek) *n.* [< Afrik.] [S Afr.] bacon

speleology (spē′lē ol′ə jē) *n.* [< Gr. *spēlaion*, cave] the scientific study and exploration of caves **—spe′leolog′ical** *adj.* **—spe′leol′ogist** *n.*

spell[1] (spel) *n.* [OE., a saying] **1.** a word or formula supposed to have some magic power **2.** irresistible influence; charm; fascination **—cast a spell on** to enchant

spell[2] *vt.* **spelled** or **spelt, spell′ing** [< OFr. *espeller*, explain] **1.** to name, write, etc., esp. correctly, the letters of (a word, etc.) **2.** to make up (a word, etc.): said of specified letters **3.** to mean [*red spells* danger] —*vi.* to spell words, etc. **—spell out 1.** to read with difficulty **2.** to explain in detail

spell[3] *n.* [OE. *spelian*] **1.** a period of work, duty, etc. **2.** a period (*of* being in some state) **3.** a period of specified weather **4.** [Colloq.] a period of time that is indefinite, short, etc. —*vt.* **spelled,**

spell'ing to work in place of another while he rests

spellbind *vt.* **-bound′, -bind′ing** to hold or affect as by a spell; fascinate

spelt[1] (spelt) *alt. pt. & pp. of* SPELL[2]

spelt[2] *n.* [< LL. *spelta*] a species of wheat with grains that do not thresh free of chaff

spend (spend) *vt.* **spent, spend′ing** [< L. *expendere*, expend] 1. to pay out (money) 2. to give or devote (time, effort, etc.) to something 3. to pass (time) 4. to use up, exhaust, etc. 5. to waste; squander —*vi.* to pay out or use up money, etc. —**spend a penny** [Colloq.] to expel bodily wastes —**spend′able** *adj.* —**spend′er** *n.*

spendthrift *n.* a person who spends money carelessly; squanderer —*adj.* wasteful; extravagant

spent (spent) *pt. & pp. of* SPEND —*adj.* 1. tired out 2. used up; worn out

sperm (spurm) *n.* [< Gr. *sperma*, seed] 1. semen 2. *same as* SPERMATOZOON

spermaceti (spur′mə set′ē) *n.* [< LL. *sperma*, SPERM + L. *cetus*, a whale] a white, waxlike substance from a sperm whale used in making cosmetics, etc.

spermatozoon (spur′mə tə zō′on) *n., pl.* **-zo′a** [< Gr. *sperma*, seed + *zōion*, animal] the male germ cell, found in semen

spermicide (spur′mə sīd′) *n.* [SPERM + -i- + -CIDE] an agent that kills spermatozoa —**sperm′ici′dal** *adj.*

sperm oil a lubricating oil from the sperm whale

sperm whale a large, toothed whale of warm seas: a closed cavity in its roughly square head contains sperm oil

spew (spyo͞o) *vt., vi.* [OE. *spiwan*] 1. to vomit 2. to flow or gush forth

sp. gr. specific gravity

sphagnum (sfag′nəm) *n.* [< Gr. *sphagnos*, kind of moss] 1. a spongelike moss found in bogs 2. a mass of such mosses, used to improve soil, to pot plants, etc.

sphere (sfēər) *n.* [< Gr. *sphaira*] 1. any round body with a surface equally distant from the centre at all points; globe; ball 2. a star or planet 3. the visible heavens; sky 4. *short for* CELESTIAL SPHERE 5. any of a series of transparent shells imagined as revolving one within another around the earth and containing the stars, planets, sun, and moon 6. the place or range of action, knowledge, etc. 7. place in society

spherical (sfer′i k′l) *adj.* 1. shaped like a sphere 2. of a sphere or spheres —**spher′-ically** *adv.*

spheroid (sfēər′oid) *n.* a body that is almost but not quite a sphere —*adj.* of this shape: also **spheroi′dal**

sphincter (sfiŋk′tər) *n.* [< Gr. *sphingein*, to draw close] *Anat.* a ring-shaped muscle at a body orifice that can open or close it by expanding or contracting

sphinx (sfiŋks) *n.,* pl. **sphinx′es** [< Gr. *sphinx*, strangler] 1. any Egyptian statue having a lion's body and the head of

a man, ram, or hawk; specif., [S-] such a statue with a man's head, near Cairo, Egypt 2. *a*) [S-] *Gr. Myth.* a winged monster with a lion's body and a woman's head and breasts who killed passers-by unable to solve its riddle *b*) a person who is hard to understand

spice (spīs) *n.* [< L. *species*, sort] 1. any of several vegetable substances, as clove, pepper, etc., used to season food 2. that which adds zest or interest —*vt.* **spiced, spic′ing** 1. to flavour with spice 2. to add zest to

spick-and-span (spik′′n span′) *adj.* [< SPIKE[1] + ON. *spānn*, a chip] 1. neat and clean 2. new or fresh

spicy (spi′sē) *adj.* **-ier, -iest** 1. containing spices 2. having the flavour or aroma of spice 3. lively, interesting, etc. 4. risqué —**spic′iness** *n.*

spider (spi′dər) *n.* [< OE. *spinnan*, to spin] 1. any of various small arachnids with eight legs, that spins silk thread, as for webs 2. any implement or device shaped like a spider —**spi′dery** *adj.*

spider monkey a monkey of South and Central America with long, spidery limbs and a long tail

spiel (spēl) *n.* [G., play] [Chiefly U.S. Slang] a talk or harangue, as in selling —*vi.* [Chiefly U.S. Slang] to give a spiel —**spiel′er** *n.*

spigot (spig′ət) *n.* [ME. *spigote*] 1. a plug or peg used to stop the vent in a barrel, etc. 2. a tap

spike[1] (spīk) *n.* [prob. < ON. *spīkr*] 1. a long, heavy nail 2. a sharp-pointed projection, as along the top of an iron fence 3. *a*) any of the pointed metal projections on the bottoms of shoes used in athletics, golf, etc. *b*) [pl.] a pair of such shoes —*vt.* **spiked, spik′ing** 1. to fasten or fit as with spikes 2. to pierce with, or impale on, a spike 3. [Slang] to add alcohol to (a drink) —**spike someone's guns** to thwart someone's plans, etc. —**spik′y** *adj.*

spike[2] *n.* [L. *spica*] 1. an ear of grain 2. a long flower cluster with flowers attached directly to the stalk

spikelet *n.* a small spike, as in a flower cluster

spikenard (spīk′närd) *n.* [< L. *spica*, ear of grain + *nardus*, NARD] 1. a fragrant ointment used in ancient times 2. the Asiatic plant from which it is made

spill[1] (spil) *vt.* **spilled** or **spilt, spill′ing** [OE. *spillan*, destroy] 1. to let fall or flow over from a container, esp. without intending to 2. to shed (blood) 3. [Colloq.] to let (a secret) become known 4. [Colloq.] to make (a rider, load, etc.) fall off —*vi.* to be spilled from a container —*n.* 1. a spilling 2. what is spilled 3. [Colloq.] a fall; tumble —**spill over** to overflow —**spill the beans** to disclose a secret

spill[2] *n.* [< ?] a thin roll of paper, thin stick, etc. set on fire to light a pipe, candle, etc.

spillikin (spil′i k'n) *n.* [< MDu. *spille*, a splinter] 1. any of the strips used in playing spillikins **2.** [*pl. with sing. v.*] a game played by trying to remove strips in a jumbled heap without moving any of the others

spillway (spil′wā′) *n.* a channel to carry off excess water

spin (spin) *vt.* **spun, spin′ning** [OE. *spinnan*] **1.** to cause to rotate **2.** *a)* to draw out and twist fibres of (wool, cotton, etc.) into thread *b)* to make (thread, etc.) thus **3.** to make (a web, etc.): said of spiders, etc. **4.** to produce in a way that suggests spinning **5.** to draw *out* (a story, etc.) to great length **6.** to make (wheels of a vehicle) rotate without traction, as on ice **7.** to extract water from (clothes), as in a spin dryer —*vi.* **1.** to whirl **2.** to spin thread, etc. **3.** to feel dizzy and seem to be spinning **4.** to go into a spin: said of an aircraft **5.** to move along swiftly and smoothly **6.** to rotate freely without traction —*n.* **1.** the spinning or rotating of something, as a cricket ball **2.** a ride in a motor vehicle, on a bicycle, etc. **3.** the descent of an aircraft nose first along a spiral path —**spin out** to extend; prolong

spina bifida (spī′nə bif′ə də) a defect in which the spine fails to fuse in the embryonic stage

spinach (spin′ij) *n.* [< Per. *aspanākh*] **1.** a plant with large, dark-green, edible leaves **2.** the leaves

spinal (spī′n′l) *adj.* of the spine or spinal cord

spinal column the series of joined vertebrae forming the axial support for the skeleton; spine

spinal cord the thick cord of nerve tissue of the central nervous system, in the spinal column

spin bowler *Cricket* a bowler who imparts a twisted motion to the balls he bowls

spindle (spin′d′l) *n.* [< OE. *spinnan,* to spin] **1.** a slender rod or pin for twisting, winding, or holding the thread in spinning **2.** something spindle-shaped, as a slender rod in some chair backs **3.** any rod, pin, or shaft that revolves or serves as an axis for a revolving part —*adj.* of or like a spindle —*vi.* **-dled, -dling** to grow in a long, slender shape

spindlelegs *n.pl.* **1.** thin legs **2.** [with sing. v.] [Colloq.] a person with thin legs —**spin′dle-leg′ged, spin′dle-shanked′** *adj.*

spindly (spin′dlē) *adj.* **-dlier, -dliest** long or tall and very thin or slender

spindrift (spin′drift) *n.* [Scot. < obs. *spoon,* to scud + DRIFT] spray blown from a rough sea

spindry (spin′drī′) *vt.* **-dried′, -dry′ing** to dry washing by centrifugal force in a spin dryer

spin dryer a device that extracts water from clothes, etc. by spinning them in a perforated drum: also **spin drier**

spine (spīn) *n.* [< L. *spina,* thorn] **1.** the spinal column **2.** anything like this, as the back of a book **3.** any of the short, sharp projections on a cactus, etc.

4. any of the sharp, stiff projections on certain animals, as a porcupine quill **5.** anything like this

spine-chilling *adj.* thrilling; lurid; frightening

spineless *adj.* **1.** having no spine or spines **2.** lacking courage, willpower, etc. —**spine′lessly** *adv.* —**spine′lessness** *n.*

spinet (spin′et′) *n.* [< It. prob. < *spina,* thorn] an obsolete, small harpsichord

spinnaker (spin′ə kər) *n.* [< ?] a large, triangular forward sail used on some racing yachts

spinner (spin′ər) *n.* a person or thing that spins; specif., *a)* a fishing lure having blades that revolve when drawn through the water *b)* a spin bowler

spinneret (spin′ə ret′) *n.* [< SPINNER] the organ used by spiders, caterpillars, etc. to spin their silky threads

spinney, spinny (spin′ē) *n.,* pl. **-neys, -nies** [see SPINE] a copse or small grove of trees

spinning (spin′iŋ) *n.* the act of making thread, etc. from fibres or filaments —*adj.* that spins

spinning jenny an early spinning machine with several spindles, for spinning more than one thread at a time

spinning wheel a simple spinning machine with a single spindle driven by a large wheel

spin-off (spin′of′) *n.* a secondary, often unforeseen, benefit, etc.

spinster (spin′stər) *n.* [ME. < *spinnen,* to spin] an unmarried woman, esp. an older one —**spin′sterish** *adj.*

spiny (spī′nē) *adj.* **-ier, -iest** **1.** covered with spines or thorns **2.** full of difficulties; troublesome

spiracle (spī′rə k′l) *n.* [< L. *spirare,* breathe] *Zool.* an opening for breathing

spiral (spī′rəl) *adj.* [< Gr. *speira*] circling or coiling around a central point in a curve that constantly increases (or decreases) in size —*n.* **1.** a spiral curve or coil; helix **2.** something having a spiral form **3.** a spiral path **4.** a continuous, widening decrease or increase —*vi., vt.* **-ralled, -ralling** to move in or form (into) a spiral —**spi′rally** *adv.*

spirant (spī′rənt) *n., adj.* [< L. *spirare,* breathe] *same as* FRICATIVE

spire (spīər) *n.* [OE. *spir*] **1.** anything that tapers to a point, as a steeple **2.** the top part of a pointed, tapering object or structure, as a mountain peak

spirea (spī rē′ə) *n.* [< Gr. *speira,* a coil] a shrub of the rose family, with dense clusters of small, pink or white flowers: also sp. **spirae′a**

spirit (spir′it) *n.* [< L. *spirare,* breathe] **1.** the soul **2.** the thinking, feeling part of man **3.** [*also* S-] life, will, thought, etc., regarded as separate from matter **4.** a supernatural being, as a ghost, angel, etc. **5.** an individual person [a brave *spirit*] **6.** [*usually pl.*] disposition; mood [high *spirits*] **7.** vivacity, courage, etc. **8.** enthusiasm and loyalty [school *spirit*] **9.** real meaning [the *spirit* of the law]

10. an essential quality *[the spirit of the Renaissance]* **11.** *[usually pl.]* distilled alcoholic liquor **12.** *[often pl.]* any liquid produced by distillation —*vt.* to carry (*away, off,* etc.) secretly and swiftly —*adj.* **1.** of spirits or spiritualism **2.** operating by the burning of alcohol *[a spirit lamp]* —not corporeal —**out of spirits** sad; depressed —**the Spirit** same as HOLY SPIRIT —**spir'itless** *adj.*

spirited *adj.* **1.** full of spirit; lively; animated **2.** having a (specified) character, mood, or disposition *[low-spirited]* —**spir'itedly** *adv.*

spirit gum a solution of gum arabic in ether used to attach false hair, whiskers, etc. to the face

spirit lamp a lamp in which alcohol, usually methylated spirits, is burned

spirit level same as LEVEL (*n.* 2)

spiritual (spir'i tyoo wəl) *adj.* **1.** of the spirit or soul **2.** of or consisting of spirit; not corporeal **3.** refined in thought or feeling **4.** religious; sacred —*n.* a religious folk song of U.S. Negro origin —**spir'itual'ity** (-wal'ə tē) *n.* —**spir'itually** *adv.*

spiritualism *n.* **1.** the belief that the dead survive as spirits which can communicate with the living **2.** the philosophical doctrine that all reality is spiritual —**spir'itualist** *n.*

spirituous (spir'i tyoo wəs) *adj.* of, like, or containing alcohol: said of distilled beverages

spirt (spʉrt) *n., vt., vi.* same as SPURT

spit¹ (spit) *n.* [OE. *spitu*] **1.** a thin, pointed rod on which meat is roasted over a fire **2.** a narrow point of land extending into a body of water —*vt.* **spit'ted, spit'ting** to impale as on a spit —**spit'ter** *n.*

spit² *vt.* **spit** or **spat, spit'ting** [OE. *spittan*] **1.** to eject from the mouth **2.** to throw (*out*) or emit explosively —*vi.* **1.** to eject saliva from the mouth **2.** to make an explosive hissing noise, as an angry cat **3.** to sputter, as frying fat **4.** to rain very lightly —*n.* **1.** the act of spitting **2.** saliva **3.** a salivalike secretion of certain insects **4.** [Colloq.] the perfect likeness, as of a person: in **spit and image** —**spit it out 1.** to speak with venom **2.** to divulge some information without more delay

spit and polish formal or ceremonial, sometimes superficial, orderliness, neatness, etc. as in the military

spite (spīt) *n.* [see DESPITE] ill will; malice; grudge —*vt.* **spit'ed, spit'ing** to show one's spite for by hurting, frustrating, etc. —**in spite of** regardless of —**spite'ful** *adj.* —**spite'fully** *adv.* —**spite'fulness** *n.*

spitfire (spit'fīər') *n.* a person, esp. a woman or girl, who is easily aroused to violent outbursts of temper

spitting image alteration of SPIT AND IMAGE: see SPIT²

spittle (spit''l) *n.* [< OE. *spatl*] saliva; spit

spittoon (spi toon') *n.* a container to spit into

spiv (spiv) *n.* [< ?] [Colloq.] a man who lives by his wits, without doing any honest work

splake (splāk) *n.* [< *sp(eckled)* + *lake(trout)*] a type of hybrid trout bred by Canadian zoologists

splash (splash) *vt.* [echoic] **1.** to cause (a liquid) to scatter **2.** to dash or scatter a liquid, mud, etc. on, so as to wet or soil **3.** to make (one's way) by splashing **4.** to mark as by splashing **5.** to display conspicuously —*vi.* to move, fall, strike, or scatter with a splash —*n.* **1.** the act or sound of splashing **2.** a mass of splashed water, mud, etc. **3.** a spot or mark made as by splashing **4.** a patch of colour, light, etc. **5.** [Colloq.] a small quantity *[a splash of soda]* —**make a splash** [Colloq.] to attract great attention —**splash'y** *adj.*

splashdown *n.* the landing of a spacecraft on water

splatter (splat'ər) *n., vt., vi.* [< SPATTER] spatter or splash

splay (splā) *vt., vi.* [< ME. *displaien,* to display] to spread out or apart —*n.* a sloping surface or angle —*adj.* spreading outwards

spleen (splēn) *n.* [< Gr. *splen*] **1.** a large, vascular organ in the upper left part of the abdomen: it modifies the blood structure **2.** malice; spite; bad temper

spleenwort (splēn'wʉrt') *n.* any of various ferns

splendid (splen'did) *adj.* [< L. *splendere,* to shine] **1.** shining; brilliant **2.** magnificent; gorgeous **3.** worthy of high praise; grand **4.** [Colloq.] very good; excellent —**splen'didly** *adv.*

splendiferous (splen dif'ər əs) *adj.* [Colloq.] gorgeous; splendid: used jokingly —**splendif'erously** *adv.*

splendour (splen'dər) *n.* [< L. *splendere,* to shine] **1.** great lustre; brilliance **2.** magnificent richness or glory; pomp; grandeur Also, U.S. sp., **splen'dor**

splenetic (spli net'ik) *adj.* **1.** of the spleen **2.** irritable; peevish

splenic (splen'ik) *adj.* [< Gr. *splēnikos*] **1.** of or having to do with the spleen **2.** in or near the spleen

splice (splīs) *vt.* **spliced, splic'ing** [MDu. *splissen*] **1.** to join (ropes) by weaving together the end strands **2.** to join the ends of (timbers) by overlapping and binding together **3.** to fasten the ends of (wire, film, tape, etc.) together, as by cementing, twisting, etc. **4.** [Colloq.] to join in marriage —*n.* a joint or joining made by splicing —**splic'er** *n.*

splint (splint) *n.* [MDu. *splinte*] **1.** a thin strip of wood, etc. used to keep a broken bone in place **2.** a thin strip of wood or cane woven together with others to make baskets, chair seats, etc. —*vt.* to support or hold in place as with a splint or splints

splinter *vt., vi.* [MDu., akin to prec.] to break or split into thin, sharp pieces —*n.* a thin, sharp piece of wood, bone, etc., made by splitting —*adj.* designating a group that separates from a main party, church, etc. because of opposing views —**splin'tery** *adj.*

split (split) *vt.* **split, split′ting** [MDu. *splitten*] 1. to separate along the grain or length into two or more parts 2. to break or tear apart 3. to divide into parts 4. to cause (a group, party, etc.) to separate into factions 5. *a*) to break (a molecule) into atoms *b*) to produce nuclear fission in (an atom) —*vi.* 1. to separate lengthwise into two or more parts 2. to break apart; burst 3. [Slang] to divulge secrets; inform —*n.* 1. a splitting 2. a break; crack 3. a division in a group, between persons, etc. 4. a confection made of a split banana or other fruit with ice cream, etc. 5. [*pl.*] the feat of spreading the legs apart until they lie flat on the floor 6. [Colloq.] a small bottle of wine, etc., usually about six ounces 7. [Colloq.] a share —*adj.* separated —**split off** to break off or separate as by splitting —**split up** 1. to divide or separate 2. to become parted through disagreement

split infinitive *Gram.* an infinitive with the verb and the *to* separated by an adverb (Ex.: he decided *to gradually change* his style)

split-level *adj.* of a type of house with floor levels so staggered that each level is about a half storey above or below the adjacent one

split pea a green or yellow pea that has been shelled, dried, and split

split personality *a popular name for* SCHIZOPHRENIA

split second a fraction of a second —**split′-sec′ond** *adj.*

splitting *adj.* 1. that splits 2. severe, as a headache

splotch (sploch) *n.* [< ?] an irregular spot, splash, or stain —*vt., vi.* to mark with splotches —**splotch′y** *adj.*

splurge (splurj) *n.* [echoic] [Colloq.] 1. any showy display 2. a spending spree —*vi.* **splurged, splurg′ing** [Colloq.] 1. to make a splurge 2. to spend money extravagantly

splutter (splut′ər) *vi.* [var. of SPUTTER] 1. to make hissing or spitting sounds 2. to speak hurriedly and confusedly —*vt.* 1. to utter hurriedly and confusedly 2. to spatter —*n.* a spluttering sound

Spode (spōd) *n.* a fine porcelain or chinaware produced by Josiah Spode (1754-1827), British potter

spoil (spoil) *vt.* **spoiled** or **spoilt, spoil′-ing** [< L. *spolium*, plunder] 1. to damage so as to make useless, etc. 2. to impair the enjoyment, etc. of 3. to let (a person) have his own way so much that he demands or expects it —*vi.* to be damaged; decay, as food —*n.* 1. [*usually pl.*] *a*) goods, territory, etc. taken by plunder *b*) advantages gained as a result of being successful 2. an object of plunder; prey —**be spoiling for a fight** to be aggressively eager for a fight, etc. —**spoil′able** *adj.*

spoilage *n.* 1. a spoiling or being spoiled 2. something spoiled or the amount spoiled

spoiler *n.* a device on an aircraft or vehicle to increase drag and reduce lift

spoilsport *n.* a person who behaves in such a way as to ruin the pleasure of others

spoils system [Chiefly U.S.] the practice of treating public offices as the booty of the political party that wins

spoke¹ (spōk) *n.* [OE. *spaca*] 1. *a*) any of the braces extending from the hub to the rim of a wheel *b*) any of the thin metal rods in an umbrella 2. a ladder rung

spoke² *pt. & archaic pp.* of SPEAK

spoken (spō′k'n) *pp.* of SPEAK —*adj.* 1. uttered; oral 2. characterized by a (specified) kind of voice [*soft-spoken*]

spokeshave *n.* a planing tool used for shaping rounded surfaces, as spokes

spokesman *n.* a person who speaks or gives information for another or for a group

spoliation (spō′lē ā′shən) *n.* [L. *spoliatio*] robbery; plundering

spondee (spon′dē) *n.* [< Gr. *spondē*, libation] a metrical foot consisting of two long or heavily accented syllables —**sponda′ic** (-dā′ik) *adj.*

sponge (spunj) *n.* [< Gr. *spongia*] 1. a plantlike sea animal having a porous structure 2. the skeleton of such animals, light in weight and highly absorbent, used for washing surfaces, etc. 3. a piece of spongy cellulose, etc. 4. a light, porous pudding 5. *same as* SPONGECAKE 6. [Colloq.] a person who lives upon others as a parasite —*vt.* **sponged, spong′ing** 1. to use a sponge on so as to dampen, wipe clean, etc. 2. to remove as with a damp sponge (with *out, off*, etc.) 3. to absorb with or like a sponge (often with *up*) 4. [Colloq.] to obtain, as by begging —*vi.* 1. to take up liquid like a sponge 2. [Colloq.] to be a parasite (often with *off* or *on*) —**throw** (or **toss,** etc.) **in the sponge** [Colloq.] to admit defeat —**spong′er** *n.* —**spon′giness** *n.* —**spon′gy** *adj.*

sponge bag a small bag, usually made of plastic, that holds toilet articles, esp. for use when travelling

spongecake *n.* a light cake of spongy texture made of flour, beaten eggs, sugar, etc., but no fat

sponge rubber rubber processed to have a spongelike texture

sponsor (spon′sər) *n.* [L. < *spondere*, promise solemnly] 1. one who promotes an activity or someone taking part in an activity, either for profit or for charity 2. a legislator who presents a bill 3. a godparent 4. a business firm, etc. that pays for a radio or TV programme on which it advertises something —*vt.* to act as sponsor for —**sponso′rial** (-sôr′ē əl) *adj.* —**spon′sorship** *n.*

spontaneity (spon′tə nā′ə tē) *n.* the state or quality of being spontaneous

spontaneous (spon tā′nē əs) *adj.* [< L. *sponte*, of free will] 1. moved by a natural feeling or impulse, without constraint, effort, etc. 2. acting by internal energy, force, etc. —**sponta′neously** *adv.*

spontaneous combustion the process of catching fire as a result of heat generated by internal chemical action

spoof (spo͞of) *n.* [coinage] [Slang] 1. a hoax, joke, or deception 2. a parody —*vt., vi.* [Slang] 1. to fool; deceive 2. to satirize playfully

spook (spo͞ok) *n.* [Du.] [Colloq.] a spectre; ghost —*vt. vi.* [Colloq.] to startle or be startled, frightened, etc. —**spook′ily** *adv.* —**spook′iness** *n.* —**spook′y** *adj.*

spool (spo͞ol) *n.* [< MDu. *spoele*] 1. a cylinder upon which thread, wire, etc. is wound 2. something like a spool —*vt.* to wind on a spool

spoon (spo͞on) *n.* [OE. *spon*, a chip] 1. a utensil consisting of a small, shallow bowl with a handle, used for eating or stirring 2. something shaped like a spoon —*vt.* to take up as with a spoon —*vi.* [Colloq.] to hug and kiss: an old-fashioned term

spoonbill *n.* a wading bird with a bill that is spoon-shaped at the tip

spoonerism (spo͞on′əriz'm) *n.* [< Rev. W. A. *Spooner*] an unintentional interchange of sounds in two or more words (Ex.: "a well-boiled icicle" for "a well-oiled bicycle")

spoonfeed (spo͞on′fēd′) *vt.* **-fed′, -feed′ing** 1. to feed with a spoon 2. to treat, instruct, etc. so as to discourage independent thought and action

spoor (spo͞or) *n.* [Afrik. < MDu.] the track or trail of a wild animal hunted as game

sporadic (spə rad′ik) *adj.* [< Gr. *sporas*, scattered] 1. happening from time to time 2. appearing singly, or in isolated instances —**sporad′ically** *adv.*

sporangium (spə ran′jē əm) *n.*, *pl.* **-gia** [< Gr. *spora*, seed + *angeion*, vessel] *Bot.* an organ or single cell producing spores

spore (spôr) *n.* [< Gr. *spora*, a seed] a small reproductive body produced by bacteria, mosses, ferns, etc. and capable of giving rise to a new individual

spore case *same as* SPORANGIUM

sporran (spor′ən) *n.* [ScotGael. *sporan*] a leather pouch worn hanging from the belt in front of the kilt

sport (spôrt) *n.* [< DISPORT] 1. any recreational activity 2. such an activity requiring bodily exertion and carried on according to a set of rules, as golf, bowling, etc. 3. fun or play 4. a) an object of ridicule b) a plaything 5. [Colloq.] a person who is sportsmanlike 6. a plant or animal showing some variation from the normal type —*vt.* [Colloq.] to wear or display —*vi.* 1. to play or frolic 2. a) to joke b) to trifle or play (with) —**in** (or **for**) **sport** in joke or jest —**make sport of** to ridicule

sporting *adj.* 1. of, interested in, or taking part in sports 2. sportsmanlike; fair —**sport′ingly** *adv.*

sporting chance [Colloq.] a fair or even chance

sportive *adj.* 1. full of sport or merriment 2. done in fun or play —**spor′tively** *adv.* —**spor′tiveness** *n.*

sports *adj.* 1. of or for sports, esp. athletics

[*sports* day] 2. suitable for informal, casual wear

sports car a low, small motor car, typically with seats for two and a high-compression engine

sportscast *n.* a radio or TV broadcast of sports news —**sports′cast′er** *n.*

sportsman *n.* 1. a man who takes part in sports, esp. in hunting, fishing, etc. 2. a person who plays fair and can take defeat without complaint —**sports′manlike′** *adj.* —**sports′manship′** *n.*

sportswear *n.* clothes worn while engaging in sports or for informal, casual wear

sportswoman *n.* a woman who takes part in sports

sporty *adj.* **-ier, -iest** [Colloq.] 1. sportsmanlike 2. loud, flashy, or showy, as clothes —**sport′ily** *adv.* —**sport′iness** *n.*

spot (spot) *n.* [< MDu. *spotte*] 1. a small area differing from the surrounding area, as in colour 2. a stain, speck, etc. 3. a) a pimple b) a flaw; fault 4. a locality; place 5. *shortened form of* SPOTLIGHT 6. [Colloq.] a small quantity; bit 7. [Colloq.] a position or job 8. [Colloq.] a position in a schedule —*vt.* **spot′ted, spot′ting** 1. to pick out; recognize 2. to mark with spots 3. to stain; blemish 4. to place; locate 5. to look out for and note (trains, talent, etc.) 6. to rain slightly; spit —*vi.* 1. to become marked with spots 2. to make a stain, as ink, etc. —*adj.* 1. ready [*spot* cash] 2. made at random [a *spot* survey] —**hit the spot** [Colloq.] to satisfy a craving —**in a** (**bad** or **tight**) **spot** [Colloq.] in trouble —**on the spot** 1. at the place mentioned 2. at once 3. [Colloq.] in trouble or in a demanding situation 4. [U.S. Slang] in danger —**spot′less** *adj.* —**spot′lessly** *adv.*

spot-check *vt.* to check or examine at random —*n.* an act or instance of such checking

spotlight *n.* 1. a strong beam of light focused on a particular person, thing, etc. 2. a lamp used to project such a light 3. public attention —*vt.* to focus a spotlight on

spot-on *adj.* absolutely correct; very accurate

spotted *adj.* 1. marked with spots 2. blemished

spotted dick a steamed suet pudding containing dried fruit: also **spotted dog**

spotter *n.* 1. a person who watches for and notes down something specific, as locomotive engine numbers 2. a person who watches for, and reports, enemy aircraft

spotty *adj.* **-tier, -tiest** 1. having, occurring in, or marked with spots 2. not uniform or consistent

spot welding a process in which metal pieces are welded by a powerful surge of current —**spot′-weld′er** *n.*

spouse (spous) *n.* [see SPONSOR] a partner in marriage

spout (spout) *n.* [< ME. *spouten*, to spout]

1. a lip or projecting tube, as of a teapot, drinking fountain, gutter, by which a liquid is poured or discharged **2.** a stream, jet, etc. as of liquid from a spout —*vt., vi.* **1.** to shoot out (liquid, etc.), as from a spout **2.** to utter in a loud, pompous, or hasty manner —**up the spout** [Slang] **1.** in pawn **2.** in trouble; ruined; lost —**spout′er** *n.*

SPQR [L. *S(enatus) P(opulus)q(ue) R(omanus)*] the Senate and the people of Rome

sprain (sprān) *vt.* [< ?] to wrench a ligament or muscle of (a joint) without dislocating the bones —*n.* an injury resulting from this

sprang (spraŋ) *pt. of* SPRING

sprat (sprat) *n.* [OE. *sprott*] a small, sardinelike fish of the herring family

sprawl (sprôl) *vi.* [OE. *spreawlian*] **1.** to sit or lie with the limbs in a relaxed or awkward position **2.** to spread out in a straggling, irregular fashion, as handwriting, etc. —*vt.* to cause to sprawl —*n.* a sprawling arrangement, movement, or position

spray¹ (sprā) *n.* [< MDu. *spraeien*, to spray] **1.** a mist of fine liquid particles **2.** *a)* a jet of such particles, as from a spray gun *b)* a device for shooting out such a jet **3.** something likened to a spray —*vt., vi.* **1.** to direct a spray (upon) **2.** to shoot out in a spray

spray² (sprā) *n.* [ME.] **1.** a small branch of a tree, etc. with leaves, berries, flowers, etc. **2.** a design like this

spray gun a device that shoots out a spray of liquid, as paint or insecticide, by air pressure

spread (spred) *vt.* **spread, spread′ing** [OE. *sprædan*] **1.** to open out; unfold; unfurl **2.** to move apart (the fingers, arms, wings, etc.) **3.** to distribute over an area; scatter; smear **4.** to extend in time **5.** to cause to be widely or more widely known, felt, existent, etc. **6.** to cover (*with* something) **7.** to set (a table) for a meal **8.** to push apart or farther apart —*vi.* **1.** to extend itself **2.** to be made widely or more widely known, felt, etc. **3.** to be pushed apart or farther apart **4.** to admit of being smeared, as butter —*n.* **1.** the act or extent of spreading **2.** an expanse; extent [*middle-aged spread*] **3.** two facing pages of a magazine, etc., treated as a single sheet **4.** a cover for a bed; bedspread **5.** any soft substance, as jam, paste, etc. **6.** [Colloq.] a meal with a wide variety of food —**spread oneself thin** to try to do too many things at once —**spread′er** *n.*

spread-eagle *adj.* with outstretched arms and legs —*vt.* **-gled, -gling** to stretch out thus

spree (sprē) *n.* [< ?] **1.** a lively frolic **2.** a drinking bout **3.** a period of unrestrained activity

sprig (sprig) *n.* [ME. *sprigge*] **1.** *a)* a little twig *b)* a design like this **2.** a young fellow —*vt.* **sprigged, sprig′ging** to decorate with a design of sprigs

sprightly (sprīt′lē) *adj.* **-lier, -liest** [< SPIRIT] gay, lively, brisk, etc. —**spright′liness** *n.*

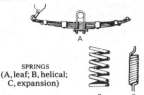

SPRINGS
(A, leaf; B, helical; C, expansion)

spring (spriŋ) *vi.* **sprang** or **sprung, sprung, spring′ing** [OE. *springan*] **1.** to leap; bound **2.** to appear suddenly **3.** to bounce **4.** to arise as from some source; grow or develop **5.** to become bent, warped, split, etc. **6.** to rise up above surrounding objects Often followed by *up* —*vt.* **1.** to cause to leap forth suddenly **2.** to cause to snap shut, as by a spring **3.** to cause to warp, bend, split, etc. **4.** to make known suddenly **5.** [Slang] to organize an escape from jail —*n.* **1.** a leap, or the distance so covered **2.** a sudden darting or flying back **3.** elasticity; resilience **4.** energy or vigour **5.** a device, as a coil of wire, that returns to its original form after being forced out of shape **6.** a flow of water from the ground, the source of a stream **7.** any source or origin **8.** that season of the year when plants begin to grow after lying dormant all winter **9.** any period of beginning —*adj.* **1.** of, for, appearing in, or planted in the spring **2.** of or like a spring **3.** having, or supported on, springs **4.** coming from a spring [*spring* water] —**spring a leak** to begin to leak suddenly

spring balance a device for measuring weight by the compression or extension of a spiral spring

springboard *n.* a flexible, springy board used as a takeoff in leaping or diving

springbok (spriŋ′bok′) *n.* [Afrik. < Du. *springen*, to spring + *bok*, a buck] **1.** a South African gazelle that leaps high in the air **2.** [Colloq.] [S-] *a)* an inhabitant of South Africa *b)* a S African athlete, esp. a rugger player **3.** in South Africa, an amateur sportsman who has gained S African colours Also **springbuck**

spring chicken 1. [Chiefly U.S.] a young chicken **2.** [Slang] a young or inexperienced person

springcleaning (spriŋ′klēn′iŋ) *n.* a thorough cleaning of the interior of a house, etc. as conventionally done in spring

springer *n.* short for SPRINGER SPANIEL

springer spaniel a breed of field spaniel used for flushing, or springing, game

spring onion an immature onion whose bulb and green leaves are eaten raw in salads

spring tide a tide occurring at the new and the full moon, normally the highest tide of the month

springtime *n.* the season of spring: also **spring′tide′**

springy *adj.* -ier, -iest flexible; elastic —**spring'ily** *adv.* —**spring'iness** *n.*

sprinkle (spriŋ'k'l) *vt.* -kled, -kling [ME. *sprinklen*] 1. to scatter (water, salt, etc.) in drops or particles 2. to scatter drops or particles upon 3. to distribute at random —*vi.* 1. to scatter in drops 2. to rain lightly —*n.* a light rain —**sprin'kler** *n.*

sprinkling *n.* 1. a small number or amount, esp. when thinly distributed 2. the act of one that sprinkles

sprint (sprint) *vi.* [< Scand.] to run or race at full speed, esp. for a short distance —*n.* 1. the act of sprinting 2. a short race at full speed —**sprint'er** *n.*

sprit (sprit) *n.* [OE. *spreot*] a spar extended upwards from a mast to the corner of a fore-and-aft sail

sprite (sprit) *n.* [see SPIRIT] an elf, pixie, fairy, or goblin

spritsail (sprit's'l) *n.* a sail extended by a sprit

SPROCKET
WHEELS

sprocket (sprok'it) *n.* [< ?] any of the teeth, as on the rim of a wheel, arranged to fit into the links of a chain

sprout (sprout) *vi.* [OE. *sprutan*] 1. to begin to grow or germinate; give off shoots or buds 2. to grow or develop rapidly —*vt.* to cause to sprout —*n.* 1. a young growth on a plant; shoot 2. a new growth from a bud, etc. 3. [*pl.*] shortened form of BRUSSELS SPROUTS

spruce¹ (sproos) *n.* [< ME., Prussia] 1. any of various evergreen trees of the pine family, having slender needles 2. its wood

spruce² *adj.* spruc'er, spruc'est [< *Spruce* leather (see prec.)] neat and trim; smart —*vt., vi.* spruced, spruc'ing to make or become spruce (usually with *up*)

sprung (spruŋ) *pp. & alt. pt.* of SPRING

spry (sprī) *adj.* spri'er or spry'er, spri'- est or spry'est [< ?] full of life; active and agile —**spry'ly** *adv.*

spud (spud) *n.* [< ?] 1. [Colloq.] a potato 2. a sharp spade for rooting out weeds, etc. —*vt., vi.* spud'ded, spud'ding to dig, etc. with a spud

spue (spyoo) *vt., vi.* spued, spu'ing *same as* SPEW

spume (spyoom) *n.* [< L. *spuma*] foam or froth —*vt., vi.* spumed, spum'ing to foam or froth —**spum'y** *adj.*

spun (spun) *pt. & pp.* of SPIN —*adj.* formed by or as if by spinning

spunk (spuŋk) *n.* [IrGael. *sponc*, tinder] 1. [Colloq.] courage; spirit 2. wood that smoulders when ignited

spunky *adj.* -ier, -iest [Colloq.] courageous; spirited —**spunk'ily** *adv.* —**spunk'iness** *n.*

spur (spur) *n.* [OE. *spura*] 1. a pointed device worn on the heel by horsemen and used to urge the horse forward 2. anything that urges or incites; stimulus 3. something like a spur, esp. a spinelike process, as on the wings or legs of certain birds 4. a ridge projecting from a mountain or mountain range 5. a short side track (**spur track**) connected with the main track of a railway —*vt.* spurred, spur'ring 1. to prick with spurs 2. to urge on; incite 3. to provide with a spur or spurs —*vi.* 1. to spur one's horse 2. to hurry; hasten —**on the spur of the moment** abruptly and impulsively —**win one's spurs** 1. to prove one's ability 2. to gain distinction —**spur'like** *adj.*

spurge (spurj) *n.* [see EXPURGATE] a plant having a milky juice and small white flowers

spurious (spyoor'ē əs) *adj.* [L. *spurius*] not genuine; false; counterfeit —**spu'riously** *adv.* —**spu'riousness** *n.*

spurn (spurn) *vt.* [OE. *spurnan*] 1. to reject in a scornful way 2. to push or drive away as with the foot

spurt (spurt) *vt., vi.* [< OE. *sprutan*, to sprout] 1. to gush forth in a stream or jet 2. to show a sudden, brief burst of energy or activity —*n.* 1. a sudden gushing forth; jet 2. a sudden, brief burst of energy, etc.

sputnik (spoot'nik) *n.* [Russ., co-traveller] an artificial satellite of the earth; specif., [S-] one put into orbit by the U.S.S.R.

sputter (sput'ər) *vi.* [Du. *sputteren*] 1. to spit out, as when talking excitedly 2. to talk in an excited, confused way, spitting out one's words 3. to make sharp, sizzling or spitting sounds —*vt.* 1. to spit out (bits or drops) in an explosive manner 2. to utter by sputtering —*n.* 1. the act or noise of sputtering 2. hasty, confused utterance

sputum (spyoot'əm) *n.*, *pl.* spu'ta [< L. *spuere*, SPIT²] saliva, usually mixed with mucus

spy (spī) *n.*, *pl.* spies [< OHG. *spehōn*, examine] a person who keeps close and secret watch on another or others, esp. one employed by a government —*vt.* spied, spy'ing to catch sight of; see —*vi.* to watch closely and secretly; act as a spy —**spy out** to discover or seek to discover by looking carefully

spyglass *n.* a small telescope

sq. 1. squadron 2. square

squab (skwob) *n.* [prob. < Scand.] 1. a very young pigeon 2. a stuffed cushion

squabble (skwob''l) *vi.* -bled, -bling [< Scand.] to quarrel noisily over a small matter —*n.* a noisy, petty quarrel; wrangle —**squab'bler** *n.*

squad (skwod) *n.* [< Fr.: see SQUARE] 1. a small group of soldiers 2. any small group of people working together [*flying squad*]

squadron *n.* [< It. *squadra*, a square] 1. a group of warships assigned to special duty 2. a unit of cavalry consisting of from two to four troops, etc. 3. in various airforces, a unit of a number of aircraft

squadron leader *see* MILITARY RANKS, table

squalid (skwol'id) *adj.* [< L. *squalere*, be foul] 1. foul; filthy 2. wretched; sordid

squall[1] (skwôl) *n.* [< Scand.] a brief, violent windstorm, usually with rain —**squall'y** *adj.*

squall[2] *vi., vt.* [ON. *skvala*, cry out] to cry or scream loudly or harshly —*n.* a harsh, shrill cry or loud scream —**squall'er** *n.*

squalor (skwol'ər) *n.* [L., foulness] filth and wretchedness

squander (skwon'dər) *vt., vi.* [< ?] to spend or use (money, time, etc.) wastefully

square (skwâər) *n.* [< L. *ex-*, out + *quadrus*, a square] 1. a plane figure having four equal sides and four right angles 2. anything shaped like or nearly like this 3. an open area bounded by several streets 4. an instrument used for drawing or testing right angles 5. the product of a number multiplied by itself 6. [Slang] a person who is square (*adj.* 11) —*adj.* 1. *a*) having four equal sides and four right angles *b*) more or less cubical, as a box 2. forming a right angle 3. straight, level, even, etc. 4. leaving no balance; balanced 5. just; fair; honest 6. clear; direct 7. of a unit of surface measure in the form of a square with sides of a specified length 8. having a shape broad for its length or height [a *square* build] 9. designating a number that is the product of another number multiplied by itself 10. [Colloq.] satisfying; substantial 11. [Slang] old-fashioned or unsophisticated —*vt.* **squared**, **squar'ing** 1. to make into a square 2. to multiply (a quantity) by itself 3. to test or adjust with regard to straightness or evenness 4. to mark off (a surface) in squares 5. to bring to or near to the form of a right angle 6. to settle; adjust 7. to make equal 8. to bring into agreement —*vi.* 1. to fit; agree; accord (*with*) —*adv.* 1. honestly; fairly 2. directly; exactly —**get square with** to settle with, esp. with a creditor —**on the square** [Colloq.] honest(ly); fair(ly) —**square off** [Chiefly U.S.] to get into position for attacking or for defending —**square the circle** 1. to find a square equal in area to a circle: an insoluble problem 2. to attempt something that seems impossible —**square up** 1. to make a settlement, as by payment 2. to assume a posture of opposition (*to* an adversary) —**square'ly** *adv.* —**square'ness** *n.*

squarebashing *n.* [Slang] military drill as performed on the parade ground

square dance a lively dance with various steps and figures, the couples forming squares, etc.

square deal [Colloq.] any dealing that is honest and fair

square leg *Cricket* a fielding position on the batsman's left

square measure a system of measuring area, esp. the system in which 10 000 square centimetres = 1 square metre and that in which 144 square inches = 1 square foot

square-rigged *adj.* having square sails as principal sails —**square'-rig'ger** *n.*

square root the number that is multiplied by itself to produce a given number [3 is the *square root* of 9]

squash[1] (skwosh) *vt.* [< L. *ex-*, intens. + *quatere*, to shake] 1. to crush into a soft or flat mass; press 2. to suppress; quash 3. [Colloq.] to silence (another) crushingly —*vi.* 1. to be squashed by pressure, etc. 2. to squelch 3. to force one's way; squeeze —*n.* 1. something squashed; crushed mass 2. the act or sound of squashing 3. either of two games (**squash rackets**, **squash tennis**) played in a four-walled court with rackets and a rubber ball 4. a drink made from fruit juice diluted with water

squash[2] *n.* [< Algonquian] [U.S.] the fleshy fruit of various plants of the gourd family, cooked as a vegetable

squashy *adj.* **-ier**, **-iest** 1. soft and wet; mushy 2. easily squashed —**squash'i-ness** *n.*

squat (skwot) *vi.* **squat'ted**, **squat'ting** [< L. *ex-*, intens. + *cogere*, to force] 1. to crouch, with the knees bent and the weight on the balls of the feet 2. to crouch close to the ground 3. to settle on land, or occupy property, without any title to it —*adj.* 1. crouched in a squatting position 2. short and thick: also **squat'ty** —*n.* 1. the act or position of squatting 2. [Colloq.] premises that are, or could be, occupied by squatters

squatter *n.* 1. someone who illegally occupies property 2. [Aust.] *a*) a person who occupies land as a tenant of the Crown *b*) a sheep farmer

squaw (skwô) *n.* [< Algonquian] a N American Indian woman, esp. a wife

squawk (skwôk) *vi.* [echoic] 1. to utter a loud, harsh cry, as a parrot 2. [Colloq.] to complain —*n.* 1. a squawking cry 2. [Colloq.] a complaint

squeak (skwēk) *vi.* [echoic] to make or utter a short, sharp, high-pitched sound or cry —*vt.* to utter with a squeak —*n.* a short, shrill sound or cry —**narrow** (or **close**) **squeak** [Colloq.] a narrow escape —**squeak through** (or **by**, etc.) [Colloq.] to barely manage to succeed, survive, etc. —**squeak'er** *n.* —**squeak'ily** *adv.* —**squeak'y** *adj.*

squeal (skwēl) *vi.* [see SQUALL[2]] 1. to make or utter a long, shrill sound or cry 2. [Slang] to inform against someone —*vt.* to utter with a squeal —*n.* a long, shrill sound or cry —**squeal'er** *n.*

squeamish (skwēm'ish) *adj.* [< ?] 1. easily nauseated 2. easily shocked 3. too fastidious or scrupulous —**squeam'ish-ness** *n.*

squeegee (skwē'jē) *n.* [prob. < SQUEEZE] a T-shaped tool with a blade of rubber, etc., for wiping liquid off a surface

squeeze (skwēz) *vt.* **squeezed**, **squeez'ing** [OE. *cwysan*] 1. to press hard, esp. from two or more sides 2. to extract (liquid, etc.) by pressure 3. to force (*into*, *out*, etc.) as by pressing 4. to get or extort by force or unfair means **5.** to put pressure on (someone) to do something **6.** to embrace closely —*vi.* **1.** to yield to pressure **2.** to exert pressure **3.** to force one's way by pushing (*in, out, through*, etc.) —*n.* **1.** a squeezing or being squeezed **2.** a close embrace; hug **3.** the state of being closely pressed or packed **4.** a difficult situation **5.** a quantity extracted by squeezing **6.** [Colloq.] pressure exerted, as in extortion: esp. in **put the squeeze on** —**squeeze through** (or **by**, etc.) [Colloq.] to barely manage to succeed, survive, etc. —**squeez'er** *n.*

squelch (skwelch) *n.* [echoic] the sound of liquid, mud, etc. moving under pressure or suction —*vt.* **1.** to crush as by stamping upon; squash **2.** [Colloq.] to suppress or silence completely and crushingly —*vi.* **1.** to walk heavily through mud, etc., making a splashing sound **2.** to make such a sound

squib (skwib) *n.* [echoic] **1.** a firework that hisses before exploding **2.** a short, witty writing that criticizes, etc. —**a damp squib** a plan or project that comes to nothing

squid (skwid) *n.* [< ?] a cephalopod mollusc having a slender body and ten arms, two arms being much longer than the others

squiffy (skwif'ē) *adj.* -fier, -fiest [< ?] [Slang] drunk; intoxicated

squiggle (skwig''l) *n.* [SQU(IRM) + (W)IGGLE] a short curved or wavy line; illegible scribble

squill (skwil) *n.* [< Gr. *skilla*] **1.** the dried bulb of a plant like the lily formerly used in medicine **2.** this plant

squint (skwint) *vi.* [? < Du. *schuinte*, a slant] **1.** to peer with the eyes partly closed **2.** to look sidelong or askance **3.** to be cross-eyed —*vt.* **1.** to keep (the eyes) partly closed in peering —*n.* **1.** a squinting **2.** a being cross-eyed **3.** [Colloq.] a glance, often sidelong —*adj.* **1.** looking sidelong or askance **2.** cross-eyed —**squint'y** *adj.*

squire (skwīer) *n.* [see ESQUIRE] **1.** a country gentleman, esp. the main landowner in a rural community **2.** a young man of high birth who attended a knight **3.** a man escorting a woman —*vt., vi.* to act as a squire (to)

squirearchy (skwīer'är kē) *n.* [< prec.] large landowners collectively: also sp. **squir'archy**

squirm (skwurm) *vi.* [prob. echoic] **1.** to twist and turn the body; wriggle **2.** to show or feel distress, as from embarrassment —*n.* a squirming —**squirm'y** *adj.*

squirrel (skwir'əl) *n.* [< Gr. *skia*, a shadow + *oura*, tail] **1.** a small, tree-dwelling rodent with heavy fur and a long, bushy tail, esp. the grey squirrel or the red squirrel **2.** its fur —*vt.* **-relled, -relling** to store or hide (*away*)

squirt (skwurt) *vt.* [prob. < LowG. *swirtjen*] **1.** to shoot out (a liquid) in a jet **2.** to wet with liquid thus shot out —*vi.* to spurt —*n.* **1.** a device for squirting, as a syringe **2.** a small amount of squirted liquid **3.** [Colloq.] a small or young person

squish (skwish) *vi.* to make a soft, splashing sound when walked on, etc. —*n.* a squishing sound —**squish'y** *adj.*

Sr *Chem.* strontium

Sr. **1.** Senior **2.** Sister

S.R.C. Science Research Council

S.R.N. State Registered Nurse

SS. [L. *Sancti*] Saints

S.S., SS, S/S steamship

SSE, S.S.E., s.s.e. south-southeast

S.S.R., SSR Soviet Socialist Republic

S.S.R.C. Social Science Research Council

SSW, S.S.W., s.s.w. south-southwest

-st *same as* -EST

St. **1.** Saint **2.** Strait **3.** Street

st. **1.** stitch **2.** stone **3.** *Cricket* stumped (by)

stab (stab) *vt.* **stabbed, stab'bing** [ME. *stabbe*] **1.** to pierce or wound as with a knife **2.** to thrust (a knife, etc.) into something —*vi.* **1.** to make a piercing wound as with a knife **2.** to feel like a stabbing knife: said of pain —*n.* **1.** a thrust, as with a knife **2.** a wound made by piercing with a knife, dagger, etc. **3.** a sharp pain —**make** (or **take**) **a stab at** to make an attempt at —**stab in the back** to harm (someone) by treachery

stabile (stā'bīl) *adj.* [L.: see STABLE[1]] stable; stationary

stability (stə bil'ə tē) *n., pl.* -ties **1.** a being stable, or fixed; steadiness **2.** firmness of character, purpose, etc. **3.** resistance to change

stabilize (stā'bə līz') *vt., vi.* -ized', -liz'-ing to make or become stable, or firm —**sta'biliza'tion** *n.*

stabilizer *n.* **1.** an aerofoil to keep an aircraft steady in flight **2.** a gyrostabilizer to steady a ship in rough waters **3.** a person or thing that stabilizes

stable[1] (stā'b'l) *adj.* **-bler, -blest** [< L. *stare*, to stand] **1.** a) firm; steady b) not likely to break down, fall apart, etc. **2.** firm in character, purpose, etc. **3.** not likely to change; enduring —**sta'bly** *adv.*

stable[2] *n.* [< L. *stare*, to stand] **1.** a building in which horses or cattle are sheltered and fed **2.** all the racehorses of one owner **3.** a source of training, as a school —*vt., vi.* **-bled, -bling** to keep or be kept in a stable

stablemate *n.* **1.** a horse from the same stable **2.** someone who has the same school, etc. as someone else Also **stable companion**

staccato (stəkät′ō) *adj.* [It.] *Music* with distinct breaks between successive tones —*adv.* so as to be staccato

stack (stak) *n.* [ON. *stakkr*] **1.** any orderly pile **2.** a large pile of straw, hay, etc., esp. one neatly arranged **3.** [*pl.*] the main area for shelving books in a library **4.** [Colloq.] a large amount **5.** *a*) a grouping of chimney flues *b*) a smokestack —*vt.* **1.** to pile in a stack **2.** to load with stacks **3.** to assign (aircraft) to various altitudes for circling before landing **4.** to arrange underhandedly for a desired result [to *stack* the cards] —**stack′able** *adj.* —**stack′er** *n.*

stacked (stakt) *adj.* [Chiefly U.S. Slang] having a full, shapely figure : said of a woman

stackup *n.* an arrangement of circling aircraft at various altitudes awaiting their turn to land

stadium (stā′dē əm) *n.* [L. < Gr. *stadion*, unit of length] a large, open structure for football, athletics, etc. with tiers of seats for spectators

staff (stäf) *n., pl.* **staffs**; also, for sense 5, **staves** [OE. *stæf*] **1.** a group of people assisting a leader [a teaching *staff*] **3.** a group of officers serving a commanding officer as advisers and administrators **4.** a stick, rod, or pole used as for support, a weapon, a symbol of authority, etc. **5.** *Music* the five horizontal lines and four intermediate spaces on which music is written —*adj.* of, by, for, or on a staff —*vt.* to provide with a staff, as of workers

staff nurse a nurse who is second in command of a ward to a sister

staff officer an officer on a staff

Staffs. Staffordshire

staff sergeant *see* MILITARY RANKS, table

stag (stag) *n.* [OE. *stagga*] **1.** a full-grown male deer **2.** *Finance* a speculator who applies to buy shares in a new company, hoping to sell immediately at a profit —*adj.* for men only

stag beetle a large beetle of which the male has long, branched mandibles

stage (stāj) *n.* [< L. *stare*, to stand] **1.** a period or degree in a process of development, change, etc. **2.** a platform **3.** *a*) an area or platform on which plays, speeches, etc. are presented *b*) the theatre as a profession (with *the*) **4.** the scene of an event **5.** a stopping point on a route **6.** the distance between two such points **7.** a stagecoach **8.** any of two or more propulsion units used in sequence as the rocket of a spacecraft, etc. —*vt.* **staged, stag′ing 1.** to present as on a stage **2.** to plan and carry out —**by easy stages** a little at a time —**stag′er** *n.*

stagecoach *n.* formerly, a horse-drawn coach moving along a set route

stage fright nervousness felt when appearing as a speaker or performer before an audience

stagehand *n.* one who moves scenery, operates the curtain, etc. for a stage performance

stage-manage *vt.* **-aged, -aging 1.** to be stage manager for **2.** to arrange with dramatic effect, esp. as if from behind scenes

stage manager an assistant to the director of a play, in overall charge backstage during an actual performance

stage-struck *adj.* having an intense desire to act

stage whisper 1. a loud whisper by an actor on the stage, thought of as being heard only by the audience and not by his fellow actors **2.** a whisper that is intended to be overheard

stagflation (stagflā′shən) *n.* [< STAGNATE + INFLATION] a period of high inflation and no increase in productivity

stagger (stag′ər) *vi.* [ON. *stakra*, to totter] **1.** to totter or reel, as from a blow, fatigue, etc. **2.** to waver in purpose, etc. —*vt.* **1.** to make stagger **2.** to affect strongly, as with astonishment **3.** to set alternately, as on either side of a line **4.** to arrange (duties, holidays, etc.) so as to avoid crowding —*n.* **1.** a staggering, tottering, etc. **2.** a staggered arrangement **3.** [*pl.*, *with sing. v.*] a disease of horses, cattle, etc., marked by staggering —**stag′gering** *adj.* —**stag′geringly** *adv.*

staging (stā′jin) *n.* **1.** scaffolding **2.** the act of presenting a play on the stage **3.** shelving used for plants in greenhouses

stagnant (stag′nənt) *adj.* **1.** not flowing or moving **2.** foul from lack of movement : said of water, etc. **3.** lacking activity, etc. —**stag′nancy** *n.* —**stag′nantly** *adv.*

stagnate (stag nāt′) *vi., vt.* **-nat′ed, -nat′ing** [< L. *stagnum*, a swamp] to become or make stagnant —**stagna′tion** *n.*

stag party a party for men only, esp. one held for a bachelor just before he is married

stagy (stā′jē) *adj.* **-ier, -iest 1.** theatrical **2.** affected; not real Also **stage′y** —**stag′ily** *adv.* —**stag′iness** *n.*

staid (stād) *adj.* [see STAY³] sober; sedate —**staid′ly** *adv.*

stain (stān) *vt.* [< L. *dis-*, from + *tingere*, to colour] **1.** to spoil the appearance of by discolouring or spotting **2.** to disgrace or dishonour **3.** to colour (wood, glass, etc.) with a dye, pigment, etc. **4.** to treat (material for microscopic study) with a colouring matter —*n.* **1.** a discolouration; spot **2.** a moral blemish; dishonour **3.** a dye for staining wood, etc. —**stain′able** *adj.* —**stain′less** *adj.*

stainless steel steel alloyed with chromium, etc., virtually immune to rust and corrosion

stair (stäər) *n.* [OE. *stæger*] **1.** [*usually pl.*] a flight of steps; staircase **2.** one of a series of steps leading from one level to another

staircase *n.* a flight of stairs with a handrail: also **stair′way′**

stairwell *n.* a vertical shaft (in a building) containing a staircase: also **stair well**

stake (stāk) *n.* [OE. *staca*] 1. a length of wood or metal pointed at one end for driving into the ground 2. the post to which a person was tied for execution by burning 3. [*often pl.*] something, esp. money, risked, as in a wager 4. [*often pl.*] a prize given a winner, as in a race 5. [*pl., with sing. v.*] a race in which a prize is offered 6. a share or interest, as in property —*vt.* **staked, stak′ing** 1. *a)* to mark the boundaries of *b)* to establish (a claim) thus 2. to support (a plant, etc.) by tying to a stake 3. to risk; gamble 4. [U.S. Colloq.] to furnish with money or resources —**at stake** being risked —**stake out** to station (police, etc.) in an attempt to capture a suspected criminal

Stakhanovism (sta khan′ə viz′m) *n.* [< A. G. *Stakhanov*] in the Soviet Union, a system of working in teams to get higher production, with bonuses, etc. given for success —**Stakha′novite′** *adj., n.*

STALACTITES

STALAGMITES

stalactite (stal′ək tīt′) *n.* [< Gr. *stalaktos*, dripping] an icicle-shaped deposit hanging from the roof of a cave, formed by evaporation of dripping water full of lime

stalagmite (stal′əg mīt′) *n.* [< Gr. *stalagmos*, a dropping] a cone-shaped deposit built up on the floor of a cave by dripping water full of lime, often from a stalactite above

stale (stāl) *adj.* **stal′er, stal′est** [prob. < LowG.] 1. having lost freshness; flat, dry, stagnant, etc. 2. no longer new or interesting 3. ineffective, weakened, etc. from too much or too little activity —*vt., vi.* **staled, stal′ing** to make or become stale —**stale′ly** *adv.* —**stale′ness** *n.*

stalemate (stāl′māt′) *n.* [< OFr. *estal*, a fixed location + CHECKMATE] 1. *Chess* any situation in which a player cannot move without placing his king in check 2. a deadlock —*vt.* **-mat′ed, -mat′ing** to bring into a stalemate

Stalinism (stä′lin iz′m) *n.* the form of government associated with Joseph Stalin (1879-1953), Soviet statesman

stalk[1] (stôk) *vi., vt.* [< OE. *stealc*, steep] 1. to walk (through) in a stiff, haughty manner 2. to pursue or approach (game, etc.) stealthily —*n.* 1. a slow, stiff, or haughty stride 2. a stalking of game, etc. —**stalk′er** *n.*

stalk[2] *n.* [OE. *stela*] 1. *Bot. a)* the main stem of a plant *b)* a lengthened part on which fruit, a flower, etc. grows 2. *Zool.* a lengthened support for an animal organ —**stalk′less** *adj.* —**stalk′y** *adj.*

stalking-horse *n.* 1. a horse, or a figure of one, used as cover by a hunter 2. anything used to hide intentions, schemes, etc.

stall[1] (stôl) *n.* [OE. *steall*] 1. a compartment for one animal in a stable 2. *a)* a booth, etc. where goods are sold, as at a fair *b)* an enclosed seat in a church *c)* a theatre seat near the stage *d)* a small, enclosed space, as for taking a shower *e)* any of the spaces marked off for parking cars in a garage, etc. 3. a protective sheath for a finger 4. a stopping or standing still due to failure to work properly, as in a car or aircraft —*vt., vi.* 1. to stop as from failure to work properly, as a motor car 2. to put (an aircraft) into a stall, or go into a stall 3. to put, keep, or be kept in a stall

stall[2] *vi.* [< obs. *stale*, a decoy] to act or speak evasively so as to deceive or delay —*vt.* to delay by stalling

stallion (stal′yən) *n.* [< Gmc. *stal*, a stall] an uncastrated male horse, esp. one used as a stud

stalwart (stôl′wərt) *adj.* [< OE. *stathol*, foundation + *wyrthe*, worth] 1. sturdy; robust 2. valiant 3. resolute; firm —*n.* 1. a stalwart person 2. a firm supporter of a cause —**stal′wartly** *adv.*

stamen (stā′mən) *n., pl.* **-mens** [< L., a thread, warp] a pollen-bearing organ in a flower

stamina (stam′ə nə) *n.* [L.: see STAMEN] resistance to fatigue, illness, hardship, etc.; endurance

stammer (stam′ər) *vt., vi.* [OE. *stamerian*] to speak or say with pauses and rapid repetitions of initial sounds, as because of excitement —*n.* the act of stammering —**stam′merer** *n.*

stamp (stamp) *vt.* [ME. *stampen*] 1. to bring (the foot) down forcibly 2. *a)* to beat, crush, etc. by treading on heavily *b)* to grind or crush 3. to imprint or cut out (a design, lettering, etc.) 4. to impress distinctly or indelibly [a face *stamped* with grief] 5. to put an official seal or a stamp on (a document, letter, etc.) 6. to characterize, as if by imprinting —*vi.* 1. to bring the foot down forcibly on the ground, etc. 2. to walk with loud, heavy steps —*n.* 1. a stamping 2. a small piece of paper, distinctively imprinted and usually gummed, sold by a government and required to be put on a letter, parcel, etc. to show that postage has been paid 3. a machine, tool, etc. for stamping 4. the mark or form made by stamping 5. a characteristic sign or impression [the *stamp* of truth *]* **6.** a mark, seal, etc. used to show officially that a tax has been paid, authority given, etc. **7.** kind; class —**stamp on** to subdue; suppress —**stamp out** **1.** to crush by treading on forcibly **2.** to crush (a revolt, etc.) —**stamp′er** *n.*

stamp-collecting *n.* same as PHILATELY —**stamp′ -collec′tor** *n.*

stampede (stam pēd′) *n.* [< Sp. *estampar*, to stamp] **1.** a sudden, headlong rush or flight, as of a herd of frightened horses, cattle, etc. **2.** [Canad.] a rodeo —*vi.* **-ped′-ed, -ped′ing** to move in a stampede —*vt.* to cause to stampede —**stamped′er** *n.*

stamping ground [Colloq.] a favourite gathering place or resort

stance (stans) *n.* [< L. *stare*, to stand] **1.** a way of standing, esp. in regard to placing the feet **2.** an attitude adopted for dealing with a situation

stanch (stänch) *vt., vi., adj.* see STAUNCH

stanchion (stän′shan) *n.* [see STANCE] **1.** an upright bar, post, etc. used as a support **2.** a restraining device in a stall, fitted loosely about a cow's neck

stand (stand) *vi.* **stood, stand′ing** [OE. *standan*] **1.** to be in, or assume, an upright position, as on the feet **2.** to rise to an upright position, as from sitting **3.** *a)* to take, or be in, a (specified) upright position *b)* to take a (specified) position or attitude *[I stand* opposed *]* **4.** to have a (specified) height when standing **5.** to be situated **6.** to gather and remain : said of a liquid **7.** to remain unchanged, valid, etc. **8.** to be in a (specified) condition *[he stands* to lose *]* **9.** to be of a (specified) rank, degree, etc. *[to stand* first *]* **10.** to make resistance **11.** *a)* to halt *b)* to remain stationary **12.** to be a candidate, as for office **13.** Naut. to take or hold a certain course —*vt.* **1.** to make stand; put upright **2.** to put up with; endure **3.** to withstand **4.** to undergo *[to stand* trial *]* **5.** [Colloq.] to bear the cost of (a meal, etc.) —*n.* **1.** a standing; esp., *a)* a halt or stop; specif., *a)* a stopping, as to counterattack *b)* a halt by a touring theatrical company to give a performance **2.** the place where one stands; position **3.** a view, opinion, etc., as on an issue **4.** a structure to stand or sit on; specif., *a)* a raised platform for a band, etc. *b)* [often *pl.*] a set of benches in tiers, as for spectators *c)* [U.S.] the witness box **5.** *a)* a booth, stall, etc. where goods are sold *b)* a parking space reserved for taxicabs, etc. **6.** a rack, small table, etc. for holding things **7.** a standing growth of trees or plants —**stand a chance** to have a chance —**stand by 1.** to be near and ready to act as needed **2.** to aid or support **3.** to keep (a promise, etc.) —**stand corrected** to admit correction by someone else —**stand for 1.** to represent **2.** to be a candidate for (office) **3.** [Colloq.] to put up with; endure —**stand in for** to substitute for —**stand off 1.** to keep at a distance **2.** to evade **3.** to discharge (an employee) temporarily —**stand on 1.** to be founded on **2.** to insist upon

(ceremony, one's rights, etc.) —**stand one's ground** to maintain one's position —**stand out 1.** to project **2.** to show up clearly **3.** to be prominent or outstanding **4.** to refuse to give in —**stand to 1.** to abide by or adhere to **2.** Mil. to be on the alert in expectation of enemy attack —**stand up 1.** to rise to or be in a standing position **2.** to prove valid, durable, etc. **3.** [Slang] to fail to keep an engagement with —**stand up for** to defend —**stand up to** to confront fearlessly

standard (stan′dard) *n.* [OFr. *estendard*] **1.** something established as a rule or basis of comparison in measuring quantity, quality, etc. **2.** a usage or practice that is generally accepted *[moral standards]* **3.** a flag, banner, etc. used as an emblem of a people, military unit, etc. **4.** an upright support **5.** a tree or shrub with a single, tall stem **6.** [S Afr.] a form or grade in school —*adj.* **1.** used as or conforming to an established rule, model, etc. **2.** generally accepted as authoritative **3.** regular or typical **4.** of or in accord with speech or writing that is more or less formal *[standard* English *]*

standard-bearer *n.* **1.** a person carrying the flag, as of a military group **2.** a leader of a movement, etc.

standard gauge a width of $56^{1}/_{2}$ inches (143.8 cm) between the rails of a railway track

standardize *vt.* **-ized′, -iz′ing** to make standard or uniform —**stand′ardiza′tion** *n.*

standard lamp an electric light fixed to a tall support standing on the floor

standard of living level of daily living, as of a person, with regard to the adequacy of necessities and comforts

standard time the time in any of the 24 time zones, each an hour apart, into which the earth is divided : it is based on distance east or west of Greenwich

standby (stand′bī′) *n., pl.* **-bys′** a person or thing that can always be depended on, or one ready to be used if needed —*adj.* of, for, or being a standby

stand-in *n.* a temporary substitute, as for an actor

standing *n.* **1.** status, rank, or reputation *[in good standing]* **2.** duration *[of long standing]* **3.** the act of one that stands —*adj.* **1.** that stands; upright **2.** in or from a standing position **3.** not flowing; stagnant **4.** permanent

standing order **1.** [often *pl.*] a rule governing procedure in a formally constituted body, as parliament **2.** an instruction to a bank requesting regular payments, as for mortgage payments, etc.

standing room room in which to stand, esp. when there are no vacant seats, as in a theatre

standoffish (stand′of′ish) *adj.* reserved and cool; aloof

standpipe *n.* a large vertical pipe for storing water

standpoint *n.* point of view

standstill *n.* a stop, halt, or cessation

stank (staŋk) *alt. pt.* of STINK

stannary (stan'ər ē) *n., pl.* **-ries** [< LL. *stannum,* tin] a region of tin mines and tinworks

stanza (stan'zə) *n.* [It.: < L. *stare,* to stand] a group of lines of verse, usually four or more and regular in pattern, forming one of the divisions of a poem or song

staphylococcus (staf'ə lō kok'əs) *n., pl.* **-coc'ci** (-kok'ī) [< Gr. *staphylē,* bunch of grapes + -COCCUS] any of a genus of spherical bacteria that generally occur in clusters or chains and cause pus to form in abscesses, etc. —**staph'ylococ'-cal** *adj.*

staple[1] *n.* [< MDu. *stapel,* mart] 1. chief; main 2. regularly stocked, produced, or consumed —*n.* 1. a chief commodity made, grown, etc. in a particular place 2. a chief item or element 3. raw material 4. a regularly stocked item of trade, as salt 5. the fibre of cotton, wool, etc.

staple[2] *n.* [OE. *stapol,* a post] 1. a U-shaped piece of metal with sharp-pointed ends, driven into a surface to hold a hook, wire, etc. in place 2. a similar piece of thin wire binding papers —*vt.* **-pled, -pling** to fasten with a staple —**sta'pler** *n.*

star (stär) *n.* [OE. *steorra*] 1. any heavenly body seen as a point of light in the night sky, esp. one that is a distant sun 2. a flat figure with five or six points, representing a star 3. a mark, emblem, etc. resembling such a figure 4. an asterisk 5. *a)* Astrol. a planet, etc. regarded as influencing human fate *b)* [*often pl.*] fate 6. a person who excels, esp. an actor or actress —*vt.* **starred, star'ring** 1. to decorate with stars 2. to mark with stars as a grade of quality 3. to present (a performer) in a leading role —*vi.* to have a leading role —*adj.* 1. excelling [a star athlete] 2. of a star or stars —**star'-less** *adj.* —**star'like'** *adj.*

starboard (stär'bərd) *n.* [< OE. *steoran,* to steer + *bord,* board] the right-hand side of a ship or aircraft as one faces forwards —*adj.* of or on the starboard

starch (stärch) *n.* [< OE. *stearc,* stiff] 1. a white, tasteless, odourless food substance found in potatoes, grain, etc.: it is a carbohydrate 2. a powdered form of this, used in laundering to stiffen cloth, etc. 3. stiff formality —*vt.* to stiffen as with starch

starchy *adj.* **-ier, -iest** 1. of or like starch 2. formal; unbending —**starch'ily** *adv.* —**starch'iness** *n.*

star-crossed (stär'krost) *adj.* ill-fated

stardom *n.* the status of a star of stage, screen, etc.

stare (stāər) *vi.* **stared, star'ing** [OE. *starian*] to look with a steady, fixed gaze, as in wonder, curiosity, etc. —*vt.* to affect in a given way by staring —*n.* a staring look —**stare down** to stare back at (another) until he looks away —**stare one in the face** to be obvious

starfish (stär'fish') *n.* a small star-shaped sea animal with a hard, spiny skeleton

stargaze *vi.* **-gazed', -gaz'ing** 1. to gaze at the stars 2. to daydream —**star'gaz'-er** *n.*

stark (stärk) *adj.* [OE. *stearc*] 1. grimly blunt [stark realism] 2. bleak; desolate 3. sheer; utter [stark terror] 4. sharply outlined 5. [Archaic] stiff or rigid 6. totally naked —*adv.* in a stark way; esp., utterly [stark mad] —**stark'ly** *adv.* —**stark'ness** *n.*

starlet (stär'lit) *n.* a young actress being promoted as a possible future star

starlight *n.* light from the stars

starling (stär'liŋ) *n.* [OE. *stær*] a short-tailed, dark-coloured bird with iridescent plumage

Star of David a six-pointed star formed of two equilateral triangles: a symbol of Judaism

starry (stär'ē) *adj.* **-rier, -riest** 1. shining like stars 2. lighted by or full of stars —**star'riness** *n.*

starry-eyed *adj.* given to naive wishes, romantic dreams, etc.; enthusiastic but gullible

Stars and Stripes the red, white, and blue flag of the United States, with 13 stripes and 50 stars

Star-Spangled Banner the United States national anthem

star-studded *adj.* 1. covered with many stars 2. containing many leading entertainers

start (stärt) *vi.* [OE. *styrtan*] 1. to go into action or motion; begin; commence 2. to make a sudden, involuntary movement, as when startled 3. to spring into being, activity, etc. 4. to be among the beginning entrants in a race, etc. 5. to stick out or seem to stick out —*vt.* 1. to begin doing, set into motion, action, etc. 2. to displace, loosen, etc. 3. to cause to be among those starting in a race, etc. 4. to rouse or flush (game) —*n.* 1. a starting, or beginning 2. *a)* the place or time of a beginning *b)* a lead or other advantage 3. a sudden, brief shock 4. a sudden, startled movement 5. an opportunity to begin a career, etc. 6. [*pl.*] brief bursts of activity: usually in **by fits and starts** —**start out** (or **off**) to begin a journey, action, etc. —**start up** 1. to spring up 2. to cause (an engine, etc.) to begin running

starter *n.* 1. any of various devices for starting an internal-combustion engine 2. one giving the signal to start 3. one starting in a race, etc. 4. the first course of a meal

startle (stärt''l) *vt.* **-tled, -tling** [< ME. *sterten,* to start] to surprise, frighten, or alarm suddenly —*vi.* to be startled —**star'tling** *adj.* —**star'tlingly** *adv.*

star turn the principal performer in an entertainment, esp. in a variety show

starve (stärv) *vi.* **starved, starv'ing** [OE. *steorfan,* to die] 1. *a)* to die from lack of food *b)* to suffer from hunger *c)* [Colloq.] to be very hungry 2. to suffer great need (with *for*) —*vt.* 1. to cause to starve 2. to force by starving —**starva'tion** *n.*

starveling *n.* a starving person or animal

stash (stash) *vt.* [prob. < STORE & CACHE] [Colloq.] to hide in a secret or safe place —*n.* [Slang] **1.** a place for hiding things **2.** something hidden away

stasis (stā'sis) *n., pl.* -**ses** (-sēz) [Gr.] a stoppage of the flow of a bodily fluid, as of blood

-**stat** (stat) [< Gr.] *a combining form meaning* stationary, making stationary [*thermostat*]

state (stāt) *n.* [< L. *stare*, to stand] **1.** a set of circumstances or attributes characterizing a person or thing; condition **2.** a particular mental or emotional condition [a *state* of bliss] **3.** condition as regards structure, form, etc. **4.** *a*) high rank *b*) ceremonious display; pomp **5.** [*sometimes* S-] a body of people politically organized under one government within a definite territory **6.** [*sometimes* S-] any of the political units together constituting a federal government **7.** the territory of a state **8.** civil government [church and *state*] —*adj.* **1.** ceremonial **2.** [*sometimes* S-] of the government or a state —*vt.* **stat'ed, stat'ing 1.** to establish by specifying **2.** to set forth or express in a specific way —**in** (or **into**) **a state** [Colloq.] in (or into) an agitated emotional condition —**lie in state** to be displayed formally to the public before burial —**the States** the United States of America

state apartment a public room in a palace used for social receptions on ceremonial occasions

stateless *adj.* without a nationality

stately *adj.* -**lier, -liest** dignified, imposing, or grand —**state'liness** *n.*

stately home a large house, esp. one open to the public

statement *n.* **1.** *a*) a stating *b*) the thing stated **2.** a summary of a financial account

State Registered Nurse a nurse who has completed extensive training

stateroom *n.* **1.** a private cabin on a ship **2.** *same as* STATE APARTMENT

state school any school which is maintained by the state

statesman *n.* one who is wise and experienced in the business of government —**states'manlike'** *adj.* —**states'man-ship'** *n.*

static (stat'ik) *adj.* [< Gr. *statikos,* causing to stand] *adj.* **1.** at rest; stationary **2.** of masses, forces, etc. at rest or in equilibrium : opposed to DYNAMIC **3.** *Elec.* designating, of, or producing stationary electrical charges, as from friction **4.** *Radio* of or having to do with static Also **stat'i-cal** —*n.* **1.** electrical discharges in the atmosphere that interfere with radio or TV reception, etc. **2.** interference produced by such discharges —**stat'ically** *adv.*

static electricity electricity at rest, as opposed to dynamic or current electricity

statics *n.pl.* [*with sing. v.*] [SEE STATIC] the branch of mechanics dealing with bodies, masses, or forces at rest or in equilibrium

station (stā'shən) *n.* [< L. *stare,* to stand] **1.** the place where a person or thing stands or is located, esp. an assigned post **2.** *a*) a regular stopping place, as on a bus route or railway *b*) the building at such a place **3.** social standing **4.** a place equipped for radio or television transmission **5.** in Australia, a sheep run or cattle ranch —*vt.* to assign to a station; post

stationary (stā'shə nər ē) *adj.* [see STATION] **1.** not moving or movable; fixed **2.** unchanging in condition, value, etc. **3.** not itinerant

stationer (stā'shə nər) *n.* [< see STATION] a person who sells office supplies, greeting cards, some books, etc.

Stationer's Hall the hall of the old Company of Stationers who formerly registered every book, etc. published in Britain

stationery *n.* [see STATION] writing materials; specif., paper and envelopes used for letters

Stationery Office in Britain, the government department responsible for the publication of all official reports

stationmaster *n.* an official in charge of a railway station

station sergeant a police sergeant in charge of a police station

station wagon [U.S.] an estate car

statism (stāt'iz'm) *n.* the doctrine of vesting economic control in a centralized state government

statistic (stə tis'tik) *n.* a statistical item or element

statistical *adj.* of, having to do with, consisting of, or based on statistics —**statis'tically** *adv.*

statistician (stat'is tish'ən) *n.* an expert in statistics

statistics (stə tis'tiks) *n.pl.* [< L. *status,* STATE] **1.** numerical facts assembled and classified so as to present significant information **2.** [*with sing. v.*] the science of compiling such facts

statuary (stat'yoo wər ē) *n., pl.* -**aries 1.** statues collectively **2.** the art of making statues —*adj.* of or suitable for statues

statue (stach'oo) *n.* [< L. *statuere,* to place] the form of a person or animal carved in stone, etc., modelled in clay, etc., or cast in bronze, etc.

statuesque (stə tyoo esk') *adj.* **1.** like a statue **2.** tall and well-proportioned —**stat'uesque'ly** *adv.*

statuette *n.* (-et') a small statue

stature (stach'ər) *n.* [< L. *statura*] **1.** the standing height of the body **2.** growth or level of attainment [moral *stature*]

status (stāt'əs) *n., pl.* -**tuses** [L.: see STATE] **1.** social or professional position, rank, etc., esp. in relation to that of others **2.** high position; prestige **3.** condition with regard to law [the *status* of a minor] **4.** state or condition, as of affairs

status quo (kwō') [L., the state in which] the existing state of affairs : also **status in quo**

status symbol a possession, practice, etc. regarded as a mark of social status

statute (stat′tyo͞ot) *n.* [see STATUE] 1. an established rule 2. a law passed by a legislative body

statute law   law established by a legislative body

statutory (stat′tyo͞ o tər ē) *adj.* 1. fixed or authorized by statute 2. declared by statute to be punishable : said of an offence

staunch (stônch) *vt.* [< OFr. *estanchier*] 1. to stop or check (the flow of blood etc.) from (a wound, etc.) 2. to stop (a drain of resources, etc.) —*adj.* 1. firm; steadfast [a *staunch* supporter] 2. strong; solid 3. watertight; seaworthy   Also **stanch**   For the *adj.*, **staunch** is usually used; for the *v.*, either **staunch** or **stanch** is used —**staunch′ly** *adv.* —**staunch′ness** *n.*

STAVE

stave (stāv) *n.* [see STAFF] 1. one of the thin, shaped strips of wood that form the wall of a barrel, bucket, etc. 2. a stanza 3. *Music* same as STAFF —*vt.* **staved** or **stove, stav′ing** 1. to puncture or smash, esp. by breaking in staves 2. to furnish with staves —**stave in** to break or crush inwards —**stave off** to ward off or hold off

staves *n.* 1. alt. pl. of STAFF 2. pl. of STAVE

stay[1] (stā) *n.* [OE. *stæg*] a heavy rope or cable used as a brace, as for a mast of a ship

stay[2] *n.* [MFr. *estaie*] 1. a support; prop 2. a strip of stiffening material used in a corset, shirt collar, etc. —*vt.* to support, or prop up

stay[3] *vi.* **stayed, stay′ing** [< L. *stare*, to stand] 1. to continue in the place or condition specified; remain 2. to live, esp. temporarily 3. to stop; halt 4. to pause; wait 5. [Colloq.] to endure; last —*vt.* 1. to stop or check 2. to hinder, impede, or detain 3. to postpone (legal action) 4. to satisfy for a time (thirst, etc.) 5. *a*) to remain through (often with *out*) *b*) to be able to last through —*n.* 1. the action of remaining, or the time spent, in a place 2. a postponement in legal action —**stay for** [Colloq.] remain waiting for —**stay put** [Colloq.] to remain in place or unchanged

stay-at-home *adj.*   domesticated; untravelled —*n.*   a person who is unadventurous

staying power   ability to last or endure; endurance

staysail (stā′s'l) *n.* a sail, esp. a triangular sail, fastened on a stay

STD 1. [L. *Sacrae Theologiae Doctor*] Doctor of Sacred Theology 2. Subscriber Trunk Dialling

stead (sted) *n.* [OE. *stede*] the place or position of a person or thing as filled by a substitute —**stand (one) in good stead** to be of use, advantage, etc. to (one)

steadfast (sted′fəst) *adj.* [OE. *stedefæste*] 1. firm; fixed 2. constant —**stead′fast′ly** *adv.* —**stead′fast′ness** *n.*

steady (sted′ē) *adj.* **-ier, -iest** [see STEAD] 1. that does not shake, totter, etc.; firm 2. constant, regular, or continuous 3. constant in behaviour, loyalty, etc. 4. habitual or regular 5. calm and controlled [*steady* nerves] 6. sober; reliable —*vt., vi.* **stead′ied, stead′ying** to make or become steady —*n.* [Colloq.] one's regular boyfriend or girlfriend —**go steady** [Colloq.] to date one person regularly —**stead′ily** *adv.* —**stead′iness** *n.*

steady-state *adj.* of a system, etc. that does not change with time

steak (stāk) *n.* [< ON. *steikja*, to roast on a spit]   a slice of meat, esp. beef, or fish, cut thick for grilling or frying

steakhouse *n.*   a restaurant that specializes in steaks

steal (stēl) *vt.* **stole, stol′en, steal′ing** [OE. *stælan*] 1. to take (another's property, etc.) dishonestly, esp. in a secret manner 2. to take slyly, etc. [to *steal* a look] 3. to gain slyly or artfully [he *stole* her heart] 4. to move, put, or convey stealthily (*in, into, from, away,* etc.) —*vi.* 1. to be a thief 2. to move, stealthily, quietly, etc. —*n.* [U.S. Colloq.] a bargain —**steal a march on** to obtain an advantage, esp. by a trick —**steal′er** *n.*

stealth (stelth) *n.* [< ME. *stelen*, to steal] secret or furtive action or behaviour —**stealth′ily** *adv.* —**stealth′iness** *n.* —**stealth′y** *adj.*

steam (stēm) *n.* [OE.] 1. water as converted into a vapour by being heated to the boiling point 2. condensed water vapour 3. the power of steam under pressure 4. [Colloq.] driving force; energy —*adj.* 1. heated, operated, etc. by steam 2. containing or conducting steam —*vi.* 1. to give off steam 2. to become covered with condensed steam, as a window (usually with *up*) 3. to generate steam 4. to move by steam power 5. [Colloq.] to proceed quickly [to *steam* ahead] —*vt.* to expose to the action of steam, as in cooking —**let** (or **blow**) **off steam** [Colloq.] to release pent-up emotion

steam engine   an engine using steam under pressure to supply mechanical energy

steamer *n.* 1. something operated by steam power, as a steamship 2. a container in which things are cooked, cleaned, etc. with steam

steam iron   an electric iron that releases steam onto material being pressed

steam radio [Colloq.] radio broadcasting considered as old-fashioned in comparison with television

steamroller *n.* 1. a heavy, steam-driven roller used in road building 2. crushing power or relentless force —*vt., vi.* to crush, override, or force as (with) a steamroller —*adj.* relentlessly overpowering

steamship *n.* a ship driven by steam power

steam train a train powered by steam rather than diesel or electricity

steamy *adj.* -ier, -lest 1. of or like steam 2. filled with steam —**steam′ily** *adv.* —**steam′iness** *n.*

stearic acid (stē ar′ik) [< Gr. *stear,* tallow] a colourless, fatty acid found in many animal and vegetable fats, and used in making candles, soaps, etc.

stearin (stēar′in) *n.* [see prec.] a white, crystalline substance found in the solid portion of most animal and vegetable fats: also **ste′arine**

steatite (stē′ə tīt′) *n.* [< Gr. *stear,* tallow] a compact, massive variety of talc; soapstone

steed (stēd) *n.* [OE. *steda*] a horse: literary term

steel (stēl) *n.* [OE. *stiele*] 1. a hard, tough metal composed of iron alloyed with carbon and often with other metals, as nickel, to produce hardness, etc. 2. something made of steel; specif., [Poet.] a sword or dagger 3. great strength or hardness 4. [Canad.] a railway track or line —*adj.* of or like steel —*vt.* to make hard, tough, unfeeling, etc. —**steel′iness** *n.* —**steel′y** *adj.*

steel band a percussion band, originating in Trinidad, using steel oil drums

steel wool long, hairlike shavings of steel in a pad or ball, used for scouring, smoothing, and polishing

steelworks *n.* a place where steel is made —**steel′work′er** *n.*

steelyard *n.* [STEEL & YARD¹] a balance scale consisting of a metal arm along which a weight is moved

steep¹ (stēp) *adj.* [OE. *steap,* lofty] 1. having a sharp rise or slope; precipitous 2. [Colloq.] a) excessive b) extreme —*n.* a steep slope —**steep′ly** *adv.* —**steep′ness** *n.*

steep² *vt.* [ME. *stepen*] to immerse, saturate, imbue, etc. —*n.* 1. a steeping 2. liquid in which something is steeped

steepen *vt., vi.* to make or become steep or steeper

steeple (stē′p'l) *n.* [OE. *stepel*] a tower rising above the main structure of a church, usually capped with a spire —**stee′pled** *adj.*

steeplechase *n.* 1. a horse race run over a prepared course obstructed with ditches, hedges, etc. 2. a similar race on foot —*vi.* -chased′, -chas′ing —**stee′plechas′er** *n.*

steeplejack *n.* a person whose work is building, painting, or repairing steeples, smokestacks, etc.

steer¹ (stēr) *vt.* [OE. *stieran*] 1. to guide (a ship, etc.) by means of a rudder 2. to direct the course of (a motor car, etc.) 3. to follow (a course) —*vi.* 1. to steer a ship, motor car, etc. 2. to be steered

3. to set and follow a course —**steer clear of** to avoid

steer² *n.* [OE. *steor*] 1. a castrated male of the cattle family 2. loosely, any male of beef cattle

steerage *n.* 1. a steering 2. formerly, a section in some ships occupied by passengers paying the lowest fare

steering committee a committee, as of a legislative body, appointed to arrange the order of business

steering wheel a wheel turned by the driver of a vehicle to change direction

steersman *n.* a person who steers a ship or boat

stein (stīn) *n.* [G.] an earthenware beer mug

stele (stē′lē) *n.* [< Gr. *stēlē,* a slab] an upright stone slab with an inscription or design, as a grave marker: also **stela** (stē′lə)

stellar (stel′ər) *adj.* [< L. *stella,* a star] of the stars or a star

stem¹ (stem) *n.* [OE. *stemn*] 1. the main stalk of a tree, shrub, or other plant bearing the leaves, flowers, etc. 2. any stalk supporting leaves, flowers, or fruit 3. a stemlike part, as of a pipe, goblet, etc. 4. the thick stroke of a letter, or vertical line of a musical note 5. the prow of a ship; bow 6. a branch of a family 7. the part of a word to which inflectional endings are added —*vt.* stemmed, stem′ming 1. to make headway against 2. to remove the stem from (a fruit, etc.) —*vi.* to originate or derive —**from stem to stern** 1. from one end of a ship to another 2. through the length of anything —**stem′less** *adj.*

stem² *vt.* stemmed, stem′ming [ON. *stemma*] to stop or check; esp., to dam (a river, etc.), or to stop or check as if by damming

stench (stench) *n.* [OE. *stenc*] an offensive smell; stink

STENCIL

stencil (sten′s'l) *vt.* -cilled, -cilling [< L. *scintilla,* a spark] to make, mark, or paint with a stencil —*n.* 1. a thin sheet, as of paper or metal, perforated or cut through in such a way that when ink, paint, etc. is applied to the sheet, the patterns, designs, letters, etc. are marked on the surface beneath 2. a design, etc. so made

sten gun a lightweight machine gun

stenographer (stə nog′rə fər) *n.* a person skilled in stenography

stenography (stə nog′rə fē) *n.* [< Gr. *stenos,* narrow + -GRAPHY] the writing of dictation, etc. in shorthand and later transcribing it, as on a typewriter —**stenographic** (sten'əgraf'ik) *adj.*

stentor (sten'tôr) *n.* [< *Stentor*, a Greek herald in the *Iliad*] [*sometimes* S-] a person having a very loud voice

stentorian (sten tôr'ē ən) *adj.* very loud

step (step) *n.* [OE. *stepe*] 1. the act of moving and placing the foot, as in walking 2. the distance covered by such a movement 3. a short distance 4. a manner of stepping; gait 5. a sequence of movements in dancing 6. the sound of stepping 7. a footprint 8. a rest for the foot in climbing, as a stair or the rung of a ladder 9. [*pl.*] a flight of stairs or a step ladder 10. a degree; level; stage 11. any of a series of acts, processes, etc. —*vi.* stepped, step'ping 1. to move by executing a step 2. to walk a short distance 3. to move quickly: often with *along* 4. to come or enter (*into* a situation, etc.) 5. to put or press the foot down (*on* something) —*vt.* 1. *a)* to set (the foot) down *b)* to move across or over by foot 2. to measure by taking steps: usually with *off* 3. to arrange in a series of degrees —**break step** 1. to stop marching in cadence 2. to cease to conform —**in step** 1. keeping to a set rhythm, as in marching 2. in conformity or agreement —**keep step** to stay in step —**out of step** not in step —**step by step** gradually —**step down** to resign (*from* an office, etc.) —**step in** to start to participate; intervene —**step on it** [Colloq.] to go faster —**step out** 1. to go outside (a building), esp. briefly 2. to begin to walk more quickly 3. to go out for a good time —**step up** 1. to approach 2. to advance 3. to increase, as in rate —**take steps** to adopt certain measures —**watch one's step** [Colloq.] to be careful: also **mind one's step**

stepbrother *n.* one's stepparent's son by a former marriage

stepchild *n.* [< OE. *steop-*, orphaned] a child (**stepdaughter** or **stepson**) that one's husband or wife had by a former marriage

stephanotis (stef'ə nōt'is) *n.* [< Gr. *stephanos*, crown] a climbing plant with white, waxy flowers

stepladder (step'lad'ər) *n.* a four-legged ladder having broad, flat steps

stepparent *n.* [see STEPCHILD] the person (**stepfather** or **stepmother**) who has married one's parent after the death or divorce of the other parent

steppe (step) *n.* [< Russ. *step'*] any of the great plains of SE Europe and Asia, having few trees

steppingstone (step'iŋ stōn') *n.* 1. a stone used to step on, as in crossing a stream 2. a means of advancement

stepsister *n.* one's stepparent's daughter by a former marriage

-ster (stər) [OE. *-estre*] a suffix meaning a person who is, does, or is associated with [*punster, gangster*]

stere (stēər) *n.* [< Gr. *stereos*, cubic] a cubic metre

stereo (ster'ē ō') *n., pl.* **-os'** 1. a stereophonic record player, radio, etc. 2. a stereoscope or a stereoscopic picture, etc. 3. shortened form of STEREOTYPE —*adj.* shortened form of STEREOPHONIC

stereo- [< Gr. *stereos*, hard] a combining form meaning solid, firm, three-dimensional [*stereoscope*]

stereophonic (ster'ē ə fon'ik) *adj.* [prec. + PHONIC] of sound reproduction, as in films, records, etc., using two or more channels to reproduce through separate speakers a blend of sounds from separate sources —**ster'eophon'ically** *adv.*

stereoscope (ster'ē ə skōp') *n.* [STEREO- + -SCOPE] an instrument that gives a three-dimensional effect to photographs viewed through it —**ster'eoscop'ic** (-skop'ik) *adj.*

stereotype (ster'ē ə tīp') *n.* [see STEREO- & -TYPE] 1. a printing plate cast in type metal from a mould (*matrix*), as of a page of set type 2. a fixed idea or popular conception —*vt.* **-typed'**, **-typ'ing** to make a stereotype of

stereotyped *adj.* 1. hackneyed; trite; not original 2. printed from stereotype plates

sterile (ster'il) *adj.* [L. *sterilis*] 1. incapable of producing others of its kind; barren 2. producing little or nothing 3. free from living microorganisms —**sterility** (stə ril'ə tē) *n.*

sterilize (ster'ə līz') *vt.* **-lized'**, **-liz'ing** 1. to make incapable of producing others of its kind 2. to free from living microorganisms —**ster'iliza'tion** *n.* —**ster'iliz'er** *n.*

sterling (stur'liŋ) *n.* [< ?] 1. British money 2. sterling silver or articles made of it —*adj.* 1. of or payable in British money 2. of standard quality: said of silver that is at least 92.5 percent pure 3. worthy; excellent

sterling area a group of countries that use sterling as a medium for international payments

stern[1] (sturn) *adj.* [OE. *styrne*] 1. severe; strict 2. grim; forbidding 3. unrelenting; firm —**stern'ly** *adv.* —**stern'ness** *n.*

stern[2] *n.* [< ON. *styra*, to steer] 1. the rear end of a ship, boat, etc. 2. the rear end of anything

sternum (stur'nəm) *n., pl.* **ster'nums, ster'na** [< Gr. *sternon*] a thin, flat structure of bone to which most of the ribs are attached in the front of the chest; breastbone

sternward (sturn'wərd) *adv., adj.* towards the stern; astern: also **stern'wards** *adv.*

steroid (stēar'oid) *n.* [see STEROL] any of a group of compounds including the sterols, sex hormones, etc.

sterol (stēar'ol) *n.* [< (CHOLE)STEROL] any of a group of solid cyclic alcohols, as cholesterol, found in plant and animal tissues

stertorous (stur'tə rəs) *adj.* [< L. *stertere*, to snore] characterized by loud, laboured breathing

stet (stet) [L.] let it stand: a printer's term used to indicate that matter previously struck out is to remain —*vt.* **stet′ted, stet′-ting** to mark with "stet"

STETHOSCOPE

stethoscope (steth′ə skōp′) *n.* [< Gr. *stēthos,* the chest + -SCOPE] *Med.* a hearing instrument placed against the body for examining the heart, lungs, etc. by listening to the sounds they make —**steth′o-scop′ic** (-skop′ik) *adj.*
Stetson (stet′s′n) *n.* [U.S.] [*often* s-] a man's hat, worn esp. by cowboys, usually of felt, with a broad brim and a high crown
stevedore (stē′və dôr′) *n.* [< L. *stipare,* to cram] a person employed at loading and unloading ships
stew (styo͞o) *vt.* [ult. < L. *ex,* out + Gr. *typhos,* steam] to cook by simmering slowly for a long time —*vi.* **1.** to undergo cooking in this way **2.** [Colloq.] to swelter —*n.* **1.** a dish, esp. of meat and vegetables, cooked by stewing **2.** a state of anxiety or worry, esp. in phrase **in a stew** —**stew in one's own juice** to suffer from one's own actions
steward (styo͞o′ərd) *n.* [< OE. *stig,* enclosure + *weard,* keeper] **1.** a person in charge of the affairs of a large household, who supervises the kitchen and servants, manages the accounts, etc. **2.** a person variously responsible for the food and drink, etc. in a club, restaurant, etc. **3.** a person in charge of arrangements for a ball, race, etc. **4.** an attendant on a ship, aircraft, etc. who looks after the passengers' comfort —**stew′ardship** *n.*
stewardess *n.* a woman steward (esp. sense 4)
stewed (styo͞od) *adj.* **1.** cooked by stewing, as food **2.** [Slang] drunk; intoxicated **3.** tasting bitter through infusing too long : said of tea
stick (stik) *n.* [OE. *sticca*] **1.** a twig or small branch broken or cut off **2.** a long, slender piece of wood, as a staff, club, cane, etc. **3.** a stalk, as of celery **4.** something shaped like a stick **5.** a separate article [every *stick* of furniture] **6.** an implement for striking a ball, puck, etc. [a hockey *stick*] **7.** punishment, esp. beating **8.** [*usually pl.*] something made of sticks, as a racing hurdle **9.** [Colloq.] a dull or stupid person —*vt.* **stuck, stick′-ing 1.** to pierce, as with a pointed instrument **2.** to pierce something with (a knife, pin, etc.) **3.** to thrust or push (in, out, etc.) **4.** to fasten or attach by gluing, pinning, etc. **5.** to transfix or impale **6.** to obstruct, bog down, etc.; also, to detain, delay, etc. [the wheels were *stuck,*

he was *stuck* in town] **7.** [Colloq.] to place; put; set **8.** [Slang] to impose something unpleasant, as paying a bill [I was *stuck* with the bill] **9.** [Slang] endure; bear; tolerate —*vi.* **1.** to be fixed by a pointed end, as a nail, etc. **2.** to be attached by adhesion; adhere **3.** to remain; stay [to *stick* at home] **4.** to keep or stay close [*stick* to the trail] **5.** to persevere [to *stick* at a job] **6.** to remain firm; endure **7.** to become fixed, blocked, embedded, jammed, etc. **8.** to be puzzled **9.** to hesitate; scruple [he'll *stick* at nothing] **10.** to protrude (with *out, up,* etc.) —**stick around** [Slang] to stay near at hand —**stick by** (or to) to remain loyal to —**stick it out** [Slang] to endure something to the end —**stick out a mile** [Colloq.] to be very obvious —**stick to someone's fingers** [Colloq.] to be stolen, embezzled, etc.: usually said of money —**stick up** [Slang] to commit armed robbery upon —**stick up for** [Colloq.] to uphold; defend —**stuck with** [Colloq.] unable to dispose of —**the sticks** [Colloq.] the rural districts
sticker *n.* a person or thing that sticks; specif., a gummed label
sticking plaster adhesive material for covering a slight wound, usually a thin cloth with gum on one side
stick insect an insect resembling a twig
stick-in-the-mud *n.* [Colloq.] a person who resists change or progress
stickleback (stik′'l bak′) *n.* [< OE. *sticel,* a prick] a small, scaleless fish with sharp spines
stickler (stik′lər) *n.* [< OE. *stihtan,* arrange] a person who insists on strict observance of something [a *stickler* for discipline]
stick-up (stik′up′) *n.* slang term for HOLDUP (sense 2)
sticky *adj.* **-ier, -iest 1.** adhesive; clinging **2.** covered with an adhesive substance **3.** [Colloq.] hot and humid **4.** [Colloq.] difficult; troublesome **5.** [Colloq.] very unpleasant, esp. in to **come to a sticky end** —**stick′iness** *n.*
sticky wicket a difficult or awkward situation
stiff (stif) *adj.* [OE. *stif*] **1.** hard to bend; rigid; firm **2.** hard to move or operate **3.** sore or limited in movement : said of joints or muscles **4.** not fluid or loose; thick [a *stiff* sauce] **5.** moving swiftly, as a breeze **6.** containing much alcohol : said of a drink **7.** harsh [a *stiff* punishment] **8.** difficult [a *stiff* climb] **9.** constrained or awkward **10.** resolute or stubborn, as a person, a fight, etc. **11.** [Colloq.] high [a *stiff* price] —*adv.* **1.** to a stiff condition **2.** [Colloq.] completely [scared *stiff*] —*n.* [U.S. Slang] a corpse —**stiff′-ly** *adv.* —**stiff′ness** *n.*
stiffen *vt., vi.* to make or become stiff or stiffer
stiff-necked *adj.* stubborn; obstinate
stifle (stī′f'l) *vt.* **-fled, -fling** [< MFr. *estouffer,* smother] **1.** to suffocate; smother **2.** to suppress or check —*vi.*

to suffer or die from lack of air —**sti′‑fling** *adj.*

stigma (stig′mə) *n., pl.* **‑mas;** also, and for 2 & 3 usually, **stig′mata** [L. < Gr.] **1.** a mark of disgrace or reproach **2.** a small mark, scar, etc., as a pore, on the surface of a plant or animal **3.** [*pl.*] marks resembling the Crucifixion wounds of Jesus **4.** *Bot.* the upper tip of the style of a flower, on which pollen falls —**stig‑mat′ic** (‑mat′ik) *adj.*

stigmatize *vt.* **‑tized′, ‑tiz′ing** **1.** to mark with a stigma **2.** to mark as disgraceful —**stig′matiza′tion** *n.*

stile (stīl) *n.* [< OE. *stigan*, to climb] a step or set of steps used in climbing over a fence or wall

stiletto (sti let′ō) *n., pl.* **‑tos, ‑toes** [It. < L. *stilus*, style] **1.** a small dagger with a slender, tapering blade **2.** a sharp instrument for making eyelet holes **3.** a high, very thin heel on a woman's shoe: also **stiletto heel**

still¹ (stil) *adj.* [OE. *stille*] **1.** not moving; motionless **2.** calm; tranquil **3.** without sound; silent **4.** soft, or low in sound **5.** not effervescent: said of wine, etc. **6.** *Cinema* designating a single posed photograph for use as in publicity —*n.* **1.** silence; quiet [*the still of the night*] **2.** a still photograph —*adv.* **1.** at or up to the time indicated **2.** even; yet [*still* colder] **3.** nevertheless; yet [*rich but still* unhappy] —*conj.* nevertheless; yet —*vt., vi.* to make or become still —**still′ness** *n.*

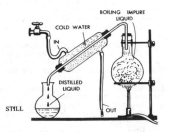

STILL

still² *n.* [< obs. *still*, DISTIL] an apparatus used for distilling liquids, esp. spirits

stillborn *adj.* **1.** dead at birth **2.** unsuccessful from the beginning —**still′‑birth′** *n.*

still life an arrangement of objects, as fruit in a bowl, flowers in a vase, etc. as the subject of a painting, drawing, etc. —**still′‑life′** *adj.*

stillroom *n.* **1.** a room containing a still **2.** a housekeeper's storeroom for preserves, etc.

stilt (stilt) *n.* [ME. *stilte*] **1.** either of a pair of poles, each with a footrest somewhere along its length, used for walking **2.** any of a number of long posts used to hold a building, etc. above the ground

stilted (stil′tid) *adj.* **1.** artificially dignified; pompous **2.** raised on stilts —**stilt′edly** *adv.* —**stilt′edness** *n.*

Stilton (cheese) (stil′t'n) [< *Stilton*, in England] a rich, crumbly cheese with veins of blue-green mould

stimulant (stim′yoo lant) *n.* anything, as a drug, that stimulates —*adj.* stimulating

stimulate (stim′yoo lāt) *vt.* **‑lat′ed, ‑lat′‑ing** [< ff.] **1.** to stir up or spur on; arouse; excite **2.** to invigorate **3.** *Med., Physiol.* to excite (an organ, etc.) to increased activity —**stim′ula′tor** *n.* —**stim′ula′tion** *n.* —**stim′ulative** *adj., n.*

stimulus (stim′yoo ləs) *n., pl.* **‑uli′** (‑lī′) [L., a goad] something that stirs to action; incentive

stimy (stī′mē) *n., pl.* **‑mies,** *vt.* **‑mied, ‑mying** same as STYMIE

sting (stiŋ) *vt.* **stung, sting′ing** [OE. *stingan*] **1.** to prick or wound with a sting **2.** to cause sharp, sudden, smarting pain to **3.** to cause to suffer mentally **4.** to stimulate suddenly and sharply **5.** [Slang] to cheat; esp., to overcharge —*vi.* **1.** to use a sting **2.** to cause or feel sharp, smarting pain —*n.* **1.** the act or power of stinging **2.** a pain or wound resulting from stinging **3.** a sharp-pointed organ, as in insects, used to prick or wound —**sting′er** *n.* —**sting′ingly** *adv.*

stinging nettle a nettle that stings

stingray *n.* a large ray (fish) having a whiplike tail with a sharp spine or spines that can inflict painful wounds

stingy (stin′jē) *adj.* **‑gier, ‑giest** [akin to STING] **1.** miserly **2.** less than needed or expected —**stin′giness** *n.*

stink (stiŋk) *vi.* **stank** or **stunk, stunk, stink′ing** [OE. *stincan*] **1.** to give off a strong, bad smell **2.** to be offensive or hateful **3.** [Slang] to be no good —*vt.* [Slang] to smell; notice the stink of —*n.* **1.** a strong, bad smell; stench **2.** [Slang] a strong public reaction, as of outrage **3.** [*pl.*] [Colloq.] chemistry —**stink out** to drive out by a strong, bad smell

stink bomb a device made to burn or explode and give off an offensive smell

stinker *n.* **1.** a person or thing that stinks **2.** [Slang] *a)* a person regarded with disgust *b)* a difficult task, problem, etc.

stinking *adj.* **1.** that stinks **2.** [Slang] *a)* very bad, unsatisfactory, etc. *b)* offensive, disgusting, etc. —*adv.* [Slang] to an excessive degree —**stink′ingly** *adv.*

stinkwood *n.* a S African hardwood of great value, used esp. for furniture

stint (stint) *vt.* [OE. *styntan*, to blunt] to limit to a certain, usually small, quantity or share —*vi.* to be sparing in giving or using —*n.* **1.** restriction; limit **2.** a task to be done —**stint′er** *n.*

stipend (stī′pend) *n.* [< L. *stips*, small coin + *pendere*, to pay] a regular or fixed payment, as a salary, esp. of a clergyman

stipendiary (stī pen′dē ər ē) *adj.* receiving, or performing services for, a stipend —*n., pl.* **‑aries** a person who receives a stipend

stipple (stip′'l) *vt.* **‑pled, ‑pling** [< Du. *stippel*, a speckle] **1.** to paint, draw, engrave, or apply in small dots **2.** to form a roughened pattern on (paint, plaster, etc.) —*n.* **1.** the art of painting, drawing, etc. in dots **2.** the effect so produced Also **stip′pling** *n.*

stipulate (stip′yoolāt′) *vt.* **-lat′ed, -lat′ing** [< L. *stipulari,* to bargain] **1.** to specify as an essential condition of an agreement **2.** to arrange definitely, as in a contract —*vi.* to make a specific demand (*for* something) as a condition of an agreement —**stip′ula′tion** *n.* —**stip′-ula′tor** *n.*

stipule (stip′yool) *n.* [< L. *stipula,* a stalk] either of a pair of small, leaflike parts at the base of some leafstalks —**stip′u-lar** (-yoo lər) *adj.* —**stip′ulat′ed** *adj.*

stir[1] (stur) *vt.* **stirred, stir′ring** [OE. *styrian*] **1.** to mix (a liquid, etc.) by moving a spoon, etc. around **2.** to move, esp. slightly **3.** to move deeply **4.** to make move or be active **5.** to rouse from sleep, lethargy, etc. **6.** to provoke (often with *up*) —*vi.* **1.** to move, esp. slightly **2.** to be busy and active **3.** to begin to show signs of activity —*n.* **1.** a stirring, or the sound of this **2.** movement; activity **3.** excitement or commotion —**stir one′s stumps** [Colloq.] to move, esp. faster —**stir′rer** *n.*

stir[2] *n.* [< ?] [Slang] a prison

stirk (sturk) *n.* [< OE. *stirc*] [Dial.] a bullock or heifer

stirring (stur′iŋ) *adj.* **1.** active; busy **2.** moving; rousing

stirrup (stir′əp) *n.* [OE. *stigrap*] a flat-bottomed ring hung by a strap (**stirrup leather**) from a saddle and used as a footrest

stirrup cup a drink taken by a departing guest, esp. one on horseback

stirrup pump a hand pump for putting out fires, set in a bucket and held by a stirrup or bracket, for one foot

stitch (stich) *n.* [OE. *stice,* a puncture] **1.** a single complete in-and-out movement of a threaded needle in sewing **2.** a single loop of yarn worked off a needle in knitting, etc. **3.** a loop, etc. made by stitching **4.** a particular kind of stitch **5.** a sudden, sharp pain, as in the side **6.** a piece, as of clothing [not wearing a *stitch*] —*vi.* to make stitches; sew —*vt.* to fasten, repair, adorn, etc. with stitches; sew —**in stitches** laughing uproariously —**stitch′-ing** *n.*

stitchery *n.* [Chiefly U.S.] ornamental needlework

stoat (stōt) *n.* [ME. *stote*] a large European weasel, esp. in its brown summer coat

stock (stok) *n.* [OE. *stocc*] **1.** *a)* the total amount of goods on hand in a store, etc.; inventory *b)* all the animals, equipment, etc. kept on a farm **2.** raw material **3.** *a)* the capital invested in a company or corporation by individuals through the purchase of shares *b)* the certificates showing the amount invested **4.** reputation; estimation **5.** the trunk of a tree **6.** a plant stem into which a graft is inserted **7.** any of certain plants of the cabbage family **8.** *a)* a line of

descent; family *b)* a strain, race, or other related group of animals or plants **9.** a main part, as of an implement, etc., to which the working parts are attached, as the part of a rifle holding the barrel **10.** [*pl.*] *a)* a former instrument of punishment consisting of a wooden frame with holes for confining an offender's ankles and, sometimes, his wrists *b)* a frame of timbers supporting a ship during construction **11.** water in which meat, fish, etc. has been boiled or stewed, used as a base for soup or gravy **12.** a former type of wide, stiff cravat —*vt.* **1.** *a)* to furnish (a farm) with stock or (a shop, etc.) with stock *b)* to supply with [to *stock* a pond with fish] **2.** to keep a supply of, as for future use —*vi.* to put in a stock, or supply (often with *up*) —*adj.* **1.** continually kept in stock [*stock* sizes] **2.** common, hackneyed, or trite **3.** that deals with stock [a *stock* boy] —**in** (or **out of**) **stock** (not) available for sale or use —**on the stocks** in preparation —**take stock 1.** to inventory the stock on hand **2.** to examine the situation before deciding or acting

stockade (sto kād′) *n.* [< Pr. *estaca,* a stake] **1.** a barrier of stakes driven into the ground side by side, for defence against attack **2.** an enclosure made with such stakes —*vt.* **-ad′ed, -ad′ing** to surround with a stockade

stockbreeder (stok′brēd′ər) *n.* a breeder of livestock

stockbroker *n.* a person who acts as an agent for others in buying and selling stocks —**stock′bro′king** *n.*

stock car a passenger motor car of standard make, modified in various ways for use in racing

stock exchange 1. a place where stocks and shares are regularly bought and sold **2.** an association of stockbrokers, esp. [S- E-] the group who occupy the Stock Exchange building in London

stockholder *n.* a person owning stock or shares in a given company

stockinette, stockinet (stok′ə net′) *n.* [prob. < *stocking net*] an elastic, machine-knitted cloth

stocking (stok′iŋ) *n.* [< obs. sense of STOCK] **1.** a closefitting covering, usually knitted, for the foot and, usually, most of the leg **2.** something like this, as a patch of colour on an animal's leg —**in one's stocking feet** wearing no shoes

stocking mask a nylon stocking pulled over a criminal's head for disguise

stock in trade 1. tools, materials, etc. used in carrying on a trade **2.** any of the practices or devices always in use by a person or group

stockist (stok′ist) *n.* one who keeps a supply of certain goods

stockjobber *n.* an operator in the stock exchange who deals only with brokers —**stock′job′bing** *n.*

stock market 1. *same as* STOCK EXCHANGE **2.** the business carried on at a stock exchange **3.** the prices quoted on stocks and shares

stockpile *n.* a supply of goods, etc., stored up in anticipation of future shortage —*vt., vi.* **-piled´, -pil´ing** to accumulate a stockpile (of)

stockpot *n.* a pot used for preparing soup stock

stockroom *n.* a room in which a store of goods, materials, etc. is kept: also **stock room**

stock-still (stok´stil´) *adj.* perfectly motionless

stocktaking *n.* the act of preparing an inventory of goods in a shop, etc.

stocky *adj.* **-ier, -iest** heavily built; sturdy; short and thickest —**stock´iness** *n.*

stockyard *n.* an enclosure with pens, sheds, etc. for cattle, pigs, etc.

stodge (stoj) *n.* [< ?] [Colloq.] **1.** heavy, filling food **2.** a boring person or thing —*vi., vt.* [Colloq.] to cram (oneself) with food

stodgy *adj.* **-ier, -iest** [< prec.] **1.** heavy and uninteresting: said of food **2.** dull; uninteresting **3.** drab, unfashionable, or unattractive —**stodg´ily** *adv.* —**stodg´iness** *n.*

stoep (stoop) *n.* [Du.] in S Africa, a veranda in front of a house

Stoic (stō´ik) *n.* [< Gr. *stoa,* colonnade] **1.** a member of a Greek school of philosophy holding that the wise man should be indifferent to the external world and to passion or emotion **2.** [s-] a stoical person —*adj.* **1.** of the Stoics or their philosophy **2.** [s-] *same as* STOICAL

stoical *adj.* showing indifference to joy, grief, pain, etc. —**sto´ically** *adv.*

Stoicism *n.* **1.** the philosophy of the Stoics **2.** [s-] indifference to pleasure or pain

stoke (stōk) *vt., vi.* **stoked, stok´ing** [< STOKER] **1.** to stir up and feed fuel to (a fire) **2.** to eat large quantities of food

stokehold *n.* **1.** the room containing the boilers on a ship **2.** *same as* STOKEHOLE

stokehole *n.* the opening in a furnace or boiler through which the fuel is put

stoker *n.* [Du. < *stoken,* to poke] a man who tends a furnace, specif. of a steam boiler, as on a ship

STOLE

stole[1] (stōl) *n.* [< Gr. *stolē,* garment] **1.** a woman's long scarf of cloth or fur worn around the shoulders **2.** a long,

decorated strip of cloth worn like a scarf by clergymen

stole[2] *pt.* of STEAL

stolen *pp.* of STEAL

stolid (stol´id) *adj.* [L. *stolidus,* slow] having or showing little or no emotion or sensitivity —**stolidity** (stə lid´ə tē) *n.*

stoma (stō´mə) *n., pl.* **-mata** (-mə tə), **-mas** [< Gr. *stoma,* mouth] a mouth or mouthlike opening in plants, animals, etc.

stomach (stum´ək) *n.* [ult. < Gr. *stoma,* mouth] **1.** the large, saclike organ of vertebrates into which food passes while undergoing digestion **2.** the abdomen, or belly **3.** appetite for food **4.** desire or inclination of any kind —*vt.* **1.** to be able to eat or digest **2.** to tolerate; bear

stomachache *n.* pain in the stomach or abdomen

stomacher *n.* a triangular piece of cloth formerly worn, esp. by women, as a covering for the chest and abdomen

stomach pump a suction pump with a flexible tube that can be placed in the stomach to remove the contents

stomach upset a slight digestive disorder

stomp (stomp) *vt., vi. var.* of STAMP —*n.* formerly, a jazz tune with a lively rhythm and a strong beat

stone (stōn) *n.* [OE. *stan*] **1.** the hard, solid, nonmetallic mineral matter of which rock is composed **2.** a small piece of rock **3.** a piece of rock shaped for some purpose, as a building block or a gravestone **4.** the seed of certain fruits **5.** a precious stone **6.** *pl.* **stone** formerly, a unit of weight equal to 14 pounds **7.** *Med. same as* CALCULUS (sense 2) —*vt.* **stoned, ston´ing** **1.** to throw stones at or kill with stones **2.** to remove the stone from (a peach, etc.) —*adj.* of stone or stoneware —**cast the first stone** to be the first to criticize —**leave no stone unturned** to do everything possible —**stone the crows** [Slang] an expression of surprise

Stone Age the early period in human culture during which stone implements were used

stonechat *n.* a small, insect-eating bird

stone-cold (stōn´kōld´) *adj.* quite or completely cold

stonecrop *n. popular name for* SEDUM

stonecutter *n.* a person or machine that cuts stone and makes it smooth —**stone´-cut´ting** *n.*

stoned *adj.* **1.** having the stones removed **2.** [Slang] *a)* drunk *b)* under the influence of a drug

stone-dead (stōn´ded´) *adj.* completely dead; lifeless

stone-deaf (stōn´def´) *adj.* completely deaf

stone fruit any fruit, as a plum, having a stone

stonemason *n.* a person who cuts stone to shape and uses it in making walls, buildings, etc.

stone's throw a relatively short distance

stonewall (stōn´wôl´) *vi.* **1.** *Cricket* to play a defensive game **2.** [Colloq.] to obstruct a debate, etc., esp. by giving noncommittal answers

stoneware *n.* a coarse, dense pottery containing much silica or sand and flint

stonework *n.* **1.** the art or process of working in stone **2.** something made or built in stone

stony *adj.* **-ier, -iest 1.** covered with or having many stones **2.** *a)* hard *b)* unfeeling; pitiless *c)* cold; fixed —**ston′ily** *adv.* —**ston′iness** *n.*

stony-broke *adj.* [Slang] having no money at all

stood (stood) *pt. & pp. of* STAND

stooge (stōōj) *n.* [< ?] [Colloq.] **1.** an actor who aids a comedian by feeding him lines, etc. **2.** anyone who acts as a foil, underling, etc. —*vi.* **stooged, stoog′ing** [Colloq.] to be a stooge (*for* someone)

stool (stōōl) *n.* [OE. *stol*] **1.** a single seat having no back or arms **2.** *same as* FOOTSTOOL **3.** a water closet **4.** the faecal matter eliminated in a single bowel movement

stool ball an early form of cricket played with a short-handled bat

stool pigeon 1. a pigeon or other bird used as a decoy **2.** [Colloq.] a police informer

stoop¹ (stōōp) *vi.* [OE. *stupian*] **1.** to bend the body forward or in a crouch **2.** to carry the head and shoulders habitually bent forward **3.** to do something beneath one's dignity —*n.* the act or position of stooping the body —**stoop′ingly** *adv.*

stoop² *n.* [Du. *stoep*] [U.S.] a small porch or platform with steps, at the door of a house

stop (stop) *vt.* **stopped, stop′ping** [ult. < Gr. *styppē*, tow fibres] **1.** to cease [*stop* talking] **2.** to cause to cease motion, activity, etc. **3.** to halt the progress of (a person, vehicle, etc.) **4.** to prevent the passage of; block **5.** to block up; obstruct: often with *up* **6.** to close by filling, shutting off, etc. **7.** *a)* to check (a blow, etc.) *b)* to defeat (an opponent) **8.** to fill (a decayed tooth) **9.** to close (a finger hole of a wind instrument) or press down (a violin string, etc.) to produce a desired pitch **10.** to keep from acting, etc.; prevent **11.** to notify one's bank to withhold payment on (one's cheque): also **stop payment** —*vi.* **1.** to cease moving, etc.; halt **2.** to leave off doing something **3.** to cease operating **4.** to come to an end **5.** to stay for a while (often with *at* or *in*) —*n.* **1.** a stopping or being stopped **2.** a finish; end **3.** a stay or brief visit **4.** a place stopped at, as on a bus route **5.** an obstruction, plug, stopper, etc. **6.** a mechanical part that stops or regulates motion **7.** a punctuation mark, esp. a full stop **8.** a stopping of a violin string, finger hole of a wind instrument, etc. to produce a desired pitch **9.** *a)* a tuned set of organ pipes, reeds, or electronic devices of the same type and tone quality *b)* a pull, lever, or key for putting such a set into operation **10.** *Phonet. a)* a stopping of the outgoing breath, as with the lips, tongue, or velum *b)* a

consonant formed in this way, as *p, b, k, g, t,* and *d* —*adj.* that stops or is meant to stop [a *stop* signal] —**pull out all the stops** to make an all-out effort —**put a stop to** to cause to cease —**stop at nothing** to be merciless or ruthless —**stop off** to stop for a short visit on the way to a place

stopcock *n.* a valve for stopping or regulating the flow of a fluid, as through a pipe

stopgap *n.* a temporary substitute

stoppage *n.* **1.** an obstructed condition; block **2.** a period during which a factory, etc. is inactive, as because of a strike **3.** [often *pl.*] a deduction at source from wages, esp. for tax purposes

stopper *n.* something inserted to close an opening; plug

stopping train a train which stops at most of the minor stations as well as the major ones

stop press 1. the news put into a newspaper after printing has begun **2.** the space left blank for such news

stopwatch *n.* a watch with a hand that can be started and stopped instantly so as to indicate fractions of seconds

storage (stôr′ij) *n.* **1.** a storing or being stored **2.** *a)* a place or space for storing goods *b)* the cost of keeping goods stored **3.** *same as* MEMORY (sense 7)

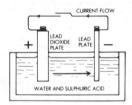

STORAGE BATTERY CELL
(current flowing when charging)

storage battery a battery of rechargeable electrochemical cells for providing electric current

storage heater a heater that stores off-peak electricity, etc. for later use

store (stôr) *vt.* **stored, stor′ing** [< L. *instaurare,* restore] **1.** to put aside for use when needed **2.** to furnish with a supply **3.** to put in a warehouse, etc. for safekeeping **4.** to put (information) in a computer memory unit —*n.* **1.** a supply (*of* something) for use when needed; reserve **2.** [*pl.*] supplies, esp. of food, clothing, etc. **3.** a large shop where a variety of goods are regularly offered for sale **4.** a storehouse —**in store** set aside for, or awaiting one in, the future —**set store by** to value; esteem

storehouse *n.* a place where things are stored

storeroom *n.* a room where things are stored

storey (stôr'ē) *n., pl.* **-reys** [see HISTORY: prob. < "storied" windows] 1. a horizontal division of a building extending from a floor to the ceiling directly above [*ten storeys tall*] 2. all the rooms on the same level of a building

storied *adj.* [< STORY] 1. ornamented with designs showing scenes in history, etc. 2. famous in story or history

stork (stôrk) *n.* [OE. *storc*] a large, long-legged wading bird, having a long neck and bill

storm (stôrm) *n.* [OE.] 1. a disturbance of the atmosphere with a strong wind, and usually rain, snow, thunder, etc. 2. any heavy fall of snow, rain, etc. 3. anything resembling a storm 4. a strong emotional outburst 5. a strong disturbance of a political or social nature 6. *a*) a discharge or shower, as of missiles *b*) a violent outbreak, as of abuse 7. a sudden, strong attack on a fortified place —*vi.* 1. to rage; rant 2. to move violently [*to storm* into a room] 3. to blow violently, rain, snow, etc. —*vt.* to capture or attempt to capture (a fortified place) with a sudden, strong attack

storm centre 1. the shifting centre of a cyclone 2. a centre or focus of trouble or disturbance

storm door (or **window**) an extra door (or window) outside the ordinary one as added protection

storm trooper a member of Hitler's Nazi party militia

stormy *adj.* **-ier, -iest** 1. of or characterized by storms 2. violent, raging, etc.

stormy petrel 1. a small petrel whose presence is thought to warn of coming storms: also **storm petrel** 2. a person thought to bring trouble wherever he goes

story (stôr'ē) *n., pl.* **-ries** [see HISTORY] 1. the telling of an event or series of events; account; narration 2. an anecdote or joke 3. a fictitious literary composition shorter than a novel 4. the plot of a novel, play, etc.: also **story line** 5. [Colloq.] a falsehood 6. a news event or a report of it

storybook *n.* a book of stories, esp. one for children —*adj.* typical of romantic tales in storybooks

stoup (stōōp) *n.* [ON. *staup*] 1. [Obs.] a drinking cup 2. a basin for holy water in a church

stout (stout) *adj.* [OFr. *estout*, bold] 1. rather fat 2. strong; sturdy; firm 3. courageous; brave —*n.* a heavy, dark-brown brew like porter, but with a higher percentage of hops —**stout'ish** *adj.*

stouthearted *adj.* courageous; brave

stove[1] (stōv) *n.* [MDu., a heated room] an apparatus using electricity, gas, coal, etc. for heating, cooking, etc.

stove[2] *alt. pt. & pp. of* STAVE

stovepipe *n.* a metal pipe used to carry off smoke or fumes from a stove

stow (stō) *vt.* [OE. *stow*, a place] 1. to pack in an orderly, compact way 2.

to fill by packing thus 3. [Slang] to stop [*stow* the chatter!] —**stow away** 1. to put or hide away 2. to be a stowaway

stowage *n.* 1. a stowing or being stowed 2. place or room for stowing 3. charges for stowing

stowaway *n.* a person who hides aboard a ship, aircraft, etc. to get free passage, evade port officials, etc.

STP 1. [L. *Sanctae Theologiae Professor*] Professor of Sacred Theology 2. Standard Temperature and Pressure

strabismus (strə biz'məs) *n.* [< Gr. *strabizein*, to squint] a disorder of the muscles of the eyes, as cross-eye, in which both eyes cannot be focused on the same point at the same time

straddle (strad'l) *vt.* **-dled, -dling** [< STRIDE] 1. to place oneself with a leg on either side of 2. to spread (the legs) wide apart —*vi.* 1. to sit, stand, or walk with the legs wide apart 2. to be spread apart: said of the legs —*n.* the act or position of straddling

Stradivarius (strad'ə vãer'ē əs) *n.* a stringed instrument, esp. a violin, made by A. Stradivari or his sons

strafe (sträf) *vt.* **strafed, straf'ing** [< G. *Gott strafe England* (God punish England!)] to attack with machine-gun fire from low-flying aircraft —**straf'er** *n.*

straggle (strag'l) *vi.* **-gled, -gling** [< ?] 1. to stray from the course or wander from the main group 2. to be scattered over a wide area 3. to leave, arrive, etc. at scattered, irregular intervals 4. to hang in an untidy way, as hair —**strag'-gler** *n.* —**strag'gly** *adj.*

straight (strāt) *adj.* [< ME. *strecchen*, to stretch] 1. having the same direction throughout its length [*a straight* line] 2. not crooked, wavy, etc. 3. upright; erect 4. direct, uninterrupted, etc. [*to hold a straight* course] 5. in order; properly arranged, etc. 6. honest; sincere 7. outspoken; frank 8. without anything added; undiluted 9. not qualified [*a straight* denial] 10. serious; without music, dancing, etc.: said of drama 11. [Slang] normal or conventional; specif., not a homosexual, drug addict, etc. —*adv.* 1. in a straight line 2. upright; erectly 3. without detour, delay, etc. —*n.* something straight; specif., *a*) the straight part of a race track *b*) Poker a hand consisting of any five cards in sequence —**go straight** to reform, esp. to abandon former criminal activities —**straight away** (or **off**) at once —**the straight and narrow** (**path**) a strict code of morals

straighten *vt., vi.* to make or become straight —**straighten out** to make or become less confused, easier to deal with, etc.

straight face a facial expression showing no amusement or other emotion —**straight'-faced'** *adj.*

straight fight a contest between two participants only

straightforward (strāt'fôr'wərd) *adj.* 1. honest; frank 2. simple; uncomplicated;

said of a task —*adv.* in a straightforward manner: also **straight′for′wards**

straight man an actor who serves as a foil for a comedian, feeding him lines

straightway *adv.* at once; without delay

strain[1] (strān) *vt.* [< L. *stringere*, draw tight] 1. to draw or stretch tight 2. to exert, use, or tax to the utmost 3. to injure by overexertion [to *strain* a muscle] 4. to injure or weaken by force, pressure, etc. 5. to stretch beyond the normal limits 6. *a)* to pass through a screen, sieve, etc.; filter *b)* to remove by filtration, etc. —*vi.* 1. to make violent efforts; strive hard 2. to become strained 3. to be subjected to great stress or pressure 4. to pull with force 5. to filter —*n.* 1. a straining or being strained 2. great effort, exertion, etc. 3. an injury as a result of overexertion [heart *strain*] 4. stress or force 5. a great or excessive demand on one's emotions, resources, etc.

strain[2] *n.* [< OE. *strynan*, to produce] 1. ancestry; lineage 2. the descendants of a common ancestor; race; stock 3. a group of organisms within a species, different from others in the species 4. a trace; streak 5. the tone of a speech, action, etc. 6. [*often pl.*] a tune; air

strained *adj.* 1. unnatural; forced 2. tense

strainer *n.* a person or thing that strains; specif., a device for straining, sifting, or filtering

strait (strāt) *n.* [see STRICT] 1. [*often pl.*] a narrow waterway connecting two large bodies of water 2. [*often pl.*] difficulty; distress —*adj.* [Archaic] narrow; strict

straiten *vt.* 1. esp. formerly, to restrict 2. to bring into difficulties: usually in the phrase **in straitened circumstances,** lacking sufficient money

straitjacket *n.* a coatlike device that binds the arms tight against the body: used to restrain persons in a violent state

strait-laced *adj.* narrowly strict in behaviour or moral views

strand[1] (strand) *vt., vi.* [OE.] 1. to run or drive aground [a ship *stranded* by the storm] 2. to leave or be put into a difficult, helpless position [*stranded* in a strange city with no money] —*n.* a shore, esp. a sea shore

strand[2] *n.* [< ?] 1. any of the threads, fibres, wires, etc. that are twisted together to form a string, rope, or cable 2. a ropelike length of anything [a *strand* of pearls]

strange (strānj) *adj.* **strang′er, strang′-est** [< L. *extraneus*, foreign] 1. unusual; extraordinary 2. peculiar; odd 3. not previously known, seen, heard, etc.; unfamiliar 4. lacking experience; unaccustomed [*strange* to the job] 5. foreign; alien

stranger *n.* 1. an outsider or newcomer 2. a person not known or familiar to one 3. a person unaccustomed (*to* something) [a *stranger* to hatred]

strangle (straŋ′g'l) *vt.* **-gled, -gling** [< Gr. *strangalē,* halter] 1. to kill by squeezing the throat as with the hands, a noose, etc., so as to shut off the breath 2. to choke or suffocate in any way 3. to suppress, stifle, or repress —**stran′gler** *n.*

stranglehold *n.* 1. an illegal wrestling hold that chokes off an opponent's breath 2. any force that restricts or suppresses freedom

strangulate (straŋ′gyo͞olāt′) *vt.* **-lat′ed, -lat′ing** [< L. *strangulare*] 1. *same as* STRANGLE 2. *Med.* to cause (an intestine or other tube) to become squeezed so that a flow, as of blood, is cut off —**stran′gula′tion** *n.*

strap (strap) *n.* [dial. < STROP] 1. a narrow strip of leather, plastic, cloth, etc. often with a buckle at one end, for tying or holding things 2. a straplike thing, as a shoulder strap 3. punishment with a strap —*vt.* **strapped, strap′ping** 1. to fasten with a strap 2. to beat with a strap —**strap′less** *adj.*

straphanger *n.* [Colloq.] a standing passenger, as on a crowded bus, who supports himself by holding onto a hanging strap

strapping *adj.* [Colloq.] tall and sturdy; robust

strata (strāt′ə) *n.* *alt. pl.* of STRATUM

stratagem (strat′ə jəm) *n.* [< Gr. *stratos,* army + *agein,* to lead] 1. a trick or plan for deceiving an enemy in war 2. any trick or scheme

strategic (strə tē′jik) *adj.* 1. of strategy 2. sound in strategy; advantageous 3. *a)* needed for carrying on war [*strategic* materials] *b)* directed against the military and industrial installations of the enemy [*strategic* bombing] —**strate′gically** *adv.*

strategy (strat′ə jē) *n.,* *pl.* **-gies** [see STRATAGEM] 1. *a)* the science of planning and directing military operations *b)* a plan or action based on this 2. skill in managing or planning, esp. by using stratagems —**strat′egist** *n.*

strath (strath) *n.* [< ScotGael. *srath*] a wide river valley

strathspey (strath′spā′) *n.* [< STRATH + *Spey,* river in E⋅ Scotland] 1. a slow Scottish dance with gliding steps 2. music for this

stratify (strat′ə fī′) *vt.* **-fied′, -fy′ing** [< L. *stratum,* layer + *facere,* make] to form or arrange in layers or strata —**strat′ifica′tion** (-fi kā′shən) *n.*

stratosphere (strat′ə sfēər′) *n.* [< Fr. < ModL. *stratum,* STRATUM + Fr. *sphère,* SPHERE] the atmospheric zone extending from about 9 kilometres to about 24 kilometres above the earth's surface, in which the temperature ranges from about -45°C to -75°C —**strat′ospher′ic** (-sfer′ik) *adj.*

stratum (strāt′əm) *n.,* *pl.* **stra′ta, -tums** [< L. *sternere,* to spread] 1. a horizontal layer of material, specif., *Geol.* a single layer of sedimentary rock 2. a section, level, or division 3. any of the socioeconomic groups of a society

stratus (strāt′əs) *n.,* *pl.* **stra′ti** (-ī) [L. :

see prec.] a cloud type extending in a long, low, grey layer

straw (strô) *n.* [OE. *strēaw*] 1. hollow stalks of grain after threshing, used for bedding, for weaving baskets, etc. 2. a single one of such stalks 3. a tube used for sucking beverages 4. a worthless trifle —*adj.* 1. straw-coloured; yellowish 2. made of straw —**a straw in the wind** a sign of what may happen —**grasp** (or **clutch, catch**) **at a straw** (or **straws**) to try anything that offers even the slightest hope

strawberry *n.*, *pl.* **-ries** [< OE. *strēaw, straw* + *berige,* berry] 1. the small, red, fleshy fruit of a low plant of the rose family that puts out runners 2. this plant

strawberry blonde reddish blonde

strawberry mark a red birthmark

strawflower *n.* a plant whose brightly coloured flower heads are dried for winter arrangements

straw vote [Chiefly U.S.] an unofficial vote or poll for sampling popular opinion: also **straw poll**

stray (strā) *vi.* [prob. < L. *extra vagari,* wander outside] 1. to wander from a given place, course, etc.; roam 2. to deviate (*from* what is right) 3. to wander from the subject; digress —*n.* a person or thing that strays; esp., a domestic animal wandering at large —*adj.* 1. having strayed; lost 2. isolated or incidental [a few *stray* words]

streak (strēk) *n.* [OE. *strica*] 1. a long, thin mark; stripe 2. a ray of light or a flash, as of lightning 3. a thin layer, as of fat in meat or ore in rock 4. a tendency in one's nature [a jealous *streak*] 5. a period or series [a *streak* of victories] —*vt.* to mark with streaks —*vi.* 1. to become streaked 2. to move swiftly 3. to make a short dash, naked, in public —**streak'y** *adj.*

streaker *n.* one who makes a short dash, naked, in a public place

streaky bacon bacon with alternating strips of fat and lean meat

stream (strēm) *n.* [OE.] 1. a current or flow of water; specif., a small river 2. a steady flow of any fluid or of rays of energy [a *stream* of light] 3. a moving line of things 4. a trend [the *stream* of events] 5. *Educ.* any of the sections formed by grouping children of similar ability together —*vi.* 1. to flow as in a stream 2. to flow (*with*) [eyes *streaming* with tears] 3. to move swiftly 4. to float, as a flag in the breeze —*vt. Educ.* to arrange children in streams

streamer *n.* 1. a long, narrow flag 2. any long, narrow, flowing strip of material 3. a newspaper headline across the full page

streamline *vt.* **-lined', -lin'ing** to make streamlined —*adj. same as* STREAMLINED

streamlined *adj.* 1. having a contour designed to offer the least resistance in moving through air, water, etc. 2. arranged so as to be more efficient [a *streamlined* programme] 3. trim [a *streamlined* figure]

stream of consciousness a literary technique presenting the thoughts, inner feelings, etc. of a character in a natural, unrestrained flow

street (strēt) *n.* [< L. *strata* (*via*), paved (road)] 1. a public road in a city or town; esp., a paved thoroughfare with buildings along the sides 2. the people living, working, etc. in the buildings along a given street —(**right**) **up one's street** [Colloq.] (just) what one knows or likes best —**streets ahead** [Colloq.] far superior to

streetcar *n.* [U.S.] a tram (sense 2)

streetwalker *n.* a prostitute who solicits customers in the street

strength (streŋth) *n.* [OE. *strengthu*] 1. the state or quality of being strong; power; force 2. toughness; durability 3. the power to resist attack 4. legal, moral, or intellectual force 5. potency, as of drugs 6. intensity, as of colour 7. force as measured in numbers [an army at full *strength*] 8. a source of strength —**on the strength of** based or relying on

strengthen *vt., vi.* to make or become stronger

strenuous (stren'yŏŏ wəs) *adj.* [L. *strenuus*] requiring or characterized by great effort or energy

streptococcus (strep'tō kok'əs) *n., pl.* **-coc'ci** (-kok'ī) [< Gr. *streptos,* twisted + COCCUS] any of a group of spherical bacteria that occur generally in chains: some species cause serious diseases —**strep'tococ'cal** *adj.*

streptomycin (strep'tō mī'sin) *n.* [< Gr. *streptos,* twisted + *mykēs,* fungus] an antibiotic drug used in the treatment of various bacterial diseases, as tuberculosis

stress (stres) *n.* [< L. *strictus,* STRICT] 1. emphasis; importance 2. the relative force of utterance given a syllable or word 3. strain; specif., force that strains or deforms 4. *a)* mental or physical tension *b)* urgency, pressure, etc. causing this —*vt.* 1. to emphasize 2. to give stress to 3. to put pressure or strain on —**stress'ful** *adj.*

stretch (strech) *vt.* [OE. *streccan*] 1. to reach out; extend 2. to cause (the body or limbs) to reach out to full length, as in relaxing, etc. 3. to pull or spread out to full extent or to a greater size 4. to strain in interpretation, scope, etc. to questionable or unreasonable limits —*vi.* 1. *a)* to spread out to full extent or beyond normal limits *b)* to extend over a given space, distance, or time 2. *a)* to extend the body or limbs to full length *b)* to lie down (usually *with out*) 3. to become stretched to greater size, as any elastic substance —*n.* 1. a stretching or being stretched 2. an unbroken length, tract, etc. [a *stretch* of beach] 3. *a)* an unbroken period [a *stretch* of ten days] *b)* [Slang] a term served in prison —*adj.* made of elasticized fabric —**stretch a point** to make a concession —**stretch one's legs** to go for a short walk

stretcher *n.* 1. a light frame covered with canvas, etc. and used for carrying the sick, injured, or dead 2. one that stretches; specif., *a)* a brick or stone laid lengthwise in the face of a wall b) a device for stretching or shaping garments, etc.

stretcherbearer n. a person who helps carry a stretcher

strew (strōō) vt. strewed, strewed or strewn, strew'ing [OE. streawian] 1. to spread about here and there; scatter 2. to cover as by scattering 3. to be scattered over (a surface)

strewth (strōōth) interj. [< God's truth] an exclamation of surprise, indignation, etc.

stria (strī'ə) n., pl. stri'ae (-ē) [L.] 1. a narrow groove or channel 2. any of a number of parallel lines, stripes, furrows, etc.

striated (strī āt'id) adj. striped, furrowed, etc.

stricken (strik''n) alt. pp. of STRIKE —adj. 1. struck or wounded 2. suffering, as from pain, trouble, etc.

strict (strikt) adj. [< L. stringere, draw tight] 1. a) enforcing rules with great care b) closely enforced or rigidly maintained c) disciplining severely 2. exact or precise 3. absolute [the strict truth]

stricture (strik'chər) n. [< L. stringere, draw tight] 1. strong criticism; censure 2. Med. an abnormal narrowing of a passage in the body

stride (strīd) vi., vt. strode, strid'den, strid'ing [OE. stridan] 1. to walk with long steps 2. to cross with a single, long step [he strode over the log] 3. to straddle —n. 1. the act of striding 2. a long step 3. a) a full step in a gait, as of a horse b) the distance covered by such a step 4. [usually pl.] progress; advancement [great strides in industry] —get into one's stride to reach one's normal level of efficiency —take in one's stride to cope with easily

strident (strīd''nt) adj. [< L. stridere, to rasp] harsh-sounding; shrill; grating —stri'dency n.

strife (strīf) n. [OFr. estrif] 1. fighting or quarrelling; conflict 2. contention or competition

strike (strīk) vt. struck, struck or occas. (but for vt. 7 & 11 usually) strick'en, strik'-ing [OE. strican, to go] 1. a) to give a blow to; hit b) to give (a blow, etc.) 2. to come or cause to come into forceful contact 3. to attack 4. to ignite (a match) or produce (a light, etc.) by friction 5. to produce (a tone or chord) on a musical instrument 6. to announce (time), as with a bell: said of clocks, etc. 7. to afflict, as with disease 8. to come upon [we struck the main road] 9. to discover, as after drilling [to strike oil] 10. to affect as if by contact, a blow, etc.; specif., a) to occur to [struck by an idea] b) to impress (one's fancy, etc.) c) to seem to [it strikes me as silly] d) to cause to become suddenly [to be struck dumb] e) to overcome suddenly [to be struck with amazement] 11. to remove (from a list, record, etc.) 12. to make (a bargain, etc.) 13. a) to lower (a sail, flag, etc.) b) to take down (a tent, etc.) 14. to make by stamping, printing, etc. [to strike

coins] 15. to assume (a pose, etc.) 16. to put forth (roots): said of plants —vi. 1. to hit (at) 2. to attack 3. a) to make sounds as by being struck: said of a bell, clock, etc. b) to be announced thus [six o'clock struck] 4. a) to hit; collide (against, on, or upon) b) to make an impression on the mind 5. to ignite, as a match 6. to seize a bait: said of a fish 7. to dart in an attempt to wound, as a snake 8. to come suddenly (on or upon) 9. to run upon a reef, rock, etc.: said of a ship 10. a) to lower sail b) to lower a flag in token of surrender 11. to refuse to continue to work until certain demands are met 12. to take root: said of a plant —n. 1. the act of striking; blow; specif., a military attack 2. a) a concerted refusal by employees to go on working, in an attempt to get higher wages, better conditions, etc. b) any similar refusal to do something, undertaken as a form of protest [a hunger strike] 3. the discovery of a rich deposit of oil, coal, etc. 4. any sudden success 5. the pull on the line by a fish seizing bait —(out) on strike striking (vi. 11) —strike back to retaliate —strike camp to take down all tents at the end of a period of encampment —strike home 1. to deliver an effective blow 2. to have the desired effect —strike off 1. to erase or remove from a list, record, etc. 2. to remove as by a cut or blow —strike out 1. to remove from a record, etc. 2. to start out —strike up 1. to begin playing, singing, etc. 2. to begin (a friendship, etc.)

strikebreaker n. a person who tries to break up a strike, as by working —strike'break'ing n.

strike pay an allowance paid by a trade union to workers on strike

striker n. 1. a person who strikes; specif., a) a worker who is on strike b) in football, an attacking player whose main function is to score goals 2. a thing that strikes, as the clapper in a bell, etc.

striking adj. 1. that strikes or is on strike 2. impressive; outstanding; remarkable —strik'ingly adv.

Strine (strīn) n. [< supposed pronun. of Australian] a humorous transliteration of Australian speech

string (striŋ) n. [OE. streng] 1. a length of fibre or wire, nylon, etc. used for tying, pulling, lacing, etc. 2. a length of things on a string [a string of pearls] 3. a line, row, or series of things 4. a) a slender cord of wire, gut, etc., stretched on a violin, guitar, etc., and bowed, plucked, or struck to make a musical sound b) [pl.] all the stringed instruments of an orchestra, or their players 5. a fibre of a plant 6. [Colloq.] a condition attached to a plan, offer, etc.: usually used in pl. —vt. strung, strung, string'-ing 1. to provide with strings 2. to thread on a string 3. to tie, pull, hang, etc. with a string 4. to adjust or tune the strings of (a musical instrument) 5. to make nervous or keyed (up) 6. to remove the strings from (beans, etc.) 7.

to arrange in a row —**vi.** to stretch out in a line —**on a string** completely under one's control —**pull strings** 1. to get someone to use influence on one's behalf, often secretly 2. to direct action of others, often secretly —**string along** [Colloq.] to deceive —**string along with** [Colloq.] 1. to accompany 2. to agree —**string up** [Colloq.] to kill by hanging

stringcourse n. a decorative, horizontal band of brick or stone set in the wall of a building

stringed rare pp. of STRING —**adj.** having strings, as certain musical instruments

stringent (strin′jənt) **adj.** [< L. stringere, draw tight] 1. strict; severe 2. tight in loan or investment money [a stringent money market] —**strin′gency** n.

stringer (strin′ər) n. 1. a long piece of timber used as a support, as to connect upright posts in a frame 2. a long structural member of an aircraft fuselage, wing, etc. 3. a journalist retained by a newspaper to cover events in a particular area

string quartet a quartet of or for players on stringed instruments

string vest an undergarment made from a large-meshed material

stringy adj. -ier, -iest 1. like or consisting of strings or fibres 2. having tough fibres [stringy meat]

strip¹ (strip) **vt.** stripped, strip′ping [OE. strypan] 1. to remove (the clothing, etc.) from (a person) 2. to dispossess (a person) of (honours, titles, etc.) 3. to plunder; rob 4. to make bare or clear by taking away removable parts, etc. [to strip a room of furniture] 5. to break or damage the thread of (a nut, bolt, etc.) or the teeth of (a gear) —**vi.** 1. to take off all clothing; undress 2. to perform a striptease —**strip down** 1. to remove paint from a surface so as to prepare it for repainting 2. to take an engine apart so as to clean or repair it

strip² n. [STRIPE] 1. a long, narrow piece, as of land, ribbon, etc. 2. a runway for aircraft; landing strip 3. [Colloq.] the clothes worn by members of a team, esp. a football team

strip cartoon same as COMIC STRIP

strip club a nightclub, etc. that has regular performances of striptease

stripe (strip) n. [MDu. strīpe] 1. a long, narrow band, mark, or streak, differing as in colour from the area around it 2. a strip of cloth on the sleeve of a uniform to show rank, years served, etc. 3. [Archaic] a stroke with a whip —**vt.** **striped, strip′ing** to mark with stripes

strip lighting electric lighting by means of fluorescent tubes

stripling (strip′liŋ) n. a grown boy; youth

stripper (strip′ər) n. 1. a striptease artist 2. a solvent or device for removing paint, varnish etc.

striptease n. an act, as in clubs, etc., in which a woman takes off her clothes slowly —**strip′tease′** vi.

stripy (strī′pē) **adj.** strip′ier, strip′iest characterized by, like, or marked with stripes

strive (strīv) **vi.** strove, striven (striv′'n), striv′ing [< OFr. estrif, effort] 1. to try very hard [to strive to win] 2. to struggle; contend [to strive against tyranny]

strobe (strōb) n. 1. shortened form of STROBOSCOPE 2. an electronic tube that can emit extremely rapid, brief flashes of light: used in photography, the theatre, etc.

stroboscope (strō′bəskōp′) n. [< Gr. strobos, a twisting round + -SCOPE] 1. an instrument for studying motion by illuminating a moving body, machine, etc. very briefly at frequent intervals 2. same as STROBE

strode (strōd) pt. of STRIDE

stroke (strōk) n. [akin to OE. strican, to hit] 1. a striking of one thing against another; blow 2. a sudden action resulting as if from a blow [a stroke of luck] 3. a sudden attack, esp. of apoplexy 4. a) a single effort to do something, esp. a successful one b) something accomplished by such an effort 5. the sound of striking, as of a clock 6. a) a single movement, as with some tool, club, pen, etc. b) any of a series of repeated rhythmic motions made against water, air, etc. c) a type, manner, or rate of such a movement 7. a mark made by a pen, etc. 8. a gentle, caressing motion with the hand 9. Mech. any of the continuous, reciprocating movements of a piston, etc. 10. Rowing the rower who sits nearest the stern and sets the rate of rowing —**vt.** **stroked, strok′ing** 1. to draw one's hand, a tool, etc. gently over 2. to hit (a ball), as in tennis etc. 3. to set the rate of rowing for (a crew) —**at a stroke** by a single action —**on the stroke** punctually

stroll (strōl) **vi.** [< ?] 1. to walk in an idle, leisurely manner; saunter 2. to go from place to place; wander —n. a leisurely walk

strong (stroŋ) **adj.** [OE. strang] 1. a) physically powerful b) healthy; sound 2. not easily upset [a strong stomach] 3. morally or intellectually powerful [a strong will] 4. governing firmly 5. firm; durable 6. having many resources; powerful in wealth, numbers, etc. 7. of a specified number [a force 6000 strong] 8. having a powerful effect [strong measures] 9. having a large amount of its essential quality [strong coffee] 10. affecting the senses powerfully [strong light, odour, etc.] 11. rancid; rank [strong butter] 12. intense in degree or quality 13. forthright [strong language] 14. moving rapidly and with force [a strong wind] 15. Chem. having a high ion concentration, as some acids and bases 16. Gram. expressing variation in tense by internal change of vowel rather than by inflectional endings; irregular (Ex.: swim, swam, swum) —**come on strong** [Slang] to make a striking impression

strong-arm *adj.* [Colloq.] using physical force

strongbox *n.* a heavily made box for storing valuables

strong drink alcoholic drink

stronghold *n.* 1. a fortified place 2. a place where a group having certain views, attitudes, etc. is concentrated

strong language emphatic language; specif., swearing

strong-minded *adj.* having a strong, unyielding will; determined

strongroom *n.* a strongly built room used for the safekeeping of valuables

strontium (stron′tē əm) *n.* [< *Strontian*, Scotland, where first found] a pale-yellow, metallic chemical element: symbol, Sr : a deadly radioactive isotope of strontium (**strontium 90**) is present in the fallout of nuclear explosions

strop (strop) *n.* [ME.] a device, esp. a thick leather band, used for putting a fine edge on razors —*vt.* **stropped, strop′- ping** to sharpen on a strop

stroppy (strop′ē) *adj.* [< OBSTREPEROUS] [Slang] angry, irritated, or awkward

strove (strōv) *alt. pt. of* STRIVE

struck (struk) *pt. & pp. of* STRIKE

structural (struk′chər əl) *adj.* 1. of or having structure 2. used in construction or building 3. integral to a structure; load bearing: said of a wall

structure (struk′chər) *n.* [< L. *struere*, arrange] 1. something constructed, as a building or dam 2. the arrangement of all the parts of a whole [the *structure* of the atom] 3. something composed of interrelated parts 4. manner of building, constructing, or organizing —*vt.* **-tured, -turing** to put together according to a system; organize

strudel (strōō′d'l) *n.* [G.] a kind of pastry made of a very thin dough filled usually with apple

struggle (strug′'l) *vi.* **-gled, -gling** [< ?] 1. to make great efforts; strive 2. to fight violently with an opponent 3. to make one's way with difficulty —*n.* 1. great effort; exertion 2. conflict; strife

strum (strum) *vt., vi.* **strummed, strum′- ming** [echoic] to play (a guitar, banjo, etc.), esp. in a casual way, or without much skill —*n.* the act or sound of this

strumpet (strum′pit) *n.* [< ?] [Obs.] a prostitute

strung (strun) *pt. & alt. pp. of* STRING

strut (strut) *vi.* **strut′ted, strut′ting** [OE. *strutian*, stand rigid] to walk in a stiff, swaggering manner —*vt.* to provide with a strut , —*n.* 1. a brace fitted into a framework to resist lengthwise pressure 2. a vain, swaggering walk

’struth (strōōth) *interj.* same as STREWTH

strychnine (strik′nēn) *n.* [< Gr. *strychnos*, nightshade] a highly poisonous crystalline alkaloid, used in small doses as a stimulant

STUB

stub (stub) *n.* [OE. *stybb*] 1. a short piece remaining after the main part has been removed or used up [a cigar *stub*] 2. a short piece of a ticket or cheque kept as a record 3. a tree stump —*vt.* **stubbed, stub′bing** 1. to strike (one's toe, etc.) against something by accident 2. to put out (a cigarette, etc.) by pressing the end against a surface: often with *out*

stubble (stub′'l) *n.* [< L. *stipula*, stalk] 1. the short stumps of grain left standing after harvesting 2. any growth like this [a *stubble* of beard] —**stub′bly** *adj.*

stubborn (stub′ərn) *adj.* [< ?] 1. refusing to yield, obey, or comply; obstinate 2. done in an obstinate or persistent manner [a *stubborn* campaign] 3. hard to handle, treat, or deal with [a *stubborn* cold]

stubby (stub′ē) *adj.* **stub′bier, stub′biest** 1. short and heavy or dense 2. short and thickset 3. covered with stubs or stubble —**stub′biness** *n.*

stucco (stuk′ō) *n., pl.* **-coes, -cos** [It.] plaster or cement used for surfacing inside or outside walls, etc. —*vt.* **stuc′coed, stuc′- coing** to cover with stucco

stuck (stuk) *pt. & pp. of* STICK —*adj.* 1. baffled, nonplussed 2. [Slang] keen on [I'm not really *stuck* on the idea] —**get stuck in** [Slang] 1. to start working hard 2. to start eating

stuck-up *adj.* [Colloq.] snobbish; conceited

stud[1] (stud) *n.* [OE. *studu*, post] 1. a small knob or rounded nailhead used to ornament a surface 2. a rounded projection on the sole of a boot or shoe to give better grip 3. a small, buttonlike device used as an ornament or fastener on a shirt 4. an upright piece in the frame of a building, to which panels, laths, etc. are nailed 5. a projecting pin or peg used as a support, pivot, etc. —*vt.* **stud′- ded, stud′ding** 1. to set or decorate with studs or studlike objects 2. to be set thickly on [rocks *stud* the hillside] 3. to scatter (something) thickly

stud[2] *n.* [OE. *stod*] 1. a) a number of horses kept for breeding b) the place where these are kept 2. any male animal used for breeding, esp. a stallion 3. [Slang] a virile, sexually promiscuous man —**at stud** available for breeding: said of male animals

studbook *n.* a register of purebred animals, esp. racehorses

student (styōō′dənt) *n.* [< L. *studere*, to study] 1. a person who is enrolled for study in a university, college, etc. 2. a person who studies something

studied (stud′ēd) *adj.* 1. prepared by careful study 2. deliberate [*studied* indifference]

studio (styo͞o′dē ō′) *n., pl.* **-dios′** [It.] **1.** a place where an artist or photographer does his work **2.** a place where films are made **3.** a place where radio or television programmes are produced or where recordings are made

studio couch a kind of couch that can be opened into a full-sized bed

studious (styo͞o′dē əs) *adj.* **1.** fond of study **2.** showing close attention **3.** zealous; wholehearted

study (stud′ē) *vt.* **stud′ied, stud′ying** [< L. *studere*, to study] **1.** to try to learn by reading, etc. **2.** *a)* to investigate carefully *b)* to scrutinize [to *study* a map] **3.** to read (a book, lesson, etc.) so as to know and understand it **4.** to take a course in at a university or college **5.** to give attention or thought to —*vi.* **1.** to study something **2.** to be a student —*n., pl.* **stud′ies 1.** the application of the mind to acquire knowledge, as by reading **2.** careful examination of a subject, event, etc. **3.** a branch of learning **4.** [*pl.*] formal education; schooling **5.** a work of literature or art treating a subject in careful detail **6.** a first sketch for a story, picture, etc. **7.** *same as* ÉTUDE **8.** earnest effort or deep absorption **9.** a room designed for study, writing, etc. **10.** the object, etc. to be studied [the *study* of mankind is man]

stuff (stuf) *n.* [< OFr. *estoffer*] **1.** the material out of which anything is made **2.** essence; character **3.** any kind of matter, unspecified **4.** cloth, esp. woollen cloth **5.** *a)* personal belongings *b)* things; objects **6.** worthless objects; junk **7.** foolish or worthless ideas, words, etc. [*stuff* and nonsense] **8.** [Slang] money —*vt.* **1.** to fill (something); pack; specif., *a)* to fill the skin of (a dead animal, etc.) in order to mount and preserve it *b)* to fill (a fowl, etc.) with seasoning, bread crumbs, etc. before roasting **2.** to fill too full, esp. with food **3.** to pack or cram with **4.** to plug; block; stop up **5.** to push [to *stuff* money into a purse] —*vi.* to eat too much —**do one's stuff** do what is expected of one

stuffed shirt [Colloq.] a pompous, pretentious person

stuffing *n.* **1.** soft, springy material used as padding in cushions, etc. **2.** a seasoned mixture for stuffing fowl, etc.

stuffy *adj.* **stuff′ier, stuff′iest 1.** poorly ventilated; close **2.** having the nasal passages stopped up, as from a cold **3.** [Colloq.] *a)* dull; old-fashioned *b)* prim; strait-laced *c)* pompous; pretentious —**stuff′ily** *adv.* —**stuff′iness** *n.*

stultify (stul′tə fī′) *vt.* **-fied′, -fy′ing** [< L. *stultus*, foolish + *facere*, make] **1.** to render worthless or useless **2.** *a)* to cause to appear foolish, absurd, etc. *b)* to make dull or sluggish —**stul′tifica′tion** *n.*

stumble (stum′b'l) *vi.* **-bled, -bling** [< Scand.] **1.** to trip in walking, running, etc. **2.** to walk unsteadily **3.** to speak, act, etc. in a confused, blundering manner **4.** to come by chance [to *stumble* across

a clue] —*n.* a stumbling —**stum′blingly** *adv.*

stumbling block an obstacle or difficulty

stump (stump) *n.* [prob. < MLowG. *stump*] **1.** the lower end of a tree left in the ground after most of the trunk has been cut off **2.** *a)* the part of an arm, tooth, etc. left after the rest has been removed *b)* a butt; stub [the *stump* of a pencil] **3.** [Chiefly U.S.] the place where a political speech is made **4.** *Cricket* any of the three upright sticks of a wicket —*vt.* **1.** [Colloq.] to puzzle; baffle **2.** *Cricket* to dismiss (a batsman) by hitting the stumps with a bat **3.** [Chiefly U.S.] to travel over (a district) making political speeches —*vi.* **1.** to walk heavily or clumsily **2.** [U.S.] to travel about making political speeches —**stump up** [Colloq.] to hand over money due; pay up

stumpy *adj.* **-ier, -iest** short and thickset; stubby —**stump′iness** *n.*

stun (stun) *vt.* **stunned, stun′ning** [see ASTONISH] **1.** to make senseless or unconscious, as by a blow **2.** to shock deeply; daze

stung (stuŋ) *pt. & pp.* of STING

stunk (stuŋk) *pp. & alt. pt.* of STINK

stunner (stun′ər) *n.* [Colloq.] a remarkably attractive, excellent, etc. person or thing

stunning *adj.* **1.** that stuns **2.** [Colloq.] remarkably attractive, excellent, etc.

stunt¹ (stunt) *vt.* [OE. *stunt*, stupid] **1.** to check the growth or development of; dwarf **2.** to hinder (growth or development)

stunt² *n.* [< ?] **1.** a display of skill or daring; trick **2.** something done to attract attention —*vi.* to perform stunts

stunt man a professional acrobat who takes the place of an actor when dangerous scenes involving falls, leaps, etc. are filmed

stupefy (styo͞o′pə fī′) *vt.* **-fied′, -fy′ing** [< L. *stupere*, be stunned + *facere*, make] **1.** to make dull or lethargic; stun **2.** to astonish; bewilder —**stu′pefac′tion** *n.*

stupendous (styo͞o pen′dəs) *adj.* [< L. *stupere*, be stunned] **1.** astonishing **2.** astonishingly great

stupid (styo͞o′pid) *adj.* [see *prec.*] **1.** showing or resulting from a lack of intelligence **2.** dazed; stupefied **3.** lacking normal intelligence; slow-witted **4.** dull and boring [a *stupid* party] —**stupid′ity** *n.*

stupor (styo͞o′pər) *n.* [L.] a state in which the mind and senses are so dulled, as by a drug, that one can barely think, act, feel, etc.

sturdy (stur′dē) *adj.* **-dier, -diest** [OFr. *estourdi*, stunned] **1.** strong; hardy **2.** strongly built —**stur′dily** *adv.* —**stur′diness** *n.*

sturgeon (stur′jən) *n.* [OFr. *esturjon*] any of several large food fishes, valuable as a source of caviar and isinglass

stutter (stut′ər) *vt., vi.* [< ME. *stutten*] **1.** *same as* STAMMER **2.** to make (a series of repeated sounds) [*stuttering* machine guns] —*n.* the act of stuttering

sty¹ (stī) *n., pl.* **sties** [OE. *sti*] **1.** a pen for pigs **2.** any foul or depraved place

sty², **stye** *n., pl.* **sties** [< OE. *stigan*, to climb] a small, inflamed swelling of a sebaceous gland on the rim of the eyelid

Stygian (stij′ē ən) *adj.* 1. of the river Styx and the infernal regions 2. [*also* **s-**] a) infernal or hellish b) dark or gloomy

style (stīl) *n.* [< L. *stilus*, writing implement] 1. sort; kind 2. the way in which anything is made or done; manner 3. *a)* manner of expression in writing or speaking b) characteristic manner of expression or design in any art, period, etc. 4. distinction, originality, etc. in artistic or literary expression [this author lacks *style*] 5. a) the current fashion b) a fashionable, luxurious manner [to dine in *style*] 6. elegance of manner 7. form of address; title [entitled to the *style* of Mayor] 8. a pointed instrument for engraving, writing, or drawing 9. *Bot.* the stalklike part of a carpel between the stigma and the ovary —*vt.* **styled, styl′-ing** 1. to design the style of 2. to name; call

stylish *adj.* smart; fashionable

stylist *n.* 1. a writer, etc. whose work has style (sense 4) 2. a person who designs current styles, as in dress 3. a hairdresser who styles hair —**stylis′tic** *adj.* —**stylis′tically** *adv.*

stylize *vt.* **-ized, -izing** to make conform to a given style rather than to nature; conventionalize —**styl′iza′tion** *n.*

stylus (stī′ləs) *n., pl.* **-luses, -li** (-lī) [< L. *stilus*, pointed instrument] 1. a style or other needlelike marking device 2. *a)* a sharp, pointed device for cutting the grooves of a gramophone record b) a gramophone needle

stymie (stī′mē) *n.* [< ?] 1. *Golf* the situation on a putting green when an opponent's ball lies in a direct line between the player's ball and the hole 2. any frustrating situation —*vt.* **-mied, -mieing** 1. to obstruct with a stymie 2. to block; impede

styptic (stip′tik) *adj.* [< Gr. *styphein*, to contract] tending to halt bleeding by contracting the tissues or blood vessels —*n.* any styptic substance

styrene (stī′rēn) *n.* [< L. *styrax*, a kind of tree] a colourless or yellowish, aromatic liquid used in the manufacture of synthetic rubber and plastics

suasion (swā′zhən) *n.* [< L. *suadere*, persuade] persuasion: chiefly in **moral suasion**, a persuading by appealing to one's sense of morality —**sua′vity** *n.*

suave (swäv) *adj.* [< L. *suavis*, sweet] smoothly gracious or polite; polished; urbane —**suavity** *n.*

sub (sub) *n.* 1. *shortened form of:* a) SUBMARINE b) SUBSCRIPTION c) SUBSTITUTE 2. [Colloq.] an advance payment of wages or salary —*vi.* **subbed, sub′bing** [Colloq.] 1. to be a substitute (*for* someone) 2. to grant or receive (an advance payment of wages or salary)

sub- [< L. *sub*, under] a prefix meaning: 1. beneath [*subsoil*] 2. lower in rank than [*subaltern*] 3. to a lesser degree than [*subtropical*] 4. by or forming a division into smaller parts [*subsection*] *Sub-* is often assimilated to *suc-* before c, *suf-* before f, *sug-* before g, *sum-* before m, *sup-* before p, and *sur-* before r: *sub-* often changes to *sus-* before c, p, and t

subaltern (sub′əl tərn) *adj.* [< L. *sub-*, under + *alternus*, alternate] holding an army commission below that of captain —*n.* a subaltern officer

subaqua (sub′a′kwä) *adj.* of underwater sports

subaqueous (sub ā′kwē əs) *adj.* [< SUB + AQUA] 1. adapted for underwater use or existence 2. living or occurring underwater

subatom (sub at′əm) *n.* one of the parts that make up an atom —**sub′atom′ic** (-ə tom′ik) *adj.*

subcommittee (sub′kə mit′ē) *n.* a small committee with special duties chosen from a main committee

subconscious (sub′kon′shəs) *adj.* occurring with little or no conscious perception on the part of the individual: said of mental processes and reactions —the **subconscious** subconscious mental activity

subcontinent (sub kon′tə nənt) *n.* a large land mass, smaller than a continent

subcontract (sub kon′trakt; *for v.,* sub′-kən trakt′) *n.* a secondary contract undertaking some or all of the obligations of a primary or previous contract —*vt., vi.* to make a subcontract (for) —**subcon-trac′tor** *n.*

subculture (sub′kul′chər) *n.* 1. a distinctive social group within a larger group 2. the distinct cultural patterns of such a group

subcutaneous (sub′kyoo tā′nē əs) *adj.* beneath the skin

subdivide (sub′di vīd′) *vt., vi.* **-vid′ed, -vid′ing** to divide further after previous division —**sub′divi′sion** *n.*

subdominant (sub dom′ə nənt) *n. Music* the fourth tone of a diatonic scale

subdue (səb dyoo′) *vt.* **-dued′, -du′ing** [< L. *subducere*, remove] 1. to win control of; conquer 2. to overcome, as by training; control 3. to make less intense; diminish; soften —**subdued′** *adj.*

subeditor (sub′ed′i tər) *n.* a person who writes and checks copy, esp. on a newspaper

subfusc (sub′fusk) *adj.* [< L. *sub-*, below + *fuscus*, dark brown] having a dull or dark, often drab, colour —*n.* subfusc clothing

subhuman (sub′hyoo′mən) *adj.* 1. less than human 2. nearly human

subj. 1. subjective 2. subjunctive

subjacent (sub jā′sənt) *adj.* [< L. *sub-*, under + *jacere*, to lie] underlying

subject (sub′jikt; *for v.* səb jekt′) *n.* [< L. *sub-*, under + *jacere*, to throw] 1. something dealt with in discussion, study, painting, etc.; theme 2. a branch of learning 3. *Gram.* the noun, noun phrase, or noun substitute in a sentence about which something is said 4. one undergoing a treatment, experiment, etc. 5. a person under the authority of another; esp., a person who owes allegiance to a ruler **6.** a main theme of a musical composition **7.** a cause; reason —*adj.* **1.** under the authority or control of, or owing allegiance to, another **2.** having a tendency (*to*) [*subject* to fits] **3.** liable to receive [*subject* to censure] **4.** contingent upon [*subject* to his approval] —*vt.* **1.** to cause to undergo something **2.** to make liable or vulnerable [to *subject* one to contempt] **3.** to bring under the authority or control of —**subjec′tion** *n.*

subjective (səb jek′tiv) *adj.* **1.** of or resulting from the feelings of the person thinking; not objective; personal [a *subjective* opinion] **2.** determined by and emphasizing the ideas, feelings, etc. of the artist or writer **3.** *Gram.* same as NOMINATIVE —**subjectivity** (sub′jek-tiv′ə tē) *n.*

subjoin (səb join′) *vt.* [SUB- & JOIN] to add (something) at the end of a statement

sub judice (sub jōō′də sē) [L., under judgement] before the court; under judicial consideration but not yet decided

subjugate (sub′jōō gāt′) *vt.* -**gat′ed, -gat′- ing** [< L. *sub-*, under + *jugum*, a yoke] to bring under control or subjection; conquer —**sub′juga′tion** *n.*

subjunctive (səb juŋk′tiv) *adj.* [< L. *subjungere*, to SUBJOIN] designating or of that mood of a verb used to express supposition, desire, possibility, etc. [*were* in "if I *were* you" is in the *subjunctive* mood] —*n.* **1.** the subjunctive mood **2.** a verb in this mood

sublease (sub′lēs′; *for v.* sub lēs′) *n.* a lease granted by a lessee to another person —*vt.* -**leased′, -leas′ing** to grant or hold a sublease of

sublet (sub let′) *vt.* -**let′, -let′ting** to let to another (property which one is renting)

sublieutenant (sub′lef ten′ənt) *n.* see MILITARY RANKS, table

sublimate (sub′lə māt′; *for adj. & n.,* -mət) *vt.* -**mat′ed, -mat′ing** [see ff.] **1.** to express (impulses, esp. sexual impulses, regarded as unacceptable) in ways that are acceptable **2.** to sublime (a substance) **3.** to have an ennobling effect on —*n.* a substance that is the product of subliming —**sub′lima′tion** *n.*

sublime (sə blīm′) *adj.* [< L. *sub-*, up to + *limen*, lintel] **1.** noble; exalted **2.** inspiring awe or admiration through grandeur, beauty, etc. —*vt.* -**limed′, -lim′- ing 1.** to make sublime **2.** to purify (a solid) by heating directly to a gaseous state and condensing the vapour back into solid form —*vi.* to go through this process —**sublimity** (sə blim′ə tē) *n.*

subliminal (sub lim′ən'l) *adj.* [< SUB- + L. *limen*, threshold] below the threshold of consciousness; specif., involving stimuli intended to take effect subconsciously through repetition —**sublim′inally** *adv.*

submachine gun (sub′mə shēn′) a portable, automatic firearm fired from the shoulder or hip

submarine (sub′mə rēn′) *n.* a kind of

warship, armed with torpedoes, etc., that can operate under water —*adj.* being, living, used, etc. beneath the surface of the sea

submerge (səb murj′) *vt.* -**merged′, -merg′ing** [< L. *sub-*, under + *mergere*, to plunge] **1.** to place under or as under water, etc. **2.** to cover over; suppress —*vi.* to sink beneath the surface of water, etc. —**submer′gence** *n.*

submerse (səb murs′) *vt.* -**mersed′, -mers′ing** same as SUBMERGE —**submer′- sion** *n.*

submersible *adj.* that can be submersed —*n.* any of various ships that can operate under water

submission (səb mish′ən) *n.* **1.** a submitting; surrendering **2.** resignation; obedience **3.** a submitting of something to another for decision, consideration, etc.

submissive *adj.* yielding; docile —**sub-mis′siveness** *n.*

submit (səb mit′) *vt.* -**mit′ted, -mit′ting** [< L. *sub-*, under + *mittere*, send] **1.** to yield to the control of another **2.** to allow to be subjected to treatment, analysis, etc.: often used reflexively **3.** to present to others for decision, consideration, etc. **4.** to suggest —*vi.* **1.** to yield to the control of another **2.** to allow oneself to be subjected (*to* treatment, etc.) **3.** to defer to another's judgment **4.** to be submissive

subnormal (sub nôr′m'l) *adj.* below the normal, esp. in intelligence —*n.* a subnormal person —**sub′normal′ity** (-mal′ə tē) *n.* —**subnor′mally** *adv.*

subordinate (sə bôr′də nit; *for v.* -nāt′) *adj.* [< L. *sub-*, under + *ordinare*, to order] **1.** below another in rank, importance, etc.; secondary **2.** under the power or authority of another **3.** *Gram.* functioning as a noun, adjective, or adverb within a sentence [a *subordinate* phrase]: cf. SUBORDINATE CLAUSE —*n.* a subordinate person or thing —*vt.* -**nat′- ed, -nat′ing 1.** to place in a subordinate position **2.** to make obedient or subservient (*to*) —**subor′dina′tion** *n.*

subordinate clause in a complex sentence, a clause that cannot function syntactically as a complete sentence by itself; dependent clause (Ex.: She will visit us *if she can*)

suborn (su bôrn′) *vt.* [< L. *sub-*, under + *ornare*, furnish] **1.** to get by bribery or other illegal methods **2.** to induce or urge (another) to do something illegal, esp. to commit perjury

subplot (sub′plot′) *n.* a subordinate plot in a play, novel, etc.

subpoena (səb pē′nə) *n.* [< L. *sub poena*, under penalty] a written legal order directing a person to appear in court —*vt.* -**naed, -naing** to summon with such an order

sub rosa (sub rō′zə) [L., under the rose] secretly; privately

subscribe (səb skrīb′) *vt.* -**scribed′, -scrib′ing** [see SUB- & SCRIBE] **1.** to promise to contribute (money) **2.** to write one's signature on (a document, etc.) as an indication of consent **3.** to sign (one's name) at the end of a document, etc. —*vi.* **1.** to promise to contribute a sum of money **2.** to agree to receive and pay for a periodical, etc. for a specified period (*to*) **3.** to give support (*to*) **4.** to sign one's name to a document, etc. —**subscrib'er** *n.*

subscriber trunk dialling in Britain, a service by which telephone users can obtain trunk calls by dialling direct without the aid of the operator

subscript (sub'skript) *adj.* [< 'SUB- & SCRIBE] written below —*n.* a figure, letter, or symbol written below and to the side of another [in Y₃ and X₂, 3 and *a* are *subscripts*]

subscription (səb skrip'shən) *n.* **1.** a subscribing **2.** something subscribed; specif., *a*) an amount of money subscribed *b*) a formal agreement to receive and pay for a periodical, etc. for a specified period *c*) the membership fee paid to a club

subsequent (sub'si kwənt) *adj.* [< L. *sub-*, after + *sequi*, follow] following in time, or order —**subsequent to** after

subservient (səb sur'vē ənt) *adj.* **1.** submissive; obsequious **2.** that is useful in a subordinate capacity —**subser'vience** *n.*

subset (sub'set') *n.* a mathematical set containing some or all of the elements of a given set

subside (səb sīd') *vi.* -**sid'ed**, -**sid'ing** [< L. *sub-*, under + *sidere*, settle] **1.** to sink to the bottom or to a lower level **2.** to sink or collapse, as because of mining operations below : said of the earth's surface **3.** to become less active, intense, etc. —**subsid'ence** (-sīd''ns, sub'si dəns) *n.*

subsidiary (səb sid'ē ær ē) *adj.* [see SUBSIDY] **1.** giving aid, service, etc.; auxiliary **2.** being in a subordinate capacity —*n., pl.* -**aries** a person or thing that is subsidiary; specif., a company (**subsidiary company**) controlled by another company

subsidize (sub'sə dīz') *vt.* -**dized**, -**diz'-ing** to support with a subsidy —**sub'sidiza'tion** *n.*

subsidy (sub'sə dē) *n., pl.* -**dies** [< L. *subsidium*, reserve troops] financial aid given by a government, as to an industry considered of benefit to the public

subsist (səb sist') *vi.* [< L. *sub-*, under + *sistere*, to stand] **1.** to continue to be; exist **2.** to continue to live (*on* or *by*)

subsistence *n.* **1.** means of support or livelihood; specif., the barest means needed to sustain life **2.** existence

subsistence farming a type of farming in which most of the produce is eaten by the farmer leaving little to sell

subsoil (sub'soil') *n.* the layer of soil beneath the surface soil

subsonic (sub son'ik) *adj.* [SUB- + SONIC] of a velocity less than the speed of sound

substance (sub'stəns) *n.* [< L. *sub-*, under + *stare*, to stand] **1.** the physical matter of which a thing consists; material **2.** the real or essential part of anything;

essence **3.** *a*) solid quality *b*) consistency; body **4.** the real content or meaning of something said or written **5.** property; wealth —**in substance** essentially

substandard (sub stan'dərd) *adj.* below standard

substantial (səb stan'shəl) *adj.* **1.** ample; large **2.** important **3.** well-to-do **4.** strong; firm **5.** real; actual **6.** with regard to essential elements **7.** of or having substance —**substan'tial'ity** (-shē al'-ə tē) *n.*

substantiate (səb stan'shē āt') *vt.* -**at'ed**, -**at'ing** to show to be true or real by giving evidence; prove —**substan'tia'tion** *n.*

substantive (sub'stən tiv) *adj.* [see SUBSTANCE] **1.** existing independently; permanent **3.** actual; real —*n.* a noun —**sub'stanti'val** (-tī'v'l) *adj.*

substitute (sub'stə tyōot') *n.* [< L. *sub-*, under + *statuere*, to put] a person or thing serving or used in place of another —*vt., vi.* -**tut'ed**, -**tut'ing** to put, use, or serve in place of another —*adj.* being a substitute —**sub'stitu'tion** *n.*

subsume (səb syōom') *vt.* -**sumed'**, -**sum'-ing** [< L. *sub-*, under + *sumere*, take] **1.** to include within a larger class, group, etc. **2.** to show (an idea, instance, etc.) to be covered by a rule, principle, etc.

subtenant (sub'ten'ənt) *n.* one who rents from a tenant

subtend (səb tend') *vt.* [< L. *sub-*, under + *tendere*, to stretch] to extend under or be opposite to [each side of a triangle *subtends* the opposite angle]

subterfuge (sub'tər fyōoj') *n.* [< L. *subter-*, below + *fugere*, flee] any plan, action, etc. used to hide one's true objective, evade a difficult situation, etc.

subterranean (sub'tə rā'nē ən) *adj.* [< L. *sub-*, under + *terra*, earth] **1.** underground **2.** secret; hidden Also **sub'-terra'neous**

subtitle (sub'tīt''l) *n.* **1.** a secondary title of a book, play, etc. **2.** a dialogue, esp. translated, or description flashed on a cinema or TV screen —*vt.* -**ti'tled**, -**ti'-tling** to add a subtitle or subtitles to

subtle (sut''l) *adj.* **sub'tler**, **sub'tlest** [< L. *subtilis*, closely woven] **1.** not grossly obvious [a *subtle* hint] **2.** not easily detected [a *subtle* poison] **3.** making fine distinctions or marked by mental keeness **4.** delicately skilful **5.** crafty; sly **6.** tenuous; not dense —**sub'tly** *adv.*

subtlety (sut''l tē) *n.* **1.** the quality or condition of being subtle **2.** *pl.* -**ties** something subtle, as a fine distinction

subtonic (sub ton'ik) *n. Music* the seventh tone of a diatonic scale

subtract (səb trakt') *vt., vi.* [< L. *sub-*, under + *trahere*, draw] to take away (a part from a whole) or (one number or quantity from another)

subtraction *n.* a subtracting or being subtracted; esp., the mathematical process of finding the difference between two numbers or quantities

subtropical (sub trop'i k'l) *adj.* of or

characteristic of regions bordering on the tropics; nearly tropical

suburb (sub'ərb) *n.* [< L. *sub-*, under, near + *urbs*, town] 1. a residential district on the outskirts of a city or town 2. [*pl.*] a region of such districts (with *the*)

suburban (sə bʉr'bən) *adj.* 1. of or living in a suburb or the suburbs 2. characteristic of the suburbs or suburbanites —**subur'banize'** *vt., vi.*

suburbanite *n.* a person living in a suburb

suburbia (sə bʉr'bē ə) *n.* the suburbs or suburbanites collectively: used to connote suburban values, attitudes, etc.

subvention (səb ven'shən) *n.* [< L. *sub-*, under + *venire*, come] a grant of money; subsidy

subversive (səb vʉr'siv) *adj.* tending or seeking to subvert —*n.* a person regarded as subversive

subvert (səb vʉrt') *vt.* [< L. *sub-*, under + *vertere*, to turn] 1. to overthrow or destroy (something established) 2. to corrupt, as in morals —**subver'sion** *n.*

subway (sub'wā') *n.* 1. an underground way, esp. for pedestrians 2. [U.S.] an underground railway

suc- same as SUB-: used before *c*

succeed (sək sēd') *vi.* [< L. *sub-*, under + *cedere*, go] 1. to accomplish something planned or tried 2. to happen or turn out as planned 3. to have success; do well 4. *a)* to come next after another *b)* to follow another into office, etc., as by inheritance (often with *to*) —*vt.* 1. to follow into office, etc. 2. to come after

success (sək ses') *n.* 1. *a)* a favourable outcome *b)* something having a favourable outcome 2. the gaining of wealth, fame, etc. 3. a successful person

successful *adj.* 1. turning out to be as was hoped 2. having gained wealth, fame, etc. —**success'fully** *adv.*

succession (sək sesh'ən) *n.* 1. a succeeding or coming after another 2. the right to succeed to an office, etc. 3. a number of persons or things coming one after another; series 4. *a)* a series of heirs or rightful successors *b)* the order of such a series —**in succession** one after another

successive *adj.* coming one after another; consecutive

successor *n.* a person or thing that succeeds another; esp., one who succeeds to a throne, title, etc.

succinct (sək siŋkt') *adj.* [< L. *sub-*, under + *cingere*, gird] clearly and briefly stated; concise —**succinct'ness** *n.*

succour (suk'ər) *vt.* [< L. *sub-*, under + *currere*, to run] to aid in time of need or distress —*n.* 1. aid; help 2. one that succours

succubus (suk'yoo bəs) *n.*, *pl.* **-bi'** (-bī') [< L. *sub-*, under + *cubare*, to lie] a female demon thought in medieval times to have sexual intercourse with sleeping men

succulent (suk'yoo lənt) *adj.* [< L. *sucus*, juice] 1. juicy 2. full of interest, vigour, etc. 3. *Bot.* having thick, fleshy tissues

for storing water, as a cactus —*n.* a succulent plant —**suc'culence** *n.*

succumb (sə kum') *vi.* [< L. *sub-*, under + *cumbere*, to lie] 1. to give way (*to*); yield 2. to die [to succumb to a plague]

such (such) *adj.* [OE. *swilc*] 1. *a)* of the kind mentioned or implied [one such as he] *b)* of the same or a similar kind [pens, pencils, and *such* supplies] 2. certain but not specified; whatever [such time as you go] 3. so extreme, so much, etc. [such fun!] —*adv.* to so great a degree [such good news] —*pron.* such a one or ones —**as such** 1. as being what is indicated 2. in itself —**such as** 1. for example 2. like or similar to

such and such (being) something particular but not specified [he went to such and such a place]

suck (suk) *vt.* [OE. *sucan*] 1. to draw (liquid) into the mouth with the lips and tongue 2. to take up or in as by sucking; absorb, inhale, etc. 3. to suck liquid from (fruit, etc.) 4. to hold (a sweet, etc.) in the mouth and lick it 5. to place (the thumb, etc.) in the mouth and draw on —*vi.* 1. to suck milk from the breast or udder 2. to make a sucking sound or movement —*n.* the act or sound of sucking —**suck up to** [Slang] to flatter or fawn upon

·SUCKERS

sucker *n.* 1. one that sucks 2. a part used for sucking or holding fast to a surface by suction 3. [Colloq.] *a)* a person easily fooled *b)* a person readily drawn to specified attractions 4. *Bot.* a shoot from a root bud

suckle (suk''l) *vt.* **-led, -ling** to give milk to from a breast or udder; nurse

suckling (suk'liŋ) *n.* [SUCK & -LING[1]] an unweaned child or animal

sucrose (syoo'krōs) *n.* [< Fr. *sucre*, sugar] *Chem.* pure crystalline sugar extracted from sugar cane or sugar beets

suction (suk'shən) *n.* [< L. *sugere*, suck] 1. the act or process of sucking 2. the drawing of air out of a space to make a vacuum that will suck in surrounding air, liquid, etc. or cause something to stick to the surface 3. the force so created —*adj.* operating by suction

Sudanese (soo də nēz') *adj.* of the Sudan —*n.*, *pl.* **-nese'** a native of the Sudan

sudatory (syoo'də tər ē) *adj.* [< L. *sudor*, sweat] of perspiration —*n.*, *pl.* **-ries** an agent that causes sweating

sudden (sud''n) *adj.* [ult. < L. *sub-*, under

+ *ire*, go] **1.** *a)* happening or coming unexpectedly *b)* sharp or abrupt *[a sudden turn]* **2.** done, coming, or taking place quickly or abruptly —**all of a sudden** without any warning; quickly —**sud'denly** *adv.* —**sud'denness** *n.*

sudorific (syoo'də rif'ik) *adj.* [< L. *sudor*, sweat + *facere*, make] causing sweating —*n.* a sudorific drug, etc.

suds (sudz) *n.pl.* [prob. < MDu. *sudse*, marsh water] **1.** soapy water **2.** foam or lather —**suds'y** *adj.*

sue (syoo) *vt.* **sued, su'ing** [< L. *sequi*, follow] **1.** to bring a lawsuit in court against **2.** to appeal to; petition —*vi.* **1.** to bring legal suit **2.** to plead (*for*)

suede, suède (swâd) *n.* [< Fr. *gants de Suède*, Swedish gloves] **1.** tanned leather with the flesh side buffed into a nap **2.** a kind of cloth made to resemble this

suet (soo'it) *n.* [< L. *sebum*, fat] hard fat from around the kidneys and loins of cattle and sheep —**su'ety** *adj.*

suf- *same as* SUB-: used before *f*

suffer (suf'ər) *vt.* [< L. *sub-*, under + *ferre*, to bear] **1.** to undergo (something painful or unpleasant) **2.** to undergo (any process) **3.** to allow **4.** to endure —*vi.* to undergo pain, harm, loss, punishment, etc. —**suf'ferer** *n.* —**suf'fering** *n.*

sufferance *n.* consent, toleration, etc. implied by failure to interfere or prohibit —**on sufferance** allowed but not supported or encouraged

suffice (sə fis') *vi.* **-ficed', -fic'ing** [< L. *sub-*, under + *facere*, make] to be enough —*vt.* [Archaic] to be enough for

sufficiency (sə fish'ən sē) *n.* **1.** sufficient means, ability, or resources **2.** a being sufficient; adequacy

sufficient (sə fish''nt) *adj.* enough

suffix (suf'iks) *n.* [< L. *sub-*, under + *figere*, fix] a syllable or group of syllables added at the end of a word or word base to change its meaning or give it grammatical function (Ex.: *-ish* in *smallish*, *-ed* in *walked*) —*vt.* to add as a suffix

suffocate (suf'ə kāt') *vt.* **-cat'ed, -cat'-ing** [< L. *sub-*, under + *fauces*, throat] **1.** to kill by cutting off the supply of oxygen to the lungs, gills, etc. **2.** to hinder the free breathing of **3.** to smother, suppress, etc. —*vi.* **1.** to die by being suffocated **2.** to be unable to breathe freely; choke, etc. —**suf'foca'tingly** *adv.* —**suf'foca'tion** *n.*

suffragan (suf'rə gən) *n.* [< L. *suffragari*, to support] **1.** a bishop assisting another bishop **2.** a bishop as a subordinate of his archbishop

suffrage (suf'rij) *n.* [< L. *suffragium*, a vote] **1.** the right to vote in political elections **2.** a short prayer of supplication

suffragette (suf'rə jet') *n.* formerly, a woman who worked for women's right to vote

suffuse (sə fyooz') *vt.* **-fused', -fus'ing** [< L. *sub-*, under + *fundere*, pour] to overspread so as to fill with a glow, colour,

fluid, etc.: said of light, a blush, air, etc. —**suffu'sion** *n.*

sug- *same as* SUB-: used before *g*

sugar (shoog'ər) *n.* [ult. < Sans. *śárkarâ*] **1.** any of a class of sweet, soluble, crystalline carbohydrates, including sucrose, glucose, fructose, etc. **2.** sucrose in crystalline or powdered form, used to sweeten food **3.** a lump or spoonful of sugar *[three sugars please]* —*vt.* **1.** to put sugar on or in **2.** to make seem pleasant or less bad

sugar beet a variety of beet with a white root from which common sugar is obtained

SUGAR CANE

sugar cane a tall tropical grass cultivated as the main source of common sugar

sugaring off [Canad.] the boiling down of maple sap to produce sugar, traditionally a social event in early spring

sugar loaf a conical mass of crystallized sugar

sugary *adj.* **1.** of, like, or containing sugar **2.** too sweet or sentimental —**sug'-ariness** *n.*

suggest (sə jest') *vt.* [< L. *sub-*, under + *gerere*, carry] **1.** to mention as something to think over, act on, etc. **2.** to call to mind through association of ideas **3.** to propose as a possibility **4.** to imply; intimate

suggestible *adj.* easily influenced by suggestion —**suggest'ibil'ity** *n.*

suggestion *n.* **1.** a suggesting or being suggested **2.** something suggested **3.** a trace **4.** *Psychol.* the inducing of an idea that is accepted or acted on readily without questioning

suggestive *adj.* **1.** that suggests ideas **2.** tending to suggest something considered improper or indecent

suicidal (soo'ə sid'əl) *adj.* **1.** of, involving, or leading to suicide **2.** having an urge to commit suicide **3.** rash to the point of being dangerous —**su'ici'dally** *adv.*

suicide (soo'ə sid') *n.* [L. *sui*, of oneself + -CIDE] **1.** the intentional killing of oneself **2.** ruin of one's interests through one's own actions **3.** a person who has committed suicide

suit (soot) *n.* [< L. *sequi*, follow] **1.** *a)* a set of clothes to be worn together; esp., a coat and trousers (or skirt) *b)*

any complete outfit [a *suit* of armour]
c) an outfit worn for a specific purpose
[a *spacesuit*] **2.** a set of similar things;
specif., any of the four sets of thirteen
playing cards each (*spades, clubs, hearts,
diamonds*) **3.** a lawsuit **4.** a suing,
pleading, or wooing —*vt.* **1.** to be right
for or becoming to **2.** to make fit; adapt
[a dance *suited* to the music] **3.** to please;
satisfy —*vi.* to be convenient or
satisfactory —**follow suit** **1.** to play a
card of the same suit as the card led
2. to follow the example set —**suit oneself**
to do as one pleases

suitable *adj.* right for the purpose,
occasion, etc.; fitting; appropriate —**suit'-
abil'ity** *n.*

suitcase *n.* a travel case for clothes,
etc., esp. a rectangular one that opens
into two hinged compartments

suite (swēt) *n.* [Fr.: see SUIT] **1.** a set
of related things; specif., *a*) a unit of
connected rooms *b*) a set of matched
furniture for a room **2.** a group of
attendants; retinue **3.** *Music* an
instrumental composition made up of
several movements

suitor (sōōt'ər) *n.* **1.** a person who sues,
petitions, etc. **2.** a man courting a woman

sulk (sulk) *vi.* [< ff.] to be sulky —*n.*
1. a sulky mood or state: also **the sulks**
2. a sulky person

sulky *adj.* -**ier**, -**iest** [prob. < OE. *solcen*,
idle] sullen in a pouting or peevish way
—*n.*, *pl.* **sulk'ies** a light, two-wheeled
carriage for one person —**sulk'ily** *adv.*
—**sulk'iness** *n.*

sullen (sul'ən) *adj.* [ult. < L. *solus*, alone]
1. silent and keeping to oneself because
one feels angry, bitter, hurt, etc. **2.** gloomy;
sombre; dull —**sul'lenness** *n.*

sully (sul'ē) *vt.* -**lied**, -**lying** [< OFr.
souiller] to soil, stain, etc., now esp.
by disgracing

sulpha (sul'fə) *adj.* designating or of a
family of drugs that are sulphonamides,
used in combating certain bacterial
infections: also, esp. U.S., **sulfa**

sulphate (sul'fāt) *n.* a salt or ester of
sulphuric acid

sulphide (sul'fīd) *n.* a compound of
sulphur with another element or a radical

sulphite (sul'fīt) *n.* a salt or ester of
sulphurous acid

sulphonamide (sul fon'ə mīd) *n.* [<
sulphon(yl), the radical SO₂ + AMIDE]
any of various compounds, as
sulphadiazine, containing the univalent
radical -SO₂NH₂: many are used as drugs

sulphur (sul'fər) *n.* [L.] **1.** a pale-yellow,
nonmetallic chemical element: it burns
with a blue flame and a stifling odour:
symbol, S **2.** any of numerous butterflies
with yellow or orange wings **3.** a greenish-
yellow colour

sulphur dioxide a heavy, colourless,
suffocating gas

sulphureous (sul fyo͞oər'ē əs) *adj.* **1.** of,
like, or containing sulphur **2.** greenish-
yellow

sulphuric (sul fyo͞oər'ik) *adj.* of or

containing sulphur, esp. sulphur with a
valence of six

sulphuric acid an oily, colourless,
corrosive liquid used in making explosives,
fertilizers, chemicals, etc.

sulphurize (sul'fyo͞o rīz') *vt.* -**rized'**, -**riz'-
ing** to combine or treat with sulphur or
a sulphur compound

sulphurous (sul'fər əs) *adj.* **1.** of or
containing sulphur, esp. sulphur with a
valence of four **2.** like burning sulphur
in odour, colour, etc. **3.** of or suggesting
the fires of hell

sultan (sul't'n) *n.* [Fr. < Ar. *sultān*] a
Moslem ruler

sultana (sul tä'nə) *n.* **1.** a small seedless
raisin **2.** a sultan's wife, mother, sister,
or daughter

sultanate (sul'tan ət) *n.* the authority,
office, reign, or dominion of a sultan

sultry (sul'trē) *adj.* -**trier**, -**triest** [see
SWELTER] **1.** oppressively hot and moist;
sweltering **2.** inflamed with passion, lust,
etc. —**sul'triness** *n.*.

sum (sum) *n.* [< L. *summus*, highest]
1. a series of numbers to be added up,
or any problem in arithmetic **2.** an amount
of money **3.** gist; summary **4.** the whole
amount; totality [the *sum* of one's
experiences] —*vt.*, *vi.* summed, sum'ming
to get, or come to, a total —**in sum** to
put it briefly —**sum up** **1.** to add up
into a total **2.** to summarize **3.** to form
a quick opinion of

sum- *same as* SUB-: used before *m*

sumac, sumach (sho͞o'mak) *n.* [Ar.
summāq] any of various plants with leaves
which can be powdered and used in tanning
and dyeing

Sumerian (so͞o mēər'ē ən) *adj.* designating or of an ancient people of Sumer
—*n.* **1.** any of the Sumerian people **2.**
the language of the Sumerians

summarize (sum'ə rīz') *vt.* -**rized'**, -**riz'-
ing** to make or be a summary of —**sum'ma-
riza'tion** *n.*

summary (sum'ə rē) *n.*, *pl.* -**ries** [< L.
summa, a sum] a brief account covering
the main points —*adj.* **1.** *a*) prompt and
informal *b*) hasty and arbitrary **2.** briefly
giving the general idea; concise —**sum'mar-
ily** *adv.*

summation (su mā'shən) *n.* **1.** a summing
up **2.** a total or aggregate

summer (sum'ər) *n.* [OE. *sumor*] **1.** the
warmest season of the year, following
spring **2.** any period regarded as a time
of growth, development, etc. —*adj.* of,
typical of, or suitable for summer —**sum'-
mery** *adj.*

summerhouse *n.* a small, open structure
in a garden, park, etc., for providing a
shady rest

summersault (sum'ər sôlt') *n.*, *vi.* var.
of SOMERSAULT

summer school a session at a college
or university held during the summer (or
long) vacation

summer solstice the time in the
Northern Hemisphere when the sun is

farthest north of the celestial equator; June 21 or 22

summertime *n.* **1.** the season of summer **2.** any daylight-saving time, esp. British Summer Time

summingup (sum'iŋ up') *n.* a summarizing

summit (sum'it) *n.* [< L. *summus*, highest] **1.** the highest point; top **2.** the highest degree or state **3.** *a)* a top level of officials, esp. of heads of government *b)* a conference at this level: also **summit meeting**

summon (sum'ən) *vt.* [< L. *sub-*, secretly + *monere*, warn] **1.** to call for or send for with authority **2.** to order, as by a summons, to appear in court **3.** to call upon to do something **4.** to call together; order to meet **5.** to call forth; rouse (often with *up*)

summons (sum'ənz) *n.*, *pl.* **-monses** [see prec.] **1.** an order to come or do something; specif., *Law a)* an official order to appear in court *b)* the writ containing such an order **2.** a call, knock, etc. that summons —*vt.* to serve a court summons upon

sump (sump) *n.* [ME. *sompe*, a swamp] a pit, cistern, cesspool, etc. for draining or collecting liquid, esp. oil from a motor vehicle engine

sumptuary (sump'tyooə wər ē) *adj.* [< L. *sumptus*, expense] of or regulating expenditure

sumptuous (sump'tyoo wəs) *adj.* [see prec.] **1.** involving great expense; costly; lavish **2.** magnificent, as in furnishings

sum total 1. the total arrived at by adding up a sum or sums **2.** everything involved or included

sun (sun) *n.* [OE. *sunne*] **1.** *a)* the self-luminous, gaseous sphere about which the earth and other planets revolve and which furnishes light, heat, and energy for the solar system *b)* its heat or light **2.** any star that is the centre of a planetary system —*vt.*, *vi.* **sunned, sun'ning** to expose or be exposed to the sun so as to warm, tan, etc. —**place in the sun** a favourable position —**under the sun** on earth; in the world

Sun. Sunday

sun bath exposure of the body to sunlight or a sunlamp

sunbathe *vi.* **-bathed', -bath'ing** to take a sun bath —**sun'bath'er** *n.*

sunbeam *n.* a ray or beam of sunlight

sunburn *n.* an inflammation of the skin resulting from prolonged exposure to the sun's rays —**sun'burnt'** *adj.*

sunburst *n.* a decoration suggesting the sun and its rays

sundae (sun'dā) *n.* [prob. < SUNDAY] a serving of ice cream covered with syrup, fruit, nuts, etc.

Sunday (sun'dē) *n.* [OE. *sunnandæg*, day of the sun] the first day of the week, observed by most Christians as a day of worship or rest —*adj.* done, worn, etc. on Sunday

Sunday best [Colloq.] one's best clothes

Sundays *adv.* [Colloq.] on or during every Sunday

Sunday school a school giving religious instruction on Sunday at a church or synagogue

sunder (sun'dər) *vt.*, *vi.* [< OE. *sundor*, asunder] to break apart; split

SUNDIAL

sundial *n.* an instrument that shows time by the shadow of a pointer cast by the sun on a dial marked in hours

sundown *n.* same as SUNSET

sundowner *n.* **1.** [Aust. Colloq.] a tramp **2.** [Colloq.] an alcoholic drink taken at sunset

sundries (sun'drēz) *n.pl.* sundry items; miscellaneous things

sundry (sun'drē) *adj.* [< OE. *sundor*, apart] various; miscellaneous —*pron.* [with pl. v.] sundry persons or things: chiefly in **all and sundry** everybody

sunfish *n.* a large sea fish with a globelike body

sunflower *n.* a tall plant with large, yellow, daisylike flowers

sung (suŋ) *pp. & rare pt. of* SING

sunglasses (sun'gläs'iz) *n.pl.* eyeglasses with special lenses, usually tinted, to protect the eyes from the sun's glare

sun god the sun personified and worshipped as a god

sunk (suŋk) *pp. & alt. pt. of* SINK —*adj.* **1.** same as SUNKEN **2.** [Colloq.] utterly ruined, disgraced, etc.

sunken *obs. pp. of* SINK —*adj.* **1.** submerged [a *sunken* ship] **2.** below the level of the surrounding area [a *sunken* patio] **3.** hollow [*sunken* cheeks]

sunk fence same as HA-HA

sunlamp (sun'lamp') *n.* an electric lamp that radiates ultraviolet rays like those of sunlight

sunless *adj.* without sun or sunlight; dark

sunlight *n.* the light of the sun

sunlit *adj.* lighted by the sun

sun lounge a room or porch with large windows positioned so as to receive as much sunlight as possible

sunny *adj.* **sun'nier, sun'niest 1.** bright with sunlight **2.** bright and cheerful **3.** of or suggestive of the sun —**on the sunny side of** somewhat younger than (a specified age) —**sun'nily** *adv.* —**sun'niness** *n.*

sunrise *n.* **1.** the daily appearance of the sun above the eastern horizon **2.** the time of this **3.** the colour of the sky at this time

sunroof *n.* a panel in the roof of a car that may be opened

sunset *n.* **1.** the daily disappearance of

the sun below the western horizon **2.** the time of this **3.** the colour of the sky at this time

sunshade *n.* a parasol, awning, etc. used for protection against the sun's rays

sunshine *n.* **1.** the shining of the sun, or its light and heat **2.** cheerfulness, joy, etc., or a source of this

sunspot *n.* any temporarily cooler region appearing from time to time as a dark spot on the sun

sunstroke *n.* heatstroke caused by excessive exposure to the sun

suntan *n.* a darkened condition of the skin resulting from exposure to the sun or a sunlamp —**sun'-tanned'** *adj.*

sunup *n.* [U.S.] *same as* SUNRISE

sup[1] (sup) *n., vt., vi.* **supped, sup'ping** [OE. *supan,* to drink] *same as* SIP

sup[2] *vi.* **supped, sup'ping** [< OFr. *soupe, soup*] [Obs.] to have supper

sup- *same as* SUB-: used before *p*

sup. 1. superior **2.** superlative **3.** supplement **4.** supplementary **5.** supply

super (sōo'pər) *n.* [< ff.] *shortened form of:* **1.** SUPERNUMERARY **2.** SUPERINTENDENT —*adj.* [Colloq.] outstanding; exceptionally fine

super- [L. < *super,* above] *a prefix meaning:* **1.** over, above [*superstructure*] **2.** superior to [*superintendent*] **3.** surpassing [*superfine*] **4.** greater than others of its kind [*supermarket*] **5.** additional [*supertax*]

superable (sōo'pər ə b'l) *adj.* that can be overcome

superabundant (sōo'pər ə bun'dənt) *adj.* excessively abundant —**su'perabun'dance** *n.*

superannuate (sōo'pər an'yoo wāt') *vt.* **-at'ed, -at'ing 1.** to retire, esp. with a pension, because of old age or infirmity **2.** to set aside as old-fashioned or obsolete

superannuated *adj.* [< L. *super,* beyond + *annus,* year] **1.** *a)* too old for further work *b)* retired because of old age or infirmity **2.** old-fashioned; outdated

superannuation (sōo'pər an'yoo wā'shən) *n.* **1.** the amount deducted regularly from employees' incomes in a contributory pension scheme **2.** the pension paid

superb (sōo purb') *adj.* [< L. *super,* above] **1.** [Colloq.] excellent **2.** noble; majestic **3.** rich; splendid

supercargo (sōo'pər kär'gō) *n., pl.* **-goes, -gos** [< Sp. *sobre,* over + *cargo,* CARGO] an officer on a merchant ship who has charge of the cargo, representing the shipowner

supercharge (sōo'pər chärj') *vt.* **-charged', -charg'ing 1.** to increase the power of (an engine), as with a supercharger **2.** *same as* PRESSURIZE (sense 1)

supercharger *n.* a blower or compressor used to increase the power of an internal-combustion engine by increasing the supply of air or fuel mixture to the cylinders

supercilious (sōo'pər sil'ē əs) *adj.* [< L. *super-,* above + *cilium,* eyelid] full of or showing pride or contempt; haughty

superconductivity (sōo'pər kon'dək-tiv'ə tē) *n.* Physics the ability of certain metals and alloys to conduct electricity continuously without resistance when chilled to near absolute zero

supercool (sōo'pər kōol') *vt.* to lower the temperature of (a liquid) to below its freezing point without causing solidification

superego (sōo'pər ē'gō) *n., pl.* **-gos** Psychoanalysis that part of the psyche which is critical of the self or ego and enforces moral standards

supererogation (sōo'pər er'ə gā'shən) *n.* [< L. *super,* above + *erogare,* to pay out] the act of doing more than what is required or expected

superficial (sōo'pər fish'əl) *adj.* [< L. *super-,* above + *facies,* face] **1.** of or being on the surface **2.** concerned with and understanding only the obvious; shallow **3.** quick and cursory **4.** merely apparent [a *superficial* resemblance] —**su'perfi'cial'ity** (-ē al'ə tē) *n.*

superfine (sōo'pər fīn') *adj.* **1.** too subtle, delicate, or refined **2.** of very fine quality

superfluous (sōo pur'floo wəs) *adj.* [< L. *super-,* above + *fluere,* to flow] more than is needed or wanted; excessive; unnecessary —**superfluity** (sōo'pər floo'-ə tē) *n.*

superheat (sōo'pər hēt') *vt.* **1.** to heat (steam not in contact with water) beyond its saturation point, so that a drop in temperature will not cause it to turn back to water **2.** to heat (a liquid) above its boiling point without its vaporizing **3.** to make too hot

superhuman (sōo'pər hyōo'mən) *adj.* **1.** having a nature above that of man; divine **2.** greater than normal for a human being

superimpose (sōo'pər im pōz') *vt.* **-posed', -pos'ing 1.** to put on top of something else **2.** to add as a feature that dominates or does not properly fit with the rest

superinduce (sōo'pər in dyōos') *vt.* **-duced', -duc'ing** to bring in as an addition

superintend (sōo'pər in tend') *vt.* to act as superintendent of; supervise —**su'perintend'ence** *n.*

superintendent *n.* [see SUPER- & INTEND] **1.** a person in charge of a department, institution, etc.; supervisor **2.** a police officer ranking above an inspector

superior (sōo pēar'ē ər) *adj.* [< L. *superus,* that is above] **1.** higher in order, status, quality, numbers, etc. (with *to*) **2.** above average; excellent **3.** haughty **4.** not influenced or affected by **5.** higher in space; placed higher up —*n.* **1.** a superior person or thing **2.** the head of a religious community —**supe'rior'ity** (-or'ə tē) *n.*

superlative (sōo pur'lə tiv) *adj.* [< L. *super-,* above + *latus,* carried] **1.** excelling all others; supreme **2.** excessive **3.** Gram. designating the extreme degree of comparison of adjectives and adverbs: usually indicated by *-est* (*hardest*) or *most* (*most beautiful*) —*n.* **1.** the highest degree **2.** Gram. *a)* the superlative degree *b)* a word or form in this degree

superman (so͞o′pər man′) *n.* **1.** in Nietzsche's philosophy, a type of superior man regarded as the goal of the evolutionary struggle **2.** an apparently superhuman man

supermarket (so͞o′pər mär′kit) *n.* a large, self-service, retail store selling food, household goods, etc.

supernal (so͞o pur′n'l) *adj.* [< L. *supernus*, upper] celestial, heavenly, or divine

supernatural (so͞o′pər nach′rəl) *adj.* existing outside man's normal experience or the known laws of nature; specif., of or involving God or a god, or ghosts, the occult, etc. —**the supernatural** supernatural beings, forces, happenings, etc.

supernova (so͞o′pər nō′və) *n., pl.* **-vae** (-vē), **-vas** [see SUPER- & NOVA] an extremely bright nova that suddenly increases 10 million to 100 million times in brightness

supernumerary (so͞o′pər nyo͞o′mə rər ē) *adj.* [< L. *super*, above + *numerus*, number] extra or superfluous —*n., pl.* **-aries** **1.** a supernumerary person or thing **2.** *Theatre* a person with a small, nonspeaking part

superphosphate (so͞o′pər fos′fāt) *n.* an acid phosphate; esp. one made by treating phosphate rock with sulphuric acid, and used as a fertilizer

superpose (so͞o′pər pōz′) *vt.* **-posed′**, **-pos′ing** [see SUPER- & POSE[1]] to lay or place on, over, or above something else

superpower (so͞o′pər pou′ər) *n.* any of the few most powerful nations of the world

supersaturate (so͞o′pər sach′ə rāt′) *vt.* **-rat′ed**, **-rat′ing** to saturate beyond the normal point for the given temperature

superscribe (so͞o′pər skrīb′) *vt.* **-scribed′**, **-scrib′ing** [see SUPER- & SCRIBE] to write (an inscription, name, etc.) at the top or on an outer surface of —**su′perscrip′tion** (-skrip′shən) *n.*

superscript (so͞o′pər skript′) *adj.* written above —*n.* a figure, letter, or symbol written above and to the side of another [in y^2 and x^n, *2* and *n* are *superscripts*]

supersede (so͞o′pər sēd′) *vt.* **-sed′ed**, **-sed′ing** [< L. *super-*, above + *sedere*, sit] **1.** to succeed; replace; supplant **2.** to cause to be set aside as inferior or obsolete

supersensitive (so͞o′pər sen′sə tiv) *adj.* highly sensitive or too sensitive

supersonic (so͞o′pər son′ik) *adj.* [SUPER- + SONIC] designating or moving at a speed greater than that of sound —**su′person′ically** *adv.*

supersonics *n.pl.* [*with sing. v.*] the science dealing with supersonic phenomena

superstition (so͞o′pər stish′ən) *n.* [< L. *super-*, over + *stare*, to stand] **1.** any belief, based on fear or ignorance, that is not in accord with the known facts or rational thought; esp., such a belief in charms, the supernatural, etc. **2.** any action or practice based on such a belief **3.** such beliefs collectively —**su′persti′tious** *adj.*

superstructure (so͞o′pər struk′chər) *n.* a structure built on top of another, as that part of a ship above the main deck

supertanker (so͞o′pər taŋ′kər) *n.* an extremely large tanker

supertax (so͞o′pər taks′) *n.* an additional tax; esp., a surtax

supervene (so͞o′pər vēn′) *vi.* **-vened′**, **-ven′ing** [< L. *super-*, over + *venire*, come] to happen as something added or not expected —**su′perven′tion** (-ven′shən) *n.*

supervise (so͞o′pər vīz′) *vt., vi.* **-vised′**, **-vis′ing** [< L. *super-*, over + *videre*, see] to oversee or direct (work, workers, etc.); superintend —**su′pervi′sion** (-vizh′ən) *n.* —**su′pervi′sor** *n.*

supine (so͞o pīn′) *adj.* [L. *supinus*] **1.** lying on the back, face upwards **2.** showing no concern about matters

supper (sup′ər) *n.* [< OFr. *soupe*, soup] an evening meal, esp. a light one

supplant (sə plänt′) *vt.* [< L. *sub-*, under + *planta*, sole of the foot] to take the place of, esp. through plotting

supple (sup′'l) *adj.* [< L. *supplex*, humble] **1.** bending easily; flexible **2.** lithe; limber **3.** adaptable or yielding —**sup′plely** *adv.* —**sup′pleness** *n.*

supplement (sup′lə mənt; *for v. also* -ment′) *n.* [see SUPPLY[1]] **1.** something added, esp. to make up for a lack **2.** a section added to a book, etc., to give additional information **3.** a separate newspaper section containing feature stories, illustrations, etc. **4.** *Math.* the number of degrees to be added to an angle or arc to make 180 degrees —*vt.* to provide a supplement to —**sup′plemen′tary** *adj.* —**sup′plementa′tion** *n.*

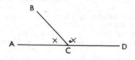

SUPPLEMENTARY ANGLES

supplementary angle either of two angles that together form 180 degrees

supplementary benefits in Britain, an allowance paid by the state to various categories of people to bring their income up to a certain minimum level

suppliant (sup′lē ənt) *n.* a person who supplicates —*adj.* supplicating; beseeching

supplicate (sup′lə kāt′) *vt., vi.* **-cat′ed**, **-cat′ing** [< L. *sub-*, under + *plicare*, to fold] **1.** to ask for (something) humbly **2.** to make a humble request (of) —**sup′plica′tion** *n.* —**sup′plicatory** *adj.*

supply[1] (sə plī′) *vt.* **-plied′**, **-ply′ing** [< L. *sub-*, under + *plere*, to fill] **1.** to furnish or provide **2.** to meet the needs of **3.** to make up for (a deficiency, etc.) —*vi.* to serve as a substitute —*n., pl.* **-plies′** **1.** the act of supplying **2.** a stock;

store **3.** [*pl.*] materials, provisions, etc. for supplying an army, a business, etc. **4.** a substitute, as for a minister, teacher, etc. —*adj.* serving as a substitute —**suppli'er** *n.*

supply[2] (sup'lē) *adv.* in a supple manner; supplely

support (sə pôrt') *vt.* [< L. *sub-*, under + *portare*, carry] **1.** to carry or bear the weight of; hold up **2.** to give courage or faith to **3.** to be in favour of; uphold **4.** to provide for (a person, institution, etc.) with money **5.** to help prove or vindicate **6.** to bear; endure **7.** to keep up; maintain **8.** *Theatre* to act a subordinate role with (a specified star) —*n.* **1.** a supporting or being supported **2.** a person or thing that supports

supporter *n.* a person or thing who supports, esp., one who supports a team, club, etc.

supporting film a film that is not the main attraction but forms part of a cinema programme

supportive *adj.* that gives support or help

suppose (sə pōz') *vt.* **-posed', -pos'ing** [< L. *sub-*, under + *ponere*, to place] **1.** to believe, think, guess, etc. **2.** to take to be true, as for the sake of argument [*suppose* A equals B] **3.** to consider as a possibility [*suppose* he doesn't come] **4.** to presuppose **5.** to expect: always in the passive [*she's supposed* to telephone]

supposed *adj.* **1.** regardèd as true, possible, etc., without actual knowledge **2.** merely imagined —**suppos'edly** *adv.*

supposition (sup'ə zish'ən) *n.* **1.** the act of supposing **2.** something supposed; assumption

suppositious (sup'ə zish'əs) *adj.* [see SUPPOSE] **1.** hypothetical **2.** substituted with intent to deceivę Also **supposititious** (sə poz'ə tish'əs)

suppository (sə poz'ə tər ē) *n.*, pl. **-ries** [see SUPPOSE] a piece of medicated substance, inserted into the rectum, vagina, etc., where it is melted and spread by the body heat

suppress (sə pres') *vt.* [< L. *sub-*, under + *premere*, to press] **1.** to put an end to; prohibit **2.** to restrain; check [to *suppress* a laugh] **3.** to keep from being known, published, etc. **4.** to put down by force; quell **5.** *Electronics, Radio,* etc. to eliminate (an unwanted signal, etc.) —**suppres'sion** *n.* —**suppres'sor** *n.*

suppurate (sup'yoo rāt') *vi.* **-rat'ed, -rat'ing** [< L. *sub-*, under + *pus,* pus] to form or discharge pus; fester —**sup'pura'tion** *n.* —**sup'purative** *adj.*

supra- [< L. *supra,* above] a prefix meaning above, over, beyond [*suprarenal*]

supranational (sōō'prə nash'ə n'l) *adj.* of or involving all or a number of nations

supremacy (soo prem'ə sē) *n.*, pl. **-cies** **1.** the quality or state of being supreme **2.** supreme power or authority

supreme (soo prēm') *adj.* [< L. *superus,* that is above] **1.** highest in rank, power, etc. **2.** highest in quality, achievement, etc. **3.** highest in degree [a *supreme* fool] **4.** final; ultimate —**supreme'ly** *adv.*

Supreme Being God

supremo (soo prēm'ō) *n.* [< SUPREM(E) + *-o*] a person with overall authority or control

Supt., supt. Superintendent

sur-[1] [OFr. < L. *super,* over] a prefix meaning over, upon, above, beyond [*surcharge*]

sur-[2] *same as* SUB-: used before *r*

surcease (sur sēs') *n.* [< L. *supersedere,* refrain from] [Archaic] end

surcharge (sur'chärj; *for v.* sur chärj') *vt.* **-charged', -charg'ing** [see SUR-[1] & CHARGE] **1.** *a)* to charge an additional sum *b)* to overcharge **2.** to overload **3.** to mark (a postage stamp) with a surcharge —*n.* **1.** an additional charge **2.** an overcharge **3.** a new face value overprinted on a postage stamp

surcoat (sur'kōt') *n.* [< MFr.: see SUR-[1] & COAT] an outer coat; esp., a short cloak worn over a knight's armour

surd (surd) *n.* [L. *surdus,* deaf] **1.** *Math.* an irrational number or quantity, as a root that cannot be determined exactly **2.** *Phonet.* a voiceless sound —*adj. same as:* **1.** *Math.* IRRATIONAL **2.** *Phonet.* VOICELESS

sure (shoоər) *adj.* **sur'er, sur'est** [see SECURE] **1.** having no doubt; confident **2.** that cannot be doubted, questioned, etc. **3.** that can be counted on to be or happen [a *sure* defeat] **4.** that will not fail; reliable **5.** never missing [a *sure* aim] **6.** bound to do, experience, etc. [*sure* to lose] —*adv.* [Chiefly U.S. Colloq.] surely —**for sure** certain(ly) —**make sure** to be or cause to be certain —**sure enough** [Colloq.] certainly —**to be sure** surely; certainly —**sure'ness** *n.*

sure-fire *adj.* [Colloq.] sure to be successful

sure-footed (shoоər'foot'id) *adj.* not likely to stumble, fall, or err

surely *adv.* **1.** without a doubt; certainly **2.** with confidence

surety (shoоər'ə tē) *n.*, pl. **-ties** **1.** a person who makes himself responsible for another; specif., *Law* one who makes himself liable for another's debts **2.** something that makes sure, protects, etc.; security **3.** a being sure **4.** something sure; certainty

surf (surf) *n.* [< ?] the foam caused by waves breaking on the shore or a reef —*vi.* to engage in the sport of surfing —**surf'er** *n.*

surface (sur'fis) *n.* [Fr. < *sur-,* over + *face,* a face] **1.** *a)* the outer face of a thing *b)* any side of a thing having several sides **2.** outward appearance **3.** *Geom.* an extent having length and breadth, but no thickness —*adj.* **1.** of, on, or at the surface **2.** functioning or carried on land or sea, rather than in the air [*surface* mail] **3.** seeming such in appearance, superficial —*vt.* **-faced', -fac-**

ing 1. to bring (a submarine, etc.) to the surface **2.** to treat the surface of, esp. so as to make smooth —*vi.* **1.** to rise to the surface **2.** to become known, esp. after being concealed

surface tension a property of liquids in which the surface tends to contract to the smallest possible area, so that it seems like a thin, elastic film under tension

surfboard (surf´bôrd´) *n.* a long, narrow board used in the sport of surfing —**surf´-board´er** *n.*

surfeit (sur´fit) *n.* [< L. *super,* over + *facere,* make] **1.** too great an amount or supply **2.** an indulging in too much food, drink, etc. **3.** disgust, nausea, etc. resulting from this —*vt.* to feed or supply to excess

surfing (sur´fiŋ) *n.* the sport of riding in towards shore on the crest of a wave, esp. on a surfboard: also **surfriding**

surg. 1. surgeon **2.** surgery **3.** surgical

surge (surj) *n.* [< L. *surgere,* to rise] **1.** any sudden strong rush [*a surge* of energy, the *surge* of the crowd*]* **2.** a large wave of water, or the swelling or rushing motion of such a wave —*vi.* **surged, surg´ing** to move in a surge

surgeon (sur´jən) *n.* a doctor who specializes in surgery

surgery (sur´jər ē) *n., pl.* **-geries** [< Gr. *cheir,* hand + *ergein,* to work] **1.** a) the treatment of disease, injury, etc. by operations with the hands or instruments, as the removal of diseased parts by cutting b) the branch of medicine dealing with this **2.** the consulting rooms of a dentist, doctor, etc. **3.** [Colloq.] the place or time when members of parliament can be visited by their constituents

surgical *adj.* **1.** of surgeons or surgery **2.** used in surgery **3.** resulting from surgery —**sur´gically** *adv.*

surgical spirit methylated spirit for use as a cleanser in operations, etc.

surly (sur´lē) *adj.* **-lier, -liest** [earlier *sirly,* imperious < SIR] bad-tempered; sullenly rude; uncivil —**sur´liness** *n.*

surmise (sur mīz´; *for n. also* sur´mīz) *n.* [< L. *super,* upon + *mittere,* send] **1.** a guess; conjecture **2.** the act of surmising —*vt., vi.* **-mised´, -mis´ing** to imagine or infer (something) without conclusive evidence; guess

surmount (sur mount´) *vt.* [see SUR-[1] & MOUNT[2]] **1.** to overcome (a difficulty) **2.** to be or lie at the top of; be or rise above

surmounted *adj.* topped with; capped; crowned (*with* or *by*)

surname (sur´nām´) *n.* [< OFr. *sur-,* over + *nom,* name] the family name, or last name, as distinguished from a Christian name —*vt.* **-named´, -nam´ing** to give a surname to

surpass (sər päs´) *vt.* [< MFr.: see SUR-[1] + PASS[2]] **1.** to be better than; excel **2.** to exceed in quantity, degree, etc. **3.** to go beyond the limit, capacity, etc. of —**surpass´ing** *adj.*

SURPLICE

surplice (sur´plis) *n.* [ult. < L. *super-,* above + *pellicium,* fur robe] a loose, white, wide-sleeved outer vestment worn by the clergy and choir in some churches —**sur´pliced** *adj.*

surplus (sur´pləs) *n.* [OFr. < *sur-,* above + L. *plus,* more] **1.** a quantity over and above what is needed or used; excess **2.** the excess of the assets of a business over its liabilities —*adj.* that is a surplus; excess

surprise (sər prīz´) *vt.* **-prised´, -pris´ing** [< OFr. *sur-,* over + *prendre,* take] **1.** a) to cause to feel astonishment by being unexpected b) to present (someone) unexpectedly with a gift, etc. **2.** to cause by some unexpected action to do or say something unintended: often with *into* **3.** to come upon suddenly or unexpectedly **4.** to attack without warning —*n.* **1.** a being surprised; astonishment **2.** something that surprises because unexpected, unusual, etc. **3.** an unexpected attack —**take by surprise 1.** to come upon suddenly **2.** to amaze —**surpris´-ing adj.**

surrealism (sə rē´ə liz'm) *n.* [< Fr.: see SUR-[1] & REALISM] a modern movement in art and literature, in which an attempt is made to portray the workings of the subconscious mind, as by arranging material in unexpected, fantastic ways —**surre´al, surre´alis´tic** *adj.* —**surre´alist** *adj., n.* —**surre´alis´tically** *adv.*

surrender (sə ren´dər) *vt.* [< MFr. < *sur-* (see SUR-[1]) + *rendre,* RENDER] **1.** to give up possession of; yield **2.** to give up or abandon *[to surrender* all hope*]* **3.** to yield (oneself) to an emotion, etc. —*vi.* to give oneself up, esp. as a prisoner; yield —*n.* the act of surrendering

surreptitious (sur´əp tish´əs) *adj.* [< L. *sub-,* under + *rapere,* seize] **1.** done, got, etc. in a secret, stealthy way **2.** acting in a secret, stealthy way

surrogate (sur´ə git) *n.* [< L. *sub-,* in place of + *rogare,* to elect] a deputy or substitute, esp. a clergyman acting as a deputy of a bishop in granting special licences for marriages

surround (sə round´) *vt.* [< L. *super,* over + *undare,* to rise] **1.** to encircle on all or nearly all sides; enclose **2.** to cut off (a military unit, etc.) from retreat by encircling —*n.* something that surrounds —**surround´ing** *adj.*

surroundings *n.pl.* the things,

conditions, influences, etc. that surround a given place or person; environment

surtax (sur'taks) *n.* an extra tax on something already taxed, esp., a graduated tax on the amount by which an income exceeds a given figure —*vt.* to levy a surtax on

surtout (sur'tōō) *n.* [Fr. < *sur*, over + *tout*, all] formerly, a man's long, closefitting overcoat

surveillance (sər vā'ləns) *n.* [Fr. < *sur-*, over + *veiller*, to watch] watch kept over a person, esp. a suspect

survey (sər vā'; *for n. usually* sur'vā) *vt.* [< OFr. *sur-*, over + *veoir*, see] 1. to examine or consider carefully or in a comprehensive way 2. to determine the location, form, or boundaries of (a tract of land) —*vi.* to survey land —*n.*, *pl.* -veys 1. a detailed study made by gathering and analysing information 2. a comprehensive study [a *survey* of Italian art] 3. *a)* the process of surveying a tract of land *b)* a plan or written description of the area surveyed

surveying (sər vā'iŋ) *n.* 1. the act of one who surveys 2. the science or profession of surveying land

surveyor *n.* a person who surveys, esp. one whose work is surveying land

survival (sər vī'v'l) *n.* 1. the act of surviving 2. someone or something that survives, esp. an ancient belief, custom, etc

survival of the fittest *popular term for* NATURAL SELECTION

survive (sər vīv') *vt.* -vived', -viv'ing [< L. *super-*, above + *vivere*, to live] 1. to exist longer than; outlive 2. to continue to live after [to *survive* a wreck] —*vi.* to continue existing —**survi'vor** *n.*

sus (sus) *n.* [SUS(PICION), SUS(PECT)] [Colloq.] suspicion —*vt.* [Colloq.] to suspect —**sus out** [Colloq.] to puzzle out

susceptibility (sə sep'tə bil'ə ātē) *n.*, *pl.* -ties 1. a being susceptible 2. [*pl.*] sensitive feelings 3. a susceptible temperament

susceptible (sə sep'tə b'l) *adj.* [< L. *sus-*, under + *capere*, take] easily affected emotionally; sensitive —**susceptible of** allowing [testimony *susceptible of* error] —**susceptible to** easily influenced by or affected with [*susceptible to* disease] —**suscep'tibly** *adv.*

suspect (sə spekt'; *for adj. & n.* sus'pekt) *vt.* [< L. *sus-*, under + *spicere*, to look] 1. to believe to be guilty of something specified, on little or no evidence 2. to believe to be bad, harmful, etc.; distrust 3. to think likely; suppose —*adj.* viewed with suspicion —*n.* one suspected, esp. of a crime

suspend (sə spend') *vt.* [< L. *sus-*, under + *pendere*, hang] 1. to hang by a support from above 2. to hold (dust in the air, etc.) in suspension 3. to make inoperative for a time 4. to defer (judgment, a sentence, etc.) 5. to remove (someone) from a position, school, etc., for a time, as a punishment —**suspen'sory** *adj.*

suspended animation a temporary

cessation of the vital functions, resembling death

suspended sentence a prison sentence that is only served if the guilty party commits another offence

suspender belt a belt, usually of elastic fibre, with suspenders hanging from it, worn by women

suspenders *n.pl.* 1. elastic straps with fasteners at the ends for holding up stockings 2. [U.S.] braces

suspense (sə spens') *n.* [see SUSPEND] 1. the state of being undecided 2. a state of usually anxious uncertainty, as in awaiting a decision 3. the growing excitement felt as a story, play, etc. builds to a climax

suspension *n.* 1. a suspending or being suspended; specif., *a)* a temporary removal from a position, privilege, etc. *b)* a temporary stoppage or cancelling *c)* a deferring of action on a sentence 2. a supporting device upon or from which something is suspended 3. the system of springs, etc. supporting a vehicle upon its undercarriage 4. *Chem. a)* the condition of a substance whose particles are dispersed through a fluid but not dissolved in it *b)* a substance in this condition

suspension bridge a bridge suspended from cables anchored at either end and supported by towers at intervals

suspicion (sə spish'ən) *n.* [see SUSPECT] 1. a suspecting or being suspected 2. the feeling or state of mind of a person who suspects 3. a trace —**above suspicion** not to be suspected; honourable —**under suspicion** suspected

suspicious *adj.* 1. arousing suspicion 2. showing suspicion 3. *a)* feeling suspicion *b)* tending habitually to suspect evil, etc. —**suspi'ciously** *adv.*

sustain (sə stān') *vt.* [< L. *sus-*, under + *tenere*, hold] 1. to keep in existence; maintain or prolong [to *sustain* a mood] 2. to provide for the support of; specif., to provide nourishment for 3. to support; carry the weight of 4. to comfort; encourage 5. to endure; withstand 6. to suffer (an injury, loss, etc.) 7. to uphold the validity of [to *sustain* a verdict] 8. to confirm; corroborate

sustenance (sus'ti nəns) *n.* 1. nourishment; food 2. means of support 3. a sustaining or being sustained

susurrate (syōō'sə rāt') *vi.* -rat'ed, -rat'-ing [< L. *susurrare*] to whisper; murmur; rustle —**susurration** (sōō'sə rā'shən) *n.*

sutler (sut'lər) *n.* [< ModDu. *soetelen*, do dirty work] formerly, a person following an army to sell food, drink, esp. alcohol, etc. to its soldiers

suttee (sut'ē) *n.* [< Sans. *satī*, virtuous wife] 1. a Hindu widow who threw herself alive onto her husband's funeral pyre 2. the former custom of such self-cremation

suture (sōō'chər) *n.* [< L. *suere*, sew] 1. *Surgery a)* the stitching together of the two edges of a wound or incision *b)* the gut, thread, etc. used, or any of the stitches made **2.** *Anat.* the line of junction of two bones, esp. of the skull —*vt.* **-tured, -turing** to join together as with sutures

suzerain (sōō′zə rān′) *n.* [Fr. < *sus*, above + (*sou*)*verain*, SOVEREIGN] **1.** a state in its relation to another state over which it has political control **2.** a feudal lord —**su′zerainty** *n.*

svelte (svelt) *adj.* [Fr.] slender and graceful

SW, S.W., s.w. 1. southwest **2.** southwestern

Sw. 1. Sweden **2.** Swedish

swab (swob) *n.* [< ModDu. *zwabben*, do dirty work] **1.** *a*) a small piece of cottonwool, etc. used to apply medicine to or clean the throat, mouth, etc. *b*) matter collected in this way **2.** a mop for cleaning decks, floors, etc. **3.** [Slang] a clumsy, loutish person —*vt.* **swabbed, swab′bing** to clean, medicate, etc. with a swab

swaddle (swod′′l) *vt.* **-dled, -dling** [OE. *swethel*] to wrap (a newborn baby) in long, narrow bands of cloth (**swaddling clothes** or **bands**), as in former times

swag (swag) *n.* [< ?] **1.** [Slang] *a*) loot; plunder *b*) goods; valuables; money **2.** a curtain, garland, chain, etc. hanging decoratively in a loop or curve **3.** [Aust. Colloq.] a bundle containing one's personal belongings

swagger (swag′ər) *vi.* [prob. < Norw. *svagga*, to sway] **1.** to walk with a bold, arrogant stride; strut **2.** to boast, brag, or show off in a loud, superior manner —*n.* swaggering walk or manner —**swag′geringly** *adv.*

swagger stick a short stick or cane as carried by some army officers, etc.: also **swagger cane**

swagman (swag′mən) *n.* [Aust. Colloq.] a vagrant worker, carrying his possessions on his back

Swahili (swä hē′lē) *n.* **1.** *pl.* **-lis, -ii** any of a Bantu people of Zanzibar and the nearby mainland **2.** their Bantu language, widely used as a lingua franca in E and C Africa

swain (swān) *n.* [< ON. *sveinn*, boy] [Poet. or Archaic] **1.** a country youth **2.** a young rustic lover **3.** a lover

SWALLOW (to 19 cm)

swallow¹ (swol′ō) *n.* [OE. *swealwe*] a

small, swift-flying, migratory bird with long, pointed wings and a forked tail

swallow² *vt.* [OE. *swelgan*] **1.** to pass (food, etc.) from the mouth into the stomach **2.** to take in; absorb (often with *up*) **3.** to take back (words said) **4.** to tolerate [to *swallow* insults] **5.** to suppress [to *swallow* one's pride] **6.** to utter (words) indistinctly **7.** [Colloq.] to accept as true without question —*vi.* to move the muscles of the throat as in swallowing —*n.* **1.** the act of swallowing **2.** the amount swallowed at one time

swallow dive a dive in which the legs are held straight, the back is arched, and the arms are stretched out to the sides

swallowtail *n.* **1.** something having a forked shape like that of a swallow's tail **2.** a butterfly having taillike points on the hind wings

swam (swam) *pt.* of SWIM¹ & SWIM²

swami (swä′mē) *n., pl.* **-mis** [< Sans. *svāmin*, lord] master: a title of respect for a Hindu religious teacher

swamp (swomp) *n.* [< ME. *sompe*, SUMP] a piece of wet, spongy land; marsh; bog —*adj.* of or native to a swamp —*vt.* **1.** to plunge in a swamp, deep water, etc. **2.** to flood as with water **3.** to overwhelm [*swamped* by debts] —**swamp′y** *adj.*

swan (swon) *n.* [OE.] **1.** a large-bodied water bird with webbed feet, a long, graceful neck, and, usually, pure white feathers **2.** [Poet.] a poet or singer —*vi.* [Colloq.] to wander idly; stroll —**swan′like′** *adj.*

swank (swaŋk) *n.* [akin to OE. *swancor*, pliant] [Colloq.] ostentation or showiness in dress, behaviour, speech, etc. —*vi.* [Slang] to show off; boast —**swank′y** *adj.*

swan's-down (swonz′doun′) *n.* **1.** the soft, fine underfeathers of a swan **2.** a soft, thick fabric of wool and silk, rayon, or cotton Also **swans′down′**

swan song 1. the last act, work, etc. of a person **2.** the sweet song supposed to be sung by a dying swan

swan-upping *n.* [see SWAN + UP, *v.*] the practice of marking young swans with a notch in the upper beak as a sign of ownership

swap (swop) *vt., vi.* **swapped, swap′ping** [ME. *swappen*, to strike] [Colloq.] to exchange or barter —*n.* [Colloq.] *a*) an exchange, or barter *b*) the thing exchanged

sward (swôrd) *n.* [OE. *sweard*, skin] grass-covered soil; turf

swarm¹ (swôrm) *n.* [OE. *swearm*] **1.** a large number of bees, led by a queen, leaving a hive to start a new colony **2.** a moving mass or crowd —*vi.* **1.** to fly off in a swarm: said of bees **2.** to move, collect, etc. in large numbers **3.** to be filled or crowded (*with*) —*vt.* to crowd; throng

swarm² *vi., vt.* [< ?] to climb (a tree, mast, etc.); shin (*up*)

swarthy (swôr′the) *adj.* **-ier, -iest** [< OE. *sweart*] having a dark complexion; dusky —**swarth′ily** *adv.* —**swarth′iness** *n.*

swashbuckler (swosh′buk′lər) *n.* [<

swash, swagger + BUCKLER] a blustering, swaggering fighting man —**swash'buck'- ling** *n., adj.*

swastika (swos'ti kə) *n.* [< Sans. *svasti,* well-being] **1.** a design of ancient origin in the form of a cross with four equal arms, each bent in a right-angle extension **2.** this design with the extensions bent clockwise: used as the Nazi emblem

swat (swot) *vt.* **swat'ted, swat'ting** [see SQUAT] [Colloq.] to hit with a quick, sharp blow —*n.* [Colloq.] a quick, sharp blow —**swat'ter** *n.*

swatch (swoch) *n.* [< ?] **1.** a sample piece of cloth **2.** a small amount in a bunch or patch

swath (swôth) *n.* [OE. *swathu,* a track] **1.** the area covered with one cut of a scythe, etc. **2.** the strip of grass, wheat, etc. cut in a single strip by a mower, etc. **3.** any long strip

swathe[1] (swāth) *vt.* **swathed, swath'ing** [OE. *swathian*] **1.** to wrap or bind up in a bandage **2.** to wrap (a bandage, etc.) around something **3.** to envelop

swathe[2] *n.* same as SWATH

sway (swā) *vi.* [ON. *sveigja,* to bend] **1.** to swing or move from side to side or to and fro **2.** to vacillate in position, judgment or opinion —*vt.* **1.** to cause to sway **2.** to influence in a certain direction [*swayed* by promises] —*n.* **1.** a swaying or being swayed **2.** influence or control **3.** [Archaic] rule; dominion —**hold sway** to reign or prevail

swear (swâər) *vi.* **swore, sworn, swear'- ing** [OE. *swerian*] **1.** to make a solemn declaration, supporting it with an appeal to God or to something held sacred **2.** to make a solemn promise; vow **3.** to use profane or offensive language; curse **4.** *Law* to give evidence under oath —*vt.* **1.** to declare, pledge, or vow on oath **2.** to assert with great emphasis **3.** to administer a legal oath to —**swear by 1.** to name (something held sacred) in taking an oath **2.** to have great faith in —**swear in** to administer an oath to (a person taking office, a witness, etc.) —**swear off** to promise to give up —**swear to** to be certain of [I couldn't *swear to* his presence]

swearword *n.* a word or phrase used in swearing or cursing; profane or offensive word

sweat (swet) *vi.* **sweat'ed, sweat'ing** [OE. *swat*] **1.** to give out a salty moisture through the pores of the skin; perspire **2.** *a)* to give out moisture in droplets on its surface *b)* to condense water in droplets on its surface **3.** to work hard enough to cause sweating **4.** [Colloq.] to suffer distress, anxiety, etc. —*vt.* **1.** *a)* to give out (moisture) through a porous surface *b)* to condense (moisture) on the surface **2.** to cause to perspire, as by drugs, exercise, etc. **3.** *a)* to cause to work so hard as to sweat *b)* to cause (employees) to work long hours at low wages under poor working conditions **4.** [Colloq.] to get information from by torture or gruelling questioning —*n.* **1.** the clear,

salty liquid given out through the pores in the skin **2.** moisture given out or collected in droplets on a surface **3.** a sweating **4.** a condition of eagerness, impatience, etc. **5.** hard work; drudgery —**sweat blood** [Slang] **1.** to work very hard **2.** to be impatient, anxious, etc. —**sweat out** [Slang] **1.** to endure **2.** to wait anxiously or impatiently —**sweat'y** *adj.*

sweatband *n.* **1.** a band of leather, etc. inside a hat to protect it against sweat **2.** a piece of cloth tied round the forehead, or a band worn round the wrist, to absorb sweat, as in sport

sweater *n.* a knitted outer garment for the upper part of the body

sweat shirt a heavy, long-sleeved cotton jersey

sweatshop *n.* a place where employees work long hours at low wages under poor working conditions

Swed. **1.** Sweden **2.** Swedish

Swede (swēd) *n.* a native or inhabitant of Sweden

swede (swēd) *n.* a turnip with a large, yellow root

Swedish *adj.* of Sweden, its people, their language, etc. —*n.* the North Germanic language of the Swedes

sweep (swēp) *vt.* **swept, sweep'ing** [OE. *swapan*] **1.** to clean as by brushing with a broom [to *sweep* a floor] **2.** to remove (dirt, etc.) as with a broom **3.** to strip, carry away, or destroy with forceful movement **4.** to touch lightly in moving across **5.** to pass swiftly over or across **6.** to rake with gunfire **7.** to win overwhelmingly —*vi.* **1.** to clean a surface, room, etc. as with a broom **2.** to move or progress steadily with speed, force, or gracefulness **3.** to trail, as the train of a gown **4.** to extend in a long curve [a road *sweeping* up the hill] —*n.* **1.** the act of sweeping **2.** a steady sweeping movement **3.** range or scope **4.** extent or stretch [a *sweep* of meadow] **5.** a line, contour, curve, etc. that gives an impression of flow or movement **6.** a chimney sweep **7.** complete victory or success **8.** a long oar —**sweep the board** to win all the possible prizes, etc. —**sweep'- er** *n.*

sweeping *adj.* **1.** that sweeps **2.** extending over a wide range **3.** *a)* extensive; comprehensive *b)* complete *c)* indiscriminate —*n.* [*pl.*] things swept up, as dirt from a floor

sweepstakes *n., pl.* **-stakes' 1.** a lottery in which each participant puts up money in a common fund from which the prizes come **2.** *a)* a contest, esp. a horse race, which determines the winners of such a lottery *b)* the prize or prizes won Also **sweep'stake'**, **sweeps**

sweet (swēt) *adj.* [OE. *swete*] **1.** *a)* having a taste of, or like that of, sugar *b)* containing sugar in some form [*sweet* wines] **2.** *a)* pleasant in taste, looks, etc. *b)* gratifying [*sweet* praise] *c)* having a friendly, pleasing disposition *d)* sentimental *e)* [Colloq.] good, delightful, etc. **3.** *a)* not rancid, spoiled, or sour [*sweet* milk] *b)* not salty or salted —*n.* 1. something sweet; specif., *a)* a small piece of sweet food, usually made from sugar or syrup, with flavouring, nuts, etc. added *b)* a sweet dessert *c)* [*usually pl.*] pleasure or a pleasurable experience 2. a sweetheart; darling —**be sweet on** [Colloq.] to be in love with —**sweet′ish** *adj.* —**sweet′-ness** *n.*

sweetbread *n.* the thymus or the pancreas of a calf, lamb, etc., when used as food

sweetbrier, sweetbriar *n.* same as EGLANTINE

sweet corn any of various strains of maize with kernels rich in sugar, eaten as a cooked vegetable

sweeten *vt.* 1. to make sweet 2. to make pleasant or agreeable 3. to make less harsh, less acidic, etc. —*vi.* to become sweet

sweetener *n.* a sweetening agent, esp. a synthetic substance, such as saccharin

sweetheart *n.* 1. a lover 2. darling: a term of endearment

sweetmeat *n.* a sweetened delicacy such as candied fruit, a sweet, etc.

sweet pea a climbing annual plant of the legume family, with butterfly-shaped flowers

sweet potato a tropical, trailing plant with a fleshy tuberlike root used as a vegetable

sweet-talk *vt., vi.* [U.S. Colloq.] to talk in a flattering or blandishing way (to)

sweet tooth [Colloq.] a fondness or craving for sweets

sweetveld (swit′felt′) *n.* [< Afrik.] in South Africa, a particular type of grazing

sweet william, sweet William a perennial pink with dense, flat clusters of small flowers

swell (swel) *vi.* **swelled, swelled** or **swoll′-len, swell′ing** [OE. *swellan*] 1. to become larger as a result of pressure from within; expand 2. to curve out; bulge 3. to extend above the normal level 4. to form large waves: said of the sea 5. to be filled (*with* pride, etc.) 6. to increase in size, force, intensity, or loudness —*vt.* to cause to swell —*n.* 1. a part that swells; specif., *a)* a large wave that moves steadily without breaking *b)* a piece of rising ground 2. a swelling or being swollen 3. an increase in size, amount, degree, etc. 4. [Old Colloq.] a person, esp. a man, of wealth and fashion 5. *Music a)* a crescendo *b)* a device for controlling the loudness of tones, as in an organ —*adj.* [Chiefly U.S. Slang] first-rate; excellent

swelled head [Colloq.] great self-con-ceit: also **swollen head**

swelling *n.* 1. an increasing or being increased in size, volume, etc. 2. a swollen part, as on the body

swelter (swel′tər) *vi.* [OE. *sweltan*, die] to be or feel oppressively hot —*n.* a sweltering

sweltering *adj.* very hot, sweaty, sticky, etc.

swept (swept) *pt. & pp.* of SWEEP

sweptwing *adj.* *Aeron.* having wings swept backwards

swerve (swurv) *vi., vt.* **swerved, swerv′-ing** [OE. *sweorfan*, to scour] to turn aside suddenly from a straight line, course, etc. —*n.* the act or degree of swerving

swift (swift) *adj.* [OE.] 1. moving with great speed; fast 2. coming, happening, or done quickly 3. acting or responding quickly [*swift* to help] —*n.* an insect-eating, swift-flying bird resembling the swallow

swig (swig) *vt., vi.* **swigged, swig′ging** [< ?] [Colloq.] to drink in big gulps —*n.* [Colloq.] a big gulp, esp. of alcoholic liquor

swill (swil) *vt.* [OE. *swilian*] 1. to flood with water so as to wash 2. to drink greedily 3. to feed swill to (pigs, etc.) —*vi.* to drink in large quantities —*n.* 1. liquid refuse fed to pigs, etc. 2. refuse or slop 3. the act of swilling 4. a swig

swim¹ (swim) *vi.* **swam, swum, swim′-ming** [OE. *swimman*] 1. to move through water by movements of the arms, legs, fins, etc. 2. to move along smoothly 3. to float on or be immersed in a liquid 4. to overflow [eyes *swimming* with tears] —*vt.* 1. to move in or across (a body of water) by swimming 2. to perform (a specified stroke) in swimming —*n.* an act, spell, or distance of swimming —**in the swim** active in the main current of affairs —**swim with the tide** to side with the majority opinion —**swim′mer** *n.*

swim² *n.* [OE. *swima*] the condition of being dizzy —*vi.* **swam, swum, swim′ming** 1. to be dizzy 2. to have a hazy, reeling, or whirling appearance

swim bladder a gas-filled sac in the body cavity of most bony fishes, giving buoyancy to the body

swimming bath an indoor swimming pool: often used in pl.

swimmingly *adv.* easily and with success

swimming pool a pool of water for swimming; esp., a tank specially built for the purpose

swimsuit *n.* a garment worn for swimming: also **swimming costume**

swindle (swin′d'l) *vt.* **-dled, -dling** [< G. *schwindeln*, to cheat] 1. to get money or property from (another) under false pretences; cheat; defraud 2. to get by fraud —*n.* an act of swindling —**swin′-dler** *n.*

swine (swin) *n., pl.* **swine** [OE. *swin*] 1. a pig 2. a contemptible or disgusting person —**swin′ish** *adj.*

swine fever an infectious disease of pigs

swineherd *n.* one who tends swine

swing (swiŋ) *vi.* **swung, swing′ing** [OE. *swingan*] 1. to sway or move backwards and forwards 2. to walk, trot, etc. with freely swaying movements 3. to stride (*at*) 4. to turn, as on a hinge 5. *a)* to hang *b)* [Colloq.] to be hanged in execution 6. to move on a swing (*n.* 7) 7. to have an exciting rhythmic quality [music that really *swings*] 8. [Slang] to be very fashionable, active, etc., esp. in the pursuit of pleasure —*vt.* **1.** to move (a weapon, bat, etc.) with a sweeping motion **2.** to cause (a freely hanging object) to move backwards and forwards **3.** to cause to turn, pivot, or hang freely **4.** to cause to move in a curve *[to swing a car around a corner]* **5.** [Colloq.] to cause to come about successfully *[to swing a vote]* —*n.* **1.** the act of swinging **2.** the arc through which something swings **3.** a relaxed motion, as in walking **4.** a sweeping blow or stroke **5.** the course of some activity, etc. **6.** rhythm **7.** a seat hanging from ropes or chains, on which one can sit and swing **8.** the amount that a thing swings *[the swing to Labour in the election]* **9.** a style of jazz music c 1935 to 1945, characterized by large bands **10.** [Canad.] a train of freight sleighs or canoes —**in full swing 1.** in complete and active operation **2.** going on without restraint —**swing the lead** [Colloq.] to try and evade a job, duty, etc.

swing boat　a boat-shaped gondola, suspended from a frame, used for swinging in at a fair

swingeing (swinj'iŋ) *adj.* [OE. *swengan*, to shake] [Colloq.] very large or severe

swingletree (swiŋ'g'ltrē') *n.* [< ME. *swingle*, rod + *tre*, tree] a pivoted crossbar at the front of a wagon, etc., to which the traces of a horse's harness are hooked

swipe (swīp) *n.* [see SWEEP] [Colloq.] a hard, sweeping blow —*vt.* **swiped, swip'ing** [Colloq.] **1.** to hit with a hard, sweeping blow **2.** to steal —*vi.* [Colloq.] to make a sweeping blow

swirl (swurl) *vi., vt.* [ME. *swyrl*] to move or cause to move with a whirling motion —*n.* **1.** a whirl; eddy **2.** a twist; curl —**swirl'y** *adj.*

swish (swish) *vi.* [echoic] **1.** to move with a sharp, hissing sound, as a cane swung through the air **2.** to rustle, as skirts —*vt.* to cause to swish —*n.* **1.** a hissing or rustling sound **2.** a movement that makes this sound —*adj.* [Colloq.] fashionable; smart

Swiss (swis) *adj.* of Switzerland, its people, or its culture —*n., pl.* **Swiss** a native or inhabitant of Switzerland

swiss roll　a flat sponge cake rolled up while hot with jam or cream inside

switch (swich) *n.* [prob. < MDu. or LowG.] **1.** a device used to open, close, or divert an electric circuit **2.** a shift; change **3.** a thin, flexible twig, stick, etc. used for whipping **4.** a sharp, lashing movement, as with a whip **5.** a tress of detached hair used as part of a coiffure **6.** the bushy part of the tail of a cow, etc. —*vt.* **1.** to shift; change **2.** [Colloq.] to exchange *[to switch places]* **3.** to transfer (a train, etc.) from one line to another by means of a switch **4.** to turn (an electric light, etc.) *on* or *off* by using a switch **5.** to swing sharply *[a cow switches its tail]* **6.** to whip as with a switch —*vi.* to shift; transfer

switchback *n.* **1.** a steep road or railway

with hairpin bends **2.** an amusement ride in which small, open cars move on tracks that dip and curve sharply

switchboard *n.* a panel equipped with apparatus for controlling the operation of a system of electric circuits, as in a telephone exchange

switch-over *n.* a changeover; exchange

swither (swith'ər) *vi.* [< ?] to hesitate; vacillate

swivel (swiv''l) *n.* [< OE. *swifan*, revolve] a coupling device that allows free turning of the parts attached to it —*vi., vt.* **-elled, -elling** to turn or cause to turn as on a swivel

swivel chair　a chair whose seat turns horizontally on a pivot

swizz (swiz) *n.* [< ?] [Slang] a fraud; a great disappointment: also **swiz**

swizzle (swiz''l) *n.* [< ?] **1.** an alcoholic drink containing rum or gin **2.** [Slang] same as SWIZZ

swizzle stick [< ?]　a small rod for stirring mixed drinks

swob (swob) *n., vt.* **swobbed, swob'bing** var. sp. of SWAB

swollen (swō'lən) alt. pp. of SWELL —*adj.* blown up; distended; bulging

swoon (swōōn) *vi.* [< OE. *geswogen*, unconscious] **1.** to faint **2.** to feel rapturous emotion —*n.* a faint

swoop (swōōp) *vt.* [OE. *swapan*, sweep along] to snatch or seize suddenly: often with *up* —*vi.* to pounce or sweep (*down* or *upon*) —*n.* the act of swooping

swoosh (swōōsh) *vi., vt.* [echoic] to move, pour, etc. with a sharp, rustling or whistling sound —*n.* such a sound

swop (swop) *n., vt., vi.* **swopped, swop'ping** var. sp. of SWAP

sword (sôrd) *n.* [OE. *sweord*] **1.** a hand weapon having a long, sharp, pointed blade, set in a hilt **2.** a) power; esp., military power b) war —**cross swords 1.** to fight **2.** to argue —**put to the sword** to kill

sword-bearer *n.* the person who carries the sword of state on ceremonial occasions

sword dance　a dance in which the performers dance over swords laid on the ground, or brandish swords in the air —**sword dancer**

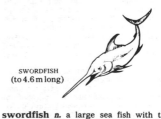

SWORDFISH
(to 4.6 m long)

swordfish *n.* a large sea fish with the upper jawbone extending in a long, flat, swordlike projection

sword of Damocles (dam'ə klēz') [after the courtier of ancient Syracuse who was

seated at a feast under a sword hanging from a hair] any imminent danger

swordplay *n.* the act or skill of using a sword in fencing or fighting

swordsman *n.* 1. a person who uses a sword in fencing or fighting 2. a person skilled in using a sword —**swords'man·ship'** *n.*

swordstick *n.* a walking stick that contains a slender sword

swordswallower *n.* someone who swallows, or appears to swallow, swords in a circus, etc.

swore (swôr) *pt. of* SWEAR

sworn (swôrn) *pp. of* SWEAR —*adj.* bound, promised, etc. as by an oath

swot[1] (swot) *n., vt.* swot'ted, swot'ting *var. sp. of* SWAT

swot[2] *vi., vt.* swot'ted, swot'ting [< SWEAT] [Colloq.] to study hard —*n.* [Colloq.] 1. a person who studies hard 2. something demanding hard study

swum (swum) *pp. of* SWIM[1] & SWIM[2]

swung (swuŋ) *pp. & pt. of* SWING

Sx. Sussex

sybarite (sib'ə rīt') *n.* [< Sybaris, ancient Greek city in S Italy] anyone very fond of luxury and self-indulgence —**syb'arit'ic** (-rit'ik) *adj.* —**syb'arit'ically** *adv.*

sycamore (sik'ə môr') *n.* [< Gr. *sykomoros*] a tree of the maple family found in Europe and Asia

sycophant (sik'ə fant) *n.* [< Gr. *sykophantēs*, informer] a person who seeks favour by flattering people of wealth or influence —**syc'ophancy** *n.* —**syc'o·phan'tic** *adj.* —**syc'ophan'tically** *adv.*

syllabic (si lab'ik) *adj.* 1. of a syllable or syllables 2. forming a syllable by itself, as the *l* in *tattle* —**syllab'ically** *adv.*

syllabify (si lab'ə fī') *vt.* -fied', -fy'ing to form or divide into syllables —**syllab'ifi·ca'tion** *n.*

syllable (sil'ə b'l) *n.* [< Gr. *syn-*, together + *lambanein*, to take] 1. a word or part of a word pronounced with a single, uninterrupted sounding of the voice 2. any of the parts into which a written word is divided, in fairly close relation to its spoken syllables, to show where the word can be broken at the end of a line 3. the least bit, as of something said

syllabub (sil'ə bub') *n.* [< ?] a dessert made of sweetened milk or cream mixed with wine and beaten to a froth

syllabus (sil'ə bəs) *n., pl.* -buses, -bi' (-bī') [< Gr. *sillybos*, parchment label] a summary or outline, esp. of a course of study

syllogism (sil'ə jiz'm) *n.* [< Gr. *syn-*, together + *logizesthai*, to reason] a form of reasoning in which two statements are made and a logical conclusion drawn from them Ex: All mammals are warm-blooded (*major premise*); whales are mammals (*minor premise*); therefore, whales are warmblooded (*conclusion*)

sylph (silf) *n.* [< L., spirit] 1. an imaginary being supposed to live in the air 2. a slender, graceful woman or girl —**sylph'-like'** *adj.*

sylvan (sil'vən) *adj.* [< L. *silva*, wood] 1. of, characteristic of, or living in woods or forests 2. wooded

symbiosis (sim'bi ō'sis) *n.* [< Gr. *syn-*, together + *bioun*, to live] the living together of two kinds of organisms to their mutual advantage —**sym'biot'ic** (-ot'ik) *adj.*

symbol (sim'b'l) *n.* [< Gr. *syn-*, together + *ballein*, to throw] 1. an object used to represent something abstract [the dove is a *symbol* of peace] 2. a mark, letter, abbreviation, etc. standing for a quality, process, etc., as in music, mathematics, etc.

symbolic (sim bol'ik) *adj.* 1. of or expressed in a symbol or symbols 2. that serves as a symbol (of) 3. using symbolism —**symbol'ically** *adv.*

symbolism (sim'bəl iz'm) *n.* 1. the representation of things by use of symbols, esp. in art or literature 2. symbolic meaning

symbolize *vt.* -ized', -iz'ing 1. to be a symbol of; stand for 2. to represent by a symbol or symbols

symmetry (sim'ə trē) *n., pl.* -tries [< Gr., *syn-*, together + *metron*, a measure] 1. correspondence of opposite parts in size, shape, and position 2. balance or beauty of form resulting from such correspondence —**symmetrical** (si met'-ri k'l), **symmet'ric** *adj.* —**symmet'rically** *adv.*

sympathetic (sim'pə thet'ik) *adj.* 1. of, feeling, or showing sympathy 2. in agreement with one's tastes, mood, etc.; congenial 3. showing favour, approval, etc. [to be *sympathetic* to a plan] 4. similar to and caused by the action of another, related thing [*sympathetic* vibrations] —**sym'pathet'ically** *adv.*

sympathetic magic a type of magic in which a small-scale ceremony is thought to produce a large-scale effect, as pouring water on an altar to induce rain

sympathize (sim'pə thīz') *vi.* -thized', -thiz'ing 1. to share or understand the feelings or ideas of another 2. to feel or express sympathy, esp. in pity or compassion; commiserate 3. to be in accord

sympathy (sim'pə thē) *n., pl.* -thies [< Gr. *syn-*, together + *pathos*, feeling] 1. a sharing of, or the ability to share, another's emotions, etc.; esp., [often *pl.*] pity or compassion 2. sameness of feeling; affinity 3. agreement in qualities; accord 4. a mutual liking or understanding arising from sameness of feeling, ability to share, another's emotions 5. approval of an idea, cause, etc.

symphonic poem a piece of music for full symphony orchestra, interpreting particular poetic or descriptive ideas

symphony (sim'fə nē) *n., pl.* -nies [< Gr. *syn-*, together + *phōnē*, a sound] 1. *Music* a) an extended composition for full orchestra, having several movements b) [U.S.] *short for* SYMPHONY ORCHESTRA

2. harmony, as of colour or sound —**symphonic** (sim fon'ik) *adj.* —**symphon'ically** *adv.*

symphony orchestra a large orchestra of string, wind, and percussion sections for playing symphonic works

symposium (sim pō'zē əm) *n.,* pl. -**siums,** -**sia** [L. < Gr. *syn-*, together + *posis,* a drinking] **1.** any meeting at which ideas are freely exchanged **2.** a conference for the discussion of some particular subject **3.** a collection of opinions or essays on a given subject

symptom (simp'təm) *n.* [< Gr. *syn-*, together + *piptein,* to fall] any circumstance or condition that accompanies something and indicates its existence; sign; specif., *Med.* any condition accompanying a disease and serving as an aid in diagnosis —**symp'tomat'ic** (-tə mat'ik) *adj.* —**symp'tomat'ically** *adv.*

syn- [Gr. < *syn,* with] *a prefix meaning* with, together with, at the same time, by means of: *syn-* is assimilated to *syl-* before *l; sym-* before *m, p, b;* and *sys-* before *s* and aspirate *h*

synagogue (sin'ə gog') *n.* [< Gr. *syn-*, together + *agein,* bring] **1.** a building or place used for worship in the Jewish faith **2.** an assembly of Jews meeting for worship and religious study —**syn'a-gog'al, syn'agog'ical** (-goj'ik'l) *adj.*

synchromesh (siŋ'krō mesh') *adj.* designating or employing a device by which gears to be meshed are automatically brought to the same speed of rotation before the change is completed —*n.* a synchromesh gear system

synchronism (siŋ'krə niz'm) *n.* **1.** occurrence at the same time **2.** a chronological listing of persons or events in history, showing existence or occurrence at the same time —**syn'chronis'tic** *adj.*

synchronize (siŋ'krə nīz') *vi.* -**nized'**, -**niz'ing** [< Gr. *syn-*, together + *chronos,* time] to move or occur at the same time or rate —*vt.* to cause to agree in time or rate; regulate (clocks, action and dialogue, etc.) so as to make synchronous —**syn'chroniza'tion** *n.*

synchronous *adj.* [see prec.] **1.** happening at the same time; simultaneous **2.** having the same rate and phase, as vibrations

syncopate (siŋ'kə pāt') *vt.* -**pat'ed, -pat'ing** [see SYNCOPE] *Music* **1.** to shift (the regular accent) as by beginning a tone on an unaccented beat and continuing it through the next accented beat **2.** to use such shifted accents in (a composition, etc.) —**syn'copa'tion** *n.*

syncope (siŋ'kə pē) *n.* [< Gr. *syn-*, together + *koptein,* to cut] **1.** the dropping of sounds or letters from the middle of a word, as in *Wooster* for *Worcester* **2.** a fainting caused by an inadequate flow of blood to the brain

syncretize (siŋ'krə tīz') *vt., vi.* -**tized'**, -**tiz'ing** [< Gr. *synkrētizein*] to combine, unite, or reconcile

syndic (sin'dik) *n.* [< Gr. *syn-*, together + *dikē,* justice] a business manager, esp. of a university

syndicalism (sin'di kə liz'm) *n.* a theory in which all means of production and distribution would be brought under the control of federations of trade unions —**syn'dicalist** *adj., n.*

syndicate (sin'də kit; *for v.* -kāt') *n.* [see SYNDIC] **1.** *a)* an association of individuals or corporations formed to carry out some financial project requiring much capital *b)* any group organized to further some undertaking [*crime syndicate*] **2.** an organization that sells articles or features for publication by many newspapers —*vt.* -**cat'ed, -cat'ing 1.** to manage as or form into a syndicate **2.** to sell (an article, etc.) through a syndicate for publication in many newspapers, etc. —**syn'dica'tion** *n.*

syndrome (sin'drōm) *n.* [< Gr. *syn-*, with + *dramein,* to run] **1.** a set of symptoms characterizing a disease **2.** any set of characteristics identifying a type, condition, etc.

synecdoche (si nek'də kē) *n.* [< Gr. *syn-*, together + *ekdechesthai,* receive] a figure of speech in which a part is used for a whole, an individual for a class, a material for a thing, or the reverse of any of these (Ex.: *bread* for *food, the army* for *a soldier,* or *copper* for *a penny*)

synod (sin'əd) *n.* [< Gr. *syn-*, together + *hodos,* way] a council of churches or church officials; specif., a high governing body in any of certain Christian churches —**syn'odal** *adj.*

synonym (sin'ə nim) *n.* [< Gr. *syn-*, together + *onyma,* a name] a word having the same or nearly the same meaning as another in the same language

synonymous (si non'ə məs) *adj.* of the same or nearly the same meaning —**synon'ymously** *adv.*

synopsis (si nop'sis) *n.,* pl. -**ses** (-sēz) [< Gr. *syn-*, together + *opsis,* a seeing] a short outline or summary

synoptic *adj.* **1.** of or giving a synopsis or general view **2.** giving an account from the same point of view: said, esp. [*often S-*] of the first three Gospels —**synop'tically** *adv.*

synovia (sī nō'vē ə) *n.* [< ?] the clear lubricating fluid secreted by the membranes of joint cavities, etc. —**syno'vial** *adj.*

syntactic (sin tak'tik) *adj.* of or in accordance with syntax: also **syntac'tical** —**syntac'tically** *adv.*

syntax (sin'taks) *n.* [< Gr. *syn-*, together + *tassein,* arrange] *Gram.* the organization and relationship of words, phrases, and clauses in sentences; sentence structure

synthesis (sin'thə sis) *n.,* pl. -**ses'** (-sēz') [Gr. < *syn-*, together + *tithenai,* to place] **1.** the putting together of parts or elements so as to form a whole **2.** a whole formed in this way **3.** *Chem.* the formation of a complex compound by the combining of two or more simpler compounds, elements, or radicals

synthesize *vt.* **-sized′, -siz′ing** to bring together into a whole by synthesis

synthesizer *n.* a person or thing that synthesizes; specif., an electronic music device that produces sounds not made by ordinary musical instruments

synthetic (sin thet′ik) *adj.* **1.** produced by chemical synthesis, rather than of natural origin **2.** artificial; insincere **3.** of or using synthesis —*n.* a synthetic substance —**synthet′ically** *adv.*

synthetic resin any of a large class of complex organic compounds formed from simpler molecules by polymerization, used in making plastics

syphilis (sif′ə lis) *n.* [< *Syphilus*, hero of a L. poem] an infectious venereal disease, usually passed on during sexual intercourse or contracted in the womb before birth —**syph′ilit′ic** *adj., n.*

syphon (sī′fən) *n., vi., vt.* var. *sp. of* SIPHON

Syriac (sir′ē ak′) *n.* the ancient Aramaic language of Syria, used from the 3rd cent. to the 13th

Syrian (sir′ē ən) *adj.* of Syria, its people, their language, etc. —*n.* a member of the Semitic people of Syria

syringa (sə riŋ′gə) *n.* [see ff.] **1.** same as LILAC **2.** same as MOCK ORANGE

syringe (sir′inj) *n.* [< Gr. *syrinx*, a pipe] **1.** short for HYPODERMIC SYRINGE **2.** a device consisting of a narrow tube fitted at one end with a rubber bulb or piston by means of which a liquid can be drawn in and then pushed out in a stream —*vt.* **-ringed′, -ring′ing** to cleanse, inject, etc. with a syringe

syrup (sir′əp) *n.* [< Ar. *sharāb*, a drink] **1.** any sweet, thick liquid; specif., *a)* a solution made by boiling sugar with water and, often, flavoured *b)* any such solution used in preparing medicines **2.** cloying sentimentality —**syr′upy** *adj.*

system (sis′təm) *n.* [< Gr. *syn-*, together + *histanai*, to set] **1.** a group of things or parts working together or connected in some way so as to form a whole [a solar *system*, *system* of motorways] **2.** a set of principles, rules, etc. [an economic *system*] **3.** a method of classification or arrangement [the metric *system*] **4.** orderly procedure; method **5.** *a)* the body considered as a functioning organism *b)* a number of organs acting together to perform one of the main bodily functions [the nervous *system*] **6.** *Geol.* a major division of stratified rocks —**get it out of one's system** [Colloq.] to free oneself of an obsession, etc.

systematic (sis′tə mat′ik) *adj.* **1.** based on or forming a system **2.** according to a system, method, or plan; regular; orderly —**sys′temat′ically** *adv.*

systematize (sis′təm ə tīz′) *vt.* **-tized′, -tiz′ing** to form into a system; make systematic

systemic (sis tem′ik) *adj.* of or affecting the entire organism or bodily system —*n.* any of a group of pesticides that are absorbed into the tissues of plants, making the plants poisonous to insects, etc. that feed on them —**system′ically** *adv.*

systems analysis the analysis of the methods involved in scientific or industrial operations, usually with a computer, so that an improved system can be designed —**systems analyst**

systole (sis′tə lē′) *n.* [< Gr. *syn-*, together + *stellein*, send] the usual rhythmic contraction of the heart, during which the blood is driven onward from the chambers —**systolic** (sis tol′ik) *adj.*

T

T, t (tē) *n., pl.* **T's, t's** the twentieth letter of the English alphabet

T (tē) *n.* an object shaped like *T* —*adj.* shaped like T —**to a T** to perfection; exactly

T 1. temperature 2. tenor

t tonne(s)

t. 1. temperature 2. time 3. ton(s)

ta (tä) *interj.* [Colloq.] thank you: orig. a child's term

Ta *Chem.* tantalum

taal (täl) *n.* [< Afrik.] [S Afr.] language, esp. Afrikaans

tab¹ (tab) *n.* [< ?] a small, flat loop, strap, or strip fastened to something for pulling it, hanging it up, identification, etc. —*vt.* **tabbed, tab'bing** to provide with tabs

tab² *n.* [prob. < TABULATE] [U.S. Colloq.] a bill for a meal or drinks, esp. in a restaurant —**keep tabs** (or **a tab**) **on** [Colloq.] to watch every move of

tab³ *n.* shortened form of: 1. TABLET 2. TABULATOR

tabard (tab'ərd) *n.* [OFr. *tabart*] 1. a short-sleeved cloak, as worn by a knight over his armour 2. a woman's garment of similar shape 3. a herald's official coat

Tabasco (təbas'kō) [< *Tabasco*, a Mexican state] *Trademark* a hot sauce made from a kind of red pepper

tabby (tab'ē) *n., pl.* **-bies** [< Fr. < Ar. *'attābi*] a grey or brown cat with dark stripes —*adj.* having dark stripes over grey or brown

tabernacle (tab'ərnak''l) *n.* [< L. *tabernaculum*, tent] 1. [T-] the portable sanctuary carried by the Jews in their wanderings from Egypt 2. a place of worship 3. a cabinetlike enclosure on an altar, for consecrated Hosts

table (tā'b'l) *n.* [< L. *tabula*, a board] 1. a) a piece of furniture consisting of a flat top set on legs *b)* such a table set with food for a meal *c)* food served at table *d)* the people seated at a table 2. a large, flat-topped piece of furniture or equipment used for games, etc. [billiard *table*] 3. a) a compact, orderly list of details, contents, etc. *b)* a compact, orderly arrangement of facts, figures, etc. 4. any of various flat surfaces, layers, or parts 5. a thin slab of stone, etc.; tablet —*adj.* 1. of, for, or on a table 2. fit for serving at table [*table* salt] —*vt.* **-bled, -bling** 1. to put on a table 2. to put up for consideration (a motion, bill, etc.) 3. to set aside the consideration of (a motion, bill, etc.) —**at table** at a meal —**the tables** laws, as the Ten Commandments, inscribed on flat stone slabs —**turn the tables** to reverse a situation completely —**under the table** [Colloq.] very drunk

tableau (tab'lō) *n., pl.* **-leaux** (-lōz), **-leaus** [Fr.: see prec.] 1. a striking, dramatic scene or picture 2. a representation of a scene, etc. by a group posed in costume

tablecloth (tā'b'lkloth') *n.* a cloth for covering a table

table d'hôte (tä'b'ldōt') *pl.* **ta'bles d'hote'** (-b'lz) [Fr., table of the host] a complete meal served at a restaurant for a set price: distinguished from À LA CARTE

tableland (tā'b'lland') *n.* a high, broad, level region; plateau

table licence a licence permitting alcoholic drinks to be served with meals only

table linen tablecloths, napkins, etc.

tablespoon *n.* 1. a large spoon used for serving at table 2. a spoon used as a measuring unit in cookery —**ta'ble-spoon'ful** *n.*

tablet (tab'lit) *n.* [see TABLE] 1. a small, flat piece of some hard substance, as medicine, soap, etc. 2. a flat, thin piece of stone, metal, etc. 3. a writing pad containing sheets of paper fastened at one edge

table tennis a game, like tennis in miniature, played on a table, with a small ball and short-handled bats

tabloid (tab'loid) *n.* [< TABLET] a newspaper with small pages having many pictures and short, often sensational, news stories

taboo (təbōō') *n.* [Tongan *tabu*] 1. among some Polynesian peoples, a sacred prohibition which makes certain people or things untouchable, unmentionable, etc. 2. any social restriction resulting from convention —*adj.* forbidden by taboo —*vt.* 1. to put under taboo 2. to prohibit or forbid

tabor (tā'bər) *n.* [< Per. *tabīrah*] a small drum, formerly used by a fife player to beat out his own accompaniment

tabu (təbōō') *n., adj., vt.* var. sp. of TABOO

tabular (tab'yələr) *adj.* [see TABLE] 1. of or arranged in tables or columns 2. calculated by using tables

tabulate (tab'yoolāt') *vt.* **-lat'ed, -lat'-ing** [< L. *tabula*, TABLE] to put (facts, statistics, etc.) in a table or columns —**tab'-ula'tion** *n.*

tabulator *n.* a person or thing that tabulates; specif., a device or key for setting stops on a typewriter carriage, as for typing columns

tachograph (tak'ōgräf') *n.* [< Gr. *tachos*, speed + -GRAPH] an instrument for recording the speed and distance travelled by a motor vehicle

tachometer (takom'ətər) *n.* [< Gr.

tachos, speed + -METER] a device that measures the revolutions per minute of a revolving shaft

tacit (tas′it) *adj.* [< L. *tacere,* to be silent] not expressed openly, but implied or understood —**tac′itly** *adv.*

taciturn (tas′ə turn′) *adj.* [see prec.] almost always silent; not liking to talk —**tac′itur′nity** *n.*

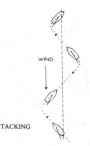

WIND

TACKING

tack¹ (tak) *n.* [MDu. *tacke,* twig] 1. a short nail with a sharp point and a large, flat head 2. *Sewing* a) a stitch for marking darts, etc. from a pattern, clipped and later removed: in full, **tailor's tack** *b)* a loose temporary stitch 3. stickiness 4. a course of action or policy 5. *Naut.* a) the direction in which a ship is moving in relation to the position of the sails *b)* a change of direction made by changing the position of the sails *c)* any of a series of zigzag movements caused by such changes —*vt.* 1. to fasten with tacks 2. to attach temporarily, as with long stitches 3. to attach as a supplement (*to, onto*) 4. *Naut.* to manoeuvre (a ship) against the wind by a series of tacks —*vi.* 1. to change its course by being tacked : said of a ship 2. to change suddenly one's course of action

tack² *n.* [< TACKLE] a horse's equipment, as saddles, bridles, etc.

tackie *n.* [S Afr.] a plimsoll; gym shoe

tackle (tak′'l) *n.* [MDu. *takel,* pulley, rope] 1. equipment; gear [*fishing tackle*] 2. a system of ropes and pulleys, used to lower, raise, or move weights 3. the act or an instance of tackling, as in football 4. *Naut.* the running rigging and pulleys used to operate a ship's sails —*vt.* **tack′led, tack′ling** 1. to undertake (a task, problem, etc.) 2. to confront (a person) about an unpleasant matter 3. to take hold of; seize 4. *Football, etc.* to stop or obstruct (an opponent in possession of the ball) —*vi.* *Football, etc.* to tackle an opponent —**tack′ler** *n.*

tacky (tak′ē) *adj.* **-ier, -iest** [see TACK] sticky, as varnish, glue, etc. before completely dry —**tack′iness** *n.*

taco (tä′kō) *n.,* pl. **-cos** [AmSp.] a fried, folded tortilla filled with chopped meat, lettuce, etc.

tact (takt) *n.* [< L. *tangere,* to touch] a sense of the right thing to say or do without offending

tactful *adj.* having or showing tact —**tact′fully** *adv.* —**tact′fulness** *n.*

tactic (tak′tik) *n.* [see TACTICS] a tactical move

tactical *adj.* 1. of tactics, esp. in military or naval manoeuvres 2. showing skill in tactics —**tac′tically** *adv.*

tactician (tak tish′ən) *n.* an expert in tactics

tactics *n.pl.* [< Gr. *tassein,* arrange] 1. *a)* [*with sing. v.*] the science of manoeuvring military and naval forces in action *b)* actions in accord with this science 2. any methods used to gain an end

tactile (tak′tīl) *adj.* [< L. *tangere,* to touch] 1. that can be perceived by the touch;, tangible 2. of or related to the sense of touch —**tactil′ity** (-til′ə tē) *n.*

tactless (takt′lis) *adj.* not having or showing tact —**tact′lessly** *adv.* —**tact′lessness** *n.*

tadpole (tad′pōl′) *n.* [ME. *tadde,* toad + *poll,* head] the larva of certain amphibians, as frogs and toads, having gills and a tail and living in water

taffeta (taf′itə) *n.* [< Per. *tāftan,* to weave] a fine, rather stiff fabric of silk, nylon, etc., with a sheen

taffrail (taf′rāl′) *n.* [< Du. *tafereel,* a panel] the rail around a ship's stern

Taffy (taf′ē) *n.* [< *Dafydd,* W. form of *David*] [Colloq.] a Welshman

tag (tag) *n.* [< ?] 1. a card, paper, ticket, etc. attached to something as a label or for identification, etc. 2. any hanging part or loosely attached end 3. a hard-tipped end, as of metal, on a cord or lace 4. an epithet 5. the sentence or sentences ending a speech, story, play, etc. 6. a children's game in which one player, called "it," chases the others until he touches, or tags, one of them, making him "it" in turn —*vt.* **tagged, tag′ging** 1. to provide with a tag; put a tag on 2. to identify by an epithet 3. to choose or select 4. [Colloq.] to follow close behind —*vi.* [Colloq.] to follow close behind (usually with *along, after,* etc.)

Tagalog (tə gä′log) *n.* 1. pl. **-logs, -log** a member of a Malayan people of the Philippine Islands 2. their Indonesian language

tag end the last part of anything

tagetes (ta jē′tēz) *n.* [< L. *Tages,* Etruscan god] a plant of the aster family, with yellow or orange flowers, as the marigold

tail¹ (tāl) *n.* [OE. *tægel*] 1. the rear end of an animal's body, esp. when forming a distinct, flexible appendage to the trunk 2. anything like an animal's tail in form or position [*the tail of a shirt*] 3. a luminous train behind a comet 4. the hind, last, bottom, or inferior part of anything 5. [*often pl.*] the reverse side of a coin 6. the rear section of an aircraft, rocket, etc. 7. [*pl.*] [Colloq.] *a)* a swallow-tailed coat *b)* full-dress attire for men 8. [Colloq.] a person or vehicle that follows another, esp. in surveillance —*adj.* 1.

at the rear 2. from the rear [a *tail* wind]
—*vt.* 1. to provide with a tail 2. to
remove the stalk of gooseberries, etc. 3.
[Colloq.] to follow stealthily —*vi.* 1. to
become gradually smaller or fainter (with
off or *away*) 2. [Colloq.] to follow close
behind —**on one's tail** following one closely
—**turn tail** to run from danger, difficulty,
etc. —**with one's tail between one's legs**
in defeat, esp. with fear or dejection

tail² *n.* [see TAILOR] *same as* ENTAIL
—*adj.* limited in a specific way as to
inheritance

tailback *n.* an accumulation or buildup
of vehicles in a traffic jam

tailboard *n.* a board or gate at the back
of a lorry, etc.

tail coat a man's full-dress coat, with
long, tapering tails at the back

tailgate *n.* 1. [Chiefly U.S.] *same as*
TAILBOARD 2. a door at the rear of a
hatchback vehicle

taillight *n.* a light, usually red, at the
rear of a vehicle to warn vehicles coming
from behind

tailor (tā′lər) *n.* [< L. *talea*, twig] a
person who makes, repairs, or alters
clothes, esp. men's suits, coats, etc. —*vt.*
1. to form, alter, etc. so as to meet certain
conditions 2. to make (clothes) high to tailor's
work 3. to make clothes for —*vi.* to
work as a tailor —**tai′loring** *n.*

tailorbird *n.* any of several small Asiatic
and African birds that stitch leaves together
to camouflage and hold their nests

tailored *adj.* 1. having trim, simple lines,
as some women's garments 2. specially
fitted, as loose covers

tailor-made *adj.* 1. having trim, simple
lines; tailored 2. made-to-measure 3.
exactly suited to its purpose

tailpiece *n.* 1. a part forming the end
of something 2. an ornamental design
at the end of a chapter, etc.

tailpipe *n.* an exhaust pipe at the rear
of a motor vehicle

tailplane *n.* a horizontal aerofoil at the
tail of an aircraft to provide longitudinal
stability

tailspin *n.* 1. *same as* SPIN: also **tail
spin** 2. [Colloq.] a state of rapidly
increasing confusion

tail wind a wind blowing in the same
direction as the course of a ship or aircraft

taint (tānt) *vt.* [ult. < L. *tingere*, to wet]
to affect with something injurious,
unpleasant, etc.; infect —*vi.* to become
tainted —*n.* 1. a trace of corruption,
disgrace, etc. 2. an infectious or
contaminating trace

take (tāk) *vt.* **took, tak′en, tak′ing** [<
ON. *taka*] 1. *a*) to get possession of;
capture, seize, etc. *b*) to hold 2. *a*) to
win (a trick at cards, etc.) *b*) to capture
(an opponent's piece in chess) 3. to get
hold of 4. to affect; attack 5. to capture
the fancy of 6. to obtain, acquire, assume,
etc. 7. to eat, drink, etc. for nourishment
or as medicine 8. to enter into a special
relationship with [to *take* a wife] 9.
to rent, lease, etc. 10. to get regularly

by paying for [to *take* a newspaper] 11.
to assume as a responsibility, task, etc.
[to *take* a job] 12. to join or support
(one side in a contest, disagreement, etc.)
13. to get, adopt, etc. by selection or
choice 14. to use [*take* a mop to the
floor] 15. to travel by [to *take* a bus]
16. to go to for shelter, etc. [to *take*
cover] 17. to consider 18. to occupy
[*take* a chair] 19. to require; need [it
takes money] 20. to derive (a name,
quality, etc.) from something or someone
21. to extract, as for quotation 22. to
obtain by observation, etc. [*take* a vote]
23. to be studying as a student in (a
course, etc.) 24. to write down 25. to
make (a photograph, picture, etc.) 26.
to make an impression of 27. to undergo
28. to engage in [to *take* a nap] 29.
to accept (an offer, bet, etc.) 30. to have
a specified reaction to [to *take* a joke
in earnest] 31. to be affected by [he
took cold] 32. to understand 33. to
suppose [he *took* her to be a clerk] 34.
to feel [*take* pity] 35. to conduct; lead
36. to escort 37. to carry 38. to remove
as by stealing 39. to remove by death
40. to subtract 41. [Colloq.] to aim (a
specified action) [he took a jab at me]
42. *Gram.* to be used with in construction
[a transitive verb *takes* an object] —*vi.*
1. to take root: said of a plant 2. to
catch [the fire *took* rapidly] 3. to be
popular 4. to be effective [the vaccination
took] 5. to detract (*from*) [nothing *took*
from the scene's beauty] 6. to go [to
take to the hills] 7. [Colloq. or Dial.]
to become (ill) —*n.* 1. the amount taken
[the day's *take* of fish] 2. a film scene
photographed with an uninterrupted run
of the camera —**have what it takes**
[Colloq.] to possess the attributes
necessary for success, etc. —**take after**
to be, act, or look like —**take a person
up on** to accept someone's offer —**take
as read** to accept (minutes, etc.) without
the formality of reading or further
discussion —**take back** to retract
(something said, etc.) —**take down** 1.
to put in writing; record 2. to take apart
3. to humble (a person) —**take for** to
consider to be —**take in** 1. to understand
2. to include 3. to visit 4. to admit;
receive 5. to make smaller 6. to cheat;
trick —**take it** [Slang] to withstand
hardship, ridicule, etc. —**take it or leave
it** [Colloq.] accept it or not —**take it
out of** to sap the energy of —**take it
out on** [Colloq.] to make (another) suffer
for one's own anger, etc. —**taken short**
[Colloq.] to be in sudden need of evacuating
the bowels —**take off** 1. to remove (a
garment, etc.) 2. to deduct 3. to leave
the ground or water in flight: said of
an aircraft 4. to spend as a holiday 5.
[Colloq.] to start 6. [Colloq.] to mimic
7. [Colloq.] to depart —**take on** 1. to
acquire; assume 2. to employ 3. to
undertake (a task, etc.) 4. to play against;
oppose 5. [Colloq.] to show violent
emotion —**take oneself off** [Colloq.] to
go away; leave —**take one's time** to be

unhurried —**take out** 1. to remove 2. to apply for and get 3. [Colloq.] to escort —**take over** to begin controlling, managing, etc. —**take the biscuit** (or **cake**) [Colloq.] to exceed all others (used ironically) —**take to** 1. to become fond of 2. to develop a habit of doing —**take up** 1. to become interested in (an occupation, etc.) 2. to make tighter or shorter 3. to accept (a challenge, etc.) 4. to resume (something interrupted) 5. to absorb (a liquid) 6. to occupy (space or time) —**take upon** (or **on**) **oneself** 1. to take the responsibility for 2. to undertake Also **take upon** (or **on**) **one** —**tak′able** adj. —**tak′er** n.

takeaway adj. designating food sold by a restaurant to be eaten away from the premises —n. an establishment which sells such food

take-home pay wages or salary after deductions for income tax, etc. have been made

taken pp. of TAKE

takeoff n. 1. the act of leaving the ground, as in jumping or flight 2. the place from which one leaves the ground 3. [Colloq.] an amusing or mocking imitation Also **take′-off′**

takeover n. the act of assuming control, management, etc.: also **take′-o′ver**

taking adj. attractive; winning —n. 1. the act of one that takes 2. [pl.] earnings; profits

talc (talk) n. [Fr. < Ar. talq] 1. shortened form of TALCUM POWDER 2. a soft mineral, magnesium silicate, used to make talcum powder, etc.

talcum (**powder**) (tal′kəm) a powder for the body made of powdered, purified talc, usually perfumed

tale (tāl) n. [OE. talu] 1. a story of true or fictitious events; narrative 2. a piece of idle or malicious gossip 3. a lie

talebearer n. a person who spreads gossip, tells secrets, etc. —**tale′bear′ing** adj., n.

talent (tal′ənt) n. [< Gr. talanton, a weight] 1. a special, superior ability in an art, science, craft, etc. 2. people who have talent 3. an ancient unit of weight or money 4. [Slang] people of the opposite sex —**tal′ented** adj.

talent scout a person whose work is recruiting persons of superior ability in the theatre, sports, etc.

talisman (tal′iz mən) n., pl. -**mans** [< MGr. telesma, a consecrated object] a ring, stone, etc., bearing engraved figures supposed to bring good luck or to have magic power —**tal′isman′ic** adj.

talk (tôk) vi. [ME. talken] 1. to put ideas into words; speak 2. to express ideas by speech substitutes [talk by signs] 3. to chatter 4. to gossip 5. to confer; consult 6. to reveal secret information —vt. 1. to use in speaking; utter [to talk nonsense] 2. to discuss 3. to put into a specified condition by talking —n. 1. a) the act of talking b) conversation 2. an informal speech 3. [often pl.] a

conference 4. gossip 5. the subject of conversation, gossip, etc. 6. frivolous discussion 7. a particular kind of speech —**now you're talking** [Colloq.] you are proposing something acceptable —**talk back** to answer impertinently —**talk down** 1. to silence by talking louder, longer, or more effectively than 2. to instruct (an aircraft pilot) by radio to enable him to land in poor visibility —**talk down to** to talk to (a person) as if he were one's inferior in rank, intellect, etc. —**talk into** to persuade —**talk out** 1. to discuss (a problem, etc.) at length in an effort to reach understanding 2. to block (a bill, etc.) in a legislative body by lengthy discussion —**talk over** to discuss —**talk shop** to speak about one's work, esp. when meeting socially rather than at work —**you can** (or **can't**) **talk** [Colloq.] you are not in a position to comment, criticize, etc. —**talk′er** n.

talkative adj. talking, or fond of talking, a great deal; loquacious —**talk′ativeness** n.

talking book a recording of a reading of a book, etc. for use esp. by the blind

talking-to n. [Colloq.] a rebuke; scolding

tall (tôl) adj. [< OE. (ge)tæl, swift] 1. of more than normal height 2. having a specified height [five feet tall] 3. [Colloq.] hard to believe [a tall story]

tallboy n. a high chest of drawers, sometimes in two parts, one above the other, or supported on legs

tall order a demand which is difficult to fulfil

tallow (tal′ō) n. [< MLowG. talg] the pale yellow solid fat extracted from cattle, sheep, etc., used in making candles, soaps, etc. —**tal′lowy** adj.

tally (tal′ē) vi. -**lied**, -**lying** [< L. talea, a stick] to agree; correspond —vt. 1. to count (usually with up) 2. to put on or as on a tally —n., pl. -**lies** 1. an account, reckoning, or score 2. an identifying tag or label 3. orig., a stick with notches representing the amount of a debt

tallyho (tal′ē hō′) interj. [< Fr. taiaut] the cry of a hunter on sighting the fox —n., pl. -**hos′** a cry of "tallyho" —vi. to cry "tallyho"

Talmud (tal′mood) n. [< Heb. lāmadh, learn] the writings constituting the Jewish civil and religious law —**Talmud′ic**, **Talmud′ical** adj. —**Tal′mudist** n.

talon (tal′ən) n. [< L. talus, ankle] the claw of a bird of prey, or, sometimes, of an animal

tam (tam) n. short for TAM-O'-SHANTER

tamarind (tam′ə rind) n. [< Sp. < Ar. tamr hindī, date of India] 1. a tropical tree with yellow flowers and brown pods 2. its fruit, used in medicine, etc.

tamarisk (tam′ə risk) n. [< L. tamarix] any of a genus of trees or shrubs with slender branches and feathery flower clusters, common near salt water

tambour (tam′boŏər) n. [< Ar. tanbūr, stringed instrument] 1. an embroidery frame of two hoops, one closely fitting inside the other, that hold the cloth stretched between them **2.** a door, panel, etc. as in a cabinet, made of narrow, wooden slats that glide flexibly in grooves, as around curves **3.** a drum

TAMBOURINE

tambourine (tam′bə rēn′) *n.* [see TAMBOUR] a shallow, single-headed hand drum having jingling metal discs in the rim : played by shaking, hitting, etc. —**tam′-bourin′ist** *n.*

tame (tām) *adj.* **tam′er, tam′est** [OE. *tam*] **1.** changed from a wild state, as an animal, for use by man **2.** gentle; docile **3.** without force or spirit; dull —*vt.* **tamed, tam′ing 1.** to make tame **2.** to make gentle, docile, or spiritless **3.** to make less intense; soften —**tam′able, tame′able** *adj.* —**tame′ly** *adv.* —**tame′ness** *n.* —**tam′er** *n.*

Tamil (tam′il) *n.* **1.** any of a people of S India and N Sri Lanka **2.** their language

tam-o′-shanter (tam′ə shan′tər) *n.* [< R. Burns's poem] a Scottish cap with a round, flat top

tamp (tamp) *vt.* [< ?] to pack or pound (*down*) by a series of blows or taps

tamper (tam′pər) *vi.* [var. of TEMPER] [Archaic] to plot —**tamper with 1.** to meddle with, esp. so as to damage, etc. **2.** to make secret, illegal arrangements with, as by bribing

tampon (tam′pon) *n.* [< Fr. *tapon*, a plug] a plug, as of cotton put into a body cavity, wound, etc. to stop bleeding, etc. —*vt.* to put a tampon into

tan[1] (tan) *n.* [< ML. *tannum*] **1.** a yellowish-brown colour *b)* such a colour given to fair skin by exposure to the sun **2.** tannin or a solution made from it —*adj.* **tan′ner, tan′nest** yellowish-brown —*vt.* **tanned, tan′ning 1.** to produce a tan colour in, as by exposure to the sun **2.** to change (hide) into leather by soaking in tannin **3.** [Colloq.] to whip severely —*vi.* to become tanned

tan[2] *Math.* tangent

tandem (tan′dəm) *n.* [< L. *tandem*, at length] **1.** a bicycle with two seats and sets of pedals placed tandem **2.** a two-wheeled carriage drawn by horses harnessed tandem —*adv.* one behind another; in single file

tang (taŋ) *n.* [ON. *tangi*, a sting] **1.** a strong, penetrating taste or odour **2.** a touch or trace (*of*) **3.** a special flavour, quality, etc. **4.** a projecting prong on a knife, etc. that fits into the handle —**tang′y** *adj.*

tangent (tan′jənt) *n.* [< L. *tangere*, to touch] **1.** *Geom.* a tangent line, curve, or surface **2.** *Trigonometry* the ratio of the side opposite a given acute angle in a right-angled triangle to the adjacent side —*adj.* **1.** *Geom.* touching and not intersecting a curve or surface at one point only : said of a line or plane **2.** touching —**go** (or **fly**) **off at** (or **on**) **a tangent** to change suddenly from one line of action, etc. to another

tangential (tan jen′shəl) *adj.* **1.** of or like a tangent **2.** going off at a tangent **3.** merely touching on a subject —**tangen′-tially** *adv.*

tangerine (tan′jə rēn′) *n.* [< Fr. *Tanger*, Tangier] **1.** an orange with a reddish-yellow colour and segments that are easily separated **2.** reddish yellow

tangible (tan′jə b′l) *adj.* [< L. *tangere*, to touch] **1.** that can be touched or felt by touch **2.** that can be appraised for value [*tangible* assets] **3.** definite; objective —**tan′gibil′ity** *n.* —**tan′gibly** *adv.*

tangle (taŋ′g′l) *n.* [< ?] **1.** an intertwisted, confused mass, as of string, branches, etc. **2.** a jumbled, confused condition —*vi.* **-gled, -gling 1.** to become tangled **2.** [Colloq.] to quarrel or fight —*vt.* **1.** to make a confused muddle of; intertwist **2.** to catch as in a net or snare —**tan′gly** *adj.*

tango (taŋ′gō) *n.*, *pl.* **-gos** [AmSp.] **1.** a S American dance with long gliding steps **2.** music for this —*vi.* **-goed, -going** to dance the tango

tank (taŋk) *n.* [< Sp. & Port. *estancar*, stop the flow of] **1.** any large container for liquid or gas **2.** an armoured, self-propelled combat vehicle armed with guns and moving on tractor treads —**tank up** [Colloq.] **1.** to supply with or get a full tank of petrol **2.** to drink much liquor —**tank′ful′** *n.*

tankard (taŋ′kərd) *n.* [ME.] a large drinking cup with a handle and, often, a hinged lid

tanker (taŋ′kər) *n.* a ship, lorry or aeroplane carrying oil or other liquids in large tanks

tank farming *same as* HYDROPONICS

tanner (tan′ər) *n.* a person whose work is tanning hides

tannery *n.*, *pl.* **-neries** a place where hides are tanned

tannic (tan′ik) *adj.* of, like, or obtained from tannin

tannic acid a yellowish, astringent substance, derived from oak bark, etc. and used in tanning, etc.

tannin (tan′in) *n.* *same as* TANNIC ACID

Tannoy (tan′oi) *Trademark* a public-address system

tansy (tan′zē) *n.*, *pl.* **-sies** [< Gr. *athanasia*, immortality] a strong-smelling plant with clusters of small, yellow flowers

tantalize (tan′tə līz′) *vt.* **-lized′, -liz′ing** [see TANTALUS] to tease or disappoint by promising or showing something and then withholding it —**tan′taliza′tion** *n.* —**tan′taliz′er** *n.* —**tan′taliz′ingly** *adv.*

tantalum (tan′tə ləm) *n.* [see TANTALUS : from the difficulty in extracting it] a rare, steel-blue, metallic chemical element that resists corrosion : symbol, Ta

tantalus (tan'tə ləs) *n.* [< *Tantalus*, in Gr. Myth. a king surrounded by inaccessible water and fruit in Hades] a stand in which bottles may be locked with their contents visible

tantamount (tan'tə mount') *adj.* [< OFr. *tant*, so much + *amonter*, amount] equivalent (*to*)

tantra (tan'trə) *n.* [Sans., doctrine] [*often* T-] any of a class of mystical Hindu or Buddhist writings

tantrum (tan'trəm) *n.* [< ?] a violent, wilful outburst of annoyance, rage, etc.; childish fit of bad temper

tanyard (tan'yärd') *n.* a tannery

Taoism (tä'ō iz'm) *n.* [< Chin. *tao*, the way] a Chinese religion and philosophy advocating simplicity, selflessness, etc. —**Tao'ist** *n., adj.*

tap¹ (tap) *vt.* **tapped, tap'ping** [OFr. *taper*] 1. to strike lightly 2. to strike something lightly with 3. to make or do by tapping [to *tap* a message] —*vi.* 1. to strike a light, rapid blow 2. to move with a tapping sound —*n.* 1. a light, rapid blow, or the sound made by it 2. a small metal plate attached to a shoe, as for tap dancing —**tap'per** *n.*

tap² *n.* [OE. *tæppa*] 1. a device for controlling the flow of liquid from a pipe, etc. 2. a plug, cork, etc. for stopping a hole in a container holding a liquid 3. a draining of liquid from a body cavity 4. the act of wiretapping 5. a place in an electrical circuit where a connection can be made —*vt.* **tapped, tap'ping** 1. to make a hole in for drawing off liquid 2. to draw (liquid) from a container, cavity, etc. 3. to make use of [to *tap* new resources] 4. to make a connection in (an electric circuit, telephone line, etc.); specif., to wiretap (a telephone line) 5. [Slang] to borrow or get money from —**on tap** 1. in a tapped cask and ready to be drawn 2. [Colloq.] ready for consideration or action

tap dance a dance performed with sharp, loud taps of the foot, toe, or heel at each step —**tap'-dance'** *vi.* —**tap'-danc'er** *n.*

tape (tāp) *n.* [OE. *tæppe*, fillet] 1. a strong, narrow, woven strip of cloth, paper, etc. used for binding, tying, etc. 2. a strip of cloth stretched above the finishing line of a race 3. *short for* TAPE MEASURE 4. a) *short for* MAGNETIC TAPE b) a recording on magnetic tape —*vt.* **taped, tap'ing** 1. to put tape on or around, as for binding, tying, etc. 2. to measure by using a tape measure 3. to record (sound, computer data, etc.) on magnetic tape —**have** (someone or something) **taped** to have a shrewd idea of (a character's nature, etc.) —**tap'er** *n.*

tape deck a simplified magnetic-tape assembly, having tape reels and recording and playback heads

tape machine a telegraphic device that records stock market quotations, etc., on paper tape

tape measure a tape with marks showing lengths, used for measuring

taper (tā'pər) *vt., vi.* [OE. *tapur*] 1. to decrease gradually in width or thickness 2. to lessen; diminish Often with *off* —*n.* 1. a slender candle 2. a long wick coated with wax, used for lighting candles, etc. 3. a gradual decrease in width, thickness, power, etc.

tape-record *vt.* to record on magnetic tape

tape recorder a device for recording sound on magnetic tape

tape recording 1. the act of recording on magnetic tape 2. the magnetic tape used in recording 3. the sounds recorded on magnetic tape

tapestry (tap'is trē) *n., pl.* **-tries** [< Gr. *tapēs*, carpet] a heavy woven cloth with decorative designs and pictures, used as a wall hanging, etc. —**tap'estried** *adj.*

tapeworm (tāp'wurm') *n.* a flatworm that lives as a parasite in the intestines of man and other vertebrates

tapioca (tap'ē ō'kə) *n.* [< Tupi] a starchy, granular substance prepared from the root of the cassava plant, used for puddings, etc.

tapir (tā'pər) *n.* [< Tupi *tapyra*] a large, piglike mammal found in tropical America: tapirs have flexible snouts

tappet (tap'it) *n.* [see TAP¹] in a machine, a projection that is moved by recurring contact, as with a cam

taproom (tap'room') *n.* a room with a bar at which alcoholic drinks are served

taproot (tap'root') *n.* [TAP² + ROOT¹] a main root, growing almost vertically downwards, from which branch roots spread out

taps (taps) *n.* [< TAP¹, because orig. an army drum signal] a song sung at the conclusion of an evening gathering by Girl Guides and Scouts

tapster (tap'stər) *n.* [< OE. *tæppestre*, barmaid] [Now Rare] a barman

tar¹ (tär) *n.* [OE. *teru*] 1. a thick, sticky, black liquid obtained by the destructive distillation of wood, coal, etc. 2. loosely, any of the solids in smoke, as from tobacco —*vt.* **tarred, tar'ring** to cover or smear with or as with tar —*adj.* 1. of or like tar 2. **tarred** —**tar and feather** to cover (a person) with tar and feathers, as in punishment by mob action —**tarred with the same brush** (or **stick**) having the same faults

tar² *n.* [< TAR(PAULIN)] [Colloq.] a sailor

tarantella (tar'ən tel'ə) *n.* [It., < *Taranto*, town of Italy] 1. a fast, whirling southern Italian dance for couples 2. music for this

tarantula (tə ran'tyoo lə) *n., pl.* **-las, -lae** (-lē) [< prec.] 1. a large, hairy, somewhat poisonous spider of S Europe 2. a large, hairy tropical spider

tarboosh (tär boosh') *n.* [Ar. *ṭarbūsh*] a brimless cap of felt shaped like a truncated cone

tardy (tär'dē) *adj.* **-dier, -diest** [< L. *tardus*, slow] 1. late, delayed, or dilatory 2. slow in moving, acting, etc. —**tar'dily** *adv.* —**tar'diness** *n.*

tare[1] (tãer) *n.* [< ?] 1. any of several vetches 2. *Bible* a weed

tare[2] *n.* [< Ar. *taraha*, to reject] deduction of the weight of a container, etc. from the total weight to determine the weight of the contents

target (tär′git) *n.* [< MFr. *targe*, a shield] 1. *a)* a round, flat board, straw coil, etc., marked as with concentric circles, aimed at in archery, etc. *b)* any object that is shot at, bombarded, etc. 2. an objective 3. an object of attack, criticism, or ridicule

tariff (tar′if) *n.* [< Ar. *ta'rif*, information] 1. a list or system of taxes upon exports or imports 2. a tax of this kind, or its rate 3. any list of prices, charges, etc.

tarlatan, tarletan (tär′lə tən) *n.* [Fr. *tarlatane*] a thin, stiff, open-weave muslin

tarmac (tär′mak) *n.* [< TAR[1] & J. L. McAdam] 1. *Trademark* a paving material of crushed stone rolled and bound with tar: also **tar′macad′am** 2. a road, runway, etc. paved with tarmac —*vt.* to cover (a surface) with tarmac

tarn (tärn) *n.* [ON. *tjörn*] a small mountain lake

tarnish (tär′nish) *vt.* [< MFr. *ternir*, make dim] 1. to dull the lustre of (a metal) by exposure to the air 2. to sully (a reputation, etc.) —*vi.* to lose lustre; discolour —*n.* 1. a being tarnished; dullness 2. the film of discolouration on a tarnished surface 3. a stain; blemish —**tar′nishable** *adj.*

taro (tä′rō) *n., pl.* -**ros** [Tahitian] a large, tropical Asiatic plant, cultivated for its edible tubers

tarot (tar′ō) *n.* [Fr., ? *ult.* < Ar. *taraha*, to remove] [*often* T-] any of a set of playing cards used in fortunetelling

tarpaulin (tär pô′lin) *n.* [TAR[1] + PALL[2]] 1. canvas coated with a waterproofing compound 2. a sheet of this spread over something to keep it dry

tarragon (tar′ə gən) *n.* [Sp. < Gr. *drakōn*, dragon] 1. a herb whose fragrant leaves are used for seasoning 2. these leaves

tarry[1] (tar′ē) *vi.* -**ried, -rying** [prob. < L. *tardus*, slow] 1. to delay, linger, etc. 2. to stay for a time, esp. longer than intended 3. to wait

tarry[2] (tär′ē) *adj.* **tar′rier, tar′riest** 1. of or like tar 2. covered or smeared with tar —**tar′riness** *n.*

tarsal (tär′s'l) *adj.* of the tarsus —*n.* a tarsal bone

tarsus (tär′səs) *n., pl.* -**si** (-sī) [< Gr. *tarsos*, flat of the foot] 1. the human ankle, consisting of seven bones 2. *Zool.* the corresponding group of bones in the vertebrates having four limbs

tart[1] (tärt) *adj.* [OE. *teart*] 1. sharp in taste; sour; acid 2. cutting [a *tart* answer] —**tart′ly** *adv.*

tart[2] *n.* [MFr. *tarte*] 1. a small shell of pastry filled with jam, custard, etc. 2. a pie filled with fruit or other sweet filling often having a top crust

tart[3] *n.* [< prec.] [Colloq.] a prostitute or any woman of loose morals —**tart up**

[Slang] to clothe, decorate, etc., often in a cheap and showy way

tartan (tär′t'n) *n.* [prob. < MFr. *tiretaine*, a cloth of mixed fibres] woollen cloth with a woven plaid pattern, esp. as worn in the Scottish Highlands, where each clan has its own pattern —*adj.* of or made of tartan

tartar[1] (tär′tər) *n.* [< Per. *Tātār*] 1. a bad-tempered person hard to deal with 2. [T-] *same as* TATAR

tartar[2] *n.* [< MGr. *tartaron*] 1. a hard deposit on the teeth 2. a potassium salt forming a reddish, crustlike deposit in wine casks: in purified form called CREAM OF TARTAR

tartaric (tär tar′ik) *adj.* of, containing, or derived from tartar or tartaric acid

tartaric acid a colourless, crystalline acid found in fruit juices, etc. and obtained from tartar

tartar sauce [< Fr.] a sauce, as for seafood, consisting of mayonnaise with chopped pickles, olives, capers, etc.: also sp. **tartare sauce**

Tarzan (tär′zan) *n.* [< *Tarzan*, hero of stories by E. R. Burroughs] [*also* t-] a very strong, virile, and agile man

task (täsk) *n.* [< L. *taxare*, to tax] 1. a piece of work that one must do 2. any difficult undertaking —*vt.* to put a strain on; tax —**take to task** to reprimand or scold

task force a specially trained, self-contained military unit assigned a specific mission or task

taskmaster *n.* a person who assigns tasks to others, esp. when exacting or severe

Tasmanian devil (taz mā′nē ən) a badgerlike, voracious, flesh-eating marsupial of Tasmania

Tasmanian wolf (or **tiger**) a fierce, flesh-eating marsupial of Tasmania

Tass (tas) [< the initial letters of the full name] a Soviet agency for gathering and distributing news

tass (tas) *n.* [< Per. *tast*, cup] [Obs. or Scot.] a small cup

tassel (tas′'l) *n.* [OFr., knob] 1. an ornamental tuft of threads, cords, etc. of equal length, hanging loosely from a knot 2. something resembling this, as a tuft of corn silk —**tas′selled** *adj.*

taste (tāst) *n.* [OFr. *taster*] 1. the sense by which the taste buds on the tongue, when stimulated by a substance, distinguish it as sweet, sour, salty, or bitter 2. the quality perceived through this sense 3. a small amount put into the mouth to test the flavour 4. a slight experience of something 5. *a)* the ability to appreciate and judge what is beautiful, appropriate, etc. *b)* a specific preference 6. a liking; inclination —*vt.* **tast′ed, tast′ing** 1. to detect the flavour of by the sense of taste 2. to test the flavour of by putting a little in one's mouth 3. to eat or drink, esp. a small amount of 4. to experience —*vi.* 1. to have the specific flavour (*of*) 2. to tell flavours by the sense of taste —**in bad, poor**, etc. (or **good, excellent,**

etc.) **taste** in a form, style, or manner showing a bad (or good) sense of beauty, excellence, etc. —**to one's taste** 1. pleasing to one 2. so as to please one

taste bud any of the cells in the tongue that are the sense organs of taste

tasteful adj. having or showing good taste [*tasteful* décor] —**taste′fully** adv. —**taste′fulness** n.

tasteless adj. 1. without taste; insipid 2. in poor taste —**taste′lessly** adv. —**taste′lessness** n.

taster n. one employed to test the quality of wines, teas, etc. by tasting

tasty adj. -**ier**, -**iest** that tastes good; appetizing —**tast′ily** adv. —**tast′iness** n.

tat (tat) vt. **tat′ted**, **tat′ting** to make by tatting —vi. to do tatting

ta-ta (tä tä′) interj. [Colloq.] goodbye: orig. a child's term

Tatar (tät′ər) n. [Per.] 1. a member of any of the tribes that invaded W Asia and E Europe in the Middle Ages 2. any of a Turkic people living in a region of EC Russia and in parts of Asia 3. any of their Turkic languages —adj. of the Tatars or their languages

'tater, tater (tät′ər) n. dial. form of POTATO: also **tatie** (-tē), **tattie** (tat′ē)

tatter (tat′ər) n. [< ON. *töturr*, rags] 1. a torn and hanging shred or piece, as of a garment 2. [pl.] torn, ragged clothes —**tat′tered** adj.

tatting (tat′iŋ) n. [< ?] 1. a fine lace made by looping and knotting thread that is wound on a hand shuttle 2. the act of making this

tattle (tat′'l) vi. -**tled**, -**tling** [echoic] 1. to chatter 2. to tell others' secrets —n. chatter —**tat′tler** n.

tattletale n. an informer; talebearer

tattoo[1] (ta tōō′) vt. -**tooed**, -**too′ing** [< Tahitian *tatau*] 1. to puncture (the skin) with a needle and insert colours so as to leave permanent marks 2. to make (marks or designs) on the skin this way —n., pl. -**toos′** a tattooed mark or design

tattoo[2] n., pl. -**toos′** [< Du. < *tap toe*, shut the tap: a signal for closing barrooms] 1. a) a signal on a drum, bugle, etc. summoning soldiers, etc. to their quarters at night b) a military spectacle featuring marching, etc. 2. any continuous drumming, rapping, etc.

tatty (tat′ē) adj. **tat′tier**, **tat′tiest** [? < OE. *taetteca*, a rag] shabby, decrepit, tawdry, etc. —**tat′tily** adv.

tau (tou) n. the nineteenth letter of the Greek alphabet (T, τ)

taught (tôt) pt. & pp. of TEACH

taunt (tônt) vt. [< Fr. *tant pour tant*, tit for tat] 1. to reproach scornfully or sarcastically 2. to provoke by taunting —n. a scornful or jeering remark —**taunt′ingly** adv.

taupe (tōp) n. [Fr. < L. *talpa*, mole] a dark, brownish-grey, the colour of moleskin —adj. of such a colour

Taurus (tôr′əs) [L., bull] 1. a N constellation containing the Pleiades 2. the second sign of the zodiac

taut (tôt) adj. [ME. *toght*, tight] 1. tightly stretched, as a rope 2. strained; tense [a *taut* smile] 3. trim, tidy, etc. [a *taut* ship] —**taut′ly** adv. —**taut′ness** n.

tauten vt., vi. to make or become taut

tauto- [< Gr. *to auto*, the same] a combining form meaning the same [*tautology*]

tautology (tô tol′ə jē) n., pl. -**gies** [see TAUTO- & -LOGY] 1. needless repetition of an idea in a different word, phrase, etc. (Ex.: "necessary essentials") 2. Math. a statement, etc., that cannot be denied (Ex.: *a circle is round*) —**tau′tolog′ical** adj.

tavern (tav′ərn) n. [< L. *taberna*] 1. Literary an inn 2. [U.S.] a place where wines, spirits, beer, etc. are sold and drunk

tawdry (tô′drē) adj. -**drier**, -**driest** [< St. Audrey laces, sold at St. Audrey's fair] cheap and showy —**taw′drily** adv. —**taw′driness** n.

tawny (tô′nē) adj. -**nier**, -**niest** [< OFr. *tanner*, to tan] brownish-yellow; tan —**taw′niness** n.

tawny owl a common owl with short wings and a hooting call

tawse (tôz) n. [prob. < *taw*, a thong] [Scot.] a leather thong used for corporal punishment: also sp. **taws**

tax (taks) vt. [< L. *taxare*, appraise] 1. to require (a person) to pay a percentage of his income, etc. for the use of a government 2. to assess a tax on (income, purchases, etc.) 3. to put a burden or strain on 4. to accuse; charge —n. 1. a compulsory payment, usually a percentage of income, purchase price, etc., for the use of a government 2. a heavy demand; burden —**tax′abil′ity** n. —**tax′able** adj.

taxation (tak sā′shən) n. 1. a taxing or being taxed 2. a tax or tax levy 3. revenue from taxes

tax-deductible adj. allowed as a deduction in computing income tax

tax-free adj. exempt from taxation

taxi (tak′sē) n., pl. **tax′is** shortened form of TAXICAB —vi. **tax′ied**, **tax′iing** or **tax′ying** 1. to move slowly along the ground as an aircraft does when approaching a runway to begin its takeoff 2. to go in a taxi —vt. 1. to cause (an aircraft) to taxi 2. to carry in a taxi

taxicab n. [< *taxi*(*meter*) *cab*] a motor car in which passengers are carried for a fare shown on a meter

taxidermy (tak′si dur′mē) n. [< Gr. *taxis*, arrangement + *derma*, skin] the art of preparing, stuffing, and mounting the skins of animals so as to give a lifelike effect —**tax′ider′mist** n.

taximeter (tak′sē mēt′ər) n. [< ML. *taxa*, a tax + -*meter*, -METER] an automatic device in taxicabs that registers fares due

taxi rank a place where taxicabs are stationed for hire

taxonomy (tak son′ə mē) n. [< Gr. *taxis*, arrangement + *nomos*, law] the science of classification, esp. of plants and animals —**tax′onom′ic** (-sə nom′ik), **tax′onom′ical** adj. —**taxon′omist** n.

taxpayer (taks′pā′ər) *n.* a person who pays taxes

tax return *see* RETURN

Tb *Chem.* niobium

TB, T.B., tb, t.b. tuberculosis

T-bone steak a steak from the loin, with a T-shaped bone

tbs., tbsp. tablespoon; tablespoons

Tc *Chem.* technetium

tch *interj., n.* a clicking sound made with the tongue, to express disapproval, sympathy, etc. —*vi.* to utter "tchs"

Te *Chem.* tellurium

te (tē) *n.* *same as* TI

tea (tē) *n.* [Chin. dial. *t'e*] 1. an evergreen shrub grown in warm parts of Asia for its young leaves, which are prepared by drying, etc. for use in making a drink 2. the dried, prepared leaves 3. the drink made by steeping these in hot water, etc. 4. a tealike beverage [camomile *tea*, beef *tea*] 5. a light meal, usually with tea, in the late afternoon: also **afternoon tea** —**tea and sympathy** [Colloq.] kind treatment of someone in trouble

tea bag a small, porous bag with tea leaves in it, as for making an individual cup of tea

tea ball a hollow, perforated metal ball used to hold tea leaves in making tea

teacake *n.* a flat, round, slightly sweetened bun, usually served hot and buttered

teach (tēch) *vt.* **taught, teach′ing** [OE. *tæcan*] 1. to show how to do something; instruct 2. to give lessons to 3. to give lessons in (a subject) 4. to give knowledge, insight, etc. to —*vi.* to be a teacher —**teach′able** *adj.*

teacher *n.* a person who teaches, esp. in a school

tea-chest (tē′chest′) *n.* a large, square wooden box lined with foil, for exporting tea, for storage, etc.

teaching (tē′ching) *n.* 1. the art or profession of a teacher 2. something taught: *usually in pl.*

tea-cloth (tē′kloth′) *n.* 1. a small tablecloth 2. a towel for drying dishes: also **tea towel**

tea-cosy *n.* a padded cover for a teapot to keep the contents hot

teacup *n.* a cup for drinking tea, etc. —**a storm in a teacup** a great commotion over a small problem —**tea′cupful′** *n.*

teahouse *n.* in the Orient, a place where tea is served

teak (tēk) *n.* [< Port. < native word *tēkka*] 1. a large East Indian tree with hard, yellowish-brown wood used for shipbuilding, furniture, etc. 2. its wood: also **teak′wood′**

teal (tēl) *n.* [ME. *tele*] a small freshwater wild duck

team (tēm) *n.* [OE., offspring] 1. a group of people working or playing together 2. two or more horses, oxen, etc. harnessed to the same vehicle or plough —*vt., vi.* to join together in a team (often with *up*)

teammate *n.* a fellow team member

team spirit concern for the benefit of the group as a whole rather than for individual interest

teamster *n.* 1. a driver of a team of horses 2. [U.S.] a lorry driver

teamwork *n.* the action or effort of people working together as a group

tea party a social gathering at which tea is served

teapot (tē′pot′) *n.* a pot with a spout, handle, and lid, for brewing and pouring tea

tear[1] (tãr) *vt.* **tore, torn, tear′ing** [OE. *teran*] 1. to pull apart by force; rend 2. to make (a hole, etc.) by tearing 3. to lacerate 4. to split into factions; disrupt 5. to divide by doubt, etc. 6. to remove as by tearing, etc. (with *up, out, off,* etc.) —*vi.* 1. to be torn 2. to move with force or speed —*n.* 1. a tearing 2. a torn place; rip —**tear at** to pull at violently —**tear down** to take apart; wreck, etc. —**tear into** [Colloq.] to attack or criticize violently

tear[2] (tēr) *n.* [OE.] 1. a drop of the salty fluid that keeps the eyeball moist and flows from the eye in weeping 2. [*pl.*] sorrow; grief —**in tears** weeping

tearaway (tãr′ə wā) *n.* a reckless young man; hooligan

teardrop (tēr′drop′) *n.* a tear —*adj.* tear-shaped

tearful *adj.* 1. in tears; weeping 2. causing tears; sad —**tear′fully** *adv.* —**tear′fulness** *n.*

tear gas (tēr) a gas that makes the eyes sore and blinds them with tears —**tear′-gas′** *vt.* **-gassed′, -gas′sing**

tearing (tãr′iŋ) *adj.* violent or furious

tear-jerker (tēr′jur′kər) *n.* [Colloq.] a play, film, etc. that is sad in a too sentimental way —**tear′-jerk′ing** *adj.*

tearoom (tē′room′) *n.* a restaurant that serves tea, coffee, light lunches, etc.: also **tea-shop**

tease (tēz) *vt.* **teased, teas′ing** [OE. *tæsan*] 1. to bother or annoy by mocking, poking fun, etc. 2. to tantalize 3. *a)* to card or comb (flax, wool, etc.) *b)* to raise a nap on (cloth) with teasels —*vi.* to tease someone —*n.* 1. a teasing or being teased 2. a person who teases

teasel (tē′z'l) *n.* [< OE. *tæsan,* to tease] 1. a bristly plant with prickly, cylindrical flower heads 2. a dried flower used to raise a nap on cloth 3. any device for raising a nap on cloth

teaser (tē′zər) *n.* [Colloq.] an annoying or puzzling problem

teaspoon (tē′spoon′) *n.* a spoon for stirring tea, coffee, etc. —**tea′spoonful′** *n.*

teat (tēt) *n.* [< OFr. *tete*] 1. the nipple of a breast or udder 2. a rubber device resembling this

teazel, teazle (tē′z'l) *n.* *same as* TEASEL

Tech (tek) *n.* [Colloq.] technical college

tech. 1. technical 2. technology

technetium (tek nē′shē əm) *n.* [< Gr. *technē,* an art] a metallic chemical element obtained in the fission of uranium: symbol, Tc

technic (tek′nik; tek nēk′) *n.* [< Gr. *technē,* an art] *same as* TECHNIQUE

technical (tek′ni k'l) *adj.* 1. dealing with the practical, industrial, or mechanical arts 2. of, used in, or peculiar to a specific science, art, craft, etc. 3. of or showing technique 4. according to principles or rules 5. involving or using technicalities —**tech′nically** *adv.*

technical drawing drawing done, as by a draughtsman, with T squares, scales, compasses, etc.

technicality (tek′nə kal′ə tē) *n.*, *pl.* **-ties** 1. the state or quality of being technical 2. a technical point, term, method, etc. 3. a minute point or detail brought to bear upon a main issue

technical knockout *Boxing* a victory won when the opponent is so badly hurt that the referee stops the match

technician (tek nish′ən) *n.* one skilled in the technicalities or in the technique of some art or science

Technicolor (tek′ni kul′ər) *Trademark* a certain process of making colour films —*n.* [t-] bright colours —**tech′nicol′ored** *adj.*

technique (tek nēk′) *n.* [see TECHNIC] 1. the method of procedure in artistic work, scientific operation, etc. 2. the degree of expertness shown in this 3. any method of doing a thing

techno- [< Gr. *technē*, an art] *a combining form meaning* art, science, skill

technocracy (tek nok′rə sē) *n.* [prec. + -CRACY] government by scientists and engineers —**tech′nocrat′**(-nə krat′) *n.* —**tech′nocrat′ic** *adj.*

technological (tek′nə loj′i k'l) *adj.* of or resulting from technology

technology (tek nol′ə jē) *n.* [Gr. *technologia*] 1. the science or study of the practical or industrial arts, applied sciences, etc. 2. the methods used in a science, art, etc. 3. applied science —**technol′ogist** *n.*

tectonics (tek ton′iks) *n.pl.* [*with sing. v.*] [< Gr. *tektōn*, builder] *Geol.* the study of the earth's crystal structure and the forces that changes in it

Ted (ted) *n.* *short form of* TEDDY BOY

teddy bear (ted′ē) [< *Teddy* (*Theodore*) *Roosevelt*] a child's stuffed toy made to look like a bear cub

Teddy Boy [< *Edward*, referring to the Edwardian dress] a youth of the 1950's who wore mock Edwardian fashions

Te Deum (tē dē′əm) [LL.] a Christian hymn beginning *Te Deum laudamus* (We praise thee, O God)

tedious (tē′dē əs) *adj.* full of tedium; tiresome; boring —**te′diously** *adv.* —**te′diousness** *n.*

tedium (tē′dē əm) *n.* [< L. *taedet*, it offends] the condition or quality of being tiresome or monotonous

tee¹ (tē) *n.*, *pl.* **tees** 1. the letter T, t 2. anything shaped like a T —*adj.* shaped like a T —**to a tee** exactly

tee² *n.* [< ?] a mark aimed at in quoits, curling, etc.

tee³ *n.* [prob. < Scot. dial. *teaz*] 1. a small, pointed holder of wood, etc. on which a golf ball is put to be driven 2. the place at each hole from which a golfer makes his first stroke —**tee off** 1. to play a golf ball from a tee 2. to begin

tee-hee (tē′hē′) *interj., n.* [echoic] the sound of a titter or snicker

teem¹ (tēm) *vi.* [< OE. *team*, progeny] to be full; abound; swarm (*with*)

teem² *vi.* [ON. *tæma*] to pour [a *teeming* rain]

teenage (tēn′āj) *adj.* 1. in one's teens 2. of, like, or for persons in their teens

teenager *n.* a person in his teens

teens (tēnz) *n.pl.* [< OE. *tien*, ten] 1. the years from thirteen to nineteen (of a person's age) 2. the numbers thirteen to nineteen

teeny (tē′nē) *adj.* **-nier, -niest** *colloq.* var. *of* TINY

teeny-bopper (tē′nē bop′ər) *n.* [< TEENS + BOP] [Slang] a teenager, esp. a girl following the latest fads

teeny-weeny *adj.* [Colloq.] very small; tiny

teepee (tē′pē) *n.* alt. sp. *of* TEPEE

tee shirt same as T-SHIRT

teeter (tēt′ər) *vi.* [dial.] to totter, wobble, etc. —*vt.* to cause to teeter

teeth (tēth) *n.* pl. *of* TOOTH

teethe (tēth) *vi.* **teethed, teeth′ing** to grow teeth; cut one's teeth

teething (tēth′in) *n.* the stage during which a baby cuts teeth

teething ring a ring of ivory, plastic, etc. for teething babies to bite on

teething troubles difficulties experienced in the early stages of a project, etc.

teetotal (tē tōt′'l) *adj.* [< redupl. of initial letter of TOTAL] of or in favour of teetotalism —**teeto′taller** *n.*

teetotalism *n.* the principle or practice of never drinking any alcoholic liquor —**teeto′talist** *n.*

Teflon (tef′lon) *Trademark* a tough polymer used for nonstick coatings for cooking utensils, etc.

te-hee (tē′hē′) *interj., n.* var. *of* TEE-HEE

tel- same as TELE-

tel. 1. telegram 2. telegraph 3. telephone

tele- *a combining form meaning:* 1. [< Gr. *tēle*, far off] at, over, from, or to a distance 2. [< TELE(VISION)] of or by television

telecast (tel′ə kast) *vt., vi.* **-cast′** or **-cast′ed, -cast′ing** [TELE- + (BROAD)CAST] to broadcast by television —*n.* a television broadcast —**tel′ecast′er** *n.*

telecommunication (tel′ə kə myōo̅′nə kā′shən) *n.* [also *pl.*, *with sing. or* *pl. v.*] communication by radio, telephone, telegraph, television, etc.

telegram (tel′ə gram′) *n.* [TELE- + -GRAM] a message transmitted by telegraph

telegraph (tel′ə gräf′) *n.* [TELE- & -GRAPH] an apparatus or system for sending messages by electric impulses through a wire or by means of radio waves —*vt.* **1.** to send (a message) by telegraph to (someone) **2.** [Canad. Colloq.] to cast (votes) illegally by impersonating registered voters —*vi.* to send a telegram —**telegrapher** (tə leg′rə fər), **teleg′raphist** *n.* —**tel′egraph′ic** *adj.* —**tel′egraph′ically** *adv.*

telegraphy (tə leg′rə fē) *n.* **1.** the operation of telegraph apparatus **2.** the sending of messages by telegraph

telekinesis (tel′ə kī nē′sis) *n.* [< TELE- + Gr. *kinēsis*, motion] the causing of an object to move supposedly by means of psychic forces

telemeter (tel′ə mēt′ər) *n.* [TELE- + -METER] a device for measuring temperature, radiation, etc. at a remote point and transmitting the information by radio —**tel′emet′ric** (-met′rik) *adj.* —**telemetry** (tə lem′ə trē) *n.*

teleology (tel′ē ol′ə jē) *n.* [< Gr. *telos*, an end + -LOGY] **1.** the fact or quality of having an ultimate purpose **2.** a belief that what happens in nature is determined by an overall design or purpose —**te′leolog′ical** (-ə loj′i k'l) *adj.*

telepathy (tə lep′ə thē) *n.* [TELE- + -PATHY] supposed communication between minds by some means other than the normal functioning of the senses —**telepathic** (tel′ə path′ik) *adj.* —**telep′athist** *n.*

telephone (tel′ə fōn′) *n.* [TELE- + -PHONE] an instrument for conveying speech over distances by converting sound into electric impulses sent through a wire —*vi.* **-phoned′, -phon′ing** to talk over a telephone —*vt.* **1.** to convey (a message) by telephone **2.** to speak to or reach (a person) by telephone —**tel′ephon′ic** (-fon′ik) *adj.* —**tel′ephon′ically** *adv.*

telephone box a booth in a public place containing a telephone, usually operated by inserting coins: also **telephone booth, telephone kiosk**

telephone directory a book in which are listed alphabetically the names of persons, businesses, etc. having telephones in a specified area

telephonist (tə lef′ə nist) *n.* a telephone switchboard operator

telephony (tə lef′ə nē) *n.* the science of communication by telephone

telephoto (tel′ə fōt′ō) *adj.* designating a camera lens producing a large image of a distant object

telephotography (tel′ə fə tog′rə fē) *n.* **1.** photography done with a telephoto lens **2.** the process of transmitting photographs over distances using telephone wires or radio channels —**tel′epho′tograph′ic** (-fōt′ə graf′ik) *adj.*

teleprinter (tel′ə print′ər) *n.* a form of telegraph in which the message is typed

on a keyboard that sends electric signals to a machine that prints the words

Teleprompter (tel′ə promp′tər) *Trademark* an electronic device that unrolls a prepared script line by line for a speaker on television

telescope (tel′ə skōp′) *n.* [TELE- & -SCOPE] an instrument for making distant objects, as stars, appear nearer and larger: it consists of tubes containing lenses —*vi.,* *vt.* **-scoped′, -scop′ing** to slide or be forced one inside another like tubes of a collapsible telescope —**tel′escop′ic** (-skop′ik) *adj.*

teletext (tel′ē tekst) *n.* [TELE- & TEXT] a computer-based service which shows news and information on subscribers' specially equipped televisions

Teletype (tel′ə tīp′) *Trademark* a form of teleprinter —*vt.,* *vi.* **-typed′, -typ′ing** [*often* t-] to send (messages) by Teletype

televise (tel′ə vīz′) *vt.,* *vi.* **-vised′, -vis′ing** to transmit by television —**tel′evi′sor** *n.*

television (tel′ə vizh′ən) *n.* [TELE- + VISION] **1.** the process of transmitting scenes or views by converting light rays into electric signals that are transmitted to a receiver that reconverts the signals, reproducing the original image **2.** television broadcasting as an industry, art, etc. **3.** a television receiving set **4.** programmes watched on a television set —*adj.* of, in, or by television

telex (tel′eks) *n.* [TEL(ETYPE) + EX-(CHANGE)] **1.** an international telegraph service in which teleprinters are rented out to subscribers for direct communication **2.** a message sent by telex —*vt.* to send (a message) by telex

tell (tel) *vt.* **told, tell′ing** [OE. *tellan*, lit., to calculate] **1.** to let know; inform **2.** to request; order **3.** to give an account of (a story, etc.) in speech or writing **4.** to express in words; utter **5.** to report; announce **6.** to make known; disclose **7.** to recognize; distinguish **8.** to know; decide **9.** to assure emphatically —*vi.* **1.** to give an account or description (of something) **2.** to have a marked effect —**tell a tale** reveal something of interest or importance —**tell it to the marines** [Colloq.] an expression of disbelief —**tell off** [Colloq.] to rebuke severely —**tell on 1.** to make weary, worn-out, etc. **2.** [Colloq.] to inform against —**you're telling me** [Slang] I know that very well already —**tell′able** *adj.*

teller *n.* a person who counts; specif., *a)* one who counts votes *b)* a bank clerk

telling *adj.* **1.** having an effect; forceful; striking **2.** that tells or reveals much —**tell′ingly** *adv.*

telltale *n.* **1.** a talebearer or informer **2.** an outward indication of a secret —*adj.* revealing a secret

tellurium (te lyooər′ē əm) *n.* [< L. *tellus,* the earth] a rare, tin-white, brittle, nonmetallic chemical element: symbol, Te

telly (tel′ē) *n.* [Colloq.] television

temerity (tə mer′ə tē) *n.* [< L. *temere,*

rashly]   foolish or rash boldness; recklessness

temp (temp) *n.* [< TEMPORARY] [Colloq.] a temporary employee

temp. 1. temperature 2. temporary

temper (tem'pər) *n.* [< L. *temperare*, regulate] 1. frame of mind; disposition 2. anger; rage 3. a tendency to get angry 4. mental calm; composure : now only in **lose** (or **keep**) **one's temper, out of temper** 5. the degree of hardness and resiliency of a metal —*vt.* 1. to moderate [*temper* criticism with reason *]* 2. *a)* to bring to the proper texture, hardness, etc. by treating in some way [to *temper* steel by heating and sudden cooling *] b)* to toughen 3. *Music* to tune (a note, instrument, etc.)

tempera (tem'pər ə) *n.* [It.: see prec.] 1. a way of painting that uses pigments mixed with size or egg to produce a dull finish 2. the paint so used

temperament (tem'prə mənt) *n.* [see TEMPER] 1. one's customary frame of mind or natural disposition 2. a nature that is excitable, moody, etc.

temperamental (tem'prə men't'l) *adj.* 1. easily upset 2. of or caused by temperament 3. erratic in behaviour —**tem'peramen'tally** *adv.*

temperance (tem'pər əns) *n.* [see TEMPER] 1. moderation; self-restraint 2. moderation in drinking alcoholic liquor, or, esp., the avoiding of alcoholic liquor completely

temperate (tem'pər ət) *adj.* [see TEMPER] 1. neither very hot nor very cold : said of a climate, etc. 2. moderate in one's actions, speech, etc. 3. moderate, esp. in using alcoholic liquor —**tem'perately** *adv.*

Temperate Zone either of two zones of the earth (**North Temperate Zone** and **South Temperate Zone**) between the tropics and the polar circles

temperature (tem'prə chər) *n.* [< L. *temperatus*, temperate] the degree of hotness or coldness of anything, usually as measured on a thermometer; specif., *a)* the degree of heat of a living body; also, an excess of this over the normal (about 98.4 °F or 36.8 °C in man) *b)* the degree of heat of the atmosphere

tempered (tem'pərd) *adj.* 1. having been given the desired texture, etc. 2. modified by other qualities, etc. 3. having a (specified) temper

tempest (tem'pist) *n.* [< L. *tempus*, time] a violent storm with high winds, esp. one accompanied by rain or snow

tempestuous (tem pes'tyoo wəs) *adj.* 1. of or like a tempest 2. violent; turbulent —**tempes'tuously** *adv.*

template, templet (tem'plit) *n.* [< L. *templum*, small timber] a pattern, usually a thin plate, for forming an accurate copy of an object or shape

temple[1] (tem'p'l) *n.* [< L. *templum*] 1. a building for the worship of a god or gods 2. [T-] any of three buildings for worshiping Jehovah, successively built by the Jews in ancient Jerusalem 3. a building, usually of imposing size, serving some special purpose

temple[2] *n.* [< L. *tempus*] the flat area at either side of the forehead

tempo (tem'pō) *n., pl.* **-pos, -pi** (-pē) [< L. *tempus*, time] 1. the speed at which a piece of music is performed 2. rate of activity; pace

temporal[1] (tem'pər əl) *adj.* [< L. *tempus*, time] 1. of or limited by time; not eternal 2. of this world; not spiritual 3. civil or secular —**tem'porally** *adv.*

temporal[2] *adj.* [see TEMPLE[2]] of or near the temple or temples (of the head)

temporal bone either of a pair of compound bones forming the sides of the skull

temporary (tem'pə rer ē) *adj.* [< L. *tempus*, time] lasting only for a time; not permanent —**tem'porarily** *adv.* —**tem'porariness** *n.*

temporize (tem'pə rīz') *vi.* **-rized', -riz'- ing** [< L. *tempus*, time] 1. to act or speak in a way one thinks is expedient 2. to put off making a decision so as to gain time —**tem'poriz'er** *n.*

tempt (tempt) *vt.* [< L. *temptare*, to test] 1. to entice (a person) to do or want something that is wrong, forbidden, etc. 2. to be inviting or enticing to 3. to provoke or risk provoking (fate, etc.) 4. to cause to be inclined to [*tempted* to leave] —**tempt'er** *n.* —**tempt'ress** *n.fem.*

temptation (temp tā'shən) *n.* 1. a tempting or being tempted 2. something that tempts

tempting (temp'tiŋ) *adj.* enticing; attractive —**tempt'ingly** *adv.*

‡tempus fugit (tem'pəs fyoo͞o'jit) [L.] time flies

ten (ten) *adj., n.* [OE.] totalling one more than nine; 10; X

ten. 1. tenor 2. *Music* tenuto

tenable (ten'ə b'l) *adj.* [see TENANT] that can be held, defended, or believed —**ten'a-bil'ity** *n.*

tenacious (tə nā'shəs) *adj.* [< L. *tenere*, to hold] 1. holding firmly 2. that retains well 3. strongly cohesive or adhesive 4. persistent —**tena'ciously** *adv.* —**tena'- ciousness** *n.*

tenacity (tə nas'ə tē) *n.* a being tenacious

tenancy (ten'ən sē) *n., pl.* **-cies** occupancy or duration of occupancy by a tenant

tenant (ten'ənt) *n.* [< L. *tenere*, to hold] 1. a person who pays rent to occupy or use land, a building, etc. 2. an occupant of a specified place —**ten'antless** *adj.*

tenant farmer a person who farms land owned by another and pays rent in cash or in a share of the crops

tenantry *n., pl.* **-ries** 1. a body of tenants 2. occupancy by a tenant

tench (tench) *n.* [< L. *tinca*] a common freshwater fish of the carp family

Ten Commandments *Bible* the ten laws forming the fundamental moral code of Israel : Ex. 20 :2-17; Deut. 5 :6-22

tend[1] (tend) *vt.* [see ATTEND] 1. to take

care of; watch over; attend to **2.** to be in charge of; manage

tend² *vi.* [< L. *tendere*, to stretch] **1.** to be likely or apt; incline **2.** to lead (*to* or *towards* a specified result) **3.** to move or extend [*to tend* eastwards]

tendency (ten'dən sē) *n., pl.* **-cies** [< L. *tendere*, to stretch] **1.** an inclination to move or act in a particular direction or way **2.** a course towards some purpose, object, or result

tendentious (ten den'shəs) *adj.* [see TENDENCY] advancing a definite point of view —**tenden'tiously** *adv.*

tender¹ (ten'dər) *adj.* [< L. *tener*, soft] **1.** easily chewed, broken, cut, etc. **2.** physically weak; frail **3.** immature; young [the *tender* age of five] **4.** needing careful handling **5.** gentle or light, as a touch **6.** affectionate, loving, etc. **7.** *a)* that feels pain easily; sensitive *b)* sensitive to others' feelings; compassionate —**ten'derly** *adv.* —**ten'derness** *n.*

tender² [< L. *tendere*, to stretch] to present for acceptance; offer (an invitation, apology, etc.) —*vi.* to make an offer or estimate for a particular job (with *for*) —*n.* a formal offer to supply specified goods or services at a stated cost —**put out to tender** to invite and compare tenders for a particular job

tender³ *n.* **1.** a person who has charge of something **2.** a ship to supply or service another ship, a submarine, etc. **3.** the vehicle behind a steam locomotive for carrying its coal and water

tenderfoot *n., pl.* **-foots'**, **-feet'** **1.** a newcomer, specif. to the hardships of ranching in the W U.S. **2.** formerly, a beginner in the Boy Scouts

tenderize *vt.* **-ized'**, **-iz'ing** to make (meat) tender, as by beating

tenderloin *n.* the tenderest muscle of a loin of pork

tendon (ten'dən) *n.* [< Gr. *teinein*, to stretch] any of the cords of tough, fibrous tissue connecting muscles to bones or other parts; sinew

TENDRIL

tendril (ten'drəl) *n.* [prob. < L. *tener*, soft] a threadlike, clinging part of a climbing plant, serving to support it

tenebrous (ten'ə brəs) *adj.* [< L. *tenebrae*, darkness] dark; gloomy

tenement (ten'i mənt) *n.* [< L. *tenere*, to hold] **1.** a large building divided into rooms or flats for rent, now often one

that is run-down and overcrowded; also **tenement building** **2.** a separately tenanted room or flat

tenet (ten'it, tē'net) *n.* [L., he holds] a doctrine or belief held as a truth, as by some group

tenfold (ten'fōld') *adj.* **1.** having ten parts **2.** having ten times as much or as many —*adv.* ten times as much or as many

ten-gallon hat a wide-brimmed felt hat with a high, round crown, orig. worn by cowboys

tenner (ten'ər) *n.* [Colloq.] a ten-pound note

tennis (ten'is) *n.* [< OFr. *tenir*, to hold] **1.** a game (officially **lawn tennis**), usually played outdoors, in which two or four players using rackets hit a ball back and forth over a net dividing a marked rectangular area (**tennis court**) **2.** a similar indoor game (**real tennis**), the ball being in addition bounced against walls

tenon (ten'ən) *n.* [see TENANT] a part of a piece of wood, etc. cut to stick out so that it will fit into a hole (*mortise*) in another piece to make a joint

tenor (ten'ər) *n.* [< L. *tenere*, to hold] **1.** *a)* the highest usual adult male voice, or its range *b)* a part for this voice *c)* a singer or instrument having this range **2.** general meaning **3.** general course or tendency —*adj.* of, in, or for the tenor

tenpin bowling a form of bowling in which bowls are rolled down a lane to knock over ten target pins

tense¹ (tens) *adj.* **tens'er**, **tens'est** [< L. *tendere*, to stretch] **1.** stretched tight; taut **2.** feeling, showing, or causing mental strain —*vt.*, *vi.* **tensed**, **tens'ing** to make or become tense —**tense'ly** *adv.* —**tense'ness** *n.*

tense² *n.* [< L. *tempus*, time] any of the forms of a verb that show the time of the action or condition

tensile (ten'sīl) *adj.* **1.** of or under tension **2.** capable of being stretched —**tensil'ity** (-sil'ə tē) *n.*

tensile strength the lengthwise stress that a given substance can bear without tearing apart

tension (ten'shən) *n.* **1.** a tensing or being tensed **2.** mental or nervous strain **3.** a state of strained relations **4.** voltage **5.** stress on a material by forces tending to cause extension —**ten'sional** *adj.*

tent (tent) *n.* [< L. *tendere*, to stretch] **1.** a portable shelter consisting of canvas, etc. stretched over poles and attached to stakes **2.** anything like a tent —*adj.* of or like a tent

tentacle (ten'tə k'l) *n.* [< L. *tentare*, to touch] a slender, flexible growth near the head or mouth, as of some invertebrates, used for grasping, feeling, etc. —**ten'tacled** *adj.*

tentative (ten'tə tiv) *adj.* [< L. *tentare*, to try] made or done as a test; not definite or final —**ten'tatively** *adv.* —**ten'tativeness** *n.*

tenter (ten'tər) *n.* [see TENT] a frame to stretch cloth on for even drying

tenterhook *n.* any of the hooked nails that hold cloth stretched on a tenter —**on tenterhooks** in suspense

tenth (tenth) *adj.* [OE. *teogotha*] **1.** preceded by nine others in a series; 10th **2.** designating any of ten equal parts —*n.* **1.** the one following the ninth **2.** any of the ten equal parts of something; 1/10 —**tenth'ly** *adv.*

tent stitch an embroidery stitch forming a series of parallel slanting lines

tenuous (ten'yoo wəs) *adj.* [< L. *tenuis*, thin] **1.** slight; flimsy **2.** slender or fine **3.** not dense; rare, as air high up —**tenuity** (tənyoō'ətē) *n.* —**ten'uously** *adv.*

tenure (ten'yooər) *n.* [see TENANT] **1.** the act or right of holding property, an office, etc. **2.** the period or condition of this **3.** [U.S.] the holding of a position in teaching, etc. on a permanent basis

tenuto (tənyoō'tō) *adj.* [It.] *Music* held for the full value, as a note

TEPEE

tepee (tē'pē) *n.* [< Siouan *ti*, to dwell + *pi*, used for] a cone-shaped tent of animal skins, used by the American Indians

tepid (tep'id) *adj.* [< L. *tepere*, be slightly warm] **1.** lukewarm **2.** unenthusiastic —**tepidity** (təpid'ətē) *n.* —**tep'idly** *adv.*

tequila (təkē'lə) *n.* [< *Tequila*, a Mexican district] a strong alcoholic liquor of Mexico

ter. **1.** terrace **2.** territory

terbium (tur'bē əm) *n.* [< *Ytterby*, town in Sweden] a metallic chemical element of the rare-earth group: symbol, Tb

tercel (tur's'l) *n.* var. of TIERCEL

tercentenary (tur'sentēn'ərē) *adj., n., pl.* **-naries** [< L. *ter*, three times + CENTENARY] *same as* TRICENTENNIAL: *also* **ter'centen'nial** (-ten'ē əl)

tercet (tur'sit) *n.* [< L. *tertius*, third] a group of three lines that rhyme with an adjacent triplet

teredo (tərē'dō) *n., pl.* **-dos** [< Gr. *terēdon*, borer] a marine mollusc that bores into and destroys submerged wood

tergiversate (tur'jivursāt') *vi.* **-sat'ed, -sat'ing** [< L. *tergum*, the back + *versari*, turn] **1.** to desert a cause, party, etc. **2.** to be evasive —**ter'giversa'tion** *n.*

term (turm) *n.* [< L. *terminus*, a limit] **1.** a word or phrase having definite meaning in some science, art, etc. **2.** a word or phrase of a specified kind [a colloquial *term*] **3.** [*pl.*] words that express ideas in a specified form [to speak in derogatory

terms] **4.** [*pl.*] personal relations [on speaking *terms*] **5.** [*pl*] conditions of a contract, sale, etc. that limit or define it **6.** *a)* a set period of time [a *term* of office] *b)* a division of an academic year, during which a school, etc., is in session **7.** a set date, as for payment **8.** *Law* the time a court is in session **9.** *Logic* any one of the three parts of a syllogism **10.** *Math.* a) either of the two quantities of a fraction or ratio *b)* each quantity in a series or in an algebraic expression —*vt.* to call by a term; name —**bring to terms** to force to agree —**come to terms** to arrive at an agreement —**in terms of** **1.** regarding; concerning **2.** used as a basis for expression —**term'less** *adj.*

termagant (tur'məgənt) *n.* [< OFr. *Tervagant*, alleged Moslem deity] a quarrelsome, scolding woman; shrew

terminable (tur'mi nə b'l) *adj.* **1.** that can be terminated **2.** that terminates after a specified time

terminal (tur'mə n'l) *adj.* [L. *terminalis*] **1.** of, at, or forming the end or extremity of something **2.** concluding; final **3.** terminating in death: said of a disease **4.** in or of a term or set period of time **5.** of, at, or forming the end of a transport route —*n.* **1.** an end; extremity **2.** a connective point on an electric circuit **3.** a device having input/output links with a computer **4.** *a)* a terminus for trains or long-distance buses *b)* a building at an airport where passengers await departure —**ter'minally** *adv.*

terminal velocity *Physics* the unchanging velocity reached by a falling body when there is no frictional resistance

terminate (tur'mə nāt') *vt.* **-nat'ed, -nat'ing** [< L. *terminus*, a limit] **1.** to form the end or limit of **2.** to put an end to; stop —*vi.* to come to an end —**ter'mina'tor** *n.*

termination (tur'mə nā'shən) *n.* **1.** a terminating or being terminated **2.** the end or limit **3.** an inflectional ending of a word —**ter'mina'tional** *adj.*

terminology (tur'mə nol'ə jē) *n., pl.* **-gies** the terms or special words used in some science, art, work, etc. —**ter'minolog'ical** (-nə loj'ik'l) *adj.*

terminus (tur'mə nəs) *n., pl.* **-ni'** (-nī'), **-nuses** [L., a limit] **1.** a final point or goal **2.** *a)* either end of a railway line, bus route, etc. *b)* a station or town at such a point

termitarium (tur mi tāə'rē əm) *n.* [< ff.] **1.** a colony of termites **2.** the conical mound-dwelling built by termites

termite (tur'mīt) *n.* [< L. *termes*, wood-boring worm] a pale-coloured, soft-bodied, antlike insect that lives in colonies

terms of trade the ratio of export prices to import prices

tern (turn) *n.* [ON. *therna*] a sea bird related to the gull, but smaller, with a forked tail

ternary (tur'nər ē) *adj.* [< L. *terni*, three each] **1.** threefold; triple **2.** third in rank, etc.

Terpsichore (turp sik′ə rē′) *Gr. Myth.* the Muse of dancing

terpsichorean (turp′si kə rē′ən) *adj.* 1. [T-] of Terpsichore 2. having to do with dancing

terrace (ter′əs) *n.* [< L. *terra*, earth] 1. *a)* a raised, flat mound of earth with sloping sides *b)* any of a series of flat platforms of earth, as on a hillside *c)* [*usually pl.*] unroofed tiers round a football pitch on which the spectators stand 2. an unroofed, paved area adjoining a house and overlooking a lawn or garden 3. *a)* a row of identical houses, usually with common walls *b)* a street in front of such houses —*vt.* **-raced, -racing** to form into a terrace

terraced house a house forming one of a row of identical houses with common dividing walls

terra cotta (ter′ə kot′ə) [It., baked earth] 1. a hard, brown-red, usually unglazed earthenware used for pottery, sculpture, etc. 2. its brown-red colour

terra firma (fur′mə) [L.] firm earth; solid ground

terrain (tə rān′) *n.* [< L. *terra*, earth] a tract of ground, esp. with regard to its features or fitness for some use

terra incognita (ter′ə iŋ kog′ni tə) [L.] an unknown or unexplored area

terrapin (ter′ə pin) *n.* [< Algonquian] 1. an American freshwater turtle 2. its edible flesh

terrarium (tə rāar′ē əm) *n., pl.* **-iums, -ia** [< L. *terra*, earth + *-arium* as in *aquarium*] 1. an enclosure for keeping small land animals 2. a glass container for a garden of small plants

terrazzo (tə rat′sō) *n.* [It.] flooring of small chips of marble set in cement and polished

terrene (te rēn′) *adj.* [< L. *terra*, earth] 1. of earth; earthy 2. worldly; mundane

terrestrial (tə res′tre əl) *adj.* [< L. *terra*, earth] 1. of this world; worldly 2. constituting the earth 3. consisting of land as distinguished from water 4. living on land rather than in water, in the air, etc. —**terres′trially** *adv.*

terrible (ter′ə b'l) *adj.* [< L. *terrere*, frighten] 1. [Colloq.] extreme; intense 2. [Colloq.] very bad, unpleasant, etc. 3. causing terror; dreadful —**ter′ribly** *adv.*

terrier (ter′ē ər) *n.* [ult. < L. *terra*, earth] a type of small, active dog, orig. bred to burrow after game

terrific (tə rif′ik) *adj.* [< L. *terrere*, frighten] 1. [Colloq.] *a)* unusually great, intense, etc. *b)* unusually fine, enjoyable, etc. 2. causing great fear —**terrif′ically** *adv.*

terrify (ter′ə fī′) *vt.* **-fied′, -fy′ing** to fill with terror; frighten greatly; alarm —**ter′rify′ingly** *adv.*

terrine (te rēn′) *n.* [Fr.: see TUREEN] 1. a small earthenware container 2. a paté

territorial (ter′ə tôr′ē əl) *adj.* 1. of territory or land 2. [*often* T-] organized regionally for home defence —*n.* [T-] a member of a Territorial force —**ter′rito′- rially** *adv.*

Territorial Army in Britain, a locally recruited volunteer reserve force

Territorial Council [Canad.] an elected body responsible for local government in the Northwest Territories or the Yukon

territorial waters the area of sea over which a nation has jurisdiction

territory (ter′ə tər ē) *n., pl.* **-ries** [< L. *terra*, earth] 1. any large tract of land; region 2. the land and waters under the jurisdiction of a nation, state, ruler, etc. 3. an assigned area, as of a travelling salesman 4. the area occupied by an animal or pair of animals, as for breeding 5. a sphere of action, existence, etc. 6. a part of a country or empire without the full status of a principal division

terror (ter′ər) *n.* [< L. *terrere*, frighten] 1. intense fear 2. a person or thing causing intense fear 3. [Colloq.] a very annoying person, esp. a child

terrorism *n.* the use of force and violence to intimidate, subjugate, etc., esp. as a political policy —**ter′rorist** *n., adj.*

terrorize *vt.* **-ized′, -iz′ing** 1. to coerce, make submit, etc. by filling with terror 2. to fill with terror —**ter′roriza′tion** *n.*

terry (ter′ē) *n., pl.* **-ries** [< ?] cloth having a pile in which the loops are left uncut: also **terry cloth**

terse (turs) *adj.* **ters′er, ters′est** [< L. *tergere*, wipe] free of superfluous words; concise; succinct

tertiary (tur′shə rē) *adj.* [< L. *tertius*, third] 1. of the third rank, order, formation, etc.; third 2. [T-] *Geol.* designating or of the first period in the Cainozoic Era

Terylene (ter′ə lēn′) [< *ter*(*ephthalate*) + (*polyeth*)*ylene*] *Trademark* a synthetic, polyester, textile fibre

tessellate (tes′ə lāt′) *vt.* **-lat′ed, -lat′ing** [< L. *tessella*, little square stone] to lay out or pave in a mosaic pattern of small, square blocks

tessera (tes′ər ə) *n., pl.* **-serae** (-ē) [< Gr. *tesseres*, four] any of the small pieces used in mosaic work

test¹ (test) *n.* [< L. *testa*, shell] 1. *a)* an examination or trial, as to prove the value of something *b)* a method or criterion used in this 2. an event, situation, etc. that tries a person's qualities 3. a set of questions, problems, etc. for determining a person's knowledge, abilities, etc. 4. [Colloq.] *same as* TEST MATCH 5. *Chem.* a trial or reaction for identifying a substance —*vt.* to subject to a test; try —**test′a- ble** *adj.* —**test′er** *n.*

test² *n.* [see prec.] the hard outer covering of certain invertebrate animals, as the shell of clams

Test. Testament

testa (tes′tə) *n., pl.* **-tae** (-tē) [< L., shell] *Bot.* the hard outer covering of a seed

testaceous (tes tā′shəs) *adj.* [< L. *testaceus*, made of shell or tile] 1. of or like shells 2. hard-shelled

testament (tes′tə mənt) *n.* [< L. *testis*,

a witness] **1.** orig., a covenant **2.** [T-] either of the two parts of the Christian Bible, the *Old Testament* and the *New Testament* **3.** a proof; testimonial *[a testament* to liberty] **4.** *Law* a will, esp. in **last will and testament** —**tes'tamen'tary** (-men'tə rē) *adj.*

testate (tes'tāt) *adj.* [< L. *testari,* make a will] having made and left a legally valid will

testator (tes tāt'ər) *n.* a person who has made a will —**testa'trix** *n.fem.*

test case *Law* a case that is likely to be used as a precedent

testicle (tes'ti k'l) *n.* [< L. *testis*] either of two oval sex glands in the male that are suspended in the scrotum and secrete spermatozoa

testify (tes'tə fī') *vi.* **-fied'**, **-fy'ing** [< L. *testis,* a witness + *facere,* make] **1.** to give evidence, esp. under oath in court **2.** to be evidence or an indication *[his look testifies* to his rage] —*vt.* **1.** to affirm; give as evidence, esp. under oath in court **2.** to be evidence of; indicate

testimonial (tes'tə mō'nē əl) *n.* **1.** a statement testifying to a person's qualifications, etc. or to the merits of some product **2.** something given or done as an expression of gratitude or appreciation

testimony (tes'tə mə nē) *n.,* *pl.* **-nies** [< L. *testis,* witness] **1.** a statement made under oath in court to establish a fact **2.** any affirmation or declaration **3.** any form of evidence; indication **4.** public avowal, as of faith

testis (tes'tis) *n.,* *pl.* **-tes** (-tēz) [L.] same as TESTICLE

test match a cricket or Rugby League match which is one of a series between international sides

testosterone (tes tos'tə rōn') *n.* [see TESTIS & STEROL] a male sex hormone

test paper **1.** a paper on which a test has been written **2.** paper, as litmus paper, prepared with a reagent for making chemical tests

test pilot a pilot who tests new or newly designed aircraft in flight, to determine their fitness for use

test-tube *adj.* **1.** made in or as in a test tube; experimental **2.** produced by artificial insemination

test tube a tube of thin, clear glass closed at one end, used in chemical experiments, etc.

testy *adj.* **-tier, -tiest** [< OFr. *teste,* head] irritable; touchy; peevish —**tes'tily** *adv.* —**tes'tiness** *n.*

tetanus (tet'ən əs) *n.* [L. < Gr. *tetanos,* spasm] an acute infectious disease, often fatal, caused by the toxin of a bacillus which usually enters the body through wounds; lockjaw

tetchy (tech'ē) *adj.* **-ier, -iest** [prob. < OFr. *teche,* a spot] touchy; irritable —**tetch'ily** *adv.* —**tetch'iness** *n.*

tête-à-tête (tāt'ə tāt') *n.* [Fr., head-to-head] a private conversation between two people —*adj.* for or of two people in private —*adv.* together privately

tether (teth'ər) *n.* [prob. < ON. *tjöthr*] a rope or chain fastened to an animal so as to keep it within certain bounds —*vt.* to fasten with a tether —**at the end of one's tether** at the end of one's endurance, etc.

tetra- [< Gr.] *a combining form meaning* four

tetrad (tet'rad) *n.* [< Gr. *tetras,* four] a group of four

tetraethyl lead (tet'rə ēth'il) a heavy, colourless, poisonous compound of lead, added to petrol to increase power and prevent engine knock

tetragon (tet'rə gon') *n.* [see TETRA- + -GON] a plane figure with four angles and four sides —**tetrag'onal** (te trag'ə n'l) *adj.*

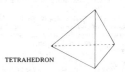

TETRAHEDRON

tetrahedron (tet'rə hē'drən) *n.,* *pl.* **-drons, -dra** [see TETRA- & -HEDRON] a solid figure with four triangular faces —**tet'rahe'dral** *adj.*

tetralogy (te tral'ə jē) *n.,* *pl.* **-gies** [see TETRA- & -LOGY] any series of four related plays, novels, etc.

tetrameter (te tram'ə tar) *n.* [see TETRA- & -METER] **1.** a line of verse containing four metrical feet **2.** verse consisting of tetrameters

Teut. **1.** Teuton **2.** Teutonic

Teuton (tyōōt'ən) *n.* a member of any Teutonic people; esp., a German

Teutonic (tyōō ton'ik) *adj.* designating or of a group of north European peoples including the Germans, Scandinavians, Dutch, English, etc.

text (tekst) *n.* [< L. *texere,* to weave] **1.** the principal matter on a printed page, as distinguished from pictures, etc. **2.** any form in which a written work exists **3.** the exact or original words of an author as distinguished from notes, etc. **4.** a Biblical passage used as the topic of a sermon **5.** a play or book that is to be studied

textbook *n.* a book giving instructions in the principles of a subject of study

textile (teks'tīl) *n.* [see TEXT] a fabric made by weaving, knitting, etc.; cloth —*adj.* **1.** having to do with weaving or woven fabrics **2.** that has been or can be woven

textual (teks'tyōo wəl) *adj.* of, contained in, or based on a text —**tex'tually** *adv.*

textualism *n.* strict adherence to the text, esp. of the Scriptures

texture (teks'chər) *n.* [see TEXT] **1.** the character of a fabric as determined by the arrangement, size, etc. of its threads **2.** the structure or composition of anything, esp. in the way it looks or feels —*vt.*

-tured, -turing to cause to have a particular texture —**tex′tural** adj.

T.G.W.U. Transport and General Workers' Union

Th Chem. thorium

Th. Thursday

Thai (tī) n. 1. a group of Asian languages considered to belong to the Sino-Tibetan language family 2. pl. **Thais, Thai** a native or inhabitant of Thailand —adj. of Thailand, its people, culture, etc.

thalidomide (thə lid′ə mīd′) n. [< (ph)thali(mi)do (glutari)mide] a drug formerly used as a sedative and hypnotic: found to be responsible for severe birth deformities when taken during pregnancy

thallium (thal′ē əm) n. [< Gr. thallos, green shoot: from its green spectrum line] a rare, bluish-white, soft, metallic chemical element: symbol, Tl

than (thən; unstressed thən, th'n) [< OE. thanne] a particle used: a) to introduce the second element in a comparison [A is taller than B] b) to express exception [none other than Sam]

thane (thān) n. [OE. thegen] 1. in early England, one of a class of freemen who held land of the king 2. in early Scotland, a person of rank who held land of the king Also **thegn**

thank (thaŋk) vt. [OE. thancian] 1. to express appreciation to, as by saying "thank you" 2. to hold responsible: an ironic use —**thank you** shortened form of I thank you

thankful adj. feeling or expressing thanks —**thank′fully** adv. —**thank′fulness** n.

thankless adj. 1. unappreciated 2. not feeling or expressing thanks —**thank′lessly** adv. —**thank′lessness** n.

thanks n.pl. an expression of gratitude —interj. I thank you —**thanks to** 1. thanks be given to 2. on account of

thanksgiving 1. a formal, public expression of thanks to God 2. [T-] a) a U.S. holiday on the fourth Thursday in November b) a Canadian holiday on the second Monday of October in full, **Thanksgiving Day**

that (thət; unstressed thət) pron., pl. **those** [OE. thæt] 1. the person or thing mentioned [that is John] 2. the thing further away [this is larger than that] 3. something being contrasted [this is more likely than that] 4. who, whom, or which [the road (that) we took] 5. where [the cupboard that I found it in] 6. when [the year that he died] —adj., pl. **those** 1. designating the one mentioned [that man is John] 2. designating the thing farther away 3. designating something being contrasted —conj. used to introduce: 1. a noun clause [that he's gone is obvious] 2. an adverbial clause expressing purpose [they died that we might live], result [he ran so fast that I lost him], or cause [I'm sorry that I won] 3. an incomplete sentence expressing surprise, desire, etc. [oh, that he were here!] —adv. 1. to that extent; so [I can't see that far] 2. [Colloq.]

very [I don't like skating that much] —all that [Colloq.] 1. so very [he isn't all that rich] 2. everything of the same sort [sex and all that] —at that [Colloq.] 1. at that point: also with that 2. even so —that is 1. to be specific 2. in other words —that's that! that is settled!

thatch (thach) n. [OE. thæc] 1. a) roof or roofing of straw, rushes, etc. b) material for such a roof: also **thatch′ing** 2. [Colloq.] the hair of the head —vt. to cover with or as with thatch —**thatch′-er** n. —**thatch′y** adj.

thaw (thô) vi. [OE. thawian] 1. a) to melt: said of ice, snow, etc. b) to pass to an unfrozen state: said of frozen foods 2. to become warmer, so that snow, etc. melts [it thawed today] 3. to lose coldness or reserve of manner —vt. to cause to thaw —n. 1. a thawing 2. a spell of weather warm enough to allow thawing

Th.D. [L. Theologiae Doctor] Doctor of Theology

the (thə; before vowels thi, thē) adj., definite article [OE. se, the] 1. the (as opposed to a, an) refers to a particular person or thing, as a) that (one) being spoken of [the Queen; the story ended] b) that (one) considered outstanding, etc. [that's the hotel in town]: usually italicized in print 2. the is used to refer to that one of a number of persons or things which is identified by a modifier [the red hat] 3. the is used to refer to a person or thing considered generically [the cow is a domestic animal, the good, the true] —adv. 1. that much; to that extent [the better to see you with] 2. by how much . . . by that much [the sooner, the better]

theatre (thē′ə tər) n. [< Gr. theasthai, to view] 1. a place or structure where plays, films, etc. are presented 2. any place like a theatre, having ascending rows of seats 3. any scene of events 4. a) the art of writing or putting on plays b) people engaged in putting on plays

theatre sister a nurse who assists a surgeon in the operating theatre

theatrical (thē at′ri k'l) adj. 1. having to do with the theatre 2. dramatic; esp. (in disparagement), melodramatic —**theat′rical′ity** (-kal′ə tē) n. —**theat′rically** adv.

theatricals n.pl. performances of stage plays, esp. by amateurs

thee (thē) pron. [OE. the] objective case of THOU[1]

theft (theft) n. [OE. thiefth] the act or an instance of stealing; larceny

their (thâar; unstressed thər) possessive pronominal adj. [ON. theirra] of, belonging to, made by, or done by them

theirs pron. that or those belonging to them: used without a following noun [that cat is theirs]: also used after of to indicate possession [a friend of theirs]

theism (thē′iz'm) n. [< Gr. theos, god] 1. belief in a god or gods 2. belief in one God who is creator —**the′ist** n., adj. —**theis′tic** adj. —**theis′tically** adv.

them (*th*em; *unstressed th*əm, *th*'m) *pron.* [ON. *theim*] *objective case* of THEY

theme (thēm) *n.* [< Gr. *tithenai*, to put] **1.** *a)* a topic, as of a lecture *b)* a motif **2.** *a)* a short melody used as the subject of a musical composition *b)* a musical phrase upon which variations are developed **3.** [U.S.] a short essay —**thematic** (thē mat'ik) *adj.*

themselves (*th*əm selvz') *pron.* **1.** an intensive form of they [they went *themselves*] **2.** a reflexive form of they [they hurt *themselves*] **3.** their true selves [they are not *themselves* today]

then (*th*en) *adv.* [see THAN] **1.** at that time [he was young *then*] **2.** next in time or order [first comes one and *then* two] **3.** in that case; accordingly [if it rains, *then* I will get wet] **4.** besides; moreover [I like to walk, and *then* it's cheaper] **5.** at another time [now it's warm, *then* cold] —*adj.* being such at that time [the *then* director] —*n.* that time [by *then*, they were gone] —**but then** but on the other hand —**then and there** at once —**what then?** what would happen in that case?

thence (*th*ens) *adv.* [OE. *thanan*] **1.** from that place **2.** from that time **3.** on that account

thenceforth *adv.* from that time onwards; thereafter: also **thence'for'ward**, **thence'for'wards**

theo- [< Gr.] *a combining form meaning* a god or God

theocracy (thē ok'rə sē) *n., pl.* **-cies** [see THEO- & -CRACY] **1.** lit., the rule of a state by God or a god **2.** government by priests claiming to rule with divine authority —**the'ocrat'ic** *adj.* —**the'ocrat'ically** *adv.*

THEODOLITE
(A, vertical angles;
B, horizontal angles)

theodolite (thē od'əl īt') *n.* [ModL. *theodelitus*] a surveying instrument used to measure vertical and horizontal angles

theol. **1.** theologian **2.** theology

theologian (thē'ə lō'jən) *n.* a student of or a specialist in theology

theology (thē ol'ə jē) *n., pl.* **-gies** [see THEO- & -LOGY] **1.** the study of God and of religious doctrines and matters of divinity **2.** a specific system of this study —**the'olog'ical** (-ə loj'i k'l) *adj.*

theorem (thēər'əm) *n.* [< Gr. *theōrein*, to view] **1.** a proposition that can be proved from accepted premises; law or principle **2.** *Math., Physics* a proposition embodying something to be proved

theoretical (thēə'ret'i k'l) *adj.* **1.** of or constituting theory **2.** limited to or based on theory; hypothetical **3.** tending to theorize; speculative —**the'oret'ically** *adv.*

theoretician (thēə'rə tish'ən) *n.* a person who specializes in the theory of some art, science, etc.: also **the'orist**

theorize (thēə'rīz') *vi.* **-rized'**, **-riz'ing** to form a theory or theories; speculate —**the'oriza'tion** *n.*

theory (thēər'ē) *n., pl.* **-ries** [< Gr. *theōrein*, to view] **1.** a speculative idea or plan as to how something might be done **2.** a systematic statement of principles involved **3.** a formulation of underlying principles of certain observed phenomena which has been verified to some degree **4.** the principles of an art or science rather than its practice **5.** popularly, a guess

theosophy (thē os'ə fē) *n., pl.* **-phies** [< Gr. *theos*, god + *sophos*, wise] any of various philosophies or religions that propose to establish direct contact with divine principle through contemplation, revelation, etc. —**the'osoph'ical** (-ə sof'-i k'l) *adj.* —**theos'ophist** *n.*

therapeutic (ther'ə pyoot'ik) *adj.* [< Gr. *therapeuein*, to nurse] **1.** serving to cure, or preserve health **2.** of therapeutics —**ther'apeu'tically** *adv.*

therapeutics *n.pl.* [with *sing. v.*] the branch of medicine that deals with the treatment and cure of diseases

therapy (ther'ə pē) *n., pl.* **-pies** [< Gr. *therapeuein*, to nurse] the treatment of any physical or mental disorder by medical or physical means —**ther'apist** *n.*

there (*th*āər) *adv.* [OE. *ther*] **1.** to or into that place [go *there*] **2.** at that point **3.** in that respect [*there* you are wrong] **4.** right now [*there* goes the whistle] **5.** at or in that place: often used as an intensive [John *there* is a good boy] *There* is also used: *a)* in interjectional phrases of approval, etc. [*there's* a fine fellow!] *b)* in constructions in which the real subject follows the verb [*there* are three men here] —*n.* that place [we left *there* at six] —*interj.* an exclamation expressing defiance, dismay, sympathy, etc. —**(not) all there** [Colloq.] (not) mentally sound

thereabouts *adv.* **1.** near that place **2.** near that time, number, amount, degree, etc. Also **there'about'**

thereafter (*th*āər af'tər) *adv.* after that; subsequently

thereat (*th*āər'at') *adv.* **1.** at that place; there **2.** at that time **3.** for that reason

thereby *adv.* **1.** by that means **2.** connected with that [*thereby* hangs a tale]

therefor (*th*āər'fôr') *adv.* [Archaic] for this; for that; for it

therefore (*th*er'fôr') *adv.* for this reason; consequently; hence: often used as a conjunction

therefrom (*th*āər from') *adv.* from this; from that; from it

therein (*th*āər'in') *adv.* **1.** in or into that place or thing **2.** in that matter, detail, etc.

thereinto (*th*âer in'tōō) *adv.* [Archaic]
1. into that place or thing 2. into that
matter, condition, etc.
thereof (*th*âer'ov') *adv.* 1. of that 2.
concerning that 3. from that as a cause,
reason, etc.
thereon (*th*âer'on') *adv.* [Archaic] 1.
on that 2. *same as* THEREUPON
there's (*th*âerz) 1. there is 2. there has
thereto (*th*âer tōō') *adv.* 1. to that place,
thing, etc.: also **there'un'to** 2. [Archaic]
besides
theretofore (*th*âer'tə fôr') *adv.* until
that time; before that
thereunder (*th*âer un'dər) *adv.* [Archaic]
1. under that; under it 2. under the terms
stated there
thereupon (*th*âer'ə pon') *adv.* 1.
immediately immediately following that
2. as a consequence of that 3. concerning
that subject, etc.
therewith (*th*âer with') *adv.* [Archaic] 1.
along with that 2. in addition to that
3. immediately thereafter
therewithal (*th*âer'with ôl') *adv.* in
addition; besides
therm (*th*urm) *n.* a unit of heat equal
to 100 000 British thermal units (105 506 000
joules)
thermal (thur'm'l) *adj.* [< Gr. *thermē,*
heat] having to do with heat, hot springs,
etc. —*n.* a rising column of warm air,
caused by the uneven heating of the earth
or sea by the sun —**ther'mally** *adv.*
thermic (thur'mik) *adj.* of or caused by
heat
thermionic valve (thurm'ē on'ik) [see
THERMO- & ION] an electron tube having
a cathode electrically heated in order to
cause electron or ion emission: also [esp.
U.S.] **thermionic tube**
thermo- [< Gr. *thermē,* heat] a
combining form meaning: 1. heat
[*thermodynamics*] 2. thermoelectric
thermocouple (thur'mō kup''l) *n.* a
junction of two dissimilar metals which
produces electric current when heated:
also called **thermoelectric couple**
thermodynamics (thur'mō dī nam'iks)
n.pl. [with *sing. v.*] the branch of physics
dealing with the reversible transformation
of heat into other forms of energy
thermoelectric (thur'mō i lek'trik) *adj.*
of or using electricity produced when the
junctions between two metals are
maintained at different temperatures
thermometer (thər mom'ə tər) *n.* [see
THERMO- & -METER] an instrument for
measuring temperatures, as a graduated
glass tube in which mercury rises or falls
as it expands or contracts from changes
in temperature: see FAHRENHEIT, CELSIUS
thermonuclear (thur'mō nyōō'klē ər)
adj. Physics 1. designating a reaction
in which light atomic nuclei fuse at very
high temperatures into heavier nuclei 2.
of or employing the heat energy released
in nuclear fusion
thermoplastic (thur'mō plas'tik) *adj.*
soft and mouldable when subjected to heat:
said of certain plastics

Thermos (thur'məs) [Gr. *thermos,* hot]
Trademark a type of flask or jug used
for keeping liquids at almost their original
temperature for several hours: in full
Thermos flask (or **jug**)
thermosetting (thur'mō set'iŋ) *adj.*
becoming unmouldable when subjected to
heat: said of certain plastics
thermostat (thur'mō stat') *n.* [THERMO-
+ -STAT] an apparatus for regulating
temperature, esp. one that automatically
controls a heating unit —**ther'mostat'ic**
adj. —**ther'mostat'ically** *adv.*
thesaurus (thi sôr'əs) *n., pl.* **-ri** (-ī), **-ruses**
[L. < Gr. *thēsauros,* a treasure] a book
containing a store of words; specif., a
book of synonyms and antonyms
these (*th*ēz) *pron., adj.* pl. *of* THIS
thesis (*th*ē'sis) *n., pl.* **the'ses** (-sēz) [<
Gr. *tithenai,* to put] 1. a research paper,
esp. one presented as part of the
requirements for a degree 2. a proposition
defended in argument 3. *Logic* an
unproved statement assumed as a premise
Thespian (thes'pē ən) *adj.* [< *Thespis,*
Greek poet] [often t-] having to do
with drama —*n.* [often t-] an actor or
actress
Thess. Thessalonians
theta (*th*ēt'ə) *n.* the eighth letter of the
Greek alphabet (Θ, θ)
thews (thyōōz) *n.pl., sing.* **thew** [OE.
theaw, habit] 1. muscular power 2.
muscles or sinews
they (*th*ā) *pron.* for sing. see HE, SHE,
IT [ON. *their*] 1. the persons, animals,
or things previously mentioned 2. people
in general [*they* say it's so]
they'd (*th*ād) 1. they had 2. they would
they'll (*th*āl) 1. they will 2. they shall
they're (*th*âer) they are
they've (*th*āv) they have
thiamine (thī'ə mēn') *n.* [THI(O)- +
(VIT)AMIN] vitamin B₁, a white, crystalline
compound found in cereal grains, egg yolk,
liver, etc.: a deficiency of this vitamin
results in beriberi
thick (thik) *adj.* [OE. *thicce*] 1. of relatively
great depth from one surface or side to
the other 2. measured between opposite
surfaces [nine centimetres *thick*] 3. a)
dense; luxuriant [*thick* woods] b) great
in number and close together [a *thick*
crowd] c) having much body [*thick* soup]
d) dense and heavy [*thick* smoke] 4.
dark or obscure [*thick* shadows] 5.
slurred, muffled, or husky [*thick* speech]
b) strongly marked [a *thick* accent] c)
muzzy; fuddled [a *thick* head] 6. [Colloq.]
stupid 7. [Colloq.] close in friendship
8. [Colloq.] too much to be tolerated [that's
a bit *thick*] —*adv.* in a thick way —*n.*
the thickest part or the period of greatest
activity [in the *thick* of the fight] —**lay
it on thick** [Slang] to exaggerate —the
thick end of the stick the inferior part
of any transaction, etc. —**through thick
and thin** in good times and bad times
—**thick'ish** *adj.* —**thick'ly** *adv.*
thicken *vt., vi.* 1. to make or become

thicker 2. to make or become more complex —**thick′ener** n.

thickening n. 1. the action of one that thickens 2. a substance used to thicken 3. the thickened part

thicket (thĭk′it) n. [< OE. *thicce*, thick] a thick growth of shrubs or small trees

thickheaded adj. stupid —**thick′head′-edness** n.

thickness n. 1. a being thick 2. the measure of how thick a thing is 3. a layer [three *thicknesses* of cloth]

thickset adj. 1. thick in body; stocky 2. planted thickly or closely

thick-skinned adj. 1. not easily hurt by criticism, insults, etc. 2. having a thick skin

thief (thēf) n., pl. **thieves** (thēvz) [OE. *theof*] a person who steals, esp. secretly

thieve (thēv) vt., vi. **thieved, thiev′ing** [OE. *theofian*] to steal —**thiev′ish** adj. —**thiev′ishly** adv.

thievery n., pl. **-eries** the act or practice of stealing or an instance of this; theft

thigh (thī) n. [OE. *theoh*] the part of the leg between the knee and the hip

thighbone n. the largest and longest bone in the body, from the hip to the knee; femur: also **thigh bone**

thimble (thim′b'l) n. [< OE. *thuma*, thumb] a small cap of metal, plastic, etc. worn as a protection on the finger that pushes the needle in sewing —**thim′-bleful** n.

thimblerig n. a swindling game in which the victim bets that a pea is under one of three thimble-shaped containers manipulated by sleight of hand —vt., vi. **-rigged′, -rig′ging** to cheat or swindle, as in this game —**thim′blerig′ger** n.

thin (thin) adj. **thin′ner, thin′nest** [OE. *thynne*] 1. of relatively little depth from one surface or side to the other 2. having little fat or flesh; slender 3. a) scanty in growth; sparse [thin hair] b) small in size or number [thin receipts] c) lacking body; watery [thin soup] d) rarified, as air at high altitudes 4. not deep and strong [a thin voice] 5. light or sheer, as fabric 6. easily seen through; flimsy [a thin excuse] 7. [Colloq.] dull; miserable [a thin time] —adv. in a thin way —vt., vi. **thinned, thin′ning** to make or become thin or thinner: often with out, down, etc. —**thin on the ground** [Colloq.] small in number —**thin on top** [Colloq.] going bald —**thin′ly** adv. —**thin′ness** n. —**thin′-nish** adj.

thine (thīn) pron. [OE. *thin*] possessive form of THY —adj. [Archaic or Poet.] thy: used before a vowel

thing (thing) n. [OE., a council] 1. any matter, affair, or concern 2. a) a tangible object, as distinguished from a quality, concept, etc. b) a lifeless object c) an item, detail, etc. 3. something mentioned but unnamed 4. a person or creature 5. a happening, act, incident, etc. 6. an end to be achieved 7. a) [pl.] personal belongings b) a dress, garment, etc. [not a *thing* to wear] 8. [Colloq.] a point of dispute; issue 9. [Colloq.] a strong fear, aversion, etc. [to have a *thing* about flying] 10. [Colloq.] something remarkable [there's a *thing*] —**do one's (own) thing** [Colloq.] to express one's personality in one's own way of life —**see things** [Colloq.] to have hallucinations —**the thing** 1. that which is wise, essential, etc. 2. that which is the height of fashion

thingamabob, thingumabob (thing′ə-mə bob′) n. [Colloq.] same as THINGAMAJIG: also **thing′ummy**

thingamajig, thingumajig (thing′ə mə jig′) n. [see THING] [Colloq.] any device or gadget: jocular substitute for a name not known or forgotten

think (think) vt. **thought, think′ing** [OE. *thencan*] 1. to believe; expect [I think I can go] 2. to judge; consider 3. to form or have in the mind [think good thoughts] 4. to determine, work out, etc. by reasoning 5. a) to form an idea of [think what may be] b) to recall; recollect —vi. 1. to use the mind; reflect or reason 2. to have an opinion, belief, judgment, etc. 3. to remember (with of or about) 4. to consider or be considerate (with of or about) 5. to invent; conceive (of) 6. to focus the attention on being [think big] —n. [Colloq.] the act of thinking [give it a good *think*] —**think better of** 1. to form a more favourable opinion of 2. to make a more sensible decision about, after reconsidering —**think fit** to regard as proper —**think little (or nothing) of** 1. to attach little (or no) importance to 2. to have little (or no) hesitancy about —**think out** 1. to think about to a conclusion: also **think through** 2. to work out by thinking —**think out loud** to speak one's thoughts as they occur: also **think aloud** —**think over** to give thought to —**think twice** to consider carefully before deciding —**think up** to invent, contrive, etc. by thinking —**think′able** adj. —**think′-er** n.

thinking adj. 1. that thinks or can think 2. reflective —n. thought —**put on one's thinking cap** to give serious consideration to a matter

think tank [Colloq.] a group of experts organized to do intensive research and problem solving

thinner (thin′ər) n. a substance added, as turpentine to paint, for thinning

thin-skinned (thin′skind′) adj. 1. easily hurt by criticism, insults, etc. 2. having a thin skin

thio- [< Gr. *theion*, brimstone] a combining form meaning sulphur, used to indicate the replacement of oxygen by sulphur

thiopental (sodium) (thī′ə pen′tal) [< THIO- + PENTA-] a yellowish-white powder, injected intravenously in solution as a general anaesthetic

thiosulphuric acid (thī′ə sul fyoōar′ik) [THIO- + SULPHURIC] an unstable acid whose salts are used in photography, bleaching, etc.

third (thurd) *adj.* [OE. *thridda*] **1.** preceded by two others in a series; 3rd **2.** designating any of the three equal parts of something —*adv.* in the third place, rank, group, etc. —*n.* **1.** the one following the second **2.** any of the three equal parts of something; 1/3 **3.** an honours degree of the third, and usually the lowest, class **4.** *Music* the third tone of an ascending scale, or a tone two degrees above or below any given tone in such a scale —**third′ly** *adv.*

third-class *adj.* of the class, rank, excellence, etc. next below the second; inferior

third degree [Colloq.] harsh treatment and questioning of a prisoner to force a confession or information —**third′-degree′** *adj.*

third dimension **1.** the quality of having, or of seeming to have, depth, or solidity **2.** the quality of being true to life or seeming real

third man *Cricket* a fielding position on the off side near the boundary behind the batsman's wicket

third party a person other than the principals in a case or matter

third person that form of a pronoun (as *he*) or verb (as *is*) which refers to the person or thing spoken of

third-rate *adj.* **1.** inferior; very poor **2.** third in quality or other rating; third-class —**third′-rat′er** *n.*

third world [*often* T- W-] the underdeveloped or emergent countries of the world, esp. of Africa and Asia

thirst (thurst) *n.* [OE. *thurst*] **1.** the discomfort caused by a desire for water, characterized generally by dryness in the mouth and throat **2.** [Colloq.] a craving for a liquid **3.** any strong desire; craving —*vi.* **1.** to be thirsty **2.** to have a strong desire

thirsty (thur′stē) *adj.* **-ier, -iest 1.** feeling thirst **2.** lacking moisture; dry [*thirsty* fields] **3.** [Colloq.] causing thirst [*thirsty* work] **4.** having a strong desire; craving —**thirst′ily** *adv.* —**thirst′iness** *n.*

thirteen (thur′tēn′) *adj., n.* [OE. *threotyne*] three more than ten; 13; XIII —**thir′teenth′** *adj.,n.*

thirty (thur′tē) *adj.,n.* [OE. *thritig*] three times ten; 30; XXX —**the thirties** the numbers or years, as of a century, from thirty to thirty-nine —**thir′tieth** *adj.,n.*

Thirty-nine Articles a set of formulas defining the doctrinal position of the Church of England

this (this) *pron., adj. pl.* **these** [OE. *thes*] **1.** (designating) the person or thing mentioned or understood [*this* (man) is John] **2.** (designating) the thing that is nearer than another referred to as "that" [*this* box is larger than that] **3.** (designating) the fact, idea, etc. that is being, or is about to be, presented, etc. [now listen to *this* (news)] —*adv.* to this extent; so [it was *this* big]

THISTLE

thistle (this′'l) *n.* [OE. *thistel*] a plant with prickly leaves and white or purple, flowers —**this′tly** *adj.*

thistledown *n.* the down attached to the flower head of a thistle

thither (thith′ər) *adv.* [OE. *thider*] to or towards that place; there —*adj.* on or towards that side

tho, tho' (thō) *conj., adv.* shortened sp. of THOUGH

thole (thōl) *n.* [OE. *thol*] a pin or either of a pair of pins set vertically in the gunwale of a boat to serve as a fulcrum for an oar: also **thole′pin′**

Thompson submachine gun (tomp′sən) [< J. T. *Thompson*] *Trademark* a type of submachine gun

thong (thoŋ) *n.* [OE. *thwang*] a narrow strip of leather, etc. used as a lace, strap, etc.

thoracic (thô ras′ik) *adj.* of, in, or near the thorax

thorax (thôr′aks) *n., pl.* **-raxes, -races′** (-ə sēz′) [L. < Gr.] **1.** in man and other vertebrates, the part of the body between the neck and the abdomen **2.** the middle one of the three main segments of an insect's body

thorium (thôr′ē əm) *n.* [< Thor, Scand. god] a rare, greyish, radioactive chemical element, used in making electronic equipment and as a nuclear fuel: symbol, Th

thorn (thôrn) *n.* [OE.] **1.** *a)* a very short, hard, leafless branch or stem with a sharp point *b)* any small tree or shrub bearing thorns **2.** anything that keeps troubling, vexing, or irritating one: usually in **thorn in one's side** (or **flesh**) —**thorn′y** *adj.*

thorough (thur′ə) *adj.* [var. of THROUGH] **1.** done or proceeding through to the end; complete **2.** absolute [a *thorough* rascal] **3.** very exact, accurate, or painstaking —**thor′oughly** *adv.* —**thor′oughness** *n.*

thoroughbred *adj.* purebred, as a horse or dog; pedigreed —*n.* a thoroughbred animal; specif., [T-] any of a breed of racehorses

thoroughfare *n.* a public street open at both ends, esp. one through which there is much traffic

thoroughgoing *adj.* very thorough; specif., *a)* precise and painstaking *b)* absolute; out-and-out

Thos. Thomas

those (thōz) *adj., pron.* [OE. *thas*] *pl.* of THAT

thou¹ (thou) *pron.* [OE. *thu*] the second person singular of the personal pronoun: now replaced by *you* except in poetic, religious, and some dialectal use

thou² (thou) *n.* [Colloq.] 1. a thousand 2. a thousandth

though (thō) *conj.* [< OE. *theah*] 1. in spite of the fact that [*though* it rained, he went] 2. and yet; nevertheless; however 3. even if; supposing that [*though* he may fail, he will have tried] —*adv.* however; nevertheless

thought¹ (thôt) *n.* [OE. *thoht*] 1. the act or process of thinking 2. the power of reasoning; intellect 3. what one thinks; idea, opinion, plan, etc. 4. the ideas, opinions, etc. prevailing at a given time or place or among a given people 5. attention; consideration 6. intention or expectation 7. a little; trifle [be a *thought* more careful]

thought² *pt. & pp.* of THINK¹

thoughtful *adj.* 1. considerate of others 2. characterized by thought; serious 3. full of thought; meditative —**thought′fully** *adv.* —**thought′fulness** *n.*

thoughtless *adj.* 1. not considerate of others 2. not stopping to think; careless 3. not given thought; rash —**thought′lessly** *adv.* —**thought′lessness** *n.*

thought-reading *n.* the supposed ability to know another person's thoughts by telepathy —**thought′-read′er** *n.*

thousand (thou′z'nd) *n.* [OE. *thusend*] 1. ten hundred; 1000; M 2. a large number 3. [Colloq.] a thousand pounds —*adj.* amounting to one thousand in number —**thou′sandth** *adj., n.*

thousandfold *adj., adv.* a thousand times as much or as many

thrall (thrôl) *n.* [OE. *thræl* < ON.] 1. orig., a slave 2. slavery

thralldom, thraldom *n.* the condition of being a thrall; servitude; slavery

thrash (thrash) *vt.* [OE. *therscan*] 1. to give a severe beating to; flog 2. to make move wildly 3. to overwhelm; surpass 4. same as THRESH —*vi.* 1. same as THRESH 2. to move about violently [*thrashing* in agony] —**thrash out** to settle by much discussion —**thrash′er** *n.*

thread (thred) *n.* [OE. *thræd*] 1. a) a light, fine, stringlike length of two or more fibres of cotton, silk, etc. twisted together and used in sewing b) a similar fine length of material, as glass 2. any thin line, vein, ray, etc. 3. something like a thread in its length, sequence, etc. 4. the spiral ridge of a screw, bolt, nut, etc. —*vt.* 1. to put a thread through the eye of (a needle, etc.) 2. to string (beads, etc.) on or as if on a thread 3. to fashion a thread (sense 4) on or in (a screw, etc.) 4. a) to pass through by twisting, turning, or weaving in and out [to *thread* the streets] b) to make (one's way) in this fashion —**thread′er** *n.* —**thread′-like′** *adj.*

threadbare *adj.* 1. worn down so that the threads show 2. wearing worn-out clothes 3. stale; trite

threat (thret) *n.* [OE. *threat*, a throng] 1. an expression of intention to hurt, destroy, punish, etc., as in intimidation 2. a) a sign of something dangerous [the

threat of war] b) a source of possible danger, harm, etc.

threaten *vt.* [OE. *threatnian*] 1. to make threats against 2. a) to be a sign of (danger, harm, etc.) [clouds *threatening* snow] b) to be a source of possible danger, harm, etc. to —*vi.* 1. to make threats etc. —**threat′eningly** *adv.*

three (thrē) *adj., n.* [OE. *threo, thrie*] totalling one more than two; 3; III

3-D (thrē′dē′) *adj.* producing an effect of three dimensions [a 3-D film]

three-decker (thrē′dek′ər) *n.* 1. a ship with three decks 2. any structure with three levels 3. [Colloq.] a sandwich made with three slices of bread

three-dimensional (thrē′də men′shən 'l) *adj.* 1. of or having three dimensions 2. appearing to have depth or thickness in addition to height and width

threefold *adj., adv.* 1. three times as much or as many 2. having three parts

three-legged race a race in which competitors run in pairs with their adjoining legs tied together

threepenny (throop′ə nē) *adj.* 1. worth or costing threepence 2. of small worth; cheap

threepenny bit a former British coin, twelve-sided, and worth three (old) pennies

three-ply *adj.* having three thicknesses, strands, etc.

three-point turn a complete turn of a motor vehicle, usually made in three backwards-and-forwards movements

three-quarter *adj.* of or involving three fourths —*n.* Rugby any of the players between the full back and the half backs

threescore *adj.* sixty

threesome *n.* a group of three persons

threnody (thren′ə dē) *n.*, *pl.* -dies [< Gr. *thrēnos*, lament + *ōidē*, song] a song of lamentation; dirge

thresh (thresh) *vt., vi.* [earlier form of THRASH] 1. to beat out (grain) from (husks) as with a flail 2. to thrash

thresher *n.* 1. one who threshes 2. a machine for threshing grain: also **threshing machine**

threshold (thresh′ōld) *n.* [OE. *therscold*] 1. a) a length of wood, stone, etc. placed beneath a door b) a doorway 2. the beginning point of something 3. Physiol., Psychol. the point at which a stimulus is just strong enough to produce a response [the *threshold* of pain]

threw (throo) *pt.* of THROW

thrice (thrīs) *adv.* [ME. *thries*] 1. three times 2. greatly; highly

thrift (thrift) *n.* [< ON. *thrifast*, to thrive] 1. careful management of one's money or resources; frugality 2. a small plant with narrow leaves and small white, pink, red, or purplish flowers —**thrift′less** *adj.*

thrifty *adj.* -ier, -iest practising thrift; economical —**thrift′ily** *adv.* —**thrift′iness** *n.*

thrill (thril) *vi., vt.* [< OE. *thurh*, through] 1. to feel or cause to feel keen emotional excitement 2. to quiver or cause to quiver;

tremble —n. 1. a thrilling or being thrilled 2. the quality of thrilling 3. a tremor; quiver

thriller n. a novel, film, etc., of suspense, esp. one dealing with crime and detection

thrips (thrips) n., pl. **thrips** [Gr., woodworm] a small, winged insect that sucks the juices of plants

thrive (thrīv) vi. thrived, or throve, thrived or thriven (thriv''n), thriv'ing [< ON. thrifa, to grasp] 1. to prosper or flourish 2. to grow vigorously or luxuriantly

thro', thro (thrōō) prep., adv., adj. shortened sp. of THROUGH

throat (thrōt) n. [OE. throte] 1. the front part of the neck 2. the upper part of the passage from the mouth and nose to the stomach and lungs 3. any narrow, throatlike passage —cut one another's throats [Colloq.] to ruin each other, as by underselling in business —jump down someone's throat [Colloq.] to reply to sharply and critically —thrust (or ram) down a person's throat to insist that someone listens, pays attention, etc., to something

throaty adj. -ier, -iest 1. produced in the throat, as some sounds or tones 2. husky [a throaty voice] —throat'ily adv. —throat'iness n.

throb (throb) vi. throbbed, throb'bing [ME. throbben] 1. to beat, pulsate, vibrate, etc. 2. to beat strongly or fast 3. to quiver with excitement —n. 1. the act of throbbing 2. a beat or pulsation, esp. a strong one of the heart —throb'bingly adv.

throe (thrō) n. [< OE. thrawu, pain] a spasm or pang of pain: usually used in pl. [death throes] —in the throes of in the act of struggling with (a problem, etc.)

thrombosis (throm bō'sis) n. [< Gr. thrombos, a clot] coagulation of the blood in the heart or a blood vessel, forming a clot —thrombot'ic (-bät'ik) adj.

throne (thrōn) n. [< Gr. thronos, seat] 1. the chair on which a king, cardinal, etc. sits on formal occasions 2. the power or rank of a king, etc. 3. a sovereign ruler, etc. —vt. throned, thron'ing to enthrone

throng (thrôŋ) n. [< OE. thringan, to crowd] 1. a crowd 2. any great number of things massed together —vi. to gather together in a throng; crowd —vt. to crowd into

throstle (thros''l) n. [OE.] same as SONG THRUSH

throttle (throt''l) n. [< THROAT] 1. the valve that regulates the amount of fuel vapour entering an engine 2. the pedal that controls this valve 3. [Dial.] the throat —vt. -tled, -tling 1. to choke; strangle 2. to censor or suppress 3. a) to reduce the flow of (fuel vapour, etc.) by means of a throttle b) to lessen the speed of (an engine, vehicle, etc.) by this means (often with back or down) —throt'tler n.

through (thrōō) prep. [OE. thurh] 1. in one side and out the other side of 2. in the midst of; among 3. by way of

4. over the entire extent of 5. to various places in; around [touring through France] 6. a) from the beginning to the end of b) [U.S.] up to and including 7. without making a stop for [to go through a red light] 8. as a result of —adv. 1. in one side and out the other 2. from the beginning to the end 3. completely to the end [see it through] 4. thoroughly; completely: also **through and through** —adj. 1. extending from one place to another [a through road] 2. travelling to the destination without stops [a through train] 3. finished 4. [Colloq.] at the end of one's usefulness, etc. [through as a politician] 5. [Colloq.] having no further dealings, etc. (with someone or something) 6. connected (on a telephone line)

throughout (thrōō out') prep. all the way through —adv. 1. everywhere 2. in every respect

throughput n. the amount of material put through a process in a given period, as by a computer

throve (thrōv) alt. pt. of THRIVE

throw (thrō) vt. threw, thrown, throw'ing [OE. thrawan, to twist] 1. to cause to fly through the air by releasing from the hand; cast; hurl 2. to cause to fall; upset 3. to send rapidly [they threw troops into the battle] 4. to put suddenly into a specified state [thrown into confusion] 5. a) to cast (dice) b) to make (a specified cast) at dice [to throw a five] 6. to move (a switch, etc.) so as to connect, disconnect, etc. 7. to direct, cast, etc. [to throw a glance] 8. to cause (one's voice) to seem to come from some other source 9. [U.S. Colloq.] to lose (a game, race, etc.) deliberately 10. [Colloq.] to give (a party, etc.) 11. [Colloq.] to have (a fit, tantrum, etc.) 12. [Colloq.] to confuse or disconcert 13. Ceramics to shape on a potter's wheel —vi. to cast or hurl something —n. 1. a throwing; cast 2. the distance something is or can be thrown —throw a spanner in the works to obstruct by interference —throw away 1. to rid oneself of; discard 2. to waste 3. to fail to make use of 4. to deliver (a line or lines) in an offhand way: said of an actor or comedian —throw back 1. to stop from advancing 2. to revert to the type of an ancestor —throw back on to force (someone) to depend on [thrown back on his own resources] —throw in 1. to interpolate (a remark, suggestion, etc.) 2. to add extra or free 3. to throw (a football, etc.) from a side line, after it has gone out of play —throw in one's lot with to give one's allegiance to —throw off 1. to rid oneself of 2. to recover from 3. to write or utter quickly, in an offhand manner —throw on to put on (a garment) hastily —throw oneself at to try very hard to win the affection or love of —throw oneself into to engage in with great vigour —throw oneself on (or upon) 1. to rely on for support for aid 2. to assault —throw one's hand in to give up all attempt to succeed —throw open 1. to open completely and suddenly

2. to remove all restrictions from —**throw out 1.** to discard **2.** to reject or remove **3.** to put forth or utter (a hint or suggestion) —**throw over 1.** to abandon **2.** to jilt —**throw together 1.** to make or assemble hurriedly **2.** to cause to become acquainted —**throw up 1.** to give up or abandon **2.** to vomit **3.** to construct rapidly **4.** to mention repeatedly (*to* someone), as in reproach —**throw′er** *n.*

throwaway *adj.* **1.** designed to be discarded after use **2.** said or done incidentally [*a throwaway* remark]

throwback *n.* a person, animal, or plant that has the characteristics of an earlier type

thru (thrōō) *prep., adv., adj.* shortened U.S. *sp.* of THROUGH

thrum[1] (thrum) *n.* [OE., ligament] **1.** the row of warp thread ends left on a loom when the web is cut off **2.** any of these ends

thrum[2] *vt., vi.* **thrummed, thrum′ming** [echoic] **1.** to strum (a guitar, banjo, etc.) **2.** to drum (on) with the fingers —*n.* the act or sound of thrumming

thrush[1] (thrush) *n.* [OE. *thrysce*] any of a large group of songbirds, including the blackbird, etc., esp. the song thrush

thrush[2] *n.* [< ?] **1.** a fungus disease, esp. of infants that forms milky white lesions on the mouth and throat **2.** a disease of the frog of a horse's foot

thrust (thrust) *vt.* **thrust, thrust′ing** [< ON. *thrysta*] **1.** to push with sudden force **2.** to pierce; stab **3.** to force or impose (oneself or another) upon someone else —*vi.* **1.** to push or shove against something **2.** to make a stab or lunge, as with a sword **3.** to force one's way (*into, through,* etc.) —*n.* **1.** *a)* a sudden, forceful push *b)* a stab *c)* a remark intended to annoy someone **2.** continuous pressure of one part against another, as of a rafter against a wall **3.** *a)* the driving force of a propeller *b)* the forward force produced by a jet or rocket engine **4.** forward movement; impetus

thud (thud) *vi.* **thud′ded, thud′ding** [prob. < OE. *thyddan,* to strike] to hit with a dull sound —*n.* a dull sound, as of a heavy object dropping on a soft, solid surface

thug (thug) *n.* [< Hindi *thag,* rogue] **1.** a rough, brutal gangster, robber, etc. **2.** [*also* T-] a member of a former religious organization in India that murdered and robbed —**thug′gery** *n.*

thulium (thyōō′lē əm) *n.* [< *ultima Thule,* the northernmost region of the world for the ancients] a metallic chemical element of the rare-earth group: symbol, Tm

thumb (thum) *n.* [OE. *thuma*] **1.** the short, thick finger of the human hand that is nearest the wrist **2.** that part of a glove, etc. which covers the thumb —*vt.* **1.** to handle, turn, soil, etc. as with the thumb **2.** [Colloq.] to ask for or get (a ride) or make (one's way) in hitchhiking by gesturing with the thumb extended —**all thumbs** clumsy; fumbling —**thumbs down** a signal of disapproval —**under one's thumb** under one's influence

thumb index a series of rounded notches cut in the front edge of a book with a labelled tab at the base of each notch

thumbnail *n.* the nail of the thumb —*adj.* very small or brief [*a thumbnail* sketch]

thumbscrew *n.* a former instrument of torture for squeezing the thumbs

thump (thump) *n.* [echoic] **1.** a blow with something heavy and blunt **2.** the dull sound made by such a blow —*vt.* **1.** to strike with a thump **2.** to thrash; beat severely —*vi.* **1.** to hit or fall with a thump **2.** to make a dull, heavy sound; pound; throb —**thump′er** *n.*

thumping *adj.* [Colloq.] very large; whopping

thunder (thun′dər) *n.* [OE. *thunor*] **1.** the sound that is heard after a flash of lightning, caused by the sudden heating and expansion of air by electrical discharge **2.** any sound like this —*vi.* **1.** to produce thunder [*it is thundering*] **2.** to make strong denunciations, etc. —*vt.* to utter, attack, etc. with a thundering sound —**steal someone's thunder** to lessen the effectiveness of someone's statement by anticipating him —**thun′derer** *n.*

thunderbolt *n.* **1.** a flash of lightning with the thunder heard after it **2.** something that stuns or acts with sudden force or violence **3.** the imagined agency of destruction produced by a flash of lightning

thunderclap *n.* **1.** a clap, or loud crash, of thunder **2.** anything like this in being sudden, startling, etc.

thundercloud *n.* a storm cloud charged with electricity and producing lightning and thunder

thundering *adj.* [Colloq.] very large or excessive

thunderous *adj.* **1.** full of or making thunder **2.** making a noise like thunder —**thun′derously** *adv.*

thunderstorm *n.* a storm with thunder and lightning

thunderstruck *adj.* amazed or shocked as if struck by a thunderbolt : also **thun′der-strick′en**

thurible (thyōōar′ə b'l) *n.* [< Gr. *thyos,* sacrifice] a censer

Thurs., Thur. Thursday

Thursday (thurz′dē) *n.* [< ON. *Thorsdagr,* Thor's day] the fifth day of the week

Thursdays *adv.* [Colloq.] on or during every Thursday

thus (*th*us) *adv.* [OE.] **1.** in this or that manner **2.** to this or that degree or extent; so **3.** consequently; therefore

thwack (thwak) *vt.* [echoic] to strike with something flat; whack —*n.* a blow with something flat

thwart (thwôrt) *vt.* [ON. *thvert,* transverse] to keep from being; hinder (a person, plans, etc.) —*n.* **1.** a rower's seat extending across a boat **2.** a brace extending across a canoe

thy (*th*ī) *possessive pronominal adj.* [ME. *thin*] of, belonging to, or done by thee : archaic or poet. var. of *your*

thyme (tīm) *n.* [< Gr. *thymon*] an

thymol (thī′mol) *n.* a colourless compound extracted from thyme: used as an antiseptic

thymus (thī′məs) *n.* [< Gr. *thymos*] a ductless, glandlike body near the throat: also **thymus gland**

thyroid (thī′roid) *adj.* [< Gr. *thyreos,* door-shaped shield] **1.** designating a large ductless gland near the trachea, secreting a hormone which regulates growth **2.** designating the principal cartilage of the larynx, forming the Adam's apple —*n.* **1.** the thyroid gland **2.** the thyroid cartilage **3.** a preparation of the thyroid gland of certain animals, used in treating goitre, etc.

thyself (*th*ī self′) *pron.* reflexive or intensive form of THOU: an archaic or poet. var. of *yourself*

ti (tē) *n.* Music a syllable representing the seventh tone of the diatonic scale

Ti Chem. titanium

tiara (tē är′ə) *n.* [L. < Gr.] **1.** a woman's coronetlike headdress, often jewelled **2.** the Pope's triple crown

tibia (tib′ē ə) *n., pl.* **-iae′** (-i ē′), **-ias** the inner and thicker of the two bones of the leg below the knee; shinbone —**tib′-ial** *adj.*

tic (tik) *n.* [Fr. < ?] a twitching of a muscle, esp. of the face, that is not consciously controlled

tick¹ (tik) *n.* [echoic] **1.** a light clicking sound, as of a clock **2.** a mark made to check off items **3.** [Colloq.] a moment; instant —*vi.* **1.** to make a tick or ticks, as a clock **2.** [Colloq.] to function *[* what makes him *tick?]* —*vt.* to check off (an item in a list, etc.) with a tick (usually with *off*) —**tick off** [Colloq.] to reprimand —**tick over** to idle: said of an engine, etc.

TICK
(c. 0.5 cm long)

tick² *n.* [OE. *ticia*] any of a large group of bloodsucking arachnids that are parasitic on man, cattle, sheep, etc.

tick³ *n.* [ult. < Gr. *thēkē,* a case] **1.** the cloth case that is filled with cotton, feathers, etc. to form a mattress or pillow **2.** [Colloq.] same as TICKING

tick⁴ *n.* [< TICKET] [Colloq.] credit *[* to buy something on *tick]*

ticker *n.* **1.** [Slang] the heart **2.** [Old Slang] a watch

ticker tape a continuous paper ribbon on which a tape machine prints

ticket (tik′it) *n.* [< obs. Fr. *étiquet*] **1.** a printed card or piece of paper that gives one a specified right, as to attend a theatre, ride on a bus, etc. **2.** a label or tag, as on a piece of merchandise, giving the size, price, etc. **3.** [Colloq.] a summons to court for a traffic violation **4.** a licence or certificate, as of a ship's captain **5.** [U.S.] the list of candidates nominated by a political party in an election —*vt.* to label or tag with a ticket —**that's the ticket!** [Colloq.] that's the correct thing

tickey *n.* an obsolete S African threepenny piece —**turn on a tickey** [S Afr.] turn in a small space

ticking (tik′iŋ) *n.* [see TICK³] a strong, heavy cloth, often striped, used for casings of mattresses, pillows, etc.

tickle (tik′'l) *vt.* **-led, -ling** [ME. *tikelen*] **1.** to touch or stroke lightly so as to cause twitching, laughter, etc. **2.** to please, gratify, etc. —*vi.* to have a scratching or tingling sensation —*n.* **1.** a tickling or being tickled **2.** a tickling sensation **3.** [Canad.] a narrow strait

tickler (tik′lər) *n.* a person or thing that tickles

ticklish *adj.* **1.** sensitive to tickling **2.** needing careful handling; delicate

tick-tack *n.* a system of signalling with the hands and arms used by bookmakers at race courses

ticktock *n.* the sound made by a clock

tidal (tīd′'l) *adj.* of, having, caused by, determined by, or dependent on a tide or tides —**tid′ally** *adv.*

tidal wave 1. an unusually great, destructive wave sent inshore by an earthquake or a very strong wind **2.** any great, widespread movement, feeling, etc.

tiddler (tid′lər) *n.* [< ?] [Colloq.] **1.** a stickleback or other small fish **2.** anything very small

tiddly, tiddley (tid′lē) *adj.* [< ?] [Slang] **1.** little **2.** slightly drunk

tiddlywinks (tid′lē wiŋks′) *n.* a game in which the players try to snap little coloured discs into a cup by pressing their edges with a larger disc: also **tid′dledy-winks′**

tide (tīd) *n.* [OE. *tid,* time] **1.** the alternate rise and fall of the surface of oceans, seas, etc., caused by the attraction of the moon and sun **2.** something that rises and falls like the tide **3.** a stream, current, trend, etc. *[* the *tide* of public opinion *]* **4.** a period of time: now only in combination *[Eastertide]* —*adj.* same as TIDAL —*vt.* **tid′ed, tid′ing** to carry as with the tide —**tide over** to help along temporarily, as through a period of difficulty —**turn the tide** to reverse a condition

tidemark *n.* **1.** the high-water mark of the tide **2.** [Colloq.] a dirty line indicating the extent of washing

tide-table *n.* a table giving times of high and low water at a particular place

tidings (tī′diŋz) *n.pl.* [sometimes with sing. v.] [OE. *tidung*] news; information

tidy (tī′dē) *adj.* **-dier, -diest** [< OE. *tid,* time] **1.** neat in appearance, arrangement, etc.; orderly **2.** [Colloq.] rather large; considerable *[* a tidy sum *]* —*vt., vi.* **-died, -dying** to make (things) tidy (often with *up*) —*n., pl.* **-dies 1.** a small receptacle for scraps or oddments 2. *same as* ANTIMACASSAR —**ti′dily** *adv.* —**ti′diness** *n.*

tie (tī) *vt.* **tied, ty′ing** [< OE. *teag*, rope] 1. to bind, as with thread, rope, etc. 2. to knot the laces, strings, etc. of 3. to make (a knot) in 4. to join or bind in any way [*tied* by common interests] 5. to confine; restrict 6. to equal (the score, record, etc.) of (opponents, a rival, etc.) —*vi.* to make a tie —*n.* 1. something that joins, binds, etc. 2. something that confines or restricts [legal *ties*] 3. a string, cord, etc. used to tie things 4. a long piece of material worn, esp. by men, round the neck, and tied in front 5. a beam, rod, etc. that holds together and strengthens parts of a building 6. *a)* an equality of scores, votes, etc. in a contest *b)* a contest in which scores, etc. are equal 7. *Music* a curved line joining two notes of the same pitch, indicating that the tone is to be held unbroken —**tie down** to confine; restrict —**tie up** 1. to wrap up and tie with string, etc. 2. to moor (a ship or boat) to a dock 3. to block or hinder 4. to cause to be already in use, committed, etc.

tie beam a horizontal beam serving as a tie (n. 5)

tied cottage a dwelling occupied by a tenant only as long as he is employed by its owner

tied house a public house restricted to dealing with one particular brewery

tie-dye *n.* 1. a method of dyeing designs on cloth by tightly tying bunches of it with thread, etc. so that the dye affects only exposed parts 2. cloth so decorated or a design so made —*vt.* -**dyed′**, -**dye′- ing** to dye in this way

tiepin *n.* an ornamental pin used to fasten a necktie to a shirt front

tier (tēar) *n.* [< MFr. *tire*, order] any of a series of rows, as of seats, arranged one above another —**tiered** *adj.*

tiercel (tur′səl) *n.* [< L. *tertius*, third] *Falconry* a male hawk, esp. the male peregrine

tie-up (tī′up′) *n.* connection, relation, or involvement

tiff (tif) *n.* [< ?] a slight quarrel

tiffin (tif′in) *n.*, *vi.* Anglo-Ind. term for LUNCH

tiger (tī′gər) [< Gr. *tigris*] 1. a large, flesh-eating animal of the cat family, native to Asia, having a tawny coat striped with black 2. *a)* a very energetic or persevering person *b)* a fierce, belligerent person —**ti′- gerish** *adj.*

tiger lily a lily having orange flowers with purplish-black spots

tiger moth a stout-bodied moth with brightly striped or spotted wings

tiger's eye a semiprecious, yellow-brown stone

tight (tīt) *adj.* [< OE. *-thight*, strong] 1. fully stretched; taut 2. fitting so closely as to be uncomfortable 3. made so that water, air, etc. cannot pass through [a *tight* boat] 4. drawn, spaced, etc. closely together [a *tight* weave] 5. fixed securely; firm [a *tight* joint] 6. strict [*tight* control] 7. difficult to manage: esp. in the phrase **a tight corner** (or **squeeze**, etc.), a difficult situation 8. showing strain [a *tight* smile] 9. almost even or tied [a *tight* race] 10. sharp: said of a spiral, turn, etc. 11. difficult to get; scarce 12. [Colloq.] stingy 13. [Colloq.] drunk —*adv.* 1. securely or firmly [hold *tight*] 2. [Colloq.] soundly [sleep *tight*] —**sit tight** to maintain one's opinion or position —**tight′ly** *adv.* —**tight′- ness** *n.*

-tight (tīt) [< prec.] *a combining form meaning* not letting (something specified) in or out [watertight, airtight]

tighten *vt.*, *vi.* to make or become tight or tighter

tightfisted *adj.* stingy

tightfitting *adj.* fitting very tightly

tightknit (tīt′nit′) *adj.* 1. closely integrated 2. well organized or put together in an efficient way

tight-lipped (tīt′lipt′) *adj.* 1. not saying much; secretive 2. having the lips closed tightly

tightrope *n.* a tightly-stretched rope on which acrobats do balancing acts

tights *n.pl.* 1. a tightly-fitting garment covering the body from waist to feet, worn by woman 2. a similar garment worn by acrobats, dancers, etc.

tigress (tī′gris) *n.* a female tiger

tike (tīk) *n.* *same as* TYKE

tilde (til′də) *n.* [Sp. < L. *titulus*, title] a diacritical mark (~) used in various ways, as in Spanish over an *n* to indicate a palatal nasal sound (ny), as in *señor*

tile (tīl) *n.* [< L. *tegula*] 1. *a)* a thin piece of glazed or unglazed, fired clay, stone, etc. used for roofing, flooring, bathroom walls, etc. *b)* a similar piece of plastic, cork, etc. 2. a drain of semicircular tiles or earthenware pipe 3. any of the pieces in mah-jongg or some other games —*vt.* **tiled, til′ing** to cover with tiles —**til′er** *n.*

tiling *n.* 1. the action of a person who tiles 2. tiles collectively

till[1] (til) *prep.*, *conj.* [OE. *til*] *same as* UNTIL

till[2] *vt.*, *vi.* [OE. *tilian*, strive for] to work (land) in raising crops, as by ploughing, etc. —**till′able** *adj.*

till[3] *n.* [< ?] a drawer or tray, as in a shop counter, for keeping money

tillage *n.* 1. the tilling of land 2. land that is tilled

tiller *n.* [< ML. *telarium*, weaver's beam] a bar or handle for turning a boat's rudder

tilt (tilt) *vt.* [prob. < OE. *tealt*, shaky] to cause to slope or slant; tip —*vi.* 1. to slope; incline 2. to poise or thrust one's lance (*at* one's opponent) in a tilt 3. to take part in a tilt or joust 4. to dispute, argue, contend, etc. —*n.* 1. a slope or slant 2. a medieval contest in which two horsemen thrust with lances in an attempt to unseat each other 3. any spirited contest, dispute, etc. between persons —(**at**) **full tilt** with the greatest force —**tilt′er** *n.*

tilth (tilth) *n.* [see TILL[2]] **1.** a tilling of land **2.** tilled land

Tim. Timothy

timber (tim'bər) *n.* [OE.] **1.** wood for building houses, ships, etc. **2.** a wooden beam used in building **3.** wood sawn into planks, boards, etc. of convenient sizes **4.** trees collectively **5.** a wooden rib of a ship —**tim'bered** *adj.* —**tim'bering** *n.*

timber limit [Canad.] **1.** the area to which rights of cutting timber, granted by a government licence, are limited **2.** same as TIMBERLINE

timberline *n.* the line above or beyond which trees do not grow, as on mountains

timbre (tam'brə) *n.* [Fr. ult. < Gr. *tympanon*, drum] the quality of sound that makes one voice or musical instrument different from another

timbrel (tim'brəl) *n.* [< OFr.: see prec.] an ancient type of tambourine

Timbuktu (tim'buk too') *n.* [< *Timbuktu*, town in W Africa] [Colloq.] any very distant place

time (tim) *n.* [OE. *tima*] **1.** duration in which things happen in the past, present, and future; every minute there has been or ever will be **2.** a system of measuring the passing of hours **3.** the period during which something exists, happens, or acts **4.** [*usually pl.*] a period of history **5.** *a)* a period characterized by a prevailing condition [a good *time*] *b)* [*usually pl.*] prevailing conditions [*times* are bad] **6.** a set period, as a term of imprisonment, apprenticeship, etc. **7.** a period necessary, sufficient, measured, etc. for something [a baking *time* of ten minutes] **8.** the period worked or to be worked by an employee **9.** a precise instant, minute, hour, day, year, etc., as determined by a clock **10.** the point at which something happens; occasion **11.** the usual, suitable, or appointed moment for something [*time* to get up] **12.** any one of a series of moments at which something recurs [for the fifth *time*] **13.** *Music a)* the grouping of rhythmic beats into measures of equal length *b)* the characteristic rhythm of a piece of music in terms of this grouping *c)* the speed at which a composition is played *d)* the duration of a note or rest —*interj.* a word called out by a publican indicating that it is closing time —*vt.* **timed, tim'ing 1.** to arrange the time of so as to be suitable, opportune, etc. **2.** to adjust, set, etc. so as to coincide in time **3.** to record the pace, speed, etc. of [to *time* a runner] —*adj.* **1.** having to do with time **2.** set to explode, open, etc. at a given time —**against time** trying to finish in a given time —**ahead of time** sooner than due —**at one time 1.** together **2.** formerly —**at the same time 1.** together **2.** nonetheless; however —**at times** sometimes —**behind the times** out of date —**do time** [Colloq.] to serve a prison term —**for the time being** for the present —**from time to time** now and then —**have no time for** [Colloq.] to dislike —**in no time** very quickly —**in**

time 1. eventually **2.** before it is too late **3.** keeping the set tempo, pace, etc. —**make time** to find occasion or opportunity (with *for*) —**many a time** often —**on time** at the appointed time —**pass the time of day** to exchange a few words of greeting, etc. —**time after time** again and again: also **time and again** —**time of one's life** [Colloq.] an experience of great pleasure for one —**time on one's hands** an interval with nothing to do —**time out of mind** time so long past as to be vague: also **time immemorial** —**time was** there was a time

time and a half a rate of payment one and a half times the usual rate, as for working overtime

time and motion study the study of operational or production procedures and the time consumed by them, with the intention of increasing efficiency

time clock a clock with a mechanism for recording on a card (**timecard**) the time at which an employee begins and ends a work period

time exposure 1. a relatively long exposure of photographic film, generally for more than half a second **2.** a photograph taken in this way

time-honoured *adj.* honoured because in existence or usage for a long time

timekeeper *n.* **1.** one who keeps account of the hours worked by employees or the elapsed time in certain sports **2.** *a)* a watch, clock, etc. judged in terms of its accuracy [good *timekeeper*] *b)* an employee judged in terms of his punctuality

timeless *adj.* **1.** eternal **2.** always valid or true —**time'lessly** *adv.* —**time'lessness** *n.*

time limit a fixed period of time during which something must be done or ended

timely *adj.* **-lier, -liest** happening, done, said, etc. at a suitable time; well-timed; opportune —**time'liness** *n.*

timeout *n.* [Chiefly U.S.] a period of rest or leisure; break

timepiece *n.* any apparatus for measuring and recording time; esp., a clock or watch

timer *n.* a device for timing, or automatically starting and stopping, some mechanism

times *prep.* multiplied by: symbol, × [two *times* three is six]

timeserver *n.* a person who seeks to advance himself by altering his principles to gain support or favour

time signature *Music* a sign, usually like a numerical fraction, after the key signature, indicating the tempo

timetable *n.* **1.** a schedule of the times of arrival and departure of planes, trains, buses, etc. **2.** a tabulated list of the periods allotted to different subjects at school, etc.

timeworn *adj.* **1.** showing signs of wear or disrepair because of long use **2.** hackneyed; trite

time zone a region throughout which the same standard time is used

timid (tim'id) *adj.* [< L. *timere*, to fear] **1.** easily frightened; shy **2.** showing lack of self-confidence —**timidity** (tə mid′-ə tē) n.

timing (tī′miŋ) n. the regulation of the speed with which something is performed so as to produce the most effective results

timorous (tim′ər əs) adj. [< L. timor, fear] 1. full of or subject to fear 2. showing or caused by timidity —**tim′orously** adv. —**tim′orousness** n.

timpani (tim′pə nē) n.pl., sing. -pano′ (-nō′) [It.: see TYMPANUM] kettledrums; esp., a set played by one performer —**tim′panist** n.

tin (tin) n. [OE.] 1. a soft, silver-white, metallic chemical element, easily shaped at ordinary temperatures: symbol, Sn 2. same as TIN PLATE 3. a container made of tinned iron or other metal, in which foods are sealed for preservation 4. the contents of a tin 5. a container made of tin and used for storing food, etc. [a biscuit tin] —vt. **tinned, tin′ning** 1. to put in tins for preservation 2. to plate with tin

tin can a tin used for preserving food

tincture (tiŋk′chər) n. [< L. tingere, to dye] 1. a light colour; tint; tinge 2. a slight trace, smattering, etc. 3. a medicinal substance in a solution of alcohol —vt. **-tured, -turing** 1. to colour lightly; tint 2. to give a slight trace to

tinder (tin′dər) n. [OE. tynder] any dry, easily flammable material, esp. as formerly used for starting a fire from a spark made by flint and steel struck together

tinderbox n. 1. formerly, a metal box for holding tinder, flint, and steel 2. any place or situation in which trouble, war, etc. is likely to flare up

tine (tīn) n. [OE. tind] a sharp, projecting point; prong [the tines of a fork] —**tined** adj.

tinfoil (tin′foil′) n. a very thin sheet or sheets of tin or an alloy of tin and lead, etc. used as a wrapping for food products, in insulation, etc.

ting (tiŋ) n. [echoic] a single, light, ringing sound, as of a small bell being struck

ting-a-ling n. the sound of a small bell ringing repeatedly

tinge (tinj) vt. **tinged, tinge′ing** or **ting′-ing** [L. tingere, to dye] 1. to colour slightly 2. to give a trace, slight flavour, shade, etc. to —n. 1. a slight colouring; tint 2. a slight trace, flavour, etc.

tingle (tiŋ′g′l) vi. **-gled, -gling** [< ME. tinklen, to tinkle] to have a prickling or stinging feeling, as from cold, excitement, etc. —n. this feeling —**tin′gly** adj.

tin god a person unworthy of the honour or respect he demands or receives

tinker (tiŋ′kər) n. [< ?] 1. a person who mends pots, pans, etc. 2. [Colloq.] a mischievous child, animal, etc. —vi. 1. to potter aimlessly 2. to make clumsy attempts to mend something 3. to work as a tinker —**tin′kerer** n.

tinker's damn (or **dam** or **cuss**) [< prec. + DAMN] something of no value: esp. in **not worth a tinker's damn**

tinkle (tiŋ′k′l) vi. **-kled, -kling** [echoic] to make a series of light, clinking sounds like those of a small bell —vt. to cause to tinkle —n. the act or sound of tinkling —**give someone a tinkle** [Colloq.] to phone someone up —**tin′kly** adj.

tin lizzie [orig. nickname of an early model of Ford car] any cheap or old car

tinny (tin′ē) adj. **tin′nier, tin′niest** 1. of tin 2. like tin; bright but cheap 3. of or like the sound made in striking a tin object —**tin′niness** n.

tin plate thin sheets of iron or steel plated with tin —**tin′-plate′** vt.

tinpot (tin′pot′) adj. [Colloq.] 1. worthless; inferior 2. insignificant

tinsel (tin′s′l) n. [see STENCIL] 1. thin sheets, strips, or threads of tin, metal foil, etc., used for decoration, as on Christmas trees 2. something that looks showy and fine but is really of little value —adj. 1. of or decorated with tinsel 2. showy; gaudy —**tin′selled** adj. —**tin′selly** adj.

tinsmith (tin′smith′) n. a person who works in tin or tin plate; maker of tinware: also **tin′man**

tint (tint) n. [< L. tingere, to dye] 1. a colour or shading of a colour 2. a delicate colour 3. a dye for the hair —vt. to give a tint to

tintinnabulation (tin′ti nab′yoo lā′shən) n. [< L. tintinnabulum, little bell] the ringing sound of bells

tiny (tī′nē) adj. **-nier, -niest** [< ?] very small; diminutive —**ti′nily** adv. —**ti′niness** n.

-tion (shən) [< L.] a suffix meaning: 1. the act of [correction] 2. the state of being [elation] 3. the thing that is [creation]

-tious (shəs) [< L.] a suffix used to form adjectives from nouns ending in -TION [cautious]

tip¹ (tip) n. [ME. tippe] 1. the pointed or rounded end or top of something 2. something attached to the end, as a cap 3. a top or apex, as of a mountain —vt. **tipped, tip′ping** 1. to make a tip on 2. to cover the tip or tips of (with something)

tip² vt. **tipped, tip′ping** [< ?] 1. to give a small present of money to (a waiter, etc.) for some service 2. [Colloq.] to give secret information to (often with off) 3. to strike lightly and sharply —vi. to give a tip or tips —n. 1. a small present of money given to a waiter, etc. for services 2. a hint, warning, etc. 3. a piece of secret information 4. a light, sharp blow —**tip′per** n.

tip³ vt., vi. **tipped, tip′ping** [< ?] 1. to overturn or upset (often with over) 2. to tilt or slant —vi. 1. to tilt or slant 2. to overturn or topple (often with over) —n. 1. a tilt; slant 2. a place where rubbish is deposited —**tip one's hat** to greet by raising one's hat slightly

tip-off n. a giving of secret information; a hint, warning, etc.

tippet (tip′it) n. [prob. < TIP¹] a scarflike garment of fur, wool, etc. for the neck and shoulders, hanging down in front

tipple (tip′′l) vi., vt. **-pled, -pling** [< ?]

to drink (alcoholic liquor) habitually —n. strong drink —**tip′pler** n.

tipstaff (tip′stäf) n., pl. **-staffs, -staves** 1. an official in a law court 2. formerly, a metal-tipped staff used as a badge of office

tipster (tip′stər) n. [Colloq.] one who sells tips, as to people betting on horse races, speculating in stocks, etc.

tipsy (tip′sē) adj. **-sier, -siest** 1. somewhat drunk 2. that tips easily; not steady —**tip′-sily** adv. —**tip′siness** n.

tiptoe (tip′tō′) vi. **-toed′, -toe′ing** to walk stealthily or cautiously on one's tiptoes —n. the tip of a toe —adj. standing on one's tiptoes —adv. on tiptoe —**on tiptoe** 1. on one's tiptoes 2. eager or eagerly 3. silently

tiptop adj., adv. 1. [Colloq.] at the highest point of excellence, etc. 2. at the highest point —n. 1. [Colloq.] the highest in quality or excellence 2. the highest point

tirade (tīrād′) n. [Fr. < It. tirare, to fire] a long, vehement speech or denunciation; harangue

tire[1] (tīər) vt., vi. **tired, tir′ing** [OE. tiorian] 1. to make or become weary or fatigued, as by exertion 2. to make or become bored or impatient, as by dull talk

tire[2] n. U.S. sp. of TYRE

tired adj. 1. fatigued; weary 2. hackneyed —**tired′ly** adv. —**tired′ness** n.

tireless adj. that does not become tired —**tire′lessly** adv. —**tire′lessness** n.

tiresome adj. 1. tiring; boring 2. annoying; irksome —**tire′somely** adv. —**tire′someness** n.

tiro (tīə′rō) n., pl. **-ros** var. sp. of TYRO

'tis (tiz) it is

tissue (tish′ōō) n. [< L. texere, to weave] 1. Biol. the substance of an organic body, consisting of cells and the material between them 2. a piece of soft, absorbent paper, used as a disposable handkerchief, etc. 3. same as TISSUE PAPER 4. a tangled mass or series; mesh; web [a tissue of lies] 5. cloth; esp., light, thin cloth

tissue paper very thin, unglazed, nearly transparent paper, as for wrapping things, making tracings, etc.

tissue-type vt. Med. to determine the genetic constitution of body tissue for transplants, etc.

tit[1] (tit) n. [see TIT(MOUSE)] any of various small birds, as the blue tit, coal tit, etc.

tit[2] n. [OE.] 1. same as TEAT 2. [Vulg.] breast

Tit. Titus

titan (tīt′n) n. [< the Titans, in Gr. Myth. giants] any person or thing of great size or power —**Ti′taness** n.fem.

Titanic (tītan′ik) adj. 1. of or like the Titans 2. [t-] of great size, strength, or power —**titan′ically** adv.

titanium (tītä′nēəm) n. [< Titan] a silvery or dark-grey, lustrous, metallic chemical element found in various minerals and used as a deoxidizing agent in molten steel: symbol, Ti

titbit (tit′bit′) n. [< dial tid, small object] a choice piece of food, gossip, etc.

titfer (tit′fər) n. [< ff.: rhyming slang] [Slang] a hat

tit for tat [< tip for tap: see TIP[2]] this in return for that, as blow for blow

tithe (tīth) n. [OE. teothe, a tenth] 1. one tenth of the annual produce of one's land or of one's annual income, paid as a contribution to support a church or its clergy 2. a tenth part —vt., vi. **tithed, tith′-ing** to pay a tithe of (one's income, etc.) —**tith′er** n.

tithe barn a barn where the parish tithe corn was stored

titian (tish′ən) adj., n. [from the hair colour in many of Titian's portraits] reddish yellow

titillate (tit′əlāt′) vt. **-lat′ed, -lat′ing** [< L. titillare, to tickle] 1. to excite or stimulate pleasurably 2. to tickle —**tit′illa′tion** n.

titivate (tit′əvāt′) vt., vi. **-vat′ed, -vat′-ing** [prob. < TIDY] to dress up; spruce up —**tit′iva′tion** n.

title (tīt′'l) n. [< L. titulus] 1. the name of a book, poem, picture, etc. 2. a) short for TITLE PAGE b) a literary work having a particular title [50 new titles published in the autumn] 3. an epithet 4. a word used to show the rank, office, occupation, etc. of a person 5. a claim or right 6. Law a) a right to ownership, esp. of real estate b) evidence of such right c) a title deed 7. a championship, esp. in sports

titleholder n. the winner of a championship, as in some sport

title page the page in the front of a book that gives the title, author, publisher, etc.

title role (or **part** or **character**) the character in a play, film, etc. whose name is used as or in its title

titmouse (tit′mous′) n., pl. **-mice′** [< ME. tit-, little + OE. mase, titmouse] same as TIT[1]

titrate (tī′trāt) vt., vi. **-trated, -trating** [< Fr. titre, a standard] to test by or be subjected to titration

titration (tītrā′shən) n. Chem. the process of finding out how much of a substance is in a known volume of a solution by measuring the volume of a solution of known concentration added to produce a given reaction

titter (tit′ər) vi. [echoic] to laugh in a half-suppressed way; giggle —n. a tittering —**tit′terer** n.

tittle (tit′'l) n. [ME. titel] a very small particle; iota; jot

tittle-tattle (tit′'l tat′'l) n., vi. **-tled, -tling** [redupl. of TATTLE] gossip; chatter

tittup (tit′əp) n. [echoic] a lively movement; caper —vi. **-tuped** or **-tupped, -tuping** or **-tupping** to move in a frolicsome way; prance

titular (tit′yoolər) adj. [< L. titulus, title] 1. of a title 2. having a title 3. in name only [a titular leader]

tizzy (tiz′ē) n., pl. **-zies** [< ?] [Colloq.] a state of frenzied excitement, esp. over some trivial matter

Tl Chem. thallium

Tm *Chem.* thulium

tn. ton(s)

TNT, T.N.T. trinitrotoluene

to (tōō; *unstressed* too, tə) *prep.* [OE.] **1.** a) towards [turn *to* the left] b) in the direction of and reaching [he went *to* London] **2.** as far as [wet *to* the skin] **3.** into a condition of [a rise *to* fame] **4.** on, onto, at, etc. [tie it *to* the post] **5.** a) until [from noon *to* night] b) before [ten *to* six] **6.** for the purpose of [come *to* my aid] **7.** as concerns; in respect of [open *to* attack] **8.** producing [torn *to* pieces] **9.** along with [add this *to* the rest] **10.** belonging with [the key *to* this house] **11.** as compared with [a score of 7 *to* 0] **12.** in agreement or correspondence with [not *to* my taste] **13.** constituting [ten *to* the pound] **14.** with (a specified person or thing) as the recipient of the action [give the book *to* her] **15.** in honour of [a toast *to* you] *To* is also a sign of the infinitive (Ex.: it is easy *to* read) —*adv.* **1.** forward **2.** shut or closed [the door was blown *to*] **3.** to the matter at hand [fall *to*] —**to and fro** back and forth

TOAD (to 22 cm long)

toad (tōd) *n.* [OE. *tade*] **1.** a tailless, leaping amphibian with a rough, warty skin, that lives on moist land **2.** a person regarded as loathsome

toadflax *n.* a perennial plant with yellow-orange flowers: also called **butter and eggs**

toad in the hole sausages baked in batter

toadstool *n.* a fungus with a cap-like top, esp., in popular usage, any poisonous mushroom

toady *n., pl.* **toad'ies** [< *toadeater*, quack doctor's assistant] a person who flatters and serves others in any way to gain favour: also **toad'eat'er** —*vt., vi.* **toad'-ied, toad'ying** to be a toady (to)

to-and-fro *adv.* moving forwards and backwards

toast[1] (tōst) *n.* [< L. *torrere*, parch] sliced bread browned by heat —*vt.* **1.** to brown the surface of (bread, etc.) by heating **2.** to warm thoroughly —*vi.* to become toasted —**toast'er** *n.*

toast[2] *n.* [< the toasted spiced bread formerly put in the wine] **1.** a person, thing, idea, etc. in honour of which glasses of wine, etc. are raised and drunk **2.** a) a proposal to drink to some person, etc. b) such a drink —*vt., vi.* to propose or drink a toast (to)

toastmaster *n.* the person at a banquet who proposes toasts, introduces after-dinner speakers, etc.

toast-rack *n.* a small, partitioned stand of metal, china, etc., for serving toasted bread

tobacco (təbak'ō) *n., pl.* **-cos** [Sp. *tobacco* < WInd., pipe] **1.** a plant of the nightshade family, with large leaves and white or yellow flowers, widely cultivated for its leaves **2.** these leaves, prepared for smoking, chewing, or snuffing **3.** cigars, cigarettes, snuff, etc.

tobacconist (təbak'ənist) *n.* a dealer in tobacco and other smoking supplies

toboggan (təbog'ən) *n.* [CanadFr. *tabagan* < Algonquian] a long, narrow, flat sledge without runners, curved back at the front end: used for riding downhill —*vi.* to ride on a toboggan —**tobog'ganist** *n.*

Toby (tō'bē) *n., pl.* **-bies** [< *Tobias*, masculine name] a beer mug shaped like a stout man with a three-cornered hat: also **Toby jug**

toccata (təkät'ə) *n.* [It.] a composition in free style for the organ, etc., often used as a prelude of a fugue

Toc H (tok'äch') [< the former telegraphic code for *T.H.*, initials of *Talbot House, Belgium, the original headquarters*] a society formed after World War I to promote a greater spirit of Christian comradeship

tocsin (tok'sin) *n.* [Fr. < Pr. *toc*, a stroke + *senh*, a bell] **1.** an alarm bell **2.** its sound

tod (tod) *n.* [< ?] [Colloq.] only in **on one's tod** on one's own

today (tədā') *adv.* [OE. *to dæg*] **1.** on or during the present day **2.** in the present time or age —*n.* **1.** the present day **2.** the present time or period Also **to-day**

toddle (tod'l) *vi.* **-dled, -dling** [? < TOTTER] to walk with short, uncertain steps, as a child —*n.* a toddling

toddler *n.* a young child, usually one who has recently learnt to walk

toddy (tod'ē) *n., pl.* **tod'dies** [< Hindi *tāṛ*, palm tree] a drink of brandy, whisky, etc. mixed with hot water, sugar, etc.: also **hot toddy**

to-do (tədōō') *n.* [Colloq.] a commotion; fuss

toe (tō) *n.* [OE. *ta*] **1.** a) any of the digits of the foot b) the forepart of the foot c) that part of a shoe, sock, etc. which covers the toes **2.** anything like a toe in location, shape, or function —*vt.* **toed, toe'ing** to touch, kick, etc. with the toes —**on one's toes** [Colloq.] alert —**step** (or **tread**) **on someone's toes** to offend someone, esp. by intruding on his rights —**toe the line** (or **mark**) to follow orders, etc. strictly —**turn up one's toes** [Slang] to die

toecap *n.* a reinforced covering on the toe of a shoe

toed *adj.* having (a specified kind or number of) toes [pigeon-toed]

toehold *n.* **1.** a small space for supporting the toe of the foot in climbing, etc. **2.** any means of surmounting obstacles, gaining entry, etc. **3.** a slight advantage

toenail *n.* the nail of a toe —*vt. Carpentry* to fasten with a nail driven slantingly

toff (tof) *n.* [see TUFT] [Slang] a fashionable, upper-class person

toffee, toffy (to′fē) *n.* [< obs. *taffy*] a hard, chewy sweet made from sugar, butter, etc. **—for toffee** [Colloq.] at all [he can't dance *for toffee*]

toffee apple a toffee-coated apple held on a stick

toffee-nosed *adj.* [Slang] snobbish; pretentious

tog (tog) *n.* [prob. ult. < L. *toga*, TOGA] [*pl.*] [Colloq.] clothes **—vt., vi. togged, tog′ging** [Colloq.] to dress (usually with *up* or *out*)

tog. together

toga (tō′gə) *n.* [L. < *tegere*, to cover] in ancient Rome, a loose, one-piece outer garment worn in public by citizens **—to′-gaed** *adj.*

together (tə geth′ər) *adv.* [< OE. < *to*, TO + *gædre*, together] **1.** in or into one group or place [we ate *together*] **2.** in or into contact, collision, etc. [the cars skidded *together*] **3.** considered collectively [he won more than all of us *together*] **4.** with one another; in association [to live *together*] **5.** at the same time [shots fired *together*] **6.** continuously [he worked for two days *together*] **7.** in or into agreement, cooperation, etc. [let's get *together*]

togetherness *n.* a feeling of closeness; unity

toggle (tog′'l) *n.* [prob. < TUG] a rod, pin, or bolt for insertion through a loop of a rope, a link of a chain, etc. to make an attachment, prevent slipping, etc.

TOGGLE JOINT
(arrows indicate direction of pressure)

toggle joint a knee-shaped joint consisting of two pivoted bars: pressure put on the joint to straighten it transmits outward pressure to the open ends

toggle switch a switch consisting of a projecting lever moved back and forth through a small arc to open or close an electric circuit

toil (toil) *vi.* [< L. *tudiculare*, stir about] **1.** to work hard and continuously **2.** to go or move slowly with pain or effort **—n. 1.** hard, exhausting work or effort **2.** a task performed by such effort **—toil′-er** *n.*

toilet (toi′lit) *n.* [< MFr. *toile*, cloth] **1.** *a)* a room with a bowl-shaped fixture for defecation and urination *b)* such a fixture **2.** the act of dressing or grooming oneself **3.** dress; attire **—adj.** for a toilet

toilet paper (or **tissue**) soft, absorbent paper, for cleaning oneself after discharging waste from the body

toilet roll a roll of toilet paper

toiletry (toi′lə trē) *n., pl.* **-ries** soap, lotion, cologne, etc. used in cleaning and grooming oneself

toilette (twä let′) *n.* [Fr.: see TOILET] the process of grooming oneself, including bathing, hairdressing, dressing, etc.

toilet training the training of a young child to use a toilet when he needs to discharge bodily waste

toilet water a perfumed, slightly alcoholic liquid applied to the skin after bathing, etc.

toils *n.pl.* [< L. *tela*, web] snares suggestive of nets

toilsome (toil′səm) *adj.* requiring toil; laborious **—toil′somely** *adv.* **—toil′someness** *n.*

toilworn *adj.* worn out by toil

Tokay (tō kā′) *n.* a sweet, rich wine made in Tokay, Hungary

token (tō′k'n) *n.* [OE. *tacn*] **1.** a sign, indication, or symbol [a *token* of one's affection] **2.** a distinguishing mark or feature **3.** a keepsake **4.** a metal disc with a face value higher than its real value, issued as a substitute for currency, for use in a slot machine, etc. **5.** a voucher which can be exchanged for goods of a particular value **—adj.** merely simulated; slight [*token* resistance] **—by the same** (or **this**) **token** following from this

tokenism *n.* a pretence of acting on a principle by doing so in a very small way

tokoloshe (tok′o losh′, -losh′ē) *n.* [< Xhosa] a malevolent imp of Bantu folklore

toktokkie (tok′tok′ē) *n.* [Afrik.] a large S African beetle

told (tōld) *pt. & pp. of* TELL **—all told** in all [there were ten *all told*]

tolerable (tol′ər ə b'l) *adj.* **1.** endurable **2.** fairly good; passable **—tol′erably** *adv.*

tolerance (tol′ər əns) *n.* **1.** the quality of respecting others' beliefs, practices, etc. **2.** the capacity to endure something, as pain, hardship, etc. **3.** the amount of variation allowed from a standard, accuracy, etc., esp. in a mechanical part **4.** *Med.* the ability to resist the effects of a continued or increasing dose of a drug, etc.

tolerant *adj.* having or showing tolerance of others' beliefs, practices, etc. **—tol′erantly** *adv.*

tolerate (tol′ə rāt′) *vt.* **-at′ed, -at′ing** [< L. *tolerare*, to bear] **1.** to allow; permit **2.** to recognize and respect (others' beliefs, practices, etc.) without sharing them **3.** to put up with **4.** *Med.* to have tolerance for (a drug, etc.)

toleration (tol′ə rā′shən) *n.* tolerance; esp., freedom to hold religious views that differ from the established ones

toll[1] (tōl) *n.* [prob. ult. < Gr. *telos*, tax] **1.** a tax or charge for a privilege, as for the use of a bridge **2.** a charge for some service **3.** the number lost, taken, etc. [the storm took a heavy *toll* of lives]

toll² *vt.* [ME.] **1.** to ring (a church bell, etc.) slowly with regular strokes, as for announcing a death **2.** to announce, summon, etc. by this —*vi.* to sound or ring slowly: said of a bell —*n.* the act or sound of tolling a bell

toll bar a bar, gate, etc. for stopping travel at a point where toll is taken

toll bridge a bridge at which toll is paid for passage

tollgate *n.* a gate for stopping travel at a point where toll is taken

tollie (tol′ē) *n.* [Afrik.] [S Afr.] a steer calf

tollkeeper *n.* a person who collects tolls at a tollgate

toll road a road on which toll must be paid

tolu (balsam) (tōlōō′) [< *Tolú*, in Colombia] a fragrant resin obtained from a S American tree: it is used in cough syrups, etc.

toluene (tol′yōōwēn′) *n.* [TOLU + (BENZ)ENE] a liquid hydrocarbon formerly obtained from tolu balsam: it is used in making dyes, explosives, etc.: also **tol′uol**

tom (tom) *n.* [< the name *Thomas*] the male of some animals, esp. of the cat —*adj.* male

tomahawk (tom′ə hôk′) *n.* [< AmInd.] a light axe with a head of stone, used by North American Indians as a tool and a weapon

tomato (tə māt′ō) *n., pl.* **-toes** [< SAmInd. *tomatl*] **1.** a red fruit with a juicy pulp, used as a vegetable: botanically it is a berry **2.** the plant that it grows on

tomb (tōōm) *n.* [< Gr. *tymbos*] **1.** a vault or grave for the dead **2.** a burial monument —**the tomb** death

tombola (tom bō′lə) *n.* [It. < *tombolare*, to tumble] a kind of lottery in which numbered tickets are bought, some of which entitle the possessor to prizes

tomboy (tom′boi′) *n.* a girl who behaves or plays like an active boy —**tom′boy′ish** *adj.* —**tom′boy′ishly** *adv.*

tombstone (tōōm′stōn′) *n.* a stone, usually with an inscription, marking a tomb or grave

Tom, Dick, and Harry everyone; anyone: usually preceded by *every*

tome (tōm) *n.* [Fr. < Gr. *tomos*, piece cut off] a book, esp. a large or ponderous one

tomfoolery (tom fōōl′ər ē) *n., pl.* **-eries** foolish behaviour; nonsense

Tommy (tom′ē) *n., pl.* **-mies** [< *Tommy Atkins* (for *Thomas Atkins*, fictitious name used in Brit. army sample forms)] [*also* **t-**] epithet for a private in the British army

Tommy gun alternate trademark for THOMPSON SUBMACHINE GUN —*n.* a submachine gun

tommyrot *n.* [Slang] nonsense; foolishness

tomorrow (tə mor′ō) *adv.* [OE. *to morgen*] **1.** on the day after today **2.** at some time in the future —*n.* **1.** the day after today **2.** some time in the future Also **to-morrow**

Tom Thumb any midget or small person

tomtit (tom′tit′) *n.* any of various tits, esp. the blue tit

tom-tom (tom′tom′) *n.* [Hindi *tam-tam*] a simple kind of deep drum with a small head, usually beaten with the hands

ton (tun) *n.* [var. of TUN] **1.** a unit of weight equal to 2,240 pounds avoirdupois, or 1016 kilograms, used, esp. formerly, in Britain: in full, **long ton 2.** a unit of weight equal to 2,000 pounds avoirdupois, or 907.18 kilograms, used in the U.S., Canada, etc.: in full, **short ton 3.** short for METRIC TON **4.** a unit of internal capacity of ships, equal to 100 cubic feet **5.** a unit of carrying capacity of ships, usually equal to 40 cubic feet **6.** a unit for measuring displacement of ships, equal to 35 cubic feet **7.** [often *pl.*] [Colloq.] a very large amount or number **8.** [Slang] a) £100 b) a speed of 100 m.p.h.

tonal (tō′n'l) *adj.* of a tone or tonality —**ton′ally** *adv.*

tonality (tō nal′ə tē) *n., pl.* **-ties 1.** Art the colour scheme in a painting **2.** Music a) same as KEY¹ b) tonal character as determined by the relationship of the tones to the keynote

tone (tōn) *n.* [< Gr. *teinein*, to stretch] **1.** a) a vocal or musical sound b) its quality **2.** an intonation, etc. of the voice that expresses a particular feeling [a tone of contempt] **3.** a way of expressing things that shows a certain attitude [the friendly tone of her letter] **4.** a) the style, character, spirit, etc. of a place or period b) distinctive style; elegance **5.** a quality of colour **6.** Music a) a sound of distinct pitch (as distinguished from a noise) b) any one of the full intervals of a diatonic scale **7.** Painting the effect produced by the combination of light, shade, and colour **8.** Physiol. the condition of an organism, organ, muscle, etc. with reference to its normal, healthy functioning —*vt.* **toned,** **ton′ing** to give a tone to —*vi.* to take on a tone —**tone down 1.** to make or become less bright, sharp, etc.; soften **2.** to make (something written or said) less harsh —**tone in with** to harmonize with —**tone up 1.** to give a more intense tone to **2.** to become strengthened —**tone′less** *adj.*

tone-deaf *adj.* not able to distinguish accurately differences in musical pitch —**tone′-deaf′ness** *n.*

tone poem same as SYMPHONIC POEM

tong (toŋ) *n.* [Chin. *t'ang*, meeting place] a Chinese association, society, etc.

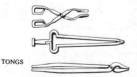

TONGS

tongs (toŋz) *n.pl.* [sometimes with sing. v.] [OE. *tange*] a device for seizing or lifting objects, with two arms pivoted or hinged together

tongue (tuŋ) *n.* [OE. *tunge*] **1.** the movable muscular structure in the mouth: it is used in eating, tasting, and (in man) speaking **2.** an animal's tongue used as food **3.** *a*) speech *b*) a manner of speaking [a glib *tongue*] **4.** a language or dialect **5.** something like a tongue in shape, position, or use; specif., *a*) the flap under the laces of a shoe *b*) the clapper of a bell *c*) a narrow strip of land extending into a sea, river, etc. *d*) a long, narrow flame —*vt.* **tongued, tongu'ing 1.** to touch, lick, etc. with the tongue **2.** *Music* to play by tonguing: see TONGUING —**find one's tongue** to recover the ability to talk, as after shock —**hold one's tongue** to keep from speaking —**on everyone's tongue** spoken as common gossip —**on the tip of one's** (or **the**) **tongue** almost said or remembered —**with one's tongue in one's cheek** ironically; humorously

tongue-and-groove joint a kind of joint in which a tongue or tenon on one board fits exactly into a groove in another

tongue-tie *n.* limited motion of the tongue, caused by a short folded membrane under the tongue

tongue-tied *adj.* speechless from embarrassment, etc.

tongue twister a phrase or sentence difficult to say quickly (Ex.: six sick sheiks)

tonguing *n.* the use of the tongue in playing a wind instrument, esp. for more accurate intonation of rapid notes

tonic (ton'ik) *n.* [see TONE] **1.** a drug, medicine, etc. for improving bodily health **2.** anything that restores energy, cheerfulness, etc. **3.** a carbonated beverage flavoured with a little quinine and served in a mixed drink with gin, vodka, etc.; tonic water **4.** *Music* the basic tone of a diatonic scale; keynote —*adj.* **1.** invigorating to the body or mind **2.** *Music* designating or based on a keynote

tonight (tə nīt') *adv.* [OE. *to niht*] on or during the present or coming night —*n.* this night or the night about to come Also **to-night**

tonnage (tun'ij) *n.* **1.** the total shipping, in tons, of a country or port **2.** the amount in tons a ship can carry **3.** weight in tons

tonne (tun, tun'ē) *n.* a measure of weight equal to 1000 kilograms

tonsil (ton's'l) *n.* [L. *tonsillae, pl.*] either of a pair of oval masses of lymphoid tissue, one on each side of the throat at the back of the mouth

tonsillectomy (ton'sə lek'tə mē) *n., pl.* **-mies** the surgical removal of the tonsils

tonsillitis (ton'sə līt'əs) *n.* inflammation of the tonsils

tonsorial (ton sôr'ē əl) *adj.* [< L. *tondere*, to clip] of a barber or barbering: often used humorously

tonsure (ton'shər) *n.* [< L. *tondere*, to clip] **1.** the act of shaving a man's head, esp. on top, when he becomes a priest or monk **2.** the part of the head left

bare by doing this —*vt.* **-sured, -suring** to shave the head or crown of

ton-up boy (tun'up) *n.* [Colloq.] a motorcyclist who habitually rides very fast

too (tōō) *adv.* [< TO] **1.** in addition; also **2.** more than enough; [the hat is *too* big] **3.** very; extremely [it's *too* good!] Often used as an adjective with *much, many* [*too* much to see]

took (took) *pt. of* TAKE

tool (tōōl) *n.* [OE. *tol*] **1.** any implement, instrument, etc. held in the hand and used for some work, as a knife, saw, or shovel **2.** *a*) the working part of a power-driven machine, as a drill *b*) the whole machine **3.** any means, agent [books are *tools* of education] **4.** a person used by another to accomplish his purposes —*vt.* **1.** to shape or work with a tool **2.** to provide tools or machinery for (a factory, etc.): often with *up* **3.** to impress designs, etc. on (leather, etc.) with tools —**tool'er** *n.* —**tool'ing** *n.*

toolmaker *n.* a machinist who makes, maintains, and repairs machine tools —**tool'mak'ing** *n.*

toot (tōōt) *vi.,vt.* [echoic] to sound (a horn, whistle, etc.) in short blasts —*n.* a short blast of a horn, etc.

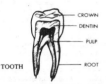

CROWN
DENTIN
PULP
TOOTH
ROOT

tooth (tōōth) *n., pl.* **teeth** (tēth) [OE. *toth*] **1.** any of a set of hard, bonelike structures in the jaws of most vertebrates, used for biting, tearing, and chewing **2.** a toothlike part, as on a saw, comb, gearwheel, etc. **3.** an appetite or taste [a sweet *tooth*] **4.** an effective means of enforcing something [to put *teeth* into a law] —**armed** (or **dressed**) **to the teeth** as armed (or dressed up) as one can be —**by the skin of one's teeth** narrowly; only just —**get** (or **sink**) **one's teeth into** to become fully occupied with —**in the teeth of 1.** directly against **2.** defying —**long in the tooth** [Colloq.] old —**tooth and nail** with all one's strength or resources —**tooth'less** *adj.*

toothache *n.* pain in or near a tooth

toothbrush *n.* a brush for cleaning the teeth

tooth-comb *n.* a small comb with teeth close together —**to go through** (something) **with a fine tooth-comb** to examine (something) with meticulous care

toothpaste *n.* a paste used in cleaning the teeth with a toothbrush

toothpick *n.* a very small, pointed stick for removing bits of food from between the teeth

tooth powder   a powder used like toothpaste

toothsome *adj.*   pleasing to the taste; tasty

toothy *adj.* **-ier, -iest** showing prominent teeth

tootle (tōōt'′l) *vi.* **-tled, -tling** [< TOOT] to keep tooting softly —*n.* the act or sound of tootling

top[1] (top) *n.* [OE.] **1.** the highest part, point, or surface of anything **2.** the highest degree, pitch, rank, position, etc. **3.** the part of a plant growing above the ground **4.** an uppermost part or covering; specif., *a)* a lid, cap, cover, etc. *b)* any garment, esp. for women, which extends from the shoulder to the waist or hips **5.** a person of highest rank, etc. **6.** the head or the crown **7.** the beginning, as of a piece of music [take it from the *top*] —*adj.* of or at the top; highest, greatest, foremost, etc. —*vt.* **topped, top′ping** **1.** to take off the top of (a plant, etc.) **2.** to put a top on [to top a cake with icing] **3.** to be a top for **4.** to reach or go over the top of **5.** to exceed in amount, height, etc. [the fund topped £75] **6.** to be at the top of; head; lead —**off the top of one's head** speaking without preparation or careful thought —**on top** at the top; successful —**on top of 1.** resting upon **2.** in addition to; besides **3.** right after **4.** controlling successfully —**over the top 1.** over the front of a trench, as in attacking **2.** exceeding the quota or goal —(**the**) **tops** [Slang] the very best —**top off** to complete by adding a finishing touch —**top out** to complete the skeleton of a building, esp. by adding the highest part —**top up** to raise the level of a liquid, etc., in a container, usually filling it

top[2] *n.* [OE.] a child's cone-shaped toy, spun on its pointed end —**sleep like a top** to sleep soundly

topaz (tō′paz) *n.* [< Gr. *topazos*] a crystalline mineral esp., a clear, yellow variety used as a gem

top brass [Colloq.] **1.** high-ranking army officers **2.** important officials

topcoat (top′kōt′) *n.* a lightweight overcoat

top dog [Colloq.] the leader or chief of a group

top-drawer *adj.* of first importance

top-dressing (top′dres′iŋ) *n.* material applied to a surface, as fertilizer —**top′-dress**′ *vt.*

tope[1] (tōp) *vt., vi.* **toped, top′ing** [< ?] [Archaic] to drink much (alcohol)

tope[2] *n.* [< ?] a small, grey shark

topee (tō′pē) *n.* [Hindi *topi*] in India, a pith helmet worn as protection against the sun

toper (tō′pər) *n.* a person who topes; drunkard

top-flight (top′flīt′) *adj.* [Colloq.] best; first-rate

topgallant (top′gal′ənt; *naut.* tə gal′-) *adj.* next above the topmast —*n.* a topgallant mast, sail, etc.

top gear   the gear ratio of a motor vehicle transmission which produces the highest speed

top hat   a tall, black, cylindrical hat, usually of silk, worn by men in formal dress

top-heavy (top′hev′ē) *adj.* too heavy at the top and so likely to fall over —**top′-heav′iness** *n.*

top-hole (top′hōl′) *adj.* [Old Slang] excellent

topi (tō′pē) *n. same as* TOPEE

topiary (tō′pē ər ē) *adj.* of the art of trimming and training shrubs or trees into ornamental shapes —*n., pl.* **-aries** topiary work

topic (top′ik) *n.* [< Gr. *topos*, a place] the subject of a writing, speech, discussion, etc.

topical (top′i k'l) *adj.* **1.** of current or local interest **2.** of a particular place; local **3.** of, using, or arranged by topics —**top′ical′ity** (-kal′ə tē) *n.* —**top′ically** *adv.*

topknot (top′not′) *n.* **1.** a knot of feathers, ribbons, etc. worn as a headdress **2.** a tuft of hair or feathers on the crown of the head

topless *adj.* without a top; specif., designating or wearing a costume that exposes the breasts

top-level *adj.* of the highest office or rank

topmast *n.* the second mast above the deck of a sailing ship, supported by the lower mast

topmost *adj.* at the very top

top-notch (top′noch′) *adj.* [Colloq.] first-rate; excellent

topography (tə pog′rə fē) *n., pl.* **-phies** [see TOPIC & -GRAPHY] **1.** *a)* the science of showing on maps, charts etc. the surface features of a region, such as hills, rivers, and roads *b)* such features **2.** surveying done to discover and measure such features —**topog′rapher** *n.* —**topographic** (top′-ə graf′ik) *adj.* —**top′ograph′ically** *adv.*

topology (tə pol′ə jē) *n., pl.* **-gies** [< Gr. *topos*, a place + -LOGY] *Math.* the study of those properties of geometric figures that remain unchanged even when under distortion —**topological** (top′ə loj′i k'l) *adj.* —**topol′ogist** *n.*

topper (top′ər) *n.* [Colloq.] *same as* TOP HAT

topping *n.* something that is put on top of something else, as a sauce on food —*adj.* [Colloq.] excellent; first-rate

topple (top′′l) *vi.* **-pled, -pling** [< TOP[1], *v.*] to fall (*over*) from top-heaviness, etc. —*vt.* **1.** to cause to topple **2.** to overthrow

topsail (top′s′l) *n.* in a square-rigged vessel, the square sail next above the lowest sail on a mast

top-secret *adj.* designating or of the most highly restricted military or government information

topside *n.* **1.** [*usually pl.*] the part of a ship's side above the waterline **2.** a lean cut of beef from the thigh containing no bone

topsoil *n.* the upper layer of soil, usually darker and richer than the subsoil

topsy-turvy (top′sē tur′vē) *adv., adj.*

[prob. < *top*, highest part + ME. *terven*, to roll] **1.** upside down **2.** in confusion or disorder —**top′sy-tur′vily** *adv.*

toque (tōk) *n.* [Fr.] **1.** a woman's small, round hat **2.** [Canad.] a knitted cap with a round tassel on top

tor (tôr) *n.* [OE. *torr*] a high, rocky hill; crag

torah (tō′rə) *n.* [Heb.] *Judaism* [*also* T-] the whole of Jewish religious literature, including the Scripture, the Talmud, etc.

torch (tôrch) *n.* [< L. *torquere*, to twist] **1.** a portable electric light, usually operated by batteries **2.** a portable light consisting of a long piece of resinous wood, etc. flaming at one end **3.** anything viewed as enlightening, inspiring, etc. —**carry a (or the) torch for** [Slang] to love (someone), esp. without having one's love returned

torchbearer *n.* **1.** a person who carries a torch **2.** a person or leader who enlightens or inspires others

torchlight *n.* the light of a torch or torches —*adj.* done or carried on by torchlight

tore (tôr) *pt. of* TEAR[1]

toreador (tôr′ē ə dôr′) *n.* [Sp. < L. *taurus*, bull] a bullfighter

torero (tō rāe′ō) *n.*, *pl.* **-ros** [Sp. < L. *taurus*, bull] a bullfighter, esp. a matador

torment (tôr′ment; *for v.*, *usually* tôr ment′) *n.* [< L. *torquere*, to twist] **1.** great pain, physical or mental; agony **2.** a source of pain, anxiety, or annoyance —*vt.* **1.** to make suffer greatly, in body or mind **2.** to annoy or tease —**tormen′tor** *n.*

tormentil (tôr′men til′) *n.* [< ML. *tormentilla*] a perennial plant with yellow flowers; used in tanning and dyeing

torn (tôrn) *pp. of* TEAR[1]

tornado (tôr nā′dō) *n.*, *pl.* **-does, -dos** [< Sp. < L. *tonare*, to thunder] a rapidly whirling column of air, usually seen as a funnel-shaped cloud that destroys everything in its narrow path

torpedo (tôr pē′dō) *n.*, *pl.* **-does** [L., numbness < *torpere*, be stiff] a large, cigar-shaped, self-propelled projectile launched under water against enemy ships as from a submarine: it explodes on contact —*vt.* **-doed, -doing** to attack, destroy, etc. as with a torpedo

torpedo boat a small, fast warship armed with torpedoes

torpid (tôr′pid) *adj.* [< L. *torpere*, be numb] **1.** sluggish or slow and dull **2.** dormant; inactive and unfeeling as a hibernating animal —**torpid′ity** *n.* —**tor′pidly** *adv.*

torpor (tôr′pər) *n.* **1.** sluggishness; dullness; apathy **2.** a state of being dormant or inactive

torque (tôrk) *n.* [< L. *torques*, twisted metal necklace] **1.** *Physics* a twisting effect exerted on a body by a force acting at a distance **2.** popularly, any force that causes rotation **3.** an ancient Celtic necklace or armband of twisted metal

torr (tôr) *n.* [< E. *Torricelli*] a unit of pressure sufficient to support a column

of mercury one millimetre high under standard conditions

torrent (tôr′ənt) *n.* [Fr. < L. *torrere*, parch] **1.** a swift, violent stream, esp. of water **2.** a flood or rush of words, questions, etc. **3.** [*often pl.*] a very heavy fall of rain —**torrential** (tə ren′shəl) *adj.*

torrid (tôr′id) *adj.* [< L. *torrere*, parch] **1.** dried by or subjected to intense heat, esp. of the sun; scorched; arid **2.** so hot as to scorch **3.** highly passionate, ardent, etc. —**tor′ridly** *adv.*

Torrid Zone the area of the earth's surface between the Tropic of Cancer & the Tropic of Capricorn

torsion (tôr′shən) *n.* [< L. *torquere*, to twist] **1.** a twisting or being twisted **2.** the tendency of a twisted rod, etc. to untwist again —**tor′sional** *adj.*

torso (tôr′sō) *n.*, *pl.* **-sos, -si** (-sē) [< Gr. *thyrsos*, a stem] **1.** the trunk of the human body **2.** a statue representing this, esp. one lacking head and limbs

tort (tôrt) *n.* [< L. *torquere*, to twist] *Law* a wrongful act (not involving a breach of contract) for which a civil action can be brought

tortilla (tôr tē′ə) *n.* [Sp. < *torta*, cake] a griddlecake of unleavened maize : a staple food throughout Mexico

tortoise (tôr′təs) *n.* [< ML. *tortuca*] a toothless land reptile having a soft body encased in a dome-shaped shell, and clawed limbs: cf. TURTLE

tortoise shell the hard, mottled, yellow-and-brown shell of some turtles used, esp. formerly, in making combs, etc. —**tor′toise-shell′** *adj.*

tortuous (tôr′tyoo wəs) *adj.* [< L. *torquere*, to twist] **1.** full of twists and turns; winding **2.** devious or deceitful —**tor′tuos′ity** (-wos′ə tē) *n.* —**tor′tuously** *adv.*

torture (tôr′chər) *n.* [Fr. < L. *torquere*, to twist] **1.** the inflicting of severe pain, as to force information or confession **2.** any severe physical or mental pain, or a cause of it —*vt.* **-tured, -turing** **1.** to subject to torture **2.** to twist (meaning, etc.) —**tor′turer** *n.* —**tor′turous** *adj.*

Tory (tôr′ē) *n.*, *pl.* **-ries** [< Ir. *tōruidhe*, robber] **1.** a member of the Conservative Party in Britain or Canada **2.** formerly, a member of one of the two major political parties of England: changed officially c. 1830 to *Conservative* **3.** [*often* t-] any very conservative person —*adj.* [*also* t-] of or being a Tory —**To′ryism** *n.*

toss (tos) *vt.* [prob. < Scand.] **1.** to throw upwards lightly from the hand **2.** to throw or pitch about [tossed by a storm] **3.** to jerk upwards [tossed her head] **4.** to throw in or bandy (ideas, remarks, etc.) **5.** to disturb; agitate **6.** to toss up with a coin, etc. **7.** to mix (a salad, etc.) lightly so as to coat the ingredients with a dressing —*vi.* **1.** to be tossed or thrown about **2.** to fling oneself about in sleep, etc. —*n.* **1.** a tossing or being tossed **2.** a tossing up: see phrase below **3.** a fall from a horse

—**toss a pancake** to fling a pancake up so that it returns to the pan on its other side —**toss off** 1. to make, do, write, etc. quickly and casually 2. to drink up in one draught —**toss up** to toss a coin to decide something according to which side lands uppermost —**toss'er** *n.*

tossup *n.* 1. the act of tossing a coin to decide something 2. an even chance

tot¹ (tot) *n.* [prob. < Scand.] 1. a young child 2. a small drink of alcohol

tot² *vt., vi.* **tot'ted, tot'ting** [< TOTAL] [Colloq.] to add; total (usually with *up*)

total (tōt'l) *adj.* [< L. *totus*, all] 1. constituting the (or a) whole; entire 2. complete; utter —*n.* the whole amount or number —*vt.* **-talled, -talling** 1. to add up to 2. to find the total of; add —*vi.* to amount (*to*) as a whole —**to'- tally** *adv.*

totalitarian (tōtal'ə tãar'ē ən) *adj.* [TOTAL + (AUTHOR)ITARIAN] designating a government or state in which one political group maintains complete control and bans all others —*n.* a person favouring such a government or state —**total'itar'ianism** *n.*

totality (tō tal'ə tē) *n., pl.* **-ties** 1. the total amount or sum 2. the fact or condition of being total

totalizator (tōt'əl i zāt'ər) *n.* a machine used in parimutuel betting to register bets and, usually, compute odds and payoffs while bets are being placed: also **to'talisa'- tor, to'taliz'er**

tote¹ (tōt) *vt.* **tot'ed, tot'ing** [< ?] [Colloq.] 1. to carry or haul 2. to be armed with (a gun, etc.)

tote² *n.* shortened form of TOTALIZATOR

tote bag a large, open bag of cloth, straw, etc.: also **tote**

totem (tōt'əm) *n.* [< AmInd.] 1. among primitive peoples, an animal or natural object taken as a symbol of a family or clan 2. an image of this —**totemic** (tō tem'ik) *adj.* —**to'temism** *n.*

TOTEM POLE

totem pole a pole carved and painted with totems, often erected in front of their dwellings, by Indian tribes of northwestern N America

tother, t'other, (tuth'ər) *adj., pron.* [Chiefly Dial.] that (or the) other

totter (tot'ər) *vi.* [prob. < Scand.] 1.

to rock or shake as if about to fall 2. to be on the point of collapse 3. to be unsteady on one's feet; stagger —*n.* a tottering —**tot'tering** *adj.* —**tot'tery** *adj.*

toucan (tōō'kan) *n.* [Tupi *tucana*] a brightly coloured, fruit-eating bird of tropical America, with a very large beak

touch (tuch) *vt.* [OFr. *tochier*] 1. to put the hand, finger, etc. on, so as to feel 2. to bring into contact with something else 3. to be or come into contact with 4. to border on 5. to strike lightly 6. to affect by contact 7. to injure slightly 8. to give a light tint, aspect, etc. to [*touched* with pink] 9. to stop at: said of a ship 10. to handle; use 11. to partake of [*didn't touch* his supper] 12. to come up to; reach 13. to compare with 14. to deal with, esp. in passing 15. to affect; concern 16. to arouse an emotion in, esp. one of sympathy or gratitude 17. [Slang] to ask for a loan or gift of money from 18. *Geom.* to be tangent to —*vi.* 1. to touch a person or thing 2. to be or come into contact 3. to verge (*on, upon*) 4. to pertain; bear (*on, upon*) 5. to treat in passing (*with on, upon*) 6. *Geom.* to be tangent —*n.* 1. a touching or being touched; specif., a light tap, stroke, etc. 2. the sense by which physical objects are felt 3. a sensation so caused; feel 4. a special quality, skill, or manner [he lost his *touch*] 5. *a*) a mark, impression, etc. left by touching *b*) a subtle change or addition in a painting, story, etc. 6. *a*) a trace, tinge, etc. [a *touch* of humour] *b*) a slight attack [a *touch* of the flu] 7. contact or communication [keep in *touch*] 8. [Slang] *a*) the act of asking for a loan *b*) a person with regard to how easily money can be so obtained from him [he's a soft *touch*] 9. *Music* the way that a performer strikes the keys of a piano, etc. —**touch down** 1. to land: said of an aircraft 2. *Rugby* to place the ball behind the goal line, as when scoring a try —**touch off** 1. to make explode; fire 2. to produce (esp. a violent reaction, etc.) —**touch up** to improve (a painting, story, etc.) by minor additions —**touch wood** to place one's hand on a wooden object in the superstitious hope of averting ill fortune —**touch'able** *adj.* —**touch'er** *n.*

touch and go an uncertain, risky, or dangerous situation —**touch-and-go** *adj.*

touchdown *n.* 1. a landing 2. *Rugby* the act of touching down

touché (tōō shā') *interj.* [Fr.] *Fencing* touched: said when one's opponent scores a point: also used in congratulating someone on his witty reply, etc.

touched (tucht) *adj.* 1. emotionally moved 2. [Colloq.] unbalanced mentally: also **touched in the head**

touching *adj.* arousing tender emotion —*prep.* with regard to —**touch'ingly** *adv.*

touch judge one of the two linesmen in rugby

touch-line *n.* either of the lines marking the sides of a football or rugby pitch

touch-paper *n.* paper soaked in saltpetre to make it burn slowly

touchstone *n.* 1. a stone formerly used to test the purity of gold or silver 2. any test of genuineness

touch-type *vi.* **-typed′**, **-typ′ing** to type without looking at the keys —**touch′-typ′-ist** *n.*

touchwood *n.* something, esp. dry wood, used as tinder

touchy *adj.* **-ier, -iest** easily offended or irritated —**touch′ily** *adv.* —**touch′iness** *n.*

tough (tuf) *adj.* [OE. *toh*] 1. that will bend, twist, etc. without tearing or breaking 2. not easily cut or chewed [*tough steak*] 3. not easily moulded, worked, etc. [*tough putty*] 4. strong; hardy 5. stubborn 6. overaggressive; rough 7. *a*) very difficult *b*) violent [a *tough* fight] 8. [Colloq.] unfavourable; bad [a *tough* time] —*n.* a tough person; thug —**tough′ly** *adv.* —**tough′ness** *n.*

toughen *vt., vi.* to make or become tough or tougher

toupee (too′pā) *n.* [< Fr. *toupet*, tuft of hair] a man's wig, esp. one for a small bald spot

tour (tooar) *n.* [< OFr. *tourner*, to TURN] 1. a long journey for sightseeing 2. turn or shift of work; esp., a period of military service at one place 3. a journey, as by a theatrical company, to give performances, etc. in various cities —*vi., vt.* to go on a tour (through) —**on tour** touring

tour de force (tooar′də fôrs′) *pl.* **tours′-de force′** (tooar) [Fr.] an unusually skilful or ingenious achievement, performance, etc.

tourism (tooar′iz′m) *n.* tourist travel, esp. when regarded as a business —**touris′-tic** *adj.*

tourist *n.* one who makes a tour, esp. for pleasure —*adj.* 1. of or for tourists 2. designating or of the lowest-priced accommodation, as on a ship: also **tourist class**

touristy *adj.* [Colloq.] designed to be attractive to tourists: often a derogatory term

tourmaline (tooar′mə lin) *n.* [Fr.] a crystalline mineral, usually black, used as a gemstone and in optical equipment

tournament (tooar′nə mənt) *n.* [< OFr. *torneier:* see TURN] 1. a series of contests in a sport, chess, or bridge, usually a competition for championship 2. in the Middle Ages, a contest in which knights on horseback tried to unseat one another with lances

‡tournedos (tooar′nə dō) *n., pl.* **-dos′**(-dō′) [Fr.] a thick round beefsteak, served in a variety of ways

tourniquet (tooar′nə kā′) *n.* [Fr. < L. *tunica*, tunic] any device for compressing a blood vessel to stop bleeding, as a bandage twisted about a limb

tousle (tou′z′l) *vt.* **-sled, -sling** [< ME. *tusen*, to pull] to disorder, dishevel, rumple, etc.

tout (tout) *vi., vt.* [OE. *totian*, to peep] [Colloq.] 1. to solicit (customers, votes, etc.) (often with *for*) 2. to spy on (racehorses) to get betting tips —*n.* [Colloq.] a person who touts —**tout′er** *n.*

tow¹ (tō) *vt.* [OE. *togian*] to pull as by a rope —*n.* 1. a towing or being towed 2. something towed —**in tow** 1. being towed 2. as one's companion or follower

tow² *n.* [OE. *tow-*, spinning] the coarse and broken fibres of hemp, flax, etc. before spinning

toward (tō′ərd; *also, and for prep. usually,* tə wôrd′) *adj.* [OE. *toweard*] [Archaic] 1. favourable 2. in progress —*prep.* same as TOWARDS

towards (tə wôrdz′) *prep.* [see prec.] 1. in the direction of 2. aimed at or tending to [steps *towards* peace] 3. concerning; regarding 4. close to [*towards* noon] 5. in order to get [saving *towards* a car]

towbar *n.* a rigid metal bar used for towing vehicles, esp. one attached to a car

towel (tou′l) *n.* [< OFr. *toaille*] a piece of absorbent cloth or paper for wiping or drying things —*vt.* **-elled, -elling** to wipe or dry with a towel —**throw** (or **toss,** etc.) **in the towel** [Colloq.] to admit defeat

towelling *n.* material for making towels

tower (tou′ər) *n.* [< L. *turris*] 1. a tall structure often part of another building 2. such a structure used as a fortress or prison 3. a person or thing like a tower in height, strength, etc. —*vi.* to rise high or stand high like a tower —**a tower of strength** an unfailing support in time of trouble —**tow′ered** *adj.*

tower block a building of many storeys, as for offices or flats

towering *adj.* 1. very high or tall 2. very great, intense, etc. [a *towering* rage]

towhead (tō′hed′) *n.* 1. a head of pale-yellow hair 2. a person having such hair —**tow′head′ed** *adj.*

towline (tō′lin′) *n.* a rope, chain, etc. for towing

town (toun) *n.* [OE. *tun*] 1. a group of houses and buildings, larger than a village but smaller than a city 2. a city or other thickly-populated urban area 3. the business centre of a city 4. the people of a town —*adj.* of or for a town —**go to town** [Colloq.] to act enthusiastically —**on the town** [Colloq.] out for a good time

town clerk the chief administrative officer of a town

town crier a person who formerly cried public announcements through the streets of a village or town

townee *n.* [Derog. Colloq.] a town dweller

town gas a manufactured gas for domestic and industrial use, made from coal gas mixed with natural gas

town hall a building in a town, housing the offices of public officials, the council chamber, etc.

town house 1. a city residence, esp. of a person who also owns a country residence **2.** a terraced dwelling, usually of two or more storeys

town planning the comprehensive planning of the physical and social development of a town

township n. **1.** orig., in England, a parish or division of a parish **2.** in parts of the U.S., a division of a county constituting a unit of local government **3.** in Australia, a small town **4.** in Canada, a land-survey area, usually 36 square miles (93 km²)

townsman n. a person who lives in, or has been reared in, a town

townspeople n.pl. **1.** the people of a town **2.** people reared in a town or city Also **towns'folk'**

towpath (tō'păth') n. a path beside a canal, for men or animals towing canal boats

towrope n. a rope used in towing

toxaemia (tok sē'mē ə) n. [ModL.: see TOXIC & -AEMIA] a condition in which poisonous substances, esp. toxins from bacteria, etc., are in the bloodstream

toxic (tok'sik) adj. [< L. toxicum, a poison] **1.** of, affected by, or caused by a toxin **2.** acting as a poison —**tox'ically** adv. —**toxic'ity** (-sis'ə tē) n.

toxicology (tok'si kol'ə jē) n. [see TOXIC & -LOGY] the science of poisons, their effects, antidotes, etc. —**tox'icolog'ic** (-kə loj'ik) adj. —**tox'icolog'ically** adv. —**tox'icol'ogist** n.

toxin (tok'sin) n. [< TOXIC] **1.** any of various poisonous compounds produced by some microorganisms and causing certain diseases **2.** any of various similar poisons produced by certain plants or animals

toy (toi) n. [< ?] **1.** a plaything, esp. one for children **2.** a thing of little value or importance; trifle **3.** anything small; specif., a dog of a small breed —adj. **1.** being or like a toy **2.** of or for toys **3.** made as a toy —vi. to play or trifle (with a thing, idea, etc.)

trace¹ (trās) n. [< L. trahere, draw] **1.** a mark, footprint, etc. left by the passage of a person, animal, or thing **2.** a mark left by a past person, thing, or event [traces of war] **3.** a barely perceptible amount [a trace of anger] —vt. **traced, trac'ing 1.** to follow the trail of; track **2.** to follow the development or history of **3.** to draw, outline, etc. **4.** to copy (a drawing, etc.) by following its lines on a transparent sheet placed over it **5.** to record by a curved, broken, or wavy line, as in a seismograph —vi. to go back or date back (to something past) —**trace'abil'ity, n.** —**trace'able adj.**

trace² n. [see TRAIT] either of two straps, etc. connecting a draught animal's harness to the vehicle drawn —**kick over the traces** to shake off control

trace element 1. a chemical element, as iron, copper, zinc, etc., essential in nutrition, but only in minute quantities **2.** any element present in minute quantities in an organism, soil, water, etc.

tracer n. **1.** one that traces; specif., a person who traces designs, etc. on

transparent paper **2.** an element or other substance used to follow biochemical reactions, as to locate diseased cells

tracer bullet (or **shell**) a bullet or shell that leaves a trail of smoke to mark its course and help in adjusting aim

tracery n., pl. **-eries** [< TRACE¹] any graceful design of lines that come together or 'cross in various ways, as in a stained glass window

trachea (trə kē'ə) n., pl. **-cheae** (-ē'), **-cheas** [< Gr. tracheia (arteria), rough (windpipe)] **1.** the tube that conveys air from the larynx to the bronchi; windpipe **2.** any of the minute tubes branching through the bodies of insects, etc. and bringing in air

tracheotomy (trā'kē ot'ə mē) n., pl. **-mies** surgical incision of the trachea

tracing (trā'sin) n. something made by tracing, as a copy of a drawing, or a line traced by a recording instrument

track (trak) n. [MFr. trac] **1.** a mark or marks left by a person, animal, or thing, as a footprint **2.** a beaten path or trail **3.** a course or line of motion or action **4.** a sequence of ideas, events, etc. **5.** a course or circuit laid out for running, horse racing, etc. **6.** a pair of parallel metal rails on which trains, etc. run **7.** either of the two endless belts on tanks, some tractors, etc. on which they move **8.** a) same as SOUND TRACK b) the part of a magnetic tape passing under a recording or reading head c) any of the bands of a gramophone record —vt. **1.** a) to follow the track or footprints of b) to follow (a path, etc.) **2.** to trace by means of vestiges, evidence, etc. **3.** to plot the path of and record data from (an aircraft, spacecraft, etc.) using a telescope, radar, etc. —**in one's tracks** exactly where one is; immediately —**keep** (or **lose**) **track of** to follow (or fail to follow) the course, progress, etc. of —**make tracks** [Colloq.] to go or leave hurriedly —**on** (or **off**) **the track** keeping to (or straying from) the subject or goal —**track down 1.** to pursue until caught **2.** to investigate fully —**track'er n.**

track event an athletic sport performed on a track, as running, hurdling, etc.

track record [Colloq.] the past performance of a person or organization, esp. when put to the test

track shoe a spiked shoe worn by athletes in track events

track suit a warm suit worn over their sports kit by athletes, as before a race

tract¹ (trakt) n. [< L. trahere, draw] **1.** a continuous expanse of land, etc. **2.** Anat., Zool. a system of parts or organs having some special function [the digestive tract]

tract² n. [see ff.] a pamphlet, esp. one on a religious or political subject

tractable (trak'tə b'l) adj. [< L. trahere, to draw] **1.** easily managed, taught, etc. **2.** easily worked —**trac'tabil'ity n.**

traction (trak'shən) n. [< L. trahere, draw] **1.** a pulling or drawing, as of a load, or a being pulled **2.** the power used by a locomotive, etc. **3.** the power, as of tyres on a road, to grip a surface while moving, without slipping

traction engine a steam locomotive for pulling heavy wagons, farm equipment, etc. on roads or in fields

tractor (trak′tər) *n.* [see TRACTION] **1.** a powerful, motor-driven vehicle with large rear wheels for pulling farm machinery, etc. **2.** a vehicle with a driver's cab for hauling one or more trailers

trad (trad) *n.* [Colloq.] traditional jazz —*adj.* [Colloq.] traditional

trade (trād) *n.* [MLowG., a track] **1.** buying and selling; commerce **2.** *a)* an occupation *b)* skilled work; craft *c)* all the persons or companies in a particular line of business **3.** business of a specified kind [the tourist *trade*] **4.** customers **5.** an exchange; swap **6.** [*pl.*] the trade winds —*adj.* **1.** of trade or commerce **2.** of, by, or for the trade [a *trade* journal] **3.** of the members in the trades, or crafts, etc. [*trade* unions] —*vi.* trad′ed, trad′-ing **1.** to carry on a business **2.** to have business dealings (*with* someone) **3.** to make an exchange (*with* someone) —*vt.* **1.** to buy and sell (stocks, etc.) **2.** to exchange; barter —**trade in** to give (one's used car, etc.) as part of the purchase price of a new one —**trade on** (or **upon**) to take advantage of

trade-in *n.* a used car, etc. given or taken as part payment towards another one

trademark *n.* a symbol, design, word, etc. used by a manufacturer to distinguish his products from those of competitors: usually registered and protected by law

trade name **1.** the name by which a commodity is commonly known in trade **2.** a name, often a trademark, used by a company to describe a product **3.** the name under which a company carries on business

trade price the price of commodities as sold by wholesalers to retailers

trader *n.* **1.** a person who trades; merchant **2.** a ship used in trade

tradescantia (trad′es kan′shē ə) *n.* [ModL., < John *Tradescant*] a widely cultivated house plant with variegated leaves

trade secret a secret formula, process, etc. known to and used to advantage by only one manufacturer or trade

tradesman (trādz′mən) *n.* a person engaged in trade; esp., a shopkeeper —**trades′wom′an** *n.fem.*

Trades Union Congress the major association of British trade unions

trade union an association of workers to promote and protect the welfare, interests and rights of its members, mainly by collective bargaining: also **trades union** —**trade′-un′ion** *adj.* —**trade unionism** —**trade unionist**

trade wind a wind that blows steadily towards the equator from the northeast in the tropics north of the equator and

from the southeast in the tropics south of the equator

trading estate *same as* INDUSTRIAL ESTATE

trading stamp a stamp given by some retailers as a premium, redeemable in merchandise

tradition (trə dish′ən) *n.* [< L. *tradere*, deliver] **1.** the handing down orally of beliefs, customs, stories, etc. from generation to generation **2.** a belief, custom, etc. so handed down

traditional *adj.* of, handed down by, or conforming to tradition; conventional —**tradi′tionally** *adv.*

traduce (trə dyōōs′) *vt.* -duced′, -duc′ing [< L. *tra(ns)*, across + *ducere*, to lead] to defame; slander —**traduc′er** *n.*

traffic (traf′ik) *n.* [< L. *trans*, across + It. *ficcare*, bring] **1.** *a)* the movement or number of cars in a street, pedestrians along a pavement, etc. *b)* the cars, pedestrians, etc. **2.** trade, sometimes of a wrong or illegal kind [*traffic* in drugs] **3.** dealings or business (*with* someone) **4.** the amount of business done in a given period —*adj.* of traffic or its regulation —*vi.* **traf′ficked, traf′ficking 1.** to carry on traffic (*in* something) **2.** to have dealings (*with* someone) —**traf′ficker** *n.*

trafficator (traf′i kā′tər) *n.* formerly, a small arm at the side of a motor vehicle which could be raised to indicate a turn to right or left

traffic island a small, raised area in the middle of a road to separate lanes of traffic and serve as a stopping place for pedestrians

traffic light (or **signal**) a set of signal lights at intersections of streets to regulate traffic

traffic warden an official who aids the police in duties concerning the controlling of road traffic

tragedian (trə jē′dē ən) *n.* an actor of tragedy

tragedienne (trə jē′dē en′) *n.* an actress of tragedy

tragedy (traj′ə dē) *n.*, *pl.* -dies [< Gr. *tragos*, goat + *ōidē*, song] **1.** a serious play having a sad or disastrous ending brought about by fate, moral weakness, etc. **2.** a very sad or tragic event

tragic (traj′ik) *adj.* **1.** of, like, or having to do with tragedy **2.** very sad, disastrous, etc. **3.** suitable to tragedy [a *tragic* voice] Also **trag′ical** —**trag′ically** *adv.*

tragicomedy (traj′ə kom′ə dē) *n.*, *pl.* -dies a play, novel, etc. combining tragic and comic elements —**trag′icom′ic, trag′i-com′ical** *adj.*

trail (trāl) *vt.* [< L. *trahere*, drag] **1.** *a)* to drag or let drag behind one *b)* to bring along behind [*trailing* exhaust fumes] **2.** to follow the tracks of **3.** to hunt by tracking **4.** to follow or lag behind **5.** *Mil.* to carry (a rifle, etc.) at the full length of one arm, in a horizontal position with the muzzle to the fore —*vi.* **1.** to be drawn along behind one, as the train of a gown **2.** to grow along the ground, etc., as some plants **3.** to straggle **4.** to flow behind in a long, thin stream, wisp, etc., as smoke **5.** to follow or lag behind **6.** to grow gradually weaker, dimmer, etc. (with *off* or *away*) **7.** to move wearily or aimlessly —*n.* **1.** a mark, scent, etc. left by a person, animal, or thing that has passed **2.** a rough path made across country, as by repeated passage **3.** a train of events, etc. following something [a *trail* of debts] **4.** something that trails behind

trailblazer *n.* **1.** a pioneer in any field **2.** a person who blazes a trail —**trail′blaz′-ing** *n.*

trailer *n.* **1.** a cart or van designed to be pulled by a motor vehicle **2.** a selection of scenes from a coming film used to advertise it **3.** one that trails another **4.** [U.S.] a caravan

trailing arbutus an evergreen N American plant with pink or white flowers, the floral emblem of Nova Scotia

train (trān) *n.* [< L. *trahere*, to pull] **1.** a line of connected railway coaches or wagons pulled or pushed by a locomotive **2.** a series of events that follow some happening [war brought famine in its *train*] **3.** any connected sequence; series [a *train* of thought] **4.** a group of followers or attendants in a procession **5.** a procession; caravan **6.** something that drags along behind, as a part of a gown that trails **7.** a line of gunpowder used to set off an explosive charge —*vt.* **1.** to teach so as to make fully skilled [to *train* aircraft pilots] **2.** to subject to certain action, exercises, etc. so as to bring to a desired condition **3.** to bring up; rear **4.** to guide the growth of (a plant) by tying, pruning, etc. **5.** to make fit for some sport, as by exercise, practice, etc. **6.** to discipline (animals) to do tricks or obey commands **7.** to aim (a gun, binoculars, etc.) at something (usually with *on*) —*vi.* to give or get training —**train′able** *adj.*

trainee (trā nē′) *n.* a person undergoing vocational training, military training, etc. —**trainee′ship′** *n.*

trainer *n.* **1.** *a)* a person who trains animals, as racehorses *b)* a person who trains athletes, etc. **2.** an apparatus used in training, as, in aeronautics, a flight simulator

training *n.* the process of being trained, esp. for some sport, as by exercise, practice, etc.

train spotter a person who collects the numbers of railway locomotives

traipse (trāps) *vi., vt.* **traipsed, traips′-ing** [< ?] [Colloq.] to walk heavily or tiredly —*n.* [Colloq.] the act of traipsing

trait (trā) *n.* [Fr. < L. *trahere*, draw] a distinct quality or feature, as of personality

traitor (trāt′ər) *n.* [< L. *tradere*, betray] a person who betrays his country, cause, friends, etc. —**trai′torous** *adj.* —**trai′tress** *n.fem.*

trajectory (traj′ik tə rē, trə jek′-) *n., pl.* **-ries** [< L. *tra(ns)*, across + *jacere*, to throw] the curved path of something

hurtling through space, esp. that of a projectile

tram (tram) *n.* [prob. < LowG. *traam*, a beam] **1.** a public vehicle running on rails laid in the road **2.** an open railway car used in mines: also **tram′car′**

tramline *n.* **1.** [often *pl.*] the tracks on which a tram runs: also **tram′way′ 2.** [often *pl.*] the parallel markings along the sides of a tennis court

trammel (tram′′l) *n.* [< L. *tres*, three + *macula*, a mesh] **1.** [usually *pl.*] something that hinders freedom of action **2.** a three-ply fishing net: also **trammel net** —*vt.* **-melled -melling 1.** to hinder, restrain, or shackle **2.** to entangle as in a trammel

tramp (tramp) *vi.* [< LowG. *trampen*, trample] **1.** to walk firmly or heavily **2.** to travel about on foot, esp. as a vagabond —*vt.* **1.** to step on heavily; trample **2.** to walk or ramble through —*n.* **1.** a person who travels about on foot doing odd jobs or begging; vagrant **2.** the sound of heavy steps **3.** a journey on foot; hike **4.** a freight ship that has no regular schedule **5.** [Slang] a sexually promiscuous woman

trample (tram′p′l) *vi.* **-pled, -pling** [see prec.] to tread heavily —*vt.* to crush, destroy, etc. as by treading heavily on —**trample under foot** to crush or hurt by or as by trampling: also **trample on** (or **upon**) —**tram′pler** *n.*

trampoline (tram′pə lin) *n.* [< It. *trampolino*, springboard] a sheet of strong canvas stretched tightly on a frame, used as a kind of springboard in acrobatic tumbling, gymnastics, etc. —**tram′polin′-ist** *n.*

trance (trāns) *n.* [see TRANSIT] **1.** a state brought on by hysteria, hypnosis, etc., in which a person seems to be conscious but is unable to move or act of his own will **2.** any daze, stupor, etc. **3.** the condition of being completely lost in thought

trannie (tran′ē) *n.* [Colloq.] a transistor radio

tranquil (traŋ′kwəl) *adj.* [L. *tranquillus*] free from disturbance or agitation; calm [tranquil waters]

tranquillity (traŋ kwil′ə tē) *n.* the quality or state of being tranquil; calmness, etc.

tranquillize (traŋ′kwə liz′) *vt., vi.* **-ized′, -iz′ing** to calm by the use of a tranquillizer

tranquillizer *n.* any of certain drugs used in calming persons suffering from tension, anxiety, etc.

trans- [L. < *trans*, across] a prefix meaning: **1.** over, across, through **2.** so as to change thoroughly [transliterate] **3.** above and beyond

trans. 1. transaction(s) **2.** transitive **3.** translated **4.** translation **5.** transport

transact (tran zakt′) *vt.* [< L. *trans-*, across + *agere*, drive] to carry on, conduct, or complete (business, etc.) —**transac′tor** *n.*

transaction *n.* **1.** a transacting or being transacted **2.** *a)* a business deal *b)* [*pl.*] a record of the proceedings of a society, etc.

transalpine (tranz al'pīn) *adj.* on the other (the northern) side of the Alps, from Rome

transatlantic (tranz'ət lan'tik) *adj.* 1. crossing the Atlantic 2. on the other side of the Atlantic

transceiver (tran sē'vər) *n.* [< TRANS (MITTER) + (RE)CEIVER] an apparatus in a single housing, functioning alternately as a radio transmitter and receiver

transcend (tran send') *vt.* [< L. *trans-*, over + *scandere*, to climb] 1. to go beyond the limits of [his story *transcends* belief] 2. to surpass; excel

transcendent *adj.* 1. transcending; surpassing; excelling 2. *Theol.* existing apart from the material universe —**transcend'ence, transcend'ency** *n.*

transcendental (tran'sen den't'l) *adj.* 1. *same as:* a) TRANSCENDENT (sense 1) b) SUPERNATURAL 2. abstract 3. of transcendentalism —**tran'scenden'tally** *adv.*

transcendentalism *n.* any of various philosophies seeking to discover the nature of reality by investigating the process of thought rather than the things that are thought about —**tran'scenden'talist** *n., adj.*

transcendental meditation intense meditation with the object of increasing awareness

transcribe (tran skrīb') *vt.* -**scribed'**, -**scrib'ing** [< L. *trans-*, over + *scribere*, write] 1. to write or type out in full (shorthand notes, a speech, etc.) 2. to arrange (a piece of music) for an instrument, etc. other than that for which it was originally written 3. *Radio & TV* to record (a programme, commercial, etc.) for broadcast later —**transcrib'er** *n.*

transcript (tran'skript') *n.* something made by transcribing; written, typewritten, or printed copy

transcription (tran skrip'shən) *n.* 1. the act or process of transcribing 2. a transcript 3. an arrangement of a piece of music for an instrument, voice, etc. other than that for which it was originally written

transducer (tranz dyōōs'ər) *n.* [< L. *transducere*, lead across] any of various devices that transmit energy from one system to another, sometimes one that converts the energy in form

transept (tran'sept) *n.* [< L. *trans-*, across + *septum*, enclosure] 1. the part of a cross-shaped church at right angles to the nave 2. either arm of this part

transfer (trans fur'; *for n.,* trans'fər) *vt.* -**ferred'**, -**fer'ring** [< L. *trans-*, across + *ferre*, to bear] 1. to convey, carry, send, etc. from one person or place to another 2. to make over (title to property, etc.) to another 3. to move (a design, etc.) from one surface to another 4. *Football* to sell or release a player to another club —*vi.* 1. to transfer oneself or be transferred 2. to change from one group, football club, etc. to another —*n.* 1. a transferring or being transferred 2. a picture or design transferred or to be

transferred from one surface to another 3. a document effecting a transfer 4. a person who transfers or is transferred —**transfer'able, transfer'rable** *adj.* —**transfer'ence** *n.*

transfiguration (trans'fig yōō rā'shən) *n.* a transfiguring or being transfigured —[T-] 1. *Bible* the change in the appearance of Jesus on the mountain 2. a church festival (Aug. 6) commemorating this

transfigure (trans fig'ər) *vt.* -**ured**, -**uring** [see TRANS- & FIGURE] 1. to transform 2. to transform so as to glorify

transfix (trans fiks') *vt.* [< L. *trans-*, through + *figere*, to fix] 1. to pierce through as with something pointed 2. to fasten in this way; impale 3. to make unable to move, as from fright, shock, etc.

transform (trans fôrm') *vt.* [< L. *trans-*, over + *forma*, a shape] 1. to change the form or appearance of 2. to change the condition, character, or function of 3. *Elec.* to change (voltage, current, etc.) by use of a transformer 4. *Math.* to change (an algebraic expression or equation) in form but not in value —**transform'able** *adj.* —**trans'forma'tion** *n.* —**trans'forma'tional** *adj.*

transformer *n.* *Elec.* a device for transferring electric energy from one alternating-current circuit to another, usually with a change in voltage, current, etc.

transfuse (trans fyōōz') *vt.* -**fused'**, -**fus'-ing** [< L. *trans-*, across + *fundere*, pour] 1. to pour in or spread through 2. *Med.* to transfer or introduce (blood, saline solution, etc.) into a blood vessel, usually a vein —**transfus'er** *n.* —**transfu'sion** *n.*

transgress (trans gres') *vt.* [< L. *trans-*, over + *gradi*, to step] 1. to overstep or break (a law, etc.) 2. to go beyond (a limit, boundary, etc.) —*vi.* to break a law, etc.; sin —**transgres'sion** *n.* —**transgres'sor** *n.*

transient (tran'zē ənt) *adj.* [see TRANSIT] 1. temporary; transitory 2. passing quickly; fleeting; ephemeral —**tran'sience, tran'siency** *n.*

transistor (tran sis'tər) *n.* [TRAN(SFER) + (RE)SISTOR] 1. a small, solid-state electronic device used instead of a thermionic valve 2. *same as* TRANSISTOR RADIO

transistorize *vt.* -**ized'**, -**iz'ing** to equip with transistors

transistor radio a portable radio powered by transistors

transit (tran'sit) *n.* [< L. *trans-*, over + *ire*, go] 1. a) passage through or across b) a transition; change 2. a being carried from one place to another 3. *Astron.* the apparent passage of a heavenly body across a given meridian

transit camp a camp in which refugees, soldiers, etc. live temporarily

transition (tran sizh'ən) *n.* 1. a) a passing from one condition, activity, place, etc. to another b) the period of this 2. *Archit.* the change from Norman to Early English style **3.** *Music* a shifting from one key to another —transi'tional *adj.*

transitive (tran'sə tiv) *adj.* taking a direct object to complete the meaning: said of certain verbs

transitory (tran'sə tər ē) *adj.* not enduring; temporary; fleeting —tran'sitorily *adv.* —tran'sitoriness *n.*

translate (trans lāt') *vt.* -lat'ed, -lat'ing [< L. *transferre*, to TRANSFER] **1.** to put into the words of a different language **2.** to change into another medium or form **3.** to put into different words; rephrase **4.** to change from one place or condition to another **5.** to interpret; infer —*vi.* **1.** to make a translation into another language **2.** to be capable of being translated —translat'able *adj.* —transla'tor *n.*

translation *n.* **1.** a translating or being translated **2.** writing or speech translated into another language **3.** *Mech.* motion in which every point of an object moves simultaneously

transliterate (tranz lit'ə rāt') *vt.* -at'ed, -at'ing [< TRANS- + L. *litera*, letter] to write or spell (words, etc.) in corresponding characters of another alphabet —translit'era'tion *n.* —translit'erator *n.*

translucent (tranz lōō'sənt) *adj.* [< L. *trans-*, through + *lucere*, to shine] letting light pass but diffusing it so that objects on the other side cannot be clearly distinguished —translu'cence, translu'cency *n.*

transmigrate (tranz'mī grāt') *vi.* -grat'ed, -grat'ing [see TRANS- & MIGRATE] **1.** to move from one country, etc. to another **2.** to pass into another body at death: said of the soul —trans'migra'tion *n.* —transmi'gratory *adj.*

transmissible (tranz mis'ə b'l) *adj.* capable of being transmitted —transmis'sibil'ity *n.*

transmission (tranz mish'ən) *n.* **1.** a transmitting or being transmitted **2.** something transmitted, esp. a radio or TV programme **3.** the part of a motor car, etc. that transmits motive force from the engine to the wheels, as by gears

transmit (tranz mit') *vt.* -mit'ted, -mit'-ting [< L. *trans-*, over + *mittere*, send] **1.** to cause to go from one person or place to another; transfer **2.** to pass along (a disease, etc.) **3.** to pass on to others by heredity, inheritance, etc. **4.** to communicate (news, etc.) **5.** *a)* to cause (light, heat, etc.) to pass through some medium *b)* to conduct [water *transmits* sound] **6.** to send out (radio or television broadcasts, etc.) by electromagnetic waves —transmit'table *adj.* —transmit'tal *n.*

transmitter (tranz mit'ər) *n.* one that transmits; specif., the apparatus that generates, modulates, and sends out radio waves

transmogrify (tranz mog'rə fī') *vt.* -fied', -fy'ing [< ?] to transform, esp. in a grotesque or strange manner

transmute (tranz myōōt') *vt., vi.* -mut'-ed, -mut'ing [< L. *trans-*, over + *mutare*, to change] to change from one form, nature, substance, etc. into another; transform —trans'muta'tion *n.*

transom (tran'səm) *n.* [prob. < L. *transtrum*, crossbeam] **1.** a horizontal crossbar across a window or at the top of a door **2.** a small window directly over a door or window

transparency (trans par'ən sē) *n.* **1.** a transparent state or quality: also transpar'-ence **2.** *pl.* -cies something transparent, specif., a positive photograph to be projected or viewed against the light

transparent *adj.* [< L. *trans-*, through + *parere*, appear] **1.** transmitting light rays so that objects on the other side may be distinctly seen **2.** so fine in texture as to be seen through **3.** easily understood or detected; obvious **4.** open; frank —transpar'ently *adv.*

transpire (tran spīr') *vi.* -spired', -spir'-ing [< L. *trans*, through + *spirare*, breathe] **1.** to become known **2.** [Colloq.] to come to pass; happen: regarded by some as a loose usage **3.** to give off vapour, moisture, etc. as through pores —*vt.* to cause (vapour, moisture, etc.) to pass through tissue, esp. through pores —tran'-spira'tion (-spə rā'shən) *n.*

transplant (trans plănt'; *for n.* trans'-plănt') *vt.* [see TRANS- & PLANT] **1.** to remove from one place and plant or put in another **2.** to remove (people) from one place and resettle in another **3.** *Surgery* to transfer (tissue or an organ) from one individual or part of the body to another —*n.* **1.** a transplanting **2.** something transplanted, as a body organ or seedling —trans'planta'tion *n.*

transponder (tran spon'dər) *n.* [TRAN(SMITTER) + (RE)SPOND + -er] a transceiver that automatically transmits electrical signals when actuated by a specific signal

transport (trans pôrt'; *for n.* trans'pôrt) *vt.* [< L. *trans-*, over + *portare*, carry] **1.** to carry from one place to another, esp. over long distances **2.** to carry away with emotion **3.** *Hist.* to deport to a penal colony, etc. —*n.* **1.** a means or system of conveyance **2.** a ship, aircraft, etc. used for transporting soldiers, etc. **3.** a transporting **4.** strong emotion, esp. of delight or joy —transport'abil'ity *n.* —transport'er *n.*

transportation (trans'pər tā'shən) *n.* **1.** a transporting **2.** *Hist.* banishment for crime, as to a penal colony

transport café a cheap eating place on a main road, used chiefly by long-distance lorry drivers

transpose (trans pōz') *vt.* -posed', -pos'-ing [see TRANS- & POSE[1]] **1.** to change the usual or relative order or position of **2.** to rewrite or play (a musical composition) in a different key —transpos'able *adj.* —trans'posi'tion *n.*

transsexual (tranz sek'syōō wəl) *n.* a person who tends to identify with the opposite sex —transsex'ualism *n.*

transsship (trans ship') *vt.* -shipped', -ship'ping to transfer from one ship, train, etc. to another for reshipment —**transship′ment** n.

transubstantiation (tran′səb stan′shē-ā′shən) n. [< L. trans-, over + substantia, substance] R.C. & Orthodox Eastern Ch. the doctrine that, in the Eucharist, the whole substance of the bread and wine is changed into the body and blood of Christ

transuranic (tranz′yoo ran′ik) adj. designating or of the elements, as plutonium, having atomic numbers higher than that of uranium

transverse (tranz vʉrs′) adj. [see TRAVERSE] lying, situated, placed, etc. across; crosswise —**transverse′ly** adv.

transvestite (tranz ves′tīt) n. [< TRANS- + L. vestire, to clothe] a person who derives sexual pleasure from dressing in the clothes of the opposite sex

trap¹ (trap) n. [OE. træppe] 1. any device for catching animals; gin, snare, etc. 2. any stratagem or ambush designed to trick unsuspecting persons 3. any of various devices for preventing the escape of gas, offensive odours, etc. 4. an apparatus for throwing discs into the air to be shot at in clay-pigeon shooting 5. a light, two-wheeled carriage with springs 6. same as TRAPDOOR 7. [Slang] the mouth 8. Golf same as BUNKER 9. Greyhound Racing a box-like stall from which the greyhound is released —vt. **trapped, trap′ping** 1. to catch as in a trap 2. to hold back or seal off by a trap 3. to furnish with a trap or traps

trap² n. [< Sw. trappa, stair] any of several dark-coloured, igneous rocks; esp., such a rock, as basalt, used in road making

trap³ vt. **trapped, trap′ping** [< OFr. drap, cloth] to cover with trappings —n. [pl.] [Colloq.] personal belongings, clothes, etc.

trapdoor n. a hinged door in a ceiling or floor

trapeze (trə pēz′) n. [see ff.] a short horizontal bar, hung at a height by two ropes, on which gymnasts, acrobats, etc. swing and perform acrobatics

TRAPEZIUM

trapezium (trə pē′zē əm) n., pl. **-ziums, -zia** [< Gr. tetra, four + peza, foot] 1. a plane figure with four sides only two of which are parallel 2. [U.S.] same as TRAPEZOID

TRAPEZOID

trapezoid (trap′ə zoid′) n. [see prec.] 1. a plane figure with four sides no two of which are parallel 2. [U.S.] same as TRAPEZIUM —adj. shaped like a trapezoid: also **trap′ezoi′dal**

trapper (trap′ər) n. one who traps fur-bearing animals for their skins

trappings n.pl. [see TRAP³] 1. the pleasant accompaniments that usually symbolize a condition, office, etc. [trappings of success] 2. a highly decorated covering for a horse

Trappist (trap′ist) n. [< Fr. (La) Trappe, abbey in Normandy] a monk of a branch of the Cistercian order, living under a vow of silence —adj. of the Trappists

trash (trash) n. [prob. < Scand.] 1. discarded or worthless things; rubbish 2. [Chiefly U.S.] a person or people regarded as disreputable —**trash′y** adj.

‡**trattoria** (trät′tô rē′ä) n., pl. **-ie** (-e) [It.] a small, inexpensive restaurant in Italy

trauma (trô′mə) n., pl. **-mas, -mata** [Gr.] 1. Psychiatry an emotional shock which has a lasting effect on the mind 2. Med. a bodily injury, wound, or shock —**traumat′ic** (-mat′ik) adj. —**traumat′ically** adv.

travail (trav′āl) n. [OFr. < VL. tria, three + palus, a stake] [Obs.] 1. very hard work 2. the pains of childbirth —vi. [Obs.] 1. to toil 2. to suffer the pains of childbirth

travel (trav′'l) vi. **-elled, -elling** [var. of prec.] 1. to go from one place to another; make a journey 2. to go from place to place as a travelling salesman 3. to move, pass, or be transmitted 4. to move in a given course: said of mechanical parts, etc. 5. to be capable of withstanding deterioration, etc. if transported 6. [Colloq.] to move with speed —vt. to make a journey over or through —n. 1. the act or process of travelling 2. [pl.] journeys, tours, etc. 3. a) mechanical motion b) the distance of a mechanical stroke, etc. —**trav′eller** n.

travel agency an agency that makes travel arrangements for tourists or other travellers —**travel agent**

traveller's cheque a cheque for a fixed amount, usually one of a set, issued by a bank, etc. and sold to a traveller who signs it when it is issued and again in the presence of the one cashing it

traveller's tale an exaggerated account; a tall story

travelling salesman same as COMMERCIAL TRAVELLER

travelogue (trav′ə log′) n. 1. an illustrated lecture on travels 2. a film of travels

traverse (trav′ərs) vt. **-ersed, -ersing** [< L. trans-, over + vertere, to turn] 1. a) to pass over, across, or through b) to go back and forth over or along 2. to survey or examine carefully 3. to turn (a gun, etc.) laterally —vi. 1. to cross over 2. to move back and forth over a place, etc. 3. to swivel or pivot 4. to move across a mountain slope, as in skiing, in an oblique direction —n. 1. something that traverses or crosses; specif., a crossbar, crossbeam, etc. 2. a traversing or passing across 3. a way across 4.

a zigzag course taken by a vessel —*adj.* extending across —**travers'al** *n.*

travesty (trav'is tē) *n., pl.* **-ties** [< Fr. < L. *trans-*, over + *vestire*, to dress] a grotesque or exaggerated imitation for purposes of ridicule; burlesque —*vt.* **-tied, -tying** to make a travesty of

travois (trə voi') *n., pl.* **-vois** (-voiz') [< OFr. *trave*, beam] [Canad.] 1. *Hist.* a sled made of two poles joined by a frame, used by Plains Indians 2. a similar sled used for dragging logs

trawl (trôl) *n.* [< ?] a large, baglike net dragged by a boat along the bottom of a fishing bank: also **trawl'net'** —*vt., vi.* to fish or catch with a trawl

trawler *n.* a boat used in trawling

tray (trā) *n.* [OE. *treg,* wooden board] 1. a flat receptacle with low sides, for holding or carrying articles 2. a tray with its contents 3. a shallow, removable compartment of a trunk, cabinet, etc.

treacherous (trech'ər əs) *adj.* 1. full of or showing treachery 2. dangerous; deceptive *[treacherous* rocks *]*

treachery (trech'ər ē) *n., pl.* **-eries** [< OFr. *trichier,* to cheat] 1. betrayal of trust, faith, or allegiance; disloyalty or treason 2. an act of disloyalty or treason

treacle (trē'k'l) *n.* [< Gr. *thēriakē,* remedy for venomous bites] 1. a thick, usually dark brown syrup produced during the refining of sugar: also called **black treacle** 2. anything sweet and cloying —**trea'cly** *adj.*

tread (tred) *vt.* **trod, trod'den** or **trod, tread'ing** [OE. *tredan*] 1. to walk on, in, along, over, etc. 2. to do or follow by walking, dancing, etc. 3. to press or beat with the feet 4. to copulate with: said of male birds —*vi.* 1. to walk 2. to set one's foot (*on, across,* etc.) 3. to trample (*on* or *upon*) —*n.* 1. the manner or sound of treading 2. something on which a person or thing treads or moves, as a shoe sole, the horizontal surface of a stair step, etc. 3. a) the thick outer layer of a motor car tyre b) the depth or pattern of grooves in this layer —**tread the boards** to act in plays —**tread on air** to be very happy —**tread on a person's toes** (or **corns**) to encroach on someone's sphere of action, feelings, etc. —**tread water** to keep the body upright and the head above water in swimming by moving the legs up and down

treadle (tred''l) *n.* [see prec.] a pedal moved by the foot to turn a wheel

treadmill (tred'mil') *n.* 1. a mill wheel turned as by an animal treading an endless belt 2. any monotonous routine of duties, work, etc.

treason (trē'z'n) *n.* [< L. *trans-*, over + *dare,* give] betrayal of one's country, esp. by helping the enemy in time of war

treasonable *adj.* of or involving treason; traitorous: also **trea'sonous** —**trea'sonably** *adv.*

treasure (trezh'ər) *n.* [< Gr. *thēsauros*] 1. accumulated wealth, as money, gold, jewels, etc. 2. any person or thing considered valuable —*vt.* **-ured, -uring** 1. to cherish 2. to save up (money, etc.) for future use

treasure hunt a game in which successive clues direct players to a hidden prize

treasurer *n.* an officer in charge of the funds of a company, society, etc.

treasure-trove *n.* [< OFr. *tresor,* treasure + *trover,* to find] treasure found hidden, the original owner of which is not known

treasury *n., pl.* **-uries** 1. a place where treasure or funds are kept, recorded, etc. 2. the funds or revenues of a country, company, etc. 3. [T-] the governmental department in charge of revenue, taxation, etc. 4. a collection of treasures in literature, etc.

Treasury Bench the front row of seats to the right of the speaker in the British House of Commons, occupied by the principal members of the government

treasury bill a short-term bill of exchange issued by the government to raise money for temporary purposes

treat (trēt) *vt.* [< L. *trahere,* to draw] 1. to act towards (a person, animal, etc.) in a specified manner 2. to regard in a specified way *[he treated* it as a joke *]* 3. to deal with (a subject) in writing, etc. in a specified style 4. to pay for the food, drink, etc. of (another) 5. to subject to some process, as in a chemical procedure 6. to give medical care to (someone) or for some disorder —*vi.* 1. to discuss terms (*with* a person or *for* a settlement) 2. to speak or write (*of*) 3. to stand the cost of another's entertainment: also **stand treat** —*n.* 1. a meal, drink, etc. paid for by someone else 2. anything that gives great pleasure 3. the act of treating —**treat'able** *adj.* —**treat'er** *n.*

treatise (trēt'iz) *n.* [see TREAT] a formal, systematic article or book dealing with some subject in a detailed way

treatment (trēt'mənt) *n.* 1. act, manner, method, etc. of treating 2. medical or surgical care

treaty (trēt'ē) *n., pl.* **-ties** [< L. *tractare,* manage] 1. a formal agreement between two or more nations, relating to peace, alliance, trade, etc. 2. [Canad.] any of the formal agreements between Indians and the Canadian government by which Indians surrender their land rights in return for aid

treble (treb''l) *adj.* [< L. *triplus,* triple] 1. threefold; triple 2. of, for, or performing the treble —*n.* 1. the highest part in musical harmony; soprano 2. a high-pitched voice or sound 3. treble the amount, size, etc. —*vt., vi.* **-bled, -bling** to make or become threefold —**tre'bly** *adv.*

treble chance a method of competing in the football pools, by selecting from a list of matches those that will end in a draw, home and away wins counting less

treble clef *Music* a sign on a staff, indicating the position of G above middle C on the second line

tree (trē) *n.* [OE. *treow*] 1. a large, woody

perennial plant with one main trunk which develops many branches **2.** a treelike bush or shrub **3.** anything resembling a tree, as a family tree —*vt.* **treed, tree'-ing** to chase up a tree —**up a tree** [Colloq.] in a situation without escape —**tree'less** *adj.* —**tree'like'** *adj.*

tree creeper a small long-beaked bird that climbs tree-trunks in search of insects

tree line *same as* TIMBERLINE

tree surgery treatment of damaged trees by filling cavities, pruning, etc. —**tree surgeon**

trefoil (trē'foil) *n.* [< L. *tri-*, three + *folium*, leaf] **1.** a plant with leaves divided into three leaflets, as the clover **2.** any ornamental figure shaped like this

trek (trek) *n.* [Afrik. < Du. *trekken*, draw] **1.** a long and often difficult journey **2.** in South Africa, a journey made by ox wagon **3.** a migration —*vi.* **trekked, trek'-king 1.** to travel slowly and laboriously **2.** [Colloq.] to go, esp. on foot **3.** in South Africa, to travel by ox wagon —**trek'-ker** *n.*

trellis (trel'is) *n.* [< L. *trilix*, triple-twilled] an openwork structure of thin, crossed strips, esp. of wood, on which climbing plants are trained

tremble (trem'b'l) *vi.* **-bled, -bling** [< L. *tremere*] **1.** to shake involuntarily from cold, fear, etc.; shiver **2.** to feel great fear or anxiety **3.** to quake, vibrate, quaver, etc. —*n.* **1.** a trembling **2.** [*sometimes pl.*] a fit of trembling —**trem'bly** *adj.*

trembler *n.* a trembling spring that makes electrical contact when shaken

tremendous (tri men'dəs) *adj.* [< L. *tremere*, tremble] **1.** very large; great **2.** [Colloq.] wonderful, amazing, etc. —**tremen'dously** *adv.*

tremolo (trem'ə lō') *n.,* pl. **-los'** [It.] a trembling effect produced by rapidly repeating the same musical tone

tremor (trem'ər) *n.* [< L. *tremere*, tremble] **1.** a trembling, shaking, etc. **2.** a vibratory motion **3.** a nervous thrill **4.** a minor earthquake

tremulous (trem'yoo ləs) *adj.* [< L. *tremere*, tremble] **1.** trembling; quivering **2.** fearful; timid —**trem'ulously** *adv.* —**trem'ulousness** *n.*

trench (trench) *n.* [< OFr.] a long, narrow ditch with earth banked in front as a parapet, used in battle for cover, etc. —*vt.* to dig a ditch or ditches in —*vi.* **1.** to dig a ditch **2.** [Archaic] to infringe (*on* or *upon* another's land, rights, etc.)

trenchant (tren'chənt) *adj.* [see prec.] **1.** keen; incisive [*trenchant* words] **2.** forceful; vigorous [a *trenchant* argument] —**trench'ancy** *n.*

trench coat a belted raincoat in a military style

trencher *n.* *Hist.* a wooden platter for carving and serving meat

trencherman *n.* one who eats much and heartily

trend (trend) *n.* [OE. *trendan*] **1.** general tendency or direction **2.** fashion; mode —*vi.* to take a certain trend

trend-setter *n.* any person or innovation that is likely to create a new trend —**trend'-set'ting** *adj.*

trendy *adj.* **-ier, -iest** [Colloq.] of or in the latest style or trend —**trend'ily** *adv.* —**trend'iness** *n.*

trepidation (trep'ə dā'shən) *n.* [< L. *trepidus*, disturbed] fearful uncertainty or anxiety

trespass (tres'pəs) *vi.* [< L. *trans-*, across + *passus*, a step] **1.** to go on another's property without permission or right **2.** to go beyond the limits of what is considered right or moral **3.** to intrude; encroach **4.** *Law* to commit a trespass —*n.* *Law* an illegal act done with force against another's person, rights, or property —**tres'passer** *n.*

tress (tres) *n.* [< ?] **1.** a lock of human hair **2.** [*pl.*] a woman's hair, esp. when long and falling loosely

TRESTLE

trestle (tres''l) *n.* [< L. *transtrum*, beam] **1.** a horizontal beam fastened to two pairs of spreading legs, used as a support, to form a table, etc. **2.** a framework of uprights and crosspieces, supporting a bridge, etc.

trews (trooz) *n.pl.* [ScotGael. *triubhus*] [Scot.] close-fitting trousers, orig. of tartan

T.R.H. Their Royal Highnesses

tri- [< Fr., L., or Gr.] *a combining form meaning:* **1.** having or involving three [*triangular*] **2.** in three ways [*trilingual*] **3.** into three [*trisect*] **4.** every third [*triannual*]

Triad (trī'əd) *n.* a Chinese secret society, esp. one involved with drug smuggling

triad (trī'əd) *n.* [< Gr. *treis*, three] **1.** a group of three persons, things, etc. **2.** a musical chord of three tones, esp. one consisting of a root tone and its third and fifth —**triad'ic** *adj.*

trial (trī'əl) *n.* [Anglo-Fr. < *trier*, to try] **1.** a) a trying, testing, etc.; test b) an experiment **2.** a) a being tried by suffering, temptation, etc. b) suffering, hardship, etc. **3.** a formal examination of the facts of a case by a court of law to decide the validity of a charge or claim **4.** [*often pl.*] a competition for individuals —*adj.* **1.** of a trial **2.** of or for trying, testing, etc. —**on trial** in the process of being tried

trial and error a trying or testing over and over again until the right result is found —**tri'al-and-er'ror** *adj.*

trial balance a statement of the debit and credit balances in a double-entry bookkeeping ledger

trial run an initial test or rehearsal of something new or untried, as a vehicle, a play, etc., to gauge its effectiveness

TRIANGLES

triangle (trī'aŋ'g'l) *n.* [see TRI- & ANGLE¹]
1. a plane figure having three angles and
three sides 2. any three-sided or three-
cornered figure, area, etc. 3. a situation
involving three persons 4. a musical
percussion instrument consisting of a steel
rod bent in a triangle —**trian'gular** (-aŋ'-
gyoolər) *adj.* —**trian'gular'ity** (-lar'ətē) *n.*
triangulate (trī'aŋ'gyoolāt') *vt.* 1. to
survey using triangulation 2. to measure
by trignometry
triangulation (trī'aŋ'gyoolā'shən) *n.*
Surveying the determining of distance
between points on the earth's surface by
dividing an area into connected triangles
Triassic (trī'as'ik) *adj.* [< LL. *trias*, TRIAD]
designating or of the first period of the
Mesozoic Era
tribe (trīb) *n.* [L. *tribus*] 1. a group of
persons or clans believed to have a common
ancestor 2. any group of people with
the same occupation, ideas, etc. 3. a
subdivision of a subfamily of plants or
animals 4. loosely, any group of plants
or animals classified together 5. [Colloq.]
a) a family b) [pl.] large numbers —**trib'-
al** *adj.*
tribesman *n.* a member of a tribe
tribulation (trib'yoolā'shən) *n.* [< L.
tribulare, afflict] 1. great misery or
distress 2. the cause of this; affliction; trial
tribunal (trībyoo͞o'n'l) *n.* [L.: see TRIBUNE¹]
1. in Britain a) a special court, convened
by the government to inquire into a specific
matter b) a board of people called together
to adjudicate on a particular problem 2.
a court of justice 3. the judge's bench
tribune¹ (trib'yoon) *n.* [< L. *tribus*, tribe]
1. in ancient Rome, any of several
magistrates whose duty it was to protect
the rights and interests of the plebeians
2. a champion of the people
tribune² *n.* [Fr. < It. < L.: see TRIBUNAL,
sense 3] a raised platform or dais for
speakers
Tribunite *n.* a member of the left-wing
Tribune group of the Labour Party
tributary (trib'yootərē) *n.*, *pl.* -**taries**
1. a tributary stream or river 2. a tributary
nation or ruler —*adj.* 1. *a*) flowing into
a larger one [a tributary stream] b) making
additions; contributory 2. subject [a
tributary nation] 3. paying tribute
tribute (trib'yoot) *n.* [< L. *tribuere*, allot]
1. something given, done, or said to show
gratitude, honour, or praise 2. money
that one nation is forced to pay to another,
more powerful nation 3. any forced
payment
trice (trīs) *n.* [< MDu. *trisen*, to pull]
an instant: now only in **in a trice**
tricentennial (trī'senten'ē əl) *adj.*

happening once in, or lasting for, 300
years —*n.* a 300th anniversary
triceps (trī'seps) *n.*, *pl.* -**cepses, -ceps**
[< L. *tri-*, three + *caput*, head] a muscle
having three points of origin, esp. the
muscle at the back of the upper arm
trichina (tri kī'nə) *n.*, *pl.* -**nae** (-nē) [<
Gr. *trichinos*, hairy] a very small worm
whose larvae cause trichinosis
trichinosis (trik'ənō'sis) *n.* a disease
marked by fever, diarrhoea, muscular pains,
etc. and usually acquired by eating
undercooked infested pork
trichromatic (trī'krō mat'ik) *adj.* [TRI-+
CHROMATIC] of, having, or using three
colours
trick (trik) *n.* [< OFr. *trichier*, to cheat]
1. something that is done to fool, cheat,
outwit, etc. 2. *a*) a piece of playful mischief;
prank *b*) a deception or illusion 3. a
clever or skilful act intended to amuse;
specif., *a*) an act of jugglery, sleight of
hand, etc. *b*) a feat done by a trained
animal 4. the art or knack of doing a
thing easily, skilfully, etc. 5. a personal
mannerism 6. *Card Games* the cards
played and won in a single round —*vt.*
to deceive, cheat, outwit, fool, etc. —*adj.*
1. of, for, or using tricks 2. that tricks
—**do the trick** [Colloq.] to bring about
the desired result —**how's tricks?** [Slang]
how are things going? —**trick out** (or **up**)
to dress up —**trick'ery** *n.*
trickle (trik''l) *vi.* -**led,** -**ling** [ME. *triklen*]
1. to flow slowly in a thin stream or
fall in drops 2. to move little by little
—*vt.* to cause to trickle —*n.* 1. a trickling
2. a thin flow or drip
trickster (trik'stər) *n.* a person who
tricks; cheat
tricky *adj.* -**ier,** -**iest** 1. intricate; difficult
2. needing skill or care 3. given to or
full of trickery —**trick'ily** *adv.* —**trick'i-
ness** *n.*
tricolour (trī'kələr) *n.* a flag consisting
of three stripes, each of a different colour,
esp. the flag of France
tricot (trē'kō) *n.* [Fr. < *tricoter*, knit]
a knitted fabric
tricycle (trī'si k'l) *n.* [Fr.] a light, three-
wheeled vehicle worked by pedals, esp.
one for children —**tri'cyclist** *n.*
trident (trīd''nt) *n.* [< L. *tri-*, three +
dens, tooth] a three-pronged spear
Tridentine (trī den'tīn) *adj.* [< ML.
Tridentum, Trent] of the Council of Trent,
held intermittently at Trent, 1545-63, or
its decrees
tried (trīd) *pt.* & *pp.* of TRY —*adj.* 1.
tested; proved 2. trustworthy; faithful 3.
having endured trials and troubles
triennial (trīen'ē əl) *adj.* [< L. *tri-*, three
+ *annus*, year] 1. happening every three
years 2. lasting three years
trier (trī'ər) *n.* a person or thing that tries
trifle (trī'f'l) *n.* [< OFr. *truffe*, deception]
1. something of little value or importance
2. a small amount or sum 3. a cold
dessert of sponge cake soaked in sherry
and covered with custard and cream —*vi.*
-**fled,** -**fling** 1. to deal lightly [not a person

to *trifle* with *]* **2.** to play or toy (*with* something) —**tri′fler** *n.*

trifling *adj.* **1.** trivial **2.** frivolous; fickle

triforium (trī fôr′ē əm) *n., pl.* **-ria** [< L. *tri*, TRI- + *foris*, door] an arcade in the wall above the arches of the nave, choir, or transept of a church

trig. **1.** trigonometric(al) **2.** trigonometry

trigger (trig′ər) *n.* [< Du. *trekken*, to pull] a lever pulled or pressed to release a catch, etc.; esp., the small lever pressed back by the finger in firing a gun —*vt.* **1.** to set into action with a trigger **2.** to set off (an action) (often with *off*) —**quick on the trigger** [Colloq.] quick to act, retort, etc.

trigger-happy *adj.* [Colloq.] quick to resort to force, make war, etc.

trigonometry (trig′ə nom′ə trē) *n.* [< Gr. *trigōnon*, triangle + -*metria*, measurement] the branch of mathematics dealing with the relations between the sides or angles of triangles —**trig′onomet′ric** (-nə met′-rik), **trig′onomet′rical** *adj.* —**trig′onomet′rically** *adv.*

trig point [Colloq.] a point on a hilltop, etc., used for triangulation by a surveyor: also **trig station**

trike (trīk) *n.* [Colloq.] *same as* TRICYCLE

trilby (tril′bē) *n.* [< novel *Trilby*, by George Du Maurier] a man's soft, felt hat with an indented crown

trill (tril) *n.* [< It.: echoic] **1.** a rapid alternation of a tone with one just above it **2.** a bird's warble **3.** a rapid vibration of the tongue or uvula, as in pronouncing *r* in some languages —*vt., vi.* to sound with a trill

trillion (tril′yən) *n.* [Fr.] **1.** in Britain and Germany, the number represented by 1 followed by 18 zeros **2.** in the U.S. and France, the number represented by 1 followed by 12 zeros —**tril′lionth** *adj., n.*

trillium (tril′yəm) *n.* [< Swed. *trilling*, triplet] a plant with three leaves at the top of the stem enclosing a single flower: the floral emblem of Ontario

trilobite (trī′lō bīt′) *n.* [< ModL.: see TRI- + LOBE] an extinct sea arthropod, a common fossil in Paleozoic rocks

trilogy (tril′ə jē) *n., pl.* **-gies** [Gr.: see TRI- & -LOGY] a set of three plays, novels, etc. which form a related group, although each is a complete work

trim (trim) *vt.* **trimmed, trim′ming** [OE. *trymman*, make firm] **1.** to make neat or tidy, esp. by clipping, etc. **2.** to clip, lop, cut, etc. **3.** to cut (something) down to the required size or shape **4.** to decorate with ornaments, colourful materials, etc. **5.** *a)* to balance (a ship or aircraft) by shifting cargo, adjusting stabilizers, etc. *b)* to put (sails, etc.) in order for sailing **6.** [Colloq.] *a)* to scold *b)* to beat *c)* to defeat —*vi.* **1.** to change one's opinions, policy, etc. in a way that is expedient **2.** to keep a ship, etc. in balance —*n.* **1.** condition or order **2.** good condition or order **3.** a trimming by clipping, cutting, etc. **4.** *a)* decorative moulding around windows and doors *b)* the interior

furnishings of a motor car —*adj.* **trim′-mer, trim′mest 1.** orderly; neat **2.** well-proportioned **3.** in good condition —**trim one's sails** to adjust one's opinions, actions, etc. to meet changing conditions —**trim′ly** *adv.* —**trim′ness** *n.*

trimaran (trī′mə ran′) *n.* [TRI- + (CATA)MARAN] a boat resembling a catamaran, but with three parallel hulls

trimming (trim′iŋ) *n.* that which trims; specif., *a)* decoration *b)* [*pl.*] vegetables, sauces, etc. served as the usual accompaniments of a main dish

Trinitarian (trin′ə tãr′ē ən) *adj.* of or believing in the Trinity —*n.* one who believes in the Trinity

trinitrotoluene (trī nī′trō tol′yoo wēn′) *n.* [TRI- + NITRE + TOLUENE] a high explosive derived from toluene and used for blasting, in artillery shells, etc.: also **tri-ni′trotol′uol′**: abbrev. **TNT**

trinity (trin′ə tē) *n., pl.* **-ties** [< L. *trinus*, triple] **1.** a unit formed of three persons or things **2.** [T-] *Christian Theol.* the union of the three divine persons (Father, Son, and Holy Spirit) in one Godhead

Trinity Brethren the members of **Trinity House**, an association responsible for the licensing of pilots, and the upkeep and inspection of lighthouses, buoys, etc. along the British coast

Trinity Sunday the Sunday after Whit-sunday, dedicated to the Trinity

trinket (triŋ′kit) *n.* [< ?] a small piece of cheap jewellery, etc.

trio (trē′ō) *n., pl.* **tri′os** [< It. *tri-*, TRI-] **1.** a group of three **2.** *Music a)* a composition for three voices or instruments *b)* the three performers of such a composition

trip (trip) *n.* [OFr. *treper*] **1.** *a)* a journey *b)* a pleasant excursion **2.** *a)* a stumble *b)* a manoeuvre to cause this **3.** a light, quick tread **4.** a contrivance, as a pawl, to trip a part **5.** [Slang] the hallucinations, sensations, etc. produced by a psychedelic drug, esp. LSD —*vi., vt.* **tripped, trip′-ping 1.** to stumble or cause to stumble **2.** to make or cause to make a mistake **3.** to move or perform with light, rapid steps **4.** to release (a spring, wheel, etc.), as by going past an escapement catch —**trip up** to catch in a lie, error, etc.

tripartite (trī pär′tīt) *adj.* [< L. *tri-*, three + *partire*, part] **1.** having three parts **2.** made between three parties, as an agreement

tripe (trīp) *n.* [< ?] **1.** part of the stomach of an ox, etc., used as food **2.** [Colloq.] nonsense; rubbish

triple (trip′'l) *adj.* [Fr. < L. *triplus*] **1.** consisting of three; threefold **2.** done, said, etc. three times **3.** three times as much, as many, etc. **4.** *Music* having three beats to the bar [*triple* time] —*n.* a triple amount, number, etc. —*vt., vi.* **tri′-pled, tri′pling** to make or be three times as much or as many —**tri′ply** *adv.*

triple jump an athletic event in which the competitor has to perform a hop, a step, and a jump in a continuous movement

triple point *Chem.* the temperature and pressure at which the three phases of a substance are in equilibrium

triplet (trip′lit) *n.* [TRIPL(E) + -ET] 1. a group of three, usually of one kind; specif., *a)* a group of three lines of poetry *b)* a group of three musical notes 2. any of three offspring born at a single birth

triplicate (trip′lə kit; *for v.* -kāt′) *adj.* [< L. *triplex,* threefold] threefold —*n.* any of three identical copies —*vt.* -cat′ed, -cat′-ing to make three identical copies of —**in triplicate** in three identical copies —trip′lica′tion *n.*

tripod (trī′päd) *n.* [< Gr. *tri-,* three + *pous,* foot] 1. a three-legged support for a camera, etc. 2. a three-legged cauldron, stool, etc.

tripos (trī′pos) *n.* [< L. *tripus,* tripod: after three-legged stool used formerly at graduation] the final examination at Cambridge University

tripper (trip′ər) *n.* one who makes an excursion; tourist

tripping *adj.* moving lightly and quickly —trip′pingly *adv.*

triptych (trip′tik) *n.* [< Gr. *tri-,* three + *ptychē,* a fold] a set of three hinged panels with pictures, carvings, etc.

trireme (trī′rēm) *n.* [< L. *tri-,* three + *remus,* oar] an ancient Greek or Roman galley with three banks of oars on each side

trisect (trī sekt′) *vt.* [< TRI- + L. *secare,* to cut] to cut into three, usually equal, parts —trisec′tion *n.*

‡**triste** (trēst) *adj.* [Fr.] sad

trite (trīt) *adj.* trit′er, trit′est [< L. *terere,* wear out] no longer fresh, original, etc. —trite′ly *adv.* —trite′ness *n.*

tritium (trit′ē əm) *n.* [< Gr. *tritos,* third] a radioactive isotope of hydrogen with an atomic weight of 3

Triton (trīt′'n) *Gr. Myth.* a sea god with the head and upper body of a man and the tail of a fish

triumph (trī′əmf) *n.* [< L. *triumphus*] 1. exultation or joy over a victory, etc. 2. a victory; success 3. in ancient Rome, a procession celebrating a victorious general's return —*vi.* 1. to be victorious, etc. 2. to rejoice over victory, etc. —**trium′-phal** *adj.*

triumphant (trī um′fant) *adj.* 1. victorious; successful 2. exulting in victory, etc. —**trium′phantly** *adv.*

triumvir (trī um′vər) *n.,* pl. **-virs, -viri′** (-vī rē′) [L. < *trium virum,* of three men] in ancient Rome, any of three administrators sharing authority equally

triumvirate *n.* 1. government by three men 2. any association of three in authority 3. any group of three

trivalent (trī vā′lənt) *adj.* [TRI- + -VALENT] 1. having a valence of three 2. having three valences

trivet (triv′it) *n.* [< L. *tripes,* tripod] 1. a three-legged stand for holding pots, kettles, etc. over or near a fire 2. a short-legged plate for hot dishes to rest on —**as right as a trivet** in perfect condition

trivia (triv′ē ə) *n.pl.* [often with sing.

v.] [ModL. < ff.] unimportant matters; trivialities

trivial (triv′ē əl) *adj.* [< L. *tri-,* three + *via,* road] of little value or importance; trifling —triv′ial′ity *n.* —triv′ially *adv.*

trochee (trō′kē) *n.* [< Gr. *trechein,* to run] a metrical foot of two syllables, the first accented and the other unaccented —**trocha′ic** (-kā′ik) *adj.*

trod (träd) *pt. & alt. pp. of* TREAD

trodden *alt. pp. of* TREAD

trode (trōd) *archaic pt. of* TREAD

troglodyte (träg′lə dīt′) *n.* [< Gr. *trōglē,* cave + *dyein,* enter] a cave dweller, esp. any of the prehistoric people who lived in caves

troika (troi′kə) *n.* [Russ. < *troe,* three] 1. a Russian vehicle drawn by three horses abreast 2. any group of three; esp., an association of three in authority

Trojan (trō′jən) *adj.* of ancient Troy, its people, etc. —*n.* 1. an inhabitant of ancient Troy 2. a strong, hard-working, determined person

Trojan horse [< the hollow, wooden horse filled with Greek soldiers and left at the gates of Troy] a person, device, etc. intended as a trap to deceive or undermine an enemy

troll[1] (trōl) *vt., vi.* [ME. *trollen,* to roll] 1. to fish (*for* or *in*) with a moving line, esp. with a revolving bait trailed from a moving boat 2. to sing the parts of (a round, etc.) in succession

troll[2] *n.* [ON.] in Scandinavian folklore, any of certain supernatural beings, giants or dwarfs, living underground or in caves

trolley (träl′ē) *n.,* pl. **-leys** [< TROLL[1]] 1. a small table on castors used for conveying food and drink 2. a low, wheeled stand for transporting luggage, etc. 3. a low cart, as for carrying groceries in a supermarket 4. a wheeled carriage, etc. that runs suspended from an overhead track 5. a device to carry electric current from an overhead wire to the motor of an electric tram, etc.

trolley bus an electric bus that gets its power from overhead wires by means of trolleys but does not run on tracks

trolley car [U.S.] an electric tram that gets its power from an overhead wire by means of a trolley

trollop (träl′əp) *n.* [< ?] a sexually promiscuous woman; specif., a prostitute

trolly (träl′ē) *n.* var. of TROLLEY

trombone (träm bōn′) *n.* [It. < *tromba,* trumpet] a large brass instrument with a bell mouth and a long tube bent parallel to itself twice and having either a section that slides in or out (**slide trombone**) or valves (**valve trombone**) —trombon′ist *n.*

‡**trompe l'oeil** (trōnp lē′y′) [Fr., trick of the eye] a painting, etc. so realistic that it gives the illusion of being the actual thing depicted

tronk (tronk) *n.* [< Afrik.] [S Afr. Slang] a prison

troop (trō̄op) *n.* [< ML. *troppus,* a flock] 1. a group of persons or animals; band, herd, etc. 2. loosely, a great number;

lot **3.** [*pl.*] soldiers **4.** a subdivision of a cavalry regiment **5.** a unit of Boy Scouts under an adult leader —*vi.* **1.** to gather or go as in a group **2.** to walk, go, etc. —**trooping the colour** a ceremony held at the public mounting of garrison guards when colours are transferred

trooper *n.* **1.** a cavalryman **2.** a cavalry horse **3.** a troopship **4.** [U.S. & formerly Aust.] a mounted policeman

troopship *n.* a ship for carrying troops

trope (trōp) *n.* [< Gr. *tropos*, a turning] the use of figures of speech

trophy (trō'fē) *n.*, *pl.* **-phies** [< Gr. *tropaion*, token of an enemy's defeat] **1.** a prize, usually a silver cup, awarded in a sports contest, etc. **2.** something taken from a defeated enemy and kept as a memorial of victory

-trophy (trə fē) [< Gr. *trephein*, nourish] *a combining form meaning* nutrition, growth [*hypertrophy*]

tropic (trop'ik) *n.* [< Gr. *tropikos*, of a turn (of the sun at the solstices)] **1.** either of two parallels of latitudes, one, the **Tropic of Cancer**, c. 23$\frac{1}{2}$° north of the equator and the other, the **Tropic of Capricorn**, c. 23$\frac{1}{2}$° south of the equator **2.** [*also* T-] [*pl.*] the region of the earth between these latitudes, noted for its hot climate —*adj.* tropical

tropical *adj.* of, in, characteristic of, or suitable for the tropics —**trop'ically** *adv.*

tropical fish any of various usually brightly coloured fish, orig. from the tropics

Tropical Zone *same as* TORRID ZONE

tropism (trō'piz'm) *n.* [< Gr. *tropos*, a turning] the tendency of a plant or animal to grow or turn towards or away from an external stimulus such as light

troposphere (trop'ə sfēar') *n.* [< Gr. *tropos*, a turning + SPHERE] the atmosphere from the earth's surface to the stratosphere, reaching from 9 to 18 km, in which temperature usually decreases as altitude increases

‡**troppo** (trop'ō) *adv.* [It.] *Music* too; too much so

Trot (trot) *n.* [Colloq.] a Trotskyite

trot (trot) *vi.*, *vt.* **trot'ted, trot'ting** [< OHG. *trottōn*, to tread] **1.** to move, ride, go, etc. at a trot **2.** to hurry; run —*n.* **1.** a gait of a horse, etc. in which the legs are lifted in alternating diagonal pairs **2.** a person's gait between a walk and a run **3.** [*pl.*] [Colloq.] an attack of diarrhoea —**on the trot** [Colloq.] **1.** busy; moving about **2.** one after the other; successively —**trot out** [Colloq.] to present for, or as for, others to see, or admire, or consider

troth (trōth) *n.* [< OE. *treowth*, truth] [Archaic] **1.** faithfulness; loyalty **2.** truth: chiefly in **in troth**, truly **3.** a promise, esp. to marry

Trotskyite (trot'skē īt') *adj.* of the theories of Leon Trotsky (1879-1940), Russian revolutionist and writer —*n.* a follower of Trotsky —**Trot'skyism** *n.*

trotter (trot'ər) *n.* **1.** a horse bred and

trained for trotting races **2.** the foot of a sheep or pig used as food

troubadour (trōō'bə dooar') *n.* [Fr. < Pr. *trobar*, compose in verse] any of a class of medieval lyric poets who lived in southern France in the 11th, 12th, and 13th cent.

trouble (trub''l) *n.* [< L. *turbidus*, turbid] **1.** a state of mental distress; worry **2.** public disturbance **3.** *a*) a misfortune or mishap *b*) a difficult situation **4.** a cause of annoyance, distress, etc. **5.** effort; care —*vt.* **-bled, -bling 1.** to worry; perturb **2.** to disturb or agitate **3.** to cause pain or discomfort to [*troubled* by headaches] **4.** to cause difficulty to **5.** to annoy, tease, etc. —*vi.* to take pains; bother [don't *trouble* to return it] —**in(to) trouble** [Colloq.] pregnant when unmarried

troublemaker *n.* a person who habitually makes trouble for others —**trou'blemak'-ing** *n.*

trouble-shooter *n.* a person whose work is to find and repair or eliminate mechanical breakdowns or other sources of trouble —**trou'ble-shoot'ing** *n.*

troublesome *adj.* full of or causing trouble

troublous (trub'ləs) *adj.* [Literary] **1.** troubled; disturbed **2.** *same as* TROUBLE-SOME

trough (trof) *n.* [OE. *trog*] **1.** a long, narrow, open container for holding water or food for animals **2.** a vessel of similar shape **3.** a long, narrow hollow, as between waves **4.** a long, narrow area of low barometric pressure

trounce (trouns) *vt.* **trounced, trounc'ing** [< ?] **1.** to beat; thrash **2.** [Colloq.] to defeat —**trounc'er** *n.*

troupe (trōōp) *n.* [Fr.] a group, esp. of actors, singers, etc.; company —**troup'-er** *n.*

trousers (trou'zərz) *n.pl.* [< ScotGael. *triubhas*] a two-legged outer garment, esp. for men and boys, reaching from the waist usually to the ankles

trousseau (trōō'sō) *n.*, *pl.* **-seaux** (-sōz), **-seaus** [< OFr. *trousse*, a bundle] a bride's outfit of clothes, linen, etc.

trout (trout) *n.* [< Gr. *trōgein*, gnaw] any of various food and game fishes related to the salmon and found chiefly in fresh water

trove (trōv) *n.* *short for* TREASURE-TROVE

trow (trō) *vi.*, *vt.* [< OE. *treow*, faith] [Archaic] to believe, think, suppose, etc.

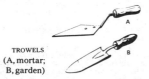

TROWELS
(A, mortar;
B, garden)

trowel (trou'əl) *n.* [< L. *trua*, ladle] **1.** a hand tool with a flat blade for smoothing plaster or applying mortar **2.** a tool with a pointed scoop for digging holes in a garden

troy (troi) *adj.* by or in troy weight

troy weight [< *Troyes*, in France] a system of weights for gold, silver, precious stones, etc., in which one pound equals twelve ounces

trs. transpose

truant (trōō′ənt) *n.* [OFr., beggar] **1.** a pupil who stays away from school without permission **2.** a person who shirks his duties —*adj.* **1.** that is a truant **2.** idle; shiftless **3.** errant; straying —**tru′ancy** *n.*

truce (trōōs) *n.* [OE. *treow*, faith] **1.** a period during a war in which the nations or peoples engaged in it agree to stop fighting for a time **2.** any pause in quarrelling, conflict, etc.

truck¹ (truk) *n.* [prob. < Gr. *trochos*, a wheel] **1.** an open railway wagon **2.** [Chiefly U.S.] a lorry **3.** a swivelling frame, with two or more pairs of wheels, under each end of a railway carriage, etc. **4.** a frame or platform on wheels, with handles at one end, used to carry trunks, crates, etc. —*vt.* to carry on a truck

truck² *vt., vi.* [MFr. *troquer*] to exchange; barter —*n.* **1.** barter **2.** payment of wages in goods instead of money **3.** [Colloq.] dealings [to have no *truck* with]

trucking *n.* [U.S.] The business of carrying goods by lorry

truckle (truk′'l) *n.* [< Gr. *trochos*, wheel] a low bed on castors, that can be rolled under a higher bed when not in use: also **truckle bed** —*vi.* **-led, -ling** to give in or yield too easily (*to*)

truculent (truk′yoo lənt) *adj.* [< L. *trux*] **1.** defiantly aggressive or obstreperous **2.** [Archaic] fierce; savage —**truc′ulence, truc′ulency** *n.* —**truc′ulently** *adv.*

trudge (truj) *vi.* trudged, trudg′ing [< ?] to walk, esp. wearily or laboriously —*n.* a trudging

true (trōō) *adj.* tru′er, tru′est [OE. *treowe*] **1.** in accordance with fact; not false **2.** genuine; authentic **3.** faithful; loyal **4.** conforming to a standard, etc.; accurate **5.** rightful; lawful **6.** accurately fitted, placed, or shaped **7.** determined by the poles of the earth's axis, not by the earth's magnetic poles [*true* north] —*adv.* truly, truthfully, accurately, etc. —**come true** to happen as predicted or expected —**in** (or **out of**) **true** that is (or is not) properly set, adjusted, etc.

true-blue (trōō′blōō′) *adj.* **1.** very loyal; staunch **2.** staunchly Conservative in politics

true-life (trōō′līf′) *adj.* like that which happens in real life; true to reality [a *true-life* story]

truelove *n.* (one's) sweetheart; a loved one

truffle (truf′'l) *n.* [< Fr. < L. *tuber*, knob] **1.** a fleshy, edible fungi that grows underground **2.** a soft sweet flavoured with chocolate and rum

trug (trug) *n.* [< ?] a shallow, broad, gardener's basket made of strips of wood

truism (trōō′iz'm) *n.* a statement the truth of which is obvious and well known —**truis′tic** *adj.*

truly (trōō′lē) *adv.* **1.** in a true manner; genuinely, faithfully, rightfully, etc. **2.** really; indeed

trump¹ (trump) *n.* [< TRIUMPH] **1.** any playing card of a suit that ranks higher than any other suit during the playing of a hand **2.** [occas. pl. with sing. v.] a suit of trumps **3.** any advantage held in reserve —*vt.* **1.** to take (a trick, etc.) with a trump **2.** to outdo; surpass —*vi.* to play a trump —**trump up** to make up (a charge against someone, etc.) in order to deceive —**turn up trumps** to end more favourably than was expected

trump² *n., vi., vt.* [OFr. *trompe*] archaic or poet. var. of TRUMPET

trumpery (trum′pər ē) *n., pl.* **-eries** [< MFr. *tromper*, deceive] **1.** something showy but worthless **2.** nonsense —*adj.* showy but worthless

TRUMPET

trumpet (trum′pit) *n.* [< OFr. *trompe*] **1.** a brass instrument with a blaring tone, consisting of a looped tube flared at the end opposite the mouthpiece **2.** something shaped like a trumpet; esp., *same as* EAR TRUMPET **3.** a sound like that of a trumpet —*vi.* **1.** to blow a trumpet **2.** to make a sound like a trumpet —*vt.* **1.** to sound on or as on a trumpet **2.** to proclaim loudly —**trum′peter** *n.*

trumpet major the head trumpeter in a cavalry regiment

truncate (truŋ kāt′) *vt.* **-cat′ed, -cat′ing** [< L. *truncus*, stem] to shorten by cutting; lop —**trunca′tion** *n.*

truncated *adj.* cut short or appearing as if cut short

truncheon (trun′chən) *n.* [< L. *truncus*, stem] **1.** a policeman's stick **2.** a staff carried as a symbol of authority

trundle (trun′d'l) *vt., vi.* **-dled, -dling** [< OE. *trendan*, to roll] to roll along

trunk (truŋk) *n.* [< L. *truncus*] **1.** the main stem of a tree **2.** a human body or animal body, not including the head and limbs **3.** the thorax of an insect **4.** a long, flexible snout, as of an elephant **5.** a large, reinforced box for carrying a traveller's clothes, etc. **6.** [pl.] men's shorts worn as for boxing, swimming, etc. **7.** *short for* TRUNK LINE **8.** [U.S.] the boot of a motor vehicle

trunk call a long-distance telephone call

trunk line a main line of a railway, telephone system, etc.

trunk road a main road connecting important centres

trunnion (trun′yən) *n.* [Fr. *trognon*, a stump] 1. either of two projecting pins on each side of a cannon, on which it pivots 2. either of two similar pins in machinery

truss (trus) *vt.* [OFr. *trousser*] 1. to tie or bind (often with *up*) 2. to skewer or bind the wings, etc. of (a fowl) before cooking 3. to support or strengthen with a truss —*n.* 1. a rigid framework of beams, struts, etc. for supporting a roof, bridge, etc. 2. an appliance worn for supporting a hernia 3. a flower cluster 4. a bundle or pack

trust (trust) *n.* [ON. *traust*] 1. firm belief in the honesty, reliability, etc. of another 2. confident expectation, hope, etc. 3. *a)* the fact of having confidence placed in one *b)* the responsibility resulting from this 4. care; custody 5. something entrusted to one 6. confidence in a purchaser's intention to pay for goods etc. 7. a business combination of companies, with control vested in a single board of trustees who are able to eliminate competition, etc. 8. *Law a)* the fact of having nominal ownership of property to keep, use, or administer for another's benefit *b)* the property involved —*vi.* 1. to have trust or faith 2. to hope (*for*) 3. to give business credit —*vt.* 1. to have trust in 2. to commit (*to* a person's care) 3. to put something confidently in the charge of 4. to believe or suppose 5. to hope 6. to grant business credit to —*adj.* 1. relating to a trust or trusts 2. held in trust —**in trust** in the condition of being entrusted to another's care —**take on trust** to accept without requiring corroboration —**trust to** to rely on —**trust′able** *adj.*

trustee (trus tē′) *n.* 1. one to whom another's property or the management of another's property is entrusted 2. any of a group of persons appointed to manage the affairs of a charity, etc. —**trustee′-ship′** *n.*

trustful *adj.* full of confidence in others; trusting

trust fund money, stock, etc. held in trust

trusting *adj.* that trusts; trustful

trust territory a territory placed by the United Nations under the control of a country that manages the affairs of the territory

trustworthy *adj.* -thier, -thiest worthy of trust; dependable; reliable —**trust′wor′-thiness** *n.*

trusty *adj.* -ier, -iest that can be relied upon —*n., pl.* **trust′ies** a convict granted special privileges as a trustworthy person —**trust′iness** *n.*

truth (trōōth) *n., pl.* **truths** (trōōthz) [OE. *treowth*] 1. the quality of being true; specif., *a)* sincerity *b)* the quality of being in agreement with facts *c)* reality *d)* correctness 2. that which is true 3. an established or verified fact, etc. —**in truth** truly; in fact

truthful *adj.* 1. telling the truth; honest 2. agreeing with fact or reality —**truth′-fully** *adv.* —**truth′fulness** *n.*

try (trī) *vt.* **tried, try′ing** [< ?] 1. to attempt; endeavour 2. to put to the proof; test 3. to test the effect of 4. to subject to a severe test or strain 5. to test the faith, patience, etc. of 6. *a)* to examine and decide (a case) in a law court *b)* to determine legally the guilt or innocence of (a person) —*vi.* to make an effort, attempt, etc. —*n., pl.* **tries** 1. an attempt; effort; trial 2. *Rugby* a score made by placing the ball behind the opponent's goal-line —**try it on** [Colloq.] to see how far one can go before being reprimanded —**try on** to test the fit, etc. of (a garment) by putting it on —**try one's hand at** to attempt (to do something), esp. for the first time —**try out** to test the quality, value, etc. of

trying *adj.* that tries one's patience; annoying

try-on *n.* [Colloq.] an attempt to do something forbidden without being detected, prevented, or punished

tryout *n.* [Colloq.] a chance to prove, or a test to determine, one's fitness to be in a team, act a role, etc.

trysail (trī′s′l, -sāl′) *n.* [< a *try*, position of lying to in a storm] a small, stout, fore-and-aft sail used for keeping a vessel's head to the wind in a storm

tryst (trist, trīst) *n.* [OFr. *triste*, hunting station] 1. an appointment to meet, esp. one made secretly by lovers 2. *a)* the meeting *b)* the place of such a meeting: also **trysting place**

tsar (zär) *n.* 1. an emperor: title of any of the former emperors of Russia 2. an absolute ruler; despot —**tsar′dom** *n.* —**tsar′ist** *adj., n.*

tsarevitch (zär′ə vich′) *n.* [< Russ.] the eldest son of a tsar of Russia

tsarina (zä rē′nə) *n.* [< Russ.] the wife of a tsar; empress of Russia: also **tsarit′-za** (-rit′sə)

TSE, T.S.E. Toronto Stock Exchange

tsetse fly (tset′sē) [Afrik. < Bantu] any of several small flies of central and southern Africa, including the one that carries sleeping sickness

T-shirt (tē′shurt′) *n.* [so named because T-shaped] a collarless pullover shirt with short sleeves

tsk *interj., n.* a clicking or sucking sound made with the tongue, to express disapproval, sympathy, etc.

tsotsi (tsot′sē) *n.* [< ?] [S Afr. Colloq.] a young criminal, often given to violence, operating mainly in black African townships

tsp. 1. teaspoon(s) 2. teaspoonful(s)

T square a T-shaped ruler for drawing parallel lines

T.T. 1. teetotal 2. teetotaller 3. Tourist Trophy 4. tuberculin tested

T.U., TU trade union

Tu. Tuesday

tub (tub) *n.* [MDu. *tubbe*] 1. *a)* a round, open, flat-bottomed wooden container *b)* any large, open container of metal, etc., as for washing c) a small, plastic container, with a lid, for margarine, etc. **2.** [Colloq.] a bath **3.** [Colloq.] a slow-moving boat —*vt., vi.* **tubbed, tub′bing 1.** [Colloq.] to wash in a tub **2.** [Colloq.] to bath (oneself)

tuba (tyōō′bə) *n., pl.* **tu′bas, tu′bae** (-bē) [L., trumpet] a large, brass musical instrument

tubby (tub′ē) *adj.* **tub′bier, tub′biest** short and fat —**tub′biness** *n.*

tube (tyōōb) *n.* [Fr. < L. *tubus*, a pipe] **1.** *a)* a slender, hollow cylinder or pipe of metal, glass, rubber, etc., in which gases and liquids can flow or be kept *b)* an instrument, part, organ, etc. resembling a tube **2.** a rubber casing inflated with air and used, esp. formerly, with an outer casing to form a tyre for a motor vehicle **3.** a screw-topped, pliable cylinder for holding pastes or semiliquids [*tube* of toothpaste] **4.** short for ELECTRON TUBE **5.** [Colloq.] [*often* T-] an underground railway system, esp. that in London (often preceded by *the*) —*vt.* **tubed, tub′ing** to provide with or pass through a tube or tubes

tuber (tyōō′bər) *n.* [L., a swelling] a short, thickened, fleshy part of an underground stem, as a potato

tubercle *n.* [see prec.] **1.** a small, rounded part growing out from a bone or from the root of a plant **2.** any abnormal hard swelling; specif., that of tuberculosis

tubercular (tyōō bur′kyoo lər) *adj.* **1.** of or having tuberculosis **2.** of, like, or having tubercles Also **tuber′culous**

tuberculin (tyōō bur′kyoo lin) *n.* a sterile solution prepared from a culture of the tubercle bacillus and injected into the skin as a test for tuberculosis

tuberculin tested produced by cows that have been certified as free of tuberculosis: said of milk, etc.

tuberculosis (tyōō bur′kyoo lō′sis) *n.* [ModL.: see TUBER & -OSIS] an infectious disease causing tubercles to form, esp. in the lungs; consumption

tuberous (tyōō′bər əs) *adj.* [see TUBER] **1.** covered with rounded swellings; knobby **2.** of, like, or having a tuber Also **tu′berose′**

tubing (tyōō′biŋ) *n.* **1.** a series or system of tubes **2.** material in the form of a tube **3.** a piece or length of tube

tubthumper (tub′thum′pər) [Colloq.] a ranting public speaker

tubular (tyōō′byoo lər) *adj.* [< L. *tubus*, a pipe] **1.** of or shaped like a tube **2.** made with tubes

tubule (tyōōb′yool) *n.* a small tube

T.U.C. Trades Union Congress

tuck (tuk) *vt.* [< MDu. *tucken*] **1.** to put snugly into a small space; cram **2.** *a)* to thrust the edges of (a sheet, napkin, etc.) under or in, in order to secure *b)* to cover or wrap snugly (with *up*) **3.** to pull up or gather up in a fold or folds, as to make shorter **4.** to sew a fold or folds in (a garment) —*n.* **1.** a sewn fold in a garment **2.** [Slang] food, esp. sweets, cakes, etc. —**tuck away** to eat

or drink heartily —**tuck in 1.** to pull in or contract (one's chin, stomach, etc.) **2.** to eat or drink heartily

tucker¹ *n.* **1.** a neck and shoulder covering formerly worn with a low-cut bodice by women **2.** [Aust. Slang] food

tucker² *vt.* [< ?] [U.S. Colloq.] to tire (*out*)

tuck-in *n.* [Slang] a large meal

tuck shop a shop selling sweets, cakes, etc., esp. to schoolchildren

Tudor (tyōō′dər) *adj.* **1.** designating or of the Tudors (1485-1603) **2.** of a style of architecture characterized by extensive panelling, half-timbering, etc.

Tues. Tuesday

Tuesday (tyōōz′dē) *n.* [OE. *Tiwes dæg*, day of the god of war *Tiw*] the third day of the week

Tuesdays *adv.* [Colloq.] on or during every Tuesday

tufa (tyōō′fə) *n.* [It. < L. *tofus*] a porous rock formed of calcium carbonate, etc. deposited by springs

tuff (tuf) *n.* [< TUFA] a porous rock formed from volcanic ash, dust, etc.

tuffet (tuf′ət) *n.* [< TUFT] a tuft of grass

tuft (tuft) *n.* [OFr. *tufe*] a bunch of hairs, feathers, grass, etc. growing or tied closely together —*vt.* to provide with a tuft or tufts —*vi.* to grow in or form into tufts —**tuft′ed** *adj.* —**tuft′y** *adj.*

tug (tug) *vi.* **tugged, tug′ging** [ME. *tuggen*] to pull hard —*vt.* **1.** to pull at **2.** to tow with a tugboat —*n.* **1.** a hard pull **2.** *shortened form of* TUGBOAT —**tug′ger** *n.*

tugboat *n.* a small, powerful boat used for towing or pushing ships, barges, etc.

tug of war 1. a contest in which two teams pull at opposite ends of a rope, each trying to drag the other across a central line **2.** any power struggle between two parties

tuition (tyōō wish′ən) *n.* [< L. *tueri*, protect] **1.** teaching **2.** the fee for instruction, esp. at a college

tulip (tyōō′lip) *n.* [< Fr. < Turk. *tülbend*, TURBAN] **1.** any of various spring-blooming bulb plants, with a large, cup-shaped flower **2.** the flower or bulb

tulip tree a tree of the magnolia family with tulip-shaped, greenish-yellow flowers

tulle (tyōōl) *n.* [< *Tulle*, in France] a thin, fine netting of silk, rayon, etc., used for veils, etc.

tullibee (tul′əbē) *n.* [< AmInd.] a type of N American whitefish

tumble (tum′b'l) *vi.* **-bled, -bling** [OE. *tumbian*, to jump] **1.** *a)* to fall suddenly *b)* to undergo a sudden drop [*prices tumbled*] **2.** to stumble or trip **3.** to toss or roll about **4.** to perform somersaults, etc. **5.** [Colloq.] to understand suddenly (with *to*) —*vt.* **1.** to cause to tumble **2.** to put into disorder as by tossing here and there —*n.* **1.** *a)* a somersault, etc. *b)* a fall **2.** disorder; confusion

tumbledown *adj.* dilapidated

tumbler *n.* **1.** an ordinary drinking glass with no stem **2.** an acrobat or gymnast who does somersaults, etc. **3.** a part of the mechanism of a lock **4.** a kind of pigeon that does somersaults in flight

tumbler-drier (tum′blər drī′ər) *n.* a machine which dries laundered articles by tumbling them about in hot air : also **tum′ble-dri′er**

tumbrel, tumbril (tum′brəl) *n.* [< MFr. *tomber*, to fall] any of the carts used to carry the condemned to the guillotine during the French Revolution

tumescence (tyo͞o mes′′ns) *n.* [< L. *tumescere*, swell up] **1.** a swelling **2.** a swollen part —**tumes′cent** *adj.*

tumid (tyo͞o′mid) *adj.* [< L. *tumere*, to swell] **1.** swollen; bulging **2.** pompous —**tumid′ity** *n.*

tummy (tum′ē) *n.*, *pl.* **-mies** [Colloq.] stomach: also **tum**

tummy button [Colloq.] the navel

tumour (tyo͞o′mər) *n.* [< L. *tumere*, to swell] an abnormal growth of tissue in some part of the body, that is either benign or malignant: U.S. sp. **tu′mor**

tumult (tyo͞o′mult) *n.* [< L. *tumultus*] **1.** noisy commotion; uproar **2.** confusion; disturbance **3.** great emotional disturbance

tumultuous (tyo͞o mul′tyo͞o wəs) *adj.* **1.** wild and noisy; uproarious **2.** making a tumult **3.** greatly disturbed —**tumul′tuously** *adv.*

tumulus (tyo͞o′myo͞o ləs) *n.*, *pl.* **-li′**(-lī′), **-luses** [L.] an ancient burial mound

tun (tun) *n.* [< ML. *tunna*] **1.** a large cask for liquids **2.** a measure of capacity for liquids

tuna (tyo͞o′nə) *n.* [AmSp. < Sp.: see TUNNY] **1.** a large, sea food and game fish of the mackerel group **2.** the flesh of the tuna, often tinned for food: also called **tuna fish**

tundra (tun′drə) *n.* [Russ.] any of the vast, nearly level, treeless plains of the arctic regions

tune (tyo͞on) *n.* [< TONE] **1.** a succession of musical tones; melody; air **2.** correct musical pitch: now chiefly in phrases **in tune, out of tune** —*vt.* **tuned, tun′ing 1.** to adjust (a musical instrument) to some standard of pitch **2.** to adapt (music, the voice, etc.) to some pitch, tone, etc. **3.** to adapt to some condition, mood, etc. **4.** to adjust (a motor, etc.) to the proper or desired performance —**call the tune** to be in control —**change one's tune** to change one's attitude or manner: also **sing a different tune** —**to the tune of** [Colloq.] to the amount of —**tune in** to adjust a radio or television so as to receive (a specified station, programme, etc.) —**tune up 1.** to adjust (musical instruments) to the same pitch **2.** to put (an engine) into good working condition —**tun′able, tune′able** *adj.* —**tun′er** *n.*

tuneful *adj.* musical; melodious —**tune′fully** *adv.*

tuneup, tune-up *n.* an adjusting, as of an engine, to the proper condition

tungsten (tuŋ′stən) *n.* [Sw. < *tung*, heavy + *sten*, stone] a hard, heavy, grey-white, metallic chemical element, used in some steel, electric lamp filaments, etc.: symbol, W

tunic (tyo͞o′nik) *n.* [L. *tunica*] **1.** a blouselike garment extending to the hips or lower, often belted **2.** a short coat forming part of the uniform of soldiers, policemen, etc. **3.** a loose, gownlike garment worn by men and women in ancient Greece and Rome

tuning fork a small steel instrument with two prongs, which when struck sounds a certain fixed tone

tunnel (tun′′l) *n.* [< OFr. *tonne*, tun] **1.** an underground passageway **2.** any tunnellike passage **3.** an animal's burrow —*vt.* **-nelled, -nelling 1.** to make a tunnel through or under **2.** to make (one's way) by digging a tunnel —*vi.* to make a tunnel —**tun′neller** *n.*

tunny (tun′ē) *n.* [< Gr. *thynnos*] same as TUNA

tup (tup) *n.* [ME. *tupe*] a male sheep; ram

Tupi (to͞o pē′) *n.* [Tupi, comrade] **1.** *pl.* **Tupis′, Tupi′** any member of a group of S American Indian tribes living along the lower Amazon **2.** their language

tupik (to͞o′pək) *n.* [< Eskimo] [Canad.] a tent of seal or caribou skin used for shelter by the Inuit in the summer

tuppence (tup′′ns) *n.* same as TWOPENCE

tuque (to͞ok) *n.* [< TOQUE] [Canad.] a knitted cap with a long tapering end

TURBAN

turban (tur′bən) *n.* [ult. < Per. *dulbänd*] **1.** a headdress of Moslem origin, consisting of a cloth wound in folds about the head, often over a cap **2.** any hat made like or resembling this

turbid (tur′bid) *adj.* [< L. *turba*, a crowd] **1.** muddy or cloudy from having the sediment stirred up **2.** thick or dark, as clouds or smoke **3.** muddled —**turbid′ity** *n.*

turbine (tur′bin) *n.* [< L. *turbo*, a whirl] an engine driven by the pressure of steam, water, air, etc. against the vanes of a wheel on a shaft

turbo- [< TURBINE] *a combining form meaning* consisting of or driven by a turbine

turbofan (tur′bō fan′) *n.* a turbojet engine in which additional thrust is obtained from air that bypasses the engine and is accelerated by a fan

turbojet *n.* a jet engine with a turbine-driven air compressor that compresses air for fuel combustion, the resulting hot gases being used to rotate the turbine before forming the propulsive jet

turboprop *n.* [TURBINE + PROP(ELLER)] a turbojet engine whose turbine shaft drives a propeller that develops most of the thrust

turbot (tur′bət) *n.* [< OFr. *tourbout*] a large European flatfish, highly regarded as food

turbulent (tur′byoo lənt) *adj.* [Fr. < L. *turba*, a crowd] full of commotion or wild disorder; specif., a) disorderly b) violently agitated or excited c) marked by wildly irregular motion —**tur′bulence**, **tur′bulency** *n.*

turd (turd) *n.* [< OE. *tord*] [Vulg.] a piece of excrement

tureen (tə rēn′) *n.* [MFr. *terrine*, earthen vessel] a large, deep dish with a lid, for serving soup, etc.

turf (turf) *n.*, *pl.* **turfs**, **turves** (turvz) [OE.] 1. a) a surface layer of earth containing grass plants with their matted roots b) a piece of this 2. peat —*vt.* to cover with turf —**the turf** 1. a track for horse racing 2. the sport of horse racing —**turf out** [Colloq.] to throw out

turf accountant *same as* BOOKMAKER

turgescent (tur jes′'nt) *adj.* [< L. *turgescere*, swell up] becoming turgid or swollen —**turges′cence** *n.*

turgid (tur′jid) *adj.* [< L. *turgere*, to swell] 1. swollen; distended 2. grandiloquent —**turgid′ity** *n.*

Turk (turk) *n.* 1. a native or inhabitant of Turkey 2. a member of any of the peoples speaking Turkic languages

Turk. 1. Turkey 2. Turkish

turkey (tur′kē) *n.* [< the guinea fowl, imported through Turkey] a) a large, wild or domesticated, N American bird with a small head and spreading tail, bred as poultry in many countries b) its flesh

Turkey carpet a deep-piled, soft, woollen carpet, usually brightly patterned

turkey cock 1. a male turkey 2. an arrogant, conceited person

Turkic (tur′kik) *adj.* 1. designating or of a subfamily of Altaic languages, including Turkish 2. designating or of the peoples who speak any of these languages

Turkish (tur′kish) *adj.* of Turkey, the Turks, their language, etc. —*n.* the Turkic language of Turkey

Turkish bath 1. a public bath in which the bather, after a period of heavy perspiration in a room of hot air or steam, is washed and massaged 2. [*sometimes pl.*] an establishment for such baths

Turkish coffee very strong, black, sweetened coffee

Turkish delight a jelly-like sweet, usually cube-shaped, delicately flavoured and covered in icing sugar

Turkish towel [*also* t-] a thick cotton towel of terry cloth

turmeric (tur′mər ik) *n.* [< ML. *terra merita*, deserving earth] 1. an East Indian plant whose rhizome in powdered form is used as a yellow dye, seasoning, etc. 2. powder made from this

turmoil (tur′moil) *n.* [< ?] a very excited or confused condition; tumult; uproar

turn (turn) *vt.* [ult. < Gr. *tornos*, lathe] 1. to make (a wheel, etc.) move about a centre; rotate 2. to move round [to turn a key] 3. to do (a somersault, etc.) 4. to give a rounded shape to, as on a lathe 5. to give a graceful form to [to turn a compliment] 6. to change the position or direction of 7. to ponder (often with *over*) 8. to bend, fold, twist, etc. 9. to reverse; invert [to turn pages, a collar, the soil, etc.] 10. to make topsy-turvy 11. to upset (the stomach) 12. to deflect; divert 13. to convert or persuade 14. to go round (a corner, etc.) 15. to reach or pass (a certain age, amount, etc.) 16. to drive, set, let go, etc. in some way [the dog was turned loose] 17. to direct, point, aim, etc. [thoughts turned to the past] 18. to put to a specified use [he turned his hand to writing] 19. to change from one form, condition, etc. to another [to turn cream into butter] 20. to exchange for [to turn produce into hard cash] 21. to translate 22. to derange, distract, or infatuate 23. to make sour 24. to affect in some way —*vi.* 1. to rotate, revolve, pivot, etc. 2. to reel; whirl [my head is turning] 3. to become curved or bent 4. to become reversed 5. to become upset, as the stomach 6. to change or reverse one's or its course or direction [the tide turned] 7. to refer (*to*) 8. to go or apply (*to*) for help 9. to direct one's attention, abilities, etc. [he turned to music] 10. to make a sudden attack (*on* or *upon*) 11. to reverse one's feelings, allegiance, etc. [he turned against his sister] 12. to depend or hinge (*on* or *upon*) 13. to become [to turn bitter with age] 14. to change into another form 15. to become sour, etc. 16. to change colour, as leaves in the autumn —*n.* 1. a turning round; rotation 2. a single twist, coil, winding, etc. 3. a musical ornament of four tones, with the tones above and below the principal tone alternating with it 4. a change or reversal of position, course, or direction 5. a short walk or ride around an area, as for exercise 6. the place where a change in direction occurs; bend; curve; angle or corner 7. a change in trend, events, health, etc. 8. the time of change [the turn of the century] 9. a sudden, brief shock 10. an action or deed [a good turn] 11. a spell of activity 12. an attack of illness, dizziness, etc. 13. the right, duty, or chance to do something [his turn to bat] 14. an act in a variety show 15. a distinctive form, manner, detail, etc. [a quaint turn of speech] 16. natural inclination —**at every turn** constantly —**by turns** one after another in regular order —**in turn** in proper sequence or succession —**out of turn** 1. not in proper sequence or order 2. imprudently [to talk out of turn] —**take turns** to speak, do, etc. one after another in regular order —**to a turn** perfectly —**turn and turn about** alternately —**turn down** 1. to reject (the request, etc. of someone) **2.** to lessen the volume of **3.** to fold down (a page, sheet, etc.) —**turn in 1.** to deliver; hand in **2.** to inform on, as to the police **3.** to give back **4.** [Colloq.] to go to bed **5.** [Colloq.] to give up —**turn off 1.** *a)* to leave (a road, etc.) *b)* to branch off: said of a road, etc. **2.** to stop from functioning **3.** to stop displaying suddenly [to *turn off* a smile] **4.** [Slang] to cause (someone) to become uninterested, annoyed, etc. —**turn on 1.** to start; make go on or start functioning **2.** to display suddenly [to *turn on* the charm] **3.** [Slang] to stimulate with or as with a psychedelic drug —**turn out 1.** to put out (a light) **2.** to put outside **3.** to dismiss **4.** to come or gather [to *turn out* for a picnic] **5.** to produce **6.** to result **7.** to prove to be **8.** to become **9.** to equip, dress, etc. **10.** [Colloq.] to get out of bed **11.** to clean out the contents of [he *turned out* his pockets] —**turn over 1.** to change or reverse the position of **2.** to change one's position **3.** to begin, or make begin, to operate, as an engine **4.** to consider **5.** to hand over —**turn up 1.** to fold back or over upon itself **2.** to lift up or turn face up **3.** to increase the speed, intensity, etc. of, as by turning a control **4.** to have an upward direction **5.** to happen **6.** to arrive **7.** to be found —**turn′er** *n.*

turnabout *n.* **1.** a turning about, as to face the other way **2.** a shift or reversal of allegiance, opinion, etc.

TURNBUCKLE

turnbuckle *n.* a mechanical device with a swivel at one end and a thread at the other to enable a threaded wire or rope to be tightened

turncoat *n.* a renegade; traitor

turndown *adj.* **1.** that can be turned down **2.** having the upper part folded down [a *turndown* collar]

turning *n.* **1.** the action of a person or thing that turns **2.** *a)* a road that joins another *b)* the point where this occurs **3.** the process of shaping things on a lathe

turning circle the smallest circle in which it is possible to turn a motor vehicle round in one forward movement

turning point a point in time at which a decisive change occurs; crisis

turnip (tur′nip) *n.* [< L. *napus*, turnip] **1.** *a)* a plant of the cabbage family, with edible, hairy leaves and a roundish, light-coloured root used as a vegetable *b)* same as SWEDE **2.** the root of either of these plants

turnkey (turn′kē′) *n.*, *pl.* **-keys′** a warder; jailer

turnout *n.* **1.** *a)* a gathering of people, as for a meeting *b)* the number of people **2.** an amount produced **3.** a carriage with its horse or horses **4.** a set of clothes

turnover *n.* **1.** *a)* the amount of business done during a given period *b)* the selling out and replacing of a stock of goods **2.** a small, semi-circular pastry made by folding one half of the crust over the other with a filling in between **3.** the rate at which staff leave a firm, occupation, etc., and have to be replaced **4.** a turning over; upset

turnpike *n.* [ME. *turnpyke*, spiked road barrier] **1.** *same as* TOLLGATE **2.** [U.S.] a road, esp. an expressway, for the use of which a toll is charged

turnstile *n.* a post with revolving horizontal bars, used at an entrance to admit persons one at a time

turntable *n.* **1.** a platform for supporting a gramophone record being played **2.** a platform carrying tracks to turn a locomotive round

turnup *n.* something turned up, specif., a turned-up fold at the bottom of a trouser leg —**a turnup for the book** [Colloq.] an unexpected happening

turpentine (tur′pən tīn′) *n.* [< Gr. *terebinthos*, a tree yielding turpentine] **1.** any of the various oleoresins obtained from pines and other coniferous trees: in full, **gum turpentine 2.** a colourless, volatile oil distilled from such oleoresins and used in paints, etc.: in full, **spirits (or oil) of turpentine**

turpitude (tur′pə tyōod′) *n.* [< L. *turpis*, vile] the condition of being wicked, evil, or depraved

turps (turps) *n.pl.* [*with sing. v.*] same as TURPENTINE (*sense* 2)

turquoise (tur′kwoiz) *n.* [< OFr. *turqueis*, Turkish] **1.** a greenish-blue, semiprecious stone, a phosphate of aluminium and copper **2.** a greenish blue —*adj.* greenish-blue

turret (tur′it) *n.* [see TOWER] **1.** a small tower projecting from a building, usually at a corner **2.** a low, armoured, usually revolving, towerlike structure for guns, as on a warship, tank, etc. **3.** an attachment for a lathe, etc., consisting of a block holding several cutting tools, which may be rotated to present any of the tools to the work —**tur′reted** *adj.*

turtle (tur′t′l) *n.* [< Fr. *tortue*, tortoise] **1.** any of various land and water reptiles having a toothless beak and a soft body encased in a hard shell into which, in most species, it can pull its head, tail, and four legs: popularly, the term is restricted to the marine species, land species being usually called *tortoise* **2.** the flesh of some turtles, used as food —**turn turtle** to turn upside down

turtledove (tur′t′l duv′) *n.* [< L. *turtur*, echoic] any of several wild doves noted for their sad cooing and their devotion to their mates

turtleneck *n.* **1.** a round, high, snugly fitting collar on a sweater, etc. **2.** a sweater, etc. with such a neck

tusk (tusk) *n.* [OE. *tucs*] in elephants, wild boars, etc., a long, pointed tooth, usually one of a pair, that sticks out of the mouth —**tusked** *adj.* —**tusk′like′** *adj.*

tussle (tus′'l) *n., vi.* **-sled, -sling** [< ME. *tusen,* to pull] struggle; wrestle; scuffle

tussock (tus′ək) *n.* [< ?] a thick tuft or clump of grass, twigs, etc. —**tus′socky** *adj.*

tut (tut) *interj., n.* an exclamation of impatience, annoyance, etc. —*vi.* **tut′ted, tut′ting** to utter "tuts"

tutelage (tyoot′əl ij) *n.* [< L. *tutela,* protection] **1.** guardianship; care, protection, etc. **2.** teaching **3.** a being under a guardian or tutor —**tu′telary** *adj.*

tutor (tyoot′ər) *n.* [< L. *tueri,* to guard] **1.** a private teacher who usually teaches one student at a time **2.** in some universities, etc., *a)* a member of staff in charge of the studies of a number of students *b)* a member of staff responsible for the general welfare of a number of students —*vt.* to act as a tutor to; esp., to teach (students) one at a time —*vi.* to act as a tutor —**tu′torage, tu′torship′** *n.*

tutorial (tyoo tôr′ē əl) *n.* a period of intensive tuition given by a tutor to an individual student or a small group of students —*adj.* of a tutor

tutti (toot′ē) *adj.* [It.] *Music* for all instruments or voices

tutti-frutti (toot′ē froot′ē) *n.* [It., all fruits] ice cream or other sweet food containing bits of candied fruits

tutu (too′too) *n.* [Fr.] a very short, full, projecting skirt worn by women ballet dancers

tu-whit tu-whoo (too wit′too woo′) the sound made by an owl

tuxedo (tuk sē′dō) *n., pl.* **-dos** [< country club near *Tuxedo* Lake, New York State] [U.S.] a dinner jacket

TV (tē′vē′) *n., pl.* **TVs, TV's** television or a television receiving set

twaddle (twod′'l) *n.* [prob. akin to TATTLE] foolish, empty talk or writing —*vt., vi.* **-dled, -dling** to talk or write in a foolish manner

twain (twān) *n., adj.* [OE. *twegen*] archaic *var. of* TWO

twang (twaŋ) *n.* [echoic] **1.** a quick, sharp, vibrating sound, as of a plucked string **2.** *a)* a sharp, nasal speech sound *b)* a dialect using such sounds —*vi., vt.* **1.** to make or cause to make a twang, as a bowstring, banjo, etc. **2.** to speak or say with a twang —**twang′y** *adj.*

'twas (twoz; *unstressed* twəz) it was

twat (twot) *n.* [< ?] **1.** [Vulg.] the female genitals **2.** [Vulg. Slang] a stupid person

tweak (twēk) *vt.* [OE. *twiccan,* to twitch] to give a sudden, twisting pinch to (someone's nose, etc.) —*n.* such a pinch

twee (twē) *adj.* [< *tweet,* child's pronun. of SWEET] [Colloq.] affectedly pretty, dainty, or quaint

tweed (twēd) *n.* [< misreading of *tweel,* Scot. form of TWILL] **1.** a wool fabric with a rough surface, in a twill weave of two or more colours **2.** [*pl.*] clothes of tweed

tweedy *adj.* **-ier, -iest 1.** of or like tweed **2.** having the heartiness, fondness for the outdoors, etc. of a person given to wearing tweeds —**tweed′iness** *n.*

'tween (twēn) *prep.* [Poet.] between

tweet (twēt) *n., interj.* [echoic] the thin, chirping sound of a small bird —*vi.* to make this sound

twee-talig (twēə′tä′ləkh) *adj.* [< Afrik.] [S Afr.] bilingual

tweeter *n.* a small, high-fidelity loudspeaker for reproducing high-frequency sounds: cf. WOOFER

tweezers (twē′zərz) *n.pl.* [*with sing. or pl. v.*] [< Fr. *étui,* case] small pincers for plucking out hairs, handling little objects, etc.: also **pair of tweezers**

twelfth (twelfth) *adj.* [OE. *twelfta*] **1.** preceded by eleven others in a series; 12th **2.** designating any of the twelve equal parts of something —*n.* **1.** the one following the eleventh **2.** any of the twelve equal parts of something; 1/12

Twelfth Day the twelfth day (Jan. 6) after Christmas; Epiphany: the evening before, or sometimes the evening of, this day is called **Twelfth Night**

twelfth man a reserve player in a cricket team

twelve (twelv) *adj., n.* [OE. *twelf*] two more than ten; 12; XII —**the Twelve** the Twelve Apostles —**twelve′fold** *adj., adv.*

Twelve Apostles the twelve disciples chosen by Jesus to go forth to teach the gospel

twelvemonth *n.* a year

twelve-tone (twelv′tōn′) *adj.* *Music* designating or of a system of composition in which the twelve tones of the chromatic scale are arranged as a basis for further thematic development

twenty (twen′tē) *adj., n., pl.* **-ties** [OE. *twegentig*] two times ten; 20; XX —**the twenties** the numbers or years, as of a century, from twenty to twenty-nine —**twen′tieth** *adj., n.*

'twere (twur) [Poet.] it were

twerp (twurp) *n.* [< ?] [Colloq.] a person regarded as insignificant, contemptible, etc.

twice (twīs) *adv.* [OE. *twiga*] two times

twiddle (twid′'l) *vt.* **-dled, -dling** [< ?] to twirl or play with lightly —**twiddle one's thumbs 1.** to twirl one's thumbs idly around one another **2.** to be idle —**twid′dler** *n.* —**twid′dly** *adj.*

twig (twig) *n.* [OE. *twigge*] a small branch or shoot of a tree or shrub —*vi., vt.* **twigged, twigging** [Colloq.] to understand (something) —**twigged** *adj.* —**twig′gy** *adj.*

twilight (twī′līt′) *n.* [ME.] **1.** *a)* the soft, dim light just after sunset or, sometimes, just before sunrise *b)* the period from sunset to dark **2.** any growing darkness **3.** a condition of gradual decline —*adj.* of or like twilight

twilight zone 1. an inner city area that has deteriorated **2.** any indefinite condition or area

twilit (twī′lit) *adj.* full of or bathed in the soft, dim light of twilight

twill (twil) *n.* [OE. *twilic,* double-threaded] **1.** a cloth woven so as to have parallel diagonal lines or ribs **2.** the pattern of this weave —**twilled** *adj.*

'twill (twil) [Poet.] it will

twin (twin) *adj.* [OE. *twinn*, double] **1.** consisting of, or being one of a pair of, two separate, similar things **2.** being two, or either of two, that have been born at the same birth —*n.* **1.** either of two born at the same birth : twins are either *identical* (produced from the same ovum) or *fraternal* (produced from separate ova) **2.** either of two persons or things very much alike —*vi., vt* twinned, twin'ning to pair or be paired

twine (twin) *n.* [OE. *twin*] a strong thread, string, or cord of strands twisted together —*vt.* twined, twin'ing **1.** to twist together; intertwine **2.** to wreathe or wind (one thing) around or with another **3.** to enfold, embrace, etc. —*vi.* **1.** to twist, interlace, etc. **2.** to twist and turn

twin-engined (twin'en'jənd) *adj.* powered by two engines: said of an aeroplane: also **twin'-en'gine**

twinge (twinj) *n.* [OE. *twengan*, squeeze] **1.** a sudden, brief, darting pain or pang **2.** a sudden, brief feeling of remorse, shame, etc. —*vt., vi.* twinged, twing'ing to have or cause to have a sudden, brief, darting pain or pang

twinkle (twin'k'l) *vi.* -kled, -kling [OE. *twinclian*] **1.** to shine with quick flashes of light at intervals, as some stars **2.** to light up, as with amusement: said of the eyes **3.** to move about quickly and lightly, as a dancer's feet —*vt.* to make twinkle —*n.* **1.** a quick flash of light **2.** a quick flash of amusement, etc. in the eye **3.** a wink of the eye —**twin'-kler** *n.*

twinkling *n.* **1.** the action of a thing that twinkles **2.** *a)* the winking of an eye *b)* an instant

twinset (twin'set') *n.* a woman's matching cardigan and jumper

twin towns two towns in different countries which have created social and cultural links

twirl (twurl) *vt., vi.* [< ?] **1.** to rotate rapidly; spin **2.** to whirl in a circle **3.** to twist or coil —*n.* a twirling or being twirled —**twirl'er** *n.*

twist (twist) *vt.* [< OE. *twist*, rope] **1.** to cause to turn round **2.** *a)* to contort or distort (the face, etc.) *b)* to cause to be malformed **3.** to wind (strands of cotton, silk, etc.) around one another **4.** to wreathe; twine **5.** to wind (thread, rope, etc.) around something **6.** to give spiral shape to **7.** *a)* to subject to torsion *b)* to wrench; sprain **8.** to distort the meaning of **9.** to make (one's or its way) by turning one way and then another **10.** to break off by turning the end (often with *off*) —*vi.* **1.** to undergo twisting **2.** to spiral, coil, twine, etc. (*round* or *about* something) **3.** to revolve or rotate **4.** to turn to one side **5.** to wind or meander, as a path **6.** to squirm; writhe —*n.* **1.** a twisting or being twisted **2.** a knot, etc. made by twisting **3.** a turn; bend **4.** a place at which something twists **5.** an

eccentricity; quirk **6.** distortion, as of meaning **7.** a different or unexpected meaning, slant, etc. **8.** stress due to torsion, or the degree of this **9.** a contortion, as of the face **10.** a wrench or sprain **11.** a strong, closely twisted silk thread **12.** a twisted roll of tobacco leaves **13.** a loaf of bread made of twisted pieces of dough **14.** a sliver of peel from a lemon, etc. twisted and added to a drink —**round the twist** [Slang] mad —**twist a person's arm 1.** to hurt someone by wrenching his arm **2.** to bring moral pressure to bear on someone in order to compel him to do something —**twist (a person) round one's little finger** to have complete dominance over (a person) —**twist'y** *adj.*

twister *n.* **1.** a swindler; cheat **2.** a person or thing that twists

twit¹ (twit) *vt.* **twit'ted, twit'ting** [OE. *ætwitan*] to reproach, tease, taunt, etc., esp. by reminding of a fault —*n.* a reproach or taunt

twit² *n.* [? < prec.] [Colloq.] a foolish, contemptible person

twitch (twich) *vt., vi.* [< OE. *twiccian*, pluck] **1.** to pull (at) with a quick, slight jerk **2.** to move with a quick, slight jerk, often due to muscle spasm —*n.* **1.** a quick, slight jerk **2.** a sudden, quick motion, esp. one caused by muscle spasm

twitter (twit'ər) *vi.* [echoic] **1.** to make a series of light, sharp vocal sounds; chirp, as birds do **2.** *a)* to chatter *b)* to giggle —*vt.* to say in a twittering manner —*n.* **1.** the act or sound of twittering **2.** a condition of trembling excitement —**twit'-tery** *adj.*

'twixt (twikst) *prep.* [Poet.] betwixt

two (tōō) *adj., n.* [OE. *twa*] totalling one more than one; 2; II —**in two** in two parts —**put two and two together** to reach an obvious conclusion by considering several facts together —**that makes two of us** [Colloq.] that applies equally to me

two-edged *adj.* **1.** that has two cutting edges **2.** that can have two different meanings, as a remark

two-faced (tōō'fāst') *adj.* **1.** deceitful; hypocritical **2.** having two faces —**two'-fac'edly** (-fās'id lē) *adv.*

twofold *adj.* **1.** having two parts **2.** having twice as much or as many —*adv.* twice as much or as many

two-handed (tōō'han'did) *adj.* **1.** that needs to be used or wielded with both hands **2.** worked by two people **3.** for two people, as a card game

twopence (tōō'pens'; *for 3 also* tup''ns) *n.* **1.** the sum of two pennies **2.** a British coin worth one fiftieth of a pound **3.** something of little value

twopenny (tup'ə nē, tup'nē) *adj.* **1.** cheap; worthless **2.** worth or costing twopence

two-piece (tōō'pēs') *adj.* consisting of two separate parts [a *two-piece* bathing suit] —*n.* such a garment

two-ply *adj.* **1.** having two thicknesses, layers, strands, etc. **2.** woven double

two-sided *adj.* **1.** having two sides **2.** having two aspects *[a two-sided question]*

twosome *n.* **1.** two people; a couple **2.** *Golf* a game involving two players

two-step *n.* **1.** a dance in 2/4 time **2.** a piece of music for this dance

two-time *vt.* **-timed´, -tim´ing** [Colloq.] to deceive (someone) by carrying on a relationship with another —**two´-tim´er** *n.*

'twould (twood) [Poet.] it would

two-way *adj.* **1.** moving, permitting movement, or operating in either of two opposite directions **2.** involving reciprocity *[a two-way cultural exchange]* **3.** used for both transmitting and receiving

-ty¹ (tē, ti) [< L. *-tas*] *a suffix meaning* quality, condition of *[novelty]*

-ty² (tē, ti) [OE. *-tig*] *a suffix meaning* tens, times ten

tycoon (tīkoon´) *n.* [< Chin. *ta*, great + *kiun*, prince] a wealthy and powerful industrialist, financier, etc.

tyee (tī´ē´) *n.* [< Amlnd.] [Canad.] chief; champion; boss

tyee salmon *same as* CHINOOK SALMON

tying (tī´iŋ) *prp. of* TIE

tyke (tīk) *n.* [ON. *tik*, bitch] **1.** [Chiefly N Dial.] *a)* a dog, esp. a mongrel *b)* a boor **2.** [Slang] a Yorkshireman: often derogatory Also sp. **tike**

tympani (tim´pə nē) *n.pl., sing.* **-no´** (-nō´) *var. of* TIMPANI —**tym´panist** *n.*

tympanic membrane (tim pan´ik) a thin membrane that separates the middle ear from the external ear and vibrates when struck by sound waves

tympanum (tim´pə nəm) *n., pl.* **-nums, -na** [L. < Gr. *tympanon*, a drum] **1.** *Anat. same as: a)* MIDDLE EAR *b)* TYMPANIC MEMBRANE **2.** a drum or drumhead —**tympan´ic** (-pan´ik) *adj.*

Tynwald (tin´wəld) [< ON. *thing*, assembly + *vollr*, field] the parliament of the Isle of Man

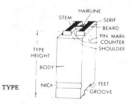

TYPE

labels: HAIRLINE, STEM, SERIF, BEARD, PIN MARK, COUNTER, SHOULDER, TYPE HEIGHT, BODY, NICK, FEET, GROOVE

type (tīp) *n.* [< Gr. *typos*, figure] **1.** a class, group, etc. having characteristics in common **2.** the characteristic form, plan, style, etc. of a particular class or group **3.** one that is representative or characteristic of a class or group **4.** a model; pattern **5.** a person, thing, or event that represents another, esp. another that it is thought will appear later **6.** the device on either side of a coin **7.** [Colloq.] a person *[he's a strange type]*

8. *Printing a)* a rectangular piece of metal or, sometimes, wood, with a raised letter, figure, etc. in reverse on its upper end *b)* such pieces collectively *c)* a printed or photographically reproduced character or characters —*vt.* **typed, typ´ing 1.** to write with a typewriter; typewrite **2.** to classify according to type —*vi.* to use a typewriter

-type (tīp) [see TYPE] *a combining form meaning:* **1.** example *[prototype]* **2.** print, printing type *[monotype]*

typecast (tīp´kast´) *vt.* **-cast´, -cast´ing** to cast (an actor) repeatedly in the same type of part

typeface *n. same as* FACE (*n.* 9)

type-script *n.* any typed document

typescript *n.* any typed document

typesetter *n.* **1.** a person who sets type; compositor **2.** a machine for setting type —**type´set´ting** *n., adj.*

typewrite *vt., vi.* **-wrote´, -writ´ten, -writ´ing** to write with a typewriter: now usually shortened to *type*

typewriter *n.* a writing machine with a keyboard for reproducing letters, figures, etc. that resemble printed ones

typhoid (tī´foid) *n.* [< TYPHUS] an infectious disease caused by a bacillus and acquired by eating food or drinking water contaminated by excreta: it causes fever, intestinal disorders, etc.: in full, **typhoid fever**

typhoon (tīfoon´) *n.* [< Chin. dial. *tai-fung*, great wind] any violent tropical cyclone originating in the W Pacific, esp. in the South China Sea —**typhon´ic** (-fon´ik) *adj.*

typhus (tī´fəs) *n.* [< Gr. *typhos*, fever] an acute infectious disease caused by a rickettsia transmitted to man by fleas, lice, etc., and causing fever, red spots on the skin, etc.: in full, **typhus fever** —**ty´phous** *adj.*

typical (tip´ik'l) *adj.* **1.** having the distinguishing characteristics, qualities, etc. of a class, group, etc. **2.** characteristic **3.** symbolic —**typ´ically** *adv.*

typify (tip´ə fī´) *vt.* **-fied´, -fy´ing** [see TYPE] **1.** to be typical of **2.** to be a type or emblem of; symbolize

typist (tīp´ist) *n.* a person whose work is typing

typo (tī´pō) *n., pl.* **-pos** [Colloq.] **1.** a typographer **2.** [U.S.] a typographical error

typo- [see TYPE] *a combining form meaning* type

typography (tīpog´rə fē) *n.* [see TYPE- & -GRAPHY] **1.** the art or process of setting and arranging type for printing **2.** the arrangement, style, or appearance of matter printed from type —**typog´rapher** *n.* —**ty´pograph´ical** *adj.*

tyrannical (ti ran´i k'l) *adj.* **1.** arbitrary; despotic **2.** harsh, cruel, unjust, etc. —**tyran´nically** *adv.*

tyrannize (tir´ə nīz´) *vi.* **-nized´, -niz´ing 1.** to govern as a tyrant **2.** to use authority harshly or cruelly —*vt.* to oppress —**tyr′-anniz′er** *n.*

tyrannosaur (ti ran′ə sôr′) *n.* [< Gr. *tyrannos*, tyrant + -SAURUS] any of various huge, twofooted, flesh-eating dinosaurs of the Cretaceous Period in N America : also **tyran′nosaur′us**

tyrannous (tir′ə nəs) *adj.* tyrannical; despotic, oppressive, unjust, etc. —**tyr′annously** *adv.*

tyranny (tir′ə nē) *n., pl.* **-rannies** 1. the office, authority, government, etc. of a tyrant, or absolute ruler 2. oppressive and unjust government 3. very cruel and unjust use of power 4. a tyrannical act

tyrant (tī′rənt) *n.* [< Gr. *tyrannos*] 1. an absolute ruler 2. a cruel, oppressive ruler

tyre (tīər) *n.* [prob. < ME. *atir*, equipment] a hoop of iron or rubber, or a rubber tube filled with air, fixed around the wheel of a vehicle to form a tread

tyre-gauge *n.* a small instrument for measuring air pressure in tyres

Tyrian (tir′ē ən) *adj.* designating or of Tyre, a seaport in SW Lebanon, and centre of ancient Phoenician culture

Tyrian purple (or **dye**) a purple or crimson dye used by the ancient Romans and Greeks : it was made from certain molluscs, orig. at Tyre

tyro (tī′rō) *n., pl.* **-ros** [< L. *tiro*, recruit] a beginner in learning something; novice

tzar (zär) *n.* *var. of* TSAR —**tzar′dom** *n.* —**tzar′ism** *n.* —**tzar′ist** *adj., n.*

tzarina (zä rē′nə) *n.* *var. of* TSARINA : also **tzarit′za** (-rit′sə)

tzetze fly (tset′sē) *var. of* TSETSE FLY

U

U, u (yōō) *n., pl.* **U's, u's** the twenty-first letter of the English alphabet

U (yōō) *n.* **1.** something shaped like U **2.** *Cinema* [< *universal*] a film to which a person of any age may be admitted —*adj.* [Colloq.] of the upper class, as supposedly characterized by behaviour, tastes, etc.

U *Chem.* uranium

U.A.R. United Arab Republic

ubiquitous (yōō bik′wə təs) *adj.* [see ff.] present, or seeming to be present, everywhere at the same time

ubiquity (yōō bik′wə tē) *n.* [< L. *ubique,* everywhere] the state, fact, or capacity of being, or seeming to be, everywhere at the same time

U-boat (yōō′bōt′) *n.* [< G. *Unterseeboot,* undersea boat] a German submarine

u.c. *Printing* upper case

U.C.C.A. Universities Central Council on Admissions

udder (ud′ər) *n.* [OE. *udr*] a mammary gland with two or more teats, as in cows

U.D.I. unilateral declaration of independence

UEFA (yōō ā′fə) Union of European Football Associations

UFO (yōō′fō, yōō′ef ō′) *n., pl.* **UFOs, UFO's** [*u(nidentified) f(lying) o(bject)*] any of a number of unidentified objects reported to have been seen flying at varying heights and speeds and variously regarded as hallucinations, spacecraft from another planet, etc.

ugh (ŏŏkh, *etc.*) *interj.* [echoic] an exclamation of disgust, horror, etc.

ugli (ug′lē) *n.* [< UGLY] a Jamaican citrus fruit that is a cross between a grapefruit, orange, and tangerine

ugly (ug′lē) *adj.* **-lier, -liest** [< ON. *uggr,* fear] **1.** unpleasing to look at **2.** vile, offensive, etc. *[an ugly lie]* **3.** ominous; dangerous *[ugly storm clouds]* **4.** [Colloq.] ill-tempered *[an ugly disposition]* —**ug′liness** *n.*

ugly duckling [< story by H. C. Andersen] a plain child or unpromising thing that in time becomes beautiful, important, etc.

uh (u, un) *interj.* **1.** *same as* HUH **2.** a prolonged sound made in speaking, as while searching for a word

UHF, U.H.F., uhf, u.h.f. ultrahigh frequency

uh-huh (ə hu′) *interj.* an exclamation indicating: a) an affirmative response b) that one is listening attentively

UHT ultra heat treated

Uitlander (āt′lan′dər) *n.* [Afrik. < Du. *uit,* out + *land,* land] in South Africa, a foreigner; specif., one not a Boer in the Transvaal

U.K. United Kingdom

U.K.A.E.A. United Kingdom Atomic Energy Authority

ukase (yōō kāz′) *n.* [Russ. *ukaz,* edict] **1.** in Czarist Russia, an imperial decree **2.** any official, esp. arbitrary, decree

Ukrainian (yōō krā′nē ən) *adj.* of the Ukraine, its people, their language, etc. —*n.* **1.** a native of the Ukraine **2.** the Slavic language of the Ukrainians

ukulele (yōō′kə lā′lē) *n.* [Haw., flea] a musical instrument with four strings, like a small guitar

ulcer (ul′sər) *n.* [L. *ulcus*] an open sore that festers, damages the tissue, etc.

ulcerate *vt., vi.* **-at′ed, -at′ing** to make or become ulcerous —**ul′cera′tion** *n.*

ulcerous *adj.* of, like, or characterized by an ulcer or ulcers

-ule (yōōl, yool) [< L.] *a suffix meaning* little *[sporule]*

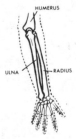

HUMERUS

ULNA ——RADIUS

ulna (ul′nə) *n., pl.* **-nae** (-nē), **-nas** [L., elbow] **1.** the larger of the two bones of the forearm, on the side opposite the thumb **2.** a corresponding bone in the forelimb of other vertebrates —**ul′nar** *adj.*

ulster (ul′stər) *n.* [< *Ulster,* in Ireland] a long, loose, heavy overcoat

Ulsterman *n.* a native of Ulster —**Ulsterwoman** *n.fem.*

ult. **1.** ultimate(ly) **2.** ultimo

ulterior (ul tēər′ē ər) *adj.* [L., beyond] **1.** beyond what is openly seen, said, or made known *[an ulterior motive]* **2.** lying beyond or on the further side

ultimate (ul′tə mit) *adj.* [< L. *ultimus,* last] **1.** beyond which it is impossible to go; farthest **2.** final; last **3.** fundamental; primary **4.** greatest possible

—n. something ultimate [the *ultimate* in pleasure] **—ul′timately adv.**

ultima Thule (ul′ti mə thōō′lē) [L.] **1.** among the ancients, the northernmost region of the world **2.** any far-off, unknown region

ultimatum (ul′tə māt′əm) **n.**, pl. **-tums**, **-ta** [see ULTIMATE] a final offer or demand, esp. with a threat to break off relations, use force, etc.

ultimo (ul′tə mō′) **adv.** [L. *ultimo* (*mense*), (in the) last (month)] in the preceding month

ultra (ul′trə) **adj.** [L., beyond] going beyond the usual limit; extreme

ultra- [L.] *a prefix meaning:* **1.** beyond [*ultraviolet*] **2.** to an extreme degree [*ultramodern*] **3.** beyond the range of [*ultramicroscopic*]

ultraconservative (ul′trə kən sur′və tiv) **adj.** conservative to an extreme degree **—n.** an ultraconservative person

ultrahigh frequency any radio frequency between 300 and 3000 megahertz

ultramarine (ul′trə mə rēn′) **n.** [see ULTRA- & MARINE] **1.** a blue pigment orig. made from powdered lapis lazuli **2.** a deep blue **—adj.** deep-blue

ultramontane (ul′trə mon′tān) **adj.** [< L. *ultra*, beyond + *mons*, mountain] **1.** beyond the mountains, specif., the Alps **2.** of the doctrine of papal supremacy **—n. 1.** a person living south of the Alps **2.** a person holding ultramontane principles **—ul′tramon′tanism** (-tə niz′m) **n.**

ultrasonic (ul′trə son′ik) **adj.** [ULTRA- + SONIC] designating or of a frequency of mechanical vibrations above the range audible to the human ear **—ul′trason′ically adv.**

ultrasonics n.pl. [*with sing. v.*] the science dealing with ultrasonic phenomena

ultrasound (ul′trə sound′) **n.** ultrasonic waves, used in surgery, etc.

ultraviolet (ul′trə vī′ə lit) **adj.** lying just beyond the violet end of the visible spectrum **—n.** ultraviolet radiation

ululate (yōōl′yoo lāt′) **vi. -lat′ed, -lat′ing** [< L. *ululare*] **1.** to howl or hoot **2.** to wail **—ul′ula′tion n.**

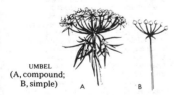

UMBEL
(A, compound;
B, simple)

umbel (um′b'l) **n.** [L. *umbella*, parasol] a cluster of flowers with stalks of nearly equal length which spring from the same point **—um′bellate adj.**

umbelliferous (um′be lif′ər əs) **adj.** [< UMBEL + -FEROUS] having an umbel, as plants of the parsley family

umber (um′bər) **n.** [< It. (*terra d′*)*ombra*, (earth of) shade] **1.** a kind of earth containing oxides of manganese and iron, used as a pigment : raw umber is yellowish-brown ; burnt umber is reddish-brown **2.** a yellowish-brown or reddish-brown colour **—adj.** of the colour of umber

umbilical (um bil′i k'l, um′bi li′k'l) **adj.** of the navel **—n. 1.** *same as* UMBILICAL CORD **2.** any vital link or connection

umbilical cord a cordlike structure that connects a foetus with the placenta : it is severed at birth

umbilicus (um bil′i kəs) **n.**, pl. **-ci′**(-sī′) [L.] *same as* NAVEL

umbra (um′brə) **n.**, pl. **-brae** (-brē), **-bras** [L.] **1.** a shadow **2.** the dark cone of shadow projecting from a planet or satellite on the side opposite the sun

umbrage (um′brij) **n.** [< L. *umbra*, a shade] offence or resentment [to take *umbrage* at a remark]

umbrella (um brel′ə) **n.** [< L. *umbra*, shade] **1.** cloth, plastic, etc. stretched over a folding radial frame at the top of a stick, carried for protection against the rain or sun **2.** any comprehensive, protective organization, alliance, etc. **—adj.** embracing a variety of items; comprehensive [delegates of various firms were included under the *umbrella* title "commercial"]

umbrella tree any of various trees that have an umbrellalike shape

umfazi (oom′fä′zē) **n.** [< Bantu] [S Afr.] a black married woman

umiak (ōō′mē ak′) **n.** [< Eskimo] an open Eskimo boat made of skins stretched on a wooden frame

umlaut (oom′lout) **n.** [G. < *um*, about + *Laut*, a sound] Linguis. **1.** a change in the sound of a vowel, caused by its assimilation to another vowel in the next syllable **2.** the diacritical mark (¨) placed over such a vowel, esp. in German

umlungu (oom′loon′goo) **n.** [< Bantu] [S Afr.] a white man : used esp. as a term of address

umpire (um′pīər) **n.** [< MFr. *nomper*, uneven, hence third person] **1.** an official who administers the rules of a game, as in cricket **2.** one who gives a decision in a dispute; arbiter **—vt., vi. -pired, -piring** to act as umpire (in or of)

umpteen (ump′tēn′) **adj.** [Colloq.] very many **—ump′teenth′ adj.**

'un (ən) **pron.** [Colloq.] one [that's a big *'un*]

un- (un; *unstressed, also* ən) [< OE.] *a prefix meaning:* **1.** not, lack of, the opposite of [*unhappy, untruth*] **2.** the reverse or removal of [*unfasten, unchain*]; sometimes *un-* is merely intensive [*unloosen*] The list at the bottom of the following pages includes many of the more common compounds formed with *un-* that do not have special meanings

UN, U.N. United Nations

unable (un ā′b'l) **adj.** not able; lacking the ability, means, or power to do something

unabridged (un′ə brijd′) **adj.** not abridged, or shortened

unaccountable (un′ə koun′tə b'l) **adj. 1.** that cannot be explained or accounted for; strange **2.** not responsible —**un′ac-count′ably** *adv.*

unadopted (un′ə dopt′id) *adj.* **1.** not adopted **2.** (of roads) not maintained by a local authority

unadvised (un′əd vīzd′) *adj.* **1.** thoughtlessly hasty; indiscreet **2.** without advice —**un′advis′edly** (-vīz′id lē) *adv.*

unaffected (un′ə fek′tid) *adj.* **1.** not influenced **2.** without affectation; sincere and natural —**un′affect′edly** *adv.*

unanimous (yōō nan′ə məs) *adj.* [< L. *unus,* one + *animus,* the mind] **1.** agreeing completely **2.** showing, or based on, complete agreement —**unanimity** (yōō′-nə nim′ə tē) *n.*

unapproachable (un′ə prōch′ə b'l) *adj.* **1.** not accessible, friendly, etc. **2.** having no rival or equal

unarmed (un′ärmd′) *adj.* having no weapons

unassailable (un′ə sāl′ə b'l) *adj.* **1.** that cannot be successfully attacked **2.** that cannot be successfully denied —**un′assail′-ably** *adv.*

unassuming (un′ə syōō′miŋ) *adj.* not pretentious or forward; modest —**un′as-sum′ingly** *adv.*

unattached (un′ə tacht′) *adj.* **1.** not fastened **2.** not connected with any organization **3.** not engaged or married

unaware (un′ə wâr′) *adj.* not aware or conscious [*unaware* of danger] —*adv.* same as UNAWARES

unawares *adv.* unexpectedly; by surprise

unbalanced (un′bal′ənst) *adj.* **1.** not balanced **2.** not sane

unbearable (un′bâar′ə b'l) *adj.* that cannot be endured

unbeaten (un′bēt′ən) *adj.* undefeated or unsurpassed

unbecoming (un′bi kum′iŋ) *adj.* not suited to one's appearance, status, character, etc. [*unbecoming* behaviour] —**un′becom′ingly** *adv.*

unbeknown (un′bi nōn′) *adj.* without one's knowledge (usually with *to*): also **un′-beknownst′**

unbelievable (un′bə lēv′ə b'l) *adj.* beyond belief; astounding; incredible —**un′-believ′ably** *adv.*

unbeliever *n.* **1.** a doubter **2.** a person who does not accept any religious belief

unbelieving *adj.* doubting; sceptical; incredulous —**un′believ′ingly** *adv.*

unbend (un′bend′) *vt., vi.* -bent′, -bend′-ing **1.** to make or become less tense, less formal, etc. **2.** to make or become straight again

unbending *adj.* **1.** rigid; stiff **2.** firm; resolute **3.** aloof; austere

unbidden (un′bid′'n) *adj.* **1.** not commanded **2.** not invited

unbind (un′bīnd′) *vt.* -bound, -bind′ing **1.** to untie; unfasten **2.** to release from restraints

unblushing (un′blush′iŋ) *adj.* shameless —**unblush′ingly** *adv.*

unbolt (un′bōlt′) *vt., vi.* to draw back the bolt or bolts of (a door, etc.); unbar; open

unborn (un′bôrn′) *adj.* **1.** not born **2.** still within the mother's womb **3.** yet to come or be; future

unbosom (un′booz′əm) *vt., vi.* to reveal (one's feelings, secrets, etc.) —**unbosom oneself** to express (oneself) openly about one's feelings, etc.

unbounded (un′boun′did) *adj.* **1.** without bounds or limits **2.** not restrained; uncontrolled

unbowed (un′boud′) *adj.* **1.** not bowed or bent **2.** not yielding; unsubdued

unbridled (un′brī′d'ld) *adj.* not controlled; unrestrained

unbroken (un′brō′k'n) *adj.* **1.** whole; intact **2.** not tamed **3.** uninterrupted **4.** not surpassed [an *unbroken* record]

unburden (un′bʉrd′'n) *vt.* **1.** to free from a burden **2.** to relieve (oneself or one's mind) by disclosing (something hard to bear)

uncalled-for (un kôld′fôr′) *adj.* unnecessary and out of place; impertinent

uncanny (un′kan′ē) *adj.* **1.** mysterious in an eerie way; weird **2.** so remarkable

unabashed	unalterable	unattended	unburied
unabated	unaltered	unattested	unburned
unabsorbed	unambiguous	unattractive	unburnt
unacademic	unambitious	unauthenticated	unbusinesslike
unacceptable	unamiable	unauthorized	uncaring
unaccommodating	unamusing	unavailable	uncarpeted
unaccompanied	unannounced	unavenged	unceasing
unaccomplished	unanswerable	unavowed	unchain
unaccounted-for	unapologetic	unawed	unchallenged
unacknowledged	unappealing	unbathed	unchangeable
unacquainted	unappeasable	unbefitting	unchanged
unadaptable	unappetizing	unbiased	unchaperoned
unadjustable	unappreciated	unbleached	uncharacteristic
unadorned	unappreciative	unblemished	uncharted
unadulterated	unarguable	unblinking	unchartered
unadventurous	unashamed	unblock	unchastened
unadvertised	unasked	unbound	unchecked
unaffiliated	unaspiring	unbreakable	unchilled
unafraid	unassigned	unbreathable	unchivalrous
unaided	unassimilated	unbridgeable	unclaimed
unalike	unassisted	unbruised	unclarified
unalloyed	unattainable	unbuilt	unclassified

as to seem unnatural —**uncan'nily** *adv.*
—**uncan'niness** *n.*
uncared-for (un'kãard'fôr') *adj.* neglected
unceremonious (un'ser ə mō'nē əs) *adj.*
1. informal 2. so curt or abrupt as to be discourteous
uncertain (un surt''n) *adj.* 1. *a*) not surely or certainly known *b*) not sure or certain in knowledge; doubtful 2. not definite; vague 3. not dependable or reliable 4. not steady or constant; varying —**uncer'tainty** *n.*
uncharitable (un'char'i tə b'l) *adj.* unforgiving, ungenerous, or faultfinding —**unchar'itableness** *n.* —**unchar'itably** *adv.*
unchristian (un'kris'chən) *adj.* 1. not practising a Christian religion 2. not in accord with the principles of Christianity
uncial (un'si əl) *adj.* [< L. *uncia*, an inch] designating or of a form of large, rounded letter used in manuscripts between 300 and 900 A.D. —*n.* an uncial letter or manuscript
uncircumcised (un'sur'kəm sīzd') *adj.* 1. not circumcised; specif., not Jewish 2. [Archaic] heathen
uncivil (un'siv''l) *adj.* 1. not civil or courteous; ill-mannered 2. [Obs.] not civilized; barbarous —**unciv'illy** *adv.*
unclasp (un'klãsp') *vt.* 1. to unfasten the clasp of 2. to release from a clasp —*vi.* to become unfastened
uncle (uŋ'k'l) *n.* [< L. *avunculus*] 1. the brother of one's father or mother 2. the husband of one's aunt 3. [Old Slang] a pawnbroker
unclean *adj.* 1. dirty; filthy 2. not pure according to religious laws 3. morally impure; unchaste
Uncle Sam [< abbrev. U.S.] [Colloq.] the U.S. government or people
unclose (un'klōz') *vt., vi.* -**closed', -clos'ing** to reveal
unclothe (un'klōth') *vt.* -**clothed' or -clad', -cloth'ing** to strip of or as of clothes; uncover

uncoil (un'koil') *vt., vi.* to unwind
uncomfortable (un'kumf'tər b'l) *adj.* 1. feeling discomfort 2. causing discomfort 3. ill at ease —**uncom'fortableness** *n.* —**uncom'fortably** *adv.*
uncommitted (un'kə mit'id) *adj.* 1. not bound to a specific opinion, cause, etc. 2. not having taken a position; neutral
uncommon (un kom'ən) *adj.* 1. rare; not usual 2. strange; remarkable
uncommunicative (un'kə myoo'ni kə tiv) *adj.* not communicative; reserved; taciturn
uncompromising (un kom'prə mī'ziŋ) *adj.* not yielding; firm; inflexible
unconcern (un'kən surn') *n.* 1. lack of interest; indifference 2. lack of concern, or worry
unconcerned *adj.* 1. not interested 2. not anxious 3. not involved —**un'concern'edly** (-sur'nid lē) *adv.*
unconditional (un'kən dish'ən 'l) *adj.* without conditions or stipulations —**un'condi'tionally** *adv.*
unconscionable (un kon'shən ə b'l) *adj.* 1. not guided or restrained by conscience; unscrupulous 2. unreasonable, excessive, etc. —**uncon'scionably** *adv.*
unconscious (un'kon'shəs) *adj.* 1. deprived of consciousness 2. not aware (*of*) 3. not realized or intended [*uncon'scious* humour] —**the unconscious** *Psychoanalysis* the sum of all memories, feelings, etc. of which the individual is not conscious but which influence his behaviour —**uncon'sciously** *adv.* —**uncon'sciousness** *n.*
unconstitutional (un'kon stə tyoo'shən 'l) *adj.* not in accordance with a constitution, as of a state —**un'constitu'tional'ity** (-shə nal'ə tē) *n.*
unconventional (un'kən ven'shən 'l) *adj.* not conforming to customary, formal, or accepted practices, standards, etc. —**un'conven'tional'ity** (-shə nal'ə tē) *n.*
uncork (un'kôrk') *vt.* to pull the cork out of
uncounted (un'koun'tid) *adj.* 1. not

uncleared	unconquered	uncurbed	undigested
unclog	unconsecrated	uncured	undignified
unclouded	unconsidered	uncurl	undiluted
uncluttered	unconsolidated	undamaged	undiminished
uncollected	unconstrained	undated	undimmed
uncollectible	uncontaminated	undecipherable	undiplomatic
uncoloured	uncontested	undeclared	undiscernible
uncombined	uncontrollable	undecorated	undischarged
uncomforted	uncontrolled	undefeated	undisciplined
uncommissioned	unconvinced	undefended	undisclosed
uncomplaining	unconvincing	undefiled	undiscouraged
uncompleted	uncooked	undemanding	undiscriminating
uncomplicated	uncooperative	undemocratic	undisguised
uncomplimentary	uncoordinated	undemonstrative	undismayed
uncomprehending	uncorrected	undependable	undisputed
unconcealed	uncorroborated	undeserving	undistinguished
unconfessed	uncountable	undesired	undisturbed
unconfined	uncritical	undestroyed	undivided
unconfirmed	uncross	undetected	undocumented
uncongenial	uncrowned	undeterred	undrinkable
unconnected	uncultivated	undeveloped	undutiful
unconquerable	uncultured	undeviating	undyed

counted **2.** too many to be counted; innumerable

uncouple (un'kup''l) *vt.* **-pled, -pling** to unfasten (things coupled); disconnect —*vi.* to become unfastened

uncouth (un kōōth') *adj.* [< OE. *un-*, not + *cunnan*, know] awkward; clumsy; boorish —**uncouth'ness** *n.*

uncover (un kuv'ər) *vt.* **1.** to disclose **2.** to remove the cover or protection from **3.** to remove the hat from (the head) —*vi.* to bare the head, as in showing respect

unction (unk'shən) *n.* [< L. *ungere*, anoint] **1.** *a)* the act of anointing, as in a religious ceremony *b)* the oil, etc. used **2.** anything that soothes **3.** *a)* a very earnest manner of speaking or behaving *b)* such a manner when it seems put on

unctuous (unk'tyōōəs) *adj.* [< L. *ungere*, anoint] **1.** oily or greasy **2.** characterized by a smug, smooth pretence of spiritual feeling or earnestness —**unc'tuousness** *n.*

undaunted (un'dôn'tid) *adj.* not afraid or discouraged

undeceive (un'di sēv') *vt.* **-ceived', -ceiv'ing** to cause to be no longer deceived, mistaken, or misled

undecided (un'di sīd'id) *adj.* **1.** not decided or settled **2.** not having come to a decision

undeniable (un'di nī'ə b'l) *adj.* that cannot be denied or disputed —**un'deni'ably** *adv.*

under (un'dər) *prep.* [OE.] **1.** in, at, or to a position down from; below **2.** less than **3.** beneath the surface of [*under* water] **4.** below and to the other side of [to drive *under* a bridge] **5.** covered or concealed by [a jumper *under* a coat] **6.** *a)* lower in authority, position, value, amount, etc. than *b)* lower than the required degree of [*under* age] **7.** *a)* subject to the control, government, etc. of *b)* bound by [*under* oath] *c)* undergoing [*under* repair] **8.** with the character, disguise, etc. of [*under* an alias] **9.** in (the designated category) **10.** during the rule of [France

under Louis XV] **11.** being the subject of [the question *under* discussion] **12.** because of [*under* the circumstances] **13.** authorized by [*under* her signature] **14.** planted with [an acre *under* barley] **15.** driven by [*under* sail] —*adv.* **1.** in or to a lower position; beneath **2.** beneath the surface **3.** in or to a subordinate condition **4.** so as to be covered or concealed **5.** less in amount, value, etc. —*adj.* lower in position, authority, amount, etc.

under- [OE.] *a prefix meaning:* **1.** beneath or below [*undershirt*] **2.** in an inferior position or rank [*undergraduate*] **3.** too little, below normal [*underdeveloped*]

underachieve (un'dər ə chēv') *vi.* **-chieved', -chiev'ing** to fail to do as well in school studies as might be expected from scores made on intelligence tests

underage (un'dər āj') *adj.* **1.** not of full or mature age **2.** below the age required by law

underarm *adj.* **1.** under the arm **2.** same as UNDERHAND (sense 1) —*adv.* same as UNDERHAND

underbid (un'dər bid') *vt., vi.* **-bid', -bid'-ding** **1.** to bid lower than (another person) **2.** to bid less than the worth of

undercarriage *n.* **1.** the part of an aircraft containing the wheels, etc. used for landing and taking off **2.** a supporting frame or structure, as of a motor car

undercharge (un'dər chärj') *vt., vi.* **-charged', -charg'ing** **1.** to charge too low a price (to) **2.** to provide with too little or low a charge

undercliff *n.* a lesser cliff beneath a higher one, formed by debris from the latter

underclothes *n.pl.* same as UNDERWEAR: also **un'dercloth'ing**

undercoat *n.* **1.** a coat of paint, varnish, etc. applied before the final coat: also **un'dercoat'ing** **2.** the soft fur under the outer coat of some animals **3.** a coat worn under an overcoat —*vt.* to apply an undercoat (of paint, etc.) to

undercover *adj.* acting or done in secret

undercroft *n.* [< obs. *croft*, vault] a crypt

undercurrent *n.* 1. a current flowing below the surface 2. a hidden or underlying tendency, opinion, etc.

undercut (un′dər kut′) *vt.* -cut′, -cut′ting 1. to undersell or work for lower wages than 2. to cut out the under part of 3. *Sports* to strike (a ball) with an oblique downward motion, as in golf, esp. so as to impart backspin

underdeveloped (un′dər di vel′əpt) *adj.* not developed to a desirable degree; specif., a) inadequately developed economically and industrially [*underdeveloped* nations] b) *Photog.* processed in developer for less than the required time: said of a film

underdo (un′dər do͞o′) *vt.* -did′, -done′, -do′ing to do less than is usual, needed, or desired

underdog (un′dər dôg′) *n.* 1. the one that is losing, as in a contest 2. a person who is handicapped or a victim of injustice, discrimination, etc.

underdone (un′dər dun′) *adj.* not cooked enough

underemployed (un′dər im ploid′) *adj.* 1. employed at less than full time 2. working at low-skilled, poorly paid jobs when one can do more skilled work

underestimate (un′dər es′tə māt′; for *n.* -mit) *vt.* -mat′ed, -mat′ing to set too low an estimate on or for —*n.* an estimate that is too low —un′deres′tima′tion *n.*

underexpose (un′dər ik spōz′) *vt.* -posed′, -pos′ing to expose (a photographic film, etc.) to inadequate light or for too short a time —un′derexpo′sure *n.*

underfelt *n.* felt laid underneath a carpet as an underlay

underfoot (un′dər foot′) *adv., adj.* 1. under the feet 2. in the way, as of one walking

undergarment *n.* an item of underwear

undergo (un′dər gō′) *vt.* -went′, -gone′, -go′ing to experience; endure

undergraduate (un′dər grad′yoo it) *n.* a student at a university or college who has not yet received a bachelor's degree

underground (un′dər ground′; *for adv.* un′dər ground′) *adj.* 1. occurring, working, etc. beneath the surface of the earth 2. secret; undercover 3. designating newspapers, films, etc. that are unconventional, radical, etc. —*adv.* 1. beneath the surface of the earth 2. in or into secrecy or hiding —*n.* 1. the region beneath the surface of the earth 2. a secret movement organized to oppose the government in power or enemy forces of occupation 3. an underground electric railway for passenger travel 4. any radical or avant-garde group, movement, etc. that operates outside the establishment

undergrowth *n.* small trees, shrubs, etc. that grow beneath large trees in woods or forests

underhand *adj.* 1. performed with the hand below the level of the elbow or shoulder 2. *same as* UNDERHANDED —*adv.* with an underhand motion

underhanded *adj.* secret, sly, deceitful, etc.

underlay (un′dər lā′; *for n.* un′dər lā′) *vt.* -laid′, -lay′ing to raise or support with something laid underneath —*n.* something laid underneath; specif., a layer of felt, rubber, etc. laid under a carpet to increase insulation and resilience

underlie (un′dər lī′) *vt.* -lay′, -lain′, -ly′ing 1. to lie under or beneath 2. to form the basis or foundation of

underline (un′dər līn′) *vt.* -lined′, -lin′ing 1. to draw a line beneath 2. to emphasize

underling (un′dər liŋ) *n.* [OE.: see UNDER- & -LING] a person who must carry out the orders of others above him; inferior: a disparaging term

underlying (un′dər lī′iŋ) *adj.* 1. not clearly evident, but implicit 2. fundamental; basic 3. placed beneath

undermine (un′dər mīn′) *vt.* -mined′, -min′ing 1. to wear away and weaken the supports of 2. to weaken or impair, esp. in a slow or stealthy way 3. to dig beneath

unilluminated	uninsured	unlovely	unneighbourly
unillustrated	unintelligent	unmanageable	unnoticeable
unimaginable	unintelligible	unmarked	unnoticed
unimaginably	unintentional	unmarred	unobjectionable
unimaginative	uninterested	unmarried	unobliging
unimpaired	uninteresting	unmeasured	unobservant
unimpeded	uninterrupted	unmelodious	unobserved
unimportant	unintimidated	unmended	unobstructed
unimposing	uninventive	unmentioned	unobtainable
unimpressed	uninvited	unmerited	unobtrusive
unimpressionable	uninviting	unmixed	unoffending
unimpressive	uninvolved	unmodified	unofficial
unindustrialized	unjustifiable	unmolested	unopen
uninfected	unknot	unmollified	unopened
uninflected	unladylike	unmoor	unopposed
uninformed	unlamented	unmourned	unoriginal
uninhabitable	unleavened	unmovable	unorthodox
uninhabited	unlicensed	unmoved	unostentatious
uninitiated	unlined	unmoving	unpacified
uninjured	unlink	unmusical	unpaid
uninspired	unlovable	unnamed	unpainted
uninspiring	unloved	unnavigable	unpalatable

underneath (un'dər nēth') *adv., prep.* under; below —*n.* the underpart

undernourish (un'dər nur'ish) *vt.* to provide with less food than is needed for health and growth

underpants *n.pl.* a man's undergarment for the lower part of the body, with a separate opening for each leg

underpass *n.* a passageway under something; esp., a road that runs under a railway or another road

underpin (un'dər pin') *vt.* **-pinned'**, **-pin'-ning** to support or strengthen from beneath, as with props —*un'derpin'ning n.*

underplay (un'dər plā') *vt., vi.* **1.** to act (a role or scene) in an intentionally restrained manner **2.** *Cards* to play a low card deliberately instead of a higher one

underprivileged (un'dər priv'lijd) *adj.* deprived of basic social rights and security through poverty, discrimination, etc.

underproduce (un'dər prə dyoos') *vt., vi.* **-duced'**, **-duc'ing** to produce in a quantity that is below full capacity or that fails to meet the need or demand —*un'derpro-duc'tion n.*

underscore (un'dər skôr') *vt.* **-scored'**, **-scor'ing** *same as* UNDERLINE

undersea *adj., adv.* beneath the surface of the sea

underseal *n.* a coating of tarlike material applied to the undersurface of a car, etc. to retard the development of rust —*vt.* to apply an underseal to

undersecretary (un'dər sek'rə tər ē) *n., pl.* **-taries** any of various senior civil servants in certain government departments

undersexed (un'dər sekst') *adj.* having a weaker than normal sexual drive or interest

undershirt *n.* [Chiefly U.S.] a usually sleeveless undergarment worn under a shirt by men

undershoot (un'dər shoot') *vt.* **-shot'**, **-shoot'ing 1.** to shoot or fall short of (a target, mark, etc.) **2.** to bring an aircraft down short of (the runway, etc.)

undershot *adj.* **1.** with the lower part jutting out past the upper [an *undershot* jaw] **2.** driven by water flowing along the lower part [an *undershot* water wheel]

underside *n.* the side or surface underneath

undersign (un'dər sīn') *vt.* to sign one's name at the end of (a letter, document, etc.) —**the undersigned** the person or persons undersigning

undersized (un'dər sīzd') *adj.* smaller in size than is usual, average, or proper

underskirt *n.* a garment worn under a skirt

understaffed (un'dər staft') *adj.* having fewer personnel than needed

understand (un'dər stand') *vt.* **-stood'**, **-stand'ing** [OE. *understandan*, to stand under] **1.** to get or know the meaning of **2.** to gather or assume from what is heard, known, etc. **3.** to take as meaning; interpret **4.** to take as a fact **5.** to supply mentally (an idea, word, etc.), as for grammatical completeness **6.** to learn **7.** to know the nature, character, etc. of **8.** to have a sympathetic rapport with [no one *understands* me] —*vi.* to have understanding, comprehension, etc. —*un'-derstand'able adj.* —*un'derstand'ably adv.*

understanding *n.* **1.** comprehension **2.** sympathetic awareness **3.** sense **4.** an explanation or interpretation [one's *understanding* of the matter] **5.** *a*) mutual comprehension, as of intentions *b*) an agreement, esp. one that is informal —*adj.* having or showing comprehension, sympathy, etc. —*un'derstand'ingly adv.*

understate (un'dər stāt') *vt.* **-stat'ed**, **-stat'ing 1.** to express in a restrained style **2.** to make a weaker statement of than is warranted by truth, accuracy, or importance —*un'derstate'ment n.*

understudy *n., pl.* **-stud'ies 1.** an actor who learns the part of another actor so that he can serve as a substitute **2.** anyone who is trained to take the place of another —*vt., vi.* **-stud'ied, -stud'ying 1.** to act

unpardonable	unpresentable	unquotable	unremorseful
unpatriotic	unpressed	unrealized	unremovable
unpaved	unpretentious	unreasoned	unremunerative
unperceived	unpriced	unrebuked	unrenewed
unpersuadable	unprivileged	unreceptive	unrenowned
unperturbed	unproductive	unreciprocated	unrepairable
unpicked	unprofitable	unreclaimed	unrepentant
unpitied	unpromising	unrecognizable	unrepenting
unpitying	unprompted	unrecognized	unrepresentative
unplaced	unpronounceable	unreconciled	unrepresented
unplanned	unpropitious	unrecorded	unrepressed
unplayable	unprotected	unredeemed	unreprimanded
unpleasing	unproved	unrefined	unrequested
unploughed	unproven	unreflecting	unrequited
unplucked	unprovided	unregarded	unresisting
unplug	unprovoked	unregistered	unresolved
unpolished	unpublished	unregretted	unresponsive
unpolluted	unpunctual	unregulated	unrested
unpredictable	unpunished	unrelated	unrestful
unpremeditated	unquenchable	unreliability	unrestrained
unprepared	unquenched	unreliable	unrestricted
unprepossessing	unquestioning	unrelieved	unretentive

as an understudy (to) **2.** to learn (a part) as an understudy

undertake (un'dər tāk') *vt.* **-took', -tak'-en, -tak'ing 1.** to take upon oneself; agree to do **2.** to promise; guarantee

undertaker (un'dər tā'kər) *n.* a contractor who makes all the necessary arrangements for a burial or cremation

undertaking (un'dər tā'kiŋ; *for 3,* un'-dər tā'kiŋ) *n.* **1.** something undertaken; task; enterprise **2.** a promise; guarantee **3.** the business of an undertaker

under-the-counter *adj.* [Colloq.] done, sold, given, etc. secretly in an unlawful or unethical way

underthings *n.pl.* women's or girls' underwear

undertone *n.* **1.** a low tone of sound or voice **2.** any underlying quality, factor, element, etc. [an *undertone* of horror] **3.** a subdued or background colour

undertow *n.* [UNDER- + TOW¹] a current of water moving beneath the surface water and in a different direction, as seawards under the incoming tide

undervalue (un'dər val'yōō) *vt.* **-ued, -uing 1.** to value too low, or below the real worth **2.** to regard too lightly

underwater (un'dər wôt'ər) *adj.* being, done, used, or for use under water —*adv.* beneath the surface of the water

underway (un'dər wā') *adj. Naut.* not at anchor or moored or aground

underwear *n.* clothing worn under one's outer clothes, usually next to the skin

underweight (un'dər wāt') *adj.* below the normal, desirable, or allowed weight

underwood *n. same as* UNDERGROWTH

underworld *n.* **1.** the criminal members of society, regarded as a group **2.** the mythical world of the dead; Hades

underwrite *vt.* **-wrote', -writ'ten, -writ'-ing 1.** to agree to buy at a fixed price any unsold portion of (an issue of shares, etc.) **2.** to pledge to support (an under-taking, etc.) financially **3.** a) to sign one's

name to (an insurance policy) thus assuming liability, esp. in shipping b) to insure c) to assume liability to the amount of (a specified sum) —*vi.* to practise insurance, esp. in shipping —**un'derwrit'-er** *n.*

undesirable (un'di zīər'ə b'l) *adj.* not desirable; objectionable —*n.* an undesir-able —**un'desir'ably** *adv.*

undies (un'dēz) *n.pl.* [Colloq.] women's or girls' underwear

undine (un'dēn) *n.* [< Mod.L. *unda,* a wave] *Folklore* a female water spirit who could acquire a soul by marrying, and having a child by, a mortal

undo (un'dōō') *vt.* **-did', -done', -do'ing 1.** to untie or open **2.** to reverse or do away with (something done or its effect) **3.** to ruin or destroy —**undo'er** *n.*

undoing *n.* **1.** ruin or the cause of ruin **2.** a reversal of something done or its effect

undone¹ (un'dun') *pp. of* UNDO —*adj.* ruined, disgraced, etc.

undone² *adj.* not performed, accom-plished, etc.

undoubted (un dout'id) *adj.* certain —**undoubt'edly** *adv.*

undreamed (un drēmd') *adj.* not even dreamed (*of*) or imagined; inconceivable: also **undreamt'**

undress (un'dres') *vt.* to take off the clothing of —*vi.* to take off one's clothes —*n.* **1.** the state of being naked, partly clothed, etc. **2.** ordinary or informal dress, as opposed to uniform, etc.

undue (un dyōō') *adj.* **1.** excessive [*undue* haste] **2.** not suitable; improper [*undue* flippancy]

undulant (un'dyoo lənt) *adj.* moving in or as in waves

undulate (un'dyoo lāt'; *for adj. usually* -lit) *vi., vt.* **-lat'ed, -lat'ing** [< L. *unda,* a wave] **1.** to move or cause to move in waves **2.** to have or cause to have a wavy form, surface, etc. —*adj.* wavy: also **un'dulat'ed**

undulation (un'dyoo lā'shən) *n.* **1.** an

unretrieved	unscholarly	unshaven	unsold
unreturned	unscientific	unshed	unsolicited
unrevenged	unscorched	unsheltered	unsolidified
unrevised	unscratched	unshielded	unsolved
unrewarding	unscriptural	unshockable	unsought
unrhymed	unseasoned	unshorn	unsown
unrhythmic	unseaworthy	unshrinkable	unspecialized
unromantic	unseeing	unshrinking	unspecific
unsafe	unseen	unshuffled	unspecified
unsalable	unsegmented	unshuttered	unspectacular
unsalaried	unsegregated	unsighted	unspoiled
unsaleable	unselective	unsigned	unspoken
unsalted	unsentimental	unsimplified	unsporting
unsanctified	unserviceable	unsingable	unsportsmanlike
unsanctioned	unsewn	unsinkable	unspotted
unsatisfactory	unshadowed	unslackened	unstained
unsatisfied	unshakable	unslaked	unsterilized
unsatisfying	unshakeable	unsleeping	unstinted
unscalable	unshaken	unsliced	unstoppable
unscarred	unshamed	unsmiling	unstressed
unscented	unshapely	unsmoked	unsubstantiated
unscheduled	unshared	unsoiled	unsuccessful

undulating **2.** a wavy form or outline, esp. one of a series

unduly (un'dyōō'lē) *adv.* too much [*unduly* alarmed]

undying (un'dī'iŋ) *adj.* immortal or eternal

unearned *adj.* **1.** not earned by work or service; specif., obtained as a return on an investment [*unearned* income] **2.** not deserved

unearth (un'urth') *vt.* **1.** to dig up **2.** to discover or disclose

unearthly *adj.* **1.** supernatural **2.** weird; mysterious **3.** [Colloq.] absurd, unreasonable, etc. —**unearth'liness** *n.*

uneasy (un ē'zē) *adj.* **-eas'ier, -eas'iest 1.** worried; anxious **2.** disturbing; disquieting [an *uneasy* feeling] **3.** precarious [an *uneasy* truce] —**uneas'iness** *n.* —**uneas'ily** *adv.*

unemployed (un'im ploid') *adj.* **1.** without work **2.** not being used —**the unemployed** people who are out of work —**un'em ploy'ment** *n.*

unequal (un'ē'kwəl) *adj.* **1.** not equal, as in size, strength, etc. **2.** *a)* not balanced *b)* that matches unequal contestants [an *unequal* battle] **3.** not even, regular, etc.; variable **4.** not adequate [*unequal* to the task] —**une'qually** *adv.*

unequalled *adj.* unmatched; unrivalled

unequivocal (un'i kwiv'ək'l) *adj,* not equivocal; plain; clear —**un'equiv'ocally** *adv.*

unerring (un'ur'iŋ) *adj.* free from error; sure; exact

UNESCO (yōō nes'kō) United Nations Educational, Scientific, and Cultural Organization

uneven (un'ē'vən) *adj.* **1.** not level, smooth, or flat **2.** not equal in size, amount, etc. **3.** not uniform; varying **4.** not equally balanced or matched **5.** *Math.* not evenly divisible by two

unexampled (un'ig zam'p'ld) *adj.* with nothing like it before; unprecedented

unexceptionable (un'ik sep'shə nə b'l) *adj.* without flaw or fault; not warranting even the slightest criticism

unexceptional (un'ik sep'shən 'l) *adj.* **1.**

not uncommon; ordinary **2.** not admitting of any exception

unfailing (un fāl'iŋ) *adj.* **1.** not failing **2.** never ceasing or falling short; inexhaustible **3.** always reliable

unfair (un'fãar') *adj.* **1.** not just or impartial; biased; inequitable **2.** dishonest or unethical in business dealings

unfaithful (un fāth'fəl) *adj.* **1.** failing to stay loyal or to keep a vow, promise, etc. **2.** not true, accurate, etc. **3.** guilty of adultery —**unfaith'fulness** *n.*

unfamiliar (un'fə mil'yər) *adj.* **1.** not well-known; strange [*unfamiliar* lands] **2.** not acquainted (*with* something)

unfeeling (un fēl'iŋ) *adj.* without sympathy; hardhearted; cruel

unfeigned (un fānd') *adj.* genuine; sincere —**unfeign'edly** (-fān'id lē) *adv.*

unfinished *adj.* **1.** not finished or completed **2.** having no finish, or final coat, as of paint

unfit (un'fit') *adj.* **1.** not meeting requirements **2.** not physically or mentally fit —**unfit'ness** *n.*

unflappable (un'flap'ə b'l) *adj.* [Colloq.] not easily excited or upset; calm

unflinching (un flin'chiŋ) *adj.* resolute; unyielding

unfold (un'fōld') *vt.* **1.** to open and spread out (something folded) **2.** to reveal, disclose, display, or explain —*vi.* **1.** to become unfolded **2.** to develop fully

unfortunate (un fôr'chə nit) *adj.* **1.** *a)* unlucky *b)* bringing, or coming by, bad luck **2.** regrettable; unsuitable [an *unfortunate* remark] —*n.* an unfortunate person —**unfor'tunately** *adv.*

unfounded (un'foun'did) *adj.* **1.** not founded on fact or truth; baseless **2.** not established

unfreeze (un'frēz') *vt.* **-froze', -froz'en, -freez'ing 1.** to cause to thaw **2.** to remove financial controls from (prices, wages, etc.)

unfrock (un'frok') *vt.* to deprive of the rank of priest

unfurl (un'furl') *vt., vi.* to open or unfold from a furled state

ungainly (un gān'lē) *adj.* awkward; clumsy —**ungain'liness** *n.*

unsuited	untalented	untreated	unwashed
unsullied	untamed	untried	unwatered
unsupervised	untapped	untroubled	unwavering
unsupportable	untarnished	untrustworthy	unwearable
unsupported	untasted	untuned	unwearying
unsuppressed	unthanked	unturned	unweeded
unsure	unthought-of	untypical	unwelcome
unsurpassable	untiring	unusable	unwincing
unsurpassed	untorn	unvaccinated	unwinking
unsusceptible	untouched	unvaried	unwished-for
unsuspecting	untraceable	unvarying	unwithered
unsustained	untraced	unventilated	unwitnessed
unswayed	untrained	unverified	unworkable
unsweetened	untrammelled	unversed	unworn
unswept	untransferable	unvisited	unworried
unswerving	untranslatable	unwanted	unwounded
unsymmetrical	untransmitted	unwarned	unwoven
unsympathetic	untravelled	unwarrantable	unwrinkled
unsystematic	untraversed	unwarranted	unyielding

ungodly (un'god'lē) *adj.* 1. impious 2. sinful; wicked —**ungod'liness** *n.*

ungovernable (un'guv'ər nə b'l) *adj.* that cannot be governed or controlled; unruly

ungracious (un'grā'shəs) *adj.* rude; discourteous

unguarded (un'gärd'id) *adj.* 1. unprotected 2. without guile or cunning; open 3. careless; thoughtless

unguent (uŋ'gwənt) *n.* [< L. *unguere*, anoint] a salve or ointment

ungulate (un'gyoo lāt') *adj.* [< L. *ungula*, hoof] having hoofs —*n.* a mammal having hoofs

unhallowed (un'hal'ōd) *adj.* 1. not consecrated; unholy 2. wicked; profane

unhand (un'hand') *vt.* to loose from one's grasp; let go of

unhappy (un hap'ē) *adj.* -hap'pier, -hap'-piest 1. sad; sorrowful 2. unlucky 3. not suitable —**unhap'pily** *adv.* —**unhap'piness** *n.*

unhealthy (un hel'thē) *adj.* -health'ier, -health'iest 1. having poor health; sickly 2. harmful to health 3. dangerous or risky [an *unhealthy* situation] —**unhealth'ily** *adv.* —**unhealth'iness** *n.*

unheard (un'hurd') *adj.* 1. not perceived by the ear 2. not given a hearing

unheard-of *adj.* 1. unprecedented 2. unacceptable or outrageous [*unheard-of* behaviour]

unhinge (un'hinj') *vt.* -hinged', -hing'-ing 1. to remove from the hinges 2. to throw (the mind) into confusion; unbalance

unholy (un'hō'lē) *adj.* -lier, -liest 1. not sacred or consecrated 2. wicked; profane 3. [Colloq.] dreadful —**unho'liness** *n.*

unhook (un'hook') *vt.* 1. to remove or loosen from a hook 2. to undo or unfasten the hooks of

unhorse (un'hôrs') *vt.* -horsed', -hors'-ing to throw (a rider) from a horse

uni- [< L.] *a combining form meaning* having or consisting of one only

Uniat (yoo'nē'at) *n.* [< Russ. < L. *unus*, one] a member of the Eastern Church: also **Uniate**

unicameral (yoo'nə kam'ər əl) *adj.* [< UNI- + LL. *camera*, chamber] having a single legislative chamber

UNICEF (yoo'nə sef') United Nations International Children's Emergency Fund

unicellular (yoo'nə sel'yoo lər) *adj.* having or consisting of a single cell

UNICORN

unicorn (yoo'nə kôrn') *n.* [< L. *unus*, one + *cornu*, horn] a mythical horse-like animal with a single horn growing from the centre of its forehead

UNIDO United Nations Industrial Development Organization

unification (yoo'nə fi kā'shən) *n.* the act of unifying or the state of being unified

uniform (yoo'nə fôrm') *n.* [< L. *unus*, one + *-formis*, -form] the official or distinctive clothes for members of a particular group, as soldiers or schoolchildren —*adj.* 1. not varying in form, degree, manner, etc. 2. having the same form, appearance, etc. as others of the same class 3. consistent in action, effect, etc. —*vt.* to clothe with a uniform —**u'niform'ity** *n.* —**u'niform'ly** *adv.*

unify (yoo'nə fī') *vt., vi.* -fied', -fy'ing [< LL. *unificare*] to combine into one

unilateral (yoo'nə lat'ər əl) *adj.* [UNI- + LATERAL] 1. of, occurring on, or affecting one side only 2. done by one only [*unilateral* disarmament]

unimpeachable (un'im pēch'ə b'l) *adj.* that cannot be doubted, questioned, or discredited —**un'impeach'ably** *adv.*

uninhibited (un'in hib'it id) *adj.* without inhibition; esp., free from the usual social or psychological restraints

union (yoon'yən) *n.* [< L. *unus*, one] 1. a uniting or being united; combination 2. a grouping together of nations, political groups, etc. for some specific purpose 3. marriage 4. something united; a whole made up of united parts 5. *short for* TRADE UNION 6. a device symbolizing political union, used in a flag 7. [often U-] *a)* a facility for social recreation at a university *b)* the buildings of such an organization In full, **student union** 8. harmony; concord 9. formerly, *a)* a combination of parishes for the administration of the poor law *b)* a workhouse 10. *Math.* a set containing all the elements of two or more given sets, with no element listed more than once —**un'ionism** *n.*

unionist *n.* 1. a supporter of the principle of union 2. a member of a trade union 3. [U-] a supporter of the union of Great Britain and Ireland, esp. N Ireland

unionize *vt.* -ized', -iz'ing 1. to organize (workers) into a trade union 2. to bring into conformity with the rules, etc. of a trade union —**un'ioniza'tion** *n.*

Union Jack the national flag of the United Kingdom, consisting of the crosses of St. George, St. Andrew and St. Patrick

unique (yoo nēk') *adj.* [Fr. < L. *unicus*, single] 1. one and only, having no like or equal 2. highly unusual, extraordinary, etc.: a usage objected to by many —**unique'ly** *adv.*

unisex (yoo'nə seks') *adj.* [Colloq.] designating or of a fashion, as in garments, hair styles, etc., adopted by persons of either sex

unison (yoo'nə zən) *n.* [< L. *unus*, one + *sonus*, a sound] 1. identity of musical pitch, as of two or more voices **2.** agreement; harmony **—in unison 1.** with all the voices or instruments performing the same part **2.** in agreement

unit (yōō′nit) *n.* [< UNITY] **1.** the smallest whole number; one **2.** any fixed quantity, measure, etc. used as a standard **3.** a single person or group, esp. as distinguished from others or as part of a whole **4.** a single, distinct part, esp. one used for a specific purpose [the lens *unit* of a camera] **5.** a piece of furniture designed to form a whole with other, matching parts **6.** a subdivision of a military formation **7.** a complete system, organization, etc. that performs a specific function [a production *unit*]

Unitarian (yōō′nə tãər′ē ən) *n.* a member of a Christian sect holding that God exists as one person or being **—U′nitar′ianism** *n.*

unitary (yōō′nə tər ē) *adj.* **1.** of a unit or units **2.** of, or characterized by unity

unite (yoo nīt′) *vt., vi.* **-nit′ed, -nit′ing** [< L. *unus,* one] **1.** to put or join together so as to make one; combine **2.** to bring or come together in common cause, interest, etc.

united *adj.* **1.** combined; joined **2.** of or resulting from joint action or association **3.** in agreement

United Empire Loyalist *Canad. Hist.* any of the American colonists who settled in Canada during or after the War of American Independence because of loyalty to the British Crown

United Kingdom Great Britain and Northern Ireland

United Nations an international organization of nations pledged to promote world peace and security

unit price the price per unit, as per lb., as distinct from the total price of an item

unit trust a company formed by public subscriptions which are pooled to buy stocks and shares in a number of companies, under the supervision of a trustee

unity (yōō′nə tē) *n., pl.* **-ties** [< L. *unus,* one] **1.** the state of being united; oneness **2.** something complete in itself **3.** harmony; agreement **4.** a complex that is a union of related parts **5.** a harmonious unified arrangement of parts in an artistic work **6.** *Math.* any quantity, magnitude, etc. identified as a unit, or 1

Univ. 1. Universalist **2.** University

univalent (yōō′nə vā′lənt) *adj. Chem.* **1.** having one valence **2.** having a valence of one

universal (yōō′nə vʉr′s'l) *adj.* [see UNIVERSE] **1.** present or occurring everywhere **2.** of, for, or including all or the whole **3.** that can be used for all kinds, forms, sizes, etc. **4.** used, intended to be used, or understood by all **5.** *Logic* predicating something of every member of a specified class

universality (yōō′nə vʉr sal′ə tē) *n., pl.*

-ties the quality, state, or instance of being universal

UNIVERSAL JOINT

universal joint (or **coupling**) a joint or coupling that permits a swing of limited angle in any direction, esp. one used to transmit rotary motion from one shaft to another not in line with it

universally (yōō′nə vʉr′sə lē) *adv.* **1.** in every instance **2.** in every part or place

universal suffrage suffrage for all adult citizens

universe (yōō′nə vʉrs′) *n.* [< L. *unus,* one + *vertere,* to turn] **1.** all the things that exist **2.** the world

university (yōō′nə vʉr′sə tē) *n., pl.* **-ties** [see prec.] **1.** an educational institution of the highest level authorized to confer various degrees **2.** the buildings, students, faculty, or administrators of a university

unjust (un′just′) *adj.* not just or right; unfair

unkempt (un′kempt′) *adj.* [UN- + dial. *kemben,* to comb] not tidy, neat, or groomed **—unkempt′ness** *n.*

unkind (un′kīnd′) *adj.* not kind; harsh, severe, cruel, etc. **—unkind′ness** *n.*

unknown (un′nōn′) *adj.* **1.** not in one's knowledge, acquaintance, etc.; unfamiliar (*to*) **2.** not discovered, identified, etc. **—n.** an unknown person, thing, or quantity

unknown quantity someone or something whose influence cannot be predicted; an enigma

unlatch (un′lach′) *vt., vi.* to open by release of a latch

unlawful (un′lô′fəl) *adj.* **1.** against the law; illegal **2.** illicit **—unlaw′fully** *adv.*

unlearn (un′lʉrn′) *vt., vi.* to forget (something learned) by a conscious effort, as in retraining

unlearned (-lʉr′nid; *for* 2 -lʉrnd′) *adj.* **1.** showing a lack of learning or education **2.** acquired without conscious study [*unlearned* tact]

unleash (un′lēsh′) *vt.* to release from or as from a leash

unless (ən les′) *conj.* [< ME. *on lesse that,* at less than] in any case other than; except if

unlettered (un′let′ərd) *adj.* **1.** uneducated **2.** illiterate

unlike (un′līk′) *adj.* not alike; different **—prep. 1.** different from **2.** not characteristic of [it's *unlike* her to cry]

unlikely adj. not likely to happen or be true; improbable —**unlike'liness** n.

unlimited (un lim'it id) adj. 1. without limits or restrictions 2. without boundaries

unload (un'lōd') vt. 1. a) to remove (a load, cargo, etc.) b) to take a load, etc. from 2. to remove the charge from (a gun) 3. to get rid of

unlock (un'lok') vt. 1. a) to open (a lock) b) to open the lock of (a door, etc.) 2. to let loose by or as if by opening a lock

unlooked-for (un lookt'fôr') adj. not expected

unloose (un'lōōs') vt. -loosed', -loos'ing to make or set loose: also **unloos'en**

unlucky (un luk'ē) adj. -luck'ier, -luck'i-est having or marked by bad luck; unfortunate —**unluck'ily** adv.

unmake (un'māk') vt. -made', -mak'ing 1. to cause to be as before 2. to ruin; destroy 3. to depose from a position or authority

unman (un'man') vt. -manned', -man'-ning 1. to deprive of manly courage, confidence, etc. 2. to castrate

unmanned adj. not manned; specif., operating automatically or by remote control

unmannerly (un man'ər lē) adj. having or showing poor manners; rude —**unman'-nerliness** n.

unmask (un'mäsk') vt., vi. 1. to remove a mask or disguise (from) 2. to show or appear in true character

unmeaning (un mēn'iŋ) adj. 1. lacking in meaning or sense 2. showing no sense or intelligence

unmentionable (un men'shən ə b'l) adj. not fit to be mentioned —n. [pl.] unmentionable things; specif., underwear: a humorous usage

unmerciful (un mur'si fəl) adj. having or showing no mercy; cruel; relentless; pitiless —**unmer'cifully** adv.

unmistakable (un'mis tāk'ə b'l) adj. that cannot be misunderstood; clear; plain —**un'mistak'ably** adv.

unmitigated (un mit'ə gāt'id) adj. 1. not lessened or eased 2. absolute [an unmitigated fool]

unmoral (un'mor''l) adj. var. of AMORAL

unmuzzle (un'muz''l) vt. -zled, -zling 1. to free (a dog, etc.) from a muzzle 2. to stop restraining or censoring

unnatural (un nach'ər əl) adj. 1. abnormal; strange 2. artificial; strained 3. abnormally evil or cruel —**unnat'urally** adv. —**unnat'uralness** n.

unnecessary (un nes'ə sər ē) adj. not necessary or required; needless —**unnec'-essarily** adv.

unnerve (un'nurv') vt. -nerved', -nerv'-ing to cause to lose one's courage, confidence, etc.

unnumbered (un'num'bərd) adj. 1. innumerable 2. having no number

U.N.O. United Nations Organization

unoccupied (un'ok'yə pīd') adj. 1. vacant; empty 2. at leisure; idle

unorganized (un'ôr'gə nīzd') adj. 1. not having or following any regular order or system 2. not having or belonging to a trade union

unpack (un'pak') vt. 1. to open and remove the packed contents of 2. to take from a crate, trunk, etc. —vi. to empty a packed trunk, etc.

unparalleled (un par'ə leld') adj. that has no equal or counterpart; unmatched

unparliamentary (un'pär'lə men'tər ē) adj. contrary to parliamentary law or usage

unperson (un'pur's'n) n. [< George Orwell's 1984] a person who was formerly a public figure and who has been intentionally removed from public recognition

unpick (un'pik') vt. to undo the stitches of a piece of sewing or knitting

unpin (un'pin') vt. -pinned', -pin'ning 1. to remove a pin or pins from 2. to unfasten or detach in this way

unpleasant (un plez''nt) adj. offensive; disagreeable —**unpleas'antly** adv. —**unpleas'antness** n.

unplumbed (un'plumd') adj. 1. not sounded or measured with a plumb 2. not fully understood

unpopular (un'pop'yoo lər) adj. not liked by the public or the majority —**un'popu-lar'ity** (-yoo lar'ə tē) n.

unpractised (un prak'tist) adj. not skilled or experienced

unprecedented (un pres'ə den'tid) adj. having no precedent or parallel; unheard-of

unprincipled (un prin'sə p'ld) adj. unscrupulous

unprintable (un'print'ə b'l) adj. not printable; not fit to be printed, as because of obscenity

unprofessional (un'prə fesh'ən 'l) adj. 1. violating the ethical code of a given profession 2. not belonging to a profession

unqualified (un kwol'ə fīd') adj. 1. lacking the necessary qualifications 2. not limited; absolute [an unqualified success] —**unqual'ified'ly** adv.

unquestionable (un kwes'chən ə b'l) adj. not to be doubted or disputed; certain —**unques'tionably** adv.

unquiet (un kwī'ət) adj. restless, disturbed, uneasy, anxious, etc.

unquote (un'kwōt') interj. I end the quotation : used in speech after a quotation

unravel (un rav''l) vt. -elled, -elling 1. to undo (something woven, tangled, etc.); separate the threads of 2. to make clear; solve —vi. to become unravelled

unread (un'red') adj. 1. not read, as a book 2. having read little or nothing 3. unlearned (in a subject)

unready (un'red'ē) adj. 1. not ready; unprepared 2. not prompt or alert —**unread'iness** n.

unreal (un're'əl) adj. not real; imaginary, false, etc. —**un'real'ity** (-rē al'ə tē) n.

unrealistic (un'rē ə lis'tik) *adj.* not realistic; impractical; visionary —**un'realis'tically** *adv.*

unreasonable (un rē'z'n ə b'l) *adj.* 1. excessive; immoderate 2. having or showing little sense —**unrea'sonably** *adv.*

unreasoning *adj.* lacking reason or judgment

unregenerate (un'ri gen'ər ət) *adj.* 1. unrepentant, unreformed 2. obstinate, recalcitrant

unrelenting (un'ri len'tiŋ) *adj.* 1. refusing to yield or relent 2. without mercy 3. not relaxing, as in effort

unremitting (un'ri mit'iŋ) *adj.* not stopping, relaxing, or slackening; persistent —**un'remit'tingly** *adv.*

unreserved (un'ri zurvd') *adj.* 1. frank; open 2. unlimited 3. not set aside for advance sale, as seats —**un'reserv'edly** (-zur'vid lē) *adv.*

unrest (un'rest') *n.* a troubled or disturbed state; specif., a state of discontent close to revolt

unrighteous (un rī'chəs) *adj.* 1. wicked; sinful 2. unjust

unrip (un rip') *vt.* **-ripped', -rip'ping** to rip open

unripe (un'rīp') *adj.* 1. not ripe or mature; green 2. not yet fully developed

unrivalled (un rī'v'ld) *adj.* having no equal

unroll (un'rōl') *vt.* 1. to open or extend (something rolled up) 2. to present to view; display —*vi.* to become unrolled

unruffled (un'ruf''ld) *adj.* not disturbed or agitated

unruly (un rōō'lē) *adj.* **-rul'ier, -rul'iest** [< ME. *un-*, not + *reuly*, orderly] hard to control; disobedient, disorderly, etc. —**unrul'iness** *n.*

unsaddle (un sad''l) *vt.* **-dled, -dling** 1. to take the saddle off (a horse, etc.) 2. to throw from the saddle; unhorse

unsaid (un'sed') *pt. & pp.* of UNSAY —*adj.* not expressed

unsaturated (un sach'ə rāt'id) *adj. Chem.* 1. capable of dissolving more of the solute 2. designating an organic compound with a double or triple bond between carbon atoms

unsavoury (un'sā'vər ē) *adj.* 1. morally offensive 2. unpleasant to taste or smell

unsay (un'sā') *vt.* **-said', -say'ing** to take back or retract (what has been said)

unscathed (un'skāth*d*') *adj.* unharmed

unscramble (un skram'b'l) *vt.* **-bled, -bling** to cause to be no longer scrambled, disordered, etc.; specif., *Electronics* to make (incoming scrambled signals) intelligible

unscrew (un'skrōō') *vt.* 1. to remove a screw or screws from 2. to remove or loosen by removing a screw or screws, or by turning

unscrupulous (un skrōō'pyoo ləs) *adj.* heedless of what is right, just, etc.; unprincipled

unseasonable (un sē'z'n ə b'l) *adj.* 1. not usual for the season 2. untimely; inopportune

unseat (un'sēt') *vt.* 1. to throw or dislodge from a seat, saddle, etc. 2. to remove from office, deprive of rank, etc.

unseemly (un sēm'lē) *adj.* not proper; unbecoming —**unseem'liness** *n.*

unselfish (un'sel'fish) *adj.* not selfish; altruistic; generous —**unself'ishly** *adv.* —**unself'ishness** *n.*

unsettle (un'set''l) *vt.* **-tled, -tling** to make unsettled, insecure, etc.; disturb, displace, disorder, etc.

unsettled *adj.* 1. not settled; not in order, not stable, etc. 2. troubled or restless 3. not established in a place or abode 4. not paid, as a debt 5. having no settlers

unshackle (un'shak''l) *vt.* **-led, -ling** 1. to loosen or remove the shackles from 2. to free

unsheathe (un'shēth') *vt.* **-sheathed', -sheath'ing** to remove (a sword, knife, etc.) from a sheath

unsightly (un sīt'lē) *adj.* ugly —**unsight'liness** *n.*

unskilful (un'skil'fəl) *adj.* awkward; clumsy

unskilled *adj.* having, showing, or requiring no special skill or training

unsociable (un sō'shə b'l) *adj.* 1. avoiding others; not sociable 2. not conducive to sociability —**unso'ciably** *adv.*

unsocial (un sō'shəl) *adj.* 1. having or showing a dislike for the society of others 2. falling outside the normal working day [*unsocial* hours] —**unso'cially** *adv.*

unsophisticated (un'sə fis'tə kāt'id) *adj.* artless, simple, unworldly, etc.

unsound (un'sound') *adj.* 1. not normal or healthy 2. not safe or secure 3. not safe and secure financially 4. not accurate, sensible, etc.

unsparing (un spār'iŋ) *adj.* 1. not sparing or stinting; lavish 2. not merciful; severe —**unspar'ingly** *adv.*

unspeakable (un spēk'ə b'l) *adj.* 1. indescribably bad, evil, etc. 2. marvellous, awesome, etc. beyond expression 3. that cannot be spoken —**unspeak'ably** *adv.*

unstable (un'stā'b'l) *adj.* not stable; specif., *a*) easily upset *b*) changeable *c*) unreliable; fickle *d*) *Chem., Physics* readily decomposing

unsteady (un'sted'ē) *adj.* not steady; specif., *a*) not firm or stable *b*) changeable or erratic —*vt.* **-stead'ied, -stead'ying** to make unsteady —**unstead'ily** *adv.*

unstring (un'striŋ') *vt.* **-strung, -string'-ing** 1. to loosen or remove the string or strings of 2. to remove from a string

unstructured (un struk'chərd) *adj.* not formally or systematically organized

unstrung (un'struŋ') *adj.* 1. nervous, upset, etc. 2. having the string(s) loosened or detached, as a bow

unstudied (un'stud'ēd) *adj.* 1. spontaneous; natural; unaffected 2. unlearned or unversed (*in*)

unsubstantial (un'səb stan'shəl) *adj.* 1.

having no material substance **2.** flimsy; light **3.** unreal; visionary —**un'substan'ti·al'ity** (-stan'shē al'ə tē) *n.*

unsuitable (un soot'ə b'l) *adj.* not suitable; unbecoming; inappropriate —**unsuit'ably** *adv.*

unsung (un'suŋ') *adj.* not honoured or celebrated

unsuspected (un'sə spek''tid) *adj.* **1.** not believed guilty, harmful, etc. **2.** not under suspicion **3.** not known to exist

untangle (un taŋ'g'l) *vt.* -gled, -gling **1.** to free from a tangle; disentangle **2.** to free from confusion

untaught (un tôt') *adj.* **1.** not taught or educated **2.** acquired without being taught; natural

unthankful (un thaŋk'fəl) *adj.* **1.** ungrateful **2.** thankless; unappreciated

unthinkable (un thiŋk'ə b'l) *adj.* **1.** not to be considered; impossible **2.** beyond thought or imagination; inconceivable —**unthink'ably** *adv.*

unthinking (un'thiŋk'iŋ) *adj.* **1.** showing no consideration; thoughtless **2.** lacking the ability to think; not rational —**unthink'ingly** *adv.*

unthrone (un thrōn') *vt.* -throned', -thron'ing *same as* DETHRONE

untidy (un tī'dē) *adj.* -dier, -diest not neat; slovenly; messy —**unti'dily** *adv.* —**unti'diness** *n.*

untie (un'tī') *vt.* -tied', -ty'ing **1.** to loosen or undo (something tied or knotted) **2.** to free, as from restraint

until (ən til') *prep.* [ME. *untill*] **1.** up to the time of; till [*until* payday] **2.** before (a specified time) [not *until* tomorrow] —*conj.* **1.** up to the time when or that [*until* I go] **2.** to the point, degree, etc. that [heat water *until* it boils] **3.** before [don't leave *until* he does]

untimely (un tīm'lē) *adj.* **1.** before the usual or expected time; premature [his *untimely* death] **2.** at the wrong time; inopportune —**untime'liness** *n.*

unto (un'too) *prep.* [ME.] *archaic or poet. var. of* TO

untold (un'tōld') *adj.* **1.** too great, numerous, etc. to be counted or described **2.** not told or revealed

untouchable (un tuch'ə b'l) *adj.* that cannot or should not be touched —*n.* in India, formerly, one whose touch was regarded as defiling to higher-caste Hindus

untoward (un'tə wôrd') *adj.* **1.** inappropriate, unseemly, etc. [an *untoward* remark] **2.** not favourable [untoward circumstances]

untrue (un'troo') *adj.* **1.** not correct; false **2.** not agreeing with a standard or rule **3.** not faithful or loyal

untruthful (un'trooth'fəl) *adj.* **1.** not in accordance with the truth **2.** telling a lie or lies, esp. habitually —**untruth'fully** *adv.* —**untruth'fulness** *n.*

untutored (un'tyoot'ərd) *adj.* **1.** not tutored or taught; uneducated **2.** simple; naive

untwine (un twīn') *vt.* -twined', -twin'ing to undo (something twined or twisted); disentangle

unused (un'yoozd'; *for 3,* -yoost') *adj.* **1.** not in use **2.** that has never been used **3.** unaccustomed (*to*)

unusual (un yoo'zhoo wal) *adj.* not usual or common; rare —**unu'sually** *adv.* —**unu'sualness** *n.*

unutterable (un ut'ər ə b'l) *adj.* that cannot be expressed —**unut'terably** *adv.*

unvarnished (un vär'nisht) *adj.* **1.** not varnished **2.** plain; simple; unadorned [the *unvarnished* truth]

unveil (un'vāl') *vt.* to reveal as by removing a veil from —*vi.* to take off a veil; reveal oneself

unveiling *n.* a formal or ceremonial removal of a covering from a new statue, tombstone, etc.

unvoiced (un'voist') *adj.* **1.** not uttered or expressed **2.** *Phonet. same as* VOICELESS

unwary (un wãer'ē) *adj.* not wary; not alert to possible danger, trickery, etc. —**unwar'ily** *adv.* —**unwar'iness** *n.*

unwell (un'wel') *adj.* not well; ailing; ill; sick

unwept (un'wept') *adj.* **1.** not wept for; unmourned

unwholesome (un'hōl'səm) *adj.* **1.** harmful to body or mind **2.** unhealthy or unhealthy-looking **3.** morally bad —**unwhole'someness** *n.*

unwieldy (un'wēl'dē) *adj.* hard to manage, handle, etc. because of weight, shape, etc. —**unwield'iness** *n.*

unwilling (un'wil'iŋ) *adj.* **1.** not willing; reluctant **2.** done, given, etc. against one's will —**unwill'ingly** *adv.*

unwind (un'wīnd') *vt.* -wound', -wind'ing **1.** to wind off or undo (something wound) **2.** to uncoil **3.** to untangle **4.** to relax —*vi.* **1.** to become unwound, relaxed, etc.

unwise (un'wīz') *adj.* foolish or imprudent

unwitting (un wit'iŋ) *adj.* **1.** not knowing; unaware **2.** not intended; unintentional —**unwit'tingly** *adv.*

unwonted (un wōn'tid) *adj.* not usual or habitual

unworldly (un'wurld'lē) *adj.* **1.** not concerned with material values **2.** unsophisticated **3.** not of this world

unworthy (un wur'thē) *adj.* -thier, -thiest **1.** not deserving (of) **2.** not fit (of) **3.** worthless **4.** not deserved —**unwor'thily** *adv.* —**unwor'thiness** *n.*

unwrap (un'rap') *vt.* -wrapped', -wrap'ping to take off the wrapping of; open or undo —*vi.* to become unwrapped

unwritten (un'rit''n) *adj.* **1.** not written or printed **2.** operating only through custom or tradition [an *unwritten* law]

unzip (un zip') *vt., vi.* -zipped', -zip'ping to open (a zip fastener), or the zip fastener of (a garment, etc.)

up (up) *adv.* [OE.] **1.** to, in, or on a higher position or level **2.** to a later period [from childhood *up*] **3.** to a higher condition or rank **4.** to a higher amount, degree, etc. **5.** *a)* in or into an upright position *b)* out of bed **6.** in or into action, consideration, etc. *[to bring a matter up]* **7.** aside; away; by *[lay up grain]* **8.** so as to be even with in time, degree, etc. **9.** so as to be tightly closed, bound, etc. *[tie it up]* **10.** so as to stop *[to rein up a horse]* **11.** above the horizon **12.** ahead (by a specified number or amount) —*prep.* **1.** to, towards, or at a higher place on or in **2.** along —*adj.* **1.** of a high or higher position **2.** going towards a more important place from a less important one *[an up train]* **3.** above the horizon **4.** higher in amount, degree, etc. *[rents are up]* **5.** *a)* standing *b)* out of bed **6.** active, excited, etc. *[her temper was up]* **7.** at an end. *[time is up]* **8.** [Colloq.] happening *[what's up?]* —*n.* a period of prosperity, luck, etc. —*vi.* **upped, up'ping** [Colloq.] to do something suddenly or abruptly *[he up and left]* —*vt.* [Colloq.] to raise or increase *Up* is also used with some verbs to indicate intensity or completion *[drink up]* —**on the up and up** [Colloq.] **1.** honest **2.** making steady progress; improving —**up against** [Colloq.] faced with —**up and around** out of bed and again active, as after an illness —**up and doing** busy; active —**up for 1.** presented or considered for (an elective office, election, sale, etc.) **2.** before a court for —**ups and downs** good periods and bad periods —**up to** [Colloq.] **1.** occupied with; scheming *[up to mischief]* **2.** capable of **3.** as many as **4.** as far as **5.** dependent upon —**well up on** [Colloq.] well-informed about

up- *a combining form meaning* up *[uphill]*

up-and-coming *adj.* **1.** enterprising, alert, and promising **2.** gaining in importance

upbeat *n. Music* an upward stroke made by a conductor to show an unaccented beat —*adj.* lively; cheerful

upbraid (up brād´) *vt.* [< OE. *up-*, up + *bregdan*, to pull] to rebuke; censure

upbringing *n.* the training and education received while growing up

upcast *n. Mining* a ventilating shaft through which air is returned to the surface

upcountry (up´kun´trē) *adj., adv.* in or towards the interior of a country

update (up dāt´) *vt.* **-dat'ed, -dat'ing** to bring up to date so as to conform to the most recent facts, methods, ideas, etc.

upend (up end´) *vt., vi.* **1.** to turn or stand on end **2.** to upset

upgrade (up grād´) *vt.* **-grad'ed, -grad'ing** **1.** to promote to a more skilled job at higher pay **2.** to raise in importance, value, etc.

upheaval (up hē´v'l) *n.* a sudden, violent change

uphill *adv.* towards the top of a hill —*adj.* **1.** going or sloping up **2.** requiring great effort

uphold (up hōld´) *vt.* **-held´, -hold´ing 1.**

to defend or maintain against opposition **2.** to give moral support to —**uphold'er** *n.*

upholster (up hōl´star) *vt.* [< ME. *upholder*, dealer in small wares] to fit (furniture, etc.) with covering, padding, springs, etc. —**uphol'sterer** *n.*

upholstery *n., pl.* **-steries 1.** the materials used in upholstering **2.** the work of upholstering

upkeep *n.* **1.** maintenance **2.** the cost of this **3.** state of repair

upland *n.* land elevated above other land —*adj.* of or situated in upland

uplift (up lift´; *for n.* up´lift´) *vt.* **1.** to lift up **2.** to raise to a higher moral, social, or cultural level —*n.* **1.** an uplifting **2.** any influence, movement, etc. aimed at uplifting society

upmost *adj. same as* UPPERMOST

upon (ə pon´) *prep.* on, or up and on: generally interchangeable with *on*

upper (up´ər) *adj.* **1.** higher in place or position **2.** farther north or inland **3.** [U-] *Geol.* later: used of a division of a period —*n.* the part of a shoe above the sole —**on one's uppers** [Colloq.] in need; poor

Upper Canada 1. *Hist.* the official name of the part of Canada southwest of the Ottawa River and north of the lower Great Lakes **2.** *another name for* Ontario

upper case capital-letter type used in printing, as distinguished from small letters (*lower case*) —**up'per-case´** *adj.*

upper class the social class above the middle class; rich, socially prominent, or aristocratic class

uppercut *n. Boxing* a short, swinging blow directed upwards

upper hand the position of advantage or control

Upper House [*often* u- h-] the smaller and less representative branch of a legislature having two branches

uppermost *adj.* highest in place, power, authority, etc. —*adv.* in the highest place, rank, etc.

uppish *adj.* [Colloq.] arrogant, snobbish, etc.: also **up'pity** —**up'pishly** *adv.* —**up'-pishness** *n.*

upright (up´rīt´; *also for adv.* up rīt´) *adj.* **1.** standing or directed straight up; erect **2.** honourable —*adv.* in an upright position —*n.* **1.** something having an upright position, esp. a vertical support **2.** *short for* UPRIGHT PIANO —**up'right'ness** *n.*

upright piano a piano with a vertical rectangular body

uprising *n.* a rising up; specif., a revolt

uproar *n.* [Du. *oproer*, a stirring up] **1.** a violent disturbance; tumult **2.** loud, confused noise

uproarious (up rôr´ē əs) *adj.* **1.** making, or marked by, an uproar **2.** *a)* loud and boisterous, as laughter *b)* causing such laughter

uproot (up rōōt´) *vt.* **1.** to tear up by the roots **2.** to destroy or remove entirely; eradicate **3.** to displace (a person) from his habitual or native surroundings

upset (up set´; *for n. and occas. adj.* up´-

set') *vt.* **-set'**, **-set'ting** 1. *a)* to tip over; overturn *b)* to defeat, esp. unexpectedly 2. *a)* to disturb the functioning of *b)* to disturb emotionally —*vi.* to become overturned —*n.* an upsetting or being upset —*adj.* 1. overturned 2. defeated 3. disturbed, esp. emotionally —**upset'ter** *n.*

upshot *n.* [< the final shot in an archery match] the conclusion; outcome

upside down 1. with the top side or part underneath 2. in disorder; topsy-turvy —**up'side'-down'** *adj.*

upsilon (yōōp sī'lən) *n.* the twentieth letter of the Greek alphabet (Υ, υ)

upstage (up'stāj') *adv.* towards or at the rear of a stage —*adj.* 1. of the rear of a stage 2. haughty and aloof —*vt.* **-staged'**, **-stag'ing** to draw attention, as of an audience, to oneself at the expense of (another)

upstairs *adv.* 1. up the stairs 2. on or to an upper floor —*adj.* situated on an upper floor —*n.* an upper floor or floors

upstanding (up stan'diŋ) *adj.* 1. honourable 2. standing straight; erect

upstart *n.* a person who has recently come into wealth, power, etc., esp. one who is aggressive; parvenu

upstream (up'strēm') *adv., adj.* in the direction against the current of a stream

upswing *n.* a swing or trend upwards; specif., an upward trend in business

upsy-daisy (up'sə dā'zē) *interj.* [< UP] up you go: used playfully in lifting a baby

uptake *n.* a drawing up, absorbing, etc. —**quick** (or **slow**) **on the uptake** [Colloq.] quick (or slow) to understand

upthrust *n.* 1. an upward push 2. an upheaval of a part of the earth's crust

uptight *adj.* [Colloq.] 1. having repressed feelings of irritation, anger, etc. 2. very conventional or repressed in attitudes

up-to-date *adj.* 1. keeping up with what is most recent, modern, etc. 2. keeping up to one's schedule

upturn (up turn'; *for n.* up'turn') *vt., vi.* to turn up, upwards, or over —*n.* an upward turn, curve, or trend

upward *adv., adj.* 1. towards a higher place, position, degree, etc. 2. from an earlier to a later time 3. beyond (an indicated price, amount, etc.) *[tickets cost upward of £1]* Also **up'wards** *adv.*

upward mobility movement from a lower to a higher social and economic status

upwind (up'wind') *adv., adj.* in the direction from which the wind is blowing or usually blows

uraemia (yooa rēm'ya) *n* [< Gr. *ouron*, urine + *haima*, blood] a toxic condition caused by the presence in the blood of waste products normally eliminated in the urine —**urae'mic** *adj.*

uraeus (yoo rē'əs) *n.*, *pl.* **-rae'i** (-ī) [< Mod.L. < Gr. *ouraios*, cobra] the sacred serpent on the headdress of ancient Egyptian rulers

uranium (yoo rā'nē əm) *n.* [ModL. < URANUS, the planet] a very hard, heavy, radioactive metallic chemical element: it is found only in combination, and its

isotopes are important in work on atomic energy: symbol, U

Uranus (yoor'ə nəs, yoo rā'nəs) 1. *Gr. Myth.* a god who personified the heavens 2. a planet of the solar system, seventh in distance from the sun

urban (ur'bən) *adj.* [< L. *urbs*, city] of, in, or characteristic of a city or town

urban district formerly, an urban division of an administrative county, with an elected council

urbane (ur bān') *adj.* [see URBAN] polite and courteous in a smooth, polished way; refined

urban guerrilla a guerrilla operating in an urban environment, using terrorist methods of intimidation

urbanity (ur ban'ə tē) *n.*, *pl.* **-ties** the quality of being urbane

urbanize (ur'bə nīz') *vt.* **-ized'**, **-iz'ing** to change from rural to urban —**ur'baniza'-tion** *n.*

urban renewal the renewal of urban areas suffering from neglect and decay, as by clearing slums and constructing new housing, etc.

urchin (ur'chin) *n.* [< L. *ericius*, hedgehog] 1. a small mischievous child, esp. one who is poor or ragged 2. *same as* SEA URCHIN

Urdu (ooar'dōō) *n.* [Hindi] an Indic language, a variant of Hindi and an official language of Pakistan

-ure (ər) [< L.] *a suffix meaning:* 1. act or result of being *[exposure]* 2. agent of *[legislature]* 3. state *[composure]*

urea (yooar'ēə) *n.* [< Gr. *ouron*, urine] a soluble, crystalline solid, found in urine or produced synthetically: used in making plastics, etc.

ureter (yooa rēt'ər) *n.* [< Gr. *ourein*, urinate] a tube that carries urine from a kidney to the bladder

urethra (yooa rē'thra) *n.*, *pl.* **-thrae** (-thrē), **-thras** [< Gr. *ouron*, urine] the canal through which urine is discharged from the bladder in most mammals

urge (urj) *vt.* **urged**, **urg'ing** [L. *urgere*, press hard] 1. to plead with; try to persuade 2. to recommend earnestly and strongly 3. to drive or force onwards —*vi.* to make an earnest presentation of arguments, claims, etc. —*n.* an impulse to do a certain thing

urgency *n.*, *pl.* **-cies** 1. an urgent quality or state 2. insistence; importunity

urgent *adj.* 1. calling for haste, immediate action, etc. 2. insistent —**ur'gently** *adv.*

-urgy (ur'jē) [< Gr. *ergon*, work] *a combining form meaning* a working with or by means of (something specified) *[zymurgy]*

uric (yooar'ik) *adj.* of, contained in, or derived from urine

uric acid a white, odourless, crystalline substance found in urine

urinal (yooar'ə n'l, yoo rī'-) *n.* 1. a receptacle for urine 2. a place for urinating

urinary (yooar'ə nər ē) *adj.* 1. of urine 2. of the organs involved in secreting and discharging urine

urinate (yoŏər'ə nāt') vi. **-nat'ed, -nat'-**
ing to discharge urine from the body —**u'ri-**
na'tion n.

urine (yoŏər'in) n. [< L. urina] in
mammals, the yellowish fluid containing
urea and other waste products, secreted
from the blood by the kidneys, passed
to the bladder, and periodically discharged
through the urethra

urn (urn) n. [L. urna] 1. a) a vase, esp.
one with a foot or pedestal b) a container
for the ashes of a cremated body 2.
a metal container with a tap, used for
making or serving coffee, tea, etc.

urogenital (yoŏər'ō jen'ə t'l) adj. designating or of the urinary and genital organs

urology (yoŏ rol'ə jē) n. the branch of
medicine dealing with the urogenital or
urinary system —**u'rolog'ical** adj. —**urol'-**
ogist n.

Ursa Major (ur'sə) [L., Great Bear] the
most conspicuous constellation in the
northern sky: it contains the Plough

Ursa Minor [L., Little Bear] the
northernmost constellation: it contains the
North Star

ursine (ur'sīn) adj. [< L. ursus, bear]
of or like a bear

Ursuline (ur'syoo lin') n. [< Saint Ursula]
R.C.Ch. any member of a teaching order
of nuns founded c. 1537 —adj. of this order

us (us) pron. [OE.] objective case of WE

U.S., US United States

USA, U.S.A. 1. United States of America
2. United States Army

usable, useable (yoŏ'zə b'l) adj. that
can be used; fit for use —**us'abil'ity, us'a-**
bleness n.

usage (yoŏ'zij) n. 1. manner or extent
of using; treatment 2. custom; habit 3.
the way in which a word, phrase, etc.
is used, or an instance of this

use (yoŏz; for n. yoŏs) vt. **used, us'ing**
[L. uti, to use] 1. to put or bring into
action or service 2. to practise; exercise
[use your judgment] 3. to treat [to use
a friend badly] 4. to consume, expend,
etc. [to use up one's energy] 5. to take
(drugs etc.) habitually 6. to accustom
(used in the passive with to) [used to
certain ways] 7. to exploit (a person)
—vi. to be accustomed (meaning "did
at one time") [he used to live in Oxford]
—n. 1. a using or being used 2. the
ability to use 3. the right to use 4.
the need or opportunity to use 5. a way
of using 6. usefulness 7. the object or
purpose for which something is used 8.
custom; practice 9. Eccles. a distinctive
form of liturgical observance, as of a diocese
—**have no use for** 1. to have no need
of 2. to dislike strongly —**in use** being
used —**make use of** 1. to have occasion
to use 2. to exploit —**u'ser** n.

used adj. secondhand

useful adj. 1. serviceable; helpful 2.
[Colloq.] capable or desirable [he's a useful
member of the team] —**use'fully** adv.
—**use'fulness** n.

useless adj. 1. unserviceable; worthless
2. to no purpose; ineffectual —**use'lessly**
adv. —**use'lessness** n.

U-shaped adj. having the shape of a U

usher (ush'ər) n. [< L. ostium, door]
1. one who shows people to their seats
in a theatre, church, etc. 2. any of the
groom's attendants at a wedding 3. an
official who maintains order in a law court
4. an official who precedes a person of
rank in a procession —vt. 1. to escort
(others) to seats, etc. 2. to herald or
bring (in)

usherette (ush'ə ret') n. a woman usher,
as in a cinema

U.S.S.R., USSR Union of Soviet
Socialist Republics

usual (yoŏ'zhoo wəl) adj. [see USE] such
as is most often seen, heard, used, etc.;
common; ordinary; customary —**as usual**
in the usual way —**u'sually** adv.

usurious (yoŏ zhooar'ē əs) adj. 1.
practising usury 2. of or involving usury

usurp (yoŏ zurp') vt., vi. [< L. usus, a
use + rapere, seize] to take or assume
(power, position, rights, etc.) by force or
without right —**usurpa'tion** n. —**usurp'-**
er n.

usury (yoŏ'zhoo rē) n., pl. **-ries** [see USE]
1. the lending of money at interest, now
specif. at a rate of interest that is excessively
high 2. interest at such a high rate —**u'-**
surer n.

utensil (yoŏ ten's'l) n. [< L. uti, to use]
an implement or container used for a
particular purpose, now esp. one used in
a kitchen

uterine (yoŏ'tə rīn') adj. of the uterus

uterus (yoŏt'ər əs) n., pl. **u'teri'** (-ī') [L.]
a hollow, muscular organ of female
mammals in which the ovum is deposited
and the embryo and foetus are developed;
womb

utilidor (yoŏ til'ə dôr') n. [Canad.] above-
ground, insulated casing for pipes carrying
water, etc. in permafrost regions

utilitarian (yoŏ til'ə tāər'ē ən) adj. 1.
designed for use rather than beauty 2.
of or believing in utilitarianism —n. a
person who believes in utilitarianism

utilitarianism n. 1. the doctrine that
the value of anything is determined solely
by its utility 2. the doctrine that the
purpose of all action should be to bring
about the greatest happiness of the greatest
number

utility (yoŏ til'ə tē) n., pl. **-ties** [< L.
uti, to use] 1. usefulness 2. something
useful 3. something useful to the public,
esp. the service of electricity, gas, water,
etc. —adj. for practical use with little
attention to beauty

utility room a room containing various
household appliances and equipment, for
heating, laundry, etc.

utilize (yoŏt'əl īz') vt. **-lized', -liz'ing** to
make practical or profitable use of —**u'tili-**
za'tion n.

utmost (ut'mōst') adj. [< OE. ut, out]
1. farthest 2. greatest —n. the most
that is possible

Utopia (yoŏ tō'pē ə) n. [< Gr. ou, not

+ *topos*, a place] an imaginary island described by Sir Thomas More as having a perfect political and social system : any idealized place, state, or situation of perfection —Uto′**pian** *adj.*

utricle (yōō′tri k'l) *n.* [< L. *uter*, leather bag] a small sac, vesicle, or baglike part

utter[1] (ut′ər) *adj.* [< OE. compar. of *ut*, out] 1. complete; total 2. unqualified; absolute —ut′**terly** *adv.*

utter[2] *vt.* [< ME. < *utter*, outward < *ut*, out] 1. to express with the voice 2. to pass (counterfeit money, forged cheques, etc.)

utterance *n.* 1 something uttered 2. the act or power of uttering

uttermost *adj., n.* *same as* UTMOST

U-turn *n.* a turning completely around, esp. of a vehicle within the width of a street or road

UV, uv ultraviolet

UVULA

uvula (yōō′vyoo lə) *n., pl.* **-las, -lae**′(-lē′) [< L. *uva*, grape] the small, fleshy part of the soft palate hanging down above the back of the tongue —u′**vular** *adj.*

uxorious (uk sôr ē əs) *adj.* [< L. *uxor*, wife] dotingly fond of or submissive to one's wife

V

V, v (vē) *n., pl.* **V's, v's** the twenty-second letter of the English alphabet

V (vē) *n.* **1.** something shaped like V **2.** a Roman numeral for 5

V 1. *Chem.* vanadium **2.** *Physics the symbol for* volt

V v 1. velocity **2.** victory **3.** volt

v. 1. [G. *von*] of **2.** [L. *vide*] see **3.** verb **4.** verse **5.** verso **6.** versus **7.** very **8.** violin **9.** voice **10.** volume

VA, V.A. 1. Vicar Apostolic **2.** Vice-Admiral **3.** (Royal Order of) Victoria and Albert

vac (vak) *n.* [Colloq.] vacation

vacancy (vā'kən sē) *n., pl.* **-cies 1.** a being vacant; emptiness **2.** empty space **3.** an unoccupied position or office **4.** a room, etc. available for rent

vacant (vā'kənt) *adj.* [< L. *vacare*, be empty] **1.** having nothing in it; empty **2.** not held, filled, or occupied, as a position, seat, house, etc. **3.** without thought, interest, etc. [*a vacant mind*] **4.** free from work or activity —**va'cantly** *adv.*

vacate (və kāt') *vt.* **-cat'ed, -cat'ing** [< prec.] **1.** to make (an office, house, etc.) vacant **2.** *Law* to make void; annul

vacation (və kā'shən) *n.* [< L. *vacatio*] **1.** a period of the year when law courts or universities are closed **2.** [U.S.] a holiday —*vi* [U.S.] to take a holiday

vaccinate (vak'si nāt') *vt., vi.* **-nat'ed, -nat'ing** to inoculate with a vaccine in order to prevent a disease, esp. smallpox —**vac'cina'tion** *n.*

vaccine (vak'sēn) *n.* [< L. *vacca*, cow: from use of cowpox virus in smallpox vaccine] any preparation of killed or weakened organisms introduced into the body to produce immunity to a specific disease

vacillate (vas'i lāt') *vi.* **-lat'ed, -lat'ing** [< L. *vacillare*] **1.** to show indecision **2.** to sway to and fro —**vac'illat'ing** *adj.* —**vac'illa'tion** *n.*

vacuity (və kyōo'ə tē) *n., pl.* **-ties** [< L. *vacuus*, empty] **1.** emptiness **2.** an empty space; void **3.** lack of intelligence, interest, or thought **4.** inanity

vacuous (vak'yoo wəs) *adj.* [L. *vacuus*] **1.** empty **2.** stupid; senseless —**vac'uousness** *n.*

vacuum (vak'yooəm) *n., pl.* **-uums, -ua** [L.] **1.** a space with nothing at all in it **2.** an enclosed space, as that inside a vacuum tube, out of which most of the air or gas has been taken, as by pumping **3.** a void **4.** *short for* VACUUM

CLEANER —*vt., vi.* to clean with a vacuum cleaner

vacuum cleaner a machine for cleaning carpets, floors, upholstery, etc. by suction

vacuum flask (or **jug**) *same as* THERMOS

vacuum-packed *adj.* packed in an airtight container to keep the contents fresh

vacuum pump a pump used to draw air or gas out of a sealed space

vacuum tube a sealed tube, which has been made a partial vacuum, for observing the effect of a discharge of electricity through rarefied gas, as a neon tube

V.A.D. Voluntary Aid Detachment

vade mecum (vā'dē mē'kəm) [L., go with me] something carried about for constant use, reference, etc., as a handbook

vagabond (vag'ə bond') *n.* [< L. *vagari*, wander] **1.** a person who wanders from place to place **2.** a tramp **3.** an idle or shiftless person —*adj.* **1.** wandering **2.** vagrant; shiftless —**vag'abond'age, vag'abond'ism** *n.*

vagary (və'gər ē) *n., pl.* **-garies** [< L. *vagari*, wander] an odd, whimsical, or eccentric idea or action —**vagar'ious** (və gāər'ē əs) *adj.*

vagina (və jī'nə) *n., pl.* **-nas, -nae** (-nē) [L., a sheath] in female mammals, the canal leading from the vulva to the uterus —**vagi'nal** *adj.*

vagrant (vā'grənt) *n.* [prob. < OFr. *walcrer*, wander] a person who wanders from place to place; esp., one without a regular job, supporting himself by begging, etc.; tramp —*adj.* **1.** wandering; nomadic **2.** of or like a vagrant **3.** following no fixed direction or course —**va'grancy** *n.*

vague (vāg) *adj.* **va'guer, va'guest** [< L. *vagus*, wandering] **1.** not explicit; imprecise **2.** indefinite in shape or form **3.** not sharp, certain, or precise in thought or expression **4.** not known or determined —**vague'ly** *adv.* —**vague'ness** *n.*

vain (vān) *adj.* [< L. *vanus*, empty] **1.** excessively proud of one's appearance, etc.; conceited **2.** having no real value; worthless [*vain pomp*] **3.** without effect; futile [*a vain attempt*] —**in vain 1.** unsuccessfully **2.** profanely —**vain'ly** *adv.* —**vain'ness** *n.*

vainglory (vān glôr'ē) *n.* [< L. *vana gloria*, empty boasting] **1.** extreme self-pride and boastfulness **2.** vain show —**vain'glo'rious** *adj.*

VALANCE

valance (val′əns) *n.* [< ?] **1.** a short curtain hanging from the edge of a bed, shelf, etc. **2.** a short drapery or facing across the top of a window Also **valence**

vale (vāl) *n.* [< L. *vallis*] [Poet.] a valley

valediction (val′i dik′shən) *n.* [< L. *vale,* farewell + *dicere,* say] **1.** a bidding farewell **2.** something said in parting —**val′edic′tory** *adj.*

valence (vā′ləns) *n.* [< L. *valere,* be strong] *Chem.* the combining capacity of an element or radical, as measured by the number of hydrogen or chlorine atoms which one radical or atom of the element will combine with or replace: also **va′lency**

valency *n.* any of the units of valence which an element may have

-valent (vā′lənt) [< L. *valens*] *Chem.* a suffix meaning: **1.** having a specified valence **2.** having a specified number of valences

valentine (val′ən tīn′) *n.* **1.** a greetings card or gift sent to one's sweetheart on St. Valentine's Day **2.** a sweetheart selected for such greeting

valerian (və lēər′ē ən) *n.* [< ML. *valeriana*] **1.** a plant with white, pink, red, or purplish flowers **2.** a drug made from its roots, formerly used as a sedative

valet (val′it) *n.* [Fr.] **1.** a man's personal manservant who takes care of his clothes, etc. **2.** an employee, as of a hotel, who cleans or presses clothes, etc. —*vt., vi.* to serve (a person) as a valet

valetudinarian (vai′i tyoo′di näar′ē ən) *n.* [< L. *valere,* be strong] **1.** a person in poor health **2.** a person who worries constantly about his health —*adj.* **1.** in poor health **2.** anxiously concerned about one's health Also **val′etu′dinary**

Valhalla (val hal′ə) *n.* *Norse Myth* the abode of dead heroes

valiant (val′yənt) *adj.* [< L. *valere,* be strong] courageous; brave —**val′iance** *n.*

valid (val′id) *adj.* [< L. *valere,* be strong] **1.** well-grounded on principles or evidence, as an argument; sound **2.** having legal force —**val′idly** *adv.*

validate (val′i dāt′) *vt.* -dat′ed, -dat′ing **1.** to prove to be valid **2.** to declare legally valid —**val′ida′tion** *n.*

validity (və lid′ə tē) *n., pl.* -ties the state, quality, or fact of being valid in law or in argument, proof, etc.

valise (və lēz′) *n.* [Fr.] a piece of hand luggage

Valkyrie (val kēar′ē) *n.* one of several Norse war-goddesses who conduct the dead to Valhalla

valley (val′ē) *n., pl.* -leys [< L. *vallis*] **1.** low land lying between hills or mountains **2.** the land drained by a river system **3.** any long dip or hollow

valour (val′ər) *n.* [< L. *valere,* be strong] great courage or bravery: U.S. sp., **val′-or** —**val′orous** *adj.*

valuable (val′yoo wə b'l) *adj.* **1.** *a)* being worth money *b)* having great monetary value **2.** highly regarded as precious, useful, etc. —*n.* [*usually pl.*] an article of value, as a piece of jewellery —**val′uably** *adv.*

valuation (val′yoo wā′shən) *n.* **1.** the act of determining the value of anything, esp., assessment by a professional valuer **2.** determined or estimated value **3.** estimation of the worth, merit, etc. of anything

value (val′yoo) *n.* [< L. *valere*] **1.** the worth of a thing in money or goods **2.** estimated worth **3.** purchasing power **4.** that quality of a thing that makes it more or less desirable, useful, etc. **5.** [*pl.*] the social principles, goals, or standards held by an individual, class, society, etc. **6.** numerical order assigned to a playing card, etc. **7.** relative duration, intensity, etc. **8.** *Math.* the quantity for which a symbol stands —*vt.* -ued, -uing **1.** to estimate the value of; appraise **2.** to place an estimate of worth on [*to value* health above wealth*]* **3.** to think highly of; prize —**val′ueless** *adj.* —**val′uer** *n.*

value-added tax a tax levied on the difference between a commodity's pretax selling price per unit and its materials' cost per unit

valued *adj.* **1.** estimated; appraised **2.** highly thought of; esteemed

value judgment a subjective estimate of the worth, goodness, etc. of a person, action, event, etc.

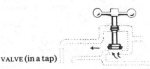

VALVE (in a tap)

valve (valv) *n.* [L. *valva,* leaf of a folding door] **1.** *Mech. a)* any device in a pipe, etc. that regulates the flow by means of a flap, lid, plug, etc. *b)* this flap, lid, plug, etc. **2.** *Anat.* a membranous structure which permits body fluids to flow in one direction only, or opens and closes a tube, etc. **3.** *same as* THERMIONIC VALVE **4.** *Music* a device, as in the trumpet, that opens an auxiliary to the main tube, lengthening the air column and lowering the pitch **5.** *Zool.* one of the parts making up the shell of a mollusc, clam, etc. —**valve′less** *adj.* —**valve′like′** *adj.*

valvular (val′vyoo lər) *adj.* **1.** having the form or function of a valve **2.** having a valve or valves 3. of a valve or valves; esp., of the valves of the heart

vamoose (və mōōs′) *vi., vt.* **-moosed′, -moos′ing** [Sp. *vamos*, let us go] [Old Slang] to leave quickly: also **vamose′** (-mōs′) **-mosed′, -mos′ing**

vamp¹ (vamp) *n.* [< OFr. *avant*, before + *pié*, foot] 1. something patched up to seem new 2. the part of a boot or shoe covering the instep and, in some styles, the toes 3. *Music* an improvised accompaniment —*vt.* 1. to patch (*up*); repair 2. *Music* to improvise

vamp² *n.* [< VAMPIRE] a seductive woman who exploits men by use of her sexual charms —*vt., vi.* to seduce or beguile (a man) by the use of feminine charms

vampire (vam′pīər) *n.* [< Slav.] 1. *Folklore* a corpse that comes alive at night and sucks the blood of sleeping persons 2. a person who preys on others in a dishonest or wicked way —**vam′pirism** *n.*

vampire bat a tropical American bat that lives on the blood of animals

van¹ (van) *n.* the vanguard

van² *n.* [< CARAVAN] 1. a closed vehicle for carrying goods, etc. 2. a closed railway carriage for luggage or goods, or for the guard

vanadium (və nā′dē əm) *n.* [< ON. *Vanadis*, goddess of love] a rare, ductile metallic chemical element used in steel alloys: symbol, V

Van Allen (radiation) belt (van al′ən) [< J. A. *Van Allen*] either of two belts of high intensity radiation encircling the earth at varying altitudes

vandal (van′d'l) *n.* [< the *Vandals*, an E Gmc. tribe that sacked Rome (455 A.D.)] a person who destroys or spoils things on purpose, esp. works of art or public property, etc. —**van′dalism** *n.*

vandalize *vt.* **-ized′, -iz′ing** to destroy or damage (public or private property) on purpose

Vandyke beard (van dīk′) a closely trimmed, pointed beard, as seen in portraits by Van Dyck

vane (vān) *n.* [OE. *fana*, a flag] 1. *same as* WEATHER VANE 2. any of the flat blades set around an axle and rotated about it by moving air, water, etc. [the *vanes* of a windmill] or mechanically rotated to move the air, water, etc. [the *vanes* of a turbine]

vanguard (van′gärd′) *n.* [< OFr. *avant*, before + *garde*, guard] 1. the front part of an army in an advance 2. the leading position or persons in a movement

vanilla (və nil′ə) *n.* [< Sp. *vaina*, pod] 1. a tropical climbing orchid with fragrant flowers and podlike capsules (**vanilla beans**) 2. a flavouring made from these capsules —**vanil′lic** *adj.*

vanish (van′ish) *vi.* [see EVANESCE] 1. to go or pass suddenly from sight 2. to cease to exist; come to an end

vanishing cream a cosmetic cream which sinks into the skin leaving no trace of grease

vanishing point the point where parallel

lines receding from the observer seem to come together

vanity (van′ə tē) *n., pl.* **-ties** [< L. *vanus*, vain] 1. excessive pride in oneself, one's possessions, etc. 2. a being vain, or excessively proud of oneself, one's possessions, etc. 3. anything that is vain or futile 4. worthlessness; futility

vanity case a woman's small travelling case fitted for carrying cosmetics, toilet articles, etc.

vanity unit a wash basin built into a tiled, etc. surface, usually with storage space beneath it

vanquish (vaŋ′kwish) *vt.* [< L. *vincere*] 1. to conquer or defeat 2. to overcome (a feeling, condition, etc.); suppress —**van′-quisher** *n.*

vantage (vän′tij) *n.* [see ADVANTAGE] 1. an advantageous position 2. a position that allows a clear and broad view: also **vantage point** 3. *Tennis same as* ADVANTAGE

vapid (vap′id) *adj.* [L. *vapidus*] 1. having no taste or flavour 2. lifeless; dull; boring —**vapid′ity** *n.*

vaporize (vā′pə rīz′) *vt., vi.* **-ized′, -iz′-ing** to change into vapour, as by heating or spraying —**va′poriza′tion** *n.* —**va′por-iz′er** *n.*

vaporous (vā′pər əs) *adj.* 1. forming vapour 2. full of vapour 3. like vapour 4. fleeting, fanciful, etc. Also **va′poury**

vapour (vā′pər) *n.* [L. *vapor*] 1. *a)* visible particles of moisture floating in the air, as fog or steam *b)* anything, as smoke, fumes, etc., given off in a cloud 2. the gaseous form of any substance that is usually a liquid or solid 3. [*pl.*] [Obs.] depressed spirits (often with *the*) U.S. sp. vapor

var. 1. variant(s) 2. various

variable (vãar′ē ə b'l) *adj.* 1. apt to change or vary; changeable, inconstant, etc. 2. that can be changed or varied 3. *Math.* having no fixed value —*n.* 1. anything changeable; thing that varies 2. *Math.* a quantity that may have a number of different values or a symbol for this —**var′i-abil′ity** *n.* —**var′iably** *adv.*

variance (vãar′ē əns) *n.* 1. a varying or being variant 2. degree of change or difference; discrepancy 3. a quarrel; dispute —**at variance** not in agreement; conflicting

variant *adj.* varying; different in some way from others of the same kind —*n.* anything variant, as a different spelling of the same word

variation (vãar′ē ā′shən) *n.* 1. *a)* a change in form, condition, extent, etc. *b)* the degree of such change 2. a thing that is somewhat different from another of the same kind 3. *Music* the repetition of a melody or theme with changes in harmony, rhythm, key, etc. —**var′ia′tional** *adj.*

varicoloured (vãar′i kul′ərd) *adj.* of several or many colours

varicose (var′i kōs′) *adj.* [< L. *varix*, enlarged vein] abnormally and irregularly

varied (vãr'id) *adj.* 1. of different kinds; various 2. variegated 3. changed; altered —**var'iedly** *adv.*

variegated (vãr'i gāt'id) *adj.* displaying differently coloured spots, patches, streaks, etc. —**var'iega'tion** *n.*

variety (və rī'ə tē) *n., pl.* -ties [< L. *varietas*] 1. a being various or varied; absence of sameness 2. any of the various forms of something; sort [*varieties* of cloth] 3. a number of different kinds [a *variety* of fruits] 4. a subdivision of a species —*adj.* of or in a variety show

variety show a show made up of different kinds of acts, as comic skits, songs, dances, etc.

variorum (vãr'ē ôr'əm) *n.* [L., of various (scholars)] 1. an edition, as of a literary work, with notes by various editors, etc. 2. an edition containing variant texts

various (vãr'ē əs) *adj.* [L. *varius*, diverse] 1. differing one from another; of several kinds 2. several or many —**var'iously** *adv.*

varlet (vär'lit) *n.* [OFr.: see VALET] [Archaic] a scoundrel; knave

varmint, varment (vär'mint) *n.* [< VERMIN] [Dial. or Colloq.] a person or animal regarded as objectionable

varnish (vär'nish) *n.* [< ML. *veronix*, resin] 1. a preparation made of resinous substances dissolved in oil, alcohol, etc., used to give a hard, glossy surface to wood, etc. 2. the hard, glossy surface produced 3. a surface gloss or smoothness, as of manner —*vt.* 1. to cover with varnish 2. to smooth over in a false way

varsity (vär'sə tē) *n., pl.* -ties [< UNIVERSITY] [Colloq.] university

varve (värv) *n.* [Swed. *varv*, layer] an annual layer of glacial sediment deposited in lakes and fiords

vary (vãr'ē) *vt.* **var'ied, var'ying** [< L. *varius*, various] 1. to change; alter 2. to make different from one another 3. to give variety to —*vi.* 1. to differ or change 2. to deviate or depart (*from*)

vas (vas) *n., pl.* **vasa** (vā'sə) [L.] *Anat., Biol.* a vessel or duct —**vasal** (vā's'l) *adj.*

vascular (vas'kyoo lər) *adj.* [< L. *vas*, vessel] of or having vessels or special cells for carrying blood, sap, etc.

vas deferens (vas'def'ə renz') *pl.* **vasa deferentia** (vā'sə def'ə ren'shē ə) [L.] the duct that carries sperm from the testicle to the ejaculatory duct of the penis

vase (vāz) *n.* [< L. *vas*, vessel] an open container used for decoration, holding flowers, etc.

vasectomy (va sek'tə mē) *n., pl.* -mies [< VAS + -ECTOMY] the cutting, tying, and removing of part of the vas deferens for the purpose of sterilizing sexually

Vaseline (vas'i lēn') [< G. *Was(ser)*, water + Gr. *el(aion)*, oil] *Trademark* petroleum jelly used in ointments, etc.

vassal (vas''l) *n.* [< ML. *vassus*, servant] 1. a person in the feudal system who held land in return for fealty, military help, etc. to an overlord 2. a subordinate, servant, slave, etc. —**vas'salage** *n.*

vast (väst) *adj.* [L. *vastus*] very great in size, extent, amount, degree, etc. —**vast'ly** *adv.* —**vast'ness** *n.*

vat (vat) *n.* [OE. *fæt*] a large tank, tub, or cask for holding liquids, as for use in a manufacturing process

V.A.T. value-added tax

Vatican (vat'i kən) 1. the papal palace in Vatican City 2. the papal government or authority

vaudeville (vō'də vil) *n.* [Fr. < *Vau-de-Vire*, a valley in Normandy, famous for light songs] a stage show consisting of mixed speciality acts, including songs, dances, comic skits, etc. —**vaudevil'lian** *n., adj.*

vault[1] (vôlt) *n.* [< L. *volvere*, to roll] 1. an arched roof or ceiling 2. an arched chamber or space, esp. when underground 3. a cellar room used for storage 4. a burial chamber 5. a secure room for the safekeeping of valuables, as in a bank 6. the sky as a vaultlike canopy —*vt.* 1. to cover with a vault 2. to build as a vault —*vi.* to curve like a vault —**vault'ed** *adj.*

vault[2] *vi.* [< L. *volvere*, to roll] to leap as over a barrier, esp. putting the hands on the barrier or using a long pole —*vt.* to vault over —*n.* a vaulting —**vault'er** *n.*

vaulting[1] *n.* the arched work forming a vault

vaulting[2] *adj.* 1. that vaults or leaps 2. reaching too far [*vaulting* ambition]

vaunt (vônt) *vi., vt.* [< L. *vanus*, vain] to boast or brag (of) —*n.* a boast —**vaunt'ed** *adj.*

vb. 1. verb 2. verbal

V.C. 1. Vice Chairman 2. Vice Chancellor 3. Vice-Consul 4. Victoria Cross

VD, V.D. venereal disease

VDU visual display unit

VE Victory in Europe —**V-E Day** (vē'ē') May 8, 1945, the official date of Germany's surrender ending the European phase of World War II

've *contraction of* HAVE [we've seen it]

veal (vēl) *n.* [< L. *vitulus*, calf] the flesh of a young calf, used as food

vector (vek'tər) *n.* [L., carrier] 1. *Math.* a) a physical quantity with magnitude and direction, such as a force or velocity b) a line representing such a quantity 2. a carrier, as an insect, of a disease-producing organism

Veda (vā'də) *n.* [Sans. *veda*, knowledge] the ancient sacred books of Hinduism —**Vedaic** (vi dā'ik), **Ve'dic** *adj.*

veer (vēər) *vi.* [< Fr. *virer*, turn round] 1. to change direction; turn 2. to change sides, as from one opinion to another 3. to turn clockwise: said of the wind —*n.* a change of direction

veg (vej) *n.* [Colloq.] a vegetable or vegetables

Vega (vē′gə) [ML. < Ar.] a very bright star in the constellation Lyra

vegan (vē′gən) *n.* [< VEGETARIAN] a person who eats no animal product

vegetable (vej′tə b'l) *n.* [see VEGETATE] 1. any plant that is eaten whole or in part, raw or cooked, as the potato, pea, celery, lettuce, etc. 2. [Colloq.] a person who has lost control of his mental faculties, limbs, etc. as from an injury —*adj.* 1. of, like, or from vegetables [*vegetable oil*] 2. of plants in general [*vegetable kingdom*]

vegetable marrow 1. a plant yielding long, green striped fruit 2. the fruit of the marrow eaten as a vegetable

vegetable oil any of various liquid fats derived from the fruits or seeds of plants

vegetal (vej′it'l) *adj.* *same as* VEGETABLE

vegetarian (vej′i tãr′ē ən) *n.* a person who eats no meat; strictly, one who believes in a vegetable diet —*adj.* 1. of vegetarians, their principles, etc. 2. consisting only of vegetables, fruits, etc. —**veg′etar′ianism** *n.*

vegetate (vej′i tāt′) *vi.* -**tat′ed**, -**tat′ing** [< L. *vegere*, quicken] 1. to grow as plants 2. to lead a dull, inactive life

vegetation (vej′i tā′shən) *n.* plant life in general

vegetative (vej′i tə tiv) *adj.* 1. of plants or plant growth 2. growing as plants 3. helping plant growth [*vegetative* loams]

vehement (vē′i mənt) *adj.* [< L. *vehemens*, eager] full of or showing very strong feeling; intense, fervent, impassioned, etc. —**ve′hemence, ve′hemency** *n.* —**ve′hemently** *adv.*

vehicle (vē′i k'l) *n.* [< L. *vehere*, to carry] 1. a means of carrying persons or things, as a motor car, bicycle, etc. 2. a means of expressing ideas 3. *Painting* a liquid, as water or oil, with which pigments are mixed for use 4. a substance, as a syrup, in which medicines are given —**vehicular** (vi hik′yoo lər) *adj.*

veil (vāl) *n.* [< L. *velum*, cloth] 1. a piece of light fabric, as net, worn, esp. by women, over the face or head to hide the features or as an ornament 2. a part of a nun's headdress, falling round the face and over the shoulders 3. anything used to separate, cover, or conceal [a *veil* of silence] —*vt.* to cover, conceal, etc. with or as with a veil —**take the veil** to become a nun

veiled *adj.* 1. wearing or covered with a veil 2. concealed, disguised, etc. [a *veiled* threat]

vein (vān) *n.* [L. *vena*] 1. any blood vessel bringing blood back to the heart 2. any riblike support in an insect wing 3. any of the fine lines in a leaf 4. a layer of mineral, rock, etc. in a fissure or zone of different rock; lode 5. a streak of a different colour, etc., as in marble 6. a distinctive quality or strain [a *vein*

of humour] 7. a temporary state of mind; mood —*veined adj.*

veiny *adj.* -**ier**, -**iest** full of veins or veinlike markings

Velcro (vel′krō) [< VEL(VET)] *Trademark* a nylon material made with a surface of tiny hooks and one of pile: matching strips are used in garments, etc. as fasteners, easily pressed together or pulled apart

veld, veldt (velt, felt) *n.* [Afrik. < MDu. *veld*, field] in South Africa, open grassy country

veldskoen (felt′skoon′) *n.* [< Afrik.] [S Afr.] an ankle-high boot, orig. of rawhide

veleta (və lē′tə) *n.* [Sp., weather cock] an old-time dance in slow triple time: also **vale′ta**

vellum (vel′əm) *n.* [see VEAL] 1. a fine parchment used for writing on or for binding books 2. a manuscript on vellum 3. a strong paper resembling vellum

velocipede (vi los′i pēd′) *n.* [< L. *velox*, swift + *pes*, foot] an early bicycle or tricycle

velocity (vi los′ə tē) *n.*, *pl.* -**ties** [< L. *velox*, swift] 1. quickness of motion or action; speed 2. rate of motion in relation to time

velour, velours (və looər′) *n.*, *pl.* **velours′** [< L. *villus*, shaggy hair] a fabric with a soft nap like velvet

velvet (vel′vit) *n.* [< L. *villus*, shaggy hair] 1. a rich fabric of silk, cotton, nylon, etc. with a soft, thick pile 2. the soft, furry covering of the newly-formed antlers of a deer —*adj.* 1. made of velvet 2. smooth or soft like velvet —**on velvet** in a position of ease or advantage —**vel′vety** *adj.*

velveteen (vel′vi tēn′) *n.* a velvetlike cotton cloth

Ven. Venerable

vena cava (vē′nə kā′və) *pl.* **ve′nae ca′vae** (vē′nē kā′vē) [< L. *vena*, vein + *cava*, hollow] *Anat.* either of two large veins carrying blood to the right atrium of the heart

venal (vē′n'l) *adj.* [< L. *venum*, sale] open to, or characterized by, bribery or corruption —**venal′ity** (-nal′ə tē) *n.* —**ve′nally** *adv.*

venation (vē nā′shən) *n.* [< L. *vena*, vein] 1. an arrangement or system of veins, as in an insect's wing or a leaf 2. such veins collectively

vend (vend) *vt.*, *vi.* [< L. *venum dare*, offer for sale] to sell, esp. by peddling

vendetta (ven det′ə) *n.* [It. < L. *vindicta*, vengeance] 1. a feud in which relatives of a murdered or wronged person seek vengeance on the guilty person or his family 2. any bitter feud —**vendet′tist** *n.*

vendible (ven′də b'l) *adj.* [see VEND] capable of being sold

vending machine a coin-operated machine for selling certain kinds of articles, refreshments, etc.

vendor, vender (ven′dôr) *n.* 1. one who sells 2. *same as* VENDING MACHINE

veneer (və nēər′) *n.* [< Fr. *fournir,* furnish] 1. a thin layer used to veneer something 2. a surface appearance that hides what is below —*vt.* 1. to cover with a thin layer of finer material; esp., to cover (wood) with wood of a finer quality 2. to make outwardly attractive

venerable (ven′ər ə b'l) *adj.* 1. worthy of respect or reverence by reason of age, dignity, etc. 2. *a) Anglican Ch.* an archdeacon's title *b) R.C.Ch.* a title indicating the lowest of the three degrees of sanctity —**ven′erabil′ity** *n.* —**ven′erably** *adv.*

venerate (ven′ə rāt′) *vt.* -at′ed, -at′ing [< L. *venerari,* to worship] to feel or show deep respect for

veneration (ven′ə rā′shən) *n.* 1. deep respect and reverence 2. an act showing this

venereal (və nēər′ē əl) *adj.* [< L. *venus,* love] 1. *a)* transmitted only or chiefly by sexual intercourse with an infected individual, as syphilis and gonorrhoea *b)* infected with a venereal disease *c)* of venereal disease 2. relating to sexual love or intercourse

Venetian (və nē′shən) *adj.* of Venice, its people, culture, etc. —*n.* a native or inhabitant of Venice

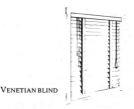

VENETIAN BLIND

Venetian blind [*also* v- b-] a window blind made of a number of thin, horizontal slats that can be set at any angle to regulate the light passing through

vengeance (ven′jəns) *n.* [see VINDICATE] 1. the return of an injury for an injury, in punishment; revenge 2. the desire to make such a return —**with a vengeance** 1. with great force or fury 2. to an excessive or unusual extent

vengeful *adj.* seeking vengeance; vindictive

venial (vē′nē el) *adj.* [< L. *venia,* grace] 1. that can be forgiven, pardoned, or excused 2. *R.C.Ch.* not causing spiritual death : said of sins not regarded as serious —**ve′nially** *adv.*

venison (ven′zən, ven′i s'n) *n.* [< L. *venari,* to hunt] the flesh of deer, used as food

Venn diagrams (ven) [< J. *Venn*] *Math.* diagrams using overlapping circles to show relationships between sets

venom (ven′əm) *n.* [< L. *venenum,* a poison] 1. the poison secreted by some snakes, spiders, etc., injected into the victim by bite or sting 2. spite; malice

venomous *adj.* 1. full of venom; poisonous 2. full of ill will; malicious 3. *Zool.* able to inject venom —**ven′omously** *adv.* —**ven′omousness** *n.*

venous (vē′nəs) *adj.* [L. *venosus*] 1. of or having veins 2. designating blood carried in veins

vent[1] (vent) *n.* [< L. *ventus,* a wind] 1. a small opening to let gas, etc. out 2. *Zool.* the excretory opening in animals 3. a means of escaping; outlet 4. expression; release [giving vent to emotion] —*vt.* 1. to give release or expression to 2. to make a vent in 3. to let (steam, gas, etc.) out through an opening

vent[2] *n.* [< L. *findere,* to split] a vertical slit in a garment, as one in the back of a jacket

ventilate (ven′ti lāt′) *vt.* -lat′ed, -lat′ing [< L. *ventus,* a wind] 1. to circulate fresh air in (a room, etc.) 2. to put a vent in, to let air, gas, etc. escape 3. to examine and discuss (a grievance, etc.) openly —**ven′tila′tion** *n.*

ventilator *n.* any device used to bring in fresh air and drive out foul air

ventral (ven′trəl) *adj.* [< L. *venter,* belly] of, on, or near the belly —**ven′trally** *adv.*

ventricle (ven′tri k'l) *n.* [< L. *venter,* belly] 1. either of the two lower chambers of the heart which receive blood from the atria and pump it into the arteries 2. a small cavity in the brain —**ventric′ular** *adj.*

ventriloquism (ven tril′ə kwiz′m) *n.* [< L. *venter,* belly + *loqui,* speak] the art of speaking so that the voice seems to come from some source other than the speaker : also **ventril′oquy** (-kwè) —**ventril′oquist** *n.* —**ventril′oquize′** *vi., vt.*

venture (ven′chər) *n.* [see ADVENTURE] 1. a risky undertaking, as in business 2. something on which a risk is taken —*vt.* -tured, -turing 1. to risk; hazard 2. to take the risk of; brave 3. to express (an opinion, etc.) at the risk of being criticized, etc. —*vi.* to do or go at some risk —**ven′turer** *n.* —**at a venture** by mere chance

venturesome *adj.* 1. inclined to venture; daring 2. risky; hazardous Also **ven′turous**

venue (ven′yōō) *n.* [< L. *venire,* come] 1. *a)* a meeting place *b)* the scene of an action or event 2. *Law a)* the locality in which a cause of action or crime occurs *b)* the locality in which a jury is drawn and a case tried —**change of venue** 1. a change of rendezvous 2. *Law* the substitution of another place of trial, as when the jury or court is likely to be prejudiced

Venus (vē′nəs) [L., love] 1. *Rom. Myth.* the goddess of love and beauty 2. a planet in the solar system, second in distance from the sun

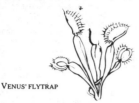

VENUS' FLYTRAP

Venus' flytrap a swamp plant having leaves with two hinged blades that snap shut and so trap insects

veracious (vərā′shəs) *adj.* [< L. *verus*, true] 1. habitually truthful; honest 2. true; accurate

veracity (vəras′ətē) *n., pl.* -ties 1. honesty 2. accuracy or precision 3. truth

veranda, verandah (vəran′də) *n.* [< Port. *varanda*, balcony] an open gallery, usually roofed, along the outside of a building

verb (vʉrb) *n.* [< L. *verbum*, word] a word expressing action, existence, or occurrence —*adj.* of, or functioning as, a verb

verbal (vʉr′b'l) *adj.* 1. of, in, or by means of words 2. concerned merely with words rather than with facts, ideas, or actions 3. oral rather than written 4. *Gram.* of, like, or derived from a verb —*n. Gram.* a verbal noun or other word derived from a verb : in English, gerunds, infinitives, and participles are verbals —**ver′bally** *adv.*

verbalism *n.* 1. a word or word phrase 2. words only, without any real meaning

verbalize *vi., vt.* -ized′, -iz′ing 1. to be wordy, or verbose 2. to express in words —**ver′baliza′tion** *n.*

verbal noun *Gram.* a noun derived from a verb, esp. a gerund or an infinitive (Ex.: *walking* is healthy)

verbatim (vʉr bāt′im) *adv., adj.* [< L. *verbum*, word] word for word

verbena (vʉr bē′nə) *n.* [< L., foliage] any of a group of ornamental plants with spikes or clusters of red, white, or purplish flowers

verbiage (vʉr′bē ij) *n.* [< L. *verbum*, word] an excess of words; wordiness

verbose (vər bōs′) *adj.* [< L. *verbum*, word] using too many words; wordy —**ver-bos′ity** (-bos′ə tē) *n.*

verdant (vʉr′d'nt) *adj.* [prob. < VERDURE] 1. covered with green vegetation 2. green 3. inexperienced; immature —**ver′dancy** *n.*

verdict (vʉr′dikt) *n.* [< L. *vere*, truly + *dicere*, say] 1. *Law* the decision reached by a jury 2. any decision or judgment

verdigris (vʉr′di gris) *n.* [< OFr. *verd*, green + *de*, of + *Grece*, Greece] a green

or greenish-blue coating that forms on brass, bronze, or copper

verdure (vʉr′jər) *n.* [OFr. < *verd*, green] 1. the fresh green colour of growing things 2. green vegetation —**ver′dured** *adj.* —**ver′durous** *adj.*

verge[1] (vʉrj) *n.* [< L. *virga*, rod] 1. the edge, brink, or margin 2. a grassy border, as along a road —*vi.* **verged, verg′-ing** to be on the verge, brink, or border (with *on* or *upon*)

verge[2] *vi.* **verged, verg′ing** [L. *vergere*] 1. to tend or incline (*to* or *towards*) 2. to pass gradually (*into*) [dawn *verging* into daylight]

verger (vʉr′jər) *n.* [see VERGE[1]] 1. a church caretaker or usher 2. a person who carries a staff of office before a bishop, etc.

Vergilian (vʉr jil′ē ən) *adj.* var. of VIRGILIAN

veriest (ver′ē ist) *adj.* [< VERY] being such to the highest degree; utter [the *veriest* nonsense]

verify (ver′i fī′) *vt.* -fied′, -fy′ing [< L. *verus*, true + *facere*, make] 1. to prove to be true by evidence, etc.; confirm 2. to test the accuracy of, as by comparison —**ver′ifi′able** *adj.* —**ver′ifica′tion** *n.*

verily (ver′ə lē) *adv.* [Archaic] in very truth; truly

verisimilar (ver′i sim′i lər) *adj.* [< L. *verus*, true + *similis*, like] seeming to be true· or real; likely

verisimilitude (ver′i si mil′i tyo̅o̅d′) *n.* [see prec.] the appearance of being true or real

veritable (ver′i tə b'l) *adj.* [< L. *veritas*, truth] true; aptly named [a *veritable* feast] —**ver′itably** *adv.*

verity (ver′ə tē) *n., pl.* -ties [< L. *verus*, true] 1. conformity to truth or fact 2. a principle, belief, etc. taken to be fundamentally and permanently true

verkrampte (far kram′tə) *n.* [< Afrik.] in South Africa, a person of extreme right wing views, often an Afrikaner Nationalist

verligte (far ləkh′tə) *n.* [< Afrik.] in South Africa, a person of moderate or liberal views, esp. an Afrikaner

vermi- [< L. *vermis*] *a combining form meaning* worm

vermicelli (vʉr′mi sel′ē) *n.* [It., little worms] 1. pasta like spaghetti, but in thinner strings 2. tiny chocolate strands used to decorate cakes, etc.

vermicide (vʉr′mi sīd′) *n.* [VERMI- + -CIDE] a drug or other agent used to kill worms, esp. intestinal worms

vermicular (vʉr mik′yoo lər) *adj.* [< L. *vermis*, a worm] 1. wormlike in shape or movement 2. of or caused by worms

vermiform (vʉr′mi fôrm′) *adj.* [VERMI- + -FORM] shaped like a worm

vermiform appendix *see* APPENDIX

vermilion (vər mil′yən) *n.* [< L. *vermis*, a worm] 1. a bright red pigment 2.

a bright red or scarlet —*adj.* of the colour vermilion

vermin (vur′min) *n., pl.* **-min** [< L. *vermis,* a worm] **1.** (*functioning as pl*) *a*) insects, bugs, or small animals regarded as pests because they are destructive, disease-carrying, etc., as flies, lice, or rats *b*) birds or animals that kill game on reserves **2.** a vile, loathsome person —**ver′minous** *adj.*

vermouth (vur′məth) *n.* [Fr. < G. *Wermut,* wormwood] a sweet or dry, fortified white wine flavoured with aromatic herbs

vernacular (vər nak′yoo lər) *n.* [L. *vernaculus,* native] **1.** the native language or dialect of a country or place **2.** the common, everyday language of ordinary people in a particular locality **3.** the shoptalk of a profession or trade —*adj.* **1.** of, in, or using the native language of a place **2.** native to a place —**vernac′ularism** *n.*

vernal (vur′n'l) *adj.* [< L. *ver,* spring] **1.** of the spring **2.** springlike **3.** youthful —**ver′nally** *adv.*

vernier (vur′nē ər) *n.* [< P. *Vernier*] a short scale that slides along a longer instrument and is used to indicate fractional parts of divisions: also **vernier scale**

Veronal (ver′ə n'l) [G., < *Verona,* in Italy] *Trademark* barbitone

veronica (vi ron′i kə) *n.* [< ?] same as SPEEDWELL

verruca (və rōō′kə) *n., pl.* **-cas, -cae** (-sē) [L.] **1.** a wart **2.** a wartlike elevation, as on a toad's back

versatile (vur′sə tīl′) *adj.* [< L. *vertere,* to turn] **1.** competent in many things; able to turn easily from one subject or occupation to another **2.** adaptable to many uses or functions —**ver′satil′ity** (-til′ə tē) *n.*

verse (vurs) *n.* [< L. *vertere,* to turn] **1.** a stanza or other short division of a poem **2.** *a*) poetry in general; sometimes, specif., poems of a light nature *b*) poetry of a specified kind [blank *verse*] **3.** a single line of poetry **4.** a single poem **5.** any of the short divisions of a chapter of the Bible

versed (vurst) *adj.* [< L. *versari,* be busy] skilled or learned (in a subject)

versification (vur′si fi kā′shən) *n.* the art, practice, or theory of poetic composition

versify (vur′si fī′) *vi.* **-fied′, -fy′ing** to compose verses —*vt.* **1.** to tell in verse **2.** to put into verse form —**ver′sifi′er** *n.*

version (vur′shən) *n.* [see VERSE] **1.** an account giving one point of view **2.** a translation, esp. one of the Bible **3.** a particular form [the film *version* of the novel]

verso (vur′sō) *n., pl.* **-sos** [see VERSE] *Printing* any left-hand page of a book; back of a leaf

versus (vur′səs) *prep.* [L.] **1.** in contest against [our team *versus* theirs] **2.** in contrast with

VERTEBRAE
(A, spinal column;
B, single vertebra)

vertebra (vur′ti brə) *n., pl.* **-brae** (-brē′), **-bras** [L. < *vertere,* to turn] any of the single bones of the spinal column —**ver′tebral** *adj.*

vertebrate *n.* any of a large group of animals that have a backbone and a brain and cranium —*adj.* **1.** having a backbone, or spinal column **2.** of the vertebrates

vertex (vur′teks) *n., pl.* **-texes, -tices** (-ti sēz′) [L. < *vertere,* to turn] **1.** the highest point; top **2.** *Geom. a*) the point where the two sides of an angle intersect *b*) a corner point of a triangle, square, cube, etc.

vertical (vur′ti k'l) *adj.* **1.** perpendicular to a level surface; upright; straight up or down **2.** of or at the vertex —*n.* a vertical line, plane, etc. —**ver′tically** *adv.*

vertiginous (vur tij′i nəs) *adj.* **1.** of, affected by, or causing vertigo **2.** whirling; spinning **3.** unstable

vertigo (vur′ti gō′) *n., pl.* **-goes′, vertigines** (vur tij′i nēz′) [L. < *vertere,* to turn] a sensation of dizziness

vertu (vur tōō′) *n.* same as VIRTU

vervain (vur′vān) *n.* [< L. *verbena,* foliage] any of a number of verbenas

verve (vurv) *n.* [Fr. < L. *verba,* words] vigour; vivacity; spirit

very (ver′ē) *adv.* [< L. *verus,* true] **1.** exceedingly **2.** truly; really : used as an intensive [the *very* same man] —*adj.* —**ver′ier, ver′iest 1.** complete; utter [the *very* opposite] **2.** same [the *very* hat he lost] **3.** exactly right, suitable, etc. **4.** even (the): used as an intensive [the *very* rafters shook] **5.** actual [caught in the *very* act]

very high frequency any radio frequency between 30 and 300 megahertz

very low frequency any radio frequency between 10 and 30 kilohertz

Very signal (or light) (ver′ē) [< E.W. *Very*] a coloured flare fired from a special pistol (**Very pistol**)

vesicle (ves′i k'l) *n.* [< L. *vesica,* bladder] a small, membranous cavity, sac, or cyst; specif., a blister —**vesicular** (və sik′yoo lər) *adj.*

vesper (ves′pər) *n.* [L.] **1.** *a*) orig., evening *b*) [Poet.] [V-] same as EVENING STAR **2.** [*pl.*] an evening prayer or service

vessel (ves′'l) *n.* [< L. *vas*] **1.** a utensil for holding something, as a bowl, pot, etc. **2.** a ship or large boat **3.** a tube or duct containing or circulating a body fluid

vest (vest) *n.* [< L. *vestis*, garment] **1.** an undergarment covering the body from the shoulders to the hips **2.** [U.S.] a waistcoat —*vt.* **1.** to place (some right, power, or property) in the control of a person or group (with *in*) **2.** to provide or invest (a person or group) (*with* some right, power, or property) —*vi.* to become vested (*in* a person), as property

vesta (ves′tə) *n.* [< *Vesta*, Roman goddess of the hearth] a short, wooden, or, orig., wax, match

vestal (ves′t'l) *adj.* **1.** chaste; pure **2.** of or sacred to Vesta —*n.* a chaste woman; specif., a virgin

vestal virgin in ancient Rome, any of the virgin priestesses of Vesta, who tended the sacred fire in her temple

vested interest **1.** an established right, as to some future benefit **2.** a strong personal concern in a state of affairs, system, etc., usually resulting in private gain **3.** a person or group that has such an interest

vestibule (ves′tibyōōl′) *n.* [L. *vestibulum*] a small entrance hall, either to a building or a room

vestige (ves′tij) *n.* [< L. *vestigium*, footprint] **1.** a trace or remaining bit of something once present or whole **2.** *Biol.* an organ or part not so fully developed or functional as it once was in the embryo or species —**vestig′ial** *adj.*

vestment (vest′mənt) *n.* [< L. *vestire*, clothe] an official robe or gown, esp. one worn by clergymen, etc. during religious services

vestry (ves′trē) *n.*, *pl.* **-tries** [< L. *vestis*, garment] **1.** a room in a church, where vestments and sacred vessels are kept **2.** a room in a church, used for meetings, Sunday school, etc.

vesture (ves′chər) *n.* [< L. *vestire*, clothe] [Now Rare] clothing

vet (vet) *n.* shortened form of VETERINARY SURGEON —*vt.* **vet′ted, vet′ting** **1.** to examine or evaluate thoroughly **2.** to examine or treat (an animal)

vet. **1.** veteran **2.** veterinary (surgeon)

vetch (vech) *n.* [< L. *vicia*] any of a number of leafy, climbing or trailing plants, used chiefly as fodder

veteran (vet′ər ən) *n.* [< L. *vetus*, old] **1.** a person with much experience in some kind of work, esp. in the armed forces of a country **2.** [U.S.] an ex-serviceman

veteran car a car made before 1916, or, strictly, before 1905

veterinary (vet′ər in ər ē) *adj.* [< L. *veterina*, beasts of burden] designating or of the treatment of diseases and injuries in animals, esp. domestic animals —*n.*, *pl.* **-naries** a veterinary surgeon

veterinary surgeon a person who practises veterinary medicine or surgery: also, chiefly U.S., **veterinarian**

veto (vē′tō) *n.*, *pl.* **-toes** [L., I forbid] **1.** *a)* an order forbidding some act *b)* the power to prevent action thus **2.** the

right of a ruler or legislature to reject bills passed by another branch of the government **3.** [U.S.] a document giving the reasons for rejecting a bill **4.** the power of any of the five permanent members of the Security Council of the United Nations to prevent an action by casting a negative vote —*vt.* **-toed, -toing** **1.** to prevent (a bill) from becoming law by veto **2.** to forbid

vex (veks) *vt.* [< L. *vexare*, agitate] **1.** to disturb, irritate, etc., esp. in a petty, nagging way **2.** to distress or afflict —**vexed question** a difficult matter which is much debated

vexation (vek sā′shən) *n.* **1.** a vexing or being vexed **2.** a cause of annoyance or distress —**vexa′tious** *adj.*

vexing *adj.* that vexes —**vex′ingly** *adv.*

VHF, V.H.F., vhf, v.h.f. very high frequency

vi., v.i. intransitive verb

V.I. **1.** Vancouver Island **2.** Virgin Islands

via (vī′ə) *prep.* [L., abl. sing. of *via*, a way] **1.** by way of [from Rome to London *via* Paris] **2.** by means of [*via* airmail]

viable (vī′ə b'l) *adj.* [Fr. < L. *vita*, life] **1.** practicable; likely to survive [a *viable* economy, *viable* ideas] **2.** able to live; specif., developed enough to be able to live outside the uterus —**vi′abil′ity** *n.* —**vi′ably** *adv.*

viaduct (vī′ə dukt′) *n.* [L. *via* (see VIA) + (AQUE)DUCT] a bridge consisting of a series of short spans supported on piers or towers, usually to carry a road or railway over a valley, gorge, etc.

vial (vī′əl) *n.* [< Gr. *phialē*, shallow cup] a small bottle, usually of glass, for holding medicine or other liquids

viand (vī′ənd) *n.* [< L. *vivere*, to live] **1.** an article of food **2.** [*pl.*] food; esp., choice dishes

viaticum (vī at′i kəm) *n.*, *pl.* **-ca, -cums** [L. < *via*, way] [*often* V-] the Eucharist as given to a person dying or in danger of death

vibes (vībz) *n.pl.* **1.** [Colloq.] a vibraphone **2.** [< VIBRATION(S)] [Slang] qualities in a person or thing that produce an emotional response in one

vibrant (vī′brənt) *adj.* [< L. *vibrare*, vibrate] **1.** quivering; vibrating **2.** produced by vibration; resonant: said of sound **3.** energetic, vivacious, etc.

vibraphone (vī′brə fōn′) *n.* [VIBRA(TE) + -PHONE] a musical instrument resembling the marimba, but with electrically operated valves in the resonators that produce a gentle vibrato —**vi′braphon′ist** *n.*

vibrate (vī brāt′) *vt.* **-brat′ed, -brat′ing** [< L. *vibrare*] **1.** to set in to-and-fro motion; oscillate **2.** to cause to quiver —*vi.* **1.** to swing back and forth **2.** to move rapidly back and forth; quiver **3.** to resound **4.** to feel very excited; thrill

vibration *n.* **1.** a vibrating; esp., rapid movement back and forth; quivering **2.** [*pl.*] *same as* VIBES (sense 2) **3.** *Physics* rapid, periodic, to-and-fro motion or oscillation of an elastic body or the particles of a fluid, as in transmitting sound

vibrato (vi brät′ō) *n.,* *pl.* **-tos** [It.] *Music* the pulsating effect of a rapid, hardly noticeable variation in pitch

vibrator (vī′brāt′ər) *n.* something that vibrates, as an electrical device used in massage, etc.

vicar (vik′ər) *n.* [< L. *vicis,* a change] 1. *Anglican Ch.* a priest in charge of a parish in which, formerly, the tithes belonged to a layman, monastery, etc. 2. *R.C.Ch* a church officer acting as a deputy of a bishop 3. a deputy —**vicarial** (vi kãr′ē əl) *adj.*

vicarage *n.* 1. the residence of a vicar 2. the benefice or salary of a vicar

vicar apostolic *pl.* **vicars apostolic** *R.C.Ch.* a titular bishop in a region where no regular see has yet been organized

vicar-general *n.,* *pl.* **vic′ars-gen′eral** 1. *Anglican Ch.* a layman serving as administrative deputy to an archbishop or bishop 2. *R.C.Ch.* a priest, etc. acting as administrative deputy to a bishop

vicarious (vi kãr′ē əs) *adj.* [< L. *vicis,* a change] 1. *a)* done or undergone by one person in place of another *b)* felt as if one were actually taking part in another's experience [a *vicarious* thrill] 2. *a)* taking the place of another *b)* delegated —**vicar′iously** *adv.*

Vicar of Christ the Pope

vice¹ (vīs) *n.* [< L. *vitium*] 1. *a)* an evil or wicked action, habit, etc. *b)* depravity *c)* prostitution 2. any fault, defect, etc.

vice² (vī′sē) *prep.* [L.: see VICE-] in the place of; as the deputy or successor of

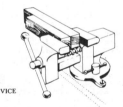

VICE

vice³ (vīs) *n.* [< L. *vitis,* vine] a device consisting of two jaws opened and closed by a screw, lever, etc., used for holding firmly an object being worked on

vice- [< L. *vice,* in the place of another] a prefix meaning subordinate; deputy [*vice-*president]

vice admiral *see* MILITARY RANKS, table

vice-consul (vīs′kon′s′l) *n.* an officer who is subordinate to or a substitute for a consul

vicegerent (vīs′jer′ənt) *n.* [< *vice,* VICE- + *gerere,* to direct] a deputy —**vice′ge′-rency** *n.*

vice-president (vīs′prez′i dənt) *n.* an officer next in rank below a president,

acting in his place during his absence or incapacity

viceroy (vīs′roi) *n.* [MFr.: < VICE- + *roy,* king] a person ruling a country, province, etc. as the deputy of a sovereign —**vice′roy′alty** *n.* —**vicereine** (vīs′rān′) *n.fem.*

vice squad a police squad assigned to the suppression or control of prostitution, gambling, etc.

vice versa (vī′sē vur′sə) [L.] the order or relation being reversed; conversely

Vichy (**water**) (vē′shē) a mineral water found at Vichy, in C France

vicinage (vis′i nij) *n.* [see ff.] 1. *same as* VICINITY 2. the people living in a particular neighbourhood

vicinity (vi sin′ə tē) *n.* *pl.* **-ties** [< L. *vicinus,* near] 1. surrounding region; neighbourhood 2. nearness

vicious (vish′əs) *adj.* [< L. *vitium,* vice] 1. characterized by, or done with, cruelty, brutality, etc. 2. very intense, sharp, etc. [a *vicious* wind] 3. malicious; spiteful [a *vicious* rumour] 4. bad-tempered; dangerous [a *vicious* horse] 5. ruined by defects, flaws, etc. [a *vicious* argument] —**vi′ciously** *adv.* —**vi′ciousness** *n.*

vicious circle 1. a situation in which the solution of one problem gives rise to another, but the solution of this brings back the first, etc. 2. *Logic* an argument which is not valid because its conclusion rests on a premise which itself depends on the conclusion

vicissitudes (vi sis′i tyōōdz′) *n.pl.* [Fr. < L. *vicis,* a turn] unpredictable changes in life, fortune, etc.; ups and downs

victim (vik′tim) *n.* [L. *victima*] 1. someone or something killed, destroyed, sacrificed, etc. 2. a person who suffers some loss, esp. by being swindled

victimize *vt.* **-ized′, -iz′ing** 1. to punish or discriminate against selectively or unfairly 2. to make a victim of —**vic′timi-za′tion** *n.*

victor (vik′tər) *n.* [L. < *vincere,* conquer] the winner in a battle, struggle, etc.

VICTORIA

victoria (vik tôr′ē ə) *n.* [< Queen *Victoria*] a four-wheeled carriage for two, with a folding top

Victoria Cross the highest British military decoration, given for deeds of exceptional valour

Victoria Day the Monday preceding May 24th, in Canada a national holiday to commemorate Queen Victoria's birthday

Victorian *adj.* 1. of or characteristic of the time when Victoria was queen of England 2. showing the respectability, prudery, etc. regarded as typical of Victorians —*n.* a person, esp. a British writer, of the time of Queen Victoria

victoria plum a large, sweet, red or yellow plum

victorious (vik tôr′ē əs) *adj.* 1. having won a victory; triumphant 2. of or bringing about victory

victory (vik′tər ē) *n., pl.* -**ries** [< VICTOR] 1. the decisive winning of a battle or war 2. success in any contest or struggle

victual (vit′′l) *n.* [< L. *victus,* food] [*pl.*] [Dial. or Colloq.] articles of food —*vt.* -**ualled,** -**ualling** to supply with victuals —*vi.* to lay in a supply of food —**vict′ual-ler** *n.*

vicuña (vi kyōōn′ə) *n.* [SAmInd.] 1. a S American animal related to the llama and alpaca, with soft, shaggy wool 2. a fabric made from this wool or in imitation of it

‡**vide** (vī′dē) [L.] see: used to direct attention to a particular page, book, etc.

‡**videlicet** (vi dē′li set′) *adv.* [L. < *videre licet,* it is permitted to see] that is; namely

video (vid′ē ō′) *adj.* [L., I see] of télevision, esp. of the picture portion of a television broadcast —*n.* 1. apparatus for recording and replaying television broadcasts etc. 2. [U.S.] *same as* TELEVISION

videophone *n.* [VIDEO + (TELE)PHONE] a telephone combined with television so that users can see, as well as speak to, each other

videotape *n.* a magnetic tape on which a television broadcast can be recorded

vie (vī) *vi.* **vied, vy′ing** [< L. *invitare,* invite] to be a rival or rivals; compete (*with* someone)

vies (fis) *adj.* [< Afrik.] [S Afr. Slang] angry

Vietnamese (vyet′nə mēz′) *adj.* designating or of Vietnam, in SE Asia —*n., pl.* **Vietnamese** 1. a native or inhabitant of Vietnam 2. the language of Vietnam

view (vyōō) *n.* [< L. *videre,* see] 1. a seeing or looking 2. sight or vision; esp., range of vision 3. mental examination or survey 4. *a*) a scene or prospect, as of a landscape *b*) a picture of such a scene 5. visual appearance of something 6. manner of regarding something; opinion 7. an object; aim; goal —*vt.* 1. to see; behold 2. to regard in a particular way 3. to inspect; scrutinize 4. to consider —**in view** 1. in sight 2. under consideration 3. as an object aimed at —**in view of** 1. because of 2. in a position from which one can see something, or from which one can be seen —**on view** displayed publicly —**with a view to** 1. with the purpose of 2. looking forward to

viewdata *n.* *same as* TELETEXT

viewer *n.* 1. a person who views something, esp. television 2. an optical device for viewing of slides, etc.

viewfinder *n.* *same as* FINDER (sense 2)

viewpoint *n.* the mental position from which things are viewed and judged; point of view

vigil (vij′il) *n.* [< L. *vigere,* be lively] 1. *a*) a watchful staying awake during the usual hours of sleep *b*) a watch kept 2. *Eccles.* the evening or day before a festival

vigilance committee [U.S.] a group that sets itself up, without legal authority, to punish crime, etc.

vigilant (vij′i lənt) *adj.* [< L. *vigil,* awake] staying watchful and alert to danger or trouble —**vig′ilance** *n.* —**vig′ilantly** *adv.*

vigilante (vij′i lan′tē) *n.* [Sp., vigilant] [U.S.] a member of a vigilance committee

vignette (vin yet′) *n.* [Fr. < *vigne,* vine] 1. an ornamental design used in a book, etc., as at the beginning or end of a chapter 2. a photograph shading off gradually at the edges 3. a short, delicate literary sketch

vigorous (vig′ər əs) *adj.* 1. strong; robust 2. of, characterized by, or requiring vigour 3. forceful; energetic; powerful —**vig′orously** *adv.* —**vig′orousness** *n.*

vigour (vig′ər) *n.* [< L. *vigere,* be strong] 1. active physical or mental force 2. active or healthy growth 3. intensity, force, or energy Also, U.S. sp., **vig′or**

Viking (vī′kiŋ) *n.* [ON. *vikingr*] any of the Scandinavian pirates who ravaged the coasts of Europe from the 8th to the 10th centuries

vile (vīl) *adj.* [< L. *vilis,* cheap, base] 1. morally evil; wicked 2. disgusting 3. degrading; low 4. very bad [*vile* weather] —**vile′ly** *adv.* —**vile′ness** *n.*

vilify (vil′i fī′) *vt.* -**fied**′, -**fy′ing** [see VILE] to use abusive language about; revile —**vil′ifica′tion** *n.*

villa (vil′ə) *n.* [It. < L̇.] 1. a country house or estate, esp. when large 2. a small suburban house 3. a house, as at the seaside, which is rented to holiday makers

village (vil′ij) *n.* [< L. *villa,* country house] 1. a group of houses in the country, larger than a hamlet and smaller than a town 2. the people of a village, collectively —*adj.* of a village —**vil′lager** *n.*

villain (vil′ən) *n.* [< VL. *villanus,* farm servant] 1. an evil person; scoundrel 2. a wicked character in a novel, play, etc. 3. [Colloq.] a rogue; rascal: used humorously

villainous *adj.* 1. of or like a villain; evil; wicked 2. very bad or disagreeable —**vil′lainously** *adv.*

villainy *n., pl.* -**lainies** 1. a being villainous 2. villainous conduct 3. a wicked, detestable, or criminal deed

villein (vil′ən) *n.* [see VILLAIN] in medieval times, an unfree peasant attached to a lord, to whom he paid dues and services in return for his land —**vil′leinage, vil′lenage** *n.*

vim (vim) *n.* [L. < *vis,* strength] [Colloq.] energy

vinaigrette (vin′ā gret′) *n.* [Fr. < *vinaigre,* vinegar] a small ornamental box or bottle used for holding smelling salts, etc.

vinaigrette sauce a savoury sauce made of vinegar, oil, herbs, etc. and used on salads, etc.

vinculum (viŋ′kyoo ləm) *n., pl.* **-la** [L. < *vincere,* bind] *Math.* a line drawn over two or more terms of a compound quantity to show that they are to be treated together (Ex.: a - $\overline{x+y}$)

vindicable (vin′di kə b'l) *adj.* justifiable

vindicate (vin′di kāt′) *vt.* **-cat′ed, -cat′- ing** [< L. *vis,* force + *dicere,* say] **1.** to clear from criticism, blame, etc. **2.** to defend (a cause, etc.) against opposition **3.** to justify —**vin′dicative, vin′dica′tory** *adj.* —**vin′dica′tor** *n.*

vindication (vin′di kā′shən) *n.* **1.** a vindicating or being vindicated **2.** a fact or circumstance that vindicates

vindictive (vin dik′tiv) *adj.* [< L. *vindicta,* revenge] **1.** revengeful in spirit **2.** said or done in revenge —**vindic′tively** *adv.* —**vindic′tiveness** *n.*

vine (vīn) *n.* [< L. *vinum,* wine] **1.** any of a genus of climbing perennial plants, esp. the grapevine **2.** [Aust. & N.Z.] any climbing or trailing plant

vinegar (vin′i gər) *n.* [< MFr. *vin,* wine + *aigre,* sour] **1.** a sour liquid containing acetic acid, made by fermenting cider, wine, etc.: it is used as a condiment and preservative **2.** ill-tempered speech, character, etc. —**vin′egary** *adj.*

vinery (vīn′ər ē) *n., pl.* **-eries 1.** an enclosed area or building in which grapevines are grown **2.** vines collectively

vineyard (vin′yərd) *n.* land devoted to cultivating grapevines

‡**vingt-et-un** (van tā ën′) *n.* [Fr., twenty-one] a gambling game at cards, in which each player's aim is to obtain from the dealer cards totalling twenty-one points or as near as possible to that total without exceeding it

vini- [< L. *vinum,* wine] *a combining form meaning* wine grapes or wine [*viniculture*]

viniculture (vin′i kul′chər) *n.* [prec. + CULTURE] the cultivation of wine grapes —**vin′icul′turist** *n.*

vinous (vī′nəs) *adj.* [< L. *vinum,* wine] of, having the nature of, or characteristic of wine

vintage (vin′tij) *n.* [< L. *vinum,* wine + *demere,* remove] **1.** *a)* the crop of grapes of a vineyard or grape-growing region in a single season *b)* the wine of a particular region and year **2.** the type or model of a particular year or period —*adj.* **1.** of choice vintage [*vintage* wine] **2.** dating from a period long past

vintage car an old car made between 1917 and 1930

vintner (vint′nər) *n.* [< L. *vinetum,* vineyard] a wine merchant

vinyl (vī′n'l) *n.* [< L. *vinum,* wine] **1.** the univalent radical, $CH_2:CH-$, derived from ethylene **2.** any of various plastics made from polymerized vinyl compounds

viol (vī′əl) *n.* [MFr. *viole*] any of an early family of stringed instruments, usually with six strings, frets, and a flat back

viola[1] (viō′lə) *n.* [It.] a stringed instrument of the violin family, slightly larger than a violin and tuned a fifth lower

viola[2] (vī′ələ) *n.* [< L., a violet] any of various violets developed from a pansy

violable (vī′ə ləb'l) *adj.* that can be, or is likely to be, violated

viola da gamba (də gam′bə) *n.* [It., viol for the leg] an early instrument of the viol family, held between the knees and comparable in range to the cello

violate (vī′ə lāt′) *vt.* **-lat′ed, -lat′ing** [< L. *violare,* use force] **1.** to break (a law, rule, promise, etc.) **2.** to assault sexually; esp., to rape (a woman) **3.** to desecrate or profane (something sacred) **4.** to break in on; disturb **5.** to offend, insult, etc. —**vi′ola′tor** *n.*

violation (vī′ə lā′shən) *n.* **1.** infringement **2.** rape **3.** desecration of something sacred **4.** disturbance

violence (vī′ələns) *n.* [< L. *violentus,* violent] **1.** physical force used so as to injure or damage **2.** intense, powerful force, as of a storm, etc. **3.** harm done by unjust or callous use of force or power, as in violating another's privacy, etc. **4.** vehemence; fury **5.** a violent deed or act —**do violence to 1.** to outrage **2.** to act contrary to **3.** to distort the meaning of

violent *adj.* **1.** acting with or characterized by great physical force, so as to injure, etc. **2.** caused by violence **3.** furious; passionate; immoderate [*violent* language] **4.** extreme; intense [a *violent* storm]

violet (vī′ə lət) *n.* [< L. *viola*] **1.** a short plant with white, blue, purple, or yellow flowers: the purple violet is the floral emblem of New Brunswick **2.** a bluish-purple colour —*adj.* bluish-purple

VIOLIN
(A, scroll; B, pegs; C, neck; D, fingerboard; E, waist; F, tailpiece; G, chinboard)

violin (vī′ə lin′) *n.* [< It. *viola,* viol] **1.** an instrument having four strings and no frets, and played with a bow **2.** a violinist [first *violin*]

violinist *n.* a violin player

violist (vī′əl ist; *for 2* vi ō′list) *n.* **1.** a viol player **2.** a viola player

violoncello (vī′ə lən chel′ō) *n., pl.* **-los** [It.] *same as* CELLO —**vi′oloncel′list** *n.*

VIP, V.I.P. [Colloq.] very important person

viper (vī'pər) *n.* [< L. *vivus*, living + *parere*, to bear] **1.** any of a family of venomous snakes found in Europe, Africa, and Asia, including the adder **2.** a malicious or treacherous person —**vi'perous** *adj.*

virago (vi rä'gō) *n., pl.* **-goes, -gos** [< L. *vir*, man] a quarrelsome, shrewish woman

viral (vī'rəl) *adj.* of or caused by a virus

Virgilian (vər jil'ē ən) *adj.* of, or in the style of, Virgil (70-19 B.C.), Roman poet

virgin (vur'jin) *n.* [< L. *virgo*, a maiden] a person, esp. a woman, who has not had sexual intercourse —[V-] *Astron.* same as VIRGO —*adj.* **1.** being a virgin **2.** chaste; modest **3.** untouched, pure, clean, etc. [*virgin* snow] **4.** as yet unused, untrod, unexplored, etc. by man [a *virgin* forest] —**the Virgin** Mary, the mother of Jesus

virginal[1] (vur'ji n'l) *adj.* **1.** of or like a virgin; maidenly **2.** pure; fresh; unsullied —**vir'ginally** *adv.*

virginal[2] *n.* [prob. akin to prec.] [*sometimes pl.*] a small, rectangular harpsichord of the 16th cent., placed on a table or in the lap to be played: also **pair of virginals**

Virgin Birth *Christian Theol.* the doctrine that Jesus was born to Mary, a virgin, and that she was his only human parent

Virginia creeper (vər jin'yə) a plant native to North America, with leaves that turn bright red in autumn

virginity (vər jin'ə tē) *n.* the state or fact of being a virgin; maidenhood; chastity

Virgin Mary Mary, the mother of Jesus

Virgo (vur'gō) [L., virgin] **1.** a large constellation between Leo and Libra **2.** the sixth sign of the zodiac

virgule (vur'gyōōl) *n.* [< L. *virga*, a twig] a short, diagonal line (/) placed between two words to show that either can be used (and/or), in dates or fractions (3/8), to express "per" (kilometres/hour), etc.

virile (vir'il) *adj.* [< L. *vir*, man] **1.** of or characteristic of a man; masculine **2.** having manly strength or vigour **3.** sexually potent —**virility** (vi ril'ə tē) *n.*

virology (vīə rol'ər jē) *n.* [< VIRUS + -LOGY] the study of viruses and virus diseases —**virol'ogist** *n.*

virtu (vur tōō') *n.* [It. < L. *virtus*, virtue] **1.** a love of, or taste for, artistic objects **2.** such objects, collectively **3.** the quality of being so artistic, beautiful, rare, etc. as to interest a collector

virtual (vur'choo wəl) *adj.* being such practically or in effect, although not in actual fact or name —**vir'tually** *adv.*

virtue (vur'tyōō) *n.* [< L. *virtus*, manliness, worth] **1.** general moral excellence **2.** a specific moral quality regarded as good **3.** chastity **4.** *a)* excellence in general *b)* a good quality **5.** efficacy, as of a medicine —**by (or in) virtue of** because of

virtuosity (vur'tyoo wos'ə tē) *n., pl.* **-ties** [< ff.] great technical skill in some fine art, esp. in the performance of music

virtuoso (vur'tyoo wō'zō) *n., pl.* **-sos, -si** [It., skilled] a person having great

technical skill in some fine art, esp. in the performance of music —*adj.* of or like that of a virtuoso

virtuous (vur'tyoo wəs) *adj.* **1.** having, or characterized by, moral virtue **2.** chaste: said of a woman —**vir'tuously** *adv.* —**vir'tuousness** *n.*

virulent (vir'oo lənt) *adj.* [< L. *virus*, a poison] **1.** *Med. a)* violent and rapid in its course: said of a disease *b)* highly infectious: said of a microorganism **2.** *a)* extremely poisonous *b)* full of hate and enmity —**vir'ulence** *n.*

virus (vī'ə rəs) *n.* [L., a poison] **1.** *a)* any of a group of ultramicroscopic infective agents that cause various diseases in animals or plants *b)* a disease caused by a virus **2.** a harmful influence

visa (vē'zə) *n.* [Fr. < L. *videre*, see] an endorsement on a passport, showing that it has been examined by the proper officials of a country and granting entry into that country —**vi'saed** *adj.*

visage (viz'ij) *n.* [< L. *videre*, to see] **1.** the face; countenance **2.** appearance; aspect

vis-à-vis (vē'zä vē) *adj., adv.* [Fr.] face to face —*prep.* **1.** face to face with **2.** in relation to —*n.* one opposite, or corresponding to, another

viscera (vis'ə rə) *n.pl., sing.* **vis'cus** [L.] the internal organs of the body, as the heart, lungs, liver, intestines, etc.

visceral *adj.* **1.** of or affecting the viscera **2.** emotional rather than intellectual

viscid (vis'əd) *adj.* sticky; viscous; glutinous

viscose (vis'kōs) *n.* a syruplike solution made by treating cellulose with sodium hydroxide and carbon disulphide: used in making cellophane and rayon thread and fabrics (**viscose rayon**) —*adj.* **1.** same as VISCOUS **2.** of viscose

viscosity (vis kos'ə tē) *n., pl.* **-ties** **1.** a viscous quality or state **2.** *Physics* the internal friction of a fluid, caused by molecular attraction

viscount (vī'kount) *n.* [see VICE-COUNT[2]] a nobleman below an earl or count and above a baron —**vis'countcy, vis'county** *n.* —**vis'countess** *n.fem.*

viscous (vis'kəs) *adj.* [< L. *viscum*, birdlime] being a cohesive and sticky fluid; viscid

vise (vīs) *n., vt.* Chiefly U.S. *sp.* of VICE[3]

visibility (viz'i bil'ə tē) *n., pl.* **-ties** **1.** the relative possibility of being seen under the prevailing conditions of distance, light, and atmosphere **2.** range of vision

visible (viz'ə b'l) *adj.* [< L. *videre*, see] **1.** that can be seen **2.** that can be perceived; evident **3.** on hand [*visible* supply] —**vis'ibly** *adv.*

vision (vizh'ən) *n.* [< L. *videre*, see] **1.** the power of seeing **2.** something supposedly seen in a dream, trance, etc. **3.** a mental image [*visions* of power] **4.** *a)* the ability to perceive something not actually visible, as through mental acuteness *b)* force or power of imagination [a statesman of great *vision*]

visionary *adj.* 1. of, having the nature of, or seen in a vision 2. *a)* imaginary *b)* not realistic; impractical 3. seeing visions —*n., pl.* **-aries** 1. a person who sees visions 2. a dreamer

visit (viz′it) *vt.* [< L. *videre,* see] 1. to go or come to see (someone) out of friendship or for professional reasons 2. to stay with as a guest 3. to go or come to (a place) as in order to inspect or look at 4. to come upon or afflict [a drought *visited* the land] —*vi.* to visit someone or something, esp. socially —*n.* a visiting; specif., *a)* a social call *b)* a stay as a guest *c)* an official call, as of a doctor, etc.

visitant *n.* 1. a supernatural being supposedly seen 2. a visitor 3. a migratory bird in any of its temporary resting places

visitation (viz′i tā′shən) *n.* 1. an official visit as to inspect 2. any trouble looked on as punishment sent by God —**the Visitation** R.C.Ch. 1. the visit of the Virgin Mary to Elizabeth: Luke 1:39-56 2. a church feast (July 2) commemorating this

visitor (viz′it ər) *n.* a person making a visit

VISORS

visor (vī′zər) *n.* [< OFr. *vis,* a face] 1. *a)* in armour, the movable part of a helmet covering the face *b)* a movable section of safety glass, that is part of a protective head covering 2. the projecting brim of a cap, for shading the eyes 3. an adjustable shade in a car, over the windscreen

vista (vis′ta) *n.* [It. < L. *videre,* see] 1. a view, esp. one seen through a long passage, as between rows of trees 2. a comprehensive mental view of a series of events —**vis′taed** *adj.*

visual (viz′yoo wəl) *adj.* [< L. *videre,* see] 1. of, connected with, based on, or used in seeing 2. that is or can be seen; visible —**vis′ually** *adv.*

visual aids films, slides, charts, etc. (but not books) used in teaching, etc.

visualize *vt.* **-ized′, -iz′ing** to form a mental image of (something not visible) —**vis′ualiza′tion** *n.*

vital (vīt′'l) *adj.* [< L. *vita,* life] 1. *a)* essential to life [*vital* organs] *b)* fatal 2. *a)* essential; indispensable *b)* of crucial importance 3. of or concerned with life 4. affecting the validity, truth, etc. of something [a *vital* error] 5. full of life and vigour —*n.* [*pl.*] the vital organs, as the heart, brain, etc. —**vi′tally** *adv.*

vitality (vī tal′ə tē) *n., pl.* **-ties** 1. mental or physical energy 2. power to live or go on living 3. power to endure or survive

vitalize (vīt′əl īz′) *vt.* **-ized′, -iz′ing** 1.

to make vital; give life to 2. to give vigour or animation to

vital statistics 1. data on births, deaths, etc. 2. [Colloq.] the measurements of a woman's bust, waist, and hips

vitamin (vit′ə min) *n.* [< L. *vita,* life] any of a number of complex organic substances found variously in foods and essential for the normal functioning of the body

vitamin A a fat-soluble alcohol found in fish-liver oil, egg yolk, butter, etc. or derived from carrots and other vegetables: a deficiency of this vitamin results in night blindness

vitamin B (complex) a group of unrelated water-soluble substances, including: *a)* **vitamin B₁** (*see* THIAMINE) *b)* **vitamin B₂** (*see* RIBOFLAVIN) *c)* NIACIN *d)* **vitamin B₁₂** a complex vitamin, essential for normal growth and used esp. in treating anaemia

vitamin C same as ASCORBIC ACID

vitamin D any of several fat-soluble vitamins occurring in fish-liver oils, milk, egg yolk, etc.: a deficiency of this vitamin tends to produce rickets

vitamin E the four related oils which occur in wheat germ, lettuce, etc.: necessary for fertility in some animals

vitamin K a fat-soluble vitamin that promotes blood-clotting, found in fish meal, etc.

vitiate (vish′ē āt′) *vt.* **-at′ed, -at′ing** [< L. *vitium,* VICE¹] 1. to make imperfect or faulty 2. to weaken morally 3. to make legally ineffective —**vi′tia′tion** *n.* —**vi′tia′tor** *n.*

viticulture (vit′i kul′chər) *n.* [< L. *vitis,* vine + CULTURE] the cultivation of grapes —**vit′icul′turist** *n.*

vitreous (vit′rē əs) *adj.* [< L. *vitrum,* glass] 1. of, like, or derived from glass 2. of the vitreous humour

vitreous body (or **humour**) the transparent, colourless, jellylike substance that fills the eyeball between the retina and lens

vitrify (vit′ri fī′) *vt., vi.* **-fied′, -fy′ing** [< L. *vitrum,* glass + *facere,* make] to change into glass or a glasslike substance by fusion due to heat —**vit′rifica′tion, vit′-rifac′tion** *n.*

vitriol (vit′rē əl) *n.* [< L. *vitreus,* glassy] 1. *a)* any of several sulphates of metals, as of copper (*blue vitriol*), of iron (*green vitriol*) etc. *b)* same as SULPHURIC ACID: in full, **oil of vitriol** 2. sharpness or bitterness, as in speech

vitriolic (vit′rē ol′ik) *adj.* 1. of, like, or derived from a vitriol 2. extremely biting or caustic [*vitriolic* talk]

vituperate (vi tyoo′pə rāt′) *vt.* **-at′ed, -at′-ing** [< L. *vitium,* a fault + *parare,* prepare] to speak abusively to or about —**vitu′pera′-tion** *n.* —**vitu′perative** *adj.*

viva (vī′və) *n.* [Colloq.] *same as* VIVA VOCE

‡**viva** (vē′vä) *interj.* [It., Sp.] (long) live (someone or something specified)!

vivace (vi vä′chā) *adj., adv.* [It.] *Music* in a lively, spirited manner

vivacious (vi vā′shəs) *adj.* [< L. *vivere,*

to live] full of animation; spirited —**viva'- ciousness** n.

vivacity (vi vas'ə tē) n. the quality or state of being vivacious; liveliness; animation

vivarium (vī vāer'ē əm) n., pl. **-iums, -ia** [L. < vivere, to live] an enclosed place for animals to live as if in their natural environment

viva voce (vī'və vō'sē) [ML., with living voice] by word of mouth; orally —n. an oral examination

vivid (viv'id) adj. [< L. vivere, to live] 1. bright; intense: said of colours, light, etc. 2. forming or suggesting clear or striking mental images [a vivid imagination] 3. full of life; lively, striking —**viv'- idly** adv.

vivify (viv'i fī') vt. **-fied'**, **-fy'ing** [< L. vivus, alive + facere, make] 1. to give life to; animate 2. to make more lively, active, striking, etc.

viviparous (vi vip'ər əs) adj. [< L. vivus, alive + parere, to produce] bearing living young (as most mammals) instead of laying eggs

vivisect (viv'i sekt') vt., vi. to practise vivisection (on) —**viv'isec'tor** n.

vivisection (viv'i sek'shən) n. [< L. vivus, alive + SECTION] medical research consisting of surgical operations or other experiments done on living animals —**viv'- isec'tionist** n.

vixen (vik's'n) n. [< OE. fyxe, she-fox] 1. a female fox 2. an ill-tempered, shrewish woman

viz., viz (viz; often read "namely") [< L. videlicet] that is; namely

vizier (vi zē'ər) n. [< Ar. wazīr, porter] in Moslem countries, a high officer in the government

vizor (vī'zər) n. alt. sp. of VISOR

V-J Day the day on which the fighting with Japan officially ended in World War II (Aug. 15, 1945)

VL. Vulgar Latin

vlei (flā) n. [< Afrik.] [S Afr.] low, marshy ground

VLF, V.L.F., vlf, v.l.f. very low frequency

V neck a neckline V-shaped in front —**V'-neck'** adj.

voc. vocative

vocab. vocabulary

vocable (vō'kəb'l) n. [< L. vocare, to call] a word; esp., a word regarded as a unit of sounds rather than as a unit of meaning

vocabulary (vō kab'yoo lər ē) n., pl. **-lar- ies** [< L.: see prec.] 1. a list of words, usually arranged in alphabetical order and defined as in a dictionary or glossary 2. all the words of a language 3. a) all the words used by a particular person, class, profession, etc. b) all the words recognized and understood by a particular person

vocal (vō'k'l) adj. [< L. vox, voice] 1. a) uttered by the voice; oral [vocal sounds] b) sung [vocal music] 2. able to speak or make oral sounds 3. of, used in, or belonging to the voice [vocal organs] 4. speaking freely or strongly —n. a piece of pop or jazz music that is sung —**vo'- cally** adv.

vocal cords either of two pairs of membranous cords or folds in the larynx: voice is produced when air from the lungs causes the lower cords to vibrate

vocalist n. a singer

vocalize vt. **-ized'**, **-iz'ing** 1. a) to express with the voice b) to make capable of vocal expression 2. Phonet. a) to change into or use as a vowel b) to voice —vi. to speak or sing —**vo'caliza'tion** n.

vocation (vō kā'shən) n. [< L. vocare, to call] 1. any trade, profession, or occupation 2. a) a call to enter a certain career, esp. a religious one b) the work or career towards which one believes oneself to be called —**voca'tional** adj.

vocational guidance the work of testing and interviewing persons in order to guide them towards the choice of a suitable vocation

vocative (vok'ə tiv) adj. [< L. vocare, to call] Gram. in certain inflected languages, designating or of the case indicating the person or things addressed —n. the vocative case

vociferate (vō sif'ə rāt') vt., vi. **-at'ed, -at'ing** [< L. vox, voice + ferre, to bear] to utter or shout loudly or vehemently; bawl —**vocif'era'tion** n. —**vocif'era'tor** n.

vociferous (vō sif'ər əs) adj. loud, noisy, or vehement; clamorous —**vocif'erously** adv.

vodka (vod'kə) n. [Russ., < voda, water] a colourless spirit distilled from wheat, rye, etc.

voetsek (foot'sek) interj. [S Afr. Slang] be off; go away: used when chasing away animals; offensive when addressed to humans

voetstoets (foot'stoots) adj. [< Afrik.] [S Afr.] denoting a sale in which the vendor is freed from all responsibility for the condition of the goods sold —adv. without responsibility for the condition of goods sold

vogue (vōg) n. [Fr., a rowing] 1. the accepted fashion at any particular time 2. general acceptance; popularity —adj. in vogue: also **voguish** (vō'gish)

voice (vois) n. [< L. vox] 1. sound made through the mouth, esp. by human beings in talking, singing, etc. 2. the ability to make such sounds 3. any sound, influence, etc. regarded as like vocal utterance [the voice of one's conscience] 4. a specified or distinctive quality of vocal sound [an angry voice] 5. a) an expressed wish, opinion, etc. b) the right to express one's choice, opinion, etc.; vote 6. utterance or expression [giving voice to his joy] 7. the means by which something is expressed 8. Gram. a form of a verb showing it as active or passive 9. Music the quality of a person's singing [a good voice] 10. Phonet. sound made by vibrating the vocal cords with air forced from the lungs, as in pronouncing all vowels

and such consonants as *b, d, g, m,* etc.
—*vt.* **voiced, voic′ing** to utter or express in words —**in voice** with the voice in good condition, as for singing —**with one voice** unanimously

voiced *adj.* 1. having (a specified kind of) voice *[deep-voiced]* 2. expressed by the voice 3. *Phonet.* made by vibrating the vocal cords : said of certain consonants

voiceless *adj.* 1. having no voice; mute 2. not speaking or spoken 3. *Phonet.* uttered without voice, as *p, t, k,* etc. —**voice′lessly** *adv.*

voice-over *n.* the voice commenting or narrating off camera, as for a television commercial

voice print *n.* a pattern of wavy lines and whorls recorded by a device actuated by the sound of a person's voice and distinctive for each individual

void (void) *adj.* [< L. *vacare,* be empty] 1. *a)* having nothing in it; empty; vacant *b)* lacking; devoid (*of*) *[void of sense]* 3. useless; ineffective 4. *Law* not binding; invalid —*n.* 1. an empty space or vacuum 2. *a)* total absence of something normally present *b)* a feeling of emptiness —*vt.* 1. *a)* to empty (the contents of something) *b)* to discharge (urine or faeces) 2. to make void —*vi.* to defecate or, esp., to urinate

voile (voil) *n.* [Fr., a veil] a thin, sheer fabric, as of cotton

vol. 1. volcano 2. *pl.* **vols.** volume 3. volunteer

volatile (vol′ə til) *adj.* [< L. *volare,* to fly] 1. vaporizing or evaporating quickly, as alcohol 2. *a)* unstable or explosive *b)* moving capriciously from one idea, interest, etc. to another; fickle —**vol′atil′-ity** (-til′ə tē) *n.*

volatilize (vo lat′i līz′) *vt., vi.* **-ized′, -iz′-ing** to make or become volatile; evaporate —**vol′atiliza′tion** *n.*

vol-au-vent (vol′ō von) *n.* [Fr.] a puff-pastry case with a filling of meat, fish, etc. in a thick sauce

volcanic (vol kan′ik) *adj.* 1. of, from, or produced by a volcano 2. having volcanoes 3. likely to explode; violent —**volcan′ically** *adv.*

volcano (vol kā′nō) *n., pl.* **-noes, -nos** [< L. *Volcanus,* Vulcan, god of fire] 1. a vent in the earth's crust through which molten rock (*lava*), gases, ashes, etc. burst from the earth's interior 2. a cone-shaped mountain of volcanic materials built up around the vent

vole (vōl) *n.* [< *vole mouse* < Norw. *voll,* field + MOUSE] a small rodent with a stout body and short tail

volition (vō lish′ən) *n.* [< L. *velle,* to will] the act or power of using the will

Volk (folk) *n.* [< Afrik.] [S Afr.] the Afrikaner nation

Volksraad (folks′rät′) *n.* [< Afrik.] in S Africa, the former Legislative Assemblies of the Transvaal and Orange Free State republics

volley (vol′ē) *n., pl.* **-leys** [< L. *volare,* to fly] 1. *a)* the simultaneous discharge

of a number of guns or other weapons *b)* the missiles discharged in this way 2. a burst of words or acts suggestive of this 3. *Sports* a return of a ball, etc. before it touches the ground —*vt., vi.* **-leyed, -leying** 1. to discharge or be discharged as in a volley 2. *Sports* to return (the ball, etc.) as a volley —**vol′-leyer** *n.*

volleyball *n.* a game played on a court by two teams who hit a large, light, inflated ball back and forth over a high net with the hands, each team trying to return the ball before it touches the ground

vols. volumes

volt (vōlt) *n.* [< A. *Volta*] the SI unit of electromotive force or difference in potential

voltage *n.* electromotive force, or difference in electrical potential, expressed in volts

voltaic (vol tā′ik) *adj.* designating or of electricity produced by chemical action

volte-face (volt fäs′) *n.* [Fr.] a sudden reversal of opinion or direction; about-face

voltmeter (vōlt′mēt′ər) *n.* an instrument for measuring voltage

voluble (vol′yㅎㅎ b'l) *adj.* [< L. *volvere,* to roll] talking very much and easily —**vol′ubil′ity** *n.* —**vol′ubly** *adv.*

volume (vol′yㅎㅎm) *n.* [< L. *volumen,* scroll] 1. the amount of space occupied in three dimensions 2. *a)* a quantity, bulk, mass, or amount *b)* a large quantity 3. the strength or loudness of sound 4. *a)* a collection of written or printed sheets bound together; book *b)* any of the books of a set 5. a set of the issues of a periodical over a fixed period of time —**speak volumes** to be very meaningful

volumetric (vol′yㅎㅎ met′rik) *adj.* of or based on the measurement of volume : also **vol′umet′rical**

voluminous (və lyㅎㅎ′mi nəs) *adj.* 1. large; bulky; full 2. writing, producing, or consisting of enough to fill volumes —**volu′-minously** *adv.*

voluntary (vol′ən tər ē) *adj.* [< L. *voluntas,* free will] 1. given or done of one's own free will 2. acting willingly or of one's own accord 3. controlled by the will *[voluntary muscles]* 4. having the power of free choice 5. *a)* supported by freewill contributions *b)* done by, or composed of, volunteers —*n., pl.* **-taries** an organ solo played for a church service —**vol′untarily** *adv.*

Voluntary Service Overseas a British organization which provides skilled volunteers to help in underdeveloped areas of the world

volunteer (vol′ən tēər′) *n.* 1. a person who offers to do something of his own free will 2. a person who enlists in the armed forces of his own free will —*adj.* 1. of or made up of volunteers 2. serving as a volunteer —*vt.* to offer or give of one's own free will —*vi.* to enter or offer to enter into any service of one's own free will; enlist

voluptuary (və lup′tyㅎㅎ wər ē) *n., pl.* **-aries**

[see ff.] a person devoted to luxurious living and sensual pleasures

voluptuous (-ty‌oo‌was) *adj.* [< L. *voluptas*, pleasure] **1.** full of, producing, or fond of sensual pleasures **2.** suggesting, or arising from, sensual pleasure **3.** sexually attractive because of a full, shapely figure —**volup′tuousness** *n.*

volute (və lyoo‌t′) *n.* [< L. *volvere*, to roll] a spiral or twisting form; whorl —*adj.* spiralled: also **volut′ed** —**volu′- tion** *n.*

vomit (vom′it) *vi., vt.* [< L. *vomere*, to vomit] **1.** to throw up (the contents of the stomach) through the mouth **2.** to throw out or be thrown out with force —*n.* matter thrown up from the stomach

voodoo (voo‌′doo‌) *n., pl.* **-doos** [Creole Fr. < a WAfr. word] a primitive religion based on a belief in sorcery, fetishism, etc.: it originated in Africa and is still practised, chiefly by natives of the West Indies —*adj.* of voodoos or their practices, beliefs, etc. —**voo′dooism** *n.* —**voo′doo- ist** *n.*

voorkamer (foo‌ar′kä′mar) *n.* [< Afrik.][S Afr.] the front room of a house

voorlaaier (foo‌ar′li′ar) *n.* [< Afrik. *voor*, front + *laai*, load] [S Afr.] a muzzle loading gun

voorskot (foo‌ar′skot′) *n.* [< Afrik.] in South Africa, an advance payment made to a farmer's cooperative for a crop or wool clip

voortrekker (foo‌ar′trek′ar) *n.* [< Afrik.] in South Africa, **1.** any of the original Afrikaner settlers of the Transvaal and Orange Free State who migrated from the Cape Colony in the 1830's **2.** a member of the Afrikaner youth movement founded in 1931

voracious (və rā′shəs) *adj.* [< L. *vorare*, devour] **1.** greedy in eating; ravenous; gluttonous **2.** very greedy or eager in some desire or pursuit —**vora′ciously** *adv.* —**vorac′ity** (-ras′ə tē), **vora′ciousness** *n.*

-vorous (və rəs) [< L. *vorare*, devour] *a combining form meaning* feeding on, eating [*omnivorous*]

vortex (vôr′teks) *n., pl.* **vor′texes, vor′ti- ces′** (-tə sēz′) [L. < *vertere*, to turn] **1.** a whirling mass of water, air, etc. forming a vacuum at its centre, into which anything caught in the motion is drawn **2.** any situation like this in its engulfing effect, catastrophic power, etc. —**vor′tical** *adj.*

votary (vōt′ə rē) *n., pl.* **-ries** [< L. *vovere*, to vow] **1.** *a)* a person bound by religious vows, as a monk *b)* a devout worshipper **2.** one devoted to some cause or interest —**vo′taress** *n.fem.*

vote (vōt) *n.* [< L. *votum*, a vow] **1.** a decision on a proposal, etc., or a choice between candidates for office **2.** *a)* the expression of such a decision or choice *b)* the ballot, etc. by which it is expressed **3.** the right to exercise such a decision, etc. **4.** *a)* votes collectively *b)* a specified group of voters [the Scottish *vote*] —*vi.* **vot′ed, vot′ing** to express preference in a matter by ballot, etc. —*vt.* **1.** to decide,

choose, or authorize by vote **2.** to declare by general opinion **3.** [Colloq.] to suggest (often with *that*) —**vote down** to defeat by voting —**vote in** to elect —**vote out** to defeat (an incumbent) in an election

voter *n.* a person who has a right to vote, esp. one who actually votes

votive (vōt′iv) *adj.* [see VOTE] given, done, etc. in fulfilment of a vow

vouch (vauch) *vi.* [< L. *vocare*, to call] **1.** to give assurance, a guarantee, etc. (with *for*) **2.** to serve as evidence or assurance (*for*)

voucher (vau′chər) *n.* **1.** a paper giving evidence of the expenditure or receipt of money, the accuracy of an account, etc. **2.** a ticket or card entitling the holder to receive goods or services of a specific value

vouchsafe (vauch sāf′) *vt.* **-safed′, -saf′- ing** [< ME. *vouchen safe*, vouch as safe] to be kind or gracious enough to give or grant

vow (vau) *n.* [see VOTE] **1.** a solemn promise or pledge, as one made to God or with God as one's witness **2.** a solemn affirmation —*vt.* **1.** to promise solemnly **2.** to declare in a forceful or earnest way —*vi.* to make a vow —**take vows** to enter a religious order

vowel (vau′əl) *n.* [< L. *vocalis*, vocal] **1.** any speech sound made by letting the voiced breath pass in a continuous stream through the pharynx and opened mouth **2.** a letter, as *a, e, i, o, u,* and sometimes *y,* representing such a sound

‡**vox** (voks) *n., pl.* **voces** (vō′sēz) [L.] voice

‡**vox populi** (pop′yoo li′) [L.] the voice of the people; public opinion or sentiment: abbrev. **vox pop.**

voyage (voi′ij) *n.* [< L. *via*, way] **1.** a relatively long journey by water or, formerly, by land **2.** a journey by aircraft or spacecraft —*vi.* **-aged, -aging** to travel —**voy′ager** *n.*

voyageur (vwä yä zhur′) *n.* [Canad.] a guide, trapper, boatman, etc., esp. in the North

voyeur (vwä yur′) *n.* [Fr. < *voir*, see] a person who has an exaggerated interest in viewing sexual objects or scenes —**voy- eur′ism** *n.*

V.Rev. Very Reverend

vrou (frō) *n.* [Afrik.] [S Afr.] an Afrikaner woman, esp. a married woman

vrystater (frä′stä′tər) *n.* [< Afrik.] [S Afr.] a native inhabitant of the Free State, esp. one who is white

vs. versus

V.S. veterinary surgeon

V-shaped *adj.* shaped like the letter V

V-sign *n.* `1. an offensive sign made with the index and middle finger, the palm facing inwards **2.** a similar sign meaning victory or peace, the palm facing outwards

V.S.O. Voluntary Service Overseas

V.S.O.P. very superior (or special) old pale: said of brandy

vt., v.t. transitive verb

VTOL [v(*ertical*) t(*ake*)o(*ff and*) l(*anding*)]

an aircraft, usually other than a helicopter, that can take off and land vertically

VTR video tape recorder

vulcanite (vul′kə nīt′) *n.* [< *Vulcan,* Roman god of fire and metalworking] a hard rubber made by heating crude rubber with a large amount of sulphur: used in combs, electrical insulation, etc.

vulcanize *vt., vi.* **-ized′**, **-iz′ing** [see prec.] to heat (crude rubber) with sulphur in order to increase its strength and elasticity —**vul′caniza′tion** *n.*

Vulg. Vulgate

vulgar (vul′gər) *adj.* [< L. *vulgus,* the common people] **1.** *a)* characterized by a lack of culture, refinement, taste, etc.; crude; boorish *b)* indecent or obscene **2.** of the great mass of people in general; common; popular [a *vulgar* superstition] —**vul′garly** *adv.*

vulgar fraction *same as* SIMPLE FRACTION

vulgarian (vul gāər′ē ən) *n.* a vulgar person; esp., a rich person with coarse, showy manners or tastes

vulgarism (vul′gər iz′m) *n.* a word, phrase, etc. that is used widely but is regarded as coarse or obscene

vulgarity (vul gar′ə tē) *n.* **1.** the state or quality of being vulgar, crude, etc. **2.** *pl.* **-ties** a vulgar act, habit, usage in speech, etc.

vulgarize (vul′gə rīz′) *vt.* **-ized′**, **-iz′ing 1.** to popularize **2.** to make coarse, crude, etc. —**vul′gariza′tion** *n.*

Vulgar Latin the everyday speech of the Roman people, from which the Romance languages developed

Vulgate (vul′gāt) *n.* [ML. *vulgata* (*editio*), popular (edition)] a Latin version of the Bible prepared in the 4th cent., serving as an authorized version of the Roman Catholic Church

vulnerable (vul′nər ə b'l) *adj.* [< L. *vulnus,* a wound] **1.** that can be wounded or physically injured **2.** *a)* open to, or easily hurt by, criticism or attack *b)* affected by a specified influence, etc. **3.** open to attack by armed forces **4.** *Bridge* open to increased penalties or increased bonuses: said of a team which has won one game —**vul′nerabil′ity** *n.* —**vul′nerably** *adv.*

vulpine (vul′pīn) *adj.* [< L. *vulpes,* fox] **1.** of or like a fox **2.** clever, cunning, etc.

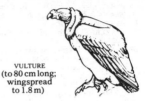

VULTURE
(to 80 cm long;
wingspread
to 1.8 m)

vulture (vul′chər) *n.* [L. *vultur*] **1.** a large bird related to the eagles and hawks, with a naked head **2.** a greedy, ruthless person who preys on others

vulva (vul′və) *n., pl.* **-vae** (-vē), **-vas** [< L., womb] the external genital organs of the female

vv. **1.** verses **2.** violins

v.v. vice versa

vying (vī′iŋ) *adj.* that competes

W

W, w (dub′′l yōō) *n., pl.* **W's, w's** the twenty-third letter of the English alphabet
W 1. *Chem.* tungsten 2. *Physics the symbol for* watt
W, W., w, w. 1. west 2. western
W. 1. Wales 2. Welsh 3. women's (size)
W., w. 1. weight 2. width 3. won
w. 1. week(s) 2. wide 3. wife 4. with
W.A. Western Australia
Waac (wak) *n.* a member of the Women's Army Auxiliary Corps
WAAC Women's Army Auxiliary Corps
Waaf (waf) *n.* a member of the Women's Auxiliary Air Force
WAAF Women's Auxiliary Air Force
wacky (wak′ē) *adj.* **wack′ier, wack′iest** [< ?] [Slang] odd, silly, or crazy —**wack′ily** *adv.*
wad (wod) *n.* [< ?] 1. a small, soft mass or ball, as a handful of cottonwool 2. a lump or small, compact mass 3. a mass of soft material used for padding, packing, etc. 4. a roll or bundle, esp. of bank notes —*vt.* **wad′ded, wad′ding** 1. to roll up into a wad 2. to plug or stuff with a wad 3. to pad with wadding
wadding *n.* any soft material for use in padding, stuffing, etc.; esp., loose, fluffy sheets of cotton
waddle (wod′'l) *vi.* **-dled, -dling** [< WADE] to walk with short steps, swaying from side to side —*n.* a waddling gait —**wad′-dler** *n.*
wade (wād) *vi.* **wad′ed, wad′ing** [OE. *waden*, go] 1. to walk through a substance, as water, mud, etc., that slows one down 2. to get through with difficulty 3. [Colloq.] to start or attack with vigour (with *in* or *into*) —*vt.* to go across or through by wading —*n.* an act of wading —**wad′able** *adj.*
wader *n.* 1. *same as* WADING BIRD 2. [*pl.*] long waterproof boots
wadi (wod′ē) *n., pl.* **-dis, -dies** [Ar. *wādī*] in N Africa, etc., a valley, ravine, etc. that is dry except during the rainy season Also sp. **wa′dy**
wading bird any of various long-legged birds that wade in shallow water and marshes for food, as the heron
wafer (wā′fər) *n.* [< MDu. *wafel*] 1. a thin, crisp sweetened biscuit 2. a thin cake of unleavened bread used in the Eucharist 3. a small disc of sticky paper, used as a seal on letters, etc.
waffle¹ (wof′'l) *n.* [Du. *wafel*] a crisp batter cake with small, square hollows, baked in a waffle iron
waffle² *vi.* **-fled, -fling** [orig., to yelp] [Colloq.] to speak or write in a wordy or indecisive manner —*n.* [Colloq.] talk or writing of this kind
waffle iron an appliance for cooking waffles, having two flat, studded plates pressed together so that the waffle bakes between them
waft (wäft) *vt.* [< Du. *wachter*, watcher] to carry or move (sounds, etc.) lightly through the air or over water —*vi.* 1. to float, as in the air 2. to blow gently: said of breezes —*n.* 1. an odour, sound, etc. carried through the air 2. a gust of wind 3. a wafting movement
wag¹ (wag) *vt.* **wagged, wag′ging** [OE. *wagian*] 1. to cause to move rapidly back and forth, up and down, etc. 2. to move (the tongue) in talking, esp. in idle gossip —*vi.* 1. to move rapidly back and forth, up and down, etc. 2. to keep moving in talk: said of the tongue —*n.* the act of wagging
wag² *n.* [prob. < obs. *waghalter*, a rogue] a comical or humorous person; joker; wit
wage (ẉāj) *n.* [< OFr. *gage*, a pledge] 1. [*often pl.*] money paid to an employee for work done, as on an hourly or weekly basis 2. [*usually pl., formerly with sing. v.*] what is given in return; recompense ["The *wages* of sin is death"] *vt.* **waged, wag′ing** to engage in (a war, etc.)
wager *n., vi., vt.* [see WAGE] bet —**wa′-gerer** *n.*
waggish (wag′ish) *adj.* 1. roguishly merry 2. playful; jesting [a *waggish* remark] —**wag′gishly** *adv.*
waggle (wag′'l) *vt.* **-gled, -gling** [< WAG¹] to wag, esp. with short, quick movements —*n.* a waggling —**wag′gly** *adj.*
wag-n-bietjie (väkh′'n bi′ki) *n.* [< Afrik. *wag*, wait + *n*, a + *bietjie*, bit] [S Afr.] any of various thorn bushes or trees
Wagnerian (väg nēar′ē ən) *adj.* of or like Richard Wagner or his music, theories, etc.
wagon, waggon (wag′ən) *n.* [Du. *wagen*] 1. a four-wheeled vehicle for hauling heavy loads 2. a railway goods vehicle, esp. an open one —**hitch one's wagon to a star** 1. to set oneself an ambitious goal 2. to attach oneself to a person of greater importance, etc. —**on** (or **off**) **the wagon** [Slang] no longer (or once again) drinking alcohol —**wag′oner, wag′goner** *n.*
wagonette, waggonette (wag′ə net′) *n.* [< WAGON] a four-wheeled carriage with two seats set lengthwise facing each other behind the driver's seat
wagtail (wag′tāl′) *n.* a small bird having a long tail that wags up and down
waif (wāf) *n.* [prob. < ON.] 1. a person without home or friends esp., a homeless

child **2.** anything found that is without an owner .

wail (wāl) *vi.* [< ON. *væ*, woe] **1.** to express grief or pain by long, loud cries **2.** to make a sad, crying sound —*n.* **1.** a long cry of grief or pain **2.** a sound like this **3.** the act of wailing —**wail'-ful** *adj.*

wain (wān) *n.* [OE. *wægn*] [Archaic] a wagon

wainscot (wān'skət) *n.* [< MDu. *wagenschot*] a lining or panelling of wood, etc. on the walls of a room, often on the lower part only —*vt.* **-scoted** or **-scotted**, **-scoting** or **-scotting** to line (a wall, etc.) with wainscoting

wainscoting, wainscotting *n.* **1.** *same as* WAINSCOT **2.** material used to wainscot

waist (wāst) *n.* [< OE. *weaxan*, grow] **1.** the part of the body between the ribs and the hips **2.** the part of a garment that covers the waist **3.** the middle, narrow part of something —**waist'ed** *adj.*

waistband *n.* a band encircling the waist, esp. one at the top of a skirt, trousers, etc.

waistcoat *n.* a short, tight-fitting, sleeveless garment worn, esp. under a suit jacket, by men

waistline *n.* **1.** the line of the waist, between the ribs and the hips **2.** the narrow part of a woman's dress, etc., worn at the waist or above or below it as styles change **3.** the distance round the waist

wait (wāt) *vi.* [ONormFr. *waitier*] **1.** to remain in readiness or in anticipation (often with *until* or *for*) **2.** to be ready [dinner is *waiting* for us] **3.** to remain undone for a time **4.** to serve food (with *at* or *on*) [to *wait* at table] —*vt.* **1.** to be, remain, or delay in expectation of **2.** [Colloq.] to delay serving (a meal) [to *wait* dinner] —*n.* **1.** the act or a period of waiting **2.** [*pl.*] itinerant carol singers at Christmas —**lie in wait (for)** to wait so as to catch after planning an ambush (for) —**wait on (or upon) 1.** to serve (a customer, etc.) as a waiter, etc. **2.** to act as a servant to **3.** to call on or visit (esp. a superior) in order to pay one's respects, etc. —**wait up** to put off going to bed until someone expected arrives or something expected happens (often with *for*) —**you wait!** [Colloq.] I will have my revenge: also **just you wait!**

waiter *n.* a man who waits at table, as in a restaurant

waiting *adj.* **1.** that waits **2.** of or for a wait —*n.* **1.** the act of one that waits **2.** a period of waiting —**in waiting** in attendance, as on a king

waiting game a delaying action until one has the advantage

waiting list a list of applicants, as for a vacancy, in the order of their application

waiting room a room in which people wait, as at a railway station, dentist's surgery, etc.

waitress (wā'tris) *n.* a woman who waits at table, as in a restaurant

waive (wāv) *vt.* **waived, waiv'ing** [< ON. *veifa*, fluctuate] **1.** to give up or forgo (a right, claim, etc.) **2.** to refrain from insisting on **3.** to defer

waiver *n.* *Law* a giving up voluntarily, of a right, claim, etc.

wake¹ (wāk) *vi.* **woke, wok'en** or, occas. **woke, wak'ing** [< OE. *wacian*, be awake & *wacan*, arise] **1.** to come out of sleep (often with *up*) **2.** to be or stay awake **3.** to become active again (often with *up*) **4.** to become alert (*to* a danger, etc.) —*vt.* **1.** to cause to wake from or as from sleep (often with *up*) **2.** to arouse or excite (passions, etc.) —*n.* **1.** an all-night vigil over a corpse before burial **2.** [*usually pl.*] [N Eng. Dial.] an annual holiday

wake² *n.* [ON. *vŏk*, hole in the ice] **1.** the track left in the water by a moving ship **2.** any track left behind —**in the wake of** following close behind

wakeful *adj.* **1.** unable to sleep **2.** keeping awake **3.** alert; watchful —**wake'fully** *adv.*

waken *vi., vt.* [OE. *wæcnian*] to become awake or cause to wake

waking *adj.* of the period when one is not asleep

wale (wāl) *n.* [OE. *walu*, weal] **1.** a ridge on the surface of cloth, as corduroy **2.** [*pl.*] heavy planks fastened to the outside of the hull of a wooden ship —*vt.* **waled, wal'ing** to make (cloth, etc.) with wales

walk (wôk) *vi.* [OE. *wealcan*, to roll] **1.** to move along on foot at a moderate pace by placing one foot on the ground before lifting the other **2.** to appear after death as a ghost **3.** to follow a certain course, way of life, etc. —*vt.* **1.** to go along, over, etc. by walking **2.** to cause (a horse, dog, etc.) to walk, as for exercise **3.** to go along with (a person) on a walk **4.** to bring to a specified state by walking —*n.* **1.** the act of walking **2.** a stroll or hike **3.** a route taken in walking **4.** a distance to walk **5.** the pace of one who walks **6.** a way of walking [I knew her by her *walk*] **7.** a particular station in life, sphere of activity, etc. **8.** a path, avenue, etc. set apart for walking —**walk (all) over** [Colloq.] **1.** to defeat decisively **2.** to take advantage of —**walk a person off his feet** to tire someone out by walking —**walk away from** to outdistance easily —**walk away with** to win easily —**walk into** [Colloq.] to become involved in an awkward situation through lack of caution —**walk off 1.** to go away, esp. without warning **2.** to get rid of (fat, etc.) by walking —**walk off with 1.** to steal **2.** to win easily —**walk out 1.** to leave suddenly esp. in anger **2.** to go on strike —**walk out on** [Colloq.] to desert —**walk the streets 1.** to pace the streets aimlessly, or in search of work **2.** to be a prostitute —**walk'ing** *adj., n.*

walkabout *n.* **1.** an Australian Aborigine's periodic nomadic excursion into the bush **2.** an occasion when members of the royal family, etc. walk among and meet the public informally

walker *n.* **1.** one that walks **2.** a frame

on wheels for babies learning to walk
3. a similar frame used as a support in
walking by convalescents, etc.

walkie-talkie (wôk′ē tôk′ē) *n.* a
compact radio transmitter and receiver
that can be carried by one person: also
walk′y-talk′y, *pl.* **-talk′ies**

walk-on *n.* a minor role in which an
actor has no speaking lines

walkout *n.* **1.** a strike of workers **2.**
an abrupt departure of people as a show
of protest

walkover *n.* an easily won victory

walkway *n.* a path, passage, etc. for
pedestrians, esp. one that is sheltered

wall (wôl) *n.* [< L. *vallum,* rampart] **1.**
an upright structure of wood, stone, etc.,
serving to enclose, divide, support, or
protect **2.** [*usually pl.*] a fortification
3. anything like a wall in appearance or
function [a *wall* of silence] *—adj.* of,
on, in, or along a wall *—vt.* **1.** to enclose,
etc. with or as with a wall (often with
off, in, etc.) **2.** to close up (an opening)
with a wall (usually with *up*) *—***drive** (or
push) to the wall **1.** to place in a desperate
position *—***drive** (or **send,** etc.) **up the
wall** [Colloq.] to make frantic, tense,
etc. *—***go to the wall 1.** to fail in business
2. to suffer defeat *—***run** (or **bang) one's
head against a brick wall** to try to deal
with an impossibly difficult problem
*—***walled** *adj.*

wallaby (wol′ə bē) *n.* [< Abor. name]
a small or medium-sized marsupial related
to the kangaroo

wallah (wol′ə) *n.* [< Hindu -*wālā*] [orig.
Anglo-Indian] a person connected with
a particular thing or function: also sp. **wal′la**

wallboard (wôl′bôrd′) *n.* fibrous
material made up into thin slabs for use
in making or covering walls, etc.

wallet (wol′it) *n.* [ME. *walet*] a flat case,
as of leather, with compartments for
banknotes, cards, etc.

walleye (wôl′ī′) *n.* [< ON. *vagl,* beam
+ *eygr,* having eyes] **1.** an eye that
turns outwards, showing more white than
is normal **2.** any of several fishes with
large, staring eyes *—***wall′eyed′** *adj.*

wallflower *n.* **1.** any of a number of
garden plants having racemes of yellow,
orange, etc. flowers **2.** [Colloq.] a girl
who merely looks on at a dance from
lack of a partner

Walloon (wo loōn′) *n.* [Fr. *Wallon*] a
member of a people living mostly in S
and SE Belgium

wallop (wol′əp) *vt.* [< OFr. *galoper,* to
gallop] [Colloq.] **1.** to beat soundly **2.**
to strike hard *—vi.* [Dial.] **1.** to move
along in a rapid, awkward way **2.** to
boil vigorously *—n.* [Colloq.] a hard blow
*—***wal′loper** *n.*

walloping *adj.* [Colloq.] enormous *—n.*
1. a thrashing **2.** a crushing defeat

wallow (wol′ō) *vi.* [OE. *wealwian*] **1.**
to roll about, as in mud, dust, etc. **2.**
to revel in some feeling, etc. [to *wallow*
in self-pity] *—n.* **1.** a wallowing **2.** a
place where animals wallow

wallpaper (wôl′pā′pər) *n.* paper for
covering the walls or ceiling of a room
—vt. to put wallpaper on or in

Wall Street [< street in New York City:
main U.S. financial centre] U.S. financiers
or the U.S. money market

wall-to-wall *adj.* that completely covers
a floor [*wall-to-wall* carpeting]

walnut (wôl′nut′) *n.* [< OE. *wealh,* foreign
+ *hnutu,* nut] **1.** any of a number of
related trees, valued for their nuts and
wood **2.** their edible nut, having a hard,
crinkled shell **3.** their wood, used for
furniture, etc.

WALRUS
(to 3.5 m long
& 1.5 m high)

walrus (wôl′rəs) *n.* [< ON. *hrosshvalr,*
horse whale] a massive sea mammal
having two tusks jutting from the upper
jaw, a thick moustache, a thick hide, and
a heavy layer of blubber *—adj.* like that
of a walrus [a *walrus* moustache]

waltz (wôls) *n.* [< G. *walzen,* dance about]
1. a ballroom dance for couples, in 3/4
time **2.** music for this dance or in its
characteristic rhythm *—adj.* of, for, or
characteristic of a waltz *—vi.* **1.** to dance
a waltz **2.** to move lightly and nimbly
3. [Colloq.] to progress effortlessly (usually
with *through*) *—vt.* to dance with in
a waltz

wampum (wom′pəm) *n.* [< Algonquian]
small beads made of shells and used by
N American Indians as money, for
ornament, etc.

wan (won) *adj.* **wan′ner, wan′nest** [OE.
wann, dark] **1.** sickly pale; pallid **2.**
suggestive of a sickly condition; feeble
[a *wan* smile] *—***wan′ness** *n.*

wand (wond) *n.* [ON. *vondr*] **1.** a rod
carried as a symbol of authority **2.** any
rod of supposed magic power **3.** a
conductor's baton

wander (won′dər) *vi.* [OE. *wandrian*] **1.**
to move or go about aimlessly **2.** to
go to a place in a casual or indirect way
3. *a)* to stray (*from* a path, course, etc.)
b) to stray from home, friends, etc. (often
with *off*) **4.** to go astray in mind or
purpose **5.** to meander, as a river **6.**
to move idly from one object to another:
said of the eyes, etc. *—vt.* to roam through,
in, or over *—***wan′derer** *n.* *—***wan′dering**
adj., n.

Wandering Jew 1. in medieval folklore,
a Jew condemned to wander the earth
because he insulted Christ **2.** [w- j-]
any of several trailing plants, including
tradescantia

wanderlust *n.* [G.] an impulse, longing,
or urge to wander or travel

wane (wān) *vi.* **waned, wan′ing** [OE.
wanian] **1.** to show a gradually decreasing

area of illuminated surface: said of the moon **2.** to grow dim or faint: said of light, etc. **3.** to decline in power, etc. **—on the wane** declining, decreasing, etc.

wangle (waŋ′g'l) *vt.* **-gled, -gling** [< ?] [Colloq.] to get, make, or bring about by persuasion, manipulation, etc. **—vi.** [Colloq.] to make use of tricky and indirect methods to achieve one's aims **—wan′-gler** *n.*

wanigan, wannigan (won′i gən) *n.* [< AmInd.] [Canad.] **1.** a lumberjack's chest or box **2.** a cabin, caboose, or houseboat

Wankel engine (waŋ′k′l) [< F. *Wankel*] a rotary combustion engine requiring fewer parts and less fuel than a comparable turbine engine

want (wont) *vt.* [ON. *vanta*] **1.** to feel the need of; crave **2.** to desire or wish [to *want* to travel] **3.** to require; need *Want* is also used colloquially as an auxiliary meaning ought or should [you *want* to be careful] **4. a)** to wish to see or speak with (someone) **b)** to wish to apprehend, as for arrest **5.** to have too little of; lack **6.** to be short by (a specified amount) [it *wants* two minutes of noon] **—vi.** **1.** to have a need or lack (usually with *for*) **2.** to be destitute **—n.** **1.** a scarcity; shortage **2.** poverty; destitution **3.** a wish for something; craving **4.** something needed; need

wanting *adj.* **1.** absent; lacking **2.** not up to some standard [found *wanting*] **—prep.** **1.** lacking (something) **2.** minus **—wanting in** having not enough of (some quality, etc.)

wanton (won′t'n) *adj.* [< OE. *wan*, lacking + *teon*, bring up] **1.** senseless, unprovoked, or deliberately malicious **2.** sexually loose **3.** [Poet.] frisky; playful **4.** recklessly ignoring justice, morality, etc. **5.** lavish, luxurious, or extravagant **—n.** a wanton person; esp., a sexually loose woman **—vi.** to be wanton **—wan′tonly** *adv.* **—wan′tonness** *n.*

wapiti (wop′ə tē) *n.* [< Algonquian] the American elk, the largest N American deer

war (wôr) *n.* [ONormFr. *werre*, strife] **1.** open armed conflict between countries or between factions within the same country **2.** any period of such conflict **3.** any active hostility, contention, or struggle **4.** military operations as a science **—adj.** of, used in, or resulting from war **—vi.** **warred, war′ring** to carry on war **—at war** in a state of active armed conflict **—carry the war into the enemy's camp** (or **country**) to resort to offensive measures in any conflict **—declare war (on)** **1.** to make a formal declaration of being at war (with) **2.** to announce one's hostility (to), and intention to attack **—go to war** **1.** to enter into a war **2.** to join the armed forces during a war **—to have been in the wars** to have injuries or marks of ill-treatment **—war′ring** *adj.*

War. Warwickshire

warble (wôr′b'l) *vt., vi.* **-bled, -bling** [ONormFr. *werbler*] to sing with trills, etc., as a bird **—n.** **1.** an act of warbling **2.** a warbling sound; trill

warbler *n.* **1.** a bird or person that warbles **2.** a small songbird related to the thrush

war crime any crime committed in war in violation of accepted rules of war **—war criminal**

war cry **1.** a name, phrase, etc. shouted in a charge or battle **2.** a slogan adopted by a party in any contest

ward (wôrd) *n.* [OE. *weardian*, to guard] **1.** a division of a city or town, for purposes of administration, voting, etc. **2.** a division of a hospital [a maternity *ward*] **3. a)** a child or person not able to manage his own affairs [*ward* in chancery] **b)** any person under another's care **4.** a being under guard **5.** a guarding: now only in **watch and ward** **6.** a ridge or notch in a lock or key that allows only the right key to enter **—vt.** to turn aside; fend off (usually with *off*)

-ward (wərd) [OE.] a suffix forming adjectives meaning in a (specified) direction [*backward*]

warden (wôr′d'n) *n.* [< OFr. *gardein*] **1.** a person who guards, or has charge of, something [a traffic *warden*] **2.** a governing officer in certain hospitals, colleges, etc. **—war′denship** *n.*

warder (wôr′dər) *n.* a prison officer **—ward′ress** *n.fem.*

wardrobe (wôrd′rōb′) *n.* **1.** a cupboard or cabinet with hangers for holding clothes **2.** a room where clothes are kept, as in a theatre **3.** one's supply of clothes

wardrobe mistress the person in charge of the costumes of a theatrical company

wardroom (wôrd′rōōm′) *n.* in a warship, a compartment used for eating and relaxing in by commissioned officers, except, usually, the captain

-wards (wərdz) a suffix forming adverbs meaning in a (specified) direction [*backwards*]: also sometimes **-ward**

wardship (wôrd′ship′) *n.* **1.** guardianship **2.** the condition of being a ward

ware (wãr) *n.* [OE. *waru*] **1.** any thing or service that one has to sell: usually used in pl. **2.** things that are for sale, esp. a (specified) kind of merchandise [*hardware, glassware*] **3.** a specified kind of pottery

warehouse (wãr′hous′; for v., -houz′) *n.* **1.** a building where goods are stored **2.** a wholesale store **—vt. -housed′, -hous′-ing** to place or store in a warehouse **—ware′house′man** *n.*

warfare (wôr′fãr′) *n.* **1.** the action of waging war **2.** conflict of any kind

war game **1.** training in military tactics in which maps and small figures are used to represent terrain, troops, etc. **2.** [pl.] practice manoeuvres for troops

warhead *n.* the front section of a self-propelled projectile, etc. containing the explosive charge

war horse **1.** a horse used in battle **2.** [Colloq.] a person who has engaged in many struggles For 2 now usually **war′-horse′** *n.*

warily (wãr′ə lē) *adv.* cautiously

wariness *n.* the quality or state of being wary

warlike (wôr′līk′) *adj.* 1. fond of or ready for war; bellicose 2. of or appropriate to war 3. threatening war

warlock (wôr′lok′) *n.* [OE. *wærloga*, traitor] a sorcerer or wizard

warm (wôrm) *adj.* [OE. *wearm*] 1. *a)* having or giving off a moderate degree of heat *b)* giving off pleasurable heat *[a warm fire]* 2. *a)* overheated, as with exercise *b)* such as to make one heated *[warm work]* 3. effective in keeping body heat in *[warm clothing]* 4. marked by liveliness or disagreement, as an argument 5. ardent; enthusiastic 6. *a)* cordial or sincere *[a warm welcome]* *b)* sympathetic or loving 7. suggesting warmth : said of yellow, orange, or red colours 8. newly made; fresh, as a scent or trail 9. [Colloq.] close to discovering something 10. [Colloq.] disagreeable *[we'll make it warm for him]* —*vt., vi.* to make or become warm —*n.* [Colloq.] 1. a warming or being warmed *[have a warm by the fire]* 2. a warm place *[come into the warm]* —**warm up** 1. to make or become warm, esp. warm enough to operate efficiently 2. to reheat (cooked food, etc.) 3. *Sports* to practise before going into a game 4. to make or become more lively —**warm′er** *n.* —**warm′ish** *adj.* —**warm′ly** *adv.* —**warm′ness** *n.*

warmblooded *adj.* 1. having a relatively constant body temperature, usually warmer than that of the surroundings 2. ardent —**warm′blood′edness** *n.*

war memorial a monument erected in a public place and bearing the names of those killed in war

warm front *Meteorol.* the edge of an advancing mass of warm air replacing colder air

warmhearted *adj.* kind, sympathetic, friendly, etc. —**warm′heart′edly** *adv.* —**warm′heart′edness** *n.*

warming pan a long-handled, covered pan for holding live coals : formerly used to warm beds

warmonger (wôr′muŋ′gər) *n.* one that advocates or tries to bring war —**war′mon′gering** *adj., n.*

warmth (wôrmth) *n.* 1. *a)* a being warm *b)* mild heat 2. *a)* enthusiasm *b)* affectionate feelings *c)* slight anger

warn (wôrn) *vt.* [OE. *wearnian*] 1. to tell (a person) of a danger, coming evil, etc. 2. to caution about certain acts 3. to notify in advance —**warn off** to give notice to stay away or keep off —**warn′er** *n.*

warning *n.* 1. the act of one that warns, or the state of being warned 2. something that serves to warn —*adj.* that warns —**warn′ingly** *adv.*

warp (wôrp) *vt.* [OE. *weorpan*, to throw] 1. to bend or twist out of shape 2. to distort, pervert, bias, etc. 3. to move (a ship) by hauling on a line fastened to a dock, etc. —*vi.* to become bent or twisted out of shape —*n.* 1. *a)* a

distortion, as a twist or bend in wood *b)* any similar distortion 2. a mental twist, quirk, etc. 3. a rope run from a ship to a dock, etc., used to haul the vessel into position 4. *Weaving* the threads running lengthwise in the loom —**warp′ed** *adj.* —**warp′er** *n.*

war paint 1. a pigment applied to the face and body, as by some American Indian tribes, in preparation for war 2. [Colloq.] *a)* ceremonial dress *b)* women's cosmetics

warpath (wôr′päth′) *n.* the path taken by American Indians on a warlike expedition —**on the warpath** 1. ready for war 2. angry; ready to fight

warrant (wor′ənt) *n.* [< OFr. *garant*] 1. *a)* authorization, as by the law *b)* justification for some act, belief, etc. 2. something that serves as a guarantee of some event or result 3. *a)* *Law* a writ authorizing an officer to make an arrest, search, etc. *b)* *Mil.* the certificate of appointment to the grade of warrant officer —*vt.* 1. to serve as justification for (an act, belief, etc.) 2. to authorize 3. *a)* to guarantee the quality, quantity, etc. of (goods) to a purchaser *b)* to guarantee to (the purchaser) that goods sold are as represented 4. [Colloq.] to state with confidence *[I warrant he'll be late]* —**war′rantable** *adj.*

warrant officer *see* MILITARY RANKS, table : in the army the rank has two classes : regimental sergeant major and company sergeant major

warrantor (wôr′ən tôr′) *n.* *Law* a person who warrants, or gives warranty : also **war′ranter**

warranty *n., pl.* **-ties′** [*see* WARRANT] 1. *Law* a guarantee; specif., a guarantee of something in a contract 2. official authorization 3. justification

warren (wor′ən) *n.* [< OFr. *warir*, to preserve] 1. an area containing many interconnected tunnels in which rabbits live and breed 2. any building crowded like a rabbit warren

warrior (wo′rē ər) *n.* [< ONormFr. *werre*, WAR] a man experienced in conflict or war

wart (wôrt) *n.* [OE. *wearte*] 1. a small, usually hard, tumorous growth on the skin 2. a small growth on a plant —**warts and all** [Colloq.] with all defects and blemishes revealed —**wart′y** *adj.*

wart hog a wild African pig with large, incurved tusks, and a number of warts below the eyes

wartime (wôr′tīm′) *n.* a time of war —*adj.* of or characteristic of such a time

wary (wāar′ē) *adj.* **war′ier, war′iest** [OE. *wær*] 1. cautious; on one's guard 2. characterized by caution —**wary of** careful of

was (woz; *unstressed* wəz) [OE. *wæs*] 1st and 3rd pers. sing., *pt.,* of BE

wash (wosh) *vt.* [OE. *wæscan*] 1. to clean by means of water or other liquid, often with soap, etc. 2. to purify 3. to moisten 4. to cleanse by licking, as a cat does 5. to flow over, past, or against : said of a sea, waves, etc. 6. to soak (*out*), flush (*off*), or carry (*away*) by the action of water **7.** to erode [the flood *washed* out the tracks] **8.** to cover with a thin coating of paint or metal **9.** *Mining* to pass water through or over (earth, etc.) in order to separate (ore, etc.) —*vi.* **1.** to wash oneself or one's hands, face, etc. **2.** to wash clothes **3.** to undergo washing, esp. without fading, etc. **4.** to be removed by washing **5.** to be worn away by the action of water **6.** [Colloq.] to withstand a test [his story won't *wash*] —*n.* **1.** *a*) a washing *b*) a place where something is washed [a car *wash*] **2.** a quantity of clothes, etc. washed, or to be washed **3.** a thin coating of paint or metal **4.** any of various liquids for cosmetic or medicinal use **5.** *a*) the rush or surge of water or waves *b*) the sound of this *c*) the eddy of water caused by a propeller, oars, etc. *d*) a slipstream **6.** refuse liquid food; swill **7.** low ground which is flooded part of the time and partly dry the rest —**come out in the wash** [Colloq.] to be revealed eventually —**wash down 1.** to clean by washing **2.** to follow (food, a drink of whisky, etc.) with a drink, as of water —**wash one's hands (of)** to disclaim all responsibility for —**wash up** to wash eating and cooking utensils after use

washable *adj.* that can be washed without damage

wash-and-wear *adj.* designating or of fabrics or garments that need little or no ironing after washing

washboard *n.* a ridged board or frame used for scrubbing dirt out of clothes

wash drawing a painting done in transparent watercolours, usually in shades of black or grey

washed-out *adj.* **1.** faded in colour, specif. from washing **2.** [Colloq.] tired; pale

washed-up *adj.* [Slang] finished; done for

washer *n.* **1.** a person who washes **2.** a flat disc or ring of metal, rubber, etc., used to make a seal for a tap valve, to provide packing, etc. **3.** [Colloq.] a washing machine

washerwoman *n.* a woman whose work is washing clothes, etc.

washing *n.* **1.** clothes, etc. washed or to be washed, esp. at one time **2.** matter obtained or removed by washing **3.** a thin coating, as of metal, put on in liquid form

washing machine a machine for washing clothes, linens, etc.

washing-up *n.* **1.** the washing of dishes, cutlery, etc. after a meal **2.** the dishes, cutlery, etc. that are to be washed up

wash leather a piece of leather, usually chamois, used for washing windows, etc.

washout *n.* **1.** the washing away of soil, rocks, etc. by a strong flow of water **2.** a hole made by such washing away, as in a road **3.** [Colloq.] a complete failure

washy *adj.* **wash'ier, wash'iest 1.** watery; weak **2.** pale **3.** insipid —**wash'iness** *n.*

WASP, Wasp (wosp) *n.* [U.S. Derog.] a white Anglo-Saxon Protestant

wasp (wosp) *n.* [OE. *wæsp*] a winged insect with a slender body, biting mouthparts, and, in the females and workers, a sharp sting —**wasp'like'** *adj.* —**wasp'y** *adj.*

waspish *adj.* bad-tempered; snappish —**wasp'ishly** *adv.*

wasp waist a very slender or tightly corseted waist —**wasp'-waist'ed** *adj.*

wassail (wo'săl) *n.* [< ON. *ves heill*, be hearty] **1.** a toast formerly given in drinking healths **2.** the spiced ale with which such healths were drunk **3.** a celebration with much drinking, esp. at Christmas time —*vi.* **1.** to drink wassails **2.** to go from house to house carol singing at Christmas —*vt.* to drink to the health of —**was'sailer** *n.*

wastage (wās'tij) *n.* **1.** loss by use, decay, etc. **2.** the process of wasting **3.** anything wasted, or the amount of this —**natural wastage** loss of personnel in the normal course of events, as from retirement

waste (wāst) *vt.* **wast'ed, wast'ing** [< L. *vastare*, lay waste] **1.** to use up or spend without need, gain, or purpose **2.** to fail to take advantage of **3.** to make weak or feeble **4.** to wear away; use up **5.** to devastate —*vi.* **1.** to lose strength, health, flesh, etc., as by disease (often with *away*) **2.** to be used up —*adj.* **1.** left over; no longer of use **2.** excreted from the body, as faeces or urine **3.** used to carry off or hold waste [a *waste* pipe] **4.** uncultivated or uninhabited —*n.* **1.** *a*) a squandering, as of money, time, etc. *b*) a failure to take advantage (*of* something) *c*) a gradual loss or decrease by use, wear, etc. **2.** useless or discarded material, as refuse **3.** matter excreted from the body, as faeces **4.** uncultivated or uninhabited land, as a desert **5.** *a*) a desolate or devastated area *b*) a vast expanse, as of the sea —**go to waste** to be or become wasted —**lay waste (to)** to devastate —**waste breath** (or **words**) to give advice which will not be heeded —**wast'er** *n.*

wasteful *adj.* in the habit of wasting or characterized by waste; extravagant —**waste'fully** *adv.*

wasteland *n.* land that is uncultivated, barren, unproductive, devastated, etc.

wastepaper *n.* paper thrown away after use or as useless: also **waste paper**

wasting *adj.* destructive to health, as a disease

wastrel (wās'trəl) *n.* **1.** a spendthrift **2.** a good-for-nothing

watap (wa tap') *n.* [< AmInd.] thread made by N American Indians from conifer roots and used for sewing, etc.

watch (woch) *n.* [OE. *wæcce*] **1.** a small timepiece carried in the pocket, worn on the wrist, etc. **2.** the act or fact of keeping awake, esp. in order to guard **3.** close observation for a time, as to find out something **4.** a person or group on duty to protect or guard **5.** [*pl.*] hours (of the night): only in **watches of the night 6.** the period of duty of a guard **7.** *Naut.* any of the periods of duty (usually four hours) into which the day is divided on board ship —*vi.* 1. to look; observe 2. to be looking or waiting attentively (with *for*) 3. to be on the alert 4. to stay awake at night —*vt.* 1. to observe carefully and constantly 2. to wait and look for 3. to keep watch over 4. to keep informed about 5. to guard —**on the watch** on the lookout —**watch it!** [Colloq.] be careful! —**watch one's step** to be circumspect in one's behaviour —**watch out** to be alert and on one's guard —**watch over** to protect from harm —**watch'er** *n.*

watchdog *n.* 1. a dog kept to guard property 2. a person or group that keeps watch to prevent waste, dishonest practices, etc.

watch fire a fire kept burning at night as a signal or for the use of those staying awake to guard

watchful *adj.* alert; vigilant —**watch'fully** *adv.* —**watch'fulness** *n.*

watching brief an instruction to observe proceedings in a law court on behalf of a client only indirectly concerned

watchmaker *n.* a person who makes or repairs watches —**watch'mak'ing** *n.*

watchman *n.* a person hired to watch or guard, esp. at night

watch night a religious service held on New Year's Eve: also **watch meeting** or **watch-night service**

watch-spring *n.* the mainspring of a watch

watchstrap *n.* a band of leather, metal, cloth, etc. for holding a watch on the wrist

watchtower *n.* a high tower from which a sentinel watches for enemies, forest fires, etc.

watchword *n.* 1. a password 2. a slogan

water (wôt'ər) *n.* [OE. *wæter*] 1. the colourless, transparent liquid occurring on earth as rivers, lakes, etc., and falling as rain: a compound of hydrogen and oxygen, H_2O 2. an area of this liquid, as a lake 3. [*often pl.*] an area of a sea [*international waters*] 4. water with reference to its depth, its surface, its level, etc. [*high water*] 5. [*pl.*] the water of mineral springs 6. any body fluid or secretion, as urine, saliva, tears, etc. 7. a solution of any substance, often a gas, in water 8. the degree of transparency of a precious stone —*vt.* 1. to give (animals) water to drink 2. to give water to (soil, crops, etc.), as by sprinkling, irrigating, etc. 3. to moisten with water 4. to dilute with water (often with *down*) —*vi.* 1. to fill with tears: said of the eyes 2. to secrete or fill with saliva 3. to take on a supply of water 4. to drink water: said of animals —*adj.* 1. of or having to do with water 2. in, on, or near water 3. operated by water [*a water wheel*] —**by water** by ship or boat —**hold water** to remain sound, logical, etc. —**like water** lavishly; freely —**make one's mouth water** to create a desire or appetite in one —**make** (or **pass**) **water** to urinate —**water down** to weaken the effectiveness of —**water under the bridge** past history —**wa'terless'** *adj.*

water bed a heavy vinyl bag filled with water and used as a bed

water biscuit a thin, crisp, plain biscuit, usually served with butter or cheese

water buffalo a slow, powerful, oxlike draught animal native to S Asia

water bus a small river craft used as a form of public transport

water butt a large barrel with one end open, used for collecting and storing rainwater

water cannon a powerful hose which fires water at high pressure

water chestnut 1. a Chinese sedge, growing in clumps in water 2. its button-shaped tuber, used in cooking

water clock a mechanism for measuring time by the fall or flow of water

water closet *same as* TOILET (*n.* 1)

watercolour *n.* 1. a pigment or colouring matter mixed with water for use as a paint 2. a painting done with such paints —*adj.* painted in watercolours

water-cooled *adj.* kept from overheating by having water circulated around or through it

watercourse *n.* 1. a stream, river, etc. 2. a channel for water, as a canal or stream bed

watercress *n.* a plant grown generally in running water: its leaves are used in salads, etc.

water diviner a person able to locate the presence of water, esp. underground, with a divining rod

waterfall *n.* a steep fall of water, as of a stream, from a height

waterfowl *n.* a bird that lives on or near the water, esp. one that swims

waterfront *n.* the land or part of a city or town adjoining a body of water, as a harbour, lake, etc.

water gate 1. a gate controlling the flow of water; floodgate 2. a gate giving access to a body of water

water gauge a device, as a glass tube, that shows the water level in a tank, boiler, etc.

water glass 1. a drinking glass; tumbler 2. *same as* WATER GAUGE 3. sodium silicate or, sometimes, potassium silicate, usually dissolved in water to form a syrupy liquid used as a preservative for eggs, etc.

water hole a dip or hole in the surface of the ground, in which water collects; pool

water ice water and sugar flavoured and frozen

wateriness *n.* the state or quality of being watery

watering can a container with a spout, often having a perforated nozzle, for watering plants

watering place 1. a place at a stream, lake, etc. where animals go to drink 2. a spa with mineral springs for drinking 3. a seaside resort

water jump a strip, ditch, or channel of water that a horse must jump, as in a steeplechase

water level 1. *a*) the surface of still

water *b)* the height of this   **2.** *same as* WATERLINE

WATERLILY

waterlily *n., pl.* **-lil′ies**   **1.** any of various water plants having large, flat, floating leaves and showy flowers   **2.** the flower of such a plant

waterline *n.* the line to which the surface of the water comes on the side of a boat

waterlogged *adj.*   **1.** soaked with water   **2.** soaked or filled with water so as to be sluggish in movement: said of boats

Waterloo (wôt ər lōō′) *n.* [< the town in C Belgium; scene of Napoleon's final defeat (1815)] any disastrous defeat

water main a main pipe in a system of water pipes

waterman *n.* a person who works on or with boats

watermark *n.*   **1.** a faint mark in paper, produced by pressure of a projecting design, as in the mould   **2.** the design —*vt.* to mark (paper) with a watermark

water-meadow *n.* a meadow which is kept fertile by periodic flooding by a stream

watermelon *n.*   **1.** a large, edible fruit with a hard, green rind and juicy, pink or red pulp having many seeds   **2.** the plant on which it grows

water nymph *Gr. & Rom. Myth.* a goddess having the form of a lovely young girl, supposed to dwell in a stream, pool, etc.

water pipe   **1.** a pipe for carrying water   **2.** a hookah

water pistol a toy gun that shoots water in a stream

water polo a water game played with a round, partly inflated ball by two teams of seven swimmers

water power the power of running or falling water, used to drive machinery, etc.

waterproof *adj.* that keeps out water completely —*n.*   **1.** waterproof material   **2.** a raincoat, etc. of waterproof material —*vt.* to make waterproof —**wa′terproof′-er** *n.*

water rat any of various rodents that live on the banks of streams and ponds, esp. the water vole

water rate a charge levied for the public supplying of water

water-repellent *adj.* that repels water but is not thoroughly waterproof

water seal a bend in a pipe which holds water and prevents the passage of odours or gas

watershed *n.*   **1.** a ridge dividing the areas drained by different river systems   **2.** popularly, the area drained by a river

system   **3.** a crucial period that serves as a dividing line

waterside *n.* land at the edge of a body of water —*adj.* of, at, or on the waterside

water-ski *vi.* **-skied′**, **-ski′ing** to be towed, as a sport, on skilike boards (**water skis**) by a line attached to a speedboat —**wa′terski′er** *n.*

water snake any of numerous saltwater or freshwater snakes

water softener   **1.** a chemical compound, added to hard water to make it soft   **2.** a tank, etc. in which water is filtered through chemicals to make it soft

waterspout *n.*   **1.** a tornado occurring over water, appearing as a rapidly rotating column of spray   **2.** a pipe or spout from which water runs

water table the level below which the ground is saturated with water

watertight *adj.*   **1.** so snugly put together that no water can get in or through   **2.** well thought out, with no weak points: said of an argument, plan, etc.

water tower an elevated tank used for water storage and for keeping equal pressure on a water system

water vapour water in the form of mist or tiny diffused particles, esp. when below the boiling point, as in the air

waterway *n.* any body of water wide enough and deep enough for boats, ships, etc.

water wheel   **1.** a wheel with paddles turned by running water, used to give power   **2.** a wheel with buckets on its rim, used for lifting water

water wings a device, inflated with air, used to keep one afloat while learning to swim

waterworks *n.pl.* [*often with sing. v.*]   **1.** a system of reservoirs, pumps, etc. used to bring a water supply to a city, etc.   **2.** a pumping station in such a system   **3.** [Slang] tears: usually in **turn on the waterworks,** to weep   **4.** [Colloq.] the urinary system

watery *adj.*   **1.** of or like water   **2.** containing or full of water   **3.** thin, diluted, weak, etc.   **4.** tearful   **5.** in or consisting of water [a *watery* grave]

watt (wot) *n.* [< James *Watt*] the SI unit of power

wattage *n.*   **1.** amount of electrical power, expressed in watts   **2.** the number of watts required to operate a given appliance

WATTLES

wattle (wot′′l) *n.* [OE. *watul*] **1.** a woven work of sticks intertwined with twigs or branches, used for walls, roofs, etc. **2.** in Australia, any of various acacias **3.** a fleshy, often brightly coloured piece of skin that hangs from the throat of a cock, etc. —*adj.* made of or roofed with wattle —*vt.* **-tled, -tling** to intertwine (sticks, twigs, etc.) so as to form an interwoven structure

wattle and daub a form of wall construction consisting of a framework of interwoven twigs plastered with a mixture of clay, etc.

waul (wôl) *vi., n.* wail, squall, or howl

wave (wāv) *vi.* **waved, wav′ing** [OE. *wafian*] **1.** to move up and down or back and forth in a curving motion **2.** to signal by moving a hand, etc. to and fro **3.** to have the form of a series of curves —*vt.* **1.** to cause to wave or sway to and fro **2.** *a)* to move or swing (something) as a signal *b)* to signal (something) by doing this *c)* to signal to (someone) by doing this [he *waved* us on] **3.** to arrange (hair, etc.) in a series of curves —*n.* **1.** *a)* a ridge or swell moving along the surface of a body of water, etc. *b)* something that suggests this **2.** a curve or series of curves, as in the hair **3.** a motion to and fro or up and down, as that made by the hand in signalling **4.** *a)* an upsurge or rise [a crime *wave*, a *wave* of emotion] *b)* a movement of people, etc., in groups [a *wave* of settlers] **5.** *Physics* a state of motion that periodically advances and retreats as it is transmitted progressively from one particle in a medium to the next in a given direction, as in the propagation of light —**wave down** to signal to the driver of a vehicle to stop —**wave′less** *adj.* —**wave′like** *adj.*

wave band *Radio & TV* a specific range of wave frequencies

wavelength *n.* *Physics* the distance from any given point in a wave to the next point characterized by the same phase **2.** the wavelength used by a particular broadcasting station —**on someone's** (or **the same**) **wavelength** [Colloq.] having similar thoughts, views, etc. as another

wavelet *n.* a little wave; ripple

waver (wā′vər) *vi.* [see WAVE] **1.** to show indecision **2.** to become unsteady **3.** to tremble: said of the voice, etc. **4.** to flicker: said of light **5.** to sway to and fro; flutter —**wa′veringly** *adv.*

wavy (wā′vē) *adj.* **wav′ier, wav′iest** **1.** having or forming waves **2.** moving in a wavelike motion **3.** wavering; fluctuating —**wav′ily** *adv.*

wax¹ (waks) *n.* [OE. *weax*] **1.** an easily moulded, dull yellow substance secreted by bees for building cells; beeswax **2.** any substance like this —*vt.* to rub, polish, cover, or treat with wax —*adj.* made of wax —**be wax in a person's hands** to be completely under the control of another person —**wax′like′** *adj.*

wax² *vi.* [OE. *weaxan*, grow] **1.** to increase in strength, intensity, etc. **2.** to become gradually full: said of the moon

wax³ *n.* [< ?] [Old Slang] a fit of temper

waxen *adj.* **1.** made of, or covered with, wax **2.** like wax, as in being pale, soft, easily moulded, etc.

wax light a candle or wax taper

wax paper a kind of paper made moisture-proof by a wax, or paraffin, coating: also **waxed paper**

waxwing *n.* a bird with scarlet spines, suggesting sealing wax, at the ends of the secondary quill feathers

waxwork *n.* **1.** work, as objects, figures, etc., made of wax **2.** a human figure made of wax

waxworks *n.pl.* [with *sing. v.*] an exhibition of wax figures made to look like famous people

waxy *adj.* **wax′ier, wax′iest** **1.** full of, covered with, or made of wax **2.** like wax in nature or appearance —**wax′iness** *n.*

way (wā) *n.* [OE. *weg*] **1.** a method of doing something **2.** a customary manner of living, etc. [to change one's *ways*] **3.** *a)* manner; style [a pleasant *way*] *b)* power of pleasing **4.** a course from one place to another **5.** a specified route **6.** room for passing; an opening, as in a crowd **7.** distance [a long *way* off] **8.** direction of movement, etc. [look this *way*] **9.** course or habits of life [evil *ways*] **10.** respect; point; particular **11.** a road, street path, etc. **12.** wish [to get one's *way*] **13.** range, as of experience [that never came my *way*] **14.** relationship as to those taking part [a four-*way* agreement] **15.** [Colloq.] a (specified) state or condition [he is in a bad *way*] **16.** [Colloq.] a locality [out our *way*] —*adv.* [Colloq.] far [*way* behind] —**by the way** incidentally —**by way of 1.** as a way, method, or means of **2.** passing through —**give way 1.** to yield **2.** to break down —**give way to** to yield to —**go out of the** (or **one's**) **way** to make a special effort —**in the way** in such a position as to obstruct, hinder, etc. —**lead the way** to be a guide —**look the other way** to feign ignorance of something which one ought to deal with —**on the way 1.** progressing; approaching **2.** (of baby) expected —**on the way out** becoming unfashionable —**out of the way 1.** in a position so as not to hinder, etc. **2.** disposed of **3.** not on the usual route **4.** *a)* improper *b)* unusual —**the way** according to the way that [with things *the way* they are] —**under way** moving; advancing

waybill *n.* a paper giving a list of goods and instructions, sent with the goods being transported

wayfarer *n.* a person who travels, esp. from place to place on foot —**way′far′ing** *adj., n.*

waylay (wā′lā′) *vt.* **-laid′, -lay′ing 1.**

to lie in wait for and attack **2.** to wait for and accost (a person) on the way —**way'lay'er** n.

wayleave n. a right of way granted by a land-owner for a specific purpose in return for a payment

way-out (wā'out') adj. [Colloq.] very unusual, unconventional, etc.

-ways (wāz) [< WAY] a suffix meaning in a (specified) direction, position, or manner [endways]

ways and means **1.** methods and resources at the disposal of a person, company, etc. **2.** methods of raising money, as for government

wayside n. the area close to the side of a road —adj. on, near, or along the side of a road —**go by the wayside** to be discarded

wayward adj. [see AWAY & -WARD] **1.** insistent upon having one's own way **2.** unpredictable; erratic —**way'wardly** adv.

Wb Physics the symbol for weber

W.B., W/B waybill

w.c. **1.** water closet: also **W.C.** **2.** without charge

W/Cdr. Wing Commander

we (wē) pron. for sing. see I [OE.] the persons speaking or writing: sometimes used by a person in referring to a group of which he is one, or by a monarch, editor, etc. in referring to himself

W.E.A. Workers' Educational Association

weak (wēk) adj. [ON. veikr] **1.** a) not physically strong b) lacking vitality **2.** easily broken, bent, etc. **3.** lacking in moral strength or willpower **4.** lacking in mental power **5.** lacking in skill or strength for combat or competition **6.** having few resources, little wealth, etc. **7.** lacking in force, or credibility [a weak argument] **8.** a) not functioning normally or well: said of a body organ or part b) easily upset; queasy [a weak stomach] **9.** lacking in volume, intensity, etc. **10.** lacking the usual strength [weak tea] **11.** poor or deficient in something specified **12.** ineffective [a weak argument] **13.** Gram. inflected by adding a suffix such as -ed, -d rather than by an internal vowel change: said of regular verbs —**weak'-ish** adj.

weaken vt., vi. to make or become weak or weaker

weak-kneed (wēk'nēd') adj. lacking courage, determination, etc.

weakling n. **1.** a person or animal low in physical strength **2.** a person of weak character

weakly adj. -lier, -liest sickly; feeble; weak —adv. in a weak way —**weak'liness** n.

weak-minded adj. **1.** not firm of mind; indecisive **2.** mentally retarded —**weak'-mind'edness** n.

weakness n. **1.** a being weak **2.** a weak point **3.** a liking (for something)

weal[1] (wēl) n. [see WALE] a mark, line, or ridge raised on the skin, as by a blow

weal[2] n. [OE. wela] [Archaic] well-being

weald (wēld) n. [OE.] [Poet.] **1.** a forest **2.** open country —**The Weald** region in SE England, in Surrey, Kent, and Sussex

wealth (welth) n. [see WEAL[2]] **1.** a) much money or property; riches b) the state of being rich **2.** a large amount; abundance **3.** valuable products, contents, or derivatives **4.** Econ. everything having value in money or a price

wealth tax a tax on personal property

wealthy adj. wealth'ier, wealth'iest **1.** having wealth; rich **2.** of or suggestive of wealth **3.** abounding (in something) —**wealth'iness** n.

wean (wēn) vt. [OE. wenian] **1.** to accustom (a child or young animal) to food other than its mother's milk **2.** to withdraw (a person) by degrees (from a habit, etc.) as by substituting something else

weapon (wep'ən) n. [OE. wæpen] **1.** any device used for fighting, esp. in warfare **2.** any part (of an animal or plant) used for attacking or defending **3.** any means of attack or defence

weaponry n. weapons collectively

wear (wāar) vt. wore, worn, wear'ing [OE. werian] **1.** to have or carry (clothing, jewellery, etc.) on the body **2.** to have or show in one's expression or appearance; display **3.** to damage, diminish, etc., as by constant use or friction (often with away) **4.** to bring by use to a specified state **5.** to make by the friction of rubbing, flowing, etc. **6.** to tire or exhaust **7.** [Colloq.] to accept; tolerate —vi. **1.** to become damaged, diminished, etc., as by constant use or friction **2.** to hold up in spite of use; last **3.** to grow gradually [courage wearing thin] **4.** to pass away gradually: said of time **5.** to have an irritating effect (on) —n. **1.** a wearing or being worn **2.** things, esp. clothes, worn [men's wear, sportswear] **3.** damage, loss, etc., as from use or friction **4.** the ability to last in spite of use —**wear down** **1.** to lose or cause to lose thickness or height by use, friction, etc. **2.** to overcome by constant effort —**wear off** to diminish by degrees —**wear out** **1.** to make or become useless from continued use **2.** to exhaust —**wear the trousers** [Colloq.] to be master of the house —**wear thin** to be almost exhausted: said of one's patience —**wear'er** n.

wear and tear loss and damage resulting from use

wearing adj. causing fatigue; tiring

wearisome (wēar'ē səm) adj. causing weariness; tiring —**wea'risomely** adv.

weary (wēar'ē) adj. -rier, -riest [OE. werig] **1.** tired; worn out **2.** no longer liking, patient, etc.; bored (with of) **3.** tiring **4.** tedious —vt., vi. -ried, -rying to make or become weary —**wea'rily** adv. —**wea'riness** n.

WEASEL (15-35 cm long, including tail)

weasel (wē′z'l) *n.* [OE. *wesle*] an agile, flesh-eating mammal with a long, slender body, short legs, and a long, bushy tail: it feeds on rats, birds, eggs, etc. —**weaselly** *adj.*

weather (weth′ər) *n.* [OE. *weder*] 1. the general condition (as to temperature, moisture, cloudiness, etc.) of the atmosphere at a particular time and place 2. storm, rain, etc. [protected against the *weather*] —*vt.* 1. to expose to the weather, as for drying 2. to wear away by exposure to the atmosphere 3. to get through safely [to *weather* a storm] 4. *Naut.* to pass to the windward of (a cape, etc.) —*vi.* to become worn, discoloured, etc. by exposure to the weather —*adj.* of the side of a ship, etc. towards the wind; windward —**under the weather** [Colloq.] not feeling well

weather-beaten (weth′ər bēt′'n) *adj.* showing the effect of weather

weatherboard *n.* 1. a sloping plank, as at the bottom of a door, to deflect rain 2. [*pl.*] feather-edged, overlapping boards fixed horizontally

weather-bound *adj.* delayed or halted by bad weather, as a ship, aircraft, etc.

weathercock *n.* 1. a weather vane in the form of a cock 2. a changeable person or thing

weather eye 1. an eye alert to signs of changing weather 2. a close watch for any change —**keep a weather eye open** to be on the alert

weather forecast prediction of future weather for a particular period based on scientific data collected by a meteorological office

weather-house *n.* an ornament with the figures of a man and a woman attached to a piece of catgut affected by moisture, so that one emerges in wet weather and the other in dry

weathering *n.* *Geol.* the effects of the forces of weather on rock surfaces, as in forming soil, sand, etc.

weatherman *n.* a person who forecasts the weather

weather office [Canad.] the Atmospheric Environment Service of the Federal Department of Environment, Canada, which prepares weather forecasts; also, esp. U.S., **weather bureau**

weatherproof *adj.* that can be exposed to wind, rain, etc. without being damaged

weatherstrip *n.* a thin strip of metal, felt, etc. used to cover the joint between a door or window and its casing, so as to keep out draughts, rain, etc.

weather vane a shaped piece of metal, etc., set up high to swing in the wind and show which way it is blowing

weather-wise *adj.* skilled in predicting the weather

weatherworn *adj.* *same as* WEATHER-BEATEN

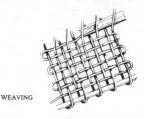

WEAVING

weave (wēv) *vt.* **wove** or for *vt.* 6 & *vi.* 3, **weaved, wo′ven** or for *vt.* 6 & *vi.* 3, **weaved, weav′ing** [OE. *wefan*] 1. a) to make (a fabric), esp. on a loom, by interlacing threads or yarns b) to form (threads) into a fabric 2. to form (incidents, etc.) into a story, poem, etc. 3. to make by interlacing twigs, straw, etc. [to *weave* baskets] 4. to twist (something) into, through, or among [to *weave* flowers into one's hair] 5. to spin (a web): said of spiders, etc. 6. a) to cause (a vehicle, etc.) to move from side to side or in and out b) to make (one's way) by moving thus —*vi.* 1. to do weaving 2. to become interlaced 3. to move from side to side or in and out —*n.* a method or pattern of weaving —**get weaving** [Colloq.] to hurry —**weav′er** *n.*

weaverbird *n.* a tropical, finchlike bird that weaves an elaborate domed nest of sticks, grass, etc.

web (web) *n.* [OE. *webb*] 1. the network spun by a spider or by the larvae of certain insects 2. any woven fabric; esp., a length of cloth being woven on a loom or just taken off 3. a tissue or membrane, esp. that joining the digits of various water birds or water animals 4. *Printing* a large roll of paper for continuously feeding a type of rotary press (**web press**) 5. a carefully woven trap 6. anything contrived in an intricate way [a *web* of lies] —**webbed** *adj.* —**web′like** *adj.*

webbing *n.* a strong, tough fabric, as of jute, woven in strips and used for belts, in upholstery, etc.

weber (vā′bər) *n.* [< Wilhelm *Weber*] the SI unit of magnetic flux

webfoot (web′foot′) *n., pl.* -**feet′** a foot with the toes webbed —**web′-foot′ed** *adj.*

wed (wed) *vt.* **wed′ded, wed′ded** or **wed, wed′ding** [OE. *weddian*] 1. to marry; specif., a) to take as husband or wife b) to join in marriage 2. to join closely —*vi.* to get married

we'd (wēd) 1. we had 2. we should 3. we would

Wed. Wednesday

wedded (wed′id) *adj.* 1. married 2. devoted [*wedded* to one's work]

wedding *n.* [OE. *weddung*] 1. the act

or ceremony of getting married, or the festivities that go with it **2.** a marriage anniversary

wedding breakfast the meal at the reception following a marriage ceremony

wedding cake a rich iced fruit cake, usually with several tiers, served at a wedding reception

wedding ring a ring worn to indicate that one is married

wedge (wej) *n.* [OE. *wecg*] **1.** a piece of wood, metal, etc. tapering to a thin edge that can be driven into a narrow opening, as to split wood **2.** anything with a wedgelike shape or part **3.** any action or procedure used to open the way for a change —*vt.* **wedged, wedg′ing 1.** to fix in place by driving a wedge under, beside, etc. **2.** to pack (*in*) or crowd together **3.** to split as with a wedge —**the thin end of the wedge** anything unimportant in itself that implies the start of something much larger —**wedge′-like′** *adj.* —**wedg′y** *adj.*

Wedgwood (ware) (wej′wood′) [< J. *Wedgwood*] *Trademark* a fine pottery with neoclassical relief figures

wedlock (wed′lok′) *n.* [< OE. *wed*, a pledge + *-lac*, an offering] the state of being married

Wednesday (wenz′dē) *n.* [OE. *Wodnes dæg*, Woden's day] the fourth day of the week

Wednesdays *adv.* [Colloq.] on or during every Wednesday

wee (wē) *adj.* **we′er, we′est** [ME. *we*] **1.** very small; tiny **2.** very early [the *wee* hours]

weed (wēd) *n.* [OE. *weod*] **1.** any undesired, uncultivated plant, esp. one growing in profusion and crowding out a desired crop **2.** [Colloq.] *a*) tobacco: with *the b*) a cigar or cigarette *c*) a marijuana cigarette **3.** a horse unfit for racing or breeding **4.** [Slang] a thin, scrawny person —*vt.* **1.** to remove weeds from (a garden, etc.) **2.** to remove as useless, harmful, etc.: often with *out* —*vi.* to remove weeds, etc. —**weed′er** *n.*

weedkiller *n.* a substance, usually a chemical or hormone, used for destroying weeds

weeds *n.pl.* [< OE. *wæde*, garment] black mourning clothes, esp. those worn by a widow

weedy *adj.* **weed′ier, weed′iest 1.** full of weeds **2.** of or like a weed **3.** [Colloq.] weak; lanky —**weed′iness** *n.*

week (wēk) *n.* [OE. *wicu*] **1.** a period of seven days, esp. one beginning with Sunday and ending with Saturday **2.** the hours or days of work in a seven-day period —*adv.* seven days from a specified day [Monday *week*] —**week by week** each week —**week in, week out** every week

weekday *n.* **1.** any day of the week except Sunday **2.** any day not in the weekend —*adj.* of or on a weekday

weekdays *adv.* [Colloq.] on or during every weekday or most weekdays

weekend (wēk′end′) *n.* the period from Friday night or Saturday to Monday morning —*adj.* of or on a weekend

weekends (wēk′endz′) *adv.* [Colloq.] on or during every weekend or most weekends

weekly *adj.* **1.** done, happening, appearing, etc. once a week or every week **2.** continuing or lasting for a week —*adv.* once a week; every week —*n., pl.* **-lies** a periodical published once a week

weeny (wē′nē) *adj.* **-nier, -niest** [WEE + (TI)NY] [Colloq.] small; tiny

weep (wēp) *vi.* **wept, weep′ing** [OE. *wepan*] **1.** to show or express strong emotion, usually grief or sorrow, by shedding tears **2.** to lament or mourn (with *for*) **3.** to drip or form liquid drops **4.** to exude liquid —*vt.* **1.** to weep for **2.** to shed (tears, etc.) —*n.* a fit of weeping —**weep′er** *n.*

weeping *n.* the act of one who or that which weeps —*adj.* **1.** that weeps tears or other liquid **2.** having graceful, drooping branches [*weeping* willow] —**weep′ingly** *adv.*

weepy *adj.* **weep′ier, weep′iest** inclined to weep; tearful —**weep′iness** *n.*

weevil (wē′v'l) *n.* [OE. *wifel*] any of numerous beetles, esp. those with projecting beaks, that feed, esp. as larvae, on grain —**wee′vily, wee′villy** *adj.*

weft (weft) *n.* [OE. *wefan*, to weave] **1.** in weaving, the horizontal threads crossing the warp **2.** something woven

weigh[1] (wā) *vt.* [OE. *wegan*, carry] **1.** to determine the weight of **2.** to have a (specified) weight [it *weighs* ten kilograms] **3.** to lift or balance (an object) in the hand(s) in order to estimate its heaviness **4.** to measure out as by weight (often with *out*) **5.** to consider and choose carefully [to *weigh* one's words] **6.** *Naut.* to hoist (an anchor) —*vi.* **1.** to have significance, importance, or influence **2.** to be a burden (with *on* or *upon*) **3.** *Naut.* to hoist anchor —**weigh down** to burden or bear down on —**weigh in** to weigh (a boxer, jockey, etc.) before or after a contest so as to verify his declared weight —**weigh in with** to contribute an argument (to a discussion, etc.) —**weigh up** to form a judgment of —**weigh′er** *n.*

weigh[2] *n.* var. of WAY, in **under welgh**, progressing; advancing: cf. UNDERWAY

weighbridge *n.* a machine onto which a vehicle can be driven to be weighed with its contents

weight (wāt) *n.* [OE. *wiht*] **1.** a quantity weighing a specified amount **2.** heaviness as a quality; specif., the force of gravity acting on a body **3.** how much a thing weighs or should weigh **4.** *a*) any unit of heaviness *b*) any system of such units [*troy weight*] *c*) a piece of metal, etc. of a specific standard heaviness, used in weighing **5.** any block or mass used for its heaviness [*paperweight*] **6.** *a*) any heavy thing or load *b*) a burden of responsibility, sorrow, etc. **7.** importance or consequence **8.** influence, power, or authority **9.** the relative thickness or heaviness of a fabric —*vt.* **1.** to add weight to **2.** to load down; burden **3.** to manipulate so as to favour a particular side **—by weight** as determined by weighing **—carry weight** to be important, influential, etc. **—pull one's weight** to do one's share **—throw one's weight around** to act in an overauthoritarian, aggressive manner

weighting *n.* extra money given in particular cases, as with a job located in an area of high living costs

weightless *adj.* having little or no apparent weight; specif., free of the pull of gravity **—weight'lessness** *n.*

weight lifting the athletic exercise or competitive sport of lifting barbells **—weight lifter**

weighty *adj.* **weight'ier, weight'iest** 1. very heavy **2.** burdensome; oppressive **3.** significant; important **—weight'ily** *adv.* **—weight'iness** *n.*

weir (wêər) *n.* [OE. *wer*] **1.** a low dam built in a river to back up or divert water, as for a mill **2.** a fence built in a stream or channel to catch fish

weird (wêərd) *adj.* [< OE. *wyrd*, fate] **1.** of or suggestive of ghosts or other supernatural things **2.** [Colloq.] strikingly odd, strange, etc. **—weird'ly** *adv.* **—weird'-ness** *n.*

welch (welsh) *vt., vi.* [Slang] *var. of* WELSH

welcome (wel'kəm) *adj.* [< OE. *wilcuma*, a welcome guest] **1.** gladly received *[a welcome guest]* **2.** agreeable or gratifying **3.** willingly permitted or invited *[welcome to use the library]* **4.** under no obligation *[you're welcome]* **—n.** an act or expression of welcoming **—interj.** you are welcome **—vt. -comed, -coming 1.** to greet with pleasure and hospitality **2.** to receive with pleasure **—bid welcome** to receive with cordial greetings **—wear out** (or **outstay**) **one's welcome** to come too often or stay too long **—wel'comer** *n.*

weld (weld) *vt.* [< obs. *well*] **1.** to unite (pieces of metal, etc.) by heating until fused or until soft enough to hammer together **2.** to unite closely **—n.** the joint formed by welding **—weld'able** *adj.* **—weld'er** *n.*

welfare (wel'fâər') *n.* [see WELL² & FARE] **1.** a condition of health, happiness, and comfort **2.** financial or other assistance, esp. that given by the state for the poor, unemployed, etc. **—on welfare** [Chiefly U.S.] receiving government aid because of poverty, unemployment, etc.

welfare state a nation in which the government assumes responsibility for the welfare of the citizens, with regard to employment, medical care, etc.

welkin (wel'kin) *n.* [OE. *wolcen*] [Archaic or Poet.] the sky, or the upper air

well¹ (wel) *n.* [OE. *wella*] **1.** a hole sunk into the earth to obtain water, gas, oil, etc. **2.** a natural spring and pool **3.** an abundant source **4.** *a)* an open shaft in a building for a staircase *b)* a shaft to let light and air into a building or between buildings *c)* a lift shaft **5.** any cavity, space or container for liquid, as

an inkwell **6.** the space in a lawcourt where solicitors sit **—vi., vt.** to pour forth as from a well; gush (*up, forth, down, out,* etc.)

well² *adv.* **bet'ter, best** [OE. *wel*] **1.** in a desirable way; satisfactorily **2.** *a)* in a proper way *b)* in a kind or favourable way **3.** skilfully **4.** fittingly **5.** in comfort and plenty **6.** with good reason **7.** thoroughly **8.** with certainty; definitely *[you know very well why]* **9.** intimately; closely *Well* is used in hyphenated compounds, to mean *properly, thoroughly,* etc. *[well-defined]* **—adj. 1.** in good health, condition, etc. **2.** proper, right, etc. **—interj.** an exclamation used to express surprise, agreement, etc. **—as well 1.** in addition **2.** with equal effect **—as well as** in addition to **—leave** (or **let**) **well alone** refrain from interfering in a situation which appears satisfactory **—well away** [Slang] drunk **—well up in** [Colloq.] knowing thoroughly **—wish someone well** to wish someone success

we'll (wēl) **1.** we shall **2.** we will

well-appointed (wel'ə poin'tid) *adj.* excellently furnished or equipped

well-balanced *adj.* **1.** carefully balanced, adjusted, etc. **2.** sane; sensible

well-behaved *adj.* behaving well; polite

well-being (wel'bē'iŋ) *n.* the state of being well, happy, or prosperous; welfare

wellborn (wel'bôrn') *adj.* born into a family of high social position

well-bred (wel'bred') *adj.* **1.** showing good breeding **2.** of good stock: said of animals

well-connected *adj.* having influential or well-born relatives

well-disposed (wel'dis pōzd') *adj.* inclined to be friendly or favourable (*towards* a person) or receptive (*to* an idea, etc.)

well-done *adj.* **1.** performed with skill and efficiency **2.** thoroughly cooked: said esp. of meat **—interj.** an exclamation of approval

well-fed *adj.* **1.** having a nutritious diet; well nourished **2.** plump or fat

well-groomed *adj.* clean and neat; carefully washed, combed, dressed, etc.

well-grounded (wel'groun'did) *adj.* **1.** having a thorough basic knowledge of a subject **2.** based on good reasons

wellhead *n.* **1.** the source of a spring of water; spring **2.** any source; fountain-head

well-heeled (wel'hēld') *adj.* [Slang] rich; prosperous

wellie (wel'ē) *n.* [Colloq.] a wellington boot

well-informed (wel'in fôrmd') *adj.* **1.** having thorough knowledge of a subject **2.** having considerable knowledge of many subjects

Wellington (boot) (wel'iŋ tən) [< 1st Duke of *Wellington*] [*also* **w-b-**] a knee-length boot usually made from rubber

well-intentioned (wel'in ten'shənd) *adj.* having or showing good or kindly intentions, but often with bad results

well-known *adj.* 1. widely or generally known; famous 2. thoroughly known

well-made *adj.* 1. skilfully and strongly built 2. shapely

well-meaning (wel′mē′niŋ) *adj.* having good or kindly intentions but often with bad results: also **well′-meant′**

well-nigh (wel′nī′) *adv.* very nearly; almost

well-off (wel′of′) *adj.* 1. in a favourable or fortunate condition 2. prosperous; well-to-do

well-preserved *adj.* in good condition or of good appearance, in spite of age

well-read *adj.* 1. having read much (*in* a subject) 2. having a wide knowledge of books

well-rounded (wel′roun′did) *adj.* 1. well planned for proper balance 2. showing interest, ability, etc. in many fields 3. shapely

well set up [Colloq.] well built; sturdy

well spent achieving satisfactory results; not wasted

well-spoken *adj.* 1. speaking fluently, graciously, etc. 2. properly or aptly spoken

wellspring *n.* 1. a spring or fountainhead 2. a source of abundant supply

well-thought-of *adj.* having a good reputation; of good repute

well-timed *adj.* timely; opportune

well-to-do *adj.* prosperous; well-off; wealthy

well-tried (wel′trīd′) *adj.* proved to be satisfactory by long experience

well-wisher *n.* a person who wishes well to another or to a cause, etc. —**well′-wish′ing** *adj., n.*

well-worn *adj.* 1. much worn; much used 2. overused; trite

Welsh (welsh) *adj.* of Wales, its people, their language, etc. —*n.* the language spoken in Wales —**the Welsh** the people of Wales —**Welsh′man** *n.*

welsh (welsh) *vt., vi.* [< ?] [Slang] 1. to cheat by failing to pay a bet or other debt 2. to evade (an obligation) Often with *on* —**welsh′er** *n.*

Welsh rabbit a dish of melted cheese served on toast

welt (welt) *n.* [ME. *welte*] 1. a strip of material at an edge or seam of a garment, etc. 2. a ridge raised on the skin by the blow of a whip etc. 3. a strip of leather in the seam between the sole and upper of a shoe —*vt.* 1. to furnish with a welt 2. to beat severely; thrash

welter *vi.* [MDu. *welteren*] 1. to roll about or wallow, as a pig in mud 2. to be soaked, stained, etc. [to welter in blood] —*n.* 1. a turmoil 2. a confused mass; jumble

welterweight (wel′tər wāt′) *n.* [< ?] *see* TABLE OF BOXING AND WRESTLING WEIGHTS

wen (wen) *n.* [OE. *wenn*] a harmless skin tumour

wench (wench) *n.* [OE. *wencel*, child] 1. a girl or young woman : now a somewhat derogatory or jocular term 2. [Archaic]

a) a country girl *b)* a female servant *c)* a loose woman

wend (wend) *vt.* [OE. *wendan*, to turn] to proceed on (one's way)

wendigo (wen′di gou′) *n.* [< AmInd.] [Canad.] *same as* SPLAKE

Wensleydale (wenz′lē dāl) *n.* [< *Wensleydale* in N Yorkshire] a type of blue-veined or white cheese

went (went) [old pt. of WEND] *pt. of* GO

wept (wept) *pt. & pp. of* WEEP

were (wur; *unstressed* wər) [OE. *wǣron*] *pl. & 2nd pers. sing., past indic., and subj., of* BE

we're (wēr) we are

weren't (wurnt) were not

werewolf (wēər′woolf′) *n., pl.* **-wolves′** [< OE. *wer*, man + *wulf*, wolf] *Folklore* a person changed into a wolf: also sp. **wer′wolf′**

wert (wurt; *unstressed* wərt) *archaic 2nd pers. sing., past indic. & subj., of* BE: *used with* thou

Wesleyan (wez′lē ən) *adj.* of John Wesley or the Methodist Church —*n.* a follower of John Wesley; Methodist —**Wes′leyanism** *n.*

west (west) *n.* [OE.] 1. the direction in which sunset occurs (270° on the compass, opposite east) 2. a region in this direction 3. [W-] the Western Hemisphere, or the Western Hemisphere and Europe —*adj.* 1. in, of, to, or towards the west 2. from the west —*adv.* in or towards the west —**go west** [Colloq.] 1. to be lost, ruined, etc. 2. to die

westbound *adj.* going westwards

West Country the southwest of England, esp. Cornwall, Devon, and Somerset

West End the part of London containing the main shopping and entertainment areas

westerly *adj., adv.* towards or from the west

western *adj.* 1. in, of, or towards the west 2. from the west 3. [W-] of the West —*n.* a story, film, etc. about cowboys in the western U.S. —**west′ernmost′** *adj.*

westerner *n.* a native or inhabitant of the west

Western Hemisphere that half of the earth that includes North & South America

westernize *vt.* **-ized′, -iz′ing** to make western in character, etc. —**west′erniza′-tion** *n.*

Westminster (west′min′star) [< *Westminster* in London] the British parliament

west-northwest *n.* the direction halfway between due west and northwest

west-southwest *n.* the direction halfway between due west and southwest

westward *adv., adj.* towards the west: also **west′wards** *adv.* —*n.* a westward direction or region —**west′wardly** *adv.*

wet (wet) *adj.* **wet′ter, wet′test** [OE. *wǣt*] 1. covered or soaked with water or other liquid 2. rainy; misty 3. not yet dry 4. [Colloq.] feeble, ineffectual —*n.* 1. water; moisture 2. rain or rainy weather 3. [Colloq.] a feeble, ineffectual person —*vt., vi.* **wet** or **wet′ted, wet′ting** 1.

to make or become wet (often with *through* or *down*) **2.** to urinate (in, on, something) —**wet behind the ears** [Colloq.] young and inexperienced —**wet′ly** *adv.* —**wet′- ness** *n.* —**wet′ter** *n.* —**wet′tish** *adj.*

wet blanket a person or thing that dampens or lessens the enthusiasm or gaiety of others

wet dream an involuntary emission of semen by men during sleep, usually accompanying a sexual dream

wether (weth′ər) *n.* [OE.] a castrated male sheep

wet nurse a woman hired to suckle another woman's child —**wet-nurse** *vt.*

wet suit a closefitting, usually one-piece suit of rubber, worn by skin divers for warmth

we've (wēv) we have

Wg. Cdr. Wing Commander

WGmc. West Germanic

whack (wak) *vt., vi.* [echoic] [Colloq.] to strike with a sharp, resounding blow —*n.* **1.** [Colloq.] a sharp, resounding blow, or its sound **2.** [Colloq.] a share —**have** (or **take**) **a whack at** [Colloq.] to make an attempt at —**out of whack** [Colloq.] not in proper condition

whacked *adj.* [Colloq.] tired out; exhausted

whacking *adj.* [Colloq.] big; great

whale (wāl) *n.* [OE. *hwæl*] a large fishlike mammal that lives in the sea and has a flat, horizontal tail and front limbs modified into flippers —*vi.* **whaled, whal′- ing** to hunt whales —**a whale of a** [Colloq.] an exceptionally large, fine, etc. example of (a class of persons or things)

whaleboat *n.* a long rowing boat, pointed at both ends: used formerly by whalers

whalebone *n.* **1.** horny, elastic material hanging from the upper jaw of whalebone whales and straining the tiny sea animals they feed on **2.** something made of this, as a corset stay

whaler *n.* **1.** a ship used in whaling **2.** a man whose work is whaling: also **whale′man**

whaling *n.* the work or trade of hunting and killing whales for their blubber, whalebone, etc.

wham (wam) *interj.* a sound imitating a heavy blow or explosion —*vt., vi.* **whammed, wham′ming** to strike loudly

wharf (wôrf) *n., pl.* **wharves** (wôrvz), **wharfs** [OE. *hwerf*, a dam] a platform built along or out from the shore, where ships can dock and load or unload —*vt.* **1.** to bring to a wharf **2.** to unload on a wharf

wharfage *n.* **1.** the use of a wharf **2.** a fee charged for this

wharfinger (wôr′fin jər) *n.* one who owns or manages a wharf

what (wot; *unstressed* wət) *pron.* [< OE. *hwa, who*] **1.** which thing, event, etc. [*what* is that object? you told him *what*?] **2.** that which or those which [to know *what* one wants] —*adj.* **1.** which or which kind of [*what* man told you that? I know *what* books you like] **2.** as much, or

as many, as [take *what* time (or men) you need] **3.** how great, surprising, etc. [*what* joy!] —*adv.* **1.** in what respect? to what degree? how? [*what* does it matter?] **2.** in some manner or degree; partly (usually with *with*) [*what* with singing and joking, the time passed quickly] **3.** how greatly, surprisingly, etc. [*what* sad news!] —*interj.* an exclamation of surprise, anger, etc. [*what*! no dinner?] —**what about** what do you think, know, etc. concerning? —**what for** why? —**what have you** [Colloq.] anything similar [games, toys, or *what have you*] —**what's what** [Colloq.] the true state of affairs —**what's yours?** [Colloq.] what would you like to drink? —**what the (heck, devil,** etc.) **1.** an exclamation of surprise **2.** what: used emphatically —**what though** no matter if

whatever *pron.* **1.** *a)* which thing, event, etc. [*whatever* can it be?] *b)* anything that [tell her *whatever* you like] *c)* no matter what [*whatever* you do, don't rush] **2.** [Colloq.] anything of the sort —*adj.* **1.** of no matter what type, degree, etc. [make *whatever* repairs are needed] **2.** being who it may be [*whatever* man told you that, it isn't true] **3.** of any kind Also [Poet.] **whate′er′**

whatnot *n.* a set of open shelves, as for bric-a-brac —**or** (or **and**) **whatnot** or (or and) any other such things

whatsoever *pron., adj.* whatever: also [Poet.] **what′soe′er′**

WHEAT

wheat (wēt) *n.* [OE. *hwæte*] **1.** a cereal grass with dense spikes that bear grain **2.** such grain, used for flour, cereals, pasta, etc.

wheatear (wēt′ēər′) *n.* [< WHITE + ARSE] a small, upland, migratory bird of the thrush family, with a white rump

wheaten *adj.* made of wheat or wheat flour

wheat germ **1.** the wheat-kernel embryo, rich in vitamins, milled out as an oily flake **2.** the milled flakes

wheatmeal *n.* wholemeal flour made from wheat

wheedle (wē′d'l) *vt., vi.* **-dled, -dling** [< ?] **1.** to influence or persuade (a person) by flattery, coaxing, etc. **2.** to get (something) by coaxing or flattery —**whee′dler** *n.*

wheel (wēl) *n.* [OE. *hweol*] **1.** a solid disc, or a circular frame connected by spokes to a central hub, capable of turning on a central axis **2.** anything like a wheel in shape, movement, etc. **3.** a steering wheel of a car **4.** a medieval torture instrument that was a circular frame on which a victim was painfully stretched **5.** [*usually pl.*] propelling or controlling forces [the *wheels* of progress] **6.** a turning movement **7.** [*pl.*] [Colloq.] a car —*vt.*, *vi.* **1.** to rotate, revolve, pivot, etc. **2.** to turn so as to reverse direction, attitude, etc. (often with *about* or *round*) **3.** to move on wheels or in a wheeled vehicle —**at the wheel 1.** steering a ship, motor vehicle, etc. **2.** in charge —**wheel of fortune** the changes, good and bad, that occur in life —**wheels within wheels** a series of intricately connected events, plots, etc. devolving on one another —**wheeled** *adj.*

wheelbarrow *n.* a shallow, open box for moving small loads, having a single wheel in front and two shafts with handles for pushing or pulling it

wheelbase *n.* in a motor vehicle, the distance in inches from the centre of the hub of a front wheel to the centre of the hub of the corresponding back wheel

wheelchair *n.* a chair mounted on large wheels, used in moving about by persons unable to walk

wheeler *n.* **1.** a horse, etc. nearest the wheel **2.** something with a specified number of wheels [*two-wheeler*]

wheelhouse *n.* an enclosed place on the upper deck of a ship, for the helmsman

wheelrace *n.* the area of a millrace where the water wheel is fixed

wheel-spin *n.* the revolution of wheels without full grip of the road

wheelwright *n.* a person who makes and repairs wagon and carriage wheels

wheeze (wēz) *vi.* wheezed, wheez'ing [ON. *hvæsa*, to hiss] to breathe with a whistling, breathy sound, as in asthma —*n.* **1.** the sound of wheezing **2.** [Slang] a clever idea or plan —**wheez'er** *n.* —**wheez'ingly** *adv.* —**wheez'y** *adj.*

WHELK
(7.5 cm long)

whelk (welk) *n.* [OE. *wioluc*] any of various large sea snails with spiral shells, esp. those species used for food

whelm (welm) *vt.* [ME. *whelmen*] to submerge or engulf

whelp (welp) *n.* [OE. *hwelp*] **1.** a puppy **2.** a young lion, wolf, etc. **3.** [Derog.] a youth or child —*vt.*, *vi.* to give birth to whelps

when (wen; *unstressed* wən) *adv.* [OE. *hwænne*] **1.** at what time? **2.** on what occasion or under what circumstances? **3.** at what point? —*conj.* **1.** at the time or point that [he told us *when* we sat down] **2.** at which [it is a time *when*

action must be taken] **3.** as soon as **4.** at whatever time that [he rested *when* he could] **5.** although [to object *when* there's no reason to do so] —*pron.* what time or which time [until *when* will you stay?] —**say when** [Colloq.] to indicate at what point to stop: used of pouring a drink

whence (wens) *adv.* [OE. *hwanan*] from what place, source, cause, etc. [*whence* did he come?] —*conj.* to the place from which [return *whence* you came]

whencesoever (wens'sō ev'ər) *adv., conj.* [Archaic] from whatever place, source, or cause

whenever (wen ev'ər) *adv.* [Colloq.] when [*whenever* will he learn?] —*conj.* at whatever time [visit us *whenever* you can] Also [Poet.] **when'e'er'**

whensoever (wen'sō ev'ər) *adv., conj.* whenever: also [Poet.] **when'soe'er'**

where (wāar) *adv.* [OE. *hwær*] **1.** in or at what place? [*where* is the car?] **2.** to or towards what place? [*where* did he go?] **3.** in what situation? [*where* will we be if we lose?] **4.** in what respect? [*where* is she to blame?] **5.** from what place or source? [*where* did you find out?] —*conj.* **1.** in or at what place [he knows *where* it is] **2.** in or at which place **3.** in or at the place in which [he is *where* he should be] **4.** in whatever place, situation, or respect in which **5.** to the place to which [he'll go *where* we go] **6.** to or towards whatever place [go *where* you please] —*pron.* **1.** the place at which [it is a mile from *where* he lives] **2.** what or which place

whereabouts *adv.* where —*n.* the place where a person or thing is [do you know his *whereabouts*?]

whereas (wāar az') *conj.* **1.** but on the other hand; while **2.** in view of the fact that

whereat (wāar at') *adv.* [Archaic] at what? —*conj.* [Archaic] at which point

whereby (wāar bī') *conj.* by means of which [a plan *whereby* to make money]

wherefore (wāar'fôr') *n.* the reason; cause —*conj.* **1.** for which **2.** because of which; therefore —*adv.* [Archaic] for what reason or purpose? why?

wherein (wāar in') [Archaic] *adv.* in what way? how? —*conj.* in which [the room *wherein* he lay]

whereof (wāar ov') *adv., conj.* of what, which, or whom

whereon (wāar on') *conj.* on which —*adv.* [Archaic] on what?

wheresoever (wāar'sō ev'ər) *adv., conj.* wherever: also [Poet.] **where'soe'er'**

whereupon (wāar'ə pon') *conj.* **1.** upon which **2.** at which —*adv.* [Archaic] upon what? whereon?

wherever (wāar ev'ər) *conj.* in, at, or to whatever place [he thinks of us, *wherever* he is] —*adv.* [Colloq.] where Also [Poet.] **where'er'**

wherewithal (wāar'with ôl) *n.* necessary means, esp. money (usually with *the*) [the *wherewithal* to continue one's education]

wherry (wer'ē) *n.,* *pl.* **-ries** [< ?] **1.**

a light rowing boat used on rivers **2.** a large, broad, but light barge **—wher′ry·man** n.

whet (wet) vt. **whet′ted, whet′ting** [OE. hwæt, keen] **1.** to sharpen by rubbing or grinding (the edge of a knife or tool) **2.** to stimulate **—whet′ter** n.

whether (weth′ər) conj. [OE. hwæther] **1.** if it be the case or fact that **2.** in case; in either case that [whether it rains or snows] **3.** either [whether by accident or design] **—whether or no** in any case

whetstone (wet′stōn′) n. an abrasive stone for sharpening knives or other edged tools

whew (wyōō) interj. [echoic] an exclamation of relief, surprise, dismay, etc.

whey (wā) n. [OE. hwæg] the thin, watery part of milk, which separates from the curds after clotting

whey·faced adj. having a pale or pallid face

which (wich) pron. [OE. hwylc] **1.** what one (or ones) of the persons, things, or events mentioned or implied? [which do you want?] **2.** the one (or ones) that [he knows which he wants] **3.** that: used as a relative referring to the thing or event specified [the boat which sank] **4.** any that; whichever [take which you like] **—adj. 1.** what one or ones (of the number mentioned or implied) [which man (or men) came?] **2.** whatever [try which plan you like] **3.** being the one just mentioned [he is old, which fact is important]

whichever (wich ev′ər) pron., adj. **1.** any one (of two or more) **2.** no matter which

whiff (wif) n. [echoic] **1.** a light puff or gust of air or wind **2.** a slight gust of odour **3.** an inhaling or exhaling of tobacco smoke **4.** a suggestion; trace

whiffle vi. **-fled, -fling** [< WHIFF] **1.** to shift; vacillate **2.** to blow in gusts: said of the wind **—whif′fler** n.

Whig (wig) n. [< whiggamores, Scot. Presbyterians who marched on Edinburgh in 1648] a member of the English political party which supported the Hanoverian succession, and (18th - mid 19th cent.) championed popular rights: it later became the Liberal Party **—adj.** of or being a Whig **—Whig′gish** adj. **—Whig′gism, Whig′gery** n.

while (wīl) conj. [OE. hwil] **1.** during or throughout the time that **2.** at the same time that [while you're up, close the door] **3.** a) although [while she isn't pretty, she is charming] b) whereas [the walls are green, while the ceiling is white] **—vt. whiled, whil′ing** to spend (time) in a pleasant way [to while away the hours] **—n.** a period of time [a short while] **—between whiles** at intervals **—worth (one's) while** worth one's time

whilom (wī′ləm) adv. [< OE. hwil, while] [Archaic] at one time; formerly **—adj.** former [their whilom friends]

whilst (wilst) conj. same as WHILE

whim (wim) n. [< ?] a sudden fancy; idle and passing notion

whimper (wim′pər) vi., vt. [echoic] to cry or utter with low, whining, broken sounds **—n.** a whimpering sound or cry **—whim′perer** n.

whimsical (wim′zi k'l) adj. **1.** spontaneously playful **2.** different in an odd way; quaint, fantastic **3.** full of whims or whimsy; having odd notions **—whim′si·cal′ity** (-kal′ə tē), **whim′sicalness** n. **—whim′sically** adv.

whimsy (wim′zē) n., pl. **-sies** [< ?] **1.** a whim **2.** a quaint or fanciful humour Also sp. **whim′sey,** pl. **-seys**

whin¹ (win) n. [prob. < Scand.] same as FURZE

whin² n. [< ?] any of several hard, igneous or basaltic rocks: also **whin′stone**

whinchat (win′chat′) n. [< WHIN¹ + chat, warbler] a brown and buff songbird

whine (wīn) vi. **whined, whin′ing** [OE. hwinan] **1.** a) to utter a peevish, high-pitched sound, as in complaint b) to make a drawn-out, high-pitched sound **2.** to complain in a childish way **—n. 1.** the act or sound of whining **2.** a complaint uttered in a whining tone **—whin′er** n. **—whin′iness** n. **—whin′ingly** adv. **—whin′y** adj.

whinny (win′ē) vi. **whin′nied, whin′ny·ing** [< WHINE] to neigh in a low, gentle way: said of a horse **—n.,** pl. **whinnies** the whinnying of a horse, or a similar sound

whip (wip) vt. **whipped, whip′ping** [MDu. wippen, to swing] **1.** to strike, as with a strap; beat **2.** to move, pull, throw, etc. suddenly [to whip out a knife] **3.** to strike as a whip does [the rain whipped her face] **4.** to drive, urge, etc. by or as by whipping **5.** to wind (cord or thread) round (a rope, etc.), so as to prevent fraying **6.** to beat (eggs, cream, etc.) into a froth with a fork, mixer, etc. **7.** to sew (a seam, etc.) with a loose, overhand stitch **8.** [Colloq.] to defeat or outdo **9.** [Colloq.] to steal **—vi. 1.** to move, go, etc. quickly and suddenly **2.** to flap about in a whiplike manner **—n. 1.** an instrument for striking or flogging, consisting of a rod with a lash attached to one end **2.** a blow, etc. made as with a whip **3.** a person who uses a whip, as a coachman **4.** a) an officer of a political party in parliament, etc. who enforces party discipline, etc.: also **party whip** b) in the British Parliament, a notice issued to members to be in attendance at a certain time, underlined to indicate the degree of importance [a three-line whip] **5.** a whipping motion **6.** a dessert made of sugar and whipped cream, beaten egg whites, etc., and often fruit **—whip into shape** [Colloq.] to bring by vigorous action into a desired condition **—whip up 1.** to rouse; excite **2.** [Colloq.] to prepare quickly and efficiently **—whip′-like′** adj. **—whip′per** n.

whipcord n. **1.** a strong worsted cloth with a hard, diagonally ribbed surface **2.** hard, twisted cord used for whiplashes

whip hand 1. the hand in which a driver holds his whip **2.** the position of advantage or control

whiplash n. **1.** the lash of a whip **2.**

a sudden, severe jolting of the neck backwards and then forwards, as in a rear-end motor car collision : also **whiplash injury**

whipper-in (wip'ər in') *n.*, *pl.* **whippers-in** a huntsman's assistant who keeps the hounds together

whippersnapper (wip'ər snap'ər) *n.* a young or unimportant person who appears impertinent or presumptuous

whippet (wip'it) *n.* [< obs. *whippet*, move fast] a swift dog resembling a small greyhound

whipping *n.* a flogging or beating, as in punishment

whipping boy 1. a scapegoat 2. orig., a boy brought up with a young prince and required to take punishment for the latter's misdeeds

whipping top a toy top which is kept spinning by strokes from a whip

whippoorwill (wip'poo'wil') *n.* [echoic] a greyish nightjar of eastern N America

whip-round *n.* [Colloq.] an impromptu collection of money, as to buy a present for someone

whipstock *n.* the handle of a whip

whir, whirr (wur) *vi.*, *vt.* **whirred, whir'-ring** [prob. < Scand.] to fly, revolve, vibrate, etc. with a whizzing or buzzing sound —*n.* a sound like this, as of a propeller

whirl (wurl) *vi.* [ON. *hvirfla*] 1. to move rapidly in a circular manner 2. to rotate or spin fast; gyrate 3. to seem to spin; reel —*vt.* to cause to rotate, revolve, etc. rapidly —*n.* 1. the act of whirling 2. a whirling motion 3. something whirling or being whirled 4. a confused or giddy condition 5. a tumult; uproar 6. a round of parties, etc. —**give it a whirl** [Colloq.] to make an attempt —**whirl'er** *n.*

whirligig *n.* [see WHIRL & GIG[1]] 1. a child's toy that whirls or spins 2. a merry-go-round 3. something that seems to whirl

whirlpool *n.* water in rapid, violent, whirling motion tending to form a circle into which floating objects are drawn

whirlwind *n.* 1. a current of air whirling violently upwards in a spiral that has a forward motion 2. anything resembling a whirlwind, as in destructive force, etc. —*adj.* carried on as fast as possible [a *whirlwind* courtship]

whirlybird *n.* colloq. term for HELICOPTER

whisk (wisk) *vt.* [ON. *visk*, brush] 1. to move, remove, brush (*away*, *off*, *out*, etc.) with a quick, sweeping motion 2. to whip (eggs, cream, etc.) —*vi.* to move quickly, nimbly, or briskly —*n.* 1. a brushing with a quick, light, sweeping motion 2. a kitchen utensil for whipping eggs, etc. 3. a small bunch of straw, hair, etc. used for brushing

whisker (wis'kər) *n.* [see WHISK] 1. a) any of the long, bristly hairs growing on the upper lip of a cat, rat, etc. b) a hair of a man's beard 2. [pl.] the hair growing on a man's face —**by a whisker** [Colloq.] only just —**whisk'ered, whisk'ery** *adj.*

whiskey jack [Canad.] *same as* CANADA JAY

whisky (wis'kē) *n.*, *pl.* **-kies** [< IrGael. *uisce*, water + *beathadh*, life] 1. a strong alcoholic liquor distilled from the fermented mash of grain, esp. barley 2. a drink of whisky *Note*: in the U.S. and Ireland, the usual spelling is **whiskey**

whisper (wis'pər) *vi.* [OE. *hwisprian*] 1. to speak very softly 2. to talk in a quiet or furtive way, as in gossiping 3. to make a soft, rustling sound —*vt.* 1. to say very softly, esp. by whispering 2. to tell as a secret —*n.* 1. soft, low, breathy speech 2. something whispered 3. a soft, rustling sound —**whis'perer** *n.* —**whis'pering** *adj.*, *n.* —**whis'peringly** *adv.* —**whis'pery** *adj.*

whist[1] (wist) *interj.* [echoic] [Archaic or Dial.] hush!

whist[2] *n.* [< earlier *whisk*] a card game usually played by two pairs of players, similar to, and the forerunner of, bridge

whistle (wis'l) *vi.* **-tled, -tling** [OE. *hwistlian*] 1. to make a clear, shrill sound by forcing breath through a small opening 2. to make a clear, shrill cry: said of some birds and animals 3. to move with a high, shrill sound, as the wind 4. a) to blow a whistle b) to have its whistle blown, as a train —*vt.* 1. to produce (a tune, etc.) by whistling 2. to summon, signal, etc. by whistling —*n.* 1. an instrument for making whistling sounds 2. the act or sound of whistling —**wet one's whistle** [Colloq.] to take a drink —**whistle for** to seek or expect in vain —**whistle in the dark** to pretend to be confident —**whis'tler** *n.* —**whis'tling** *adj.*, *n.*

whit (wit) *n.* [OE. *wiht*, wight] the least bit; jot; iota [not a *whit* the wiser]

white (wīt) *adj.* **whit'er, whit'est** [OE. *hwīt*] 1. having the colour of pure snow or milk; of the colour of reflected light containing all of the visible rays of the spectrum: opposite to black 2. of a light or pale colour 3. pale; wan [a face *white* with terror] 4. pure; innocent 5. free from evil intent [*white* magic] 6. a) having a light-coloured skin; Caucasoid b) of or controlled by Caucasoids —*n.* 1. white colour 2. a white or light-coloured part or thing, as the albumen of an egg, the white part of the eyeball, a white garment, white wine, white pigment, etc. 3. a person with a light-coloured skin; Caucasoid —**bleed white** to drain (a person) completely of money, resources, etc. —**white'ly** *adv.* —**white'ness** *n.*

white ant *same as* TERMITE

whitebait *n.*, *pl.* **-bait** any of various small, silvery fishes, as young herring, used as food

white blood cell *same as* LEUCOCYTE: also called **white blood corpuscle**

whitecap *n.* a wave with its crest broken into white foam

white coffee coffee made with milk or cream

white-collar *adj.* designating or of clerical or professional workers

white dwarf any of a class of small, extremely dense stars of low luminosity

white elephant 1. something that is of little use but costs a lot to maintain 2. any object that its owner no longer wants to keep but that others may want to own or buy

white feather an indication of cowardice : chiefly in **show the white feather**

whitefish any of various food fishes with white, non-oily flesh, as the cod, plaice, etc.

white flag a white banner hoisted as a signal of truce or surrender

whitefly *n., pl.* **-flies**′ any of various tiny whitish insects, often harmful to plants

White Friar a Carmelite friar : so called from the white mantle worn by these friars

white gold gold alloyed with nickel, zinc, etc., to give it a white, platinumlike appearance for use in jewellery

white-haired *adj.* having white or very light hair

Whitehall (wīt′hôl) *n.* [< a street in London, site of several government offices] the British government or its central administration

white-headed boy one who is treated with special favour

white heat 1. the degree of intense heat at which metal, etc. glows white 2. a state of intense excitement, etc.

white hope any person who is expected to bring honour and glory to a place, group, etc.

white horse 1. a white-crested wave 2. the figure of a horse on a hillside, formed by removing the turf and exposing the underlying chalk

white-hot *adj.* 1. glowing white with heat 2. extremely angry, excited, enthusiastic, etc.

White House, the [< the white mansion in Washington, official residence of the president of the U.S.] the executive branch of the U.S. government

white lead a poisonous, heavy, white powder, basic lead carbonate, used as a paint pigment, etc.

white lie a lie about something unimportant, often one told to spare someone's feelings

white light *Physics* light, as sunlight, composed of rays of all the wavelengths ranging from red to violet

white man's burden the supposed duty of the white men to bring their civilization to the non-white inhabitants of their colonies

white matter whitish nerve tissue of the brain and spinal cord, consisting chiefly of nerve fibres

white meat any light-coloured meat, as veal, pork, the breast of poultry, etc.

white monk a Cistercian

whiten *vt., vi.* to make or become white or whiter —**whit′ener** *n.* —**whit′ening** *n.*

white noise a sound containing a blend of all the audible frequencies distributed equally over the range of the frequency band

white paper an official government report that defines or supports the ministry's policy on a specific matter

white pepper pepper ground from the husked, dried seeds of the nearly ripe pepper berry

White Russian a native or inhabitant of White Russia; Byelorussian

white sale a sale of sheets, towels, linens, etc. held in a department store

white sauce a sauce for vegetables, meat, fish, etc., made of fat or butter, flour, milk or stock, and seasoning

white slave a woman forced into prostitution for the profit of others —**white slaver** —**white slavery**

white spirit a light-coloured mixture of petroleum hydrocarbons used as a solvent, etc.

white tie 1. a white bow tie, properly worn with a tail coat 2. a swallow-tailed coat and its accessories

whitewash *n.* 1. a mixture of lime, whiting, size, water, etc., for whitening walls, etc. 2. a concealing of faults or defects as in an effort to avoid blame —*vt.* 1. to cover with whitewash 2. to conceal the faults or defects of —**white′wash′er** *n.* —**white′wash′ing** *n.*

white whale *same as* BELUGA (sense 2)

whitewood *n.* 1. any of a number of trees with light-coloured wood 2. the wood of such a tree —*adj.* made of such a wood [*whitewood* furniture]

whither (wi*th*′ər) *adv.* [OE. *hwider*] to what place, condition, etc.? —*conj.* 1. to which place, condition, etc. 2. wherever *Where* is now almost always used in place of *whither*

whithersoever (wi*th*′ər sō ev′ər) *adv., conj.* [Archaic or Poet.] to whatever place

whiting[1] (wīt′iŋ) *n.* [MDu. *wijting*] a small, edible, European seafish

whiting[2] *n.* [see WHITE, *v.*] powdered chalk used in making paints, inks, etc.

whitish *adj.* somewhat white

whitlow (wit′lō) *n.* [ME. *whitflawe*] an inflamed sore on a finger or toe

Whitsun (wit′s'n) *adj.* of or observed on Whitsunday or at Whitsuntide

Whitsunday (wit′sun′dē) *n.* [OE. *Hwita Sunnandæg*, white Sunday] *same as* PENTECOST

whittle (wit′'l) *vt.* **-tled**, **-tling** [OE. *thwitan*, to cut] 1. *a)* to cut thin shavings from (wood) with a knife *b)* to carve (an object) in this manner 2. to reduce, destroy, etc. gradually : usually with *down, away*, etc. —**whit′tler** *n.*

whiz, whizz (wiz) *vi.* **whizzed, whiz′zing** [echoic] 1. to make the buzzing sound of something moving swiftly through the air 2. to speed by with or as with this sound —*n.* a whizzing sound —**whiz′zingly** *adv.*

whiz kid, whizz kid [Colloq.] an outstandingly able and successful, or potentially successful, young person

who (hōō) *pron.*, objective **whom**, poss.
whose [OE. *hwa*] **1.** what or which person
or persons [*who* is he? I don't know *who*
he is] **2.** *a)* the person (or, a, person or persons)
that [the man *who* came to dinner] *b)*
any person or persons that [*"who* steals
my purse steals nought"] The use of
who rather than *whom* as the object of
a verb or preposition although widespread,
is objected to by some —**who's who** who
the important people are

WHO World Health Organization

whoa (wō) *interj.* [< HO] stop!: used
esp. in directing a horse to stand still

whodunit (hōō dun'it) *n.* [Colloq.] a
mystery novel, play, etc.

whoever (hōō ev'ər) *pron.* **1.** any person
that **2.** no matter what person [*whoever*
said it, it's not so] **3.** what person? who?
[*whoever* told you that?]

whole (hōl) *adj.* [OE. *hal*] **1.** complete
2. not divided up; in a single unit **3.**
constituting the entire amount, extent, etc.
[the *whole* week] **4.** not broken, damaged,
defective, etc. **5.** healthy **6.** *Arith.* not
mixed or fractional [25 is a *whole* number]
—*n.* **1.** the entire amount, etc.; totality
2. a complete organization of parts —**as
a whole** altogether —**on the whole** all
things considered —**whole'ness** *n.*

wholehearted (hōl'här'tid) *adj.* doing
or done with all one's energy, enthusiasm,
etc. —**whole'heart'edly** *adv.* —**whole'-
heart'edness** *n.*

wholemeal *adj.* **1.** made of the entire
wheat kernel **2.** made of wholemeal flour
[*wholemeal* bread]

whole note *Music U.S. name for*
SEMIBREVE

whole number zero or any positive
or negative multiple of 1; integer [28 is
a *whole number*]

wholesale *n.* the selling of goods in
relatively large quantities, esp. to retailers
who then sell them at higher prices to
consumers —*adj.* **1.** of, or engaged in
such selling **2.** extensive or sweeping
—*adv.* extensively or sweepingly [to reject
proposals *wholesale*] —*vt.*, *vi.* **-saled'**,
-sal'ing to sell wholesale —**whole'sal'-
er** *n.*

wholesome *adj.* [see WHOLE] **1.** good
for one's health or well-being **2.** tending
to improve the mind or character **3.** having
or showing health and vigour **4.** suggesting
health —**whole'somely** *adv.* —**whole'-
someness** *n.*

who'll (hōōl) **1.** who shall **2.** who will

wholly (hōl'lē) *adv.* to the whole amount
or extent; totally; entirely

whom (hōōm) *pron. objective case of* WHO

whomever (hōōm ev'ər) *pron. objective
case of* WHOEVER

whomsoever (hōōm'sō ev'ər) *pron.
objective case of* WHOSOEVER

whoop (hōōp, wōōp) *n.* [OFr. *houper*, cry
out] **1.** a loud shout, cry, etc., as of
excitement, joy, etc. **2.** the gasping sound
made following a fit of coughing in

whooping cough —*vi.*, *vt.* to utter, or
utter with, a whoop or whoops —**whoop
it (or things) up** [Slang] **1.** to celebrate
noisily **2.** to create enthusiasm (for)
—**whoop'er** *n.*

whoopee (wōō'pē) *interj.* [< prec.] an
exclamation of great joy, etc. —*n.* a shout
of "whoopee!" —**make whoopee** [Colloq.]
1. to have fun in a noisy way **2.** to
be lightheartedly amorous

whooping cough (hōō'piŋ) an acute
infectious disease with coughing fits that
end in a whoop

whoops (wōōps) *interj.* an exclamation
of surprise or apology

whop (wop) *vt.*, *vi.* whopped, whop'ping
[echoic] [Colloq.] **1.** to beat, strike,
etc. **2.** to defeat decisively —*n.* [Colloq.]
a sharp, loud blow, thump, etc.

whopper *n.* [Colloq.] **1.** anything
extraordinarily large **2.** a great lie

whopping *adj.* [Colloq.] colossal; very
large

whore (hôr) *n.* [OE. *hore*] a sexually
promiscuous woman, esp., a prostitute —*vi.*
whored, whor'ing **1.** to be a whore **2.**
to fornicate with whores —**whor'ish** *adj.*

who're (hōō'ər) who are

whorehouse (hôr'hous') *n.* a brothel

whorl (wurl) *n.* [< WHIRL] **1.** any of
the circular ridges that form the design
of a fingerprint **2.** *Bot.* a circular growth
of leaves, petals, etc. about the same point
on a stem **3.** *Zool.* any of the turns
in a spiral shell —**whorled** *adj.*

whortleberry (wur't'l bar ē) *n.*, *pl.* -ries
[< OE. *horta*] *same as* BILBERRY

who's (hōōz) **1.** who is **2.** who has

whose (hōōz) *pron.* [OE. *hwæs*] that
or those belonging to whom [*whose* is
this?] —**possessive pronominal** *adj.* of,
belonging to, made, or done by whom
or which [the man *whose* car was stolen]

whosoever (hōō'sō ev'ər) *pron.* whoever

why (wī) *adv.* [OF. *hwi*, < *hwæt*, what]
for what reason, cause, or purpose? [*why*
go?] —*conj.* **1.** because of which [there
is no reason *why* you should go] **2.** the
reason for which [that is *why* he went]
—*n.*, *pl.* whys the reason, cause, etc.
[never mind the *why* and wherefore]
—*interj.* an exclamation used to show
surprise, impatience, etc.

W.I. 1. West Indies **2.** Women's Institute

wick (wik) *n.* [OE. *weoce*] a piece of
cord or tape in a candle, oil lamp, etc.,
that absorbs the fuel and, when lighted,
burns —**get on a person's wick** [Colloq.]
to cause extreme irritation to a person

wicked (wik'id) *adj.* [ME. < *wikke*, evil]
1. morally bad; evil **2.** generally painful,
unpleasant, etc. **3.** naughty; mischievous
[a *wicked* smile] —**wick'edly** *adv.*
—**wick'edness** *n.*

wicker (wik'ər) *n.* [< Scand.] **1.** a thin,
flexible twig **2.** such twigs or long, woody
strips woven together, as in making baskets
—*adj.* made of wicker

wickerwork *n.* **1.** things made of wicker **2.** the art or craft of making wicker objects

wicket (wik′it) *n.* [ONormFr. *wiket*] **1.** *Cricket* a) either of two sets of three stumps each with two bails resting on top of them b) the playing space between the two wickets [a fast *wicket*] c) a player's turn at batting, or the period during which two batsmen bat d) the instance of a batsman being got out **2.** a small door or gate, esp. one set in or near a large one **3.** a small gate for regulating the flow of water, as to a water wheel

wicketkeeper *n.* *Cricket* the fielder stationed immediately behind the wicket

widdershins (wid′ər shinz′) *adv.* var. of WITHERSHINS

wide (wīd) *adj.* **wid′er**, **wid′est** [OE. *wid*] **1.** extending over a large area; esp. from side to side **2.** of a specified extent from side to side [two kilometres *wide*] **3.** of great extent, range, etc. **4.** roomy; full **5.** opened as far as possible **6.** far from the point, issue, etc. aimed at [*wide* of the mark] **7.** [Slang] shrewd and unscrupulous [a *wide* boy] —*adv.* **1.** over a relatively large area [to travel far and *wide*] **2.** to a large or full extent [*wide* open] **3.** so as to miss the point, issue, etc. [his shot went *wide*] —*n.* *Cricket* a ball bowled out of the batsman's reach —**give a wide berth (to)** to steer clear of (something) —**wide of the mark** mistaken —**wide′ly** *adv.* —**wide′ness** *n.*

-wide (wīd) *a combining form meaning* existing or extending throughout [*nationwide*]

wide-angle *adj.* designating or of a kind of camera lens covering a wide angle of view

wide-awake (wīd′ə wāk′) *adj.* **1.** completely awake **2.** alert **3.** [Colloq.] knowing; wise —**wide′-awake′ness** *n.*

wide-eyed (wīd′īd′) *adj.* with the eyes wide open, as in credulous surprise

widen *vt., vi.* to make or become wide or wider

wide-open *adj.* **1.** opened wide **2.** exposed to attack

widespread *adj.* spread widely; esp., a) widely extended b) occurring over a wide area or extent

widgeon (wij′ən) *n.* [< ?] any of various wild, freshwater ducks

widow (wid′ō) *n.* [OE. *widewe*] **1.** a woman whose husband has died and who has not remarried **2.** [Colloq.] a woman whose husband is often away indulging in a specified hobby or activity [a golf *widow*] —*vt.* to cause to become a widow [*widowed* by the war] —**wid′owhood′** *n.*

widower *n.* a man whose wife has died and who has not remarried

widow's peak a point formed by hair growing down in the middle of a forehead

width (width) *n.* **1.** a being wide; wideness **2.** the distance from side to side **3.** a piece of something of a certain width [two *widths* of cloth]

wield (wēld) *vt.* [OE. *wealdan*] **1.** to handle (a tool, etc.), esp. with skill **2.** to exercise (power, influence, etc.) —**wield′er** *n.*

wife (wīf) *n., pl.* **wives** (wīvz) [OE. *wif*] **1.** a man's partner in marriage **2.** [Archaic] a woman [*housewife*] —**wife′less** *adj.* —**wife′ly** *adj.*

wig (wig) *n.* [< PERIWIG] a false covering of real or synthetic hair for the head —*vt.* **wigged, wig′ging** [Colloq.] to scold, rebuke, etc. —**wigged** *adj.* —**wig′less** *adj.*

wigeon (wij′ən) *n.* var. of WIDGEON

wigging (wig′iŋ) *n.* [Colloq.] a scolding

wiggle (wig′'l) *vt., vi.* **-gled, -gling** [< MDu. & MLowG. *wiggelen*] to move with short, jerky or twisting motions from side to side —*n.* the act or an instance of wiggling —**wig′gler** *n.*

wiggly *adj.* **-glier, -gliest 1.** that wiggles; wiggling **2.** wavy [a *wiggly* line]

wight (wīt) *n.* [OE. *wiht*] [Archaic] a human being

WIGWAM

wigwam (wig′wam) *n.* [< Algonquian] a N American Indian dwelling consisting of a framework of arched poles covered with bark

wilco (wil′kō′) *interj.* [*wil*(*l*) *co*(*mply*)] I will comply with your request: used in radiotelephony

wild (wīld) *adj.* [OE. *wilde*] **1.** living or growing in its original, natural state **2.** not lived in or cultivated; waste **3.** not civilized; savage **4.** unruly, rough, lawless, etc. **5.** dissolute, orgiastic, etc. [a *wild* party] **6.** turbulent; stormy **7.** a) [Colloq.] excited or enthusiastic b) angered, frantic, etc. **8.** disordered, dishevelled **9.** fantastically impractical; reckless **10.** missing the target [a *wild* shot] —*adv.* in a wild manner —*n.* [usually *pl.*] a wilderness or wasteland —**out in the wilds** far from civilization —**run wild** to behave in an uncontrolled way —**wild horses wouldn't drag it from me** [Colloq.] I will keep the secret at all costs —**wild′ly** *adv.* —**wild′ness** *n.*

wild carrot a common weed, with umbels of white flowers: also called **Queen Anne's lace**

wildcat *n.* **1.** an undomesticated cat, resembling the domestic tabby, but larger and having a bushy tail **2.** a fierce, aggressive person **3.** [Chiefly U.S.] an oil well drilled in an area not known before to have oil —*adj.* **1.** unsound or financially risky **2.** illegal or unauthorized [a *wildcat* strike]

wildebeest (wil'də bēst') *n.* [Afrik.] *same as* GNU

wilderness (wil'dər nis) *n.* [< OE. *wilde*, wild + *deor*, animal] 1. an uncultivated, uninhabited region 2. a confused mass or tangle

wildfire *n.* 1. a fire that spreads fast and is hard to put out [rumours spread like *wildfire*] 2. *same as* GREEK FIRE 3. lightning without audible thunder

wild flower any flowering plant growing without cultivation Also **wild'flower**

wildfowl *n.* a game bird

wild-goose chase any futile search or undertaking

wildlife *n.* wild animals and birds, collectively

wild oats any of several wild grasses —**sow one's wild oats** to be dissolute in youth before settling down

Wild West the western U.S. in its early frontier period of lawlessness

wile (wīl) *n.* [OE. *wil*] a sly stratagem or coquettish trick: *usually used in pl.* —*vt.* **wiled, wil'ing** to beguile; lure —**wile away** to while away (time): by confusion with *while*

wilful (wil'fəl) *adj.* 1. done deliberately or intentionally 2. always wanting one's own way; self-willed U.S. sp. **willful** —**wil'fully** *adv.* —**wil'fulness** *n.*

will¹ (wil) *n.* [OE. *willa*] 1. the power of making a reasoned choice or of controlling one's own actions 2. *a)* the legal statement of a person's wishes concerning the disposal of his property after death *b)* the document containing this 3. *a)* the desire, purpose, etc. [what is your *will?*] *b)* a compelling command or decree [the *will* of the people] 4. *a)* determination *b)* energy and enthusiasm 5. attitude towards others —*vt.* 1. to have as the object of one's will 2. to control by the power of the will 3. to bequeath by a will —*vi.* to decree, choose, or prefer —**at will** when one wishes

will² (wil; *unstressed* wəl) *v.*, *pt.* **would** [OE. *willan*] 1. an auxiliary used to express the future: strictly *will* is used in the second and third persons for simple future and in the first person to show determination or obligation, and *shall* is to be used in the first person for simple future and in the second and third persons to show determination or obligation 2. an auxiliary used to express: *a)* willingness [*will* you do me a favour?] *b)* ability or capacity [it *will* hold another quart] *c)* habit, inclination, etc. [boys *will* be boys] —*vt.*, *vi.* to wish; desire [do what (or as) you *will*]

willies (wil'ēz) *n.pl.* [< ?] [Slang] a state of nervousness; jitters: with *the*

willing (wil'iŋ) *adj.* 1. ready or agreeing (to do something) 2. doing, giving, etc. or done, given, etc. readily or gladly —**wil'-ingly** *adv.* —**wil'ingness** *n.*

will-o'-the-wisp *n.* [earlier *Will*(personal name) *with the wisp*] 1. a light seen

moving over marshes at night 2. any person or thing that allures and misleads

willow (wil'ō) *n.* [OE. *welig*] 1. *a)* a tree or shrub bearing catkins and having flexible twigs used in weaving baskets, etc. *b)* the wood 2. [orig. made of willow] [Colloq.] a cricket bat

willow herb a plant with narrow leaves and purple flowers

willow pattern a design for china picturing a river, pagoda, willow trees, etc., usually in blue on a white ground

willowy *adj.* 1. gracefully slender; supple, lithe, etc. 2. shaded with willows

willpower (wil'pou'ər) *n.* strength of will, mind, or determination

willy-nilly (wil'ē nil'ē) *adv.*, *adj.* [< *will I*, *nill I: nill I: <* OE. *nyllan*, be unwilling] (happening) whether one wishes it or not

wilt (wilt) *vi.* [< obs. *welk*, wither] 1. to become limp; wither; droop: said of plants 2. to become weak or faint —*vt.* to cause to wilt —*n.* any of various plant diseases characterized by wilting

Wilts. Wiltshire

wily (wī'lē) *adj.* **wil'ier, wil'iest** crafty; sly —**wil'iness** *n.*

WIMPLE

wimple (wim'p'l) *n.* [OE. *wimpel*] a woman's head covering of medieval times consisting of a cloth arranged about the head and neck

Wimpy (wim'pē) *n.* [< a cartoon-strip character who ate hamburgers] *Trademark* a hamburger in a soft bread-roll

win (win) *vi.* **won, win'ning** [OE. *winnan*, to fight] 1. *a)* to gain a victory *b)* to finish in first place in a race, contest, etc. 2. to succeed in reaching or achieving [to *win* back to health] —*vt.* 1. *a)* to get by effort, struggle, etc. [to *win* distinction] *b)* to achieve (one's demands, etc.) *c)* to gain (a prize) in competition *d)* to earn (a livelihood, etc.) 2. to be victorious in (a contest, dispute, etc.) 3. to influence or persuade: often with *over* 4. to gain the sympathy, favour, etc. of —*n.* 1. [Colloq.] a victory, as in a contest 2. anything won, as a sum of money

wince (wins) *vi.* **winced, winc'ing** [< OFr. *guenchir*] to draw back slightly, usually grimacing, as in pain —*n.* a wincing

winceyette (win'sē et') *n.* [< *wincey*, a kind of fabric + -ETTE] a soft flannelette material

winch (winch) *n.* [OE. *wince*] 1. a crank

with a handle for transmitting motion **2.** a hoisting or hauling apparatus consisting of a drum or cylinder round which is wound a cable attached to the object to be lifted or moved —*vt.* to hoist or haul with a winch

wind¹ (wind) *vt.* **wound, wind′ing** [OE. *windan*] **1.** a) to coil (string, ribbon, etc.) round itself or round something else [*winding* a bandage round his toe] b) to cover by encircling with something **2.** to make (one's way) or move (something) in a winding or twisting course **3.** to insinuate [*winding* his way into her heart] **4.** to turn, or make revolve **5.** to hoist or haul as with a winch (often with *up*) **6.** to tighten the spring of (a clock, etc.) as by turning a stem —*vi.* **1.** to move or go in a twisting or curving course **2.** to coil or spiral (*about* or *round* something) —*n.* **1.** the act of winding **2.** a single turn of something wound **3.** a turn; twist; bend —**wind up 1.** to wind into a ball, etc. **2.** to tighten the spring of (a clockwork mechanism) **3.** to become tense, nervous, etc. **4.** to bring or come to an end **5.** [Colloq.] to liquidate (a company) **6.** [Colloq.] to come to (a specified condition or place) —**wind′er** *n.*

wind² (wind) *n.* [OE.] **1.** a current of air sometimes of considerable force **2.** an air current regarded as bearing a scent [to lose (the) *wind* of the fox] **3.** [Colloq.] a hint [we got *wind* that you were coming] **4.** breath or the power of breathing **5.** idle or empty talk **6.** gas in the stomach or intestines; indigestion **7.** the wind instruments of an orchestra, or the players of these —*vt.* **1.** to get the scent of **2.** to put out of breath [to be *winded* by a long run] **3.** to rest (a horse, etc.) so as to allow recovery of breath —**break wind** to expel gas from the bowels —**get the wind up** [Colloq.] to become alarmed —**how the wind blows** what the trend of affairs, public opinion, etc. is —**in the wind** happening or about to happen —**put the wind up** [Colloq.] to alarm —**take the wind out of one's sails** to remove one's advantage, nullify one's argument, etc. suddenly —**wind′less** *adj.*

windbag *n.* [Colloq.] a person who talks much but says little of importance

windblown *adj.* **1.** blown by the wind **2.** twisted in growth by the prevailing wind: said of a tree

wind-borne *adj.* carried by the wind, as pollen

windbreak *n.* a hedge, fence, or row of trees, etc. that serves as a protection from wind

windcheater *n.* a short, warm jacket with a closefitting elastic waistband and cuffs: also **windjammer**

wind cone *same as* WINDSOCK

wind-down (wīnd′doun′) *n.* a gradual reduction

windfall (wind′fôl′) *n.* **1.** something blown down by the wind, as fruit from a tree **2.** any unexpected gain, esp. financial

windflower *n.* *same as* ANEMONE

wind gauge *same as* ANEMOMETER

winding (wīn′diŋ) *adj.* twisting, turning, bending etc.

winding sheet a cloth in which the body of a dead person is wrapped for burial; shroud

wind instrument (wind) a musical instrument sounded by blowing air, esp. breath, through it, as an oboe

windjammer (wind′jam′ər) *n.* **1.** a large merchant sailing ship **2.** *same as* WINDCHEATER

WINDLASS

windlass (wind′ləs) *n.* [< ON. *vinda*, WIND¹ + *ass*, beam] a winch, esp. a simple one worked by a crank —*vt.,vi.* to hoist with a windlass

windmill (win′mil′) *n.* **1.** a machine for grinding or pumping, worked by the wind blowing on vanes fixed on a shaft at the top of a tower **2.** a toy consisting of a stick with coloured vanes which revolve in the wind —**fight (or tilt at) windmills** to fight imaginary opponents —**throw one's cap over the windmill** to behave in a reckless or unorthodox fashion

window (win′dō) *n.* [< ON. *vindr*, WIND² + *auga*, eye] **1.** a) an opening in a building, vehicle, etc., to let in light or air, usually having a pane or panes of glass set in a frame b) any such pane or frame **2.** any similar opening **3.** the display area behind the window of a shop —**win′dow-less** *adj.*

window box a long, narrow box on a window ledge, for growing plants

window dressing 1. the display in a shop window to attract customers **2.** any attempt to make something seem better than it really is

window envelope an envelope with a transparent panel, through which the address on the enclosure can be seen

window ledge *same as* WINDOWSILL

windowpane *n.* a pane of glass in a window

window seat a seat built in beneath a window or windows and usually containing storage space

window-shop *vi.* **-shopped′, -shop′ping** to look at displays of goods in shop windows without entering the shops to buy —**win′-dow-shop′per** *n.*

windowsill *n.* the sill of a window

windpipe (wind′pīp′) *n.* *same as* TRACHEA

windproof *adj.* that the wind cannot blow through

windscreen *n.* the sheet of glass forming the front window of a motor vehicle: U.S. **wind′shield**

windscreen wiper a rubber-edged blade which can be electrically operated to clear a windscreen of rainwater, etc.: also **wiper**

windsock *n.* a long, cone-shaped cloth bag, open at both ends and attached to the top of a mast to show wind direction: also called **wind sleeve**

WINDSOR CHAIR

Windsor chair (win′zər) a style of wooden chair, with spreading legs, a spindle back, and usually a saddlelike seat

Windsor knot a form of double slipknot in a necktie, resulting in a wider, bulkier knot

wind-swept (wind′swept′) *adj.* swept by or exposed to winds

wind tunnel a tunnellike chamber through which air is forced and in which scale models of aircraft, etc. are tested to determine the effects of wind pressure

windup (wīnd′up′) *n.* a conclusion; end

windward (wind′wərd) *n.* the direction from which the wind blows —*adv.* towards the wind —*adj.* on the side from which the wind blows

windy (win′dē) *adj.* -ier, -iest 1. characterized by wind *[a windy day]* 2. swept by strong winds 3. violent like wind 4. *a)* without substance; empty, flimsy, etc. *b)* long-winded, pompous, etc. 5. flatulent 6. [Slang] frightened; cowardly

wine (wīn) *n.* [< L. *vinum*] 1. the fermented juice of grapes as an alcoholic drink 2. the fermented juice of other fruits or plants *[dandelion wine]* 3. a dark, purplish red —*vt., vi.* **wined, win′-ing** to provide with or drink wine: usually in **wine and dine,** to entertain lavishly

winebibber *n.* a person given to drinking much or too much wine —**wine′bib′bing** *adj., n.*

wine cellar 1. a cellar where wine is stored 2. a stock of wine

wine-coloured *adj.* dark purplish-red

wineglass *n.* a small glass, usually stemmed, for serving wine

wine press any equipment for pressing grapes to extract the juice for making wine

wineskin *n.* a large bag for holding wine, made of the skin of an animal

wine-tasting *n.* the assessing of the qualities of wines by tasting small samples —**wine′taster** *n.*

wing (wiŋ) *n.* [< ON. *vaengr*] 1. either of the paired organs of flight of a bird, bat, insect, etc. 2. something like a wing in use or position; esp., *a)* (or the) main supporting surface of an aeroplane *b)* a distinct part of a building, often at one side or having a special use *c)* either side of a theatre stage out of sight of the audience *d)* the part of a car body that surrounds the wheels 3. a group; section, esp., *a)* a faction of a political party, viewed as more extreme than the main part *b)* either end of a battle formation 4. in soccer, hockey, etc. *a)* either of the two sides of the pitch near the touchline *b)* a player stationed there: also **winger** 5. *a)* R.A.F. a unit larger than a squadron *b)* [*pl.*] the insignia worn by pilots of military aircraft —*vt.* 1. *a)* to cause to speed as on wings *b)* to make (one's way) by flying 2. to wound, as with a bullet, in the wing or arm 3. to provide with wings —*vi.* to go swiftly as on wings —**give wing** (or **wings**) **to** to enable to fly on or as if on wings —**on the wing** 1. flying 2. travelling —**spread one's wings** to develop one's capabilities fully —**take wing** to fly away —**under one's wing** under one's protection, patronage, etc. —**winged** *adj.* —**wing′less** *adj.*

wing chair an armchair with a high back from each side of which high sides, or wings, extend forwards

wing commander *see* MILITARY RANKS, table

wing nut a nut with flared sides for turning with the thumb and forefinger

wingspan *n.* the distance between the wing tips of an aircraft, bird, etc.: also **wingspread**

wink (wiŋk) *vi.* [OE. *wincian*] 1. to close and open an eyelid quickly so as to signal, etc. 2. to close the eyelids and open them again quickly 3. to twinkle —*vt.* to make (an eye) wink —*n.* a winking, or the instant of time it takes —**wink at** to pretend not to notice (some wrongdoing)

winker *n.* a flashing light indicator on a motor vehicle

winkle[1] (wiŋ′k'l) *n.* an edible saltwater snail

winkle[2] *vt.* -kled, -kling [Colloq.] to pry or rout from cover, secrecy, etc. (with *out,* etc.)

winkle-picker *n.* a shoe with a narrow, sharply-pointed toe

winner (win′ər) *n.* one that wins; esp., [Colloq.] one that seems destined to win or be successful

winning *adj.* 1. victorious 2. attractive; charming —*n.* [*pl.*] something won, esp. money —**win′ningly** *adv.*

Winnipeg couch (win′i peg′) [Canad.] a couch with no arms or back, opening out into a double bed

winnow (win′ō) *vt.* [OE. *windwian*] 1. *a)* to blow the chaff from (grain) *b)* to blow off (chaff) 2. to scatter 3. to analyse carefully so as to separate the various elements —*vi.* to winnow grain

wino (wī′nō) *n.* [Colloq.] one who habitually gets drunk on wine

winsome (win′səm) *adj.* [OE. *wynsum,* pleasant] sweetly attractive; charming —**win′someness** *n.*

winter (win′tər) *n.* [OE.] 1. the coldest

season of the year, following autumn **2.** any period of decline, dreariness, etc. —*adj.* of or suitable for winter —*vi.* to pass the winter —*vt.* to keep or maintain during the winter

wintergreen *n.* **1.** any of several evergreen plants, esp. an American shrub with small, rounded leaves **2.** an aromatic compound (**oil of wintergreen**) made from these leaves

winter quarters a place where troops, etc. settle in for the winter

winter solstice the time in the Northern Hemisphere when the sun is farthest south of the celestial equator; December 21 or 22

winter sports open-air sports on ice or snow

wintertime *n.* the season of winter

wintry *adj.* **-trier, -triest** of or like winter; cold, bleak, etc. [a *wintry* day, a *wintry* stare] —**win′triness** *n.*

winy (wī′nē) *adj.* **-ier, -iest** like wine in taste, smell, colour, etc.

wipe (wīp) *vt.* **wiped, wip′ing** [OE. *wipian*] **1.** to clean or dry by rubbing with a cloth, etc. **2.** to rub (a cloth, etc.) over something **3.** to apply by wiping **4.** to remove as by wiping (with *away*, *off*, etc.) —*n.* a wiping —**wipe out 1.** to erase **2.** to kill **3.** to destroy —**wipe the floor with** [Slang] to defeat utterly —**wip′er** *n.*

wire (wīar) *n.* [OE. *wir*] **1.** metal that has been drawn into a long thread **2.** a length of this, used for conducting electric current, etc. **3.** wire netting or other wirework **4.** anything made of wire, as a telephone cable, etc. **5.** a telegram —*adj.* made of wire or wirework —*vt.* **wired, wir′ing 1.** to furnish, connect, bind, etc. with wire **2.** to supply with a system of wires for electric current **3.** to telegraph —*vi.* to telegraph

wire cutter an instrument for cutting wire

wire gauge a device for measuring the diameter of wire, thickness of sheet metal, etc.: usually a disc with notches of graduated sizes along its edge

wire-haired *adj.* having coarse, or wiry, hair

wireless *n., adj., vt., vi.* *old-fashioned term for* RADIO

wireless telegraphy (or **telegraph**) telegraphy by radio-transmitted signals

wire netting netting of woven wire, used for fences, etc.

wirepuller *n.* [Chiefly U.S.] a person who gets what he wants through his friends' influence, esp. in politics —**wire′pull′ing** *n.*

wire service [Chiefly U.S.] an organization that sends news by direct telegraph to subscribing newspapers and radio and television stations

wiretap *vi., vt.* **-tapped′, -tap′ping** to tap (a telephone wire, etc.) to get information secretly —*n.* **1.** wiretapping **2.** a device used in wiretapping

wire wool a pad of fine wire used esp. in scrubbing cooking utensils

wireworm *n.* the destructive wormlike larva of various beetles

wiring *n.* a system of wires, as to provide a house with electricity

wiry *adj.* **wir′ier, wir′iest 1.** lean, sinewy, and strong **2.** of or like wire —**wir′ily** *adv.* —**wir′iness** *n.*

wisdom (wiz′dəm) *n.* **1.** the quality of being wise **2.** learning; knowledge **3.** wise teaching

wisdom tooth the back tooth on each side of each jaw in human beings, appearing usually between the ages of 17 and 25

wise¹ (wīz) *adj.* **wis′er, wis′est** [OE. *wis*] **1.** having or showing good judgment; sagacious **2.** judicious; sound [a *wise* saying] **3.** informed [none the *wiser*] **4.** learned; erudite **5.** shrewd; cunning —**be** (or **get**) **wise to** [Slang] to be (or become) aware of —**be wise after the event** to realize when it is too late what should have been done when it is too late —**wise′ly** *adv.*

wise² *n.* [OE.] way; manner : used chiefly in phrases, as **in no wise, in this wise,** etc.

-wise (wīz) [< prec.] *a suffix meaning :* **1.** a (specified) direction, position, or manner [*lengthwise*] **2.** in the same way as [*clockwise*] **3.** [Colloq.] with regard to [*weatherwise*]

wiseacre (wīz′ā′kər) *n.* [< OHG. *wizzago*, prophet] a person who acts as though he were much wiser than he really is

wisecrack *n.* [Colloq.] a flippant gibe or sardonic remark —*vi.* [Colloq.] to make wisecracks

wise guy [Slang] a person who is brashly and annoyingly conceited, knowing, etc.; smart alec

wish (wish) *vt.* [OE. *wyscan*] **1.** to have a longing for; want **2.** to express a desire concerning [to *wish* her good luck] **3.** to bid [to *wish* a person good morning] **4.** to impose [he *wished* the job on me] —*vi.* **1.** to long; yearn **2.** to make a wish —*n.* **1.** a wishing **2.** something wished for [he got his *wish*] **3.** a polite request with some of the force of an order **4.** [*pl.*] expressed desire for a person's health, etc. [best *wishes*] —**wish′- er** *n.*

wishbone *n.* the forked bone in front of the breastbone of most birds

wishful *adj.* desirous; longing

wishful thinking thinking in which one interprets facts in terms of what one would like to believe

wishy-washy (wish′ē wosh′ē) *adj.* [< WASHY] [Colloq.] **1.** watery; insipid **2.** not strong or decisive in character; weak

wisp (wisp) *n.* [< ?] **1.** a small bunch or tuft [a *wisp* of straw] **2.** a thin, filmy bit [a *wisp* of smoke] **3.** something delicate, frail, etc. [a *wisp* of a girl] —**wisp′y** *adj.*

wist (wist) *pt. & pp.* of WIT²

wisteria (wis tēar′ē ə) *n.* [ModL. < C. *Wistar*] a twining shrub with clusters of bluish, white, pink, or purple flowers: also **wistar′ia** (-tāar′-)

wistful (wist′fəl) *adj.* [< earlier *wistly*, attentive] showing or expressing vague yearnings or pensive longing —**wist′fully** *adv.* —**wist′fulness** *n.*

wit¹ (wit) *n.* [OE.] **1.** *a)* the ability to make clever remarks in a surprising, epigrammatic, or ironic way *b)* a person having this ability **2.** alert, practical intelligence; good sense **3.** [*pl.*] powers of thinking and reasoning —**at one's wits′ end** at a loss as to what to do —**keep** (or **have**) **one's wits about one** to remain mentally alert —**live by one's wits** to live by trickery

wit² *vt., vi.* **wist, wit′ting** [OE. *witan*] [Archaic] to know or learn —**to wit** that is to say; namely

witblitz (vit′blits′) *n.* [< Afrik. *wit*, white + *blits*, lightning] [S Afr.] alcoholic drink illegally distilled

witch (wich) *n.* [OE. *wicce*] **1.** a woman who is supposed to have magic power, esp. with the help of evil spirits **2.** an ugly and ill-tempered old woman **3.** [Colloq.] a fascinating woman

witchcraft *n.* **1.** black magic; sorcery **2.** bewitching attraction

witch doctor among certain tribes, a person who practises a type of primitive medicine supposedly involving magic

witch elm *var. of* WYCH ELM

witchery *n., pl.* **-eries** **1.** witchcraft; sorcery **2.** bewitching charm; fascination

witches′ Sabbath a midnight meeting of witches, sorcerers and demons, supposed in medieval times to have been held annually

witch hazel [OE. *wice*] **1.** an American shrub with yellow flowers **2.** an alcoholic lotion made from its leaves and bark

witch hunt a public campaign carried out to expose and discredit people holding unorthodox or dissenting views, on the pretext of safeguarding the public welfare

witenagemot, witenagemote (wit′ən-ə gə mōt′) *n.* [< OE. *wita*, wise man + (ge)*mot*, a meeting] the king's council of the Anglo-Saxons

with (with) *prep.* [OE. against] **1.** *a)* by means of [stir *with* a spoon] *b)* by [filled *with* air] **2.** *a)* near to *b)* in the company of *c)* into; among [mix blue *with* red] **3.** as a member of [to sing *with* a quartet] **4.** working for [*with* the firm 20 years] **5.** concerning [pleased *with* her gift] **6.** compared to [equal *with* the others] **7.** as well as [he can run *with* the best] **8.** *a)* of the same opinions as [I'm *with* you] *b)* on the same side as ′ **9.** following the drift of someone's thoughts **10.** in the opinion of [it's all right *with* me] **11.** as a result of [faint *with* hunger] **12.** against [to argue *with* a friend] **13.** having received [*with* your permission] **14.** having or showing [to play *with* skill] **15.** in the care, of [leave the baby *with* me] **16.** including [*with* the newcomers, the class is large] **17.** in spite of [*with* all her faults, I love her still] **18.** at the same time as **19.** in proportion to [wages varying *with* skills] **20.** from [to part *with* money] **21.** after [*with* that remark, he left] —**with**

child [Archaic] pregnant —**with it** [Colloq.] fashionable; up to date

with- [OE. < prec.] *a combining form meaning:* **1.** away, back [*withdraw*] **2.** against, from [*withhold*]

withal (with ôl′) *adv.* **1.** besides **2.** notwithstanding **3.** [Archaic] with that —*prep.* [Archaic] with: used following its object

withdraw (with drô′) *vt.* -**drew′**, -**drawn′**, -**draw′ing** **1.** to take back; remove **2.** to take back (something said, offered, etc.) —*vi.* **1.** to move back; go away; retreat **2.** to remove oneself (*from* an organization, association with other people, etc.)

withdrawal *n.* **1.** the act of withdrawing **2.** a giving up the use of a narcotic drug, typically accompanied by distress of body and mind (**withdrawal symptoms**)

withdrawn *pp. of* WITHDRAW —*adj.* shy, reserved, unsociable, etc.

withe (with, with, wīth) *n.* [OE. *withthe*] a tough, flexible twig of willow, etc., used for binding things

wither (with′ər) *vi.* [< ME. *wederen*, to weather] **1.** to dry up; shrivel **2.** to fade; waste away [our hopes soon *withered*] —*vt.* **1.** to cause to wither **2.** to make feel abashed, as by a scornful glance —**with′ering** *adj.*

withers (with′ərz) *n.pl.* [< OE. *wither*, against] the highest part of the back of a horse, etc., between the shoulder blades

withershins (with′ər shinz′) *adv.* [< MHG. *wider*, against + *sin*, direction] [Chiefly Scot.] in a direction contrary to the apparent course of the sun; anticlockwise

withhold (with hōld′) *vt.* -**held′**, -**hold′ing** **1.** to keep from giving; refuse [to *withhold* approval] **2.** to hold back; restrain

within (with in′) *prep.* [OE. *withinnan*] **1.** inside **2.** not more than [*within* a mile of home] **3.** inside the limits of [*within* the law] —*adv.* inside

without (with out′) *prep.* [OE. *withutan*] **1.** lacking [shoes *without* laces] **2.** not accompanied by **3.** free from [a man *without* fear] **4.** with avoidance of [to pass *without* speaking] **5.** [Archaic] outside —*adv.* [Archaic] outside —**go** (or **do**) **without** to manage although lacking something

withstand (with stand′) *vt., vi.* -**stood′**, -**stand′ing** to oppose, resist, or endure, esp. in a successful way

witless (wit′lis) *adj.* foolish —**wit′lessness** *n.*

witness (wit′nis) *n.* [OE. *gewitnes*, testimony] **1.** a person who saw, or can give a firsthand account of, something **2.** evidence; testimony **3.** a person who testifies in court **4.** a person who watches a will, etc. being signed and then, as proof that he did, signs it himself —*vt.* **1.** to be present at **2.** to serve as evidence of **3.** to be the scene of [this field *witnessed* a battle] **4.** to testify to **5.** to act as witness of (a contract, will, etc.) —**bear witness** to be or give evidence

witness box the place from which a witness gives his testimony in a law court: *U.S. name* **witness stand**

witticism (wit′i siz′m) *n.* a witty remark

witting (wit′iŋ) *adj.* [ME. *wytting*] intentional —**wit′tingly** *adv.*

witty (wit′ē) *adj.* **wit′tier, wit′tiest** [OE. *wittig*] cleverly amusing —**wit′tily** *adv.* —**wit′tiness** *n.*

wives (wīvz) *n. pl. of* WIFE

wizard (wiz′ərd) *n.* [ME. *wisard*] **1.** a magician; sorcerer **2.** [Colloq.] a person exceptionally gifted at a specified activity —*adj.* [Slang] outstanding; excellent

wizardry *n.* magic; sorcery

wizen (wiz′'n) *vt., vi.* [OE. *wisnian*] to dry up; wither; shrivel —**wiz′ened** *adj.*

wk. *pl.* **wks. 1.** week **2.** work

WNW, W.N.W., w.n.w. west-north-west

woad (wōd) *n.* [OE. *wad*] **1.** a plant with leaves that yield a blue dye **2.** this dye

wobble (wob′'l) *vi.* **-bled, -bling** [< LowG. *wabbeln*] **1.** to move from side to side in an unsteady way **2.** to shake; tremble **3.** to waver in mind —*vt.* to cause to wobble —*n.* an unsteady wobbling motion or sound —**wob′bliness** *n.* —**wob′bly** *adj.*

wodge (woj) *n.* [Colloq.] a thick lump or chunk

woe (wō) *n.* [OE. *wa*] **1.** great sorrow; grief **2.** [*often pl.*] misfortune —*interj.* alas!

woebegone (wō′bi gon′) *adj.* sad or mournful

woeful *adj.* **1.** sad; mournful **2.** of, causing, or involving woe **3.** pitiful; wretched —**woe′fully** *adv.* —**woe′fulness** *n.*

wog (wog) *n.* [< ?] [Derog. Slang] a foreigner, esp. one who is not white

woke (wōk) *alt. pt. & pp. of* WAKE[1]

woken *pp. of* WAKE[1]

wold (wōld) *n.* [OE. *wald*] a treeless, rolling plain, esp. a high one —**the Wolds** a range of chalk hills in NE England

wolf (woolf) *n., pl.* **wolves** [OE. *wulf*] **1.** any of a group of wild, flesh-eating, doglike mammals formerly widespread throughout the Northern Hemisphere **2.** [Colloq.] a man who boldly approaches women for sexual purposes —*vt.* to eat greedily (often with *down*) —**cry wolf** to give a false alarm —**keep the wolf from the door** to provide the necessities of life —**wolf in sheep's clothing** a malicious person in a harmless or friendly guise —**wolf′ish** *adj.*

Wolf Cub *former name of* CUB SCOUT

wolfhound *n.* a large dog of any of several breeds formerly used for hunting wolves

wolfram (wool′frəm) *n.* [G.] *same as* TUNGSTEN

wolframite *n.* [< G.] a brownish or blackish mineral, a compound of tungsten, iron, and manganese

wolfsbane (woolfs′bān′) *n.* *same as* ACONITE

wolf whistle a two-note whistle made by a man to express admiration of a woman and attract her attention

wolverine (wool′və rēn′) *n.* [< WOLF] a flesh-eating mammal found in the northern U.S.: the European variety is the GLUTTON Also *sp.* **wol′verene′**

wolves (woolvz) *n. pl. of* WOLF

woman (woom′ən) *n., pl.* **wom′en** (wim′-in) [< OE. *wif*, a female + *mann*, human being] **1.** an adult, female human being **2.** women as a group **3.** [Colloq.] a female domestic help —*adj.* female

womanhood *n.* **1.** the condition of being a woman **2.** womanly qualities **3.** womankind

womanish *adj.* like or suitable to a woman; feminine or effeminate

womanize *vi.* **-ized′, -iz′ing** [Colloq.] to be sexually promiscuous with women —**wom′aniz′er** *n.*

womanly *adj.* **1.** like a woman **2.** characteristic of or fit for a woman —**wom′-anliness** *n.*

womb (woom) *n.* [OE. *wamb*] **1.** *same as* UTERUS **2.** any place in which something is contained, developed, etc.

wombat (wom′bat) *n.* [< Abor. name] a burrowing Australian marsupial that looks like a small bear

women (wim′in) *n. pl. of* WOMAN

Women's Institute a society for women chiefly in rural areas, with regular meetings for craft and cultural activities

Women's Liberation a movement among women to eradicate all inequalities in social and economic life that are based on the assumption that men are superior to women: also **Women's Lib**

women's rights the rights claimed by and for women of equal privileges and opportunities with men

won (wun) *pt. & pp. of* WIN

wonder (wun′dər) *n.* [OE. *wundor*] **1.** the feeling of surprise, amazement, etc. caused by something strange, remarkable, etc. **2.** a person, thing, or event so unusual as to cause this feeling **3.** a miracle —*vi.* **1.** to feel wonder; marvel **2.** to have curiosity, sometimes mixed with doubt —*vt.* to have curiosity or doubt about *[I wonder what he meant]* —**no wonder!** now I know why! —**won′derment** *n.*

wonderful *adj.* **1.** marvellous; amazing **2.** [Colloq.] very good; excellent —**won′-derfully** *adv.*

wonderland *n.* an imaginary place full of wonders, or a real place like this

wonder-struck *adj.* struck with wonder, surprise, admiration, etc.

wondrous (wun′drəs) *adj., adv.* [Now Rare] wonderful(ly) —**won′drously** *adv.*

wonky (woŋ′kē) *adj.* **-kier, -kiest** [< OE. *wancal*, shaky] [Slang] shaky; unsteady; unreliable

wont (wōnt) *adj.* [< OE. *wunian*, be used to] accustomed *[he was wont to rise early]* —*n.* usual practice; habit

wonted (wōn′tid) *adj.* customary; accustomed

woo (woo) *vt.* [OE. *wogian*] **1.** to try to get the love of; court **2.** to seek *[to* *woo* fame*]* **3.** to coax; urge —*vi.* to court a person —**woo′er** *n.*

wood (wood) *n.* [OE. *wudu*] **1.** the hard, fibrous substance beneath the bark of trees and shrubs **2.** timber **3.** [*usually pl.*] a thick growth of trees; forest **4.** firewood **5.** *a)* a wooden cask [whisky aged in *wood*] *b)* any of the biased wooden bowls used in the game of bowls *c)* *Golf* any of a set of numbered clubs with wooden heads —*adj.* **1.** wooden **2.** for cutting, shaping, or holding wood **3.** growing or living in woods —**cannot see the wood for the trees** lose sight of larger issues in a mass of detail —**out of the wood** [Colloq.] out of difficulty, danger, etc.

woodbine *n.* [see WOOD & BIND] the wild honeysuckle

woodcarving *n.* **1.** the art or craft of carving wood by hand **2.** an object so made —**wood′carv′er** *n.*

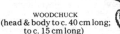

WOODCHUCK
(head & body to c. 40 cm long;
to c. 15 cm long)

woodchuck (wood′chuk′) *n.* [< Algonquian name] a N American animal that burrows in the ground and sleeps all winter

woodcock *n.* a game bird with short legs and a long bill

woodcraft *n.* **1.** matters relating to the woods, as camping, hunting, etc. **2.** same as: *a)* WOODWORKING *b)* WOODCARVING

woodcut *n.* **1.** a wooden block engraved with a design, etc. **2.** a print made from this

woodcutter *n.* a person who fells trees, cuts wood, etc.

wooded *adj.* covered with trees

wooden *adj.* **1.** made of wood **2.** stiff; clumsy **3.** dull; insensitive —**wood′enly** *adv.* —**wood′enness** *n.*

woodenheaded *adj.* [Colloq.] dull; stupid —**wood′enhead′edness** *n.*

woodland *n.* land covered with woods or trees —*adj.* of or living in woods

woodlouse *n.,* *pl.* **-lice** a small, terrestrial crustacean with a flat, oval body, living in damp places, as under rocks

woodpecker *n.* a tree-climbing bird with a strong, pointed bill used to drill holes in bark to get insects

wood pigeon a common pigeon, resembling the domestic pigeon, but larger, with white patches on the wings and neck: also called **ring′dove**

woodpile *n.* a pile of wood, esp. of firewood

wood pulp pulp made from wood fibre, used in paper manufacture

woodruff (wood′ruf′) *n.* [OE. *wudurofe*]

a plant with small white, sweet-scented flowers

woodshed *n.* a shed for storing firewood

wood sorrel any of a group of plants with white, pink, or yellow, five-petalled flowers

woodwind *n.* the wind instruments of an orchestra made, esp. originally, of wood —*adj.* of or for such instruments

woodwork *n.* **1.** work done in wood **2.** things made of wood, esp. the interior mouldings, doors, stairs, etc. of a house

woodworking *n.* the art or work of making things out of wood —**wood′work′er** *n.*

woodworm *n.* any of a number of insect larvae that live on and burrow in wood

woody *adj.* **-ier, -iest** **1.** covered with trees; wooded **2.** consisting of or like wood —**wood′iness** *n.*

woody nightshade a plant of the nightshade family with purple flowers and poisonous, red berries

woof[1] (woof) *n.* [< OE. *wefan*, to weave] *same as* WEFT

woof[2] (woof) *n.* a gruff barking sound of or like that of a dog —*vi.* to make such a sound

woofer (woof′ər) *n.* [< prec.] in an assembly of two or more loudspeakers, a large speaker for reproducing low-frequency sounds

wool (wool) *n.* [OE. *wull*] **1.** the soft, curly hair of sheep or of some other animals, as the goat **2.** *a)* yarn spun from the fibres of such hair *b)* cloth, clothing, etc. made of this yarn **3.** anything that looks or feels like wool —*adj.* of wool or woollen goods —**pull the wool over someone's eyes** to deceive someone —**wool′like′** *adj.*

wool fat **1.** the natural grease found in a sheep's wool, yielding lanolin **2.** *same as* LANOLIN

woolgathering *n.* absent-mindedness or daydreaming

woolgrower *n.* a person who raises sheep for wool —**wool′grow′ing** *n.*

woollen *adj.* **1.** made of wool **2.** of or relating to wool or woollen cloth —*n.* [*pl.*] woollen goods or clothing U.S. sp. **wool′en**

woolly *adj.* **wool′lier, wool′liest** **1.** of or like wool **2.** bearing wool **3.** covered with wool or something like wool in texture **4.** confused; fuzzy [*woolly* ideas] —*n.,* *pl.* **wool′lies** a knitted garment, as a cardigan —**wool′liness** *n.*

woolpack *n.* **1.** a large bag in which to pack wool for sale **2.** a bale of wool so packed

woolsack *n.* **1.** in Britain, a cushion stuffed with wool, on which the Lord Chancellor sits in the House of Lords **2.** the office of Lord Chancellor

woozy (woo′zē) *adj.* **-ier, -iest** [Colloq.] **1.** dizzy, faint, and sickish **2.** befuddled, as from drink —**wooz′ily** *adv.* —**wooz′iness** *n.*

wop (wop) *n.* [< ?] [Derog. Slang] a member of a Latin people, esp. an Italian

Worcester sauce (woos′tər) [orig. made

in *Worcester*] a spicy sauce for meats, poultry, etc.

word (wurd) *n.* [OE.] **1.** *a*) a speech sound, or series of speech sounds, serving to communicate meaning *b*) a letter or group of letters representing such a unit of language **2.** a remark *[a word of advice]* **3.** a promise **4.** news; information *[no word from home]* **5.** *a*) a password *b*) a command **6.** [*usually pl.*] *a*) talk; speech *b*) lyrics; text **7.** [*pl.*] a quarrel **8.** an ordered combination of characters with meaning, regarded as a unit and stored in a computer —*vt.* to express in words; phrase —**a good word** a commendation —**by word of mouth** by speech; orally —**in a word** in short —**in so many words** precisely; explicitly —**of many** (or **few**) **words** talkative (or untalkative) —**put words into a person's mouth 1.** to impute a statement to a person who has not said it **2.** to tell a person what to say —**take a person at his word** take action in the belief that someone meant what he said —**take the words out of one's mouth** to have someone else say what one was about to say oneself —**the Word** the Bible : also **Word of God** —**(upon) my word!** indeed! really! —**word for word** in precisely the same words —**word′less** *adj.* —**word′-lessly** *adv.*

word blindness *same as:* **1.** ALEXIA **2.** DYSLEXIA

word game any game involving the formation, discovery, or alteration of a word or words

wording *n.* choice and arrangement of words

word of honour pledged word; solemn promise

word order the arrangement of words in a phrase, clause, or sentence

word-perfect (wurd′pur′fikt) *adj.* knowing one's lesson, theatrical role, etc. perfectly by heart

word processing the storage and organization of language by electronic means, esp. for business purposes —**word processor**

wordy *adj.* **-ier, -iest** containing or using too many words; verbose —**word′iness** *n.*

wore (wôr) *pt. of* WEAR[1]

work (wurk) *n.* [OE. *weorc*] **1.** physical or mental effort exerted to do or make something; labour; toil **2.** *a*) employment at a job *[out of work]* *b*) one's place of employment **3.** occupation, profession, business, trade, etc. **4.** something one is making or doing; task **5.** something made or done; specif., *a*) an act; deed *[good works]* *b*) [*pl.*] collected writings *c*) [*pl.*] engineering structures, as bridges, dams, etc. *d*) a fortification *e*) needlework **6.** [*pl., with sing. v.*] a place where something is manufactured, as a factory **7.** workmanship **8.** *Mech.* transference of force from one body or system to another, measured by the product of the force and the amount of displacement in the line of force —*adj.* of, for, or used in work —*vi.* **1.** to do work; labour; toil **2.** to

be employed **3.** *a*) to function; operate *b*) to operate effectively **4.** to undergo fermentation **5.** to produce results or exert an influence **6.** to be manipulated, kneaded, etc. **7.** to move, proceed, etc. slowly and with difficulty **8.** to move, twitch, etc. as from agitation *[his face worked with emotion]* **9.** to change into a specified condition, as by repeated movement *[the handle worked loose]* —*vt.* **1.** to carry on activity in, along, etc.; cover *[a salesman working his territory]* **2.** to cause to work **3.** to operate; use **4.** to cultivate (soil) **5.** to manipulate; knead **6.** to mould; shape **7.** to bring into a specified condition, as by moving back and forth *[to work a nail loose]* **8.** to influence; persuade **9.** to provoke; rouse *[to work oneself into a rage]* **10.** to cause; bring about *[his idea worked wonders]* **11.** to make (one's way, etc.) by effort **12.** to sew, embroider, etc. **13.** [Colloq.] to manipulate to one's own advantage —**at work** working —**get** (or **give one**) **the works** [Slang] to be (or cause one to be) the victim of an ordeal —**have one's work cut out (for one)** to have difficulty in accomplishing one's task —**make short** (or **quick**) **work of** to deal with quickly —**out of work** unemployed —**the works 1.** the working parts (*of* a watch, clock, etc.) **2.** everything —**work in** to insert or be inserted —**work off 1.** to get rid of, as by exertion **2.** to pay (a debt or obligation) by work instead of money —**work on 1.** to influence **2.** to try to persuade —**work out 1.** to accomplish **2.** to solve **3.** to exhaust (a mine, etc.) **4.** to result in some way **5.** to calculate **6.** to reach a total *[it works out at £1 each]* **7.** to develop; elaborate —**work over** [Colloq.] to subject to harsh or cruel treatment —**work to rule** to adhere strictly to all working regulations in order to reduce the rate of working, as a form of industrial action —**work up 1.** to advance; rise **2.** to develop; elaborate **3.** to arouse; excite

workable *adj.* **1.** practicable; feasible **2.** that can be worked

workaday *adj.* **1.** commonplace; ordinary **2.** of or suitable for working days

workbasket *n.* a container for sewing equipment

workbench *n.* a table at which work is done, as by a mechanic, carpenter, etc.

worker *n.* **1.** one who works for a living **2.** a person who works for a cause, etc. **3.** any of various sterile female ants, bees, etc. that do work for the colony

work force the total number of workers actively employed in, or available for, work

workhouse *n.* formerly, a poorhouse

work-in *n.* a form of industrial action in which a factory that is to be closed is occupied and run by its workers

working *adj.* **1.** that works **2.** used in work **3.** sufficient to get work done *[a working majority]* **4.** on which further work may be based *[a working hypothesis]* —*n.* **1.** the act or process of a person or thing that works **2.** [*usually pl.*] a part of a mine, quarry, etc. where work is or has been done —**in working order** fit or ready to operate

working class workers as a class; esp., industrial or manual workers —**work′ing-class′** *adj.*

working day 1. a day on which work is done 2. the part of a day during which work is done

workingman *n.* a worker; esp., an industrial or manual worker; wage earner; labourer

working party a body appointed to investigate a problem, question, etc.

workload *n.* the amount of work assigned to be completed within a given time

workman *n.* 1. *same as* WORKINGMAN 2. a craftsman

workmanlike *adj.* characteristic of a good workman; skilful

workmanship *n.* 1. skill of a workman; craftsmanship 2. something produced by this skill

work of art 1. something produced in one of the fine arts, as a painting, sculpture, etc. 2. anything made, performed, etc. with great skill and beauty

work-out *n.* a session of physical exercise, esp. for training

workroom *n.* a room in which work is done

workshop *n.* 1. a room or building where work is done 2. a seminar or series of meetings for intensive study, work, etc. in some field [a writers' *workshop*]

work-shy *adj.* avoiding work; lazy

worktable *n.* a table at which work is done, esp. one with drawers for tools, materials, etc.

work-to-rule *n.* a form of industrial action in which employees adhere strictly to all working regulations, in order to reduce their rate of working and efficiency

world (wurld) *n.* [OE. *werold*] 1. *a*) the planet earth *b*) the whole universe 2. the earth and its inhabitants 3. *a*) mankind *b*) people generally 4. *a*) [*also* W-] some part of the earth [the Old *World*] *b*) some period of its history, society, etc. [the ancient *world*] *c*) any sphere or domain [the animal *world*] 5. experience, outlook, etc. [his *world* is narrow] 6. secular life and interests 7. [*often pl.*] great deal [to do a *world* (or *worlds*) of good] —**come into the world** to be born —**dead to the world** unaware of one's surroundings, esp. asleep or drunk —**on top of the world** very happy; elated

World Bank an agency (officially **International Bank for Reconstruction and Development**) of the UN, established in 1945 to make loans to member nations

worldbeater *n.* [Colloq.] one that is, or has the qualities needed to become, a great success

World Cup an award given in a competition held every four years between football teams of various countries

worldly *adj.* **-lier, -liest** 1. of this world; temporal or secular 2. concerned with the affairs, pleasures, etc. of this world 3. worldly-wise —**world′liness** *n.*

worldly-wise *adj.* wise in the ways of the world; sophisticated

world-shaking *adj.* of great importance; momentous

World War I the war (1914–18) between the Allies (Great Britain, France, Russia, the U.S., Italy, Japan, etc.) and the Central Powers (Germany, Austria-Hungary, etc.)

World War II the war (1939–45) between the Allies (Great Britain, France, the Soviet Union, the U.S., etc.) and the Axis (Germany, Italy, Japan, etc.)

world-weary *adj.* bored with living

worldwide *adj.* extending throughout the world

worm (wurm) *n.* [OE. *wyrm*, serpent] 1. a long, slender, soft-bodied, limbless invertebrate 2. popularly, an insect larva, as a grub or maggot 3. any of various wormlike animals, as the glow worm 4. a person looked down on as being too meek, wretched, etc. 5. a short, rotating screw that meshes with the teeth of a worm wheel or a rack 6. [*pl.*] *Med.* any disease caused by parasitic worms in the intestines, etc. —*vi.* to move, proceed, etc. like a worm, in a winding, creeping, or roundabout manner —*vt.* 1. to bring about, get, make, etc. in a winding, creeping, or roundabout manner 2. to purge of intestinal worms —**the worm will turn** a hitherto meek, yielding person will suddenly assert his will if provoked too far —**worm′like′** *adj.*

wormcast *n.* a coil of earth that has been excreted by an earthworm

worm-eaten *adj.* eaten into by worms, termites, etc.

worm gear 1. *same as* WORM WHEEL 2. a gear consisting of a worm and worm wheel

wormhole *n.* a hole made, as in wood, by a worm, termite, etc.

worm wheel a toothed wheel designed to gear with the thread of a worm

wormwood (wurm′wood′) *n.* [< OE. *wermod*] 1. a plant that yields a bitter-tasting, dark-green oil (**wormwood oil**) used in making absinthe 2. a bitter, unpleasant experience

wormy *adj.* **-ier, -iest** 1. worm-infested 2. *same as* WORM-EATEN 3. like a worm 4. debased; grovelling —**worm′iness** *n.*

worn (wôrn) *pp.* of WEAR[1] —*adj.* 1. damaged by use or wear 2. showing the effects of worry or anxiety 3. exhausted; spent

worn-out *adj.* 1. used or worn until no longer effective, usable, or serviceable 2. exhausted; tired out

worrisome (wur′ē səm) *adj.* causing worry or anxiety

worry (wur′ē) *vt.* **-ried, -rying** [OE. *wyrgan*, strangle] 1. to make troubled or uneasy 2. to annoy; bother 3. *a*) to treat roughly, as with continual biting [a dog *worrying* a bone] *b*) to pluck at, touch, etc. repeatedly in a nervous way —*vi.* 1. to be anxious, troubled, etc. 2. to manage to get (*along or through*) difficulties 3. to bite, pull, or tear (*at*

an object) with the teeth —*n., pl.* **-ries**
1. a troubled state of mind; anxiety **2.**
something that causes anxiety —**wor′ri·er** *n.*
worry beads a string of beads that when
fingered or played with supposedly relieves
nervous tension
worse (wʉrs) *adj. compar.* of BAD[1] &
ILL [OE. *wiersa*] **1.** *a)* bad, evil, harmful,
etc. in a greater degree *b)* of inferior
quality **2.** in poorer health **3.** in a less
satisfactory situation —*adv. compar.* of
BADLY & ILL in a worse manner; to a
worse extent —*n.* that which is worse
—**for the worse** to a worse condition
—**worse off** financially poorer
worsen *vt., vi.* to make or become worse
worship (wʉr′ship) *n.* [< OE.: see WORTH
& -SHIP] **1.** *a)* reverence or devotion for
a deity *b)* a church service or other rite
showing this **2.** intense love or admiration
3. a title of honour (preceded by *your*
or *his*) used in addressing magistrates,
etc. —*vt.* **-shipped, -shipping 1.** to show
religious reverence for **2.** to have intense
love or admiration for —*vi.* to engage
in worship —**wor′shipper** *n.*
worshipful *adj.* **1.** honourable; respected
2. feeling or offering great devotion or
respect
worst (wʉrst) *adj. superl.* of BAD[1] & ILL
[OE. *wyrsta*] **1.** *a)* bad, evil, harmful,
etc. in the greatest degree *b)* of the lowest
quality or condition **2.** in the least
satisfactory situation —*adv. superl.* of
BADLY & ILL in the worst manner; to
the worst extent —*n.* that which is worst
—*vt.* to get the better of; defeat —**if
the worst comes to the worst** if the
worst possible thing happens
worsted (woos′tid) *n.* [< *Worstead,*
Norfolk] **1.** a smooth, hard-twisted
woollen yarn **2.** fabric made from this
—*adj.* made of worsted
wort[1] (wʉrt) *n.* [< OE. *wyrt-*] a liquid
prepared with malt which, after fermenting,
becomes beer, ale, etc.
wort[2] *n.* [OE. *wyrt,* a root] a plant or
herb: now usually in compounds [*liverwort*]
worth (wʉrth) *adj.* [OE. *weorth*] [with
prepositional force] **1.** deserving or
worthy of **2.** equal in value to **3.** having
wealth amounting to —*n.* **1.** material value,
esp. as expressed in money **2.** importance;
value **3.** the quantity of something that
may be had for a given sum [*four pounds'
worth* of petrol] —**for all one is worth**
to the utmost
worthless *adj.* useless, valueless, etc.
—**worth′lessness** *n.*
worthwhile (wʉrth′wīl′) *adj.* important
or valuable enough to repay time or effort
spent
worthy (wʉr′thē) *adj.* **-thier, -thiest 1.**
deserving; meriting (often with *of* or an
infinitive) **2.** having worth, value, or merit
—*n., pl.* **-thies** a person of outstanding
worth or importance —**wor′thily** *adv.*
—**wor′thiness** *n.*
would (wood; *unstressed* wəd) *v.* [OE.
wolde] **1.** *pt.* of WILL[2] **2.** an auxiliary

used to express *a)* condition [if you *would*]
b) futurity [he said he *would* come] *c)*
habitual action [on Sundays he *would* sleep
late] *d)* a request [*would* you please leave?]
3. I wish [*would* that she were here]
would-be *adj.* wishing or pretending to be
wound[1] (woond) *n.* [OE. *wund*] **1.** an
injury in which the skin or other tissue
is broken, cut, torn, etc. **2.** any hurt
to the feelings, honour, etc. —*vt., vi.* to
inflict a wound (*on* or *upon*); injure
wound[2] (wound) *pt. & pp.* of WIND[1]
wove (wōv) *pt. & alt. pp.* of WEAVE
woven *alt. pp.* of WEAVE
wow (wou) *interj.* an exclamation of
surprise, pleasure, pain, etc. —*n.* [Chiefly
U.S. Slang] a remarkable, exciting, etc.
person or thing —*vt.* [Chiefly U.S. Slang]
to be a great success with
wpm words per minute
W.R.A.C. Women's Royal Army Corps
wrack (rak) *n.* [< OE. *wræc,* misery]
1. ruin; destruction : now chiefly in **wrack
and ruin 2.** seaweed, etc. cast up on shore
W.R.A.F. Women's Royal Air Force
wraith (rāth) *n.* [Scot.] **1.** a ghostlike
figure of a person supposedly seen just
before his death **2.** a ghost
wrangle (raŋ′g'l) *vi.* **-gled, -gling** [< ME.
wringen, to WRING] to quarrel angrily
and noisily —*vt.* [US & Canad.) to herd
(cattle or horses) —*n.* an angry, noisy
quarrel
wrap (rap) *vt.* **wrapped, wrap′ping** [ME.
wrappen] **1.** to wind or fold (a covering)
round something **2.** to envelop; conceal
[a town *wrapped* in fog] **3.** to enclose
and fasten in paper, etc. —*vi.* to twine,
extend, coil, etc. (usually with *over, round,*
etc.) —*n.* an outer covering or garment
—**wrapped up in** absorbed in —**wrap up
1.** to enfold in a covering **2.** to put on
warm clothing **3.** *a)* [Colloq.] to bring
to an end *b)* [Slang] to be quiet
wraparound *adj.* **1.** that is wrapped
around the body [a *wraparound* skirt]
2. moulded, etc. so as to curve
wrapper *n.* **1.** the covering of paper,
polythene, etc., in which a sweet, biscuit,
etc. is enclosed **2.** the dust jacket of
a book **3.** the paper in which a magazine,
etc. is enclosed for posting **4.** a loose
garment, as a woman's dressing gown
wrapping *n.* [often *pl.*] the material,
as paper, in which something is wrapped
wrath (roth) *n.* [OE., *wroth*] intense
anger; rage —**wrath′ful** *adj.*
wreak (rēk) *vt.* [OE. *wrecan,* to revenge]
1. to inflict (vengeance), cause (havoc),
etc. **2.** to give free play to (anger, malice,
etc.)
wreath (rēth) *n., pl.* **wreaths** (rēthz) [OE.
writhan, to twist] **1.** a twisted band or
ring of leaves, flowers, etc. **2.** something
suggesting this in shape [*wreaths* of smoke]
wreathe (rēth) *vt.* **wreathed, wreath′ing
1.** to form into a wreath **2.** to entwine
round; encircle [clouds *wreathe* the hills]
3. to cover [a face *wreathed* in smiles]
—*vi.* to have a twisting or coiling
movement

wreck (rek) *vt.* [< ON. *vrek*, driftwood]
1. to destroy or damage badly 2. to
overthrow; thwart —*vi.* to be wrecked
—*n.* 1. a shipwreck 2. the remains of
anything that has been destroyed or badly
damaged 3. a person in very poor health
4. a wrecking or being wrecked; ruin

wreckage *n.* 1. the remains of something
that has been wrecked 2. a wrecking
or being wrecked

wrecker *n.* 1. a person or thing that
wrecks 2. formerly, a person who lured
ships to destruction on rocky coasts in
order to plunder the wreckage

Wren (ren) *n.* [< initials *W.R.N.S.*] a
member of the Women's Royal Naval
Service

wren (ren) *n.* [OE. *wrenna*] a small,
songbird having a long bill, rounded wings,
and a stubby, erect tail

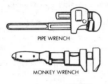

PIPE WRENCH

MONKEY WRENCH

TYPES OF
WRENCH

MOLE WRENCH

wrench (rench) *n.* [OE. *wrenc*, a trick]
1. a sudden, sharp twist or pull 2. an
injury caused by a twist or jerk, as to
the back 3. a sudden feeling of grief,
etc., as at parting from someone 4. a
tool for holding and turning nuts, bolts,
etc. —*vt.* 1. to twist, pull, or jerk violently
2. to injure (a part of the body) by wrenching
—*vi.* to pull (*at* something) with a
wrenching movement

wrest (rest) *vt.* [OE. *wræstan*] 1. to
pull or force away violently with a twisting
motion 2. to take by force; usurp —*n.*
a wresting; twist; wrench

wrestle (res′l) *vi.*, *vt.* -tled, -tling [<
OE. *wræstan*, to twist] 1. to struggle
hand to hand with (an opponent) in an
attempt to throw or force him to the
ground without striking blows 2. to
struggle hard (*with* a problem, etc.) —*n.*
1. a wrestling; wrestling bout 2. a struggle
or contest —**wres′tler** *n.*

wrestling (res′liŋ) *n.* a sport in which
the opponents wrestle

wretch (rech) *n.* [OE. *wrecca*, an outcast]
1. a miserable or unhappy person 2. a
person who is despised or scorned

wretched (rech′id) *adj.* [OE. *wræcc*] 1.
very unhappy 2. causing misery [*wretched*
slums] 3. very inferior 4. deserving to
be despised —**wretch′edly** *adv.* —**wretch′-
edness** *n.*

wrick (rik) *vt.*, *n.* [< ME. *wrikken*, move
jerkily] sprain or wrench

wriggle (rig′l) *vi.* **wrig′gled, wrig′gling**
[MLowG. *wriggeln*] 1. to twist and turn;
squirm 2. to move along with a twisting
motion 3. to make one's way by subtle
or shifty means —*vt.* to cause to wriggle
—*n.* a wriggling —**wrig′gly** *adj.*

wright (rīt) *n.* [OE. *wyrcan*, to work]
a person who makes: used chiefly in
compounds [*shipwright*]

wring (riŋ) *vt.* **wrung, wring′ing** [OE.
wringan] 1. *a*) to squeeze, press, or twist,
esp. so as to force out water *b*) to force
out (water, etc.) 2. to twist (the hands)
together as an expression of distress 3.
to clasp (another's hand) forcefully in
greeting 4. to extract by force, threats,
persistence, etc. 5. to afflict with anguish,
pity, etc. [the story *wrung* her heart]
—*vi.* to squirm or twist with great effort
—*n.* a wringing —**wringing wet** soaked;
drenched

wringer *n.* a device with two rollers
close together between which wet clothes
are run to squeeze out the water

wrinkle[1] (riŋ′k'l) *n.* [< OE. (*ge*)*wrinclian*,
to wind] 1. a small ridge or furrow in
a normally smooth surface 2. a crease
or pucker in the skin —*vt.*, *vi.* **-kled,
-kling** to contract or pucker into small
ridges or creases —**wrin′kly** *adj.*

wrinkle[2] *n.* [prob. < OE. *wrenc*, a trick]
[Colloq.] a piece of useful information; tip

wrist (rist) *n.* [OE.] the joint or part
of the arm between the hand and the forearm

wristwatch *n.* a watch worn on a strap
or band round the wrist

writ (rit) *n.* [OE. < *writan*, write] a formal
legal document ordering or prohibiting
some action

write (rīt) *vt.* **wrote, writ′ten, writ′ing**
[OE. *writan*] 1. *a*) to form (words, letters,
etc.) on a surface, esp. with a pen or
pencil *b*) to form the words, letters, etc.
of [*write* your name] 2. to spell (a word,
etc.) 3. to be the author or composer
of 4. to fill in (a cheque, form, etc.)
with the writing required 5. to
communicate in writing [he *wrote* that
he was ill] 6. [Colloq. & U.S.] to
communicate with in writing [*write* me
every day] 7. to record in writing, etc.
8. to leave signs or evidence of [greed
was *written* on his face] —*vi.* 1. to write
words 2. to write books, etc. 3. to write
a letter 4. to produce writing of a specified
kind [to *write* legibly] —**write down** 1.
to put into written form 2. to discredit
in writing 3. to write in a very simple
style so as to be easily understood —**write
off** 1. to cancel or remove from accounts
(bad debts, etc.) 2. to drop from
consideration 3. to cause, or acknowledge,
the complete destruction of —**write out**
1. to put into writing 2. to write in
full —**write up** 1. to write an account
of 2. to praise in writing 3. to bring
a piece of writing, as a diary, up to date

writer *n.* a person who writes, esp. as
a business or occupation; author,
journalist, etc.

write-off *n.* [Colloq.] something
damaged beyond repair, esp. a car

write-up *n.* a published account of something; review

writhe (ri*th*) *vt.* **writhed, writh'ing** [OE. *writhan,* to twist] to cause to twist or turn; contort —*vi.* **1.** to make twisting movements; squirm **2.** to suffer great emotional distress —*n.* a writhing movement

writing (rīt'iŋ) *n.* **1.** letters or symbols written on a surface **2.** the act of a person who writes **3.** a letter, document, etc. **4.** *short for* HANDWRITING **5.** a literary work **6.** the profession of a writer **7.** the art, style, etc. of literary composition —*adj.* **1.** that writes **2.** used in writing —**the writing on the wall** signs of approaching disaster

writing desk a piece of furniture with a writing surface and drawers and compartments for papers, etc.

written (rit''n) *pp. of* WRITE —*adj.* put down in a form to be read

W.R.N.S. (renz) Women's Royal Naval Service

wrong (rôŋ) *adj.* [< ON. *rangr,* twisted] **1.** *a)* incorrect *b)* mistaken **2.** not just, moral, etc. **3.** not in accordance with an established standard, etc. [the *wrong* method] **4.** not suitable or appropriate **5.** in an unsatisfactory or bad condition **6.** not functioning properly [what's *wrong* with the light?] **7.** designating the unfinished, inner, or under side [the *wrong* side of a fabric] —*adv.* in a wrong manner, direction, etc. —*n.* **1.** something wrong, esp. an unjust or immoral act **2.** *Law* a violation of a legal right —*vt.* **1.** to treat badly or unjustly **2.** to think badly of without real justification —**get hold of the wrong end of the stick** to misunderstand completely —**get (someone or something) wrong** [Colloq.] to fail to understand (someone or something) —**in the wrong** not on the side supported by truth, justice, etc. —**wrong'ly** *adv.* —**wrong'ness** *n.*

wrongdoing *n.* any act or behaviour that is wrong —**wrong'do'er** *n.*

wrongful *adj.* **1.** unjust, unfair, or injurious **2.** unlawful [*wrongful* dismissal] —**wrong'fully** *adv.*

wrongheaded (roŋ'hed'id) *adj.* stubborn in sticking to wrong opinions, ideas, etc.; perverse

wrong' un 1. [Colloq.] a bad character **2.** *Cricket* a googly

wrote (rôt) *pt. of* WRITE

wroth (rôth) *adj.* [OE. *wrath*] [Obs.] angry; wrathful

wrought (rôt) *archaic pt. & pp. of* WORK —*adj.* **1.** shaped by hammering: said of metals **2.** formed; fashioned **3.** elaborated with care

wrought iron a kind of iron that contains very little carbon: it is tough but easy to work or shape —**wrought'-i'ron** *adj.*

wrung (ruŋ) *pt. & pp. of* WRING

W.R.V.S. Women's Royal Voluntary Service

wry (rī) *adj.* **wri'er, wri'est** [OE. *wrigian,* to turn] **1.** twisted; distorted **2.** made by twisting or distorting the features **3.** perverse; ironic [*wry* humour] —*vt., vi.* **wried, wry'ing** to writhe or twist —**wry'-ly** *adv.* —**wry'ness** *n.*

wryneck *n.* **1.** a bird related to the woodpecker, noted for its habit of twisting its neck **2.** a condition in which the neck is twisted by a muscle spasm

WSW, W.S.W., w.s.w. west-south-west

wt. weight

wych-elm (wich'elm') *n.* [< OE. *wice,* pliant + ELM] a small variety of elm native to Europe and N Asia

wynd (wīnd) *n.* [< ME. *winden,* WIND[1]] [Scot.] a narrow lane or alley

WX women's extra large size

X

X, x (eks) *n., pl.* **X's, x's** the twenty-fourth letter of the English alphabet

X (eks) *n.* **1.** a mark shaped like X, used to represent the signature of a person who cannot write, to mark a particular point on a map, etc. **2.** the Roman numeral for 10 **3.** a person or thing unknown **4.** *Cinema* a film to which no one under the age of eighteen may be admitted —*adj.* shaped like X

x *Math.* a symbol for: *a)* an unknown quantity *b)* times (in multiplication) [3 × 3 = 9]

xanthein (zan′thē in) *n.* [Fr. *xanthéine*] the water-soluble part of the yellow pigment in some plants

xanthine (zan′thēn) *n.* [Fr.] a white, crystalline nitrogenous compound present in blood, urine, and certain plants

Xanthippe (zan thip′ē) *n.* [< wife of Socrates] a nagging or quarrelsome wife: also **Xantippe** (zan tip′ē)

x-axis *n., pl.* **x′-ax′es** *Math.* the horizontal axis along which the abscissa is measured

X chromosome see SEX CHROMOSOME

Xe *Chem.* xenon

xebec (zē′bek) *n.* [< Fr. < Ar. *shabbāk*] a small, three-masted ship, once common in the Mediterranean

xeno- [< Gr.] *a combining form meaning:* **1.** stranger, foreigner **2.** strange, foreign

xenon (ze′non) *n.* [Gr., strange] a heavy, colourless, gaseous chemical element present in the air in minute quantities: symbol, Xe

xenophobia (zen′ə fō′bē ə) *n.* [see XENO- & -PHOBIA] fear or hatred of strangers or foreigners —**xen′opho′bic** *adj.*

xerography (zēə rog′rə fē) *n.* [< Gr. *xēros*, dry + -GRAPHY] a process for copying printed material, etc., in which an image of the material is electrically charged on a surface and attracts oppositely charged dry ink particles, which are then fused in place

Xerox (zēar′oks) *Trademark* a device for copying printed material, etc. by xerography —*n.* a copy made by such a device —*vt., vi.* to reproduce by such a device

Xhosa (kô′sə) *n.* **1.** *pl.* **Xho′sas, Xho′-** sa any member of a people living in Cape Province, South Africa **2.** their language, characterized by clicks

xi (zī, sī) *n.* the fourteenth letter of the Greek alphabet (Ξ, ξ)

XL extra large size

Xmas (kris′məs; *occas.* eks′məs) *n.* [X (chi), 1st letter in Gr. *Christos*, Christ + -MAS] *same as* CHRISTMAS

X-ray *n.* **1.** an electromagnetic ray or radiation of very short wavelength produced by the bombardment of a metal by a stream of electrons, as in a vacuum tube: X-rays can penetrate solid substances and are widely used in medicine to study the bones, organs, etc. inside the body and to diagnose and treat certain disorders **2.** a photograph made by means of X-rays —*vt.* to examine, treat, or photograph with X-rays Also **x-ray**

xylem (zī′ləm) *n.* [G. < Gr. *xylon*, wood] the woody tissue of a plant, which contains cells that conduct water, minerals, etc.

xylene (zī′lēn) *n.* [< Gr. *xylon*, wood] any of three isomeric, colourless hydrocarbons, with the characteristics of benzene and derived from coal tar, and petroleum: used as solvents, antiseptics, etc.

XYLOPHONE

xylophone (zī′lə fōn′) *n.* [< Gr. *xylon*, wood + -PHONE] a musical instrument consisting of a series of graduated wooden bars struck with small wooden hammers —**xyloph′onist** (zī lof′ə nist) *n.*

xylose (zī′lōs) *n.* [< Gr. *xylon*, wood] a colourless sugar derived from wood, straw, etc. and used in dyeing, diabetic foods, etc.

Y

Y, y (wī) *n.,* *pl.* **Y's, y's** the twenty-fifth letter of the English alphabet

Y (wī) *n.* something shaped like Y

Y *Chem.* yttrium

y *Math. a symbol for:* **1.** the second of a set of unknown quantities, *x* usually being the first **2.** an ordinate

-y¹ (ē, i) [< ME.] *a suffix meaning* little, dear: used in forming diminutives, nicknames, etc. [*kitty, Billy*]

-y² [< OE.] *a suffix meaning:* **1.** having, full of [*dirty*] **2.** rather [*chilly*] **3.** tending to [*sticky*] **4.** suggestive of [*wavy*]

-y³ [< L. *-ia*] *a suffix meaning:* **1.** quality or condition of (being) [*jealousy*] **2.** a shop, group, etc. of a specified kind [*bakery*]

-y⁴ [< L. *-ium*] *a suffix meaning* action of [*inquiry*]

y. year(s)

yabber (ya'bər) *vi., n.* [Abor.] [Chiefly Aust. Colloq.] talk; jabber

yacht (yot) *n.* [Du. *jacht*] a large boat or small ship for pleasure cruises, races, etc. —*vi.* to sail in a yacht —**yacht'ing** *n.*

yachtsman *n.* a person who owns or sails a yacht

yack, yack-yack, yackety-yack *var. of* YAK², etc.

yah (yä) *interj.* a shout of scorn, defiance, etc.

Yahoo (yə hōō') *n.* **1.** in Swift's *Gulliver's Travels,* any of a race of coarse, brutish creatures **2.** [y-] a vicious, coarse person

Yahweh, Yahwe (yä'wä) God: a form of the Hebrew name in the Scriptures

yak¹ (yak) *n.* [Tibetan *gyak*] a stocky, long-haired wild ox of Tibet and C Asia

yak² *vi.* **yakked, yak'king** [echoic] [Slang] to talk much or idly; chatter —*n.* [Slang] idle talk or chatter Also **yak'-yak', yakety-yak** (yak'ə tē yak')

Yale (**lock**) (yāl) [< Linus *Yale*] *Trademark* a type of cylinder lock using a flat serrated key

yam (yam) *n.* [Port. *inhame*] **1.** the edible, starchy root of a climbing plant grown in tropical regions **2.** [U.S.] the sweet potato

yammer (yam'ər) *vi.* [< OE. *geomor,* mournful] [Colloq. or Dial.] **1.** to whine; wail **2.** to talk incoherently —*n.* the act of yammering

yang (yaŋ) *n.* [< Chin. dial.] in Chinese philosophy, the active, positive, masculine force in the universe

Yank (yaŋk) *n.* [Slang] a Yankee; esp., a U.S. soldier in World Wars I and II

yank (yaŋk) *n., vt., vi.* [<?] [Colloq.] jerk

Yankee (yaŋ'kē) *n.* [< ? Du. *Jan Kees,* a disparaging nickname] **1.** a native or inhabitant of the U.S. **2.** [U.S.] a native or inhabitant of New England or of a Northern state —*adj.* of or like Yankees

yap (yap) *vi.* **yapped, yap'ping** [echoic] **1.** to make a sharp, shrill bark **2.** [Colloq.] to talk noisily and stupidly —*n.* **1.** a sharp, shrill bark **2.** [Colloq.] noisy, stupid talk —**yap'per** *n.*

yapp (yap) *n.* [< *Yapp,* Brit. bookseller] a style of bookbinding in limp leather in which the cover projects beyond the edges of the book

Yarborough (yär'bər ə) *n.* [< second Earl of *Yarborough*] a bridge or whist hand containing no card higher than a nine

yard¹ (yärd) *n.* [OE. *gierd,* rod] **1.** *a)* a measure of length, equal to 3 feet (0.914 m) *b)* a cubic yard **2.** *Naut.* a slender rod or spar fastened across a mast to support a sail or to hold signal flags, lights, etc.

yard² *n.* [OE. *geard,* enclosure] **1.** a piece of enclosed ground, esp. one adjoining or surrounded by a building **2.** a place in the open used for a particular purpose [*shipyard*] **3.** an area with a network of railway lines where trains are made up, serviced, etc.: also **railway yard 4.** [U.S. & Canad.] the winter pasture of deer, moose, etc. —**the Yard** *short for* SCOTLAND YARD

yardage *n.* **1.** measurement in yards **2.** the extent of something so measured

yardarm *n.* *Naut.* either end of a yard supporting a square sail, signal lights, etc.

yardstick *n.* **1.** any standard used in judging, comparing, etc. **2.** a measuring stick one yard long

yarmulke (yär'məl kə) *n.* [Yid. < Pol.] a skullcap often worn by Jewish men at prayer, etc.

yarn (yärn) *n.* [OE. *gearn*] **1.** a continuous strand of spun wool, silk, cotton, nylon, glass, etc., for weaving, knitting, etc. **2.** [Colloq.] a tale, esp. one that seems exaggerated —*vi.* [Old Colloq.] to tell yarns

yarrow (yar'ō) *n.* [OE. *gearwe*] a plant with finely divided leaves and clusters of small, pink or white flower heads

yashmak (yash'mak) *n.* [Ar. *yashmaq*] the double veil worn by Moslem women in public

yatter (yat'ər) *vi.* [prob. < YA(K)² + (CHA)TTER] [Colloq.] to talk idly about trivial things —*n.* [Colloq.] a yattering

yaw (yô) *vi.* [<?] **1.** to swing back and forth across its course, as a ship pushed by high waves **2.** to swing about

the vertical axis, as an aircraft —*n.* a yawing

yawl (yôl) *n.* [< MLowG. *jolle* or Du. *jol*] 1. a sailing boat like a ketch, but with the short mizzenmast behind the rudderpost 2. a ship's boat

yawn (yôn) *vi.* [< OE. *ganian*, gape] 1. to open the mouth wide and breathe in deeply, as one often does automatically when sleepy 2. to gape [a *yawning* chasm] —*n.* a yawning

yaws (yôz) *n.pl.* [with sing. v.] [< Carib] a tropical infectious disease characterized by raspberrylike skin eruptions

y-axis *n.*, *pl.* **y'-ax'es** *Math.* the vertical axis along which the ordinate is measured

Yb *Chem.* ytterbium

Y chromosome see SEX CHROMOSOME

yclept, ycleped (i klept') *pp.* [< OE. *clipian*, to call] [Archaic] called; named

yd. *pl.* **yd., yds.** yard

Y.D.T. [U.S. & Canad.] Yukon Daylight Time

ye¹ (*thē*, yē) *adj.* archaic form of THE

ye² (yē) *pron.* [OE. *ge*] [Archaic] you

yea (yā) *adv.* [OE. *gea*] 1. yes 2. [Archaic] indeed; truly —*n.* an answer or vote of "yes"

year (yēar) *n.* [OE. *gear*] 1. a period of 365 days (in leap year, 366 days) divided into 12 months (from Jan. 1 to Dec. 31) 2. the period (365 days, 5 hours, 48 minutes, 46 seconds) of one revolution of the earth round the sun 3. the period in which any planet makes its revolution around the sun 4. any period of 12 calendar months [six *years* ago] 5. a calendar year of a specified number in an era [the *year* 500 B.C.] 6. a specific period, not necessarily corresponding with a calendar year [a school *year*] 7. the total intake of students, etc., admitted to an educational establishment in any one academic year 8. [pl.] a) age [old for his *years*] b) a long time [*years* ago] —**year in, year out** with long and monotonous regularity

yearbook *n.* a reference book of facts and statistics, published yearly

yearling *n.* an animal in its second year

yearlong (yēar'lôŋ') *adj.* continuing for a full year

yearly *adj.* 1. happening once a year, or every year 2. lasting a year 3. of a year, or each year —*adv.* every year

yearn (yʉrn) *vi.* [OE. *georn*, eager] 1. to be filled with longing 2. to feel tenderness or sympathy —**yearn'ing** *n., adj.*

yeast (yēst) *n.* [OE. *gist*] a yellowish, moist mass of minute fungi that ferment sugars to form alcohol and carbon dioxide, and are used in making beer, etc. and as a leavening in baking

yeasty *adj.* **-ier, -iest** 1. of, like, or containing yeast 2. frothy; foamy 3. in a ferment; restless —**yeast'iness** *n.*

yell (yel) *vi., vt.* [OE. *giellan*] to cry out loudly; shout; scream —*n.* a shout; scream

yellow (yel'ō) *adj.* [OE. *geolu*] 1. of

the colour of butter, or ripe lemons 2. having a yellowish skin 3. [Colloq.] cowardly —*n.* a yellow colour, pigment or dye —*vt., vi.* to make or become yellow —**yel'lowish** *adj.* —**yel'lowness** *n.*

yellow-belly *n.*, *pl.* **-lies** [Slang] a coward

yellow fever a tropical disease caused by a virus carried to man by the **yellow-fever mosquito**, and marked by fever, jaundice, etc.

yellow flag a flag indicating that a ship is in quarantine

yellowhammer (yel'ō ham'ər) *n.* [< OE. *geolu*, yellow + *amore*, kind of finch] a small finch, having a yellow head, neck, and breast

Yellow Pages [also y- p-] the section or volume of a telephone directory, on yellow paper, containing classified listings of subscribers according to business, profession, etc.

yellow streak a tendency to be cowardly

yellowwood *n.* any of several trees with yellow wood, esp. a S African conifer with wood used for furniture, building, etc.

yelp (yelp) *vi.* [OE. *gielpan*, to boast] 1. to utter a short, sharp cry or bark 2. to cry out sharply, as in pain —*n.* a short, sharp cry or bark

yen¹ (yen) *n.*, *pl.* **yen** [Jap. < Chin. *yüan*, round] the monetary unit of Japan

yen² *n.* [Chin. *yán*] [Colloq.] a strong longing or desire —*vi.* **yenned, yen'ning** [Colloq.] to have a yen (*for*)

yeoman (yō'mən) *n.* [ME. *yeman*] *Hist.* 1. a small landowner 2. orig., a) a manservant in a royal or noble household b) a freeholder of a class below the gentry

yeoman of the (royal) guard any of the 100 men forming a ceremonial guard for the British royal family

yeomanry *n.* 1. yeomen collectively 2. a British volunteer cavalry force, organized in 1761 for home defence

yeoman's service very useful or loyal service: also **yeoman service**

yep (yep) *adv.* [Chiefly U.S. Slang] yes

-yer (yər) same as -IER: usually after *w*, as in *lawyer*

yerba (yʉr'bə) *n.* [Sp.] same as MATÉ

yes (yes) *adv.* [OE. *gese*] 1. aye; it is so: used to express agreement, consent, affirmation, etc. 2. not only that, but more [ready, yes, eager to help] *Yes* is sometimes used to signify "What is it?" or as a polite expression of interest —*n.*, *pl.* **yes'es** an affirmative vote, voter, etc.

yes man [Colloq.] a person who indicates approval of every suggestion or opinion offered by his superior

yesterday (yes'tər dē) *n.* [< OE. *geostran*, yesterday + *dæg*, day] 1. the day before today 2. a recent day or time 3. [usually pl.] time gone by —*adv.* 1. on the day before today 2. recently

yesteryear (yes'tər yēar') *n.*, *adv.* [Poet.] 1. last year 2. (in) recent years

yet (yet) *adv.* [OE. *giet*] 1. up to now; thus far [he hasn't gone *yet*] 2. at the present time [we can't leave *yet*] 3. still; even now [there is *yet* a chance] 4. sooner or later [she will thank you *yet*] 5. in addition; still [he was *yet* more kind] 6. even [he did not come, nor *yet* write] 7. now, after all the time that has elapsed [hasn't he finished *yet*?] 8. nevertheless [he was rich, *yet* lonely] —*conj.* nevertheless [she seems happy, *yet* she is troubled] —**as yet** up to now

yeti (yet'ē) *n.* [Tibetan] [*often* Y-] same as ABOMINABLE SNOWMAN

yew (yo̅o̅) *n.* [OE. *iw*] 1. an evergreen tree with a fine-grained, elastic wood 2. the wood

Y.H.A. Youth Hostels Association

yid (yid) *n.* [Derog. Slang] a Jew

Yiddish (yid'ish) *n.* [< MHG. *jüdisch*, < L. *Judaeus*, Jew] a language derived from medieval High German, spoken by East European Jews: it is written in the Hebrew alphabet —*adj.* of or in this language

yield (yēld) *vt.* [OE. *gieldan*, to pay] 1. to produce crop, result, profit, etc. 2. to give up; surrender 3. to concede; grant —*vi.* 1. to produce or bear 2. to give up; surrender 3. to give way to physical force 4. to give place (often with *to*) —*n.* the amount yielded

yielding *adj.* 1. submissive; obedient 2. pliable; flexible

yin (yin) *n.* [< Chin. dial.] in Chinese philosophy, the passive, negative, feminine force in the universe

yip (yip) *n., vi.* yipped, yip'ping [echoic] [Colloq.] yelp

yippee (yip ē') *interj.* an exclamation of joy, delight, etc.

YMCA, Y.M.C.A. Young Men's Christian Association

yob (yob) *n.* [back slang for BOY] [Slang] an aggressive, surly youth; lout: also **yobbo** (yo'bō)

yodel (yō'd'l) *vt., vi.* -delled, -delling [G. *jodeln*] to sing with sudden changes back and forth between the normal chest voice and the falsetto —*n.* a yodelling —**yo'del-ler** *n.*

yoga (yō'gə) *n.* [Sans., union] 1. *Hinduism* a discipline by which one seeks to achieve union with the universal soul through deep meditation, prescribed postures, controlled breathing, etc. 2. a system of exercising involving such postures, breathing, etc. —**yo'gic** *adj.*

yogi (yō'gē) *n., pl.* -gis a person who is a master of yoga

yogurt (yo'gərt) *n.* [Turk. *yōghurt*] a thick, semisolid food made from milk fermented by a bacterium: also sp. **yo'ghurt**

yo-heave-ho *interj.* a chant formerly used by sailors while pulling or lifting together in rhythm

yoicks (yoiks) *interj.* a cry used for urging on the hounds in fox hunting

YOKE (on pair of oxen)

yoke (yōk) *n., pl.* **yokes**; for 2, usually **yoke** [OE. *geoc*] 1. a wooden frame fitted round the necks of a pair of oxen, etc. to harness them 2. a pair of animals harnessed together 3. bondage 4. something that binds, unites, etc. 5. something like a yoke, as a frame fitting over the shoulders for carrying pails 6. a part of a garment fitted closely round the shoulders or hips to support the gathered parts below —*vt.* **yoked, yok'ing** 1. to put a yoke on 2. to harness (an animal) to (a plough, etc.) 3. to join —*vi.* to be joined

yokel (yō'k'l) *n.* [prob. < dial. *yokel*, green woodpecker] a country person; rustic: a contemptuous term

yolk (yōk) *n.* [OE. *geolca*] the yellow, principal substance of an egg

Yom Kippur (yom kip'ər) a Jewish holiday, the Day of Atonement, a fast day

yon (yon) *adj., adv.* [OE. *geon*] [Archaic or Dial.] yonder —*pron.* [Archaic or Dial.] yonder person or thing

yonder (yon'dər) *adj.* [ME.] 1. more distant (with *the*) 2. being at a distance, but within sight —*adv.* over there

yoo-hoo (yo̅o̅'ho̅o̅') *interj., n.* a call to attract someone's attention

yore (yôr) *n.* [OE. *geara*] time long past: now only in **of yore,** formerly

york (yôrk) *vt.* *Cricket* to bowl or try to bowl (a batsman) with a yorker

yorker *n.* [prob. < *Yorkshire* County Cricket Club] *Cricket* a ball bowled so as to pitch just under or just beyond the bat

Yorkist (yôr'kist) *n.* a member or supporter of the English royal house of York —*adj.* of or supporting the house of York, esp. in the Wars of the Roses

Yorks. Yorkshire

Yorkshire pudding (yôrk'shər) a batter of flour, eggs, and milk baked in the drippings of roasting meat

Yorkshire terrier a long-haired toy terrier

you (yo̅o̅; *unstressed* yo̅o̅, yə) *pron.* [OE. *eow*, dat. & acc. pl. of *ge*, YE²] 1. the person or persons to whom one is speaking 2. people generally [*you* never can tell!]

you'd (yo̅o̅d; *unstressed* yo̅o̅d, yəd) 1. you had 2. you would

you'll (yo̅o̅l; *unstressed* yo̅o̅l, yəl) 1. you will 2. you shall

young (yuŋ) *adj.* [OE. *geong*] 1. being in an early period of life or growth 2. fresh; vigorous 3. representing a new tendency, movement, etc. [the Young

Liberals *]* **4.** of youth *[in my young days]* **5.** in an early stage **6.** lacking experience; immature —*n.* **1.** young people **2.** offspring *[a bear and her young]* —**with young** pregnant —**young′ish** *adj.*

youngster *n.* a child, youth, or young animal

your (yôr; *unstressed* yər) *possessive pronominal adj.* [OE. *eower*] **1.** of, belonging to, or done by you: also used before some titles *[your* Honour *]* **2.** [Colloq, often Derog.] indicating all things or people of a certain type *[your* average working man *]*

you're (yᴏᴏər) you are

yours (yôrz) *pron.* that or those belonging to you *[that book is yours, yours* are better*]*: also used after *of* to indicate possession *[a friend of yours]*

yourself (yôr self′) *pron., pl.* **-selves′**(-selvz′) **1.** a form of the 2nd pers. sing. pronoun, used: *a)* as an intensive *[you yourself* went *].b)* as a reflexive *[you* hurt *yourself] c)* as a quasi-noun meaning "your real or true self" *[you are not yourself* today*]* **2.** *same as* ONESELF *[it* is best to do it *yourself]*

Yours faithfully a phrase used before the signature in ending a formal letter

Yours sincerely a phrase used before the signature in ending an informal letter

Yours truly **1.** a phrase used before the signature in ending a formal letter **2.** [Colloq.] [also y- t-] I or me

youth (yᴏᴏth) *n., pl.* **youths** (yᴏᴏ*thz*) [OE. *geoguth*] **1.** the state or quality of being young **2.** the period of adolescence **3.** an early stage of development **4.** young people collectively **5.** a young man

youthful *adj.* **1.** young **2.** characteristic of, or suitable for youth **3.** fresh; vigorous **4.** new; early —**youth′fully** *adv.* —**youth′fulness** *n.*

youth hostel a place providing cheap lodging for young people on bicycle tours, hikes, etc.

you've (yᴏᴏv) you have

yowl (yaul) *vi.* [ME. *youlen*] to utter a long, mournful cry; howl —*n.* such a cry

yo-yo (yō′yō′) *n.* [< Tagalog name] a spoollike toy attached to one end of a string upon which it may be made to spin up and down

yr. **1.** year(s) **2.** younger **3.** your

yrs. **1.** years **2.** yours

Y.S.T. [U.S. & Canad.] Yukon Standard Time

Y.T. [Canad.] Yukon Territory

ytterbium (itur′bē əm) *n.* [ModL. < *Ytterby*, Sweden] a silvery, metallic chemical element of the rare-earth group: symbol, Yb

yttrium (it′rē əm) *n.* [< prec.] a rare, silvery, metallic chemical element: symbol, Y

yucca (yuk′ə) *n.* [ModL. < Sp. *yuca*] a plant of the U.S. and Latin America, having stiff, sword-shaped leaves and white flowers in an erect raceme

Yugoslav (yᴏᴏ′gō släv′) *adj.* of Yugoslavia or its people —*n.* a member of a Slavic people who live in Yugoslavia: also **Yu′gosla′vian**

yuk (yuk) *interj.* an exclamation indicating contempt or disgust —*n.* [U.S. Slang] a loud laugh

yukky, yucky (yuk′ē) *adj.* [Colloq.] messy; revolting

Yukoner (yᴏᴏ′kon ər) *n.* a native or inhabitant of Yukon

yule (yᴏᴏl) *n.* [OE. *geol*] [Archaic] Christmas

yule log **1.** a large log formerly used as a foundation for the ceremonial Christmas Eve fire **2.** a chocolate swiss roll served at Christmas

yuletide *n.* [Archaic] Christmas time

yummy (yum′ē) *adj.* **yum′mier, yum′miest** [echoic] [Colloq.] very tasty; delectable; delicious

yum-yum (yum′yum′) *interj.* [echoic] an expression indicating appreciation of food

YWCA, Y.W.C.A. Young Women's Christian Association

Z

Z, z (zed) *n., pl.* **Z's, z's** the twenty-sixth and last letter of the English alphabet

Z (zed) *n.* an object shaped like Z

z *Math. a symbol for:* the third in a set of unknown quantities, *x* and *y* usually being the first two

zany (zā′nē) *adj.* **-nier, -niest** [< It. *zanni* < *Giovanni*, John] **1.** comical in a crazy way **2.** crazy —*n., pl.* **-nies 1.** a clown or buffoon **2.** a simpleton

zap (zap) *vt., vi.* **zapped, zap′ping** [echoic] [Slang] to move, strike, kill, etc. with sudden speed and force —*n.* [Slang] energy, verve, pep, etc.

zeal (zēl) *n.* [< Gr. *zēlos*] intense enthusiasm; fervour

zealot (zel′ət) *n.* [< Gr. *zēlos*, zeal] a person who is zealous, esp. to an excessive degree; fanatic —**zeal′otry** *n.*

zealous (zel′əs) *adj.* full of zeal; fervent; enthusiastic —**zeal′ously** *adv.* —**zeal′ousness** *n.*

zebec, zebeck (zē′bek) *n.* same as XEBEC

zebra (zeb′rə, zē′brə) *n.* [Port. < Congolese] any of several swift African mammals, with dark stripes on a white or tawny body

zebra crossing a street crossing, marked with black and white bands, at which pedestrians have the right of way

zebu (zē′bōō) *n.* [Fr. *zébu*] an oxlike domestic animal of Asia and Africa: it has a large hump and short, curving horns

zed (zed) *n.* [< Gr. *zēta*] the letter Z, z

zee (zē) *n., pl.* **zees** *U.S. name for the letter* Z, z

‡**Zeitgeist** (tsīt′gīst′) *n.* [G., time spirit] the trend of thought and feeling in a period of history

Zen (zen) *n.* [Jap. < Sans. *dhyāna*, meditation] **1.** a Japanese Buddhist sect that seeks enlightenment through meditation and intuition rather than in traditional scripture **2.** the beliefs and practices of this sect

zenana (ze nä′nə) *n.* [< Per. *Zan*, woman] in India and Iran, the part of the house reserved for women

Zend-Avesta (zend′ə ves′tə) *n.* the sacred writings of the Zoroastrians

zenith (zen′ith) *n.* [< Ar. *semt*, road] **1.** the point in the sky directly overhead **2.** the highest point; peak

zephyr (zef′ər) *n.* [< Gr. *zephyros*] **1.** the west wind **2.** a soft, gentle breeze

zeppelin (zep′ə lin) *n.* [< F. von *Zeppelin*] [*often* Z-] a type of dirigible airship designed about 1900

zero (zēr′ō) *n., pl.* **-ros, -roes** [Fr. < Ar. *ṣifr*, CIPHER] **1.** the symbol 0; nought **2.** the point, marked 0, from which positive or negative quantities are reckoned on a graduated scale, as on thermometers **3.** a temperature that causes a thermometer to register zero **4.** nothing —*adj.* **1.** of or at zero **2.** without measurable value **3.** designating visibility limited to very short distances, as in flying —*vt.* **-roed, -roing** to adjust (an instrument, etc.) to a zero point from which all readings are to be made —**zero in on 1.** to adjust gunfire so as to be aiming directly at (a target) **2.** [Colloq.] to concentrate attention on **3.** [Colloq.] to converge upon

zero gravity a condition of weightlessness

zero hour the time set for the beginning of an attack, etc.; critical point

zero-rated *adj.* denoting goods on which the buyer pays no value-added tax

zest (zest) *n.* [< Fr. *zeste*, orange peel] **1.** keen enjoyment [*zest* for life] **2.** stimulating or exciting quality; piquancy **3.** something that gives flavour or relish **4.** orange or lemon peel, used as a flavouring in drinks, etc. —**zest′ful** *adj.*

zeta (zēt′ə) *n.* the sixth letter of the Greek alphabet (Z, ζ)

zeugma (zyōōg′mə) *n.* [< Gr., yoke] a figure of speech in which a word modifies two or more words, with only one of which it seems logically connected (Ex.: the room was not light, but his fingers were)

ziggurat (zig′ŏŏ rat′) *n.* [< Assyrian] a type of rectangular temple tower of ancient Mesopotamia

zigzag (zig′zag′) *n.* [Fr.] **1.** a series of short, sharp turns in alternate directions **2.** a design, path, etc. having a series of such turns —*adj.* having the form of a zigzag —*adv.* in a zigzag course —*vt., vi.* **-zagged′, -zag′ging** to move or form in a zigzag

zillion (zil′yən) *n.* [< MILLION] [U.S. Colloq.] a very large, indefinite number

zinc (ziŋk) *n.* [G. *Zink*] a bluish-white, metallic chemical element, used as a protective coating for iron, in alloys, etc.: symbol, Zn —*vt.* **zincked** or **zinced, zinck′ing** or **zinc′ing** to coat or treat with zinc; galvanize

zincography (ziŋ kog′rə fē) *n.* [ZINC + -GRAPHY] the art or process of engraving or etching on zinc plates for printing

zinc ointment an ointment containing zinc oxide

zinc oxide a white powder used as a pigment and in making glass, cosmetics, etc.

zing (ziŋ) *n.* [echoic] [Colloq.] **1.** a shrill, high-pitched sound, as of something moving at high speed **2.** vitality, zest, etc. —*vi.* [Colloq.] to make or move with a shrill sound

zinnia (zin′ē ə) *n.* [ModL., < J. G. *Zinn*]

a plant of the composite family, having colourful flowers, native to America

Zion (zī′ən) *n.* **1.** the hill in Jerusalem on which the Temple was built **2.** the land of Israel **3.** the Jewish people **4.** heaven

Zionism *n.* a movement formerly for re-establishing, now for supporting, the Jewish national state of Israel —**Zi′onist** *n., adj.*

zip (zip) *n.* [echoic] **1.** *same as* ZIP FASTENER **2.** a short, sharp hissing sound, as of a passing bullet **3.** [Colloq.] energy; vim —*vi.* **zipped, zip′ing 1.** to become fastened by means of a zip fastener **2.** [Colloq.] to act or move with speed or energy **3.** to make, or move with, a zipping sound —*vt.* to fasten with a zip fastener (often with *up*)

zip fastener a device used to fasten and unfasten two edges of material: it consists of two rows of interlocking teeth worked by a part that slides up or down: also **zip′per**

zippy *adj.* **zip′pier, zip′piest** [Colloq.] full of vim and energy

zircon (zur′kon) *n.* [G. < Per. *zar*, gold] a crystalline silicate of zirconium, coloured yellow, brown, red, etc.: transparent varieties are used as gems

zirconium (zur kō′nē əm) *n.* [ModL.: see prec.] a soft grey or black metallic chemical element used in alloys, ceramics, etc.: symbol, Zr

zither (zith′ər) *n.* [< Gr. *kithara*, lute] a musical instrument having strings stretched across a flat soundboard and played with a plectrum and the fingers

zloty (zlo′tē) *n., pl.* **-tys** [Pol., golden] the monetary unit of Poland

Zn *Chem.* zinc

zodiac (zō′dē ak′) *n.* [< Gr. *zōion*, animal]

1. an imaginary belt in the heavens extending on either side of the apparent path of the sun and including the paths of the moon and the principal planets: it is divided into twelve equal parts, or signs, named for constellations **2.** a diagram representing the zodiac and its signs: used in astrology —**zodi′acal** (-dī′ə k'l) *adj.*

zombie (zom′bē) *n.* [of Afr. origin] **1.** in West Indian superstition, a dead person brought back by magic to a form of life in which he can be made to act as he is ordered **2.** [Colloq.] a person like a zombie in seeming to be half dead, to move automatically, etc.: also **zom′bi**

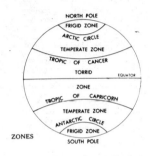

ZONES

zone (zōn) *n.* [Fr. < Gr. *zōnē*] **1.** any area or region considered with reference to its particular use, properties, features, etc. [a demilitarized *zone*] **2.** any of the five great divisions into which the

ZODIAC

earth's surface is marked off by imaginary lines **3.** an encircling band, stripe, etc. —*vt.* **zoned, zon'ing 1.** to divide into zones, as for different uses, jurisdiction, etc. **2.** to assign to a particular zone —**zon'al** *adj.*

zoo (zōō) *n.* [< *zoo(logical garden)*] a place where a collection of live animals is kept for public showing

zoo- [< Gr. *zōion,* animal] *a combining form meaning* animal, animals

zooid (zō'oid) *n.* [< ZOO] **1.** an independent animal organism produced by fission, gemmation, etc. rather than by sexual means **2.** any of the individual members of a compound organism, as the coral

zool. 1. zoological **2.** zoology

zoological garden *same as* ZOO

zoology (zō ol'ə jē) *n.* [see ZOO- & -LOGY] the branch of biology that deals with animals —**zo'olog'ical** (-ə loj'i k'l) *adj.* —**zo'olog'ically** *adv.* —**zool'ogist** *n.*

zoom (zōōm) *vi.* [echoic] **1.** to make, or move with, a loud, low-pitched, buzzing sound **2.** to move rapidly **3.** to climb suddenly and sharply: said of an aircraft **4.** to rise rapidly [prices *zoomed*] **5.** to focus a camera by using a zoom lens —*n.* **1.** a zooming **2.** *same as* ZOOM LENS

zoom lens a system of camera lenses that can be rapidly adjusted for close-up shots or distance views while keeping the image in focus

zoophyte (zō'ə fīt') *n.* [see ZOO- & Gr. *phyton,* plant] any animal, as a coral, that looks and grows somewhat like a plant

Zoroastrianism (zo'rō as'trē ən iz'm) *n.* the religious system of the ancient Persians, teaching the eventual triumph of the spirit of good over the spirit of evil

Zouave (zōō äv') *n.* [Fr. < Ar. *Zwāwa,* an Algerian tribe] a member of a former infantry unit in the French army that wore a colourful Oriental uniform

zounds (zoundz) *interj.* [< oath (by) *God's wounds*] [Archaic] a mild oath

Zr *Chem.* zirconium

zucchetto (tsōō ket'tō) *n., pl.* **-tos** [It. < *zucca,* gourd] *R.C.Ch.* a skullcap worn by clergymen

Zulu (zōō'lōō) *n.* **1.** *pl.* **-lus, -lu** any member of a cattle-owning people living in Natal, South Africa **2.** their language —*adj.* of the Zulus, their language, etc.

zygote (zī'gōt) *n.* [< Gr. *zygon,* a yoke] a cell formed by the union of male and female gametes; fertilized egg cell

zymo- [< Gr. *zymē,* a leaven] *a combining form meaning* fermentation [*zymology*]

zymotic (zī mot'ik) *adj.* [< Gr. *zymē,* a ferment] **1.** of fermentation **2.** [Obs.] designating or of any infectious disease

zymurgy (zī'mur jē) *n.* [ZYM(O)- + -URGY] the branch of chemistry dealing with fermentation, as applied in wine making, brewing, etc.

PUNCTUATION MARKS AND OTHER SYMBOLS

,	comma.
;	semicolon.
:	colon.
.	period.
—	dash.
!	exclamation mark.
?	interrogation or doubt.
-	hyphen; as in *knick-knack*.
'	apostrophe; as in *Peter's pence*.
( )	parentheses.
[ ]	brackets.
}	brace, to enclose two or more lines.
´	acute accent; as in *blasé*.
` ^	grave accent } as in circumflex } *tête-à-tête*.
~	tilde, used over *n* in certain Spanish words to denote the sound of *ny*; as in *señor*.
‚	cedilla, to denote that *c* is pronounced soft; as in *façade*.
" "	quotation marks.
' '	quotation marks, when used within a quotation; as in *"He said, 'I will go at once' and jumped into the car."*
‾	macron, to mark length of sound; as in *cōbra*.
˘	breve, marking a short sound; as in *lĭnen*.
··	diaeresis; as in *daïs*.
··	in German, used to denote modification of the vowel sound; as in *Köln* (Cologne).
∧	caret, marking a word or letter to be inserted in the line.
* *	*, ...,* — or - - - - ellipsis to indicate a break in a narrative, or an omission.
* *	or ∗ ∗ asterism, used to call attention to a particular passage.
· · ··	or - - - - leaders, to direct the eye to a certain point.
¶	paragraph.
*	star, asterisk; (1) a reference mark; (2) used in philology to denote forms assumed to have existed though not recorded.
†	dagger, obelisk; (1) a reference mark; (2) obsolete or dead.
‡	double dagger, a reference mark.
²	superior figure, used (1) as a reference mark; (2) to indicate the number of a verse or line; as in *St. Mark* 4¹⁶.
ᵃ	superior letter.
§	section mark.
‖	parallel mark.
☞	index, hand, fist.
#	number; space.
„	ditto.
&	ampersand, and.
&c	et cetera.
@	at.
℔	per.
%	per cent, per hundred.
©	copyright.
®	registered; registered trademark.
♂	male.
♀	female.

PUNCTUATION AND THE USE OF CAPITAL LETTERS

apostrophe The sign ('), used to indicate possession. In the singular -'s is used (eg *day's end*); in the plural the apostrophe is added to the end of the word (eg *the neighbours' dog*). Plurals that do not end in -s also take -'s (eg *sheep's eyes*). Except for a few traditional exceptions (like *Jesus', Keats'*) proper names ending in -s take -'s at the end (eg *Thomas's, the Jones's*).

brackets These serve to isolate part of a sentence, which could be omitted and still leave an intelligible statement. Punctuation of the rest of the sentence should run as if the bracketed portion were not there, eg *That house over there (with the blue door) is ours.* Square brackets are used where the writer inserts his own information into a quotation, eg *I knew Pitt [the Younger] as a boy.*

capital letters These are used at the beginning of a sentence or quoted speech, and for proper names and titles of people and organizations, eg *Mr Robertson, Dr Smith, South America, British Rail.* They are not used when speaking of a general topic like *the pay of miners, the manufacture of cosmetics.* If an initial is included in a title it has a capital, eg *We went to see The Tempest.*

colons and semicolons The function of these is to provide more of a break than a comma, and less than a full stop. The colon is used to make an abrupt break between two related statements, eg *Take it or leave it: the choice is yours.* It is also used to introduce a list, quotation, or summary and may be followed by a dash if the following matter begins on a separate line. Semicolons can be used instead of conjunctions to link two sentences or parts of them, eg *Two of the lights were working; two were out.*

commas 1. These make divisions or slight pauses in sentences, eg *She stormed out, slamming the door behind her.*

2. Commas are used to divide units in a series of nouns, adjectives, or phrases, eg *The cupboard was full of pots, pans, and crockery.* In such a series the last comma (ie before 'and' or 'or') is optional.

It is not usual to place a comma between the last of a series of adjectives and the noun, eg *It was a long, hot, humid day.*

3. Commas also serve to mark off a word or phrase in a sentence which can stand grammatically complete on its own, as can dashes and brackets. Commas give the lightest degree of separation, dashes produce a jerky effect, and brackets cut off part of a sentence most firmly, eg *He hurried home, taking a short cut, but still arrived too late. It's a long time — over two years — since we last met. They both went to Athens (unaware of each other's plans) and stayed in the same hotel.*

4. When two phrases are linked by a conjunction a comma is used if there is a contrast, eg *She was dark, but her brother was fair.*

5. When addressing a person, commas are used before and after the person's name or title, eg *Well, Mrs Smith, how are you today?*

exclamation marks These should only be used after genuine exclamations and not after ordinary statements.

full stops (periods) Normally, these appear only at the end of a complete sentence containing a main verb, except in reported speech and where a passage takes the form of an argument, eg *You may think you can get away with it. Not a chance.* Full stops are also used after abbreviations and initial letters standing for the whole word (as in, *fig., a.m., R.C.*) but they are often omitted after abbreviations which include the first and last letters of a word (*Dr, Mr, ft*) and in much-used titles like *BBC, USA, TUC.* As usage is currently in a state of flux the above should be taken only as a guide to common practice.

hyphens Compound words, like *lay-by* or *manor house,* or words with a prefix, like *unpick,* may or may not contain a hyphen. It is generally used when the compound is new and dropped as it becomes familiar. When a compound adjective comes before a noun it should be hyphenated to stress that the constituent parts are not to be used independently, eg *He has a half-Italian wife.*

inverted commas (quotation marks, quotes) 1. These are used for direct quotation, not for indirect speech. It is usual to have a comma before and after a quotation if the sentence is resumed, eg *He said, "Follow me", and set off down the street.*

2. Single quotation marks can be used to indicate a title or quotation within a speech, eg *"I loved 'War and Peace'," she said, "but it took so long to read."*

question marks These are used at the end of direct questions, but not after reported ones.

PLURALS OF NOUNS

Plurals are formed by adding -s except in the following cases.

1. When a word ends in -ch, -s, -sh, -ss, or -x the plural is formed by adding -es (eg *benches, gases, dishes, crosses, taxes*).

2. When a word ends in -y preceded by a consonant the plural form is -ies (eg *parties, bodies, policies*). When a word ends in -y preceded by a vowel the plural is formed by adding -s (eg *trays, joys, keys*).

3. When a word ends in -o the more common plural ending is -oes (eg *cargoes, potatoes, heroes, goes*). In many less familiar words or when the final -o is preceded by a vowel the plural ending is -os (eg *avocados, armadillos, studios, cameos*).

4. When a word ends in -f the plural is formed either by adding -s (eg *beliefs, cuffs, whiffs*) or by changing the -f to -v and adding -es (eg *wives, thieves, loaves*). Some words may take both forms (eg *scarf, hoof, wharf*).

5. When a word ends in -ex or -ix the more formal plural ending is -ices. In more general contexts -es is used (eg *appendices, appendixes; indices, indexes*).

6. When a word from Latin ends in -is the plural form is -es (eg *crises, analyses*).

With compound words (like *court-martial*) it is usually the most important part which is pluralized (eg *courts-martial, lord-justices, mothers-in-law*).

In certain cases the plural form of a word is the same as the singular (eg *deer, sheep, grouse*) and in some words both forms end in -s (eg *measles, corps, mews*).

There are two main types of plural which take either singular or plural verbs:

a. words like *media* and *data*. These are in common use as singular nouns although, strictly, this is incorrect.

b. words ending in -ics. Generally, these are treated as plural when the word relates to an individual person or thing (eg *his mathematics are poor; the hall's acoustics are good*) and as singular when it is regarded more strictly as a science (eg *mathematics is an important subject*).

forms of address Letters to men can be addressed as follows: *Mr. Bates, Mr. T. Bates,* or *Mr. Thomas Bates.* If the courtesy title *Esq.* is used the surname must be preceded by a first name or initials, and any letters must be put after the *Esq.,* eg *Thomas Bates Esq., M.A.* Young boys can be addressed as *Master.* The plural form *Messrs.* is only used with the names of business firms which contain a personal name, eg. *Messrs. Jackson and Sons.*

Unmarried women and young girls can be addressed as *Miss.* Married women are often identified by their husband's first name or initial, eg *Mrs. R(obert)* Henderson, but it is increasingly common for them to appear as in *Mrs. M(ary)* Henderson, which is also the usual form for a widow. It is possible to use *Ms.* instead of *Miss* or *Mrs.*

Professional titles are used instead of *Mr.* etc., as in *Dr. H. Stevens, The Rev. Simon Clifford.* First names are always used with the titles *Sir* and *Dame,* as in *Sir Laurence Olivier, Dame Margot Fonteyn.*

Orders, decorations, degrees, qualifications, and letters denoting professions appear in that order. Degrees start with the lowest, but orders start with the highest, eg *Joseph Halliday Esq., O.B.E., D.S.O., M.A., F.S.A., M.D.* Orders and decorations are usually included in addresses, but qualifications etc. are only used where appropriate, as when writing to a person in his official capacity.

A list of some ceremonious forms of address follows at the end of this article.

postal addresses In Britain the recommended form of postal address has the Post Town in capital letters, followed by the county in small letters, followed by the postcode (where applicable), eg

Miss Joan Bannerman
6 Overton Drive
HORSHAM
Sussex
(postcode)

address of a letter The writer's address should appear in the top right-hand corner with the date underneath. The name and address of the intended recipient should come below the date, on the left-hand side of the page.

beginnings and endings These depend on the degree of formality required. The most commonly used forms are as follows:

very formal

Sir,	I am, Sir, *or*
Gentlemen,	I remain, Sir,
Madam,	Your obedient
Mesdames,	servant,

formal

Dear Sir(s),	Yours faithfully,
Dear Madam,	
Mesdames,	Yours truly,

when correspondent is known

Dear Mr.	Yours sincerely,
(Mrs. etc.) —	Yours truly,

between friends

Dear —	Yours ever,
My dear —	Yours affectionately,

postscript This is abbreviated to PS (not P.S.). An additional postscript is labelled PPS.

CEREMONIOUS FORMS OF ADDRESS

The Queen *Address* The Queen's Most Excellent Majesty *Begin* Madam *or* May it please Your Majesty *Refer to as* Your Majesty *End* I have the honour to remain, Your Majesty's faithful subject,

Prince *Address* His Royal Highness Prince (Christian name) *Or, if a duke* His Royal Highness the Duke of — *Begin* Sir, *Refer to as* Your Royal Highness *End* I have the honour to remain, Your Royal Highness's most dutiful subject,

Princess *Address* Her Royal Highness the Princess (Christian name) *Or, if a duchess* Her Royal Highness the Duchess of — *Begin* Madam, *Refer to as* Your Royal Highness *End* I have the honour to remain, Your Royal Highness's dutiful and obedient subject,

Duke *Address* His Grace the Duke of — *Begin* My Lord Duke *Refer to as* Your Grace *End* I have the honour to be, Your Grace's most obedient servant,

Duchess *Address* Her Grace the Duchess of — *Begin* Madam, *Refer to as* Your Grace *End* I have the honour to be, Your Grace's most obedient servant,

Baronet *Address* Sir (Christian name and surname), Bt. *Begin* Sir, *End* I am, Sir, Your obedient servant,

Baronet's wife *Address* Lady (surname) *Begin* Madam *Refer to as* Your Ladyship *End* I am, Madam, Your obedient servant,

Knight *Address* Sir (Christian name and surname) K.C.B. *Begin, End* as Baronet

Knight's wife   as Baronet's wife

Prime Minister   according to rank

Privy Councillor *Address* The Rt. Hon. (name or title) *Begin etc.* according to rank

Member of Parliament *Address* according to rank, with the addition of M.P. *Begin etc.* according to rank

Secretary of State *Address* H.M. Principal Secretary of State for (Department) *Begin* Sir *End* I am, Sir, Your obedient servant,

Ambassador, British *Address* His Excellency (rank) H.B.M.'s Ambassador and Plenipotentiary *Begin* Sir, My Lord, etc. according to rank *Refer to as* Your Excellency *End* I am, etc. (according to rank), Your obedient servant,

Consul-General *Address* (name) Esq., H.B.M.'s Consul-General, Consul, Vice-Consul etc. *Begin* Sir *End* I am, Sir, Your obedient servant,

Lord Mayor (for London, York, Belfast, Dublin) *Address* The Rt. Hon. the Lord Mayor of — or The Rt. Hon. (Christian name and surname), Lord Mayor of — *Begin* My Lord, *Refer to as* Your Lordship *End* I am, my Lord Mayor, Your obedient servant,

Lord Mayor (for others) The Right Worshipful the Lord Mayor of — Otherwise as above

Lord Mayor's Wife *Address* The Rt. Hon. (or Hon. according to husband's title) The Lady Mayoress of — *Begin* My Lady Mayoress or Madam *Refer to as* Your Ladyship *End* I am, my Lady Mayoress, Your obedient servant,

Mayor *Address* (for certain cities) The Right Worshipful the Mayor of — *Begin* (Your Lordship) Sir (or Madam) *End* I am, Sir (or Madam), Your obedient servant,

GROUP NAMES & COLLECTIVE NOUNS

barren of mules
bevy of quails
bevy of roes
brace or leash of bucks
brood or covey of grouse
brood of hens or chickens
building or clamour of rooks
bunch, company or knob of wigeon (in the water)
bunch, knob or spring of teal
cast of hawks
cete of badgers
charm of goldfinches
chattering of choughs
clowder of cats
colony of gulls (breeding)
covert of coots
covey of partridges
cowardice of curs
desert of lapwings
dopping of sheldrakes
down or husk of hares
drove or herd of cattle (kine)
exaltation of larks
fall of woodcock
field or string of racehorses
flight of wigeon (in the air)
flight or dule of doves
flight of swallows
flight of dunlins
flight, rush, bunch or knob of pochards
flock or flight of pigeons
flock of sheep
flock of swifts
flock or gaggle of geese
flock, congregation, flight or volery of birds
gaggle of geese (on the ground)
gang of elk
haras (stud) of horses
herd of antelopes
herd of buffaloes
herd, sedge or siege of cranes
herd of curlews
herd of deer
herd of giraffes
herd or tribe of goats
herd or pod of seals
herd or bevy of swans
herd of ponies

herd of swine
hill of ruffs
host of sparrows
kindle of kittens
labour of moles
leap of leopards
litter of cubs
litter of pups or pigs
litter of whelps
murmuration of starlings
muster of peacocks
nest of rabbits
nye or nide of pheasants
pace or herd of asses
pack of grouse
pack, mute or cry of hounds
pack, rout or herd of wolves
paddling of ducks
plump, sord or sute of wildfowl
pod of whiting
pride or troop of lions
rag of colts
richesse of martens
run of poultry
school or run of whales
school or gam of porpoises
sedge or siege of bitterns
sedge or siege of herons
shoal or glean of herrings
shoal, draught, haul, run or catch of fish
shrewdness of apes
skein of geese (in flight)
skulk of foxes
sleuth of bears
sord or sute of mallards
sounder of boars
sounder or dryft of swine
stand or wing of plovers
stud of mares
swarm of insects
swarm or grist of bees, or flies
swarm or cloud of gnats
tok of capercailzies
team of ducks (in flight)
troop of kangaroos
troop of monkeys
walk or wisp of snipe
watch of nightingales
yoke, drove, team or herd of oxen

TABLE OF ALPHABETS

The sounds of the letters are shown in parentheses

HEBREW		GREEK Print and Script		RUSSIAN Upper and Lower Case		GERMAN Upper and Lower Case	
א Aleph	*1*	Α α Alpha	(a)	А а (a)		𝕬 𝖆	(a)
ב Bet	(b)	Β β Beta	(b)	Б б (b)		𝕬 ä	(e)
ב Vet	(v)	Γ γ Gamma	(g)	В в (v)		𝕭 𝖇	(b)
ג Gimel	(g)	Δ δ Delta	(d)	Г г (g)		𝕮 𝖈	(k, ts, s)
ד Daled	(d)	Ε ε Epsilon	(e)	Д д (d)		𝕮𝖍 𝖈𝖍	(H, kh)
ה He	(h)	Ζ ζ Zeta	(z)	Е е (ye)		𝕯 𝖉	(d)
ו Vav	(v)	Η η Eta	(ā)	Ж ж (zh)		𝕰 𝖊	(e, ā)
ז Zayin	(z)	Θ θ Theta	(th)	З з (z)		𝕱 𝖋	(f)
ח Het	(kh)	Ι ι Iota	(ē)	И и (i, ē)		𝕲 𝖌	(g, kh)
ט Tet	(t)	Κ κ Kappa	(k)	Й й (ē)		𝕳 𝖍	(h)
י Yod	(y)	Λ λ Lambda	(l)	К к (k)		𝕴 𝖎	(i, ē)
כ Kaf	(k)	Μ μ Mu	(m)	Л л (l)		𝕵 𝖏	(y)
כ Khaf	(kh)	Ν ν Nu	(n)	М м (m)		𝕶 𝖐	(k)
ל Lamed	(l)	Ξ ξ Xi	(ks)	Н н (n)		𝕷 𝖑	(l)
מם Mem	(m)	Ο ο Omicron	(o)	О о (ŏ, o)		𝕸 𝖒	(m)
נן Nun	(n)	Π π Pi	(p)	П п (p)		𝕹 𝖓	(n)
ס Samekh	(s)	Ρ ρ Rho	(r)	Р р (r)		𝕺 𝖔	(ō, ŏ)
ע Ayin	*1*	Σ σ ς Sigma	(s)	С с (s)		𝕺 ö	(ö)
פ Pe	(p)	Τ τ Tau	(t)	Т т (t)		𝕻 𝖕	(p)
פף Fe	(f)	Υ υ Upsilon	(ü, ōō)	У у (ōō)		𝕼(u) 𝖖(u)	(kv)
צץ Tsadi	(ts)	Φ φ Phi	(f)	Ф ф (f)		𝕽 𝖗	(r)
ק Kof	(k)	Χ χ Chi	(H)	Х х (kh)		𝕾 𝖘 𝖘	(s, z)
ר Resh	(r)	Ψ ψ Psi	(ps)	Ц ц (ts)		𝕾𝖈𝖍 𝖘𝖈𝖍	(sh)
ש Shin	(sh)	Ω ω Omega	(ō)	Ч ч (ch)		𝕿 𝖙	(t)
ש Sin	(s)			Ш ш (sh)		𝖀 𝖚	(ōō)
ת Tav	(t)			Щ щ (shch)		𝖀 ü	(ü)
ת Thav	(th, s)			Ъ ъ *2*		𝖁 𝖛	(f)
				Ы ы (ĕ)		𝖂 𝖜	(v)
				Ь ь *3*		𝖃 𝖝	(ks)
				Э э (e)		𝖄 𝖞	(ē, ü)
				Ю ю (yōō)		𝖅 𝖟	(ts)
				Я я (yä)			

NOTES

1. A neutral letter, either silent or sounded according to diacritical mark.

2. Indicates nonpalatalization of a preceding consonant.

3. Indicates palatalization of a preceding consonant.

GEOLOGICAL TIME CHART

Main Divisions of Geological Time

Eras	Periods or Systems	Epochs or Series	Principal Physical & Biological Features
Cainozoic	QUATERNARY	Recent 12,000*	Glaciers restricted to Antartica and Greenland; development and spread of modern human culture.
		Pleistocene 600,000	Great glaciers covered much of Northern Hemisphere; appearance of modern man late in Pleistocene.
	TERTIARY	Pliocene 10,000,000	W North America uplifted; continued development of mammals; first possible apelike men appeared in Africa.
		Miocene 25,000,000	Renewed uplift of Alpine mountains: mammals began to acquire present-day characters; dogs, solid-hoofed horses, manlike apes appeared.
		Oligocene 35,000,000	Many older types of mammals became extinct; mastodons, first monkeys, and apes appeared.
		Eocene 55,000,000	Alpine mountain building (Himalayas, Alps, Andes, Rockies); expansion of early mammals; primitive horses appeared.
		Paleocene 65,000,000	Great development of primitive mammals.
Mesozoic	CRETACEOUS 135,000,000		Chalk deposits laid down; dinosaurs reached maximum development & then became extinct; mammals small & very primitive.
	JURASSIC 180,000,000		Rocks of S and C Europe laid down; conifers & cycads dominant among plants; primitive birds appeared.
	TRIASSIC 230,000,000		Modern corals appeared & some insects of present-day types; great expansion of reptiles including earliest dinosaurs.

*Figures indicate approximate number of years since the beginning of each division.

Main Divisions of Geological Time			Principal Physical & Biological Features
Eras	Periods or Systems		Principal Physical & Biological Features
Paleozoic	PERMIAN 280,000,000		Trees of coal-forming forests declined; ferns abundant; conifers present; trilobites became extinct; reptiles surpassed amphibians.
Paleozoic	CARBONIFEROUS	UPPER CARBONIFEROUS 310,000,000	Hercynian mountain building (C Europe, E coast of North America); great coal-forming swamp forests flourished in N Hemisphere; seed-bearing ferns abundant; cockroaches & first reptiles appeared.
Paleozoic	CARBONIFEROUS	LOWER CARBONIFEROUS 345,000,000	Land plants became diversified; crinoids achieved greatest development; sharks of relatively modern types appeared; land animals little known.
Paleozoic	DEVONIAN 405,000,000		Land plants evolved rapidly, large trees appeared; brachiopods reached maximum development; many kinds of primitive fishes; first sharks, insects, & amphibians appeared.
Paleozoic	SILURIAN 425,000,000		Great mountains formed in NW Europe; first small land plants appeared; shelled cephalopods abundant; trilobites began decline; first jawed fish appeared.
Paleozoic	ORDOVICIAN 500,000,000		Caledonian mountain building; much limestone deposited in shallow seas; many marine invertebrates, first primitive jawless fish appeared.
Paleozoic	CAMBRIAN 600,000,000		Shallow seas covered parts of continents; abundant record of marine life, esp. trilobites & brachiopods; other fossils rare.
Precambrian	LATE PRECAMBRIAN** 2,000,000,000		Metamorphosed sedimentary rocks and granite formed; first evidence of life, calcareous algae & invertebrates.
Precambrian	EARLY PRECAMBRIAN** 4,500,000,000		Crust formed on molten earth; crystalline rocks much disturbed; history unknown.

**Regarded as separate eras.

NAMES AND SYMBOLS OF METRIC UNITS

Quantity	Name of Unit	Value	Symbol
LENGTH	metre	base unit	m
	centimetre	0.01 m	cm
	millimetre	0.001 m	mm
	micrometre	0.000 001 m	μm (or um)
	kilometre	1 000 m	km
	international nautical mile (for navigation)	1 852 m	n mile
MASS (weight)	kilogram	base unit	kg
	milligram	0.000 001 kg	mg
	gram	0.001 kg	g
	tonne	1 000 kg	t
TIME	second	base unit	s
	minute	60 s	min
	hour	60 min	h
	day	24 h	d
AREA	square metre	SI unit	m²
	square millimetre	0.000 001 m²	mm²
	square centimetre	0.000 1 m²	cm²
	hectare	10 000 m²	ha
	square kilometre	1 000 000 m²	km²
VOLUME	cubic metre	SI unit	m³
	cubic centimetre	0.000 001 m³	cm³
VOLUME (for fluids)	litre	0.001 m³	1
	millilitre	0.001 l	ml
	kilolitre	1 000 l (1 m³)	kl
VELOCITY	metre per second	SI unit	m/s
	kilometre per hour	0.27 m/s	km/h
	knot	1 n mile/h or o.514 m/s	kn
FORCE	newton	SI unit	N
	kilonewton	1 000 N	kN
	meganewton	1 000 000 N	MN
ENERGY	joule	SI unit	J
	kilojoule	1 000 J	kJ
	megajoule	1 000 000 J	MJ

Quantity	Name of Unit	Value	Symbol
POWER	watt	SI unit	W
	kilowatt	1 000 W	kW
	megawatt	1 000 000 W	MW
DENSITY	kilogram per cubic metre	SI unit	kg/m³
	tonne per cubic metre	1 000 kg/m³	t/m³
	gram per cubic metre	0.001 kg/m³	g/m³
DENSITY (for fluids)	kilogram per litre	1 000 kg/m³	kg/l
PRESSURE	pascal	SI unit (N/m²)	Pa
	kilopascal	1 000 Pa	kPa
	megapascal	1 000 000 Pa	MPa
PRESSURE (for meteorology)	millibar	100 Pa	mb
ELECTRIC CURRENT	ampere	base unit	A
	milliampere	0.001 A	mA
POTENTIAL DIFFERENCE	volt	SI unit	V
	microvolt	0.000 001 V	μV
	millivolt	0.001 V	mV
	kilovolt	1 000 V	kV
	megavolt	1 000 000 V	MV
ELECTRICAL RESISTANCE	ohm	SI unit	Ω
	microhm	0.000 001Ω	$\mu\Omega$
	megohm	1 000 000Ω	MΩ
FREQUENCY	hertz	SI unit	Hz
	kilohertz	1 000 Hz	kHz
	megahertz	1 000 000 Hz	MHz
	gigahertz	1 000 000 000 Hz	GHz
TEMPERATURE	kelvin	SI unit	K
	degree Celsius	K-273.15	°C

METRIC/IMPERIAL CONVERSION FACTORS

Imperial to Metric Units	Metric to Imperial Units

LENGTH

Imperial to Metric	Metric to Imperial
1 in = 25.4 mm	1 cm = 0.394 in
1 ft = 30.5 cm	1 m = 3.28 ft
1 yd = 0.914 m	1 m = 1.09 yd
1 mile = 1.61 km	1 km = 0.621 mile

MASS

1 oz = 28.3 g	1 g = 0.0353 oz
1 lb = 454 g	1 kg = 2.20 lb
1 ton = 1.02 tonne	1 tonne = 0.984 ton

AREA

1 in² = 6.45 cm²	1 cm² = 0.155 in²
1 ft² = 929 cm²	1 m² = 10.8 ft²
1 yd² = 0.836 m²	1 m² = 1.20 yd²
1 ac = 0.405 ha	1 ha = 2.47 ac
1 sq. mile = 259 ha	1 km² = 247 ac

VOLUME

1 in³ = 16.4 cm³	1 cm³ = 0.0610 in³
1 ft³ = 0.0283 m³	1 m³ = 35.3 ft³
1 yd³ = 0.765 m³	1 m³ = 1.31 yd³
1 bushel = 0.0364 m³	1 m³ = 27.5 bushels

VOLUME (fluids)

1 fl oz = 28.4 ml	1 ml = 0.0352 fl oz
1 pint = 568 ml	1 litre = 1.76 pint
1 gallon = 4.55 litre	1 m³ = 220 gallons

FORCE

1 lbf (pound-force) = 4.45 N	1 N (newton) = 0.225 lbf

PRESSURE

1 psi (lb/sq in) = 6.89 kPa	1 kPa (kilo-pascal) = 0.145 psi

VELOCITY

1 mph = 1,61 km/h	1 km/h = 0.621 mph

TEMPERATURE

$$°C = \frac{5}{9}(°F - 32)$$

$$°F = \frac{9 \times °C}{5} + 32$$

ENERGY

1 Btu (British thermal unit) = 1.06 kJ	1 kJ (kilo-joule) = 0.948 Btu

POWER

1 hp = 0.746 kW	1 kW = 1.34 hp

FUEL CONSUMPTION

$$mpg = \frac{282}{litres/100 \ km}$$

$$litres/100 \ km = \frac{282}{mpg}$$

TEMPERATURE CONVERSION TABLE

CELSIUS TO FAHRENHEIT

Conversion formulae:

See METRIC/IMPERIAL CONVERSION FACTORS

°C	°F	°C	°F	°C	°F
50	122	20	68	−10	14
49	120.2	19	66.2	−11	12.2
48	118.4	18	64.4	−12	10.4
47	116.6	17	62.6	−13	8.6
46	114.8	16	60.8	−14	6.8
45	113	15	59	−15	5
44	111.2	14	57.2	−16	3.2
43	109.4	13	55.4	−17	1.4
42	107.6	12	53.6	−18	−0.4
41	105.8	11	51.8	−19	−2.2
40	104	10	50	−20	−4
39	102.2	9	48.2	−21	−5.8
38	100.4	8	46.4	−22	−7.6
37	98.6	7	44.6	−23	−9.4
36	96.8	6	42.8	−24	−11.2
35	95	5	41	−25	−13
34	93.2	4	39.2	−26	−14.8
33	91.4	3	37.4	−27	−16.6
32	89.6	2	35.6	−28	−18.4
31	87.8	1	33.8	−29	−20.2
30	86	0	32	−30	−22
29	84.2	−1	30.2	−31	−23.8
28	82.4	−2	28.4	−32	−25.6
27	80.6	−3	26.6	−33	−27.4
26	78.8	−4	24.8	−34	−29.2
25	77	−5	23	−35	−31
24	75.2	−6	21.2	−36	−32.8
23	73.4	−7	19.4	−37	−34.6
22	71.6	−8	17.6	−38	−36.4
21	69.8	−9	15.8	−39	−38.2

MATHEMATICAL SYMBOLS

Symbol	Meaning	Symbol	Meaning
$+$	1. plus, addition sign 2. positive	$\bigcirc$	circle; circumference
$-$	1. minus, subtraction sign 2. negative	$\frown$	arc of a circle
$\times$	multiplied by	$\triangle$	triangle
$\div$	divided by; also indicated by oblique stroke (8/2) or horizontal line $\dfrac{8}{2}$	$\square$	square
		$\square$	rectangle
		$\square$	parallelogram
$=$	equals; is equal to	$\sqrt{}$	radical sign (ie square root sign)
$\neq$	is not equal to	Σ	sum
$\equiv$	is identical with; is congruent to	$\int$	integral
$\sim$	difference between; is equivalent to	$\cup$	union
$\doteqdot, \approx$	is approximately equal to	$\cap$	intersection
$>$	is greater than	$\in$	is a member of; is an element of; belongs to
$<$	is less than	$\subseteq$	is contained as subclass within
$\not>$	is not greater than	$\supseteq$	contains as subclass
$\not<$	is not less than	$\{\ \}$	set braces
$\leqslant$	less than or equal to	ϕ	the empty set
$\geqslant$	greater than or equal to	$|\ |$	absolute value of; modulus of
$\cong$	is isomorphic to	$\triangleleft$	is a normal subgroup of
$:$	is to; ratio sign	μ	mean (population)
$::$	as: used between ratios	σ	standard deviation (population)
∞	infinity	$\overline{x}$	mean (sample)
$\propto$	varies as, proportional to	s	standard deviation (sample)
$\therefore$	therefore	π	ratio of circumference of any circle to its diameter
$\because$	since, because	e	base of natural logarithms
$\angle$	angle	$\circ$	degrees of arc or temperature
$\llcorner$	right angle	$'$	minutes of arc or time; feet
$\perp$	is perpendicular to	$''$	seconds of arc or time; inches
$\parallel$	is parallel to		

CHEMICAL SYMBOLS

Each element is placed in alphabetical order of its symbol and is followed by its atomic number.

Ac actinium, 89	**Ge** germanium, 32	**Po** polonium, 84
Ag silver, 47	**H** hydrogen, 1	**Pr** praseodymium, 59
Al aluminium, 13	**Ha** hahnium, 105	**Pt** platinum, 78
Am americium, 95	**He** helium, 2	**Pu** plutonium, 94
Ar argon, 18	**Hf** hafnium, 72	**Ra** radium, 88
As arsenic, 33	**Hg** mercury, 80	**Rb** rubidium, 37
At astatine, 85	**Ho** holmium, 67	**Re** rhenium, 75
Au gold, 79	**I** iodine, 53	**Rf** rutherfordium, 104
B boron, 5	**In** indium, 49	**Rh** rhodium, 45
Ba barium, 56	**Ir** iridium, 77	**Rn** radon, 86
Be beryllium, 4	**K** potassium, 19	**Ru** ruthenium, 44
Bi bismuth, 83	**Kr** krypton, 36	**S** sulphur, 16
Bk berkelium, 97	**La** lanthanum, 57	**Sb** antimony, 51
Br bromine, 35	**Li** lithium, 3	**Sc** scandium, 21
C carbon, 6	**Lr** lawrencium, 103	**Se** selenium, 34
Ca calcium, 20	**Lu** lutetium, 71	**Si** silicon, 14
Cd cadmium, 48	**Md** mendelevium, 101	**Sm** samarium, 62
Ce cerium, 58	**Mg** magnesium, 12	**Sn** tin, 50
Cf californium, 98	**Mn** manganese, 25	**Sr** strontium, 38
Cl chlorine, 17	**Mo** molybdenum, 42	**Ta** tantalum, 73
Cm curium, 96	**N** nitrogen, 7	**Tb** terbium, 65
Co cobalt, 27	**Na** sodium, 11	**Tc** technetium, 43
Cr chromium, 24	**Nb** niobium, 41	**Te** tellurium, 52
Cs caesium, 55	**Nd** neodymium, 60	**Th** thorium, 90
Cu copper, 29	**Ne** neon, 10	**Ti** titanium, 22
Dy dysprosium, 66	**Ni** nickel, 28	**Tl** thallium, 81
Er erbium, 68	**No** nobelium, 102	**Tm** thulium, 69
Es einsteinium, 99	**Np** neptunium, 93	**U** uranium, 92
Eu europium, 63	**O** oxygen, 8	**V** vanadium, 23
F fluorine, 9	**Os** osmium, 76	**W** tungsten, 74
Fe iron, 26	**P** phosphorus, 15	**Xe** xenon, 54
Fm fermium, 100	**Pa** protactinium, 91	**Y** yttrium, 39
Fr francium, 87	**Pb** lead, 82	**Yb** ytterbium, 70
Ga gallium, 31	**Pd** palladium, 46	**Zn** zinc, 30
Gd gadolinium, 64	**Pm** promethium, 61	**Zr** zirconium, 40

COUNTRIES, RELATED NOUNS, ADJECTIVES, CURRENCIES & CAPITALS

Country	Noun/ Adjective	Currency Unit	Capital
Afghanistan	Afghan	afghani	Kabul
Albania	Albanian	lek	Tirana
Algeria	Algerian	dinar	Algiers
Andorra	Andorran	franc/ peseta	Andorra la Vella
Angola	Angolan	kwanza	Luanda
Argentina	Argentine or Argentinian	peso	Buenos Aires
Australia	Australian	dollar	Canberra
Austria	Austrian	schilling	Vienna
Bahamas	Bahamian	dollar	Nassau
Bahrain	Bahraini	dinar	Manama
Bangladesh	Bangladeshi	taka	Dacca
Barbados	Barbadian	dollar	Bridgetown
Belgium	Belgian	franc	Brussels
Benin	Beninese	franc	Porto Novo
Bermuda	Bermudan	dollar	Hamilton
Bolivia	Bolivian	peso boliviano	La Paz
Botswana		pula	Gaborone
Brazil	Brazilian	cruzeiro	Brasilia
Bulgaria	Bulgarian	lev	Sofia
Burma	Burmese	kyat	Rangoon
Burundi	Burundian	franc	Bujumbura
Cameroon	Cameroonian	franc	Yaoundé
Canada	Canadian	dollar	Ottawa
Central African Rep.		franc	Bangui
Chad	Chadian	franc	Ndjamena
Chile	Chilean	peso	Santiago
China	Chinese	yuan	Peking
China (Taiwan)	Chinese	dollar	Taipei
Colombia	Colombian	peso	Bogotá
Congo	Congolese	franc	Brazzaville
Costa Rica	Costa Rican	colon	San José
Cuba	Cuban	peso	Havana
Cyprus	Cypriot	pound	Nicosia
Czechoslovakia	Czech, Czechoslovak, or Czechoslovakian	koruna	Prague
Denmark	Dane; Danish	krone	Copenhagen
Dominica	Dominican	dollar	Roseau
Dominican Rep.	Dominican	peso	Santo Domingo
Ecuador	Ecuadorean	sucre	Quito
Egypt	Egyptian	pound	Cairo
El Salvador	Salvadorean	colon	San Salvador
Equatorial Guinea		ekpwele	Malabo
Ethiopia	Ethiopian	birr	Addis Ababa
Fiji	Fijian	dollar	Suva
Finland	Finn; Finnish	markka	Helsinki
France	Frenchman, -woman; French	franc	Paris
Gabon	Gabonese	franc	Libreville
Gambia	Gambian	dalasi	Banjul
Germany, East	East German	mark	East Berlin
Germany, West	West German	deutschmark	Bonn
Ghana	Ghanaian	cedi	Accra
Greece	Greek	drachma	Athens
Grenada	Grenadian	dollar	St. George's

Country	Noun/ Adjective	Currency Unit	Capital
Guatemala	Guatemalan	quetzal	Guatemala City
Guinea	Guinean	franc	Conakry
Guinea-Bissau		peso	Bissau
Guyana	Guyanese	dollar	Georgetown
Haiti	Haitian	gourde	Port-au-Prince
Honduras	Honduran	lempira	Tegucigalpa
Hungary	Hungarian	forint	Budapest
Iceland	Icelander; Icelandic	krona	Reykjavik
India	Indian	rupee	New Delhi
Indonesia	Indonesian	rupiah	Djakarta
Iran	Iranian	rial	Teheran
Iraq	Iraqi	dinar	Baghdad
Ireland, Republic of	Irishman, -woman; Irish	pound	Dublin
Israel	Israeli	pound	Jerusalem
Italy	Italian	lira	Rome
Jamaica	Jamaican	dollar	Kingston
Japan	Japanese	yen	Tokyo
Jordan	Jordanian	dinar	Amman
Kampuchea	Kampuchean	riel	Phnom Penh
Kenya	Kenyan	shilling	Nairobi
Korea, North	North Korean	won	Pyongyang
Korea, South	South Korean	won	Seoul
Kuwait	Kuwaiti	dinar	Kuwait
Laos	Laotian	kip	Vientiane
Lebanon	Lebanese	pound	Beirut
Lesotho		rand	Maseru
Liberia	Liberian	dollar	Monrovia
Libya	Libyan	dinar	Tripoli
Liechtenstein		franc	Vaduz
Luxembourg		franc	Luxembourg
Madagascar	Madagascan	franc	Tananarive
Malawi	Malawian	kwacha	Lilongwe
Malaysia	Malaysian	ringgit	Kuala Lumpur
Mali	Malian	franc	Bamako
Malta	Maltese	pound	Valletta
Mauritania	Mauritanian	ouguiya	Nouakchott
Mauritius	Mauritian	rupee	Port Louis
Mexico	Mexican	peso	Mexico City
Monaco	Monegasque	franc	Monaco
Mongolian People's Rep.	Mongolian	tugrik	Ulan Bator
Morocco	Moroccan	dirham	Rabat
Mozambique	Mozambican	escudo	Maputo
Nepal	Nepalese	rupee	Katmandu
Netherlands	Dutchman, -woman; Netherlander; Dutch	guilder	Amsterdam
New Zealand	New Zealander	dollar	Wellington
Nicaragua	Nicaraguan	cordoba	Managua
Niger		franc	Niamey
Nigeria	Nigerian	naira	Lagos
Norway	Norwegian	krone	Oslo
Oman	Omani	rial	Muscat
Pakistan	Pakistani	rupee	Islamabad
Panama	Panamanian	balboa	Panama City

Country	Noun/ Adjective	Currency Unit	Capital
Papua New Guinea	Papuan	kina	Port Moresby
Paraguay	Paraguayan	guarani	Asunción
Peru	Peruvian	sol	Lima
Philippines	Filipino or Philippine	peso	Quezon City
Poland	Pole; Polish	zloty	Warsaw
Portugal	Portuguese	escudo	Lisbon
Qatar	Qatari	riyal	Doha
Rumania	Rumanian	leu	Bucharest
Rwanda	Rwandan	franc	Kigali
San Marino	San Marinese or Sammarinese	lira	San Marino
Saudi Arabia	Saudi Arabian	riyal	Riyadh
Senegal	Senegalese	franc	Dakar
Sierra Leone	Sierra Leonean	leone	Freetown
Singapore	Singaporean	dollar	Singapore
Somalia	Somalian	shilling	Mogadiscio
South Africa	South African	rand	Cape Town (legislative) Pretoria (administrative)
Spain	Spaniard; Spanish	peseta	Madrid
Sri Lanka	Sri Lankan	rupee	Colombo
Sudan	Sudanese	pound	Khartoum
Surinam	Surinamese	guilder	Paramaribo
Swaziland	Swazi	lilangani	Mbabane
Sweden	Swede; Swedish	krona	Stockholm
Switzerland	Swiss	franc	Bern
Syria	Syrian	pound	Damascus
Tanzania	Tanzanian	shilling	Dar es Salaam
Thailand	Thai	baht	Bangkok
Togo	Togolese	franc	Lomé
Tonga	Tongan	pa'anga	Nuku'alofa
Trinidad and Tobago	Trinidadian, Tobagan	dollar	Port-of-Spain
Tunisia	Tunisian	dinar	Tunis
Turkey	Turk; Turkish	lira	Ankara
Uganda	Ugandan	shilling	Kampala
USSR	Russian or Soviet	ruble	Moscow
United Arab Emirates		dirham	Abu Dhabi
United Kingdom	Briton; British	pound	London
USA	American	dollar	Washington, D.C.
Uruguay	Uruguayan	peso	Montevideo
Venezuela	Venezuelan	bolivar	Caracas
Vietnam	Vietnamese	dong	Hanoi
Western Samoa	Samoan	dollar	Apia
Yemen, People's Democratic Rep.	Yemeni	dinar	Aden
Yemen Arab Rep.	Yemeni	riyal	Sanaa
Yugoslavia	Yugoslav or Yugoslavian	dinar	Belgrade
Zaire	Zairean	zaire	Kinshasa
Zambia	Zambian	kwacha	Lusaka
Zimbabwe	Zimbabwean	dollar	Salisbury

WORLD STANDARD TIMES

At noon, GMT, 1300 BST

For each degree of longitude, time differs by 4 minutes; west of Greenwich is earlier, east of Greenwich later, than GMT.

Place	Time	Place	Time
Accra	1200	Malta	1300
Adelaide	2130	Melbourne	2200
Aden	1500	Mexico City	0600
Algiers	1300	Montevideo	0830
Amsterdam	1300	Montreal	0700
Athens	1400	Moscow	1500
Auckland	2400	Nairobi	1500
Beirut	1400	New Orleans	0600
Belgrade	1300	New York	0700
Berlin	1300	Oslo	1300
Berne	1300	Ottawa	0700
Bombay	1730	Panama	0700
Brindisi	1300	Paris	1300
Brisbane	2200	Peking	2000
Brussels	1300	Perth, Australia	2000
Bucharest	1400	Prague	1300
Budapest	1300	Quebec	0700
Buenos Aires	0800	Rangoon	1830
Cairo	1400	Rio de Janeiro	0900
Calcutta	1730	Rome	1300
Cape Town	1400	St John's, Newfoundland	0830
Caracas	0800	St Louis	0600
Chicago	0600	San Francisco	0400
Colombo	1730	Santiago	0800
Copenhagen	1300	Singapore	1930
Gibraltar	1300	Sofia	1400
Helsinki	1400	Stockholm	1300
Hobart	2200	Suez	1400
Hong Kong	2000	Sydney	2200
Istanbul	1400	Tehran	1530
Jerusalem	1400	Tokyo	2100
Karachi	1700	Toronto	0700
Lagos	1300	Tunis	1300
Leningrad	1500	Vancouver	0400
Lima	0700	Vienna	1300
Lisbon	1200	Warsaw	1300
Madeira	1100	Winnipeg	0600
Madras	1730	Yokohama	2100
Madrid	1300		

DISTANCES BY AIR

The flight distances shown in the following tables are quoted in kilometres via the shortest normal airline routing from airport to airport. For cities with more than one airport a mean distance is given. An asterisk indicates a maximum distance.

from London

Accra	5086
Algiers	1650
Amsterdam	370
Auckland	24290*
Baghdad	4097
Bahrain	5084
Bangkok	9551
Barcelona	1129
Beirut	3468
Belgrade	1689
Berlin	952
Bombay	7205
Brisbane	23746*
Brussels	340
Budapest	1476
Buenos Aires	13442*
Cairo	3518
Calcutta	11111*
Cape Town	12275*
Casablanca	2062
Chicago	6364
Cologne	525
Colombo	11289*
Copenhagen	984
Dakar	4349
Darwin	18151*
Delhi	6730
Djakarta	15208*
Dubrovnik	1715
Geneva	736
Hamburg	745
Honolulu	11699*
Istanbul	2502
Jamaica	7532
Johannesburg	9059
Karachi	8494
Kuwait	4666
Lagos	4988
Lisbon	1555
Madrid	1232
Marseilles	971
Melbourne	25011*
Milan	940
Montreal	5234
Moscow	2507
Nairobi	6825
Naples	1613
New York	5564
Nice	1022
Oslo	1175
Palma	1330
Paris	336
Prague	1037
Rangoon	12255*
Rio de Janeiro	11132*
Rome	1436
Salisbury (Zimbabwe)	10707*
San Francisco	10420*
Singapore	14133*
Stockholm	1462
Sydney	24163*
Tehran	4408
Tel Aviv	3577
Tokyo	17518*
Toronto	5727
Tunis	1813
Venice	1135
Vienna	1262
Warsaw	1465
Washington	5889
Wellington	24372

from Montreal

Amsterdam	5509
Auckland	17658*
Berlin	7314*
Bombay	15340*
Cairo	10488*
Moscow	8832*
New York	531
Paris	5527
Rio de Janeiro	9942*
Rome	6601
Vancouver	3684
Zurich	6000

from Sydney

Auckland	2162
Berlin	20940*
Cairo	17475*
Johannesburg	14685*
Moscow	20933*
New York	19407*
Paris	21329*

Rome	20041*
San Francisco	14442*
Singapore	6303
Tokyo	7821
Toronto	18839*

from Auckland

Berlin	23535*
Brisbane	2297
Buenos Aires	15809*
Cairo	20069*
Honolulu	7094
Moscow	24598*
New York	17275*
Paris	23923*
Rome	24588*
San Francisco	13142*
Singapore	10157*
Tokyo	13584*

from Johannesburg

Amsterdam	10848*
Auckland	17161*
Berlin	10930*
Cape Town	1272
Montreal	16061*
Moscow	11162*
Nairobi	2914
New York	15424*
Paris	10600*
Rio de Janeiro	7150
Rome	9507*
Tel Aviv	6506

from Bombay

Auckland	14857*
Berlin	8680*
Cairo	4345
Hong Kong	4303
Johannesburg	8939*
Moscow	8671*
Paris	9068*
Rio de Janeiro	18444*
Rome	6182
San Francisco	19563*
Singapore	3916
Sydney	12262*